S0-BSV-531

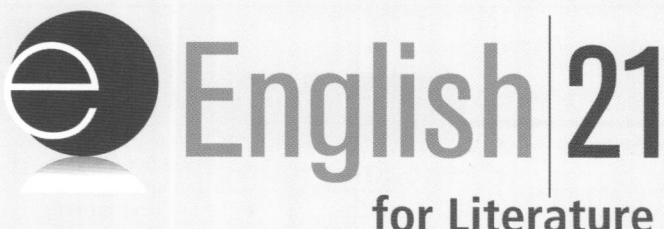

English | 21
for Literature

academic.cengage.com/english21

Supporting students through every step of the writing process

More than just the largest compilation of online resources ever organized for literature courses, English21 supports students through every step of the writing process, from assignment to final draft. This complete support system weaves robust, self-paced instruction with interactive assignments to engage students as they become better prepared and more effective writers.

OPEN HERE TO LEARN MORE ABOUT HOW English21 CAN WORK FOR YOU!

English|21

Interact with the power and simplicity of English21!

Get started at academic.cengage.com/english21.

At this website, you can view a demonstration of English21; learn more about the books and courses available with English21; and find answers to Frequently Asked Questions pertaining to registration, instructor and student training, system requirements, technical support and more.

STUDENTS

If a printed access card did not come with this text, check your local college store or go to **www.ichapters.com** to purchase instant access to English21 or English21 *Plus* at Wadsworth Cengage Learning's preferred online store.

ichapters.com

INSTRUCTORS

Contact your local Wadsworth Cengage Learning representative for English21 or English21 *Plus* packaging information.

Perrine's

Literature
Structure, Sound, and Sense

Perrine

Literature

Structure, Sound, and Sense

Perrine's

Literature

Structure, Sound, and Sense

Tenth Edition

Thomas R. Arp
Southern Methodist University

Greg Johnson
Kennesaw State University

WADSWORTH
CENGAGE Learning™

Australia • Brazil • Canada • Mexico • Singapore • Spain • United Kingdom • United States

WADSWORTH
CENGAGE Learning

Perrine's Literature:
Structure, Sound, and Sense,
Tenth Edition
Thomas R. Arp / Greg Johnson
Publisher: Lyn Uhl
Development Editor: Helen Triller
Assistant Editor: Cheryl Forman
Editorial Assistant: Lindsey Veautour
Technology Project Manager: Stephanie Gregoire
Executive Marketing Manager: Mandee Eckersley
Marketing Assistant: Kathleen Remsberg
Advertising Project Manager: Stacey Purviance
Senior Content Project Manager: Karen Stocz
Creative Director: Rob Hugel
Art Director: Cate Barr
Manufacturing Manager: Marcia Locke
Permissions Editor: Fred Courtright/ Bob Kauser
Production Service: Newgen–Austin
Cover Designer: Mark Fox

© 2009, 2006 Wadsworth Cengage Learning

ALL RIGHTS RESERVED. No part of this work covered by the copyright herein may be reproduced, transmitted, stored, or used in any form or by any means graphic, electronic, or mechanical, including but not limited to photocopying, recording, scanning, digitizing, taping, Web distribution, information networks, or information storage and retrieval systems, except as permitted under Section 107 or 108 of the 1976 United States Copyright Act, without the prior written permission of the publisher.

For product information and technology assistance, contact us at
Cengage Learning Academic Resource Center, 1-800-423-0563

For permission to use material from this text or product,
submit all requests online at **www.cengage. com/permissions.**

Library of Congress Control Number: 2007938681
ISBN-13: 978-1-4130-3308-3
ISBN-10: 1-4130-3308-3

Wadsworth Cengage Learning
25 Thomson Place
Boston, MA 02210
USA

Cengage Learning products are represented in Canada by Nelson Education, Ltd.

For your course and learning solutions, visit **academic.cengage.com.**

Purchase any of our products at your local college store or at our preferred online store **www.ichapters.com.**

Printed in the United States
1 2 3 4 5 6 7 12 11 10 09 08

Brief Contents

Contents

Fiction The Elements of Fiction   59

Chapter One Reading the Story   61

Chapter Two Plot and Structure   103

Chapter Three Characterization   161

Chapter Six Figurative Language 2: Symbol, Allegory   725

Featured Poets

The following poems appear as illustrations in various chapters of the poetry section, but these four poets are represented by a sufficient number of poems to warrant studying them as individual artists.

Poems for Further Reading   941

Drama The Elements of Drama   1021

Chapter One The Nature of Drama   1023

Preface

In preparing this tenth edition of *Perrine's Literature: Structure, Sound, and Sense*, we have striven to be true to the principles established by Laurence Perrine more than fifty years ago, while at the same time acknowledging the developing nature of literature. The book as always works to balance the classic with the contemporary, to represent a wide diversity of writers, and to emphasize the importance of the close reading of literature as the avenue to enjoying and appreciating it. While there are many flourishing approaches to literature and its effects, we believe that the initial step must be understanding the basic elements of fiction, poetry, and drama.

This book is addressed to the student who is beginning a serious study of imaginative literature. It seeks to give that student a sufficient grasp of the nature and variety of fiction, poetry, and drama; some reasonable means for reading with appreciative understanding; and a few primary ideas of how to evaluate literature. One important principle established in the earliest editions is the need for conciseness and compactness so that the book will have a friendly, welcoming appeal and will not seem daunting in its comprehensiveness. In matters of theory, in an introductory textbook some issues are undoubtedly simplified, but none we hope seriously so, and some more sophisticated theoretical approaches have had to be excluded in the interests of space. Another principle is that the elements of literature are presented in a progression in which each new topic builds on what preceded it. The separate chapters gradually introduce the student to the elements of the three genres, putting the emphasis always on *how* and *why*: How can the reader use these elements to get at the meaning of the work, to interpret it sensibly, and to respond to it adequately? *Why* does the writer use these elements? What values have they for the writer and reader?

The tenth edition of *Literature* maintains the balance between classic and modern writers, and continues to offer a wide sampling of vicarious experiences through the works of women as well as men, ethnic minorities as well as authors representing the varieties of American and world literatures. The structure of the book reflects the step-by-step approach to understanding literature. Each chapter contains two parts: (1) a discussion of the topic indicated by the chapter title, with illustrative works, and (2) a relevant selection of works with study questions for further illustration of the topic.

Although the book emphasizes the study of literature, not writers, we have continued the practice of representing some authors with a sufficient number of works to support the study of them as individual artists. In the fiction section we include three stories each by one of the classic pioneers in the short story form (James Joyce), by a great twentieth-century writer (Flannery O'Connor), and by a major contemporary author (Joyce Carol Oates). In this edition, there are also three poets amply represented: Emily Dickinson, John Donne, and Robert Frost. The table of contents gathers the titles of their poems in a boxed format for easy reference.

New to this edition is the presentation of a "Contemporary Collection," five poets represented by six poems each placed throughout the text. These, too, are identified in a boxed format in the table of contents. One of them, Adrienne Rich, does not permit us to supply study questions for her poems, but the Instructor's Manual available to teachers using the book has study questions as well as the usual explanatory discussions of the poems. In addition, to provide an introduction to the further works of individual poets, the book contains at least three poems each by eighteen poets, both classic and modern. These poems can easily be referenced in the index of the book.

In the drama section we have expanded the number of one-act plays so as to provide a wider range of dramatic styles and approaches, and to provide more contemporary playwrights of diverse backgrounds.

Again in the interests of space, we have not provided extended biographical information about the writers, but instructors and students who feel the need for such material are urged to consult Wadsworth's valuable "Literature Resource Center" at http://trials.galegroup.com/thomson.

Through the ten editions of a book that originated in the middle of the twentieth century, *Perrine's Literature: Structure, Sound, and Sense* has evolved in many ways, responding to shifts in interest, concern, and taste expressed by its users. But certain abiding principles remain as relevant to this century as they were in the last. Among these are the conviction that the close reading of a text is basic to the understanding and appreciation of literature; that to understand the means by which a work achieves its ends is an essential part of experiencing it fully; and that reading literature is important to the development of the whole person. The first assumptions of this book are that literature needs to be read carefully and thought about considerably and that, when so read, gives its readers continuing rewards in experience and understanding.

T. R. A. and G. J.

Professional Acknowledgments

The following instructors have offered helpful reactions and suggestions for this tenth edition of *Perrine's Literature: Structure, Sound, and Sense:*

Diana Aghabegian
Santa Monica College

Robert Anderson
Oakland University

Joe Angelella
Bucks County Community College

Mary Kate Azcuy
Monmouth University

Stephen Baarendse
Columbia International University

Joseph Barbarese
Rutgers University, Camden

Albert Bellais
Savannah State University

David Bergman
Towson University

Laura Brown
Central Alabama Community College

Amy Burtner
SUNY Cortland

Michele Cheung
University of Southern Maine

Cindy Childress
University of Louisiana at Lafayette

Ken Cox
Florence-Darlington Technical College

Kay Cramer
Pasco-Hernando Community College

Melissa Crofton
University of South Carolina

Larry Czer
Martin Luther College

Fred D'Astoli
College of the Canyons

Linda Desjardins
Northern Essex Community College

Robert Donahoo
Sam Houston State University

Mike Donaghe
Eastern New Mexico University

Vicki Dorshorn
University of Kansas

Richard Downing
Pasco-Hernando Community College

Ellen Dugan-Barrette
Brescia University

Patricia Flinn
New Jersey City University

Susan Gebhardt-Burns
Western Connecticut State University

Kendall Grant
Brigham Young University, Idaho

Christine Gray
Community College of Baltimore County

Susan Grimland
Collin County Community College

Christopher Healy
University of Louisiana at Lafayette

Jack Heller
Huntington University

Jeffrey Hibbert
Temple University

Eleanor Howes
Louisiana State University

Charles Israel
Columbia College, South Carolina

Eileen Johnston
United States Naval Academy

Jeff Kahan
University of La Verne

Douglas King
Gannon University

Jennifer Lenhart
Cleveland State University

Clive McClelland
Liberty University

Matt Marafino
Allegany College of Maryland

Mildred Mickle
Penn State McKeesport

D'Juana Montgomery
Southwestern Assemblies of God University

Deborah Murray
Kansas State University

Pat Newberry
University of Memphis

Richard Passon
University of Scranton

Cindy Ramage
Texarkana College

Pam Reid
Copiah-Lincoln Community College

Cindy Ross
Jefferson Community College

Ellen Shull
Palo Alto College

Ken Wolfskill
Chowan University

John Young
Gannon University

Foreword to Students

You've been reading stories ever since you learned to read; your first exposure to verse came with "Pat-a-cake, pat-a-cake, baker's man"; you've been watching dramatized life since your family planted you in front of the TV. You've developed your own tastes and your own attitudes toward what these varieties of "literature" can give you. In a sense, there's no need to take an introductory course in reading literature, because you've moved beyond the "introductory" phase. Let's say, then, that it's time to become familiar and friendly with the literary arts.

But let's take stock of where you stand. What have you been getting out of the things that you enjoy reading and watching? For most people, the first answer is "vicarious experience," the impression that you are temporarily able to live in some other world than your own private one—a world that may be as familiar as your own neighborhood or as alien to your experience as space travel in some future time or the adventures of explorers of the past. What you want is for the author to take you to where you have never been, so that you can imagine yourself as a person in a world other than your own.

You probably also want to be able to "relate" to the characters in the things you read or watch, discovering in them some features of yourself or some qualities that you would like to have. Or you like to share vicariously the excitements, joys, and sorrows of people who are not very much like you, but whose lives seem rich and interesting. Or you get a lift from watching some characters making major mistakes with their lives, and turning themselves around just in time—or maybe you are thrilled to see such people brought to justice and punished for misdeeds.

Whatever the sources of your pleasure and enjoyment from reading, you may now be ready to find both broader and deeper reasons for continuing that pastime. No matter how much experience you bring to the study of these works, you're in for a few surprises. Some of them will be the surprises that come from broadening your vicarious experience, from "traveling" with us to India and Russia and Nigeria, to Rome and Pittsburgh and Dublin, to sixteenth-century London and seventeenth-century Massachusetts and nineteenth-century Wall Street. Some will be the surprises that come from penetrating to the secret recesses of the human mind and soul in joys and agonies, from observing people whom you have never met or imagined and with whom you have nothing in common but your humanness.

And, we hope, there will be the surprises and pleasures that come from feeling yourself growing in control or even mastery of your responses and reactions as you learn *how* literature does what it does. This, of course, is what the formal study of literature can bring you. We all know how we *feel* when we first read through a work. We probably start by thinking "I like this" or "it doesn't say much to me" or "what in the world is that supposed to mean?" If you could, you'd act on your first reaction and read the work again, or try to see what it's trying to say, or drop it and go on to do something more pleasurable.

But you're in a special situation. You're taking a course (either by your own choice or because you're required to), and one of the rules of the game is that you're supposed to move from your initial reaction to some sort of "serious" response that will satisfy your teacher. If you like something and want to reread it, your teacher will pester you with wanting to know *why* you liked it, and might even insist that you offer reasons why other people should like it too. If you are only a little bit curious about it, or think that it is a waste of time, your teacher will lead (or nudge, or bash) you into finding things in it that might change your first opinion. In any case, the terms of your special situation, as a student in a course with a grade on the horizon, make it necessary for you to have more than an initial reaction. You'll need to have a developing understanding of the work, and you'll need to show in discussion or writing both what you understand and how the work itself led to that understanding.

That's where this book will help. In addition to a systematic guide for discovering how and what a literary work means, we've provided you with suggestions for writing at the ends of the chapters and standards for your written work in the first section of the book.

Why is writing so important? It's the most straightforward way of sorting out your feelings and ideas, putting them into shape, nailing down your own experience. All writing about literature has a double motive—it sharpens your grasp of the work, and it helps you to lead other people to share your experience. Writing about literature is writing persuasively, and persuading others to see what you see helps you to see it more clearly.

So at the most basic level, we want to help you with reading and writing. But you have every right to ask, "Why literature?" That's a good question, because in our world there are so many ways of gaining experience and insight into our lives and the lives of others that focusing on one resource based on the spoken and written word may seem narrow and old-fashioned. We're willing to grant that, and we'll go even further: in a sense, it is also elitist, and turning to literature as a source of experience will set you apart from the majority of people. Thus, literature provides not only vicarious experience and opportunities to relate to others' lives, but it also permits you to join a special group of scholars, instructors, critics, and other students who share in the wealth of enjoyment and intellectual challenge that it has to offer.

Writing
about
Literature

I. Why Write about Literature?

Written assignments in a literature class have two purposes: (1) to give you additional practice in writing clearly and persuasively, and (2) to deepen your understanding of literary works by leading you to read and think about a few works more searchingly than you might otherwise do. But these two purposes are private. To be successful, your paper must have a public purpose as well: it should be written to enlighten others besides yourself. Even if no one else ever reads your paper, you should never treat it as a private note to your instructor. You should write every paper as if it were intended for publication.

II. For Whom Do You Write?

The audience for whom you write will govern both the content and the expression of your paper. You need to know something about your readers' backgrounds—national, racial, social, religious—and be able to make intelligent guesses about their knowledge, interests, and previous reading. In writing about George Herbert's "Peace" (page 735) for a Hindu audience, you would need to include explanations of Christian belief and biblical stories that would be unnecessary for a western European or American audience. In presenting Graham Greene's "The Destructors" (page 111), your editors have felt it necessary to provide information (in footnotes) that would not be needed by a British audience; for "Los Vendidos" by Luis Valdez (page 1207), footnotes provide translations and explanations that would not be necessary for an audience familiar with the Spanish-language slang of contemporary America. But the most crucial question about an audience is: *Has it read the work you are writing about?* The book reviewer in your Sunday paper generally writes about a newly published book that the audience has not read. A reviewer's purpose is to let readers know something of what the book is about and to give them some notion of whether they will enjoy or profit from reading it. At an opposite extreme, the scholar writing in a specialized scholarly journal can generally assume an audience that *has* read the work, that has a knowledge of previous interpretations of the work, and that is familiar with other works in its period or genre. The scholar's purpose, not infrequently, is to persuade this audience that some new information or some new way of looking at the work appreciably deepens or alters its meaning or significance.

Clearly, essays written for such different audiences and with such different purposes differ considerably in content, organization, and style. Book reviewers reviewing a new novel will include a general idea of its plot while being careful not to reveal the outcome. Scholars will assume that readers already know the plot, and will have no compunction about discussing its outcome. Reviewers will try to write interestingly and engagingly about the novel and to persuade readers that they have valid grounds for their opinions of its worth, but their manner will generally be informal. Scholars are more interested in presenting a cogent argument, logically arranged and solidly based on evidence. They will be more formal, and may use critical terms and refer to related works that would be unfamiliar to nonspecialized readers. In documentation the two types of essays will be quite different. Reviewers' only documentation is normally the identification of the novel's title, author, publisher, and price, at the top of the review. For other information and opinions, they hope that a reader will rely on their intelligence, knowledge, and judgment. Scholars, on the other hand, may furnish an elaborate array of citations of other sources of information, allowing the reader to verify the accuracy or basis of any important part of their argument. Scholars expect to be challenged, and they see to it that all parts of their arguments are buttressed.

For whom, then, should *you* write? Unless your instructor stipulates (or you request) a different audience, the best plan is to assume that you are writing for the other members of your class. Pretend that your class publishes a journal of which it also constitutes the readership. Your instructor is the editor and determines editorial policy. If you write on a work that has been assigned for class reading, you assume that your audience is familiar with it. (This kind of paper is generally of the greatest educational value, for it is most open to challenge and class discussion and places on you a heavier burden of proof.) If you compare an assigned work with one that has not been assigned, you must gauge what portion of your audience is familiar with the unassigned work and proceed accordingly. If the unassigned story were A. Conan Doyle's "The Adventure of the Speckled Band," you would probably not need to explain that "Sherlock Holmes is a detective" and that "Dr. Watson is his friend," for you can assume that *this* audience, through movies, TV, or reading, is familiar with these characters; but you could not assume familiarity with this particular story. You know that, as members of the same class, your readers have certain backgrounds and interests in common and are at comparable levels of education. Anything you know about your audience may be important for how you write your paper and what you put in it.

Assuming members of your class as your audience carries another advantage: you can also assume that they are familiar with the definitions and examples given in this book, and therefore you can avoid wasting space by quoting or paraphrasing the book. There will be no need to tell them that an indeterminate ending is one in which the central conflict is left unresolved, or that Emily Dickinson's poems are untitled, or that Miss Brill is an unmarried Englishwoman living in France.

III. Two Basic Approaches

In a beginning study of literature, most writing will focus on a careful reading of details of the assigned work as the basis for any further exploration. Traditionally, the approach will be structured as an *explication* or an *analysis*.

1. Explication

An *explication* (literally, an "unfolding") is a detailed elucidation of a work, sometimes line by line or word by word, which is interested not only in *what* that work means but in *how* it means what it means. It thus considers all relevant aspects of a work—speaker or point of view, connotative words and double meanings, images, figurative language, allusions, form, structure, sound, rhythm—and discusses, if not all of these, at least the most important. (There is no such thing as exhausting the meanings and the ways to those meanings in a complex piece of literature, and the explicator must settle for something less than completeness.) Explication follows from what we sometimes call "close reading"—looking at a piece of writing, as it were, through a magnifying glass.

Clearly, the kinds of literature for which an explication is appropriate are limited. First, the work must be rich enough to repay the kind of close attention demanded. One would not think of explicating "Little Jack Horner" (page 785) unless for purposes of parody, for it has no meanings that need elucidation and no "art" worthy of comment. Second, the work must be short enough to be encompassed in a relatively brief discussion. A thorough explication of *Othello* would be much longer than the play itself and would tire the patience of the most dogged reader. Explications work best with short poems. (Sonnets like Shakespeare's "That time of year" [page 885] and Frost's "Design" [page 790] almost beg for explication.) Explication sometimes may also be appropriate for passages in long poems, as, for example, the lines spoken by Macbeth after the death of his wife (page 774) or the "sonnet" from *Romeo and Juliet* (page 889), and occasionally for exceptionally rich or crucial passages of prose, perhaps the final paragraphs of stories like "Paul's Case" (page 244) or "Miss Brill" (page 174). But explication as a critical form should perhaps be separated from explication as a method. Whenever you elucidate even a small part of a literary work by a close examination that relates it to the whole, you are essentially explicating (unfolding). For example, if you point out the multiple meanings in the title of "Time Flies" (page 1071) as they relate to that play's themes, you are explicating the title.

For examples of explication, see the three sample essays in Part XII of this section (pages 40–58). The discussions in this book display the explicative method frequently, but except for the sample essays, there are no pure examples of explication. The discussions of "A Noiseless Patient Spider" (pages 727–728) and "Digging" (pages 730–733) come close to being explications and might have been so had they included answers to the study questions and one or two other matters. The exercises provided in "Understanding and Evaluating Poetry" on page 641 should be helpful to you in writing an explication of a poem. Not all the questions will be applicable to every poem, and you need not answer all those that are applicable, but you should start by considering all that apply and then work with those that are central and important for your explication.

2. Analysis

An *analysis* (literally a "breaking up" or separation of something into its constituent parts), instead of trying to examine all parts of a work in relation to the whole, selects for examination *one* aspect or element or part that relates to the whole. Clearly, an analysis is a better approach to longer works and to prose works than is an explication. A literary work may be usefully approached through almost any of its elements—point of view, characterization, plot, setting, symbolism, structure, and the like—so long as you relate this element to the central meaning or the whole. (An analysis of meter is meaningless unless it shows how meter serves the meaning; an analysis of the vocabulary and grammar of "The Gilded Six-Bits" [page 553] or "The Sandbox" [page 1064] would be pointless unless related to the characterization of the speakers.) The list of exercises on pages 100–102 may suggest approaches to stories, plays, and narrative poems; the list on page 641 to anything written in verse;

and that on pages 1027–1028 to dramas. As always, it is important to choose a topic appropriate to the space available. "Characterization in Flannery O'Connor's 'Greenleaf'" is too large a topic to be usefully treated in a few pages, but a character analysis of Mrs. May or of her two sons might fit the space neatly. For examples of analyses of three literary forms, see the sample essays in Part XII of this section (pages 40–58).

IV. Choosing a Topic

As editor of this imaginary publication, your instructor is responsible for the nature of its contents. Instructors may be very specific in their assignments, or they may be very general, inviting you to submit a paper on any subject within a broadly defined area of interest. They will also have editorial policies concerning length of papers, preparation of manuscripts, and deadlines for submission (all of which should be meticulously heeded). Instructors may further specify whether the paper should be entirely the work of your own critical thinking, or whether it is to be an investigative assignment—that is, one involving research into what other writers have written concerning your subject and the use of their findings, where relevant, to help you support your own conclusions.

Let us consider four kinds of papers you might write: (1) papers that focus on a single literary work, (2) papers of comparison and contrast, (3) papers on a number of works by a single author, and (4) papers on a number of works having some feature other than authorship in common.

1. Papers That Focus on a Single Literary Work

If your assignment is a specific one (How is the landscape symbolic in "The Guest"? [page 356] What emotions are evoked by the imagery in "The Widow's Lament in Springtime"? [page 693] How does music contribute to the effect of *Death of a Salesman*? [page 1449]), your task is clear-cut. You have only to read the selection carefully (obviously more than once), formulate your answer, and support it with corroborating evidence from within the text as cogently and convincingly as possible. In order to convince your readers that your answer is the best one, you will need to examine and account for apparently contrary evidence as well as clearly supportive evidence; otherwise, skeptical readers, reluctant to change their minds, might simply refer to "important points" that you have "overlooked."

Specific questions like these, when they are central to the work and may be a matter of dispute, make excellent topics for papers. You may discover them for yourself when you disagree with a classmate about the interpretation of a story or poem or play. The study questions following many of the selections in this anthology frequently suggest topics of this kind.

If your assignment is more general, and if you are given some choice as to what selection you wish to write on, it is usually best to choose one you enjoyed, whether or not you entirely understood it. (You are more likely to write a good paper on a selection you liked than on one you disliked, and you should arrive at a fuller understanding of it while thinking through your paper.) You must then decide what kind of paper you will write, taking into account the length and kind of selection you have chosen and the amount of space at your disposal.

2. Papers of Comparison and Contrast

The comparison and contrast of two stories, poems, or plays having one or more features in common may be an illuminating exercise because the similarities highlight the differences, or vice versa, and thus lead to a better understanding not only of both pieces but of literary processes in general. The works selected may be similar in plot but different in theme, similar in subject but different in tone, similar in theme but different in literary value, or, conversely, different in plot but similar in theme, different in subject but similar in tone, and so on. In writing such a paper, it is usually best to decide first whether the similarities or the differences are more significant, begin with a brief summary of the less significant, and then concentrate on the more significant.

A number of selections in this collection have been included to encourage just this kind of study: "The Most Dangerous Game" and "Hunters in the Snow" in chapter 1 of the Fiction section; "Roman Fever" and "A New Leaf" in chapter 8; in the Poetry section, "Terence, this is stupid stuff" and "Ars Poetica" in chapter 1; "Spring" and "The Widow's Lament in Springtime" in chapter 4; "The Unknown Citizen" and "A Considerable Speck" in chapter 7; except for "Little Jack Horner," all seven pairs of poems in chapter 9; "For a Lamb" and "Apparently with no surprise," "Crossing the Bar" and "The Oxen," "One dignity delays for all" and "'Twas warm—at first—like Us," "The Apparition" and "The Flea," and "Dover Beach" and "Church Going" in chapter 10; "Had I the Choice" and "The Aim Was Song" in chapter 12; and all seven pairs of poems in chapter 15. In addition, many of the Suggestions for Writing at the ends of chapters group together comparable works.

3. Papers on a Number of Works by a Single Author

Most readers, when they discover a work they particularly like, look for other works by the same author. The paper that focuses on a single author rather than a single work is the natural corollary of such an interest. The most common concern in a paper of this type is to identify the characteristics that make this author different from other authors and therefore of particular interest to the writer. What are the author's characteristic subjects, settings, attitudes, or themes? With what kinds of life does the author characteristically deal? What are the author's preferred literary forms? Is the author's approach ironic, witty, serious, comic, tragic? Is the author's vision directed principally inward or outward? In short, what configuration of patterns makes the author's fingerprints unique? Your paper may consider one or more of these questions.

Several writers are represented in this book by a sufficient number of works to support such a paper without turning to outside sources. In the Fiction section, three stories each by James Joyce, Flannery O'Connor, and Joyce Carol Oates are grouped together for comparative study. In the Poetry section, there are numerous poems by John Donne, Emily Dickinson, and Robert Frost, six poems each by authors listed in the table of contents as a "Contemporary Collection," and at least three poems each by twenty poets, both classic and modern. The author listings in the index will help you locate the multiple poems by a single author.

A more ambitious type of paper on a single author examines the works for signs of development. The attitudes that any person, especially an author, takes toward the world may change with the passing from adolescence to adulthood to old age. So also may the author's means of expressing attitudes and judgments. Though some writers are remarkably consistent in outlook and expression throughout their careers, others manifest surprising changes. To write a paper on the development of an author's work, you must have accurate information about the dates when works were written, and the works must be read in chronological order. When you have mastered the differences, you may be able to illustrate them through close examination of two or three works, one for each stage.

When readers become especially interested in the works of a particular author, they may develop a curiosity about that author's life as well. This is a legitimate interest, and, if there is sufficient space and your editor/instructor permits it, you may want to incorporate biographical information into your paper. If so, however, you should heed three caveats. First, your main interest should be in the literature itself: the biographical material should be subordinated to and used in service of your examination of the work. In general, discuss only those aspects of the author's life that bear directly on the work: biography should not be used as "filler." Second, you should be extremely cautious about identifying an event in a work with an event in the life of the author. Almost never is a story, poem, or play an exact transcription of its author's personal experience. Authors fictionalize themselves when they put themselves into imaginative works. If you consider that even in autobiographies (where they intend to give accurate accounts of their lives) writers must select incidents from the vast complexity of their experiences, that the memory of past events may be defective, and that at best writers work from their own points of view—in short, when you realize that even autobiography cannot be an absolutely reliable transcription of historical fact—you should be more fully prepared not to expect such an equation in works whose object is imaginative truth. Third, you must document the sources of your information about the author's life (see pages 23–31).

4. Papers on a Number of Works with Some Feature Other Than Authorship in Common

You might also write a successful paper on works by various authors that have some features in common, such as subject matter, form, setting, point of view, literary devices, and the like; discovering the ways in which different works employ a particular feature can be illuminating. Probably the most familiar paper of this type is the one that treats works having a similar thematic concern (love, war, religious belief or doubt, art, adolescence, initiation, maturity, old age, death, parents and children, racial conflict, social injustice). But a paper may also examine particular forms of literature, for example, the Italian sonnet, the dramatic monologue, the short story with an unreliable narrator. Topics of this kind may be further limited by time or place or number—four attitudes toward death; Elizabethan love lyrics; poetry on the experience of war; satires of bureaucracy.

V. Proving Your Point

In writing about literature, your object generally is to convince your readers that your understanding of a work is valid and important and to lead them to share that understanding. When writing about other subjects, it may be appropriate to persuade your readers through various rhetorical means—through eloquent diction, structural devices that create suspense, analogies, personal anecdotes, and the like. But readers of essays about literature usually look for "proof." They want you to show them *how* the work, or the element you are discussing, does what you claim it does. Like scientists who require proof of the sort that they can duplicate in their own laboratories, readers of criticism want access to the process of inference, analysis, and deduction that has led to your conclusions, so that they may respond as you have done.

To provide this proof is no easy task, for it requires the development of your own reading and writing skills. In addition, you must have developed a responsible interpretation of the work and of the way it achieves its effect; you should be able to point out precisely how it communicates its meanings; and you should be able to present your experiences of it clearly and directly. When you have spent considerable time in coming to understand and respond to a work of literature, it may become so familiar that it seems self-evident to you, and you will need to "back off" sufficiently to be able to put yourself in your readers' position—they may have vague feelings about the work ("I like it" or "It moves me deeply"), without knowing what it is that produced those feelings. It is your job to refine the feelings and define away the vagueness.

Some forms of "proof" rarely do the job. Precision does not result from explaining a metaphor metaphorically ("When Shakespeare's Juliet calls parting from Romeo a 'sweet sorrow,' the reader is reminded of taking bitter-tasting medicine"). Nor can you prove anything about a work by hypothesizing about what it might have been if it did not contain what it does ("If Desdemona had not lost her handkerchief, Othello would never have murdered her" —this is equivalent to saying, "If the play were not what it is, it would not be what it is"). Your own personal experiences will rarely help your readers ("My anxiety, excitement, and awkwardness at my first skiing lesson were like the mixed feelings Prufrock imagines for himself at the tea party"—*your* reader hasn't shared your experience of that lesson). Even your personal history of coming to understand a literary work will seldom help, though you present it in more general terms ("At a first reading, the opening paragraphs of 'Eveline' are confusing because they do not explain Eveline's reason for reminiscing about her childhood"—most literature does not yield up its richness on a first reading, so this approach has nothing to add to your reader's understanding). Just as argument by analogy is not regarded as valid in formal logic, so in critical discourse analogies are usually unconvincing ("Desdemona's ignorance about adultery is like a child's inability to balance a checkbook"). These strategies all have in common the looseness and vagueness of trying to define something by saying what it is not, or what it is like, rather than dealing with what it *is*.

"Proof" in writing about literature is primarily an exercise in strict definition. Juliet's phrase "sweet sorrow" (quoted in the preceding paragraph) derives its feeling from the paradoxical linking of sweetness and grief as a representation of the conflicting emotions of love. To provide an appropriate definition of the effect of the phrase, you would need to identify the figure of speech as paradox and to investigate the way in which love can simultaneously inflict pain and give pleasure, and you might find it useful to point to the alliteration that ties these opposites together. Obviously, comparing this kind of proof to that required by science is inexact, since what you are doing is reminding your readers, or perhaps informing them, of feelings that are associated with language, not of the properties of chemical compounds. Furthermore, a scientific proof is incomplete if it does not present every step in a process. If that requirement were placed on literary analysis, a critical essay would be interminable, since more can always be said about any interpretive point. So, rather than attempting to prove every point that you make, you should aim to demonstrate that your *method* of analysis is valid by providing persuasive proof of your major point or points. If you have shown that your handling of a major point is sound, your readers will tend to trust your judgment on lesser matters.

VI. Writing the Paper

The general procedures for writing a good paper on literature are much the same as the procedures for writing a good paper on any subject.

1. As soon as possible after receiving the assignment, read carefully and thoughtfully the literary materials on which it is based, mulling over the problem to be solved or—if the assignment is general—a good choice of subject, jotting down notes, and sidelining or underlining important passages if the book is your own. (If you use a library book, note the page or line numbers of such passages so that you can readily find them again.) Be sure to read the assigned material more than once.

2. Then, rather than proceeding directly to the writing of the paper, put the materials aside for several days and let them steep in your mind. The advantage of this is that your subconscious mind, if you have truly placed the problem in it, will continue to work on the problem while you are engaged in other activities, indeed even while you are asleep. Repeated investigations into the psychology of creativity have shown that great solutions to scientific and artistic problems frequently occur while the scientist or artist is thinking of something else; the answer pops into consciousness as if out of nowhere but really out of the hidden recesses of the mind, where it has been quietly incubating. Whether this apparent "miracle" happens to you or not, it is probable that you will have more ideas when you sit down to write after a period of incubation than you will if you try to write your paper immediately after reading the materials.

3.   When you are ready to write (allow yourself as long an incubation period as possible, but also allow ample time for writing, looking things up, revising, copying your revision, and correcting your final copy), jot down a list of the ideas you have, select connecting ideas relevant to your problem or to a single acceptable subject, and formulate a thesis statement that will clearly express in one sentence what you wish to say about that subject. Make a rough outline, rearranging your ideas in the order that will best support your thesis. Do they make a coherent case? Have you left out anything necessary to demonstrate your thesis? If so, add it in the proper place. Then begin to write, using your rough outline as a guide. Write this first draft as swiftly as possible, not bothering about sentence structure, grammar, diction, spelling, or verification of sources. Concentrate on putting on paper what is in your head and on your outline without interrupting the flow of thought for any other purpose. If alternative ways of expressing a thought occur to you, put them all down for a later decision. Nothing is more unprofitable than staring at a blank sheet of paper, chewing on a pencil—or staring at a blank monitor, hearing the computer's hum—wondering, "How shall I begin?" Just begin. Get something down on paper. It may look awful, but you can shape and polish it later.

4.   Once you have something on paper, it is much easier to see what should be done with it. The next step is to revise. Does your paper proceed from an introductory paragraph that either defines the problem to be solved or states your thesis, through a series of logically arranged paragraphs that advance toward a solution of the problem or demonstrate your thesis, to a final paragraph that either solves the problem or sums up and restates your thesis but in somewhat different words? If not, analyze the difficulty. Do the paragraphs need reorganization or amplification? Are more examples needed? Does the thesis itself need modification? Make whatever adjustments are necessary for a logical and convincing demonstration. This may require a rewriting of the paper, or it may call only for deletions, insertions, and circlings with arrows showing that a sentence or paragraph should be shifted from one place to another.

Notice that you are expected to organize your paper according to *your* purpose or thesis. This frequently will mean that you will not be moving paragraph-by-paragraph through a story, line-by-line through a poem, or speech-by-speech through a play, following the structure that the author created, but rather ordering your paper in the most effective way to make your point. If you do discuss a work following the order in which its materials are presented, your reader will naturally expect your thesis to include some comment on the structure of the work. The exception to this is a paper devoted entirely to explication, since in that case you will be expected to follow the structure of the poem or the passage you are explicating.

5.   In your revision (if not earlier), make sure that the stance expressed in your statements and judgments is firm and forthright, not weak and wishy-washy. Don't allow your paper to become a sump of phrases like "it seems to me that," "I think [or feel] that," "this word might connote," "this line could mean," and "in my opinion." Your readers know that the content of your paper expresses your thoughts; you need to warn them only when it expresses someone else's. And don't be weak-kneed in expressing your opinion. Even though you are not 100 percent sure of your rightness, write as if you are presenting a truth. Realizing beforehand that you will need to state your interpretations and conclusions confidently should also help you to strive for a greater degree of certainty as you read and interpret.

6.   Having revised your paper for the logic, coherence, confidence, and completeness of its argument, your next step is to revise it for effectiveness of expression. Do this slowly and carefully. How many words can you cut out without loss of meaning? Are your sentences constructed for maximum force and economy? Are they correctly punctuated? Do the pronouns have clear antecedents? Do the verbs agree with their subjects? Are the tenses consistent? Have you chosen the most exact words and spelled them correctly? Now is the time to use the dictionary, to verify quotations and other references, and to supply whatever documentation is needed. A conscientious writer may put a paper through several revisions.

7.   After all is in order, type your final copy, being sure to follow the editorial policies of your instructor for the submission of manuscripts.

8.   Read over your final copy slowly and carefully, and correct any mistakes (omissions, repetitions, typographical errors) you may have made in copying from your draft. This final step—too often omitted due to haste or fatigue—is extremely important and may make the difference between an A or a C paper, or between a C paper and an F.

It is easy to make careless mistakes in copying, but your reader should not be counted on to recognize the difference between a copying error and one of ignorance. Moreover, the smallest error may utterly destroy the sense of what you have written: omission of a "not" may make your paper say exactly the opposite of what you meant it to say. Few instructors require or want you to recopy or retype a whole page of your paper at this stage. It is enough to make neat corrections in ink on the paper itself.

VII. Writing In-Class Essays or Essay Tests

You will often be asked in your literature courses to write essays in class or to write essay tests. The topic or assignment may be given to you in advance so that you can prepare for writing in the classroom, or you may be given the topic in the class when you will do the writing. If you have the topic early enough to prepare, you will want to follow the preparatory suggestions offered for writing a formal out-of-class essay. If the topic for your essay or test is not given out in advance, the following general approaches may be useful.

1.   Analyze the topic. If you are asked to compare characters, or to discuss the implications of an event, or to define a concept and exemplify it, be sure that you do so. Pay attention to key words and such instructions as *compare, show how*, and especially *define*. If asked to compare, be sure you are drawing the comparison and not just giving two summaries; if asked to define, be sure your statement is in the form of a definition and does not just give examples. And be sure that you answer all parts of a question: consider whether it contains two or even three tasks within a single instruction.

2.   For each question, take a little time to jot down a few key words or ideas that seem to be essential in answering the question, to keep yourself from spending all your time on one of the points but leaving out others of equal importance. If you can, decide which points are the *most* important, to be sure to include them.

3.   Try to begin your answer with a topic sentence that includes all the major points you intend to use in your essay. You can often get a good topic sentence out of the question itself: if it says "Show how the frame story of Gordimer's 'Once upon a Time' is related to the main story," you might begin your essay, "The frame story involving a writer awakened by a frightening noise in the night introduces fear, the central topic of the main story, but the kinds of fear are distinctly different."

4. Don't give summaries of actions and plots unless you need to do so. You may need to give a brief summary, for example, in order to support a point; but be sure you are doing that rather than assuming that a summary will *make* a point. An essay test is not usually the place to prove that you have read the assigned material, but that you can *use* your reading.

5. Be specific and concrete. Prove your points with facts—named characters, specific actions, concrete details of plot, and even paraphrases or quotations from speeches if you can recall them (but don't quote unless you have indeed memorized them, and do not place quotation marks around paraphrases).

6. Keep an eye on the clock and budget your time. If you are asked to write two essays with equal time allotments, and you answer only one, then your maximum score can be no more than 50%—no matter how well you answer the one. If you have time, review and revise your writing, making corrections as neatly as you can. When moving whole paragraphs or blocks of writing, be sure your final intention is clear. And take all the time that is allotted to you—if you think you have said everything you can, then spend the time in revision.

VIII. Introducing Quotations

In writing about literature it is often desirable, sometimes imperative, to quote from the work under discussion. Quoted material is needed (1) to provide essential evidence in support of your argument, and (2) to set before your reader any passage that you are going to examine in detail. It will also keep your reader in contact with the text and allow you to use felicitous phrasing from the text to enhance your own presentation. You must, however, be careful not to overquote. If a paper consists of more than 20 percent quotation, it loses the appearance of closely knit argument and seems instead merely a collection of quotations strung together like clothes hung out on a line to dry. Avoid, especially, unnecessary use of long quotations. Readers tend to skip them. Consider carefully whether the quoted material may not be more economically presented by paraphrase, or whether the quotation, if judged necessary, may not be effectively shortened by ellipsis (see Q9 below). Readers faced with a long quotation may reasonably expect you to examine it in some detail; that is, the longer your quotation, the more you should do with it.

As a general rule in analytical writing, quotation should be included for the purpose of supporting or proving a point, not for the purpose of re-creating the experience of a work for your reader. You may assume that your reader has already read the work and does not need to have it summarized—but on the other hand, you should not send your reader back to the book to reread in order to understand what you are referring to. Analysis is the process of demonstrating how the parts work together to create the whole; it must examine these parts in detail and show how they work together. Quoting presents details, and analysis shows how the details do what you say they do. If a quotation seems entirely self-evident to you, so that you have nothing to explain about it, then it is not really worth quoting. If it is self-evident, your reader has already understood all there is to know about it.

As with every other aspect of good writing, the use of quotation is a matter of intelligence and tact. There are no hard-and-fast rules, since the amount of material you quote and the way you explain the significance of your quotations will vary, depending on the work you are writing about and the kind of paper you are writing. In general, however, you should limit direct quotation to words, phrases, or short passages that are so well written and illuminating that to paraphrase them would dilute the force of your argument. Such quotation strengthens your own writing by showing that you have mastered the material and can offer the crucial evidence directly from the text. On the other hand, if the *content* of a passage (especially a long passage) is more significant than the specific language the author uses, then a paraphrase is probably adequate. Either way, be sure that you quote or paraphrase selectively, keeping your own ideas about the work in the foreground; and also be sure that your quotation or paraphrase directly supports your argument.

Principles and Guidelines

There is no legislative body that establishes laws governing the formal aspects of quoting, documenting, or any other aspect of writing. The only "rules" are the editorial policies of the publisher to whom you submit your work. (In the case of papers being written as class assignments, your "publisher" is your instructor.) There is, however, a national organization—the Modern Language Association of America—that is so influential that its policies for its own publications and its recommendations for others are adopted by most journals of literary criticism and scholarship. The instructions below are in general accord with those stated in the *MLA Handbook for Writers of Research Papers*, 6th edition, by Joseph Gibaldi (New York: MLA, 2003). In your course, your instructor will inform you of any editorial policies in effect that differ from those given here or in the *MLA Handbook*. The examples we use here are all drawn from act 5, scene 2 of *Othello*.

Q1.   If the quotation is short (normally not more than four typed lines of prose or not more than two or three lines of verse), put it in quotation marks and introduce it directly into the text of your essay.

> a   Othello, before stabbing himself, reminds his listeners, "I have done the state some service and they know 't."
>
> b   He speaks of himself as "one that loved not wisely but too well" and compares himself to "the base Indian"
>
> c   who "threw a pearl away / Richer than all his tribe" (5.2.338–47).

Q2.   If the quotation is long (normally more than four typed lines of prose or more than three lines of verse), begin it on a new line (and resume the text of your essay on a new line also); double-space it (like the rest of your paper); and indent it twice as far from the left margin (ten spaces or one inch) as you do for a new paragraph indentation (five spaces or one-half inch). If it is verse and has lines either too long or too short to look good with a ten-space indentation, center the quotation between the margins. Whether verse or prose, *do not enclose it in quotation marks.* Since the indentation and the line arrangement both signal a quotation, the use of quotation marks would be redundant.

> In the final scene, convinced that Desdemona is entirely innocent and having decided to kill himself, Othello says to his auditors:
>
> > I pray you, in your letters,
> > When you shall these unlucky deeds relate,
> > Speak of me as I am, nothing extenuate,
> > Nor set down aught in malice. (5.2.339–42)

The two boxed examples illustrate the "run-in" quotation (Q1), where the quotation is "run in" with the writer's own text, and the "set-off" or "block" quotation (Q2), which is separated from the writer's text.

Q3.   In quoting verse, it is extremely important to preserve the line arrangement of the original because the verse line is a rhythmical unit and thus affects meaning. When more than one line of verse is run in, the lines are separated by a virgule (or diagonal slash) with one letter-space on each side, and capitalization after the first line follows that of the original. (See Q1.c above.)

Q4.   In general, sentences containing a quotation are punctuated as they would be if there were no quotation. In Q1.a above, a comma precedes the quoted statement as it would if there were no quotation marks. In Q2, a colon precedes the quoted sentence because it is long and complex. In Q1.b and Q1.c, there is no punctuation at all before the quotation. Do not put punctuation before a quotation unless it is otherwise called for.

Q5.   Your quotation must combine with its introduction to make a grammatically correct sentence. The normal processes of grammar and syntax, like the normal processes of punctuation, are unaffected by quoting. Subjects must agree with their verbs, verbs must be consistent in tense, pronouns must have their normal relation with antecedents.

WRONG	Othello says, "One that loved not wisely but too well" (5.2.343).
	(Incomplete sentence)
RIGHT	Othello speaks of himself as "one that loved not wisely but too well" (5.2.343).

WRONG	Othello asks his auditors to "speak of me as I am" (5.2.341).
	(The pronouns "me" and "I" do not agree in person with their antecedent.)
RIGHT	Othello bids his auditors,
	Speak of me as I am, nothing extenuate,
	Nor set down aught in malice. Then must you speak
	Of one that loved not wisely but too well.
	(5.2.341–43)

WRONG	Othello says that "I have done the state some service" (5.2.338). *(Incorrect mixture of direct and indirect quotation)*
RIGHT	Othello says, "I have done the state some service" (5.2.338).

WRONG	Othello says that he "have done the state some service" (5.2.338). *(Subject and verb of subordinate clause lack agreement.)*
RIGHT	Othello says that he has "done the state some service" (5.2.338).

Q6.   Your introduction must supply enough context to make the quotation meaningful. Be careful that all pronouns in the quotation have clearly identifiable antecedents.

WRONG	In the final speech of the play, Lodovico says, "Look on the tragic loading of this bed: / This is thy work" (5.2.362–63). *(Whose work?)*
RIGHT	In the final speech of the play, Lodovico says to Iago, "Look on the tragic loading of this bed: / This is thy work" (5.2.362–63).

Q7.   The words within your quotation marks must be quoted *exactly* from the original.

WRONG	Though Iago bids his wife to "hold her peace," Emilia declares, "I will speak as liberally as the north wind" (5.2.218–19).

Q8.   It is permissible to insert or supply words in a quotation *if* you enclose them within brackets. Brackets (parentheses with square corners) indicate *your* changes or additions. If parentheses were used, the reader might interpret the enclosed material as the *author's* (as part of what you are quoting). Avoid excessive use of brackets: they make quotations more difficult to read and comprehend. Often paraphrase will serve as well as quotation, particularly if you are not explicitly analyzing the language of a passage.

CORRECT	Though Iago bids his wife to "hold [her] peace," Emilia declares, "I will speak as liberal[ly] as the north [wind]" (5.2.218–19).
BETTER	Though Iago bids his wife to hold her peace, Emilia declares that she will speak as liberally as the north wind.

Notice that a word within brackets can either replace a word in the original (as in the substitution of *her* for "your" above) or be added to explain or complete the original (as with *-ly* and *wind* above). Since a reader understands that brackets signal either substitutions or additions, it is superfluous to include the words for which substitutions have been made.

WRONG	Iago bids his wife to "hold your [her] peace" (5.2.218).

Your sentences, including bracketed words, must read as if there were no brackets:

RIGHT   After Iago's treachery has been completely exposed, Lodovico tells Othello:

You must forsake this room, and go with us.
Your power and your command is taken off.
And Cassio rules in Cyprus. For this slave [Iago],
If there can be any cunning cruelty
That can torment him much and hold him long,
It shall be his. (5.2.329–34)

Q9. It is permissible to omit words from quoted material, but *only if* the omission is indicated. Three *spaced* periods are used to indicate the omission (technically they are called "ellipsis points"). If there are four periods, the first is the normal period at the end of a sentence; the other three indicate the ellipsis.

The statement just concluded, if quoted, might be shortened in the following way: "It is permissible to omit words . . . *if* the omission is indicated. Three *spaced* periods are used to indicate the omission. . . . If there are four periods, the first is the normal period at the end of a sentence."

It is usually not necessary to indicate ellipsis at the beginning or ending of a quotation (the very act of quoting implies that something precedes and follows)—unless what you quote is in some way contradicted by its context, as for example by a "not" preceding the material you quote.

Q10. Single quotation marks are used for quotations within quotations. Thus, if the material you are quoting in a run-in quotation includes a quotation, you should reduce the original double quote marks to single quote marks. (In a block quotation, the quotation marks would remain unchanged.)

In her dying speech, Emilia asks her dead mistress, "Hark, canst thou hear me? I will play the swan, / And die in music. 'Willow, willow, willow' " (5.2.246–47)

Single quotation marks are not used for any other purposes and should not be substituted for double quotes.

Q11. At the conclusion of a run-in quotation, commas and periods are conventionally placed *within* quotation marks; semicolons and colons are placed outside. (The convention is based on appearance, not on logic.) Question marks and exclamation marks are placed inside if they belong to the quoted sentence, outside if they belong to your sentence. (This *is* based on logic.) Special rules apply when the quotation is followed by parenthetical documentation (see PD3 and PD4, page 27). The following examples are all correct:

"I am not valiant neither," says Othello (5.2.242).

Othello says, "I am not valiant neither" (5.2.242).

"Who can control his fate?" cries Othello (5.2.264).

Does Shakespeare endorse Othello's implication that no one "can control his fate"? (5.2.264).

IX. Documentation

Documentation is the process of identifying the sources of materials used in your paper. The sources are of two kinds: primary and secondary. *Primary* sources are materials written *by* the author being studied, and may be confined to the single work being discussed. *Secondary* sources are materials by other writers *about* the author or work being discussed, or materials having some bearing on that work. Documentation serves two purposes: (1) it enables your readers to check any material they may think you have misinterpreted; (2) it enables you to make proper acknowledgment of information, ideas, opinions, or phraseology that are not your own.

It is difficult to overemphasize the second of these purposes. The use of someone else's ideas or insights in your own words, since it does not require quotation marks, makes an even heavier demand for acknowledgment than does quoted material. Although you need not document matters of common knowledge, your use without acknowledgment of material that is uniquely someone else's is not only dishonest but also illegal (plagiarism), and could result in penalties ranging from an F on the paper through expulsion from school to a term in jail, depending on the magnitude of the offense.

Documentation may be given in (1) the text of your essay; (2) parentheses placed within the text of your essay; or (3) a list of Works Cited placed at the end of your essay but keyed to parenthetical references within the essay. The three methods are progressively more formal.

In any case, the type of documentation required in your class will be chosen by your instructor, who may wish to have you practice several methods so that you will learn their use.

1. Textual Documentation

Every literary essay contains textual documentation. A title like "Dramatic Irony in *Oedipus Rex*" identifies the play that will furnish the main materials in the paper. A paragraph beginning "In scene 2 . . ." locates more specifically the source of what follows. An informally documented essay is one that relies on textual documentation exclusively. Perhaps the majority of articles published in newspapers and periodicals with wide circulation are of this kind. Informal documentation works best for essays written on a single short work, without use of secondary sources, for readers without great scholarly expectations. A first-rate paper might be written on Herman Melville's "Bartleby the Scrivener" using only textual documentation. The author's name and the title of the story mentioned somewhere near the beginning of the essay, plus a few phrases like "In the opening paragraph" or "When Bartleby answers the lawyer's advertisement for additional scriveners" or "At the story's conclusion" might provide all the documentation needed for this audience. The action of the story is straightforward enough that the reader can easily locate any detail within it. If the essay is intended for our hypothetical journal published by your literature class (all of whose members are using the same anthology and have presumably read the story), its readers can readily locate the story and its events. But textual documentation, although less appropriate, can also be used for more complex subjects, and can even accommodate secondary sources with phrases like "As Yvor Winters points out in his essay on Melville in *In Defense of Reason*. . . ."

Principles and Guidelines

TD1.   Enclose titles of short stories, articles, one-act plays, and poems (unless they are book-length) in quotation marks; underline titles of full-length plays, magazines, newspapers, and books. Do not underline or put the title of your own paper in quotation marks. The general principle is that titles of separate publications are underlined; titles of selections or parts of books are put within quotation marks. Full-length plays, like *Othello* and *Oedipus Rex*, though often reprinted as part of an anthology, are elsewhere published as separate books and should be underlined. Underlining, in manuscripts, is equivalent to italics in printed matter. Many word-processing programs include italic fonts, so you should check with your instructor for the preferred style.

TD2.   Capitalize the first word and all important words in titles. Do not capitalize articles, prepositions, and conjunctions except when they begin the title ("The Lottery," "Hunters in the Snow," "To the Virgins, to Make Much of Time").

TD3.   When the title above a poem is identical with its first line or a major part of its first line, there is a strong presumption that the poet left the poem untitled and the editor or anthologist has used the first line or part of it to serve as a title. In such a case you may *use* the first line as a title, but should not *refer* to it as a title. For example, you might write that "Dickinson's 'There's a certain slant of Light' is a powerful poem about a depressed psychological state." But you should not write, "Dickinson repeats her title in the first line of 'There's a certain slant of Light' because she wants to emphasize her main point." In using it as a title, capitalize only those words that are capitalized in the first line.

TD4.   Never use page numbers in the body of your discussion because a page is not a structural part of a story, poem, or play. You may refer in your discussions to paragraphs, sections, stanzas, lines, acts, or scenes, as appropriate, but use page numbers *only* in parenthetical documentation where a specific edition of the work has been named.

TD5.   Spell out numerical references when they precede the unit they refer to; use numbers when they follow the unit (the fifth act, or act 5; the second paragraph, or paragraph 2; the fourth line, or line 4; the tenth stanza, or stanza 10). Use the first of these alternative forms sparingly, and only with small numbers. Never write "In the thirty-fourth and thirty-fifth lines . . . ," for to do so is to waste good space and irritate your reader; write "In lines 34–35. . . ."

2. Parenthetical Documentation

Parenthetical documentation makes possible fuller and more precise accrediting without a forbidding apparatus of footnotes or an extensive list of Works Cited. With a full-length play like Tennessee Williams's *The Glass Menagerie*, a phrase like "midway through scene 4" is insufficient to allow the reader to locate the passage readily. This can be done by giving a page number, within parentheses, after the passage cited. But the reader needs to know also what book or edition the page number refers to, so this information must be supplied the first time such a citation is made.

Parenthetical documentation is the method most often required for a paper using only the primary source, or, at most, two or three sources—as, for example, most of the writing assigned in an introductory literature course. The information given in parenthetical documentation should enable your reader to turn easily to the exact source of a quotation or a reference. At the first mention of a work (which may well precede the first quotation from it), full publishing details should be given, but parenthetical documentation should supplement textual documentation; that is, information provided in the text of your essay should not be repeated within the parentheses. For the readers of our hypothetical class journal, the first reference in a paper on Williams's play might look like this:

> In Tennessee Williams's *The Glass Menagerie* (reprinted in Thomas R. Arp and Greg Johnson, *Perrine's Literature: Structure, Sound, and Sense*, 10th ed. [Boston: Wadsworth, 2009] 1153–1204), Tom occasionally addresses the audience directly.

Notice in this entry that brackets are used for parentheses within parentheses. In subsequent references, provided no other source intervenes, only the page number need be given:

> Amanda defines her fear that she and Laura will be deserted when she compares Tom to his father: "He was out all hours without explanation!—Then *left! Good-bye!* And me with the bag to hold" (1171).

If you use more than one source, each must be identified—if referred to a second time, by an abbreviated version of the first citation; normally this will be the author's last name or, if you cite several works by a single author, the work's title or a shortened version of it; in any case, use the shortest identification that will differentiate the source from all others.

Principles and Guidelines

PD1.   For the first citation from a book, give the author's name; the title of the selection; the name of the book from which it is taken; the editor (preceded by the abbreviation *ed.* for "edited by") or the translator (preceded by the abbreviation *trans.* for "translated by"); the edition (designated by a number) if there has been more than one; the city of publication (the first one will suffice if there is more than one); the publisher (this may be given in shortened form, dropping all but the first name); the year of publication or of most recent copyright; and the page number. The following example correctly combines textual with parenthetical documentation:

> In "Home Burial," Frost has a husband complain, "'A man must partly give up being a man/With womenfolk'" (*The Poetry of Robert Frost*, ed. Edward Connery Lathem [New York: Holt, 1969] 52).

PD2.   For your principal primary source, after the first reference, only a page number is required. Since the paragraphs of the stories in this book are numbered, your instructor may prefer you to supply the paragraph number rather than the page number. For long poems, it may be useful to give line numbers or stanza numbers rather than page numbers. If a poem is short, line numbers are unnecessary and should be omitted. For plays in verse, citation by line number (preceded by act and scene number) will usually be more useful than citation by page number—for example, *Othello* (5.2.133).

PD3.   Documentation for run-in quotations always follows the quotation marks. If the quotation ends with a period, move it to the end of the documentation. If it ends with an exclamation point or question mark, leave it, but put a period after the documentation as well. The following examples are from *Othello*:

> "She was false as water" (5.2.133).

> "Alas, what cry is that?" (5.2.116).

PD4.   With block quotations, parenthetical documentation follows the last mark of punctuation without further punctuation after the parentheses:

> Out and alas! That was my lady's voice.
> Help! Help, ho! Help! O lady, speak again!
> Sweet Desdemona! O sweet mistress, speak!
>   (5.2.118–20)

PD5.   Avoid cluttering your paper with excessive documentation. When possible, use one note to cover a series of short quotations. (See example, Q1.) Remember that short poems need no parenthetical documentation at all after the first reference. Do not document well-known sayings or proverbs that you use for stylistic purposes and that form no part of the substance of your investigation (and of course be wary of including hackneyed commonplaces in your formal writing).

PD6. It is customary in a formal paper to document all quoted materials. Do not, however, assume that *only* quotations need documentation. The first purpose of documentation (see page 23) is to allow the reader to check the primary text concerning any major or possibly controversial interpretation. If you declare that the turning point in a long story occurs with an apparently minor event, it may be more important for the reader to have a page number for that event than for any quotation from the story. Judgment must be exercised. You cannot and should not provide page numbers for every detail of a story; but neither should you think that you have necessarily done your duty if you only document all quotations.

3. Documentation by Works Cited

When your assignment involves the use of secondary sources, your instructor may require you to create a list of "Works Cited," to be located at the end of your paper. Any book, article, website, or other source you use or quote from must be referenced parenthetically in the body of your paper so that the reader can easily locate the source in your Works Cited list.

Your first step should be to create the Works Cited list (no longer called a "bibliography") in the format detailed in the *MLA Handbook for Writers of Research Papers* mentioned earlier. Then you should locate each instance in your paper where you have quoted from or paraphrased a source or where your ideas have been formed by reading a source. In order to identify the source, you should normally give the author's last name and the page number to which you are indebted.

For example, let's say you are writing a research paper on Emily Dickinson and one of your sources is David Porter's book *The Art of Emily Dickinson's Early Poetry*. Typically you would cite a reference to the book in this manner: (Porter 141). There are some instances, however, where more information might be needed. David Porter wrote a second book on Dickinson called *Dickinson: The Modern Idiom*. If both of Porter's titles are in your Works Cited list, you need to identify the source parenthetically with an abbreviation of the particular book you are citing. These might read as follows: (Porter, *Early Poetry*, 141) or (Porter,

Modern Idiom, 252). The key principle is that you should keep the parenthetical citations both as brief and as clear as possible, so that the reader will have no trouble finding the particular source you are citing.

Here is another example of when you must provide some information in addition to the last name and page number: you might have two authors on your Works Cited list with the last name of Smith. In this case, you need to be specific about which of the two authors you are quoting. Thus the parenthetical citations might read (Mary Smith 88) or (John Smith 138). Note that the first name is required only when there are two sources on the Works Cited list whose authors have the same last name.

Always keep nearby the *MLA Handbook* when preparing the parenthetical documentation and the Works Cited list. Different types of sources—for instance, a newspaper story or an article from an anthology with multiple editors—require different formats, and examples of all these are located in the *Handbook*.

Here is a sample Works Cited page from a paper on Emily Dickinson. Note that the list should start on a new page and be double-spaced, and note the proper method of abbreviation for publishers' names—for example, "Harvard UP" rather than "Harvard University Press." Also remember to indent after the first line of an entry. When two titles are by the same author, like the entries for David Porter here, the second and any subsequent listings of the author's name should be replaced by a straight line.

Works Cited

Buckingham, Willis J. Emily Dickinson: An Annotated Bibliography. Bloomington: Indiana UP, 1970.

Cameron, Sharon. Lyric Time: Dickinson and the Limits of Genre. Baltimore: Johns Hopkins UP, 1979.

Diehl, Joanne Feit. "Dickinson and Bloom: An Antithetical Reading of Romanticism." Texas Studies in Literature and Language Vol. 23 (1981): 414–41.

Porter, David. The Art of Dickinson's Early Poetry. Cambridge: Harvard UP, 1966.

—————. Dickinson: The Modern Idiom. Cambridge: Harvard UP, 1981.

Wilson, Suzanne M. "Structural Patterns in the Poetry of Emily Dickinson." American Literature Vol. 35 (1963): 53–59.

4. Documentation of Electronic Sources

If your instructor encourages or permits you to do research on the Internet or other electronic sources, you need to be sure that the information is reliable, since much of what is available is uncredited or incorrect. As with all research, the quality of your paper will be directly affected by the quality of its sources.

Electronic sources are cited in your paper as parenthetical references and then included in your list of Works Cited. Examples include personal websites; online books, magazines, and newspapers; and materials obtained from a library subscription service such as Lexis-Nexis or Expanded Academic ASAP. Unlike textual sources, which usually clearly state author, title, date of publication, and publisher, electronic sources may or may not provide such information. Whatever the format, you will need to provide information that enables your reader to access the exact source of your materials.

Your parenthetical citations normally will include the name of the author and a page number. If the source is not paginated, the name of the author may suffice; if it is divided by paragraphs, sections, or screen numbers, after the author's name use the abbreviations "par.," "sec.," or the word "screen" followed by the appropriate number. Here are some examples from a paper on James Joyce's "Araby":

A *scholarly project or information database:*
According to many scholars, James Joyce's "Araby" is best understood if studied at both a realistic and a symbolic level (Gray 1).

A *document within a scholarly project or information database:*
"Araby" was first published in *Irish Homestead* in 1904 ("James Joyce").

An *article in a scholarly journal:*
Most scholars contend that "Araby" is an initiation story recounting a young man's first bitter taste of reality (Coulthard).

An *article in an encyclopedia:*
Joyce often used stream of consciousness, a technique that allows authors to capture their character's complete flow of interior thoughts and feelings ("Stream of Consciousness" par. 2).

Works from online services:
Often lacking courage and honesty, the anti-hero reflects modern man's ambivalence towards traditional social mores ("Anti-hero" sec. 2). Dublin,

and its long history of legal and cultural repression, heavily influenced Joyce's writing ("Dublin" par. 2).

A CD-ROM *nonperiodical publication:*
According to the *Oxford English Dictionary*, the word "araby" is a romantic word for the Middle East ("Araby").

In your list of Works Cited, Internet sources should include both the date of the electronic publication (if available) and the date you accessed the source, and should also include the URL. These are the Works Cited for the examples above:

Gray, Wallace. "James Joyce's Dubliners: An Introduction by Wallace Gray." World Wide Dubliners by James Joyce. Ed. Roger B. Blumberg and Wallace Gray. 1997. Brown U. 5 Sep. 2004 <http://www.mendele.com/WWD/home.html>.

"James Joyce." Contemporary Authors. 2003. Gale Group. 3 Sep. 2004. <http://www.galenet.com/servlet/LitIndex/>.

Coulthard, A.R. "Joyce's 'Araby'." Explicator 52 (1994): 97-100.

Academic Search Premier. EBSCOhost. U Texas Lib. Austin, TX. 6 Sep. 2004 <http://www.lib.utexas.edu/indexes/s-literaturesinenglish. html>.

"Stream of Consciousness." Britannica Online. 2004. Encyclopedia Britannica. 2 Sep. 2004 <http://www.britannica.com>.

"Anti-hero." Encyclopedia. 2004. Infoplease.com. 1 Sep. 2004. Keyword: James Joyce.

"Dublin." Encyclopedia. 2004. Infoplease.com. 6 Sep. 2004. Path: James Joyce; Irish Literary Renaissance; History; Republic of Ireland.

"Araby." The Oxford English Dictionary. 2nd ed. CD-ROM. Oxford: Oxford UP, 2001.

The Internet and other electronic sources provide a great variety of materials, and there are many complex variations on the examples we have given you. For the fullest possible range of correct references, consult the *MLA Handbook*.

X. Stance and Style

In section II, "For Whom Do You Write?" we discussed the assumed audience for your critical writing. Now we must consider the other half of the reader/writer equation. We might ask the parallel question "Who Are You?" except that that would imply that we are asking about your own personal identity. Rather, since we defined your audience hypothetically as members of your class, we need to define "you" in terms of the voice that your audience will expect and appreciate. There are certain conventional expectations that are aroused when we read critical analyses of literature, and the following suggestions may lead you to adopt the stance that your readers will expect. If these sound prescriptive (or if your instructor suggests others), remember that writing about literature is essentially persuasive writing, its purpose being to persuade your readers to agree with your interpretation; the means of persuasion are many, and the writer's stance is only one of them. What we advise here are a few "hints" that have been valuable to students in the past, and may be helpful to you.

S1. *Avoid first-person pronouns.* This injunction warns you away from unnecessarily intruding yourself into your critical statements, with a consequent loss of power and precision. Consider the relative force of these approaches:

POOR	It seems to me that Welty uses the name Phoenix to symbolize endurance and persistence.
GOOD	Welty uses the name Phoenix to symbolize endurance and persistance.
BETTER	The name Phoenix symbolizes endurance and persistence.

The first example dilutes the statement by making it sound tentative and opinionated. It allows your reader to respond, "Why should I consider that seriously, since the writer confesses that it's only a private opinion rather than a fact?" As a critic, you should adopt the stance of the sensitive person who is confident of the accuracy of her or his insights—even when in your heart you may *feel* tentative or unsure. Say it with an air of confidence.

The third example is "better" because it observes the following suggestion:

S2. *Write about the work.* When analyzing a work of literature or some aspect of it, you should be sure that the thesis or topic of a paragraph or essay (and its thesis sentence) focuses on your topic. You will usually not be writing about an *author* but about a *work*, so try to avoid using the author's name as the subject:

POOR	Welty uses the name to symbolize endurance. *(This focuses on* Welty *[subject] and* uses *[verb].)*
GOOD	The name symbolizes endurance. (*Subject,* name; *verb,* symbolizes.)

Try also to avoid the verb *uses*, since your focus is not on a writer using a technical device but on the result of that use; not on an author selecting a device to achieve a purpose but on the result of that selection. The easiest way to get rid of the word *use* or the idea of *using* is simply to delete them:

POOR	Welty uses the name to symbolize . . .
GOOD	The name symbolizes . . .

The revised version cuts the wordiness and is more direct.

S3. *Be cautious about passive constructions.* In analyzing literature, the passive voice presents three potential problems: (1) it may fail to identify its subject and thus (2) may introduce vagueness, and (3) it is often a weak and wordy way to say something that you can say directly and forcefully. It may also be a roundabout way to write about an author rather than a work:

POOR	The plot is structured on Phoenix's journey.
GOOD	Phoenix's journey gives structure to the plot.

S4. *Be cautious about praise.* Praising a work or writer with such adverbs as *cleverly, remarkably, beautifully,* and so forth, is much less effective than presenting and analyzing the details that you find praiseworthy. Your opinion is important, but your reader wants the opportunity to share it—and such labeling doesn't really afford that opportunity.

S5. *Avoid preparatory circumlocution.* Don't write a "table of contents" as an introductory paragraph, and eliminate such phrases as "in order to understand X we must examine Y." Just go ahead and examine Y, and trust your reader to recognize its relevance. Another example: "Z is a significant aspect of the poem" (or, a little worse, "It is interesting to note that Z is a significant aspect"). If Z is significant, just go ahead and say what it signifies; if it is interesting, let what is interesting about it be your topic.

Such circumlocution is sometimes called "treading water," since it is generally only a way of keeping afloat on the page until you get a good idea of the direction you really want to swim. You wouldn't walk into a room and announce, "I am now going to tell you that I'm here," or "I will tell you how interested you'll be to notice that I'm here." You'd say, "Here I am!"

It is perfectly all right to use such space-wasters in preliminary drafts—as ways of keeping your pen or keyboard in action while you are figuring out which way you are going to swim. Just be sure to edit them from your finished text.

S6. *Avoid negative hypotheses.* Negative hypothesis is introduced with an example on page 34, "Proving Your Point." Here's another: "If Phoenix Jackson's grandson had not swallowed lye, she would not have made her trip to the city." But he did, so a critical analysis can neither speculate about what might have happened under other circumstances, nor prove by comparison that what happens is better or worse—there is nothing to compare.

On the other hand, in the process of coming to understand a work (as distinct from presenting the results of that process in your writing), it can be valuable to entertain such hypotheses. For example, in discussing connotation, we suggest that imagining possible alternative words can sharpen your appreciation of the poet's actual choice (see study questions for Dickinson, "There is no Frigate like a Book" [page 674] or Kay, "Pathedy of Manners" [page 677]).

XI. Grammar, Punctuation, and Usage: Common Problems

1. Grammar

G1. In discussing the action of a literary work, rely primarily on the present tense (even when the work itself uses the past), keeping the past, future, and perfect tenses available for prior or subsequent actions; for example,

> When Mrs. May imagines that the bull may have gored Greenleaf and killed him, and thinks of this as the "perfect ending" for a story she has been telling her friends, the situation is highly ironic, for she does not guess that the bull will cause her own death.

G2. Do not let pronouns refer to nouns in the possessive case. Antecedents of pronouns should always hold a strong grammatical position: a possessive is a mere modifier, like an adjective:

WRONG	In Shakespeare's play *Othello,* he writes . . .
	(Antecedent of "he" is in possessive case.)
RIGHT	In his play *Othello,* Shakespeare writes . . .
	(Antecedent of "his" is the subject of the sentence.)

2. Punctuation

P1. The insertion of a parenthetical phrase in your sentence structure (as, for example, in parenthetical documentation) does not alter the normal punctuation of the rest of the sentence. Do not, as the preceding sentence doesn't, place a comma after a parenthetical phrase unless it belonged there before the parenthesis was inserted. You wouldn't write, "Welty's story, touches upon racial issues," so don't include that comma when you insert a parenthesis.

WRONG	Welty's "A Worn Path" (rpt. in Thomas R. Arp and Greg Johnson, *Perrine's Literature: Structure, Sound and Sense,* 10th ed. [Boston: Wadsworth, 2009] 223–230), touches upon racial issues in the early twentieth century. *(Delete the comma after the parenthesis.)*

And it is an inflexible rule of punctuation: never place a comma immediately before a parenthesis.

P2.   Do not set off restrictive appositives with commas. A restrictive appositive is one necessary to the meaning of the sentence; a nonrestrictive appositive could be left out without changing the meaning.

WRONG	In her story, "A Worn Path," Welty . . . *(The title of the story is necessary to the meaning of the statement. As punctuated, the sentence falsely implies that Welty wrote only one story.)*
RIGHT	In her story "A Worn Path," Welty . . .
RIGHT	In her story in chapter 4 of *Perrine's Literature,* "A Worn Path," Welty . . . *(The chapter number identifies the story. The title simply supplies additional information and could be omitted without changing the meaning.)*

P3.   Words used simply as words should be either underlined or italicized or put in quotation marks.

WRONG	The word describing the seal and frame is gold. *(This statement is false; all the words in the story are* *black.)*
RIGHT	The word describing the seal and frame is "gold."

Since the word "gold" is quoted from the story, it has here been put in quotation marks. However, if you list a series of words from various parts of the story, you may prefer underlining for the sake of appearance. Whichever system you choose, be consistent throughout your paper.

P4. Observe the conventions of typed manuscripts: (1) put a space after an abbreviating period (p. 7, not p.7; pp. 10–13, not pp.10–13); (2) use two hyphens to represent a dash--and do not put spaces before and after them.

P5. Observe the standard for forming possessives. For a singular noun, add an apostrophe and an *s* (a student's duty, yesterday's mail, the dress's hemline). For a plural noun, add only an apostrophe (the students' duties, seven days' mail). For proper nouns, the same rules apply (Camus's "The Guest," Chekhov's "The Darling," Ives's play).

Do not confuse the contraction *it's* (it is) with the possessive *its* (belonging to it). *Its* is an exception to the general rule requiring apostrophes for possessives.

3. Usage

U1. Though accepted usage changes with time, and the distinctions between the following pairs of words are fading, many instructors will bless you if you try to preserve them.

convince, persuade   *Convince* pertains to belief (conviction); *persuade* pertains to either action or belief. The following sentences observe the distinction. "In 'Eveline,' Frank persuades Evvie to sail away with him." "In 'Eveline,' Frank seems to have convinced Evvie that she will be happy in Argentina." "Although Eveline has been persuaded to leave, finally she is not convinced that she should go."

describe, define   *Describe* means to delineate the visual appearance of something; *define* means to state the meaning of a word or phrase, or to explain the essential quality of something. Reserve *describe* and *description* for talking about how things look.

disinterested, uninterested   A disinterested judge is one who has no stake or personal interest in the outcome of a case and can therefore judge fairly; an uninterested judge goes to sleep on the bench. A good judge is interested in the case but disinterested in its outcome. An uninterested reader finds reading boring. A disinterested reader? Perhaps one who can enjoy a good book whatever its subject matter.

imply, infer   A writer or speaker implies; a reader or listener infers. An implication is a meaning hinted at but not stated outright. An inference is a conclusion drawn from evidence not complete enough for proof. If you imply that I am a snob, I may infer that you do not like me.

lover, beloved   In older literature, the word *lover* usually meant one of two things—a man who is sexually involved, or any person who feels affection or esteem for another person or persons. In the case of the former, *lover* generally designated the male partner and *beloved* his female partner. In the case of the latter usage, no sexual implications are involved.

quote, quotation   The word *quote* was originally only a verb. Today the use of the terms "single quotes" and "double quotes" in reference to quotation marks is almost universally accepted; but, although the use of "quote" for the noun "quotation" is common in informal speech, it is still unacceptable in formal writing.

Note also that quoting is an act performed by the writer *about* literature, not by the writer *of* literature:

WRONG	Shakespeare's famous quotation "To be or not to be" . . .
RIGHT	The famous quotation from Shakespeare, "To be or not to be" . . .

sensuous, sensual   *Sensuous* normally pertains to the finer senses, *sensual* to the appetites. Good poetry is sensuous: it appeals through the imagination to the senses. A voluptuous woman, an attractive man, or a rich dessert may have a sensual appeal that stirs a desire for possession.

U2.   Some words and phrases to avoid are the following.

center around   A geometrical impossibility. A story may perhaps center *on* a certain feature, but to make it center *around* that feature is to make the hub surround the wheel.

just as   This phrase as a term of comparison is too precise for literary analysis because the adjective *just* means *exactly* or *identical in every possible way*, almost an impossibility when discussing literature. You should take the trouble to establish the points of similarity and dissimilarity between things that you are comparing.

lifestyle   An overused neologism, especially inappropriate for use with older literature, that is too general to mean much. One dictionary defines it as "a person's typical approach to living, including his moral attitudes, preferred entertainment, fads, fashions, etc." If you wish to define someone's moral attitudes, do so; if you try to define a person's "lifestyle," you have a monumental task of all-inclusive definition. It's easier just to avoid it.

society   The problem with this word is that it is too often used only vaguely as a substitute for some more precise idea. Any story, poem, or play that does deal with "society" will clearly indicate a *particular* society—the world of segregated white middle-class people in South Africa's apartheid system in "Once upon a Time," or the paternalistic society of Norway in the late nineteenth century in *A Doll House.* In those cases, once one has defined the particular society and its characteristics, the term might legitimately be used. But don't use it simply to mean "people in general at that time in that place." And it is important to avoid the glib assumption that *society* makes a person do something. A person's desire to be a member of a social group may lead to actions that appear to be imposed or forced, but what makes a person conform is the desire to be or remain a member, not the fact that there are codes of behavior. See Ellen Kay's "Pathedy of Manners" (page 677).

somewhat (also *rather, more or less, as it were, in a manner*).   All of these terms are specifically designed to avoid or evade precision—to create a sense of vagueness. Since clarity and precision are the goals of critical analysis, these terms should be avoided. They also sound wishy-washy, while you should strive to sound firm and convinced.

upset   As an adjective to define an emotional condition, the word is just too vague. Your dictionary will tell you that its synonyms are "distressed, disturbed, agitated, perturbed, irritated," and so forth. All of those terms are more precise than *upset*, and the one that most nearly indicates your meaning should be chosen.

what the author is trying to say is   The implication of this expression is that the author *failed* to say it. You don't say "I'm trying to get to Boston" if you are already there; give the author credit for having got where he or she was going.

Others suggested by your instructor:

_____   _____

_____   _____

_____   _____

_____   _____

XII. Writing Samples

1. Fiction Explication

The Indeterminate Ending in "Where Are You Going, Where Have You Been?"

The concluding paragraphs of Joyce Carol Oates's "Where Are You Going, Where Have You Been?" (rpt. in Thomas R. Arp and Greg Johnson, Perrine's Story and Structure, 12th ed. [Boston: Wadsworth, 2009] 469–483) have frequently been explicated by critics, in part because of their seeming indeterminacy. After her long, frightening encounter with Arnold Friend, the protagonist Connie finally submits to his wishes that she open the back screen door and join him and his sinister friend, Ellie Oscar, in Friend's bizarre golden jalopy. What happens next is unknown, however, for we are left suspended at her moment of submission, and similarly unknown is her true motive for acquiescing to Friend. Has she simply become entranced by Friend's hypnotically suggestive insistence that she submit? Is she acting out of a kind of altruism, in order to spare her family the gruesome fate at which Arnold Friend has hinted if she refuses to comply? These questions give the ending paragraphs an aura of mystery that helps make this story a perennially fascinating one for discussion and debate.

The story, it should be pointed out, has carefully prepared for this ending. Connie, only fifteen, is perhaps a "typical" teenager of her time and place, and we have seen her characterized appealingly as being naïve as well as rebellious, both of which are appropriate to her age. Arnold Friend, by contrast, is a considerably older (around thirty) and threatening, even demonic figure who tries to make himself look younger by the evident use of makeup and hair dye, and by using slang expressions popular with the teenagers with whom he mingles. In the second half of the story, after Friend arrives at Connie's house and begins his drawn-out seduction of her, wanting her to come with him and Oscar in the jalopy, Connie's mood shifts from wise-cracking dismissal and skepticism, to slow-building anxiety, and finally, by the end, to outright terror.

The final couple of pages show Connie in a state of fear so extreme that she becomes detached from her surroundings and unable to resist Friend's persistent suggestions that she open the screen door and come outside to join him. We are told of her "pounding heart" and, in a careful choice of words on the narrator's part, we are told that "She watched herself push the door slowly open" (483). Such descriptions suggest that Connie now suffers a fearfulness so extreme that she is numbed both physically and mentally, and that she no longer quite understands the possible consequences of her acquiescence to Friend.

Rather than using rough language or violent means to attain his ends, Friend continues to cajole her; his self-possession during the final scene is in marked contrast to Connie's zombie-like compliance. He calls her "My sweet little blue-eyed girl"—even though Connie has brown eyes—and speaks in a "half-sung sigh" (483). This seeming gentleness as a prelude to rape and likely murder (the story is based on the case of a serial killer who operated in Arizona and was dubbed by the media "the Pied Piper of Tucson") gives the final scene its powerfully macabre and sinister impact. The scene suggests, above all, Connie's helplessness; she knows that if Friend wanted, he could easily force his way through the screen door, and it is clear that Ellie Oscar is brandishing a gun.

The final paragraph confirms Connie's fatal detachment from her surroundings even as it provides the story's indeterminate ending. Connie fails to recognize the surrounding land she sees outside, even though she's in her own house and has viewed the landscape countless times in the past. Yet the narrator insists that this was "so much land that Connie had never seen before and did not recognize except to know that she was going to it" (483). What will happen next, however, remains outside the story's purview: Oates could have narrated a rape and murder, but the suggestiveness of the indeterminate ending is in fact more powerful, and has given rise to other interpretations of what will happen. For instance, in the film version of the story, entitled Smooth Talk and directed by Joyce Chopra, Arnold Friend takes Connie away in his jalopy, almost certainly for a sexual tryst, but then brings her back home, where she has the brief conversation with her sister, June, which ends the film. One can understand Chopra's predicament, for as Oates later said, the text itself provides an "unfilmable" conclusion because its effect is based on its lack of a visually presented, definite, determined fate for Connie. The director thus chose a "happy ending" rather than the tragic implications most readers take from the text itself.

By withholding a neatly determined closure in the final paragraphs, "Where Are You Going, Where Have You Been?" is in line with contemporary fiction generally, which prefers not to provide tidy narrative packages but privileges a rich suggestiveness and ambiguity that leave much to the reader's imagination. However one imagines Connie's ultimate fate, this story's ending is clearly a triumph of careful and effective storytelling that powerfully haunts the imagination and forces the reader to confront the lack of certainty and determinacy that characterizes life itself.

Comments

While this essay does not provide a line-by-line explication of the passage, its handling of key words and phrases and its limitation to one paragraph for its evidence qualify it as explicative. It summarizes the major event in the story not for purposes of narration but in order to provide necessary background material for explicating the mystery that it presents. Since there is only one documented source, the citations from the story need not use the author's name. The date of publication of the story is not documented since it is known to the hypothetical readers of the essay who have read the introductory footnote in the text.

2. Fiction Analysis

The Function of the Frame Story in "Once upon a Time"

Nadine Gordimer's "Once upon a Time" (rpt. in Thomas R. Arp and Greg Johnson, *Perrine's Literature: Structure, Sound, and Sense*, 10th ed. [Boston: Wadsworth, 2009] 231–236) is a complex, ironic presentation of the results of fear and hatred. This "children's story," so flat in its tone, characterization, and reporting of events, proceeds by gradual steps to show a family systematically barricading itself behind various security devices, the last of which has an effect opposite of what was intended in destroying the child that the parents are trying to protect.

The tale is especially harrowing because of the tone hinted at in the title. This is an easy, casual narration that repeats such standard storybook phrases as "living happily ever after" (233) and identifies its characters only by their functions and relationships, never exploring motivations or revealing the steps of their decision making. The deeper causes for fear are not defined in the tale. All these qualities, and others, establish the tone of fairy tales and other stories for children. In this story, however, no one lives "happily ever after," for in attempting to safeguard themselves, the parents destroy their lives.

But that tale doesn't begin until the ninth paragraph of Gordimer's story. What precedes it is the frame story of a writer who has been asked to write a story for a children's collection, who refuses to contribute, and then is awakened in the night by some noise that frightens her. Her fear first chillingly conjures up a burglar or murderer "moving from room to room, coming up the passage—to [her] door" (231). Then the actual cause of her waking comes to her: deep down, "three thousand feet below" her house, some rock face has fallen in the gold mine beneath (232). She is not in personal danger, then. Yet she cannot return to sleep, so she tells herself "a bedtime story" to relax her mind—and the story is of the family that grows obsessed with security and protection, the awful story of the mutilation of the little boy.

The frame story initially seems little more than an introductory explanation of how the tale came to be written, against the writer's will and purpose. Its details are unrelated to the children's tale—explicitly so, as the writer, despite her knowledge of two recent murders in her neighborhood, and the rational fears that such events arouse, has "no burglar bars, no gun under the pillow" (231), in contrast to the precautions taken in the tale. There is no fairy-tale gold mine in her life, only the knowledge of the mining of gold a half-mile beneath her. So what does this frame have to do with the tale, other than to place the reader within the literal reality of a writer's time and place, from which the imagination journeys to "once upon a time"? Is it more than an ironic contrast in subject and tone?

For answers, we need to consider the writer's time and place as parallels to those of the tale. Both are located in South Africa, both are in the present (even though the phrase "once upon a time" normally signals a long time ago, in a far-off place). The family in the tale, with their burglar bars, walls, alarms, and finally "the razor-bladed coils all round the walls of the house," are like those people in the writer's world who *do* keep guns under their pillows. Like the real people of the writer's neighborhood, the family focuses its fears on the black African populace who surround and outnumber them. On the one hand, in the writer's world, the fears focus on "a casual laborer . . . dismissed without pay" who returns to strangle the watchdogs and knife the man who treated him unfairly (231); on the other hand, in the children's story, the fears focus on the hungry, out-of-work, and begging multitudes who fill and spoil the suburban streets of the fictitious family's neighborhood. In both worlds, unfairness, want, and deprivation mark the blacks, while the whites feel surrounded and threatened by them.

Why cannot the writer return to sleep after she has discovered the innocent cause of her awakening? Because the comforting natural explanation, which removes her from personal danger, is in fact more horrifying than a murderous prowler. She thinks of

> the Chopi and Tsonga migrant miners who might [be] down there, under [her] in the earth at that moment. The stope where the [rock] fall was could have been disused, dripping water from its ruptured veins; or men might now be interred there in the most profound of tombs. (232)

Two possibilities occur to her—one of no harm to men, the other of burial alive—both a consequence of the wage-slavery of "migrant miners" over whose heads (literally and figuratively) the white society lives in "uneasy strain . . . of brick, cement, wood and glass" (232). If no miner has been harmed by *this* rock fall, others have been and will be; and moreover, being killed in that subterranean world of "ruptured veins" is not the only harm that the whites have inflicted on the original inhabitants of the country they control, nor on their own sensitivities and consciences.

The frame story of "Once upon a Time," then, foreshadows the fear, the violence, and the pain of the children's tale, and points to the ultimate cause of its terrible sacrifice of a child—the systematic maltreatment of one race by another and the brutality and self-destruction that are its result.

Comments

This analysis has as its subject an aspect of the story that the writer can fully develop in the limited space. It is written for our hypothetical class journal, as indicated by the way in which the writer refrains from giving a detailed summary of the tale enclosed in the frame (since the audience is known to be familiar with the story), and presents details from the frame narration as they support the writer's argument. It employs some information about the author that is common knowledge to the class (her nationality and her contemporaneity are in the intro-ductory footnote to the story). Quotations are integrated into the writer's sentence structures, and the writer interpolates words within the extended quotation.

3. Poetry Explication

"A Study of Reading Habits"

The first noteworthy feature of Philip Larkin's "A Study of Reading Habits" (rpt. in Thomas R. Arp and Greg Johnson, *Perrine's Literature: Structure, Sound, and Sense*, 10th ed. [Boston: Wadsworth, 2009] 658) is the ironic discrepancy between the formal language of its title and the colloquial, slangy, even vulgar language of the poem itself. The title by its tone implies a formal sociological research paper, possibly one that samples a cross section of a population and draws conclusions about people's reading. The poem presents, instead, the confessions of one man whose attitudes toward reading have progressively deteriorated to the point where books seem to him "a load of crap." The poem's real subject, moreover, is not the man's reading habits but the revelation of life and character they provide.

The poem is patterned in three stanzas having an identical rhyme scheme (*abcbac*) and the same basic meter (iambic trimeter). The stanzaic division of the poem corresponds to the internal structure of meaning, for the three stanzas present the speaker at three stages of his life: as schoolboy, adolescent, and adult. Larkin signals the chronological progression in the first lines of the stanzas by the words "When," "Later," and "now." The "now" is the present out of which the adult speaks, recalling the two earlier periods.

The boy he remembers in stanza 1 was unhappy, both in his home and, even more so, at school. Perhaps small and bullied by bigger boys, probably an indifferent student, making poor grades, and scolded by teachers, he found a partial escape from his miseries through reading. The books he read—tales of action and adventure, pitting good guys against bad guys, full of physical conflict, and ending with victory for the good guy— enabled him to construct a fantasy life in which he identified with the virtuous hero and in his imagination beat up villains twice his size, thus reversing the situations of his real life.

In stanza 2 the speaker recalls his adolescence when his dreams were of sexual rather than muscular prowess. True to the prediction of "ruining [his] eyes" in stanza 1, he had to wear spectacles, which he describes hyperbolically as "inch-thick"—a further detriment to his social life. To compensate for his lack of success with girls, he envisioned himself as a Dracula figure with cloak and fangs, enjoying a series of sexual triumphs. His reading continued to feed his fantasy life, but, instead of identifying with the virtuous hero, he identified with the glamorous, sexually ruthless villain. The poet puns on the word "ripping" (the speaker "had ripping times in the dark"), implying both the British slang meaning of "splendid" and the violence of the rapist who rips the clothes off his victim.

In stanza 3 the speaker, now a young adult, confesses that he no longer reads much. His accumulated experience of personal failure and his long familiarity with his shortcomings have made it impossible for him to identify, even in fantasy, with the strong virtuous hero or the viciously potent villain. He can no longer hide from himself the truth that he resembles more closely the weak secondary characters of the escapist tales he picks up. He recognizes himself in the undependable dude who fails the heroine, or the cowardly storekeeper who knuckles under to the bad guys. He therefore has turned to a more powerful means of escape, one that protects him from dwelling on what he knows about himself: drunkenness. His final words are memorable—so "unpoetical" in a traditional sense, so poetically effective in characterizing this speaker. "Get stewed," he tells himself. "Books are a load of crap."

It would be a serious mistake to identify the speaker of the poem, or his attitudes or his language, with the poet. Poets, unless they are in a cynical or depressed mood, do not think that "books are a load of crap." Philip Larkin, moreover, an English poet and a graduate of Oxford, was for many years until his death a university librarian (Ian Hamilton, ed., *Oxford Companion to Twentieth-Century Poetry* [Oxford: Oxford UP, 1994] 288). "A Study of Reading Habits" is both dramatic and ironic. It presents a first-person speaker who has been unable to cope with the reality of his life in any of its stages and has therefore turned toward various means of escaping it. His confessions reveal a progressive deterioration of values (from good to evil to sodden indifference) and a decline in reading tastes (from adventure stories to prurient sexual novels to none) that reflect his downward slide.

Comments

The title of this paper is enclosed in quotation marks because the writer has used the title of the poem for the title of the paper. The paper uses textual and parenthetical documentation. Line numbers for quotations from the poem are not supplied because the poem is too short to require them: they would serve no useful purpose. Notice that in quoting from stanza 1, the writer has changed the phrase "ruining my eyes" to fit the essay's syntax, but has indicated the alteration by putting the changed word within brackets. The paper is written for an American audience; if it had been written for an English audience, the writer would not have needed to explain that "ripping" is British slang or to have made it a point that the poet is English. The paper is documented for an audience using this textbook. If it were directed toward a wider audience, the writer would want to refer for his text of the poem not to a textbook or anthology but to the volume of Larkin's poetry containing this poem (*Collected Poems*, ed. Anthony Thwaite [London: Faber, 1988] 31). Also, the writer would probably wish to include the poet's name in the title: Philip Larkin's "A Study of Reading Habits" (or) An Examination of Larkin's "A Study of Reading Habits." Since Larkin's nationality and his profession as a librarian are not common knowledge, the paper documents a biographical source where that information is found.

4. Poetry Analysis

Diction in "Pathedy of Manners"

Ellen Kay's "Pathedy of Manners" (rpt. in Thomas R. Arp and Greg Johnson, *Perrine's Literature: Structure, Sound, and Sense*, 10th ed. [Boston: Wadsworth, 2009] 677–678) surprisingly shifts its time focus after the first four stanzas. Until the beginning of the fifth stanza, the poem reads as a biographical narrative summarizing the development of a young woman; stanzas 5–8 shift to the present and future for a summary evaluation of the consequences of the woman's choices and a definition of her life as a "pathedy"—a pathetic drama, in the poet's coined term.

From the fifth stanza to the end, the poem straightforwardly defines the emotional condition of a woman who chooses a course of life that ultimately brings neither contentment nor happiness. She is alone, widowed, and separated from her children, and has begun entertaining the idea of recapturing her missed opportunities. However, as the speaker explains it, she is

> Toying with plots to kill time and re-wed
> Illusions of lost opportunity.

The diction in these lines, along with the structural placement of the word "re-wed" at the end of a line, creates a complexity of feeling that goes beyond what the woman herself is willing to confront. The phrase "Toying with plots"—particularly when it goes on "to kill"—combines the superficiality of idle conjecture with the melodramatic action suggested by "plots to kill." The phrase continues: it's only "time" that she is plotting to kill, and the whole project seems to collapse with the cliché "to kill time." Thus in her daydreaming the woman spans the contrasts contained in the superficiality of "Toying," the violence of "plots to kill," and the blandness of the cliché for escaping boredom—killing time.

The concluding phrase contains the misleading implication that she might escape her boredom by remarrying—misleading, because the object of the verb "re-wed" is not a second husband, but rather her youthful "illusions." One way to "kill [the passage of] time" is to return to one's past, and this seems to be her desire. But the phrase "Illusions of lost opportunity" presents further complications of feeling. One might easily sympathize with a person who thinks her life has gone sour because she was denied the opportunity to achieve "all that wealth and mind had offered her" (as the next stanza says). However, that is not the issue here. The woman wants to recapture "illusions" that she has missed her opportunities. It's an odd idea—the desire to get back to the point where she might pretend that her failures in life amounted to missing out on what was offered to her. She wants to comfort herself with the thought that she was not responsible for her choices.

In order to test this interpretation, we may turn to the kind of language that showed the woman moving from her early brilliance to the emptiness of the present. What we find is a purposeful progression from opportunities to the fulfillment of them—a woman who made her choices based on her desire to seem a part of the well-bred social elite. As the first stanza implies, she was "brilliant" in two ways: she was extraordinarily intelligent and spectacularly resplendent in appearance. She was elected (as a junior) to the honor society for liberal arts graduates, and she was enormously popular on the social scene. All her opportunities seemed to point to a doubly successful life growing out of the doubleness of her brilliance.

But she made a choice: "when she might have thought, [she] conversed instead." She chose the path of social brilliance over the development of her mind. Knowing that she was not "bred to" the appreciation of beautiful, expensive objects, she set out to learn the tastes of those who had been raised among them. The diction again provides a double-edged valuation. As line 5 puts it, "She learned the *cultured jargon*" of the class to which she aspired. "Cultured" denotes both the taste and intellect of the elite and the artificiality of imitations (as in *cultured pearls*, a second meaning later reinforced when she marries a man for his "real . . . pearl cufflinks"). "Jargon" denotes both the specialized language of a particular group and the meaningless gibberish of empty repetition. In their opposed denotations, the two words also bear contrasted connotations, each of them both positive and negative. What was it, then, that the young woman set out to learn—a language that would offer her entry into a higher social class, or empty artificialities? Pathetically, what she attained was both, a dulling of her brilliant mind in order to reach social brilliance.

Such ambivalent and ambiguous diction pervades the first five stanzas, which ironically show the woman deteriorating intellectually while she climbs the social ladder. Lines 5–6 focus this irony by calling her children both "ideal" (by what standards?) and "lonely." In light of her accumulation of the trappings of class, one of her lessons has an even sharper point: she who has become a fraud "learned to tell real Wedgwood [china] from a fraud."

In effect, then, there were no "lost" opportunities, for she seems to have seized every one that she desired. For this unhappy woman, it would be most comforting to suppose that there were some that she missed—but that would be an "illusion." She began in possibilities, "brilliant and adored," but she will end "alone in brilliant circles." She will be surrounded by the glitterati, going round and round with them in meaningless circling. By her own actions, she limited her brilliance to a single denotative meaning—a shiny surface—without the intellectual keenness that she discarded.

Comments

The title of this paper is not enclosed in quotation marks—the writer uses them only to set off the title of the poem. The paper uses textual and parenthetical documentation, but line numbers are not included for each quoted word or phrase because the poem is too short to require them. When the paper does focus on a pair of lines, numbers in the text locate them. Because this is an analysis, the writer does not feel constrained to follow the order of presentation of materials in the poem, but rather organizes the paper according to the progression of its topics. Also as an analysis, the paper does not attempt commentary on every detail, but selects a few from various places in the poem to support the thesis, and analyzes them from the perspective of their denotative and connotative meanings. The paper includes the general meaning of the poem as an orientation for the meaningful presentation of the details, but its main focus is on the quality of language as that contributes to the general meaning.

5. Drama Explication

Iago's First Soliloquy

At the end of the first act of *Othello, the Moor of Venice* (rpt. in Thomas R. Arp and Greg Johnson, *Perrine's Literature: Structure, Sound, and Sense,* 10th ed. [Boston: Wadsworth, 2009], 1273–1366), Iago delivers the first of his several soliloquies (1.3.363–84). In this act Iago has initiated the action by leading Roderigo to announce to her father Desdemona's elopement with Othello. The result is Brabantio's violent accusation of Othello and his estrangement from his daughter. Most of Iago's time on the stage has been with Roderigo, whom he manipulates first in inducing him to cause trouble for Othello and dismay to Brabantio, and then at length in persuading him to pursue Desdemona to Cyprus (having first gathered up as much money as he can).

Iago begins the soliloquy justifying to himself spending time with such a fool as Roderigo:

> Thus do I ever make my fool my purse,
> For I mine own gained knowledge should profane
> If I would time expend with such a snipe
> But for my sport and profit.   (363–66)

That he feels the need to justify such an association is implied by the terms he uses to describe him—"fool," "snipe," and, at the end of the soliloquy, "ass." Roderigo is no fit companion for a man of such "gained knowledge"—that is, a man of Iago's accomplishments and wisdom. We may sense in this not only his contempt for Roderigo, but pride in his own superiority, a pride that is evidenced elsewhere in this soliloquy as well. For example, he alludes to Roderigo at the end when he says that Othello "will be as tenderly led by the nose / As asses are." What he gains from associating with this "snipe" is "sport and profit"—the pleasure of manipulating and controlling someone, and the monetary gain that he plans to receive. How Roderigo's money becomes Iago's we learn much later: he persuades Roderigo to give him cash to purchase jewels to bribe Desdemona into sleeping with the young man, but of course he pockets the money rather than buying her presents (see 4.2.184–88 and 5.1.15–17).

After these four lines of self-justification, Iago turns to Othello. He has already at length told Roderigo of his duplicity in serving the general, and has given a reason for hating him: Othello has promoted Cassio ahead of Iago, thus thwarting his ambitions (1.1.8–65). In the soliloquy, ambition takes a back seat to other motives:

> I hate the Moor,
> And it is thought abroad that 'twixt my sheets
> He's done my office. I know not if 't be true,
> But I for mere suspicion in that kind
> Will do as if for surety.   (366–70)

We must not read this too quickly, or we might miss the disconnect between the first line and what follows. He does not say "I hate the Moor" *because* I suspect him of sleeping with my wife; rather, those appear as two distinct motives, one explicit, the other general and vague. His hatred is almost abstract, a flat statement of loathing without a supporting cause. His jealousy, on the other hand, though based merely on rumors (and vigorously refuted by Emilia later in the play), is at least a humanly comprehensible motivation. And he does not repeat what he has told Roderigo, that he hates Othello because he bypassed him for promotion. Rather, that comes in as he begins to plot his revenge for having been cuckolded:

> [Othello] holds me well,
> The better shall my purpose work on him.
> Cassio's a proper man. Let me see now,
> To get his place, and to plume up my will
> In double knavery.—How, how?—Let's see.— (370–74)

He enjoys the irony that Othello's admiration for him will make the general more vulnerable to his plotting. But even more delightful to him is the proud prospect of "double knavery," taking revenge on Othello and supplanting Cassio as lieutenant, and thus "plum[ing] up [his] will" by creating a two-part plot that will bring down Cassio as well as Othello. What he has against Cassio personally (as opposed to his professional jealousy) is implied in the brief sentence referring to Cassio's handsomeness. As he explains much later, Cassio "hath a daily beauty in his life / That makes me ugly" (5.1.19–20). He is jealous of Cassio's social and physical superiority; Cassio is as far above him in grace as he himself is superior to Roderigo in craft and intelligence. And as he goes on to say, Cassio

> hath a person and a smooth dispose
> To be suspected, framed to make women false.
>
> (377–78)

It is characteristic of Iago that he perceives the virtues in others, and in his thinking twists them into weaknesses or vices. Othello esteems him, which will make him less suspicious; Cassio is handsome, which makes him a threat to women. He goes on in this vein:

> The Moor is of a free and open nature
> That thinks men honest that but seem to be so.
>
> (379–80)

Othello's lack of guile, his own honesty, make him the more vulnerable to a guileful, dishonest schemer like Iago. He concludes the soliloquy with an echo of an earlier remark of his:

> I have 't. It is engendered. Hell and night
> Must bring this monstrous birth to the world's light.
>
> (383–84)

In advising Roderigo to prepare for his trip to Cyprus, Iago tells him, "There are many events in the womb of time which will be delivered" (1.3.353–54). He ends the soliloquy proudly announcing that he himself has impregnated that "womb of time," and the offspring will be "monstrous."

The essence of the plot is expressed with great simplicity:

> After some time, to abuse Othello's ear
> That [Cassio] is too familiar with [Othello's] wife.
>
> (375–76)

This monstrous lie seems to Iago a perfect revenge—and one that inadvertently suggests Iago is not in fact jealous of Othello's sleeping with Emilia, for this perfect circle of wife-for-wife will culminate not in Desdemona's infidelity but in the illusion of it. We may well wonder if Iago does in fact believe in his own wife's disloyalty, since he is plotting a lie about Desdemona's.

There is one more example of Iago's proud self-estimation in the soliloquy, his assertion of his strong will. Of Othello's supposed sexual relations with Emilia, he says,

> I know not if 't be true,
> But I for mere suspicion in that kind
> Will do as if for surety.   (368–70)

His boast is that he is not the sort of man who waits and investigates (a man of "gained knowledge"), but one who will take drastic action even on "mere suspicion." It is a curious assertion, since the subsequent events seem to show the opposite—and may even be contradicted here by his plan to induce Othello's jealousy only "After some time."

What this soliloquy reveals is that Iago takes great pride in his manipulative abilities, that he has a mixture of motives, and that he is not entirely consistent. These are traits that we can follow throughout the play.

Comments

The essay restricts its references to the text of the play, so parenthetical documentation is appropriate. While it explicates the whole soliloquy, it does not simply "read" the speech from beginning to end, but rather structures its argument according to the writer's several points that characterize Iago. Its conclusion draws attention to the importance of the speech in establishing character traits that can be observed in the rest of the play.

6. Drama Analysis

Othello's Race

The subtitle of *Othello* is *The Moor of Venice*, a term that can be misleading if we rely on a standard desk dictionary for a definition of "moor." For example, the *Random House College Dictionary* defines it thus: "Moor . . . a Muslim of mixed Berber and Arab people inhabiting NW Africa." *The American Heritage Dictionary* agrees with that definition and adds an alternative: "one of the Saracens who invaded Spain in the eighth century A.D." But these definitions do not match the facts in the play.

Othello is presented as a Christian, not a Muslim. Iago refers to his "baptism" (2.3.308), and in his first meeting with Desdemona on Cyprus he clearly alludes to their shared belief in Christian salvation (2.1.184–90).

But more importantly, he is throughout the play characterized as a black African. A fuller definition of the word "moor" can be found in the *Oxford English Dictionary*: "in the Middle Ages, and as late as the 17 c., Moors were commonly supposed to be mostly black, . . . and hence the word was often used for 'negro.'"

In the opening scene Roderigo refers to Othello's negroid features by calling him "the thick-lips" (1.1.66), and Iago insultingly refers to his race ("an old black ram," "a Barbary horse" [1.1.88, 110–11]). Brabantio's public denunciation of him in 1.3 is clearly calling him black. He himself in his soliloquy trying to cope with Desdemona's supposed rejection of him in favor of Cassio explicitly calls himself "black" (3.3.264), and later in that scene in referring to Desdemona's supposed sinful lust says:

> Her name, that was as fresh
> As Dian's visage, is now begrimed and black
> As mine own face.   (3.3.387–89)

The play also establishes a racist bigotry about Othello's color, chiefly in the assumptions revealed by Brabantio in his distress over Desdemona's marriage to the Moor. When he learns of it from Iago and Roderigo in 1.1, he declares to Roderigo "would you had had her" (1.1.173), though he has already reminded Roderigo that he had rejected him as a suitor for his daughter—that is, *any* white man would be preferable to a black. This attitude is supported by his assumption that a mixed marriage is "in spite of nature" and "against all rules of nature" (1.3.96, 101). That she is aware of her father's prejudices is implied in Desdemona's defense of her choice: "I saw Othello's visage in his mind" (1.3.249), not in the superficial coloring of his skin. That the racism is not limited to Brabantio is indicated by the nature of the insults mouthed to him by Iago and Roderigo, and even by the goodhearted Duke who tries to patch up the quarrel between Brabantio and Othello. He says to Brabantio, "If virtue no delighted beauty lack / Your son-in-law is far more fair than black" (1.3.286–87), by which he means that Othello's virtues outweigh his unfortunate blackness.

Surprisingly, Othello himself seems partially to subscribe to the racist argument that it is unnatural for whites and blacks to marry. Having been reminded by Iago of Brabantio's warning that Desdemona had deceived her father and therefore could deceive her husband, Othello echoes Brabantio: "nature erring from itself" (3.3.228) he says of his wife's accepting him as a husband.

The importance of correctly identifying Othello's race and recognizing the social attitude toward it is that we can more clearly see the deeply ironic reversal of expectations enacted in this tragedy. By tradition, black was the color ascribed to the devil (hence Emilia's charge that by murdering Desdemona Othello has shown himself to be "a blacker devil" [5.2.130]). Evil itself was popularly referred to as a black deed. Again, the *OED* provides full and useful definitions of two figurative meanings of the word "black":

> Having dark or deadly purposes, malignant; pertaining to or involving death, deadly; baneful, disastrous, sinister . . . Foul, iniquitous, atrocious, horribly wicked.

But in the play, the "horribly wicked" character is Iago, the white Venetian, and Othello is a great, virtuous man who makes the terrible mistake of supposing his wife to be a criminal deserving execution at the hands of "justice." The dramatic effect is overwhelming, as we see the viciousness of white Iago overcoming the virtue of black Othello.

Works Cited

"Black," "Moor." The Compact Edition of the Oxford English Dictionary.
    1971.
"Moor." The American Heritage Dictionary of the English Language.
    1981.

"Moor." <u>The Random House College Dictionary</u>. Rev. ed. 1980.

Shakespeare, William. <u>Othello, the Moor of Venice</u>. Rpt. in Thomas
    R. Arp and Greg Johnson, <u>Perrine's Literature: Structure, Sound,
    and Sense</u>. 10th ed. Boston: Wadsworth, 2009.

Comments

This analysis makes use of references from four sources, three dictionaries and the text of the play, so a Works Cited list is appropriate. The textual material is not presented in the order of its appearance in the play but is instead arranged according to the writer's thesis. The essay proceeds by defining Othello's race, then establishing the prevailing attitudes toward it, and finally reaching a conclusion about the effect of reversing racial expectations.

Fiction

The Elements
of Fiction

Chapter One

Reading the Story

Before embarking on a study of fiction, we might ask a basic question: Why bother to read it? With so many pressing demands on our time, and with so many nonfiction books of history, memoir, politics, and cultural discussion competing for our attention, why should we spend our scarce free time on works of imagination?

The eternal answers to this question are two: enjoyment and understanding.

Since the invention of language, human beings have enjoyed hearing and reading stories, participating in the fictional experiences and adventures of imaginary people. The bedtime stories read to children, the thrillers and romances many adults take to the beach, the historical novels and inspirational fiction elderly people often enjoy—any such harmless activity that helps make life less tedious or stressful surely needs nothing else to recommend it. Simple enjoyment has always been a primary aim and justification for reading fiction.

Fiction whose sole purpose is to entertain, however, requires no serious or intensive study. Unless a story expands or refines our thinking on a significant topic or quickens our sense of life, its value is not appreciably greater than that of video games or crossword puzzles. A story written with serious artistic intentions, on the other hand, must yield not only enjoyment but also understanding.

Like all serious art, fiction of this latter kind provides an imagined experience that yields authentic insights into some significant aspect of life. "Art is a lie," Picasso said, "that leads to the truth," and since a short story is a fiction, and thus a kind of "lie," this statement perfectly sums up the kind of story that provides entertainment but also may become part of an enduring literature. Most fiction, of course, is of the other sort: it has no aspirations beyond merely entertaining the reader. In order to distinguish these types of fiction, therefore, we should begin by defining two broad classifications, employing the terms most often used today: **commercial fiction**, the kind intended solely to entertain; and **literary fiction**, which is the primary subject of this book.

Commercial fiction, such as the legal thrillers and romance novels that make up best-seller lists and the easy-to-read short stories that appear in mass-market magazines, is written and published primarily to make money, and it makes money because it helps large numbers of people escape the tedium and stress of their lives. Literary fiction, however, is written by someone with serious artistic intentions who hopes to broaden, deepen, and sharpen the reader's awareness of life. Commercial fiction takes us *away* from the real world: it helps us temporarily to forget our troubles. Literary fiction plunges us, through the author's imaginative vision and artistic ability, more deeply *into* the real world, enabling us to understand life's difficulties and to empathize with others. While commercial fiction has the reader's immediate plea-sure as its object, literary fiction hopes to provide a complex, lasting aesthetic and intellectual pleasure rather than a simple, escapist diver-sion; its object is to offer pleasure *plus* understanding.

We should immediately make the point that these two categories of fiction are not clear-cut. Not every given story can simply be tossed into one of two bins marked "commercial" or "literary." Rather the two categories suggest opposite ends of a spectrum; some works may fall close to the middle rather than to one end, and genres normally associated with commercial purposes and categories are sometimes used successfully by authors with literary intentions. A famous work such as Harriet Beecher Stowe's *Uncle Tom's Cabin* (1852), for instance, seems to straddle the line between commercial and literary fiction; immensely popular in its own time, it was written with serious intentions but is marred by significant aesthetic flaws. Because it does have some literary quality, however, and because it is an historically important work of its century, it is still read today by general readers and scholars alike. Another example of the occasional blending of our two broad categories is Charlotte Brontë's novel *Jane Eyre* (1847), which adheres to certain conventions of the romance novel and has been commercially successful since it was first published; but it also remains one of the finest literary novels ever written. Similarly, writers such as Charles Dickens, Edith Wharton, and John Updike have published novels that were simultaneously best-sellers and highly praised by literary critics.

The terms "commercial" and "literary" should be applied to novels or stories themselves, not necessarily to their authors. Dickens, in fact, is a good example of a single author capable of writing different works that fall into one category or the other. His novel *Martin Chuzzlewit* (1844), for instance, had disappointing sales when first published but today is greatly admired and discussed by literary scholars; on the other hand, his sentimental but hugely popular *A Christmas Carol* (1843) is essentially a commercial work. More recently, Graham Greene wrote some novels he subtitled "entertainments" as a way of setting them apart from his more serious, literary novels.

It should likewise be stressed that the difference between commercial and literary fiction does not necessarily relate to the absence or presence of a "moral." A story whose incidents and characters are notably shallow may have an unimpeachable moral, while a literary story or novel may have no "moral" at all in the conventional sense; it may choose to dramatize human experience rather than to moralize about it. Similarly, the difference between commercial and literary fiction does not lie in the absence or presence of "facts." An historical romance may be packed with reliable information and yet be pure escape in its depiction of human behavior. Nor does the difference lie in the presence or absence of an element of fantasy. Commercial fiction may have the surface appearance of everyday reality—a police detective novel is a good example—but have little significance beyond the reality depicted; on the other hand, a wildly fanciful tale may impress the reader with a profound and surprising truth. The differences between the two kinds of fiction are deeper and more subtle than any of these distinctions.

Perhaps we can clarify the difference by analogy. Commercial writers are like inventors who devise a contrivance for our diversion. When we push a button, lights flash, bells ring, and cardboard figures move jerkily across a painted horizon. Such writers are full of tricks and surprises: they pull rabbits out of hats, saw beautiful women in two, and juggle brightly colored balls in the air. By contrast, literary writers are more like explorers: they take us out into the midst of life and say, "Look, here is the world in all its complexity." They also take us behind the scenes, where they show us the props and mirrors and seek to dispel the illusions. This is not to say that literary writers are merely reporters. More surely than commercial writers, they carefully shape their materials. But they shape them always with the intent that we may see, feel, and understand them better, not for the primary purpose of furnishing entertainment. In short, any fiction that illuminates some aspect of human life or behavior with genuine originality and power may be called "literary." Such a story presents an insight—whether large or small—into the nature and condition of our existence. It gives us a keener awareness of our humanity within a universe that is sometimes friendly, sometimes hostile. It helps us to understand our world, our neighbors, and ourselves.

The distinctions we have drawn between the two types of fiction are true of both the full-length novel and the short story. Since the latter form is the focus of this text, however, we should stress that the short story, by its very nature, is a more literary genre. Writers hoping to succeed as commercial authors usually work in the novel form, which has proved more popular with large masses of people than has the more refined and subtle art of the story. (A collection of short stories appearing on any best-seller list is an extremely rare event.) Although there are types of commercial short stories that appear in men's adventure magazines, mystery and horror anthologies, and women's publications, the majority of short fiction published today appears in journals that are called, in fact, "literary magazines." Because of their serious intentions and their brevity, short stories provide the ideal vehicle for studying those elements of storytelling common to all literary fiction.

As you read and reread the stories in this book, you will become aware that the term "short story" is a highly elastic one. While brevity is an obvious characteristic of the genre, short narratives have always been part of the human storytelling impulse and have shown an impressive diversity throughout history. Ancient fairy tales and fables were the precursors of the modern short story, but only in the last two centuries has the short story assumed the generally accepted characteristics, outlined in the following chapters, which constitute its uniqueness as a literary genre. Authors of short stories continually seek new ways to exploit the genre, however, using fresh techniques and storytelling approaches in order to advance and refine this sophisticated form. A seemingly conventional tale may veer in an unexpected direction; a fragmented structure may help to mirror the world of one story, while an experimental approach to language or style may distinguish another from anything you have read before. The short story's lack of commercial appeal has, in a way, helped its development as an art form, for writers of short fiction, unconstrained by the demands of the marketplace and a mass audience, are able to give free rein to their creativity and imagination. Noting the "freedom and promise of the form," author Joyce Carol Oates has observed that "radical experimentation, which might be ill-advised in the novel, is well suited for the short story." This outlook, shared by most literary writers, has helped to maintain the status of the short story as a genre capable of ongoing diversity, richness, and self-renewal.

Before beginning a serious study of fiction, you should be aware that literary fiction requires a different way of reading than commercial fiction does. When we take a novel by Stephen King or Danielle Steel to the beach, we do not want to have to think much, if at all, about what we are reading; we simply want a diverting way of passing the time. When we read a literary novel or story, however, we are seeking something different. We expect a serious work to offer some of the immediate pleasures of a well-told story—an original premise and intriguing characters, for instance; but we also know that a literary work may be more demanding of the reader in terms of its language, structure, and complexity. Ultimately we expect to come away from a literary work with an enhanced understanding of life.

In order to appreciate how it operates as a work of narrative art, we should read any piece of literary fiction *at least twice* before we can fully grasp what it has to offer. This is another reason the short story represents an ideal medium for the intensive study of fiction, since its length enables us to reread a story without making unreasonable demands on our time. As you read the stories included in this book, try following this general procedure: (1) read the story the first time simply to enjoy and familiarize yourself with it; (2) read the story a second time, more slowly and deliberately, in the attempt to understand its full artistic significance and achievement. As you proceed through the chapters, learning about plot, characterization, theme, and so forth, you will gradually develop the instincts of a serious reader: it is important to ask, for instance, why a story is constructed in a certain way, or why an author explores a specific character's inner life. With commercial fiction, such questions are irrelevant: there the focus is usually on what happens next, not on the techniques the author uses to tell the story. But with literary fiction, we are willing to invest more time and energy into reading more deliberately, and into careful rereading, because we know the personal rewards will be greater.

When we speak of different kinds of reading, of course, we aren't necessarily talking about different kinds of people. Avid readers may read both commercial and literary fiction at different times, just as an individual may sometimes want fast food, or "junk food," and at other times be willing to invest considerable time and money in savoring a gourmet meal. An English professor may buy a paperback thriller to enjoy during a vacation, while a factory worker might read *Jane Eyre* during her work breaks. So the primary distinction is between kinds of reading, not kinds of readers.

We also bring different expectations to our reading of these two different types of fiction. When we pick up a commercial novel, we come to the book with specific, fixed expectations and will feel frustrated and disappointed unless those expectations are met. Depending on the genre, some of these expectations may include (1) a sympathetic hero or heroine—someone with whom the reader can identify and whose adventures and triumphs the reader can share; (2) a defined plot in which something exciting is always happening and in which there is a strong element of suspense (thus the term "page-turner," often applied to a successful commercial novel); (3) a happy ending that sends the reader away undisturbed and optimistic about life; (4) a general theme, or "message," that affirms widely held, conventional views of the world.

By contrast, when we come to a novel or story with literary intentions, we approach the work with a different set of expectations. For one thing, we are willing to expect the unexpected: instead of adopting a conventional way of storytelling, a literary author may create a unique style or angle of vision in order to express his or her artistic truth; and instead of a happy or conventional ending in which everything is tied together in a neat package, a literary work may end in an unsettling or even unresolved way, forcing us to examine our own expectations about the story itself, about the way the story is told, and about our ingrained, perhaps unconscious way of viewing a certain topic or idea that may have been challenged or changed by what we have read. In short, when reading literary fiction we must keep an open mind and stay receptive to the author's imaginative vision, however different it may be from our own habits of perceiving and "reading" the world.

Reading effectively, it should be stressed, involves evaluating what we read. A typical library contains thousands of books, and any individual has time to read only a fraction of them. To choose our reading wisely, we need to know two things: (1) how to get the most out of any book we read and (2) how to choose the books that will best repay the time and attention we devote to them. The assumption of this book is that a proper selection will include both fiction and nonfiction—nonfiction as an indispensable fund of information and ideas that constitute one kind of knowledge of the world; literary fiction as an equally indispensable source of a different kind of knowledge, a knowledge of experience, felt in the emotions as well as apprehended by the mind. One aim of this book is to help you develop your understanding and judgment in evaluating what you read.

If we approach a literary story in a serious, committed way, after all, we will probably have a more memorable and satisfying reading experience than the kind we derive from commercial fiction, which we tend to forget as soon as we have consumed it. Especially if you are accustomed to reading fiction quickly and without much thought about its possible complex meanings, try to adopt a slower, more thoughtful approach as you read the stories in this and later chapters. Inevitably, as with different commercial works, you will find some of the stories in this book more appealing than others. They have been chosen carefully, however, to help you explore the elements of fiction and to illustrate the diversity of the short-story form as practiced by a broad range of writers. Ideally, a careful reading of these stories will convince you that while nonfiction may be an indispensable fund of information and ideas, and one way of knowing about the world, fiction is an equally indispensable source of knowledge, and a knowledge apprehended not only by your intellect but by your emotions and imagination as well. Through the act of reading a story and sharing an author's imaginative vision, you will gain not only a pleasurable experience but growth in your understanding of the world and of the human condition.

REVIEWING CHAPTER ONE

1. Differentiate between commercial fiction and literary fiction.
2. Explain the purposes of literary fiction.
3. Review the different types of short stories.
4. Describe the best way to read a short story for the purpose of serious study.
5. List the differing expectations we bring to the reading of commercial and literary fiction.

Richard Connell
The Most Dangerous Game

"Off there to the right—somewhere—is a large island," said Whitney. "It's rather a mystery—"

"What island is it?" Rainsford asked.

"The old charts call it 'Ship-Trap Island,'" Whitney replied. "A suggestive name, isn't it? Sailors have a curious dread of the place. I don't know why. Some superstition—"

"Can't see it," remarked Rainsford, trying to peer through the dank tropical night that was palpable as it pressed its thick warm blackness in upon the yacht.

"You've good eyes," said Whitney, with a laugh, "and I've seen you   5
pick off a moose moving in the brown fall bush at four hundred yards, but even you can't see four miles or so through a moonless Caribbean night."

THE MOST DANGEROUS GAME   First published in 1924. Richard Connell (1893–1949) was a native of New York State, graduated from Harvard, and served a year in France with the United States Army during World War I.

"Nor four yards," admitted Rainsford. "Ugh! It's like moist black velvet."

"It will be light in Rio," promised Whitney. "We should make it in a few days. I hope the jaguar guns have come from Purdey's. We should have some good hunting up the Amazon. Great sport, hunting."

"The best sport in the world," agreed Rainsford.

"For the hunter," amended Whitney. "Not for the jaguar."

10   "Don't talk rot, Whitney," said Rainsford. "You're a big-game hunter, not a philosopher. Who cares how a jaguar feels?"

"Perhaps the jaguar does," observed Whitney.

"Bah! They've no understanding."

"Even so, I rather think they understand one thing—fear. The fear of pain and the fear of death."

"Nonsense," laughed Rainsford. "This hot weather is making you soft, Whitney. Be a realist. The world is made up of two classes—the hunters and the huntees. Luckily, you and I are the hunters. Do you think we've passed that island yet?"

15   "I can't tell in the dark. I hope so."

"Why?" asked Rainsford.

"The place has a reputation—a bad one."

"Cannibals?" suggested Rainsford.

"Hardly. Even cannibals wouldn't live in such a God-forsaken place. But it's gotten into sailor lore, somehow. Didn't you notice that the crew's nerves seemed a bit jumpy today?"

20   "They were a bit strange, now you mention it. Even Captain Nielsen—"

"Yes, even that tough-minded old Swede, who'd go up to the devil himself and ask him for a light. Those fishy blue eyes held a look I never saw there before. All I could get out of him was: 'This place has an evil name among seafaring men, sir.' Then he said to me, very gravely: 'Don't you feel anything?'—as if the air about us was actually poisonous. Now, you mustn't laugh when I tell you this—I did feel something like a sudden chill.

"There was no breeze. The sea was as flat as a plate-glass window. We were drawing near the island then. What I felt was a—a mental chill; a sort of sudden dread."

"Pure imagination," said Rainsford. "One superstitious sailor can taint the whole ship's company with his fear."

"Maybe. But sometimes I think sailors have an extra sense that tells them when they are in danger. Sometimes I think evil is a tangible thing—with wave lengths, just as sound and light have. An evil place can, so to speak, broadcast vibrations of evil. Anyhow, I'm glad we're getting out of this zone. Well, I think I'll turn in now, Rainsford."

"I'm not sleepy," said Rainsford. "I'm going to smoke another pipe   25
on the after deck."

"Good night, then, Rainsford. See you at breakfast."

"Right. Good night, Whitney."

There was no sound in the night as Rainsford sat there, but the muffled throb of the engine that drove the yacht swiftly through the darkness, and the swish and ripple of the wash of the propeller.

Rainsford, reclining in a steamer chair, indolently puffed on his favorite brier. The sensuous drowsiness of the night was on him. "It's so dark," he thought, "that I could sleep without closing my eyes; the night would be my eyelids—"

An abrupt sound startled him. Off to the right he heard it, and his   30
ears, expert in such matters, could not be mistaken. Again he heard the sound, and again. Somewhere, off in the blackness, some one had fired a gun three times.

Rainsford sprang up and moved quickly to the rail, mystified. He strained his eyes in the direction from which the reports had come, but it was like trying to see through a blanket. He leaped upon the rail and balanced himself there, to get greater elevation; his pipe, striking a rope, was knocked from his mouth. He lunged for it; a short, hoarse cry came from his lips as he realized he had reached too far and had lost his balance. The cry was pinched off short as the blood-warm waters of the Caribbean Sea closed over his head.

He struggled up to the surface and tried to cry out, but the wash from the speeding yacht slapped him in the face and the salt water in his open mouth made him gag and strangle. Desperately he struck out with strong strokes after the receding lights of the yacht, but he stopped before he had swum fifty feet. A certain cool-headedness had come to him; it was not the first time he had been in a tight place. There was a chance that his cries could be heard by some one aboard the yacht, but that chance was slender, and grew more slender as the yacht raced on. He wrestled himself out of his clothes, and shouted with all his power. The lights of the yacht became faint and ever-vanishing fireflies; then they were blotted out entirely by the night.

Rainsford remembered the shots. They had come from the right, and doggedly he swam in that direction, swimming with slow, deliberate strokes, conserving his strength. For a seemingly endless time he fought the sea. He began to count his strokes; he could do possibly a hundred more and then—

Rainsford heard a sound. It came out of the darkness, a high screaming sound, the sound of an animal in an extremity of anguish and terror.

35   He did not recognize the animal that made the sound; he did not try to; with fresh vitality he swam toward the sound. He heard it again; then it was cut short by another noise, crisp, staccato.

"Pistol shot," muttered Rainsford, swimming on.

Ten minutes of determined effort brought another sound to his ears—the most welcome he had ever heard—the muttering and growling of the sea breaking on a rocky shore. He was almost on the rocks before he saw them; on a night less calm he would have been shattered against them. With his remaining strength he dragged himself from the swirling waters. Jagged crags appeared to jut into the opaqueness; he forced himself upward, hand over hand. Gasping, his hands raw, he reached a flat place at the top. Dense jungle came down to the very edge of the cliffs. What perils that tangle of trees and underbrush might hold for him did not concern Rainsford just then. All he knew was that he was safe from his enemy, the sea, and that utter weariness was on him. He flung himself down at the jungle edge and tumbled headlong into the deepest sleep of his life.

When he opened his eyes he knew from the position of the sun that it was late in the afternoon. Sleep had given him new vigor; a sharp hunger was picking at him. He looked about him, almost cheerfully.

"Where there are pistol shots, there are men. Where there are men, there is food," he thought. But what kind of men, he wondered, in so forbidding a place? An unbroken front of snarled and ragged jungle fringed the shore.

40   He saw no sign of a trail through the closely knit web of weeds and trees; it was easier to go along the shore, and Rainsford floundered along by the water. Not far from where he had landed, he stopped.

Some wounded thing, by the evidence a large animal, had thrashed about in the underbrush; the jungle weeds were crushed down and the moss was lacerated; one patch of weeds was stained crimson. A small, glittering object not far away caught Rainsford's eye and he picked it up. It was an empty cartridge.

"A twenty-two," he remarked. "That's odd. It must have been a fairly large animal too. The hunter had his nerve with him to tackle it with a light gun. It's clear that the brute put up a fight. I suppose the first three shots I heard was when the hunter flushed his quarry and wounded it. The last shot was when he trailed it here and finished it."

He examined the ground closely and found what he had hoped to find—the print of hunting boots. They pointed along the cliff in the direction he had been going. Eagerly he hurried along, now slipping on a rotten log or a loose stone, but making headway; night was beginning to settle down on the island.

Bleak darkness was blacking out the sea and jungle when Rainsford sighted the lights. He came upon them as he turned a crook in the coast line, and his first thought was that he had come upon a village, for there were many lights. But as he forged along he saw to his great astonishment that all the lights were in one enormous building—a lofty structure with pointed towers plunging upward into the gloom. His eyes made out the shadowy outlines of a palatial château; it was set on a high bluff, and on three sides of it cliffs dived down to where the sea licked greedy lips in the shadows.

"Mirage," thought Rainsford. But it was no mirage, he found, when   45 he opened the tall spiked iron gate. The stone steps were real enough; the massive door with a leering gargoyle for a knocker was real enough; yet about it all hung an air of unreality.

He lifted the knocker, and it creaked up stiffly, as if it had never before been used. He let it fall, and it startled him with its booming loudness. He thought he heard steps within; the door remained closed. Again Rainsford lifted the heavy knocker, and let it fall. The door opened then, opened as suddenly as if it were on a spring, and Rainsford stood blinking in the river of glaring gold light that poured out. The first thing Rainsford's eyes discerned was the largest man Rainsford had ever seen—a gigantic creature, solidly made and black-bearded to the waist. In his hand the man held a long-barreled revolver, and he was pointing it straight at Rainsford's heart.

Out of the snarl of beard two small eyes regarded Rainsford.

"Don't be alarmed," said Rainsford, with a smile which he hoped was disarming. "I'm no robber. I fell off a yacht. My name is Sanger Rainsford of New York City."

The menacing look in the eyes did not change. The revolver pointed as rigidly as if the giant were a statue. He gave no sign that he understood Rainsford's words, or that he had even heard them. He was dressed in uniform, a black uniform trimmed with gray astrakhan.

"I'm Sanger Rainsford of New York," Rainsford began again. "I fell   50 off a yacht. I am hungry."

The man's only answer was to raise with his thumb the hammer of his revolver. Then Rainsford saw the man's free hand go to his forehead in a military salute, and he saw him click his heels together and stand at attention. Another man was coming down the broad marble steps, an erect, slender man in evening clothes. He advanced to Rainsford and held out his hand.

In a cultivated voice marked by a slight accent that gave it added precision and deliberateness, he said: "It is a very great pleasure and honor to welcome Mr. Sanger Rainsford, the celebrated hunter, to my home."

Automatically Rainsford shook the man's hand.

"I've read your book about hunting snow leopards in Tibet, you see," explained the man. "I am General Zaroff."

55   Rainsford's first impression was that the man was singularly handsome; his second was that there was an original, almost bizarre quality about the general's face. He was a tall man past middle age, for his hair was a vivid white; but his thick eyebrows and pointed military mustache were as black as the night from which Rainsford had come. His eyes, too, were black and very bright. He had high cheek bones, a sharp-cut nose, a spare, dark face, the face of a man used to giving orders, the face of an aristocrat. Turning to the giant in uniform, the general made a sign. The giant put away his pistol, saluted, withdrew.

"Ivan is an incredibly strong fellow," remarked the general, "but he has the misfortune to be deaf and dumb. A simple fellow, but, I'm afraid, like all his race, a bit of a savage."

"Is he Russian?"

"He is a Cossack," said the general, and his smile showed red lips and pointed teeth. "So am I.

"Come," he said, "we shouldn't be chatting here. We can talk later. Now you want clothes, food, rest. You shall have them. This is a most restful spot."

60   Ivan had reappeared, and the general spoke to him with lips that moved but gave forth no sound.

"Follow Ivan, if you please, Mr. Rainsford," said the general. "I was about to have my dinner when you came. I'll wait for you. You'll find that my clothes will fit you, I think."

It was to a huge, beam-ceilinged bedroom with a canopied bed big enough for six men that Rainsford followed the silent giant. Ivan laid out an evening suit, and Rainsford, as he put it on, noticed that it came from a London tailor who ordinarily cut and sewed for none below the rank of duke.

The dining room to which Ivan conducted him was in many ways remarkable. There was a medieval magnificence about it; it suggested a baronial hall of feudal times with its oaken panels, its high ceiling, its vast refectory table where twoscore men could sit down to eat. About the hall were the mounted heads of many animals—lions, tigers, elephants, moose, bears; larger or more perfect specimens Rainsford had never seen. At the great table the general was sitting, alone.

"You'll have a cocktail, Mr. Rainsford," he suggested. The cocktail was surpassingly good; and, Rainsford noted, the table appointments were of the finest—the linen, the crystal, the silver, the china.

They were eating *borsch*, the rich, red soup with whipped cream so   65
dear to Russian palates. Half apologetically General Zaroff said: "We do our best to preserve the amenities of civilization here. Please forgive any lapses. We are well off the beaten track, you know. Do you think the champagne has suffered from its long ocean trip?"

"Not in the least," declared Rainsford. He was finding the general a most thoughtful and affable host, a true cosmopolite. But there was one small trait of the general's that made Rainsford uncomfortable. Whenever he looked up from his plate he found the general studying him, appraising him narrowly.

"Perhaps," said General Zaroff, "you were surprised that I recognized your name. You see, I read all books on hunting published in English, French, and Russian. I have but one passion in my life, Mr. Rainsford, and it is the hunt."

"You have some wonderful heads here," said Rainsford as he ate a particularly well cooked filet mignon. "That Cape buffalo is the largest I ever saw."

"Oh, that fellow. Yes, he was a monster."

"Did you charge you?"   70

"Hurled me against a tree," said the general. "Fractured my skull. But I got the brute."

"I've always thought," said Rainsford, "that the Cape buffalo is the most dangerous of all big game."

For a moment the general did not reply; he was smiling his curious red-lipped smile. Then he said slowly: "No. You are wrong, sir. The Cape buffalo is not the most dangerous big game." He sipped his wine. "Here in my preserve on this island," he said in the same slow tone, "I hunt more dangerous game."

Rainsford expressed his surprise. "Is there big game on this island?"

The general nodded. "The biggest."   75

"Really?"

"Oh, it isn't here naturally, of course. I have to stock the island."

"What have you imported, general?" Rainsford asked. "Tigers?"

The general smiled. "No," he said. "Hunting tigers ceased to interest me some years ago. I exhausted their possibilities, you see. No thrill left in tigers, no real danger. I live for danger, Mr. Rainsford."

The general took from his pocket a gold cigaret case and offered his   80
guest a long black cigaret with a silver tip; it was perfumed and gave off a smell like incense.

"We will have some capital hunting, you and I," said the general. "I shall be most glad to have your society."

"But what game—" began Rainsford.

"I'll tell you," said the general. "You will be amused, I know. I think I may say, in all modesty, that I have done a rare thing. I have invented a new sensation. May I pour you another glass of port, Mr. Rainsford?"

"Thank you, general."

85   The general filled both glasses, and said: "God makes some men poets. Some He makes kings, some beggars. Me He made a hunter. My hand was made for the trigger, my father said. He was a very rich man with a quarter of a million acres in the Crimea, and he was an ardent sportsman. When I was only five years old he gave me a little gun, specially made in Moscow for me, to shoot sparrows with. When I shot some of his prize turkeys with it, he did not punish me; he complimented me on my marksmanship. I killed my first bear in the Caucasus when I was ten. My whole life has been one prolonged hunt. I went into the army—it was expected of noblemen's sons—and for a time commanded a division of Cossack cavalry, but my real interest was always the hunt. I have hunted every kind of game in every land. It would be impossible for me to tell you how many animals I have killed."

The general puffed at his cigaret.

"After the debacle in Russia I left the country, for it was imprudent for an officer of the Czar to stay there. Many noble Russians lost everything. I, luckily, had invested heavily in American securities, so I shall never have to open a tea room in Monte Carlo or drive a taxi in Paris. Naturally, I continued to hunt—grizzlies in your Rockies, crocodiles in the Ganges, rhinoceroses in East Africa. It was in Africa that the Cape buffalo hit me and laid me up for six months. As soon as I recovered I started for the Amazon to hunt jaguars, for I had heard they were unusually cunning. They weren't." The Cossack sighed. "They were no match at all for a hunter with his wits about him, and a high-powered rifle. I was bitterly disappointed. I was lying in my tent with a splitting headache one night when a terrible thought pushed its way into my mind. Hunting was beginning to bore me! And hunting, remember, had been my life. I have heard that in America businessmen often go to pieces when they give up the business that has been their life."

"Yes, that's so," said Rainsford.

The general smiled. "I had no wish to go to pieces," he said. "I must do something. Now, mine is an analytical mind, Mr. Rainsford. Doubtless that is why I enjoy the problems of the chase."

90   "No doubt, General Zaroff."

"So," continued the general, "I asked myself why the hunt no longer fascinated me. You are much younger than I am, Mr. Rainsford, and have not hunted as much, but you perhaps can guess the answer."

"What was it?"

"Simply this: hunting had ceased to be what you call 'a sporting proposition.' It had become too easy. I always got my quarry. Always. There is no greater bore than perfection."

The general lit a fresh cigaret.

"No animal had a chance with me any more. That is no boast; it is a   95
mathematical certainty. The animal had nothing but his legs and his instinct. Instinct is no match for reason. When I thought of this it was a tragic moment for me, I can tell you."

Rainsford leaned across the table, absorbed in what his host was saying.

"It came to me as an inspiration what I must do," the general went on.

"And that was?"

The general smiled the quiet smile of one who has faced an obstacle and surmounted it with success. "I had to invent a new animal to hunt," he said.

"A new animal? You're joking."   100

"Not at all," said the general. "I never joke about hunting. I needed a new animal. I found one. So I bought this island, built this house, and here I do my hunting. The island is perfect for my purposes—there are jungles with a maze of trails in them, hills, swamps—"

"But the animal, General Zaroff?"

"Oh," said the general, "it supplies me with the most exciting hunting in the world. No other hunting compares with it for an instant. Every day I hunt, and I never grow bored now, for I have a quarry with which I can match my wits."

Rainsford's bewilderment showed in his face.

"I wanted the ideal animal to hunt," explained the general. "So I   105
said: 'What are the attributes of an ideal quarry?' And the answer was, of course: 'it must have courage, cunning, and, above all, it must be able to reason.'"

"But no animal can reason," objected Rainsford.

"My dear fellow," said the general, "there is one that can."

"But you can't mean—" gasped Rainsford.

"And why not?"

"I can't believe you are serious, General Zaroff. This is a grisly joke."   110

"Why should I not be serious? I am speaking of hunting."

"Hunting? Good God, General Zaroff, what you speak of is murder."

The general laughed with entire good nature. He regarded Rainsford quizzically. "I refuse to believe that so modern and civilized a young man as you seem to be harbors romantic ideas about the value of human life. Surely your experiences in the war—"

"Did not make me condone cold-blooded murder," finished Rainsford stiffly.

115   Laughter shook the general. "How extraordinarily droll you are!" he said. "One does not expect nowadays to find a young man of the educated class, even in America, with such a naive, and, if I may say so, mid-Victorian point of view. It's like finding a snuff-box in a limousine. Ah, well, doubtless you had Puritan ancestors. So many Americans appear to have had. I'll wager you'll forget your notions when you go hunting with me. You've a genuine new thrill in store for you, Mr. Rainsford."

"Thank you, I'm a hunter, not a murderer."

"Dear me," said the general, quite unruffled, "again that unpleasant word. But I think I can show you that your scruples are quite ill founded."

"Yes?"

"Life is for the strong, to be lived by the strong, and, if need be, taken by the strong. The weak of the world were put here to give the strong pleasure. I am strong. Why should I not use my gift? If I wish to hunt, why should I not? I hunt the scum of the earth—sailors from tramp ships—lascars, blacks, Chinese, whites, mongrels—a thoroughbred horse or hound is worth more than a score of them."

120   "But they are men," said Rainsford hotly.

"Precisely," said the general. "That is why I use them. It gives me pleasure. They can reason, after a fashion. So they are dangerous."

"But where do you get them?"

The general's left eyelid fluttered down in a wink. "This island is called Ship-Trap," he answered. "Sometimes an angry god of the high seas sends them to me. Sometimes, when Providence is not so kind, I help Providence a bit. Come to the window with me."

Rainsford went to the window and looked out toward the sea.

125   "Watch! Out there!" exclaimed the general, pointing into the night. Rainsford's eyes saw only blackness, and then, as the general pressed a button, far out to sea Rainsford saw the flash of lights.

The general chuckled. "They indicate a channel," he said, "where there's none: giant rocks with razor edges crouch like a sea monster with wide-open jaws. They can crush a ship as easily as I crush this nut." He dropped a walnut on the hardwood floor and brought his heel grinding down on it. "Oh, yes," he said, casually, as if in answer to a question, "I have electricity. We try to be civilized here."

"Civilized? And you shoot down men?"

A trace of anger was in the general's black eyes, but it was there for but a second, and he said, in his most pleasant manner: "Dear me, what a righteous young man you are! I assure you I do not do the thing you suggest. That would be barbarous. I treat these visitors with every consideration. They get plenty of good food and exercise. They get into splendid physical condition. You shall see for yourself tomorrow."

"What do you mean?"

"We'll visit my training school," smiled the general. "It's in the   130
cellar. I have about a dozen pupils down there now. They're from the Spanish bark *San Lucar* that had the bad luck to go on the rocks out there. A very inferior lot, I regret to say. Poor specimens and more accustomed to the deck than to the jungle."

He raised his hand, and Ivan, who served as waiter, brought thick Turkish coffee. Rainsford, with an effort, held his tongue in check.

"It's a game, you see," pursued the general blandly. "I suggest to one of them that we go hunting. I give him a supply of food and an excellent hunting knife. I give him three hours' start. I am to follow, armed only with a pistol of the smallest caliber and range. If my quarry eludes me for three whole days, he wins the game. If I find him"—the general smiled—"he loses."

"Suppose he refuses to be hunted?"

"Oh," said the general, "I give him his option, of course. He need not play that game if he doesn't wish to. If he does not wish to hunt, I turn him over to Ivan. Ivan once had the honor of serving as official knouter to the Great White Czar, and he has his own ideas of sport. Invariably, Mr. Rainsford, invariably they choose the hunt."

"And if they win?"   135

The smile on the general's face widened. "To date I have not lost," he said.

Then he added, hastily: "I don't wish you to think me a braggart, Mr. Rainsford. Many of them afford only the most elementary sort of problem. Occasionally I strike a tartar. One almost did win. I eventually had to use the dogs."

"The dogs?"

"This way, please. I'll show you."

The general steered Rainsford to a window. The lights from the   140
windows sent a flickering illumination that made grotesque patterns on the courtyard below, and Rainsford could see moving about there a

dozen or so huge black shapes; as they turned toward him, their eyes glittered greenly.

"A rather good lot, I think," observed the general. "They are let out at seven every night. If anyone should try to get into my house—or out of it—something extremely regrettable would occur to him." He hummed a snatch of song from the Folies Bergère.

"And now," said the general, "I want to show you my new collection of heads. Will you come with me to the library?"

"I hope," said Rainsford, "that you will excuse me tonight, General Zaroff. I'm really not feeling at all well."

"Ah, indeed?" the general inquired solicitously. "Well, I suppose that's only natural, after your long swim. You need a good, restful night's sleep. Tomorrow you'll feel like a new man, I'll wager. Then we'll hunt, eh? I've one rather promising prospect—"

145   Rainsford was hurrying from the room.

"Sorry you can't go with me tonight," called the general. "I expect rather fair sport—a big, strong black. He looks resourceful—Well, good night, Mr. Rainsford; I hope you have a good night's rest."

The bed was good, and the pajamas of the softest silk, and he was tired in every fiber of his being, but nevertheless Rainsford could not quiet his brain with the opiate of sleep. He lay, eyes wide open. Once he thought he heard stealthy steps in the corridor outside his room. He sought to throw open the door; it would not open. He went to the window and looked out. His room was high up in one of the towers. The lights of the château were out now, and it was dark and silent, but there was a fragment of sallow moon, and by its wan light he could see, dimly, the courtyard; there, weaving in and out in the pattern of shadow, were black, noiseless forms; the hounds heard him at the window and looked up, expectantly, with their green eyes. Rainsford went back to the bed and lay down. By many methods he tried to put himself to sleep. He had achieved a doze when, just as morning began to come, he heard, far off in the jungle, the faint report of a pistol.

General Zaroff did not appear until luncheon. He was dressed faultlessly in the tweeds of a country squire. He was solicitous about the state of Rainsford's health.

"As for me," sighed the general, "I do not feel so well. I am worried, Mr. Rainsford. Last night I detected traces of my old complaint."

150   To Rainsford's questioning glance the general said: "Ennui. Boredom."

Then, taking a second helping of Crêpes Suzette, the general explained: "The hunting was not good last night. The fellow lost his head. He made a straight trail that offered no problems at all. That's the trouble with these sailors; they have dull brains to begin with, and they do not know how to get about in the woods. They do excessively stupid and obvious things. It's most annoying. Will you have another glass of Chablis, Mr. Rainsford?"

"General," said Rainsford firmly, "I wish to leave this island at once."

The general raised his thickets of eyebrows; he seemed hurt. "But, my dear fellow," the general protested, "you've only just come. You've had no hunting—"

"I wish to go today," said Rainsford. He saw the dead black eyes of the general on him, studying him. General Zaroff's face suddenly brightened.

He filled Rainsford's glass with venerable Chablis from a dusty bottle.   155

"Tonight," said the general, "we will hunt—you and I."

Rainsford shook his head. "No, general," he said. "I will not hunt."

The general shrugged his shoulders and delicately ate a hothouse grape. "As you wish, my friend," he said. "The choice rests entirely with you. But may I not venture to suggest that you will find my idea of sport more diverting than Ivan's?"

He nodded toward the corner to where the giant stood, scowling, his thick arms crossed on his hogshead of chest.

"You don't mean—" cried Rainsford.   160

"My dear fellow," said the general, "have I not told you I always mean what I say about hunting? This is really an inspiration. I drink to a foeman worthy of my steel—at last."

The general raised his glass, but Rainsford sat staring at him.

"You'll find this game worth playing," the general said enthusiastically. "Your brain against mine. Your woodcraft against mine. Your strength and stamina against mine. Outdoor chess! And the stake is not without value, eh?"

"And if I win—" began Rainsford huskily.

"I'll cheerfully acknowledge myself defeated if I do not find you by   165
midnight of the third day," said General Zaroff. "My sloop will place you on the mainland near a town."

The general read what Rainsford was thinking.

"Oh, you can trust me," said the Cossack. "I will give you my word as a gentleman and a sportsman. Of course you, in turn, must agree to say nothing of your visit here."

"I'll agree to nothing of the kind," said Rainsford.

"Oh," said the general, "in that case— But why discuss that now? Three days hence we can discuss it over a bottle of Veuve Cliquot, unless—"

170   The general sipped his wine.

Then a businesslike air animated him. "Ivan," he said to Rainsford, "will supply you with hunting clothes, food, a knife. I suggest you wear moccasins; they leave a poorer trail. I suggest too that you avoid the big swamp in the southeast corner of the island. We call it Death Swamp. There's quicksand there. One foolish fellow tried it. The deplorable part of it was that Lazarus followed him. You can imagine my feelings, Mr. Rainsford. I loved Lazarus; he was the finest hound in my pack. Well, I must beg you to excuse me now. I always take a siesta after lunch. You'll hardly have time for a nap, I fear. You'll want to start, no doubt. I shall not follow till dusk. Hunting at night is so much more exciting than by day, don't you think? Au revoir, Mr. Rainsford, au revoir."

General Zaroff, with a deep, courtly bow, strolled from the room.

From another door came Ivan. Under one arm he carried khaki hunting clothes, a haversack of food, a leather sheath containing a long-bladed hunting knife; his right hand rested on a cocked revolver thrust in the crimson sash about his waist. . . .

Rainsford had fought his way through the bush for two hours. "I must keep my nerve. I must keep my nerve," he said through tight teeth.

175   He had not been entirely clear-headed when the château gates snapped shut behind him. His whole idea at first was to put distance between himself and General Zaroff, and, to this end, he had plunged along, spurred on by the sharp rowels of something very like panic. Now he had got a grip on himself, had stopped, and was taking stock of himself and the situation.

He saw that straight flight was futile; inevitably it would bring him face to face with the sea. He was in a picture with a frame of water, and his operations, clearly, must take place within that frame.

"I'll give him a trail to follow," muttered Rainsford, and he struck off from the rude paths he had been following into the trackless wilderness. He executed a series of intricate loops; he doubled on his trail again and again, recalling all the lore of the fox hunt, and all the dodges of the fox. Night found him leg-weary, with hands and face lashed by the branches, on a thickly wooded ridge. He knew it would be insane to blunder on through the dark, even if he had the strength. His need for rest was imperative and he thought: "I have played the fox, now I must play the cat of the fable." A big tree with a thick trunk and outspread branches was nearby, and, taking care to leave not the slightest mark, he climbed up into the crotch, and stretching out on one of the broad limbs, after a fashion, rested. Rest brought him new confidence and almost a feeling of security. Even so zealous a hunter as General Zaroff could not trace him there, he told himself; only the devil himself could follow that complicated trail through the jungle after dark. But, perhaps, the general was a devil—

An apprehensive night crawled slowly by like a wounded snake, and sleep did not visit Rainsford, although the silence of a dead world was on the jungle. Toward morning when a dingy gray was varnishing the sky, the cry of some startled bird focused Rainsford's attention in that direction. Something was coming through the bush, coming slowly, carefully, coming by the same winding way Rainsford had come. He flattened himself down on the limb, and through a screen of leaves almost as thick as tapestry, he watched. The thing that was approaching was a man.

It was General Zaroff. He made his way along with his eyes fixed in utmost concentration on the ground before him. He paused, almost beneath the tree, dropped to his knees and studied the ground. Rainsford's impulse was to hurl himself down like a panther, but he saw the general's right hand held something metallic—a small automatic pistol.

The hunter shook his head several times, as if he were puzzled.   180
Then he straightened up and took from his case one of his black cigarets; its pungent incense-like smoke floated up to Rainsford's nostrils.

Rainsford held his breath. The general's eyes had left the ground and were traveling inch by inch up the tree. Rainsford froze there, every muscle tensed for a spring. But the sharp eyes of the hunter stopped before they reached the limb where Rainsford lay; a smile spread over his brown face. Very deliberately he blew a smoke ring into the air; then he turned his back on the tree and walked carelessly away, back along the trail he had come. The swish of the underbrush against his hunting boots grew fainter and fainter.

The pent-up air burst hotly from Rainsford's lungs. His first thought made him feel sick and numb. The general could follow a trail through the woods at night; he could follow an extremely difficult trail; he must have uncanny powers; only by the merest chance had the Cossack failed to see his quarry.

Rainsford's second thought was even more terrible. It sent a shudder of cold horror through his whole being. Why had the general smiled? Why had he turned back?

Rainsford did not want to believe what his reason told him was true, but the truth was as evident as the sun that had by now pushed through the morning mists. The general was playing with him! The general was saving him for another day's sport! The Cossack was the cat; he was the mouse. Then it was that Rainsford knew the full meaning of terror.

185   "I will not lose my nerve. I will not."

He slid down from the tree, and struck off again into the woods. His face was set and he forced the machinery of his mind to function. Three hundred yards from his hiding place he stopped where a huge dead tree leaned precariously on a smaller, living one. Throwing off his sack of food, Rainsford took his knife from its sheath and began to work with all his energy.

The job was finished at last, and he threw himself down behind a fallen log a hundred feet away. He did not have to wait long. The cat was coming again to play with the mouse.

Following the trail with the sureness of a bloodhound, came General Zaroff. Nothing escaped those searching black eyes, no crushed blade of grass, no bent twig, no mark, no matter how faint, in the moss. So intent was the Cossack on his stalking that he was upon the thing Rainsford had made before he saw it. His foot touched the protruding bough that was the trigger. Even as he touched it, the general sensed his danger and leaped back with the agility of an ape. But he was not quick enough; the dead tree, delicately adjusted to rest on the cut living one, crashed down and struck the general a glancing blow on the shoulder as it fell; but for his alertness, he must have been smashed beneath it. He staggered, but he did not fall; nor did he drop his revolver. He stood there, rubbing his injured shoulder, and Rainsford, with fear again gripping his heart, heard the general's mocking laugh ring through the jungle.

"Rainsford," called the general, "if you are within the sound of my voice, as I suppose you are, let me congratulate you. Not many men know how to make a Malay man-catcher. Luckily, for me, I too have hunted in Malacca. You are proving interesting, Mr. Rainsford. I am going now to have my wound dressed; it's only a slight one. But I shall be back. I shall be back."

190   When the general, nursing his bruised shoulder, had gone, Rainsford took up his flight again. It was flight now, a desperate, hopeless flight, that carried him on for some hours. Dusk came, then darkness, and still he pressed on. The ground grew softer under his moccasins; the vegetation grew ranker, denser; insects bit him savagely. Then, as he stepped forward, his foot sank in the ooze. He tried to wrench it back, but the muck sucked viciously at his foot as if it were a giant leech. With

a violent effort, he tore loose. He knew where he was now. Death Swamp and its quicksand.

His hands were tight closed as if his nerve were something tangible that some one in the darkness was trying to tear from his grip. The softness of the earth had given him an idea. He stepped back from the quicksand a dozen feet or so, and, like some huge prehistoric beaver, he began to dig.

Rainsford had dug himself in in France when a second's delay meant death. That had been a placid pastime compared to his digging now. The pit grew deeper; when it was above his shoulders, he climbed out and from some hard saplings cut stakes and sharpened them to a fine point. These stakes he planted at the bottom of the pit with the points sticking up. With flying fingers he wove a rough carpet of weeds and branches and with it he covered the mouth of the pit. Then, wet with sweat and aching with tiredness, he crouched behind the stump of a lightning-charred tree.

He knew his pursuer was coming; he heard the padding sound of feet on the soft earth, and the night breeze brought him the perfume of the general's cigaret. It seemed to Rainsford that the general was coming with unusual swiftness; he was not feeling his way along, foot by foot. Rainsford, crouching there, could not see the general, nor could he see the pit. He lived a year in a minute. Then he felt an impulse to cry aloud with joy, for he heard the sharp crackle of the breaking branches as the cover of the pit gave way; he heard the sharp scream of pain as the pointed stakes found their mark. He leaped up from his place of concealment. Then he cowered back. Three feet from the pit a man was standing, with an electric torch in his hand.

"You've done well, Rainsford," the voice of the general called. "Your Burmese tiger pit has claimed one of my best dogs. Again you score. I think, Mr. Rainsford, I'll see what you can do against my whole pack. I'm going home for a rest now. Thank you for a most amusing evening."

At daybreak Rainsford, lying near the swamp, was awakened by the sound that made him know that he had new things to learn about fear. It was a distant sound, faint and wavering, but he knew it. It was the baying of a pack of hounds.   195

Rainsford knew he could do one of two things. He could stay where he was and wait. That was suicide. He could flee. That was postponing the inevitable. For a moment he stood there, thinking. An idea that held a wild chance came to him, and, tightening his belt, he headed away from the swamp.

The baying of the hounds drew nearer, then still nearer, nearer, ever nearer. On a ridge Rainsford climbed a tree. Down a watercourse, not a quarter of a mile away, he could see the bush moving. Straining his eyes, he saw the lean figure of General Zaroff; just ahead of him Rainsford made out another figure whose wide shoulders surged through the tall jungle weeds; it was the giant Ivan, and he seemed pulled forward by some unseen force; Rainsford knew that Ivan must be holding the pack in leash.

They would be on him any minute now. His mind worked frantically. He thought of a native trick he had learned in Uganda. He slid down the tree. He caught hold of a springy young sapling and to it he fastened his hunting knife, with the blade pointing down the trail; with a bit of wild grapevine he tied back the sapling. Then he ran for his life. The hounds raised their voices as they hit the fresh scent. Rainsford knew now how an animal at bay feels.

He had to stop to get his breath. The baying of the hounds stopped abruptly, and Rainsford's heart stopped too. They must have reached the knife.

200 He shinnied excitedly up a tree and looked back. His pursuers had stopped. But the hope that was in Rainsford's brain when he climbed died, for he saw in the shallow valley that General Zaroff was still on his feet. But Ivan was not. The knife, driven by the recoil of the springing tree, had not wholly failed.

"Nerve, nerve, nerve!" he panted, as he dashed along. A blue gap showed between the trees dead ahead. Ever nearer drew the hounds. Rainsford forced himself on toward that gap. He reached it. It was the shore of the sea. Across a cove he could see the gloomy gray stone of the château. Twenty feet below him the sea rumbled and hissed. Rainsford hesitated. He heard the hounds. Then he leaped far out into the sea. . . .

When the general and his pack reached the place by the sea, the Cossack stopped. For some minutes he stood regarding the blue-green expanse of water. He shrugged his shoulders. Then he sat down, took a drink of brandy from a silver flask, lit a perfumed cigaret, and hummed a bit from *Madame Butterfly*.

General Zaroff had an exceedingly good dinner in his great paneled dining hall that evening. With it he had a bottle of Pol Roger and half a bottle of Chambertin. Two slight annoyances kept him from perfect enjoyment. One was the thought that it would be difficult to replace Ivan; the other was that his quarry had escaped him; of course the American hadn't played the game—so thought the general as he tasted his after-dinner liqueur. In his library he read, to soothe himself, from the works of Marcus Aurelius. At ten he went up to his bedroom. He was deliciously tired, he said to himself, as he locked himself in. There was a little moonlight, so, before turning on his light, he went to the window and looked down at the courtyard. He could see the great hounds, and he called: "Better luck another time," to them. Then he switched on the light.

A man, who had been hiding in the curtains of the bed, was standing there.

"Rainsford!" screamed the general. "How in God's name did you get   205
here?"

"Swam," said Rainsford. "I found it quicker than walking through the jungle."

The general sucked in his breath and smiled. "I congratulate you," he said. "You have won the game."

Rainsford did not smile. "I am still a beast at bay," he said, in a low, hoarse voice. "Get ready, General Zaroff."

The general made one of his deepest bows. "I see," he said. "Splendid! One of us is to furnish a repast for the hounds. The other will sleep in this very excellent bed. On guard, Rainsford. . . ."

He had never slept in a better bed, Rainsford decided.   210

QUESTIONS

1. Discuss the two meanings of the title.
2. How important is suspense in the story? How is it developed and sustained? What roles do chance and coincidence play in the story?
3. Discuss the characterizations of Rainsford and General Zaroff. Which one is more fully characterized? Are both characters plausible?
4. Why does Connell include the "philosophical" discussion between Whitney and Rainsford at the beginning of the story (paragraphs 7–24)? Does it reveal a personal limitation on Rainsford's part? Does Rainsford undergo any significant changes in the course of the story? Do we come to know him better as the story proceeds?
5. Compare the discussion between Whitney and Rainsford and the after-dinner conversation between Rainsford and Zaroff (paragraphs 68–145). In these discussions, is Rainsford more like Whitney or Zaroff? How does he differ from Zaroff? Does the end of the story resolve that difference?
6. As you read the story, do you develop any expectations of how it might be resolved? Are these expectations met or overturned?
7. As you go through the story a second time, do you find more significance in any of the action or description than you noticed during the first reading?
8. Would you describe this story as commercial fiction or literary fiction? Support your answer.

Tobias Wolff
Hunters in the Snow

Tub had been waiting for an hour in the falling snow. He paced the sidewalk to keep warm and stuck his head out over the curb whenever he saw lights approaching. One driver stopped for him but before Tub could wave the man on he saw the rifle on Tub's back and hit the gas. The tires spun on the ice.

The fall of snow thickened. Tub stood below the overhang of a building. Across the road the clouds whitened just above the rooftops, and the street lights went out. He shifted the rifle strap to his other shoulder. The whiteness seeped up the sky.

A truck slid around the corner, horn blaring, rear end sashaying. Tub moved to the sidewalk and held up his hand. The truck jumped the curb and kept coming, half on the street and half on the sidewalk. It wasn't slowing down at all. Tub stood for a moment, still holding up his hand, then jumped back. His rifle slipped off his shoulder and clattered on the ice, a sandwich fell out of his pocket. He ran for the steps of the building. Another sandwich and a package of cookies tumbled onto the new snow. He made the steps and looked back.

The truck had stopped several feet beyond where Tub had been standing. He picked up his sandwiches and his cookies and slung the rifle and went up to the driver's window. The driver was bent against the steering wheel, slapping his knees and drumming his feet on the floorboards. He looked like a cartoon of a person laughing, except that his eyes watched the man on the seat beside him. "You ought to see yourself," the driver said. "He looks just like a beach ball with a hat on, doesn't he? Doesn't he, Frank?"

5   The man beside him smiled and looked off.

"You almost ran me down," Tub said. "You could've killed me."

"Come on, Tub," said the man beside the driver. "Be mellow. Kenny was just messing around." He opened the door and slid over to the middle of the seat.

HUNTERS IN THE SNOW   First published in 1981. Tobias Wolff (b. 1945), a winner of the PEN/Faulkner award, has also won many awards for his short fiction, including places in the annual *Prize Stories: The O. Henry Awards* and *The Best American Short Stories* volumes. Raised in the state of Washington, he dropped out of high school and worked as an apprentice seaman, then later served as a paratrooper in Vietnam. He then earned degrees at Oxford University and Stanford, where he now teaches.

Tub took the bolt out of his rifle and climbed in beside him. "I waited an hour," he said. "If you meant ten o'clock why didn't you say ten o'clock?"

"Tub, you haven't done anything but complain since we got here," said the man in the middle. "If you want to piss and moan all day you might as well go home and bitch at your kids. Take your pick." When Tub didn't say anything he turned to the driver. "Okay, Kenny, let's hit the road."

Some juvenile delinquents had heaved a brick through the wind- 10 shield on the driver's side, so the cold and snow tunneled right into the cab. The heater didn't work. They covered themselves with a couple of blankets Kenny had brought along and pulled down the muffs on their caps. Tub tried to keep his hands warm by rubbing them under the blanket but Frank made him stop.

They left Spokane and drove deep into the country, running along black lines of fences. The snow let up, but still there was no edge to the land where it met the sky. Nothing moved in the chalky fields. The cold bleached their faces and made the stubble stand out on their cheeks and along their upper lips. They stopped twice for coffee before they got to the woods where Kenny wanted to hunt.

Tub was for trying someplace different; two years in a row they'd been up and down this land and hadn't seen a thing. Frank didn't care one way or the other, he just wanted to get out of the goddamned truck. "Feel that," Frank said, slamming the door. He spread his feet and closed his eyes and leaned his head way back and breathed deeply. "Tune in on that energy."

"Another thing," Kenny said. "This is open land. Most of the land around here is posted."

"I'm cold," Tub said.

Frank breathed out."Stop bitching, Tub. Get centered."   15

"I wasn't bitching."

"Centered," Kenny said. "Next thing you'll be wearing a nightgown, Frank. Selling flowers out at the airport."

"Kenny," Frank said, "you talk too much."

"Okay," Kenny said. "I won't say a word. Like I won't say anything about a certain babysitter."

"What babysitter?" Tub asked.   20

"That's between us," Frank said, looking at Kenny. "That's confi- dential. You keep your mouth shut."

Kenny laughed.

"You're asking for it," Frank said.

"Asking for what?"

25   "You'll see."
            "Hey," Tub said, "are we hunting or what?"
            They started off across the field. Tub had trouble getting through
     the fences. Frank and Kenny could have helped him; they could have
     lifted up on the top wire and stepped on the bottom wire, but they
     didn't. They stood and watched him. There were a lot of fences and Tub
     was puffing when they reached the woods.
            They hunted for over two hours and saw no deer, no tracks, no sign.
     Finally they stopped by the creek to eat. Kenny had several slices of pizza
     and a couple of candy bars; Frank had a sandwich, an apple, two carrots,
     and a square of chocolate; Tub ate one hard-boiled egg and a stick of
     celery.
            "You ask me how I want to die today," Kenny said, "I'll tell you burn
     me at the stake." He turned to Tub. "You still on that diet?" He winked
     at Frank.
30   "What do you think? You think I like hard-boiled eggs?"
            "All I can say is, it's the first diet I ever heard of where you gained
     weight from it."
            "Who said I gained weight?"
            "Oh, pardon me. I take it back. You're just wasting away before my
     very eyes. Isn't he, Frank?"
            Frank had his fingers fanned out, tips against the bark of the stump
     where he'd laid his food. His knuckles were hairy. He wore a heavy
     wedding band and on his right pinky another gold ring with a flat face
     and an "F" in what looked like diamonds. He turned the ring this way
     and that. "Tub," he said, "you haven't seen your own balls in ten years."
35   Kenny doubled over laughing. He took off his hat and slapped his
     leg with it.
            "What am I supposed to do?" Tub said. "It's my glands."

            They left the woods and hunted along the creek. Frank and Kenny
     worked one bank and Tub worked the other, moving upstream. The
     snow was light but the drifts were deep and hard to move through.
     Wherever Tub looked the surface was smooth, undisturbed, and after a
     time he lost interest. He stopped looking for tracks and just tried to
     keep up with Frank and Kenny on the other side. A moment came
     when he realized he hadn't seen them in a long time. The breeze was
     moving from him to them; when it stilled he could sometimes hear
     Kenny laughing but that was all. He quickened his pace, breasting hard
     into the drifts, fighting away the snow with his knees and elbows. He
     heard his heart and felt the flush on his face but he never once
     stopped.

Tub caught up with Frank and Kenny at a bend of the creek. They were standing on a log that stretched from their bank to his. Ice had backed up behind the log. Frozen reeds stuck out, barely nodding when the air moved.

"See anything?" Frank asked.

Tub shook his head.   40

There wasn't much daylight left and they decided to head back toward the road. Frank and Kenny crossed the log and they started downstream, using the trail Tub had broken. Before they had gone very far Kenny stopped. "Look at that," he said, and pointed to some tracks going from the creek back into the woods. Tub's footprints crossed right over them. There on the bank, plain as day, were several mounds of deer sign. "What do you think that is, Tub?" Kenny kicked at it. "Walnuts on vanilla icing?"

"I guess I didn't notice."

Kenny looked at Frank.

"I was lost."

"You were lost. Big deal."   45

They followed the tracks into the woods. The deer had gone over a fence half buried in drifting snow. A no hunting sign was nailed to the top of one of the posts. Frank laughed and said the son of a bitch could read. Kenny wanted to go after him but Frank said no way, the people out here didn't mess around. He thought maybe the farmer who owned the land would let them use it if they asked. Kenny wasn't so sure. Anyway, he figured that by the time they walked to the truck and drove up the road and doubled back it would be almost dark.

"Relax," Frank said. "You can't hurry nature. If we're meant to get that deer, we'll get it. If we're not, we won't."

They started back toward the truck. This part of the woods was mainly pine. The snow was shaded and had a glaze on it. It held up Kenny and Frank but Tub kept falling through. As he kicked forward, the edge of the crust bruised his shins. Kenny and Frank pulled ahead of him, to where he couldn't even hear their voices any more. He sat down on a stump and wiped his face. He ate both the sandwiches and half the cookies, taking his own sweet time. It was dead quiet.

When Tub crossed the last fence into the road the truck started moving. Tub had to run for it and just managed to grab hold of the tailgate and hoist himself into the bed. He lay there, panting. Kenny looked out the rear window and grinned. Tub crawled into the lee of the cab to get out of the freezing wind. He pulled his earflaps low and pushed his chin into the collar of his coat. Someone rapped on the window but Tub would not turn around.

50   He and Frank waited outside while Kenny went into the farmhouse to ask permission. The house was old and paint was curling off the sides. The smoke streamed westward off the top of the chimney, fanning away into a thin gray plume. Above the ridge of the hills another ridge of blue clouds was rising.

"You've got a short memory," Tub said.

"What?" Frank said. He had been staring off.

"I used to stick up for you."

"Okay, so you used to stick up for me. What's eating you?"

55   "You shouldn't have just left me back there like that."

"You're a grown-up, Tub. You can take care of yourself. Anyway, if you think you're the only person with problems I can tell you that you're not."

"Is something bothering you, Frank?"

Frank kicked at a branch poking out of the snow. "Never mind," he said.

"What did Kenny mean about the babysitter?"

60   "Kenny talks too much," Frank said. "You just mind your own business."

Kenny came out of the farmhouse and gave the thumbs-up and they began walking back toward the woods. As they passed the barn a large black hound with a grizzled snout ran out and barked at them. Every time he barked he slid backwards a bit, like a cannon recoiling. Kenny got down on all fours and snarled and barked back at him, and the dog slunk away into the barn, looking over his shoulder and peeing a little as he went.

"That's an old-timer," Frank said. "A real graybeard. Fifteen years if he's a day."

"Too old," Kenny said.

Past the barn they cut off through the fields. The land was unfenced and the crust was freezing up thick and they made good time. They kept to the edge of the field until they picked up the tracks again and followed them into the woods, farther and farther back toward the hills. The trees started to blur with the shadows and the wind rose and needled their faces with the crystals it swept off the glaze. Finally they lost the tracks.

65   Kenny swore and threw down his hat. "This is the worst day of hunting I ever had, bar none." He picked up his hat and brushed off the snow. "This will be the first season since I was fifteen I haven't got my deer."

"It isn't the deer," Frank said. "It's the hunting. There are all these forces out here and you just have to go with them."

"You go with them," Kenny said. "I came out here to get me a deer, not listen to a bunch of hippie bullshit. And if it hadn't been for dimples here I would have, too."

"That's enough," Frank said.

"And you—you're so busy thinking about that little jailbait of yours you wouldn't know a deer if you saw one."

"Drop dead," Frank said, and turned away.   70

Kenny and Tub followed him back across the fields. When they were coming up to the barn Kenny stopped and pointed. "I hate that post," he said. He raised his rifle and fired. It sounded like a dry branch cracking. The post splintered along its right side, up towards the top. "There," Kenny said. "It's dead."

"Knock it off," Frank said, walking ahead.

Kenny looked at Tub. He smiled. "I hate that tree," he said, and fired again. Tub hurried to catch up with Frank. He started to speak but just then the dog ran out of the barn and barked at them. "Easy, boy," Frank said.

"I hate that dog." Kenny was behind them.

"That's enough," Frank said. "You put that gun down."   75

Kenny fired. The bullet went in between the dog's eyes. He sank right down into the snow, his legs splayed out on each side, his yellow eyes open and staring. Except for the blood he looked like a small bearskin rug. The blood ran down the dog's muzzle into the snow.

They all looked at the dog lying there.

"What did he ever do to you?" Tub asked. "He was just barking."

Kenny turned to Tub. "I hate you."

Tub shot from the waist. Kenny jerked backward against the fence   80
and buckled to his knees. He folded his hands across his stomach. "Look," he said. His hands were covered with blood. In the dusk his blood was more blue than red. It seemed to belong to the shadows. It didn't seem out of place. Kenny eased himself onto his back. He sighed several times, deeply. "You shot me," he said.

"I had to," Tub said. He knelt beside Kenny. "Oh God," he said. "Frank. Frank."

Frank hadn't moved since Kenny killed the dog.

"Frank!" Tub shouted.

"I was just kidding around," Kenny said. "It was a joke. Oh!" he said, and arched his back suddenly. "Oh!" he said again, and dug his heels into the snow and pushed himself along on his head for several feet. Then he stopped and lay there, rocking back and forth on his heels and head like a wrestler doing warm-up exercises.

85   Frank roused himself. "Kenny," he said. He bent down and put his gloved hand on Kenny's brow. "You shot him," he said to Tub.

"He made me," Tub said.

"No no no," Kenny said.

Tub was weeping from the eyes and nostrils. His whole face was wet. Frank closed his eyes, then looked down at Kenny again. "Where does it hurt?"

"Everywhere," Kenny said, "just everywhere."

90   "Oh God," Tub said.

"I mean where did it go in?" Frank said.

"Here." Kenny pointed at the wound in his stomach. It was welling slowly with blood.

"You're lucky," Frank said. "It's on the left side. It missed your appendix. If it had hit your appendix you'd really be in the soup." He turned and threw up onto the snow, holding his sides as if to keep warm.

"Are you all right?" Tub said.

95   "There's some aspirin in the truck," Kenny said.

"I'm all right," Frank said.

"We'd better call an ambulance," Tub said.

"Jesus," Frank said. "What are we going to say?"

"Exactly what happened," Tub said. "He was going to shoot me but I shot him first."

100   "No sir!" Kenny said. "I wasn't either!"

Frank patted Kenny on the arm. "Easy does it, partner." He stood. "Let's go."

Tub picked up Kenny's rifle as they walked down toward the farmhouse. "No sense leaving this around," he said. "Kenny might get ideas."

"I can tell you one thing," Frank said. "You've really done it this time. This definitely takes the cake."

They had to knock on the door twice before it was opened by a thin man with lank hair. The room behind him was filled with smoke. He squinted at them. "You get anything?" he asked.

105   "No," Frank said.

"I knew you wouldn't. That's what I told the other fellow."

"We've had an accident."

The man looked past Frank and Tub into the gloom. "Shoot your friend, did you?"

Frank nodded.

110   "I did," Tub said.

"I suppose you want to use the phone."

"If it's okay."

The man in the door looked behind him, then stepped back. Frank and Tub followed him into the house. There was a woman sitting by the stove in the middle of the room. The stove was smoking badly. She looked up and then down again at the child asleep in her lap. Her face was white and damp; strands of hair were pasted across her forehead. Tub warmed his hands over the stove while Frank went into the kitchen to call. The man who had let them in stood at the window, his hands in his pockets.

"My friend shot your dog," Tub said.

The man nodded without turning around. "I should have done it   115
myself. I just couldn't."

"He loved that dog so much," the woman said. The child squirmed and she rocked it.

"You asked him to?" Tub said. "You asked him to shoot your dog?"

"He was old and sick. Couldn't chew his food any more. I would have done it myself but I don't have a gun."

"You couldn't have anyway," the woman said. "Never in a million years."

The man shrugged.   120

Frank came out of the kitchen. "We'll have to take him ourselves. The nearest hospital is fifty miles from here and all their ambulances are out anyway."

The woman knew a shortcut but the directions were complicated and Tub had to write them down. The man told them where they could find some boards to carry Kenny on. He didn't have a flashlight but he said he would leave the porch light on.

It was dark outside. The clouds were low and heavy-looking and the wind blew in shrill gusts. There was a screen loose on the house and it banged slowly and then quickly as the wind rose again. They could hear it all the way to the barn. Frank went for the boards while Tub looked for Kenny, who was not where they had left him. Tub found him farther up the drive, lying on his stomach. "You okay?" Tub said.

"It hurts."

"Frank says it missed your appendix."   125

"I already had my appendix out."

"All right," Frank said, coming up to them. "We'll have you in a nice warm bed before you can say Jack Robinson." He put the two boards on Kenny's right side.

"Just as long as I don't have one of those male nurses," Kenny said.

"Ha ha," Frank said. "That's the spirit. Get ready, set, *over you go*," and he rolled Kenny onto the boards. Kenny screamed and kicked his legs in the air. When he quieted down Frank and Tub lifted the boards and carried him down the drive. Tub had the back end, and with the snow blowing into his face he had trouble with his footing. Also he was tired and the man inside had forgotten to turn the porch light on. Just past the house Tub slipped and threw out his hands to catch himself. The boards fell and Kenny tumbled out and rolled to the bottom of the drive, yelling all the way. He came to rest against the right front wheel of the truck.

130   "You fat moron," Frank said. "You aren't good for diddly."

Tub grabbed Frank by the collar and backed him hard up against the fence. Frank tried to pull his hands away but Tub shook him and snapped his head back and forth and finally Frank gave up.

"What do you know about fat," Tub said. "What do you know about glands." As he spoke he kept shaking Frank. "What do you know about me."

"All right," Frank said.

"No more," Tub said.

135   "All right."

"No more talking to me like that. No more watching. No more laughing."

"Okay, Tub. I promise."

Tub let go of Frank and leaned his forehead against the fence. His arms hung straight at his sides.

"I'm sorry, Tub." Frank touched him on the shoulder. "I'll be down at the truck."

140   Tub stood by the fence for a while and then got the rifles off the porch. Frank had rolled Kenny back onto the boards and they lifted him into the bed of the truck. Frank spread the seat blankets over him. "Warm enough?" he asked.

Kenny nodded.

"Okay. Now how does reverse work on this thing?"

"All the way to the left and up." Kenny sat up as Frank started forward to the cab. "Frank!"

"What?"

145   "If it sticks don't force it."

The truck started right away. "One thing," Frank said, "you've got to hand it to the Japanese. A very ancient, very spiritual culture and they can still make a hell of a truck." He glanced over at Tub. "Look, I'm sorry. I didn't know you felt that way, honest to God I didn't. You should have said something."

"I did."

"When? Name one time."

"A couple of hours ago."

"I guess I wasn't paying attention."   150

"That's true, Frank," Tub said. "You don't pay attention very much."

"Tub," Frank said, "what happened back there, I should have been more sympathetic. I realize that. You were going through a lot. I just want you to know it wasn't your fault. He was asking for it."

"You think so?"

"Absolutely. It was him or you. I would have done the same thing in your shoes, no question."

The wind was blowing into their faces. The snow was a moving   155
white wall in front of their lights; it swirled into the cab through the hole in the windshield and settled on them. Tub clapped his hands and shifted around to stay warm, but it didn't work.

"I'm going to have to stop," Frank said. "I can't feel my fingers."

Up ahead they saw some lights off the road. It was a tavern. Outside in the parking lot there were several jeeps and trucks. A couple of them had deer strapped across their hoods. Frank parked and they went back to Kenny. "How you doing, partner," Frank said.

"I'm cold."

"Well, don't feel like the Lone Ranger. It's worse inside, take my word for it. You should get that windshield fixed."

"Look," Tub said, "he threw the blankets off." They were lying in a   160
heap against the tailgate.

"Now look, Kenny," Frank said, "it's no use whining about being cold if you're not going to try and keep warm. You've got to do your share." He spread the blankets over Kenny and tucked them in at the corners.

"They blew off."

"Hold on to them then."

"Why are we stopping, Frank?"

"Because if me and Tub don't get warmed up we're going to freeze   165
solid and then where will you be?" He punched Kenny lightly in the arm. "So just hold your horses."

The bar was full of men in colored jackets, mostly orange. The waitress brought coffee. "Just what the doctor ordered," Frank said, cradling the steaming cup in his hand. His skin was bone white. "Tub, I've been thinking. What you said about me not paying attention, that's true."

"It's okay."

"No. I really had that coming. I guess I've just been a little too interested in old number one. I've had a lot on my mind. Not that that's any excuse."

"Forget it, Frank. I sort of lost my temper back there. I guess we're all a little on edge."

170 Frank shook his head. "It isn't just that."

"You want to talk about it?"

"Just between us, Tub?"

"Sure, Frank. Just between us."

"Tub, I think I'm going to be leaving Nancy."

175 "Oh, Frank. Oh, Frank." Tub sat back and shook his head.

Frank reached out and laid his hand on Tub's arm. "Tub, have you ever been really in love?"

"Well—"

"I mean *really* in love." He squeezed Tub's wrist. "With your whole being."

"I don't know. When you put it like that, I don't know."

180 "You haven't then. Nothing against you, but you'd know it if you had." Frank let go of Tub's arm. "This isn't just some bit of fluff I'm talking about."

"Who is she, Frank?"

Frank paused. He looked into his empty cup. "Roxanne Brewer."

"Cliff Brewer's kid? The babysitter?"

"You can't just put people into categories like that, Tub. That's why the whole system is wrong. And that's why this country is going to hell in a rowboat."

185 "But she can't be more than—" Tub shook his head.

"Fifteen. She'll be sixteen in May." Frank smiled. "May fourth, three twenty-seven p.m. Hell, Tub, a hundred years ago she'd have been an old maid by that age. Juliet was only thirteen."

"Juliet? Juliet Miller? Jesus, Frank, she doesn't even have breasts. She doesn't even wear a top to her bathing suit. She's still collecting frogs."

"Not Juliet Miller. The real Juliet. Tub, don't you see how you're dividing people up into categories? He's an executive, she's a secretary, he's a truck driver, she's fifteen years old. Tub, this so-called babysitter, this so-called fifteen-year-old has more in her little finger than most of us have in our entire bodies. I can tell you this little lady is something special."

Tub nodded. "I know the kids like her."

190 "She's opened up whole worlds to me that I never knew were there."

"What does Nancy think about all of this?"

"She doesn't know."

"You haven't told her?"

"Not yet. It's not so easy. She's been damned good to me all these years. Then there's the kids to consider." The brightness in Frank's eyes

trembled and he wiped quickly at them with the back of his hand. "I
guess you think I'm a complete bastard."

"No, Frank. I don't think that."   195

"Well, you *ought* to."

"Frank, when you've got a friend it means you've always got someone on your side, no matter what. That's the way I feel about it, anyway."

"You mean that, Tub?"

"Sure I do."

Frank smiled. "You don't know how good it feels to hear you say   200
that."

Kenny had tried to get out of the truck but he hadn't made it. He
was jackknifed over the tailgate, his head hanging above the bumper.
They lifted him back into the bed and covered him again. He was
sweating and his teeth chattered. "It hurts, Frank."

"It wouldn't hurt so much if you just stayed put. Now we're going to
the hospital. Got that? Say it—I'm going to the hospital."

"I'm going to the hospital."

"Again."

"I'm going to the hospital."   205

"Now just keep saying that to yourself and before you know it we'll
be there."

After they had gone a few miles Tub turned to Frank. "I just pulled a
real boner," he said.

"What's that?"

"I left the directions on the table back there."

"That's okay. I remember them pretty well."   210

The snowfall lightened and the clouds began to roll back off the
fields, but it was no warmer and after a time both Frank and Tub were
bitten through and shaking. Frank almost didn't make it around a curve,
and they decided to stop at the next roadhouse.

There was an automatic hand-dryer in the bathroom and they took
turns standing in front of it, opening their jackets and shirts and letting
the jet of hot air breathe across their faces and chests.

"You know," Tub said, "what you told me back there, I appreciate it.
Trusting me."

Frank opened and closed his fingers in front of the nozzle. "The way
I look at it, Tub, no man is an island. You've got to trust someone."

"Frank—"   215

Frank waited.

"When I said that about my glands, that wasn't true. The truth is I
just shovel it in."

"Well, Tub—"

"Day and night, Frank. In the shower. On the freeway." He turned and let the air play over his back. "I've even got stuff in the paper towel machine at work."

220 "There's nothing wrong with your glands at all?" Frank had taken his boots and socks off. He held first his right, then his left foot up to the nozzle.

"No. There never was."

"Does Alice know?" The machine went off and Frank started lacing up his boots.

"Nobody knows. That's the worst of it, Frank. Not the being fat, I never got any big kick out of being thin, but the lying. Having to lead a double life like a spy or a hit man. This sounds strange but I feel sorry for those guys, I really do. I know what they go through. Always having to think about what you say and do. Always feeling like people are watching you, trying to catch you at something. Never able to just be yourself. Like when I make a big deal about only having an orange for breakfast and then scarf all the way to work. Oreos, Mars Bars, Twinkies. Sugar Babies. Snickers." Tub glanced at Frank and looked quickly away. "Pretty disgusting, isn't it?"

"Tub. Tub." Frank shook his head. "Come on." He took Tub's arm and led him into the restaurant half of the bar. "My friend is hungry," he told the waitress. "Bring four orders of pancakes, plenty of butter and syrup."

225 "Frank—"

"Sit down."

When the dishes came Frank carved out slabs of butter and just laid them on the pancakes. Then he emptied the bottle of syrup, moving it back and forth over the plates. He leaned forward on his elbows and rested his chin in one hand. "Go on, Tub."

Tub ate several mouthfuls, then started to wipe his lips. Frank took the napkin away from him. "No wiping," he said. Tub kept at it. The syrup covered his chin; it dripped to a point like a goatee. "Weigh in, Tub," Frank said, pushing another fork across the table. "Get down to business." Tub took the fork in his left hand and lowered his head and started really chowing down. "Clean your plate," Frank said when the pancakes were gone, and Tub lifted each of the four plates and licked it clean. He sat back, trying to catch his breath.

"Beautiful," Frank said. "Are you full?"

230 "I'm full," Tub said. "I've never been so full."

Kenny's blankets were bunched up against the tailgate again.
"They must have blown off," Tub said.

"They're not doing him any good," Frank said. "We might as well get some use out of them."

Kenny mumbled. Tub bent over him. "What? Speak up."

"I'm going to the hospital," Kenny said.   235

"Attaboy," Frank said.

The blankets helped. The wind still got their faces and Frank's hands but it was much better. The fresh snow on the road and the trees sparkled under the beam of the headlight. Squares of light from farmhouse windows fell onto the blue snow in the fields.

"Frank," Tub said after a time, "you know that farmer? He told Kenny to kill the dog."

"You're kidding!" Frank leaned forward, considering. "That Kenny. What a card." He laughed and so did Tub. Tub smiled out the back window. Kenny lay with his arms folded over his stomach, moving his lips at the stars. Right overhead was the Big Dipper, and behind, hanging between Kenny's toes in the direction of the hospital, was the North Star, Pole Star, Help to Sailors. As the truck twisted through the gentle hills the star went back and forth between Kenny's boots, staying always in his sight. "I'm going to the hospital," Kenny said. But he was wrong. They had taken a different turn a long way back.

QUESTIONS

1. Discuss the way Tub is presented in the opening scene. Does your assessment of his character change in the later scenes?

2. How does the cold, hostile environment in the story relate to its meaning?

3. Which is the most sympathetic of the three characters? The story deals, in part, with the power struggle among the characters. Which character is the most powerful? Do the balance of power and alliances between the characters shift as the story proceeds?

4. How do the physical descriptions of the characters help us to understand them? For example, how is Tub's obesity relevant to his character?

5. The second half of the story includes some surprising twists and turns. How are these more meaningful and substantial than the random plot twists one might find in a purely commercial work of fiction?

6. What other elements of the story suggest that this is a serious, literary work rather than merely an entertaining yarn about three hapless hunters?

7. What is the purpose of the scene in which Frank and Tub stop at the tavern for food and coffee, leaving the wounded Kenny in the back of the truck? During their conversation, Frank analyzes his own character and expresses remorse. Are his insights and remorse genuine? Why or why not?

8. The final plot twist comes in the last two sentences of the story. Here the narrator speaks directly to the reader, giving us information the characters don't know. How is this an appropriate conclusion to the story? What final statement is being made about the characters?

Understanding and Evaluating Fiction

Most of the stories in this book are accompanied by study questions that are by no means exhaustive. The following is a list of questions that you may apply to any story. You may be unable to answer many of them until you have read further in the book.

Plot and Structure

1. Who is the protagonist of the story? What are the conflicts? Are they physical, intellectual, moral, or emotional? Is the main conflict between sharply differentiated good and evil, or is it more subtle and complex?

2. Does the plot have unity? Are all the episodes relevant to the total meaning or effect of the story? Does each incident grow logically out of the preceding incident and lead naturally to the next? Is the ending happy, unhappy, or indeterminate? Is it fairly achieved?

3. What use does the story make of chance and coincidence? Are these occurrences used to initiate, to complicate, or to resolve the story? How improbable are they?

4. How is suspense created in the story? Is the interest confined to "What happens next?" or are larger concerns involved? Can you find examples of mystery? Of dilemma?

5. What use does the story make of surprise? Are the surprises achieved fairly? Do they serve a significant purpose? Do they divert the reader's attention from weaknesses in the story?

6. To what extent is this a "formula" story?

Characterization

7. What means does the author use to reveal character? Are the characters sufficiently dramatized? What use is made of character contrasts?

8. Are the characters consistent in their actions? Adequately motivated? Plausible? Does the author successfully avoid stock characters?

9. Is each character fully enough developed to justify its role in the story? Are the main characters round or flat?

10. Is any of the characters a developing character? If so, is the change a large or a small one? Is it a plausible change for such a person? Is it sufficiently motivated? Is it given sufficient time?

Theme

11. Does the story have a theme? What is it? Is it implicit or explicit?
12. Does the theme reinforce or oppose popular notions of life? Does it furnish a new insight or refresh or deepen an old one?

Point of View

13. What point of view does the story use? Is it consistent in its use of this point of view? If shifts are made, are they justified?
14. What advantages has the chosen point of view? Does it furnish any clues as to the purpose of the story?
15. If the point of view is that of one of the characters, does this character have any limitations that affect her or his interpretation of events or persons?
16. Does the author use point of view primarily to reveal or conceal? Is important information known to the focal character ever unfairly withheld?

Symbol, Allegory, and Fantasy

17. Does the story make use of symbols? If so, do the symbols carry or merely reinforce the meaning of the story?
18. Does the story make use of symbolic settings?
19. Does the story employ allegory? Is the use of allegory clear-cut or ambiguous?
20. Does the story contain any elements of fantasy? If so, what is the initial assumption? Does the story operate logically from this assumption?
21. Is the fantasy employed for its own sake or to express some human truth? If the latter, what truth?

Humor and Irony

22. If the story employs humor, is the humor present merely for its own sake or does it contribute to the meaning?
23. Does the story anywhere use irony of situation? Dramatic irony? Verbal irony? What functions do the ironies serve?

General

24. Is the primary interest of the story in plot, character, theme, or some other element?
25. What contribution to the story is made by its setting? Is the particular setting essential, or could the story have happened anywhere?

26. What are the characteristics of the author's style? Are they appropriate to the nature of the story?
27. What light is thrown on the story by its title?
28. Do all the elements of the story work together to support a central purpose? Is any part irrelevant or inappropriate?
29. What do you conceive to be the story's central purpose? How fully has it achieved that purpose?
30. Is the story commercial or literary? How significant is the story's purpose?
31. Is the story more or less impressive on a second reading?

SUGGESTIONS FOR WRITING

1. After reviewing the distinguishing characteristics of literary and commercial fiction, and bearing in mind that the two types of fiction represent a spectrum of qualities rather than hard-and-fast opposites, examine one of the following stories for its mix of literary and commercial characteristics:
   a. Fitzgerald, "A New Leaf" (page 385).
   b. Hurston, "The Gilded Six-Bits" (page 553).
   c. Poe, "The Cask of Amontillado" (page 617).
   d. Wharton, "Roman Fever" (page 373).

   On balance, determine whether your choice is predominantly commercial or literary.
2. Connell's "The Most Dangerous Game" and Wolff's "Hunters in the Snow" both deal with the "sport" of hunting. In a comparative essay, determine which is the literary and which is the commercial story.

Chapter Two

Plot and Structure

Plot is the sequence of incidents or events through which an author constructs a story; skilled authors are careful to present the sequence in a significant order. When described in isolation, the plot bears about the same relationship to a story that a map does to a journey. Just as a map may be drawn on a finer or grosser scale, so may a plot be recounted with lesser or greater detail. A plot summary may include what characters say or think, as well as what they do, but it leaves out description and analysis and concentrates primarily on major events.

Plot should not be confused with the content of the work. The plot is not the action itself, but the way the author *arranges* the action toward a specific end. In commercial fiction, the plot may include many surprising twists and turns and a culminating, climactic incident; because the main goal is to keep the reader turning the pages, a commercial author is likely to use a tried-and-true, fairly conventional **structure** in arranging the plot elements. The story may follow a standard chronology, for instance, and may employ familiar structural patterns. Connell's "The Most Dangerous Game" has a chronological structure and includes the familiar structural tactic (one as old as the story of Goldilocks and the Three Bears) of using a three-part sequence in narrating Rainsford's attempts to entrap General Zaroff: first he tries the Malay man-catcher, and fails; then he tries the Burmese tiger pit, and fails; but on the third try, with the "native trick" learned in Uganda, he manages to kill Ivan and ultimately outwit Zaroff. Although Wolff's "Hunters in the Snow" also employs a chronological structure, the plot elements are arranged in a complex way in order to explore the relationships among the three principal characters. Compared with "The Most Dangerous Game," the plot structure in "Hunters in the Snow" is more experimental and unpredictable, taking unexpected excursions into the thought processes of all three characters. For a literary writer, a complex structure is often required to convey complex meanings. In Wolff's story, the *significance* of the action is more important than the action itself, and subtle exchanges of words among characters may be just as significant as the more action-oriented sequences of the hunting expeditions.

Ordinarily, however, both the surface excitement required in commercial fiction and the significant meaning found in literary fiction arise out of some sort of **conflict**—a clash of actions, ideas, desires, or wills. Characters may be pitted against some other person or group of persons (conflict of person against person); they may be in conflict with some external force—physical nature, society, or "fate" (conflict of person against environment); or they may be in conflict with some elements in their own natures (conflict of person against himself or herself). The conflict may be physical, mental, emotional, or moral. There is conflict in a chess game—during which the competitors sit quite still for hours— as surely as in a wrestling match; emotional conflict may be raging within a person sitting alone in a silent room.

The central character in a conflict, whether sympathetic or unsympathetic as a person, is called the **protagonist**; occasionally there may be more than one protagonist in a story. (The technical term "protagonist" is preferable to the popular term "hero" or "heroine" because it is less ambiguous. The protagonist is simply the central character; the term "hero" or "heroine" implies that the central character has heroic qualities, which is often not the case.) Any force arranged against the protagonist—whether persons, things, conventions of society, or the protagonist's own character traits—is the **antagonist**. In some stories the conflict is single, clear-cut, and easily identifiable. In others it is multiple, various, and subtle. A person may be in conflict with other individuals, with social norms or nature, and with herself or himself all at the same time, and sometimes may be involved in conflict without being aware of it.

"The Most Dangerous Game" illustrates most of these kinds of conflict. Rainsford, the protagonist, is pitted first against other men— against Whitney and General Zaroff in the discussions preceding the manhunt, against Zaroff and Ivan during the manhunt. Early in the story he is pitted against nature when he falls into the sea and cannot get back to the yacht. At the beginning of the manhunt, he is in conflict with himself when he tries to fight off panic by repeating to himself, "I must keep my nerve. I must keep my nerve." The various conflicts illuminated in this story are physical (Rainsford against the sea and Zaroff), mental (Rainsford's initial conflict of ideas with Whitney and his battle of wits with Zaroff during the manhunt, which Zaroff refers to as "outdoor chess"), emotional (Rainsford's efforts to control his terror), and moral (Rainsford's refusal to "condone cold-blooded murder," in contrast to Zaroff's contempt for "romantic ideas about the value of human life").

Excellent literary fiction has been written utilizing all four of these major kinds of conflict. Much commercial fiction, however, emphasizes only the confrontation between man and man, depending on the element of physical conflict to supply the primary excitement. For instance, it is hard to conceive of a western story without a fistfight or a gunfight. Even in the most formulaic kinds of fiction, however, something more will be found than mere physical action. Good people will be arrayed against bad ones, and thus the conflict will also be between moral values. In commercial fiction this conflict often is clearly defined in terms of moral absolutes: the "good guy" versus the "bad guy." In literary fiction, the contrasts are usually less distinct. Good may be opposed to good, or half-truth to half-truth. There may be difficulty in determining what *is* good or bad, causing internal conflict rather than physical confrontation. In the real world, of course, significant moral issues are seldom sharply defined—judgments are difficult, and choices are complex rather than simple. Literary writers are aware of this complexity and are more concerned with displaying its various shadings of moral values than with presenting glaring, simplistic contrasts of good and evil, right and wrong.

Suspense is the quality in a story that makes readers ask "What's going to happen next?" or "How will this turn out?" Such questions compel them to keep reading. Suspense increases when a reader's curiosity is combined with anxiety about the fate of a likable, sympathetic character. Thus, in old serial movies—often appropriately called "cliffhangers"—a strong element of suspense was created at the end of each episode by leaving the hero hanging from the edge of a cliff or the heroine tied to railroad tracks with an express train rapidly approaching. In murder mysteries—often called "whodunits"—the main element of suspense is the reader's desire to know who committed the murder. In love stories the reader wants to know if the boy will win the girl, or if the lovers will be reunited.

In more literary forms of fiction the suspense often involves not so much the question *what* as the question *why*—not "What will happen next?" but "Why is the protagonist behaving this way? How is the protagonist's behavior to be explained in terms of human personality and character?" The forms of suspense range from crude to subtle and may involve not only actions but psychological considerations and moral issues as well. There are two common devices writers use to create suspense: they introduce an element of **mystery** (an unusual set of circumstances for which the reader craves an explanation) or they place the protagonist in a **dilemma** (a position in which he or she must choose between two courses of action, both undesirable). But suspense can readily be created for most readers by placing *anybody* on a seventeenth-story window ledge or simply by bringing together two attractive, sexy young people.

In "The Most Dangerous Game," the author initiates suspense in the opening sentences with Whitney's account of the mystery of "Ship-Trap Island," of which sailors "have a curious dread"—a place that seems to emanate evil. The mystery grows when, in this out-of-the-way spot, Rainsford discovers an enormous château with a leering gargoyle knocker on its massive door and confronts a bearded giant pointing a long-barreled revolver straight at his heart. Connell introduces a second mystery when General Zaroff tells Rainsford that he hunts "more dangerous game" on this island than the Cape buffalo. He then frustrates Rainsford's (and the reader's) curiosity for some thirty-six paragraphs before revealing what the game is. Meanwhile, by placing the protagonist in physical danger, Connell introduces a second kind of suspense. Initiated by Rainsford's fall into the sea and his confrontation with Ivan, this second kind becomes the principal source of suspense in the second half of the story. Simply put, the issues of whether Rainsford will escape and how he will escape are what keep the reader absorbed in the story. The manhunt itself begins with a dilemma. Rainsford must choose among three undesirable courses of action: he can hunt men with Zaroff; he can let himself be hunted; or he can submit to a presumably torturous death at the hands of Ivan. During the hunt, he is faced with other dilemmas. For instance, on the third day, pursued by Zaroff's hounds, "Rainsford knew he could do one of two things. He could stay where he was and wait. That was suicide. He could flee. That was postponing the inevitable."

Suspense is usually the most important criterion for good commercial fiction; unless a story makes us want to keep reading it, it can have little merit. In literary fiction, however, suspense is less important than other elements the author uses to engage the reader's interest: such a story may be amusing, well written, morally penetrating, peopled by intriguing characters; or it may feature some combination of all these elements. One test of a literary story is to determine whether it creates a desire to read it again. Like a play by Shakespeare, a successful literary story should create an even richer reading experience on the second or third encounter—even though we already know what is going to happen—than on a first reading. By contrast, when an author creates suspense artificially—by the simple withholding of vital information, for instance—readers will feel that the author's purpose is simply to keep them guessing what will happen next, not to reveal some insight into human experience. Either a commercial or a literary story could be written, for example, about the man on the seventeenth-story window ledge; but the literary story would focus less upon whether the man will jump than upon the psychological factors and life experiences that brought him to the ledge in the first place. The commercial story would keep us asking, "What happens next?" The literary story will make us wonder, "*Why* do things happen as they do?" or "What is the significance of this event?"

Closely connected with the element of suspense in fiction is the element of **surprise**. If we know ahead of time exactly what is going to happen in a story and why, there can be no suspense; as long as we do not know, whatever happens comes with an element of surprise. The surprise is proportional to the unexpectedness of what happens; it becomes pronounced when the story departs radically from our expectation. In the short story such radical departure is most often found in a **surprise ending**: one that features a sudden, unexpected turn or twist. In this book, Kate Chopin's "The Story of an Hour" (page 524) is a good example of a tale with such an ending.

As with physical action and suspense, commercial fiction tends to feature a surprise ending more frequently than literary fiction. But in either type of story, there are two ways by which the legitimacy and value of a surprise ending may be judged: (1) by the fairness with which the surprise is achieved and (2) by the purpose that it serves. If the surprise is contrived through an improbable coincidence or series of coincidences, or by the planting of false clues (details whose only purpose is to mislead the reader), or through the arbitrary withholding of information, then we may well dismiss it as a cheap trick. If, on the other hand, the ending that at first is such a surprise comes to seem, the more we think about it and look back over the story, perfectly logical and natural, we will feel the surprise was achieved fairly. Again, a surprise ending may be judged as trivial if it exists simply for its own sake—to shock or to titillate the reader. We may judge it as a fraud if it serves, as it does in more formulaic commercial fiction, to conceal earlier weaknesses in the story by giving us a shiny bauble at the end to absorb and concentrate our attention. We will consider a surprise ending justified, however, when it serves to broaden or to reinforce the meaning of the story. In literary fiction, the surprise is one that furnishes meaningful illumination, not just a reversal of expectation.

Whether or not a commercial story has a surprise ending, it almost always has a **happy ending**: the protagonist must solve her problems, defeat an adversary, win her man, "live happily ever after." A common obstacle confronting readers who are making their first attempt to enjoy literary fiction is that such fiction often (though certainly not always) ends unhappily. They are likely to label such stories as "depressing" and to complain that "real life has enough troubles of its own" or, conversely, that "real life is seldom as unhappy as all that."

Two justifications may be made for the **unhappy ending**. First, many situations in real life do have unpleasant outcomes; therefore, if fiction is to reflect and illuminate life, it must acknowledge human defeats as well as triumphs. Commercial writers of sports fiction usually write of how an individual or a team achieves victory against formidable odds. Yet if one team wins the pennant, thirteen others must lose it; if a golfer wins a tournament, fifty or a hundred others must fail to win. In situations like these, at least, success is much less frequent than failure. Varying the formula, a sports writer might tell how an individual lost the game but learned some important moral lesson—for instance, the importance of fair play. But here again, in real life, people achieve such compensations only occasionally. Defeat, in fact, sometimes embitters people and makes them less able to cope with life than before. Thus we need to understand and perhaps expect defeat as well as victory.

The second justification for an unhappy ending is its value in forcing us to ponder the complexities of life. The story with a happy ending has been "wrapped up" for us: it sends the reader away feeling pleasantly and vaguely satisfied with the world, and it requires no further thought. The unhappy ending, on the other hand, may cause readers to brood over the outcome, to relive the story in their minds, and by searching out its implications to get much more meaning and significance from it. Just as we can judge individuals better when we see how they behave in times of trouble, so we can see deeper into life when it is pried open for inspection. The unhappy ending is also more likely to raise significant issues. Shakespeare's tragedies reverberate in our minds much longer and more resonantly than his comedies. The ending of "The Most Dangerous Game" resolves all our anxieties, but the ending of "Hunters in the Snow" forces us to think about the mysteries and contradictions of human nature.

Readers of literary fiction evaluate an ending not by whether it is happy or unhappy but by whether it is logical within the story's own terms and whether it affords a full, believable revelation. An ending that meets these tests can be profoundly satisfying, whether happy or unhappy. In fact, some artistically satisfying stories have no ending at all in the sense that the central conflict is resolved in favor of protagonist or antagonist. In real life some problems are never solved and some battles never permanently won. A story, therefore, may have an **indeterminate ending**, one in which no definitive conclusion is reached. There must be some kind of conclusion, of course; a story, which must have artistic unity, cannot simply stop. But the conclusion need not be in terms of a resolved conflict. We cannot be sure whether Tub and Frank in "Hunters in the Snow" will maintain their alliance, or what the ultimate fate of their "friendship" might be. But the story is more effective without a definite resolution, for it leaves us to ponder the complex psychological dynamics that operate within human relationships.

Artistic unity is essential to a good plot. There must be nothing in the story that is irrelevant, that does not contribute to the meaning; there should be nothing there for its own sake or its own excitement. Good writers exercise rigorous selection: they include nothing that does not advance the central intention of the story. But they not only select; they also arrange. Authors place the story's incidents and scenes in the most effective order, which is not necessarily the chronological order (although, when we place them in chronological order, they must form a logical progression). In a carefully unified story each event grows out of the preceding one and leads logically to the next. The author links scenes together in a chain of cause and effect. With such a story the reader should not feel that events might as easily have taken one turn as another; at the same time, the author's handling of plot should not be heavy-handed but should have a quality of natural inevitability, given the specific set of characters and the initial situation.

An author who includes a turn in the plot that is unjustified by the situation or the characters is indulging in **plot manipulation**. An unmotivated action is one instance of such manipulation. Similarly, the reader feels manipulated if the plot relies too heavily on chance or on coincidence to provide a resolution to a story. This kind of resolution is sometimes called a **deus ex machina** (Latin for "god from a machine") after the practice of some ancient Greek dramatists in having a god descend from heaven at the last minute (presented in the theater by means of a mechanical stage device) to rescue the protagonist from some impossible situation. But while this was an accepted convention in Greek drama, such a resolution is seldom convincing in fiction. The action should grow organically out of the plot rather than end with an arbitrary, chance resolution for which the author has laid no groundwork earlier in the story.

Chance cannot be barred from fiction, of course, any more than it can be barred from life; the same is true of **coincidence**. Chance is the occurrence of an event that has no apparent cause in previous events or in predisposition of character, while coincidence is the chance occurrence of *two* events that may have a peculiar correspondence. But if an author uses an improbable chance event to resolve a story, the story loses its sense of conviction and thus its power to move the reader. The use of coincidence in fiction is even more problematic, since coincidence is chance compounded. Coincidence may justifiably be used to initiate a story, and occasionally to complicate it, but not to resolve it. Its use is objectionable in proportion to its improbability, its importance to the story, and its nearness to the ending. If two characters in a story both start talking of the same topic at once, it may be a coincidence but not necessarily an objectionable one. But if both decide suddenly and at the same time to kill their mothers, the coincidence would be less believable. The use of even a highly improbable coincidence may be perfectly appropriate at the start of a story. Just as a chemist may wonder what will happen if he places certain chemical elements together in a test tube, an author may wonder what will happen if two former lovers accidentally meet in Majorca, where they longed as young lovers to go, many years after they have each married someone else. The improbable initial situation is justified because it offers a chance to observe human nature in conditions that may be particularly revealing, and readers of literary fiction should demand only that the author develop a story logically from that initial situation. But the writer who uses a similar coincidence to resolve a story is imposing an unlikely pattern on human experience rather than revealing any human truth. It is often said that fact is stranger than fiction: in fact, convincing fiction often cannot include some of the more bizarre occurrences (including chance and coincidence) that sometimes happen in life. In life, almost any sequence of events is possible; but in a story the sequence must be plausible in order to convince and hold the reader.

There are various approaches to the analysis of plot. We may, if we wish, draw diagrams of different kinds of plots or trace the development of **rising action**, **climax**, and **falling action**. Tracing such structural patterns, however, if they are concerned only with examining the plot in isolation, will not take us very far into the story. A more profitable approach is to consider the *function* of plot in trying to understand the relationship of each incident to the larger meaning of the story. In literary fiction, plot is important for what it reveals. Analyzing a story by focusing on its central conflict may be especially fruitful, for this quickly takes the reader to the primary issue in the story. In evaluating fiction for its quality, it is useful to examine the way incidents and scenes are connected as a way of testing the story's plausibility and unity. In any good story, plot is inextricable from other elements of fiction to be considered in later chapters: characterization, point of view, and so forth. It provides a kind of map, or guide, but it cannot serve as a substitute for the reader's journey into the author's fictional landscape.

REVIEWING CHAPTER TWO

1. Define the term "plot."
2. Describe the importance of conflict in fiction.
3. Differentiate between the protagonist and the antagonist in a story.
4. Explore the importance of the element of surprise in fiction.
5. Consider the differences between a happy, an unhappy, and an indeterminate ending.
6. Review the importance of artistic unity in literary fiction.

Graham Greene

The Destructors

1

It was the eve of August Bank Holiday° that the latest recruit became the leader of the Wormsley Common Gang. No one was surprised except Mike, but Mike at the age of nine was surprised by everything. "If you don't shut your mouth," somebody once said to him, "you'll get a frog down it." After that Mike had kept his teeth tightly clamped except when the surprise was too great.

The new recruit had been with the gang since the beginning of the summer holidays, and there were possibilities about his brooding silence that all recognized. He never wasted a word even to tell his name until that was required of him by the rules. When he said "Trevor" it was a statement of fact, not as it would have been with the others a statement of shame or defiance. Nor did anyone laugh except Mike, who finding himself without support and meeting the dark gaze of the newcomer

THE DESTRUCTORS   First published in 1954. The setting is London nine years after the conclusion of World War II (1939–1945). During the first sustained bombing attacks on London ("the first blitz") from September 1940 to May 1941, many families slept in the Underground (i.e., subway) stations, which were used as bomb shelters. "Trevor" was typically an upper-class English name. Sir Christopher Wren (1632–1723), England's most famous architect, designed St. Paul's Cathedral and many other late seventeenth- and early eighteenth-century buildings. Graham Greene (1904–1991), who was born just outside London, lived in that city at various stages of his life.

Bank Holiday: three-day weekend in Britain, one of several during the year opened his mouth and was quiet again. There was every reason why T., as he was afterwards referred to, should have been an object of mockery—there was his name (and they substituted the initial because otherwise they had no excuse not to laugh at it), the fact that his father, a former architect and present clerk, had "come down in the world" and that his mother considered herself better than the neighbors. What but an odd quality of danger, of the unpredictable, established him in the gang without any ignoble ceremony of initiation?

The gang met every morning in an impromptu car-park, the site of the last bomb of the first blitz. The leader, who was known as Blackie, claimed to have heard it fall, and no one was precise enough in his dates to point out that he would have been one year old and fast asleep on the down platform of Wormsley Common Underground Station. On one side of the car-park leant the first occupied house, No. 3, of the shattered Northwood Terrace—literally leant, for it had suffered from the blast of the bomb and the side walls were supported on wooden struts. A smaller bomb and some incendiaries had fallen beyond, so that the house stuck up like a jagged tooth and carried on the further wall relics of its neighbor, a dado, the remains of a fireplace. T., whose words were almost confined to voting "Yes" or "No" to the plan of operations proposed each day by Blackie, once startled the whole gang by saying broodingly, "Wren built that house, father says."

"Who's Wren?"

5   "The man who built St. Paul's."

"Who cares?" Blackie said. "It's only Old Misery's."

Old Misery—whose real name was Thomas—had once been a builder and decorator. He lived alone in the crippled house, doing for himself: once a week you could see him coming back across the common with bread and vegetables, and once as the boys played in the car-park he put his head over the smashed wall of his garden and looked at them.

"Been to the lav," one of the boys said, for it was common knowledge that since the bombs fell something had gone wrong with the pipes of the house and Old Misery was too mean to spend money on the property. He could do the redecorating himself at cost price, but he had never learnt plumbing. The lav was a wooden shed at the bottom of the narrow garden with a star-shaped hole in the door: it had escaped the blast which had smashed the house next door and sucked out the window-frames of No. 3.

The next time the gang became aware of Mr. Thomas was more surprising. Blackie, Mike and a thin yellow boy, who for some reason was called by his surname Summers, met him on the common coming back from the market. Mr. Thomas stopped them. He said glumly, "You belong to the lot that play in the car-park?"

Mike was about to answer when Blackie stopped him. As the leader   10
he had responsibilities. "Suppose we are?" he said ambiguously.

"I got some chocolates," Mr. Thomas said. "Don't like 'em myself. Here you are. Not enough to go round, I don't suppose. There never is," he added with somber conviction. He handed over three packets of Smarties.

The gang were puzzled and perturbed by this action and tried to explain it away. "Bet someone dropped them and he picked 'em up," somebody suggested.

"Pinched 'em and then got in a bleeding funk," another thought aloud.

"It's a bribe," Summers said. "He wants us to stop bouncing balls on his wall."

"We'll show him we don't take bribes," Blackie said, and they   15
sacrificed the whole morning to the game of bouncing that only Mike was young enough to enjoy. There was no sign from Mr. Thomas.

Next day T. astonished them all. He was late at the rendezvous, and the voting for the day's exploit took place without him. At Blackie's suggestion the gang was to disperse in pairs, take buses at random and see how many free rides could be snatched from unwary conductors (the operation was to be carried out in pairs to avoid cheating). They were drawing lots for their companions when T. arrived.

"Where you been, T.?" Blackie asked. "You can't vote now. You know the rules."

"I've been *there*," T. said. He looked at the ground, as though he had thoughts to hide.

"Where?"

"At Old Misery's." Mike's mouth opened and then hurriedly closed   20
again with a click. He had remembered the frog.

"At Old Misery's?" Blackie said. There was nothing in the rules against it, but he had a sensation that T. was treading on dangerous ground. He asked hopefully, "Did you break in?"

"No. I rang the bell."

"And what did you say?"

"I said I wanted to see his house."

"What did he do?"   25

"He showed it to me."

"Pinch anything?"

"No."

"What did you do it for then?"

30   The gang had gathered round: it was as though an impromptu court were about to form and to try some case of deviation. T. said, "It's a beautiful house," and still watching the ground, meeting no one's eyes, he licked his lips first one way, then the other.

"What do you mean, a beautiful house?" Blackie asked with scorn.

"It's got a staircase two hundred years old like a corkscrew. Nothing holds it up."

"What do you mean, nothing holds it up. Does it float?"

"It's to do with opposite forces, Old Misery said."

35   "What else?"

"There's paneling."

"Like in the Blue Boar?"

"Two hundred years old."

"Is Old Misery two hundred years old?"

40   Mike laughed suddenly and then was quiet again. The meeting was in a serious mood. For the first time since T. had strolled into the car-park on the first day of the holidays his position was in danger. It only needed a single use of his real name and the gang would be at his heels.

"What did you do it for?" Blackie asked. He was just, he had no jealousy, he was anxious to retain T. in the gang if he could. It was the word "beautiful" that worried him—that belonged to a class world that you could still see parodied at the Wormsley Common Empire° by a man wearing a top hat and a monocle, with a haw-haw accent. He was tempted to say, "My dear Trevor, old chap," and unleash his hell hounds. "If you'd broken in," he said sadly—that indeed would have been an exploit worthy of the gang.

"This was better," T. said. "I found out things." He continued to stare at his feet, not meeting anybody's eye, as though he were absorbed in some dream he was unwilling—or ashamed—to share.

"What things?"

"Old Misery's going to be away all tomorrow and Bank Holiday."

45   Blackie said with relief, "You mean we could break in?"

"And pinch things?" somebody asked.

Blackie said, "Nobody's going to pinch things. Breaking in—that's good enough, isn't it? We don't want any court stuff."

"I don't want to pinch anything," T. said. "I've got a better idea."

"What is it?"

50   T. raised his eyes, as grey and disturbed as the drab August day. "We'll pull it down," he said. "We'll destroy it."

Wormsley Common Empire: a music hall for revues and popular entertainments

Blackie gave a single hoot of laughter and then, like Mike, fell quiet, daunted by the serious implacable gaze. "What'd the police be doing all the time?" he asked.

"They'd never know. We'd do it from inside. I've found a way in." He said with a sort of intensity, "We'd be like worms, don't you see, in an apple. When we came out again there'd be nothing there, no staircase, no panels, nothing but just walls, and then we'd make the walls fall down—somehow."

"We'd go to jug," Blackie said.

"Who's to prove? And anyway we wouldn't have pinched anything." He added without the smallest flicker of glee, "There wouldn't be anything to pinch after we'd finished."

"I've never heard of going to prison for breaking things," Summers said.   55

"There wouldn't be time," Blackie said. "I've seen housebreakers at work."

"There are twelve of us," T. said. "We'd organize."

"None of us know how . . ."

"I know," T. said. He looked across at Blackie. "Have you got a better plan?"

"Today," Mike said tactlessly, "we're pinching free rides . . ."   60

"Free rides," T. said. "You can stand down, Blackie, if you'd rather . . ."

"The gang's got to vote."

"Put it up then."

Blackie said uneasily, "It's proposed that tomorrow and Monday we destroy Old Misery's house."

"Here, here," said a fat boy called Joe.   65

"Who's in favor?"

T. said, "It's carried."

"How do we start?" Summers asked.

"He'll tell you," Blackie said. It was the end of his leadership. He went away to the back of the car-park and began to kick a stone, dribbling it this way and that. There was only one old Morris in the park, for few cars were left there except lorries: without an attendant there was no safety. He took a flying kick at the car and scraped a little paint off the rear mudguard. Beyond, paying no more attention to him than to a stranger, the gang had gathered round T.; Blackie was dimly aware of the fickleness of favor. He thought of going home, of never returning, of letting them all discover the hollowness of T.'s leadership, but suppose after all what T. proposed was possible—nothing like it had ever been done before. The fame of the Wormsley Common car-park gang would surely reach around London. There would be headlines in the papers. Even the grown-up gangs who ran the betting at the all-in wrestling and the barrow-boys would hear with respect of how Old Misery's house had been destroyed. Driven by the pure, simple and altruistic ambition of fame for the gang, Blackie came back to where T. stood in the shadow of Misery's wall.

70   T. was giving his orders with decision: it was as though this plan had been with him all his life, pondered through the seasons, now in his fifteenth year crystallized with the pain of puberty. "You," he said to Mike, "bring some big nails, the biggest you can find, and a hammer. Anyone else who can better bring a hammer and a screwdriver. We'll need plenty of them. Chisels too. We can't have too many chisels. Can anybody bring a saw?"

"I can," Mike said.

"Not a child's saw," T. said. "A real saw."

Blackie realized he had raised his hand like any ordinary member of the gang.

"Right, you bring one, Blackie. But now there's a difficulty. We want a hacksaw."

75   "What's a hacksaw?" someone asked.

"You can get 'em at Woolworth's," Summers said.

The fat boy called Joe said gloomily, "I knew it would end in a collection."

"I'll get one myself," T. said. "I don't want your money. But I can't buy a sledge-hammer."

Blackie said, "They are working on No. 15. I know where they'll leave their stuff for Bank Holiday."

80   "Then that's all," T. said. "We meet here at nine sharp."

"I've got to go to church," Mike said.

"Come over the wall and whistle. We'll let you in."

2

On Sunday morning all were punctual except Blackie, even Mike. Mike had had a stroke of luck. His mother felt ill, his father was tired after Saturday night, and he was told to go to church alone with many warnings of what would happen if he strayed. Blackie had had difficulty in smuggling out the saw, and then in finding the sledge-hammer at the back of No. 15. He approached the house from a lane at the rear of the garden, for fear of the policeman's beat along the main road. The tired evergreens kept off a stormy sun: another wet Bank Holiday was being prepared over the Atlantic, beginning in swirls of dust under the trees. Blackie climbed the wall into Misery's garden.

There was no sign of anybody anywhere. The lav stood like a tomb in a neglected graveyard. The curtains were drawn. The house slept. Blackie lumbered nearer with the saw and the sledge-hammer. Perhaps after all nobody had turned up: the plan had been a wild invention: they had woken wiser. But when he came close to the back door he could hear a confusion of sound hardly louder than a hive in swarm: a clickety-clack, a bang bang, a scraping, a creaking, a sudden painful crack. He thought: it's true, and whistled.

They opened the back door to him and he came in. He had at once   85 the impression of organization, very different from the old happy-go-lucky ways under his leadership. For a while he wandered up and down stairs looking for T. Nobody addressed him: he had a sense of great urgency, and already he could begin to see the plan. The interior of the house was being carefully demolished without touching the outer walls. Summers with hammer and chisel was ripping out the skirting-boards in the ground floor dining-room: he had already smashed the panels of the door. In the same room Joe was heaving up the parquet blocks, exposing the soft wood floor-boards over the cellar. Coils of wire came out of the damaged skirting and Mike sat happily on the floor clipping the wires.

On the curved stairs two of the gang were working hard with an inadequate child's saw on the banisters—when they saw Blackie's big saw they signaled for it wordlessly. When he next saw them a quarter of the banisters had been dropped into the hall. He found T. at last in the bathroom—he sat moodily in the least cared-for room in the house, listening to the sounds coming up from below.

"You've really done it," Blackie said with awe. "What's going to happen?"

"We've only just begun," T. said. He looked at the sledgehammer and gave his instructions. "You stay here and break the bath and the wash-basin. Don't bother about the pipes. They come later."

Mike appeared at the door. "I've finished the wires, T.," he said.

"Good. You've just got to go wandering round now. The kitchen's   90 in the basement. Smash all the china and glass and bottles you can lay hold of. Don't turn on the taps—we don't want a flood—yet. Then go into all the rooms and turn out drawers. If they are locked get one of the others to break them open. Tear up any papers you find and smash all the ornaments. Better take a carving-knife with you from the kitchen. The bedroom's opposite here. Open the pillows and tear up the sheets. That's enough for the moment. And you, Blackie, when you've finished in here crack the plaster in the passage up with your sledge-hammer."

"What are you going to do?" Blackie asked.

"I'm looking for something special," T. said.

It was nearly lunch-time before Blackie had finished and went in search of T. Chaos had advanced. The kitchen was a shambles of broken glass and china. The dining-room was stripped of parquet, the skirting was up, the door had been taken off its hinges, and the destroyers had moved up a floor. Streaks of light came in through the closed shutters where they worked with the seriousness of creators—and destruction after all is a form of creation. A kind of imagination had seen this house as it had now become.

Mike said, "I've got to go home for dinner."

95   "Who else?" T. asked, but all the others on one excuse or another had brought provisions with them.

They squatted in the ruins of the room and swapped unwanted sandwiches. Half an hour for lunch and they were at work again. By the time Mike returned, they were on the top floor, and by six the superficial damage was completed. The doors were all off, all the skirtings raised, the furniture pillaged and ripped and smashed—no one could have slept in the house except on a bed of broken plaster. T. gave his orders—eight o'clock next morning, and to escape notice they climbed singly over the garden wall, into the car-park. Only Blackie and T. were left: the light had nearly gone, and when they touched a switch, nothing worked—Mike had done his job thoroughly.

"Did you find anything special?" Blackie asked.

T. nodded. "Come over here," he said, "and look." Out of both pockets he drew bundles of pound notes. "Old Misery's savings," he said. "Mike ripped out the mattress, but he missed them."

"What are you going to do? Share them?"

100   "We aren't thieves," T. said. "Nobody's going to steal anything from this house. I kept these for you and me—a celebration." He knelt down on the floor and counted them out—there were seventy in all. "We'll burn them," he said, "one by one," and taking it in turns they held a note upwards and lit the top corner, so that the flame burnt slowly towards their fingers. The grey ash floated above them and fell on their heads like age. "I'd like to see Old Misery's face when we are through," T. said.

"You hate him a lot?" Blackie asked.

"Of course I don't hate him," T. said. "There'd be no fun if I hated him." The last burning note illuminated his brooding face. "All this hate and love," he said, "it's soft, it's hooey. There's only things, Blackie," and he looked round the room crowded with the unfamiliar shadows of half things, broken things, former things. "I'll race you home, Blackie," he said.

3

Next morning the serious destruction started. Two were missing—
Mike and another boy whose parents were off to Southend and Brighton
in spite of the slow warm drops that had begun to fall and the rumble of
thunder in the estuary like the first guns of the old blitz. "We've got to
hurry," T. said.

Summers was restive. "Haven't we done enough?" he said. "I've
been given a bob for slot machines. This is like work."

"We've hardly started," T. said. "Why, there's all the floor left, and   105
the stairs. We haven't taken out a single window. You voted like the
others. We are going to *destroy* this house. There won't be anything left
when we've finished."

They began again on the first floor picking up the top floorboards
next to the outer wall, leaving the joists exposed. Then they sawed
through the joists and retreated into the hall, as what was left of the floor
heeled and sank. They had learnt with practice, and the second floor
collapsed more easily. By the evening an odd exhilaration seized them as
they looked down the great hollow of the house. They ran risks and
made mistakes: when they thought of the windows it was too late to
reach them. "Cor," Joe said, and dropped a penny down in the dry
rubble-filled well. It cracked and span among the broken glass.

"Why did we start this?" Summers asked with astonishment; T. was
already on the ground, digging at the rubble, clearing a space along the
outer wall. "Turn on the taps," he said. "It's too dark for anyone to see
now, and in the morning it won't matter." The water overtook them on
the stairs and fell through the floorless rooms.

It was then they heard Mike's whistle at the back. "Something's
wrong," Blackie said. They could hear his urgent breathing as they
unlocked the door.

"The bogies?"° Summers asked.

"Old Misery," Mike said. "He's on his way." He put his head   110
between his knees and retched. "Ran all the way," he said with pride.

"But why?" T. said. "He told me . . ." He protested with the fury of
the child he had never been, "It isn't fair."

"He was down at Southend," Mike said, "and he was on the train
coming back. Said it was too cold and wet." He paused and gazed at the
water. "My, you've had a storm here. Is the roof leaking?"

"How long will he be?"

"Five minutes. I gave Ma the slip and ran."

bogies: police

115   "We better clear," Summers said. "We've done enough, anyway."

"Oh, no, we haven't. Anybody could do this—" "This" was the shattered hollowed house with nothing left but the walls. Yet the walls could be preserved. Façades were valuable. They could build inside again more beautifully than before. This could again be a home. He said angrily, "We've got to finish. Don't move. Let me think."

"There's no time," a boy said.

"There's got to be a way," T. said. "We couldn't have got this far . . ."

"We've done a lot," Blackie said.

120   "No. No, we haven't. Somebody watch the front."

"We can't do any more."

"He may come in at the back."

"Watch the back too." T. began to plead. "Just give me a minute and I'll fix it. I swear I'll fix it." But his authority had gone with his ambiguity. He was only one of the gang. "Please," he said.

"Please," Summers mimicked him, and then suddenly struck home with the fatal name. "Run along home, Trevor."

125   T. stood with his back to the rubble like a boxer knocked groggy against the ropes. He had no words as his dreams shook and slid. Then Blackie acted before the gang had time to laugh, pushing Summers backward. "I'll watch the front, T.," he said, and cautiously he opened the shutters of the hall. The grey wet common stretched ahead, and the lamps gleamed in the puddles. "Someone's coming, T. No, it's not him. What's your plan, T.?"

"Tell Mike to go out to the lav and hide close beside it. When he hears me whistle he's got to count ten and start to shout."

"Shout what?"

"Oh, 'Help,' anything."

"You hear, Mike," Blackie said. He was the leader again. He took a quick look between the shutters. "He's coming, T."

130   "Quick, Mike. The lav. Stay here, Blackie, all of you till I yell."

"Where are you going, T.?"

"Don't worry. I'll see to this. I said I would, didn't I?"

Old Misery came limping off the common. He had mud on his shoes and he stopped to scrape them on the pavement's edge. He didn't want to soil his house, which stood jagged and dark between the bombsites, saved so narrowly, as he believed, from destruction. Even the fan-light had been left unbroken by the bomb's blast. Somewhere somebody whistled. Old Misery looked sharply round. He didn't trust whistles. A child was shouting: it seemed to come from his own garden. Then a boy ran into the road from the car-park. "Mr. Thomas," he called. "Mr. Thomas."

"What is it?"

"I'm terribly sorry, Mr. Thomas. One of us got taken short, and we   135
thought you wouldn't mind, and now he can't get out."

"What do you mean, boy?"

"He's got stuck in your lav."

"He'd no business . . . Haven't I seen you before?"

"You showed me your house."

"So I did. So I did. That doesn't give you the right to . . ."   140

"Do hurry, Mr. Thomas. He'll suffocate."

"Nonsense. He can't suffocate. Wait till I put my bag in."

"I'll carry your bag."

"Oh no, you don't. I carry my own."

"This way, Mr. Thomas."   145

"I can't get in the garden that way. I've got to go through the
house."

"But you *can* get in the garden this way, Mr. Thomas. We often do."

"You often do?" He followed the boy with a scandalized fascination.
"When? What right? . . ."

"Do you see . . .? The wall's low."

"I'm not going to climb walls into my own garden. It's absurd."   150

"This is how we do it. One foot here, one foot there, and over." The
boy's face peered down, an arm shot out, and Mr. Thomas found his bag
taken and deposited on the other side of the wall.

"Give me back my bag," Mr. Thomas said. From the loo° a boy
yelled and yelled. "I'll call the police."

"Your bag's all right, Mr. Thomas. Look. One foot there. On your
right. Now just above. To your left." Mr. Thomas climbed over his own
garden wall. "Here's your bag, Mr. Thomas."

"I'll have the wall built up," Mr. Thomas said. "I'll not have you boys
coming over here, using my loo." He stumbled on the path, but the boy
caught his elbow and supported him. "Thank you, thank you, my boy,"
he murmured automatically. Somebody shouted again through the dark.
"I'm coming, I'm coming," Mr. Thomas called. He said to the boy beside
him, "I'm not unreasonable. Been a boy myself. As long as things are
done regular. I don't mind you playing round the place Saturday mornings. Sometimes I like company. Only it's got to be regular. One of you
asks leave and I say Yes. Sometimes I'll say No. Won't feel like it. And
you come in at the front door and out at the back. No garden walls."

"Do get him out, Mr. Thomas."   155

"He won't come to any harm in my loo," Mr. Thomas said, stumbling slowly down the garden. "Oh, my rheumatics," he said. "Always

loo: outdoor toilet (an older term for "lav")

get 'em on Bank Holiday. I've got to go careful. There's loose stones here. Give me your hand. Do you know what my horoscope said yesterday? 'Abstain from any dealings in first half of week. Danger of serious crash.' That might be on this path," Mr. Thomas said. "They speak in parables and double meanings." He paused at the door of the loo. "What's the matter in there?" he called. There was no reply.

"Perhaps he's fainted," the boy said.

"Not in my loo. Here, you come out," Mr. Thomas said, and giving a great jerk at the door he nearly fell on his back when it swung easily open. A hand first supported him and then pushed him hard. His head hit the opposite wall and he sat heavily down. His bag hit his feet. A hand whipped the key out of the lock and the door slammed. "Let me out," he called, and heard the key turn in the lock. "A serious crash," he thought, and felt dithery and confused and old.

A voice spoke to him softly through the star-shaped hole in the door. "Don't worry, Mr. Thomas," it said, "we won't hurt you, not if you stay quiet."

160   Mr. Thomas put his head between his hands and pondered. He had noticed that there was only one lorry in the car-park, and he felt certain that the driver would not come for it before the morning. Nobody could hear him from the road in front, and the lane at the back was seldom used. Anyone who passed there would be hurrying home and would not pause for what they would certainly take to be drunken cries. And if he did call "Help," who, on a lonely Bank Holiday evening, would have the courage to investigate? Mr. Thomas sat on the loo and pondered with the wisdom of age.

After a while it seemed to him that there were sounds in the silence—they were faint and came from the direction of his house. He stood up and peered through the ventilation-hole—between the cracks in one of the shutters he saw a light, not the light of a lamp, but the wavering light that a candle might give. Then he thought he heard the sound of hammering and scraping and chipping. He thought of burglars—perhaps they had employed the boy as a scout, but why should burglars engage in what sounded more and more like a stealthy form of carpentry? Mr. Thomas let out an experimental yell, but nobody answered. The noise could not even have reached his enemies.

4

Mike had gone home to bed, but the rest stayed. The question of leadership no longer concerned the gang. With nails, chisels, screwdrivers, anything that was sharp and penetrating, they moved around the inner walls worrying at the mortar between the bricks. They started too high, and it was Blackie who hit on the damp course and realized the work could be halved if they weakened the joints immediately above. It was a long, tiring, unamusing job, but at last it was finished. The gutted house stood there balanced on a few inches of mortar between the damp course and the bricks.

There remained the most dangerous task of all, out in the open at the edge of the bomb-site. Summers was sent to watch the road for passers-by, and Mr. Thomas, sitting on the loo, heard clearly now the sound of sawing. It no longer came from his house, and that a little reassured him. He felt less concerned. Perhaps the other noises too had no significance.

A voice spoke to him through the hole. "Mr. Thomas."

"Let me out," Mr. Thomas said sternly.   165

"Here's a blanket," the voice said, and a long grey sausage was worked through the hole and fell in swathes over Mr. Thomas's head.

"There's nothing personal," the voice said. "We want you to be comfortable tonight."

"Tonight," Mr. Thomas repeated incredulously.

"Catch," the voice said. "Penny buns—we've buttered them, and sausage-rolls. We don't want you to starve, Mr. Thomas."

Mr. Thomas pleaded desperately. "A joke's a joke, boy. Let me   170
out and I won't say a thing. I've got rheumatics. I got to sleep comfortable."

"You wouldn't be comfortable, not in your house, you wouldn't. Not now."

"What do you mean, boy?" but the footsteps receded. There was only the silence of night: no sound of sawing. Mr. Thomas tried one more yell, but he was daunted and rebuked by the silence—a long way off an owl hooted and made away again on its muffled flight through the soundless world.

At seven next morning the driver came to fetch his lorry. He climbed into the seat and tried to start the engine. He was vaguely aware of a voice shouting, but it didn't concern him. At last the engine responded and he backed the lorry until it touched the great wooden shore that supported Mr. Thomas's house. That way he could drive right out and down the street without reversing. The lorry moved forward, was momentarily checked as though something were pulling it from behind, and then went on to the sound of a long rumbling crash. The driver was astonished to see bricks bouncing ahead of him, while stones hit the roof of his cab. He put on his brakes. When he climbed out the whole landscape had suddenly altered. There was no house beside the car-park, only a hill of rubble. He went round and examined the back of his car for damage, and found a rope tied there that was still twisted at the other end round part of a wooden strut.

The driver again became aware of somebody shouting. It came from the wooden erection which was the nearest thing to a house in that desolation of broken brick. The driver climbed the smashed wall and unlocked the door. Mr. Thomas came out of the loo. He was wearing a grey blanket to which flakes of pastry adhered. He gave a sobbing cry. "My house," he said. "Where's my house?"

175 "Search me," the driver said. His eye lit on the remains of a bath and what had once been a dresser and he began to laugh. There wasn't anything left anywhere.

"How dare you laugh," Mr. Thomas said. "It was my house. My house."

"I'm sorry," the driver said, making heroic efforts, but when he remembered the sudden check to his lorry, the crash of bricks falling, he became convulsed again. One moment the house had stood there with such dignity between the bomb-sites like a man in a top hat, and then, bang, crash, there wasn't anything left—not anything. He said, "I'm sorry. I can't help it, Mr. Thomas. There's nothing personal, but you got to admit it's funny."

QUESTIONS

1. Who is the protagonist in this story—Trevor, Blackie, or the gang? Who or what is the antagonist? Identify the conflicts of the story.
2. How is suspense created?
3. This story uses the most common basic formula of commercial fiction: protagonist aims at a goal, is confronted with various obstacles between himself and his goal, overcomes the obstacles, and achieves his goal. How does this story differ from commercial fiction in its use of this formula? Does the story have a happy ending?
4. Discuss the gang's motivations, taking into account (a) the age and beauty of the house, (b) Blackie's reasons for not going home after losing his position of leadership, (c) the seriousness with which the boys work at their task, and their loss of concern over their leadership, (d) the burning of the pound notes, (e) their consideration for Old Misery, (f) the lorry driver's reaction. What characteristics do the gang's two named exploits—pinching free rides and destroying the house—have in common?
5. Of what significance, if any, is the setting of this story in blitzed London? Does the story have anything to say about the consequences of war? About the causes of war?

6. Explain as fully as you can the causes of the gang's delinquency, taking into account (a) their reaction to the name Trevor, (b) their reaction to Old Misery's gift of chocolates, (c) Blackie's reaction to the word "beautiful," (d) Trevor's comments on "hate and love," (e) Summers's reaction to the word "Please," (f) the setting.

7. What good qualities do the delinquents in this story have? Do they differ as a group from other youth gangs you have read or know about? If so, account for the differences.

8. On the surface this is a story of action, suspense, and adventure. At a deeper level it is about delinquency, war, and human nature. Try to sum up what the story says about human nature in general.

Alice Munro

How I Met My Husband

We heard the plane come over at noon, roaring through the radio news, and we were sure it was going to hit the house, so we all ran out into the yard. We saw it come over the treetops, all red and silver, the first close-up plane I ever saw. Mrs. Peebles screamed.

"Crash landing," their little boy said. Joey was his name.

"It's okay," said Dr. Peebles. "He knows what he's doing." Dr. Peebles was only an animal doctor, but had a calming way of talking, like any doctor.

This was my first job—working for Dr. and Mrs. Peebles, who had bought an old house out on the Fifth Line, about five miles out of town. It was just when the trend was starting of town people buying up old farms, not to work them but to live on them.

We watched the plane land across the road, where the fairgrounds   5 used to be. It did make a good landing field, nice and level for the old race track, and the barns and display sheds torn down now for scrap lumber so there was nothing in the way. Even the old grandstand bays had burned.

"All right," said Mrs. Peebles, snappy as she always was when she got over her nerves. "Let's go back in the house. Let's not stand here gawking like a set of farmers."

She didn't say that to hurt my feelings. It never occurred to her.

How I Met My Husband   First published in her collection *Something I've Been Meaning to Tell You* in 1974. Alice Munro (b. 1931) grew up in rural southwestern Ontario, where much of her fiction is set. She attended the University of Western Ontario for two years and moved to British Columbia, where she lived until 1972; she now lives in Clinton, Ontario. She is the author of ten collections of short fiction, most recently *The View from Castle Rock* (2006).

I was just setting the dessert down when Loretta Bird arrived, out of breath, at the screen door.

"I thought it was going to crash into the house and kill youse all!"

10   She lived on the next place and the Peebleses thought she was a country-woman, they didn't know the difference. She and her husband didn't farm, he worked on the roads and had a bad name for drinking. They had seven children and couldn't get credit at the HiWay Grocery. The Peebleses made her welcome, not knowing any better, as I say, and offered her dessert.

Dessert was never anything to write home about, at their place. A dish of Jell-O or sliced bananas or fruit out of a tin. "Have a house without a pie, be ashamed until you die," my mother used to say, but Mrs. Peebles operated differently.

Loretta Bird saw me getting the can of peaches.

"Oh, never mind," she said. "I haven't got the right kind of a stomach to trust what comes out of those tins, I can only eat home canning."

I could have slapped her. I bet she never put down fruit in her life.

15   "I know what he's landed here for," she said. "He's got permission to use the fairgrounds and take people up for rides. It costs a dollar. It's the same fellow who was over at Palmerston last week and was up the lakeshore before that. I wouldn't go up, if you paid me."

"I'd jump at the chance," Dr. Peebles said. "I'd like to see this neighborhood from the air."

Mrs. Peebles said she would just as soon see it from the ground. Joey said he wanted to go and Heather did, too. Joey was nine and Heather was seven.

"Would you, Edie?" Heather said.

I said I didn't know. I was scared, but I never admitted that, especially in front of children I was taking care of.

20   "People are going to be coming out here in their cars raising dust and trampling your property, if I was you I would complain," Loretta said. She hooked her legs around the chair rung and I knew we were in for a lengthy visit. After Dr. Peebles went back to his office or out on his next call and Mrs. Peebles went for her nap, she would hang around me while I was trying to do the dishes. She would pass remarks about the Peebleses in their own house.

"She wouldn't find time to lay down in the middle of the day, if she had seven kids like I got."

She asked me did they fight and did they keep things in the dresser drawer not to have babies with. She said it was a sin if they did. I pretended I didn't know what she was talking about.

I was fifteen and away from home for the first time. My parents had made the effort and sent me to high school for a year, but I didn't like it. I was shy of strangers and the work was hard, they didn't make it nice for you or explain the way they do now. At the end of the year the averages were published in the paper, and mine came out at the very bottom, 37 percent. My father said that's enough and I didn't blame him. The last thing I wanted, anyway, was to go on and end up teaching school. It happened the very day the paper came out with my disgrace in it, Dr. Peebles was staying at our place for dinner, having just helped one of our cows have twins, and he said I looked smart to him and his wife was looking for a girl to help. He said she felt tied down, with the two children, out in the country. I guess she would, my mother said, being polite, though I could tell from her face she was wondering what on earth it would be like to have only two children and no barn work, and then to be complaining.

When I went home I would describe to them the work I had to do, and it made everybody laugh. Mrs. Peebles had an automatic washer and dryer, the first I ever saw. I have had those in my own home for such a long time now it's hard to remember how much of a miracle it was to me, not having to struggle with the wringer and hang up and haul down. Let alone not having to heat water. Then there was practically no baking. Mrs. Peebles said she couldn't make pie crust, the most amazing thing I ever heard a woman admit. I could, of course, and I could make light biscuits and a white cake and dark cake, but they didn't want it, she said they watched their figures. The only thing I didn't like about working there, in fact, was feeling half hungry a lot of the time. I used to bring back a box of doughnuts made out at home, and hide them under my bed. The children found out, and I didn't mind sharing, but I thought I better bind them to secrecy.

The day after the plane landed Mrs. Peebles put both children in   25
the car and drove over to Chesley, to get their hair cut. There was a good woman then at Chesley for doing hair. She got hers done at the same place, Mrs. Peebles did, and that meant they would be gone a good while. She had to pick a day Dr. Peebles wasn't going out into the country, she didn't have her own car. Cars were still in short supply then, after the war.

I loved being left in the house alone, to do my work at leisure. The kitchen was all white and bright yellow, with fluorescent lights. That was before they ever thought of making the appliances all different colors and doing the cupboards like dark old wood and hiding the lighting. I loved light. I loved the double sink. So would anybody new-come from washing dishes in a dishpan with a rag-plugged hole on an oilcloth-covered table by light of a coal-oil lamp. I kept everything shining.

The bathroom too. I had a bath in there once a week. They wouldn't have minded if I took one oftener, but to me it seemed like asking too much, or maybe risking making it less wonderful. The basin and the tub and the toilet were all pink, and there were glass doors with flamingos painted on them, to shut off the tub. The light had a rosy cast and the mat sank under your feet like snow, except that it was warm. The mirror was three-way. With the mirror all steamed up and the air like a perfume cloud, from things I was allowed to use, I stood up on the side of the tub and admired myself naked, from three directions. Sometimes I thought about the way we lived out at home and the way we lived here and how one way was so hard to imagine when you were living the other way. But I thought it was still a lot easier, living the way we lived at home, to picture something like this, the painted flamingos and the warmth and the soft mat, than it was anybody knowing only things like this to picture how it was the other way. And why was that?

I was through my jobs in no time, and had the vegetables peeled for supper and sitting in cold water besides. Then I went into Mrs. Peebles' bedroom. I had been in there plenty of times, cleaning, and I always took a good look in her closet, at the clothes she had hanging there. I wouldn't have looked in her drawers, but a closet is open to anybody. That's a lie. I would have looked in drawers, but I would have felt worse doing it and been more scared she could tell.

Some clothes in her closet she wore all the time, I was quite familiar with them. Others she never put on, they were pushed to the back. I was disappointed to see no wedding dress. But there was one long dress I could just see the skirt of, and I was hungering to see the rest. Now I took note of where it hung and lifted it out. It was satin, a lovely weight on my arm, light bluish-green in color, almost silvery. It had a fitted, pointed waist and a full skirt and an off-the-shoulder fold hiding the little sleeves.

30   Next thing was easy. I got out of my own things and slipped it on. I was slimmer at fifteen than anybody would believe who knows me now and the fit was beautiful. I didn't, of course, have a strapless bra on, which was what it needed, I just had to slide my straps down my arms under the material. Then I tried pinning up my hair, to get the effect. One thing led to another. I put on rouge and lipstick and eyebrow pencil from her dresser. The heat of the day and the weight of the satin and all the excitement made me thirsty, and I went out to the kitchen, got-up as I was, to get a glass of ginger ale with ice cubes from the refrigerator. The

Peebleses drank ginger ale, or fruit drinks, all day, like water, and I was getting so I did too. Also there was no limit on ice cubes, which I was so fond of I would even put them in a glass of milk.

I turned from putting the ice tray back and saw a man watching me through the screen. It was the luckiest thing in the world I didn't spill the ginger ale down the front of me then and there.

"I never meant to scare you. I knocked but you were getting the ice out, you didn't hear me."

I couldn't see what he looked like, he was dark the way somebody is pressed up against a screen door with the bright daylight behind them. I only knew he wasn't from around here.

"I'm from the plane over there. My name is Chris Watters and what I was wondering was if I could use that pump."

There was a pump in the yard. That was the way the people used to   35
get their water. Now I noticed he was carrying a pail.

"You're welcome," I said. "I can get it from the tap and save you pumping." I guess I wanted him to know we had piped water, didn't pump ourselves.

"I don't mind the exercise." He didn't move, though, and finally he said, "Were you going to a dance?"

Seeing a stranger there had made me entirely forget how I was dressed.

"Or is that the way ladies around here generally get dressed up in the afternoon?"

I didn't know how to joke back then. I was too embarrassed.   40

"You live here? Are you the lady of the house?"

"I'm the hired girl."

Some people change when they find that out, their whole way of looking at you and speaking to you changes, but his didn't.

"Well, I just wanted to tell you you look very nice. I was so surprised when I looked in the door and saw you. Just because you looked so nice and beautiful."

I wasn't even old enough then to realize how out of the common it is,   45
for a man to say something like that to a woman, or somebody he is treating like a woman. For a man to say a word like *beautiful*. I wasn't old enough to realize or to say anything back, or in fact to do anything but wish he would go away. Not that I didn't like him, but just that it upset me so, having him look at me, and me trying to think of something to say.

He must have understood. He said good-bye, and thanked me, and went and started filling his pail from the pump. I stood behind the Venetian blinds in the dining room, watching him. When he had gone, I went into the bedroom and took the dress off and put it back in the same place. I dressed in my own clothes and took my hair down and washed my face, wiping it on Kleenex, which I threw in the wastebasket.

The Peebleses asked me what kind of man he was. Young, middle-aged, short, tall? I couldn't say.

"Good-looking?" Dr. Peebles teased me.

I couldn't think a thing but that he would be coming to get his water again, he would be talking to Dr. or Mrs. Peebles, making friends with them, and he would mention seeing me that first afternoon, dressed up. Why not mention it? He would think it was funny. And no idea of the trouble it would get me into.

50   After supper the Peebleses drove into town to go to a movie. She wanted to go somewhere with her hair fresh done. I sat in my bright kitchen wondering what to do, knowing I would never sleep. Mrs. Peebles might not fire me, when she found out, but it would give her a different feeling about me altogether. This was the first place I ever worked but I really had picked up things about the way people feel when you are working for them. They like to think you aren't curious. Not just that you aren't dishonest, that isn't enough. They like to feel you don't notice things, that you don't think or wonder about anything but what they liked to eat and how they liked things ironed, and so on. I don't mean they weren't kind to me, because they were. They had me eat my meals with them (to tell the truth I expected to, I didn't know there were families who don't) and sometimes they took me along in the car. But all the same.

I went up and checked on the children being asleep and then I went out. I had to do it. I crossed the road and went in the old fairgrounds gate. The plane looked unnatural sitting there, and shining with the moon. Off at the far side of the fairgrounds, where the bush was taking over, I saw his tent.

He was sitting outside it smoking a cigarette. He saw me coming.

"Hello, were you looking for a plane ride? I don't start taking people up till tomorrow." Then he looked again and said, "Oh, it's you. I didn't know you without your long dress on."

My heart was knocking away, my tongue was dried up. I had to say something. But I couldn't. My throat was closed and I was like a deaf-and-dumb.

55   "Did you want to ride? Sit down. Have a cigarette."

I couldn't even shake my head to say no, so he gave me one.

"Put it in your mouth or I can't light it. It's a good thing I'm used to shy ladies."

I did. It wasn't the first time I had smoked a cigarette, actually. My girl friend out home, Muriel Lowe, used to steal them from her brother.

"Look at your hand shaking. Did you just want to have a chat, or what?"

In one burst I said, "I wisht you wouldn't say anything about that   60
dress."

"What dress? Oh, the long dress."

"It's Mrs. Peebles'."

"Whose? Oh, the lady you work for? Is that it? She wasn't home so you got dressed up in her dress, eh? You got dressed up and played queen. I don't blame you. You're not smoking the cigarette right. Don't just puff. Draw it in. Did anybody ever show you how to inhale? Are you scared I'll tell on you? Is that it?"

I was so ashamed at having to ask him to connive this way I couldn't nod. I just looked at him and he saw *yes*.

"Well I won't. I won't in the slightest way mention it or embarrass   65
you. I give you my word of honor."

Then he changed the subject, to help me out, seeing I couldn't even thank him.

"What do you think of this sign?"

It was a board sign lying practically at my feet.

SEE THE WORLD FROM THE SKY. ADULTS $1.00, CHILDREN 50¢. QUALIFIED
PILOT.

"My old sign was getting pretty beat up, I thought I'd make a new   70
one. That's what I've been doing with my time today."

The lettering wasn't all that handsome, I thought. I could have done a better one in half an hour.

"I'm not an expert at sign making."

"It's very good," I said.

"I don't need it for publicity, word of mouth is usually enough. I turned away two carloads tonight. I felt like taking it easy. I didn't tell them ladies were dropping in to visit me."

Now I remembered the children and I was scared again, in case one   75
of them had waked up and called me and I wasn't there.

"Do you have to go so soon?"

I remembered some manners. "Thank you for the cigarette."

"Don't forget. You have my word of honor."

I tore off across the fairgrounds, scared I'd see the car heading home from town. My sense of time was mixed up, I didn't know how long I'd been out of the house. But it was all right, it wasn't late, the children were asleep. I got in bed myself and lay thinking what a lucky end to the day, after all, and among things to be grateful for I could be grateful Loretta Bird hadn't been the one who caught me.

80   The yard and borders didn't get trampled, it wasn't as bad as that. All the same it seemed very public, around the house. The sign was on the fairgrounds gate. People came mostly after supper but a good many in the afternoon, too. The Bird children all came without fifty cents between them and hung on the gate. We got used to the excitement of the plane coming in and taking off, it wasn't excitement anymore. I never went over, after that one time, but would see him when he came to get his water. I would be out on the steps doing sitting-down work, like preparing vegetables, if I could.

"Why don't you come over? I'll take you up in my plane."

"I'm saving my money," I said, because I couldn't think of anything else.

"For what? For getting married?"

I shook my head.

85   "I'll take you up for free if you come sometime when it's slack. I thought you would come, and have another cigarette."

I made a face to hush him, because you never could tell when the children would be sneaking around the porch, or Mrs. Peebles herself listening in the house. Sometimes she came out and had a conversation with him. He told her things he hadn't bothered to tell me. But then I hadn't thought to ask. He told her he had been in the war, that was where he learned to fly a plane, and now he couldn't settle down to ordinary life, this was what he liked. She said she couldn't imagine anybody liking such a thing. Though sometimes, she said, she was almost bored enough to try anything herself, she wasn't brought up to living in the country. It's all my husband's idea, she said. This was news to me.

"Maybe you ought to give flying lessons," she said.

"Would you take them?"

She just laughed.

90   Sunday was a busy flying day in spite of it being preached against from two pulpits. We were all sitting out watching. Joey and Heather were over on the fence with the Bird kids. Their father had said they could go, after their mother saying all week they couldn't.

A car came down the road past the parked cars and pulled up right in the drive. It was Loretta Bird who got out, all importance, and on the driver's side another woman got out, more sedately. She was wearing sunglasses.

"This is a lady looking for the man that flies the plane," Loretta Bird said. "I heard her inquire in the hotel coffee shop where I was having a Coke and I brought her out."

"I'm sorry to bother you," the lady said. "I'm Alice Kelling, Mr. Watters' fiancée."

This Alice Kelling had on a pair of brown and white checked slacks and a yellow top. Her bust looked to me rather low and bumpy. She had a worried face. Her hair had had a permanent, but had grown out, and she wore a yellow band to keep it off her face. Nothing in the least pretty or even young-looking about her. But you could tell from how she talked she was from the city, or educated, or both.

Dr. Peebles stood up and introduced himself and his wife and me   95
and asked her to be seated.

"He's up in the air right now, but you're welcome to sit and wait. He gets his water here and he hasn't been yet. He'll probably take his break about five."

"That is him, then?" said Alice Kelling, wrinkling and straining at the sky.

"He's not in the habit of running out on you, taking a different name?" Dr. Peebles laughed. He was the one, not his wife, to offer iced tea. Then she sent me into the kitchen to fix it. She smiled. She was wearing sunglasses too.

"He never mentioned his fiancée," she said.

I loved fixing iced tea with lots of ice and slices of lemon in tall   100
glasses. I ought to have mentioned before, Dr. Peebles was an abstainer, at least around the house, or I wouldn't have been allowed to take the place. I had to fix a glass for Loretta Bird too, though it galled me, and when I went out she had settled in my lawn chair, leaving me the steps.

"I knew you was a nurse when I first heard you in that coffee shop."

"How would you know a thing like that?"

"I get my hunches about people. Was that how you met him, nursing?"

"Chris? Well yes. Yes, it was."

"Oh, were you overseas?" said Mrs. Peebles.   105

"No, it was before he went overseas. I nursed him when he was stationed at Centralia and had a ruptured appendix. We got engaged and then he went overseas. My, this is refreshing, after a long drive."

"He'll be glad to see you," Dr. Peebles said. "It's a rackety kind of life, isn't it, not staying one place long enough to really make friends."

"Youse've had a long engagement," Loretta Bird said.

Alice Kelling passed that over. "I was going to get a room at the hotel, but when I was offered directions I came on out. Do you think I could phone them?"

110   "No need," Dr. Peebles said. "You're five miles away from him if you stay at the hotel. Here, you're right across the road. Stay with us. We've got rooms on rooms, look at this big house."

Asking people to stay, just like that, is certainly a country thing, and maybe seemed natural to him now, but not to Mrs. Peebles, from the way she said, oh yes, we have plenty of room. Or to Alice Kelling, who kept protesting, but let herself be worn down. I got the feeling it was a temptation to her, to be that close. I was trying for a look at her ring. Her nails were painted red, her fingers were freckled and wrinkled. It was a tiny stone. Muriel Lowe's cousin had one twice as big.

Chris came to get his water, late in the afternoon just as Dr. Peebles had predicted. He must have recognized the car from a way off. He came smiling.

"Here I am chasing after you to see what you're up to," called Alice Kelling. She got up and went to meet him and they kissed, just touched, in front of us.

"You're going to spend a lot on gas that way," Chris said.

115   Dr. Peebles invited Chris to stay for supper, since he had already put up the sign that said: NO MORE RIDES TILL 7 P.M. Mrs. Peebles wanted it served in the yard, in spite of the bugs. One thing strange to anybody from the country is this eating outside. I had made a potato salad earlier and she had made a jellied salad, that was one thing she could do, so it was just a matter of getting those out, and some sliced meat and cucumbers and fresh leaf lettuce. Loretta Bird hung around for some time saying, "Oh, well, I guess I better get home to those yappers," and, "It's so nice just sitting here, I sure hate to get up," but nobody invited her, I was relieved to see, and finally she had to go.

That night after rides were finished Alice Kelling and Chris went off somewhere in her car. I lay awake till they got back. When I saw the car lights sweep my ceiling I got up to look down on them through the slats of my blind. I don't know what I thought I was going to see. Muriel Lowe and I used to sleep on her front veranda and watch her sister and her sister's boy friend saying good night. Afterward we couldn't get to sleep, for longing for somebody to kiss us and rub up against us and we would talk about suppose you were out in a boat with a boy and he wouldn't bring you in to shore unless you did it, or what if somebody got you trapped in a barn, you would have to, wouldn't you, it wouldn't be your fault. Muriel said her two girl cousins used to try with a toilet paper roll that one of them was a boy. We wouldn't do anything like that; just lay and wondered.

All that happened was that Chris got out of the car on one side and she got out on the other and they walked off separately—him toward the fairgrounds and her toward the house. I got back in bed and imagined about me coming home with him, not like that.

Next morning Alice Kelling got up late and I fixed a grapefruit for her the way I had learned and Mrs. Peebles sat down with her to visit and have another cup of coffee. Mrs. Peebles seemed pleased enough now, having company. Alice Kelling said she guessed she better get used to putting in a day just watching Chris take off and come down, and Mrs. Peebles said she didn't know if she should suggest it because Alice Kelling was the one with the car, but the lake was only twenty-five miles away and what a good day for a picnic.

Alice Kelling took her up on the idea and by eleven o'clock they were in the car, with Joey and Heather and a sandwich lunch I had made. The only thing was that Chris hadn't come down, and she wanted to tell him where they were going.

"Edie'll go over and tell him," Mrs. Peebles said. "There's no   120
problem."

Alice Kelling wrinkled her face and agreed.

"Be sure and tell him we'll be back by five!"

I didn't see that he would be concerned about knowing this right away, and I thought of him eating whatever he ate over there, alone, cooking on his camp stove, so I got to work and mixed up a crumb cake and baked it, in between the other work I had to do; then, when it was a bit cooled, wrapped it in a tea towel. I didn't do anything to myself but take off my apron and comb my hair. I would like to have put some makeup on, but I was too afraid it would remind him of the way he first saw me, and that would humiliate me all over again.

He had come and put another sign on the gate: NO RIDES THIS P.M. APOLOGIES. I worried that he wasn't feeling well. No sign of him outside and the tent flap was down. I knocked on the pole.

"Come in," he said, in a voice that would just as soon have said   125
Stay out.

I lifted the flap.

"Oh, it's you. I'm sorry. I didn't know it was you."

He had been just sitting on the side of the bed, smoking. Why not at least sit and smoke in the fresh air?

"I brought a cake and hope you're not sick," I said.

"Why would I be sick? Oh—that sign. That's all right. I'm just tired   130
of talking to people. I don't mean you. Have a seat." He pinned back the tent flap. "Get some fresh air in here."

I sat on the edge of the bed, there was no place else. It was one of those fold-up cots, really: I remembered and gave him his fiancée's message.

He ate some of the cake. "Good."

"Put the rest away for when you're hungry later."

"I'll tell you a secret. I won't be around here much longer."

135   "Are you getting married?"

"Ha ha. What time did you say they'd be back?"

"Five o'clock."

"Well, by that time, this place will have seen the last of me. A plane can get further than a car." He unwrapped the cake and ate another piece of it, absentmindedly.

"Now you'll be thirsty."

140   "There's some water in the pail."

"It won't be very cold. I could bring some fresh. I could bring some ice from the refrigerator."

"No," he said. "I don't want you to go. I want a nice long time of saying good-bye to you."

He put the cake away carefully and sat beside me and started those little kisses, so soft, I can't ever let myself think about them, such kindness in his face and lovely kisses, all over my eyelids and neck and ears, all over, then me kissing back as well as I could (I had only kissed a boy on a dare before, and kissed my own arms for practice) and we lay back on the cot and pressed together, just gently, and he did some other things, not bad things or not in a bad way. It was lovely in the tent, that smell of grass and hot tent cloth with the sun beating down on it, and he said, "I wouldn't do you any harm for the world." Once, when he had rolled on top of me and we were sort of rocking together on the cot, he said softly, "Oh, no," and freed himself and jumped up and got the water pail. He splashed some of it on his neck and face, and the little bit left, on me lying there.

"That's to cool us off, miss."

145   When we said good-bye I wasn't at all sad, because he held my face and said, "I'm going to write you a letter. I'll tell you where I am and maybe you can come and see me. Would you like that? Okay then. You wait." I was really glad I think to get away from him, it was like he was piling presents on me I couldn't get the pleasure of till I considered them alone.

No consternation at first about the plane being gone. They thought he had taken somebody up, and I didn't enlighten them. Dr. Peebles had phoned he had to go to the country, so there was just us having supper, and then Loretta Bird thrusting her head in the door and saying, "I see he's took off."

"What?" said Alice Kelling, and pushed back her chair.

"The kids come and told me this afternoon he was taking down his tent. Did he think he'd run through all the business there was round here? He didn't take off without letting you know, did he?"

"He'll send me word," Alice Kelling said. "He'll probably phone tonight. He's terribly restless, since the war."

"Edie, he didn't mention to you, did he?" Mrs. Peebles said. "When you took over the message?"   150

"Yes," I said. So far so true.

"Well why didn't you say?" All of them were looking at me. "Did he say where he was going?"

"He said he might try Bayfield," I said. What made me tell such a lie? I didn't intend it.

"Bayfield, how far is that?" said Alice Kelling.

Mrs. Peebles said, "Thirty, thirty-five miles."   155

"That's not far. Oh, well, that's really not far at all. It's on the lake, isn't it?"

You'd think I'd be ashamed of myself, setting her on the wrong track. I did it to give him more time, whatever time he needed. I lied for him, and also, I have to admit, for me. Women should stick together and not do things like that. I see that now, but didn't then. I never thought of myself as being in any way like her, or coming to the same troubles, ever.

She hadn't taken her eyes off me. I thought she suspected my lie.

"When did he mention this to you?"

"Earlier."   160

"When you were over at the plane?"

"Yes."

"You must've stayed and had a chat." She smiled at me, not a nice smile. "You must've stayed and had a little visit with him."

"I took a cake," I said, thinking that telling some truth would spare me telling the rest.

"We didn't have a cake," said Mrs. Peebles rather sharply.   165

"I baked one."

Alice Kelling said, "That was very friendly of you."

"Did you get permission," said Loretta Bird. "You never know what these girls'll do next," she said. "It's not they mean harm so much, as they're ignorant."

"The cake is neither here nor there," Mrs. Peebles broke in. "Edie, I wasn't aware you knew Chris that well."

I didn't know what to say.   170

"I'm not surprised," Alice Kelling said in a high voice. "I knew by the look of her as soon as I saw her. We get them at the hospital all the time." She looked hard at me with her stretched smile. "Having their babies. We have to put them in a special ward because of their diseases. Little country tramps. Fourteen and fifteen years old. You should see the babies they have, too."

"There was a bad woman here in town had a baby that pus was running out of its eyes," Loretta Bird put in.

"Wait a minute," said Mrs. Peebles. "What is this talk? Edie. What about you and Mr. Watters? Were you intimate with him?"

"Yes," I said. I was thinking of us lying on the cot and kissing, wasn't that intimate? And I would never deny it.

175   They were all one minute quiet, even Loretta Bird.

"Well," said Mrs. Peebles. "I am surprised. I think I need a cigarette. This is the first of any such tendencies I've seen in her," she said, speaking to Alice Kelling, but Alice Kelling was looking at me.

"Loose little bitch." Tears ran down her face. "Loose little bitch, aren't you? I knew as soon as I saw you. Men despise girls like you. He just made use of you and went off, you know that, don't you? Girls like you are just nothing, they're just public conveniences, just filthy little rags!"

"Oh, now," said Mrs. Peebles.

"Filthy," Alice Kelling sobbed. "Filthy little rags!"

180   "Don't get yourself upset," Loretta Bird said. She was swollen up with pleasure at being in on this scene. "Men are all the same."

"Edie, I'm very surprised," Mrs. Peebles said. "I thought your parents were so strict. You don't want to have a baby, do you?"

I'm still ashamed of what happened next. I lost control, just like a six-year-old, I started howling. "You don't get a baby from just doing that!"

"You see. Some of them are that ignorant," Loretta Bird said.

But Mrs. Peebles jumped up and caught my arms and shook me.

185   "Calm down. Don't get hysterical. Calm down. Stop crying. Listen to me. Listen. I'm wondering, if you know what being intimate means. Now tell me. What did you think it meant?"

"Kissing," I howled.

She let go. "Oh, Edie. Stop it. Don't be silly. It's all right. It's all a misunderstanding. Being intimate means a lot more than that. Oh, I wondered."

"She's trying to cover up, now," said Alice Kelling. "Yes. She's not so stupid. She sees she got herself in trouble."

"I believe her," Mrs. Peebles said. "This is an awful scene."

190   "Well there is one way to find out," said Alice Kelling, getting up. "After all, I am a nurse."

Mrs. Peebles drew a breath and said, "No. No. Go to your room, Edie. And stop that noise. This is too disgusting."

I heard the car start in a little while. I tried to stop crying, pulling back each wave as it started over me. Finally I succeeded, and lay heaving on the bed.

Mrs. Peebles came and stood in the doorway.

"She's gone," she said. "That Bird woman too. Of course, you know you should never have gone near that man and that is the cause of all this trouble. I have a headache. As soon as you can, go and wash your face in cold water and get at the dishes and we will not say any more about this."

Nor we didn't. I didn't figure out till years later the extent of what I had been saved from. Mrs. Peebles was not very friendly to me afterward, but she was fair. Not very friendly is the wrong way of describing what she was. She had never been very friendly. It was just that now she had to see me all the time and it got on her nerves, a little.

As for me, I put it all out of my mind like a bad dream and concentrated on waiting for my letter. The mail came every day except Sunday, between one-thirty and two in the afternoon, a good time for me because Mrs. Peebles was always having her nap. I would get the kitchen all cleaned and then go up to the mailbox and sit in the grass, waiting. I was perfectly happy, waiting, I forgot all about Alice Kelling and her misery and awful talk and Mrs. Peebles and her chilliness and the embarrassment of whether she had told Dr. Peebles and the face of Loretta Bird, getting her fill of other people's troubles. I was always smiling when the mailman got there, and continued smiling even after he gave me the mail and I saw today wasn't the day. The mailman was a Carmichael. I knew by his face because there are a lot of Carmichaels living out by us and so many of them have a sort of sticking-out top lip. So I asked his name (he was a young man, shy, but good-humored, anybody could ask him anything) and then I said, "I knew by your face!" He was pleased by that and always glad to see me and got a little less shy. "You've got the smile I've been waiting on all day!" he used to holler out the car window.

It never crossed my mind for a long time a letter might not come. I believed in it coming just like I believed the sun would rise in the morning. I just put off my hope from day to day, and there was the goldenrod out around the mailbox and the children gone back to school, and the leaves turning, and I was wearing a sweater when I went to wait. One day walking back with the hydro bill stuck in my hand, that was all, looking across at the fairgrounds with the full-blown milkweed and dark teasels, so much like fall, it just struck me: *No letter was ever going to come*. It was an impossible idea to get used to. No, not impossible. If I thought about Chris's face when he said he was going to write to me, it was impossible, but if I forgot that and thought about the actual tin mailbox, empty, it was plain and true. I kept on going to meet the mail, but my heart was heavy now like a lump of lead. I only smiled because I thought of the mailman counting on it, and he didn't have an easy life, with the winter driving ahead.

Till it came to me one day there were women doing this with their lives, all over. There were women just waiting and waiting by mailboxes for one letter or another. I imagined me making this journey day after day and year after year, and my hair starting to go gray, and I thought, I was never made to go on like that. So I stopped meeting the mail. If there were women all through life waiting, and women busy and not waiting, I knew which I had to be. Even though there might be things the second kind of women have to pass up and never know about, it still is better.

I was surprised when the mailman phoned the Peebleses' place in the evening and asked for me. He said he missed me. He asked if I would like to go to Goderich, where some well-known movie was on, I forget now what. So I said yes, and I went out with him for two years and he asked me to marry him, and we were engaged a year more while I got my things together, and then we did marry. He always tells the children the story of how I went after him by sitting by the mailbox every day, and naturally I laugh and let him, because I like for people to think what pleases them and makes them happy.

QUESTIONS

1. Describe the plot structure in the story. How is the arrangement of the plot elements effective? At which points were your expectations as a reader overturned?
2. How does the story generate suspense? Which developments of the plot help to increase the suspense?
3. How do minor characters like Loretta Bird and Mrs. Peebles help advance the plot? What else do they add to the story?
4. Is Edie a sympathetic character? How does her status as "the hired girl" affect the way you respond to her as a reader?
5. Evaluate Chris Watters as a potential husband for Edie. Does her evaluation of him differ from the reader's?
6. The title "How I Met My Husband" suggests a reminiscence told from a much later, more mature vantage point. Can you detect the voice of an older, wiser Edie who is distinct from the young girl working for Dr. and Mrs. Peebles?

7. Discuss the role of Alice Kelling in advancing the plot and in the story as a whole. Could she be described as the antagonist? Why or why not?
8. Discuss the effectiveness of the surprise ending. How does Carmichael differ from Chris Watters? Can it be argued that the surprise ending is also inevitable and appropriate?

Jhumpa Lahiri
Interpreter of Maladies

At the tea stall Mr. and Mrs. Das bickered about who should take Tina to the toilet. Eventually Mrs. Das relented when Mr. Das pointed out that he had given the girl her bath the night before. In the rearview mirror Mr. Kapasi watched as Mrs. Das emerged slowly from his bulky white Ambassador, dragging her shaved, largely bare legs across the back seat. She did not hold the little girl's hand as they walked to the rest room.

They were on their way to see the Sun Temple at Konarak. It was a dry, bright Saturday, the mid-July heat tempered by a steady ocean breeze, ideal weather for sightseeing. Ordinarily Mr. Kapasi would not have stopped so soon along the way, but less than five minutes after he'd picked up the family that morning in front of Hotel Sandy Villa, the little girl had complained. The first thing Mr. Kapasi had noticed when he saw Mr. and Mrs. Das, standing with their children under the portico of the hotel, was that they were very young, perhaps not even thirty. In addition to Tina they had two boys, Ronny and Bobby, who appeared very close in age and had teeth covered in a network of flashing silver wires. The family looked Indian but dressed as foreigners did, the children in stiff, brightly colored clothing and caps with translucent visors. Mr. Kapasi was accustomed to foreign tourists; he was assigned to them regularly because he could speak English. Yesterday he had driven an elderly couple from Scotland, both with spotted faces and fluffy white hair so thin it exposed their sunburnt scalps. In comparison, the tanned, youthful faces of Mr. and Mrs. Das were all the more striking. When he'd introduced himself, Mr. Kapasi had pressed his palms together in

INTERPRETER OF MALADIES   First published in her 1999 collection *Interpreter of Maladies*, which won the 2000 Pulitzer Prize for fiction. Lahiri's book conducts an incisive exploration of Indian culture, especially as it collides with the values of western Europe and the United States. This story takes place in the state of Orissa on the eastern coast of India; the "Sun Temple at Konarak" is located on the coast near the city of Puri, where the Das family is staying. Of Indian ancestry, Jhumpa Lahiri (b. 1967) was born in London, grew up in Rhode Island, and earned an M.A. in creative writing and a Ph.D. in Renaissance Studies from Boston University. She now lives in New York City.

greeting, but Mr. Das squeezed hands like an American so that Mr. Kapasi felt it in his elbow. Mrs. Das, for her part, had flexed one side of her mouth, smiling dutifully at Mr. Kapasi, without displaying any interest in him.

As they waited at the tea stall, Ronny, who looked like the older of the two boys, clambered suddenly out of the back seat, intrigued by a goat tied to a stake in the ground.

"Don't touch it," Mr. Das said. He glanced up from his paperback tour book, which said "INDIA" in yellow letters and looked as if it had been published abroad. His voice, somehow tentative and a little shrill, sounded as though it had not yet settled into maturity.

5   "I want to give it a piece of gum," the boy called back as he trotted ahead.

Mr. Das stepped out of the car and stretched his legs by squatting briefly to the ground. A clean-shaven man, he looked exactly like a magnified version of Ronny. He had a sapphire blue visor, and was dressed in shorts, sneakers, and a T-shirt. The camera slung around his neck, with an impressive telephoto lens and numerous buttons and markings, was the only complicated thing he wore. He frowned, watching as Ronny rushed toward the goat, but appeared to have no intention of intervening. "Bobby, make sure that your brother doesn't do anything stupid."

"I don't feel like it," Bobby said, not moving. He was sitting in the front seat beside Mr. Kapasi, studying a picture of the elephant god taped to the glove compartment.

"No need to worry," Mr. Kapasi said. "They are quite tame." Mr. Kapasi was forty-six years old, with receding hair that had gone completely silver, but his butterscotch complexion and his unlined brow, which he treated in spare moments to dabs of lotus-oil balm, made it easy to imagine what he must have looked like at an earlier age. He wore gray trousers and a matching jacket-style shirt, tapered at the waist, with short sleeves and a large pointed collar, made of a thin but durable synthetic material. He had specified both the cut and the fabric to his tailor—it was his preferred uniform for giving tours because it did not get crushed during his long hours behind the wheel. Through the windshield he watched as Ronny circled around the goat, touched it quickly on its side, then trotted back to the car.

"You left India as a child?" Mr. Kapasi asked when Mr. Das had settled once again into the passenger seat.

10   "Oh, Mina and I were both born in America," Mr. Das announced with an air of sudden confidence. "Born and raised. Our parents live here now, in Assansol. They retired. We visit them every couple years." He turned to watch as the little girl ran toward the car, the wide purple

bows of her sundress flopping on her narrow brown shoulders. She was holding to her chest a doll with yellow hair that looked as if it had been chopped, as a punitive measure, with a pair of dull scissors. "This is Tina's first trip to India, isn't it, Tina?"

"I don't have to go to the bathroom anymore," Tina announced.

"Where's Mina?" Mr. Das asked.

Mr. Kapasi found it strange that Mr. Das should refer to his wife by her first name when speaking to the little girl. Tina pointed to where Mrs. Das was purchasing something from one of the shirtless men who worked at the tea stall. Mr. Kapasi heard one of the shirtless men sing a phrase from a popular Hindi love song as Mrs. Das walked back to the car, but she did not appear to understand the words of the song, for she did not express irritation, or embarrassment, or react in any other way to the man's declarations.

He observed her. She wore a red-and-white-checkered skirt that stopped above her knees, slip-on shoes with a square wooden heel, and a close-fitting blouse styled like a man's undershirt. The blouse was decorated at chest-level with a calico appliqué in the shape of a strawberry. She was a short woman, with small hands like paws, her frosty pink fingernails painted to match her lips, and was slightly plump in her figure. Her hair, shorn only a little longer than her husband's, was parted far to one side. She was wearing large dark brown sunglasses with a pinkish tint to them, and carried a big straw bag, almost as big as her torso, shaped like a bowl, with a water bottle poking out of it. She walked slowly, carrying some puffed rice tossed with peanuts and chili peppers in a large packet made from newspapers. Mr. Kapasi turned to Mr. Das.

"Where in America do you live?"   15

"New Brunswick, New Jersey."

"Next to New York?"

"Exactly. I teach middle school there."

"What subject?"

"Science. In fact, every year I take my students on a trip to the   20 Museum of Natural History in New York City. In a way we have a lot in common, you could say, you and I. How long have you been a tour guide, Mr. Kapasi?"

"Five years."

Mrs. Das reached the car. "How long's the trip?" she asked, shutting the door.

"About two and a half hours," Mr. Kapasi replied.

At this Mrs. Das gave an impatient sigh, as if she had been traveling her whole life without pause. She fanned herself with a folded Bombay film magazine written in English.

25   "I thought that the Sun Temple is only eighteen miles north of Puri," Mr. Das said, tapping on the tour book.

"The roads to Konarak are poor. Actually it is a distance of fifty-two miles," Mr. Kapasi explained.

Mr. Das nodded, readjusting the camera strap where it had begun to chafe the back of his neck.

Before starting the ignition, Mr. Kapasi reached back to make sure the cranklike locks on the inside of each of the back doors were secured. As soon as the car began to move the little girl began to play with the lock on her side, clicking it with some effort forward and backward, but Mrs. Das said nothing to stop her. She sat a bit slouched at one end of the back seat, not offering her puffed rice to anyone. Ronny and Tina sat on either side of her, both snapping bright green gum.

"Look," Bobby said as the car began to gather speed. He pointed with his finger to the tall trees that lined the road. "Look."

30   "Monkeys!" Ronny shrieked. "Wow!"

They were seated in groups along the branches, with shining black faces, silver bodies, horizontal eyebrows, and crested heads. Their long gray tails dangled like a series of ropes among the leaves. A few scratched themselves with black leathery hands, or swung their feet, staring as the car passed.

"We call them the hanuman,"° Mr. Kapasi said. "They are quite common in the area."

As soon as he spoke, one of the monkeys leaped into the middle of the road, causing Mr. Kapasi to brake suddenly. Another bounced onto the hood of the car, then sprang away. Mr. Kapasi beeped his horn. The children began to get excited, sucking in their breath and covering their faces partly with their hands. They had never seen monkeys outside of a zoo, Mr. Das explained. He asked Mr. Kapasi to stop the car so that he could take a picture.

While Mr. Das adjusted his telephoto lens, Mrs. Das reached into her straw bag and pulled out a bottle of colorless nail polish, which she proceeded to stroke on the tip of her index finger.

35   The little girl stuck out a hand. "Mine too. Mommy, do mine too."

"Leave me alone," Mrs. Das said, blowing on her nail and turning her body slightly. "You're making me mess up."

The little girl occupied herself by buttoning and unbuttoning a pinafore on the doll's plastic body.

"All set," Mr. Das said, replacing the lens cap.

---

hanuman: a gray monkey venerated by Hindus

The car rattled considerably as it raced along the dusty road, causing them all to pop up from their seats every now and then, but Mrs. Das continued to polish her nails. Mr. Kapasi eased up on the accelerator, hoping to produce a smoother ride. When he reached for the gearshift the boy in front accommodated him by swinging his hairless knees out of the way. Mr. Kapasi noted that this boy was slightly paler than the other children. "Daddy, why is the driver sitting on the wrong side in this car, too?" the boy asked.

"They all do that here, dummy," Ronny said.   40

"Don't call your brother a dummy," Mr. Das said. He turned to Mr. Kapasi. "In America, you know . . . it confuses them."

"Oh yes, I am well aware," Mr. Kapasi said. As delicately as he could, he shifted gears again, accelerating as they approached a hill in the road. "I see it on *Dallas*, the steering wheels are on the left-hand side."

"What's *Dallas*?" Tina asked, banging her now naked doll on the seat behind Mr. Kapasi.

"It went off the air," Mr. Das explained. "It's a television show."

They were all like siblings, Mr. Kapasi thought as they passed a row   45
of date trees. Mr. and Mrs. Das behaved like an older brother and sister, not parents. It seemed that they were in charge of the children only for the day; it was hard to believe they were regularly responsible for anything other than themselves. Mr. Das tapped on his lens cap, and his tour book, dragging his thumbnail occasionally across the pages so that they made a scraping sound. Mrs. Das continued to polish her nails. She had still not removed her sunglasses. Every now and then Tina renewed her plea that she wanted her nails done, too, and so at one point Mrs. Das flicked a drop of polish on the little girl's finger before depositing the bottle back inside her straw bag.

"Isn't this an air-conditioned car?" she asked, still blowing on her hand. The window on Tina's side was broken and could not be rolled down.

"Quit complaining," Mr. Das said. "It isn't so hot."

"I told you to get a car with air-conditioning," Mrs. Das continued. "Why do you do this, Raj, just to save a few stupid rupees. What are you saving us, fifty cents?"

Their accents sounded just like the ones Mr. Kapasi heard on American television programs, though not like the ones on *Dallas*.

"Doesn't it get tiresome, Mr. Kapasi, showing people the same   50
thing every day?" Mr. Das asked, rolling down his own window all the way. "Hey, do you mind stopping the car. I just want to get a shot of this guy."

Mr. Kapasi pulled over to the side of the road as Mr. Das took a picture of a barefoot man, his head wrapped in a dirty turban, seated on top of a cart of grain sacks pulled by a pair of bullocks. Both the man and the bullocks were emaciated. In the back seat Mrs. Das gazed out another window, at the sky, where nearly transparent clouds passed quickly in front of one another.

"I look forward to it, actually," Mr. Kapasi said as they continued on their way. "The Sun Temple is one of my favorite places. In that way it is a reward for me. I give tours on Fridays and Saturdays only. I have another job during the week."

"Oh? Where?" Mr. Das asked.

"I work in a doctor's office."

55   "You're a doctor?"

"I am not a doctor. I work with one. As an interpreter."

"What does a doctor need an interpreter for?"

"He has a number of Gujarati° patients. My father was Gujarati, but many people do not speak Gujarati in this area, including the doctor. And so the doctor asked me to work in his office, interpreting what the patients say."

"Interesting. I've never heard of anything like that," Mr. Das said.

60   Mr. Kapasi shrugged. "It is a job like any other."

"But so romantic," Mrs. Das said dreamily, breaking her extended silence. She lifted her pinkish brown sunglasses and arranged them on top of her head like a tiara. For the first time, her eyes met Mr. Kapasi's in the rearview mirror: pale, a bit small, their gaze fixed but drowsy.

Mr. Das craned to look at her. "What's so romantic about it?"

"I don't know. Something." She shrugged, knitting her brows together for an instant. "Would you like a piece of gum, Mr. Kapasi?" she asked brightly. She reached into her straw bag and handed him a small square wrapped in green-and-white-striped paper. As soon as Mr. Kapasi put the gum in his mouth a thick sweet liquid burst onto his tongue.

"Tell us more about your job, Mr. Kapasi," Mrs. Das said.

65   "What would you like to know, madame?"

"I don't know," she shrugged, munching on some puffed rice and licking the mustard oil from the corners of her mouth. "Tell us a typical situation." She settled back in her seat, her head tilted in a patch of sun, and closed her eyes. "I want to picture what happens."

"Very well. The other day a man came in with a pain in his throat."

"Did he smoke cigarettes?"

Gujarati: from Gujarat, a state in western India

"No. It was very curious. He complained that he felt as if there were long pieces of straw stuck in his throat. When I told the doctor he was able to prescribe the proper medication."

"That's so neat."   70

"Yes," Mr. Kapasi agreed after some hesitation.

"So these patients are totally dependent on you," Mrs. Das said. She spoke slowly, as if she were thinking aloud. "In a way, more dependent on you than the doctor."

"How do you mean? How could it be?"

"Well, for example, you could tell the doctor that the pain felt like a burning, not straw. The patient would never know what you had told the doctor, and the doctor wouldn't know that you had told the wrong thing. It's a big responsibility."

"Yes, a big responsibility you have there, Mr. Kapasi," Mr. Das   75
agreed.

Mr. Kapasi had never thought of his job in such complimentary terms. To him it was a thankless occupation. He found nothing noble in interpreting people's maladies, assiduously translating the symptoms of so many swollen bones, countless cramps of bellies and bowels, spots on people's palms that changed color, shape, or size. The doctor, nearly half his age, had an affinity for bell-bottom trousers and made humorless jokes about the Congress party. Together they worked in a stale little infirmary where Mr. Kapasi's smartly tailored clothes clung to him in the heat, in spite of the blackened blades of a ceiling fan churning over their heads.

The job was a sign of his failings. In his youth he'd been a devoted scholar of foreign languages, the owner of an impressive collection of dictionaries. He had dreamed of being an interpreter for diplomats and dignitaries, resolving conflicts between people and nations, settling disputes of which he alone could understand both sides. He was a self-educated man. In a series of notebooks, in the evenings before his parents settled his marriage, he had listed the common etymologies of words, and at one point in his life he was confident that he could converse, if given the opportunity, in English, French, Russian, Portuguese, and Italian, not to mention Hindi, Bengali, Orissi, and Gujarati. Now only a handful of European phrases remained in his memory, scattered words for things like saucers and chairs. English was the only non-Indian language he spoke fluently anymore. Mr. Kapasi knew it was not a remarkable talent. Sometimes he feared that his children knew better English than he did, just from watching television. Still, it came in handy for the tours.

He had taken the job as an interpreter after his first son, at the age of seven, contracted typhoid—that was how he had first made the acquaintance of the doctor. At the time Mr. Kapasi had been teaching English in a grammar school, and he bartered his skills as an interpreter to pay the increasingly exorbitant medical bills. In the end the boy had died one evening in his mother's arms, his limbs burning with fever, but then there was the funeral to pay for, and the other children who were born soon enough, and the newer, bigger house, and the good schools and tutors, and the fine shoes and the television, and the countless other ways he tried to console his wife and to keep her from crying in her sleep, and so when the doctor offered to pay him twice as much as he earned at the grammar school, he accepted. Mr. Kapasi knew that his wife had little regard for his career as an interpreter. He knew it reminded her of the son she'd lost, and that she resented the other lives he helped, in his own small way, to save. If ever she referred to his position, she used the phrase "doctor's assistant," as if the process of interpretation were equal to taking someone's temperature, or changing a bedpan. She never asked him about the patients who came to the doctor's office, or said that his job was a big responsibility.

For this reason it flattered Mr. Kapasi that Mrs. Das was so intrigued by his job. Unlike his wife, she had reminded him of its intellectual challenges. She had also used the word "romantic." She did not behave in a romantic way toward her husband, and yet she had used the word to describe him. He wondered if Mr. and Mrs. Das were a bad match, just as he and his wife were. Perhaps they, too, had little in common apart from three children and a decade of their lives. The signs he recognized from his own marriage were there—the bickering, the indifference, the protracted silences. Her sudden interest in him, an interest she did not express in either her husband or her children, was mildly intoxicating. When Mr. Kapasi thought once again about how she had said "romantic," the feeling of intoxication grew.

80   He began to check his reflection in the rearview mirror as he drove, feeling grateful that he had chosen the gray suit that morning and not the brown one, which tended to sag a little in the knees. From time to time he glanced through the mirror at Mrs. Das. In addition to glancing at her face he glanced at the strawberry between her breasts, and the golden brown hollow in her throat. He decided to tell Mrs. Das about another patient, and another: the young woman who had complained of a sensation of raindrops in her spine, the gentleman whose birthmark had begun to sprout hairs. Mrs. Das listened attentively, stroking her hair with a small plastic brush that resembled an oval bed of nails, asking more questions, for yet another example. The children were quiet, intent on spotting more monkeys in the trees, and Mr. Das was absorbed by his tour book, so it seemed like a private conversation between

Mr. Kapasi and Mrs. Das. In this manner the next half hour passed, and when they stopped for lunch at a roadside restaurant that sold fritters and omelette sandwiches, usually something Mr. Kapasi looked forward to on his tours so that he could sit in peace and enjoy some hot tea, he was disappointed. As the Das family settled together under a magenta umbrella fringed with white and orange tassels, and placed their orders with one of the waiters who marched about in tricornered caps, Mr. Kapasi reluctantly headed toward a neighboring table.

"Mr. Kapasi, wait. There's room here," Mrs. Das called out. She gathered Tina onto her lap, insisting that he accompany them. And so, together, they had bottled mango juice and sandwiches and plates of onions and potatoes deep-fried in graham-flour batter. After finishing two omelette sandwiches Mr. Das took more pictures of the group as they ate.

"How much longer?" he asked Mr. Kapasi as he paused to load a new roll of film in the camera.

"About half an hour more."

By now the children had gotten up from the table to look at more monkeys perched in a nearby tree, so there was a considerable space between Mrs. Das and Mr. Kapasi. Mr. Das placed the camera to his face and squeezed one eye shut, his tongue exposed at one corner of his mouth. "This looks funny. Mina, you need to lean in closer to Mr. Kapasi."

She did. He could smell a scent on her skin, like a mixture of whiskey and rosewater. He worried suddenly that she could smell his perspiration, which he knew had collected beneath the synthetic material of his shirt. He polished off his mango juice in one gulp and smoothed his silver hair with his hands. A bit of the juice dripped onto his chin. He wondered if Mrs. Das had noticed.   85

She had not. "What's your address, Mr. Kapasi?" she inquired, fishing for something inside her straw bag.

"You would like my address?"

"So we can send you copies," she said. "Of the pictures." She handed him a scrap of paper which she had hastily ripped from a page of her film magazine. The blank portion was limited, for the narrow strip was crowded by lines of text and a tiny picture of a hero and heroine embracing under a eucalyptus tree.

The paper curled as Mr. Kapasi wrote his address in clear, careful letters. She would write to him, asking about his days interpreting at the doctor's office, and he would respond eloquently, choosing only the most entertaining anecdotes, ones that would make her laugh out loud as she read them in her house in New Jersey. In time she would reveal the disappointment of her marriage, and he his. In this way their friendship would grow, and flourish. He would possess a picture of the two of them, eating fried onions under a magenta umbrella, which he would keep, he decided, safely tucked between the pages of his Russian grammar. As his mind raced, Mr. Kapasi experienced a mild and pleasant shock. It was similar to a feeling he used to experience long ago when, after months of translating with the aid of a dictionary, he would finally read a passage from a French novel, or an Italian sonnet, and understand the words, one after another, unencumbered by his own efforts. In those moments Mr. Kapasi used to believe that all was right with the world, that all struggles were rewarded, that all of life's mistakes made sense in the end. The promise that he would hear from Mrs. Das now filled him with the same belief.

90   When he finished writing his address Mr. Kapasi handed her the paper, but as soon as he did so he worried that he had either misspelled his name, or accidentally reversed the numbers of his postal code. He dreaded the possibility of a lost letter, the photograph never reaching him, hovering somewhere in Orissa, close but ultimately unattainable. He thought of asking for the slip of paper again, just to make sure he had written his address accurately, but Mrs. Das had already dropped it into the jumble of her bag.

They reached Konarak at two-thirty. The temple, made of sandstone, was a massive pyramid-like structure in the shape of a chariot. It was dedicated to the great master of life, the sun, which struck three sides of the edifice as it made its journey each day across the sky. Twenty-four giant wheels were carved on the north and south sides of the plinth. The whole thing was drawn by a team of seven horses, speeding as if through the heavens. As they approached, Mr. Kapasi explained that the temple had been built between A.D. 1243 and 1255, with the efforts of twelve hundred artisans, by the great ruler of the Ganga dynasty, King Narasimhadeva the First, to commemorate his victory against the Muslim army.

"It says the temple occupies about a hundred and seventy acres of land," Mr. Das said, reading from his book.

"It's like a desert," Ronny said, his eyes wandering across the sand that stretched on all sides beyond the temple.

"The Chandrabhaga River once flowed one mile north of here. It is dry now," Mr. Kapasi said, turning off the engine.

95   They got out and walked toward the temple, posing first for pictures by the pair of lions that flanked the steps. Mr. Kapasi led them next to one of the wheels of the chariot, higher than any human being, nine feet in diameter.

"'The wheels are supposed to symbolize the wheel of life,'" Mr. Das read. "'They depict the cycle of creation, preservation, and achievement of realization.' Cool." He turned the page of his book. "'Each wheel is divided into eight thick and thin spokes, dividing the day into eight equal parts. The rims are carved with designs of birds and animals, whereas the medallions in the spokes are carved with women in luxurious poses, largely erotic in nature.'"

What he referred to were the countless friezes of entwined naked bodies, making love in various positions, women clinging to the necks of men, their knees wrapped eternally around their lovers' thighs. In addition to these were assorted scenes from daily life, of hunting and trading, of deer being killed with bows and arrows and marching warriors holding swords in their hands.

It was no longer possible to enter the temple, for it had filled with rubble years ago, but they admired the exterior, as did all the tourists Mr. Kapasi brought there, slowly strolling along each of its sides. Mr. Das trailed behind, taking pictures. The children ran ahead, pointing to figures of naked people, intrigued in particular by the Nagamithunas, the half-human, half-serpentine couples who were said, Mr. Kapasi told them, to live in the deepest waters of the sea. Mr. Kapasi was pleased that they liked the temple, pleased especially that it appealed to Mrs. Das. She stopped every three or four paces, staring silently at the carved lovers, and the processions of elephants, and the topless female musicians beating on two-sided drums.

Though Mr. Kapasi had been to the temple countless times, it occurred to him, as he, too, gazed at the topless women, that he had never seen his own wife fully naked. Even when they had made love she kept the panels of her blouse hooked together, the string of her petticoat knotted around her waist. He had never admired the backs of his wife's legs the way he now admired those of Mrs. Das, walking as if for his benefit alone. He had, of course, seen plenty of bare limbs before, belonging to the American and European ladies who took his tours. But Mrs. Das was different. Unlike the other women, who had an interest only in the temple, and kept their noses buried in a guidebook, or their eyes behind the lens of a camera, Mrs. Das had taken an interest in him.

Mr. Kapasi was anxious to be alone with her, to continue their private conversation, yet he felt nervous to walk at her side. She was lost behind her sunglasses, ignoring her husband's requests that she pose for another picture, walking past her children as if they were strangers. Worried that he might disturb her, Mr. Kapasi walked ahead, to admire, as he always did, the three life-sized bronze avatars of Surya, the sun god, each emerging from its own niche on the temple facade to greet the sun

100

at dawn, noon, and evening. They wore elaborate headdresses, their languid, elongated eyes closed, their bare chests draped with carved chains and amulets. Hibiscus petals, offerings from previous visitors, were strewn at their gray-green feet. The last statue, on the northern wall of the temple, was Mr. Kapasi's favorite. This Surya had a tired expression, weary after a hard day of work, sitting astride a horse with folded legs. Even his horse's eyes were drowsy. Around his body were smaller sculptures of women in pairs, their hips thrust to one side.

"Who's that?" Mrs. Das asked. He was startled to see that she was standing beside him.

"He is the Astachala-Surya," Mr. Kapasi said. "The setting sun."

"So in a couple of hours the sun will set right here?" She slipped a foot out of one of her square-heeled shoes, rubbed her toes on the back of her other leg.

"That is correct."

105   She raised her sunglasses for a moment, then put them back on again. "Neat."

Mr. Kapasi was not certain exactly what the word suggested, but he had a feeling it was a favorable response. He hoped that Mrs. Das had understood Surya's beauty, his power. Perhaps they would discuss it further in their letters. He would explain things to her, things about India, and she would explain things to him about America. In its own way this correspondence would fulfill his dream, of serving as an interpreter between nations. He looked at her straw bag, delighted that his address lay nestled among its contents. When he pictured her so many thousands of miles away he plummeted, so much so that he had an overwhelming urge to wrap his arms around her, to freeze with her, even for an instant, in an embrace witnessed by his favorite Surya. But Mrs. Das had already started walking.

"When do you return to America?" he asked, trying to sound placid.

"In ten days."

He calculated: A week to settle in, a week to develop the pictures, a few days to compose her letter, two weeks to get to India by air. According to his schedule, allowing room for delays, he would hear from Mrs. Das in approximately six weeks' time.

110   The family was silent as Mr. Kapasi drove them back, a little past four-thirty, to Hotel Sandy Villa. The children had bought miniature granite versions of the chariot's wheels at a souvenir stand, and they turned them round in their hands. Mr. Das continued to read his book. Mrs. Das untangled Tina's hair with her brush and divided it into two little ponytails.

Mr. Kapasi was beginning to dread the thought of dropping them off. He was not prepared to begin his six-week wait to hear from Mrs. Das. As he stole glances at her in the rearview mirror, wrapping elastic bands around Tina's hair, he wondered how he might make the tour last a little longer. Ordinarily he sped back to Puri using a shortcut, eager to return home, scrub his feet and hands with sandalwood soap, and enjoy the evening newspaper and a cup of tea that his wife would serve him in silence. The thought of that silence, something to which he'd long been resigned, now oppressed him. It was then that he suggested visiting the hills at Udayagiri and Khandagiri, where a number of monastic dwellings were hewn out of the ground, facing one another across a defile. It was some miles away, but well worth seeing, Mr. Kapasi told them.

"Oh yeah, there's something mentioned about it in this book," Mr. Das said. "Built by a Jain king or something."

"Shall we go then?" Mr. Kapasi asked. He paused at a turn in the road. "It's to the left."

Mr. Das turned to look at Mrs. Das. Both of them shrugged.

"Left, left," the children chanted.   115

Mr. Kapasi turned the wheel, almost delirious with relief. He did not know what he would do or say to Mrs. Das once they arrived at the hills. Perhaps he would tell her what a pleasing smile she had. Perhaps he would compliment her strawberry shirt, which he found irresistibly becoming. Perhaps, when Mr. Das was busy taking a picture, he would take her hand.

He did not have to worry. When they got to the hills, divided by a steep path thick with trees, Mrs. Das refused to get out of the car. All along the path, dozens of monkeys were seated on stones, as well as on the branches of the trees. Their hind legs were stretched out in front and raised to shoulder level, their arms resting on their knees.

"My legs are tired," she said, sinking low in her seat. "I'll stay here."

"Why did you have to wear those stupid shoes?" Mr. Das said. "You won't be in the pictures."

"Pretend I'm there."   120

"But we could use one of these pictures for our Christmas card this year. We didn't get one of all five of us at the Sun Temple. Mr. Kapasi could take it."

"I'm not coming. Anyway, those monkeys give me the creeps."

"But they're harmless," Mr. Das said. He turned to Mr. Kapasi. "Aren't they?"

"They are more hungry than dangerous," Mr. Kapasi said. "Do not provoke them with food, and they will not bother you."

125   Mr. Das headed up the defile with the children, the boys at his side, the little girl on his shoulders. Mr. Kapasi watched as they crossed paths with a Japanese man and woman, the only other tourists there, who paused for a final photograph, then stepped into a nearby car and drove away. As the car disappeared out of view some of the monkeys called out, emitting soft whooping sounds, and then walked on their flat black hands and feet up the path. At one point a group of them formed a little ring around Mr. Das and the children. Tina screamed in delight. Ronny ran in circles around his father. Bobby bent down and picked up a fat stick on the ground. When he extended it, one of the monkeys approached him and snatched it, then briefly beat the ground.

"I'll join them," Mr. Kapasi said, unlocking the door on his side. "There is much to explain about the caves."

"No. Stay a minute," Mrs. Das said. She got out of the back seat and slipped in beside Mr. Kapasi. "Raj has his dumb book anyway." Together, through the windshield, Mrs. Das and Mr. Kapasi watched as Bobby and the monkey passed the stick back and forth between them.

"A brave little boy," Mr. Kapasi commented.

"It's not so surprising," Mrs. Das said.

130   "No?"

"He's not his."

"I beg your pardon?"

"Raj's. He's not Raj's son."

Mr. Kapasi felt a prickle on his skin. He reached into his shirt pocket for the small tin of lotus-oil balm he carried with him at all times, and applied it to three spots on his forehead. He knew that Mrs. Das was watching him, but he did not turn to face her. Instead he watched as the figures of Mr. Das and the children grew smaller, climbing up the steep path, pausing every now and then for a picture, surrounded by a growing number of monkeys.

135   "Are you surprised?" The way she put it made him choose his words with care.

"It's not the type of thing one assumes," Mr. Kapasi replied slowly. He put the tin of lotus-oil balm back in his pocket.

"No, of course not. And no one knows, of course. No one at all. I've kept it a secret for eight whole years." She looked at Mr. Kapasi, tilting her chin as if to gain a fresh perspective. "But now I've told you."

Mr. Kapasi nodded. He felt suddenly parched, and his forehead was warm and slightly numb from the balm. He considered asking Mrs. Das for a sip of water, then decided against it.

"We met when we were very young," she said. She reached into her straw bag in search of something, then pulled out a packet of puffed rice. "Want some?"

"No, thank you."   140

She put a fistful in her mouth, sank into the seat a little, and looked away from Mr. Kapasi, out the window on her side of the car. "We married when we were still in college. We were in high school when he proposed. We went to the same college, of course. Back then we couldn't stand the thought of being separated, not for a day, not for a minute. Our parents were best friends who lived in the same town. My entire life I saw him every weekend, either at our house or theirs. We were sent upstairs to play together while our parents joked about our marriage. Imagine! They never caught us at anything, though in a way I think it was all more or less a setup. The things we did those Friday and Saturday nights, while our parents sat downstairs drinking tea . . . I could tell you stories, Mr. Kapasi."

As a result of spending all her time in college with Raj, she continued, she did not make many close friends. There was no one to confide in about him at the end of a difficult day, or to share a passing thought or a worry. Her parents now lived on the other side of the world, but she had never been very close to them, anyway. After marrying so young she was overwhelmed by it all, having a child so quickly, and nursing, and warming up bottles of milk and testing their temperature against her wrist while Raj was at work, dressed in sweaters and corduroy pants, teaching his students about rocks and dinosaurs. Raj never looked cross or harried, or plump as she had become after the first baby.

Always tired, she declined invitations from her one or two college girlfriends, to have lunch or shop in Manhattan. Eventually the friends stopped calling her, so that she was left at home all day with the baby, surrounded by toys that made her trip when she walked or wince when she sat, always cross and tired. Only occasionally did they go out after Ronny was born, and even more rarely did they entertain. Raj didn't mind; he looked forward to coming home from teaching and watching television and bouncing Ronny on his knee. She had been outraged when Raj told her that a Punjabi friend, someone whom she had once met but did not remember, would be staying with them for a week for some job interviews in the New Brunswick area.

Bobby was conceived in the afternoon, on a sofa littered with rubber teething toys, after the friend learned that a London pharmaceutical company had hired him, while Ronny cried to be freed from his playpen. She made no protest when the friend touched the small of her back as she was about to make a pot of coffee, then pulled her against his crisp navy suit. He made love to her swiftly, in silence, with an expertise she had never known, without the meaningful expressions and smiles Raj always insisted on afterward. The next day Raj drove the friend to JFK. He was married now, to a Punjabi girl, and they lived in London still, and every year they exchanged Christmas cards with Raj and Mina, each couple tucking photos of their families into the envelopes. He did not know that he was Bobby's father. He never would.

145   "I beg your pardon, Mrs. Das, but why have you told me this information?" Mr. Kapasi asked when she had finally finished speaking, and had turned to face him once again.

"For God's sake, stop calling me Mrs. Das. I'm twenty-eight. You probably have children my age."

"Not quite." It disturbed Mr. Kapasi to learn that she thought of him as a parent. The feeling he had had toward her, that had made him check his reflection in the rearview mirror as they drove, evaporated a little.

"I told you because of your talents." She put the packet of puffed rice back into her bag without folding over the top.

"I don't understand," Mr. Kapasi said.

150   "Don't you see? For eight years I haven't been able to express this to anybody, not to friends, certainly not to Raj. He doesn't even suspect it. He thinks I'm still in love with him. Well, don't you have anything to say?"

"About what?"

"About what I've just told you. About my secret, and about how terrible it makes me feel. I feel terrible looking at my children, and at Raj, always terrible. I have terrible urges, Mr. Kapasi, to throw things away. One day I had the urge to throw everything I own out the window, the television, the children, everything. Don't you think it's unhealthy?"

He was silent.

"Mr. Kapasi, don't you have anything to say? I thought that was your job."

155   "My job is to give tours, Mrs. Das."

"Not that. Your other job. As an interpreter."

"But we do not face a language barrier. What need is there for an interpreter?"

"That's not what I mean. I would never have told you otherwise. Don't you realize what it means for me to tell you?"

"What does it mean?"

160   "It means that I'm tired of feeling so terrible all the time. Eight years, Mr. Kapasi, I've been in pain eight years. I was hoping you could help me feel better, say the right thing. Suggest some kind of remedy."

He looked at her, in her red plaid skirt and strawberry T-shirt, a woman not yet thirty, who loved neither her husband nor her children, who had already fallen out of love with life. Her confession depressed him, depressed him all the more when he thought of Mr. Das at the top of the path, Tina clinging to his shoulders, taking pictures of ancient monastic cells cut into the hills to show his students in America, unsuspecting and unaware that one of his sons was not his own. Mr. Kapasi felt insulted that Mrs. Das should ask him to interpret her common, trivial little secret. She did not resemble the patients in the doctor's office, those who came glassy-eyed and desperate, unable to sleep or breathe or urinate with ease, unable, above all, to give words to their pains. Still, Mr. Kapasi believed it was his duty to assist Mrs. Das. Perhaps he ought to tell her to confess the truth to Mr. Das. He would explain that honesty was the best policy. Honesty, surely, would help her feel better, as she'd put it. Perhaps he would offer to preside over the discussion, as a mediator. He decided to begin with the most obvious question, to get to the heart of the matter, and so he asked, "Is it really pain you feel, Mrs. Das, or is it guilt?"

She turned to him and glared, mustard oil thick on her frosty pink lips. She opened her mouth to say something, but as she glared at Mr. Kapasi some certain knowledge seemed to pass before her eyes, and she stopped. It crushed him; he knew at that moment that he was not even important enough to be properly insulted. She opened the car door and began walking up the path, wobbling a little on her square wooden heels, reaching into her straw bag to eat handfuls of puffed rice. It fell through her fingers, leaving a zigzagging trail, causing a monkey to leap down from a tree and devour the little white grains. In search of more, the monkey began to follow Mrs. Das. Others joined him, so that she was soon being followed by about half a dozen of them, their velvety tails dragging behind.

Mr. Kapasi stepped out of the car. He wanted to holler, to alert her in some way, but he worried that if she knew they were behind her, she would grow nervous. Perhaps she would lose her balance. Perhaps they would pull at her bag or her hair. He began to jog up the path, taking a fallen branch in his hand to scare away the monkeys. Mrs. Das continued walking, oblivious, trailing grains of puffed rice. Near the top of the incline, before a group of cells fronted by a row of squat stone pillars, Mr. Das was kneeling on the ground, focusing the lens of his camera. The children stood under the arcade, now hiding, now emerging from view.

"Wait for me," Mrs. Das called out. "I'm coming."

Tina jumped up and down. "Here comes Mommy!"   165

"Great," Mr. Das said without looking up. "Just in time. We'll get Mr. Kapasi to take a picture of the five of us."

Mr. Kapasi quickened his pace, waving his branch so that the monkeys scampered away, distracted, in another direction.

"Where's Bobby?" Mrs. Das asked when she stopped.

Mr. Das looked up from the camera. "I don't know. Ronny, where's Bobby?"

170   Ronny shrugged. "I thought he was right here."

"Where is he?" Mrs. Das repeated sharply. "What's wrong with all of you?"

They began calling his name, wandering up and down the path a bit. Because they were calling, they did not initially hear the boy's screams. When they found him, a little farther down the path under a tree, he was surrounded by a group of monkeys, over a dozen of them, pulling at his T-shirt with their long black fingers. The puffed rice Mrs. Das had spilled was scattered at his feet, raked over by the monkeys' hands. The boy was silent, his body frozen, swift tears running down his startled face. His bare legs were dusty and red with welts from where one of the monkeys struck him repeatedly with the stick he had given to it earlier.

"Daddy, the monkey's hurting Bobby," Tina said.

Mr. Das wiped his palms on the front of his shorts. In his nervousness he accidentally pressed the shutter on his camera; the whirring noise of the advancing film excited the monkeys, and the one with the stick began to beat Bobby more intently. "What are we supposed to do? What if they start attacking?"

175   "Mr. Kapasi," Mrs. Das shrieked, noticing him standing to one side. "Do something, for God's sake, do something!"

Mr. Kapasi took his branch and shooed them away, hissing at the ones that remained, stomping his feet to scare them. The animals retreated slowly, with a measured gait, obedient but unintimidated. Mr. Kapasi gathered Bobby in his arms and brought him back to where his parents and siblings were standing. As he carried him he was tempted to whisper a secret into the boy's ear. But Bobby was stunned, and shivering with fright, his legs bleeding slightly where the stick had broken the skin. When Mr. Kapasi delivered him to his parents, Mr. Das brushed some dirt off the boy's T-shirt and put the visor on him the right way. Mrs. Das reached into her straw bag to find a bandage which she taped over the cut on his knee. Ronny offered his brother a fresh piece of gum. "He's fine. Just a little scared, right, Bobby?" Mr. Das said, patting the top of his head.

"God, let's get out of here," Mrs. Das said. She folded her arms across the strawberry on her chest. "This place gives me the creeps."

"Yeah. Back to the hotel, definitely," Mr. Das agreed.

"Poor Bobby," Mrs. Das said. "Come here a second. Let Mommy fix your hair." Again she reached into her straw bag, this time for her hairbrush, and began to run it around the edges of the translucent visor. When she whipped out the hairbrush, the slip of paper with Mr. Kapasi's address on it fluttered away in the wind. No one but Mr. Kapasi noticed. He watched as it rose, carried higher and higher by the breeze, into the trees where the monkeys now sat, solemnly observing the scene below. Mr. Kapasi observed it too, knowing that this was the picture of the Das family he would preserve forever in his mind.

QUESTIONS

1. Define the central conflict in this story. Is the conflict resolved in the story's conclusion?

2. How does the plot help to illuminate the differing cultural viewpoints of Mr. Kapasi and of Mr. and Mrs. Das? Which cultural viewpoint is presented with greater sympathy?

3. How does Mr. Kapasi's job as an "interpreter of maladies" relate to the action in this story? Does he have the occasion to use his diagnostic ability in his interactions with the Das family?

4. Discuss the significance of Mrs. Das's requesting, and then losing, Mr. Kapasi's address. Apart from its function in the plot, how does this suggest a resolution to the story?

5. How do the characters' views of one another differ from the way the reader is encouraged to view them? How does this ironic technique help to generate suspense?

6. How do the monkeys that the group encounters in the hill country serve as a plot element, helping to advance the story?

7. Discuss the function of the "secret" Mrs. Das reveals to Mr. Kapasi. Does this scene make Mrs. Das more sympathetic?

8. What does the ending suggest about Mr. Kapasi's future? Has his encounter with the Das family created any permanent change in his outlook on life or his view of himself? Is the ending happy or unhappy?

SUGGESTIONS FOR WRITING

1. In Wolff's "Hunters in the Snow," the plot helps to illuminate the struggle for power among the three principal characters. Write an essay in which you show how this struggle for power is elucidated by some of the elements of fiction presented in Chapter Two—such as suspense, mystery, surprise, and conflict.

2. Write an essay on the ending of one of the following stories, determining whether it is happy, unhappy, or indeterminate and how the type of ending helps define the story as an example of commercial or literary fiction:

   a. Wolff, "Hunters in the Snow" (page 86).

      b. Achebe, "Civil Peace" (page 509).
      c. Chopin, "The Story of an Hour" (page 524).
      d. Jackson, "The Lottery" (page 261).
3. Write an essay defining the type(s) of conflict in one of these stories:
      a. Achebe, "Civil Peace" (page 509).
      b. Hurston, "The Gilded Six-Bits" (page 553).
      c. Hemingway, "Hills Like White Elephants" (page 278).
      d. Wharton, "Roman Fever" (page 373).

Chapter Three

Characterization

The preceding chapter considered plot apart from characterization, as if the two were separable. Actually, along with the other elements of fiction discussed in later chapters, plot and characterization work together in any good story. In commercial fiction, plot is usually more important than in-depth characterization, while literary writers are usually more concerned with complex characters than with the mechanics of plot. Many literary fiction writers, in fact, consider characterization to be the most important element of their art.

Analyzing **characterization** is more difficult than describing plot, for human character is infinitely complex, variable, and ambiguous. Anyone can summarize what a person in a story has done, but a writer needs considerable skill and insight into human beings to describe convincingly *who* a person is. Even the most complicated plot in a detective story puts far less strain on our understanding than does human nature. This is why commercial fiction may feature an elaborate plot but offer characters who are simple and two-dimensional, even stereotypical. In such fiction the characters must be easily identifiable and clearly labeled as good or bad; the commercial author's aim is to create characters who can carry the plot forward, not to explore human psychology and motivation.

The main character in a commercial work must also be someone attractive or sympathetic. If the protagonist is male, he need not be perfect, but usually he must be fundamentally decent—honest, good-hearted, and preferably good-looking. He may also have larger-than-life qualities, showing himself to be daring, dashing, or gallant. He may defy laws made for "ordinary" people, but this makes him even more likable because he breaks the rules for a good reason: to catch a criminal, or to prevent a disaster. In commercial fiction, the reader enjoys identifying with such a protagonist, vicariously sharing his adventures, escapes, and triumphs. If the protagonist has vices, they must be the kind a typical reader would not mind or would enjoy having. For instance, the main character in successful commercial

fiction may be sexually promiscuous—James Bond is a good example—
and thus allow readers to indulge imaginatively in pleasures they might
not allow themselves in real life.

Literary fiction does not necessarily renounce the attractive character. Jane Eyre, Huckleberry Finn, and Holden Caulfield are literary
characters beloved by millions of readers; both Mr. Kapasi in "Interpreter of Maladies" and Edie in "How I Met My Husband" are likable
characters as well. But literary protagonists are less easily labeled and
pigeonholed than their counterparts in commercial fiction. Sometimes
they may be wholly unsympathetic, even despicable. But because human
nature is not often entirely bad or perfectly good, literary fiction deals
usually with characters who are composed of both good and evil
impulses, three-dimensional human beings who live in our memory as
"real" people long after we have stopped reading.

Such fiction offers an exciting opportunity to observe human nature
in all its complexity and multiplicity. It enables us to know people, to
understand them, and to develop compassion for them in a way we
might not do without reading serious fiction. In some respects, we can
know fictional characters even better than we know real people in our
lives. For one thing, we observe fictional people in situations that are
always significant and that serve to illuminate their characters in a way
that our daily, routine exposure to real people seldom does. We can also
view a character's inner life in a way that's impossible in ordinary life.
Authors can show us, if they wish, exactly what is happening in a
character's mind and emotions. In real life, of course, we can only
guess at another person's thoughts and feelings from external behavior,
which may be designed to conceal the person's inner life. Because of the
opportunity literary fiction affords us of knowing its characters so thoroughly, it also enables us to understand the motives and behavior of
people in real life.

Authors present their characters either directly or indirectly. In
direct presentation they tell us straight out, by exposition or analysis,
what the characters are like, or they have another character in the
story describe them. In **indirect presentation** the author *shows* us the
characters through their actions; we determine what they are like by
what they say or do. Graham Greene uses direct presentation when he
tells us about Blackie: "He was just, he had no jealousy." He uses
indirect presentation when he shows Blackie allowing the gang to vote
on Trevor's project, accepting the end of his leadership fairly calmly,
taking orders from Trevor without resentment, burning banknotes
with Trevor, and racing him home. In this story, of course, the word
"just" has a slight ironic twist—it applies only to behavior within the

gang—and Greene presents this indirectly. Alice Munro relies on indirect presentation to show that Chris Watters is a charming but irresponsible barnstormer; Edie never directly criticizes him, but we feel her disillusionment as she waits day after day for a letter that will never come.

Sometimes the method of direct presentation has the advantages of being clear and economical, but good writers use it sparingly. In order to involve the reader in a character, the author must *show* the character in action; the axiom "show, don't tell" is therefore one of the basics of fiction writing. If characters are merely described, then the story will read more like an essay. The direct method usually has little emotional impact unless it is bolstered by the indirect. It will give us only the explanation of a character, not the impression of a living, breathing human being. In almost all good fiction, therefore, the characters are **dramatized**. They are shown speaking and behaving, as in a stage play. If we are really to believe in the selfishness of a character, we must see the character acting selfishly. Instead of telling us that Frank in "Hunters in the Snow" is a selfish, self-deluding man, Wolff gives us dramatic scenes in which Frank exhibits his selfishness and self-delusions through his dialogue and actions. Most literary writers rely on indirect presentation and may even use it exclusively.

Good fiction follows three other principles of characterization. First, the characters are consistent in their behavior: they do not behave one way on one occasion and a different way on another unless there is a clear and sufficient reason for the change. Second, the characters' words and actions spring from **motivations** the reader can understand and believe; if we can't understand why they behave in a certain way immediately, that understanding comes by the end of the story. Finally, the characters must be plausible or lifelike. They cannot be perfectly virtuous or monsters of evil; nor can they have some impossible combination of contradictory traits. In short, the author must convince the reader that the character might well have existed so that, at least while we're reading, we have the illusion that the person is real and forget we are reading fiction at all.

In his book *Aspects of the Novel* (1927), the British novelist E. M. Forster introduced terms that have become standard in discussing types of characters; he wrote that a literary character is either "flat" or "round." **Flat characters** usually have only one or two predominant traits; they can be summed up in a sentence or two. Richard Connell's character Ivan, for instance, is a fearsome thug, and that is all we need to know about him. By contrast, **round characters** are complex and many-sided; they have the three-dimensional quality of real people. Huck Finn, for example, because Mark Twain imagined and dramatized him so success-fully as an individual, lives vigorously in the imagination of millions of readers. This is not to say that flat characters cannot be memorable. Though essentially two-dimensional, they too may be made memorable in the hands of an expert author who creates some vivid detail of their appearance, gestures, or speech. Ebenezer Scrooge, in Dickens's *A Christmas Carol*, could be defined as a stereotype of the miserly misan-thrope; but his "Bah! Humbug!" has helped make him an immortal character.

Whether round or flat, all characters in good fiction are dramatized to whatever extent needed to make them convincing and to fulfill their roles in the story. Most short stories, of course, will have room for only one or two round characters. Minor characters must necessarily remain flat. There are some literary stories, of course, where the exploration of individual character is not the main focus of interest—Shirley Jackson's "The Lottery" (page 261) is an example—and in such stories none of the characters may be developed fully. Such instances, however, are rela-tively rare.

A special kind of flat character is the **stock character**. These are stereotyped figures who have recurred so often in fiction that we recognize them at once: the strong silent sheriff, the brilliant detective with eccentric habits, the mad scientist who performs fiendish experi-ments on living people, the glamorous international spy of mysterious background, the comic Englishman with a monocle, the cruel step-mother, and so forth. Commercial authors often rely on such stock characters for precisely the reason that they can be grasped quickly and easily by the reader. Such characters are like interchangeable parts that might be transferred from one story to another. When literary writers employ a conventional type, however, they usually add individualizing touches to help create a fresh and memorable character. Conan Doyle's Sherlock Holmes follows a stock pattern of the detective, but he remains more memorable than hundreds of other fictional detectives who have come and gone since he was created. Similarly, Wolff's character Tub in "Hunters in the Snow" embodies the stereo-types of the fat, comic buffoon; but certain details about him—his insecurity, his habit of hiding the food he eats so compulsively—help to make him distinctive.

Fictional characters may also be classified as either static or devel-oping. The **static character** remains essentially the same person from the beginning of the story to the end. The **developing** (or dynamic) **charac-ter**, on the other hand, undergoes some distinct change of character, personality, or outlook. The change may be a large or a small one; it may be positive or negative; but it is something significant and basic, not some minor change of habit or opinion. The Irish writer James Joyce used a term that has become widely adopted today, noting that a character in a story often experiences an **epiphany**, which he termed a moment of spiritual insight into life or into the character's own circumstances. This epiphany or insight usually defines the moment of the developing character's change.

Edie in Munro's "How I Met My Husband" is a dynamic character, for she learns a painful lesson about romance and growing up that alters the entire course of her life. Many stories show a change in the protagonist as the result of some crucial situation in his or her life. This change is usually at the heart of the story, and defining and explaining the change will be the best way to arrive at its meaning. In commercial fiction, changes in character are likely to be relatively superficial, intended mainly to effect a happy ending. Readers of literary fiction, however, usually expect that a convincing change in a character meet three conditions: (1) it must be consistent with the individual's characterization as dramatized in the story; (2) it must be sufficiently motivated by the circumstances in which the character is placed; and (3) the story must offer sufficient time for the change to take place and still be believable. Essential changes in human character, after all, do not usually occur suddenly. For this reason, good fiction will not give us a confirmed criminal who miraculously reforms at the end of a story, or a lifelong racist who wakes up one day and decides to be tolerant and open-minded. If fiction is to be convincing, it must show us believable, dynamic, but often quiet changes or turning points in a character's life. When an author has carefully laid the groundwork earlier in the story, we believe in the character's change and experience the moment of epiphany as a possibly small but significant marker in the life of an individual human being.

Ultimately it is the quality of characterization by which a literary story stands or falls. Long after we have read even the greatest novels and short stories, we tend to remember not the incidents of plot but the unforgettable characters who made our reading such a rich, vibrant experience. Through the creation of character, an author can summon up a new personality, a new voice, and an entirely new and original way of seeing the world. Such characters come alive each time a reader takes up the story, renewing the miracle of the human imagination.

REVIEWING CHAPTER THREE

1. Describe the significance of characterization in literary fiction vs. commercial fiction.
2. Distinguish between direct and indirect presentation of character in fiction.
3. Review the terms "flat character," "round character," and "stock character."
4. Consider the difference between a static character and a dynamic character.
5. Explore the authors' use of characterization in the following stories.

Alice Walker

Everyday Use

for your grandmama

I will wait for her in the yard that Maggie and I made so clean and wavy yesterday afternoon. A yard like this is more comfortable than most people know. It is not just a yard. It is like an extended living room. When the hard clay is swept clean as a floor and the fine sand around the edges lined with tiny, irregular grooves, anyone can come and sit and look up into the elm tree and wait for the breezes that never come inside the house.

Maggie will be nervous until after her sister goes: she will stand hopelessly in corners, homely and ashamed of the burn scars down her arms and legs, eying her sister with a mixture of envy and awe. She thinks her sister has held life always in the palm of one hand, that "no" is a word the world never learned to say to her.

EVERYDAY USE   First published in 1973. Alice Walker was born in Georgia in 1944, attended Spelman College for two years, earned her B.A. from Sarah Lawrence, and was active in the civil rights movement. She has taught and been writer-in-residence at various colleges including Jackson State, Tougaloo, Wellesley, the University of California at Berkeley, and Brandeis. The names adopted by two of the characters in the story reflect the practice among some members of the black community of rejecting names inherited from the period of slavery and selecting others more in keeping with their African heritage. The greetings used by Hakim and Wangero ("Asalamalakim" and "Wa-su-zo-Tean-o") are apparently adaptations of Arabic and African languages.

You've no doubt seen those TV shows where the child who has "made it" is confronted, as a surprise, by her own mother and father, tottering in weakly from backstage. (A pleasant surprise, of course: What would they do if parent and child came on the show only to curse out and insult each other?) On TV mother and child embrace and smile into each other's faces. Sometimes the mother and father weep, the child wraps them in her arms and leans across the table to tell how she would not have made it without their help. I have seen these programs.

Sometimes I dream a dream in which Dee and I are suddenly brought together on a TV program of this sort. Out of a dark and soft-seated limousine I am ushered into a bright room filled with many people. There I meet a smiling, gray, sporty man like Johnny Carson° who shakes my hand and tells me what a fine girl I have. Then we are on the stage and Dee is embracing me with tears in her eyes. She pins on my dress a large orchid, even though she had told me once that she thinks orchids are tacky flowers.

In real life I am a large, big-boned woman with rough, man-working   5
hands. In the winter I wear flannel nightgowns to bed and overalls during the day. I can kill and clean a hog as mercilessly as a man. My fat keeps me hot in zero weather. I can work outside all day, breaking ice to get water for washing; I can eat pork liver cooked over the open fire minutes after it comes steaming from the hog. One winter I knocked a bull calf straight in the brain between the eyes with a sledge hammer and had the meat hung up to chill before nightfall. But of course all this does not show on television. I am the way my daughter would want me to be: a hundred pounds lighter, my skin like an uncooked barley pancake. My hair glistens in the hot bright lights. Johnny Carson has much to do to keep up with my quick and witty tongue.

But that is a mistake. I know even before I wake up. Who ever knew a Johnson with a quick tongue? Who can even imagine me looking a strange white man in the eye? It seems to me I have talked to them always with one foot raised in flight, with my head turned in whichever way is farthest from them. Dee, though. She would always look anyone in the eye. Hesitation was no part of her nature.

"How do I look, Mama?" Maggie says, showing just enough of her thin body enveloped in pink skirt and red blouse for me to know she's there, almost hidden by the door.

"Come out into the yard," I say.

Have you ever seen a lame animal, perhaps a dog run over by some careless person rich enough to own a car, sidle up to someone who is

Johnny Carson: former host of *The Tonight Show* on NBC

ignorant enough to be kind to him? That is the way my Maggie walks. She has been like this, chin on chest, eyes on ground, feet in shuffle, ever since the fire that burned the other house to the ground.

10   Dee is lighter than Maggie, with nicer hair and a fuller figure. She's a woman now, though sometimes I forget. How long ago was it that the other house burned? Ten, twelve years? Sometimes I can still hear the flames and feel Maggie's arms sticking to me, her hair smoking and her dress falling off her in little black papery flakes. Her eyes seemed stretched open, blazed open by the flames reflected in them. And Dee. I see her standing off under the sweet gum tree she used to dig gum out of; a look of concentration on her face as she watched the last dingy gray board of the house fall in toward the red-hot brick chimney. Why don't you do a dance around the ashes? I'd wanted to ask her. She had hated the house that much.

I used to think she hated Maggie, too. But that was before we raised the money, the church and me, to send her to Augusta to school. She used to read to us without pity; forcing words, lies, other folks' habits, whole lives upon us two, sitting trapped and ignorant underneath her voice. She washed us in a river of make-believe, burned us with a lot of knowledge we didn't necessarily need to know. Pressed us to her with the serious way she read, to shove us away at just the moment, like dimwits, we seemed about to understand.

Dee wanted nice things. A yellow organdy dress to wear to her graduation from high school; black pumps to match a green suit she'd made from an old suit somebody gave me. She was determined to stare down any disaster in her efforts. Her eyelids would not flicker for minutes at a time. Often I fought off the temptation to shake her. At sixteen she had a style of her own: and knew what style was.

I never had an education myself. After second grade the school was closed down. Don't ask me why: in 1927 colored asked fewer questions than they do now. Sometimes Maggie reads to me. She stumbles along good-naturedly but can't see well. She knows she is not bright. Like good looks and money, quickness passed her by. She will marry John Thomas (who has mossy teeth in an earnest face) and then I'll be free to sit here and I guess just sing church songs to myself. Although I never was a good singer. Never could carry a tune. I was always better at a man's job. I used to love to milk till I was hooked in the side in '49. Cows are soothing and slow and don't bother you, unless you try to milk them the wrong way.

I have deliberately turned my back on the house. It is three rooms, just like the one that burned, except the roof is tin; they don't make shingle roofs any more. There are no real windows, just some holes cut in the sides, like the portholes in a ship, but not round and not square, with rawhide holding the shutters up on the outside. This house is in a pasture, too, like the other one. No doubt when Dee sees it she will want to tear it down. She wrote me once that no matter where we "choose" to live, she will manage to come see us. But she will never bring her friends. Maggie and I thought about this and Maggie asked me, "Mama, when did Dee ever *have* any friends?"

She had a few. Furtive boys in pink shirts hanging about on washday   15 after school. Nervous girls who never laughed. Impressed with her, they worshipped the well-turned phrase, the cute shape, the scalding humor that erupted like bubbles in lye. She read to them.

When she was courting Jimmy T she didn't have much time to pay to us, but turned all her faultfinding power on him. He *flew* to marry a cheap city girl from a family of ignorant flashy people. She hardly had time to recompose herself.

When she comes I will meet—but there they are!

Maggie attempts to make a dash for the house, in her shuffling way, but I stay her with my hand. "Come back here," I say. And she stops and tries to dig a well in the sand with her toe.

It is hard to see them clearly through the strong sun. But even the first glimpse of leg out of the car tells me it is Dee. Her feet were always neat-looking, as if God himself had shaped them with a certain style. From the other side of the car comes a short, stocky man. Hair is all over his head a foot long and hanging from his chin like a kinky mule tail. I hear Maggie suck in her breath. "Uhnnnh," is what it sounds like. Like when you see the wriggling end of a snake just in front of your foot on the road. "Uhnnnh."

Dee next. A dress down to the ground, in this hot weather. A   20 dress so loud it hurts my eyes. There are yellows and oranges enough to throw back the light of the sun. I feel my whole face warming from the heat waves it throws out. Earrings gold, too, and hanging down to her shoulders. Bracelets dangling and making noises when she moves her arm up to shake the folds of the dress out of her armpits. The dress is loose and flows, and as she walks closer, I like it. I hear Maggie go "Uhnnnh" again. It is her sister's hair. It stands straight up like the wool on a sheep. It is black as night and around the edges are two long pigtails that rope about like small lizards disappearing behind her ears.

"Wa-su-zo-Tean-o!" she says, coming on in that gliding way the dress makes her move. The short stocky fellow with the hair to his navel is all grinning and he follows up with "Asalamalakim, my mother and sister!" He moves to hug Maggie but she falls back, right up against the back of my chair. I feel her trembling there and when I look up I see the perspiration falling off her chin.

"Don't get up," says Dee. Since I am stout it takes something of a push. You can see me trying to move a second or two before I make it. She turns, showing white heels through her sandals, and goes back to the car. Out she peeks next with a Polaroid. She stoops down quickly and lines up picture after picture of me sitting there in front of the house with Maggie cowering behind me. She never takes a shot without making sure the house is included. When a cow comes nibbling around the edge of the yard she snaps it and me and Maggie and the house. Then she puts the Polaroid in the back seat of the car, and comes up and kisses me on the forehead.

Meanwhile Asalamalakim is going through motions with Maggie's hand. Maggie's hand is as limp as a fish, and probably as cold, despite the sweat, and she keeps trying to pull it back. It looks like Asalamalakim wants to shake hands but wants to do it fancy. Or maybe he don't know how people shake hands. Anyhow, he soon gives up on Maggie.

"Well," I say. "Dee."

25   "No, Mama," she says. "Not 'Dee,' Wangero Leewanika Kemanjo!"

"What happened to 'Dee'?" I wanted to know.

"She's dead," Wangero said. "I couldn't bear it any longer, being named after the people who oppress me."

"You know as well as me you was named after your aunt Dicie," I said. Dicie is my sister. She named Dee. We called her "Big Dee" after Dee was born.

"But who was she named after?" asked Wangero.

30   "I guess after Grandma Dee," I said.

"And who was she named after?" asked Wangero.

"Her mother," I said, and saw Wangero was getting tired. "That's about as far back as I can trace it," I said. Though, in fact, I probably could have carried it back beyond the Civil War through the branches.

"Well," said Asalamalakim, "there you are."

"Uhnnnh," I heard Maggie say.

35   "There I was not," I said, "before 'Dicie' cropped up in our family, so why should I try to trace it that far back?"

He just stood there grinning, looking down on me like somebody inspecting a Model A car. Every once in a while he and Wangero sent eye signals over my head.

"How do you pronounce this name?" I asked.

"You don't have to call me by it if you don't want to," said Wangero.

"Why shouldn't I?" I asked. "If that's what you want us to call you, we'll call you."

"I know it might sound awkward at first," said Wangero.   40

"I'll get used to it," I said. "Ream it out again."

Well, soon we got the name out of the way. Asalamalakim had a name twice as long and three times as hard. After I tripped over it two or three times he told me to just call him Hakim-a-barber. I wanted to ask him was he a barber, but I didn't really think he was, so I didn't ask.

"You must belong to those beef-cattle peoples down the road," I said. They said "Asalamalakim" when they met you, too, but they didn't shake hands. Always too busy: feeding the cattle, fixing the fences, putting up salt-lick shelters, throwing down hay. When the white folks poisoned some of the herd the men stayed up all night with rifles in their hands. I walked a mile and a half just to see the sight.

Hakim-a-barber said, "I accept some of their doctrines, but farming and raising cattle is not my style." (They didn't tell me, and I didn't ask, whether Wangero (Dee) had really gone and married him.)

We sat down to eat and right away he said he didn't eat collards and   45
pork was unclean. Wangero, though, went on through the chitlins and corn bread, the greens and everything else. She talked a blue streak over the sweet potatoes. Everything delighted her. Even the fact that we still used the benches her daddy made for the table when we couldn't afford to buy chairs.

"Oh, Mama!" she cried. Then turned to Hakim-a-barber. "I never knew how lovely these benches are. You can feel the rump prints," she said, running her hands underneath her and along the bench. Then she gave a sigh and her hand closed over Grandma Dee's butter dish. "That's it!" she said. "I knew there was something I wanted to ask you if I could have." She jumped up from the table and went over in the corner where the churn stood, the milk in it clabber by now. She looked at the churn and looked at it.

"This churn top is what I need," she said. "Didn't Uncle Buddy whittle it out of a tree you all used to have?"

"Yes," I said.

"Uh huh," she said happily. "And I want the dasher, too."

"Uncle Buddy whittle that, too?" asked the barber.   50

Dee (Wangero) looked up at me.

"Aunt Dee's first husband whittled the dash," said Maggie so low you almost couldn't hear her. "His name was Henry, but they called him Stash."

"Maggie's brain is like an elephant's," Wangero said, laughing. "I can use the churn top as a centerpiece for the alcove table," she said, sliding a plate over the churn, "and I'll think of something artistic to do with the dasher."

When she finished wrapping the dasher the handle stuck out. I took it for a moment in my hands. You didn't even have to look close to see where hands pushing the dasher up and down to make butter had left a kind of sink in the wood. In fact, there were a lot of small sinks; you could see where thumbs and fingers had sunk into the wood. It was beautiful light yellow wood, from a tree that grew in the yard where Big Dee and Stash had lived.

55   After dinner Dee (Wangero) went to the trunk at the foot of my bed and started rifling through it. Maggie hung back in the kitchen over the dishpan. Out came Wangero with two quilts. They had been pieced by Grandma Dee and then Big Dee and me had hung them on the quilt frames on the front porch and quilted them. One was in the Lone Star pattern. The other was Walk Around the Mountain. In both of them were scraps of dresses Grandma Dee had worn fifty and more years ago. Bits and pieces of Grandpa Jarrell's Paisley shirts. And one teeny faded blue piece, about the size of a penny matchbox, that was from Great Grandpa Ezra's uniform that he wore in the Civil War.

"Mama," Wangero said sweet as a bird. "Can I have these old quilts?"

I heard something fall in the kitchen, and a minute later the kitchen door slammed.

"Why don't you take one or two of the others?" I asked. "These old things was just done by me and Big Dee from some tops your grandma pieced before she died."

"No," said Wangero. "I don't want those. They are stitched around the borders by machine."

60   "That'll make them last better," I said.

"That's not the point," said Wangero. "These are all pieces of dresses Grandma used to wear. She did all this stitching by hand. Imagine!" She held the quilts securely in her arms, stroking them.

"Some of the pieces, like those lavender ones, come from old clothes her mother handed down to her," I said, moving up to touch the quilts. Dee (Wangero) moved back just enough so that I couldn't reach the quilts. They already belonged to her.

"Imagine!" she breathed again, clutching them closely to her bosom.

"The truth is," I said, "I promised to give them quilts to Maggie, for when she marries John Thomas."

65   She gasped like a bee had stung her.

"Maggie can't appreciate these quilts!" she said. "She'd probably be backward enough to put them to everyday use."

"I reckon she would," I said. "God knows I been saving 'em for long enough with nobody using 'em. I hope she will!" I didn't want to bring up how I had offered Dee (Wangero) a quilt when she went away to college. Then she had told me they were old-fashioned, out of style.

"But they're *priceless!*" she was saying now, furiously; for she has a temper. "Maggie would put them on the bed and in five years they'd be in rags. Less than that!"

"She can always make some more," I said. "Maggie knows how to quilt."

Dee (Wangero) looked at me with hatred. "You just will not   70
understand. The point is these quilts, *these* quilts!"

"Well," I said, stumped. "What would *you* do with them?"

"Hang them," she said. As if that was the only thing you *could* do with quilts.

Maggie by now was standing in the door. I could almost hear the sound her feet made as they scraped over each other.

"She can have them, Mama," she said, like somebody used to never winning anything, or having anything reserved for her. "I can 'member Grandma Dee without the quilts."

I looked at her hard. She had filled her bottom lip with checker-   75
berry snuff and it gave her face a kind of dopey, hangdog look. It was Grandma Dee and Big Dee who taught her how to quilt herself. She stood there with her scarred hands hidden in the folds of her skirt. She looked at her sister with something like fear but she wasn't mad at her. This was Maggie's portion. This was the way she knew God to work.

When I looked at her like that something hit me in the top of my head and ran down to the soles of my feet. Just like when I'm in church and the spirit of God touches me and I get happy and shout. I did something I never had done before: hugged Maggie to me, then dragged her on into the room, snatched the quilts out of Miss Wangero's hands and dumped them into Maggie's lap. Maggie just sat there on my bed with her mouth open.

"Take one or two of the others," I said to Dee.

But she turned without a word and went out to Hakim-a-barber.

"You just don't understand," she said, as Maggie and I came out to the car.

"What don't I understand?" I wanted to know.   80

"Your heritage," she said. And then she turned to Maggie, kissed her, and said, "You ought to try to make something of yourself, too, Maggie. It's really a new day for us. But from the way you and Mama still live you'd never know it."

She put on some sunglasses that hid everything above the tip of her nose and her chin.

Maggie smiled; maybe at the sunglasses. But a real smile, not scared. After we watched the car dust settle I asked Maggie to bring me a dip of snuff. And then the two of us sat there just enjoying, until it was time to go in the house and go to bed.

QUESTIONS

1. Characterize the speaker and evaluate her reliability as a reporter and interpreter of events. Where does she refrain from making judgments? Where does she present less than the full truth? Do these examples of reticence undercut her reliability?

2. Describe as fully as possible the lives of the mother, Dee, and Maggie prior to the events of the story. How are the following incidents from the past also reflected in the present actions: (a) Dee's hatred of the old house; (b) Dee's ability "to stare down any disaster"; (c) Maggie's burns from the fire; (d) the mother's having been "hooked in the side" while milking a cow; (e) Dee's refusal to accept a quilt when she went away to college?

3. As evidence of current social movements and as innovations that the mother responds to, what do the following have in common: (a) Dee's new name and costume; (b) Hakim's behavior and attitudes; (c) the "beef-cattle peoples down the road"; (d) Dee's concern for her "heritage"?

4. Does the mother's refusal to let Dee have the quilts indicate a permanent or temporary change of character? Why has she never done anything like it before? Why does she do it now? What details in the story prepare for and foreshadow that refusal?

5. How does the physical setting give support to the contrasting attitudes of both the mother and Dee? Does the author indicate that one or the other of them is entirely correct in her feelings about the house and yard?

6. Is Dee wholly unsympathetic? Is the mother's victory over her altogether positive? What emotional ambivalence is there in the final scene between Maggie and her mother in the yard?

Katherine Mansfield

Miss Brill

Although it was so brilliantly fine—the blue sky powdered with gold and great spots of light like white wine splashed over the Jardins Publiques—Miss Brill was glad that she had decided on her fur. The air was motionless, but when you opened your mouth there was just a faint chill, like a chill from a glass of iced water before you sip, and now and

MISS BRILL   Written in 1921; first published in 1922. "Jardins Publiques" is French for Public Gardens. Katherine Mansfield (1888–1923) was born and grew up in New Zealand but lived her adult life in London, with various sojourns on the Continent.

again a leaf came drifting—from nowhere, from the sky. Miss Brill put up her hand and touched her fur. Dear little thing! It was nice to feel it again. She had taken it out of its box that afternoon, shaken out the moth powder, given it a good brush, and rubbed the life back into the dim little eyes. "What has been happening to me?" said the sad little eyes. Oh, how sweet it was to see them snap at her again from the red eiderdown! . . . But the nose, which was of some black composition, wasn't at all firm. It must have had a knock, somehow. Never mind—a little dab of black sealing-wax when the time came—when it was absolutely necessary . . . Little rogue! Yes, she really felt like that about it. Little rogue biting its tail just by her left ear. She could have taken it off and laid it on her lap and stroked it. She felt a tingling in her hands and arms, but that came from walking, she supposed. And when she breathed, something light and sad—no, not sad, exactly—something gentle seemed to move in her bosom.

There were a number of people out this afternoon, far more than last Sunday. And the band sounded louder and gayer. That was because the Season had begun. For although the band played all the year round on Sundays, out of season it was never the same. It was like some one playing with only the family to listen; it didn't care how it played if there weren't any strangers present. Wasn't the conductor wearing a new coat, too? She was sure it was new. He scraped with his foot and flapped his arms like a rooster about to crow, and the bandsmen sitting in the green rotunda blew out their cheeks and glared at the music. Now there came a little "flutey" bit—very pretty!—a little chain of bright drops. She was sure it would be repeated. It was; she lifted her head and smiled.

Only two people shared her "special" seat: a fine old man in a velvet coat, his hands clasped over a huge carved walking-stick, and a big old woman, sitting upright, with a roll of knitting on her embroidered apron. They did not speak. This was disappointing, for Miss Brill always looked forward to the conversation. She had become really quite expert, she thought, at listening as though she didn't listen, at sitting in other people's lives just for a minute while they talked round her.

She glanced, sideways, at the old couple. Perhaps they would go soon. Last Sunday, too, hadn't been as interesting as usual. An Englishman and his wife, he wearing a dreadful Panama hat and she button boots. And she'd gone on the whole time about how she ought to wear spectacles; she knew she needed them; but that it was no good getting any; they'd be sure to break and they'd never keep on. And he'd been so patient. He'd suggested everything—gold rims, the kind that curve round your ears, little pads inside the bridge. No, nothing would please her. "They'll always be sliding down my nose!" Miss Brill had wanted to shake her.

5   The old people sat on the bench, still as statues. Never mind, there was always the crowd to watch. To and fro, in front of the flower beds and the band rotunda, the couples and groups paraded, stopped to talk, to greet, to buy a handful of flowers from the old beggar who had his tray fixed to the railings. Little children ran among them, swooping and laughing; little boys with big white silk bows under their chins, little girls, little French dolls, dressed up in velvet and lace. And sometimes a tiny staggerer came suddenly rocking into the open from under the trees, stopped, stared, as suddenly sat down "flop," until its small high-stepping mother, like a young hen, rushed scolding to its rescue. Other people sat on the benches and green chairs, but they were nearly always the same, Sunday after Sunday, and—Miss Brill had often noticed—there was something funny about nearly all of them. They were odd, silent, nearly all old, and from the way they stared they looked as though they'd just come from dark little rooms or even—even cupboards!

Behind the rotunda the slender trees with yellow leaves down drooping, and through them just a line of sea, and beyond the blue sky with gold-veined clouds.

Tum-tum-tum tiddle-um! tiddle-um! tum tiddley-um tum ta! blew the band.

Two young girls in red came by and two young soldiers in blue met them, and they laughed and paired and went off arm-in-arm. Two peasant women with funny straw hats passed, gravely, leading beautiful smoke-colored donkeys. A cold, pale nun hurried by. A beautiful woman came along and dropped her bunch of violets, and a little boy ran after to hand them to her, and she took them and threw them away as if they'd been poisoned. Dear me! Miss Brill didn't know whether to admire that or not! And now an ermine toque and a gentleman in gray met just in front of her. He was tall, stiff, dignified, and she was wearing the ermine toque she'd bought when her hair was yellow. Now everything, her hair, her face, even her eyes, was the same color as the shabby ermine, and her hand, in its cleaned glove, lifted to dab her lips, was a tiny yellowish paw. Oh, she was so pleased to see him—delighted! She rather thought they were going to meet that afternoon. She described where she'd been—everywhere, here, there, along by the sea. The day was so charming—didn't he agree? And wouldn't he, perhaps? . . . But he shook his head, lighted a cigarette, slowly breathed a great deep puff into her face, and, even while she was still talking and laughing, flicked the match away and walked on. The ermine toque was alone; she smiled more brightly than ever. But even the band seemed to know what she was feeling and played more softly, played tenderly, and the drum beat, "The Brute! The Brute!" over and over. What would she do? What was going to happen now? But as Miss Brill wondered, the ermine toque turned, raised her hand as though she'd seen some one else, much nicer, just over there, and pattered away. And the band changed again and played more quickly, more gayly than ever, and the old couple on Miss Brill's seat got up and marched away, and such a funny old man with long whiskers hobbled along in time to the music and was nearly knocked over by four girls walking abreast.

Oh, how fascinating it was! How she enjoyed it! How she loved sitting here, watching it all! It was like a play. It was exactly like a play. Who could believe the sky at the back wasn't painted? But it wasn't till a little brown dog trotted on solemn and then slowly trotted off, like a little "theater" dog, a little dog that had been drugged, that Miss Brill discovered what it was that made it so exciting. They were all on stage. They weren't only the audience, not only looking on; they were acting. Even she had a part and came every Sunday. No doubt somebody would have noticed if she hadn't been there; she was part of the performance after all. How strange she'd never thought of it like that before! And yet it explained why she made such a point of starting from home at just the same time each week—so as not to be late for the performance—and it also explained why she had quite a queer, shy feeling at telling her English pupils how she spent her Sunday afternoons. No wonder! Miss Brill nearly laughed out loud. She was on the stage. She thought of the old invalid gentleman to whom she read the newspaper four afternoons a week while he slept in the garden. She had got quite used to the frail head on the cotton pillow, the hollowed eyes, the open mouth and the high pinched nose. If he'd been dead she mightn't have noticed for weeks; she wouldn't have minded. But suddenly he knew he was having the paper read to him by an actress! "An actress!" The old head lifted; two points of light quivered in the old eyes. "An actress—are ye?" And Miss Brill smoothed the newspaper as though it were the manuscript of her part and said gently: "Yes, I have been an actress for a long time."

The band had been having a rest. Now they started again. And what   10
they played was warm, sunny, yet there was just a faint chill—a some-thing, what was it?—not sadness—no, not sadness—a something that made you want to sing. The tune lifted, lifted, the light shone; and it seemed to Miss Brill that in another moment all of them, all the whole company, would begin singing. The young ones, the laughing ones who were moving together, they would begin, and the men's voices, very resolute and brave, would join them. And then she too, she too, and the others on the benches—they would come in with a kind of accom-paniment—something low, that scarcely rose or fell, something so beau-tiful—moving . . . And Miss Brill's eyes filled with tears and she looked

smiling at all the other members of the company. Yes, we understand, we understand, she thought—though what they understood she didn't know.

Just at that moment a boy and girl came and sat down where the old couple had been. They were beautifully dressed; they were in love. The hero and heroine, of course, just arrived from his father's yacht. And still soundlessly singing, still with that trembling smile, Miss Brill prepared to listen.

"No, not now," said the girl. "Not here, I can't."

"But why? Because of that stupid old thing at the end there?" asked the boy. "Why does she come here at all—who wants her? Why doesn't she keep her silly old mug at home?"

"It's her fu-fur which is so funny," giggled the girl. "It's exactly like a fried whiting."

"Ah, be off with you!" said the boy in an angry whisper. Then: "Tell me, ma petite chère—"

"No, not here," said the girl. "Not yet."

On her way home she usually bought a slice of honeycake at the baker's. It was her Sunday treat. Sometimes there was an almond in her slice, sometimes not. It made a great difference. If there was an almond it was like carrying home a tiny present—a surprise—something that might very well not have been there. She hurried on the almond Sundays and struck the match for the kettle in quite a dashing way.

But today she passed the baker's by, climbed the stairs, went into the little dark room—her room like a cupboard—and sat down on the red eiderdown. She sat there for a long time. The box that the fur came out of was on the bed. She unclasped the necklet quickly; quickly, without looking, laid it inside. But when she put the lid on she thought she heard something crying.

QUESTIONS

1. We view the people and events of this story almost entirely through the eyes and feelings of its protagonist. The author relies upon indirect presentation for her characterization of Miss Brill. After answering the following questions, write as full an account as you can of the nature and temperament of the story's main character.

2. What nationality is Miss Brill? What is the story's setting? Why is it important?

3. How old is Miss Brill? What are her circumstances? Why does she listen in on conversations?

4. Why does Miss Brill enjoy her Sundays in the park? Why especially this Sunday?

5. Of what importance to the story is the woman in the ermine toque?

6. What is Miss Brill's mood at the beginning of the story? What is it at the end? Why? Is she a static or a developing character?
7. What function does Miss Brill's fur serve in the story? What is the meaning of the final sentence?
8. Does Miss Brill come to a realization about her life and habits, or does she manage to suppress the truths that have been presented to her?

Richard Wright

The Man Who Was Almost a Man

Dave struck out across the fields looking homeward through paling light. Whut's the use talking wid em niggers in the field? Anyhow, his mother was putting supper on the table. Them niggers can't understan nothing. One of these days he was going to get a gun and practice shooting, then they couldn't talk to him as though he were a little boy. He slowed, looking at the ground. Shucks, Ah ain scareda them even ef they are biggern me! Aw, Ah know whut Ahma do. Ahm going by ol Joe's sto n git that Sears Roebuck catlog n look at them guns. Mebbe Ma will lemme buy one when she gits mah pay from ol man Hawkins. Ahma beg her t gimme some money. Ahm ol ernough to hava gun. Ahm seventeen. Almost a man. He strode, feeling his long loose-jointed limbs. Shucks, a man oughta hava little gun aftah he done worked hard all day.

He came in sight of Joe's store. A yellow lantern glowed on the front porch. He mounted steps and went through the screen door, hearing it bang behind him. There was a strong smell of coal oil and mackerel fish. He felt very confident until he saw fat Joe walk in through the rear door, then his courage began to ooze.

"Howdy, Dave! Wutcha want?"

"How yuh, Mistah Joe? Aw, Ah don wanna buy nothing. Ah jus wanted t see ef yuhd lemme look at that catlog erwhile."

"Sure! You wanna see it here?"   5

"Nawsuh. Ah wans t take it home wid me. Ah'll bring it back termorrow when Ah come in from the fiels."

"You plannin on buying something?"

THE MAN WHO WAS ALMOST A MAN   First published in 1938. Richard Wright (1908–1960) grew up in rural Mississippi and ran away from home at age fifteen, leading a rootless existence and supporting himself through menial jobs. His first book was *Uncle Tom's Children* (1938), which dealt largely with poor blacks confronting a racist South in the first half of the twentieth century. Wright is best known for his novel *Native Son* (1940) and his autobiographical work *Black Boy* (1945).

"Yessuh."

"Your ma lettin you have your own money now?"

10   "Shucks. Mistah Joe, Ahm gittin t be a man like anybody else!"

Joe laughed and wiped his greasy white face with a red bandanna.

"Whut you plannin on buyin?"

Dave looked at the floor, scratched his head, scratched his thigh, and smiled. Then he looked up shyly.

"Ah'll tell yuh, Mistah Joe, ef yuh promise yuh won't tell."

15   "I promise."

"Waal, Ahma buy a gun."

"A gun? Whut you want with a gun?"

"Ah wanna keep it."

"You ain't nothing but a boy. You don't need a gun."

20   "Aw, lemme have the catlog, Mistah Joe. Ah'll bring it back."

Joe walked through the rear door. Dave was elated. He looked around at barrels of sugar and flour. He heard Joe coming back. He craned his neck to see if he were bringing the book. Yeah, he's got it. Gawddog, he's got it!

"Here, but be sure you bring it back. It's the only one I got."

"Sho, Mistah Joe."

"Say, if you wanna buy a gun, why don't you buy one from me? I gotta gun to sell."

25   "Will it shoot?"

"Sure it'll shoot."

"Whut kind is it?"

"Oh, it's kinda old . . . a left-handed Wheeler. A pistol. A big one."

"Is it got bullets in it?"

30   "It's loaded."

"Kin Ah see it?"

"Where's your money?"

"What you wan fer it?"

"I'll let you have it for two dollars."

35   "Just two dollahs! Shucks, Ah could buy tha when Ah git mah pay."

"I'll have it here when you want it."

"Awright, suh. Ah be in fer it."

He went through the door, hearing it slam again behind him. Ahma git some money from Ma n buy me a gun! Only two dollahs! He tucked the thick catalogue under his arm and hurried.

"Where yuh been, boy?" His mother held a steaming dish of black-eyed peas.

40   "Aw, Ma, Ah just stopped down the road t talk wid the boys."

"Yuh know bettah t keep suppah waitin."

He sat down, resting the catalogue on the edge of the table.

"Yuh git up from there and git to the well n wash yoself! Ah ain feedin no hogs in mah house!"

She grabbed his shoulder and pushed him. He stumbled out of the room, then came back to get the catalogue.

"Whut this?"   45

"Aw, Ma, it's jusa catlog."

"Who yuh git it from?"

"From Joe, down at the sto."

"Waal, thas good. We kin use it in the outhouse."

"Naw, Ma." He grabbed for it. "Gimme ma catlog, Ma."   50

She held onto it and glared at him.

"Quit hollerin at me! Whut's wrong wid yuh? Yuh crazy?"

"But, Ma, please. It ain mine! It's Joe's! He tol me t bring it back tim termorrow."

She gave up the book. He stumbled down the back steps, hugging the thick book under his arm. When he had splashed water on his face and hands, he groped back to the kitchen and fumbled in a corner for the towel. He bumped into a chair; it clattered to the floor. The catalogue sprawled at his feet. When he had dried his eyes he snatched up the book and held it again under his arm. His mother stood watching him.

"Now, ef yuh gonna act a fool over that ol book, Ah'll take it n burn   55
it up."

"Naw, Ma, please."

"Waal, set down n be still!"

He sat down and drew the oil lamp close. He thumbed page after page, unaware of the food his mother set on the table. His father came in. Then his small brother.

"Whutcha got there, Dave?" his father asked.

"Jusa catlog," he answered, not looking up.   60

"Yeah, here they is!" His eyes glowed at blue-and-black revolvers. He glanced up, feeling sudden guilt. His father was watching him. He eased the book under the table and rested it on his knees. After the blessing was asked, he ate. He scooped up peas and swallowed fat meat without chewing. Buttermilk helped to wash it down. He did not want to mention money before his father. He would do much better by cornering his mother when she was alone! He looked at his father uneasily out of the edge of his eye.

"Boy, how come yuh don quit foolin wid tha book n eat yo suppah?"

"Yessuh."

"How you n ol man Hawkins gitten erlong?"

65   "Suh?"

"Can't yuh hear! Why don yuh lissen? Ah ast yu how wuz yuh n ol man Hawkins gittin erlong?"

"Oh, swell, Pa. Ah plows mo lan than anybody over there."

"Waal, yuh oughta keep yo mind on whut yuh doin."

"Yessuh."

70   He poured his plate full of molasses and sopped it up slowly with a chunk of cornbread. When his father and brother had left the kitchen, he still sat and looked again at the guns in the catalogue, longing to muster courage enough to present his case to his mother. Lawd, ef Ah only had tha pretty one! He could almost feel the slickness of the weapon with his fingers. If he had a gun like that he would polish it and keep it shining so it would never rust. N Ah'd keep it loaded, by Gawd!

"Ma?" His voice was hesitant.

"Hunh?"

"Ol man Hawkins give yuh mah money yit?"

"Yeah, but ain no usa yuh thinking bout throwin nona it erway. Ahm keeping tha money sos yuh kin have cloes t go to school this winter."

75   He rose and went to her side with the open catalogue in his palms. She was washing dishes, her head bent low over a pan. Shyly he raised the book. When he spoke, his voice was husky, faint.

"Ma, Gawd knows Ah wans one of these."

"One of whut?" she asked, not raising her eyes.

"One of these," he said again, not daring even to point. She glanced up at the page, then at him with wide eyes.

"Nigger, is yuh gone plumb crazy?"

80   "Aw, Ma —"

"Git outta here! Don yuh talk t me bout no gun! Yuh a fool!"

"Ma, Ah kin buy one fer two dollahs."

"Not ef Ah knows it, yuh ain't!"

"But yuh promised me one —"

85   "Ah don care whut Ah promised! Yuh ain nothing but a boy yit!"

"Ma, ef yuh lemme buy one Ah'll *never* ast yuh fer nothing no mo."

"Ah tol yuh t git outta here! Yuh ain gonna toucha penny of tha money fer no gun! Thas how come Ah has Mistah Hawkins t pay yo wages to me, cause Ah knows yuh ain got no sense."

"But, Ma, we needa gun. Pa ain got no gun. We needa gun in the house. Yuh kin never tell whut might happen."

"Now don yuh try to maka fool outta me, boy! Ef we did hava gun, yuh wouldn't have it!"

He laid the catalogue down and slipped his arm around her   90
waist.

"Aw, Ma, Ah done worked hard alla summer n ain ast yuh fer
nothing, is Ah, now?"

"Thas whut yuh spose t do!"

"But Ma, Ah wans a gun. Yuh kin lemme have two dollahs outta mah
money. Please, Ma. I kin give it to Pa . . . Please Ma! Ah loves yuh, Ma."

When she spoke her voice came soft and low.

"Whut yu wan wida gun, Dave? Yuh don need no gun. Yuh'll git in   95
trouble. N ef yo pa just thought Ah let yuh have money t buy a gun he'd
hava fit."

"Ah'll hide it, Ma. It ain but two dollahs."

"Lawd, chil, whut's wrong wid yuh?"

"Ain nothin wrong, Ma. Ahm almos a man now. Ah wans a gun."

"Who gonna sell yuh a gun?"

"Ol Joe at the sto."   100

"N it don cos but two dollahs?"

"Thas all, Ma. Jus two dollahs. Please, Ma."

She was stacking the plates away; her hands moved slowly, reflectively. Dave kept an anxious silence. Finally, she turned to him.

"Ah'll let yuh git tha gun ef yuh promise me one thing."

"Whut's tha, Ma?"   105

"Yuh bring it straight back t me, yuh hear? It be fer Pa."

"Yessum! Lemme go now, Ma."

She stooped, turned slightly to one side, raised the hem of her dress,
rolled down the top of her stocking, and came up with a slender wad of
bills.

"Here," she said. "Lawd knows yuh don need no gun. But yer pa
does. Yuh bring it right back t me, yuh hear? Ahma put it up. Now ef yuh
don, Ahma have yuh pa lick yuh so hard yuh won fergit it."

"Yessum."   110

He took the money, ran down the steps, and across the yard.

"Dave! Yuuuuuh Daaaaave!"

He heard, but he was not going to stop now. "Naw, Lawd!"

The first movement he made the following morning was to reach
under his pillow for the gun. In the gray light of dawn he held it loosely,
feeling a sense of power. Could kill a man with a gun like this. Kill
anybody, black or white. And if he were holding his gun in his hand,
nobody could run over him; they would have to respect him. It was a big
gun, with a long barrel and a heavy handle. He raised and lowered it in
his hand, marveling at its weight.

115   He had not come straight home with it as his mother had asked; instead he had stayed out in the fields, holding the weapon in his hand, aiming it now and then at some imaginary foe. But he had not fired it; he had been afraid that his father might hear. Also he was not sure he knew how to fire it.

To avoid surrendering the pistol he had not come into the house until he knew that they were all asleep. When his mother had tiptoed to his bedside late that night and demanded the gun, he had first played possum; then he had told her that the gun was hidden outdoors, that he would bring it to her in the morning. Now he lay turning it slowly in his hands. He broke it, took out the cartridges, felt them, and then put them back.

He slid out of bed, got a long strip of old flannel from a trunk, wrapped the gun in it, and tied it to his naked thigh while it was still loaded. He did not go in to breakfast. Even though it was not yet daylight, he started for Jim Hawkins' plantation. Just as the sun was rising he reached the barns where the mules and plows were kept.

"Hey! That you, Dave?"

He turned. Jim Hawkins stood eying him suspiciously.

120   "What're yuh doing here so early?"

"Ah didn't know Ah wuz gittin up so early, Mistah Hawkins. Ah wuz fixin t hitch up ol Jenny n take her t the fiels."

"Good. Since you're so early, how about plowing that stretch down by the woods?"

"Suits me, Mistah Hawkins."

"O.K. Go to it!"

125   He hitched Jenny to a plow and started across the fields. Hot dog! This was just what he wanted. If he could get down by the woods, he could shoot his gun and nobody would hear. He walked behind the plow, hearing the traces creaking, feeling the gun tied tight to his thigh.

When he reached the woods, he plowed two whole rows before he decided to take out the gun. Finally, he stopped, looked in all directions, then he untied the gun and held it in his hand. He turned to the mule and smiled.

"Know whut this is, Jenny? Naw, yuh wouldn know! Yuhs jusa ol mule! Anyhow, this is a gun, n it kin shoot, by Gawd!"

He held the gun at arm's length. Whut t hell, Ahma shoot this thing! He looked at Jenny again.

"Lissen here, Jenny! When Ah pull this ol trigger, Ah don wan yuh t run n acka fool now!"

Jenny stood with head down, her short ears pricked straight. Dave   130
walked off about twenty feet, held the gun far out from him at arm's
length, and turned his head. Hell, he told himself, Ah ain afraid. The
gun felt loose in his fingers; he waved it wildly for a moment. Then he
shut his eyes and tightened his forefinger. Bloom! A report half deafened
him and he thought his right hand was torn from his arm. He heard
Jenny whinnying and galloping over the field, and he found himself on
his knees, squeezing his fingers hard between his legs. His hand was
numb; he jammed it into his mouth, trying to warm it, trying to stop the
pain. The gun lay at his feet. He did not quite know what had happened.
He stood up and stared at the gun as though it were a living thing. He
gritted his teeth and kicked the gun. Yuh almos broke mah arm! He
turned to look for Jenny; she was far over the fields, tossing her head and
kicking wildly.

"Hol on there, ol mule!"

When he caught up with her she stood trembling, walling her big
white eyes at him. The plow was far away; the traces had broken. Then
Dave stopped short, looking, not believing. Jenny was bleeding. Her left
side was red and wet with blood. He went closer. Lawd, have mercy!
Wondah did Ah shoot this mule? He grabbed for Jenny's mane. She
flinched, snorted, whirled, tossing her head.

"Hol on now! Hol on."

Then he saw the hole in Jenny's side, right between the ribs. It was
round, wet, red. A crimson stream streaked down the front leg, flowing
fast. Good Gawd! Ah wuzn't shootin at tha mule. He felt panic. He
knew he had to stop that blood, or Jenny would bleed to death. He had
never seen so much blood in all his life. He chased the mule for a half
mile, trying to catch her. Finally she stopped, breathing hard, stumpy tail
half arched. He caught her mane and led her back to where the plough
and gun lay. Then he stooped and grabbed handfuls of damp black earth
and tried to plug the bullet hole. Jenny shuddered, whinnied, and broke
from him.

"Hol on! Hol on now!"   135

He tried to plug it again, but blood came anyhow. His fingers were
hot and sticky. He rubbed dirt into his palms, trying to dry them. Then
again he attempted to plug the bullet hole, but Jenny shied away,
kicking her heels high. He stood helpless. He had to do something.
He ran at Jenny; she dodged him. He watched a red stream of blood flow
down Jenny's leg and form a bright pool at her feet.

"Jenny . . . Jenny," he called weakly.

His lips trembled. She's bleeding t death! He looked in the direction
of home, wanting to go back, wanting to get help. But he saw the pistol

lying in the damp black clay. He had a queer feeling that if he only did something, this would not be; Jenny would not be there bleeding to death.

When he went to her this time, she did not move. She stood with sleepy, dreamy eyes; and when he touched her she gave a low-pitched whinny and knelt to the ground, her front knees slopping in blood.

140   "Jenny . . . Jenny . . ." he whispered.

For a long time she held her neck erect; then her head sank, slowly. Her ribs swelled with a mighty heave and she went over.

Dave's stomach felt empty, very empty. He picked up the gun and held it gingerly between his thumb and fore-finger. He buried it at the foot of a tree. He took a stick and tried to cover the pool of blood with dirt—but what was the use? There was Jenny lying with her mouth open and her eyes walled and glassy. He could not tell Jim Hawkins he had shot his mule. But he had to tell something. Yeah, Ah'll tell em Jenny started gittin wil n fell on the joint of the plow. . . . But that would hardly happen to a mule. He walked across the field slowly, head down.

It was sunset. Two of Jim Hawkins' men were over near the edge of the woods digging a hole in which to bury Jenny. Dave was surrounded by a knot of people, all of whom were looking down at the dead mule.

"I don't see how in the world it happened," said Jim Hawkins for the tenth time.

145   The crowd parted and Dave's mother, father, and small brother pushed into the center.

"Where Dave?" his mother called.

"There he is," said Jim Hawkins.

His mother grabbed him.

"Whut happened, Dave? Whut yuh done?"

150   "Nothin."

"C mon, boy, talk," his father said.

Dave took a deep breath and told the story he knew nobody believed.

"Waal," he drawled. "Ah brung ol Jenny down here sos Ah could do mah plowin. Ah plowed bout two rows, just like yuh see." He stopped and pointed at the long rows of upturned earth. "Then somethin musta been wrong wid ol Jenny. She wouldn ack right a-tall. She started snortin n kickin her heels. Ah tried t hol her, but she pulled erway, rearin n going in. Then when the point of the plow was stickin up in the air, she swung erroun n twisted herself back on it . . . She stuck herself n started t bleed. N fo Ah could do anything, she wuz dead."

"Did you ever hear of anything like that in all your life?" asked Jim Hawkins.

There were white and black standing in the crowd. They murmured. 155
Dave's mother came close to him and looked hard into his face. "Tell the truth, Dave," she said.

"Looks like a bullet hole to me," said one man.

"Dave, whut yuh do wid the gun?" his mother asked.

The crowd surged in, looking at him. He jammed his hands into his pockets, shook his head slowly from left to right, and backed away. His eyes were wide and painful.

"Did he hava gun?" asked Jim Hawkins.

"By Gawd, Ah tol yuh tha wuz a gun wound," said a man, slapping 160
his thigh. His father caught his shoulders and shook him till his teeth rattled.

"Tell whut happened, yuh rascal! Tell whut . . ."

Dave looked at Jenny's stiff legs and began to cry.

"Whut yuh do wid the gun?" his mother asked.

"Whut wuz he doin wida gun?" his father asked.

"Come on and tell the truth," said Hawkins. "Ain't nobody going to 165
hurt you . . ."

His mother crowded close to him.

"Did yuh shoot tha mule, Dave?"

Dave cried, seeing blurred white and black faces.

"Ahh ddinn gggo tt sshooot hher . . . Ah ssswear ffo Gawd Ah ddin. . . . Ah wuz a-tryin t sssee ef the old gggun would sshoot—"

"Where yuh git the gun from?" his father asked. 170

"Ah got it from Joe, at the sto."

"Where yuh git the money?"

"Ma give it t me."

"He kept worryin me, Bob. Ah had t. Ah tol im t bring the gun right back t me . . . It was fer yuh, the gun."

"But how yuh happen to shoot that mule?" asked Jim Hawkins. 175

"Ah wuzn shootin at the mule, Mistah Hawkins. The gun jumped when Ah pulled the trigger . . . N fo Ah knowed anythin Jenny was there a-bleedin."

Somebody in the crowd laughed. Jim Hawkins walked close to Dave and looked into his face.

"Well, looks like you have bought you a mule, Dave."

"Ah swear fo Gawd, Ah didn go t kill the mule, Mistah Hawkins!"

"But you killed her!" 180

All the crowd was laughing now. They stood on tiptoe and poked heads over one another's shoulders.

"Well, boy, looks like yuh done bought a dead mule! Hahaha!"

"Ain tha ershame."

"Hohohohoho."

185   Dave stood, head down, twisting his feet in the dirt.

"Well, you needn't worry about it, Bob," said Jim Hawkins to Dave's father. "Just let the boy keep on working and pay me two dollars a month."

"What yuh wan fer yo mule, Mistah Hawkins?"

Jim Hawkins screwed up his eyes.

"Fifty dollars."

190   "Whut yuh do wid tha gun?" Dave's father demanded.

Dave said nothing.

"Yuh wan me t take a tree n beat yuh till yuh talk!"

"Nawsuh!"

"Whut yuh do wid it?"

195   "Ah throwed it erway."

"Where?"

"Ah . . . ah throwed it in the creek."

"Waal, c mon home. N firs thing in the mawnin git to tha creek n fin tha gun."

"Yessuh."

200   "Whut yuh pay fer it?"

"Two dollahs."

"Take tha gun n git yo money back n carry it t Mistah Hawkins, yuh hear? N don fergit Ahma lam you black bottom good fer this! Now march yosef on home, suh!"

Dave turned and walked slowly. He heard people laughing. Dave glared, his eyes welling with tears. Hot anger bubbled in him. Then he swallowed and stumbled on.

That night Dave did not sleep. He was glad that he had gotten out of killing the mule so easily, but he was hurt. Something hot seemed to turn over inside him each time he remembered how they had laughed. He tossed on his bed, feeling his hard pillow. N Pa says he's gonna beat me . . . He remembered other beatings, and his back quivered. Naw, naw, Ah sho don wan im t beat me tha way no mo. Dam em all! Nobody ever gave him anything. All he did was work. They treat me like a mule, n then they beat me. He gritted his teeth. N Ma had t toll on me.

205   Well, if he had to, he would take old man Hawkins that two dollars. But that meant selling the gun. And he wanted to keep that gun. Fifty dollars for a dead mule.

He turned over, thinking how he fired the gun. He had an itch to fire it again. Ef other men kin shoota gun, by Gawd, Ah kin! He was still, listening. Mebbe they all sleepin now. The house was still. He heard the soft breathing of his brother. Yes, now! He would go down and get that gun and see if he could fire it! He eased out of bed and slipped into overalls.

The moon was bright. He ran almost all the way to the edge of the woods. He stumbled over the ground, looking for the spot where he had buried the gun. Yeah, here it is. Like a hungry dog scratching for a bone, he pawed it up. He puffed his black cheeks and blew dirt from the trigger and barrel. He broke it and found four cartridges unshot. He looked around; the fields were filled with silence and moonlight. He clutched the gun stiff and hard in his fingers. But, as soon as he wanted to pull the trigger, he shut his eyes and turned his head. Naw, Ah can't shoot wid mah eyes closed n mah head turned. With effort he held his eyes open; then he squeezed. *Blooooom!* He was stiff, not breathing. The gun was still in his hands. Dammit, he'd done it! He fired again. *Blooooom!* He smiled. *Blooooom! Blooooom! Click, click.* There! It was empty. If anybody could shoot a gun, he could. He put the gun into his hip pocket and started across the fields.

When he reached the top of a ridge he stood straight and proud in the moonlight, looking at Jim Hawkins' big white house, feeling the gun sagging in his pocket. Lawd, ef Ah had just one mo bullet Ah'd taka shot at tha house. Ah'd like t scare ol man Hawkins jusa little . . . Jusa enough t let im know Dave Saunders is a man.

To his left the road curved, running to the tracks of the Illinois Central. He jerked his head, listening. From far off came a faint *hoooof-hoooof; hoooof-hoooof; hoooof-hoooof.* . . . He stood rigid. Two dollahs a mont. Les see now . . . Tha mean it'll take bout two years. Shucks! Ah'll be dam!

He started down the road, toward the tracks. Yeah, here she comes! 210 He stood beside the track and held himself stiffly. Here she comes, erroun the ben . . . C mon, yuh slow poke! C mon! He had his hand on his gun; something quivered in his stomach. Then the train thundered past, the gray and brown box cars rumbling and clinking. He gripped the gun tightly; then he jerked his hand out of his pocket. Ah betcha Bill wouldn't do it! Ah betcha . . . The cars slid past, steel grinding upon steel. Ahm ridin yuh ternight, so hep me Gawd! He was hot all over. He hesitated just a moment; then he grabbed, pulled atop of a car, and lay flat. He felt his pocket; the gun was still there. Ahead the long rails glinting in the moonlight, stretching away, away to somewhere, somewhere where he could be a man . . .

QUESTIONS

1. Analyze the way in which Dave's characterization is developed in this story. In what sense is he "almost a man"? In what ways is he still a boy?
2. What function does the gun play in developing the plot? How does the plot structure in general help to reinforce our view of Dave's character?
3. Identify the protagonist and antagonist in the story. How is the antagonist developed?
4. Discuss the role and characterization of Dave's parents. Are they sympathetic characters? Why or why not?
5. Does the story have an indeterminate ending? Why or why not? How does the ending suggest what Dave's ultimate fate will be?

SUGGESTIONS FOR WRITING

1. Write an essay on the direct or indirect presentation of character in one of the following:
   a. Connell, "The Most Dangerous Game" (page 67).
   b. Greene, "The Destructors" (page 111).
   c. Lahiri, "Interpreter of Maladies" (page 141).
2. Considering the three criteria that are necessary for developing a convincing character, write an essay in which you determine whether one of the following characters meets these criteria:
   a. Rainsford in Connell, "The Most Dangerous Game" (page 67).
   b. Blackie in Greene, "The Destructors" (page 111).
   c. Mr. Kapasi in Lahiri, "Interpreter of Maladies" (page 141).
   d. Dave in Wright, "The Man Who Was Almost a Man" (page 179).

Theme

"Daddy, the man next door kisses his wife every morning when he leaves for work. Why don't you do that?"

"Are you kidding? I don't even know the woman."

"Daughter, your young man stays until a very late hour. Hasn't your mother said anything to you about this habit of his?"

"Yes, father. Mother says men haven't altered a bit."

For readers who contemplate the two jokes above, a significant difference emerges between them. The first joke depends only upon a reversal of expectation. We expect the man to explain why he doesn't kiss his wife; instead he explains why he doesn't kiss his neighbor's wife. The second joke, though it contains a reversal of expectation, depends as much or more for its effectiveness on a truth about human life, namely, that *people tend to grow more conservative as they grow older* or that *parents often scold their children for doing exactly what they did themselves when young.* This truth, which might be stated in different ways, is the *theme* of the joke.

The **theme** of a piece of fiction is its controlling idea or its central insight. It is the unifying generalization about life stated or implied by the story. To derive the theme of a story, we must determine what its central *purpose* is: what view of life it supports or what insight into life it reveals.

Not all stories have a significant theme. The purpose of a horror story may be simply to scare readers, to give them gooseflesh. The purpose of an adventure story may be simply to carry readers through a series of exciting escapades. The purpose of a murder mystery may be simply to pose a problem for readers to try to solve (and to prevent them from solving it, if possible, until the last paragraph). The purpose of some stories may be simply to provide suspense or to make readers laugh or to surprise them with a sudden twist at the end. Theme exists only (1) when an author has seriously attempted to record life accurately or to reveal some truth about it or (2) when an author has deliberately introduced as a unifying element some concept or theory of life that the story illuminates. Theme exists in virtually all literary fiction but only in some commercial fiction. In literary fiction it is the primary purpose of the story; in commercial fiction, it is usually less important than such elements as plot and suspense.

In many stories the theme may be equivalent to the revelation of human character. If a story has as its central purpose to exhibit a certain kind of human being, our statement of theme may be no more than a concentrated description of the person revealed, with the addition, "Some people are like this." Frequently, however, a story through its portrayal of specific persons in specific situations will have something to say about the nature of all human beings or about their relationship to each other or to the universe. Whatever central generalization about life arises from the specifics of the story constitutes theme.

The theme of a story, like its plot, may be stated very briefly or at greater length. With a simple or very brief story, we may be satisfied to sum up the theme in a single sentence. With a more complex story, if it is successfully unified, we can still state the theme in a single sentence, but we may feel that a paragraph—or occasionally even an essay—is needed to state it adequately. A rich story will give us many and complex insights into life. In stating the theme in a sentence, we must pick the *central* insight, the one that explains the greatest number of elements in the story and relates them to each other. For theme is what gives a story its unity. In any story at all complex, however, we are likely to feel that a one-sentence statement of theme leaves out a great part of the story's meaning. Though the theme of *Othello* may be expressed as "Jealousy exacts a terrible cost," such a statement does not begin to suggest the range and depth of Shakespeare's play. Any successful story is a good deal more and means a good deal more than any one-sentence statement of theme that we may extract from it, for the story will modify and expand this statement in various and subtle ways.

We must never think, once we have stated the theme of a story, that the whole purpose of the story has been to yield up this abstract statement. If this were so, there would be no reason for the story: we could stop with the abstract statement. The function of literary writers is not to state a theme but to vivify it. They wish to deliver it not simply to our intellects but to our emotions, our senses, and our imaginations. The theme of a story may be little or nothing except as it is embodied and vitalized by the story. Unembodied, it is a dry backbone, without flesh or life.

Sometimes the theme of a story is explicitly stated somewhere in the story, either by the author or by one of the characters. More often, however, the theme is implied. Story writers, after all, are story writers, not essayists or philosophers. Their first business is to reveal life, not to comment on it. They may well feel that unless the story somehow expresses its own meaning, without their having to point it out, they have not told the story well. Or they may feel that if the story is to have its maximum emotional effect, they must refrain from interrupting it or making remarks about it. They are also wary of spoiling a story for perceptive readers by "explaining" it, just as some people ruin jokes by explaining them. For these reasons theme is more often left implicit than stated explicitly. Good writers do not ordinarily write a story for the sole purpose of "illustrating" a theme, as do the writers of parables or fables. They write stories to bring alive some segment of human existence. When they do so searchingly and coherently, theme arises naturally out of what they have written. Good readers may state the generalizations for themselves.

Some readers—especially inexperienced readers—look for a "moral" in everything they read, some rule of conduct that they regard as applicable to their lives. They consider the words "theme" and "moral" to be interchangeable. Sometimes the words are interchangeable. Occasionally the theme of a story may be expressed as a moral principle without doing violence to the story. More frequently, however, the word "moral" is too narrow to fit the kind of illumination provided by a first-rate story. It is hardly suitable, for instance, for the kind of story that simply displays human character. Such nouns as "moral," "lesson," and "message" are therefore best avoided in the discussion of fiction. The critical term theme is preferable for several reasons. First, it is less likely to obscure the fact that a story is not a preachment or a sermon: a story's *first* object is enjoyment. Second, it should keep us from trying to wring from every story a didactic pronouncement about life. The person who seeks a moral in every story is likely to oversimplify and conventionalize it—to reduce it to some dusty platitude like "Be kind to animals" or "Look before you leap" or "Crime does not pay." The purpose of literary story writers is to give us a greater awareness and a greater understanding of life, not to inculcate a code of moral rules for regulating daily conduct. In getting at the theme of the story it is better to ask not *What does this story teach?* but *What does this story reveal?* Readers who analyze Lahiri's "Interpreter of Maladies" as being simply about the danger of keeping secrets in a marriage have missed nine-tenths of the story. The theme could be stated more accurately this way: "The human search for love can result in a 'malady' when unaccompanied by honest emotion (as is the case with Mrs. Das) or when inspired by naïve infatuation (as is the case with Mr. Kapasi). Different sets of cultural and moral values often result in comic but also poignant failures to connect meaningfully with another person." Obviously, this dry statement is a poor thing beside the living reality of the story. But it is a more faithful abstracting of the story's content than any pat, cut-and-dried "moral."

The revelation offered by a good story may be something fresh or something old. The story may bring us some insight into life that we had not had before, and thus expand our horizons, or it may make us *feel* or *feel again* some truth of which we have long been merely intellectually aware. We may know in our minds, for instance, that "War is horrible" or that "Old age is often pathetic and in need of understanding," but these are insights that need to be periodically renewed. *Emotionally* we may forget them, and if we do, we are less alive and complete as human beings. Story writers perform a service for us—interpret life for us—whether they give us new insights or refresh and extend old ones.

The themes of commercial and literary stories may be identical, but frequently they are different. Commercial stories, for the most part, confirm their readers' prejudices, endorse their opinions, ratify their feelings, and satisfy their wishes. Usually, therefore, the themes of such stories are widely accepted platitudes of experience that may or may not be supported by the life around us. They represent life as we would like it to be, not always as it is. We should certainly like to believe, for instance, that "motherhood is sacred," that "true love always wins through," that "virtue and hard work are rewarded in the end," that "cheaters never win," that "old age brings a mellow wisdom that compensates for its infirmity," and that "every human being has a soft spot in him somewhere." Literary writers, however, being thoughtful observers of life, are likely to question these beliefs and often to challenge them. Their ideas about life are not simply taken over ready-made from what they were taught in Sunday school or from the books they read as children; they are the formulations of sensitive and independent observers who have collated all that they have read and been taught by life itself. The themes of their stories therefore do not often correspond to the pretty little sentiments we find inscribed in greeting cards. They may sometimes represent rather somber truths. Much of the process of maturing as a reader lies in the discovery that there may be more nourishment and deeper enjoyment in these somber truths than in the warm and fuzzy optimism found in so-called "inspirational" fiction.

We do not, however, have to accept the theme of a literary story any more than we do that of a commercial story. Though we should never summarily dismiss it without reflection, we may find that the theme of a story represents a judgment on life with which, on examination, we cannot agree. If it is the reasoned view of a seasoned and serious artist, nevertheless, it cannot be without value to us. There is value in knowing what the world looks like to others, and we can thus use a judgment to expand our knowledge of human experience even though we cannot ourselves accept it. Genuine artists and thoughtful observers, moreover, can hardly fail to present us with partial insights along the way, although we disagree with the total view. Careful readers, therefore, will not reject a story because they reject its theme. They can enjoy any story that arises from sufficient depth of observation and reflection and is artistically composed, though they disagree with its theme; and they will prefer it to a shallower, less thoughtful, or less successfully integrated story that presents a theme they endorse.

Discovering and stating the theme of a story is often a delicate task. Sometimes we will *feel* what the story is about strongly enough and yet find it difficult to put this feeling into words. If we are skilled readers, it is perhaps unnecessary that we do so. The bare statement of the theme, so lifeless and impoverished when abstracted from the story, may seem to diminish the story to something less than it is. Often, however, the attempt to state a theme will reveal to us aspects of a story that we should otherwise not have noticed and will thereby lead to more thorough understanding. The ability to state theme, moreover, is a test of our understanding of a story. Careless readers often think they understand a story when in actuality they have misunderstood it. They understand the events but not what the events add up to. Or, in adding up the events, they arrive at an erroneous total. People sometimes miss the point of a joke. It is not surprising that they should occasionally miss the point of a good piece of fiction, which is many times more complex than a joke.

There is no prescribed method for discovering theme. Sometimes we can best get at it by asking in what way the main character has changed in the course of the story and what, if anything, the character has learned before its end. Sometimes the best approach is to explore the nature of the central conflict and its outcome. Sometimes the title will provide an important clue. At all times we should keep in mind the following principles:

1. Theme should be expressible in the form of a statement with a subject and a predicate. It is insufficient to say that the theme of a story is motherhood or loyalty to country. Motherhood and loyalty are simply subjects. Theme must be a statement *about* the subject. For instance, "Motherhood sometimes has more frustrations than rewards" or "Loyalty to country often inspires heroic self-sacrifice." If we express the theme in the form of a phrase, the phrase must be convertible to sentence form. A phrase such as "the futility of envy," for instance, may be converted to the statement "Envy is futile": it may therefore serve as a statement of theme.

2. The theme should be stated as a *generalization* about life. In stating theme we do not use the names of the characters or refer to precise places or events, for to do so is to make a specific rather than a general statement. The theme of "The Destructors" is not that "The Wormsley Common Gang of London, in the aftermath of World War II, found a creative outlet in destroying a beautiful two-hundred-year-old house designed by Sir Christopher Wren." Rather, it is something like this: "The dislocations caused by a devastating war may produce among the young a conscious or unconscious rebellion against all the values of the reigning society—a rebellion in which the creative instincts are channeled into destructive enterprises."

3. We must be careful not to make the generalization larger than is justified by the terms of the story. Terms like *every*, *all*, *always* should be used very cautiously; terms like *some*, *sometimes*, *may* are often more accurate. The theme of "Everyday Use" is not that "Habitually compliant and tolerant mothers will eventually stand up to their bullying children," for we have only one instance of such behavior in the story. But the story does sufficiently present this event as a climactic change in a developing character. Because the story's narrator recalls precise details of her previous behavior that she brings to bear on her present decision, we can safely infer that this decision will be meaningful and lasting, and should feel that we can generalize beyond the specific situation. The theme might be expressed thus: "A person whose honesty and tolerance have long made her susceptible to the strong will of another may reach a point where she will exert her own will for the sake of justice," or more generally, "Ingrained habits can be given up if justice makes a greater demand." Notice that we have said *may* and *can*, not *will* and *must*. Only occasionally will the theme of a story be expressible as a universal generalization. The bleak, darkly humorous ending of "Hunters in the Snow" lets us know that Wolff views all three of his characters as hopelessly "lost" in both the geographical and moral senses of the word. The world contains many people who are essentially predatory, the story seems to say, entirely self-interested "hunters" in a cold universe; even when two individuals form temporary alliances, these are symbiotic relationships in which each person is simply trying to fulfill a selfish need through the other.

4. Theme is the *central* and *unifying* concept of a story. Therefore (a) it accounts for all the major details of the story. If we cannot explain the bearing of an important incident or character on the theme, either

in exemplifying it or modifying it in some way, it is probable that our interpretation is partial and incomplete, that at best we have got hold only of a subtheme. Another alternative, though it must be used with caution, is that the story itself is imperfectly constructed and lacks unity. (b) The theme is not contradicted by any detail of the story. If we have to overlook or blink at or "force" the meaning of some significant detail in order to frame our statement, we may be sure that our statement is defective. (c) The theme cannot rely upon supposed facts—facts not actually stated or clearly implied by the story. The theme exists *inside*, not *outside*, the story. The statement of it must be based on the data of the story itself, not on assumptions supplied from our own experience.

   5. There is no *one* way of stating the theme of a story. The story is not a guessing game or an acrostic that is supposed to yield some magic verbal formula that won't work if a syllable is changed. It merely presents a view of life, and, as long as the above conditions are fulfilled, that view may surely be stated in more than one way. Here, for instance, are three possible ways of stating the theme of "Miss Brill": (a) A person living alone may create a protective fantasy life by dramatizing insignificant activities, but such a life can be jeopardized when she is forced to see herself as others see her. (b) Isolated elderly people, unsupported by a network of family and friends, may make a satisfying adjustment through a pleasant fantasy life, but when their fantasy is punctured by the cold claw of reality, the effect can be devastating. (c) Loneliness is a pitiable emotional state that may be avoided by refusing to acknowledge that one feels lonely, though such an avoidance may also require one to create unrealistic fantasies about oneself.

   6. We should avoid any statement that reduces the theme to some familiar saying that we have heard all our lives, such as "You can't judge a book by its cover" or "A stitch in time saves nine." Although such a statement *may* express the theme accurately, too often it is simply a lazy shortcut that impoverishes the essential meaning of the story in order to save mental effort. When readers force every new experience into an old formula, they lose the chance for a fresh perception. Beware of using clichès when attempting to summarize a story's theme. To decide that "love is blind" is the theme of "How I Met My Husband" is to indulge in a reductive absurdity. When a ready-made phrase comes to mind as the theme of a story, this may be a sign that the reader should think more deeply and thoroughly about the author's central purpose.

1. Review the definition of "theme" in fiction.
2. Describe the best way(s) in which the theme of a story may be stated.
3. Distinguish between the theme of a story and the central purpose of a story.
4. Differentiate between the typical themes of commercial vs. literary stories.
5. Review the six principles relating to theme as described in this chapter.

Tim Gautreaux
Welding with Children

Tuesday was about typical. My four daughters, not a one of them married, you understand, brought over their kids, one each, and explained to my wife how much fun she was going to have looking after them again. But Tuesday was her day to go to the casino, so guess who got to tend the four babies? My oldest daughter also brought over a bed rail that the end broke off of. She wanted me to weld it. Now, what the hell you can do in a bed that'll cause the end of a iron rail to break off is beyond me, but she can't afford another one on her burger-flipping salary, she said, so I got to fix it with four little kids hanging on my coveralls. Her kid is seven months, nicknamed Nu-Nu, a big-head baby with a bubbling tongue always hanging out his mouth. My second-oldest, a flight attendant on some propeller airline out of Alexandria, has a little six-year-old girl named Moonbean, and that ain't no nick-name. My third-oldest, who is still dating, dropped off Tammynette, also six, and last to come was Freddie, my favorite because he looks like those

WELDING WITH CHILDREN   First published in 1999. Tim Gautreaux (b. 1947) is the author of two novels, most recently *The Clearing* (2004), and two collections of short fiction. His stories have appeared in major American magazines such as *The Atlantic Monthly* and *Harper's*, and in the anthology *Best American Short Stories*. He lives in Hammond, Louisiana, and teaches English at Southeastern Louisiana University.

old photographs of me when I was seven, a round head with copper bristle for hair, cut about as short as Velcro. He's got that kind of papery skin like me, too, except splashed with a handful of freckles.

When everybody was on deck, I put the three oldest in front the TV and rocked Nu-Nu off and dropped him in the Portacrib. Then I dragged the bed rail and the three awake kids out through the trees, back to my tin workshop. I tried to get something done, but Tammynette got the big grinder turned on and jammed a file against the stone just to laugh at the sparks. I got the thing unplugged and then started to work, but when I was setting the bed rail in the vise and clamping on the ground wire from the welding machine, I leaned against the iron and Moonbean picked the electric rod holder off the cracker box and struck a blue arc on the zipper of my coveralls, low. I jumped back like I was hit with religion and tore those coveralls off and shook the sparks out of my drawers. Moonbean opened her goat eyes wide and sang, "Whoo. Grendaddy can bust a move." I decided I better hold off trying to weld with little kids around.

I herded them into the yard to play, but even though I got three acres, there ain't much for them to do at my place, so I sat down and watched Freddie climb on a Oldsmobile engine I got hanging from a willow oak on a long chain. Tammynette and Moonbean pushed him like he was on a swing, and I yelled at them to stop, but they wouldn't listen. It was a sad sight, I guess. I shouldn't have that old greasy engine hanging from that Kmart chain in my side yard. I know better. Even in this central Louisiana town of Gumwood, which is just like any other red-dirt place in the South, trash in the yard is trash in the yard. I make decent money as a now-and-then welder.

I think sometimes about how I even went to college once. I went a whole semester to LSU. Worked overtime at a sawmill for a year to afford the tuition and showed up in my work boots to be taught English 101 by a black guy from Pakistan who couldn't understand one word we said, much less us him. He didn't teach me a damn thing and would sit on the desk with his legs crossed and tell us to write nonstop in what he called our "portfolios," which he never read. For all I know, he sent our tablets back to Pakistan for his relatives to use as stove wood.

The algebra teacher talked to us with his eyes rolled up like his lecture was printed out on the ceiling. He didn't even know we were in the room, most of the time, and for a month I thought the poor bastard was stone-blind. I never once solved for X. 5

The chemistry professor was a fat drunk who heated Campbell's soup on one of those little burners and ate it out the can while he talked. There was about a million of us in that classroom, and I couldn't get the hang of what he wanted us to do with the numbers and names. I sat way in the back next to some fraternity boys who called me "Uncle Jed." Time or two, when I could see the blackboard off on the horizon, I almost got the hang of something, and I was glad of that.

I kind of liked the history professor and learned to write down a lot of what he said, but he dropped dead one hot afternoon in the middle of the pyramids and was replaced by a little porch lizard that looked down his nose at me where I sat in the front row. He bit on me pretty good because I guess I didn't look like nobody else in that class, with my short red hair and blue jeans that were blue. I flunked out that semester, but I got my money's worth learning about people that don't have hearts no bigger than bird shot.

Tammynette and Moonbean gave the engine a long shove, got distracted by a yellow butterfly playing in a clump of pig-weed, and that nine-hundred-pound V-8 kind of ironed them out on the back-swing. So I picked the squalling girls up and got everybody inside, where I cleaned them good with Go-Jo.

"I want a Icee," Tammynette yelled while I was getting the motor oil from between her fingers. "I ain't had a Icee all day."

10   "You don't need one every day, little miss," I told her.

"Don't you got some money?" She pulled a hand away and flipped her hair with it like a model on TV.

"Those things cost most of a dollar. When I was a kid, I used to get a nickel for candy, and that only twice a week."

"Icee," she yelled in my face, Moonbean taking up the cry and calling out from the kitchen in her dull little voice. She wasn't dull in the head; she just talked low, like a bad cowboy actor. Nu-Nu sat up in the Portacrib and gargled something, so I gathered everyone up, put them in the Caprice, and drove them down to the Gumwood Pak-a-Sak. The baby was in my lap when I pulled up, Freddie tuning in some rock music that sounded like hail on a tin roof. Two guys I know, older than me, watched us roll to the curb. When I turned the engine off, I could barely hear one of them say, "Here comes Bruton and his bastardmobile." I grabbed the steering wheel hard and looked down on the top of Nu-Nu's head, feeling like someone just told me my house burned down. I'm naturally tanned, so the old men couldn't see the shame rising in my face. I got out, pretending I didn't hear anything, Nu-Nu in the crook of my arm like a loaf of bread. I wanted to punch the older guy and break his upper plate, but I could see the article in the local paper. I could imagine the memories the kids would have of their grandfather whaling away at two snuff-dripping geezers. I looked them in the eye and smiled, surprising even myself. Bastardmobile. Man.

"Hey, Bruton," the younger one said, a Mr. Fordlyson, maybe sixty-five. "All them kids yours? You start over?"

"Grandkids," I said, holding Nu-Nu over his shoes so maybe he'd   15
drool on them.

The older one wore a straw fedora and was nicked up in twenty places with skin cancer operations. He snorted. "Maybe you can do better with this batch," he told me. I remembered then that he was also a Mr. Fordlyson, the other guy's uncle. He used to run the hardwood sawmill north of town, was a deacon in the Baptist church, and owned about 1 percent of the pissant bank down next to the gin. He thought he was king of Gumwood, but then, every old man in town who had five dollars in his pocket and an opinion on the tip of his tongue thought the same.

I pushed past him and went into the Pak-a-Sak. The kids saw the candy rack and cried out for Mars Bars and Zeroes. Even Nu-Nu put out a slobbery hand toward the Gummy Worms, but I ignored their whining and drew them each a small Coke Icee. Tammynette and Moonbean grabbed theirs and headed for the door. Freddie took his carefully when I offered it. Nu-Nu might be kind of wobble-headed and plain as a melon, but he sure knew what an Icee was and how to go after a straw. And what a smile when that Coke syrup hit those bald gums of his.

Right then, Freddie looked up at me with his green eyes in that speckled face and said, "What's a bastardmobile?"

I guess my mouth dropped open. "I don't know what you're talking about."

"I thought we was in a Chevrolet," he said.   20

"We are."

"Well, that man said we was in a—"

"Never mind what he said. You must have misheard him." I nudged him toward the door and we went out. The older Mr. Fordlyson was watching us like we were a parade. I was trying to look straight ahead. In my mind, the newspaper bore the headline, LOCAL MAN ARRESTED WITH GRANDCHILDREN FOR ASSAULT. I got into the car with the kids and looked back out at the Fordlysons where they sat on a bumper rail, sweating through their white shirts and staring at us all. Their kids owned sawmills, ran fast-food franchises, were on the school board. They were all married. I guess the young Fordlysons were smart, though looking at that pair, you'd never know where they got their brains. I started my car and backed out onto the highway, trying not to think, but to me the word was spelled out in chrome script on my fenders: BASTARDMOBILE.

On the way home, Tammynette stole a suck on Freddie's straw, and he jerked it away and called her something I'd only heard the younger workers at the plywood mill say. The words hit me in the back of the head like a brick, and I pulled off the road onto the gravel shoulder. "What'd you say, boy?"

25   "Nothing." But he reddened. I saw he cared what I thought.

"Kids your age don't use language like that."

Tammynette flipped her hair and raised her chin. "How old you got to be?"

I gave her a look. "Don't you care what he said to you?"

"It's what they say on the comedy program," Freddie said. "Everybody says that."

30   "What comedy program?"

"It comes on after the nighttime news."

"What you doing up late at night?"

He just stared at me, and I saw that he had no idea of what *late* was. Glendine, his mamma, probably lets him fall asleep in front of the set every night. I pictured him crumpled up on that smelly shag rug his mamma keeps in front of the TV to catch the spills and crumbs.

When I got home, I took them all out on our covered side porch. The girls began to struggle with jacks, their little ball bouncing crooked on the slanted floor, Freddie played tunes on his Icee straw, and Nu-Nu fell asleep in my lap. I stared at my car and wondered if its name had spread throughout the community, if everywhere I drove people would call out, "Here comes the bastardmobile." Gumwood is one of those towns where everybody looks at everything that moves. I do it myself. If my neighbor Miss Hanchy pulls out of her lane, I wonder, Now, where is the old bat off to? It's two-thirty, so her soap opera must be over. I figure her route to the store and then somebody different will drive by and catch my attention, and I'll think after them. This is not all bad. It makes you watch how you behave, and besides, what's the alternative? Nobody giving a flip about whether you live or die? I've heard those stories from the big cities about how people will sit in an apartment window six stories up, watch somebody take ten minutes to kill you with a stick, and not even reach for the phone.

35   I started thinking about my four daughters. None of them has any religion to speak of. I thought they'd pick it up from their mamma, like I did from mine, but LaNelle always worked so much, she just had time to cook, clean, transport, and fuss. The girls grew up watching cable and videos every night, and that's where they got their view of the world, and that's why four dirty blondes with weak chins from St. Helena Parish thought they lived in a Hollywood soap opera. They also thought the married pulpwood truck drivers and garage mechanics they dated

were movie stars. I guess a lot of what's wrong with my girls is my fault, but I don't know what I could've done different.

Moonbean raked in a gaggle of jacks, and a splinter from the porch floor ran up under her nail. "Shit dog," she said, wagging her hand like it was on fire and coming to me on her knees.

"Don't say that."

"My finger hurts. Fix it, Paw-Paw."

"I will if you stop talking like white trash."

Tammynette picked up on fivesies. "Mamma's boyfriend, Melvin,   40
says *shit dog.*"

"Would you do everything your mamma's boyfriend does?"

"Melvin can drive," Tammynette said. "I'd like to drive."

I got out my penknife and worked the splinter from under Moonbean's nail while she jabbered to Tammynette about how her mamma's Toyota cost more than Melvin's teeny Dodge truck. I swear I don't know how these kids got so complicated. When I was their age, all I wanted to do was make mud pies or play in the creek. I didn't want anything but a twice-a-week nickel to bring to the store. These kids ain't eight years old and already know enough to run a casino. When I finished, I looked down at Moonbean's brown eyes, at Nu-Nu's pulsing head. "Does your mammas ever talk to y'all about, you know, God?"

"My mamma says *God* when she's cussing Melvin," Tammynette said.

"That's not what I mean. Do they read Bible stories to y'all at   45
bedtime?"

Freddie's face brightened. "She rented *Conan the Barbarian* for us once. That movie kicked ass."

"That's not a Bible movie," I told him.

"It ain't? It's got swords and snakes in it."

"What's that got to do with anything?"

Tammynette came close and grabbed Nu-Nu's hand and played the   50
fingers like they were piano keys. "Ain't the Bible full of swords and snakes?"

Nu-Nu woke up and peed on himself, so I had to go for a plastic diaper. On the way back from the bathroom, I saw our little book rack out the corner of my eye. I found my old Bible stories hardback and brought it out on the porch. It was time somebody taught them something about something.

They gathered round, sitting on the floor, and I got down amongst them. I started into Genesis and how God made the earth, and how he made us and gave us a soul that would live forever. Moonbean reached into the book and put her hand on God's beard. "If he shaved, he'd look just like that old man down at the Pak-a-Sak," she said.

My mouth dropped a bit. "You mean Mr. Fordlyson? That man don't look like God."

Tammynette yawned. "You just said God made us to look like him."

55   "Never mind," I told them, going on into Adam and Eve and the Garden. Soon as I turned the page, they saw the snake and began to squeal.

"Look at the size of that sucker," Freddie said.

Tammynette wiggled closer. "I knew they was a snake in this book."

"He's a bad one," I told them. "He lied to Adam and Eve and said not to do what God told them to do."

Moonbean looked up at me slow. "This snake can talk?"

60   "Yes."

"How about that. Just like on cartoons. I thought they was making that up."

"Well, a real snake can't talk, nowadays," I explained.

"Ain't this garden snake a real snake?" Freddie asked.

"It's the devil in disguise," I told them.

65   Tammynette flipped her hair. "Aw, that's just a old song. I heard it on the reddio."

"That Elvis Presley tune's got nothing to do with the devil making himself into a snake in the Garden of Eden."

"Who's Elvis Presley?" Moonbean sat back in the dust by the weatherboard wall and stared out at my overgrown lawn.

"He's some old singer died a million years ago," Tammynette told her.

"Was he in the Bible, too?"

70   I beat the book on the floor. "No, he ain't. Now pay attention. This is important." I read the section about Adam and Eve disobeying God, turned the page, and all hell broke loose. An angel was holding a long sword over Adam and Eve's downturned heads as he ran them out of the Garden. Even Nu-Nu got excited and pointed a finger at the angel.

"What's that guy doing?" Tammynette asked.

"Chasing them out of Paradise. Adam and Eve did a bad thing, and when you do bad, you get punished for it." I looked down at their faces and it seemed that they were all thinking about something at the same time. It was scary, the little sparks I saw flying in their eyes. Whatever you tell them at this age stays forever. You got to be careful. Freddie looked up at me and asked, "Did they ever get to go back?"

"Nope. Eve started worrying about everything and Adam had to work every day like a beaver just to get by."

"Was that angel really gonna stick Adam with that sword?" Moonbean asked.

"Forget about that darned sword, will you?"   75

"Well, that's just mean" is what she said.

"No it ain't," I said. "They got what was coming to them." Then I went into Noah and the Flood, and in the middle of things, Freddie piped up.

"You mean all the bad people got drownded at once? All right!"

I looked down at him hard and saw that the Bible was turning into one big adventure film for him. Freddie had already watched so many movies that any religion he would hear about would nest in his brain on top of *Tanga the Cave Woman* and *Bikini Death Squad*. I got everybody a cold drink and jelly sandwiches, and after that I turned on a window unit, handed out Popsicles, and we sat inside on the couch because the heat had waked up the yellow flies outside. I tore into how Abraham almost stabbed Isaac, and the kids' eyes got big when they saw the knife. I hoped that they got a sense of obedience to God out of it, but when I asked Freddie what the point of the story was, he just shrugged and looked glum. Tammynette, however, had an opinion. "He's just like O. J. Simpson!"

Freddie shook his head. "Naw. God told Abraham to do it just as a   80
test."

"Maybe God told O. J. to do what he did," Tammynette sang.

"Naw. O. J. did it on his own," Freddie told her. "He didn't like his wife no more."

"Well, maybe Abraham didn't like his son no more neither, so he was gonna kill him dead and God stopped him." Tammynette's voice was starting to rise the way her mother's did when she'd been drinking.

"Daddies don't kill their sons when they don't like them," Freddie told her. "They just pack up and leave." He broke apart the two halves of his Popsicle and bit one, then the other.

Real quick, I started in on Sodom and Gomorrah and the burning   85
of the towns full of wicked people. Moonbean was struck with Lot's wife. "I saw this movie once where Martians shot a gun at you and turned you into a statue. You reckon it was Martians burnt down those towns?"

"The Bible is not a movie," I told her.

"I think I seen it down at Blockbuster," Tammynette said.

I didn't stop to argue, just pushed on through Moses and the Ten Commandments, spending a lot of time on number six, since that one give their mammas so much trouble. Then Nu-Nu began to rub his nose with the backs of his hands and started to tune up, so I knew it was time to put the book down and wash faces and get snacks and play crawl-around. I was determined not to turn on TV again, but Freddie hit the button when I was in the kitchen. When Nu-Nu and me came into the living room, they were in a half circle around a talk show. On the set were several overweight, tattooed, frowning, slouching individuals who, the announcer told us, had tricked their parents into signing over ownership of their houses, and then evicted them. The kids watched like they were looking at cartoons, which is to say, they gobbled it all up. At a commercial, I asked Moonbean, who has the softest heart, what she thought of kids that threw their parents in the street. She put a finger in an ear and said through a long yawn that if the parents did mean things, then the kids could do what they wanted to them. I shook my head, went in the kitchen, found the Christmas vodka, and poured myself a long drink. I stared out in the yard to where my last pickup truck lay dead and rusting in a pile of wisteria at the edge of the lot. I formed a little fantasy about gathering all these kids into my Caprice and heading out northwest to start over, away from their mammas, TVs, mildew, their casino-mad grandmother, and Louisiana in general. I could get a job, raise them right, send them to college so they could own sawmills and run car dealerships. A drop of sweat rolled off the glass and hit my right shoe, and I looked down at it. The leather lace-ups I was wearing were paint-spattered and twenty years old. They told me I hadn't held a steady job in a long time, that whatever bad was gonna happen was partly my fault. I wondered then if my wife had had the same fantasy: leaving her scruffy, sunburned, failed-welder husband home and moving away with these kids, maybe taking a course in clerical skills and getting a job in Utah, raising them right, sending them off to college. Maybe even each of their mammas had the same fantasy, pulling their kids out of their parents' gassy-smelling old house and heading away from the heat and humidity. I took another long swallow and wondered why one of us didn't do it. I looked out to my Caprice sitting in the shade of a pecan tree, shadows of leaves moving on it, making it wiggle like a dark green flame, and I realized we couldn't drive away from ourselves. We couldn't escape in the bastardmobile.

In the pantry, I opened the house's circuit panel and rotated out a fuse until I heard a cry from the living room. I went in and pulled down a storybook, something about a dog chasing a train. My wife bought it twenty years ago for one of our daughters but never read it to her. I sat in front of the dark television.

90   "What's wrong with the TV, Paw-Paw?" Moonbean rasped.

"It died," I said, opening the book. They squirmed and complained, but after a few pages they were hooked. It was a good book, one I'd read myself one afternoon during a thunderstorm. But while I was reading, this blue feeling got me. I was thinking, What's the use? I'm just one old man with a little brown book of Bible stories and a doggy-hero book. How can that compete with daily MTV, kids' programs that make big people look like fools, the Playboy Channel, the shiny magazines their mammas and their boyfriends leave around the house, magazines like *Me*, and *Self*, and *Love Guides*, and rental movies where people kill one another with no more thought than it would take to swat a fly, nothing at all like what Abraham suffered before he raised that knife? But I read on for a half hour, and when that dog stopped the locomotive before it pulled the passenger train over the collapsed bridge, even Tammynette clapped her sticky hands.

The next day, I didn't have much on the welding schedule, so after one or two little jobs, including the bed rail that my daughter called and ragged me about, I went out to pick up a window grate the town marshal wanted me to fix. It was hot right after lunch, and Gumwood was wiggling with heat. Across from the cypress railroad station was our little redbrick city hall with a green copper dome on it, and on the grass in front of that was a pecan tree with a wooden bench next to its trunk. Old men sometimes gathered under the cool branches and told one another how to fix tractors that hadn't been made in fifty years, or how to make grits out of a strain of corn that didn't exist anymore. That big pecan was a landmark, and locals called it the "Tree of Knowledge." When I walked by going to the marshal's office, I saw the older Mr. Fordlyson seated in the middle of the long bench, blinking at the street like a chicken. He called out to me.

"Bruton," he said. "Too hot to weld?" I didn't think it was a friendly comment, though he waved for me to come over.

"Something like that." I was tempted to walk on, but he motioned for me to sit next to him, which I did. I looked across the street for a long time. "The other day at the store," I began, "you said my car was a bastardmobile."

Fordlyson blinked twice but didn't change his expression. Most 95
local men would be embarrassed at being called down for a lack of politeness, but he sat there with his face as hard as a plowshare. "Is that not what it is?" he said at last.

I should have been mad, and I was mad, but I kept on. "It was a mean thing to let me hear." I looked down and wagged my head. "I need help with those kids, not your meanness."

He looked at me with his little nickel-colored eyes glinting under that straw fedora with the black silk hatband. "What kind of help you need?"

I picked up a pecan that was still in its green pod. "I'd like to fix it so those grandkids do right. I'm thinking of talking to their mammas and—"

"Too late for their mammas." He put up a hand and let it fall like an ax. "They'll have to decide to straighten out on their own or not at all. Nothing you can tell those girls now will change them a whit." He said this in a tone that hinted I was stupid for not seeing this. Dumb as a post. He looked off to the left for half a second, then back. "You got to deal directly with those kids."

100   "I'm trying." I cracked the nut open on the edge of the bench.

"Tryin' won't do shit. You got to bring them to Sunday school every week. You go to church?"

"Yeah."

"Don't eat that green pecan—it'll make you sick. Which church you go to?"

"Bonner Straight Gospel."

105   He flew back as though he'd just fired a twelve-gauge at the dog sleeping under the station platform across the street. "Bruton, your wild-man preacher is one step away from taking up serpents. I've heard he lets the kids come to the main service and yells at them about frying in hell like chicken parts. You got to keep them away from that man. Why don't you come to First Baptist?"

I looked at the ground. "I don't know."

The old man bobbed his head once. "I know damned well why not. You won't tithe."

That hurt deep. "Hey, I don't have a lot of extra money. I know the Baptists got good Sunday-school programs, but . . ."

Fordlyson waved a finger in the air like a little sword. "Well, join the Methodists. The Presbyterians." He pointed up the street. "Join those Catholics. Some of them don't put more than a dollar a week in the plate, but there's so many of them, and the church has so many services a weekend, the priests can run the place on volume like Wal-Mart."

110   I knew several good mechanics who were Methodists. "How's the Methodists' children's programs?"

The old man spoke out of the side of his mouth. "Better'n you got now."

"I'll think about it," I told him.

"Yeah, bullshit. You'll go home and weld together a log truck, and tomorrow you'll go fishing, and you'll never do nothing for them kids, and they'll all wind up serving time in Angola or on their backs in New Orleans."

It got me hot the way he thought he had all the answers, and I turned on him quick. "Okay, wise man. I came to the Tree of Knowledge. Tell me what to do."

He pulled down one finger on his right hand with the forefinger of   115
the left. "Go join the Methodists." Another finger went down and he told me, "Every Sunday, bring them children to church." A third finger, and he said, "And keep 'em with you as much as you can."

I shook my head. "I already raised my kids."

Fordlyson looked at me hard and didn't have to say what he was thinking. He glanced down at the ground between his smooth-toe lace-ups. "And clean up your yard."

"What's that got to do with anything?"

"It's got everything to do with everything."

"Why?"   120

"If you don't know, I can't tell you." Here he stood up, and I saw his daughter at the curb in her Lincoln. One leg wouldn't straighten all the way out, and I could see the pain in his face. I grabbed his arm, and he smiled a mean little smile and leaned in to me for a second and said, "Bruton, everything worth doing hurts like hell." He toddled off and left me with his sour breath on my face and a thought forming in my head like a rain cloud.

After a session with the Methodist preacher, I went home and stared at the yard, then stared at the telephone until I got up the strength to call Famous Amos Salvage. The next morning, a wrecker and a gondola came down my road, and before noon, Amos loaded up four derelict cars, six engines, four washing machines, ten broken lawn mowers, and two and one-quarter tons of scrap iron. I begged and borrowed Miss Hanchy's Super-A and bush-hogged the three acres I own and then some. I cut the grass and picked up around the workshop. With the money I got from the scrap, I bought some aluminum paint for the shop and some first-class stuff for the outside of the house. The next morning, I was up at seven replacing screens on the little porch, and on the big porch on the side, I began putting down a heavy coat of glossy green deck enamel. At lunch, my wife stuck her head through the porch door to watch me work. "The kids are coming over again. How you gonna keep 'em off of all this wet paint?"

My knees were killing me, and I couldn't figure how to keep Nu-Nu from crawling where he shouldn't. "I don't know."

She looked around at the wet glare. "What's got into you, changing our religion and all?"

125   "Time for a change, I guess." I loaded up my brush.

She thought about this a moment, then pointed. "Careful you don't paint yourself in a corner."

"I'm doing the best I can."

"It's about time," she said under her breath, walking away.

I backed off the porch and down the steps, then stood in the pine straw next to the house, painting the ends of the porch boards. I heard a car come down the road and watched my oldest daughter drive up and get out with Nu-Nu over her shoulder. When she came close, I looked at her dyed hair, which was the color and texture of fiberglass insulation, the dark mascara, and the olive skin under her eyes. She smelled of cigarette smoke, stale smoke, like she hadn't had a bath in three days. Her tan blouse was tight and tied in a knot above her navel, which was a lardy hole. She passed Nu-Nu to me like he was a ham. "Can he stay the night?" she asked. "I want to go hear some music."

130   "Why not?"

She looked around slowly. "Looks like a bomb hit this place and blew everything away." The door to her dusty compact creaked open, and a freckled hand came out. "I forgot to mention that I picked up Freddie on the way in. Hope you don't mind." She didn't look at him as she mumbled this, hands on her cocked hips. Freddie, who had been sleeping, I guess, sat on the edge of the car seat and rubbed his eyes like a drunk.

"He'll be all right here," I said.

She took in a deep, slow breath, so deathly bored that I felt sorry for her. "Well, guess I better be heading on down the road." She turned, then whipped around on me. "Hey, guess what?"

"What?"

135   "Nu-Nu finally said his first word yesterday." She was biting the inside of her cheek. I could tell.

I looked at the baby, who was going after my shirt buttons. "What'd he say?"

"Da-da." And her eyes started to get red, so she broke and ran for her car.

"Wait," I called, but it was too late. In a flash, she was gone in a cloud of gravel dust, racing toward the most cigarette smoke, music, and beer she could find in one place.

I took Freddie and the baby around to the back steps by the little screen porch and sat down. We tickled and goo-gooed at Nu-Nu until finally he let out a "Da-da"—real loud, like a call.

Freddie looked back toward the woods, at all the nice trees in the   140
yard, which looked like what they were now that the trash had been
carried off. "What happened to all the stuff?"

"Gone," I said. "We gonna put a tire swing on that tall willow oak
there, first off."

"All right. Can you cut a drain hole in the bottom so the rainwater
won't stay in it?" He came close and put a hand on top of the baby's
head.

"Yep."

"A big steel-belt tire?"

"Sounds like a plan." Nu-Nu looked at me and yelled, "Da-da," and   145
I thought how he'll be saying that in one way or another for the rest of
his life and never be able to face the fact that Da-da had skipped town,
whoever Da-da was. The baby brought me in focus, somebody's blue eyes
looking at me hard. He blew spit over his tongue and cried out, "Da-da,"
and I put him on my knee, facing away toward the cool green branches
of my biggest willow oak.

"Even Nu-Nu can ride the tire," Freddie said.

"He can fit the circle in the middle," I told him.

QUESTIONS

1. Identify the theme of the story. How do the major scenes help to illustrate
   the theme?
2. The story portrays three generations of Southerners: the oldest generation,
   represented by the narrator; the next generation, represented by his daughters; and the youngest generation, represented by the narrator's small grandchildren. What specific values does each generation represent? How does the
   narrator attempt to bridge the wide "generation gap" between himself and his
   grandchildren?
3. How are the narrator's daughters portrayed? Are they sympathetic or unsympathetic characters? What values do they represent?
4. Why does the narrator attempt to get his grandchildren interested in Bible
   stories?
5. The narrator's acquaintance Mr. Fordlyson calls the narrator's car a "bastardmobile." How does the narrator react to this? Why is his reaction such an
   important component to the story?
6. What is the significance of the children's unusual names? How do their
   names reflect their identities and the values of their parents?
7. Discuss the change the narrator undergoes in the last few pages. Why does
   he clean up his place so thoroughly? What permanent changes does he
   plan to make to the way he lives and to the way he relates to his
   grandchildren?

Anton Chekhov
The Darling

Olenka, the daughter of the retired collegiate assessor, Plemyannia-kov, was sitting in her back porch, lost in thought. It was hot, the flies were persistent and teasing, and it was pleasant to reflect that it would soon be evening. Dark rainclouds were gathering from the east, and bringing from time to time a breath of moisture in the air.

Kukin, who was the manager of an open air theater called the Tivoli, and who lived in the lodge, was standing in the middle of the garden looking at the sky.

"Again!" he observed despairingly. "It's going to rain again! Rain every day, as though to spite me. I might as well hang myself! It's ruin! Fearful losses everyday."

He flung up his hands, and went on, addressing Olenka:

5   "There! that's the life we lead, Olga Semyonovna. It's enough to make one cry. One works and does one's utmost; one wears oneself out, getting no sleep at night, and racks one's brain what to do for the best. And then what happens? To begin with, one's public is ignorant, boorish. I give them the very best operetta, a dainty masque, first rate music hall artists. But do you suppose that's what they want! They don't understand anything of that sort. They want a clown; what they ask for is vulgarity. And then look at the weather! Almost every evening it rains. It started on the tenth of May, and it's kept it up all May and June. It's simply awful! The public doesn't come, but I've to pay the rent just the same, and pay the artists."

The next evening the clouds would gather again, and Kukin would say with an hysterical laugh:

"Well, rain away, then! Flood the garden, drown me! Damn my luck in this world and the next! Let the artists have me up!° Send me to prison!—to Siberia!—the scaffold! Ha, ha, ha!"

And next day the same thing.

Olenka listened to Kukin with silent gravity, and sometimes tears came into her eyes. In the end his misfortunes touched her; she grew to love him. He was a small thin man, with a yellow face, and curls

THE DARLING   First published in 1898. Translated from the Russian by Constance Garnett. Anton Chekhov (1860–1904) was raised in semipoverty in the town of Taganrog, on the Black Sea. A scholarship enabled him to take a medical degree from Moscow University, but writing plays, stories, and sketches was his main source of income. Along with James Joyce, Chekhov is often considered one of the founders of the modern short story.

have me up: take me to court

combed forward on his forehead. He spoke in a thin tenor; as he talked his mouth worked on one side, and there was always an expression of despair on his face; yet he aroused a deep and genuine affection in her. She was always fond of someone, and could not exist without loving. In earlier days she had loved her papa, who now sat in a darkened room, breathing with difficulty; she had loved her aunt who used to come every other year from Bryansk; and before that, when she was at school, she had loved her French master. She was a gentle, soft-hearted, compassionate girl, with mild, tender eyes and very good health. At the sight of her full rosy cheeks, her soft white neck with a little dark mole on it, and the kind, naive smile, which came into her face when she listened to anything pleasant, men thought, "Yes, not half bad," and smiled too, while lady visitors could not refrain from seizing her hand in the middle of a conversation, exclaiming in a gush of delight, "You darling!"

The house in which she had lived from her birth upwards, and   10
which was left her in her father's will, was at the extreme end of the town, not far from the Tivoli. In the evenings and at night she could hear the band playing, and the crackling and banging of fireworks, and it seemed to her that it was Kukin struggling with his destiny, storming the entrenchments of his chief foe, the indifferent public; there was a sweet thrill at her heart, she had no desire to sleep, and when he returned home at daybreak, she tapped softly at her bedroom window, and showing him only her face and one shoulder through the curtain, she gave him a friendly smile. . . .

He proposed to her, and they were married. And when he had a closer view of her neck and her plump, fine shoulders, he threw up his hands, and said:

"You darling!"

He was happy, but as it rained on the day and night of his wedding, his face still retained an expression of despair.

They got on very well together. She used to sit in his office, to look after things in the Tivoli, to put down the accounts and pay the wages. And her rosy cheeks, her sweet, naive, radiant smile, were to be seen now at the office window, now in the refreshment bar or behind the scenes of the theater. And already she used to say to her acquaintances that the theater was the chief and most important thing in life, and that it was only through the drama that one could derive true enjoyment and become cultivated and humane.

"But do you suppose the public understands that?" she used to say.   15
"What they want is a clown. Yesterday we gave 'Faust Inside Out,' and almost all the boxes were empty; but if Vanitchka and I had been

producing some vulgar thing, I assure you the theater would have been packed. Tomorrow Vanitchka and I are doing 'Orpheus in Hell.' Do come."

And what Kukin said about the theater and the actors she repeated. Like him she despised the public for their ignorance and their indifference to art; she took part in the rehearsals, she corrected the actors, she kept an eye on the behavior of the musicians, and when there was an unfavorable notice in the local paper, she shed tears, and then went to the editor's office to set things right.

The actors were fond of her and used to call her "Vanitchka and I," and "the darling"; she was sorry for them and used to lend them small sums of money, and if they deceived her, she used to shed a few tears in private, but did not complain to her husband.

They got on well in the winter too. They took the theater in the town for the whole winter, and let it for short terms to a Little Russian° company, or to a conjurer, or to a local dramatic society. Olenka grew stouter, and was almost always beaming with satisfaction, while Kukin grew thinner and yellower, and continually complained of their terrible losses, although he had not done badly all the winter. He used to cough at night, and she used to give him hot raspberry tea or lime-flower water, to rub him with eau de Cologne and to wrap him in her warm shawls.

"You're such a sweet pet!" she used to say with perfect sincerity, stroking his hair. "You're such a pretty dear!"

20   Towards Lent he went to Moscow to collect a new troupe, and without him she could not sleep, but sat all night at her window, looking at the stars, and she compared herself with the hens, who are awake all night and uneasy when the cock is not in the hen house. Kukin was detained in Moscow, and wrote that he would be back at Easter, adding some instructions about the Tivoli. But on the Sunday before Easter, late in the evening, came a sudden ominous knock at the gate; someone was hammering on the gate as though on a barrel—boom, boom, boom! The drowsy cook went flopping with her bare feet through the puddles, as she ran to open the gate.

"Please open," said someone outside in a thick bass. "There is a telegram for you."

Olenka had received telegrams from her husband before, but this time for some reason she felt numb with terror. With shaking hands she opened the telegram and read as follows:

"Ivan Petrovitch died suddenly today. Awaiting immate instructions fufuneral Tuesday."

Little Russian: Ukrainian

That was how it was written in the telegram—"fufuneral," and the utterly incomprehensible word "immate." It was signed by the stage manager of the operatic company.

"My darling!" sobbed Olenka. "Vanitchka, my precious, my darling! Why did I ever meet you! Why did I know you and love you! Your poor heartbroken Olenka is all alone without you!"

Kukin's funeral took place on Tuesday in Moscow, Olenka returned home on Wednesday, and as soon as she got indoors she threw herself on her bed and sobbed so loudly that it could be heard next door, and in the street.   25

"Poor darling!" the neighbors said, as they crossed themselves. "Olga Semyonovna, poor darling! How she does take on!"

Three months later Olenka was coming home from mass, melancholy and in deep mourning. It happened that one of her neighbors, Vassily Andreitch Pustovalov, returning home from church, walked back beside her. He was the manager at Babakayev's, the timber merchant's. He wore a straw hat, a white waistcoat, and a gold watch chain, and looked more like a country gentleman than a man in trade.

"Everything happens as it is ordained, Olga Semyonovna," he said gravely, with a sympathetic note in his voice; "and if any of our dear ones die, it must be because it is the will of God, so we ought to have fortitude and bear it submissively."

After seeing Olenka to her gate, he said goodbye and went on. All day afterwards she heard his sedately dignified voice, and whenever she shut her eyes she saw his dark beard. She liked him very much. And apparently she had made an impression on him too, for not long afterwards an elderly lady, with whom she was only slightly acquainted, came to drink coffee with her, and as soon as she was seated at table began to talk about Pustovalov, saying that he was an excellent man whom one could thoroughly depend upon, and that any girl would be glad to marry him. Three days later Pustovalov came himself. He did not stay long, only about ten minutes, and he did not say much, but when he left, Olenka loved him—loved him so much that she lay awake all night in a perfect fever, and in the morning she sent for the elderly lady. The match was quickly arranged, and then came the wedding.

Pustovalov and Olenka got on very well together when they were married.   30

Usually he sat in the office till dinner° time, then he went out on business, while Olenka took his place, and sat in the office till evening, making up accounts and booking orders.

dinner: the midday meal

"Timber gets dearer every year; the price rises twenty percent," she would say to her customers and friends. "Only fancy we used to sell local timber, and now Vassitchka always has to go for wood to the Mogilev district. And the freight!" she would add, covering her cheeks with her hands in horror. "The freight!"

It seemed to her that she had been in the timber trade for ages and ages, and that the most important and necessary thing in life was timber; and there was something intimate and touching to her in the very sound of words such as "baulk," "post," "beam," "pole," "scantling," "batten," "lath," "plank," etc.

At night when she was asleep she dreamed of perfect mountains of planks and boards, and long strings of wagons, carting timber somewhere far away. She dreamed that a whole regiment of six-inch beams forty feet high, standing on end, was marching upon the timber yard; that logs, beams, and boards knocked together with the resounding crash of dry wood, kept falling and getting up again, piling themselves on each other. Olenka cried out in her sleep, and Pustovalov said to her tenderly: "Olenka, what's the matter, darling? Cross yourself!"

35   Her husband's ideas were hers. If he thought the room was too hot, or that business was slack, she thought the same. Her husband did not care for entertainments, and on holidays he stayed at home. She did likewise.

"You are always at home or in the office," her friends said to her. "You should go to the theater, darling, or to the circus."

"Vassitchka and I have no time to go to theaters," she would answer sedately. "We have no time for nonsense. What's the use of these theaters?"

On Saturdays Pustovalov and she used to go to the evening service; on holidays to early mass, and they walked side by side with softened faces as they came home from church. There was a pleasant fragrance about them both, and her silk dress rustled agreeably. At home they drank tea, with fancy bread and jams of various kinds, and afterwards they ate pie. Every day at twelve o'clock there was a savory smell of beetroot soup and of mutton or duck in their yard, and on fast days of fish, and no one could pass the gate without feeling hungry. In the office the samovar was always boiling, and customers were regaled with tea and cracknels. Once a week the couple went to the baths and returned side by side, both red in the face.

"Yes, we have nothing to complain of, thank God," Olenka used to say to her acquaintances. "I wish everyone were as well off as Vassitchka and I."

When Pustovalov went away to buy wood in the Mogilev district,   40
she missed him dreadfully, lay awake and cried. A young veterinary
surgeon in the army, called Smirnin, to whom they had let their lodge,
used sometimes to come in the evening. He used to talk to her and play
cards with her, and this entertained her in her husband's absence. She
was particularly interested in what he told her of his home life. He was
married and had a little boy, but was separated from his wife because she
had been unfaithful to him, and now he hated her and used to send her
forty rubles a month for the maintenance of their son. And hearing of all
this, Olenka sighed and shook her head. She was sorry for him.

"Well, God keep you," she used to say to him at parting, as she
lighted him down the stairs with a candle. "Thank you for coming to
cheer me up, and may the Mother of God give you health."

And she always expressed herself with the same sedateness and
dignity, the same reasonableness, in imitation of her husband. As
the veterinary surgeon was disappearing behind the door below, she
would say:

"You know, Vladimir Platonitch, you'd better make it up with your
wife. You should forgive her for the sake of your son. You may be sure the
little fellow understands."

And when Pustovalov came back, she told him in a low voice about
the veterinary surgeon and his unhappy home life, and both sighed and
shook their heads and talked about the boy, who, no doubt, missed his
father, and by some strange connection of ideas, they went up to the
holy icons, bowed to the ground before them and prayed that God would
give them children.

And so the Pustovalovs lived for six years quietly and peaceably in   45
love and complete harmony.

But behold! one winter day after drinking hot tea in the office,
Vassily Andreitch went out into the yard without his cap on to see about
sending off some timber, caught cold and was taken ill. He had the best
doctors, but he grew worse and died after four months' illness. And
Olenka was a widow once more.

"I've nobody, now you've left me, my darling," she sobbed, after her
husband's funeral. "How can I live without you, in wretchedness and
misery! Pity me, good people, all alone in the world!"

She went about dressed in black with long "weepers,"° and gave up
wearing hat and gloves for good. She hardly ever went out, except to
church, or to her husband's grave, and led the life of a nun. It was not till
six months later that she took off the weepers and opened the shutters of

"weepers": white cuffs indicating mourning

the windows. She was sometimes seen in the mornings, going with her cook to market for provisions, but what went on in her house and how she lived now could only be surmised. People guessed, from seeing her drinking tea in her garden with the veterinary surgeon, who read the newspaper aloud to her, and from the fact that, meeting a lady she knew at the post office, she said to her:

"There is no proper veterinary inspection in our town, and that's the cause of all sorts of epidemics. One is always hearing of people's getting infection from the milk supply, or catching diseases from horses and cows. The health of domestic animals ought to be as well cared for as the health of human beings."

50   She repeated the veterinary surgeon's words, and was of the same opinion as he about everything. It was evident that she could not live a year without some attachment, and had found new happiness in the lodge. In anyone else this would have been censured, but no one could think ill of Olenka; everything she did was so natural. Neither she nor the veterinary surgeon said anything to other people of the change in their relations, and tried, indeed, to conceal it, but without success, for Olenka could not keep a secret. When he had visitors, men serving in his regiment, and she poured out tea or served the supper, she would begin talking of the cattle plague, of the foot and mouth disease, and of the municipal slaughterhouses. He was dreadfully embarrassed, and when the guests had gone, he would seize her by the hand and hiss angrily:

"I've asked you before not to talk about what you don't understand. When we veterinary surgeons are talking among ourselves, please don't put your word in. It's really annoying."

And she would look at him with astonishment and dismay, and ask him in alarm: "But, Voloditchka, what *am* I to talk about?"

And with tears in her eyes she would embrace him, begging him not to be angry, and they were both happy.

But this happiness did not last long. The veterinary surgeon departed, departed forever with his regiment, when it was transferred to a distant place—to Siberia, it may be. And Olenka was left alone.

55   Now she was absolutely alone. Her father had long been dead, and his armchair lay in the attic, covered with dust and lame of one leg. She got thinner and plainer, and when people met her in the street they did not look at her as they used to, and did not smile to her; evidently her best years were over and left behind, and now a new sort of life had begun for her, which did not bear thinking about. In the evening Olenka sat in the porch, and heard the band playing and the fireworks popping in the Tivoli, but now the sound stirred no response. She

looked into her yard without interest, thought of nothing, wished for nothing, and afterwards, when night came on she went to bed and dreamed of her empty yard. She ate and drank as it were unwillingly.

And what was worst of all, she had no opinions of any sort. She saw the objects about her and understood what she saw, but could not form any opinion about them, and did not know what to talk about. And how awful it is not to have any opinions! One sees a bottle, for instance, or the rain, or a peasant driving in his cart, but what the bottle is for, or the rain, or the peasant, and what is the meaning of it, one can't say, and could not even for a thousand rubles. When she had Kukin, or Pustovalov, or the veterinary surgeon, Olenka could explain everything, and give her opinion about anything you like, but now there was the same emptiness in her brain and in her heart as there was in her yard outside. And it was as harsh and as bitter as wormwood in the mouth.

Little by little the town grew in all directions. The road became a street, and where the Tivoli and the timber yard had been, there were new turnings and houses. How rapidly time passes! Olenka's house grew dingy, the roof got nasty, the shed sank on one side, and the whole yard was overgrown with docks and stinging nettles. Olenka herself had grown plain and elderly; in summer she sat in the porch, and her soul, as before, was empty and dreary and full of bitterness. In winter she sat at her window and looked at the snow. When she caught the scent of spring, or heard the chime of the church bells, a sudden rush of memories from the past came over her, there was a tender ache in her heart, and her eyes brimmed over with tears; but this was only for a minute, and then came emptiness again and the sense of the futility of life. The black kitten, Briska, rubbed against her and purred softly, but Olenka was not touched by these feline caresses. That was not what she needed. She wanted a love that would absorb her whole being, her whole soul and reason—that would give her ideas and an object in life, and would warm her old blood. And she would shake the kitten off her skirt and say with vexation:

"Get along; I don't want you!"

And so it was, day after day and year after year, and no joy, and no opinions. Whatever Mavra, the cook, said she accepted.

One hot July day, towards evening, just as the cattle were being driven away, and the whole yard was full of dust, someone suddenly knocked at the gate. Olenka went to open it herself and was dumbfounded when she looked out: she saw Smirnin, the veterinary surgeon, gray headed, and dressed as a civilian. She suddenly remembered everything. She could not help crying and letting her head fall on his breast

60

without uttering a word, and in the violence of her feeling she did not notice how they both walked into the house and sat down to tea.

"My dear Vladimir Platonitch! What fate has brought you?" she muttered, trembling with joy.

"I want to settle here for good, Olga Semyonovna," he told her. "I have resigned my post, and have come to settle down and try my luck on my own account. Besides, it's time for my boy to go to school. He's a big boy. I am reconciled with my wife, you know."

"Where is she?" asked Olenka.

"She's at the hotel with the boy, and I'm looking for lodgings."

65   "Good gracious, my dear soul! Lodgings? Why not have my house? Why shouldn't that suit you? Why, my goodness, I wouldn't take any rent!" cried Olenka in a flutter, beginning to cry again. "You live here, and the lodge will do nicely for me. Oh dear! how glad I am!"

Next day the roof was painted and the walls were whitewashed, and Olenka, with her arms akimbo, walked about the yard giving directions. Her face was beaming with her old smile, and she was brisk and alert as though she had waked from a long sleep. The veterinary's wife arrived— a thin, plain lady, with short hair and a peevish expression. With her was her little Sasha, a boy of ten, small for his age, blue-eyed, chubby, with dimples in his cheeks. And scarcely had the boy walked into the yard when he ran after the cat, and at once there was the sound of his gay, joyous laugh.

"Is that your puss, auntie?" he asked Olenka. "When she has little ones, do give us a kitten. Mamma is awfully afraid of mice."

Olenka talked to him, and gave him tea. Her heart warmed and there was a sweet ache in her bosom, as though the boy had been her own child. And when he sat at the table in the evening, going over his lessons, she looked at him with deep tenderness and pity as she murmured to herself:

"You pretty pet! . . . my precious! . . . Such a fair little thing, and so clever."

70   "'An island is a piece of land which is entirely surrounded by water,'" he read aloud.

"An island is a piece of land," she repeated, and this was the first opinion to which she gave utterance with positive conviction after so many years of silence and dearth of ideas.

Now she had opinions of her own, and at supper she talked to Sasha's parents, saying how difficult the lessons were at the high schools, but that yet the high school was better than a commercial one, since with a high school education all careers were open to one, such as being a doctor or an engineer.

Sasha began going to the high school. His mother departed to Harkov to her sister's and did not return; his father used to go off every day to inspect cattle, and would often be away from home for three days together, and it seemed to Olenka as though Sasha was entirely abandoned, that he was not wanted at home, that he was being starved, and she carried him off to her lodge and gave him a little room there.

And for six months Sasha had lived in the lodge with her. Every morning Olenka came into his bedroom and found him fast asleep, sleeping noiselessly with his hand under his cheek. She was sorry to wake him.

"Sashenka," she would say mournfully, "get up, darling. It's time for   75
school."

He would get up, dress and say his prayers, and then sit down to breakfast, drink three glasses of tea, and eat two large cracknels and half a buttered roll. All this time he was hardly awake and a little ill-humored in consequence.

"You don't quite know your fable, Sashenka," Olenka would say, looking at him as though he were about to set off on a long journey. "What a lot of trouble I have with you! You must work and do your best, darling, and obey your teachers."

"Oh, do leave me alone!" Sasha would say.

Then he would go down the street to school, a little figure, wearing a big cap and carrying a satchel on his shoulder. Olenka would follow him noiselessly.

"Sashenka!" she would call after him, and she would pop into his   80
hand a date or a caramel. When he reached the street where the school was, he would feel ashamed of being followed by a tall, stout woman; he would turn round and say:

"You'd better go home, auntie. I can go the rest of the way alone."

She would stand still and look after him fixedly till he had disappeared at the school gate.

Ah, how she loved him! Of her former attachments not one had been so deep; never had her soul surrendered to any feeling so spontaneously, so disinterestedly, and so joyously as now that her maternal instincts were aroused. For this little boy with the dimple in his cheek and the big school cap, she would have given her whole life, she would have given it with joy and tears of tenderness. Why? Who can tell why?

When she had seen the last of Sasha, she returned home, contented and serene, brimming over with love; her face, which had grown younger during the last six months, smiled and beamed; people meeting her looked at her with pleasure.

85   "Good morning, Olga Semyonovna, darling. How are you, darling?"

"The lessons at the high school are very difficult now," she would relate at the market. "It's too much; in the first class yesterday they gave him a fable to learn by heart, and a Latin translation and a problem. You know it's too much for a little chap."

And she would begin talking about the teachers, the lessons, and the school books, saying just what Sasha said.

At three o'clock they had dinner together: in the evening they learned their lessons together and cried. When she put him to bed, she would stay a long time making the Cross over him and murmuring a prayer; then she would go to bed and dream of that faraway misty future when Sasha would finish his studies and become a doctor or an engineer, would have a big house of his own with horses and a carriage, would get married and have children. . . . She would fall asleep still thinking of the same thing, and tears would run down her cheeks from her closed eyes, while the black cat lay purring beside her: "Mrr, mrr, mrr."

Suddenly there would come a loud knock at the gate.

90   Olenka would wake up breathless with alarm, her heart throbbing. Half a minute later would come another knock.

"It must be a telegram from Harkov," she would think, beginning to tremble from head to foot. "Sasha's mother is sending for him from Harkov. . . . Oh, mercy on us!"

She was in despair. Her head, her hands, and her feet would turn chill, and she would feel that she was the most unhappy woman in the world. But another minute would pass, voices would be heard: it would turn out to be the veterinary surgeon coming home from the club.

"Well, thank God!" she would think.

And gradually the load in her heart would pass off, and she would feel at ease. She would go back to bed thinking of Sasha, who lay sound asleep in the next room, sometimes crying out in his sleep:

95   "I'll give it you! Get away! Shut up!"

QUESTIONS

1. Identify the theme of "The Darling." How do Olenka's several relationships with male characters help to elucidate the theme?
2. Analyze the characterization of Olenka. Is she admirable or unsympathetic? Are there passages in the text that can support either view? Cite the passages that support your own view of her character.
3. Other than telling the story in chronological order, how does Chekhov provide structure to the narrative? How does the structure contribute to the meaning?

4. What is the significance of the ending, which focuses on a young boy rather than on one of Olenka's husbands? How does this unexpected ending help emphasize the story's theme?
5. Is Olenka a static or a developing character? Give specific evidence from the text for your opinion.
6. Discuss the use of humor in the story. Could it be argued that the humor makes the story more rather than less "serious" as an example of literary fiction?

Eudora Welty
A Worn Path

It was December—a bright frozen day in the early morning. Far out in the country there was an old Negro woman with her head tied in a red rag, coming along a path through the pinewoods. Her name was Phoenix Jackson. She was very old and small and she walked slowly in the dark pine shadows, moving a little from side to side in her steps, with the balanced heaviness and lightness of a pendulum in a grandfather clock. She carried a thin, small cane made from an umbrella, and with this she kept tapping the frozen earth in front of her. This made a grave and persistent noise in the still air, that seemed meditative like the chirping of a solitary little bird.

She wore a dark striped dress reaching down to her shoe tops, and an equally long apron of bleached sugar sacks, with a full pocket: all neat and tidy, but every time she took a step she might have fallen over her shoelaces, which dragged from her unlaced shoes. She looked straight ahead. Her eyes were blue with age. Her skin had a pattern all its own of numberless branching wrinkles and as though a whole little tree stood in the middle of her forehead, but a golden color ran underneath, and the two knobs of her cheeks were illumined by a yellow burning under the dark. Under the red rag her hair came down on her neck in the frailest of ringlets, still black, and with an odor like copper.

Now and then there was a quivering in the thicket. Old Phoenix said, "Out of my way, all you foxes, owls, beetles, jack rabbits, coons, and wild animals! . . . Keep out from under these feet, little bobwhites. . . . Keep the big wild hogs out of my path. Don't let none of those come

A WORN PATH   First published in 1941. Eudora Welty (1909–2001) was born in Jackson, Mississippi, where she was raised and to which she returned after studying at the University of Wisconsin and Columbia University. In the mid-1930s she was employed by the federal Work Projects Administration (WPA) to travel throughout Mississippi writing newspaper copy and taking photographs, a job that enabled her to observe many varieties of rural life in her native state.

running my direction. I got a long way." Under her small black-freckled hand her cane, limber as a buggy whip, would switch at the brush as if to rouse up any hiding things.

On she went. The woods were deep and still. The sun made the pine needles almost too bright to look at, up where the wind rocked. The cones dropped as light as feathers. Down in the hollow was the mourning dove—it was not too late for him.

5   The path ran up a hill. "Seem like there is chains about my feet, time I get this far," she said, in the voice of argument old people keep to use with themselves. "Something always take a hold of me on this hill—pleads I should stay."

After she got to the top she turned and gave a full, severe look behind her where she had come. "Up through pines," she said at length. "Now down through oaks."

Her eyes opened their widest, and she started down gently. But before she got to the bottom of the hill a bush caught her dress.

Her fingers were busy and intent, but her skirts were full and long, so that before she could pull them free in one place they were caught in another. It was not possible to allow the dress to tear. "I in the thorny bush," she said. "Thorns, you doing your appointed work. Never want to let folks pass, no sir. Old eyes thought you was a pretty little *green* bush."

Finally, trembling all over, she stood free, and after a moment dared to stoop for her cane.

10   "Sun so high!" she cried, leaning back and looking, while the thick tears went over her eyes. "The time getting all gone here."

At the foot of this hill was a place where a log was laid across the creek.

"Now comes the trial," said Phoenix.

Putting her right foot out, she mounted the log and shut her eyes. Lifting her skirt, leveling her cane fiercely before her, like a festival figure in some parade, she began to march across. Then she opened her eyes and she was safe on the other side.

"I wasn't as old as I thought," she said.

15   But she sat down to rest. She spread her skirts on the bank around her and folded her hands over her knees. Up above her was a tree in a pearly cloud of mistletoe. She did not dare to close her eyes, and when a little boy brought her a plate with a slice of marble-cake on it she spoke to him. "That would be acceptable," she said. But when she went to take it there was just her own hand in the air.

So she left that tree, and had to go through a barbed-wire fence. There she had to creep and crawl, spreading her knees and stretching her fingers like a baby trying to climb the steps. But she talked loudly to herself: she could not let her dress be torn now, so late in the day, and she could not pay for having her arm or her leg sawed off if she got caught fast where she was.

At last she was safe through the fence and risen up out in the clearing. Big dead trees, like black men with one arm, were standing in the purple stalks of the withered cotton field. There sat a buzzard.

"Who you watching?"

In the furrow she made her way along.

"Glad this not the season for bulls," she said, looking sideways,   20
"and the good Lord made his snakes to curl up and sleep in the winter. A pleasure I don't see no two-headed snake coming around that tree, where it come once. It took a while to get by him, back in the summer."

She passed through the old cotton and went into a field of dead corn. It whispered and shook and was taller than her head. "Through the maze now," she said, for there was no path.

Then there was something tall, black, and skinny there, moving before her.

At first she took it for a man. It could have been a man dancing in the field. But she stood still and listened, and it did not make a sound. It was as silent as a ghost.

"Ghost," she said sharply, "who be you the ghost of? For I have heard of nary death close by."

But there was no answer—only the ragged dancing in the wind.   25

She shut her eyes, reached out her hand, and touched a sleeve. She found a coat and inside that an emptiness, cold as ice.

"You scarecrow," she said. Her face lighted. "I ought to be shut up for good," she said with laughter. "My senses is gone. I too old. I the oldest people I ever know. Dance, old scarecrow," she said, "while I dancing with you."

She kicked her foot over the furrow, and with mouth drawn down, shook her head once or twice in a little strutting way. Some husks blew down and whirled in streamers about her skirts.

Then she went on, parting her way from side to side with the cane, through the whispering field. At last she came to the end, to a wagon track where the silver grass blew between the red ruts. The quail were walking around like pullets, seeming all dainty and unseen.

"Walk pretty," she said. "This the easy place. This the easy going."   30

She followed the track, swaying through the quiet bare fields, through the little strings of trees silver in their dead leaves, past cabins silver from weather, with the doors and windows boarded shut, all like old women under a spell sitting there. "I walking in their sleep," she said, nodding her head vigorously.

In a ravine she went where a spring was silently flowing through a hollow log. Old Phoenix bent and drank. "Sweet-gum makes the water sweet," she said, and drank more. "Nobody know who made this well, for it was here when I was born."

The track crossed a swampy part where the moss hung as white as lace from every limb. "Sleep on, alligators, and blow your bubbles." Then the track went into the road.

Deep, deep the road went down between the high green-colored banks. Overhead the live-oaks met, and it was as dark as a cave.

35   A black dog with a lolling tongue came up out of the weeds by the ditch. She was meditating, and not ready, and when he came at her she only hit him a little with her cane. Over she went in the ditch, like a little puff of milkweed.

Down there, her senses drifted away. A dream visited her, and she reached her hand up, but nothing reached down and gave her a pull. So she lay there and presently went to talking. "Old woman," she said to herself, "that black dog come up out of the weeds to stall you off, and now there he sitting on his fine tail, smiling at you."

A white man finally came along and found her—a hunter, a young man, with his dog on a chain.

"Well, Granny!" he laughed. "What are you doing there?"

"Lying on my back like a June-bug waiting to be turned over, mister," she said, reaching up her hand.

40   He lifted her up, gave her a swing in the air, and set her down. "Anything broken, Granny?"

"No sir, them old dead weeds is springy enough," said Phoenix, when she had got her breath. "I thank you for your trouble."

"Where do you live, Granny?" he asked, while the two dogs were growling at each other.

"Away back yonder, sir, behind the ridge. You can't even see it from here."

"On your way home?"

45   "No sir, going to town."

"Why, that's too far! That's as far as I walk when I come out myself, and I get something for my trouble." He patted the stuffed bag he carried, and there hung down a little closed claw. It was one of the bobwhites, with its beak hooked bitterly to show it was dead. "Now you go on home, Granny!"

"I bound to go to town, mister," said Phoenix. "The time come around."

He gave another laugh, filling the whole landscape. "I know you old colored people! Wouldn't miss going to town to see Santa Claus!"

But something held old Phoenix very still. The deep lines in her face went into a fierce and different radiation. Without warning, she had seen with her own eyes a flashing nickel fall out of the man's pocket onto the ground.

"How old are you, Granny?" he was saying.   50

"There is no telling, mister," she said, "no telling."

Then she gave a little cry and clapped her hands and said, "Git on away from here, dog! Look! Look at that dog!" She laughed as if in admiration. "He ain't scared of nobody. He a big black dog." She whispered, "Sic him!"

"Watch me get rid of that cur," said the man. "Sic him, Pete! Sic him!"

Phoenix heard the dogs fighting, and heard the man running and throwing sticks. She even heard a gunshot. But she was slowly bending forward by that time, further and further forward, the lids stretched down over her eyes, as if she were doing this in her sleep. Her chin was lowered almost to her knees. The yellow palm of her hand came out from the fold of her apron. Her fingers slid down and along the ground under the piece of money with the grace and care they would have in lifting an egg from under a setting hen. Then she slowly straightened up, she stood erect, and the nickel was in her apron pocket. A bird flew by. Her lips moved. "God watching me the whole time. I come to stealing."

The man came back, and his own dog panted about them. "Well, I   55 scared him off that time," he said, and then he laughed and lifted his gun and pointed it at Phoenix.

She stood straight and faced him.

"Doesn't the gun scare you?" he said, still pointing it.

"No, sir, I seen plenty go off closer by, in my day, and for less than what I done," she said, holding utterly still.

He smiled, and shouldered the gun. "Well, Granny," he said, "you must be a hundred years old, and scared of nothing. I'd give you a dime if I had any money with me. But you take my advice and stay home, and nothing will happen to you."

"I bound to go on my way, mister," said Phoenix. She inclined her   60 head in the red rag. Then they went in different directions, but she could hear the gun shooting again and again over the hill.

She walked on. The shadows hung from the oak trees to the road like curtains. Then she smelled wood-smoke, and smelled the river, and she saw a steeple and the cabins on their steep steps. Dozens of little black children whirled around her. There ahead was Natchez shining. Bells were ringing. She walked on.

In the paved city it was Christmas time. There were red and green electric lights strung and crisscrossed everywhere, and all turned on in the daytime. Old Phoenix would have been lost if she had not distrusted her eyesight and depended on her feet to know where to take her.

She paused quietly on the sidewalk where people were passing by. A lady came along in the crowd, carrying an armful of red-, green-, and silver-wrapped presents; she gave off perfume like the red roses in hot summer, and Phoenix stopped her.

"Please, missy, will you lace up my shoe?" She held up her foot.

65   "What do you want, Grandma?"

"See my shoe," said Phoenix. "Do all right for out in the country, but wouldn't look right to go in a big building."

"Stand still then, Grandma," said the lady. She put her packages down on the sidewalk beside her and laced and tied both shoes tightly.

"Can't lace 'em with a cane," said Phoenix. "Thank you, missy. I doesn't mind asking a nice lady to tie up my shoe, when I gets out on the street."

Moving slowly and from side to side, she went into the big building, and into a tower of steps, where she walked up and around and around until her feet knew to stop.

70   She entered a door, and there she saw nailed up on the wall the document that had been stamped with the gold seal and framed in the gold frame, which matched the dream that was hung up in her head.

"Here I be," she said. There was a fixed and ceremonial stiffness over her body.

"A charity case, I suppose," said an attendant who sat at the desk before her.

But Phoenix only looked above her head. There was sweat on her face, the wrinkles in her skin shone like a bright net.

"Speak up, Grandma," the woman said. "What's your name? We must have your history, you know. Have you been here before? What seems to be the trouble with you?"

75   Old Phoenix only gave a twitch to her face as if a fly were bothering her.

"Are you deaf?" cried the attendant.

But then the nurse came in.

"Oh, that's just old Aunt Phoenix," she said. "She doesn't come for herself—she has a little grandson. She makes these trips just as regular as clockwork. She lives away back off the Old Natchez Trace." She bent down. "Well, Aunt Phoenix, why don't you just take a seat? We won't keep you standing after your long trip." She pointed.

The old woman sat down, bolt upright in the chair.

"Now, how is the boy?" asked the nurse.   80

Old Phoenix did not speak.

"I said, how is the boy?"

But Phoenix only waited and stared straight ahead, her face very solemn and withdrawn into rigidity.

"Is his throat any better?" asked the nurse. "Aunt Phoenix, don't you hear me? Is your grandson's throat any better since the last time you came for the medicine?"

With her hands on her knees, the old woman waited, silent, erect   85 and motionless, just as if she were in armor.

"You mustn't take up our time this way, Aunt Phoenix," the nurse said. "Tell us quickly about your grandson, and get it over. He isn't dead, is he?"

At last there came a flicker and then a flame of comprehension across her face, and she spoke.

"My grandson. It was my memory had left me. There I sat and forgot why I made my long trip."

"Forgot?" The nurse frowned. "After you came so far?"

Then Phoenix was like an old woman begging a dignified forgive-   90 ness for waking up frightened in the night. "I never did go to school, I was too old at the Surrender," she said in a soft voice. "I'm an old woman without an education. It was my memory fail me. My little grandson, he is just the same, and I forgot it in the coming."

"Throat never heals, does it?" said the nurse, speaking in a loud, sure voice to old Phoenix. By now she had a card with something written on it, a little list. "Yes. Swallowed lye. When was it?—January—two, three years ago—?"

Phoenix spoke unasked now. "No, missy, he not dead, he just the same. Every little while his throat begin to close up again, and he not able to swallow. He not get his breath. He not able to help himself. So the time come around, and I go on another trip for the soothing medicine."

"All right. The doctor said as long as you came to get it, you could have it," said the nurse. "But it's an obstinate case."

"My little grandson, he sit up there in the house all wrapped up, waiting by himself," Phoenix went on. "We is the only two left in the world. He suffer and it don't seem to put him back at all. He got a sweet look. He going to last. He wear a little patch quilt and peep out holding his mouth open like a little bird. I remembers so plain now. I not going to forget him again, no, the whole enduring time. I could tell him from all the others in creation."

95   "All right." The nurse was trying to hush her now. She brought her a bottle of medicine. "Charity," she said, making a check mark in a book.

Old Phoenix held the bottle close to her eyes, and then carefully put it into her pocket.

"I thank you," she said.

"It's Christmas time, Grandma," said the attendant. "Could I give you a few pennies out of my purse?"

"Five pennies is a nickel," said Phoenix stiffly.

100   "Here's a nickel," said the attendant.

Phoenix rose carefully and held out her hand. She received the nickel and then fished the other nickel out of her pocket and laid it beside the new one. She stared at her palm closely, with her head on one side.

Then she gave a tap with her cane on the floor.

"This is what come to me to do," she said. "I going to the store and buy my child a little windmill they sells, made out of paper. He going to find it hard to believe there such a thing in the world. I'll march myself back where he waiting, holding it straight up in this hand."

She lifted her free hand, gave a little nod, turned around, and walked out of the doctor's office. Then her slow step began on the stairs, going down.

QUESTIONS

1. Write a precise, well-developed sentence that states as fully as possible the theme of the story. Remember to avoid clichès or oversimplification.
2. Apart from the story's major theme, can you isolate minor themes that help give the story richness and depth? List as many as you can.
3. Discuss the way the characterization of Phoenix contributes to the theme.
4. Analyze the minor characters. What do they reveal about Phoenix and about the world in which she lives?
5. Like many classic works of literature, "A Worn Path" features a journey and a quest. Discuss the elements of plot and structure that dramatize Phoenix's journey. What are the obstacles to her quest, and how does she overcome them?
6. In answer to a student who wrote to ask her, "Is the grandson really dead?" Welty responded, "My best answer would be: *Phoenix* is alive." What might have led the student to ask that question? How can the author's remark be seen as an answer?

Nadine Gordimer

Once upon a Time

Someone has written to ask me to contribute to an anthology of stories for children. I reply that I don't write children's stories; and he writes back that at a recent congress/book fair/seminar a certain novelist said every writer ought to write at least one story for children. I think of sending a postcard saying I don't accept that I "ought" to write anything.

And then last night I woke up—or rather was awakened without knowing what had roused me.

A voice in the echo-chamber of the subconscious?

A sound.

A creaking of the kind made by the weight carried by one foot after   5
another along a wooden floor. I listened. I felt the apertures of my ears distend with concentration. Again: the creaking. I was waiting for it; waiting to hear if it indicated that feet were moving from room to room, coming up the passage—to my door. I have no burglar bars, no gun under the pillow, but I have the same fears as people who do take these precautions, and my windowpanes are thin as rime, could shatter like a wineglass. A woman was murdered (how do they put it) in broad daylight in a house two blocks away, last year, and the fierce dogs who guarded an old widower and his collection of antique clocks were strangled before he was knifed by a casual laborer he had dismissed without pay.

I was staring at the door, making it out in my mind rather than seeing it, in the dark. I lay quite still—a victim already—the arrhythmia of my heart was fleeing, knocking this way and that against its body-cage. How finely tuned the senses are, just out of rest, sleep! I could never listen intently as that in the distractions of the day; I was reading every faintest sound, identifying and classifying its possible threat.

But I learned that I was to be neither threatened nor spared. There was no human weight pressing on the boards, the creaking was a buckling, an epicenter of stress. I was in it. The house that surrounds me while I sleep is built on undermined ground; far beneath my bed, the floor, the house's foundations, the stopes and passages of gold mines

Once upon a Time   First published in 1989. Nadine Gordimer was born in 1923 in a small town near Johannesburg, South Africa, and graduated from the University of Witwatersrand. She has taught at several American universities but continues to reside in her native country. A prolific writer, Gordimer has published more than twenty books of fiction (novels and short story collections). In addition to England's prestigious Booker Prize for Fiction, she received the Nobel Prize for literature in 1991.

have hollowed the rock, and when some face trembles, detaches and falls, three thousand feet below, the whole house shifts slightly, bringing uneasy strain to the balance and counterbalance of brick, cement, wood and glass that hold it as a structure around me. The misbeats of my heart tailed off like the last muffled flourishes on one of the wooden xylophones made by the Chopi and Tsonga° migrant miners who might have been down there, under me in the earth at that moment. The stope where the fall was could have been disused, dripping water from its ruptured veins; or men might now be interred there in the most profound of tombs.

I couldn't find a position in which my mind would let go of my body—release me to sleep again. So I began to tell myself a story; a bedtime story.

In a house, in a suburb, in a city, there were a man and his wife who loved each other very much and were living happily ever after. They had a little boy, and they loved him very much. They had a cat and a dog that the little boy loved very much. They had a car and a caravan trailer for holidays, and a swimming-pool which was fenced so that the little boy and his playmates would not fall in and drown. They had a housemaid who was absolutely trustworthy and an itinerant gardener who was highly recommended by the neighbors. For when they began to live happily ever after they were warned, by that wise old witch, the husband's mother, not to take on anyone off the street. They were inscribed in a medical benefit society, their pet dog was licensed, they were insured against fire, flood damage and theft, and subscribed to the local Neighborhood Watch, which supplied them with a plaque for their gates lettered YOU HAVE BEEN WARNED over the silhouette of a would-be intruder. He was masked; it could not be said if he was black or white, and therefore proved the property owner was no racist.

10   It was not possible to insure the house, the swimming-pool or the car against riot damage. There were riots, but these were outside the city, where people of another color were quartered. These people were not allowed into the suburb except as reliable housemaids and gardeners, so there was nothing to fear, the husband told the wife. Yet she was afraid that some day such people might come up the street and tear off the plaque YOU HAVE BEEN WARNED and open the gates and stream in . . . Nonsense, my dear, said the husband, there are police and soldiers and tear-gas and guns to keep them away. But to please her—for he loved her very much and buses were being burned, cars stoned, and

---

Chopi and Tsonga: two peoples from Mozambique, northeast of South Africa schoolchildren shot by the police in those quarters out of sight and hearing of the suburb—he had electronically controlled gates fitted. Anyone who pulled off the sign YOU HAVE BEEN WARNED and tried to open the gates would have to announce his intentions by pressing a button and speaking into a receiver relayed to the house. The little boy was fascinated by the device and used it as a walkie-talkie in cops and robbers play with his small friends.

The riots were suppressed, but there were many burglaries in the suburb and somebody's trusted housemaid was tied up and shut in a cupboard by thieves while she was in charge of her employers' house. The trusted housemaid of the man and wife and little boy was so upset by this misfortune befalling a friend left, as she herself often was, with responsibility for the possessions of the man and his wife and the little boy that she implored her employers to have burglar bars attached to the doors and windows of the house, and an alarm system installed. The wife said, She is right, let us take heed of her advice. So from every window and door in the house where they were living happily ever after they now saw the trees and sky through bars, and when the little boy's pet cat tried to climb in by the fanlight to keep him company in his little bed at night, as it customarily had done, it set off the alarm keening through the house.

The alarm was often answered—it seemed—by other burglar alarms, in other houses, that had been triggered by pet cats or nibbling mice. The alarms called to one another across the gardens in shrills and bleats and wails that everyone soon became accustomed to, so that the din roused the inhabitants of the suburb no more than the croak of frogs and musical grating of cicadas' legs. Under cover of the electronic harpies' discourse intruders sawed the iron bars and broke into homes, taking away hi-fi equipment, television sets, cassette players, cameras and radios, jewelry and clothing, and sometimes were hungry enough to devour everything in the refrigerator or paused audaciously to drink the whiskey in the cabinets or patio bars. Insurance companies paid no compensation for single malt,° a loss made keener by the property owner's knowledge that the thieves wouldn't even have been able to appreciate what it was they were drinking.

Then the time came when many of the people who were not trusted housemaids and gardeners hung about the suburb because they were unemployed. Some importuned for a job: weeding or painting a roof; anything, baas,° madam. But the man and his wife remembered the warning about taking on anyone off the street. Some drank liquor and

single malt: an expensive Scotch whiskey   **baas:** boss

fouled the street with discarded bottles. Some begged, waiting for the
man or his wife to drive the car out of the electronically operated gates.
They sat about with their feet in the gutters, under the jacaranda trees
that made a green tunnel of the street—for it was a beautiful suburb,
spoilt only by their presence—and sometimes they fell asleep lying right
before the gates in the midday sun. The wife could never see anyone go
hungry. She sent the trusted housemaid out with bread and tea, but the
trusted housemaid said these were loafers and *tsotsis*,° who would come
and tie her and shut her in a cupboard. The husband said, She's right.
Take heed of her advice. You only encourage them with your bread and
tea. They are looking for their chance . . . And he brought the little boy's
tricycle from the garden into the house every night, because if the house
was surely secure, once locked and with the alarm set, someone might
still be able to climb over the wall or the electronically closed gates into
the garden.

   You are right, said the wife, then the wall should be higher. And the
wise old witch, the husband's mother, paid for the extra bricks as her
Christmas present to her son and his wife—the little boy got a Space
Man outfit and a book of fairy tales.

15   But every week there were more reports of intrusion: in broad
daylight and the dead of night, in the early hours of the morning, and
even in the lovely summer twilight—a certain family was at dinner
while the bedrooms were being ransacked upstairs. The man and his
wife, talking of the latest armed robbery in the suburb, were distracted by
the sight of the little boy's pet cat effortlessly arriving over the seven-
foot wall, descending first with a rapid bracing of extended forepaws
down on the sheer vertical surface, and then a graceful launch, landing
with swishing tail within the property. The whitewashed wall was
marked with the cat's comings and goings; and on the street side of
the wall there were larger red-earth smudges that could have been made
by the kind of broken running shoes, seen on the feet of unemployed
loiterers, that had no innocent destination.

   When the man and wife and little boy took the pet dog for its walk
round the neighborhood streets they no longer paused to admire this
show of roses or that perfect lawn; these were hidden behind an array of
different varieties of security fences, walls and devices. The man, wife,
little boy and dog passed a remarkable choice: there was the low-cost
option of pieces of broken glass embedded in cement along the top of
walls, there were iron grilles ending in lance-points, there were attempts
at reconciling the aesthetics of prison architecture with the Spanish

tsotsis: hooligans

Villa style (spikes painted pink) and with the plaster urns of neoclassical façades (twelve-inch pikes finned like zigzags of lightning and painted pure white). Some walls had a small board affixed, giving the name and telephone number of the firm responsible for the installation of the devices. While the little boy and the pet dog raced ahead, the husband and wife found themselves comparing the possible effectiveness of each style against its appearance; and after several weeks when they paused before this barricade or that without needing to speak, both came out with the conclusion that only one was worth considering. It was the ugliest but the most honest in its suggestion of the pure concentration-camp style, no frills, all evident efficacy. Placed the length of walls, it consisted of a continuous coil of stiff and shining metal serrated into jagged blades, so that there would be no way of climbing over it and no way through its tunnel without getting entangled in its fangs. There would be no way out, only a struggle getting bloodier and bloodier, a deeper and sharper hooking and tearing of flesh. The wife shuddered to look at it. You're right, said the husband, anyone would think twice . . . And they took heed of the advice on a small board fixed to the wall: Consult DRAGON'S TEETH The People For Total Security.

Next day a gang of workmen came and stretched the razor-bladed coils all round the walls of the house where the husband and wife and little boy and pet dog and cat were living happily ever after. The sunlight flashed and slashed, off the serrations, the cornice of razor thorns encircled the home, shining. The husband said, Never mind. It will weather. The wife said, You're wrong. They guarantee it's rust-proof. And she waited until the little boy had run off to play before she said, I hope the cat will take heed . . . The husband said, Don't worry, my dear, cats always look before they leap. And it was true that from that day on the cat slept in the little boy's bed and kept to the garden, never risking a try at breaching security.

One evening, the mother read the little boy to sleep with a fairy story from the book the wise old witch had given him at Christmas. Next day he pretended to be the Prince who braves the terrible thicket of thorns to enter the palace and kiss the Sleeping Beauty back to life: he dragged a ladder to the wall, the shining coiled tunnel was just wide enough for his little body to creep in, and with the first fixing of its razor-teeth in his knees and hands and head he screamed and struggled deeper into its tangle. The trusted housemaid and the itinerant gardener, whose "day" it was, came running, the first to see and to scream with him, and the itinerant gardener tore his hands trying to get at the little boy. Then the man and his wife burst wildly into the garden and for some reason (the cat, probably) the alarm set up wailing against the screams while the bleeding mass of the little boy was hacked out of the security coil with saws, wire-cutters, choppers, and they carried it—the man, the wife, the hysterical trusted housemaid and the weeping gardener—into the house.

QUESTIONS

1. The opening section of the story is told by a writer awakened by a frightening sound in the night. What two causes for the sound does she consider? Ultimately, which is the more significant cause for fear? How do these together create an emotional background for the "children's story" she tells?
2. What stylistic devices create the atmosphere of children's stories? How is this atmosphere related to the story's theme?
3. To what extent does the story explore the motives for the behavior of the wife and husband, the husband's mother, the servants, and the people who surround the suburb and the house? What motives can you infer for these people? What ironies do they display in their actions?
4. Can you fix the blame for the calamity that befalls the child? What are the possible meanings of the repeated phrase "YOU HAVE BEEN WARNED"?
5. What details in the introductory section and in the children's story imply the nature of the social order in which both occur?
6. Analyze the story's final paragraph in detail. How does it help to elucidate the theme?

SUGGESTIONS FOR WRITING

1. Bearing in mind point 5 in the introduction to this chapter ("there is no *one* way of stating the theme of a story"), write out three alternative statements of theme for one or more of the following:
   a. Wolff, "Hunters in the Snow" (page 86).
   b. Munro, "How I Met My Husband" (page 125).
   c. Chekhov, "The Darling" (page 212).
2. The theme of a story often is displayed in the development of the protagonist or in the epiphany that the protagonist experiences. But in some stories, there may be more than one focal character, and the theme must therefore be inferred by examining the different experiences of more than one person. Demonstrate the validity of this statement by examining the three main characters in one of the following:
   a. Wolff, "Hunters in the Snow" (page 86).
   b. Walker, "Everyday Use" (page 166).
   c. Hurston, "The Gilded Six-Bits" (page 553).

Chapter Five

Point of View

Primitive storytellers, unbothered by considerations of form, simply spun their tales. "Once upon a time," they began, and proceeded to narrate the story to their listeners, describing the characters when necessary, telling what the characters thought and felt as well as what they did, and interjecting comments and ideas of their own. Modern fiction writers are artistically more self-conscious. They realize that there are many ways of telling a story; they decide upon a method before they begin, or discover one while in the act of writing, and may even set up rules for themselves. Instead of telling the story themselves, they may let one of the characters tell it; they may tell it by means of letters or diaries; they may confine themselves to recording the thoughts of one of the characters. With the growth of artistic consciousness, the question of **point of view**—of who tells the story, and, therefore, of how it gets told—has assumed special importance.

To determine the point of view of a story, we ask, "Who tells the story?" and "How much is this person allowed to know?" and, especially, "To what extent does the narrator look inside the characters and report their thoughts and feelings?"

Though many variations and combinations are possible, the basic points of view are four, as follows:

---

1. Omniscient

2. Third-person limited   (a) Major character
                                             (b) Minor character

3. First person   (a) Major character
                                             (b) Minor character

4. Objective

---

1. In the **omniscient point of view**, the story is told in the third person by a narrator whose knowledge and prerogatives are unlimited. Such narrators are free to go wherever they wish, to peer inside the minds and hearts of characters at will and tell us what they are thinking or feeling. These narrators can interpret behavior and can comment, if they wish, on the significance of their stories. They know all. They can tell us as much or as little as they please.

The following version of Aesop's fable "The Ant and the Grasshopper" is told from the omniscient point of view. Notice that in it we are told not only what both characters do and say, but also what they think and feel; notice also that the narrator comments at the end on the significance of the story. (The phrases in which the narrator enters into the thoughts or feelings of the ant and the grasshopper have been italicized; the comment by the author is printed in small capitals.)

> *Weary in every limb*, the ant tugged over the snow a piece of corn he had stored up last summer. *It would taste mighty good at dinner tonight.*
>
> A grasshopper, *cold and hungry*, looked on. *Finally he could bear it no longer.* "Please, friend ant, may I have a bite of corn?"
>
> "What were you doing all last summer?" asked the ant. He looked the grasshopper up and down. *He knew its kind.*
>
> "I sang from dawn till dark," replied the grasshopper, *happily unaware of what was coming next.*
>
> "Well," said the ant, *hardly bothering to conceal his contempt,* "since you sang all summer, you can dance all winter."
>
> HE WHO IDLES WHEN HE'S YOUNG
> WILL HAVE NOTHING WHEN HE'S OLD

Stories told from the omniscient point of view may vary widely in the amount of omniscience the narrator is allowed. In "Hunters in the Snow," we are frequently allowed into the mind of Tub, but near the end of the story the omniscient narrator takes over and gives us information none of the characters could know. In "The Destructors," though we are taken into the minds of Blackie, Mike, the gang as a group, Old Misery, and the lorry driver, we are not taken into the mind of Trevor—the most important character. In "The Most Dangerous Game," we are confined to the thoughts and feelings of Rainsford, except for the brief passage between Rainsford's leap into the sea and his waking in Zaroff's bed, during which the point of view shifts to General Zaroff.

The omniscient is the most flexible point of view and permits the widest scope. It is also the most subject to abuse. It offers constant danger that the narrator may come between the readers and the story, or that the continual shifting of viewpoint from character to character may cause a breakdown in coherence or unity. Used skillfully, it enables the author to achieve simultaneous breadth and depth. Unskillfully used, it can destroy the illusion of reality that the story attempts to create.

2. In the **third-person limited point of view**, the story is told in the third person, but from the viewpoint of one character in the story. Such point-of-view characters are filters through whose eyes and minds writers look at the events. Authors employing this perspective may move both inside and outside these characters but never leave their sides. They tell us what these characters see and hear and what they think and feel; they possibly interpret the characters' thoughts and behavior. They know everything about their point-of-view characters—often more than the characters know about themselves. But they limit themselves to these characters' perceptions and show no direct knowledge of what *other* characters are thinking or feeling or doing, except for what the point-of-view character knows or can infer about them. The chosen character may be either a major or a minor character, a participant or an observer, and this choice also will be a very important one for the story. "Interpreter of Maladies," "Miss Brill," and "A Worn Path" are told from the third-person limited point of view, from the perspective of the main character. The use of this viewpoint with a minor character is rare in the short story, and is not illustrated in this book.

Here is "The Ant and the Grasshopper" told, in the third person, from the point of view of the ant. Notice that this time we are told nothing of what the grasshopper thinks or feels. We see and hear and know of him only what the ant sees and hears and knows.

> *Weary in every limb*, the ant tugged over the snow a piece of corn he had stored up last summer. *It would taste mighty good at dinner tonight. It was then that he noticed the grasshopper, looking cold and pinched.*
>
> "Please, friend ant, may I have a bite of your corn?" asked the grasshopper.
>
> He looked the grasshopper up and down. "What were you doing all last summer?" he asked. *He knew its kind.*
>
> "I sang from dawn till dark," replied the grasshopper.
>
> "Well," said the ant, *hardly bothering to conceal his contempt,* "since you sang all summer, you can dance all winter."

The third-person limited point of view, since it acquaints us with the world through the mind and senses of only one character, approximates more closely than the omniscient the conditions of real life; it also offers a ready-made unifying element, since all details of the story are the experience of one character. And it affords an additional device of characterization, since what a point-of-view character does or does not find noteworthy, and the inferences that such a character draws about other characters' actions and motives, may reveal biases or limitations in the observer. At the same time it offers a limited field of observation, for the readers can go nowhere except where the chosen character goes, and there may be difficulty in having the character naturally cognizant of all important events. Clumsy writers will constantly have the focal character listening at keyholes, accidentally overhearing important conversations, or coincidentally being present when important events occur.

A variant of third-person limited point of view, illustrated in this chapter by Porter's "The Jilting of Granny Weatherall," is called **stream of consciousness**. Stream of consciousness presents the apparently random thoughts going through a character's head within a certain period of time, mingling memory and present experiences, and employing transitional links that are psychological rather than strictly logical. (First-person narrators might also tell their stories through stream of consciousness, though first-person use of this technique is relatively rare.)

3. In the **first-person point of view**, the author disappears into one of the characters, who tells the story in the first person. This character, again, may be either a major or a minor character, protagonist or observer, and it will make considerable difference whether the protagonist tells the story or someone else tells it. In "How I Met My Husband," the protagonist tells the story in the first person. In "A Rose for Emily," presented in Part 4, the story is told in the unusual first-person plural, from the vantage point of the townspeople observing Emily's life through the years.

Our fable is retold below in the first person from the point of view of the grasshopper. (The whole story is italicized because it all comes out of the grasshopper's mind.)

> *Cold and hungry, I watched the ant tugging over the snow a piece of corn he had stored up last summer. My feelers twitched, and I was conscious of a tic in my left hind leg. Finally I could bear it no longer.*
>
> *"Please, friend ant," I asked, "may I have a bite of your corn?"*
>
> *He looked me up and down. "What were you doing all last summer?" he asked, rather too smugly it seemed to me.*
>
> *"I sang from dawn till dark," I said innocently, remembering the happy times.*

"Well," he said, with a priggish sneer, "since you sang all summer, you can dance all winter."

The first-person point of view shares the virtues and limitations of the third-person limited. It offers, sometimes, a gain in immediacy and reality, since we get the story directly from a participant, the author as intermediary being eliminated. It offers no opportunity, however, for *direct* interpretation by the author, and there is constant danger that narrators may be made to transcend their own sensitivity, their knowledge, or their powers of language in telling a story. Talented authors, however, can make tremendous literary capital out of the very limitations of their narrators. The first-person point of view offers excellent opportunities for dramatic irony and for studies in limited or blunted human perceptiveness. In "How I Met My Husband," for instance, there is an increasingly clear difference between what the narrator perceives and what the reader perceives as the story proceeds. Even though Edie is clearly narrating her story from the vantage point of maturity—ultimately we know this from the ending and from the title itself—she rarely allows her mature voice to intrude or to make judgments on Edie's thoughts and feelings as a fifteen-year-old girl infatuated with a handsome pilot. The story gains in emotional power because of the poignancy of youthful romanticism that Edie's hopes and wishes represent, and because of the inevitable disillusionment she must suffer. By choosing this point of view, Munro offers an interpretation of the material *indirectly*, through her dramatization of Edie's experiences. In other stories, like "A Rose for Emily," the author intends the first-person viewpoint to suggest a conventional set of perceptions and attitudes, perhaps including those of the author and the reader. Identifications of a narrator's attitudes with the author's, however, must always be undertaken with extreme caution; they are justified only if the total material of the story supports them, or if outside evidence (for example, a statement by the author) supports such an identification. In "A Rose for Emily" the narrative detachment does reflect the author's own; nevertheless, much of the interest of the story arises from the limited viewpoint of the townspeople and the cloak of mystery surrounding Emily and her life inside the house.

4. In the **objective point of view**, the narrator disappears into a kind of roving sound camera. This camera can go anywhere but can record only what is seen and heard. It cannot comment, interpret, or enter a character's mind. With this point of view (sometimes called also the **dramatic point of view**) readers are placed in the position of spectators at a movie or play. They see what the characters do and hear what they say but must infer what they think or feel and what they are like. Authors are not there to explain. The purest example of a story told from the objective point of view would be one written entirely in dialogue, for as soon as authors add words of their own, they begin to interpret through their very choice of words. Actually, few stories using this point of view are antiseptically pure, for the limitations it imposes on the author are severe. Shirley Jackson's "The Lottery," presented in this chapter, is essentially objective in its narration.

The following version of "The Ant and the Grasshopper" is also told from the objective point of view. (Since we are nowhere taken into the thoughts or feelings of the characters, none of this version is printed in italics.)

The ant tugged over the snow a piece of corn he had stored up last summer, perspiring in spite of the cold.

A grasshopper, his feelers twitching and with a tic in his left hind leg, looked on for some time. Finally he asked, "Please, friend ant, may I have a bite of your corn?"

The ant looked the grasshopper up and down. "What were you doing all last summer?" he snapped.

"I sang from dawn till dark," replied the grasshopper, not changing his tone.

"Well," said the ant, and a faint smile crept into his face, "since you sang all summer, you can dance all winter."

The objective point of view requires readers to draw their own inferences. But it must rely heavily on external action and dialogue, and it offers no opportunities for direct interpretation by the author.

Each of the points of view has its advantages, its limitations, and its peculiar uses. Ideally the choice of the author will depend upon the materials and the purpose of a story. Authors choose the point of view that enables them to present their particular materials most effectively in terms of their purposes. Writers of murder mysteries with suspense and thrills as the purpose will ordinarily avoid using the point of view of the murderer or the brilliant detective: otherwise they would have to reveal at the beginning the secrets they wish to conceal till the end. On the other hand, if they are interested in exploring criminal psychology, the murderer's point of view might be by far the most effective. In the Sherlock Holmes stories, A. Conan Doyle effectively uses the somewhat imperceptive Dr. Watson as his narrator, so that the reader may be kept in the dark as long as possible and then be as amazed as Watson is by Holmes's deductive powers. In Dostoevsky's *Crime and Punishment*, however, the author is interested not in mystifying and surprising but in illuminating the moral and psychological operations of the human soul in the act of taking life; he therefore tells the story from the viewpoint of a sensitive and intelligent murderer.

For readers, the examination of point of view may be important both for understanding and for evaluating the story. First, they should know whether the events of the story are being interpreted by a narrator or by one of the characters. If the latter, they must ask how this character's mind and personality affect the interpretation, whether the character is perceptive or imperceptive, and whether the interpretation can be accepted at face value or must be discounted because of ignorance, stupidity, or self-deception.

Next, readers should ask whether the writer has chosen the point of view for maximum revelation of the material or for another reason. The author may choose the point of view mainly to conceal certain information till the end of the story and thus maintain suspense and create surprise. The author may even deliberately mislead readers by presenting the events through a character who puts a false interpretation on them. Such a false interpretation may be justified if it leads eventually to more effective revelation of character and theme. If it is there merely to trick readers, it is obviously less justifiable.

Finally, readers should ask whether the author has used the selected point of view fairly and consistently. Even in commercial fiction we have a right to demand fair treatment. If the person to whose thoughts and feelings we are admitted has pertinent information that is not revealed, we legitimately feel cheated. To have a chance to solve a murder mystery, we must know what the detective learns. A writer also should be consistent in the point of view; if it shifts, it should do so for a just artistic reason. Serious literary writers choose and use point of view so as to yield ultimately the greatest possible insight, either in fullness or in intensity.

REVIEWING CHAPTER FIVE

1. Explain how to determine the point of view in a story.
2. Describe the characteristics of omniscient point of view.
3. Review the definition of third-person limited point of view.
4. Consider the virtues and limitations of first-person point of view.
5. Explore the use of objective point of view in Hemingway's "Hills Like White Elephants," presented in this chapter.

Willa Cather
Paul's Case

It was Paul's afternoon to appear before the faculty of the Pittsburgh High School to account for his various misdemeanors. He had been suspended a week ago, and his father had called at the Principal's office and confessed his perplexity about his son. Paul entered the faculty room suave and smiling. His clothes were a trifle outgrown, and the tan velvet on the collar of his open overcoat was frayed and worn; but for all that there was something of a dandy about him, and he wore an opal pin in his neatly knotted black four-in-hand, and a red carnation in his buttonhole. This latter adornment the faculty somehow felt was not properly significant of the contrite spirit befitting a boy under the ban of suspension.

Paul was tall for his age and very thin, with high, cramped shoulders and a narrow chest. His eyes were remarkable for a certain hysterical brilliancy, and he continually used them in a conscious, theatrical sort of way, peculiarly offensive in a boy. The pupils were abnormally large, as though he were addicted to belladonna, but there was a glassy glitter about them which that drug does not produce.

When questioned by the Principal as to why he was there, Paul stated, politely enough, that he wanted to come back to school. This was a lie, but Paul was quite accustomed to lying; found it, indeed, indispensable for overcoming friction. His teachers were asked to state their respective charges against him, which they did with such a rancor and aggrievedness as evinced that this was not a usual case. Disorder and impertinence were among the offences named, yet each of his instructors felt that it was scarcely possible to put into words the real cause of the trouble, which lay in a sort of hysterically defiant manner of the boy's; in the contempt which they all knew he felt for them, and which he seemingly made not the least effort to conceal. Once, when he had been making a synopsis of a paragraph at the blackboard, his English teacher had stepped to his side and attempted to guide his hand. Paul had started back with a shudder and thrust his hands violently behind him. The astonished woman could scarcely have been more hurt and embarrassed had he struck at her. The insult was so involuntary and

PAUL'S CASE   Written in 1904, first published in 1905. Willa Cather (1873–1947) was born in Virginia and grew up and was educated in Nebraska. From 1895 to 1905 she lived and worked in Pittsburgh, first as a journalist, writing drama and music criticism, later as a teacher of English and Latin in two Pittsburgh high schools. In 1902 she traveled in Europe.

definitely personal as to be unforgettable. In one way and another, he had made all his teachers, men and women alike, conscious of the same feeling of physical aversion. In one class he habitually sat with his hand shading his eyes; in another he always looked out of the window during the recitation; in another he made a running commentary on the lecture, with humorous intent.

His teachers felt this afternoon that his whole attitude was symbolized by his shrug and his flippantly red carnation flower, and they fell upon him without mercy, his English teacher leading the pack. He stood through it smiling, his pale lips parted over his white teeth. (His lips were continually twitching, and he had a habit of raising his eyebrows that was contemptuous and irritating to the last degree.) Older boys than Paul had broken down and shed tears under that ordeal, but his set smile did not once desert him, and his only sign of discomfort was the nervous trembling of the fingers that toyed with the buttons of his overcoat, and an occasional jerking of the other hand which held his hat. Paul was always smiling, always glancing about him, seeming to feel that people might be watching him and trying to detect something. This conscious expression, since it was as far as possible from boyish mirthfulness, was usually attributed to insolence or "smartness."

As the inquisition proceeded, one of his instructors repeated an   5
impertinent remark of the boy's, and the Principal asked him whether he thought that a courteous speech to make to a woman. Paul shrugged his shoulders slightly and his eyebrows twitched.

"I don't know," he replied. "I didn't mean to be polite or impolite, either. I guess it's a sort of way I have, of saying things regardless."

The Principal asked him whether he didn't think that a way it would be well to get rid of. Paul grinned and said he guessed so. When he was told that he could go, he bowed gracefully and went out. His bow was like a repetition of the scandalous red carnation.

His teachers were in despair, and his drawing-master voiced the feeling of them all when he declared there was something about the boy which none of them understood. He added: "I don't really believe that smile of his comes altogether from insolence; there's something sort of haunted about it. The boy is not strong for one thing. There is something wrong about the fellow."

The drawing-master had come to realize that, in looking at Paul, one saw only his white teeth and the forced animation of his eyes. One warm afternoon the boy had gone to sleep at his drawing-board, and his master had noted with amazement what a white, blue-veined face it was; drawn and wrinkled like an old man's about the eyes, the lips twitching even in his sleep.

10   His teachers left the building dissatisfied and unhappy; humiliated to have felt so vindictive toward a mere boy, to have uttered this feeling in cutting terms, and to have set each other on, as it were, in the gruesome game of intemperate reproach. One of them remembered having seen a miserable street cat set at bay by a ring of tormentors.

As for Paul, he ran down the hill whistling the Soldiers' Chorus from *Faust*, looking behind him now and then to see whether some of his teachers were not there to witness his light-heartedness. As it was now late in the afternoon and Paul was on duty that evening as usher at Carnegie Hall, he decided that he would not go home to supper.

When he reached the concert hall, the doors were not yet open. It was chilly outside, and he decided to go up into the picture gallery—always deserted at this hour—where there were some of Raffelli's gay studies of Paris streets and an airy blue Venetian scene or two that always exhilarated him. He was delighted to find no one in the gallery but the old guard, who sat in the corner, a newspaper on his knee, a black patch over one eye and the other closed. Paul possessed himself of the place and walked confidently up and down, whistling under his breath. After a while he sat down before a blue Rico and lost himself. When he bethought him to look at his watch, it was after seven o'clock and he rose with a start and ran downstairs, making a face at Augustus Caesar, peering out from the cast-room, and an evil gesture at the Venus of Milo as he passed her on the stairway.

When Paul reached the ushers' dressing-room, half a dozen boys were there already, and he began excitedly to tumble into his uniform. It was one of the few that at all approached fitting, and Paul thought it very becoming—though he knew the tight, straight coat accentuated his narrow chest, about which he was exceedingly sensitive. He was always excited while he dressed, twanging all over to the tuning of the strings and the preliminary flourishes of the horns in the music-room; but tonight he seemed quite beside himself, and he teased and plagued the boys until, telling him that he was crazy, they put him down on the floor and sat on him.

Somewhat calmed by his suppression, Paul dashed out to the front of the house to seat the early comers. He was a model usher. Gracious and smiling he ran up and down the aisles. Nothing was too much trouble for him; he carried messages and brought programs as though it were his greatest pleasure in life, and all the people in his section thought him a charming boy, feeling that he remembered and admired them. As the house filled, he grew more and more vivacious and animated, and the color came to his cheeks and lips. It was very much as though this were a great reception and Paul were the host. Just as the musicians came out to take their places, his English teacher arrived with checks for the seats which a prominent manufacturer had taken for the season. She betrayed some embarrassment when she handed Paul the tickets, and a *hauteur* which subsequently made her feel very foolish. Paul was startled for a moment, and had the feeling of wanting to put her out; what business had she here among all these fine people and gay colors? He looked her over and decided that she was not appropriately dressed and must be a fool to sit downstairs in such togs. The tickets had probably been sent her out of kindness, he reflected, as he put down a seat for her, and she had about as much right to sit there as he had.

When the symphony began, Paul sank into one of the rear seats   15
with a long sigh of relief, and lost himself as he had done before the Rico. It was not that symphonies, as such, meant anything in particular to Paul, but the first sight of the instruments seemed to free some hilarious spirit within him; something that struggled there like the Genius in the bottle found by the Arab fisherman. He felt a sudden zest of life; the lights danced before his eyes and the concert hall blazed into unimaginable splendor. When the soprano soloist came on, Paul forgot even the nastiness of his teacher's being there, and gave himself up to the peculiar intoxication such personages always had for him. The soloist chanced to be a German woman, by no means in her first youth, and the mother of many children; but she wore a satin gown and a tiara, and she had that indefinable air of achievement, that world-shine upon her, which always blinded Paul to any possible defects.

After a concert was over, Paul was often irritable and wretched until he got to sleep—and tonight he was even more than usually restless. He had the feeling of not being able to let down; of its being impossible to give up this delicious excitement which was the only thing that could be called living at all. During the last number he withdrew and, after hastily changing his clothes in the dressing-room, slipped out to the side door where the singer's carriage stood. Here he began pacing rapidly up and down the walk, waiting to see her come out.

Over yonder the Schenley, in its vacant stretch, loomed big and square through the fine rain, the windows of its twelve stories glowing like those of a lighted cardboard house under a Christmas tree. All the actors and singers of any importance stayed there when they were in Pittsburgh, and a number of the big manufacturers of the place lived there in the winter. Paul had often hung about the hotel, watching the people go in and out, longing to enter and leave schoolmasters and dull care behind him forever.

At last the singer came out, accompanied by the conductor, who helped her into her carriage and closed the door with a cordial *auf wiedersehen*—which set Paul to wondering whether she were not an old sweetheart of his. Paul followed the carriage over to the hotel, walking so rapidly as not to be far from the entrance when the singer alighted and disappeared behind the swinging glass doors which were opened by a Negro in a tall hat and a long coat. In the moment that the door was ajar, it seemed to Paul that he, too, entered. He seemed to feel himself go after her up the steps, into the warm, lighted building, into an exotic, a tropical world of shiny, glistening surfaces and basking ease. He reflected upon the mysterious dishes that were brought into the dining-room, the green bottles in buckets of ice, as he had seen them in the supper-party pictures of the Sunday supplement. A quick gust of wind brought the rain down with sudden vehemence, and Paul was startled to find that he was still outside in the slush of the gravel driveway; that his boots were letting in the water and his scanty overcoat was clinging wet about him; that the lights in front of the concert hall were out, and that the rain was driving in sheets between him and the orange glow of the windows above him. There it was, what he wanted—tangibly before him, like the fairy world of a Christmas panto-mime; as the rain beat in his face, Paul wondered whether he were destined always to shiver in the black night outside, looking up at it.

He turned and walked reluctantly toward the car tracks. The end had to come sometime; his father in his night-clothes at the top of the stairs, explanations that did not explain, hastily improvised fictions that were forever tripping him up, his upstairs room and its horrible yellow wallpaper, the creaking bureau with the greasy plush collar-box, and over his painted wooden bed the pictures of George Washington and John Calvin, and the framed motto, "Feed my Lambs," which had been worked in red worsted by his mother, whom Paul could not remember.

20   Half an hour later, Paul alighted from the Negley Avenue car and went slowly down one of the side streets off the main thoroughfare. It was a highly respectable street, where all the houses were exactly alike, and where business men of moderate means begot and reared large families of children, all of whom went to Sabbath School and learned the shorter catechism, and were interested in arithmetic; all of whom were as exactly alike as their homes, and of a piece with the monotony in which they lived. Paul never went up Cordelia Street without a shudder of loathing. His home was next to the house of the Cumberland minister. He approached it tonight with the nerveless sense of defeat, the hopeless feeling of sinking back forever into ugliness and common-ness that he had always had when he came home. The moment he

turned into Cordelia Street he felt the waters close above his head. After each of these orgies of living, he experienced all the physical depression which follows a debauch; the loathing of respectable beds, of common food, of a house permeated by kitchen odors; a shuddering repulsion for the flavorless, colorless mass of everyday existence; a morbid desire for cool things and soft lights and fresh flowers.

The nearer he approached the house, the more absolutely unequal Paul felt to the sight of it all: his ugly sleeping chamber; the old bathroom with the grimy zinc tub, the cracked mirror, the dripping spigots; his father, at the top of the stairs, his hairy legs sticking out from his nightshirt, his feet thrust into carpet slippers. He was so much later than usual that there would certainly be inquiries and reproaches. Paul stopped short before the door. He felt that he could not be accosted by his father tonight; that he could not toss again on that miserable bed. He would not go in. He would tell his father that he had no carfare, and it was raining so hard he had gone home with one of the boys and stayed all night.

Meanwhile, he was wet and cold. He went around to the back of the house and tried one of the basement windows, found it open, and raised it cautiously, and scrambled down the cellar wall to the floor. There he stood, holding his breath, terrified by the noise he had made; but the floor above him was silent, and there was no creak on the stairs. He found a soap-box, and carried it over to the soft ring of light that streamed from the furnace door, and sat down. He was horribly afraid of rats, so he did not try to sleep, but sat looking distrustfully at the dark, still terrified lest he might have awakened his father. In such reactions, after one of the experiences which made days and nights out of the dreary blanks of the calendar, when his senses were deadened, Paul's head was always singularly clear. Suppose his father had heard him getting in at the window and had come down and shot him for a burglar? Then, again, suppose his father had come down, pistol in hand, and he had cried out in time to save himself, and his father had been horrified to think how nearly he had killed him? Then again, suppose a day should come when his father would remember that night, and wish there had been no warning cry to stay his hand? With this last supposition Paul entertained himself until daybreak.

The following Sunday was fine; the sodden November chill was broken by the last flash of autumnal summer. In the morning Paul had to go to church and Sabbath School, as always. On seasonable Sunday afternoons the burghers of Cordelia Street usually sat out on their front "stoops," and talked to their neighbors on the next stoop, or called to those across the street in neighborly fashion. The men sat placidly on gay cushions placed upon the steps that led down to the sidewalk, while the women, in their Sunday "waists," sat in rockers on the cramped porches, pretending to be greatly at their ease. The children played in the streets; there were so many of them that the place resembled the recreation grounds of a kindergarten. The men on the steps—all in their shirt-sleeves, their vests unbuttoned, sat with their legs well apart, their stomachs comfortably protruding, and talked of the prices of things, or told anecdotes of the sagacity of their various chiefs and overlords. They occasionally looked over the multitude of squabbling children, listened affectionately to their high-pitched, nasal voices, smiling to see their own proclivities reproduced in their offspring, and interspersed their legends of the iron kings with remarks about their sons' progress at school, their grades in arithmetic, and the amounts they had saved in their toy banks.

On this last Sunday of November, Paul sat all afternoon on the lowest step of his "stoop," staring into the street, while his sisters, in their rockers, were talking to the minister's daughters next door about how many shirtwaists they had made in the last week, and how many waffles someone had eaten at the last church supper. When the weather was warm, and his father was in a particularly jovial frame of mind, the girls made lemonade, which was always brought out in a red-glass pitcher, ornamented with forget-me-nots in blue enamel. This the girls thought very fine, and the neighbors joked about the suspicious color of the pitcher.

25   Today Paul's father, on the top step, was talking to a young man who shifted a restless baby from knee to knee. He happened to be the young man who was daily held up to Paul as a model, and after whom it was his father's dearest hope that he would pattern. This young man was of a ruddy complexion, with a compressed, red mouth, and faded, nearsighted eyes, over which he wore thick spectacles, with gold bows that curved about his ears. He was clerk to one of the magnates of a great steel corporation, and was looked upon in Cordelia Street as a young man with a future. There was a story that, some five years ago—he was now barely twenty-six—he had been a trifle "dissipated," but in order to curb his appetites and save the loss of time and strength that a sowing of wild oats might have entailed, he had taken his chief's advice, oft reiterated to his employees, and at twenty-one had married the first woman whom he could persuade to share his fortunes. She happened to be an angular schoolmistress, much older than he, who also wore thick glasses, and who had now borne him four children, all nearsighted like herself.

The young man was relating how his chief, now cruising in the Mediterranean, kept in touch with all the details of the business, arranging his office hours on his yacht just as though he were at home, and "knocking off work enough to keep two stenographers busy." His father told, in turn, the plan his corporation was considering, of putting in an electric railway plant at Cairo. Paul snapped his teeth; he had an awful apprehension that they might spoil it all before he got there. Yet he rather liked to hear these legends of the iron kings, that were told and retold on Sundays and holidays; these stories of palaces in Venice, yachts on the Mediterranean, and high play at Monte Carlo appealed to his fancy, and he was interested in the triumphs of cash-boys who had become famous, though he had no mind for the cash-boy stage.

After supper was over, and he had helped to dry the dishes, Paul nervously asked his father whether he could go to George's to get some help in his geometry, and still more nervously asked for carfare. This latter request he had to repeat, as his father, on principle, did not like to hear requests for money, whether much or little. He asked Paul whether he could not go to some boy who lived nearer, and told him that he ought not to leave his school work until Sunday; but he gave him the dime. He was not a poor man, but he had a worthy ambition to come up in the world. His only reason for allowing Paul to usher was that he thought a boy ought to be earning a little.

Paul bounded upstairs, scrubbed the greasy odor of the dishwater from his hands with the ill-smelling soap he hated, and then shook over his fingers a few drops of violet water from the bottle he kept hidden in his drawer. He left the house with his geometry conspicuously under his arm, and the moment he got out of Cordelia Street and boarded a downtown car, he shook off the lethargy of two deadening days, and began to live again.

The leading juvenile of the permanent stock company which played at one of the downtown theaters was an acquaintance of Paul's, and the boy had been invited to drop in at the Sunday-night rehearsals whenever he could. For more than a year Paul had spent every available moment loitering about Charley Edwards's dressing-room. He had won a place among Edwards's following not only because the young actor, who could not afford to employ a dresser, often found him useful, but because he recognized in Paul something akin to what churchmen term "vocation."

It was at the theater and at Carnegie Hall that Paul really lived; the   30
rest was but a sleep and a forgetting. This was Paul's fairy tale, and it had for him all the allurement of a secret love. The moment he inhaled the gassy, painty, dusty odor behind the scenes, he breathed like a prisoner set free, and felt within him the possibility of doing or saying splendid, brilliant things. The moment the cracked orchestra beat out the

overture from *Martha*, or jerked at the serenade from *Rigoletto*, all stupid and ugly things slid from him, and his senses were deliciously, yet delicately fired.

Perhaps it was because, in Paul's world, the natural nearly always wore the guise of ugliness, that a certain element of artificiality seemed to him necessary in beauty. Perhaps it was because his experience of life elsewhere was so full of Sabbath-School picnics, petty economies, wholesome advice as to how to succeed in life, and the unescapable odors of cooking, that he found this existence so alluring, these smartly clad men and women so attractive, that he was so moved by these starry apple orchards that bloomed perennially under the limelight.

It would be difficult to put it strongly enough how convincingly the stage entrance of the theater was for Paul the actual portal of Romance. Certainly none of the company ever suspected it, least of all Charley Edwards. It was very like the old stories that used to float about London of fabulously rich Jews, who had subterranean halls, with palms, and fountains, and soft lamps and richly appareled women who never saw the disenchanting light of London day. So, in the midst of that smoke-palled city, enamored of figures and grimy toil, Paul had his secret temple, his wishing-carpet, his bit of blue-and-white Mediterranean shore bathed in perpetual sunshine.

Several of Paul's teachers had a theory that his imagination had been perverted by garish fiction; but the truth was, he scarcely ever read at all. The books at home were not such as would either tempt or corrupt a youthful mind, and as for reading the novels that some of his friends urged upon him—well, he got what he wanted much more quickly from music; any sort of music, from an orchestra to a barrel-organ. He needed only the spark, the indescribable thrill that made his imagination master of his senses, and he could make plots and pictures enough of his own. It was equally true that he was not stage-struck—not, at any rate, in the usual acceptation of the expression. He had no desire to become an actor, any more than he had to become a musician. He felt no necessity to do any of these things; what he wanted was to see, to be in the atmosphere, float on the wave of it, to be carried out, blue league after league, away from everything.

After a night behind the scenes, Paul found the schoolroom more than ever repulsive; the bare floors and naked walls; the prosy men who never wore frock coats, or violets in their buttonholes; the women with their dull gowns, shrill voices, and pitiful seriousness about prepositions that govern the dative. He could not bear to have the other pupils think, for a moment, that he took these people seriously; he must convey to them that he considered it all trivial, and was there only by the way of a joke, anyway. He had autographed pictures of all the members of the stock company which he showed his classmates, telling them the most incredible stories of his familiarity with these people, of his acquaintance with the soloists who came to Carnegie Hall, his suppers with them and the flowers he sent them. When these stories lost their effect, and his audience grew listless, he would bid all the boys goodbye, announcing that he was going to travel for a while; going to Naples, to California, to Egypt. Then, next Monday, he would slip back, conscious and nervously smiling; his sister was ill, and he would have to defer his voyage until spring.

Matters went steadily worse with Paul at school. In the itch to let his   35
instructors know how heartily he despised them, and how thoroughly he was appreciated elsewhere, he mentioned once or twice that he had no time to fool with theorems; adding—with a twitch of the eyebrows and a touch of that nervous bravado which so perplexed them—that he was helping the people down at the stock company; they were old friends of his.

The upshot of the matter was that the Principal went to Paul's father, and Paul was taken out of school and put to work. The manager at Carnegie Hall was told to get another usher in his stead; the door-keeper at the theater was warned not to admit him to the house; and Charley Edwards remorsefully promised the boy's father not to see him again.

The members of the stock company were vastly amused when some of Paul's stories reached them—especially the women. They were hard-working women, most of them supporting indolent husbands or brothers, and they laughed rather bitterly at having stirred the boy to such fervid and florid inventions. They agreed with the faculty and with his father, that Paul's was a bad case.

The east-bound train was plowing through a January snowstorm; the dull dawn was beginning to show grey when the engine whistled a mile out of Newark. Paul started up from the seat where he had lain curled in uneasy slumber, rubbed the breath-misted window-glass with his hand, and peered out. The snow was whirling in curling eddies above the white bottom lands, and the drifts lay already deep in the fields and along the fences, while here and there the tall dead grass and dried weed stalks protruded black above it. Lights shone from the scattered houses, and a gang of laborers who stood beside the track waved their lanterns.

Paul had slept very little, and he felt grimy and uncomfortable. He had made the all-night journey in a day coach because he was afraid if he took a Pullman he might be seen by some Pittsburgh business man who had noticed him in Denny and Carson's office. When the whistle woke him, he clutched quickly at his breast pocket, glancing about him with an uncertain smile. But the little, clay-bespattered Italians were still sleeping, the slatternly women across the aisle were in openmouthed oblivion, and even the crumby, crying babies were for the nonce stilled. Paul settled back to struggle with his impatience as best he could.

40   When he arrived at the Jersey City station, he hurried through his breakfast, manifestly ill at ease and keeping a sharp eye about him. After he reached the Twenty-third Street station, he consulted a cabman, and had himself driven to a men's furnishing establishment which was just opening for the day. He spent upward of two hours there, buying with endless reconsidering and great care. His new street suit he put on in the fitting-room; the frock coat and dress clothes he had bundled into the cab with his new shirts. Then he drove to a hatter's and a shoe house. His next errand was at Tiffany's, where he selected silver-mounted brushes and a scarf-pin. He would not wait to have his silver marked, he said. Lastly, he stopped at a trunk shop on Broadway, and had his purchases packed into various traveling-bags.

It was a little after one o'clock when he drove up to the Waldorf, and, after settling with the cabman, went into the office. He registered from Washington; said his mother and father had been abroad, and that he had come down to await the arrival of their steamer. He told his story plausibly and had no trouble, since he offered to pay for them in advance, in engaging his rooms; a sleeping-room, sitting-room, and bath.

Not once, but a hundred times Paul had planned this entry into New York. He had gone over every detail of it with Charley Edwards, and in his scrapbook at home there were pages of description about New York hotels, cut from the Sunday papers.

When he was shown to his sitting-room on the eighth floor, he saw at a glance that everything was as it should be; there was but one detail in his mental picture that the place did not realize, so he rang for the bell-boy and sent him down for flowers. He moved about nervously until the boy returned, putting away his new linen and fingering it delightedly as he did so. When the flowers came, he put them hastily into water, and then tumbled into a hot bath. Presently he came out of his white bathroom, resplendent in his new silk underwear, and playing with the tassels of his red robe. The snow was whirling so fiercely outside his windows that he could scarcely see across the street; but within, the air was deliciously soft and fragrant. He put the violets and jonquils on the taboret beside the couch, and threw himself down with a long sigh, covering himself with a Roman blanket. He was thoroughly tired; he had been in such haste, he had stood up to such a strain, covered so much ground in the last twenty-four hours, that he wanted to think how it had all come about. Lulled by the sound of the wind, the warm air, and the cool fragrance of the flowers, he sank into deep, drowsy retrospection.

It had been wonderfully simple; when they had shut him out of the theater and concert hall, when they had taken away his bone, the whole thing was virtually determined. The rest was a mere matter of opportunity. The only thing that at all surprised him was his own courage—for he realized well enough that he had always been tormented by fear, a sort of apprehensive dread which, of late years, as the meshes of the lies he had told closed about him, had been pulling the muscles of his body tighter and tighter. Until now, he could not remember a time when he had not been dreading something. Even when he was a little boy, it was always there—behind him, or before, or on either side. There had always been the shadowed corner, the dark place into which he dared not look, but from which something seemed always to be watching him—and Paul had done things that were not pretty to watch, he knew.

But now he had a curious sense of relief, as though he had at last   45
thrown down the gauntlet to the thing in the corner.

Yet it was but a day since he had been sulking in the traces; but yesterday afternoon that he had been sent to the bank with Denny & Carson's deposit, as usual—but this time he was instructed to leave the book to be balanced. There was above two thousand dollars in checks, and nearly a thousand in the banknotes which he had taken from the book and quietly transferred to his pocket. At the bank he had made out a new deposit slip. His nerves had been steady enough to permit of his returning to the office, where he had finished his work and asked for a full day's holiday tomorrow, Saturday, giving a perfectly reasonable pretext. The bank book, he knew, would not be returned before Monday or Tuesday, and his father would be out of town for the next week. From the time he slipped the banknotes into his pocket until he boarded the night train for New York, he had not known a moment's hesitation.

How astonishingly easy it had all been; here he was, the thing done; and this time there would be no awakening, no figure at the top of the stairs. He watched the snowflakes whirling by his window until he fell asleep.

When he awoke, it was four o'clock in the afternoon. He bounded up with a start; one of his precious days gone already! He spent nearly an hour in dressing, watching every stage of his toilet carefully in the mirror. Everything was quite perfect; he was exactly the kind of boy he had always wanted to be.

When he went downstairs, Paul took a carriage and drove up Fifth Avenue toward the Park. The snow had somewhat abated; carriages and tradesmen's wagons were hurrying soundlessly to and fro in the winter twilight; boys in woolen mufflers were shoveling off the doorsteps; the Avenue stages made fine spots of color against the white street. Here and there on the corners whole flower gardens blooming behind glass windows, against which the snowflakes stuck and melted; violets, roses, carnations, lilies-of-the-valley—somehow vastly more lovely and alluring that they blossomed thus unnaturally in the snow. The Park itself was a wonderful stage winter-piece.

50   When he returned, the pause of the twilight had ceased, and the tune of the streets had changed. The snow was falling faster, lights streamed from the hotels that reared their many stories fearlessly up into the storm, defying the raging Atlantic winds. A long, black stream of carriages poured down the Avenue, intersected here and there by other streams, tending horizontally. There were a score of cabs about the entrance of his hotel, and his driver had to wait. Boys in livery were running in and out of the awning stretched across the sidewalk, up and down the red velvet carpet laid from the door to the street. Above, about, within it all, was the rumble and roar, the hurry and toss of thousands of human beings as hot for pleasure as himself, and on every side of him towered the glaring affirmation of the omnipotence of wealth.

The boy set his teeth and drew his shoulders together in a spasm of realization; the plot of all dramas, the text of all romances, the nerve-stuff of all sensations was whirling about him like the snowflakes. He burnt like a faggot in a tempest.

When Paul came down to dinner, the music of the orchestra floated up the elevator shaft to greet him. As he stepped into the thronged corridor, he sank back into one of the chairs against the wall to get his breath. The lights, the chatter, the perfumes, the bewildering medley of color—he had, for a moment, the feeling of not being able to stand it. But only for a moment; these were his own people, he told himself. He went slowly about the corridors, through the writing-rooms, smoking-rooms, reception-rooms, as though he were exploring the chambers of an enchanted palace, built and peopled for him alone.

When he reached the dining-room he sat down at a table near a window. The flowers, the white linen, the many-colored wine-glasses, the gay toilettes of the women, the low popping of corks, the undulating repetitions of the "Blue Danube" from the orchestra, all flooded Paul's dream with bewildering radiance. When the roseate tinge of his champagne was added—that cold, precious, bubbling stuff that creamed and foamed in his glass—Paul wondered that there were honest men in the world at all. This was what all the world was fighting for, he reflected; this was what all the struggle was about. He doubted the reality of his past. Had he ever known a place called Cordelia Street, a place where fagged-looking business men boarded the early car? Mere rivets in a machine they seemed to Paul—sickening men, with combings of children's hair always hanging to their coats, and the smell of cooking in their clothes. Cordelia Street—Ah, that belonged to another time and country! Had he not always been thus, had he not sat here night after night, from as far back as he could remember, looking pensively over just such shimmering textures, and slowly twirling the stem of a glass like this one between his thumb and middle finger? He rather thought he had.

He was not in the least abashed or lonely. He had no especial desire to meet or to know any of these people; all he demanded was the right to look on and conjecture, to watch the pageant. The mere stage properties were all he contended for. Nor was he lonely later in the evening, in his loge at the Opera. He was entirely rid of his nervous misgivings, of his forced aggressiveness, of the imperative desire to show himself different from his surroundings. He felt now that his surroundings explained him. Nobody questioned the purple; he had only to wear it passively. He had only to glance down at his dress coat to reassure himself that here it would be impossible for anyone to humiliate him.

He found it hard to leave his beautiful sitting-room to go to bed that night, and sat long watching the raging storm from his turret window. When he went to sleep, it was with the lights turned on in his bedroom; partly because of his old timidity, and partly so that, if he should wake in the night, there would be no wretched moment of doubt, no horrible suspicion of yellow wallpaper, or of Washington and Calvin above his bed.   55

On Sunday morning the city was practically snowbound. Paul breakfasted late, and in the afternoon he fell in with a wild San Francisco boy, a freshman at Yale, who said he had run down for a "little flyer" over Sunday. The young man offered to show Paul the night side of the town, and the two boys went off together after dinner, not returning to the hotel until seven o'clock the next morning. They had started out in the confiding warmth of a champagne friendship, but their parting in the elevator was singularly cool. The freshman pulled himself together to make his train, and Paul went to bed. He awoke at two o'clock in the afternoon, very thirsty and dizzy, and rang for ice-water, coffee, and the Pittsburgh papers.

On the part of the hotel management, Paul excited no suspicion. There was this to be said for him, that he wore his spoils with dignity and in no way made himself conspicuous. His chief greediness lay in his ears and eyes, and his excesses were not offensive ones. His dearest pleasures were the grey winter twilights in his sitting-room; his quiet enjoyment of his flowers, his clothes, his wide divan, his cigarette, and his sense of power. He could not remember a time when he had felt so at peace with himself. The mere release from the necessity of petty lying, lying every day and every day, restored his self-respect. He had never lied for pleasure, even at school; but to make himself noticed and admired, to assert his difference from other Cordelia Street boys; and he felt a good deal more manly, more honest, even, now that he had no need for boastful pretensions, now that he could, as his actor friends used to say, "dress the part." It was characteristic that remorse did not occur to him. His golden days went by without a shadow, and he made each as perfect as he could.

On the eighth day after his arrival in New York, he found the whole affair exploited in the Pittsburgh papers, exploited with a wealth of detail which indicated that local news of a sensational nature was at a low ebb. The firm of Denny & Carson announced that the boy's father had refunded the full amount of his theft, and that they had no intention of prosecuting. The Cumberland minister had been interviewed, and expressed his hope of yet reclaiming the motherless lad, and Paul's Sabbath-School teacher declared that she would spare no effort to that end. The rumor had reached Pittsburgh that the boy had been seen in a New York hotel, and his father had gone East to find him and bring him home.

Paul had just come in to dress for dinner; he sank into the chair, weak in the knees, and clasped his head in his hands. It was to be worse than jail, even; the tepid waters of Cordelia Street were to close over him finally and forever. The grey monotony stretched before him in hopeless, unrelieved years;—Sabbath School, Young People's Meeting, the yellow-papered room, the damp dish-towels; it all rushed back upon him with sickening vividness. He had the old feeling that the orchestra had suddenly stopped, the sinking sensation that the play was over. The sweat broke out on his face, and he sprang to his feet, looked about him with his white, conscious smile, and winked at himself in the mirror. With something of the childish belief in miracles with which he had so often gone to class, all his lessons unlearned, Paul dressed and dashed whistling down the corridor to the elevator.

60   He had no sooner entered the dining-room and caught the measure of the music than his remembrance was lightened by his old elastic power of claiming the moment, mounting with it, and finding it all-sufficient. The glare and glitter about him, the mere scenic accessories had again, and for the last time, their old potency. He would show

himself that he was game, he would finish the thing splendidly. He doubted, more than ever, the existence of Cordelia Street, and for the first time he drank his wine recklessly. Was he not, after all, one of these fortunate beings? Was he not still himself, and in his own place? He drummed a nervous accompaniment to the music and looked about him, telling himself over and over that it had paid.

He reflected drowsily, to the swell of the violin and the chill sweetness of his wine, that he might have done it more wisely. He might have caught an outbound steamer and been well out of their clutches before now. But the other side of the world had seemed too far away and too uncertain then; he could not have waited for it; his need had been too sharp. If he had to choose over again, he would do the same thing tomorrow. He looked affectionately about the dining-room, now gilded with a soft mist. Ah, it had paid indeed!

Paul was awakened next morning by a painful throbbing in his head and feet. He had thrown himself across the bed without undressing, and had slept with his shoes on. His limbs and hands were lead-heavy, and his tongue and throat were parched. There came upon him one of those fateful attacks of clear-headedness that never occurred except when he was physically exhausted and his nerves hung loose. He lay still and closed his eyes and let the tide of realities wash over him.

His father was in New York; "stopping at some joint or other," he told himself. The memory of successive summers on the front stoop fell upon him like a weight of black water. He had not a hundred dollars left; and he knew now, more than ever, that money was everything, the wall that stood between all he loathed and all he wanted. The thing was winding itself up; he had thought of that on his first glorious day in New York, and had even provided a way to snap the thread. It lay on his dressing-table now; he had got it out last night when he came blindly up from dinner—but the shiny metal hurt his eyes, and he disliked the look of it, anyway.

He rose and moved about with a painful effort, succumbing now and again to attacks of nausea. It was the old depression exaggerated; all the world had become Cordelia Street. Yet somehow he was not afraid of anything, was absolutely calm; perhaps because he had looked into the dark corner at last, and knew. It was bad enough, what he saw there; but somehow not so bad as his long fear of it had been. He saw everything clearly now. He had a feeling that he had made the best of it, that he had lived the sort of life he was meant to live, and for half an hour he sat staring at the revolver. But he told himself that was not the way, so he went downstairs and took a cab to the ferry.

65   When Paul arrived at Newark, he got off the train and took another cab, directing the driver to follow the Pennsylvania tracks out of town. The snow lay heavy on the roadways and had drifted deep in the open fields. Only here and there the dead grass or dried weed stalks projected, singularly black, above it.

Once well into the country, Paul dismissed the carriage and walked, floundering along the tracks, his mind a medley of irrelevant things. He seemed to hold in his brain an actual picture of everything he had seen that morning. He remembered every feature of both his drivers, the toothless old woman from whom he had bought the red flowers in his coat, the agent from whom he had got his ticket, and all of his fellow-passengers on the ferry. His mind, unable to cope with vital matters near at hand, worked feverishly and deftly at sorting and grouping these images. They made for him a part of the ugliness of the world, of the ache in his head, and the bitter burning on his tongue. He stooped and put a handful of snow into his mouth as he walked, but that, too, seemed hot. When he reached a little hillside, where the tracks ran through a cut some twenty feet below him, he stopped and sat down.

The carnations in his coat were drooping with cold, he noticed; all their red glory over. It occurred to him that all the flowers he had seen in the show windows that first night must have gone the same way, long before this. It was only one splendid breath they had, in spite of their brave mockery at the winter outside the glass. It was a losing game in the end, it seemed, this revolt against the homilies by which the world is run. Paul took one of the blossoms carefully from his coat and scooped a little hole in the snow, where he covered it up. Then he dozed awhile, from his weak condition, seeming insensible to the cold.

The sound of an approaching train woke him and he started to his feet, remembering only his resolution, and afraid lest he should be too late. He stood watching the approaching locomotive, his teeth chattering, his lips drawn away from them in a frightened smile; once or twice he glanced nervously sidewise, as though he were being watched. When the right moment came, he jumped. As he fell, the folly of his haste occurred to him with merciless clearness, the vastness of what he had left undone. There flashed through his brain, clearer than ever before, the blue of Adriatic water, the yellow of Algerian sands.

He felt something strike his chest—his body being thrown swiftly through the air, on and on, immeasurably far and fast, while his limbs gently relaxed. Then, because the picture making mechanism was crushed, the disturbing visions flashed into black, and Paul dropped back into the immense design of things.

QUESTIONS

1. Technically we should classify the author's point of view as omniscient, for she enters into the minds of characters at will. Nevertheless, early in the story the focus changes rather abruptly. Locate the point where the change occurs. Through whose eyes do we see Paul prior to this point? Through whose eyes do we see him afterward? What is the purpose of this shift? Does it offer any clue to the purpose of the story?

2. What details of Paul's appearance and behavior, as his teachers see him, indicate that he is different from most other boys?

3. Explain Paul's behavior. Why does he lie? What does he hate? What does he want? Contrast the world of Cordelia Street with the worlds that Paul finds at Carnegie Hall, at the Schenley, at the stock theater, and in New York.

4. Is Paul artistic? Describe his reactions to music, to painting, to literature, and to the theater. What value does he find in the arts?

5. Is Paul a static or a developing character? If the latter, at what points does he change? Why?

6. What do Paul's clandestine trips to the stock theater, his trip to New York, and his suicide have in common?

7. Compare Paul and the college boy he meets in New York (paragraphs 56). Are they two of a kind? If not, how do they differ?

8. What are the implications of the title? What does the last sentence of the story do to the reader's focus of vision?

9. Are there any clues to the causes of Paul's unusual personality? How many? In what is the author chiefly interested?

10. In what two cities is the story set? Does this choice of setting have any symbolic value? Could the story have been set as validly in Cleveland and Detroit? In San Francisco and Los Angeles? In New Orleans and Birmingham?

Shirley Jackson

The Lottery

The morning of June 27th was clear and sunny, with the fresh warmth of a full-summer day; the flowers were blossoming profusely and the grass was richly green. The people of the village began to gather in the square, between the post office and the bank, around ten o'clock; in some towns there were so many people that the lottery took two days and had to be started on June 26th, but in this village, where there were only about three hundred people, the whole lottery took less than two

THE LOTTERY   First published in 1948. Shirley Jackson (1919–1965) was born in San Francisco and spent most of her early life in California. After her marriage in 1940 she lived in a quiet rural community in Vermont.

hours, so it could begin at ten o'clock in the morning and still be through in time to allow the villagers to get home for noon dinner.

The children assembled first, of course. School was recently over for the summer, and the feeling of liberty sat uneasily on most of them; they tended to gather together quietly for a while before they broke into boisterous play, and their talk was still of the classroom and the teacher, of books and reprimands. Bobby Martin had already stuffed his pockets full of stones, and the other boys soon followed his example, selecting the smoothest and roundest stones; Bobby and Harry Jones and Dickie Delacroix—the villagers pronounced this name "Dellacroy"—eventually made a great pile of stones in one corner of the square and guarded it against the raids of the other boys. The girls stood aside, talking among themselves, looking over their shoulders at the boys, and the very small children rolled in the dust or clung to the hands of their older brothers or sisters.

Soon the men began to gather, surveying their own children, speaking of planting and rain, tractors and taxes. They stood together, away from the pile of stones in the corner, and their jokes were quiet and they smiled rather than laughed. The women, wearing faded house dresses and sweaters, came shortly after their menfolk. They greeted one another and exchanged bits of gossip as they went to join their husbands. Soon the women, standing by their husbands, began to call to their children, and the children came reluctantly, having to be called four or five times. Bobby Martin ducked under his mother's grasping hand and ran, laughing, back to the pile of stones. His father spoke up sharply, and Bobby came quickly and took his place between his father and his oldest brother.

The lottery was conducted—as were the square dances, the teenage club, the Halloween program—by Mr. Summers, who had time and energy to devote to civic activities. He was a round-faced, jovial man and he ran the coal business, and people were sorry for him, because he had no children and his wife was a scold. When he arrived in the square, carrying the black wooden box, there was a murmur of conversation among the villagers, and he waved and called, "Little late today, folks." The postmaster, Mr. Graves, followed him, carrying a three-legged stool, and the stool was put in the center of the square and Mr. Summers set the black box down on it. The villagers kept their distance, leaving a space between themselves and the stool, and when Mr. Summers said, "Some of you fellows want to give me a hand?" there was a hesitation before two men, Mr. Martin and his oldest son, Baxter, came forward to hold the box steady on the stool while Mr. Summers stirred up the papers inside it.

The original paraphernalia for the lottery had been lost long ago,   5
and the black box now resting on the stool had been put into use even
before Old Man Warner, the oldest man in town, was born. Mr.
Summers spoke frequently to the villagers about making a new box,
but no one liked to upset even as much tradition as was represented by
the black box. There was a story that the present box had been made
with some pieces of the box that had preceded it, the one that had been
constructed when the first people settled down to make a village here.
Every year, after the lottery, Mr. Summers began talking again about a
new box, but every year the subject was allowed to fade off without
anything's being done. The black box grew shabbier each year; by now it
was no longer completely black but splintered badly along one side to
show the original wood color, and in some places faded or stained.

Mr. Martin and his oldest son, Baxter, held the black box securely
on the stool until Mr. Summers had stirred the papers thoroughly with
his hand. Because so much of the ritual had been forgotten or discarded,
Mr. Summers had been successful in having slips of paper substituted for
the chips of wood that had been used for generations. Chips of wood,
Mr. Summers had argued, had been all very well when the village was
tiny, but now that the population was more than three hundred and
likely to keep on growing, it was necessary to use something that would
fit more easily into the black box. The night before the lottery, Mr.
Summers and Mr. Graves made up the slips of paper and put them in the
box, and it was then taken to the safe of Mr. Summers's coal company
and locked up until Mr. Summers was ready to take it to the square next
morning. The rest of the year, the box was put away, sometimes one
place, sometimes another; it had spent one year in Mr. Graves's barn and
another year underfoot in the post office, and sometimes it was set on a
shelf in the Martin grocery and left there.

There was a great deal of fussing to be done before Mr. Summers
declared the lottery open. There were the lists to make up—of heads of
families, heads of households in each family, members of each household
in each family. There was the proper swearing-in of Mr. Summers by the
postmaster, as the official of the lottery; at one time, some people
remembered, there had been a recital of some sort, performed by the
official of the lottery, a perfunctory, tuneless chant that had been rattled
off duly each year; some people believed that the official of the lottery
used to stand just so when he said or sang it, others believed that he was
supposed to walk among the people, but years and years ago this part of
the ritual had been allowed to lapse. There had been, also, a ritual salute,
which the official of the lottery had had to use in addressing each person
who came up to draw from the box, but this also had changed with time,

until now it was felt necessary only for the official to speak to each person approaching. Mr. Summers was very good at all this; in his clean white shirt and blue jeans, with one hand resting carelessly on the black box, he seemed very proper and important as he talked interminably to Mr. Graves and the Martins.

Just as Mr. Summers finally left off talking and turned to the assembled villagers, Mrs. Hutchinson came hurriedly along the path to the square, her sweater thrown over her shoulders, and slid into place in the back of the crowd. "Clean forgot what day it was," she said to Mrs. Delacroix, who stood next to her, and they both laughed softly. "Thought my old man was out back stacking wood," Mrs. Hutchinson went on, "and then I looked out the window and the kids were gone, and then I remembered it was the twenty-seventh and came a-running." She dried her hands on her apron, and Mrs. Delacroix said, "You're in time, though. They're still talking away up there."

Mrs. Hutchinson craned her neck to see through the crowd and found her husband and children standing near the front. She tapped Mrs. Delacroix on the arm as a farewell and began to make her way through the crowd. The people separated good-humoredly to let her through; two or three people said, in voices just loud enough to be heard across the crowd, "Here comes your Missus, Hutchinson," and "Bill, she made it after all." Mrs. Hutchinson reached her husband, and Mr. Summers, who had been waiting, said cheerfully, "Thought we were going to have to get on without you, Tessie." Mrs. Hutchinson said, grinning, "Wouldn't have me leave m'dishes in the sink, now, would you, Joe?" and soft laughter ran through the crowd as the people stirred back into position after Mrs. Hutchinson's arrival.

10   "Well, now," Mr. Summers said soberly, "guess we better get started, get this over with, so's we can go back to work. Anybody ain't here?"

"Dunbar," several people said. "Dunbar, Dunbar."

Mr. Summers consulted his list. "Clyde Dunbar," he said. "That's right. He's broke his leg, hasn't he? Who's drawing for him?"

"Me, I guess," a woman said, and Mr. Summers turned to look at her. "Wife draws for her husband," Mr. Summers said. "Don't you have a grown boy to do it for you, Janey?" Although Mr. Summers and everyone else in the village knew the answer perfectly well, it was the business of the official of the lottery to ask such questions formally. Mr. Summers waited with an expression of polite interest while Mrs. Dunbar answered.

"Horace's not but sixteen yet," Mrs. Dunbar said regretfully. "Guess I gotta fill in for the old man this year."

"Right," Mr. Summers said. He made a note on the list he was   15
holding. Then he asked, "Watson boy drawing this year?"

A tall boy in the crowd raised his hand. "Here," he said. "I'm
drawing for m'mother and me." He blinked his eyes nervously and
ducked his head as several voices in the crowd said things like "Good
fellow, Jack," and "Glad to see your mother's got a man to do it."

"Well," Mr. Summers said, "guess that's everyone. Old Man Warner
make it?"

"Here," a voice said, and Mr. Summers nodded.

A sudden hush fell on the crowd as Mr. Summers cleared his
throat and looked at the list. "All ready?" he called. "Now, I'll read
the names—heads of families first—and the men come up and take a
paper out of the box. Keep the paper folded in your hand without
looking at it until everyone has had a turn. Everything clear?"

The people had done it so many times that they only half listened to   20
the directions; most of them were quiet, wetting their lips, not looking
around. Then Mr. Summers raised one hand high and said, "Adams." A
man disengaged himself from the crowd and came forward. "Hi, Steve,"
Mr. Summers said, and Mr. Adams said, "Hi, Joe." They grinned at one
another humorlessly and nervously. Then Mr. Adams reached into the
black box and took out a folded paper. He held it firmly by one corner as
he turned and went hastily back to his place in the crowd, where he
stood a little apart from his family, not looking down at his hand.

"Allen," Mr. Summers said. "Anderson . . . Bentham."

"Seems like there's no time at all between lotteries any more," Mrs.
Delacroix said to Mrs. Graves in the back row. "Seems like we got
through with the last one only last week."

"Time sure goes fast," Mrs. Graves said.

"Clark . . . Delacroix."

"There goes my old man," Mrs. Delacroix said. She held her breath   25
while her husband went forward.

"Dunbar," Mr. Summers said, and Mrs. Dunbar went steadily to the
box while one of the women said, "Go on, Janey," and another said,
"There she goes."

"We're next," Mrs. Graves said. She watched while Mr. Graves
came around from the side of the box, greeted Mr. Summers gravely,
and selected a slip of paper from the box. By now, all through the crowd
there were men holding the small folded papers in their large hands,
turning them over and over nervously. Mrs. Dunbar and her two sons
stood together, Mrs. Dunbar holding the slip of paper.

"Harburt . . . Hutchinson."

"Get up there, Bill," Mrs. Hutchinson said, and the people near her laughed.

30   "Jones."

"They do say," Mr. Adams said to Old Man Warner, who stood next to him, "that over in the north village they're talking of giving up the lottery."

Old Man Warner snorted. "Pack of crazy fools," he said. "Listening to the young folks, nothing's good enough for *them*. Next thing you know, they'll be wanting to go back to living in caves, nobody work any more, live *that* way for a while. Used to be a saying about 'Lottery in June, corn be heavy soon.' First thing you know, we'd all be eating stewed chickweed and acorns. There's *always* been a lottery," he added petulantly. "Bad enough to see young Joe Summers up there joking with everybody."

"Some places have already quit lotteries," Mrs. Adams said.

"Nothing but trouble in *that*," Old Man Warner said stoutly. "Pack of young fools."

35   "Martin." And Bobby Martin watched his father go forward. "Overdyke . . . Percy."

"I wish they'd hurry," Mrs. Dunbar said to her older son. "I wish they'd hurry."

"They're almost through," her son said.

"You get ready to run tell Dad," Mrs. Dunbar said.

Mr. Summers called his own name and then stepped forward precisely and selected a slip from the box. Then he called, "Warner."

40   "Seventy-seventh year I been in the lottery," Old Man Warner said as he went through the crowd. "Seventy-seventh time."

"Watson." The tall boy came awkwardly through the crowd. Someone said, "Don't be nervous, Jack," and Mr. Summers said, "Take your time, son."

"Zanini."

After that, there was a long pause, a breathless pause, until Mr. Summers, holding his slip of paper in the air, said, "All right, fellows." For a minute, no one moved, and then all the slips of paper were opened. Suddenly, all the women began to speak at once, saying, "Who is it?" "Who's got it?" "Is it the Dunbars?" "Is it the Watsons?" Then the voices began to say, "It's Hutchinson. It's Bill." "Bill Hutchinson's got it."

"Go tell your father," Mrs. Dunbar said to her older son.

45   People began to look around to see the Hutchinsons. Bill Hutchinson was standing quiet, staring down at the paper in his hand. Suddenly, Tessie Hutchinson shouted to Mr. Summers. "You didn't give him time enough to take any paper he wanted. I saw you. It wasn't fair."

"Be a good sport, Tessie," Mrs. Delacroix called, and Mrs. Graves said, "All of us took the same chance."

"Shut up, Tessie," Bill Hutchinson said.

"Well, everyone," Mr. Summers said, "that was done pretty fast, and now we've got to be hurrying a little more to get done in time." He consulted his next list. "Bill," he said, "you draw for the Hutchinson family. You got any other households in the Hutchinsons?"

"There's Don and Eva," Mrs. Hutchinson yelled. "Make *them* take their chance!"

"Daughters draw with their husband's families, Tessie," Mr. Sum- 50 mers said gently. "You know that as well as anyone else."

"It wasn't *fair*," Tessie said.

"I guess not, Joe," Bill Hutchinson said regretfully. "My daughter draws with her husband's family, that's only fair. And I've got no other family except the kids."

"Then, as far as drawing for families is concerned, it's you," Mr. Summers said in explanation, "and as far as drawing for households is concerned, that's you, too. Right?"

"Right," Bill Hutchinson said.

"How many kids, Bill?" Mr. Summers asked formally. 55

"Three," Bill Hutchinson said. "There's Bill, Jr., and Nancy, and little Dave. And Tessie and me."

"All right, then," Mr. Summers said. "Harry, you got their tickets back?"

Mr. Graves nodded and held up the slips of paper. "Put them in the box, then," Mr. Summers directed. "Take Bill's and put it in."

"I think we ought to start over," Mrs. Hutchinson said, as quietly as she could. "I tell you it wasn't *fair*. You didn't give him time enough to choose. *Every*body saw that."

Mr. Graves had selected the five slips and put them in the box, and 60 he dropped all the papers but those onto the ground, where the breeze caught them and lifted them off.

"Listen, everybody," Mrs. Hutchinson was saying to the people around her.

"Ready, Bill?" Mr. Summers asked, and Bill Hutchinson, with one quick glance around at his wife and children, nodded.

"Remember," Mr. Summers said, "take the slips and keep them folded until each person has taken one. Harry, you help little Dave." Mr. Graves took the hand of the little boy, who came willingly with him up to the box. "Take a paper out of the box, Davy," Mr. Summers said. Davy put his hand into the box and laughed. "Take just *one* paper," Mr. Summers said. "Harry, you hold it for him." Mr. Graves took the child's hand and removed the folded paper from the tight fist and held it while little Dave stood next to him and looked up at him wonderingly.

"Nancy next," Mr. Summers said. Nancy was twelve, and her school friends breathed heavily as she went forward, switching her skirt, and took a slip daintily from the box. "Bill, Jr.," Mr. Summers said, and Billy, his face red and his feet over-large, nearly knocked the box over as he got a paper out. "Tessie," Mr. Summers said. She hesitated for a minute, looking around defiantly, and then set her lips and went up to the box. She snatched a paper out and held it behind her.

65   "Bill," Mr. Summers said, and Bill Hutchinson reached into the box and felt around, bringing his hand out at last with the slip of paper in it.

The crowd was quiet. A girl whispered, "I hope it's not Nancy," and the sound of the whisper reached the edges of the crowd.

"It's not the way it used to be," Old Man Warner said clearly. "People ain't the way they used to be."

"All right," Mr. Summers said. "Open the papers. Harry, you open little Dave's."

Mr. Graves opened the slip of paper and there was a general sigh through the crowd as he held it up and everyone could see that it was blank. Nancy and Bill, Jr., opened theirs at the same time, and both beamed and laughed, turning around to the crowd and holding their slips of paper above their heads.

70   "Tessie," Mr. Summers said. There was a pause, and then Mr. Summers looked at Bill Hutchinson, and Bill unfolded his paper and showed it. It was blank.

"It's Tessie," Mr. Summers said, and his voice was hushed. "Show us her paper, Bill."

Bill Hutchinson went over to his wife and forced the slip of paper out of her hand. It had a black spot on it, the black spot Mr. Summers had made the night before with the heavy pencil in the coal-company office. Bill Hutchinson held it up, and there was a stir in the crowd.

"All right, folks," Mr. Summers said. "Let's finish quickly."

Although the villagers had forgotten the ritual and lost the original black box, they still remembered to use stones. The pile of stones the boys had made earlier was ready; there were stones on the ground with the blowing scraps of paper that had come out of the box. Mrs. Delacroix selected a stone so large she had to pick it up with both hands and turned to Mrs. Dunbar. "Come on," she said. "Hurry up."

75   Mrs. Dunbar had small stones in both hands, and she said, gasping for breath, "I can't run at all. You'll have to go ahead and I'll catch up with you."

The children had stones already, and someone gave little Davy Hutchinson a few pebbles.

Tessie Hutchinson was in the center of a cleared space by now, and she held her hands out desperately as the villagers moved in on her. "It isn't fair," she said. A stone hit her on the side of the head.

Old Man Warner was saying, "Come on, come on, everyone." Steve Adams was in front of the crowd of villagers, with Mrs. Graves beside him.

"It isn't fair, it isn't right," Mrs. Hutchinson screamed, and then they were upon her.

QUESTIONS

1. What is a "lottery"? How does the title lead you to expect something very different from what the story presents?
2. What is a scapegoat? Who is the scapegoat in this story? What other examples of scapegoating can you recall?
3. What normal law of probability has been suspended in this story? Granting this initial implausibility, does the story proceed naturally?
4. What is the significance of the fact that the original box has been lost and many parts of the ritual have been forgotten? Can you find a statement in the story that most likely explains the original purpose of the ritual?
5. What different attitudes toward the ritual stoning are represented by (a) Mr. Summers, (b) Old Man Warner, (c) Mr. and Mrs. Adams, (d) Mrs. Hutchinson, (e) the villagers in general? Which attitude most closely reflects the point of the story?
6. By transporting a primitivistic ritual into a modern setting, the story reveals something about human nature and human society. What?
7. Many modern customs or rituals have developed from primitive origins (for example, the decoration of a Christmas tree). Can you identify some others? What would set them apart from the ritual stoning in this story?
8. Can you support a claim that this story is presented from the objective point of view? Why is the dispassionate, matter-of-fact tone of the story so effective?

Katherine Anne Porter
The Jilting of Granny Weatherall

She flicked her wrist neatly out of Doctor Harry's pudgy careful fingers and pulled the sheet up to her chin. The brat ought to be in knee breeches. Doctoring around the country with spectacles on his nose!

THE JILTING OF GRANNY WEATHERALL   First published in 1930. Katherine Anne Porter (1890–1980) was born and grew up in Texas, was educated at convent schools in New Orleans, and lived in Chicago, Fort Worth, Mexico, and New York City before writing this story.

"Get along now, take your schoolbooks and go. There's nothing wrong with me."

Doctor Harry spread a warm paw like a cushion on her forehead where the forked green vein danced and made her eyelids twitch. "Now, now, be a good girl, and we'll have you up in no time."

"That's no way to speak to a woman nearly eighty years old just because she's down. I'd have you respect your elders, young man."

"Well, Missy, excuse me." Doctor Harry patted her cheek. "But I've got to warn you, haven't I? You're a marvel, but you must be careful or you're going to be good and sorry."

5   "Don't tell me what I'm going to be. I'm on my feet now, morally speaking. It's Cornelia. I had to go to bed to get rid of her."

Her bones felt loose, and floated around in her skin, and Doctor Harry floated like a balloon around the foot of the bed. He floated and pulled down his waistcoat and swung his glasses on a cord. "Well, stay where you are, it certainly can't hurt you."

"Get along and doctor your sick," said Granny Weatherall. "Leave a well woman alone. I'll call for you when I want you. . . . Where were you forty years ago when I pulled through milk-leg and double pneumonia? You weren't even born. Don't let Cornelia lead you on," she shouted, because Doctor Harry appeared to float up to the ceiling and out. "I pay my own bills, and I don't throw my money away on nonsense!"

She meant to wave good-by, but it was too much trouble. Her eyes closed of themselves, it was like a dark curtain drawn around the bed. The pillow rose and floated under her, pleasant as a hammock in a light wind. She listened to the leaves rustling outside the window. No, somebody was swishing newspapers: no, Cornelia and Doctor Harry were whispering together. She leaped broad awake, thinking they whispered in her ear.

"She was never like this, *never* like this!" "Well, what can we expect?" "Yes, eighty years old. . . ."

10   Well, and what if she was? She still had ears. It was like Cornelia to whisper around doors. She always kept things secret in such a public way. She was always being tactful and kind. Cornelia was dutiful; that was the trouble with her. Dutiful and good: "So good and dutiful," said Granny, "that I'd like to spank her." She saw herself spanking Cornelia and making a fine job of it.

"What'd you say, Mother?"

Granny felt her face tying up in hard knots.

"Can't a body think, I'd like to know?"

"I thought you might want something."

15   "I do. I want a lot of things. First off, go away and don't whisper."

She lay and drowsed, hoping in her sleep that the children would keep out and let her rest a minute. It had been a long day. Not that she was tired. It was always pleasant to snatch a minute now and then. There was always so much to be done, let me see: tomorrow.

Tomorrow was far away and there was nothing to trouble about. Things were finished somehow when the time came; thank God there was always a little margin over for peace: then a person could spread out the plan of life and tuck in the edges orderly. It was good to have everything clean and folded away, with the hair brushes and tonic bottles sitting straight on the white embroidered linen: the day started without fuss and the pantry shelves laid out with rows of jelly glasses and brown jugs and white stone-china jars with blue whirligigs and words painted on them: coffee, tea, sugar, ginger, cinnamon, allspice: and the bronze clock with the lion on top nicely dusted off. The dust that lion could collect in twenty-four hours! The box in the attic with all those letters tied up, well, she'd have to go through that tomorrow. All those letters—George's letters and John's letters and her letters to them both—lying around for the children to find afterwards made her uneasy. Yes, that would be tomorrow's business. No use to let them know how silly she had been once.

While she was rummaging around she found death in her mind and it felt clammy and unfamiliar. She had spent so much time preparing for death there was no need for bringing it up again. Let it take care of itself now. When she was sixty she had felt very old, finished, and went around making farewell trips to see her children and grandchildren, with a secret in her mind: This is the very last of your mother, children! Then she made her will and came down with a long fever. That was all just a notion like a lot of other things, but it was lucky too, for she had once for all got over the idea of dying for a long time. Now she couldn't be worried. She hoped she had better sense now. Her father had lived to be one hundred and two years old and had drunk a noggin of strong hot toddy on his last birthday. He told the reporters it was his daily habit, and he owed his long life to that. He had made quite a scandal and was very pleased about it. She believed she'd just plague Cornelia a little.

"Cornelia! Cornelia!" No footsteps, but a sudden hand on her cheek. "Bless you, where have you been?"

"Here, Mother."   20

"Well, Cornelia, I want a noggin of hot toddy."

"Are you cold, darling?"

"I'm chilly, Cornelia. Lying in bed stops the circulation. I must have told you that a thousand times."

Well, she could just hear Cornelia telling her husband that Mother was getting a little childish and they'd have to humor her. The thing that most annoyed her was that Cornelia thought she was deaf, dumb, and blind. Little hasty glances and tiny gestures tossed around her and over her head saying, "Don't cross her, let her have her way, she's eighty years old," and she sitting there as if she lived in a thin glass cage. Sometimes Granny almost made up her mind to pack up and move back to her own house where nobody could remind her every minute that she was old. Wait, wait, Cornelia, till your own children whisper behind your back!

25   In her day she had kept a better house and had got more work done. She wasn't too old yet for Lydia to be driving eighty miles for advice when one of the children jumped the track, and Jimmy still dropped in and talked things over: "Now, Mammy, you've a good business head, I want to know what you think of this? . . ." Old. Cornelia couldn't change the furniture around without asking. Little things, little things! They had been so sweet when they were little. Granny wished the old days were back again with the children young and everything to be done over. It had been a hard pull, but not too much for her. When she thought of all the food she had cooked, and all the clothes she had cut and sewed, and all the gardens she had made—well, the children showed it. There they were, made out of her, and they couldn't get away from that. Sometimes she wanted to see John again and point to them and say, Well, I didn't do so badly, did I? But that would have to wait. That was for tomorrow. She used to think of him as a man, but now all the children were older than their father, and he would be a child beside her if she saw him now. It seemed strange and there was something wrong in the idea. Why, he couldn't possibly recognize her. She had fenced in a hundred acres once, digging the post holes herself and clamping the wires with just a negro boy to help. That changed a woman. John would be looking for a young woman with the peaked Spanish comb in her hair and the painted fan. Digging post holes changed a woman. Riding country roads in the winter when women had their babies was another thing: sitting up nights with sick horses and sick negroes and sick children and hardly ever losing one. John, I hardly ever lost one of them! John would see that in a minute, that would be something he could understand, she wouldn't have to explain anything!

It made her feel like rolling up her sleeves and putting the whole place to rights again. No matter if Cornelia was determined to be everywhere at once, there were a great many things left undone on this place. She would start tomorrow and do them. It was good to be strong enough for everything, even if all you made melted and changed and slipped under your hands, so that by the time you finished you almost forgot what you were working for. What was it I set out to do? she asked herself intently, but she could not remember. A fog rose over the valley, she saw it marching across the creek swallowing the trees and moving up the hill like an army of ghosts. Soon it would be at the near edge of the orchard, and then it was time to go in and light the lamps. Come in, children, don't stay out in the night air.

Lighting the lamps had been beautiful. The children huddled up to her and breathed like little calves waiting at the bars in the twilight. Their eyes followed the match and watched the flame rise and settle in a blue curve, then they moved away from her. The lamp was lit, they didn't have to be scared and hang on to mother any more. Never, never, never more. God, for all my life I thank Thee. Without Thee, my God, I could never have done it. Hail, Mary, full of grace.

I want you to pick all the fruit this year and see that nothing is wasted. There's always someone who can use it. Don't let good things rot for want of using. You waste life when you waste good food. Don't let things get lost. It's bitter to lose things. Now, don't let me get to thinking, not when I am tired and taking a little nap before supper. . . .

The pillow rose about her shoulders and pressed against her heart and the memory was being squeezed out of it: oh, push down the pillow, somebody: it would smother her if she tried to hold it. Such a fresh breeze blowing and such a green day with no threats in it. But he had not come, just the same. What does a woman do when she has put on the white veil and set out the white cake for a man and he doesn't come? She tried to remember. No, I swear he never harmed me but in that. He never harmed me but in that . . . and what if he did? There was the day, the day, but a whirl of dark smoke rose and covered it, crept up and over into the bright field where everything was planted so carefully in orderly rows. That was hell, she knew hell when she saw it. For sixty years she had prayed against remembering him and against losing her soul in the deep pit of hell, and now the two things were mingled in one and the thought of him was a smoky cloud from hell that moved and crept in her head when she had just got rid of Doctor Harry and was trying to rest a minute. Wounded vanity, Ellen, said a sharp voice in the top of her mind. Don't let your wounded vanity get the upper hand of you. Plenty of girls get jilted. You were jilted, weren't you? Then stand up to it. Her eyelids wavered and let in streamers of blue-gray light like tissue paper over her eyes. She must get up and pull the shades down or she'd never sleep. She was in bed again and the shades were not down. How could that happen? Better turn over, hide from the light, sleeping in the light gave you nightmares. "Mother, how do you feel now?" and a stinging wetness on her forehead. But I don't like having my face washed in cold water!

30   Hapsy? George? Lydia? Jimmy? No, Cornelia, and her features were swollen and full of little puddles. "They're coming, darling, they'll all be here soon." Go wash your face, child, you look funny.

Instead of obeying, Cornelia knelt down and put her head on the pillow. She seemed to be talking but there was no sound. "Well, are you tongue-tied? Whose birthday is it? Are you going to give a party?"

Cornelia's mouth moved urgently in strange shapes. "Don't do that, you bother me, daughter."

"Oh, no, Mother. Oh, no. . . ."

Nonsense. It was strange about children. They disputed your every word. "No what, Cornelia?"

35   "Here's Doctor Harry."

"I won't see that boy again. He just left five minutes ago."

"That was this morning, Mother. It's night now. Here's the nurse."

"This is Doctor Harry, Mrs. Weatherall. I never saw you look so young and happy!"

"Ah, I'll never be young again—but I'd be happy if they'd let me lie in peace and get rested."

40   She thought she spoke up loudly, but no one answered. A warm weight on her forehead, a warm bracelet on her wrist, and a breeze went on whispering, trying to tell her something. A shuffle of leaves in the everlasting hand of God, He blew on them and they danced and rattled. "Mother, don't mind, we're going to give you a little hypodermic." "Look here, daughter, how do ants get in this bed? I saw sugar ants yesterday." Did you send for Hapsy too?

It was Hapsy she really wanted. She had to go a long way back through a great many rooms to find Hapsy standing with a baby on her arm. She seemed to herself to be Hapsy also, and the baby on Hapsy's arm was Hapsy and himself and herself, all at once, and there was no surprise in the meeting. Then Hapsy melted from within and turned flimsy as gray gauze and the baby was a gauzy shadow, and Hapsy came up close and said, "I thought you'd never come," and looked at her very searchingly and said, "You haven't changed a bit!" They leaned forward to kiss, when Cornelia began whispering from a long way off, "Oh, is there anything you want to tell me? Is there anything I can do for you?"

Yes, she had changed her mind after sixty years and she would like to see George. I want you to find George. Find him and be sure to tell him I forgot him. I want him to know I had my husband just the same and my children and my house like any other woman. A good house too and a good husband that I loved and fine children out of him. Better than I hoped for even. Tell him I was given back everything he took away and more. Oh, no, oh, God, no, there was something else besides the house and the man and the children. Oh, surely they were not all? What was it? Something not given back. . . . Her breath crowded down under her ribs and grew into a monstrous frightening shape with cutting edges; it bored up into her head, and the agony was unbelievable: Yes, John, get the Doctor now, no more talk, my time has come.

When this one was born it should be the last. The last. It should have been born first, for it was the one she had truly wanted. Everything came in good time. Nothing left out, left over. She was strong, in three days she would be as well as ever. Better. A woman needed milk in her to have her full health.

"Mother, do you hear me?"

"I've been telling you—"   45

"Mother, Father Connolly's here."

"I went to Holy Communion only last week. Tell him I'm not so sinful as all that."

"Father just wants to speak to you."

He could speak as much as he pleased. It was like him to drop in and inquire about her soul as if it were a teething baby, and then stay on for a cup of tea and a round of cards and gossip. He always had a funny story of some sort, usually about an Irishman who made his little mistakes and confessed them, and the point lay in some absurd thing he would blurt out in the confessional showing his struggles between native piety and original sin. Granny felt easy about her soul. Cornelia, where are your manners? Give Father Connolly a chair. She had her secret comfortable understanding with a few favorite saints who cleared a straight road to God for her. All as surely signed and sealed as the papers for the new Forty Acres. Forever . . . heirs and assigns forever. Since the day the wedding cake was not cut, but thrown out and wasted. The whole bottom dropped out of the world, and there she was blind and sweating with nothing under her feet and the walls falling away. His hand had caught her under the breast, she had not fallen, there was the freshly polished floor with the green rug on it, just as before. He had cursed like a sailor's parrot and said, "I'll kill him for you." Don't lay a hand on him, for my sake leave something to God. "Now, Ellen, you must believe what I tell you. . . ."

So there was nothing, nothing to worry about any more, except   50
sometimes in the night one of the children screamed in a nightmare, and they both hustled out shaking and hunting for the matches and calling, "There, wait a minute, here we are!" John, get the doctor now,

Hapsy's time has come. But there was Hapsy standing by the bed in a white cap. "Cornelia, tell Hapsy to take off her cap. I can't see her plain."

Her eyes opened very wide and the room stood out like a picture she had seen somewhere. Dark colors with the shadows rising towards the ceiling in long angles. The tall black dresser gleamed with nothing on it but John's picture, enlarged from a little one, with John's eyes very black when they should have been blue. You never saw him, so how do you know how he looked? But the man insisted the copy was perfect, it was very rich and handsome. For a picture, yes, but it's not my husband. The table by the bed had a linen cover and a candle and a crucifix. The light was blue from Cornelia's silk lampshades. No sort of light at all, just frippery. You had to live forty years with kerosene lamps to appreciate honest electricity. She felt very strong and she saw Doctor Harry with a rosy nimbus around him.

"You look like a saint, Doctor Harry, and I vow that's as near as you'll ever come to it."

"She's saying something."

"I heard you, Cornelia. What's all this carrying-on?"

55   "Father Connolly's saying—"

Cornelia's voice staggered and bumped like a cart in a bad road. It rounded corners and turned back again and arrived nowhere. Granny stepped up in the cart very lightly and reached for the reins, but a man sat beside her and she knew him by his hands, driving the cart. She did not look in his face, for she knew without seeing, but looked instead down the road where the trees leaned over and bowed to each other and a thousand birds were singing a Mass. She felt like singing too, but she put her hand in the bosom of her dress and pulled out a rosary, and Father Connolly murmured Latin in a very solemn voice and tickled her feet. My God, will you stop that nonsense? I'm a married woman. What if he did run away and leave me to face the priest by myself? I found another a whole world better. I wouldn't have exchanged my husband for anybody except St. Michael himself, and you may tell him that for me with a thank you in the bargain.

Light flashed on her closed eyelids, and a deep roaring shook her. Cornelia, is that lightning? I hear thunder. There's going to be a storm. Close all the windows. Call the children in. . . . "Mother, here we are, all of us." "Is that you, Hapsy?" "Oh, no, I'm Lydia. We drove as fast as we could." Their faces drifted above her, drifted away. The rosary fell out of her hands and Lydia put it back. Jimmy tried to help, their hands fumbled together, and Granny closed two fingers around Jimmy's thumb. Beads wouldn't do, it must be something alive. She was so amazed her thoughts ran round and round. So, my dear Lord, this is my death and I wasn't even thinking about it. My children have come to see me die. But I can't, it's not time. Oh, I always hated surprises. I wanted to give Cornelia the amethyst set—Cornelia, you're to have the amethyst set, but Hapsy's to wear it when she wants, and, Doctor Harry, do shut up. Nobody sent for you. Oh, my dear Lord, do wait a minute. I meant to do something about the Forty Acres, Jimmy doesn't need it and Lydia will later on, with that worthless husband of hers. I meant to finish the altar cloth and send six bottles of wine to Sister Borgia for her dyspepsia. I want to send six bottles of wine to Sister Borgia, Father Connolly, now don't let me forget.

Cornelia's voice made short turns and tilted over and crashed. "Oh, Mother, oh, Mother, oh, Mother. . . ."

"I'm not going, Cornelia. I'm taken by surprise. I can't go."

You'll see Hapsy again. What about her? "I thought you'd never   60
come." Granny made a long journey outward, looking for Hapsy. What if I don't find her? What then? Her heart sank down and down, there was no bottom to death, she couldn't come to the end of it. The blue light from Cornelia's lampshade drew into a tiny point in the center of her brain, it flickered and winked like an eye, quietly it fluttered and dwindled. Granny lay curled down within herself, amazed and watchful, staring at the point of light that was herself; her body was now only a deeper mass of shadow in an endless darkness and this darkness would curl around the light and swallow it up. God, give a sign!

For the second time there was no sign. Again no bridegroom and the priest in the house. She could not remember any other sorrow because this grief wiped them all away. Oh, no, there's nothing more cruel than this—I'll never forgive it. She stretched herself with a deep breath and blew out the light.

QUESTIONS

1. Why is stream of consciousness appropriate in this story? What character-istics of Ellen Weatherall's condition does this narrative technique represent? How effectively does it reveal events of the past? How clearly does it reflect the present? What is gained by the lack of clarity?

2. The protagonist reveals herself to be in conflict with other persons, and with her physical environment, both in the past and in the present. Identify her antagonists. To what extent has she experienced conflicts within herself? To what extent is she now experiencing such conflicts?

3. What does her memory present as the major turning points in her life? Is it more than a coincidence that one of them occurs every twenty years? Considering the many major events in a woman's life that might have been climactic, how do the ones she recalls so vividly define her character?

4. What kind of life has Granny Weatherall made for herself? What have been her characteristic activities and attitudes? Can her "jilting" be seen as a partial cause for these activities and attitudes?

5. What is the significance of Hapsy? What religious symbolism is attached to the vision of her and her infant son (paragraph 41)?

6. Most critics understand the title to refer to two "jiltings," the one by her fiancé sixty years earlier, the other by God at the moment of her death. Can you justify this interpretation? Does the story have a determinate or indeterminate ending?

Ernest Hemingway

Hills Like White Elephants

The hills across the valley of the Ebro were long and white. On this side there was no shade and no trees and the station was between two lines of rails in the sun. Close against the side of the station there was the warm shadow of the building and a curtain, made of strings of bamboo beads, hung across the open door into the bar, to keep out flies. The American and the girl with him sat at a table in the shade, outside the building. It was very hot and the express from Barcelona would come in forty minutes. It stopped at this junction for two minutes and went on to Madrid.

"What should we drink?" the girl asked. She had taken off her hat and put it on the table.

"It's pretty hot," the man said.

"Let's drink beer."

5   "Dos cervezas," the man said into the curtain.

"Big ones?" a woman asked from the doorway.

"Yes. Two big ones."

The woman brought two glasses of beer and two felt pads. She put the felt pads and beer glasses on the table and looked at the man and the girl. The girl was looking off at the line of hills. They were white in the sun and the country was brown and dry.

"They look like white elephants," she said.

10   "I've never seen one," the man drank his beer.

"No, you wouldn't have."

"I might have," the man said. "Just because you say I wouldn't have doesn't prove anything."

HILLS LIKE WHITE ELEPHANTS   First published in 1927. Ernest Hemingway (1899–1961) was born and grew up in Oak Park, Illinois, with summer vacations in northern Michigan. By the time he wrote this story he had been wounded in Italy during World War I; had traveled extensively in Europe as a newspaper correspondent and writer; had married, fathered a son, been divorced, and remarried.

The girl looked at the bead curtain. "They've painted something on it," she said "What does it say?"

"Anis del Toro. It's a drink."

"Could we try it?"

The man called "Listen" through the curtain. The woman came out from the bar.

"Four reales."

"We want two Anis del Toro."

"With water?"

"Do you want it with water?"

"I don't know," the girl said. "Is it good with water?"

"It's all right."

"You want them with water?" asked the woman.

"Yes, with water."

"It tastes like licorice," the girl said and put the glass down.

"That's the way with everything."

"Yes," said the girl. "Everything tastes of licorice. Especially all the things you've waited so long for, like absinthe."

"Oh, cut it out."

"You started it," the girl said. "I was being amused. I was having a fine time."

"Well, let's try to have a fine time."

"All right. I was trying. I said the mountains looked like white elephants. Wasn't that bright?"

"That was bright."

"I wanted to try this new drink. That's all we do, isn't it—look at things and try new drinks."

"I guess so."

The girl looked across at the hills.

"They're lovely hills," she said. "They don't really look like white elephants. I just meant the coloring of their skin through the trees."

"Should we have another drink?"

"All right."

The warm wind blew the bead curtain against the table.

"The beer's nice and cool," the man said.

"It's lovely," the girl said.

"It's really an awfully simple operation, Jig," the man said. "It's not really an operation at all."

The girl looked at the ground the table legs rested on.

"I know you wouldn't mind it, Jig. It's really not anything. It's just to let the air in."

The girl did not say anything.

"I'll go with you and I'll stay with you all the time. They just let the air in and then it's all perfectly natural."

"Then what will we do afterward?"

"We'll be fine afterward. Just like we were before."

"What makes you think so?"

50   "That's the only thing that bothers us. It's the only thing that's made us unhappy."

The girl looked at the bead curtain, put her hand out and took hold of two strings of beads.

"And you think then we'll be all right and be happy."

"I know we will. You don't have to be afraid. I've known lots of people that have done it."

"So have I," said the girl. "And afterward they were all so happy."

55   "Well," the man said, "if you don't want to you don't have to. I wouldn't have you do it if you didn't want to. But I know it's perfectly simple."

"And you really want to?"

"I think it's the best thing to do. But I don't want you to do it if you don't really want to."

"And if I do it you'll be happy and things will be like they were and you'll love me?"

"I love you now. You know I love you."

60   "I know. But if I do it, then it will be nice again if I say things are like white elephants, and you'll like it?"

"I'll love it. I love it now but I just can't think about it. You know how I get when I worry."

"If I do it you won't ever worry."

"I won't worry about that because it's perfectly simple."

"Then I'll do it. Because I don't care about me."

65   "What do you mean?"

"I don't care about me."

"Well, I care about you."

"Oh yes. But I don't care about me. And I'll do it and then everything will be fine."

"I don't want you to do it if you feel that way."

70   The girl stood up and walked to the end of the station. Across, on the other side, were fields of grain and trees along the banks of the Ebro. Far away, beyond the river, were mountains. The shadow of a cloud moved across the field of grain and she saw the river through the trees.

"And we could have all this," she said. "And we could have everything and every day we make it more impossible."

"What did you say?"

"I said we could have everything."

"We can have everything."

"No, we can't."

"We can have the whole world."   75

"No, we can't."

"We can go everywhere."

"No, we can't. It isn't ours any more."

"It's ours."   80

"No, it isn't. And once they take it away, you never get it back."

"But they haven't taken it away."

"We'll wait and see."

"Come on back in the shade," he said. "You mustn't feel that way."

"I don't feel any way," the girl said. "I just know things."   85

"I don't want you to do anything that you don't want to do—"

"Nor that isn't good for me," she said. "I know. Could we have another beer."

"All right. But you've got to realize—"

"I realize," the girl said. "Can't we stop talking?"

They sat down at the table and the girl looked across at the hills on 90
the dry side of the valley and the man looked at her and at the table.

"You've got to realize," he said, "that I don't want you to do it if you don't want to. I'm perfectly willing to go through with it if it means anything to you."

"Doesn't it mean anything to you? We could get along."

"Of course it does. But I don't want anybody but you. I don't want any one else. And I know it's perfectly simple."

"Yes, you know it's perfectly simple."

"It's all right for you to say that, but I do know it."   95

"Would you do something for me now?"

"I'd do anything for you."

"Would you please please please please please please please stop talking?"

He did not say anything but looked at the bags against the wall of the station. There were labels on them from all the hotels where they had spent nights.

"But I don't want you to," he said. "I don't care anything about it."   100

"I'll scream," said the girl.

The woman came out through the curtains with two glasses of beer and put them down on the damp felt pads. "The train comes in five minutes," she said.

"What did she say?" asked the girl.

"That the train is coming in five minutes."

105   The girl smiled brightly at the woman, to thank her.
       "I'd better take the bags over to the other side of the station," the
man said. She smiled at him.
       "All right. Then come back and we'll finish the beer."
       He picked up the two heavy bags and carried them around the
station to the other tracks. He looked up the tracks but could not see the
train. Coming back, he walked through the barroom, where people
waiting for the train were drinking. He drank an Anis at the bar and
looked at the people. They were all waiting reasonably for the train. He
went out through the bead curtain. She was sitting at the table and
smiled at him.
       "Do you feel better?" he asked.
110   "I feel fine," she said. "There's nothing wrong with me. I feel fine."

QUESTIONS

1. The main topic of discussion between the man and the girl is never named.
   What is the "awfully simple operation"? Why is it not named? What different
   attitudes are taken toward it by the man and the girl? Why?
2. What is indicated about the past life of the man and the girl? How? What has
   happened to the quality of their relationship? Why? How do we know? How
   accurate is the man's judgment about their future?
3. Though the story consists mostly of dialogue, and though it contains
   strong emotional conflict, it is entirely without adverbs indicating the
   tone of the remarks. How does Hemingway indicate tone? At what points
   are the characters insincere? Self-deceived? Ironic or sarcastic? To what
   extent do they give open expression to their feelings? Does either want an
   open conflict? Why or why not? Trace the various phases of emotion in
   the girl.
4. How sincere is the man in his insistence that he would not have the girl
   undergo the operation if she does not want to and that he is "perfectly
   willing to go through with it" if it means anything to the girl? What is "it"?
   How many times does he repeat these ideas? What significance has the
   man's drinking an Anis by himself before rejoining the girl at the end of the
   story?
5. Much of the conversation seems to be about trivial things (ordering drinks,
   the weather, and so on). What purposes does this conversation serve? What
   relevance has the girl's remark about absinthe?
6. What is the point of the girl's comparison of the hills to white elephants?
   Does the remark assume any significance for the reader beyond its significance for the characters? Why does the author use it for his title?
7. What purpose does the setting serve—the hills across the valley, the treeless
   railroad tracks and station? What is contributed by the precise information
   about time at the end of the first paragraph?

8. Which of the two characters is more "reasonable"? Which "wins" the conflict between them? The point of view is objective. Does this mean that we cannot tell whether the sympathy of the author lies more with one character than with the other? Explain your answer.

SUGGESTIONS FOR WRITING

1. Compare the effectiveness of first-person point of view in any two of the following stories. What contrasting effects do the authors achieve from the different ways they use the first person?
   a. Munro, "How I Met My Husband" (page 125).
   b. Faulkner, "A Rose for Emily" (page 526).
   c. Melville, "Bartleby the Scrivener" (page 586).
   d. Poe, "The Cask of Amontillado" (page 617).
2. Compare/contrast the use of third-person point of view in any two of the following stories. Does the author use objective, omniscient, or limited? Why is the particular point of view appropriate to each story? Focus on scenes in which the chosen point of view is especially effective.
   a. Wolff, "Hunters in the Snow" (page 86).
   b. Lahiri, "Interpreter of Maladies" (page 141).
   c. Mansfield, "Miss Brill" (page 174).
   d. Joyce, "Eveline" (page 408).
   e. Hawthorne, "Young Goodman Brown" (page 309).
   f. García Márquez, "A Very Old Man with Enormous Wings" (page 327).
   g. Oates, "Where Are You Going, Where Have You Been?" (page 469).
   h. Jackson, "The Lottery" (page 261).

Symbol, Allegory, and Fantasy

Most successful stories are characterized by compression. The writer's aim is to say as much as possible as briefly as possible. This does not mean that most good stories are brief. It means only that nothing is wasted and that the author chooses each word and detail carefully for maximum effectiveness.

Talented authors achieve compression by exercising a careful selectivity. They choose the details and incidents essential to the story they have to tell and they eliminate any that do not contribute to the unified effect of the story. Because every element in a story must do as much as possible, some details and incidents may serve a variety of purposes at once. A detail that illustrates character at the same time that it advances plot is more useful than a detail that does only one or the other.

Three of the many resources available to writers for achieving compression are symbol, allegory, and fantasy. To varying degrees, each of these techniques is a way to depart from the strict adherence to factual language and representation of the kind a journalist uses, for instance, in writing a newspaper story. By modifying, enhancing, and at times even abandoning such a factual or realistic approach to storytelling, an author can increase the emotional force and resonance of a story, suggesting a much larger and richer meaning than might be achieved with a strictly realistic approach. But such narrative strategies also require close attention on the reader's part.

A literary **symbol** is something that means *more* than what it suggests on the surface. It may be an object, a person, a situation, an action, or some other element that has a literal meaning in the story but that suggests or represents other meanings as well. A very simple illustration is that of name symbolism. Most names are simply labels. A name, for instance, does not tell much about the person to whom it is attached, except possibly the individual's nationality or, in the case of first names, the person's gender. In a story, however, authors may choose names for their characters that not only label them but also suggest something about them. In "A Worn Path," for instance, the name

"Phoenix" has several meanings that are relevant to Welty's character. In Egyptian mythology, a phoenix was a bird that consumed itself by fire after five hundred years, but then rose from its own ashes. It was also employed as a Christian symbol of death and resurrection in the art and architecture of the medieval period. Authors have often used this bird to suggest magical powers of renewal and endurance, and this meaning certainly relates to Phoenix Jackson's enduring love for her grandson. More generally, a phoenix also means a person of particular excellence, a meaning also applicable to Welty's protagonist. In "Everyday Use," Dee's rejection of her name and adoption of the alternative "Wangero" symbolizes for her a changed perspective on her heritage. The name of General Zaroff in "The Most Dangerous Game" is fitting for a former "officer of the Czar" who now behaves like a czar himself. Trevor's name in Greene's "The Destructors" suggests his upper-class origins. Equally meaningful in that story is the name of the Wormsley Common Gang. First, the word "Common," here designating a small public park or green, also suggests the "common people" or the lower middle and laboring classes as opposed to the upper class. More significant, when Trevor advocates his plan for gutting the old house—"We'd do it from inside. . . . We'd be like worms, don't you see, in an apple" (paragraph 52), we see that Greene's choice of the name Wormsley was quite deliberate and that it is appropriate also (as well as perfectly natural) that Wormsley Common should have an Underground Station. (The word "apple," in Trevor's speech, also has symbolic resonances. Though it is often a mistake to push symbolism too hard, the reader may well ask whether anything would be lost if Trevor had compared the gang's activities to those of worms in a peach or a pear.)

More important than name symbolism is the symbolic use of objects and actions. In some stories these symbols will fit so naturally into the literal context that their symbolic value will not at first be apparent except to the most perceptive reader. In other stories— usually stories with a less realistic surface—they will be so central and so obvious that they will demand symbolical interpretation if the story is to yield significant meaning. In the first kind of story the symbols *reinforce* and *add* to the meaning. In the second kind of story they *carry* the meaning.

Eudora Welty's "A Worn Path" superficially concerns a very old woman who walks from the back country into the city, encountering a variety of obstacles on her trip, in order to receive a bottle of soothing medicine from a charity clinic for her chronically ill grandson. The story has the familiar structure of a journey or quest and, in the old woman's ability to overcome or avert the dangers that she faces, a kind of mythic power that might remind us of *The Odyssey* or *Pilgrim's Progress*. It is a story of valor, purposefulness, and triumph, as the abiding love of the protagonist gives her the strength and shrewdness to achieve her goal.

But the symbolic meaning is more profound and moving. There are two predominant sets of symbols in the story, one made apparent by repetition, the other gradually developed by realistic details that build by accretion. The first is initially suggested by the symbolic name of the protagonist, "Phoenix" (not uncommon for a black woman in the south at the time of the story). In this example of name symbolism the character thus embodies such qualities as great age, pertinacity, persistence, and the magical ability to renew herself and regain strength and vigor.

Name symbolism, however, is only a beginning point in interpreting "A Worn Path." It adds grandeur to an otherwise apparently insignificant person, but it also initiates the repetitive references to birds that fill the story. At the onset of her trip, Phoenix's tapping of her cane sounds like "the chirping of a solitary little bird"; as she begins her journey, she warns "little bobwhites" to avoid being underfoot; and when she hears the "mourning dove" still crying down in the hollow, she symbolically interprets it as a parallel to herself: it too has persisted into the winter season. A buzzard among "big dead trees" she interprets as a reminder of death—and she brusquely dismisses it by asking, "'Who you watching?'" When she encounters a scarecrow, she first mistakes it for a mysterious dancing man, then for a ghost. As a bird herself she is "scared" by it, then identifies it for what it is and dances with it while corn husks "whirl in streamers about her skirts," a festive dance of triumph over this enemy of birds. Immediately after, as she escapes from the "maze" of the dead cornfield into a familiar wagon track, the "quail . . . walking around like pullets, seeming all dainty and unseen" reinforce her victory over fear and confusion.

The next bird that Phoenix sees is one of those same quail, now called "bobwhite," in the hunter's bag, with "a little closed claw" and "its beak hooked bitterly to show it was dead," a symbol of the genuine dangers that all mortal birds may face—but not Phoenix, who is not frightened by the foolish, callous hunter pointing his gun at her.

Birds thus symbolize for Phoenix the dangers and the delights of her life, both past and present. They are a well-known population of her world, and all of them embody some meaning for her. She is an interpreter of symbols. She feels protective and pitying toward the vulnerable, and she scorns and dismisses the threatening. There is one bird, however, that truly disturbs her. When by her ruse of inciting a dog-fight so as to pick up the nickel dropped by the hunter (who later lies to her about having any money, pretending he wishes to be charitable), Phoenix looks up as she puts the coin in her pocket and sees "a bird

[fly] by." Her interpretation links bird-life to faith and morality: "'God watching me the whole time. I come to stealing.'" What birds know and do is to her an intimation of God's commandments and love.

At the climax of the story, one final symbolic reference to birds reveals the central meaning of the story. After a momentary memory lapse at the charity clinic, Phoenix focuses again on the purpose of her trip, to relieve the suffering of her grandson. "'We is the only two left in the world,'" she says, meaning that the two of them are the last of their family but also implying their mutual need to sustain each other. She goes on, "He wear a little patch quilt and peep out holding his mouth open like a little bird." She is confident that the two of them are "going to last," the loving spirit of Phoenix ever renewing itself, and the innocent "sweet" child always needing and receiving her self-sacrifice.

There is another symbolic frame of reference in this story, not so obvious but perhaps just as important. While the bird symbolism enlarges the meaning of Phoenix's trip to embrace enduring human values that transcend time and place, the story also symbolizes the historical and cultural issue of racial division in America at the time of its writing and in the years before and since the Civil War. Phoenix, who "'was too old at the Surrender'" (1865) to attend school, and now at over 100 is the oldest person she knows about, spans in her lifetime the period of slavery, emancipation, its aftermath during the Reconstruction, and the era of Jim Crow laws in the south and prejudice and bigotry throughout the country. A diligent reading will reveal a constant recurrence of "black" and "white" as words, as implied appearances, and even as moral abstractions. Because they are not always easily associated with right and wrong, good and evil, the references do not constitute an allegorical system but rather a repeated reminder of black-white oppositions. The first of these will suggest the subtlety of this symbolism: in the initial description of Phoenix's appearance, the narrator points out that the hair of this centenarian, falling on her neck "in the frailest of ringlets . . . [is] still black." Contrary to natural expectations, her hair has not turned *white*, and her racial identity is intact. Following this implied contrast of black and white, the careful reader will discover many explicit or implicit references to these colors.

Symbolically, the most impressive and touching example occurs during Phoenix's dream as she rests after the ordeal of crossing the creek. She sits down, spreads out her skirts, and assumes a girlish posture as she looks around: "Up above her was a tree in a pearly cloud of mistletoe. She did not dare to close her eyes, and when a little boy brought her a plate with a slice of marble-cake on it she spoke to him. 'That would be acceptable,' she said. But when she went to take it there was just her hand in the air." Here, as if from heaven itself (where the "pearly" gates are as white as the garments of the angels themselves), a "little boy" (perhaps reminiscent of her grandson) offers her a delicacy that displays a perfect mixing of light and dark, a promised harmony of sweet equality—but not yet, not in real life. Phoenix's understated acceptance of it as a gift offered rather than a right demanded is characteristic of the humble gratitude for small advances that was all too common at the time of the story. As a black woman, she has endured and she will keep enduring the vicissitudes of social change, a reminder of love as a remedy for hatred.

Another example of symbolic setting and action is presented in Hemingway's "Hills Like White Elephants," in which a man and a girl sit waiting for the train to Madrid, where the girl is to have an abortion. But the girl is not fully persuaded that she wants an abortion (at the deepest levels of her being, she does not). The man is aware of this and seeks to reassure her: "It's really an awfully simple operation. . . . It's not really an operation at all. . . . But I don't want you to do it if you don't really want to." The man *does* want her to do it even if she doesn't really want to; nevertheless, the decision is not irrevocable. They are at a railroad junction, a place where one can change directions. Symbolically it represents a juncture where they can change the direction of their lives. Their bags, with "labels on them from all the hotels where they had spent nights," indicate the kind of rootless, pleasure-seeking existence without responsibility they have hitherto lived. The man wants the girl to have the abortion so that they can go on living as they have before.

The railway station is situated in a river valley between two mountain ranges. On one side of the valley there is no shade and no trees and the country is "brown and dry." It is on this side, "the dry side," that the station sits in the heat, "between two lines of rails." It is also this side that the couple see from their table and that prompts the girl's remark that the hills look "like white elephants." On the other side of the valley, which the girl can see when she walks to the end of the station, lies the river, with "fields of grain and trees" along its banks, the "shadow of a cloud" moving across a field of grain, and another range of mountains in the distance. Looking in this direction, the girl remarks, "And we could have all this." The two landscapes, on opposite sides of the valley, have symbolic meaning in relation to the decision that the girl is being asked to reconfirm. The hot arid side of the valley represents sterility; the other side, with water in the river and the cloud, a hint of coolness in the cloud's moving shadow, and growing things along the river banks, represents fertility. The girl's remark about this other side shows a conscious recognition of its symbolism.

But what does the girl mean by her remark that the mountains on the dry side of the valley look "like white elephants"? Perhaps nothing at all. It is intended as a "bright" remark, a clever if far-fetched comparison made to amuse the man, as it would have in their earlier days together. But whether or not the girl means anything by it, almost certainly Hemingway means something. Or perhaps several things. Clearly the child begun in the girl's womb is a "white elephant" for the man, who says, "I don't want anybody but you. I don't want any one else." For the girl, on the other hand, the abortion itself, the decision to continue living as they have been living, without responsibility, may be considered a "white elephant." We already know that this life has lost its savor for her. When she remarks that the Anis del Toro "tastes like licorice," the man's response—"that's the way with everything"—is probably meant to apply only to the drink and food in this section of the country, but the girl's confirmation of his observation seems to enlarge its meaning to the whole life they have been living together, which consists, she says, only of looking at things and trying new drinks. Thus the licorice flavor, suggesting tedium and disillusion, joins the "hills like white elephants," the opposed sides of the river valley, and the railroad junction in a network of symbols that intensify the meaning and impact of the story.

The ability to recognize and identify symbols requires perception and tact. The great danger facing readers when they first become aware of symbolic values is a tendency to run wild—to find symbols everywhere and to read into the details of a story all sorts of fanciful meanings not legitimately supported by it. But we need to remember that most stories operate almost wholly at the literal level and that even in highly symbolic stories, the majority of the details are purely literal. A story is not an excuse for an exercise in ingenuity. It is better, indeed, to miss the symbolic meanings of a story than to pervert its meaning by discovering symbols that are nonexistent. Better to miss the boat than to jump wildly for it and drown.

The ability to interpret symbols is nevertheless essential for a full understanding of literature. Readers should always be alert for symbolic meanings but should observe the following cautions:

1. The story itself must furnish a clue that a detail is to be taken symbolically. In Mansfield's story, Miss Brill's fur is given prominence at the beginning of the story, when it is taken out of its box; at the climax of the story, when the girl on the bench compares it to "a fried whiting"; and at the end of the story, when Miss Brill puts it back in the box and thinks she hears it crying. The fur is clearly a symbol for Miss Brill herself. It comes out of a box like a dark little room or a cupboard, it is old and in need of repair, it is ridiculed by the boy and the girl on the park bench, and it is returned to its box at the end of the story. Symbolically, it is herself whom Miss Brill hears crying. In Welty's story, the repetition of references to birds, including the name of the protagonist, signals the need to interpret them symbolically. The title "A Worn Path" explicitly refers to Phoenix's repeated journeys, and by implication symbolizes the journeys of her race toward love and full acceptance. Both items are emphasized and significant to the meaning of the story, but neither is essential to its plot. Even greater emphasis is given to the quilts in the story by Walker. Symbols nearly always signal their existence by *emphasis*, *repetition*, or *position*. In the absence of such signals, we should be reluctant to identify an item as symbolic.

2. The meaning of a literary symbol must be established and supported by the entire context of the story. The symbol has its meaning *in* the story, not *outside* it. For instance, in "A Worn Path," the meaning of the "pearly cloud of mistletoe" is supported by and dependent on its relation to other references within the story establishing the correlations between black and white and the dreams that Phoenix harbors. In another context a cloud of mistletoe might connote parasitism and the death of the host tree. Here, associated as it is with a proffered gift of delight from on high, the symbol reinforces Phoenix's faith and reliance on God's will.

3. To be called a symbol, an item must suggest a meaning different in *kind* from its literal meaning; a symbol is something more than the representative of a class or type. Miss Brill, for instance, is an old, odd, silent, friendless person, set in her ways, who does not realize (until the climax of the story) that she herself is old, odd, and set in her ways—like other elderly people she observes in the park each Sunday. But to say this is to say no more than that the story has a theme. Every literary story suggests a generalization about life, is more than an accounting of the specific fortunes of specific individuals. There is no point, therefore, in calling Miss Brill a *symbol* of odd, self-deluded elderly people; she *is* an odd, self-deluded elderly person: a member of the class of odd, self-deluded elderly persons. Her fur is a symbol, but she is not. We ought not to use the phrase *is a symbol of* when we can easily use *is*, or *is an example of* or *is an evidence of*. Phoenix Jackson, in "A Worn Path," through the symbolic associations attached to her name, is clearly meant to be something more than an *example* of any class or race of human beings, or of humanity in general; she is a symbol of something *within* the human spirit, of hidden possibilities latent in many people.

The quilts in Alice Walker's "Everyday Use" are *evidence* that the family has been enslaved and impoverished, evidence of a past that Dee is proud to have escaped. To her, they are valuable as artifacts of oppression. In the story, however, they *symbolize* a wealth beyond money in the family's linkages to an authentic heritage of craftsmanship and beauty.

4. A symbol may have more than one meaning. It may suggest a cluster of meanings. At its most effective, a symbol is like a many-faceted jewel: it flashes different colors when turned in the light. This is not to say that it can mean anything we want it to: the area of possible meanings is always controlled by the context. Nevertheless, this possibility of complex meaning plus concreteness and emotional power gives the symbol its peculiar compressive value. The path in Welty's story symbolizes life itself, including its obstacles, its habits, its occasional moments of humor, pain, and beauty, and above all its nature as a journey human beings must undertake with as much courage and dignity as possible, motivated by love. The quilts in Walker's story have an equally wide range of meaning—inherited values, family attachments, independence and self-reliance, the beauty of useful objects, the virtue of craftsmanship—all in contrast to the shallow, monetary meaning expressed in Dee's acquisitive demand for them. When she says, "But they're *priceless!*" she means that they are worth a great deal of money, but in the truer sense their symbolic values cannot be reckoned at any price. The meaning is not confined to any one of these qualities: it is all of them, and therein lies the symbol's value.

An **allegory** is a story that has a second meaning beneath the surface, endowing a cluster of characters, objects, or events with added significance; often the pattern relates each literal item to a corresponding abstract idea or moral principle. It is different from symbolism in that it puts less emphasis on the literal meanings and more on the ulterior meanings. Also, those ulterior meanings are more fixed, and they usually constitute a pre-existing system of ideas or principles. Medieval and Renaissance religious allegories, for instance, were intended to illustrate the progress of a typical Christian individual through life, as in the medieval play *Everyman* and in John Bunyan's *Pilgrim's Progress*, a seventeenth-century work in which a character named "Christian" journeys toward salvation, encountering along the way such temptations as despair, labeled "The Slough of Despond," and witnessing human hypocrisy in a town called "Fair Speech." Probably the most widely read allegorical work today is Nathaniel Hawthorne's novel *The Scarlet Letter* (1850). Although Hawthorne's novel, like most more modern allegories, eschews the mechanical, one-to-one correspondences found in older allegorical works (which were written more for religious or political than literary purposes), he does provide a coherent system that evokes and critiques the seventeenth-century Puritan world in which the novel is set. The novel's allegorical pattern includes the scarlet "A" for adultery that Hester Prynne wears on her dress; the names of her husband, Chillingworth, and her daughter, Pearl; Hester's uneasy residence on the border between the wilderness, representing natural impulses, and the "civilized" Puritan culture that ostracizes her. In this chapter, Hawthorne's story "Young Goodman Brown" has a similar allegorical pattern. The title character, as his name suggests, is a typical young and virtuous man; his surname "Brown," like "Smith" in America today, is the most common name during his era, again suggesting his identity as a representative individual. His wife, "Faith," represents the steadfast virtue he is leaving behind during his journey into the wilderness, just as her pink ribbons suggest her innocence. During a crisis point in the story, Brown shouts "My Faith is gone!" and the allegorical meaning is clear, for he is talking simultaneously about his literal wife and the abstraction of his religious faith. Other elements in the story— the old man's staff that begins "writhing" like a serpent, the wilderness itself with its suggestions of moral chaos and depravity—likewise fulfill roles in Hawthorne's allegory.

It should be stressed, however, that an author employing allegory usually does not intend simply to create two levels of reality, one literal and one abstract, which readers merely identify as though connecting a series of dots. Serious writers often introduce an element of ambiguity into their allegorical meanings, undercutting easy and simplistic interpretation. For example, in Hawthorne's story, Brown's innocent wife Faith pleads with her husband not to undertake the journey, observing, "A lone woman is troubled with such dreams and such thoughts that she's afeared of herself sometimes"—a bit of dialogue that suggests her identity as more than an abstract representation of faith but also as a flesh-and-blood woman who may well encounter her own temptations and psychological turmoil when separated from her husband.

The creation of an allegorical pattern of meaning enables an author to achieve power through economy. Reading a story, you should therefore be aware of an author's use of description and detail, for these may be present not only to create a sensual apprehension of a story's characters and settings, but also to suggest meanings—moral, intellectual, emotional—beyond that reality. This ability to compress a great deal of meaning into the relatively small canvas of a short story is part of what gives the best examples of this genre their powerful narrative impact.

While some stories use factual details to suggest additional, sometimes abstract, meanings, there is another type of story that abandons factual representation altogether. The nonrealistic story, or **fantasy**, is one that transcends the bounds of known reality. After all, truth in fiction is not the same as fidelity to fact. All fiction is essentially a game of make-believe in which the author imaginatively conceives characters and situations and sets them down on paper. The purpose of any literary artist is to communicate truths by means of imagined facts. While most authors, using realistic means, attempt to create an illusion of reality in telling their stories, careful to stay in the realm of the plausible and relate something that *could have happened*, sometimes an author chooses to go a step further and create a story that is entirely implausible or even impossible. Such stories require from the reader what the poet Samuel Taylor Coleridge called "a willing suspension of disbelief": that is, the reader is willing to accept the author's premise of a strange and marvelous world, in which a character falls down a rabbit hole or climbs up a beanstalk or finds himself in an alien spaceship. Such a fantasy story introduces human beings into a world where the ordinary laws of nature are suspended or superseded and where the landscape and its creatures are unfamiliar; or, on the other hand, it may introduce ghosts, fairies, dragons, werewolves, talking animals, Martian invaders, or miraculous occurrences into the recognizable, everyday world of human beings. A recently popular form of this second approach to fantasy has been called "magical realism," in which fantastic and magical events are woven into mundane and ordinary situations, creating striking and memorable effects unavailable to either realism or fantasy alone. Such popular forms of storytelling as fables, ghost stories, and science fiction are all types of fantasy. Like stories using symbolism and allegory, fantasy stories are often highly compressed, enabling the author to convey a richly textured, resonant vision within a relatively short narrative.

The story writer begins, then, by saying, "What if. . . ." "What if," for instance, "a young, somewhat naïve girl working in a farmhouse should meet a handsome pilot visiting the area and become infatuated with him." From this initial assumption the author goes on to develop a story ("How I Met My Husband"), which, though presumably imaginary in the sense that it never happened, nevertheless reveals convincingly to us some truths of human behavior.

But now, what if the author goes a step further and supposes not just something that might very well have happened (though it didn't) but something highly improbable—something that could happen, say, only as the result of a very surprising coincidence? What if he begins, "Let's suppose that a misogynist and a charming woman find themselves alone on a desert island"? This initial supposition causes us to stretch our imaginations a bit further, but is not this situation just as capable of revealing human truths as the former? The psychologist puts a rat in a maze (certainly an improbable situation for a rat), observes its reactions to the maze, and discovers some truth of rat behavior. The author may put imaginary characters on an imagined desert island, imaginatively study their reactions, and reveal some truth of human nature. The improbable initial situation may yield as much truth as the probable one.

From the improbable it is but one step further to the impossible (as we know it in this life). Why should our author not begin "Let's suppose that a miser and his termagant wife find themselves in hell" or "Let's suppose that a primitive scapegoat ritual still survives in contemporary America." Could not these situations also be used to exhibit human traits?

Like stories employing realistic characters and events, fantasies may be purely commercial entertainment or they may be serious literary works. A story about a spaceship on its way to a distant planet might be filled with stock characters or with richly imagined human beings; it may be designed chiefly to exhibit mechanical marvels and to provide thrills and adventures, or it may be a way of creating a setting in which human behavior can be sharply observed and studied. Fantasy, like other forms of fiction, may be employed sheerly for its own sake or as a means of communicating significant insights into the world of human beings. The important point to remember is that truth in fiction is not to be identified with a realistic method. Stories that fly on the wings of fantasy may be vehicles for truth that are as powerful in their own way as such realistic stories as "Hunters in the Snow" or "Interpreter of Maladies." Fantasy may employ the techniques of symbolism or allegory, or it may simply provide an exotic, nonrealistic setting as a way of observing human nature. Some of the world's greatest works of literature have been partly or wholly fantasy: *The Odyssey, The Divine Comedy, The Tempest, Pilgrim's Progress, Gulliver's Travels,* and *Alice in Wonderland* all offer profound and significant insights into the human condition.

Clearly, then, we must not judge a story as good or bad according to whether or not it stays within the limits of the possible. Rather, we should begin reading any story by suspending disbelief—that is, by granting every story its initial premise or assumption. The writer may begin with an ordinary, everyday situation or with a far-fetched, improbable coincidence. Or the writer may be allowed to suspend a law of nature or to create a marvelous being or machine or place. But once we have accepted an impossible reality as a premise, we have a right to demand probability and consistency in the author's treatment of it. Fantasy is not an excuse for haphazard writing or a poorly imagined story. We need to ask, too, for what reason the story employs fantasy. Is it used simply for its own strangeness, or for thrills or surprises or laughs? Or is it used to illuminate truths of the reader's own experience? What, finally, is the purpose of the author's fantastic invention? Is it, like a roller coaster, simply a machine for producing a temporary thrill? Or does it, like an observation balloon, provide a unique vantage point that may change our view of the world forever?

REVIEWING CHAPTER SIX

1. Review the definition of a literary symbol.
2. Explore the uses of symbolic names, objects, and actions.
3. Summarize the use of symbolism in Welty's "A Worn Path."
4. Distinguish between symbolism and allegory.
5. Describe the importance of ambiguity in a literary allegory.
6. Define the term "fantasy" and describe the prominent features of a fantastic story.

D. H. Lawrence
The Rocking-Horse Winner

There was a woman who was beautiful, who started with all the advantages, yet she had no luck. She married for love, and the love turned to dust. She had bonny children, yet she felt they had been thrust upon her, and she could not love them. They looked at her coldly, as if they were finding fault with her. And hurriedly she felt she must cover up some fault in herself. Yet what it was that she must cover up she never knew. Nevertheless, when her children were present, she always felt the center of her heart go hard. This troubled her, and in her manner she was all the more gentle and anxious for her children, as if she loved them very much. Only she herself knew that at the center of her heart was a hard little place that could not feel love, no, not for anybody. Everybody else said of her: "She is such a good mother. She adores her children." Only she herself, and her children themselves, knew it was not so. They read it in each other's eyes.

THE ROCKING-HORSE WINNER   First published in 1933. D. H. Lawrence (1885–1930), son of a coal miner and a school teacher, was born and grew up in Nottinghamshire, England, was rejected for military service in World War I because of lung trouble, and lived most of his adult life abroad, including parts of three years in New Mexico.

There were a boy and two little girls. They lived in a pleasant house, with a garden, and they had discreet servants, and felt themselves superior to anyone in the neighborhood.

Although they lived in style, they felt always an anxiety in the house. There was never enough money. The mother had a small income, and the father had a small income, but not nearly enough for the social position which they had to keep up. The father went into town to some office. But though he had good prospects, these prospects never materialized. There was always the grinding sense of the shortage of money, though the style was always kept up.

At last the mother said: "I will see if I can't make something." But she did not know where to begin. She racked her brains, and tried this thing and the other, but could not find anything successful. The failure made deep lines come into her face. Her children were growing up, they would have to go to school. There must be more money, there must be more money. The father, who was always very handsome and expensive in his tastes, seemed as if he never would be able to do anything worth doing. And the mother, who had a great belief in herself, did not succeed any better, and her tastes were just as expensive.

5   And so the house came to be haunted by the unspoken phrase: There must be more money! There must be more money! The children could hear it all the time, though nobody said it aloud. They heard it at Christmas, when the expensive and splendid toys filled the nursery. Behind the shining modern rocking horse, behind the smart doll's-house, a voice would start whispering: "There must be more money! There must be more money!" And the children would stop playing, to listen for a moment. They would look into each other's eyes, to see if they had all heard. And each one saw in the eyes of the other two that they too had heard. "There must be more money! There must be more money!"

It came whispering from the springs of the still-swaying rocking horse, and even the horse, bending his wooden, champing head, heard it. The big doll, sitting so pink and smirking in her new pram, could hear it quite plainly, and seemed to be smirking all the more self-consciously because of it. The foolish puppy, too, that took the place of the Teddy bear, he was looking so extraordinarily foolish for no other reason but that he heard the secret whisper all over the house: "There must be more money!"

Yet nobody ever said it aloud. The whisper was everywhere, and therefore no one spoke it. Just as no one ever says: "We are breathing!" in spite of the fact that breath is coming and going all the time.

"Mother," said the boy Paul one day, "why don't we keep a car of our own? Why do we always use uncle's, or else a taxi?"

"Because we're the poor members of the family," said the mother.

"But why are we, mother?"

"Well—I suppose," she said slowly and bitterly, "it's because your father has no luck."

The boy was silent for some time.

"Is luck money, mother?" he asked, rather timidly.

"No, Paul. Not quite. It's what causes you to have money."

"Oh!" said Paul vaguely. "I thought when Uncle Oscar said filthy lucker, it meant money."

"Filthy lucre° does mean money," said the mother. "But it's lucre, not luck."

"Oh!" said the boy. "Then what is luck, mother?"

"It's what causes you to have money. If you're lucky you have money. That's why it's better to be born lucky than rich. If you're rich, you may lose your money. But if you're lucky, you will always get more money."

"Oh! Will you? And is father not lucky?"

"Very unlucky, I should say," she said bitterly.

The boy watched her with unsure eyes.

"Why?" he asked.

"I don't know. Nobody ever knows why one person is lucky and another unlucky."

"Don't they? Nobody at all? Does nobody know?"

"Perhaps God. But He never tells."

"He ought to, then. And aren't you lucky either, mother?"

"I can't be, if I married an unlucky husband."

"But by yourself, aren't you?"

"I used to think I was, before I married. Now I think I am very unlucky indeed."

"Why?"

"Well—never mind! Perhaps I'm not really," she said.

The child looked at her, to see if she meant it. But he saw, by the lines of her mouth, that she was only trying to hide something from him.

"Well, anyhow," he said stoutly, "I'm a lucky person."

"Why?" said his mother, with a sudden laugh.

He stared at her. He didn't even know why he had said it.

"God told me," he asserted, brazening it out.

"I hope He did, dear!" she said, again with a laugh, but rather bitter.

"He did, mother!"

filthy lucre: See New Testament, I Timothy 3:3.

"Excellent!" said the mother, using one of her husband's exclamations.

40   The boy saw she did not believe him; or, rather, that she paid no attention to his assertion. This angered him somewhat, and made him want to compel her attention.

He went off by himself, vaguely, in a childish way, seeking for the clue to "luck." Absorbed, taking no heed of other people, he went about with a sort of stealth, seeking inwardly for luck. He wanted luck, he wanted it, he wanted it. When the two girls were playing dolls in the nursery, he would sit on his big rocking horse, charging madly into space, with a frenzy that made the little girls peer at him uneasily. Wildly the horse careered, the waving dark hair of the boy tossed, his eyes had a strange glare in them. The little girls dared not speak to him.

When he had ridden to the end of his mad little journey, he climbed down and stood in front of his rocking horse, staring fixedly into its lowered face. Its red mouth was slightly open, its big eye was wide and glassy-bright.

"Now!" he would silently command the snorting steed. "Now, take me to where there is luck! Now take me!"

And he would slash the horse on the neck with the little whip he had asked Uncle Oscar for. He knew the horse could take him to where there was luck, if only he forced it. So he would mount again, and start on his furious ride, hoping at last to get there. He knew he could get there.

45   "You'll break your horse, Paul!" said the nurse.

"He's always riding like that! I wish he'd leave off!" said his elder sister Joan.

But he only glared down on them in silence. Nurse gave him up. She could make nothing of him. Anyhow he was growing beyond her.

One day his mother and his Uncle Oscar came in when he was on one of his furious rides. He did not speak to them.

"Hallo, you young jockey! Riding a winner?" said his uncle.

50   "Aren't you growing too big for a rocking horse? You're not a very little boy any longer, you know," said his mother.

But Paul only gave a blue glare from his big, rather close-set eyes. He would speak to nobody when he was in full tilt. His mother watched him with an anxious expression on her face.

At last he suddenly stopped forcing his horse into the mechanical gallop, and slid down.

"Well, I got there!" he announced fiercely, his blue eyes still flaring, and his sturdy long legs straddling apart.

"Where did you get to?" asked his mother.

"Where I wanted to go," he flared back at her.   55

"That's right, son!" said Uncle Oscar. "Don't you stop till you get there. What's the horse's name?"

"He doesn't have a name," said the boy.

"Gets on without all right?" asked the uncle.

"Well, he has different names. He was called Sansovino last week."

"Sansovino, eh? Won the Ascot. How did you know his name?"   60

"He always talks about horse races with Bassett," said Joan.

The uncle was delighted to find that his small nephew was posted with all the racing news. Bassett, the young gardener, who had been wounded in the left foot in the war and got his present job through Oscar Cresswell, whose batman he had been, was a perfect blade of the "turf." He lived in the racing events, and the small boy lived with him.

Oscar Cresswell got it all from Bassett.

"Master Paul comes and asks me, so I can't do more than tell him, sir," said Bassett, his face terribly serious, as if he were speaking of religious matters.

"And does he ever put anything on a horse he fancies?"   65

"Well—I don't want to give him away—he's a young sport, a fine sport, sir. Would you mind asking him yourself? He sort of takes a pleasure in it, and perhaps he'd feel I was giving him away, sir, if you don't mind."

Bassett was serious as a church.

The uncle went back to his nephew, and took him off for a ride in the car.

"Say, Paul, old man, do you ever put anything on a horse?" the uncle asked.

The boy watched the handsome man closely.   70

"Why, do you think I oughtn't to?" he parried.

"Not a bit of it! I thought perhaps you might give me a tip for the Lincoln."

The car sped on into the country, going down to Uncle Oscar's place in Hampshire.

"Honor bright?" said the nephew.

"Honor bright, son!" said the uncle.   75

"Well, then, Daffodil."

"Daffodil! I doubt it, sonny. What about Mirza?"

"I only know the winner," said the boy. "That's Daffodil."

"Daffodil, eh?"

There was a pause. Daffodil was an obscure horse comparatively.   80

"Uncle!"

"Yes, son?"

"You won't let it go any further, will you? I promised Bassett."

"Bassett be damned, old man! What's he got to do with it?"

85   "We're partners. We've been partners from the first. Uncle, he lent me my first five shillings, which I lost. I promised him, honor bright, it was only between me and him; only you gave me that ten-shilling note I started winning with, so I thought you were lucky. You won't let it go any further, will you?"

The boy gazed at his uncle from those big, hot, blue eyes, set rather close together. The uncle stirred and laughed uneasily.

"Right you are, son! I'll keep your tip private. Daffodil, eh? How much are you putting on him?"

"All except twenty pounds," said the boy. "I keep that in reserve."

The uncle thought it a good joke.

90   "You keep twenty pounds in reserve, do you, you young romancer? What are you betting, then?"

"I'm betting three hundred," said the boy gravely. "But it's between you and me, Uncle Oscar! Honor bright?"

The uncle burst into a roar of laughter.

"It's between you and me all right, you young Nat Gould,"° he said, laughing. "But where's your three hundred?"

"Bassett keeps it for me. We're partners."

95   "You are, are you! And what is Bassett putting on Daffodil?"

"He won't go quite as high as I do, I expect. Perhaps he'll go a hundred and fifty."

"What, pennies?" laughed the uncle.

"Pounds," said the child, with a surprised look at his uncle. "Bassett keeps a bigger reserve than I do."

Between wonder and amusement Uncle Oscar was silent. He pursued the matter no further, but he determined to take his nephew with him to the Lincoln races.

100   "Now, son," he said, "I'm putting twenty on Mirza, and I'll put five for you on any horse you fancy. What's your pick?"

"Daffodil, uncle."

"No, not the fiver on Daffodil!"

"I should if it was my own fiver," said the child.

"Good! Good! Right you are! A fiver for me and a fiver for you on Daffodil."

Nat Gould: a journalist and novelist (1857–1919) who wrote about horse racing

The child had never been to a race meeting before, and his eyes were   105
blue fire. He pursed his mouth tight, and watched. A Frenchman just in
front had put his money on Lancelot. Wild with excitement, he flayed his
arms up and down, yelling "Lancelot! Lancelot!" in his French accent.

Daffodil came in first, Lancelot second, Mirza third. The child,
flushed and with eyes blazing, was curiously serene. His uncle brought
him four five-pound notes, four to one.

"What am I to do with these?" he cried, waving them before the
boy's eyes.

"I suppose we'll talk to Bassett," said the boy. "I expect I have fifteen
hundred now; and twenty in reserve; and this twenty."

His uncle studied him for some moments.

"Look here, son!" he said. "You're not serious about Bassett and that   110
fifteen hundred, are you?"

"Yes, I am. But it's between you and me, uncle. Honor bright!"

"Honor bright all right, son! But I must talk to Bassett."

"If you'd like to be a partner, uncle, with Bassett and me, we could
all be partners. Only, you'd have to promise, honor bright, uncle, not to
let it go beyond us three. Bassett and I are lucky, and you must be lucky,
because it was your ten shillings I started winning with . . ."

Uncle Oscar took both Bassett and Paul into Richmond Park for an
afternoon, and there they talked.

"It's like this, you see, sir," Bassett said. "Master Paul would get me   115
talking about racing events, spinning yarns, you know, sir. And he was
always keen on knowing if I'd made or if I'd lost. It's about a year since,
now, that I put five shillings on Blush of Dawn for him—and we lost.
Then the luck turned, with that ten shillings he had from you, that we
put on Singhalese. And since that time, it's been pretty steady, all things
considering. What do you say, Master Paul?"

"We're all right when we're sure," said Paul. "It's when we're not
quite sure that we go down."

"Oh, but we're careful then," said Bassett.

"But when are you sure?" smiled Uncle Oscar.

"It's Master Paul, sir," said Bassett, in a secret, religious voice. "It's as
if he had it from heaven. Like Daffodil, now, for the Lincoln. That was
as sure as eggs."

"Did you put anything on Daffodil?" asked Oscar Cresswell.   120

"Yes, sir, I made my bit."

"And my nephew?"

Bassett was obstinately silent, looking at Paul.

"I made twelve hundred, didn't I, Bassett? I told uncle I was putting
three hundred on Daffodil."

125   "That's right," said Bassett, nodding.

"But where's the money?" asked the uncle.

"I keep it safe locked up, sir. Master Paul he can have it any minute he likes to ask for it."

"What, fifteen hundred pounds?"

"And twenty! and forty, that is, with the twenty he made on the course."

130   "It's amazing!" said the uncle.

"If Master Paul offers you to be partners, sir, I would, if I were you; if you'll excuse me," said Bassett.

Oscar Cresswell thought about it.

"I'll see the money," he said.

They drove home again, and sure enough, Bassett came round to the garden-house with fifteen hundred pounds in notes. The twenty pounds reserve was left with Joe Glee, in the Turf Commission deposit.

135   "You see, it's all right, uncle, when I'm sure! Then we go strong, for all we're worth. Don't we Bassett?"

"We do that, Master Paul."

"And when are you sure?" said the uncle, laughing.

"Oh, well, sometimes I'm absolutely sure, like about Daffodil," said the boy; "and sometimes I have an idea; and sometimes I haven't even an idea, have I, Bassett? Then we're careful, because we mostly go down."

"You do, do you! And when you're sure, like about Daffodil, what makes you sure, sonny?"

140   "Oh, well, I don't know," said the boy uneasily. "I'm sure, you know, uncle; that's all."

"It's as if he had it from heaven, sir," Bassett reiterated.

"I should say so!" said the uncle.

But he became a partner. And when the Leger was coming on, Paul was "sure" about Lively Spark, which was a quite inconsiderable horse. The boy insisted on putting a thousand on the horse, Bassett went for five hundred, and Oscar Cresswell two hundred. Lively Spark came in first, and the betting had been ten to one against him. Paul had made ten thousand.

"You see," he said, "I was absolutely sure of him."

145   Even Oscar Cresswell had cleared two thousand.

"Look here son," he said, "this sort of thing makes me nervous."

"It needn't, uncle! Perhaps I shan't be sure again for a long time."

"But what are you going to do with your money?" asked the uncle.

"Of course," said the boy, "I started it for mother. She said she had no luck, because father is unlucky, so I thought if I was lucky, it might stop whispering."

"What might stop whispering?"   150

"Our house. I hate our house for whispering."

"What does it whisper?"

"Why—why"—the boy fidgeted—"why, I don't know. But it's always short of money, you know, uncle."

"I know it, son, I know it."

"You know people send mother writs, don't you, uncle?"   155

"I'm afraid I do," said the uncle.

"And then the house whispers, like people laughing at you behind your back. It's awful, that is! I thought if I was lucky . . ."

"You might stop it," added the uncle.

The boy watched him with big blue eyes that had an uncanny cold fire in them, and he said never a word.

"Well, then!" said the uncle. "What are we doing?"   160

"I shouldn't like mother to know I was lucky," said the boy.

"Why not, son?"

"She'd stop me."

"I don't think she would."

"Oh!"—and the boy writhed in an odd way—"I don't want her to   165
know, uncle."

"All right, son! We'll manage it without her knowing."

They managed it very easily. Paul, at the other's suggestion, handed over five thousand pounds to his uncle, who deposited it with the family lawyer, who was then to inform Paul's mother that a relative had put five thousand pounds into his hands, which sum was to be paid out a thousand pounds at a time, on the mother's birthday, for the next five years.

"So she'll have a birthday present of a thousand pounds for five successive years," said Uncle Oscar. "I hope it won't make it all the harder for her later."

Paul's mother had her birthday in November. The house had been "whispering" worse than ever lately, and, even in spite of his luck, Paul could not bear up against it. He was very anxious to see the effect of the birthday letter telling his mother about the thousand pounds.

When there were no visitors, Paul now took his meals with his   170
parents, as he was beyond the nursery control. His mother went into town nearly every day. She had discovered that she had an odd knack of sketching furs and dress materials, so she worked secretly in the studio of a friend who was the chief "artist" for the leading drapers. She drew the figures of ladies in furs and ladies in silk and sequins for the newspaper advertisements. This young woman artist earned several thousand pounds a year, but Paul's mother only made

several hundreds, and she was again dissatisfied. She so wanted to be first in something, and she did not succeed, even in making sketches for drapery advertisements.

She was down to breakfast on the morning of her birthday. Paul watched her face as she read her letters. He knew the lawyer's letter. As his mother read it, her face hardened and became more expressionless. Then a cold, determined look came on her mouth. She hid the letter under the pile of others, and said not a word about it.

"Didn't you have anything nice in the post for your birthday, mother?" said Paul.

"Quite moderately nice," she said, her voice cold and absent.

She went away to town without saying more.

175   But in the afternoon Uncle Oscar appeared. He said Paul's mother had had a long interview with the lawyer, asking if the whole five thousand could be advanced at once, as she was in debt.

"What do you think, uncle?" said the boy.

"I leave it to you, son."

"Oh, let her have it, then! We can get some more with the other," said the boy.

"A bird in the hand is worth two in the bush, laddie!" said Uncle Oscar.

180   "But I'm sure to know for the Grand National; or the Lincolnshire; or else the Derby. I'm sure to know for one of them," said Paul.

So Uncle Oscar signed the agreement, and Paul's mother touched the whole five thousand. Then something very curious happened. The voices in the house suddenly went mad, like a chorus of frogs on a spring evening. There were certain new furnishings, and Paul had a tutor. He was really going to Eton,° his father's school, in the following autumn. There were flowers in the winter, and a blossoming of the luxury Paul's mother had been used to. And yet the voices in the house, behind the sprays of mimosa and almond blossom, and from under the piles of iridescent cushions, simply trilled and screamed in a sort of ecstasy: "There must be more money! Oh-h-h, there must be more money. Oh, now, now-w! Now-w-w-w—there must be more money—more than ever! More than ever!"

It frightened Paul terribly. He studied away at his Latin and Greek with his tutor. But his intense hours were spent with Bassett. The Grand National had gone by: he had not "known," and had lost a hundred pounds. Summer was at hand. He was in agony for

---

Eton: England's most prestigious privately supported school

the Lincoln. But even for the Lincoln he didn't "know" and he lost fifty pounds. He became wild-eyed and strange, as if something were going to explode in him.

"Let it alone, son! Don't you bother about it!" urged Uncle Oscar. But it was as if the boy couldn't really hear what his uncle was saying.

"I've got to know for the Derby! I've got to know for the Derby!" the child reiterated, his big blue eyes blazing with a sort of madness.

His mother noticed how overwrought he was.   185

"You'd better go to the seaside. Wouldn't you like to go now to the seaside, instead of waiting? I think you'd better," she said, looking down at him anxiously, her heart curiously heavy because of him.

But the child lifted his uncanny blue eyes.

"I couldn't possibly go before the Derby, mother!" he said. "I couldn't possibly!"

"Why not?" she said, her voice becoming heavy when she was opposed. "Why not? You can still go from the seaside to see the Derby with your Uncle Oscar, if that's what you wish. No need for you to wait here. Besides, I think you care too much about these races. It's a bad sign. My family has been a gambling family, and you won't know till you grow up how much damage it has done. But it has done damage. I shall have to send Bassett away, and ask Uncle Oscar not to talk racing to you, unless you promise to be reasonable about it; go away to the seaside and forget it. You're all nerves!"

"I'll do what you like, mother, so long as you don't send me away till   190
after the Derby," the boy said.

"Send you away from where? Just from this house?"

"Yes," he said, gazing at her.

"Why, you curious child, what makes you care about this house so much, suddenly? I never knew you loved it."

He gazed at her without speaking. He had a secret within a secret, something he had not divulged, even to Bassett or to his Uncle Oscar.

But his mother, after standing undecided and a little bit sullen for   195
some moments, said:

"Very well, then! Don't go to the seaside till after the Derby, if you don't wish it. But promise me you won't let your nerves go to pieces. Promise you won't think so much about horse racing and events, as you call them!"

"Oh, no," said the boy casually. "I won't think much about them, mother. You needn't worry. I wouldn't worry, mother, if I were you."

"If you were me and I were you," said his mother, "I wonder what we should do!"

"But you know you needn't worry, mother, don't you?" the boy repeated.

200 "I should be awfully glad to know it," she said wearily.

"Oh, well, you can, you know. I mean, you ought to know you needn't worry," he insisted.

"Ought I? Then I'll see about it," she said.

Paul's secret of secrets was his wooden horse, that which had no name. Since he was emancipated from a nurse and a nursery-governess, he had had his rocking horse removed to his own bedroom at the top of the house.

"Surely, you're too big for a rocking horse!" his mother had remonstrated.

205 "Well, you see mother, till I can have a real horse, I like to have some sort of animal about," had been his quaint answer.

"Do you feel he keeps you company?" she laughed.

"Oh, yes! He's very good, he always keeps me company, when I'm there," said Paul.

So the horse, rather shabby, stood in an arrested prance in the boy's bedroom.

The Derby was drawing near, and the boy grew more and more tense. He hardly heard what was spoken to him, he was very frail, and his eyes were really uncanny. His mother had sudden seizures of uneasiness about him. Sometimes, for half-an-hour, she would feel a sudden anxiety about him that was almost anguish. She wanted to rush to him at once, and know he was safe.

210 Two nights before the Derby, she was at a big party in town, when one of her rushes of anxiety about her boy, her first-born, gripped her heart till she could hardly speak. She fought with the feeling, might and main, for she believed in common sense. But it was too strong. The children's nursery-governess was terribly surprised and startled at being rung up in the night.

"Are the children all right, Miss Wilmot?"

"Oh, yes, they are quite all right."

"Master Paul? Is he all right?"

"He went to bed as right as a trivet. Shall I run up and look at him?"

215 "No," said Paul's mother reluctantly. "No! Don't trouble. It's all right. Don't sit up. We shall be home fairly soon." She did not want her son's privacy intruded upon.

"Very good," said the governess.

It was about one o'clock when Paul's mother and father drove up to their house. All was still. Paul's mother went to her room and slipped off her white fur coat. She had told her maid not to wait up for her. She heard her husband downstairs, mixing a whiskey-and-soda.

And then, because of the strange anxiety at her heart, she stole upstairs to her son's room. Noiselessly she went along the upper corridor. Was there a faint noise? What was it?

She stood, with arrested muscles, outside his door listening. There was a strange, heavy, and yet not loud noise. Her heart stood still. It was a soundless noise, yet rushing and powerful. Something huge, in violent, hushed motion. What was it? What in God's name was it? She ought to know. She felt that she knew the noise. She knew what it was.

Yet she could not place it. She couldn't say what it was. And on and   220
on it went, like madness.

Softly, frozen with anxiety and fear, she turned the door handle.

The room was dark. Yet in the space near the window, she heard and saw something plunging to and fro. She gazed in fear and amazement.

Then suddenly she switched on the light, and saw her son, in his green pajamas, madly surging on the rocking horse. The blaze of light suddenly lit him up, as he urged the wooden horse, and lit her up, as she stood, blonde, in her dress of pale green and crystal, in the doorway.

"Paul!" she cried. "Whatever are you doing?"

"It's Malabar!" he screamed, in a powerful, strange voice. "It's   225
Malabar."

His eyes blazed at her for one strange and senseless second, as he ceased urging his wooden horse. Then he fell with a crash to the ground, and she, all her tormented motherhood flooding upon her, rushed to gather him up.

But he was unconscious, and unconscious he remained, with some brain-fever. He talked and tossed, and his mother sat stonily by his side.

"Malabar! It's Malabar! Bassett, Bassett, I know it! It's Malabar!"

So the child cried, trying to get up and urge the rocking horse that gave him his inspiration.

"What does he mean by Malabar?" asked the heart-frozen mother.   230

"I don't know," said his father stonily.

"What does he mean by Malabar?" she asked her brother Oscar.

"It's one of the horses running for the Derby," was the answer.

And, in spite of himself, Oscar Cresswell spoke to Bassett, and himself put a thousand on Malabar: at fourteen to one.

The third day of the illness was critical: they were waiting for a   235
change. The boy, with his rather long, curly hair, was tossing ceaselessly on the pillow. He neither slept nor regained consciousness, and his eyes were like blue stones. His mother sat, feeling her heart had gone, turned actually into a stone.

In the evening, Oscar Cresswell did not come, but Bassett sent a message, saying could he come up for one moment, just one moment? Paul's mother was very angry at the intrusion, but on second thought she agreed. The boy was the same. Perhaps Bassett might bring him to consciousness.

The gardener, a shortish fellow with a brown mustache, and sharp little brown eyes, tiptoed into the room, touched his imaginary cap to Paul's mother, and stole to the bedside, staring with glittering, smallish eyes, at the tossing, dying child.

"Master Paul!" he whispered. "Master Paul! Malabar came in first all right, a clean win. I did as you told me. You've made over seventy thousand pounds, you have; you've got over eighty thousand. Malabar came in all right, Master Paul."

"Malabar! Malabar! Did I say Malabar, mother? Did I say Malabar? Do you think I'm lucky, mother? I knew Malabar, didn't I? Over eighty thousand pounds! I call that lucky, don't you, mother? Over eighty thousand pounds! I knew, didn't I know I knew? Malabar came in all right. If I ride my horse till I'm sure, then I tell you, Bassett, you can go as high as you like. Did you go for all you were worth, Bassett?"

240   "I went a thousand on it, Master Paul."

"I never told you, mother, that if I can ride my horse, and get there, then I'm absolutely sure—oh, absolutely! Mother, did I ever tell you? I'm lucky."

"No, you never did," said the mother.

But the boy died in the night.

And even as he lay dead, his mother heard her brother's voice saying to her: "My God, Hester, you're eighty-odd thousand to the good and a poor devil of a son to the bad. But, poor devil, poor devil, he's best gone out of a life where he rides his rocking horse to find a winner."

QUESTIONS

1. In the phraseology of its beginning ("There was a woman . . ."), its simple style, its direct characterization, and its use of the wish motif—especially that of the wish that is granted only on conditions that nullify its desirability (compare the story of King Midas)—this story has the qualities of a fairy tale. Its differences, however—in characterization, setting, and ending—are especially significant. What do they tell us about the purpose of the story?

2. Characterize the mother fully. How does she differ from the stepmothers in fairy tales like "Cinderella" and "Hansel and Gretel"? How does the boy's mistake about *filthy lucker* (paragraph 15) clarify her thinking and her motivations? Why had her love for her husband turned to dust? Why is she "unlucky"?

3. What kind of a child is Paul? What are his motivations?
4. The initial assumptions of the story are that (a) a boy might get divinatory powers by riding a rocking horse, and (b) a house can whisper. Could the second of these be accepted as little more than a metaphor? Once we have granted these initial assumptions, does the story develop plausibly?
5. It is ironic that the boy's attempt to stop the whispers should only increase them. Is this a plausible irony? Why? What does it tell us about the theme of the story? Why is it ironic that the whispers should be especially audible at Christmas time? What irony is contained in the boy's last speech?
6. In what way is the boy's furious riding on the rocking horse an appropriate symbol for materialistic pursuits?
7. How might a commercial writer have ended the story?
8. How many persons in the story are affected (or infected) by materialism?
9. What is the theme of the story?

Nathaniel Hawthorne

Young Goodman Brown

Young Goodman Brown came forth at sunset into the street of Salem village, but put his head back, after crossing the threshold, to exchange a parting kiss with his young wife. And Faith, as the wife was aptly named, thrust her own pretty head into the street, letting the wind play with the pink ribbons of her cap while she called to Goodman Brown.

"Dearest heart," whispered she softly and rather sadly when her lips were close to his ear, "prithee, put off your journey until sunrise, and sleep in your own bed tonight. A lone woman is troubled with such dreams and such thoughts that she's afeard of herself, sometimes. Pray, tarry with me this night, dear husband, of all nights in the year!"

"My love and my Faith," replied young Goodman Brown, "of all nights in the year this one must I tarry away from thee. My journey, as thou callest it, forth and back again must needs be done 'twixt now and

YOUNG GOODMAN BROWN   First published in 1835. "Goodman" was a title of respect, but at a social rank lower than "gentleman." "Goody" (or "Goodwife") was the feminine equivalent. Deacon Gookin in the story is a historical personage (1612–1687), as are also Goody Cloyse, Goody Cory, and Martha Carrier, all three executed at the Salem witchcraft trials in 1692. Nathaniel Hawthorne (1804–1864) was born and grew up in Salem, Massachusetts, where Hawthornes had lived since the seventeenth century. One ancestor had been a judge at the Salem witch trials; another had been a leader in the persecution of Quakers. "Young Goodman Brown" is one of several stories in which Hawthorne explored the Puritan past of New England.

sunrise. What, my sweet, pretty wife, dost thou doubt me already, and we but three months married!"

"Then God bless you!" said Faith with the pink ribbons, "and may you find all well when you come back."

5   "Amen!" cried Goodman Brown. "Say thy prayers, dear Faith, and go to bed at dusk, and no harm will come to thee."

So they parted; and the young man pursued his way until, being about to turn the corner by the meeting-house, he looked back and saw the head of Faith still peeping after him with a melancholy air in spite of her pink ribbons.

"Poor little Faith!" thought he, for his heart smote him. "What a wretch am I, to leave her on such an errand! She talks of dreams, too. Methought, as she spoke, there was trouble in her face, as if a dream had warned her what work is to be done tonight. But no, no! 'twould kill her to think it. Well; she's a blessed angel on earth and after this one night I'll cling to her skirts and follow her to Heaven."

With this excellent resolve for the future, Goodman Brown felt himself justified in making more haste on his present evil purpose. He had taken a dreary road, darkened by all the gloomiest trees of the forest, which barely stood aside to let the narrow path creep through, and closed immediately behind. It was all as lonely as could be; and there is this peculiarity in such a solitude, that the traveler knows not who may be concealed by the innumerable trunks and the thick boughs overhead, so that with lonely footsteps he may be passing through an unseen multitude.

"There may be a devilish Indian behind every tree," said Goodman Brown to himself; and he glanced fearfully behind him as he added, "What if the devil himself should be at my very elbow!"

10   His head being turned back, he passed a crook of the road, and looking forward again beheld the figure of a man in grave and decent attire, seated at the foot of an old tree. He rose at Goodman Brown's approach and walked onward side by side with him.

"You are late, Goodman Brown," said he. "The clock of the Old South was striking as I came through Boston, and that is full fifteen minutes agone."°

"Faith kept me back awhile," replied the young man with a tremor in his voice caused by the sudden appearance of his companion, though not wholly unexpected.

---

full fifteen minutes agone: The distance from the center of Boston to the forest was over twenty miles.

It was now deep dusk in the forest, and deepest in that part of it where these two were journeying. As nearly as could be discerned, the second traveler was about fifty years old, apparently in the same rank of life as Goodman Brown, and bearing a considerable resemblance to him, though perhaps more in expression than features. Still, they might have been taken for father and son. And yet, though the elder person was as simply clad as the younger, and as simple in manner too, he had an indescribable air of one who knew the world and would not have felt abashed at the governor's dinner table or in King William's court,° were it possible that his affairs should call him thither. But the only thing about him that could be fixed upon as remarkable was his staff, which bore the likeness of a great black snake, so curiously wrought that it might almost be seen to twist and wriggle itself like a living serpent. This, of course, must have been an ocular deception, assisted by the uncertain light.

"Come, Goodman Brown!" cried his fellow-traveler, "this is a dull pace for the beginning of a journey. Take my staff if you are so soon weary."

"Friend," said the other, exchanging his slow pace for a full stop,   15
"having kept covenant by meeting thee here, it is my purpose now to return whence I came. I have scruples touching the matter thou wot'st of."

"Sayest thou so?" replied he of the serpent, smiling apart. "Let us walk on nevertheless, reasoning as we go, and if I convince thee not, thou shalt turn back. We are but a little way in the forest yet."

"Too far, too far!" exclaimed the goodman, unconsciously resuming his walk. "My father never went into the woods on such an errand, nor his father before him. We have been a race of honest men and good Christians since the days of the martyrs. And shall I be the first of the name of Brown that ever took this path and kept—"

"Such company, thou wouldst say," observed the elder person interrupting his pause. "Well said, Goodman Brown! I have been as well acquainted with your family as with ever a one among the Puritans, and that's no trifle to say. I helped your grandfather the constable when he lashed the Quaker woman so smartly through the streets of Salem. And it was I that brought your father a pitch-pine knot kindled at my own hearth, to set fire to an Indian village, in King Philip's war.° They were my good friends, both; and many a pleasant walk have we had along this path and returned merrily after midnight. I would fain be friends with you, for their sake."

King William's court: William III, King of England, 1689–1702   **King Philip's war:** a war between the colonists and Indians, 1675–1676

"If it be as thou sayest," replied Goodman Brown, "I marvel they never spoke of these matters. Or, verily, I marvel not, seeing that the least rumor of the sort would have driven them from New England. We are a people of prayer, and good works to boot, and abide no such wickedness."

20   "Wickedness or not," said the traveler with twisted staff, "I have a general acquaintance here in New England. The deacons of many a church have drunk the communion wine with me, the selectmen of divers towns make me their chairman, and a majority of the Great and General Court° are firm supporters of my interest. The governor and I, too—but these are state secrets."

"Can this be so!" cried Goodman Brown with a stare of amazement at his undisturbed companion. "Howbeit, I have nothing to do with the governor and council; they have their own ways and are no rule for a simple husbandman like me. But were I to go on with thee, how should I meet the eye of that good old man, our minister, at Salem village? Oh, his voice would make me tremble, both Sabbath-day and lecture-day!"

Thus far, the elder traveler had listened with due gravity but now burst into a fit of irrepressible mirth, shaking himself so violently that his snakelike staff actually seemed to wriggle in sympathy.

"Ha! ha! ha!" shouted he, again and again; then composing himself, "Well, go on, Goodman Brown, go on; but prithee, don't kill me with laughing!"

"Well, then, to end the matter at once," said Goodman Brown, considerably nettled, "there is my wife, Faith. It would break her dear little heart, and I'd rather break my own!"

25   "Nay, if that be the case," answered the other, "e'en go thy ways, Goodman Brown. I would not for twenty old women like the one hobbling before us that Faith should come to any harm."

As he spoke he pointed his staff at a female figure on the path in whom Goodman Brown recognized a very pious and exemplary dame who had taught him his catechism in youth and was still his moral and spiritual adviser, jointly with the minister and Deacon Gookin.

"A marvel, truly, that Goody Cloyse should be so far in the wilderness at nightfall!" said he. "But with your leave, friend, I shall take a cut through the woods until we have left this Christian woman behind. Being a stranger to you, she might ask whom I was consorting with and whither I was going."

"Be it so," said his fellow-traveler. "Betake you to the woods and let me keep the path."

Great and General Court: the legislature of the Massachusetts Bay Colony

Accordingly, the young man turned aside, but took care to watch his companion who advanced softly along the road until he had come within a staff's length of the old dame. She, meanwhile, was making the best of her way, with singular speed for so aged a woman, and mumbling some indistinct words, a prayer, doubtless, as she went. The traveler put forth his staff and touched her withered neck with what seemed the serpent's tail.

"The devil!" screamed the pious old lady.   30

"Then Goody Cloyse knows her old friend?" observed the traveler, confronting her and leaning on his writhing stick.

"Ah, forsooth, and is it your worship indeed?" cried the good dame. "Yea, truly is it, and in the very image of my old gossip, Goodman Brown, the grandfather of the silly fellow that now is. But would your worship believe it? my broomstick hath strangely disappeared, stolen as I suspect by that unhanged witch, Goody Cory, and that, too, when I was all anointed with the juice of smallage and cinque-foil and wolf's-bane—"

"Mingled with fine wheat and the fat of a new-born babe," said the shape of old Goodman Brown.

"Ah, your worship knows the recipe," cried the old lady, cackling aloud. "So, as I was saying, being all ready for the meeting, and no horse to ride on, I made up my mind to foot it; for they tell me there is a nice young man to be taken into communion tonight. But now your good worship will lend me your arm and we shall be there in a twinkling."

"That can hardly be," answered her friend. "I may not spare you my   35
arm, Goody Cloyse, but here is my staff, if you will."

So saying, he threw it down at her feet where, perhaps, it assumed life, being one of the rods which its owner had formerly lent to the Egyptian Magi. Of this fact, however, Goodman Brown could not take cognizance. He had cast up his eyes in astonishment, and looking down again beheld neither Goody Cloyse nor the serpentine staff, but his fellow-traveler alone, who waited for him as calmly as if nothing had happened.

"That old woman taught me my catechism!" said the young man, and there was a world of meaning in this simple comment.

They continued to walk onward while the elder traveler exhorted his companion to make good speed and persevere in the path, discoursing so aptly that his arguments seemed rather to spring up in the bosom of his auditor than to be suggested by himself. As they went he plucked a branch of maple to serve for a walking-stick, and began to strip it of the twigs and little boughs which were wet with evening dew. The moment his fingers touched them they became strangely withered and dried up, as with a week's sunshine. Thus the pair proceeded at a good free pace, until suddenly, in a gloomy hollow of the road, Goodman Brown sat himself down on the stump of a tree and refused to go any farther.

"Friend," said he stubbornly, "my mind is made up. Not another step will I budge on this errand. What if a wretched old woman do choose to go to the devil when I thought she was going to Heaven! Is that any reason why I should quit my dear Faith and go after her?"

40   "You will think better of this by and by," said his acquaintance composedly. "Sit here and rest yourself awhile, and when you feel like moving again, there is my staff to help you along."

Without more words, he threw his companion the maple stick and was as speedily out of sight as if he had vanished into the deepening gloom. The young man sat a few moments by the roadside, applauding himself greatly and thinking with how clear a conscience he should meet the minister in his morning walk, nor shrink from the eye of good old Deacon Gookin. And what calm sleep would be his that very night, which was to have been spent so wickedly, but purely and sweetly now, in the arms of Faith! Amidst these pleasant and praiseworthy meditations, Goodman Brown heard the tramp of horses along the road and deemed it advisable to conceal himself within the verge of the forest, conscious of the guilty purpose that had brought him thither, though now so happily turned from it.

On came the hoof-tramps and the voices of the riders, two grave old voices conversing soberly as they drew near. These mingled sounds appeared to pass along the road within a few yards of the young man's hiding place; but owing, doubtless, to the depth of the gloom at that particular spot, neither the travelers nor their steeds were visible. Though their figures brushed the small boughs by the wayside, it could not be seen that they intercepted even for a moment the faint gleam from the strip of bright sky athwart which they must have passed. Goodman Brown alternately crouched and stood on tiptoe, pulling aside the branches and thrusting forth his head as far as he durst, without discerning so much as a shadow. It vexed him the more because he could have sworn, were such a thing possible, that he recognized the voices of the minister and Deacon Gookin, jogging along quietly as they were wont to do when bound to some ordination or ecclesiastical council. While yet within hearing, one of the riders stopped to pluck a switch.

"Of the two, reverend Sir," said the voice like the deacon's, "I had rather miss an ordination dinner than tonight's meeting. They tell me that some of our community are to be here from Falmouth and beyond, and others from Connecticut and Rhode Island, besides several of the Indian powwows who, after their fashion, know almost as much deviltry as the best of us. Moreover, there is a goodly young woman to be taken into communion."

"Mighty well, Deacon Gookin!" replied the solemn old tones of the minister. "Spur up, or we shall be late. Nothing can be done, you know, until I get on the ground."

The hoofs clattered again, and the voices talking so strangely in the empty air passed on through the forest where no church had ever been gathered nor solitary Christian prayed. Whither, then, could these holy men be journeying, so deep into the heathen wilderness? Young Good-man Brown caught hold of a tree for support, being ready to sink down on the ground, faint and over-burthened with the heavy sickness of his heart. He looked up to the sky, doubting whether there really was a Heaven above him. Yet there was the blue arch, and the stars brightening in it.

"With Heaven above, and Faith below, I will yet stand firm against the devil!" cried Goodman Brown.

While he still gazed upward into the deep arch of the firmament and had lifted his hands to pray, a cloud, though no wind was stirring, hurried across the zenith and hid the brightening stars. The blue sky was still visible except directly overhead, where this black mass of cloud was sweeping swiftly northward. Aloft in the air, as if from the depths of the cloud, came a confused and doubtful sound of voices. Once the listener fancied that he could distinguish the accents of townspeople of his own, men and women, both pious and ungodly, many of whom he had met at the communion-table, and had seen others rioting at the tavern. The next moment, so indistinct were the sounds, he doubted whether he had heard aught but the murmur of the old forest whispering without a wind. Then came a stronger swell of those familiar tones heard daily in the sunshine at Salem village, but never, until now, from a cloud at night. There was one voice, of a young woman uttering lamentations yet with an uncertain sorrow, and entreating for some favor, which, perhaps, it would grieve her to obtain. And all the unseen multitude, both saints and sinners, seemed to encourage her onward.

"Faith!" shouted Goodman Brown in a voice of agony and despera-tion; and the echoes of the forest mocked him, crying "Faith! Faith!" as if bewildered wretches were seeking her all through the wilderness.

The cry of grief, rage, and terror was yet piercing the night when the unhappy husband held his breath for a response. There was a scream, drowned immediately in a louder murmur of voices fading into far-off laughter as the dark cloud swept away leaving the clear and silent sky above Goodman Brown. But something fluttered lightly down through the air and caught on the branch of a tree. The young man seized it and beheld a pink ribbon.

50   "My Faith is gone!" cried he, after one stupefied moment. "There is no good on earth, and sin is but a name. Come, devil! for to thee is this world given."

And maddened with despair, so that he laughed loud and long, did Goodman Brown grasp his staff and set forth again at such a rate that he seemed to fly along the forest path rather than to walk or run. The road grew wilder and drearier and more faintly traced, and vanished at length, leaving him in the heart of the dark wilderness, still rushing onward with the instinct that guides mortal man to evil. The whole forest was peopled with frightful sounds—the creaking of the trees, the howling of wild beasts, and the yell of Indians; while sometimes the wind tolled like a distant church bell, and sometimes gave a broad roar around the traveler, as if all Nature were laughing him to scorn. But he was himself the chief horror of the scene, and shrank not from its other horrors.

"Ha! ha! ha!" roared Goodman Brown when the wind laughed at him. "Let us hear which will laugh loudest! Think not to frighten me with your deviltry! come witch, come wizard, come Indian powwow, come devil himself! and here comes Goodman Brown. You may as well fear him as he fear you!"

In truth, all through the haunted forest there could be nothing more frightful than the figure of Goodman Brown. On he flew among the black pines, brandishing his staff with frenzied gestures, now giving vent to an inspiration of horrid blasphemy, and now shouting forth such laughter as set all the echoes of the forest laughing like demons around him. The fiend in his own shape is less hideous than when he rages in the breast of man. Thus sped the demoniac on his course until, quivering among the trees, he saw a red light before him, as when the felled trunks and branches of a clearing have been set on fire and throw up their lurid blaze against the sky at the hour of midnight. He paused in a lull of the tempest that had driven him onward, and heard the swell of what seemed a hymn rolling solemnly from a distance with the weight of many voices. He knew the tune. It was a familiar one in the choir of the village meeting-house. The verse died heavily away, and was lengthened by a chorus not of human voices but of all the sounds of the benighted wilderness pealing in awful harmony together. Goodman Brown cried out, and his cry was lost to his own ear by its unison with the cry of the desert.

In the interval of silence he stole forward until the light glared full upon his eyes. At one extremity of an open space, hemmed in by the dark wall of the forest, arose a rock bearing some rude, natural resemblance either to an altar or a pulpit, and surrounded by four blazing pines, their tops aflame, their stems untouched, like candles at an evening meeting. The mass of foliage that had overgrown the summit of the rock was all on fire, blazing high into the night and fitfully illuminating the whole field. Each pendent twig and leafy festoon was in a blaze. As the red light arose and fell, a numerous congregation alternately shone forth, then disappeared in shadow, and again grew, as it were, out of the darkness, peopling the heart of the solitary woods at once.

"A grave and dark-clad company!" quoth Goodman Brown.   55

In truth they were such. Among them, quivering to and fro between gloom and splendor, appeared faces that would be seen next day at the council-board of the province, and others which Sabbath after Sabbath looked devoutly heavenward and benignantly over the crowded pews from the holiest pulpits in the land. Some affirm that the lady of the governor was there. At least, there were high dames well known to her, and wives of honored husbands, and widows a great multitude, and ancient maidens, all of excellent repute, and fair young girls who trembled lest their mothers should espy them. Either the sudden gleams of light flashing over the obscure field bedazzled Goodman Brown, or he recognized a score of the church members of Salem village famous for their especial sanctity. Good old Deacon Gookin had arrived and waited at the skirts of that venerable saint, his reverend pastor. But irreverently consorting with these grave, reputable, and pious people, these elders of the church, these chaste dames and dewy virgins, there were men of dissolute lives and women of spotted fame, wretches given over to all mean and filthy vice and suspected even of horrid crimes. It was strange to see that the good shrank not from the wicked, nor were the sinners abashed by the saints. Scattered also among their pale-faced enemies were the Indian priests or powwows who had often scared their native forest with more hideous incantations than any known to English witchcraft.

"But where is Faith?" thought Goodman Brown; and as hope came into his heart he trembled.

Another verse of the hymn arose, a slow and mournful strain such as the pious love, but joined to words which expressed all that our nature can conceive of sin, and darkly hinted at far more. Unfathomable to mere mortals is the lore of fiends. Verse after verse was sung, and still the chorus of the desert swelled between, like the deepest tone of a mighty organ. And with the final peal of that dreadful anthem, there came a sound as if the roaring wind, the rushing streams, the howling beasts, and every other voice of the unconverted wilderness were mingling and according with the voice of guilty man in homage to the prince of all. The four blazing pines threw up a loftier flame and obscurely discovered shapes and visages of horror on the smoke-wreaths above the impious assembly. At the same moment the fire on the rock shot redly forth and formed a glowing arch above its base, where now appeared a figure. With reverence be it spoken, the apparition bore no slight similitude both in garb and manner to some grave divine of the New England churches.

"Bring forth the converts!" cried a voice that echoed through the field and rolled into the forest.

60   At the word, Goodman Brown stepped forth from the shadow of the trees and approached the congregation, with whom he felt a loathful brotherhood by the sympathy of all that was wicked in his heart. He could have well-nigh sworn that the shape of his own dead father beckoned him to advance, looking downward from a smoke-wreath, while a woman with dim features of despair threw out her hand to warn him back. Was it his mother? But he had no power to retreat one step nor to resist, even in thought, when the minister and good old Deacon Gookin seized his arms and led him to the blazing rock. Thither came also the slender form of a veiled female led between Goody Cloyse, that pious teacher of the catechism, and Martha Carrier, who had received the devil's promise to be queen of hell. A rampant hag was she! And there stood the proselytes beneath the canopy of fire.

"Welcome, my children," said the dark figure, "to the communion of your race! Ye have found, thus young, your nature and your destiny. My children, look behind you!"

They turned, and flashing forth as it were in a sheet of flame, the fiend-worshippers were seen; the smile of welcome gleamed darkly on every visage.

"There," resumed the sable form, "are all whom ye have reverenced from youth. Ye deemed them holier than yourselves and shrank from your own sin, contrasting it with their lives of righteousness and prayerful aspirations heavenward. Yet here are they all in my worshipping assembly! This night it shall be granted you to know their secret deeds: how hoary-bearded elders of the church have whispered wanton words to the young maids of their households; how many a woman eager for widow's weeds has given her husband a drink at bedtime, and let him sleep his last sleep in her bosom; how beardless youths have made haste to inherit their father's wealth; and how fair damsels—blush not, sweet ones!—have dug little graves in the garden and bidden me, the sole guest, to an infant's funeral. By the sympathy of your human hearts for sin, ye shall scent out all the places—whether in church, bedchamber, street, field, or forest—where crime has been committed, and shall exult to behold the whole earth one stain of guilt, one mighty blood-spot. Far more than this! It shall be yours to penetrate in every bosom the deep mystery of sin, the fountain of all wicked arts, and which inexhaustibly supplies more evil impulses than human power—than my power, at its utmost!—can make manifest in deeds. And now, my children, look upon each other."

They did so, and by the blaze of the hell-kindled torches the wretched man beheld his Faith, and the wife her husband trembling before that unhallowed altar.

"Lo! there ye stand, my children," said the figure in a deep solemn   65
tone, almost sad with its despairing awfulness, as if his once angelic nature could yet mourn for our miserable race. "Depending upon one another's hearts, ye had still hoped that virtue were not all a dream! Now are ye undeceived—Evil is the nature of mankind. Evil must be your only happiness. Welcome, again, my children, to the communion of your race!"

"Welcome!" repeated the fiend-worshippers in one cry of despair and triumph.

And there they stood, the only pair as it seemed who were yet hesitating on the verge of wickedness in this dark world. A basin was hollowed naturally in the rock. Did it contain water, reddened by the lurid light? or was it blood? or, perchance, a liquid flame? Herein did the Shape of Evil dip his hand and prepare to lay the mark of baptism upon their foreheads, that they might be partakers of the mystery of sin, more conscious of the secret guilt of others both in deed and thought than they could now be of their own. The husband cast one look at his pale wife, and Faith at him. What polluted wretches would the next glance show them to each other, shuddering alike at what they disclosed and what they saw!

"Faith! Faith!" cried the husband. "Look up to Heaven, and resist the Wicked One!"

Whether Faith obeyed he knew not. Hardly had he spoken when he found himself amid calm night and solitude, listening to a roar of the wind which died heavily away through the forest. He staggered against the rock and felt it chill and damp, while a hanging twig that had been all on fire besprinkled his cheek with the coldest dew.

The next morning, young Goodman Brown came slowly into the   70
street of Salem village staring around him like a bewildered man. The good old minister was taking a walk along the graveyard to get an appetite for breakfast and meditate his sermon, and bestowed a blessing as he passed on Goodman Brown. He shrank from the venerable saint as if to avoid an anathema. Old Deacon Gookin was at domestic worship, and

the holy words of his prayer were heard through the open window. "What God doth the wizard pray to?" quoth Goodman Brown. Goody Cloyse, that excellent old Christian, stood in the early sunshine at her own lattice catechizing a little girl who had brought her a pint of morning's milk. Goodman Brown snatched away the child as from the grasp of the fiend himself. Turning the corner by the meeting-house, he spied the head of Faith with the pink ribbons gazing anxiously forth, and bursting into such joy at sight of him that she skipped along the street and almost kissed her husband before the whole village. But Goodman Brown looked sternly and sadly into her face and passed on without a greeting.

Had Goodman Brown fallen asleep in the forest and only dreamed a wild dream of a witch-meeting?

Be it so, if you will. But, alas! it was a dream of evil omen for young Goodman Brown. A stern, a sad, a darkly meditative, a distrustful, if not a desperate man did he become from the night of that fearful dream. On the Sabbath-day when the congregation were singing a holy psalm, he could not listen because an anthem of sin rushed loudly upon his ear and drowned all the blessed strain. When the minister spoke from the pulpit with power and fervid eloquence and with his hand on the open Bible, of the sacred truths of our religion, and of saint-like lives and triumphant deaths, and of future bliss or misery unutterable, then did Goodman Brown turn pale, dreading lest the roof should thunder down upon the gray blasphemer and his hearers. Often awaking suddenly at midnight, he shrank from the bosom of Faith, and at morning or eventide when the family knelt down at prayer, he scowled and muttered to himself and gazed sternly at his wife and turned away. And when he had lived long and was borne to his grave a hoary corpse, followed by Faith, an aged woman, and children and grandchildren, a goodly procession, besides neighbors not a few, they carved no hopeful verse upon his tombstone, for his dying hour was gloom.

QUESTIONS

1. What does Hawthorne gain by including the names of actual persons (Goody Cloyse, Goody Cory, Deacon Gookin, Martha Carrier) and places (Salem village, Boston, Old South Church)? What religion is practiced by the townspeople?

2. What is the point of view? Where does it change, and what is the result of the change?

3. What allegorical meanings may be given to Goodman Brown? His wife? The forest? Night (as opposed to day)? Brown's journey?

4. What is Brown's motive for going into the forest? What results does he expect from his journey? What does he expect the rest of his life to be like?

5. After he keeps his appointment with the traveler in the forest, Brown announces that he plans to return home. Why does he not do so immediately, and why at each stage when he renews his intention to do so does he proceed deeper into the forest? Is there any reason to suppose he does not actually see and hear what he thinks he perceives?
6. What details of the "witch-meeting" parallel those of a church communion service? Why does the congregation include "grave, reputable, and pious people" as well as known sinners (paragraph 56)?
7. What prevents Goodman Brown from receiving baptism? What does the devil promise as the result of baptism? Is that what you usually suppose is the reward for selling your soul to the devil? Why is it an appropriate reward for Goodman Brown? Since he does not receive baptism, how do you account for his behavior when he returns to the village?
8. "Had Goodman Brown . . . only dreamed a wild dream of a witch-meeting?" (paragraph 71). How are we to answer this question? Point out other places where Hawthorne leaves the interpretation of the story ambiguous. How is such ambiguity related to the story's theme?
9. Characterize the behavior of Faith and the other townspeople after Brown's return to the village. Are Brown's attitude and behavior thereafter the result of conviction or doubt? Is he completely misanthropic?
10. Does the story demonstrate the devil's claim that "Evil is the nature of mankind" (paragraph 65)?

Ursula K. Le Guin

The Ones Who Walk Away from Omelas

With a clamor of bells that set the swallows soaring, the Festival of Summer came to the city. Omelas, bright-towered by the sea. The rigging of the boats in harbor sparkled with flags. In the streets between houses with red roofs and painted walls, between old moss-grown gardens and under avenues of trees, past great parks and public buildings, processions moved. Some were decorous: old people in long stiff robes of mauve and grey, grave master workmen, quiet, merry women carrying their babies and chatting as they walked. In other streets the music beat faster, a shimmering of gong and tambourine, and the people went dancing, the procession was a dance. Children dodged in and out, their high calls rising like the swallows' crossing flights over the music and the singing. All the processions wound towards the north side of the

THE ONES WHO WALK AWAY FROM OMELAS   First published in 1973. Ursula K. Le Guin (b. 1929) is a prolific author of science fiction and fantasy novels and short stories. Educated at Radcliffe College and Columbia University, she lives in Oregon. Her best-known works are the novels *The Left Hand of Darkness* (1969) and *The Dispossessed* (1974).

city, where on the great water-meadow called the Green Fields boys and girls, naked in the bright air, with mud-stained feet and ankles and long, lithe arms, exercised their restive horses before the race. The horses wore no gear at all but a halter without bit. Their manes were braided with streamers of silver, gold, and green. They flared their nostrils and pranced and boasted to one another; they were vastly excited, the horse being the only animal who has adopted our ceremonies as his own. Far off to the north and west the mountains stood up half encircling Omelas on her bay. The air of morning was so clear that the snow still crowning the Eighteen Peaks burned with white-gold fire across the miles of sunlit air, under the dark blue of the sky. There was just enough wind to make the banners that marked the racecourse snap and flutter now and then. In the silence of the broad green meadows one could hear the music winding through the city streets, farther and nearer and ever approaching, a cheerful faint sweetness of the air that from time to time trembled and gathered together and broke out into the great joyous clanging of the bells.

Joyous! How is one to tell about joy? How describe the citizens of Omelas?

They were not simple folk, you see, though they were happy. But we do not say the words of cheer much any more. All smiles have become archaic. Given a description such as this one tends to make certain assumptions. Given a description such as this one tends to look next for the King, mounted on a splendid stallion and surrounded by his noble knights, or perhaps in a golden litter borne by great-muscled slaves. But there was no king. They did not use swords, or keep slaves. They were not barbarians. I do not know the rules and laws of their society, but I suspect that they were singularly few. As they did without monarchy and slavery, so they also got on without the stock exchange, the advertisement, the secret police, and the bomb. Yet I repeat that these were not simple folk, not dulcet shepherds, noble savages, bland utopians. They were not less complex than us. The trouble is that we have a bad habit, encouraged by pedants and sophisticates, of considering happiness as something rather stupid. Only pain is intellectual, only evil interesting. This is the treason of the artist: a refusal to admit the banality of evil and the terrible boredom of pain. If you can't lick 'em, join 'em. If it hurts, repeat it. But to praise despair is to condemn delight, to embrace violence is to lose hold of everything else. We have almost lost hold; we can no longer describe a happy man, nor make any celebration of joy. How can I tell you about the people of Omelas? They were not naïve and happy children—though their children were, in fact, happy. They were mature, intelligent, passionate adults whose lives were not wretched.

O miracle! but I wish I could describe it better. I wish I could convince you. Omelas sounds in my words like a city in a fairy tale, long ago and far away, once upon a time. Perhaps it would be best if you imagined it as your own fancy bids, assuming it will rise to the occasion, for certainly I cannot suit you all. For instance, how about technology? I think that there would be no cars or helicopters in and above the streets; this follows from the fact that the people of Omelas are happy people. Happiness is based on a just discrimination of what is necessary, what is neither necessary nor destructive, and what is destructive. In the middle category, however—that of the unnecessary but undestructive, that of comfort, luxury, exuberance, etc.—they could perfectly well have central heating, subway trains, washing machines, and all kinds of marvelous devices not yet invented here, floating light-sources, fuel-less power, a cure for the common cold. Or they could have none of that: it doesn't matter. As you like it. I incline to think that people from towns up and down the coast have been coming in to Omelas during the last days before the Festival on very fast little trains and double-decked trams and that the train station of Omelas is actually the handsomest building in town, though plainer than the magnificent Farmers' Market. But even granted trains, I fear that Omelas so far strikes some of you as goody-goody. Smiles, bells, parades, horses, bleh. If so, please add an orgy. If an orgy would help, don't hesitate. Let us not, however, have temples from which issue beautiful nude priests and priestesses already half in ecstasy and ready to copulate with any man or woman, lover or stranger, who desires union with the deep godhead of the blood, although that was my first idea. But really it would be better not to have any temples in Omelas—at least, not manned temples. Religion yes, clergy no. Surely the beautiful nudes can just wander about, offering themselves like divine soufflés to the hunger of the needy and the rapture of the flesh. Let them join the processions. Let tambourines be struck above the copulations, and the glory of desire be proclaimed upon the gongs, and (a not unimportant point) let the offspring of these delightful rituals be beloved and looked after by all. One thing I know there is none of in Omelas is guilt. But what else should there be? I thought at first there were no drugs, but that is puritanical. For those who like it, the faint insistent sweetness of *drooz* may perfume the ways of the city, *drooz* which first brings a great lightness and brilliance to the mind and limbs, and then after some hours a dreamy languor, and wonderful visions at last of the very arcana and inmost secrets of the Universe, as well as exciting the pleasure of sex beyond all belief; and it is not habit-forming. For more modest tastes I think there ought to be beer. What else, what else belongs in the joyous city? The sense of victory, surely, the celebration of courage. But as we did without clergy, let us do without soldiers. The joy built upon successful slaughter is not the right kind of joy; it will not do; it is fearful and it is trivial. A boundless and generous contentment, a magnanimous triumph felt not against some outer enemy but in communion with the finest and fairest in the souls of all men everywhere and the splendor of the world's summer: this is what swells the hearts of the people of Omelas, and the victory they celebrate is that of life. I really don't think many of them need to take *drooz*.

Most of the processions have reached the Green Fields by now. A marvelous smell of cooking goes forth from the red and blue tents of the provisioners. The faces of small children are amiably sticky; in the benign grey beard of a man a couple of crumbs of rich pastry are entangled. The youths and girls have mounted their horses and are beginning to group around the starting line of the course. An old woman, small, fat, and laughing, is passing out flowers from a basket, and tall young men wear her flowers in their shining hair. A child of nine or ten sits at the edge of the crowd, alone, playing on a wooden flute. People pause to listen, and they smile, but they do not speak to him, for he never ceases playing and never sees them, his dark eyes wholly rapt in the sweet, thin magic of the tune.

5   He finishes, and slowly lowers his hands holding the wooden flute.

As if that little private silence were the signal, all at once a trumpet sounds from the pavillion near the starting line: imperious, melancholy, piercing. The horses rear on their slender legs, and some of them neigh in answer. Sober-faced, the young riders stroke the horses' necks and soothe them, whispering, "Quiet, quiet, there my beauty, my hope. . . ." They begin to form in rank along the starting line. The crowds along the racecourse are like a field of grass and flowers in the wind. The Festival of Summer has begun.

Do you believe? Do you accept the festival, the city, the joy? No? Then let me describe one more thing.

In a basement under one of the beautiful public buildings of Omelas, or perhaps in the cellar of one of its spacious private homes, there is a room. It has one locked door, and no window. A little light seeps in dustily between cracks in the boards, secondhand from a cobwebbed window somewhere across the cellar. In one corner of the little room a couple of mops, with stiff, clotted, foul-smelling heads, stand near a rusty bucket. The floor is dirt, a little damp to the touch, as cellar dirt usually is. The room is about three paces long and two wide: a mere broom closet or disused tool room. In the room a child is sitting. It could be a boy or a girl. It looks about six, but actually is nearly ten. It is feeble-

minded. Perhaps it was born defective, or perhaps it has become imbecile through fear, malnutrition, and neglect. It picks its nose and occasionally fumbles vaguely with its toes or genitals, as it sits hunched in the
corner farthest from the bucket and the two mops. It is afraid of the
mops. It finds them horrible. It shuts its eyes, but it knows the mops are
still standing there; and the door is locked; and nobody will come. The
door is always locked; and nobody ever comes, except that sometimes—
the child has no understanding of time or interval—sometimes the door
rattles terribly and opens, and a person, or several people, are there. One
of them may come in and kick the child to make it stand up. The others
never come close, but peer in at it with frightened, disgusted eyes. The
food bowl and the water jug are hastily filled, the door is locked, the eyes
disappear. The people at the door never say anything, but the child, who
has not always lived in the tool room, and can remember sunlight and its
mother's voice, sometimes speaks. "I will be good," it says. "Please let me
out. I will be good!" They never answer. The child used to scream for
help at night, and cry a good deal, but now it only makes a kind of
whining, "eh-haa, eh-haa," and it speaks less and less often. It is so thin
there are no calves to its legs; its belly protrudes; it lives on a half-bowl of
corn meal and grease a day. It is naked. Its buttocks and thighs are a mass
of festered sores, as it sits in its own excrement continually.

They all know it is there, all the people of Omelas. Some of them
have come to see it, others are content merely to know it is there. They
all know that it has to be there. Some of them understand why, and
some do not, but they all understand that their happiness, the beauty of
their city, the tenderness of their friendships, the health of their children, the wisdom of their scholars, the skill of their makers, even the
abundance of their harvest and the kindly weathers of their skies,
depend wholly on this child's abominable misery.

This is usually explained to children when they are between eight   10
and twelve, whenever they seem capable of understanding; and most of
those who come to see the child are young people, though often enough
an adult comes, or comes back, to see the child. No matter how well the
matter has been explained to them, these young spectators are always
shocked and sickened at the sight. They feel disgust, which they had
thought themselves superior to. They feel anger, outrage, impotence,
despite all the explanations. They would like to do something for the
child. But there is nothing they can do. If the child were brought up into
the sunlight out of that vile place, if it were cleaned and fed and
comforted, that would be a good thing, indeed; but if it were done, in
that day and hour all the prosperity and beauty and delight of Omelas
would wither and be destroyed. Those are the terms. To exchange all the

goodness and grace of every life in Omelas for that single, small improvement: to throw away the happiness of thousands for the chance of the happiness of one: that would be to let guilt within the walls indeed.

The terms are strict and absolute; there may not even be a kind word spoken to the child.

Often the young people go home in tears, or in a tearless rage, when they have seen the child and faced this terrible paradox. They may brood over it for weeks or years. But as time goes on they begin to realize that even if the child could be released, it would not get much good of its freedom: a little vague pleasure of warmth and food, no doubt, but little more. It is too degraded and imbecile to know any real joy. It has been afraid too long ever to be free of fear. Its habits are too uncouth for it to respond to humane treatment. Indeed, after so long it would probably be wretched without walls about it to protect it, and darkness for its eyes, and its own excrement to sit in. Their tears at the bitter injustice dry when they begin to perceive the terrible justice of reality and to accept it. Yet it is their tears and anger, the trying of their generosity and the acceptance of their helplessness, which are perhaps the true source of the splendor of their lives. Theirs is no vapid, irresponsible happiness. They know that they, like the child, are not free. They know compassion. It is the existence of the child, and their knowledge of its existence, that makes possible the nobility of their architecture, the poignancy of their music, the profundity of their science. It is because of the child that they are so gentle with children. They know that if the wretched one were not there snivelling in the dark, the other one, the flute-player, could make no joyful music as the young riders line up in their beauty for the race in the sunlight of the first morning of summer.

Now do you believe in them? Are they not more credible? But there is one more thing to tell, and this is quite incredible.

At times one of the adolescent girls or boys who go to see the child does not go home to weep or rage, does not, in fact, go home at all. Sometimes also a man or woman much older falls silent for a day or two, and then leaves home. These people go out into the street, and walk down the street alone. They keep walking, and walk straight out of the city of Omelas, through the beautiful gates. They keep walking across the farmlands of Omelas. Each one goes alone, youth or girl, man or woman. Night falls; the traveler must pass down village streets, between the houses with yellow-lit windows, and on out into the darkness of the fields. Each alone, they go west or north, towards the mountains. They go on. They leave Omelas, they walk ahead into the darkness, and they do not come back. The place they go towards is a place even less imaginable to most of us than the city of happiness. I cannot describe it at all. It is possible that it does not exist. But they seem to know where they are going, the ones who walk away from Omelas.

QUESTIONS

1. Describe the fantasy elements in this story. How does the fantasy reflect the conditions of the real world?
2. Why does the story contain no scenes, dialogue, or conventional plot?
3. How would you describe the narrator? Is the narrator reliable or unreliable? How does the narrator seem to regard Omelas and its social conditions?
4. What is the theme of the story? Compare this story to Shirley Jackson's "The Lottery." Though the two realities presented in the stories are very different, in what ways are they similar? What common themes do the stories share?
5. What does the miserable child represent? Is the child's misery inevitable or preventable?
6. What kinds of people are those who "walk away" from Omelas? Does the narrator seem to approve or disapprove of these people?

Gabriel García Márquez

A Very Old Man with Enormous Wings

On the third day of rain they had killed so many crabs inside the house that Pelayo had to cross his drenched courtyard and throw them into the sea, because the newborn child had a temperature all night and they thought it was due to the stench. The world had been sad since Tuesday. Sea and sky were a single ash-gray thing and the sands of the beach, which on March nights glimmered like powdered light, had become a stew of mud and rotten shellfish. The light was so weak at noon that when Pelayo was coming back to the house after throwing away the crabs, it was hard for him to see what it was that was moving and groaning in the rear of the courtyard. He had to go very close to see that it was an old man, a very old man, lying face down in the mud, who, in spite of his tremendous efforts, couldn't get up, impeded by his enormous wings.

Frightened by that nightmare, Pelayo ran to get Elisenda, his wife, who was putting compresses on the sick child, and he took her to the

A VERY OLD MAN WITH ENORMOUS WINGS   First published in 1955. Translated by Gregory Rabassa. Born in Colombia in 1928, Gabriel García Márquez studied law and worked as a newspaper reporter before publishing his first book of stories, *Leaf Storm* (1955). His best-known novels, which exemplify the unique blend of realistic and fantastic detail known as magical realism, include *One Hundred Years of Solitude* (1969) and *Love in the Time of Cholera* (1988). He won the Nobel Prize for literature in 1982.

rear of the courtyard. They both looked at the fallen body with mute stupor. He was dressed like a ragpicker. There were only a few faded hairs left on his bald skull and very few teeth in his mouth, and his pitiful condition of a drenched great-grandfather had taken away any sense of grandeur he might have had. His huge buzzard wings, dirty and half-plucked, were forever entangled in the mud. They looked at him so long and so closely that Pelayo and Elisenda very soon overcame their surprise and in the end found him familiar. Then they dared speak to him, and he answered in an incomprehensible dialect with a strong sailor's voice. That was how they skipped over the inconvenience of the wings and quite intelligently concluded that he was a lonely castaway from some foreign ship wrecked by the storm. And yet, they called in a neighbor woman who knew everything about life and death to see him, and all she needed was one look to show them their mistake.

"He's an angel," she told them. "He must have been coming for the child, but the poor fellow is so old that the rain knocked him down."

On the following day everyone knew that a flesh-and-blood angel was held captive in Pelayo's house. Against the judgment of the wise neighbor woman, for whom angels in those times were the fugitive survivors of a celestial conspiracy, they did not have the heart to club him to death. Pelayo watched over him all afternoon from the kitchen, armed with his bailiff's club, and before going to bed he dragged him out of the mud and locked him up with the hens in the wire chicken coop. In the middle of the night, when the rain stopped, Pelayo and Elisenda were still killing crabs. A short time afterward the child woke up without a fever and with a desire to eat. Then they felt magnanimous and decided to put the angel on a raft with fresh water and provisions for three days and leave him to his fate on the high seas. But when they went out into the courtyard with the first light of dawn, they found the whole neighborhood in front of the chicken coop having fun with the angel, without the slightest reverence, tossing him things to eat through the openings in the wire as if he weren't a supernatural creature but a circus animal.

5   Father Gonzaga arrived before seven o'clock, alarmed at the strange news. By that time onlookers less frivolous than those at dawn had already arrived and they were making all kinds of conjectures concerning the captive's future. The simplest among them thought that he should be named mayor of the world. Others of sterner mind felt that he should be promoted to the rank of five-star general in order to win all wars. Some visionaries hoped that he could be put to stud in order to implant on earth a race of winged wise men who could take charge of the universe. But Father Gonzaga, before becoming a priest,

had been a robust woodcutter. Standing by the wire, he reviewed his catechism in an instant and asked them to open the door so that he could take a close look at that pitiful man who looked more like a huge decrepit hen among the fascinated chickens. He was lying in a corner drying his open wings in the sunlight among the fruit peels and breakfast leftovers that the early risers had thrown him. Alien to the impertinences of the world, he only lifted his antiquarian eyes and murmured something in his dialect when Father Gonzaga went into the chicken coop and said good morning to him in Latin. The parish priest had his first suspicion of an impostor when he saw that he did not understand the language of God or know how to greet His ministers. Then he noticed that seen close up he was much too human: he had an unbearable smell of the outdoors, the back side of his wings was strewn with parasites and his main feathers had been mistreated by terrestrial winds, and nothing about him measured up to the proud dignity of angels. Then he came out of the chicken coop and in a brief sermon warned the curious against the risks of being ingenuous. He reminded them that the devil had the bad habit of making use of carnival tricks in order to confuse the unwary. He argued that if wings were not the essential element in determining the difference between a hawk and an airplane, they were even less so in the recognition of angels. Nevertheless, he promised to write a letter to his bishop so that the latter would write to his primate so that the latter would write to the Supreme Pontiff in order to get the final verdict from the highest courts.

His prudence fell on sterile hearts. The news of the captive angel spread with such rapidity that after a few hours the courtyard had the bustle of a marketplace and they had to call in troops with fixed bayonets to disperse the mob that was about to knock the house down. Elisenda, her spine all twisted from sweeping up so much marketplace trash, then got the idea of fencing in the yard and charging five cents admission to see the angel.

The curious came from far away. A traveling carnival arrived with a flying acrobat who buzzed over the crowd several times, but no one paid any attention to him because his wings were not those of an angel but, rather, those of a sidereal bat. The most unfortunate invalids on earth came in search of health: a poor woman who since childhood had been counting her heartbeats and had run out of numbers; a Portuguese man who couldn't sleep because the noise of the stars disturbed him; a sleepwalker who got up at night to undo the things he had done while awake; and many others with less serious ailments. In the midst of that shipwreck disorder that made the earth tremble, Pelayo and Elisenda were happy with fatigue, for in less than a week they had crammed their rooms with money and the line of pilgrims waiting their turn to enter still reached beyond the horizon.

The angel was the only one who took no part in his own act. He spent his time trying to get comfortable in his borrowed nest, befuddled by the hellish heat of the oil lamps and sacramental candles that had been placed along the wire. At first they tried to make him eat some mothballs, which, according to the wisdom of the wise neighbor woman, were the food prescribed for angels. But he turned them down, just as he turned down the papal lunches that the penitents brought him, and they never found out whether it was because he was an angel or because he was an old man that in the end he ate nothing but eggplant mush. His only supernatural virtue seemed to be patience. Especially during the first days, when the hens pecked at him, searching for the stellar parasites that proliferated in his wings, and the cripples pulled out feathers to touch their defective parts with, and even the most merciful threw stones at him, trying to get him to rise so they could see him standing. The only time they succeeded in arousing him was when they burned his side with an iron for branding steers, for he had been motionless for so many hours that they thought he was dead. He awoke with a start, ranting in his hermetic language and with tears in his eyes, and he flapped his wings a couple of times, which brought on a whirlwind of chicken dung and lunar dust and a gale of panic that did not seem to be of this world. Although many thought that his reaction had been one not of rage but of pain, from then on they were careful not to annoy him, because the majority understood that his passivity was not that of a hero taking his ease but that of a cataclysm in repose.

Father Gonzaga held back the crowd's frivolity with formulas of maidservant inspiration while awaiting the arrival of a final judgment on the nature of the captive. But the mail from Rome showed no sense of urgency. They spent their time finding out if the prisoner had a navel, if his dialect had any connection with Aramaic, how many times he could fit on the head of a pin, or whether he wasn't just a Norwegian with wings. Those meager letters might have come and gone until the end of time if a providential event had not put an end to the priest's tribulations.

10   It so happened that during those days, among so many other carnival attractions, there arrived in town the traveling show of the woman who had been changed into a spider for having disobeyed her parents. The admission to see her was not only less than the admission to see the angel, but people were permitted to ask her all manner of questions about her absurd state and to examine her up and down so that no one would ever doubt the truth of her horror. She was a frightful

tarantula the size of a ram and with the head of a sad maiden. What was most heart-rending, however, was not her outlandish shape but the sincere affliction with which she recounted the details of her misfortune. While still practically a child she had sneaked out of her parents' house to go to a dance, and while she was coming back through the woods after having danced all night without permission, a fearful thunderclap rent the sky in two and through the crack came the lightning bolt of brimstone that changed her into a spider. Her only nourishment came from the meatballs that charitable souls chose to toss into her mouth. A spectacle like that, full of so much human truth and with such a fearful lesson, was bound to defeat without even trying that of a haughty angel who scarcely deigned to look at mortals. Besides, the few miracles attributed to the angel showed a certain mental disorder, like the blind man who didn't recover his sight but grew three new teeth, or the paralytic who didn't get to walk but almost won the lottery, and the leper whose sores sprouted sunflowers. Those consolation miracles, which were more like mocking fun, had already ruined the angel's reputation when the woman who had been changed into a spider finally crushed him completely. That was how Father Gonzaga was cured forever of his insomnia and Pelayo's courtyard went back to being as empty as during the time it had rained for three days and crabs walked through the bedrooms.

The owners of the house had no reason to lament. With the money they saved they built a two-story mansion with balconies and gardens and high netting so that crabs wouldn't get in during the winter, and with iron bars on the windows so that angels wouldn't get in. Pelayo also set up a rabbit warren close to town and gave up his job as bailiff for good, and Elisenda bought some satin pumps with high heels and many dresses of iridescent silk, the kind worn on Sunday by the most desirable women in those times. The chicken coop was the only thing that didn't receive any attention. If they washed it down with creolin and burned tears of myrrh inside it every so often, it was not in homage to the angel but to drive away the dungheap stench that still hung everywhere like a ghost and was turning the new house into an old one. At first, when the child learned to walk, they were careful that he not get too close to the chicken coop. But then they began to lose their fears and got used to the smell, and before the child got his second teeth he'd gone inside the chicken coop to play, where the wires were falling apart. The angel was no less standoffish with him than with other mortals, but he tolerated the most ingenious infamies with the patience of a dog who had no illusions. They both came down with chicken pox at the same time. The doctor who took care of the child couldn't resist the temptation to listen to the angel's heart, and he found so much whistling in the heart and so many sounds in his kidneys that it seemed impossible for him to be alive. What surprised him most, however, was the logic of his wings. They seemed so natural on that completely human organism that he couldn't understand why other men didn't have them too.

When the child began school it had been some time since the sun and rain had caused the collapse of the chicken coop. The angel went dragging himself about here and there like a stray dying man. They would drive him out of the bedroom with a broom and a moment later find him in the kitchen. He seemed to be in so many places at the same time that they grew to think that he'd been duplicated, that he was reproducing himself all through the house, and the exasperated and unhinged Elisenda shouted that it was awful living in that hell full of angels. He could scarcely eat and his antiquarian eyes had also become so foggy that he went about bumping into posts. All he had left were the bare cannulae of his last feathers. Pelayo threw a blanket over him and extended him the charity of letting him sleep in the shed, and only then did they notice that he had a temperature at night, and was delirious with the tongue twisters of an old Norwegian. That was one of the few times they became alarmed, for they thought he was going to die and not even the wise neighbor woman had been able to tell them what to do with dead angels.

And yet he not only survived his worst winter, but seemed improved with the first sunny days. He remained motionless for several days in the farthest corner of the courtyard, where no one would see him, and at the beginning of December some large, stiff feathers began to grow on his wings, the feathers of a scarecrow, which looked more like another misfortune of decrepitude. But he must have known the reason for those changes, for he was quite careful that no one should notice them, that no one should hear the sea chanteys that he sometimes sang under the stars. One morning Elisenda was cutting some bunches of onions for lunch when a wind that seemed to come from the high seas blew into the kitchen. Then she went to the window and caught the angel in his first attempts at flight. They were so clumsy that his fingernails opened a furrow in the vegetable patch and he was on the point of knocking the shed down with the ungainly flapping that slipped on the light and couldn't get a grip on the air. But he did manage to gain altitude. Elisenda let out a sigh of relief, for herself and for him, when she saw him pass over the last houses, holding himself up in some way with the risky flapping of a senile vulture. She kept watching him even when she was through cutting the onions and she kept on watching until it was no longer possible for her to see him, because then he was no longer an annoyance in her life but an imaginary dot on the horizon of the sea.

QUESTIONS

1. At what point in the story did you first know that it included elements of fantasy? Discuss the effect of the second sentence: "The world had been sad since Tuesday."
2. What is the symbolic significance of the old man and his enormous wings? Since he's called an "angel," is there a religious significance to his physical appearance? Why does the narrator stress such details as his "dirty and half-plucked" wings and his grossly physical, animalistic traits? How is the oxymoron "flesh-and-blood angel" central to the meaning?
3. The author wrote that this was "a tale for children." In what ways is it a tale for children but also a story for adults?
4. Discuss the blend of realistic and fantastic details. Does this blend make the story more or less effective? Does it require a different way of reading than other stories you've read that contain no elements of fantasy?
5. The story contains almost no dialogue. Why is this appropriate? How does it relate to the point of view the author has chosen?
6. What is the major theme of the story? How do the fantastic elements help provide insights into the way human beings actually think and behave?

SUGGESTIONS FOR WRITING

1. Compare the use of symbolism in any two of the following stories, clarifying how each achieves compression through the use of symbols:
   a. Mansfield, "Miss Brill" (page 174).
   b. Joyce, "Eveline" (page 408).
   c. Gordimer, "Once upon a Time" (page 231).
   d. Faulkner, "A Rose for Emily" (page 526).
   e. Hurston, "The Gilded Six-Bits" (page 553).
   f. Poe, "The Cask of Amontillado" (page 617).
2. Argue that any one of the following stories does, or does not, contain elements of fantasy. Carefully support your argument.
   a. Connell, "The Most Dangerous Game" (page 67).
   b. Mansfield, "Miss Brill" (page 174).
   c. Porter, "The Jilting of Granny Weatherall" (page 269).
   d. Lawrence, "The Rocking-Horse Winner" (page 295).
   e. Hawthorne, "Young Goodman Brown" (page 309).
   f. Jackson, "The Lottery" (page 261).
   g. Poe, "The Cask of Amontillado" (page 617).

Chapter Seven

Humor and Irony

In previous chapters, we have sometimes used the term "serious" to describe a story or writer whose intentions are literary and artistic rather than primarily commercial. In this context, however, it's important to understand that a serious story is not necessarily a solemn one. In fact, many of the world's great works of serious literature have employed humor in conveying major truths about the human condition. The ancient Greek and Roman dramatists wrote raucous comic plays; Shakespeare's humor is an important dimension of his work, in tragedies such as *Hamlet* and *King Lear* as well as in his famous comedies. Writers as diverse as Geoffrey Chaucer, Jonathan Swift, Jane Austen, Charles Dickens, Mark Twain, and Flannery O'Connor have used humor as a central element in their art.

Novels and short stories that employ humor often use the technique we call **irony**, a term which has a range of meanings that all involve some sort of discrepancy or incongruity. All the above-named writers are master ironists, employing incongruous situations and characters that evoke laughter in the reader even as they express a significant insight into human nature. Irony should not be equated with mere sarcasm, which is simply language one person uses to belittle or ridicule another. Irony is far more complex, a technique used to convey a truth about human experience by exposing some incongruity of a character's behavior or a society's traditions. Operating through careful, often subtle indirection, irony helps to critique the world in which we live by laughing at the many varieties of human eccentricity and folly. It may be useful here to distinguish three distinct kinds of irony found in literary fiction.

Verbal irony, usually the simplest kind, is a figure of speech in which the speaker says the opposite of what he or she intends to say. (This form of irony is, in fact, often employed to create sarcasm.) In "Hunters in the Snow," when Kenny says to Tub, "You're just wasting away before my very eyes," he is speaking ironically—and sarcastically—for of course Tub is obese.

In **dramatic irony** the contrast is between what a character says or thinks and what the reader knows to be true. The value of this kind of irony lies in the truth it conveys about the character or the character's expectations. In "How I Met My Husband," for instance, Loretta Bird says about Mrs. Peebles, "She wouldn't find time to lay down in the middle of the day, if she had seven kids like I got." The reader grasps the irony of this remark, since Loretta herself often "finds time" to sit gossiping at the Peebles farm instead of staying home with her children. Another effective example comes when Miss Brill, sitting in the park, thinks about the other people around her:

> Other people sat on the benches and green chairs, but they were nearly always the same, Sunday after Sunday, and—Miss Brill had often noticed—there was something funny about nearly all of them . . . from the way they stared they looked as though they'd just come from dark little rooms or even—even cupboards!

It is ironic that the judgment she makes of them is exactly the same one the story makes of her—even including the word "funny," which the young girl later uses about her beloved fur. Miss Brill is unaware that her phrase "nearly always the same, Sunday after Sunday" describes her own behavior, which she unwittingly reveals when she thinks that she "had *often* noticed" them. And of course the irony of the statement about the "cupboards" they must have come from becomes overt when she returns at the end of the story to "her room like a cupboard." Perhaps the most poignant of the dramatic ironies involving Miss Brill lies in her boastful thought, "Yes, I have been an actress for a long time," for she has indeed created a fictitious role for herself—not that of a glamorous stage actress in a romantic musical play, but that of a perceptive, happy, and self-sufficient woman. First-person stories similarly use dramatic irony to suggest that the narrator is not reliable. In Porter's "The Jilting of Granny Weatherall," for example, Granny confusedly reports that ants are biting her when she is actually receiving a hypodermic injection, and that the priest is tickling her feet when really he is administering extreme unction (the last rites in Roman Catholicism). The result is an ironic portrayal of Granny's bewildered mental state.

In **irony of situation**, usually the most important kind for the fiction writer, the discrepancy is between appearance and reality, or between expectation and fulfillment, or between what is and what would seem appropriate. In "The Most Dangerous Game," it is ironic that Rainsford, "the celebrated hunter," should become the hunted, for this is a reversal of his expected and appropriate role. In "The Destruc-tors," it is ironic that Old Misery's horoscope should read, "Abstain from any dealings in first half of week. Danger of serious crash," for the horoscope is valid in a sense that is quite different from what the words appear to indicate. In "Interpreter of Maladies," it is ironic that Mr. Das's guidebook to India "looked as if it had been published abroad," and that the Indian tour guide Mr. Kapasi watches the Ameri-can television show *Dallas* but the American-born Tina Das has never heard of the program. In "Hunters in the Snow," it is ironic that inside the diner Frank and Tub encourage one another's self-indulgent behav-ior—Frank's lust for a teenage babysitter, Tub's gluttony—and view themselves as forming a noble, trusting alliance, when all the while their companion Kenny is lying wounded and freezing outside in the back of their truck.

Irony, like symbol and allegory, is often a means for the author to achieve compression. By creating an ironic situation or perspective, the author can suggest complex meanings without stating them. In "Miss Brill," we do not need to be told how difficult it is for an aging, solitary woman to cope with her aloneness; we witness her plight and the incongruous means by which she attempts to deny it and therefore endure it. In "Hunters in the Snow," we do not need to be told that these three hunting buddies are not "friends" in any meaningful sense of that word; we witness their cruel, self-absorbed behavior. In these and other stories, the ironic contrast between appearances and reality gen-erates a complex set of meanings.

One reason that irony is such an important technique is that a story, like other art forms, achieves its effects through indirection. "Tell all the truth," Emily Dickinson advised, "but tell it slant"—advice as valid for fiction writers as for poets. In art, the truth must be produced indirectly because a flat statement—as in an essay, or a dry plot summa-ry—can have no emotional impact on the reader. We must *feel* the truth a story conveys with our whole being, not simply understand it with our intellect. If a story has no emotional impact, it has failed as a work of art.

Humor and irony are important because they help an author to achieve such an impact. A reader will not respond to a story, for instance, that contrives its emotions and attempts to "play upon" the reader's feelings directly. An ironic method can help to temper and control the emotional content of a story, evoking responses that are intellectual and emotional at once. At the end of "Interpreter of Maladies," we feel Mr. Kapasi's disillusionment even as we understand the hopelessness of his attraction to Mrs. Das. The narrator's cool, dispassionate stance, complete with its ironic observations and its undercurrent of humor, helps to keep the story's emotional content more honest, genuine, and believable.

By contrast, stories that try to elicit easy or unearned emotional responses are guilty of **sentimentality**. Sentimentality in fiction is not the same as genuine emotion; rather, it is contrived or excessive emotion. A novel such as Harriet Beecher Stowe's *Uncle Tom's Cabin* (1852), for instance, often tries to wring tears from the reader over the plight of African American slaves; for this reason, the novel is much less powerful as a work of art than Toni Morrison's *Beloved* (1987), which uses carefully restrained, artful language and a frequently biting irony in its castigation of slavery. A narrative contains genuine emotion when it treats life faithfully and perceptively. A sentimental narrative oversimplifies and exaggerates emotion in the attempt to arouse a similarly excessive emotion in the reader.

Genuine emotion, like character, is presented indirectly—it is dramatized. It cannot be produced by words that identify emotions, like *angry, sad, pathetic, heart-breaking,* or *passionate.* A writer draws forth genuine emotion by producing a character in a situation that deserves our sympathy and showing us enough about the character and the situation to make them real and convincing.

Sentimental writers are recognizable by a number of characteristics. First, they often try to make words do what the situation faithfully presented by itself will not do. They **editorialize**—that is, comment on the story and, in a manner, instruct us how to feel. Or they overwrite and **poeticize**—use an immoderately heightened and distended language to accomplish their effects. Second, they make an excessively selective use of detail. All artists, of course, must be selective in their use of detail, but good writers use representative details while sentimentalists use details that all point one way—toward producing emotion rather than conveying truth. The little child who dies will be shown as always uncomplaining and cheerful under adversity, never as naughty, querulous, or ungrateful. It will possibly be an orphan or the only child of a mother who loves it dearly; in addition, it may be lame, hungry, ragged, and possessed of one toy, from which it cannot be parted. The villain will be *all* villain, with a cruel laugh and a sharp whip, though he may reform at the end, for sentimentalists are firm believers in the heart of gold beneath the rough exterior. In short, reality will be unduly heightened and drastically oversimplified. Third, sentimentalists rely heavily on the stock response—an emotion that has its source outside the facts established by the story. In some readers certain situations and objects—babies, mothers, grandmothers, young love, patriotism, worship—

produce an almost automatic response, whether the immediate situation warrants it or not. Sentimental writers, to affect such readers, have only to draw out certain stops, as on an organ, to produce an easily anticipated effect. They depend on stock materials to produce a stock response. They thus need not go to the trouble of picturing the situation in realistic and convincing detail. Finally, sentimental writers present, nearly always, a fundamentally "sweet" picture of life. They rely not only on stock characters and situations but also on stock themes. For them every cloud has its silver lining, every bad event its good side, every storm its rainbow. If the little child dies, it goes to heaven or makes some life better by its death. Virtue is characteristically triumphant: the villain is defeated, the ne'er-do-well redeemed. True love is rewarded in some fashion; it is love—never hate—that makes the world go round. In short, sentimental writers specialize in the sad but sweet. The tears called for are warm tears, never bitter. There is always sugar at the bottom of the cup.

The writers we value most are able to look at human experience in a clear-eyed, honest way and to employ literary techniques such as humor and irony as a way to enhance, not reduce, the emotional impact of their stories. Though not every first-rate story contains humor—Joyce's "Eveline," for instance, presents a relentlessly bleak portrait of its heroine's plight—there are few that do not involve some blend on the author's part of human empathy and ironic detachment. After reading "Hills Like White Elephants," "Miss Brill," and "A Rose for Emily," for example, we experience a similarly blended response to the protagonists of these stories. A complex human reality requires a complex narrative technique, and in this way the best storytellers always have attempted to portray the whole of human experience—from its most tragic misery to its most absurd folly—in a single, integrated artistic vision.

REVIEWING CHAPTER SEVEN

1. Distinguish between verbal irony and dramatic irony.
2. Define the term "irony of situation."
3. Explore the reasons why sentimentality is an undesirable trait in literary fiction.
4. List the major characteristics of sentimental writing.
5. Describe the particular types of irony found in the following stories.

Frank O'Connor
The Drunkard

It was a terrible blow to Father when Mr. Dooley on the terrace died. Mr. Dooley was a commercial traveler with two sons in the Dominicans and a car of his own, so socially he was miles ahead of us, but he had no false pride. Mr. Dooley was an intellectual, and, like all intellectuals, the thing he loved best was conversation, and in his own limited way Father was a well-read man and could appreciate an intelligent talker. Mr. Dooley was remarkably intelligent. Between business acquaintances and clerical contacts, there was very little he didn't know about what went on in town, and evening after evening he crossed the road to our gate to explain to Father the news behind the news. He had a low, palavering voice and a knowing smile, and Father would listen in astonishment, giving him a conversational lead now and again, and then stump triumphantly in to Mother with his face aglow and ask: "Do you know what Mr. Dooley is after telling me?" Ever since, when somebody has given me some bit of information off the record I have found myself on the point of asking: "Was it Mr. Dooley told you that?"

Till I actually saw him laid out in his brown shroud with the rosary beads entwined between his waxy fingers I did not take the report of his death seriously. Even then I felt there must be a catch and that some summer evening Mr. Dooley must reappear at our gate to give us the lowdown on the next world. But Father was very upset, partly because Mr. Dooley was about one age with himself, a thing that always gives a distinctly personal turn to another man's demise; partly because now he would have no one to tell him what dirty work was behind the latest scene at the Corporation.° You could count on your fingers the number of men in Blarney Lane who read the papers as Mr. Dooley did, and none of these would have overlooked the fact that Father was only a laboring man. Even Sullivan, the carpenter, a mere nobody, thought he was a cut above Father. It was certainly a solemn event.

"Half past two to the Curragh," Father said meditatively, putting down the paper.

THE DRUNKARD   First published in 1948. Frank O'Connor (1903–1966) was born Michael O'Donovan, the only child of very poor, Roman Catholic parents in Cork, Ireland. He used his mother's maiden name as a pseudonym when he began to publish. "The Drunkard" is based on an incident from his boyhood in Cork, as revealed in the first two chapters of his autobiographical volume, *An Only Son* (1961).

Corporation: the officials of the city (mayor, aldermen, councillors)

"But you're not thinking of going to the funeral?" Mother asked in alarm.

5 "'Twould be expected," Father said, scenting opposition. "I wouldn't give it to say to them."

"I think," said Mother with suppressed emotion, "it will be as much as anyone will expect if you go to the chapel with him."

("Going to the chapel," of course, was one thing, because the body was removed after work, but going to a funeral meant the loss of a half-day's pay.)

"The people hardly know us," she added.

"God between us and all harm," Father replied with dignity, "we'd be glad if it was our own turn."

10 To give Father his due, he was always ready to lose a half day for the sake of an old neighbor. It wasn't so much that he liked funerals as that he was a conscientious man who did as he would be done by, and nothing could have consoled him so much for the prospect of his own death as the assurance of a worthy funeral. And, to give Mother her due, it wasn't the half-day's pay she begrudged, badly as we could afford it.

Drink, you see, was Father's great weakness. He could keep steady for months, even for years, at a stretch, and while he did he was as good as gold. He was first up in the morning and brought the mother a cup of tea in bed, stayed home in the evenings and read the paper; saved money and bought himself a new blue serge suit and bowler hat. He laughed at the folly of men who, week in, week out, left their hard-earned money with the publicans; and sometimes, to pass an idle hour, he took pencil and paper and calculated precisely how much he saved each week through being a teetotaller. Being a natural optimist he sometimes continued this calculation through the whole span of his prospective existence and the total was breathtaking. He would die worth hundreds.

If I had only known it, this was a bad sign; a sign he was becoming stuffed up with spiritual pride and imagining himself better than his neighbors. Sooner or later, the spiritual pride grew till it called for some form of celebration. Then he took a drink—not whiskey, of course; nothing like that—just a glass of some harmless drink like lager beer. That was the end of Father. By the time he had taken the first he already realized that he had made a fool of himself, took a second to forget it and a third to forget that he couldn't forget, and at last came home reeling drunk. From this on it was "The Drunkard's Progress," as in the moral prints. Next day he stayed in from work with a sick head while Mother went off to make his excuses at the works, and inside a fortnight he was poor and savage and despondent again. Once he began he drank steadily through everything down to the kitchen clock. Mother and I knew all the phases and dreaded all the dangers. Funerals were one.

"I have to go to Dunphy's to do a half-day's work," said Mother in distress. "Who's to look after Larry?"

"I'll look after Larry," Father said graciously. "The little walk will do him good."

There was no more to be said, though we all knew I didn't need anyone to look after me, and that I could quite well have stayed home and looked after Sonny, but I was being attached to the party to act as a brake on Father. As a brake I had never achieved anything, but Mother still had great faith in me.

Next day, when I got home from school, Father was there before me and made a cup of tea for both of us. He was very good at tea, but too heavy in the hand for anything else; the way he cut bread was shocking. Afterwards, we went down the hill to the church, Father wearing his best blue serge and a bowler cocked to one side of his head with the least suggestion of the masher. To his great joy he discovered Peter Crowley among the mourners. Peter was another danger signal, as I knew well from certain experiences after Mass on Sunday morning: a mean man, as Mother said, who only went to funerals for the free drinks he could get at them. It turned out that he hadn't even known Mr. Dooley! But Father had a sort of contemptuous regard for him as one of the foolish people who wasted their good money in public-houses when they could be saving it. Very little of his own money Peter Crowley wasted!

It was an excellent funeral from Father's point of view. He had it all well studied before we set off after the hearse in the afternoon sunlight.

"Five carriages!" he exclaimed. "Five carriages and sixteen covered cars! There's one alderman, two councillors and 'tis unknown how many priests. I didn't see a funeral like this from the road since Willie Mack, the publican, died."

"Ah, he was well liked," said Crowley in his husky voice.

"My goodness, don't I know that?" snapped Father. "Wasn't the man my best friend? Two nights before he died—only two nights—he was over telling me the goings-on about the housing contract. Them fellows in the Corporation are night and day robbers. But even I never imagined he was as well connected as that."

Father was stepping out like a boy, pleased with everything: the other mourners, and the fine houses along Sunday's Well. I knew danger signals were there in full force: a sunny day, a fine funeral and a distinguished company of clerics and public men were bringing out all the natural vanity and flightiness of Father's character. It was with something like genuine pleasure that he saw his old friend lowered into the grave; with the sense of having performed a duty and the pleasant awareness that however much he would miss poor Mr. Dooley in the long summer evenings, it was he and not poor Mr. Dooley who would do the missing.

"We'll be making tracks before they break up," he whispered to Crowley as the gravediggers tossed in the first shovelfuls of clay, and away he went, hopping like a goat from grassy hump to hump. The drivers, who were probably in the same state as himself, though without months of abstinence to put an edge on it, looked up hopefully.

"Are they nearly finished, Mick?" bawled one.

"All over now bar the last prayers," trumpeted Father in the tone of one who brings news of great rejoicing.

25   The carriages passed us in a lather of dust several hundred yards from the public-house, and Father, whose feet gave him trouble in hot weather, quickened his pace, looking nervously over his shoulder for any sign of the main body of mourners crossing the hill. In a crowd like that a man might be kept waiting.

When we did reach the pub the carriages were drawn up outside, and solemn men in black ties were cautiously bringing out consolation to mysterious females whose hands reached out modestly from behind the drawn blinds of the coaches. Inside the pub there were only the drivers and a couple of shawly women. I felt if I was to act as a brake at all, this was the time, so I pulled Father by the coattails.

"Dadda, can't we go home now?" I asked.

"Two minutes now," he said, beaming affectionately. "Just a bottle of lemonade and we'll go home."

This was a bribe, and I knew it, but I was always a child of weak character. Father ordered lemonade and two pints. I was thirsty and swallowed my drink at once. But that wasn't Father's way. He had long months of abstinence behind him and an eternity of pleasure before. He took out his pipe, blew through it, filled it, and then lit it with loud pops, his eyes bulging above it. After that he deliberately turned his back on the pint, leaned one elbow on the counter in the attitude of a man who did not know there was a pint behind him, and deliberately brushed the tobacco from his palms. He had settled down for the evening. He was steadily working through all the important funerals he had ever attended. The carriages departed and the minor mourners drifted in till the pub was half full.

30   "Dadda," I said, pulling his coat again, "can't we go home now?"

"Ah, your mother won't be in for a long time yet," he said benevolently enough. "Run out in the road and play, can't you."

It struck me very cool, the way grown-ups assumed that you could play all by yourself on a strange road. I began to get bored as I had so often been bored before. I knew Father was quite capable of lingering there till nightfall. I knew I might have to bring him home, blind drunk, down Blarney Lane, with all the old women at their doors, saying: "Mick Delaney is on it again." I knew that my mother would be half crazy with anxiety; that next day Father wouldn't go out to work; and before the end of the week she would be running down to the pawn with the clock under her shawl. I could never get over the lonesomeness of the kitchen without a clock.

I was still thirsty. I found if I stood on tiptoe I could just reach Father's glass, and the idea occurred to me that it would be interesting to know what the contents were like. He had his back to it and wouldn't notice. I took down the glass and sipped cautiously. It was a terrible disappointment. I was astonished that he could even drink such stuff. It looked as if he had never tried lemonade.

I should have advised him about lemonade but he was holding forth himself in great style. I heard him say that bands were a great addition to a funeral. He put his arms in the position of someone holding a rifle in reverse and hummed a few bars of Chopin's Funeral March. Crowley nodded reverently. I took a longer drink and began to see that porter might have its advantages. I felt pleasantly elevated and philosophic. Father hummed a few bars of the Dead March in *Saul*. It was a nice pub and a very fine funeral, and I felt sure that poor Mr. Dooley in Heaven must be highly gratified. At the same time I thought they might have given him a band. As Father said, bands were a great addition.

But the wonderful thing about porter was the way it made you stand aside, or rather float aloft like a cherub rolling on a cloud, and watch yourself with your legs crossed, leaning against a bar counter, not worrying about trifles but thinking deep, serious, grown-up thoughts about life and death. Looking at yourself like that, you couldn't help thinking after a while how funny you looked, and suddenly you got embarrassed and wanted to giggle. But by the time I had finished the pint, that phase too had passed; I found it hard to put back the glass, the counter seemed to have grown so high. Melancholia was supervening again. 35

"Well," Father said reverently, reaching behind him for his drink, "God rest the poor man's soul, wherever he is!" He stopped, looked first at the glass, and then at the people around him. "Hello," he said in a fairly good-humored tone, as if he were just prepared to consider it a joke, even if it was in bad taste, "who was at this?"

There was silence for a moment while the publican and the old women looked first at Father and then at his glass.

"There was no one at it, my good man," one of the women said with an offended air. "Is it robbers you think we are?"

"Ah, there's no one here would do a thing like that, Mick," said the publican in a shocked tone.

40   "Well, someone did it," said Father, his smile beginning to wear off.

"If they did, they were them that were nearer it," said the woman darkly, giving me a dirty look; and at the same moment the truth began to dawn on Father. I suppose I must have looked a bit starry-eyed. He bent and shook me.

"Are you all right, Larry?" he asked in alarm.

Peter Crowley looked down at me and grinned.

"Could you beat that?" he exclaimed in a husky voice.

45   I could and without difficulty. I started to get sick. Father jumped back in holy terror that I might spoil his good suit, and hastily opened the back door.

"Run! run! run!" he shouted.

I saw the sunlit wall outside with the ivy overhanging it, and ran. The intention was good but the performance was exaggerated, because I lurched right into the wall, hurting it badly, as it seemed to me. Being always very polite, I said "Pardon" before the second bout came on me. Father, still concerned for his suit, came up behind and cautiously held me while I got sick.

"That's a good boy!" he said encouragingly. "You'll be grand when you get that up."

Begor, I was not grand! Grand was the last thing I was. I gave one unmerciful wail out of me as he steered me back to the pub and put me sitting on the bench near the shawlies. They drew themselves up with an offended air, still sore at the suggestion that they had drunk his pint.

50   "God help us!" moaned one, looking pityingly at me. "Isn't it the likes of them would be fathers?"

"Mick," said the publican in alarm, spraying sawdust on my tracks, "that child isn't supposed to be in here at all. You'd better take him home quick in case a bobby would see him."

"Merciful God!" whimpered Father, raising his eyes to heaven and clapping his hands silently as he only did when distraught. "What misfortune was on me? Or what will his mother say? . . . If women might stop at home and look after their children themselves!" he added in a snarl for the benefit of the shawlies. "Are them carriages all gone, Bill?"

"The carriages are finished long ago, Mick," replied the publican.

"I'll take him home," Father said despairingly. . . . "I'll never bring you out again," he threatened me. "Here," he added, giving me the clean handkerchief from his breast pocket, "put that over your eye."

The blood on the handkerchief was the first indication I got that I   55
was cut, and instantly my temple began to throb and I set up another howl. "Whisht, whisht, whisht!" Father said testily, steering me out the door. "One'd think you were killed. That's nothing. We'll wash it when we get home."

"Steady now, old scout!" Crowley said, taking the other side of me. "You'll be all right in a minute."

I never met two men who knew less about the effects of drink. The first breath of fresh air and the warmth of the sun made me groggier than ever and I pitched and rolled between wind and tide till Father started to whimper again.

"God Almighty, and the whole road out! What misfortune was on me didn't stop at my work! Can't you walk straight?"

I couldn't. I saw plain enough that, coaxed by the sunlight, every woman old and young in Blarney Lane was leaning over her half-door or sitting on her doorstep. They all stopped gabbling to gape at the strange spectacle of two sober, middle-aged men bringing home a drunken small boy with a cut over his eye. Father, torn between the shamefast desire to get me home as quick as he could, and the neighborly need to explain that it wasn't his fault, finally halted outside Mrs. Roche's. There was a gang of old women outside a door at the opposite side of the road. I didn't like the look of them from the first. They seemed altogether too interested in me. I leaned against the wall of Mrs. Roche's cottage with my hands in my trousers pockets, thinking mournfully of poor Mr. Dooley in his cold grave on the Curragh, who would never walk down the road again, and, with great feeling, I began to sing a favorite song of Father's.

> Though lost to Mononia and cold in the grave
> He returns to Kincora no more.

"Wisha, the poor child!" Mrs. Roche said, "Haven't he a lovely   60
voice, God bless him!"

That was what I thought myself, so I was the more surprised when Father said "Whisht!" and raised a threatening finger at me. He didn't seem to realize the appropriateness of the song, so I sang louder than ever.

"Whisht, I tell you!" he snapped, and then tried to work up a smile for Mrs. Roche's benefit. "We're nearly home now. I'll carry you the rest of the way."

But, drunk and all as I was, I knew better than to be carried home ignominiously like that.

"Now," I said severely, "can't you leave me alone? I can walk all right. 'Tis only my head. All I want is a rest."

65 "But you can rest at home in bed," he said viciously, trying to pick me up, and I knew by the flush on his face that he was very vexed.

"Ah, Jasus," I said crossly, "what do I want to go home for? Why the hell can't you leave me alone?"

For some reason the gang of old women at the other side of the road thought this was very funny. They nearly split their sides over it. A gassy fury began to expand in me at the thought that a fellow couldn't have a drop taken without the whole neighborhood coming out to make game of him.

"Who are ye laughing at?" I shouted, clenching my fists at them. "I'll make ye laugh at the other side of yeer faces if ye don't let me pass."

They seemed to think this funnier still; I had never seen such ill-mannered people.

70 "Go away, ye bloody bitches!" I said.

"Whisht, whisht, whisht, I tell you!" snarled Father, abandoning all pretense of amusement and dragging me along behind him by the hand. I was maddened by the women's shrieks of laughter. I was maddened by Father's bullying. I tried to dig in my heels but he was too powerful for me, and I could only see the women by looking back over my shoulder.

"Take care or I'll come back and show ye!" I shouted. "I'll teach ye to let decent people pass. Fitter for ye to stop at home an wash yeer dirty faces."

"'Twill be all over the road," whimpered Father. "Never again, never again, not if I live to be a thousand!"

To this day I don't know whether he was forswearing me or the drink. By way of a song suitable to my heroic mood I bawled "The Boys of Wexford," as he dragged me in home. Crowley, knowing he was not safe, made off and Father undressed me and put me to bed. I couldn't sleep because of the whirling in my head. It was very unpleasant, and I got sick again. Father came in with a wet cloth and mopped up after me. I lay in a fever, listening to him chopping sticks to start a fire. After that I heard him lay the table.

75 Suddenly the front door banged open and Mother stormed in with Sonny in her arms, not her usual gentle, timid self, but a wild, raging woman. It was clear that she had heard it all from the neighbors.

"Mick Delaney," she cried hysterically, "what did you do to my son?"

"Whisht, woman, whisht, whisht!" he hissed, dancing from one foot to the other. "Do you want the whole road to hear?"

"Ah," she said with a horrifying laugh, "the road knows all about it by this time. The road knows the way you filled your unfortunate innocent child with drink to make sport for you and that other rotten, filthy brute."

"But I gave him no drink," he shouted, aghast at the horrifying interpretation the neighbors had chosen to give his misfortune. "He took it while my back was turned. What the hell do you think I am?"

"Ah," she replied bitterly, "everyone knows what you are now. God   80 forgive you, wasting our hard-earned few ha'pence on drink, and bringing up your child to be a drunken corner-boy like yourself."

Then she swept into the bedroom and threw herself on her knees by the bed. She moaned when she saw the gash over my eye. In the kitchen Sonny set up a loud bawl on his own, and a moment later Father appeared in the bedroom door with his cap over his eyes, wearing an expression of the most intense self-pity.

"That's a nice way to talk to me after all I went through," he whined. "That's a nice accusation, that I was drinking. Not one drop of drink crossed my lips the whole day. How could it when he drank it all? I'm the one that ought to be pitied, with my day ruined on me, and I after being made a show for the whole road."

But the next morning, when he got up and went out quietly to work with his dinner-basket, Mother threw herself on me in the bed and kissed me. It seemed it was all my doing, and I was being given a holiday till my eye got better.

"My brave little man!" she said with her eyes shining. "It was God did it you were there. You were his guardian angel."

QUESTIONS

1. What are the sources of humor in this story? Does the humor arise from observation of life or from distortion of life? What elements of the story seem to you funniest?
2. Is this a purely humorous story, or are there undertones of pathos in it? If the latter, from what does the pathos arise?
3. List what seem to you the chief insights into life and character presented by the story.
4. Is the title seriously meant? To whom does it refer?
5. The boy's drunkenness is seen from four perspectives. What are they, and how do they differ?
6. What is the principal irony in the story?

7. The story is told in retrospect by a man recalling an incident from his boyhood. What does this removal in time do to the treatment of the material?

8. *Did* Larry's father forswear liquor? Support your answer with evidence from the story.

Margaret Atwood

Rape Fantasies

The way they're going on about it in the magazines you'd think it was just invented, and not only that but it's something terrific, like a vaccine for cancer. They put it in capital letters on the front cover, and inside they have these questionnaires like the ones they used to have about whether you were a good enough wife or an endomorph or an ectomorph, remember that? with the scoring upside down on page 73, and then these numbered do-it-yourself dealies, you know? RAPE, TEN THINGS TO DO ABOUT IT, like it was ten new hairdos or something. I mean, what's so new about it?

So at work they all have to talk about it because no matter what magazine you open, there it is, staring you right between the eyes, and they're beginning to have it on the television, too. Personally I'd prefer a June Allyson° movie anytime but they don't make them any more and they don't even have them that much on the Late Show. For instance, day before yesterday, that would be Wednesday, thank god it's Friday as they say, we were sitting around in the women's lunch room—the *lunch* room, I mean you'd think you could get some peace and quiet in there—and Chrissy closes up the magazine she's been reading and says, "How about it, girls, do you have rape fantasies?"

The four of us were having our game of bridge the way we always do, and I had a bare twelve points counting the singleton with not that much of a bid in anything. So I said one club, hoping Sondra would remember about the one club convention, because the time before when I used that she thought I really meant clubs and she bid us up to three, and all I had was four little ones with nothing higher than a six, and we went down two and on top of that we were vulnerable. She is not the world's best bridge player. I mean, neither am I but there's a limit.

RAPE FANTASIES   First published in 1977. Margaret Atwood was born in 1939 in Ottawa, and grew up there, in Sault Ste. Marie, and in Toronto, all in Ontario. She was educated at the University of Toronto, Radcliffe, and Harvard. She has published several novels, collections of short stories, and volumes of poetry.

June Allyson: American film and television actress popular in the 1940s and 1950s

Darlene passed but the damage was done, Sondra's head went round like it was on ball bearings and she said, "*What* fantasies?"

"Rape fantasies," Chrissy said. She's a receptionist and she looks like one; she's pretty but cool as a cucumber, like she's been painted all over with nail polish, if you know what I mean. Varnished. "It says here all women have rape fantasies."

"For Chrissake, I'm eating an egg sandwich," I said, "and I bid one club and Darlene passed."

"You mean, like some guy jumping you in an alley or something," Sondra said. She was eating her lunch, we all eat our lunches during the game, and she bit into a piece of that celery she always brings and started to chew away on it with this thoughtful expression in her eyes and I knew we might as well pack it in as far as the game was concerned.

"Yeah, sort of like that," Chrissy said. She was blushing a little, you could see it even under her makeup.

"I don't think you should go out alone at night," Darlene said, "you put yourself in a position," and I may have been mistaken but she was looking at me. She's the oldest, she's forty-one though you wouldn't know it and neither does she, but I looked it up in the employees' file. I like to guess a person's age and then look it up to see if I'm right. I let myself have an extra pack of cigarettes if I am, though I'm trying to cut down. I figure it's harmless as long as you don't tell. I mean, not everyone has access to that file, it's more or less confidential. But it's all right if I tell you, I don't expect you'll ever meet her, though you never know, it's a small world. Anyway.

"For *heaven's* sake, it's only *Toronto*," Greta said. She worked in Detroit for three years and she never lets you forget it, it's like she thinks she's a war hero or something, we should all admire her just for the fact that she's still walking this earth, though she was really living in Windsor the whole time, she just worked in Detroit. Which for me doesn't really count. It's where you sleep, right?

"Well, do you?" Chrissy said. She was obviously trying to tell us about hers but she wasn't about to go first, she's cautious, that one.

"I certainly don't," Darlene said, and she wrinkled up her nose, like this, and I had to laugh. "I think it's disgusting." She's divorced, I read that in the file too, she never talks about it. It must've been years ago anyway. She got up and went over to the coffee machine and turned her back on us as though she wasn't going to have anything more to do with it.

"Well," Greta said. I could see it was going to be between her and Chrissy. They're both blondes, I don't mean that in a bitchy way but they do try to outdress each other. Greta would like to get out of Filing, she'd like to be a receptionist too so she could meet more people. You don't meet much of anyone in Filing except other people in Filing. Me, I don't mind it so much, I have outside interests.

"Well," Greta said, "I sometimes think about, you know my apartment? It's got this little balcony, I like to sit out there in the summer and I have a few plants out there. I never bother that much about locking the door to the balcony, it's one of those sliding glass ones, I'm on the eighteenth floor for heaven's sake, I've got a good view of the lake and the CN Tower and all. But I'm sitting around one night in my housecoat, watching TV with my shoes off, you know how you do, and I see this guy's feet, coming down past the window, and the next thing you know he's standing on the balcony, he's let himself down by a rope with a hook on the end of it from the floor above, that's the nineteenth, and before I can even get up off the chesterfield he's inside the apartment. He's all dressed in black with black gloves on"—I knew right away what show she got the black gloves off because I saw the same one—"and then he, well, you know."

15   "You know what?" Chrissy said, but Greta said, "And afterwards he tells me that he goes all over the outside of the apartment building like that, from one floor to another, with his rope and his hook . . . and then he goes out to the balcony and tosses his rope, and he climbs up it and disappears."

"Just like Tarzan," I said, but nobody laughed.

"Is that all?" Chrissy said. "Don't you ever think about, well, I think about being in the bathtub, with no clothes on . . ."

"So who takes a bath in their clothes?" I said, you have to admit it's stupid when you come to think of it, but she just went on, ". . . with lots of bubbles, what I use is Vitabath, it's more expensive but it's so relaxing, and my hair pinned up, and the door opens and this fellow's standing there. . . ."

"How'd he get in?" Greta said.

20   "Oh, I don't know, through a window or something. Well, I can't very well get out of the bathtub, the bathroom's too small and besides he's blocking the doorway, so I just *lie* there, and he starts to very slowly take his own clothes off, and then he gets into the bathtub with me."

"Don't you scream or anything?" said Darlene. She'd come back with her cup of coffee, she was getting really interested. "I'd scream like bloody murder."

"Who'd hear me?" Chrissy said. "Besides, all the articles say it's better not to resist, that way you don't get hurt."

"Anyway you might get bubbles up your nose," I said, "from the deep breathing," and I swear all four of them looked at me like I was in bad taste, like I'd insulted the Virgin Mary or something. I mean, I don't see what's wrong with a little joke now and then. Life's too short, right?

"Listen," I said, "those aren't *rape* fantasies. I mean, you aren't getting *raped*, it's just some guy you haven't met formally who happens to be more attractive than Derek Cummins"—he's the Assistant Manager, he wears elevator shoes or at any rate they have these thick soles and he has this funny way of talking, we call him Derek Duck—"and you have a good time. Rape is when they've got a knife or something and you don't want to."

"So what about you, Estelle," Chrissy said, she was miffed because I   25
laughed at her fantasy, she thought I was putting her down. Sondra was miffed too, by this time she'd finished her celery and she wanted to tell about hers, but she hadn't got in fast enough.

"All right, let me tell you one," I said. "I'm walking down this dark street at night and this fellow comes up and grabs my arm. Now it so happens that I have a plastic lemon in my purse, you know how it always says you should carry a plastic lemon in your purse? I don't really do it, I tried it once but the darn thing leaked all over my checkbook, but in this fantasy I have one, and I say to him, "You're intending to rape me, right?" and he nods, so I open my purse to get the plastic lemon, and I can't find it! My purse is full of all this junk, Kleenex and cigarettes and my change purse and my lipstick and my driver's license, you know the kind of stuff: so I ask him to hold out his hands, like this, and I pile all this junk into them and down at the bottom there's the plastic lemon, and I can't get the top off. So I hand it to him and he's very obliging, he twists the top off and hands it back to me, and I squirt him in the eye."

I hope you don't think that's too vicious. Come to think of it, it is a bit mean, especially when he was so polite and all.

"*That's* your rape fantasy?" Chrissy says, "I don't believe it."

"She's a card," Darlene says, she and I are the ones that've been here the longest and she never will forget the time I got drunk at the office party and insisted I was going to dance under the table instead of on top of it, I did a sort of Cossack number but then I hit my head on the bottom of the table—actually it was a desk—when I went to get up, and I knocked myself out cold. She's decided that's the mark of an original mind and she tells everyone new about it and I'm not sure that's fair. Though I did do it.

"I'm being totally honest," I say. I always am and they know it.   30
There's no point in being anything else, is the way I look at it, and sooner or later the truth will out so you might as well not waste the time, right? "You should hear the one about the Easy-Off Cleaner."

But that was the end of the lunch hour, with one bridge game shot to hell, and the next day we spent most of the time arguing over whether to start a new game or play out the hands we had left over from the day before, so Sondra never did get a chance to tell about her rape fantasy.

It started me thinking though, about my own rape fantasies. Maybe I'm abnormal or something, I mean I have fantasies about handsome strangers coming in through the window too, like Mr. Clean, I wish one would, please god somebody without flat feet and big sweat marks on his shirt, and over five feet five, believe me being tall is a handicap though it's getting better, tall guys are starting to like someone whose nose reaches higher than their belly button. But if you're being totally honest you can't count those as rape fantasies. In a real rape fantasy, what you should feel is this anxiety, like when you think about your apartment building catching on fire and whether you should use the elevator or the stairs or maybe just stick your head under a wet towel, and you try to remember everything you've read about what to do but you can't decide.

For instance, I'm walking along this dark street at night and this short, ugly fellow comes up and grabs my arm, and not only is he ugly, you know, with a sort of puffy nothing face, like those fellows you have to talk to in the bank when your account's overdrawn—of course I don't mean they're all like that—but he's absolutely covered in pimples. So he gets me pinned against the wall, he's short but he's heavy, and he starts to undo himself and the zipper gets stuck. I mean, one of the most significant moments in a girl's life, it's almost like getting married or having a baby or something, and he sticks the zipper.

So I say, kind of disgusted, "Oh for Chrissake," and he starts to cry. He tells me he's never been able to get anything right in his entire life, and this is the last straw, he's going to go jump off a bridge.

35   "Look," I say, I feel so sorry for him, in my rape fantasies I always end up feeling sorry for the guy, I mean there has to be something *wrong* with them, if it was Clint Eastwood it'd be different but worse luck it never is. I was the kind of little girl who buried dead robins, know what I mean? It used to drive my mother nuts, she didn't like me touching them, because of the germs I guess. So I say, "Listen, I know how you feel. You really should do something about those pimples, if you got rid of them you'd be quite good looking, honest; then you wouldn't have to go around doing stuff like this. I had them myself once," I say, to comfort him, but in fact I did, and it ends up I give him the name of my old dermatologist, the one I had in high school, that was back in Leamington, except I used to go to St. Catharine's for the dermatologist. I'm telling you, I was really

lonely when I first came here; I thought it was going to be such a big adventure and all, but it's a lot harder to meet people in a city. But I guess it's different for a guy.

Or I'm lying in bed with this terrible cold, my face is all swollen up, my eyes are red and my nose is dripping like a leaky tap, and this fellow comes in through the window and *he* has a terrible cold too, it's a new kind of flu that's been going around. So he says, "I'b goig do rabe you"—I hope you don't mind me holding my nose like this but that's the way I imagine it—and he lets out this terrific sneeze, which slows him down a bit, also I'm no object of beauty myself, you'd have to be some kind of pervert to want to rape someone with a cold like mine, it'd be like raping a bottle of LePages mucilage the way my nose is running. He's looking wildly around the room, and I realize it's because he doesn't have a piece of Kleenex! "Id's ride here," I say, and I pass him the Kleenex, god knows why he even bothered to get out of bed, you'd think if you were going to go around climbing in windows you'd wait till you were healthier, right? I mean, that takes a certain amount of energy. So I ask him why doesn't he let me fix him a NeoCitran and scotch, that's what I always take, you still have the cold but you don't feel it, so I do and we end up watching the Late Show together. I mean, they aren't all sex maniacs, the rest of the time they must lead a normal life. I figure they enjoy watching the Late Show just like anybody else.

I do have a scarier one though . . . where the fellow says he's hearing angel voices that're telling him he's got to kill me, you know, you read about things like that all the time in the papers. In this one I'm not in the apartment where I live now, I'm back in my mother's house in Leamington and the fellow's been hiding in the cellar, he grabs my arm when I go downstairs to get a jar of jam and he's got hold of the axe too, out of the garage, that one is really scary. I mean, what do you say to a nut like that?

So I start to shake but after a minute I get control of myself and I say, is he sure the angel voices have got the right person, because I hear the same angel voices and they've been telling me for some time that I'm going to give birth to the reincarnation of St. Anne who in turn has the Virgin Mary and right after that comes Jesus Christ and the end of the world, and he wouldn't want to interfere with that, would he? So he gets confused and listens some more, and then he asks for a sign and I show him my vaccination mark, you can see it's sort of an odd-shaped one, it got infected because I scratched the top off, and that does it, he apologizes and climbs out the coal chute again, which is how he got in in the first place, and I say to myself there's some advantage in having been brought up a Catholic even though I haven't been to church since they changed the service into English, it just isn't the same, you might as well be a Protestant. I must write to Mother and tell her to nail up that coal chute, it always has bothered me. Funny, I couldn't tell you at all what this man looks like but I know exactly what kind of shoes he's wearing, because that's the last I see of him, his shoes going up the coal chute, and they're the old-fashioned kind that lace up the ankles, even though he's a young fellow. That's strange, isn't it?

Let me tell you though I really sweat until I see him safely out of there and I go upstairs right away and make myself a cup of tea. I don't think about that one much. My mother always said you shouldn't dwell on unpleasant things and I generally agree with that, I mean, dwelling on them doesn't make them go away. Though not dwelling on them doesn't make them go away either, when you come to think of it.

40   Sometimes I have these short ones where the fellow grabs my arm but I'm really a Kung-Fu expert, can you believe it, in real life I'm sure it would just be a conk on the head and that's that, like getting your tonsils out, you'd wake up and it would be all over except for the sore places, and you'd be lucky if your neck wasn't broken or something, I could never even hit the volleyball in gym and a volleyball is fairly large, you know?—and I just go *zap* with my fingers into his eyes and that's it, he falls over, or I flip him against a wall or something. But I could never really stick my fingers in anyone's eyes, could you? It would feel like hot jello and I don't even like cold jello, just thinking about it gives me the creeps. I feel a bit guilty about that one, I mean how would you like walking around knowing someone's been blinded for life because of you?

But maybe it's different for a guy.

The most touching one I have is when the fellow grabs my arm and I say, sad and kind of dignified, "You'd be raping a corpse." That pulls him up short and I explain that I've just found out I have leukemia and the doctors have only given me a few months to live. That's why I'm out pacing the streets alone at night, I need to think, you know, come to terms with myself. I don't really have leukemia but in the fantasy I do, I guess I chose that particular disease because a girl in my grade four class died of it, the whole class sent her flowers when she was in the hospital. I didn't understand then that she was going to die and I wanted to have leukemia too so I could get flowers. Kids are funny, aren't they? Well, it turns out that he has leukemia himself, and *he* only has a few months to live, that's why he's going around raping people, he's very bitter because he's so young and his life is being taken from him before he's really lived it. So we walk along gently under the street lights, it's spring and sort of misty, and we end up going for coffee, we're happy we've found the only other person in the world who can understand what we're going through, it's almost like fate, and after a while we just sort of look at each other and our hands touch, and he comes back with me and moves into my apartment and we spend our last months together before we die, we just sort of don't wake up in the morning, though I've never decided which one of us gets to die first. If it's him I have to go on and fantasize about the funeral, if it's me I don't have to worry about that, so it just about depends on how tired I am at the time. You may not believe this but sometimes I even start crying. I cry at the end of movies, even the ones that aren't all that sad, so I guess it's the same thing. My mother's like that too.

The funny thing about these fantasies is that the man is always someone I don't know, and the statistics in the magazines, well, most of them anyway, they say it's often someone you do know, at least a little bit, like your boss or something—I mean, it wouldn't be *my* boss, he's over sixty and I'm sure he couldn't rape his way out of a paper bag, poor old thing, but it might be someone like Derek Duck, in his elevator shoes, perish the thought—or someone you just met, who invites you up for a drink, it's getting so you can hardly be sociable any more, and how are you supposed to meet people if you can't trust them even that basic amount? You can't spend your whole life in the Filing Department or cooped up in your own apartment with all the doors and windows locked and the shades down. I'm not what you would call a drinker but I like to go out now and then for a drink or two in a nice place, even if I am by myself, I'm with Women's Lib on that even though I can't agree with a lot of the other things they say. Like here for instance, the waiters all know me and if anyone, you know, bothers me . . . I don't know why I'm telling you all this, except I think it helps you get to know a person, especially at first, hearing some of the things they think about. At work they call me the office worry wart, but it isn't so much like worrying, it's more like figuring out what you should do in an emergency, like I said before.

Anyway, another thing about it is that there's a lot of conversation, in fact I spend most of my time, in the fantasy that is, wondering what I'm going to say and what he's going to say, I think it would be better if you could get a conversation going. Like, how could a fellow do that to a person he's just had a long conversation with, once you let them know you're human, you have a life too, I don't see how they could go ahead with it, right? I mean, I know it happens but I just don't understand it, that's the part I really don't understand.

QUESTIONS

1. Consider the use of humor and irony in this story. Why is humor appropriate in a story titled "Rape Fantasies"?
2. Characterize Estelle, the narrator. Include as much information as you can about her age, education, background, physical characteristics, attitudes, social and professional life. How does the point of view of this story both hinder and aid you in drawing up your characterization?
3. To whom is Estelle speaking? Where, and on what occasion? How long has Estelle been acquainted with the person she is addressing? What can you infer about Estelle's reasons for talking about this subject?
4. What do the "rape fantasies" of Greta and Chrissy have in common? Why does Estelle object to her coworkers' fantasies?
5. What are the common characteristics of Estelle's own "rape fantasies"? How, taken together, do they reveal her personality?
6. Is this story concerned with rape? In what way is the title appropriate?

Albert Camus

The Guest

The schoolmaster was watching the two men climb toward him. One was on horseback, the other on foot. They had not yet tackled the abrupt rise leading to the schoolhouse built on the hillside. They were toiling onward, making slow progress in the snow, among the stones, on the vast expanse of the high, deserted plateau. From time to time the horse stumbled. Without hearing anything yet, he could see the breath issuing from the horse's nostrils. One of the men, at least, knew the region. They were following the trail although it had disappeared days ago under a layer of dirty white snow. The schoolmaster calculated that it would take them half an hour to get onto the hill. It was cold; he went back into the school to get a sweater.

THE GUEST   First published in 1957. Translated into English by Justin O'Brien. Algeria, now a republic, was until midcentury a French territory with a population about 88 percent Muslim (either Arab or Berber). Daru and Balducci, in the story, are French civil servants. Algeria gained its independence as a result of the Algerian War, 1954–1962, a Muslim revolt against French rule. Albert Camus (1913–1960), though a Frenchman, was born in northeastern Algeria, was educated in Algiers, and did not see France until 1939. In 1940, with the fall of France to Germany, he returned to Algiers and taught for two years in a private school in Oran, on the seacoast. In 1942 he returned to Paris and engaged actively in the Resistance movement by writing for the underground press. He continued his residence in Paris after World War II.

He crossed the empty, frigid classroom. On the blackboard the four rivers of France, drawn with four different colored chalks, had been flowing toward their estuaries for the past three days. Snow had suddenly fallen in mid-October after eight months of drought without the transition of rain, and the twenty pupils, more or less, who lived in the villages scattered over the plateau had stopped coming. With fair weather they would return. Daru now heated only the single room that was his lodging, adjoining the classroom and giving also onto the plateau to the east. Like the class windows, his window looked to the south too. On that side the school was a few kilometers from the point where the plateau began to slope toward the south. In clear weather could be seen the purple mass of the mountain range where the gap opened onto the desert.

Somewhat warmed, Daru returned to the window from which he had first seen the two men. They were no longer visible. Hence they must have tackled the rise. The sky was not so dark, for the snow had stopped falling during the night. The morning had opened with a dirty light which had scarcely become brighter as the ceiling of clouds lifted. At two in the afternoon it seemed as if the day were merely beginning. But still this was better than those three days when the thick snow was falling amidst unbroken darkness with little gusts of wind that rattled the double door of the classroom. Then Daru had spent long hours in his room, leaving it only to go to the shed and feed the chickens or get some coal. Fortunately the delivery truck from Tadjid, the nearest village to the north, had brought his supplies two days before the blizzard. It would return in forty-eight hours.

Besides, he had enough to resist a siege, for the little room was cluttered with bags of wheat that the administration left as a stock to distribute to those of his pupils whose families had suffered from the drought. Actually they had all been victims because they were all poor. Every day Daru would distribute a ration to the children. They had missed it, he knew, during these bad days. Possibly one of the fathers or big brothers would come this afternoon and he could supply them with grain. It was just a matter of carrying them over to the next harvest. Now shiploads of wheat were arriving from France and the worst was over. But it would be hard to forget that poverty, that army of ragged ghosts wandering in the sunlight, the plateaus burned to a cinder month after month, the earth shriveled up little by little, literally scorched, every stone bursting into dust under one's foot. The sheep had died then by thousands and even a few men, here and there, sometimes without anyone's knowing.

In contrast with such poverty, he who lived almost like a monk in his remote schoolhouse, nonetheless satisfied with the little he had and with the rough life, had felt like a lord with his whitewashed walls, his

5

narrow couch, his unpainted shelves, his well, and his weekly provision of water and food. And suddenly this snow, without warning, without the foretaste of rain. This is the way the region was, cruel to live in, even without men—who didn't help matters either. But Daru had been born here. Everywhere else, he felt exiled.

He stepped out onto the terrace in front of the schoolhouse. The two men were now halfway up the slope. He recognized the horseman as Balducci, the old gendarme he had known for a long time. Balducci was holding on the end of a rope an Arab who was walking behind him with hands bound and head lowered. The gendarme waved a greeting to which Daru did not reply, lost as he was in contemplation of the Arab dressed in a faded blue jellaba, his feet in sandals but covered with socks of heavy raw wool, his head surmounted by a narrow, short *chèche*. They were approaching. Balducci was holding back his horse in order not to hurt the Arab, and the group was advancing slowly.

Within earshot, Balducci shouted: "One hour to do the three kilometers from El Ameur!" Daru did not answer. Short and square in his thick sweater, he watched them climb. Not once had the Arab raised his head. "Hello," said Daru when they got up onto the terrace. "Come in and warm up." Balducci painfully got down from his horse without letting go the rope. From under his bristling mustache he smiled at the schoolmaster. His little dark eyes, deep-set under a tanned forehead, and his mouth surrounded with wrinkles made him look attentive and studious. Daru took the bridle, led the horse to the shed, and came back to the two men, who were now waiting for him in the school. He led them into his room. "I am going to heat up the classroom," he said. "We'll be more comfortable there." When he entered the room again, Balducci was on the couch. He had undone the rope tying him to the Arab, who had squatted near the stove. His hands still bound, the *chèche* pushed back on his head, he was looking toward the window. At first Daru noticed only his huge lips, fat, smooth, almost Negroid; yet his nose was straight, his eyes were dark and full of fever. The *chèche* revealed an obstinate forehead and, under the weathered skin now rather discolored by the cold, the whole face had a restless and rebellious look that struck Daru when the Arab, turning his face toward him, looked him straight in the eyes. "Go into the other room," said the schoolmaster, "and I'll make you some mint tea." "Thanks," Balducci said. "What a chore! How I long for retirement." And addressing his prisoner in Arabic: "Come on, you." The Arab got up and, slowly, holding his bound wrists in front of him, went into the classroom.

With the tea, Daru brought a chair. But Balducci was already enthroned on the nearest pupil's desk and the Arab had squatted against the teacher's platform facing the stove, which stood between the desk and the window. When he held out the glass of tea to the prisoner, Daru hesitated at the sight of his bound hands. "He might perhaps be untied." "Sure," said Balducci. "That was for the trip." He started to get to his feet. But Daru, setting the glass on the floor, had knelt beside the Arab. Without saying anything, the Arab watched him with his feverish eyes. Once his hands were free, he rubbed his swollen wrists against each other, took the glass of tea, and sucked up the burning liquid in swift little sips.

"Good," said Daru. "And where are you headed?"

Balducci withdrew his mustache from the tea. "Here, son."   10

"Odd pupils! And you're spending the night?"

"No. I'm going back to El Ameur. And you will deliver this fellow to Tinguit. He is expected at police headquarters."

Balducci was looking at Daru with a friendly little smile.

"What's this story?" asked the schoolmaster. "Are you pulling my leg?"

"No, son. Those are the orders."   15

"The orders? I'm not . . ." Daru hesitated, not wanting to hurt the old Corsican. "I mean, that's not my job."

"What! What's the meaning of that? In wartime people do all kinds of jobs."

"Then I'll wait for the declaration of war!"

Balducci nodded.

"O.K. But the orders exist and they concern you too. Things are   20 brewing, it appears. There is talk of a forthcoming revolt. We are mobilized, in a way."

Daru still had his obstinate look.

"Listen, son," Balducci said. "I like you and you must understand. There's only a dozen of us at El Ameur to patrol throughout the whole territory of a small department and I must get back in a hurry. I was told to hand this guy over to you and return without delay. He couldn't be kept there. His village was beginning to stir; they wanted to take him back. You must take him to Tinguit tomorrow before the day is over. Twenty kilometers shouldn't faze a husky fellow like you. After that, all will be over. You'll come back to your pupils and your comfortable life."

Behind the wall the horse could be heard snorting and pawing the earth. Daru was looking out the window. Decidedly, the weather was clearing and the light was increasing over the snowy plateau. When all the snow was melted, the sun would take over again and once more would burn the fields of stone. For days, still, the unchanging sky would shed its dry light on the solitary expanse where nothing had any connection with man.

"After all," he said, turning around toward Balducci, "what did he do?" And, before the gendarme had opened his mouth, he asked: "Does he speak French?"

25   "No, not a word. We had been looking for him for a month, but they were hiding him. He killed his cousin."

"Is he against us?"

"I don't think so. But you can never be sure."

"Why did he kill?"

"A family squabble, I think. One owed the other grain, it seems. It's not at all clear. In short, he killed his cousin with a billhook. You know, like a sheep, *kreezk!*"

30   Balducci made the gesture of drawing a blade across his throat and the Arab, his attention attracted, watched him with a sort of anxiety. Daru felt a sudden wrath against the man, against all men with their rotten spite, their tireless hates, their blood lust.

But the kettle was singing on the stove. He served Balducci more tea, hesitated, then served the Arab again, who, a second time, drank avidly. His raised arms made the jellaba fall open and the schoolmaster saw his thin, muscular chest.

"Thanks, kid," Balducci said. "And now, I'm off."

He got up and went toward the Arab, taking a small rope from his pocket.

"What are you doing?" Daru asked dryly.

35   Balducci, disconcerted, showed him the rope.

"Don't bother."

The old gendarme hesitated. "It's up to you. Of course, you are armed?"

"I have my shotgun."

"Where?"

40   "In the trunk."

"You ought to have it near your bed."

"Why? I have nothing to fear."

"You're crazy, son. If there's an uprising, no one is safe, we're all in the same boat."

"I'll defend myself. I'll have time to see them coming."

45   Balducci began to laugh, then suddenly the mustache covered the white teeth.

"You'll have time? O.K. That's just what I was saying. You have always been a little cracked. That's why I like you, my son was like that."

At the same time he took out his revolver and put it on the desk.

"Keep it; I don't need two weapons from here to El Ameur."

The revolver shone against the black paint of the table. When the gendarme turned toward him, the schoolmaster caught the smell of leather and horseflesh.

"Listen, Balducci," Daru said suddenly, "every bit of this disgusts me,   50
and first of all your fellow here. But I won't hand him over. Fight, yes, if I have to. But not that."

The old gendarme stood in front of him and looked at him severely.

"You're being a fool," he said slowly. "I don't like it either. You don't get used to putting a rope on a man even after years of it, and you're even ashamed—yes, ashamed. But you can't let them have their way."

"I won't hand him over," Daru said again.

"It's an order, son, and I repeat it."

"That's right. Repeat to them what I've said to you: I won't hand   55
him over."

Balducci made a visible effort to reflect. He looked at the Arab and at Daru. At last he decided.

"No, I won't tell them anything. If you want to drop us, go ahead; I'll not denounce you. I have an order to deliver the prisoner and I'm doing so. And now you'll just sign this paper for me."

"There's no need. I'll not deny that you left him with me."

"Don't be mean with me. I know you'll tell the truth. You're from hereabouts and you are a man. But you must sign, that's the rule."

Daru opened his drawer, took out a little square bottle of purple ink,   60
the red wooden penholder with the "sergeant-major" pen he used for making models of penmanship, and signed. The gendarme carefully folded the paper and put it into his wallet. Then he moved toward the door.

"I'll see you off," Daru said.

"No," said Balducci. "There's no use being polite. You insulted me." He looked at the Arab, motionless in the same spot, sniffed peevishly, and turned away toward the door. "Good-by, son," he said. The door shut behind him. Balducci appeared suddenly outside the window and then disappeared. His footsteps were muffled by the snow. The horse stirred on the other side of the wall and several chickens fluttered in fright. A moment later Balducci reappeared outside the window leading the horse by the bridle. He walked toward the little rise without turning around and disappeared from sight with the horse following him. A big stone could be heard bouncing down. Daru walked back toward the prisoner, who, without stirring, never took his eyes off him. "Wait," the schoolmaster said in Arabic and went toward the bedroom. As he was going through the door, he had a second thought, went to the desk, took the revolver, and stuck it in his pocket. Then, without looking back, he went into his room.

For some time he lay on his couch watching the sky gradually close over, listening to the silence. It was this silence that had seemed painful to him during the first days here, after the war. He had requested a post in the little town at the base of the foothills separating the upper plateaus from the desert. There, rocky walls, green and black to the north, pink and lavender to the south, marked the frontier of eternal summer. He had been named to a post farther north, on the plateau itself. In the beginning, the solitude and the silence had been hard for him on these wastelands peopled only by stones. Occasionally, furrows suggested cultivation, but they had been dug to uncover a certain kind of stone good for building. The only plowing here was to harvest rocks. Elsewhere a thin layer of soil accumulated in the hollows would be scraped out to enrich paltry village gardens. This is the way it was: bare rock covered three quarters of the region. Towns sprang up, flourished, then disappeared; men came by, loved one another or fought bitterly, then died. No one in this desert, neither he nor his guest, mattered. And yet, outside this desert neither of them, Daru knew, could have really lived.

65   When he got up, no noise came from the classroom. He was amazed at the unmixed joy he derived from the mere thought that the Arab might have fled and that he would be alone with no decision to make. But the prisoner was there. He had merely stretched out between the stove and the desk. With eyes open, he was staring at the ceiling. In that position, his thick lips were particularly noticeable, giving him a pouting look. "Come," said Daru. The Arab got up and followed him. In the bedroom, the schoolmaster pointed to a chair near the table under the window. The Arab sat down without taking his eyes off Daru.

"Are you hungry?"

"Yes," the prisoner said.

Daru set the table for two. He took flour and oil, shaped a cake in a frying-pan, and lighted the little stove that functioned on bottled gas. While the cake was cooking, he went out to the shed to get cheese, eggs, dates, and condensed milk. When the cake was done he set it on the window sill to cool, heated some condensed milk diluted with water, and beat up the eggs into an omelette. In one of his motions he knocked against the revolver stuck in his right pocket. He set the bowl down, went into the classroom, and put the revolver in his desk drawer. When he came back to the room, night was falling. He put on the light and served the Arab. "Eat," he said. The Arab took a piece of the cake, lifted it eagerly to his mouth, and stopped short.

"And you?" he asked.

"After you. I'll eat too."   70

The thick lips opened slightly. The Arab hesitated, then bit into the cake determinedly.

The meal over, the Arab looked at the schoolmaster. "Are you the judge?"

"No, I'm simply keeping you until tomorrow."

"Why do you eat with me?"

"I'm hungry."   75

The Arab fell silent. Daru got up and went out. He brought back a folding bed from the shed, set it up between the table and the stove, perpendicular to his own bed. From a large suitcase which, upright in a corner, served as a shelf for papers, he took two blankets and arranged them on the camp bed. Then he stopped, felt useless, and sat down on his bed. There was nothing more to do or to get ready. He had to look at this man. He looked at him, therefore, trying to imagine his face bursting with rage. He couldn't do so. He could see nothing but the dark yet shining eyes and the animal mouth.

"Why did you kill him?" he asked in a voice whose hostile tone surprised him.

The Arab looked away.

"He ran away. I ran after him."

He raised his eyes to Daru again and they were full of a sort of woeful   80
interrogation. "Now what will they do to me?"

"Are you afraid?"

He stiffened, turning his eyes away.

"Are you sorry?"

The Arab stared at him openmouthed. Obviously he did not understand. Daru's annoyance was growing. At the same time he felt awkward and self-conscious with his big body wedged between the two beds.

"Lie down there," he said impatiently. "That's your bed."   85

The Arab didn't move. He called to Daru:

"Tell me!"

The schoolmaster looked at him.

"Is the gendarme coming back tomorrow?"

"I don't know."   90

"Are you coming with us?"

"I don't know. Why?"

The prisoner got up and stretched out on top of the blankets, his feet toward the window. The light from the electric bulb shone straight into his eyes and he closed them at once.

"Why?" Daru repeated, standing beside the bed.

95   The Arab opened his eyes under the blinding light and looked at him, trying not to blink.

"Come with us," he said.

In the middle of the night, Daru was still not asleep. He had gone to bed after undressing completely; he generally slept naked. But when he suddenly realized that he had nothing on, he hesitated. He felt vulnerable and the temptation came to him to put his clothes back on. Then he shrugged his shoulders; after all, he wasn't a child and, if need be, he could break his adversary in two. From his bed he could observe him, lying on his back, still motionless with his eyes closed under the harsh light. When Daru turned out the light, the darkness seemed to coagulate all of a sudden. Little by little, the night came back to life in the window where the starless sky was stirring gently. The schoolmaster soon made out the body lying at his feet. The Arab still did not move, but his eyes seemed open. A faint wind was prowling around the schoolhouse. Perhaps it would drive away the clouds and the sun would reappear.

During the night the wind increased. The hens fluttered a little and then were silent. The Arab turned over on his side with his back to Daru, who thought he heard him moan. Then he listened for his guest's breathing, become heavier and more regular. He listened to that breath so close to him and mused without being able to go to sleep. In this room where he had been sleeping alone for a year, this presence bothered him. But it bothered him also by imposing on him a sort of brotherhood he knew well but refused to accept in the present circumstances. Men who share the same rooms, soldiers or prisoners, develop a strange alliance as if, having cast off their armor with their clothing, they fraternized every evening, over and above their differences, in the ancient community of dream and fatigue. But Daru shook himself; he didn't like such musings, and it was essential to sleep.

A little later, however, when the Arab stirred slightly, the schoolmaster was still not asleep. When the prisoner made a second move, he stiffened, on the alert. The Arab was lifting himself slowly on his arms with almost the motion of a sleepwalker. Seated upright in bed, he waited motionless without turning his head toward Daru, as if he were listening attentively. Daru did not stir; it had just occurred to him that the revolver was still in the drawer of his desk. It was better to act at once. Yet he continued to observe the prisoner, who, with the same slithery motion, put his feet on the ground, waited again, then began to stand up slowly. Daru was about to call out to him when the Arab began to walk, in a quite natural but extraordinarily silent way. He was heading toward the door at the end of the room that opened into the shed. He lifted the latch with precaution and went out, pushing the door behind him but without shutting it. Daru had not stirred. "He is running away," he merely thought. "Good riddance!" Yet he listened attentively. The hens were not fluttering; the guest must be on the plateau. A faint sound of water reached him, and he didn't know what it was until the Arab again stood framed in the doorway, closed the door carefully, and came back to bed without a sound. Then Daru turned his back on him and fell asleep. Still later he seemed, from the depths of his sleep, to hear furtive steps around the schoolhouse. "I'm dreaming! I'm dreaming!" he repeated to himself. And he went on sleeping.

When he awoke, the sky was clear; the loose window let in a cold, pure air. The Arab was asleep, hunched up under the blankets now, his mouth open, utterly relaxed. But when Daru shook him, he started dreadfully, staring at Daru with wild eyes as if he had never seen him and such a frightened expression that the schoolmaster stepped back. "Don't be afraid. It's me. You must eat." The Arab nodded his head and said yes. Calm had returned to his face, but his expression was vacant and listless.

The coffee was ready. They drank it seated together on the folding bed as they munched their pieces of the cake. Then Daru led the Arab under the shed and showed him the faucet where he washed. He went back into the room, folded the blankets and the bed, made his own bed and put the room in order. Then he went through the classroom and out onto the terrace. The sun was already rising in the blue sky; a soft, bright light was bathing the deserted plateau. On the ridge the snow was melting in spots. The stones were about to reappear. Crouched on the edge of the plateau, the schoolmaster looked at the deserted expanse. He thought of Balducci. He had hurt him, for he had sent him off in a way as if he didn't want to be associated with him. He could still hear the gendarme's farewell and, without knowing why, he felt strangely empty and vulnerable. At that moment, from the other side of the schoolhouse, the prisoner coughed. Daru listened to him almost despite himself and then, furious, threw a pebble that whistled through the air before sinking into the snow. That man's stupid crime revolted him, but to hand him over was contrary to honor. Merely thinking of it made him smart with humiliation. And he cursed at one and the same time his own people who had sent him this Arab and the Arab too who had dared to kill and not managed to get away. Daru got up, walked in a circle on the terrace, waited motionless, and then went back into the schoolhouse.

The Arab, leaning over the cement floor of the shed, was washing his teeth with two fingers. Daru looked at him and said: "Come." He went back into the room ahead of the prisoner. He slipped a hunting-jacket on over his sweater and put on walking-shoes. Standing, he waited until the Arab had put on his *chèche* and sandals. They went into the classroom and the schoolmaster pointed to the exit, saying: "Go ahead." The fellow didn't budge. "I'm coming," said Daru. The Arab went out. Daru went back into the room and made a package of pieces of rusk, dates, and sugar. In the classroom, before going out, he hesitated a second in front of his desk, then crossed the threshold and locked the door. "That's the way," he said. He started toward the east, followed by the prisoner. But, a short distance from the schoolhouse, he thought he heard a slight sound behind them. He retraced his steps and examined the surroundings of the house; there was no one there. The Arab watched him without seeming to understand. "Come on," said Daru.

They walked for an hour and rested beside a sharp peak of limestone. The snow was melting faster and faster and the sun was drinking up the puddles at once, rapidly cleaning the plateau, which gradually dried and vibrated like the air itself. When they resumed walking, the ground rang under their feet. From time to time a bird rent the space in front of them with a joyful cry. Daru breathed in deeply the fresh morning light. He felt a sort of rapture before the vast familiar expanse, now almost entirely yellow under its dome of blue sky. They walked an hour more, descending toward the south. They reached a level height made up of crumbly rocks. From there on, the plateau sloped down, eastward, toward a low plain where there were a few spindly trees and, to the south, toward outcroppings of rock that gave the landscape a chaotic look.

Daru surveyed the two directions. There was nothing but the sky on the horizon. Not a man could be seen. He turned toward the Arab, who was looking at him blankly. Daru held out the package to him. "Take it," he said. "There are dates, bread, and sugar. You can hold out for two days. Here are a thousand francs too." The Arab took the package and the money but kept his full hands at chest level as if he didn't know what to do with what was being given him. "Now look," the schoolmaster said as he pointed in the direction of the east, "there's the way to Tinguit. You have a two-hour walk. At Tinguit you'll find the administration and the police. They are expecting you." The Arab looked toward the east, still holding the package and the money against his chest. Daru took his elbow and turned him rather roughly toward the south. At the foot of the height on which they stood could be seen a faint path. "That's the trail across the plateau. In a day's walk from here you'll find pasturelands and the first nomads. They'll take you in and shelter you according to their law." The Arab had now turned toward Daru and a sort of panic was visible in his expression. "Listen," he said. Daru shook his head: "No, be quiet. Now I'm leaving you." He turned his back on him, took two long steps in the direction of the school, looked hesitantly at the motionless Arab, and started off again. For a few minutes he heard nothing but his own step resounding on the cold ground and did not turn his head. A moment later, however, he turned around. The Arab was still there on the edge of the hill, his arms hanging now, and he was looking at the schoolmaster. Daru felt something rise in his throat. But he swore with impatience, waved vaguely, and started off again. He had already gone some distance when he again stopped and looked. There was no longer anyone on the hill.

Daru hesitated. The sun was now rather high in the sky and was   105
beginning to beat down on his head. The schoolmaster retraced his steps, at first somewhat uncertainly, then with decision. When he reached the little hill, he was bathed in sweat. He climbed it as fast as he could and stopped, out of breath, at the top. The rock-fields to the south stood out sharply against the blue sky, but on the plain to the east a steamy heat was already rising. And in that slight haze, Daru, with heavy heart, made out the Arab walking slowly on the road to prison.

A little later, standing before the window of the classroom, the schoolmaster was watching the clear light bathing the whole surface of the plateau, but he hardly saw it. Behind him on the blackboard, among the winding French rivers, sprawled the clumsily chalked-up words he had just read: "You handed over our brother. You will pay for this." Daru looked at the sky, the plateau, and, beyond, the invisible lands stretching all the way to the sea. In this vast landscape he had loved so much, he was alone.

QUESTIONS

1. What is the central conflict of the story? Is it external or internal? Can it be defined in terms of dilemma?
2. Compare and contrast the attitudes of Daru and Balducci toward the prisoner and the situation. What is their attitude toward each other? Is either a bad or a cruel man? How does the conflict between Daru and Balducci intensify the central conflict?
3. Why does Daru give the prisoner his freedom? What reasons are there for not giving him his freedom?
4. In what respect is the title ironic? Why does "The Guest" make a better title than "The Prisoner"? And why does the French title "L'Hôte" (which can mean either "The Guest" or "The Host") make an even better title than its English translation?
5. This story contains the materials of explosive action—a revolver, a murderer, a state of undeclared war, an incipient uprising, a revenge note—but no violence occurs in the story. In what aspect of the situation is Camus principally interested?

6. This story has as its background a specific political situation—the French Algerian crisis in the years following World War II. How does Daru reflect France's plight? Is the story's meaning limited to this situation? What does the story tell us about good and evil and the nature of moral choice? How does the story differ in its treatment of these things from the typical Western story or the patriotic editorial?

7. In what respect is the ending of the story ironic? What kind of irony is this? What does it contribute to the meaning of the story?

8. Besides the ironies of the title and the ending, there are other ironies in the story. Find and explain them. Daru uses verbal irony in paragraph 11 when he exclaims, "Odd pupils!" Is verbal irony the same thing as sarcasm?

9. Comment on the following: (a) Daru's behavior toward firearms and how it helps reveal him; (b) Camus's reason for making the Arab a murderer; (c) the Arab's reason for taking the road to prison.

SUGGESTIONS FOR WRITING

1. Write an essay exploring the use of irony in one of the following stories, or compare the use of irony in any two of the stories:
   a. Wolff, "Hunters in the Snow" (page 86).
   b. Munro, "How I Met My Husband" (page 125).
   c. Lahiri, "Interpreter of Maladies" (page 141).
   d. Walker, "Everyday Use" (page 166).
   e. O'Connor, "The Drunkard" (page 339).
   f. Atwood, "Rape Fantasies" (page 348).
   g. O'Connor, "Everything That Rises Must Converge" (page 434).
   h. Melville, "Bartleby the Scrivener" (page 586).

2. Discuss the effect of humor in any of the following. Apart from its entertainment value, how does the humor contribute to the theme and significance of the story?
   a. Wolff, "Hunters in the Snow" (page 86).
   b. Walker, "Everyday Use" (page 166).
   c. O'Connor, "The Drunkard" (page 339).
   d. Atwood, "Rape Fantasies" (page 348).
   e. Hurston, "The Gilded Six-Bits" (page 553).
   f. Melville, "Bartleby the Scrivener" (page 586).
   g. O'Connor, "A Good Man Is Hard to Find" (page 420).

Evaluating Fiction

Our purpose in the preceding chapters has been to develop not literary critics but proficient readers—readers who choose wisely and read well. Yet good reading involves the ability to evaluate what we read, and making wise choices necessitates sound judgment. This does not mean that in order to read well we must decide whether Welty's "A Worn Path" or Lawrence's "The Rocking-Horse Winner" is the "better" story, or whether Willa Cather is a "better" writer than Katherine Anne Porter. Any such judgments would be unpredictable, since in both these pairings equally intelligent readers might choose one or the other based on personal tastes and preferences. We do need, however, to be able to discriminate between the genuine and the spurious, the consequential and the trivial, the significant and the merely entertaining. Where such distinct categories are the issue, good readers will almost always reach the same conclusions.

There are no simple rules for literary judgment. Such judgment depends ultimately on our sensitivity, intelligence, and experience; it is a product of how much and how alertly we have lived and how much and how well we have read. Yet there are at least two basic principles that may serve to help you form your own evaluations. First, *every story should be judged initially by how fully it achieves its central purpose*. In a first-rate story, every element works with every other element to accomplish the central purpose as economically and powerfully as possible. For this reason, no single element in a story should be judged in isolation.

In fact, isolating a single element for evaluation without considering the other fictional elements in a story can lead to a flawed evaluation. It would be a mistake, for instance, to criticize "The Guest" for not revealing what ultimately happens to Daru, since the theme of the story involves the unpredictability of the consequences of human choices in unfriendly conditions. We cannot say that "Miss Brill" and "Eveline" are poor stories because they do not have exciting plots full of action and conflict: the effectiveness of a story's plot can be judged only in relation to the other elements in a story and to its central purpose. In "Miss Brill" and "Eveline," of course, the relatively plotless quality of the narratives reflects the uneventful nature of these two women's lives.

Every first-rate story is an organic whole. All its parts should be related and all should be essential to the central purpose. We might ask, for example, whether the plot and characterizations of "The Most Dangerous Game" help to elucidate an important theme. Near the beginning of the story, there *is* a suggestion of theme. When Whitney declares that hunting is a great sport—for the hunter, not for the jaguar—Rainsford replies, "Who cares how a jaguar feels? . . . They've no understanding." To this, Whitney counters: "I rather think they understand one thing—fear. The fear of pain and the fear of death." Evidently Rainsford has something to learn about how it feels to be hunted, and presumably during the hunt he learns it, for when General Zaroff turns back the first time—playing cat and mouse—we are told, "Then it was that Rainsford knew the full meaning of terror." Later, on the morning of the third day, Rainsford awakens to the baying of hounds—"a sound that made him know that he had new things to learn about fear." But little is made of Rainsford's terror during the hunt. The story focuses instead on Malay man-catchers, Burmese tiger pits, Ugandan knife-throwers—in short, on the colorful and entertaining action. The story ends with the physical triumph of Rainsford over Zaroff, but has Rainsford been altered by the experience? Has he learned anything significant? Has he changed his attitudes toward hunting? We cannot answer, for the author's major purpose has been not to develop these themes but to entertain the reader. There is no clear thematic connection between the final sentence—"He had never slept in a better bed, Rainsford decided"—and the question "Who cares how a jaguar feels?" Rather, the ending merely provokes a smile from the reader at Rainsford's victory and at the cleverness of the author's concluding flourish; it does not, however, encourage the reader to think further about the story as an artistic statement of any real import.

By contrast, Wolff's "Hunters in the Snow" is a far more thematically unified story. Throughout a varied group of scenes, the story develops the idea that human beings, like animals in the wild, engage constantly in a struggle for power. Tub is overweight and the most sympathetic of the three major characters, and both Frank and Kenny treat him cruelly at several key points. Once Kenny is wounded, however, and thereby becomes the "weakest" of the characters, Frank and Tub form a new alliance and Kenny becomes the odd man out. Ultimately the story makes clear that the more powerful individual in any relationship will behave in a cruel and callous way toward the weaker individual. The reader finishes this masterful story thinking not about the bleak setting or the hunting trip it depicts but about the dark complexity of human relationships.

Once you have judged a story as successful in achieving its central purpose, you may consider a second principle of judgment: *a story should also be judged by the significance of its purpose*. Once you determine that a story successfully integrates its materials into an organic unity, you should then evaluate the depth, the range, and the significance of what the story has achieved. This principle returns us to our distinction between commercial and literary fiction. If a story's chief aim is to entertain, we may judge it to have less stature and significance than a story whose aim is to reveal important truths of human experience. "The Most Dangerous Game" and "Hunters in the Snow," it could be argued, are equally successful in achieving their central purposes. But Wolff's story is far more ambitious and significant than Connell's. A critical consensus has developed that "Hunters in the Snow" is a contemporary masterpiece of short fiction, while Connell's story is less highly regarded. Using other stories from the preceding chapters, we might also argue that "Once upon a Time" has a more ambitious, significant purpose than "The Drunkard," and that "Young Goodman Brown" has a more ambitious, significant purpose than "Miss Brill." This is not to disparage either "The Drunkard" or "Miss Brill," both of which are excellent stories, but to suggest that certain stories stake out larger thematic terrain and plumb the depths of human experience more profoundly than others.

A related evaluative principle is simply one of length. Most fiction takes the form of novels, not short stories, and while all the aspects of fiction we have discussed are represented in both longer and shorter forms, there is no doubt that a novel has the room to explore more varieties of human experience than does the short story, and that it has the leisure to explore them in greater depth. Obviously, then, Hawthorne's *The Scarlet Letter* is a greater work than his short story "Young Goodman Brown," simply by virtue of its greater length and therefore its greater richness of characterization, plot, and language. It should be stressed, however, that length alone is not a significant criterion in evaluating a work of fiction. The very brief "Eveline" is a more significant literary work, of course, than any 500-page romance or horror novel found on a best-seller list. But a serious literary author practicing the long form of the novel inevitably has greater opportunities for developing varieties of characters, exploring multiple themes, and providing richer and fuller artistic visions than the short story affords.

Again, as we stressed in discussing literary versus commercial fiction, we cannot evaluate stories by placing them into artificial categories; the evaluation of individual stories and novels is an ongoing process, and even the most informed evaluations do not remain fixed in time. For instance, the finest work of Herman Melville, author of *Moby-Dick* and "Bartleby the Scrivener," received scathing critical assessments and was virtually forgotten at the time of his death; yet today he is considered one of the most significant fiction writers of his era. Conversely, a short story called "Circumstance," published by Harriet Prescott Spofford in 1860, was one of the most famous stories of the nineteenth century, highly praised by such discriminating readers as Emily Dickinson and Henry James; but today the story is seldom read except by scholars and historians. When we evaluate a work of fiction, therefore, we must be aware that we are judging it according to the aesthetic criteria of our own time and that such criteria evolve and change. Similarly, individual readers—including professional critics—may evaluate works differently at different points in their own lives. Some readers, for instance, might respond enthusiastically to a particular novel in their twenties, but in their fifties might reread the beloved novel and wonder why they rated it so highly. While evaluating what we read is essential to developing our skill and insight, we must also be aware that any evaluation of a given work—our own, or that of the culture at large—may well change over time.

Ultimately, however, we must rely on our own judgments, based on our accumulated experience with both literature and life.

REVIEWING CHAPTER EIGHT

1. Review the two basic principles required for evaluating fiction.
2. Describe the elements that make up a first-rate story.
3. Analyze the literary quality of Connell's "The Most Dangerous Game" vs. Wolff's "Hunters in the Snow."
4. Describe the importance of length in evaluating fiction.
5. Choose any two stories in this book and evaluate them comparatively.

EXERCISE

The two stories that follow both deal with the experiences of Americans in Europe, with social and moral standards of sexual behavior, and with contrasts between past actions and present behavior. Which story, in your estimation, deserves the higher ranking? Which gives the greater insight into significant

has certainly given us a good deal of time to kill; and sometimes I get tired just looking—even at this." Her gesture was now addressed to the stupendous scene at their feet.

The dark lady laughed again, and they both relapsed upon the view, contemplating it in silence, with a sort of diffused serenity which might have been borrowed from the spring effulgence of the Roman skies. The luncheon hour was long past, and the two had their end of the vast terrace to themselves. At its opposite extremity a few groups, detained by a lingering look at the outspread city, were gathering up guidebooks and fumbling for tips. The last of them scattered, and the two ladies were alone on the air-washed height.

"Well, I don't see why we shouldn't just stay here," said Mrs. Slade, the lady of the high color and energetic brows. Two derelict basket chairs stood near, and she pushed them into the angle of the parapet, and settled herself in one, her gaze upon the Palatine. "After all, it's still the most beautiful view in the world."

"It always will be, to me," assented her friend Mrs. Ansley, with so slight a stress on the "me" that Mrs. Slade, though she noticed it, wondered if it were not merely accidental, like the random underlinings of old-fashioned letter writers.

"Grace Ansley was always old-fashioned," she thought; and added aloud, with a retrospective smile: "It's a view we've both been familiar with for a good many years. When we first met here we were younger than our girls are now. You remember?"

"Oh, yes, I remember," murmured Mrs. Ansley, with the same undefinable stress. "There's that headwaiter wondering," she interpolated. She was evidently far less sure than her companion of herself and of her rights in the world.

"I'll cure him of wondering," said Mrs. Slade, stretching her hand toward a bag as discreetly opulent-looking as Mrs. Ansley's. Signing to the headwaiter, she explained that she and her friend were old lovers of Rome, and would like to spend the end of the afternoon looking down on the view—that is, if it did not disturb the service? The headwaiter, bowing over her gratuity, assured her that the ladies were most welcome, and would be still more so if they would condescend to remain for dinner. A full-moon night, they would remember. . . .

Mrs. Slade's black brows drew together, as though references to the moon were out of place and even unwelcome. But she smiled away her frown as the headwaiter retreated. "Well, why not? We might do worse. There's no knowing, I suppose, when the girls will be back. Do you even know back from *where*? I don't!"

Mrs. Ansley again colored slightly. "I think those young Italian aviators we met at the Embassy invited them to fly to Tarquinia for tea. I suppose they'll want to wait and fly back by moonlight."

"Moonlight—moonlight! What a part it still plays. Do you suppose   15
they're as sentimental as we were?"

"I've come to the conclusion that I don't in the least know what they are," said Mrs. Ansley. "And perhaps we didn't know much more about each other."

"No; perhaps we didn't."

Her friend gave her a shy glance. "I never should have supposed you were sentimental, Alida."

"Well, perhaps I wasn't." Mrs. Slade drew her lids together in retrospect; and for a few moments the two ladies, who had been intimate since childhood, reflected how little they knew each other. Each one, of course, had a label ready to attach to the other's name; Mrs. Delphin Slade, for instance, would have told herself, or anyone who asked her, that Mrs. Horace Ansley, twenty-five years ago, had been exquisitely lovely—no, you wouldn't believe it, would you? . . . though, of course, still charming, distinguished. . . . Well, as a girl she had been exquisite; far more beautiful than her daughter Barbara, though certainly Babs, according to the new standards at any rate, was more effective—had more *edge*, as they say. Funny where she got it, with those two nullities as parents. Yes; Horace Ansley was—well, just the duplicate of his wife. Museum specimens of old New York. Good-looking, irreproachable, exemplary. Mrs. Slade and Mrs. Ansley had lived opposite each other—actually as well as figuratively—for years. When the drawing-room curtains in No. 20 East 73rd Street were renewed, No. 23, across the way, was always aware of it. And of all the movings, buyings, travels, anniversaries, illnesses—the tame chronicle of an estimable pair. Little of it escaped Mrs. Slade. But she had grown bored with it by the time her husband made his big *coup* in Wall Street, and when they bought in upper Park Avenue had already begun to think: "I'd rather live opposite a speakeasy for a change; at least one might see it raided." The idea of seeing Grace raided was so amusing that (before the move) she launched it at a woman's lunch. It made a hit, and went the rounds—she sometimes wondered if it had crossed the street, and reached Mrs. Ansley. She hoped not, but didn't much mind. Those were the days when respectability was at a discount, and it did the irreproachable no harm to laugh at them a little.

A few years later, and not many months apart, both ladies lost their   20
husbands. There was an appropriate exchange of wreaths and condolences, and a brief renewal of intimacy in the half-shadow of their

mourning; and now, after another interval, they had run across each other in Rome, at the same hotel, each of them the modest appendage of a salient daughter. The similarity of their lot had again drawn them together, lending itself to mild jokes, and the mutual confession that, if in old days it must have been tiring to "keep up" with daughters, it was now, at times, a little dull not to.

No doubt, Mrs. Slade reflected, she felt her unemployment more than poor Grace ever would. It was a big drop from being the wife of Delphin Slade to being his widow. She had always regarded herself (with a certain conjugal pride) as his equal in social gifts, as contributing her full share to the making of the exceptional couple they were: but the difference after his death was irremediable. As the wife of the famous corporation lawyer, always with an international case or two on hand, every day brought its exciting and unexpected obligation: the impromptu entertaining of eminent colleagues from abroad, the hurried dashes on legal business to London, Paris or Rome, where the entertaining was so handsomely reciprocated; the amusement of hearing in her wake: "What, that handsome woman with the good clothes and the eyes is Mrs. Slade—*the* Slade's wife? Really? Generally the wives of celebrities are such frumps."

Yes; being *the* Slade's widow was a dullish business after that. In living up to such a husband all her faculties had been engaged; now she had only her daughter to live up to, for the son who seemed to have inherited his father's gifts had died suddenly in boyhood. She had fought through that agony because her husband was there, to be helped and to help; now, after the father's death, the thought of the boy had become unbearable. There was nothing left but to mother her daughter; and dear Jenny was such a perfect daughter that she needed no excessive mothering. "Now with Babs Ansley I don't know that I *should* be so quiet," Mrs. Slade sometimes half-enviously reflected; but Jenny, who was younger than her brilliant friend, was that rare accident, an extremely pretty girl who somehow made youth and prettiness seem as safe as their absence. It was all perplexing—and to Mrs. Slade a little boring. She wished that Jenny would fall in love—with the wrong man, even; that she might have to be watched, out-maneuvered, rescued. And instead, it was Jenny who watched her mother, kept her out of drafts, made sure that she had taken her tonic. . . .

Mrs. Ansley was much less articulate than her friend, and her mental portrait of Mrs. Slade was slighter, and drawn with fainter touches. "Alida Slade's awfully brilliant; but not as brilliant as she thinks," would have summed it up; though she would have added, for the enlightenment of strangers, that Mrs. Slade had been an extremely dashing girl; much more so than her daughter, who was pretty, of course, and clever in a way, but had none of her mother's—well, "vividness," someone had once called it. Mrs. Ansley would take up current words like this, and cite them in quotation marks, as unheard-of audacities. No; Jenny was not like her mother. Sometimes Mrs. Ansley thought Alida Slade was disappointed; on the whole she had had a sad life. Full of failures and mistakes; Mrs. Ansley had always been rather sorry for her. . . .

So these two ladies visualized each other, each through the wrong end of her little telescope.

2

For a long time they continued to sit side by side without speaking.   25 It seemed as though, to both, there was a relief in laying down their somewhat futile activities in the presence of the vast Memento Mori° which faced them. Mrs. Slade sat quite still, her eyes fixed on the golden slope of the Palace of the Caesars, and after a while Mrs. Ansley ceased to fidget with her bag, and she too sank into meditation. Like many intimate friends, the two ladies had never before had occasion to be silent together, and Mrs. Ansley was slightly embarrassed by what seemed, after so many years, a new stage in their intimacy, and one with which she did not yet know how to deal.

Suddenly the air was full of that deep clangor of bells which periodically covers Rome with a roof of silver. Mrs. Slade glanced at her wristwatch. "Five o'clock already," she said, as though surprised.

Mrs. Ansley suggested interrogatively: "There's bridge at the Embassy at five." For a long time Mrs. Slade did not answer. She appeared to be lost in contemplation, and Mrs. Ansley thought the remark had escaped her. But after a while she said, as if speaking out of a dream: "Bridge, did you say? Not unless you want to. . . . But I don't think I will, you know."

"Oh, no," Mrs. Ansley hastened to assure her. "I don't care to at all. It's so lovely here; and so full of old memories, as you say." She settled herself in her chair, and almost furtively drew forth her knitting. Mrs. Slade took sideway note of this activity, but her own beautifully cared-for hands remained motionless on her knee.

"I was just thinking," she said slowly, "what different things Rome stands for to each generation of travelers. To our grandmothers, Roman fever; to our mothers, sentimental dangers—how we used to be

---

Memento Mori: reminder of mortality (Latin: literally, "remember that you must die")

guarded! —to our daughters, no more dangers than the middle of Main
Street. They don't know it—but how much they're missing!"

30   The long golden light was beginning to pale, and Mrs. Ansley
lifted her knitting a little closer to her eyes. "Yes; how we were
guarded!"

"I always used to think," Mrs. Slade continued, "that our mothers
had a much more difficult job than our grandmothers. When Roman
fever stalked the streets it must have been comparatively easy to
gather in the girls at the danger hour; but when you and I were
young, with such beauty calling us, and the spice of disobedience
thrown in, and no worse risk than catching cold during the cool hour
after sunset, the mothers used to be put to it to keep us in—didn't
they?"

She turned again toward Mrs. Ansley, but the latter had reached a
delicate point in her knitting. "One, two, three—slip two; yes, they must
have been," she assented, without looking up.

Mrs. Slade's eyes rested on her with a deepened attention. "She can
knit—in the face of *this!* How like her. . . ."

Mrs. Slade leaned back, brooding, her eyes ranging from the ruins
which faced her to the long green hollow of the Forum, the fading glow
of the church fronts beyond it, and the outlying immensity of the
Colosseum. Suddenly she thought: "It's all very well to say that our
girls have done away with sentiment and moonlight. But if Babs Ansley
isn't out to catch that young aviator—the one who's a Marchese—then
I don't know anything. And Jenny has no chance beside her. I know
that too. I wonder if that's why Grace Ansley likes the two girls to go
everywhere together? My poor Jenny as a foil—!" Mrs. Slade gave a
hardly audible laugh, and at the sound Mrs. Ansley dropped her
knitting.

35   "Yes—?"

"I—oh, nothing. I was only thinking how your Babs carries everything before her. That Campolieri boy is one of the best matches in
Rome. Don't look so innocent, my dear—you know he is. And I was
wondering, ever so respectfully, you understand . . . wondering how two
such exemplary characters as you and Horace had managed to produce
anything quite so dynamic." Mrs. Slade laughed again, with a touch of
asperity.

Mrs. Ansley's hands lay inert across her needles. She looked straight
out at the great accumulated wreckage of passion and splendor at her
feet. But her small profile was almost expressionless. At length she said:
"I think you overrate Babs, my dear."

Mrs. Slade's tone grew easier. "No; I don't. I appreciate her. And perhaps envy you. Oh, my girl's perfect; if I were a chronic invalid I'd—well, I think I'd rather be in Jenny's hands. There must be times . . . but there! I always wanted a brilliant daughter . . . and never quite understood why I got an angel instead."

Mrs. Ansley echoed her laugh in a faint murmur. "Babs is an angel too."

"Of course—of course! But she's got rainbow wings. Well, they're   40 wandering by the sea with their young men; and here we sit . . . and it all brings back the past a little too acutely."

Mrs. Ansley had resumed her knitting. One might almost have imagined (if one had known her less well, Mrs. Slade reflected) that, for her also, too many memories rose from the lengthening shadows of those august ruins. But no; she was simply absorbed in her work. What was there for her to worry about? She knew that Babs would almost certainly come back engaged to the extremely eligible Campolieri. "And she'll sell the New York house, and settle down near them in Rome, and never be in their way . . . she's much too tactful. But she'll have an excellent cook, and just the right people in for bridge and cocktails . . . and a perfectly peaceful old age among her grandchildren."

Mrs. Slade broke off this prophetic flight with a recoil of self-disgust. There was no one of whom she had less right to think unkindly than of Grace Ansley. Would she never cure herself of envying her? Perhaps she had begun too long ago.

She stood up and leaned against the parapet, filling her troubled eyes with the tranquilizing magic of the hour. But instead of tranquilizing her the sight seemed to increase her exasperation. Her gaze turned toward the Colosseum. Already its golden flank was drowned in purple shadow, and above it the sky curved crystal clear, without light or color. It was the moment when afternoon and evening hang balanced in midheaven.

Mrs. Slade turned back and laid her hand on her friend's arm. The gesture was so abrupt that Mrs. Ansley looked up, startled.

"The sun's set. You're not afraid, my dear?"   45

"Afraid—?"

"Of Roman fever or pneumonia? I remember how ill you were that winter. As a girl you had a very delicate throat, hadn't you?"

"Oh, we're all right up here. Down below, in the Forum, it does get deathly cold, all of a sudden . . . but not here."

"Ah, of course you know because you had to be so careful." Mrs. Slade turned back to the parapet. She thought: "I must make one more effort not to hate her." Aloud she said: "Whenever I look at the Forum from up here, I remember that story about a great-aunt of yours, wasn't she? A dreadfully wicked great-aunt?"

50   "Oh, yes; great-aunt Harriet. The one who was supposed to have sent her young sister out to the Forum after sunset to gather a night-blooming flower for her album. All our great-aunts and grandmothers used to have albums of dried flowers."

Mrs. Slade nodded. "But she really sent her because they were in love with the same man——"

"Well, that was the family tradition. They said Aunt Harriet con-fessed it years afterward. At any rate, the poor little sister caught the fever and died. Mother used to frighten us with the story when we were children."

"And you frightened *me* with it, that winter when you and I were here as girls. The winter I was engaged to Delphin."

Mrs. Ansley gave a faint laugh. "Oh, did I? Really frightened you? I don't believe you're easily frightened."

55   "Not often; but I was then. I was easily frightened because I was too happy. I wonder if you know what that means?"

"I—yes . . ." Mrs. Ansley faltered.

"Well, I suppose that was why the story of your wicked aunt made such an impression on me. And I thought: 'There's no more Roman fever, but the Forum is deathly cold after sunset—especially after a hot day. And the Colosseum's even colder and damper.'"

"The Colosseum—?"

"Yes. It wasn't easy to get in, after the gates were locked for the night. Far from easy. Still, in those days it could be managed; it *was* managed, often. Lovers met there who couldn't meet elsewhere. You knew that?"

60   "I—I dare say. I don't remember."

"You don't remember? You don't remember going to visit some ruins or other one evening, just after dark, and catching a bad chill? You were supposed to have gone to see the moon rise. People always said that expedition was what caused your illness."

There was a moment's silence; then Mrs. Ansley rejoined: "Did they? It was all so long ago."

"Yes. And you got well again—so it didn't matter. But I suppose it struck your friends—the reason given for your illness, I mean—because everybody knew you were so prudent on account of your throat, and your mother took such care of you. . . . You *had* been out late sight-seeing, hadn't you, that night?"

"Perhaps I had. The most prudent girls aren't always prudent. What made you think of it now?"

Mrs. Slade seemed to have no answer ready. But after a moment she broke out: "Because I simply can't bear it any longer—!"   65

Mrs. Ansley lifted her head quickly. Her eyes were wide and very pale. "Can't bear what?"

"Why—your not knowing that I've always known why you went."

"Why I went—?"

"Yes. You think I'm bluffing, don't you? Well, you went to meet the man I was engaged to—and I can repeat every word of the letter that took you there."

While Mrs. Slade spoke Mrs. Ansley had risen unsteadily to her feet.   70
Her bag, her knitting and gloves, slid in a panic-stricken heap to the ground. She looked at Mrs. Slade as though she were looking at a ghost.

"No, no—don't," she faltered out.

"Why not? Listen, if you don't believe me. 'My one darling, things can't go on like this. I must see you alone. Come to the Colosseum immediately after dark tomorrow. There will be somebody to let you in. No one whom you need fear will suspect'—but perhaps you've forgotten what the letter said?"

Mrs. Ansley met the challenge with an unexpected composure. Steadying herself against the chair she looked at her friend, and replied: "No; I know it by heart too."

"And the signature? 'Only *your* D.S.' Was that it? I'm right, am I? That was the letter that took you out that evening after dark?"

Mrs. Ansley was still looking at her. It seemed to Mrs. Slade that a   75
slow struggle was going on behind the voluntarily controlled mask of her small quiet face. "I shouldn't have thought she had herself so well in hand," Mrs. Slade reflected, almost resentfully. But at this moment Mrs. Ansley spoke. "I don't know how you knew. I burnt that letter at once."

"Yes; you would, naturally—you're so prudent!" The sneer was open now. "And if you burnt the letter you're wondering how on earth I know what was in it. That's it, isn't it?"

Mrs. Slade waited, but Mrs. Ansley did not speak.

"Well, my dear, I know what was in that letter because I wrote it!"

"You wrote it?"

"Yes."   80

The two women stood for a minute staring at each other in the last golden light. Then Mrs. Ansley dropped back into her chair. "Oh," she murmured, and covered her face with her hands.

Mrs. Slade waited nervously for another word or movement. None came, and at length she broke out: "I horrify you."

Mrs. Ansley's hands dropped to her knee. The face they uncovered was streaked with tears. "I wasn't thinking of you. I was thinking—it was the only letter I ever had from him!"

"And I wrote it. Yes; I wrote it! But I was the girl he was engaged to. Did you happen to remember that?"

85   Mrs. Ansley's head drooped again. "I'm not trying to excuse myself . . . I remembered. . . ."

"And still you went?"

"Still I went."

Mrs. Slade stood looking down on the small bowed figure at her side. The flame of her wrath had already sunk, and she wondered why she had ever thought there would be any satisfaction in inflicting so purposeless a wound on her friend. But she had to justify herself.

"You do understand? I'd found out—and I hated you, hated you. I knew you were in love with Delphin—and I was afraid; afraid of you, of your quiet ways, your sweetness . . . your . . . well, I wanted you out of the way, that's all. Just for a few weeks; just till I was sure of him. So in a blind fury I wrote that letter . . . I don't know why I'm telling you now."

90   "I suppose," said Mrs. Ansley slowly, "it's because you've always gone on hating me."

"Perhaps. Or because I wanted to get the whole thing off my mind." She paused. "I'm glad you destroyed the letter. Of course I never thought you'd die."

Mrs. Ansley relapsed into silence, and Mrs. Slade, leaning above her, was conscious of a strange sense of isolation, of being cut off from the warm current of human communion. "You think me a monster!"

"I don't know. . . . It was the only letter I had, and you say he didn't write it?"

"Ah, how you care for him still!"

95   "I cared for that memory," said Mrs. Ansley.

Mrs. Slade continued to look down on her. She seemed physically reduced by the blow—as if, when she got up, the wind might scatter her like a puff of dust. Mrs. Slade's jealousy suddenly leapt up again at the sight. All these years the woman had been living on that letter. How she must have loved him, to treasure the mere memory of its ashes! The letter of the man her friend was engaged to. Wasn't it she who was the monster?

"You tried your best to get him away from me, didn't you? But you failed; and I kept him. That's all."

"Yes. That's all."

"I wish now I hadn't told you. I'd no idea you'd feel about it as you do; I thought you'd be amused. It all happened so long ago, as you say; and you must do me the justice to remember that I had no reason to think you'd ever taken it seriously. How could I, when you were married to Horace Ansley two months afterward? As soon as you could get out of bed your mother rushed you off to Florence and married you. People were rather surprised—they wondered at its being done so quickly; but I thought I knew. I had an idea you did it out of *pique*—to be able to say you'd got ahead of Delphin and me. Girls have such silly reasons for doing the most serious things. And your marrying so soon convinced me that you'd never really cared."

"Yes. I suppose it would," Mrs. Ansley assented.   100

The clear heaven overhead was emptied of all its gold. Dusk spread over it, abruptly darkening the Seven Hills. Here and there lights began to twinkle through the foliage at their feet. Steps were coming and going on the deserted terrace—waiters looking out of the doorway at the head of the stairs, then reappearing with trays and napkins and flasks of wine. Tables were moved, chairs straightened. A feeble string of electric lights flickered out. Some vases of faded flowers were carried away, and brought back replenished. A stout lady in a dust coat suddenly appeared, asking in broken Italian if anyone had seen the elastic band which held together her tattered Baedeker.° She poked with her stick under the table at which she had lunched, the waiters assisting.

The corner where Mrs. Slade and Mrs. Ansley sat was still shadowy and deserted. For a long time neither of them spoke. At length Mrs. Slade began again: "I suppose I did it as a sort of joke—"

"A joke?"

"Well, girls are ferocious sometimes, you know. Girls in love especially. And I remember laughing to myself all that evening at the idea that you were waiting around there in the dark, dodging out of sight, listening for every sound, trying to get in— Of course I was upset when I heard you were so ill afterward."

Mrs. Ansley had not moved for a long time. But now she turned   105
slowly toward her companion. "But I didn't wait. He'd arranged everything. He was there. We were let in at once," she said.

Mrs. Slade sprang up from her leaning position. "Delphin there? They let you in?—Ah, now you're lying!" she burst out with violence.

Mrs. Ansley's voice grew clearer, and full of surprise. "But of course he was there. Naturally he came—"

Baedeker: tourist guidebook (one of a series issued by the German publisher Karl Baedeker)

"Came? How did he know he'd find you there? You must be raving!"

Mrs. Ansley hesitated, as though reflecting. "But I answered the letter. I told him I'd be there. So he came."

110   Mrs. Slade flung her hands up to her face. "Oh, God—you answered! I never thought of your answering. . . ."

"It's odd you never thought of it, if you wrote the letter."

"Yes. I was blind with rage."

Mrs. Ansley rose, and drew her fur scarf about her. "It is cold here. We'd better go . . . I'm sorry for you," she said, as she clasped the fur about her throat.

The unexpected words sent a pang through Mrs. Slade. "Yes; we'd better go." She gathered up her bag and cloak. "I don't know why you should be sorry for me," she muttered.

115   Mrs. Ansley stood looking away from her toward the dusky secret mass of the Colosseum. "Well—because I didn't have to wait that night."

Mrs. Slade gave an unquiet laugh. "Yes; I was beaten there. But I oughtn't to begrudge it to you, I suppose. At the end of all these years. After all, I had everything; I had him for twenty-five years. And you had nothing but that one letter that he didn't write."

Mrs. Ansley was again silent. At length she turned toward the door of the terrace. She took a step, and turned back, facing her companion.

"I had Barbara," she said, and began to move ahead of Mrs. Slade toward the stairway.

QUESTIONS

1. Characterize Grace Ansley and Alida Slade as fully as you can. By what characterizing devices does the story imply the superiority of Mrs. Slade (what gestures, what statements, what unspoken thoughts)? At what point does Mrs. Ansley begin to seem the superior person?
2. What is the meaning of the comment about "the wrong end of [the] little telescope" (paragraph 24)? How is that comment a suitable conclusion for the first part of the story?
3. Trace the revelation of the animosity that Mrs. Slade feels for Mrs. Ansley. Is Mrs. Ansley doing anything on this evening to provoke her envy? Why has Mrs. Slade always harbored negative feelings about her friend?
4. What purpose is served by the discussion of the different meanings of Rome to mothers and daughters of different generations (paragraphs 29–31)? What standards of behavior have changed from one generation to the next? What standards have remained the same? How does this discussion expand the meaning of the title of the story?

F. Scott Fitzgerald
A New Leaf

1

It was the first day warm enough to eat outdoors in the Bois de Boulogne, while chestnut blossoms slanted down across the tables and dropped impudently into the butter and the wine. Julia Ross ate a few with her bread and listened to the big goldfish rippling in the pool and the sparrows whirring about an abandoned table. You could see everybody again—the waiters with their professional faces, the watchful Frenchwomen all heels and eyes, Phil Hoffman opposite her with his heart balanced on his fork, and the extraordinarily handsome man just coming out on the terrace.

> —the purple noon's transparent might.
> The breath of the moist air is light
> Around each unexpanded bud—

Julia trembled discreetly; she controlled herself; she didn't spring up and call, "Yi-yi-yi-yi! Isn't this grand?" and push the maître d'hôtel into the lily pond. She sat there, a well-behaved woman of twenty-one, and discreetly trembled.

Phil was rising, napkin in hand. "Hi there, Dick!"

"Hi, Phil!"

It was the handsome man; Phil took a few steps forward and they   5
talked apart from the table.

"——seen Carter and Kitty in Spain——"

"——poured on to the Bremen——"

"——so I was going to——"

The man went on, following the head waiter, and Phil sat down.

"Who is that?" she demanded.   10

"A friend of mine—Dick Ragland."

A NEW LEAF   First published in 1931. The lines of poetry are slightly misquoted from Shelley's "Stanzas Written in Dejection—December 1818, Near Naples," lines 4–6; Shelley wrote "Blue isles and snowy mountains wear / The purple noon's transparent might, / The breath of the moist earth is light / Around its unexpanded buds" (3–6). F. Scott Fitzgerald (1896–1940) published dozens of short stories during the 1920s and 1930s. Their popularity helped him earn huge sums from such magazines as *The Saturday Evening Post*, providing Fitzgerald and his wife, Zelda, with an affluent lifestyle. Fitzgerald struggled with alcoholism for most of his adult life; he and Zelda lived for several years in France before returning permanently to the United States in 1931.

"He's without doubt the handsomest man I ever saw in my life."

"Yes, he's handsome," he agreed without enthusiasm.

"Handsome! He's an archangel, he's a mountain lion, he's something to eat. Just why didn't you introduce him?"

15   "Because he's got the worst reputation of any American in Paris."

"Nonsense; he must be maligned. It's all a dirty frame-up—a lot of jealous husbands whose wives got one look at him. Why, that man's never done anything in his life except lead cavalry charges and save children from drowning."

"The fact remains he's not received anywhere—not for one reason but for a thousand."

"What reasons?"

"Everything. Drink, women, jails, scandals, killed somebody with an automobile, lazy, worthless——"

20   "I don't believe a word of it," said Julia firmly. "I bet he's tremendously attractive. And you spoke to him as if you thought so too."

"Yes," he said reluctantly, "like so many alcoholics, he has a certain charm. If he'd only make his messes off by himself somewhere—except right in people's laps. Just when somebody's taken him up and is making a big fuss over him, he pours the soup down his hostess' back, kisses the serving maid and passes out in the dog kennel. But he's done it too often. He's run through about everybody, until there's no one left."

"There's me," said Julia.

There was Julia, who was a little too good for anybody and sometimes regretted that she had been quite so well endowed. Anything added to beauty has to be paid for—that is to say, the qualities that pass as substitutes can be liabilities when added to beauty itself. Julia's brilliant hazel glance was enough, without the questioning light of intelligence that flickered in it; her irrepressible sense of the ridiculous detracted from the gentle relief of her mouth, and the loveliness of her figure might have been more obvious if she had slouched and postured rather than sat and stood very straight, after the discipline of a strict father.

Equally perfect young men had several times appeared bearing gifts, but generally with the air of being already complete, of having no space for development. On the other hand, she found that men of larger scale had sharp corners and edges in youth, and she was a little too young herself to like that. There was, for instance, this scornful young egotist, Phil Hoffman, opposite her, who was obviously going to be a brilliant lawyer and who had practically followed her to Paris. She liked him as well as anyone she knew, but he had at present all the overbearance of the son of a chief of police.

"Tonight I'm going to London, and Wednesday I sail," he said.   25
"And you'll be in Europe all summer, with somebody new chewing on
your ear every few weeks."

"When you've been called for a lot of remarks like that you'll begin
to edge into the picture," Julia remarked. "Just to square yourself, I want
you to introduce that man Ragland."

"My last few hours!" he complained.

"But I've given you three whole days on the chance you'd work out a
better approach. Be a little civilized and ask him to have some coffee."

As Mr. Dick Ragland joined them, Julia drew a little breath of
pleasure. He was a fine figure of a man, in coloring both tan and
blond, with a peculiar luminosity to his face. His voice was quietly
intense; it seemed always to tremble a little with a sort of gay despair;
the way he looked at Julia made her feel attractive. For half an hour, as
their sentences floated pleasantly among the scent of violets and snowdrops, forget-me-nots and pansies, her interest in him grew. She was
even glad when Phil said:

"I've just thought about my English visa. I'll have to leave you two   30
incipient love birds together against my better judgment. Will you meet
me at the Gare St. Lazare° at five and see me off?"

He looked at Julia hoping she'd say, "I'll go along with you now."
She knew very well she had no business being alone with this man, but
he made her laugh, and she hadn't laughed much lately, so she said: "I'll
stay a few minutes; it's so nice and springy here."

When Phil was gone, Dick Ragland suggested a *fine* champagne.

"I hear you have a terrible reputation?" she said impulsively.

"Awful. I'm not even invited out any more. Do you want me to slip
on my false mustache?"

"It's so odd," she pursued. "Don't you cut yourself off from all   35
nourishment? Do you know that Phil felt he had to warn me about
you before he introduced you? And I might very well have told him
not to."

"Why didn't you?"

"I thought you seemed so attractive and it was such a pity."

His face grew bland; Julia saw that the remark had been made so
often that it no longer reached him.

"It's none of my business," she said quickly. She did not realize
that his being a sort of outcast added to his attraction for her—not
the dissipation itself, for never having seen it, it was merely an
abstraction—but its result in making him so alone. Something atavistic

Gare St. Lazare: a railroad station

in her went out to the stranger to the tribe, a being from a world with
different habits from hers, who promised the unexpected—promised
adventure.

40   "I'll tell you something else," he said suddenly. "I'm going permanently on the wagon on June fifth, my twenty-eighth birthday. I don't
have fun drinking any more. Evidently I'm not one of the few people
who can use liquor."

"You sure you can go on the wagon?"

"I always do what I say I'll do. Also I'm going back to New York and
go to work."

"I'm really surprised how glad I am." This was rash, but she let it
stand.

"Have another *fine?*" Dick suggested. "Then you'll be gladder still."

45   "Will you go on this way right up to your birthday?"

"Probably. On my birthday I'll be on the Olympic in mid-ocean."

"I'll be on that boat too!" she exclaimed.

"You can watch the quick change; I'll do it for the ship's concert."

The tables were being cleared off. Julia knew she should go now, but
she couldn't bear to leave him sitting with that unhappy look under his
smile. She felt, maternally, that she ought to say something to help him
keep his resolution.

50   "Tell me why you drink so much. Probably some obscure reason you
don't know yourself."

"Oh, I know pretty well how it began."

He told her as another hour waned. He had gone to the war at
seventeen and, when he came back, life as a Princeton freshman with a
little black cap was somewhat tame. So he went up to Boston Tech and
then abroad to the Beaux Arts; it was there that something happened
to him.

"About the time I came into some money I found that with a few
drinks I got expansive and somehow had the ability to please people,
and the idea turned my head. Then I began to take a whole lot of drinks
to keep going and have everybody think I was wonderful. Well, I got
plastered a lot and quarreled with most of my friends, and then I met a
wild bunch and for a while I was expansive with them. But I was
inclined to get superior and suddenly think 'What am I doing with
this bunch?' They didn't like that much. And when a taxi that I was
in killed a man, I was sued. It was just a graft, but it got in the papers, and
after I was released the impression remained that I'd killed him. So all
I've got to show for the last five years is a reputation that makes mothers
rush their daughters away if I'm at the same hotel."

An impatient waiter was hovering near and she looked at her watch.

"Gosh, we're to see Phil off at five. We've been here all the   55
afternoon."

As they hurried to the Gare St. Lazare, he asked: "Will you let me see you again; or do you think you'd better not?"

She returned his long look. There was no sign of dissipation in his face, in his warm cheeks, in his erect carriage.

"I'm always fine at lunch," he added, like an invalid.

"I'm not worried," she laughed. "Take me to lunch day after tomorrow."

They hurried up the steps of the Gare St. Lazare, only to see the last   60
carriage of the Golden Arrow disappearing toward the Channel. Julia was remorseful, because Phil had come so far.

As a sort of atonement, she went to the apartment where she lived with her aunt and tried to write a letter to him, but Dick Ragland intruded himself into her thoughts. By morning the effect of his good looks had faded a little; she was inclined to write him a note that she couldn't see him. Still, he had made her a simple appeal and she had brought it all on herself. She waited for him at half-past twelve on the appointed day.

Julia had said nothing to her aunt, who had company for luncheon and might mention his name—strange to go out with a man whose name you couldn't mention. He was late and she waited in the hall, listening to the echolalia of chatter from the luncheon party in the dining room. At one she answered the bell.

There in the outer hall stood a man whom she thought she had never seen before. His face was dead white and erratically shaven, his soft hat was crushed bunlike on his head, his shirt collar was dirty, and all except the band of his tie was out of sight. But at the moment when she recognized the figure as Dick Ragland she perceived a change which dwarfed the others into nothing; it was in his expression. His whole face was one prolonged sneer—the lids held with difficulty from covering the fixed eyes, the drooping mouth drawn up over the upper teeth, the chin wabbling like a madeover chin in which the paraffin had run—it was a face that both expressed and inspired disgust.

"H'lo," he muttered.

For a minute she drew back from him; then, at a sudden silence from   65
the dining room that gave on the hall, inspired by the silence in the hall itself, she half pushed him over the threshold, stepped out herself and closed the door behind them.

"Oh-h-h!" she said in a single, shocked breath.

"Haven't been home since yest'day. Got involve' on a party at——"

With repugnance, she turned him around by his arm and stumbled with him down the apartment stairs, passing the concierge's wife, who peered out at them curiously from her glass room. Then they came out into the bright sunshine of the Rue Guynemer.

Against the spring freshness of the Luxembourg Gardens opposite, he was even more grotesque. He frightened her; she looked desperately up and down the street for a taxi, but one turning the corner of the Rue de Vaugirard disregarded her signal.

70   "Where'll we go lunch?" he asked.

"You're in no shape to go to lunch. Don't you realize? You've got to go home and sleep."

"I'm all right. I get a drink I'll be fine."

A passing cab slowed up at her gesture.

"You go home and go to sleep. You're not fit to go anywhere."

75   As he focused his eyes on her, realizing her suddenly as something fresh, something new and lovely, something alien to the smoky and turbulent world where he had spent his recent hours, a faint current of reason flowed through him. She saw his mouth twist with vague awe, saw him make a vague attempt to stand up straight. The taxi yawned.

"Maybe you're right. Very sorry."

"What's your address?"

He gave it and then tumbled into a corner, his face still struggling toward reality. Julia closed the door.

When the cab had driven off, she hurried across the street and into the Luxembourg Gardens as if someone were after her.

2

80   Quite by accident, she answered when he telephoned at seven that night. His voice was strained and shaking:

"I suppose there's not much use apologizing for this morning. I didn't know what I was doing, but that's no excuse. But if you could let me see you for a while somewhere tomorrow—just for a minute—I'd like the chance of telling you in person how terribly sorry——"

"I'm busy tomorrow."

"Well, Friday then, or any day."

"I'm sorry, I'm very busy this week."

85   "You mean you don't ever want to see me again?"

"Mr. Ragland, I hardly see the use of going any further with this. Really, that thing this morning was a little too much. I'm very sorry. I hope you feel better. Good-by."

She put him entirely out of her mind. She had not even associated his reputation with such a spectacle—a heavy drinker was someone who sat up late and drank champagne and maybe in the small hours rode home singing. This spectacle at high noon was something else again. Julia was through.

Meanwhile there were other men with whom she lunched at Ciro's and danced in the Bois. There was a reproachful letter from Phil Hoffman in America. She liked Phil better for having been so right about this. A fortnight passed and she would have forgotten Dick Ragland, had she not heard his name mentioned with scorn in several conversations. Evidently he had done such things before.

Then, a week before she was due to sail, she ran into him in the booking department of the White Star Line. He was as handsome— she could hardly believe her eyes. He leaned with an elbow on the desk, his fine figure erect, his yellow gloves as stainless as his clear, shining eyes. His strong, gay personality had affected the clerk who served him with fascinated deference; the stenographers behind looked up for a minute and exchanged a glance. Then he saw Julia; she nodded, and with a quick, wincing change of expression he raised his hat.

They were together by the desk a long time and the silence was oppressive.   90

"Isn't this a nuisance?" she said.

"Yes," he said jerkily, and then: "You going by the Olympic?"

"Oh, yes."

"I thought you might have changed."

"Of course not," she said coldly.   95

"I thought of changing; in fact, I was here to ask about it."

"That's absurd."

"You don't hate the sight of me? So it'll make you seasick when we pass each other on the deck?"

She smiled. He seized his advantage:

"I've improved somewhat since we last met."   100

"Don't talk about that."

"Well then, you have improved. You've got the loveliest costume on I ever saw."

This was presumptuous, but she felt herself shimmering a little at the compliment.

"You wouldn't consider a cup of coffee with me at the café next door, just to recover from this ordeal?"

How weak of her to talk to him like this, to let him make advances.   105
It was like being under the fascination of a snake.

"I'm afraid I can't." Something terribly timid and vulnerable came into his face, twisting a little sinew in her heart. "Well, all right," she shocked herself by saying.

Sitting at the sidewalk table in the sunlight, there was nothing to remind her of that awful day two weeks ago. Jekyll and Hyde. He was courteous, he was charming, he was amusing. He made her feel, oh, so attractive! He presumed on nothing.

"Have you stopped drinking?" she asked.

"Not till the fifth."

"Oh!"

"Not until I said I'd stop. Then I'll stop."

When Julia rose to go, she shook her head at his suggestion of a further meeting.

"I'll see you on the boat. After your twenty-eighth birthday."

"All right; one more thing: It fits in with the high price of crime that I did something inexcusable to the one girl I've ever been in love with in my life."

She saw him the first day on board, and then her heart sank into her shoes as she realized at last how much she wanted him. No matter what his past was, no matter what he had done. Which was not to say that she would ever let him know, but only that he moved her chemically more than anyone she had ever met, that all other men seemed pale beside him.

He was popular on the boat; she heard that he was giving a party on the night of his twenty-eighth birthday. Julia was not invited; when they met they spoke pleasantly, nothing more.

It was the day after the fifth that she found him stretched in his deck chair looking wan and white. There were wrinkles on his fine brow and around his eyes, and his hand, as he reached out for a cup of bouillon, was trembling. He was still there in the late afternoon, visibly suffering, visibly miserable. After three times around, Julia was irresistibly impelled to speak to him:

"Has the new era begun?"

He made a feeble effort to rise, but she motioned him not to and sat on the next chair.

"You look tired."

"I'm just a little nervous. This is the first day in five years that I haven't had a drink."

"It'll be better soon."

"I know," he said grimly.

"Don't weaken."

"I won't."

"Can't I help you in any way? Would you like a bromide?"

"I can't stand bromides," he said almost crossly. "No, thanks, I mean."

Julia stood up: "I know you feel better alone. Things will be brighter tomorrow."

"Don't go, if you can stand me."

Julia sat down again.   130

"Sing me a song—can you sing?"

"What kind of a song?"

"Something sad—some sort of blues."

She sang him Libby Holman's "This is how the story ends," in a low, soft voice.

"That's good. Now sing another. Or sing that again."   135

"All right. If you like, I'll sing to you all afternoon."

3

The second day in New York he called her on the phone. "I've missed you so," he said. "Have you missed me?"

"I'm afraid I have," she said reluctantly.

"Much?"

"I've missed you a lot. Are you better?"   140

"I'm all right now. I'm still just a little nervous, but I'm starting work tomorrow. When can I see you?"

"When you want."

"This evening then. And look—say that again."

"What?"

"That you're afraid you have missed me."   145

"I'm afraid that I have," Julia said obediently.

"Missed me," he added.

"I'm afraid I have missed you."

"All right. It sounds like a song when you say it."

"Good-by, Dick."   150

"Good-by, Julia dear."

She stayed in New York two months instead of the fortnight she had intended, because he would not let her go. Work took the place of drink in the daytime, but afterward he must see Julia.

Sometimes she was jealous of his work when he telephoned that he was too tired to go out after the theater. Lacking drink, night life was less than nothing to him—something quite spoiled and well lost. For Julia, who never drank, it was a stimulus in itself—the music and the parade of dresses and the handsome couple they made dancing

together. At first they saw Phil Hoffman once in a while; Julia considered that he took the matter rather badly; then they didn't see him
any more.

A few unpleasant incidents occurred. An old schoolmate, Esther
Cary, came to her to ask if she knew of Dick Ragland's reputation.
Instead of growing angry, Julia invited her to meet Dick and was
delighted with the ease with which Esther's convictions were changed.
There were other, small, annoying episodes, but Dick's misdemeanors
had, fortunately, been confined to Paris and assumed here a far-away
unreality. They loved each other deeply now—the memory of that
morning slowly being effaced from Julia's imagination—but she wanted
to be sure.

155   "After six months, if everything goes along like this, we'll announce
our engagement. After another six months we'll be married."

"Such a long time," he mourned.

"But there were five years before that," Julia answered. "I trust you
with my heart and with my mind, but something else says wait. Remember, I'm also deciding for my children."

Those five years—oh, so lost and gone.

In August, Julia went to California for two months to see her family.
She wanted to know how Dick would get along alone. They wrote every
day; his letters were by turns cheerful, depressed, weary and hopeful. His
work was going better. As things came back to him, his uncle had begun
really to believe in him, but all the time he missed his Julia so. It was
when an occasional note of despair began to appear that she cut her visit
short by a week and came East to New York.

160   "Oh, thank God you're here!" he cried as they linked arms and
walked out of the Grand Central station. "It's been so hard. Half a dozen
times lately I've wanted to go on a bust and I had to think of you, and
you were so far away."

"Darling—darling, you're so tired and pale. You're working too
hard."

"No, only that life is so bleak alone. When I go to bed my mind
churns on and on. Can't we get married sooner?"

"I don't know; we'll see. You've got your Julia near you now, and
nothing matters."

After a week, Dick's depression lifted. When he was sad, Julia made
him her baby, holding his handsome head against her breast, but she
liked it best when he was confident and could cheer her up, making her
laugh and feel taken care of and secure. She had rented an apartment
with another girl and she took courses in biology and domestic science
in Columbia. When deep fall came, they went to football games and the

new shows together, and walked through the first snow in Central Park, and several times a week spent long evenings together in front of her fire. But time was going by and they were both impatient. Just before Christmas, an unfamiliar visitor—Phil Hoffman—presented himself at her door. It was the first time in many months. New York, with its quality of many independent ladders set side by side, is unkind to even the meetings of close friends; so, in the case of strained relations, meetings are easy to avoid.

And they were strange to each other. Since his expressed skepticism   165
of Dick, he was automatically her enemy; on another count, she saw that he had improved, some of the hard angles were worn off; he was now an assistant district attorney, moving around with increasing confidence through his profession.

"So you're going to marry Dick?" he said. "When?"

"Soon now. When mother comes East."

He shook his head emphatically. "Julia, don't marry Dick. This isn't jealousy—I know when I am licked—but it seems awful for a lovely girl like you to take a blind dive into a lake full of rocks. What makes you think that people change their courses? Sometimes they dry up or even flow into a parallel channel, but I've never known anybody to change."

"Dick's changed."

"Maybe so. But isn't that an enormous 'maybe'? If he was unattrac-   170
tive and you liked him, I'd say go ahead with it. Maybe I'm all wrong, but it's so darn obvious that what fascinates you is that handsome pan of his and those attractive manners."

"You don't know him," Julia answered loyally. "He's different with me. You don't know how gentle he is, and responsive. Aren't you being rather small and mean?"

"Hm." Phil thought for a moment. "I want to see you again in a few days. Or perhaps I'll speak to Dick."

"You let Dick alone," she cried. "He has enough to worry him without your nagging him. If you were his friend you'd try to help him instead of coming to me behind his back."

"I'm your friend first."

"Dick and I are one person now."   175

But three days later Dick came to see her at an hour when he would usually have been at the office.

"I'm here under compulsion," he said lightly, "under threat of exposure by Phil Hoffman."

Her heart dropping like a plummet. "Has he given up?" she thought. "Is he drinking again?"

"It's about a girl. You introduced me to her last summer and told me to be very nice to her—Esther Cary."

180   Now her heart was beating slowly.

"After you went to California I was lonesome and I ran into her. She'd liked me that day, and for a while we saw quite a bit of each other. Then you came back and I broke it off. It was a little difficult; I hadn't realized that she was so interested."

"I see." Her voice was starved and aghast.

"Try and understand. Those terribly lonely evenings. I think if it hadn't been for Esther, I'd have fallen off the wagon. I never loved her—I never loved anybody but you—but I had to see somebody who liked me."

He put his arm around her, but she felt cold all over and he drew away.

185   "Then any woman would have done," Julia said slowly. "It didn't matter who."

"No!" he cried.

"I stayed away so long to let you stand on your own feet and get back your self-respect by yourself."

"I only love you, Julia."

"But any woman can help you. So you don't really need me, do you?"

190   His face wore that vulnerable look that Julia had seen several times before; she sat on the arm of his chair and ran her hand over his cheek.

"Then what do you bring me?" she demanded. "I thought that there'd be the accumulated strength of having beaten your weakness. What do you bring me now?"

"Everything I have."

She shook her head. "Nothing. Just your good looks—and the head waiter at dinner last night had that."

They talked for two days and decided nothing. Sometimes she would pull him close and reach up to his lips that she loved so well, but her arms seemed to close around straw.

195   "I'll go away and give you a chance to think it over," he said despairingly. "I can't see any way of living without you, but I suppose you can't marry a man you don't trust or believe in. My uncle wanted me to go to London on some business——"

The night he left, it was sad on the dim pier. All that kept her from breaking was that it was not an image of strength that was leaving her; she would be just as strong without him. Yet as the murky lights fell on the fine structure of his brow and chin, as she saw the faces turn toward him, the eyes that followed him, an awful emptiness seized her and she wanted to say: "Never mind, dear; we'll try it together."

But try what? It was human to risk the toss between failure and success, but to risk the desperate gamble between adequacy and disaster——

"Oh, Dick, be good and be strong and come back to me. Change, change, Dick—change!"

"Good-by, Julia—good-by."

She last saw him on the deck, his profile cut sharp as a cameo   200
against a match as he lit a cigarette.

4

It was Phil Hoffman who was to be with her at the beginning and the end. It was he who broke the news as gently as it could be broken. He reached her apartment at half-past eight and carefully threw away the morning paper outside. Dick Ragland had disappeared at sea.

After her first wild burst of grief, he became purposely a little cruel.

"He knew himself. His will had given out; he didn't want life any more. And, Julia, just to show you how little you can possibly blame yourself, I'll tell you this: He'd hardly gone to his office for four months—since you went to California. He wasn't fired because of his uncle; the business he went to London on was of no importance at all. After his first enthusiasm was gone he'd given up."

She looked at him sharply. "He didn't drink, did he? He wasn't drinking?"

For a fraction of a second Phil hesitated. "No, he didn't drink; he   205
kept his promise—he held on to that."

"That was it," she said. "He kept his promise and he killed himself doing it."

Phil waited uncomfortably.

"He did what he said he would and broke his heart doing it," she went on chokingly. "Oh, isn't life cruel sometimes—so cruel, never to let anybody off. He was so brave—he died doing what he said he'd do."

Phil was glad he had thrown away the newspaper that hinted of Dick's gay evening in the bar—one of many gay evenings that Phil had known of in the past few months. He was relieved that was over, because Dick's weakness had threatened the happiness of the girl he loved; but he was terribly sorry for him—even understanding how it was necessary for him to turn his maladjustment to life toward one mischief or another—but he was wise enough to leave Julia with the dream that she had saved out of wreckage.

210   There was a bad moment a year later, just before their marriage, when she said:

"You'll understand the feeling I have and always will have about Dick, won't you, Phil? It wasn't just his good looks. I believed in him— and I was right in a way. He broke rather than bent; he was a ruined man, but not a bad man. In my heart I knew when I first looked at him."

Phil winced, but he said nothing. Perhaps there was more behind it than they knew. Better let it all alone in the depths of her heart and the depths of the sea.

QUESTIONS

1. The title alludes to the familiar phrase "turning over a new leaf." What does that mean? In the story, how might it apply to both Julia Ross and Dick Ragland? To what extent does either of them live up to the meaning of the phrase? Which of them would you call the protagonist?

2. From what point of view is the story told? For what purposes does the point of view shift? Pick out several examples to support your interpretation. Compare the contribution of point of view here to that in "Roman Fever."

3. As fully as possible, explain what causes Julia to fall in love with Dick, and what causes Dick to fall in love with Julia. Does either of them have a more mature or sound basis for loving the other? Compare their emotional lives with those of Mrs. Ansley and Mrs. Slade in "Roman Fever."

4. What causes Julia to reject Dick, twice? What in his behavior causes her rejections, and what in her character causes them?

5. What is the function of Phil Hoffman in the plot? Why does Julia reject him, and why does she finally marry him?

6. What are the connotations of the settings of the story—Paris, the steamship Olympia, and New York—and how do they reinforce your understanding of the social class and attitudes of the characters? Compare the role of settings in this story to that in "Roman Fever." Which story more fully integrates the setting into its meanings and emotional effects?

7. How do we learn about the emotional reactions of the characters to each other and to their own situations? Find several examples for analysis to support your answer. How does this story differ from "Roman Fever" in the way it presents the emotional lives of its characters?

8. What is the theme of "A New Leaf"? By comparison, is it more or less significant than that of "Roman Fever"?

SUGGESTIONS FOR WRITING

1. Write an essay evaluating the relative quality of any of the following pairs of stories. Decide which is the better story, and support your argument fully:
   a. Connell, "The Most Dangerous Game" (page 67) and Glaspell, "A Jury of Her Peers" (page 534).

b. Walker, "Everyday Use" (page 166) and Hurston, "The Gilded Six-Bits" (page 553).
c. O'Connor, "The Drunkard" (page 339) and Cheever, "The Swimmer" (page 514).
d. Wharton, "Roman Fever" (page 373) and Fitzgerald, "A New Leaf" (page 385).
e. Lahiri, "Interpreter of Maladies" (page 141) and Gautreaux, "Welding with Children" (page 198).
f. Porter, "The Jilting of Granny Weatherall" (page 269) and Oates, "June Birthing" (page 498).

2. Write an essay in which you argue for the literary quality of any one of the following stories, detailing its successful use of the elements of fiction:
   a. Lahiri, "Interpreter of Maladies" (page 141).
   b. Joyce, "Eveline" (page 408).
   c. Gordimer, "Once upon a Time" (page 231).
   d. Hawthorne, "Young Goodman Brown" (page 309).
   e. Melville, "Bartleby the Scrivener" (page 586).
   f. Oates, "Where Are You Going, Where Have You Been?" (page 469).
   g. Wharton, "Roman Fever" (page 373).

Three Featured Writers

James Joyce
Flannery O'Connor
Joyce Carol Oates

James Joyce
Araby

North Richmond Street, being blind,° was a quiet street except at the hour when the Christian Brothers' School set the boys free. An uninhabited house of two storeys stood at the blind end, detached from its neighbours in a square ground. The other houses of the street, conscious of decent lives within them, gazed at one another with brown imperturbable faces.

The former tenant of our house, a priest, had died in the back drawing-room. Air, musty from having been long enclosed, hung in all the rooms, and the waste room behind the kitchen was littered with old useless papers. Among these I found a few paper-covered books, the pages of which were curled and damp: *The Abbot*, by Walter Scott, *The Devout Communicant* and *The Memoirs of Vidocq*.° I liked the last best because its leaves were yellow. The wild garden behind the house contained a central apple-tree and a few straggling bushes under one of which I found the late tenant's rusty bicycle-pump. He had been a very charitable priest; in his will he had left all his money to institutions and the furniture of his house to his sister.

When the short days of winter came dusk fell before we had well eaten our dinners. When we met in the street the houses had grown somber. The space of sky above us was the color of ever-changing violet and towards it the lamps of the street lifted their feeble lanterns. The cold air stung us and we played till our bodies glowed. Our shouts echoed in the silent street. The career of our play brought us through the dark muddy lanes behind the houses where we ran the gauntlet of the rough tribes from the cottages, to the back doors of the dark dripping gardens where odors arose from the ashpits, to the dark odorous stables where a coachman smoothed and combed the horse or shook music from the buckled harness. When we returned to the street, light from the kitchen windows had filled the areas. If my uncle was seen turning the corner we hid in the shadow until we had seen him safely housed. Or if Mangan's

ARABY   First published in 1914. James Joyce (1882–1941) was born and lived in Dublin, Ireland, until 1904 when he went to Paris, and for the rest of his life he lived abroad and wrote about Dublin. He attended Jesuit school and graduated from University College in Dublin. The short stories collected in his first book, *Dubliners*, are among the most celebrated and influential of the genre in the modern era.

blind: a dead-end street   **The Abbot:** an 1820 novel by Sir Walter Scott (1771–1834); **The Devout Communicant:** a Roman Catholic tract published in 1813; **The Memoirs of Vidocq:** memoirs by a French detective, Francois Vidocq (1775–1857) sister came out on the doorstep to call her brother in to his tea we watched her from our shadow peer up and down the street. We waited to see whether she would remain or go in and, if she remained, we left our shadow and walked up to Mangan's steps resignedly. She was waiting for us, her figure defined by the light from the half-opened door. Her brother always teased her before he obeyed and I stood by the railings looking at her. Her dress swung as she moved her body and the soft rope of her hair tossed from side to side.

Every morning I lay on the floor in the front parlor watching her door. The blind was pulled down to within an inch of the sash so that I could not be seen. When she came out on the doorstep my heart leaped. I ran to the hall, seized my books and followed her. I kept her brown figure always in my eye and, when we came near the point at which our ways diverged, I quickened my pace and passed her. This happened morning after morning. I had never spoken to her, except for a few casual words, and yet her name was like a summons to all my foolish blood.

5   Her image accompanied me even in places the most hostile to romance. On Saturday evenings when my aunt went marketing I had to go to carry some of the parcels. We walked through the flaring streets, jostled by drunken men and bargaining women, amid the curses of laborers, the shrill litanies of shop-boys who stood on guard by the barrels of pigs' cheeks, the nasal chanting of street-singers, who sang a come-all-you° about O'Donovan Rossa,° or a ballad about the troubles in our native land. These noises converged in a single sensation of life for me: I imagined that I bore my chalice safely through a throng of foes. Her name sprang to my lips at moments in strange prayers and praises which I myself did not understand. My eyes were often full of tears (I could not tell why) and at times a flood from my heart seemed to pour itself out into my bosom. I thought little of the future. I did not know whether I would ever speak to her or not or, if I spoke to her, how I could tell her of my confused adoration. But my body was like a harp and her words and gestures were like fingers running upon the wires.

One evening I went into the back drawing-room in which the priest had died. It was a dark rainy evening and there was no sound in the house. Through one of the broken panes I heard the rain impinge upon the earth, the fine incessant needles of water playing in the sodden beds. Some distant lamp or lighted window gleamed below me. I was thankful that I could see so little. All my senses seemed to desire to veil themselves and,

come-all-you: an Irish patriotic song   O'Donovan Rossa: Jeremiah O'Donovan (1831–1915), an Irish nationalist feeling that I was about to slip from them, I pressed the palms of my hands together until they trembled, murmuring: O *love!* O *love!* many times.

At last she spoke to me. When she addressed the first words to me I was so confused that I did not know what to answer. She asked me was I going to *Araby.* I forget whether I answered yes or no. It would be a splendid bazaar, she said; she would love to go.

"And why can't you?" I asked.

While she spoke she turned a silver bracelet round and round her wrist. She could not go, she said, because there would be a retreat that week in her convent. Her brother and two other boys were fighting for their caps and I was alone at the railings. She held one of the spikes, bowing her head towards me. The light from the lamp opposite our door caught the white curve of her neck, lit up her hair that rested there and, falling, lit up the hand upon the railing. It fell over one side of her dress and caught the white border of a petticoat, just visible as she stood at ease.

"It's well for you," she said.   10

"If I go," I said, "I will bring you something."

What innumerable follies laid waste my waking and sleeping thoughts after that evening! I wished to annihilate the tedious intervening days. I chafed against the work of school. At night in my bedroom and by day in the classroom her image came between me and the page I strove to read. The syllables of the word *Araby* were called to me through the silence in which my soul luxuriated and cast an Eastern enchantment over me. I asked for leave to go to the bazaar Saturday night. My aunt was surprised and hoped it was not some Freemason° affair. I answered few questions in class. I watched my master's face pass from amiability to sternness; he hoped I was not beginning to idle. I could not call my wandering thoughts together. I had hardly any patience with the serious work of life which, now that it stood between me and my desire, seemed to me child's play, ugly monotonous child's play.

On Saturday morning I reminded my uncle that I wished to go to the bazaar in the evening. He was fussing at the hallstand, looking for the hat-brush, and answered me curtly:

"Yes, boy, I know."

As he was in the hall I could not go into the front parlor and lie   15
at the window. I left the house in bad humor and walked slowly towards the school. The air was pitilessly raw and already my heart misgave me.

When I came home to dinner my uncle had not yet been home. Still it was early. I sat staring at the clock for some time and, when its ticking began to irritate me, I left the room. I mounted the staircase and

Freemason: member of a highly secretive fraternal organization gained the upper part of the house. The high cold empty gloomy rooms liberated me and I went from room to room singing. From the front window I saw my companions playing below in the street. Their cries reached me weakened and indistinct and, leaning my forehead against the cool glass, I looked over at the dark house where she lived. I may have stood there for an hour, seeing nothing but the brown-clad figure cast by my imagination, touched discreetly by the lamplight at the curved neck, at the hand upon the railings and at the border below the dress.

When I came downstairs again I found Mrs. Mercer sitting at the fire. She was an old garrulous woman, a pawnbroker's widow, who collected used stamps for some pious purpose. I had to endure the gossip of the tea-table. The meal was prolonged beyond an hour and still my uncle did not come. Mrs. Mercer stood up to go: she was sorry she couldn't wait any longer, but it was after eight o'clock and she did not like to be out late, as the night air was bad for her. When she had gone I began to walk up and down the room, clenching my fists. My aunt said:

"I'm afraid you may put off your bazaar for this night of Our Lord."

At nine o'clock I heard my uncle's latchkey in the halldoor. I heard him talking to himself and heard the hallstand rocking when it had received the weight of his overcoat. I could interpret these signs. When he was midway through his dinner I asked him to give me the money to go to the bazaar. He had forgotten.

20   "The people are in bed and after their first sleep now," he said.

I did not smile. My aunt said to him energetically:

"Can't you give him the money and let him go? You've kept him late enough as it is."

My uncle said he was very sorry he had forgotten. He said he believed in the old saying: *All work and no play makes Jack a dull boy.* He asked me where I was going and, when I had told him a second time he asked me did I know *The Arab's Farewell to his Steed.*° When I left the kitchen he was about to recite the opening lines of the piece to my aunt.

I held a florin° tightly in my hand as I strode down Buckingham Street towards the station. The sight of the streets thronged with buyers and glaring with gas recalled to me the purpose of my journey. I took my seat in a third-class carriage of a deserted train. After an intolerable delay the train moved out of the station slowly. It crept onward among ruinous houses and over the twinkling river. At

The Arab's Farewell to His Steed: a popular nineteenth-century song   **florin:** a coin worth two shillings

Westland Row Station a crowd of people pressed to the carriage doors; but the porters moved them back, saying that it was a special train for the bazaar. I remained alone in the bare carriage. In a few minutes the train drew up beside an improvised wooden platform. I passed out on to the road and saw by the lighted dial of a clock that it was ten minutes to ten. In front of me was a large building which displayed the magical name.

I could not find any sixpenny entrance and, fearing that the bazaar   25 would be closed, I passed in quickly through a turnstile, handing a shilling to a weary-looking man. I found myself in a big hall girdled at half its height by a gallery. Nearly all the stalls were closed and the greater part of the hall was in darkness. I recognized a silence like that which pervades a church after a service. I walked into the center of the bazaar timidly. A few people were gathered about the stalls which were still open. Before a curtain, over which the words *Café Chantant*° were written in colored lamps, two men were counting money on a salver. I listened to the fall of the coins.

Remembering with difficulty why I had come I went over to one of the stalls and examined porcelain vases and flowered tea-sets. At the door of the stall a young lady was talking and laughing with two young gentlemen. I remarked their English accents and listened vaguely to their conversation.

"O, I never said such a thing!"

"O, but you did!"

"O, but I didn't!"

"Didn't she say that?"   30

"Yes, I heard her."

"O, there's a . . . fib!"

Observing me the young lady came over and asked me did I wish to buy anything. The tone of her voice was not encouraging; she seemed to have spoken to me out of a sense of duty. I looked humbly at the great jars that stood like eastern guards at either side of the dark entrance to the stall and murmured:

"No, thank you."

The young lady changed the position of one of the vases and went   35 back to the two young men. They began to talk of the same subject. Once or twice the young lady glanced at me over her shoulder.

I lingered before her stall, though I knew my stay was useless, to make my interest in her wares seem the more real. Then I turned away slowly and walked down the middle of the bazaar. I allowed the two

Café Chantant: a café with music

pennies to fall against the sixpence in my pocket. I heard a voice call from one end of the gallery that the light was out. The upper part of the hall was now completely dark.

Gazing up into the darkness I saw myself as a creature driven and derided by vanity; and my eyes burned with anguish and anger.

QUESTIONS

1. Discuss the setting and the way it is described in the opening paragraphs. How is the setting related to the boy's state of mind?
2. How is the boy characterized? Roughly how old is he and how would you describe his temperament and personality?
3. Analyze the role of Mangan's sister. Why is she not given a name? How does her physical description relate to the boy's state of mind?
4. Describe the role of the boy's uncle. Can he be called the antagonist? When the uncle returns home, he is talking to himself and moving awkwardly. What are these "signs" the boy says he is able to interpret?
5. How is the bazaar described? How is it different from the reader's and the boy's expectations?
6. At the bazaar, there is an inconsequential conversation between the young salesgirl and two Englishmen. Why is this dialogue important? How does the boy react to it?
7. Why does the boy decide not to buy anything for Mangan's sister? Where in the text would you locate the moment of "epiphany"?
8. Analyze the boy's feelings as described in the story's last paragraph. Are his feelings justified? How will he be changed as a result of his experience at the bazaar?

James Joyce

Eveline

She sat at the window watching evening invade the avenue. Her head was leaned against the window curtains and in her nostrils was the odor of dusty cretonne. She was tired.

Few people passed. The man out of the last house passed on his way home; she heard his footsteps clacking along the concrete pavement and afterwards crunching on the cinder path before the new red houses. One

EVELINE   First published in 1904. Eveline's weekly wages working as a sales clerk in "the Stores" are the equivalent of less than ten dollars. The "night boat" that she and Frank are planning to take departed from a dock called "the North Wall" for Liverpool, England; presumably Frank has planned to take a ship from there to Argentina with her.

time there used to be a field there in which they used to play every evening with other people's children. Then a man from Belfast bought the field and built houses in it—not like their little brown houses but bright brick houses with shining roofs. The children of the avenue used to play together in that field—the Devines, the Waters, the Dunns, little Keogh the cripple, she and her brothers and sisters. Ernest, however, never played: he was too grown up. Her father used often to hunt them in out of the field with his blackthorn stick; but usually little Keogh used to keep *nix* and call out when he saw her father coming. Still they seemed to have been rather happy then. Her father was not so bad then; and besides, her mother was alive. That was a long time ago; she and her brothers and sisters were all grown up; her mother was dead. Tizzie Dunn was dead, too, and the Waters had gone back to England. Everything changes. Now she was going to go away like the others, to leave her home.

Home! She looked round the room, reviewing all its familiar objects which she had dusted once a week for so many years, wondering where on earth all the dust came from. Perhaps she would never see again those familiar objects from which she had never dreamed of being divided. And yet during all those years she had never found out the name of the priest whose yellowing photograph hung on the wall above the broken harmonium beside the colored print of the promises made to Blessed Margaret Mary Alacoque.° He had been a school friend of her father. Whenever he showed the photograph to a visitor her father used to pass it with a casual word:

"He is in Melbourne now."

She had consented to go away, to leave her home. Was that wise? 5 She tried to weigh each side of the question. In her home anyway she had shelter and food; she had those whom she had known all her life about her. Of course she had to work hard both in the house and at business. What would they say of her in the Stores when they found out that she had run away with a fellow? Say she was a fool, perhaps; and her place would be filled up by advertisement. Miss Gavan would be glad. She had always had an edge on her, especially whenever there were people listening.

"Miss Hill, don't you see these ladies are waiting?"

"Look lively, Miss Hill, please."

She would not cry many tears at leaving the Stores.

Blessed Margaret Mary Alacoque: now a saint in the Roman Catholic church (canonized in 1920), Margaret Mary Alacoque (1647–1690) reported visions of Christ and suffered much illness during her brief life

But in her new home, in a distant unknown country, it would not be like that. Then she would be married—she, Eveline. People would treat her with respect then. She would not be treated as her mother had been. Even now, though she was over nineteen, she sometimes felt herself in danger of her father's violence. She knew it was that that had given her the palpitations. When they were growing up he had never gone for her, like he used to go for Harry and Ernest, because she was a girl; but latterly he had begun to threaten her and say what he would do to her only for° her dead mother's sake. And now she had nobody to protect her. Ernest was dead and Harry, who was in the church decorating business, was nearly always down somewhere in the country. Besides, the invariable squabble for money on Saturday nights had begun to weary her unspeakably. She always gave her entire wages—seven shillings—and Harry always sent up what he could but the trouble was to get any money from her father. He said she used to squander the money, that she had no head, that he wasn't going to give her his hard-earned money to throw about the streets, and much more, for he was usually fairly bad of a Saturday night. In the end he would give her the money and ask her had she any intention of buying Sunday's dinner. Then she had to rush out as quickly as she could and do her marketing, holding her black leather purse tightly in her hand as she elbowed her way through the crowds and returning home late under her load of provisions. She had hard work to keep the house together and to see that the two young children who had been left to her charge went to school regularly and got their meals regularly. It was hard work—a hard life—but now that she was about to leave it she did not find it a wholly undesirable life.

10   She was about to explore another life with Frank. Frank was very kind, manly, open-hearted. She was to go away with him by the night-boat to be his wife and to live with him in Buenos Aires where he had a home waiting for her. How well she remembered the first time she had seen him; he was lodging in a house on the main road where she used to visit. It seemed a few weeks ago. He was standing at the gate, his peaked cap pushed back on his head and his hair tumbled forward over a face of bronze. Then they had come to know each other. He used to meet her outside the Stores every evening and see her home. He took her to see *The Bohemian Girl*° and she felt elated as she sat in an unaccustomed part of the theater with him. He was awfully fond of music and sang a little. People knew that they were courting and, when he sang about the lass

only for: except for   ***The Bohemian Girl:*** an opera by the Irish composer Michael William Balfe, first produced in 1843 that loves a sailor, she always felt pleasantly confused. He used to call her Poppens out of fun. First of all it had been an excitement for her to have a fellow and then she had begun to like him. He had tales of distant countries. He had started as a deck boy at a pound a month on a ship of the Allan Line going out to Canada. He told her the names of the ships he had been on and the names of the different services. He had sailed through the Straits of Magellan and he told her stories of the terrible Patagonians. He had fallen on his feet in Buenos Aires, he said, and had come over to the old country just for a holiday. Of course, her father had found out the affair and had forbidden her to have anything to say to him.

"I know these sailor chaps," he said.

One day he had quarrelled with Frank and after that she had to meet her lover secretly.

The evening deepened in the avenue. The white of two letters in her lap grew indistinct. One was to Harry; the other was to her father. Ernest had been her favorite but she liked Harry too. Her father was becoming old lately, she noticed; he would miss her. Sometimes he could be very nice. Not long before, when she had been laid up for a day, he had read her out a ghost story and made toast for her at the fire. Another day, when their mother was alive, they had all gone for a picnic to the Hill of Howth.° She remembered her father putting on her mother's bonnet to make the children laugh.

Her time was running out but she continued to sit by the window, leaning her head against the window curtain, inhaling the odor of dusty cretonne. Down far in the avenue she could hear a street organ playing. She knew the air. Strange that it should come that very night to remind her of the promise to her mother, her promise to keep the home together as long as she could. She remembered the last night of her mother's illness; she was again in the close dark room at the other side of the hall and outside she heard a melancholy air of Italy. The organ-player had been ordered to go away and given sixpence. She remembered her father strutting back into the sickroom saying:

"Damned Italians! coming over here!"   15

As she mused the pitiful vision of her mother's life laid its spell on the very quick of her being—that life of commonplace sacrifices closing in final craziness. She trembled as she heard again her mother's voice saying constantly with foolish insistence:

"Derevaun Seraun! Derevaun Seraun!"°

The Hill of Howth: located nine miles northeast of Dublin, this hill overlooks Dublin Bay   **Derevaun Seraun!:** interpreted as a slurred Gaelic phrase meaning either "the end of pleasure is pain" or "the end of song is raving madness"

She stood up in a sudden impulse of terror. Escape! She must escape! Frank would save her. He would give her life, perhaps love, too. But she wanted to live. Why should she be unhappy? She had a right to happiness. Frank would take her in his arms, fold her in his arms. He would save her.

She stood among the swaying crowd in the station at the North Wall. He held her hand and she knew that he was speaking to her, saying something about the passage over and over again. The station was full of soldiers with brown baggages. Through the wide doors of the sheds she caught a glimpse of the black mass of the boat, lying in beside the quay wall, with illumined portholes. She answered nothing. She felt her cheek pale and cold and, out of a maze of distress, she prayed to God to direct her, to show her what was her duty. The boat blew a long mournful whistle into the mist. If she went, tomorrow she would be on the sea with Frank, steaming towards Buenos Aires. Their passage had been booked. Could she still draw back after all he had done for her? Her distress awoke a nausea in her body and she kept moving her lips in silent fervent prayer.

20   A bell clanged upon her heart. She felt him seize her hand:
"Come!"

All the seas of the world tumbled about her heart. He was drawing her into them: he would drown her. She gripped with both hands at the iron railing.

"Come!"

No! No! No! It was impossible. Her hands clutched the iron in frenzy. Amid the seas she sent a cry of anguish!

25   "Eveline! Evvy!"

He rushed beyond the barrier and called to her to follow. He was shouted at to go on but he still called to her. She set her white face to him, passive, like a helpless animal. Her eyes gave him no sign of love or farewell or recognition.

QUESTIONS

1. Analyze the first brief paragraph in detail. How does it help to introduce the story's theme? Why does the narrator use the unexpected word "invade" in the first sentence? Why is the second sentence written in passive voice?

2. What in Eveline's present circumstances makes it desirable for her to escape her home? Characterize her father and Miss Gavan, her supervisor. What does the memory of her mother contribute to her decision to leave?

3. At just about the middle of the story (end of paragraph 9), Eveline sums up her life in Dublin: "It was hard work—a hard life—but now that she was about to leave it she did not find it a wholly undesirable life." What about it makes it attractive to her?

4. What kind of man is Frank? Why does Eveline's father forbid her to see him? Is there any evidence to support her father's suspicion about Frank?

5. Look closely at the descriptions of Eveline's life in Dublin and contrast them with Frank's destination in Buenos Aires. How do these two settings aid our understanding of Eveline's situation and her ultimate fate?

6. To what extent is Eveline's refusal to board the ship based on her judgment and will? Has she *decided* not to go?

7. Is Eveline a sympathetic or unsympathetic character? Is she a victim of her character or of circumstances beyond her control? How do these issues contribute to the major theme?

8. Joyce said that this and other stories he wrote about Dublin dealt with the "spiritual paralysis" of its citizens. What evidence in this story supports that idea as a major theme?

James Joyce

The Boarding House

Mrs. Mooney was a butcher's daughter. She was a woman who was quite able to keep things to herself: a determined woman. She had married her father's foreman and opened a butcher's shop near Spring Gardens. But as soon as his father-in-law was dead Mr. Mooney began to go to the devil. He drank, plundered the till, ran headlong into debt. It was no use making him take the pledge: he was sure to break out again a few days after. By fighting his wife in the presence of customers and by buying bad meat he ruined his business. One night he went for his wife with the cleaver and she had to sleep in a neighbor's house.

After that they lived apart. She went to the priest and got a separation from him with care of the children. She would give him neither money nor food nor house-room; and so he was obliged to enlist himself as a sheriff's man. He was a shabby stooped little drunkard with a white face and a white moustache and white eyebrows, penciled above his little eyes, which were pink-veined and raw; and all day long he sat in the bailiff's room, waiting to be put on a job. Mrs. Mooney, who had taken what remained of her money out of the butcher business and set up a boarding house in Hardwicke Street, was a big imposing woman. Her house had a floating population made up of tourists from Liverpool

THE BOARDING HOUSE   First published in 1914. Hardwicke Street, where Mrs. Mooney's boarding house is located, is in the vicinity of Mountjoy Square, a formerly fashionable district that had grown shabby. "George's Church" is the Protestant church of St. George, and when Mrs. Mooney thinks of "catching short twelve at Marlborough Street," she is planning to attend the abbreviated noon mass at the chief Catholic church in Dublin, the Metropolitan Pro-Cathedral.

and the Isle of Man and, occasionally, *artistes* from the music halls. Its resident population was made up of clerks from the city. She governed her house cunningly and firmly, knew when to give credit, when to be stern and when to let things pass. All the resident young men spoke of her as *The Madam*.

Mrs. Mooney's young men paid fifteen shillings a week for board and lodgings (beer or stout at dinner excluded). They shared in common tastes and occupations and for this reason they were very chummy with one another. They discussed with one another the chances of favorites and outsiders. Jack Mooney, the Madam's son, who was clerk to a commission agent in Fleet Street, had the reputation of being a hard case. He was fond of using soldiers' obscenities: usually he came home in the small hours. When he met his friends he had always a good one to tell them as he was always sure to be on to a good thing—that is to say, a likely horse or a likely *artiste*. He was also handy with the mitts and sang comic songs. On Sunday nights there would often be a reunion in Mrs. Mooney's front drawing-room. The music-hall *artistes* would oblige; and Sheridan played waltzes and polkas and vamped accompaniments. Polly Mooney, the Madam's daughter, would also sing. She sang:

> I'm a . . . naughty girl.
> You needn't sham:
> You know I am.

Polly was a slim girl of nineteen, she had light soft hair and a small full mouth. Her eyes, which were grey with a shade of green through them, had a habit of glancing upwards when she spoke with anyone, which made her look like a little perverse madonna. Mrs. Mooney had first sent her daughter to be a typist in a corn-factor's office but, as a disreputable sheriff's man used to come every other day to the office, asking to be allowed to say a word to his daughter, she had taken her daughter home again and set her to do housework. As Polly was very lively the intention was to give her the run of the young men. Besides, young men like to feel that there is a young woman not very far away. Polly, of course, flirted with the young men but Mrs. Mooney, who was a shrewd judge, knew that the young men were only passing the time away: none of them meant business. Things went on so for a long time and Mrs. Mooney began to think of sending Polly back to typewriting when she noticed that something was going on between Polly and one of the young men. She watched the pair and kept her own counsel.

5   Polly knew that she was being watched, but still her mother's persistent silence could not be misunderstood. There had been no open complicity between mother and daughter, no open understanding

but, though people in the house began to talk of the affair, still Mrs. Mooney did not intervene. Polly began to grow a little strange in her manner and the young man was evidently perturbed. At last, when she judged it to be the right moment, Mrs. Mooney intervened. She dealt with moral problems as a cleaver deals with meat: and in this case she had made up her mind.

It was a bright Sunday morning of early summer, promising heat, but with a fresh breeze blowing. All the windows of the boarding house were open and the lace curtains ballooned gently towards the street beneath the raised sashes. The belfry of George's Church sent out constant peals and worshippers, singly or in groups, traversed the little circus before the church, revealing their purpose by their self-contained demeanor no less than by the little volumes in their gloved hands. Breakfast was over in the boarding house and the table of the breakfast-room was covered with plates on which lay yellow streaks of eggs with morsels of bacon-fat and bacon-rind. Mrs. Mooney sat in the straw armchair and watched the servant Mary remove the breakfast things. She made Mary collect the crusts and pieces of broken bread to help to make Tuesday's bread-pudding. When the table was cleared, the broken bread collected, the sugar and butter safe under lock and key, she began to reconstruct the interview which she had had the night before with Polly. Things were as she had suspected: she had been frank in her questions and Polly had been frank in her answers. Both had been somewhat awkward, of course. She had been made awkward by her not wishing to receive the news in too cavalier a fashion or to seem to have connived and Polly had been made awkward not merely because allusions of that kind always made her awkward but also because she did not wish it to be thought that in her wise innocence she had divined the intention behind her mother's tolerance.

Mrs. Mooney glanced instinctively at the little gilt clock on the mantelpiece as soon as she had become aware through her revery that the bells of George's Church had stopped ringing. It was seventeen minutes past eleven: she would have lots of time to have the matter out with Mr. Doran and then catch short twelve at Marlborough Street. She was sure she would win. To begin with she had all the weight of social opinion on her side: she was an outraged mother. She had allowed him to live beneath her roof, assuming that he was a man of honor, and he had simply abused her hospitality. He was thirty-four or thirty-five years of age, so that youth could not be pleaded as his excuse; nor could ignorance be his excuse since he was a man who had seen something of the world. He had simply taken advantage of Polly's youth and inexperience: that was evident. The question was: What reparation would he make?

There must be reparation made in such cases. It is all very well for the man: he can go his ways as if nothing had happened, having had his moment of pleasure, but the girl has to bear the brunt. Some mothers would be content to patch up such an affair for a sum of money; she had known cases of it. But she would not do so. For her only one reparation could make up for the loss of her daughter's honor: marriage.

She counted all her cards again before sending Mary up to Mr. Doran's room to say that she wished to speak with him. She felt sure she would win. He was a serious young man, not rakish or loud-voiced like the others. If it had been Mr. Sheridan or Mr. Meade or Bantam Lyons her task would have been much harder. She did not think he would face publicity. All the lodgers in the house knew something of the affair; details had been invented by some. Besides, he had been employed for thirteen years in a great Catholic wine-merchant's office and publicity would mean for him, perhaps, the loss of his sit.° Whereas if he agreed all might be well. She knew he had a good screw° for one thing and she suspected he had a bit of stuff put by.

10   Nearly the half-hour! She stood up and surveyed herself in the pier-glass. The decisive expression of her great florid face satisfied her and she thought of some mothers she knew who could not get their daughters off their hands.

Mr. Doran was very anxious indeed this Sunday morning. He had made two attempts to shave but his hand had been so unsteady that he had been obliged to desist. Three days' reddish beard fringed his jaws and every two or three minutes a mist gathered on his glasses so that he had to take them off and polish them with his pocket-handkerchief. The recollection of his confession of the night before was a cause of acute pain to him; the priest had drawn out every ridiculous detail of the affair and in the end had so magnified his sin that he was almost thankful at being afforded a loophole of reparation. The harm was done. What could he do now but marry her or run away? He could not brazen it out. The affair would be sure to be talked of and his employer would be certain to hear of it. Dublin is such a small city: everyone knows everyone else's business. He felt his heart leap warmly in his throat as he heard in his excited imagination old Mr. Leonard calling out in his rasping voice: *Send Mr. Doran here, please.*

All his long years of service gone for nothing! All his industry and diligence thrown away! As a young man he had sown his wild oats, of course; he had boasted of his free-thinking and denied the existence of God to his companions in public-houses. But that was all passed and

sit: slang for "situation," job   screw: slang for salary or wages done with . . . nearly. He still bought a copy of *Reynolds's Newspaper* every week but he attended to his religious duties and for nine-tenths of the year lived a regular life. He had money enough to settle down on; it was not that. But the family would look down on her. First of all there was her disreputable father and then her mother's boarding house was beginning to get a certain fame. He had a notion that he was being had. He could imagine his friends talking of the affair and laughing. She *was* a little vulgar; sometimes she said *I seen* and *If I had've known.* But what would grammar matter if he really loved her? He could not make up his mind whether to like her or despise her for what she had done. Of course, he had done it too. His instinct urged him to remain free, not to marry. Once you are married you are done for, it said.

While he was sitting helplessly on the side of the bed in shirt and trousers she tapped lightly at his door and entered. She told him all, that she had made a clean breast of it to her mother and that her mother would speak with him that morning. She cried and threw her arms round his neck, saying:

"O, Bob! Bob! What am I to do? What am I to do at all?"

She would put an end to herself, she said.   15

He comforted her feebly, telling her not to cry, that it would be all right, never fear. He felt against his shirt the agitation of her bosom.

It was not altogether his fault that it had happened. He remembered well, with the curious patient memory of the celibate, the first casual caresses her dress, her breath, her fingers had given him. Then late one night as he was undressing for bed she had tapped at his door, timidly. She wanted to relight her candle at his for hers had been blown out by a gust. It was her bath night. She wore a loose open combing-jacket of printed flannel. Her white instep shone in the opening of her furry slippers and the blood glowed warmly behind her perfumed skin. From her hands and wrists too as she lit and steadied her candle a faint perfume arose.

On nights when he came in very late it was she who warmed up his dinner. He scarcely knew what he was eating, feeling her beside him alone, at night, in the sleeping house. And her thoughtfulness! If the night was anyway cold or wet or windy there was sure to be a little tumbler of punch ready for him. Perhaps they could be happy together. . . .

They used to go upstairs together on tiptoe, each with a candle, and on the third landing exchange reluctant good-nights. They used to kiss. He remembered well her eyes, the touch of her hand and his delirium. . . .

But delirium passes. He echoed her phrase, applying it to himself: 20
What am I to do? The instinct of the celibate warned him to hold back. But the sin was there; even his sense of honor told him that reparation must be made for such a sin.

While he was sitting with her on the side of the bed Mary came to the door and said that the missus wanted to see him in the parlor. He stood up to put on his coat and waistcoat, more helpless than ever. When he was dressed he went over to her to comfort her. It would be all right, never fear. He left her crying on the bed and moaning softly: O my God!

Going down the stairs his glasses became so dimmed with moisture that he had to take them off and polish them. He longed to ascend through the roof and fly away to another country where he would never hear again of his trouble, and yet a force pushed him downstairs step by step. The implacable faces of his employer and of the Madam stared upon his discomfiture. On the last flight of stairs he passed Jack Mooney who was coming up from the pantry nursing two bottles of *Bass*. They saluted coldly; and the lover's eyes rested for a second or two on a thick bulldog face and a pair of thick short arms. When he reached the foot of the staircase he glanced up and saw Jack regarding him from the door of the return-room.

Suddenly he remembered the night when one of the music-hall *artistes*, a little blond Londoner, had made a rather free allusion to Polly. The reunion had been almost broken up on account of Jack's violence. Everyone tried to quiet him. The music-hall *artiste*, a little paler than usual, kept smiling and saying that there was no harm meant: but Jack kept shouting at him that if any fellow tried that sort of a game on with *his* sister he'd bloody well put his teeth down his throat, so he would.

Polly sat for a little time on the side of the bed, crying. Then she dried her eyes and went over to the looking-glass. She dipped the end of the towel in the water-jug and refreshed her eyes with the cool water. She looked at herself in profile and readjusted a hairpin above her ear. Then she went back to the bed again and sat at the foot. She regarded the pillows for a long time and the sight of them awakened in her mind secret amiable memories. She rested the nape of her neck against the cool iron bed-rail and fell into a revery. There was no longer any perturbation visible on her face.

25   She waited on patiently, almost cheerfully, without alarm, her memories gradually giving place to hopes and visions of the future. Her hopes and visions were so intricate that she no longer saw the white pillows on which her gaze was fixed or remembered that she was waiting for anything.

At last she heard her mother calling. She started to her feet and ran to the banisters.

"Polly! Polly!"

"Yes, mamma?"

"Come down, dear. Mr. Doran wants to speak to you." Then she remembered what she had been waiting for.

QUESTIONS

1. Characterize Mrs. Mooney. What clues to her character are provided by the account of her first marriage? What kind of landlady does she prove to be? What are the connotations attached to her identity as a "butcher's daughter"? Why do her boarders refer to her as "the Madam"? What are her motivations in actions concerning her daughter?
2. Consider the role of Mrs. Mooney's son. Why is he included in the story?
3. What kind of young woman is Polly? In what ways is she like or unlike her mother? To what extent does she collaborate with her mother?
4. Characterize Mr. Doran. To what extent has he "taken advantage" of Polly? What qualities in himself and in his situation make him peculiarly vulnerable? Did you find him to be a sympathetic character?
5. What is the function of dramatic irony in this story? Point out examples, and discuss.

Flannery O'Connor

A Good Man Is Hard to Find

The grandmother didn't want to go to Florida. She wanted to visit some of her connections in east Tennessee and she was seizing at every chance to change Bailey's mind. Bailey was the son she lived with, her only boy. He was sitting on the edge of his chair at the table, bent over the orange sports section of the *Journal*. "Now look here, Bailey," she said, "see here, read this," and she stood with one hand on her thin hip and the other rattling the newspaper at his bald head. "Here this fellow that calls himself The Misfit is aloose from the Federal Pen and headed toward Florida and you read here what it says he did to these people. Just you read it. I wouldn't take my children in any direction with a criminal like that aloose in it. I couldn't answer to my conscience if I did."

Bailey didn't look up from his reading so she wheeled around then and faced the children's mother, a young woman in slacks, whose face was as broad and innocent as a cabbage and was tied around with a green head-kerchief that had two points on the top like a rabbit's ears. She was sitting on the sofa, feeding the baby his apricots out of a jar. "The children have been to Florida before," the old lady said. "You all ought to take them somewhere else for a change so they would see different parts of the world and be broad. They never have been to east Tennessee."

The children's mother didn't seem to hear her but the eight-year-old boy, John Wesley, a stocky child with glasses, said, "If you don't want to go to Florida, why dontcha stay at home?" He and the little girl, June Star, were reading the funny papers on the floor.

"She wouldn't stay at home to be queen for a day," June Star said without raising her yellow head.

5   "Yes and what would you do if this fellow, The Misfit, caught you?" the grandmother asked.

"I'd smack his face," John Wesley said.

"She wouldn't stay at home for a million bucks," June Star said. "Afraid she'd miss something. She has to go everywhere we go."

A GOOD MAN IS HARD TO FIND   First published in 1953. Flannery O'Connor (1925–1964) spent most of her writing life in Milledgeville, Georgia. Though a devout Roman Catholic, she wrote about the denizens of the rural South, most of whom were fundamentalist Protestants. O'Connor's people are often prideful, hardheaded southerners whose confrontation with violence and death forces them to test their capacity for grace. O'Connor insisted that her Christian vision of human life and destiny informed all her writing.

"All right, Miss," the grandmother said. "Just remember that the next time you want me to curl your hair."

June Star said her hair was naturally curly.

The next morning the grandmother was the first one in the car, ready to go. She had her big black valise that looked like the head of a hippopotamus in one corner, and underneath it she was hiding a basket with Pitty Sing, the cat, in it. She didn't intend for the cat to be left alone in the house for three days because he would miss her too much and she was afraid he might brush against one of the gas burners and accidentally asphyxiate himself. Her son, Bailey, didn't like to arrive at a motel with a cat.

She sat in the middle of the back seat with John Wesley and June Star on either side of her. Bailey and the children's mother and the baby sat in front and they left Atlanta at eight forty-five with the mileage on the car at 55890. The grandmother wrote this down because she thought it would be interesting to say how many miles they had been when they got back. It took them twenty minutes to reach the outskirts of the city.

The old lady settled herself comfortably, removing her white cotton gloves and putting them up with her purse on the shelf in front of the back window. The children's mother still had on slacks and still had her head tied up in a green kerchief, but the grandmother had on a navy blue straw sailor hat with a bunch of white violets on the brim and a navy blue dress with a small white dot in the print. Her collars and cuffs were white organdy trimmed with lace and at her neckline she had pinned a purple spray of cloth violets containing a sachet. In case of an accident, anyone seeing her dead on the highway would know at once that she was a lady.

She said she thought it was going to be a good day for driving, neither too hot nor too cold, and she cautioned Bailey that the speed limit was fifty-five miles an hour and that the patrolmen hid themselves behind billboards and small clumps of trees and sped out after you before you had a chance to slow down. She pointed out interesting details of the scenery: Stone Mountain; the blue granite that in some places came up to both sides of the highway; the brilliant red clay banks slightly streaked with purple; and the various crops that made rows of green lace-work on the ground. The trees were full of silver-white sunlight and the meanest of them sparkled. The children were reading comic magazines and their mother had gone back to sleep.

"Let's go through Georgia fast so we won't have to look at it much," John Wesley said.

10

15   "If I were a little boy," said the grandmother, "I wouldn't talk about my native state that way. Tennessee has the mountains and Georgia has the hills."

"Tennessee is just a hillbilly dumping ground," John Wesley said, "and Georgia is a lousy state too."

"You said it," June Star said.

"In my time," said the grandmother, folding her thin veined fingers, "children were more respectful of their native states and their parents and everything else. People did right then. Oh look at the cute little pickaninny!" she said and pointed to a Negro child standing in the door of a shack. "Wouldn't that make a picture, now?" she asked and they all turned and looked at the little Negro out of the back window. He waved.

"He didn't have any britches on," June Star said.

20   "He probably didn't have any," the grandmother explained. "Little niggers in the country don't have things like we do. If I could paint, I'd paint that picture," she said.

The children exchanged comic books.

The grandmother offered to hold the baby and the children's mother passed him over the front seat to her. She set him on her knee and bounced him and told him about the things they were passing. She rolled her eyes and screwed up her mouth and stuck her leathery thin face into his smooth bland one. Occasionally he gave her a faraway smile. They passed a large cotton field with five or six graves fenced in the middle of it, like a small island. "Look at the graveyard!" the grandmother said, pointing it out. "That was the old family burying ground. That belonged to the plantation."

"Where's the plantation?" John Wesley asked.

"Gone With the Wind," said the grandmother. "Ha. Ha."

25   When the children finished all the comic books they had brought, they opened the lunch and ate it. The grandmother ate a peanut butter sandwich and an olive and would not let the children throw the box and the paper napkins out the window. When there was nothing else to do they played a game by choosing a cloud and making the other two guess what shape it suggested. John Wesley took one the shape of a cow and June Star guessed a cow and John Wesley said, no, an automobile, and June Star said he didn't play fair, and they began to slap each other over the grandmother.

The grandmother said she would tell them a story if they would keep quiet. When she told a story, she rolled her eyes and waved her head and was very dramatic. She said once when she was a maiden lady she had been courted by a Mr. Edgar Atkins Teagarden from Jasper, Georgia.

She said he was a very good-looking man and a gentleman and that he brought her a watermelon every Saturday afternoon with his initials cut in it, E. A. T. Well, one Saturday, she said, Mr. Teagarden brought the watermelon and there was nobody at home and he left it on the front porch and returned in his buggy to Jasper, but she never got the watermelon, she said, because a nigger boy ate it when he saw the initials, E. A. T.! This story tickled John Wesley's funny bone and he giggled and giggled but June Star didn't think it was any good. She said she wouldn't marry a man that just brought her a watermelon on Saturday. The grandmother said she would have done well to marry Mr. Teagarden because he was a gentleman and had bought Coca-Cola stock when it first came out and that he had died only a few years ago, a very wealthy man.

They stopped at The Tower for barbecued sandwiches. The Tower was a part stucco and part wood filling station and dance hall set in a clearing outside of Timothy. A fat man named Red Sammy Butts ran it and there were signs stuck here and there on the building and for miles up and down the highway saying, TRY RED SAMMY'S FAMOUS BARBECUE. NONE LIKE FAMOUS RED SAMMY'S! RED SAM! THE FAT BOY WITH THE HAPPY LAUGH! A VETERAN! RED SAMMY'S YOUR MAN!

Red Sammy was lying on the bare ground outside The Tower with his head under a truck while a gray monkey about a foot high, chained to a small chinaberry tree, chattered nearby. The monkey sprang back into the tree and got on the highest limb as soon as he saw the children jump out of the car and run toward him.

Inside, The Tower was a long dark room with a counter at one end and tables at the other and dancing space in the middle. They all sat down at a board table next to the nickelodeon and Red Sam's wife, a tall burnt-brown woman with hair and eyes lighter than her skin, came and took their order. The children's mother put a dime in the machine and played "The Tennessee Waltz," and the grandmother said that tune always made her want to dance. She asked Bailey if he would like to dance but he only glared at her. He didn't have a naturally sunny disposition like she did and trips made him nervous. The grandmother's brown eyes were very bright. She swayed her head from side to side and pretended she was dancing in her chair. June Star said play something she could tap to so the children's mother put in another dime and played a fast number and June Star stepped out onto the dance floor and did her tap routine.

"Ain't she cute?" Red Sam's wife said, leaning over the counter. "Would you like to come be my little girl?"   30

"No I certainly wouldn't," June Star said. "I wouldn't live in a broken-down place like this for a million bucks!" and she ran back to the table.

"Ain't she cute?" the woman repeated, stretching her mouth politely.

"Aren't you ashamed?" hissed the grandmother.

Red Sam came in and told his wife to quit lounging on the counter and hurry up with these people's order. His khaki trousers reached just to his hip bones and his stomach hung over them like a sack of meal swaying under his shirt. He came over and sat down at a table nearby and let out a combination sigh and yodel. "You can't win," he said. "You can't win," and he wiped his sweating red face off with a gray handkerchief. "These days you don't know who to trust," he said. "Ain't that the truth?"

35   "People are certainly not nice like they used to be," said the grandmother.

"Two fellers come in here last week," Red Sammy said, "driving a Chrysler. It was a old beat-up car but it was a good one and these boys looked all right to me. Said they worked at the mill and you know I let them fellers charge the gas they bought? Now why did I do that?"

"Because you're a good man!" the grandmother said at once.

"Yes'm, I suppose so," Red Sam said as if he were struck with this answer.

His wife brought the orders, carrying the five plates all at once without a tray, two in each hand and one balanced on her arm. "It isn't a soul in this green world of God's that you can trust," she said. "And I don't count nobody out of that, not nobody," she repeated, looking at Red Sammy.

40   "Did you read about that criminal, The Misfit, that's escaped?" asked the grandmother.

"I wouldn't be a bit surprised if he didn't attact this place right here," said the woman. "If he hears about it being here, I wouldn't be none surprised to see him. If he hears it's two cent in the cash register, I wouldn't be a tall surprised if he . . ."

"That'll do," Red Sam said. "Go bring these people their Co'-Colas," and the woman went off to get the rest of the order.

"A good man is hard to find," Red Sammy said. "Everything is getting terrible. I remember the day you could go off and leave your screen door unlatched. Not no more."

He and the grandmother discussed better times. The old lady said that in her opinion Europe was entirely to blame for the way things were now. She said the way Europe acted you would think we were made of money and Red Sam said it was no use talking about it, she was exactly right. The children ran outside into the white sunlight and looked at the monkey in the lacy chinaberry tree. He was busy catching fleas on himself and biting each one carefully between his teeth as if it were a delicacy.

They drove off again into the hot afternoon. The grandmother took   45
cat naps and woke up every few minutes with her own snoring. Outside of Toombsboro she woke up and recalled an old plantation that she had visited in this neighborhood once when she was a young lady. She said the house had six white columns across the front and that there was an avenue of oaks leading up to it and two little wooden trellis arbors on either side in front where you sat down with your suitor after a stroll in the garden. She recalled exactly which road to turn off to get to it. She knew that Bailey would not be willing to lose any time looking at an old house, but the more she talked about it, the more she wanted to see it once again and find out if the little twin arbors were still standing. "There was a secret panel in this house," she said craftily, not telling the truth but wishing that she were, "and the story went that all the family silver was hidden in it when Sherman came through but it was never found . . ."

"Hey!" John Wesley said. "Let's go see it! We'll find it! We'll poke all the woodwork and find it! Who lives there? Where do you turn off at? Hey Pop, can't we turn off there?"

"We never have seen a house with a secret panel!" June Star shrieked. "Let's go to the house with the secret panel! Hey Pop, can't we go see the house with the secret panel!"

"It's not far from here, I know," the grandmother said. "It wouldn't take over twenty minutes."

Bailey was looking straight ahead. His jaw was as rigid as a horseshoe. "No," he said.

The children began to yell and scream that they wanted to see the   50
house with the secret panel. John Wesley kicked the back of the front seat and June Star hung over her mother's shoulder and whined desperately into her ear that they never had any fun even on their vacation, that they could never do what THEY wanted to do. The baby began to scream and John Wesley kicked the back of the seat so hard that his father could feel the blows in his kidney.

"All right!" he shouted and drew the car to a stop at the side of the road. "Will you all shut up? Will you all just shut up for one second? If you don't shut up, we won't go anywhere."

"It would be very educational for them," the grandmother murmured.

"All right," Bailey said, "but get this: this is the only time we're going to stop for anything like this. This is the one and only time."

"The dirt road that you have to turn down is about a mile back," the grandmother directed. "I marked it when we passed."

55   "A dirt road," Bailey groaned.

After they had turned around and were headed toward the dirt road, the grandmother recalled other points about the house, the beautiful glass over the front doorway and the candle-lamp in the hall. John Wesley said that the secret panel was probably in the fireplace.

"You can't go inside this house," Bailey said. "You don't know who lives there."

"While you all talk to the people in front, I'll run around behind and get in a window," John Wesley suggested.

"We'll all stay in the car," his mother said.

60   They turned onto the dirt road and the car raced roughly along in a swirl of pink dust. The grandmother recalled the times when there were no paved roads and thirty miles was a day's journey. The dirt road was hilly and there were sudden washes in it and sharp curves on dangerous embankments. All at once they would be on a hill, looking down over the blue tops of trees for miles around, then the next minute, they would be in a red depression with the dust-coated trees looking down on them.

"This place had better turn up in a minute," Bailey said, "or I'm going to turn around."

The road looked as if no one had traveled on it in months.

"It's not much farther," the grandmother said and just as she said it, a horrible thought came to her. The thought was so embarrassing that she turned red in the face and her eyes dilated and her feet jumped up, upsetting her valise in the corner. The instant the valise moved, the newspaper top she had over the basket under it rose with a snarl and Pitty Sing, the cat, sprang onto Bailey's shoulder.

The children were thrown to the floor and their mother, clutching the baby, was thrown out the door onto the ground; the old lady was thrown into the front seat. The car turned over once and landed right-side-up in a gulch off the side of the road. Bailey remained in the driver's seat with the cat—gray-striped with a broad white face and an orange nose—clinging to his neck like a caterpillar.

65   As soon as the children saw they could move their arms and legs, they scrambled out of the car, shouting, "We've had an ACCIDENT!" The grandmother was curled up under the dashboard, hoping she was injured so that Bailey's wrath would not come down on her all at once. The horrible thought she had had before the accident was that the house she had remembered so vividly was not in Georgia but in Tennessee.

Bailey removed the cat from his neck with both hands and flung it out the window against the side of a pine tree. Then he got out of the car and started looking for the children's mother. She was sitting against the side of the red gutted ditch, holding the screaming baby, but she only had a cut down her face and a broken shoulder. "We've had an ACCI-DENT!" the children screamed in a frenzy of delight.

"But nobody's killed," June Star said with disappointment as the grandmother limped out of the car, her hat still pinned to her head but the broken front brim standing up at a jaunty angle and the violet spray hanging off the side. They all sat down in the ditch, except the children, to recover from the shock. They were all shaking.

"Maybe a car will come along," said the children's mother hoarsely.

"I believe I have injured an organ," said the grandmother, pressing her side, but no one answered her. Bailey's teeth were clattering. He had on a yellow sport shirt with bright blue parrots designed in it and his face was as yellow as the shirt. The grandmother decided that she would not mention that the house was in Tennessee.

The road was about ten feet above and they could see only the tops   70
of the trees on the other side of it. Behind the ditch they were sitting in there were more woods, tall and dark and deep. In a few minutes they saw a car some distance away on top of a hill, coming slowly as if the occupants were watching them. The grandmother stood up and waved both arms dramatically to attract their attention. The car continued to come on slowly, disappeared around a bend and appeared again, moving even slower, on top of the hill they had gone over. It was a big black battered hearse-like automobile. There were three men in it.

It came to a stop just over them and for some minutes, the driver looked down with a steady expressionless gaze to where they were sitting, and didn't speak. Then he turned his head and muttered some-thing to the other two and they got out. One was a fat boy in black trousers and a red sweat shirt with a silver stallion embossed on the front of it. He moved around on the right side of them and stood staring, his mouth partly open in a kind of loose grin. The other had on khaki pants and a blue striped coat and a gray hat pulled down very low, hiding most of his face. He came around slowly on the left side. Neither spoke.

The driver got out of the car and stood by the side of it, looking down at them. He was an older man than the other two. His hair was just beginning to gray and he wore silver-rimmed spectacles that gave him a scholarly look. He had a long creased face and didn't have on any shirt or undershirt. He had on blue jeans that were too tight for him and was holding a black hat and a gun. The two boys also had guns.

"We've had an ACCIDENT!" the children screamed.

The grandmother had the peculiar feeling that the bespectacled man was someone she knew. His face was as familiar to her as if she had known him all her life but she could not recall who he was. He moved away from the car and began to come down the embankment, placing his feet carefully so that he wouldn't slip. He had on tan and white shoes and no socks, and his ankles were red and thin. "Good afternoon," he said. "I see you all had you a little spill."

75   "We turned over twice!" said the grandmother.

"Oncet," he corrected. "We seen it happen. Try their car and see will it run, Hiram," he said quietly to the boy with the gray hat.

"What you got that gun for?" John Wesley asked. "Whatcha gonna do with that gun?"

"Lady," the man said to the children's mother, "would you mind calling them children to sit down by you? Children make me nervous. I want all you all to sit down right together there where you're at."

"What are you telling US what to do for?" June Star asked.

80   Behind them the line of woods gaped like a dark open mouth. "Come here," said their mother.

"Look here now," Bailey began suddenly, "we're in a predicament! We're in . . ."

The grandmother shrieked. She scrambled to her feet and stood staring. "You're The Misfit!" she said. "I recognized you at once!"

"Yes'm," the man said, smiling slightly as if he were pleased in spite of himself to be known, "but it would have been better for all of you, lady, if you hadn't of reckernized me."

Bailey turned his head sharply and said something to his mother that shocked even the children. The old lady began to cry and The Misfit reddened.

85   "Lady," he said, "don't you get upset. Sometimes a man says things he don't mean. I don't reckon he meant to talk to you thataway."

"You wouldn't shoot a lady, would you?" the grandmother said and removed a clean handkerchief from her cuff and began to slap at her eyes with it.

The Misfit pointed the toe of his shoe into the ground and made a little hole and then covered it up again. "I would hate to have to," he said.

"Listen," the grandmother almost screamed, "I know you're a good man. You don't look a bit like you have common blood. I know you must come from nice people!"

"Yes mam," he said, "finest people in the world." When he smiled he showed a row of strong white teeth. "God never made a finer woman than my mother and my daddy's heart was pure gold," he said. The boy with the red sweat shirt had come around behind them and was standing with his gun at his hip. The Misfit squatted down on the ground. "Watch them children, Bobby Lee," he said. "You know they make me nervous." He looked at the six of them huddled together in front of him and he seemed to be embarrassed as if he couldn't think of anything to say. "Ain't a cloud in the sky," he remarked, looking up at it. "Don't see no sun but don't see no cloud neither."

"Yes, it's a beautiful day," said the grandmother. "Listen," she said, "you shouldn't call yourself The Misfit because I know you're a good man at heart. I can just look at you and tell."   90

"Hush!" Bailey yelled. "Hush! Everybody shut up and let me handle this!" He was squatting in the position of a runner about to sprint forward but he didn't move.

"I pre-chate that, lady," The Misfit said and drew a little circle in the ground with the butt of his gun.

"It'll take a half a hour to fix this here car," Hiram called, looking over the raised hood of it.

"Well, first you and Bobby Lee get him and that little boy to step over yonder with you," The Misfit said, pointing to Bailey and John Wesley. "The boys want to ast you something," he said to Bailey. "Would you mind stepping back in them woods there with them?"

"Listen," Bailey began, "we're in a terrible predicament! Nobody   95 realizes what this is," and his voice cracked. His eyes were as blue and intense as the parrots in his shirt and he remained perfectly still.

The grandmother reached up to adjust her hat brim as if she were going to the woods with him but it came off in her hand. She stood staring at it and after a second she let it fall on the ground. Hiram pulled Bailey up by the arm as if he were assisting an old man. John Wesley caught hold of his father's hand and Bobby Lee followed. They went off toward the woods and just as they reached the dark edge, Bailey turned and supporting himself against a gray naked pine trunk, he shouted, "I'll be back in a minute, Mamma, wait on me!"

"Come back this instant!" his mother shrilled but they all disappeared into the woods.

"Bailey Boy!" the grandmother called in a tragic voice but she found she was looking at The Misfit squatting on the ground in front of her. "I just know you're a good man," she said desperately. "You're not a bit common!"

"Nome, I ain't a good man," The Misfit said after a second as if he had considered her statement carefully, "but I ain't the worst in the world neither. My daddy said I was a different breed of dog from my brothers and sisters. 'You know,' Daddy said, 'it's some that can live their whole life out without asking about it and it's others has to know why it is, and this boy is one of the latters. He's going to be into everything!'" He put on his black hat and looked up suddenly and then away deep into the woods as if he were embarrassed again. "I'm sorry I don't have on a shirt before you ladies," he said, hunching his shoulders slightly. "We buried our clothes that we had on when we escaped and we're just making do until we can get better. We borrowed these from some folks we met," he explained.

100   "That's perfectly all right," the grandmother said. "Maybe Bailey has an extra shirt in his suitcase."

"I'll look and see terrectly," The Misfit said.

"Where are they taking him?" the children's mother screamed.

"Daddy was a card himself," The Misfit said. "You couldn't put anything over on him. He never got in trouble with the Authorities though. Just had the knack of handling them."

"You could be honest too if you'd only try," said the grandmother. "Think how wonderful it would be to settle down and live a comfortable life and not have to think about somebody chasing you all the time."

105   The Misfit kept scratching in the ground with the butt of his gun as if he were thinking about it. "Yes'm, somebody is always after you," he murmured.

The grandmother noticed how thin his shoulder blades were just behind his hat because she was standing up looking down on him. "Do you ever pray?" she asked.

He shook his head. All she saw was the black hat wiggle between his shoulder blades. "Nome," he said.

There was a pistol shot from the woods, followed closely by another. Then silence. The old lady's head jerked around. She could hear the wind move through the tree tops like a long satisfied insuck of breath. "Bailey Boy!" she called.

"I was a gospel singer for a while," The Misfit said. "I been most everything. Been in the arm service, both land and sea, at home and abroad, been twict married, been an undertaker, been with the railroads, plowed Mother Earth, been in a tornado, seen a man burnt alive oncet," and looked up at the children's mother and the little girl who were sitting close together, their faces white and their eyes glassy; "I even seen a woman flogged," he said.

110   "Pray, pray," the grandmother began, "pray, pray . . ."

"I never was a bad boy that I remember of," The Misfit said in an almost dreamy voice, "but somewheres along the line I done something wrong and got sent to the penitentiary. I was buried alive," and he looked up and held her attention to him by a steady stare.

"That's when you should have started to pray," she said. "What did you do to get sent to the penitentiary that first time?"

"Turn to the right, it was a wall," The Misfit said, looking up again at the cloudless sky. "Turn to the left, it was a wall. Look up it was a ceiling, look down it was a floor. I forget what I done, lady. I set there and set there, trying to remember what it was I done and I ain't recalled it to this day. Oncet in a while, I would think it was coming to me, but it never come."

"Maybe they put you in by mistake," the old lady said vaguely.

"Nome," he said. "It wasn't no mistake. They had the papers   115
on me."

"You must have stolen something," she said.

The Misfit sneered slightly. "Nobody had nothing I wanted," he said. "It was a head-doctor at the penitentiary said what I had done was kill my daddy but I known that for a lie. My daddy died in nineteen ought nineteen of the epidemic flu and I never had a thing to do with it. He was buried in the Mount Hopewell Baptist churchyard and you can go there and see for yourself."

"If you would pray," the old lady said, "Jesus would help you."

"That's right," The Misfit said.

"Well then, why don't you pray?" she asked trembling with delight   120
suddenly.

"I don't want no hep," he said. "I'm doing all right by myself."

Bobby Lee and Hiram came ambling back from the woods. Bobby Lee was dragging a yellow shirt with bright blue parrots in it.

"Thow me that shirt, Bobby Lee," The Misfit said. The shirt came flying at him and landed on his shoulder and he put it on. The grandmother couldn't name what the shirt reminded her of. "No, lady," The Misfit said while he was buttoning it up, "I found out the crime don't matter. You can do one thing or you can do another, kill a man or take a tire off his car, because sooner or later you're going to forget what it was you done and just be punished for it."

The children's mother had begun to make heaving noises as if she couldn't get her breath. "Lady," he asked, "would you and that little girl like to step off yonder with Bobby Lee and Hiram and join your husband?"

"Yes, thank you," the mother said faintly. Her left arm dangled   125
helplessly and she was holding the baby, who had gone to sleep, in the other. "Hep that lady up, Hiram," The Misfit said as she struggled to climb out of the ditch, "and Bobby Lee, you hold onto that little girl's hand."

"I don't want to hold hands with him," June Star said. "He reminds me of a pig."

The fat boy blushed and laughed and caught her by the arm and pulled her off into the woods after Hiram and her mother.

Alone with The Misfit, the grandmother found that she had lost her voice. There was not a cloud in the sky nor any sun. There was nothing around her but woods. She wanted to tell him that he must pray. She opened and closed her mouth several times before anything came out. Finally she found herself saying, "Jesus, Jesus," meaning, Jesus will help you, but the way she was saying it, it sounded as if she might be cursing.

"Yes'm," The Misfit said as if he agreed. "Jesus thown everything off balance. It was the same case with Him as with me except He hadn't committed any crime and they could prove I had committed one because they had the papers on me. Of course," he said, "they never shown me my papers. That's why I sign myself now. I said long ago, you get you a signature and sign everything you do and keep a copy of it. Then you'll know what you done and you can hold up the crime to the punishment and see do they match and in the end you'll have something to prove you ain't been treated right. I call myself The Misfit," he said, "because I can't make what all I done wrong fit what all I gone through in punishment."

130   There was a piercing scream from the woods, followed closely by a pistol report. "Does it seem right to you, lady, that one is punished a heap and another ain't punished at all?"

"Jesus!" the old lady cried. "You've got good blood! I know you wouldn't shoot a lady! I know you come from nice people! Pray! Jesus, you ought not to shoot a lady. I'll give you all the money I've got!"

"Lady," The Misfit said, looking beyond her far into the woods, "there never was a body that give the undertaker a tip."

There were two more pistol reports and the grandmother raised her head like a parched old turkey hen crying for water and called, "Bailey Boy, Bailey Boy!" as if her heart would break.

"Jesus was the only One that ever raised the dead." The Misfit continued, "and He shouldn't have done it. He thown everything off balance. If He did what He said, then it's nothing for you to do but thow away everything and follow Him, and if He didn't, then it's nothing for you to do but enjoy the few minutes you got left the best way you can— by killing somebody or burning down his house or doing some other meanness to him. No pleasure but meanness," he said and his voice had become almost a snarl.

135   "Maybe He didn't raise the dead," the old lady mumbled, not knowing what she was saying and feeling so dizzy that she sank down in the ditch with her legs twisted under her.

"I wasn't there so I can't say He didn't," The Misfit said. "I wisht I had of been there," he said, hitting the ground with his fist. "It ain't right I wasn't there because if I had of been there I would of known. Listen lady," he said in a high voice, "if I had of been there I would of known and I wouldn't be like I am now." His voice seemed about to crack and the grandmother's head cleared for an instant. She saw the man's face twisted close to her own as if he were going to cry and she murmured, "Why you're one of my babies. You're one of my own children!" She reached out and touched him on the shoulder. The Misfit sprang back as if a snake had bitten him and shot her three times through the chest. Then he put his gun down on the ground and took off his glasses and began to clean them.

Hiram and Bobby Lee returned from the woods and stood over the ditch, looking down at the grandmother who half sat and half lay in a puddle of blood with her legs crossed under her like a child's and her face smiling up at the cloudless sky.

Without his glasses, The Misfit's eyes were red-rimmed and pale and defenseless-looking. "Take her off and thow her where you thown the others," he said, picking up the cat that was rubbing itself against his leg.

"She was a talker, wasn't she?" Bobby Lee said, sliding down the ditch with a yodel.

"She would of been a good woman," The Misfit said, "if it had been   140 somebody there to shoot her every minute of her life."

"Some fun!" Bobby Lee said.

"Shut up, Bobby Lee," The Misfit said. "It's no real pleasure in life."

QUESTIONS

1. The family members surrounding the grandmother are carefully portrayed. Discuss their characterizations and the way they affect our perceptions of the grandmother.

2. Some readers have found the grandmother sympathetic and others have found her a figure of evil, portrayed with imagery often associated with witches. How can these conflicting responses be resolved? Is she more or less sympathetic than the other members of her family?

3. What is the function of the scene at Red Sammy's barbecue place? How does it advance the plot? the theme?

4. During the conversation between the grandmother and Red Sammy, they discuss the difficulty of finding a "good man" in the modern world. Is this a plain statement of the theme, or does the context of their conversation make the dialogue ironic? How does their discussion relate to the larger dramatization of good and evil in the story?

5. The story makes extensive use of animal symbolism. Find the many references to animals and discuss the overall significance of this motif.

6. Analyze The Misfit's motivation for killing the family and for his criminal behavior in general. Unlike his sidekicks, he has a philosophical temperament and carefully rationalizes his behavior. What do his remarks contribute to the theme of the story?

7. Why do the murders of the grandmother's family members take place "off-stage," out in the woods? Could it be argued that this heightens the effect of the violence?

8. At the end of the story, what does The Misfit mean when he says of the grandmother, "She would of been a good woman . . . if it had been somebody there to shoot her every minute of her life" (paragraph 140)?

9. Reread the description of the grandmother after she has been murdered and is lying in the ditch (paragraph 137). Why is she described in this way?

10. In an essay, "A Reasonable Use of the Unreasonable," O'Connor argues that just before the grandmother's death "Her head clears for an instant and she realizes, even in her limited way, that she is responsible for the man before her and joined to him by ties of kinship. . . . And at this point she does the right thing, she makes the right gesture." Compare these comments with your own initial sense of the climactic scene. Does O'Connor's "reading" of this scene differ from your own? Does her commentary change your understanding of the story?

11. In the same essay, O'Connor argues that not only is The Misfit more intelligent than the grandmother but his "capacity for grace" is greater than hers. Do you agree with this remark? Why or why not?

Flannery O'Connor

Everything That Rises Must Converge

Her doctor had told Julian's mother that she must lose twenty pounds on account of her blood pressure, so on Wednesday nights Julian had to take her downtown on the bus for a reducing class at the Y. The reducing class was designed for working girls over fifty, who weighed from 165 to 200 pounds. His mother was one of the slimmer ones, but she said ladies did not tell their age or weight. She would not ride the buses by herself at night since they had been integrated, and because the reducing class was one of her few pleasures, necessary for her health, and *free*, she said Julian could at least put himself out to take her, considering all she did for him. Julian did not like to consider all she did for him, but every Wednesday night he braced himself and took her.

She was almost ready to go, standing before the hall mirror, putting on her hat, while he, his hands behind him, appeared pinned to the door frame, waiting like Saint Sebastian for the arrows to begin piercing him.

EVERYTHING THAT RISES MUST CONVERGE   First published in 1965.

The hat was new and had cost her seven dollars and a half. She kept saying, "Maybe I shouldn't have paid that for it. No, I shouldn't have. I'll take it off and return it tomorrow. I shouldn't have bought it."

Julian raised his eyes to heaven. "Yes, you should have bought it," he said. "Put it on and let's go." It was a hideous hat. A purple velvet flap came down on one side of it and stood up on the other; the rest of it was green and looked like a cushion with the stuffing out. He decided it was less comical than jaunty and pathetic. Everything that gave her pleasure was small and depressed him.

She lifted the hat one more time and set it down slowly on top of her head. Two wings of gray hair protruded on either side of her florid face, but her eyes, sky-blue, were as innocent and untouched by experience as they must have been when she was ten. Were it not that she was a widow who had struggled fiercely to feed and clothe and put him through school and who was supporting him still, "until he got on his feet," she might have been a little girl that he had to take to town.

"It's all right, it's all right," he said. "Let's go." He opened the door   5
himself and started down the walk to get her going. The sky was a dying violet and the houses stood out darkly against it, bulbous liver-colored monstrosities of a uniform ugliness though no two were alike. Since this had been a fashionable neighborhood forty years ago, his mother persisted in thinking they did well to have an apartment in it. Each house had a narrow collar of dirt around it in which sat, usually, a grubby child. Julian walked with his hands in his pockets, his head down and thrust forward and his eyes glazed with the determination to make himself completely numb during the time he would be sacrificed to her pleasure.

The door closed and he turned to find the dumpy figure, surmounted by the atrocious hat, coming toward him. "Well," she said, "you only live once and paying a little more for it, I at least won't meet myself coming and going."

"Some day I'll start making money," Julian said gloomily—he knew he never would—"and you can have one of those jokes whenever you take the fit." But first they would move. He visualized a place where the nearest neighbors would be three miles away on either side.

"I think you're doing fine," she said, drawing on her gloves. "You've only been out of school a year. Rome wasn't built in a day."

She was one of the few members of the Y reducing class who arrived in hat and gloves and who had a son who had been to college: "It takes time," she said, "and the world is in such a mess. This hat looked better on me than any of the others, though when she brought it out I said, 'Take that thing back. I wouldn't have it on my head,' and she said, 'Now wait till you see it on,' and when she put it on me, I said, 'We-ull,' and she said, 'If you ask me, that hat does something for you and you do something for the hat, and besides,' she said, 'with that hat, you won't meet yourself coming and going.'"

10   Julian thought he could have stood his lot better if she had been selfish, if she had been an old hag who drank and screamed at him. He walked along, saturated in depression, as if in the midst of his martyrdom he had lost his faith. Catching sight of his long, hopeless, irritated face, she stopped suddenly with a grief-stricken look, and pulled back on his arm. "Wait on me," she said. "I'm going back to the house and take this thing off and tomorrow I'm going to return it. I was out of my head. I can pay the gas bill with that seven-fifty."

He caught her arm in a vicious grip. "You are not going to take it back," he said. "I like it."

"Well," she said, "I don't think I ought . . ."

"Shut up and enjoy it," he muttered, more depressed than ever.

"With the world in the mess it's in," she said, "it's a wonder we can enjoy anything. I tell you, the bottom rail is on the top."

15   Julian sighed.

"Of course," she said, "if you know who you are, you can go anywhere." She said this every time he took her to the reducing class. "Most of them in it are not our kind of people," she said, "but I can be gracious to anybody. I know who I am."

"They don't give a damn for your graciousness," Julian said savagely. "Knowing who you are is good for one generation only. You haven't the foggiest idea where you stand now or who you are."

She stopped and allowed her eyes to flash at him. "I most certainly do know who I am," she said, "and if you don't know who you are, I'm ashamed of you."

"Oh hell," Julian said.

20   "Your great-grandfather was a former governor of this state," she said. "Your grandfather was a prosperous landowner. Your grandmother was a Godhigh."

"Will you look around you," he said tensely, "and see where you are now?" and he swept his arm jerkily out to indicate the neighborhood, which the growing darkness at least made less dingy.

"You remain what you are," she said. "Your great-grandfather had a plantation and two hundred slaves."

"There are no more slaves," he said irritably.

"They were better off when they were," she said. He groaned to see that she was off on that topic. She rolled onto it every few days like a train on an open track. He knew every stop, every junction, every swamp along the way, and knew the exact point at which her conclusion would roll majestically into the station: "It's ridiculous. It's simply not realistic. They should rise, yes, but on their own side of the fence."

"Let's skip it," Julian said.   25

"The ones I feel sorry for," she said, "are the ones that are half white. They're tragic."

"Will you skip it?"

"Suppose we were half white. We would certainly have mixed feelings."

"I have mixed feelings now," he groaned.

"Well let's talk about something pleasant," she said. "I remember   30 going to Grandpa's when I was a little girl. Then the house had double stairways that went up to what was really the second floor—all the cooking was done on the first. I used to like to stay down in the kitchen on account of the way the walls smelled. I would sit with my nose pressed against the plaster and take deep breaths. Actually the place belonged to the Godhighs but your grandfather Chestny paid the mortgage and saved it for them. They were in reduced circumstances," she said, "but reduced or not, they never forgot who they were."

"Doubtless that decayed mansion reminded them," Julian muttered. He never spoke of it without contempt or thought of it without longing. He had seen it once when he was a child before it had been sold. The double stairways had rotted and been torn down. Negroes were living in it. But it remained in his mind as his mother had known it. It appeared in his dreams regularly. He would stand on the wide porch, listening to the rustle of oak leaves, then wander through the high-ceilinged hall into the parlor that opened onto it and gaze at the worn rugs and faded draperies. It occurred to him that it was he, not she, who could have appreciated it. He preferred its threadbare elegance to anything he could name and it was because of it that all the neighborhoods they had lived in had been a torment to him—whereas she had hardly known the difference. She called her insensitivity "being adjustable."

"And I remember the old darky who was my nurse, Caroline. There was no better person in the world. I've always had a great respect for my colored friends," she said. "I'd do anything in the world for them and they'd . . ."

"Will you for God's sake get off that subject?" Julian said. When he got on a bus by himself, he made it a point to sit down beside a Negro, in reparation as it were for his mother's sins.

"You're mighty touchy tonight," she said. "Do you feel all right?"

"Yes I feel all right," he said. "Now lay off."   35

She pursed her lips. "Well, you certainly are in a vile humor," she observed. "I just won't speak to you at all."

They had reached the bus stop. There was no bus in sight and Julian, his hands still jammed in his pockets and his head thrust forward, scowled down the empty street. The frustration of having to wait on the bus as well as ride on it began to creep up his neck like a hot hand. The presence of his mother was borne in upon him as she gave a pained sigh. He looked at her bleakly. She was holding herself very erect under the preposterous hat, wearing it like a banner of her imaginary dignity. There was in him an evil urge to break her spirit. He suddenly unloosened his tie and pulled it off and put it in his pocket.

She stiffened. "Why must you look like *that* when you take me to town?" she said. "Why must you deliberately embarrass me?"

"If you'll never learn where you are," he said, "you can at least learn where I am."

40   "You look like a—thug," she said.

"Then I must be one," he murmured.

"I'll just go home," she said. "I will not bother you. If you can't do a little thing like that for me . . ."

Rolling his eyes upward, he put his tie back on. "Restored to my class," he muttered. He thrust his face toward her and hissed, "True culture is in the mind, the *mind*," he said, and tapped his head, "the mind."

"It's in the heart," she said, "and in how you do things and how you do things is because of who you *are*."

45   "Nobody in the damn bus cares who you are."

"I care who I am," she said icily.

The lighted bus appeared on top of the next hill and as it approached, they moved out into the street to meet it. He put his hand under her elbow and hoisted her up on the creaking step. She entered with a little smile, as if she were going into a drawing room where everyone had been waiting for her. While he put in the tokens, she sat down on one of the broad front seats for three which faced the aisle. A thin woman with protruding teeth and long yellow hair was sitting on the end of it. His mother moved up beside her and left room for Julian beside herself. He sat down and looked at the floor across the aisle where a pair of thin feet in red and white canvas sandals were planted.

His mother immediately began a general conversation meant to attract anyone who felt like talking. "Can it get any hotter?" she said and removed from her purse a folding fan, black with a Japanese scene on it, which she began to flutter before her.

"I reckon it might could," the woman with the protruding teeth said, "but I know for a fact my apartment couldn't get no hotter."

"It must get the afternoon sun," his mother said. She sat forward and   50
looked up and down the bus. It was half filled. Everybody was white. "I
see we have the bus to ourselves," she said. Julian cringed.

"For a change," said the woman across the aisle, the owner of the red
and white canvas sandals. "I come on one the other day and they were
thick as fleas—up front and all through."

"The world is in a mess everywhere," his mother said. "I don't know
how we've let it get in this fix."

"What gets my goat is all those boys from good families stealing
automobile tires," the woman with the protruding teeth said. "I told my
boy, I said you may not be rich but you been raised right and if I ever
catch you in any such mess, they can send you on to the reformatory. Be
exactly where you belong."

"Training tells," his mother said. "Is your boy in high school?"

"Ninth grade," the woman said.   55

"My son just finished college last year. He wants to write but he's
selling typewriters until he gets started," his mother said.

The woman leaned forward and peered at Julian. He threw her such
a malevolent look that she subsided against the seat. On the floor across
the aisle there was an abandoned newspaper. He got up and got it and
opened it out in front of him. His mother discreetly continued the
conversation in a lower tone but the woman across the aisle said in a
loud voice, "Well that's nice. Selling typewriters is close to writing. He
can go right from one to the other."

"I tell him," his mother said, "that Rome wasn't built in a day."

Behind the newspaper Julian was withdrawing into the inner compartment of his mind where he spent most of his time. This was a kind of
mental bubble in which he established himself when he could not bear
to be a part of what was going on around him. From it he could see out
and judge but in it he was safe from any kind of penetration from
without. It was the only place where he felt free of the general idiocy
of his fellows. His mother had never entered it but from it he could see
her with absolute clarity.

The old lady was clever enough and he thought that if she had   60
started from any of the right premises, more might have been expected
of her. She lived according to the laws of her own fantasy world, outside
of which he had never seen her set foot. The law of it was to sacrifice
herself for him after she had first created the necessity to do so by making
a mess of things. If he had permitted her sacrifices, it was only because
her lack of foresight had made them necessary. All of her life had been a
struggle to act like a Chestny without the Chestny goods, and to give
him everything she thought a Chestny ought to have; but since, said she,

it was fun to struggle, why complain? And when you had won, as she had won, what fun to look back on the hard times! He could not forgive her that she had enjoyed the struggle and that she thought she had won.

What she meant when she said she had won was that she had brought him up successfully and had sent him to college and that he had turned out so well—good looking (her teeth had gone unfilled so that his could be straightened), intelligent (he realized he was too intelligent to be a success), and with a future ahead of him (there was of course no future ahead of him). She excused his gloominess on the grounds that he was still growing up and his radical ideas on his lack of practical experience. She said he didn't yet know a thing about "life," that he hadn't even entered the real world—when already he was as disenchanted with it as a man of fifty.

The further irony of all this was that in spite of her, he had turned out so well. In spite of going to only a third-rate college, he had, on his own initiative, come out with a first-rate education; in spite of growing up dominated by a small mind, he had ended up with a large one; in spite of all her foolish views, he was free of prejudice and unafraid to face facts. Most miraculous of all, instead of being blinded by love for her as she was for him, he had cut himself emotionally free of her and could see her with complete objectivity. He was not dominated by his mother.

The bus stopped with a sudden jerk and shook him from his meditation. A woman from the back lurched forward with little steps and barely escaped falling in his newspaper as she righted herself. She got off and a large Negro got on. Julian kept his paper lowered to watch. It gave him a certain satisfaction to see injustice in daily operation. It confirmed his view that with a few exceptions there was no one worth knowing within a radius of three hundred miles. The Negro was well dressed and carried a briefcase. He looked around and then sat down on the other end of the seat where the woman with the red and white canvas sandals was sitting. He immediately unfolded a newspaper and obscured himself behind it. Julian's mother's elbow at once prodded insistently into his ribs. "Now you see why I won't ride on these buses by myself," she whispered.

The woman with the red and white canvas sandals had risen at the same time the Negro sat down and had gone further back in the bus and taken the seat of the woman who had got off. His mother leaned forward and cast her an approving look.

65   Julian rose, crossed the aisle, and sat down in the place of the woman with the canvas sandals. From this position, he looked serenely across at his mother. Her face had turned an angry red. He stared at her,

making his eyes the eyes of a stranger. He felt his tension suddenly lift as if he had openly declared war on her.

He would have liked to get in conversation with the Negro and to talk with him about art or politics or any subject that would be above the comprehension of those around them, but the man remained entrenched behind his paper. He was either ignoring the change of seating or had never noticed it. There was no way for Julian to convey his sympathy.

His mother kept her eyes fixed reproachfully on his face. The woman with the protruding teeth was looking at him avidly as if he were a type of monster new to her.

"Do you have a light?" he asked the Negro.

Without looking away from his paper, the man reached in his pocket and handed him a packet of matches.

"Thanks," Julian said. For a moment he held the matches foolishly. 70 A NO SMOKING sign looked down upon him from over the door. This alone would not have deterred him; he had no cigarettes. He had quit smoking some months before because he could not afford it. "Sorry," he muttered and handed back the matches. The Negro lowered the paper and gave him an annoyed look. He took the matches and raised the paper again.

His mother continued to gaze at him but she did not take advantage of his momentary discomfort. Her eyes retained their battered look. Her face seemed to be unnaturally red, as if her blood pressure had risen. Julian allowed no glimmer of sympathy to show on his face. Having got the advantage, he wanted desperately to keep it and carry it through. He would have liked to teach her a lesson that would last her a while, but there seemed no way to continue the point. The Negro refused to come out from behind his paper.

Julian folded his arms and looked stolidly before him, facing her but as if he did not see her, as if he had ceased to recognize her existence. He visualized a scene in which, the bus having reached their stop, he would remain in his seat and when she said, "Aren't you going to get off?" he would look at her as at a stranger who had rashly addressed him. The corner they got off on was usually deserted, but it was well lighted and it would not hurt her to walk by herself the four blocks to the Y. He decided to wait until the time came and then decide whether or not he would let her get off by herself. He would have to be at the Y at ten to bring her back, but he could leave her wondering if he was going to show up. There was no reason for her to think she could always depend on him.

He retired again into the high-ceilinged room sparsely settled with large pieces of antique furniture. His soul expanded momentarily but then he became aware of his mother across from him and the vision shriveled. He studied her coldly. Her feet in little pumps dangled like a child's and did not quite reach the floor. She was training on him an exaggerated look of reproach. He felt completely detached from her. At that moment he could with pleasure have slapped her as he would have slapped a particularly obnoxious child in his charge.

He began to imagine various unlikely ways by which he could teach her a lesson. He might make friends with some distinguished Negro professor or lawyer and bring him home to spend the evening. He would be entirely justified but her blood pressure would rise to 300. He could not push her to the extent of making her have a stroke, and moreover, he had never been successful at making any Negro friends. He had tried to strike up an acquaintance on the bus with some of the better types, with ones that looked like professors or ministers or lawyers. One morning he had sat down next to a distinguished-looking dark brown man who had answered his questions with a sonorous solemnity but who had turned out to be an undertaker. Another day he had sat down beside a cigar-smoking Negro with a diamond ring on his finger, but after a few stilted pleasantries, the Negro had rung the buzzer and risen, slipping two lottery tickets into Julian's hand as he climbed over him to leave.

75   He imagined his mother lying desperately ill and his being able to secure only a Negro doctor for her. He toyed with that idea for a few minutes and then dropped it for a momentary vision of himself participating as a sympathizer in a sit-in demonstration. This was possible but he did not linger with it. Instead, he approached the ultimate horror. He brought home a beautiful suspiciously Negroid woman. Prepare yourself, he said. There is nothing you can do about it. This is the woman I've chosen. She's intelligent, dignified, even good, and she's suffered and she hasn't thought it *fun*. Now persecute us, go ahead and persecute us. Drive her out of here, but remember, you're driving me too. His eyes were narrowed and through the indignation he had generated, he saw his mother across the aisle, purple-faced, shrunken to the dwarf-like proportions of her moral nature, sitting like a mummy beneath the ridiculous banner of her hat.

He was tilted out of his fantasy again as the bus stopped. The door opened with a sucking hiss and out of the dark a large, gaily dressed, sullen-looking colored woman got on with a little boy. The child, who might have been four, had on a short plaid suit and a Tyrolean hat with a blue feather in it. Julian hoped that he would sit down beside him and that the woman would push in beside his mother. He could think of no better arrangement.

As she waited for her tokens, the woman was surveying the seating possibilities—he hoped with the idea of sitting where she was least wanted. There was something familiar-looking about her but Julian could not place what it was. She was a giant of a woman. Her face was set not only to meet opposition but to seek it out. The downward tilt of her large lower lip was like a warning sign: DON'T TAMPER WITH ME. Her bulging figure was encased in a green crepe dress and her feet overflowed in red shoes. She had on a hideous hat. A purple velvet flap came down on one side of it and stood up on the other; the rest of it was green and looked like a cushion with the stuffing out. She carried a mammoth red pocketbook that bulged throughout as if it were stuffed with rocks.

To Julian's disappointment, the little boy climbed up on the empty seat beside his mother. His mother lumped all children, black and white, into the common category, "cute," and she thought little Negroes were on the whole cuter than little white children. She smiled at the little boy as he climbed on the seat.

Meanwhile the woman was bearing down upon the empty seat beside Julian. To his annoyance, she squeezed herself into it. He saw his mother's face change as the woman settled herself next to him and he realized with satisfaction that this was more objectionable to her than it was to him. Her face seemed almost gray and there was a look of dull recognition in her eyes, as if suddenly she had sickened at some awful confrontation. Julian saw that it was because she and the woman had, in a sense, swapped sons. Though his mother would not realize the symbolic significance of this, she would feel it. His amusement showed plainly on his face.

The woman next to him muttered something unintelligible to   80
herself. He was conscious of a kind of bristling next to him, a muted growling like that of an angry cat. He could not see anything but the red pocketbook upright on the bulging green thighs. He visualized the woman as she had stood waiting for her tokens—the ponderous figure, rising from the red shoes upward over the solid hips, the mammoth bosom, the haughty face, to the green and purple hat.

His eyes widened.

The vision of the two hats, identical, broke upon him with the radiance of a brilliant sunrise. His face was suddenly lit with joy. He could not believe that Fate had thrust upon his mother such a lesson. He gave a loud chuckle so that she would look at him and see that he saw. She turned her eyes on him slowly. The blue in them seemed to have turned a bruised purple. For a moment he had an uncomfortable sense of her innocence, but it lasted only a second before principle rescued him. Justice entitled him to laugh. His grin hardened until it said to her as plainly as if he were saying aloud: Your punishment exactly fits your pettiness. This should teach you a permanent lesson.

Her eyes shifted to the woman. She seemed unable to bear looking at him and to find the woman preferable. He became conscious again of the bristling presence at his side. The woman was rumbling like a volcano about to become active. His mother's mouth began to twitch slightly at one corner. With a sinking heart, he saw incipient signs of recovery on her face and realized that this was going to strike her suddenly as funny and was going to be no lesson at all. She kept her eyes on the woman and an amused smile came over her face as if the woman were a monkey that had stolen her hat. The little Negro was looking up at her with large fascinated eyes. He had been trying to attract her attention for some time.

"Carver!" the woman said suddenly. "Come heah!"

85   When he saw that the spotlight was on him at last, Carver drew his feet up and turned himself toward Julian's mother and giggled.

"Carver!" the woman. "You heah me? Come heah!"

Carver slid down from the seat but remained squatting with his back against the base of it, his head turned slyly around toward Julian's mother, who was smiling at him. The woman reached a hand across the aisle and snatched him to her. He righted himself and hung backwards on her knees, grinning at Julian's mother. "Isn't he cute?" Julian's mother said to the woman with the protruding teeth.

"I reckon he is," the woman said without conviction.

The Negress yanked him upright but he eased out of her grip and shot across the aisle and scrambled, giggling wildly, onto the seat beside his love.

90   "I think he likes me," Julian's mother said, and smiled at the woman. It was the smile she used when she was being particularly gracious to an inferior. Julian saw everything lost. The lesson had rolled off her like rain on a roof.

The woman stood up and yanked the little boy off the seat as if she were snatching him from contagion. Julian could feel the rage in her at having no weapon like his mother's smile. She gave the child a sharp slap across his leg. He howled once and then thrust his head into her stomach and kicked his feet against her shins. "Be-have," she said vehemently.

The bus stopped and the Negro who had been reading the newspaper got off. The woman moved over and set the little boy down with a thump between herself and Julian. She held him firmly by the knee. In a moment he put his hands in front of his face and peeped at Julian's mother through his fingers.

"I see yoooooooo!" she said and put her hand in front of her face and peeped at him.

The woman slapped his hand down. "Quit yo' foolishness," she said, "before I knock the living Jesus out of you!"

Julian was thankful that the next stop was theirs. He reached up and pulled the cord. The woman reached up and pulled it at the same time. Oh my God, he thought. He had the terrible intuition that when they got off the bus together, his mother would open her purse and give the little boy a nickel. The gesture would be as natural to her as breathing. The bus stopped and the woman got up and lunged to the front, dragging the child, who wished to stay on, after her. Julian and his mother got up and followed. As they neared the door, Julian tried to relieve her of her pocketbook.

"No," she murmured. "I want to give the little boy a nickel."

"No!" Julian hissed. "No!"

She smiled down at the child and opened her bag. The bus door opened and the woman picked him up by the arm and descended with him, hanging at her hip. Once in the street she set him down and shook him.

Julian's mother had to close her purse while she got down the bus step but as soon as her feet were on the ground, she opened it again and began to rummage inside. "I can't find but a penny," she whispered, "but it looks like a new one."

"Don't do it!" Julian said fiercely between his teeth. There was a streetlight on the corner and she hurried to get under it so that she could better see into her pocketbook. The woman was heading off rapidly down the street with the child still hanging backward on her hand.

"Oh little boy!" Julian's mother called and took a few quick steps and caught up with them just beyond the lamppost. "Here's a bright new penny for you," and she held out the coin, which shone bronze in the dim light.

The huge woman turned and for a moment stood, her shoulders lifted and her face frozen with frustrated rage, and stared at Julian's mother. Then all at once she seemed to explode like a piece of machinery that had been given one ounce of pressure too much. Julian saw the black fist swing out with the red pocketbook. He shut his eyes and cringed as he heard the woman shout, "He don't take nobody's pennies!" When he opened his eyes, the woman was disappearing down the street with the little boy staring wide-eyed over her shoulder. Julian's mother was sitting on the sidewalk.

"I told you not to do that," Julian said angrily. "I told you not to do that!"

He stood over her for a minute, gritting his teeth. Her legs were stretched out in front of her and her hat was on her lap. He squatted down and looked her in the face. It was totally expressionless. "You got exactly what you deserved," he said. "Now get up."

105   He picked up her pocketbook and put what had fallen out back in it. He picked the hat up off her lap. The penny caught his eye on the sidewalk and he picked that up and let it drop before her eyes into the purse. Then he stood up and leaned over and held his hands out to pull her up. She remained immobile. He sighed. Rising above them on either side were black apartment buildings, marked with irregular rectangles of light. At the end of the block a man came out of a door and walked off in the opposite direction. "All right," he said, "suppose somebody happens by and wants to know why you're sitting on the sidewalk?"

She took the hand and, breathing hard, pulled heavily up on it and then stood for a moment, swaying slightly as if the spots of light in the darkness were circling around her. Her eyes, shadowed and confused, finally settled on his face. He did not try to conceal his irritation. "I hope this teaches you a lesson," he said. She leaned forward and her eyes raked his face. She seemed trying to determine his identity. Then, as if she found nothing familiar about him, she started off with a headlong movement in the wrong direction.

"Aren't you going on to the Y?" he asked.

"Home," she muttered.

"Well, are we walking?"

110   For answer she kept going. Julian followed along, his hands behind him. He saw no reason to let the lesson she had had go without backing it up with an explanation of its meaning. She might as well be made to understand what had happened to her. "Don't think that was just an uppity Negro woman," he said. "That was the whole colored race which will no longer take your condescending pennies. That was your black double. She can wear the same hat as you, and to be sure," he added gratuitously (because he thought it was funny), "it looked better on her than it did on you. What all this means," he said, "is that the old world is gone. The old manners are obsolete and your graciousness is not worth a damn." He thought bitterly of the house that had been lost for him. "You aren't who you think you are," he said.

She continued to plow ahead, paying no attention to him. Her hair had come undone on one side. She dropped her pocketbook and took no notice. He stooped and picked it up and handed it to her but she did not take it.

"You needn't act as if the world had come to an end," he said, "because it hasn't. From now on you've got to live in a new world and face a few realities for a change. Buck up," he said, "it won't kill you."

She was breathing fast.

"Let's wait on the bus," he said.

"Home," she said thickly.   115

"I hate to see you behave like this," he said. "Just like a child. I should be able to expect more of you." He decided to stop where he was and make her stop and wait for a bus. "I'm not going any farther," he said, stopping. "We're going on the bus."

She continued to go on as if she had not heard him. He took a few steps and caught her arm and stopped her. He looked into her face and caught his breath. He was looking into a face he had never seen before. "Tell Grandpa to come get me," she said.

He stared, stricken.

"Tell Caroline to come get me," she said.

Stunned, he let her go and she lurched forward again, walking as if   120
one leg were shorter than the other. A tide of darkness seemed to be sweeping her from him. "Mother!" he cried. "Darling, sweetheart, wait!" Crumpling, she fell to the pavement. He dashed forward and fell at her side, crying, "Mamma, Mamma!" He turned her over. Her face was fiercely distorted. One eye, large and staring, moved slightly to the left as if it had become unmoored. The other remained fixed on him, raked his face again, found nothing and closed.

"Wait here, wait here!" he cried and jumped up and began to run for help toward a cluster of lights he saw in the distance ahead of him. "Help, help!" he shouted, but his voice was thin, scarcely a thread of sound. The lights drifted farther away the faster he ran and his feet moved numbly as if they carried him nowhere. The tide of darkness seemed to sweep him back to her, postponing from moment to moment his entry into the world of guilt and sorrow.

QUESTIONS

1. Discuss the mother-son relationship in the story. What values does each generation represent? Which character is more dependent on the other, the mother or Julian? Which character is more admirable, and why?

2. Roughly what historical time period in the American South does the story examine? How is the issue of race presented differently here than if the story were set in the present?

3. Why is it significant that Julian's mother and Carver's mother are wearing identical hats? How does this coincidence help elucidate the theme?

4. How does O'Connor use humor effectively in the story? Isolate the passages you found particularly humorous and consider the ways in which these passages represent a serious intention on the author's part.

5. In the concluding paragraphs, Julian undergoes a remarkable change. What is the nature of this change, or "epiphany," and what does it say about him? In what ways will he be a different person in his future life?
6. Compare the ending of this story to that of "A Good Man Is Hard to Find." How are the endings similar?

Flannery O'Connor

Greenleaf

Mrs. May's bedroom window was low and faced on the east and the bull, silvered in the moonlight, stood under it, his head raised as if he listened—like some patient god come down to woo her—for a stir inside the room. The window was dark and the sound of her breathing too light to be carried outside. Clouds crossing the moon blackened him and in the dark he began to tear at the hedge. Presently they passed and he appeared again in the same spot, chewing steadily, with a hedge-wreath that he had ripped loose for himself caught in the tips of his horns. When the moon drifted into retirement again, there was nothing to mark his place but the sound of steady chewing. Then abruptly a pink glow filled the window. Bars of light slid across him as the venetian blind was slit. He took a step backward and lowered his head as if to show the wreath across his horns.

For almost a minute there was no sound from inside, then as he raised his crowned head again, a woman's voice, guttural as if addressed to a dog, said, "Get away from here, Sir!" and in a second muttered, "Some nigger's scrub bull."

The animal pawed the ground and Mrs. May, standing bent forward behind the blind, closed it quickly lest the light make him charge into the shrubbery. For a second she waited, still bent forward, her nightgown hanging loosely from her narrow shoulders. Green rubber curlers sprouted neatly over her forehead and her face beneath them was smooth as concrete with an egg-white paste that drew the wrinkles out while she slept.

She had been conscious in her sleep of a steady rhythmic chewing as if something were eating one wall of the house. She had been aware that whatever it was had been eating as long as she had the place and had eaten everything from the beginning of her fence line up to the house and now was eating the house and calmly with the same steady rhythm would continue through the house, eating her and the boys, and then on, eating everything but the Greenleafs, on and on, eating everything

GREENLEAF   First published in 1956.

until nothing was left but the Greenleafs on a little island all their own in the middle of what had been her place. When the munching reached her elbow, she jumped up and found herself, fully awake, standing in the middle of her room. She identified the sound at once: a cow was tearing at the shrubbery under the window. Mr. Greenleaf had left the lane gate open and she didn't doubt that the entire herd was on her lawn. She turned on the dim pink table lamp and then went to the window and slit the blind. The bull, gaunt and long-legged, was standing about four feet from her, chewing calmly like an uncouth country suitor.

For fifteen years, she thought as she squinted at him fiercely, she had been having shiftless people's hogs root up her oats, their mules wallow on her lawn, their scrub bulls breed her cows. If this one was not put up now, he would be over the fence, ruining her herd before morning—and Mr. Greenleaf was soundly sleeping a half mile down the road in the tenant house. There was no way to get him unless she dressed and got in her car and rode down there and woke him up. He would come but his expression, his whole figure, his every pause, would say: "Hit looks to me like one or both of them boys would not make their maw ride out in the middle of the night thisaway. If hit was my boys, they would have got the bull up theirself." 5

The bull lowered his head and shook it and the wreath slipped down to the base of his horns where it looked like a menacing prickly crown. She had closed the blind then; in a few seconds she heard him move off heavily.

Mr. Greenleaf would say, "If hit was my boys they would never have allowed their maw to go after the hired help in the middle of the night. They would have did it theirself."

Weighing it, she decided not to bother Mr. Greenleaf. She returned to bed thinking that if the Greenleaf boys had risen in the world it was because she had given their father employment when no one else would have him. She had had Mr. Greenleaf fifteen years but no one else would have had him five minutes. Just the way he approached an object was enough to tell anybody with eyes what kind of a worker he was. He walked with a high-shouldered creep and he never appeared to come directly forward. He walked on the perimeter of some invisible circle and if you wanted to look him in the face, you had to move and get in front of him. She had not fired him because she had always doubted she could do better. He was too shiftless to go out and look for another job; he didn't have the initiative to steal, and after she had told him three or four times to do a thing, he did it; but he never told her about a sick cow until it was too late to call the veterinarian and if her barn had caught fire, he would have called his wife to see the flames before he began to put them out. And of the wife, she didn't even like to think. Beside the wife, Mr. Greenleaf was an aristocrat.

"If hit had been my boys," he would have said, "they would have cut off their right arm before they would have allowed their maw to . . ."

10   "If your boys had any pride, Mr. Greenleaf," she would like to say to him some day, "there are many things that they would not *allow* their mother to do."

The next morning as soon as Mr. Greenleaf came to the back door, she told him there was a stray bull on the place and that she wanted him penned up at once.

"Done already been here three days," he said, addressing his right foot which he held forward, turned slightly as if he were trying to look at the sole. He was standing at the bottom of the three back steps while she leaned out the kitchen door, a small woman with pale nearsighted eyes and grey hair that rose on top like the crest of some disturbed bird.

"Three days!" she said in the restrained screech that had become habitual with her.

Mr. Greenleaf, looking into the distance over the near pasture, removed a package of cigarets from his shirt pocket and let one fall into his hand. He put the package back and stood for a while looking at the cigaret. "I put him in the bull pen but he torn out of there," he said presently. "I didn't see him none after that." He bent over the cigaret and lit it and then turned his head briefly in her direction. The upper part of his face sloped gradually into the lower which was long and narrow, shaped like a rough chalice. He had deep-set fox-colored eyes shadowed under a grey felt hat that he wore slanted forward following the line of his nose. His build was insignificant.

15   "Mr. Greenleaf," she said, "get the bull up this morning before you do anything else. You know he'll ruin the breeding schedule. Get him up and keep him up and the next time there's a stray bull on this place, tell me at once. Do you understand?"

"Where do you want him put at?" Mr. Greenleaf asked.

"I don't care where you put him," she said. "You are supposed to have some sense. Put him where he can't get out. Whose bull is he?"

For a moment Mr. Greenleaf seemed to hesitate between silence and speech. He studied the air to the left of him. "He must be some-body's bull," he said after a while.

"Yes, he must!" she said and shut the door with a precise little slam.

20   She went into the dining room where the two boys were eating breakfast and sat down on the edge of her chair at the head of the table.

She never ate breakfast but she sat with them to see that they had what they wanted. "Honestly!" she said, and began to tell about the bull, aping Mr. Greenleaf saying, "It must be *somebody's* bull."

Wesley continued to read the newspaper folded beside his plate but Scofield interrupted his eating from time to time to look at her and laugh. The two boys never had the same reaction to anything. They were as different, she said, as night and day. The only thing they did have in common was neither of them cared what happened on the place. Scofield was a business type and Wesley was an intellectual.

Wesley, the younger child, had had rheumatic fever when he was seven and Mrs. May thought that this was what had caused him to be an intellectual. Scofield, who had never had a day's sickness in his life, was an insurance salesman. She would not have minded his selling insurance if he had sold a nicer kind but he sold the kind that only Negroes buy. He was what Negroes call a "policy man." He said there was more money in nigger-insurance than any other kind, and before company, he was very loud about it. He would shout, "Mama don't like to hear me say it but I'm the best nigger-insurance salesman in this county!"

Scofield was thirty-six and he had a broad pleasant face but he was not married. "Yes," Mrs. May would say, "and if you sold decent insurance, some *nice* girl would be willing to marry you. What nice girl wants to marry a nigger-insurance man? You'll wake up some day and it'll be too late."

And at this Scofield would yodel and say, "Why Mamma, I'm not going to marry until you're dead and gone and then I'm going to marry me some nice fat girl that can take over this place!" And once he had added, "—some nice lady like Mrs. Greenleaf." When he had said this Mrs. May had risen from her chair, her back stiff as a rake handle, and had gone to her room. There she had sat down on the edge of her bed for some time with her small face drawn. Finally she had whispered, "I work and slave, I struggle and sweat to keep this place for them and as soon as I'm dead, they'll marry trash and bring it in here and ruin everything. They'll marry trash and ruin everything I've done," and she had made up her mind at that moment to change her will. The next day she had gone to her lawyer and had had the property entailed so that if they married, they could not leave it to their wives.

The idea that one of them might marry a woman even remotely like 25
Mrs. Greenleaf was enough to make her ill. She had put up with Mr. Greenleaf for fifteen years, but the only way she had endured his wife had been by keeping entirely out of her sight. Mrs. Greenleaf was large and loose. The yard around her house looked like a dump and her five girls were always filthy; even the youngest one dipped snuff. Instead of

making a garden or washing their clothes, her preoccupation was what she called "prayer healing."

Every day she cut all the morbid stories out of the newspaper—the accounts of women who had been raped and criminals who had escaped and children who had been burned and of train wrecks and plane crashes and the divorces of movie stars. She took these to the woods and dug a hole and buried them and then she fell on the ground over them and mumbled and groaned for an hour or so, moving her huge arms back and forth under her and out again and finally just lying down flat and, Mrs. May suspected, going to sleep in the dirt.

She had not found out about this until the Greenleafs had been with her a few months. One morning she had been out to inspect a field that she wanted planted in rye but that had come up in clover because Mr. Greenleaf had used the wrong seeds in the grain drill. She was returning through a wooded path that separated two pastures, muttering to herself and hitting the ground methodically with a long stick she carried in case she saw a snake. "Mr. Greenleaf," she was saying in a low voice, "I cannot afford to pay for your mistakes. I am a poor woman and this place is all I have. I have two boys to educate. I cannot . . ."

Out of nowhere a guttural agonized voice groaned, "Jesus! Jesus!" In a second it came again with a terrible urgency. "Jesus! Jesus!"

Mrs. May stopped still, one hand lifted to her throat. The sound was so piercing that she felt as if some violent unleashed force had broken out of the ground and was charging toward her. Her second thought was more reasonable: somebody had been hurt on the place and would sue her for everything she had. She had no insurance. She rushed forward and turning a bend in the path, she saw Mrs. Greenleaf sprawled on her hands and knees off the side of the road, her head down.

30   "Mrs. Greenleaf!" she shrilled, "what's happened?"

Mrs. Greenleaf raised her head. Her face was a patchwork of dirt and tears and her small eyes, the color of two field peas, were red-rimmed and swollen, but her expression was as composed as a bulldog's. She swayed back and forth on her hands and knees and groaned, "Jesus, Jesus."

Mrs. May winced. She thought the word, Jesus, should be kept inside the church building like other words inside the bedroom. She was a good Christian woman with a large respect for religion, though she did not, of course, believe any of it was true. "What is the matter with you?" she asked sharply.

"You broke my healing," Mrs. Greenleaf said, waving her aside. "I can't talk to you until I finish."

Mrs. May stood, bent forward, her mouth open and her stick raised off the ground as if she were not sure what she wanted to strike with it.

"Oh, Jesus, stab me in the heart!" Mrs. Greenleaf shrieked. "Jesus, 35 stab me in the heart!" and she fell back flat in the dirt, a huge human mound, her legs and arms spread out as if she were trying to wrap them around the earth.

Mrs. May felt as furious and helpless as if she had been insulted by a child. "Jesus," she said, drawing herself back, "would be *ashamed* of you. He would tell you to get up from there this instant and go wash your children's clothes!" and she had turned and walked off as fast as she could.

Whenever she thought of how the Greenleaf boys had advanced in the world, she had only to think of Mrs. Greenleaf sprawled obscenely on the ground, and say to herself, "Well, no matter how far they go, they *came* from that."

She would like to have been able to put in her will that when she died, Wesley and Scofield were not to continue to employ Mr. Greenleaf. She was capable of handling Mr. Greenleaf; they were not. Mr. Greenleaf had pointed out to her once that her boys didn't know hay from silage. She had pointed out to him that they had other talents, that Scofield was a successful businessman and Wesley a successful intellectual. Mr. Greenleaf did not comment, but he never lost an opportunity of letting her see, by his expression or some simple gesture, that he held the two of them in infinite contempt. As scrub-human as the Greenleafs were, he never hesitated to let her know that in any like circumstance in which his own boys might have been involved, they—O. T. and E. T. Greenleaf—would have acted to better advantage.

The Greenleaf boys were two or three years younger than the May boys. They were twins and you never knew when you spoke to one of them whether you were speaking to O. T. or E. T., and they never had the politeness to enlighten you. They were long-legged and raw-boned and red-skinned, with bright grasping fox-colored eyes like their father's. Mr. Greenleaf's pride in them began with the fact that they were twins. He acted, Mrs. May said, as if this were something smart they had thought of themselves. They were energetic and hard-working and she would admit to anyone that they had come a long way—and that the Second World War was responsible for it.

They had both joined the service and, disguised in their uniforms, 40 they could not be told from other people's children. You could tell, of course, when they opened their mouths but they did that seldom. The smartest thing they had done was to get sent overseas and there to marry

French wives. They hadn't married French trash either. They had married nice girls who naturally couldn't tell that they murdered the king's English or that the Greenleafs were who they were.

Wesley's heart condition had not permitted him to serve his country but Scofield had been in the army for two years. He had not cared for it and at the end of his military service, he was only a Private First Class. The Greenleaf boys were both some kind of sergeants, and Mr. Greenleaf, in those days, had never lost an opportunity of referring to them by their rank. They had both managed to get wounded and now they both had pensions. Further, as soon as they were released from the army, they took advantage of all the benefits and went to the school of agriculture at the university—the taxpayers meanwhile supporting their French wives. The two of them were living now about two miles down the highway on a piece of land that the government had helped them to buy and in a brick duplex bungalow that the government had helped to build and pay for. If the war had made anyone, Mrs. May said, it had made the Greenleaf boys. They each had three little children apiece, who spoke Greenleaf English and French, and who, on account of their mothers' background, would be sent to the convent school and brought up with manners. "And in twenty years," Mrs. May asked Scofield and Wesley, "do you know what those people will be?

"*Society*," she said blackly.

She had spent fifteen years coping with Mr. Greenleaf and, by now, handling him had become second nature with her. His disposition on any particular day was as much a factor in what she could and couldn't do as the weather was, and she had learned to read his face the way real country people read the sunrise and sunset.

She was a country woman only by persuasion. The late Mr. May, a businessman, had bought the place when land was down, and when he died it was all he had to leave her. The boys had not been happy to move to the country to a broken-down farm, but there was nothing else for her to do. She had the timber on the place cut and with the proceeds had set herself up in the dairy business after Mr. Greenleaf had answered her ad. "i seen yor add and i will come have 2 boys," was all his letter said, but he arrived the next day in a pieced-together truck, his wife and five daughters sitting on the floor in the back, himself and the two boys in the cab.

45   Over the years they had been on her place, Mr. and Mrs. Greenleaf had aged hardly at all. They had no worries, no responsibilities. They lived like the lilies of the field, off the fat that she struggled to put into the land. When she was dead and gone from overwork and worry, the

Greenleafs, healthy and thriving, would be just ready to begin draining Scofield and Wesley.

Wesley said the reason Mrs. Greenleaf had not aged was because she released all her emotions in prayer healing. "You ought to start praying, Sweetheart," he had said in the voice that, poor boy, he could not help making deliberately nasty.

Scofield only exasperated her beyond endurance but Wesley caused her real anxiety. He was thin and nervous and bald and being an intellectual was a terrible strain on his disposition. She doubted if he would marry until she died but she was certain that then the wrong woman would get him. Nice girls didn't like Scofield but Wesley didn't like nice girls. He didn't like anything. He drove twenty miles every day to the university where he taught and twenty miles back every night, but he said he hated the twenty-mile drive and he hated the second-rate university and he hated the morons who attended it. He hated the country and he hated the life he lived; he hated living with his mother and his idiot brother and he hated hearing about the damn dairy and the damn help and the damn broken machinery. But in spite of all he said, he never made any move to leave. He talked about Paris and Rome but he never went even to Atlanta.

"You'd go to those places and you'd get sick," Mrs. May would say. "Who in Paris is going to see that you get a salt-free diet? And do you think if you married one of those odd numbers you take out that *she* would cook a salt-free diet for you? No indeed, she would not!" When she took this line, Wesley would turn himself roughly around in his chair and ignore her. Once when she had kept it up too long, he had snarled, "Well, why don't you do something practical, Woman? Why don't you pray for me like Mrs. Greenleaf would?"

"I don't like to hear you boys make jokes about religion," she had said. "If you would go to church, you would meet some nice girls."

But it was impossible to tell them anything. When she looked at the two of them now, sitting on either side of the table, neither one caring the least if a stray bull ruined her herd—which was their herd, their future—when she looked at the two of them, one hunched over a paper and the other teetering back in his chair, grinning at her like an idiot, she wanted to jump up and beat her fist on the table and shout, "You'll find out one of these days, you'll find out what *Reality* is when it's too late!"

"Mamma," Scofield said, "don't you get excited now but I'll tell you whose bull that is." He was looking at her wickedly. He let his chair drop forward and he got up. Then with his shoulders bent and his hands held up to cover his head, he tiptoed to the door. He backed into the hall and

50

pulled the door almost to so that it hid all of him but his face. "You want to know, Sugar-pie?" he asked.

Mrs. May sat looking at him coldly.

"That's O. T. and E. T.'s bull," he said. "I collected from their nigger yesterday and he told me they were missing it," and he showed her an exaggerated expanse of teeth and disappeared silently.

Wesley looked up and laughed.

55   Mrs. May turned her head forward again, her expression unaltered. "I am the only *adult* on this place," she said. She leaned across the table and pulled the paper from the side of his plate. "Do you see how it's going to be when I die and you boys have to handle him?" she began. "Do you see why he didn't know whose bull that was? Because it was theirs. Do you see what I have to put up with? Do you see that if I hadn't kept my foot on his neck all these years, you boys might be milking cows every morning at four o'clock?"

Wesley pulled the paper back toward his plate and staring at her full in the face, he murmured, "I wouldn't milk a cow to save your soul from hell."

"I know you wouldn't," she said in a brittle voice. She sat back and began rapidly turning her knife over at the side of her plate. "O. T. and E. T. are fine boys," she said. "They ought to have been my sons." The thought of this was so horrible that her vision of Wesley was blurred at once by a wall of tears. All she saw was his dark shape, rising quickly from the table. "And you two," she cried, "you two should have belonged to that woman!"

He was heading for the door.

"When I die," she said in a thin voice, "I don't know what's going to become of you."

60   "You're always yapping about when-you-die," he growled as he rushed out, "but you look pretty healthy to me."

For some time she sat where she was, looking straight ahead through the window across the room into a scene of indistinct grays and greens. She stretched her face and her neck muscles and drew in a long breath but the scene in front of her flowed together anyway into a watery gray mass. "They needn't think I'm going to die any time soon," she muttered, and some more defiant voice in her added: I'll die when I get good and ready.

She wiped her eyes with the table napkin and got up and went to the window and gazed at the scene in front of her. The cows were grazing on two pale green pastures across the road and behind them, fencing them in, was a black wall of trees with a sharp sawtooth edge that held off the indifferent sky. The pastures were enough to calm her. When she looked out any window in her house, she saw the reflection of her own character. Her city friends said she was the most remarkable woman they knew, to go, practically penniless and with no experience, out to a rundown farm and make a success of it. "Everything is against you," she would say, "the weather is against you and the dirt is against you and the help is against you. They're all in league against you. There's nothing for it but an iron hand!"

"Look at Mamma's iron hand!" Scofield would yell and grab her arm and hold it up so that her delicate blue-veined little hand would dangle from her wrist like the head of a broken lily. The company always laughed.

The sun, moving over the black and white grazing cows, was just a little brighter than the rest of the sky. Looking down, she saw a darker shape that might have been its shadow cast at an angle, moving among them. She uttered a sharp cry and turned and marched out of the house.

Mr. Greenleaf was in the trench silo, filling a wheelbarrow. She   65
stood on the edge and looked down at him. "I told you to get up that bull. Now he's in with the milk herd."

"You can't do two thangs at oncet," Mr. Greenleaf remarked.

"I told you to do that first."

He wheeled the barrow out of the open end of the trench toward the barn and she followed close behind him. "And you needn't think, Mr. Greenleaf," she said, "that I don't know exactly whose bull that is or why you haven't been in any hurry to notify me he was here. I might as well feed O. T. and E. T.'s bull as long as I'm going to have him here ruining my herd."

Mr. Greenleaf paused with the wheelbarrow and looked behind him. "Is that them boys' bull?" he asked in an incredulous tone.

She did not say a word. She merely looked away with her mouth   70
taut.

"They told me their bull was out but I never known that was him," he said.

"I want that bull put up now," she said, "and I'm going to drive over to O. T. and E. T.'s and tell them they'll have to come get him today. I ought to charge for the time he's been here—then it wouldn't happen again."

"They didn't pay but seventy-five dollars for him," Mr. Greenleaf offered.

"I wouldn't have had him as a gift," she said.

"They was just going to beef him," Mr. Greenleaf went on, "but he   75
got loose and run his head into their pickup truck. He don't like cars and

trucks. They had a time getting his horn out the fender and when they finally got him loose, he took off and they was too tired to run after him—but I never known that was him there."

"It wouldn't have paid you to know, Mr. Greenleaf," she said. "But you know now. Get a horse and get him."

In a half hour, from her front window she saw the bull, squirrel-colored, with jutting hips and long light horns, ambling down the dirt road that ran in front of the house. Mr. Greenleaf was behind him on the horse. "That's a Greenleaf bull if I ever saw one," she muttered. She went out on the porch and called, "Put him where he can't get out."

"He likes to bust loose," Mr. Greenleaf said, looking with approval at the bull's rump. "This gentleman is a sport."

"If those boys don't come for him, he's going to be a dead sport," she said. "I'm just warning you."

80   He heard her but he didn't answer.

"That's the awfullest looking bull I ever saw," she called but he was too far down the road to hear.

It was mid-morning when she turned into O. T. and E. T.'s drive-way. The house, a new red-brick, low-to-the-ground building that looked like a warehouse with windows, was on top of a treeless hill. The sun was beating down directly on the white roof of it. It was the kind of house that everybody built now and nothing marked it as belonging to Greenleafs except three dogs, part hound and part spitz, that rushed out from behind it as soon as she stopped her car. She reminded herself that you could always tell the class of people by the class of dog, and honked her horn. While she sat waiting for someone to come, she continued to study the house. All the windows were down and she wondered if the government could have air-conditioned the thing. No one came and she honked again. Presently a door opened and several children appeared in it and stood looking at her, making no move to come forward. She recognized this as a true Greenleaf trait—they could hang in the door, looking at you for hours.

"Can't one of you children come here?" she called.

After a minute they all began to move forward, slowly. They had on overalls and were barefooted but they were not as dirty as she might have expected. There were two or three that looked distinctly like Greenleafs; the others not so much so. The smallest child was a girl with untidy black hair. They stopped about six feet from the automobile and stood looking at her.

85   "You're mighty pretty," Mrs. May said, addressing herself to the smallest girl.

There was no answer. They appeared to share one dispassionate expression between them.

"Where's your Mamma?" she asked.

There was no answer to this for some time. Then one of them said something in French. Mrs. May did not speak French.

"Where's your daddy?" she asked.

After a while, one of the boys said, "He ain't hyar neither."   90

"Ahhhh," Mrs. May said as if something had been proven. "Where's the colored man?"

She waited and decided no one was going to answer. "The cat has six little tongues," she said. "How would you like to come home with me and let me teach you how to talk?" She laughed and her laugh died on the silent air. She felt as if she were on trial for her life, facing a jury of Greenleafs. "I'll go down and see if I can find the colored man," she said.

"You can go if you want to," one of the boys said.

"Well, thank you," she murmured and drove off.

The barn was down the lane from the house. She had not seen it   95
before but Mr. Greenleaf had described it in detail for it had been built according to the latest specifications. It was a milking parlor arrangement where the cows are milked from below. The milk ran in pipes from the machines to the milk house and was never carried in no bucket, Mr. Greenleaf said, by no human hand. "When you gonter get you one?" he had asked.

"Mr. Greenleaf," she had said, "I have to do for myself. I am not assisted hand and foot by the government. It would cost me $20,000 to install a milking parlor. I barely make ends meet as it is."

"My boys done it," Mr. Greenleaf had murmured and then—"but all boys ain't alike."

"No indeed!" she had said. "I thank God for that!"

"I thank Gawd for ever-thang," Mr. Greenleaf had drawled.

You might as well, she had thought in the fierce silence that   100
followed; you've never done anything for yourself.

She stopped by the side of the barn and honked but no one appeared. For several minutes she sat in the car, observing the various machines parked around, wondering how many of them were paid for. They had a forage harvester and a rotary hay baler. She had those too. She decided that since no one was here, she would get out and have a look at the milking parlor and see if they kept it clean.

She opened the milking room door and stuck her head in and for the first second she felt as if she were going to lose her breath. The spotless white concrete room was filled with sunlight that came from a row of windows head-high along both walls. The metal stanchions gleamed ferociously and she had to squint to be able to look at all. She drew her head out the room quickly and closed the door and leaned against it, frowning. The light outside was not so bright but she was conscious that the sun was directly on top of her head, like a silver bullet ready to drop into her brain.

A Negro carrying a yellow calf-feed bucket appeared from around the corner of the machine shed and came toward her. He was a light yellow boy dressed in the cast-off army clothes of the Greenleaf twins. He stopped at a respectable distance and set the bucket on the ground.

"Where's Mr. O. T. and Mr. E. T.?" she asked.

105   "Mist O. T. he in town, Mist E. T. he off yonder in the field," the Negro said, pointing first to the left and then to the right as if he were naming the position of two planets.

"Can you remember a message?" she asked, looking as if she thought this doubtful.

"I'll remember it if I don't forget it," he said with a touch of sullenness.

"Well, I'll write it down then," she said. She got in her car and took a stub of pencil from her pocket book and began to write on the back of an empty envelope. The Negro came and stood at the window. "I'm Mrs. May," she said as she wrote. "Their bull is on my place and I want him off *today*. You can tell them I'm furious about it."

"That bull lef here Sareday," the Negro said, "and none of us ain't seen him since. We ain't knowed where he was."

110   "Well, you know now," she said, "and you can tell Mr. O. T. and Mr. E. T. that if they don't come get him today, I'm going to have their daddy shoot him the first thing in the morning. I can't have that bull ruining my herd." She handed him the note.

"If I knows Mist O. T. and Mist E. T.," he said, taking it, "they goin to say go ahead on and shoot him. He done busted up one of our trucks already and we be glad to see the last of him."

She pulled her head back and gave him a look from slightly bleared eyes. "Do they expect me to take my time and my worker to shoot their bull?" she asked. "They don't want him so they just let him loose and expect somebody else to kill him? He's eating my oats and ruining my herd and I'm expected to shoot him too?"

"I speck you is," he said softly. "He done busted up . . ."

She gave him a very sharp look and said, "Well, I'm not surprised. That's just the way some people are," and after a second she asked, "Which is boss, Mr. O. T. or Mr. E. T.?" She had always suspected that they fought between themselves secretly.

"They never quarls," the boy said. "They like one man in two skins."   115
"Hmp. I expect you just never heard them quarrel."

"Nor nobody else heard them neither," he said, looking away as if this insolence were addressed to someone else.

"Well," she said, "I haven't put up with their father for fifteen years not to know a few things about Greenleafs."

The Negro looked at her suddenly with a gleam of recognition. "Is you my policy man's mother?" he asked.

"I don't know who your policy man is," she said sharply. "You   120 give them that note and tell them if they don't come for that bull today, they'll be making their father shoot it tomorrow," and she drove off.

She stayed at home all afternoon waiting for the Greenleaf twins to come for the bull. They did not come. I might as well be working for them, she thought furiously. They are simply going to use me to the limit. At the supper table, she went over it again for the boys' benefit because she wanted them to see exactly what O. T. and E. T. would do. "They don't want that bull," she said, "—pass the butter—so they simply turn him loose and let somebody else worry about getting rid of him for them. How do you like that? I'm the victim. I've always been the victim."

"Pass the butter to the victim," Wesley said. He was in a worse humor than usual because he had had a flat tire on the way home from the university.

Scofield handed her the butter and said, "Why, Mamma, ain't you ashamed to shoot an old bull that ain't done nothing but give you a little scrub strain in your herd? I declare," he said, "with the Mamma I got it's a wonder I turned out to be such a nice boy!"

"You ain't her boy, Son," Wesley said.

She eased back in her chair, her fingertips on the edge of the table.   125

"All I know is," Scofield said, "I done mighty well to be as nice as I am seeing what I come from."

When they teased her they spoke Greenleaf English but Wesley made his own particular tone come through it like a knife edge. "Well lemme tell you one thang, Brother," he said, leaning over the table, "that if you had half a mind you would already know."

"What's that, Brother?" Scofield asked, his broad face grinning into the thin constricted one across from him.

"That is," Wesley said, "that neither you nor me is her boy. . . . ," but he stopped abruptly as she gave a kind of hoarse wheeze like an old horse lashed unexpectedly. She reared up and ran from the room.

"Oh, for God's sake," Wesley growled, "what did you start her off   130 for?"

"I never started her off," Scofield said. "You started her off."

"Hah."

"She's not as young as she used to be and she can't take it."

"She can only give it out," Wesley said. "I'm the one that takes it."

135   His brother's pleasant face had changed so that an ugly family resemblance showed between them. "Nobody feels sorry for a lousy bastard like you," he said and grabbed across the table for the other's shirtfront.

From her room she heard a crash of dishes and she rushed back through the kitchen into the dining room. The hall door was open and Scofield was going out of it. Wesley was lying like a large bug on his back with the edge of the over-turned table cutting him across the middle and broken dishes scattered on top of him. She pulled the table off him and caught his arm to help him rise but he scrambled up and pushed her off with a furious charge of energy and flung himself out the door after his brother.

She would have collapsed but a knock on the door stiffened her and she swung around. Across the kitchen and back porch, she could see Mr. Greenleaf peering eagerly through the screenwire. All her resources returned in full strength as if she had only needed to be challenged by the devil himself to regain them. "I heard a thump," he called, "and I thought the plastering might have fell on you."

If he had been wanted someone would have had to go on a horse to find him. She crossed the kitchen and the porch and stood inside the screen and said, "No, nothing happened but the table turned over. One of the legs was weak," and without pausing, "the boys didn't come for the bull so tomorrow you'll have to shoot him."

The sky was crossed with thin red and purple bars and behind them the sun was moving down slowly as if it were descending a ladder. Mr. Greenleaf squatted down on the step, his back to her, the top of his hat on a level with her feet. "Tomorrow I'll drive him home for you," he said.

140   "Oh no, Mr. Greenleaf," she said in a mocking voice, "you drive him home tomorrow and next week he'll be back here. I know better than that." Then in a mournful tone, she said, "I'm surprised at O. T. and E. T. to treat me this way. I thought they'd have more gratitude. Those boys spent some mighty happy days on this place, didn't they, Mr. Greenleaf?"

Mr. Greenleaf didn't say anything.

"I think they did," she said. "I think they did. But they've forgotten all the nice little things I did for them now. If I recall, they wore my boys' old clothes and played with my boys' old toys and hunted with my boys' old guns. They swam in my pond and shot my birds and fished in my stream and I never forgot their birthday and Christmas seemed to roll around very often if I remember it right. And do they think of any of those things now?" she asked. "NOOOOO," she said.

For a few seconds she looked at the disappearing sun and Mr. Greenleaf examined the palms of his hands. Presently as if it had just occurred to her, she asked, "Do you know the real reason they didn't come for that bull?"

"Naw I don't," Mr. Greenleaf said in a surly voice.

"They didn't come because I'm a woman," she said. "You can get   145
away with anything when you're dealing with a woman. If there were a man running this place . . ."

Quick as a snake striking Mr. Greenleaf said, "You got two boys. They know you got two men on the place."

The sun had disappeared behind the tree line. She looked down at the dark crafty face, upturned now, and at the wary eyes, bright under the shadow of the hatbrim. She waited long enough for him to see that she was hurt and then she said, "Some people learn gratitude too late, Mr. Greenleaf, and some never learn it at all," and she turned and left him sitting on the steps.

Half the night in her sleep she heard a sound as if some large stone were grinding a hole on the outside wall of her brain. She was walking on the inside, over a succession of beautiful rolling hills, planting her stick in front of each step. She became aware after a time that the noise was the sun trying to burn through the tree line and she stopped to watch, safe in the knowledge that it couldn't, that it had to sink the way it always did outside of her property. When she first stopped it was a swollen red ball, but as she stood watching it began to narrow and pale until it looked like a bullet. Then suddenly it burst through the tree line and raced down the hill toward her. She woke up with her hand over her mouth and the same noise, diminished but distinct, in her ear. It was the bull munching under her window. Mr. Greenleaf had let him out.

She got up and made her way to the window in the dark and looked out through the slit blind, but the bull had moved away from the hedge and at first she didn't see him. Then she saw a heavy form some distance away, paused as if observing her. This is the last night I am going to put up with this, she said, and watched until the iron shadow moved away in the darkness.

The next morning she waited until exactly eleven o'clock. Then she   150
got in her car and drove to the barn. Mr. Greenleaf was cleaning milk cans. He had seven of them standing up outside the milk room to get the

sun. She had been telling him to do this for two weeks. "All right, Mr. Greenleaf," she said, "go get your gun. We're going to shoot that bull."

"I thought you wanted theseyer cans . . ."

"Go get your gun, Mr. Greenleaf," she said. Her voice and face were expressionless.

"That gentleman torn out of there last night," he murmured in a tone of regret and bent again to the can he had his arm in.

"Go get your gun, Mr. Greenleaf," she said in the same triumphant toneless voice. "The bull is in the pasture with the dry cows. I saw him from my upstairs window. I'm going to drive you up to the field and you can run him into the empty pasture and shoot him there."

155   He detached himself from the can slowly. "Ain't nobody ever ast me to shoot my boys' own bull!" he said in a high rasping voice. He removed a rag from his back pocket and began to wipe his hands violently, then his nose.

She turned as if she had not heard this and said, "I'll wait for you in the car. Go get your gun."

She sat in the car and watched him stalk off toward the harness room where he kept a gun. After he had entered the room, there was a crash as if he had kicked something out of his way. Presently he emerged again with the gun, circled behind the car, opened the door violently and threw himself onto the seat beside her. He held the gun between his knees and looked straight ahead. He'd like to shoot me instead of the bull, she thought, and turned her face away so that he could not see her smile.

The morning was dry and clear. She drove through the woods for a quarter of a mile and then out into the open where there were fields on either side of the narrow road. The exhilaration of carrying her point had sharpened her senses. Birds were screaming everywhere, the grass was almost too bright to look at, the sky was an even piercing blue. "Spring is here!" she said gaily. Mr. Greenleaf lifted one muscle somewhere near his mouth as if he found this the most asinine remark ever made. When she stopped at the second pasture gate, he flung himself out of the car door and slammed it behind him. Then he opened the gate and she drove through. He closed it and flung himself back in, silently, and she drove around the rim of the pasture until she spotted the bull, almost in the center of it, grazing peacefully among the cows.

"The gentleman is waiting on you," she said and gave Mr. Greenleaf's furious profile a sly look. "Run him into that next pasture and when you get him in, I'll drive in behind you and shut the gate myself."

160   He flung himself out again, this time deliberately leaving the car door open so that she had to lean across the seat and close it. She sat smiling as she watched him make his way across the pasture toward the

opposite gate. He seemed to throw himself forward at each step and then pull back as if he were calling on some power to witness that he was being forced. "Well," she said aloud as if he were still in the car, "it's your own boys who are making you do this, Mr. Greenleaf." O. T. and E. T. were probably splitting their sides laughing at him now. She could hear their identical nasal voices saying, "Made Daddy shoot our bull for us. Daddy don't know no better than to think that's a fine bull he's shooting. Gonna kill Daddy to shoot that bull!"

"If those boys cared a thing about you, Mr. Greenleaf," she said, "they would have come for that bull. I'm surprised at them."

He was circling around to open the gate first. The bull, dark among the spotted cows, had not moved. He kept his head down, eating constantly. Mr. Greenleaf opened the gate and then began circling back to approach him from the rear. When he was about ten feet behind him, he flapped his arms at his sides. The bull lifted his head indolently and then lowered it again and continued to eat. Mr. Greenleaf stooped again and picked up something and threw it at him with a vicious swing. She decided it was a sharp rock for the bull leapt and then began to gallop until he disappeared over the rim of the hill. Mr. Greenleaf followed at his leisure.

"You needn't think you're going to lose him!" she cried and started the car straight across the pasture. She had to drive slowly over the terraces and when she reached the gate, Mr. Greenleaf and the bull were nowhere in sight. This pasture was smaller than the last, a green arena, encircled almost entirely by woods. She got out and closed the gate and stood looking for some sign of Mr. Greenleaf but he had disappeared completely. She knew at once that his plan was to lose the bull in the woods. Eventually, she would see him emerge somewhere from the circle of trees and come limping toward her and when he finally reached her, he would say, "If you can find that gentleman in them woods, you're better than me."

She was going to say, "Mr. Greenleaf, if I have to walk into those woods with you and stay all afternoon, we are going to find that bull and shoot him. You are going to shoot him if I have to pull the trigger for you." When he saw she meant business, he would return and shoot the bull quickly himself.

She got back into the car and drove to the center of the pasture where he would not have so far to walk to reach her when he came out of the woods. At this moment she could picture him sitting on a stump, making lines in the ground with a stick. She decided she would wait exactly ten minutes by her watch. Then she would begin to honk. She got out of the car and walked around a little and then sat down on the

165

front bumper to wait and rest. She was very tired and she lay her head back against the hood and closed her eyes. She did not understand why she should be so tired when it was only mid-morning. Through her closed eyes, she could feel the sun, red-hot overhead. She opened her eyes slightly but the white light forced her to close them again.

For some time she lay back against the hood, wondering drowsily why she was so tired. With her eyes closed, she didn't think of time as divided into days and nights but into past and future. She decided she was tired because she had been working continuously for fifteen years. She decided she had every right to be tired, and to rest for a few minutes before she began working again. Before any kind of judgment seat, she would be able to say: I've worked, I have not wallowed. At this very instant while she was recalling a lifetime of work, Mr. Greenleaf was loitering in the woods and Mrs. Greenleaf was probably flat on the ground, asleep over her holeful of clippings. The woman had got worse over the years and Mrs. May believed that now she was actually demented. "I'm afraid your wife has let religion warp her," she said once tactfully to Mr. Greenleaf. "Everything in moderation, you know."

"She cured a man oncet that half his gut was eat out with worms," Mr. Greenleaf said, and she had turned away, half-sickened. Poor souls, she thought now, so simple. For a few seconds she dozed.

When she sat up and looked at her watch, more than ten minutes had passed. She had not heard any shot. A new thought occurred to her; suppose Mr. Greenleaf had aroused the bull chunking stones at him and the animal had turned on him and run him up against a tree and gored him? The irony of it deepened: O. T. and E. T. would then get a shyster lawyer and sue her. It would be the fitting end to her fifteen years with the Greenleafs. She thought of it almost with pleasure as if she had hit on the perfect ending for a story she was telling her friends. Then she dropped it, for Mr. Greenleaf had a gun with him and she had insurance.

She decided to honk. She got up and reached inside the car window and gave three sustained honks and two or three shorter ones to let him know she was getting impatient. Then she went back and sat down on the bumper again.

170   In a few minutes something emerged from the tree line, a black heavy shadow that tossed its head several times and then bounded forward. After a second she saw it was the bull. He was crossing the pasture toward her at a slow gallop, a gay almost rocking gait as if he were overjoyed to find her again. She looked beyond him to see if Mr. Greenleaf was coming out of the woods too but he was not. "Here he is, Mr. Greenleaf!" she called and looked on the other side of the pasture

to see if he could be coming out there but he was not in sight. She looked back and saw that the bull, his head lowered, was racing toward her. She remained perfectly still, not in fright, but in a freezing disbelief. She stared at the violent black streak bounding toward her as if she had no sense of distance, as if she could not decide at once what his intention was, and the bull had buried his head in her lap, like a wild tormented lover, before her expression changed. One of his horns sank until it pierced her heart and the other curved around her side and held her in an unbreakable grip. She continued to stare straight ahead but the entire scene in front of her had changed—the tree line was a dark wound in a world that was nothing but sky—and she had the look of a person whose sight has been suddenly restored but who finds the light unbearable.

Mr. Greenleaf was running toward her from the side with his gun raised and she saw him coming though she was not looking in his direction. She saw him approaching on the outside of some invisible circle, the tree line gaping behind him and nothing under his feet. He shot the bull four times through the eye. She did not hear the shots but she felt the quake in the huge body as it sank, pulling her forward on its head, so that she seemed, when Mr. Greenleaf reached her, to be bent over whispering some last discovery into the animal's ear.

QUESTIONS

1. The characters and events of the story are almost entirely reflected through Mrs. May's mind. How objective are her evaluations? How far are they reliable testimony and how far only an index of her own mind?
2. What is Mrs. May's mental image of herself? How does it compare with the image her sons have of her? How does it compare with the reader's image?
3. What is Mrs. May's dominant emotion? What is the consuming preoccupation of her mind? Are there any occasions on which she feels joy? What are they?
4. Describe the behavior of Mrs. May and Greenleaf toward each other. Why does Mrs. May keep Greenleaf on when she despises him so?
5. The two families—the Mays and the Greenleafs—are obviously contrasted. Describe this contrast as fully as possible, considering especially the following: (a) their social and economic status—past, present, and future; (b) their religious attitudes; (c) the attitudes of Mrs. May and Greenleaf respectively toward their children; and (d) Wesley and Scofield versus O. T. and E. T. What are the reasons for Mrs. May's feelings toward the Greenleafs?
6. The turning point of the story comes when Mrs. May commands Greenleaf to get his gun. What emotional reversal takes place at this point? What are Mrs. May's motivations in having the bull shot?

7. "[S]uppose [thinks Mrs. May in paragraph 168] Mr. Greenleaf had aroused the bull chunking stones at him and the animal had turned on him and run him up against a tree and gored him? . . . She thought of it almost with pleasure as if she had hit on the perfect ending for a story she was telling her friends." From what perspective is the actual ending of the story a perfect ending? Is the ending of the story purely chance, or is there a sense in which Mrs. May has brought this on herself?

8. What symbolic implications, if any, have the following: (a) the name Greenleaf; (b) the bull; (c) the sun; (d) Mrs. May's two dreams (paragraphs 4 and 148); and (e) the name May? How important is symbolism to the final effect of the story?

9. What kinds of irony predominate in the story? Identify examples of each of the three kinds of irony. How important is irony to the final effect of the story?

Joyce Carol Oates
Where Are You Going, Where Have You Been?

Her name was Connie. She was fifteen and she had a quick nervous giggling habit of craning her neck to glance into mirrors, or checking other people's faces to make sure her own was all right. Her mother, who noticed everything and knew everything and who hadn't much reason any longer to look at her own face, always scolded Connie about it. "Stop gawking at yourself, who are you? You think you're so pretty?" she would say. Connie would raise her eyebrows at these familiar complaints and look right through her mother, into a shadowy vision of herself as she was right at that moment: she knew she was pretty and that was everything. Her mother had been pretty once too, if you could believe those old snapshots in the album, but now her looks were gone and that was why she was always after Connie.

"Why don't you keep your room clean like your sister? How've you got your hair fixed—what the hell stinks? Hair spray? You don't see your sister using that junk."

Her sister June was twenty-four and still lived at home. She was a secretary in the high school Connie attended, and if that wasn't bad enough—with her in the same building—she was so plain and chunky and steady that Connie had to hear her praised all the time by her mother and her mother's sisters. June did this, June did that, she saved money and helped clean the house and cooked and Connie couldn't do a thing, her mind was all filled with trashy daydreams. Their father was away at work most of the time and when he came home he wanted supper and he read the newspaper at supper and after supper he went to bed. He didn't bother talking much to them, but around his bent head Connie's mother kept picking at her until Connie wished her mother was dead and she herself was dead and it was all over. "She makes me want to throw up sometimes," she complained to her friends. She had a high, breathless, amused voice which made everything she said sound a little forced, whether it was sincere or not.

WHERE ARE YOU GOING, WHERE HAVE YOU BEEN?   First published in 1966. Joyce Carol Oates (b. 1938), one of contemporary America's most prolific writers, is the author of more than eighty volumes of fiction, literary criticism, poetry, and drama. She grew up in rural New York and since 1978 has taught creative writing at Princeton University. Concerning "Where Are You Going, Where Have You Been?" Oates has written that "every third or fourth story of mine is probably in this mode—'realistic allegory,' it might be called. It is Hawthornean, romantic, shading into parable."

There was one good thing: June went places with girl friends of hers, girls who were just as plain and steady as she, and so when Connie wanted to do that her mother had no objections. The father of Connie's best girl friend drove the girls the three miles to town and left them off at a shopping plaza, so that they could walk through the stores or go to a movie, and when he came to pick them up again at eleven he never bothered to ask what they had done.

5   They must have been familiar sights, walking around that shopping plaza in their shorts and flat ballerina slippers that always scuffed the sidewalk, with charm bracelets jingling on their thin wrists; they would lean together to whisper and laugh secretly if someone passed by who amused or interested them. Connie had long dark blond hair that drew anyone's eye to it, and she wore part of it pulled up on her head and puffed out and the rest of it she let fall down her back. She wore a pull-over jersey blouse that looked one way when she was at home and another way when she was away from home. Everything about her had two sides to it, one for home and one for anywhere that was not home: her walk that could be childlike and bobbing, or languid enough to make anyone think she was hearing music in her head, her mouth which was pale and smirking most of the time, but bright and pink on these evenings out, her laugh which was cynical and drawling at home—"Ha, ha, very funny"—but high-pitched and nervous anywhere else, like the jingling of the charms on her bracelet.

Sometimes they did go shopping or to a movie, but sometimes they went across the highway, ducking fast across the busy road, to a drive-in restaurant where older kids hung out. The restaurant was shaped like a big bottle, though squatter than a real bottle, and on its cap was a revolving figure of a grinning boy who held a hamburger aloft. One night in mid-summer they ran across, breathless with daring, and right away someone leaned out a car window and invited them over, but it was just a boy from high school they didn't like. It made them feel good to be able to ignore him. They went up through the maze of parked and cruising cars to the bright-lit, fly-infested restaurant, their faces pleased and expectant as if they were entering a sacred building that loomed out of the night to give them what haven and what blessing they yearned for. They sat at the counter and crossed their legs at the ankles, their thin shoulders rigid with excitement, and listened to the music that made everything so good: the music was always in the background like music at a church service, it was something to depend upon.

A boy named Eddie came in to talk with them. He sat backwards on his stool, turning himself jerkily around in semi-circles and then stopping and turning again, and after a while he asked Connie if she would like something to eat. She said she did and so she tapped her friend's arm on her way out—her friend pulled her face up into a brave droll look—and Connie said she would meet her at eleven, across the way. "I just hate to leave her like that," Connie said earnestly, but the boy said that she wouldn't be alone for long. So they went out to his car and on the way Connie couldn't help but let her eyes wander over the windshields and faces all around her, her face gleaming with a joy that had nothing to do with Eddie or even this place; it might have been the music. She drew her shoulders up and sucked in her breath with the pure pleasure of being alive, and just at that moment she happened to glance at a face just a few feet from hers. It was a boy with shaggy black hair, in a convertible jalopy painted gold. He stared at her and then his lips widened into a grin. Connie slit her eyes at him and turned away, but she couldn't help glancing back and there he was still watching her. He wagged a finger and laughed and said, "Gonna get you, baby," and Connie turned away again without Eddie noticing anything.

She spent three hours with him, at the restaurant where they ate hamburgers and drank Cokes in wax cups that were always sweating, and then down an alley a mile or so away, and when he left her off at five to eleven only the movie house was still open at the plaza. Her girl friend was there, talking with a boy. When Connie came up the two girls smiled at each other and Connie said, "How was the movie?" and the girl said, "*You* should know." They rode off with the girl's father, sleepy and pleased, and Connie couldn't help but look at the darkened shopping plaza with its big empty parking lot and its signs that were faded and ghostly now, and over at the drive-in restaurant where cars were still circling tirelessly. She couldn't hear the music at this distance.

Next morning June asked her how the movie was and Connie said, "So-so."

She and that girl and occasionally another girl went out several times a week that way, and the rest of the time Connie spent around the house—it was summer vacation—getting in her mother's way and thinking, dreaming, about the boys she met. But all the boys fell back and dissolved into a single face that was not even a face, but an idea, a feeling, mixed up with the urgent insistent pounding of the music and the humid night air of July. Connie's mother kept dragging her back to the daylight by finding things for her to do or saying, suddenly, "What's this about the Pettinger girl?"

And Connie would say nervously, "Oh, her. That dope." She always drew thick clear lines between herself and such girls, and her mother was simple and kindly enough to believe her. Her mother was

10

so simple, Connie thought, that it was maybe cruel to fool her so much. Her mother went scuffling around the house in old bedroom slippers and complained over the telephone to one sister about the other, then the other called up and the two of them complained about the third one. If June's name was mentioned her mother's tone was approving, and if Connie's name was mentioned it was disapproving. This did not really mean she disliked Connie and actually Connie thought that her mother preferred her to June because she was prettier, but the two of them kept up a pretense of exasperation, a sense that they were tugging and struggling over something of little value to either of them. Sometimes, over coffee, they were almost friends, but something would come up—some vexation that was like a fly buzzing suddenly around their heads—and their faces went hard with contempt.

One Sunday Connie got up at eleven—none of them bothered with church—and washed her hair so that it could dry all day long, in the sun. Her parents and sister were going to a barbecue at an aunt's house and Connie said no, she wasn't interested, rolling her eyes to let her mother know just what she thought of it. "Stay home alone then," her mother said sharply. Connie sat out back in a lawn chair and watched them drive away, her father quiet and bald, hunched around so that he could back the car out, her mother with a look that was still angry and not at all softened through the windshield, and in the back seat poor old June all dressed up as if she didn't know what a barbecue was, with all the running yelling kids and the flies. Connie sat with her eyes closed in the sun, dreaming and dazed with the warmth about her as if this were a kind of love, the caresses of love, and her mind slipped over onto thoughts of the boy she had been with the night before and how nice he had been, how sweet it always was, not the way someone like June would suppose but sweet, gentle, the way it was in movies and promised in songs; and when she opened her eyes she hardly knew where she was, the back yard ran off into weeds and a fence-line of trees and behind it the sky was perfectly blue and still. The asbestos "ranch house" that was now three years old startled her—it looked small. She shook her head as if to get awake.

It was too hot. She went inside the house and turned on the radio to drown out the quiet. She sat on the edge of her bed, barefoot, and listened for an hour and a half to a program called XYZ Sunday Jamboree, record after record of hard, fast, shrieking songs she sang along with, interspersed by exclamations from "Bobby King": "An' look here you girls at Napoleon's—Son and Charley want you to pay real close attention to this song coming up!"

And Connie paid close attention herself, bathed in a glow of slow-pulsed joy that seemed to rise mysteriously out of the music itself and lay languidly about the airless little room, breathed in and breathed out with each gentle rise and fall of her chest.

After a while she heard a car coming up the drive. She sat up at   15
once, startled, because it couldn't be her father so soon. The gravel kept crunching all the way in from the road—the driveway was long—and Connie ran to the window. It was a car she didn't know. It was an open jalopy, painted a bright gold that caught the sunlight opaquely. Her heart began to pound and her fingers snatched at her hair, checking it, and she whispered "Christ. Christ," wondering how bad she looked. The car came to a stop at the side door and the horn sounded four short taps as if this were a signal Connie knew.

She went into the kitchen and approached the door slowly, then hung out the screen door, her bare toes curling down off the step. There were two boys in the car and now she recognized the driver: he had shaggy, shabby black hair that looked crazy as a wig and he was grinning at her.

"I ain't late, am I?" he said.

"Who the hell do you think you are?" Connie said.

"Toldja I'd be out, didn't I?"

"I don't even know who you are."   20

She spoke sullenly, careful to show no interest or pleasure, and he spoke in a fast bright monotone. Connie looked past him to the other boy, taking her time. He had fair brown hair, with a lock that fell onto his forehead. His sideburns gave him a fierce, embarrassed look, but so far he hadn't even bothered to glance at her. Both boys wore sunglasses. The driver's glasses were metallic and mirrored everything in miniature.

"You wanta come for a ride?" he said.

Connie smirked and let her hair fall loose over one shoulder.

"Don'tcha like my car? New paint job," he said. "Hey."

"What?"   25

"You're cute."

She pretended to fidget, chasing flies away from the door.

"Don'tcha believe me, or what?" he said.

"Look, I don't even know who you are," Connie said in disgust.

"Hey, Ellie's got a radio, see. Mine's broke down." He lifted his   30
friend's arm and showed her the little transistor the boy was holding, and now Connie began to hear the music. It was the same program that was playing inside the house.

"Bobby King?" she said.

"I listen to him all the time. I think he's great."

"He's kind of great," Connie said reluctantly.

"Listen, that guy's *great*. He knows where the action is."

35   Connie blushed a little, because the glasses made it impossible for her to see just what this boy was looking at. She couldn't decide if she liked him or if he was just a jerk, and so she dawdled in the doorway and wouldn't come down or go back inside. She said, "What's all that stuff painted on your car?"

"Can'tcha read it?" He opened the door very carefully, as if he was afraid it might fall off. He slid out just as carefully, planting his feet firmly on the ground, the tiny metallic world in his glasses slowing down like gelatine hardening and in the midst of it Connie's bright green blouse. "This here is my name, to begin with," he said. ARNOLD FRIEND was written in tarlike black letters on the side, with a drawing of a round grinning face that reminded Connie of a pumpkin, except it wore sunglasses. "I wanta introduce myself, I'm Arnold Friend and that's my real name and I'm gonna be your friend, honey, and inside the car's Ellie Oscar, he's kinda shy." Ellie brought his transistor radio up to his shoulder and balanced it there. "Now these numbers are a secret code, honey," Arnold Friend explained. He read off the numbers 33, 19, 17 and raised his eyebrows at her to see what she thought of that, but she didn't think much of it. The left rear fender had been smashed and around it was written, on the gleaming gold background: DONE BY CRAZY WOMAN DRIVER. Connie had to laugh at that. Arnold Friend was pleased at her laughter and looked up at her. "Around the other side's a lot more—you wanta come and see them?"

"No."

"Why not?"

"Why should I?"

40   "Don'tcha wanta see what's on the car? Don'tcha wanta go for a ride?"

"I don't know."

"Why not?"

"I got things to do."

"Like what?"

45   "Things."

He laughed as if she had said something funny. He slapped his thighs. He was standing in a strange way, leaning back against the car as if he were balancing himself. He wasn't tall, only an inch or so taller than she would be if she came down to him. Connie liked the way he was dressed, which was the way all of them dressed: tight faded jeans stuffed into black, scuffed boots, a belt that was a little soiled and showed how lean he was, and a white pull-over shirt that was a little soiled and showed the hard small muscles of his arms and shoulders. He looked as if he probably did hard work, lifting and carrying things. Even his neck looked muscular. And his face was a familiar face, somehow: the jaw and chin and cheeks slightly darkened, because he hadn't shaved for a day or two, and the nose long and hawk-like, sniffing as if she were a treat he was going to gobble up and it was all a joke.

"Connie, you ain't telling the truth. This is your day set aside for a ride with me and you know it," he said, still laughing. The way he straightened and recovered from his fit of laughing showed that it had been all fake.

"How do you know what my name is?" she said suspiciously.

"It's Connie."

"Maybe and maybe not."   50

"I know my Connie," he said, wagging his finger. Now she remembered him even better, back at the restaurant, and her cheeks warmed at the thought of how she sucked in her breath just at the moment she passed him—how she must have looked to him. And he had remembered her. "Ellie and I come out here especially for you," he said. "Ellie can sit in back. How about it?"

"Where?"

"Where what?"

"Where're we going?"

He looked at her. He took off the sunglasses and she saw how pale   55
the skin around his eyes was, like holes that were not in shadow but instead in light. His eyes were chips of broken glass that catch the light in an amiable way. He smiled. It was as if the idea of going for a ride somewhere, to some place, was a new idea to him.

"Just for a ride, Connie sweetheart."

"I never said my name was Connie," she said.

"But I know what it is. I know your name and all about you, lots of things," Arnold Friend said. He had not moved yet but stood still leaning back against the side of the jalopy. "I took a special interest in you, such a pretty girl, and found out all about you like I know your parents and sister are gone somewheres and I know where and how long they're going to be gone, and I know who you were with last night, and your best girl friend's name is Betty. Right?"

He spoke in a simple lilting voice, exactly as if he were reciting the words to a song. His smile assured her that everything was fine. In the car Ellie turned up the volume on his radio and did not bother to look around at them.

"Ellie can sit in the back seat," Arnold Friend said. He indicated his   60
friend with a casual jerk of his chin, as if Ellie did not count and she should not bother with him.

"How'd you find out all that stuff?" Connie said.

"Listen: Betty Schultz and Tony Fitch and Jimmy Pettinger and Nancy Pettinger," he said, in a chant. "Raymond Stanley and Bob Hutter—"

"Do you know all those kids?"

"I know everybody."

65 "Look, you're kidding. You're not from around here."

"Sure."

"But—how come we never saw you before?"

"Sure you saw me before," he said. He looked down at his boots, as if he were a little offended. "You just don't remember."

"I guess I'd remember you," Connie said.

70 "Yeah?" He looked up at this, beaming. He was pleased. He began to mark time with the music from Ellie's radio, tapping his fists lightly together. Connie looked away from his smile to the car, which was painted so bright it almost hurt her eyes to look at it. She looked at that name, ARNOLD FRIEND. And up at the front fender was an expression that was familiar—MAN THE FLYING SAUCERS. It was an expression kids had used the year before, but didn't use this year. She looked at it for a while as if the words meant something to her that she did not yet know.

"What're you thinking about? Huh?" Arnold Friend demanded. "Not worried about your hair blowing around in the car, are you?"

"No."

"Think I maybe can't drive good?"

"How do I know?"

75 "You're a hard girl to handle. How come?" he said. "Don't you know I'm your friend? Didn't you see me put my sign in the air when you walked by?"

"What sign?"

"My sign." And he drew an X in the air, leaning out toward her. They were maybe ten feet apart. After his hand fell back to his side the X was still in the air, almost visible. Connie let the screen door close and stood perfectly still inside it, listening to the music from her radio and the boy's blend together. She stared at Arnold Friend. He stood there so stiffly relaxed, pretending to be relaxed, with one hand idly on the door handle as if he were keeping himself up that way and had no intention of ever moving again. She recognized most things about him, the tight jeans that showed his thighs and buttocks and the greasy leather boots and the tight shirt, and even that slippery friendly smile of his, that sleepy dreamy smile that all the boys used to get across ideas they didn't want to put into words. She recognized all this and also the singsong way he talked, slightly mocking, kidding, but serious and a little melancholy, and she recognized the way he tapped one fist against the other in homage to the perpetual music behind him. But all these things did not come together.

She said suddenly, "Hey, how old are you?"

His smile faded. She could see then that he wasn't a kid, he was much older—thirty, maybe more. At this knowledge her heart began to pound faster.

"That's a crazy thing to ask. Can'tcha see I'm your own age?"   80

"Like hell you are."

"Or maybe a coupla years older, I'm eighteen."

"Eighteen?" she said doubtfully.

He grinned to reassure her and lines appeared at the corners of his mouth. His teeth were big and white. He grinned so broadly his eyes became slits and she saw how thick the lashes were, thick and black as if painted with a black tar-like material. Then he seemed to become embarrassed, abruptly, and looked over his shoulder at Ellie. "*Him,* he's crazy," he said. "Ain't he a riot, he's a nut, a real character." Ellie was still listening to the music. His sunglasses told nothing about what he was thinking. He wore a bright orange shirt unbuttoned halfway to show his chest, which was a pale, bluish chest and not muscular like Arnold Friend's. His shirt collar was turned up all around and the very tips of the collar pointed out past his chin as if they were protecting him. He was pressing the transistor radio up against his ear and sat there in a kind of daze, right in the sun.

"He's kinda strange," Connie said.   85

"Hey, she says you're kinda strange! Kinda strange!" Arnold Friend cried. He pounded on the car to get Ellie's attention. Ellie turned for the first time and Connie saw with shock that he wasn't a kid either—he had a fair, hairless face, cheeks reddened slightly as if the veins grew too close to the surface of his skin, the face of a forty-year-old baby. Connie felt a wave of dizziness rise in her at this sight and she stared at him as if waiting for something to change the shock of the moment, make it all right again. Ellie's lips kept shaping words, mumbling along with the words blasting in his ear.

"Maybe you two better go away," Connie said faintly.

"What? How come?" Arnold Friend cried. "We come out here to take you for a ride. It's Sunday." He had the voice of the man on the radio now. It was the same voice, Connie thought. "Don'tcha know it's Sunday all day and honey, no matter who you were with last night today you're with Arnold Friend and don't you forget it!—Maybe you better step out here," he said, and this last was in a different voice. It was a little flatter, as if the heat was finally getting to him.

"No. I got things to do."

90   "Hey."

"You two better leave."

"We ain't leaving until you come with us."

"Like hell I am—"

"Connie, don't fool around with me. I mean, I mean, don't fool *around*," he said, shaking his head. He laughed incredulously. He placed his sunglasses on top of his head, carefully, as if he were indeed wearing a wig, and brought the stems down behind his ears. Connie stared at him, another wave of dizziness and fear rising in her so that for a moment he wasn't even in focus but was just a blur, standing there against his gold car, and she had the idea that he had driven up the driveway all right but had come from nowhere before that and belonged nowhere and that everything about him and even about the music that was so familiar to her was only half real.

95   "If my father comes and sees you—"

"He ain't coming. He's at a barbecue."

"How do you know that?"

"Aunt Tillie's. Right now they're—uh—they're drinking. Sitting around," he said vaguely, squinting as if he were staring all the way to town and over to Aunt Tillie's backyard. Then the vision seemed to get clear and he nodded energetically. "Yeah. Sitting around. There's your sister in a blue dress, huh? And high heels, the poor sad bitch—nothing like you sweetheart! And your mother's helping some fat woman with the corn, they're cleaning the corn—husking the corn—"

"What fat woman?" Connie cried.

100   "How do I know what fat woman. I don't know every goddam fat woman in the world!" Arnold Friend laughed.

"Oh, that's Mrs. Hornby. . . . Who invited her?" Connie said. She felt a little light-headed. Her breath was coming quickly.

"She's too fat. I don't like them fat. I like them the way you are, honey," he said, smiling sleepily at her. They stared at each other for a while, through the screen door. He said softly, "Now what you're going to do is this: you're going to come out that door. You're going to sit up front with me and Ellie's going to sit in the back, the hell with Ellie, right? This isn't Ellie's date. You're my date. I'm your lover, honey."

"What? You're crazy—"

"Yes, I'm your lover. You don't know what that is but you will," he said. "I know that too. I know all about you. But look: it's real nice and you couldn't ask for nobody better than me, or more polite. I always keep my word. I'll tell you how it is, I'm always nice at first, the first time. I'll hold you so tight you won't think you have to try to get away or pretend anything because you'll know you can't. And I'll come inside you where it's all secret and you'll give in to me and you'll love me—"

"Shut up! You're crazy!" Connie said. She backed away from the door. She put her hands against her ears as if she'd heard something terrible, something not meant for her. "People don't talk like that, you're crazy," she muttered. Her heart was almost too big now for her chest and its pumping made sweat break out all over her. She looked out to see Arnold Friend pause and then take a step toward the porch, lurching. He almost fell. But, like a clever drunken man, he managed to catch his balance. He wobbled in his high boots and grabbed hold of one of the porch posts.

"Honey?" he said. "You still listening?"

"Get the hell out of here!"

"Be nice, honey. Listen."

"I'm going to call the police—"

He wobbled again and out of the side of his mouth came a fast spat curse, an aside not meant for her to hear. But even this "Christ!" sounded forced. Then he began to smile again. She watched this smile come, awkward as if he were smiling from inside a mask. His whole face was a mask, she thought wildly, tanned down to his throat but then running out as if he had plastered makeup on his face but had forgotten about his throat.

"Honey—? Listen, here's how it is. I always tell the truth and I promise you this: I ain't coming in that house after you."

"You better not! I'm going to call the police if you—if you don't—"

"Honey," he said, talking right through her voice, "honey, I'm not coming in there but you are coming out here. You know why?"

She was panting. The kitchen looked like a place she had never seen before, some room she had run inside but which wasn't good enough, wasn't going to help her. The kitchen window had never had a curtain, after three years, and there were dishes in the sink for her to do—probably—and if you ran your hand across the table you'd probably feel something sticky there.

"You listening, honey? Hey?"

"—going to call the police—"

"Soon as you touch the phone I don't need to keep my promise and can come inside. You won't want that."

She rushed forward and tried to lock the door. Her fingers were shaking. "But why lock it," Arnold Friend said gently, talking right into her face. "It's just a screen door. It's just nothing." One of his boots was at a strange angle, as if his foot wasn't in it. It pointed out to the left,

105

110

115

bent at the ankle. "I mean, anybody can break through a screen door and glass and wood and iron or anything else if he needs to, anybody at all and specially Arnold Friend. If the place got lit up with a fire honey you'd come running out into my arms, right into my arms and safe at home—like you knew I was your lover and'd stopped fooling around. I don't mind a nice shy girl but I don't like no fooling around." Part of those words were spoken with a slight rhythmic lilt, and Connie somehow recognized them—the echo of a song from last year, about a girl rushing into her boyfriend's arms and coming home again—

Connie stood barefoot on the linoleum floor, staring at him. "What do you want?" she whispered.

120   "I want you," he said.

"What?"

"Seen you that night and thought, that's the one, yes sir. I never needed to look any more."

"But my father's coming back. He's coming to get me. I had to wash my hair first—" She spoke in a dry, rapid voice, hardly raising it for him to hear.

"No, your daddy is not coming and yes, you had to wash your hair and you washed it for me. It's nice and shining and all for me, I thank you, sweetheart," he said, with a mock bow, but again he almost lost his balance. He had to bend and adjust his boots. Evidently his feet did not go all the way down; the boots must have been stuffed with something so that he would seem taller. Connie stared out at him and behind him Ellie in the car, who seemed to be looking off toward Connie's right, into nothing. This Ellie said, pulling the words out of the air one after another as if he were just discovering them, "You want me to pull out the phone?"

125   "Shut your mouth and keep it shut," Arnold Friend said, his face red from bending over or maybe from embarrassment because Connie had seen his boots. "This ain't none of your business."

"What—what are you doing? What do you want?" Connie said. "If I call the police they'll get you, they'll arrest you—"

"Promise was not to come in unless you touch that phone, and I'll keep that promise," he said. He resumed his erect position and tried to force his shoulders back. He sounded like a hero in a movie, declaring something important. He spoke too loudly and it was as if he were speaking to someone behind Connie. "I ain't made plans for coming in that house where I don't belong but just for you to come out to me, the way you should. Don't you know who I am?"

"You're crazy," she whispered. She backed away from the door but did not want to go into another part of the house, as if this would give him permission to come through the door. "What do you . . . You're crazy, you. . . ."

"Huh? What're you saying, honey?"

Her eyes darted everywhere in the kitchen. She could not remember   130
what it was, this room.

"This is how it is, honey: you come out and we'll drive away, have a nice ride. But if you don't come out we're gonna wait till your people come home and then they're all going to get it."

"You want that telephone pulled out?" Ellie said. He held the radio away from his ear and grimaced, as if without the radio the air was too much for him.

"I toldja shut up, Ellie," Arnold Friend said, "you're deaf, get a hearing aid, right? Fix yourself up. This little girl's no trouble and's gonna be nice to me, so Ellie keep to yourself, this ain't your date—right? Don't hem in on me, don't hog, don't crush, don't bird dog, don't trail me," he said in a rapid meaningless voice, as if he were running through all the expressions he'd learned but was no longer sure which one of them was in style, then rushing on to new ones, making them up with his eyes closed, "Don't crawl under my fence, don't squeeze in my chipmunk hole, don't sniff my glue, suck my Popsicle, keep your own greasy fingers on yourself!" He shaded his eyes and peered in at Connie, who was backed against the kitchen table. "Don't mind him honey he's just a creep. He's a dope. Right? I'm the boy for you and like I said you come out here nice like a lady and give me your hand, and nobody else gets hurt, I mean, your nice old bald-headed daddy and your mummy and your sister in her high heels. Because listen: why bring them in this?"

"Leave me alone," Connie whispered.

"Hey, you know that old woman down the road, the one with the   135
chickens and stuff—you know her?"

"She's dead!"

"Dead? What? You know her?" Arnold Friend said.

"She's dead—"

"Don't you like her?"

"She's dead—she's—she isn't here any more—"   140

"But don't you like her, I mean, you got something against her? Some grudge or something?" Then his voice dipped as if he were conscious of a rudeness. He touched the sunglasses perched on top of his head as if to make sure they were still there. "Now you be a good girl."

"What are you going to do?"

"Just two things, or maybe three," Arnold Friend said. "But I promise it won't last long and you'll like me that way you get to like people you're close to. You will. It's all over for you here, so come on out. You don't want your people in any trouble, do you?"

She turned and bumped against a chair or something, hurting her leg, but she ran into the back room and picked up the telephone. Something roared in her ear, a tiny roaring, and she was so sick with fear that she could do nothing but listen to it—the telephone was clammy and very heavy and her fingers groped down to the dial but were too weak to touch it. She began to scream into the phone, into the roaring. She cried out, she cried for her mother, she felt her breath start jerking back and forth in her lungs as if it were something Arnold Friend were stabbing her with again and again with no tenderness. A noisy sorrowful wailing rose all about her and she was locked inside it the way she was locked inside the house.

145   After a while she could hear again. She was sitting on the floor with her wet back against the wall.

Arnold Friend was saying from the door, "That's a good girl. Put the phone back."

She kicked the phone away from her.

"No, honey. Pick it up. Put it back right."

She picked it up and put it back. The dial tone stopped.

150   "That's a good girl. Now you come outside."

She was hollow with what had been fear, but what was now just an emptiness. All that screaming had blasted it out of her. She sat, one leg cramped under her, and deep inside her brain was something like a pinpoint of light that kept going and would not let her relax. She thought, I'm not going to see my mother again. She thought, I'm not going to sleep in my bed again. Her bright green blouse was all wet.

Arnold Friend said, in a gentle-loud voice that was like a stage voice, "The place where you came from ain't there any more, and where you had in mind to go is cancelled out. This place you are now—inside your daddy's house—is nothing but a cardboard box I can knock down any time. You know that and always did know it. You hear me?"

She thought, I have got to think. I have to know what to do.

"We'll go out to a nice field, out in the country here where it smells so nice and it's sunny," Arnold Friend said. "I'll have my arms around you so you won't need to try to get away and I'll show you what love is like, what it does. The hell with this house! It looks solid all right," he said. He ran a fingernail down the screen and the noise did not make Connie shiver, as it would have the day before. "Now put your hand on your heart, honey. Feel that? That feels solid too but we know better, be nice to me, be sweet like you can because what else is there for a girl like you but to be sweet and pretty and give in?—and get away before her people come back?"

She felt her pounding heart. Her hand seemed to enclose it. She thought for the first time in her life that it was nothing that was hers, that belonged to her, but just a pounding, living thing inside this body that wasn't really hers either.   155

"You don't want them to get hurt," Arnold Friend went on. "Now get up, honey. Get up all by yourself."

She stood.

"Now turn this way. That's right. Come over here to me—Ellie, put that away, didn't I tell you? You dope. You miserable creepy dope," Arnold Friend said. His words were not angry but only part of an incantation. The incantation was kindly. "Now come out through the kitchen to me honey and let's see a smile, try it, you're a brave sweet little girl and now they're eating corn and hotdogs cooked to bursting over an outdoor fire, and they don't know one thing about you and never did and honey you're better than them because not a one of them would have done this for you."

Connie felt the linoleum under her feet; it was cool. She brushed her hair back out of her eyes. Arnold Friend let go of the post tentatively and opened his arms for her, his elbows pointing in toward each other and his wrists limp, to show that this was an embarrassed embrace and a little mocking, he didn't want to make her self-conscious.

She put out her hand against the screen. She watched herself push the door slowly open as if she were safe back somewhere in the other doorway, watching this body and this head of long hair moving out into the sunlight where Arnold Friend waited.   160

"My sweet little blue-eyed girl," he said, in a half-sung sigh that had nothing to do with her brown eyes but was taken up just the same by the vast sunlit reaches of the land behind him and on all sides of him, so much land that Connie had never seen before and did not recognize except to know that she was going to it.

QUESTIONS

1. Oates has called this story a "realistic allegory." What are the allegorical elements in the story?
2. Describe the characterization of Connie. Is she a typical teenage girl of her time and place? What techniques does Oates employ to make her an individual, three-dimensional character?
3. Why is Connie's sister June included in the story? How does her characterization serve to highlight Connie's own?

4. Do the descriptions of Arnold Friend—his face, his clothing, his dialogue— have symbolic meaning? Is his name symbolic?
5. Discuss the symbolic importance of music in the story. Why is music so important to Connie and to the story as a whole?
6. What is the significance of the title? Does it point to an allegorical interpretation?
7. Describe the ways in which the story generates suspense. At which points is an increase of suspense particularly noticeable?
8. Why does Connie agree to go with Arnold Friend? Is she motivated by altruism and a love for her family, or by simple fear and hysteria? What is her ultimate fate?

Joyce Carol Oates
Life after High School

"Sunny? Sun-ny?"

On that last night of March 1959, in soiled sheepskin parka, unbuckled overshoes, but bare-headed in the lightly falling snow, Zachary Graff, eighteen years old, six feet one and a half inches tall, weight 203 pounds, IQ 160, stood beneath Sunny Burhman's second-story bedroom window, calling her name softly, urgently, as if his very life depended upon it. It was nearly midnight: Sunny had been in bed for a half hour, and woke from a thin dissolving sleep to hear her name rising mysteriously out of the dark, low, gravelly, repetitive as the surf. "*Sun-ny—?*" She had not spoken with Zachary Graff since the previous week, when she'd told him, quietly, tears shining in her eyes, that she did not love him; she could not accept his engagement ring, still less marry him. This was the first time in the twelve weeks of Zachary's pursuit of her that he'd dared to come to the rear of the Burhmans' house, by day or night; the first time, as Sunny would say afterward, he'd ever appealed to her in such a way.

They would ask, In what way?

Sunny would hesitate, and say, So—emotionally. In a way that scared me.

5   So you sent him away?

She did. She'd sent him away.

* * *

LIFE AFTER HIGH SCHOOL   First published in 1995. See the footnote to "Where Are You Going, Where Have You Been?" for more information on Oates and her career.

It was much talked-of, at South Lebanon High School, how, in this spring of their senior year, Zachary Graff, who had never to anyone's recollection asked a girl out before, let alone pursued her so publicly and with such clumsy devotion, seemed to have fallen in love with Sunny Burhman.

Of all people—Sunny Burhman.

Odd too that Zachary should seem to have discovered Sunny, when the two had been classmates in the South Lebanon, New York, public schools since first grade, back in 1947.

Zachary, whose father was Homer Graff, the town's preeminent   10 physician, had, since ninth grade, cultivated a clipped, mock-gallant manner when speaking with female classmates; his Clifton Webb style. He was unfailingly courteous, but unfailingly cool; measured; formal. He seemed impervious to the giddy rise and ebb of adolescent emotion, moving, clumsy but determined, like a grizzly bear on its hind legs, through the school corridors, rarely glancing to left or right: his gaze, its myopia corrected by lenses encased in chunky black plastic frames, was firmly fixed on the horizon. Dr. Graff's son was not unpopular so much as feared, thus disliked.

If Zachary's excellent academic record continued uninterrupted through final papers, final exams, and there was no reason to suspect it would not, Zachary would be valedictorian of the Class of 1959. Barbara ("Sunny") Burhman, later to distinguish herself at Cornell, would graduate only ninth, in a class of eighty-two.

Zachary's attentiveness to Sunny had begun, with no warning, immediately after Christmas recess, when classes resumed in January. Suddenly, a half-dozen times a day, in Sunny's vicinity, looming large, eyeglasses glittering, there Zachary *was.* His Clifton Webb pose had dissolved, he was shy, stammering, yet forceful, even bold, waiting for the advantageous moment (for Sunny was always surrounded by friends) to push forward and say, "Hi, Sunny!" The greeting, utterly commonplace in content, sounded, in Zachary's mouth, like a Latin phrase tortuously translated.

Sunny, so-named for her really quite astonishing smile, that dazzling white Sunny-smile that transformed a girl of conventional freckled snub-nosed prettiness to true beauty, might have been surprised, initially, but gave no sign, saying, "Hi, Zach!"

In those years, the corridors of South Lebanon High School were lyric crossfires of *Hi!* and *H'lo!* and *Good to see ya!* uttered hundreds of times daily by the golden girls, the popular, confident, good-looking girls, club officers, prom queens, cheerleaders like Sunny Burhman and her friends, tossed out indiscriminately, for that was the style.

15   Most of the students were in fact practicing Christians, of Lutheran, Presbyterian, Methodist stock.

Like Sunny Burhman, who was, or seemed, even at the time of this story, too good to be true.

That's to say—*good*.

So, though Sunny soon wondered why on earth Zachary Graft was hanging around her, why, again, at her elbow, or lying in wait for her at the foot of a stairs, why, for the nth time that week, *him*, she was too *good* to indicate impatience, or exasperation; too *good* to tell him, as her friends advised, to get lost.

He telephoned her too. Poor Zachary. Stammering over the phone, his voice lowered as if he were in terror of being overheard, "Is S-Sunny there, Mrs. B-Burhman? May I speak with her, please?" And Mrs. Burhman, who knew Dr. Graff and his wife, of course, since everyone in South Lebanon, population 3,800, knew everyone else or knew of them, including frequently their family histories and facts about them of which their children were entirely unaware, hesitated, and said, "Yes, I'll put her on, but I hope you won't talk long—Sunny has homework tonight." Or, apologetically but firmly: "No, I'm afraid she isn't here. May I take a message?"

20   "N-no message," Zachary would murmur, and hurriedly hang up.

Sunny, standing close by, thumbnail between her just perceptibly gap-toothed front teeth, expression crinkled in dismay, would whisper, "Oh Mom. I feel so *bad*. I just feel so—*bad*."

Mrs. Burhman said briskly, "You don't have time for all of them, honey."

Still, Zachary was not discouraged, and with the swift passage of time it began to be observed that Sunny engaged in conversations with him—the two of them sitting, alone, in a corner of the cafeteria, or walking together after a meeting of the Debate Club, of which Zachary was president, and Sunny a member. They were both on the staff of the South Lebanon High Beacon, and the South Lebanon High Yearbook 1959, and the South Lebanon Torch (the literary magazine). They were both members of the National Honor Society and the Quill & Scroll Society. Though Zachary Graff in his aloofness and impatience with most of his peers would be remembered as antisocial, a "loner," in fact, as his record of activities suggested, printed beneath his photograph in the yearbook, he had time, or made time, for things that mattered to him.

He shunned sports, however. High school sports, at least.

25   His life's game, he informed Sunny Burhman, unaware of the solemn pomposity with which he spoke, would be *golf*. His father had been instructing him, informally, since his twelfth birthday.

Said Zachary, "I have no natural talent for it, and I find it profoundly boring, but golf will be my game." And he pushed his chunky black glasses roughly against the bridge of his nose, as he did countless times a day, as if they were in danger of sliding off.

Zachary Graff had such a physical presence, few of his contemporaries would have described him as unattractive, still less homely, ugly. His head appeared oversized, even for his massive body; his eyes were deep-set, with a look of watchfulness and secrecy; his skin was tallow-colored, and blemished, in wavering patches like topographical maps. His big teeth glinted with filaments of silver, and his breath, oddly for one whose father was a doctor, was stale, musty, cobwebby—not that Sunny Burhman ever alluded to this fact, to others.

Her friends began to ask of her, a bit jealously, reproachfully, "What do you two talk about so much?—you and *him?*" and Sunny replied, taking care not to hint, with the slightest movement of her eyebrows, or rolling of her eyes, that, yes, she found the situation peculiar too, "Oh— Zachary and I talk about all kinds of things. *He* talks, mainly. He's brilliant. He's—" pausing, her forehead delicately crinkling in thought, her lovely brown eyes for a moment clouded, "—well, *brilliant.*"

In fact, at first, Zachary spoke, in his intense, obsessive way, of impersonal subjects: the meaning of life, the future of Earth, whether science or art best satisfies the human hunger for self-expression. He said, laughing nervously, fixing Sunny with his shyly bold stare, "Just to pose certain questions is, I guess, to show your hope they can be answered."

Early on, Zachary seemed to have understood that, if he expressed doubt, for instance about "whether God exists" and so forth, Sunny Burhman would listen seriously; and would talk with him earnestly, with the air of a nurse giving a transfusion to a patient in danger of expiring for loss of blood. She was not a religious fanatic, but she *was* a devout Christian—the Burhmans were members of the First Presbyterian Church of South Lebanon, and Sunny was president of her youth group, and, among other good deeds, did YWCA volunteer work on Saturday afternoons; she had not the slightest doubt that Jesus Christ, that's to say His spirit, dwelled in her heart, and that, simply by speaking the truth of what she believed, she could convince others.

Though one day, and soon, Sunny would examine her beliefs, and question the faith into which she'd been born; she had not done so by the age of seventeen and a half. She was a virgin, and virginal in all, or most, of her thoughts.

Sometimes, behind her back, even by friends, Sunny was laughed at, gently—never ridiculed, for no one would ridicule Sunny.

30

Once, when Sunny Burhman and her date and another couple were gazing up into the night sky, standing in the parking lot of the high school, following a prom, Sunny had said in a quavering voice, "It's so big it would be terrifying, wouldn't it?—except for Jesus, who makes us feel at home."

When popular Chuck Crueller, a quarterback for the South Lebanon varsity football team, was injured during a game, and carried off by ambulance to undergo emergency surgery, Sunny mobilized the other cheerleaders, tears fierce in her eyes. "We can do it for Chuck—we can pray." And so the eight girls in their short-skirted crimson jumpers and starched white cotton blouses had gripped one another's hands tight, weeping, on the verge of hysteria, had prayed, prayed, *prayed*—hidden away in the depths of the girls' locker room for hours. Sunny had led the prayers, and Chuck Crueller recovered.

35   So you wouldn't ridicule Sunny Burhman, somehow it wouldn't have been appropriate.

As her classmate Tobias Shanks wrote of her, as one of his duties as literary editor of the 1959 South Lebanon yearbook: *"Sunny" Burhman!— an all-American girl too good to be true who is nonetheless TRUE!*

If there was a slyly mocking tone to Tobias Shanks's praise, a hint that such goodness was predictable, and superficial, and of no genuine merit, the caption, mere print, beneath Sunny's dazzlingly beautiful photograph, conveyed nothing of this.

Surprisingly, for all his pose of skepticism and superiority, Zachary Graff too was a Christian. He'd been baptized Lutheran, and never failed to attend Sunday services with his parents at the First Lutheran Church. Amid the congregation of somber, somnambulant worshippers, Zachary Graff's frowning young face, the very set of his beefy shoulders, drew the minister's uneasy eye; it would be murmured of Dr. Graff's precocious son, in retrospect, that he'd been perhaps too *serious*.

Before falling in love with Sunny Burhman, and discussing his religious doubts with her, Zachary had often discussed them with Tobias Shanks, who'd been his friend, you might say his only friend, since seventh grade. (But only sporadically since seventh grade, since the boys, each highly intelligent, inclined to impatience and sarcasm, got on each other's nerves.) Once, Zachary confided in Tobias that he prayed every morning of his life—immediately upon waking he scrambled out of bed, knelt, hid his face in his hands, and prayed. For his sinful soul, for his sinful thoughts, deeds, desires. He lacerated his soul the way he'd been taught by his mother to tug a fine-toothed steel comb through his coarse, oily hair, never less than once a day.

Tobias Shanks, a self-professed agnostic since the age of fourteen,   40
laughed, and asked derisively, "Yes, but what do you pray *for*, exactly?"
and Zachary had thought a bit, and said, not ironically, but altogether
seriously, "To get through the day. Doesn't everyone?"
This melancholy reply, Tobias was never to reveal.

Zachary's parents were urging him to go to Muhlenberg College,
which was church-affiliated; Zachary hoped to go elsewhere. He said,
humbly, to Sunny Burhman, "If you go to Cornell, Sunny, I—maybe I'll
go there too?"
Sunny hesitated, then smiled. "Oh. That would be nice."
"You wouldn't mind, Sunny?"
"Why would I *mind*, Zachary?" Sunny laughed, to hide her impa-   45
tience. They were headed for Zachary's car, parked just up the hill from
the YM-YWCA building. It was a gusty Saturday afternoon in early
March. Leaving the YWCA, Sunny had seen Zachary Graff standing at
the curb, hands in the pockets of his sheepskin parka, head lowered, but
eyes nervously alert. Standing there, as if accidentally.
It was impossible to avoid him, she had to allow him to drive her
home. Though she was beginning to feel panic, like darting tongues of
flame, at the prospect of Zachary Graff always *there*.
Tell the creep to get lost, her friends counseled. Even her nice
friends were without sentiment regarding Zachary Graff.
Until sixth grade, Sunny had been plain little Barbara Burhman.
Then, one day, her teacher had said, to all the class, in one of those
moments of inspiration that can alter, by whim, the course of an entire
life, "Tell you what, boys and girls—let's call Barbara 'Sunny' from now
on—that's what she *is*."
Ever afterward, in South Lebanon, she was "Sunny" Burhman. Plain
little Barbara had been left behind, seemingly forever.
So, of course, Sunny could not tell Zachary Graff to get lost. Such   50
words were not part of her vocabulary.
Zachary owned a plum-colored 1956 Plymouth which other boys
envied—it seemed to them distinctly unfair that Zachary, of all people,
had his own car, when so few of them, who loved cars, did. But Zachary
was oblivious of their envy, as, in a way, he seemed oblivious of his
own good fortune. He drove the car as if it were an adult duty, with
middle-aged fussiness and worry. He drove the car as if he were its own
chauffeur. Yet, driving Sunny home, he talked—chattered—continuously. Speaking of college, and of religious "obligations," and of his
parents' expectations of him; speaking of medical school; the future;
the life—"beyond South Lebanon."

He asked again, in that gravelly, irksomely humble voice, if Sunny would mind if he went to Cornell. And Sunny said, trying to sound merely reasonable, "Zachary, it's a *free world*."

Zachary said, "Oh no it isn't, Sunny. For some of us, it isn't."

This enigmatic remark Sunny was determined not to follow up.

55   Braking to a careful stop in front of the Burhmans' house, Zachary said, with an almost boyish enthusiasm, "So—Cornell? In the fall? We'll both go to Cornell?"

Sunny was quickly out of the car before Zachary could put on the emergency brake and come around, ceremoniously, to open her door. Gaily, recklessly, infinitely relieved to be out of his company, she called back over her shoulder, "Why not?"

Sunny's secret vanity must have been what linked them.

For several times, gravely, Zachary had said to her, "When I'm with you, Sunny, it's possible for me to believe."

He meant, she thought, in God. In Jesus. In the life hereafter.

60   The next time Zachary maneuvered Sunny into his car, under the pretext of driving her home, it was to present the startled girl with an engagement ring.

He'd bought the ring at Stern's Jewelers, South Lebanon's single good jewelry store, with money secretly withdrawn from his savings account; that account to which, over a period of more than a decade, he'd deposited modest sums with a painstaking devotion. This was his "college fund," or had been—out of the $3,245 saved, only $1,090 remained. How astonished, upset, furious his parents would be when they learned—Zachary hadn't allowed himself to contemplate.

The Graffs knew nothing about Sunny Burhman. So far as they might have surmised, their son's frequent absences from home were nothing out of the ordinary—he'd always spent time at the public library, where his preferred reading was reference books. He'd begin with Volume One of an encyclopedia, and make his diligent way through each successive volume, like a horse grazing a field, rarely glancing up, uninterested in his surroundings.

"Please—will you accept it?"

Sunny was staring incredulously at the diamond ring, which was presented to her, not in Zachary's big clumsy fingers, with the dirt-edged nails, but in the plush-lined little box, as if it might be more attractive that way, more like a gift. The ring was 24-karat gold and the diamond was small but distinctive, and coldly glittering. A beautiful ring, but Sunny did not see it that way.

She whispered, "Oh. Zachary. Oh *no*—there must be some   65
misunderstanding."

Zachary seemed prepared for her reaction, for he said, quickly, "Will
you just try it on?—see if it fits?"

Sunny shook her head. No she couldn't.

"They'll take it back to adjust it, if it's too big," Zachary said. "They
promised."

"Zachary, no," Sunny said gently. "I'm so sorry."

Tears flooded her eyes and spilled over onto her cheeks.   70

Zachary was saying, eagerly, his lips flecked with spittle, "I realize
you don't l-love me, Sunny, at least not yet, but—you could wear the
ring, couldn't you? Just—wear it?" He continued to hold the little box
out to her, his hand visibly shaking. "On your right hand, if you don't
want to wear it on your left? Please?"

"Zachary, no. That's impossible."

"Just, you know, as a, a gift—? Oh Sunny—"

They were sitting in the plum-colored Plymouth, parked, in an
awkwardly public place, on Upchurch Avenue three blocks from Sunny's house. It was 4:25 P.M., March 26, a Thursday: Zachary had lingered
after school in order to drive Sunny home after choir practice. Sunny
would afterward recall, with an odd haltingness, as if her memory of the
episode were blurred with tears, that, as usual, Zachary had done most of
the talking. He had not argued with her, nor exactly begged, but spoke
almost formally, as if setting out the basic points of his debating strategy:
If Sunny did not love him, he could love enough for both; and, If Sunny
did not want to be "officially" engaged, she could wear his ring anyway,
couldn't she?

It would mean so much to him, Zachary said.   75

Life or death, Zachary said.

Sunny closed the lid of the little box, and pushed it from her, gently.
She was crying, and her smooth pageboy was now disheveled. "Oh
Zachary, I'm *sorry*. I *can't*."

Sunny knelt by her bed, hid her face in her hands, prayed.

Please help Zachary not to be in love with me. Please help me not to
be cruel. Have mercy on us both O God.

O God help him to realize he doesn't love me—doesn't know *me*.   80

Days passed, and Zachary did not call. If he was absent from school,
Sunny did not seem to notice.

Sunny Burhman and Zachary Graff had two classes together, English
and physics; but, in the busyness of Sunny's high school life, surrounded by
friends, mesmerized by her own rapid motion as if she were lashed to

the prow of a boat bearing swiftly through the water, she did not seem to notice.

She was not a girl of secrets. She was not a girl of stealth. Still, though she had confided in her mother all her life, she did not tell her mother about Zachary's desperate proposal; perhaps, so flattered, she did not acknowledge it as desperate. She reasoned that if she told either of her parents they would have telephoned Zachary's parents immediately. I can't betray him, she thought.

Nor did she tell her closest girlfriends, or the boy she was seeing most frequently at the time, knowing that the account would turn comical in the telling, that she and her listeners would collapse into laughter, and this too would be a betrayal of Zachary.

85   She happened to see Tobias Shanks, one day, looking oddly at *her*. That boy who might have been twelve years old, seen from a short distance. Sunny knew that he was, or had been, a friend of Zachary Graff's; she wondered if Zachary confided in him; yet made no effort to speak with him. He didn't like her, she sensed.

No, Sunny didn't tell anyone about Zachary and the engagement ring. Of all sins, she thought, betrayal is surely the worst.

"Sunny? Sun-ny?"

She did not believe she had been sleeping but the low, persistent, gravelly sound of Zachary's voice penetrated her consciousness like a dream-voice—felt, not heard.

Quickly, she got out of bed. Crouched at her window without turning on the light. Saw, to her horror, Zachary down below, standing in the shrubbery, his large head uplifted, face round like the moon, and shadowed like the moon's face. There was a light, damp snowfall; blossomlike clumps fell on the boy's broad shoulders, in his matted hair. Sighting her, he began to wave excitedly, like an impatient child.

90   "Oh. Zachary. My God."

In haste, fumbling, she put on a bulky-knit ski sweater over her flannel nightgown, kicked on bedroom slippers, hurried downstairs. The house was already darkened; the Burhmans were in the habit of going to bed early. Sunny's only concern was that she could send Zachary away without her parents knowing he was there. Even in her distress she was not thinking of the trouble Zachary might make for her: she was thinking of the trouble he might make for himself.

Yet, as soon as she saw him close up, she realized that something was gravely wrong. Here was Zachary Graff—yet not Zachary.

He told her he had to talk with her, and he had to talk with her now. His car was parked in the alley, he said.

He made a gesture as if to take her hand, but Sunny drew back. He loomed over her, his breath steaming. She could not see his eyes.

She said no she couldn't go with him. She said he must go home, at once, before her parents woke up.

He said he couldn't leave without her, he had to talk with her. There was a raw urgency, a forcefulness, in him, that Sunny had never seen before, and that frightened her.

She said no. He said yes.

He reached again for her hand, this time taking hold of her wrist. His fingers were strong.

"I told you — I can love enough for both!"

Sunny stared up at him, for an instant mute, paralyzed, seeing not Zachary Graff's eyes but the lenses of his glasses which appeared, in the semidark, opaque. Large snowflakes were falling languidly, there was no wind. Sunny saw Zachary Graff's face which was pale and clenched as a muscle, and she heard his voice which was the voice of a stranger, and she felt him tug at her so roughly her arm was strained in its very socket, and she cried, "No! no! go away! no!"—and the spell was broken, the boy gaped at her another moment, then released her, turned, and ran.

No more than two or three minutes had passed since Sunny unlocked the rear door and stepped outside, and Zachary fled. Yet, afterward, she would recall the encounter as if it had taken a very long time, like a scene in a protracted and repetitive nightmare.

It would be the last time Sunny Burhman saw Zachary Graff alive.

Next morning, all of South Lebanon talked of the death of Dr. Graff's son Zachary: he'd committed suicide by parking his car in a garage behind an unoccupied house on Upchurch Avenue, and letting the motor run until the gas tank was emptied. Death was diagnosed as the result of carbon monoxide poisoning, the time estimated at approximately 4:30 A.M. of April 1, 1959.

Was the date deliberate?—Zachary had left only a single note behind, printed in firm block letters and taped to the outside of the car windshield:

April Fool's Day 1959

To Whom It May (Or May Not) Concern:

I, Zachary A. Graff, being of sound mind & body, do hereby declare that I have taken my own life of my own free will & I hereby declare all others guiltless as they are ignorant of the death of the aforementioned & the life.

(signed)
ZACHARY A. GRAFF

Police officers, called to the scene at 7:45 A.M., reported finding Zachary, lifeless, stripped to his underwear, in the rear seat of the car; the sheepskin parka was oddly draped over the steering wheel, and the interior of the car was, again oddly, for a boy known for his fastidious habits, littered with numerous items: a Bible, several high school textbooks, a pizza carton and some uneaten crusts of pizza, several empty Pepsi bottles, an empty bag of M&M's candies, a pair of new, unlaced gym shoes (size eleven), a ten-foot length of clothesline (in the glove compartment), and the diamond ring in its plush-lined little box from Stern's Jewelers (in a pocket of the parka).

Sunny Burhman heard the news of Zachary's suicide before leaving for school that morning, when a friend telephoned. Within earshot of both her astonished parents, Sunny burst into tears, and sobbed, "Oh my God—it's my fault."

So the consensus in South Lebanon would be, following the police investigation, and much public speculation, not that it was Sunny Burhman's fault, exactly, not that the girl was to blame, exactly, but, yes, poor Zachary Graff, the doctor's son, had killed himself in despondency over her: her refusal of his engagement ring, her rejection of his love.

That was the final season of her life as "Sunny" Burhman.

110   She was out of school for a full week following Zachary's death, and, when she returned, conspicuously paler, more subdued, in all ways less sunny, she did not speak, even with her closest friends, of the tragedy; nor did anyone bring up the subject with her. She withdrew her name from the balloting for the senior prom queen, she withdrew from her part in the senior play, she dropped out of the school choir, she did not participate in the annual statewide debating competition—in which, in previous years, Zachary Graff had excelled. Following her last class of the day she went home immediately, and rarely saw her friends on weekends. Was she in mourning?—or was she simply ashamed? Like the bearer of a deadly virus, herself unaffected, Sunny knew how, on all sides, her classmates and her teachers were regarding her: She was the girl for whose love a boy had thrown away his life, she was an unwitting agent of death.

Of course, her family told her that it wasn't her fault that Zachary Graff had been mentally unbalanced.

Even the Graffs did not blame her—or said they didn't.

Sunny said, "Yes. But it's my fault he's dead."

The Presbyterian minister, who counseled Sunny, and prayed with her, assured her that Jesus surely understood, and that there could be no sin in *her*—it wasn't her fault that Zachary Graff had been mentally unbalanced. And Sunny replied, not stubbornly, but matter-of-factly, sadly, as if stating a self-evident truth, "Yes. But it's my fault he's dead."

Her older sister, Helen, later that summer, meaning only well, said, in exasperation, "Sunny, when are you going to cheer *up*?" and Sunny turned on her with uncharacteristic fury, and said, "Don't call me that idiotic name ever again—I want it *gone!*"

When in the fall she enrolled at Cornell University, she was "Barbara Burhman."

She would remain "Barbara Burhman" for the rest of her life.

Barbara Burhman excelled as an undergraduate, concentrating on academic work almost exclusively; she went on to graduate school at Harvard, in American studies; she taught at several prestigious universities, rising rapidly through administrative ranks before accepting a position, both highly paid and politically visible, with a well-known research foundation based in Manhattan. She was the author of numerous books and articles; she was married, and the mother of three children; she lectured widely, she was frequently interviewed in the popular press, she lent her name to good causes. She would not have wished to think of herself as extraordinary—in the world she now inhabited, she was surrounded by similarly active, energetic, professionally engaged men and women—except in recalling as she sometimes did, with a mild pang of nostalgia, her old, lost self, sweet "Sunny" Burhman of South Lebanon, New York

She hadn't been queen of the senior prom. She hadn't even continued to be a Christian.

The irony had not escaped Barbara Burhman that, in casting away his young life so recklessly, Zachary Graff had freed her for hers.

With the passage of time, grief had lessened. Perhaps in fact it had disappeared. After twenty, and then twenty-five, and now thirty-one years, it was difficult for Barbara, known in her adult life as an exemplar of practical sense, to feel a kinship with the adolescent girl she'd been, or that claustrophobic high school world of the late 1950s. She'd never returned for a single reunion. If she thought of Zachary Graff—about whom, incidentally, she'd never told her husband of twenty-eight years—it was with the regret we think of remote acquaintances, lost to us by accidents of fate. Forever, Zachary Graff, the most brilliant member of the class of 1959 of South Lebanon High, would remain a high school boy, trapped, aged eighteen.

Of that class, the only other person to have acquired what might be called a national reputation was Tobias Shanks, now known as T. R. Shanks, a playwright and director of experimental drama; Barbara Burhman had followed Tobias's career with interest, and had sent him a telegram congratulating him on his most recent play, which went on to win a number of awards, dealing, as it did, with the vicissitudes of gay life in the 1980s. In the winter of 1990 Barbara and Tobias began to encounter each other socially, when Tobias was playwright-in-residence at Bard College, close by Hazelton-on-Hudson where Barbara lived. At first they were strangely shy of each other; even guarded; as if, in even this neutral setting, their South Lebanon ghost-selves exerted a powerful influence. The golden girl, the loner. The splendidly normal, the defiantly "odd." One night Tobias Shanks, shaking Barbara Burhman's hand, had smiled wryly, and said, "It *is* Sunny, isn't it?" and Barbara Burhman, laughing nervously, hoping no one had overheard, said, "No, in fact it isn't. It's Barbara."

They looked at each other, mildly dazed. For one saw a small-boned but solidly built man of youthful middle-age, sweet-faced, yet with ironic, pouched eyes, thinning gray hair, and a close-trimmed gray beard; the other saw a woman of youthful middle-age, striking in appearance, impeccably well-groomed, with fading hair of no distinctive color and faint, white, puckering lines at the edges of her eyes. Their ghost-selves *were* there—not aged, or not aged merely, but transformed, as the genes of a previous generation are transformed by the next.

Tobias stared at Barbara for a long moment, as if unable to speak. Finally he said, "I have something to tell you, Barbara. When can we meet?"

125   Tobias Shanks handed the much-folded letter across the table to Barbara Burhman, and watched as she opened it, and read it, with an expression of increasing astonishment and wonder.

"*He* wrote this? Zachary? To you?"

"He did."

"And you— Did you—?"

Tobias shook his head.

130   His expression was carefully neutral, but his eyes swam suddenly with tears.

"We'd been friends, very close friends, for years. Each other's only friend, most of the time. The way kids that age can be, in certain restricted environments—kids who aren't what's called 'average' or 'normal.' We talked a good deal about religion—Zachary was afraid of hell. We both liked science fiction. We both had very strict parents.

I suppose I might have been attracted to Zachary at times—I knew I was attracted to other guys—but of course I never acted upon it; I wouldn't have dared. Almost no one dared, in those days." He laughed, with a mild shudder. He passed a hand over his eyes. "I couldn't have *loved* Zachary Graff as he claimed he loved me, because—I couldn't. But I could have allowed him to know that he wasn't sick, crazy, 'perverted' as he called himself in that letter." He paused. For a long painful moment Barbara thought he wasn't going to continue. Then he said, with that same mirthless shuddering laugh, "I could have made him feel less lonely. But I didn't. I failed him. My only friend."

Barbara had taken out a tissue, and was dabbing at her eyes.

She felt as if she'd been dealt a blow so hard she could not gauge how she'd been hurt—if there was hurt at all.

She said, "Then it hadn't ever been 'Sunny'—she was an illusion."

Tobias said thoughtfully, "I don't know. I suppose so. There was the sense, at least as I saw it at the time, that, yes, he'd chosen you; decided upon you." 135

"As a symbol."

"Not just a symbol. We all adored you—we were all a little in love with you." Tobias laughed, embarrassed. "Even me."

"I wish you'd come to me and told me, back then. After—it happened."

"I was too cowardly. I was terrified of being exposed, and, maybe, doing to myself what he'd done to himself. Suicide is so very attractive to adolescents." Tobias paused, and reached over to touch Barbara's hand. His fingertips were cold. "I'm not proud of myself, Barbara, and I've tried to deal with it in my writing, but—that's how I was, back then." Again he paused. He pressed a little harder against Barbara's hand. "Another thing—after Zachary went to you, that night, he came to me."

"To you?" 140

"To me."

"And—?"

"And I refused to go with him too. I was furious with him for coming to the house like that, risking my parents discovering us. I guess I got a little hysterical. And he fled."

"He fled."

"Then, afterward, I just couldn't bring myself to come forward. Why I saved that letter, I don't know—I'd thrown away some others that were less incriminating. I suppose I figured—no one knew about me, everyone knew about you. 'Sunny' Burhman." 145

They were at lunch—they ordered two more drinks—they'd forgotten their surroundings—they talked.

After an hour or so Barbara Burhman leaned across the table, as at one of her professional meetings, to ask, in a tone of intellectual curiosity, "What do you think Zachary planned to do with the clothesline?"

QUESTIONS

1. Analyze the characterizations of the three principal figures: Sunny, Zachary, and Tobias. Which of them are developing characters?
2. This story is set in 1959. Today Zachary's behavior would be considered "stalking." Can it be argued that he is a sympathetic character nonetheless? Is he more sympathetic as a boy in 1959 than if the story were set in 1999?
3. What do you infer about the relationship between Zachary and Tobias? Cite evidence from the text for your opinion.
4. After learning the contents of Zachary's letter to Tobias, Barbara Burhman "felt as if she'd been dealt a blow." What is the reason for her discomfort?
5. Discuss the significance of the title. Does it have a different meaning by the end of the story than it has at first glance?
6. Discuss the adult Barbara Burhman's final question. How is this question an appropriate closure to the story?

Joyce Carol Oates

June Birthing

She was one of those who had always believed that mere chance is unworthy of changing a life. But this is how it happened.

Driving home from work that sun-splotched June afternoon thinking how orderly, how newly happy her life, quiet, private, protected from hurt; smooth as the asphalt country highway over which she drove her car so frequently she had almost ceased to see her surroundings—hilly farmland bordered by deciduous trees, fields luminous at this time of year with white-blooming wild rose, the deep ditch beside the road dense with cattails. She was thirty-seven years old and believed she had earned this privacy, this protection. And turning onto the narrower gravel road that led, in a sequence of uphill curves, another two miles to her house, she saw something moving by the side of the road, and at once braked the car to a stop. Something moving, something living. Her first panicked thought was *A baby? Abandoned?*

There, in damp flattened grass at the shoulder of the road, was a new-born fawn.

JUNE BIRTHING   First published in 1996. See the footnote to "Where Are You Going, Where Have You Been?" for more information on Oates and her career.

Kathe approached the creature in amazement. Incredibly, it was no larger than an adult cat. The smallest deer she had ever seen. It was motionless now, though alive; regarding her with large, unperturbed moist brown eyes; its smooth furry coat was freckled and streaked with white. It seemed to be lying on its knees, its head lifted. "Poor thing!" Kathe murmured. "Where is your mother?" She crouched beside the fawn, uncertain what to do. It did not appear to be injured but it was obviously too young to be separated from its mother. Had it been abandoned? Had the mother deer been injured, frightened away by dogs, struck by a car? Hunting was forbidden in this part of north central New Jersey but deer were frequently struck by cars on rural and even suburban roads, the deer population had so increased in recent years.

Kathe was crouched trembling with excitement on the shoulder of   5
the road, staring at the baby fawn which in turn stared back at her. So small! So vulnerable! It could not have been more than a few hours old. Kathe saw no sign of any other deer, no movement in a field of tall grasses and wild rose that lifted to a woods some distance away. She was thinking, *I must do something, I must do something*, but the immediacy of the tiny creature, its extraordinary physical beauty and terrible frailty distracted her, scattered her thoughts like a flock of birds frightened by a gunshot. Strange how she was trembling, as if for a moment she'd actually thought the fawn might be a human baby, abandoned here by the side of the road; delivered, by the madness of chance, to *her*.

Another vehicle approached, taking the curve fast; seeing Kathe's car, the driver hit his brakes, his van skidded a few yards and stopped. A door swung open, a man called out angrily, "Goddamn, what's going on here? This curve is blind—I almost hit you."

The stranger appeared behind Kathe, breathing quickly. A big man in work clothes, torso like the trunk of a thick tree, brawny bare forearms and a broad, heavy-jawed face, dark-tinted glasses flashing light. There was something familiar about him and his mud-splattered Toyota van but Kathe did not know him and his ferocity, his male disgust, made her wince. When he drew nearer, however, and saw the baby fawn in the grass, his expression softened. "Is that a *deer*? Is it alive? My God."

Kathe said quickly, "It's alive, it hasn't been injured. It's just *small*." The man whistled, squatting nearby. "It sure *is*."

Kathe was greatly relieved that the man was sympathetic. He was   10
even willing to confer with her about what should be done. Clearly, the fawn couldn't be left here by itself—it would shortly die, or be killed. The man suggested an animal shelter in Schuylersville, a country town seven miles away—"They'd know what to do with it." Kathe was

surprised and grateful that this stranger should be taking an interest in the tiny creature as intense, or nearly, as her own.

It seemed they would go to the animal shelter together. Neither had exactly agreed yet here was Kathe removing the keys from her car ignition and locking the doors.

When she tried to lift the fawn in her arms, however, it began to tremble violently and made a frantic bleating sound. Kathe was in a sudden terror it would die at her touch, its tiny heart might stop.

The man squatted beside her making cajoling clucking sounds to comfort the fawn. After a moment he carefully slid his hands, which were big work-callused hands, beneath the fawn, and gently lifted it. The fawn was small enough to fit in the palms of his cupped hands.

He has been a father, Kathe thought. He's had experience with babies.

15   Kathe climbed eagerly into the Toyota van, whose motor was still running. The van was mud-splattered along its passenger's side and it was not a recent model but it appeared otherwise in good condition. Kathe pushed aside a jacket, and sat on the high front seat, positioning her knees so that the man, his breath still audible, as if he were mildly asthmatic, set the fawn tenderly into her lap. She was not thinking of the strangeness of this adventure, its dreamlike abruptness and shifts of action. She was not thinking there might be some danger to herself in so trustingly climbing into a stranger's van. Instead she stared as if hypnotized by the tiny creature entrusted to her, trembling in her lap. It had ceased to struggle and was gazing at her with fine-lashed liquid-brown eyes. So beautiful!—the miniature eyes, nose, muzzle, pert upright ears— the smooth fine honey-colored fur—the slender folded legs, no more than six inches long, and the perfect miniature hooves—the animal's blood-warmth and the pulse of its rapidly beating heart: Kathe had never seen, had never held, in her arms, anything so extraordinary.

The man, the burly stranger, climbed up beside her into the van with a grunt and backed the van around so that he could continue on the country highway north and east to Schuylersville. It was past six o'clock but the summer sky was flooded with light as if it were midday. A warm fragrant breeze smelling of wild rose blew through the van's open windows, cooling Kathe's warm skin. She felt feverish. Her heart was beating uncomfortably hard and her mouth had gone dry. As if to relieve the tension the man was speaking casually, commenting on how developed the area was getting; he'd lived out here for the past twelve years, and he'd seen dozens of new houses go up, old farmhouses converted. In fact he'd been involved in some of this—he was a self-employed carpenter and a cabinetmaker. He bred horses for the pleasure of it. His name was—

Kathe was only half listening, staring at the fawn. She sat hunched carefully forward, securing the creature with both hands, pressing it against her belly and thighs; if the van struck a pothole, the fawn could not slip from her grasp.

She said, "I guess I'm a little upset right now, I don't know why. If you don't mind I'd rather not talk."

They rode in silence to the animal shelter in Schuylersville.

Where, as soon as the young woman receptionist sighted them entering with the fawn in Kathe's arms, they were rebuffed. 20

Sorry, no deer, it was state policy. Absolutely no deer.

Kathe confronted the young woman, leaning against the counter, the fawn in her arms blinking in the harsh fluorescent light. She pleaded, she was angry, she was persistent—the fawn was newly born, it was lost from its mother, lying by the side of a road, we can't just let it die, can we? The man too spoke aggressively, arguing that it was the shelter's duty to take in lost and injured animals—wasn't it tax-supported? Her face flushed, the young woman repeated it was policy and there was nothing she could do about it: the deer population in the state was five times denser than it had been in the 1700s—think of that. Anxiously, beginning to be frightened, Kathe held the fawn up for the young woman to see. "But—look how beautiful it is, how tiny and helpless! Look at these eyes! See how it's trembling, it doesn't want to die." The young woman said sullenly, "Sure, I know, all baby animals are darling, but I can't help it, the vet's on duty in the back and he'll tell you the same thing: it's state policy." Kathe asked desperately, "What can I do with it, then? Can I feed it milk, cow's milk, would it drink milk from a baby's bottle?"

The young woman avoided looking at the fawn. The flush in her face, rising from her throat, was deeper. She said, "Frankly, I'd take it back where I found it if I were you. If nothing has happened to the mother deer she'll return to her fawn." The man objected, "But now we've handled the fawn, the doe will smell our scent," and the young woman said, "That won't matter. It really won't. If the doe is all right she won't have forgotten where she left the fawn and she'll come back to get it, probably after dark," and Kathe said, "But it was by the side of a road we found it, in a dangerous place," and the young woman said, patiently, as if speaking to a frightened child or a hysterical person, "Then leave it a few yards away, in a safer place. The doe will find it, I'm sure." Kathe was trembling, hugging the fawn to her breasts. A sudden sense of hopelessness in the face of the world's cold logic struck her; she felt weak, desolate. Absurdly, she was almost in tears. "Please, you wouldn't be lying to us, would you?" she asked. The young woman said curtly, "You shouldn't have taken the fawn away in the first place. Next time, you'll know better."

So the man, now Kathe's infuriated companion, drove them back to the exact spot where Kathe had found the fawn. And there was her car, startling to her eye, as if unexpected, parked at a crooked angle on the shoulder. "Poor thing," Kathe murmured, stepping down from the cab with the fawn in her arms, "I hope your mother hasn't forgotten you." She crossed the ditch, making her way cautiously, and lowered the fawn into a patch of chicory and wild grass. Her heart was beating so hard now that she could scarcely catch her breath. *No, I can't, I can't do this* but wisely, practically, she turned back to the man, who was out of the van, at the side of the road, watching her, and said, "Should we wait a while? And see what happens? In case there's some danger?" She was trying to speak normally and she believed she was speaking normally though her voice quavered and her eyes stung with tears. "In case there are dogs?—or—" The man said quickly, "We can wait a while, sure," surprising her with his reasonableness.

25   Kathe thought, He has had experience with women, or girls, or children, in just such a state. He knows, but he doesn't judge.

So they waited in the van a short distance away. Cars passed from time to time but the fawn, on the far side of the ditch, was safe. Dusk came slowly, by degrees lifting from the earth; out of the woods, out of the undersides of hills, out of the ditch choked with cattails and wild rose. It was nearly eight o'clock and the sky in the west was a brilliant dreamlike wash of pale orange and blue. The man had introduced himself as Lyle Carter, and this time Kathe retained the name, and offered her own, Kathe Connor, which was her maiden name, her unmarried name, startling her ear with its freshness. But she was staring at the fawn, and distracted from Lyle Carter's conversation, she could not concentrate, jamming her knuckles against her mouth and waiting, praying *Let the doe come! God, please! Just this once and I will never ask again.* Several times she had to restrain herself from getting out of the van and going to check to see if the fawn was all right—that small, almost indiscernible shape in the gathering shadows.

It was as if she were hypnotized. She was aware of Lyle Carter's presence, and she could hear his low-pitched, casual voice, and she understood that her behavior was not fully within her control, yet she could not remove her eyes from the fawn, or from the hilly field lifting behind it. An eighth of a mile away there was a woods, and near this woods, at dusk, or very early in the morning, she'd sometimes noticed a small herd of deer when she'd driven by. She narrowed her eyes and tried to see deer there now, or a single deer, a doe; but there was nothing.

Lyle Carter said, "Why don't we go somewhere and wait? Then, when we come back, after dark, the doe will probably have taken away the fawn."

Kathe did not answer at first. Then she said, for she knew she must be reasonable, "If you think the fawn will be safe. If we're not abandoning it . . ."

Lyle Carter said, turning the key in the ignition, "Sure the fawn will   30
be safe. We're not abandoning it."

So they drove now in Lyle Carter's van to the Horseshoe Tavern on the highway which Kathe had passed numerous times but had never entered, nor thought of entering. Inside, the bartender and several men at the bar called out hello to Lyle Carter and he greeted them cheerfully in turn. Kathe noticed that he had a slight limp, favoring his right leg. He led Kathe to a booth by a front window where they had a view of the slow-dissolving sky at dusk and where Kathe ordered a club soda for her first drink and then switched to beer since beer was what Lyle Carter was drinking. She was anxious, but she smiled and responded to Lyle Carter's conversation; by degrees she became more relaxed, and dared to look fully at him. He'd removed his dark glasses and was looking at her. It was not clear if he was smiling or frowning. His eyes were shadowed deep in their sockets, intelligent, watchful, curious. His face was weathered with the sun-creases of early middle age; Kathe guessed him to be in his mid-forties, one of those fair-skinned men who look older than their age. Yet he had an air of good humor, generosity. He was telling her that he knew what it was to feel strongly about an animal—one of his daughters had been distraught for weeks after a young horse of hers died. Kathe did not know how to reply, and so sat silent; she wondered why this information was being offered to her. After a moment Lyle Carter asked Kathe did she have a family?—which was his way, she surmised, of asking if she was married. She told him yes, a family, but no, not a marriage, no longer; and no children. And what about him? Lyle Carter shrugged, and sucked at his beer, as if the effort of self-assessment was physically taxing. He said finally that he'd become accustomed to being alone in this phase of his life and he didn't know if it was good for him, or not so good; or if he had much choice. He laughed, he seemed genuinely amused. "Some things happen, and then other things happen," he said. He seemed about to say more, but did not.

He ordered two more beers for them. Suddenly it was dark. Kathe said, "Should we go back and check? The fawn . . ." and Lyle Carter said, "Let's give the doe another half-hour. Our headlights might scare her off." Kathe looked at the man, raising her eyes to his face, which seemed to her familiar, yes probably she'd been seeing Lyle Carter, and his battered Toyota van, for months, even for years, in and around the country towns in the vicinity, and she smiled at him, for he had such good sense; she guessed him one of those men who pride themselves on their manual dexterity, their physical strength, their moral stubbornness, their rock-bottom common good sense.

She said, "You wouldn't think a single fawn would matter so much, would you?"

QUESTIONS

1. Identify the theme of this story. How does the title help to clarify the theme?
2. Describe Kathe's characterization. Why is she so concerned about the fawn?
3. What are the reader's expectations when Lyle Carter appears on the scene? How are these expectations either met or overturned? What is the significance of Lyle's physical description and characterization? Is he a flat or a developing character?
4. What is the significance of the final conversation between Kathe and Lyle in the tavern? What does Kathe mean by her final question to Lyle that ends the story? How is this an appropriate ending?
5. Despite the brevity of this story, it is a *story* rather than a mere sketch or anecdote. In what way does the story constitute a complete narrative, including a change in the protagonist?

SUGGESTIONS FOR WRITING

The following are suggestions for essays on the featured authors. Use of secondary sources, widely available for the three authors, should assist you in developing your ideas.

1. Compare the characterizations of Connie in "Where Are You Going, Where Have You Been?" and Eveline in "Eveline." In what ways are they typical girls of their era? How do they differ?
2. Study the use of settings in "Greenleaf" and in "The Boarding House." How do the authors employ the settings differently in each story? How are the characters related to the settings of each?
3. Analyze and compare the plot structures of each of the three O'Connor stories. How are the plots similar? How do the main characters' fates elucidate a common theme?
4. Discuss the depiction of the intergenerational relationships in the three O'Connor stories, focusing on Bailey and the grandmother, Mrs. May and her sons Scofield and Wesley, and Julian and his mother. What are the primary similarities and differences in these relationships in the three stories?

5. Write an essay on family dysfunction as dramatized in O'Connor's "A Good Man Is Hard to Find" and Joyce's "Eveline." What do these stories say about family interactions and the relationship of the family to the larger world? What comparisons and contrasts can you identify between the depictions of family in the two stories?

6. Discuss the theme of romantic love in Joyce's "Araby" and "Eveline." What do these stories say about the satisfactions and frustrations of romantic relationships? How are healthy and unhealthy forms of love contrasted and dramatized?

7. Write an essay on one of the following characters, elucidating his or her significance within the story.
   a. Mangan's sister in "Araby"
   b. Frank in "Eveline"
   c. The Misfit in "A Good Man Is Hard to Find"
   d. Red Sammy in "A Good Man Is Hard to Find"
   e. Carver's mother in "Everything That Rises Must Converge"
   f. Mrs. Greenleaf in "Greenleaf"
   g. Mr. Greenleaf in "Greenleaf"
   h. Ellie Oscar in "Where Are You Going, Where Have You Been?"
   i. Tobias Shanks in "Life After High School"
   j. Lyle Carter in "June Birthing"

8. Compare/contrast the relationships of Frank and Eveline in "Eveline" and Kathe and Lyle in "June Birthing." Which relationship has more potential, and why?

9. Compare/contrast the use of irony in any two of the O'Connor stories. In addition to providing humor, how does the use of irony help clarify the theme in each story? How do the characters' stated opinions and judgments and the narrators' implied judgments differ in each?

10. Discuss the use of the following symbols: religious symbolism in "Araby"; the boarding house in "The Boarding House"; the bull in "Greenleaf"; the purple hat in "Everything That Rises Must Converge"; animal symbolism in "A Good Man Is Hard to Find"; the golden car in "Where Are You Going, Where Have You Been?"

Stories for
Further Reading

Chinua Achebe
Civil Peace

Jonathan Iwegbu counted himself extraordinarily lucky. "Happy survival!" meant so much more to him than just a current fashion of greeting old friends in the first hazy days of peace. It went deep to his heart. He had come out of the war with five inestimable blessings— his head, his wife Maria's head, and the heads of three out of their four children. As a bonus he also had his old bicycle—a miracle too but naturally not to be compared to the safety of five human heads.

The bicycle had a little history of its own. One day at the height of the war it was commandeered "for urgent military action." Hard as its loss would have been to him he would still have let it go without a thought had he not had some doubts about the genuineness of the officer. It wasn't his disreputable table rags, nor the toes peeping out of one blue and one brown canvas shoes, nor yet the two stars of his rank done obviously in a hurry in biro,° that troubled Jonathan; many good and heroic soldiers looked the same or worse. It was rather a certain lack of grip and firmness in his manner. So Jonathan, suspecting he might be amenable to influence, rummaged in his raffia bag° and produced the two pounds with which he had been going to buy firewood which his wife, Maria, retailed to camp officials for extra stock-fish and corn meal, and got his bicycle back. That night he buried it in the little clearing in the bush where the dead of the camp, including his own youngest son, were buried. When he dug it up again a year later after the surrender all it needed was a little palm-oil greasing. "Nothing puzzles God," he said in wonder.

He put it to immediate use as a taxi and accumulated a small pile of Biafran money ferrying camp officials and their families across the four-mile stretch to the nearest tarred road. His standard charge per trip was six pounds and those who had the money were only glad to be rid of

CIVIL PEACE   First published in 1972. Chinua Achebe (b. 1930) grew up in eastern Nigeria. From early childhood he was bilingual, speaking both English and Igbo, the language of the Ibo tribe. He studied at London University and earned a B.A. degree from the University College of Ibadan. During the violent seven-year Nigerian Civil War, he served for two years (1967–69) on diplomatic missions for Biafra. Achebe is best known for his 1958 novel, *Things Fall Apart*. He has taught at Nigerian universities and at the University of Massachusetts (Amherst), the University of Connecticut, and UCLA.

biro: ball-point pen   **raffia bag:** bag made from palm tree leaves some of it in this way. At the end of a fortnight he had made a small fortune of one hundred and fifteen pounds.

Then he made the journey to Enugu and found another miracle waiting for him. It was unbelievable. He rubbed his eyes and looked again and it was still standing there before him. But, needless to say, even that monumental blessing must be accounted also totally inferior to the five heads in the family. This newest miracle was his little house in Ogui Overside. Indeed nothing puzzles God! Only two houses away a huge concrete edifice some wealthy contractor had put up just before the war was a mountain of rubble. And here was Jonathan's little zinc house of no regrets built with mud blocks quite intact! Of course the doors and windows were missing and five sheets off the roof. But what was that? And anyhow he had returned to Enugu early enough to pick up bits of old zinc and wood and soggy sheets of cardboard lying around the neighborhood before thousands more came out of their forest holes looking for the same things. He got a destitute carpenter with one old hammer, a blunt plane, and a few bent and rusty nails in his tool bag to turn this assortment of wood, paper, and metal into door and window shutters for five Nigerian shillings or fifty Biafran pounds. He paid the pounds, and moved in with his overjoyed family carrying five heads on their shoulders.

5   His children picked mangoes near the military cemetery and sold them to soldiers' wives for a few pennies—real pennies this time—and his wife started making breakfast akara balls° for neighbors in a hurry to start life again. With his family earnings he took his bicycle to the villages around and bought fresh palm-wine which he mixed generously in his rooms with the water which had recently started running again in the public tap down the road, and opened up a bar for soldiers and other lucky people with good money.

At first he went daily, then every other day, and finally once a week, to the offices of the Coal Corporation where he used to be a miner, to find out what was what. The only thing he did find out in the end was that that little house of his was even a greater blessing than he had thought. Some of his fellow ex-miners who had nowhere to return at the end of the day's waiting just slept outside the doors of the offices and cooked what meal they could scrounge together in Bournvita° tins. As the weeks lengthened and still nobody could say what was what Jonathan discontinued his weekly visits altogether and faced his palm-wine bar.

---

akara balls: made from ground black beans fried in oil   **Bournvita:** a type of candy

But nothing puzzles God. Came the day of the windfall when after five days of endless scuffles in queues and counter-queues in the sun outside the Treasury he had twenty pounds counted into his palms as ex-gratia award° for the rebel money he had turned in. It was like Christmas for him and for many others like him when the payments began. They called it (since few could manage its proper official name) *egg-rasher*.

As soon as the pound notes were placed in his palm Jonathan simply closed it tight over them and buried fist and money inside his trouser pocket. He had to be extra careful because he had seen a man a couple of days earlier collapse into near-madness in an instant before that oceanic crowd because no sooner had he got his twenty pounds than some heartless ruffian picked it off him. Though it was not right that a man in such an extremity of agony should be blamed yet many in the queues that day were able to remark quietly on the victim's carelessness, especially after he pulled out the innards of his pocket and revealed a hole in it big enough to pass a thief's head. But of course he had insisted that the money had been in the other pocket, pulling it out too to show its comparative wholeness. So one had to be careful.

Jonathan soon transferred the money to his left hand and pocket so as to leave his right free for shaking hands should the need arise, though by fixing his gaze at such an elevation as to miss all approaching human faces he made sure that the need did not arise, until he got home.

He was normally a heavy sleeper but that night he heard all the   10
neighborhood noises die down one after another. Even the night watch-man who knocked the hour on some metal somewhere in the distance had fallen silent after knocking one o'clock. That must have been the last thought in Jonathan's mind before he was finally carried away himself. He couldn't have been gone for long, though, when he was violently awakened again.

"Who is knocking?" whispered his wife lying beside him on the floor.

"I don't know," he whispered back breathlessly.

The second time the knocking came it was so loud and imperious that the rickety old door could have fallen down.

"Who is knocking?" he asked then, his voice parched and trembling.

---

ex-gratia award: monetary reward given freely rather than required by law

15   "Na tief-man and him people," came the cool reply. "Make you hopen de door." This was followed by the heaviest knocking of all.

Maria was the first to raise the alarm, then he followed and all their children.

"Police-o! Thieves-o! Neighbors-o! Police-o! We are lost! We are dead! Neighbors, are you asleep? Wake up! Police-o!"

This went on for a long time and then stopped suddenly. Perhaps they had scared the thief away. There was total silence. But only for a short while.

"You done finish?" asked the voice outside. "Make we help you small.° Oya, everybody!"

20   *"Police-o! Tief-man-o! Neighbors-o! we done loss-o! Police-o! . . ."*

There were at least five other voices besides the leader's.

Jonathan and his family were now completely paralyzed by terror. Maria and the children sobbed inaudibly like lost souls. Jonathan groaned continuously.

The silence that followed the thieves' alarm vibrated horribly. Jonathan all but begged their leader to speak again and be done with it.

"My frien," said he at long last, "we don try our best for call dem but I tink say dem all done sleep-o . . . So wetin we go do now? Sometaim you wan call soja? Or you wan make we call dem for you? Soja better pass police. No be so?"

25   "Na so!" replied his men. Jonathan thought he heard even more voices now than before and groaned heavily. His legs were sagging under him and his throat felt like sandpaper.

"My frien, why you no de talk again. I de ask you say you wan make we call soja?"

"No."

"Awrighto. Now make we talk business. We no be bad tief. We no like for make trouble. Trouble done finish. War done finish and all the katakata wey de for inside. No Civil War again. This time na Civil Peace. No be so?"

"Na so!" answered the horrible chorus.

30   "What do you want from me? I am a poor man. Everything I had went with this war. Why do you come to me? You know people who have money. We . . ."

"Awright! We know say you no get plenty money. But we sef no get even anini. So derefore make you open dis window and give us one

"**Make we help you small**": "Let us help you a little" (spoken sarcastically)

hundred pound and we go commot. Orderwise we de come for inside now to show you guitar-boy like dis . . ."

A volley of automatic fire rang through the sky. Maria and the children began to weep aloud again.

"Ah, missisi de cry again. No need for dat. We done talk say we na good tief. We just take our small money and go nwayorly. No molest. Abi we de molest?"

"At all!" sang the chorus.

"My friends," began Jonathan hoarsely. "I hear what you say and I thank you. If I had one hundred pounds . . ."   35

"Lookia my frien, no be play we come play for your house. If we make mistake and step for inside you no go like am-o. So derefore . . ."

"To God who made me; if you come inside and find one hundred pounds, take it and shoot me and shoot my wife and children. I swear to God. The only money I have in this life is this twenty pounds *egg-rasher* they gave me today . . ."

"OK. Time de go. Make you open dis window and bring the twenty pound. We go manage am like dat."

There were now loud murmurs of dissent among the chorus: "Na lie de man de lie; e get plenty money . . . Make we go inside and search properly well . . . Wetin be twenty pound? . . ."

"Shurrup!" rang the leader's voice like a lone shot in the sky and   40
silenced the murmuring at once. "Are you dere? Bring the money quick!"

"I am coming," said Jonathan fumbling in the darkness with the key of the small wooden box he kept by his side on the mat.

At the first sign of light as neighbors and others assembled to commiserate with him he was already strapping his five-gallon demijohn° to his bicycle carrier and his wife, sweating in the open fire, was turning over akara balls in a wide clay bowl of boiling oil. In the corner his eldest son was rinsing out dregs of yesterday's palm-wine from old beer bottles.

"I count it as nothing," he told his sympathizers, his eyes on the rope he was tying. "What is *egg-rasher?* Did I depend on it last week? Or is it greater than other things that went with the war? I say, let *egg-rasher* perish in the flames! Let it go where everything else has gone. Nothing puzzles God."

demijohn: a large, narrow-necked bottle

John Cheever
The Swimmer

It was one of those midsummer Sundays when everyone sits around saying "I *drank* too much last night." You might have heard it whispered by the parishioners leaving church, heard it from the lips of the priest himself, struggling with his cassock in the *vestiarium*, heard it from the golf links and the tennis courts, heard it from the wildlife preserve where the leader of the Audubon group was suffering from a terrible hangover. "I *drank* too much," said Donald Westerhazy. "We all *drank* too much," said Lucinda Merrill. "It must have been the wine," said Helen Westerhazy. "I *drank* too much of that claret."

This was at the edge of the Westerhazys' pool. The pool, fed by an artesian well with a high iron content, was a pale shade of green. It was a fine day. In the west there was a massive stand of cumulus clouds so like a city seen from a distance—from the bow of an approaching ship—that it might have had a name. Lisbon. Hackensack. The sun was hot. Neddy Merrill sat by the green water, one hand in it, one around a glass of gin. He was a slender man—he seemed to have the especial slenderness of youth—and while he was far from young he had slid down his banister that morning and given the bronze backside of Aphrodite on the hall table a smack, as he jogged toward the smell of coffee in his dining room. He might have been compared to a summer's day, particularly the last hours of one, and while he lacked a tennis racket or a sail bag the impression was definitely one of youth, sport, and clement weather. He had been swimming and now he was breathing deeply, stertorously as if he could gulp into his lungs the components of that moment, the heat of the sun, the intenseness of his pleasure. It all seemed to flow into his chest. His own house stood in Bullet Park, eight miles to the south, where his four beautiful daughters would have had their lunch and might be playing tennis. Then it occurred to him that by taking a dogleg to the southwest he could reach his home by water.

His life was not confining and the delight he took in this observation could not be explained by its suggestion of escape. He seemed to see, with a cartographer's eye, that string of swimming pools, that quasi-subterranean stream that curved across the county. He had made a

THE SWIMMER   First published in 1964. John Cheever (1912–1982) was born in Quincy, Massachusetts. After being expelled from a private school at seventeen, he went to New York City and published his first story later that year. He lived in various New England and New York towns, especially in commuter towns near New York City.

discovery, a contribution to modern geography; he would name the stream Lucinda after his wife. He was not a practical joker nor was he a fool but he was determinedly original and had a vague and modest idea of himself as a legendary figure. The day was beautiful and it seemed to him that a long swim might enlarge and celebrate its beauty.

He took off a sweater that was hung over his shoulders and dove in. He had an inexplicable contempt for men who did not hurl themselves into pools. He swam a choppy crawl, breathing either with every stroke or every fourth stroke and counting somewhere well in the back of his mind the one-two one-two of a flutter kick. It was not a serviceable stroke for long distances but the domestication of swimming had saddled the sport with some customs and in his part of the world a crawl was customary. To be embraced and sustained by the light green water was less a pleasure, it seemed, than the resumption of a natural condition, and he would have liked to swim without trunks, but this was not possible, considering his project. He hoisted himself up on the far curb—he never used the ladder—and started across the lawn. When Lucinda asked where he was going he said he was going to swim home.

The only maps and charts he had to go by were remembered or imaginary but these were clear enough. First there were the Grahams, the Hammers, the Lears, the Howlands, and the Crosscups. He would cross Ditmar Street to the Bunkers and come, after a short portage, to the Levys, the Welchers, and the public pool in Lancaster. Then there were the Hallorans, the Sachses, the Biswangers, Shirley Adams, the Gilmartins, and the Clydes. The day was lovely, and that he lived in a world so generously supplied with water seemed like a clemency, a beneficence. His heart was high and he ran across the grass. Making his way home by an uncommon route gave him the feeling that he was a pilgrim, an explorer, a man with a destiny, and he knew that he would find friends all along the way; friends would line the banks of the Lucinda River.

He went through a hedge that separated the Westerhazys' land from the Grahams', walked under some flowering apple trees, passed the shed that housed their pump and filter, and came out at the Grahams' pool. "Why, Neddy," Mrs. Graham said, "what a marvelous surprise. I've been trying to get you on the phone all morning. Here, let me get you a drink." He saw then, like any explorer, that the hospitable customs and traditions of the natives would have to be handled with diplomacy if he was ever going to reach his destination. He did not want to mystify or seem rude to the Grahams nor did he have the time to linger there. He swam the length of their pool and joined them in the sun and was rescued, a few minutes later, by the arrival of two carloads of friends from

5

Connecticut. During the uproarious reunions he was able to slip away. He went down by the front of the Grahams' house, stepped over a thorny hedge, and crossed a vacant lot to the Hammers'. Mrs. Hammer, looking up from her roses, saw him swim by although she wasn't quite sure who it was. The Lears heard him splashing past the open windows of their living room. The Howlands and the Crosscups were away. After leaving the Howlands' he crossed Ditmar Street and started for the Bunkers', where he could hear, even at that distance, the noise of a party.

The water refracted the sound of voices and laughter and seemed to suspend it in midair. The Bunkers' pool was on a rise and he climbed some stairs to a terrace where twenty-five or thirty men and women were drinking. The only person in the water was Rusty Towers, who floated there on a rubber raft. Oh, how bonny and lush were the banks of the Lucinda River! Prosperous men and women gathered by the sapphire-colored waters while caterer's men in white coats passed them cold gin. Overhead a red de Haviland trainer was circling around and around and around in the sky with something like the glee of a child in a swing. Ned felt a passing affection for the scene, a tenderness for the gathering, as if it was something he might touch. In the distance he heard thunder. As soon as Enid Bunker saw him she began to scream: "Oh, look who's here! What a marvelous surprise! When Lucinda said that you couldn't come I thought I'd *die*." She made her way to him through the crowd, and when they had finished kissing she led him to the bar, a progress that was slowed by the fact that he stopped to kiss eight or ten other women and shake the hands of as many men. A smiling bartender he had seen at a hundred parties gave him a gin and tonic and he stood by the bar for a moment, anxious not to get stuck in any conversation that would delay his voyage. When he seemed about to be surrounded he dove in and swam close to the side to avoid colliding with Rusty's raft. At the far end of the pool he bypassed the Tomlinsons with a broad smile and jogged up the garden path. The gravel cut his feet but this was the only unpleasantness. The party was confined to the pool, and as he went toward the house he heard the brilliant, watery sound of voices fade, heard the noise of a radio from the Bunkers' kitchen, where someone was listening to a ball game. Sunday afternoon. He made his way through the parked cars and down the grassy border of their driveway to Alewives Lane. He did not want to be seen on the road in his bathing trunks but there was no traffic and he made the short distance to the Levys' driveway, marked with a PRIVATE PROPERTY sign and a green tube for *The New York Times*. All the doors and windows of the big house were open but there were no signs of life; not even a dog barked. He went around the side of the house to the pool and saw that the Levys had only recently left. Glasses and bottles and dishes of nuts were on a table at the deep end, where there was a bathhouse or gazebo, hung with Japanese lanterns. After swimming the pool he got himself a glass and poured a drink. It was his fourth or fifth drink and he had swum nearly half the length of the Lucinda River. He felt tired, clean, and pleased at that moment to be alone; pleased with everything.

It would storm. The stand of cumulus cloud—that city—had risen and darkened, and while he sat there he heard the percussiveness of thunder again. The de Haviland trainer was still circling overhead and it seemed to Ned that he could almost hear the pilot laugh with pleasure in the afternoon; but when there was another peal of thunder he took off for home. A train whistle blew and he wondered what time it had gotten to be. Four? Five? He thought of the provincial station at that hour, where a waiter, his tuxedo concealed by a raincoat, a dwarf with some flowers wrapped in newspaper, and a woman who had been crying would be waiting for the local. It was suddenly growing dark; it was that moment when the pinheaded birds seem to organize their song into some acute and knowledgeable recognition of the storm's approach. Then there was a fine noise of rushing water from the crown of an oak at his back, as if a spigot there had been turned. Then the noise of fountains came from the crowns of all the tall trees. Why did he love storms, what was the meaning of his excitement when the door sprang open and the rain wind fled rudely up the stairs, why had the simple task of shutting the windows of an old house seemed fitting and urgent, why did the first watery notes of a storm wind have for him the unmistakable sound of good news, cheer, glad tidings? Then there was an explosion, a smell of cordite, and rain lashed the Japanese lanterns that Mrs. Levy had bought in Kyoto the year before last, or was it the year before that?

He stayed in the Levys' gazebo until the storm had passed. The rain had cooled the air and he shivered. The force of the wind had stripped a maple of its red and yellow leaves and scattered them over the grass and the water. Since it was midsummer the tree must be blighted, and yet he felt a peculiar sadness at this sign of autumn. He braced his shoulders, emptied his glass, and started for the Welchers' pool. This meant crossing the Lindleys' riding ring and he was surprised to find it overgrown with grass and all the jumps dismantled. He wondered if the Lindleys had sold their horses or gone away for the summer and put them out to board. He seemed to remember having heard something about the Lindleys and their horses but the memory was unclear. On he went, barefoot through the wet grass, to the Welchers', where he found their pool was dry.

10   This breach in his chain of water disappointed him absurdly, and he felt like some explorer who seeks a torrential headwater and finds a dead stream. He was disappointed and mystified. It was common enough to go away for the summer but no one ever drained his pool. The Welchers had definitely gone away. The pool furniture was folded, stacked, and covered with a tarpaulin. The bathhouse was locked. All the windows of the house were shut, and when he went around to the driveway in front he saw a FOR SALE sign nailed to a tree. When had he last heard from the Welchers—when, that is, had he and Lucinda last regretted an invitation to dine with them? It seemed only a week or so ago. Was his memory failing or had he so disciplined it in the repression of unpleasant facts that he had damaged his sense of the truth? Then in the distance he heard the sound of a tennis game. This cheered him, cleared away all his apprehensions and let him regard the overcast sky and the cold air with indifference. This was the day that Neddy Merrill swam across the county. That was the day! He started off then for his most difficult portage.

Had you gone for a Sunday afternoon ride that day you might have seen him, close to naked, standing on the shoulders of Route 424, waiting for a chance to cross. You might have wondered if he was the victim of foul play, had his car broken down, or was he merely a fool. Standing barefoot in the deposits of the highway—beer cans, rags, and blowout patches—exposed to all kinds of ridicule, he seemed pitiful. He had known when he started that this was a part of his journey—it had been on his maps—but confronted with the lines of traffic, worming through the summery light, he found himself unprepared. He was laughed at, jeered at, a beer can was thrown at him, and he had no dignity or humor to bring to the situation. He could have gone back, back to the Westerhazys', where Lucinda would still be sitting in the sun. He had signed nothing, vowed nothing, pledged nothing, not even to himself. Why, believing as he did, that all human obduracy was susceptible to common sense, was he unable to turn back? Why was he determined to complete his journey even if it meant putting his life in danger? At what point had this prank, this joke, this piece of horseplay become serious? He could not go back, he could not even recall with any clearness the green water at the Westerhazys', the sense of inhaling the day's components, the friendly and relaxed voices saying that they had *drunk* too much. In the space of an hour, more or less, he had covered a distance that made his return impossible.

An old man, tooling down the highway at fifteen miles an hour, let him get to the middle of the road, where there was a grass divider. Here he was exposed to the ridicule of the northbound traffic, but after ten or fifteen minutes he was able to cross. From here he had only a short walk to the Recreation Center at the edge of the village of Lancaster, where there were some handball courts and a public pool.

The effect of the water on voices, the illusion of brilliance and suspense, was the same here as it had been at the Bunkers' but the sounds here were louder, harsher, and more shrill, and as soon as he entered the crowded enclosure he was confronted with regimentation. "ALL SWIMMERS MUST TAKE A SHOWER BEFORE USING THE POOL. ALL SWIMMERS MUST USE THE FOOTBATH. ALL SWIMMERS MUST WEAR THEIR IDENTIFICATION DISKS." He took a shower, washed his feet in a cloudy and bitter solution, and made his way to the edge of the water. It stank of chlorine and looked to him like a sink. A pair of lifeguards in a pair of towers blew police whistles at what seemed to be regular intervals and abused the swimmers through a public address system. Neddy remembered the sapphire water at the Bunkers' with longing and thought that he might contaminate himself—damage his own prosperousness and charm—by swimming in this murk, but he reminded himself that he was an explorer, a pilgrim, and that this was merely a stagnant bend in the Lucinda River. He dove, scowling with distaste, into the chlorine and had to swim with his head above water to avoid collisions, but even so he was bumped into, splashed, and jostled. When he got to the shallow end both lifeguards were shouting at him: "Hey, you, you without the identification disk, get outa the water." He did, but they had no way of pursuing him and he went through the reek of suntan oil and chlorine out through the hurricane fence and passed the handball courts. By crossing the road he entered the wooded part of the Halloran estate. The woods were not cleared and the footing was treacherous and difficult until he reached the lawn and the clipped beech hedge that encircled their pool.

The Hallorans were friends, an elderly couple of enormous wealth who seemed to bask in the suspicion that they might be Communists. They were zealous reformers but they were not Communists, and yet when they were accused, as they sometimes were, of subversion, it seemed to gratify and excite them. Their beech hedge was yellow and he guessed this had been blighted like the Levys' maple. He called hullo, hullo, to warn the Hallorans of his approach, to palliate his invasion of their privacy. The Hallorans, for reasons that had never been explained to him, did not wear bathing suits. No explanations were in order, really. Their nakedness was a detail in their uncompromising zeal for reform and he stepped politely out of his trunks before he went through the opening in the hedge.

15   Mrs. Halloran, a stout woman with white hair and a serene face, was reading the *Times*. Mr. Halloran was taking beech leaves out of the water with a scoop. They seemed not surprised or displeased to see him. Their pool was perhaps the oldest in the county, a fieldstone rectangle, fed by a brook. It had no filter or pump and its waters were the opaque gold of the stream.

"I'm swimming across the county," Ned said.

"Why, I didn't know one could," exclaimed Mrs. Halloran.

"Well, I've made it from the Westerhazys'," Ned said. "That must be about four miles."

He left his trunks at the deep end, walked to the shallow end, and swam this stretch. As he was pulling himself out of the water he heard Mrs. Halloran say, "We've been *terribly* sorry to hear about all your misfortunes, Neddy."

20   "My misfortunes?" Ned asked. "I don't know what you mean."

"Why, we heard that you'd sold the house and that your poor children . . ."

"I don't recall having sold the house," Ned said, "and the girls are at home."

"Yes," Mrs. Halloran sighed. "Yes . . ." Her voice filled the air with an unseasonable melancholy and Ned spoke briskly. "Thank you for the swim."

"Well, have a nice trip," said Mrs. Halloran.

25   Beyond the hedge he pulled on his trunks and fastened them. They were loose and he wondered if, during the space of an afternoon, he could have lost some weight. He was cold and he was tired and the naked Hallorans and their dark water had depressed him. The swim was too much for his strength but how could he have guessed this, sliding down the banister that morning and sitting in the Westerhazys' sun? His arms were lame. His legs felt rubbery and ached at the joints. The worst of it was the cold in his bones and the feeling that he might never be warm again. Leaves were falling down around him and he smelled wood smoke on the wind. Who would be burning wood at this time of year?

He needed a drink. Whiskey would warm him, pick him up, carry him through the last of his journey, refresh his feeling that it was original and valorous to swim across the county. Channel swimmers took brandy. He needed a stimulant. He crossed the lawn in front of the Hallorans' house and went down a little path to where they had built a house for their only daughter, Helen, and her husband, Eric Sachs. The Sachses' pool was small and he found Helen and her husband there.

"Oh, *Neddy*," Helen said. "Did you lunch at Mother's?"

"Not *really*," Ned said. "I *did* stop to see your parents." This seemed to be explanation enough. "I'm terribly sorry to break in on you like this but I've taken a chill and I wonder if you'd give me a drink."

"Why, I'd *love* to," Helen said, "but there hasn't been anything in this house to drink since Eric's operation. That was three years ago."

Was he losing his memory, had his gift for concealing painful facts   30
let him forget that he had sold his house, that his children were in trouble, and that his friend had been ill? His eyes slipped from Eric's face to his abdomen, where he saw three pale, sutured scars, two of them at least a foot long. Gone was his navel, and what, Neddy thought, would the roving hand, bed-checking one's gifts at 3 A.M., make of a belly with no navel, no link to birth, this breach in the succession?

"I'm sure you can get a drink at the Biswangers'," Helen said. "They're having an enormous do. You can hear it from here. Listen!"

She raised her head and from across the road, the lawns, the gardens, the woods, the fields, he heard again the brilliant noise of voices over water. "Well, I'll get wet," he said, still feeling that he had no freedom of choice about his means of travel. He dove into the Sachses' cold water and, gasping, close to drowning, made his way from one end of the pool to the other. "Lucinda and I want *terribly* to see you," he said over his shoulder, his face set toward the Biswangers'. "We're sorry it's been so long and we'll call you *very* soon."

He crossed some fields to the Biswangers' and the sounds of revelry there. They would be honored to give him a drink, they would be happy to give him a drink. The Biswangers invited him and Lucinda for dinner four times a year, six weeks in advance. They were always rebuffed and yet they continued to send out their invitations, unwilling to comprehend the rigid and undemocratic realities of their society. They were the sort of people who discussed the price of things at cocktails, exchanged market tips during dinner, and after dinner told dirty stories to mixed company. They did not belong to Neddy's set—they were not even on Lucinda's Christmas card list. He went toward their pool with feelings of indifference, charity, and some unease, since it seemed to be getting dark and these were the longest days of the year. The party when he joined it was noisy and large. Grace Biswanger was the kind of hostess who asked the optometrist, the veterinarian, the real-estate dealer, and the dentist. No one was swimming and the twilight, reflected on the water of the pool, had a wintry gleam. There was a bar and he started for this. When Grace Biswanger saw him she came toward him, not affectionately as he had every right to expect, but bellicosely.

"Why, this party has everything," she said loudly, "including a gate crasher."

35   She could not deal him a social blow—there was no question about this and he did not flinch. "As a gate crasher," he asked politely, "do I rate a drink?"

"Suit yourself," she said. "You don't seem to pay much attention to invitations."

She turned her back on him and joined some guests, and he went to the bar and ordered a whiskey. The bartender served him but he served him rudely. His was a world in which the caterer's men kept the social score, and to be rebuffed by a part-time barkeep meant that he had suffered some loss of social esteem. Or perhaps the man was new and uninformed. Then he heard Grace at his back say: "They went for broke overnight—nothing but income—and he showed up drunk one Sunday and asked us to loan him five thousand dollars. . . ." She was always talking about money. It was worse than eating your peas off a knife. He dove into the pool, swam its length and went away.

The next pool on his list, the last but two, belonged to his old mistress, Shirley Adams. If he had suffered any injuries at the Biswangers' they would be cured here. Love—sexual roughhouse in fact—was the supreme elixir, the pain killer, the brightly colored pill that would put the spring back into his step, the joy of life in his heart. They had had an affair last week, last month, last year. He couldn't remember. It was he who had broken it off, his was the upper hand, and he stepped through the gate of the wall that surrounded her pool with nothing so considered as self-confidence. It seemed in a way to be his pool, as the lover, particularly the illicit lover, enjoys the possessions of his mistress with an authority unknown to holy matrimony. She was there, her hair the color of brass, but her figure, at the edge of the lighted, cerulean water, excited in him no profound memories. It had been, he thought, a lighthearted affair, although she had wept when he broke it off. She seemed confused to see him and he wondered if she was still wounded. Would she, God forbid, weep again?

"What do you want?" she asked.

40   "I'm swimming across the county."

"Good Christ. Will you ever grow up?"

"What's the matter?"

"If you've come here for money," she said, "I won't give you another cent."

"You could give me a drink."

45   "I could but I won't. I'm not alone."

"Well, I'm on my way."

He dove in and swam the pool, but when he tried to haul himself up onto the curb he found that the strength in his arms and shoulders had gone, and he paddled to the ladder and climbed out. Looking over his shoulder he saw, in the lighted bathhouse, a young man. Going out onto the dark lawn he smelled chrysanthemums or marigolds—some stubborn autumnal fragrance—on the night air, strong as gas. Looking overhead he saw that the stars had come out, but why should he seem to see Andromeda, Cepheus, and Cassiopeia? What had become of the constellations of midsummer? He began to cry.

It was probably the first time in his adult life that he had ever cried, certainly the first time in his life that he had ever felt so miserable, cold, tired, and bewildered. He could not understand the rudeness of the caterer's barkeep or the rudeness of a mistress who had come to him on her knees and showered his trousers with tears. He had swum too long, he had been immersed too long, and his nose and his throat were sore from the water. What he needed then was a drink, some company, and some clean, dry clothes, and while he could have cut directly across the road to his home he went on to the Gilmartins' pool. Here, for the first time in his life, he did not dive but went down the steps into the icy water and swam a hobbled sidestroke that he might have learned as a youth. He staggered with fatigue on his way to the Clydes' and paddled the length of their pool, stopping again and again with his hand on the curb to rest. He climbed up the ladder and wondered if he had the strength to get home. He had done what he wanted, he had swum the county, but he was so stupefied with exhaustion that his triumph seemed vague. Stooped, holding on to the gateposts for support, he turned up the driveway of his own house.

The place was dark. Was it so late that they had all gone to bed? Had Lucinda stayed at the Westerhazys' for supper? Had the girls joined her there or gone someplace else? Hadn't they agreed, as they usually did on Sunday, to regret all their invitations and stay at home? He tried the garage doors to see what cars were in but the doors were locked and rust came off the handles onto his hands. Going toward the house, he saw that the force of the thunderstorm had knocked one of the rain gutters loose. It hung down over the front door like an umbrella rib, but it could be fixed in the morning. The house was locked, and he thought that the stupid cook or the stupid maid must have locked the place up until he remembered that it had been some time since they had employed a maid or a cook. He shouted, pounded on the door, tried to force it with his shoulder, and then, looking in at the windows, saw the place was empty.

Kate Chopin

The Story of an Hour

Knowing that Mrs. Mallard was afflicted with a heart trouble, great care was taken to break to her as gently as possible the news of her husband's death.

It was her sister Josephine who told her, in broken sentences, veiled hints that revealed in half concealing. Her husband's friend Richards was there, too, near her. It was he who had been in the newspaper office when intelligence of the railroad disaster was received, with Brently Mallard's name leading the list of "killed." He had only taken the time to assure himself of its truth by a second telegram, and had hastened to forestall any less careful, less tender friend in bearing the sad message.

She did not hear the story as many women have heard the same, with a paralyzed inability to accept its significance. She wept at once, with sudden, wild abandonment, in her sister's arms. When the storm of grief had spent itself she went away to her room alone. She would have no one follow her.

There stood, facing the open window, a comfortable, roomy armchair. Into this she sank, pressed down by a physical exhaustion that haunted her body and seemed to reach into her soul.

5   She could see in the open square before her house the tops of trees that were all aquiver with the new spring life. The delicious breath of rain was in the air. In the street below a peddler was crying his wares. The notes of a distant song which some one was singing reached her faintly, and countless sparrows were twittering in the eaves.

There were patches of blue sky showing here and there through the clouds that had met and piled one above the other in the west facing her window.

She sat with her head thrown back upon the cushion of the chair, quite motionless, except when a sob came up into her throat and shook her, as a child who has cried itself to sleep continues to sob in its dreams.

She was young, with a fair, calm face, whose lines bespoke repression and even a certain strength. But now there was a dull stare in her eyes, whose gaze was fixed away off yonder on one of those patches of

---

THE STORY OF AN HOUR   First published in 1894. Kate Chopin (1851–1904) is best known for her novel *The Awakening* (1899), which scandalized nineteenth-century critics with its frank treatment of adultery and of a woman's sexual awakening. Chopin was also a prolific short-story writer who often wrote about women trapped in stifling, unhappy marriages.

blue sky. It was not a glance of reflection, but rather indicated a suspension of intelligent thought.

There was something coming to her and she was waiting for it, fearfully. What was it? She did not know; it was too subtle and elusive to name. But she felt it, creeping out of the sky, reaching toward her through the sounds, the scents, the color that filled the air.

Now her bosom rose and fell tumultuously. She was beginning to   10
recognize this thing that was approaching to possess her, and she was striving to beat it back with her will—as powerless as her two white slender hands would have been.

When she abandoned herself a little whispered word escaped her slightly parted lips. She said it over and over under her breath: "Free, free, free!" The vacant stare and the look of terror that had followed it went from her eyes. They stayed keen and bright. Her pulses beat fast, and the coursing blood warmed and relaxed every inch of her body.

She did not stop to ask if it were not a monstrous joy that held her. A clear and exalted perception enabled her to dismiss the suggestion as trivial.

She knew that she would weep again when she saw the kind, tender hands folded in death; the face that had never looked save with love upon her, fixed and gray and dead. But she saw beyond that bitter moment a long procession of years to come that would belong to her absolutely. And she opened and spread her arms out to them in welcome.

There would be no one to live for during those coming years; she would live for herself. There would be no powerful will bending her in that blind persistence with which men and women believe they have a right to impose a private will upon a fellow creature. A kind intention or a cruel intention made the act seem no less a crime as she looked upon it in that brief moment of illumination.

And yet she had loved him—sometimes. Often she had not. What   15
did it matter! What could love, the unsolved mystery, count for in face of this possession of self-assertion which she suddenly recognized as the strongest impulse of her being.

"Free! Body and soul free!" she kept whispering.

Josephine was kneeling before the closed door with her lips to the keyhole, imploring for admission. "Louise, open the door! I beg; open the door—you will make yourself ill. What are you doing, Louise? For heaven's sake open the door."

"Go away. I am not making myself ill." No; she was drinking in a very elixir of life through that open window.

Her fancy was running riot along those days ahead of her. Spring days, and summer days, and all sorts of days that would be her own. She breathed a quick prayer that life might be long. It was only yesterday she had thought with a shudder that life might be long.

20   She arose at length and opened the door to her sister's importunities. There was a feverish triumph in her eyes, and she carried herself unwittingly like a goddess of Victory. She clasped her sister's waist, and together they descended the stairs. Richards stood waiting for them at the bottom.

Some one was opening the front door with a latchkey. It was Brently Mallard who entered, a little travel-stained, composedly carrying his gripsack and umbrella. He had been far from the scene of the accident, and did not even know there had been one. He stood amazed at Josephine's piercing cry; at Richards' quick motion to screen him from the view of his wife.

But Richards was too late.

When the doctors came they said she had died of heart disease—of joy that kills.

William Faulkner
A Rose for Emily

1

When Miss Emily Grierson died, our whole town went to her funeral: the men through a sort of respectful affection for a fallen monument, the women mostly out of curiosity to see the inside of her house, which no one save an old manservant—a combined gardener and cook—had seen in at least ten years.

It was a big, squarish frame house that had once been white, decorated with cupolas and spires and scrolled balconies in the heavily lightsome style of the seventies, set on what had once been our most select street. But garages and cotton gins had encroached and obliterated even the august names of that neighborhood; only Miss Emily's house was left, lifting its stubborn and coquettish decay above the cotton wagons and the gasoline pumps—an eyesore among eyesores. And

A ROSE FOR EMILY   First published in 1930. William Faulkner (1897–1962) spent most of his life in Oxford, Mississippi, the small town he mythologized as "Jefferson" in his fiction. Faulkner's novels and stories often portray small-town southerners isolated psychologically—sometimes to an extreme degree—from the modern world. He won the Nobel Prize for literature in 1950.

now Miss Emily had gone to join the representatives of those august names where they lay in the cedar-bemused cemetery among the ranked and anonymous graves of Union and Confederate soldiers who fell at the battle of Jefferson.

Alive, Miss Emily had been a tradition, a duty, and a care; a sort of hereditary obligation upon the town, dating from that day in 1894 when Colonel Sartoris, the mayor—he who fathered the edict that no Negro woman should appear on the streets without an apron—remitted her taxes, the dispensation dating from the death of her father on into perpetuity. Not that Miss Emily would have accepted charity. Colonel Sartoris invented an involved tale to the effect that Miss Emily's father had loaned money to the town, which the town, as a matter of business, preferred this way of repaying. Only a man of Colonel Sartoris' generation and thought could have invented it, and only a woman could have believed it.

When the next generation, with its more modern ideas, became mayors and aldermen, this arrangement created some little dissatisfaction. On the first of the year they mailed her a tax notice. February came, and there was no reply. They wrote her a formal letter, asking her to call at the sheriff's office at her convenience. A week later the mayor wrote her himself, offering to call or to send his car for her, and received in reply a note on paper of an archaic shape, in a thin, flowing calligraphy in faded ink, to the effect that she no longer went out at all. The tax notice was also enclosed, without comment.

They called a special meeting of the Board of Aldermen. A deputation waited upon her, knocked at the door through which no visitor had passed since she ceased giving china-painting lessons eight or ten years earlier. They were admitted by the old Negro into a dim hall from which a stairway mounted into still more shadow. It smelled of dust and disuse—a close, dank smell. The Negro led them into the parlor. It was furnished in heavy, leather-covered furniture. When the Negro opened the blinds of one window, a faint dust rose sluggishly about their thighs, spinning with slow motes in the single sun-ray. On a tarnished gilt easel before the fireplace stood a crayon portrait of Miss Emily's father.

They rose when she entered—a small, fat woman in black, with a thin gold chain descending to her waist and vanishing into her belt, leaning on an ebony cane with a tarnished gold head. Her skeleton was small and spare; perhaps that was why what would have been merely plumpness in another was obesity in her. She looked bloated, like a body long submerged in motionless water, and of that pallid hue. Her eyes, lost in the fatty ridges of her face, looked like two small pieces of coal

5

pressed into a lump of dough as they moved from one face to another while the visitors stated their errand.

She did not ask them to sit. She just stood in the door and listened quietly until the spokesman came to a stumbling halt. Then they could hear the invisible watch ticking at the end of the gold chain.

Her voice was dry and cold. "I have no taxes in Jefferson. Colonel Sartoris explained it to me. Perhaps one of you can gain access to the city records and satisfy yourselves."

"But we have. We are the city authorities, Miss Emily. Didn't you get a notice from the sheriff, signed by him?"

10   "I received a paper, yes," Miss Emily said. "Perhaps he considers himself the sheriff. . . . I have no taxes in Jefferson."

"But there is nothing on the books to show that, you see. We must go by the—"

"See Colonel Sartoris. I have no taxes in Jefferson."

"But, Miss Emily—"

"See Colonel Sartoris." (Colonel Sartoris had been dead almost ten years.) "I have no taxes in Jefferson. Tobe!" The Negro appeared. "Show these gentlemen out."

2

15   So she vanquished them, horse and foot, just as she had vanquished their fathers thirty years before about the smell. That was two years after her father's death and a short time after her sweetheart—the one we believed would marry her—had deserted her. After her father's death she went out very little; after her sweetheart went away, people hardly saw her at all. A few of the ladies had the temerity to call, but were not received, and the only sign of life about the place was the Negro man—a young man then—going in and out with a market basket.

"Just as if a man—any man—could keep a kitchen properly," the ladies said; so they were not surprised when the smell developed. It was another link between the gross, teeming world and the high and mighty Griersons.

A neighbor, a woman, complained to the mayor, Judge Stevens, eighty years old.

"But what will you have me do about it, madam?" he said.

"Why, send her word to stop it," the woman said. "Isn't there a law?"

20   "I'm sure that won't be necessary," Judge Stevens said. "It's probably just a snake or a rat that nigger of hers killed in the yard. I'll speak to him about it."

The next day he received two more complaints, one from a man who came in diffident deprecation. "We really must do something about it, Judge. I'd be the last one in the world to bother Miss Emily, but we've got to do something." That night the Board of Aldermen met—three gray-beards and one younger man, a member of the rising generation.

"It's simple enough," he said. "Send her word to have her place cleaned up. Give her a certain time to do it in, and if she don't . . ."

"Dammit, sir," Judge Stevens said, "will you accuse a lady to her face of smelling bad?"

So the next night, after midnight, four men crossed Miss Emily's lawn and slunk about the house like burglars, sniffing along the base of the brickwork and at the cellar openings while one of them performed a regular sowing motion with his hand out of a sack slung from his shoulder. They broke open the cellar door and sprinkled lime there, and in all the outbuildings. As they recrossed the lawn, a window that had been dark was lighted and Miss Emily sat in it, the light behind her, and her upright torso motionless as that of an idol. They crept quietly across the lawn and into the shadow of the locusts that lined the street. After a week or two the smell went away.

That was when people had begun to feel really sorry for her. People in our town, remembering how old lady Wyatt, her great-aunt, had gone completely crazy at last, believed that the Griersons held themselves a little too high for what they really were. None of the young men were quite good enough for Miss Emily and such. We had long thought of them as a tableau; Miss Emily a slender figure in white in the background, her father a spraddled silhouette in the foreground, his back to her and clutching a horsewhip, the two of them framed by the back-flung front door. So when she got to be thirty and was still single, we were not pleased exactly, but vindicated; even with insanity in the family she wouldn't have turned down all of her chances if they had really materialized. 25

When her father died, it got about that the house was all that was left to her; and in a way, people were glad. At last they could pity Miss Emily. Being left alone, and a pauper, she had become humanized. Now she too would know the old thrill and the old despair of a penny more or less.

The day after his death all the ladies prepared to call at the house and offer condolence and aid, as is our custom. Miss Emily met them at the door, dressed as usual and with no trace of grief on her face. She told them that her father was not dead. She did that for three days, with the ministers calling on her, and the doctors, trying to persuade her to let them dispose of the body. Just as they were about to resort to law and force, she broke down, and they buried her father quickly.

We did not say she was crazy then. We believed she had to do that. We remembered all the young men her father had driven away, and we knew that with nothing left, she would have to cling to that which had robbed her, as people will.

3

She was sick for a long time. When we saw her again, her hair was cut short, making her look like a girl, with a vague resemblance to those angels in colored church windows—sort of tragic and serene.

30   The town had just let the contracts for paving the sidewalks, and in the summer after her father's death they began to work. The construction company came with niggers and mules and machinery, and a foreman named Homer Barron, a Yankee—a big, dark, ready man, with a big voice and eyes lighter than his face. The little boys would follow in groups to hear him cuss the niggers, and the niggers singing in time to the rise and fall of picks. Pretty soon he knew everybody in town. Whenever you heard a lot of laughing anywhere about the square, Homer Barron would be in the center of the group. Presently we began to see him and Miss Emily on Sunday afternoons driving in the yellow-wheeled buggy and the matched team of bays from the livery stable.

At first we were glad that Miss Emily would have an interest, because the ladies all said, "Of course a Grierson would not think seriously of a Northerner, a day laborer." But there were still others, older people, who said that even grief could not cause a real lady to forget *noblesse oblige*—without calling it *noblesse oblige*. They just said, "Poor Emily. Her kinsfolk should come to her." She had some kin in Alabama; but years ago her father had fallen out with them over the estate of old lady Wyatt, the crazy woman, and there was no communication between the two families. They had not even been represented at the funeral.

And as soon as the old people said, "Poor Emily," the whispering began. "Do you suppose it's really so?" they said to one another. "Of course it is. What else could . . ." This behind their hands; rustling of craned silk and satin behind jalousies closed upon the sun of Sunday afternoon as the thin, swift clop-clop-clop of the matched team passed: "Poor Emily."

She carried her head high enough—even when we believed that she was fallen. It was as if she demanded more than ever the recognition of her dignity as the last Grierson; as if it had wanted that touch of earthiness to reaffirm her imperviousness. Like when she bought the rat poison, the arsenic. That was over a year after they had begun to say "Poor Emily," and while the two female cousins were visiting her.

"I want some poison," she said to the druggist. She was over thirty then, still a slight woman, though thinner than usual, with cold, haughty black eyes in a face the flesh of which was strained across the temples and about the eyesockets as you imagine a lighthouse-keeper's face ought to look. "I want some poison," she said.

"Yes, Miss Emily. What kind? For rats and such? I'd recom—"   35

"I want the best you have. I don't care what kind."

The druggist named several. "They'll kill anything up to an elephant. But what you want is—"

"Arsenic," Miss Emily said. "Is that a good one?"

"Is . . . arsenic? Yes ma'am. But what you want—"

"I want arsenic."   40

The druggist looked down at her. She looked back at him, erect, her face like a strained flag. "Why, of course," the druggist said. "If that's what you want. But the law requires you to tell what you are going to use it for."

Miss Emily just stared at him, her head tilted back in order to look him eye for eye, until he looked away and went and got the arsenic and wrapped it up. The Negro delivery boy brought her the package; the druggist didn't come back. When she opened the package at home there was written on the box, under the skull and bones: "For rats."

4

So the next day we all said, "She will kill herself"; and we said it would be the best thing. When she had first begun to be seen with Homer Barron, we had said, "She will marry him." Then we said, "She will persuade him yet," because Homer himself had remarked—he liked men, and it was known that he drank with the younger men in the Elk's Club—that he was not a marrying man. Later we said, "Poor Emily," behind the jalousies as they passed on Sunday afternoon in the glittering buggy, Miss Emily with her head high and Homer Barron with his hat cocked and a cigar in his teeth, reins and whip in a yellow glove.

Then some of the ladies began to say that it was a disgrace to the town and a bad example to the young people. The men did not want to interfere, but at last the ladies forced the Baptist minister—Miss Emily's people were Episcopal—to call upon her. He would never divulge what happened during that interview, but he refused to go back again. The next Sunday they again drove about the streets, and the following day the minister's wife wrote to Miss Emily's relations in Alabama.

45   So she had blood-kin under her roof again and we sat back to watch developments. At first nothing happened. Then we were sure that they were to be married. We learned that Miss Emily had been to the jeweler's and ordered a man's toilet set in silver, with the letters H. B. on each piece. Two days later we learned that she had bought a complete outfit of men's clothing, including a nightshirt, and we said, "They are married." We were really glad. We were glad because the two female cousins were even more Grierson than Miss Emily had ever been.

So we were not surprised when Homer Barron—the streets had been finished some time since—was gone. We were a little disappointed that there was not a public blowing-off, but we believed that he had gone on to prepare for Miss Emily's coming, or to give her a chance to get rid of the cousins. (By that time it was a cabal, and we were all Miss Emily's allies to help circumvent the cousins.) Sure enough, after another week they departed. And, as we had expected all along, within three days Homer Barron was back in town. A neighbor saw the Negro man admit him at the kitchen door at dusk one evening.

And that was the last we saw of Homer Barron. And of Miss Emily for some time. The Negro man went in and out with the market basket, but the front door remained closed. Now and then we would see her at a window for a moment, as the men did that night when they sprinkled the lime, but for almost six months she did not appear on the streets. Then we knew that this was to be expected too; as if that quality of her father which had thwarted her woman's life so many times had been too virulent and too furious to die.

When we next saw Miss Emily, she had grown fat and her hair was turning gray. During the next few years it grew grayer and grayer until it attained an even pepper-and-salt iron-gray, when it ceased turning. Up to the day of her death at seventy-four it was still that vigorous iron-gray, like the hair of an active man.

From that time on her front door remained closed, save for a period of six or seven years, when she was about forty, during which she gave lessons in china-painting. She fitted up a studio in one of the downstairs rooms, where the daughters and grand-daughters of Colonel Sartoris' contemporaries were sent to her with the same regularity and in the same spirit that they were sent on Sundays with a twenty-five cent piece for the collection plate. Meanwhile her taxes had been remitted.

50   Then the newer generation became the backbone and the spirit of the town, and the painting pupils grew up and fell away and did not send their children to her with boxes of color and tedious brushes and pictures cut from the ladies' magazines. The front door closed upon the last one and remained closed for good. When the town got free postal delivery

Miss Emily alone refused to let them fasten the metal numbers above her door and attach a mailbox to it. She would not listen to them.

Daily, monthly, yearly we watched the Negro grow grayer and more stooped, going in and out with the market basket. Each December we sent her a tax notice, which would be returned by the post office a week later, unclaimed. Now and then we would see her in one of the downstairs windows—she had evidently shut up the top floor of the house—like the carven torso of an idol in a niche, looking or not looking at us, we could never tell which. Thus she passed from generation to generation—dear, inescapable, impervious, tranquil, and perverse.

And so she died. Fell ill in the house filled with dust and shadows, with only a doddering Negro man to wait on her. We did not even know she was sick; we had long since given up trying to get any information from the Negro. He talked to no one, probably not even to her, for his voice had grown harsh and rusty, as if from disuse.

She died in one of the downstairs rooms, in a heavy walnut bed with a curtain, her gray head propped on a pillow yellow and moldy with age and lack of sunlight.

5

The Negro met the first of the ladies at the front door and let them in, with their hushed, sibilant voices and their quick, curious glances, and then he disappeared. He walked right through the house and out the back and was not seen again.

The two female cousins came at once. They held the funeral on the second day, with the town coming to look at Miss Emily beneath a mass of bought flowers, with the crayon face of her father musing profoundly above the bier and the ladies sibilant and macabre; and the very old men—some in their brushed Confederate uniforms—on the porch and the lawn, talking of Miss Emily as if she had been a contemporary of theirs, believing that they had danced with her and courted her perhaps, confusing time with its mathematical progression, as the old do, to whom all the past is not a diminishing road, but, instead, a huge meadow which no winter ever quite touches, divided from them now by the narrow bottleneck of the most recent decade of years.

Already we knew that there was one room in that region above stairs which no one had seen in forty years, and which would have to be forced. They waited until Miss Emily was decently in the ground before they opened it.

The violence of breaking down the door seemed to fill this room with pervading dust. A thin, acrid pall as of the tomb seemed to lie everywhere upon this room decked and furnished as for a bridal: upon

55

the valance curtains of faded rose color, upon the rose-shaded lights, upon the dressing table, upon the delicate array of crystal and the man's toilet things backed with tarnished silver, silver so tarnished that the monogram was obscured. Among them lay a collar and tie, as if they had just been removed, which, lifted, left upon the surface a pale crescent in the dust. Upon a chair hung the suit, carefully folded; beneath it the two mute shoes and the discarded socks.

The man himself lay in the bed.

For a long while we just stood there, looking down at the profound and fleshless grin. The body had apparently once lain in the attitude of an embrace, but now the long sleep that outlasts love, that conquers even the grimace of love, had cuckolded him. What was left of him, rotted beneath what was left of the nightshirt, had become inextricable from the bed in which he lay; and upon him and upon the pillow beside him lay that even coating of the patient and biding dust.

60   Then we noticed that in the second pillow was the indentation of a head. One of us lifted something from it, and leaning forward, that faint and invisible dust dry and acrid in the nostrils, we saw a long strand of iron-gray hair.

Susan Glaspell

A Jury of Her Peers

When Martha Hale opened the storm door and got a cut of the north wind, she ran back for her big woolen scarf. As she hurriedly wound that round her head her eye made a scandalized sweep of her kitchen. It was no ordinary thing that called her away—it was probably farther from ordinary than anything that had ever happened in Dickson County. But what her eye took in was that her kitchen was in no shape for leaving: her bread all ready for mixing, half the flour sifted and half unsifted.

She hated to see things half done; but she had been at that when the team from town stopped to get Mr. Hale, and then the sheriff came running in to say his wife wished Mrs. Hale would come too—adding, with a grin, that he guessed she was getting scarey and wanted another woman along. So she had dropped everything right where it was.

A JURY OF HER PEERS   First published in 1917, the story is based on the author's one-act play *Trifles* (page 1029), written in 1916 for the Provincetown Players. Susan Glaspell (1882–1948) lived for the first thirty-two years of her life in Iowa. She said that *Trifles* (and hence this short story) was suggested to her by an experience she had while working for a Des Moines newspaper.

"Martha!" now came her husband's impatient voice. "Don't keep folks waiting out here in the cold."

She again opened the storm door, and this time joined the three men and the one woman waiting for her in the big two-seated buggy.

After she had the robes tucked around her she took another look at the woman who sat beside her on the back seat. She had met Mrs. Peters the year before at the county fair, and the thing she remembered about her was that she didn't seem like a sheriff's wife. She was small and thin and didn't have a strong voice. Mrs. Gorman, sheriff's wife before Gorman went out and Peters came in, had a voice that somehow seemed to be backing up the law with every word. But if Mrs. Peters didn't look like a sheriff's wife, Peters made it up in looking like a sheriff. He was to a dot the kind of man who could get himself elected sheriff—a heavy man with a big voice, who was particularly genial with the law-abiding, as if to make it plain that he knew the difference between criminals and non-criminals. And right there it came into Mrs. Hale's mind, with a stab, that this man who was so pleasant and lively with all of them was going to the Wrights' now as a sheriff.

"The country's not very pleasant this time of year," Mrs. Peters at last ventured, as if she felt they ought to be talking as well as the men.

Mrs. Hale scarcely finished her reply, for they had gone up a little hill and could see the Wright place now, and seeing it did not make her feel like talking. It looked very lonesome this cold March morning. It had always been a lonesome-looking place. It was down in a hollow, and the poplar trees around it were lonesome-looking trees. The men were looking at it and talking about what had happened. The county attorney was bending to one side of the buggy, and kept looking steadily at the place as they drew up to it.

"I'm glad you came with me," Mrs. Peters said nervously, as the two women were about to follow the men in through the kitchen door.

Even after she had her foot on the doorstep, her hand on the knob, Martha Hale had a moment of feeling she could not cross the threshold. And the reason it seemed she couldn't cross it now was simply because she hadn't crossed it before. Time and time again it had been in her mind, "I ought to go over and see Minnie Foster"—she still thought of her as Minnie Foster, though for twenty years she had been Mrs. Wright. And then there was always something to do and Minnie Foster would go from her mind. But *now* she could come.

The men went over to the stove. The women stood close together by the door. Young Henderson, the county attorney, turned around and said, "Come up to the fire, ladies."

Mrs. Peters took a step forward, then stopped. "I'm not—cold," she said.

And so the two women stood by the door, at first not even so much as looking around the kitchen.

The men talked for a minute about what a good thing it was the sheriff had sent his deputy out that morning to make a fire for them, and then Sheriff Peters stepped back from the stove, unbuttoned his outer coat, and leaned his hands on the kitchen table in a way that seemed to mark the beginning of official business. "Now, Mr. Hale," he said in a sort of semiofficial voice, "before we move things about, you tell Mr. Henderson just what it was you saw when you came here yesterday morning."

The county attorney was looking around the kitchen,

15   "By the way," he said, "has anything been moved?" He turned to the sheriff. "Are things just as you left them yesterday?"

Peters looked from cupboard to sink; from that to a small worn rocker a little to one side of the kitchen table.

"It's just the same."

"Somebody should have been left here yesterday," said the county attorney.

"Oh—yesterday," returned the sheriff, with a little gesture as of yesterday having been more than he could bear to think of. "When I had to send Frank to Morris Center for that man who went crazy—let me tell you, I had my hands full *yesterday*. I knew you could get back from Omaha by today, George, and as long as I went over everything here myself—"

20   "Well, Mr. Hale," said the county attorney, in a way of letting what was past and gone go, "tell just what happened when you came here yesterday morning."

Mrs. Hale, still leaning against the door, had that sinking feeling of the mother whose child is about to speak a piece. Lewis often wandered along and got things mixed up in a story. She hoped he would tell this straight and plain, and not say unnecessary things that would just make things harder for Minnie Foster. He didn't begin at once, and she noticed that he looked queer—as if standing in that kitchen and having to tell what he had seen there yesterday morning made him almost sick.

"Yes, Mr. Hale?" the county attorney reminded.

"Harry and I had started to town with a load of potatoes," Mrs. Hale's husband began.

Harry was Mrs. Hale's oldest boy. He wasn't with them now, for the very good reason that those potatoes never got to town yesterday and he was taking them this morning, so he hadn't been home when the sheriff stopped to say he wanted Mr. Hale to come over to the Wright place and tell the county attorney his story there, where he could point it all out. With all Mrs. Hale's other emotions came the fear that maybe Harry wasn't dressed warm enough—they hadn't any of them realized how that north wind did bite.

"We come along this road," Hale was going on, with a motion of his   25 hand to the road over which they had just come, "and as we got in sight of the house I says to Harry, 'I'm goin' to see if I can't get John Wright to take a telephone.' You see," he explained to Henderson, "unless I can get somebody to go in with me they won't come out this branch road except for a price I can't pay. I'd spoke to Wright about it once before; but he put me off, saying folks talked too much anyway, and all he asked was peace and quiet—guess you know about how much he talked himself. But I thought maybe if I went to the house and talked about it before his wife, and said all the women-folks liked the telephones, and that in this lonesome stretch of road it would be a good thing—well, I said to Harry that that was what I was going to say—though I said at the same time that I didn't know as what his wife wanted made much difference to John—"

Now, there he was!—saying things he didn't need to say. Mrs. Hale tried to catch her husband's eye, but fortunately the county attorney interrupted with:

"Let's talk about that a little later, Mr. Hale. I do want to talk about that, but I'm anxious now to get along to just what happened when you got here."

When he began this time, it was very deliberately and carefully:

"I didn't see or hear anything. I knocked at the door. And still it was all quiet inside. I knew they must be up—it was past eight o'clock. So I knocked again, louder, and I thought I heard somebody say 'Come in.' I wasn't sure—I'm not sure yet. But I opened the door—this door," jerking a hand toward the door by which the two women stood, "and there, in that rocker"—pointing to it—"sat Mrs. Wright."

Every one in the kitchen looked at the rocker. It came into   30 Mrs. Hale's mind that that rocker didn't look in the least like Minnie Foster—the Minnie Foster of twenty years before. It was a dingy red, with wooden rungs up the back, and the middle rung was gone, and the chair sagged to one side.

"How did she—look?" the county attorney was inquiring.

"Well," said Hale, "she looked—queer."

"How do you mean—queer?"

As he asked it he took out a notebook and pencil. Mrs. Hale did not like the sight of that pencil. She kept her eye fixed on her husband, as if to keep him from saying unnecessary things that would go into that notebook and make trouble.

35   Hale did speak guardedly, as if the pencil had affected him too.

"Well, as if she didn't know what she was going to do next. And kind of—done up."

"How did she seem to feel about your coming?"

"Why, I don't think she minded—one way or other. She didn't pay much attention. I said, 'Ho' do, Mrs. Wright? It's cold, ain't it?' And she said, 'Is it?'—and went on pleatin' at her apron.

"Well, I was surprised. She didn't ask me to come up to the stove, or to sit down, but just set there, not even lookin' at me. And so I said: 'I want to see John.'

40   "And then she—laughed. I guess you would call it a laugh.

"I thought of Harry and the team outside, so I said, a little sharp, 'Can I see John?' 'No,' says she—kind of dull like. 'Ain't he home?' says I. Then she looked at me. 'Yes,' says she, 'he's home.' 'Then why can't I see him?' I asked her, out of patience with her now. ''Cause he's dead,' says she, just as quiet and dull—and fell to pleatin' her apron. 'Dead?' says I, like you do when you can't take in what you've heard.

"She just nodded her head, not getting a bit excited, but rockin' back and forth.

"'Why—where is he?' says I, not knowing *what* to say.

"She just pointed upstairs—like this"—pointing to the room above.

45   "I got up, with the idea of going up there myself. By this time I—didn't know what to do. I walked from there to here; then I says: 'Why, what did he die of?'

"'He died of a rope around his neck,' says she; and just went on pleatin' at her apron."

Hale stopped speaking, and stood staring at the rocker, as if he were still seeing the woman who had sat there the morning before. Nobody spoke; it was as if every one were seeing the woman who had sat there the morning before.

"And what did you do then?" the county attorney at last broke the silence.

"I went out and called Harry. I thought I might—need help. I got Harry in, and we went upstairs." His voice fell almost to a whisper. "There he was—lying over the—"

50   "I think I'd rather have you go into that upstairs," the county attorney interrupted, "where you can point it all out. Just go on now with the rest of the story."

"Well, my first thought was to get that rope off. It looked—"

He stopped, his face twitching.

"But Harry, he went up to him, and he said, 'No, he's dead all right, and we'd better not touch anything.' So we went downstairs.

"She was still sitting that same way. 'Has anybody been notified?' I asked. 'No,' says she, unconcerned."

"'Who did this, Mrs. Wright?' said Harry. He said it businesslike, and she stopped pleatin' at her apron. 'I don't know,' she says. 'You don't *know?*' says Harry. 'Weren't you sleepin' in the bed with him?' 'Yes,' says she, 'but I was on the inside,' 'Somebody slipped a rope round his neck and strangled him, and you didn't wake up?' says Harry. 'I didn't wake up,' she said after him.   55

"We may have looked as if we didn't see how that could be, for after a minute she said, 'I sleep sound.'

"Harry was going to ask her more questions, but I said maybe that weren't our business; maybe we ought to let her tell her story first to the coroner or the sheriff. So Harry went fast as he could over to High Road—the Rivers's place, where there's a telephone."

"And what did she do when she knew you had gone for the coroner?" The attorney got his pencil in his hand all ready for writing.

"She moved from that chair to this one over here"—Hale pointed to a small chair in the corner—"and just sat there with her hands held together and looking down. I got a feeling that I ought to make some conversation, so I said I had come in to see if John wanted to put in a telephone; and at that she started to laugh, and then she stopped and looked at me—scared."

At the sound of a moving pencil the man who was telling the story looked up.   60

"I dunno—maybe it wasn't scared," he hastened; "I wouldn't like to say it was. Soon Harry got back, and then Dr. Lloyd came, and you, Mr. Peters, and so I guess that's all I know that you don't."

He said that last with relief, and moved a little, as if relaxing. Every one moved a little. The county attorney walked toward the stair door.

"I guess we'll go upstairs first—then out to the barn and around there."

He paused and looked around the kitchen.

"You're convinced there was nothing important here?" he asked the sheriff. "Nothing that would—point to any motive?"   65

The sheriff too looked all around, as if to re-convince himself.

"Nothing here but kitchen things," he said, with a little laugh for the insignificance of kitchen things.

The county attorney was looking at the cupboard—a peculiar, ungainly structure, half closet and half cupboard, the upper part of it being built in the wall, and the lower part just the old-fashioned kitchen cupboard. As if its queerness attracted him, he got a chair and opened the upper part and looked in. After a moment he drew his hand away sticky.

"Here's a nice mess," he said resentfully.

70   The two women had drawn nearer, and now the sheriff's wife spoke.

"Oh—her fruit," she said, looking to Mrs. Hale for sympathetic understanding. She turned back to the county attorney and explained: "She worried about that when it turned so cold last night. She said the fire would go out and her jars might burst."

Mrs. Peters's husband broke into a laugh.

"Well, can you beat the women! Held for murder, and worrying about her preserves!"

The young attorney set his lips.

75   "I guess before we're through with her she may have something more serious than preserves to worry about."

"Oh, well," said Mrs. Hale's husband, with good-natured superiority, "women are used to worrying over trifles."

The two women moved a little closer together. Neither of them spoke. The county attorney seemed suddenly to remember his manners—and think of his future.

"And yet," said he, with the gallantry of a young politician, "for all their worries, what would we do without the ladies?"

The women did not speak, did not unbend. He went to the sink and began washing his hands. He turned to wipe them on the roller wheel—whirled it for a cleaner place.

80   "Dirty towels! Not much of a housekeeper, would you say, ladies?"

He kicked his foot against some dirty pans under the sink.

"There's a great deal of work to be done on a farm," said Mrs. Hale stiffly.

"To be sure. And yet"—with a little bow to her—"I know there are some Dickson County farmhouses that do not have such roller towels." He gave it a pull to expose its full length again.

"Those towels get dirty awful quick. Men's hands aren't always as clean as they might be."

85   "Ah, loyal to your sex, I see," he laughed. He stopped and gave her a keen look. "But you and Mrs. Wright were neighbors. I suppose you were friends, too."

Martha Hale shook her head.

"I've seen little enough of her of late years. I've not been in this house—it's more than a year."

"And why was that? You didn't like her?"

"I liked her well enough," she replied with spirit. "Farmers' wives have their hands full, Mr. Henderson. And then—" She looked around the kitchen.

"Yes?" he encouraged.   90

"It never seemed a very cheerful place," said she, more to herself than to him.

"No," he agreed; "I don't think any one would call it cheerful. I shouldn't say she had the homemaking instinct."

"Well, I don't know as Wright had, either," she muttered.

"You mean they didn't get on very well?" he was quick to ask.

"No; I don't mean anything," she answered, with decision. As she   95
turned a little away from him, she added: "But I don't think a place would be any the cheerfuler for John Wright's bein' in it."

"I'd like to talk to you about that a little later, Mrs. Hale," he said. "I'm anxious to get the lay of things upstairs now."

He moved toward the stair door, followed by the two men.

"I suppose anything Mrs. Peters does'll be all right?" the sheriff inquired. "She was to take in some clothes for her, you know—and a few little things. We left in such a hurry yesterday."

The county attorney looked at the two women whom they were leaving alone there among the kitchen things.

"Yes—Mrs. Peters," he said, his glance resting on the woman who   100
was not Mrs. Peters, the big farmer woman who stood behind the sheriff's wife. "Of course Mrs. Peters is one of us," he said, in a manner of entrusting responsibility. "And keep your eye out, Mrs. Peters, for anything that might be of use. No telling; you women might come upon a clue to the motive—and that's the thing we need."

Mr. Hale rubbed his face after the fashion of a show man getting ready for a pleasantry.

"But would the women know a clue if they did come upon it!" he said; and, having delivered himself of this, he followed the others through the stair door.

The women stood motionless and silent, listening to the footsteps, first upon the stairs, then in the room above them.

Then, as if releasing herself from something strange, Mrs. Hale began to arrange the dirty pans under the sink, which the county attorney's disdainful push of the foot had deranged.

"I'd hate to have men comin' into my kitchen," she said testily—   105
"snoopin' round and criticizin'."

"Of course it's no more than their duty," said the sheriff's wife, in her manner of timid acquiescence.

"Duty's all right," replied Mrs. Hale bluffly; "but I guess that deputy sheriff that come out to make the fire might have got a little of this on." She gave the roller towel a pull. "Wish I'd thought of that sooner! Seems mean to talk about her for not having things slicked up, when she had to come away in such a hurry."

She looked around the kitchen. Certainly it was not "slicked up." Her eye was held by a bucket of sugar on a low shelf. The cover was off the wooden bucket, and beside it was a paper bag—half full.

Mrs. Hale moved toward it.

110   "She was putting this in here," she said to herself—slowly.

She thought of the flour in her kitchen at home—half sifted, half not sifted. She had been interrupted, and had left things half done. What had interrupted Minnie Foster? Why had that work been left half done? She made a move as if to finish it,—unfinished things always bothered her,—and then she glanced around and saw that Mrs. Peters was watching her—and she didn't want Mrs. Peters to get that feeling she had got of work begun and then—for some reason—not finished.

"It's a shame about her fruit," she said, and walked toward the cupboard that the county attorney had opened, and got on the chair, murmuring: "I wonder if it's all gone."

It was a sorry enough looking sight, but "Here's one that's all right," she said at last. She held it toward the light. "This is cherries, too." She looked again. "I declare I believe that's the only one."

With a sigh, she got down from the chair, went to the sink, and wiped off the bottle.

115   "She'll feel awful bad, after all her hard work in the hot weather. I remember the afternoon I put up my cherries last summer!"

She set the bottle on the table, and, with another sigh, started to sit down in the rocker. But she did not sit down. Something kept her from sitting down in that chair. She straightened—stepped back, and, half turned away, stood looking at it, seeing the woman who sat there "pleatin' at her apron."

The thin voice of the sheriff's wife broke in upon her: "I must be getting those things from the front room closet." She opened the door into the other room, started in, stepped back. "You coming with me, Mrs. Hale?" she asked nervously. "You—you could help me get them."

They were soon back—the stark coldness of that shut-up room was not a thing to linger in.

"My!" said Mrs. Peters, dropping the things on the table and hurrying to the stove.

Mrs. Hale stood examining the clothes the woman who was being   120
detained in town had said she wanted.

"Wright was close!" she exclaimed, holding up a shabby black skirt
that bore the marks of much making over. "I think maybe that's why she
kept so much to herself. I s'pose she felt she couldn't do her part; and
then, you don't enjoy things when you feel shabby. She used to wear
pretty clothes and be lively—when she was Minnie Foster, one of the
town girls, singing in the choir. But that—oh, that was twenty years ago."

With a carefulness in which there was something tender, she folded
the shabby clothes and piled them at one corner of the table. She looked
at Mrs. Peters, and there was something in the other woman's look that
irritated her.

"She don't care," she said to herself. "Much difference it makes to
her whether Minnie Foster had pretty clothes when she was a girl."

Then she looked again, and she wasn't so sure; in fact, she hadn't at
any time been perfectly sure about Mrs. Peters. She had that shrinking
manner, and yet her eyes looked as if they could see a long way into things.

"This all you was to take in?" asked Mrs. Hale.   125

"No," said the sheriff's wife; "she said she wanted an apron. Funny
thing to want," she ventured in her nervous little way, "for there's not
much to get you dirty in jail, goodness knows. But I suppose just to make
her feel more natural. If you're used to wearing an apron—. She said they
were in the bottom drawer of this cupboard. Yes—here they are. And
then her little shawl that always hung on the stair door."

She took the small gray shawl from behind the door leading upstairs,
and stood a minute looking at it.

Suddenly Mrs. Hale took a quick step toward the other woman.

"Mrs. Peters!"

"Yes, Mrs. Hale?"   130

"Do you think she—did it?"

A frightened look blurred the other things in Mrs. Peters's eyes.

"Oh, I don't know," she said, in a voice that seemed to shrink away
from the subject.

"Well, I don't think she did," affirmed Mrs. Hale stoutly. "Asking
for an apron, and her little shawl. Worryin' about her fruit."

"Mr. Peters says—." Footsteps were heard in the room above; she   135
stopped, looked up, then went on in a lowered voice: "Mr. Peters says—
it looks bad for her. Mr. Henderson is awful sarcastic in a speech, and
he's going to make fun of her saying she didn't—wake up."

For a moment Mrs. Hale had no answer. Then, "Well, I guess John
Wright didn't wake up—when they was slippin' that rope under his
neck," she muttered.

"No, it's *strange*," breathed Mrs. Peters. "They think it was such a—funny way to kill a man."

She began to laugh; at the sound of the laugh, abruptly stopped.

"That's just what Mr. Hale said," said Mrs. Hale, in a resolutely natural voice. "There was a gun in the house. He says that's what he can't understand."

140   "Mr. Henderson said, coming out, that what was needed for the case was a motive. Something to show anger—or sudden feeling."

"Well, I don't see any signs of anger around here," said Mrs. Hale. "I don't—"

She stopped. It was as if her mind tripped on something. Her eye was caught by a dish-towel in the middle of the kitchen table. Slowly she moved toward the table. One half of it was wiped clean, the other half messy. Her eyes made a slow, almost unwilling turn to the bucket of sugar and the half empty bag beside it. Things begun—and not finished.

After a moment she stepped back, and said, in that manner of releasing herself:

"Wonder how they're finding things upstairs? I hope she had it a little more red up° up there. You know,"—she paused, and feeling gathered,—"it seems kind of *sneaking*; locking her up in town and coming out here to get her own house to turn against her!"

145   "But, Mrs. Hale," said the sheriff's wife, "the law is the law."

"I s'pose 'tis," answered Mrs. Hale shortly.

She turned to the stove, saying something about that fire not being much to brag of. She worked with it a minute, and when she straightened up she said aggressively:

"The law is the law—and a bad stove is a bad stove. How'd you like to cook on this?"—pointing with the poker to the broken lining. She opened the oven door and started to express her opinion of the oven; but she was swept into her own thoughts, thinking of what it would mean, year after year, to have that stove to wrestle with. The thought of Minnie Foster trying to bake in that oven—and the thought of her never going over to see Minnie Foster—.

She was startled by hearing Mrs. Peters say: "A person gets discouraged—and loses heart."

150   The sheriff's wife had looked from the stove to the sink—to the pail of water which had been carried in from outside. The two women stood there silent, above them the footsteps of the men who were looking for evidence against the woman who had worked in that kitchen. That look of seeing into things, of seeing through a thing to something else, was in

red up: neatened, readied (dialect)

the eyes of the sheriff's wife now. When Mrs. Hale next spoke to her, it was gently:

"Better loosen up your things, Mrs. Peters. We'll not feel them when we go out."

Mrs. Peters went to the back of the room to hang up the fur tippet she was wearing. A moment later she exclaimed, "Why, she was piecing a quilt," and held up a large sewing basket piled high with quilt pieces.

Mrs. Hale spread some of the blocks on the table.

"It's log-cabin pattern," she said, putting several of them together. "Pretty, isn't it?"

They were so engaged with the quilt that they did not hear the footsteps on the stairs. Just as the stair door opened Mrs. Hale was saying: 155

"Do you suppose she was going to quilt it or just knot it!"

The sheriff threw up his hands.

"They wonder whether she was going to quilt it or just knot it!"

There was a laugh for the ways of women, a warming of hands over the stove, and then the county attorney said briskly:

"Well, let's go right out to the barn and get that cleared up."   160

"I don't see as there's anything so strange," Mrs. Hale said resentfully, after the outside door had closed on the three men—"our taking up our time with little things while we're waiting for them to get the evidence. I don't see as it's anything to laugh about!"

"Of course they've got awful important things on their minds," said the sheriff's wife apologetically.

They returned to an inspection of the blocks for the quilt. Mrs. Hale was looking at the fine, even sewing, and preoccupied with thoughts of the woman who had done that sewing, when she heard the sheriff's wife say, in a queer tone:

"Why, look at this one."

She turned to take the block held out to her.   165

"The sewing," said Mrs. Peters, in a troubled way. "All the rest of them have been so nice and even—but—this one. Why, it looks as if she didn't know what she was about!"

Their eyes met—something flashed to life, passed between them; then, as if with an effort, they seemed to pull away from each other. A moment Mrs. Hale sat there, her hands folded over that sewing which was so unlike all the rest of the sewing. Then she had pulled a knot and drawn the threads.

"Oh, what are you doing, Mrs. Hale?" asked the sheriff's wife, startled.

"Just pulling out a stitch or two that's not sewed very good," said Mrs. Hale mildly.

170   "I don't think we ought to touch things," Mrs. Peters said, a little helplessly.

"I'll just finish up this end," answered Mrs. Hale, still in that mild, matter-of-fact fashion.

She threaded a needle and started to replace bad sewing with good. For a little while she sewed in silence. Then, in that thin, timid voice, she heard:

"Mrs. Hale!"

"Yes, Mrs. Peters?"

175   "What do you suppose she was so—nervous about?"

"Oh, I don't know," said Mrs. Hale, as if dismissing a thing not important enough to spend much time on. "I don't know as she was—nervous. I sew awful queer sometimes when I'm just tired."

She cut a thread, and out of the corner of her eye looked up at Mrs. Peters. The small, lean face of the sheriff's wife seemed to have tightened up. Her eyes had that look of peering into something. But the next moment she moved, and said in her thin, indecisive way:

"Well, I must get those clothes wrapped. They may be through sooner than we think. I wonder where I could find a piece of paper—and string."

"In that cupboard, maybe," suggested Mrs. Hale, after a glance around.

180   One piece of the crazy sewing remained unripped. Mrs. Peters's back turned, Martha Hale now scrutinized that piece, compared it with the dainty, accurate sewing of the other blocks. The difference was startling. Holding this block made her feel queer, as if the distracted thoughts of the woman who had perhaps turned to it to try and quiet herself were communicating themselves to her.

Mrs. Peters's voice roused her.

"Here's a birdcage," she said. "Did she have a bird, Mrs. Hale?"

"Why, I don't know whether she did or not!" She turned to look at the cage Mrs. Peters was holding up. "I've not been here in so long." She sighed. "There was a man round last year selling canaries cheap—but I don't know as she took one. Maybe she did. She used to sing real pretty herself."

Mrs. Peters looked around the kitchen.

185   "Seems kind of funny to think of a bird here." She half laughed—an attempt to put up a barrier. "But she must have had one—or why would she have a cage? I wonder what happened to it."

"I suppose maybe the cat got it," suggested Mrs. Hale, resuming her sewing.

"No, she didn't have a cat. She's got that feeling some people have about cats—being afraid of them. When they brought her to our house yesterday, my cat got in the room, and she was real upset and asked me to take it out."

"My sister Bessie was like that," laughed Mrs. Hale.

The sheriff's wife did not reply. The silence made Mrs. Hale turn around. Mrs. Peters was examining the birdcage.

"Look at this door," she said slowly. "It's broke. One hinge has been pulled apart."   190

Mrs. Hale came nearer.

"Looks as if some one must have been—rough with it."

Again their eyes met—startled, questioning, apprehensive. For a moment neither spoke nor stirred. Then Mrs. Hale, turning away, said brusquely:

"If they're going to find any evidence, I wish they'd be about it. I don't like this place."

"But I'm awful glad you came with me, Mrs. Hale." Mrs. Peters put   195
the birdcage on the table and sat down. "It would be lonesome for me—sitting here alone."

"Yes, it would, wouldn't it?" agreed Mrs. Hale, a certain determined naturalness in her voice. She picked up the sewing, but now it dropped in her lap, and she murmured in a different voice: "But I tell you what I *do* wish, Mrs. Peters. I wish I had come over sometimes when she was here. I wish—I had."

"But of course you were awful busy, Mrs. Hale. Your house—and your children."

"I could've come," retorted Mrs. Hale shortly. "I stayed away because it weren't cheerful—and that's why I ought to have come. I"—she looked around—"I've never liked this place. Maybe because it's down in a hollow and you don't see the road. I don't know what it is, but it's a lonesome place, and always was. I wish I had come over to see Minnie Foster sometimes. I can see now—" She did not put it into words.

"Well, you musn't reproach yourself," counseled Mrs. Peters. "Somehow, we just don't see how it is with other folks till—something comes up."

"Not having children makes less work," mused Mrs. Hale, after a   200
silence, "but it makes a quiet house—and Wright out to work all day—and no company when he did come in. Did you know John Wright, Mrs. Peters?"

"Not to know him. I've seen him in town. They say he was a good man."

"Yes—good," conceded John Wright's neighbor grimly. "He didn't drink, and kept his word as well as most, I guess, and paid his debts. But he was a hard man, Mrs. Peters. Just to pass the time of day with him—." She stopped, shivered a little. "Like a raw wind that gets to the bone." Her eye fell upon the cage on the table before her, and she added, almost bitterly: "I should think she would've wanted a bird!"

Suddenly she leaned forward, looking intently at the cage. "But what do you s'pose went wrong with it?"

"I don't know," returned Mrs. Peters; "unless it got sick and died."

205   But after she said it she reached over and swung the broken door. Both women watched it as if somehow held by it.

"You didn't know—her?" Mrs. Hale asked, a gentler note in her voice.

"Not till they brought her yesterday," said the sheriff's wife.

"She—come to think of it, she was kind of like a bird herself. Real sweet and pretty, but kind of timid and—fluttery. How—she—did—change."

That held her for a long time. Finally, as if struck with a happy thought and relieved to get back to everyday things, she exclaimed:

210   "Tell you what, Mrs. Peters, why don't you take the quilt in with you? It might take up her mind."

"Why, I think that's a real nice idea, Mrs. Hale," agreed the sheriff's wife, as if she too were glad to come into the atmosphere of a simple kindness. "There couldn't possibly be any objection to that, could there? Now, just what will I take? I wonder if her patches are in here—and her things."

They turned to the sewing basket.

"Here's some red," said Mrs. Hale, bringing out a roll of cloth. Underneath that was a box. "Here, maybe her scissors are in here— and her things." She held it up. "What a pretty box! I'll warrant that was something she had a long time ago—when she was a girl."

She held it in her hand a moment; then, with a little sigh, opened it.

215   Instantly her hand went to her nose.

"Why—!"

Mrs. Peters drew nearer—then turned away.

"There's something wrapped up in this piece of silk," faltered Mrs. Hale.

"This isn't her scissors," said Mrs. Peters in a shrinking voice.

220   Her hand not steady, Mrs. Hale raised the piece of silk. "Oh, Mrs. Peters!" she cried. "It's—"

Mrs. Peters bent closer.

"It's the bird," she whispered.

"But, Mrs. Peters!" cried Mrs. Hale. "*Look* at it! Its neck—look at its neck! It's all—other side *to*."

She held the box away from her.

The sheriff's wife again bent closer.

"Somebody wrung its neck," said she, in a voice that was slow and deep.

225

And then again the eyes of the two women met—this time clung together in a look of dawning comprehension, of growing horror. Mrs. Peters looked from the dead bird to the broken door of the cage. Again their eyes met. And just then there was a sound at the outside door.

Mrs. Hale slipped the box under the quilt pieces in the basket, and sank into the chair before it. Mrs. Peters stood holding to the table. The county attorney and the sheriff came in from outside.

"Well, ladies," said the county attorney, as one turning from serious things to little pleasantries, "have you decided whether she was going to quilt it or knot it?"

"We think," began the sheriff's wife in a flurried voice, "that she was going to—knot it."

230

He was too preoccupied to notice the change that came in her voice on that last.

"Well, that's very interesting, I'm sure," he said tolerantly. He caught sight of the birdcage. "Has the bird flown?"

"We think the cat got it," said Mrs. Hale in a voice curiously even.

He was walking up and down, as if thinking something out.

"Is there a cat?" he asked absently.

235

Mrs. Hale shot a look up at the sheriff's wife.

"Well, not *now*," said Mrs. Peters. "They're superstitious, you know; they leave."

She sank into the chair.

The county attorney did not heed her. "No sign at all of any one having come in from the outside," he said to Peters, in the manner of continuing an interrupted conversation. "Their own rope. Now let's go upstairs again and go over it, piece by piece. It would have to have been some one who knew just the—"

The stair door closed behind them and their voices were lost.

240

The two women sat motionless, not looking at each other, but as if peering into something and at the same time holding back. When they spoke now it was as if they were afraid of what they were saying, but as if they could not help saying it.

"She liked the bird," said Martha Hale, low and slowly. "She was going to bury it in that pretty box."

"When I was a girl," said Mrs. Peters, under her breath, "my kitten —there was a boy took a hatchet, and before my eyes—before I could get there—" She covered her face an instant. "If they hadn't held me back I would have"—she caught herself, looked upstairs where footsteps were heard, and finished weakly—"hurt him."

Then they sat without speaking or moving.

245   "I wonder how it would seem," Mrs. Hale at last began, as if feeling her way over strange ground—"never to have had any children around?" Her eyes made a slow sweep of the kitchen, as if seeing what that kitchen had meant through all the years. "No, Wright wouldn't like the bird," she said after that—"a thing that sang. She used to sing. He killed that too." Her voice tightened.

Mrs. Peters moved uneasily.

"Of course we don't know who killed the bird."

"I knew John Wright," was Mrs. Hale's answer.

"It was an awful thing was done in this house that night, Mrs. Hale," said the sheriff's wife. "Killing a man while he slept—slipping a thing round his neck that choked the life out of him."

250   Mrs. Hale's hand went out to the birdcage.

"His neck. Choked the life out of him."

"We don't *know* who killed him," whispered Mrs. Peters wildly. "We don't *know*."

Mrs. Hale had not moved. "If there had been years and years of—nothing, then a bird to sing to you, it would be awful—still—after the bird was still."

It was as if something within her not herself had spoken, and it found in Mrs. Peters something she did not know as herself.

255   "I know what stillness is," she said, in a queer, monotonous voice. "When we homesteaded in Dakota, and my first baby died—after he was two years old—and me with no other then—"

Mrs. Hale stirred.

"How soon do you suppose they'll be through looking for evidence?"

"I know what stillness is," repeated Mrs. Peters, in just that same way. Then she too pulled back. "The law has got to punish crime, Mrs. Hale," she said in her tight little way.

"I wish you'd seen Minnie Foster," was the answer, "when she wore a white dress with blue ribbons, and stood up there in the choir and sang."

260   The picture of that girl, the fact that she had lived neighbor to that girl for twenty years, and had let her die for lack of life, was suddenly more than she could bear.

"Oh, I *wish* I'd come over here once in a while!" she cried. "That was a crime! That was a crime! Who's going to punish that?"

"We mustn't take on," said Mrs. Peters, with a frightened look toward the stairs.

"I might 'a' *known* she needed help! I tell you, it's *queer*, Mrs. Peters. We live close together, and we live far apart. We all go through the same things—it's all just a different kind of the same thing! If it weren't—why do you and I *understand?* Why do we *know*—what we know this minute?"

She dashed her hand across her eyes. Then, seeing the jar of fruit on the table, she reached for it and choked out:

"If I was you I wouldn't *tell* her her fruit was gone! Tell her it *ain't.* 265 Tell her it's all right—all of it. Here—take this in to prove it to her! She —she may never know whether it was broke or not."

She turned away.

Mrs. Peters reached out for the bottle of fruit as if she were glad to take it—as if touching a familiar thing, having something to do, could keep her from something else. She got up, looked about for something to wrap the fruit in, took a petticoat from the pile of clothes she had brought from the front room, and nervously started winding that round the bottle.

"My!" she began, in a high, false voice, "it's a good thing the men couldn't hear us! Getting all stirred up over a little thing like a—dead canary." She hurried over that. "As if that could have anything to do with—with— My, wouldn't they *laugh?*"

Footsteps were heard on the stairs.

"Maybe they would," muttered Mrs. Hale—"maybe they wouldn't." 270

"No, Peters," said the county attorney incisively; "it's all perfectly clear, except the reason for doing it. But you know juries when it comes to women. If there was some definite thing—something to show. Something to make a story about. A thing that would connect up with this clumsy way of doing it!"

In a covert way Mrs. Hale looked at Mrs. Peters. Mrs. Peters was looking at her. Quickly they looked away from each other. The outer door opened and Mr. Hale came in.

"I've got the team round now," he said. "Pretty cold out there."

"I'm going to stay here awhile by myself," the county attorney suddenly announced. "You can send Frank out for me, can't you?" he asked the sheriff. "I want to go over everything. I'm not satisfied we can't do better."

Again, for one brief moment, the two women's eyes found one 275 another.

The sheriff came up to the table.

"Did you want to see what Mrs. Peters was going to take in?"

The county attorney picked up the apron. He laughed.

"Oh, I guess they're not very dangerous things the ladies have picked out."

280   Mrs. Hale's hand was on the sewing basket in which the box was concealed. She felt that she ought to take her hand off the basket. She did not seem able to. He picked up one of the quilt blocks which she had piled on to cover the box. Her eyes felt like fire. She had a feeling that if he took up the basket she would snatch it from him.

But he did not take it up. With another little laugh, he turned away, saying:

"No; Mrs. Peters doesn't need supervising. For that matter, a sheriff's wife is married to the law. Ever think of it that way, Mrs. Peters?"

Mrs. Peters was standing beside the table. Mrs. Hale shot a look up at her; but she could not see her face. Mrs. Peters had turned away. When she spoke, her voice was muffled.

"Not—just that way," she said.

285   "Married to the law!" chuckled Mrs. Peters's husband. He moved toward the door into the front room, and said to the county attorney:

"I just want you to come in here a minute, George. We ought to take a look at these windows."

"Oh—windows," said the county attorney scoffingly.

"We'll be right out, Mr. Hale," said the sheriff to the farmer, who was still waiting by the door.

Hale went to look after the horses. The sheriff followed the county attorney into the other room. Again—for one moment—the two women were alone in that kitchen.

290   Martha Hale sprang up, her hands tight together, looking at that other woman, with whom it rested. At first she could not see her eyes, for the sheriff's wife had not turned back since she turned away at that suggestion of being married to the law. But now Mrs. Hale made her turn back. Her eyes made her turn back. Slowly, unwillingly, Mrs. Peters turned her head until her eyes met the eyes of the other woman. There was a moment when they held each other in a steady, burning look in which there was no evasion nor flinching. Then Martha Hale's eyes pointed the way to the basket in which was hidden the thing that would make certain the conviction of the other woman—that woman who was not there and yet who had been there with them all through the hour.

For a moment Mrs. Peters did not move. And then she did it. With a rush forward, she threw back the quilt pieces, got the box, tried to put it in her handbag. It was too big. Desperately she opened it, started to take the bird out. But there she broke—she could not touch the bird. She stood helpless, foolish.

There was the sound of a knob turning in the inner door. Martha Hale snatched the box from the sheriff's wife, and got it in the pocket of her big coat just as the sheriff and the county attorney came back into the kitchen.

"Well, Henry," said the county attorney facetiously, "at least we found out that she was not going to quilt it. She was going to—what is it you call it, ladies?"

Mrs. Hale's hand was against the pocket of her coat.

"We call it—knot it, Mr. Henderson."   295

Zora Neale Hurston
The Gilded Six-Bits

It was a Negro yard around a Negro house in a Negro settlement that looked to the payroll of the G and G Fertilizer works for its support.

But there was something happy about the place. The front yard was parted in the middle by a sidewalk from gate to door-step, a sidewalk edged on either side by quart bottles driven neck down into the ground on a slant. A mess of homey flowers planted without a plan but blooming cheerily from their helter-skelter places. The fence and house were whitewashed. The porch and steps scrubbed white.

The front door stood open to the sunshine so that the floor of the front room could finish drying after its weekly scouring. It was Saturday. Everything clean from the front gate to the privy house. Yard raked so that the strokes of the rake would make a pattern. Fresh newspaper cut in fancy edge on the kitchen shelves.

Missie May was bathing herself in the galvanized washtub in the bedroom. Her dark-brown skin glistened under the soapsuds that skittered down from her wash rag. Her stiff young breasts thrust forward aggressively like broad-based cones with the tips lacquered in black.

THE GILDED SIX-BITS   First published in 1933. Zora Neale Hurston (1891–1960), the daughter of a preacher and of a teacher who died when Hurston was thirteen, was raised in Eatonville, Florida, the setting of this story. Her schooling was repeatedly interrupted, but included a high school diploma in 1918 and college studies at Howard University in Washington, D.C., and Barnard College in New York. She did extensive field research in the folkways of African Americans in the south and in the Caribbean; by the time she wrote this story, she had married and divorced her first husband. In slang, a "bit" was twelve and a half cents, but was used only in multiples of two; "six-bits" refers to the two gilded coins used for ornaments by Mr. Slemmons, his twenty-five-cent stickpin and the fifty-cent coin on his watch chain.

5   She heard men's voices in the distance and glanced at the dollar
clock on the dresser.

"Humph! Ah'm way behind time t'day! Joe gointer be heah 'fore Ah
git mah clothes on if Ah don't make haste."

She grabbed the clean meal sack at hand and dried herself hurriedly
and began to dress. But before she could tie her slippers, there came the
ring of singing metal on wood. Nine times.

Missie May grinned with delight. She had not seen the big tall man
come stealing in the gate and creep up the walk grinning happily at the
joyful mischief he was about to commit. But she knew that it was her
husband throwing silver dollars in the door for her to pick up and pile
beside her plate at dinner. It was this way every Saturday afternoon. The
nine dollars hurled into the open door, he scurried to a hiding place
behind the cape jasmine bush and waited.

Missie May promptly appeared at the door in mock alarm.

10   "Who dat chunkin' money in mah do'way?" she demanded. No
answer from the yard. She leaped off the porch and began to search the
shrubbery. She peeped under the porch and hung over the gate to look
up and down the road. While she did this, the man behind the jasmine
darted to the chinaberry tree. She spied him and gave chase.

"Nobody ain't gointer be chunkin' money at me and Ah not do 'em
nothin'," she shouted in mock anger. He ran around the house with
Missie May at his heels. She overtook him at the kitchen door. He ran
inside but could not close it after him before she crowded in and locked
with him in a rough and tumble. For several minutes the two were a
furious mass of male and female energy. Shouting, laughing, twisting,
turning, tussling, tickling each other in the ribs; Missie May clutching
onto Joe and Joe trying, but not too hard, to get away.

"Missie May, take yo' hand out mah pocket!" Joe shouted out
between laughs.

"Ah ain't, Joe, not lessen you gwine gimme whateve' it is good you
got in yo' pocket. Turn it go, Joe, do Ah'll tear yo' clothes."

"Go on tear 'em. You de one dat pushes de needles round heah.
Move yo' hand Missie May."

15   "Lemme git dat paper sack out yo' pocket. Ah bet it's candy kisses."

"Tain't. Move yo' hand. Woman ain't got no business in a man's
clothes no how. Go way."

Missie May gouged way down and gave an upward jerk and
triumphed.

"Unhhunh! Ah got it. It 'tis so candy kisses. Ah knowed you had
somethin' for me in yo' clothes. Now Ah got to see whut's in every
pocket you got."

Joe smiled indulgently and let his wife go through all of his pockets and take out the things that he had hidden there for her to find. She bore off the chewing gum, the cake of sweet soap, the pocket handkerchief as if she had wrested them from him, as if they had not been bought for the sake of this friendly battle.

"Whew! dat play-fight done got me all warmed up," Joe exclaimed.   20
"Got me some water in de kittle?"

"Yo' water is on de fire and yo' clean things is cross de bed. Hurry up and wash yo'self and git changed so we kin eat. Ah'm hongry." As Missie said this, she bore the steaming kettle into the bedroom.

"You ain't hongry, sugar," Joe contradicted her. "Youse jes' a little empty. Ah'm de one whut's hongry. Ah could eat up camp meetin', back off 'ssociation, and drink Jurdan dry. Have it on de table when Ah git out de tub."

"Don't you mess wid mah business, man. You git in yo' clothes. Ah'm a real wife, not no dress and breath. Ah might not look lak one, but if you burn me, you won't git a thing but wife ashes."

Joe splashed in the bedroom and Missie May fanned around in the kitchen. A fresh red and white checked cloth on the table. Big pitcher of buttermilk beaded with pale drops of butter from the churn. Hot fried mullet, crackling bread, ham hock atop a mound of string beans and new potatoes, and perched on the window-sill a pone of spicy potato pudding.

Very little talk during the meal but that little consisted of banter   25
that pretended to deny affection but in reality flaunted it. Like when Missie May reached for a second helping of the tater pone. Joe snatched it out of her reach.

After Missie May had made two or three unsuccessful grabs at the pan, she begged, "Aw, Joe gimme some mo' dat tater pone."

"Nope, sweetenin' is for us men-folks. Y'all pritty lil frail eels don't need nothin' lak dis. You too sweet already."

"Please, Joe."

"Naw, naw. Ah don't want you to git no sweeter than whut you is already. We goin' down de road a lil piece t'night so you go put on yo' Sunday-go-to-meetin' things."

Missie May looked at her husband to see if he was playing some   30
prank. "Sho nuff, Joe?"

"Yeah. We goin' to de ice cream parlor."

"Where de ice cream parlor at, Joe?"

"A new man done come heah from Chicago and he done got a place and took and opened it up for a ice cream parlor, and bein' as it's real swell, Ah wants you to be one de first ladies to walk in dere and have some set down."

"Do Jesus, Ah ain't knowed nothin' 'bout it. Who de man done it?"

35   "Mister Otis D. Slemmons, of spots and places—Memphis, Chicago, Jacksonville, Philadelphia and so on."

"Dat heavy-set man wid his mouth full of gold teethes?"

"Yeah. Where did you see 'im at?"

"Ah went down to de sto' tuh git a box of lye and Ah seen 'im standin' on de corner talkin' to some of de mens, and Ah come on back and went to scrubbin' de floor, and he passed and tipped his hat whilst Ah was scourin' de steps. Ah thought Ah never seen *him* befo'."

Joe smiled pleasantly. "Yeah, he's up to date. He got de finest clothes Ah ever seen on a colored man's back."

40   "Aw, he don't look no better in his clothes than you do in yourn. He got a puzzlegut on 'im and he so chuckle-headed, he got a pone behind his neck."

Joe looked down at his own abdomen and said wistfully, "Wisht Ah had a build on me lak he got. He ain't puzzlegutted, honey. He jes' got a corporation. Dat make 'm look lak a rich white man. All rich mens is got some belly on 'em."

"Ah seen de pitchers of Henry Ford and he's a spare-built man and Rockefeller look lak he ain't got but one gut. But Ford and Rockefeller and dis Slemmons and all de rest kin be as many-gutted as dey please, Ah'm satisfied wid you jes' lak you is, baby. God took pattern after a pine tree and built you noble. Youse a pritty man, and if Ah knowed any way to make you mo' pritty still Ah'd take and do it."

Joe reached over gently and toyed with Missie May's ear. "You jes' say dat cause you love me, but Ah know Ah can't hold no light to Otis D. Slemmons. Ah ain't never been nowhere and Ah ain't got nothin' but you."

Missie May got on his lap and kissed him and he kissed back in kind. Then he went on. "All de womens is crazy 'bout 'im everywhere he go."

45   "How you know dat, Joe?"

"He tole us so hisself."

"Dat don't make it so. His mouf is cut cross-ways, ain't it? Well, he kin lie jes' lak anybody else."

"Good Lawd, Missie! You womens sho is hard to sense into things. He's got a five-dollar gold piece for a stick-pin and he got a ten-dollar gold piece on his watch chain and his mouf is jes' crammed full of gold teethes. Sho wisht it wuz mine. And whut make it so cool, he got money 'cumulated. And womens give it all to 'im."

"Ah don't see whut de womens see on 'im. Ah wouldn't give 'im a wink if de sheriff wuz after 'im."

"Well, he tole us how de white womens in Chicago give 'im all dat   50
gold money. So he don't 'low nobody to touch it at all. Not even put dey finger on it. Dey tole 'im not to. You kin make 'miration at it, but don't tetch it."

"Whyn't he stay up dere where dey so crazy 'bout 'im?"

"Ah reckon dey done made 'im vast-rich and he wants to travel some. He say dey wouldn't leave 'im hit a lick of work. He got mo' lady people crazy 'bout him than he kin shake a stick at."

"Joe, Ah hates to see you so dumb. Dat stray nigger jes' tell y'all anything and y'all b'lieve it."

"Go 'head on now, honey and put on yo' clothes. He talkin' 'bout his pritty womens—Ah want 'im to see *mine*."

Missie May went off to dress and Joe spent the time trying to make   55
his stomach punch out like Slemmons' middle. He tried the rolling swagger of the stranger, but found that his tall bone-and-muscle stride fitted ill with it. He just had time to drop back into his seat before Missie May came in dressed to go.

On the way home that night Joe was exultant. "Didn't Ah say ole Otis was swell? Can't he talk Chicago talk? Wuzn't dat funny whut he said when great big fat ole Ida Armstrong come in? He asted me, 'Who is dat broad wid de forte shake?' Dat's a new word. Us always thought forty was a set of figgers but he showed us where it means a whole heap of things. Sometimes he don't say forty, he jes' say thirty-eight and two and dat mean de same thing. Know whut he tole me when Ah wuz payin' for our ice cream? He say, 'Ah have to hand it to you, Joe. Dat wife of yours is jes' thirty-eight and two. Yessuh, she's forte!' Ain't he killin'?"

"He'll do in case of a rush. But he sho is got uh heap uh gold on 'im. Dat's de first time Ah ever seed gold money. It lookted good on him sho nuff, but it'd look a whole heap better on you."

"Who, me? Missie May youse crazy! Where would a po' man lak me git gold money from?"

Missie May was silent for a minute, then she said, "Us might find some goin' long de road some time. Us could."

"Who would be losin' gold money round heah? We ain't even seen   60
none dese white folks wearin' no gold money on dey watch chain. You must be figgerin' Mister Packard or Mister Cadillac goin' pass through heah."

"You don't know whut been lost 'round heah. Maybe somebody way back in memorial times lost they gold money and went on off and it ain't never been found. And then if we wuz to find it, you could wear some 'thout havin' no gang of womens lak dat Slemmons say he got."

Joe laughed and hugged her. "Don't be so wishful 'bout me. Ah'm satisfied de way Ah is. So long as Ah be yo' husband, Ah don't keer 'bout nothin' else. Ah'd ruther all de other womens in de world to be dead than for you to have de toothache. Less we go to bed and git our night rest."

It was Saturday night once more before Joe could parade his wife in Slemmons' ice cream parlor again. He worked the night shift and Saturday was his only night off. Every other evening around six o'clock he left home, and dying dawn saw him hustling home around the lake where the challenging sun flung a flaming sword from east to west across the trembling water.

That was the best part of life—going home to Missie May. Their whitewashed house, the mock battle on Saturday, the dinner and ice cream parlor afterwards, church on Sunday nights when Missie out-dressed any woman in town—all, everything was right.

65   One night around eleven the acid ran out at the G and G. The foreman knocked off the crew and let the steam die down. As Joe rounded the lake on his way home, a lean moon rode the lake in a silver boat. If anybody had asked Joe about the moon on the lake, he would have said he hadn't paid it any attention. But he saw it with his feelings. It made him yearn painfully for Missie. Creation obsessed him. He thought about children. They had been married more than a year now. They had money put away. They ought to be making little feet for shoes. A little boy child would be about right.

He saw a dim light in the bedroom and decided to come in through the kitchen door. He could wash the fertilizer dust off himself before presenting himself to Missie May. It would be nice for her not to know that he was there until he slipped into his place in bed and hugged her back. She always liked that.

He eased the kitchen door open slowly and silently, but when he went to set his dinner bucket on the table he bumped it into a pile of dishes, and something crashed to the floor. He heard his wife gasp in fright and hurried to reassure her.

"Iss me, honey. Don't git skeered."

There was a quick, large movement in the bedroom. A rustle, a thud, and a stealthy silence. The light went out.

70   What? Robbers? Murderers? Some varmint attacking his helpless wife, perhaps? He struck a match, threw himself on guard and stepped over the door-sill into the bedroom.

The great belt on the wheel of Time slipped and eternity stood still. By the match light he could see the man's legs fighting with his breeches in his frantic desire to get them on. He had both chance and time to kill the intruder in his helpless condition—half in and half out of his pants —but he was too weak to take action. The shapeless enemies of humanity that live in the hours of Time had waylaid Joe. He was assaulted in his weakness. Like Samson awakening after his haircut. So he just opened his mouth and laughed.

The match went out and he struck another and lit the lamp. A howling wind raced across his heart, but underneath its fury he heard his wife sobbing and Slemmons pleading for his life. Offering to buy it with all that he had. "Please, suh, don't kill me. Sixty-two dollars at de sto'. Gold money."

Joe just stood. Slemmons looked at the window, but it was screened. Joe stood out like a rough-backed mountain between him and the door. Barring him from escape, from sunrise, from life.

He considered a surprise attack upon the big clown that stood there laughing like a chessy cat. But before his fist could travel an inch, Joe's own rushed out to crush him like a battering ram. Then Joe stood over him.

"Git into yo' damn rags, Slemmons, and dat quick." 75

Slemmons scrambled to his feet and into his vest and coat. As he grabbed his hat, Joe's fury overrode his intentions and he grabbed at Slemmons with his left hand and struck at him with his right. The right landed. The left grazed the front of his vest. Slemmons was knocked a somersault into the kitchen and fled through the open door. Joe found himself alone with Missie May, with the golden watch charm clutched in his left fist. A short bit of broken chain dangled between his fingers.

Missie May was sobbing. Wails of weeping without words. Joe stood, and after awhile he found out that he had something in his hand. And then he stood and felt without thinking and without seeing with his natural eyes. Missie May kept on crying and Joe kept on feeling so much and not knowing what to do with all his feelings, he put Slemmons' watch charm in his pants pocket and took a good laugh and went to bed.

"Missie May, whut you cryin' for?"

"Cause Ah love you so hard and Ah know you don't love *me* no mo'."

Joe sank his face into the pillow for a spell then he said huskily, "You 80 don't know de feelings of dat yet, Missie May."

"Oh Joe, honey, he said he wuz gointer give me dat gold money and he jes' kept on after me——"

Joe was very still and silent for a long time. Then he said, "Well, don't cry no mo', Missie May. Ah got yo' gold piece for you."

The hours went past on their rusty ankles. Joe still and quiet on one bed-rail and Missie May wrung dry of sobs on the other. Finally the sun's tide crept upon the shore of night and drowned all its hours. Missie May with her face stiff and streaked towards the window saw the dawn come into her yard. It was day. Nothing more. Joe wouldn't be coming home as usual. No need to fling open the front door and sweep off the porch, making it nice for Joe. Never no more breakfast to cook; no more washing and starching of Joe's jumper-jackets and pants. No more nothing. So why get up?

With this strange man in her bed, she felt embarrassed to get up and dress. She decided to wait till he had dressed and gone. Then she would get up, dress quickly and be gone forever beyond reach of Joe's looks and laughs. But he never moved. Red light turned to yellow, then white.

85   From beyond the no-man's land between them came a voice. A strange voice that yesterday had been Joe's.

"Missie May, ain't you gonna fix me no breakfus'?"

She sprang out of bed. "Yeah, Joe. Ah didn't reckon you wuz hongry."

No need to die today. Joe needed her for a few more minutes anyhow.

Soon there was a roaring fire in the cook stove. Water bucket full and two chickens killed. Joe loved fried chicken and rice. She didn't deserve a thing and good Joe was letting her cook him some breakfast. She rushed hot biscuits to the table as Joe took his seat.

90   He ate with his eyes in his plate. No laughter, no banter.

"Missie May, you ain't eatin' yo' breakfus'."

"Ah don't choose none, Ah thank yuh."

His coffee cup was empty. She sprang to refill it. When she turned from the stove and bent to set the cup beside Joe's plate, she saw the yellow coin on the table between them.

She slumped into her seat and wept into her arms.

95   Presently Joe said calmly, "Missie May, you cry too much. Don't look back lak Lot's wife and turn to salt."

The sun, the hero of every day, the impersonal old man that beams as brightly on death as on birth, came up every morning and raced across the blue dome and dipped into the sea of fire every evening. Water ran down hill and birds nested.

Missie knew why she didn't leave Joe. She couldn't. She loved him too much, but she could not understand why Joe didn't leave her. He was polite, even kind at times, but aloof.

There were no more Saturday romps. No ringing silver dollars to stack beside her plate. No pockets to rifle. In fact the yellow coin in his trousers was like a monster hiding in the cave of his pockets to destroy her.

She often wondered if he still had it, but nothing could have induced her to ask nor yet to explore his pockets to see for herself. Its shadow was in the house whether or no.

One night Joe came home around midnight and complained of pains in the back. He asked Missie to rub him down with liniment. It had been three months since Missie had touched his body and it all seemed strange. But she rubbed him. Grateful for the chance. Before morning, youth triumphed and Missie exulted. But the next day, as she joyfully made up their bed, beneath her pillow she found the piece of money with the bit of chain attached.

Alone to herself, she looked at the thing with loathing, but look she must. She took it into her hands with trembling and saw first thing that it was no gold piece. It was a gilded half dollar. Then she knew why Slemmons had forbidden anyone to touch his gold. He trusted village eyes at a distance not to recognize his stick-pin as a gilded quarter, and his watch charm as a four-bit piece.

She was glad at first that Joe had left it there. Perhaps he was through with her punishment. They were man and wife again. Then another thought came clawing at her. He had come home to buy from her as if she were any woman in the long house. Fifty cents for her love. As if to say that he could pay as well as Slemmons. She slid the coin into his Sunday pants pocket and dressed herself and left his house.

Half way between her house and the quarters she met her husband's mother, and after a short talk she turned and went back home. Never would she admit defeat to that woman who prayed for it nightly. If she had not the substance of marriage she had the outside show. Joe must leave *her*. She let him see she didn't want his gold four-bits too.

She saw no more of the coin for some time though she knew that Joe could not help finding it in his pocket. But his health kept poor, and he came home at least every ten days to be rubbed.

The sun swept around the horizon, trailing its robes of weeks and days. One morning as Joe came in from work, he found Missie May chopping wood. Without a word he took the ax and chopped a huge pile before he stopped.

"You ain't got no business choppin' wood, and you know it."

"How come? Ah been choppin' it for de last longest."

"Ah ain't blind. You makin' feet for shoes."

"Won't you be glad to have a lil baby chile, Joe?"

100

105

110   'You know dat 'thout astin' me."
"Iss gointer be a boy chile and de very spit of you."
"You reckon, Missie May?"
"Who else could it look lak?"
Joe said nothing, but he thrust his hand deep into his pocket and
fingered something there.

115   It was almost six months later Missie May took to bed and Joe went
and got his mother to come wait on the house.
Missie May was delivered of a fine boy. Her travail was over when
Joe came in from work one morning. His mother and the old women
were drinking great bowls of coffee around the fire in the kitchen.
The minute Joe came into the room his mother called him aside.
"How did Missie May make out?" he asked quickly.
"Who, dat gal? She strong as a ox. She gointer have plenty mo'. We
done fixed her wid de sugar and lard to sweeten her for de nex' one."

120   Joe stood silent awhile.
"You ain't ast 'bout de baby, Joe. You oughter be mighty proud cause
he sho is de spittin' image of yuh, son. Dat's yourn all right, if you never
git another one, dat un is yourn. And you know Ah'm mighty proud too,
son, cause Ah never thought well of you marryin' Missie May cause her
ma used tuh fan her foot round° right smart and Ah been mighty skeered
dat Missie May wuz gointer git misput on her road."
Joe said nothing. He fooled around the house till late in the day
then just before he went to work, he went and stood at the foot of the
bed and asked his wife how she felt. He did this every day during the
week.
On Saturday he went to Orlando to make his market. It had been a
long time since he had done that.
Meat and lard, meal and flour, soap and starch. Cans of corn and
tomatoes. All the staples. He fooled around town for awhile and bought
bananas and apples. Way after while he went around to the candy store.

125   "Hello, Joe," the clerk greeted him. "Ain't seen you in a long time."
"Nope, Ah ain't been heah. Been round in spots and places."
"Want some of them molasses kisses you always buy?"
"Yessuh." He threw the gilded half dollar on the counter. "Will dat
spend?"
"Whut is it, Joe? Well, I'll be doggone! A gold-plated four-bit piece.
Where'd you git it, Joe?"

130   "Offen a stray nigger dat come through Eatonville. He had it on his
watch chain for a charm—goin' round making out iss gold money. Ha

fan . . . round: run around on her husband

ha! He had a quarter on his tie pin and it wuz all golded up too. Tryin' to fool people. Makin' out he so rich and everything. Ha! Ha! Tryin' to tole off folkses wives from home."

"How did you git it, Joe? Did he fool you, too?"

"Who, me? Naw suh! He ain't fooled me none. Know whut Ah done? He come round me wid his smart talk. Ah hauled off and knocked 'im down and took his old four-bits way from 'im. Gointer buy my wife some good ole lasses kisses wid it. Gimme fifty cents worth of dem candy kisses."

"Fifty cents buys a mighty lot of candy kisses, Joe. Why don't you split it up and take some chocolate bars, too. They eat good, too."

"Yessuh, dey do, but Ah wants all dat in kisses. Ah got a lil boy chile home now. Tain't a week old yet, but he kin suck a sugar tit and maybe eat one them kisses hisself."

Joe got his candy and left the store. The clerk turned to the next   135
customer. "Wisht I could be like these darkies. Laughin' all the time. Nothin' worries 'em."

Back in Eatonville, Joe reached his own front door. There was the ring of singing metal on wood. Fifteen times. Missie May couldn't run to the door, but she crept there as quickly as she could.

"Joe Banks, Ah hear you chunkin' money in mah do'way. You wait till Ah got mah strength back and Ah'm gointer fix you for dat.'

Henry James
The Real Thing

1

When the porter's wife, who used to answer the house-bell, announced "A gentleman and a lady, sir," I had, as I often had in those days—the wish being father to the thought—an immediate vision of sitters. Sitters my visitors in this case proved to be; but not in the sense I should have preferred. There was nothing at first however to indicate

THE REAL THING   First published in 1891. Henry James (1843–1916) published numerous novels and short stories during his illustrious career, including such classics as *The Portrait of a Lady* (1881) and *The Ambassadors* (1903). Considered one of America's premier masters of the fictional art, James came from an intellectual family—his father was a religious philosopher, his brother William a brilliant psychologist and philosopher, and his sister Alice a talented diarist—and though born in New York, he spent most of his adult life in England. His fiction often dealt with the theme of the artist's place in society.

that they mightn't have come for a portrait. The gentleman, a man of fifty, very high and very straight, with a moustache slightly grizzled and a dark grey walking-coat admirably fitted, both of which I noted professionally—I don't mean as a barber or yet as a tailor—would have struck me as a celebrity if celebrities often were striking. It was a truth of which I had for some time been conscious that a figure with a good deal of frontage was, as one might say, almost never a public institution. A glance at the lady helped to remind me of this paradoxical law: she also looked too distinguished to be a "personality." Moreover one would scarcely come across two variations together.

Neither of the pair immediately spoke—they only prolonged the preliminary gaze suggesting that each wished to give the other a chance. They were visibly shy; they stood there letting me take them in—which, as I afterwards perceived, was the most practical thing they could have done. In this way their embarrassment served their cause. I had seen people painfully reluctant to mention that they desired anything so gross as to be represented on canvas; but the scruples of my new friends appeared almost insurmountable. Yet the gentleman might have said "I should like a portrait of my wife," and the lady might have said "I should like a portrait of my husband." Perhaps they weren't husband and wife—this naturally would make the matter more delicate. Perhaps they wished to be done together—in which case they ought to have brought a third person to break the news.

"We come from Mr. Rivet," the lady finally said with a dim smile that had the effect of a moist sponge passed over a "sunk"° piece of painting, as well as of a vague allusion to vanished beauty. She was as tall and straight, in her degree, as her companion, and with ten years less to carry. She looked as sad as a woman could look whose face was not charged with expression; that is her tinted oval mask showed waste as an exposed surface shows friction. The hand of time had played over her freely, but to an effect of elimination. She was slim and stiff, and so welldressed, in dark blue cloth, with lappets and pockets and buttons, that it was clear she employed the same tailor as her husband. The couple had an indefinable air of prosperous thrift—they evidently got a good deal of luxury for their money. If I was to be one of their luxuries it would behoove me to consider my terms.

"Ah Claude Rivet recommended me?" I echoed; and I added that it was very kind of him, though I could reflect that, as he only painted landscape, this wasn't a sacrifice.

"sunk": faded

The lady looked very hard at the gentleman, and the gentleman looked round the room. Then staring at the floor a moment and stroking his moustache, he rested his pleasant eyes on me with the remark: "He said you were the right one."

"I try to be, when people want to sit."

"Yes, we should like to," said the lady anxiously.

"Do you mean together?"

My visitors exchanged a glance. "If you could do anything with *me* I suppose it would be double," the gentleman stammered.

"Oh yes, there's naturally a higher charge for two figures than for one."

"We should like to make it pay," the husband confessed.

"That's very good of you," I returned, appreciating so unwonted a sympathy—for I supposed he meant pay the artist.

A sense of strangeness seemed to dawn on the lady. "We mean for the illustrations—Mr. Rivet said you might put one in."

"Put in—an illustration?" I was equally confused.

"Sketch her off, you know," said the gentleman, coloring.

It was only then that I understood the service Claude Rivet had rendered me; he had told them how I worked in black-and-white, for magazines, for storybooks, for sketches of contemporary life, and consequently had copious employment for models. These things were true, but it was not less true—I may confess it now; whether because the aspiration was to lead to everything or to nothing I leave the reader to guess—that I couldn't get the honors, to say nothing of the emoluments, of a great painter of portraits out of my head. My "illustrations" were my pot-boilers; I looked to a different branch of art—far and away the most interesting it had always seemed to me—to perpetuate my fame. There was no shame in looking to it also to make my fortune; but that fortune was by so much further from being made from the moment my visitors wished to be "done" for nothing. I was disappointed; for in the pictorial sense I had immediately *seen* them. I had seized their type—I had already settled what I would do with it. Something that wouldn't absolutely have pleased them, I afterwards reflected.

"Ah you're—you're—a?" I began as soon as I had mastered my surprise. I couldn't bring out the dingy word "models": it seemed so little to fit the case.

"We haven't had much practice," said the lady.

"We've got to *do* something, and we've thought that an artist in your line might perhaps make something of us," her husband threw off. He further mentioned that they didn't know many artists and that they had gone first, on the off-chance—he painted views of course, but sometimes put in figures; perhaps I remembered—to Mr. Rivet, whom they had met a few years before at a place in Norfolk where he was sketching.

20   "We used to sketch a little ourselves," the lady hinted.

"It's very awkward, but we absolutely *must* do something," her husband went on.

"Of course we're not so *very* young," she admitted with a wan smile.

With the remark that I might as well know something more about them the husband had handed me a card extracted from a neat new pocket-book—their appurtenances were all of the freshest—and inscribed with the words "Major Monarch." Impressive as these words were they didn't carry my knowledge much further; but my visitor presently added: "I've left the army and we've had the misfortune to lose our money. In fact our means are dreadfully small."

"It's awfully trying—a regular strain," said Mrs. Monarch.

25   They evidently wished to be discreet—to take care not to swagger because they were gentlefolk. I felt them willing to recognize this as something of a drawback, at the same time that I guessed at an underlying sense—their consolation in adversity—that they *had* their points. They certainly had; but these advantages struck me as preponderantly social; such for instance as would help to make a drawing-room look well. However, a drawing-room was always, or ought to be, a picture.

In consequence of his wife's allusion to their age Major Monarch observed: "Naturally, it's more for the figure that we thought of going in. We can still hold ourselves up." On the instant I saw that the figure was indeed their strong point. His "naturally" didn't sound vain, but it lighted up the question. "*She* has got the best," he continued, nodding at his wife, with a pleasant after-dinner absence of circumlocution. I could only reply, as if we were in fact sitting over our wine, that this didn't prevent his own from being very good; which led him in turn to rejoin: "We thought that if you ever have to do people like us, we might be something like it. *She*, particularly—for a lady in a book, you know."

I was so amused by them that, to get more of it, I did my best to take their point of view; and though it was an embarrassment to find myself appraising physically, as if they were animals on hire or useful blacks, a pair whom I should have expected to meet only in one of the relations in which criticism is tacit, I looked at Mrs. Monarch judicially enough to be able to exclaim, after a moment, with conviction: "Oh yes, a lady in a book!" She was singularly like a bad illustration.

"We'll stand up, if you like," said the Major; and he raised himself before me with a really grand air.

I could take his measure at a glance—he was six feet two and a perfect gentleman. It would have paid any club in process of formation and in want of a stamp to engage him at a salary to stand in the principal window. What struck me immediately was that in coming to me they had rather missed their vocation; they could surely have been turned to better account for advertising purposes. I couldn't of course see the thing in detail, but I could see them make someone's fortune—I don't mean their own. There was something in them for a waistcoat-maker, an hotel-keeper, or a soap-vendor. I could imagine "We always use it" pinned on their bosoms with the greatest effect; I had a vision of the promptitude with which they would launch a table d'hôte.°

Mrs. Monarch sat still, not from pride but from shyness, and presently her husband said to her: "Get up my dear and show how smart you are." She obeyed, but she had no need to get up to show it. She walked to the end of the studio, and then she came back blushing, with her fluttered eyes on her husband. I was reminded of an incident I had accidentally had a glimpse of in Paris—being with a friend there, a dramatist about to produce a play—when an actress came to him to ask to be intrusted with a part. She went through her paces before him, walked up and down as Mrs. Monarch was doing. Mrs. Monarch did it quite as well, but I abstained from applauding. It was very odd to see such people apply for such poor pay. She looked as if she had ten thousand a year. Her husband had used the word that described her: she was in the London current jargon essentially and typically "smart." Her figure was, in the same order of ideas, conspicuously and irreproachably "good." For a woman of her age her waist was surprisingly small; her elbow moreover had the orthodox crook. She held her head at the conventional angle, but why did she come to *me*? She ought to have tried on jackets at a big shop. I feared my visitors were not only destitute but "artistic"—which would be a great complication. When she sat down again I thanked her, observing that what a draughtsman most valued in his model was the faculty of keeping quiet.

"Oh *she* can keep quiet," said Major Monarch. Then he added jocosely: "I've always kept her quiet."

"I'm not a nasty fidget, am I?" It was going to wring tears from me, I felt, the way she hid her head, ostrich-like, in the other broad bosom.

The owner of this expanse addressed his answer to me. "Perhaps it isn't out of place to mention—because we ought to be quite businesslike, oughtn't we?—that when I married her she was known as the Beautiful Statue."

a table d'hôte: a restaurant

"Oh dear!" said Mrs. Monarch ruefully.

35 "Of course I should want a certain amount of expression," I rejoined.

"Of *course!*"—and I had never heard such unanimity.

"And then I suppose you know that you'll get awfully tired."

"Oh, we *never* get tired!" they eagerly cried.

"Have you had any kind of practice?"

40 They hesitated—they looked at each other. "We've been photographed—*immensely*," said Mrs. Monarch.

"She means the fellows have asked us themselves," added the Major.

"I see—because you're so good-looking."

"I don't know what they thought, but they were always after us."

"We always got our photographs for nothing," smiled Mrs. Monarch.

45 "We might have brought some, my dear," her husband remarked.

"I'm not sure we have any left. We've given quantities away," she explained to me.

"With our autographs and that sort of thing," said the Major.

"Are they to be got in the shops?" I enquired as a harmless pleasantry.

"Oh yes, *hers*—they used to be."

50 "Not now," said Mrs. Monarch, with her eyes on the floor.

2

I could fancy the "sort of thing" they put on the presentation copies of their photographs, and I was sure they wrote a beautiful hand. It was odd how quickly I was sure of everything that concerned them. If they were now so poor as to have to earn shillings and pence they could never have had much of a margin. Their good looks had been their capital, and they had good-humoredly made the most of the career that this resource marked out for them. It was in their faces, the blankness, the deep intellectual repose of the twenty years of country-house visiting that had given them pleasant intonations. I could see the sunny drawing-rooms, sprinkled with periodicals she didn't read, in which Mrs. Monarch had continually sat; I could see the wet shrubberies in which she had walked, equipped to admiration for either exercise. I could see the rich covers the Major had helped to shoot and the wonderful garments in which, late at night, he repaired to the smoking-room to talk about them. I could imagine their leggings and waterproofs, their knowing tweeds and rugs, their rolls of sticks and cases of tackle and neat umbrellas; and I could evoke the exact appearance of their servants and the compact variety of their luggage on the platforms of country stations.

They gave small tips, but they were liked; they didn't do anything themselves, but they were welcome. They looked so well everywhere; they gratified the general relish for stature, complexion, and "form." They knew it without fatuity or vulgarity, and they respected themselves in consequence. They weren't superficial; they were thorough and kept themselves up—it had been their line. People with such a taste for activity had to have some line. I could feel how even in a dull house they could have been counted on for the joy of life. At present something had happened—it didn't matter what, their little income had grown less, it had grown least—and they had to do something for pocket-money. Their friends could like them, I made out, without liking to support them. There was something about them that represented credit—their clothes, their manners, their type; but if credit is a large empty pocket in which an occasional chink reverberates, the chink at least must be audible. What they wanted of me was to help to make it so. Fortunately they had no children—I soon divined that. They would also perhaps wish our relations to be kept secret: this was why it was "for the figure"—the reproduction of the face would betray them.

I liked them—I felt, quite as their friends must have done—they were so simple; and I had no objection to them if they would suit. But somehow with all their perfections I didn't easily believe in them. After all they were amateurs, and the ruling passion of my life was the detestation of the amateur. Combined with this was another perversity—an innate preference for the represented subject over the real one: the defect of the real one was so apt to be a lack of representation. I like things that appeared; then one was sure. Whether they *were* or not was a subordinate and almost always a profitless question. There were other considerations, the first of which was that I already had two or three recruits in use, notably a young person with big feet, in alpaca, from Kilburn, who for a couple of years had come to me regularly for my illustrations and with whom I was still—perhaps ignobly—satisfied. I frankly explained to my visitors how the case stood, but they had taken more precautions than I supposed. They had reasoned out their opportunity, for Claude Rivet had told them of the projected *édition de luxe* of one of the writers of our day—the rarest of the novelists—who, long neglected by the multitudinous vulgar and dearly prized by the attentive (need I mention Philip Vincent?), had had the happy fortune of seeing, late in life, the dawn and then the full light of a higher criticism; an estimate in which on the part of the public there was something really of expiation. The edition preparing, planned by a publisher of taste, was practically an act of high reparation; the woodcuts with which it was to be enriched were the homage of English art to one of the most independent representatives of English letters. Major and Mrs. Monarch confessed to me they had hoped I might be able to work *them* into my branch of the enterprise. They knew I was to do the first of the books, "Rutland Ramsay," but I had to make clear to them that my participation in the rest of the affair—this first book was to be a test—must depend on the satisfaction I should give. If this should be limited my employers would drop me with scarce common forms. It was therefore a crisis for me, and naturally I was making special preparations, looking about for new people, should they be necessary, and securing the best types. I admitted however that I should like to settle down to two or three good models who would do for everything.

"Should we have often to—a—put on special clothes?" Mrs. Monarch timidly demanded.

55   "Dear yes—that's half the business."

"And should we be expected to supply our own costumes?"

"Oh no; I've got a lot of things. A painter's models put on—or put off—anything he likes."

"And you mean—a—the same?"

"The same?"

60   Mrs. Monarch looked at her husband again.

"Oh she was just wondering," he explained, "if the costumes are in *general* use." I had to confess that they were, and I mentioned further that some of them—I had a lot of genuine greasy last-century things— had served their time, a hundred years ago, on living world-stained men and women; on figures not perhaps so far removed, in that vanished world, from *their* type, the Monarchs', *quoi!*° of a breeched and bewigged age. "We'll put on anything that *fits*," said the Major.

"Oh I arrange that—they fit in the pictures."

"I'm afraid I should do better for the modern books. I'd come as you like," said Mrs. Monarch.

"She has got a lot of clothes at home: they might do for contemporary life," her husband continued.

65   "Oh I can fancy scenes in which you'd be quite natural." And indeed I could see the slipshod rearrangements of stale properties—the stories I tried to produce pictures for without the exasperation of reading them—whose sandy tracts the good lady might help to people. But I had to return to the fact that for this sort of work—the daily mechanical grind—I was already equipped: the people I was working with were fully adequate.

quoi!: French for "what!"

"We only thought we might be more like *some* characters," said Mrs. Monarch mildly, getting up.

Her husband also rose; he stood looking at me with a dim wistfulness that was touching in so fine a man. "Wouldn't it be rather a pull sometimes to have—a—to have—?" He hung fire; he wanted me to help him by phrasing what he meant. But I couldn't—I didn't know. So he brought it out awkwardly: "The *real* thing; a gentleman, you know, or a lady." I was quite ready to give a general assent—I admitted that there was a great deal in that. This encouraged Major Monarch to say, following up his appeal with an unacted gulp: "It's awfully hard—we've tried everything." The gulp was communicative; it proved too much for his wife. Before I knew it Mrs. Monarch had dropped again upon a divan and burst into tears. Her husband sat down beside her, holding one of her hands; whereupon she quickly dried her eyes with the other, while I felt embarrassed as she looked up at me. "There isn't a confounded job I haven't applied for—waited for—prayed for. You can fancy we'd be pretty bad first. Secretaryships and that sort of thing? You might as well ask for a peerage. I'd be *anything*—I'm strong; a messenger or a coal-heaver. I'd put on a gold-laced cap and open carriage doors in front of the haberdasher's; I'd hang about a station to carry portmanteaux; I'd be a postman. But they won't *look* at you; there are thousands as good as yourself already on the ground. *Gentlemen*, poor beggars, who've drunk their wine, who've kept their hunters!"

I was as reassuring as I knew how to be, and my visitors were presently on their feet again while, for the experiment, we agreed on an hour. We were discussing it when the door opened and Miss Churm came in with a wet umbrella. Miss Churm had to take the omnibus to Maida Vale and then walk half a mile. She looked a trifle blowsy and slightly splashed. I scarcely ever saw her come in without thinking afresh how odd it was that, being so little in herself, she should yet be so much in others. She was a meagre little Miss Churm, but was such an ample heroine of romance. She was only a freckled cockney, but she could represent everything, from a fine lady to a shepherdess; she had the faculty as she might have had a fine voice or long hair. She couldn't spell and she loved beer, but she had two or three "points," and practice, and a knack, and mother-wit, and a whimsical sensibility, and a love of the theater, and seven sisters, and not an ounce of respect, especially for the *h*. The first thing my visitors saw was that her umbrella was wet, and in their spotless perfection they visibly winced at it. The rain had come on since their arrival.

"I'm all in a soak; there *was* a mess of people in the 'bus. I wish you lived near a stytion," said Miss Churm. I requested her to get ready as quickly as possible, and she passed into the room in which she always changed her dress. But before going out she asked me what she was to get into this time.

70   "It's the Russian princess, don't you know?" I answered; "the one with the 'golden eyes,' in black velvet, for the long thing in the *Cheapside.*°

"Golden eyes? I *say*!" cried Miss Churm, while my companions watched her with intensity as she withdrew. She always arranged herself, when she was late, before I could turn round; and I kept my visitors a little on purpose, so that they might get an idea, from seeing her, what would be expected of themselves. I mentioned that she was quite my notion of an excellent model—she was really very clever.

"Do you think she looks like a Russian princess?" Major Monarch asked with lurking alarm.

"When I make her, yes."

"Oh if you have to *make* her—!" he reasoned, not without point.

75   "That's the most you can ask. There are so many who are not makeable."

"Well now, *here's* a lady"—and with a persuasive smile he passed his arm into his wife's—"who's already made!"

"Oh I'm not a Russian princess," Mrs. Monarch protested a little coldly. I could see she had known some and didn't like them. There at once was a complication of a kind I never had to fear with Miss Churm.

This young lady came back in black velvet—the gown was rather rusty and very low on her lean shoulders—and with a Japanese fan in her red hands. I reminded her that in the scene I was doing she had to look over some one's head. "I forget whose it is; but it doesn't matter. Just look over a head."

"I'd rather look over a stove," said Miss Churm; and she took her station near the fire. She fell into position, settled herself into a tall attitude, gave a certain backward inclination to her head and a certain forward droop to her fan, and looked, at least to my prejudiced sense, distinguished and charming, foreign and dangerous. We left her looking so while I went downstairs with Major and Mrs. Monarch.

80   "I believe I could come about as near it as that," said Mrs. Monarch.

"Oh you think she's shabby, but you must allow for the alchemy of art."

the *Cheapside*: a London magazine

However, they went off with an evident increase of comfort founded on their demonstrable advantage in being the real thing. I could fancy them shuddering over Miss Churm. She was very droll about them when I went back, for I told her what they wanted.

"Well, if *she* can sit I'll tyke to book-keeping," said my model.

"She's very ladylike," I replied as an innocent form of aggravation.

"So much the worse for *you*. That means she can't turn round."   85

"She'll do for the fashionable novels."

"Oh yes, she'll *do* for them!" my model humorously declared. "Ain't they bad enough without her?" I had often sociably denounced them to Miss Churm.

3

It was for the elucidation of a mystery in one of these works that I first tried Mrs. Monarch. Her husband came with her, to be useful if necessary—it was sufficiently clear that as a general thing he would prefer to come with her. At first I wondered if this were for "propriety's" sake—if he were going to be jealous and meddling. The idea was too tiresome, and if it had been confirmed it would speedily have brought our acquaintance to a close. But I soon saw there was nothing in it and that if he accompanied Mrs. Monarch it was—in addition to the chance of being wanted—simply because he had nothing else to do. When they were separate his occupation was gone and they never *had* been separate. I judged rightly that in their awkward situation their close union was their main comfort and that this union had no weak spot. It was a real marriage, an encouragement to the hesitating, a nut for pessimists to crack. Their address was humble—I remember afterwards thinking it had been the only thing about them that was really professional—and I could fancy the lamentable lodgings in which the Major would have been left alone. He could sit there more or less grimly with his wife—he couldn't sit there anyhow without her.

He had too much tact to try and make himself agreeable when he couldn't be useful; so when I was too absorbed in my work to talk he simply sat and waited. But I liked to hear him talk—it made my work, when not interrupting it, less mechanical, less special. To listen to him was to combine the excitement of going out with the economy of staying at home. There was only one hindrance—that I seemed not to know any of the people this brilliant couple had known. I think he wondered extremely, during the term of our intercourse, whom the deuce I *did* know. He hadn't a stray sixpence of an idea to fumble for, so we didn't spin it very fine; we confined ourselves to questions of leather and even of liquor—saddlers and breeches-makers and how to get excellent claret cheap—and matters like "good trains" and the habits of small game. His lore on these last subjects was astonishing—he managed to interweave the station-master with the ornithologist. When he couldn't talk about greater things he could talk cheerfully about smaller, and since I couldn't accompany him into reminiscences of the fashionable world he could lower the conversation without a visible effort to my level.

90   So earnest a desire to please was touching in a man who could so easily have knocked one down. He looked after the fire and had an opinion on the draught of the stove without my asking him, and I could see that he thought many of my arrangements not half knowing. I remember telling him that if I were only rich I'd offer him a salary to come and teach me how to live. Sometimes he gave a random sigh of which the essence might have been: "Give me even such a bare old barrack as *this*, and I'd do something with it!" When I wanted to use him he came alone; which was an illustration of the superior courage of women. His wife could bear her solitary second floor, and she was in general more discreet; showing by various small reserves that she was alive to the propriety of keeping our relations markedly professional—not letting them slide into sociability. She wished it to remain clear that she and the Major were employed, not cultivated, and if she approved of me as a superior, who could be kept in his place, she never thought me quite good enough for an equal.

She sat with great intensity, giving the whole of her mind to it, and was capable of remaining for an hour almost as motionless as before a photographer's lens. I could see she had been photographed often, but somehow the very habit that made her good for that purpose unfitted her for mine. At first I was extremely pleased with her ladylike air, and it was a satisfaction, on coming to follow her lines, to see how good they were and how far they could lead the pencil. But after a little skirmishing I began to find her too insurmountably stiff; do what I would with it my drawing looked like a photograph or a copy of a photograph. Her figure had no variety of expression—she herself had no sense of variety. You may say that this was my business and was only a question of placing her. Yet I placed her in every conceivable position and she managed to obliterate their differences. She was always a lady certainly, and into the bargain was always the same lady. She was the real thing, but always the same thing. There were moments when I rather writhed under the serenity of her confidence that she *was* the real thing. All her dealings with me and all her husband's were an implication that this was lucky for *me*. Meanwhile I found myself trying to invent types that approached her own, instead of making her own transform itself—in the clever way that was not impossible for instance to poor Miss Churm. Arrange as I would and take the precautions I would, she always came out, in my pictures, too tall—landing me in the dilemma of having represented a fascinating woman as seven feet high, which (out of respect perhaps to my own very much scantier inches) was far from my idea of such a personage.

The case was worse with the Major—nothing I could do would keep *him* down, so that he became useful only for the representation of brawny giants. I adored variety and range, I cherished human accidents, the illustrative note; I wanted to characterize closely, and the thing in the world I most hated was the danger of being ridden by a type. I had quarreled with some of my friends about it; I had parted company with them for maintaining that one *had* to be, and that if the type was beautiful—witness Raphael and Leonardo°—the servitude was only a gain. I was neither Leonardo nor Raphael—I might only be a presumptuous young modern searcher; but I held that everything was to be sacrificed sooner than character. When they claimed that the obsessional form could easily *be* character I retorted, perhaps superficially, "Whose?" It couldn't be everybody's—it might end in being nobody's.

After I had drawn Mrs. Monarch a dozen times I felt surer even than before that the value of such a model as Miss Churm resided precisely in the fact that she had no positive stamp, combined of course with the other fact that what she did have was a curious and inexplicable talent for imitation. Her usual appearance was like a curtain which she could draw up at request for a capital performance. This performance was simply suggestive; but it was a word to the wise—it was vivid and pretty. Sometimes even I thought it, though she was plain herself, too insipidly pretty; I made it a reproach to her that the figures drawn from her were monotonously (*bêtement*, as we used to say) graceful. Nothing made her more angry; it was so much her pride to feel she could sit for characters that had nothing in common with each other. She would accuse me at such moments of taking away her "reputyion."

It suffered a certain shrinkage, this queer quantity, from the repeated visits of my new friends. Miss Churm was greatly in demand, never in want of employment, so I had no scruple in putting her off occasionally, to try them more at my ease. It was certainly amusing at first to do the real thing—it was amusing to do Major Monarch's trousers. They *were* the real thing, even if he did come out colossal. It was amusing to do his

Raphael and Leonardo: Raphael Sanzio (1483-1520) and Leonardo da Vinci (1452-1519), Italian artists of the Renaissance period wife's back hair—it was so mathematically neat—and the particular "smart" tension of her tight stays. She lent herself especially to positions in which the face was somewhat averted or blurred; she abounded in ladylike back views and *profils perdus.*° When she stood erect she took naturally one of the attitudes in which court-painters represent queens and princesses; so that I found myself wondering whether, to draw out this accomplishment, I couldn't get the editor of the *Cheapside* to publish a really royal romance, "A Tale of Buckingham Palace." Sometimes however the real thing and the make-believe came into contact; by which I mean that Miss Churm, keeping an appointment or coming to make one on days when I had much work in hand, encountered her invidious rivals. The encounter was not on their part, for they noticed her no more than if she had been the housemaid; not from intentional loftiness, but simply because as yet, professionally, they didn't know how to fraternize, as I could imagine they would have liked—or at least that the Major would. They couldn't talk about the omnibus—they always walked; and they didn't know what else to try—she wasn't interested in good trains or cheap claret. Besides, they must have felt—in the air— that she was amused at them, secretly derisive of their ever knowing how. She wasn't a person to conceal the limits of her faith if she had had a chance to show them. On the other hand Mrs. Monarch didn't think her tidy; for why else did she take pains to say to me—it was going out of the way, for Mrs. Monarch—that she didn't like dirty women?

95   One day when my young lady happened to be present with my other sitters—she even dropped in, when it was convenient, for a chat—I asked her to be so good as to lend a hand in getting tea, a service with which she was familiar and which was one of a class that, living as I did in a small way, with slender domestic resources, I often appealed to my models to render. They liked to lay hands on my property, to break the sitting, and sometimes the china—it made them feel Bohemian. The next time I saw Miss Churm after this incident she surprised me greatly by making a scene about it—she accused me of having wished to humiliate her. She hadn't resented the outrage at the time, but had seemed obliging and amused, enjoying the comedy of asking Mrs. Monarch, who sat vague and silent, whether she would have cream and sugar, and putting an exaggerated simper into the question. She had tried intonations—as if she too wished to pass for the real thing—till I was afraid my other visitors would take offense.

---

profils perdus: French for, literally, "lost profiles," meaning profiles in which the face is averted and unseen

Oh they were determined not to do this, and their touching patience was the measure of their great need. They would sit by the hour, uncomplaining, till I was ready to use them; they would come back on the chance of being wanted and would walk away cheerfully if it failed. I used to go to the door with them to see in what magnificent order they retreated. I tried to find other employment for them—I introduced them to several artists. But they didn't "take," for reasons I could appreciate, and I became rather anxiously aware that after such disappointments they fell back upon me with a heavier weight. They did me the honor to think me most *their* form. They weren't romantic enough for the painters, and in those days there were few serious workers in black-and-white. Besides, they had an eye to the great job I had mentioned to them—they had secretly set their hearts on supplying the right essence for my pictorial vindication of our fine novelist. They knew that for this undertaking I should want no costume-effects, none of the frippery of past ages—that it was a case in which everything would be contemporary and satirical and presumably genteel. If I could work them into it their future would be assured, for the labor would of course be long and the occupation steady.

One day Mrs. Monarch came without her husband—she explained his absence by his having had to go to the City. While she sat there in her usual relaxed majesty there came at the door a knock which I immediately recognized as the subdued appeal of a model out of work. It was followed by the entrance of a young man whom I at once saw to be a foreigner and who proved in fact an Italian acquainted with no English word but my name, which he uttered in a way that made it seem to include all others. I hadn't then visited his country, nor was I proficient in his tongue; but as he was not so meanly constituted—what Italian is?—as to depend only on that member for expression he conveyed to me, in familiar but graceful mimicry, that he was in search of exactly the employment in which the lady before me was engaged. I was not struck with him at first, and while I continued to draw I dropped few signs of interest or encouragement. He stood his ground however—not importunately, but with a dumb dog-like fidelity in his eyes that amounted to innocent impudence, the manner of a devoted servant—he might have been in the house for years—unjustly suspected. Suddenly it struck me that this very attitude and expression made a picture; whereupon I told him to sit down and wait till I should be free. There was another picture in the way he obeyed me, and I observed as I worked that there were others still in the way he looked wonderingly, with his head thrown back, about the high studio. He might have been crossing himself in

Saint Peter's. Before I finished I said to myself "The fellow's a bankrupt orange-monger, but a treasure."

When Mrs. Monarch withdrew he passed across the room like a flash to open the door for her, standing there with the rapt pure gaze of the young Dante spellbound by the young Beatrice.° As I never insisted, in such situations, on the blankness of the British domestic, I reflected that he had the making of a servant—and I needed one, but couldn't pay him to be only that—as well as of a model; in short I resolved to adopt my bright adventurer if he would agree to officiate in the double capacity. He jumped at my offer, and in the event my rashness—for I had really known nothing about him—wasn't brought home to me. He proved a sympathetic though a desultory ministrant, and had in a wonderful degree the *sentiment de la pose*.° It was uncultivated, instinctive, a part of the happy instinct that had guided him to my door and helped him to spell out my name on the card nailed to it. He had had no other introduction to me than a guess, from the shape of my high north window, seen outside, that my place was a studio and that as a studio it would contain an artist. He had wandered to England in search of fortune, like other itinerants, and had embarked, with a partner and a small green hand-cart, on the sale of penny ices. The ices had melted away and the partner had dissolved in their train. My young man wore tight yellow trousers with reddish stripes and his name was Oronte. He was sallow but fair, and when I put him into some old clothes of my own he looked like an Englishman. He was as good as Miss Churm, who could look, when requested, like an Italian.

4

I thought Mrs. Monarch's face slightly convulsed when, on her coming back with her husband, she found Oronte installed. It was strange to have to recognize in a scrap of a lazzarone° a competitor to her magnificent Major. It was she who scented danger first, for the Major was anecdotally unconscious. But Oronte gave us tea, with a hundred eager confusions—he had never been concerned in so queer a process— and I think she thought better of me for having at last an "establishment." They saw a couple of drawings that I had made of the establishment, and Mrs. Monarch hinted that it never would have struck her he

Beatrice: Beatrice Portinari (1266–1290), a Florentine woman who served as an inspiration for the poet Dante   *sentiment de la pose:* an inborn knack for posing (French)   **lazzarone:** Italian for "beggar"

had sat for them. "Now the drawings you make from *us*, they look exactly like us," she reminded me, smiling in triumph; and I recognized that this was indeed just their defect. When I drew the Monarchs I couldn't anyhow get away from them—get into the character I wanted to represent; and I hadn't the least desire my model should be discoverable in my picture. Miss Churm never was, and Mrs. Monarch thought I hid her, very properly, because she was vulgar; whereas if she was lost it was only as the dead who go to heaven are lost—in the gain of an angel the more.

By this time I had got a certain start with "Rutland Ramsay," the first novel in the great projected series; that is I had produced a dozen drawings, several with the help of the Major and his wife, and I had sent them in for approval. My understanding with the publishers, as I have already hinted, had been that I was to be left to do my work, in this particular case, as I liked, with the whole book committed to me; but my connection with the rest of the series was only contingent. There were moments when, frankly, it *was* a comfort to have the real thing under one's hand; for there were characters in "Rutland Ramsay" that were very much like it. There were people presumably as erect as the Major and women of as good a fashion as Mrs. Monarch. There was a great deal of country-house life—treated, it is true, in a fine fanciful ironical generalized way—and there was a considerable implication of knickerbockers and kilts. There were certain things I had to settle at the outset; such things for instance as the exact appearance of the hero and the particular bloom and figure of the heroine. The author of course gave me a lead, but there was a margin for interpretation. I took the Monarchs into my confidence, I told them frankly what I was about, I mentioned my embarrassments and alternatives. "Oh take *him*!" Mrs. Monarch murmured sweetly, looking at her husband; and "What could you want better than my wife?" the Major enquired with the comfortable candor that now prevailed between us.

I wasn't obliged to answer these remarks—I was only obliged to place my sitters. I wasn't easy in mind, and I postponed a little timidly perhaps the solving of my question. The book was a large canvas, the other figures were numerous, and I worked off at first some of the episodes in which the hero and the heroine were not concerned. When once I had set *them* up I should have to stick to them—I couldn't make my young man seven feet high in one place and five feet nine in another. I inclined on the whole to the latter measurement, though the Major more than once reminded me that *he* looked about as young as any one. It was indeed quite possible to arrange him, for the figure, so that it would have been difficult to detect his age. After the spontaneous

100

Oronte had been with me a month, and after I had given him to understand several times over that his native exuberance would presently constitute an insurmountable barrier to our further intercourse, I waked to a sense of his heroic capacity. He was only five feet seven, but the remaining inches were latent. I tried him almost secretly at first, for I was really rather afraid of the judgment my other models would pass on such a choice. If they regarded Miss Churm as little better than a snare what would they think of the representation by a person so little the real thing as an Italian street-vendor of a protagonist formed by a public school?

If I went a little in fear of them it wasn't because they bullied me, because they had got an oppressive foothold, but because in their really pathetic decorum and mysteriously permanent newness they counted on me so intensely. I was therefore very glad when Jack Hawley came home: he was always of such good counsel. He painted badly himself, but there was no one like him for putting his finger on the place. He had been absent from England for a year; he had been somewhere—I don't remember where—to get a fresh eye. I was in a good deal of dread of any such organ, but we were old friends; he had been away for months and a sense of emptiness was creeping into my life. I hadn't dodged a missile for a year.

He came back with a fresh eye, but with the same old black velvet blouse, and the first evening he spent in my studio we smoked cigarettes till the small hours. He had done no work himself, he had only got the eye; so the field was clear for the production of my little things. He wanted to see what I had produced for the *Cheapside*, but he was disappointed in the exhibition. That at least seemed the meaning of two or three comprehensive groans which, as he lounged on my big divan, his leg folded under him, looking at my latest drawings, issued from his lips with the smoke of the cigarette.

"What's the matter with you?" I asked.

105 "What's the matter with *you*?"

"Nothing save that I'm mystified."

"You are indeed. You're quite off the hinge. What's the meaning of this new fad?" And he tossed me, with visible irreverence, a drawing in which I happened to have depicted both my elegant models. I asked if he didn't think it good, and he replied that it struck him as execrable, given the sort of thing I had always represented myself to him as wishing to arrive at; but I let that pass—I was so anxious to see exactly what he meant. The two figures in the picture looked colossal, but I supposed this was *not* what he meant, inasmuch as, for aught he knew to the contrary, I might have been trying for some such effect. I maintained that I was working exactly in the same way as when he last had done me the honor to tell me I might do something some day. "Well, there's a screw loose somewhere," he answered; "wait a bit and I'll discover it." I depended upon him to do so: where else was the fresh eye? But he produced at last nothing more luminous than "I don't know—I don't like your types." This was lame for a critic who had never consented to discuss with me anything but the question of execution, the direction of strokes, and the mystery of values.

"In the drawings you've been looking at I think my types are very handsome."

"Oh they won't do!"

"I've been working with new models."   110

"I see you have. *They* won't do."

"Are you very sure of that?"

"Absolutely—they're stupid."

"You mean *I* am—for I ought to get round that."

"You *can't*—with such people. Who are they?"   115

I told him, so far as was necessary, and he concluded heartlessly: *"Ce sont des gens qu'il faut mettre à la porte.°*

"You've never seen them; they're awfully good"—I flew to their defense.

"Not seen them? Why all this recent work of yours drops to pieces with them. It's all I want to see of them."

"No one else has said anything against it—the *Cheapside* people are pleased."

"Every one else is an ass, and the *Cheapside* people the biggest asses 120
of all. Come, don't pretend at this time of day to have pretty illusions about the public, especially about publishers and editors. It's not for *such* animals you work—it's for those you know, *coloro che sanno;*° so keep straight for *me* if you can't keep straight for yourself. There was a certain sort of thing you used to try for—and a very good thing it was. But this twaddle isn't *in* it." When I talked with Hawley later about "Rutland Ramsay" and its possible successors he declared that I must get back into my boat again or I should go to the bottom. His voice in short was the voice of warning.

I noted the warning, but I didn't turn my friends out of doors. They bored me a good deal; but the very fact that they bored me admonished me not to sacrifice them—if there was anything to be done with them— simply to irritation. As I look back at this phase they seem to me to

Ce sont . . . la porte: French for "You'll have to show them to the door"   *coloro che sanno:*
Italian for "the ones who know"

have pervaded my life not a little. I have a vision of them as most of the
time in my studio, seated against the wall on an old velvet bench to be
out of the way, and resembling the while a pair of patient courtiers in a
royal ante-chamber. I'm convinced that during the coldest weeks of the
winter they held their ground because it saved them fire. Their newness
was losing its gloss, and it was impossible not to feel them objects of
charity. Whenever Miss Churm arrived they went away, and after I was
fairly launched in "Rutland Ramsay" Miss Churm arrived pretty often.
They managed to express to me tacitly that they supposed I wanted her
for the low life of the book, and I let them suppose it, since they had
attempted to study the work—it was lying about the studio—without
discovering that it dealt only with the highest circles. They had dipped
into the most brilliant of our novelists without deciphering many passages. I still took an hour from them, now and again, in spite of Jack
Hawley's warning: it would be time enough to dismiss them, if dismissal
should be necessary, when the rigor of the season was over. Hawley had
made their acquaintance—he had met them at my fireside—and
thought them a ridiculous pair. Learning that he was a painter they
tried to approach him, to show him too that they were the real thing; but
he looked at them, across the big room, as if they were miles away: they
were a compendium of everything he most objected to in the social
system of his country. Such people as that, all convention and patent-
leather, with ejaculations that stopped conversation, had no business in
a studio. A studio was a place to learn to see, and how could you see
through a pair of featherbeds?

The main inconvenience I suffered at their hands was that at first I
was shy of letting it break upon them that my artful little servant had
begun to sit to me for "Rutland Ramsay." They knew I had been odd
enough—they were prepared by this time to allow oddity to artists—to
pick a foreign vagabond out of the streets when I might have had a
person with whiskers and credentials; but it was some time before they
learned how high I rated his accomplishments. They found him in an
attitude more than once, but they never doubted I was doing him as an
organ-grinder. There were several things they never guessed, and one of
them was that for a striking scene in the novel, in which a footman
briefly figured, it occurred to me to make use of Major Monarch as
the menial. I kept putting this off, I didn't like to ask him to don the
livery—besides the difficulty of finding a livery to fit him. At last, one
day late in the winter, when I was at work on the despised Oronte, who
caught one's idea on the wing, and was in the glow of feeling myself go
very straight, they came in, the Major and his wife, with their society
laugh about nothing (there was less and less to laugh at); came in like

country-callers—they always reminded me of that—who have walked across the park after church and are presently persuaded to stay to luncheon. Luncheon was over, but they could stay to tea—I knew they wanted it. The fit was on me, however, and I couldn't let my ardor cool and my work wait, with the fading daylight, while my model prepared it. So I asked Mrs. Monarch if she would mind laying it out—a request which for an instant brought all the blood to her face. Her eyes were on her husband's for a second, and some mute telegraphy passed between them. Their folly was over the next instant; his cheerful shrewdness put an end to it. So far from pitying their wounded pride, I must add, I was moved to give it as complete a lesson as I could. They bustled about together and got out the cups and saucers and made the kettle boil. I know they felt as if they were waiting on my servant, and when the tea was prepared I said: "He'll have a cup, please—he's tired." Mrs. Monarch brought him one where he stood, and he took it from her as if he had been a gentleman at a party squeezing a crush-hat with an elbow.

Then it came over me that she had made a great effort for me— made it with a kind of nobleness—and that I owed her a compensation. Each time I saw her after this I wondered what the compensation could be. I couldn't go on doing the wrong thing to oblige them. Oh it *was* the wrong thing, the stamp of the work for which they sat—Hawley was not the only person to say it now. I sent in a large number of the drawings I had made for "Rutland Ramsay," and I received a warning that was more to the point than Hawley's. The artistic adviser of the house for which I was working was of opinion that many of my illustrations were not what had been looked for. Most of these illustrations were the subjects in which the Monarchs had figured. Without going into the question of what *had* been looked for, I had to face the fact that at this rate I shouldn't get the other books to do. I hurled myself in despair on Miss Churm—I put her through all her paces. I not only adopted Oronte publicly as my hero, but one morning when the Major looked in to see if I didn't require him to finish a *Cheapside* figure for which he had begun to sit the week before, I told him I had changed my mind— I'd do the drawing from my man. At this my visitor turned pale and stood looking at me. "Is *he* your idea of an English gentleman?" he asked.

I was disappointed, I was nervous, I wanted to get on with my work; so I replied with irritation: "Oh my dear Major—I can't be ruined for *you*!"

It was a horrid speech, but he stood another moment—after which, without a word, he quitted the studio. I drew a long breath,

125

for I said to myself that I shouldn't see him again. I hadn't told him definitely that I was in danger of having my work rejected, but I was vexed at his not having felt the catastrophe in the air, read with me the moral of our fruitless collaboration, the lesson that in the deceptive atmosphere of art even the highest respectability may fail of being plastic.

I didn't owe my friends money, but I did see them again. They reappeared together three days later; and, given all the other facts, there was something tragic in that one. It was a clear proof they could find nothing else in life to do. They had threshed the matter out in a dismal conference—they had digested the bad news that they were not in for the series. If they weren't useful to me for the *Cheapside* their function seemed difficult to determine, and I could only judge at first that they had come, forgivingly, decorously, to take a last leave. This made me rejoice in secret that I had little leisure for a scene; for I had placed both my other models in position together and I was pegging away at a drawing from which I hoped to derive glory. It had been suggested by the passage in which Rutland Ramsay, drawing up a chair to Artemisia's piano-stool, says extraordinary things to her while she ostensibly fingers out a difficult piece of music. I had done Miss Churm at the piano before—it was an attitude in which she knew how to take on an absolutely poetic grace. I wished the two figures to "compose" together with intensity, and my little Italian had entered perfectly into my conception. The pair were vividly before me, the piano had been pulled out; it was a charming show of blended youth and murmured love, which I had only to catch and keep. My visitors stood and looked at it, and I was friendly to them over my shoulder.

They made no response, but I was used to silent company and went on with my work, only a little disconcerted—even though exhilarated by the sense that *this* was at least the ideal thing—at not having got rid of them after all. Presently I heard Mrs. Monarch's sweet voice beside or rather above me: "I wish her hair were a little better done." I looked up and she was staring with a strange fixedness at Miss Churm, whose back was turned to her. "Do you mind my just touching it?" she went on—a question which made me spring up for an instant as with the instinctive fear that she might do the young lady a harm. But she quieted me with a glance I shall never forget—I confess I should like to have been able to paint *that*—and went for a moment to my model. She spoke to her softly, laying a hand on her shoulder and bending over her; and as the girl, understanding, gratefully assented, she disposed her rough curls, with a few quick passes, in such a way as to make Miss Churm's head twice as charming. It was one of the most heroic personal services I've ever seen rendered. Then Mrs. Monarch turned away with a low sigh and, looking about her as if for something to do, stooped to the floor with a noble humility and picked up a dirty rag that had dropped out of my paint-box.

The Major meanwhile had also been looking for something to do, and, wandering to the other end of the studio, saw before him my breakfast-things neglected, unremoved. "I say, can't I be useful *here?*" he called out to me with an irrepressible quaver. I assented with a laugh that I fear was awkward, and for the next ten minutes, while I worked, I heard the light clatter of china and the tinkle of spoons and glass. Mrs. Monarch assisted her husband—they washed up my crockery, they put it away. They wandered off into my little scullery, and I afterwards found that they had cleaned my knives and that my slender stock of plate had an unprecedented surface. When it came over me, the latent eloquence of what they were doing, I confess that my drawing was blurred for a moment—the picture swam. They had accepted their failure, but they couldn't accept their fate. They had bowed their heads in bewilderment to the perverse and cruel law in virtue of which the real thing could be so much less precious than the unreal; but they didn't want to starve. If my servants were my models, then my models might be my servants. They would reverse the parts—the others would sit for the ladies and gentlemen and *they* would do the work. They would still be in the studio—it was an intense dumb appeal to me not to turn them out. "Take us on," they wanted to say, "we'll do *anything.*"

My pencil dropped from my hand; my sitting was spoiled and I got rid of my sitters, who were also evidently rather mystified and awestruck. Then, alone with the Major and his wife I had a most uncomfortable moment. He put their prayer into a single sentence: "I say, you know— just let *us* do for you, can't you?" I couldn't—it was dreadful to see them emptying my slops; but I pretended I could, to oblige them, for about a week. Then I gave them a sum of money to go away, and I never saw them again. I obtained the remaining books, but my friend Hawley repeats that Major and Mrs. Monarch did me a permanent harm, got me into false ways. If it be true I'm content to have paid the price—for the memory.

Herman Melville

Bartleby the Scrivener

A Story of Wall Street

I am a rather elderly man. The nature of my avocations for the last thirty years has brought me into more than ordinary contact with what would seem an interesting and somewhat singular set of men of whom as yet nothing that I know of has ever been written—I mean the law-copyists or scriveners. I have known very many of them, professionally and privately, and if I pleased could relate diverse histories at which good-natured gentlemen might smile and sentimental souls might weep. But I waive the biographies of all other scriveners for a few passages in the life of Bartleby, who was a scrivener the strangest I ever saw or heard of. While of other law-copyists I might write the complete life, of Bartleby nothing of that sort can be done. I believe that no materials exist for a full and satisfactory biography of this man. It is an irreparable loss to literature. Bartleby was one of those beings of whom nothing is ascertainable except from the original sources, and in his case those are very small. What my own astonished eyes saw of Bartleby, *that* is all I know of him except, indeed, one vague report which will appear in the sequel.

Ere introducing the scrivener as he first appeared to me, it is fit I make some mention of myself, my employees, my business, my chambers, and general surroundings, because some such description is indispensable to an adequate understanding of the chief character about to be presented.

Imprimis: I am a man who from his youth upwards has been filled with a profound conviction that the easiest way of life is the best. Hence, though I belong to a profession proverbially energetic and nervous, even to turbulence at times, yet nothing of that sort have I ever suffered to

BARTLEBY THE SCRIVENER   First published in 1853. Herman Melville (1819–1891) was born in New York City. After working as a farmhand, clerk, bookkeeper, and teacher, he went to sea in 1837, where his adventures and observations supplied him with the material for several novels of the sea including *Moby-Dick* (1851). The lack of financial success of that book and later works of fiction, including *Piazza Tales*, which reprinted "Bartleby the Scrivener," led Melville eventually to write poetry instead. By the time of the story, Wall Street had become the financial and business center of New York City. In the days before the invention of the typewriter, official documents and legal papers had to be copied by hand—the job of a "scrivener." "The Tombs" (paragraph 11 and thereafter) was the vivid nickname of the city prison, properly called the Halls of Justice.

invade my peace. I am one of those unambitious lawyers who never addresses a jury or in any way draws down public applause, but in the cool tranquility of a snug retreat do a snug business among rich men's bonds and mortgages and title-deeds. All who know me consider me an eminently *safe* man. The late John Jacob Astor, a personage little given to poetic enthusiasm, had no hesitation in pronouncing my first grand point to be prudence; my next, method. I do not speak it in vanity but simply record the fact that I was not unemployed in my profession by the late John Jacob Astor, a name which, I admit, I love to repeat, for it hath a rounded and orbicular sound to it and rings like unto bullion. I will freely add that I was not insensible to the late John Jacob Astor's good opinion.

Sometime prior to the period at which this little history begins, my avocations had been largely increased. The good old office now extinct in the State of New York of a Master in Chancery had been conferred upon me. It was not a very arduous office but very pleasantly remunerative. I seldom lose my temper; much more seldom indulge in dangerous indignation at wrongs and outrages; but I must be permitted to be rash here and declare that I consider the sudden and violent abrogation of the office of Master in Chancery by the new Constitution as a _____ premature act, inasmuch as I had counted upon a life-lease of the profits, whereas I only received those of a few short years. But this is by the way.

My chambers were upstairs at No. ___ Wall Street. At one end they looked upon the white wall of the interior of a spacious skylight shaft penetrating the building from top to bottom. This view might have been considered rather tame than otherwise, deficient in what landscape painters call "life." But if so, the view from the other end of my chambers offered at least a contrast, if nothing more. In that direction my windows commanded an unobstructed view of a lofty brick wall, black by age and everlasting shade, which wall required no spy-glass to bring out its lurking beauties, but for the benefit of all near-sighted spectators was pushed up to within ten feet of my window panes. Owing to the great height of the surrounding buildings, and my chambers being on the second floor, the interval between this wall and mine not a little resembled a huge square cistern.

At the period just preceding the advent of Bartleby, I had two persons as copyists in my employment and a promising lad as an office boy. First, Turkey; second, Nippers; third, Ginger Nut. These may seem names the like of which are not usually found in the Directory. In truth they were nicknames mutually conferred upon each other by my three clerks, and were deemed expressive of their respective persons or characters. Turkey was a short, pursy Englishman of about my own age, that

5

is, somewhere not far from sixty. In the morning, one might say, his face was of a fine florid hue, but after twelve o'clock, meridian—his dinner hour—it blazed like a grate full of Christmas coals, and continued blazing—but as it were with a gradual wane—till 6 o'clock P.M. or thereabouts, after which I saw no more of the proprietor of the face, which gaining its meridian with the sun, seemed to set with it, to rise, culminate, and decline the following day, with the like regularity and undiminished glory. There are many singular coincidences I have known in the course of my life, not the least among which was the fact that exactly when Turkey displayed his fullest beams from his red and radiant countenance, just then, too, at the critical moment began the daily period when I considered his business capacities as seriously disturbed for the remainder of the twenty-four hours. Not that he was absolutely idle or averse to business then; far from it. The difficulty was, he was apt to be altogether too energetic. There was a strange, inflamed, flurried, flighty recklessness of activity about him. He would be incautious in dipping his pen into his inkstand. All his blots upon my documents were dropped there after twelve o'clock, meridian. Indeed not only would he be reckless and sadly given to making blots in the afternoon, but some days he went further and was rather noisy. At such times, too, his face flamed with augmented blazonry, as if cannel coal had been heaped on anthracite. He made an unpleasant racket with his chair; spilled his sand-box;° in mending his pens, impatiently split them all to pieces, and threw them on the floor in a sudden passion; stood up and leaned over his table, boxing his papers about in a most indecorous manner, very sad to behold in an elderly man like him. Nevertheless, as he was in many ways a most valuable person to me, and all the time before twelve o'clock, meridian, was the quickest, steadiest creature too, accomplishing a great deal of work in a style not easy to be matched—for these reasons, I was willing to overlook his eccentricities, though indeed occasionally I remonstrated with him. I did this very gently, however, because though the civilest, nay, the blandest and most reverential of men in the morning, yet in the afternoon he was disposed upon provocation to be slightly rash with his tongue, in fact insolent. Now valuing his morning services as I did, and resolved not to lose them; yet at the same time made uncomfortable by his inflamed ways after twelve o'clock; and being a man of peace, unwilling by my admonitions to call forth unseemly retorts from him, I took upon me one Saturday noon (he was always worse on Saturdays) to hint to him very kindly that perhaps now that he was growing old, it might be well to abridge his

sand-box: sand kept in a shaker and used for blotting wet ink labors; in short, he need not come to my chambers after twelve o'clock but, dinner over, had best go home to his lodgings and rest himself till tea-time. But no; he insisted upon his afternoon devotions. His countenance became intolerably fervid as he oratorically assured me—gesticulating with a long ruler at the other end of the room—that if his services in the morning were useful, how indispensable, then, in the afternoon?

"With submission, sir," said Turkey on this occasion. "I consider myself your right-hand man. In the morning I but marshal and deploy my columns, but in the afternoon I put myself at their head and gallantly charge the foe, thus!"—and he made a violent thrust with the ruler.

"But the blots, Turkey," intimated I.

"True,—but, with submission, sir, behold these hairs! I am getting old. Surely, sir, a blot or two of a warm afternoon is not to be severely urged against gray hairs. Old age—even if it blot the page—is honorable. With submission, sir, we *both* are getting old."

This appeal to my fellow-feeling was hardly to be resisted. At all   10
events, I saw that go he would not. So I made up my mind to let him stay, resolving nevertheless to see to it that during the afternoon he had to do with my less important papers.

Nippers, the second on my list, was a whiskered, sallow, and upon the whole rather piratical-looking young man of about five and twenty. I always deemed him the victim of two evil powers—ambition and indigestion. The ambition was evinced by a certain impatience of the duties of a mere copyist, an unwarrantable usurpation of strictly professional affairs such as the original drawing up of legal documents. The indigestion seemed betokened in an occasional nervous testiness and grinning irritability causing the teeth to audibly grind together over mistakes committed in copying; unnecessary maledictions hissed rather than spoken in the heat of business; and especially by a continual discontent with the height of the table where he worked. Though of a very ingenious mechanical turn, Nippers could never get this table to suit him. He put chips under it, blocks of various sorts, bits of paste-board, and at last went so far as to attempt an exquisite adjustment by final pieces of folded blotting-paper. But no invention would answer. If for the sake of easing his back he brought the table lid at a sharp angle well up towards his chin, and wrote there like a man using the steep roof of a Dutch house for his desk, then he declared that it stopped the circulation in his arms. If now he lowered the table to his waistbands and stooped over it in writing, then there was a sore aching in his back. In short, the truth of the matter was Nippers knew not what he wanted. Or if he wanted anything, it was to be rid of a scrivener's table altogether. Among the manifestations of his diseased ambition was a fondness he had for receiving visits from certain ambiguous-looking fellows in seedy coats, whom he called his clients. Indeed I was aware that not only was he at times considerable of a ward-politician, but he occasionally did a little business at the Justices' courts and was not unknown on the steps of the Tombs. I have good reason to believe however that one individual who called upon him at my chambers and who with a grand air he insisted was his client was no other than a dun, and the alleged title-deed, a bill. But with all his failings, and the annoyances he caused me, Nippers, like his compatriot Turkey, was a very useful man to me; wrote a neat, swift hand; and, when he chose, was not deficient in a gentle-manly sort of deportment. Added to this, he always dressed in a gentle-manly sort of way, and so incidentally reflected credit upon my chambers. Whereas with respect to Turkey, I had much ado to keep him from being a reproach to me. His clothes were apt to look oily and smell of eating-houses. He wore his pantaloons very loose and baggy in the summer. His coats were execrable, his hat not to be handled. But while the hat was a thing of indifference to me inasmuch as his natural civility and deference as a dependent Englishman always led him to doff it the moment he entered the room, yet his coat was another matter. Concerning his coats, I reasoned with him, but with no effect. The truth was I suppose that a man with so small an income could not afford to sport such a lustrous face and a lustrous coat at one and the same time. As Nippers once observed, Turkey's money went chiefly for red ink. One winter day I presented Turkey with a highly respectable looking coat of my own, a padded gray coat of a most comfortable warmth and which buttoned straight up from the knee to the neck. I thought Turkey would appreciate the favor and abate his rashness and obstreperousness of afternoons. But no. I verily believe that buttoning himself up in so downy and blanket-like a coat had a pernicious effect upon him, upon the same principle that too much oats are bad for horses. In fact, precisely as a rash, restive horse is said to feel his oats, so Turkey felt his coat. It made him insolent. He was a man whom prosperity harmed.

Though concerning the self-indulgent habits of Turkey I had my own private surmises, yet touching Nippers I was well persuaded that whatever might be his faults in other respects, he was at least a temperate young man. But indeed, nature herself seemed to have been his vintner and at his birth charged him so thoroughly with an irritable, brandy-like disposition that all subsequent potations were needless. When I consider how amid the stillness of my chambers Nippers would sometimes impa-tiently rise from his seat and stooping over his table spread his arms wide apart, seize the whole desk, and move it, and jerk it, with a grim, grinding motion on the floor, as if the table were a perverse voluntary agent intent on thwarting and vexing him, I plainly perceive that for Nippers, brandy and water were altogether superfluous.

It was fortunate for me that, owing to its peculiar cause—indigestion—the irritability and consequent nervousness of Nippers were mainly observable in the morning, while in the afternoon he was comparatively mild. So that Turkey's paroxysms only coming on about twelve o'clock, I never had to do with their eccentricities at one time. Their fits relieved each other like guards. When Nippers's was on, Turkey's was off, and vice versa. This was a good natural arrangement under the circumstances.

Ginger Nut, the third on my list, was a lad some twelve years old. His father was a carman,° ambitious of seeing his son on the bench instead of a cart before he died. So he sent him to my office as student at law, errand boy, and cleaner and sweeper, at the rate of one dollar a week. He had a little desk to himself but he did not use it much. Upon inspection, the drawer exhibited a great array of the shells of various sorts of nuts. Indeed, to this quick-witted youth the whole noble science of the law was contained in a nutshell. Not the least among the employments of Ginger Nut, as well as one which he discharged with the most alacrity, was his duty as cake and apple purveyor for Turkey and Nippers. Copying law papers being proverbially a dry, husky sort of business, my two scriveners were fain to moisten their mouths very often with Spitzenbergs° to be had at the numerous stalls nigh the Custom House and Post Office. Also, they sent Ginger Nut very frequently for that peculiar cake—small, flat, round, and very spicy—after which he had been named by them. Of a cold morning when business was but dull, Turkey would gobble up scores of these cakes as if they were mere wafers—indeed they sell them at the rate of six or eight for a penny—the scrape of his pen blending with the crunching of the crisp particles in his mouth. Of all the fiery afternoon blunders and flurried rashnesses of Turkey was his once moistening a ginger cake between his lips and clapping it on to a mortgage for a seal. I came within an ace of dismissing him then. But he mollified me by making an oriental bow and saying—"With submission, sir, it was generous of me to find you in stationery on my own account."

Now my original business—that of a conveyancer and title hunter, and drawer-up of recondite documents of all sorts—was considerably increased by receiving the master's office. There was now great work for scriveners. Not only must I push the clerks already with me, but I must have additional help. In answer to my advertisement, a motionless

15

carman: a cart driver   Spitzenbergs: a variety of apple

young man one morning stood upon my office threshold, the door being open, for it was summer. I can see that figure now—pallidly neat, pitiably respectable, incurably forlorn! It was Bartleby.

After a few words touching his qualifications I engaged him, glad to have among my corps of copyists a man of so singularly sedate an aspect, which I thought might operate beneficially upon the flighty temper of Turkey and the fiery one of Nippers.

I should have stated before that ground glass folding doors divided my premises into two parts, one of which was occupied by my scriveners, the other by myself. According to my humor I threw open these doors, or closed them. I resolved to assign Bartleby a corner by the folding doors, but on my side of them so as to have this quiet man within easy call in case any trifling thing was to be done. I placed his desk close up to a small side window in that part of the room, a window which originally had afforded a lateral view of certain grimy backyards and bricks, but which owing to subsequent erections commanded at present no view at all, though it gave some light. Within three feet of the panes was a wall, and the light came down from far above between two lofty buildings as from a very small opening in a dome. Still further to a satisfactory arrangement, I procured a high green folding screen which might entirely isolate Bartleby from my sight though not remove him from my voice. And thus, in a manner privacy and society were conjoined.

At first Bartleby did an extraordinary quantity of writing. As if long famishing for something to copy, he seemed to gorge himself on my documents. There was no pause for digestion. He ran a day and night line, copying by sunlight and by candlelight. I should have been quite delighted with his application had he been cheerfully industrious. But he wrote on silently, palely, mechanically.

It is of course an indispensable part of a scrivener's business to verify the accuracy of his copy, word by word. Where there are two or more scriveners in an office, they assist each other in this examination, one reading from the copy, the other holding the original. It is a very dull, wearisome, and lethargic affair. I can readily imagine that to some sanguine temperaments it would be altogether intolerable. For example, I cannot credit that the mettlesome poet Byron would have contentedly sat down with Bartleby to examine a law document of, say, five hundred pages closely written in a crimpy hand.

20   Now and then in the haste of business, it had been my habit to assist in comparing some brief document myself, calling Turkey or Nippers for this purpose. One object I had in placing Bartleby so handy to me behind the screen was to avail myself of his services on such trivial occasions. It was on the third day, I think, of his being with

me, and before any necessity had arisen for having his own writing examined, that being much hurried to complete a small affair I had in hand, I abruptly called to Bartleby. In my haste and natural expectancy of instant compliance, I sat with my head bent over the original on my desk and my right hand sideways and somewhat nervously extended with the copy, so that immediately upon emerging from his retreat Bartleby might snatch it and proceed to business without the least delay.

In this very attitude did I sit when I called to him, rapidly stating what it was I wanted him to do—namely, to examine a small paper with me. Imagine my surprise, nay my consternation, when without moving from his privacy Bartleby in a singularly mild, firm voice replied, "I would prefer not to."

I sat awhile in perfect silence, rallying my stunned faculties. Immediately it occurred to me that my ears had deceived me, or Bartleby had entirely misunderstood my meaning. I repeated my request in the clearest tone I could assume. But in quite as clear a one came the previous reply, "I would prefer not to."

"Prefer not to," echoed I, rising in high excitement and crossing the room with a stride. "What do you mean? Are you moonstruck? I want you to help me compare this sheet here—take it," and I thrust it towards him.

"I would prefer not to," said he.

I looked at him steadfastly. His face was leanly composed, his gray eye dimly calm. Not a wrinkle of agitation rippled him. Had there been the least uneasiness, anger, impatience or impertinence in his manner, in other words had there been anything ordinarily human about him, doubtless I should have violently dismissed him from the premises. But as it was, I should have as soon thought of turning my pale plaster-of-paris bust of Cicero out of doors. I stood gazing at him awhile as he went on with his own writing, and then reseated myself at my desk. This is very strange, thought I. What had one best do? But my business hurried me. I concluded to forget the matter for the present, reserving it for my future leisure. So calling Nippers from the other room, the paper was speedily examined.

A few days after this Bartleby concluded four lengthy documents, being quadruplicates of a week's testimony taken before me in my High Court of Chancery. It became necessary to examine them. It was an important suit and great accuracy was imperative. Having all things arranged I called Turkey, Nippers and Ginger Nut from the next room, meaning to place the four copies in the hands of my four clerks while I should read from the original. Accordingly Turkey, Nippers and

Ginger Nut had taken their seats in a row, each with his document in hand, when I called to Bartleby to join this interesting group.

"Bartleby! quick, I am waiting."

I heard a slow scrape of his chair legs on the unscraped floor, and soon he appeared standing at the entrance of his hermitage.

"What is wanted?" said he mildly.

30   "The copies, the copies," said I hurriedly. "We are going to examine them. There"—and I held towards him the fourth quadruplicate.

"I would prefer not to," he said, and gently disappeared behind the screen.

For a few moments I was turned into a pillar of salt° standing at the head of my seated column of clerks. Recovering myself, I advanced towards the screen and demanded the reason for such extraordinary conduct.

"Why do you refuse?"

"I would prefer not to."

35   With any other man I should have flown outright into a dreadful passion, scorned all further words, and thrust him ignominiously from my presence. But there was something about Bartleby that not only strangely disarmed me, but in a wonderful manner touched and disconcerted me. I began to reason with him.

"These are your own copies we are about to examine. It is labor saving to you, because one examination will answer for your four papers. It is common usage. Every copyist is bound to help examine his copy. Is it not so? Will you not speak? Answer!"

"I prefer not to," he replied in a flute-like tone. It seemed to me that while I had been addressing him, he carefully revolved every statement that I made, fully comprehended the meaning, could not gainsay the irresistible conclusion, but at the same time some paramount consideration prevailed with him to reply as he did.

"You are decided, then, not to comply with my request—a request made according to common usage and common sense?"

He briefly gave me to understand that on that point my judgment was sound. Yes: his decision was irreversible.

40   It is not seldom the case that when a man is browbeaten in some unprecedented and violently unreasonable way he begins to stagger in his own plainest faith. He begins, as it were, vaguely to surmise that wonderful as it may be, all the justice and all the reason is on the other side. Accordingly, if any disinterested persons are present he turns to them for some reinforcement for his own faltering mind.

pillar of salt: See Genesis 19.26.

"Turkey," said I, "what do you think of this? Am I not right?"

"With submission, sir," said Turkey with his blandest tone, "I think that you are."

"Nippers," said I, "what do *you* think of it?"

"I think I should kick him out of the office."

(The reader of nice perceptions will here perceive that, it being morning, Turkey's answer is couched in polite and tranquil terms, but Nippers replies in ill-tempered ones. Or, to repeat a previous sentence, Nippers's ugly mood was on duty, and Turkey's off.)   45

"Ginger Nut," said I, willing to enlist the smallest suffrage in my behalf, "what do *you* think of it?"

"I think, sir, he's a little *loony*," replied Ginger Nut, with a grin.

"You hear what they say," said I, turning towards the screen, "come forth and do your duty."

But he vouchsafed no reply. I pondered a moment in sore perplexity. But once more business hurried me. I determined again to postpone the consideration of this dilemma to my future leisure. With a little trouble we made out to examine the papers without Bartleby, though at every page or two, Turkey deferentially dropped his opinion that this proceeding was quite out of the common, while Nippers, twitching in his chair with a dyspeptic nervousness, ground out between his set teeth occasional hissing maledictions against the stubborn oaf behind the screen. And for his (Nippers's) part, this was the first and the last time he would do another man's business without pay.

Meanwhile Bartleby sat in his hermitage, oblivious to everything but his own peculiar business there.   50

Some days passed, the scrivener being employed upon another lengthy work. His late remarkable conduct led me to regard his way narrowly. I observed that he never went to dinner, indeed that he never went anywhere. As yet I had never of my personal knowledge known him to be outside of my office. He was a perpetual sentry in the corner. At about eleven o'clock though, in the morning, I noticed that Ginger Nut would advance toward the opening in Bartleby's screen as if silently beckoned thither by a gesture invisible to me where I sat. That boy would then leave the office jingling a few pence and reappear with a handful of ginger nuts which he delivered in the hermitage, receiving two of the cakes for his trouble.

He lives then on ginger nuts, thought I; never eats a dinner, properly speaking; he must be a vegetarian then, but no, he never eats even vegetables, he eats nothing but ginger nuts. My mind then ran on in reveries concerning the probable effects upon the human constitution of living entirely on ginger nuts. Ginger nuts are so called because they contain ginger as one of their peculiar constituents, and the final flavoring one. Now what was ginger? A hot, spicy thing. Was Bartleby hot and spicy? Not at all. Ginger, then, had no effect upon Bartleby. Probably he preferred it should have none.

Nothing so aggravates an earnest person as a passive resistance. If the individual so resisted be of a not inhumane temper, and the resisting one perfectly harmless in his passivity, then in the better moods of the former, he will endeavor charitably to construe to his imagination what proves impossible to be solved by his judgment. Even so for the most part I regarded Bartleby and his ways. Poor fellow! thought I, he means no mischief; it is plain he intends no insolence; his aspect sufficiently evinces that his eccentricities are involuntary. He is useful to me. I can get along with him. If I turn him away, the chances are he will fall in with some less indulgent employer, and then he will be rudely treated and perhaps driven forth miserably to starve. Yes. Here I can cheaply purchase a delicious self-approval. To befriend Bartleby, to humor him in his strange wilfulness, will cost me little or nothing, while I lay up in my soul what will eventually prove a sweet morsel for my conscience. But this mood was not invariable with me. The passiveness of Bartleby sometimes irritated me. I felt strangely goaded on to encounter him in new opposition, to elicit some angry spark from him answerable to my own. But indeed I might as well have essayed to strike fire with my knuckles against a bit of Windsor soap. But one afternoon the evil impulse in me mastered me, and the following little scene ensued:

"Bartleby," said I, "when those papers are all copied I will compare them with you."

55   "I would prefer not to."

"How? Surely you do not mean to persist in that mulish vagary?"

No answer.

I threw open the folding doors nearby, and turning upon Turkey and Nippers, exclaimed in an excited manner—

"He says, a second time, he won't examine his papers. What do you think of it, Turkey?"

60   It was afternoon, be it remembered. Turkey sat glowing like a brass boiler, his bald head steaming, his hands reeling among his blotted papers.

"Think of it?" roared Turkey, "I think I'll just step behind his screen and black his eyes for him!"

So saying, Turkey rose to his feet and threw his arms into a pugilistic position. He was hurrying away to make good his promise when I detained him, alarmed at the effect of incautiously rousing Turkey's combativeness after dinner.

"Sit down, Turkey," said I, "and hear what Nippers has to say. What do you think of it, Nippers? Would I not be justified in immediately dismissing Bartleby?"

"Excuse me, that is for you to decide, sir. I think his conduct quite unusual, and indeed unjust as regards Turkey and myself. But it may only be a passing whim."

"Ah," exclaimed I, "you have strangely changed your mind then— you speak very gently of him now." 65

"All beer," cried Turkey, "gentleness is effects of beer—Nippers and I dined together today. You see how gentle *I* am, sir. Shall I go and black his eyes?"

"You refer to Bartleby, I suppose. No, not today, Turkey," I replied, "pray, put up your fists."

I closed the doors, and again advanced towards Bartleby. I felt additional incentives tempting me to my fate. I burned to be rebelled against again. I remembered that Bartleby never left the office.

"Bartleby," said I, "Ginger Nut is away; just step round to the post office, won't you? (it was but a three minutes walk) and see if there is anything for me."

"I would prefer not to." 70

"You *will* not?"

"I *prefer* not."

I staggered to my desk and sat there in a deep study. My blind inveteracy returned. Was there any other thing in which I could procure myself to be ignominiously repulsed by this lean, penniless wight?—my hired clerk? What added thing is there, perfectly reasonable, that he will be sure to refuse to do?

"Bartleby!"

No answer. 75

"Bartleby," in a louder tone.

No answer.

"Bartleby," I roared.

Like a very ghost, agreeably to the laws of magical invocation, at the third summons he appeared at the entrance of his hermitage.

"Go to the next room, and tell Nippers to come to me." 80

"I prefer not to," he respectfully and slowly said, and mildly disappeared.

"Very good, Bartleby," said I, in a quiet sort of serenely severe self-possessed tone, intimating the unalterable purpose of some terrible retribution very close at hand. At the moment I half intended something of the kind. But upon the whole, as it was drawing towards my dinner hour, I thought it best to put on my hat and walk home for the day, suffering much from perplexity and distress of mind.

Shall I acknowledge it? The conclusion of this whole business was that it soon became a fixed fact of my chambers that a pale young scrivener by the name of Bartleby had a desk there; that he copied for me at the usual rate of four cents a folio (one hundred words); but he was permanently exempt from examining the work done by him, that duty being transferred to Turkey and Nippers, one of compliment doubtless to their superior acuteness; moreover, said Bartleby was never on any account to be dispatched on the most trivial errand of any sort, and that even if entreated to take upon him such a matter, it was generally understood that he would prefer not to—in other words, that he would refuse point-blank.

As days passed on, I became considerably reconciled to Bartleby. His steadiness, his freedom from all dissipation, his incessant industry (except when he chose to throw himself into a standing revery behind his screen), his great stillness, his unalterableness of demeanor under all circumstances, made him a valuable acquisition. One prime thing was this—*he was always there*—first in the morning, continually through the day, and the last at night. I had a singular confidence in his honesty. I felt my most precious papers perfectly safe in his hands. Sometimes to be sure I could not for the very soul of me avoid falling into sudden spasmodic passions with him. For it was exceeding difficult to bear in mind all the time those strange peculiarities, privileges, and unheard of exemptions forming the tacit stipulations on Bartleby's part under which he remained in my office. Now and then in the eagerness of dispatching pressing business, I would inadvertently summon Bartleby, in a short rapid tone, to put his finger, say, on the incipient tie of a bit of red tape with which I was about compressing some papers. Of course, from behind the screen the usual answer, "I prefer not to," was sure to come, and then how could a human creature with the common infirmities of our nature, refrain from bitterly exclaiming upon such perverseness—such unreasonableness? However, every added repulse of this sort which I received only tended to lessen the probability of my repeating the inadvertence.

85   Here it must be said that according to the custom of most legal gentlemen occupying chambers in densely populated law buildings, there were several keys to my door. One was kept by a woman residing in the attic, which person weekly scrubbed and daily swept and dusted my apartments. Another was kept by Turkey for convenience sake. The third I sometimes carried in my own pocket. The fourth I knew not who had.

Now one Sunday morning I happened to go to Trinity Church° to hear a celebrated preacher, and finding myself rather early on the ground I thought I would walk round to my chambers for a while. Luckily I had my key with me, but upon applying it to the lock, I found it resisted by something inserted from the inside. Quite surprised, I called out, when to my consternation a key was turned from within, and thrusting his lean visage at me and holding the door ajar, the apparition of Bartleby appeared, in his shirt sleeves, and otherwise in a strangely tattered dishabille, saying quietly that he was sorry but he was deeply engaged just then and—preferred not admitting me at present. In a brief word or two, he moreover added that perhaps I had better walk round the block two or three times, and by that time he would probably have concluded his affairs.

Now, the utterly unsurmised appearance of Bartleby tenanting my law-chambers of a Sunday morning with his cadaverously gentlemanly nonchalance, yet withal firm and self-possessed, had such a strange effect upon me that incontinently I slunk away from my own door and did as desired. But not without sundry twinges of impotent rebellion against the mild effrontery of this unaccountable scrivener. Indeed it was his wonderful mildness chiefly which not only disarmed me but unmanned me, as it were. For I consider that one, for the time, is a sort of unmanned when he tranquilly permits his hired clerk to dictate to him and order him away from his own premises. Furthermore, I was full of uneasiness as to what Bartleby could possibly be doing in my office in his shirt sleeves and in an otherwise dismantled condition of a Sunday morning. Was anything amiss going on? Nay, that was out of the question. It was not to be thought of for a moment that Bartleby was an immoral person. But what could he be doing there?—copying? Nay again, whatever might be his eccentricities, Bartleby was an eminently decorous person. He would be the last man to sit down to his desk in any state approaching to nudity. Besides, it was Sunday, and there was something about Bartleby that forbade the supposition that he would by any secular occupation violate the proprieties of the day.

Nevertheless, my mind was not pacified; and full of a restless curiosity, at last I returned to the door. Without hindrance I inserted my key, opened it, and entered. Bartleby was not to be seen. I looked round anxiously, peeped behind his screen, but it was very plain that he was gone. Upon more closely examining the place, I surmised that for an indefinite period Bartleby must have ate, dressed, and slept in my office, and that too without plate, mirror, or bed. The cushioned seat of a

Trinity Church: located at the corner of Broadway and Wall Street rickety old sofa in one corner bore the faint impress of a lean, reclining form. Rolled away under his desk I found a blanket; under the empty grate, a blacking box and brush; on a chair, a tin basin with soap and a ragged towel; in a newspaper a few crumbs of ginger nuts and a morsel of cheese. Yes, thought I, it is evident enough that Bartleby has been making his home here, keeping bachelor's hall all by himself. Immediately then the thought came sweeping across me, what miserable friendlessness and loneliness are here revealed! His poverty is great; but his solitude, how horrible! Think of it. Of a Sunday, Wall Street is deserted as Petra, and every night of every day it is an emptiness. This building too which of weekdays hums with industry and life at nightfall echoes with sheer vacancy, and all through Sunday is forlorn. And here Bartleby makes his home, sole spectator of a solitude which he has seen all populous—a sort of innocent and transformed Marius brooding among the ruins of Carthage!

For the first time in my life a feeling of overpowering stinging melancholy seized me. Before I had never experienced aught but a not unpleasing sadness. The bond of a common humanity now drew me irresistibly to gloom. A fraternal melancholy! For both I and Bartleby were sons of Adam. I remembered the bright silks and sparkling faces I had seen that day in gala trim, swan-like sailing down the Mississippi of Broadway; and I contrasted them with the pallid copyist, and thought to myself, Ah, happiness courts the light, so we deem the world is gay; but misery hides aloof, so we deem that misery there is none. These sad fancyings—chimeras doubtless of a sick and silly brain—led on to other and more special thoughts concerning the eccentricities of Bartleby. Presentiments of strange discoveries hovered round me. The scrivener's pale form appeared to me laid out, among uncaring strangers, in its shivering winding sheet.

90   Suddenly I was attracted by Bartleby's closed desk, the key in open sight left in the lock.

I mean no mischief, seek the gratification of no heartless curiosity, thought I; besides, the desk is mine, and its contents too, so I will make bold to look within. Everything was methodically arranged, the papers smoothly placed. The pigeon holes were deep, and removing the files of documents, I groped into their recesses. Presently I felt something there and dragged it out. It was an old bandanna handkerchief, heavy and knotted. I opened it, and saw it was a savings bank.

I now recalled all the quiet mysteries which I had noted in the man. I remembered that he never spoke but to answer; that though at intervals he had considerable time to himself, yet I had never seen him reading—no, not even a newspaper; that for long periods he would stand looking out, at his pale window behind the screen, upon the dead brick wall; I was quite sure he never visited any refectory or eating house, while his pale face clearly indicated that he never drank beer like Turkey, or tea and coffee even, like other men; that he never went anywhere in particular that I could learn, never went out for a walk, unless indeed that was the case at present; that he had declined telling who he was or whence he came or whether he had any relatives in the world; that though so thin and pale, he never complained of ill health. And more than all, I remembered a certain unconscious air of pallid— how shall I call it?—of pallid haughtiness, say, or rather an austere reserve about him, which had positively awed me into my tame compliance with his eccentricities when I had feared to ask him to do the slightest incidental thing for me, even though I might know from his long-continued motionlessness that behind his screen he must be standing in one of those dead-wall reveries of his.

Revolving all these things, and coupling them with the recently discovered fact that he made my office his constant abiding place and home, and not forgetful of his morbid moodiness; revolving all these things, a prudential feeling began to steal over me. My first emotions had been those of pure melancholy and sincerest pity; but just in proportion as the forlornness of Bartleby grew and grew to my imagination, did that same melancholy merge into fear, that pity into repulsion. So true it is, and so terrible too, that up to a certain point the thought or sight of misery enlists our best affections; but in certain special cases, beyond that point it does not. They err who would assert that invariably this is owing to the inherent selfishness of the human heart. It rather proceeds from a certain hopelessness of remedying excessive and organic ill. To a sensitive being, pity is not seldom pain. And when at last it is perceived that such pity cannot lead to effectual succor, common sense bids the soul be rid of it. What I saw that morning persuaded me that the scrivener was the victim of innate and incurable disorder. I might give alms to his body, but his body did not pain him; it was his soul that suffered, and his soul I could not reach.

I did not accomplish the purpose of going to Trinity Church that morning. Somehow, the things I had seen disqualified me for the time from church-going. I walked homeward, thinking what I would do with Bartleby. Finally I resolved upon this:—I would put certain calm questions to him the next morning, touching his history, &c., and if he declined to answer them openly and unreservedly (and I supposed he would prefer not), then to give him a twenty dollar bill over and above whatever I might owe him, and tell him his services were no longer required; but that if in any other way I could assist him, I would be happy to do so, especially if he desired to return to his native place, wherever that might be, I would willingly help to defray the expenses. Moreover, if after reaching home he found himself at any time in want of aid, a letter from him would be sure of a reply.

95   The next morning came.

"Bartleby," said I, gently calling to him behind his screen.

No reply.

"Bartleby," said I, in a still gentler tone, "come here; I am not going to ask you to do anything you would prefer not to do—I simply wish to speak to you."

Upon this he noiselessly slid into view.

100   "Will you tell me, Bartleby, where you were born?"

"I would prefer not to."

"Will you tell me *anything* about yourself?"

"I would prefer not to."

"But what reasonable objection can you have to speak to me? I feel friendly towards you."

105   He did not look at me while I spoke, but kept his glance fixed upon my bust of Cicero, which as I then sat was directly behind me, some six inches above my head.

"What is your answer, Bartleby?" said I, after waiting a considerable time for a reply, during which his countenance remained immovable, only there was the faintest conceivable tremor of the white attenuated mouth.

"At present I prefer to give no answer," he said, and retired into his hermitage.

It was rather weak in me I confess, but his manner on this occasion nettled me. Not only did there seem to lurk in it a certain disdain, but his perverseness seemed ungrateful, considering the undeniable good usage and indulgence he had received from me.

Again I sat ruminating what I should do. Mortified as I was at his behavior, and resolved as I had been to dismiss him when I entered my office, nevertheless I strangely felt something superstitious knocking at my heart, and forbidding me to carry out my purpose, and denouncing me for a villain if I dared to breathe one bitter word against this forlornest of mankind. At last, familiarly drawing my chair behind his screen, I sat down and said: "Bartleby, never mind then about revealing your history; but let me entreat you, as a friend, to comply as far as may be with the usages of this office. Say now you will help to examine papers tomorrow or next day: in short, say now that in a day or two you will begin to be a little reasonable:—say so, Bartleby."

"At present I would prefer not to be a little reasonable," was his   110
mildly cadaverous reply.

Just then the folding doors opened, and Nippers approached. He
seemed suffering from an unusually bad night's rest, induced by severer
indigestion than common. He overheard those final words of Bartleby.

"*Prefer not*, eh?" gritted Nippers—"I'd *prefer* him, if I were you, sir,"
addressing me—"I'd *prefer* him; I'd give him preferences, the stubborn
mule! What is it, sir, pray, that he *prefers* not to do now?"

Bartleby moved not a limb.

"Mr. Nippers," said I, "I'd prefer that you would withdraw for the
present."

Somehow, of late I had got into the way of involuntarily using this   115
word "prefer" upon all sorts of not exactly suitable occasions. And I
trembled to think that my contact with the scrivener had already and
seriously affected me in a mental way. And what further and deeper
aberration might it not yet produce? This apprehension had not been
without efficacy in determining me to summary means.

As Nippers, looking very sour and sulky, was departing, Turkey
blandly and deferentially approached.

"With submission, sir," said he, "yesterday I was thinking about
Bartleby here, and I think that if he would but prefer to take a quart
of good ale every day, it would do much towards mending him and
enabling him to assist in examining his papers."

"So you have got the word too," said I, slightly excited.

"With submission, what word, sir?" asked Turkey, respectfully
crowding himself into the contracted space behind the screen, and by
so doing making me jostle the scrivener. "What word, sir?"

"I would prefer to be left alone here," said Bartleby, as if offended at   120
being mobbed in his privacy.

"*That's* the word, Turkey," said I—"*that's* it."

"Oh, *prefer*? oh yes—queer word. I never use it myself. But, sir, as I
was saying, if he would but prefer—"

"Turkey," interrupted I, "you will please withdraw."

"Oh certainly, sir, if you prefer that I should."

As he opened the folding door to retire, Nippers at his desk caught   125
a glimpse of me and asked whether I would prefer to have a certain
paper copied on blue paper or white. He did not in the least roguishly
accent the word prefer. It was plain that it involuntarily rolled from his
tongue. I thought to myself, surely I must get rid of a demented man
who already has in some degree turned the tongues if not the heads of
myself and clerks. But I thought it prudent not to break the dismission
at once.

The next day I noticed that Bartleby did nothing but stand at his window in his dead-wall revery. Upon my asking him why he did not write, he said that he had decided upon doing no more writing.

"Why, how now? what next?" exclaimed I, "do no more writing?"

"No more."

"And what is the reason?"

130   "Do you not see the reason for yourself?" he indifferently replied.

I looked steadfastly at him, and perceived that his eyes looked dull and glazed. Instantly it occurred to me that his unexampled diligence in copying by his dim window for the first few weeks of his stay with me might have temporarily impaired his vision.

I was touched. I said something in condolence with him. I hinted that of course he did wisely in abstaining from writing for a while, and urged him to embrace that opportunity of taking wholesome exercise in the open air. This, however, he did not do. A few days after this, my other clerks being absent, and being in a great hurry to dispatch certain letters by the mail, I thought that, having nothing else earthly to do, Bartleby would surely be less inflexible than usual and carry these letters to the post office. But he blankly declined. So, much to my inconvenience, I went myself.

Still added days went by. Whether Bartleby's eyes improved or not, I could not say. To all appearance, I thought they did. But when I asked him if they did, he vouchsafed no answer. At all events, he would do no copying. At last, in reply to my urgings, he informed me that he had permanently given up copying.

"What!" exclaimed I; "suppose your eyes should get entirely well— better than ever before—would you not copy then?"

135   "I have given up copying," he answered, and slid aside.

He remained as ever, a fixture in my chamber. Nay—if that were possible—he became still more of a fixture than before. What was to be done? He would do nothing in the office: why should he stay there? In plain fact, he had now become a millstone to me, not only useless as a necklace but afflictive to bear. Yet I was sorry for him. I speak less than truth when I say that on his own account, he occasioned me uneasiness. If he would but have named a single relative or friend, I would instantly have written and urged their taking the poor fellow away to some convenient retreat. But he seemed alone, absolutely alone in the universe. A bit of wreck in the mid-Atlantic. At length, necessities connected with my business tyrannized over all other considerations. Decently as I could, I told Bartleby that in six days' time he must unconditionally leave the office. I warned him to take measures, in the interval, for procuring some other abode. I offered to assist him in this endeavor, if he himself would but take the first step towards a removal. "And when you finally quit me, Bartleby," added I, "I shall see that you go not away entirely unprovided. Six days from this hour, remember."

At the expiration of that period I peeped behind the screen, and lo! Bartleby was there.

I buttoned up my coat, balanced myself, advanced slowly towards him, touched his shoulder, and said, "The time has come; you must quit this place; I am sorry for you; here is money; but you must go."

"I would prefer not," he replied, with his back still towards me.

"You *must*."   140

He remained silent.

Now I had an unbounded confidence in this man's common honesty. He had frequently restored to me six pences and shillings carelessly dropped upon the floor, for I am apt to be very reckless in such shirt-button affairs. The proceeding then which followed will not be deemed extraordinary.

"Bartleby," said I, "I owe you twelve dollars on account; here are thirty-two; the odd twenty are yours. Will you take it?" and I handed the bills towards him.

But he made no motion.

"I will leave them here then," putting them under a weight on the   145
table. Then taking my hat and cane and going to the door I tranquilly turned and added, "After you have removed your things from these offices, Bartleby, you will of course lock the door—since every one is now gone for the day but you—and if you please, slip your key underneath the mat so that I may have it in the morning. I shall not see you again, so good-bye to you. If hereafter in your new place of abode I can be of any service to you, do not fail to advise me by letter. Good-bye, Bartleby, and fare you well."

But he answered not a word; like the last column of some ruined temple, he remained standing mute and solitary in the middle of the otherwise deserted room.

As I walked home in a pensive mood, my vanity got the better of my pity. I could not but highly plume myself on my masterly management in getting rid of Bartleby. Masterly I call it, and such it must appear to any dispassionate thinker. The beauty of my procedure seemed to consist in its perfect quietness. There was no vulgar bullying, no bravado of any sort, no choleric hectoring and striding to and fro across the apartment, jerking out vehement commands for Bartleby to bundle himself off with his beggarly traps.° Nothing of the kind. Without loudly bidding Bartleby depart—as an inferior genius might have done—I *assumed* the ground that depart he must, and upon the assumption built all I had to say. The more I thought over my procedure, the more I was charmed with it. Nevertheless, next morning, upon awakening, I had my doubts—I had somehow slept off the fumes of vanity. One of the coolest and wisest hours a man has is just after he awakes in the morning. My procedure seemed as sagacious as ever—but only in theory. How it would prove in practice—there was the rub. It was truly a beautiful thought to have assumed Bartleby's departure; but after all, that assumption was simply my own, and none of Bartleby's. The great point was not whether I had assumed that he would quit me, but whether he would prefer so to do. He was more a man of preferences than assumptions.

After breakfast, I walked downtown, arguing the probabilities *pro* and *con*. One moment I thought it would prove a miserable failure, and Bartleby would be found all alive at my office as usual; the next moment it seemed certain that I should see his chair empty. And so I kept veering about. At the corner of Broadway and Canal Street, I saw quite an excited group of people standing in earnest conversation.

"I'll take odds he doesn't," said a voice as I passed.

"Doesn't go?—done!" said I, "put up your money."

150   I was instinctively putting my hand in my pocket to produce my own, when I remembered that this was an election day. The words I had overheard bore no reference to Bartleby, but to the success or non-success of some candidate for the mayoralty. In my intent frame of mind, I had, as it were, imagined that all Broadway shared in my excitement and were debating the same question with me. I passed on, very thankful that the uproar of the street screened my momentary absentmindedness.

As I had intended, I was earlier than usual at my office door. I stood listening for a moment. All was still. He must be gone. I tried the knob. The door was locked. Yes, my procedure had worked to a charm; he indeed must be vanished. Yet a certain melancholy mixed with this: I was almost sorry for my brilliant success. I was fumbling under the door mat for the key which Bartleby was to have left there for me when accidentally my knee knocked against a panel, producing a summoning sound, and in response a voice came to me from within—"Not yet; I am occupied."

It was Bartleby.

I was thunderstruck. For an instant I stood like the man who, pipe in mouth, was killed one cloudless afternoon long ago in Virginia, by

traps: belongings

summer lightning; at his own warm open window he was killed, and remained leaning out there upon the dreamy afternoon till someone touched him, when he fell.

"Not gone!" I murmured at last. But again obeying that wondrous   155 ascendancy which the inscrutable scrivener had over me, and from which ascendancy, for all my chafing, I could not completely escape, I slowly went downstairs and out into the street, and while walking round the block, considered what I should next do in this unheard of perplexity. Turn the man out by an actual thrusting I could not; to drive him away by calling him hard names would not do; calling in the police was an unpleasant idea; and yet, permit him to enjoy his cadaverous triumph over me?—this too I could not think of. What was to be done? or if nothing could be done, was there anything further that I could *assume* in the matter? Yes, as before I had prospectively assumed that Bartleby would depart, so now I might retrospectively assume that departed he was. In the legitimate carrying out of this assumption, I might enter my office in a great hurry, and pretending not to see Bartleby at all, walk straight against him as if he were air. Such a proceeding would in a singular degree have the appearance of a home-thrust. It was hardly possible that Bartleby could withstand such an application of the doctrine of assumptions. But upon second thoughts the success of the plan seemed rather dubious. I resolved to argue the matter over with him again.

"Bartleby," said I, entering the office with a quietly severe expression, "I am seriously displeased. I am pained, Bartleby. I had thought better of you. I had imagined you of such a gentlemanly organization that in my delicate dilemma a slight hint would suffice—in short, an assumption. But it appears I am deceived. Why," I added, unaffectedly starting, "you have not even touched that money yet," pointing to it just where I had left it the evening previous.

He answered nothing.

"Will you, or will you not, quit me?" I now demanded in a sudden passion, advancing close to him.

"I would prefer *not* to quit you," he replied, gently emphasizing the not.

"What earthly right have you to stay here? Do you pay any rent?   160 Do you pay my taxes? Or is this property yours?"

He answered nothing.

"Are you ready to go on and write now? Are your eyes recovered? Could you copy a small paper for me this morning? or help examine a few lines? or step round to the post office? In a word, will you do anything at all to give a coloring to your refusal to depart the premises?"

He silently retired into his hermitage.

I was now in such a state of nervous resentment that I thought it but prudent to check myself at present from further demonstrations. Bartleby and I were alone. I remembered the tragedy of the unfortunate Adams and the still more unfortunate Colt° in the solitary office of the latter; and how poor Colt, being dreadfully incensed by Adams, and imprudently permitting himself to get wildly excited, was at unawares hurried into his fatal act—an act which certainly no man could possibly deplore more than the actor himself. Often it had occurred to me in my ponderings upon the subject that had that altercation taken place in the public street, or at a private residence, it would not have terminated as it did. It was the circumstance of being alone in a solitary office, upstairs, of a building entirely unhallowed by humanizing domestic associations— an uncarpeted office, doubtless, of a dusty haggard sort of appearance— this it must have been which greatly helped to enhance the irritable desperation of the hapless Colt.

165   But when this old Adam of resentment rose in me and tempted me concerning Bartleby, I grappled him and threw him. How? Why, simply by recalling the divine injunction: "A new commandment° give I unto you, that ye love one another." Yes, this it was that saved me. Aside from higher considerations, charity often operates as a vastly wise and prudent principle—a great safeguard to its possessor. Men have committed murder for jealousy's sake, and anger's sake, and hatred's sake, and selfishness' sake, and spiritual pride's sake; but no man that ever I heard of ever committed a diabolical murder for sweet charity's sake. Mere self-interest, then, if no better motive can be enlisted, should, especially with high-tempered men, prompt all beings to charity and philanthropy. At any rate, upon the occasion in question, I strove to drown my exasperated feelings towards the scrivener by benevolently construing his conduct. Poor fellow, poor fellow! thought I, he don't mean anything; and besides, he has seen hard times, and ought to be indulged.

I endeavored also immediately to occupy myself, and at the same time to comfort my despondency. I tried to fancy that in the course of the morning, at such time as might prove agreeable to him, Bartleby of his own free accord would emerge from his hermitage and take up some decided line of march in the direction of the door. But no. Half-past twelve o'clock came; Turkey began to glow in the face, overturn his inkstand, and become generally obstreperous; Nippers abated down into

Colt: In a famous murder case in 1841, John Colt used a hatchet to kill Samuel Adams, who owed him money. **commandment:** See John 15.12.

quietude and courtesy; Ginger Nut munched his noon apple; and Bartleby remained standing at his window in one of his profoundest dead-wall reveries. Will it be credited? Ought I to acknowledge it? That afternoon I left the office without saying one further word to him.

Some days now passed, during which at leisure intervals I looked a little into "Edwards on the Will," and "Priestly on Necessity."° Under the circumstances, those books induced a salutary feeling. Gradually I slid into the persuasion that these troubles of mine touching the scrivener had been all predestinated from eternity, and Bartleby was billeted upon me for some mysterious purpose of an all-wise Providence which it was not for a mere mortal like me to fathom. Yes, Bartleby, stay there behind your screen, thought I; I shall persecute you no more; you are harmless and noiseless as any of these old chairs; in short, I never feel so private as when I know you are here. At least I see it, I feel it; I penetrate to the predestinated purpose of my life. I am content. Others may have loftier parts to enact; but my mission in this world, Bartleby, is to furnish you with office-room for such period as you may see fit to remain.

I believe that this wise and blessed frame of mind would have continued with me had it not been for the unsolicited and uncharitable remarks obtruded upon me by my professional friends who visited the rooms. But thus it often is, that the constant friction of illiberal minds wears out at last the best resolves of the more generous. Though to be sure, when I reflected upon it, it was not strange that people entering my office should be struck by the peculiar aspect of the unaccountable Bartleby, and so be tempted to throw out some sinister observations concerning him. Sometimes an attorney having business with me, and calling at my office, and finding no one but the scrivener there, would undertake to obtain some sort of precise information from him touching my whereabouts; but without heeding his idle talk, Bartleby would remain standing immovable in the middle of the room. So after contemplating him in that position for a time, the attorney would depart, no wiser than he came.

Also, when a reference was going on, and the room full of lawyers and witnesses and business was driving fast, some deeply occupied legal gentleman present seeing Bartleby wholly unemployed would request him to run round to his (the legal gentleman's) office and fetch some papers for him. Thereupon, Bartleby would tranquilly decline, and remain idle as before. Then the lawyer would give a great stare and turn to me. And what could I say? At last I was made aware that all

---

"Edwards . . . Necessity": writings by eighteenth-century philosophers who took the position that free will does not exist through the circle of my professional acquaintance, a whisper of wonder was running round having reference to the strange creature I kept at my office. This worried me very much. And as the idea came upon me of his possibly turning out a long-lived man, and keep occupying my chambers, and denying my authority, and perplexing my visitors, and scandalizing my professional reputation, and casting a general gloom over the premises, keeping soul and body together to the last upon his savings (for doubtless he spent but half a dime a day), and in the end perhaps outliving me, and claiming possession of my office by right of his perpetual occupancy: as all these dark anticipations crowded upon me more and more, and my friends continually intruded their relentless remarks upon the apparition in my room, a great change was wrought in me. I resolved to gather all my faculties together, and forever rid me of this intolerable incubus.

170   Ere revolving any complicated project, however, adapted to this end, I first simply suggested to Bartleby the propriety of his permanent departure. In a calm and serious tone, I commended the idea to his careful and mature consideration. But having taken three days to meditate upon it, he apprised me that his original determination remained the same, in short, that he still preferred to abide with me.

What shall I do? I now said to myself, buttoning up my coat to the last button. What shall I do? what ought I do? what does conscience say I *should* do with this man, or rather ghost? Rid myself of him, I must; go, he shall. But how? You will not thrust him, the poor, pale, passive mortal—you will not thrust such a helpless creature out of your door? you will not dishonor yourself by such cruelty? No, I will not, I cannot do that. Rather would I let him live and die here, and then mason up his remains in the wall. What then will you do? For all your coaxing, he will not budge. Bribes he leaves under your own paperweight on your table; in short, it is quite plain that he prefers to cling to you.

Then something severe, something unusual must be done. What! surely you will not have him collared by a constable, and commit his innocent pallor to the common jail? And upon what ground could you procure such a thing to be done?—a vagrant, is he? What! he a vagrant, a wanderer, who refuses to budge? It is because he will *not* be a vagrant, then, that you seek to count him *as* a vagrant. That is too absurd. No visible means of support: there I have him. Wrong again: for indubitably he *does* support himself, and that is the only unanswerable proof that any man can show of his possessing the means so to do. No more then. Since he will not quit me, I must quit him. I will change my offices; I will move elsewhere, and give him fair notice that if I find him on my new premises I will then proceed against him as a common trespasser.

Acting accordingly, next day I thus addressed him: "I find these chambers too far from the City Hall; the air is unwholesome. In a word, I propose to remove my offices next week, and shall no longer require your services. I tell you this now, in order that you may seek another place."

He made no reply, and nothing more was said.

On the appointed day I engaged carts and men, proceeded to my chambers, and having but little furniture, everything was removed in a few hours. Throughout, the scrivener remained standing behind the screen, which I directed to be removed the last thing. It was withdrawn, and being folded up like a huge folio, left him the motionless occupant of a naked room. I stood in the entry watching him a moment, while something from within me upbraided me.   175

I re-entered, with my hand in my pocket—and—and my heart in my mouth.

"Good-bye, Bartleby; I am going—good-bye, and God some way bless you; and take that," slipping something in his hand. But it dropped upon the floor, and then—strange to say—I tore myself from him whom I had so longed to be rid of.

Established in my new quarters, for a day or two I kept the door locked, and started at every footfall in the passages. When I returned to my rooms after any little absence, I would pause at the threshold for an instant, and attentively listen ere applying my key. But these fears were needless. Bartleby never came nigh me.

I thought all was going well, when a perturbed looking stranger visited me inquiring whether I was the person who had recently occupied rooms at No. ___ Wall Street.

Full of forebodings, I replied that I was.   180

"Then sir," said the stranger, who proved a lawyer, "you are responsible for the man you left there. He refuses to do any copying; he refuses to do anything; he says he prefers not to; and he refuses to quit the premises."

"I am very sorry, sir," said I, with assumed tranquility, but an inward tremor, "but, really, the man you allude to is nothing to me—he is no relation or apprentice of mine, that you should hold me responsible for him."

"In mercy's name, who is he?"

"I certainly cannot inform you. I know nothing about him. Formerly I employed him as a copyist, but he has done nothing for me now for some time past."

"I shall settle him then—good morning, sir."   185

Several days passed, and I heard nothing more; and though I often felt a charitable prompting to call at the place and see poor Bartleby, yet a certain squeamishness of I know not what withheld me.

All is over with him by this time, thought I at last, when through another week no further intelligence reached me. But coming to my room the day after, I found several persons waiting at my door in a high state of nervous excitement.

"That's the man—here he comes," cried the foremost one, whom I recognized as the lawyer who had previously called upon me alone.

"You must take him away, sir, at once," cried a portly person among them, advancing upon me, and whom I knew to be the landlord of No. ___ Wall Street. "These gentlemen, my tenants, cannot stand it any longer; Mr. B—" pointing to the lawyer, "has turned him out of his room, and he now persists in haunting the building generally, sitting upon the banisters of the stairs by day, and sleeping in the entry by night. Everybody is concerned; clients are leaving the offices; some fears are entertained of a mob; something you must do, and that without delay."

190   Aghast at this torrent, I fell back before it, and would fain have locked myself in my new quarters. In vain I persisted that Bartleby was nothing to me—no more than to anyone else. In vain—I was the last person known to have anything to do with him, and they held me to the terrible account. Fearful then of being exposed in the papers (as one person present obscurely threatened), I considered the matter, and at length said that if the lawyer would give me a confidential interview with the scrivener, in his (the lawyer's) own room, I would that afternoon strive my best to rid them of the nuisance they complained of.

Going upstairs to my old haunt, there was Bartleby silently sitting upon the banister at the landing.

"What are you doing here, Bartleby?" said I.

"Sitting upon the banister," he mildly replied.

I motioned him into the lawyer's room, who then left us.

195   "Bartleby," said I, "are you aware that you are the cause of great tribulation to me, by persisting in occupying the entry after being dismissed from the office?"

No answer.

"Now one of two things must take place. Either you must do something or something must be done to you. Now what sort of business would you like to engage in? Would you like to re-engage in copying for someone?"

"No; I would prefer not to make any change."

"Would you like a clerkship in a dry-goods store?"

"There is too much confinement about that. No, I would not like a   200
clerkship; but I am not particular."

"Too much confinement," I cried, "why you keep yourself confined
all the time!"

"I would prefer not to take a clerkship," he rejoined, as if to settle
that little item at once.

"How would a bar-tender's business° suit you? There is no trying of
the eyesight in that."

"I would not like it at all; though, as I said before, I am not
particular."

His unwonted wordiness inspirited me. I returned to the charge.   205

"Well then, would you like to travel through the country collecting
bills for the merchants? That would improve your health."

"No, I would prefer to be doing something else."

"How then would going as a companion to Europe, to entertain
some young gentleman with your conversation—how would that suit
you?"

"Not at all. It does not strike me that there is anything definite
about that. I like to be stationary. But I am not particular."

"Stationary you shall be then," I cried, now losing all patience, and   210
for the first time in all my exasperating connection with him fairly flying
into a passion. "If you do not go away from these premises before night, I
shall feel bound—indeed I *am* bound—to—to—to quit the premises
myself!" I rather absurdly concluded, knowing not with what possible
threat to try to frighten his immobility into compliance. Despairing of all
further efforts, I was precipitately leaving him, when a final thought
occurred to me—one which had not been wholly unindulged before.

"Bartleby," said I, in the kindest tone I could assume under such
exciting circumstances, "will you go home with me now—not to my
office, but my dwelling—and remain there till we can conclude upon
some convenient arrangement for you at our leisure? Come, let us start
now, right away."

"No: at present I would prefer not to make any change at all."

I answered nothing, but effectually dodging everyone by the sud-
denness and rapidity of my flight, rushed from the building, ran up Wall
Street towards Broadway, and jumping into the first omnibus was soon
removed from pursuit. As soon as tranquility returned I distinctly perceived that I had now done all that I possibly could, both in respect to
the demands of the landlord and his tenants, and with regard to my own
desire and sense of duty, to benefit Bartleby and shield him from rude

---

bar-tender's business: work as an attendant in a courtroom persecution. I now strove to be entirely carefree and quiescent; and my conscience justified me in the attempt though indeed it was not so successful as I could have wished. So fearful was I of being again hunted out by the incensed landlord and his exasperated tenants that, surrendering my business to Nippers, for a few days I drove about the upper part of the town and through the suburbs in my rockaway; crossed over to Jersey City and Hoboken, and paid fugitive visits to Manhattanville and Astoria. In fact I almost lived in my rockaway for the time.

When again I entered my office, lo, a note from the landlord lay upon the desk. I opened it with trembling hands. It informed me that the writer had sent to the police and had Bartleby removed to the Tombs as a vagrant. Moreover, since I knew more about him than anyone else, he wished me to appear at that place and make a suitable statement of the facts. These tidings had a conflicting effect upon me. At first I was indignant, but at last almost approved. The landlord's energetic, summary disposition had led him to adopt a procedure which I do not think I would have decided upon myself; and yet as a last resort, under such peculiar circumstances, it seemed the only plan.

215   As I afterwards learned, the poor scrivener, when told that he must be conducted to the Tombs, offered not the slightest obstacle, but in his pale unmoving way, silently acquiesced.

Some of the compassionate and curious bystanders joined the party; and headed by one of the constables arm in arm with Bartleby, the silent procession filed its way through all the noise, and heat, and joy of the roaring thoroughfares at noon.

The same day I received the note I went to the Tombs or, to speak more properly, the Halls of Justice. Seeking the right officer, I stated the purpose of my call, and was informed that the individual I described was indeed within. I then assured the functionary that Bartleby was a perfectly honest man, and greatly to be compassionated, however unaccountably eccentric. I narrated all I knew, and closed by suggesting the idea of letting him remain in as indulgent confinement as possible till something less harsh might be done—though indeed I hardly knew what. At all events, if nothing else could be decided upon, the almshouse must receive him. I then begged to have an interview.

Being under no disgraceful charge, and quite serene and harmless in all his ways, they had permitted him freely to wander about the prison, and especially in the inclosed grass-platted yards thereof. And so I found him there, standing all alone in the quietest of the yards, his face towards a high wall, while all around, from the narrow slits of the jail windows, I thought I saw peering out upon him the eyes of murderers and thieves.

"Bartleby!"

"I know you," he said, without looking around—"and I want noth-   220
ing to say to you."

"It was not I that brought you here, Bartleby," said I, keenly pained
at his implied suspicion. "And to you, this should not be so vile a place.
Nothing reproachful attaches to you by being here. And see, it is not so
sad a place as one might think. Look, there is the sky, and here is the
grass."

"I know where I am," he replied, but would say nothing more, and so
I left him.

As I entered the corridor again, a broad meat-like man in an apron
accosted me, and jerking his thumb over his shoulder said—"Is that your
friend?"

"Yes."

"Does he want to starve? If he does, let him live on the prison fare,   225
that's all."

"Who are you?" asked I, not knowing what to make of such an
unofficially speaking person in such a place.

"I am the grub-man. Such gentlemen as have friends here, hire me
to provide them with something good to eat."

"Is this so?" said I, turning to the turnkey.

He said it was.

"Well, then," said I, slipping some silver into the grub-man's hands   230
(for so they called him), "I want you to give particular attention to my
friend there; let him have the best dinner you can get. And you must be
as polite to him as possible."

"Introduce me, will you?" said the grub-man, looking at me with an
expression which seemed to say he was all impatience for an opportunity
to give a specimen of his breeding.

Thinking it would prove of benefit to the scrivener, I acquiesced,
and asking the grub-man his name, went up with him to Bartleby.

"Bartleby, this is a friend; you will find him very useful to you."

"Your sarvant, sir, your sarvant," said the grub-man making a low
salutation behind his apron. "Hope you find it pleasant here, sir—
spacious grounds—cool apartments, sir—hope you'll stay with us some
time—try to make it agreeable. What will you have for dinner today?"

"I prefer not to dine today," said Bartleby, turning away. "It would   235
disagree with me; I am unused to dinners." So saying he slowly moved to
the other side of the enclosure, and took up a position fronting the dead
wall.

"How's this?" said the grub-man, addressing me with a stare of
astonishment. "He's odd, ain't he?"

"I think he is a little deranged," said I, sadly.

"Deranged? deranged is it? Well now, upon my word, I thought that friend of yourn was a gentleman forger; they are always pale and genteel-like, them forgers. I can't help pity 'em—can't help it, sir. Did you know Monroe Edwards?" he added touchingly, and paused. Then, laying his hand pityingly on my shoulder, sighed, "he died of consumption at Sing-Sing. So you weren't acquainted with Monroe?"

"No, I was never socially acquainted with any forgers. But I cannot stop longer. Look to my friend yonder. You will not lose by it. I will see you again."

240   Some few days after this, I again obtained admission to the Tombs, and went through the corridors in quest of Bartleby, but without finding him.

"I saw him coming from his cell not long ago," said a turnkey, "maybe he's gone to loiter in the yards."

So I went in that direction.

"Are you looking for the silent man?" said another turnkey passing me. "Yonder he lies—sleeping in the yard there. 'Tis not twenty minutes since I saw him lie down."

The yard was entirely quiet. It was not accessible to the common prisoners. The surrounding walls, of amazing thickness, kept off all sound behind them. The Egyptian character of the masonry weighed upon me with its gloom. But a soft imprisoned turf grew under foot. The heart of the eternal pyramids, it seemed, wherein, by some strange magic, through the clefts, grass-seed dropped by birds had sprung.

245   Strangely huddled at the base of the wall, his knees drawn up, and lying on his side, his head touching the cold stones, I saw the wasted Bartleby. But nothing stirred. I paused; then went close up to him; stooped over, and saw that his dim eyes were open; otherwise he seemed profoundly sleeping. Something prompted me to touch him. I felt his hand, when a tingling shiver ran up my arm and down my spine to my feet.

The round face of the grub-man peered upon me now. "His dinner is ready. Won't he dine today, either? Or does he live without dining?"

"Lives without dining," said I, and closed the eyes.

"Eh!—He's asleep, ain't he?"

"With kings and counselors,"° murmured I.

250   There would seem little need for proceeding further in this history. Imagination will readily supply the meager recital of poor Bartleby's interment. But ere parting with the reader, let me say that if this little

"With . . . counselors": Job 3.14

narrative has sufficiently interested him to awaken curiosity as to who Bartleby was, and what manner of life he led prior to the present narrator's making his acquaintance, I can only reply that in such curiosity I fully share, but am wholly unable to gratify it. Yet here I hardly know whether I should divulge one little item of rumor which came to my ear a few months after the scrivener's decease. Upon what basis it rested, I could never ascertain; and hence how true it is I cannot now tell. But inasmuch as this vague report has not been without a certain strange suggestive interest to me, however sad, it may prove the same with some others; and so I will briefly mention it. The report was this: that Bartleby had been a subordinate clerk in the Dead Letter Office at Washington, from which he had been suddenly removed by a change in the administration. When I think over this rumor, I cannot adequately express the emotions which seize me. Dead letters! does it not sound like dead men? Conceive a man by nature and misfortune prone to a pallid hopelessness, can any business seem more fitted to heighten it than that of continually handling these dead letters and assorting them for the flames? For by the cart-load they are annually burned. Sometimes from out the folded paper the pale clerk takes a ring—the finger it was meant for, perhaps, moulders in the grave; a bank note sent in swiftest charity —he whom it would relieve, nor eats nor hungers any more; pardon for those who died despairing; hope for those who died unhoping; good tidings for those who died stifled by unrelieved calamities. On errands of life, these letters speed to death.

Ah, Bartleby! Ah, humanity!

Edgar Allan Poe

The Cask of Amontillado

The thousand injuries of Fortunato I had borne as I best could; but when he ventured upon insult, I vowed revenge. You, who so well know the nature of my soul, will not suppose, however, that I gave utterance to

THE CASK OF AMONTILLADO   First published in 1846. Edgar Allan Poe (1809–1849) was one of the first modern practitioners and theorists of the short story as a literary form, prescribing as its highest goal the creation of "a certain unique or single effect." His own achievement best matches his theory in his horror tales, of which this is an example. Poe was born in Boston, abandoned at the age of three by his father after the death of his mother, and raised by adoptive parents in Virginia. As a young man he failed in attempts at education at the University of Virginia and at West Point. Difficulty with alcohol combined with nervous sensitivity led to continuing health problems and perhaps to his early death. "Amontillado" is a dry Spanish sherry wine; "carnival" is the festive season preceding Lent.

a threat. At *length* I would be avenged; this was a point definitively settled—but the very definitiveness with which it was resolved precluded the idea of risk. I must not only punish, but punish with impunity. A wrong is unredressed when retribution overtakes its redresser. It is equally unredressed when the avenger fails to make himself felt as such to him who has done the wrong.

It must be understood, that neither by word nor deed had I given Fortunato cause to doubt my good will. I continued, as was my wont, to smile in his face, and he did not perceive that my smile *now* was at the thought of his immolation.

He had a weak point—this Fortunato—although in other regards he was a man to be respected and even feared. He prided himself on his connoisseurship in wine. Few Italians have the true virtuoso spirit. For the most part their enthusiasm is adopted to suit the time and opportunity—to practice imposture upon the British and Austrian *millionaires*. In painting and gemmary Fortunato, like his countrymen, was a quack—but in the matter of old wines he was sincere. In this respect I did not differ from him materially: I was skillful in the Italian vintages myself, and bought largely whenever I could.

It was about dusk, one evening during the supreme madness of the carnival season, that I encountered my friend. He accosted me with excessive warmth, for he had been drinking much. The man wore motley. He had on a tight-fitting parti-striped dress, and his head was surmounted by the conical cap and bells. I was so pleased to see him, that I thought I should never have done wringing his hand.

5   I said to him—"My dear Fortunato, you are luckily met. How remarkably well you are looking today! But I have received a pipe of what passes for Amontillado, and I have my doubts."

"How?" said he. "Amontillado? A pipe? Impossible! And in the middle of the carnival!"

"I have my doubts," I replied; "and I was silly enough to pay the full Amontillado price without consulting you in the matter. You were not to be found, and I was fearful of losing a bargain."

"Amontillado!"

"I have my doubts."

10   "Amontillado!"

"And I must satisfy them."

"Amontillado!"

"As you are engaged, I am on my way to Luchesi. If anyone has a critical turn, it is he. He will tell me—"

"Luchesi cannot tell Amontillado from Sherry."

"And yet some fools will have it that his taste is a match for your own."   15

"Come, let us go."

"Whither?"

"To your vaults."

"My friend, no; I will not impose upon your good nature. I perceive you have an engagement. Luchesi—"

"I have no engagement;—come."   20

"My friend, no. It is not the engagement, but the severe cold with which I perceive you are afflicted. The vaults are insufferably damp. They are encrusted with niter."

"Let us go, nevertheless. The cold is merely nothing. Amontillado! You have been imposed upon. And as for Luchesi, he cannot distinguish Sherry from Amontillado."

Thus speaking, Fortunato possessed himself of my arm. Putting on a mask of black silk, and drawing a *roquelaire°* closely about my person, I suffered him to hurry me to my palazzo.

There were no attendants at home; they had absconded to make merry in honor of the time. I had told them that I should not return until the morning, and had given them explicit orders not to stir from the house. These orders were sufficient, I well knew, to insure their immediate disappearance, one and all, as soon as my back was turned.

I took from their sconces two flambeaux, and giving one to Fortunato, bowed him through several suites of rooms to the archway that   25
led into the vaults. I passed down a long and winding staircase, requesting him to be cautious as he followed. We came at length to the foot of the descent, and stood together on the damp ground of the catacombs of the Montresors.

The gait of my friend was unsteady, and the bells upon his cap jingled as he strode.

"The pipe," said he.

"It is farther on," said I; "but observe the white web-work which gleams from these cavern walls."

He turned towards me, and looked into my eyes with two filmy orbs that distilled the rheum of intoxication.

"Niter?" he asked, at length.   30

"Niter," I replied. "How long have you had that cough?"

"Ugh! ugh! ugh!—ugh! ugh! ugh!—ugh! ugh! ugh!—ugh! ugh! ugh!—ugh! ugh! ugh!"

---

roquelaire: a knee-length cloak worn in the eighteenth century

My poor friend found it impossible to reply for many minutes.

"It is nothing," he said, at last.

35   "Come," I said, with decision, "we will go back; your health is precious. You are rich, respected, admired, beloved; you are happy, as once I was. You are a man to be missed. For me it is no matter. We will go back; you will be ill, and I cannot be responsible. Beside, there is Luchesi—"

"Enough," he said; "the cough is a mere nothing; it will not kill me. I shall not die of a cough."

"True—true," I replied; "and, indeed, I had no intention of alarming you unnecessarily—but you should use all proper caution. A draught of this Medoc will defend us from the damps."

Here I knocked off the neck of a bottle which I drew from a long row of its fellows that lay upon the mold.

"Drink," I said, presenting him the wine.

40   He raised it to his lips with a leer. He paused and nodded to me familiarly, while his bells jingled.

"I drink," he said, "to the buried that repose around us."

"And I to your long life."

He again took my arm, and we proceeded.

"These vaults," he said, "are extensive."

45   "The Montresors," I replied, "were a great and numerous family."

"I forget your arms."

"A huge human foot d'or, in a field azure; the foot crushes a serpent rampant whose fangs are imbedded in the heel."

"And the motto?"

"*Nemo me impune lacessit.*"°

50   "Good!" he said.

The wine sparkled in his eyes and the bells jingled. My own fancy grew warm with the Medoc. We had passed through walls of piled bones, with casks and puncheons intermingling, into the inmost recesses of the catacombs. I paused again, and this time I made bold to seize Fortunato by an arm above the elbow.

"The niter!" I said; "see, it increases. It hangs like moss upon the vaults. We are below the river's bed. The drops of moisture trickle among the bones. Come, we will go back ere it is too late. Your cough—"

"It is nothing," he said; "let us go on. But first, another draught of the Medoc."

Nemo . . . lacessit: No one can provoke me and get away with it.

I broke and reached him a flacon of De Grâve. He emptied it at a breath. His eyes flashed with a fierce light. He laughed and threw the bottle upwards with a gesticulation I did not understand.

I looked at him in surprise. He repeated the movement—a gro-   55
tesque one.

"You do not comprehend?" he said.

"Not I," I replied.

"Then you are not of the brotherhood."

"How?"

"You are not of the masons."   60

"Yes, yes," I said, "yes, yes."

"You? Impossible! A mason?"

"A mason," I replied.

"A sign," he said.

"It is this," I answered, producing a trowel from beneath the folds of   65
my *roquelaire*.

"You jest," he exclaimed, recoiling a few paces. "But let us proceed to the Amontillado."

"Be it so," I said, replacing the tool beneath the cloak, and again offering him my arm. He leaned upon it heavily. We continued our route in search of the Amontillado. We passed through a range of low arches, descended, passed on, and descending again, arrived at a deep crypt, in which the foulness of the air caused our flambeaux rather to glow than flame.

At the most remote end of the crypt there appeared another less spacious. Its walls had been lined with human remains, piled to the vault overhead, in the fashion of the great catacombs of Paris. Three sides of this interior crypt were still ornamented in this manner. From the fourth the bones had been thrown down, and lay promiscuously upon the earth, forming at one point a mound of some size. Within the wall thus exposed by the displacing of the bones, we perceived a still interior recess, in depth about four feet, in width three, in height six or seven. It seemed to have been con-structed for no especial use within itself, but formed merely the interval between two of the colossal supports of the roof of the catacombs, and was backed by one of their circumscribing walls of solid granite.

It was in vain that Fortunato, uplifting his dull torch, endeavored to pry into the depth of the recess. Its termination the feeble light did not enable us to see.

"Proceed," I said; "herein is the Amontillado. As for Luchesi—"   70

"He is an ignoramus," interrupted my friend, as he stepped unsteadily forward, while I followed immediately at his heels. In an instant he had reached the extremity of the niche, and finding his progress arrested by the rock, stood stupidly bewildered. A moment more and I had fettered him to the granite. In its surface were two iron staples, distant from each other about two feet, horizontally. From one of these depended a short chain, from the other a padlock. Throwing the links about his waist, it was but the work of a few seconds to secure it. He was too much astounded to resist. Withdrawing the key I stepped back from the recess.

"Pass your hand," I said, "over the wall; you cannot help feeling the niter. Indeed it is *very* damp. Once more let me *implore* you to return. No? Then I must positively leave you. But I must first render you all the little attentions in my power."

"The Amontillado!" ejaculated my friend, not yet recovered from his astonishment.

"True," I replied; "the Amontillado."

75   As I said these words, I busied myself among the pile of bones of which I have before spoken. Throwing them aside, I soon uncovered a quantity of building stone and mortar. With these materials and with the aid of my trowel, I began vigorously to wall up the entrance of the niche.

I had scarcely laid the first tier of the masonry when I discovered that the intoxication of Fortunato had in a great measure worn off. The earliest indication I had of this was a low moaning cry from the depth of the recess. It was *not* the cry of a drunken man. There was then a long and obstinate silence. I laid the second tier, and the third, and the fourth; and then I heard the furious vibrations of the chain. The noise lasted for several minutes, during which, that I might harken to it with the more satisfaction, I ceased my labors and sat down upon the bones. When at last the clanking subsided, I resumed the trowel, and finished without interruption the fifth, the sixth, and the seventh tier. The wall was now nearly upon a level with my breast. I again paused, and holding the flambeaux over the masonwork, threw a few feeble rays upon the figure within.

A succession of loud and shrill screams, bursting suddenly from the throat of the chained form, seemed to thrust me violently back. For a brief moment I hesitated—I trembled. Unsheathing my rapier, I began to grope with it about the recess: but the thought of an instant reassured me. I placed my hand upon the solid fabric of the catacombs, and felt satisfied. I reapproached the wall. I replied to the yells of him who clamored. I re-echoed—I aided—I surpassed them in volume and in strength. I did this, and the clamorer grew still.

It was now midnight, and my task was drawing to a close. I had completed the eighth, the ninth, and the tenth tier. I had finished a portion of the last and the eleventh; there remained but a single stone to be fitted and plastered in. I struggled with its weight; I placed it partially in its destined position. But now there came from out the niche a low laugh that erected the hairs upon my head. It was succeeded by a sad voice, which I had difficulty in recognising as that of the noble Fortunato. The voice said—

"Ha! ha! ha!—he! he!—a very good joke indeed—an excellent jest. We will have many a rich laugh about it at the palazzo—he! he! he!— over our wine—he! he! he!"

"The Amontillado!" I said.   80

"He! he! he!—he! he! he!—yes, the Amontillado. But is it not getting late? Will not they be awaiting us at the palazzo, the Lady Fortunato and the rest? Let us be gone."

"Yes," I said, "let us be gone."

"*For the love of God, Montresor!*"

"Yes," I said, "for the love of God!"

But to these words I harkened in vain for a reply. I grew impatient. I   85
called aloud—

"Fortunato!"

No answer. I called again—

"Fortunato!"

No answer still. I thrust a torch through the remaining aperture and let it fall within. There came forth in return only a jingling of the bells. My heart grew sick—on account of the dampness of the catacombs. I hastened to make an end of my labor. I forced the last stone into its position; I plastered it up. Against the new masonry I re-erected the old rampart of bones. For the half of a century no mortal has disturbed them. *In pace requiescat!*°

In pace requiescat: May he rest in peace!

John Updike
A & P

In walks these three girls in nothing but bathing suits. I'm in the third check-out slot, with my back to the door, so I don't see them until they're over by the bread. The one that caught my eye first was the one in the plaid green two-piece. She was a chunky kid, with a good tan and a sweet broad soft-looking can with those two crescents of white just under it, where the sun never seems to hit, at the top of the backs of her legs. I stood there with my hand on a box of HiHo crackers trying to remember if I rang it up or not. I ring it up again and the customer starts giving me hell. She's one of these cashregister-watchers, a witch about fifty with rouge on her cheekbones and no eyebrows, and I know it made her day to trip me up. She'd been watching cash registers for fifty years and probably never seen a mistake before.

By the time I got her feathers smoothed and her goodies into a bag—she gives me a little snort in passing, if she'd been born at the right time they would have burned her over in Salem—by the time I get her on her way the girls had circled around the bread and were coming back, without a push-cart, back my way along the counters, in the aisle between the check-outs and the Special bins. They didn't even have shoes on. There was this chunky one, with the two-piece—it was bright green and the seams on the bra were still sharp and her belly was still pretty pale so I guessed she just got it (the suit)—there was this one, with one of those chubby berry-faces, the lips all bunched together under her nose, this one, and a tall one, with black hair that hadn't quite frizzed right, and one of these sunburns right across under the eyes, and a chin that was too long—you know, the kind of girl other girls think is very "striking" and "attractive" but never quite makes it, as they very well know, which is why they like her so much—and then the third one, that wasn't quite so tall. She was the queen. She kind of led them, the other two peeking around and making their shoulders round. She didn't look around, not this queen, she just walked straight on slowly, on these long white primadonna legs. She came down a little hard on her heels, as if

---

A & P   First published in 1960. John Updike (b. 1932) is one of America's most celebrated contemporary writers and a highly prolific, equally adept practitioner in many genres: the novel, the short story, poetry, and criticism. Born in Shillington, Pennsylvania, he attended Harvard University and shortly after his graduation began publishing short stories in the *New Yorker*, the magazine with which his work is strongly identified. In his most characteristic fiction, he portrays the anxieties of middle-class life in a style of luminous clarity and realism.

she didn't walk in her bare feet that much, putting down her heels and then letting the weight move along to her toes as if she was testing the floor with every step, putting a little deliberate extra action into it. You never know for sure how girls' minds work (do you really think it's a mind in there or just a little buzz like a bee in a glass jar?) but you got the idea she had talked the other two into coming in here with her, and now she was showing them how to do it, walk slow and hold yourself straight.

She had on a kind of dirty-pink—beige maybe, I don't know—bathing suit with a little nubble all over it and, what got me, the straps were down. They were off her shoulders looped loose around the cool tops of her arms, and I guess as a result the suit had slipped a little on her, so all around the top of the cloth there was this shining rim. If it hadn't been there you wouldn't have known there could have been anything whiter than those shoulders. With the straps pushed off, there was nothing between the top of the suit and the top of her head except just *her*, this clean bare plane of the top of her chest down from the shoulder bones like a dented sheet of metal tilted in the light. I mean, it was more than pretty.

She had sort of oaky hair that the sun and salt had bleached, done up in a bun that was unraveling, and a kind of prim face. Walking into the A&P with your straps down, I suppose it's the only kind of face you *can* have. She held her head so high her neck, coming up out of those white shoulders, looked kind of stretched, but I didn't mind. The longer her neck was, the more of her there was.

She must have felt in the corner of her eye me and over my shoulder   5
Stokesie in the second slot watching, but she didn't tip. Not this queen. She kept her eyes moving across the racks, and stopped, and turned so slow it made my stomach rub the inside of my apron, and buzzed to the other two, who kind of huddled against her for relief, and they all three of them went up the cat-and-dog-food-breakfast-cereal-macaroni-rice-raisins-seasonings-spreads-spaghetti-soft-drinks-crackers-and-cookies aisle. From the third slot I look straight up this aisle to the meat counter, and I watched them all the way. The fat one with the tan sort of fumbled with the cookies, but on second thought she put the packages back. The sheep pushing their carts down the aisle—the girls were walking against the usual traffic (not that we have one-way signs or anything)—were pretty hilarious. You could see them, when Queenie's white shoulders dawned on them, kind of jerk, or hop, or hiccup, but their eyes snapped back to their own baskets and on they pushed. I bet you could set off dynamite in an A&P and the people would by and large keep reaching and checking oatmeal off their lists and muttering "Let me see, there was a third thing, began with A, asparagus, no, ah, yes, applesauce!" or

whatever it is they do mutter. But there was no doubt, this jiggled them. A few houseslaves in pin curlers even looked around after pushing their carts to make sure what they had seen was correct.

You know, it's one thing to have a girl in a bathing suit down on the beach, where what with the glare nobody can look at each other much anyway, and another thing in the cool of the A&P, under the fluorescent lights, against all those stacked packages, with her feet paddling along naked over our checkerboard green-and-cream rubber-tile floor.

"Oh Daddy," Stokesie said beside me. "I feel so faint."

"Darling," I said. "Hold me tight." Stokesie's married, with two babies chalked up on his fuselage already, but as far as I can tell that's the only difference. He's twenty-two, and I was nineteen this April.

"Is it done?" he asks, the responsible married man finding his voice. I forgot to say he thinks he's going to be manager some sunny day, maybe in 1990 when it's called the Great Alexandrov and Petrooshki Tea Company or something.

10   What he meant was, our town is five miles from a beach, with a big summer colony out on the Point, but we're right in the middle of town, and the women generally put on a shirt or shorts or something before they get out of the car into the street. And anyway these are usually women with six children and varicose veins mapping their legs and nobody, including them, could care less. As I say, we're right in the middle of town, and if you stand at our front doors you can see two banks and the Congregational church and the newspaper store and three real-estate offices and about twenty-seven old freeloaders tearing up Central Street because the sewer broke again. It's not as if we're on the Cape; we're north of Boston and there's people in this town haven't seen the ocean for twenty years.

The girls had reached the meat counter and were asking McMahon something. He pointed, they pointed, and they shuffled out of sight behind a pyramid of Diet Delight peaches. All that was left for us to see was old McMahon patting his mouth and looking after them sizing up their joints. Poor kids, I began to feel sorry for them, they couldn't help it.

Now here comes the sad part of the story, at least my family says it's sad but I don't think it's sad myself. The store's pretty empty, it being Thursday afternoon, so there was nothing much to do except lean on the register and wait for the girls to show up again. The whole store was like a pinball machine and I didn't know which tunnel they'd come out of. After a while they come around out of the far aisle, around the light bulbs, records at discount of the Caribbean Six or Tony Martin Sings or some such gunk you wonder they waste the wax on, sixpacks of candy bars, and plastic toys done up in cellophane that fall apart when a kid looks at them anyway. Around they come, Queenie still leading the way, and holding a little gray jar in her hand. Slots Three through Seven are unmanned and I could see her wondering between Stokes and me, but Stokesie with his usual luck draws an old party in baggy gray pants who stumbles up with four giant cans of pineapple juice (what do these bums *do* with all that pineapple juice? I've often asked myself) so the girls come to me. Queenie puts down the jar and I take it into my fingers icy cold. Kingfish Fancy Herring Snacks in Pure Sour Cream: 49¢. Now her hands are empty, not a ring or a bracelet, bare as God made them, and I wonder where the money's coming from. Still with that prim look she lifts a folded dollar bill out of the hollow at the center of her nubbled pink top. The jar went heavy in my hand. Really, I thought that was so cute.

Then everybody's luck begins to run out. Lengel comes in from haggling with a truck full of cabbages on the lot and is about to scuttle into that door marked MANAGER behind which he hides all day when the girls touch his eye. Lengel's pretty dreary, teaches Sunday school and the rest, but he doesn't miss that much. He comes over and says, "Girls, this isn't the beach."

Queenie blushes, though maybe it's just a brush of sunburn I was noticing for the first time, now that she was so close. "My mother asked me to pick up a jar of herring snacks." Her voice kind of startled me, the way voices do when you see the people first, coming out so flat and dumb yet kind of tony, too, the way it ticked over "pick up" and "snacks." All of a sudden I slid right down her voice into her living room. Her father and the other men were standing around in ice-cream coats and bow ties and the women were in sandals picking up herring snacks on toothpicks off a big plate and they were all holding drinks the color of water with olives and sprigs of mint in them. When my parents have somebody over they get lemonade and if it's a real racy affair Schlitz in tall glasses with "They'll Do It Every Time" cartoons stencilled on.

"That's all right," Lengel said. "But this isn't the beach." His repeating this struck me as funny, as if it had just occurred to him, and he had been thinking all these years the A&P was a great big dune and he was the head lifeguard. He didn't like my smiling—as I say he doesn't miss much—but he concentrates on giving the girls that sad Sunday-school-superintendent stare.

Queenie's blush is no sunburn now, and the plump one in plaid, that I liked better from the back—a really sweet can—pipes up, "We weren't doing any shopping. We just came in for the one thing."

15

"That makes no difference," Lengel tells her, and I could see from the way his eyes went that he hadn't noticed she was wearing a two-piece before. "We want you decently dressed when you come in here."

"We *are* decent," Queenie says suddenly, her lower lip pushing, getting sore now that she remembers her place, a place from which the crowd that runs the A&P must look pretty crummy. Fancy Herring Snacks flashed in her very blue eyes.

"Girls, I don't want to argue with you. After this come in here with your shoulders covered. It's our policy." He turns his back. That's policy for you. Policy is what the kingpins want. What the others want is juvenile delinquency.

20   All this while, the customers had been showing up with their carts but, you know, sheep, seeing a scene, they had all bunched up on Stokesie, who shook open a paper bag as gently as peeling a peach, not wanting to miss a word. I could feel in the silence everybody getting nervous, most of all Lengel, who asks me, "Sammy, have you rung up this purchase?"

I thought and said "No" but it wasn't about that I was thinking. I go through the punches, 4, 9, GROC, TOT—it's more complicated than you think, and after you do it often enough, it begins to make a little song, that you hear words to, in my case "Hello (*bing*) there, you (*gung*) hap-py *pee*-pul (*splat*)!"—the *splat* being the drawer flying out. I uncrease the bill, tenderly as you may imagine, it just having come from between the two smoothest scoops of vanilla I had ever known were there, and pass a half and a penny into her narrow pink palm, and nestle the herrings in a bag and twist its neck and hand it over, all the time thinking.

The girls, and who'd blame them, are in a hurry to get out, so I say "I quit" to Lengel quick enough for them to hear, hoping they'll stop and watch me, their unsuspected hero. They keep right on going, into the electric eye; the door flies open and they flicker across the lot to their car, Queenie and Plaid and Big Tall Goony-Goony (not that as raw material she was so bad), leaving me with Lengel and a kink in his eyebrow.

"Did you say something, Sammy?"

"I said I quit."

25   "I thought you did."

"You didn't have to embarrass them."

"It was they who were embarrassing us."

I started to say something that came out "Fiddle-de-doo." It's a saying of my grandmother's, and I know she would have been pleased.

"I don't think you know what you're saying," Lengel said.

"I know you don't," I said. "But I do." I pull the bow at the back of   30
my apron and start shrugging it off my shoulders. A couple customers
that had been heading for my slot begin to knock against each other,
like scared pigs in a chute.

Lengel sighs and begins to look very patient and old and gray. He's
been a friend of my parents for years. "Sammy, you don't want to do this
to your Mom and Dad," he tells me. It's true, I don't. But it seems to me
that once you begin a gesture it's fatal not to go through with it. I fold
the apron, "Sammy" stitched in red on the pocket, and put it on the
counter, and drop the bow tie on top of it. The bow tie is theirs, if you've
ever wondered. "You'll feel this for the rest of your life," Lengel says, and
I know that's true, too, but remembering how he made that pretty girl
blush makes me so scrunchy inside I punch the No Sale tab and the
machine whirs "pee-pul" and the drawer splats out. One advantage to
this scene taking place in summer, I can follow this up with a clean exit,
there's no fumbling around getting your coat and galoshes, I just saunter
into the electric eye in my white shirt that my mother ironed the night
before, and the door heaves itself open, and outside the sunshine is
skating around the asphalt.

I look around for my girls, but they're gone, of course. There wasn't
anybody but some young married screaming with her children about
some candy they didn't get by the door of a powder-blue Falcon station
wagon. Looking back in the big windows, over the bags of peat moss
and aluminum lawn furniture stacked on the pavement, I could see
Lengel in my place in the slot, checking the sheep through. His face
was dark gray and his back stiff, as if he'd just had an injection of iron,
and my stomach kind of fell as I felt how hard the world was going to be
to me hereafter.

Poetry

The Elements of Poetry

What Is Poetry?

Poetry is as universal as language and almost as ancient. The most primitive peoples have used it, and the most civilized have cultivated it. In all ages and in all countries, poetry has been written, and eagerly read or listened to, by all kinds and conditions of people—by soldiers, statesmen, lawyers, homemakers, farmers, doctors, scientists, clergy, philosophers, kings, and queens. In all ages it has been especially the concern of the educated, the intelligent, and the sensitive, and it has appealed, in its simpler forms, to the uneducated and to children. Why? First, because it has given pleasure. People have read it, listened to it, or recited it because they liked it—because it gave them enjoyment. But this is not the whole answer. Poetry in all ages has been regarded as important, not simply as one of several alternative forms of amusement, as one person might choose bowling, another chess, and another poetry. Rather, it has been regarded as something central to existence, something having unique value to the fully realized life, something that we are better off for having and without which we are spiritually impoverished. To understand the reasons for this, we need to have at least a provisional understanding of what poetry is—provisional, because people have always been more successful at appreciating poetry than at defining it.

Initially, poetry might be defined as a kind of language that says *more* and says it *more intensely* than does ordinary language. To understand this fully, we need to understand what poetry "says." For language is employed on different occasions to say quite different kinds of things; in other words, language has different uses.

Perhaps the commonest use of language is to communicate *information*. We say that it is nine o'clock, that we liked a certain movie, that George Washington was the first president of the United States, that bromine and iodine are members of the halogen group of chemical elements. This we might call the *practical* use of language; it helps us with the ordinary business of living.

But it is not primarily to communicate information that novels, short stories, plays, and poems are written. These exist to bring us a sense and a perception of life, to widen and sharpen our contacts with existence. Their concern is with *experience*. We all have an inner need to live more deeply and fully and with greater awareness, to know the experience of others, and to understand our own experience better. Poets, from their own store of felt, observed, or imagined experiences, select, combine, and reorganize. They create significant new experiences for their readers—significant because focused and formed—in which readers can participate and from which they may gain a greater awareness and understanding of their world. Literature, in other words, can be used as a gear for stepping up the intensity and increasing the range of our experience and as a glass for clarifying it. This is the *literary* use of language, for literature is not only an aid to living but a means of living.

In advertisements, sermons, political speeches, and even some poems we find a third use of language: as an instrument of *persuasion*, or argument. But the distinctions among these three uses—the practical, the literary, and the argumentative—are not always clear-cut, since some written language simultaneously performs two or even all three functions. For example, an excellent poem we consider "literary" may convey information and may also try to persuade us to share a particular point of view. Effectiveness in communicating experience, however, is the one essential criterion for any poem aspiring to the condition of literature.

Suppose, for instance, that we are interested in eagles. If we want simply to acquire information about eagles, we may turn to an encyclopedia or a book of natural history. We would find that there are about fifty-five species of eagles and that most have hooked bills, curved claws, broad wings, and powerfully developed breast muscles. We would also learn that eagles vary in length from about sixteen inches to as long as forty inches; that most hunt while flying, though some await their prey on a high perch; that they nest in tall trees or on inaccessible cliffs; that they lay only one or two eggs; and that for human beings eagles "symbolize power, courage, freedom, and immortality and have long been used as national, military, and heraldic emblems and as symbols in religion."*

But unless we are interested in this information only for practical purposes, we are likely to feel a little disappointed, as though we had grasped the feathers of the eagle but not its soul. True, we have learned many facts about the eagle, but we have missed somehow its lonely majesty, its power, and the wild grandeur of its surroundings that would make the eagle a living creature rather than a mere museum specimen. For the living eagle we must turn to literature.

Encyclopedia Americana, International Edition, Vol. 9 (1995) 520–22.

The Eagle

He clasps the crag with crooked hands;
Close to the sun in lonely lands,
Ringed with the azure world, he stands.

The wrinkled sea beneath him crawls;
He watches from his mountain walls,   5
And like a thunderbolt he falls.

Alfred, Lord Tennyson (1809–1892)

QUESTIONS

1. What is peculiarly effective about the expressions "crooked hands," "Close to the sun," "Ringed with the azure world," "wrinkled," "crawls," and "like a thunderbolt"?
2. Notice the formal pattern of the poem, particularly the contrast of "he stands" in the first stanza and "he falls" in the second. Is there any other contrast between the two stanzas?

When "The Eagle" has been read well, readers will feel that they have enjoyed a significant experience and understand eagles better, though in a different way, than they did from the encyclopedia article alone. For while the article *analyzes* our experience of eagles, the poem in some sense *synthesizes* such an experience. Indeed, we may say the two approaches to experience—the scientific and the literary—complement each other. And we may contend that the kind of understanding we get from the second is at least as valuable as the kind we get from the first.

Literature, then, exists to communicate significant experience—significant because it is concentrated and organized. Its function is not to tell us *about* experience but to allow us imaginatively to *participate* in it. It is a means of allowing us, through the imagination, to live more fully, more deeply, more richly, and with greater awareness. It can do this in two ways: by *broadening* our experience—that is, by making us acquainted with a range of experience with which in the ordinary course of events we might have no contact, or by *deepening* our experience—that is, by making us feel more poignantly and more understandingly the everyday experiences all of us have. It enlarges our perspectives and breaks down some of the limits we may feel.

We can avoid two limiting approaches to poetry if we keep this conception of literature firmly in mind. The first approach always looks for a lesson or a bit of moral instruction. The second expects to find poetry always beautiful. Let us consider one of the songs from Shakespeare's *Love's Labor's Lost* (Act 5, scene 2).

Winter

When icicles hang by the wall,
And Dick the shepherd blows his nail,
And Tom bears logs into the hall,
And milk comes frozen home in pail,
When blood is nipped and ways be foul,   5
Then nightly sings the staring owl,
"Tu-whit, tu-who!"
    A merry note,
    While greasy Joan doth keel° the pot.   skim

When all aloud the wind doth blow,   10
And coughing drowns the parson's saw,
And birds sit brooding in the snow,
And Marian's nose looks red and raw,
When roasted crabs° hiss in the bowl,   crab apples
Then nightly sings the staring owl,   15
"Tu-whit, tu-who!"
    A merry note,
    While greasy Joan doth keel the pot.

William Shakespeare (1564–1616)

QUESTIONS

1. Vocabulary: *saw* (11), *brooding* (12).
2. Is the owl's cry really a "merry" note? How are this adjective and the verb "sings" employed?
3. In what way does the owl's cry contrast with the other details of the poem?

In this poem Shakespeare communicates the quality of winter life around a sixteenth-century English country house. But he does not do so by telling us flatly that winter in such surroundings is cold and in many respects unpleasant, though with some pleasant features too (the adjectives *cold, unpleasant,* and *pleasant* are not even used in the poem). Instead, he provides a series of concrete, homely details that suggest these qualities and enable us, imaginatively, to experience this winter life ourselves. The shepherd blows on his fingernails to warm his hands; the milk freezes in the pail between the cowshed and the kitchen; the cook is slovenly and unclean, "greasy" either from spattered cooking fat or from her own sweat as she leans over the hot fire; the roads are muddy; the folk listening to the parson have colds; the birds "sit brooding in the snow"; and the servant girl's nose is raw from a cold. But pleasant things are in prospect. Tom is bringing in logs for the fire, the hot cider or ale is ready for drinking, and the soup or stew will soon be ready. In contrast to all these familiar details of country life is the mournful and eerie note of the owl.

Obviously, the poem contains no moral. If we limit ourselves to looking in poetry for some lesson, message, or noble truth about life, we are bound to be disappointed. This limited approach sees poetry as a kind of sugarcoated pill—a wholesome truth or lesson made palatable by being put into pretty words. What this narrow approach really wants is a sermon—not a poem, but something inspirational. Yet "Winter," which has appealed to readers for more than four centuries, is not inspirational and contains no moral preachment.

Neither is the poem "Winter" beautiful. Though it is appealing in its way and contains elements of beauty, there is little that is really beautiful in red, raw noses, coughing in chapel, nipped blood, foul roads, and greasy cooks. Yet the second limiting approach may lead us to feel that poetry deals exclusively with beauty—with sunsets, flowers, butterflies, love, God—and that the one appropriate response to any poem is, after a moment of awed silence, "Isn't that beautiful!" But this narrow approach excludes a large proportion of poetry. The function of poetry is sometimes to be ugly rather than beautiful. And poetry may deal with common colds and greasy cooks as legitimately as with sunsets and flowers. Consider another example:

Dulce et Decorum Est

> Bent double, like old beggars under sacks,
> Knock-kneed, coughing like hags, we cursed through sludge,
> Till on the haunting flares we turned our backs,
> And towards our distant rest began to trudge.
> Men marched asleep. Many had lost their boots,   5
> But limped on, blood-shod. All went lame, all blind;
> Drunk with fatigue; deaf even to the hoots
> Of gas-shells dropping softly behind.
>
> Gas! GAS! Quick, boys!—An ecstasy of fumbling,
> Fitting the clumsy helmets just in time,   10

But someone still was yelling out and stumbling
And flound'ring like a man in fire or lime.—
Dim through the misty panes and thick green light,
As under a green sea, I saw him drowning.

In all my dreams before my helpless sight   15
He plunges at me, guttering, choking, drowning.

If in some smothering dreams, you too could pace
Behind the wagon that we flung him in,
And watch the white eyes writhing in his face,
His hanging face, like a devil's sick of sin,   20
If you could hear, at every jolt, the blood
Come gargling from the froth-corrupted lungs
Bitter as the cud
Of vile, incurable sores on innocent tongues,—
My friend, you would not tell with such high zest   25
To children ardent for some desperate glory,
The old lie: *Dulce et decorum est*
Pro patria mori.

Wilfred Owen (1893–1918)

QUESTIONS

1. The Latin quotation, from the Roman poet Horace, means "It is sweet and becoming to die for one's country." What is the poem's comment on this statement?
2. List the elements of the poem that seem not beautiful and therefore "unpoetic." Are there any elements of beauty in the poem?
3. How do the comparisons in lines 1, 14, 20, and 23–24 contribute to the effectiveness of the poem?
4. What does the poem gain by moving from plural pronouns and the past tense to singular pronouns and the present tense?

Poetry takes all life as its province. Its primary concern is not with beauty, not with philosophical truth, not with persuasion, but with experience. Beauty and philosophical truth are aspects of experience, and the poet is often engaged with them. But poetry as a whole is concerned with all kinds of experience—beautiful or ugly, strange or common, noble or ignoble, actual or imaginary. Paradoxically, an artist can transform even the most unpleasant or painful experiences into works of great beauty and emotional power. Encountered in real life, pain and death are not pleasurable for most people; but we might read and reread poems about these subjects because of their ability to enlighten and move us. A real-life experience that makes us cry is usually an unhappy one; but if we cry while reading a great novel or poem it is because we are deeply moved, our humanity affirmed. Similarly, we do not ordinarily like to be frightened in real life, but we sometimes seek out books or movies that will terrify us. Works of art focus and organize experiences of all kinds, conveying the broad spectrum of human life and evoking a full range of emotional and intellectual responses. Even the most tragic literature, through its artistry of language, can help us to see and feel the significance of life, appealing to our essential humanity in a way that can be intensely pleasurable and affirming.

There is no sharp distinction between poetry and other forms of imaginative literature. Although some inexperienced readers may believe that poetry can be recognized by the arrangement of its lines on the page or by its use of rhyme and meter, such superficial signs are of little worth. The Book of Job in the Bible and Melville's *Moby-Dick* are highly poetical, but the familiar verse that begins "Thirty days hath September, / April, June, and November . . ." is not. The difference between poetry and other literature is one of degree. Poetry is the most condensed and concentrated form of literature. It is language whose individual lines, either because of their own brilliance or because they focus so powerfully on what has gone before, have a higher voltage than most language. It is language that grows frequently incandescent, giving off both light and heat.

Ultimately, therefore, poetry can be recognized only by the response made to it by a practiced reader, someone who has acquired some sensitivity to poetry. But there is a catch here. We are not all equally experienced readers. To some readers, poetry may often seem dull and boring, a fancy way of writing something that could be said more simply. So might a color-blind person deny that there is such a thing as color.

The act of communication involved in reading poetry is like the act of communication involved in receiving a message by radio. Two devices are required: a transmitting station and a receiving set. The completeness of the communication depends both on the power and clarity of the transmitter and on the sensitivity and tuning of the receiver. When a person reads a poem and no experience is received, either the poem is not a good poem or the reader is not properly tuned. With new poetry, we cannot always be sure which is at fault. With older poetry, if it has acquired critical acceptance—has been enjoyed and admired by generations of good readers—we may assume that the receiving set is at fault. Fortunately, the fault is not irremediable.

Though we cannot all become expert readers, we can become good enough to find both pleasure and value in much good poetry, or we can increase the amount of pleasure we already find in poetry and the number of kinds of poetry in which we find it. The purpose of this book is to help you increase your sensitivity and range as a receiving set.

Poetry, finally, is a kind of multidimensional language. Ordinary language—the kind that we use to communicate information—is one-dimensional. It is directed at only part of the listener, the understanding. Its one dimension is intellectual. Poetry, which is language used to communicate experience, has at least four dimensions. If it is to communicate experience, it must be directed at the *whole* person, not just at your understanding. It must involve not only your intelligence but also your senses, emotions, and imagination. To the intellectual dimension, poetry adds a sensuous dimension, an emotional dimension, and an imaginative dimension.

Poetry achieves its extra dimensions—its greater pressure per word and its greater tension per poem—by drawing more fully and more consistently than does ordinary language on a number of language resources, none of which is peculiar to poetry. These various resources form the subjects of a number of the following chapters. Among them are connotation, imagery, metaphor, symbol, paradox, irony, allusion, sound repetition, rhythm, and pattern. Using these resources and the materials of life, the poet shapes and makes a poem. Successful poetry is never effusive language. If it is to come alive it must be as cunningly put together and as efficiently organized as a tree. It must be an organism whose every part serves a useful purpose and cooperates with every other part to preserve and express the life that is within it.

REVIEWING CHAPTER ONE

1. Differentiate between ordinary language and poetic language.
2. Describe the uses of language: information, experience, persuasion.
3. Consider how looking for moral instruction or beauty are limiting approaches.
4. Explain the distinctions between poetry and other imaginative literature.
5. Review the four dimensions of experience that poetry involves.
6. Determine which ideas in this chapter are exemplified in the following poems.

Understanding and Evaluating Poetry

Most of the poems in this book are accompanied by study questions that are by no means exhaustive. The following is a list of questions that you may apply to any poem. You may be unable to answer many of them until you have read further into the book.

1. Who is the speaker? What kind of person is the speaker?
2. Is there an identifiable audience for the speaker? What can we know about it (her, him, or them)?
3. What is the occasion?
4. What is the setting in time (hour, season, century, and so on)?
5. What is the setting in place (indoors or out, city or country, land or sea, region, nation, hemisphere)?
6. What is the central purpose of the poem?
7. State the central idea or theme of the poem in a sentence.
8. a. Outline the poem to show its structure and development, or
   b. Summarize the events of the poem.
9. Paraphrase the poem.
10. Discuss the diction of the poem. Point out words that are particularly well chosen and explain why.
11. Discuss the imagery of the poem. What kinds of imagery are used? Is there a structure of imagery?
12. Point out examples of metaphor, simile, personification, and metonymy, and explain their appropriateness.
13. Point out and explain any symbols. If the poem is allegorical, explain the allegory.
14. Point out and explain examples of paradox, overstatement, understatement, and irony. What is their function?
15. Point out and explain any allusions. What is their function?
16. What is the tone of the poem? How is it achieved?
17. Point out significant examples of sound repetition and explain their function.
18. a. What is the meter of the poem?
    b. Copy the poem and mark its scansion.
19. Discuss the adaptation of sound to sense.
20. Describe the form or pattern of the poem.
21. Criticize and evaluate the poem.

Shall I compare thee to a summer's day?*

Shall I compare thee to a summer's day?
Thou art more lovely and more temperate:
Rough winds do shake the darling buds of May,
And summer's lease hath all too short a date.
Sometimes too hot the eye of heaven shines,   5
And often is his gold complexion dimmed;
And every fair° from fair sometimes declines   beauty
By chance of nature's changing course untrimmed;°   stripped bare
But thy eternal summer shall not fade
Nor lose possession of that fair thou ow'st,°   own   10
Nor shall death brag thou wand'rest in his shade
When in eternal lines to time thou grow'st.
So long as men can breathe or eyes can see,
So long lives this,° and this gives life to thee.   this poem

William Shakespeare (1564–1616)

QUESTIONS

1. Vocabulary: *temperate* (2), *shade* (11). What different meanings does "temperate" have when used to describe a person or "a summer's day"?
2. What details show that "a summer's day" is lacking in loveliness and is intemperate?
3. What are "the eye of heaven" (5) and "his gold complexion"(6)?
4. The poem begins more or less literally comparing the person being addressed to "a summer's day," but at line 9 it departs from what is literally possible into what is impossible. What does the poem gain by this shift in meaning?
5. Explain the logic behind lines 13–14. Is this a valid proof? Why or why not?

The Whipping

The old woman across the way
    is whipping the boy again
and shouting to the neighborhood
    her goodness and his wrongs.

---

*Whenever a heading duplicates the first line of the poem or a substantial portion thereof, with typically only the first word capitalized, it is probable that the poet left the poem untitled and that the anthologist has substituted the first line or part of it as an editorial convenience. Such a heading is not referred to as the title of the poem.

Wildly he crashes through elephant-ears,   5
    pleads in dusty zinnias,
while she in spite of crippling fat
    pursues and corners him.

She strikes and strikes the shrilly circling
    boy till the stick breaks   10
in her hand. His tears are rainy weather
    to woundlike memories:

My head gripped in bony vise
    of knees, the writhing struggle
to wrench free, the blows, the fear   15
    worse than blows that hateful

Words could bring, the face that I
    no longer knew or loved . . .
Well, it is over now, it is over,
    and the boy sobs in his room,   20

And the woman leans muttering against
    a tree, exhausted, purged—
avenged in part for lifelong hidings
    she has had to bear.

Robert Hayden (1913–1980)

QUESTIONS

1. What similarities connect the old woman, the boy, and the speaker? Can you
   say that one of them is the main subject of the poem?
2. Does this poem express any beauty? What human truth does it embody?
   Could you argue against the claim that "it is over now, it is over" (19)?

The last Night that She lived

The last Night that She lived
It was a Common Night
Except the Dying—this to Us
Made Nature different

We noticed smallest things—   5
Things overlooked before
By this great light upon our Minds
Italicized—as 'twere.

As We went out and in
Between Her final Room   10
And Rooms where Those to be alive
Tomorrow were, a Blame

That Others could exist
While She must finish quite
A Jealousy for Her arose   15
So nearly infinite—

We waited while She passed—
It was a narrow time—
Too jostled were Our Souls to speak
At length the notice came.   20

She mentioned, and forgot—
Then lightly as a Reed
Bent to the Water, struggled scarce—
Consented, and was dead—

And We—We placed the Hair—   25
And drew the Head erect—
And then an awful leisure was
Belief to regulate—

Emily Dickinson (1830–1886)

QUESTIONS

1. Vocabulary: *Italicized* (8), *awful* (27).
2. Lines 11–12 and 12–15 depart from common word order and grammar. Rephrase them so that their plain sense is clear (e.g., "Rooms where Those to be alive / Tomorrow were" means "Rooms in which there were people who would be alive tomorrow"). Notice that both "a Blame" (12) and "A Jealousy" (15) are subjects of the verb "arose" (15).
3. What do the images of "a narrow time" (18) and "Too jostled" (19) contribute to the emotions of the poem?

4. Why is the comparison in lines 22–23 particularly effective?
5. Explain the emotional and spiritual adjustments expressed in the last four lines.

Ballad of Birmingham

(On the bombing of a church in Birmingham, Alabama, 1963)

"Mother dear, may I go downtown
Instead of out to play,
And march the streets of Birmingham
In a Freedom March today?"

"No, baby, no, you may not go,   5
For the dogs are fierce and wild,
And clubs and hoses, guns and jails
Aren't good for a little child."

"But, mother, I won't be alone.
Other children will go with me,   10
And march the streets of Birmingham
To make our country free."

"No, baby, no, you may not go,
For I fear those guns will fire.
But you may go to church instead   15
And sing in the children's choir."

She has combed and brushed her night-dark hair,
And bathed rose petal sweet,
And drawn white gloves on her small brown hands,
And white shoes on her feet.   20

The mother smiled to know her child
Was in the sacred place,
But that smile was the last smile
To come upon her face.

For when she heard the explosion,   25
Her eyes grew wet and wild.
She raced through the streets of Birmingham
Calling for her child.

She clawed through bits of glass and brick,
Then lifted out a shoe.   30
"O, here's the shoe my baby wore,
But, baby, where are you?"

Dudley Randall (1914–2000)

QUESTIONS

1. This poem is based on a historical incident. Throughout 1963, Birmingham, Alabama, was the site of demonstrations and marches protesting the racial segregation of schools and other public facilities. Although they were intended as peaceful protests, these demonstrations often erupted in violence as police attempted to disperse them with fire hoses and police dogs. On the morning of September 15, 1963, a bomb exploded during Sunday School at the 16th Street Baptist Church, killing four children and injuring fourteen. How does the poem differ from what you would expect to find in a newspaper account of such an incident? In an encyclopedia entry? In a speech calling for the elimination of racial injustice?
2. What do the details in the fifth stanza (17–20) contribute to the effect of the poem? Is "She" (17) the mother or the child?
3. In form, this poem shares certain characteristics with the **folk ballad** (see Glossary and Index of Literary Terms, page 1657). Why do you think this twentieth-century poet chose to write in a form that recalls the ballad tradition?
4. What purpose does the poem have beyond simply telling a story? How does the irony help achieve that purpose?

Kitchenette Building

We are things of dry hours and the involuntary plan,
Grayed in, and gray. "Dream" makes a giddy sound, not strong
Like "rent," "feeding a wife," "satisfying a man."

But could a dream send up through onion fumes
Its white and violet, fight with fried potatoes   5
And yesterday's garbage ripening in the hall,
Flutter, or sing an aria down these rooms

Even if we were willing to let it in,
Had time to warm it, keep it very clean,
Anticipate a message, let it begin?   10

We wonder. But not well! not for a minute!
Since Number Five is out of the bathroom now,
We think of lukewarm water, hope to get in it.

                                    Gwendolyn Brooks (1917–2000)

QUESTIONS

1. Vocabulary: *aria* (7). A "kitchenette" (title) is a small kitchen or an alcove or part of a room fitted as a kitchen. What, then, is a "kitchenette building"? Who do you suppose is "Number Five" (12)?
2. Who is the "We" of the poem? Why is the use of plural speakers effective?
3. Why would these speakers refer to themselves as "things" (1)? If a dream rose through the cooking fumes and smell of garbage, why might these people not be "willing to let it in" (8)?

The Red Wheelbarrow

so much depends
upon

a red wheel
barrow

glazed with rain   5
water

beside the white
chickens.

                                    William Carlos Williams (1883–1963)

QUESTIONS

1. The speaker asserts that "so much depends upon" the objects he refers to, leading the reader to ask: *How much* and *why?* This glimpse of a farm scene implies one kind of answer. What is the importance of the wheelbarrow, rain, and chicken to a farmer? To all of us?
2. What further importance can you infer from the references to color, shape, texture, and the juxtaposition of objects? Does the poem itself have a shape? What two ways of observing and valuing the world does the poem imply?

3. What are the possible reasons for "experimental" qualities in this poem—for instance, its lack of capitalization, its very short lines, and its plain, even homely images? Do these qualities give the poem a greater emotional power than a more conventional and decorative poem on the same topic might have achieved?

Constantly risking absurdity

Constantly risking absurdity
                              and death
        whenever he performs
                above the heads
                              of his audience   5
    the poet like an acrobat
                climbs on rime
                      to a high wire of his own making
and balancing on eyebeams
                      above a sea of faces   10
            paces his way
                  to the other side of day
        performing entrechats
                  and sleight-of-foot tricks
and other high theatrics   15
                  and all without mistaking
        any thing
            for what it may not be
    For he's the super realist
                  who must perforce perceive   20
        taut truth
            before the taking of each stance or step
    in his supposed advance
                  toward that still higher perch
where Beauty stands and waits   25
                  with gravity
                      to start her death-defying leap
    And he
        a little charleychaplin man
                  who may or may not catch   30
        her fair eternal form
                  spreadeagled in the empty air
            of existence

Lawrence Ferlinghetti (b. 1919)

QUESTIONS

1. Vocabulary: *entrechats* (13). Explain the meanings of "above the heads" (4), "sleight-of-foot tricks" (14), "high theatrics" (15), and "with gravity" (26).
2. The poet "climbs on rime" (7), the poem asserts. To what extent does this poem utilize rhyme and other musical devices?
3. What statement does the poem make about poetry, truth, and beauty?
4. How do the rhythms created by the length and placement of lines reinforce the meanings of the poem? Does this poem take poets and poetry seriously? solemnly?

Suicide's Note

The calm,
Cool face of the river
Asked me for a kiss.

Langston Hughes (1902–1967)

QUESTIONS

1. How is the speaker's desire for death like the desire expressed in the comparison of the river to a person? How are they unlike? Explore the frame of mind that would create this comparison.
2. Does the repeated "k" sound seem beautiful to you? Can you explain the repetition in terms that reflect the speaker's frame of mind?

Terence, this is stupid stuff

"Terence, this is stupid stuff:
You eat your victuals fast enough;
There can't be much amiss, 'tis clear,
To see the rate you drink your beer.
But oh, good Lord, the verse you make,   5
It gives a chap the belly-ache.
The cow, the old cow, she is dead;
It sleeps well, the horned head:
We poor lads, 'tis our turn now
To hear such tunes as killed the cow.   10
Pretty friendship 'tis to rhyme
Your friends to death before their time

Moping melancholy mad:
Come, pipe a tune to dance to, lad."

    Why, if 'tis dancing you would be,   15
There's brisker pipes than poetry.
Say, for what were hop-yards meant,
Or why was Burton built on Trent?
Oh many a peer of England brews
Livelier liquor than the Muse,   20
And malt does more than Milton can
To justify God's ways to man.
Ale, man, ale's the stuff to drink
For fellows whom it hurts to think:
Look into the pewter pot   25
To see the world as the world's not.
And faith, 'tis pleasant till 'tis past:
The mischief is that 'twill not last.
Oh I have been to Ludlow fair
And left my necktie God knows where,   30
And carried half-way home, or near,
Pints and quarts of Ludlow beer:
Then the world seemed none so bad,
And I myself a sterling lad;
And down in lovely muck I've lain,   35
Happy till I woke again.
Then I saw the morning sky:
Heigho, the tale was all a lie;
The world, it was the old world yet,
I was I, my things were wet,   40
And nothing now remained to do
But begin the game anew.

    Therefore, since the world has still
Much good, but much less good than ill,
And while the sun and moon endure   45
Luck's a chance, but trouble's sure,
I'd face it as a wise man would,
And train for ill and not for good.
'Tis true, the stuff I bring for sale
Is not so brisk a brew as ale: 50
Out of a stem that scored the hand
I wrung it in a weary land.

But take it: if the smack is sour,
The better for the embittered hour;
It should do good to heart and head   55
When your soul is in my soul's stead;
And I will friend you, if I may,
In the dark and cloudy day.

  There was a king reigned in the East:
There, when kings will sit to feast,   60
They get their fill before they think
With poisoned meat and poisoned drink.
He gathered all that springs to birth
From the many-venomed earth;
First a little, thence to more,   65
He sampled all her killing store;
And easy, smiling, seasoned sound,
Sate the king when healths went round.
They put arsenic in his meat
And stared aghast to watch him eat;   70
They poured strychnine in his cup
And shook to see him drink it up:
They shook, they stared as white's their shirt:
Them it was their poison hurt.
—I tell the tale that I heard told.   75
Mithridates, he died old.

A. E. Housman (1859–1936)

QUESTIONS

1. The poem opens with the speaker quoting another person whose remarks he
   then refutes. What is the relationship between the two? Of what is the other
   person complaining? What request does he make of the speaker?
2. Hops (17) and "malt" (21) are principal ingredients of beer and ale. Burton-
   upon-Trent (18) is an English city famous for its breweries. Milton (21), in
   the invocation of his epic poem *Paradise Lost*, declares that his purpose is to
   "justify the ways of God to men." What, in Terence's eyes, is the efficacy of
   liquor in helping one live a difficult life? What is the "stuff" *he* brings "for
   sale" (49)?
3. "Mithridates" (76) was a king of Pontus and a contemporary of Julius Caesar;
   his "tale" is told in Pliny's *Natural History*. The poem is structured by its line
   spacing into four verse paragraphs. What is the connection of this last verse
   paragraph with the rest of the poem? What is the function of each of the
   other three?

4. Essentially, Terence assesses the value of three possible aids for worthwhile living. What are they? Which does Terence consider the best? What six lines of the poem best sum up his philosophy?
5. Many people like reading material that is cheerful and optimistic; they argue that "there's enough suffering and unhappiness in the world already." What, for Housman, is the value of pessimistic and tragic literature?

Ars Poetica

A poem should be palpable and mute
As a globed fruit,

Dumb
As old medallions to the thumb,

Silent as the sleeve-worn stone   5
Of casement ledges where the moss has grown—

A poem should be wordless
As the flight of birds.

                                    *

A poem should be motionless in time
As the moon climbs,   10

Leaving, as the moon releases
Twig by twig the night-entangled trees,

Leaving, as the moon behind the winter leaves,
Memory by memory the mind—

A poem should be motionless in time   15
As the moon climbs

                                    *

A poem should be equal to:
Not true.

For all the history of grief
An empty doorway and a maple leaf.   20

For love
The leaning grasses and two lights above the sea—

A poem should not mean
But be.

Archibald MacLeish (1892–1982)

QUESTIONS

1. How can a poem be "wordless" (7)? How can it be "motionless in time" (15)?
2. The Latin title, literally translated "The Art of Poetry," is a traditional title for works on the philosophy of poetry. What is *this* poet's philosophy of poetry? What does he mean by saying that a poem should not "mean" (23) and should not be "true" (18)?

SUGGESTIONS FOR WRITING

"Writing about Literature," the first section of this book, offers practical advice about the formal requirements and style that are usually expected in student papers. While many of the suggestions presented there may be familiar to you, reviewing them when you prepare to complete these writing assignments should help you to write more effectively.

1. The following pairs of poems deal with similar subject matter treated in very different ways. Yet in each case the two poems employ the multidimensional language that is one criterion of poetic excellence. Choose one pair and discuss the ways in which both poems qualify as poetry, even though they take different approaches to similar topics.
   a. Tennyson, "The Eagle" (page 635) and Hardy, "The Darkling Thrush" (page 972).
   b. Owen, "Dulce et Decorum Est" (page 637) and Stevens, "The Death of a Soldier" (page 1006).
   c. Hopkins, "Spring" (page 692) and Dickinson, "A Light exists in Spring" (page 955).
   d. Olds, "35/10" (page 687) and Cardiff, "Combing" (page 949).
   e. Hayden, "The Whipping" (page 642) and Roethke, "My Papa's Waltz" (page 1000).
   f. Hughes, "Suicide's Note" (page 649) and Robinson, "Richard Cory" (page 998).

2. According to "Ars Poetica" by Archibald MacLeish, "A poem should not mean / But be" (23–24). Relate this assertion to one or more of the following:
   a. Williams, "The Red Wheelbarrow" (page 647).

b. Keats, "Ode on a Grecian Urn" (page 917).
c. Blake, "The Tiger" (page 794).
d. Hughes, "Thistles" (page 832).
e. Stevens, "Disillusionment of Ten O'Clock" (page 1006).
f. Williams, "Poem" (page 1012).
g. Wordsworth, "I wandered lonely as a cloud" (page 1015).

Reading the Poem

How can you develop your understanding and appreciation of poetry? Here are some preliminary suggestions:

1. Read a poem more than once. A good poem will no more yield its full meaning on a single reading than will a Beethoven symphony on a single hearing. Two readings may be necessary simply to let you get your bearings. And if the poem is a work of art, it will repay repeated and prolonged examination. One does not listen to a good piece of music once and forget it; one does not look at a good painting once and throw it away. A poem is not like a newspaper, to be hastily read and discarded. It is to be hung on the wall of one's mind.

2. Keep a dictionary by you and use it. It is futile to try to understand poetry without troubling to learn the meanings of the words of which it is composed. You might as well attempt to play tennis without a ball. One of the benefits of studying literature is an enlarged vocabulary, and the study of poetry offers an excellent opportunity. A few other reference books also will be invaluable, particularly a good book on mythology (your instructor may recommend one) and a Bible.

3. Read so as to hear the sounds of the words in your mind. Poetry is written to be heard: its meanings are conveyed through sound as well as through print. Every word is therefore important. The best way to read a poem may be just the opposite of the best way to read a newspaper. One might read a newspaper article rapidly, and probably only once, before putting the paper into the recycling bag; but a poem should be read slowly, and most poems must be read many times before their full complexity and meaning can be experienced. When you cannot read a poem aloud so as to hear its sounds, lip-read it: form the words with your tongue and mouth even though you do not utter sounds. With ordinary reading material, lip-reading is a bad habit; with poetry, it is a good habit.

4. Always pay careful attention to what the poem is saying. Though you should be conscious of the sounds of the poem, you should never be so exclusively conscious of them that you pay no attention to what the poem means. For some readers, reading a poem is like getting on board a rhythmical roller coaster. The car starts and off they go, up and down, paying no attention to the landscape flashing past them, arriving at the end of the poem breathless, with no idea of what it has been about. This is the wrong way to read a poem. One should make the utmost effort to follow the thought continuously and to grasp the full implications and suggestions. Because a poem says so much, several readings may be necessary, but on the very first reading you should determine the subjects of the verbs, the antecedents of the pronouns, and other normal grammatical facts.

5. Practice reading poems aloud. When you find one you especially like, have friends listen to your reading of it. Try to read it to them in such a way that they will like it too. (a) Read it affectionately, but not affectedly. The two extremes that oral readers often fall into are equally deadly: one is to read as if one were reading a tax report or a railroad timetable, unexpressively, in a monotone; the other is to elocute, with artificial flourishes and vocal histrionics. It is not necessary to put emotion into reading a poem. The emotion is already there. It wants only a fair chance to get out. It will express *itself* if the poem is read naturally and sensitively. (b) Of the two extremes, reading too fast offers greater danger than reading too slow. Read slowly enough that each word is clear and distinct and that the meaning has time to sink in. Remember that your friends do not have the advantage, as you do, of having the text before them. Your ordinary rate of reading will probably be too fast. (c) Read the poem so that the rhythmical pattern is felt but not exaggerated. Remember that poetry, with few exceptions, is written in sentences, just as prose is, and that punctuation is a signal as to how it should be read. Give all grammatical pauses their full due. Do not distort the natural pronunciation of words or a normal accentuation of the sentence to fit into what you have decided is its metrical pattern. One of the worst ways to read a poem is to read it ta-DUM ta-DUM ta-DUM, with an exaggerated emphasis on every other syllable. On the other hand, it should not be read as if it were prose. An important test of your reading will be how you handle the end of a line that lacks line-ending punctuation. A frequent mistake of the beginning reader is to treat each line as if it were a complete thought, whether grammatically complete or not, and to drop the voice at the end of it. A frequent mistake of the sophisticated reader is to take a running start upon approaching the end of a line and fly over it as if it were not there. The line is a rhythmical unit, and its end should be observed whether there is punctuation or not. If there is no punctuation, you ordinarily should observe the end of the line by the slightest of pauses or by holding on to the last word in the line just a little longer than usual, without dropping your voice. In line 12 of the following poem, you should hold on to the word "although" longer than if it occurred elsewhere in the line. But do not lower your voice on it: it is part of the clause that follows in the next stanza.

The Man He Killed

Had he and I but met
By some old ancient inn,
We should have sat us down to wet
Right many a nipperkin!°   half-pint cup

But ranged as infantry,   5
And staring face to face,
I shot at him as he at me,
And killed him in his place.

I shot him dead because—
Because he was my foe,   10
Just so: my foe of course he was;
That's clear enough; although

He thought he'd 'list, perhaps,
Off-hand-like—just as I—
Was out of work—had sold his traps—°   belongings 15
No other reason why.

Yes; quaint and curious war is!
You shoot a fellow down
You'd treat, if met where any bar is,
Or help to half-a-crown.   20

Thomas Hardy (1840–1928)

QUESTIONS

1. Vocabulary: *half-a-crown* (20).
2. In informational prose the repetition of a word like "because" (9–10) would be an error. What purpose does the repetition serve here? Why does the speaker repeat to himself his "clear" reason for killing a man (10–11)? The word "although" (12) gets more emphasis than it would ordinarily because it

comes not only at the end of a line but at the end of a stanza. What purpose does this emphasis serve? Can the redundancy of "old ancient" (2) be poetically justified?

3. Poetry has been defined as "the expression of elevated thought in elevated language." Comment on the adequacy of this definition in the light of Hardy's poem.

One starting point for understanding a poem at the simplest level, and for clearing up misunderstanding, is to paraphrase its content or part of its content. To **paraphrase** a poem means to restate it in different language, so as to make its prose sense as plain as possible. The paraphrase may be longer or shorter than the poem, but it should contain all the ideas in the poem in such a way as to make them clear and to make the central idea, or **theme**, of the poem more accessible.

A Study of Reading Habits

When getting my nose in a book
Cured most things short of school,
It was worth ruining my eyes
To know I could still keep cool,
And deal out the old right hook   5
To dirty dogs twice my size.

Later, with inch-thick specs,
Evil was just my lark:
Me and my cloak and fangs
Had ripping times in the dark.   10
The women I clubbed with sex!
I broke them up like meringues.

Don't read much now: the dude
Who lets the girl down before
The hero arrives, the chap   15
Who's yellow and keeps the store,
Seem far too familiar. Get stewed:
Books are a load of crap.

Philip Larkin (1922–1985)

QUESTIONS

1. The three stanzas delineate three stages in the speaker's life. Describe each.
2. What kind of person is the speaker? What kinds of books does he read? May we identify him with the poet?
3. Contrast the speaker's advice in stanza 3 with Terence's counsel in "Terence, this is stupid stuff" (page 649). Are A. E. Housman and Philip Larkin at odds in their attitudes toward drinking and reading?

Larkin's poem may be paraphrased as follows:

> There was a time when reading was one way I could avoid almost all my troubles—except for school. It seemed worth the danger of ruining my eyes to read stories in which I could imagine myself maintaining my poise in the face of threats and having the boxing skill and experience needed to defeat bullies who were twice my size.

> Later, already having to wear thick glasses because my eyesight had become so poor, I found my delight in stories of sex and evil: imagining myself with Dracula cloak and fangs, I relished vicious nocturnal adventures. I identified myself with sexual marauders whose inexhaustible potency was like a weapon wielded against women who were sweet and fragile.

> I don't read much any more because now I can identify myself only with the flawed secondary characters, such as the flashy dresser who wins the heroine's confidence and then betrays her in a moment of crisis before the cowboy hero comes to her rescue, or the cowardly storekeeper who cringes behind the counter at the first sign of danger. Getting drunk is better than reading—books are just full of useless lies.

Notice that in a paraphrase, figurative language gives way to literal language (similes replace metaphors) and normal word order supplants inverted syntax. But a paraphrase retains the speaker's use of first, second, and third person, and the tenses of verbs. Though it is neither necessary nor possible to avoid using some of the words found in the original, a paraphrase should strive for plain, direct diction. And since a paraphrase is prose, it does not maintain the length and position of poetic lines.

A paraphrase is useful only if you understand that it is the barest, most inadequate approximation of what the poem really "says" and is no more equivalent to the poem than a corpse is to a person. After you have paraphrased a poem, you should endeavor to see how far short of the poem it falls, and why. In what respects does Larkin's poem say more, and say it more memorably, than the paraphrase? Does the phrase "full of useless lies" capture the impact of "a load of crap"? Furthermore, a paraphrase may fall far short of revealing the theme of a poem. "A Study of Reading Habits" represents a man summing up his reading experience and evaluating it—but in turn the poem itself evaluates *him* and his defects. A statement of the theme of the poem might be this:

> A person who turns to books as a source of self-gratifying fantasies may, in the course of time, discover that escapist reading no longer protects him from his awareness of his own reality, and he may out of habit have to find other, more potent, and perhaps more self-destructive means of escaping.

Notice that in stating a theme, we should be careful not to phrase it as a moral or lesson—not "you shouldn't" but "a person may."

To aid us in the understanding of a poem, we may ask ourselves a number of questions about it. Two of the most important are *Who is the speaker?* and *What is the occasion?* A cardinal error of some readers is to assume that a speaker who uses the first-person pronouns (*I, my, mine, me*) is always the poet. A less risky course would be to assume always that the speaker is someone other than the poet. Poems, like short stories, novels, and plays, belong to the world of fiction, an imaginatively conceived world that at its best is "truer" than the factually "real" world that it reflects. When poets put themselves or their thoughts into a poem, they present a *version* of themselves; that is, they present a person who in many ways is *like* themselves but who, consciously or unconsciously, is shaped to fit the needs of the poem. We must be very careful, therefore, about identifying anything in a poem with the biography of the poet.

However, caution is not prohibition. Sometimes events or ideas in a poem will help us to understand some episodes in the poet's life. More importantly for us, knowledge of the poet's life may help us understand a poem. There can be little doubt, when all the evidence is in, that "Terence, this is stupid stuff" (page 649) is Housman's defense of the kind of poetry he writes, and that the six lines in which Terence sums up his beliefs about life and the function of poetry closely echo Housman's own beliefs. On the other hand, it would be folly to suppose that Housman ever got drunk at "Ludlow fair" and once lay down in "lovely muck" and slept all night in a roadside ditch. It may seem paradoxical that Philip Larkin, a poet and novelist and for many years the chief administrator of a university library, would end a poem with the line, "Books are a load of crap." But poems often feature a persona, or speaker, who expresses a viewpoint the poet presumably does not share.

We may well think of every poem, therefore, as being to some degree *dramatic*—that is, the utterance not of the person who wrote the poem but of a fictional character in a particular situation that may be inferred. Many poems are expressly dramatic.

In "The Man He Killed" the speaker is a soldier; the occasion is his having been in battle and killed a man—obviously for the first time in his life. We can tell a good deal about him. He is not a career soldier: he enlisted only because he was out of work. He is a workingman: he speaks a simple and colloquial language ("nipperkin," "'list," "off-hand-like," "traps"). He is a friendly, kindly sort who enjoys a neighborly drink of ale in a bar and will gladly lend a friend a half-a-crown when he has it. He has known what it is to be poor. In any other circumstances he would have been horrified at taking a human life. It gives him pause even now. He is trying to figure it out. But he is not a deep thinker and thinks he has supplied a reason when he has only supplied a name: "I killed the man . . . because he was my foe." The critical question, of course, is *why* was the man his "foe"? Even the speaker is left unsatisfied by his answer, though he is not analytical enough to know what is wrong with it. Obviously this poem is expressly dramatic. We need know nothing about Thomas Hardy's life (he was never a soldier and never killed a man) to realize that the poem is dramatic. The internal evidence of the poem tells us so.

A third important question that we should ask ourselves upon reading any poem is *What is the central purpose of the poem?** The purpose may be to tell a story, to reveal human character, to impart a vivid impression of a scene, to express a mood or an emotion, or to convey vividly some idea or attitude. Whatever the purpose is, we must determine it for ourselves and define it mentally as precisely as possible. Only by relating the various details in the poem to the central purpose or theme can we fully understand their function and meaning. Only then can we begin to assess the value of the poem and determine whether it is a good one or a poor one. In "The Man He Killed" the central purpose is quite clear: it is to make us realize more keenly the irrationality of war.

---

*Our only reliable evidence of the poem's purpose, of course, is the poem itself. External evidence, when it exists, though often helpful, may also be misleading. Some critics have objected to the use of such terms as "purpose" and "intention" altogether; we cannot know, they maintain, what was *attempted* in the poem; we can only know what was *done*. We are concerned, however, not with the *poet's* purpose, but with the *poem's* purpose; that is, with the theme (if it has one), and this is determinable from the poem itself.

The puzzlement of the speaker may be our puzzlement. But even if we are able to give a more sophisticated answer than his as to why men kill each other, we ought still to have a greater awareness, after reading the poem, of the fundamental irrationality in war that makes men kill who have no grudge against each other and who might under different circumstances show each other considerable kindness.

Is my team plowing

"Is my team plowing,
That I was used to drive
And hear the harness jingle
When I was man alive?"

Aye, the horses trample,   5
The harness jingles now;
No change though you lie under
The land you used to plow.

"Is football playing
Along the river shore,   10
With lads to chase the leather,
Now I stand up no more?"

Aye, the ball is flying,
The lads play heart and soul;
The goal stands up, the keeper   15
Stands up to keep the goal.

"Is my girl happy,
That I thought hard to leave,
And has she tired of weeping
As she lies down at eve?"   20

Aye, she lies down lightly,
She lies not down to weep:
Your girl is well contented.
Be still, my lad, and sleep.

"Is my friend hearty,   25
Now I am thin and pine;

And has he found to sleep in
A better bed than mine?"

Yes, lad, I lie easy,
I lie as lads would choose;   30
I cheer a dead man's sweetheart,
Never ask me whose.

A. E. Housman (1859–1936)

QUESTIONS

1. How many actual speakers are there in this poem? What is meant by "whose" in line 32?
2. Is this poem cynical in its observation of human nature?
3. The word *sleep* (24, 27) in the concluding stanzas suggests three different meanings. What are they? How many meanings are suggested by the word *bed?*

Once we have answered the question *What is the central purpose of the poem?* we can consider another question, equally important to full understanding: *By what means is that purpose achieved?* It is important to distinguish means from ends. A student on an examination once used the poem "Is my team plowing" as evidence that A. E. Housman believed in immortality because in it a man speaks from the grave. This is as much a misconstruction as to say that Thomas Hardy joined the army because he was out of work. The purpose of Housman's poem is to communicate poignantly a certain truth about human life: life goes on after our deaths pretty much as it did before—our dying does not disturb the universe. Further, it dramatizes that irrational sense of betrayal and guilt that may follow the death of a friend. The poem achieves this purpose by means of a fanciful dramatic framework in which a dead man converses with his still-living friend. The framework tells us nothing about whether Housman believed in immortality (as a matter of fact, he did not). It is simply an effective means by which we *can* learn how Housman felt a man's death affected the life he left behind. The question *By what means is that purpose achieved?* is partially answered by describing the poem's dramatic framework, if it has any. The complete answer requires an accounting of various resources of communication that we will discuss in this book.

The most important preliminary advice we can give for reading poetry is to maintain always, while reading it, the utmost mental alertness. The most harmful idea one can get about poetry is that its purpose is to soothe and relax and that the best place to read it is lying in a hammock with a cool drink while low music plays in the background. You *can* read poetry lying in a hammock, but only if you refuse to put your mind in the same attitude as your body. Its purpose is not to soothe and relax but to arouse and awake, to shock us into life, to make us more alive.

An analogy can be drawn between reading poetry and playing tennis. Both offer great enjoyment if the game is played hard. Good tennis players must be constantly on the tips of their toes, concentrating on their opponent's every move. They must be ready for a drive to the right or left, a lob overhead, or a drop shot barely over the net. They must be ready for topspin or underspin, a ball that bounces crazily to the left or right. They must jump for the high ones and run for the long ones. And they will enjoy the game almost exactly in proportion to the effort they put into it. The same is true of reading poetry. Great enjoyment is there, but this enjoyment demands a mental effort equivalent to the physical effort one puts into tennis.

The reader of poetry has one advantage over the tennis player: poets are not trying to win matches. They may expect the reader to stretch for their shots, but they *want* the reader to return them.

REVIEWING CHAPTER TWO

1. Review the five preliminary suggestions for reading poems.
2. List steps in paraphrasing, and create paraphrases of several poems, showing how paraphrase helps to clarify the theme.
3. Explain how identifying the speaker and the occasion of the poem shows the dramatic quality of poetry.
4. Explore the concept of a "central purpose" of a poem.
5. Consider the difference between the means and the ends in determining the central purpose of a poem.
6. Determine which ideas in this chapter are exemplified in the following poems.

Break of Day

'Tis true, 'tis day; what though it be?
Oh, wilt thou therefore rise from me?

Why should we rise because 'tis light?
Did we lie down because 'twas night?
Love which in spite of darkness brought us hither   5
Should, in despite of light, keep us together.

Light hath no tongue, but is all eye;
If it could speak as well as spy,
This were the worst that it could say:
That, being well, I fain would stay,   10
And that I loved my heart and honor so,
That I would not from him that had them go.

Must business thee from hence remove?
Oh, that's the worst disease of love;
The poor, the foul, the false, love can   15
Admit, but not the busied man.
He which hath business and makes love, doth do
Such wrong as when a married man doth woo.

John Donne (1572–1631)

QUESTIONS

1. Who is the speaker? Who is addressed? What is the situation? Can the speaker be identified with the poet?
2. Explain the comparison in line 7. To whom does "I" (10–12) refer? Is "love" (15) the subject or object of "can admit"?
3. Summarize the arguments used by the speaker to keep the person addressed from leaving. What does the speaker value most?
4. Are the two persons married or unmarried? Justify your answer.

There's been a Death, in the Opposite House

There's been a Death, in the Opposite House,
As lately as Today—
I know it, by the numb look
Such Houses have—alway—

The Neighbors rustle in and out—   5
The Doctor—drives away—
A Window opens like a Pod—
Abrupt—mechanically—

Somebody flings a Mattress out—
The Children hurry by—
They wonder if it died—on that—   10
I used to—when a Boy—

The Minister—goes stiffly in—
As if the House were His—
And He owned all the Mourners—now—   15
And little Boys—besides—

And then the Milliner—and the Man
Of the Appalling Trade—
To take the measure of the House—

There'll be that Dark Parade—   20

Of Tassels—and of Coaches—soon—
It's easy as a Sign—
The Intuition of the News—
In just a Country Town—

Emily Dickinson (1830–1886)

QUESTIONS

1. What can we know about the speaker in the poem?
2. By what signs does the speaker "intuit" that a death has occurred? Explain them stanza by stanza. What does it mean that the speaker must intuit rather than simply *know* that death has taken place?
3. Comment on the words "Appalling" (18) and "Dark" (20).
4. What shift in the poem is signaled by the separation of line 20 from the end of stanza 5?
5. What is the speaker's attitude toward death?

When in Rome

Mattie dear
the box is full
take
whatever you like
to eat   5
        (an egg
        or soup
        . . . there ain't no meat.)

there's endive there
and   10
cottage cheese
            (whew! If I had some
            black-eyed peas . . .)
there's sardines
on the shelves   15
and such
but
don't
get my anchovies
they cost   20
too much!
            (me get the
            anchovies indeed!
            what she think, she got—
            a bird to feed?)   25
there's plenty in there
to fill you up.
            (yes'm. just the
            sight's
            enough!   30

Hope I lives till I get
home
I'm tired of eatin'
what they eats in Rome . . .)

Mari Evans

QUESTIONS

1. Who are the two speakers? What is the situation? Why are the second
   speaker's words enclosed in parentheses?
2. What are the attitudes of the two speakers toward one another? What is the
   attitude of each to herself?
3. What implications have the title and the last two lines?

Animals Are Passing from Our Lives

It's wonderful how I jog
on four honed-down ivory toes
my massive buttocks slipping
like oiled parts with each light step.

I'm to market. I can smell   5
the sour, grooved block, I can smell
the blade that opens the hole
and the pudgy white fingers

that shake out the intestines
like a hankie. In my dreams   10
the snouts drool on the marble,
suffering children, suffering flies,

suffering the consumers
who won't meet their steady eyes
for fear they could see. The boy   15
who drives me along believes

that any moment I'll fall
on my side and drum my toes
like a typewriter or squeal
and shit like a new housewife   20

discovering television,
or that I'll turn like a beast
cleverly to hook his teeth
with my teeth. No. Not this pig.

Philip Levine (b. 1928)

QUESTIONS

1. Who or what is the speaker? What end is served by means of the choice of speaker?
2. What are the relevant meanings of the word "suffering" (12–13)?
3. What attitude of the speaker is reflected in the final sentence of the poem (24)?

Question

Body my house
my horse my hound
what will I do
when you are fallen

Where will I sleep   5
How will I ride
What will I hunt

Where can I go
without my mount
all eager and quick   10
How will I know
in thicket ahead
is danger or treasure
when Body my good
bright dog is dead   15

How will it be
to lie in the sky
without roof or door
and wind for an eye

With cloud for shift   20
how will I hide?

May Swenson (1919–1989)

QUESTIONS

1. Who or what is the speaker that is addressing "Body"? To what various things
   is body compared?
2. The poem consists of a number of questions. How in their variety do they
   imply the single question to which the title refers?

Mirror

I am silver and exact. I have no preconceptions.
Whatever I see I swallow immediately
Just as it is, unmisted by love or dislike.
I am not cruel, only truthful—
The eye of a little god, four-cornered.   5
Most of the time I meditate on the opposite wall.
It is pink, with speckles. I have looked at it so long
I think it is a part of my heart. But it flickers.
Faces and darkness separate us over and over.

Now I am a lake. A woman bends over me,   10
Searching my reaches for what she really is.

Then she turns to those liars, the candles or the moon.
I see her back, and reflect it faithfully.
She rewards me with tears and an agitation of hands.
I am important to her. She comes and goes.   15
Each morning it is her face that replaces the darkness.
In me she has drowned a young girl, and in me an old woman
Rises toward her day after day, like a terrible fish

Sylvia Plath (1932–1963)

QUESTIONS

1. Who is the speaker? What is the central purpose of the poem, and by what means is it achieved?
2. In what ways is the mirror like and unlike a person (stanza 1)? In what ways is it like a lake (stanza 2)?
3. What is the meaning of the last two lines?

The Clod and the Pebble

"Love seeketh not Itself to please,
Nor for itself hath any care;
But for another gives its ease,
And builds a Heaven in Hell's despair."

So sang a little Clod of Clay,   5
Trodden with the cattle's feet;
But a Pebble of the brook,
Warbled out these meters meet:

"Love seeketh only Self to please,
To bind another to its delight,   10
Joys in another's loss of ease,
And builds a Hell in Heaven's despite."

William Blake (1757–1827)

QUESTIONS

1. Vocabulary: *Clod* (title). Explore the literal physical contrasts between a clod and a pebble. Why are these suitable "characters" to carry out this debate?

2. Paraphrase lines 4 and 12. What do "Heaven" and "Hell" have to do with this debate? Are they to be taken literally?
3. The Pebble gets the last word here. Does that mean that its philosophy is the poet's?

Ethics

In ethics class so many years ago
our teacher asked this question every fall:
if there were a fire in a museum
which would you save, a Rembrandt painting
or an old woman who hadn't many   5
years left anyhow? Restless on hard chairs
caring little for pictures or old age
we'd opt one year for life, the next for art
and always half-heartedly. Sometimes
the woman borrowed my grandmother's face   10
leaving her usual kitchen to wander
some drafty, half-imagined museum.
One year, feeling clever, I replied
why not let the woman decide herself?
Linda, the teacher would report, eschews   15
the burdens of responsibility.
This fall in a real museum I stand
before a real Rembrandt, old woman,
or nearly so, myself. The colors
within this frame are darker than autumn,   20
darker even than winter—the browns of earth,
though earth's most radiant elements burn
through the canvas. I know now that woman
and painting and season are almost one
and all beyond saving by children.   25

Linda Pastan (b. 1932)

QUESTIONS

1. Explore the fictitious time frame the poem creates—how often a girl takes the same class with the same teacher. What does this element of fantasy add to the poem?
2. Does the poem answer its central ethical question? If so, what is that answer; if not, what is the value of asking? What is the central purpose of the poem?

Storm Warnings

The glass has been falling all the afternoon,
And knowing better than the instrument
What winds are walking overhead, what zone
Of gray unrest is moving across the land,
I leave the book upon a pillowed chair   5
And walk from window to closed window, watching
Boughs strain against the sky

And think again, as often when the air
Moves inward toward a silent core of waiting,
How with a single purpose time has traveled   10
By secret currents of the undiscerned
Into this polar realm. Weather abroad
And weather in the heart alike come on
Regardless of prediction.

Between foreseeing and averting change   15
Lies all the mastery of elements
Which clocks and weatherglasses cannot alter.
Time in the hand is not control of time,
Nor shattered fragments of an instrument
A proof against the wind; the wind will rise,   20
We can only close the shutters.

I draw the curtains as the sky goes black
And set a match to candles sheathed in glass
Against the keyhole draught, the insistent whine
Of weather through the unsealed aperture.   25
This is our sole defense against the season;
These are the things that we have learned to do
Who live in troubled regions.

Adrienne Rich (b. 1929)

SUGGESTIONS FOR WRITING

1. Here are four definitions of poetry, all framed by poets themselves. Which
   definition best fits the poems you have so far read?
   a. I wish our clever young poets would remember my homely definitions of
      prose and poetry: that is, prose = words in their best order; poetry = the
      best words in the best order.   *Samuel Taylor Coleridge*

b. It is not meters, but a meter-making argument, that makes a poem—a thought so passionate and alive that, like the spirit of a plant or an animal, it has an architecture of its own, and adorns nature with a new thing.   *Ralph Waldo Emerson*

c. If I read a book and it makes my whole body so cold no fire can warm me, I know that is poetry. If I feel physically as if the top of my head were taken off, I know that is poetry. These are the only ways I know it. Is there any other way?   *Emily Dickinson*

d. A poem begins in delight, it inclines to the impulse, it assumes a direction with the first line laid down, it runs a course of lucky events, and ends in a clarification of life—not necessarily a great clarification, such as sects and cults are founded on, but in a momentary stay against confusion.   *Robert Frost*

2. Using two or three poems from this chapter, or poems from the following list, write an essay that supports the definition you have chosen.
   a. Atwood, "Siren Song" (page 780).
   b. Clifton, "good times" (page 950).
   c. Dickinson, "A narrow Fellow in the Grass" (page 956).
   d. Donne, "Song: Go and catch a falling star" (page 958).
   e. Joseph, "Warning" (page 978).
   f. Olds, "The Victims" (page 989).

Chapter Three

Denotation and Connotation

A primary distinction between the practical use of language and the literary use is that in literature, especially in poetry, a *fuller* use is made of individual words. To understand this, we need to examine the composition of a word.

The average word has three component parts: sound, denotation, and connotation. It begins as a combination of tones and noises, uttered by the lips, tongue, and throat, for which the written word is a notation. But it differs from a musical tone or a noise in that it has a meaning attached to it. The basic part of this meaning is its **denotation** or denotations: that is, the dictionary meaning or meanings of the word. Beyond its denotations, a word may also have connotations. The **connotations** are what it suggests beyond what it expresses: its overtones of meaning. It acquires these connotations from its past history and associations, from the way and the circumstances in which it has been used. The word *home*, for instance, by denotation means only a place where one lives, but by connotation it suggests security, love, comfort, and family. The words *childlike* and *childish* both mean "characteristic of a child," but *childlike* suggests meekness, innocence, and wide-eyed wonder, while *childish* suggests pettiness, willfulness, and temper tantrums. If we list the names of different coins—nickel, peso, euro, sen, doubloon—the word *doubloon*, to four out of five readers, immediately will suggest pirates, though a dictionary definition includes nothing about pirates. Pirates are part of its connotation.

Connotation is very important in poetry, for it is one of the means by which the poet can concentrate or enrich meaning—say more in fewer words. Consider, for instance, the following short poem:

There is no Frigate like a Book

There is no Frigate like a Book
To take us Lands away
Nor any Coursers like a Page

Of prancing Poetry—
This Traverse may the poorest take   5
Without oppress of Toll—
How frugal is the Chariot
That bears the Human soul.

Emily Dickinson (1830–1886)

This poem considers the power of a book or of poetry to carry us away, to take us from our immediate surroundings into a world of the imagination. To do this it compares literature to various means of transportation: a boat, a team of horses, a wheeled land vehicle. But the poet has been careful to choose kinds of transportation and names for them that have romantic connotations. "Frigate" suggests exploration and adventure; "coursers," beauty, spirit, and speed; "chariot," speed and the ability to go through the air as well as on land. (Compare "Swing Low, Sweet Chariot" and the myth of Phaëthon, who tried to drive the chariot of Apollo, and the famous painting of Aurora with her horses, once hung in almost every school.) How much of the meaning of the poem comes from this selection of vehicles and words is apparent if we substitute *steamship* for "frigate," *horses* for "coursers," and *streetcar* for "chariot."

QUESTIONS

1. What is lost if *miles* is substituted for "Lands" (2) or *cheap* for "frugal" (7)?
2. How is "prancing" (4) peculiarly appropriate to poetry as well as to coursers? Could the poet without loss have compared a book to coursers and poetry to a frigate?
3. Is this account appropriate to all kinds of poetry or just to certain kinds? That is, was the poet thinking of poems like Wilfred Owen's "Dulce et Decorum Est" (page 637) or of poems like Coleridge's "Kubla Khan" (page 951) and Keats's "La Belle Dame sans Merci" (page 980)?

Just as a word has a variety of connotations, so may it have more than one denotation. If we look up the word *spring* in the dictionary, for instance, we will find that it has between twenty-five and thirty distinguishable meanings: it may mean (1) a pounce or leap, (2) a season of the year, (3) a natural source of water, (4) a coiled elastic wire, and so forth. This variety of denotation, complicated by additional tones of connotation, makes language confusing and difficult to use. Any person using words must be careful to define precisely by context the denotation that is intended. But the difference between the writer using language to communicate and the poet is this: the practical writer will usually attempt to confine words to one denotation at a time; the poet will often take advantage of the fact that the word has more than one meaning by using it to mean more than one thing at the same time. Thus, when Edith Sitwell in one of her poems writes, "this is the time of the wild spring and the mating of the tigers,"* she uses the word "spring" to denote both a season of the year and a sudden leap (and she uses the word "tigers" rather than *deer* or *birds* because it has a connotation of fierceness and wildness that the others lack). The two denotations of "spring" are also appropriately possessed of contrasting connotations: the season is positive in its implications, while a sudden leap may connote the pouncing of a beast of prey. Similarly, in "Mirror" (page 669), the word "swallow" in line 2 denotes both accepting without question and consuming or devouring, and so connotes both an inability to think and an obliteration or destruction.

When my love swears that she is made of truth

When my love swears that she is made of truth,
I do believe her, though I know she lies,
That she might think me some untutored youth,
Unlearnèd in the world's false subtleties.
Thus vainly thinking that she thinks me young,   5
Although she knows my days are past the best,
Simply I credit her false-speaking tongue;
On both sides thus is simple truth supprest.
But wherefore says she not she is unjust?°   unfaithful
And wherefore say not I that I am old?   10
Oh, love's best habit is in seeming trust,
And age in love loves not to have years told:
Therefore I lie with her and she with me,
And in our faults by lies we flattered be.

William Shakespeare (1564–1616)

QUESTIONS

1. How old is the speaker? How old is his beloved? What is the nature of their relationship?
2. How is the contradiction in line 2 to be resolved? In lines 5–6? Who is lying to whom?

Collected Poems (New York: Vanguard, 1968) 392.

3. How do "simply" (7) and "simple" (8) differ in meaning? The words "vainly" (5), "habit" (11), "told" (12), and "lie" (13) all have double denotative meanings. What are they?
4. What is the tone of the poem—that is, the attitude of the speaker toward his situation? Should line 11 be taken as an expression of (a) wisdom, (b) conscious rationalization, or (c) self-deception? In answering these questions, consider both the situation and the connotations of all the important words beginning with "swears" (1) and ending with "flattered" (14).

A frequent misconception of poetic language is that poets seek always the most beautiful or noble-sounding words. What they really seek are the most *meaningful* words, and these vary from one context to another. Language has many levels and varieties, and poets may choose from all of them. Their words may be grandiose or humble, fanciful or matter-of-fact, romantic or realistic, archaic or modern, technical or everyday, monosyllabic or polysyllabic. Usually a poem will be pitched pretty much in one key: the words in Emily Dickinson's "There is no Frigate like a Book" (page 674) and those in Thomas Hardy's "The Man He Killed" (page 657) are chosen from quite different areas of language, but both poets have chosen the words most meaningful for their own poetic context. It is always important to determine the level of diction employed in a poem, for it may provide clear insight into the purpose of the poem by helping to characterize the speaker. Sometimes a poet may import a word from one level or area of language into a poem composed mostly of words from a different level or area. If this is done clumsily, the result will be incongruous and sloppy; if it is done skillfully, the result will be a shock of surprise and an increment of meaning for the reader. In fact, the many varieties of language open to poets provide their richest resource. Their task is one of constant exploration and discovery. They search always for the secret affinities of words that allow them to be brought together with soft explosions of meaning.

Pathedy of Manners

At twenty she was brilliant and adored,
Phi Beta Kappa, sought for every dance;
Captured symbolic logic and the glance
Of men whose interest was their sole reward.

She learned the cultured jargon of those bred   5
To antique crystal and authentic pearls,

Scorned Wagner, praised the Degas dancing girls,
And when she might have thought, conversed instead.

She hung up her diploma, went abroad,
Saw catalogues of domes and tapestry,   10
Rejected an impoverished marquis,
And learned to tell real Wedgwood from a fraud.

Back home her breeding led her to espouse
A bright young man whose pearl cufflinks were real.
They had an ideal marriage, and ideal   15
But lonely children in an ideal house.

I saw her yesterday at forty-three,
Her children gone, her husband one year dead,
Toying with plots to kill time and re-wed
Illusions of lost opportunity.   20

But afraid to wonder what she might have known
With all that wealth and mind had offered her,
She shuns conviction, choosing to infer
Tenets of every mind except her own.

A hundred people call, though not one friend,   25
To parry a hundred doubts with nimble talk.
Her meanings lost in manners, she will walk
Alone in brilliant circles to the end.

Ellen Kay (b. 1931)

QUESTIONS

1. The title alludes to the type of drama called "comedy of manners" and coins a
   word combining the suffix -edy with the Greek root path- (as in pathetic,
   sympathy, pathology). How does the poem narrate a story with both comic and
   pathetic implications? For what might the central character be blamed?
   What arouses our pity for her?
2. Explore the multiple denotations and the connotations attached to each
   denotation of "brilliant" (both in 1 and 28), "interest" and "reward" (4),
   "cultured" and "jargon" (5), "circles" (28).
3. Why are the poet's words more effective than these possible synonyms: "captured"
   (3) rather than *learned*; "conversed" (8) rather than *chatted, gossiped,* or *talked*;
   "catalogues" (10) rather than *volumes* or *multitudes*; "espouse" (13) rather than
   marry? Discuss the momentary ambiguity presented by the word "re-wed" (19).

4. At what point in the poem does the speaker shift from language that represents the way the woman might have talked about herself to language that reveals how the speaker judges her? Point out examples of both kinds of language.

People using language only to convey information are usually indifferent to the sounds of the words and may feel frustrated by their connotations and multiple denotations. They would rather confine each word to a single, exact meaning. They use, one might say, a fraction of the word and throw away the rest. Poets, on the other hand, use as much of the word as possible. They are interested in connotation and use it to enrich and convey meaning. And they may rely on more than one denotation.

Perhaps the purest form of practical language is scientific language. Scientists need a precise language to convey information precisely. The existence of multiple denotations and various overtones of meaning may interfere with this purpose. As a result of this, scientists have even devised special "languages" such as the following:

$$SO_2 + H_2O = H_2SO_3$$

In such a statement the symbols are entirely unambiguous; they have been stripped of all connotation and of all denotations but one. The word *sulfurous*, if it occurred in poetry, might have all kinds of connotations: fire, smoke, brimstone, hell, damnation. But H_2SO_3 means one thing and one thing only: sulfurous acid.

The ambiguity and multiplicity of meanings possessed by words might be an obstacle to the scientist, but they are an advantage for the poet who seeks richness of meaning. One resource for that is a multidimensional language using a multidimensional vocabulary, in which the dimensions of connotation and sound are added to the dimension of denotation.

The poet, we may say, plays on a many-stringed instrument and sounds more than one note at a time.

The first task in reading poetry, therefore, as in reading any kind of literature, is to develop a sense of language, a feeling for words. One needs to become acquainted with their shape, their color, and their flavor. Two of the ways of doing this are extensive use of the dictionary and extensive reading.

EXERCISES

1. Which word in each group has the most "romantic" connotations: (a) horse, steed, nag; (b) king, ruler, tyrant, autocrat; (c) Chicago, Pittsburgh, Samarkand, Detroit?

2. Which word in each group is the most emotionally connotative: (a) female parent, mother, dam; (b) offspring, children, progeny; (c) brother, sibling?

3. Arrange the words in each of the following groups from most positive to most negative in connotation: (a) skinny, thin, gaunt, slender; (b) prosperous, loaded, moneyed, affluent; (c) brainy, intelligent, eggheaded, smart.

4. Of the following, which should you be less offended at being accused of: (a) having acted foolishly, (b) having acted like a fool?

5. In any competent piece of writing, the possible multiple denotations and connotations of the words used are controlled by context. The context screens out irrelevant meanings while allowing the relevant meanings to pass through. What denotation has the word *fast* in the following contexts: fast runner, fast color, fast living, fast day? What are the varying connotations of these four denotations of *fast?*

6. Explain how in the following examples the denotation of the word *white* remains the same, but the connotations differ: (a) The young princess had blue eyes, golden hair, and a breast as white as snow; (b) Confronted with the evidence, the false princess turned as white as a sheet.

REVIEWING CHAPTER THREE

1. Distinguish between connotation and denotation as components of words.

2. Explain how words accumulate their connotations.

3. Explore the ways in which a word may have multiple denotations, and multiple connotations, showing that different denotations may have different connotations.

4. Explore the ways in which the context will determine which denotations and which connotations are relevant in a poem.

5. Show how levels of diction may characterize the speaker in a poem.

Naming of Parts

Today we have naming of parts. Yesterday,
We had daily cleaning. And tomorrow morning,
We shall have what to do after firing. But today,
Today we have naming of parts. Japonica
Glistens like coral in all of the neighboring gardens,   5
    And today we have naming of parts.

This is the lower sling swivel. And this
Is the upper sling swivel, whose use you will see,
When you are given your slings. And this is the piling swivel,
Which in your case you have not got. The branches   10
Hold in the gardens their silent, eloquent gestures,
    Which in our case we have not got.

This is the safety-catch, which is always released
With an easy flick of the thumb. And please do not let me
See anyone using his finger. You can do it quite easy   15
If you have any strength in your thumb. The blossoms
Are fragile and motionless, never letting anyone see
    Any of them using their finger.

And this you can see is the bolt. The purpose of this
Is to open the breech, as you see. We can slide it   20
Rapidly backwards and forwards: we call this
Easing the spring. And rapidly backwards and forwards
The early bees are assaulting and fumbling the flowers:
    They call it easing the Spring.

They call it easing the Spring: it is perfectly easy   25
If you have any strength in your thumb: like the bolt,
And the breech, and the cocking-piece, and the point of balance,
Which in our case we have not got; and the almond-blossom
Silent in all of the gardens and the bees going backwards and forwards,
    For today we have naming of parts.   30

Henry Reed (1914–1986)

QUESTIONS

1. Who is the speaker (or speakers) in the poem, and what is the situation?
2. What basic contrasts are represented by the trainees and by the gardens?
3. What is it that trainees "have not got" (28)? How many meanings have the phrases "easing the spring" (22, 24, 25) and "point of balance" (27)?
4. What differences in language and rhythm do you find between the lines that involve the "naming of parts" and those that describe the gardens?
5. Does the repetition of certain phrases throughout the poem have any special function or does it merely create a kind of refrain?
6. What statement does the poem make about war as it affects men and their lives?

Cross

My old man's a white old man
And my old mother's black.
If ever I cursed my white old man
I take my curses back.

If ever I cursed my black old mother   5
And wished she were in hell,
I'm sorry for that evil wish
And now I wish her well.

My old man died in a fine big house.
My ma died in a shack.   10
I wonder where I'm gonna die,
Being neither white nor black?

Langston Hughes (1902–1967)

QUESTIONS

1. What different denotations does the title have? What connotations are
   linked to each of them?
2. The language in this poem, such as "old man" (1, 3, 9), "ma" (10), and
   "gonna" (11), is plain, and even colloquial. Is it appropriate to the subject?
   Why or why not?

The world is too much with us

The world is too much with us; late and soon,
Getting and spending, we lay waste our powers:
Little we see in nature that is ours;
We have given our hearts away, a sordid boon!
This sea that bares her bosom to the moon,   5
The winds that will be howling at all hours,
And are up-gathered now like sleeping flowers,
For this, for everything, we are out of tune;
It moves us not. —Great God! I'd rather be
A pagan suckled in a creed outworn;   10
So might I, standing on this pleasant lea,
Have glimpses that would make me less forlorn;

Have sight of Proteus rising from the sea;
Or hear old Triton blow his wreathèd horn.

William Wordsworth (1770–1850)

QUESTIONS

1. Vocabulary: *boon* (4), *Proteus* (13), *Triton* (14). What two relevant denotations has "wreathèd" (14)?
2. Explain why the poet's words are more effective than these possible alternatives: *earth* for "world" (1); *selling and buying* for "getting and spending" (2); *exposes* for "bares" (5); *dozing* for "sleeping" (7); *posies* for "flowers" (7); *nourished* for "suckled" (10); *visions* for "glimpses" (12); *sound* for "blow" (14).
3. Is "Great God!" (9) a vocative (term of address) or an expletive (exclamation)? Or something of both?
4. State the theme (central idea) of the poem in a sentence.

Desert Places

Snow falling and night falling fast, oh, fast
In a field I looked into going past,
And the ground almost covered smooth in snow,
But a few weeds and stubble showing last.

The woods around it have it—it is theirs.   5
All animals are smothered in their lairs.
I am too absent-spirited to count;
The loneliness includes me unawares.

And lonely as it is that loneliness
Will be more lonely ere it will be less—   10
A blanker whiteness of benighted snow
With no expression, nothing to express.

They cannot scare me with their empty spaces
Between stars—on stars where no human race is.
I have it in me so much nearer home   15
To scare myself with my own desert places.

Robert Frost (1874–1963)

QUESTIONS

1. Examine the poem for examples of words or phrases with negative or positive connotations. Which stanza is most negative? Considering its possible synonyms, how emotionally powerful is the word "scare" (13 and 16)?

2. What multiple denotations of the word "benighted" (11) are functional in the poem? How does the etymology of "blanker" add to its force in this context?
3. "Absent-spirited" (7) is coined from the common phrase "absent-minded." What denotations of "spirit" are relevant here?
4. Who are "They" (13) who can create fear by talking about the emptiness of space? Fear of what? What are the "desert places" (16) within the speaker that may be compared to literal emptiness of space?
5. In the first publication of the poem, line 14 concluded "on stars void of human races." Frost's final version calls attention to the potentially comic effect of rhyming *spaces/race is/places*, a device called feminine rhyme often used in humorous verse (see page 821). Is the speaker feeling comical? Can you relate this effect to what you determined about the word "scare" in question 1?

Let No Charitable Hope

Now let no charitable hope
Confuse my mind with images
Of eagle and of antelope:
I am in nature none of these.

I was, being human, born alone;   5
I am, being woman, hard beset;
I live by squeezing from a stone
The little nourishment I get.

In masks outrageous and austere
The years go by in single file;   10
But none has merited my fear,
And none has quite escaped my smile.

Elinor Wylie (1885–1928)

QUESTIONS

1. Of all the natural creatures the speaker might have chosen in line 3, why did she choose "eagle" and "antelope"? What are the connotations of these particular creatures?
2. Stanza 2 suggests the kind of life the woman speaker is living. How would you describe her life?

3. Consider the phrase "outrageous and austere" (9). What are the connotations of these words?
4. Does the final stanza suggest a negative or an affirmative resolution to the speaker's argument?

A Hymn to God the Father

Wilt thou forgive that sin where I begun,
    Which is my sin, though it were done before?
Wilt thou forgive those sins through which I run,°   ran
    And do them still, though still I do deplore?
      When thou hast done, thou hast not done,   5
        For I have more.

Wilt thou forgive that sin by which I won
    Others to sin, and made my sin their door?
Wilt thou forgive that sin which I did shun
    A year or two, but wallowed in a score?
      When thou hast done, thou hast not done,   10
        For I have more.

I have a sin of fear, that when I have spun
    My last thread, I shall perish on the shore;
Swear by thyself that at my death thy Sun   15
    Shall shine as it shines now, and heretofore;
      And having done that, thou hast done.
        I have no more.

John Donne (1572–1631)

QUESTIONS

1. In 1601, John Donne at 29 secretly married Anne More, age 17, infuriating her upper-class father, who had him imprisoned for three days. Because of the marriage, Donne lost his job as private secretary to an important official at court, and probably ruined his chances for the career at court that he desired. It was, however, a true love match. In 1615 Donne entered the church. In 1617 his wife, then 33, died after bearing twelve children. In 1621 he was appointed Dean of St. Paul's Cathedral in London and quickly won a reputation for his eloquent sermons. His religious poems differ markedly in tone from the often cynical, sometimes erotic poems of his youth. The foregoing poem was probably written during a severe illness in 1623. Is this information of any value to a reader of the poem?

2. What sin is referred to in lines 1–2? What is meant by "when I have spun / My last thread" (13–14)? By "I shall perish on the shore" (14)?
3. How do the puns on "done" (5, 11, 17) and "Sun" (15) give structure and meaning to the poem? Explain the relevance of the meanings generated by the puns.

One Art

The art of losing isn't hard to master;
so many things seem filled with the intent
to be lost that their loss is no disaster.

Lose something every day. Accept the fluster
of lost door keys, the hour badly spent.   5
The art of losing isn't hard to master.

Then practice losing farther, losing faster:
places, and names, and where it was you meant
to travel. None of these will bring disaster.

I lost my mother's watch. And look! my last, or   10
next-to-last, of three loved houses went.
The art of losing isn't hard to master.

I lost two cities, lovely ones. And, vaster,
some realms I owned, two rivers, a continent.
I miss them, but it wasn't a disaster.   15

—Even losing you (the joking voice, a gesture
I love) I shan't have lied. It's evident
the art of losing's not too hard to master
though it may look like (*Write* it!) like disaster.

Elizabeth Bishop (1911–1979)

QUESTIONS

1. What various denotations of "lose" and its derivative forms are relevant to the context? What connotations are attached to the separate denotative meanings?

2. Explain how "owned" (14) and "lost" (13) shift the meanings of possessing and losing.
3. What seems to be the purpose of the speaker in the first three tercets (three-line units)? How is the advice given there supported by the personal experiences related in the next two tercets?
4. The concluding quatrain (four-line unit) contains direct address to a person, as well as a command the speaker addresses to herself. How do these details reveal the real purpose of the poem? *Can* all kinds of losses be mastered with one "art of losing"?

35/10

Brushing out our daughter's brown
silken hair before the mirror
I see the grey gleaming on my head,
the silver-haired servant behind her. Why is it
just as we begin to go   5
they begin to arrive, the fold in my neck
clarifying as the fine bones of her
hips sharpen? As my skin shows
its dry pitting, she opens like a moist
precise flower on the tip of a cactus;   10
as my last chances to bear a child
are falling through my body, the duds among them,
her full purse of eggs, round and
firm as hard-boiled yolks, is about
to snap its clasp. I brush her tangled   15
fragrant hair at bedtime. It's an old
story—the oldest we have on our planet—
the story of replacement.

Sharon Olds (b. 1942)

QUESTIONS

1. What does the title mean?
2. Much of the poem consists of contrasts between physical characteristics of the mother and daughter. What connotations give emotional weight to these contrasts?
3. Is the last sentence (lines 16–18) regretful or resigned, or can it be seen to be positive?

SUGGESTIONS FOR WRITING

Consider the denotative meaning(s) of the following titles. Then read each poem carefully and note the multiple connotations that attach to the title phrase as the poem progresses. Choose two or three titles, then write a short essay comparing the denotative and connotative meanings of each.

1. Williams, "The Red Wheelbarrow" (page 647).
2. Frost, "Fire and Ice" (page 739).
3. Piercy, "Barbie Doll" (page 754).
4. Pastan, "To a Daughter Leaving Home" (page 856).
5. Baca, "Main Character" (page 943).
6. Donne, "The Good-Morrow" (page 957).
7. Roethke, "My Papa's Waltz" (page 1000).
8. Soto, "Small Town with One Road" (page 1003).
9. Wordsworth, "The Solitary Reaper" (page 1016).

Chapter Four

Imagery

Experience comes to us largely through the senses. Our experiences of a spring day, for instance, may consist partly of certain emotions we feel and partly of certain thoughts we think, but most of it will be a cluster of sense impressions. It will consist of *seeing* blue sky and white clouds, budding leaves and daffodils; of *hearing* robins and bluebirds singing in the early morning; of *smelling* damp earth and blossoming hyacinths; and of *feeling* a fresh wind against one's cheek. A poet seeking to express the experience of a spring day therefore provides a selection of sense impressions. Similarly, to present a winter day (page 636), Shakespeare gives us hanging "icicles," milk "frozen," blood "nipped," and Marian's "red and raw" nose as well as the melancholy "'Tu-whit, tu-who'" of the owl. Had he not done so, he might have failed to evoke the emotions that accompany these sensations. The poet's language, then, is more *sensuous* than ordinary language. It is richer in imagery.

Imagery may be defined as the representation through language of sense experience. Poetry appeals directly to our senses, of course, through its music and rhythms, which we actually hear when it is read aloud. But indirectly it appeals to our senses through imagery, the representation to the imagination of sense experience. The word *image* perhaps most often suggests a mental picture, something seen in the mind's eye—and *visual* imagery is the kind of imagery that occurs most frequently in poetry. But an image may also represent a sound (*auditory imagery*); a smell (*olfactory imagery*); a taste (*gustatory imagery*); touch, such as hardness, softness, wetness, or heat and cold (*tactile imagery*); an internal sensation, such as hunger, thirst, fatigue, or nausea (*organic imagery*); or movement or tension in the muscles or joints (*kinesthetic imagery*). If we wished to be scientific, we could extend this list further, for psychologists no longer confine themselves to five or even six senses, but for purposes of discussing poetry the preceding classification should ordinarily be sufficient.

Meeting at Night

The gray sea and the long black land;
And the yellow half-moon large and low;
And the startled little waves that leap
In fiery ringlets from their sleep,
As I gain the cove with pushing prow,   5
And quench its speed i' the slushy sand.

Then a mile of warm sea-scented beach;
Three fields to cross till a farm appears;
A tap at the pane, the quick sharp scratch
And blue spurt of a lighted match,   10
And a voice less loud, through its joys and fears,
Than the two hearts beating each to each!

Robert Browning (1812–1889)

"Meeting at Night" is a poem about love. It makes, one might say, a number of statements about love: being in love is a sweet and exciting experience; when one is in love everything seems beautiful, and the most trivial things become significant; when one is in love one's beloved seems the most important thing in the world. But the poet actually *tells* us none of these things directly. He does not even use the word *love* in his poem. His business is to communicate experience, not information. He does this largely in two ways. First, he presents us with a specific situation, in which a lover goes to meet his love. Second, he describes the lover's journey so vividly in terms of sense impressions that the reader virtually sees and hears what the lover saw and heard and seems to share his anticipation and excitement.

Every line in the poem contains some image, some appeal to the senses: the gray sea, the long black land, the yellow half-moon, the startled little waves with their fiery ringlets, the blue spurt of the lighted match—all appeal to our sense of sight and convey not only shape but also color and motion. The warm sea-scented beach appeals to the senses of both smell and touch. The pushing prow of the boat on the slushy sand, the tap at the pane, the quick scratch of the match, the low speech of the lovers, and the sound of their hearts beating—all appeal to the sense of hearing.

Parting at Morning

Round the cape of a sudden came the sea,
And the sun looked over the mountain's rim:
And straight was a path of gold for him,
And the need of a world of men for me.

Robert Browning (1812–1889)

QUESTIONS

1. This poem is a sequel to "Meeting at Night." "[H]im" (3) refers to the sun. Does the last line mean that the lover needs the world of men or that the world of men needs the lover? Or both?

2. Does the sea *actually* come suddenly around the cape or *appear* to? Why does Browning mention the *effect* before its *cause* (the sun looking over the mountain's rim)?

3. Do these two poems, taken together, suggest any larger truths about love? Browning, in answer to a question, said that the second poem is the man's confession of "how fleeting is the belief (implied in the first part) that such raptures are self-sufficient and enduring—as for the time they appear."

The sharpness and vividness of any image will ordinarily depend on how specific it is and on the poet's use of effective detail. The word *hummingbird*, for instance, conveys a more definite image than does *bird*, and *ruby-throated hummingbird* is sharper and more specific still. However, to represent something vividly a poet need not describe it completely. One or two especially sharp and representative details will often serve, inviting the reader's imagination to fill in the rest. Tennyson in "The Eagle" (page 635) gives only one visual detail about the eagle itself—that he clasps the crag with "crooked hands"—but this detail is an effective and memorable one. Brooks in "Kitchenette Building" (page 646) offers no visual description of the tenement, but the smells of "onion fumes," "fried potatoes," and "garbage ripening in the hall" speak volumes about the conditions of life there. Browning, in "Meeting at Night," calls up a whole scene with "A tap at the pane, the quick sharp scratch / And blue spurt of a lighted match."

Since imagery is a peculiarly effective way of evoking vivid experience, and since it may be used to convey emotion and suggest ideas as well as to cause a mental reproduction of sensations, it is an invaluable resource for the poet. In general, the poet will seek concrete or image-bearing words in preference to abstract or nonimage-bearing words. We cannot evaluate a poem, however, by the amount or quality of its imagery alone.

Sense impression is only one of the elements of experience. Poetry may attain its ends by other means. We should never judge any single element of a poem except in reference to the total intent of that poem.

EXERCISES

In the following images, what sense is being evoked, and what does the image contribute to its context?

1. "Dulce et Decorum Est" (page 637): "deaf even to the hoots / Of gas-shells" (7–8); "He plunges at me, guttering, choking, drowning" (16); "gargling from the froth-corrupted lungs" (22).
2. "Shall I compare thee to a summer's day?" (page 642): "Rough winds do shake the darling buds of May" (3); "Sometimes too hot the eye of heaven shines" (5); "often is his gold complexion dimmed" (6).
3. "Ballad of Birmingham" (page 645): "her night-dark hair" (17); "rose petal sweet" (18); "clawed through bits of glass and brick" (29).
4. "Kitchenette Building" (page 646): "Grayed in, and gray" (2); "yesterday's garbage ripening" (6); "sing an aria down these rooms" (7); "lukewarm water" (13).

REVIEWING CHAPTER FOUR

1. State the definition of poetic imagery.
2. Relate imagery to its uses in conveying emotion, suggesting ideas, and mentally evoking sense experience.
3. Select individual images that demonstrate these three uses of imagery, and explain how they work.
4. Show that specificity in an image contributes to its sharpness and vividness.
5. Draw the distinction between abstract statements and concrete, image-bearing statements, providing examples.
6. Demonstrate that ambiguity and multiplicity of meanings contribute to the richness of poetic language.

Spring

Nothing is so beautiful as spring—
    When weeds, in wheels, shoot long and lovely and lush;
    Thrush's eggs look little low heavens, and thrush
Through the echoing timber does so rinse and wring
The ear, it strikes like lightnings to hear him sing;   5

The glassy peartree leaves and blooms, they brush
The descending blue; that blue is all in a rush
With richness; the racing lambs too have fair their fling.

What is all this juice and all this joy?
    A strain of the earth's sweet being in the beginning   10
In Eden garden. —Have, get, before it cloy,

    Before it cloud, Christ, lord, and sour with sinning
Innocent mind and Mayday in girl and boy,
    Most, O maid's child, thy choice and worthy the winning.

                  Gerard Manley Hopkins (1844–1889)

QUESTIONS

1. The first line makes an abstract statement. How is this statement brought to carry conviction?
2. The sky is described as being "all in a rush / With richness" (7–8). In what other respects is the poem "rich"?
3. To what two things does the speaker compare the spring in lines 9–14? In what ways are the comparisons appropriate?
4. Lines 11–14 might be made clearer by paraphrasing them thus: "Christ, lord, child of the Virgin: save the innocent mind of girl and boy before sin taints it, since it is most like yours and worth saving." Why are Hopkins's lines more effective, both in imagery and in syntax?

The Widow's Lament in Springtime

Sorrow is my own yard
where the new grass
flames as it has flamed
often before but not
with the cold fire   5
that closes round me this year.
Thirtyfive years
I lived with my husband.
The plumtree is white today
with masses of flowers.   10
Masses of flowers
load the cherry branches
and color some bushes

yellow and some red
but the grief in my heart   15
is stronger than they
for though they were my joy
formerly, today I notice them
and turned away forgetting.
Today my son told me   20
that in the meadows,
at the edge of the heavy woods
in the distance, he saw
trees of white flowers.
I feel that I would like   25
to go there
and fall into those flowers
and sink into the marsh near them.

                                      William Carlos Williams (1883–1963)

QUESTIONS

1. Why is springtime so poignant a time for this lament? What has been the speaker's previous experience at this time of year?
2. Why does the speaker's son tell her of the flowering trees "in the distance" (23)? What does he want her to do? Contrast the two locations in the poem—"yard" (1) versus "meadows" (21), "woods" (22), and "marsh" (28). What does the widow desire?
3. Imagery may have degrees of vividness, depending on its particularity, concreteness, and specific detail. What is the result of the contrast between the vividness of lines 2–3 and the relative flatness of lines 13–14? How does the fact that "masses" (10, 11) appeals to two senses relate to the speaker's emotional condition?

The Man with Night Sweats

I wake up cold, I who
Prospered through dreams of heat
Wake to their residue,
Sweat, and a clinging sheet.

My flesh was its own shield: 5
Where it was gashed, it healed.

I grew as I explored
The body I could trust
Even while I adored
The risk that made robust,   10

A world of wonders in
Each challenge to the skin.

I cannot but be sorry
The given shield was cracked,
My mind reduced to hurry,   15
My flesh reduced and wrecked.

I have to change the bed,
But catch myself instead

Stopped upright where I am
Hugging my body to me   20
As if to shield it from
The pains that will go through me,

As if hands were enough
To hold an avalanche off.

Thom Gunn (1929–2004)

QUESTIONS

1. "Night sweats" (title) are one of the symptoms of AIDS, an infection that
   gradually destroys the body's immune system. How does the poem represent
   that destruction?
2. Why is the imagery of the noun and verb "shield" (5, 14, 21) effective?
   What contrasts are involved between "dreams of heat" (2) and "avalanche"
   (24)?

I felt a Funeral, in my Brain

I felt a Funeral, in my Brain,
And Mourners to and fro
Kept treading—treading—till it seemed
That Sense was breaking through—

And when they all were seated,   5
A Service, like a Drum—
Kept beating—beating—till I thought
My Mind was going numb—

And then I heard them lift a Box
And creak across my Soul   10
With those same Boots of Lead, again,
Then Space—began to toll,

As all the Heavens were a Bell,
And Being, but an Ear,
And I, and Silence, some strange Race   15
Wrecked, solitary, here—

And then a Plank in Reason, broke,
And I dropped down, and down—
And hit a World, at every plunge,
And Finished knowing—then—   20

Emily Dickinson (1830–1886)

QUESTIONS

1. What senses are being evoked by the imagery? Can you account for the fact that one important sense is absent from the poem?
2. In sequence, what aspects of a funeral and burial are represented in the poem? Is it possible to define the sequence of mental events that are being compared to them?
3. With respect to the funeral activities in stanzas 1–3, where is the speaker imaginatively located?
4. What finally happens to the speaker?

Living in Sin

She had thought the studio would keep itself,
no dust upon the furniture of love.
Half heresy, to wish the taps less vocal,
the panes relieved of grime. A plate of pears,
a piano with a Persian shawl, a cat   5
stalking the picturesque amusing mouse
had risen at his urging.
Not that at five each separate stair would writhe

under the milkman's tramp; that morning light
so coldly would delineate the scraps   10
of last night's cheese and three sepulchral bottles;
that on the kitchen shelf among the saucers
a pair of beetle-eyes would fix her own—
envoy from some village in the moldings . . .
Meanwhile, he, with a yawn,   15
sounded a dozen notes upon the keyboard,
declared it out of tune, shrugged at the mirror,
rubbed at his beard, went out for cigarettes;
while she, jeered by the minor demons,
pulled back the sheets and made the bed and found   20
a towel to dust the table-top,
and let the coffee-pot boil over on the stove.
By evening she was back in love again,
though not so wholly but throughout the night
she woke sometimes to feel the daylight coming   25
like a relentless milkman up the stairs.

Adrienne Rich (b. 1929)

The Forge

All I know is a door into the dark.
Outside, old axles and iron hoops rusting;
Inside, the hammered anvil's short-pitched ring,
The unpredictable fantail of sparks
Or hiss when a new shoe toughens in water.   5
The anvil must be somewhere in the center,
Horned as a unicorn, at one end square,
Set there immovable: an altar
Where he expends himself in shape and music.
Sometimes, leather-aproned, hairs in his nose,   10
He leans out on the jamb, recalls a clatter
Of hoofs where traffic is flashing in rows;
Then grunts and goes in, with a slam and flick
To beat real iron out, to work the bellows.

Seamus Heaney (b. 1939)

QUESTIONS

1. What does the speaker mean when he says that "all" he knows is "a door into the dark" (1)? What more does he know, and how does he make his knowledge evident?
2. How do the images describing the blacksmith (10–11) relate to his attitude toward his work and toward the changing times?
3. The speaker summarizes the smith's world as "shape and music" (9), terms that suggest visual and auditory imagery. What do the contrasts between visual images contribute? The contrasts between auditory images?

After Apple-Picking

My long two-pointed ladder's sticking through a tree
Toward heaven still,
And there's a barrel that I didn't fill
Beside it, and there may be two or three
Apples I didn't pick upon some bough.   5
But I am done with apple-picking now.
Essence of winter sleep is on the night,
The scent of apples: I am drowsing off.
I cannot rub the strangeness from my sight
I got from looking through a pane of glass   10
I skimmed this morning from the drinking trough
And held against the world of hoary grass.
It melted, and I let it fall and break.
But I was well
Upon my way to sleep before it fell,   15
And I could tell
What form my dreaming was about to take.
Magnified apples appear and disappear,
Stem end and blossom end,
And every fleck of russet showing clear.   20
My instep arch not only keeps the ache,
It keeps the pressure of a ladder-round.
I feel the ladder sway as the boughs bend.
And I keep hearing from the cellar bin
The rumbling sound   25
Of load on load of apples coming in.
For I have had too much
Of apple-picking: I am overtired

Of the great harvest I myself desired.
There were ten thousand thousand fruit to touch,   30
Cherish in hand, lift down, and not let fall.
For all
That struck the earth,
No matter if not bruised or spiked with stubble,
Went surely to the cider-apple heap   35
As of no worth.
One can see what will trouble
This sleep of mine, whatever sleep it is.
Were he not gone,
The woodchuck could say whether it's like his   40
Long sleep, as I describe its coming on,
Or just some human sleep.

                              Robert Frost (1874–1963)

QUESTIONS

1. How does the poet convey so vividly the experience of "apple-picking"? Point out effective examples of each kind of imagery used. What emotional responses do the images evoke?
2. How does the speaker regard his work? Has he done it well or poorly? Does he find it enjoyable or tedious? Is he dissatisfied with its results?
3. The speaker predicts what he will dream about in his sleep. Why does he shift to the present tense (18) when he begins describing a dream he has not yet had? How sharply are real experience and dream experience differentiated in the poem?
4. The poem uses the word *sleep* six times. Does it, through repetition, come to suggest a meaning beyond the purely literal? If so, what attitude does the speaker take toward this second signification? Does he fear it? Does he look forward to it? What does he expect of it?
5. If sleep is symbolic (both literal and metaphorical), other details also may take on additional meaning. If so, how would you interpret (a) the ladder, (b) the season of the year, (c) the harvesting, (d) the "pane of glass" (10)? What denotations has the word "Essence" (7)?
6. How does the woodchuck's sleep differ from "just some human sleep" (42)?

Those Winter Sundays

Sundays too my father got up early
and put his clothes on in the blueblack cold,
then with cracked hands that ached

from labor in the weekday weather made
banked fires blaze. No one ever thanked him.   5

I'd wake and hear the cold splintering, breaking.
When the rooms were warm, he'd call,
and slowly I would rise and dress,
fearing the chronic angers of that house,

Speaking indifferently to him,   10
who had driven out the cold
and polished my good shoes as well.
What did I know, what did I know
of love's austere and lonely offices?

                                        Robert Hayden (1913–1980)

QUESTIONS

1. Vocabulary: *offices* (14).
2. What kind of imagery is central to the poem? How is this imagery related to the emotional concerns of the poem?
3. How do the subsidiary images relate to the central images?
4. From what point in time does the speaker view the subject matter of the poem? What has happened to him in the interval?

An August Night

His hands were warm and small and knowledgeable.
When I saw them again last night, they were two ferrets,
Playing all by themselves in a moonlit field.

                                        Seamus Heaney (b. 1939)

QUESTIONS

1. What are "ferrets" (2)? What is the speaker suggesting by comparing hands to ferrets?
2. Describe the general mood of the poem. How does the imagery help create the mood?

The Snow Man

One must have a mind of winter
To regard the frost and the boughs
Of the pine-trees crusted with snow;

And have been cold a long time
To behold the junipers shagged with ice,   5
The spruces rough in the distant glitter

Of the January sun; and not to think
Of any misery in the sound of the wind,
In the sound of a few leaves,

Which is the sound of the land   10
Full of the same wind
That is blowing in the same bare place

For the listener, who listens in the snow,
And, nothing himself, beholds
Nothing that is not there and the nothing that is.   15

Wallace Stevens (1879–1955)

QUESTIONS

1. The poem presents two kinds of "mind"—one that is cold and unmoved, the other emotional and responsive. What advantages does each of them have? Does the poem promote one or the other?
2. What emotional meanings are presented in the visual imagery in lines 2–3 and 5–7?
3. What emotional meanings are presented in the auditory imagery in lines 8–11?
4. How is the snow man "nothing himself" (14)? What is the meaning of what he "beholds" (14–15)? Paraphrase the poem.

To Autumn

Season of mists and mellow fruitfulness,
    Close bosom-friend of the maturing sun;
Conspiring with him how to load and bless
    With fruit the vines that round the thatch-eaves run;
To bend with apples the mossed cottage-trees,   5

And fill all fruit with ripeness to the core;
    To swell the gourd, and plump the hazel shells
With a sweet kernel; to set budding more,
    And still more, later flowers for the bees,
    Until they think warm days will never cease,   10
        For summer has o'er-brimmed their clammy cells.

Who hath not seen thee oft amid thy store?
    Sometimes whoever seeks abroad may find
Thee sitting careless on a granary floor,
    Thy hair soft-lifted by the winnowing wind;   15
Or on a half-reaped furrow sound asleep,
    Drowsed with the fume of poppies, while thy hook
        Spares the next swath and all its twinèd flowers:
And sometimes like a gleaner thou dost keep
    Steady thy laden head across a brook;   20
    Or by a cider-press, with patient look,
        Thou watchest the last oozings hours by hours.

Where are the songs of spring? Ay, where are they?
    Think not of them, thou hast thy music too,—
While barred clouds bloom the soft-dying day,   25
    And touch the stubble-plains with rosy hue;
Then in a wailful choir the small gnats mourn
    Among the river sallows, borne aloft
        Or sinking as the light wind lives or dies;
And full-grown lambs loud bleat from hilly bourn;   30
    Hedge-crickets sing; and now with treble soft
    The red-breast whistles from a garden-croft;
        And gathering swallows twitter in the skies.

John Keats (1795–1821)

QUESTIONS

1. Vocabulary: *hook* (17), *barred* (25), *sallows* (28), *bourn* (30), *croft* (32).
2. How many kinds of imagery do you find in the poem? Give examples of each.
3. Are the images arranged haphazardly or are they carefully organized? In answering this question, consider (a) what aspect of autumn each stanza particularly concerns, (b) what kind of imagery dominates each stanza, and (c) what time of the season each stanza presents. Is there any progression in time of day?

4. What is autumn personified as in stanza 2? Is there any suggestion of personification in the other two stanzas?
5. Although the poem is primarily descriptive, what attitude toward transience and passing beauty is implicit in it?

SUGGESTIONS FOR WRITING

Analyze the imagery in one of the following poems, drawing some conclusions as to whether individual images function primarily to evoke vivid experience, convey emotion, or suggest ideas (see page 691). Be sure in each case to identify the sense reference of the imagery—visual, auditory, and so forth.

1. Berry, "On Reading Poems to a Senior Class at South High" (page 945).
2. Crane, "Voyages [1]" (page 952).
3. Dickinson, "A narrow Fellow in the Grass" (page 956).
4. Forché, "The Colonel" (page 962).
5. Frost, "Once by the Pacific" (page 966).
6. Hardy, "The Darkling Thrush" (page 972).
7. Hughes, "Thistles" (page 832).
8. Plath, "Spinster" (page 992).
9. Roethke, "My Papa's Waltz" (page 1000).
10. Yeats, "The Wild Swans at Coole" (page 1019).

Figurative Language 1

Simile, Metaphor, Personification, Apostrophe, Metonymy

> *Poetry provides the one permissible way*
> *of saying one thing and meaning another.*
>
> Robert Frost

Let us assume that your brother has just come in out of a rainstorm and you say to him, "Well, you're a pretty sight! Got slightly wet, didn't you?" And he replies, "Wet? I'm drowned! It's raining cats and dogs, and my raincoat's like a sieve!"

You and your brother probably understand each other well enough; yet if you examine this conversation literally, that is to say unimaginatively, you will find that you have been speaking nonsense. Actually you have been speaking figuratively. You have been saying less than what you mean, or more than what you mean, or the opposite of what you mean, or something other than what you mean. You did not mean that your brother was a pretty sight but that he was a wretched sight. You did not mean that he got slightly wet but that he got very wet. Your brother did not mean that he got drowned but that he got drenched. It was not raining cats and dogs; it was raining water. And your brother's raincoat is so unlike a sieve that not even a child would confuse them.

If you are familiar with Molière's play *Le Bourgeois Gentilhomme*, you will remember how delighted M. Jourdain is to discover that he has been speaking prose all his life. Many people might be equally surprised to learn that they have been speaking a kind of subpoetry all their lives. The difference between their figures of speech and the poet's is that theirs are probably worn and trite, the poet's fresh and original.

On first examination, it might seem absurd to say one thing and mean another. But we all do it—and with good reason. We do it because we can say what we want to say more vividly and forcefully by figures of speech than we can by saying it directly. And we can say more by figurative statement than we can by literal statement. Figures of speech offer another way of adding extra dimensions to language.

Broadly defined, a **figure of speech** is any way of saying something other than the ordinary way, and some rhetoricians have classified as many as 250 separate figures. For our purposes, however, a figure of speech is more narrowly definable as a way of saying one thing and meaning another, and we need to be concerned with no more than a dozen. **Figurative language**—language using figures of speech—is language that cannot be taken literally (or should not be taken literally only).

Simile and **metaphor** are both used as a means of comparing things that are essentially unlike. The only distinction between them is that in simile the comparison is *expressed* by the use of some word or phrase, such as *like, as, than, similar to, resembles,* or *seems*; in metaphor, the comparison is not expressed but is created when a figurative term is *substituted for* or *identified with* the literal term.

Harlem

What happens to a dream deferred?

Does it dry up
like a raisin in the sun?
Or fester like a sore—
And then run?   5
Does it stink like rotten meat?
Or crust and sugar over—
like a syrupy sweet?

Maybe it just sags
like a heavy load.   10

Or does it explode?

Langston Hughes (1902–1967)

QUESTIONS

1. Of the six images, five are similes. Which is a metaphor? Comment on its position and its effectiveness.
2. What specific denotation has the word "dream"? Since the poem does not reveal the contents of the dream, the poem is general in its implication. What happens to your understanding of it on learning that its author was a black American?

Metaphors may take one of four forms, depending on whether the literal and figurative terms are respectively *named* or *implied*. In the first form of metaphor, as in simile, *both* the literal and figurative terms are *named*. In Williams's "The Widow's Lament in Springtime" (page 693), for example, the literal term is "sorrow" and the figurative term is "yard." In the second form, shown in Hughes's "Harlem," the literal term "dream" is *named* and the figurative term, bomb, is *implied*.

Bereft

Where had I heard this wind before
Change like this to a deeper roar?
What would it take my standing there for,
Holding open a restive door,
Looking down hill to a frothy shore?   5
Summer was past and day was past.
Somber clouds in the west were massed.
Out in the porch's sagging floor,
Leaves got up in a coil and hissed,
Blindly struck at my knee and missed.   10
Something sinister in the tone
Told me my secret must be known:
Word I was in the house alone
Somehow must have gotten abroad,
Word I was in my life alone,   15
Word I had no one left but God.

Robert Frost (1874–1963)

QUESTIONS

1. Describe the situation precisely. What time of day and year is it? Where is the speaker? What is happening to the weather?
2. How does the comparison in lines 9–10 reflect the state of mind of the speaker?
3. The word "hissed" (9) is onomatopoetic (see **onomatopeia** in Glossary and Index of Literary Terms). How is its effect reinforced in the lines following?
4. Though lines 9–10 present the clearest example of the second form of metaphor, there are others. To what is the wind ("it") compared in line 3? Why is the door "restive" (4) and what does this do (figuratively) to the door? To what is the speaker's "life" (15) compared?
5. What is the tone of the poem? How reassuring is the last line?

In the third form of metaphor, the literal term is *implied* and the figurative term is *named*. In the fourth form, *both* the literal *and* figurative terms are *implied*. The following poem exemplifies both forms:

It sifts from Leaden Sieves

It sifts from Leaden Sieves—
It powders all the Wood.
It fills with Alabaster Wool
The Wrinkles of the Road—

It makes an Even Face   5
Of Mountain, and of Plain—
Unbroken Forehead from the East
Unto the East again—

It reaches to the Fence—
It wraps it Rail by Rail   10
Till it is lost in Fleeces—
It deals Celestial Veil

To Stump, and Stack—and Stem—
A Summer's empty Room—
Acres of Joints, where Harvests were,   15
Recordless,° but for them—   unrecorded

It Ruffles Wrists of Posts
As Ankles of a Queen—
Then stills its Artisans—like Ghosts—
Denying they have been—   20

Emily Dickinson (1830–1886)

QUESTIONS

1. This poem consists essentially of a series of metaphors with the same literal term identified only as "It." What is "It"?
2. In several of these metaphors the figurative term is named—"Alabaster Wool" (3), "Fleeces" (11), "Celestial Veil" (12). In two of them, however, the figurative term as well as the literal term is left unnamed. To what is "It" compared in lines 1–2? In lines 17–18?

3. Comment on the additional metaphorical expressions or complications contained in "Leaden Sieves" (1), "Alabaster Wool" (3), "Even Face" (5), "Unbroken Forehead" (7), "A Summer's empty Room" (14), "Artisans" (19).

Metaphors of the fourth form, as one might guess, are comparatively rare. An extended example, however, is provided by Dickinson's "I like to see it lap the Miles" (page 911).

Using some examples from the poems discussed in this and the preceding chapters, the chart below provides a visual demonstration of the figures of comparison (simile and the four forms of metaphor).

		Poet	Literal Term	Figurative Term
Similes (*like, as, seems*, etc.)		Hughes	named dream	named raisin
Metaphors (*is, are*, etc.)	Form 1	Williams	named sorrow	named yard
	Form 2	Frost	named leaves	implied [snake] hissed
	Form 3	Dickinson	implied it [snow]	named wool
	Form 4	Dickinson	implied it [snow]	implied [flour] sifts

Personification consists in giving the attributes of a human being to an animal, an object, or a concept. It is really a subtype of metaphor, an implied comparison in which the figurative term of the comparison is always a human being. When Sylvia Plath makes a mirror speak and think (page 669), she is personifying an object. When Keats describes autumn as a harvester "sitting careless on a granary floor" or "on a half-reaped furrow sound asleep" (page 702), he is personifying a season. Personifications differ in the degree to which they ask the reader actually to visualize the literal term in human form. In Keats's comparison, we are asked to make a complete identification of autumn with a human being. In Sylvia Plath's, though the mirror speaks and thinks, we continue to visualize it as a mirror; similarly, in Frost's "Bereft" (page 706), the "restive" door remains in appearance a door tugged by the wind. In Browning's reference to "the startled little waves" (page 690), a personification is barely suggested; we would make a mistake if we tried to visualize the waves in human form or even, really, to think of them as having human emotions.

The Author to Her Book

Thou ill-formed offspring of my feeble brain,
Who after birth did'st by my side remain,
Till snatched from thence by friends, less wise than true,
Who thee abroad exposed to public view;
Made thee in rags, halting, to the press to trudge,   5
Where errors were not lessened, all may judge.
At thy return my blushing was not small,
My rambling brat (in print) should mother call;
I cast thee by as one unfit for light,
Thy visage was so irksome in my sight;   10
Yet being mine own, at length affection would
Thy blemishes amend, if so I could:
I washed thy face, but more defects I saw,
And rubbing off a spot, still made a flaw.
I stretched thy joints to make thee even feet,   15
Yet still thou run'st more hobbling than is meet;
In better dress to trim thee was my mind,
But nought save homespun cloth in the house I find.
In this array, 'mongst vulgars may'st thou roam;
In critics' hands beware thou dost not come;   20
And take thy way where yet thou are not known.
If for thy Father asked, say thou had'st none;
And for thy Mother, she alas is poor,
Which caused her thus to send thee out of door.

Anne Bradstreet (1612?–1672)

QUESTIONS

1. Vocabulary: *halting* (5), *feet* (15), *meet* (16), *vulgars* (19). Lines 3–4 refer to the fact that Bradstreet's book *The Tenth Muse* was published in 1650 without her permission.
2. The poem is an extended personification addressing her book as a child. What similarities does the speaker find between a child and a book of poems? What does she plan to do now that her child has been put on public display?
3. Trace the developing attitudes of the speaker toward the child/book. Why does she instruct the child to deny it has a father (22)?

The various figures of speech blend into each other, and it is sometimes difficult to classify a specific example as definitely metaphor or simile, symbol or allegory, understatement or irony, irony or paradox (some of these topics will be examined in the next two chapters). Often a given example may exemplify two or more figures at once. In Words-worth's "The world is too much with us" (page 682), when the winds are described as calm, "like sleeping flowers," the flowers function as part of a simile and are also personified as something that can sleep. The following poem shows how a simile may develop into a personification. The important consideration in reading poetry is not that we classify figures but that we construe them correctly.

The Telephone

It comes in black
and blue, indecisive
beige. In red and chaperons my life.
Sitting like a strict
and spinstered aunt   5
spiked between my needs
and need.

It tats the day, crocheting
other people's lives
in neat arrangements,   10
ignoring me,
busy with the hemming
of strangers' overlong affairs or
the darning of my
neighbors' worn-out   15
dreams.

From Monday, the morning of the week,
through mid-times
noon and Sunday's dying
light. It sits silent.   20
Its needle sound
does not transfix my ear
or draw my longing to
a close.

Ring. Damn you!   25

Maya Angelou (b. 1928)

QUESTIONS

1. Most home telephones were black before the innovation of a variety of "designer" colors. What are the connotations of the colors in lines 1–3?
2. Line 4 introduces a simile. Explain how a telephone might resemble a "spinstered aunt" (5). What would such an aunt have to do with the speaker's "needs / and need" (6–7)?
3. Beginning in line 8, the simile is developed into a personification. To what is the telephone compared? How are its activities a development of the "aunt" simile? Be sure you understand the denotations of "tats" and "crocheting" (8), "hemming" (12), "darning" (14), and "needle sound" (21).
4. How does the last line provide a conclusion to the poem?

Closely related to personification is **apostrophe**, which consists in addressing someone absent or dead or something nonhuman as if that person or thing were present and alive and could reply to what is being said. The speaker in A. E. Housman's "To an Athlete Dying Young" (page 974) apostrophizes a dead runner. William Blake apostrophizes a tiger throughout his famous poem (page 794) but does not otherwise personify it. In the poem printed below, Keats apostrophizes *and* personifies a star, as he does with autumn in "To Autumn" (page 701).

Personification and apostrophe are both ways of giving life and immediacy to one's language, but since neither requires great imaginative power on the part of the poet—apostrophe especially does not—they may degenerate into mere mannerisms and occur as often in bad and mediocre poetry as in good, a fact that Shakespeare parodies in Bottom's apostrophe to night in *A Midsummer Night's Dream* (Act 5, scene 1):

> O grim-looked night! O night with hue so black!
> O night, which ever art when day is not!
> O night, O night! Alack, alack, alack.

We need to distinguish between their effective use and their merely conventional use.

Bright Star

> Bright star, would I were steadfast as thou art—
> Not in lone splendor hung aloft the night,
> And watching, with eternal lids apart,
> Like nature's patient, sleepless Eremite,°   hermit

The moving waters at their priestlike task   5
   Of pure ablution° round earth's human shores,   cleansing
Or gazing on the new soft fallen mask
   Of snow upon the mountains and the moors—
No—yet still steadfast, still unchangeable,
   Pillowed upon my fair love's ripening breast,   10
To feel forever its soft fall and swell,
   Awake forever in a sweet unrest,
Still, still to hear her tender-taken breath,
And so live ever—or else swoon to death.

John Keats (1795–1821)

QUESTIONS

1. The speaker longs to be as "steadfast" (1) as the star, yet lines 2–8 express his wish to be unlike the star in important ways. What are the qualities of the star that he would not want to emulate? Why would these be wrong for him in his situation?
2. Explore the apparent contradictions in the phrase "sweet unrest" (12). How do they anticipate the final line?
3. The speaker repeats "still" (13). What relevant denotations does the word evoke, and how does the repetition add intensity and meaning to this apostrophe?
4. Why is an apostrophe more effective here than a description of the star that does not address it?

    In contrast to the preceding figures that compare *unlike* things are two figures that rest on congruences or correspondences. **Synecdoche** (the use of the part for the whole) and **metonymy** (the use of something closely related for the thing actually meant) are alike in that both substitute some significant detail or quality of an experience for the experience itself. Thus Randall uses metonymy when he says "those guns will fire" (page 645), for he means "the police will fire their guns." Kay uses synecdoche when she refers to "catalogues of domes" (page 678), because what she means is "enough domed buildings to fill a catalogue," and Housman's Terence (page 649) uses synecdoche when he declares that "malt does more than Milton can / To justify God's ways to man" (page 650), for "malt" means beer or ale, of which malt is an essential ingredient. On the other hand, when Terence advises "fellows whom it hurts to think" to "Look into the pewter pot / To see the world as the world's not," he is using metonymy, for by "pewter pot" he means the ale *in* the pot, not the pot itself, and by "world" he means human life and the conditions under which it is lived. Robert Frost uses metonymy in "'Out, Out—'" (page 773) when he describes an injured boy holding up his cut hand "as if to keep / The life from spilling," for literally he means to keep the blood from spilling. In each case, however, the poem gains in compactness, vividness, or meaning. Kay, by substituting one architectural detail for whole buildings, suggests the superficiality and boredom of a person who looks at many but appreciates none. Frost tells us both that the boy's hand is bleeding and that his life is in danger.

Many synecdoches and metonymies, of course, like many metaphors, have become so much a part of the language that they no longer strike us as figurative; this is the case with *redhead* for a red-haired person, *hands* for manual workers, *highbrow* for a sophisticate, *tongues* for languages, and a boiling *kettle* for the water in the kettle. Such figures are often called *dead metaphors* (where the word *metaphor* is itself a metonymy for all figurative speech). Synecdoche and metonymy are so much alike that it is hardly worthwhile to distinguish between them, and the latter term is increasingly used for both. In this book *metonymy* will be used for both figures—that is, for any figure in which a part or something closely related is substituted for the thing literally meant.

We said at the beginning of this chapter that figurative language often provides a more effective means of saying what we mean than does direct statement. What are some of the reasons for that effectiveness?

First, figurative language affords us imaginative pleasure. Imagination might be described in one sense as that faculty or ability of the mind that proceeds by sudden leaps from one point to another, that goes up a stair by leaping in one jump from the bottom to the top rather than by climbing up one step at a time.* The mind takes delight in these sudden leaps, in seeing likenesses between unlike things. We have all probably taken pleasure in staring into a fire and seeing castles and cities and armies in it, or in looking into the clouds and shaping them into animals or faces, or in seeing a man in the moon. We name our plants and flowers after fancied resemblances: jack-in-the-pulpit, baby's breath, Queen Anne's lace. Figures of speech are therefore satisfying in themselves, providing us with a source of pleasure in the exercise of the imagination.

Second, figures of speech are a way of bringing additional imagery into verse, of making the abstract concrete, of making poetry more sensuous. When Tennyson's eagle falls "like a thunderbolt" (page 635),

---

*It is also the faculty of mind that is able to "picture" or "image" absent objects as if they were present. It was with imagination in this sense that we were concerned in the chapter on imagery.

his swooping down for his prey is charged with energy, speed, and power; the simile also recalls that the Greek god Zeus was accompanied by an eagle and armed with lightning. When Emily Dickinson compares poetry to prancing coursers (page 675), she objectifies imaginative and rhythmical qualities by presenting them in visual terms. When Robert Browning compares the crisping waves to "fiery ringlets" (page 690), he starts with one image and transforms it into three. Figurative language is a way of augmenting the sense appeal of poetry.

Third, figures of speech are a way of adding emotional intensity to otherwise merely informative statements and of conveying attitudes along with information. If we say, "So-and-so is a rat" or "My feet are killing me," our meaning is as much emotional as informative. When Philip Larkin's pathetic escapist metaphorically compares books to "a load of crap" (page 658), the vulgar language not only expresses his distaste for reading, but intensifies the characterization of him as a man whose intellectual growth was stunted. As this example shows, the use of figures may be a poet's means of revealing the characteristics of a speaker—*how* he or she expresses a thought will define the attitudes or qualities as much as *what* that thought is. When Frost's speaker in "Bereft" (page 706) sees a striking snake in an eddy of leaves he shows that he is fearful. When Wilfred Owen compares a soldier caught in a gas attack to a man drowning under a green sea (page 638), he conveys a feeling of despair and suffocation as well as a visual image.

Fourth, figures of speech are an effective means of concentration, a way of saying much in brief compass. Like words, they may be multidimensional. Consider, for instance, the merits of comparing life to a candle, as Shakespeare does in a passage from *Macbeth* (page 774). Life is like a candle in that it begins and ends in darkness; in that while it burns, it gives off light and energy, is active and colorful; in that it gradually consumes itself, gets shorter and shorter; in that it can be snuffed out at any moment; in that it is brief at best, burning only for a short duration. Possibly your imagination can suggest other similarities. But at any rate, Macbeth's compact, metaphorical description of life as a "brief candle" suggests certain truths about life that would require dozens of words to state in literal language. At the same time it makes the abstract concrete, provides imaginative pleasure, and adds a degree of emotional intensity.

It is as important, when analyzing and discussing a poem, to decide what it is that the figures accomplish as it is to identify them. Seeing a personification or a simile should lead to analytical questions: *What use is being made of this figure? How does it contribute to the experience of the poem?*

If we are to read poetry well, we must be able to respond to figurative language. Every use of figurative language involves a risk of misinterpretation, though the risk is well worth taking. For the person who can interpret the figure, the dividends are immense. Fortunately all people have imagination to some degree, and imagination can be cultivated. Through practice, one's ability to interpret figures of speech can be enhanced.

EXERCISE

Decide whether the following quotations are literal or figurative. If figurative, identify the figure, explain what is being compared to what, and explain the appropriateness of the comparison. EXAMPLE: "Talent is a cistern; genius is a fountain." ANSWER: Metaphor. Talent = cistern; genius = fountain. Talent exists in finite supply, and can be used up. Genius is inexhaustible, ever renewing.

1. O tenderly the haughty day
   Fills his blue urn with fire.   *Ralph Waldo Emerson*
2. It is with words as with sunbeams—the more
   they are condensed, the deeper they burn.   *Robert Southey*
3. Joy and Temperance and Repose
   Slam the door on the doctor's nose.   *Anonymous*
4. The pen is mightier than the sword.   *Edward Bulwer-Lytton*
5. The strongest oaths are straw
   To the fire i' the blood.   *William Shakespeare*
6. The Cambridge ladies . . . live in furnished souls.   *e. e. cummings*
7. Dorothy's eyes, with their long brown lashes,
   looked very much like her mother's.   *Laetitia Johnson*
8. The tawny-hided desert crouches watching her.   *Francis Thompson*
9. Let us eat and drink, for tomorrow we shall die.   *Isaiah 22.13*
10. Let us eat and drink, for tomorrow we may die.
                                    Common misquotation of the above

REVIEWING CHAPTER FIVE

1. Distinguish between language used literally and language used figuratively, and consider why poetry is often figurative.
2. Define the figures of comparison (simile and metaphor, personification and apostrophe), and rank them in order of their emotional effectiveness.
3. Define the figures of congruence or correspondence (synecdoche and metonymy).
4. Review the four major contributions of figurative language.

Mind

Mind in its purest play is like some bat
That beats about in caverns all alone,
Contriving by a kind of senseless wit
Not to conclude against a wall of stone.

It has no need to falter or explore;   5
Darkly it knows what obstacles are there,
And so may weave and flitter, dip and soar
In perfect courses through the blackest air.

And has this simile a like perfection?
The mind is like a bat. Precisely. Save   10
That in the very happiest intellection
A graceful error may correct the cave.

Richard Wilbur (b. 1921)

QUESTIONS

1. A poet may use a variety of metaphors and similes in developing a subject
   or may, as Wilbur does here, develop a single figure at length (this poem is
   an example of an **extended simile**). Identify in this chapter a poem
   containing a variety of figures and define the advantages of each type of
   development.
2. Explore the similarities between the two things compared in this poem. In
   line 12, what is meant by "A graceful error" and by "correct the cave"?

I taste a liquor never brewed

I taste a liquor never brewed—
From Tankards scooped in Pearl—
Not all the Vats upon the Rhine
Yield such an Alcohol!

Inebriate of Air—am I—   5
And Debauchee of Dew—
Reeling—thro endless summer days—
From inns of Molten Blue—

When "Landlords" turn the drunken Bee
Out of the Foxglove's door—   10
When Butterflies—renounce their "drams"—
I shall but drink the more!

Till Seraphs swing their snowy Hats—
And Saints—to windows run—
To see the little Tippler   15
Leaning against the—Sun—

Emily Dickinson (1830–1886)

QUESTIONS

1. Vocabulary: *debauchee* (6), *foxglove* (10).
2. In this **extended metaphor**, what is being compared to alcoholic intoxication? The clues are given in the variety of "liquors" named or implied—"Air" (5), "Dew" (6), and the nectar upon which birds and butterflies feed.
3. What figurative meanings have the following details: "Tankards scooped in Pearl" (2), "inns of Molten Blue" (8), "snowy Hats" (13)?
4. The last stanza creates a stereotypical street scene in which neighbors observe the behavior of a drunkard. What do comic drunks lean against in the street? What unexpected attitude do the seraphs and saints display?

Metaphors

I'm a riddle in nine syllables,
An elephant, a ponderous house,
A melon strolling on two tendrils.
O red fruit, ivory, fine timbers!
This loaf's big with its yeasty rising.   5
Money's new-minted in this fat purse.
I'm a means, a stage, a cow in calf.
I've eaten a bag of green apples,
Boarded the train there's no getting off.

Sylvia Plath (1932–1963)

QUESTIONS

1. Like its first metaphor, this poem is a riddle to be solved by identifying the literal terms of its metaphors. After you have identified the speaker ("riddle," "elephant," "house," "melon," "stage," "cow"), identify the literal meanings

of the related metaphors ("syllables," "tendrils," "fruit," "ivory," "timbers," "loaf," "yeasty rising," "money," "purse," "train"). How do you interpret line 8?

2. How does the form of the poem relate to its content? Is this poem a complaint?

Toads

Why should I let the toad *work*
    Squat on my life?
Can't I use my wit as a pitchfork
    And drive the brute off?

Six days of the week it soils   5
    With its sickening poison—
Just for paying a few bills!
    That's out of proportion.

Lots of folk live on their wits:
    Lecturers, lispers,   10
Losels,° loblolly-men,° louts—;   *scoundrels; bumpkins*
    They don't end as paupers;

Lots of folk live up lanes
    With fires in a bucket,
Eat windfalls and tinned sardines—   15
    They seem to like it.

Their nippers° have got bare feet,   *children*
    Their unspeakable wives
Are skinny as whippets—and yet
    No one actually *starves*.   20

Ah, were I courageous enough
    To shout *Stuff your pension!*
But I know, all too well, that's the stuff
    That dreams are made on;

For something sufficiently toad-like   25
    Squats in me, too;
Its hunkers° are heavy as hard luck,   *haunches*
    And cold as snow,

And will never allow me to blarney
My way to getting   30
The fame and the girl and the money
All at one sitting.

I don't say, one bodies the other
One's spiritual truth;
But I do say it's hard to lose either,   35
When you have both.

Philip Larkin (1922–1985)

QUESTIONS

1. The poem describes two "toads." Where is each located? How are they described? What are the antecedents of the pronouns "one" and "the other / One's" (33–34) respectively?
2. What characteristics in common have the people mentioned in lines 9–12? Those mentioned in lines 13–20?
3. Explain the pun in lines 22–23 and the literary allusion it leads into. (If you don't recognize the allusion, check Shakespeare's *The Tempest*, Act 4, scene 1, lines 156–58.)
4. The first "toad" is explicitly identified as *"work"*(1). The literal term for the second "toad" is not named. Why not? What do you take it to be?
5. What kind of person is the speaker? What are his attitudes toward work?

Ghost of a Chance

You see a man
trying to think.

You want to say
to everything:
Keep off! Give him room!   5
But you only watch,
terrified
the old consolations
will get him at last
like a fish   10
half-dead from flopping
and almost crawling
across the shingle,°   gravel beach
almost breathing
the raw, agonizing   15

air
till a wave
pulls it back blind into the triumphant
sea.

Adrienne Rich (b. 1929)

A Valediction: Forbidding Mourning

As virtuous men pass mildly away,
   And whisper to their souls to go,
While some of their sad friends do say,
   The breath goes now, and some say, no:

So let us melt, and make no noise,   5
   No tear-floods, nor sigh-tempests move;
'Twere profanation of our joys
   To tell the laity our love.

Moving of th' earth brings harms and fears,
   Men reckon what it did and meant,   10
But trepidation of the spheres,
   Though greater far, is innocent.

Dull sublunary lovers' love
   (Whose soul is sense) cannot admit
Absence, because it doth remove   15
   Those things which elemented it.

But we by a love so much refined,
   That ourselves know not what it is,
Inter-assurèd of the mind,
   Care less, eyes, lips, and hands to miss.   20

Our two souls therefore, which are one,
   Though I must go, endure not yet
A breach, but an expansion,
   Like gold to airy thinness beat.

If they be two, they are two so   25
   As stiff twin compasses are two;

Thy soul, the fixed foot, makes no show
  To move, but doth, if th' other do.

And though it in the center sit,
  Yet when the other far doth roam,   30
It leans, and hearkens after it,
  And grows erect, as that comes home.

Such wilt thou be to me, who must
  Like th' other foot, obliquely run;
Thy firmness makes my circle just,   35
  And makes me end, where I begun.

John Donne (1572–1631)

QUESTIONS

1. Vocabulary: *valediction* (title), *mourning* (title), *profanation* (7), *laity* (8), *trepidation* (11), *innocent* (12), *sublunary* (13), *elemented* (16). Line 11 is a reference to the spheres of the Ptolemaic cosmology, whose movements caused no such disturbance as does a movement of the earth—that is, an earthquake.
2. Is the speaker in the poem about to die? Or about to leave on a journey? (The answer may be found in a careful analysis of the simile in the last three stanzas and by noticing that the idea of dying in stanza 1 is introduced in a simile.)
3. The poem is organized around a contrast of two kinds of lovers: the "laity" (8) and, as their implied opposite, the priesthood. Are these terms literal or metaphorical? What is the essential difference between their two kinds of love? How, according to the speaker, does their behavior differ when they must separate from each other? What is the motivation of the speaker in this "valediction"?
4. Find and explain three similes and one metaphor used to describe the parting of true lovers. The figure in the last three stanzas is one of the most famous in English literature. Demonstrate its appropriateness by obtaining a drawing compass or by using two pencils to imitate the two legs.

To His Coy Mistress

Had we but world enough, and time,
This coyness, lady, were no crime.
We would sit down, and think which way
To walk, and pass our long love's day.
Thou by the Indian Ganges' side   5
Shouldst rubies find; I by the tide

Of Humber would complain. I would
Love you ten years before the Flood,
And you should, if you please, refuse
Till the conversion of the Jews.   10
My vegetable love should grow
Vaster than empires, and more slow;
An hundred years should go to praise
Thine eyes, and on thy forehead gaze;
Two hundred to adore each breast,   15
But thirty thousand to the rest;
An age at least to every part,
And the last age should show your heart.
For, lady, you deserve this state,
Nor would I love at lower rate.   20
     But at my back I always hear
Time's wingèd chariot hurrying near;
And yonder all before us lie
Deserts of vast eternity.
Thy beauty shall no more be found,   25
Nor, in thy marble vault, shall sound
My echoing song; then worms shall try
That long-preserved virginity,
And your quaint honor turn to dust,
And into ashes all my lust: 30
The grave's a fine and private place,
But none, I think, do there embrace.
     Now therefore, while the youthful hue
Sits on thy skin like morning dew,
And while thy willing soul transpires   35
At every pore with instant fires,
Now let us sport us while we may,
And now, like amorous birds of prey,
Rather at once our time devour
Than languish in his slow-chapped power.   40
Let us roll all our strength and all
Our sweetness up into one ball,
And tear our pleasures with rough strife
Thorough° the iron gates of life.   through
Thus, though we cannot make our sun   45
Stand still, yet we will make him run.

Andrew Marvell (1621–1678)

QUESTIONS

1. Vocabulary: *coy* (title), *Humber* (7), *transpires* (35). "Mistress" (title) has the now archaic meaning of *sweetheart;* "slow-chapped" (40) derives from *chap,* meaning *jaw.*
2. What is the speaker urging his sweetheart to do? Why is she being "coy"?
3. Outline the speaker's argument in three sentences that begin with the words *If, But,* and *Therefore.* Is the argument valid?
4. Explain the appropriateness of "vegetable love" (11). What simile in the third section contrasts with it and how? What image in the third section contrasts with the distance between the Ganges and the Humber? Of what would the speaker be "complaining" by the Humber (7)?
5. Explain the figures in lines 22, 24, and 40 and their implications.
6. Explain the last two lines. For what is "sun" a metonymy?
7. Is this poem principally about love or about time? If the latter, what might making love represent? What philosophy is the poet advancing here?

Introduction to Poetry

I ask them to take a poem
and hold it up to the light
like a color slide

or press an ear against its hive.

I say drop a mouse into a poem   5
and watch him probe his way out,

or walk inside the poem's room
and feel the walls for a light switch.

I want them to water-ski
across the surface of a poem   10
waving at the author's name on the shore.

But all they want to do
is tie the poem to a chair with rope
and torture a confession out of it.

They begin beating it with a hose   15
to find out what it really means.

Billy Collins (b. 1941)

QUESTIONS

1. What is the basic situation of the poem? Who are "I" (1) and "them" (1)?
2. Explain the simile in line 3. From that point onward through line 11, the speaker invents a series of metaphors. For each of them, define what a poem is being compared to and how the metaphor expresses some characteristic quality of poetry. For example, how is a poem like a "hive" (4) full of buzzing bees?
3. The last five lines present a single extended metaphor to express what "they want to do" when they encounter a poem. What are "they" and "the poem" compared to, and how do these comparisons reflect a different attitude toward poetry from the ones expressed in the first 11 lines? What, ultimately, does this poem express about poetry and its readers?

SUGGESTIONS FOR WRITING

1. Robert Frost has said that "poetry is what evaporates from all translations." Why might this be true? How much of a word can be translated?
2. Ezra Pound has defined great literature as "simply language charged with meaning to the utmost possible degree." Would this be a good definition of poetry? The word "charged" is roughly equivalent to *filled*. Why is "charged" a better word in Pound's definition?
3. In each of the following the title announces a metaphor that dominates the poem. Write an essay describing the pair of objects and/or concepts compared in one of these poems. How does the figurative language help to communicate an idea with greater vividness or force than an ordinary, prosaic description could have achieved?
   a. Stevens, "The Snow Man" (page 701).
   b. Larkin, "Toads" (page 718).
   c. Angelou, "Harlem Hopscotch" (page 740).
   d. Frost, "A Considerable Speck" (page 765).
   e. Atwood, "Landcrab" (page 874).
   f. Herbert, "The Pulley" (page 882).

Figurative Language 2

Symbol, Allegory

The Road Not Taken

Two roads diverged in a yellow wood,
And sorry I could not travel both
And be one traveler, long I stood
And looked down one as far as I could
To where it bent in the undergrowth;   5

Then took the other, as just as fair,
And having perhaps the better claim,
Because it was grassy and wanted wear;
Though as for that the passing there
Had worn them really about the same,   10

And both that morning equally lay
In leaves no step had trodden black.
Oh, I kept the first for another day!
Yet knowing how way leads on to way,
I doubted if I should ever come back.   15

I shall be telling this with a sigh
Somewhere ages and ages hence:
Two roads diverged in a wood, and I—
I took the one less traveled by,
And that has made all the difference.   20

Robert Frost (1874–1963)

QUESTIONS

1. Does the speaker feel that he has made the wrong choice in taking the road "less traveled by" (19)? If not, why will he "sigh" (16)? What does he regret?
2. Why will the choice between two roads that seem very much alike make such a big difference many years later?

A **symbol** may be roughly defined as something that means *more* than what it is. "The Road Not Taken," for instance, concerns a choice made between two roads by a person out walking in the woods. He would like to explore both roads. He tells himself that he will explore one and then come back and explore the other, but he knows that he will probably be unable to do so. By the last stanza, however, we realize that the poem is about something more than the choice of paths in a wood, for that choice would be relatively unimportant, whereas this choice, the speaker believes, is one that will make a great difference in his life and is one that he will remember "with a sigh . . . ages and ages hence." We must interpret his choice of a road as a symbol for any choice in life between alternatives that appear almost equally attractive but will result through the years in a large difference in the kind of experience one knows.

Image, metaphor, and symbol shade into each other and are sometimes difficult to distinguish. In general, however, an image means only what it is; the figurative term in a metaphor means something other than what it is; and a symbol means what it is and something more, too. A symbol, that is, functions literally and figuratively at the same time.* If I say that a shaggy brown dog was rubbing its back against a white picket fence, I am talking about nothing but a dog (and a picket fence) and am therefore presenting an image. If I say, "Some dirty dog stole my wallet at the party," I am not talking about a dog at all and am therefore using a metaphor. But if I say, "You can't teach an old dog new tricks," I am talking not only about dogs but about living creatures of any species and am therefore speaking symbolically. Images, of course, do not cease to be images when they become incorporated in metaphors or symbols. If we are discussing the sensuous qualities of "The Road Not Taken," we should refer to the two leaf-strewn roads in the yellow wood as an image; if we are discussing the significance of the poem, we talk about the roads as symbols.

---

*This account does not hold for nonliterary symbols such as the letters of the alphabet and algebraic signs (the symbol ∞ for infinity or = for equals). With these, the symbol is meaningless except as it stands for something else, and the connection between the sign and what it stands for is purely arbitrary.

The symbol is the richest and at the same time the most difficult of the poetic figures. Both its richness and its difficulty result from its imprecision. Although the poet may pin down the meaning of a symbol to something fairly definite and precise, more often the symbol is so general in its meaning that it can suggest a great variety of specific meanings. It is like an opal that flashes out different colors when slowly turned in the light. "The Road Not Taken," for instance, concerns some choice in life, but what choice? Was it a choice of profession? A choice of residence? A choice of mate? It might be any, all, or none of these. We cannot determine what particular choice the poet had in mind, if any, and it is not important that we do so. It is enough if we see in the poem an expression of regret that the possibilities of life experience are so sharply limited. The speaker in the poem would have liked to explore both roads, but he could explore only one. The person with a craving for life, whether satisfied or dissatisfied with the choices he has made, will always long for the realms of experience that he had to forgo. Because the symbol is a rich one, the poem suggests other meanings too. It affirms a belief in the possibility of choice and says something about the nature of choice—how each choice narrows the range of possible future choices, so that we make our lives as we go, both freely choosing and being determined by past choices. Though not a philosophical poem, it obliquely comments on the issue of free will and determinism and indicates the poet's own position. It can do all these things, concretely and compactly, by its use of an effective symbol.

Symbols vary in the degree of identification and definition given them by their authors. In this poem Frost forces us to interpret the choice of roads symbolically by the degree of importance he gives it in the last stanza. Sometimes poets are much more specific in identifying their symbols. Sometimes they do not identify them at all. Consider, for instance, the next two poems.

A Noiseless Patient Spider

A noiseless patient spider,
I marked where on a little promontory it stood isolated,
Marked how to explore the vacant vast surrounding,
It launched forth filament, filament, filament, out of itself,
Ever unreeling them, ever tirelessly speeding them.   5

And you, O my soul where you stand,
Surrounded, detached, in measureless oceans of space,

Ceaselessly musing, venturing, throwing, seeking the spheres to
   connect them,
Till the bridge you will need be formed, till the ductile anchor hold,
Till the gossamer thread you fling catch somewhere, O my soul.   10

Walt Whitman (1819–1892)

In the first stanza the speaker describes a spider's apparently tireless
effort to attach its thread to some substantial support so that it can
begin constructing a web. The speaker reveals his attentive interest by
the hinted personification of the spider, and his sympathy with it is
expressed in the overstatement of size and distance—he is trying to
perceive the world as a spider sees it from a "promontory" surrounded
by vast space. He even attributes a human motive to the spider: exploration, rather than instinctive web-building. Nevertheless, the first
stanza is essentially literal—the close observation of an actual spider at
its task. In the second stanza the speaker explicitly interprets the symbolic meaning of what he has observed: his soul (personified by apostrophe and by the capabilities assigned to it) is like the spider in its constant
striving. But the soul's purpose is to find spiritual or intellectual certainties in the vast universe it inhabits. The symbolic meaning is richer than
a mere comparison; while a spider's actual purpose is limited to its
instinctive drives, the human soul strives for much more, in a much
more complex "surrounding." And, of course, the result of the soul's
symbolized striving is much more open-ended than is the attempt of a
spider to spin a web, as the paradoxical language ("Surrounded, detached," "ductile anchor") implies. *Can* the human soul connect the
celestial spheres?

QUESTIONS

1. In "Harlem" (page 705) Langston Hughes compares a frustrated dream to a
   bomb. Whitman compares the striving human soul to a spider. Why is
   Hughes's comparison a metaphor and Whitman's a symbol? What additional
   comparison does Whitman make to the soul's quest? What figure of speech
   is it?
2. In what ways are the spider and the soul contrasted? What do the contrasts
   contribute to the meaning of the symbol?
3. Can the questing soul represent human actions other than the search for
   spiritual certainties?

The Sick Rose

O Rose, thou art sick!
The invisible worm
That flies in the night,
In the howling storm,

Has found out thy bed   5
Of crimson joy,
And his dark secret love
Does thy life destroy.

William Blake (1757–1827)

QUESTIONS

1. What figures of speech do you find in the poem in addition to symbol? How do they contribute to its force or meaning?
2. Several symbolic interpretations of this poem are given below. Can you think of others?
3. Should symbolic meanings be sought for the night and the storm? If so, what meanings would you suggest?

In "A Noiseless Patient Spider" the symbolic meaning of the spider is identified and named. By contrast, in "The Sick Rose" no meanings are explicitly indicated for the rose and the worm. Indeed, we are not *compelled* to assign them specific meanings. The poem might literally be read as being about a rose that has been attacked on a stormy night by a cankerworm.

The organization of "The Sick Rose" is so rich, however, and its language so powerful that the rose and the worm refuse to remain *merely* a flower and an insect. The rose, apostrophized and personified in the first line, has traditionally been a symbol of feminine beauty and love, as well as of sensual pleasures. "Bed" can refer to a woman's bed as well as to a flower bed. "Crimson joy" suggests the intense pleasure of passionate lovemaking as well as the brilliant beauty of a red flower. The "dark secret love" of the "invisible worm" is more strongly suggestive of a concealed or illicit love affair than of the feeding of a cankerworm on a plant, though it fits that too. For all these reasons the rose almost immediately suggests a woman and the worm her secret lover—and the poem suggests the corruption of innocent but physical love by concealment and deceit. But the possibilities do not stop there. The worm is a common symbol or metonymy for death; and for readers steeped in Milton (as Blake was) it recalls the "undying worm" of

Paradise Lost, Milton's metaphor for the snake (or Satan in the form of a snake) that tempted Eve. Meanings multiply also for the reader who is familiar with Blake's other writings. Thus "The Sick Rose" has been variously interpreted as referring to the destruction of joyous physical love by jealousy, deceit, concealment, or the possessive instinct; of innocence by experience; of humanity by Satan; of imagination and joy by analytic reason; of life by death. We cannot say what specifically the poet had in mind, nor need we do so. A symbol defines an *area* of meaning, and any interpretation that falls within that area is permissible. In Blake's poem the rose stands for something beautiful, or desirable, or good. The worm stands for some corrupting agent. Within these limits, the meaning is largely "open." And because the meaning is open, the reader is justified in bringing personal experience to its interpretation. Blake's poem, for instance, might remind someone of a gifted friend whose promise has been destroyed by drug addiction.

Between the extremes exemplified by "A Noiseless Patient Spider" and "The Sick Rose" a poem may exercise all degrees of control over the range and meaning of its symbolism. Consider another example.

Digging

Between my finger and my thumb
The squat pen rests; snug as a gun.

Under my window, a clean rasping sound
When the spade sinks into gravelly ground:
My father, digging. I look down   5

Till his straining rump among the flowerbeds
Bends low, comes up twenty years away
Stooping in rhythm through potato drills
Where he was digging.

The coarse boot nestled on the lug, the shaft   10
Against the inside knee was levered firmly.
He rooted out tall tops, buried the bright edge deep
To scatter new potatoes that we picked
Loving their cool hardness in our hands.

By God, the old man could handle a spade.   15
Just like his old man.

My grandfather cut more turf in a day
Than any other man on Toner's bog.
Once I carried him milk in a bottle
Corked sloppily with paper. He straightened up   20
To drink it, then fell to right away

Nicking and slicing neatly, heaving sods
Over his shoulder, going down and down
For the good turf. Digging.

The cold smell of potato mould, the squelch and slap   25
Of soggy peat, the curt cuts of an edge
Through living roots awaken in my head.
But I've no spade to follow men like them.

Between my finger and my thumb
The squat pen rests.   30
I'll dig with it.

Seamus Heaney (b. 1939)

QUESTIONS

1. Vocabulary: *drills* (8), *fell to* (21). In Ireland, "turf" (17) is a block of peat dug from a bog; when dried, it is used as fuel.
2. What emotional responses are evoked by the imagery?

On the literal level, this poem presents a writer who interrupts himself to have a look at his father digging in a flower garden below his window. He is reminded of his father twenty years earlier digging potatoes for harvesting, and by that memory he is drawn farther back to his grandfather digging peat from a bog for fuel. The memories are vivid and appealing and rich in imagery, but the writer is not like his forebears; he has "no spade to follow" their examples. And so, with a trace of regret, he decides that his writing will have to be his substitute for their manual tasks.

But the title and the emphasis on varieties of the same task carried out in several different ways over a span of generations alert the reader to the need to discover the further significance of this literal statement. The last line is metaphorical, comparing digging to writing (and thus is itself not symbolic, for on a literal level one cannot dig with a pen). The metaphor, however, suggesting that the writer will commit himself to exploring the kinds of memories in this poem, invites an interpretation of the literal forms of digging. We notice then that the father has been involved in two sorts—the practical, backbreaking task of digging up potatoes to be gathered by the children, and twenty years later the relatively easy chore of digging in flowerbeds so as to encourage the growth of ornamental plants. There is a progression represented in the father's activities, from the necessary and arduous earlier life to the leisurely growing of flowers. Farther back in time, the grandfather's labors were deeper, heavier, and more essential, cutting and digging the material that would be used for heating and cooking—cooking potatoes, we should assume. The grandfather digs deeper and deeper, always in quest of the best peat, "the good turf."

Symbolically, then, digging has meanings that relate to basic needs—for warmth, for sustenance, for beauty, and for the personal satisfaction of doing a job well. In the concluding metaphor, another basic need is implied, the need to remember and confront one's origins, to find oneself in a continuum of meaningful activities, to assert the relevance and importance of one's vocation. And it is not coincidental that an Irish poet should find symbolic meanings in a confluence of Irish materials—from peat bogs to potatoes to poets and writers, that long-beleaguered island has asserted its special and distinct identity. Nor is it coincidental that Heaney selected this to be the opening poem in his first book of poetry: "Digging" is what his poetry does.

Meanings ray out from a symbol, like the corona around the sun or like connotations around a richly suggestive word. But the very fact that a symbol may be so rich in meanings requires that we use the greatest tact in its interpretation. Although Blake's "The Sick Rose" might, because of personal association, remind us of a friend destroyed by drug addiction, it would be unwise to say that Blake uses the rose to symbolize a gifted person succumbing to drug addiction, for this inter-pretation is private, idiosyncratic, and narrow. The poem allows it, but does not itself suggest it.

Moreover, we should never assume that because the meaning of a symbol is more or less open, we may make it mean anything we choose. We would be wrong, for instance, in interpreting the choice in "The Road Not Taken" as some choice between good and evil, for the poem tells us that the two roads are much alike and that both lie "In leaves no step had trodden black." Whatever the choice is, it is a choice between two goods. Whatever our interpretation of a symbolic poem, it must be tied firmly to the facts of the poem. We must not let loose of the string and let our imaginations go ballooning up among the clouds. Because the symbol is capable of adding so many dimensions to a poem, it is a peculiarly effective resource for the poet, but it is also peculiarly susceptible to misinterpretation by the incautious reader.

Accurate interpretation of the symbol requires delicacy, tact, and good sense. The reader must maintain balance while walking a tightrope between too little and too much—between underinterpretation and overinterpretation. If the reader falls off, however, it is much more desirable to fall off on the side of too little. Someone who reads "The Road Not Taken" as being only about a choice between two roads in a wood has at least understood part of the experience that the poem communicates, but the reader who reads into it anything imaginable might as well discard the poem and simply daydream.

Above all, we should avoid the tendency to indulge in symbol-hunting and to see virtually anything in a poem as symbolic. It is preferable to miss a symbol than to try to find one in every line of a poem.

To the Virgins, to Make Much of Time

Gather ye rosebuds while ye may,
    Old Time is still a-flying;
And this same flower that smiles today
    Tomorrow will be dying.

The glorious lamp of heaven, the Sun,   5
    The higher he's a-getting,
The sooner will his race be run,
    And nearer he's to setting.

That age is best which is the first,
    When youth and blood are warmer;   10
But being spent, the worse, and worst
    Times still succeed the former.

Then be not coy, but use your time;
    And while ye may, go marry;
For having lost but once your prime,   15
    You may forever tarry.

Robert Herrick (1591–1674)

QUESTIONS

1. The first two stanzas might be interpreted literally if the third and fourth stanzas did not force us to interpret them symbolically. What do the "rose-buds" symbolize (stanza 1)? What does the course of a day symbolize (stanza 2)? Does the poet narrow the meaning of the rosebud symbol in the last stanza or merely name *one* of its specific meanings?
2. How does the title help us interpret the meaning of the symbol? Why is "virgins" a more meaningful word than, for example, *maidens*?
3. Why is such haste necessary in gathering the rosebuds? True, the blossoms die quickly, but others will replace them. Who *really* is dying?
4. What are "the worse, and worst" times (11)? Why?
5. Why is the wording of the poem better than these possible alternatives: *blooms* for "smiles" (3); *course* for "race" (7); *used* for "spent" (11); *spend* for "use" (13)?

Allegory is a narrative or description that has a second meaning beneath the surface. Although the surface story or description may have its own interest, the author's major interest is in the ulterior meaning. When Pharoah in the Bible, for instance, has a dream in which seven fat kine are devoured by seven lean kine, the story does not really become significant until Joseph interprets its allegorical meaning: that Egypt is to enjoy seven years of fruitfulness and prosperity followed by seven years of famine. Allegory has been defined sometimes as an extended metaphor and sometimes as a series of related symbols. But it is usually distinguishable from both of these. It is unlike extended metaphor in that it involves a *system* of related comparisons rather than one comparison drawn out. It differs from symbolism in that it puts less emphasis on the images for their own sake and more on their ulterior meanings. Also, these meanings are more fixed. In allegory there is usually a one-to-one correspondence between the details and a single set of ulterior meanings. In complex allegories the details may have more than one meaning, but these meanings tend to be definite. Meanings do not ray out from allegory as they do from a symbol.

Allegory is less popular in modern literature than it was in medieval and Renaissance writing, and it is much less often found in short poems than in long narrative works such as *The Faerie Queene, Everyman*, and *Pilgrim's Progress*. It has sometimes, especially with political allegory, been used to disguise meaning rather than reveal it (or, rather, to disguise it from some people while revealing it to others). Though less rich than the symbol, allegory is an effective way of making the abstract concrete and has occasionally been used effectively even in fairly short poems.

Peace

Sweet Peace, where dost thou dwell? I humbly crave,
    Let me once know.
     I sought thee in a secret cave,
      And asked if Peace were there.
A hollow wind did seem to answer, "No,   5
    Go seek elsewhere."

I did, and going did a rainbow note.
    "Surely," thought I,
     "This is the lace of Peace's coat;
      I will search out the matter."   10
But while I looked, the clouds immediately
    Did break and scatter.

Then went I to a garden, and did spy
    A gallant flower,
     The Crown Imperial. "Sure," said I,   15
      "Peace at the root must dwell."
But when I digged, I saw a worm devour
    What showed so well.

At length I met a reverend good old man,
    Whom when for Peace   20
     I did demand, he thus began:
      "There was a prince of old
At Salem dwelt, who lived with good increase
    Of flock and fold.

"He sweetly lived; yet sweetness did not save   25
    His life from foes.
     But after death out of his grave
      There sprang twelve stalks of wheat;
Which many wondering at, got some of those
    To plant and set.   30

"It prospered strangely, and did soon disperse
    Through all the earth,
     For they that taste it do rehearse°   declare
      That virtue lies therein,

A secret virtue, bringing peace and mirth   35
          By flight of sin.

"Take of this grain, which in my garden grows,
          And grows for you;
      Make bread of it; and that repose
      And peace, which everywhere   40
With so much earnestness you do pursue,
          Is only there."

George Herbert (1593–1633)

QUESTIONS

1. Vocabulary: *gallant* (14), *virtue* (34). "Crown Imperial" (15) is a garden flower, fritillary; "Salem" (23) is Jerusalem.
2. Identify the "prince" (22), his "flock and fold" (24), the "twelve stalks of wheat" (28), the "grain" (37), and the "bread" (39).
3. Should the "secret cave" (stanza 1), the "rainbow" (stanza 2), and the flower "garden" (stanza 3) be understood merely as places where the speaker searched or do they have more precise meanings?
4. Who is the "reverend good old man" (19), and what is *his* garden (37)?

EXERCISES

1. Determine whether "sleep" in the following poems is literal, a symbol, or a metaphor (or simile).
   a. "Stopping by Woods on a Snowy Evening" (page 787).
   b. "The Chimney Sweeper" (page 756).
   c. "Is my team plowing" (page 662).
   d. "The Second Coming" (page 1018).
2. Donne's "The Flea" (page 812) and Dickinson's "I heard a Fly buzz—when I died" (page 869) deal with common insect pests. Which of them is symbolic? Explain your choice.
3. What do Blake's lamb and tiger symbolize (pages 793–794)?
4. Determine whether the following poems are predominantly symbolic or literal.
   a. "Because I could not stop for Death" (page 742).
   b. "The Snow Man" (page 701).
   c. "The Darkling Thrush" (page 972).
   d. "Song: Go and catch a falling star" (page 958).
   e. "Blackberry Eating" (page 877).
   f. "Musée des Beaux Arts" (page 943).
   g. "Richard Cory" (page 998).

h. "The Wild Swans at Coole" (page 1019).
i. "Poem: As the cat" (page 1012).
j. "Desert Places" (page 683).
k. "Constantly risking absurdity" (page 648).

REVIEWING CHAPTER SIX

1. Using examples from the poems that follow, explore how symbols must read both literally and figuratively.
2. Show that the context of a poem determines the limits of its symbolic meanings (as an exercise, you might want to examine the multiple possible meanings of a particular symbol, and eliminate those that are ruled out by the context).
3. Discuss the difference between symbol and allegory, if possible accounting for the fact that allegory is no longer as popular a figure as it once was.

The Writer

In her room at the prow of the house
Where light breaks, and the windows are tossed with linden,
My daughter is writing a story.

I pause in the stairwell, hearing
From her shut door a commotion of typewriter-keys   5
Like a chain hauled over a gunwale.

Young as she is, the stuff
Of her life is a great cargo, and some of it heavy:
I wish her a lucky passage.

But now it is she who pauses,   10
As if to reject my thought and its easy figure.
A stillness greatens, in which

The whole house seems to be thinking,
And then she is at it again with a bunched clamor
Of strokes, and again is silent.   15

I remember the dazed starling
Which was trapped in that very room, two years ago;
How we stole in, lifted a sash

And retreated, not to affright it;
And how for a helpless hour, through the crack of the door,   20
We watched the sleek, wild, dark

And iridescent creature
Batter against the brilliance, drop like a glove
To the hard floor, or the desk-top,

And wait then, humped and bloody,   25
For the wits to try it again; and how our spirits
Rose when, suddenly sure,

It lifted off from a chair-back,
Beating a smooth course for the right window
And clearing the sill of the world.   30

It is always a matter, my darling,
Of life or death, as I had forgotten. I wish
What I wished you before, but harder.

                                        Richard Wilbur (b. 1921)

QUESTIONS

1. What "easy figure" (11) of speech is presented by such language as "prow" (1), "chain hauled over a gunwale" (6), "cargo" (8), "passage" (9)? What is being compared to what? Why would "the writer"—either the daughter or the speaker—be justified in rejecting that figure?
2. The daughter seems to be rejecting both the figure of speech and the thought that it represents (11). Why might the thought be as unacceptable as the figure that expresses it?
3. Lines 16 through 30 develop the image of the trapped starling. Why should it be interpreted as a symbol? How is its meaning more complex than that of the figure developed in lines 1–15?
4. The poem symmetrically divides into two 15-line units, each developing a different figure of speech. What is the function of the additional three lines with which the poem ends?

Fire and Ice

Some say the world will end in fire,
Some say in ice.
From what I've tasted of desire
I hold with those who favor fire.
But if it had to perish twice,   5
I think I know enough of hate
To say that for destruction ice
Is also great
And would suffice.

Robert Frost (1874–1963)

QUESTIONS

1. Who are "Some" (1–2)? To which two theories do lines 1–2 refer? (In answering, it might help you to know that the poem was published in 1920.)
2. What do "fire" and "ice" respectively symbolize? What two meanings has "the world"?
3. The poem ends with an *understatement* (see Chapter 7). How does it affect the tone of the poem?

Up-Hill

Does the road wind up-hill all the way?
    Yes, to the very end.
Will the day's journey take the whole long day?
    From morn to night, my friend.

But is there for the night a resting-place?   5
    A roof for when the slow dark hours begin.
May not the darkness hide it from my face?
    You cannot miss that inn.

Shall I meet other wayfarers at night?
    Those who have gone before.   10
Then must I knock, or call when just in sight?
    They will not keep you waiting at that door.

Shall I find comfort, travel-sore and weak?
  Of labor you shall the sum.
Will there be beds for me and all who seek?   15
  Yea, beds for all who come.

Christina Rossetti (1830–1894)

QUESTIONS

1. How many speakers are there in this poem? Who are they? What does the poem gain from not using quotation marks to indicate the change from one speaker to another?
2. What are the key symbols in the poem? What clues prompt the reader to interpret them as symbols? What do they symbolize?
3. What evidence would you offer in categorizing this poem as either symbolic or allegorical?

Harlem Hopscotch

One foot down, then hop! It's hot.
  Good things for the ones that's got.
Another jump, now to the left.
  Everybody for hisself.

In the air, now both feet down.   5
  Since you black, don't stick around.
Food is gone, the rent is due,
  Curse and cry and then jump two.

All the people out of work,
  Hold for three, then twist and jerk.   10
Cross the line, they count you out.
  That's what hopping's all about.

Both feet flat, the game is done.
They think I lost. I think I won.

Maya Angelou (b. 1928)

QUESTIONS

1. What does the game of hopscotch represent in this poem, symbolically? What lines or phrases give clues to the symbolic meaning?

2. Why are some words and phrases—such as "Everybody for hisself" (4) and "Since you black" (6)—deliberately ungrammatical?
3. Why does the speaker, by the end of the poem, claim that she has "won" the game? In what sense has she won, if her playmates think she has lost?

I Saw in Louisiana a Live-Oak Growing

I saw in Louisiana a live-oak growing,
All alone stood it and the moss hung down from the branches,
Without any companion it grew there uttering joyous
    leaves of dark green,
And its look, rude, unbending, lusty, made me think of myself,
But I wonder'd how it could utter joyous leaves standing   5
    alone there without its friend near, for I knew I could not,
And I broke off a twig with a certain number of leaves
    upon it, and twined around it a little moss,
And brought it away, and I have placed it in sight in my room,
It is not needed to remind me as of my own dear friends,
(For I believe lately I think of little else than of them),
Yet it remains to me a curious token, it makes me think   10
    of manly love;
For all that, and though the live-oak glistens there in
    Louisiana solitary in a wide flat space,
Uttering joyous leaves all its life without a friend a lover near,
I know very well I could not.

Walt Whitman (1819–1892)

QUESTIONS

1. Vocabulary: *rude* (4). *Uttering* (3, 12) has an archaic meaning, "sending or shooting out."
2. What does the personified live-oak symbolize to the speaker? Does it have positive or negative connotations for him? How is he like and unlike the tree?
3. What more common denotation of "uttering" suggests that the speaker might be a poet? What other denotation of "joyous leaves" contributes to that suggestion?

Because I could not stop for Death

Because I could not stop for Death—
He kindly stopped for me—
The Carriage held but just Ourselves—
And Immortality.

We slowly drove—He knew no haste   5
And I had put away
My labor and my leisure too,
For His Civility—

We passed the School, where Children strove
At Recess—in the Ring—   10
We passed the Fields of Gazing Grain—
We passed the Setting Sun—

Or rather—He passed Us—
The Dews drew quivering and chill—
For only Gossamer, my Gown—   15
My Tippet—only Tulle—

We paused before a House that seemed
A Swelling of the Ground—
The Roof was scarcely visible—
The Cornice—in the Ground—   20

Since then—'tis Centuries—and yet
Feels shorter than the Day
I first surmised the Horses' Heads
Were toward Eternity—

Emily Dickinson (1830–1886)

QUESTIONS

1. Vocabulary: *Gossamer* (15); *Tippet, Tulle* (16); *surmised* (23).
2. Define the stages of this journey—where it begins, what events occur on the way, and its destination. Where is the speaker *now*? What is her present emotional condition?
3. To what is "Death" (1) being compared?

f

4. Identify the allegorical implications of the events. For example, what aspects of human life are implied by the three items that are "passed" in stanza 3? What is the "House" (17) before which the carriage pauses, and why does it pause there?

5. Explore the three time references in the concluding stanza. Can you explain why in the passage of "Centuries . . . Feels shorter than the Day" the speaker guessed that her journey was proceeding "toward Eternity"? For what is "Eternity" a metonymy? Has the carriage reached that destination yet?

Hymn to God My God, in My Sickness

Since I am coming to that holy room
　　Where, with thy choir of saints for evermore,
I shall be made thy music, as I come
　　　I tune the instrument here at the door,
　　　And what I must do then, think now before.　　　　5

Whilst my physicians by their love are grown
　　Cosmographers, and I their map, who lie
Flat on this bed, that by them may be shown
　　　That this is my southwest discovery,
Per fretum febris,° by these straits to die,　　　　through the 10
　　　　　　　　　　　　　　　　　　　　　raging of fever

I joy that in these straits I see my west;
　　For though those currents yield return to none,
What shall my west hurt me? As west and east
　　　In all flat maps (and I am one) are one,
　　　So death doth touch the resurrection.　　　　15

Is the Pacific Sea my home? Or are
　　The eastern riches? Is Jerusalem?
Anyan° and Magellan and Gibraltar,　　　　Bering Strait
　　　All straits, and none but straits, are ways to them,
　　　Whether where Japhet dwelt, or Cham, or Shem.　　20

We think that Paradise and Calvary,
　　Christ's cross and Adam's tree, stood in one place;
Look, Lord, and find both Adams met in me;
　　　As the first Adam's sweat surrounds my face,
　　　May the last Adam's blood my soul embrace.　　25

So, in his purple wrapped receive me, Lord;
  By these his thorns give me his other crown;
And as to others' souls I preached thy word,
  Be this my text, my sermon to mine own:
Therefore that he may raise, the Lord throws down.   30

John Donne (1572–1631)

QUESTIONS

1. Vocabulary: *Cosmographers* (7).
2. What is the speaker doing in stanza 1? What are "that holy room" (1) and "the instrument" (4)? For what is the speaker preparing himself?
3. In Donne's time explorers were seeking a Northwest Passage to Asia to match discovery of a southwest passage, the Straits of Magellan. Why is "southwest" more appropriate to the speaker's condition than "northwest"? In what ways is his fever like a strait? What denotations of "straits" (10) are relevant? What do the straits symbolize?
4. In what ways does the speaker's body resemble a map? Although the map is metaphorical, its parts are symbolic. What do west and east symbolize? Explain how the west and east "are one" (14).
5. Japhet, Cham (or Ham), and Shem (20)—sons of Noah—were in Christian legend the ancestors of the races of man, roughly identified as European, African, and Asian. In what ways are the Pacific Ocean, the East Indies, and Jerusalem (16–17) fitting symbols for the speaker's destination?
6. According to early Christian thinking, the Garden of Eden and Calvary were located in the same place. How does this tie in with the poem's geographical symbolism? Because Adam is said to prefigure Christ (Romans 5.12–21), Christ is called the second Adam. What connection is there between Adam's "sweat" (24) and Christ's "blood" (25)? How do the two Adams meet in the speaker? What do blood and sweat (together and separately) symbolize?
7. For what are "eastern riches" (17), "his purple" (26), and "his thorns" (27) metonymies? What do "purple" and "thorns" symbolize? What is Christ's "other crown" (27)?
8. How does this poem explain human suffering and give it meaning?

Weighing the Dog

It is awkward for me and bewildering for him
as I hold him in my arms in the small bathroom,
balancing our weight on the shaky blue scale,

but this is the way to weigh a dog and easier
than training him to sit obediently on one spot   5
with his tongue out, waiting for the cookie.

With pencil and paper I subtract my weight
from our total to find out the remainder that is his,
and I start to wonder if there is an analogy here.

It could not have to do with my leaving you   10
though I never figured out what you amounted to
until I subtracted myself from our combination.

You held me in your arms more than I held you
through all those awkward and bewildering months
and now we are both lost in strange and distant neighborhoods. 15

Billy Collins (b. 1941)

QUESTIONS

1. In this poem, the ordinary act of weighing the dog is made to symbolize a failed relationship. Is the symbolism appropriate? Why or why not?
2. What is the general tone of the poem? What attitude on the speaker's part is suggested by the symbolic "analogy" (9) he makes?
3. Discuss the phrase, "strange and distant neighborhoods" in the final line. How does this phrase—including its connotation and imagery—help to clarify the poem's symbolic meaning?

Ulysses

It little profits that an idle king,
By this still hearth, among these barren crags,
Matched with an agèd wife, I mete and dole
Unequal laws unto a savage race,
That hoard, and sleep, and feed, and know not me.   5
I cannot rest from travel; I will drink
Life to the lees. All times I have enjoyed
Greatly, have suffered greatly, both with those
That loved me, and alone; on shore, and when
Through scudding drifts the rainy Hyades   10
Vext the dim sea. I am become a name;
For always roaming with a hungry heart

Much have I seen and known,—cities of men,
And manners, climates, councils, governments,
Myself not least, but honored of them all;   15
And drunk delight of battle with my peers,
Far on the ringing plains of windy Troy.
I am a part of all that I have met;
Yet all experience is an arch wherethrough
Gleams that untraveled world, whose margin fades   20
For ever and for ever when I move.
How dull it is to pause, to make an end,
To rust unburnished, not to shine in use!
As though to breathe were life! Life piled on life
Were all too little, and of one to me   25
Little remains; but every hour is saved
From that eternal silence, something more,
A bringer of new things; and vile it were
For some three suns to store and hoard myself,
And this gray spirit yearning in desire   30
To follow knowledge like a sinking star,
Beyond the utmost bound of human thought.

This is my son, mine own Telemachus,
To whom I leave the scepter and the isle—
Well-loved of me, discerning to fulfil   35
This labor, by slow prudence to make mild
A rugged people, and through soft degrees
Subdue them to the useful and the good.
Most blameless is he, centered in the sphere
Of common duties, decent not to fail   40
In offices of tenderness, and pay
Meet adoration to my household gods,
When I am gone. He works his work, I mine.

There lies the port; the vessel puffs her sail:
There gloom the dark, broad seas. My mariners,   45
Souls that have toiled, and wrought, and thought with me—
That ever with a frolic welcome took
The thunder and the sunshine, and opposed
Free hearts, free foreheads—you and I are old;
Old age hath yet his honor and his toil.   50
Death closes all; but something ere the end,
Some work of noble note, may yet be done,

Not unbecoming men that strove with Gods.
The lights begin to twinkle from the rocks;
The long day wanes; the slow moon climbs; the deep   55
Moans round with many voices. Come, my friends,
'Tis not too late to seek a newer world.
Push off, and sitting well in order smite
The sounding furrows; for my purpose holds
To sail beyond the sunset, and the baths   60
Of all the western stars, until I die.
It may be that the gulfs will wash us down;
It may be we shall touch the Happy Isles,
And see the great Achilles, whom we knew.
Though much is taken, much abides; and though   65
We are not now that strength which in old days
Moved earth and heaven, that which we are, we are:
One equal temper of heroic hearts,
Made weak by time and fate, but strong in will
To strive, to seek, to find, and not to yield.   70

Alfred, Lord Tennyson (1809–1892)

QUESTIONS

1. Vocabulary: *lees* (7), *Hyades* (10), *meet* (42).
2. Ulysses, king of Ithaca, is a legendary Greek hero, a major figure in Homer's *Iliad*, the hero of Homer's *Odyssey*, and a minor figure in Dante's *Divine Comedy*. After ten years at the siege of Troy, Ulysses set sail for home but, having incurred the wrath of the god of the sea, he was subjected to storms and vicissitudes and was forced to wander for another ten years, having many adventures and seeing most of the Mediterranean world before again reaching Ithaca, his wife, and his son. Once back home, according to Dante, he still wished to travel and "to follow virtue and knowledge." In Tennyson's poem, Ulysses is represented as about to set sail on a final voyage from which he will not return. Locate Ithaca on a map. Where exactly, in geographical terms, does Ulysses intend to sail (59–64)? (The Happy Isles were the Elysian fields, or Greek paradise; Achilles was another Greek prince, the hero of the *Iliad*, who was killed at the siege of Troy.)
3. Ulysses's speech is divided into three sections, beginning at lines 1, 33, and 44. What is the topic or purpose of each section? To whom, specifically, is the third section addressed? To whom, would you infer, are sections 1 and 2 addressed? Where do you visualize Ulysses as standing during his speech?
4. Characterize Ulysses. What kind of person is he as Tennyson represents him?

5. What way of life is symbolized by Ulysses? Find as many evidences as you can that Ulysses's desire for travel represents something more than mere wanderlust and wish for adventure.
6. Give two symbolic implications of the westward direction of Ulysses's journey.
7. Interpret lines 18–21 and 26–29. What metaphor is implied in line 23? What is symbolized by "The thunder and the sunshine" (48)? What do the two metonymies in line 49 stand for?

SUGGESTIONS FOR WRITING

The following poems may be regarded as character sketches, but in each case the richness and suggestiveness of the presentation point to the symbolic nature of the sketch. Of what are the characters symbolic, and what clues does each poem present that make a symbolic interpretation valid?

1. Kay, "Pathedy of Manners" (page 677).
2. Gunn, "The Man with Night Sweats" (page 694).
3. Frost, "After Apple-Picking" (page 698).
4. Dickinson, "I died for Beauty—but was scarce" (page 956).
5. Joseph, "Warning" (page 978).
6. Plath, "Spinster" (page 992).
7. Robinson, "Richard Cory" (page 998).

Figurative Language 3

Paradox, Overstatement, Understatement, Irony

Aesop tells the tale of a traveler who sought refuge with a Satyr on a bitter winter night. On entering the Satyr's lodging, he blew on his fingers, and was asked by the Satyr why he did it. "To warm them up," he explained. Later, on being served a piping-hot bowl of porridge, he blew also on it, and again was asked why he did it. "To cool it off," he explained. The Satyr thereupon thrust him out of doors, for he would have nothing to do with a man who could blow hot and cold with the same breath.

A **paradox** is an apparent contradiction that is nevertheless somehow true. It may be either a situation or a statement. Aesop's tale of the traveler illustrates a **paradoxical situation**. As a figure of speech, paradox is a statement. When Alexander Pope wrote that a literary critic of his time would "damn with faint praise," he was using a **verbal paradox**, for how can a man damn by praising?

When we understand all the conditions and circumstances involved in a paradox, we find that what at first seemed impossible is actually entirely plausible and not strange at all. The paradox of the cold hands and hot porridge is not strange to anyone who knows that a stream of air directed upon an object of different temperature will tend to bring that object closer to its own temperature. And Pope's paradox is not strange when we realize that *damn* is being used figuratively, and that Pope means only that a too reserved praise may damage an author with the public almost as much as adverse criticism. In a **paradoxical statement** the contradiction usually stems from one of the words being used figuratively or with more than one denotation.

The value of paradox is its shock value. Its seeming impossibility startles the reader into attention and, by the fact of its apparent absurdity, underscores the truth of what is being said.

Much Madness is divinest Sense

Much Madness is divinest Sense—
To a discerning Eye—
Much Sense—the starkest Madness—
'Tis the Majority
In this, as All, prevail—   5
Assent—and you are sane—
Demur—you're straightway dangerous—
And handled with a Chain—

Emily Dickinson (1830–1886)

QUESTIONS

1. This poem presents the two sides of a paradoxical proposition: that insanity is
   good sense, and that good sense is insane. How do the concepts implied by
   the words "discerning" (2) and "Majority" (4) provide the resolution of this
   paradox?
2. How do we know that the speaker does not believe that the majority is
   correct? How do the last five lines extend the subject beyond a contrast
   between sanity and insanity?

Overstatement, understatement, and verbal irony form a continuous series, for they consist, respectively, of saying more, saying less, and
saying the opposite of what one really means.

Overstatement, or *hyperbole,* is simply exaggeration, but exaggeration in the service of truth. It is not the same as a fish story. If you say,
"I'm starved!" or "You could have knocked me over with a feather!" or
"I'll die if I don't pass this course!" you do not expect to be taken
literally; you are merely adding emphasis to what you really mean.
(And if you say, "There were literally millions of people at the beach!"
you are merely piling one overstatement on top of another, for you really
mean, "There were figuratively millions of people at the beach," or,
literally, "The beach was very crowded.") Like all figures of speech,
overstatement may be used with a variety of effects. It may be humorous
or grave, fanciful or restrained, convincing or unconvincing. When
Tennyson says of his eagle (page 635) that it is "*Close* to the sun in
lonely lands," he says what appears to be literally true, though we know
from our study of astronomy that it is not. When Kay reports that her
character in "Pathedy of Manners" (page 677) "Saw *catalogues* of domes"
on her European trip, she implies the superficiality of a person for whom

visiting a few churches and palaces seemed like enough architecture to fill catalogues. When Frost says, at the conclusion of "The Road Not Taken" (page 725),

> I shall be telling this with a sigh
> Somewhere *ages and ages hence*

we are scarcely aware of the overstatement, so quietly is the assertion made. Unskillfully used, however, overstatement may seem strained and ridiculous, leading us to react as Gertrude does to the player-queen's speeches in *Hamlet*: "The lady doth protest too much."

It is paradoxical that one can emphasize a truth either by overstating it or by understating it. **Understatement**, or saying less than one means, may exist in what one says or merely in how one says it. If, for instance, upon sitting down to a loaded dinner plate, you say, "This looks like a nice snack," you are actually stating less than the truth; but if you say, with the humorist Artemus Ward, that a man who holds his hand for half an hour in a lighted fire will experience "a sensation of excessive and disagreeable warmth," you are stating what is literally true but with a good deal less force than the situation warrants.

The Sun Rising

> Busy old fool, unruly sun,
>   Why dost thou thus
> Through windows and through curtains call on us?
> Must to thy motions lovers' seasons run?
>   Saucy pedantic wretch, go chide   5
>   Late schoolboys and sour 'prentices,
>   Go tell court-huntsmen that the king will ride,
>   Call country ants to harvest offices;
> Love, all alike, no season knows, nor clime,
> Nor hours, days, months, which are the rags of time.   10
>
>   Thy beams so reverend and strong
>   Why shouldst thou think?
> I could eclipse and cloud them with a wink,
> But that I would not lose her sight so long;
>   If her eyes have not blinded thine,   15
>   Look, and tomorrow late tell me

Whether both th' Indias of spice and mine
    Be where thou left'st them, or lie here with me.
Ask for those kings whom thou saw'st yesterday,
And thou shalt hear, "All here in one bed lay."   20

        She's all states, and all princes I;
            Nothing else is.
    Princes do but play us; compared to this,
    All honor's mimic, all wealth alchemy.
        Thou, sun, art half as happy as we,   25
            In that the world's contracted thus;
        Thine age asks ease, and since thy duties be
        To warm the world, that's done in warming us.
    Shine here to us, and thou art everywhere;
    This bed thy center is, these walls thy sphere.   30

                                        John Donne (1572–1631)

QUESTIONS

1. Vocabulary: *offices* (8), *alchemy* (24).
2. As precisely as possible, identify the time of day and the locale. What three "persons" does the poem involve?
3. What is the speaker's attitude toward the sun in stanzas 1 and 2? How and why does it change in stanza 3?
4. Does the speaker understate or overstate the actual qualities of the sun? Point out specific examples. Identify the overstatements in lines 9–10, 13, 15, 16–20, 21–24, 29–30. What do these overstatements achieve?
5. Line 17 introduces a geographical image referring to the East and West Indies, sources respectively of spices and gold. What relationship between the lovers and the rest of the world is expressed in lines 15–22?
6. Who is actually the intended listener for this extended apostrophe? What is the speaker's purpose? What is the poem's purpose?

Incident

Once riding in old Baltimore
    Heart-filled, head-filled with glee,
I saw a Baltimorean
    Keep looking straight at me.

Now I was eight and very small,   5
    And he was no whit bigger,

And so I smiled, but he poked out
  His tongue, and called me, "Nigger."

I saw the whole of Baltimore
  From May until December;   10
Of all the things that happened there
  That's all that I remember.

Countee Cullen (1903–1946)

QUESTIONS

1. What accounts for the effectiveness of the last stanza? Comment on the title. Is it in key with the meaning of the poem?

Like paradox, **irony** has meanings that extend beyond its use merely as a figure of speech.

Verbal irony, saying the opposite of what one means, is often confused with sarcasm and with satire, and for that reason it may be well to look at the meanings of all three terms. Sarcasm and satire both imply ridicule, one on the colloquial level, the other on the literary level. **Sarcasm** is simply bitter or cutting speech, intended to wound the feelings (it comes from a Greek word meaning to tear flesh). **Satire** is a more formal term, usually applied to written literature rather than to speech and ordinarily implying a higher motive: it is ridicule (either bitter or gentle) of human folly or vice, with the purpose of bringing about reform or at least of keeping other people from falling into similar folly or vice. Irony, on the other hand, is a literary device or figure that may be used in the service of sarcasm or ridicule or may not. It is popularly confused with sarcasm and satire because it is so often used as their tool; but irony may be used without either sarcastic or satirical intent, and sarcasm and satire may exist (though they do not usually) without irony. If, for instance, one of the members of your class raises his hand on the discussion of this point and says, "I don't understand," and your instructor replies, with a tone of heavy disgust in his voice, "Well, I wouldn't expect *you* to," he is being sarcastic but not ironic; he means exactly what he says. But if, after you have done particularly well on an examination, your instructor brings your test papers into the classroom saying, "Here's some *bad* news for you: you all got A's and B's!" he is being ironic but not sarcastic. Sarcasm, we may say, is cruel, as a bully is cruel: it intends to give hurt. Satire is both cruel and kind, as a surgeon is cruel and kind: it gives hurt in the interest of the patient or of society. Irony is neither cruel nor kind: it is simply a device, like a surgeon's scalpel, for performing any operation more skillfully.

Though verbal irony always implies the opposite of what is said, it has many gradations, and only in its simplest forms does it mean *only* the opposite of what is said. In more complex forms it means both what is said and the opposite of what is said, at once, though in different ways and with different degrees of emphasis. When Terence's critic, in Housman's "Terence, this is stupid stuff" (page 649) says, "'*Pretty* friendship 'tis to rhyme / Your friends to death before their time'" (11–12), we may substitute the literal *sorry* for the ironic "pretty" with little or no loss of meaning. When Terence speaks in reply, however, of the pleasure of drunkenness—"And down in *lovely* muck I've lain, / Happy till I woke again" (35–36)—we cannot substitute *loathsome* for "lovely" without considerable loss of meaning, for while muck is actually extremely unpleasant to lie in, it may *seem* lovely to an intoxicated person. Thus two meanings—one the opposite of the other—operate at once.

Like all figures of speech, verbal irony runs the danger of being misunderstood. With irony, the risks are perhaps greater than with other figures, for if metaphor is misunderstood, the result may be simply bewilderment; but if irony is misunderstood, the reader goes away with an idea exactly the opposite of what the user meant to convey. The results of misunderstanding if, for instance, you ironically called someone a numbskull might be calamitous. For this reason the user of irony must be very skillful in its use, conveying by an altered tone, or by a wink of the eye or pen, that irony is intended; and the reader of literature must be always alert to recognize the subtle signs of irony.

No matter how broad or obvious the irony, a number of people in any large audience always will misunderstand. Artemus Ward used to protect himself against these people by writing at the bottom of his newspaper column, "This is writ ironical." But irony is most delightful and most effective when it is subtlest. It sets up a special understanding between writer and reader that may add either grace or force. If irony is too obvious, it sometimes seems merely crude. But if effectively used, it, like all figurative language, is capable of adding extra dimensions to meaning.

Barbie Doll

This girlchild was born as usual
and presented dolls that did pee-pee
and miniature GE stoves and irons
and wee lipsticks the color of cherry candy.
Then in the magic of puberty, a classmate said: 5
You have a great big nose and fat legs.

She was healthy, tested intelligent,
possessed strong arms and back,
abundant sexual drive and manual dexterity.
She went to and fro apologizing.   10
Everyone saw a fat nose on thick legs.

She was advised to play coy,
exhorted to come on hearty,
exercise, diet, smile and wheedle.
Her good nature wore out   15
like a fan belt.
So she cut off her nose and her legs
and offered them up.

In the casket displayed on satin she lay
with the undertaker's cosmetics painted on,   20
a turned-up putty nose,
dressed in a pink and white nightie.
Doesn't she look pretty? everyone said.
Consummation at last.
To every woman a happy ending.   25

Marge Piercy (b. 1936)

QUESTIONS

1. In what ways is the girl described in this poem different from a Barbie doll? Discuss the poem's contrast of the living girl, a human being with intelligence and healthy appetites, and the doll, an inanimate object.
2. The poem contains a surprising but apt simile: "Her good nature wore out / like a fan belt" (15–16). Why is the image of the fan belt appropriate here?
3. Why does the speaker mention the girl's "strong arms and back" (8) and her "manual dexterity" (9)? How do these qualities contribute to her fate?
4. Discuss the verbal irony in the phrase "the magic of puberty" (5) and in the last three lines. What is the target of this satire?

    The term *irony* always implies some sort of discrepancy or incongruity. In verbal irony the discrepancy is between what is said and what is meant. In other forms the discrepancy may be between appearance and reality or between expectation and fulfillment. These other forms of irony are, on the whole, more important resources for the poet than is verbal irony. Two types are especially important.

In **dramatic irony** the discrepancy is not between what the speaker says and what the speaker means but between what the speaker says and what the poem means. The speaker's words may be perfectly straightforward, but the author, by putting these words in a particular speaker's mouth, may be indicating to the reader ideas or attitudes quite opposed to those the speaker is voicing. This form of irony is more complex than verbal irony and demands a more complex response from the reader. It may be used not only to convey attitudes but also to illuminate character, for the author who uses it is indirectly commenting not only upon the value of the ideas uttered but also upon the nature of the person who utters them. Such comment may be harsh, gently mocking, or sympathetic.

The Chimney Sweeper

When my mother died I was very young,
And my father sold me while yet my tongue
Could scarcely cry "'weep! 'weep! 'weep! 'weep!"
So your chimneys I sweep, and in soot I sleep.

There's little Tom Dacre, who cried when his head,   5
That curled like a lamb's back, was shaved; so I said,
"Hush, Tom! never mind it, for, when your head's bare,
You know that the soot cannot spoil your white hair."

And so he was quiet, and that very night,
As Tom was asleeping, he had such a sight!   10
That thousands of sweepers, Dick, Joe, Ned, and Jack,
Were all of them locked up in coffins of black.

And by came an Angel who had a bright key,
And he opened the coffins and set them all free;
Then down a green plain leaping, laughing, they run,   15
And wash in a river, and shine in the sun.

Then naked and white, all their bags left behind,
They rise upon clouds and sport in the wind;
And the Angel told Tom, if he'd be a good boy,
He'd have God for his father, and never want joy.   20

And so Tom awoke, and we rose in the dark,
And got with our bags and our brushes to work.

Though the morning was cold, Tom was happy and warm;
So if all do their duty they need not fear harm.

William Blake (1757–1827)

QUESTIONS

1. In the eighteenth century small boys, sometimes no more than four or five years old, were employed to climb up the narrow chimney flues and clean them, collecting the soot in bags. Such boys, sometimes sold to the master sweepers by their parents, were miserably treated by their masters and often suffered disease and physical deformity. Characterize the boy who speaks in this poem. How do his and the poet's attitudes toward his lot in life differ? How, especially, are the meanings of the poet and the speaker different in lines 3, 7–8, and 24?

2. The dream in lines 11–20, besides being a happy dream, can be interpreted allegorically. Point out possible significances of the sweepers' being "locked up in coffins of black" (12) and the Angel's releasing them with a bright key to play upon green plains.

A third type of irony, **irony of situation**, occurs when a discrepancy exists between the actual circumstances and those that would seem appropriate or between what one anticipates and what actually comes to pass. If a man and his second wife, on the first night of their honeymoon, are accidentally seated at the theater next to the man's first wife, we should call the situation ironic. When, in O. Henry's famous short story "The Gift of the Magi," a poor young husband pawns his gold watch, in order to buy his wife a set of combs for her hair for Christmas, and his wife sells her long brown hair, in order to buy a fob for her husband's watch, the situation is ironic. When King Midas in the famous fable is granted his wish that anything he touch turn to gold, and then finds that he cannot eat because even his food turns to gold, the situation is ironic. When Coleridge's Ancient Mariner finds himself in the middle of the ocean with "Water, water, everywhere" but not a "drop to drink," the situation is ironic. In each case the circumstances are not what would seem appropriate or what we would expect.

Dramatic irony and irony of situation are powerful devices for poetry, for, like symbol, they enable a poem to suggest meanings without stating them—to communicate a great deal more than is said. We have seen one effective use of irony of situation in "The Widow's Lament in Springtime" (page 693). Another is in "Ozymandias," which follows.

Ozymandias

I met a traveler from an antique land
Who said: Two vast and trunkless legs of stone
Stand in the desert . . . Near them, on the sand,
Half sunk, a shattered visage lies, whose frown,
And wrinkled lip, and sneer of cold command   5
Tell that its sculptor well those passions read
Which yet survive, stamped on these lifeless things,
The hand that mocked them, and the heart that fed;
And on the pedestal these words appear:
"My name is Ozymandias, king of kings;   10
Look on my works, ye Mighty, and despair!"
Nothing beside remains. Round the decay
Of that colossal wreck, boundless and bare
The lone and level sands stretch far away.

Percy Bysshe Shelley (1792–1822)

QUESTIONS

1. "[S]urvive" (7) is a transitive verb with "hand" and "heart" as direct objects. Whose hand? Whose heart? What figure of speech is exemplified in "hand" and "heart"?
2. Characterize Ozymandias.
3. Ozymandias was an ancient Egyptian tyrant. This poem was first published in 1817. Of what is Ozymandias a *symbol*? What contemporary reference might the poem have had in Shelley's time?
4. What is the theme of the poem and how is it "stated"?

Irony and paradox may be trivial or powerful devices, depending on their use. At their worst they may degenerate into mere mannerism and mental habit. At their best they may greatly extend the dimensions of meaning in a work of literature. Because irony and paradox demand an exercise of critical intelligence, they are particularly valuable as safeguards against sentimentality.

EXERCISES

Identify the figure in each of the following quotations as paradox, overstatement, understatement, or irony—and explain the use to which the figure is put (emotional emphasis, humor, satire, etc.).

1. Poetry is a language that tells us, through a more or less emotional reaction, something that cannot be said.   *Edwin Arlington Robinson*

2. Christians have burnt each other, quite persuaded
   That all the Apostles would have done as they did.   *Lord Byron*
3. A man who could make so vile a pun would not scruple to pick a pocket.
                                                             John Dennis
4. Last week I saw a woman flayed, and you will hardly believe how much it
   altered her person for the worse.   *Jonathan Swift*
5. . . . Where ignorance is bliss, / 'Tis folly to be wise. *Thomas Gray*
6. All night I made my bed to swim; with my tears I dissolved my couch.
                                                             Psalms 6.6
7. Believe him, he has known the world too long,
   And seen the death of much immortal song.   *Alexander Pope*
8. Cowards die many times before their deaths;
   The valiant never taste of death but once.   *William Shakespeare*
9. . . . all men would be cowards if they durst.   *John Wilmot, Earl of Rochester*

REVIEWING CHAPTER SEVEN

1. Distinguish between paradoxical actions and paradoxical statements, and explain how paradoxical statements may usually be
   resolved—that is, how their underlying validity is determined.
2. Define overstatement and understatement, and draw the distinction between stating what is less than is true and underemphasiz-
   ing what is true.
3. Review the definitions of sarcasm and satire.
4. Using examples from the poems that follow in this chapter, define
   the three principal forms of irony and demonstrate how the ironies
   contribute meaning or forcefulness to the poems.

Lady Luncheon Club

Her counsel was accepted: the times are grave.
A man was needed who would make them think,
And pay him from the petty cash account.

Our woman checked her golden watch,
The speaker has a plane to catch.
Dessert is served (and just in time).   5

The lecturer leans, thrusts forth his head
And neck and chest, arms akimbo

On the lectern top. He summons up
Sincerity as one might call a favored   10
Pet.

He understands the female rage,
Why Eve was lustful and
Delilah's
Grim deceit.   15

Our woman thinks:
(This cake is much too sweet).

He sighs for youthful death
And rape at ten, and murder of
The soul stretched over long.   20

Our woman notes:
(This coffee's much too strong).

The jobless streets of
Wine and wandering when
Mornings promise no bright relief.   25

She claps her hands and writes
Upon her pad: (Next time the
Speaker must be brief).

Maya Angelou (b. 1928)

QUESTIONS

1. What ironic discrepancy exists between lines 1–2 and line 3? Between lines 3 and 4?
2. What other ironies do you detect?
3. Could you make the case that the sentence in lines 9–11 might represent the central theme of the poem? Does it apply to more than the guest speaker?

Batter my heart, three-personed God

Batter my heart, three-personed God; for you
As yet but knock, breathe, shine, and seek to mend;
That I may rise and stand, o'erthrow me, and bend

Your force to break, blow, burn, and make me new.
I, like an usurped town, to another due,   5
Labor to admit you, but oh, to no end;
Reason, your viceroy in me, me should defend,
But is captived, and proves weak or untrue.
Yet dearly I love you and would be lovèd fain,°   gladly
But am betrothed unto your enemy;   10
Divorce me, untie or break that knot again,
Take me to you, imprison me, for I,
Except° you enthrall me, never shall be free,   unless
Nor ever chaste, except you ravish me.

John Donne (1572–1631)

QUESTIONS

1. In this sonnet (one in a group called "Holy Sonnets") the speaker addresses
   God in a series of metaphors and paradoxes. What is the paradox in the first
   quatrain? To what is the "three-personed God" metaphorically compared? To
   what is the speaker compared? Can the first three verbs of the parallel lines
   2 and 4 be taken as addressed to specific "persons" of the Trinity (Father, Son,
   Holy Spirit)? If so, to which are "knock" and "break" addressed? "breathe" and
   "blow"? "shine" and "burn"? (What concealed pun helps in the attribution of
   the last pair? What etymological pun in the attribution of the second pair?)
2. To what does the speaker compare himself in the second quatrain? To what is
   God compared? Who is the usurper? What role does "Reason" (7) play in this
   political metaphor, and why is it a weak one?
3. To what does the speaker compare himself in the sestet (lines 9–14)? To
   what does he compare God? Who is the "enemy" (10)? Resolve the paradox
   in lines 12–13 by explaining the double meaning of "enthrall." Resolve the
   paradox in line 14 by explaining the double meaning of "ravish."

Sorting Laundry

Folding clothes,
I think of folding you
into my life.

Our king-sized sheets
like tablecloths
for the banquets of giants,   5

pillowcases, despite so many
washings, seams still
holding our dreams.

Towels patterned orange and green,   10
flowered pink and lavender,
gaudy, bought on sale,

reserved, we said, for the beach,
refusing, even after years,
to bleach into respectability.   15

So many shirts and skirts and pants
recycling week after week, head over heels
recapitulating themselves.

All those wrinkles
to be smoothed, or else   20
ignored; they're in style.

Myriad uncoupled socks
which went paired into the foam
like those creatures in the ark.

And what's shrunk   25
is tough to discard
even for Goodwill.

In pockets, surprises:
forgotten matches,
lost screws clinking on enamel;   30

paper clips, whatever they held
between shiny jaws, now
dissolved or clogging the drain;

well-washed dollars, legal tender
for all debts public and private,   35
intact despite agitation;

and, gleaming in the maelstrom,
one bright dime,
broken necklace of good gold

you brought from Kuwait,   40
the strangely tailored shirt
left by a former lover. . . .

If you were to leave me,
if I were to fold
only my own clothes,   45

the convexes and concaves
of my blouses, panties, stockings, bras
turned upon themselves,

a mountain of unsorted wash
could not fill   50
the empty side of the bed.

Elisavietta Ritchie (b. 1932)

QUESTIONS

1. Explain the metaphor in the first stanza. Where does the poem explicitly
   return to it? What psychological association connects lines 41–42 to
   line 43?
2. Explain how the length of the poem supports the overstatement in line 49.
   What is the speaker's attitude toward the "you" in the poem, and toward her
   role as housekeeper?

The History Teacher

Trying to protect his students' innocence
he told them the Ice Age was really just
the Chilly Age, a period of a million years
when everyone had to wear sweaters.

And the Stone Age became the Gravel Age   5
named after the long driveways of the time.

The Spanish Inquisition was nothing more
than an outbreak of questions such as
"How far is it from here to Madrid?"
"What do you call the matador's hat?"   10

The War of the Roses took place in a garden,
and the Enola Gay dropped one tiny atom
on Japan.

The children would leave his classroom
for the playground to torment the weak   15
and the smart,
mussing up their hair and breaking their glasses,

while he gathered up his notes and walked home
past flower beds and white picket fences,
wondering if they would believe that soldiers   20
in the Boer War told long, rambling stories
designed to make the enemy nod off.

Billy Collins (b. 1941)

QUESTIONS

1. Vocabulary: *Spanish Inquisition* (7), *War of the Roses* (11) (usually with the plural "Wars"), *Boer War* (21). Enola Gay (12) was the name of the mother of the pilot who dropped the atomic bomb on Hiroshima and who named his plane in her honor.
2. The first two references are to extended periods of prehistory, both of them made humorous by the anachronistic references to "sweaters" (4) and "driveways" (6). What do the remaining four historical references have in common? How does the speaker bring humor to them?
3. This poem employs a particular kind of understatement called "euphemism," the substitution of a less offensive or severe term for one that might give offense. In the first line, the speaker explains why the teacher uses this device. What situational irony is revealed in lines 14–17? Considering lines 18–19, who is actually innocent in this poem?
4. Beyond the humor of the poem, what serious meanings can you discern?

Mid-Term Break

I sat all morning in the college sick bay
Counting bells knelling classes to a close.
At two o'clock our neighbors drove me home.

In the porch I met my father crying—
He had always taken funerals in stride—   5
And Big Jim Evans saying it was a hard blow.

The baby cooed and laughed and rocked the pram
When I came in, and I was embarrassed
By old men standing up to shake my hand

And tell me they were 'sorry for my trouble.'   10
Whispers informed strangers I was the eldest,
Away at school, as my mother held my hand

In hers and coughed out angry tearless sighs.
At ten o'clock the ambulance arrived
With the corpse, stanched and bandaged by the nurses.   15

Next morning I went up into the room. Snowdrops
And candles soothed the bedside; I saw him
For the first time in six weeks. Paler now,

Wearing a poppy bruise on his left temple,
He lay in the four-foot box as in his cot.   20
No gaudy scars, the bumper knocked him clear.

A four-foot box, a foot for every year.

Seamus Heaney (b. 1939)

QUESTIONS

1. Vocabulary: *knelling* (2), *stanched* (15), *Snowdrops* (16).
2. Describe in your own words the "story" being told in this narrative poem. Who is the speaker, and what is his attitude toward this event of his distant past?
3. How would you describe the general tone of the poem? Is the speaker making use of understatement or overstatement in conveying his emotion?
4. Discuss the impact of the final line. Why is the line set off in a separate stanza by itself?

A Considerable Speck

(Microscopic)

A speck that would have been beneath my sight
On any but a paper sheet so white
Set off across what I had written there.
And I had idly poised my pen in air
To stop it with a period of ink   5

When something strange about it made me think.
This was no dust speck by my breathing blown,
But unmistakably a living mite
With inclinations it could call its own.
It paused as with suspicion of my pen,   10
And then came racing wildly on again
To where my manuscript was not yet dry;
Then paused again and either drank or smelt—
With loathing, for again it turned to fly.
Plainly with an intelligence I dealt.   15
It seemed too tiny to have room for feet,
Yet must have had a set of them complete
To express how much it didn't want to die.
It ran with terror and with cunning crept.
It faltered: I could see it hesitate;   20
Then in the middle of the open sheet
Cower down in desperation to accept
Whatever I accorded it of fate.
I have none of the tenderer-than-thou
Collectivistic regimenting love   25
With which the modern world is being swept.
But this poor microscopic item now!
Since it was nothing I knew evil of
I let it lie there till I hope it slept.

I have a mind myself and recognize   30
Mind when I meet with it in any guise.
No one can know how glad I am to find
On any sheet the least display of mind.

Robert Frost (1874–1963)

QUESTIONS

1. Who is the speaker in this poem?
2. How would you describe the speaker's attitude toward the "speck" he sees on his manuscript sheet? How do lines 24–29 help clarify his attitude? At what is the irony in these lines directed?
3. Analyze the connotations of the following phrases: "beneath my sight" (1), "a period of ink" (5), "a living mite" (8), "On any sheet the least display of mind" (33).
4. What does the poem finally suggest is the significance of the mite? How does the irony in the last four lines articulate the larger theme of the poem?

The Unknown Citizen

(To JS/07/M/378 This Marble Monument Is Erected
by the State)

He was found by the Bureau of Statistics to be
One against whom there was no official complaint,
And all the reports on his conduct agree
That, in the modern sense of an old-fashioned word,
    he was a saint,
For in everything he did he served the Greater Community   5
Except for the War till the day he retired
He worked in a factory and never got fired,
But satisfied his employers, Fudge Motors Inc.
Yet he wasn't a scab or odd in his views,
For his Union reports that he paid his dues   10
(Our report on his Union shows it was sound),
And our Social Psychology workers found
That he was popular with his mates and liked a drink.
The Press are convinced that he bought a paper every day
And that his reactions to advertisements were normal   15
    in every way.
Policies taken out in his name prove that he was fully insured,
And his Health-card shows he was once in hospital
    but left it cured.
Both Producers Research and High-Grade Living declare
He was fully sensible to the advantages of the Installment Plan
And had everything necessary to the Modern Man,   20
A phonograph, a radio, a car and a frigidaire.
Our researchers into Public Opinion are content
That he held the proper opinions for the time of year;
When there was peace, he was for peace; when there was war,
    he went.
He was married and added five children to the population,   25
Which our Eugenist says was the right number for a parent
    of his generation,
And our teachers report that he never interfered with their
    education.
Was he free? Was he happy? The question is absurd:
Had anything been wrong, we should certainly have heard.

             W. H. Auden (1907–1973)

QUESTIONS

1. Vocabulary: *scab* (9), *Eugenist* (26).
2. Explain the allusion and the irony in the title. Why was the citizen "unknown"?
3. This obituary of an unknown state "hero" was apparently prepared by a functionary of the state. Give an account of the citizen's life and character from Auden's own point of view.
4. What trends in modern life and social organization does the poem satirize?

in the inner city

in the inner city
or
like we call it
home
we think a lot about uptown   5
and the silent nights
and the houses straight as
dead men
and the pastel lights
and we hang on to our no place   10
happy to be alive
and in the inner city
or
like we call it
home   15

Lucille Clifton (b. 1936)

QUESTIONS

1. In what contexts is the term "inner city" most often used, and what is it usually meant to imply?
2. What are the connotations of "silent nights" (6), "straight as / dead men" (7–8), and "pastel lights" (9)? By implication, what contrasting qualities might be found in the life of the inner city?
3. Is the irony in this poem verbal or dramatic?

My Last Duchess

Ferrara

That's my last duchess painted on the wall,
Looking as if she were alive. I call
That piece a wonder, now; Fra Pandolf's hands

Worked busily a day, and there she stands.
Will 't please you sit and look at her? I said   5
"Fra Pandolf" by design, for never read
Strangers like you that pictured countenance,
The depth and passion of its earnest glance,
But to myself they turned (since none puts by
The curtain I have drawn for you, but I)   10
And seemed as they would ask me, if they durst,
How such a glance came there; so, not the first
Are you to turn and ask thus. Sir, 'twas not
Her husband's presence only, called that spot
Of joy into the Duchess' cheek; perhaps   15
Fra Pandolf chanced to say, "Her mantle laps
Over my lady's wrist too much," or, "Paint
Must never hope to reproduce the faint
Half-flush that dies along her throat." Such stuff
Was courtesy, she thought, and cause enough   20
For calling up that spot of joy. She had
A heart—how shall I say?—too soon made glad,
Too easily impressed; she liked whate'er
She looked on, and her looks went everywhere.
Sir, 'twas all one! My favor at her breast,   25
The dropping of the daylight in the West,
The bough of cherries some officious fool
Broke in the orchard for her, the white mule
She rode with round the terrace—all and each
Would draw from her alike the approving speech,   30
Or blush, at least. She thanked men—good! but thanked
Somehow—I know not how—as if she ranked
My gift of a nine-hundred-years-old name
With anybody's gift. Who'd stoop to blame
This sort of trifling? Even had you skill   35
In speech—which I have not—to make your will
Quite clear to such an one, and say, "Just this
Or that in you disgusts me; here you miss,
Or there exceed the mark"—and if she let
Herself be lessoned so, nor plainly set   40
Her wits to yours, forsooth, and made excuse,
—E'en then would be some stooping; and I choose
Never to stoop. Oh, sir, she smiled, no doubt,
Whene'er I passed her; but who passed without
Much the same smile? This grew; I gave commands;   45

Then all smiles stopped together. There she stands
As if alive. Will 't please you rise? We'll meet
The company below, then. I repeat,
The Count your master's known munificence
Is ample warrant that no just pretense   50
Of mine for dowry will be disallowed;
Though his fair daughter's self, as I avowed
At starting, is my object. Nay, we'll go
Together down, sir. Notice Neptune, though,
Taming a sea-horse, thought a rarity,   55
Which Claus of Innsbruck cast in bronze for me!

Robert Browning (1812–1889)

QUESTIONS

1. Vocabulary: *favor* (25), *officious* (27), *munificence* (49).
2. Ferrara is in Italy. The time is during the Renaissance, probably the sixteenth century. To whom is the Duke speaking? What is the occasion? Are the Duke's remarks about his last Duchess a digression, or do they have some relation to the business at hand?
3. Characterize the Duke as fully as you can. How does your characterization differ from the Duke's opinion of himself? What kind of irony is this?
4. Why was the Duke dissatisfied with his last Duchess? Was it sexual jealousy? What opinion do you get of the Duchess's personality, and how does it differ from the Duke's opinion?
5. What characteristics of the Italian Renaissance appear in the poem (marriage customs, social classes, art)? What is the Duke's attitude toward art? Is it insincere?
6. What happened to the Duchess? Should Browning have told us?

SUGGESTIONS FOR WRITING

1. Discuss the irony in one of the following poems. Does the poem employ verbal irony, dramatic irony, or irony of situation? How does the ironic content of the poem heighten its impact?
   a. Byron, "Stanzas" (page 853).
   b. Jonson, "Still to be neat" (page 900).
   c. Crane, "War Is Kind" (page 953).
   d. Dickinson, "I died for Beauty—but was scarce" (page 956).
   e. Larkin, "Aubade" (page 984).

2. Each of the following poems deals, at least in part, with the relationship between the individual human being and a society that imposes a dehumanizing conformity. Choose any two of the poems and compare their use(s) of irony in conveying this theme.

  a. Angelou, "Harlem Hopscotch" (page 740).

  b. Dickinson, "Much Madness is divinest Sense" (page 750).

  c. Piercy, "Barbie Doll" (page 754).

  d. Auden, "The Unknown Citizen" (page 767).

  e. Atwood, "Siren Song" (page 780).

  f. Hughes, "Theme for English B" (page 976).

Chapter Eight

Allusion

The famous English diplomat and letter writer Lord Chesterfield once was invited to a great dinner given by the Spanish ambassador. At the conclusion of the meal the host rose and proposed a toast to his master, the king of Spain, whom he compared to the sun. The French ambassador followed with a health to the king of France, whom he likened to the moon. It was then Lord Chesterfield's turn. "Your excellencies have taken from me," he said, "all the greatest luminaries of heaven, and the stars are too small for me to make a comparison of my royal master; I therefore beg leave to give your excellencies—Joshua!"*

A reader familiar with the Bible—that is, one who recognizes the biblical allusion—will recognize the witty point of Lord Chesterfield's story. For an **allusion**—a reference to something in history or previous literature—is, like a richly connotative word or a symbol, a means of suggesting far more than it says. The one word "Joshua," in the context of Chesterfield's toast, calls up in the reader's mind the whole biblical story of how the Israelite captain stopped the sun and the moon in order that the Israelites might finish a battle and conquer their enemies before nightfall (Josh. 10.12–14). The force of the toast lies in its extreme economy; it says so much in so little, and it exercises the minds of the readers to make the connection for themselves.

The effect of Chesterfield's allusion is chiefly humorous or witty, but allusions also may have a powerful emotional effect. The essayist William Hazlitt writes of addressing a fashionable audience about the lexicographer Samuel Johnson. Speaking of Johnson's great heart and of his charity to the unfortunate, Hazlitt recounted how, finding a drunken prostitute lying in Fleet Street late at night, Johnson carried her on his broad back to the address she managed to give him. The audience, unable to face the picture of the famous dictionary-maker doing such a thing, broke out in titters and expostulations, whereupon Hazlitt simply said: "I remind you, ladies and gentlemen, of the parable of the Good Samaritan." The audience was promptly silenced.†

*Samuel Shellabarger, *Lord Chesterfield and His World* (Boston: Little, Brown, 1951) 132.
†Jacques Barzun, *Teacher in America* (Boston: Little, Brown, 1945) 160.

Allusions are a means of reinforcing the emotion or the ideas of one's own work with the emotion or ideas of another work or occasion. Because they may compact so much meaning in so small a space, they are extremely useful to the poet.

"Out, Out—"

The buzz-saw snarled and rattled in the yard
And made dust and dropped stove-length sticks of wood,
Sweet-scented stuff when the breeze drew across it.
And from there those that lifted eyes could count
Five mountain ranges one behind the other   5
Under the sunset far into Vermont.
And the saw snarled and rattled, snarled and rattled,
As it ran light, or had to bear a load.
And nothing happened: day was all but done.
Call it a day, I wish they might have said   10
To please the boy by giving him the half hour
That a boy counts so much when saved from work.
His sister stood beside them in her apron
To tell them "Supper." At the word, the saw,
As if to prove saws knew what supper meant,   15
Leaped out at the boy's hand, or seemed to leap—
He must have given the hand. However it was,
Neither refused the meeting. But the hand!
The boy's first outcry was a rueful laugh,
As he swung toward them holding up the hand   20
Half in appeal, but half as if to keep
The life from spilling. Then the boy saw all—
Since he was old enough to know, big boy
Doing a man's work, though a child at heart—
He saw all spoiled. "Don't let him cut my hand off—   25
The doctor, when he comes. Don't let him, sister!"
So. But the hand was gone already.
The doctor put him in the dark of ether.
He lay and puffed his lips out with his breath.
And then—the watcher at his pulse took fright.   30
No one believed. They listened at his heart.
Little—less—nothing!—and that ended it.
No more to build on there. And they, since they
Were not the one dead, turned to their affairs.

Robert Frost (1874–1963)

QUESTIONS

1. How does this poem differ from a newspaper account that might have dealt with the same incident?
2. To whom does "they" (33) refer? The boy's family? The doctor and medical attendants? Casual onlookers? Need we assume that all these people—whoever they are—turned immediately "to their affairs" (34)? Does the ending of this poem seem to you callous or merely realistic? Would a more tearful and sentimental ending have made the poem better or worse?
3. What is the figure of speech in lines 21–22?

Allusions vary widely in the burden put on them by the poet to convey meaning. Lord Chesterfield risked his whole meaning on his hearers' recognizing his allusion. Robert Frost in "'Out, Out—'" makes his meaning entirely clear even for the reader who does not recognize the allusion contained in the poem's title. His theme is the uncertainty and unpredictability of life, which may end accidentally at any moment, and the tragic waste of human potentiality that takes place when such premature deaths occur. A boy who is already "Doing a man's work" and gives every promise of having a useful life ahead of him is suddenly wiped out. There seems no rational explanation for either the accident or the death. The only comment to be made is, "No more to build on there."

Frost's title, however, is an allusion to one of the most famous passages in all English literature, and it offers a good illustration of how a poet may use allusion not only to reinforce emotion but also to help define his theme. The passage is that in *Macbeth* in which Macbeth has just been informed of his wife's death. A good many readers will recall the key phrase, "Out, out, brief candle!" with its underscoring of the tragic brevity and uncertainty of life. For some readers, however, the allusion will summon up the whole passage in Act 5, scene 5, in which Macbeth uses this phrase:

> She should have died hereafter;
> There would have been a time for such a word.
> Tomorrow, and tomorrow, and tomorrow
> Creeps in this petty pace from day to day
> To the last syllable of recorded time;   5
> And all our yesterdays have lighted fools
> The way to dusty death. Out, out, brief candle!
> Life's but a walking shadow, a poor player,
> That struts and frets his hour upon the stage
> And then is heard no more. It is a tale   10
> Told by an idiot, full of sound and fury,
> Signifying nothing.

William Shakespeare (1564–1616)

QUESTION

1. Examine Macbeth's speech for examples of personification, apostrophe, and metonymy. How many metaphors for an individual human life does it present?

Macbeth's first words underscore the theme of premature death. The boy also "should have died hereafter." The rest of the passage, with its marvelous evocation of the vanity and meaninglessness of life, expresses neither Shakespeare's philosophy nor, ultimately, Frost's, but it is Macbeth's philosophy at the time of his bereavement, and it is likely to express the feelings of us all when such tragic accidents occur. Life does indeed seem cruel and meaningless, "a tale / Told by an idiot, . . . / Signifying nothing," when human life and potentiality are thus without explanation so suddenly ended.

Allusions also vary widely in the number of readers to whom they will be familiar. Poets, in using an allusion, as in using a figure of speech, are always in danger of being misunderstood. What appeals powerfully to one reader may lose another reader altogether. But poets must assume a certain fund of common experience in readers. They could not even write about the ocean unless they could assume that readers have seen the ocean or pictures of it. In the same way poets assume a certain common fund of literary experience, most frequently of classical mythology, Shakespeare, or the Bible—particularly the King James Version. Poets are often justified in expecting a rather wide range of literary experience in readers, for the people who read poetry for pleasure are generally intelligent and well-read. But, obviously, beginning readers will not have this range, just as they will not know the meanings of as many words as will more experienced readers. Students should therefore be prepared to look up certain allusions, just as they should look up in their dictionaries the meanings of unfamiliar words. They will find that every increase in knowledge broadens their base for understanding both literature and life.

REVIEWING CHAPTER EIGHT

1. Show how allusion is similar in its effect to connotative language as well as to symbolism.
2. Using examples from the poems that follow in this chapter, draw clear distinctions between allusions that reinforce the ideas in a poem and allusions that intensify the emotions being expressed—and note those allusions that carry both intellectual and emotional meanings.

in Just—

in Just-
spring   when the world is mud-
luscious the little
lame balloonman

whistles   far   and wee   5

and eddieandbill come
running from marbles and
piracies and it's
spring

when the world is puddle-wonderful   10

the queer
old balloonman whistles
far   and   wee
and bettyandisbel come dancing

from hop-scotch and jump-rope and   15

it's
spring
and
        the

                goat-footed   20

balloonMan   whistles
far
and
wee

e. e. cummings (1894–1962)

QUESTION

1. Why is the balloonman called "goat-footed" (20)? How does the identification made by this mythological allusion enrich the meaning of the poem?

Yet Do I Marvel

I doubt not God is good, well-meaning, kind,
And did He stoop to quibble could tell why
The little buried mole continues blind,
Why flesh that mirrors Him must some day die,
Make plain the reason tortured Tantalus   5
Is baited by the fickle fruit, declare
If merely brute caprice dooms Sisyphus
To struggle up a never-ending stair.
Inscrutable His ways are, and immune
To catechism by a mind too strewn   10
With petty cares to slightly understand
What awful brain compels His awful hand.
Yet do I marvel at this curious thing:
To make a poet black and bid him sing!

Countee Cullen (1903–1946)

QUESTIONS

1. Vocabulary: *quibble* (2), *caprice* (7), *catechism* (10), *awful* (12). If you are
   unfamiliar with the allusions to Tantalus (5) and Sisyphus (7), consult a
   reference book on Greek mythology.
2. The poem presents a series of indirect questions about God's reasons and
   purposes. Restate them as direct questions, and determine the order of their
   relative importance. Why does the poet use the last of these questions as the
   conclusion of the poem?
3. Identify the ironies in the poem. What is the effect of the understated phrase
   "curious thing" (13)?

On His Blindness

When I consider how my light is spent
    Ere half my days in this dark world and wide,
    And that one talent which is death to hide
    Lodged with me useless, though my soul more bent
To serve therewith my Maker, and present   5
    My true account, lest he returning chide,
    "Doth God exact day-labor, light denied?"
    I fondly ask. But Patience, to prevent

That murmur, soon replies, "God doth not need
  Either man's work or his own gifts. Who best   10
  Bear his mild yoke, they serve him best. His state
Is kingly: thousands at his bidding speed,
  And post o'er land and ocean without rest;
  They also serve who only stand and wait."

John Milton (1608–1674)

QUESTIONS

1. Vocabulary: *spent* (1), *fondly* (8), *prevent* (8), *post* (13).
2. What two meanings has "talent" (3)? What is Milton's "one talent"?
3. The poem is unified and expanded in its dimensions by a biblical allusion that Milton's original readers would have recognized immediately. What is it? If you do not know, look up Matthew 25.14–30. In what ways is the situation in the poem similar to that in the parable? In what ways is it different?
4. What is the point of the poem?

Miniver Cheevy

Miniver Cheevy, child of scorn,
  Grew lean while he assailed the seasons;
He wept that he was ever born,
  And he had reasons.

Miniver loved the days of old   5
  When swords were bright and steeds were prancing;
The vision of a warrior bold
  Would set him dancing.

Miniver sighed for what was not,
  And dreamed, and rested from his labors;   10
He dreamed of Thebes and Camelot,
  And Priam's neighbors.

Miniver mourned the ripe renown
  That made so many a name so fragrant;
He mourned Romance, now on the town,   15
  And Art, a vagrant.

Miniver loved the Medici,
  Albeit he had never seen one;

He would have sinned incessantly
  Could he have been one.   20

Miniver cursed the commonplace
  And eyed a khaki suit with loathing;
He missed the medieval grace
  Of iron clothing.

Miniver scorned the gold he sought,   25
  But sore annoyed was he without it;
Miniver thought, and thought, and thought,
  And thought about it.

Miniver Cheevy, born too late,
  Scratched his head and kept on thinking;   30
Miniver coughed, and called it fate,
  And kept on drinking.

Edwin Arlington Robinson (1869–1935)

QUESTIONS

1. Vocabulary: *khaki* (22). The phrase "on the town" (15) means "on charity" or "down and out."
2. Identify Thebes (11), Camelot (11), Priam (12), and the Medici (17). What names and what sort of life does each call up? What does Miniver's love of these names tell about him?
3. Discuss the phrase "child of scorn" (1). What does it mean? In how many ways is it applicable to Miniver?
4. What is Miniver's attitude toward material wealth?
5. The phrase "rested from his labors" (10) alludes to the Bible *and* to Greek mythology. Explore the ironic effect of comparing Miniver to the Creator (Genesis 2.2) and to Hercules. Point out other examples of irony in the poem and discuss their importance.
6. Can we call this a poem about a man whose "fate" was to be "born too late"? Explain your answer.

My Son the Man

Suddenly his shoulders get a lot wider,
the way Houdini would expand his body
while people were putting him in chains. It seems
no time since I would help him put on his sleeper,

guide his calves into the shadowy interior,   5
zip him up and toss him up and
catch his weight. I cannot imagine him
no longer a child, and I know I must get ready,
get over my fear of men now my son
is going to be one. This was not   10
what I had in mind when he pressed up through me like a
sealed trunk through the ice of the Hudson,
snapped the padlock, unsnaked the chains,
appeared in my arms. Now he looks at me
the way Houdini studied a box   15
to learn the way out, then smiled and let himself be manacled.

Sharon Olds (b. 1942)

QUESTIONS

1. "Harry Houdini" was the stage name of Erich Weiss (1874–1926), an escape
   artist whose most famous stunt was freeing himself after being chained, sealed
   in a padlocked trunk, and dropped into deep water.
2. To what event does the speaker compare Houdini's escape?
3. How does this allusion express the speaker's feelings about her son? Are they
   mixed feelings?

Siren Song

This is the one song everyone
would like to learn: the song
that is irresistible:

the song that forces men
to leap overboard in squadrons   5
even though they see the beached skulls

the song nobody knows
because anyone who has heard it
is dead, and the others can't remember.

Shall I tell you the secret   10
and if I do, will you get me
out of this bird suit?

I don't enjoy it here
squatting on this island
looking picturesque and mythical   15

with these two feathery maniacs,
I don't enjoy singing
this trio, fatal and valuable.

I will tell the secret to you,
to you, only to you.   20
Come closer. This song

is a cry for help: Help me!
Only you, only you can,
you are unique

at last. Alas   25
it is a boring song
but it works every time.

Margaret Atwood (b. 1939)

QUESTIONS

1. Vocabulary: *Siren* (title).
2. What weakness in men does the siren exploit? How is this allusive poem about relations between women and men?

Journey of the Magi

"A cold coming we had of it,
Just the worst time of the year
For a journey, and such a long journey:
The ways deep and the weather sharp,
The very dead of winter."   5
And the camels galled, sore-footed, refractory,
Lying down in the melting snow.
There were times we regretted
The summer palaces on slopes, the terraces,
And the silken girls bringing sherbet.   10
Then the camel men cursing and grumbling

And running away, and wanting their liquor and women,
And the night-fires going out, and the lack of shelters,
And the cities hostile and the towns unfriendly
And the villages dirty and charging high prices: 15
A hard time we had of it.
At the end we preferred to travel all night,
Sleeping in snatches,
With the voices singing in our ears, saying
That this was all folly.   20

Then at dawn we came down to a temperate valley,
Wet, below the snow line, smelling of vegetation;
With a running stream and a water-mill beating the darkness,
And three trees on the low sky,
And an old white horse galloped away in the meadow.   25
Then we came to a tavern with vine-leaves over the lintel,
Six hands at an open door dicing for pieces of silver,
And feet kicking the empty wine-skins.
But there was no information, and so we continued
And arrived at evening, not a moment too soon   30
Finding the place; it was (you may say) satisfactory.

All this was a long time ago, I remember,
And I would do it again, but set down
This set down
This: were we led all that way for   35
Birth or Death? There was a Birth, certainly,
We had evidence and no doubt. I had seen birth and death,
But had thought they were different; this Birth was
Hard and bitter agony for us, like Death, our death.
We returned to our places, these Kingdoms,   40
But no longer at ease here, in the old dispensation,
With an alien people clutching their gods.
I should be glad of another death.

                                          T. S. Eliot (1888–1965)

QUESTIONS

1. The biblical account of the journey of the Magi, or wise men, to Bethlehem is
   given in Matthew 2:1–12 and has since been elaborated by numerous
   legendary accretions. It has been made familiar through countless pageants
   and Christmas cards. How does this account differ from the familiar one?

Compare it with the biblical account. What has been added? What has been left out? What is the poet doing? (Lines 1–5 are in quotation marks because they are taken, with very slight modification, from a Christmas sermon [1622] by the Anglican bishop Lancelot Andrewes.)

2. Who is the speaker? Where and when is he speaking? What is the "old dispensation" (41) to which he refers, and why are the people "alien" (42)? Why does he speak of the "Birth" (38) as being "like Death" (39)? Of whose "Birth" and "Death" is he speaking? How does his life differ from the life he lived before his journey? What does he mean by saying that he would be "glad of another death" (43)?

3. This poem was written while the poet was undergoing religious conversion. (Eliot published it in 1927, the year he was confirmed in the Anglican Church.) Could the poem be considered a parable of the conversion experience? If so, how does this account differ from popular conceptions of this experience?

4. How do the images in the second section differ from those of the first? Do any of them suggest connections with the life of Christ?

Leda and the Swan

A sudden blow: the great wings beating still
Above the staggering girl, her thighs caressed
By the dark webs, her nape caught in his bill,
He holds her helpless breast upon his breast.

How can those terrified vague fingers push   5
The feathered glory from her loosening thighs?
And how can body, laid in that white rush,
But feel the strange heart beating where it lies?

A shudder in the loins engenders there
The broken wall, the burning roof and tower   10
And Agamemnon dead.
                    Being so caught up,
So mastered by the brute blood of the air,
Did she put on his knowledge with his power
Before the indifferent beak could let her drop?   15

William Butler Yeats (1865–1939)

QUESTIONS

1. What is the connection between Leda and "The broken wall, the burning roof and tower / And Agamemnon dead" (10–11)? If you do not know, look up the myth of Leda and the story of Agamemnon.

2. How does this poem do more than evoke an episode out of mythology? What is the significance of the question asked in the last two lines? How would you answer it?

SUGGESTIONS FOR WRITING

An allusion may present a comparison or parallel, or it may create an ironic contrast. Choosing one or more of the following examples, write an essay demonstrating that the poem(s) use allusion positively, to enrich the theme, or ironically, to undercut the speaker's ideas.

1. Larkin, "A Study of Reading Habits" (page 658) (allusions to types of cheap fiction).
2. Keats, "On the Sonnet" (page 792) (allusions to Andromeda and Midas).
3. Collins, "Sonnet" (page 793) (allusions to Petrarch and Laura).
4. Dickinson, "One dignity delays for all" (page 809, line 15) (allusion to Matthew 5.5).
5. Ferlinghetti, "Constantly risking absurdity" (page 648, line 29) (allusion to Charlie Chaplin).
6. Atwood, "Siren Song" (page 780) (allusion to Greek mythology).
7. Dove, "Persephone, Falling" (page 959) (allusion to Greek mythology).
8. Gwynn, "Snow White and the Seven Deadly Sins" (page 968) (allusion to Disney film and Christian tradition).
9. Hardy, "Channel Firing" (page 970) (historical and legendary allusions).
10. Keats, "Ode to a Nightingale" (page 981, line 66) (allusion to the Book of Ruth).

Chapter Nine

Meaning and Idea

Little Jack Horner

Little Jack Horner
Sat in a corner
Eating a Christmas pie.
He stuck in his thumb
And pulled out a plum   5
And said, "What a good boy am I!"

Anonymous

The meaning of a poem is the experience it expresses—nothing less. But readers who, baffled by a particular poem, ask perplexedly, "What does it *mean*?" are usually after something more specific than this. They want something they can grasp entirely with their minds. We may therefore find it useful to distinguish the **total meaning** of a poem— the experience it communicates (and which can be communicated in no other way)—from its **prose meaning**—the ingredient that can be separated out in the form of a prose paraphrase (see chapter 2). If we make this distinction, however, we must be careful not to confuse the two kinds of meaning. The prose meaning is no more the poem than a plum is a pie or a prune is a plum.

The prose meaning will not necessarily or perhaps even usually be an idea. It may be a story, a description, a statement of emotion, a presentation of human character, or some combination of these. "Porphyria's Lover" (page 857) tells a story; "The Eagle" (page 635) is primarily descriptive; "The Widow's Lament in Springtime" (page 693) is an expression of emotion; "My Last Duchess" (page 768) is an account of human character. None of these poems is directly concerned with ideas. Message-hunters will be baffled and disappointed by poetry of this kind because they will not find what they are looking for, and they may attempt to read some idea into the poem that is really not there. Yet ideas are also part of human experience, and therefore many poems are concerned, at least partially, with presenting ideas. But with these poems message-hunting is an even more dangerous activity, for the message-hunters are likely to think that the whole object of reading the poem is to find the message—that the idea is really the only important thing in it. Like Little Jack Horner, they will reach in and pluck out the idea and say, "What a good boy am I!" as if the pie existed for the plum.

The idea in a poem is only part of the total experience that it communicates. The value and worth of the poem are determined by the value of the total experience, not by the truth or the nobility of the idea itself. This is not to say that the truth of the idea is unimportant, or that its validity should not be examined and appraised. But a good idea alone will not make a good poem, nor will an idea with which the reader does not agree ruin one. Readers of poetry are receptive to all kinds of experience. They are able to make that "willing suspension of disbelief" that Coleridge characterized as constituting poetic faith. When one attends a performance of *Hamlet*, one is willing to forget for the time being that such a person as Hamlet never existed and that the events on the stage are fictions. Likewise, poetry readers should be willing to entertain imaginatively, for the time being, ideas they objectively regard as untrue. It is one way of better understanding these ideas and of enlarging the reader's own experience. The person who believes in God should be able to enjoy a good poem expressing atheistic ideas, just as the atheist should be able to appreciate a good poem in praise of God. The optimist should be able to find pleasure in pessimistic poetry, and the pessimist in optimistic poetry. The teetotaler should be able to enjoy *The Rubáiyát of Omar Khayyám*, and the winebibber a good poem in praise of abstinence. The primary value of a poem depends not so much on the truth of the idea presented as on the power with which it is communicated and on its being made a convincing part of a meaningful total experience. We must feel that the idea has been truly and deeply *felt* by the poet, and that the poet is doing something more than merely moralizing. The plum must be made part of a pie. If the plum is properly combined with other ingredients and if the pie is well baked, it should be enjoyable even for persons who do not care for the type of plums from which it is made. Consider, for instance, the following two poems.

Loveliest of Trees

> Loveliest of trees, the cherry now
> Is hung with bloom along the bough,
> And stands about the woodland ride
> Wearing white for Eastertide.

Now, of my threescore years and ten,   5
Twenty will not come again,
And take from seventy springs a score,
It only leaves me fifty more.

And since to look at things in bloom
Fifty springs are little room,   10
About the woodlands I will go
To see the cherry hung with snow.

A. E. Housman (1859–1936)

QUESTIONS

1. Very briefly, this poem presents a philosophy of life. In a sentence, what is it?
2. How old is the speaker? Why does he assume that his life will be seventy years in length? What is surprising about the words "only" (8) and "little" (10)?
3. A good deal of ink has been spilt over whether "snow" (12) is literal or figurative. What do you say? Justify your answer.

Stopping by Woods on a Snowy Evening

Whose woods these are I think I know.
His house is in the village though;
He will not see me stopping here
To watch his woods fill up with snow.

My little horse must think it queer   5
To stop without a farmhouse near
Between the woods and frozen lake
The darkest evening of the year.

He gives his harness bells a shake
To ask if there is some mistake.   10
The only other sound's the sweep
Of easy wind and downy flake.

The woods are lovely, dark and deep,
But I have promises to keep,
And miles to go before I sleep,   15
And miles to go before I sleep.

Robert Frost (1874–1963)

QUESTIONS
1. How do these two poems differ in idea?
2. What contrasts are suggested between the speaker in the second poem and
   (a) his horse and (b) the owner of the woods?

Both of these poems present ideas, the first more or less explicitly, the second symbolically. Perhaps the best way to get at the idea of the second poem is to ask two questions. First, why does the speaker stop? Second, why does he go on? He stops, we answer, to watch the woods fill up with snow—to observe a scene of natural beauty. He goes on, we answer, because he has "promises to keep"—that is, he has obligations to fulfill. He is momentarily torn between his love of beauty and these other various and complex claims that life has upon him. The small conflict in the poem is symbolic of a larger conflict in life. One part of the sensitive, thinking person would like to give up his life to the enjoyment of beauty and art. But another part is aware of larger duties and responsibilities—responsibilities owed, at least in part, to other human beings. The speaker in the poem would like to satisfy both impulses. But when the two conflict, he seems to suggest, the "promises" must take precedence.

The first poem also presents a philosophy but it is an opposing one. For the twenty-year-old speaker, the appreciation of beauty is of such importance that he will make it his lifelong dedication, filling his time with enjoying whatever the seasons bring. The metaphor comparing white cherry blossoms to snow suggests that each season has its own special beauty, though the immediate season is spring. In a limited life, one should seek out and delight in whatever beauty is present. Thoughtful readers will have to choose between these two philosophies—to commit themselves to one or the other—but this commitment should not destroy for them their enjoyment of either poem. If it does, they are reading for plums and not for pies.

Nothing we have said so far in this chapter should be construed as meaning that the truth or falsity of the idea in a poem is a matter of no importance. *Other things being equal*, good readers naturally will, and properly should, value more highly the poem whose idea they feel to be more mature and nearer to the heart of human experience. Some ideas, moreover, may seem so vicious or so foolish or so beyond the pale of normal human decency as to discredit *by themselves* the poems in which they are found. A rotten plum may spoil a pie. But good readers strive for intellectual flexibility and tolerance, and are able to entertain sympathetically ideas other than their own. They often will like a poem whose idea they disagree with better than one with an idea they accept. And, above all, they will not confuse the prose meaning of any poem with its total meaning. They will not mistake plums for pies.

REVIEWING CHAPTER NINE

1. The second paragraph of this chapter identifies four poems as not being "directly concerned with ideas"; examine those poems and demonstrate that although that statement is true of the prose meaning of each, the total meaning does in fact express an idea.
2. Explain how a poem that expresses an idea with which you do not agree may, nevertheless, be a source of appreciation and enjoyment.
3. The poems that follow in this chapter are paired in terms of their contrasted ideas; as you read them, practice discriminating between their ideas as we have done with the pair of poems by Housman and Frost, and determine which of the contrasted ideas more closely reflects your own beliefs.
4. Having determined where your beliefs are reflected, explain how the contrasting poem nevertheless has qualities you can admire.

The Rhodora:

On Being Asked, Whence Is the Flower?

In May, when sea-winds pierced our solitudes,
I found the fresh Rhodora in the woods,
Spreading its leafless blooms in a damp nook,
To please the desert and the sluggish brook.
The purple petals, fallen in the pool,   5
Made the black water with their beauty gay;
Here might the red-bird come his plumes to cool,
And court the flower that cheapens his array.
Rhodora! if the sages ask thee why
This charm is wasted on the earth and sky,   10
Tell them, dear, that if eyes were made for seeing,
Then Beauty is its own excuse for being:
Why thou wert there, O rival of the rose!

I never thought to ask, I never knew;
But, in my simple ignorance, suppose   15
The self-same Power that brought me there brought you.

Ralph Waldo Emerson (1803–1882)

QUESTIONS

1. Vocabulary: *Whence* (subtitle), *desert* (4), *cheapens* (8), *array* (8). The
rhodora (title) is a shrub that bears its rose-purple flowers before its leaves
appear.
2. Notice that the rhyme pattern of the first eight lines is repeated in the second
eight, providing an implied break after line 8. What else creates a break or
shift at that point?
3. The speaker credits himself with "simple ignorance." Why is that phrase
ironic?

Design

I found a dimpled spider, fat and white,
On a white heal-all, holding up a moth
Like a white piece of rigid satin cloth—
Assorted characters of death and blight
Mixed ready to begin the morning right,   5
Like the ingredients of a witches' broth—
A snow-drop spider, a flower like a froth,
And dead wings carried like a paper kite.

What had that flower to do with being white,
The wayside blue and innocent heal-all?   10
What brought the kindred spider to that height,
Then steered the white moth thither in the night?
What but design of darkness to appall?—
If design govern in a thing so small.

Robert Frost (1874–1963)

QUESTIONS

1. Vocabulary: *characters* (4), *snow-drop* (7).
2. The heal-all is a wildflower, usually blue or violet but occasionally white,
found blooming along roadsides in the summer. It was once supposed to have
healing qualities, hence its name. Of what significance, scientific and poetic,

is the fact that the spider, the heal-all, and the moth are all white? Of what poetic significance is the fact that the spider is "dimpled" and "fat" and like a "snow-drop," and that the flower is "innocent" and named "heal-all"?

3. The "argument from design"—that the manifest existence of design in the universe implies the existence of a Great Designer—was a favorite eighteenth-century argument for the existence of God. What twist does Frost give the argument? What answer does he suggest to the question in lines 11–12? How comforting is the apparent concession in line 14?

4. Contrast Frost's poem in content and emotional effect with "The Rhodora." Is it possible to like both?

I never saw a Moor

I never saw a Moor—
I never saw the Sea—
Yet know I how the Heather looks
And what a Billow be.

I never spoke with God   5
Nor visited in Heaven—
Yet certain am I of the spot
As if the Checks° were given—   tickets

Emily Dickinson (1830–1886)

QUESTIONS

1. If the speaker never saw the moors or the ocean, how might she still know what they look like? What enables her to be "certain" (7) of heaven as her eventual destination?

2. Dickinson did not title her poems, but if you were to give a title to this one, what would it be? Discuss the appropriateness of your choice.

"Faith" is a fine invention

"Faith" is a fine invention
When Gentlemen can *see*—
But *Microscopes* are prudent
In an Emergency.

Emily Dickinson (1830–1886)

QUESTIONS

1. Discuss the images of vision in this poem. What different kinds of "seeing" do these images encompass?
2. To what kind of an "Emergency" (4) might this speaker be referring?
3. Though dealing with a serious subject, the poem has a humorous tone. Discuss the effectiveness and appropriateness of the poem's wit and humor.
4. How does the assertion here compare with that in the preceding poem? Must the reader assume that Dickinson is employing a fictitious persona in one of the poems? How could both poems represent one person's point of view?

On the Sonnet

If by dull rhymes our English must be chained,
And like Andromeda, the sonnet sweet
Fettered, in spite of painéd loveliness,
Let us find, if we must be constrained,
Sandals more interwoven and complete   5
To fit the naked foot of Poesy:
Let us inspect the lyre, and weigh the stress
Of every chord, and see what may be gained
By ear industrious, and attention meet;
Misers of sound and syllable, no less   10
Than Midas of his coinage, let us be
Jealous of dead leaves in the bay-wreath crown;
So, if we may not let the Muse be free,
She will be bound with garlands of her own.

John Keats (1795–1821)

QUESTIONS

1. Vocabulary: *Andromeda* (2), *meet* (9), *Midas* (11).
2. The poem prescribes a specific approach to writing sonnets. What qualities does the speaker suggest a good sonnet should have?
3. The speaker compares poetry to a foot and the sonnet form to a sandal. What does he mean by suggesting that the sonnet-sandals should be "more interwoven and complete" (5)?
4. What negative qualities does the poem imply that bad sonnets display?

Sonnet

All we need is fourteen lines, well, thirteen now,
and after this one just a dozen
to launch a little ship on love's storm-tossed seas,
then only ten more left like rows of beans.
How easily it goes unless you get Elizabethan   5
and insist the iambic bongos must be played
and rhymes positioned at the ends of lines,
one for every station of the cross.
But hang on here while we make the turn
into the final six where all will be resolved,   10
where longing and heartache will find an end,
where Laura will tell Petrarch to put down his pen,
take off those crazy medieval tights,
blow out the lights, and come at last to bed.

Billy Collins (b. 1941)

QUESTIONS

1. In line 12, "Laura will tell Petrarch to put down his pen," the poem alludes to the Italian poet Francesco Petrarch (1304–1374), who wrote a sequence of sonnets to his idealized lady-love, Laura. What attitude does the speaker take toward Petrarch and the Petrarchan sonnet?
2. The phrase "love's storm-tossed seas" (3) is a deliberate cliché. Why is the cliché appropriate here?
3. What is the effect of images such as "rows of beans" (4) and "iambic bongos" (6)? How do they help create the speaker's distinctive voice?
4. While this and the preceding poem differ greatly in language and emotion, they may be compared as statements about the sonnet. What are their essential ideas about this poetic form?

The Lamb

Little Lamb, who made thee?
    Dost thou know who made thee?
Gave thee life and bid thee feed
By the stream and o'er the mead;
Gave thee clothing of delight,   5
Softest clothing wooly bright;

Gave thee such a tender voice,
Making all the vales rejoice!
   Little Lamb, who made thee?
   Dost thou know who made thee?   10

   Little Lamb, I'll tell thee,
   Little Lamb, I'll tell thee!
He is callèd by thy name,
For he calls himself a Lamb;
He is meek and he is mild,   15
He became a little child;
I a child and thou a lamb,
We are callèd by his name.
   Little Lamb, God bless thee.
   Little Lamb, God bless thee.   20

William Blake (1757–1827)

QUESTIONS

1. Why does the speaker address the "Little Lamb" (1) directly? What effects does the poem gain from this use of apostrophe?
2. What is the relationship between the two stanzas? Why is the poem constructed in this way?
3. What is the significance of the "lamb" imagery? What connotations does it have?

The Tiger

Tiger! Tiger! burning bright
In the forests of the night,
What immortal hand or eye
Could frame thy fearful symmetry?

In what distant deeps or skies   5
Burnt the fire of thine eyes?
On what wings dare he aspire?
What the hand dare seize the fire?

And what shoulder, and what art,
Could twist the sinews of thy heart?   10

And when thy heart began to beat,
What dread hand forged thy dread feet?

What the hammer? what the chain?
In what furnace was thy brain?
What the anvil? what dread grasp   15
Dare its deadly terrors clasp?

When the stars threw down their spears,
And watered heaven with their tears,
Did he smile his work to see?
Did he who made the Lamb make thee?   20

Tiger! Tiger! burning bright
In the forests of the night,
What immortal hand or eye
Dare frame thy fearful symmetry?

William Blake (1757–1827)

QUESTIONS

1. Discuss the relationship of this poem to Blake's "The Lamb." How do the
   poems make a distinctive and meaningful pairing?
2. What is the meaning of the various questions the speaker asks of the tiger?
   What are the implications of these questions?
3. What is the symbolic meaning of the tiger? What connotations are associated
   with this symbol?

The Indifferent

"I can love both fair and brown,
Her whom abundance melts, and her whom want betrays,
Her who loves loneness best, and her who masks and plays,
    Her whom the country formed, and whom the town,
        Her who believes, and her who tries,°   tests 5
        Her who still weeps with spongy eyes,
And her who is dry cork and never cries;
I can love her, and her, and you, and you;
I can love any, so she be not true.°   faithful

"Will no other vice content you?   10
Will it not serve your turn to do as did your mothers?
Or have you all old vices spent, and now would find out others?
    Or doth a fear that men are true torment you?
        Oh, we are not; be not you so.
        Let me, and do you, twenty know.   15
    Rob me, but bind me not, and let me go.
    Must I, who came to travail thorough° you,   through
    Grow your fixed subject because you are true?"

Venus heard me sigh this song,
And by love's sweetest part, variety, she swore   20
She heard not this till now, and that it should be so no more.
    She went, examined, and returned ere long,
        And said, "Alas, some two or three
        Poor heretics in love there be,
    Which think to 'stablish dangerous constancy,   25
    But I have told them, 'Since you will be true,
    You shall be true to them who are false to you.' "

                                            John Donne (1572–1631)

QUESTIONS

1. Vocabulary: *Indifferent* (title), *know* (15), *travail* (17).
2. Who is the speaker? To whom is he speaking? About what is he "indifferent"?
   What one qualification does he insist on in a lover? Why?
3. Of what vice does he accuse the women of his generation in line 10? How, in
   his opinion, do they differ from their mothers? Why?
4. Why does Venus investigate the speaker's complaint? Does her investigation
   confirm or refute his accusation? Who are the "heretics in love" (24) whom
   she discovers? What punishment does she decree for them?

Love's Deity

I long to talk with some old lover's ghost
    Who died before the god of love was born.
I cannot think that he who then loved most
    Sunk so low as to love one which did scorn.
But since this god produced a destiny,   5
And that vice-nature, custom, lets it be,
        I must love her that loves not me.

Sure, they which made him god meant not so much,
    Nor he in his young godhead practiced it.
But when an even flame two hearts did touch,   10
    His office was indulgently to fit
Actives to passives. Correspondency
Only his subject was. It cannot be
    Love till I love her that loves me.

But every modern god will° now extend   wants to 15
    His vast prerogative as far as Jove.
To rage, to lust, to write to, to commend,
    All is the purlieu of the god of love.
Oh, were we wakened by this tyranny
To ungod this child again, it could not be   20
    I should love her who loves not me.

Rebel and atheist too, why murmur I
    As though I felt the worst that Love could do?
Love might make me leave loving, or might try
    A deeper plague, to make her love me too,   25
Which, since she loves before, I am loath to see.
Falsehood is worse than hate, and that must be
    If she whom I love should love me.

John Donne (1572–1631)

QUESTIONS

1. Vocabulary: *vice-* (6), *even* (10), *purlieu* (18).
2. Who is the modern "god of love" (2)? Why is he called a "child" (20)? What did "they which made him god" (8) intend to be his duties? How has he gone beyond these duties? Why does the speaker long to talk with some lover's ghost who died before this god was born (1–2)?
3. What is the speaker's situation? Whom does the speaker call "Rebel and atheist" (22)? Why?
4. Why does the speaker rebuke himself for "murmuring" in the final stanza? What two things could Love do to him that have not been done already? Why are they worse? Explain the words "before" (26) and "Falsehood" (27). To which word in the first stanza does "hate" (27) correspond?
5. How does the speaker define "love" in this poem? Is he consistent in his use of the term? How does he differ from the speaker in "The Indifferent" in his conception of love?
6. How do you explain the fact that "Love's Deity" and "The Indifferent," though both by the same poet, express opposite opinions about the value of fidelity in love?

My Number

Is Death miles away from this house,
reaching for a widow in Cincinnati
or breathing down the neck of a lost hiker
in British Columbia?

Is he too busy making arrangements,   5
tampering with air brakes,
scattering cancer cells like seeds,
loosening the wooden beams of roller coasters

to bother with my hidden cottage
that visitors find so hard to find?   10

Or is he stepping from a black car
parked at the dark end of the lane,
shaking open the familiar cloak,
its hood raised like the head of a crow;
and removing the scythe from the trunk?   15

Did you have any trouble with the directions?
I will ask, as I start talking my way out of this.

Billy Collins (b. 1941)

QUESTIONS

1. What human characteristics does the poem ascribe to the personified
   "Death"? Are some references more frightening than others?
2. How do the two two-line stanzas cope with the idea of dying? Are these defenses
   against death reassuring? To what common phrase does the title allude?
3. What does the poem have to say about fear and apprehension of death?

I had heard it's a fight

I had heard it's a fight. At the first clammy touch
You yell, you wrestle with it, it kicks you
In the stomach, squeezes your eyes, in agony you clutch
At a straw, you rattle, and that will fix you.

I don't know. The afternoon it touched me   5
It sneaked up like it was a sweet thrill

Inside my arms and back so I let it come just a wee
Mite closer, though I knew what it was, hell.

Was it sweet! Then like a cute schoolkid
Who does it the first time, I decided it was bad,   10
Cut out the liquor, went to the gym, and did
What a man naturally does, as I mostly had.

The crazy thing, so crazy it gives me a kick:
I can't get over that minute of dying so quick.

Edwin Denby (1903–1983)

QUESTIONS

1. Vocabulary: multiple denotations of *quick* (14).
2. What does the colloquial and slangy diction add to the poem? Does this diction imply that the topic of one's death is not so serious?
3. In line 8 the word "hell" grammatically might be an emphatic exclamation, or it might be a definition of "it" in the preceding phrase. Does the third stanza help you to decide between these possibilities—or to decide that both are appropriate?
4. Compare the attitude toward one's death as expressed here with that in the preceding poem. Does one poem have more "meaning" than the other?

SUGGESTIONS FOR WRITING

Explore the contrasting ideas in the following pairs or groups of poems:
1. Brooks, "Kitchenette Building" (page 646) and Clifton, "good times" (page 950).
2. Hayden, "Those Winter Sundays" (page 699) and Roethke, "My Papa's Waltz" (page 1000).
3. Hopkins, "Spring" (page 692), Housman, "Loveliest of Trees" (page 786), and Williams, "Spring and All" (page 1012).
4. Pastan, "To a Daughter Leaving Home" (page 856) and Wilbur, "The Writer" (page 737).
5. Clifton, "in the inner city" (page 768) and Brooks, "a song in the front yard" (page 948).
6. Angelou, "Woman Work" (page 828) and Piercy, "A Work of Artifice" (page 990).
7. Owen, "Anthem for Doomed Youth" (page 873) and Stevens, "The Death of a Soldier" (page 1006).
8. Cardiff, "Combing" (page 949) and Olds, "35/10" (page 687).
9. Crane, "Voyages [1]" (page 952), Frost, "Once by the Pacific" (page 966), Gunn, "From the Wave" (page 967), and Winters, "The Slow Pacific Swell" (page 1013).

Chapter Ten

Tone

Tone, in literature, may be defined as the writer's or speaker's attitude toward the subject, the reader, or herself or himself. It is the emotional coloring, or the emotional meaning, of the work and is an extremely important part of the full meaning. In spoken language it is indicated by the inflections of the speaker's voice. If, for instance, a friend tells you, "I'm going to get married today," the facts of the statement are entirely clear. But the emotional meaning of the statement may vary widely according to the tone of voice with which it is uttered. The tone may be ecstatic ("Hooray! I'm going to get married today!"); it may be incredulous ("I can't believe it! I'm going to get married today"); it may be despairing ("Horrors! I'm going to get married today"); it may be resigned ("Might as well face it. I'm going to get married today"). Obviously, a correct interpretation of the tone will be an important part of understanding the full meaning. It may even have rather important consequences. If someone calls you a fool, your interpretation of the tone may determine whether you take it as an insult or as playful banter. If a person says "No" to your proposal of marriage, your interpretation of the tone may determine whether you ask again or start going with someone else.

In poetry tone is likewise important. We have not really understood a poem unless we have accurately sensed whether the attitude it manifests is playful or solemn, mocking or reverent, calm or excited. But the correct determination of tone in literature is a much more delicate matter than it is in spoken language, for we do not have the speaker's voice to guide us. We must learn to recognize tone by other means. Almost all of the elements of poetry help to indicate its tone: connotation, imagery, and metaphor; irony and understatement; rhythm, sentence construction, and formal pattern. There is therefore no simple formula for recognizing tone. It is an end product of all the elements in a poem. The best we can do is illustrate.

Robert Frost's "Stopping by Woods on a Snowy Evening" (page 787) seems a simple poem, but it has always afforded trouble to beginning readers. A very good student, asked to interpret it, once wrote this:

"The poem means that we are forever passing up pleasures to go onward to what we wrongly consider our obligations. We would like to watch the snow fall on the peaceful countryside, but we always have to rush home to supper and other engagements. Frost feels that the average person considers life too short to stop and take time to appreciate true pleasures." This student did a good job in recognizing the central conflict of the poem but went astray in recognizing its tone. Let's examine why.

In the first place, the fact that the speaker in the poem *does* stop to watch the snow fall in the woods immediately establishes him as a human being with more sensitivity and feeling for beauty than most. He is not one of the people of Wordsworth's sonnet (page 682) who, "Getting and spending," have laid waste their powers and lost the capacity to be stirred by nature. Frost's speaker is contrasted with his horse, who, as a creature of habit and an animal without esthetic perception, cannot understand the speaker's reason for stopping. There is also a suggestion of contrast with the "owner" of the woods, who, if he saw the speaker stopping, might be as puzzled as the horse. (Who most truly "profits" from the woods—its absentee owner or the person who can enjoy its beauty?) The speaker goes on because he has "promises to keep." But the word "promises," though it may here have a wry ironic undertone of regret, has a favorable connotation: people almost universally agree that promises ought to be kept. If the poet had used a different term, say, "things to do," or "business to attend to," or "financial affairs to take care of," or "money to make," the connotations would have been quite different. As it is, the tone of the poem tells us that the poet is sympathetic to the speaker; Frost is endorsing rather than censuring the speaker's action. Perhaps we may go even further. In the concluding two lines, because of their climactic position, because they are repeated, and because "sleep" in poetry often figuratively refers to death, there is a suggestion of symbolic interpretation: "and many years to live before I die." If we accept this interpretation, it poses a parallel between giving oneself up to contemplation of the woods and dying. The poet's total implication would seem to be that beauty is a distinctively human value that deserves its place in a full life, but to devote one's life to its pursuit, at the expense of other obligations and duties, is tantamount to one's death as a responsible being. The poet therefore accepts the choice the speaker makes, though not without a touch of regret.

Differences in tone, and their importance, are most apparent in poems with similar content. Consider, for instance, the following pair.

For a Lamb

I saw on the slant hill a putrid lamb,
Propped with daisies. The sleep looked deep,
The face nudged in the green pillow
But the guts were out for crows to eat.

Where's the lamb? whose tender plaint   5
Said all for the mute breezes.
Say he's in the wind somewhere,
Say, there's a lamb in the daisies.

Richard Eberhart (b. 1904–2005)

QUESTION

1. What connotative force do these words possess: "putrid" (1), "guts" (4),
   "mute" (6), "lamb" (1), "daisies" (2), "pillow" (3), "tender" (5)? Give two
   relevant denotations of "a lamb in the daisies" (8).

Apparently with no surprise

Apparently with no surprise
To any happy Flower
The Frost beheads it at its play—
In accidental power—
The blonde Assassin passes on—   5
The Sun proceeds unmoved
To measure off another Day
For an Approving God.

Emily Dickinson (1830–1886)

QUESTIONS

1. What is the "blonde Assassin" (5)?
2. What ironies are involved in this poem?

Both of these poems are concerned with natural process; both use
contrast as their basic organizing principle—a contrast between life and
death, innocence and destruction, joy and tragedy. But in tone the two
poems are sharply different. The first is realistic and resigned; its tone is
wistful but not pessimistic. The second, though superficially fanciful, is basically grim, almost savage; its tone is horrified. Let's examine the difference.

The title, "For a Lamb," invites associations of innocent, frolic-some youthfulness, with the additional force of traditional Christian usage. These expectations are shockingly halted by the word "putrid." Though the speaker tries to overcome the shock with the more comforting personification implied in "face" and "pillow," the truth is undeniable: the putrefying animal is food for scavengers. The second stanza comes to grips with this truth, and also with the speak-er's desire that the lamb might still represent innocence and purity in nature. It mingles fact and desire by hoping that what the lamb represented is still "somewhere" in the wind, that the lamb is both lying in the daisy field and will, in nature's processes, be transformed into the daisies. The reader shares the speaker's sad acceptance of reality.

The second poem makes the same contrast between joyful inno-cence ("happy Flower . . . at its play") and fearful destruction ("beheads it"). The chief difference would seem to be that the cause of destruc-tion—"the blonde Assassin"—is specifically identified, while the lamb seems to have died in its sleep, pillowed as it is in grass and surrounded by flowers. But the metaphorical sleep is no less a death than that delivered by an assassin—lambs *do* die, and frost actually *does* destroy flowers. In the second poem, what makes the horror of the killing worse is that nothing else in nature is disturbed by it or seems even to notice it. The sun "proceeds unmoved / To measure off another Day." Nothing in nature stops or pauses. The flower itself is not surprised. And even God—the God who we have been told is benevolent and concerned over the least sparrow's fall—seems to approve of what has happened, for He shows no displeasure, and He supposedly created the frost as well as the flower. Further irony lies in the fact that the "Assassin" (the word's connotations are of terror and violence) is not dark but "blonde," or white (the connotations here are of innocence and beauty). The destructive agent, in other words, is among God's most exquisite crea-tions. The speaker suggests a random, amoral universe in which a flower's premature beheading may be "accidental" (4); but the behead-ing is witnessed by a "Sun" who is "unmoved" (6) and by an "Approving God" (8) who is satisfied with the flower's fate. And if we think that the speaker is unduly disturbed over the death of a flower, we may consider that what is true for the flower is true throughout nature. Death—even early or accidental death, in terrible juxtaposition with beauty—is its constant condition; the fate that befalls the flower befalls us all. In Dickinson's poem, that is the end of the process. In Eberhart's, the potentially terrible irony is directed into a bittersweet acceptance of both death and beauty as natural.

These two poems, then, though superficially similar, are completely different. And the difference is primarily one of tone.

We have been discussing tone as if every poem could be distinguished by a single tone. But varying or shifting tones in a single poem are often a valuable means for achieving the poet's purpose, and indeed may create the dramatic structure of a poem. Consider the following.

Since there's no help

Since there's no help, come let us kiss and part;
Nay, I have done, you get no more of me,
And I am glad, yea, glad with all my heart
That thus so cleanly I myself can free;
Shake hands forever, cancel all our vows,   5
And when we meet at any time again,
Be it not seen in either of our brows
That we one jot of former love retain.
Now, at the last gasp of Love's latest breath,
When, his pulse failing, Passion speechless lies,   10
When Faith is kneeling by his bed of death,
And Innocence is closing up his eyes,
Now, if thou wouldst, when all have given him over,
From death to life thou mightst him yet recover.

Michael Drayton (1563–1631)

QUESTIONS

1. What difference in tone do you find between the first eight lines and the last six? In which part is the speaker more sincere? What differences in rhythm and language help to establish the difference in tone?
2. How many figures are there in the allegorical scene in lines 9–12? What do the pronouns "his" and "him" in lines 10–14 refer to? What is dying? Why? How might the person addressed still restore it from death to life?
3. Define the dramatic situation as precisely as possible, taking into consideration both the man's attitude and the woman's.

Accurately determining tone, whether it be the tone of a rejected marriage proposal or of an insulting remark, is extremely important when interpreting language in poetry as well as in everyday conversations. For the experienced reader it will be instinctive and automatic. For the inexperienced reader it will require study. But beyond the general suggestions for reading that we already have made, there are no specific instructions we can give. Recognition of tone requires an increasing familiarity with the meanings and connotations of words, alertness to the presence of irony and other figures, and, above all, careful reading.

Picnic, Lightning

My very photogenic mother died in a freak accident
(picnic, lightning) when I was three.

Lolita

It is possible to be struck by a meteor
or a single-engine plane
while reading in a chair at home.
Safes drop from rooftops
and flatten the odd pedestrian   5
mostly within the panels of the comics,
but still, we know it is possible,
as well as the flash of summer lightning,
the thermos toppling over,
spilling out on the grass.   10

And we know the message
can be delivered from within.
The heart, no valentine,
decides to quit after lunch,
the power shut off like a switch,   15
or a tiny dark ship is unmoored
into the flow of the body's rivers,
the brain a monastery,
defenseless on the shore.

This is what I think about   20
when I shovel compost
into a wheelbarrow,
and when I fill the long flower boxes,
then press into rows
the limp roots of red impatiens—   25
the instant hand of Death
always ready to burst forth
from the sleeve of his voluminous cloak.

Then the soil is full of marvels,
bits of leaf like flakes off a fresco,   30

red-brown pine needles, a beetle quick
to burrow back under the loam.
Then the wheelbarrow is a wider blue,
the clouds a brighter white,
and all I hear is the rasp of the steel edge   35
against a round stone,
the small plants singing
with lifted faces, and the click
of the sundial
as one hour sweeps into the next.   40

Billy Collins (b. 1941)

QUESTIONS

1. Vocabulary: *unmoored* (16), *voluminous* (28).
2. What is the meaning of the epigraph taken from Vladimir Nabokov's *Lolita*?
   How does the epigraph help us to focus and understand the poem?
3. Various kinds of accidents are discussed in the poem, both external and internal.
   What is the poem saying about the perilous and provisional nature of life's
   experiences? What tone does the speaker adopt in writing about this topic?
4. Why does the speaker use gardening metaphors from line 21 to the end of the
   poem? How do these metaphors enrich the poem's meaning?

REVIEWING CHAPTER TEN

1. Consider the ways in which tone is part of the total meaning of a
   poem (you might think of the total meaning as a compound of the
   intellectual and the emotional).
2. The second paragraph of this chapter lists many of the elements of
   poetry that contribute to tone; as you examine the first two poems
   presented in the chapter, try to identify which of the elements are
   particularly significant in each of them.
3. Tone is customarily identified by an adjective (*wistful, pessimistic,
   horrified* in the discussion of the first two poems). Choose adjectives to identify the two contrasting tones in "Since there's no
   help." (Do not settle for the first adjective that pops into mind—
   this is good opportunity to exercise your vocabulary and strive for
   precision.)

My mistress' eyes

My mistress' eyes are nothing like the sun;
Coral is far more red than her lips' red;
If snow be white, why then her breasts are dun;
If hairs be wires, black wires grow on her head.
I have seen roses damasked,° red and white,   of different 5
                                                            colors
But no such roses see I in her cheeks;
And in some perfumes is there more delight
Than in the breath that from my mistress reeks.°   exhales
I love to hear her speak, yet well I know
That music hath a far more pleasing sound;   10
I grant I never saw a goddess go,—
My mistress, when she walks, treads on the ground.
And yet, by heaven, I think my love as rare
As any she belied with false compare.

William Shakespeare (1564–1616)

QUESTIONS

1. The speaker draws a contrast between the qualities often praised in exaggerated love poetry and the reality of his mistress' physical attributes. Construct the series of "false compar[isons]" that this poem implies that other poets have used (eyes as bright as the sun, hair like spun gold, etc.).
2. What is the speaker's tone in lines 1–12? Is there anything about those lines that his mistress might find pleasing? (In Shakespeare's time the word "reeks" did not have its modern denotation of "stinks.")
3. The tone clearly shifts with line 13—signaled by the simple phrase "And yet." What is the tone of the last two lines? The last line might be paraphrased "as any woman who has been lied to with false comparisons." How important are truth and lies as subjects in the poem?

Crossing the Bar

Sunset and evening star,
    And one clear call for me!
And may there be no moaning of the bar
    When I put out to sea,

But such a tide as moving seems asleep,   5
    Too full for sound and foam,

When that which drew from out the boundless deep
    Turns again home.

Twilight and evening bell,
    And after that the dark!   10
And may there be no sadness of farewell
    When I embark;

For though from out our bourne of Time and Place
    The flood may bear me far,
I hope to see my Pilot face to face   15
    When I have crossed the bar.

Alfred, Lord Tennyson (1809–1892)

QUESTIONS

1. Vocabulary: *bourne* (13).
2. What two sets of figures does Tennyson use for approaching death? What is the precise moment of death in each set?
3. In troubled weather the wind and waves above the sandbar across a harbor's mouth make a moaning sound. What metaphorical meaning has the "moaning of the bar" (3) here? For what kind of death is the speaker wishing? Why does he want "no sadness of farewell" (11)?
4. What is "that which drew from out the boundless deep" (7)? What is "the boundless deep"? To what is it opposed in the poem? Why is "Pilot" (15) capitalized?

The Oxen

Christmas Eve, and twelve of the clock.
    "Now they are all on their knees,"
An elder said as we sat in a flock
    By the embers in hearthside ease.

We pictured the meek mild creatures where   5
    They dwelt in their strawy pen,
Nor did it occur to one of us there
    To doubt they were kneeling then.

So fair a fancy few would weave
    In these years! Yet, I feel,   10

If someone said on Christmas Eve,
   "Come; see the oxen kneel

"In the lonely barton° by yonder coomb°;   farm; valley
   Our childhood used to know,"
I should go with him in the gloom,   15
   Hoping it might be so.

Thomas Hardy (1840–1928)

QUESTIONS

1. Is the simple superstition referred to in this poem opposed to, or identified with, religious faith? With what implications for the meaning of the poem?
2. What are "these years" (10), and how do they contrast with the years of the poet's boyhood? What event in intellectual history between 1840 and 1915 (the date Hardy composed this poem) was most responsible for the change?
3. Both "Crossing the Bar" and "The Oxen" in their last lines use a form of the verb *hope*. By fully discussing tone, establish the precise meaning of hope in each poem. What degree of expectation does it imply? How should the word be handled in reading Tennyson's poem aloud?

One dignity delays for all

One dignity delays for all—
One mitred Afternoon—
None can avoid this purple—
None evade this Crown!

Coach, it insures, and footmen—   5
Chamber, and state, and throng—
Bells, also, in the village
As we ride grand along!

What dignified Attendants!
What service when we pause!   10
How loyally at parting
Their hundred hats they raise!

How pomp surpassing ermine
When simple You, and I,

Present our meek escutcheon   15
And claim the rank to die!

Emily Dickinson (1830–1886)

QUESTIONS

1. Vocabulary: *mitred* (2), *state* (6), *escutcheon* (15).
2. What is the "dignity" that delays for all? What is its nature? What is being
   described in stanzas 2 and 3?
3. What figures of speech are combined in "our meek escutcheon" (15)? What
   does it represent metaphorically?

'Twas warm—at first—like Us

'Twas warm—at first—like Us—
Until there crept upon
A Chill—like frost upon a Glass—
Till all the scene—be gone.

The Forehead copied Stone—   5
The Fingers grew too cold
To ache—and like a Skater's Brook—
The busy eyes—congealed—

It straightened—that was all—
It crowded Cold to Cold—   10
It multiplied indifference—
As Pride were all it could—

And even when with Cords—
'Twas lowered, like a Weight—
It made no Signal, nor demurred,   15
But dropped like Adamant.

Emily Dickinson (1830–1886)

QUESTIONS

1. Vocabulary: *Adamant* (16).
2. What is "It" in the opening line? What is being described in the poem and
   between which points in time?
3. How would you describe the tone of this poem? How does it contrast with
   that of the preceding poem?

The Apparition

When by thy scorn, O murderess, I am dead,
      And that thou thinkst thee free
From all solicitation from me,
Then shall my ghost come to thy bed,
And thee, feigned vestal, in worse arms shall see;   5
Then thy sick taper° will begin to wink,   candle
And he, whose thou art then, being tired before,
Will, if thou stir, or pinch to wake him, think
      Thou call'st for more,
And in false sleep will from thee shrink.   10
And then, poor aspen wretch, neglected, thou,
Bathed in a cold quicksilver sweat, wilt lie
      A verier° ghost than I.   truer
What I will say, I will not tell thee now,
Lest that preserve thee; and since my love is spent,   15
I had rather thou shouldst painfully repent,
Than by my threatenings rest still innocent.

John Donne (1572–1631)

QUESTIONS

1. Vocabulary: *feigned* (5), *aspen* (11), *quicksilver* (12). Are the latter two words used literally or figuratively? Explain.
2. What has been the past relationship between the speaker and the woman addressed? How does a "solicitation" (3) differ from a proposal?
3. In line 15 the speaker proclaims that his love for the woman "is spent." Does the tone of the poem support this contention? Discuss.
4. In line 5 why does the speaker use the word "vestal" instead of *virgin*? Does he believe her not to be a virgin? Of what is he accusing her? (In ancient Rome the vestal virgins tended the perpetual fire in the temple of Vesta. They entered this service between the ages of six and ten, and served for a term of thirty years, during which they were bound to virginity.)
5. The implied metaphor in line 1—that a woman who will not satisfy her lover's desires is "killing" him—was a cliché of Renaissance poetry. What original twist does Donne give it to make it fresh and new?
6. In the scene imagined by the speaker of his ghost's visit to the woman's bed, he finds her "in worse arms" (5)—worse than whose? In what respect? By what will this other man have been "tired before" (7)? Of what will he think she is calling "for more" (9)? What is the speaker implying about himself and the woman in these lines?

7. What will the ghost say to her that he will not now reveal lest his telling it "preserve" (15) her? Can we know? Does *he* know? Why does he make this undefined threat?
8. For what does the speaker say he wants the woman to "painfully repent" (16)? Of what crime or sin would she remain "innocent" (17) if he revealed now what his ghost would say? What is the speaker's real objective?

The Flea

Mark but this flea, and mark in this
How little that which thou deny'st me is;
It sucked me first, and now sucks thee,
And in this flea our two bloods mingled be;
Thou know'st that this cannot be said   5
A sin, nor shame, nor loss of maidenhead;
    Yet this enjoys before it woo,
      And pampered swells with one blood made of two,
      And this, alas, is more than we would do.

Oh stay, three lives in one flea spare,   10
Where we almost, yea more than married are.
This flea is you and I, and this
Our marriage bed and marriage temple is;
Though parents grudge, and you, we are met
And cloistered in these living walls of jet.   15
    Though use° make you apt to kill me,   habit
      Let not to that, self-murder added be,
      And sacrilege, three sins in killing three.

Cruel and sudden, hast thou since
Purpled° thy nail in blood of innocence?   crimsoned   20
Wherein could this flea guilty be,
Except in that drop which it sucked from thee?
Yet thou triumph'st and say'st that thou
Find'st not thyself, nor me, the weaker now.
    'Tis true. Then learn how false fears be: 25
      Just so much honor, when thou yield'st to me,
      Will waste, as this flea's death took life from thee.

John Donne (1572–1631)

QUESTIONS

1. In many respects this poem is like a miniature play: it has two characters, dramatic conflict, dialogue (though we hear only one speaker), and stage action. The action is indicated by stage directions embodied in the dialogue. What has happened just *preceding* the first line of the poem? What happens *between* the first and second stanzas? What happens *between* the second and third? How does the female character behave and what does she say *during* the third stanza?
2. What has been the past relationship of the speaker and the woman? What has she denied him (2)? How has she habitually "kill[ed]" him (16)? Why has she done so? How does it happen that he is still alive? What is his objective in the poem?
3. According to a traditional Renaissance belief, the blood of lovers "mingled" during sexual intercourse. What is the speaker's argument in stanza 1? Reduce it to paraphrase. How logical is it?
4. What do "parents grudge, and you" in stanza 2? What are the "living walls of jet" (15)? What three things will the woman kill by crushing the flea? What three sins will she commit (18)?
5. Why and how does the woman "triumph" in stanza 3? What is the speaker's response? How logical is his concluding argument?
6. What action, if any, would you infer follows the conclusion of the poem?
7. "The Apparition" and "The Flea" may both be classified as "seduction poems." How do they differ in tone?

Dover Beach

The sea is calm tonight,
The tide is full, the moon lies fair
Upon the straits;—on the French coast the light
Gleams and is gone; the cliffs of England stand,
Glimmering and vast, out in the tranquil bay.   5
Come to the window, sweet is the night-air!
Only, from the long line of spray
Where the sea meets the moon-blanched land,
Listen! you hear the grating roar
Of pebbles which the waves draw back, and fling,   10
At their return, up the high strand,
Begin, and cease, and then again begin,
With tremulous cadence slow, and bring
The eternal note of sadness in.

Sophocles long ago   15
Heard it on the Aegean, and it brought

Into his mind the turbid ebb and flow
Of human misery; we
Find also in the sound a thought,
Hearing it by this distant northern sea.   20

The Sea of Faith
Was once, too, at the full, and round earth's shore
Lay like the folds of a bright girdle furled.
But now I only hear
Its melancholy, long, withdrawing roar,   25
Retreating, to the breath
Of the night-wind, down the vast edges drear
And naked shingles° of the world.   pebbled beaches

Ah, love, let us be true
To one another! for the world, which seems   30
To lie before us like a land of dreams,
So various, so beautiful, so new,
Hath really neither joy, nor love, nor light,
Nor certitude, nor peace, nor help for pain;
And we are here as on a darkling plain   35
Swept with confused alarms of struggle and flight,
Where ignorant armies clash by night.

Matthew Arnold (1822–1888)

QUESTIONS

1. Vocabulary: *strand* (11), *girdle* (23), *darkling* (35). Identify the physical locale of the cliffs of Dover and their relation to the French coast; identify Sophocles and the Aegean.
2. As precisely as possible, define the implied scene: What is the speaker's physical location? Whom is he addressing? What is the time of day and the state of the weather?
3. Discuss the visual and auditory images of the poem and their relation to illusion and reality.
4. The speaker is lamenting the decline of religious faith in his time. Is he himself a believer? Does he see any medicine for the world's maladies?
5. Discuss in detail the imagery in the last three lines. Are the "armies" figurative or literal? What makes these lines so effective?
6. What term or terms would you choose to describe the overall tone of the poem?

Church Going

Once I am sure there's nothing going on
I step inside, letting the door thud shut.
Another church: matting, seats, and stone,
And little books; sprawlings of flowers, cut
For Sunday, brownish now; some brass and stuff   5
Up at the holy end; the small neat organ;
And a tense, musty, unignorable silence,
Brewed God knows how long. Hatless, I take off
My cycle-clips in awkward reverence,

Move forward, run my hand around the font.   10
From where I stand, the roof looks almost new—
Cleaned, or restored? Someone would know: I don't.
Mounting the lectern, I peruse a few
Hectoring large-scale verses, and pronounce
"Here endeth" much more loudly than I'd meant.   15
The echoes snigger briefly. Back at the door
I sign the book, donate an Irish sixpence,
Reflect the place was not worth stopping for.

Yet stop I did: in fact I often do,
And always end much at a loss like this,   20
Wondering what to look for, wondering, too,
When churches fall completely out of use
What we shall turn them into, if we shall keep
A few cathedrals chronically on show,
Their parchment, plate and pyx in locked cases,   25
And let the rest rent-free to rain and sheep.
Shall we avoid them as unlucky places?

Or, after dark, will dubious women come
To make their children touch a particular stone;
Pick simples for a cancer; or on some   30
Advised night see walking a dead one?
Power of some sort or other will go on
In games, in riddles, seemingly at random;
But superstition, like belief, must die,
And what remains when disbelief has gone?   35
Grass, weedy pavement, brambles, buttress, sky,

A shape less recognizable each week,
A purpose more obscure. I wonder who
Will be the last, the very last, to seek
This place for what it was; one of the crew   40
That tap and jot and know what rood-lofts were?
Some ruin-bibber, randy for antique,
Or Christmas-addict, counting on a whiff
Of gown-and-bands and organ-pipes and myrrh?
Or will he be my representative,   45

Bored, uninformed, knowing the ghostly silt
Dispersed, yet tending to this cross of ground
Through suburb scrub because it held unspilt
So long and equably what since is found
Only in separation—marriage, and birth,   50
And death, and thoughts of these—for whom was built
This special shell? For though I've no idea
What this accoutered frowsty barn is worth,
It pleases me to stand in silence here;

A serious house on serious earth it is,   55
In whose blent air all our compulsions meet,
Are recognized, and robed as destinies.
And that much never can be obsolete,
Since someone will forever be surprising
A hunger in himself to be more serious,   60
And gravitating with it to this ground,
Which, he once heard, was proper to grow wise in,
If only that so many dead lie round.

Philip Larkin (1922–1985)

QUESTIONS

1. Vocabulary: *Hectoring* (14), *pyx* (25), *dubious* (28), *simples* (30), *accoutered*
   (53), *frowsty* (53), *blent* (56). *Large-scale* (14) indicates a print size suited to
   oral reading; an *Irish sixpence* (17) was a small coin not legal tender in
   England, the scene of the poem; *rood-lofts* (41) are architectural features
   found in many early Christian churches; *bibber* and *randy* (42) are figurative,
   literally meaning "drunkard" and "lustful"; *gown-and-bands* (44) are ornate
   robes worn by church officials in religious ceremonies.

2. Like "Dover Beach" (first published in 1867), "Church Going" (1954) is concerned with belief and disbelief. In modern England the landscape is dotted with small churches, often charming in their combination of stone (outside) and intricately carved wood (inside). Some are in ruins, some are badly in need of repair, and some are well tended by parishioners who keep them dusted and provide fresh flowers for the diminishing attendance at Sunday services. These churches invariably have by the entrance a book that visitors can sign as a record of their having been there and a collection box with a sign urging them to drop in a few coins for upkeep, repair, or restoration. In small towns and villages the church is often the chief or only building of architectural or historical interest, and tourist visitors may outnumber parishioners. To which of the three categories of churches mentioned here does Larkin's poem refer?

3. What different denotations does the title contain?

4. In what activity has the speaker been engaging when he stops to see the church? How is it revealed? Why does he stop? Is he a believer? How involved is he in inspecting this church building?

5. Compare the language used by the speakers in "Dover Beach" and "Church Going." Which speaker is more eloquent? Which is more informal and conversational? Without looking back at the texts, try to assign the following words to one poem or the other: *moon-blanched, cycle-clips, darkling, hath, snigger, whiff, drear, brownish, tremulous, glimmering, frowsty, stuff.* Then go back and check your success.

6. Define the tone of "Church Going" as precisely as possible. Compare this tone with that of "Dover Beach."

SUGGESTIONS FOR WRITING

1. Marvell's "To His Coy Mistress" (page 721), Herrick's "To the Virgins, to Make Much of Time" (page 733), and Housman's "Loveliest of Trees" (page 786) all treat a traditional poetic theme known as *carpe diem* ("seize the day"). They differ sharply in tone. Pointing out the differences in poetic technique among them, characterize the tone of each.

2. Describe and account for the differences in tone between the following pairs:
   a. Hayden, "The Whipping" (page 642) and Randall, "Ballad of Birmingham" (page 645).
   b. Hopkins, "Spring" (page 692) and Dickinson "A Light exists in Spring" (page 955)
   c. Rich, "Living in Sin" (page 696) and Gwynn, "Snow White and the Seven Deadly Sins" (page 968).
   d. Shakespeare, "My mistress' eyes" (page 807) and Mullen, "Dim Lady" (page 988).
   e. Drayton, "Since there's no help" (page 804) and Addonizio, "Sonnenizio" (page 894)
   f. Blake, "The Lamb" (page 793) and Blake, "The Tiger" (page 794).

Musical Devices

Poetry obviously makes a greater use of the "music" of language than does language that is not poetry. The poet, unlike the person who uses language to convey only information, chooses words for sound as well as for meaning, and uses the sound as a means of reinforcing meaning. So prominent is this musical quality of poetry that some writers have made it the distinguishing term in their definitions of poetry. Edgar Allan Poe, for instance, describes poetry as "music . . . combined with a pleasurable idea." Whether or not it deserves this much importance, verbal music, like connotation, imagery, and figurative language, is one of the important resources that enable the poet to do more than communicate mere information. The poet may indeed sometimes pursue verbal music for its own sake; more often, at least in first-rate poetry, it is an adjunct to the total meaning or communication of the poem.

The poet achieves musical quality in two broad ways: by the choice and arrangement of sounds and by the arrangement of accents. In this chapter we will consider the first of these.

An essential element in all music is repetition. In fact, we might say that all art consists of giving structure to two elements: repetition and variation. All things we enjoy greatly and lastingly have these two elements. We enjoy the sea endlessly because it is always the same yet always different. We enjoy a baseball game because it contains the same complex combination of pattern and variation. Our love of art, then, is rooted in human psychology. We like the familiar, we like variety, but we like them combined. If we get too much sameness, the result is monotony and tedium; if we get too much variety, the result is bewilderment and confusion. The composer of music, therefore, repeats certain musical tones; repeats them in certain combinations, or chords; and repeats them in certain patterns, or melodies. The poet likewise repeats certain sounds in certain combinations and arrangements, and thus adds musical meaning to verse. Consider the following short example.

The Turtle

The turtle lives 'twixt plated decks
Which practically conceal its sex.
I think it clever of the turtle
In such a fix to be so fertile.

Ogden Nash (1902–1971)

Here is a little joke, a paradox of animal life to which the author has cleverly drawn our attention. An experiment will show us, however, that much of its appeal lies not so much in what it says as in the manner in which it says it. If, for instance, we recast the verse as prose: "The turtle lives in a shell that almost conceals its sex. It is ingenious of the turtle, in such a situation, to be so prolific," the joke falls flat. Some of its appeal must lie in its metrical form. So now we cast it in unrhymed verse:

Because he lives between two decks,
It's hard to tell a turtle's gender.
The turtle is a clever beast
In such a plight to be so fertile.

Here, perhaps, is *some* improvement over the prose version, but still the piquancy of the original is missing. Much of that appeal must have consisted in the use of rhyme—the repetition of sound in "decks" and "sex," "turtle" and "fertile." So we try once more.

The turtle lives 'twixt plated decks
Which practically conceal its sex.
I think it clever of the turtle
In such a plight to be so fertile.

But for perceptive readers there is still something missing—they may not at first see what—but some little touch that makes the difference between a good piece of verse and a little masterpiece of its kind. And then they see it: "plight" has been substituted for "fix."

But why should "fix" make such a difference? Its meaning is little different from that of "plight"; its only important difference is in sound. But there we are. The final x in "fix" catches up the concluding consonant sound in "sex," and its initial f is repeated in the initial consonant sound of "fertile." Not only do these sound recurrences provide a subtle gratification to the ear, but they also give the verse structure; they emphasize and draw together the key words of the piece: "sex," "fix," and "fertile."

Poets may repeat any unit of sound from the smallest to the largest. They may repeat individual vowel and consonant sounds, whole syllables, words, phrases, lines, or groups of lines. In each instance, in a good poem, the repetition will serve several purposes: it will please the ear, it will emphasize the words in which the repetition occurs, and it will give structure to the poem. The popularity and initial impressiveness of such repetitions are evidenced by their becoming in many instances embedded in the language as clichés like "wild and woolly," "first and foremost," "footloose and fancy-free," "penny-wise, pound-foolish," "dead as a doornail," "might and main," "sink or swim," "do or die," "pell-mell," "helter-skelter," "harum-scarum," "hocus-pocus." Some of these kinds of repetition have names, as we will see.

A syllable consists of a vowel sound that may be preceded or followed by consonant sounds. Any of these sounds may be repeated. The repetition of initial consonant sounds, as in "tried and true," "safe and sound," "fish or fowl," "rhyme or reason," is **alliteration**. The repetition of vowel sounds, as in "mad as a hatter," "time out of mind," "free and easy," "slapdash," is **assonance**. The repetition of final consonant sounds, as in "first and last," "odds and ends," "short and sweet," "a stroke of luck," or Shakespeare's "struts and frets" (page 774) is **consonance.***

Repetitions may be used alone or in combination. Alliteration and assonance are combined in such phrases as "time and tide," "thick and thin," "kith and kin," "alas and alack," "fit as a fiddle," and Edgar Allan Poe's famous line, "The viol, the violet, and the vine." Alliteration and consonance are combined in such phrases as "crisscross," "last but not least," "lone and lorn," "good as gold," Housman's "malt does more than Milton can" (page 650), and Kay's "meanings lost in manners" (page 678).

Rhyme is the repetition of the accented vowel sound and any succeeding consonant sounds. It is called **masculine** when the rhyme sounds involve only one syllable, as in *decks* and *sex* or *support* and *retort*. It is **feminine** when the rhyme sounds involve two or more syllables, as in *turtle* and *fertile* or *spitefully* and *delightfully*. It is referred to as **internal**

---

*Different writers have defined these repetitions in various ways. *Alliteration* is used by some writers to mean any repetition of consonant sounds. *Assonance* has been used to mean the similarity as well as the identity of vowel sounds, or even the similarity of any sounds whatever. *Consonance* has often been reserved for words in which both the initial and final consonant sounds correspond, as in *green* and *groan*, *moon* and *mine*. *Rhyme* has been used to mean any sound repetition, including alliteration, assonance, and consonance. In the absence of clear agreement on the meanings of these terms, the terminology chosen here has appeared most useful, with support in usage. Labels are useful in analysis. However, the student should learn to recognize the devices and, more important, should learn to see their function, without worrying too much over nomenclature.

rhyme when one or more rhyming words are *within* the line and as **end rhyme** when the rhyming words are at the *ends* of lines. End rhyme is probably the most frequently used and most consciously sought sound repetition in English poetry. Because it comes at the end of the line, it receives emphasis as a musical effect and perhaps contributes more than any other musical resource except rhythm to give poetry its musical effect as well as its structure. There exists, however, a large body of poetry that does not employ rhyme and for which rhyme would not be appropriate. Also, there has always been a tendency, especially noticeable in modern poetry, to substitute approximate rhymes for perfect rhymes at the ends of lines. **Approximate rhymes** (also called slant rhymes) include words with any kind of sound similarity, from close to fairly remote. Under approximate rhyme we include alliteration, assonance, and consonance or their combinations when used at the end of the line; half-rhyme (feminine rhymes in which only half of the word rhymes—the accented half, as in *lightly* and *frightful,* or the unaccented half, as in *yellow* and *willow*); and other similarities too elusive to name. "'Twas warm—at first—like Us" (page 810), "Toads" (page 718), and "Mid-Term Break" (page 764), to different degrees, all employ various kinds of approximate end rhyme.

That night when joy began

That night when joy began
Our narrowest veins to flush,
We waited for the flash
Of morning's leveled gun.

But morning let us pass,   5
And day by day relief
Outgrows his nervous laugh,
Grown credulous of peace,

As mile by mile is seen
No trespasser's reproach,   10
And love's best glasses reach
No fields but are his own.

W. H. Auden (1907–1973)

QUESTIONS

1. What has been the past experience with love of the two people in the poem? What is their present experience? What precisely is the tone of the poem?

2. What basic metaphor underlies the poem? Work it out stanza by stanza. What is "the flash / Of morning's leveled gun" (3–4)? Does line 10 mean that no trespasser reproaches the lovers or that no one reproaches the lovers for being trespassers? Does "glasses" (11) refer to spectacles, tumblers, mirrors, or field glasses? Point out three personifications.
3. The rhyme pattern in the poem is intricate and exact. Work it out, considering alliteration, assonance, and consonance.

In addition to the repetition of individual sounds and syllables, the poet may repeat whole words, phrases, lines, or groups of lines. When such repetition is done according to some fixed pattern, it is called a **refrain**. The refrain is especially common in songlike poetry. Shakespeare's "Winter" (page 636) furnishes an example of a refrain.

The Waking

I wake to sleep, and take my waking slow.
I feel my fate in what I cannot fear.
I learn by going where I have to go.

We think by feeling. What is there to know?
I hear my being dance from ear to ear.   5
I wake to sleep, and take my waking slow.

Of those so close beside me, which are you?
God bless the Ground! I shall walk softly there,
And learn by going where I have to go.

Light takes the Tree; but who can tell us how?   10
The lowly worm climbs up a winding stair;
I wake to sleep, and take my waking slow.

Great Nature has another thing to do
To you and me; so take the lively air,
And, lovely, learn by going where to go.   15

This shaking keeps me steady. I should know.
What falls away is always. And is near.
I wake to sleep, and take my waking slow.
I learn by going where I have to go.

Theodore Roethke (1908–1963)

QUESTIONS

1. The refrains in lines 1 and 3 occur at patterned intervals in this example of the form called "villanelle" (see page 886 for a definition of the form). Even without the definition, you can work out the repetitive pattern—but the key question is, what do these two lines *mean*, as statements both within the first stanza and in each subsequent repetition? Starting with line 1, for what is "sleep" a common metaphor? What would be the meaning if the first phrase were "I was born to die"?

2. Paraphrase the third line, in light of the idea that the first line presents an attitude toward the fact that all living things must die. Where does the speaker "have to go" ultimately? What is the process of his present "going"?

3. Explain the clear-cut attitude toward emotive experience versus intellectual knowledge expressed in line 4. How is that attitude a basis for the ideas in the refrain lines? How does it support line 10?

4. What is it that "Great Nature has . . . to do" (13) to people? How should they live their lives, according to the speaker?

5. Explain the paradox that "shaking keeps [the speaker] steady" (16). Consider the possibility that the speaker is personifying "the Tree" (10) as himself— what then is "fall[ing] away," and how near is it (17)?

6. Is the tone of this poem melancholy? resigned? joyous? Explain.

We have not nearly exhausted the possibilities of sound repetition by giving names to a few of the more prominent kinds. The complete study of possible kinds of sound repetition in poetry would be so complex, however, that it would exceed the scope of this introductory text.

Some of the subtlest and loveliest effects escape our net of names. In as short a phrase as this from the prose of John Ruskin—"ivy as light and lovely as the vine"—we notice alliteration in *light* and *lovely*, assonance in *ivy*, *light*, and *vine*, and consonance in *ivy* and *lovely*, but we have no name to connect the *v* in *vine* with the *v*s in *ivy* and *lovely*, or the second *l* in *lovely* with the first *l*, or the final syllables of *ivy* and *lovely* with each other; yet these are all an effective part of the music of the line. Also contributing to the music of poetry is the linking of related rather than identical sounds, such as *m* and *n*, or *p* and *b*, or the vowel sounds in *boat*, *boot*, and *book*.

These various musical repetitions, for trained readers, will ordinarily make an almost subconscious contribution to their reading of the poem: readers will feel their effect without necessarily being aware of what has caused it. There is value, however, in occasionally analyzing a poem for these devices in order to increase awareness of them. A few words of caution are necessary. First, the repetitions are entirely a matter of sound; spelling is irrelevant. *Bear* and *pair* are rhymes, but *through* and *rough* are not. *Cell* and *sin, folly* and *philosophy* alliterate, but *sin* and *sugar, gun* and *gem* do not. Second, alliteration, assonance, consonance, and masculine rhyme are matters that ordinarily involve only stressed or accented syllables; for only such syllables ordinarily make enough impression on the ear to be significant in the sound pattern of the poem. For instance, we should hardly consider *which* and *its* in the second line of "The Turtle" an example of assonance, for neither word is stressed enough in the reading to make it significant as a sound. Third, the words involved in these repetitions must be close enough together that the ear retains the sound, consciously or subconsciously, from its first occurrence to its second. This distance varies according to circumstances, but for alliteration, assonance, and consonance the words ordinarily have to be in the same line or adjacent lines. End rhyme bridges a longer gap.

God's Grandeur

The world is charged with the grandeur of God.
    It will flame out, like shining from shook foil;
    It gathers to a greatness, like the ooze of oil
Crushed. Why do men then now not reck his rod?
Generations have trod, have trod, have trod;   5
    And all is seared with trade; bleared, smeared with toil;
    And wears man's smudge and shares man's smell: the soil
Is bare now, nor can foot feel, being shod.

And for all this, nature is never spent;
    There lives the dearest freshness deep down things;   10
And though the last lights off the black West went
    Oh, morning, at the brown brink eastward, springs—
Because the Holy Ghost over the bent
    World broods with warm breast and with ah! bright wings.

Gerard Manley Hopkins (1844–1889)

QUESTIONS

1. What is the theme of this sonnet?
2. The image in lines 3–4 possibly refers to olive oil being collected in great vats from crushed olives, but the image is much disputed. Explain the simile in line 2 and the symbols in lines 7–8 and 11–12.

3. Explain "reck his rod" (4), "spent" (9), "bent" (13).
4. Using different-colored pencils, encircle and connect examples of alliteration, assonance, consonance, and internal rhyme. Do these help to carry the meaning?

We should not leave the impression that the use of these musical devices is necessarily or always valuable. Like the other resources of poetry, they can be judged only in the light of the poem's total intention. Many of the greatest works of English poetry—for instance, *Hamlet* and *King Lear* and *Paradise Lost*—do not employ end rhyme. Both alliteration and rhyme, especially feminine rhyme, become humorous or silly if used excessively or unskillfully. If the intention is humorous, the result is delightful; if not, fatal. Shakespeare, who knew how to use all these devices to the utmost advantage, parodied their unskillful use in lines like "The preyful princess pierced and pricked a pretty pleasing prickett" in *Love's Labor's Lost* and

> Whereat with blade, with bloody, blameful blade,
> He bravely broached his boiling bloody breast

in *A Midsummer Night's Dream.* Swinburne parodied his own highly alliterative style in "Nephelidia" with lines like "Life is the lust of a lamp for the light that is dark till the dawn of the day when we die." Used skillfully and judiciously, however, musical devices provide a palpable and delicate pleasure to the ear and, even more important, add dimension to meaning.

EXERCISE

Discuss the various ways in which the following poems make use of refrain.
1. Shakespeare, "Winter" (page 636).
2. Shakespeare, "Blow, blow, thou winter wind" (page 826).
3. cummings, "in Just—" (page 776).
4. Donne, "A Hymn to God the Father" (page 685).
5. Blake, "The Lamb" (page 793).
6. Crane, "War Is Kind" (page 953).
7. Dunbar, "Sympathy" (page 960).
8. Clifton, "good times" (page 950).
9. Ferlinghetti, "Christ climbed down" (page 960).

REVIEWING CHAPTER ELEVEN

1. Review the terms printed in boldface, and as you read on in this chapter take note of the examples that you find (that is, make a conscious search for the materials that normally would not rise above the subconscious in their effects).
2. Musical devices do not convey meaning but reinforce meanings that are established by the other aspects of language; as you explore these musical devices, identify the ways in which emotional and intellectual meanings are conveyed so as to make it clear what the music is reinforcing and supporting.

Blow, blow, thou winter wind

Blow, blow, thou winter wind.
Thou art not so unkind
  As man's ingratitude.
Thy tooth is not so keen,
Because thou art not seen,   5
  Although thy breath be rude°   rough
Heigh-ho, sing heigh-ho, unto the green holly.
Most friendship is feigning, most loving mere folly.
  Then heigh-ho, the holly!
    This life is most jolly.   10

Freeze, freeze, thou bitter sky,
That dost not bite so nigh°   near the heart
  As benefits forgot.
Though thou the waters warp,
Thy sting is not so sharp   15
  As friend remembered not.
Heigh-ho, sing heigh-ho, unto the green holly.
Most friendship is feigning, most loving mere folly.
  Then heigh-ho, the holly!
    This life is most jolly.   20

William Shakespeare (1564–1616)

QUESTIONS

1. Vocabulary: *Heigh-ho* (7) is an expression of melancholy or disappointment; *holly* (7) is an emblem of cheerfulness (as at Christmas); *warp* (14) implies freezing into ridges.
2. This song from *As You Like It*, Act 2, scene 7, contrasts the social and natural worlds and is sung to celebrate living freely in the forest. What essential qualities does it ascribe to the two environments displayed in the behavior of people and the actions of nature? What paradox does the poem create by presenting the expression "heigh-ho" linked with "the holly"? Are we to take "heigh-ho" at its literal meaning?
3. What musical devices help to create the songlike quality of this poem?

We Real Cool

The Pool Players.
Seven At The Golden Shovel.

We real cool. We
Left school. We

Lurk late. We
Strike straight. We

Sing sin. We   5
Thin gin. We

Jazz June. We
Die soon.

Gwendolyn Brooks (1917–2000)

QUESTIONS

1. In addition to end rhyme, what other musical devices does this poem employ?
2. Try reading this poem with the pronouns at the beginning of the lines instead of at the end. What is lost?
3. English teachers in a certain urban school were once criticized for having their students read this poem: it was said to be immoral. What essential poetic device did the critics misunderstand?

Woman Work

I've got the children to tend
The clothes to mend
The floor to mop
The food to shop
Then the chicken to fry   5
The baby to dry
I got company to feed
The garden to weed
I've got the shirts to press
The tots to dress   10
The cane to be cut
I gotta clean up this hut
Then see about the sick
And the cotton to pick.

Shine on me, sunshine   15
Rain on me, rain
Fall softly, dewdrops
And cool my brow again.

Storm, blow me from here
With your fiercest wind   20
Let me float across the sky
'Til I can rest again.

Fall gently, snowflakes
Cover me with white
Cold icy kisses and   25
Let me rest tonight.

Sun, rain, curving sky
Mountain, oceans, leaf and stone
Star shine, moon glow
You're all that I can call my own.   30

Maya Angelou (b. 1928)

QUESTIONS

1. What is the pattern of rhymes in lines 1–14? What does it shift to in lines 15–30? Whom is the speaker addressing in the first 14 lines? What figurative address characterizes the rest of the poem?

2. The phrases "I've got . . . gotta" (1–12) produce a type of refrain called **anaphora**, the repetition of an opening word or phrase in a series of lines. What feeling is expressed by this repetition here? How do the varying forms of the phrase characterize the speaker?

3. Most of the chores in the first 14 lines are associated popularly with "woman['s] work," but two are not. What do these exceptions reveal about the situation of the speaker?

4. What kinds of release from "work" are presented in lines 15–30? Metaphorically, what does the speaker desire in lines 19–26?

5. Explain the statement in the last four lines.

Rite of Passage

As the guests arrive at my son's party
they gather in the living room—
short men, men in first grade
with smooth jaws and chins.
Hands in pockets, they stand around   5
jostling, jockeying for place, small fights
breaking out and calming. One says to another
How old are you? Six. I'm seven. So?
They eye each other, seeing themselves
tiny in the other's pupils. They clear their   10
throats a lot, a room of small bankers,
they fold their arms and frown. *I could beat you
up*, a seven says to a six,
the dark cake, round and heavy as a
turret, behind them on the table. My son,   15
freckles like specks of nutmeg on his cheeks,
chest narrow as the balsa keel of a
model boat, long hands
cool and thin as the day they guided him
out of me, speaks up as a host   20
for the sake of the group.
We could easily kill a two-year-old,
he says in his clear voice. The other
men agree, they clear their throats
like Generals, they relax and get down to   25
playing war, celebrating my son's life.

Sharon Olds (b. 1942)

QUESTIONS

1. Vocabulary: *Rite of Passage* (title).
2. What is the implication of the metaphor comparing the boys to "bankers" clearing their throats? of that comparing them to "Generals" (25) doing the same thing? Is there a "rite of passage" implied in the shift from one comparison to the other?
3. What tones of voice would be appropriate for the phrase "*I'm seven*" and the reply "*So?*"(8)? Explain the image in the next sentence.
4. How are the similes in lines 14–15 and 16–17 linked? How do they function in the progress from bankers to Generals?
5. What is the speaker's tone as she describes the children's violent impulses?
6. The poem displays a considerable amount of musicality—alliteration, assonance, and consonance—through line 21. Identify these devices, and discuss the implication of their absence in the remainder of the poem.

As imperceptibly as Grief

As imperceptibly as Grief
The Summer lapsed away—
Too imperceptible at last
To seem like Perfidy—
A Quietness distilled   5
As Twilight long begun,
Or Nature spending with herself
Sequestered Afternoon—
The Dusk drew earlier in—
The Morning foreign shone—   10
A courteous, yet harrowing Grace,
As Guest, that would be gone—
And thus, without a Wing
Or service of a Keel
Our Summer made her light escape   15
Into the Beautiful.

Emily Dickinson (1830–1886)

QUESTIONS

1. What are the subject and tone of the poem? Explain its opening simile.
2. Discuss the ways in which approximate rhymes, alliteration, and the consonant sounds in the last four lines contribute to the meaning and tone.
3. What possible meanings have the last two lines?

Music Lessons

Sometimes, in the middle of the lesson,
we exchanged places. She would gaze a moment at her
   hands
spread over the keys; then the small house with its knick-
   knacks,
its shut windows,

its photographs of her sons and the serious husband,   5
vanished as new shapes formed. Sound
became music, and music a white
scarp for the listener to climb

alone. I leaped rock over rock to the top
and found myself waiting, transformed,   10
and still she played, her eyes luminous and willful,
her pinned hair falling down—

forgetting me, the house, the neat green yard,
she fled in that lick of flame all tedious bonds:
supper, the duties of flesh and home,   15
the knife at the throat, the death in the metronome.

Mary Oliver (b. 1935)

QUESTIONS

1. Vocabulary: *scarp* (8), *metronome* (16).
2. What musical qualities do you see in the poem? How are they appropriate?
3. Discuss the characterization of the piano teacher. What kind of woman is she? What does the speaker, now a mature adult, see in her that she didn't see when she actually knew the teacher?
4. Why does the speaker use imagery of violence and death in the final line? What poetic effect does this imagery have on the reader?

Traveling through the dark

Traveling through the dark I found a deer
dead on the edge of the Wilson River road.
It is usually best to roll them into the canyon:
that road is narrow; to swerve might make more dead.

By glow of the tail-light I stumbled back of the car   5
and stood by the heap, a doe, a recent killing;
she had stiffened already, almost cold.
I dragged her off; she was large in the belly.

My fingers touching her side brought me the reason —
her side was warm; her fawn lay there waiting,   10
alive, still, never to be born.
Beside that mountain road I hesitated.

The car aimed ahead its lowered parking lights;
under the hood purred the steady engine.
I stood in the glare of the warm exhaust turning red;   15
around our group I could hear the wilderness listen.

I thought hard for us all —my only swerving —,
then pushed her over the edge into the river.

William Stafford (1914–1993)

QUESTIONS

1. State precisely the speaker's dilemma. What kind of person is he? Does he make the right decision? Why does he call his hesitation "my only swerving" (17), and how does this connect with the word "swerve" in line 4?
2. What different kinds of imagery and of image contrasts give life to the poem? Do any of the images have symbolic overtones?
3. At first glance this poem may appear to be without end rhyme. Looking closer, do you find any correspondences between lines 2 and 4 in each four-line stanza? between lines 1 and 3 of stanzas 2 and 3? between the final words of the concluding couplet? What one line end in the poem has no connection in sound to another line end in its stanza?

Thistles

Against the rubber tongues of cows and the hoeing hands of men
Thistles spike the summer air
Or crackle open under a blue-black pressure.

Every one a revengeful burst
Of resurrection, a grasped fistful   5
Of splintered weapons and Icelandic frost thrust up

From the underground stain of a decayed Viking.
They are like pale hair and the gutturals of dialects.
Every one manages a plume of blood.

Then they grow grey, like men.   10
Mown down, it is a feud. Their sons appear,
Stiff with weapons, fighting back over the same ground.

Ted Hughes (1930–1998)

QUESTIONS

1. What natural characteristics of thistles are included in the poem? What
   identity do the similes and metaphors create for these plants?
2. What do the allusions to the violence of the marauding Vikings add to the
   poem? How are modern-day thistles like a resurrection of those warlike
   voyagers? Is this poem about thistles, about Vikings, or about some more
   universal subject?
3. What musical devices does the poem display? How do they suit the topic?

Nothing Gold Can Stay

Nature's first green is gold,
Her hardest hue to hold.
Her early leaf's a flower;
But only so an hour.
Then leaf subsides to leaf.   5
So Eden sank to grief,
So dawn goes down to day.
Nothing gold can stay.

Robert Frost (1874–1963)

QUESTIONS

1. Explain the paradoxes in lines 1 and 3.
2. Discuss the poem as a series of symbols. What are the symbolic meanings of
   "gold" in the final line of the poem?
3. Discuss the contributions of alliteration, assonance, consonance, rhyme, and
   other repetitions to the effectiveness of the poem.

SUGGESTIONS FOR WRITING

1. Write an essay analyzing the use and effectiveness of alliteration and/or assonance in one of the following:
   a. Shakespeare, "Shall I compare thee to a summer's day?" (page 642).
   b. Dickinson, "There's a certain Slant of light" (page 919).
   c. Donne, "The Good-Morrow" (page 957).
   d. Hardy, "The Darkling Thrush" (page 972).
   e. Robinson, "Richard Cory" (page 998).
2. Discuss the rhymes in one of the following. Does the poem employ exact rhymes or approximate rhymes? How do the kind and pattern of rhyme contribute to the poem's effect?
   a. MacLeish, "Ars Poetica" (page 652).
   b. Browning, "My Last Duchess" (page 768).
   c. Dickinson, "A narrow Fellow in the Grass" (page 956).
   d. Plath, "Spinster" (page 992).
   e. Heaney, "Follower" (page 973).

Rhythm and Meter

Our love of rhythm is rooted even more deeply in us than our love of musical repetition. It is related to the beat of our hearts, the pulse of our blood, the intake and outflow of air from our lungs. Everything that we do naturally and gracefully we do rhythmically. There is rhythm in the way we walk, the way we swim, the way we ride a horse, the way we swing a golf club or a baseball bat. So native is rhythm to us that we read it, when we can, into the mechanical world around us. Our clocks go tick-tick-tick, but we hear tick-tock, tick-tock. The click of railway wheels beneath us patterns itself into a tune in our heads. There is a strong appeal for us in language that is rhythmic.

The term **rhythm** refers to any wavelike recurrence of motion or sound. In speech it is the natural rise and fall of language. All language is to some degree rhythmic, for all language involves alternations between accented and unaccented syllables. Language varies considerably, however, in the degree to which it exhibits rhythm. Sometimes in speech the rhythm is so unobtrusive or so unpatterned that we are scarcely aware of it. Sometimes, as in rap or in oratory, the rhythm is so pronounced that we may be tempted to tap our feet to it.

In every word of more than one syllable, one or more syllables are **accented** or **stressed**; that is, given more prominence in pronunciation than the rest.* We say toDAY, toMORrow, YESterday, interVENE. These accents within individual words are indicated by stress marks in dictionaries, and with many words of more than two syllables primary and secondary stresses are shown (in'-ter-vene"). When words are arranged into a sentence, we give certain words or syllables more prominence in pronunciation than the rest. We say: "He WENT to the STORE" or "ANN is DRIVing her CAR." There is nothing

---

*Though the words *accent* and *stress* generally are used interchangeably, as here, a distinction is sometimes made between them in technical discussions. **Accent**, the relative prominence given a syllable in relation to its neighbors, is then said to result from one or more of four causes: *stress*, or force of utterance, producing loudness; *duration*; *pitch*; and *juncture*, the manner of transition between successive sounds. Of these, *stress*, in verse written in English, is the most important.

mysterious about this; it is the normal process of language. The major difference between prose and verse is that in prose these accents occur more or less haphazardly; in verse the poet may arrange them to occur at regular intervals.

In poetry as in prose, the rhythmic effects depend almost entirely on what a statement means, and different intended meanings will produce different rhythms even in identical statements. If I say "I don't believe YOU," I mean something different from "*I* don't believe you" or from "I don't beLIEVE you." In speech, these are **rhetorical stresses**, which we use to make our intentions clear. Stressing "you" separates you from others whom I believe; stressing "I" separates me from others who *do* believe you; stressing "believe" intensifies my statement of disbelief. Such rhetorical stressing comes as naturally to us as language itself, and is at least as important in poetry as it is in expressive speaking. It is also basic to understanding the rhythm of poetry, for poetic rhythm depends on the plain, rhetorical stresses to communicate its meaning. We must be able to recognize the meaning of a line of poetry before we can determine its rhythm.

In addition to accent or stress, rhythm is based on pauses. In poetry, as in prose or speech, pauses are the result of natural speech rhythms and the structure of sentences. Periods and commas create pauses, but so does the normal flow of phrases and clauses. Poetry, however, adds another kind of pause arising from the fact that poetry is written in lines. The poetic line is a unit that creates pauses in the flow of speech, sometimes slight and sometimes large. Poets have at their disposal a variety of possibilities when ending a line. An **end-stopped line** is one in which the end of the line corresponds with a natural speech pause; a **run-on line** is one in which the sense of the line moves on without pause into the next line. (There are of course all degrees of end-stop and run-on. A line ending with a period or semicolon is heavily end-stopped. A line without punctuation at the end is normally considered a run-on line, but it is less forcibly run-on if it ends at a natural speech pause—as between subject and predicate—than if it ends, say, between an article and its noun, between an auxiliary and its verb, or between a preposition and its object.) In addition there are pauses that occur within lines, either grammatical or rhetorical. These are called **caesuras**, and they are another resource for varying the rhythm of lines.

The poetic line is the basic rhythmic unit in **free verse**, the predominating type of poetry now being written. Except for its line arrangement there are no necessary differences between the rhythms of free verse and the rhythms of prose, so our awareness of the line as a rhythmic unit is essential. Consider the rhythmic contrast between end-stopped lines and run-on lines in these two excerpts from poems presented earlier, and notice how the caesuras (marked ||) help to vary the rhythms:

A noiseless patient spider,
I marked where on a little promontory it stood isolated,
Marked how to explore the vacant vast surrounding,
It launched forth filament, || filament, || filament, || out of itself,
Ever unreeling them, || ever tirelessly speeding them.

(page 727)

Sorrow is my own yard
where the new grass
flames || as it has flamed
often before || but not
with the cold fire
that closes round me this year.

(page 693)

There is another sort of poetry that depends entirely on ordinary prose rhythms—the **prose poem**, exemplified by Carolyn Forché's "The Colonel" (page 962) and Harryette Mullen's "Dim Lady" (page 988). Having dispensed even with the line as a unit of rhythm, the prose poem lays its claim to being poetry by its attention to many of the poetic elements presented earlier in this book: connotation, imagery, figurative language, and the concentration of meaning in evocative language.

But most often, when people think of poetry they think of the two broad branches, free verse and metrical verse, which are distinguished mainly by the absence or presence of meter. **Meter** is the identifying characteristic of rhythmic language that we can tap our feet to. When verse is metrical, the accents of language are so arranged as to occur at apparently equal intervals of time, and it is this interval we mark off with the tap of a foot.

The study of meter is fascinating but highly complex. It is by no means an absolute prerequisite to an enjoyment, even a rich enjoyment, of poetry, any more than is the ability to identify by name the multiplicity of figures of speech. But a knowledge of the fundamentals of meter does have value. It can make the beginning reader more aware of the rhythmic effects of poetry and of how poetry should be read. It can enable the more advanced reader to analyze how certain effects are achieved, to see how rhythm interacts with meaning, and to explain what makes one poem (in this respect) better than another. The beginning student ought to have at least an elementary knowledge of the subject. And it is not so difficult as its traditional terminology might suggest.

Even for the beginner, one essential distinction must be understood: although the terms *rhythm* and *meter* are sometimes used interchangeably, they mean different things. Rhythm designates the flow of actual, pronounced sound (or sound heard in the mind's ear), whereas meter refers to the patterns that sounds follow when a poet has arranged them into metrical verse. This may be illustrated by an analogy of a well-designed building and the architect's blueprint for its construction. The building, like rhythmic sound, is actual and real; the blueprint for it is an abstract, idealized pattern, like metrical form. When we look at a building, we see the actuality, but we also recognize that it is based on a pattern. The actuality of the building goes beyond the idealized blueprint in a number of ways—it presents us with texture, with color, with varying effects depending on light and shade, with contrasts of building materials. In poetry, the actuality is language arranged in sentences, with a progression through time, with varying emotions, dramatic contrasts of meaning and tone, the revelation of the speaker's situation, and so forth. All these are expressed through the sounds of language, which are constantly shifting to create meanings and implications.

The word *meter* comes from a word meaning "measure" (the word *rhythm* from a word meaning "flow," as in waves). To measure something we must have a unit of measurement. For measuring length we use the inch, foot, yard; for measuring time we use the second, minute, hour. For measuring verse we use the foot, the line, and (sometimes) the stanza.

One basic unit of meter, the **foot**, consists normally of one accented syllable plus one or two unaccented syllables, though occasionally there may be no unaccented syllables. To determine which syllable in a foot is accented, we compare its sound with that of the other syllables *within the foot*, not with the sounds of syllables in other feet within a line. In fact, because of the varying stresses on syllables in a spoken sentence, it is very unusual for all of the stressed syllables in a line to be equally stressed.

For diagramming the metrical form of verse, various systems of visual symbols have been devised. In this book we shall use a breve (˘) to indicate an unstressed syllable, an ictus (′) to indicate a stressed syllable, and a vertical bar to indicate the division between feet. The basic kinds of feet are as follows:

Examples	Name of Foot	Adjectival Form	
ŭ ´ ŭ ´ to-day, the sun	Iamb	Iambic	⎤ ⎬ Duple meters
´ ŭ ´ ŭ dai-ly, went to	Trochee	Trochaic	⎦
ŭ ŭ ´ ŭ ŭ ´ in-ter-vene, in the dark	Anapest	Anapestic	⎤ ⎬ Triple meters
´ ŭ ŭ ´ ŭ ŭ mul-ti-ple, col-or of	Dactyl	Dactylic	⎦
´ ´ true-blue	Spondee*	Spondaic	

Two kinds of examples are given here, whole words and phrases, to indicate the fact that one must not assume that every individual word will be a foot, nor that divisions between feet necessarily fall between words. In actual lines, one might for example find the word *intervene* constituting parts of two different feet:

ŭ ´ | ŭ ´ | ŭ ´
I want to in- ter-vene.

As this example demonstrates, in diagramming meters we must sometimes acknowledge the primary and secondary stresses provided by dictionaries: the word *intervene* provides the stresses for two consecutive feet.

The other basic unit of measurement in metrical verse is the line, which has the same properties as in free verse—it may be end-stopped or run-on, and its phrasing and punctuation will create caesuras. The difference between metrical and free-verse lines is that metrical lines are measured by naming the number of feet in them. The following names indicate number:

Monometer	one foot	Tetrameter	four feet
Dimeter	two feet	Pentameter	five feet
Trimeter	three feet	Hexameter	six feet

---

*In the spondee the accent is thought of as being distributed equally or almost equally over the two syllables and is sometimes referred to as a hovering accent. No whole poems are written in spondees. Hence there are only four basic meters: iambic, trochaic, anapestic, and dactylic. Iambic and trochaic are called duple because they employ two-syllable feet, anapestic and dactylic triple because they employ three-syllable feet. Of the four standard meters, iambic is by far the most common, followed by anapestic. Trochaic occurs relatively infrequently as the meter of poems, and dactylic is so rare as to be almost a museum specimen.

The third unit of measurement, the **stanza**, consists of a group of lines whose metrical pattern is repeated throughout the poem. Since much verse is not written in stanzas, we shall save our discussion of this unit until a later chapter.

Although metrical form is potentially uniform in its regularity, the poet may introduce **metrical variations**, which call attention to some of the sounds because they depart from what is regular. Three means for varying meter are **substitution** (replacing the regular foot with another one), **extrametrical syllables** added at the beginnings or endings of lines, and **truncation** (the omission of an unaccented syllable at either end of a line). Because these represent clear changes in the pattern, they are usually obvious and striking. But even metrical regularity rarely creates a monotonous rhythm because rhythm is the actuality in sound, not the pattern or blueprint of meter. The rhythm of a line of poetry, like the actuality of a building, depends on the components of sound mentioned above—stress, duration, pitch, and juncture—as these are presented in rhetorically stressed sentences. We may diagram the metrical form of a line, but because no two sentences in English are identical in sound, there can be no formulas or mechanical systems for indicating rhythm. Rhythm must be described rather than formulated.

The process of defining the metrical form of a poem is called **scansion**. To *scan* any specimen of verse, we do three things: (1) we identify the prevailing foot; (2) we name the number of feet in a line—if this length follows any regular pattern; and (3) we describe the stanzaic pattern—if there is one. We may try out our skill on the following poem:

Virtue

> Sweet day, so cool, so calm, so bright,
>> The bridal of the earth and sky;
> The dew shall weep thy fall to night,
>> For thou must die.

> Sweet rose, whose hue, angry and brave,   5
>> Bids the rash gazer wipe his eye;
> Thy root is ever in its grave,
>> And thou must die.

> Sweet spring, full of sweet days and roses,
>> A box where sweets compacted lie;   10

My music shows ye have your closes,
    And all must die.

Only a sweet and virtuous soul,
    Like seasoned timber, never gives;
But though the whole world turn to coal,   15
    Then chiefly lives.

                        George Herbert (1593–1633)

QUESTIONS

1. Vocabulary: *bridal* (2), *brave* (5), *closes* (11), *coal* (15).
2. How are the four stanzas interconnected? How do they build to a climax?
   How does the fourth contrast with the first three?

    The first step in scanning a poem is to read it normally, according to
its prose meaning, listening to where the accents fall naturally, and
perhaps beating time with the hand. If we have any doubt about how
a line should be marked, we should skip it temporarily and go on to lines
where we feel greater confidence; that is, to those lines that seem most
regular, with accents that fall unmistakably at regular intervals—for we
are seeking the poem's pattern, which will be revealed by what is regular
in it. In "Virtue" lines 3, 10, and 14 clearly fall into this category, as do
the short lines 4, 8, and 12. Lines 3, 10, and 14 may be marked as
follows.

The dĕw | shall weep | thy fall | to night,   3

A bŏx | where sweets | com-pact- | ed lie;   10

Like sea- | soned tim- | ber, nev- | er gives   14

Lines 4, 8, and 12 are so nearly identical that we may use line 4 to
represent all three.

For thou | must die.   4

Surveying what we have done so far, we may with some confidence say
that the prevailing metrical foot of the poem is iambic; and we may
reasonably hypothesize that the second and third lines of each stanza are
tetrameter (four-foot) lines and the fourth line dimeter. What about the

first lines? Line 1 contains eight syllables, and since the poem is iambic, we may mark them into four feet. The last six syllables clearly constitute three iambic feet (as a general rule, the last few feet in a line tend to reflect the prevailing meter of a poem).

$$\text{Sweet day, | so cool, | so calm, | so bright}$$ 1

This too, then, is a tetrameter line, and the only question is whether to mark the first foot as another iamb or as a spondee—that is, whether it conforms to the norm established by the iambic meter, or is a substituted foot. The adjective "Sweet" is certainly more important in the line than the repeated adverb "so," and ought to receive more stress than the adverbs on the principle of *rhetorical stress,* by which the plain prose sense governs the pronunciation. But we must remember that in marking metrical stresses, we are only comparing the syllables *within a foot,* so the comparison with the repeated "so" is irrelevant. The real question is whether "Sweet" receives as much emphasis as "day."

As another general rule (but by no means an absolute one), a noun usually receives more stress than an adjective that modifies it, a verb more than its adverbs, and an adjective more than an adverb that modifies it—except when the modifying word points to an unusual or unexpected condition. If the phrase were "fat day" or "red day," we would probably feel that those adjectives were odd enough to warrant stressing them. "Sweet day" does not strike us as particularly unusual, so the noun ought to receive stress. Further, as we notice that each of the first three stanzas begins with "Sweet" modifying different nouns, we recognize that the statement of the poem is drawing attention to the similarities (and differences) of three things that can be called *sweet*—"day," "rose," and "spring." By its repetition before those three nouns, the word *sweet* may come to seem formulaic, and the nouns the object of attention. On the other hand, the repetition of "Sweet" may seem emphatic, and lead us to give approximately equal stress to both the noun and its adjective. As our purpose is to detect the *pattern* of sounds in the poem, the most likely result of this study will be to mark it iambic. However, judging it to be spondaic would not be incorrect, for ultimately we are reporting what we *hear,* and there is room for subjective differences.

The first feet of lines 5 and 9 raise the same problem as line 1 and should be marked in the same way. Choices of a similar sort occur in other lines (15 and 16). Many readers will quite legitimately perceive line 16 as parallel to lines 4, 8, and 12. Others, however, may argue that the word "Then"—emphasizing what happens to the virtuous soul when everything else has perished—has an importance that should be reflected in both the reading and the scansion, and will therefore mark the first foot of this line as a spondee:

Then chief-́ly li´ves.   16

These readers also will hear the third foot in line 15 as a spondee:

But though the whole world turn to coal   15

Lines 2 and 7 introduce a different problem. Most readers, if they encountered these lines in a paragraph of prose, would read them thus:

The BRIdal of the EARTH and SKY   2

Thy ROOT is EVer in its GRAVE   7

But this reading leaves us with an anomalous situation. First, we have only three stresses where our pattern calls for four. Second, we have three unaccented syllables occurring together, which is almost never found in verse of duple meter. From this situation we may learn an important principle. Though normal reading of the sentences in a poem establishes its metrical pattern, the metrical pattern so established in turn influences the reading. An interactive process is at work. In this poem the pressure of the pattern will cause most practiced readers to stress the second of the three unaccented syllables in both lines slightly more than those on either side of it. In scansion, comparing the syllables within the individual foot, we acknowledge that slight increase of stress by marking those syllables as stressed (remember, the marking of the accent does not indicate a *degree* of stress in comparison with other accents in the line). We mark them thus:

The bri-́dal of the earth and sky   2

Thy root is ev-́er in its grave   7

Line 5 presents a situation about which there can be no dispute. The word "angry," though it occurs in a position where we would expect an iamb, by virtue of its normal pronunciation *must* be accented on the first syllable, and thus must be marked a trochee:

Sweet rose, whose hue, an-gry and brave   5

There is little question also that the following line begins with a trochee, but the second foot ("rash gaz-") must be examined, for we may wonder whether the adjective *rash* presents an unexpected modification for the noun *gazer*. Since the possibilities seem about equal, we prefer to let the pattern again take precedence, although a spondee would be acceptable:

Bids the rash gaz-er wipe his eye   6

Similarly, the word "Only," beginning line 13, must be accented on the first syllable, thus introducing a trochaic substitution in the first foot of the line. Line 13 also presents another problem. A modern reader perceives the word "virtuous" as a three-syllable word, but the poet writing in the seventeenth century, when metrical requirements were stricter than they are today, would probably have meant the word to be pronounced as two syllables: *ver*-tyus. Following the tastes of this century, we mark it as three syllables, so introducing an anapest instead of the expected iamb in the last foot:

On-ly a sweet and vir-tu-ous soul   13

In doing this, however, we are consciously modernizing—altering the probable practice of the poet for the sake of a contemporary audience.

One problem of scansion remains: in the third stanza, lines 9 and 11 differ from the other lines of the poem in two respects—(a) they contain an uneven number of syllables (nine rather than the expected eight); (b) they end on unaccented syllables:

Sweet spring, full of sweet days and ros-es,   9

My mu-sic shows ye have your clos-es   11

Such leftover unaccented syllables at line ends are examples of extrametrical syllables and are not counted in identifying and naming the meter. These lines are both tetrameter, and if we tap our feet when reading them, we shall tap four times. Metrical verse will often have one and sometimes two leftover unaccented syllables. In iambic and anapestic verse they will come at the end of the lines; in trochaic and dactylic, at the beginning. They never occur in the middle of a line.

Our metrical analysis of "Virtue" is completed. Though (mainly for ease of discussion) we have skipped about, we have indicated a scansion for all its lines. "Virtue" is written in iambic meter (meaning that most of its feet are iambs), and is composed of four-line stanzas, the first three lines tetrameter, the final line dimeter. We are now ready to make a few generalizations about scansion.

1. Good readers will not ordinarily stop to scan a poem they are reading, and they certainly will not read a poem aloud with the exaggerated emphasis on accented syllables that we sometimes give them in order to make the metrical pattern more apparent. However, occasional scansion of a poem has value, as will be indicated in the next chapter, which discusses the relation of sound and meter to sense. Just one example here. The structure of meaning of "Virtue" is unmistakable; three parallel stanzas concerning things that die are followed by a contrasting fourth stanza concerning the one thing that does not die. The first three stanzas all begin with the word "Sweet" preceding a noun, and the first metrical foot in these stanzas is either an iamb or a spondee. The contrasting fourth stanza, however, begins with a trochee, thus departing both from the previous pattern and from the basic meter of the poem. This departure is significant, for the word *only* is the hinge upon which the structure of the poem turns, and the metrical reversal gives it emphasis. Thus meter serves meaning.

2. Scansion only begins to reveal the rhythmic quality of a poem. It simply involves classifying all syllables as either accented or unaccented and ignores the sometimes considerable differences between degrees of accent. Whether we call a syllable accented or unaccented depends only on its degree of accent relative to the other syllable(s) in its foot. In lines 2 and 7 of "Virtue," the accents on "of" and "in" are obviously much lighter than on the other accented syllables in the line. Further, unaccented syllables also vary in weight. In line 5 "whose" is clearly heavier than "-gry" or "and," and is arguably even heavier than the accented "of" and "in" of lines 2 and 7. It is not unusual, either, to find the unaccented syllable of a foot receiving more stress than the accented syllable immediately preceding it in another foot, as in this line by Gerard Manley Hopkins (page 824):

It will | flame out | like shin- | ing from | shook foil

The last four syllables of the line, two perfectly regular iambs, are actually spoken as a sequence of four increasingly stressed accents. A similar sequence of increasing accents occurs in lines 4, 8, and 12 of "Virtue,"

$$\text{For thŏu}'\text{mŭst diĕ}'| \qquad\qquad 4$$

since the necessity expressed in the word "must" makes it more heavily stressed than the pronoun "thou." The point is that metrical scansion is incapable of describing subtle rhythmic effects in poetry. It is nevertheless a useful and serviceable tool, for by showing us the metrical *pattern*, it draws attention to the way in which the actuality of sound follows the pattern even while departing from it; that is, recognizing the meter, we can more clearly hear rhythms. The *idea* of regularity helps us be aware of the *actuality* of sounds.

3. Notice that the divisions between feet have no meaning except to help us identify the meter. They do not correspond to the speech rhythms in the line. In the third foot of line 14 of "Virtue," a syntactical pause occurs *within* the foot; and, indeed, feet divisions often fall in the middle of a word. It is sometimes a mistake of beginners to expect the word and the foot to be identical units. We mark the feet divisions only to reveal regularity or pattern, not to indicate rhythm. But in "Virtue," if we examine all of the two-syllable words, we find that all eleven of them as isolated words removed from their lines would be called *trochaic*. Yet only two of them—"angry" (5) and "only" (3)—actually occur as trochaic feet. All the rest are divided in the middle between two iambic feet. This calls for two observations: (a) the rhythm of the poem, the *heard* sound, often runs counter to the meter—iambic feet have what is called a "rising" pattern, yet these words individually and as they are spoken have a "falling" rhythm; and (b) the trochaic hinge word "only" thus has rhythmic echoes throughout the poem, those preceding it yielding a kind of predictive power, and those following it reinforcing the fact that the sense of the poem turns at that word. This rhythmic effect is especially pronounced in the simile of line 14:

$$\text{Like sĕa-}'\text{sŏned tĭm-}'\text{bĕr, nĕv-}'\text{er gĭves}'| \qquad 14$$

Echoing the key word "only," this line contains three disyllabic words, each of them having a falling rhythm running counter to the iambic meter.

4. Finally—and this is the most important generalization of all—perfect regularity of meter is no criterion of merit. Inexperienced readers sometimes get the notion that it is. If the meter is regular and the rhythm mirrors that regularity in sound, they may feel that the poet has handled the meter successfully and deserves all credit for it. Actually there is nothing easier for any moderately talented versifier than to make language go ta-DUM ta-DUM ta-DUM. But there are two reasons why this is not generally desirable. The first is that, as we have said, all art consists essentially of repetition and variation. If a rhythm alternates too regularly between light and heavy beats, the result is to banish variation; the rhythm mechanically follows the meter and becomes monotonous. But used occasionally or emphatically, a monotonous rhythm can be very effective, as in the triumphant last line of Tennyson's "Ulysses" (page 747):

To strive, to seek, to find, and not to yield.

The second reason is that once a basic meter has been established, deviations from it become highly significant and are a means by which the poet can reinforce meaning. If a meter is too regular and the rhythm shows little deviation from it, the probability is that the poet, instead of adapting rhythm to meaning, has simply forced the meaning into a metrical straitjacket.

Actually what gives the skillful use of meter its greatest effectiveness is to be found in the distinction between meter and rhythm. Once we have determined the basic meter of a poem, say iambic tetrameter, we have an expectation that the rhythm will coincide with it—that the pattern will be identical to the actual sound. Thus a silent drumbeat is set up in our minds, and this drumbeat constitutes an **expected rhythm**. But the actual rhythm of the words—the **heard rhythm**—will sometimes confirm this expected rhythm and sometimes not. Thus the two—meter and rhythm—are counterpointed, and the appeal of the verse is magnified, just as when two melodies are counterpointed in music, or when we see two swallows flying together and around each other, following the same general course but with individual variations and so making a more eye-catching pattern than one swallow flying alone. If the heard rhythm conforms too closely to the expected rhythm (meter), the poem becomes dull and uninteresting rhythmically. If it departs too far from the meter, there ceases to be an expected rhythm and the result is likely to be a muddle.

There are several ways by which variation can be introduced into a poem's rhythm. The most obvious way, as we have said, is by the substitution of other kinds of feet for the basic foot. Such metrical variation will always be reflected as a rhythmic variation. In our scansion of line 13 of "Virtue," for instance, we found a trochee and an anapest substituted for the expected iambs in the first and last feet. A less obvious but equally important means of variation is through varying degrees of accent arising from the prose meaning of phrases—from the rhetorical stressing. Though we began our scansion of "Virtue" by marking lines 3, 10, and 14 as perfectly regular metrically, there is actually a considerable rhythmic difference between them. Line 3 is quite regular because the rhythmic phrasing corresponds to the metrical pattern, and the line can be read: ta DUM ta DUM ta DUM ta DUM (The DEW shall WEEP thy FALL to NIGHT). Line 10 is less regular, for the three-syllable word "compacted" cuts across the division between two feet. This should be read: ta DUM ta DUM ta-DUM-ta DUM (a BOX where SWEETS comPACTed LIE). Line 14 is the least regular of these three because here there is no correspondence between rhythmic phrasing and metrical division. This should be read: ta DUM-ta DUM-ta DUM-ta DUM (Like SEAsoned TIMber, NEVer GIVES). Finally, variation can be introduced by **grammatical** and **rhetorical pauses**, whether or not signaled by punctuation (punctuated pauses are usually of longer duration than those occasioned only by syntax and rhetoric, and pauses for periods are longer than those for commas). The comma in line 14, by introducing a grammatical pause (in the middle of a foot), provides an additional variation from its perfect regularity. Probably the most violently irregular line in the poem is line 5,

Sweet rose, whose hue, an-gry and brave,   5

for here the unusual trochaic substitution in the second from last foot of an iambic line (a rare occurrence) is set off and emphasized by the grammatical pause; and also, as we have noted, the unaccented "whose" is considerably heavier than the other unaccented syllables in the line. This trochee "angry" is the first unquestionable metrical substitution in the poem. It occurs in a line which, because it opens a stanza, is subconsciously compared to the first line of the first stanza—an example of regularity with its grammatical pauses separating all four of its feet. Once we have noticed that the first line of the second stanza contains a metrical variation, our attention is called to the fact that after the first, each stanza opens with a line containing a trochee—and that these trochees are moved forward one foot in each of the successive stanzas, from the third position in stanza two, to the second in four, and finally to the first in the concluding stanza. This pattern itself tends to add even more emphasis to the climactic change signaled by the final trochee, "only." Again, meter and rhythm serve meaning.

The effects of rhythm and meter are several. Like the musical repetitions of sound, the musical repetitions of accent can be pleasing for their own sake. In addition, rhythm works as an emotional stimulus and heightens our awareness of what is going on in a poem. Finally, a poet can adapt the sound of the verse to its content and thus make meter a powerful reinforcement of meaning. We should avoid, however, the notion that there is any mystical correspondence between certain meters or rhythms and certain emotions. There are no "happy" meters and no "melancholy" meters. The "falling" rhythm of line 14 of "Virtue," counterpointed against its "rising" meter, does not indicate a depression of mood or feeling—the line has quite the opposite emotional tone. Poets' choice of meter is probably less important than how they handle it after they have chosen it. In most great poetry, meter and rhythm work intimately with the other elements of the poem to produce the total effect.

And because of the importance of free verse today, we must not forget that poetry need not be metrical at all. Like alliteration and rhyme, like metaphor and irony, like even imagery, meter is simply *one* resource poets may or may not use. Their job is to employ their resources to the best advantage for the object they have in mind—the kind of experience they wish to express. And on no other basis should they be judged.

EXERCISES

1. A term that every student of poetry should know (and should be careful not to confuse with *free verse*) is blank verse. **Blank verse** has a very specific meter: it is *iambic pentameter, unrhymed.* It has a special name because it is the principal English meter; that is, the meter that has been used for a large proportion of the greatest English poetry, including the plays of Shakespeare and the epics of Milton. Iambic pentameter in English seems especially suitable for the serious treatment of serious themes. The natural movement of the English language tends to be iambic. Lines shorter than pentameter tend to be songlike, or at least less suited to sustained treatment of serious material. Lines longer than pentameter tend to break up into shorter units, the hexameter line being read as two three-foot units. Rhyme, while highly appropriate to many short poems, often proves a handicap for a long and lofty work. (The word *blank* indicates that the end of the line is bare of rhyme.)

Of the following poems, four are in blank verse, two are in other meters, and four are in free verse. Determine in which category each belongs.

a. Frost, "Birches" (page 963).
b. Donne, "Break of Day" (page 664).
c. Hughes, "Thistles" (page 832).
d. Plath, "Mirror" (page 669).
e. Tennyson, "Ulysses" (page 745).
f. Arnold, "Dover Beach" (page 813).
g. Auden, "The Unknown Citizen" (page 767).
h. Yeats, "The Second Coming" (page 1018).
i. Frost, "'Out, Out—'" (page 773).
j. Atwood, "Siren Song" (page 780).

2. Examine Browning, "My Last Duchess" (page 768) and Pope, "Sound and Sense" (page 865). Both are in the same meter, iambic pentameter rhymed in couplets, but their general rhythmic effect is markedly different. What accounts for the difference? How does the contrast support our statement that the way poets handle meter is more important than their choice of a meter?

3. Examine Williams, "The Widow's Lament in Springtime" (page 693), Angelou, "Lady Luncheon Club" (page 759), and Williams, "The Dance" (page 879). Which is the most forcibly run-on in the majority of its lines? Describe the differences in effect.

REVIEWING CHAPTER TWELVE

1. Review the terms printed in boldface, and as you read on in this chapter take note of the examples that you find; identify the poems as free verse or metrical, and write out scansions of the metrical verse.

2. Using examples from the poems that follow in this chapter, draw clear distinctions between rhythm and meter; and using appropriate adjectives, describe the rhythmic effects (jolly, somber, playful, etc.).

3. When possible, explain how the rhythms of a poem reinforce emotional or intellectual meanings.

"Introduction" to *Songs of Innocence*

Piping down the valleys wild,
Piping songs of pleasant glee,
On a cloud I saw a child,
And he laughing said to me:

"Pipe a song about a Lamb."   5
So I piped with merry cheer.
"Piper, pipe that song again."
So I piped; he wept to hear.

"Drop thy pipe, thy happy pipe;
Sing thy songs of happy cheer."   10
So I sung the same again
While he wept with joy to hear.

"Piper, sit thee down and write
In a book that all may read."
So he vanished from my sight,   15
And I plucked a hollow reed,

And I made a rural pen,
And I stained the water clear,
And I wrote my happy songs
Every child may joy to hear.   20

William Blake (1757–1827)

QUESTIONS

1. Poets have traditionally been thought of as inspired by one of the Muses (Greek female divinities whose duties were to nurture the arts). Blake's *Songs of Innocence,* a book of poems about childhood and the state of innocence, includes "The Chimney Sweeper" (page 756) and "The Lamb" (page 793). In this introductory poem to the book, what function is performed by the child upon a cloud?
2. What is symbolized by "a Lamb" (5)?
3. What three stages of poetic composition are suggested in stanzas 1–2, 3, and 4–5 respectively?
4. What features of the poems in his book does Blake hint at in this "Introduction"? Name at least four.

5. Mark the stressed and unstressed syllables in lines 1–2 and 9–10. Do they establish the basic meter of the poem? If so, is that meter iambic or trochaic? Or could it be either? Some metrists have discarded the distinction between iambic and trochaic, and between anapestic and dactylic, as being artificial. The important distinction, they feel, is between duple and triple meters. Does this poem support their claim?

Had I the Choice

Had I the choice to tally greatest bards,
To limn their portraits, stately, beautiful, and emulate at will,
Homer with all his wars and warriors—Hector, Achilles, Ajax,
Or Shakespeare's woe-entangled Hamlet, Lear, Othello—Tennyson's
    fair ladies,
Meter or wit the best, or choice conceit to wield in perfect rhyme,   5
    delight of singers;
These, these, O sea, all these I'd gladly barter,
Would you the undulation of one wave, its trick to me transfer,
Or breathe one breath of yours upon my verse,
And leave its odor there.

                          Walt Whitman (1819–1892)

QUESTIONS

1. Vocabulary: *tally* (1), *limn* (2), *conceit* (5).
2. What poetic qualities does the speaker propose to barter in exchange for what? What qualities do the sea and its waves symbolize?
3. Is this free verse, or metrical verse in duple meter? In what way might this be taken as an imitation of the rhythms of the sea?

The Aim Was Song

    Before man came to blow it right
        The wind once blew itself untaught,
    And did its loudest day and night
        In any rough place where it caught.

    Man came to tell it what was wrong: 5
        It hadn't found the place to blow;
    It blew too hard—the aim was song.
        And listen—how it ought to go!

He took a little in his mouth,
　　And held it long enough for north   10
To be converted into south,
　　And then by measure blew it forth.

By measure. It was word and note,
　　The wind the wind had meant to be—
A little through the lips and throat.   15
　　The aim was song—the wind could see.

Robert Frost (1874–1963)

QUESTIONS

1. Frost invents a myth about the origin of poetry. What implications does it suggest about the relation of man to nature and of poetry to nature?
2. Contrast the thought and form of this poem with Whitman's.
3. Scan the poem and identify its meter. How does the poet give variety to a regular metrical pattern?

Stanzas

When a man hath no freedom to fight for at home,
　　Let him combat for that of his neighbors;
Let him think of the glories of Greece and of Rome,
　　And get knocked on his head for his labors.

To do good to mankind is the chivalrous plan,   5
　　And is always as nobly requited:
Then battle for freedom wherever you can,
　　And, if not shot or hanged, you'll get knighted.

George Gordon, Lord Byron (1788–1824)

QUESTIONS

1. Vocabulary: *chivalrous* (5), *requited* (6).
2. Scan the poem. How would you describe its rhythmical effects? How do these effects relate to the poem's tone and general meaning?
3. This poem makes use of feminine rhyme. Does this particular kind of rhyme affect the way you read and understand the poem?
4. How is irony effectively used in this poem, particularly in the final line?

Old Ladies' Home

Sharded in black, like beetles,
Frail as antique earthenware
One breath might shiver to bits,
The old women creep out here
To sun on the rocks or prop   5
Themselves up against the wall
Whose stones keep a little heat.

Needles knit in a bird-beaked
Counterpoint to their voices:
Sons, daughters, daughters and sons,   10
Distant and cold as photos,
Grandchildren nobody knows.
Age wears the best black fabric
Rust-red or green as lichens.

At owl-call the old ghosts flock   15
To hustle them off the lawn.
From beds boxed-in like coffins
The bonneted ladies grin.
And Death, that bald-head buzzard,
Stalls in halls where the lamp wick   20
Shortens with each breath drawn.

Sylvia Plath (1932–1963)

QUESTIONS

1. Vocabulary: *Sharded* (1), *Stalls* (20).
2. Discuss the significance of these natural images: "beetles" (1), "bird-beaked / Counterpoint" (8–9), "Rust-red or green as lichens" (14), "owl-call" (15), "bald-head buzzard" (19). These are all metaphors or similes; in each case, what is being compared to what?
3. What is the speaker's tone?
4. This poem is an example of **syllabic verse**, which counts only the number of syllables per line, regardless of accents. (Plath's "Metaphors" [page 717] is another example.) In this case, the poem is constructed of seven-syllable lines in seven-line stanzas—but there is one line that contains only six syllables. What is the significance of the shortening of that line?
5. The poem contains some rhyme (particularly slant rhyme), and some of the lines contain duple metrical feet. Are these musical effects regular enough to call this a metrical poem?

Africa

Thus she had lain
sugarcane sweet
deserts her hair
golden her feet
mountains her breasts   5
two Niles her tears.
Thus she has lain
Black through the years.

Over the white seas
rime white and cold   10
brigands ungentled
icicle bold
took her young daughters
sold her strong sons
churched her with Jesus   15
bled her with guns.
Thus she has lain.

Now she is rising
remember her pain
remember the losses   20
her screams loud and vain
remember her riches
her history slain
now she is striding
although she had lain.   25

Maya Angelou (b. 1928)

QUESTIONS

1. What attitude toward the continent is expressed in the first stanza? To what is it compared? How does the second stanza extend that comparison?
2. The last stanza shifts from history to the present. What attitude does it express?
3. When you scan the poem, is it trochaic or iambic? How many accented syllables is the norm? Where, and with what effect, does the poem vary that norm?

To a Daughter Leaving Home

When I taught you
at eight to ride
a bicycle, loping along
beside you
as you wobbled away   5
on two round wheels,
my own mouth rounding
in surprise when you pulled
ahead down the curved
path of the park,   10
I kept waiting
for the thud
of your crash as I
sprinted to catch up,
while you grew   15
smaller, more breakable
with distance,
pumping, pumping
for your life, screaming
with laughter,   20
the hair flapping
behind you like a
handkerchief waving
goodbye.

Linda Pastan (b. 1932)

QUESTIONS

1. How does the discrepancy between the title and the event create meaning?
   Which details of the poem take on symbolic meaning?
2. Write out this poem as prose, ignoring line ends. What poetic effect has been
   lost? Which of the original line ends are particularly important to meaning
   and feeling?

A Blessing

Just off the highway to Rochester, Minnesota,
Twilight bounds softly forth on the grass.
And the eyes of those two Indian ponies

Darken with kindness.
They have come gladly out of the willows   5
To welcome my friend and me.
We step over the barbed wire into the pasture
Where they have been grazing all day, alone.
They ripple tensely, they can hardly contain their happiness
That we have come.   10
They bow shyly as wet swans. They love each other.
There is no loneliness like theirs.
At home once more,
They begin munching the young tufts of spring in the darkness.
I would like to hold the slenderer one in my arms,   15
For she has walked over to me
And nuzzled my left hand.
She is black and white,
Her mane falls wild on her forehead,
And the light breeze moves me to caress her long ear   20
That is delicate as the skin over a girl's wrist.
Suddenly I realize
That if I stepped out of my body I would break
Into blossom.

James Wright (1927–1980)

QUESTIONS

1. How does the first line persuade the reader to accept the reality of the poem? What nonrealistic figure of speech predominates in the description of the ponies? What is the actual reality of lines 9–10?
2. What is so attractive to the speaker in the ponies' behavior? As he begins to describe "the slenderer one" (15), what implicit comparison does his language create?
3. What is the meaning of the sudden realization of lines 22–24?
4. In this example of free verse, the poem mostly fits complete phrase to line length. But there are exceptions, when the meaning requires you to ignore the end of a line. Where do these exceptions occur, and what do they contribute to the effect of the poem?

Porphyria's Lover

The rain set early in tonight,
    The sullen wind was soon awake,
It tore the elm-tops down for spite,

And did its worst to vex the lake:
   I listened with heart fit to break.   5
When glided in Porphyria; straight
   She shut the cold out and the storm,
And kneeled and made the cheerless grate
   Blaze up, and all the cottage warm;
   Which done, she rose, and from her form   10
Withdrew the dripping cloak and shawl,
   And laid her soiled gloves by, untied
Her hat and let the damp hair fall,
   And, last, she sat down by my side
   And called me. When no voice replied,   15
She put my arm about her waist,
   And made her smooth white shoulder bare,
And all her yellow hair displaced,
   And, stooping, made my cheek lie there,
   And spread, o'er all, her yellow hair,   20
Murmuring how she loved me—she
   Too weak, for all her heart's endeavor,
To set its struggling passion free
   From pride, and vainer ties dissever,
   And give herself to me forever.   25
But passion sometimes would prevail,
   Nor could tonight's gay feast restrain
A sudden thought of one so pale
   For love of her, and all in vain:
   So, she was come through wind and rain.   30
Be sure I looked up at her eyes
   Happy and proud; at last I knew
Porphyria worshipped me: surprise
   Made my heart swell, and still it grew
   While I debated what to do.   35
That moment she was mine, mine, fair,
   Perfectly pure and good: I found
A thing to do, and all her hair
   In one long yellow string I wound
   Three times her little throat around,   40
And strangled her. No pain felt she;
   I am quite sure she felt no pain.
As a shut bud that holds a bee,
   I warily oped her lids: again
   Laughed the blue eyes without a stain.   45

And I untightened next the tress
  About her neck; her cheek once more
Blushed bright beneath my burning kiss:
  I propped her head up as before,
  Only, this time my shoulder bore   50
Her head, which droops upon it still:
  The smiling rosy little head,
So glad it has its utmost will,
  That all it scorned at once is fled,
  And I, its love, am gained instead!   55
Porphyria's love: she guessed not how
  Her darling one wish would be heard.
And thus we sit together now,
  And all night long we have not stirred
  And yet God has not said a word!   60

Robert Browning (1812–1889)

QUESTIONS

1. Why can Porphyria and the speaker not be together in a normal romantic relationship? What has kept them apart?
2. What is the "gay feast" mentioned in line 27?
3. The poem deals, in part, with abnormal human psychology. What kind of a person is the speaker? What does he reveal about himself as the poem proceeds? Why does he take such drastic action?
4. The final line has been read in a variety of ways. Why has God "not said a word"? Does this mean that God has countenanced the murder?
5. How would you describe the metrical pattern in this poem? How does the pattern help reinforce the poem's meaning?

Break, break, break

Break, break, break,
  On thy cold gray stones, O sea!
And I would that my tongue could utter
  The thoughts that arise in me.

O, well for the fisherman's boy,   5
  That he shouts with his sister at play!
O, well for the sailor lad,
  That he sings in his boat on the bay!

And the stately ships go on
   To their haven under the hill;   10
But O for the touch of a vanished hand,
   And the sound of a voice that is still!

Break, break, break,
   At the foot of thy crags, O sea!
But the tender grace of a day that is dead   15
   Will never come back to me.

               Alfred, Lord Tennyson (1809–1892)

QUESTIONS

1. In lines 3–4 the speaker wishes he could put his thoughts into words. Does he make those thoughts explicit in the course of the poem?
2. What aspects of life are symbolized by the two images in stanza 2? By the image in lines 9–10? How do lines 11–12 contrast with those images?
3. The basic meter of this poem is anapestic, and all but two lines are trimeter. Which two? What other variations from a strict anapestic trimeter do you find? How many lines (and which ones) display a strict anapestic pattern? With this much variation, would you be justified in calling the poem free verse? Do the departures from a strict metrical norm contribute to the meaning?

SUGGESTIONS FOR WRITING

The following suggestions are for brief writing exercises, not for full critical essays. The suggestions here could constitute a part of a full essay that includes some discussion of the contribution of rhythm and meter to the total meaning of a poem.

1. Scan one of the following metrical poems, and indicate how the rhythmic effects (including substitutions and variations from the metrical norm) contribute to meaning:
   a. Dickinson, "Because I could not stop for Death" (page 742).
   b. Shelley, "Ozymandias" (page 758); consider regular and irregular meters in lines 10–14.
   c. Frost, "Nothing Gold Can Stay" (page 833); consider how the first and last lines depart from metrical regularity.
   d. Blake, "Introduction" to *Songs of Innocence* (page 851; see question 5).
   e. Tennyson, "Break, break, break" (page 859; see question 3).
2. In the following free-verse poems, discuss how the line forms a rhythmic unit, paying particular attention to run-on and end-stopped lines:

a. Williams, "The Widow's Lament in Springtime" (page 693; particularly examine lines 20–24).

b. Pastan, "To a Daughter Leaving Home" (page 856; see question 2, and particularly examine lines 12–14, 15–16, 19–20, 21–24).

c. Ferlinghetti, "Constantly risking absurdity" (page 648; see question 4).

d. Hughes, "Theme for English B" (page 976).

e. Piercy, "A Work of Artifice" (page 990).

Sound and Meaning

Rhythm and sound cooperate to produce what we call the music of poetry. This music, as we have pointed out, may serve two general functions: it may be enjoyable in itself, or it may reinforce meaning and intensify the communication.

Pure pleasure in sound and rhythm exists from a very early age in the human being—probably from the age the baby first starts cooing in its cradle, certainly from the age that children begin chanting nursery rhymes and skipping rope. The appeal of the following verse, for instance, depends almost entirely on its "music":

> Pease porridge hot,
> Pease porridge cold,
> Pease porridge in the pot
> Nine days old.

There is very little sense here; the attraction comes from the emphatic rhythm, the emphatic rhymes (with a strong contrast between the short vowel and short final consonant of *hot–pot* and the long vowel and long final consonant combination of *cold–old*), and the heavy alliteration (exactly half the words begin with *p*). From nonsense rhymes such as this, many of us graduate to a love of more meaningful poems whose appeal resides largely in the sounds they make. Much of the pleasure that we find in poems like Vachel Lindsay's "The Congo" and Edgar Allan Poe's "The Bells" derives from their musical qualities.

The peculiar function of poetry as distinguished from music, however, is to convey not sounds but meaning or experience *through* sounds. In first-rate poetry, sound exists neither for its own sake nor for mere decoration, but to enhance the meaning. Its function is to support the leading player, not to steal the scene.

The poet may reinforce meaning through sound in numerous ways. Without claiming to exhaust them, we can include most of the chief means under four general headings.

First, the poet can choose words whose sound in some degree suggests their meaning. In its narrowest sense this is called onomatopoeia. **Onomatopoeia**, strictly defined, means the use of words that, at least supposedly, sound like what they mean, such as *hiss, snap,* and *bang*. Animal noises offer many examples—*bow-wow, cock-a-doodle-do, oink*—and sometimes poets may even invent words to represent them, as Shakespeare does in "Winter" (page 636) when the owl sings "Tu-whit, tu-who!" Poetry, of course, does not usually present the vocalized sounds made by animals, but onomatopoeia often expresses the sounds of movements or actions, as in the following examples: "The harness *jingles*" in Housman's "Is my team plowing" (page 662); "Neighbors *rustle* in and out" in Dickinson's "There's been a Death, in the Opposite House" (page 665); the mourners "*creak* across" in Dickinson's "I felt a Funeral, in my Brain" (page 695); and in Heaney's "The Forge" (page 697) we hear *ring, hiss, clatter, grunts,* and *slam*. Generally, we can detect the presence of onomatopoetic words simply by sounding them, but you can also use your dictionary to verify your discovery: most have the term "imitative" as part of the information about word origins.

The usefulness of onomatopoeia, of course, is strictly limited, because it occurs only where the poet is describing sound, and most poems do not describe sound. But by combining onomatopoeia with other devices that help convey meaning, the poet can achieve subtle or bold emotional effects.

In addition to onomatopoetic words there is another group of words, sometimes called **phonetic intensives**, whose sound, by a process as yet obscure, to some degree connects with their meaning. An initial *fl* sound, for instance, is often associated with the idea of moving light, as in *flame, flare, flash, flicker, flimmer*. An initial *gl* also frequently accompanies the idea of light, usually unmoving, as in *glare, gleam, glint, glow, glisten*. An initial *sl* often introduces words meaning "smoothly wet," as in *slippery, slick, slide, slime, slop, slosh, slobber, slushy*. An initial *st* often suggests strength, as in *staunch, stalwart, stout, sturdy, stable, steady, stocky, stern, strong, stubborn, steel*. Short *i* often goes with the idea of smallness, as in *inch, imp, thin, slim, little, bit, chip, sliver, chink, slit, sip, whit, tittle, snip, wink, glint, glimmer, flicker, pigmy, midge, chick, kid, kitten, minikin, miniature*. Long *o* or *oo* may suggest melancholy or sorrow, as in *moan, groan, woe, mourn, forlorn, toll, doom, gloom, moody*. Final *are* sometimes goes with the idea of a big light or noise, as *flare, glare, stare, blare*. Medial *att* suggests some kind of particled movement as in *spatter, scatter, shatter, chatter, rattle, prattle, clatter, batter*. Final *er* and *le* indicate repetition, as in *glitter, flutter, shimmer, whisper, jabber, chatter, clatter, sputter, flicker, twitter, mutter,* and *ripple, bubble, twinkle, sparkle, rattle, rumble, jingle.*

None of these various sounds is invariably associated with the idea that it seems to suggest and, in fact, a short *i* is found in *thick* as well as *thin,* in *big* as well as *little.* Language is a complex phenomenon. But there is enough association between these sounds and ideas to suggest some sort of intrinsic if obscure relationship. A word like *flicker,* though not onomatopoetic (because it does not refer to sound) would seem somehow to suggest its sense, with the *fl* suggesting moving light, the *i* suggesting smallness, the *ck* suggesting sudden cessation of movement (as in *crack, peck, pick, hack,* and *flick*), and the *er* suggesting repetition. The preceding list of sound-idea correspondences is only a very partial one. A complete list, though it would involve only a small proportion of words in the language, would probably be longer than that of the more strictly onomatopoetic words, to which they are related.

Eight O'Clock

> He stood, and heard the steeple
>   Sprinkle the quarters on the morning town.
> One, two, three, four, to market-place and people
>   It tossed them down.
>
> Strapped, noosed, nighing his hour,   5
>   He stood and counted them and cursed his luck;
> And then the clock collected in the tower
>   Its strength, and struck.

A. E. Housman (1859–1936)

QUESTIONS

1. Vocabulary: *quarters* (2).
2. Eight A.M. was the traditional hour in England for putting condemned criminals to death. Discuss the force of "morning" (2) and "struck" (8). Discuss the appropriateness of the image of the clock collecting its strength. Can you suggest any reason for the use of "nighing" (5) rather than *nearing?*
3. Consider the contribution to meaning of the following phonetic intensives: "steeple" and "Sprinkle" (1, 2), "stood" (1, 6), "Strapped" (5), "strength" and "struck" (8). Comment on the frequent *k* sounds leading up to "struck" in the second stanza.

A second and far more important way that the poet can reinforce meaning through sound is to choose sounds and group them so that the effect is smooth and pleasant sounding (*euphonious*) or rough and harsh sounding (*cacophonous*). Vowels are in general more pleasing than consonants, for vowels are musical tones, whereas consonants are merely noises. A line with a high percentage of vowel sounds in proportion to consonant sounds will therefore tend to be more melodious than one in which the proportion is low. The vowels and consonants themselves differ considerably in quality. The "long" vowels, such as those in *fate, reed, rhyme, coat, food,* and *dune* are fuller and more resonant than the "short" vowels, as in *fat, red, rim, cot, foot,* and *dun.* Of the consonants, some are fairly mellifluous, such as the "liquids," *l, m, n,* and *r;* the soft *v* and *f* sounds; the semivowels *w* and *y;* and such combinations as *th* and *wh.* Others, such as the "plosives," *b, d, g, k, p,* and *t,* are harsher and sharper in their effect. These differences in sound are the poet's materials. Good poets, however, will not necessarily seek out the sounds that are pleasing and attempt to combine them in melodious combinations. Rather, they will use **euphony** and **cacophony** as they are appropriate to content. Consider, for instance, the following lines.

Sound and Sense

> True ease in writing comes from art, not chance,
> As those move easiest who have learned to dance.
> 'Tis not enough no harshness gives offense,
> The sound must seem an echo to the sense:
> Soft is the strain when Zephyr gently blows,   5
> And the smooth stream in smoother numbers flows;
> But when loud surges lash the sounding shore,
> The hoarse, rough verse should like the torrent roar;
> When Ajax strives some rock's vast weight to throw,
> The line too labors, and the words move slow;   10
> Not so, when swift Camilla scours the plain,
> Flies o'er the unbending corn, and skims along the main.
> Hear how Timotheus' varied lays surprise,
> And bid alternate passions fall and rise!

Alexander Pope (1688–1744)

QUESTIONS
1. Vocabulary: *numbers* (6), *lays* (13).
2. This excerpt is from a long poem (called *An Essay on Criticism*) on the arts of writing and judging poetry. Which line states the thesis of the passage?

3. There are four classical allusions: Zephyr (5) was god of the west wind; Ajax (9), a Greek warrior noted for his strength; Camilla (11), a legendary queen reputedly so fleet of foot that she could run over a field of grain without bending the blades or over the sea without wetting her feet; Timotheus (13), a famous Greek rhapsodic poet. How do these allusions enable Pope to achieve greater economy?

4. Copy the passage and scan it. Then, considering both meter and sounds, show how Pope practices what he preaches. (Incidentally, on which syllable should "alternate" in line 14 be accented? Does the meter help you to know the pronunciation of "Timotheus" in line 13?)

There are no strictly onomatopoetic words in this passage, and yet the sound seems marvelously adapted to the sense. When the poem is about soft, smooth effects (lines 5–6), there is an abundance of alliteration (*s* in *soft, strain, smooth stream, smoother*) and consonance (the voiced *s* or *z* sound in *Zephyr, blows, numbers flows;* the voiced *th* of *smooth* and *smoother*). When harshness and loudness are the subject, the lines become cacophonous and even the pleasant smoothness of *s*-alliteration when coupled with *sh* evokes angry hissing: "surges la*sh* the *s*ounding *sh*ore, / The hoarse, rough verse *sh*ould. . . ." Heavy labor is expressed in cacophony ("Ajax strives some rock's vast weight to throw"), while lightness and speed are expressed with euphonious short *i* sounds ("swift Camilla . . . skims"). Throughout the passage there is a remarkable correspondence between the pleasant-sounding and the pleasant in idea, the unpleasant-sounding and the unpleasant in idea.

As the excerpt from Alexander Pope also demonstrates, a third way in which a poet can reinforce meaning through sound is by controlling the speed and movement of the lines by the choice and use of meter, by the choice and arrangement of vowel and consonant sounds, and by the disposition of pauses. In meter the unaccented syllables usually go faster than the accented syllables; hence the triple meters are swifter than the duple. But the poet can vary the tempo of any meter by the use of substitute feet. Generally, whenever two or more unaccented syllables come together, the effect will be to speed up the pace of the line; when two or more accented syllables come together, the effect will be to slow it down. This pace will also be affected by the vowel lengths and by whether the sounds are easily run together. The long vowels take longer to pronounce than the short ones. Some words are easily run together, while others demand that the position of the mouth be re-formed before the next word is uttered. It takes much longer, for instance, to say "Watch dogs catch much meat" than to say "My aunt is away," though the number of syllables is the same. And finally the poet can slow down the speed of a line through the introduction of grammatical and rhetorical pauses. Consider lines 54–56 from Tennyson's "Ulysses" (page 747):

> The lights | be-gin | to twin- | kle from | the rocks; |
>
> The long | day wanes; | the slow | moon climbs; | the deep | 55
>
> Moans round | with man- | y voi- | ces. . . .

In these lines Tennyson wished the movement to be slow, in accordance with the slow waning of the long day and the slow climbing of the moon. His meter is iambic pentameter. This is not a swift meter, but in lines 55–56 he slows it down further, by (a) introducing three spondaic feet, thus bringing three accented syllables together in two separate places; (b) choosing for his accented syllables words that have long vowel sounds or dipthongs that the voice hangs onto: "long," "day," "wanes," "slow," "moon," "climbs," "deep," "Moans," "round"; (c) choosing words that are not easily run together (except for "day" and "slow," each of these words begins and ends with consonant sounds that require varying degrees of readjustment of the mouth before pronunciation can continue); and (d) introducing two grammatical pauses, after "wanes" and "climbs," and a rhetorical pause after "deep." The result is an extremely effective use of the movement of the verse to accord with the movement suggested by the words.

A fourth way for a poet to fit sound to sense is to control both sound and meter in such a way as to emphasize words that are important in meaning. This can be done by highlighting such words through alliteration, assonance, consonance, or rhyme; by placing them before a pause; or by skillfully placing or displacing them in the metrical scheme. We have already seen how Ogden Nash uses alliteration and consonance to emphasize and link the three major words ("sex," "fix," and "fertile") in his little verse "The Turtle" (page 819), and how George Herbert pivots the structure of meaning in "Virtue" (page 840) on a trochaic substitution in the initial foot of his final stanza. For an additional example, let us look again at Drayton's "Since there's no help" (page 804). This poem is a sonnet—fourteen lines of iambic pentameter—in which a lover threatens to abandon his courtship if the woman he desires will not go to bed with him. In the first eight lines he pretends to be *glad* that they are parting so cleanly. In the last six lines, however, he paints a vivid picture of the death of his personified Love/Passion for her but intimates that even at this last moment ("Now") she could restore it to life—by satisfying his sexual desires:

Now, at the last gasp of Love's la- test breath,

When, his pulse failing, Passion speechless lies,   10

When Faith is kneeling by his bed of death,

And In- no-cence is clos- ing up his eyes,

Now, if thou wouldst, when all have given him o- ver,*

From death to life thou mightst him yet re-cov- er.

The emphasis is on *Now.* In a matter of seconds, the speaker indicates, it will be too late: his Love/Passion will be dead, and he himself will be gone. The word "Now" begins line 9. It also begins a new sentence and a new direction in the poem. It is separated from what has gone before by a period at the end of the preceding line. Metrically it initiates a trochee, thus breaking away from the poem's basic iambic meter (line 8 is perfectly regular). In all these ways—its initial position in line, sentence, and thought, and its metrical irregularity—the word "Now" is given extraordinary emphasis appropriate to its importance in the context. Its repetition in line 13 reaffirms this importance, and there again it is given emphasis by its positional and metrical situation. It begins both a line and the final rhyming couplet, is separated by punctuation from the line before, and participates in a metrical inversion. (The lines before and after are metrically regular.)

While Herbert and Drayton use metrical deviation to give emphasis to important words, Tennyson, in the concluding line of "Ulysses," uses marked regularity, plus skillful use of grammatical pauses, to achieve the same effect.

We are not now that strength which in old days

Moved earth and heav- en, that which we are, we are:

One e- qual tem- per of he-ro- ic hearts,

Made weak by time and fate, but strong in will

To strive, to seek, to find, and not to yield.   70

*Drayton probably intended "given" to be pronounced as one syllable (*giv'n*), and most sixteenth-century readers would have pronounced it thus in this poem.

The blank-verse rhythm throughout "Ulysses" is remarkably subtle and varied, but the last line is not only regular in its scansion but heavily regular, for a number of reasons. First, all the words are monosyllables. Second, the unaccented syllables are all very small and unimportant words—four *tos* and one *and*—whereas the accented syllables consist of four important verbs and a very important *not*. Third, each of the verbs is followed by a grammatical pause pointed off by a mark of punctuation. The result is to cause a pronounced alternation between light and heavy syllables that brings the accent down on the four verbs and the *not* with sledgehammer blows. The line rings out like a challenge, which it is.

I heard a Fly buzz—when I died

I heard a Fly buzz—when I died—
The Stillness in the Room
Was like the Stillness in the Air—
Between the Heaves of Storm—

The Eyes around—had wrung them dry—   5
And Breaths were gathering firm
For that last Onset—when the King
Be witnessed—in the Room—

I willed my Keepsakes—Signed away
What portion of me be   10
Assignable—and then it was
There interposed a Fly—

With Blue—uncertain stumbling Buzz—
Between the light—and me—
And then the Windows failed—and then   15
I could not see to see—

Emily Dickinson (1830–1886)

QUESTIONS

1. It is important to understand the sequence of events in this deathbed scene. Arrange the following events in correct chronological order: (a) the willing of keepsakes, (b) the weeping of mourners, (c) the appearance of the fly, (d) the preternatural stillness in the room.
2. What or who are the "Eyes" and the "Breaths" in lines 5–6? What figures of speech are involved in these lines? Is the speaker making out her will in lines 9–11? What *is* she doing?

3. What sort of expectation is set up by phrases like "last Onset" (7), "the King" (7), and "Be witnessed" (8)?
4. Explain "the Windows failed" (15) and "I could not see to see" (16).

We may well conclude our discussion of the adaptation of sound to sense by analyzing this poem. It consists of four four-line stanzas of alternating iambic tetrameter (first and third lines) and iambic trimeter (second and fourth); the first and third lines are unrhymed, the second and fourth display approximate rhymes in the first three stanzas. The fourth stanza uses an exact rhyme that echoes the last word in line 3 of the preceding stanza. The poem depicts a speaker's recollection of her own deathbed scene, focusing on the suspenseful interval during which she and her loved ones await the arrival of death—ironically symbolized in the closing lines as a common housefly. But the poem does not move chronologically. Surprisingly, it begins with its conclusion, the apparently trivial fact that the last conscious perception was hearing the buzzing fly; then it proceeds to summarize the events leading up to that moment.

How is the poem's sound fitted to its sense? In the opening stanzas, the pace is slow and even solemn, the rhythm perfectly matching the meter, as befits this apparently momentous occasion with its "Stillness," its quiet, breathless awaiting of "the King"—death itself. The approximate rhymes provide a formal unity even as they convey an atmosphere of unease, an uncertainty and fear in the face of imminent death; and the dashes contribute to the poem's measured, stately rhythm. Then the poem returns to the insignificant topic of its opening line and invests it with enormous meaning.

The one onomatopoetic word in the poem is *Buzz*, introduced abruptly in line 1 without capitalization and then reintroduced with intensity in line 13. In line 11, the final word, *was*, though unrhymed in its own stanza and unrhymed in the formal rhyme scheme, nevertheless is an exact rhyme for *Buzz* in the first line of the final stanza. In line 12, the word *interposed* continues the buzzing into the final stanza. In line 13 the vowel sound of *Buzz* is preceded by the identical vowel sounds in "*u*ncertain" and "st*u*mbling," making three *u* sounds in close succession. Finally, the *b* sound in *Buzz* is preceded in line 13 by the *b*s in "*B*lue" and "stum*b*ling." Thus *all* the sounds in *Buzz*—its initial and final consonants and its vowel—are heard at least three times in lines 11–13. This outburst of onomatopoetic effect consummates the aural imagery promised in the opening line, "I *heard* a Fly buzz."

But line 13 combines images of color and motion as well as sound. Though the sound imagery is the most important, the poem concludes with a reference to the speaker's dimming eyesight, and we may infer that she *saw* a blur of the bluebottle's deep metallic blue as well as hearing its buzz. This image is an example of **synesthesia**, the stimulation of two or more senses simultaneously, especially as here, where one sense perception is described in terms of another (as in a "Blue . . . Buzz"). The images of motion between "Blue" and "Buzz" also belong to both the visual and aural modes of sensing. The speaker hears and imperfectly sees the "uncertain" flight of the fly as it bumbles from one pane of glass to another, its buzzing now louder, now softer. Furthermore, the exact rhymes in the last stanza that pick up on "was" in the preceding one underscore the abrupt finality of the speaker's confrontation with death, and thus the sudden end of her human perception.

In analyzing verse for correspondence between sound and sense, we need to be very cautious not to make exaggerated claims. A great deal of nonsense has been written about the moods of certain meters and the effects of certain sounds, and it is easy to suggest correspondences that exist only in our imaginations. Nevertheless, the first-rate poet has nearly always an instinctive tact about handling sound so that it in some degree supports meaning. One of the few absolute rules that applies to the judgment of poetry is that the form should be adequate to the content. This rule does not mean that there must always be a close and easily demonstrable correspondence. It does mean that there will be no glaring discrepancies.

The selection that introduces this chapter ("Pease porridge hot") illustrates the use of sound in verse almost purely for its own sake, and it is, as significant poetry, among the most trivial passages in the whole book. But beyond this there is an abundant range of poetic possibilities where sound is pleasurable for itself without violating meaning and where sound to varying degrees corresponds with and corroborates meaning; and in this rich middle range lie many of the great pleasures of reading poetry.

EXERCISE

In each of the following paired quotations, the named poet wrote the version that more successfully adapts sound to sense. As specifically as possible, account for the superiority of the better version.

1. a. Go forth—and Virtue, ever in your sight,
      Shall be your guide by day, your guard by night.
   b. Go forth—and Virtue, ever in your sight,
      Shall point your way by day, and keep you safe at night.

   Charles Churchill

2. a. How charming is divine philosophy!
      Not harsh and rough as foolish men suppose
      But musical as is the lute of Phoebus.
   b. How charming is divine philosophy!
      Not harsh and crabbed as dull fools suppose
      But musical as is Apollo's lute.

   John Milton

3. a. All day the fleeing crows croak hoarsely over the snow.
   b. All day the out-cast crows croak hoarsely across the whiteness.

Elizabeth Coatsworth

4. a. Your talk attests how bells of singing gold
      Would sound at evening over silent water.
   b. Your low voice tells how bells of singing gold
      Would sound at twilight over silent water.   *Edwin Arlington Robinson*

5. a. A thousand streamlets flowing through the lawn,
      The moan of doves in gnarled ancient oaks,
      And quiet murmuring of countless bees.
   b. Myriads of rivulets hurrying through the lawn,
      The moan of doves in immemorial elms,
      And murmuring of innumerable bees.

Alfred, Lord Tennyson

6. a. It is the lark that sings so out of tune,
      Straining harsh discords and unpleasing sharps.
   b. It is the lark that warbles out of tune
      In harsh discordant tones with doleful flats.   *William Shakespeare*

7. a. "Artillery" and "armaments" and "implements of war"
      Are phrases too severe to please the gentle Muse.
   b. Bombs, drums, guns, bastions, batteries, bayonets, bullets,—
      Hard words, which stick in the soft Muses' gullets.   *Lord Byron*

8. a. The hands of the sisters Death and Night incessantly softly
         wash again, and ever again, this soiled world.
   b. The hands of the soft twins Death and Night repeatedly
         wash again, and ever again, this dirty world.   *Walt Whitman*

9. a. The curfew sounds the knell of parting day,
      The lowing cattle slowly cross the lea,
      The plowman goes wearily plodding his homeward way,
      Leaving the world to the darkening night and me.
   b. The curfew tolls the knell of parting day,
      The lowing herd wind slowly o'er the lea,
      The plowman homeward plods his weary way,
      And leaves the world to darkness and to me.   *Thomas Gray*

10. a. Let me chastise this odious, gilded bug,
       This painted son of dirt, that smells and bites.
    b. Yet let me flap this bug with gilded wings,
       This painted child of dirt, that stinks and stings.   *Alexander Pope*

REVIEWING CHAPTER THIRTEEN

1. Review the terms in the chapter presented in boldface.
2. The chapter presents four important means by which sound reinforces meaning; in reviewing them, decide whether the meaning being reinforced is intellectual or emotional, or both.
3. In the following poems, identify any of the devices by which sound reinforces meaning, being sure to define the meaning that is being reinforced—and identifying any elements of poetry that are employed in creating that meaning.

Anthem for Doomed Youth

What passing-bells for these who die as cattle?
Only the monstrous anger of the guns.
Only the stuttering rifles' rapid rattle
Can patter out their hasty orisons.
No mockeries now for them; no prayers nor bells,   5
Nor any voice of mourning save the choirs—
The shrill, demented choirs of wailing shells;
And bugles calling for them from sad shires.

What candles may be held to speed them all?
Not in the hands of boys, but in their eyes   10
Shall shine the holy glimmers of good-byes.
The pallor of girls' brows shall be their pall;
Their flowers the tenderness of patient minds,
And each slow dusk a drawing-down of blinds.

Wilfred Owen (1893–1918)

QUESTIONS

1. Vocabulary: *passing-bells* (1), *orisons* (4), *shires* (8), *pall* (12). It was the custom during World War I to draw down the blinds in homes where a son had been lost (14).
2. How do the octave and the sestet of this sonnet differ in (a) geographical setting, (b) subject matter, (c) kind of imagery used, and (d) tone? Who are the "boys" (10) and "girls" (12) referred to in the sestet?
3. What central metaphorical image runs throughout the poem? What secondary metaphors build up the central one?

4. Why are the "doomed youth" said to die "as cattle" (1)? Why would prayers,
   bells, and so on, be "mockeries" for them (5)?
5. Show how sound is adapted to sense throughout the poem.

Landcrab

A lie, that we come from water.
The truth is we were born
from stones, dragons, the sea's
teeth, as you testify,
with your crust and jagged scissors.   5

Hermit, hard socket
for a timid eye
you're a soft gut scuttling
sideways, a bone skull,
round bone on the prowl.   10
Wolf of treeroots and gravelly holes,
a mount on stilts,
the husk of a small demon.

Attack, voracious
eating, and flight: 15
it's a sound routine
for staying alive on edges.
Then there's the tide, and that dance
you do for the moon
on wet sand, claws raised   20
to fend off your mate,
your coupling a quick
dry clatter of rocks.
For mammals
with their lobes and bulbs,   25
scruples and warm milk,
you've nothing but contempt.

Here you are, a frozen scowl
targeted in flashlight,
then gone: a piece of what   30
we are, not all,

my stunted child, my momentary
face in the mirror,
my tiny nightmare.

Margaret Atwood (b. 1939)

QUESTIONS

1. What theory of the origin of human life is alluded to in line 1? Line 3 alludes to two Greek myths, of Deucalion strewing stones and Cadmus sowing dragon's teeth. If these are unfamiliar, look them up. What do theories about the origins of humankind have to do with the speaker's description of the landcrab? How do lines 30–34 return to that subject?
2. What do the free-verse rhythms contribute to the experience of the poem? Discuss the cacophony and euphony in lines 22–25. Where do you find other examples?

Tree at My Window

Tree at my window, window tree,
My sash is lowered when night comes on;
But let there never be curtain drawn
Between you and me.

Vague dream-head lifted out of the ground,   5
And thing next most diffuse to cloud,
Not all your light tongues talking aloud
Could be profound.

But, tree, I have seen you taken and tossed,
And if you have seen me when I slept,   10
You have seen me when I was taken and swept
And all but lost.

That day she put our heads together,
Fate had her imagination about her,
Your head so much concerned with outer,   15
Mine with inner, weather.

Robert Frost (1874–1963)

QUESTIONS

1. What is the speaker's attitude toward the tree? Is the tree symbolic of something affirmative or negative?
2. What sound effects does the poem employ in line 7? How do these effects help to characterize the tree?
3. Scan the poem. What is the rhythmical effect of the shorter fourth line in each stanza? How does the last line of the poem depart from that pattern?
4. Focusing on the last stanza, describe the distinction the speaker is making between "outer" and "inner" weather. How does the last stanza enlarge the theme of the poem?

Aunt Jennifer's Tigers

Aunt Jennifer's tigers prance across a screen,
Bright topaz denizens of a world of green.
They do not fear the men beneath the tree;
They pace in sleek chivalric certainty.

Aunt Jennifer's fingers fluttering through her wool   5
Find even the ivory needle hard to pull.
The massive weight of Uncle's wedding band
Sits heavily upon Aunt Jennifer's hand.

When Aunt is dead, her terrified hands will lie
Still ringed with ordeals she was mastered by.   10
The tigers in the panel that she made
Will go on prancing, proud and unafraid.

Adrienne Rich (b. 1929)

At the round earth's imagined corners

At the round earth's imagined corners, blow
Your trumpets, angels; and arise, arise
From death, you numberless infinities
Of souls, and to your scattered bodies go:
All whom the flood did, and fire shall, o'erthrow,   5
All whom war, dearth, age, agues, tyrannies,
Despair, law, chance hath slain, and you whose eyes
Shall behold God and never taste death's woe.
But let them sleep, Lord, and me mourn a space;
For if above all these, my sins abound,   10

'Tis late to ask abundance of thy grace
When we are there. Here on this lowly ground,
Teach me how to repent; for that's as good
As if thou hadst sealed my pardon with thy blood.

John Donne (1572–1631)

QUESTIONS

1. The poem refers to the Christian doctrine of the resurrection of the body, according to which after the destruction of the world the soul will be reunited with the body—not the imperfect body of mortal life, but a perfected, glorified body. Several lines contain biblical allusions: Revelation 7.1 (1), Job 19.25–26 (2–4), Romans 6.1 (10–11). What is the speaker calling for in lines 1–8? Why does he change his plea in lines 9–12? Where is "there" (12)?
2. Scan lines 1–8. How do the rhythms reinforce the meanings in these lines? What is the effect of the placement of "blow" (1)? Scan lines 11–12. What do the lack of a caesura in line 11 and the emphatic caesura in line 12 contribute to meaning? Comment on the trochaic substitution in line 12.

Blackberry Eating

I love to go out in late September
among fat, overripe, icy, black blackberries
to eat blackberries for breakfast,
the stalks very prickly, a penalty
they earn for knowing the black art   5
of blackberry-making; and as I stand among them
lifting the stalks to my mouth, the ripest berries
fall almost unbidden to my tongue,
as words sometimes do, certain peculiar words
like *strengths* or *squinched*,   10
many-lettered, one-syllabled lumps,
which I squeeze, squinch open, and splurge well
in the silent, startled, icy, black language
of blackberry-eating in late September.

Galway Kinnell (b. 1927)

QUESTIONS
1. Vocabulary: *black art* (5), *squinched* (10).
2. What comparison does the poet find between "certain peculiar words" (9) and blackberries? How appropriate is it?
3. Is the poem free verse or metrical? How do various musical devices reinforce its meaning?

The Health-Food Diner

No sprouted wheat and soya shoots
And brussels in a cake,
Carrot straw and spinach raw
(Today, I need a steak).

Not thick brown rice and rice pilau   5
Or mushrooms creamed on toast,
Turnips mashed and parsnips hashed
(I'm dreaming of a roast).

Health-food folks around the world
Are thinned by anxious zeal,   10
They look for help in seafood kelp
(I count on breaded veal).

No Smoking signs, raw mustard greens,
Zucchini by the ton,
Uncooked kale and bodies frail   15
Are sure to make me run

                    to

Loins of pork and chicken thighs
And standing rib, so prime,
Pork chops brown and fresh ground round   20
(I crave them all the time).

Irish stews and boiled corned beef
And hot dogs by the scores,
Or any place that saves a space
For smoking carnivores.   25

Maya Angelou (b. 1928)

QUESTIONS

1. At whom or what is this satiric poem directed? How seriously should we take its attitude toward healthful eating?
2. Scan the poem, taking note also of internal rhymes. How do the internal and end rhymes help create a comic tone? What other sound devices does it employ?
3. The poem is cast in the first person. What would be gained or lost if it were changed into third person?

The Dance

In Breughel's great picture, The Kermess,
the dancers go round, they go round and
around, the squeal and the blare and the
tweedle of bagpipes, a bugle and fiddles
tipping their bellies (round as the thick-   5
sided glasses whose wash they impound)
their hips and their bellies off balance
to turn them. Kicking and rolling about
the Fair Grounds, swinging their butts, those
shanks must be sound to bear up under such   10
rollicking measures, prance as they dance
in Breughel's great picture, The Kermess.

                              William Carlos Williams (1883–1963)

QUESTIONS

1. Peter Breughel the Elder was a sixteenth-century Flemish painter of peasant life. A *kermess* is an annual outdoor festival or fair. How would you characterize the mood of the people depicted in this poem?
2. Examine the poem for alliteration, consonance, assonance, and onomatopoeia. When you pronounce the syllable *ound* (lines 2, 3, 5, 6, 9, 10), how does the shape your mouth makes seem to intensify the effect?
3. Scan the poem. (Notice that the initial syllable in lines 2, 3, and 8 has the effect of completing the rhythm of the preceding line.) What one word in the poem echoes the prevailing metrical foot, describes the rhythm of the poem, and defines the mood of the picture?
4. How does sound reinforce content in this poem? What is the attitude of the speaker to the activities shown in the picture?

SUGGESTIONS FOR WRITING

Write a short essay discussing the relationship of the poem's sound to its meaning in one of the following.

1. Dickinson, "I felt a Funeral, in my Brain" (page 695).
2. Atwood, "Landcrab" (page 874).
3. Williams, "Poem" (page 1012).
4. Keats, "Ode on a Grecian Urn" (page 917).
5. Hardy, "Channel Firing" (page 970).
6. Owen, "Dulce et Decorum Est" (page 637).
7. Stevens, "The Snow Man" (page 701).
8. Yeats, "Sailing to Byzantium" (page 1017).

Pattern

Art, ultimately, is organization. It is a searching after order and significance. Most artists seek to transform the chaotic nature of experience into a meaningful and coherent pattern, largely by means of selection and arrangement. For this reason we evaluate a poem partially by the same criteria that an English instructor uses to evaluate an essay theme—by its unity, its coherence, and its proper placing of emphasis. A well-constructed poem contains neither too little nor too much; every part of the poem belongs where it is and could be placed nowhere else; any interchanging of two stanzas, two lines, or even two words would to some extent damage the poem and make it less effective. We come to feel, with a truly first-rate poem, that the choice and placement of every word are inevitable, that they could not be otherwise.

In addition to the internal ordering of the materials—the arrangement of ideas, images, thoughts, sentences, which we refer to as the poem's **structure**—the poet may impose some external pattern on a poem, may give it not only its internal order of materials but an external shape or **form**. Such formality appeals to the human instinct for design, the instinct that has prompted people, at various times, to tattoo and paint their bodies, to decorate their swords and armor with beautiful and complex tracery, and to choose patterned fabrics for their clothing, carpets, curtains, and wallpapers. The poet appeals to our love of the shapely.

In general, a poem may be cast in one of the three broad kinds of form: continuous form, stanzaic form, and fixed form. In **continuous form**, as illustrated by "The Widow's Lament in Springtime" (page 693), "After Apple-Picking" (page 698), "Ulysses" (page 745), and "My Last Duchess" (page 768), the element of design is slight. The lines follow each other without formal grouping, the only breaks being dictated by units of meaning, as paragraphs are in prose. But even here there are degrees of pattern. "The Widow's Lament in Springtime" has neither regular meter nor rhyme. "After Apple-Picking," on the other hand, is metrical; it has no regularity of length of line, but the meter is predominantly iambic; in addition, every line rhymes with another, though not according to any fixed pattern. "Ulysses" is regular in both meter and length of line: it is unrhymed iambic pentameter, or blank verse. And to these regularities "My Last Duchess" adds regularity of rhyme, for it is written in rhyming pentameter couplets. Thus, in increasing degrees, the authors of "After Apple-Picking," "Ulysses," and "My Last Duchess" have chosen a predetermined pattern in which to cast their work.

In **stanzaic form** the poet writes in a series of **stanzas**; that is, repeated units having the same number of lines, usually the same metrical pattern, and often an identical **rhyme scheme**. The poet may choose some traditional stanza pattern or invent an original one. The traditional stanza patterns (for example, terza rima, ballad meter, rhyme royal, Spenserian stanza) are many, and the student specializing in literature will wish to become familiar with some of them; the general student should know that they exist. Often the use of one of these traditional stanza forms constitutes a kind of literary allusion. When we are aware of the traditional use of a stanza form, or of its previous use by a great poet for a particular subject or experience, we may find additional subtleties of meaning in its later use. Robert Frost employs the same verse form for his poem about a moral quest as Dante uses for his great poem about moral truth, *The Divine Comedy*, with meaningful results (see "Acquainted with the Night," page 894).

Stanzaic form, like continuous form, exhibits degrees of formal pattern. The poem "in Just—" (page 776) is divided into alternating stanzas of four lines and one line, but the four-line stanzas have no formal resemblance to each other except for the number of lines, and the one-line stanzas are similarly disparate. In "Naming of Parts" (page 680) the stanzas are alike in number of lines and in meter, but they have no rhyme pattern. In "The Aim Was Song" (page 852) a rhyme scheme is added to a metrical pattern. In "Winter" (page 636) and "Blow, blow, thou winter wind" (page 826) Shakespeare employs a refrain in addition to the patterns of meter and rhyme. The following poem illustrates additional elements of design.

The Pulley

> When God at first made man,
> Having a glass of blessings standing by,
>   "Let us," said he, "pour on him all we can:
> Let the world's riches, which dispersèd lie,
>   Contract into a span."   5

> So Strength first made a way;
> Then Beauty flowed; then Wisdom, Honor, Pleasure.
>   When almost all was out, God made a stay,
> Perceiving that alone of all his treasure
>   Rest in the bottom lay.   10
>
>   "For if I should," said he,
> "Bestow this jewel also on my creature,
>   He would adore my gifts instead of me,
> And rest in Nature, not the God of Nature;
>   So both should losers be.   15
>
>   "Yet let him keep the rest,
> But keep them with repining restlessness:
>   Let him be rich and weary, that at least,
> If goodness lead him not, yet weariness
>   May toss him to my breast."   20

George Herbert (1593–1633)

QUESTIONS

1. Vocabulary: *span* (5, archaic meaning).
2. The words "riches" (4), "treasure" (9), "jewel" (12), and "gifts" (13) create an extended metaphor. What is being compared to things of material value? Does the word "rich" in line 18 refer to the same thing as "riches" in line 4?
3. The title "The Pulley" refers to a simple mechanical device for lifting weights. How does a pulley work? How does it metaphorically express the meaning of the last stanza?
4. To what does "both" (15) refer? What are God's final intentions?

A stanza form may be described by designating four things: the rhyme scheme (if there is one), the position of the refrain (if there is one), the prevailing metrical foot, and the number of feet in each line. Rhyme scheme is traditionally designated by using letters of the alphabet to indicate the rhyming lines, and x for unrhymed lines. Refrain lines may be indicated by a capital letter, and the number of feet in the line by a numerical exponent after the letter. Thus the stanza pattern of Browning's "Meeting at Night" (page 690) is iambic tetrameter $abccba$ (or iambic $abccba^4$); that of Donne's "A Hymn to God the Father" (page 685) is iambic $abab^5A^4B^2$; that of "The Pulley" is iambic $a^3bab^5a^3$.

A **fixed form** is a traditional pattern that applies to a whole poem. In French poetry many fixed forms have been widely used: rondeaus, rondels, villanelles, triolets, sestinas, ballades, double ballades, and others. In English poetry, though most of the fixed forms have been experimented with, perhaps only two—the sonnet and the villanelle—have really taken hold.

Although it is classified as a fixed form, through centuries of practice the **sonnet** has attained a degree of flexibility. It must be fourteen lines in length, and it almost always is iambic pentameter, but in structure and rhyme scheme there may be considerable leeway. Most sonnets, however, conform more or less closely to one of two general models or types: the Italian or the English.

The **Italian** or *Petrarchan* **sonnet** (so-called because the Italian poet Petrarch practiced it so extensively) is divided usually between eight lines called the **octave**, using two rhymes arranged *abbaabba*, and six lines called the **sestet**, using any arrangement of either two or three rhymes: *cdcdcd* and *cdecde* are common patterns. The division between octave and sestet in the Italian sonnet (indicated by the rhyme scheme and sometimes marked off in printing by a space) usually corresponds to a division of thought. The octave may, for instance, present a situation and the sestet a comment, or the octave an idea and the sestet an example, or the octave a question and the sestet an answer. Thus the form reflects the structure.

On First Looking into Chapman's Homer

Much have I traveled in the realms of gold,
    And many goodly states and kingdoms seen;
    Round many western islands have I been
Which bards in fealty to Apollo hold.
Oft of one wide expanse had I been told   5
    That deep-browed Homer ruled as his demesne;
    Yet did I never breathe its pure serene
Till I heard Chapman speak out loud and bold:
Then felt I like some watcher of the skies
    When a new planet swims into his ken;   10
Or like stout Cortez when with eagle eyes
    He stared at the Pacific—and all his men
Looked at each other with a wild surmise—
    Silent, upon a peak in Darien.

John Keats (1795–1821)

QUESTIONS

1. Vocabulary: *fealty* (4), *Apollo* (4), *demesne* (6), *ken* (10). *Darien* (14) is an ancient name for the Isthmus of Panama.

2. John Keats, at twenty-one, could not read Greek and was probably acquainted with Homer's *Iliad* and *Odyssey* only through the translations of Alexander Pope, which to him very likely seemed prosy and stilted. Then one day he and a friend found a vigorous poetic translation by the Elizabethan poet George Chapman. Keats and his friend, enthralled, sat up late at night excitedly reading aloud to each other from Chapman's book. Toward morning Keats walked home and, before going to bed, wrote the above sonnet and sent it to his friend. What common ideas underlie the three major figures of speech in the poem?
3. What is the rhyme scheme? What division of thought corresponds to the division between octave and sestet?
4. Balboa, not Cortez, discovered the Pacific. How seriously does this mistake detract from the value of the poem?

The **English** or *Shakespearean* **sonnet** (invented by the English poet Surrey and made famous by Shakespeare) consists of three **quatrains** and a concluding **couplet**, rhyming *abab cdcd efef gg*. Again, the units marked off by the rhymes and the development of the thought often correspond. The three quatrains, for instance, may present three examples and the couplet a conclusion, or (as in the following example) the quatrains three metaphorical statements of one idea and the couplet an application.

That time of year

That time of year thou mayst in me behold
When yellow leaves, or none, or few, do hang
Upon those boughs which shake against the cold,
Bare ruined choirs where late the sweet birds sang.
In me thou see'st the twilight of such day   5
As after sunset fadeth in the west,
Which by and by black night doth take away,
Death's second self, that seals up all in rest.
In me thou see'st the glowing of such fire,
That on the ashes of his youth doth lie   10
As the deathbed whereon it must expire,
Consumed with that which it was nourished by.
This thou perceivest, which makes thy love more strong,
To love that well which thou must leave ere long.

William Shakespeare (1564–1616)

QUESTIONS

1. What are the three major images introduced by the three quatrains? What do they have in common? Can you see any reason for presenting them in this particular order, or might they be rearranged without loss?

2. Each of the images is to some degree complicated rather than simple. For instance, what additional image is introduced by "Bare ruined choirs" (4)? Explain its appropriateness.

3. What additional comparisons are introduced in the second and third quatrains? Explain line 12.

4. Whom does the speaker address? What assertion does he make in the concluding couplet, and with what degree of confidence? Paraphrase these lines so as to state their meaning as clearly as possible.

The tradition of the sonnet has proved useful because it seems effective or appropriate for certain types of subject matter and treatment. By its history as the vehicle for love poetry in the sixteenth century, the sonnet is particularly effective when used for the serious treatment of love. But it has also been used for the discussion of death, religion, political situations, and various other serious subjects. There is, of course, no magical or mysterious identity between certain forms and certain types of content, but there may be more or less correspondence. A form may seem appropriate or inappropriate. Excellent sonnets have been written outside the traditional areas.

The **villanelle**, with its complex pattern of repetition and rhyme, has become a significant form in English only in the past hundred years or so, but of the fixed forms it probably now ranks second to the sonnet. The form requires only two rhyme sounds, and its nineteen lines are divided into five three-line stanzas (**tercets**) and a four-line concluding quatrain. The first and third lines of the first stanza serve as refrain lines entwined with the rhyme pattern—the first line repeated at the ends of the second and fourth stanzas, and the third repeated at the ends of the third and fifth stanzas. In the concluding stanza, the refrains are repeated as lines 18 and 19. We can express the pattern thus: $A^1bA^2abA^1\ abA^2\ abA^1\ abA^2\ abA^1A^2$.

Poets have been attracted to villanelles partly because they are notoriously difficult to compose effectively, thus posing a challenge to a poet's technical skill, and partly because the varying emphases given to repeated lines, along with the repetition itself, can achieve haunting, unforgettable effects. The original French models were usually light-hearted and witty, exploiting the potential for cleverness and humor inherent in the form, but modern poets often have employed the villanelle for serious subject matter. The following example, composed when the poet's father was near death, is perhaps the most famous villanelle in English.

Do Not Go Gentle into That Good Night

Do not go gentle into that good night,
Old age should burn and rave at close of day;
Rage, rage against the dying of the light.

Though wise men at their end know dark is right,
Because their words had forked no lightning they   5
Do not go gentle into that good night.

Good men, the last wave by, crying how bright
Their frail deeds might have danced in a green bay,
Rage, rage against the dying of the light.

Wild men who caught and sang the sun in flight,   10
And learn, too late, they grieved it on its way,
Do not go gentle into that good night.

Grave men, near death, who see with blinding sight
Blind eyes could blaze like meteors and be gay,
Rage, rage against the dying of the light.   15

And you, my father, there on the sad height,
Curse, bless, me now with your fierce tears, I pray.
Do not go gentle into that good night.
Rage, rage against the dying of the light.

Dylan Thomas (1914–1953)

QUESTIONS

1. Discuss the various meanings in this poem of the common phrase "good night."
2. Apart from the fixed form, the poem creates another structural principle in stanzas two through six by describing in turn "wise men" (4), "Good men" (7), "Wild men" (10), and "Grave men" (13). How does the speaker view these various types of men in their differing stances toward both life and death?

3. There are several paradoxical expressions in the poem: "dark is right" (4), "blinding sight" (13), "the sad height" (16), and "Curse, bless, me now" (17). How do these contribute to the poem's meaning?

A good villanelle avoids the potentially monotonous effects of repetition by varying the stress patterns and the meaning of the repeated lines. In Thomas's poem, for example, the third line is a direct address by the speaker to his father, while the repetition in line 9 describes the rage "Good men" feel just before their deaths. Similarly, the poem deftly alternates lines containing grammatical pauses, such as line 7, with lines having no pauses, such as line 8; the blend of run-on and end-stopped lines likewise helps to vary the rhythm. The fixed form also serves the poem's meaning, since the repetition and the circular quality of the villanelle, its continued reiteration of the same two lines, emphasizes the speaker's emotional treadmill, his desperate and perhaps hopeless prayer that his father might rage against death. As in all good poetry, a fixed form like the villanelle does not merely display the poet's technical ability but appropriately supports the tone and meaning of the poem.

Initially, it may seem absurd that poets should choose to confine themselves in an arbitrary formal mold with prescribed meter and rhyme scheme. They do so partly from the desire to carry on a tradition, as all of us carry out certain traditions for their own sake, else why should we bring a tree indoors at Christmas time? Traditional forms are also useful because they have provided a challenge to the poet, and good poets are inspired by the challenge: it will call forth ideas and images that might not otherwise have come. They will subdue the form rather than be subdued by it; they will make it do what they require. There is no doubt that the presence of a net makes good tennis players more precise in their shots than they otherwise might be. And finally, for the poet and for the reader, there is the pleasure of form itself.

EXERCISE

The typographical shape of a poem on the page (whether, for example, printed with a straight left-hand margin or with a system of indentations) is determined sometimes by the poet, sometimes by the printer, sometimes by an editor. Examine each of the following poems and try to deduce what *principle* (if any) determined its typographical design:
1. Shakespeare, "Winter" (page 636).
2. Marvell, "To His Coy Mistress" (page 721).
3. Hughes, "Harlem" (page 705).
4. Evans, "When in Rome" (page 666).
5. cummings, "in Just—" (page 776).

6. Wilbur, "The Writer" (page 737).
7. Yeats, "Leda and the Swan" (page 783).
8. Donne, "The Flea" (page 812).
9. Ferlinghetti, "Constantly risking absurdity" (page 648).
10. Blake, "The Lamb" (page 794).

REVIEWING CHAPTER FOURTEEN

1. Distinguish between structure and form, and review the definitions of the three broad types of form in poetry; using examples from the following poems in the chapter, define both the form and the structure of the poem.
2. Examine the definitions of the two types of sonnet, and explore the way in which the form of each seems to promote the structure of materials in the poem.
3. The villanelle also suggests the structure of the poem's materials; using examples from the following poems, define that implied structure.
4. Poetic forms may rely on the reader's familiarity with the subjects customarily presented in such forms—and poets may employ a form either to fulfill a reader's expectations or ironically to play against them. Find examples of both uses of the forms of the sonnet and the villanelle.

From *Romeo and Juliet*

ROMEO   If I profane with my unworthiest hand
         This holy shrine, the gentle sin is this:
         My lips, two blushing pilgrims, ready stand
         To smooth that rough touch with a tender kiss.
JULIET   Good pilgrim, you do wrong your hand too much,   5
         Which mannerly devotion shows in this;
         For saints have hands that pilgrims' hands do touch,
         And palm to palm is holy palmers' kiss.
ROMEO   Have not saints lips, and holy palmers too?
JULIET   Ay, pilgrim, lips that they must use in prayer.   10
ROMEO   O! then, dear saint, let lips do what hands do;
         They pray, "Grant thou, lest faith turn to despair."

| JULIET | Saints do not move,° though grant for prayer's sake. | propose, |
| ROMEO | Then move not, while my prayer's effect I take. | instigate |

William Shakespeare (1564–1616)

QUESTIONS

1. These fourteen lines occur in Act 1, scene 5, of Shakespeare's play. They are the first words exchanged between Romeo and Juliet, who are meeting, for the first time, at a masquerade ball given by her father. Struck by Juliet's beauty, Romeo has come up to greet her. What stage action accompanies this passage?
2. What is the basic metaphor created by such religious terms as "profane" (1), "shrine" (2), "pilgrims" (3), "holy palmers" (8)? How does this metaphor affect the tone of the relationship between Romeo and Juliet?
3. What play on words do you find in lines 8 and 13–14? What two meanings has line 11?
4. By meter and rhyme scheme, these lines form a sonnet. Do you think this was coincidental or intentional on Shakespeare's part? Discuss.

Death, be not proud

Death, be not proud, though some have callèd thee
Mighty and dreadful, for thou art not so;
For those whom thou think'st thou dost overthrow
Die not, poor death, nor yet canst thou kill me.
From rest and sleep, which but thy pictures be,   5
Much pleasure—then, from thee much more must flow;
And soonest° our best men with thee do go,   readiest
Rest of their bones and soul's delivery.
Thou art slave to fate, chance, kings, and desperate men,
And dost with poison, war, and sickness dwell;   10
And poppy or charms can make us sleep as well,
And better than thy stroke. Why swell'st thou then?
One short sleep passed, we wake eternally,
And death shall be no more; death, thou shalt die.

John Donne (1572–1631)

QUESTIONS

1. What two figures of speech dominate the poem?
2. Why should death not be proud? List the speaker's major reasons. Are they consistent? Logical? Persuasive?

3. Discuss the tone of the poem. Is the speaker (a) a man of assured faith with a firm conviction that death is not to be feared or (b) a man desperately trying to convince himself that there is nothing to fear in death?
4. In form, this sonnet blends the English and Italian models. Explain. Is its organization of thought closer to the Italian or the English sonnet?

The Sheaves

Where long the shadows of the wind had rolled,
Green wheat was yielding to the change assigned;
And as by some vast magic undivined
The world was turning slowly into gold.
Like nothing that was ever bought or sold   5
It waited there, the body and the mind;
And with a mighty meaning of a kind
That tells the more the more it is not told.

So in a land where all days are not fair,
Fair days went on till on another day   10
A thousand golden sheaves were lying there,
Shining and still, but not for long to stay—
As if a thousand girls with golden hair
Might rise from where they slept and go away.

Edwin Arlington Robinson (1869–1935)

QUESTIONS

1. Although it describes a perfectly natural process (the ripening of a wheat-field), the poem imbues that process with mythic or magical meanings. Explore the following phrases as examples: "the change assigned" (2), "some vast magic" (3), "turning . . . into gold" (4), "the body and the mind" (6), "a thousand girls with golden hair" (13). Which of these are similes, and which are metaphors?
2. What are the multiple denotations of "told" (8)? What connotations are attached to them? What other highly connotative words do you find?
3. How does the poem reveal the emotional price of viewing a natural process as if it were beyond human understanding? What is gained by so viewing it, and what lost?
4. What does the form of the sonnet contribute to the structure of the poem?

The White City

I will not toy with it nor bend an inch.
Deep in the secret chambers of my heart
I muse my life-long hate, and without flinch
I bear it nobly as I live my part.
My being would be a skeleton, a shell,   5
If this dark Passion that fills my every mood,
And makes my heaven in the white world's hell,
Did not forever feed me vital blood.
I see the mighty city through a mist—
The strident trains that speed the goaded mass,   10
The poles and spires and towers vapor-kissed,
The fortressed port through which the great ships pass,
The tides, the wharves, the dens I contemplate,
Are sweet like wanton loves because I hate.

Claude McKay (1890–1948)

QUESTIONS

1. Claude McKay was a native black Jamaican who as an adult lived in New York. Why does the speaker "hate" (3) the city?
2. Traditionally, sonnets originated as love poems. Why might McKay have cast this poem in sonnet form?
3. How does the city feed the speaker with "vital blood" (8)?
4. Why are the elements of the New York landscape described in the last line as "sweet like wanton loves" (14)?

America

Although she feeds me bread of bitterness,
And sinks into my throat her tiger's tooth,
Stealing my breath of life, I will confess
I love this cultured hell that tests my youth!
Her vigor flows like tides into my blood,   5
Giving me strength erect against her hate.
Her bigness sweeps my being like a flood.
Yet as a rebel fronts a king in state,
I stand within her walls with not a shred
Of terror, malice, not a word of jeer.   10
Darkly I gaze into the days ahead,

And see her might and granite wonders there,
Beneath the touch of Time's unerring hand,
Like priceless treasures sinking in the sand.

Claude McKay (1890–1948)

QUESTIONS

1. How is "America" characterized? Is the country depicted as a positive or a
   negative place, or both? Consider the meaning of the oxymoron (a compact
   paradox in which two successive words seemingly contradict each other)
   "cultured hell" (4).
2. Why does the speaker say that he loves America, even though the country
   has fed him "bread of bitterness" (1)?
3. Would you characterize the speaker's attitude as being rebellious or resigned
   to his fate?
4. How does the sonnet form relate to the meaning of the poem?

We Wear the Mask

We wear the mask that grins and lies,
It hides our cheeks and shades our eyes,—
This debt we pay to human guile;
With torn and bleeding hearts we smile,
And mouth with myriad subtleties.   5
Why should the world be over-wise,
In counting all our tears and sighs?
Nay, let them only see us, while
          We wear the mask.

We smile, but, O great Christ, our cries   10
To thee from tortured souls arise.
We sing, but oh the clay is vile
Beneath our feet, and long the mile;
But let the world dream otherwise,
          We wear the mask!   15

Paul Laurence Dunbar (1872–1906)

QUESTIONS

1. The poet was African American. What racial theme is implied in the poem?
   What kind of "mask" is the speaker describing?

2. How would you define the tone of this poem? Is the speaker angry? Who are the "tortured souls" (11)?
3. How do the departures from the strict sonnet form contribute to the effect of the poem?

Sonnenizio on a Line from Drayton

Since there's no help, come let us kiss and part;
or kiss anyway, let's start with that, with the kissing part,
because it's better than the parting part, isn't it—
we're good at kissing, we like how that part goes:
we part our lips, our mouths get near and nearer,   5
then we're close, my breasts, your chest, our bodies partway
to making love, so we might as well, part of me thinks—
the wrong part, I know, the bad part, but still
let's pretend we're at that party where we met
and scandalized everyone, remember that part? Hold me   10
like that again, unbutton my shirt, part of you
wants to I can tell, I'm touching that part and it says
yes, the ardent partisan, let it win you over,
it's hopeless, come, we'll kiss and part forever.

Kim Addonizio (b. 1954)

QUESTIONS

1. This "sonnenizio" alludes to Drayton's poem with the same first line (page 804). How does it differ in tone and in level of diction from that poem?
2. What word of Drayton's occurs in some form in every line of this poem? How is Drayton's meaning of it transformed?
3. Does this poem have the same theme as Drayton's?

Acquainted with the Night

I have been one acquainted with the night.
I have walked out in rain—and back in rain.
I have outwalked the furthest city light.

I have looked down the saddest city lane.
I have passed by the watchman on his beat   5
And dropped my eyes, unwilling to explain.

I have stood still and stopped the sound of feet
When far away an interrupted cry
Came over houses from another street,

But not to call me back or say good-by;   10
And further still at an unearthly height,
One luminary clock against the sky

Proclaimed the time was neither wrong nor right.
I have been one acquainted with the night.

Robert Frost (1874–1963)

QUESTIONS

1. How does the speaker reveal the strength of his purpose in his night-walking? Can you specify what that purpose is? What symbolic meanings does the night hold?
2. How is the poem structured into sentences? What is the effect of repeating the phrase "I have"? of repeating line 1 at the conclusion? How do these repetitions affect the tone of the poem?
3. Some critics have interpreted the "luminary clock" (12) literally—as the illuminated dial of a tower clock; others have interpreted it figuratively as the full moon. Of what, in either case, is it a symbol? Does the clock tell accurate chronometric time? What kind of "time" is it proclaiming in line 13? Is knowing *that* kind of time the speaker's quest?
4. The poem contains 14 lines—like a sonnet. But its rhyme scheme is **terza rima**, an interlocking scheme with the pattern *aba bcb cdc*, etc., a formal arrangement that implies continual progression. How does Frost bring the progression to an end? Terza rima was the form memorably employed by Dante for his *Divine Comedy*, of which the *Inferno* is the best-known section. In what ways does Frost's poem allude to the subject and framework of that poem?

In Memory of the Unknown Poet, Robert Boardman Vaughn

> But the essential advantage for a poet is not, to have a beautiful world with which to deal: it is to be able to see beneath both beauty and ugliness; to see the boredom, and the horror, and the glory.

> —*T.S. Eliot*

It was his story. It would always be his story.
It followed him; it overtook him finally—
The boredom, and the horror, and the glory.

Probably at the end he was not yet sorry,
Even as the boots were brutalizing him in the alley.   5
It was his story. It would always be his story,

Blown on a blue horn, full of sound and fury,
But signifying, O signifying magnificently
The boredom, and the horror, and the glory.

I picture the snow as falling without hurry   10
To cover the cobbles and the toppled ashcans completely.
It was his story. It would always be his story.

Lately he had wandered between St. Mark's Place and the Bowery,
Already half a spirit, mumbling and muttering sadly.
O the boredom, and the horror, and the glory!   15

All done now. But I remember the fiery
Hypnotic eye and the raised voice blazing with poetry.
It was his story and would always be his story—
The boredom, and the horror, and the glory.

Donald Justice (1925–2004)

QUESTIONS

1. What is the meaning of the epigraph from T. S. Eliot? How does the epigraph relate to the fate of the "unknown poet"?
2. What are the poetic effects of repetition in this villanelle? How does the speaker keep from making the repetition monotonous?
3. Why does the speaker allude to the passage from Shakespeare's *Macbeth*, quoted in this text on page 774? How does the allusion contribute meaning to the poem?

Villanelle for an Anniversary

A spirit moved, John Harvard walked the yard,
The atom lay unsplit, the west unwon,
The books stood open and the gates unbarred.

The maps dreamt on like moondust. Nothing stirred.
The future was a verb in hibernation.   5
A spirit moved, John Harvard walked the yard.

Before the classic style, before the clapboard,
All through the small hours on an origin,
The books stood open and the gates unbarred.

Night passage of a migratory bird.   10
Wingflap. Gownflap. Like a homing pigeon
A spirit moved, John Harvard walked the yard.

Was that his soul (look) sped to its reward
By grace or works? A shooting star? An omen?
The books stood open and the gates unbarred.   15

Begin again where frosts and tests were hard.
Find yourself or founder. Here, imagine
A spirit moved, John Harvard walked the yard,
The books stand open and the gates unbarred.

Seamus Heaney (b. 1939)

QUESTIONS

1. John Harvard (1607–1638), an English clergyman who arrived in
   Massachusetts in 1637, bequeathed his library and a sum of money to the
   new college at Cambridge which was then named in his honor.
2. How do the refrain lines of this villanelle help to reinforce its meaning?
3. How do you interpret line 3, "The books stood open and the gates unbarred"?
   In line 14, what is the meaning of the phrase "grace or works"? How is this an
   important distinction?
4. What is the impact of the final stanza? What additional meanings have the
   refrain lines gathered by the end of the poem?

The House on the Hill

They are all gone away,
    The House is shut and still,
There is nothing more to say.

Through broken walls and gray
    The winds blow bleak and shrill: 5
They are all gone away.

Nor is there one today
  To speak them good or ill:
There is nothing more to say.

Why is it then we stray   10
  Around that sunken sill?
They are all gone away,

And our poor fancy-play
  For them is wasted skill:
There is nothing more to say.   15

There is ruin and decay
  In the House on the Hill:
They are all gone away,
There is nothing more to say.

Edwin Arlington Robinson (1869–1935)

QUESTIONS

1. If "there is nothing more to say," why does the speaker return to this empty house? What answer can you give to the question in lines 10–11?
2. How is the form of this poem different from that of the other villanelles in this chapter? How does that make the two refrain lines even more haunting?

These are the days when Birds come back

These are the days when Birds come back—
A very few—a Bird or two—
To take a backward look.

These are the days when skies resume
The old—old sophistries of June—   5
A blue and gold mistake.

Oh fraud that cannot cheat the Bee—
Almost thy plausibility
Induces my belief.

Till ranks of seeds their witness bear—   10
And softly thro' the altered air
Hurries a timid leaf.

Oh Sacrament of summer days,
Oh Last Communion in the Haze—
Permit a child to join.   15

Thy sacred emblems to partake—
Thy consecrated bread to take
And thine immortal wine!

Emily Dickinson (1830–1886)

QUESTIONS

1. Vocabulary: *sophistries* (5). The "fraud that cannot cheat the Bee" (7) is probably an allusion to one of the apocryphal tales of Solomon, who distinguished between real and artificial flowers by putting a bee into the room; the bee of course flew to the real.
2. The time of year represented in the poem is "Indian summer" (if you are unfamiliar with the term, consult a dictionary). How is the identity of this time period implied by the terms "backward" (3) and "resume" (4), and by the evidence of "seeds" and "leaf" (10–12)? Why is that time of year a "fraud" (7)? What is it pretending to be? In the final metaphor, how is Indian summer like a "Last Communion" (14)?
3. The rhyme scheme, although complicated by an inconsistency in the first stanza and approximate rhymes throughout, divides the poem into three two-stanza units. The device of repeating the opening phrase in lines 1 and 4, as well as the pattern of repeated words in stanzas 5 and 6, reinforce this division into two-stanza units. How is the *structure* of the poem linked to the formal division into three two-stanza units?
4. What three distinct tones do you observe in the three two-stanza units? What in the development of ideas accounts for the shifts in tone?

Delight in Disorder

A sweet disorder in the dress
Kindles in clothes a wantonness.
A lawn° about the shoulders thrown   linen scarf
Into a fine distractïon;
An erring lace, which here and there   5
Enthralls the crimson stomacher;

A cuff neglected, and thereby
Ribbons to flow confusedly;
A winning wave, deserving note,
In the tempestuous petticoat;   10
A careless shoestring, in whose tie
I see a wild civility;
Do more bewitch me than when art
Is too precise in every part.

Robert Herrick (1591–1674)

QUESTIONS

1. Vocabulary: *wantonness* (2), *stomacher* (6).
2. The phrase "wild civility" (12) is another example of **oxymoron.** Discuss the effectiveness of this device in this phrase and examine the poem for other examples.
3. Consider the relationship of form to structure in this poem. How does this contribute to the meaning?

Still to be neat

Still° to be neat, still to be dressed,   always
As you were going to a feast;
Still to be powdered, still perfumed;
Lady, it is to be presumed,
Though art's hid causes are not found,   5
All is not sweet, all is not sound.

Give me a look, give me a face
That makes simplicity a grace;
Robes loosely flowing, hair as free;
Such sweet neglect more taketh me   10
Than all th' adulteries of art.
They strike mine eyes, but not my heart.

Ben Jonson (1572–1637)

QUESTIONS

1. Does the speaker admire the woman he is addressing in this poem? What lines provide clues to his attitude?
2. What contrast is defined by the separation of the poem into two stanzas? What does the speaker prefer to the "adulteries of art"?

3. How does the oxymoron "sweet neglect" (10) help to elucidate the poem's theme?

4. What are the similarities and differences in theme between this poem and Herrick's "Delight in Disorder"? How are they structured differently?

SUGGESTIONS FOR WRITING

Following are two lists, one of sonnets and the other of villanelles. Using one or two examples of either form, explore the effectiveness of the relationship of structure to form. In particular, be alert for variations or departures from the form and what these contribute to meaning and emotional effect.

Sonnets
Wordsworth, "The world is too much with us" (page 682)
Shelley, "Ozymandias" (page 758)
Donne, "Batter my heart, three-personed God" (page 760)
Yeats, "Leda and the Swan" (page 783)
Frost, "Design" (page 790)
Drayton, "Since there's no help" (page 804)
Shakespeare, "My mistress' eyes" (page 807)
Owen, "Anthem for Doomed Youth" (page 873)

Villanelles
Bishop, "One Art" (page 686)
Roethke, "The Waking" (page 822)
Plath, "Mad Girl's Love Song" (page 991)

Evaluating Poetry 1

Sentimental, Rhetorical, Didactic Verse

The attempt to evaluate a poem should never be made before the poem is understood; and, unless one has developed the capacity to experience poetry intellectually and emotionally, any judgments one makes will be of little worth. A person who likes no wines can hardly be a judge of them. But the ability to make judgments, to discriminate between good and bad, great and good, good and half-good, is surely a primary object of all liberal education, and one's appreciation of poetry is incomplete unless it includes discrimination.

In judging a poem, as in judging any work of art, we need to ask three basic questions: (1) *What is its central purpose?* (2) *How fully has this purpose been accomplished?* (3) *How important is this purpose?* We need to answer the first question in order to understand the poem. Questions 2 and 3 are those by which we evaluate it. Question 2 judges the poem on a scale of perfection. Question 3 judges it on a scale of significance.

For answering the first of our evaluative questions, *How fully has the poem's purpose been accomplished?* there are no easy yardsticks that we can apply. We cannot ask: Is the poem melodious? Does it have smooth rhythm? Does it use good grammar? Does it contain figures of speech? Are the rhymes perfect? Excellent poems exist without any of these attributes. We can judge any element in a poem only as it contributes or fails to contribute to the achievement of the central purpose; and we can judge the total poem only as these elements work together to form an integrated whole. But we can at least attempt a few generalizations. A wholly successful poem contains no excess words, no words that do not bear their full weight in contributing to the total experience, and no words that are used just to fill out the meter. Each word is the best word for expressing the total meaning: there are no inexact words forced by the rhyme scheme or the metrical pattern. The word order is the best order for expressing the author's total meaning; distortions or departures from normal order are for emphasis or some other meaningful purpose. The diction, the images, and the figures of speech are fresh, not trite (except, of course, when the poet uses trite language deliberately for purposes of irony). The sound of the poem does not clash with its sense, or the form with its content; and in general both sound and pattern are used to support meaning. The organization of the poem is the best possible organization: images and ideas are so effectively arranged that any rearrangement would be harmful to the poem. Always remember, however, that a good poem may have flaws. We should never damn a poem for its flaws if these flaws are amply compensated for by positive excellence.

What constitutes excellence in poetry? One criterion is that its combination of thought, emotion, language, and sound must be fresh and original. As the poet and critic Ezra Pound insisted, good writing must "make it new." An excellent poem will neither be merely imitative of previous literature nor appeal to stock, pre-established ways of thinking and feeling. The following discussion highlights three particular ways in which a poem can fail to achieve excellence: if a poem is sentimental, excessively rhetorical, or purely didactic, in fact, we would probably call it "verse" rather than true poetry.

Sentimentality is indulgence in emotion for its own sake, or expression of more emotion than an occasion warrants. Sentimentalists are gushy, stirred to tears by trivial or inappropriate causes; they weep at all weddings and all funerals; they are made ecstatic by manifestations of young love; they clip locks of hair, gild baby shoes, and talk baby talk. Sentimental *literature* is "tear-jerking" literature. It aims primarily at stimulating the emotions directly rather than at communicating experience truly and freshly; it depends on trite and well-tried formulas for exciting emotion; it revels in old oaken buckets, rocking chairs, mother love, and the pitter-patter of little feet; it oversimplifies; it is unfaithful to the full complexity of human experience

Rhetorical poetry uses a language more glittering and high-flown than its substance warrants. It offers a spurious vehemence of language— language without a corresponding reality of emotion or thought underneath. It is oratorical, overelegant, artificially eloquent. It is superficial and, again, often basically trite. It loves rolling phrases like "from the rocky coast of Maine to the sun-washed shores of California" and "our heroic dead" and "Old Glory." It deals in generalities. At its worst it is bombast. In this book an example is offered by the two lines quoted from the play within a play in the fifth act of Shakespeare's *A Midsummer Night's Dream:*

Whereat with blade, with bloody, blameful blade,
He bravely broached his boiling bloody breast.

Another example may be found in the player's recitation in *Hamlet* (in Act 2, scene 2):

> Out, out, thou strumpet Fortune! All you gods,
> In general synod take away her power,
> Break all the spokes and fellies from her wheel,
> And bowl the round nave down the hill of heaven
> As low as to the fiends!

Didactic poetry has as a primary purpose to teach or preach. It is probable that all the very greatest poetry teaches in subtle ways, without being expressly didactic; and much expressly didactic poetry ranks high in poetic excellence: that is, it accomplishes its teaching without ceasing to be poetry. But when the didactic purpose supersedes the poetic purpose, when the poem communicates information or moral instruction only, then it ceases to be didactic poetry and becomes didactic verse. Such verse appeals to people who read poetry primarily for noble thoughts or inspiring lessons and like them prettily expressed. It is recognizable often by its lack of any specific situation, the flatness of its diction, the poverty of its imagery and figurative language, its emphasis on moral platitudes, its lack of poetic freshness. It is either very trite or has little to distinguish it from informational prose except rhyme or meter. Emerson's "The Rhodora" (page 789) is an example of didactic *poetry*. The familiar couplet

> Early to bed and early to rise,
> Makes a man healthy, wealthy, and wise

is more aptly characterized as didactic *verse*.

Undoubtedly, so far in this chapter, we have spoken too categorically, have made our distinctions too sharp and definite. All poetic excellence is a matter of degree. There are no absolute lines between sentimentality and true emotion, artificial and genuine eloquence, didactic verse and didactic poetry. Though the difference between extreme examples is easy to recognize, subtler discriminations are harder to make.

A final caution to students: when making judgments on literature, always be honest. Do not pretend to like what you do not like. Do not be afraid to admit a liking for what you do like. A genuine enthusiasm for the second-rate is much better than false enthusiasm or no enthusiasm at all. Be neither hasty nor timorous in making your judgments. When you have attentively read a poem and thoroughly considered it, decide what you think. Do not hedge, equivocate, or try to find out others' opinions before forming your own. But, having formed an opinion and expressed it, do not allow it to harden into a narrow-minded bias. Compare your opinion *then* with the opinions of others; allow yourself to change it when convinced of its error: in this way you learn.

In the pairs of poems for comparison that follow in this chapter, the distinction to be made is not always between bad and good; it may be between varying degrees of poetic merit.

REVIEWING CHAPTER FIFTEEN

1. Review the three basic questions to be answered in evaluating a poem.
2. Explore the three weaknesses that may lead us to judge a poem less than excellent, finding examples of each in the poems that follow in this chapter.

God's Will for You and Me

Just to be tender, just to be true,
Just to be glad the whole day through,
Just to be merciful, just to be mild,
Just to be trustful as a child,
Just to be gentle and kind and sweet,   5
Just to be helpful with willing feet,
Just to be cheery when things go wrong,
Just to drive sadness away with a song,
Whether the hour is dark or bright,
Just to be loyal to God and right,   10
Just to believe that God knows best,
Just in his promises ever to rest—
Just to let love be our daily key,
That is God's will for you and me.

Pied Beauty

Glory be to God for dappled things—
　　For skies of couple-color as a brinded cow;
　　　　For rose-moles all in stipple upon trout that swim;

Fresh-firecoal chestnut-falls; finches' wings;
Landscape plotted and pieced—fold, fallow and plow;   5
And all trades, their gear and tackle and trim.
All things counter, original, spare, strange;
Whatever is fickle, freckled (who knows how?)
With swift, slow; sweet, sour; adazzle, dim;
He fathers-forth whose beauty is past change: 10
Praise him.

QUESTION

1. Which is the superior poem? Explain in full.

A Poison Tree

I was angry with my friend:
I told my wrath, my wrath did end.
I was angry with my foe:
I told it not, my wrath did grow.

And I watered it in fears,   5
Night and morning with my tears;
And I sunnèd it with smiles,
And with soft deceitful wiles.

And it grew both day and night
Till it bore an apple bright;   10
And my foe beheld it shine,
And he knew that it was mine,

And into my garden stole
When the night had veiled the pole:°   sky
In the morning glad I see   15
My foe outstretched beneath the tree.

The Most Vital Thing in Life

When you feel like saying something
That you know you will regret,
Or keenly feel an insult

Not quite easy to forget,
That's the time to curb resentment   5
    And maintain a mental peace,
For when your mind is tranquil
    All your ill-thoughts simply cease.

It is easy to be angry
    When defrauded or defied,   10
To be peeved and disappointed
    If your wishes are denied;
But to win a worthwhile battle
    Over selfishness and spite,
You must learn to keep strict silence   15
    Though you know you're in the right.

So keep your mental balance
    When confronted by a foe,
Be it enemy in ambush
    Or some danger that you know.   20
If you are poised and tranquil
    When all around is strife,
Be assured that you have mastered
    The most vital thing in life.

QUESTION

1. Which poem has more poetic merit? Explain.

Lower New York: at Dawn

Here is the dawn a hopeless thing to see:
    Sordid and pale as is the face of one
    Who sinks exhausted in oblivion
    After a night of deep debauchery.
Here, as the light reveals relentlessly   5
    All that the soul has lost and greed has won,
    Scarce we believe that somewhere now the sun
    Dawns overseas in stainless majesty.
Yet the day comes!—ghastly and harsh and thin
    Down the cold street; and now, from far away,   10

We hear a vast and sullen rumor run,
As of the tides of ocean turning in . . .
And know, for yet another human day,
The world's dull, dreadful labor is begun!

Composed upon Westminster Bridge, September 3, 1802

Earth has not anything to show more fair:
Dull would he be of soul who could pass by
A sight so touching in its majesty:
This City now doth, like a garment, wear
The beauty of the morning; silent, bare,   5
Ships, towers, domes, theaters, and temples lie
Open unto the fields, and to the sky,
All bright and glittering in the smokeless air.
Never did sun more beautifully steep
In his first splendor, valley, rock, or hill;   10
Ne'er saw I, never felt, a calm so deep!
The river glideth at his own sweet will:
Dear God! the very houses seem asleep,
And all that mighty heart is lying still!

QUESTION

1. Which poem has more freshness of language?

Pitcher

His art is eccentricity, his aim
How not to hit the mark he seems to aim at,

His passion how to avoid the obvious,
His technique how to vary the avoidance.

The others throw to be comprehended. He   5
Throws to be a moment misunderstood.
Yet not too much. Not errant, arrant, wild,
But every seeming aberration willed.

Not to, yet still, still to communicate
Making the batter understand too late.   10

The Old-Fashioned Pitcher

How dear to my heart was the old-fashioned hurler
   Who labored all day on the old village green.
He did not resemble the up-to-date twirler
   Who pitches four innings and ducks from the scene.
The up-to-date twirler I'm not very strong for;   5
   He has a queer habit of pulling up lame.
And that is the reason I hanker and long for
   The pitcher who started and finished the game.

      The old-fashioned pitcher,
        The iron-armed pitcher,   10
      The stout-hearted pitcher
        Who finished the game.

QUESTION
1. Which poem is the more interesting and more meaningful? Why?

Piano

Softly, in the dusk, a woman is singing to me;
Taking me back down the vista of years, till I see
A child sitting under the piano, in the boom of the tingling
   strings
And pressing the small, poised feet of a mother who smiles as
   she sings.

In spite of myself, the insidious mastery of song   5
Betrays me back, till the heart of me weeps to belong
To the old Sunday evenings at home, with winter outside
And hymns in the cozy parlor, the tinkling piano our guide.

So now it is vain for the singer to burst into clamor
With the great black piano appassionato. The glamor   10
Of childish days is upon me, my manhood is cast
Down in the flood of remembrance, I weep like a child
   for the past.

The Days Gone By

O the days gone by! O the days gone by!
The apples in the orchard, and the pathway through the rye;
The chirrup of the robin, and the whistle of the quail
As he piped across the meadows sweet as any nightingale;
When the bloom was on the clover, and the blue was   5
    in the sky,
And my happy heart brimmed over in the days gone by.

In the days gone by, when my naked feet were tripped
By the honey-suckle's tangles where the water-lillies dipped,
And the ripples of the river lipped the moss along the brink
Where the placid-eyed and lazy-footed cattle came to drink,   10
And the tilting snipe stood fearless of the truant's
    wayward cry
And the splashing of the swimmer, in the days gone by.

O the days gone by! O the days gone by!
The music of the laughing lip, the luster of the eye;
The childish faith in fairies, and Aladdin's magic ring—   15
The simple, soul-reposing, glad belief in everything,—
When life was like a story, holding neither sob nor sigh,
In the golden olden glory of the days gone by.

QUESTION
1. Which poem is more rhetorical in treating the subject?

The Engine

Into the gloom of the deep, dark night,
    With panting breath and a startled scream,
Swift as a bird in sudden flight
    Darts this creature of steel and steam.

Awful dangers are lurking nigh,   5
    Rocks and chasms are near the track,
But straight by the light of its great white eye
    It speeds through the shadows, dense and black.

Terrible thoughts and fierce desires
  Trouble its mad heart many an hour,   10
Where burn and smoulder the hidden fires,
  Coupled ever with might and power.

It hates, as a wild horse hates the rein,
  The narrow track by vale and hill,
And shrieks with a cry of startled pain,   15
  And longs to follow its own wild will.

I like to see it lap the Miles

I like to see it lap the Miles—
And lick the Valleys up—
And stop to feed itself at Tanks—
And then—prodigious step

Around a Pile of Mountains—   5
And supercilious peer
In Shanties—by the sides of Roads—
And then a Quarry pare

To fit its Ribs
And crawl between
Complaining all the while   10
In horrid—hooting stanza—
Then chase itself down Hill—

And neigh like Boanerges—
Then—punctual as a Star   15
Stop—docile and omnipotent
At its own stable door—

QUESTION

1. Which of these poems is more rhetorical in its language?

When I have fears that I may cease to be

When I have fears that I may cease to be
  Before my pen has gleaned my teaming brain,
Before high-pilèd books, in charactery,°   written symbols
  Hold like rich garners the full-ripened grain;
When I behold, upon the night's starred face,   5
  Huge cloudy symbols of a high romance,
And think that I may never live to trace
  Their shadows, with the magic hand of chance;
And when I feel, fair creature of an hour,
  That I shall never look upon thee more,   10
Never have relish in the faery power
  Of unreflecting love—then on the shore
Of the wide world I stand alone, and think
  Till love and fame to nothingness do sink.

O Solitude!

O Solitude! if I must with thee dwell,
  Let it not be among the jumbled heap
  Of murky buildings; climb with me the steep—
Nature's observatory—whence the dell,
Its flowery slopes, its river's crystal swell,   5
  May seem a span; let me thy vigils keep
  'Mongst boughs pavilioned, where the deer's swift leap
Startles the wild bee from the fox-glove bell.
But though I'll gladly trace these scenes with thee,
  Yet the sweet converse of an innocent mind,   10
  Whose words are images of thoughts refined,
Is my soul's pleasure; and it sure must be
  Almost the highest bliss of human-kind,
When to thy haunts two kindred spirits flee.

QUESTION

Both poems are by John Keats (1795–1821). Which of them displays true excellence? Explain.

SUGGESTIONS FOR WRITING

In each of the following pairs, both poems have literary merit, but one is clearly a more ambitious and more successful poem. Choose one pair and write a short essay in which you argue which is the better of the two poems, and why.

1. Owen, "Dulce et Decorum Est" (page 637) and Crane, "War Is Kind." (page 953).
2. Whitman, "To a Stranger" (page 1010) and Ginsberg, "A Supermarket in California" (page 966).
3. Dickinson, "I felt a Funeral, in my Brain" (page 695) and Plath, "Mad Girl's Love Song" (page 991).
4. Clifton, "good times" (page 950) and Hughes, "Theme for English B" (page 976).
5. Joseph, "Warning" (page 978) and Yeats, "Sailing to Byzantium" (page 1017).
6. Donne, "The Indifferent" (page 795) and Behn, "On Her Loving Two Equally" (page 944).

Evaluating Poetry 2

Poetic Excellence

If a poem has successfully met the test of the question, *How fully has it accomplished its purpose?* we are ready to subject it to our second evaluative question: *How important is its purpose?*

Great poetry must, of course, be good poetry. Noble intent alone cannot redeem a work that does not measure high on the scale of accomplishment; otherwise the sentimental and purely didactic verse of much of the preceding chapter would stand with the world's masterpieces. But once a work has been judged as successful on the scale of execution, its final standing will depend on its significance of purpose.

Suppose, for instance, we consider three examples in our text: the anonymous verse "Little Jack Horner" (page 785); the poem "It sifts from Leaden Sieves" by Emily Dickinson (page 707); and Shakespeare's sonnet "That time of year" (page 885). Each of these would probably be judged by critics as successful in what it sets out to do. "Little Jack Horner" is a charming nursery rhyme that even displays dramatic irony (for a "good boy" doesn't stick his thumb in his pie). But what is this verse *about?* Virtually nothing. Dickinson's poem, in contrast, *is* poetry, and very good poetry. It appeals richly to our senses and to our imaginations, and it succeeds excellently in its purpose: to convey the appearance and the quality of falling and newly fallen snow as well as a sense of the magic and the mystery of nature. Yet when we compare this excellent poem with Shakespeare's, we again see important differences. Although Dickinson's poem engages the senses and the imagination and may affect us with wonder and cause us to meditate on nature, it does not deeply engage the emotions or the intellect. It does not come as close to the core of human living and suffering as does Shakespeare's sonnet. In fact, it is concerned primarily with that staple of small talk, the weather. On the other hand, Shakespeare's sonnet evokes the universal human concerns of growing old, approaching death, and love. Of these three selections, then, Shakespeare's is the greatest. It "says" more than Dickinson's poem or the nursery rhyme; it communicates a richer experience; it successfully accomplishes a more significant purpose. The reader will get from it a deeper enjoyment because it is nourishing as well as delightful.

Great poetry engages the whole person—senses, imagination, emotion, intellect; it does not touch us merely on one or two sides of our nature. Great poetry seeks not merely to entertain us but to bring us—along with pure pleasure—fresh insights, or renewed insights, and important insights, into the nature of human experience. Great poetry, we might say, gives us a broader and deeper understanding of life, of other people, and of ourselves, always with the qualification, of course, that the kind of insight literature gives is not necessarily the kind that can be summed up in a simple "lesson" or "moral." It is *knowledge—felt* knowledge, *new* knowledge—of the complexities of human nature and of the tragedies and sufferings, the excitements and joys, that characterize human experience.

Yet, after all, we have provided no easy yardsticks or rule-of-thumb measures for literary judgment. There are no mechanical tests. The final measuring rod can be only the responsiveness, the taste, and the discernment of the reader. Such taste and discernment are partly a native endowment, partly the product of experience, partly the achievement of conscious study, training, and intellectual effort. They cannot be achieved suddenly or quickly; they can never be achieved in perfection. The pull is a long and a hard one. But success, even relative success, brings enormous personal and aesthetic rewards.

The Canonization

For God's sake, hold your tongue, and let me love!
    Or chide my palsy or my gout,
My five gray hairs or ruined fortune flout;
With wealth your state, your mind with arts improve,
    Take you a course,° get you a place,   career 5
      Observe his honor° or his grace,°   judge; bishop
Or the king's real or his stamped face°   on a coin
    Contemplate; what you will, approve,°   try out
      So you will let me love.

Alas, alas, who's injured by my love?   10
    What merchant ships have my sighs drowned?
Who says my tears have overflowed his ground?
When did my colds a forward° spring remove?   early

When did the heats which my veins fill
    Add one more to the plaguy bill?   15
Soldiers find wars, and lawyers find out still
    Litigious men which quarrels move,
        Though she and I do love.

Call us what you will, we are made such by love.
    Call her one, me another fly;°   moth 20
We are tapers too, and at our own cost die;
And we in us find the eagle and the dove;
    The phoenix riddle hath more wit°   meaning
        By us; we two, being one, are it.
So to one neutral thing both sexes fit.   25
    We die and rise the same, and prove
        Mysterious by this love.

We can die by it, if not live by love,
    And if unfit for tombs and hearse
Our legend be, it will be fit for verse;   30
And if no piece of chronicle° we prove,   history
    We'll build in sonnets pretty rooms:
    As well a well-wrought urn becomes
The greatest ashes as half-acre tombs,
    And by these hymns all shall approve°   confirm 35
        Us canonized for love,

And thus invoke us: "You whom reverend love
    Made one another's hermitage,
You to whom love was peace, that now is rage,
Who did the whole world's soul contract, and drove   40
    Into the glasses of your eyes
    (So made such mirrors and such spies
That they did all to you epitomize)
    Countries, towns, courts: beg from above
    A pattern of your love!"   45

John Donne (1572–1631)

QUESTIONS

1. Vocabulary: *Canonization* (title), *tapers* (21), *phoenix* (23), *invoke* (37), *epitomize* (43). "[R]eal" (7), pronounced as two syllables, puns on *royal*. The "plaguy bill" (15) is a list of plague victims. The word "die" (21, 26, 28) in seventeenth-century slang meant to experience the sexual climax. To

understand lines 21 and 28, one also needs to be familiar with the Renaissance superstition that every act of sexual intercourse shortened one's life by one day. The "eagle" and the "dove" (22) are symbols for strength and mildness. "[P]attern" (45) is a model that one can copy.

2. Who is the speaker and what is his condition? How old is he? To whom is he speaking? What has his auditor been saying to him before the opening of the poem? What sort of values can we ascribe to the auditor by inference from the first stanza? What value does the speaker oppose to these? How does the stanzaic pattern of the poem emphasize this value?

3. The sighs, tears, fevers, and chills in the second stanza were commonplace in the love poetry of Donne's time. How does Donne make them fresh? What is the speaker's argument in this stanza? How does it begin to turn from pure defense to offense in the last three lines of the stanza?

4. How are the things to which the lovers are compared in the third stanza *arranged*? Does their ordering reflect in any way the arrangement of the whole poem? Elucidate line 21. Interpret or paraphrase lines 23–27.

5. Explain the first line of the fourth stanza. What status does the speaker claim for himself and his beloved in the last line of this stanza?

6. In what sense is the last stanza an invocation? Who speaks in it? To whom? What powers are ascribed to the lovers in it?

7. What do the following words from the poem have in common: "Mysterious" (27), "hymns" (35), "canonized" (36), "reverend" (37), "hermitage" (38)? What judgment about love does the speaker make by the use of these words?

Ode on a Grecian Urn

> Thou still unravished bride of quietness,
>> Thou foster-child of silence and slow time,
> Sylvan historian, who canst thus express
>> A flowery tale more sweetly than our rhyme:
> What leaf-fringed legend haunts about thy shape   5
>> Of deities or mortals, or of both,
>>> In Tempe or the dales of Arcady?
>> What men or gods are these? What maidens loth?
> What mad pursuit? What struggle to escape?
>> What pipes and timbrels? What wild ecstasy?   10
>
> Heard melodies are sweet, but those unheard
>> Are sweeter; therefore, ye soft pipes, play on;
> Not to the sensual ear, but, more endeared,
>> Pipe to the spirit ditties of no tone:
> Fair youth, beneath the trees, thou canst not leave   15
>> Thy song, nor ever can those trees be bare;

Bold lover, never, never canst thou kiss,
Though winning near the goal—yet, do not grieve;
    She cannot fade, though thou hast not thy bliss,
For ever wilt thou love, and she be fair!   20

Ah, happy, happy boughs! that cannot shed
    Your leaves, nor ever bid the spring adieu;
And, happy melodist, unwearièd,
    For ever piping songs for ever new;
More happy love! more happy, happy love!   25
    For ever warm and still to be enjoyed,
        For ever panting and for ever young;
All breathing human passion far above,
    That leaves a heart high-sorrowful and cloyed,
        A burning forehead, and a parching tongue.   30

Who are these coming to the sacrifice?
    To what green altar, O mysterious priest,
Lead'st thou that heifer lowing at the skies,
    And all her silken flanks with garlands drest?
What little town by river or sea shore,   35
    Or mountain-built with peaceful citadel,
        Is emptied of its folk, this pious morn?
And, little town, thy streets for evermore
    Will silent be; and not a soul to tell
        Why thou are desolate, can e'er return.   40

O Attic shape! Fair attitude! with brede
    Of marble men and maidens overwrought,
With forest branches and the trodden weed;
    Thou, silent form, dost tease us out of thought
As doth eternity: Cold Pastoral!   45
    When old age shall this generation waste,
        Thou shalt remain, in midst of other woe
    Than ours, a friend to man, to whom thou say'st,
Beauty is truth, truth beauty,—that is all
    Ye know on earth, and all ye need to know.*   50

John Keats (1795–1821)

*(49–50) In the 1820 edition of Keats's poems the words "Beauty is truth, truth beauty" were enclosed in quotation marks, and the poem is often reprinted that way. It is now generally agreed, however, on the basis of contemporary transcripts of Keats's poem, that Keats intended the entire last two lines to be spoken by the urn.

QUESTIONS

1. The poem is an extended apostrophe addressed to a painted vase from ancient Greece. There are two separate scenes on the urn; the speaker summarizes their subjects in lines 5–10, and then specifically addresses them in 11–30 and 31–40. As completely as you can, describe what each of the scenes depicts.

2. What three denotations of "still" (1) are appropriate to the metaphorical identities ascribed to the urn in lines 1–4? What modes of sensory experience and of knowledge are evoked in those lines?

3. The structure of the poem includes the speaker's shifting motivations in the spaces *between* the stanzas. For example, lines 5–10 request information about the actions depicted on the urn, but lines 11–14 dismiss the need for answers. What do you suppose motivates that change?

4. Lines 15–28 celebrate the scene because it has captured in a still moment the intensity of pursuit and desire. Explain. How is that permanence contrasted to the reality of "breathing human passion" (28)?

5. In the fourth stanza the speaker turns to the second scene, again with a series of questions requesting specific information. How do the concluding lines of the third stanza motivate this shift of subject? Lines 31–34 are questions about what the speaker *sees* on the urn; lines 34–40 refer to something he cannot see—and are expressed in a tone of desolation. What is it that leads the speaker to that tone? What has *he* done to cause it?

6. In the final stanza, the speaker does not engage himself with the subjects of the scenes but with "shape" (41), "form" (44), and "attitude" (41—in its older meaning, the posture of a painted figure). What at the end of the preceding stanza might cause the speaker to withdraw his imagination from the scenes and to comment in general on the "form" of the urn? Explain lines 44–45 and the culminating oxymoron "Cold Pastoral."

7. The footnote bases its deduction—that the last two lines in their entirety are claimed by the speaker to be the urn's advice to "man" (48)—on external evidence. Can you find internal support for this in the obsolete grammatical usage in line 50? How is the urn's message suited to the experience that the speaker has undergone?

There's a certain Slant of light

There's a certain Slant of light,
Winter Afternoons—
That oppresses, like the Heft
Of Cathedral Tunes—

Heavenly Hurt, it gives us—   5
We can find no scar,
But internal difference,
Where the Meanings, are—

None may teach it—Any—
'Tis the Seal Despair—   10
An imperial affliction
Sent us of the Air—

When it comes, the Landscape listens—
Shadows—hold their breath—
When it goes, 'tis like the Distance   15
On the look of Death—

Emily Dickinson (1830–1886)

QUESTIONS

1. This is one of Dickinson's most famous poems dealing with human psychological states. Here the speaker calls her state of mind "Despair" (10), but many today would consider it "clinical depression." What particular images help convey the speaker's depressed state of mind?

2. The scene is carefully set: a winter afternoon, a speaker attempting to describe what she feels. How does the poem relate a possibly fleeting psychological state to such issues as religious faith, self-examination, and death?

3. Could it be argued that this experience, however painful, is ultimately a positive one for the speaker? What is the significance of the oxymorons "Heavenly Hurt" (5) and "imperial affliction" (11)?

4. Discuss the use of abstractions in this poem: "Hurt" (5), "Meanings" (8), "Despair" (10), "Death" (16). How do these abstractions work to enlarge the poem's meaning beyond a mere depiction of a specific person's temporary mood?

5. The final stanza describes the moment of great tension when the "Seal" (10) of despair falls upon the speaker. Why does she imagine that the entire landscape participates in this personal crisis? Does this suggest a self-absorbed projection onto the landscape or an honest attempt to understand and describe her mental state?

6. Discuss the concluding simile, "like the Distance / On the look of Death—." Do any specific visual images come to mind as you ponder this abstract phrase? Could "Death" here be interpreted as meaning "a dead person"?

Home Burial

He saw her from the bottom of the stairs
Before she saw him. She was starting down,
Looking back over her shoulder at some fear.

She took a doubtful step and then undid it
To raise herself and look again. He spoke   5
Advancing toward her: "What is it you see
From up there always—for I want to know."
She turned and sank upon her skirts at that,
And her face changed from terrified to dull.
He said to gain time: "What is it you see,"   10
Mounting until she cowered under him.
"I will find out now—you must tell me, dear."
She, in her place, refused him any help
With the least stiffening of her neck and silence.
She let him look, sure that he wouldn't see,   15
Blind creature; and awhile he didn't see.
But at last he murmured, "Oh," and again, "Oh."

"What is it—what?" she said.

                            "Just that I see."

"You don't," she challenged. "Tell me what it is."

"The wonder is I didn't see at once.   20
I never noticed it from here before.
I must be wonted to it—that's the reason.
The little graveyard where my people are!
So small the window frames the whole of it.
Not so much larger than a bedroom, is it?   25
There are three stones of slate and one of marble,
Broad-shouldered little slabs there in the sunlight
On the sidehill. We haven't to mind *those*.
But I understand: it is not the stones,
But the child's mound—"

                            "Don't, don't, don't, don't,"
she cried.   30

She withdrew, shrinking from beneath his arm
That rested on the banister, and slid downstairs;
And turned on him with such a daunting look,
He said twice over before he knew himself:
"Can't a man speak of his own child he's lost?"   35

"Not you! Oh, where's my hat? Oh, I don't need it!
I must get out of here. I must get air.
I don't know rightly whether any man can."
"Amy! Don't go to someone else this time.
Listen to me. I won't come down the stairs."   40
He sat and fixed his chin between his fists.
"There's something I should like to ask you, dear."

"You don't know how to ask it."

                                "Help me, then."

Her fingers moved the latch for all reply.

"My words are nearly always an offense.   45
I don't know how to speak of anything
So as to please you. But I might be taught,
I should suppose. I can't say I see how.
A man must partly give up being a man
With women-folk. We could have some arrangement   50
By which I'd bind myself to keep hands off
Anything special you're a-mind to name.
Though I don't like such things 'twixt those that love.
Two that don't love can't live together without them.
But two that do can't live together with them."   55
She moved the latch a little. "Don't—don't go.
Don't carry it to someone else this time.
Tell me about it if it's something human.
Let me into your grief. I'm not so much
Unlike other folks as your standing there   60
Apart would make me out. Give me my chance.
I do think, though, you overdo it a little.
What was it brought you up to think it the thing
To take your mother-loss of a first child
So inconsolably—in the face of love.   65
You'd think his memory might be satisfied—"

"There you go sneering now!"

                                "I'm not, I'm not!
You make me angry. I'll come down to you.
God, what a woman! And it's come to this,
A man can't speak of his own child that's dead."   70

"You can't because you don't know how to speak.
If you had any feelings, you that dug
With your own hand—how could you?—his little grave;
I saw you from that very window there,
Making the gravel leap and leap in air,   75
Leap up, like that, like that, and land so lightly
And roll back down the mound beside the hole.
I thought, Who is that man? I didn't know you.
And I crept down the stairs and up the stairs
To look again, and still your spade kept lifting.   80
Then you came in. I heard your rumbling voice
Out in the kitchen, and I don't know why,
But I went near to see with my own eyes.
You could sit there with the stains on your shoes
Of the fresh earth from your own baby's grave   85
And talk about your everyday concerns.
You had stood the spade up against the wall
Outside there in the entry, for I saw it."

"I shall laugh the worst laugh I ever laughed.
I'm cursed. God, if I don't believe I'm cursed."   90

"I can repeat the very words you were saying:
'Three foggy mornings and one rainy day
Will rot the best birch fence a man can build.'
Think of it, talk like that at such a time!
What had how long it takes a birch to rot   95
To do with what was in the darkened parlor?
You *couldn't* care! The nearest friends can go
With anyone to death, comes so far short
They might as well not try to go at all.
No, from the time when one is sick to death,   100
One is alone, and he dies more alone.
Friends make pretense of following to the grave,
But before one is in it, their minds are turned
And making the best of their way back to life
And living people, and things they understand.   105
But the world's evil. I won't have grief so
If I can change it. Oh, I won't, I won't!"

"There, you have said it all and you feel better.
You won't go now. You're crying. Close the door.

The heart's gone out of it: why keep it up?   110
Amy! There's someone coming down the road!"
"You—oh, you think the talk is all. I must go—
Somewhere out of this house. How can I make you—"

"If—you—do!" She was opening the door wider.
"Where do you mean to go? First tell me that.   115
I'll follow and bring you back by force. I *will!*—"

Robert Frost (1874–1963)

QUESTIONS

1. Vocabulary: *wonted* (22).
2. The poem centers on a conflict between husband and wife. What causes the conflict? Why does Amy resent her husband? What is *his* dissatisfaction with Amy?
3. Characterize the husband and wife respectively. What is the chief difference between them? Does the poem take sides? Is either presented more sympathetically than the other?
4. The poem does not say how long the couple have been married or how long the child has been buried. Does it contain suggestions from which we may make rough inferences?
5. The husband and wife both generalize on the other's faults during the course of the poem, attributing them to all men or to all women or to people in general. Point out these generalizations. Are they valid?
6. Finish the unfinished sentences in lines 30, 66, 113, 114.
7. Comment on the function of lines 25, 39, 92–93.
8. Following are three paraphrased and abbreviated versions of statements made in published discussions of the poem. Which would you support? Why?
   a. The young wife is gradually persuaded by her husband's kind yet firm reasonableness to express her feelings in words and to recognize that human nature is limited and cannot sacrifice everything to sorrow. Though she still suffers from excess grief, the crisis is past, and she will eventually be brought back to life.
   b. At the end, the whole poem is epitomized by the door that is neither open nor shut. The wife cannot really leave; the husband cannot really make her stay. Neither husband nor wife is capable of decisive action, of either self-liberation or liberation of the other.
   c. Her husband's attempt to talk, since it is the wrong kind of talk, only leads to her departure at the poem's end.

The Love Song of J. Alfred Prufrock

S'io credesse che mia risposta fosse
A persona che mai tornasse al mondo,
Questa fiamma staria senza piu scosse.
Ma perciocche giammai di questo fondo
Non torno vivo alcun, s'i'odo il vero,
Senza tema d'infamia ti rispondo.

Let us go then, you and I,
When the evening is spread out against the sky
Like a patient etherized upon a table;
Let us go, through certain half-deserted streets,
The muttering retreats   5
Of restless nights in one-night cheap hotels
And sawdust restaurants with oyster-shells:
Streets that follow like a tedious argument
Of insidious intent
To lead you to an overwhelming question. . . .   10
Oh, do not ask, "What is it?"
Let us go and make our visit.

In the room the women come and go
Talking of Michelangelo.

The yellow fog that rubs its back upon the window-panes,   15
The yellow smoke that rubs its muzzle on the window-panes
Licked its tongue into the corners of the evening,
Lingered upon the pools that stand in drains,
Let fall upon its back the soot that falls from chimneys,
Slipped by the terrace, made a sudden leap,   20
And seeing that it was a soft October night,
Curled once about the house, and fell asleep.

And indeed there will be time
For the yellow smoke that slides along the street,
Rubbing its back upon the window-panes;   25
There will be time, there will be time
To prepare a face to meet the faces that you meet;
There will be time to murder and create,
And time for all the works and days of hands

That lift and drop a question on your plate;   30
Time for you and time for me,
And time yet for a hundred indecisions,
And for a hundred visions and revisions,
Before the taking of a toast and tea.

In the room the women come and go   35
Talking of Michelangelo.

And indeed there will be time
To wonder, "Do I dare?" and "Do I dare?"
Time to turn back and descend the stair,
With a bald spot in the middle of my hair—   40
(They will say: "How his hair is growing thin!")
My morning coat, my collar mounting firmly to the chin,
My necktie rich and modest, but asserted by a simple pin—
(They will say: "But how his arms and legs are thin!")
Do I dare   45
Disturb the universe?
In a minute there is time
For decisions and revisions which a minute will reverse.

For I have known them all already, known them all—
Have known the evenings, mornings, afternoons,   50
I have measured out my life with coffee spoons;
I know the voices dying with a dying fall
Beneath the music from a farther room.
    So how should I presume?

And I have known the eyes already, known them all—   55
The eyes that fix you in a formulated phrase,
And when I am formulated, sprawling on a pin,
When I am pinned and wriggling on the wall,
Then how should I begin
To spit out all the butt-ends of my days and ways?   60
    And how should I presume?

And I have known the arms already, known them all—
Arms that are braceleted and white and bare
(But in the lamplight, downed with light brown hair!)
Is it perfume from a dress   65

That makes me so digress?
Arms that lie along a table, or wrap about a shawl.
   And should I then presume?
   And how should I begin?

        *   *   *

Shall I say, I have gone at dusk through narrow streets   70
And watched the smoke that rises from the pipes
Of lonely men in shirt-sleeves, leaning out of windows? . . .

I should have been a pair of ragged claws
Scuttling across the floors of silent seas.

        *   *   *

And the afternoon, the evening, sleeps so peacefully!   75
Smoothed by long fingers,
Asleep . . . tired . . . or it malingers,
Stretched on the floor, here beside you and me.
Should I, after tea and cakes and ices,
Have the strength to force the moment to its crisis?   80
But though I have wept and fasted, wept and prayed,
Though I have seen my head (grown slightly bald)
   brought in upon a platter,
I am no prophet—and here's no great matter;
I have seen the moment of my greatness flicker,
And I have seen the eternal Footman hold my   85
   coat, and snicker,
And in short, I was afraid.

And would it have been worth it, after all,
After the cups, the marmalade, the tea,
Among the porcelain, among some talk of you and me,
Would it have been worth while,   90
To have bitten off the matter with a smile,
To have squeezed the universe into a ball
To roll it toward some overwhelming question,
To say: "I am Lazarus, come from the dead,
Come back to tell you all, I shall tell you all"—   95
If one, settling a pillow by her head,
   Should say: "That is not what I meant at all.
   That is not it, at all."

And would it have been worth it, after all,
Would it have been worth while,   100
After the sunsets and the dooryards and the sprinkled streets,
After the novels, after the teacups, after the skirts
    that trail along the floor—
And this, and so much more?—
It is impossible to say just what I mean!
But as if a magic lantern threw the nerves in   105
    patterns on a screen:
Would it have been worth while
If one, settling a pillow or throwing off a shawl,
And turning toward the window, should say:
    "That is not it at all,
    That is not what I meant, at all."   110

                *   *   *

No! I am not Prince Hamlet, nor was meant to be;
Am an attendant lord, one that will do
To swell a progress, start a scene or two,
Advise the prince; no doubt, an easy tool,
Deferential, glad to be of use,   115
Politic, cautious, and meticulous;
Full of high sentence, but a bit obtuse;
At times, indeed, almost ridiculous—
Almost, at times, the Fool.

I grow old . . . I grow old . . .   120
I shall wear the bottoms of my trousers rolled.°   cuffed

Shall I part my hair behind? Do I dare to eat a peach?
I shall wear white flannel trousers, and walk upon the beach.
I have heard the mermaids singing, each to each.

I do not think that they will sing to me.   125

I have seen them riding seaward on the waves
Combing the white hair of the waves blown back
When the wind blows the water white and black.

We have lingered in the chambers of the sea
By sea-girls wreathed with seaweed red and brown   130
Till human voices wake us, and we drown.

                                      T. S. Eliot (1888–1965)

QUESTIONS

1. Vocabulary: *insidious* (9), *Michelangelo* (14, 36), *muzzle* (16), *malingers* (77), *progress* (113), *Deferential* (115), *Politic* (116), *meticulous* (116), *sentence* (117).

2. This poem may be for some readers the most difficult in the book because it uses a "stream of consciousness" technique (that is, it presents the apparently random thoughts going through a person's head within a certain time interval), in which the transitional links are psychological rather than logical, and also because it uses allusions you may be unfamiliar with. Even if you do not at first understand the poem in detail, you should be able to get from it a quite accurate picture of Prufrock's character and personality. What kind of person is he (answer this as fully as possible)? From what class of society does he come? What one line especially well sums up the nature of his past life? A brief initial orientation may be helpful: Prufrock is apparently on his way, at the beginning of the poem, to a late afternoon tea, at which he wishes (or does he?) to make a declaration of love to some lady who will be present. The "you and I" of the first line are divided parts of Prufrock's own nature, for he is experiencing internal conflict. Does he or does he not make the declaration? Where does the climax of the poem come? If the portion leading up to the climax is devoted to Prufrock's effort to prepare himself psychologically to make the declaration (or to postpone such effort), what is the portion after the climax devoted to?

3. The poem contains a number of striking or unusual figures of speech. Most of them in some way reflect Prufrock's own nature or his desires or fears. From this point of view discuss lines 2–3; 15–22 and 75–78; 57–58; 73–74; and 124–131. What figure of speech is lines 73–74? In what respect is the title ironic?

4. The poem makes extensive use of literary allusion. The Italian epigraph is a passage from Dante's *Inferno* in which a man in Hell tells a visitor that he would never tell his story if there were a chance that it would get back to living ears. In line 29 the phrase "works and days" is the title of a long poem—a description of agricultural life and a call to toil—by the early Greek poet Hesiod. Line 52 echoes the opening speech of Shakespeare's *Twelfth Night*. The prophet of lines 81–83 is John the Baptist, whose head was delivered to Salome by Herod as a reward for her dancing (Matthew 14.1–11, and Oscar Wilde's play *Salome*). Line 92 echoes the closing six lines of Marvell's "To His Coy Mistress" (page 721). Lazarus (94–95) may be either the beggar Lazarus (of Luke 16) who was not permitted to return from the dead to warn a rich man's brothers about Hell, the Lazarus (of John 11) whom Christ raised from death, or both. Lines 111–119 allude to a number of characters from Shakespeare's *Hamlet:* Hamlet himself, the chamberlain Polonius, and various minor characters including probably Rosencrantz, Guildenstern, and Osric. "Full of high sentence" (117) echoes Chaucer's description of the Clerk of Oxford in the Prologue to *The Canterbury Tales*. Relate as many of these allusions as you can to the character of Prufrock. How is Prufrock particularly like Hamlet, and how is he unlike him? Contrast Prufrock with the speaker in "To His Coy Mistress."

Sunday Morning

1

Complacencies of the peignoir, and late
Coffee and oranges in a sunny chair,
And the green freedom of a cockatoo
Upon a rug mingle to dissipate
The holy hush of ancient sacrifice.   5
She dreams a little, and she feels the dark
Encroachment of that old catastrophe,
As a calm darkens among water-lights.
The pungent oranges and bright, green wings
Seem things in some procession of the dead,   10
Winding across wide water, without sound.
The day is like wide water, without sound,
Stilled for the passing of her dreaming feet
Over the seas, to silent Palestine,
Dominion of the blood and sepulchre.   15

2

Why should she give her bounty to the dead?
What is divinity if it can come
Only in silent shadows and in dreams?
Shall she not find in comforts of the sun,
In pungent fruit and bright, green wings, or else   20
In any balm or beauty of the earth,
Things to be cherished like the thought of heaven?
Divinity must live within herself:
Passions of rain, or moods in falling snow;
Grievings in loneliness, or unsubdued   25
Elations when the forest blooms; gusty
Emotions on wet roads on autumn nights;
All pleasures and all pains, remembering
The bough of summer and the winter branch.
These are the measures destined for her soul.   30

3

Jove in the clouds had his inhuman birth.
No mother suckled him, no sweet land gave

Large-mannered motions to his mythy mind.
He moved among us, as a muttering king,
Magnificent, would move among his hinds,   35
Until our blood, commingling, virginal,
With heaven, brought such requital to desire
The very hinds discerned it, in a star.
Shall our blood fail? Or shall it come to be
The blood of paradise? And shall the earth   40
Seem all of paradise that we shall know?
The sky will be much friendlier then than now,
A part of labor and a part of pain,
And next in glory to enduring love,
Not this dividing and indifferent blue.   45

4

She says, "I am content when wakened birds,
Before they fly, test the reality
Of misty fields, by their sweet questionings;
But when the birds are gone, and their warm fields
Return no more, where, then, is paradise?"   50
There is not any haunt of prophecy,
Nor any old chimera of the grave,
Neither the golden underground, nor isle
Melodious, where spirits gat them home,
Nor visionary south, nor cloudy palm   55
Remote on heaven's hill, that has endured
As April's green endures; or will endure
Like her remembrance of awakened birds,
Or her desire for June and evening, tipped
By the consummation of the swallow's wings.   60

5

She says, "But in contentment I still feel
The need of some imperishable bliss."
Death is the mother of beauty; hence from her,
Alone, shall come fulfillment to our dreams
And our desires. Although she strews the leaves   65
Of sure obliteration on our paths,
The path sick sorrow took, the many paths
Where triumph rang its brassy phrase, or love

Whispered a little out of tenderness,
She makes the willow shiver in the sun   70
For maidens who were wont to sit and gaze
Upon the grass, relinquished to their feet.
She causes boys to pile new plums and pears
On disregarded plate. The maidens taste
And stray impassioned in the littering leaves.   75

6

Is there no change of death in paradise?
Does ripe fruit never fall? Or do the boughs
Hang always heavy in that perfect sky,
Unchanging, yet so like our perishing earth,
With rivers like our own that seek for seas   80
They never find, the same receding shores
That never touch with inarticulate pang?
Why set the pear upon those river-banks
Or spice the shores with odors of the plum?
Alas, that they should wear our colors there,   85
The silken weavings of our afternoons,
And pick the strings of our insipid lutes!
Death is the mother of beauty, mystical,
Within whose burning bosom we devise
Our earthly mothers waiting, sleeplessly.   90

7

Supple and turbulent, a ring of men
Shall chant in orgy on a summer morn
Their boisterous devotion to the sun,
Not as a god, but as a god might be,
Naked among them, like a savage source.   95
Their chant shall be a chant of paradise,
Out of their blood, returning to the sky;
And in their chant shall enter, voice by voice,
The windy lake wherein their lord delights,
The trees, like serafin, and echoing hills,   100
That choir among themselves long afterward.
They shall know well the heavenly fellowship
Of men that perish and of summer morn.
And whence they came and whither they shall go
The dew upon their feet shall manifest.   105

8

She hears, upon that water without sound,
A voice that cries, "The tomb in Palestine
Is not the porch of spirits lingering.
It is the grave of Jesus, where he lay."
We live in an old chaos of the sun,   110
Or old dependency of day and night,
Or island solitude, unsponsored, free,
Of that wide water, inescapable.
Deer walk upon our mountains, and the quail
Whistle about us their spontaneous cries;   115
Sweet berries ripen in the wilderness;
And, in the isolation of the sky,
At evening, casual flocks of pigeons make
Ambiguous undulations as they sink,
Downward to darkness, on extended wings.   120

Wallace Stevens (1879–1955)

QUESTIONS

1. Vocabulary: *peignoir* (1), *hinds* (35, 38), *requital* (37), *chimera* (52), *consummation* (60), *obliteration* (66), *serafin* (seraphim) (100). "[G]at" (54) is an obsolete past tense of "get."

2. The poem presents a woman meditating on questions of death, mutability, and permanence, beginning with a stanza that sets the stage and shows her being drawn to these questions beyond her conscious will. The meditation proper is structured as a series of questions and answers stated in direct or indirect quotations, with the answer to a preceding question suggesting a further question, and so forth. In reading through the poem, paraphrase the sequence of implied or stated questions, and the answers to them.

3. The opening scene (stanza 1), in a collection of images and details, indicates the means the woman has chosen to avoid thinking of the typical "Sunday morning" topic, the Christian religion. Define the means she employs. Trace the further references to fruits and birds throughout the poem, and explain the ordering principle that ties them together (for example, what development of idea or attitude is implied in the sequence oranges/plums and pears/wild berries?).

4. What symbolic meanings are implied by the images of (a) water, (b) the sun, and (c) birds and other animals?

5. Why does the woman give up her desire for unchanging permanence? With what does she replace it? What is her final attitude toward a world that includes change and death? What is meant by "Death is the mother of beauty" (63, 88)?

6. The poet wrote, "This is not essentially a woman's meditation on religion and the meaning of life. It is anybody's meditation" (*Letters of Wallace Stevens*, ed. Holly Stevens [New York: Knopf, 1966], 250). Can you justify that claim?

The Weary Blues

Droning a drowsy syncopated tune,
Rocking back and forth to a mellow croon,
    I heard a Negro play.
Down on Lenox Avenue the other night
By the pale dull pallor of an old gas light   5
    He did a lazy sway. . . .
    He did a lazy sway. . . .
To the tune o' those Weary Blues.
With his ebony hands on each ivory key
He made that poor piano moan with melody.   10
    O Blues!
Swaying to and fro on his rickety stool
He played that sad raggy tune like a musical fool.
    Sweet Blues!
Coming from a black man's soul.   15
    O Blues!
In a deep song voice with a melancholy tone
I heard that Negro sing, that old piano moan—
    "Ain't got nobody in all this world,
    Ain't got nobody but ma self.   20
    I's gwine to quit ma frownin'
    And put ma troubles on the shelf."
Thump, thump, thump, went his foot on the floor.
He played a few chords then he sang some more—
    "I got the Weary Blues   25
    And I can't be satisfied.
    Got the Weary Blues
    And can't be satisfied—
    I ain't happy no mo'
    And I wish that I had died."   30
And far into the night he crooned that tune.
The stars went out and so did the moon.
The singer stopped playing and went to bed

While the Weary Blues echoed through his head.
He slept like a rock or a man that's dead.   35

Langston Hughes (1902–1967)

QUESTIONS

1. Vocabulary: *syncopated* (1), *raggy* (13).
2. What kind of music is the blues? Why is the form of "The Weary Blues" appropriate to a poem about this music?
3. The poem makes frequent use of repetition. What effect does this have on the reader?
4. Who is the speaker, and why does he respond so intensely to the piano player's "sad raggy tune" (13)?
5. The two quoted lyrics from the piano player's song (19–22 and 25–30) convey quite different messages and emotions. Describe these contrasting lyrics. What is the effect of this contrast on the reader's understanding of the song?
6. The piano player sings and plays "far into the night" (31). How is the music beneficial to him? Does the speaker derive a similar benefit?
7. Analyze the final line. How does the simile form an appropriate closure to the poem?

The Fish

I caught a tremendous fish
and held him beside the boat
half out of water, with my hook
fast in a corner of his mouth.
He didn't fight.   5
He hadn't fought at all.
He hung a grunting weight,
battered and venerable
and homely. Here and there
his brown skin hung in strips   10
like ancient wallpaper,
and its pattern of darker brown
was like wallpaper:
shapes like full-blown roses
stained and lost through age.   15
He was speckled with barnacles,
fine rosettes of lime,
and infested

with tiny white sea-lice,
and underneath two or three   20
rags of green weed hung down.
While his gills were breathing in
the terrible oxygen
—the frightening gills,
fresh and crisp with blood,   25
that can cut so badly—
I thought of the coarse white flesh
packed in like feathers,
the big bones and the little bones,
the dramatic reds and blacks   30
of his shiny entrails,
and the pink swim-bladder
like a big peony.
I looked into his eyes
which were far larger than mine   35
but shallower, and yellowed,
the irises backed and packed
with tarnished tinfoil
seen through the lenses
of old scratched isinglass.   40
They shifted a little, but not
to return my stare.
—It was more like the tipping
of an object toward the light.
I admired his sullen face,   45
the mechanism of his jaw,
and then I saw
that from his lower lip
—if you could call it a lip—
grim, wet, and weaponlike,   50
hung five old pieces of fish-line,
or four and a wire leader
with the swivel still attached,
with all their five big hooks
grown firmly in his mouth.   55
A green line, frayed at the end
where he broke it, two heavier lines,
and a fine black thread
still crimped from the strain and snap
when it broke and he got away.   60

Like medals with their ribbons
frayed and wavering,
a five-haired beard of wisdom
trailing from his aching jaw.
I stared and stared   65
and victory filled up
the little rented boat,
from the pool of bilge
where oil had spread a rainbow
around the rusted engine   70
to the bailer rusted orange,
the sun-cracked thwarts,
the oarlocks on their strings,
the gunnels—until everything
was rainbow, rainbow, rainbow!   75
And I let the fish go.

Elizabeth Bishop (1911–1979)

QUESTIONS

1. Explore the multiple denotations of "tremendous" (1) and the connotations attached to them. How does the richness of that word prepare you for the complexity of the poem?
2. In what ways are many of the images paradoxical in their emotional evocations? Where does the poem create imagery out of the speaker's imagination rather than her present observation?
3. Much of the imagery is elucidated by figurative comparisons or is itself figurative. Find examples of both uses of figures, and trace what they convey in the way of ideas and/or emotions.
4. Whose "victory" fills the boat (66–67)? What is the nature of that victory? Might the term apply to more than one kind of victory?
5. What literally is the "rainbow" (69)? To what is it transformed in lines 74–75? What accounts for the transformation?
6. Explain how the tone of the poem shifts and develops. What is happening to the speaker as she observes and comments upon the physical aspects of the fish?
7. Why does the speaker "let the fish go" (76)? Is the fish symbolic?

Diving into the Wreck

First having read the book of myths,
and loaded the camera,
and checked the edge of the knife-blade,

I put on
the body-armor of black rubber   5
the absurd flippers
the grave and awkward mask.
I am having to do this
not like Cousteau* with his
assiduous team   10
aboard the sun-flooded schooner
but here alone.

There is a ladder.
The ladder is always there
hanging innocently   15
close to the side of the schooner.
We know what it is for,
we who have used it.
Otherwise
it's a piece of maritime floss   20
some sundry equipment.
I go down.
Rung after rung and still
the oxygen immerses me
the blue light   25
the clear atoms
of our human air.
I go down.
My flippers cripple me,
I crawl like an insect down the ladder   30
and there is no one
to tell me when the ocean
will begin.

First the air is blue and then
it is bluer and then green and then   35
black I am blacking out and yet
my mask is powerful
it pumps my blood with power
the sea is another story
the sea is not a question of power   40

---

*Jacques Cousteau (9) (1910–1997) was a French marine scientist who led underwater exploring expeditions.

I have to learn alone
to turn my body without force
in the deep element.

And now: it is easy to forget
what I came for   45
among so many who have always
lived here
swaying their crenellated fans
between the reefs
and besides   50
you breathe differently down here.

I came to explore the wreck.
The words are purposes.
The words are maps.
I came to see the damage that was done   55
and the treasures that prevail.
I stroke the beam of my lamp
slowly along the flank
of something more permanent
than fish or weed   60

the thing I came for:
the wreck and not the story of the wreck
the thing itself and not the myth
the drowned face always staring
toward the sun   65
the evidence of damage
worn by salt and sway into this threadbare beauty
the ribs of the disaster
curving their assertion
among the tentative haunters.   70

This is the place.
And I am here, the mermaid whose dark hair
streams black, the merman in his armored body
We circle silently
about the wreck   75
we dive into the hold.
I am she: I am he

whose drowned face sleeps with open eyes
whose breasts still bear the stress
whose silver, copper, vermeil cargo lies   80
obscurely inside barrels
half-wedged and left to rot
we are the half-destroyed instruments
that once held to a course
the water-eaten log   85
the fouled compass

We are, I am, you are
by cowardice or courage
the one who find our way
back to this scene   90
carrying a knife, a camera
a book of myths
in which
our names do not appear.

Adrienne Rich (b. 1929)

Poems for
Further Reading

Musée des Beaux Arts

About suffering they were never wrong,
The Old Masters: how well they understood
Its human position; how it takes place
While someone else is eating or opening a window or just
    walking dully along;
How, when the aged are reverently, passionately waiting   5
For the miraculous birth, there always must be
Children who did not specially want it to happen, skating
On a pond at the edge of the wood:
They never forgot
That even the dreadful martyrdom must run its course   10
Anyhow in a corner, some untidy spot
Where the dogs go on with their doggy life and the
    torturer's horse
Scratches its innocent behind on a tree.

In Brueghel's *Icarus*, for instance: how everything turns away
Quite leisurely from the disaster; the plowman may   15
Have heard the splash, the forsaken cry,
But for him it was not an important failure; the sun shone
As it had to on the white legs disappearing into the green
Water; and the expensive delicate ship that must have seen
Something amazing, a boy falling out of the sky,   20
Had somewhere to get to and sailed calmly on.

W. H. Auden (1907–1973)

Main Character

I went to see
How the West Was Won
at the Sunshine Theater.
Five years old,
deep in a plush seat,   5
light turned off,
bright screen lit up
with MGM roaring lion—
        in front of me
        a drunk Indian rose,   10
        cursed

the western violins
and hurled his uncapped bagged bottle
of wine
at the rocket roaring to the moon.   15
His dark angry body
convulsed with his obscene gestures
at the screen,
and then ushers escorted him
up the aisle,   20
and as he staggered past me,
I heard his grieving sobs.
       Red wine streaked
       blue sky and take-off smoke,
       sizzled cowboys' campfires,   25
       dripped down barbwire,
       slogged the brave, daring scouts
       who galloped off to mesa buttes
       to speak peace with Apaches,
       and made the prairie   30
       lush with wine streams.
When the movie
was over,
I squinted at the bright
sunny street outside,   35
looking for the main character.

Jimmy Santiago Baca (b. 1952)

On Her Loving Two Equally

I

How strong does my passion flow,
Divided equally twixt two?
Damon had ne'er subdued my heart
Had not Alexis took his part;
Nor could Alexis powerful prove,   5
Without my Damon's aid, to gain my love.

II

When my Alexis present is,
Then I for Damon sigh and mourn;
But when Alexis I do miss,

Damon gains nothing but my scorn.   10
But if it chance they both are by,
For both alike I languish, sigh, and die.

III

Cure then, thou mighty wingéd god,
This restless fever in my blood;
One golden-pointed dart take back: 15
But which, O Cupid, wilt thou take?
If Damon's, all my hopes are crossed;
Or that of my Alexis, I am lost.

Aphra Behn (1640–1689)

On Reading Poems to a Senior Class at South High

Before
I opened my mouth
I noticed them sitting there
as orderly as frozen fish
in a package.   5

Slowly water began to fill the room
though I did not notice it
till it reached
my ears

and then I heard the sounds   10
of fish in an aquarium
and I knew that though I had
tried to drown them
with my words
that they had only opened up   15
like gills for them
and let me in.

Together we swam around the room
like thirty tails whacking words
till the bell rang   20
puncturing
a hole in the door

where we all leaked out

They went to another class
I suppose and I home   25

where Queen Elizabeth
my cat met me
and licked my fins
till they were hands again.

D. C. Berry (b. 1942)

Manners

for a Child of 1918

My grandfather said to me
as we sat on the wagon seat,
"Be sure to remember to always
speak to everyone you meet."

We met a stranger on foot.   5
My grandfather's whip tapped his hat.
"Good day, sir. Good day. A fine day."
And I said it and bowed where I sat.

Then we overtook a boy we knew
with his big pet crow on his shoulder.   10
"Always offer everyone a ride;
don't forget that when you get older,"

my grandfather said. So Willy
climbed up with us, but the crow
gave a "Caw!" and flew off. I was worried.   15
How would he know where to go?

But he flew a little way at a time
from fence post to fence post, ahead;
and when Willy whistled he answered.
"A fine bird," my grandfather said,   20

"and he's well brought up. See, he answers
nicely when he's spoken to.

Man or beast, that's good manners.
Be sure that you both always do."

When automobiles went by,   25
the dust hid the people's faces,
but we shouted "Good day! Good day!
Fine day!" at the top of our voices.

When we came to Hustler Hill,
he said that the mare was tired,   30
so we all got down and walked,
as our good manners required.

Elizabeth Bishop (1911–1979)

Sadie and Maud

Maud went to college.
Sadie stayed at home.
Sadie scraped life
With a fine-tooth comb.

She didn't leave a tangle in.   5
Her comb found every strand.
Sadie was one of the livingest chits
In all the land.

Sadie bore two babies
Under her maiden name.   10
Maud and Ma and Papa
Nearly died of shame.

When Sadie said her last so-long
Her girls struck out from home.
(Sadie had left as heritage   15
Her fine-tooth comb.)

Maud, who went to college,
Is a thin brown mouse.
She is living all alone
In this old house.   20

Gwendolyn Brooks (1917–2000)

a song in the front yard

I've stayed in the front yard all my life.
I want a peek at the back
Where it's rough and untended and hungry weed grows.
A girl gets sick of a rose.

I want to go in the back yard now   5
And maybe down the alley,
To where the charity children play.
I want a good time today.

They do some wonderful things.
They have some wonderful fun.   10
My mother sneers, but I say it's fine
How they don't have to go in at quarter to nine.
My mother, she tells me that Johnnie Mae
Will grow up to be a bad woman.
That George'll be taken to Jail soon or late   15
(On account of last winter he sold our back gate).

But I say it's fine. Honest, I do.
And I'd like to be a bad woman, too,
And wear the brave stockings of night-black lace
And strut down the streets with paint on my face.   20

Gwendolyn Brooks (1917–2000)

Tornado at Talladega

Who is that bird
reporting the storm? —
after What came through
to do some landscaping.

Certain trees   5
stick across the road.
They are unimportant now.
They cannot sass anymore.
Not a one of these, the bewildered,
can announce anymore "How fine I am!"   10

Here, roots, ire, origins exposed,
across this twig-strewn, leaf-strewn road they lie,
mute, and ashamed, and through.

It happened all of a sudden.

Certain women and men and children   15
come out to stare.

Gwendolyn Brooks (1917–2000)

Combing

Bending, I bow my head
And lay my hand upon
Her hair, combing, and think
How women do this for
Each other. My daughter's hair   5
Curls against the comb,
Wet and fragrant—orange
Parings. Her face, downcast,
Is quiet for one so young.

I take her place. Beneath   10
My mother's hands I feel
The braids drawn up tight
As a piano wire and singing,
Vinegar-rinsed. Sitting
Before the oven I hear   15
The orange coils tick
The early hour before school.

She combed her grandmother
Mathilda's hair using
A comb made out of bone.   20
Mathilda rocked her oak wood
Chair, her face downcast,
Intent on tearing rags
In strips to braid a cotton
Rug from bits of orange   25
and brown. A simple act,

Preparing hair. Something
Women do for each other,
Plaiting the generations.

Gladys Cardiff (b. 1942)

To the Ladies

Wife and servant are the same,
But only differ in the name:
For when that fatal knot is tied,
Which nothing, nothing can divide,
When she the word *Obey* has said,   5
And man by law supreme has made,
Then all that's kind is laid aside,
And nothing left but state and pride.
Fierce as an eastern prince he grows,
And all his innate rigor shows: 10
Then but to look, to laugh, or speak,
Will the nuptial contract break.
Like mutes, she signs alone must make,
And never any freedom take,
But still be governed by a nod,   15
And fear her husband as her god:
Him still must serve, him still obey,
And nothing act, and nothing say,
But what her haughty lord thinks fit,
Who, with the power, has all the wit.   20
Then shun, oh! shun that wretched state,
And all the fawning flatterers hate.
Value yourselves, and men despise:
You must be proud, if you'll be wise.

Mary, Lady Chudleigh (1656–1710)

good times

My Daddy has paid the rent
and the insurance man is gone
and the lights is back on
and my uncle Brud has hit
for one dollar straight   5

and they is good times
good times
good times

My Mama has made bread
and Grampaw has come   10
and everybody is drunk
and dancing in the kitchen
and singing in the kitchen
oh these is good times
good times   15
good times

oh children think about the
good times

Lucille Clifton (b. 1936)

Kubla Khan

In Xanadu did Kubla Khan
A stately pleasure-dome decree:
Where Alph, the sacred river, ran
Through caverns measureless to man
   Down to a sunless sea.   5
So twice five miles of fertile ground
With walls and towers were girdled round:
And here were gardens bright with sinuous rills,
Where blossomed many an incense-bearing tree;
And here were forests ancient as the hills,   10
Enfolding sunny spots of greenery.

But oh! that deep romantic chasm which slanted
Down the green hill athwart a cedarn cover!
A savage place! as holy and enchanted
As e'er beneath a waning moon was haunted   15
By woman wailing for her demon-lover!
And from this chasm, with ceaseless turmoil seething,
As if this earth in fast thick pants were breathing,
A mighty fountain momently was forced:
Amid whose swift half-intermitted burst   20
Huge fragments vaulted like rebounding hail,
Or chaffy grain beneath the thresher's flail:

And 'mid these dancing rocks at once and ever
It flung up momently the sacred river.
Five miles meandering with a mazy motion   25
Through wood and dale the sacred river ran,
Then reached the caverns measureless to man,
And sank in tumult to a lifeless ocean:
And 'mid this tumult Kubla heard from far
Ancestral voices prophesying war!   30

    The shadow of the dome of pleasure
    Floated midway on the waves;
    Where was heard the mingled measure
    From the fountain and the caves.
It was a miracle of rare device,   35
A sunny pleasure-dome with caves of ice!

    A damsel with a dulcimer
    In a vision once I saw:
    It was an Abyssinian maid,
    And on her dulcimer she played,   40
    Singing of Mount Abora.
    Could I revive within me
    Her symphony and song,
    To such a deep delight, 'twould win me,
That with music loud and long,   45
I would build that dome in air,
That sunny dome! those caves of ice!
And all who heard should see them there,
And all should cry, Beware! Beware!
His flashing eyes, his floating hair!   50
Weave a circle round him thrice,
And close your eyes with holy dread,
For he on honey-dew hath fed,
And drunk the milk of Paradise.

Samuel Taylor Coleridge (1772–1834)

Voyages [1]

    Above the fresh ruffles of the surf
    Bright striped urchins flay each other with sand.
    They have contrived a conquest for shell shucks,

And their fingers crumble fragments of baked weed
Gaily digging and scattering.   5

And in answer to their treble interjections
The sun beats lightning on the waves,
The waves fold thunder on the sand;
And could they hear me I would tell them:

O brilliant kids, frisk with your dog,   10
Fondle your shells and sticks, bleached
By time and the elements; but there is a line
You must not cross nor ever trust beyond it
Spry cordage of your bodies to caresses
Too lichen-faithful from too wide a breast.   15
The bottom of the sea is cruel.

Hart Crane (1899–1932)

War Is Kind

Do not weep, maiden, for war is kind.
Because your lover threw wild hands toward the sky
And the affrighted steed ran on alone,
Do not weep.
War is kind.   5

    Hoarse, booming drums of the regiment,
    Little souls who thirst for fight,
    These men were born to drill and die.
    The unexplained glory flies above them,
    Great is the battle god, great, and his kingdom   10
    A field where a thousand corpses lie.

Do not weep, babe, for war is kind.
Because your father tumbled in the yellow trenches,
Raged at his breast, gulped and died,
Do not weep.   15
War is kind.

    Swift blazing flag of the regiment,
    Eagle with crest of red and gold,
    These men were born to drill and die.

Point for them the virtue of slaughter,   20
Make plain for them the excellence of killing
And a field where a thousand corpses lie.

Mother whose heart hung humble as a button
On the bright splendid shroud of your son,
Do not weep.   25
War is kind.

Stephen Crane (1871–1900)

the Cambridge ladies who live in furnished souls

the Cambridge ladies who live in furnished souls
are unbeautiful and have comfortable minds
(also, with the church's protestant blessings
daughters, unscented shapeless spirited)
they believe in Christ and Longfellow, both dead,   5
are invariably interested in so many things—
at the present writing one still finds
delighted fingers knitting for the is it Poles?
perhaps. While permanent faces coyly bandy
scandal of Mrs. N and Professor D   10
. . . . the Cambridge ladies do not care, above
Cambridge if sometimes in its box of
sky lavender and cornerless, the
moon rattles like a fragment of angry candy

e. e. cummings (1894–1962)

Spring is like a perhaps hand

Spring is like a perhaps hand
(which comes carefully
out of Nowhere) arranging
a window, into which people look (while
people stare   5
arranging and changing placing
carefully there a strange
thing and a known thing here) and

changing everything carefully

spring is like a perhaps   10
Hand in a window
(carefully to
and fro moving New and
Old things, while
people stare carefully   15
moving a perhaps
fraction of flower here placing
an inch of air there) and

without breaking anything.

                              e. e. cummings (1894–1962)

A Light exists in Spring

A Light exists in Spring
Not present on the Year
At any other period—
When March is scarcely here

A Color stands abroad   5
On Solitary Fields
That Science cannot overtake
But Human Nature feels.

It waits upon the Lawn,
It shows the furthest Tree   10
Upon the furthest Slope you know
It almost speaks to you.

Then as Horizons step
Or Noons report away,
Without the Formula of sound   15
It passes and we stay—

A quality of loss
Affecting our Content
As Trade had suddenly encroached
Upon a Sacrament.   20

                              Emily Dickinson (1830–1886)

A narrow Fellow in the Grass

A narrow Fellow in the Grass
Occasionally rides—
You may have met him? Did you not
His notice sudden is—

The Grass divides as with a Comb—   5
A spotted shaft is seen—
And then it closes at your feet
And opens further on—

He likes a Boggy Acre
A Floor too cool for Corn—   10
Yet when a Boy, and Barefoot—
I more than once at Noon

Have passed, I thought, a Whip lash—
Unbraiding in the Sun
When stooping to secure it   15
It wrinkled, and was gone—

Several of Nature's People
I know, and they know me—
I feel for them a transport
Of cordiality—   20

But never met this Fellow
Attended, or alone
Without a tighter breathing
And Zero at the Bone.

Emily Dickinson (1830–1886)

I died for Beauty—but was scarce

I died for Beauty—but was scarce
Adjusted in the Tomb
When One who died for Truth, was lain
In an adjoining Room—

He questioned softly "Why I failed"?   5
"For Beauty", I replied—

"And I—for Truth—Themself are One—
We Brethren, are", He said—

And so, as Kinsmen, met a Night—   10
We talked between the Rooms—
Until the Moss had reached our lips—
And covered up—our names—

Emily Dickinson (1830–1886)

I like a look of Agony

I like a look of Agony,
Because I know it's true—
Men do not sham Convulsion,
Nor simulate, a Throe—

The Eyes glaze once—and that is Death—   5
Impossible to feign
The Beads upon the Forehead
By homely Anguish strung.

Emily Dickinson (1830–1886)

The Good-Morrow

I wonder, by my troth, what thou and I
Did till we loved? were we not weaned till then,
But sucked on country pleasures childishly?
Or snorted we in the seven sleepers' den?
'Twas so; but this, all pleasures fancies be.   5
If ever any beauty I did see,
Which I desired, and got, 'twas but a dream of thee.

And now good-morrow to our waking souls,
Which watch not one another out of fear;
For love all love of other sights controls,   10
And makes one little room an everywhere.
Let sea-discoverers to new worlds have gone;
Let maps to other,° worlds on worlds have shown;   others
Let us possess one world; each hath one, and is one.

My face in thine eye, thine in mine appears,   15
And true plain hearts do in the faces rest;
Where can we find two better hemispheres
Without sharp north, without declining west?
Whatever dies was not mixed equally;
If our two loves be one, or thou and I   20
Love so alike that none can slacken, none can die.

John Donne (1572–1631)

(4) *seven sleepers' den*: a cave where, according to Christian legend, seven youths escaped persecution and slept for two centuries.

Song: Go and catch a falling star

Go and catch a falling star,
   Get with child a mandrake root,
Tell me where all past years are,
   Or who cleft the devil's foot,
Teach me to hear mermaids singing,   5
   Or to keep off envy's stinging,
      And find
      What wind
Serves to advance an honest mind.

If thou be'st born to strange sights,   10
   Things invisible to see,
Ride ten thousand days and nights,
   Till age snow white hairs on thee;
Thou, when thou return'st, wilt tell me
   All strange wonders that befell thee,   15
      And swear
      No where
Lives a woman true and fair.

If thou find'st one, let me know;
   Such a pilgrimage were sweet.   20
Yet do not; I would not go,
   Though at next door we might meet.
Though she were true when you met her,
   And last till you write your letter,

Yet she   25
  Will be
False, ere I come, to two or three.

John Donne (1572–1631)

(2) *mandrake*: supposed to resemble a human being because of its forked root.

Nexus

I wrote stubbornly into the evening.
At the window, a giant praying mantis
rubbed his monkey wrench head against the glass,
begging vacantly with pale eyes;

and the commas leapt at me like worms   5
or miniature scythes blackened with age.
The praying mantis screeched louder,
his ragged jaws opening onto formlessness.

I walked outside;
the grass hissed at my heels.   10
Up ahead in the lapping darkness
he wobbled, magnified and absurdly green,
a brontosaurus, a poet.

Rita Dove (b. 1952)

Persephone, Falling

One narcissus among the ordinary beautiful
flowers, one unlike all the others! She pulled,
stooped to pull harder—
when, sprung out of the earth
on his glittering terrible   5
carriage, he claimed his due.
It is finished. No one heard her.
No one! She had strayed from the herd.

(Remember: go straight to school.
This is important, stop fooling around!   10
Don't answer to strangers. Stick

with your playmates. Keep your eyes down.)
This is how easily the pit
is waiting. This is how one foot sinks into the ground.

Rita Dove (b. 1952)

Sympathy

I know what the caged bird feels, alas!
  When the sun is bright on the upland slopes;
When the wind stirs soft through the springing grass,
And the river flows like a stream of glass;
  When the first bird sings and the first bud opes,   5
And the faint perfume from its chalice steals—
I know what the caged bird feels!

I know why the caged bird beats his wing
  Till its blood is red on the cruel bars;
For he must fly back to his perch and cling   10
When he fain would be on the bough a-swing;
  And a pain still throbs in the old, old scars
And they pulse again with a keener sting—
I know why he beats his wing!

I know why the caged bird sings, ah me,   15
  When his wing is bruised and his bosom sore;—
When he beats his bars and he would be free;
It is not a carol of joy or glee,
  But a prayer that he sends from his heart's deep core,
But a plea, that upward to Heaven he flings—   20
I know why the caged bird sings!

Paul Laurence Dunbar (1872–1906)

Christ climbed down

Christ climbed down
from His bare Tree
this year
and ran away to where
there were no rootless Christmas trees   5
hung with candycanes and breakable stars

Christ climbed down
from His bare Tree
this year
and ran away to where   10
there were no gilded Christmas trees
and no tinsel Christmas trees
and no tinfoil Christmas trees
and no pink plastic Christmas trees
and no gold Christmas trees   15
and no black Christmas trees
and no powderblue Christmas trees
hung with electric candles
and encircled by tin electric trains
and clever cornball relatives   20

Christ climbed down
from His bare Tree
this year
and ran away to where
no intrepid Bible salesman   25
covered the territory
in two-tone cadillacs
and where no Sears Roebuck creches
complete with plastic babe in manger
arrived by parcel post   30
the babe by special delivery
and where no televised Wise Men
praised the Lord Calvert Whiskey

Christ climbed down
from His bare Tree   35
this year
and ran away to where
no fat handshaking stranger
in a red flannel suit
and a fake beard   40
went around passing himself off
as some sort of North Pole saint
crossing the desert to Bethlehem
Pennsylvania
in a Volkswagen sled   45
drawn by rollicking Adirondack reindeer

with German names
and bearing sacks of Humble Gifts
from Saks Fifth Avenue
for everybody's imagined Christ child   50

Christ climbed down
from His bare Tree
this year
and ran away to where
no Bing Crosby carollers   55
groaned of a tight Christmas
and where no Radio City angels
iceskated wingless
thru a winter wonderland
into a jinglebell heaven   60
daily at 8:30
with Midnight Mass matinees

Christ climbed down
from His bare Tree
this year   65
and softly stole away into
some anonymous Mary's womb again
where in the darkest night
of everybody's anonymous soul
He awaits again   70
an unimaginable
and impossibly
Immaculate Reconception
the very craziest
of Second Comings   75

Lawrence Ferlinghetti (b. 1919)

The Colonel

What you have heard is true. I was in his house. His wife carried a tray of
coffee and sugar. His daughter filed her nails, his son went out for the
night. There were daily papers, pet dogs, a pistol on the cushion beside
him. The moon swung bare on its black cord over the house. On the
television was a cop show. It was in English. Broken bottles were
embedded in the walls around the house to scoop the kneecaps from a

man's legs or cut his hands to lace. On the windows there were gratings like those in liquor stores. We had dinner, rack of lamb, good wine, a gold bell was on the table for calling the maid. The maid brought green mangoes, salt, a type of bread. I was asked how I enjoyed the country. There was a brief commercial in Spanish. His wife took everything away. There was some talk then of how difficult it had become to govern. The parrot said hello on the terrace. The colonel told it to shut up, and pushed himself from the table. My friend said to me with his eyes: say nothing. The colonel returned with a sack used to bring groceries home. He spilled many human ears on the table. They were like dried peach halves. There is no other way to say this. He took one of them in his hands, shook it in our faces, dropped it into a water glass. It came alive there. I am tired of fooling around he said. As for the rights of anyone, tell your people they can go fuck themselves. He swept the ears to the floor with his arm and held the last of his wine in the air. Something for your poetry, no? he said. Some of the ears on the floor caught this scrap of his voice. Some of the ears on the floor were pressed to the ground.
May 1978

Carolyn Forché (b. 1950)

Birches

When I see birches bend to left and right
Across the lines of straighter darker trees,
I like to think some boy's been swinging them.
But swinging doesn't bend them down to stay
As ice-storms do. Often you must have seen them   5
Loaded with ice a sunny winter morning
After a rain. They click upon themselves
As the breeze rises, and turn many-colored
As the stir cracks and crazes their enamel.
Soon the sun's warmth makes them shed crystal shells   10
Shattering and avalanching on the snow-crust—
Such heaps of broken glass to sweep away
You'd think the inner dome of heaven had fallen.
They are dragged to the withered bracken by the load,
And they seem not to break; though once they are bowed   15
So low for long, they never right themselves:
You may see their trunks arching in the woods
Years afterwards, trailing their leaves on the ground
Like girls on hands and knees that throw their hair

Before them over their heads to dry in the sun.   20
But I was going to say when Truth broke in
With all her matter-of-fact about the ice-storm
I should prefer to have some boy bend them
As he went out and in to fetch the cows—
Some boy too far from town to learn baseball,   25
Whose only play was what he found himself,
Summer or winter, and could play alone.
One by one he subdued his father's trees
By riding them down over and over again
Until he took the stiffness out of them,   30
And not one but hung limp, not one was left
For him to conquer. He learned all there was
To learn about not launching out too soon
And so not carrying the tree away
Clear to the ground. He always kept his poise   35
To the top branches, climbing carefully
With the same pains you use to fill a cup
Up to the brim, and even above the brim.
Then he flung outward, feet first, with a swish,
Kicking his way down through the air to the ground.   40
So was I once myself a swinger of birches.
And so I dream of going back to be.
It's when I'm weary of considerations,
And life is too much like a pathless wood
Where your face burns and tickles with the cobwebs   45
Broken across it, and one eye is weeping
From a twig's having lashed across it open.
I'd like to get away from earth awhile
And then come back to it and begin over.
May no fate willfully misunderstand me   50
And half grant what I wish and snatch me away
Not to return. Earth's the right place for love:
I don't know where it's likely to go better.
I'd like to go by climbing a birch tree,
And climb black branches up a snow-white trunk   55
Toward heaven, till the tree could bear no more,
But dipped its top and set me down again.
That would be good both going and coming back.
One could do worse than be a swinger of birches.

Robert Frost (1874–1963)

Mending Wall

Something there is that doesn't love a wall,
That sends the frozen-ground-swell under it,
And spills the upper boulders in the sun;
And makes gaps even two can pass abreast.
The work of hunters is another thing: 5
I have come after them and made repair
Where they have left not one stone on a stone,
But they would have the rabbit out of hiding,
To please the yelping dogs. The gaps I mean,
No one has seen them made or heard them made,   10
But at spring mending-time we find them there.
I let my neighbor know beyond the hill;
And on a day we meet to walk the line
And set the wall between us once again.
We keep the wall between us as we go.   15
To each the boulders that have fallen to each.
And some are loaves and some so nearly balls
We have to use a spell to make them balance:
"Stay where you are until our backs are turned!"
We wear our fingers rough with handling them.   20
Oh, just another kind of outdoor game,
One on a side. It comes to little more:
There where it is we do not need the wall:
He is all pine and I am apple orchard.
My apple trees will never get across   25
And eat the cones under his pines, I tell him.
He only says, "Good fences make good neighbors."
Spring is the mischief in me, and I wonder
If I could put a notion in his head:
"Why do they make good neighbors? Isn't it   30
Where there are cows? But here there are no cows.
Before I built a wall I'd ask to know
What I was walling in or walling out,
And to whom I was like to give offense.
Something there is that doesn't love a wall,   35
That wants it down." I could say "Elves" to him,
But it's not elves exactly, and I'd rather
He said it for himself. I see him there,
Bringing a stone grasped firmly by the top
In each hand, like an old-stone savage armed.   40

He moves in darkness as it seems to me,
Not of woods only and the shade of trees.
He will not go behind his father's saying,
And he likes having thought of it so well
He says again, "Good fences make good neighbors."   45

Robert Frost (1874–1963)

Once by the Pacific

The shattered water made a misty din.
Great waves looked over others coming in,
And thought of doing something to the shore
That water never did to land before.
The clouds were low and hairy in the skies,   5
Like locks blown forward in the gleam of eyes.
You could not tell, and yet it looked as if
The shore was lucky in being backed by cliff,
The cliff in being backed by continent;
It looked as if a night of dark intent   10
Was coming and not only a night, an age.
Someone had better be prepared for rage.
There would be more than ocean-water broken
Before God's last *Put out the Light* was spoken.

Robert Frost (1874–1963)

A Supermarket in California

What thoughts I have of you tonight, Walt Whitman, for I walked down the sidestreets under the trees with a headache self-concious looking at the full moon.

In my hungry fatigue, and shopping for images, I went into the neon fruit supermarket, dreaming of your enumerations!   5

What peaches and what penumbras? Whole families shopping at night! Aisles full of husbands! Wives in the avocados, babies in the tomatoes!—and you, García Lorca, what were you doing down by the watermelons?

I saw you, Walt Whitman, childless, lonely old grubber, poking 10 among the meats in the refrigerator and eyeing the grocery boys.

I heard you asking questions of each: Who killed the pork chops? What price bananas? Are you my Angel?

I wandered in and out of the brilliant stacks of cans following
you, and followed in my imagination by the store detective.   15
    We strode down the open corridors together in our solitary fancy
tasting artichokes, possessing every frozen delicacy, and never passing
the cashier.

    Where are we going, Walt Whitman? The doors close in an hour.
Which way does your beard point tonight?   20
    (I touch your book and dream of our odyssey in the supermarket
and feel absurd.)
    Will we walk all night through solitary streets? The trees add
shade to shade, lights out in the houses, we'll both be lonely.
    Will we stroll dreaming of the lost America of love past blue   25
automobiles in driveways, home to our silent cottage?
    Ah, dear father, graybeard, lonely old courage-teacher, what Ameri-
ca did you have when Charon quit poling his ferry and you got out
on a smoking bank and stood watching the boat disappear on the
black waters of Lethe?   30

Allen Ginsberg (1926–1997)

From the Wave

It mounts at sea, a concave wall
   Down-ribbed with shine,
And pushes forward, building tall
   Its steep incline.

Then from their hiding rise to sight   5
   Black shapes on boards
Bearing before the fringe of white
   It mottles towards.

Their pale feet curl, they poise their weight
   With a learn'd skill.   10
It is the wave they imitate
   Keeps them so still.

The marbling bodies have become
   Half wave, half men,
Grafted it seems by feet of foam   15
   Some seconds, then,

Late as they can, they slice the face
    In timed procession:
Balance is triumph in this place,
    Triumph possession.   20

The mindless heave of which they rode
    A fluid shelf
Breaks as they leave it, falls and, slowed,
    Loses itself.

Clear, the sheathed bodies slick as seals   25
    Loosen and tingle;
And by the board the bare foot feels
    The suck of shingle.

They paddle in the shallows still;
    Two splash each other;   30
Then all swim out to wait until
    The right waves gather.

Thom Gunn (1929–2004)

Snow White and the Seven Deadly Sins

Good Catholic girl, she didn't mind the cleaning.
All of her household chores, at first, were small
And hardly labors one could find demeaning.
One's duty was one's refuge, after all.

And if she had her doubts at certain moments   5
And once confessed them to the Father, she
Was instantly referred to texts in Romans
And Peter's First Epistle, chapter III.

Years passed. More sinful every day, the *Seven*
Breakfasted, grabbed their pitchforks, donned their horns,   10
And sped to contravene the hopes of heaven,
Sowing the neighbors' lawns with tares and thorns.

She set to work. *Pride*'s wall of looking glasses
Ogled her dimly, smeared with prints of lips;

Lust's magazines lay strewn, bare tits and asses   15
Weighted by his "devices"—chains, cuffs, whips.

Gluttony's empties covered half the table,
Mingling with *Avarice's* cards and chips,
And she'd been told to sew a Bill Blass label
Inside the blazer *Envy'd* bought at Gyp's.   20

She knelt to the cold master bathroom floor as
If a petitioner before the Pope,
Retrieving several pairs of *Sloth's* soiled drawers,
A sweat-sock and a cake of hairy soap.

Then, as she wiped the Windex from the mirror   25
She noticed, and the vision made her cry,
How much she'd grayed and paled, and how much clearer
Festered the bruise of *Wrath* beneath her eye.

"No poisoned apple needed for this Princess,"
She murmured, making **X**'s with her thumb.   30
A car door slammed, bringing her to her senses:
Ho-hum. Ho-hum. It's home from work we come.

And she was out the window in a second,
In time to see a *Handsome Prince,* of course,
Who, spying her distressed condition, beckoned   35
For her to mount (What else?) his snow-white horse.

Impeccably he spoke. His smile was glowing.
So debonair! So charming! And so *Male.*
She took a step, reversed and without slowing
Beat it to St. Anne's where she took the veil.   40

R. S. Gwynn (b. 1948)

On the Death of a Child

Where is the woman to tell me
How my face is lit up by his body?

—JAMES DICKEY

It wasn't a harsh rain—
Just steady with the lights

Pinched out along the street
One after the other—

In which he put these things out   5
For the men of morning

To collect before daybreak.
The bike with the bent fender

He rolled through the breezeway,
The chain catching on itself   10

Near the kitchen table,
The box of clothes from a spring

Hike in some local mountains,
Perhaps a few other things—

Toys outgrown, scratch paper,   15
Letters posted from camp—

He wanted nothing left
To contain the empty house,

To clutter the child's-room
From which at this late hour   20

The child begins to shine.

Daniel Halpern (b. 1945)

Channel Firing

That night your great guns, unawares,
Shook all our coffins as we lay,
And broke the chancel window-squares,
We thought it was the Judgment-day

And sat upright. While drearisome   5
Arose the howl of wakened hounds:
The mouse let fall the altar-crumb,
The worms drew back into the mounds,

The glebe cow drooled. Till God called, "No;
It's gunnery practice out at sea   10
Just as before you went below;
The world is as it used to be:

"All nations striving strong to make
Red war yet redder. Mad as hatters
They do no more for Christès sake   15
Than you who are helpless in such matters.

"That this is not the judgment-hour
For some of them's a blessed thing,
For if it were they'd have to scour
Hell's floor for so much threatening. . . .   20

"Ha, ha. It will be warmer when
I blow the trumpet (if indeed
I ever do; for you are men,
and rest eternal sorely need)."

So down we lay again. "I wonder,   25
Will the world ever saner be,"
Said one, "than when He sent us under
In our indifferent century!"

And many a skeleton shook his head.
"Instead of preaching forty year,"   30
My neighbor Parson Thirdly said,
"I wish I had stuck to pipes and beer."

Again the guns disturbed the hour,
Roaring their readiness to avenge,
As far inland as Stourton Tower,   35
And Camelot, and starlit Stonehenge.

April 1914

Thomas Hardy (1840–1928)

(35–36) *Stourton Tower:* memorial at the spot where Alfred the Great resisted the invading
Danes in 879; *Camelot:* legendary capital of Arthur's kingdom; *Stonehenge:* mysterious circle of
huge stones erected in Wiltshire by very early inhabitants of Britain. The three references move
backward in time through the historic, the legendary, and the prehistoric.

The Darkling Thrush

I leant upon a coppice gate
    When Frost was specter-gray,
And Winter's dregs made desolate
    The weakening eye of day.
The tangled bine-stems scored the sky   5
    Like strings of broken lyres,
And all mankind that haunted nigh
    Had sought their household fires.

The land's sharp features seemed to be
    The Century's corpse outleant,   10
His crypt the cloudy canopy,
    The wind his death-lament.
The ancient pulse of germ and birth
    Was shrunken hard and dry,
And every spirit upon earth   15
    Seemed fervorless as I.

At once a voice arose among
    The bleak twigs overhead
In a full-hearted evensong
    Of joy illimited;   20
An aged thrush, frail, gaunt, and small,
    In blast-beruffled plume,
Had chosen thus to fling his soul
    Upon the growing gloom.

So little cause for carolings   25
    Of such ecstatic sound
Was written on terrestrial things
    Afar or nigh around,
That I could think there trembled through
    His happy good-night air   30
Some blessed Hope, whereof he knew
    And I was unaware.

31 December 1900

Thomas Hardy (1840–1928)

Neutral Tones

We stood by a pond that winter day,
And the sun was white, as though chidden of God,
And a few leaves lay on the starving sod;
    —They had fallen from an ash, and were gray.

Your eyes on me were as eyes that rove   5
Over tedious riddles of years ago;
And some words played between us to and fro
    On which lost the more by our love.

The smile on your mouth was the deadest thing
Alive enough to have strength to die;   10
And a grin of bitterness swept thereby
    Like an ominous bird a-wing. . . .

Since then, keen lessons that love deceives,
And wrings with wrong, have shaped to me
Your face, and the God-curst sun, and a tree,   15
    And a pond edged with grayish leaves.

Thomas Hardy (1840–1928)

Follower

My father worked with a horse-plow,
His shoulders globed like a full sail strung
Between the shafts and the furrow.
The horses strained at his clicking tongue.

As expert. He would set the wing   5
And fit the bright steel-pointed sock.
The sod rolled over without breaking.
At the headrig, with a single pluck

Of reins, the sweating team turned round
And back into the land. His eye   10
Narrowed and angled at the ground,
Mapping the furrow exactly.

I stumbled in his hobnailed wake,
Fell sometimes on the polished sod;
Sometimes he rode me on his back   15
Dipping and rising to his plod.

I wanted to grow up and plow,
To close one eye, stiffen my arm.
All I ever did was follow
In his broad shadow round the farm.   20

I was a nuisance, tripping, falling,
Yapping always. But today
It is my father who keeps stumbling
Behind me, and will not go away.

Seamus Heaney (b. 1939)

To an Athlete Dying Young

The time you won your town the race
We chaired you through the market-place;
Man and boy stood cheering by,
And home we brought you shoulder-high.

Today, the road all runners come,   5
Shoulder-high, we bring you home,
And set you at your threshold down,
Townsman of a stiller town.

Smart lad, to slip betimes away
From fields where glory does not stay   10
And early though the laurel grows
It withers quicker than the rose.

Eyes the shady night has shut
Cannot see the record cut,
And silence sounds no worse than cheers   15
After earth has stopped the ears:

Now you will not swell the rout
Of lads that wore their honors out,
Runners whom renown outran
And the name died before the man.   20

So set, before its echoes fade,
The fleet foot on the sill of shade,
And hold to the low lintel up
The still-defended challenge-cup.

And round that early-laureled head   25
Will flock to gaze the strengthless dead,
And find unwithered on its curls
The garland briefer than a girl's.

A. E. Housman (1859–1936)

Aunt Sue's Stories

Aunt Sue has a head full of stories.
Aunt Sue has a whole heart full of stories.
Summer nights on the front porch
Aunt Sue cuddles a brown-faced child to her bosom
And tells him stories.   5

Black slaves
Working in the hot sun,
And black slaves
Walking in the dewy night,
And black slaves   10
Singing sorrow songs on the banks of a mighty river
Mingle themselves softly
In the flow of old Aunt Sue's voice,
Mingle themselves softly
In the dark shadows that cross and recross   15
Aunt Sue's stories.

And the dark-faced child, listening,
Knows that Aunt Sue's stories are real stories.
He knows that Aunt Sue
Never got her stories out of any book at all,   20
But that they came
Right out of her own life.

And the dark-faced child is quiet
Of a summer night
Listening to Aunt Sue's stories.   25

Langston Hughes (1902–1967)

Negro Servant

All day subdued, polite,
Kind, thoughtful to the faces that are white.
    O, tribal dance!
    O, drums!
    O, veldt at night!   5
Forgotten watch-fires on a hill somewhere!
    O, songs that do not care!
At six o'clock, or seven, or eight,
    You're through.
    You've worked all day.   10
    Dark Harlem waits for you.
    The bus, the sub—
    Pay-nights a taxi
    Through the park.
O, drums of life in Harlem after dark!   15
    O, dreams!
    O, songs!
    O, saxophones at night!
O, sweet relief from faces that are white!

Langston Hughes (1902–1967)

Theme for English B

The instructor said,

    Go home, and write
    a page tonight.
    And let that page come out of you—
    Then, it will be true.   5

I wonder if it's that simple?
I am twenty-two, colored, born in Winston-Salem.
I went to school there, then Durham, then here
to this college on the hill above Harlem.
I am the only colored student in my class.   10
The steps from the hill lead down into Harlem,
through a park, then I cross St. Nicholas,

Eighth Avenue, Seventh, and I come to the Y,
the Harlem Branch Y, where I take the elevator
up to my room, sit down, and write this page: 15

It's not easy to know what is true for you or me
at twenty-two, my age. But I guess I'm what
I feel and see and hear, Harlem, I hear you:
hear you, hear me—we two—you, me, talk on this page.
(I hear New York, too.) Me—who?   20

Well, I like to eat, sleep, drink, and be in love.
I like to work, read, learn, and understand life.
I like a pipe for a Christmas present,
or records—Bessie, bop, or Bach.
I guess being colored doesn't make me *not* like   25
the same things other folks like who are other races.
So will my page be colored that I write?
Being me, it will not be white.
But it will be
a part of you, instructor.   30
You are white—
yet a part of me, as I am a part of you.
That's American.
Sometimes perhaps you don't want to be a part of me.
Nor do I often want to be a part of you.   35
But we are, that's true!
As I learn from you,
I guess you learn from me—
although you're older—and white—
and somewhat more free.   40

This is my page for English B.

Langston Hughes (1902–1967)

(24) Bessie Smith: African American blues singer (1898?–1937).

The Death of the Ball Turret Gunner

From my mother's sleep I fell into the State,
And I hunched in its belly till my wet fur froze.

Six miles from earth, loosed from its dream of life,
I woke to black flak and the nightmare fighters.
When I died they washed me out of the turret with a hose.   5

Randall Jarrell (1914–1965)

(Title) *Ball Turret:* the poet wrote, "A ball turret was a plexiglass sphere set into the belly of a
B-17 or B-24 [bomber during World War II], and inhabited by two .50 caliber machine-guns
and one man, a short small man. When this gunner tracked with his machine-guns a fighter
[plane] attacking from below, he revolved with the turret; hunched in his little sphere, he
looked like the fetus in the womb."

To Celia

Drink to me only with thine eyes,
    And I will pledge with mine;
Or leave a kiss but in the cup,
    And I'll not ask for wine.
The thirst that from the soul doth rise   5
    Doth ask a drink divine;
But might I of Jove's nectar sup,
    I would not change for thine.

I sent thee late a rosy wreath,
    Not so much honoring thee   10
As giving it a hope that there
    It could not withered be.
But thou thereon didst only breathe,
    And sent'st it back to me;
Since when it grows, and smells, I swear,   15
    Not of itself but thee.

Ben Jonson (1572–1637)

Warning

When I am an old woman I shall wear purple
With a red hat which doesn't go, and doesn't suit me.
And I shall spend my pension on brandy and summer gloves
And satin sandals, and say we've no money for butter.
I shall sit down on the pavement when I'm tired   5
And gobble up samples in shops and press alarm bells
And run my stick along the public railings
And make up for the sobriety of my youth.

I shall go out in my slippers in the rain
And pick the flowers in other people's gardens   10
And learn to spit.

You can wear terrible shirts and grow more fat
And eat three pounds of sausages at a go
Or only bread and pickle for a week
And hoard pens and pencils and beermats and things in boxes.   15

But now we must have clothes that keep us dry
And pay our rent and not swear in the street
And set a good example for the children.
We must have friends to dinner and read the papers.

But maybe I ought to practice a little now?   20
So people who know me are not too shocked and surprised
When suddenly I am old, and start to wear purple.

Jenny Joseph (b. 1932)

Men at Forty

Men at forty
Learn to close softly
The doors to rooms they will not be
Coming back to.

At rest on a stair landing,   5
They feel it
Moving beneath them now like the deck of a ship,
Though the swell is gentle.

And deep in mirrors
They rediscover   10
The face of the boy as he practices tying
His father's tie there in secret

And the face of that father,
Still warm with the mystery of lather.
They are more fathers than sons themselves now.   15
Something is filling them, something

That is like the twilight sound
Of the crickets, immense,
Filling the woods at the foot of the slope
Behind their mortgaged houses.   20

                                        Donald Justice (1925–2004)

La Belle Dame sans Merci

A Ballad

O, what can ail thee, knight-at-arms,
    Alone and palely loitering?
The sedge has withered from the lake,
    And no birds sing.

O, what can ail thee, knight-at-arms,   5
    So haggard and so woe-begone?
The squirrel's granary is full,
    And the harvest's done.

I see a lily on thy brow,
    With anguish moist and fever dew;   10
And on thy cheeks a fading rose
    Fast withereth too.

I met a lady in the meads,
    Full beautiful—a faery's child,
Her hair was long, her foot was light,   15
    And her eyes were wild.

I made a garland for her head,
    And bracelets too, and fragrant zone;
She looked at me as she did love,
    And made sweet moan.   20

I set her on my pacing steed,
    And nothing else saw all day long;
For sidelong would she bend, and sing
    A faery's song.

She found me roots of relish sweet,   25
    And honey wild, and manna dew,

And sure in language strange she said—
    "I love thee true."

She took me to her elfin grot,
    And there she wept and sighed full sore,   30
And there I shut her wild wild eyes
    With kisses four.

And there she lullèd me asleep
    And there I dreamed—Ah! woe betide!
The latest dream I ever dreamed   35
    On the cold hill side.

I saw pale kings and princes too,
    Pale warriors, death-pale were they all;
They cried—"La Belle Dame sans Merci
    Hath thee in thrall!"   40

I saw their starved lips in the gloam
    With horrid warning gapèd wide,
And I awoke and found me here
    On the cold hill's side.

And this is why I sojourn here   45
    Alone and palely loitering,
Though the sedge has withered from the lake,
    And no birds sing.

John Keats (1795–1821)

The title means "The beautiful lady without pity."

Ode to a Nightingale

My heart aches, and a drowsy numbness pains
    My sense, as though of hemlock° I had drunk,   *a poison*
Or emptied some dull opiate to the drains
    One minute past, and Lethe-wards had sunk:
'Tis not through envy of thy happy lot,   5
    But being too happy in thine happiness,—
        That thou, light-wingèd Dryad° of the trees,   *wood nymph*
        In some melodious plot

Of beechen green, and shadows numberless,
    Singest of summer in full-throated ease.   10

O for a draught of vintage! that hath been
    Cooled a long age in the deep-delved earth,
Tasting of Flora° and the country green,   goddess of flowers
    Dance, and Provençal song, and sunburnt mirth!
O for a beaker full of the warm South,   15
    Full of the true, the blushful Hippocrene,
        With beaded bubbles winking at the brim,
            And purple-stainèd mouth;
    That I might drink, and leave the world unseen,
        And with thee fade away into the forest dim: 20

Fade far away, dissolve, and quite forget
    What thou among the leaves hast never known,
The weariness, the fever, and the fret
    Here, where men sit and hear each other groan;
Where palsy shakes a few, sad, last gray hairs,   25
    Where youth grows pale, and specter-thin, and dies,
        Where but to think is to be full of sorrow
            And leaden-eyed despairs,
    Where Beauty cannot keep her lustrous eyes,
        Or new Love pine at them beyond tomorrow.   30

Away! away! for I will fly to thee,
    Not charioted by Bacchus and his pards,
But on the viewless° wings of Poesy,   invisible
    Though the dull brain perplexes and retards:
Already with thee! tender is the night,   35
    And haply the Queen-Moon is on her throne,
        Clustered around by all her starry Fays;
            But here there is no light,
    Save what from heaven is with the breezes blown
        Through verdurous glooms and winding mossy ways.   40

I cannot see what flowers are at my feet,
    Nor what soft incense hangs upon the boughs,
But, in embalmèd° darkness, guess each sweet   perfumed
    Wherewith the seasonable month endows
The grass, the thicket, and the fruit-tree wild;   45
    White hawthorn, and the pastoral eglantine;
        Fast fading violets covered up in leaves;

And mid-May's eldest child,
   The coming musk-rose, full of dewy wine,
      The murmurous haunt of flies on summer eves.   50

Darkling° I listen; and, for many a time   *in darkness*
   I have been half in love with easeful Death,
Called him soft names in many a musèd rhyme,
   To take into the air my quiet breath;
Now more than ever seems it rich to die,   55
   To cease upon the midnight with no pain,
      While thou art pouring forth thy soul abroad
        In such an ecstasy!
   Still wouldst thou sing, and I have ears in vain—
      To thy high requiem become a sod.   60

Thou wast not born for death, immortal Bird!
   No hungry generations tread thee down;
The voice I hear this passing night was heard
   In ancient days by emperor and clown:
Perhaps the self-same song that found a path   65
   Through the sad heart of Ruth, when, sick for home,
      She stood in tears amid the alien corn;
        The same that oft-times hath
   Charmed magic casements, opening on the foam
      Of perilous seas, in faery lands forlorn.   70

Forlorn! the very word is like a bell
   To toll me back from thee to my sole self!
Adieu! the fancy cannot cheat so well
   As she is famed to do, deceiving elf.
Adieu! adieu! thy plaintive anthem fades   75
   Past the near meadows, over the still stream,
      Up the hill-side; and now 'tis buried deep
        In the next valley-glades:
   Was it a vision, or a waking dream?
      Fled is that music:—Do I wake or sleep?   80

John Keats (1795–1821)

(4) *Lethe:* river of forgetfulness in the Greek underworld. (14) *Provençal:* Provence, a wine-growing region in southern France famous, in the Middle Ages, for troubadours. (16) *Hippocrene:* fountain of the Muses on Mt. Helicon in Greece. (32) *Bacchus . . . pards:* Bacchus, god of wine, had a chariot drawn by leopards. (66) *Ruth:* see Bible, Ruth 2.

To one who has been long in city pent

To one who has been long in city pent,
   'Tis very sweet to look into the fair
   And open face of heaven, —to breathe a prayer
Full in the smile of the blue firmament.
Who is more happy, when, with heart's content,   5
   Fatigued he sinks into some pleasant lair
   Of wavy grass, and reads a debonair
And gentle tale of love and languishment?

Returning home at evening, with an ear
   Catching the notes of Philomel, —an eye   10
Watching the sailing cloudlet's bright career,
   He mourns that day so soon has glided by:
E'en like the passage of an angel's tear
   That falls through the clear ether silently.

John Keats (1795–1821)

Aubade

I work all day, and get half drunk at night.
Waking at four to soundless dark, I stare.
In time the curtain-edges will grow light.
Till then I see what's really always there:
Unresting death, a whole day nearer now,   5
Making all thought impossible but how
And where and when I shall myself die.
Arid interrogation: yet the dread
Of dying, and being dead,
Flashes afresh to hold and horrify.   10

The mind blanks at the glare. Not in remorse
—The good not done, the love not given, time
Torn off unused—nor wretchedly because
An only life can take so long to climb
Clear of its wrong beginnings, and may never;   15
But at the total emptiness for ever,
The sure extinction that we travel to
And shall be lost in always. Not to be here,
Not to be anywhere,
And soon; nothing more terrible, nothing more true.   20

This is a special way of being afraid
No trick dispels. Religion used to try,
That vast moth-eaten musical brocade
Created to pretend we never die,
And specious stuff that says *No rational being*   25
Can fear a thing it will not feel, not seeing
That this is what we fear—no sight, no sound,
No touch or taste or smell, nothing to think with,
Nothing to love or link with,
The anaesthetic from which none come round.   30

And so it stays just on the edge of vision,
A small unfocused blur, a standing chill
That slows each impulse down to indecision.
Most things may never happen: this one will,
And realization of it rages out   35
In furnace-fear when we are caught without
People or drink. Courage is no good:
It means not scaring others. Being brave
Lets no one off the grave.
Death is no different whined at than withstood.   40

Slowly light strengthens, and the room takes shape.
It stands plain as a wardrobe, what we know,
Have always known, know that we can't escape,
Yet can't accept. One side will have to go.
Meanwhile telephones crouch, getting ready to ring   45
In locked-up offices, and all the uncaring
Intricate rented world begins to rouse.
The sky is white as clay, with no sun.
Work has to be done.
Postmen like doctors go from house to house.   50

Philip Larkin (1922–1985)

The Blind Man's House at the Edge of the Cliff

At the jutting rim of the land he lives,
but not from ignorance,
not from despair.
He knows one extra step from his seaward

wide-open door would be   5
a step into salt air,
and he has no longing to shatter himself
far below, where the breakers
grind granite to sand.
No, he has chosen a life   10
pitched at the brink, a nest on the swaying
tip of a branch, for good reason:

dazzling within his darkness
is the elusive deep horizon. Here
nothing intrudes, palpable shade,   15
between his eager
inward gaze
and the vast enigma.
If he could fly he would drift forever
into that veil, soft and receding.   20

He knows that if he could see
he would be no wiser.
High on the windy cliff he breathes
face to face with desire.

Denise Levertov (1923–1997)

To Lucasta, on Going to the Wars

Tell me not, Sweet, I am unkind
    That from the nunnery
Of thy chaste breast and quiet mind,
    To war and arms I fly.

True, a new mistress now I chase,   5
    The first foe in the field;
And with a stronger faith embrace
    A sword, a horse, a shield.

Yet this inconstancy is such
    As you too shall adore;   10
I could not love thee, Dear, so much,
    Loved I not Honor more.

Richard Lovelace (1618–1658)

Puberty

Remember the way we bore our bodies to the pond
like raccoons with food to wash? Onto the blue,
smooth foil of the gift-wrapped water I slid

my embarrassing self. All the water I knew
was from books. I had read of the surfless Adriatic   5
and read how the North Atlantic erected by night

its wavering cliffs of fog and cul-de-sacs of ice,
only to turn to the dawn its chill, placid cheek.
But twitch and thrash in my chair as I might,

it was true what the swimming teacher told me: 10
once you learn how to float, it's almost impossible
to go under. I tried and tried, and so I can tell you

how we greet the news by which we survive: with rage.
A bucolic boy adrift on a Xenia, Ohio, pond?
Not on your life. Like you, I gulped and learned to swim.   15

William Matthews (1942–1997)

Silence

My father used to say,
"Superior people never make long visits,
have to be shown Longfellow's grave
or the glass flowers at Harvard.
Self-reliant like the cat—   5
that takes its prey to privacy,
the mouse's limp tail hanging like a shoelace from its mouth—
they sometimes enjoy solitude
and can be robbed of speech
by speech which has delighted them.   10
The deepest feeling always shows itself in silence;
not in silence, but restraint."
Nor was he insincere in saying, "Make my house your inn."
Inns are not residences.

Marianne Moore (1887–1972)

Dim Lady

My honeybunch's peepers are nothing like neon. Today's special at Red Lobster is redder than her kisser. If Liquid Paper is white, her racks are institutional beige. If her mop were Slinkys, dishwater Slinkys would grow on her noggin. I have seen tablecloths in Shakey's Pizza Parlors, red and white, but no such picnic colors do I see in her mug. And in some minty-fresh mouthwashes there is more sweetness than in the garlic breeze my main squeeze wheezes. I love to hear her rap, yet I'm aware that Muzak has a hipper beat. I don't know any Marilyn Monroes. My ball and chain is plain from head to toe. And yet, by gosh, my scrumptious Twinkie has as much sex appeal for me as any lanky model or platinum movie idol who's hyped beyond belief.

Harryette Mullen (b. 1953)

I Go Back to May 1937

I see them standing at the formal gates of their colleges,
I see my father strolling out
under the ochre sandstone arch, the
red tiles glinting like bent
plates of blood behind his head, I   5
see my mother with a few light books at her hip
standing at the pillar made of tiny bricks with the
wrought-iron gate still open behind her, its
sword-tips black in the May air,
they are about to graduate, they are about to get married,   10
they are kids, they are dumb, all they know is they are
innocent, they would never hurt anybody.
I want to go up to them and say Stop,
don't do it—she's the wrong woman,
he's the wrong man, you are going to do things   15
you cannot imagine you would ever do,
you are going to do bad things to children,
you are going to suffer in ways you never heard of,
you are going to want to die. I want to go
up to them there in the late May sunlight and say it,   20
her hungry pretty blank face turning to me,
her pitiful beautiful untouched body,
his arrogant handsome blind face turning to me,
his pitiful beautiful untouched body,

but I don't do it. I want to live. I   25
take them up like the male and female
paper dolls and bang them together
at the hips like chips of flint as if to
strike sparks from them, I say
Do what you are going to do, and I will tell about it.   30

Sharon Olds (b. 1942)

The Planned Child

I hated the fact that they had planned me, she had taken
a cardboard out of his shirt from the laundry
as if sliding the backbone up out of his body,
and made a chart of the month and put
her temperature on it, rising and falling,   5
to know the day to make me—I would have
liked to have been conceived in heat,
in haste, by mistake, in love, in sex,
not on cardboard, the little x on the
rising line that did not fall again.   10

But when a friend was pouring wine
and said that I seem to have been a child who had been wanted,
I took the wine against my lips
as if my mouth were moving along
that valved wall in my mother's body, she was   15
bearing down, and then breathing from the mask, and then
bearing down, pressing me out into
the world that was not enough for her without me in it,
not the moon, the sun, Orion
cartwheeling across the dark, not   20
the earth, the sea—none of it
was enough, for her, without me.

Sharon Olds (b. 1942)

The Victims

When Mother divorced you, we were glad. She took it and
took it, in silence, all those years and then
kicked you out, suddenly, and her
kids loved it. Then you were fired, and we

grinned inside, the way people grinned when   5
Nixon's helicopter lifted off the South
Lawn for the last time. We were tickled
to think of your office taken away,
your secretaries taken away,
your luncheons with three double bourbons,   10
your pencils, your reams of paper. Would they take your
suits back, too, those dark
carcasses hung in your closet, and the black
noses of your shoes with their large pores?
She had taught us to take it, to hate you and take it   15
until we pricked with her for your
annihilation, Father. Now I
pass the bums in doorways, the white
slugs of their bodies gleaming through slits in their
suits of compressed silt, the stained   20
flippers of their hands, the underwater
fire of their eyes, ships gone down with the
lanterns lit, and I wonder who took it and
took it from them in silence until they had
given it all away and had nothing   25
left but this.

                                                    Sharon Olds (b. 1942)

Résumé

Razors pain you;
Rivers are damp;
Acids stain you;
And drugs cause cramp.
Guns aren't lawful;   5
Nooses give;
Gas smells awful;
You might as well live.

                                             Dorothy Parker (1893–1967)

A Work of Artifice

The bonsai tree
in the attractive pot
could have grown eighty feet tall
on the side of a mountain

till split by lightning.   5
But a gardener
carefully pruned it.
It is nine inches high.
Every day as he
whittles back the branches   10
the gardener croons,
It is your nature
to be small and cozy,
domestic and weak;
how lucky, little tree,   15
to have a pot to grow in.
With living creatures
one must begin very early
to dwarf their growth:
the bound feet,   20
the crippled brain,
the hair in curlers,
the hands you
love to touch.

Marge Piercy (b. 1936)

Mad Girl's Love Song

I shut my eyes and all the world drops dead;
I lift my lids and all is born again.
(I think I made you up inside my head.)

The stars go waltzing out in blue and red,
And arbitrary blackness gallops in: 5
I shut my eyes and all the world drops dead.

I dreamed that you bewitched me into bed
And sung me moon-struck, kissed me quite insane.
(I think I made you up inside my head.)

God topples from the sky, hell's fires fade: 10
Exit seraphim and Satan's men:
I shut my eyes and all the world drops dead.

I fancied you'd return the way you said,
But I grow old and I forget your name.
(I think I made you up inside my head.)   15

I should have loved a thunderbird instead;
At least when spring comes they roar back again.
I shut my eyes and all the world drops dead.
(I think I made you up inside my head.)

Sylvia Plath (1932–1963)

Spinster

Now this particular girl
During a ceremonious April walk
With her latest suitor
Found herself, of a sudden, intolerably struck
By the birds' irregular babel   5
And the leaves' litter.

By this tumult afflicted, she
Observed her lover's gestures unbalance the air,
His gait stray uneven
Through a rank wilderness of fern and flower.   10
She judged petals in disarray,
The whole season, sloven.

How she longed for winter then!—
Scrupulously austere in its order
Of white and black   15
Ice and rock, each sentiment within border,
And heart's frosty discipline
Exact as a snowflake.

But here—a burgeoning
Unruly enough to pitch her five queenly wits   20
Into vulgar motley—
A treason not to be borne. Let idiots
Reel giddy in bedlam spring:
She withdrew neatly.

And round her house she set   25
Such a barricade of barb and check
Against mutinous weather

As no mere insurgent man could hope to break
With curse, fist, threat
Or love, either.   30

Sylvia Plath (1932–1963)

Wuthering Heights

The horizons ring me like faggots,
Tilted and disparate, and always unstable.
Touched by a match, they might warm me,
And their fine lines singe
The air to orange   5
Before the distances they pin evaporate,
Weighting the pale sky with a solider color.
But they only dissolve and dissolve
Like a series of promises, as I step forward.

There is no life higher than the grasstops   10
Or the hearts of sheep, and the wind
Pours by like destiny, bending
Everything in one direction.
I can feel it trying
To funnel my heat away.   15
If I pay the roots of the heather
Too close attention, they will invite me
To whiten my bones among them.

The sheep know where they are,
Browsing in their dirty wool-clouds,   20
Gray as the weather.
The black slots of their pupils take me in.
It is like being mailed into space,
A thin, silly message.
They stand about in grandmotherly disguise,   25
All wig curls and yellow teeth
And hard, marbly baas.

I come to wheel ruts, and water
Limpid as the solitudes
That flee through my fingers.   30
Hollow doorsteps go from grass to grass;

Lintel and sill have unhinged themselves.
Of people the air only
Remembers a few odd syllables.
It rehearses them moaningly: 35
Black stone, black stone.

The sky leans on me, me, the one upright
Among all horizontals.
The grass is beating its head distractedly.
It is too delicate   40
For a life in such company;
Darkness terrifies it.
Now, in valleys narrow
And black as purses, the house lights
Gleam like small change.   45

Sylvia Plath (1932–1963)

Epigram from the French

Sir, I admit your general rule
That every poet is a fool:
But you yourself may serve to show it,
That every fool is not a poet.

Alexander Pope (1688–1744)

Salutation

O generation of the thoroughly smug
    and thoroughly uncomfortable,
I have seen fishermen picnicking in the sun,
I have seen them with untidy families,
I have seen their smiles full of teeth   5
    and heard ungainly laughter.
And I am happier than you are,
And they were happier than I am;
And the fish swim in the lake
    and do not even own clothing.   10

Ezra Pound (1885–1972)

Here Lies a Lady

Here lies a lady of beauty and high degree.
Of chills and fever she died, of fever and chills,
The delight of her husband, her aunt, an infant of three,
And of medicos marveling sweetly on her ills.

For either she burned, and her confident eyes would blaze,   5
And her fingers fly in a manner to puzzle their heads—
What was she making? Why, nothing; she sat in a maze
Of old scraps of laces, snipped into curious shreds—

Or this would pass, and the light of her fire decline
Till she lay discouraged and cold, like a stalk, white and blown,   10
And would not open her eyes, to kisses, to wine;
The sixth of these states was her last; the cold settled down.

Sweet ladies, long may ye bloom, and toughly I hope ye may thole,
But was she not lucky? In flowers and lace and mourning,
In love and great honor we bade God rest her soul   15
After six little spaces of chill, and six of burning.

John Crowe Ransom (1888–1974)

Poetry: I

Someone at a table under a brown metal lamp
is studying the history of poetry.
Someone in the library at closing-time
has learned to say *modernism,*
trope, vatic, text.   5
She is listening for shreds of music.
He is searching for his name
back in the old country.
They cannot learn without teachers.
They are like us   what we were   10
if you remember.
In a corner of night a voice
is crying in a kind of whisper:
More!

Can you remember?   when we thought   15
the poets taught   how to live?
That is not the voice of a critic
nor a common reader
it is someone young   in anger
hardly knowing what to ask   20
who finds our lines   our glosses
wanting   in this world.

Adrienne Rich (b. 1929)

The Mill

The miller's wife had waited long,
    The tea was cold, the fire was dead;
And there might yet be nothing wrong
    In how he went and what he said:
"There are no millers any more,"   5
    Was all that she had heard him say;
And he had lingered at the door
    So long that it seemed yesterday.

Sick with a fear that had no form
    She knew that she was there at last;   10
And in the mill there was a warm
    And mealy fragrance of the past.
What else there was would only seem
    To say again what he had meant;
And what was hanging from a beam   15
    Would not have heeded where she went.

And if she thought it followed her,
    She may have reasoned in the dark
That one way of the few there were
    Would hide her and would leave no mark: 20
Black water, smooth above the weir
    Like starry velvet in the night,
Though ruffled once, would soon appear
    The same as ever to the sight.

Edwin Arlington Robinson (1869–1935)

Mr. Flood's Party

Old Eben Flood, climbing alone one night
Over the hill between the town below
And the forsaken upland hermitage
That held as much as he should ever know
On earth again of home, paused warily.   5
The road was his with not a native near;
And Eben, having leisure, said aloud,
For no man else in Tilbury Town to hear:

"Well, Mr. Flood, we have the harvest moon
Again, and we may not have many more;   10
The bird is on the wing, the poet says,
And you and I have said it here before.
Drink to the bird." He raised up to the light
The jug that he had gone so far to fill,
And answered huskily: "Well, Mr. Flood,   15
Since you propose it, I believe I will."

Alone, as if enduring to the end
A valiant armor of scarred hopes outworn,
He stood there in the middle of the road
Like Roland's ghost winding a silent horn.   20
Below him, in the town among the trees,
Where friends of other days had honored him,
A phantom salutation of the dead
Rang thinly till old Eben's eyes were dim.

Then, as a mother lays her sleeping child   25
Down tenderly, fearing it may awake,
He set the jug down slowly at his feet
With trembling care, knowing that most things break;
And only when assured that on firm earth
It stood, as the uncertain lives of men   30
Assuredly did not, he paced away,
And with his hand extended, paused again:

"Well, Mr. Flood, we have not met like this
In a long time; and many a change has come
To both of us, I fear, since last it was   35

We had a drop together. Welcome home!"
Convivially returning with himself,
Again he raised the jug up to the light;
And with an acquiescent quaver said:
"Well, Mr. Flood, if you insist, I might.   40

"Only a very little, Mr. Flood—
For auld lang syne. No more, sir; that will do."
So, for the time, apparently it did,
And Eben evidently thought so too;
For soon amid the silver loneliness   45
Of night he lifted up his voice and sang,
Secure, with only two moons listening,
Until the whole harmonious landscape rang—

"For auld lang syne." The weary throat gave out,
The last word wavered, and the song was done.   50
He raised again the jug regretfully
And shook his head, and was again alone.
There was not much that was ahead of him,
And there was nothing in the town below—
Where strangers would have shut the many doors   55
That many friends had opened long ago.

                    Edwin Arlington Robinson (1869–1935)

(11) *bird*: Mr. Flood is quoting from *The Rubáiyát of Omar Khayyám*, "The bird of Time . . . is on the wing." (20) *Roland*: hero of the French epic poem *The Song of Roland*. He died fighting a rearguard action for Charlemagne against the Moors in Spain; before his death he sounded a call for help on his famous horn, but the king's army arrived too late.

Richard Cory

Whenever Richard Cory went down town,
We people on the pavement looked at him:
He was a gentleman from sole to crown,
Clean favored, and imperially slim.

And he was always quietly arrayed,   5
And he was always human when he talked;
But still he fluttered pulses when he said,
"Good-morning," and he glittered when he walked.

And he was rich—yes, richer than a king—
And admirably schooled in every grace: 10
In fine, we thought that he was everything
To make us wish that we were in his place.

So on we worked, and waited for the light,
And went without the meat, and cursed the bread;
And Richard Cory, one calm summer night,   15
Went home and put a bullet through his head.

Edwin Arlington Robinson (1869–1935)

I knew a woman

I knew a woman, lovely in her bones,
When small birds sighed, she would sigh back at them;
Ah, when she moved, she moved more ways than one:
The shapes a bright container can contain!
Of her choice virtues only gods should speak,   5
Or English poets who grew up on Greek
(I'd have them sing in chorus, cheek to cheek).

How well her wishes went! She stroked my chin,
She taught me Turn, and Counter-turn, and Stand;
She taught me Touch, that undulant white skin;   10
I nibbled meekly from her proffered hand;
She was the sickle; I, poor I, the rake,
Coming behind her for her pretty sake
(But what prodigious mowing we did make).

Love likes a gander, and adores a goose: 15
Her full lips pursed, the errant note to seize;
She played it quick, she played it light and loose;
My eyes, they dazzled at her flowing knees;
Her several parts could keep a pure repose,
Or one hip quiver with a mobile nose   20
(She moved in circles, and those circles moved).

Let seed be grass, and grass turn into hay:
I'm martyr to a motion not my own;
What's freedom for? To know eternity.
I swear she cast a shadow white as stone.   25

But who would count eternity in days?
These old bones live to learn her wanton ways:
(I measure time by how a body sways).

Theodore Roethke (1908–1963)

My Papa's Waltz

The whiskey on your breath
Could make a small boy dizzy;
But I hung on like death:
Such waltzing was not easy.

We romped until the pans   5
Slid from the kitchen shelf;
My mother's countenance
Could not unfrown itself.

The hand that held my wrist
Was battered on one knuckle;   10
At every step you missed
My right ear scraped a buckle.

You beat time on my head
With a palm caked hard by dirt,
Then waltzed me off to bed   15
Still clinging to your shirt.

Theodore Roethke (1908–1963)

Root Cellar

Nothing would sleep in that cellar, dank as a ditch,
Bulbs broke out of boxes hunting for chinks in the dark,
Shoots dangled and drooped,
Lolling obscenely from mildewed crates,
Hung down long yellow evil necks, like tropical snakes.   5
And what a congress of stinks!—
Roots ripe as old bait,
Pulpy stems, rank, silo-rich,

Leaf-mold, manure, lime, piled against slippery planks.
Nothing would give up life: 10
Even the dirt kept breathing a small breath.

Theodore Roethke (1908–1963)

Young

A thousand doors ago
when I was a lonely kid
in a big house with four
garages and it was summer
as long as I could remember,   5
I lay on the lawn at night,
clover wrinkling under me,
the wise stars bedding over me,
my mother's window a funnel
of yellow heat running out,   10
my father's window, half shut,
an eye where sleepers pass,
and the boards of the house
were smooth and white as wax
and probably a million leaves   15
sailed on their strange stalks
as the crickets ticked together
and I, in my brand new body,
which was not a woman's yet,
told the stars my questions   20
and thought God could really see
the heat and the painted light,
elbows, knees, dreams, goodnight.

Anne Sexton (1928–1974)

Let me not to the marriage of true minds

Let me not to the marriage of true minds
Admit impediments. Love is not love
Which alters when it alteration finds,
Or bends with the remover to remove.
O no! it is an ever-fixèd mark   5
That looks on tempests and is never shaken;

It is the star to every wandering bark,
Whose worth's unknown, although his height be taken.
Love's not Time's fool, though rosy lips and cheeks
Within his bending sickle's compass come;   10
Love alters not with his brief hours and weeks,
But bears it out even to the edge of doom.
If this be error and upon me proved,
I never writ, nor no man ever loved.

                                      William Shakespeare (1564–1616)

Watermelons

Green Buddhas
On the fruit stand.
We eat the smile
and spit out the teeth.

                                      Charles Simic (b. 1938)

Not Waving But Drowning

Nobody heard him, the dead man,
But still he lay moaning:
I was much further out than you thought
And not waving but drowning.

Poor chap, he always loved larking   5
And now he's dead
It must have been too cold for him his heart gave way,
They said.

Oh, no no no, it was too cold always
(Still the dead one lay moaning)   10
I was much too far out all my life
And not waving but drowning.

                                      Stevie Smith (1902–1971)

Small Town with One Road

We could be here. This is the valley
And its black strip of highway, big-eyed

With rabbits that won't get across.
Kids could make it, though.
They leap barefoot to the store—   5
Sweetness on their tongues, red stain of laughter.
They are the spectators of fun.
Hot dimes fall from their palms,
Chinks of light, and they eat
Candies all the way home   10
Where there's a dog for each hand,
Cats, chickens in the yard.
A pot bangs and water runs in the kitchen.
Beans, they think, and beans it will be,
Brown soup that's muscle for the field   15
And crippled steps to a ladder.
Okie or Mexican, Jew that got lost,
It's a hard life where the sun looks.
The cotton gin stands tall in the money dream
And the mill is a paycheck for   20
A wife—and perhaps my wife
Who, when she was a girl,
Boxed peaches and plums, hoed
Papa's field that wavered like a mirage
That wouldn't leave. We could go back.   25
I could lose my job, this easy one
That's only words, and pick up a shovel,
Hoe, broom that takes it away.
Worry is my daughter's story.
She touches my hand. We suck roadside   30
Snowcones in the shade
And look about. Behind sunglasses
I see where I stood: a brown kid
Getting across. "He's like me,"
I tell my daughter, and she stops her mouth.   35
He looks both ways and then leaps
Across the road where riches
Happen on a red tongue.

Gary Soto (b. 1952)

One day I wrote her name upon the strand

One day I wrote her name upon the strand,°   beach
But came the waves and washèd it away:

Again I wrote it with a second hand,
But came the tide, and made my pains his prey.
"Vain man," said she, "that dost in vain assay°   attempt 5
A mortal thing so to immortalize.
For I myself shall, like to this, decay,
And eek° my name be wipèd out likewise."   also
"Not so," quoth I, "let baser things devise
To die in dust, but you shall live by fame: 10
My verse your virtues rare shall eternize,
And in the heavens write your glorious name,
Where whenas death shall all the world subdue
Our love shall live, and later life renew."

Edmund Spenser (1552–1599)

Anecdote of the Jar

I placed a jar in Tennessee,
And round it was, upon a hill.
It made the slovenly wilderness
Surround that hill.

The wilderness rose up to it,   5
And sprawled around, no longer wild.
The jar was round upon the ground
And tall and of a port in air.

It took dominion everywhere.
The jar was gray and bare.   10
It did not give of bird or bush,
Like nothing else in Tennessee.

Wallace Stevens (1879–1955)

The Course of a Particular

Today the leaves cry, hanging on branches swept by wind,
Yet the nothingness of winter becomes a little less.
It is still full of icy shades and shapen snow.

The leaves cry . . . One holds off and merely hears the cry.
It is a busy cry, concerning someone else.   5
And though one says that one is part of everything,

There is a conflict, there is a resistance involved;
And being part is an exertion that declines:
One feels the life of that which gives life as it is.

The leaves cry. It is not a cry of divine attention,   10
Nor the smoke-drift of puffed-out heroes, nor human cry.
It is the cry of leaves that do not transcend themselves,

In the absence of fantasia, without meaning more
Than they are in the final finding of the ear, in the thing
Itself, until, at last, the cry concerns no one at all.   15

Wallace Stevens (1879–1955)

The Death of a Soldier

Life contracts and death is expected,
As in a season of autumn.
The soldier falls.

He does not become a three-days personage,
Imposing his separation,   5
Calling for pomp.

Death is absolute and without memorial,
As in a season of autumn,
When the wind stops,

When the wind stops and, over the heavens,   10
The clouds go, nevertheless,
In their direction.

Wallace Stevens (1879–1955)

Disillusionment of Ten O'Clock

The houses are haunted
By white night-gowns.
None are green,
Or purple with green rings,
Or green with yellow rings,   5
Or yellow with blue rings.
None of them are strange,

With socks of lace
And beaded ceintures.°   sashes
People are not going   10
To dream of baboons and periwinkles.
Only, here and there, an old sailor,
Drunk and asleep in his boots,
Catches tigers
In red weather.   15

Wallace Stevens (1879–1955)

A Description of the Morning

Now hardly here and there a hackney-coach
Appearing, showed the ruddy morn's approach.
Now Betty from her master's bed had flown,
And softly stole to discompose her own.
The slip-shod 'prentice from his master's door   5
Had pared the dirt, and sprinkled round the floor.
Now Moll had whirled her mop with dextrous airs,
Prepared to scrub the entry and the stairs.
The youth with broomy stumps began to trace
The kennel's edge, where wheels had worn the place.   10
The small-coal man was heard with cadence deep,
Till drowned in shriller notes of chimney-sweep.
Duns at his lordship's gate began to meet;
And Brickdust Moll had screamed through half the street.
The turnkey now his flock returning sees,   15
Duly let out a-nights to steal for fees.
The watchful bailiffs take their silent stands;
And schoolboys lag with satchels in their hands.

Jonathan Swift (1667–1745)

(9) *youth:* he is apparently searching for salvage. (10) *kennel:* gutter. (14) *Brickdust:* red-faced.

Fern Hill

Now as I was young and easy under the apple boughs
About the lilting house and happy as the grass was green,
    The night above the dingle starry,
        Time let me hail and climb
    Golden in the heydays of his eyes,   5

And honored among wagons I was prince of the apple towns
And once below a time I lordly had the trees and leaves
    Trail with daisies and barley
  Down the rivers of the windfall light.

And as I was green and carefree, famous among the barns   10
About the happy yard and singing as the farm was home,
    In the sun that is young once only,
      Time let me play and be
  Golden in the mercy of his means,
And green and golden I was huntsman and herdsman, the calves   15
Sang to my horn, the foxes on the hills barked clear and cold,
    And the sabbath rang slowly
  In the pebbles of the holy streams.

All the sun long it was running, it was lovely, the hay
Fields high as the house, the tunes from the chimneys, it was air   20
    And playing, lovely and watery
      And fire green as grass.
    And nightly under the simple stars
As I rode to sleep the owls were bearing the farm away,
All the moon long I heard, blessed among stables, the nightjars   25
    Flying with the ricks, and the horses
      Flashing into the dark.

And then to awake, and the farm, like a wanderer white
With the dew, come back, the cock on his shoulder: it was all
    Shining, it was Adam and maiden,   30
      The sky gathered again
    And the sun grew round that very day.
So it must have been after the birth of the simple light
In the first, spinning place, the spellbound horses walking warm
    Out of the whinnying green stable   35
      On to the fields of praise.

And honored among foxes and pheasants by the gay house
Under the new made clouds and happy as the heart was long,
    In the sun born over and over,
      I ran my heedless ways,   40
    My wishes raced through the house high hay
And nothing I cared, at my sky blue trades, that time allows

In all his tuneful turning so few and such morning songs
   Before the children green and golden
      Follow him out of grace,   45

Nothing I cared, in the lamb white days, that time would take me
Up to the swallow thronged loft by the shadow of my hand,
   In the moon that is always rising,
      Nor that riding to sleep
I should hear him fly with the high fields   50
And wake to the farm forever fled from the childless land.
Oh as I was young and easy in the mercy of his means,
   Time held me green and dying
   Though I sang in my chains like the sea.

Dylan Thomas (1914–1953)

The Virgins

      Down the dead streets of sun-stoned Frederiksted,
      the first free port to die for tourism,
      strolling at funeral pace, I am reminded
      of life not lost to the American dream;
      but my small-islander's simplicities   5
      can't better our new empire's civilized
      exchange of cameras, watches, perfumes, brandies
      for the good life, so cheaply underpriced
      that only the crime rate is on the rise
      in streets blighted with sun, stone arches   10
      and plazas blown dry by the hysteria
      of rumor. A condominium drowns
      in vacancy; its bargains are dusted,
      but only a jeweled housefly drones
      over the bargains. The roulettes spin   15
      rustily to the wind—the vigorous trade
      that every morning would begin afresh
      by revving up green water round the pierhead
      heading for where the banks of silver thresh.

Derek Walcott (b. 1930)

(1) *Frederiksted:* chief port of St. Croix, largest of the American Virgin Islands, a free port where goods can be bought without payment of customs duties and therefore at bargain prices. The economy of St. Croix, once based on sugar cane, is now chiefly dependent on

tourism. Like the other American Virgin Islands, St. Croix has suffered from uncontrolled growth, building booms, unevenly distributed prosperity, destruction of natural beauty, and pollution. (5) *my . . . simplicities:* The poet is a native of St. Lucia in the West Indies. (16) *trade:* cf. trade wind.

To a Stranger

Passing stranger! you do not know how longingly I look upon you,
You must be he I was seeking, or she I was seeking, (it comes to me
    as of a dream,)
I have somewhere surely lived a life of joy with you,
All is recall'd as we flit by each other, fluid, affectionate, chaste,
    matured,
You grew up with me, were a boy with me or a girl with me,   5
I ate with you and slept with you, your body has become not yours
    only nor left my body mine only,
You give me the pleasure of your eyes, face, flesh, as we pass, you
    take of my beard, breast, hands, in return,
I am not to speak to you, I am to think of you when I sit alone or
    wake at night alone,
I am to wait, I do not doubt I am to meet you again,
I am to see to it that I do not lose you.   10

Walt Whitman (1819–1892)

When I Heard the Learn'd Astronomer

When I heard the learn'd astronomer,
When the proofs, the figures, were ranged in columns before me,
When I was shown the charts and diagrams, to add,
    divide, and measure them,
When I sitting heard the astronomer where he
    lectured with much applause in the lecture-room,
How soon unaccountable I became tired and sick,   5
Till rising and gliding out I wandered off by myself,
In the mystical moist night-air, and from time to time,
Looked up in perfect silence at the stars.

Walt Whitman (1819–1892)

Whoever You Are Holding Me Now in Hand

Whoever you are holding me now in hand,
Without one thing all will be useless,
I give you fair warning before you attempt me further,
I am not what you supposed, but far different.

Who is he that would become my follower?   5
Who would sign himself a candidate for my affections?
The way is suspicious, the result uncertain, perhaps destructive,
You would have to give up all else, I alone would expect to be your
    sole and exclusive standard,
Your novitiate would even then be long and exhausting,
The whole past theory of your life and all conformity to the   10
    lives around you would have to be abandon'd,
Therefore release me now before troubling yourself any
    further, let go your hand from my shoulders,
Put me down and depart on your way.

Or else by stealth in some wood for trial,
Or back of a rock in the open air,
(For in any roof'd room of a house I emerge not, nor in   15
    company,
And in libraries I lie as one dumb, a gawk, or unborn, or dead,)
But just possibly with you on a high hill, first watching lest
    any person for miles around approach unawares,
Or possibly with you sailing at sea, or on the beach of the
    sea or some quiet island,
Here to put your lips upon mine I permit you,
With the comrade's long-dwelling kiss or the new   20
    husband's kiss,
For I am the new husband and I am the comrade.

Or if you will, thrusting me beneath your clothing,
Where I may feel the throbs of your heart or rest upon
    your hip,
Carry me when you go forth over land or sea;
For thus merely touching you is enough, is best,   25
And thus touching you would I silently sleep and be carried
    eternally.

But these leaves conning you con at peril,
For these leaves and me you will not understand,

They will elude you at first and still more afterward, I will
    certainly elude you,
Even while you should think you had unquestionably caught   30
    me, behold!
Already you see I have escaped from you.

For it is not for what I have put into it that I have written
    this book,
Nor is it by reading it you will acquire it,
Nor do those know me best who admire me and vauntingly
    praise me,
Nor will the candidates for my love (unless at most a very   35
    few) prove victorious,
Nor will my poems do good only, they will do just as much
    evil, perhaps more,
For all is useless without that which you may guess at many
    times and not hit, that which I hinted at;
Therefore release me and depart on your way.

Walt Whitman (1819–1892)

The Critic

In the Boston Public Library on Boylston Street, where all the bums
    come in stinking from the cold,
there was one who had a battered loose-leaf book he used to scribble
    in for hours on end.
He wrote with no apparent hesitation, quickly, and with
    concentration; his inspiration was inspiring:
you had to look again to realize that he was writing over words that
    were already there —
blocks of cursive etched into the softened paper, interspersed   5
    with poems in print he'd pasted in.
I hated to think of the volumes he'd violated to construct his opus,
    but I liked him anyway,
especially the way he'd often reach the end, close his work
    with weary satisfaction, then open again
and start again: page one, chapter one, his blood-rimmed eyes as
    rapt as David's doing psalms.

C. K. Williams (b. 1936)

Poem

As the cat
climbed over
the top of

the jamcloset   5
first the right
forefoot

carefully
then the hind
stepped down

into the pit of   10
the empty
flowerpot

William Carlos Williams (1883–1963)

Spring and All

By the road to the contagious hospital
under the surge of the blue
mottled clouds driven from the
northeast—a cold wind. Beyond, the
waste of broad, muddy fields   5
brown with dried weeds, standing and fallen
patches of standing water
the scattering of tall trees

All along the road the reddish
purplish, forked, upstanding, twiggy   10
stuff of bushes and small trees
with dead, brown leaves under them
leafless vines—

Lifeless in appearance, sluggish
dazed spring approaches—   15

They enter the new world naked,
cold, uncertain of all

save that they enter. All about them
the cold, familiar wind—

Now the grass, tomorrow   20
the stiff curl of wildcarrot leaf
One by one objects are defined—
It quickens: clarity, outline of leaf

But now the stark dignity of
entrance—Still, the profound change   25
has come upon them: rooted they
grip down and begin to awaken

William Carlos Williams (1883–1963)

The Slow Pacific Swell

Far out of sight forever stands the sea,
Bounding the land with pale tranquillity.
When a small child, I watched it from a hill
At thirty miles or more. The vision still
Lies in the eye, soft blue and far away: 5
The rain has washed the dust from April day;
Paint-brush and lupine lie against the ground;
The wind above the hill-top has the sound
Of distant water in unbroken sky;
Dark and precise the little steamers ply—   10
Firm in direction they seem not to stir.
That is illusion. The artificer
Of quiet, distance holds me in a vise
And holds the ocean steady to my eyes.

Once when I rounded Flattery, the sea   15
Hove its loose weight like sand to tangle me
Upon the washing deck, to crush the hull;
Subsiding, dragged flesh at the bone. The skull
Felt the retreating wash of dreaming hair.
Half drenched in dissolution, I lay bare.   20
I scarcely pulled myself erect; I came
Back slowly, slowly knew myself the same.
That was the ocean. From the ship we saw
Gray whales for miles: the long sweep of the jaw,

The blunt head plunging clean above the wave.   25
And one rose in a tent of sea and gave
A darkening shudder; water fell away;
The whale stood shining, and then sank in spray.

A landsman, I. The sea is but a sound.
I would be near it on a sandy mound,   30
And hear the steady rushing of the deep
While I lay stinging in the sand with sleep.
I have lived inland long. The land is numb.
It stands beneath the feet, and one may come
Walking securely, till the sea extends   35
Its limber margin, and precision ends.
By night a chaos of commingling power,
The whole Pacific hovers hour by hour.
The slow Pacific swell stirs on the sand,
Sleeping to sink away, withdrawing land,   40
Heaving and wrinkled in the moon, and blind;
Or gathers seaward, ebbing out of mind.

                                    Yvor Winters (1900–1968)

A Summer Commentary

When I was young, with sharper sense,
The farthest insect cry I heard
Could stay me; through the trees, intense,
I watched the hunter and the bird.

Where is the meaning that I found?   5
Or was it but a state of mind,
Some old penumbra of the ground,
In which to be but not to find?

Now summer grasses, brown with heat,
Have crowded sweetness through the air;   10
The very roadside dust is sweet;
Even the unshadowed earth is fair.

The soft voice of the nesting dove,
And the dove in soft erratic flight

Like a rapid hand within a glove,   15
Caress the silence and the light.

Amid the rubble, the fallen fruit,
Fermenting in its rich decay,
Smears brandy on the trampling boot
And sends it sweeter on its way.   20

Yvor Winters (1900–1968)

I wandered lonely as a cloud

I wandered lonely as a cloud
That floats on high o'er vales and hills,
When all at once I saw a crowd,
A host, of golden daffodils;
Beside the lake, beneath the trees,   5
Fluttering and dancing in the breeze.

Continuous as the stars that shine
And twinkle on the milky way,
They stretched in never-ending line
Along the margin of a bay: 10
Ten thousand saw I at a glance,
Tossing their heads in sprightly dance.

The waves beside them danced; but they
Outdid the sparkling waves in glee;
A poet could not but be gay,   15
In such a jocund company;
I gazed—and gazed—but little thought
What wealth the show to me had brought:

For oft, when on my couch I lie
In vacant or in pensive mood,   20
They flash upon that inward eye
Which is the bliss of solitude;
And then my heart with pleasure fills,
And dances with the daffodils.

William Wordsworth (1770–1850)

The Solitary Reaper

Behold her, single in the field,
Yon solitary Highland lass!
Reaping and singing by herself;
Stop here, or gently pass!
Alone she cuts and binds the grain,   5
And sings a melancholy strain;
O listen! for the vale profound
Is overflowing with the sound.

No nightingale did ever chant
More welcome notes to weary bands   10
Of travelers in some shady haunt
Among Arabian sands.
A voice so thrilling ne'er was heard
In springtime from the cuckoo-bird,
Breaking the silence of the seas   15
Among the farthest Hebrides.

Will no one tell me what she sings?—
Perhaps the plaintive numbers° flow   measures
For old, unhappy, far-off things,
And battles long ago.   20
Or is it some more humble lay,°   song
Familiar matter of today?
Some natural sorrow, loss, or pain
That has been, and may be again?

Whate'er the theme, the maiden sang   25
As if her song could have no ending;
I saw her singing at her work,
And o'er the sickle bending—
I listened, motionless and still;
And, as I mounted up the hill,   30
The music in my heart I bore
Long after it was heard no more.

William Wordsworth (1770–1850)

The Lake Isle of Innisfree

I will arise and go now, and go to Innisfree,
And a small cabin build there, of clay and wattles made:
Nine bean-rows will I have there, a hive for the honey-bee,
And live alone in the bee-loud glade.

And I shall have some peace there, for peace comes   5
    dropping slow,
Dropping from the veils of the morning to where the cricket sings;
There midnight's all a glimmer, and noon a purple glow,
And evening full of the linnet's wings.

I will arise and go now, for always night and day
I hear lake water lapping with low sounds by the shore;   10
While I stand on the roadway, or on the pavements gray,
I hear it in the deep heart's core.

William Butler Yeats (1865–1939)

Sailing to Byzantium

That is no country for old men. The young
In one another's arms, birds in the trees
—Those dying generations—at their song,
The salmon-falls, the mackerel-crowded seas,
Fish, flesh, or fowl, commend all summer long   5
Whatever is begotten, born, and dies.
Caught in that sensual music all neglect
Monuments of unaging intellect.

An aged man is but a paltry thing,
A tattered coat upon a stick, unless   10
Soul clap its hands and sing, and louder sing
For every tatter in its mortal dress,
Nor is there singing school but studying
Monuments of its own magnificence;
And therefore I have sailed the seas and come   15
To the holy city of Byzantium.

O sages standing in God's holy fire
As in the gold mosaic of a wall,
Come from the holy fire, perne° in a gyre,   spin
And be the singing-masters of my soul.   20
Consume my heart away; sick with desire
And fastened to a dying animal
It knows not what it is; and gather me
Into the artifice of eternity.

Once out of nature I shall never take   25
My bodily form from any natural thing,
But such a form as Grecian goldsmiths make
Of hammered gold and gold enameling
To keep a drowsy Emperor awake;
Or set upon a golden bough to sing   30
To lords and ladies of Byzantium
Of what is past, or passing, or to come.

William Butler Yeats (1865–1939)

(Title) *Byzantium:* Ancient eastern capital of the Roman Empire; in this poem symbolically a
holy city of the imagination. (1) *That:* Ireland, or the ordinary sensual world. (27–31) *such . . .
Byzantium:* The Byzantine emperor Theophilus had made for himself mechanical golden birds
that sang upon the branches of a golden tree.

The Second Coming

Turning and turning in the widening gyre
The falcon cannot hear the falconer;
Things fall apart; the center cannot hold;
Mere anarchy is loosed upon the world,
The blood-dimmed tide is loosed, and everywhere   5
The ceremony of innocence is drowned;
The best lack all conviction, while the worst
Are full of passionate intensity.

Surely some revelation is at hand;
Surely the Second Coming is at hand.   10
The Second Coming! Hardly are those words out
When a vast image out of *Spiritus Mundi*
Troubles my sight: somewhere in sands of the desert
A shape with lion body and the head of a man,
A gaze blank and pitiless as the sun,   15

Is moving its slow thighs, while all about it
Reel shadows of the indignant desert birds.
The darkness drops again; but now I know
That twenty centuries of stony sleep
Were vexed to nightmare by a rocking cradle,   20
And what rough beast, its hour come round at last,
Slouches towards Bethlehem to be born?

William Butler Yeats (1865–1939)

(Title) In Christian legend the prophesied Second Coming may refer either to Christ or to the
Antichrist. Yeats believed in a cyclical theory of history in which one historical era would be
replaced by an opposite kind of era every two thousand years. Here, the anarchy in the world
following World War I (the poem was written in 1919) heralds the end of the Christian era.
(12) *Spiritus Mundi:* the racial memory or collective unconscious mind of mankind (literally,
world spirit).

The Wild Swans at Coole

The trees are in their autumn beauty,
The woodland paths are dry,
Under the October twilight the water
Mirrors a still sky;
Upon the brimming water among the stones   5
Are nine-and-fifty swans.

The nineteenth autumn has come upon me
Since I first made my count;
I saw, before I had well finished,
All suddenly mount   10
And scatter wheeling in great broken rings
Upon their clamorous wings.

I have looked upon those brilliant creatures,
And now my heart is sore,
All's changed since I, hearing at twilight,   15
The first time on this shore,
The bell-beat of their wings above my head,
Trod with a lighter tread.

Unwearied still, lover by lover,
They paddle in the cold   20
Companionable streams or climb the air;
Their hearts have not grown old;

Passion or conquest, wander where they will,
Attend upon them still.

But now they drift on the still water,   25
Mysterious, beautiful;
Among what rushes will they build,
By what lake's edge or pool
Delight men's eyes when I awake some day
To find they have flown away?   30

William Butler Yeats (1865–1939)

(Title) Coole Park, in County Galway, Ireland, was the estate of Lady Augusta Gregory, Yeats's
patroness and friend. Beginning in 1897, Yeats regularly summered there.

Drama

The Elements
of Drama

Chapter One

The Nature of Drama

Drama, like prose fiction, makes use of plot and characters, develops themes, arouses emotional responses, and may be either literary or commercial in its representation of reality.* Like poetry, it may draw upon all the resources of language, including verse. Much drama *is* poetry. But drama has one characteristic peculiar to itself. It is written primarily to be *performed,* not read. It normally presents its action (a) *through* actors, (b) *on* a stage, and (c) *before* an audience. Each of these conditions has important consequences for the nature of drama. Each presents an author with a potentially enormous source of power, and each imposes limitations on the directions a work may take.

Because a play presents its action *through* actors, its impact is direct, immediate, and heightened by the actors' skills. Instead of responding to words on a printed page, spectators see what is done and hear what is said. The experience of the play is registered directly upon their senses. It may therefore be both fuller and more compact. Where the work of prose fiction may tell us what a man looks like in one paragraph, how he moves or speaks in a second, what he says in a third, and how his auditors respond in a fourth, the acted play presents this material all at once. Simultaneous impressions are not temporally separated. Moreover, this experience is interpreted by actors who may be highly skilled in rendering nuances of meaning and strong emotion. Through facial expression, gesture, speech rhythm, and intonation, they may be able to make a speaker's words more expressive than can the reader's unaided imagination. Thus, the performance of a play by skilled actors expertly directed gives the playwright† a tremendous source of power.

---

*Plot, character, theme, symbol, irony, and other elements of literature have been discussed in the Fiction section and the Poetry section

†The word *wright*—as in *playwright, shipwright, wheelwright, cartwright,* and the common surname *Wright*—comes from an Anglo-Saxon word meaning a workman or craftsman. It is related to the verb *wrought* (a past-tense form of *work*) and has nothing whatever to do with the verb *write.*

But playwrights pay a price for this increased power. Of the four major points of view open to the fiction writer, dramatists are practically limited to one—the *objective, or dramatic*. They cannot directly comment on the action or the characters. They cannot enter the minds of their characters and tell us what is going on there. Although there are ways around these limitations, each way has its own limitations. Authorial commentary may be placed in the mouth of a character, but only at the risk of distorting characterization and of leaving the character's reliability uncertain. (Does the character speak for the author or only for herself or himself?) Entry can be made into a character's mind through the conventions of the **soliloquy** and the **aside**. In soliloquies, characters are presented as speaking to themselves—that is, they think out loud. In asides, characters turn from the persons with whom they are conversing to speak directly to (or for the benefit of) the audience, thus letting the audience know what they are really thinking or feeling as opposed to what they pretend to be thinking or feeling. Characters speaking in soliloquy or in asides are always presumed to be telling the truth, to the extent that they know the truth. Both devices can be used very effectively in the theater, but they interrupt the action and are therefore used sparingly. Also, they are inappropriate if the play-wright is working in a strictly realistic mode.

Because a play presents its action *on* a stage, it can forcefully command the spectator's attention. The stage is lighted; the theater is dark; extraneous noises are shut out; spectators are almost literally pinned to their seats; there is nowhere they can go; there is nothing else to look at; there is nothing to distract. The playwright has extraordinary means by which to command the undivided attention of the audience. Unlike the fiction writer or the poet, the playwright is not dependent on the power of words alone.

But the necessity to confine the action to a stage, rather than to the imagination's vast arena, limits the kind of materials playwrights can easily and effectively present. For the most part, they must present human beings in spoken interaction with each other. They cannot easily use materials in which the main interest is in unspoken thoughts and reflections. They cannot present complex actions that involve nonhuman creatures such as attacking lions or charging bulls. They find it more difficult to shift scenes rapidly than writers of prose fiction do. The latter may whisk their readers from heaven to earth and back again in the twinkling of an eye, but playwrights must usually stick to one setting for an extended period of time and may feel constrained to do so for the whole play. Moreover, the events they depict must be of a magnitude appropriate to the stage. They cannot present the movements of armies and warfare on the vast scale that Tolstoy uses in *War and Peace*. They cannot easily present adventures at sea or action on a ski slope.

Conversely, they cannot depict a fly crawling around the rim of a saucer or falling into a cup of milk. At best they can present a general on a hilltop reporting the movements of a battle, or two persons bending over a cup of milk reacting to a fly that the members of the audience cannot see.

The ease, and therefore the rapidity, with which a playwright can change from one scene to another depends, first, on the elaborateness of the stage setting and, second, on the means by which one scene is separated from another. In ancient plays and in many modern ones, stage settings have been extremely simple, depending only on a few easily moved properties or even entirely on the actors' words and the spectators' imaginations. In such cases, change of scenes is made fairly easily, especially if the actors themselves are allowed to carry on and off any properties that may be needed. Various means have been used to separate scenes from each other. In Greek plays, dancing and chanting by a chorus served as a scene divider. More recently, the closing and opening or dropping and raising of a curtain has been the means used. In contemporary theater, with its command of electrical technology, increased reliance has been placed on darkening and illuminating the stage or on darkening one part of it while lighting up another. But even where there is no stage scenery and where the shift of scene is made only by a change in lighting, the playwright can seldom change the setting as rapidly as the writer of prose fiction. On the stage, too-frequent shifts of scene make a play seem jerky. A reader's imagination, on the other hand, can change from one setting to another without even shifting gears.

Because a play presents its action *before* an audience, the experience it creates is communal, and its impact is intensified. Reading a short story or a novel is a private transaction between the reader and a book, but the performance of a play is public. The spectator's response is affected by the presence of other spectators. A comedy becomes funnier when one hears others laughing, a tragedy more moving when others are present to carry the current of feeling. A dramatic experience, in fact, becomes more intense almost exactly to the extent that it is shared and the individual spectator becomes aware that others are having the same experience. This intensification is partly dependent on the size of the audience, but more on their sense of community with each other. A play will be more successful performed before a small audience in a packed auditorium than before a large audience in a half-filled hall.

But, again, the advantage given playwrights by the fact of theatrical performance is paid for by limitations on the material they can present. A play must be able to hold the attention of a group audience. A higher premium than in prose fiction is placed on a well-defined plot, swift exposition, strong conflict, dramatic confrontations. Unless the play is very brief, it is usually divided into parts separated by an intermission or intermissions, and each part works up to its own climax or point of suspense. It is written so that its central meanings may be grasped in a single performance. Spectators at a play cannot back up and rerun a passage whose import they have missed; they cannot, in one night, sit through the whole performance a second time. In addition, playwrights usually avoid extensive use of materials that are purely narrative or lyrical. Long narrative passages are usually interrupted, descriptive passages kept short or eliminated altogether. Primarily, human beings are presented in spoken interaction with each other. Clearly, many of the world's literary masterpieces—stories and poems that enthrall the reader of a book—would not hold the attention of a group audience in a theater.

Drama, then, imposes sharp limitations on its writer but holds out the opportunity for extraordinary force. The successful playwright combines the power of words, the power of fiction, and the power of dramatic technique to make possible the achievement of that force.

REVIEWING CHAPTER ONE

1. Identify the three unique qualities that drama possesses (in contrast to literature written to be read).
2. Explore the advantages and disadvantages of having actors as the medium for the presentation of the dramatic experience.
3. Review the gains and losses imposed by having a drama acted on a stage rather than being presented on the page.
4. Explain how sharing the experience of drama with other audience members is an advantage over viewing it alone, and how the presence of an audience also can impose limitations on what the dramatist can include.

Understanding and Evaluating Drama

As drama may combine the literary resources of both prose fiction and poetry, many of the "Understanding and Evaluating" exercises provided for those two genres (pages 100–102 and 641) may be applicable to drama—except for those directed toward the study of point of view in fiction, since drama always employs the objective or dramatic point of view. Even if a drama is not written in verse, the general questions about diction and figurative language supplied for the elements of poetry may be applicable to drama.

In addition, the variety of dramatic forms and the special nature of drama as a theatrical as well as a literary experience require a set of supplementary questions. Many of these questions will become more meaningful as you read further in the drama section of this book. (Some terms printed in boldface are not defined in this section but are included in the Glossary and Index of Literary Terms, page 1657.)

1. Does the play employ **realistic** or **nonrealistic** conventions? On the spectrum from literalistic imitation of reality to stylized or surrealistic representation, where is the play situated? Are there breaks from the conventions established as a norm in the play? If so, what is the dramatic effect of these departures? Are they meaningful?

2. Is the play a **tragedy** or a **comedy**, a **melodrama** or a **farce**? If a comedy, is it primarily **romantic** or **satiric**? Does it mingle aspects of these types of drama? How important to experiencing the drama is the audience's awareness of the classification of the play?

3. Identify the **protagonist(s)** and **antagonist(s)**. Are there any **foil characters?** What dramatic functions are served by the various minor characters? Do they shed light on the actions or motives of the major characters? Do they advance the **plot** by eliciting actions by others? Do they embody ideas or feelings that illuminate the major characters or the movement of the plot?

4. How is dramatic **suspense** created? Contrast the amount of information possessed by the audience as the play proceeds with the knowledge that various individual characters have: what is the effect of such a contrast?

5. What **themes** does the play present? To what extent do the thematic materials of the play have an effect on the dramatic experience? Does the power of the ideas increase or decrease the pleasure of the theatrical experience? Does the play seem either too **didactic** or insufficient in its presentation of important human concerns?

6. How do the various physical effects—theatrical components such as sets, lights, costuming, makeup, gestures, stage movements, musical effects of song or dance, and so forth—reinforce the meanings and contribute to the emotional effects? By what means does the playwright indicate the nature of these physical effects—explicitly, through stage directions and set descriptions, or implicitly, through dialogue between characters?

7. What amount of time is covered in the action? How much of the action is presented as a report rather than dramatized on stage? Is there a meaning behind the selection of events to be dramatized and those to be reported? Does the play feel loose or tight in its construction? Is that feeling appropriate to the themes and dramatic effects of the play?

8. To what extent does the play employ narration as a means of **dramatic exposition?** What other expository methods does it use? Does the exposition have a function beyond communicating information about prior events? What effects on the audience do the expository methods have?

Susan Glaspell
Trifles

Characters

GEORGE HENDERSON, *the county attorney*
HENRY PETERS, *the sheriff*
MRS. PETERS, *the sheriff's wife*
MRS. HALE, *a neighbor*
MR. HALE, *her husband, a farmer*

The kitchen in the now abandoned farmhouse of John Wright, a gloomy kitchen, and left without having been put in order—unwashed pans under the sink, a loaf of bread outside the bread-box, a dish-towel on the table—other signs of incompleted work. At the rear the outer door opens and the SHERIFF *comes in followed by the* COUNTY ATTORNEY *and* HALE. *The* SHERIFF *and* HALE *are men in middle life, the* COUNTY ATTORNEY *is a young man; all are much bundled up and go at once to the stove. They are followed by the two women—the* SHERIFF'*s wife first; she is a slight wiry woman, with a thin nervous face.* MRS. HALE *is larger and would ordinarily be called more comfortable looking, but she is disturbed now and looks fearfully about as she enters. The women have come in slowly, and stand close together near the door.*

COUNTY ATTORNEY (*rubbing his hands*).   This feels good. Come up to the fire, ladies.

MRS. PETERS (*after taking a step forward*).   I'm not—cold.

SHERIFF (*unbuttoning his overcoat and stepping away from the stove as if to mark the beginning of official business*).   Now, Mr. Hale, before we move things about, you explain to Mr. Henderson just what you saw when you came here yesterday morning.

COUNTY ATTORNEY.   By the way, has anything been moved? Are things just as you left them yesterday?

TRIFLES   First performed in 1916. Susan Glaspell (1882–1948) was born and lived in Davenport, Iowa, earned a degree from Drake University, and worked as a reporter on a newspaper in Des Moines. In that capacity, she had occasion once to visit the kitchen of a woman who was in jail awaiting trial in a murder case. In her early thirties Glaspell moved to the East Coast to concentrate on writing fiction and plays. *Trifles* was produced at Provincetown on Cape Cod, Massachusetts, and a year later Glaspell adapted it as the short story "A Jury of Her Peers" (page 534).

SHERIFF (*looking about*).   It's just the same. When it dropped below zero last night I thought I'd send Frank out this morning to make a fire for us—no use getting pneumonia with a big case on, but I told him not to touch anything except the stove—and you know Frank.

COUNTY ATTORNEY.   Somebody should have been left here yesterday.

SHERIFF.   Oh—yesterday. When I had to send Frank to Morris Center for that man who went crazy—I want you to know I had my hands full yesterday. I knew you could get back from Omaha by today and as long as I went over everything here myself—

COUNTY ATTORNEY.   Well, Mr. Hale, tell just what happened when you came here yesterday morning.

HALE.   Harry and I had started to town with a load of potatoes. We came along the road from my place and as I got here I said, "I'm going to see if I can't get John Wright to go in with me on a party telephone." I spoke to Wright about it once before and he put me off, saying folks talked too much anyway, and all he asked was peace and quiet—I guess you know about how much he talked himself; but I thought maybe if I went to the house and talked about it before his wife, though I said to Harry that I didn't know as what his wife wanted made much difference to John—

COUNTY ATTORNEY.   Let's talk about that later, Mr. Hale. I do want to talk about that, but tell now just what happened when you got to the house.

HALE.   I didn't hear or see anything; I knocked at the door, and still it was all quiet inside. I knew they must be up, it was past eight o'clock. So I knocked again, and I thought I heard somebody say "Come in." I wasn't sure, I'm not sure yet, but I opened the door—this door (*indicating the door by which the two women are still standing*) and there in that rocker— (*pointing to it*) sat Mrs. Wright. (*They all look at the rocker.*)

COUNTY ATTORNEY.   What—was she doing?

HALE.   She was rockin' back and forth. She had her apron in her hand and was kind of—pleating it.

COUNTY ATTORNEY.   And how did she—look?

HALE.   Well, she looked queer.

COUNTY ATTORNEY.   How do you mean—queer?

HALE.   Well, as if she didn't know what she was going to do next. And kind of done up.

COUNTY ATTORNEY.   How did she seem to feel about your coming?

HALE.   Why, I don't think she minded—one way or other. She didn't pay much attention. I said, "How do, Mrs. Wright, it's cold, ain't it?" And she said "Is it?"—and went on kind of pleating at her apron. Well, I was surprised; she didn't ask me to come up to the stove, or to set down, but just sat there, not even looking at me, so I said, "I want to see John." And then she—laughed. I guess you would call it a laugh. I thought of Harry and the team outside, so I said a little sharp: "Can't I see John?" "No," she says, kind o' dull like. "Ain't he home?" says I. "Yes," says she, "he's home." "Then why can't I see him?" I asked her out of patience. "'Cause he's dead," says she. *"Dead?"* says I. She just nodded her head, not getting a bit excited, but rockin' back and forth. "Why—where is he?" says I, not knowing what to say. She just pointed upstairs—like that (*himself pointing to the room above*). I got up, with the idea of going up there. I walked from there to here—then I says, "Why, what did he die of?" "He died of a rope round his neck," says she, and just went on pleatin' at her apron. Well, I went out and called Harry. I thought I might—need help. We went upstairs and there he was lyin'—

COUNTY ATTORNEY.   I think I'd rather have you go into that upstairs, where you can point it all out. Just go on now with the rest of the story.

HALE.   Well, my first thought was to get that rope off. It looked . . . (*Stops, his face twitches.*) . . . but Harry, he went up to him, and he said, "No, he's dead all right, and we'd better not touch anything." So we went back downstairs. She was still sitting that same way. "Has anybody been notified?" I asked. "No," says she, unconcerned. "Who did this, Mrs. Wright?" said Harry. He said it business-like—and she stopped pleatin' of her apron. "I don't know," she says. "You don't *know?*" says Harry. "No," says she. "Weren't you sleepin' in the bed with him?" says Harry. "Yes," says she, "but I was on the inside." "Somebody slipped a rope round his neck and strangled him and you didn't wake up?" says Harry. "I didn't wake up," she said after him. We must 'a looked as if we didn't see how that could be, for after a minute she said, "I sleep sound." Harry was going to ask her more questions, but I said maybe we ought to let her tell her story first to the coroner, or the sheriff, so Harry went fast as he could to Rivers's place, where there's a telephone.

COUNTY ATTORNEY.   And what did Mrs. Wright do when she knew that you had gone for the coroner?

HALE.   She moved from that chair to this over here . . . (*pointing to a small chair in the corner*) . . . and just sat there with her hands held together and looking down. I got a feeling that I ought to make some conversation, so I said I had come in to see if John wanted to put in a telephone, and at that she started to laugh, and then she stopped and looked at me—scared. (*The* COUNTY ATTORNEY, *who has had his notebook out, makes a note.*) I dunno; maybe it wasn't scared. I wouldn't like to say it was. Soon Harry got back, and then Dr. Lloyd came and you, Mr. Peters, and so I guess that's all I know that you don't.

COUNTY ATTORNEY (*looking around*).   I guess we'll go upstairs first —and then out to the barn and around there. (*To the* SHERIFF) You're convinced that there was nothing important here—nothing that would point to any motive?

SHERIFF.   Nothing here but kitchen things. (*The* COUNTY ATTOR-NEY, *after again looking around the kitchen, opens the door of a cupboard closet. He gets up on a chair and looks on a shelf. Pulls his hand away, sticky.*)

COUNTY ATTORNEY.   Here's a nice mess. (*The women draw nearer.*)

MRS. PETERS (*to the other woman*).   Oh, her fruit; it did freeze. (*To the* ATTORNEY) She worried about that when it turned so cold. She said the fire'd go out and her jars would break.

SHERIFF.   Well, can you beat the woman! Held for murder and worryin' about her preserves.

COUNTY ATTORNEY.   I guess before we're through she may have something more serious than preserves to worry about.

HALE.   Well, women are used to worrying over trifles. (*The two women move a little closer together.*)

COUNTY ATTORNEY (*with the gallantry of a young politician*).   And yet, for all their worries, what would we do without the ladies? (*The women do not unbend. He goes to the sink, takes a dipperful of water from the pail and, pouring it into a basin, washes his hands. Starts to wipe them on the roller-towel, turns it for a cleaner place.*) Dirty towels! (*Kicks his foot against the pans under the sink.*) Not much of a housekeeper, would you say, ladies?

MRS. HALE (*stiffly*).   There's a great deal of work to be done on a farm.

COUNTY ATTORNEY.   To be sure. And yet . . . (*with a little bow to her*) . . . I know there are some Dickson County farmhouses which do not have such roller towels. (*He gives it a pull to expose its full length again.*)

MRS. HALE.   Those towels get dirty awful quick. Men's hands aren't always as clean as they might be.

COUNTY ATTORNEY.   Ah, loyal to your sex, I see. But you and Mrs. Wright were neighbors. I suppose you were friends, too.

MRS. HALE (*shaking her head*).   I've not seen much of her of late years. I've not been in this house—it's more than a year.

COUNTY ATTORNEY.   And why was that? You didn't like her?

MRS. HALE (*shaking her head*).   I liked her all well enough. Farmers' wives have their hands full, Mr. Henderson. And then—

COUNTY ATTORNEY.   Yes—?

MRS. HALE (*looking about*).   It never seemed a very cheerful place.

COUNTY ATTORNEY.   No—it's not cheerful. I shouldn't say she had the homemaking instinct.

MRS. HALE.   Well, I don't know as Wright had, either.

COUNTY ATTORNEY.   You mean that they didn't get on very well?

MRS. HALE.   No, I don't mean anything. But I don't think a place'd be any cheerfuler for John Wright's being in it.

COUNTY ATTORNEY.   I'd like to talk more of that a little later. I want to get the lay of things upstairs now. (*He goes to the left, where three steps lead to a stair door.*)

SHERIFF.   I suppose anything Mrs. Peters does'll be all right. She was to take in some clothes for her, you know, and a few little things. We left in such a hurry yesterday.

COUNTY ATTORNEY.   Yes, but I would like to see what you take, Mrs. Peters, and keep an eye out for anything that might be of use to us.

MRS. PETERS.   Yes, Mr. Henderson. (*The women listen to the men's steps on the stairs, then look about the kitchen.*)

MRS. HALE.   I'd hate to have men coming into my kitchen, snooping around and criticizing. (*She arranges the pans under the sink which the* ATTORNEY *had shoved out of place.*)

MRS. PETERS.   Of course it's no more than their duty.

MRS. HALE.   Duty's all right, but I guess that deputy sheriff that came out to make the fire might have got a little of this on. (*Gives the roller towel a pull.*) Wish I'd thought of that sooner. Seems mean to talk about her for not having things slicked up when she had to come away in such a hurry.

MRS. PETERS (*who has gone to a small table in the left corner of the room, and lifted one end of a towel that covers a pan*).   She had bread set. (*Stands still.*)

MRS. HALE (*eyes fixed on a loaf of bread beside the bread-box, which is on a low shelf at the other side of the room. Moves slowly toward it*).   She was going to put this in there. (*Picks up loaf, then abruptly drops it. In a manner of returning to familiar things*) It's a shame about her fruit. I wonder if it's all gone. (*Gets up on the chair and looks.*) I think there's some here that's all right, Mrs. Peters. Yes—here; (*holding it toward the window*) this is cherries, too. (*Looking again*) I declare I believe that's the only one. (*Gets down, bottle in her hand. Goes to the sink and wipes it off on the outside.*) She'll feel awful bad after all her hard work in the hot weather. I remember the afternoon I put up my cherries last summer. (*She puts the bottle on the big kitchen table, center of the room, front table. With a sigh, is about to sit down in the rocking chair. Before she is seated realizes what chair it is: with a slow look at it, steps back. The chair which she has touched rocks back and forth.*)

MRS. PETERS.   Well, I must get those things from the front room closet. (*She goes to the door at the right, but after looking into the other room, steps back.*) You coming with me, Mrs. Hale? You could help me carry them. (*They go in the other room; reappear;* MRS. PETERS *carrying a dress and skirt,* MRS. HALE *following with a pair of shoes.*)

MRS. PETERS.   My, it's cold in there. (*She puts the clothes on the big table and hurries to the stove.*)

MRS. HALE (*examining the skirt*).   Wright was close. I think maybe that's why she kept so much to herself. She didn't even belong to the Ladies' Aid. I suppose she felt she couldn't do her part, and then you don't enjoy things when you feel shabby. She used to wear pretty clothes and be lively, when she was Minnie Foster, one of the town girls singing in the choir. But that—oh, that was thirty years ago. This all you was to take in?

MRS. PETERS.   She said she wanted an apron. Funny thing to want, for there isn't much to get you dirty in jail, goodness knows. But I suppose just to make her feel more natural. She said they was in the top drawer in this cupboard. Yes, here. And then her little shawl that always hung behind the door. (*Opens stair door and looks.*) Yes, here it is. (*Quickly shuts door leading upstairs.*)

MRS. HALE (*abruptly moving toward her*).   Mrs. Peters?

MRS. PETERS.   Yes, Mrs. Hale?

MRS. HALE.   Do you think she did it?

MRS. PETERS (*in a frightened voice*).   Oh, I don't know.

MRS. HALE.   Well, I don't think she did. Asking for an apron and her little shawl. Worrying about her fruit.

MRS. PETERS (*starts to speak, glances up, where footsteps are heard in the room above. In a low voice*).   Mr. Peters says it looks bad for her. Mr. Henderson is awful sarcastic in a speech and he'll make fun of her sayin' she didn't wake up.

MRS. HALE.   Well, I guess John Wright didn't wake up when they was slipping that rope under his neck.

MRS. PETERS.   No, it's strange. It must have been done awful crafty and still. They say it was such a—funny way to kill a man, rigging it all up like that.

MRS. HALE.   That's just what Mr. Hale said. There was a gun in the house. He says that's what he can't understand.

MRS. PETERS.   Mr. Henderson said coming out that what was needed for the case was a motive; something to show anger, or—sudden feeling.

MRS. HALE (*who is standing by the table*).   Well, I don't see any signs of anger around here. (*She puts her hand on the dish towel which lies on the table, stands looking down at table, one half of which is clean, the other half messy.*) It's wiped here. (*Makes a move as if to finish work, then turns and looks at loaf of bread outside the bread-box. Drops towel. In that voice of coming back to familiar things*) Wonder how they are finding things upstairs? I hope she had it a little more red-up° up there. You know, it seems kind of *sneaking*. Locking her up in town and then coming out here and trying to get her own house to turn against her!

red-up: neatened, readied (dialectal)

MRS. PETERS.   But, Mrs. Hale, the law is the law.

MRS. HALE.   I s'pose 'tis. (*Unbuttoning her coat.*) Better loosen up your things, Mrs. Peters. You won't feel them when you go out. (MRS. PETERS *takes off her fur tippet, goes to hang it on hook at back of room, stands looking at the under part of the small corner table.*)

MRS. PETERS.   She was piecing a quilt. (*She brings the large sewing basket and they look at the bright pieces.*)

MRS. HALE.   It's log cabin pattern. Pretty, isn't it? I wonder if she was goin' to quilt it or just knot it? (*Footsteps have been heard coming down the stairs. The* SHERIFF *enters, followed by* HALE *and the* COUNTY ATTORNEY.)

SHERIFF.   They wonder if she was going to quilt it or just knot it. (*The men laugh, the women look abashed.*)

COUNTY ATTORNEY (*rubbing his hands over the stove*).   Frank's fire didn't do much up there, did it? Well, let's go out to the barn and get that cleared up. (*The men go outside.*)

MRS. HALE (*resentfully*).   I don't know as there's anything so strange, our takin' up our time with little things while we're waiting for them to get the evidence. (*She sits down at the big table smoothing out a block with decision.*) I don't see as it's anything to laugh about.

MRS. PETERS (*apologetically*).   Of course they've got awful important things on their minds. (*Pulls up a chair and joins* MRS. HALE *at the table.*)

MRS. HALE (*examining another block*).   Mrs. Peters, look at this one. Here, this is the one she was working on, and look at the sewing! All the rest of it has been so nice and even. And look at this! It's all over the place! Why, it looks as if she didn't know what she was about! (*After she has said this they look at each other, then start to glance at the door. After an instant* MRS. HALE *has pulled at a knot and ripped the sewing.*)

MRS. PETERS.   Oh, what are you doing, Mrs. Hale?

MRS. HALE (*mildly*).   Just pulling out a stitch or two that's not sewed very good. (*Threading a needle.*) Bad sewing always made me fidgety.

MRS. PETERS (*nervously*).   I don't think we ought to touch things.

MRS. HALE.   I'll just finish up this end. (*Suddenly stopping and leaning forward*) Mrs. Peters?

MRS. PETERS.   Yes, Mrs. Hale?

MRS. HALE.   What do you suppose she was so nervous about?

MRS. PETERS.   Oh—I don't know. I don't know as she was nervous. I sometimes sew awful queer when I'm just tired. (MRS. HALE *starts to say something, looks at* MRS. PETERS, *then goes on sewing.*) Well, I must get these things wrapped up. They may be through sooner than we think. (*Putting apron and other things together.*) I wonder where I can find a piece of paper, and string.

MRS. HALE.   In that cupboard, maybe.

MRS. PETERS (*looking in cupboard*).   Why, here's a bird-cage. (*Holds it up.*) Did she have a bird, Mrs. Hale?

MRS. HALE.   Why, I don't know whether she did or not—I've not been here for so long. There was a man around last year selling canaries cheap, but I don't know as she took one; maybe she did. She used to sing real pretty herself.

MRS. PETERS (*glancing around*).   Seems funny to think of a bird here. But she must have had one, or why should she have a cage? I wonder what happened to it?

MRS. HALE.   I s'pose maybe the cat got it.

MRS. PETERS.   No, she didn't have a cat. She's got that feeling some people have about cats—being afraid of them. My cat got in her room and she was real upset and asked me to take it out.

MRS. HALE.   My sister Bessie was like that. Queer, ain't it?

MRS. PETERS (*examining the cage*).   Why, look at this door. It's broke. One hinge is pulled apart.

MRS. HALE (*looking too*).   Looks as if some one must have been rough with it.

MRS. PETERS.   Why, yes. (*She brings the cage forward and puts it on the table.*)

MRS. HALE.   I wish if they're going to find any evidence they'd be about it. I don't like this place.

MRS. PETERS.   But I'm awful glad you came with me, Mrs. Hale. It would be lonesome for me sitting here alone.

MRS. HALE.   It would, wouldn't it? (*Dropping her sewing.*) But I tell you what I do wish, Mrs. Peters. I wish I had come over sometimes when *she* was here. I—(*Looking around the room*)—wish I had.

MRS. PETERS.   But of course you were awful busy, Mrs. Hale—your house and your children.

MRS. HALE.   I could've come. I stayed away because it weren't cheerful—and that's why I ought to have come. I—I've never liked this place. Maybe because it's down in a hollow and you don't see the road. I dunno what it is, but it's a lonesome place and always was. I wish I had come over to see Minnie Foster sometimes. I can see now—(*Shakes her head.*)

MRS. PETERS.   Well, you mustn't reproach yourself, Mrs. Hale. Somehow we just don't see how it is with other folks until—something comes up.

MRS. HALE.   Not having children makes less work—but it makes a quiet house, and Wright out to work all day, and no company when he did come in. Did you know John Wright, Mrs. Peters?

MRS. PETERS.   Not to know him; I've seen him in town. They say he was a good man.

MRS. HALE.   Yes—good; he didn't drink, and kept his word as well as most, I guess, and paid his debts. But he was a hard man, Mrs. Peters. Just to pass the time of day with him. (*Shivers.*) Like a raw wind that gets to the bone. (*Pauses, her eye falling on the cage.*) I should think she would'a wanted a bird. But what do you suppose went wrong with it?

MRS. PETERS.   I don't know, unless it got sick and died. (*She reaches over and swings the broken door, swings it again, both women watch it.*)

MRS. HALE.   You weren't raised round here, were you? (MRS. PETERS *shakes her head.*) You didn't know—her?

MRS. PETERS.   Not till they brought her yesterday.

MRS. HALE.   She—come to think of it, she was kind of like a bird herself—real sweet and pretty, but kind of timid and—fluttery. How—she—did—change. (*Silence; then as if struck by a happy thought and relieved to get back to everyday things.*) Tell you what, Mrs. Peters, why don't you take the quilt in with you? It might take up her mind.

MRS. PETERS.   Why, I think that's a real nice idea, Mrs. Hale. There couldn't possibly be any objection to it, could there? Now, just what would I take? I wonder if her patches are in here—and her things. (*They look in the sewing basket.*)

MRS. HALE.   Here's some red. I expect this has got sewing things in it. (*Brings out a fancy box.*) What a pretty box. Looks like something somebody would give you. Maybe her scissors are in here. (*Opens box. Suddenly puts her hand to her nose.*) Why—(MRS. PETERS *bends nearer, then turns her face away.*) There's something wrapped up in this piece of silk.

MRS. PETERS.   Why, this isn't her scissors.

MRS. HALE (*lifting the silk*).   Oh, Mrs. Peters—it's—(MRS. PETERS *bends closer.*)

MRS. PETERS.   It's the bird.

MRS. HALE (*jumping up*).   But, Mrs. Peters—look at it. Its neck! Look at its neck! It's all—other side *to*.

MRS. PETERS.   Somebody—wrung—its neck. (*Their eyes meet. A look of growing comprehension, of horror. Steps are heard outside.* MRS. HALE *slips box under quilt pieces, and sinks into her chair. Enter* SHERIFF *and* COUNTY ATTORNEY. MRS. PETERS *rises.*)

COUNTY ATTORNEY (*as one turning from serious things to little pleasantries*).   Well, ladies, have you decided whether she was going to quilt it or knot it?

MRS. PETERS.   We think she was going to—knot it.

COUNTY ATTORNEY.   Well, that's interesting, I'm sure. (*Seeing the bird-cage*) Has the bird flown?

MRS. HALE (*putting more quilt pieces over the box*).   We think the— cat got it.

COUNTY ATTORNEY (*preoccupied*).   Is there a cat? (MRS. HALE *glances in a quick covert way at* MRS. PETERS.)

MRS. PETERS.   Well, not now. They're superstitious, you know. They leave.

COUNTY ATTORNEY (*to* SHERIFF PETERS, *continuing an interrupted conversation*).   No sign at all of anyone having come in from the outside. Their own rope. Now let's go up again and go over it piece by piece. (*They start upstairs.*) It would have to have been some one who knew just the—(MRS. PETERS *sits down. The two women sit there not looking at one another, but as if peering into something and at the same time holding back. When they talk now it is in the manner of feeling their way over strange ground, as if afraid of what they are saying, but as if they cannot help saying it.*)

MRS. HALE.   She liked the bird. She was going to bury it in that pretty box.

MRS. PETERS (*in a whisper*).   When I was a girl—my kitten—there was a boy took a hatchet, and before my eyes—and before I could get there—(*Covers her face an instant.*) If they hadn't held me back I would have—(*Catches herself, looks upstairs where steps are heard, falters weakly*)—hurt him.

MRS. HALE (*with a slow look around her*).   I wonder how it would seem never to have any children around. (*Pause*) No, Wright wouldn't like the bird—a thing that sang. She used to sing. He killed that, too.

MRS. PETERS (*moving uneasily*).   We don't know who killed the bird.

MRS. HALE.   I knew John Wright.

MRS. PETERS.   It was an awful thing was done in this house that night, Mrs. Hale. Killing a man while he slept, slipping a rope around his neck that choked the life out of him.

MRS. HALE.   His neck. Choked the life out of him. (*Her hand goes out and rests on the bird-cage.*)

MRS. PETERS (*with rising voice*).   We don't know who killed him. We don't *know*.

MRS. HALE (*her own feeling not interrupted*).   If there'd been years and years of nothing, then a bird to sing to you, it would be awful—still, after the bird was still.

MRS. PETERS (*something within her speaking*).   I know what stillness is. When we homesteaded in Dakota, and my first baby died—after he was two years old, and me with no other then—

MRS. HALE (*moving*). How soon do you suppose they'll be through, looking for the evidence?

MRS. PETERS. I know what stillness is. (*Pulling herself back*) The law has got to punish crime, Mrs. Hale.

MRS. HALE (*not as if answering that*). I wish you'd seen Minnie Foster when she wore a white dress with blue ribbons and stood up there in the choir and sang. (*A look around the room.*) Oh, I *wish* I'd come over here once in a while. That was a crime! That was a crime! Who's going to punish that?

MRS. PETERS (*looking upstairs*). We mustn't—take on.

MRS. HALE. I might have known she needed help! I know how things can be—for women. I tell you, it's queer, Mrs. Peters. We live close together and we live far apart. We all go through the same things—it's all just a different kind of the same thing. (*Brushes her eyes, noticing the bottle of fruit, reaches out for it.*) If I was you I wouldn't tell her her fruit was gone. Tell her it *ain't*. Tell her it's all right. Take this in to prove it to her. She—she may never know whether it was broke or not.

MRS. PETERS (*takes the bottle, looks about for something to wrap it in; takes petticoat from the clothes brought from the other room, very nervously begins winding this around the bottle. In a false voice*). My, it's a good thing the men couldn't hear us. Wouldn't they just laugh. Getting all stirred up over a little thing like a—dead canary. As if that could have anything to do with—with—wouldn't they *laugh!* (*The men are heard coming downstairs.*)

MRS. HALE (*under her breath*). Maybe they would—maybe they wouldn't.

COUNTY ATTORNEY. No, Peters, it's all perfectly clear except a reason for doing it. But you know juries when it comes to women. If there was some definite thing. Something to show—something to make a story about—a thing that would connect up with this strange way of doing it. (*The women's eyes meet for an instant. Enter HALE from outer door.*)

HALE. Well, I've got the team around. Pretty cold out there.

COUNTY ATTORNEY. I'm going to stay here a while by myself. (*To the SHERIFF*) You can send Frank out for me, can't you? I want to go over everything. I'm not satisfied that we can't do better.

SHERIFF. Do you want to see what Mrs. Peters is going to take in? (*The ATTORNEY goes to the table, picks up the apron, laughs.*)

COUNTY ATTORNEY. Oh, I guess they're not very dangerous things the ladies have picked out. (*Moves a few things about, disturbing the quilt pieces which cover the box. Steps back.*) No, Mrs. Peters doesn't need supervising. For that matter, a sheriff's wife is married to the law. Ever think of it that way, Mrs. Peters?

MRS. PETERS.   Not—just that way.

SHERIFF (*chuckling*).   Married to the law. (*Moves toward the other room.*) I just want you to come in here a minute, George. We ought to take a look at these windows.

COUNTY ATTORNEY (*scoffingly*).   Oh, windows!

SHERIFF.   We'll be right out, Mr. Hale. (HALE *goes outside. The* SHERIFF *follows the* COUNTY ATTORNEY *into the other room. Then* MRS. HALE *rises, hands tight together, looking intensely at* MRS. PETERS, *whose eyes make a slow turn, finally meeting* MRS. HALE's. *A moment* MRS. HALE *holds her, then her own eyes point the way to where the box is concealed. Suddenly* MRS. PETERS *throws back quilt pieces and tries to put the box in the handbag she is carrying. It is too big. She opens box, starts to take bird out, cannot touch it, goes to pieces, stands there helpless. Sound of a knob turning in the other room.* MRS. HALE *snatches the box and puts it in the pocket of her big coat. Enter* COUNTY ATTORNEY *and* SHERIFF.)

COUNTY ATTORNEY (*facetiously*).   Well, Henry, at least we found out that she was not going to quilt it. She was going to—what is it you call it, ladies?

MRS. HALE (*her hand against her pocket*).   We call it—knot it, Mr. Henderson.

QUESTIONS

1. What individualizing characteristics do you find in the five people in the play? What contrasts are drawn between the men as a group, and the women? In what sense does the title contribute to these contrasts?
2. What contrasts exist between the two women? Is one of them clearly the protagonist? Identify the antagonist.
3. Describe the life that Mrs. Wright must have lived. What is the importance of her having been a singer?
4. Was the murder in any way justified? Why do the women conceal the evidence?
5. It is a common practice for plays to be made out of novels or stories, but unusual for the play to precede the story. Compare this play with the story "A Jury of Her Peers" (page 534). Which is clearer in its presentation of action and feelings? Which has a more direct emotional impact on the audience or reader? Discuss the differences between hearing the short story read aloud by an experienced performer and seeing the play acted by experienced actors.

August Strindberg
The Stronger

Characters

MRS. X, *an actress, married*
MISS Y, *an actress, unmarried*
A WAITRESS

SCENE. *The corner of a ladies' café. Two little iron tables, a red velvet sofa, several chairs. Enter* MRS. X, *dressed in winter clothes, carrying a Japanese basket on her arm.* MISS Y *sits with a half-empty beer bottle before her, reading an illustrated paper, which she changes later for another.*

MRS. X.   Good afternoon, Amelia. You're sitting here alone on Christmas eve like a poor bachelor!

MISS Y.   (*Looks up, nods, and resumes her reading.*)

MRS. X.   Do you know it really hurts me to see you like this, alone, in a café, and on Christmas eve, too. It makes me feel as I did one time when I saw a bridal party in a Paris restaurant, and the bride sat reading a comic paper, while the groom played billiards with the witnesses. Huh, thought I, with such a beginning, what will follow, and what will be the end? He played billiards on his wedding eve! (MISS Y *starts to speak.*) And she read a comic paper, you mean? Well, they are not altogether the same thing. (*A* WAITRESS *enters, places a cup of chocolate before* MRS. X *and goes out.*)

MRS. X.   You know what, Amelia! I believe you would have done better to have kept him! Do you remember, I was the first to say "Forgive him"? Do you remember that? You would be married now and have a home. Remember that Christmas when you went out to visit your fiancé's parents in the country? How you gloried in the happiness of home life and really longed to quit the theater forever? Yes, Amelia dear, home is the best of all—next to the theater—and as for children—well, you don't understand that.

THE STRONGER   Written and first performed in 1889. English translation by Edith and Warner Oland. August Strindberg (1849–1912) was born in Stockholm, Sweden, published his first play in 1870, and in 1875–1876 began an intense love affair with an aspiring actress, Siri von Essen, then the Baroness Wrangel, whom he married in 1877 after her divorce. Though the marriage produced four children, it was a troubled one, largely because of Strindberg's irrational jealousies. *The Stronger,* though written while husband and wife were living apart, was done for a joint theatrical project, and Siri played Mrs. X in the opening production.

MISS Y. (*Looks up scornfully.*)

MRS. X (*sips a few spoonfuls of the cup, then opens her basket and shows Christmas presents*).   Now you shall see what I bought for my piggywigs. (*Takes up a doll.*) Look at this! This is for Lisa, ha! Do you see how she can roll her eyes and turn her head, eh? And here is Maja's popgun. (*Loads it and shoots at Miss Y.*)

MISS Y. (*Makes a startled gesture.*)

MRS. X.   Did I frighten you? Do you think I would like to shoot you, eh? On my soul, if I don't think you did! If you wanted to shoot *me* it wouldn't be so surprising, because I stood in your way—and I know you can never forget that—although I was absolutely innocent. You still believe I intrigued and got you out of the Stora theater, but I didn't. I didn't do that, although you think so. Well, it doesn't make any difference what I say to you. You still believe I did it. (*Takes up a pair of embroidered slippers.*) And these are for my better half. I embroidered them myself—I can't bear tulips, but he wants tulips on everything.

MISS Y. (*Looks up ironically and curiously.*)

MRS. X (*putting a hand in each slipper*).   See what little feet Bob has! What? And you should see what a splendid stride he has! You've never seen him in slippers! (MISS Y *laughs aloud.*) Look! (*She makes the slippers walk on the table.* MISS Y *laughs loudly.*) And when he is grumpy he stamps like this with his foot. "What! damn those servants who can never learn to make coffee. Oh, now those creatures haven't trimmed the lamp wick properly!" And then, there are drafts on the floor and his feet are cold. "Ugh, how cold it is; the stupid idiots can never keep the fire going." (*She rubs the slippers together, one sole over the other.*)

MISS Y. (*Shrieks with laughter.*)

MRS. X.   And then he comes home and has to hunt for his slippers which Marie has stuck under the chiffonier—oh, but it's sinful to sit here and make fun of one's husband this way when he is kind and a good little man. You ought to have had such a husband, Amelia. What are you laughing at? What? What? And you see he's true to me. Yes, I'm sure of that, because he told me himself—what are you laughing at?—that when I was touring in Norway that brazen Frederika came and wanted to seduce him! Can you fancy anything so infamous? (*Pause.*) I'd have torn her eyes out if she had come to see him when I was at home. (*Pause.*) It was lucky that Bob told me about it himself and that it didn't reach me through gossip. (*Pause.*) But would you believe it, Frederika wasn't the only one! I don't know why, but the women are crazy about my husband. They must think he has influence about getting them theatrical engagements, because he is connected with the government. Perhaps you were after him yourself. I didn't use to trust you any too much. But now I know he never bothered his head about you, and you always seemed to have a grudge against him someway. (*Pause. They look at each other in a puzzled way.*)

MRS. X.   Come and see us this evening, Amelia, and show us that you're not put out with us—not put out with me at any rate. I don't know, but I think it would be uncomfortable to have you for an enemy. Perhaps it's because I stood in your way (*more slowly*) or—I really—don't know why—in particular. (*Pause.* MISS Y *stares at* MRS. X *curiously.*)

MRS. X (*thoughtfully*).   Our acquaintance has been so queer. When I saw you for the first time I was afraid of you, so afraid that I didn't dare let you out of my sight; no matter when or where, I always found myself near you—I didn't dare have you for an enemy, so I became your friend. But there was always discord when you came to our house, because I saw that my husband couldn't endure you, and the whole thing seemed as awry to me as an ill-fitting gown—and I did all I could to make him friendly toward you, but with no success until you became engaged. Then came a violent friendship between you, so that it looked all at once as though you both dared show your real feelings only when you were secure—and then—how was it later? I didn't get jealous—strange to say! And I remember at the christening, when you acted as godmother, I made him kiss you—he did so, and you became so confused—as it were; I didn't notice it then—didn't think about it later either—have never thought about it until—now! (*Rises suddenly.*) Why are you silent? You haven't said a word this whole time, but you have let me go on talking! You have sat there, and your eyes have reeled out of me all these thoughts which lay like raw silk in its cocoon—thoughts—suspicious thoughts, perhaps. Let me see—why did you break your engagement? Why do you never come to our house any more? Why won't you come to see us tonight?

MISS Y.   (*Appears as if about to speak.*)

MRS. X.   Hush, you needn't speak—I understand it all! It was because—and because—and because! Yes, yes! Now all the accounts balance. That's it. Fie, I won't sit at the same table with you. (*Moves her things to another table.*) That's the reason I had to embroider tulips—which I hate—on his slippers, because you are fond of tulips; that's why (*throws slippers on the floor*) we go to Lake Mälarn in the summer, because you don't like salt water; that's why my boy is named Eskil—because it's your father's name; that's why I wear your colors, read your authors, eat your favorite dishes, drink your drinks—chocolate, for instance; that's why—oh—my God—it's terrible, when I think about it; it's terrible. Everything, everything came from you to me, even your passions. Your soul crept into mine, like a worm into an apple, ate and ate, bored and bored, until nothing was left but the rind and a little black dust within. I wanted to get away from you, but I couldn't; you lay like a snake and charmed me with your black eyes; I felt that when I lifted my wings they only dragged me down; I lay in the water with bound feet, and the stronger I strove to keep up the deeper I worked myself down, down, until I sank to the bottom, where you lay like a giant crab to clutch me in your claws—and there I am lying now.

I hate you, hate you, hate you! And you only sit there silent—silent and indifferent; indifferent whether it's new moon or waning moon, Christmas or New Year's, whether others are happy or unhappy; without power to hate or to love; as quiet as a stork by a rat hole—you couldn't scent your prey and capture it, but you could lie in wait for it! You sit here in your corner of the café—did you know it's called "The Rat Trap" for you?—and read the papers to see if misfortune hasn't befallen someone, to see if someone hasn't been given notice at the theater, perhaps; you sit here and calculate about your next victim and reckon on your chances of recompense like a pilot in a shipwreck. Poor Amelia, I pity you, nevertheless, because I know you are unhappy, unhappy like one who has been wounded, and angry because you are wounded. I can't be angry with you, no matter how much I want to be—because you come out the weaker one. Yes, all that with Bob doesn't trouble me. What is that to me, after all? And what difference does it make whether I learned to drink chocolate from you or someone else. (*Sips a spoonful from her cup.*) Besides, chocolate is very healthful. And if you taught me how to dress—*tant mieux!*°—that has only made me more attractive to my husband; so you lost and I won there. Well, judging by certain signs, I believe you have already lost him; and you certainly intended that I should leave him—do as you did with your fiancé and regret as you now regret; but, you see, I don't do that—we mustn't be too exacting. And why should I take only what no one else wants?

Perhaps, take it all in all, I am at this moment the stronger one. You received nothing from me, but you gave me much. And now I seem like a thief since you have awakened and find I possess what is your loss. How could it be otherwise when everything is worthless and sterile in your hands? You can never keep a man's love with your tulips and your passions—but I can keep it. You can't learn how to live from your authors, as I have learned. You have no little Eskil to cherish, even

---

tant mieux!: so much the better

if your father's name was Eskil. And why are you always silent, silent, silent? I thought that was strength, but perhaps it is because you have nothing to say! Because you never think about anything! (*Rises and picks up slippers.*) Now I'm going home—and take the tulips with me—*your* tulips! You are unable to learn from another; you can't bend—therefore, you broke like a dry stalk. But I won't break! Thank you, Amelia, for all your good lessons. Thanks for teaching my husband how to love. Now I'm going home to love him. (*Goes.*)

QUESTIONS

1. Much of the action of this play lies in the past, but to reconstruct that action we must separate what is true from what is untrue and from what may or may not be true in Mrs. X's account of it. Point out places where Mrs. X (a) is probably lying, (b) is clearly rationalizing, (c) has very likely or has certainly been deceived, (d) is clearly giving an accurate account. In each case, explain your reason for your opinion. To what extent can we be certain of what has happened in the past?

2. Put together as reliable an account as possible of the past relationships of Mrs. X, her husband, and Miss Y. How did the friendship between the two women start? How did it proceed? How and why did it terminate? In what two ways have the two women consciously or unconsciously been rivals? In what way and by what means has Miss Y influenced Mrs. X's behavior and her life?

3. In a sense the play has two plots, one in the past and one in the present, though the plot in the present is really only the culminating phase of that in the past. At what point does Mrs. X discover something about the past that she had not known before? What is it she discovers? How does she react to the discovery? Why can this discovery be called the turning point of the play?

4. Trace the successive attitudes expressed by Mrs. X toward Miss Y, together with the real attitudes underlying the expressed attitudes. At what points do the expressed attitudes and the real attitudes coincide? At what points do they clearly differ?

5. What kind of person is Mrs. X? Characterize her.

6. Although Miss Y says nothing during the course of the play, we can infer a good deal about her from her reactions to Mrs. X, from her past actions, and from what Mrs. X says about her (cautiously interpreted). What kind of person is she? How, especially, does she differ from Mrs. X? What is the nature of her present life? Would this role be easy or difficult to act?

7. Although Mr. X never appears, he also is an important character in the play. What kind of man is he?

8. To which character does the title refer? Consider carefully before answering, and support your answer with a reasoned argument, including a definition of what is meant by "stronger."

Jane Martin
Beauty

Characters

CARLA
BETHANY

CARLA.   In love with me? You're in love with me? Could you describe yourself again? Uh-huh. Uh-huh. And you spoke to me? (*A knock at the door.*) Listen, I always hate to interrupt a marriage proposal, but . . . could you possibly hold that thought? (*Puts phone down and goes to door.* BETHANY, *the same age as* CARLA, *and a friend is there. She carries the sort of Mideastern lamp we know of from Aladdin.*)

BETHANY.   Thank God you were home. I mean, you're not going to believe this!
CARLA.   Somebody on the phone. (*Goes back to it.*)
BETHANY.   I mean, I just had a beach urge, so I told them at work my uncle was dying . . .
CARLA (*motions to* BETHANY *for quiet*).   And you were the one in the leather jacket with the tattoo? What was the tattoo? (CARLA *again asks* BETHANY, *who is gesturing wildly that she should hang up, to cool it.*) Look, a screaming eagle from shoulder to shoulder, maybe. There were a lot of people in the bar.
BETHANY (*gesturing and mouthing*).   I have to get back to work.
CARLA (*on phone*).   See, the thing is, I'm probably not going to marry someone. I can't remember . . . particularly when I don't drink. Sorry. Sorry. Sorry. (*She hangs up.*) Madness.
BETHANY.   So I ran out to the beach . . .
CARLA.   This was some guy I never met who apparently offered me a beer . . .
BETHANY.   . . . low tide and this . . . (*The lamp.*) . . . was just sitting there, lying there . . .
CARLA.   . . . and he tracks me down . . .
BETHANY.   . . . on the beach, and I lift this lid thing . . .
CARLA.   . . . and seriously proposes marriage.
BETHANY.   . . . and a genie comes out.

BEAUTY   First performed in 2000. "Jane Martin" is the pen name of a writer who has chosen to remain anonymous. She refuses to make a public appearance, to be interviewed, or to have a photograph published. All of her plays were first produced by the Actors Theatre of Louisville at the annual Humana Festival of New American Plays beginning in 1981.

CARLA.   I mean, that's twice in a . . . what?

BETHANY.   A genie comes out of this thing.

CARLA.   A genie?

BETHANY.   I'm not kidding, the whole Disney kind of thing, swirling smoke, and then this twenty-foot-high, see-through guy in like an Arabian outfit.

CARLA.   Very funny.

BETHANY.   Yes, funny, but twenty feet high! I look up and down the beach, I'm alone. I don't have my pepper spray or my hand alarm. You know me, when I'm petrified I joke. I say his voice is too high for Robin Williams, and he says he's a castrati. Naturally. Who else would I meet?

CARLA.   What's a castrati?

BETHANY.   You know . . . (*The appropriate gesture.*)

CARLA.   Bethany, dear one, I have three modeling calls. I am meeting Ralph Lauren!

BETHANY.   Okay, good. Ralph Lauren. Look, I am not kidding!

CARLA.   You're not kidding what?!

BETHANY.   There is a genie in this thingamajig.

CARLA.   Uh-huh. I'll be back around eight.

BETHANY.   And he offered me *wishes*!

CARLA.   Is this some elaborate practical joke because it's my birthday?

BETHANY.   No, happy birthday, but I'm like crazed because I'm on this deserted beach with a twenty-foot-high, see-through genie, so like sarcastically . . . you know how I need a new car . . . I said fine, gimme 25,000 dollars . . .

CARLA.   On the beach with the genie?

BETHANY.   Yeah, right, exactly, and it rains down out of the sky.

CARLA.   Oh sure.

BETHANY (*pulling a wad out of her purse*).   Count it, those are thousands. I lost one in the surf. (CARLA *sees the top bill. Looks at* BETHANY, *who nods encouragement.* CARLA *thumbs through them.*)

CARLA.   These look real.

BETHANY.   Yeah.

CARLA.   And they rained down out of the sky?

BETHANY.   Yeah.

CARLA.   You've been really strange lately, are you dealing?

BETHANY.   Dealing what, I've even given up chocolate.

CARLA.   Let me see the genie.

BETHANY.   Wait, wait.

CARLA.   Bethany, I don't have time to screw around. Let me see the genie or let me go on my appointments.

BETHANY.   Wait! So I pick up the money . . . see, there's sand on the money . . . and I'm like nuts so I say, you know, "Okay, look, ummm, big guy, my uncle is in the hospital" . . . because as you know when I said to the people at work my uncle was dying, I was on one level telling the truth although it had nothing to do with the beach, but he was in Intensive Care after the accident, and that's on my mind, so I say, okay, Genie, heal my uncle . . . which is like impossible given he was hit by two trucks, and the genie says, "Yes, Master" . . . like they're supposed to say, and he goes into this like kind of whirlwind, kicking up sand and stuff, and I'm like, "Oh my God" and the air clears, and he bows, you know, and says, "It is done, Master," and I say, "Okay, whatever-you-are, I'm calling on my cell phone," and I get it out and I get this doctor who is like dumbstruck who says my uncle came to, walked out of Intensive Care and left the hospital! I'm not kidding, Carla.

CARLA.   On your mother's grave?

BETHANY.   On my mother's grave. (*They look at each other.*)

CARLA.   Let me see the genie.

BETHANY.   No, no look, that's the whole thing . . . I was just, like, reacting, you know, responding, and that's already two wishes . . . although I'm really pleased about my uncle, the $25,000 thing, I could have asked for $10 million, and there is only one wish left.

CARLA.   So ask for $10 million.

BETHANY.   I don't think so. I don't think so. I mean, I gotta focus in here. Do you have a sparkling water?

CARLA.   No. Bethany, I'm missing Ralph Lauren now. Very possibly my one chance to go from catalogue model to the very, very big time, so, if you are joking, stop joking.

BETHANY.   Not joking. See, see, the thing is, I know what I want. In my guts. Yes. Underneath my entire bitch of a life is this unspoken, ferocious, all-consuming urge . . .

CARLA (*trying to get her to move this along*). Ferocious, all-consuming urge . . .

BETHANY.   I want to be like you.

CARLA.   Me?

BETHANY.   Yes.

CARLA.   Half the time you don't even like me.

BETHANY.   Jealous. The ogre of jealousy.

CARLA.   You're the one with the $40,000 job straight out of school. You're the one who has published short stories. I'm the one hanging on by her fingernails in modeling. The one who has creeps calling her on the phone. The one who had to have a nose job.

BETHANY.   I want to be beautiful.

CARLA. You are beautiful.

BETHANY. Carla, I'm not beautiful.

CARLA. You have charm. You have personality. You know perfectly well you're pretty.

BETHANY. "Pretty," see, that's it. Pretty is the minor leagues of beautiful. Pretty is what people discover about you after they know you. Beautiful is what knocks them out across the room. Pretty, you get called a couple of times a year; *beautiful* is twenty-four hours a day.

CARLA. Yeah? So?

BETHANY. So?! We're talking *beauty* here. Don't say "So?" Beauty is the real deal. You are the center of any moment of your life. People stare. Men flock. I've seen you get offered discounts on makeup for no reason. Parents treat beautiful children better. Studies show your income goes up. You can have sex anytime you want it. Men have to know me. That takes up to a year. I'm continually horny.

CARLA. Bethany, I don't even like sex. I can't have a conversation without men coming on to me. I have no privacy. I get hassled on the street. They start pressuring me from the beginning. Half the time, it never occurs to them to start with a conversation. Smart guys like you. You've had three long-term relationships, and you're only twenty-three. I haven't had one. The good guys, the smart guys are scared to death of me. I'm surrounded by male bimbos who think a preposition is when you go to school away from home. I have no woman friends except you. I don't even want to talk about this!

BETHANY. I knew you'd say something like this. See, you're "in the club" so you can say this. It's the way beauty functions as an elite. You're trying to keep it all for yourself.

CARLA. I'm trying to tell you it's no picnic.

BETHANY. But it's what everybody wants. It's the nasty secret at large in the world. It's the unspoken tidal desire in every room and on every street. It's the unspoken, the soundless whisper . . . millions upon millions of people longing hopelessly and forever to stop being whatever they are and be beautiful, but the difference between those ardent multitudes and me is that I have a goddamn genie and one more wish!

CARLA. Well, it's not what I want. This is me, Carla. I have never read a whole book. Page six, I can't remember page four. The last thing I read was *The Complete Idiot's Guide to WordPerfect*. I leave dinner parties right after the dessert because I'm out of conversation. You know the dumb blond joke about the application where it says, "Sign here," she put Sagittarius? I've done that. Only beautiful guys approach me, and that's because they want to borrow my eye shadow. I barely exist outside a mirror! You don't want to *be me*.

BETHANY.   None of you tell the truth. That's why you have no friends. We can all see you're just trying to make us feel better because we aren't in your league. This only proves to me it should be my third wish. Money can only buy things. Beauty makes you the center of the universe. (BETHANY *picks up the lamp.*)

CARLA.   Don't do it. Bethany, don't wish it! I am telling you you'll regret it. (BETHANY *lifts the lid. There is a tremendous crash, and the lights go out. Then they flicker and come back up, revealing* BETHANY *and* CARLA *on the floor where they have been thrown by the explosion. We don't realize it at first, but they have exchanged places.*)

CARLA/BETHANY.   Oh God.

BETHANY/CARLA.   Oh God.

CARLA/BETHANY.   Am I bleeding? Am I dying?

BETHANY/CARLA.   I'm so dizzy. You're not bleeding.

CARLA/BETHANY.   Neither are you.

BETHANY/CARLA.   I feel so weird.

CARLA/BETHANY.   Me too. I feel . . . (*Looking at her hands.*) Oh, my God, I'm wearing your jewelry. I'm wearing your nail polish.

BETHANY/CARLA.   I know I'm over here, but I can see myself over there.

CARLA/BETHANY.   I'm wearing your dress. I have your legs!!

BETHANY/CARLA.   These aren't my shoes. I can't meet Ralph Lauren wearing these shoes!

CARLA/BETHANY.   I wanted to be beautiful, but I didn't want to be you.

BETHANY/CARLA.   Thanks a lot!!

CARLA/BETHANY.   I've got to go. I want to pick someone out and get laid.

BETHANY/CARLA.   You can't just walk out of here in my body!

CARLA/BETHANY.   Wait a minute. Wait a minute. What's eleven eighteenths of 1,726?

BETHANY/CARLA.   Why?

CARLA/BETHANY.   I'm a public accountant. I want to know if you have my brain.

BETHANY/CARLA.   One hundred thirty-two and a half.

CARLA/BETHANY.   You have my brain.

BETHANY/CARLA.   What shade of Rubenstein lipstick does Cindy Crawford wear with teal blue?

CARLA/BETHANY.   Raging Storm.

BETHANY/CARLA.   You have my brain. You poor bastard.

CARLA/BETHANY.   I don't care. Don't you see?

BETHANY/CARLA.   See what?

CARLA/BETHANY.   We both have the one thing, the one and only thing everybody wants.

BETHANY/CARLA.   What is that?

CARLA/BETHANY.   It's better than beauty for me; it's better than brains for you.

BETHANY/CARLA.   What? What?!

CARLA/BETHANY.   Different problems.

Blackout.

QUESTIONS

1. Bethany and Carla have distinctive speaking styles. Using examples, define these two styles. Can you relate them to the two main characteristics that the women possess?
2. What is the relevance of Carla's telephone conversation to the theme of the play?
3. The play presents the advantages and disadvantages of being beautiful and of being intelligent. What are they?
4. The play is in part a fantasy (review the two basic approaches to fantasy in chapter 6 of the fiction section of this book, pp. 292–294). Which of the approaches does this play employ? That discussion of fantasy asserts that although impossible, a fantasy may embody a truth. What truth lies behind the genie's granting three wishes?
5. The play ends with a "punch line," an unexpected final statement. How relevant to the events and conversations is the statement that "the one and only thing everybody wants . . . [is] different problems"?
6. The play suggests that beauty and brains are inevitably opposite qualities. Do you agree with that idea? By what means does the play make that seem plausible?

José Rivera

Tape

Characters

VISITOR
NO NAME
VOICE

(*A small, dark room. No windows. One door. A* VISITOR *is being led in by* NO NAME. *In the room is a simple wooden table and a chair. On the table is a large reel-to-reel tape recorder, a glass of water, and a pitcher of water.*)

VISITOR.   Fucking dark in here.
NO NAME.   I'm sorry.
VISITOR.   No, I know it's not your fault.
NO NAME.   Those stupid lights . . .
VISITOR.   What does it matter now?
NO NAME.   . . . not very bright.
VISITOR.   Who cares?
NO NAME.   We don't want to cause you any undue suffering. If it's too dark in here, I'll make sure one of the other attendants replaces the light bulb. (*The* VISITOR *looks at* NO NAME.)
VISITOR.   Any "undue suffering"?
NO NAME.   That's right. (*The* VISITOR *looks at the room.*)
VISITOR.   Is this where I'll be?
NO NAME.   That's right.
VISITOR.   Will you be outside?
NO NAME.   Yes.
VISITOR.   The entire time?
NO NAME.   The entire time.
VISITOR.   Is it? Boring?
NO NAME (*as if not understanding*).   I'm sorry?
VISITOR.   Is it boring?
NO NAME (*soft smile*).   It's my job. It's what I do.
VISITOR.   Oh. (*Beat*) Will I get anything to eat or drink?

TAPE   First performed in 1993 at the Actors Theatre of Louisville Humana Festival of New American Plays. José Rivera was born in 1955 in San Juan, Puerto Rico, and moved with his family to New York in 1959. He has written for the stage, television, and film, and has won two Obie Awards for plays produced off Broadway. He was the first Puerto Rican to be nominated for an Academy Award for his film adaptation of *The Motorcycle Diaries* in 2005.

No NAME.   Well, We're not, really set up for that. Most visitors don't get hungry—so we don't have what you'd call a kitchen. But we can send out for things. Little things. Cold food. Soft drinks.

VISITOR (*hopefully*).   Beer?

No NAME (*shocked*).   I hope you're joking!

VISITOR.   Not even on special occasions like my birthday?

No NAME (*thinking*).   . . . well . . . I guess, maybe, on your birthday.

VISITOR (*truly appreciative*).   Great. Thanks. (*Beat*)

No NAME.   Do you have any more questions before we start? Because, if you do, that's okay. It's okay to ask as many questions as you want. I'm sure you're very curious. I'm sure you'd like to know as much as possible, so you can figure out how it all fits together and what it all means and where you fit in. So please ask. That's why I'm here. Don't worry about the time. We have a lot of time. (*Beat*)

VISITOR.   I don't have any questions.

No NAME (*disappointed*).   You sure?

VISITOR.   There's not much I really have to know, is there? Really?

No NAME.   No, I guess not. I just thought. . . .

VISITOR.   It's okay. I appreciate it. I know you're just trying to help. Make me feel better. I guess I really want to sit.

No NAME.   Sit. (*The* VISITOR *sits on the chair and faces the tape recorder.*)

VISITOR.   Okay, I'm sitting.

No NAME (*hovering*).   Is it . . . comfortable?

VISITOR (*exploding*).   Jesus Christ! Does it matter? Does it really fucking matter if I'm comfortable or not?!

No NAME (*pulling back*).   No. I guess not. (No NAME *looks sad. The* VISITOR *looks at* No NAME *and feels bad.*)

VISITOR.   Hey, I'm sorry. I know it's not your fault. I'm being— don't know what I'm being—I'm sorry.

No NAME.   It's all right.

VISITOR.   What's your name anyway? Do you have a name?

No NAME.   Not Really. It's not allowed.

VISITOR.   Really? Who says?

No NAME.   The rules.

VISITOR.   You've actually seen these rules? They're in writing?

No NAME.   Oh, yes. *Everything's* in writing. Books! *Instructions* for everything. Laws, parables, examples, lessons—it's overwhelming sometimes—the *details*—that's why there's such a long and extensive training course.

VISITOR (*surprised*).   There is?

No NAME.   Oh, yes. It's a *killer*—I mean, it's quite rigorous.

VISITOR.   Shit.

NO NAME.   You have to be a little bit of everything in my job. Confidant, confessor, friend, stern task master. Guide.

VISITOR.   Guess that'd take a lot of time.

NO NAME.   My teachers were great. They were strong and capable. They really pushed me. I was grateful. I knew I had been chosen for something unique and exciting. Something significant. I didn't mind the hard work and sleepless nights.

VISITOR (*surprised*).   Oh? You sleep?

NO NAME (*smiles*).   When I can. (*Beat*)

VISITOR.   Do you dream? (*Beat*)

NO NAME.   No. (*Beat*) That's not allowed. (*Beat*)

VISITOR.   I'm sorry.

NO NAME.   It's something you get used to.

VISITOR (*trying to be chummy*).   I know I went years without being able to remember one single dream I had. It really scared the shit out of me when I was ten and I just woke up and I had this dream about being chased by tigers in Central Park. . . .

NO NAME.   I know. I know that story. When you were ten. The tigers. The park.

VISITOR.   Oh. Yeah. I guess you would know everything. Every story. Every secret.

NO NAME (*apologetic*).   It's part of the training. (*A long uncomfortable silence.*) Have you ever operated a reel-to-reel tape recorder before?

VISITOR (*suddenly terrified*).   No, I haven't. I mean—no.

NO NAME.   It's not hard. (*Demonstrates.*) On here.

VISITOR.   I, uhm, these things were pretty obsolete by the time I was old enough to afford stereo equipment, you know, I got into cassettes, 8-tracks, I mean I had this one copy of "Jesus Christ Superstar" I must've played a billion times, and, later, I got into CD's, but never one of these jobbies.

NO NAME (*demonstrates*).   Off here. Play. Pause. Rewind.

VISITOR (*surprised*).   Rewind?

NO NAME.   In some cases the quality of the recording is so poor . . . you'll want to rewind it until you understand.

VISITOR.   No fast forward?

NO NAME.   Was that a joke?

VISITOR (*getting progressively more frightened*).   It looks like a pretty good one! Sturdy! Is this the only tape? (NO NAME *laughs out loud—then quickly stops.*)

NO NAME.   No!

VISITOR.   I didn't think so.

No Name.   There are ten thousand boxes!

Visitor.   Ten thousand boxes? Did I really . . . did I really lie that much?

No Name.   I'm afraid you did.

Visitor.   So . . . does everyone . . . go into a room like this?

No Name.   Exactly like this. There's no differentiation. Everyone's equal.

Visitor.   For once!

No Name.   What isn't equal, of course, is the amount of time you spend here. Listening.

Visitor (*horror stricken*).   Oh, God.

No Name.   Listening, just to yourself. To your voice.

Visitor.   I know.

No Name.   Listening, word by word, to every lie you ever told while you were alive.

Visitor.   Oh God!

No Name.   Every ugly lie to every person, every single time, every betrayal, every lying thought, every time you lied to yourself, deep in your mind, we were listening, we were recording, and it's all in these tapes, ten thousand boxes of them, in your own words, one lie after the next, over and over, until we're finished. So the amount of time varies. The amount of time you spend here all depends on how many lies you told. How many boxes of tape we have to get through together.

Visitor (*almost in tears*).   I'm sorry . . .

No Name.   Too late.

Visitor.   I said I'm sorry! I said I'm sorry! I said it a million times! What happened to forgiveness?! I don't want to be here! I don't want this! I don't want to listen! I don't want to hear myself! I didn't mean to say the things I said! I don't want to listen!

No Name.   Yes, well. Neither did we. Neither did we.

(No Name *looks sadly at the* Visitor. No Name *turns on the tape recorder.* No Name *hits the "Play" button, the reels spin slowly, and tape starts snaking its way through the machine.*)

(*Silence.*)

(No Name *leaves the room, leaving the* Visitor *all alone. The* Visitor *nervously pours a glass of water. From the depths of the machine comes a long-forgotten voice.*)

Voice.   "Where have you been? Do you know I've been looking all *over*? Jesus Christ! I went to Manny's! I went to the pharmacy! The school! I even called the police! Look at me, Jesus Christ, I'm *shaking*! Now look at me—look at me and tell me where the hell you were! Tell me right now!"

(*Silence. As the* VISITOR *waits, terrified and sad, for the lying response, the lights fade to black.*)

END OF PLAY

QUESTIONS

1. The two characters are generically identified, without names. Can you infer whether one or the other is a man or a woman? Why is this ambiguity important?

2. Do you find the characters sympathetic? Does your response to either of them change in the course of the play?

3. At what point in the play did you realize that this is not a realistic situation? Reread the play to see if you can discover hints or clues that prepare you for that realization.

4. What political overtones are suggested by the emphasis on lying and by the secret taping of everyone's lies?

5. The play doesn't imply that Visitor will ultimately be punished for lying. Why is Visitor horrified by the prospect of having to listen to a lifetime of lying?

6. What was the occasion for the first of Visitor's lies? What do you imagine the lie was?

7. Why is "do not tell lies" an inadequate statement of the point of the play? What is the theme of "Tape"?

Lynn Nottage
POOF!

Characters

SAMUEL, Loureen's husband
LOUREEN, a demure housewife, early thirties
FLORENCE, Loureen's best friend, early thirties

SCENE. *The present; a kitchen.*

SAMUEL (*in the darkness*).   WHEN I COUNT TO TEN I DON'
WANT TO SEE YA! I DON' WANT TO HEAR YA! ONE, TWO,
THREE, FOUR—
LOUREEN (*in the darkness*).   DAMN YOU TO HELL, SAMUEL!
(*A bright flash. Lights rise. A huge pile of smoking ashes rests in the
middle of the kitchen.* LOUREEN, *a demure housewife in her early thirties,
stares down at the ashes incredulously. She bends and lifts a pair of spectacles
from the remains. She ever so slowly backs away.*)
Samuel? Uh! (*Places the spectacles on the kitchen table.*) Uh! . . .
Samuel? (*Looks around.*) Don't fool with me now. I'm not in the mood.
(*Whispers.*) Samuel? I didn't mean it really. I'll be good if you come
back . . . Come on now, dinner's waiting. (*Chuckles, then stops abruptly.*)
Now stop your foolishness . . . And let's sit down. (*Examines the
spectacles.*) Uh! (*Softly.*) Don't be cross with me. Sure I forgot to pick
up your shirt for tomorrow. I can wash another, I'll do it right now.
Right now! Sam? . . . (*Cautiously.*) You hear me! (*Awaits a response.*)
Maybe I didn't ever intend to wash your shirt. (*Pulls back as though
about to receive a blow; a moment.*) Uh! (*Sits down and dials the
telephone.*) Florence, honey, could you come on down for a moment.
There's been a . . . little . . . accident . . . Quickly please. Uh! (LOUREEN
*hangs up the phone. She gets a broom and a dust pan. She hesitantly
approaches the pile of ashes. She gets down on her hands and knees and takes
a closer look. A fatuous grin spreads across her face. She is startled by a
sudden knock on the door. She slowly walks across the room like a possessed
child.* LOUREEN *lets in* FLORENCE, *her best friend and upstairs neighbor.*)

POOF!   First performed in 1993 as part of the Humana Festival of New American
Plays produced by Actors Theatre of Louisville. Lynn Nottage was born in 1964 in
Brooklyn, New York, and attended Brown University and the Yale School of Drama.
She has received numerous awards for her plays, including an Obie, the NY Drama
Critics' Circle Award, and a Guggenheim Fellowship. Most recently she has taught
writing at the Yale School of Drama.

FLORENCE, *also a housewife in her early thirties, wears a floral housecoat and a pair of oversized slippers. Without acknowledgment* LOUREEN *proceeds to saunter back across the room.*)

FLORENCE.   HEY!

LOUREEN (*pointing at the ashes*).   Uh! . . . (*She struggles to formulate words, which press at the inside of her mouth, not quite realized.*) Uh! . . .

FLORENCE.   You all right? What happened? (*Sniffs the air.*) Smells like you burned something? (*Stares at the huge pile of ashes.*) What the devil is that?

LOUREEN (*hushed*).   Samuel . . . It's Samuel, I think.

FLORENCE.   What's he done now?

LOUREEN.   It's him. It's him. (*Nods her head repeatedly.*)

FLORENCE.   Chile, what's wrong with you? Did he finally drive you out your mind? I knew something was going to happen sooner or later.

LOUREEN.   Dial 911, Florence!

FLORENCE.   Why? You're scaring me!

LOUREEN.   Dial 911! (FLORENCE *picks up the telephone and quickly dials.*) I think I killed him. (FLORENCE *hangs up the telephone.*)

FLORENCE.   What?

LOUREEN (*whimpers*).   I killed him! I killed Samuel!

FLORENCE.   Come again? . . . He's dead dead? (LOUREEN *wrings her hands and nods her head twice, mouthing "dead dead."* FLORENCE *backs away.*) No, stop it, I don't have time for this. I'm going back upstairs. You know how Samuel hates to find me here when he gets home. You're not going to get me this time. (*Louder.*) Y'all can have your little joke; I'm not part of it! (*A moment. She takes a hard look into* LOUREEN'*s eyes; she squints.*) Did you really do it this time?

LOUREEN (*hushed*).   I don't know how or why it happened, it just did.

FLORENCE.   Why you whispering?

LOUREEN.   I don't want to talk too loud—something else is liable to disappear.

FLORENCE.   Where's his body?

LOUREEN.   (*points to the pile of ashes*). There! . . .

FLORENCE.   You burned him?

LOUREEN.   I DON'T KNOW! (*Covers her mouth as if to muffle her words; hushed.*) I think so.

FLORENCE.   Either you did or you didn't, what you mean you don't know? We're talking murder, Loureen, not oven settings.

LOUREEN.   You think I'm playing?

FLORENCE.   How many times have I heard you talk about being rid of him. How many times have we sat at this very table and laughed about the many ways we could do it and how many times have you done it? None.

LOUREEN (*lifting the spectacles*).   A pair of cheap spectacles, that's all that's left. And you know how much I hate these. You ever seen him without them, no! . . . He counted to four and disappeared. I swear to God!

FLORENCE.   Don't bring the Lord into this just yet! Sit down now . . . What you got to sip on?

LOUREEN.   I don't know whether to have a stiff shot of scotch or a glass of champagne. (FLORENCE *takes a bottle of sherry out of the cupboard and pours them each a glass.* LOUREEN *downs hers, then holds out her glass for more.*) He was . . .

FLORENCE.   Take your time.

LOUREEN.   Standing there.

FLORENCE.   And?

LOUREEN.   He exploded.

FLORENCE.   Did that muthafucka hit you again?

LOUREEN.   No . . . he exploded. Boom! Right in front of me. He was shouting like he does, being all colored, then he raised up that big crusty hand to hit me, and poof, he was gone . . . I barely got words out and I'm looking down at a pile of ash. (FLORENCE *belts back her sherry. She wipes her forehead and pours them both another.*)

FLORENCE.   Chile, I'll give you this, in terms of color you've matched my husband Edgar, the story king. He came in at six Sunday morning, talking about he'd hit someone with his car, and had spent all night trying to outrun the police. I felt sorry for him. It turns out he was playing poker with his paycheck no less. You don't want to know how I found out . . . But I did.

LOUREEN.   You think I'm lying?

FLORENCE.   I certainly hope so, Loureen. For your sake and my heart's.

LOUREEN.   Samuel always said if I raised my voice something horrible would happen. And it did. I'm a witch . . . the devil spawn!

FLORENCE.   You've been watching too much television.

LOUREEN.   Never seen anything like this on television. Wish I had, then I'd know what to do . . . There's no question, I'm a witch. (*Looks at her hands with disgust.*)

FLORENCE.   Chile, don't tell me you've been messing with them mojo women again? What did I tell ya. (LOUREEN, *agitated, stands and sits back down.*)

LOUREEN.   He's not coming back. Oh no, how could he? It would be a miracle! Two in one day . . . I could be canonized. Worse yet, he could be . . . All that needs to happen now is for my palms to bleed and I'll be eternally remembered as Saint Loureen, the patron of battered wives. Women from across the country will make pilgrimages to me, laying pies and pot roast at my feet and asking the good saint to make their husbands turn to dust. How often does a man like Samuel get damned to hell, and go? (*She breaks down.* FLORENCE *moves to console her friend, then realizes that* LOUREEN *is actually laughing hysterically.*)

FLORENCE.   You smoking crack?

LOUREEN.   Do I look like I am?

FLORENCE.   Hell, I've seen old biddies creeping out of crack houses, talking about they were doing church work.

FLORENCE.   Florence, please be helpful, I'm very close to the edge! . . . I don't know what to do next! Do I sweep him up? Do I call the police? Do I . . . (*The phone rings*) Oh God.

FLORENCE.   You gonna let it ring? (LOUREEN *reaches for the telephone slowly.*)

LOUREEN.   NO! (*holds the receiver without picking it up, paralyzed*). What if it's his mother? . . . She knows! (*The phone continues to ring. They sit until it stops. They both breathe a sigh of relief.*) I should be mourning, I should be praying, I should be thinking of the burial, but all that keeps popping into my mind is what will I wear on television when I share my horrible and wonderful story with a studio audience . . . (*Whimpers.*) He's made me a killer, Florence, and you remember what a gentle child I was. (*Whispers.*) I'm a killer, I'm a killer, I'm a killer.

FLORENCE.   I wouldn't throw that word about too lightly even in jest. Talk like that gets around.

LOUREEN.   You think they'll lock me up? A few misplaced words and I'll probably get the death penalty, isn't that what they do with women like me, murderesses?

FLORENCE.   Folks have done time for less.

LOUREEN.   Thank you, just what I needed to hear!

FLORENCE.   What did you expect, that I was going to throw up my arms and congratulate you? Why'd you have to go and lose your mind at this time of day, while I got a pot of rice on the stove and Edgar's about to walk in the door and wonder where his goddamn food is. (*Losing her cool.*) And he's going to start in on me about all the nothing I've been doing during the day and why I can't work and then he'll mention how clean you keep your home. And I don't know how I'm going to look him in the eye without . . .

LOUREEN.   I'm sorry, Florence. Really. It's out of my hands now. (*She takes* FLORENCE*'s hand and squeezes it.*)

FLORENCE (*regaining her composure*).   You swear on your right tit?

LOUREEN (*clutching both breasts*).   I swear on both of them!

FLORENCE.   Both your breasts, Loureen! You know what will happen if you're lying. (LOUREEN *nods; hushed.*) Both your breasts, Loureen?

LOUREEN.   Yeah!

FLORENCE (*examines the pile of ashes, then shakes her head*).   Oh sweet, sweet Jesus. He must have done something truly terrible.

LOUREEN.   No more than usual. I just couldn't take being hit one more time.

FLORENCE.   You've taken a thousand blows from that man, couldn't you've turned the cheek and waited. I'd have helped you pack. Like we talked about. (*A moment.*)

LOUREEN.   Uh! . . . I could blow on him and he'd disappear across the linoleum. (*Snaps her fingers.*) Just like that. Should I be feeling remorse or regret or some other "R" word? I'm strangely jubilant, like on prom night when Samuel and I first made love. That's the feeling! (*The women lock eyes.*) Uh!

FLORENCE.   Is it . . .

LOUREEN.   Like a ton of bricks been lifted from my shoulders, yeah.

FLORENCE.   Really?

LOUREEN.   Yeah! (FLORENCE *walks to the other side of the room.*)

FLORENCE.   You bitch!

LOUREEN.   What?

FLORENCE.   We made a pact.

LOUREEN.   I know.

FLORENCE.   You've broken it . . . We agreed that when things got real bad for both of us we'd . . . you know . . . together . . . Do I have to go back upstairs to that? . . . What next?

LOUREEN.   I thought you'd tell me! . . . I don't know!

FLORENCE.   I don't know!

LOUREEN.   I don't know! (FLORENCE *begins to walk around the room, nervously touching objects.* LOUREEN *sits, wringing her hands and mumbling softly to herself.*)

FLORENCE.   Now you got me, Loureen, I'm truly at a loss for words.

LOUREEN.   Everybody always told me, "Keep your place, Loureen." My place, the silent spot on the couch with a wine cooler in my hand and a pleasant smile that warmed the heart. All this time I didn't know why he was so afraid for me to say anything, to speak up. Poof! . . . I've never been by myself, except for them two weeks when he won the office pool and went to Reno with his cousin Mitchell. He wouldn't tell me where he was going until I got that postcard with the cowboy smoking a hundred cigarettes . . . Didn't Sonny Larkin look good last week at Caroline's? He looked good, didn't he . . . (FLORENCE *nods. She nervously picks up Samuel's jacket, which is hanging on the back of the chair. She clutches it unconsciously.*) NO! No! Don't wrinkle that, that's his favorite jacket. He'll kill me. Put it back! (FLORENCE *returns the jacket to its perch.* LOUREEN *begins to quiver.*) I'm sorry. (*She grabs the jacket and wrinkles it up.*) There! (*She then digs into the coat pockets and pulls out his wallet and a movie stub.*) Look at that, he said he didn't go to the movies last night. Working late. (*Frantically thumbs through his wallet.*) Picture of his motorcycle, Social Security card, driver's license, and look at that from our wedding. (*Smiling.*) I looked good, didn't I? (*She puts the pictures back in the wallet and holds the jacket up to her face.*) There were some good things. (*She then sweeps her hand over the jacket to remove the wrinkles, and folds it ever so carefully, and finally throws it in the garbage.*) And out of my mouth those words made him disappear. All these years and just words, Florence. That's all they were.

FLORENCE.   I'm afraid I won't ever get those words out. I'll start resenting you, honey. I'm afraid won't anything change for me.

LOUREEN.   I been to that place.

FLORENCE.   Yeah? But now I wish I could relax these old lines (*touches her forehead*) for a minute maybe. Edgar has never done me the way Samuel did you, but he sure did take the better part of my life.

LOUREEN.   Not yet, Florence.

FLORENCE (*nods*).   I have the children to think of . . . right?

LOUREEN.   You can think up a hundred things before . . .

FLORENCE.   Then come upstairs with me . . . we'll wait together for Edgar and then you can spit out your words and . . .

LOUREEN.   I can't do that.

FLORENCE.   Yes you can. Come on now. (LOUREEN *shakes her head no.*) Well, I guess my mornings are not going to be any different.

LOUREEN.   If you can say for certain, then I guess they won't be. I couldn't say that.

FLORENCE.   But you got a broom and a dust pan, you don't need anything more than that . . . He was a bastard and nobody will care that he's gone.

LOUREEN.   Phone's gonna start ringing soon, people are gonna start asking soon, and they'll care.

FLORENCE.   What's your crime? Speaking your mind?

LOUREEN.   Maybe I should mail him to his mother. I owe her that. I feel bad for her, she didn't understand how it was. I can't just throw him away and pretend like it didn't happen. Can I?

FLORENCE.   I didn't see anything but a pile of ash. As far as I know you got a little careless and burned a chicken.

LOUREEN.   He was always threatening not to come back.

FLORENCE.   I heard him.

LOUREEN.   It would've been me eventually.

FLORENCE.   Yes.

LOUREEN.   I should call the police, or someone.

FLORENCE.   Why? What are you gonna tell them? About all those times they refused to help, about all those nights you slept in my bed 'cause you were afraid to stay down here? About the time he nearly took out your eye 'cause you flipped the television channel? •

LOUREEN.   No.

FLORENCE.   You've got it, girl!

LOUREEN.   Good-bye to the fatty meats and the salty food. Good-bye to the bourbon and the bologna sandwiches. Good-bye to the smell of his feet, his breath and his bowel movements . . . (*A moment. She closes her eyes and, reliving a horrible memory, she shudders.*) Good-bye. (*Walks over to the pile of ashes.*) Samuel? . . . Just checking.

FLORENCE.   Good-bye Samuel. (*They both smile.*)

LOUREEN.   I'll let the police know that he's missing tomorrow . . .

FLORENCE.   Why not the next day?

LOUREEN.   Chicken's warming in the oven, you're welcome to stay.

FLORENCE.   Chile, I got a pot of rice on the stove, kids are probably acting out . . . and Edgar, well . . . Listen, I'll stop in tomorrow.

LOUREEN.   For dinner?

FLORENCE.   Edgar wouldn't stand for that. Cards maybe.

LOUREEN.   Cards. (*The women hug for a long moment.* FLORENCE *exits.* LOUREEN *stands over the ashes for a few moments contemplating what to do. She finally decides to sweep them under the carpet, and then proceeds to set the table and sit down to eat her dinner.*)

END OF PLAY

QUESTIONS

1. What do Loureen and Florence have in common, and what differentiates them?
2. Citing specific reported events, describe Loureen's life with Samuel.
3. What are Loureen's various emotional states as the play progresses? In particular, what do you learn about her and Samuel in the incident involving Samuel's jacket?
4. What have Loureen and Florence been planning to do if their husbands become too abusive?
5. Explore the ironic situation that leads a woman to continue to live with an abusive husband.

Edward Albee
The Sandbox

A Brief Play, in Memory of My Grandmother (1876–1959)

Players

THE YOUNG MAN, 25, *a good-looking, well-built boy in a bathing suit*
MOMMY, 55, *a well-dressed, imposing woman*
DADDY, 60, *a small man; gray, thin*
GRANDMA, 86, *a tiny, wizened woman with bright eyes*
THE MUSICIAN, *no particular age, but young would be nice*

NOTE. *When, in the course of the play, MOMMY and DADDY call each other by these names, there should be no suggestion of regionalism. These names are of empty affection and point up the pre-senility and vacuity of their characters.*

The Scene. *A bare stage, with only the following: Near the footlights, far stage-right, two simple chairs set side by side, facing the audience; near the footlights, far stage-left, a chair facing stage-right with a music stand before it; farther back, and stage-center, slightly elevated and raked, a large child's sandbox with a toy pail and shovel; the background is the sky, which alters from brightest day to deepest night.*

At the beginning, it is brightest day; the YOUNG MAN is alone on stage to the rear of the sandbox, and to one side. He is doing calisthenics; he does calisthenics until quite at the very end of the play. These calisthenics, employing the arms only, should suggest the beating and fluttering of wings. The YOUNG MAN is, after all, the Angel of Death.

THE SANDBOX   Written in 1959. Edward Albee, abandoned by his natural parents, was adopted two weeks after birth in 1928 by a wealthy couple in Westchester County, New York, and named after his adoptive grandfather, part owner of the Keith-Albee string of movie-and-vaudeville theaters. His early schooling frequently interrupted by family vacations, Albee attended a variety of private schools. Dismissed from Trinity College (Connecticut) after three semesters, he went to Greenwich Village, against his foster parents' wishes, determined to write. For about ten years he tried poetry and fiction while working at various odd jobs to supplement a weekly allowance from a trust fund established by his grandmother. After the success of his first play, Zoo Story (1959), and the completion of a second, Albee interrupted work on The American Dream when commissioned to do a short play for an international theatrical festival. For this play (The Sandbox) he used characters from the work in progress placed in a different situation and setting. Despite its overlap of characters and themes with The American Dream (1961), it is a separate play, and Albee in 1966 declared it his favorite among his plays.

MOMMY *and* DADDY *enter from stage-left,* MOMMY *first.*

MOMMY (*motioning to* DADDY).   Well, here we are; this is the beach.

DADDY (*whining*).   I'm cold.

MOMMY (*dismissing him with a little laugh*).   Don't be silly; it's as warm as toast. Look at that nice young man over there: he doesn't think it's cold. (*Waves to the* YOUNG MAN.) Hello.

YOUNG MAN (*with an endearing smile*).   Hi!

MOMMY (*looking about*).   This will do perfectly . . . don't you think so, Daddy? There's sand there . . . and the water beyond. What do you think, Daddy?

DADDY (*vaguely*).   Whatever you say, Mommy.

MOMMY (*with the same little laugh*).   Well, of course . . . whatever I say. Then, it's settled, is it?

DADDY (*shrugs*).   She's *your* mother, not mine.

MOMMY.   I know she's my mother. What do you take me for? (*A pause.*) All right, now; let's get on with it. (*She shouts into the wings, stage-left.*) You! Out there! You can come in now. (*The* MUSICIAN *enters, seats himself in the chair, stage-left, places music on the music stand, is ready to play.* MOMMY *nods approvingly.*) Very nice; very nice. Are you ready, Daddy? Let's go get Grandma.

DADDY.   Whatever you say, Mommy.

MOMMY (*leading the way out, stage-left*).   Of course, whatever I say. (*To the* MUSICIAN) You can begin now. (*The* MUSICIAN *begins playing;* MOMMY *and* DADDY *exit; the* MUSICIAN, *all the while playing, nods to the* YOUNG MAN.)

YOUNG MAN (*with the same endearing smile*).   Hi! (*After a moment,* MOMMY *and* DADDY *re-enter, carrying* GRANDMA. *She is borne in by their hands under her armpits; she is quite rigid; her legs are drawn up; her feet do not touch the ground; the expression on her ancient face is that of puzzlement and fear.*)

DADDY.   Where do we put her?

MOMMY (*with the same little laugh*).   Wherever I say, of course. Let me see . . . well . . . all right, over there . . . in the sandbox. (*Pause.*) Well, what are you waiting for, Daddy? . . . The sandbox! (*Together they carry* GRANDMA *over to the sandbox and more or less dump her in.*)

GRANDMA (*righting herself to a sitting position; her voice a cross between a baby's laugh and cry*).   Ahhhhh! Graaaaa!

DADDY (*dusting himself*).   What do we do now?

MOMMY (*to the* MUSICIAN).   You can stop now. (*The* MUSICIAN *stops.*) (*Back to* DADDY) What do you mean, what do we do now? We go over there and sit down, of course. (*To the* YOUNG MAN) Hello there.

YOUNG MAN (*again smiling*).   Hi! (MOMMY *and* DADDY *move to the chairs, stage-right, and sit down. A pause.*)

GRANDMA (*same as before*).   Ahhhhhh! Ah-haaaaaa! Graaaaaa!

DADDY.   Do you think . . . do you think she's . . . comfortable?

MOMMY (*impatiently*).   How would I know?

DADDY (*pause*).   What do we do now?

MOMMY (*as if remembering*).   We . . . wait. We . . . sit here . . . and we wait . . . that's what we do.

DADDY (*after a pause*).   Shall we talk to each other?

MOMMY (*with that little laugh; picking something off her dress*).   Well, *you* can talk, if you want to . . . if you can think of anything to say . . . if you can think of anything *new*.

DADDY (*thinks*).   No . . . I suppose not.

MOMMY (*with a triumphant laugh*).   Of course not!

GRANDMA (*banging the toy shovel against the pail*).   Haaaaaa! Ah-haaaaaa!

MOMMY (*out over the audience*).   Be quiet, Grandma . . . just be quiet, and wait. (GRANDMA *throws a shovelful of sand at* MOMMY. *Still out over the audience*) She's throwing sand at me! You stop that, Grandma; you stop throwing sand at Mommy! (*To* DADDY) She's throwing sand at me. (DADDY *looks around at* GRANDMA, *who screams at him.*)

GRANDMA.   GRAAAAAA!

MOMMY.   Don't look at her. Just . . . sit here . . . be very still . . . and wait. (*To the* MUSICIAN) You . . . uh . . . you go ahead and do whatever it is you do. (*The* MUSICIAN *plays.* MOMMY *and* DADDY *are fixed, staring out beyond the audience.* GRANDMA *looks at them, looks at the* MUSICIAN, *looks at the sandbox, throws down the shovel.*)

GRANDMA.   Ah-haaaaaa! Graaaaaa! (*Looks for reaction; gets none. Now . . . directly to the audience*) Honestly! What a way to treat an old woman! Drag her out of the house . . . stick her in a car . . . bring her out here from the city . . . dump her in a pile of sand . . . and leave her here to set. I'm eighty-six years old! I was married when I was seventeen. To a farmer. He died when I was thirty. (*To the* MUSICIAN) Will you stop that, please? (*The* MUSICIAN *stops playing.*) I'm a feeble old woman . . . how do you expect anybody to hear me over that peep! peep! peep! (*To herself*) There's no respect around here. (*To the* YOUNG MAN) There's no respect around here!

YOUNG MAN (*same smile*).   Hi!

GRANDMA (*after a pause, a mild double-take, continues, to the audience*).   My husband died when I was thirty (*indicates* MOMMY), and I had to raise that big cow over there all by my lonesome. You can imagine what *that was like*. Lordy! (*To the* YOUNG MAN) Where'd they get *you*?

YOUNG MAN.   Oh . . . I've been around for a while.

GRANDMA.   I'll bet you have! Heh, heh, heh. Will you look at you!

YOUNG MAN (*flexing his muscles*).   Isn't that something? (*Continues his calisthenics.*)

GRANDMA.   Boy, oh boy; I'll say. Pretty good.

YOUNG MAN (*sweetly*).   I'll say.

GRANDMA.   Where ya from?

YOUNG MAN.   Southern California.

GRANDMA (*nodding*).   Figgers; figgers. What's your name, honey?

YOUNG MAN.   I don't know . . .

GRANDMA (*to the audience*).   Bright, too!

YOUNG MAN.   I mean . . . I mean, they haven't given me one yet . . . the studio . . .

GRANDMA (*giving him the once-over*).   You don't say . . . you don't say. Well . . . uh, I've got to talk some more . . . don't you go 'way.

YOUNG MAN.   Oh, no.

GRANDMA (*turning her attention back to the audience*).   Fine; fine. (*Then, once more, back to the* YOUNG MAN) You're . . . you're an actor, hunh?

YOUNG MAN (*beaming*).   Yes. I am.

GRANDMA (*to the audience again; shrugs*).   I'm smart that way. Anyhow, I had to raise . . . *that* over there all by my lonesome; and what's next to her there . . . that's what she married. Rich? I tell you . . . money, money, money. They took me off the *farm* . . . which was real decent of them . . . fixed a nice place for me under the stove . . . gave me an army blanket . . . and my own dish . . . my very own dish! So, what have I got to complain about? Nothing, of course. I'm not complaining. (*She looks up at the sky, shouts to someone off stage.*) Shouldn't it be getting dark now, dear? (*The lights dim; night comes on. The* MUSICIAN *begins to play; it becomes deepest night. There are spots on all the players, including the* YOUNG MAN, *who is, of course, continuing his calisthenics.*)

DADDY (*stirring*).   It's nighttime.

MOMMY.   Shhhh. Be still . . . wait.

DADDY (*whining*).   It's so hot.

MOMMY.   Shhhhhh. Be still . . . wait.

GRANDMA (*to herself*).   That's better. Night. (*To the* MUSICIAN) Honey, do you play all through this part? (*The* MUSICIAN *nods.*) Well, keep it nice and soft; that's a good boy. (*The* MUSICIAN *nods again; plays softly.*) That's nice. (*There is an off-stage rumble.*)

DADDY (*starting*).   What was that?

MOMMY (*beginning to weep*).   It was nothing.

DADDY.   It was . . . it was . . . thunder . . . or a wave breaking . . . or something.

MOMMY (*whispering, through her tears*).   It was an off-stage rumble . . . and you know what *that* means . . .

DADDY.   I forget . . .

MOMMY (*barely able to talk*).   It means the time has come for poor Grandma . . . and I can't bear it!

DADDY (*vacantly*).   I . . . I suppose you've got to be brave.

GRANDMA (*mocking*).   That's right, kid; be brave. You'll bear up, you'll get over it. (*Another off-stage rumble . . . louder.*)

MOMMY.   Ohhhhhhhhhh . . . poor Grandma . . . poor Grandma . . .

GRANDMA (*to* MOMMY).   I'm fine! I'm all right! It hasn't happened yet! (*A violent off-stage rumble. All the lights go out, save the spot on the* YOUNG MAN; *the* MUSICIAN *stops playing.*)

MOMMY.   Ohhhhhhhhh . . . Ohhhhhhhhh . . . (*Silence.*)

GRANDMA.   Don't put the lights up yet . . . I'm not ready; I'm not quite ready. (*Silence.*) All right, dear . . . I'm about done. (*The lights come up again, to brightest day; the* MUSICIAN *begins to play.* GRANDMA *is discovered, still in the sandbox, lying on her side, propped up on an elbow, half covered, busily shoveling sand over herself.*)

GRANDMA (*muttering*).   I don't know how I'm supposed to do anything with this goddam toy shovel . . .

DADDY.   Mommy! It's daylight!

MOMMY (*brightly*).   So it is! Well! Our long night is over. We must put away our tears, take off our mourning . . . and face the future. It's our duty.

GRANDMA (*still shoveling; mimicking*).   . . . take off our mourning . . . face the future . . . Lordy! (MOMMY *and* DADDY *rise, stretch.* MOMMY *waves to the* YOUNG MAN.)

YOUNG MAN (*with that smile*).   Hi! (GRANDMA *plays dead.* [!] MOMMY *and* DADDY *go over to look at her; she is a little more than half buried in the sand; the toy shovel is in her hands, which are crossed on her breast.*)

MOMMY (*before the sandbox; shaking her head*).   Lovely! It's . . . it's hard to be sad . . . she looks . . . so happy. (*With pride and conviction*) It pays to do things well. (*To the* MUSICIAN) All right, you can stop now, if you want to. I mean, stay around for a swim, or something; it's all right with us. (*She sighs heavily*) Well, Daddy . . . off we go.

DADDY.   Brave Mommy!

MOMMY.   Brave Daddy! (*They exit, stage left.*)

GRANDMA (*after they leave; lying quite still*).   It pays to do things well . . . Boy, oh boy! (*She tries to sit up.*) . . . well, kids . . . (*But she finds she can't.*) . . . I . . . I can't get up. I . . . I can't move . . . (*The* YOUNG MAN *stops his calisthenics, nods to the* MUSICIAN, *walks over to* GRANDMA, *kneels down by the sandbox.*)

GRANDMA.   I . . . can't move . . .

YOUNG MAN.   Shhhhh . . . be very still . . .

GRANDMA.   I . . . I can't move . . .

YOUNG MAN.   Uh . . . ma'am; I . . . I have a line here.

GRANDMA.   Oh, I'm sorry, sweetie; you go right ahead.

YOUNG MAN.   I am . . . uh . . .

GRANDMA.   Take your time, dear.

YOUNG MAN (*prepares; delivers the line like a real amateur*).   I am the Angel of Death. I am . . . uh . . . I am come for you.

GRANDMA.   What . . . wha . . . (*then, with resignation*) . . . ohhhh . . . ohhhh, I see. (*The* YOUNG MAN *bends over, kisses* GRANDMA *gently on the forehead.*)

GRANDMA (*her eyes closed, her hands folded on her breast again, the shovel between her hands, a sweet smile on her face*).   Well . . . that was very nice, dear . . .

YOUNG MAN (*still kneeling*).   Shhhhh . . . be still . . .

GRANDMA.   What I meant was . . . you did that very well, dear . . .

YOUNG MAN (*blushing*).   . . . oh . . .

GRANDMA.   No; I mean it. You've got that . . . you've got a quality.

YOUNG MAN (*with his endearing smile*).   Oh . . . thank you; thank you very much . . . ma'am.

GRANDMA (*slowly; softly—as the* YOUNG MAN *puts his hands on top of* GRANDMA's).   You're . . . you're welcome . . . dear.

(*Tableau. The* MUSICIAN *continues to play as the curtain slowly comes down.*)

QUESTIONS

1. On the face of it, this little play is absurd—absurd both in the way it is presented and in what happens in it. Is it therefore simply horseplay, or does it have a serious subject? What is its subject?

2. The word **absurd**, used above, itself demands attention, since it has been much used with reference to modern drama. The word suggests two different meanings: (a) funny, (b) meaningless. Do both meanings function here? Does either meaning predominate?

3. Characterize Mommy and Daddy. In what ways are they alike? In what ways are they foils? Two of Daddy's speeches are repeated. What do they tell us about his relationship to Mommy?

4. Discuss the treatment by Mommy and Daddy, especially Mommy, of Grandma and her death and burial. What discrepancy exists between appearance and reality? Is their treatment of her in death similar to or different from their treatment of her in life? What metaphor is submerged in Grandma's account of their fixing her a place under the stove with an army blanket and her own dish? What is the function of the Musician?

5. How does the treatment accorded the Young Man by most of the characters (Mommy, the Musician, Grandma) contrast with their treatment of Grandma? What accounts for the difference? What kind of person is the Young Man?

6. What aspects of modern American life are presented in the play? In answering this question, consider your answers to Questions 3, 4, and 5. What judgment does the play make on American life?

7. Contrast Grandma with the Young Man and with Mommy and Daddy. What admirable qualities does she have? What disagreeable qualities does she have? Why? On the whole, is she presented as more, or less, worthy of respect than the other characters in the play? Why?

8. Both in the notes and in the dialogue, the Young Man is identified as the Angel of Death. How is he a very unusual Angel of Death? Is he a simple or a multiple symbol? What other meanings does he suggest?

9. What symbolic meanings are suggested by the following: (a) the bareness of the stage, (b) the sandbox, (c) the toy pail and shovel, (d) the dimming and extinguishing of the lights, (e) Grandma's burying herself with sand, (f) the fact that Grandma is buried before she is dead, (g) the Young Man's kissing Grandma? Which of them, like the Young Man, are multiple symbols?

10. At various points in the action the characters seem aware that they are performers in a play. What effect does this have on the audience's response?

David Ives
Time Flies

Characters

HORACE
MAY
DAVID ATTENBOROUGH
A FROG

SCENE: *Evening. A pond. The chirr of treetoads, and the buzz of a huge swarm of insects. Upstage, a thicket of tall cattails. Downstage, a deep green loveseat. Overhead, an enormous full moon.*

A loud cuckoo sounds, like the mechanical "cuckoo" of a clock.

Lights come up on two mayflies: HORACE *and* MAY, *buzzing as they "fly" in. They are dressed like singles on an evening out, he in a jacket and tie, she in a party dress—but they have insect-like antennae; long tube-like tails; and on their backs, translucent wings. Outsized hornrim glasses give the impression of very large eyes.* MAY *has distinctly hairy legs.*

HORACE AND MAY.   Bzzzzzzzzzzzzzzzzzz . . . (*Their wings stop fluttering, as they "settle."*)

MAY.   Well here we are. This is my place.

HORACE.   Already? That was fast.

MAY.   Swell party, huh.

HORACE.   Yeah. Quite a swarm.

MAY.   Thank you for flying me home.

HORACE.   No. Sure. I'm happy to. Absolutely. My pleasure. I mean—you're very, very, very welcome. (*Their eyes lock and they near each other as if for a kiss, their wings fluttering a little.*) Bzzzzzzzz . . .

MAY.   Bzzzzzzzz . . . (*Before their jaws can meet:* "CUCKOO!"—*and* HORACE *breaks away.*)

TIME FLIES   One of three one-act plays presented together as *Mere Mortals*, the play was first performed Off-Broadway in New York in 1998. David Ives was born in Chicago in 1951 and educated at Northwestern University and the Yale School of Drama, and in 1995 received a Guggenheim Fellowship for play writing. David Attenborough is the host of nature programs created for British television and broadcast in the United States. The phrase *carpe diem,* used several times in the play, is Latin for "seize the day," an admonition to live life fully because it is so brief—or, paraphrased, "time flies."

HORACE. It's that late, is it. Anyway, it was very nice meeting you—I'm sorry, is it April?

MAY. May.

HORACE. May. Yes. Later than I thought, huh. (*They laugh politely.*)

MAY. That's very funny, Vergil.

HORACE. It's Horace, actually.

MAY. I'm sorry. The buzz at that party was so loud.

HORACE. So you're "May the mayfly."

MAY. Yeah. Guess my parents didn't have much imagination. May, mayfly.

HORACE. You don't, ah, live with your parents, do you, May?

MAY. No, my parents died around dawn this morning.

HORACE. Isn't that funny. Mine died around dawn too.

MAY. Maybe it's fate.

HORACE. Is that what it izzzzzzzz . . . ?

MAY. Bzzzzzzzz . . .

HORACE. Bzzzzzzzzzzzzzz . . . (*They near for a kiss, but* HORACE *breaks away.*) Well I'd better be going now. Good night.

MAY. Do you want a drink?

HORACE. I'd love a drink, actually . . .

MAY. Let me just turn on a couple of fireflies. (MAY *tickles the underside of a couple of two foot-long fireflies hanging like a chandelier, and the fireflies light up.*)

HORACE. Wow. Great pond! (*Indicating the loveseat.*) I love the lilypad.

MAY. The lilypad was here. It kinda grew on me. (*Polite laugh.*) Care to take the load off your wings?

HORACE. That's all right. I'll just—you know—hover. But will you look at that . . . ! (*Turning,* HORACE *bats* MAY *with his wings.*)

MAY. Oof!

HORACE. I'm sorry. Did we collide?

MAY. No. No. It's fine.

HORACE. I've only had my wings about six hours.

MAY. Really! So have I . . . ! Wasn't molting disgusting?

HORACE. Eugh. I'm glad that's over.

MAY. Care for some music? I've got The Beatles, The Byrds, The Crickets . . .

HORACE. I love the Crickets.

MAY. Well so do I . . . (*She kicks a large, insect-shaped coffee table, and we hear the buzz of crickets.*)

HORACE (*as they boogie to that*).   So are you going out with any—I mean, are there any other mayflies in the neighborhood?

MAY.   No, it's mostly wasps.

HORACE.   So, you live here by your, um, all by yourself? Alone?

MAY.   All by my lonesome.

HORACE.   And will you look at that moon.

MAY.   You know that's the first moon I've ever seen?

HORACE.   That's the first moon *I've* ever seen . . . !

MAY.   Isn't that funny.

HORACE.   When were you born?

MAY.   About 7:30 this morning.

HORACE.   So was I! Seven thirty-three!

MAY.   Isn't that funny.

HORACE.   Or maybe it's fate. (*They near each other again, as if for a kiss.*) Bzzzzzzz . . .

MAY.   Bzzzzzzzzz . . . I think that moon is having a very emotional effect on me.

HORACE.   Me too.

MAY.   It must be nature.

HORACE.   Me too.

MAY.   Or maybe it's fate.

HORACE.   Me too . . .

MAY.   Bzzzzzzzzzz . . .

HORACE.   Bzzzzzzzzzzzzz . . .   (*They draw their tails very close. Suddenly*)

A FROG (*amplified, over loudspeaker*).   Ribbit, ribbit!

HORACE.   A frog!

MAY.   A frog!

HORACE and MAY.   The frogs are coming, the frogs are coming! (*They "fly" around the stage in a panic. Ad lib*) A frog, a frog! The frogs are coming, the frogs are coming! (*They finally stop, breathless.*)

MAY.   It's okay. It's okay.

HORACE.   Oh my goodness.

MAY.   I think he's gone now.

HORACE.   Oh my goodness, that scared me.

MAY.   That is the only drawback to living here. The frogs.

HORACE.   You know I like frog films and frog literature. I just don't like frogs.

MAY.   And they're so rude if you're not a frog yourself.

HORACE.   Look at me. I'm shaking.

MAY.   Why don't I fix you something. Would you like a grasshopper? Or a stinger?

HORACE.   Just some stagnant water would be fine.

MAY.   A little duckweed in that? Some algae?

HORACE.   Straight up is fine.

MAY (*as she pours his drink*).   Sure I couldn't tempt you to try the lily pad?

HORACE.   Well, maybe for just a second. (HORACE *flutters down onto the love seat.*) Zzzzzz . . .

MAY (*handing him a glass*).   Here you go. Cheers, Horace.

HORACE.   Long life, May. (*They clink glasses.*)

MAY.   Do you want to watch some tube?

HORACE.   Sure. What's on?

MAY.   Let's see. (*She checks a green TV Guide.*) There is . . . *The Love Bug, M. Butterfly, The Spider's Stratagem, Travels With My Ant, Angels and Insects, The Fly* . . .

HORACE.   The original, or Jeff Goldblum?

MAY.   Jeff Goldblum.

HORACE.   Euch. Too gruesome.

MAY.   *Born Yesterday* and *Life On Earth.*

HORACE.   What's on that?

MAY.   "Swamp Life," with Sir David Attenborough.

HORACE.   That sounds good.

MAY.   Shall we try it?

HORACE.   Carpe diem.

MAY.   Carpe diem? What's that?

HORACE.   I don't know. It's Latin.

MAY.   What's Latin?

HORACE.   I don't know. I'm just a mayfly. (*"Cuckoo!"*) And we're right on time for it. (MAY *presses a remote control and* DAVID ATTENBOROUGH *appears, wearing a safari jacket.*)

DAVID ATTENBOROUGH.   Hello, I'm David Attenborough. Welcome to "Swamp Life."

MAY.   Isn't this comfy.

HORACE.   Is my wing in your way?

MAY.   No. It's fine.

DAVID ATTENBOROUGH.   You may not believe it, but within this seemingly lifeless puddle, there thrives a teeming world of vibrant life.

HORACE.   May, look—isn't that your pond?

MAY.   I think that is my pond!

HORACE.   He said "puddle."

DAVID ATTENBOROUGH.   This puddle is only several inches across, but its stagnant water plays host to over 14 gazillion different species.

MAY.   It is my pond!

DAVID ATTENBOROUGH. Every species here is engaged in a constant, desperate battle for survival. Feeding—meeting—mating—breeding—dying. And mating. And meeting. And mating. And feeding. And dying. Mating. Mating. Meeting. Breeding. Brooding. Braiding—those that can braid. Feeding. Mating.

MAY.   All right, Sir Dave!

DAVID ATTENBOROUGH.   Mating, mating, mating, and mating.

HORACE.   Only one thing on his mind.

MAY.   The filth on television these days.

DAVID ATTENBOROUGH.   Tonight we start off with one of the saddest creatures of this environment.

HORACE.   The dung beetle.

MAY.   The toad.

DAVID ATTENBOROUGH.   The lowly mayfly.

HORACE.   Did he say "the mayfly?"

MAY.   I think he said the lowly mayfly.

DAVID ATTENBOROUGH.   Yes. The lowly mayfly. Like these two mayflies, for instance.

HORACE.   May—I think that's us!

MAY.   Oh my God . . .

HORACE and MAY (*together*).   We're on television!

HORACE.   I don't believe it!

MAY.   I wish my mother was here to see this!

HORACE.   This is amazing!

MAY.   Oh God, I look terrible!

HORACE.   You look very good.

MAY.   I can't look at this.

DAVID ATTENBOROUGH.   As you can see, the lowly mayfly is not one of nature's most attractive creatures.

MAY.   At least we don't wear safari jackets.

HORACE.   I wish he'd stop saying "lowly mayfly."

DAVID ATTENBOROUGH.   The lowly mayfly has a very distinctive khkhkhkhkhkhkhkhkhkkh . . . (*the sound of TV static*)

MAY.   I think there's something wrong with my antenna . . . (*She adjusts the antenna on her head.*)

HORACE.   You don't have cable?

MAY.   Not on this pond.

DAVID ATTENBOROUGH (*stops the static sound*).   . . . and sixty tons of droppings.

HORACE.   That fixed it.

MAY.   Can I offer you some food? I've got some plankton in the pond. And some very nice gnat.

HORACE.   I do love good gnat.

MAY.   I'll set it out, you can pick. (*She rises and gets some food.*)

DAVID ATTENBOROUGH.   The lowly mayfly first appeared some 350 million years ago . . .

MAY.   That's impressive.

DAVID ATTENBOROUGH.   . . . and is of the order Ephemeroptera, meaning, "living for a single day."

MAY.   I did not know that!

HORACE.   "Living for a single day." Huh . . .

MAY (*setting out a tray on the coffee table*).   There you go.

HORACE.   Gosh, May. That's beautiful.

MAY.   There's curried gnat, salted gnat, Scottish smoked gnat . . .

HORACE.   I love that.

MAY.   . . . gnat with pesto, gnat au naturelle, and Gnat King Cole.

HORACE.   I don't think I could finish a whole one.

MAY.   "Gnat" to worry. (*They laugh politely.*) That's larva dip there in the center. Just dig in.

DAVID ATTENBOROUGH.   As for the life of the common mayfly . . .

HORACE.   Oh. We're "common" now.

DAVID ATTENBOROUGH.   . . . it is a simple round of meeting, mating, meeting, mating—

MAY.   Here we go again.

DAVID ATTENBOROUGH.   —breeding, feeding, feeding . . .

HORACE.   This dip is fabulous.

DAVID ATTENBOROUGH.   . . . and dying.

MAY.   Leaf?

HORACE.   Thank you. (MAY *breaks a leaf off a plant and hands it to* HORACE.)

DAVID ATTENBOROUGH.   Mayflies are a major food source for trout and salmon.

MAY.   Will you look at that savagery?

HORACE.   That poor, poor mayfly.

DAVID ATTENBOROUGH.   Fishermen like to bait hooks with mayfly look-alikes.

MAY.   Bastards!—Excuse me.

DAVID ATTENBOROUGH.   And then there is the giant bullfrog.

FROG (*amplified, over loudspeaker*).   Ribbit, ribbit!

HORACE and MAY.   The frogs are coming, the frogs are coming! (*They "fly" around the stage in a panic—and end up "flying" right into each other's arms.*)

HORACE.   Well there.

MAY.   Hello.

DAVID ATTENBOROUGH.   Welcome to "Swamp Life." (*Exits.*)

MAY (*hypnotized by* HORACE).   Funny how we flew right into each other's wings.

HORACE.   It is funny.

MAY.   Or fate.

HORACE.   Do you think he's gone?

MAY.   David Attenborough?

HORACE.   The frog.

MAY.   What frog? Bzzzz . . .

HORACE.   Bzzzzz . . .

DAVID ATTENBOROUGH'S VOICE.   As you see, mayflies can be quite affectionate . . .

HORACE and MAY.   Bzzzzzzzzzzz . . .

DAVID ATTENBOROUGH'S VOICE.   . . . mutually palpating their proboscises.

HORACE.   You know I've been wanting to palpate your proboscis all evening?

MAY.   I think it was larva at first sight.

HORACE and MAY (*rubbing proboscises together*).   Zzzzzzzzzz zzzzzzzzzzzzzzzzzzz . . .

MAY (*very British, "Brief Encounter"*).   Oh darling, darling.

HORACE.   Oh do darling do let's always be good to each other, shall we?

MAY.   Let's do do that, darling, always, always.

HORACE.   Always?

MAY.   Always.

HORACE and MAY.   Zzzzzzzzzzzzzzzzzzzzzzzzzzzzzzz!

MAY.   Rub my antennae. Rub my antennae. (HORACE *rubs* MAY's *antennae with his hands.*)

DAVID ATTENBOROUGH'S VOICE.   Sometimes mayflies rub antennae together.

MAY.   Oh yes. Yes. Just like that. Yes. Keep going. Harder. Rub harder.

HORACE.   Rub mine now. Rub my antennae. Oh yes. Yes. Yes. Yes. There's the rub. There's the rub. Go. Go. Go!

DAVID ATTENBOROUGH'S VOICE.   Isn't that a picture. Now get a load of mating. (HORACE *gets into mounting position, behind* MAY. *He rubs her antennae while she wolfs down the gnat-food in front of her.*)

HORACE and MAY.   Bzzzzzzzzzzzzzzzzzzzzzzzzzzzzzzzzzzzzzz!

DAVID ATTENBOROUGH'S VOICE.   Unfortunately for this insect, the mayfly has a lifespan of only one day. (HORACE *and* MAY *stop buzzing, abruptly.*)

HORACE.   What was that . . . ?

DAVID ATTENBOROUGH'S VOICE.   The mayfly has a lifespan of only one day—living just long enough to meet, mate, have offspring, and die.

MAY.   Did he say "meet, mate, have offspring, and DIE"—?

DAVID ATTENBOROUGH'S VOICE.   I did. In fact, mayflies born at 7:30 in the morning will die by the next dawn. (HORACE *whimpers softly at the thought*) But so much for the lowly mayfly. Let's move on to the newt. (*"Cuckoo!"*)

HORACE and MAY.   We're going to die . . . We're going to die! Mayday, mayday! We're going to die, we're going to die! (*Weeping and wailing, they kneel, beat their breasts, cross themselves, and tear their hair:* "Cuckoo!")

HORACE.   What time is it? What time is it?

MAY.   I don't wear a watch. I'm a lowly mayfly!

HORACE (*weeping*).   Wah-ha-ha-ha!

MAY (*suddenly sober*).   Well isn't this beautiful.

HORACE (*gasping for breath*).   Oh my goodness. I think I'm having an asthma attack. Can mayflies have asthma?

MAY.   I don't know. Ask Mr. Safari Jacket.

HORACE.   Maybe if I put a paper bag over my head . . .

MAY.   So this is my sex life?

HORACE.   Do you have a paper bag?

MAY.   One bang, a bambino, and boom—that's it.

HORACE.   Do you have a paper bag?

MAY.   For the common mayfly, foreplay segues right into funeral.

HORACE.   Do you have a paper bag?

MAY.   I don't have time to look for a paper bag, I'm going to be dead very shortly, all right? (*"Cuckoo!"*)

HORACE.   Oh come on! That wasn't a whole hour! (*"Cuckoo!"*) Time is moving so fast now. (*"Cuckoo!"*)

HORACE and MAY.   Shut up! (*"Cuckoo!"*)

HORACE (*suddenly sober*).   This explains everything. We were born this morning, we hit puberty in mid-afternoon, our biological clocks went BONG, and here we are. Hot to copulate.

MAY.   For the one brief miserable time we get to do it.

HORACE.   Yeah.

MAY.   Talk about a quickie.

HORACE.   Wait a minute, wait a minute.

MAY.   Talk fast.

HORACE.   What makes you think it would be so brief?

MAY.   Oh, I'm sorry. Did I insult your vast sexual experience?

HORACE.   Are you more experienced than I am, Dr. Ruth? Luring me here to your pad?

MAY.   I see. I see. Blame me!

HORACE.   Can I remind you we only get one shot at this?

MAY.   So I can rule out multiple orgasms, is that it?

HORACE.   I'm just saying there's not a lot of time to hone one's erotic technique, okay?

MAY.   Hmp!

HORACE.   And I'm trying to sort out some very big entomontological questions here rather quickly, do you mind?

MAY.   And I'm just the babe here, is that it? I'm just a piece of tail.

HORACE.   I'm not the one who suggested TV.

MAY.   I'm not the one who wanted to watch *Life on Earth*. "Oh—Swamp Life. That sounds interesting."

FROG.   Ribbit, ribbit.

HORACE (*calmly*).   There's a frog up there.

MAY.   Oh, I'm really scared. I'm terrified.

FROG.   Ribbit, ribbit!

HORACE (*calling to the frog*).   We're right down here! Come and get us!

MAY.   Breeding. Dying. Breeding. Dying. So this is the whole purpose of mayflies? To make more mayflies?

HORACE.   Does the world *need* more mayflies?

MAY.   We're a major food source for trout and salmon.

HORACE.   How nice for the salmon.

MAY.   Do you want more food?

HORACE.   I've lost a bit of my appetite, all right?

MAY.   Oh. Excuse me.

HORACE.   I'm sorry. Really, May.

MAY (*starts to cry*).   Males!

HORACE.   Leaf? (*He plucks another leaf and hands it to her.*)

MAY.   Thank you.

HORACE.   Really. I didn't mean to snap at you.

MAY.   Oh, you've been very nice. ("*CUCKOO!*" *They jump.*) Under the circumstances.

HORACE.   I'm sorry.

MAY.   No, I'm sorry.

HORACE.   No, I'm sorry.

MAY.   No, I'm sorry.

HORACE.   No, I'm sorry.

MAY.   We'd better stop apologizing, we're going to be dead soon.

HORACE.   I'm sorry.

MAY.   Oh Horace, I had such plans. I had such wonderful plans. I wanted to see Paris.

HORACE.   What's Paris?

MAY.   I have no fucking idea.

HORACE.   Maybe we'll come back as caviar and find out. (*They laugh a little at that.*) I was just hoping to live till Tuesday.

MAY (*making a small joke*).   What's a Tuesday? (*They laugh a little more at that.*) The sun's going to be up soon. I'm scared, Horace. I'm so scared.

HORACE.   You know, May, we don't have much time, and really, we hardly know each other—but I'm going to say it. I think you're swell. I think you're divine. From your buggy eyes to the thick raspy hair on your legs to the intoxicating scent of your secretions.

MAY.   Eeeuw.

HORACE.   Eeeuw? No. I say *woof.* And I say who cares if life is a swamp and we're just a couple of small bugs in a very small pond. I say live, May! I say . . . darn it . . . live!

MAY.   But how?

HORACE.   Well I don't honestly know that . . . (ATTENBOROUGH *appears.*)

DAVID ATTENBOROUGH.   You could fly to Paris.

MAY.   We could fly to Paris!

HORACE.   Do we have time to fly to Paris?

MAY.   Carpe diem!

HORACE.   What is carpe diem?

DAVID ATTENBOROUGH.   It means "bon voyage."

HORACE and MAY.   And we're outta here!

(*They fly off to Paris as . . . Blackout.*)

QUESTIONS

1. Although Horace and May are insects, the dialogue is distinctly human. Point out examples of contemporary social conversation. To what are these mayflies being compared?

2. Mayflies do live only one day. How does that fact become symbolic of some human relationships?

3. What is the function of the voice of David Attenborough? At what points does it shift away from what you expect of the TV host of a nature program? Why?

4. Much of the humor of the play arises from insects behaving like people. In addition, there are many puns and verbal jokes. Make a list of these, and show how they distance the audience from involvement in the emotions felt by the characters. For example, "frog" is a derogatory term for the French,

and May and Horace have a bit of conversation about what they do and don't like about frogs. Translate that into trite comments on the French—and juxtapose it to the conclusion of the play. Does it matter that the audience cannot empathize with the serious emotions that the characters share?

5. Explain the pun in the title of the play. Would "carpe diem" have been as suitable as this title?

SUGGESTIONS FOR WRITING

1. Works written as short stories, novels, or poems have sometimes been dramatized for stage production. In light of the advantages and limitations discussed in this chapter, however, some are clearly more easily adapted for the stage than others. Select one or two from the following list, and explain the relative ease or difficulty—or impossibility—of a stage adaptation: "Eveline" (page 408), "Miss Brill" (page 174), "The Lottery" (page 261), "A Very Old Man with Enormous Wings" (page 327), "To Autumn" (page 701), "Home Burial" (page 920), "The Love Song of J. Alfred Prufrock" (page 925).

2. Movie and broadcast (TV and radio) productions are in many ways more flexible than stage productions and are more easily brought to a mass audience. What limitations of stage performance discussed in this chapter can be minimized or eliminated in a movie or broadcast production? Conversely, what advantages of stage performances are unavailable to media productions?

3. In view of the greater flexibility of movies and broadcasting media in dramatic representation, what accounts for the continuing popularity of stage plays?

4. If plays are written to be *performed*, what justification is there for reading them?

Realistic and Nonrealistic Drama

Literary truth in drama (as in fiction and in poetry) is not the same as fidelity to fact. Fantasy is as much the property of the theater as of poetry or the prose tale. In *A Midsummer Night's Dream* and *The Tempest*, Shakespeare has fairies and spirits and monsters as characters, and in *Hamlet* and *Macbeth* he introduces ghosts and witches. These supernatural characters, nevertheless, serve as a vehicle for truth. When Bottom, in *A Midsummer Night's Dream*, is given an ass's head, the enchantment is a visual metaphor. The witches in *Macbeth* truthfully prefigure a tragic destiny.

Because it is written to be performed, however, drama adds still another dimension of possible unreality. It may be **realistic** or **nonrealistic** in mode of production as well as in content. Staging, makeup, costuming, and acting may all be handled in such a way as to emphasize the realistic or the fanciful.

It must be recognized, however, that all stage production, no matter how realistic, involves a certain necessary artificiality. If an indoor scene is presented on a picture-frame proscenium stage, the spectator is asked to imagine that a room with only three walls is actually a room with four walls. In a thrust-stage or arena theater, in which audiences are in a semicircle around the playing area, the spectator must imagine three of the four walls, while theater-in-the-round has the audience seated on all sides of the action and spectators have to imagine all four walls—while imaginatively shutting their minds to the presence of spectators facing them from the other side of the action. All of these types of stage presentation, moreover, require adjustments in the acting. In a proscenium theater the actors must be facing the missing fourth wall most of the time. In arena or round stagings, they must not turn their backs too long on any "wall." Both types of staging, in the interests of effective presentation, require the actors to depart from an absolute realism.

Beyond these basic requirements of artificiality in stagecraft, the departure from the appearance of reality may be slight or considerable. In many late-nineteenth- and early-twentieth-century productions, an effort was made to make stage sets as realistic as possible. If the play called for a setting in a study, there had to be real bookshelves on the wall and real books on the shelves. If the room contained a wash basin, real water had to flow from the taps. On the other hand, plays have been performed on bare stages with little more than platforms and a few props.

In between these two extremes, all degrees of realism are possible. The scenery may consist of painted flats, with painted bookshelves and painted books and painted pictures on the wall, and these paintings may strive for photographic faithfulness or for an impressionistic effect. Or, instead of scenery, a play may use only a few movable properties to suggest the required setting. Thornton Wilder's *Our Town* (1938) utilized a bare stage, without curtain, with exposed ropes and backstage equipment, and with a few chairs, two ladders, and a couple of trellises as the only properties. For a scene at a soda fountain, a plank was laid across the backs of two chairs. In fact, provision of elaborately realistic stage sets has been the exception rather than the rule in the long history of the theater. Neither in Greek nor in Shakespearean theater was setting much more than suggested.

The choice of realistic or nonrealistic stage sets, costuming, and makeup may, in fact, lie with the producer rather than the playwright, and a producer may choose to disregard a playwright's directions for the sake of novelty or emphasis. When we move to the realm of language and the management of dialogue, the choice is entirely the playwright's. Here again all degrees of realism and nonrealism are possible. In the realistic theater of the last hundred years, some playwrights have made an elaborate effort to reproduce the flat quality of ordinary speech, with all its stumblings and inarticulateness, its slang and its mispronunciations. Others go even further in imitating reality, even at the risk of offending some members of the audience, and reproduce the vulgarities of the language of the streets and the contemporary habit of using obscene terms simply to add force to a statement. In real life, of course, few lovers speak with the eloquence of Romeo and Juliet, and many people, in daily conversation, have difficulty getting through a grammatically correct sentence of any length or complexity. They break off, they begin again, they repeat themselves, and sometimes, like the Young Man in "The Sandbox," they are barely articulate ("I am . . . uh . . . I am the Angel of Death. I am . . . uh . . . I am come for you." [page 1069]). Such unimaginative and inadequate speech, skillfully used by the playwright, may faithfully render the quality of human life at some levels, yet its limitations for expressing the heights and depths of human experience are obvious. Most dramatic dialogue, even at its most realistic, is more coherent and expressive than speech in actual life. Art is always a heightening or an intensification of reality; else it would have no value. The heightening may be little or great. It is greatest in poetic drama. The love exchanges of Romeo and Juliet, spoken in rhymed iambic pentameter and at one point taking the form of a perfect sonnet (see page 889), are absurdly nonrealistic if judged as an imitation of actual speech, but they vividly express the emotional truth of passionate, idealistic young love. It is no criticism of Shakespearean tragedy, therefore, to say that in real life people do not speak in blank verse. The deepest purpose of the playwright is not to imitate actual human speech but to give accurate and powerful expression to human thought and emotion.

The term **nonrealistic** used in the previous paragraph to describe the dialogue of Romeo and Juliet should not be confused with the term "unrealistic." Nonrealistic and **realistic** describe qualities of dramatic presentation; "unrealistic" is a term that judges people's actions on a scale of good sense, practicality, and insight. It is useful in discussing drama only when you are considering a character's grasp on reality—for example, a drama (whether realistic or nonrealistic) might portray a character who is unrealistic in outlook, such as a hopeless optimist or an incorrigible sentimentalist. Mrs. X in Strindberg's "The Stronger" is an unrealistic woman in a realistic play because she does not grasp the reality of her situation. In drama, realism is the attempt to reproduce or imitate the sights and sounds of real life, insofar as these can be represented on a stage. In life, realism is looking at the world with good judgment and clear vision.

All drama asks us to accept certain departures from reality—certain **dramatic conventions**. That a room with three walls or fewer may represent one with four walls, that the actors speak in the language of the audience whatever the nationality of the persons they play, that the actors stand or sit so as to face the audience most of the time—these are all necessary conventions. Other conventions are optional—for example, that the characters may reveal their inner thoughts through soliloquies and asides or may speak in the heightened language of poetry. Playwrights working in a strictly realistic mode will avoid the optional conventions, for these conflict with the realistic method that they have chosen to achieve their purposes. Playwrights working in a freer mode may choose to use any or all of them, for they make possible the revelation of dimensions of reality unreachable by a strictly realistic method. The famous speech of Hamlet that begins "To be, or not to be," in which he debates the merits of onerous life and untimely death, is nonrealistic on two counts: (1) it is spoken as a soliloquy, and (2) it is in blank verse. But despite the nonrealistic conventions, it presents Hamlet's introspective mind, his clear rationality, and his profound emotions in a powerful way. The characteristic device of Greek drama, a **chorus**— a group of actors speaking in unison, often in a chant, while going through the steps of an elaborate formalized dance—is another nonrealistic device but a useful one for conveying communal or group emotion. It has been revived, in different forms, in many modern plays. The use of a **narrator**, as in *The Glass Menagerie* (page 1153), is a related nonrealistic device that has served playwrights as a vehicle for dramatic truth.

The history of drama might be told in a history of conventions that have arisen, flourished, and been replaced; and those readers and audiences who experience plays most fully are those who have learned to understand the main conventions of its various periods and major dramatists. The less experienced reader or spectator may judge a play defective because it makes use of conventions other than those in common current acceptance (whether or not consciously recognized as such). Most contemporary audiences, for example, have been trained by their experience with movies and television, two media based on the realistic conventions of photography. Few people pause to consider that looking at a photograph, whether filmed by a still camera or a movie camera, requires the acceptance of the simple convention that three-dimensional reality is being represented two-dimensionally, or that the full spectrum of color may be represented by shades of white, gray, or black. We accept these conventions without question, as we also accept in cinema and television the emotional reinforcement that comes with a musical background even though there is no justification for the presence of an orchestra in a living room or on a beach. The study of drama requires the purposeful learning of its conventions, both realistic and nonrealistic.

In most plays, the world into which we are taken—however unreal it may be—is treated as self-contained, and we are asked to regard it temporarily as a real world. Thus David Ives's puddle of mayflies in "Time Flies" is real to us while we watch the play. We quite willingly make that "temporary suspension of disbelief" that, according to Coleridge, "constitutes poetic faith." And the step from accepting May and Horace as real insects, though we know in fact that they are only costumed actors, is an easy one because they think and talk like human beings in a fleeting romance as they erotically rub antennae and enjoy gnat snacks. But some playwrights abandon even this much attempt to give their work an illusion of reality. They deliberately violate the self-containment of the fictional world and keep reminding us that we are only seeing a play. Thus Edward Albee, in "The Sandbox," not only presents as his main character a Grandma who buries herself alive and speaks after she is presumably dead, but he also systematically breaks down the barriers between his fictional world and the real one. The Musician, instead of being concealed in an orchestra pit, is summoned onstage and told by Mommy and Grandma when to play and when not to play. Grandma addresses herself much of the time directly to the audience and at one time shouts to the electricians offstage, instructing them to dim the lights. The Young Man reminds us that he is an actor by telling Grandma that he has "a line here" and by delivering the line "like a real amateur." When Mommy and Daddy hear a noise offstage, Daddy thinks it may be thunder or a breaking wave, but Mommy says, with literal accuracy, "It was an off-stage rumble." In short, Albee keeps reminding us that this is a play—not reality—and not even an imitation of reality, but a symbolic representation of it. The effects he gains thereby are various: partly comic, partly antisentimental, partly intellectual; and the play that results is both theatrically effective and dramatically significant.

The adjective *realistic,* then, as applied to literature, must be regarded as a descriptive, not an evaluative, term. When we call a play realistic, we are saying something about its mode of presentation, not praising nor dispraising it. Realism indicates fidelity to the outer appearances of life. Serious dramatists are interested in life's inner meanings, which they may approach through either realistic or nonrealistic presentation. Great plays have been written in both the realistic and nonrealistic modes. It is not without significance, however, that the greatest plays in this book are probably *Oedipus Rex, Tartuffe,* and *Othello*—originally written in quantitative Greek verse, rhymed French hexameters, and English blank verse, respectively. Human truth, rather than fidelity to superficial fact, is the highest achievement of literary art.

REVIEWING CHAPTER TWO

1. Distinguish between realistic and nonrealistic conventions, and between the terms "nonrealistic" and "unrealistic."
2. List the important realistic conventions that may be reflected in physical appearances and in language, and consider what they may contribute to an audience's experience of a play.
3. Define the advantages gained by playwrights who employ nonrealistic conventions, both in production values and in spoken dialogue, and consider any disadvantages that may result from them.

Henrik Ibsen
A Doll House

Characters

TORVALD HELMER, a lawyer
NORA, his wife
DR. RANK
MRS. LINDE
KROGSTAD

THE HELMERS' THREE SMALL
    CHILDREN
ANNE-MARIE, the children's nurse
A HOUSEMAID
A PORTER

SCENE. The Helmers' living room.

ACT 1

A pleasant, tastefully but not expensively furnished, living room. A door on the rear wall, right, leads to the front hall, another door, left, to HELMER's study. Between the two doors a piano. A third door in the middle of the left wall; further front a window. Near the window a round table and a small couch. Towards the rear of the right wall a fourth door; further front a tile stove with a rocking chair and a couple of armchairs in front of it. Between the stove and the door a small table. Copperplate etchings on the walls. A whatnot with porcelain figurines and other small objects. A small bookcase with deluxe editions. A rug on the floor; fire in the stove. Winter day.

The doorbell rings, then the sound of the front door opening. NORA dressed for outdoors, enters, humming cheerfully. She carries several packages, which she puts down on the table, right. She leaves the door to the front hall open; there a PORTER is seen holding a Christmas tree and a basket. He gives them to the MAID who has let them in.

NORA.   Be sure to hide the Christmas tree, Helene. The children mustn't see it before tonight when we've trimmed it. (Opens her purse; to the PORTER) How much?

A DOLL HOUSE First published and then performed in 1879. English translation by Otto Reinert. Henrik Ibsen (1828–1906), widely regarded as one of the founders of modern drama, was born in Norway. Between 1851 and 1864, while employed at theaters in Bergen and Christiana (now Oslo), Ibsen gained experience but little financial success (he had known little but poverty since his early childhood, when his extravagant father went bankrupt). As a consequence of his promising achievement as a poet and playwright, a traveling grant and then a small annual stipend from the Norwegian government permitted him to move with his family to Rome, where he took up permanent residence in 1864. By the time he wrote this play, Ibsen had long been interested in women's rights.

PORTER.   Fifty øre.

NORA.   Here's a crown.° No, keep the change. (*The* PORTER *thanks her, leaves.* NORA *closes the door. She keeps laughing quietly to herself as she takes off her coat, etc. She takes a bag of macaroons from her pocket and eats a couple. She walks cautiously over to the door to the study and listens.*) Yes, he's home. (*Resumes her humming, walks over to the table, right.*)

HELMER (*in his study*).   Is that my little lark twittering out there?

NORA (*opening some packages*).   That's right.

HELMER.   My squirrel bustling about?

NORA.   Yes.

HELMER.   When did squirrel come home?

NORA.   Just now. (*Puts the bag of macaroons back in her pocket, wipes her mouth.*) Come out here, Torvald. I want to show you what I've bought.

HELMER.   I'm busy! (*After a little while he opens the door and looks in, pen in hand.*) Bought, eh? All that? So little wastrel has been throwing money around again?

NORA.   Oh but Torvald, this Christmas we can be a little extravagant, can't we? It's the first Christmas we don't have to scrimp.

HELMER.   I don't know about that. We certainly don't have money to waste.

NORA.   Yes, Torvald, we do. A little, anyway. Just a tiny little bit? Now that you're going to get that big salary and make lots and lots of money.

HELMER.   Starting at New Year's, yes. But payday isn't till the end of the quarter.

NORA.   That doesn't matter. We can always borrow.

HELMER.   Nora! (*Goes over to her and playfully pulls her ear.*) There you go being irresponsible again. Suppose I borrowed a thousand crowns today and you spent it all for Christmas and on New Year's Eve a tile hit me in the head and laid me out cold?

NORA (*putting her hand over his mouth*).   I won't have you say such horrid things.

HELMER.   But suppose it happened. Then what?

NORA.   If it did, I wouldn't care whether we owed money or not.

HELMER.   But what about the people I had borrowed from?

NORA.   Who cares about them! They are strangers.

HELMER.   Nora, Nora, you *are* a woman! No, really! You know how I feel about that. No debts! A home in debt isn't a free home, and if it isn't free it isn't beautiful. We've managed nicely so far, you and I, and that's the way we'll go on. It won't be for much longer.

Fifty øre . . . a crown: A crown was 100 øre.

NORA (*walks over toward the stove*).   All right, Torvald. Whatever you say.

HELMER (*follows her*).   Come, come, my little songbird mustn't droop her wings. What's this? Can't have a pouty squirrel in the house, you know. (*Takes out his wallet.*) Nora, what do you think I have here?

NORA (*turns around quickly*).   Money!

HELMER.   Here. (*Gives her some bills.*) Don't you think I know Christmas is expensive?

NORA (*counting*).   Ten—twenty—thirty—forty. Thank you, thank you, Torvald. This helps a lot.

HELMER.   I certainly hope so.

NORA.   It does, it does. But I want to show you what I got. It was cheap, too. Look. New clothes for Ivar. And a sword. And a horse and trumpet for Bob. And a doll and a little bed for Emmy. It isn't any good, but it wouldn't last, anyway. And here's some dress material and scarves for the maids. I feel bad about old Anne-Marie, though. She really should be getting much more.

HELMER.   And what's in here?

NORA (*cries*).   Not till tonight!

HELMER.   I see. But now what does my little prodigal have in mind for herself?

NORA.   Oh, nothing. I really don't care.

HELMER.   Of course you do. Tell me what you'd like. Within reason.

NORA.   Oh, I don't know. Really, I don't. The only thing—

HELMER.   Well?

NORA (*fiddling with his buttons, without looking at him*).   If you really want to give me something, you might—you could—

HELMER.   All right, let's have it.

NORA (*quickly*).   Some money, Torvald. Just as much as you think you can spare. Then I'll buy myself something one of these days.

HELMER.   No, really Nora—

NORA.   Oh yes, please, Torvald. Please? I'll wrap the money in pretty gold paper and hang it on the tree. Won't that be nice?

HELMER.   What's the name for little birds that are always spending money?

NORA.   Wastrels, I know. But please let's do it my way, Torvald. Then I'll have time to decide what I need most. Now that's sensible, isn't it?

HELMER (*smiling*).   Oh, very sensible. That is, if you really bought yourself something you could use. But it all disappears in the household expenses or you buy things you don't need. And then you come back to me for more.

NORA. Oh, but Torvald—

HELMER. That's the truth, dear little Nora, and you know it. (*Puts his arm around her.*) My wastrel is a little sweetheart, but she *does* go through an awful lot of money awfully fast. You've no idea how expensive it is for a man to keep a wastrel.

NORA. That's not fair, Torvald. I really save all I can.

HELMER (*laughs*). Oh, I believe that. All you can. Meaning, exactly nothing!

NORA (*hums, smiles mysteriously*). You don't know all the things we songbirds and squirrels need money for, Torvald.

HELMER. You know, you're funny. Just like your father. You're always looking for ways to get money, but as soon as you do it runs through your fingers and you can never say what you spent it for. Well, I guess I'll just have to take you the way you are. It's in your blood. Yes, that sort of thing is hereditary, Nora.

NORA. In that case, I wish I had inherited many of Daddy's qualities.

HELMER. And I don't want you any different from just what you are—my own sweet little songbird. Hey!—I think I just noticed something. Aren't you looking—what's the word?—a little—sly—?

NORA. I am?

HELMER. You definitely are. Look at me.

NORA (*looks at him*). Well?

HELMER (*wagging a finger*). Little sweet-tooth hasn't by any chance been on a rampage today, has she?

NORA. Of course not. Whatever makes you think that?

HELMER. A little detour by the pastry shop maybe?

NORA. No, I assure you, Torvald—

HELMER. Nibbled a little jam?

NORA. Certainly not!

HELMER. Munched a macaroon or two?

NORA. No, really, Torvald, I honestly—

HELMER. All right. Of course I was only joking.

NORA (*walks toward the table, right*). You know I wouldn't do anything to displease you.

HELMER. I know. And I have your promise. (*Over to her.*) All right, keep your little Christmas secrets to yourself, Nora darling. They'll all come out tonight, I suppose, when we light the tree.

NORA. Did you remember to invite Rank?

HELMER. No, but there's no need to. He knows he'll have dinner with us. Anyway, I'll see him later this morning. I'll ask him then. I did order some good wine. Oh Nora, you've no idea how much I'm looking forward to tonight!

NORA.   Me, too. And the children, Torvald! They'll have such a good time!

HELMER.   You know it *is* nice to have a good, safe job and a comfortable income. Feels good just thinking about it. Don't you agree?

NORA.   Oh, it's wonderful.

HELMER.   Remember last Christmas? For three whole weeks you shut yourself up every evening till long after midnight making ornaments for the Christmas tree and I don't know what else. Some big surprise for all of us, anyway. I'll be damned if I've ever been so bored in my whole life!

NORA.   I wasn't bored at all!

HELMER (*smiling*).   But you've got to admit you didn't have much to show for it in the end.

NORA.   Oh, don't tease me again about that! Could I help it that the cat got in and tore up everything?

HELMER.   Of course you couldn't, my poor little Nora. You just wanted to please the rest of us, and that's the important thing. But I *am* glad the hard times are behind us. Aren't you?

NORA.   Oh yes. I think it's just wonderful.

HELMER.   This year, I won't be bored and lonely. And you won't have to strain your dear eyes and your delicate little hands—

NORA (*claps her hands*).   No I won't, will I Torvald? Oh, how wonderful, how lovely, to hear you say that! (*Puts her arm under his.*) Let me tell you how I think we should arrange things, Torvald. Soon as Christmas is over— (*The doorbell rings.*) Someone's at the door. (*Straightens things up a bit.*) A caller, I suppose. Bother!

HELMER.   Remember, I'm not home for visitors.

MAID (*in the door to the front hall*).   Ma'am, there's a lady here—

NORA.   All right. Ask her to come in.

MAID (*to* HELMER).   And the Doctor just arrived.

HELMER.   Is he in the study?

MAID.   Yes, sir. (HELMER *exits into his study. The* MAID *shows* MRS. LINDE *in and closes the door behind her as she leaves.* MRS. LINDE *is in travel dress.*)

MRS. LINDE (*timid and a little hesitant*).   Good morning, Nora.

NORA (*uncertainly*).   Good morning.

MRS. LINDE.   I don't believe you know who I am.

NORA.   No— I'm not sure— Though I know I should— Of course! Kristine! It's you!

MRS. LINDE.   Yes, it's me.

NORA.   And I didn't even recognize you! I had no idea! (*In a lower voice.*) You've changed, Kristine.

MRS. LINDE.   I'm sure I have. It's been nine or ten long years.

NORA.   Has it really been that long? Yes, you're right. I've been so happy these last eight years. And now you're here. Such a long trip in the middle of winter. How brave!

MRS. LINDE.   I got in on the steamer this morning.

NORA.   To have some fun over the holidays, of course. That's lovely. For we are going to have fun. But take off your coat! You aren't cold, are you? (*Helps her.*) There, now! Let's sit down here by the fire and just relax and talk. No, you sit there. I want the rocking chair. (*Takes her hands.*) And now you've got your old face back. It was just for a minute, right at first— Though you are a little more pale, Kristine. And maybe a little thinner.

MRS. LINDE.   And much, much older, Nora.

NORA.   Maybe a little older. Just a teeny-weeny bit, not much. (*Interrupts herself, serious.*) Oh, but how thoughtless of me, chatting away like this! Sweet, good Kristine, can you forgive me?

MRS. LINDE.   Forgive you what, Nora?

NORA (*in a low voice*).   You poor dear, you lost your husband, didn't you?

MRS. LINDE.   Three years ago, yes.

NORA.   I know. I saw it in the paper. Oh please believe me, Kristine, I really meant to write you, but I never got around to it. Something was always coming up.

MRS. LINDE.   Of course, Nora. I understand.

NORA.   No, that wasn't very nice of me. You poor thing, all you must have been through. And he didn't leave you much, either, did he?

MRS. LINDE.   No.

NORA.   And no children?

MRS. LINDE.   No.

NORA.   Nothing at all, in other words?

MRS. LINDE.   Not so much as a sense of loss—a grief to live on—

NORA (*incredulous*).   But Kristine, how can that be?

MRS. LINDE (*with a sad smile, strokes NORA's hair*).   That's the way it sometimes is, Nora.

NORA.   All alone. How awful for you. I have three darling children. You can't see them right now, though; they're out with their nurse. But now you must tell me everything—

MRS. LINDE.   No, no; I'd rather listen to you.

NORA.   No, you begin. Today I won't be selfish. Today I'll think only of you. Except there's one thing I've just got to tell you first. Something marvelous that's happened to us just these last few days. You haven't heard, have you?

MRS. LINDE.   No; tell me.

NORA.   Just think. My husband's been made manager of the Mutual Bank.

MRS. LINDE.   Your husband—! Oh, I'm so glad!

NORA.   Yes, isn't that great? You see, private law practice is so uncertain, especially when you won't have anything to do with cases that aren't—you know—quite nice. And of course Torvald won't do that and I quite agree with him. Oh, you've no idea how delighted we are! He takes over at New Year's, and he'll be getting a big salary and all sorts of extras. From now on we'll be able to live in quite a different way —exactly as we like. Oh, Kristine! I feel so carefree and happy! It's lovely to have lots and lots of money and not have to worry about a thing! Don't you agree?

MRS. LINDE.   It would be nice to have enough at any rate.

NORA.   No, I don't mean just enough. I mean lots and lots!

MRS. LINDE (*smiles*).   Nora, Nora, when are you going to be sensible? In school you spent a great deal of money.

NORA (*quietly laughing*).   Yes, and Torvald says I still do. (*Raising her finger at* MRS. LINDE.) But "Nora, Nora" isn't so crazy as you all think. Believe me, we've had nothing to be extravagant with. We've both had to work.

MRS. LINDE.   You too?

NORA.   Yes. Oh, it's been little things, mostly—sewing, crocheting, embroidery—that sort of thing. (*Casually*) And other things too. You know of course, that Torvald left government service when we got married? There was no chance of promotion in his department, and of course he had to make more money than he had been making. So for the first few years he worked altogether too hard. He had to take jobs on the side and work night and day. It turned out to be too much for him. He became seriously ill. The doctors told him he needed to go south.

MRS. LINDE.   That's right, you spent a year in Italy, didn't you?

NORA.   Yes, we did. But you won't believe how hard it was to get away. Ivar had just been born. But of course we had to go. Oh, it was a wonderful trip. And it saved Torvald's life. But it took a lot of money, Kristine.

MRS. LINDE.   I'm sure it did.

NORA.   Twelve hundred specie dollars. Four thousand eight hundred crowns. That's a lot of money.

MRS. LINDE.   Yes. So it's lucky you have it when something like that happens.

NORA.   Well, actually we got the money from Daddy.

MRS. LINDE.   I see. That was about the time your father died, I believe.

NORA.   Yes, just about then. And I couldn't even go and take care of him. I was expecting little Ivar any day. And I had poor Torvald to look after, desperately sick and all. My dear, good Daddy! I never saw him again, Kristine. That's the saddest thing that's happened to me since I got married.

MRS. LINDE.   I know you were very fond of him. But then you went to Italy?

NORA.   Yes, for now we had the money and the doctors urged us to go. So we left about a month later.

MRS. LINDE.   And when you came back your husband was well again?

NORA.   Healthy as a horse!

MRS. LINDE.   But—the doctor?

NORA.   What do you mean?

MRS. LINDE.   I thought the maid said it was the doctor, that gentleman who came the same time I did.

NORA.   Oh, that's Dr. Rank. He doesn't come as a doctor. He's our closest friend. He looks in at least once every day. No, Torvald hasn't been sick once since then. And the children are strong and healthy, too, and so am I. (*Jumps up and claps her hands.*) Oh God, Kristine! Isn't it wonderful to be alive and happy! Isn't it just lovely!— But now I'm being mean again, talking only about myself and my things. (*Sits down on a footstool close to* MRS. LINDE *and puts her arms on her lap.*) Please don't be angry with me! Tell me, is it really true that you didn't care for your husband? Then why did you marry him?

MRS. LINDE.   Mother was still alive then, but she was bedridden and helpless. And I had my two younger brothers to look after. I didn't think I had the right to turn him down.

NORA.   No, I suppose not. So he had money then?

MRS. LINDE.   He was quite well off, I think. But it was an uncertain business, Nora. When he died, the whole thing collapsed and there was nothing left.

NORA.   And then—?

MRS. LINDE.   Well, I had to manage as best I could. With a little store and a little school and anything else I could think of. The last three years have been one long workday for me, Nora, without any rest. But now it's over. My poor mother doesn't need me any more. She's passed away. And the boys are on their own too. They've both got jobs and support themselves.

NORA.   What a relief for you—

MRS. LINDE.   No, not relief. Just a great emptiness. Nobody to live for any more. (*Gets up restlessly.*) That's why I couldn't stand it any longer in that little hole. Here in town it has to be easier to find something to keep me busy and occupy my thoughts. With a little luck I should be able to find a permanent job, something in an office—

NORA.   Oh but Kristine, that's exhausting work, and you look worn out already. It would be much better for you to go to a resort.

MRS. LINDE (*walks over to the window*).   I don't have a Daddy who can give me the money, Nora.

NORA (*getting up*).   Oh, don't be angry with me.

MRS. LINDE (*over to her*).   Dear Nora, don't *you* be angry with *me*. That's the worst thing about my kind of situation: you become so bitter. You've nobody to work for, and yet you have to look out for yourself, somehow. You've got to keep on living, and so you become selfish. Do you know—when you told me about your husband's new position I was delighted not so much for your sake as for my own.

NORA.   Why was that? Oh, I see. You think maybe Torvald can give you a job?

MRS. LINDE.   That's what I had in mind.

NORA.   And he will too, Kristine. Just leave it to me. I'll be ever so subtle about it. I'll think of something nice to tell him, something he'll like. Oh I so much want to help you.

MRS. LINDE.   That's very good of you, Nora—making an effort like that for me. Especially since you've known so little trouble and hardship in your own life.

NORA.   I—?—have known so little—?

MRS. LINDE (*smiling*).   Oh well, a little sewing or whatever it was. You're still a child, Nora.

NORA (*with a toss of her head, walks away*).   You shouldn't sound so superior.

MRS. LINDE.   I shouldn't?

NORA.   You're just like all the others. None of you think I'm good for anything really serious.

MRS. LINDE.   Well, now—

NORA.   That I've never been through anything difficult.

MRS. LINDE.   But Nora! You just told me all your troubles!

NORA.   That's nothing! (*Lowers her voice*) I haven't told you about *it*.

MRS. LINDE.   It? What's that? What do you mean?

NORA.   You patronize me, Kristine, and that's not fair. You're proud that you worked so long and so hard for your mother.

MRS. LINDE.   I don't think I patronize anyone. But it *is* true that I'm both proud and happy that I could make mother's last years comparatively easy.

NORA.   And you're proud of all you did for your brothers.

MRS. LINDE.   I think I have a right to be.

NORA.   And so do I. But now I want to tell you something, Kristine. I have something to be proud and happy about too.

MRS. LINDE.   I don't doubt that for a moment. But what exactly do you mean?

NORA.   Not so loud! Torvald mustn't hear—not for anything in the world. Nobody must know about this, Kristine. Nobody but you.

MRS. LINDE.   But what is it?

NORA.   Come here. (*Pulls her down on the couch beside her.*) You see, I *do* have something to be proud and happy about. I've saved Torvald's life.

MRS. LINDE.   Saved—? How do you mean—"saved"?

NORA.   I told you about our trip to Italy. Torvald would have died if he hadn't gone.

MRS. LINDE.   I understand that. And so your father gave you the money you needed.

NORA (*smiles*).   Yes, that's what Torvald and all the others think. But—

MRS. LINDE.   But what?

NORA.   Daddy didn't give us a penny. *I* raised that money.

MRS. LINDE.   *You* did? That whole big amount?

NORA.   Twelve hundred specie dollars. Four thousand eight hundred crowns. *Now* what do you say?

MRS. LINDE.   But Nora, how could you? Did you win in the state lottery?

NORA (*contemptuously*).   State lottery! (*Snorts.*) What is so great about that?

MRS. LINDE.   Where did it come from then?

NORA (*humming and smiling, enjoying her secret*).   Hmmm. Tra-la-la-la-la!

MRS. LINDE.   You certainly couldn't have borrowed it.

NORA.   Oh? And why not?

MRS. LINDE.   A wife can't borrow money without her husband's consent.

NORA (*with a toss of her head*).   Oh, I don't know—take a wife with a little bit of a head for business—a wife who knows how to manage things—

MRS. LINDE.   But Nora, I don't understand at all—

NORA.   You don't have to. I didn't say I borrowed the money, did I? I could have gotten it some other way. (*Leans back.*) An admirer may have given it to me. When you're as tolerably good-looking as I am—

MRS. LINDE.   Oh, you're crazy.

NORA.   I think you're dying from curiosity, Kristine.

MRS. LINDE.   I'm beginning to think you've done something very foolish, Nora.

NORA (*sits up*).   Is it foolish to save your husband's life?

MRS. LINDE.   I say it's foolish to act behind his back.

NORA.   But don't you see: he couldn't be told! You're missing the whole point, Kristine. We couldn't even let him know how seriously ill he was. The doctors came to *me* and told me his life was in danger, that nothing could save him but a stay in the south. Don't you think I tried to work on him? I told him how lovely it would be if I could go abroad like other young wives. I cried and begged. I said he'd better remember what condition I was in, that he had to be nice to me and do what I wanted. I even hinted he could borrow the money. But that almost made him angry with me. He told me I was being irresponsible and that it was his duty as my husband not to give in to my moods and whims—I think that's what he called it. All right, I said to myself, you've got to be saved somehow, and so I found a way—

MRS. LINDE.   And your husband never learned from your father that the money didn't come from him?

NORA.   Never. Daddy died that same week. I thought of telling him all about it and asking him not to say anything. But since he was so sick—It turned out I didn't have to—

MRS. LINDE.   And you've never told your husband?

NORA.   Of course not! Good heavens, how could I? He, with his strict principles! Besides, you know how men are. Torvald would find it embarrassing and humiliating to learn that he owed me anything. It would upset our whole relationship. Our happy, beautiful home would no longer be what it is.

MRS. LINDE.   Aren't you ever going to tell him?

NORA (*reflectively, half smiling*).   Yes—one day, maybe. Many, many years from now, when I'm no longer young and pretty. Don't laugh! I mean when Torvald no longer feels about me the way he does now, when he no longer thinks it's fun when I dance for him and put on costumes and recite for him. Then it will be good to have something in reserve— (*Interrupts herself.*) Oh, I'm just being silly! That day will never come.— Well, now, Kristine, what do you think of my great secret? Don't you think I'm good for something too?— By the way, you wouldn't believe all the worry I've had because of it. It's been very hard to meet my obligations on schedule. You see, in business there's something called quarterly interest and something called installments on the principal, and those are terribly hard to come up with. I've had to save a little here and a little there, whenever I could. I couldn't use much of the housekeeping money, for Torvald has to eat well. And I couldn't use what I got for clothes for the children. They have to look nice, and I didn't think it would be right to spend less than I got—the sweet little things!

MRS. LINDE.   Poor Nora! So you had to take it from your allowance!

NORA.   Yes, of course. After all, it was my affair. Every time Torvald gave me money for a new dress and things like that, I never used more than half of it. I always bought the cheapest, simplest things for myself. Thank God, everything looks good on me, so Torvald never noticed. But it was hard many times, Kristine, for it's fun to have pretty clothes. Don't you think?

MRS. LINDE.   Certainly.

NORA.   Anyway, I had other ways of making money too. Last winter I was lucky enough to get some copying work. So I locked the door and sat up writing every night till quite late. God! I often got so tired—! But it was great fun, too, working and making money. It was almost like being a man.

MRS. LINDE.   But how much have you been able to pay off this way?

NORA.   I couldn't tell you exactly. You see, it's very difficult to keep track of business like that. All I know is I have been paying off as much as I've been able to scrape together. Many times I just didn't know what to do. (*Smiles.*) Then I used to imagine a rich old gentleman had fallen in love with me—

MRS. LINDE.   What! What old gentleman?

NORA.   Phooey! And now he was dead and they were reading his will, and there it said in big letters, "All my money is to be paid in cash immediately to the charming Mrs. Nora Helmer."

MRS. LINDE.   But dearest Nora—who *was* this old gentleman?

NORA.   For heaven's sake, Kristine, don't you see? There *was* no old gentleman. He was just somebody I made up when I couldn't think of any way to raise the money. But never mind him. The old bore can be anyone he likes to for all I care. I have no use for him or his last will, for now I don't have a single worry in the world. (*Jumps up.*) Dear God, what a lovely thought this is! To be able to play and have fun with the children, to have everything nice and pretty in the house, just the way Torvald likes it! Not a care! And soon spring will be here, and the air will be blue and high. Maybe we can travel again. Maybe I'll see the ocean again! Oh, yes, yes!—it's wonderful to be alive and happy! (*The doorbell rings.*)

MRS. LINDE (*getting up*).   There's the doorbell. Maybe I better be going.

NORA.   No, please stay. I'm sure it's just someone for Torvald—

MAID (*in the hall door*).   Excuse me, ma'am. There's a gentleman here who'd like to see Mr. Helmer.

NORA.   You mean the bank manager.

MAID.   Sorry, ma'am; the bank manager. But I didn't know—since the Doctor is with him—

NORA.   Who is the gentleman?

KROGSTAD (*appearing in the door*).   It's just me, Mrs. Helmer. (MRS. LINDE *starts, looks, turns away toward the window.*)

NORA (*takes a step toward him, tense, in a low voice*).   You? What do you want? What do you want with my husband?

KROGSTAD.   Bank business—in a way. I have a small job in the Mutual, and I understand your husband is going to be our new boss—

NORA.   So it's just—

KROGSTAD.   Just routine business, ma'am. Nothing else.

NORA.   All right. In that case, why don't you go through the door to the office. (*Dismisses him casually as she closes the door. Walks over to the stove and tends the fire.*)

MRS. LINDE.   Nora—who was that man?

NORA.   His name is Krogstad. He's a lawyer.

MRS. LINDE.   So it *was* him.

NORA.   Do you know him?

MRS. LINDE.   I used to—many years ago. For a while he clerked in our part of the country.

NORA.   Right. He did.

MRS. LINDE.   He has changed a great deal.

NORA.   I believe he had a very unhappy marriage.

MRS. LINDE.   And now he's a widower, isn't he?

NORA.   With many children. There now; it's burning nicely again. (*Closes the stove and moves the rocking chair a little to the side.*)

MRS. LINDE.   They say he's into all sorts of business.

NORA.   Really? Maybe so. I wouldn't know. But let's not think about business. It's such a bore.

DR. RANK (*appears in the door to* HELMER'S *study*).   No, I don't want to be in the way. I'd rather talk to your wife a bit. (*Closes the door and notices* MRS. LINDE.) Oh, I beg your pardon. I believe I'm in the way here, too.

NORA.   No, not at all. (*Introduces them.*) Dr. Rank, Mrs. Linde.

RANK.   Aha. A name often heard in this house. I believe I passed you on the stairs coming up.

MRS. LINDE.   Yes. I'm afraid I climb stairs very slowly. They aren't good for me.

RANK.   I see. A slight case of inner decay, perhaps?

MRS. LINDE.   Overwork, rather.

RANK.   Oh, is that all? And now you've come to town to relax at all the parties?

MRS. LINDE.   I have come to look for a job.

RANK.   A proven cure for overwork, I take it?

MRS. LINDE.   One has to live, Doctor.

RANK.   Yes, that seems to be the common opinion.

NORA.   Come on, Dr. Rank—you want to live just as much as the rest of us.

RANK.   Of course I do. Miserable as I am, I prefer to go on being tortured as long as possible. All my patients feel the same way. And that's true of the moral invalids too. Helmer is talking with a specimen right this minute.

MRS. LINDE (*in a low voice*).   Ah!

NORA.   What do you mean?

RANK.   Oh, this lawyer, Krogstad. You don't know him. The roots of his character are decayed. But even he began by saying something about having *to live* —as if it were a matter of the highest importance.

NORA.   Oh? What did he want with Torvald?

RANK.   I don't really know. All I heard was something about the bank.

NORA.   I didn't know that Krog—that this Krogstad had anything to do with the Mutual Bank.

RANK.   Yes, he seems to have some kind of job there. (*To* MRS. LINDE) I don't know if you are familiar in your part of the country with the kind of person who is always running around trying to sniff out cases of moral decrepitude and as soon as he finds one puts the individual under observation in some excellent position or other. All the healthy ones are left out in the cold.

MRS. LINDE.   I should think it's the sick who need looking after the most.

RANK (*shrugs his shoulders*).   There we are. That's the attitude that turns society into a hospital. (NORA, *absorbed in her own thoughts, suddenly starts giggling and clapping her hands.*) What's so funny about that? Do you even know what society is?

NORA.   What do I care about your stupid society! I laughed at something entirely different—something terribly amusing. Tell me, Dr. Rank—all the employees in the Mutual Bank, from now on they'll all be dependent on Torvald, right?

RANK.   Is that what you find so enormously amusing?

NORA (*smiles and hums*).   That's my business, that's my business! (*Walks around.*) Yes, I do think it's fun that we—that Torvald is going to have so much influence on so many people's lives. (*Brings out the bag of macaroons.*) Have a macaroon, Dr. Rank.

RANK.   Well, well—macaroons. I thought they were banned around here.

NORA.   Yes, but these were some Kristine gave me.

MRS. LINDE.   What! I?

NORA.   That's all right. Don't look so scared. You couldn't know that Torvald won't let me have them. He's afraid they'll ruin my teeth. But who cares! Just once in a while—! Right, Dr. Rank? Have one! (*Puts a macaroon into his mouth.*) You too, Kristine. And one for me. A very small one. Or at most two. (*Walks around again.*) Yes, I really feel very, very happy. Now there's just one thing I'm dying to do.

RANK.   Oh? And what's that?

NORA.   Something I'm dying to say so Torvald could hear.

RANK.   And why can't you?

NORA.   I don't dare to, for it's not nice.

MRS. LINDE.   Not nice?

RANK.   In that case, I guess you'd better not. But surely to the two of us—? What is it you'd like to say for Helmer to hear?

NORA.   I want to say, "Goddammit!"

RANK.   Are you out of your mind!

MRS. LINDE.   For heaven's sakes, Nora!

RANK.   Say it. Here he comes.

NORA (*hiding the macaroons*).   Shhh! (HELMER *enters from his study, carrying his hat and overcoat.* NORA *goes to him.*) Well, dear, did you get rid of him?

HELMER.   Yes, he just left.

NORA.   Torvald, I want you to meet Kristine. She's just come to town.

HELMER.   Kristine—? I'm sorry; I don't think—

NORA.   Mrs. Linde, Torvald dear. Mrs. Kristine Linde.

HELMER.   Ah, yes. A childhood friend of my wife's, I suppose.

MRS. LINDE.   Yes, we've known each other for a long time.

NORA.   Just think; she has come all this way just to see you.

HELMER.   I'm not sure I understand—

MRS. LINDE.   Well, not really—

NORA.   You see, Kristine is an absolutely fantastic secretary, and she would so much like to work for a competent executive and learn more than she knows already—

HELMER.   Very sensible, I'm sure, Mrs. Linde.

NORA.   So when she heard about your appointment—there was a wire—she came here as fast as she could. How about it, Torvald? Couldn't you do something for Kristine? For my sake. Please?

HELMER.   Quite possibly. I take it you're a widow, Mrs. Linde?

MRS. LINDE.   Yes.

HELMER.   And you've had office experience?

MRS. LINDE.   Some—yes.

HELMER.   In that case I think it's quite likely that I'll be able to find you a position.

NORA (*claps her hands*).   I knew it! I knew it!

HELMER.   You've arrived at a most opportune time, Mrs. Linde.

MRS. LINDE.   Oh, how can I ever thank you—

HELMER.   Not at all, not at all. (*Puts his coat on.*) But today you'll have to excuse me—

RANK.   Wait a minute; I'll come with you. (*Gets his fur coat from the front hall, warms it by the stove.*)

NORA.   Don't be long, Torvald.

HELMER.   An hour or so; no more.

NORA.   Are you leaving, too, Kristine?

MRS. LINDE (*putting on her things*).   Yes, I'd better go and find a place to stay.

HELMER.   Good. Then we'll be going the same way.

NORA (*helping her*).   I'm sorry this place is so small, but I don't think we very well could—

MRS. LINDE.   Of course! Don't be silly, Nora. Goodbye, and thank you for everything.

NORA.   Goodbye. We'll see you soon. You'll be back this evening, of course. And you too, Dr. Rank; right? If you feel well enough? Of course you will. Just wrap yourself up. (*General small talk as all exit into the hall.* CHILDREN's *voices are heard on the stairs.*) There they are! There they are! (*She runs and opens the door. The nurse* ANNE-MARIE *enters with the* CHILDREN.)

NORA.   Come in! Come in! (*Bends over and kisses them.*) Oh, you sweet, sweet darlings! Look at them, Kristine! Aren't they beautiful?

RANK.   No standing around in the draft!

HELMER.   Come along, Mrs. Linde. This place isn't fit for anyone but mothers right now. (DR. RANK, HELMER, *and* MRS. LINDE *go down the stairs. The* NURSE *enters the living room with the children.* NORA *follows, closing the door behind her.*)

NORA.   My, how nice you all look! Such red cheeks! Like apples and roses. (*The* CHILDREN *all talk at the same time.*) You've had so much fun? I bet you have. Oh, isn't that nice! You pulled both Emmy and Bob on your sleigh? Both at the same time? That's very good, Ivar. Oh, let me hold her for a minute, Anne-Marie. My sweet little doll baby! (*Takes the smallest of the children from the* NURSE *and dances with her.*) Yes, yes, of course; Mama'll dance with you too, Bob. What? You threw snowballs? Oh, I wish I'd been there! No, no; *I* want to take their clothes off, Anne-Marie. Please let me; I think it's so much fun. You go on in. You look frozen. There's hot coffee on the stove. (*The* NURSE *exits into the room to the left.* NORA *takes the* CHILDREN's *wraps off and throws them all around. They all keep telling her things at the same time.*)

NORA.   Oh, really? A big dog ran after you? But it didn't bite you. Of course not. Dogs don't bite sweet little doll babies. Don't peek at the packages, Ivar! What's in them? Wouldn't you like to know! No, no; that's something terrible! Play? You want to play? What do you want to play? Okay, let's play hide-and-seek. Bob hides first. You want *me* to? All right. I'll go first. (*Laughing and shouting,* NORA *and the* CHILDREN *play in the living room and in the adjacent room, right. Finally,* NORA *hides herself under the table; the* CHILDREN *rush in, look for her, can't find her. They hear her low giggle, run to the table, lift the rug that covers it, see her. General hilarity. She crawls out, pretends to scare them. New delight. In the meantime there has been a knock on the door between the living room and the front hall, but nobody has noticed. Now the door is opened halfway;* KROGSTAD *appears. He waits a little. The play goes on.*)

KROGSTAD.   Pardon me, Mrs. Helmer—

NORA (*with a muted cry turns around, jumps up*).   Ah! What do you want?

KROGSTAD.   I'm sorry. The front door was open. Somebody must have forgotten to close it—

NORA (*standing up*).   My husband isn't here, Mr. Krogstad.

KROGSTAD.   I know.

NORA.   So what do you want?

KROGSTAD.   I'd like a word with you.

NORA.   With—? (*To the* CHILDREN) Go in to Anne-Marie. What? No, the strange man won't do anything bad to Mama. When he's gone we'll play some more. (*She takes the* CHILDREN *into the room to the left and closes the door. She turns—tense, troubled.*) You want to speak with me?

KROGSTAD.   Yes I do.

NORA.   Today—? It isn't the first of the month yet.

KROGSTAD.   No, it's Christmas Eve. It's up to you what kind of holiday you'll have.

NORA.   What do you want? I can't possibly—

KROGSTAD.   Let's not talk about that just yet. There's something else. You do have a few minutes, don't you?

NORA.   Yes. Yes, of course. That is,—

KROGSTAD.   Good. I was sitting in Olsen's restaurant when I saw your husband go by.

NORA.   Yes—?

KROGSTAD.   —with a lady.

NORA.   What of it?

KROGSTAD.   May I be so free as to ask: wasn't that lady Mrs. Linde?

NORA.   Yes.

KROGSTAD.   Just arrived in town?

NORA.   Yes, today.

KROGSTAD.   She's a good friend of yours, I understand?

NORA.   Yes, she is. But I fail to see—

KROGSTAD.   I used to know her myself.

NORA.   I know that.

KROGSTAD.   So you know about that. I thought as much. In that case, let me ask you a simple question. Is Mrs. Linde going to be employed in the bank?

NORA.   What makes you think you have the right to cross-examine me like this, Mr. Krogstad—you, one of my husband's employees? But since you ask, I'll tell you. Yes, Mrs. Linde is going to be working in the bank. And it was I who recommended her, Mr. Krogstad. Now you know.

KROGSTAD.   So I was right.

NORA (*walks up and down*).   After all, one does have a little influence, you know. Just because you're a woman, it doesn't mean that— Really, Mr. Krogstad, people in a subordinate position should be careful not to offend someone who—oh well—

KROGSTAD.   —has influence?

NORA.   Exactly.

KROGSTAD (*changing his tone*).   Mrs. Helmer, I must ask you to be good enough to use your influence on my behalf.

NORA.   What do you mean?

KROGSTAD.   I want you to make sure that I am going to keep my subordinate position in the bank.

NORA.   I don't understand. Who is going to take your position away from you?

KROGSTAD.   There's no point in playing ignorant with me, Mrs. Helmer. I can very well appreciate that your friend will find it unpleasant to run into me. So now I know who I can thank for my dismissal.

NORA.   But I assure you—

KROGSTAD.   Never mind. Just want to say you still have time. I advise you to use your influence to prevent it.

NORA.   But Mr. Krogstad, I don't have any influence—none at all.

KROGSTAD.   No? I thought you just said—

NORA.   Of course I didn't mean it that way. I! Whatever makes you think that I have any influence of that kind on my husband?

KROGSTAD.   I went to law school with your husband. I have no reason to think that the bank manager is less susceptible than other husbands.

NORA.   If you're going to insult my husband, I'll ask you to leave.

KROGSTAD.   You're brave, Mrs. Helmer.

NORA.   I'm not afraid of you any more. After New Year's I'll be out of this thing with you.

KROGSTAD (*more controlled*).   Listen, Mrs. Helmer. If necessary I'll fight as for my life to keep my little job in the bank.

NORA.   So it seems.

KROGSTAD.   It isn't just the money; that's really the smallest part of it. There is something else— Well, I guess I might as well tell you. It's like this. I'm sure you know, like everybody else, that some years ago I committed—an impropriety.

NORA.   I believe I've heard it mentioned.

KROGSTAD.   The case never came to court, but from that moment all doors were closed to me. So I took up the kind of business you know about. I had to do something, and I think I can say about myself that I have not been among the worst. But now I want to get out of all that. My sons are growing up. For their sake I must get back as much of my good name as I can. This job in the bank was like the first rung on the ladder. And now your husband wants to kick me down and leave me back in the mud again.

NORA.   But I swear to you, Mr. Krogstad; it's not at all in my power to help you.

KROGSTAD.   That's because you don't want to. But I have the means to force you.

NORA.   You don't mean you're going to tell my husband I owe you money?

KROGSTAD.   And if I did?

NORA.   That would be a mean thing to do. (*Almost crying.*) That secret, which is my joy and my pride—for him to learn about it in such a coarse and ugly manner—to learn it from *you*—! It would be terribly unpleasant for me.

KROGSTAD.   Just unpleasant?

NORA (*heatedly*).   But go ahead! Do it! It will be worse for you than for me. When my husband realizes what a bad person you are you'll be sure to lose your job.

KROGSTAD.   I asked you if it was just domestic unpleasantness you were afraid of?

NORA.   When my husband finds out, of course he'll pay off the loan, and then we won't have anything more to do with you.

KROGSTAD (*stepping closer*).   Listen, Mrs. Helmer—either you have a very bad memory, or you don't know much about business. I think I had better straighten you out on a few things.

NORA.   What do you mean?

KROGSTAD.   When your husband was ill, you came to me to borrow twelve hundred dollars.

NORA.   I knew nobody else.

KROGSTAD.   I promised to get you the money on certain conditions. At the time you were so anxious about your husband's health and so set on getting him away that I doubt very much that you paid much attention to the details of our transaction. That's why I remind you of them now. Anyway, I promised to get you the money if you would sign an I.O.U., which I drafted.

NORA.   And which I signed.

KROGSTAD.   Good. But below your signature I added a few lines making your father security for the loan. Your father was supposed to put his signature to those lines.

NORA.   Supposed to—? He did.

KROGSTAD.   I had left the date blank. That is, your father was to date his own signature. You recall that, don't you, Mrs. Helmer?

NORA.   I guess so—

KROGSTAD.   I gave the note to you. You were to mail it to your father. Am I correct?

NORA.   Yes.

KROGSTAD.   And of course you did so right away, for no more than five or six days later you brought the paper back to me, signed by your father. Then I paid you the money.

NORA.   Well? And haven't I been keeping up with the payments?

KROGSTAD.   Fairly well, yes. But to get back to what we were talking about—those were difficult days for you, weren't they, Mrs. Helmer?

NORA.   Yes, they were.

KROGSTAD.   Your father was quite ill, I believe.

NORA.   He was dying.

KROGSTAD.   And died shortly afterwards?

NORA.   That's right.

KROGSTAD.   Tell me, Mrs. Helmer; do you happen to remember the date of your father's death? I mean the exact day of the month?

NORA.   Daddy died on September 29.

KROGSTAD.   Quite correct. I have ascertained that fact. That's why there is something peculiar about this (*takes out a piece of paper*), which I can't account for.

NORA.   Peculiar? How? I don't understand—

KROGSTAD.   It seems very peculiar, Mrs. Helmer, that your father signed this promissory note three days after his death.

NORA.   How so? I don't see what—

KROGSTAD.   Your father died on September 29. Now look. He has dated his signature October 2. Isn't that odd? (NORA *remains silent.*) Can you explain it? (NORA *is still silent.*) I also find it striking that the date and the month and the year are not in your father's handwriting but in a hand I think I recognize. Well, that might be explained. Your father may have forgotten to date his signature and somebody else may have done it here, guessing at the date before he had learned of your father's death. That's all right. It's only the signature itself that matters. And that is genuine, isn't it, Mrs. Helmer? Your father *did* put his name to this note?

NORA (*after a brief silence tosses her head back and looks defiantly at him*).   No, he didn't. *I* wrote Daddy's name.

KROGSTAD.   Mrs. Helmer—do you realize what a dangerous admission you just made?

NORA.   Why? You'll get your money soon.

KROGSTAD.   Let me ask you something. Why didn't you mail this note to your father?

NORA.   Because it was impossible. Daddy was sick—you know that. If I had asked him to sign it, I would have had to tell him what the money was for. But I couldn't tell him, as sick as he was, that my husband's life was in danger. That was impossible. Surely you can see that.

KROGSTAD.   Then it would have been better for you if you had given up your trip abroad.

NORA.   No, that was impossible! That trip was to save my husband's life. I couldn't give it up.

KROGSTAD.   But didn't you realize that what you did amounted to fraud against me?

NORA.   I couldn't let that make any difference. I didn't care about you at all. I hated the way you made all those difficulties for me, even though you knew the danger my husband was in. I thought you were cold and unfeeling.

KROGSTAD.   Mrs. Helmer, obviously you have no clear idea of what you have done. Let me tell you that what I did that time was no more and no worse. And it ruined my name and reputation.

NORA.   You! Are you trying to tell me that you did something brave once in order to save your wife's life?

KROGSTAD.   The law doesn't ask motives.

NORA.   Then it's a bad law.

KROGSTAD.   Bad or not—if I produce this note in court you'll be judged according to the law.

NORA.   I refuse to believe you. A daughter shouldn't have the right to spare her dying old father worry and anxiety? A wife shouldn't have the right to save her husband's life? I don't know the laws very well, but I'm sure that somewhere they make allowances for cases like that. And you, a lawyer, don't know that? I think you must be a bad lawyer, Mr. Krogstad.

KROGSTAD.   That may be. But business—the kind of business you and I have with one another—don't you think I know something about that? Very well. Do what you like. But let me tell you this: if I'm going to be kicked out again, you'll keep me company. (*He bows and exits through the front hall.*)

NORA (*pauses thoughtfully; then, with a defiant toss of her head*). Oh, nonsense! Trying to scare me like that! I'm not all that silly. (*Starts picking up the* CHILDREN's *clothes; soon stops.*) But—? No! That's impossible! I did it for love!

THE CHILDREN (*in the door to the left*).   Mama, the strange man just left. We saw him.

NORA.   Yes, yes; I know. But don't tell anybody about the strange man. Do you hear? Not even Daddy.

CHILDREN.   We won't. But now you'll play with us again, won't you, mama?

NORA.   No, not right now.

CHILDREN.   But Mama—you promised.

NORA.   I know, but I can't just now. Go to your own room. I've so much to do. Be nice now, my little darlings. Do as I say. (*She nudges them gently into the other room and closes the door. She sits down on the couch, picks up a piece of embroidery, makes a few stitches, then stops.*) No! (*Throws the embroidery down, goes to the hall door and calls out.*) Helene! Bring the Christmas tree in here, please! (*Goes to the table, left, opens the drawer, halts.*) No—that's impossible!

MAID (*with the Christmas tree*).   Where do you want it, ma'am?

NORA.   There. The middle of the floor.

MAID.   You want anything else?

NORA.   No, thanks. I have everything I need. (*The* MAID *goes out.* NORA *starts trimming the tree.*) I want candles—and flowers— That awful man! Oh nonsense! There's nothing wrong. This will be a lovely tree. I'll do everything you want me to, Torvald. I'll sing for you— dance for you— (HELMER, *a bundle of papers under his arm, enters from outside.*) Ah—you're back already?

HELMER.   Yes. Has anybody been here?

NORA.   Here? No.

HELMER.   That's funny. I saw Krogstad leaving just now.

NORA.   Oh? Oh yes, that's right. Krogstad was here for just a moment.

HELMER.   I can tell from your face that he came to ask you to put in a word for him.

NORA.   Yes.

HELMER.   And it was supposed to be your own idea, wasn't it? You were not to tell me he'd been here. He asked you that too, didn't he?

NORA.   Yes, Torvald, but—

HELMER.   Nora, Nora, how could you! Talk to a man like that and make him promises! And lying to me about it afterward—!

NORA.   Lying—?

HELMER.   Didn't you say nobody had been here? (*Shakes his finger at her.*) My little songbird must never do that again. Songbirds are supposed to have clean beaks to chirp with—no false notes. (*Puts his arm around her waist.*) Isn't that so? Of course it is. (*Lets her go.*) And that's enough about that. (*Sits down in front of the fireplace.*) Ah, it's nice and warm in here. (*Begins to leaf through his papers.*)

NORA (*busy with the tree; after a brief pause*).   Torvald.

HELMER.   Yes.

NORA.   I'm looking forward so much to the Stenborgs' costume party day after tomorrow.

HELMER.   And I can't wait to find out what you're going to surprise me with.

NORA.   Oh, that silly idea!

HELMER.   Oh?

NORA.   I can't think of anything. It all seems so foolish and pointless.

HELMER.   Ah, my little Nora admits that?

NORA (*behind his chair, her arms on the back of the chair*).   Are you very busy, Torvald?

HELMER.   Well—

NORA.   What are all those papers?

HELMER.   Bank business.

NORA.   Already?

HELMER.   I've asked the board to give me the authority to make certain changes in organization and personnel. That's what I'll be doing over the holidays. I want it all settled before New Year's.

NORA.   So that's why this poor Krogstad—

HELMER.   Hm.

NORA (*leisurely playing with the hair on his neck*).   If you weren't so busy, Torvald, I'd ask you for a great big favor.

HELMER.   Let's hear it, anyway.

NORA.   I don't know anyone with better taste than you, and I want so much to look nice at the party. Couldn't you sort of take charge of me, Torvald, and decide what I'll wear— Help me with my costume?

HELMER.   Aha! Little Lady Obstinate is looking for someone to rescue her?

NORA.   Yes, Torvald. I won't get anywhere without your help.

HELMER.   All right. I'll think about it. We'll come up with something.

NORA.   Oh, you *are* nice! (*Goes back to the Christmas tree. A pause.*) Those red flowers look so pretty.— Tell me, was it really all that bad what this Krogstad fellow did?

HELMER.   He forged signatures. Do you have any idea what that means?

NORA.   Couldn't it have been because he felt he had to?

HELMER.   Yes, or like so many others he may simply have been thoughtless. I'm not so heartless as to condemn a man absolutely because of a single imprudent act.

NORA.   Of course not, Torvald!

HELMER.   People like him can redeem themselves morally by openly confessing their crime and taking their punishment.

NORA.   Punishment—?

HELMER.   But that was not the way Krogstad chose. He got out of it with tricks and evasions. That's what has corrupted him.

NORA.   So you think that if—?

HELMER.   Can't you imagine how a guilty person like that has to lie and fake and dissemble wherever he goes—putting on a mask before everybody he's close to, even his own wife and children. It's the thing with the children that's the worst part of it, Nora.

NORA.   Why is that?

HELMER.   Because when a man lives inside such a circle of stinking lies he brings infection into his own home and contaminates his whole family. With every breath of air his children inhale the germs of something ugly.

NORA (*moving closer behind him*).   Are you so sure of that?

HELMER.   Of course I am. I have seen enough examples of that in my work. Nearly all young criminals have had mothers who lied.

NORA.   Why mothers—particularly?

HELMER.   Most often mothers. But of course fathers tend to have the same influence. Every lawyer knows that. And yet, for years this Krogstad has been poisoning his own children in an atmosphere of lies and deceit. That's why I call him a lost soul morally. (*Reaches out for her hands.*) And that's why my sweet little Nora must promise me never to take his side again. Let's shake on that.— What? What's this? Give me your hand. There! Now that's settled. I assure you, I would find it impossible to work in the same room with that man. I feel literally sick when I'm around people like that.

NORA (*withdraws her hand and goes to the other side of the Christmas tree*).   It's so hot in here. And I have so much to do.

HELMER (*gets up and collects his papers*).   Yes, and I really should try to get some of this reading done before dinner. I must think about your costume too. And maybe just possibly I'll have something to wrap in gilt paper and hang on the Christmas tree. (*Puts his hand on her head.*) Oh my adorable little songbird! (*Enters his study and closes the door.*)

NORA (*after a pause, in a low voice*).   It's all a lot of nonsense. It's not that way at all. It's impossible. It has to be impossible.

NURSE (*in the door, left*).   The little ones are asking ever so nicely if they can't come in and be with their mamma.

NORA.   No, no, no! Don't let them in here! You stay with them, Anne-Marie.

NURSE.   If you say so, ma'am. (*Closes the door.*)

NORA (*pale with terror*).   Corrupt my little children—! Poison my home—? (*Brief pause; she lifts her head.*) That's not true. Never. Never in a million years.

ACT 2

The same room. The Christmas tree is in the corner by the piano, stripped shabby-looking, with burnt-down candles. NORA's outside clothes are on the couch. NORA is alone. She walks around restlessly. She stops by the couch and picks up her coat.

NORA (*drops the coat again*).   There's somebody now! (*Goes to the door, listens.*) No. Nobody. Of course not—not on Christmas. And not tomorrow either.*— But perhaps— (*Opens the door and looks.*) No,

*In Norway both Christmas and the day after are legal holidays.

nothing in the mailbox. All empty. (*Comes forward.*) How silly I am! Of course he isn't serious. Nothing like that could happen. After all, I have three small children. (*The* Nurse *enters from the room, left, carrying a big carton.*)

Nurse.   Well, at last I found it—the box with your costume.

Nora.   Thanks. Just put it on the table.

Nurse (*does so*).   But it's all a big mess, I'm afraid.

Nora.   Oh, I wish I could tear the whole thing to little pieces!

Nurse.   Heavens! It's not as bad as all that. It can be fixed all right. All it takes is a little patience.

Nora.   I'll go over and get Mrs. Linde to help me.

Nurse.   Going out again? In this awful weather? You'll catch a cold.

Nora.   That might not be such a bad thing. How are the children?

Nurse.   The poor little dears are playing with their presents, but—

Nora.   Do they keep asking for me?

Nurse.   Well, you know, they're used to being with their mamma.

Nora.   I know. But Anne-Marie, from now on I can't be with them as much as before.

Nurse.   Oh well. Little children get used to everything.

Nora.   You think so? Do you think they'd forget their mamma if I were gone altogether?

Nurse.   Goodness me—gone altogether?

Nora.   Listen, Anne-Marie—something I've wondered about. How could you bring yourself to leave your child with strangers?

Nurse.   But I had to, if I were to nurse you.

Nora.   Yes, but how could you *want* to?

Nurse.   When I could get such a nice place? When something like that happens to a poor young girl, she'd better be grateful for whatever she gets. For *he* didn't do a thing for me—the louse!

Nora.   But your daughter has forgotten all about you, hasn't she?

Nurse.   Oh no! Not at all! She wrote to me both when she was confirmed and when she got married.

Nora (*putting her arms around her neck*).   You dear old thing—you were a good mother to me when I was little.

Nurse.   Poor little Nora had no one else, you know.

Nora.   And if my little ones didn't, I know you'd—oh, I'm being silly! (*Opens the carton.*) Go in to them, please. I really should—. Tomorrow you'll see how pretty I'll be.

Nurse.   I know. There won't be anybody at that party half as pretty as you, ma'am. (*Goes out, left.*)

NORA (*begins to take clothes out of the carton; in a moment she throws it all down*).   If only I dared to go out. If only I knew nobody would come. That nothing would happen while I was gone.— How silly! Nobody'll come. Just don't think about it. Brush the muff. Beautiful gloves. Beautiful gloves. Forget it. Forget it. One, two, three, four, five, six— (*Cries out.*) There they are! (NORA *moves toward the door, stops irresolutely.* MRS. LINDE *enters from the hall. She has already taken off her coat.*) Oh, it's you, Kristine. There's no one else out there, is there? I'm so glad you're here.

MRS. LINDE.   They told me you'd asked for me.

NORA.   I just happened to walk by. I need your help with something—badly. Let's sit here on the couch. Look. Torvald and I are going to a costume party tomorrow night—at Consul Stenborg's upstairs—and Torvald wants me to go as a Neapolitan fisher girl and dance the tarantella. I learned it when we were on Capri.

MRS. LINDE.   Well, well! So you'll be putting on a whole show?

NORA.   Yes. Torvald thinks I should. Look, here's the costume. Torvald had it made for me while we were there. But it's all torn and everything. I just don't know—

MRS. LINDE.   Oh, that can be fixed. It's not that much. The trimmings have come loose in a few places. Do you have needle and thread? Ah, here we are. All set.

NORA.   I really appreciate it, Kristine.

MRS. LINDE (*sewing*).   So you'll be in disguise tomorrow night, eh? You know—I may come by for just a moment, just to look at you.— Oh dear. I haven't even thanked you for the nice evening last night.

NORA (*gets up, moves around*).   Oh, I don't know. I don't think last night was as nice as it usually is.— You should have come to town a little earlier, Kristine.— Yes, Torvald knows how to make it nice and pretty around here.

MRS. LINDE.   You too, I should think. After all, you're your father's daughter. By the way, is Dr. Rank always as depressed as he was last night?

NORA.   No, last night was unusual. He's a very sick man, you know—very sick. Poor Rank, his spine is rotting away. Tuberculosis, I think. You see, his father was a nasty old man with mistresses and all that sort of thing. Rank has been sickly ever since he was a little boy.

MRS. LINDE (*dropping her sewing to her lap*).   But dearest Nora, where have you learned about things like that?

NORA (*still walking about*).   Oh, you know—with three children you sometimes get to talk with—other wives. Some of them know quite a bit about medicine. So you pick up a few things.

MRS. LINDE (*resumes her sewing; after a brief pause*).   Does Dr. Rank come here every day?

NORA.   Every single day. He's Torvald's oldest and best friend, after all. And my friend too, for that matter. He's part of the family, almost.

MRS. LINDE.   But tell me, is he quite sincere? I mean, isn't he the kind of man who likes to say nice things to people?

NORA.   No, not at all. Rather the opposite, in fact. What makes you say that?

MRS. LINDE.   When you introduced me yesterday, he told me he'd often heard my name mentioned in the house. But later on it was quite obvious your husband really had no idea who I was. So how could Dr. Rank—?

NORA.   You're right, Kristine, but I can explain that. You see, Torvald loves me so very much that he wants me all to himself. That's what he says. When we were first married he got almost jealous when I as much as mentioned anybody from back home that I was fond of. So of course I soon stopped doing that. But with Dr. Rank I often talk about home. You see, he likes to listen to me.

MRS. LINDE.   Look here, Nora. In many ways you're still a child. After all, I'm quite a bit older than you and have had more experience. I want to give you a piece of advice. I think you should get out of this thing with Dr. Rank.

NORA.   Get out of what thing?

MRS. LINDE.   Several things in fact, if you want my opinion. Yesterday you said something about a rich admirer who was going to give you money—

NORA.   One who doesn't exist, unfortunately. What of it?

MRS. LINDE.   Does Dr. Rank have money?

NORA.   Yes, he does.

MRS. LINDE.   And no dependents?

NORA.   No. But—?

MRS. LINDE.   And he comes here every day?

NORA.   Yes, I told you that already.

MRS. LINDE.   But how can that sensitive man be so tactless?

NORA.   I haven't the slightest idea what you're talking about.

MRS. LINDE.   Don't play games with me, Nora. Don't you think I know who you borrowed the twelve hundred dollars from?

NORA.   Are you out of your mind! The very idea—! A friend of both of us who sees us every day—! What a dreadfully uncomfortable position that would be!

MRS. LINDE.   So it really isn't Dr. Rank?

NORA.   Most certainly not! I would never have dreamed of asking him—not for a moment. Anyway, he didn't have any money then. He inherited it afterwards.

MRS. LINDE.   Well, I still think it may have been lucky for you, Nora dear.

NORA.   The idea! It would never have occurred to me to ask Dr. Rank—. Though I'm sure that if I *did* ask him—

MRS. LINDE.   But of course you wouldn't.

NORA.   Of course not. I can't imagine that that would ever be necessary. But I am quite sure that if I told Dr. Rank—

MRS. LINDE.   Behind your husband's back?

NORA.   I must get out of—this other thing. That's also behind his back. I *must* get out of it.

MRS. LINDE.   That's what I told you yesterday. But—

NORA (*walking up and down*).   A man manages these things so much better than a woman—

MRS. LINDE.   One's husband, yes.

NORA.   Silly, silly! (*Stops.*) When you've paid off all you owe, you get your I.O.U. back; right?

MRS. LINDE.   Yes, of course.

NORA.   And you can tear it into a hundred thousand little pieces and burn it—that dirty, filthy, paper!

MRS. LINDE (*looks hard at her, puts down her sewing, rising slowly*). Nora—you're hiding something from me.

NORA.   Can you tell?

MRS. LINDE.   Something's happened to you, Nora, since yesterday morning. What is it?

NORA (*going to her*).   Kristine! (*Listens.*) Shhh. Torvald just came back. Listen. Why don't you go in to the children for a while. Torvald can't stand having sewing around. Get Anne-Marie to help you.

MRS. LINDE (*gathers some of the sewing things together*).   All right, but I'm not leaving here till you and I have talked. (*She goes out left, just as* HELMER *enters from the front hall.*)

NORA (*towards him*).   I have been waiting and waiting for you, Torvald.

HELMER.   Was that the dressmaker?

NORA.   No, it was Kristine. She's helping me with my costume. Oh Torvald, just wait till you see how nice I'll look!

HELMER.   I told you. Pretty good idea I had, wasn't it?

NORA.   Lovely! And wasn't it nice of me to go along with it?

HELMER (*his hand under her chin*).   Nice? To do what your husband tells you? All right, you little rascal; I know you didn't mean it that way. But don't let me interrupt you. I suppose you want to try it on.

NORA.   And you'll be working?

HELMER.   Yes. (*Shows her a pile of papers.*) Look. I've been down to the bank. (*Is about to enter his study.*)

NORA.   Torvald.

HELMER (*halts*).   Yes?

NORA.   What if your little squirrel asked you ever so nicely—

HELMER.   For what?

NORA.   Would you do it?

HELMER.   Depends on what it is.

NORA.   Squirrel would run around and do all sorts of fun tricks if you'd be nice and agreeable.

HELMER.   All right. What is it?

NORA.   Lark would chirp and twitter in all the rooms, up and down—

HELMER.   So what? Lark does that anyway.

NORA.   I'll be your elfmaid and dance for you in the moonlight, Torvald.

HELMER.   Nora, don't tell me it's the same thing you mentioned this morning?

NORA (*closer to him*).   Yes, Torvald. I beg you!

HELMER.   You really have the nerve to bring that up again?

NORA.   Yes. You've just got to do as I say. You *must* let Krogstad keep his job.

HELMER.   My dear Nora. It's his job I intend to give to Mrs. Linde.

NORA.   I know. And that's ever so nice of you. But can't you just fire someone else?

HELMER.   This is incredible! You just don't give up do you? Because you make some foolish promise, *I* am supposed to—!

NORA.   That's not the reason, Torvald. It's for your own sake. That man writes for the worst newspapers. You've said so yourself. There's no telling what he may do to you. I'm scared to death of him.

HELMER.   Ah, I understand. You're afraid because of what happened before.

NORA.   What do you mean?

HELMER.   You're thinking of your father, of course.

NORA.   Yes. You're right. Remember the awful things they wrote about Daddy in the newspapers. I really think they might have forced him to resign if the ministry hadn't sent you to look into the charges and if you hadn't been so helpful and understanding.

HELMER.   My dear little Nora, there is a world of difference between your father and me. Your father's official conduct was not above reproach. Mine is, and I intend for it to remain that way as long as I hold my position.

NORA.   Oh, but you don't know what vicious people like that may think of. Oh, Torvald! Now all of us could be so happy together here in our own home, peaceful and carefree. Such a good life, Torvald, for you and me and the children! That's why I implore you—

HELMER.   And it's exactly because you plead for him that you make it impossible for me to keep him. It's already common knowledge in the bank that I intend to let Krogstad go. If it gets out that the new manager has changed his mind because of his wife—

NORA.   Yes? What then?

HELMER.   No, of course, that wouldn't matter at all as long as little Mrs. Pighead here got her way! Do you want me to make myself look ridiculous before my whole staff—make people think I can be swayed by just anybody—by outsiders? Believe me, I would soon enough find out what the consequences would be! Besides, there's another thing that makes it absolutely impossible for Krogstad to stay on in the bank now that I'm in charge.

NORA.   What's that?

HELMER.   I suppose in a pinch I could overlook his moral shortcomings—

NORA.   Yes, you could; couldn't you, Torvald?

HELMER.   And I understand he's quite a good worker, too. But we've known each other for a long time. It's one of those imprudent relationships you get into when you're young that embarrass you for the rest of your life. I guess I might as well be frank with you: he and I are on a first-name basis. And that tactless fellow never hides the fact even when other people are around. Rather, he seems to think it entitles him to be familiar with me. Every chance he gets he comes out with his damn "Torvald, Torvald." I'm telling you, I find it most awkward. He would make my position in the bank intolerable.

NORA.   You don't really mean any of this, Torvald.

HELMER.   Oh? I don't? And why not?

NORA.   No, for it's all so petty.

HELMER.   What! Petty? You think I'm being petty!

NORA.   No, I *don't* think you are petty, Torvald dear. That's exactly why I—

HELMER.   Never mind. You think my reasons are petty, so it follows that I must be petty too. Petty! Indeed! By God, I'll put an end to this right now! (*Opens the door to the front hall and calls out.*) Helene!

NORA.   What are you doing?

HELMER (*searching among his papers*).   Making a decision. (*The* MAID *enters.*) Here. Take this letter. Go out with it right away. Find somebody to deliver it. But quick. The address is on the envelope. Wait. Here's money.

MAID. Very good sir. (*She takes the letter and goes out.*)

HELMER (*collecting his papers*).   There now, little Mrs. Obstinate!

NORA (*breathless*).   Torvald—what was that letter?

HELMER. Krogstad's dismissal.

NORA. Call it back, Torvald! There's still time! Oh Torvald, please—call it back! For my sake, for your own sake, for the sake of the children! Listen to me, Torvald! Do it! You don't know what you're doing to all of us!

HELMER. Too late.

NORA. Yes. Too late.

HELMER. Dear Nora, I forgive you this fear you're in, although it really is an insult to me. Yes, it is! It's an insult to think that I am scared of a shabby scrivener's revenge. But I forgive you, for it's such a beautiful proof of how much you love me. (*Takes her in his arms.*) And that's the way it should be, my sweet darling. Whatever happens you'll see that when things get really rough I have both strength and courage. You'll find out that I am man enough to shoulder the whole burden.

NORA (*terrified*).   What do you mean by that?

HELMER. All of it, I tell you—

NORA (*composed*).   You'll never have to do that.

HELMER. Good. Then we'll share the burden, Nora—like husband and wife, the way it ought to be. (*Caresses her.*) Now are you satisfied? There, there, there. Not that look in your eyes—like a frightened dove. It's all your own foolish imagination.— Why don't you practice the tarantella—and your tambourine, too. I'll be in the inner office and close both doors, so I won't hear you. You can make as much noise as you like. (*Turning in the doorway.*) And when Rank comes, tell him where to find me. (*He nods to her, enters his study carrying his papers, and closes the door.*)

NORA (*transfixed by terror, whispers*).   He would do it. He'll do it. He'll do it in spite of the whole world.— No, this mustn't happen. Anything rather than that! There must be a way—! (*The doorbell rings.*) Dr. Rank! Anything rather than that! Anything—anything at all! (*She passes her hand over her face, pulls herself together, and opens the door to the hall. DR. RANK is out there, hanging up his coat. Darkness begins to fall during the following scene.*) Hello there, Dr. Rank. I recognized your ringing. Don't go in to Torvald yet. I think he's busy.

RANK. And you?

NORA (*as he enters and she closes the door behind him*).   You know I always have time for you.

RANK. Thanks. I'll make use of that as long as I can.

NORA. What do you mean by that— As long as you can?

RANK. Does that frighten you?

NORA.   Well, it's a funny expression. As if something was going to happen.

RANK.   Something is going to happen that I've long been expecting. But I admit I hadn't thought it would come quite so soon.

NORA (*seizes his arm*).   What is it you've found out? Dr. Rank— tell me!

RANK (*sits down by the stove*).   I'm going downhill fast. There's nothing to do about that.

NORA (*with audible relief*).   So it's *you*—

RANK.   Who else? No point in lying to myself. I'm in worse shape than any of my other patients, Mrs. Helmer. These last few days I've been making up my inner status. Bankrupt. Chances are that within a month I'll be rotting up in the cemetery.

NORA.   Shame on you! Talking that horrid way!

RANK.   The thing itself is horrid—damn horrid. The worst of it, though, is all that other horror that comes first. There is only one more test I need to make. After that I'll have a pretty good idea when I'll start coming apart. There is something I want to say to you. Helmer's refined nature can't stand anything hideous. I don't want him in my sick room.

NORA.   Oh, but Dr. Rank—

RANK.   I don't want him there. Under no circumstance. I'll close my door to him. As soon as I have full certainty that the worst is about to begin I'll give you my card with a black cross on it. Then you'll know the last horror of destruction has started.

NORA.   Today you're really quite impossible. And I had hoped you'd be in a particularly good mood.

RANK.   With death on my hands? Paying for someone else's sins? Is there justice in that? And yet there isn't a single family that isn't ruled by the same law of ruthless retribution, in one way or another.

NORA (*puts her hands over her ears*).   Poppycock! Be fun! Be fun!

RANK.   Well, yes. You may just as well laugh at the whole thing. My poor, innocent spine is suffering from my father's frolics as a young lieutenant.

NORA (*over by the table, left*).   Right. He was addicted to asparagus and goose liver paté, wasn't he?

RANK.   And truffles.

NORA.   Of course. Truffles. And oysters too, I think.

RANK.   And oysters. Obviously.

NORA.   And all the port and champagne that go with it. It's really too bad that goodies like that ruin your backbone.

RANK.   Particularly an unfortunate backbone that never enjoyed any of it.

NORA.   Ah yes, that's the saddest part of all.

RANK (*looks searchingly at her*).   Hm—

NORA (*after a brief pause*).   Why did you smile just then?

RANK.   No, it was you that laughed.

NORA.   No, it was you that smiled, Dr. Rank!

RANK (*gets up*).   You're more of a mischief-maker than I thought.

NORA.   I feel in the mood for mischief today.

RANK.   So it seems.

NORA (*with both her hands on his shoulders*).   Dear, dear Dr. Rank, don't you go and die and leave Torvald and me.

RANK.   Oh, you won't miss me for very long. Those who go away are soon forgotten.

NORA (*with an anxious look*).   Do you believe that?

RANK.   You'll make new friends, and then—

NORA.   Who'll make new friends?

RANK.   Both you and Helmer, once I'm gone. You yourself seem to have made a good start already. What was this Mrs. Linde doing here last night?

NORA.   Aha—Don't tell me you're jealous of poor Kristine?

RANK.   Yes, I am. She'll be my successor in this house. As soon as I have made my excuses, that woman is likely to—

NORA.   Shh—not so loud. She's in there.

RANK.   Today too? There you are!

NORA.   She's mending my costume. My God, you really *are* unreasonable. (*Sits down on the couch.*) Now be nice, Dr. Rank. Tomorrow you'll see how beautifully I'll dance, and then you are to pretend I'm dancing just for you—and for Torvald too, of course. (*Takes several items out of the carton.*) Sit down, Dr. Rank; I want to show you something.

RANK (*sitting down*).   What?

NORA.   Look.

RANK.   Silk stockings.

NORA.   Flesh-colored. Aren't they lovely? Now it's getting dark in here, but tomorrow— No, no. You only get to see the foot. Oh well, you might as well see all of it.

RANK.   Hmm.

NORA.   Why do you look so critical? Don't you think they'll fit?

RANK.   That's something I can't possibly have a reasoned opinion about.

NORA (*looks at him for a moment*).   Shame on you. (*Slaps his ear lightly with the stocking.*) That's what you get. (*Puts the things back in the carton.*)

RANK.   And what other treasures are you going to show me?

NORA.   Nothing at all, because you're naughty. (*She hums a little and rummages in the carton.*)

RANK (*after a brief silence*).   When I sit here like this, talking confidently with you, I can't imagine—I can't possibly imagine what would have become of me if I hadn't had you and Helmer.

NORA (*smiles*).   Well, yes—I do believe you like being with us.

RANK (*in a lower voice, lost in thought*).   And then to have to go away from it all—

NORA.   Nonsense. You are not going anywhere.

RANK (*as before*).   —and not to leave behind as much as a poor little token of gratitude, hardly a brief memory of someone missed, nothing but a vacant place that anyone can fill.

NORA.   And what if I were to ask you—? No—

RANK.   Ask me what?

NORA.   For a great proof of your friendship—

RANK.   Yes, yes—?

NORA.   No, I mean—for an enormous favor—

RANK.   Would you really for once make me as happy as all that?

NORA.   But you don't even know what it is.

RANK.   Well, then; tell me.

NORA.   Oh, but I can't, Dr. Rank. It's altogether too much to ask—It's advice and help and a favor—

RANK.   So much the better. I can't even begin to guess what it is you have in mind. So for heaven's sake tell me! Don't you trust me?

NORA.   Yes, I trust you more than anyone else I know. You are my best and most faithful friend. I know that. So I will tell you. All right, Dr. Rank. There is something you can help me prevent. You know how much Torvald loves me—beyond all words. Never for a moment would he hesitate to give his life for me.

RANK (*leaning over to her*).   Nora—do you really think he's the only one?

NORA (*with a slight start*).   Who—?

RANK.   —would gladly give his life for you.

NORA (*heavily*).   I see.

RANK.   I have sworn an oath to myself to tell you before I go. I'll never find a better occasion.— All right, Nora; now you know. And now you also know that you can confide in me more than in anyone else.

NORA (*gets up; in a calm, steady voice*).   Let me get by.

RANK (*makes room for her but remains seated*).   Nora—

NORA (*in the door to the front hall*).   Helene, bring the lamp in here, please. (*Walks over to the stove.*) Oh, dear Dr. Rank. That really wasn't very nice of you.

RANK (*gets up*).   That I have loved you as much as anybody—was that not nice?

NORA.   No; not that. But that you told me. There was no need for that.

RANK.   What do you mean? Have you known—? (*The* MAID *enters with the lamp, puts it on the table, and goes out.*) Nora—Mrs. Helmer— I'm asking you: did you know?

NORA.   Oh, how can I tell what I knew and didn't know! I really can't say—But that you could be so awkward, Dr. Rank! Just when everything was so comfortable.

RANK.   Well, anyway, now you know that I'm at your service with my life and soul. And now you must speak.

NORA (*looks at him*).   After what just happened?

RANK.   I beg of you—let me know what it is.

NORA.   There is nothing I can tell you now.

RANK.   Yes, yes. You mustn't punish me this way. Please let me do for you whatever anyone *can* do.

NORA.   Now there is nothing you can do. Besides, I don't think I really need any help, anyway. It's probably just my imagination. Of course that's all it is. I'm sure of it! (*Sits down in the rocking chair, looks at him, smiles.*) Well, well, well, Dr. Rank! What a fine gentleman you turned out to be! Aren't you ashamed of yourself, now that we have light?

RANK.   No, not really. But perhaps I ought to leave—and not come back?

NORA.   Don't be silly; of course not! You'll come here exactly as you have been doing. You know perfectly well that Torvald can't do without you.

RANK.   Yes, but what about you?

NORA.   Oh, I always think it's perfectly delightful when you come.

RANK.   That's the very thing that misled me. You are a riddle to me. It has often seemed to me that you'd just as soon be with me as with Helmer.

NORA.   Well, you see, there are people you love, and then there are other people you'd almost rather be with.

RANK.   Yes, there is something in that.

NORA.   When I lived at home with Daddy, of course I loved him most. But I always thought it was so much fun to sneak off down to the maids' room, for they never gave me advice and they always talked about such fun things.

RANK.   Aha! So it's *their* place I have taken.

NORA (*jumps up and goes over to him*).   Oh dear, kind Dr. Rank, you know very well I didn't mean it that way. Can't you see that with Torvald it is the way it used to be with Daddy? (*The* MAID *enters from the front hall.*)

MAID.   Ma'am! (*Whispers to her and gives her a caller's card.*)

NORA (*glances at the card*).   Ah! (*Puts it in her pocket.*)

RANK.   Anything wrong?

NORA.   No, no; not at all. It's nothing—just my new costume—

RANK.   But your costume is lying right there!

NORA.   Oh yes, that one. But this is another one. I ordered it. Torvald mustn't know—

RANK.   Aha. So that's the great secret.

NORA.   That's it. Why don't you go in to him, please. He's in the inner office. And keep him there for a while—

RANK.   Don't worry. He won't get away. (*Enters* HELMER's *study.*)

NORA (*to the* MAID).   You say he's waiting in the kitchen?

MAID.   Yes. He came up the back stairs.

NORA.   But didn't you tell him there was somebody with me?

MAID.   Yes, but he wouldn't listen.

NORA.   He won't leave?

MAID.   No, not till he's had a word with you, ma'am.

NORA.   All right. But try not to make any noise. And, Helene—don't tell anyone he's here. It's supposed to be a surprise for my husband.

MAID.   I understand ma'am— (*She leaves.*)

NORA.   The terrible is happening. It's happening after all. No, no, no. It can't happen. It won't happen. (*She bolts the study door. The* MAID *opens the front hall door for* KROGSTAD *and closes the door behind him. He wears a fur coat for traveling, boots, and a fur hat.* NORA *goes toward him.*) Keep your voice down. My husband's home.

KROGSTAD.   That's all right.

NORA.   What do you want?

KROGSTAD.   To find out something.

NORA.   Be quick, then. What is it?

KROGSTAD.   I expect you know I've been fired.

NORA.   I couldn't prevent it, Mr. Krogstad. I fought for you as long and as hard as I could but it didn't do any good.

KROGSTAD.   Your husband doesn't love you any more than that? He knows what I can do to you, and yet he runs the risk—

NORA.   Surely you didn't think I'd tell him?

KROGSTAD.   No, I really didn't. It wouldn't be like Torvald
Helmer to show that kind of guts—

NORA.   Mr. Krogstad, I insist that you show respect for my
husband.

KROGSTAD.   By all means. All due respect. But since you're so
anxious to keep this a secret, may I assume that you are a little better
informed than yesterday about exactly what you have done?

NORA.   Better than *you* could ever teach me.

KROGSTAD.   Of course. Such a bad lawyer as I am—

NORA.   What do you want of me?

KROGSTAD.   I just wanted to find out how you are, Mrs. Helmer.
I've been thinking about you all day. You see, even a bill collector, a
pen pusher, a—anyway, someone like me—even he has a little of what
they call a heart.

NORA.   Then show it. Think of my little children.

KROGSTAD.   Have you and your husband thought of mine? Never
mind. All I want to tell you is that you don't need to take this business
too seriously. I have no intentions of bringing charges right away.

NORA.   Oh no, you wouldn't; would you? I knew you wouldn't.

KROGSTAD.   The whole thing can be settled quite amiably.
Nobody else needs to know anything. It will be between the three of us.

NORA.   My husband must never find out about this.

KROGSTAD.   How are you going to prevent that? Maybe you can
pay me the balance of your loan?

NORA.   No, not right now.

KROGSTAD.   Or do you have a way of raising the money one of
these next few days?

NORA.   None I intend to make use of.

KROGSTAD.   It wouldn't do you any good anyway. Even if you had
the cash in your hand right this minute, I wouldn't give you your note
back. It wouldn't make any difference *how* much money you offered me.

NORA.   Then you'll have to tell what you plan to use the note *for*.

KROGSTAD.   Just keep it; that's all. Have it on hand, so to speak. I
won't say a word to anybody else. So if you've been thinking about
doing something desperate—

NORA.   I have.

KROGSTAD.   —like leaving house and home—

NORA.   I have.

KROGSTAD.   —or even something worse—

NORA.   How did you know?

KROGSTAD.   —then: don't.

NORA.   How did you know I was thinking of *that?*

KROGSTAD.   Most of us do, right at first. I did, too, but when it came down to it I didn't have the courage—

NORA (*tonelessly*).   Nor do I.

KROGSTAD (*relieved*).   See what I mean? I thought so. You don't either.

NORA.   I don't. I don't.

KROGSTAD.   Besides, it would be very silly of you. Once that first domestic blowup is behind you—. Here in my pocket is a letter for your husband.

NORA.   Telling him everything?

KROGSTAD.   As delicately as possible.

NORA (*quickly*).   He mustn't get that letter. Tear it up. I'll get you the money somehow.

KROGSTAD.   Excuse me, Mrs. Helmer, I thought I just told you—

NORA.   I'm not talking about the money I owe you. Just let me know how much money you want from my husband, and I'll get it for you.

KROGSTAD.   I want no money from your husband.

NORA.   Then, what *do* you want?

KROGSTAD.   I'll tell you, Mrs. Helmer. I want to rehabilitate myself; I want to get up in the world; and your husband is going to help me. For a year and a half I haven't done anything disreputable. All that time I have been struggling with the most miserable circumstances. I was content to work my way up step by step. Now I've been kicked out, and I'm no longer satisfied just getting my old job back. I want more than that; I want to get to the top. I'm being quite serious. I want the bank to take me back but in a higher position. I want your husband to create a new job for me—

NORA.   He'll never do that!

KROGSTAD.   He will. I know him. He won't dare not to. And once I'm back inside and he and I are working together, you'll see! Within a year I'll be the manager's right hand. It will be Nils Krogstad and not Torvald Helmer who'll be running the Mutual Bank!

NORA.   You'll never see that happen!

KROGSTAD.   Are you thinking of—?

NORA.   Now I *do* have the courage

KROGSTAD.   You can't scare me. A fine, spoiled lady like you—

NORA.   You'll see, you'll see!

KROGSTAD.   Under the ice, perhaps? Down into that cold, black water? Then spring comes and you float up again—hideous, can't be identified, hair all gone—

NORA.   You don't frighten me.

KROGSTAD.   Nor you me. One doesn't do that sort of thing, Mrs. Helmer. Besides, what good would it do? He'd still be in my power.

NORA.   Afterwards? When I'm no longer—?

KROGSTAD.   Aren't you forgetting that your reputation would be in my hands? (NORA *stares at him, speechless.*) All right; now I've told you what to expect. So don't do anything foolish. When Helmer gets my letter I expect to hear from him. And don't you forget that it's your husband himself who forces me to use such means again. That I'll never forgive him. Goodbye, Mrs. Helmer. (*Goes out through the hall.*)

NORA (*at the door, opens it a little, listens*).   He's going. And no letter. Of course not! That would be impossible! (*Opens the door more.*) What's he doing? He's still there. Doesn't go down. Having second thoughts—? Will he—? (*The sound of a letter dropping into the mailbox. Then* KROGSTAD's *steps are heard going down the stairs, gradually dying away. With a muted cry* NORA *runs forward to the table by the couch; brief pause.*) In the mailbox. (*Tiptoes back to the door to the front hall.*) There it is. Torvald, Torvald—now we're lost!

MRS. LINDE (*enters from the left, carrying* NORA's *Capri costume*). There now. I think it's all fixed. Why don't we try it on you—

NORA (*in a low, hoarse voice*).   Kristine, come here.

MRS. LINDE.   What's wrong with you? You look quite beside yourself.

NORA.   Come over here. Do you see that letter? There, look—through the glass in the mailbox.

MRS. LINDE.   Yes, yes; I see it.

NORA.   That letter is from Krogstad.

MRS. LINDE.   Nora—it was Krogstad who lent you the money!

NORA.   Yes, and now Torvald will find out about it.

MRS. LINDE.   Oh believe me, Nora. That's the best thing for both of you.

NORA.   There's more to it than you know. I forged a signature—

MRS. LINDE.   Oh my God—!

NORA.   I just want to tell you this, Kristine, that you must be my witness.

MRS. LINDE.   Witness? How? Witness to what?

NORA.   If I lose my mind—and that could very well happen—

MRS. LINDE.   Nora!

NORA.   —or if something were to happen to me—something that made it impossible for me to be here—

MRS. LINDE.   Nora, Nora! You're not yourself!

NORA.   —and if someone were to take all the blame, assume the whole responsibility—Do you understand—?

MRS. LINDE.   Yes, yes; but how can you think—!

NORA.   Then you are to witness that that's not so, Kristine. I am not beside myself. I am perfectly rational, and what I'm telling you is that nobody else has known about this. I've done it all by myself, the whole thing. Just remember that.

MRS. LINDE.   I will. But I don't understand any of it.

NORA.   Oh, how could you! For it's the wonderful that's about to happen.

MRS. LINDE.   The wonderful?

NORA.   Yes, the wonderful. But it's so terrible, Kristine. It mustn't happen for anything in the whole world.

MRS. LINDE.   I'm going over to talk to Krogstad right now.

NORA.   No, don't. Don't go to him. He'll do something bad to you.

MRS. LINDE.   There was a time when he would have done anything for me.

NORA.   He!

MRS. LINDE.   Where does he live?

NORA.   Oh, I don't know— Yes, wait a minute—(*Reaches into her pocket.*) Here's his card.— But the letter, the letter—!

HELMER (*in his study, knocks on the door*).   Nora!

NORA (*cries out in fear*).   Oh, what is it? What do you want?

HELMER.   That's all right. Nothing to be scared about. We're not coming in. For one thing, you've bolted the door, you know. Are you modeling your costume?

NORA.   Yes, yes; I am. I'm going to be so pretty, Torvald!

MRS. LINDE (*having looked at the card*).   He lives just around the corner.

NORA.   Yes, but it's no use. Nothing can save us now. The letter is in the mailbox.

MRS. LINDE.   And your husband has the key?

NORA.   Yes. He always keeps it with him.

MRS. LINDE.   Krogstad must ask for his letter back, unread. He's got to think up some pretext or other—

NORA.   But this is just the time of day when Torvald—

MRS. LINDE.   Delay him. Go in to him. I'll be back as soon as I can. (*She hurries out through the hall door.*)

NORA (*walks over to* HELMER's *door, opens it, and peeks in*).   Torvald.

HELMER (*still offstage*).   Well, well! So now one's allowed in one's own living room again. Come on, Rank. Now we'll see— (*In the doorway.*) But what's this?

NORA.   What, Torvald dear?

HELMER.   Rank prepared me for a splendid metamorphosis.

RANK (*in the doorway*).   That's how I understood it. Evidently I was mistaken.

NORA.   Nobody gets to admire me in my costume before tomorrow.

HELMER.   But, dearest Nora—you look all done in. Have you been practicing too hard?

NORA.   No, I haven't practiced at all.

HELMER.   But you'll have to, you know.

NORA.   I know it, Torvald. I simply must. But I can't do a thing unless you help me. I have forgotten everything.

HELMER.   Oh it will all come back. We'll work on it.

NORA.   Oh yes, please, Torvald. You just have to help me. Promise? I am so nervous. That big party—. You mustn't do anything else tonight. Not a bit of business. Don't even touch a pen. Will you promise, Torvald?

HELMER.   I promise. Tonight I'll be entirely at your service—you helpless little thing.—Just a moment, though. First I want to— (*Goes to the door to the front hall.*)

NORA.   What are you doing out there?

HELMER.   Just looking to see if there's any mail.

NORA.   No, no! Don't, Torvald!

HELMER.   Why not?

NORA.   Torvald, I beg you. There is no mail.

HELMER.   Let me just look, anyway. (*Is about to go out.* NORA *by the piano, plays the first bars of the tarantella dance.* HELMER *halts at the door.*) Aha!

NORA.   I won't be able to dance tomorrow if I don't get to practice with you.

HELMER (*goes to her*).   Are you really all that scared, Nora dear?

NORA.   Yes, so terribly scared. Let's try it right now. There's still time before we eat. Oh please sit down and play for me, Torvald. Teach me, coach me, the way you always do.

HELMER.   Of course I will, my darling, if that's what you want. (*Sits down at the piano.* NORA *takes the tambourine out of the carton, as well as a long, many-colored shawl. She quickly drapes the shawl around herself, then leaps into the middle of the floor.*)

NORA.   Play for me! I want to dance! (HELMER *plays and* NORA *dances.* DR. RANK *stands by the piano behind* HELMER *and watches.*)

HELMER (*playing*).   Slow down, slow down!

NORA.   Can't!

HELMER.   Not so violent, Nora!

NORA.   It has to be this way.

HELMER (*stops playing*).   No, no. This won't do at all.

NORA (*laughing, swinging her tambourine*).   What did I tell you?

RANK.   Why don't you let me play?

HELMER (*getting up*).   Good idea. Then I can direct her better. (RANK *sits down at the piano and starts playing.* NORA *dances more and more wildly.* HELMER *stands over by the stove, repeatedly correcting her. She doesn't seem to hear. Her hair comes loose and falls down over her shoulders. She doesn't notice but keeps on dancing.* MRS. LINDE *enters.*)

MRS. LINDE (*stops by the door, dumbfounded*).   Ah—!

NORA (*dancing*).   We're having such fun, Kristine!

HELMER.   My dearest Nora, you're dancing as if it were a matter of life and death!

NORA.   It is! It is!

HELMER.   Rank, stop. This is sheer madness. Stop I say! (RANK *stops playing;* NORA *suddenly stops dancing.* HELMER *goes over to her.*) If I hadn't seen it I wouldn't have believed it. You've forgotten every single thing I ever taught you.

NORA (*tosses away the tambourine*).   See? I told you.

HELMER.   Well! You certainly need coaching.

NORA.   Didn't I tell you I did? Now you've seen for yourself. I'll need your help till the very minute we're leaving for the party. Will you promise, Torvald?

HELMER.   You can count on it.

NORA.   You're not to think of anything except me—not tonight and not tomorrow. You're not to read any letters—not to look in the mailbox—

HELMER.   Ah, I see. You're still afraid of that man.

NORA.   Yes—yes, that too.

HELMER.   Nora, I can tell from looking at you. There's a letter from him out there.

NORA.   I don't know. I think so. But you're not to read it now. I don't want anything ugly to come between us before it's all over.

RANK (*to* HELMER *in a low voice*).   Better not argue with her.

HELMER (*throws his arm around her*).   The child shall have her way. But tomorrow night, when you've done your dance—

NORA.   Then you'll be free.

MAID (*in the door, right*).   Dinner can be served any time, ma'am.

NORA.   We want champagne, Helene.

MAID.   Very good, ma'am. (*Goes out.*)

HELMER.   Aha! Having a party, eh?

NORA.   Champagne from now till sunrise! (*Calls out.*) And some macaroons, Helene. Lots!—just this once.

HELMER (*taking her hands*).   There, there—I don't like this wild— frenzy—Be my own sweet little lark again, the way you always are.

NORA.   Oh, I will. But you go on in. You too, Dr. Rank. Kristine, please help me put up my hair.

RANK (*in a low voice to* HELMER *as they go out*).   You don't think she is—you know—expecting—?

HELMER.   Oh no. Nothing like that. It's just this childish fear I was telling you about. (*They go out, right.*)

NORA.   Well?

MRS. LINDE.   Left town.

NORA.   I saw it in your face.

MRS. LINDE.   He'll be back tomorrow night. I left him a note.

NORA.   You shouldn't have. I don't want you to try to stop anything. You see, it's kind of ecstasy, too, this waiting for the wonderful.

MRS. LINDE.   But what is it you're waiting *for*?

NORA.   You wouldn't understand. Why don't you go in to the others. I'll be there in a minute. (MRS. LINDE *enters the dining room, right.* NORA *stands still for a little while, as if collecting herself; she looks at her watch.*) Five o'clock. Seven hours till midnight. Twenty-four more hours till next midnight. Then the tarantella is over. Twenty-four plus seven—thirty-one more hours to live.

HELMER (*in the door, right*).   What's happening to my little lark?

NORA (*to him, with open arms*).   Here's your lark!

ACT 3

The same room. The table by the couch and the chairs around it have been moved to the middle of the floor. A lighted lamp is on the table. The door to the front hall is open. Dance music is heard from upstairs.

MRS. LINDE *is seated by the table, idly leafing through the pages of a book. She tries to read but seems unable to concentrate. Once or twice she turns her head in the direction of the door, anxiously listening.*

MRS. LINDE (*looks at her watch*).   Not yet. It's almost too late. If only he hasn't— (*Listens again.*) Ah! There he is. (*She goes to the hall and opens the front door carefully. Quiet footsteps on the stairs. She whispers.*) Come in. There's nobody here.

KROGSTAD (*in the door*).   I found your note when I got home. What's this all about?

MRS. LINDE.   I've got to talk to you.

KROGSTAD.   Oh? And it has to be here?

MRS. LINDE.   It couldn't be at my place. My room doesn't have a separate entrance. Come in. We're quite alone. The maid is asleep and the Helmers are at a party upstairs.

KROGSTAD (*entering*).   Really? The Helmers are dancing tonight, are they?

MRS. LINDE.   And why not?

KROGSTAD.   You're right. Why not, indeed.

MRS. LINDE.   All right, Krogstad. Let's talk, you and I.

KROGSTAD.   I didn't know we had anything to talk about.

MRS. LINDE.   We have much to talk about.

KROGSTAD.   I didn't think so.

MRS. LINDE.   No, because you've never really understood me.

KROGSTAD.   What was there to understand? What happened was perfectly commonplace. A heartless woman jilts a man when she gets a more attractive offer.

MRS. LINDE.   Do you think I'm all that heartless? And do you think it was easy for me to break with you?

KROGSTAD.   No?

MRS. LINDE.   You really thought it was?

KROGSTAD.   If it wasn't, why did you write the way you did that time?

MRS. LINDE.   What else could I do? If I had to make a break, I also had the duty to destroy whatever feelings you had for me.

KROGSTAD (*clenching his hands*).   So that's the way it was. And you did—*that*—just for money!

MRS. LINDE.   Don't forget I had a helpless mother and two small brothers. We couldn't wait for you, Krogstad. You know yourself how uncertain your prospects were then.

KROGSTAD.   All right. But you still didn't have the right to throw me over for somebody else.

MRS. LINDE.   I don't know. I have asked myself that question many times. Did I have that right?

KROGSTAD (*in a lower voice*).   When I lost you I lost my footing. Look at me now. A shipwrecked man on a raft.

MRS. LINDE.   Rescue may be near.

KROGSTAD.   It *was* near. Then you came between.

MRS. LINDE.   I didn't know that, Krogstad. Only today did I find out it's your job I'm taking over in the bank.

KROGSTAD.   I believe you when you say so. But now that you *do* know, aren't you going to step aside?

MRS. LINDE.   No, for it wouldn't do you any good.

KROGSTAD.   Whether it would or not—*I* would do it.

MRS. LINDE.   I have learned common sense. Life and hard necessity have taught me that.

KROGSTAD.   And life has taught me not to believe in pretty speeches.

MRS. LINDE.   Then life has taught you a very sensible thing. But you do believe in actions, don't you?

KROGSTAD.   How do you mean?

MRS. LINDE.   You referred to yourself just now as a shipwrecked man.

KROGSTAD.   It seems to me I had every reason to do so.

MRS. LINDE.   And I am a shipwrecked woman. No one to grieve for, no one to care for.

KROGSTAD.   You made your choice.

MRS. LINDE.   I had no other choice that time.

KROGSTAD.   Let's say you didn't. What then?

MRS. LINDE.   Krogstad, how would it be if we two shipwrecked people got together?

KROGSTAD.   What's this!

MRS. LINDE.   Two on one wreck are better off than each on his own.

KROGSTAD.   Kristine!

MRS. LINDE.   Why do you think I came to town?

KROGSTAD.   Surely not because of me?

MRS. LINDE.   If I'm going to live at all I must work. All my life, for as long as I can remember, I have worked. That's been my one and only pleasure. But now that I'm all alone in the world I feel nothing but this terrible emptiness and desolation. There is no joy in working just for yourself. Krogstad—give me someone and something to work for.

KROGSTAD.   I don't believe this. Only hysterical females go in for that kind of high-minded self-sacrifice.

MRS. LINDE.   Did you ever know me to be hysterical?

KROGSTAD.   You really could do this? Listen—do you know about my past? All of it?

MRS. LINDE.   Yes, I do.

KROGSTAD.   Do you also know what people think of me around here?

MRS. LINDE.   A little while ago you sounded as if you thought that together with me you might have become a different person.

KROGSTAD.   I'm sure of it.

MRS. LINDE.   Couldn't that still be?

KROGSTAD.   Kristine—do you know what you are doing? Yes, I see you do. And you think you have the courage—?

MRS. LINDE.   I need someone to be a mother to, and your children need a mother. You and I need one another. Nils, I believe in you—in the real you. Together with you I dare to do anything.

KROGSTAD (*seizes her hands*).   Thanks, thanks, Kristine—now I know I'll raise myself in the eyes of others—Ah, but I forget—!

MRS. LINDE (*listening*).   Shhh!—There's the tarantella. You must go; hurry!

KROGSTAD.   Why? What is it?

MRS. LINDE.   Do you hear what they're playing up there? When that dance is over they'll be down.

KROGSTAD.   All right. I'm leaving. The whole thing is pointless, anyway. Of course you don't know what I'm doing to the Helmers.

MRS. LINDE.   Yes, Krogstad; I do know.

KROGSTAD.   Still, you're brave enough—?

MRS. LINDE.   I very well understand to what extremes despair can drive a man like you.

KROGSTAD.   If only it could be undone!

MRS. LINDE.   It could, for your letter is still out there in the mailbox.

KROGSTAD.   Are you sure?

MRS. LINDE.   Quite sure. But—

KROGSTAD (*looks searchingly at her*).   Maybe I'm beginning to understand. You want to save your friend at any cost. Be honest with me. That's it, isn't it.

MRS. LINDE.   Krogstad, you may sell yourself once for somebody else's sake, but you don't do it twice.

KROGSTAD.   I'll demand my letter back.

MRS. LINDE.   No, no.

KROGSTAD.   Yes, of course. I'll wait here till Helmer comes down. Then I'll ask him for my letter. I'll tell him it's just about my dismissal—that he shouldn't read it.

MRS. LINDE.   No, Krogstad. You are not to ask for that letter back.

KROGSTAD.   But tell me—wasn't that the real reason you wanted to meet me here?

MRS. LINDE.   At first it was, because I was so frightened. But that was yesterday. Since then I have seen the most incredible things going on in this house. Helmer must learn the whole truth. This miserable secret must come out in the open; those two must come to a full understanding. They simply can't continue with all this concealment and evasion.

KROGSTAD.   All right; if you want to take that chance. But there is one thing I *can* do, and I'll do that right now.

MRS. LINDE (*listening*).   But hurry! Go! The dance is over. We aren't safe another minute.

KROGSTAD.   I'll be waiting for you downstairs.

MRS. LINDE.   Yes, do. You must see me home.

KROGSTAD.   I've never been so happy in my whole life. (*He leaves through the front door. The door between the living room and the front hall remains open.*)

MRS. LINDE (*straightens up the room a little and gets her things ready*).   What a change! Oh yes!—what a change! People to work for —to live for—a home to bring happiness to. I can't wait to get to work —! If only they'd come soon— (*Listens.*) Ah, there they are. Get my coat on— (*Puts on her coat and hat.* HELMER's *and* NORA's *voices are heard outside. A key is turned in the lock, and* HELMER *almost forces* NORA *into the hall. She is dressed in her Italian costume, with a big black shawl over her shoulders. He is in evening dress under an open black cloak.*)

NORA (*in the door, still resisting*).   No, no, no! I don't want to! I want to go back upstairs. I don't want to leave so early.

HELMER.   But dearest Nora—

NORA.   Oh please, Torvald—please! I'm asking you as nicely as I can—just another hour!

HELMER.   Not another minute, sweet. You know we agreed. There now. Get inside. You'll catch a cold out here. (*She still resists, but he guides her gently into the room.*)

MRS. LINDE.   Good evening.

NORA.   Kristine!

HELMER.   Ah, Mrs. Linde. Still here?

MRS. LINDE.   I know. I really should apologize, but I so much wanted to see Nora in her costume.

NORA.   You've been waiting up for me?

MRS. LINDE.   Yes, unfortunately I didn't get here in time. You were already upstairs, but I just didn't feel like leaving till I had seen you.

HELMER (*removing* NORA's *shawl*).   Yes, do take a good look at her, Mrs. Linde. I think I may say she's worth looking at. Isn't she lovely?

MRS. LINDE.   She certainly is—

HELMER.   Isn't she a miracle of loveliness, though? That was the general opinion at the party, too. But dreadfully obstinate—that she is, the sweet little thing. What can we do about that? Will you believe it —I practically had to use force to get her away.

NORA.   Oh Torvald, you're going to be sorry you didn't give me even half an hour more.

HELMER.   See what I mean, Mrs. Linde? She dances the tarantella
—she is a tremendous success—quite deservedly so, though perhaps her
performance was a little too natural—I mean, more than could be
reconciled with the rules of art. But all right! The point is: she's a
success, a tremendous success. So should I let her stay after that?
Weaken the effect? Of course not. So I take my lovely little Capri girl—
I might say, my capricious little Capri girl—under my arm—a quick
turn around the room—a graceful bow in all directions, and—as they
say in the novels—the beautiful apparition is gone. A finale should
always be done for effect, Mrs. Linde, but there doesn't seem to be any
way of getting that into Nora's head. Poooh—! It's hot in here. (*Throws
his cloak down on a chair and opens the door to his room.*) Why, it's dark in
here! Of course. Excuse me— (*Goes inside and lights a couple of candles.*)

NORA (*in a hurried, breathless whisper*).   Well?

MRS. LINDE (*in a low voice*).   I have talked to him.

NORA.   And—?

MRS. LINDE.   Nora—you've got to tell your husband everything.

NORA (*no expression in her voice*).   I knew it.

MRS. LINDE.   You have nothing to fear from Krogstad. But you
must speak.

NORA.   I'll say nothing.

MRS. LINDE.   Then the letter will.

NORA.   Thank you, Kristine. Now I know what I have to do. Shh!

HELMER (*returning*).   Well, Mrs. Linde, have you looked your fill?

MRS. LINDE.   Yes. And now I'll say goodnight.

HELMER.   So soon? Is that your knitting?

MRS. LINDE (*takes it*).   Yes, thank you. I almost forgot.

HELMER.   So you knit, do you?

MRS. LINDE.   Oh yes.

HELMER.   You know—you ought to take up embroidery instead.

MRS. LINDE.   Oh? Why?

HELMER.   Because it's so much more beautiful. Look. You hold the
embroidery so—in your left hand. Then with your right you move the
needle—like this—in an easy, elongated arc—you see?

MRS. LINDE.   Maybe you're right—

HELMER.   Knitting, on the other hand, can never be anything but
ugly. Look here: arms pressed close to the sides—the needles going up
and down—there's something Chinese about it somehow—. That
really was an excellent champagne they served us tonight.

MRS. LINDE.   Well, goodnight, Nora. And don't be obstinate any
more.

HELMER.   Well said, Mrs. Linde!

MRS. LINDE.   Goodnight, sir.

HELMER (*sees her to the front door*).   Goodnight, goodnight. I hope you'll get home all right? I'd be very glad to—but of course you don't have far to walk, do you? Goodnight, goodnight. (*She leaves. He closes the door behind her and returns to the living room.*) There! At last we got rid of her. She really is an incredible bore, that woman.

NORA.   Aren't you very tired, Torvald?

HELMER.   No, not in the least.

NORA.   Not sleepy either?

HELMER.   Not at all. Quite the opposite. I feel enormously— animated. How about you? Yes, you do look tired and sleepy.

NORA.   Yes, I am very tired. Soon I'll be asleep.

HELMER.   What did I tell you? I was right, wasn't I? Good thing I didn't let you stay any longer.

NORA.   Everything you do is right.

HELMER (*kissing her forehead*).   Now my little lark is talking like a human being. But did you notice what splendid spirits Rank was in tonight?

NORA.   Was he? I didn't notice. I didn't get to talk with him.

HELMER.   Nor did I—hardly. But I haven't seen him in such a good mood for a long time. (*Looks at her, comes closer to her.*) Ah! It does feel good to be back in our own home again, to be quite alone with you—my young, lovely, ravishing woman!

NORA.   Don't look at me like that, Torvald!

HELMER.   Am I not to look at my most precious possession? All that loveliness that is mine, nobody's but mine, all of it mine.

NORA (*walks to the other side of the table*).   I won't have you talk to me like that tonight.

HELMER (*follows her*).   The tarantella is still in your blood. I can tell. That only makes you all the more alluring. Listen! The guests are beginning to leave. (*Softly.*) Nora—soon the whole house will be quiet.

NORA.   Yes, I hope so.

HELMER.   Yes, don't you, my darling? Do you know—when I'm at a party with you, like tonight—do you know why I hardly ever talk to you, why I keep away from you, only look at you once in a while—a few stolen glances—do you know why I do that? It's because I pretend that you are my secret love, my young, secret bride-to-be, and nobody has the slightest suspicion that there is anything between us.

NORA.   Yes, I know. All your thoughts are with me.

HELMER.   Then when we're leaving and I lay your shawl around your delicate young shoulders—around that wonderful curve of your neck—then I imagine you're my young bride, that we're coming away

from the wedding, that I am taking you to my home for the first time—
that I am alone with you for the first time—quite alone with you, you
young, trembling beauty! I have desired you all evening—there hasn't
been a longing in me that hasn't been for you. When you were dancing
the tarantella, chasing, inviting—my blood was on fire; I couldn't stand
it any longer—that's why I brought you down so early—

NORA.   Leave me now, Torvald. Please! I don't want all this.

HELMER.   What do you mean? You're only playing your little
teasing bird game with me; aren't you, Nora? Don't want to? I'm your
husband, aren't I? (*There is a knock on the front door.*)

NORA (*with a start*).   Did you hear that—?

HELMER (*on his way to the hall*).   Who is it?

RANK (*outside*).   It's me. May I come in for a moment?

HELMER (*in a low voice, annoyed*).   Oh, what does he want now?
(*Aloud*) Just a minute. (*Opens the door.*) Well! How good of you not to
pass by our door.

RANK.   I thought I heard your voice, so I felt like saying hello.
(*Looks around.*) Ah yes—this dear, familiar room. What a cozy,
comfortable place you have here, you two.

HELMER.   Looked to me as if you were quite comfortable upstairs
too.

RANK.   I certainly was. Why not? Why not enjoy all you can in
this world? As much as you can for as long as you can, anyway.
Excellent wine.

HELMER.   The champagne, particularly.

RANK.   You noticed that too? Incredible how much I managed to
put away.

NORA.   Torvald drank a lot of champagne tonight, too.

RANK.   Did he?

NORA.   Yes, he did, and then he's always so much fun afterwards.

RANK.   Well, why not have some fun in the evening after a well
spent day?

HELMER.   Well spent? I'm afraid I can't claim that.

RANK (*slapping him lightly on the shoulder*).   But you see, I can!

NORA.   Dr. Rank, I believe you must have been conducting a
scientific test today.

RANK.   Exactly.

HELMER.   What do you know—little Nora talking about scientific
tests.

NORA.   May I congratulate you on the result?

RANK.   You may indeed.

NORA.   It was a good one?

RANK.   The best possible for both doctor and patient—certainty.

NORA (*a quick query*).   Certainty?

RANK.   Absolute certainty. So why shouldn't I have myself an enjoyable evening afterwards?

NORA.   I quite agree with you, Dr. Rank. You should.

HELMER.   And so do I. If only you don't pay for it tomorrow.

RANK.   Oh well—you get nothing for nothing in this world.

NORA.   Dr. Rank—you are fond of costume parties, aren't you?

RANK.   Yes, particularly when there is a reasonable number of amusing disguises.

NORA.   Listen—what are the two of us going to be the next time?

HELMER.   You frivolous little thing? Already thinking about the next party!

RANK.   You and I? That's easy. You'll be Fortune's Child.

HELMER.   Yes, but what is a fitting costume for that?

RANK.   Let your wife appear just the way she always is.

HELMER.   Beautiful. Very good indeed. But how about yourself? Don't you know what you'll go as?

RANK.   Yes, my friend. I know precisely what I'll be.

HELMER.   Yes?

RANK.   At the next masquerade I'll be invisible.

HELMER.   That's a funny idea.

RANK.   There's a certain black hat—you've heard about the hat that makes you invisible, haven't you? You put that on, and nobody can see you.

HELMER (*suppressing a smile*).   I guess that's right.

RANK.   But, I'm forgetting what I came for. Helmer, give me a cigar—one of your dark Havanas.

HELMER.   With the greatest pleasure. (*Offers him his case.*)

RANK (*takes one and cuts off the tip*).   Thanks.

NORA (*striking a match*).   Let me give you a light.

RANK.   Thanks. (*She holds the match; he lights his cigar.*) And now goodbye!

HELMER.   Goodbye, goodbye, my friend.

NORA.   Sleep well, Dr. Rank.

RANK.   I thank you.

NORA.   Wish me the same.

RANK.   You? Well, if you really want me to—. Sleep well. And thanks for the light. (*He nods to both of them and goes out.*)

HELMER (*in a low voice*).   He had had quite a bit to drink.

NORA (*absently*).   Maybe so. (HELMER *takes out his keys and goes out into the hall.*) Torvald—what are you doing out there?

HELMER.   Emptying the mailbox. It is quite full. There wouldn't be room for the newspapers in the morning—

NORA.   Are you going to work tonight?

HELMER.   You know very well I won't— Say! What's this? Somebody's been at the lock.

NORA.   The lock—?

HELMER.   Yes. Why, I wonder. I hate to think that any of the maids—. Here's a broken hairpin. It's one of yours, Nora.

NORA (*quickly*).   Then it must be one of the children.

HELMER.   You better make damn sure they stop that. Hm, hm.— There! I got it open, finally. (*Gathers up the mail, calls out to the kitchen.*) Helene—Oh Helene—turn out the light here in the hall, will you? (*He comes back into the living room and closes the door.*) Look how it's been piling up. (*Shows her the bundle of letters. Starts leafing through it.*) What's this?

NORA (*by the window*).   The letter! Oh no, no, Torvald!

HELMER.   Two calling cards—from Rank.

NORA.   From Dr. Rank?

HELMER (*looking at them*).   "Doctor medicinae Rank." They were on top. He must have put them there when he left just now.

NORA.   Anything written on them?

HELMER.   A black cross above the name. What a macabre idea. Like announcing his own death.

NORA.   That's what it is.

HELMER.   Hm? You know about this? Has he said anything to you?

NORA.   That card means he has said goodbye to us. He'll lock himself up to die.

HELMER.   My poor friend. I knew of course he wouldn't be with me very long. But so soon—. And hiding himself away like a wounded animal—

NORA.   When it has to be, it's better it happens without words. Don't you think so, Torvald?

HELMER (*walking up and down*).   He'd grown so close to us. I find it hard to think of him as gone. With his suffering and loneliness he was like a clouded background for our happy sunshine. Well, it may be better this way. For him, at any rate. (*Stops.*) And perhaps for us, too, Nora. For now we have nobody but each other. (*Embraces her.*) Oh you —my beloved wife! I feel I just can't hold you close enough. Do you know, Nora—many times I have wished some great danger threatened you, so I could risk my life and blood and everything—everything, for your sake.

NORA (*frees herself and says in a strong and firm voice*).   I think you should go and read your letters now, Torvald.

HELMER.   No, no—not tonight. I want to be with you, my darling.

NORA.   With the thought of your dying friend—?

HELMER.   You are right. This has shaken both of us. Something not beautiful has come between us. Thoughts of death and dissolution. We must try to get over it—out of it. Till then—we'll each go to our own room.

NORA (*her arms around his neck*).   Torvald—goodnight! Goodnight!

HELMER (*kisses her forehead*).   Goodnight, my little songbird. Sleep well, Nora. Now I'll read my letters. (*He goes into his room, carrying the mail. Closes the door.*)

NORA (*her eyes desperate, her hands groping, finds* HELMER's *black cloak and throws it around her; she whispers, quickly, brokenly, hoarsely*).   Never see him again. Never. Never. Never. (*Puts her shawl over her head.*) And never see the children again, either. Never; never.— The black, icy water—fathomless—this—! If only it was all over.— Now he has it. Now he's reading it. No, no; not yet. Torvald —goodbye—you—the children—(*She is about to hurry through the hall, when* HELMER *flings open the door to his room and stands there with an open letter in his hand.*)

HELMER.   Nora!

NORA (*cries out*).   Ah—!

HELMER.   What is it? You know what's in this letter?

NORA.   Yes, I do! Let me go! Let me out!

HELMER (*holds her back*).   Where do you think you're going?

NORA (*trying to tear herself loose from him*).   I won't let you save me, Torvald!

HELMER (*tumbles back*).   True! Is it true what he writes? Oh my God! No, no—this can't possibly be true.

NORA.   It is true. I have loved you more than anything else in the whole world.

HELMER.   Oh, don't give me any silly excuses.

NORA (*taking a step towards him*).   Torvald—!

HELMER.   You wretch! What have you done!

NORA.   Let me go. You are not to sacrifice yourself for me. You are not to take the blame.

HELMER.   No more playacting. (*Locks the door to the front hall.*) You'll stay here and answer me. Do you understand what you have done? Answer me! Do you understand?

NORA (*gazes steadily at him with an increasingly frozen expression*). Yes. Now I'm beginning to understand.

HELMER (*walking up and down*).   What a dreadful awakening. All these years—all these eight years—she, my pride and my joy—a hypocrite, a liar—oh worse! worse!—a criminal! Oh, the bottomless ugliness in all this! Damn! Damn! Damn! (NORA, *silent, keeps gazing at him.* HELMER *stops in front of her.*) I ought to have guessed that something like this would happen. I should have expected it. All your father's loose principles— Silence! You have inherited every one of your father's loose principles. No religion, no morals, no sense of duty —. Now I am being punished for my leniency with him. I did it for your sake, and this is how you pay me back.

NORA.   Yes. This is how.

HELMER.   You have ruined all my happiness. My whole future— that's what you have destroyed. Oh, it's terrible to think about. I am at the mercy of an unscrupulous man. He can do with me whatever he likes, demand anything of me, command me and dispose of me just as he pleases— I dare not say a word! To go down so miserably, to be destroyed—all because of an irresponsible woman!

NORA.   When I am gone from the world, you'll be free.

HELMER.   No noble gestures, please. Your father was always full of such phrases too. What good would it do me if you were gone from the world, as you put it? Not the slightest good at all. He could still make the whole thing public, and if he did, people would be likely to think I had been your accomplice. They might even think it was my idea— that it was I who urged you to do it! And for all this I have you to thank —you, whom I've borne on my hands through all the years of our marriage. *Now* do you understand what you've done to me?

NORA (*with cold calm*).   Yes.

HELMER.   I just can't get it into my head that this is happening; it's all so incredible. But we have to come to terms with it somehow. Take your shawl off. Take it off, I say! I have to satisfy him one way or another. The whole affair must be kept quiet at whatever cost.— And as far as you and I are concerned, nothing must seem to have changed. I'm talking about appearances, of course. You'll go on living here; that goes without saying. But I won't let you bring up the children; I dare not trust you with them.— Oh! Having to say this to one I have loved so much, and whom I still—! But all that is past. It's not a question of happiness any more but of hanging on to what can be salvaged—pieces, appearances— (*The doorbell rings.* HELMER *jumps.*) What's that? So late. Is the worst—? Has he—! Hide, Nora! Say you're sick. (NORA *doesn't move.* HELMER *opens the door to the hall.*)

MAID (*half dressed, out in the hall*).   A letter for your wife, sir.

HELMER.   Give it to me. (*Takes the letter and closes the door.*) Yes, it's from him. But I won't let you have it. I'll read it myself.

NORA.   Yes—you read it.

HELMER (*by the lamp*).   I hardly dare. Perhaps we're lost, both you and I. No; I've got to know. (*Tears the letter open, glances through it, looks at an enclosure; a cry of joy.*) Nora! (NORA *looks at him with a question in her eyes.*) Nora!—No, I must read it again.—Yes, yes; it is so! I'm saved! Nora, I'm saved!

NORA.   And I?

HELMER.   You too, of course; we're both saved, both you and I. Look! He's returning your note. He writes that he's sorry, he regrets, a happy turn in his life—oh, it doesn't matter what he writes. We're saved, Nora! Nobody can do anything to you now. Oh Nora, Nora—. No, I want to get rid of this disgusting thing first. Let me see— (*Looks at the signature.*) No, I don't want to see it. I don't want it to be more than a bad dream, the whole thing. (*Tears up the note and both letters, throws the pieces in the stove, and watches them burn.*) There! Now it's gone.— He wrote that ever since Christmas Eve—. Good God, Nora, these must have been three terrible days for you.

NORA.   I have fought a hard fight these last three days.

HELMER.   And been in agony and seen no other way out than—. No, we won't think of all that ugliness. We'll just rejoice and tell ourselves it's over, it's all over! Oh, listen to me, Nora. You don't seem to understand. It's over. What *is* it? Why do you look like that —that frozen expression on your face? Oh my poor little Nora, don't you think I know what it is? You can't make yourself believe that I have forgiven you. But I have, Nora; I swear to you, I have forgiven you for everything. Of course I know that what you did was for love of me.

NORA.   That is true.

HELMER.   You have loved me the way a wife ought to love her husband. You just didn't have the wisdom to judge the means. But do you think I love you any less because you don't know how to act on your own? Of course not. Just lean on me. I'll advise you; I'll guide you. I wouldn't be a man if I didn't find you twice as attractive because of your womanly helplessness. You mustn't pay any attention to the hard words I said to you right at first. It was just that first shock when I thought everything was collapsing all around me. I have forgiven you, Nora. I swear to you—I really have forgiven you.

NORA.   I thank you for your forgiveness. (*She goes out through the door, right.*)

HELMER.   No, stay— (*Looks into the room she entered.*) What are you doing in there?

NORA (*within*).   Getting out of my costume.

HELMER (*by the open door*).   Good, good. Try to calm down and compose yourself, my poor little frightened songbird. Rest safely; I have broad wings to cover you with. (*Walks around near the door.*) What a nice and cozy home we have, Nora. Here's shelter for you. Here I'll keep you safe like a hunted dove I have rescued from the hawk's talons. Believe me: I'll know how to quiet your beating heart. It will happen by and by, Nora; you'll see. Why, tomorrow you'll look at all this in quite a different light. And soon everything will be just the way it was before. I won't need to keep reassuring you that I have forgiven you; you'll feel it yourself. Did you really think I could have abandoned you, or even reproached you? Oh, you don't know a real man's heart, Nora. There is something unspeakably sweet and satisfactory for a man to know deep in himself that he has forgiven his wife—forgiven her in all the fullness of his honest heart. You see, that way she becomes his very own all over again—in a double sense, you might say. He has, so to speak, given her a second birth; it is as if she had become his wife and his child, both. From now on that's what you'll be to me, you lost and helpless creature. Don't worry about a thing, Nora. Only be frank with me, and I'll be your will and your conscience.— What's this? You're not in bed? You've changed your dress—!

NORA (*in everyday dress*).   Yes, Torvald. I have changed my dress.

HELMER.   But why—now—this late?

NORA.   I'm not going to sleep tonight.

HELMER.   But my dear Nora—

NORA (*looks at her watch*).   It isn't all that late. Sit down here with me, Torvald. You and I have much to talk about. (*Sits down at the table.*)

HELMER.   Nora—what is this all about? That rigid face—

NORA.   Sit down. This will take a while. I have much to say to you.

HELMER (*sits down, facing her across the table*).   You worry me, Nora. I don't understand you.

NORA.   No, that's just it. You don't understand me. And I have never understood you—not till tonight. No, don't interrupt me. Just listen to what I have to say.— This is a settling of accounts, Torvald.

HELMER.   What do you mean by that?

NORA (*after a brief silence*).   Doesn't one thing strike you, now that we are sitting together like this?

HELMER.   What would that be?

NORA.   We have been married for eight years. Doesn't it occur to you that this is the first time that you and I, husband and wife, are having a serious talk?

HELMER.   Well—serious—. What do you mean by that?

NORA.   For eight whole years—longer, in fact—ever since we first met we have never talked seriously to each other about a single serious thing.

HELMER.   You mean I should forever have been telling you about worries you couldn't have helped me with anyway?

NORA.   I am not talking about worries. I'm saying we have never tried seriously to get to the bottom of anything together.

HELMER.   But dearest Nora, I hardly think that would have been something *you*—

NORA.   That's the whole point. You have never understood me. Great wrong has been done to me, Torvald. First by Daddy and then by you.

HELMER.   What! By us two? We who have loved you more deeply than anyone else?

NORA (*shakes her head*).   You never loved me—neither Daddy nor you. You only thought it was fun to be in love with me.

HELMER.   But, Nora—what an expression to use!

NORA.   That's the way it has been, Torvald. When I was home with Daddy, he told me all his opinions, and so they became my opinions too. If I disagreed with him I kept it to myself, for he wouldn't have liked that. He called me his little doll baby, and he played with me the way I played with my dolls. Then I came to your house—

HELMER.   What a way to talk about our marriage!

NORA (*imperturbably*).   I mean that I passed from Daddy's hands into yours. You arranged everything according to your taste, and so I came to share it—or I pretended to; I'm not sure which. I think it was a little of both, now one and now the other. When I look back on it now, it seems to me I've been living here like a pauper—just a hand-to-mouth kind of existence. I have earned my keep by doing tricks for you, Torvald. But that's the way you wanted it. You have great sins against me to answer for, Daddy and you. It's your fault that nothing has become of me.

HELMER.   Nora, you're being both unreasonable and ungrateful. Haven't you been happy here?

NORA.   No, never. I thought I was, but I wasn't.

HELMER.   Not—not happy!

NORA.   No; just having fun. And you have always been very good to me. But our home has never been more than a playroom. I have been your doll wife here, just the way I used to be Daddy's doll child. And the children have been my dolls. I thought it was fun when you played with me, just as they thought it was fun when I played with them. That's been our marriage, Torvald.

HELMER.   There is something in what you are saying—exaggerated and hysterical though it is. But from now on things will be different. Playtime is over; it's time for growing up.

NORA.   Whose growing up—mine or the children's?

HELMER.   Both yours and the children's, Nora darling.

NORA.   Oh Torvald, you're not the man to bring me up to be the right kind of wife for you.

HELMER.   How can you say that?

NORA.   And I—? What qualifications do I have for bringing up the children?

HELMER.   Nora!

NORA.   You said so yourself a minute ago—that you didn't dare to trust me with them.

HELMER.   In the first flush of anger, yes. Surely, you're not going to count that.

NORA.   But you were quite right. I am *not* qualified. Something else has to come first. Somehow I have to grow up myself. And you are not the man to help me do that. That's a job I have to do by myself. And that's why I'm leaving you.

HELMER (*jumps up*).   What did you say!

NORA.   I have to be by myself if I am to find out about myself and about all the other things too. So I can't stay here with you any longer.

HELMER.   Nora, Nora!

NORA.   I'm leaving now. I'm sure Kristine will put me up for tonight.

HELMER.   You're out of your mind! I won't let you! I forbid you!

NORA.   You can't forbid me anything any more; it won't do any good. I'm taking my own things with me. I won't accept anything from you, either now or later.

HELMER.   But this is madness!

NORA.   Tomorrow I'm going home—I mean back to my old home town. It will be easier for me to find some kind of job there.

HELMER.   Oh, you blind, inexperienced creature—!

NORA.   I must see to it that I get experience, Torvald.

HELMER.   Leaving your home, your husband, your children! Not a thought of what people will say!

NORA.   I can't worry about that. All I know is that I have to leave.

HELMER.   Oh, this is shocking! Betraying your most sacred duties like this!

NORA.   And what do you consider my most sacred duties?

HELMER.   Do I need to tell you that? They are your duties to your husband and your children.

NORA.   I have other duties equally sacred.

HELMER.   You do not. What duties would they be?

NORA.   My duties to myself.

HELMER.   You are a wife and a mother before you are anything else.

NORA.   I don't believe that any more. I believe I am first of all a human being, just as much as you—or at any rate that I must try to become one. Oh, I know very well that most people agree with you, Torvald, and that it says something like that in all the books. But what people say and what the books say is no longer enough for me. I have to think about these things myself and see if I can't find the answers.

HELMER.   You mean to tell me you don't know what your proper place in your own home is? Don't you have a reliable guide in such matters? Don't you have religion?

NORA.   Oh but Torvald—I don't really know what religion is.

HELMER.   What are you saying!

NORA.   All I know is what the Reverend Hansen told me when he prepared me for confirmation. He said that religion was *this* and it was *that*. When I get by myself, away from here, I'll have to look into that, too. I have to decide if what the Reverend Hansen said was right, or anyway if it is right for *me*.

HELMER.   Oh, this is unheard of in a young woman! If religion can't guide you, let me appeal to your conscience. For surely you have moral feelings? Or—answer me—maybe you don't?

NORA.   Well, you see, Torvald, I don't really know what to say. I just don't know. I am confused about these things. All I know is that my ideas are quite different from yours. I have just found out that the laws are different from what I thought they were, but in no way can I get it into my head that those laws are right. A woman shouldn't have the right to spare her dying old father or save her husband's life! I just can't believe that.

HELMER.   You speak like a child. You don't understand the society you live in.

NORA.   No, I don't. But I want to find out about it. I have to make up my mind who is right, society or I.

HELMER.   You are sick, Nora; you have a fever. I really don't think you are in your right mind.

NORA.   I have never felt so clearheaded and sure of myself as I do tonight.

HELMER.   And clearheaded and sure of yourself you're leaving your husband and children?

NORA.   Yes.

HELMER.   Then there is only one possible explanation.

NORA.   What?

HELMER.   You don't love me any more.

NORA.   No, that's just it.

HELMER.   Nora! Can you say that?

NORA.   I am sorry, Torvald, for you have always been so good to me. But I can't help it. I don't love you any more.

HELMER (*with forced composure*).   And this too is a clear and sure conviction?

NORA.   Completely clear and sure. That's why I don't want to stay here any more.

HELMER.   And are you ready to explain to me how I came to forfeit your love?

NORA.   Certainly I am. It was tonight, when the wonderful didn't happen. That was when I realized you were not the man I thought you were.

HELMER.   You have to explain. I don't understand.

NORA.   I have waited patiently for eight years, for I wasn't such a fool that I thought the wonderful is something that happens any old day. Then this—thing—came crashing in on me, and then there wasn't a doubt in my mind that now—now comes the wonderful. When Krogstad's letter was in that mailbox, never for a moment did it even occur to me that you would submit to his conditions. I was so absolutely certain that you would say to him: make the whole thing public—tell everybody. And when that had happened—

HELMER.   Yes, then what? When I surrendered my wife to shame and disgrace—!

NORA.   When that had happened, I was absolutely certain that you would stand up and take the blame and say, "I'm the guilty one."

HELMER.   Nora!

NORA.   You mean I never would have accepted such a sacrifice from you? Of course not. But what would my protests have counted against yours? *That* was the wonderful I was hoping for in terror. And to prevent that I was going to kill myself.

HELMER.   I'd gladly work nights and days for you, Nora—endure sorrow and want for your sake. But nobody sacrifices his *honor* for his love.

NORA.   A hundred thousand women have done so.

HELMER.   Oh, you think and talk like a silly child.

NORA.   All right. But you don't think and talk like the man I can live with. When you had gotten over your fright—not because of what threatened *me* but because of the risk to *you*—and the whole danger was past, then you acted as if nothing at all had happened. Once again I was your little songbird, your doll, just as before, only now you had to handle her even more carefully, because she was so frail and weak. (*Rises.*) Torvald—that moment I realized that I had been living here for eight years with a stranger and had borne him three children—Oh, I can't stand thinking about it! I feel like tearing myself to pieces!

HELMER (*heavily*).   I see it, I see it. An abyss has opened up between us.— Oh but Nora—surely it can be filled?

NORA.   The way I am now I am no wife for you.

HELMER.   I have it in me to change.

NORA.   Perhaps—if your doll is taken from you.

HELMER.   To part—to part from you! No, no, Nora! I can't grasp that thought!

NORA (*goes out, right*).   All the more reason why it has to be. (*She returns with her outdoor clothes and a small bag, which she sets down on the chair by the table.*)

HELMER.   Nora, Nora! Not now! Wait till tomorrow.

NORA (*putting on her coat*).   I can't spend the night in a stranger's rooms.

HELMER.   But couldn't we live here together like brother and sister —?

NORA (*tying on her hat*).   You know very well that wouldn't last long—. (*Wraps her shawl around her.*) Goodbye, Torvald. I don't want to see the children. I know I leave them in better hands than mine. The way I am now I can't be anything to them.

HELMER.   But some day, Nora—some day—?

NORA.   How can I tell? I have no idea what's going to become of me.

HELMER.   But you're still my wife, both as you are now and as you will be.

NORA.   Listen, Torvald—when a wife leaves her husband's house, the way I am doing now, I have heard he has no more legal responsibilities for her. At any rate, I now release you from all responsibility. You are not to feel yourself obligated to me for anything, and I have no obligations to you. There has to be full freedom on both sides. Here is your ring back. Now give me mine.

HELMER.   Even this?

NORA.   Even this.

HELMER.   Here it is.

NORA.   There. So now it's over. I'm putting the keys here. The maids know everything about the house—better than I. Tomorrow, after I'm gone, Kristine will come over and pack my things from home. I want them sent after me.

HELMER.   Over! It's all over! Nora, will you never think of me?

NORA.   I'm sure I'll often think of you and the children and this house.

HELMER.   May I write to you, Nora?

NORA.   No—never. I won't have that.

HELMER.   But send you things—? You must let me—

NORA.   Nothing, nothing.

HELMER.   —help you, when you need help—

NORA.   I told you, no; I won't have it. I'll accept nothing from strangers.

HELMER.   Nora—can I never again be more to you than a stranger?

NORA (*picks up her bag*).   Oh Torvald—then the most wonderful of all would have to happen—

HELMER.   Tell me what that would be—!

NORA.   For that to happen, both you and I would have to change so that— Oh Torvald, I no longer believe in the wonderful.

HELMER.   But I *will* believe. Tell me! Change, so that—?

NORA.   So that our living together would become a true marriage. Goodbye. (*She goes out through the hall.*)

HELMER (*sinks down on a chair near the door and covers his face with his hands*).   Nora! Nora! (*Looks around him and gets up.*) All empty. She's gone. (*With sudden hope.*) The most wonderful—?!

(*From downstairs comes the sound of a heavy door slamming shut.*)

QUESTIONS

1. How do the following contribute to the characterizations of Nora at the beginning of the play: (a) her husband's nicknames for her, (b) her fondness for sweets, (c) her games with her children, (d) her prodigality with money, and (e) her deceptions? What evidence is there that these characteristics may reflect both her own nature and conformity to her husband's expectations of her? What definition of marriage does she imply in her remarks to Mrs. Linde about how she may continue to act as long as she remains "young

and pretty" (page 1098)? It was socially proper at the time of the play for Norwegian wives to address their husbands by their last names; what does Nora's use of Helmer's first name suggest about their relationship?

2. What are the various functions of Nora's conversation with Mrs. Linde in Act 1? Consider it from these perspectives: (a) the exposition of prior events and the definition of Nora's dilemma; (b) further revelations of Nora's character, both in the past and during the conversation; (c) the insight into herself that Nora gains from Mrs. Linde's history; (d) definitions of legal and moral standards of the time indicated by the prior actions of both women.

3. What are the symbolic meanings of the title? Why is it more appropriate than *A Doll's House*? Is Nora the only "doll" in the play?

4. How much time passes during the present action of the play, from the opening of Act 1 to the final curtain? What events that occurred before the first act may be considered causes for the present action? What events that take place during the present are reported rather than dramatized on the stage?

5. What is the significance of Mrs. Linde's former and present relationship to Krogstad? To what extent can Krogstad be labeled "villain"? Compare his motives and actions (in the past and in the present) with those of Helmer; with those of Dr. Rank.

6. Characterize Dr. Rank. What are his strengths? his weaknesses? Structurally and morally he may be contrasted to Krogstad—but is he a model of virtue?

7. The major characters can be described thus: Nora and Helmer are protagonist and antagonist; Mrs. Linde is a foil to Nora; and both Krogstad and Dr. Rank are foils to Helmer. By evaluating the actions and motives of the foil characters, locate Nora and Helmer on a scale of human value. To what extent do the foil characters offer models for the central characters? To what extent do they offer them examples of actions to be avoided?

8. What positive gains does Nora make in the course of the action? What must she learn in order to perform her final act? Is that act a triumph, or a failure, or some of both? (For the play's first performance in Berlin, Ibsen was pressured into creating a conventionally "happy ending"—Nora is persuaded by Helmer not to leave him for the sake of their children, and so sacrifices herself to their need for a mother. Why is the present ending truer to the themes Ibsen presents?)

9. Compare Nora and Helmer as developing characters. What opportunities for change does Helmer have? How does he respond to them? Consider the extent to which Nora and Helmer share the responsibility for having created "a doll house" of their marriage. Evaluate Nora's leaving him as an opportunity for Helmer.

10. From the first moments of the play, money is a recurring topic. Consider the importance it has in the motivations and actions of the five major characters. Can you establish a rank-order of more or less admirable attitudes toward it? Can you separate examples of genuine need from examples of

desire for gain? Is the influence of money on the lives of these characters limited to the time and society in which they lived, or are there parallels to our time?

11. Consider the ways in which the marriage of Nora and Helmer is typical rather than uniquely theirs.

12. Assess the thematic importance of deception and honesty, of self-deception and self-discovery.

13. Explore the implications of this interpretation: "*A Doll House* represents a woman imbued with the idea of becoming a person, but it proposes nothing categorical about women becoming people; in fact, its real theme has nothing to do with the sexes. It is the irrepressible conflict of two different personalities which have founded themselves on two radically different estimates of reality" (Robert M. Adams, "Ibsen on the Contrary," in *Modern Drama*, ed. Anthony Caputi [New York: Norton, 1966], 345).

Tennessee Williams

The Glass Menagerie

Characters

AMANDA WINGFIELD, *the mother, a little woman of great but confused vitality clinging frantically to another time and place. Her characterization must be carefully created, not copied from type. She is not paranoiac, but her life is paranoia. There is much to admire in Amanda, and as much to love and pity as there is to laugh at. Certainly she has endurance and a kind of heroism, and though her foolishness makes her unwittingly cruel at times, there is tenderness in her slight person.*

LAURA WINGFIELD, *her daughter. AMANDA, having failed to establish contact with reality, continues to live vitally in her illusions, but LAURA's situation is even graver. A childhood illness has left her crippled, one leg slightly shorter than the other, and held in a brace. This defect need not be more than suggested on the stage. Stemming from this, LAURA's separation increases till she is like a piece of her own glass collection, too exquisitely fragile to move from the shelf.*

TOM WINGFIELD, *her son and the narrator of the play. A poet with a job in a warehouse. His nature is not remorseless, but to escape from a trap he has to act without pity.*

JIM O'CONNOR, *the gentleman caller, a nice, ordinary, young man.*

THE GLASS MENAGERIE   First performed in 1944; developed from a short story, "Portrait of a Girl in Glass" (published later in *One Arm and Other Stories*). Tennessee Williams (1911–1983) was born Thomas Lanier Williams in Mississippi, the son of a traveling salesman. In 1918 the family moved to St. Louis when the father was made a sales manager of International Shoe Company. Here, while the family lived in a succession of rented apartments, Tom published his first story at sixteen, graduated from high school, attended the University of Missouri for three years, worked at a menial job in the shoe company (1932–1935), had a nervous breakdown, and finished his education at Washington University and the University of Iowa. Adopting "Tennessee" as his writing name, he then embarked on a life that took him to Chicago, New Orleans, Los Angeles, Mexico City, New York, Key West, and other cities while he wrote steadily, supporting himself with odd jobs. *The Glass Menagerie*, his first commercial success, rescued him from penury. The play reflects his St. Louis years, although his real father (given to alcoholic excess) never disappeared from home; his sister (two years his elder) did have dates, was not handicapped, and did not have a glass collection; a younger brother (eight years Tom's junior) does not appear; and "Miss Edwina" (Williams's mother and his guest at the first performance) has written, "The only resemblance I have to Amanda is that we both like jonquils."

Scene.   *An alley in St. Louis.*

Part 1. Preparation for a gentleman caller.
Part 2. The gentleman calls.

Time: Now and the Past.

SCENE 1

The Wingfield apartment is in the rear of the building, one of those vast hive-like conglomerations of cellular living-units that flower as warty growths in overcrowded urban centers of lower middle-class population and are symptomatic of the impulse of this largest and fundamentally enslaved section of American society to avoid fluidity and differentiation and to exist and function as one interfused mass of automatism.

The apartment faces an alley and is entered by a fire-escape, a structure whose name is a touch of accidental poetic truth, for all of these huge buildings are always burning with the slow and implacable fires of human desperation. The fire-escape is part of what we see—that is, the landing of it and steps descending from it.

The scene is memory and is therefore nonrealistic. Memory takes a lot of poetic license. It omits some details; others are exaggerated, according to the emotional value of the articles it touches, for memory is seated predominantly in the heart. The interior is therefore rather dim and poetic.

At the rise of the curtain, the audience is faced with the dark, grim rear wall of the Wingfield tenement. This building is flanked on both sides by dark, narrow alleys which run into murky canyons of tangled clotheslines, garbage cans and the sinister latticework of neighboring fire-escapes. It is up and down these side alleys that exterior entrances and exits are made, during the play. At the end of Tom's *opening commentary, the dark tenement wall slowly becomes transparent and reveals the interior of the ground floor Wingfield apartment.*

Nearest the audience is the living room, which also serves as a sleeping room for Laura, *the sofa unfolding to make her bed. Just beyond, separated from the living room by a wide arch or second proscenium with transparent faded portieres (or second curtain), is the dining room. In an old-fashioned what-not in the living room are seen scores of transparent glass animals. A blown-up photograph of the father hangs on the wall of the living room to the left of the archway. It is the face of a very handsome young man in a doughboy's First World War cap. He is gallantly smiling, ineluctably smiling, as if to say, "I will be smiling forever."*

Also hanging on the wall, near the photograph, are a typewriter keyboard chart and a Gregg shorthand diagram. An upright typewriter on a small table stands beneath the charts.

The audience hears and sees the opening scene in the dining room through both the transparent fourth wall of the building and the transparent gauze portieres of the dining-room arch. It is during this revealing scene that the fourth wall slowly ascends, out of sight. This transparent exterior wall is not brought down again until the very end of the play, during TOM's final speech.

The narrator is an undisguised convention of the play. He takes whatever license with dramatic convention as is convenient to his purposes.

TOM enters, dressed as a merchant sailor, and strolls across the front of the stage to the fire-escape. There he stops and lights a cigarette. He addresses the audience.

TOM.   Yes, I have tricks in my pocket, I have things up my sleeve. But I am the opposite of a stage magician. He gives you illusion that has the appearance of truth. I give you truth in the pleasant disguise of illusion.

To begin with, I turn back time. I reverse it to that quaint period, the thirties, when the huge middle class of America was matriculating in a school for the blind. Their eyes had failed them, or they had failed their eyes, and so they were having their fingers pressed forcibly down on the fiery Braille alphabet of a dissolving economy.

In Spain there was revolution. Here there was only shouting and confusion. In Spain there was Guernica.° Here there were disturbances of labor, sometimes pretty violent, in otherwise peaceful cities such as Chicago, Cleveland, Saint Louis . . . This is the social background of the play. (*Music.*)

The play is memory. Being a memory play, it is dimly lighted, it is sentimental, it is not realistic. In memory everything seems to happen to music. That explains the fiddle in the wings.

I am the narrator of the play, and also a character in it. The other characters are my mother, Amanda, my sister, Laura, and a gentleman caller who appears in the final scenes. He is the most realistic character in the play, being an emissary from a world of reality that we were somehow set apart from. But since I have a poet's weakness for symbols, I am using this character also as a symbol; he is the long delayed but always expected something that we live for.

There is a fifth character in the play who doesn't appear except in this larger-than-life-size photograph over the mantel. This is our father who left us a long time ago. He was a telephone man who fell in love with long distances; he gave up his job with the telephone company and skipped the light fantastic out of town . . .

Guernica: A town in northern Spain destroyed in 1937 during the Spanish Civil War by German bombers, in the first mass air attack on an urban community.

The last we heard of him was a picture post-card from Mazatlán, on the Pacific coast of Mexico, containing a message of two words—"Hello —Good-bye!" and no address.

I think the rest of the play will explain itself . . . (AMANDA's *voice becomes audible through the portieres*. TOM *divides the portieres and enters the upstage area*. AMANDA *and* LAURA *are seated at a drop-leaf table. Eating is indicated by gestures without food or utensils.* AMANDA *faces the audience.* TOM *and* LAURA *are seated in profile. The interior has lit up softly and through the scrim we see* AMANDA *and* LAURA *seated at the table in the upstage area.*)

AMANDA (*calling*).   Tom?

TOM.   Yes, Mother.

AMANDA.   We can't say grace until you come to the table!

TOM.   Coming, Mother. (*He bows slightly and withdraws, reappearing a few moments later in his place at the table.*)

AMANDA (*to her son*).   Honey, don't *push* with your *fingers*. If you have to push with something, the thing to push with is a crust of bread. And chew—chew! Animals have sections in their stomachs which enable them to digest food without mastication, but human beings are supposed to chew their food before they swallow it down. Eat food leisurely, son, and really enjoy it. A well-cooked meal has lots of delicate flavors that have to be held in the mouth for appreciation. So chew your food and give your salivary glands a chance to function!

TOM (*deliberately lays his imaginary fork down and pushes his chair back from the table*).   I haven't enjoyed one bite of this dinner because of your constant directions on how to eat it. It's you that makes me rush through meals with your hawk-like attention to every bite I take. Sickening—spoils my appetite—all this discussion of—animals' secretion—salivary glands—mastication!

AMANDA (*lightly*).   Temperament like a Metropolitan star! (*He rises and crosses downstage.*) You're not excused from the table.

TOM.   I'm getting a cigarette.

AMANDA.   You smoke too much.

LAURA (*rises*).   I'll bring in the blancmange. (TOM *remains standing with his cigarette by the portieres during the following.*)

AMANDA (*rising*).   No, sister, no, sister—you be the lady this time and I'll be the darky.

LAURA.   I'm already up.

AMANDA.   Resume your seat, little sister—I want you fresh and pretty—for gentlemen callers!

LAURA.   I'm not expecting any gentlemen callers.

AMANDA (*crossing out to kitchenette. Airily*).   Sometimes they come when they are least expected! Why, I remember one Sunday afternoon in Blue Mountain—(*enters kitchenette*).

TOM.   I know what's coming!

LAURA.   Yes. But let her tell it.

TOM.   Again?

LAURA.   She loves to tell it.

AMANDA (*returning with a bowl of dessert*).   One Sunday afternoon in Blue Mountain—your mother received—*seventeen!*—gentlemen callers! Why, sometimes there weren't chairs enough to accommodate them all. We had to send a servant over to bring in folding chairs from the parish house.

TOM (*remaining at portieres*).   How did you entertain those gentlemen callers?

AMANDA.   I understood the art of conversation!

TOM.   I bet you could talk.

AMANDA.   Girls in those days *knew* how to talk, I can tell you.

TOM.   Yes?

AMANDA.   They knew how to entertain their gentlemen callers. It wasn't enough for a girl to be possessed of a pretty face and a graceful figure—although I wasn't slighted in either respect. She also needed to have a nimble wit and a tongue to meet all occasions.

TOM.   What did you talk about?

AMANDA.   Things of importance going on in the world! Never anything coarse or common or vulgar. (*She addresses* TOM *as though he were seated in the vacant chair at the table though he remains by the portieres. He plays this scene as though he held the book.*) My callers were gentlemen —all! Among my callers were some of the most prominent young planters of the Mississippi Delta—planters and sons of planters! (TOM *motions for music and a spot of light on* AMANDA. *Her eyes lift, her face glows, her voice becomes rich and elegiac.*)

There was young Champ Laughlin who later became vice-president of the Delta Planters Bank. Hadley Stevenson who was drowned in Moon Lake and left his widow one hundred and fifty thousand in Government bonds. There were the Cutrere brothers, Wesley and Bates. Bates was one of my bright particular beaux! He got in a quarrel with that wild Wainwright boy. They shot it out on the floor of Moon Lake Casino. Bates was shot through the stomach. Died in the ambulance on his way to Memphis. His widow was so well-provided for, came into eight or ten thousand acres, that's all. She married him on the rebound—never loved her—carried my picture on him the night he died! And there was that boy that every girl in the Delta had set her cap for! That beautiful, brilliant young Fitzhugh boy from Greene County!

TOM.   What did he leave his widow?

AMANDA.   He never married! Gracious, you talk as though all of my old admirers had turned up their toes to the daisies!

TOM.   Isn't this the first you've mentioned that still survives?

AMANDA.   That Fitzhugh boy went North and made a fortune—came to be known as the Wolf of Wall Street! He had the Midas touch, whatever he touched turned to gold! And I could have been Mrs. Duncan J. Fitzhugh, mind you! But—I picked your *father!*

LAURA (*rising*).   Mother, let me clear the table.

AMANDA.   No, dear, you go in front and study your typewriter chart. Or practice your shorthand a little. Stay fresh and pretty!—It's almost time for our gentlemen callers to start arriving. (*She flounces girlishly toward the kitchenette.*) How many do you suppose we're going to entertain this afternoon? (TOM *throws down the paper and jumps up with a groan.*)

LAURA (*alone in the dining room*).   I don't believe we're going to receive any, Mother.

AMANDA (*reappearing, airily*).   What? No one—not one? You must be joking! (LAURA *nervously echoes her laugh. She slips in a fugitive manner through the half-open portieres and draws them gently behind her. A shaft of very clear light is thrown on her face against the faded tapestry of the curtains. Music: "The Glass Menagerie"° under faintly. Lightly*) Not one gentleman caller? It can't be true! There must be a flood, there must have been a tornado!

LAURA.   It isn't a flood, it's not a tornado, Mother. I'm just not popular like you were in Blue Mountain . . . (TOM *utters another groan.* LAURA *glances at him with a faint, apologetic smile. Her voice catching a little.*) Mother's afraid I'm going to be an old maid. (*The scene dims out with "Glass Menagerie" music.*)

SCENE 2

LAURA *is seated in the delicate ivory chair at the small claw-foot table. She wears a dress of soft violet material for a kimono—her hair tied back from her forehead with a ribbon. She is washing and polishing her collection of glass.* AMANDA *appears on the fire-escape steps. At the sound of her ascent,* LAURA *catches her breath, thrusts the bowl of ornaments away and seats herself stiffly*

Music . . . Menagerie": Music for the play, including "The Glass Menagerie" theme, was composed by Paul Bowles (1910–1999), American composer, novelist, and short story writer.

before the diagram of the typewriter keyboard as though it held her spellbound. Something has happened to AMANDA. *It is written in her face as she climbs to the landing: a look that is grim and hopeless and a little absurd. She has on one of those cheap or imitation velvety-looking cloth coats with imitation fur collar. Her hat is five or six years old, one of those dreadful cloche hats that were worn in the late twenties, and she is clasping an enormous black patent-leather pocketbook with nickel clasps and initials. This is her full-dress outfit, the one she usually wears to the D.A.R. Before entering she looks through the door. She purses her lips, opens her eyes very wide, rolls them upward and shakes her head. Then she slowly lets herself in the door. Seeing her mother's expression* LAURA *touches her lips with a nervous gesture.*

LAURA.   Hello, Mother, I was—(*She makes a nervous gesture toward the chart on the wall.* AMANDA *leans against the shut door and stares at* LAURA *with a martyred look.*)

AMANDA.   Deception? Deception? (*She slowly removes her hat and gloves, continuing the sweet suffering stare. She lets the hat and gloves fall on the floor—a bit of acting.*)

LAURA (*shakily*).   How was the D.A.R. meeting? (AMANDA *slowly opens her purse and removes a dainty white handkerchief which she shakes out delicately and delicately touches to her lips and nostrils.*) Didn't you go to the D.A.R. meeting, Mother?

AMANDA (*faintly, almost inaudibly*).   —No.—No. (*Then more forcibly*) I did not have the strength—to go to the D.A.R. In fact, I did not have the courage! I wanted to find a hole in the ground and hide myself in it forever! (*She crosses slowly to the wall and removes the diagram of the typewriter keyboard. She holds it in front of her for a second, staring at it sweetly and sorrowfully—then bites her lips and tears it in two pieces.*)

LAURA (*faintly*).   Why did you do that, Mother? (AMANDA *repeats the same procedure with the chart of the Gregg Alphabet.*) Why are you—

AMANDA.   Why? Why? How old are you, Laura?

LAURA.   Mother, you know my age.

AMANDA.   I thought you were an adult; it seems that I was mistaken. (*She crosses slowly to the sofa and sinks down and stares at* LAURA.)

LAURA.   Please don't stare at me, Mother. (AMANDA *closes her eyes and lowers her head. There is a ten-second pause.*)

AMANDA.   What are we going to do, what is going to become of us, what is the future? (*There is another pause.*)

LAURA.   Has something happened, Mother? (AMANDA *draws a long breath and takes out the handkerchief again. Dabbing process.*) Mother, has —something happened?

AMANDA.   I'll be all right in a minute, I'm just bewildered—(*she hesitates*)—by life.

LAURA.   Mother, I wish that you would tell me what's happened!

AMANDA.   As you know, I was supposed to be inducted into my office at the D.A.R. this afternoon. But I stopped off at Rubicam's Business College to speak to your teachers about your having a cold and ask them what progress they thought were you making down there.

LAURA.   Oh . . .

AMANDA.   I went to the typing instructor and introduced myself as your mother. She didn't know who you were. "Wingfield," she said. "We don't have any such student enrolled at the school!"

I assured her she did, that you had been going to classes since early in January.

"I wonder," she said, "if you could be talking about that terribly shy little girl who dropped out of school after only a few days' attendance?"

"No," I said, "Laura, my daughter, has been going to school every day for the past six weeks!"

"Excuse me," she said. She took the attendance book out and there was your name, unmistakably printed, and all the dates you were absent until they decided that you had dropped out of school.

I still said, "No, there must have been some mistake! There must have been some mix-up in the records!"

And she said, "No—I remember her perfectly now. Her hands shook so that she couldn't hit the right keys! The first time we gave a speed-test, she broke down completely—was sick at the stomach and almost had to be carried into the wash-room! After that morning she never showed up any more. We phoned the house but never got any answer"—While I was working at Famous and Barr, I suppose, demonstrating those—

Oh! (*She indicates a brassiere with her hands.*) I felt so weak I could barely keep on my feet! I had to sit down while they got me a glass of water! Fifty dollars' tuition, all of our plans—my hopes and ambitions for you—just gone up the spout, just gone up the spout like that. (LAURA *draws a long breath and gets awkwardly to her feet. She crosses to the victrola and winds it up.*) What are you doing?

LAURA.   Oh! (*She releases the handle and returns to her seat.*)

AMANDA.   Laura, where have you been going when you've gone out pretending that you were going to business college?

LAURA.   I've just been going out walking.

AMANDA.   That's not true.

LAURA.   It is. I just went walking.

AMANDA.   Walking? Walking? In winter? Deliberately courting pneumonia in that light coat? Where did you walk to, Laura?

LAURA.   All sorts of places—mostly in the park.

AMANDA.   Even after you'd started catching that cold?

LAURA.   It was the lesser of two evils, Mother. I couldn't go back up. I—threw up—on the floor!

AMANDA.   From half past seven till after five every day you mean to tell me you walked around in the park, because you wanted me to think that you were still going to Rubicam's Business College?

LAURA.   It wasn't as bad as it sounds. I went inside places to get warmed up.

AMANDA.   Inside where?

LAURA.   I went in the art museum and the bird-houses at the Zoo. I visited the penguins every day! Sometimes I did without lunch and went to the movies. Lately I've been spending most of my afternoons in the Jewel-box, that big glass house where they raise the tropical flowers.

AMANDA.   You did all this to deceive me, just for deception? (LAURA *looks down.*) Why?

LAURA.   Mother, when you're disappointed, you get that awful suffering look on your face, like the picture of Jesus's mother in the museum!

AMANDA.   Hush!

LAURA.   I couldn't face it. (*Pause. A whisper of strings.*)

AMANDA (*hopelessly fingering the huge pocketbook*).   So what are we going to do the rest of our lives? Stay home and watch the parades go by? Amuse ourselves with the glass menagerie, darling? Eternally play those worn-out phonograph records your father left as a painful reminder of him? We won't have a business career—we've given that up because it gave us nervous indigestion! (*Laughs wearily.*) What is there left but dependency all our lives? I know so well what becomes of unmarried women who aren't prepared to occupy a position. I've seen such pitiful cases in the South—barely tolerated spinsters living upon the grudging patronage of sister's husband or brother's wife!—stuck away in some little mouse-trap of a room—encouraged by one in-law to visit another—little birdlike women without any nest—eating the crust of humility all their life!

Is that the future that we've mapped out for ourselves? I swear it's the only alternative I can think of! (*She pauses.*) It isn't a very pleasant alternative, is it? (*She pauses again.*) Of course—some girls *do* marry. (LAURA *twists her hands nervously.*) Haven't you ever liked some boy?

LAURA.   Yes. I liked one once. (*Rises.*) I came across his picture a while ago.

AMANDA (*with some interest*).   He gave you his picture?

LAURA.   No, it's in the year-book.

AMANDA (*disappointed*).   Oh—a high-school boy.

LAURA.   Yes. His name was Jim. (LAURA *lifts the heavy annual from the claw-foot table.*) Here he is in *The Pirates of Penzance.*°

AMANDA (*absently*).   The what?

LAURA.   The operetta the senior class put on. He had a wonderful voice and we sat across the aisle from each other Mondays, Wednesdays and Fridays in the Aud. Here he is with the silver cup for debating! See his grin?

AMANDA (*absently*).   He must have had a jolly disposition.

LAURA.   He used to call me—Blue Roses.

AMANDA.   Why did he call you such a name as that?

LAURA.   When I had that attack of pleurosis—he asked me what was the matter when I came back. I said pleurosis—he thought that I said Blue Roses! So that's what he always called me after that. Whenever he saw me, he'd holler, "Hello, Blue Roses!" I didn't care for the girl he went out with. Emily Meisenbach. Emily was the best-dressed girl at Soldan. She never struck me, though, as being sincere . . . It says in the Personal Section—they're engaged. That's—six years ago! They must be married by now.

AMANDA.   Girls that aren't cut out for business careers usually wind up married to some nice man. (*Gets up with a spark of revival.*) Sister, that's what you'll do! (LAURA *utters a startled, doubtful laugh. She reaches quickly for a piece of glass.*)

LAURA.   But, Mother—

AMANDA.   Yes? (*Crossing to photograph.*)

LAURA (*in a tone of frightened apology*).   I'm—crippled!

AMANDA.   Nonsense! Laura, I've told you never, never to use that word. Why, you're not crippled, you just have a little defect—hardly noticeable, even! When people have some slight disadvantage like that, they cultivate other things to make up for it—develop charm—and vivacity—and—*charm!* That's all you have to do! (*She turns again to the photograph.*) One thing your father had plenty of —was *charm!* (TOM *motions to the fiddle in the wings. The scene fades out with music.*)

SCENE 3

Tom *speaks from the fire-escape landing.*

TOM.   After the fiasco at Rubicam's Business College, the idea of getting a gentleman caller for Laura began to play a more and more important part in Mother's calculations. It became an obsession. Like some archetype of the universal unconscious, the image of the gentleman caller haunted our small apartment . . .

The . . . Penzance: comic operetta (1880) by Gilbert and Sullivan

An evening at home rarely passed without some allusion to this image, this specter, this hope . . . Even when he wasn't mentioned, his presence hung in Mother's preoccupied look and in my sister's frightened, apologetic manner—hung like a sentence passed upon the Wingfields!

Mother was a woman of action as well as words. She began to take logical steps in the planned direction. Late that winter and in the early spring—realizing that extra money would be needed to properly feather the nest and plume the bird—she conducted a vigorous campaign on the telephone, roping in subscribers to one of those magazines for matrons called *The Home-maker's Companion*, the type of journal that features the serialized sublimations of ladies of letters who think in terms of delicate cup-like breasts, slim, tapering waists, rich, creamy thighs, eyes like woodsmoke in autumn, fingers that soothe and caress like strains of music, bodies as powerful as Etruscan sculpture. (AMANDA *enters with phone on long extension cord. She is spotted in the dim stage.*)

AMANDA.   Ida Scott? This is Amanda Wingfield! We *missed* you at the D.A.R. last Monday! I said to myself: She's probably suffering with that sinus condition! How is the sinus condition?

Horrors! Heaven have mercy!—You're a Christian martyr, yes, that's what you are, a Christian martyr!

Well, I just now happened to notice that your subscription to the *Companion*'s about to expire! Yes, it expires with the next issue, honey! —just when that wonderful new serial by Bessie Mae Hopper is getting off to such an exciting start. Oh, honey, it's something that you can't miss! You remember how *Gone with the Wind* took everybody by storm? You simply couldn't go out if you hadn't read it. All everybody *talked* was Scarlett O'Hara. Well, this is a book that critics already compare to *Gone with the Wind*. It's the *Gone with the Wind* of the post–World War generation—What?—Burning?—Oh, honey, don't let them burn, go take a look in the oven and I'll hold the wire! Heavens—I think she's hung up!

(*Before the stage is lighted, the violent voices of* TOM *and* AMANDA *are heard. They are quarreling behind the portieres. In front of them stands* LAURA *with clenched hands and panicky expression. A clear pool of light on her figure throughout this scene.*)

TOM.   What in Christ's name am I—

AMANDA (*shrilly*).   Don't you use that—

TOM.   Supposed to do!

AMANDA.   Expression! Not in my—

TOM.   Ohhh!

AMANDA.   Presence! Have you gone out of your senses?

TOM.   I have, that's true, *driven* out!

AMANDA.   What is the matter with you, you—big—big—IDIOT!

TOM.   Look!—I've got *no thing*, no single thing—

AMANDA.   Lower your voice!

TOM.   In my life here that I can call my own! Everything is—

AMANDA.   Stop that shouting!

TOM.   Yesterday you confiscated my books! You have the nerve to—

AMANDA.   I took that horrible novel back to the library—yes! That hideous book by that insane Mr. Lawrence.° (TOM *laughs wildly.*) I cannot control the output of diseased minds or people who cater to them— (TOM *laughs still more wildly.*) BUT I WON'T ALLOW SUCH FILTH BROUGHT INTO MY HOUSE! No, no, no, no, no!

TOM.   House, house! Who pays rent on it, who makes a slave of himself to—

AMANDA (*fairly screeching*).   Don't you DARE to—

TOM.   No, no, I mustn't say things. *I've* got to just—

AMANDA.   Let me tell you—

TOM.   I don't want to hear any more! (*He tears the portieres open. The upstage area is lit with a turgid smoky red glow.* AMANDA's *hair is in metal curlers and she wears a very old bathrobe, much too large for her slight figure, a relic of the faithless Mr. Wingfield. An upright typewriter and a wild disarray of manuscripts is on the drop-leaf table. The quarrel was probably precipitated by* AMANDA's *interruption of his creative labor. A chair lies overthrown on the floor. Their gesticulating shadows are cast on the ceiling by the fiery glow.*)

AMANDA.   You *will* hear more, you—

TOM.   No, I won't hear more, I'm going out!

AMANDA.   You come right back in—

TOM.   Out, out, out! Because I'm—

AMANDA.   Come back here, Tom Wingfield! I'm not through talking to you!

TOM.   Oh, go—

LAURA (*desperately*).   —Tom!

AMANDA.   You're going to listen, and no more insolence from you! I'm at the end of my patience!

Mr. Lawrence: D. H. Lawrence, author of "The Rocking-Horse Winner" (page 295), emphasized in his novels the force and importance of sexuality in human life.

TOM (*comes back toward her*).   What do you think I'm at? Aren't I supposed to have any patience to reach the end of, Mother? I know, I know. It seems unimportant to you, what I'm *doing*—what I *want* to do —having a little *difference* between them! You don't think that—

AMANDA.   I think you've been doing things that you're ashamed of. That's why you act like this. I don't believe that you go every night to the movies. Nobody goes to the movies night after night. Nobody in their right minds goes to the movies as often as you pretend to. People don't go to the movies at nearly midnight, and movies don't let out at two A.M. Come in stumbling. Muttering to yourself like a maniac! You get three hours' sleep and then go to work. Oh, I can picture the way you're doing down there. Moping, doping, because you're in no condition.

TOM (*wildly*).   No, I'm in no condition!

AMANDA.   What right have you got to jeopardize your job? Jeopardize the security of all of us? How do you think we'd manage if you were—

TOM.   Listen! You think I'm crazy *about* the *warehouse*? (*He bends fiercely toward her slight figure.*) You think I'm in love with the Continental Shoemakers? You think I want to spend fifty-five *years* down there in that—*celotex interior!* with—*fluorescent* —*tubes!* Look! I'd rather somebody picked up a crowbar and battered out my brains— than go back mornings! I *go!* Every time you come in yelling that God damn "*Rise and Shine!*" "*Rise and Shine!*" I say to myself, "How *lucky dead* people are!" But I get up. I *go!* For sixty-five dollars a month I give up all that I dream of doing and being *ever!* And you say self—*self's* all I ever think of. Why, listen, if self is what I thought of, Mother, I'd be where he is—GONE! (*Pointing to father's picture.*) As far as the system of transportation reaches! (*He starts past her. She grabs his arm.*) Don't grab at me, Mother!

AMANDA.   Where are you going?

TOM.   I'm going to the *movies!*

AMANDA.   I don't believe that lie!

TOM (*crouching toward her, overtowering her tiny figure. She backs away, gasping*).   I'm going to opium dens! Yes, opium dens, dens of vice and criminals' hang-outs, Mother. I've joined the Hogan gang, I'm a hired assassin, I carry a tommy-gun in a violin case! I run a string of cat-houses in the Valley! They call me Killer, Killer Wingfield, I'm leading a double-life, a simple, honest warehouse worker by day, by night a dynamic *czar* of the *underworld*, *Mother*. I go to gambling casinos, I spin away fortunes on the roulette table! I wear a patch over one eye and a false mustache, sometimes I put on green whiskers. On those occasions they call me—*El Diablo!* Oh, I could tell you things to make you sleepless! My enemies plan to dynamite this place. They're going to blow us all sky-high some night! I'll be glad, very happy, and so will you! You'll go up, up on a broomstick, over Blue Mountain with seventeen gentlemen callers! You ugly—babbling old—*witch* . . . (*He goes through a series of violent, clumsy movements, seizing his overcoat, lunging to the door, pulling it fiercely open. The women watch him, aghast. His arm catches in the sleeve of the coat as he struggles to pull it on. For a moment he is pinioned by the bulky garment. With an outraged groan he tears the coat off again, splitting the shoulder of it, and hurls it across the room. It strikes against the shelf of* LAURA's *glass collection, there is a tinkle of shattering glass.* LAURA *cries out as if wounded. Music: "The Glass Menagerie."*)

LAURA (*shrilly*).   My glass!—menagerie . . . (*She covers her face and turns away. But* AMANDA *is still stunned and stupefied by the "ugly witch" so that she barely notices this occurrence. Now she recovers her speech.*)

AMANDA (*in an awful voice*).   I won't speak to you—until you apologize!

(*She crosses through the portieres and draws them together behind her.* TOM *is left with* LAURA. LAURA *clings weakly to the mantel with her face averted.* TOM *stares at her stupidly for a moment. Then he crosses to shelf. Drops awkwardly on knees to collect the fallen glass, glancing at* LAURA *as if he would speak but couldn't. "The Glass Menagerie" steals in as the scene dims out.*)

SCENE 4

The interior of the apartment is dark. There is a faint light in the alley. A deep-voiced bell in a church is tolling the hour of five as the scene commences.

TOM *appears at the top of the alley. After each solemn boom of the bell in the tower, he shakes a little noise-maker or rattle as if to express the tiny spasm of man in contrast to the sustained power and dignity of the Almighty. This and the unsteadiness of his advance make it evident that he has been drinking. As he climbs the few steps to the fire-escape landing, light steals up inside.* LAURA *appears in night-dress, observing* TOM's *empty bed in the front room.* TOM *fishes in his pockets for his door-key, removing a motley assortment of articles in the search, including a perfect shower of movie-ticket stubs and an empty bottle. At last he finds the key, but just as he is about to insert it, it slips from his fingers. He strikes a match and crouches below the door.*

TOM (*bitterly*).   One crack—and it falls through!
LAURA (*opens the door*).   Tom! Tom, what are you doing?
TOM.   Looking for a door-key.
LAURA.   Where have you been all this time?

TOM.   I have been to the movies.

LAURA.   All this time at the movies?

TOM.   There was a very long program. There was a Garbo picture and a Mickey Mouse and a travelogue and a newsreel and a preview of coming attractions. And there was an organ solo and a collection for the milk-fund—simultaneously—which ended up in a terrible fight between a fat lady and an usher!

LAURA (*innocently*).   Did you have to stay through everything?

TOM.   Of course! And, oh, I forgot! There was a big stage show! The headliner on this stage show was Malvolio the Magician. He performed wonderful tricks, many of them, such as pouring water back and forth between pitchers. First it turned to wine and then it turned to beer and then it turned to whiskey. I know it was whiskey it finally turned into because he needed somebody to come up out of the audience to help him, and I came up—both shows! It was Kentucky Straight Bourbon. A very generous fellow, he gave souvenirs. (*He pulls from his back pocket a shimmering rainbow-colored scarf.*) He gave me this. This is his magic scarf. You can have it, Laura. You wave it over a canary cage and you get a bowl of goldfish. You wave it over the goldfish bowl and they fly away canaries . . . But the wonderfullest trick of all was the coffin trick. We nailed him into a coffin and he got out of the coffin without removing one nail. (*He has come inside.*) There is a trick that would come in handy for me—get me out of this 2 by 4 situation! (*Flops onto bed and starts removing shoes.*)

LAURA.   Tom—Shhh!

TOM.   What're you shushing me for?

LAURA.   You'll wake up Mother.

TOM.   Goody, goody! Pay 'er back for all those "Rise an' Shines." (*Lies down, groaning.*) You know it don't take much intelligence to get yourself into a nailed-up coffin, Laura. But who in hell ever got himself out of one without removing one nail? (*As if in answer, the father's grinning photograph lights up. Scene dims out. Immediately following the church bell is heard striking six. At the sixth stroke the alarm clock goes off in* AMANDA's *room, and after a few moments we hear her calling: "Rise and Shine! Rise and Shine! Laura, go tell your brother to rise and shine!"*)

TOM (*sitting up slowly*).   I'll rise—but I won't shine. (*The light increases.*)

AMANDA.   Laura, tell your brother his coffee is ready.

LAURA (*slips into front room*).   Tom!—It's nearly seven. Don't make Mother nervous. (*He stares at her stupidly. Beseechingly*) Tom, speak to Mother this morning. Make up with her, apologize, speak to her!

TOM.   She won't to me. It's her that started not speaking.

LAURA.   If you just say you're sorry she'll start speaking.

TOM.   Her not speaking—is that such a tragedy?

LAURA.   Please—please!

AMANDA (*calling from kitchenette*).   Laura, are you going to do what I asked you to do, or do I have to get dressed and go out myself?

LAURA.   Going, going—soon as I get on my coat! (*She pulls on a shapeless felt hat with nervous, jerky movement, pleadingly glancing at* TOM. *Rushes awkwardly for coat. The coat is one of* AMANDA's, *inaccurately made-over, the sleeves too short for* LAURA.) Butter and what else?

AMANDA (*entering upstage*).   Just butter. Tell them to charge it.

LAURA.   Mother, they make such faces when I do that.

AMANDA.   Sticks and stones can break our bones, but the expression on Mr. Garfinkel's face won't harm us! Tell your brother his coffee is getting cold.

LAURA (*at door*).   Do what I asked you, will you, will you, Tom? (*He looks sullenly away.*)

AMANDA.   Laura, go now or just don't go at all!

LAURA (*rushing out*).   Going—going! (*A second later she cries out.* TOM *springs up and crosses to door.* AMANDA *rushes anxiously in.* TOM *opens the door.*)

TOM.   Laura?

LAURA.   I'm all right. I slipped, but I'm all right.

AMANDA (*peering anxiously after her*).   If anyone breaks a leg on those fire-escape steps, the landlord ought to be sued for every cent he possesses! (*She shuts door. Remembers she isn't speaking and returns to the other room.*)

(*As* TOM *enters listlessly for his coffee, she turns her back to him and stands rigidly facing the window on the gloomy gray vault of the areaway. Its light on her face with its aged but childish features is cruelly sharp, satirical as a Daumier print.*

(*Music under: "Ave Maria."*

(TOM *glances sheepishly but sullenly at her averted figure and slumps at the table. The coffee is scalding hot; he sips it and gasps and spits it back in the cup. At his gasp,* AMANDA *catches her breath and half turns. Then catches herself and turns back to window.* TOM *blows on his coffee, glancing sidewise at his mother. She clears her throat.* TOM *clears his. He starts to rise. Sinks back down again, scratches his head, clears his throat again.* AMANDA *coughs.* TOM *raises his cup in both hands to blow on it, his eyes staring over the rim of it at his mother for several moments. Then he slowly sets the cup down and awkwardly and hesitantly rises from the chair.*)

TOM (*hoarsely*).   Mother. I—I apologize, Mother. (AMANDA *draws a quick, shuddering breath. Her face works grotesquely. She breaks into childlike tears.*) I'm sorry for what I said, for everything that I said, I didn't mean it.

AMANDA (*sobbingly*).   My devotion has made me a witch and so I make myself hateful to my children!

TOM.   *No, you don't.*

AMANDA.   I worry so much, don't sleep, it makes me nervous!

TOM (*gently*).   I understand that.

AMANDA.   I've had to put up a solitary battle all these years. But you're my right-hand bower! Don't fall down, don't fail!

TOM (*gently*).   I try, Mother.

AMANDA (*with great enthusiasm*).   Try and you will succeed! (*The notion makes her breathless.*) Why, you—you're just *full* of natural endowments! Both of my children—they're *unusual* children! Don't you think I know it? I'm so—*proud!* Happy and—feel I've—so much to be thankful for but— Promise me one thing, son!

TOM.   What, Mother?

AMANDA.   Promise, son, you'll—never be a drunkard!

TOM (*turns to her grinning*).   I will never be a drunkard, Mother.

AMANDA.   That's what frightened me so, that you'd been drinking. Eat a bowl of Purina!

TOM.   Just coffee, Mother.

AMANDA.   Shredded wheat biscuit?

TOM.   No. No, Mother, just coffee.

AMANDA.   You can't put in a day's work on an empty stomach. You've got ten minutes—don't gulp! Drinking too-hot liquids makes cancer of the stomach . . . Put cream in.

TOM.   No, thank you.

AMANDA.   To cool it.

TOM.   No! No, thank you, I want it black.

AMANDA.   I know, but it's not good for you. We have to do all that we can to build ourselves up. In these trying times we live in, all that we have to cling to is—each other . . . That's why it's so important to—Tom, I—I sent out your sister so I could discuss something with you. If you hadn't spoken I would have spoken to you. (*Sits down.*)

TOM (*gently*).   What is it, Mother, that you want to discuss?

AMANDA.   *Laura!*

TOM (*puts his cup down slowly. Music: "The Glass Menagerie"*). Oh.—Laura . . .

AMANDA (*touching his sleeve*).   You know how Laura is. So quiet but —still water runs deep! She notices things and I think she—broods about them. (TOM *looks up.*) A few days ago I came in and she was crying.

TOM.   What about?

AMANDA.   You.

TOM.   Me?

AMANDA.   She has an idea that you're not happy here.

TOM.   What gave her that idea?

AMANDA.   What gives her any idea? However, you do act strangely. I—I'm not criticizing, understand *that!* I know your ambitions do not lie in the warehouse, that like everybody in the whole wide world—you've had to—make sacrifices, but—Tom—Tom—life's not easy, it calls for—Spartan endurance! There's so many things in my heart that I cannot describe to you! I've never told you but I—*loved* your father . . .

TOM (*gently*).   I know that, Mother.

AMANDA.   And you—when I see you taking after his ways! Staying out late—and—well, you *had* been drinking the night you were in that—terrifying condition! Laura says that you hate the apartment and that you go out nights to get away from it! Is that true, Tom?

TOM.   No. You say there's so much in your heart that you can't describe to me. That's true of me, too. There's so much in my heart that I can't describe to *you!* So let's respect each other's—

AMANDA.   But, why—*why,* Tom—are you always so *restless?* Where do you *go* to, nights?

TOM.   I—go to the movies.

AMANDA.   Why do you go to the movies so much, Tom?

TOM.   I go to the movies because—I like adventure. Adventure is something I don't have much of at work, so I go to the movies.

AMANDA.   But, Tom, you go to the movies *entirely* too *much!*

TOM.   I like a lot of adventure. (AMANDA *looks baffled, then hurt. As the familiar inquisition resumes he becomes hard and impatient again.* AMANDA *slips back to her querulous attitude toward him.*)

AMANDA.   Most young men find adventure in their careers.

TOM.   Then most young men are not employed in a warehouse.

AMANDA.   The world is full of young men employed in warehouses and offices and factories.

TOM.   Do all of them find adventure in their careers?

AMANDA.   They do or they do without it! Not everybody has a craze for adventure.

TOM.   Man is by instinct a lover, a hunter, a fighter, and none of those instincts are given much play at the warehouse!

AMANDA.   Man is by instinct! Don't quote instincts to me! Instinct is something that people have got away from! It belongs to animals! Christian adults don't want it!

TOM.   What do Christian adults want, then, Mother?

AMANDA.   Superior things! Things of the mind and the spirit! Only animals have to satisfy instincts! Surely your aims are somewhat higher than theirs! Than monkeys—pigs—

TOM.   I reckon they're not.

AMANDA.   You're joking. However, that isn't what I wanted to discuss.

TOM (*rising*).   I haven't much time.

AMANDA (*pushing his shoulders*).   Sit down.

TOM.   You want me to punch in red at the warehouse, Mother?

AMANDA.   You have five minutes. I want to talk about Laura.

TOM.   All right! What about Laura?

AMANDA.   We have to be making some plans and provisions for her. She's older than you, two years, and nothing has happened. She just drifts along doing nothing. It frightens me terribly how she just drifts along.

TOM.   I guess she's the type that people call home girls.

AMANDA.   There's no such type, and if there is, it's a pity! That is unless the home is hers, with a husband!

TOM.   What?

AMANDA.   Oh, I can see the handwriting on the wall as plain as I see the nose in front of my face! It's terrifying! More and more you remind me of your father! He was out all hours without explanation!— Then *left*! Goodbye! And me with the bag to hold. I saw that letter you got from the Merchant Marine. I know what you're dreaming of. I'm not standing here blindfolded. (*She pauses.*) Very well, then. Then *do* it! But not till there's somebody to take your place.

TOM.   What do you mean?

AMANDA.   I mean that as soon as Laura has got somebody to take care of her, married, a home of her own, independent—why, then you'll be free to go wherever you please, on land, on sea, whichever way the wind blows you! But until that time you've got to look out for your sister. I don't say me because I'm old and don't matter! I say your sister because she's young and dependent.

I put her in business college—a dismal failure! Frightened her so it made her sick at the stomach. I took her over to the Young People's League at the church. Another fiasco. She spoke to nobody, nobody spoke to her. Now all she does is fool with those pieces of glass and play those worn-out records. What kind of a life is that for a girl to lead?

TOM.   What can I do about it?

AMANDA.   Overcome selfishness! Self, self, self is all that you ever think of! (TOM *springs up and crosses to get his coat. It is ugly and bulky. He pulls on a cap with earmuffs.*) Where is your muffler? Put your wool muffler on! (*He snatches it angrily from the closet and tosses it about his neck and pulls both ends tight.*) Tom! I haven't said what I had in mind to ask you.

TOM.   I'm too late to—

AMANDA (*catching his arm—very importunately. Then shyly*).
Down at the warehouse, aren't there some—nice young men?

TOM.   No!

AMANDA.   There *must* be—*some* . . .

TOM.   Mother—(*Gesture.*)

AMANDA.   Find out one that's clean-living—doesn't drink and—
ask him out for sister!

TOM.   What?

AMANDA.   For *sister!* To *meet!* Get *acquainted!*

TOM (*stamping to door*).   Oh, my *go-osh!*

AMANDA.   Will you? (*He opens door. Imploringly*) Will you? (*He
starts down.*) Will you? Will you, dear?

TOM (*calling back*).   YES! (AMANDA *closes the door hesitantly and
with a troubled but faintly hopeful expression.*)

AMANDA (*moves into spotlight at the phone*).   Ella Cartwright? This
is Amanda Wingfield!

How are you, honey?

How is that kidney condition? (*There is a five-second pause.*)

Horrors! (*There is another pause.*)

You're a Christian martyr, yes, honey, that's what you are, a
Christian martyr! Well, I just now happened to notice in my little red
book that your subscription to the *Companion* has just run out! I
knew that you wouldn't want to miss out on the wonderful serial
starting in this new issue. It's by Bessie Mae Hopper, the first thing
she's written since *Honeymoon for Three.* Wasn't that a strange and
interesting story? Well, this one is even lovelier, I believe. It has a
sophisticated, society background. It's all about the horsey set on
Long Island!

SCENE 5

*It is early dusk of a spring evening. Supper has just been finished in the
Wingfield apartment.* AMANDA *and* LAURA *in light-colored dresses are removing dishes from the table, in the upstage area, which is shadowy, their movements formalized almost as a dance or ritual, their moving forms as pale and
silent as moths.* TOM, *in white shirt and trousers, rises from the table and
crosses toward the fire-escape.*

AMANDA (*as he passes her*).   Son, will you do me a favor?

TOM.   What?

AMANDA.   Comb your hair! You look so pretty when your hair is combed! (TOM *slouches on sofa with evening paper. Enormous caption "Franco Triumphs."*) There is only one respect in which I would like you to emulate your father.

TOM.   What respect is that?

AMANDA.   The care he always took of his appearance. He never allowed himself to look untidy. (*He throws down the paper and crosses to fire-escape.*) Where are you going?

TOM.   I'm going out to smoke.

AMANDA.   You smoke too much. A pack a day at fifteen cents a pack. How much would that amount to in a month? Thirty times fifteen is how much, Tom? Figure it out and you will be astounded at what you could save. Enough to give you a night-school course in accounting at Washington U! Just think what a wonderful thing that would be for you, Son!

TOM.   I'd rather smoke. (*He steps out on landing, letting the screen door slam.*)

AMANDA (*sharply*).   I know! That's the tragedy of it . . . (*Alone, she turns to look at her husband's picture. Dance music: "All the World Is Waiting for the Sunrise!"*)

TOM (*to the audience*).   Across the alley from us was the Paradise Dance Hall. On evenings in spring the windows and doors were open and the music came outdoors. Sometimes the lights were turned out except for a large glass sphere that hung from the ceiling. It would turn slowly about and filter the dusk with delicate rainbow colors. Then the orchestra played a waltz or a tango, something that had a slow and sensuous rhythm. Couples would come outside, to the relative privacy of the alley. You could see them kissing behind ash-pits and telephone poles. This was the compensation for lives that passed like mine, without any change or adventure. Adventure and change were imminent in this year. They were waiting around the corner for all these kids. Suspended in the mist over Berchtesgaden,° caught in the folds of Chamberlain's umbrella—.° In Spain there was Guernica! But here there was only hot swing music and liquor, dance halls, bars, and movies, and sex that hung in the gloom like a chandelier and flooded the world with brief, deceptive rainbows . . . All the world was waiting for bombardments! (AMANDA *turns from the picture and comes outside.*)

Berchtesgaden: Hitler's Bavarian summer retreat   **Chamberlain's umbrella:** Neville Chamberlain, British prime minister (1937–1940), who always carried a furled umbrella, and whose name has become a symbol for appeasement, returned from a conference with Hitler in Munich in 1938 with a signed agreement that he proclaimed meant "Peace in our time." One year later, German troops invaded Poland, beginning World War II.

AMANDA (*sighing*).   A fire-escape landing's a poor excuse for a porch. (*She spreads a newspaper on a step and sits down, gracefully and demurely as if she were settling into a swing on a Mississippi veranda.*) What are you looking at?

TOM.   The moon.

AMANDA.   Is there a moon this evening?

TOM.   It's rising over Garfinkel's Delicatessen.

AMANDA.   So it is! A little silver slipper of a moon. Have you made a wish on it yet?

TOM.   Um-hum.

AMANDA.   What did you wish for?

TOM.   That's a secret.

AMANDA.   A secret, huh? Well, I won't tell mine either. I will be just as mysterious as you.

TOM.   I bet I can guess what yours is.

AMANDA.   Is my head so transparent?

TOM.   You're not a sphinx.

AMANDA.   No, I don't have secrets. I'll tell you what I wished for on the moon. Success and happiness for my precious children! I wish for that whenever there's a moon, and when there isn't a moon, I wish for it, too.

TOM.   I thought perhaps you wished for a gentleman caller.

AMANDA.   Why do you say that?

TOM.   Don't you remember asking me to fetch one?

AMANDA.   I remember suggesting that it would be nice for your sister if you brought home some nice young man from the warehouse. I think that I've made that suggestion more than once.

TOM.   Yes, you have made it repeatedly.

AMANDA.   Well?

TOM.   We are going to have one.

AMANDA.   *What?*

TOM.   A gentleman caller! (*The annunciation is celebrated with music.* AMANDA *rises.*)

AMANDA.   You mean you have asked some nice young man to come over?

TOM.   Yep. I've asked him to dinner.

AMANDA.   You really did?

TOM.   I did!

AMANDA.   You did, and did he—*accept?*

TOM.   He did!

AMANDA.   Well, well—well, well! That's—lovely!

TOM.   I thought that you would be pleased.

AMANDA. It's definite, then?

TOM. Very definite.

AMANDA. Soon?

TOM. Very soon.

AMANDA. For heaven's sake, stop putting on and tell me some things, will you?

TOM. What things do you want me to tell you?

AMANDA. *Naturally* I would like to know when he's *coming!*

TOM. He's coming tomorrow.

AMANDA. *Tomorrow?*

TOM. Yep. Tomorrow.

AMANDA. But, Tom!

TOM. Yes, Mother?

AMANDA. Tomorrow gives me no time!

TOM. Time for what?

AMANDA. Preparations! Why didn't you phone me at once, as soon as you asked him, the minute that he accepted? Then, don't you see, I could have been getting ready!

TOM. You don't have to make any fuss.

AMANDA. Oh, Tom, Tom, Tom, of course I have to make a fuss! I want things nice, not sloppy! Not thrown together. I'll certainly have to do some fast thinking, won't I?

TOM. I don't see why you have to think at all.

AMANDA. You just don't know. We can't have a gentleman caller in a pig-sty! All my wedding silver has to be polished, the monogrammed table linen ought to be laundered! The windows have to be washed and fresh curtains put up. And how about clothes? We have to *wear* something, don't we?

TOM. Mother, this boy is no one to make a fuss over!

AMANDA. Do you realize he's the first young man we've introduced to your sister? It's terrible, dreadful, disgraceful that poor little sister has never received a single gentleman caller! Tom, come inside! (*She opens the screen door.*)

TOM. What for?

AMANDA. I want to ask you some things.

TOM. If you're going to make such a fuss, I'll call it off, I'll tell him not to come!

AMANDA. You certainly won't do anything of the kind. Nothing offends people worse than broken engagements. It simply means I'll have to work like a Turk! We won't be brilliant, but we'll pass inspection. Come on inside. (TOM *follows, groaning.*) Sit down.

TOM. Any particular place you would like me to sit?

AMANDA.   Thank heavens I've got the new sofa! I'm also making payments on a floor lamp I'll have sent out! And put the chintz covers on, they'll brighten things up! Of course I'd hoped to have these walls repapered . . . What is the young man's name?

TOM.   His name is O'Connor.

AMANDA.   That, of course, means fish—tomorrow is Friday! I'll have that salmon loaf—with Durkee's dressing! What does he do? He works at the warehouse?

TOM.   Of course! How else would I—

AMANDA.   Tom, he—doesn't drink?

TOM.   Why do you ask me that?

AMANDA.   Your father *did!*

TOM.   Don't get started on that!

AMANDA.   He *does* drink, then?

TOM.   Not that I know of!

AMANDA.   Make sure, be certain! The last thing I want for my daughter's a boy who drinks!

TOM.   Aren't you being a little bit premature? Mr. O'Connor has not yet appeared on the scene!

AMANDA.   But will tomorrow. To meet your sister, and what do I know about his character? Nothing! Old maids are better off than wives of drunkards!

TOM.   Oh, my God!

AMANDA.   Be still!

TOM (*leaning forward to whisper*).   Lots of fellows meet girls whom they don't marry!

AMANDA.   Oh, talk sensibly, Tom—and don't be sarcastic! (*She has gotten a hairbrush.*)

TOM.   What are you doing?

AMANDA.   I'm brushing that cow-lick down! What is this young man's position at the warehouse?

TOM (*submitting grimly to the brush and the interrogation*).   This young man's position is that of a shipping clerk, Mother.

AMANDA.   Sounds to me like a fairly responsible job, the sort of a job *you* would be in if you just had more *get-up*. What is his salary? Have you any idea?

TOM.   I would judge it to be approximately eighty-five dollars a month.

AMANDA.   Well—not princely, but—

TOM.   Twenty more than I make.

AMANDA.   Yes, how well I know! But for a family man, eighty-five dollars a month is not much more than you can just get by on . . .

TOM.   Yes, but Mr. O'Connor is not a family man.

AMANDA.   He might be, mightn't he? Some time in the future?

TOM.   I see. Plans and provisions.

AMANDA.   You are the only young man that I know of who ignores the fact that the future becomes the present, the present the past, and the past turns into everlasting regret if you don't plan for it!

TOM.   I will think that over and see what I can make of it.

AMANDA.   Don't be supercilious with your mother! Tell me some more about this—what do you call him?

TOM.   James D. O'Connor. The D. is for Delaney.

AMANDA.   Irish on *both* sides! *Gracious!* And doesn't drink?

TOM.   Shall I call him up and ask him right this minute?

AMANDA.   The only way to find out about these things is to make discreet inquiries at the proper moment. When I was a girl in Blue Mountain and it was suspected that a young man drank, the girl whose attentions he had been receiving, if any girl *was*, would sometimes speak to the minister of his church, or rather her father would if her father was living, and sort of feel him out on the young man's character. That is the way such things are discreetly handled to keep a young woman from making a tragic mistake!

TOM.   Then how did you happen to make a tragic mistake?

AMANDA.   That innocent look of your father's had everyone fooled! He *smiled*—the world was *enchanted!* No girl can do worse than put herself at the mercy of a handsome appearance! I hope that Mr. O'Connor is not too good-looking.

TOM.   No, he's not too good-looking. He's covered with freckles and hasn't too much of a nose.

AMANDA.   He's not right-down homely, though?

TOM.   Not right-down homely. Just medium homely, I'd say.

AMANDA.   Character's what to look for in a man.

TOM.   That's what I've always said, Mother.

AMANDA.   You've never said anything of the kind and I suspect you would never give it a thought.

TOM.   Don't be so suspicious of me.

AMANDA.   At least I hope he's the type that's up and coming.

TOM.   I think he really goes in for self-improvement.

AMANDA.   What reason have you to think so?

TOM.   He goes to night school.

AMANDA (*beaming*).   Splendid! What does he do, I mean study?

TOM.   Radio engineering and public speaking!

AMANDA.   Then he has visions of being advanced in the world! Any young man who studies public speaking is aiming to have an executive job some day! And radio engineering? A thing for the future!

Both of these facts are very illuminating. Those are the sort of things that a mother should know concerning any young man who comes to call on her daughter. Seriously or—not.

TOM.   One little warning. He doesn't know about Laura. I didn't let on that we had dark ulterior motives. I just said, why don't you come and have dinner with us? He said okay and that was the whole conversation.

AMANDA.   I bet it was! You're eloquent as an oyster. However, he'll know about Laura when he gets here. When he sees how lovely and sweet and pretty she is, he'll thank his lucky stars he was asked to dinner.

TOM.   Mother, you mustn't expect too much of Laura.

AMANDA.   What do you mean?

TOM.   Laura seems all those things to you and me because she's ours and we love her. We don't even notice she's crippled any more.

AMANDA.   Don't say crippled! You know that I never allow that word to be used!

TOM.   But face facts, Mother. She is and—that's not all—

AMANDA.   What do you mean "not all"?

TOM.   Laura is very different from other girls.

AMANDA.   I think the difference is all to her advantage.

TOM.   Not quite all—in the eyes of others—strangers—she's terribly shy and lives in a world of her own and those things make her seem a little peculiar to people outside the house.

AMANDA.   Don't say peculiar.

TOM.   Face the facts. She is. (*The dance-hall music changes to a tango that has a minor and somewhat ominous tone.*)

AMANDA.   In what way is she peculiar—may I ask?

TOM (*gently*).   She lives in a world of her own—a world of— little glass ornaments, Mother . . . (*Gets up.* AMANDA *remains holding the brush, looking at him, troubled.*) She plays old phonograph records and—that's about all—(*He glances at himself in the mirror and crosses to door.*)

AMANDA (*sharply*).   Where are you going?

TOM.   I'm going to the movies. (*Out screen door.*)

AMANDA.   Not to the movies, every night to the movies! (*Follows quickly to screen door.*) I don't believe you always go to the movies! (*He is gone.* AMANDA *looks worriedly after him for a moment. Then vitality and optimism return and she turns from the door, crossing to portieres.*) Laura! Laura!

LAURA (*answers from kitchenette*).   Yes, Mother.

AMANDA.   Let those dishes go and come in front! (LAURA *appears with dish towel.* AMANDA *speaks to her gaily.*) Laura, come here and make a wish on the moon!

LAURA (*entering*).   Moon—moon?

AMANDA.   A little silver slipper of a moon. Look over your left shoulder, Laura, and make a wish! (LAURA *looks faintly puzzled as if called out of sleep.* AMANDA *seizes her shoulders and turns her at an angle by the door.*)

LAURA.   What shall I wish for, Mother?

AMANDA (*her voice trembling and her eyes suddenly filled with tears*). Happiness! Good fortune! (*The sound of the violin rises and the stage dims out.*)

SCENE 6

TOM.   And so the following evening I brought Jim home to dinner. I had known Jim slightly in high school. In high school Jim was a hero. He had tremendous Irish good nature and vitality with the scrubbed and polished look of white chinaware. He seemed to move in a continual spotlight. He was a star in basketball, captain of the debating club, president of the senior class and the glee club and he sang the male lead in the annual light operas. He was always running or bounding, never just walking. He seemed always at the point of defeating the law of gravity. He was shooting with such velocity through his adolescence that you would logically expect him to arrive at nothing short of the White House by the time he was thirty. But Jim apparently ran into more interference after his graduation from Soldan. His speed had definitely slowed. Six years after he left high school he was holding a job that wasn't much better than mine.

He was the only one at the warehouse with whom I was on friendly terms. I was valuable to him as someone who could remember his former glory, who had seen him win basketball games and the silver cup in debating. He knew of my secret practice of retiring to a cabinet of the washroom to work on poems when business was slack in the warehouse. He called me Shakespeare. And while the other boys in the warehouse regarded me with suspicious hostility, Jim took a humorous attitude toward me. Gradually his attitude affected the others, their hostility wore off and they also began to smile at me as people smile at an oddly fashioned dog who trots across their paths at some distance.

I knew that Jim and Laura had known each other at Soldan, and I had heard Laura speak admiringly of his voice. I didn't know if Jim remembered her or not. In high school Laura had been as unobtrusive as Jim had been astonishing. If he did remember Laura, it was not as my sister, for when I asked him to dinner, he grinned and said, "You know, Shakespeare, I never thought of you as having folks!"

He was about to discover that I did . . .

(*The light dims out on* TOM *and comes up in the* Wingfield *living room —a delicate lemony light. It is about five on a Friday evening of late spring which comes "scattering poems in the sky."*

(AMANDA *has worked like a Turk in preparation for the gentleman caller. The results are astonishing. The new floor lamp with its rose-silk shade is in place, a colored paper lantern conceals the broken light fixture in the ceiling, new billowing white curtains are at the windows, chintz covers are on chairs and sofa, a pair of new sofa pillows make their initial appearance. Open boxes and tissue paper are scattered on the floor.*

(LAURA *stands in the middle with lifted arms while* AMANDA *crouches before her, adjusting the hem of a new dress, devout and ritualistic. The dress is colored and designed by memory. The arrangement of* LAURA's *hair is changed; it is softer and more becoming. A fragile, unearthly prettiness has come out in* LAURA: *she is like a piece of translucent glass touched by light, given a momentary radiance, not actual, not lasting.*)

AMANDA (*impatiently*).   Why are you trembling?

LAURA.   Mother, you've made me nervous!

AMANDA.   How have I made you nervous?

LAURA.   By all this fuss! You make it seem so important!

AMANDA.   I don't understand you, Laura. You couldn't be satisfied with just sitting home, and yet whenever I try to arrange something for you, you seem to resist it. (*She gets up.*) Now take a look at yourself. No, wait! Wait just a moment—I have an idea!

LAURA.   What is it now? (AMANDA *produces two powder puffs which she wraps in handkerchiefs and stuffs in* LAURA's *bosom.*)

LAURA.   Mother, what are you doing?

AMANDA.   They call them "Gay Deceivers"!

LAURA.   I won't wear them.

AMANDA.   You will!

LAURA.   Why should I?

AMANDA.   Because, to be painfully honest, your chest is flat.

LAURA.   You make it seem like we were setting a trap.

AMANDA.   All pretty girls are a trap, a pretty trap, and men expect them to be. Now look at yourself, young lady. This is the prettiest you will ever be! (*She stands back to admire* LAURA.) I've got to fix myself now! You're going to be surprised by your mother's appearance! (*She crosses through portieres, humming gaily.* LAURA *moves slowly to the long mirror and stares solemnly at herself. A wind blows the white curtain inward in a slow, graceful motion and with a faint, sorrowful sighing.* AMANDA *speaks from somewhere behind the portieres.*) It isn't dark enough yet. (LAURA *turns slowly before the mirror with a troubled look.*)

AMANDA (*laughing, still not visible*).   I'm going to show you something. I'm going to make a spectacular appearance!

LAURA.   What is it, Mother?

AMANDA.   Possess your soul in patience—you will see! Something I've resurrected from that old trunk! Styles haven't changed so terribly much after all . . . (*She parts the portieres.*) Now just look at your mother! (*She wears a girlish frock of yellow voile with a blue silk sash. She carries a bunch of jonquils—the legend of her youth is nearly revived. Now she speaks feverishly.*) This is the dress in which I led the cotillion. Won the cakewalk twice at Sunset Hill, wore one spring to the Governor's ball in Jackson! See how I sashayed around the ballroom, Laura? (*She raises her skirt and does a mincing step around the room.*) I wore it on Sundays for my gentlemen callers! I had it on the day I met your father —I had malaria fever all that spring. The change of climate from East Tennessee to the Delta—weakened resistance—I had a little temperature all the time—not enough to be serious—just enough to make me restless and giddy!—Invitations poured in—parties all over the Delta! —"Stay in bed," said Mother, "you have fever!"—but I just wouldn't.— I took quinine but kept on going, going!—Evenings, dances!— Afternoons, long, long rides! Picnics—lovely!—So lovely, that country in May.—All lacy with dogwood, literally flooded with jonquils!— That was the spring I had the craze for jonquils. Jonquils became an absolute obsession. Mother said, "Honey, there's no more room for jonquils." And still I kept on bringing in more jonquils. Whenever, wherever I saw them, I'd say, "Stop! Stop! I see jonquils!" I made the young men help me gather the jonquils! It was a joke, Amanda and her jonquils! Finally there were no more vases to hold them, every available space was filled with jonquils. No vases to hold them? All right, I'll hold them myself! And then I—(*She stops in front of the picture. Music.*) met your father! Malaria and jonquils and then—this—boy . . . (*She switches on the rose-colored lamp.*) I hope they get here before it starts to rain. (*She crosses upstage and places the jonquils in bowl on table.*) I gave your brother a little extra change so he and Mr. O'Connor could take the service car home.

LAURA (*with altered look*).   What did you say his name was?

AMANDA.   O'Connor.

LAURA.   What is his first name?

AMANDA.   I don't remember. Oh, yes, I do. It was—Jim! (*LAURA sways slightly and catches hold of a chair.*)

LAURA (*faintly*).   Not—Jim!

AMANDA.   Yes, that was it, it was Jim! I've never known a Jim that wasn't nice! (*The music becomes ominous.*)

LAURA.   Are you sure his name is Jim O'Connor?

AMANDA.   Yes. Why?

LAURA.   Is he the one that Tom used to know in high school?

AMANDA.   He didn't say so. I think he just got to know him at the warehouse.

LAURA.   There was a Jim O'Connor we both knew in high school — (*Then, with effort*) If that is the one that Tom is bringing to dinner—you'll have to excuse me, I won't come to the table.

AMANDA.   What sort of nonsense is this?

LAURA.   You asked me once if I'd ever liked a boy. Don't you remember I showed you this boy's picture?

AMANDA.   You mean the boy you showed me in the year-book?

LAURA.   Yes, that boy.

AMANDA.   Laura, Laura, were you in love with that boy?

LAURA.   I don't know, Mother. All I know is I couldn't sit at the table if it was him!

AMANDA.   It won't be him! It isn't the least bit likely. But whether it is or not, you will come to the table. You will not be excused.

LAURA.   I'll have to be, Mother.

AMANDA.   I don't intend to humor your silliness, Laura. I've had too much from you and your brother, both! So just sit down and compose yourself till they come. Tom has forgotten his key so you'll have to let them in, when they arrive.

LAURA (*panicky*).   Oh, Mother—*you* answer the door!

AMANDA (*lightly*).   I'll be in the kitchen—busy!

LAURA.   Oh, Mother, please answer the door, don't make me do it!

AMANDA (*crossing into kitchenette*).   I've got to fix the dressing for the salmon. Fuss, fuss—silliness!—over a gentleman caller! (*Door swings shut. LAURA is left alone. She utters a low moan and turns off the lamp—sits stiffly on the edge of the sofa, knotting her fingers together. TOM and JIM appear on the fire-escape steps and climb to landing. Hearing their approach, LAURA rises with a panicky gesture. She retreats to the portieres. The doorbell rings. LAURA catches her breath and touches her throat. Low drums sound. AMANDA calls.*) Laura, sweetheart! The door! (*LAURA stares at it without moving.*)

JIM.   I think we just beat the rain.

TOM.   Uh-huh. (*He rings again, nervously. JIM whistles and fishes for a cigarette.*)

AMANDA (*very, very gaily*).   Laura, that is your brother and Mr. O'Connor! Will you let them in, darling? (LAURA *crosses toward kitchenette door*.)

LAURA (*breathlessly*).   Mother—you go to the door! (AMANDA *steps out of the kitchenette and stares furiously at* LAURA. *She points imperiously at the door*.) Please, please!

AMANDA (*in a fierce whisper*).   What is the matter with you, you silly thing?

LAURA (*desperately*).   Please, you answer it, *please!*

AMANDA.   I told you I wasn't going to humor you, Laura. Why have you chosen this moment to lose your mind?

LAURA.   Please, please, please, you go!

AMANDA.   You'll have to go to the door because I can't!

LAURA (*despairingly*).   I can't either!

AMANDA.   *Why?*

LAURA.   I'm *sick!*

AMANDA.   I'm sick too—of your nonsense! Why can't you and your brother be normal people? Fantastic whims and behavior. (TOM *gives a long ring*.) Preposterous goings on! Can you give me one reason —(*She calls out lyrically*.) Coming! Just one second!—why you should be afraid to open a door? Now you answer it, Laura!

LAURA.   Oh, oh, oh . . . (*She returns through the portieres, darts to the victrola, winds it frantically and turns it on*.)

AMANDA.   Laura Wingfield, you march right to that door!

LAURA.   Yes—yes, Mother! (*A faraway, scratchy rendition of "Dardanella" softens the air and gives her strength to move through it. She slips to the door and draws it cautiously open.* TOM *enters with the caller,* JIM O'CONNOR.)

TOM.   Laura, this is Jim. Jim, this is my sister, Laura.

JIM (*stepping inside*).   I didn't know that Shakespeare had a sister!

LAURA (*retreating stiff and trembling from the door*).   How—how do you do?

JIM (*heartily extending his hand*).   Okay! (LAURA *touches it hesitantly with hers*.) Your hand's cold, Laura!

LAURA.   Yes, well—I've been playing the victrola . . .

JIM.   Must have been playing classical music on it! You ought to play a little hot swing music to warm you up!

LAURA.   Excuse me—I haven't finished playing the victrola . . . (*She turns awkwardly and hurries into the front room. She pauses a second by the victrola. Then she catches her breath and darts through the portieres like a frightened deer*.)

JIM (*grinning*).   What was the matter?

TOM.   Oh—with Laura? Laura is—terribly shy.

JIM.   Shy, huh? It's unusual to meet a shy girl nowadays. I don't believe you ever mentioned you had a sister.

TOM.   Well, now you know. I have one. Here is the *Post Dispatch.* You want a piece of it?

JIM.   Uh-huh.

TOM.   What piece? The comics?

JIM.   Sports! (*Glances at it.*) Ole Dizzy Dean is on his bad behavior.

TOM (*uninterested*).   Yeah? (*Lights a cigarette and crosses back to fire-escape door.*)

JIM.   Where are *you* going?

TOM.   I'm going out on the terrace.

JIM (*goes after him*).   You know, Shakespeare—I'm going to sell you a bill of goods!

TOM.   What goods?

JIM.   A course I'm taking.

TOM.   Huh.

JIM.   In public speaking! You and me, we're not the warehouse type.

TOM.   Thanks—that's good news. But what has public speaking got to do with it?

JIM.   It fits you for—executive positions!

TOM.   Awww.

JIM.   I tell you it's done a helluva lot for me.

TOM.   In what respect?

JIM.   In every! Ask yourself what is the difference between you an' me and men in the office down front? Brains?—No!—Ability?—No! Then what? Just one little thing—

TOM.   What is that one little thing?

JIM.   Primarily it amounts to—social poise! Being able to square up to people and hold your own on any social level!

AMANDA (*from the kitchenette*).   Tom?

TOM.   Yes, Mother?

AMANDA.   Is that you and Mr. O'Connor?

TOM.   Yes, Mother.

AMANDA.   Well, you just make yourselves comfortable in there.

TOM.   Yes, Mother.

AMANDA.   Ask Mr. O'Connor if he would like to wash his hands.

JIM.   Aw, no—no—thank you—I took care of that at the warehouse. Tom—

TOM.   Yes?

JIM.   Mr. Mendoza was speaking to me about you.

TOM.   Favorably?

JIM.   What do you think?

TOM.   Well—

JIM.   You're going to be out of a job if you don't wake up.

TOM.   I am waking up—

JIM.   You show no signs.

TOM.   The signs are interior. I'm planning to change. (*He leans over the rail speaking with quiet exhilaration. The incandescent marquees and signs of the first-run movie houses light his face from across the alley. He looks like a voyager.*) I'm right at the point of committing myself to a future that doesn't include the warehouse and Mr. Mendoza or even a night-school course in public speaking.

JIM.   What are you gassing about?

TOM.   I'm tired of the movies.

JIM.   Movies!

TOM.   Yes, movies! Look at them— (*a wave toward the marvels of Grand Avenue*) all of those glamorous people—having adventures—hogging it all, gobbling the whole thing up! You know what happens? People go to the *movies* instead of *moving*! Hollywood characters are supposed to have all the adventures for everybody in America, while everybody in America sits in a dark room and watches them have them! Yes, until there's a war. That's when adventure becomes available to the masses! *Everyone's* dish, not only Gable's! Then the people in the dark room come out of the dark room to have some adventures themselves—Goody, goody!—It's our turn now, to go to the South Sea Island—to make a safari—to be exotic, far-off!—But I'm not patient. I don't want to wait till then. I'm tired of the *movies* and I am *about* to *move*!

JIM (*incredulously*).   Move?

TOM.   Yes.

JIM.   When?

TOM.   Soon!

JIM.   Where? Where? (*The music seems to answer the question, while* TOM *thinks it over. He searches in his pockets.*)

TOM.   I'm starting to boil inside. I know I seem dreamy, but inside —well, I'm boiling!—Whenever I pick up a shoe, I shudder a little thinking how short life is and what I am doing!—Whatever that means, I know it doesn't mean shoes—except as something to wear on a traveler's feet! (*Finds paper.*) Look—

JIM.   What?

TOM.   I'm a member.

JIM (*reading*).   The Union of Merchant Seamen.

TOM.   I paid my dues this month, instead of the light bill.

JIM.   You will regret it when they turn the lights off.

TOM.   I won't be here.

JIM.   How about your mother?

TOM.   I'm like my father. The bastard son of a bastard! See how he grins? And he's been absent going on sixteen years!

JIM.   You're just talking, you drip. How does your mother feel about it?

TOM.   Shh!—Here comes Mother! Mother is not acquainted with my plans!

AMANDA (*coming through the portieres*).   Where are you all?

TOM.   On the terrace, Mother. (*They start inside. She advances to them. TOM is distinctly shocked at her appearance. Even JIM blinks a little. He is making his first contact with girlish Southern vivacity and in spite of the night-school course in public speaking is somewhat thrown off the beam by the unexpected outlay of social charm. Certain responses are attempted by JIM but are swept aside by AMANDA's gay laughter and chatter. TOM is embarrassed but after the first shock JIM reacts very warmly. He grins and chuckles, is altogether won over.*)

AMANDA (*coyly smiling, shaking her girlish ringlets*).   Well, well, well, so this is Mr. O'Connor. Introductions entirely unnecessary. I've heard so much about you from my boy. I finally said to him, Tom— good gracious!—why don't you bring this paragon to supper? I'd like to meet this nice young man at the warehouse!—Instead of just hearing him sing your praises so much! I don't know why my son is so stand-offish—that's not Southern behavior! Let's sit down and—I think we could stand a little more air in here! Tom, leave the door open. I felt a nice fresh breeze a moment ago. Where has it gone? Mmm, so warm already! And not quite summer, even. We're going to burn up when summer really gets started. However, we're having—we're having a very light supper. I think light things are better fo' this time of year. The same as light clothes are. Light clothes an' light food are what warm weather calls fo'. You know our blood gets so thick during th' winter— it takes a while fo' us to *adjust* ou'selves!—when the season changes . . . It's come so quick this year. I wasn't prepared. All of a sudden— heavens! Already summer!—I ran to the trunk an' pulled out this light dress—Terribly old! Historical almost! But feels so good—so good an' co-ol, y' know . . .

TOM.   Mother—

AMANDA.   Yes, honey?

TOM.   How about—supper?

AMANDA.   Honey, you go ask Sister if supper is ready! You know that Sister is in full charge of supper! Tell her you hungry boys are waiting for it. (*To* JIM) Have you met Laura?

JIM.   She—

AMANDA.   Let you in? Oh, good, you've met already! It's rare for a girl as sweet an' pretty as Laura to be domestic! But Laura, is, thank heavens, not only pretty but very domestic. I'm not at all. I never was a bit. I never could make a thing but angel-food cake. Well, in the south we had so many servants. Gone, gone, gone. All vestige of gracious living! Gone completely! I wasn't prepared for what the future brought me. All of my gentlemen callers were sons of planters and so of course I assumed that I would be married to one and raise my family on a large piece of land with plenty of servants. But man proposes—and woman accepts the proposal!—to vary that old, old saying° a little bit—I married no planter! I married a man who worked for the telephone company!—That gallantly smiling gentleman over there! (*Points to the picture.*) A telephone man who—fell in love with long-distance!— Now he travels and I don't even know where!—But what am I going on for about my—tribulations? Tell me yours—I hope you don't have any! Tom?

TOM (*returning*).   Yes, Mother.

AMANDA.   Is supper nearly ready?

TOM.   It looks to me like supper is on the table.

AMANDA.   Let me look—(*She rises prettily and looks through portieres.*) Oh, lovely!—But where is Sister?

TOM.   Laura is not feeling well and she says that she thinks she'd better not come to the table.

AMANDA.   What?—Nonsense!—Laura? Oh, Laura!

LAURA (*off stage, faintly*).   Yes, Mother.

AMANDA.   You really must come to the table. We won't be seated until you come to the table! Come in, Mr. O'Connor. You sit over there, and I'll—Laura? Laura Wingfield! You're keeping us waiting, honey! We can't say grace until you come to the table! (*The kitchenette door is pushed weakly open and* LAURA *comes in. She is obviously quite faint, her lips trembling, her eyes wide and staring. She moves unsteadily toward the table. Outside a summer storm is coming abruptly. The white curtains billow inward at the windows and there is a sorrowful murmur and deep blue dusk.* LAURA *suddenly stumbles—she catches at a chair with a faint moan.*)

---

old . . . saying: "Man proposes, but God disposes" (Thomas à Kempis [1380–1471], *Imitation of Christ*)

TOM.   Laura!

AMANDA.   Laura! (*There is a clap of thunder. Despairingly*) Why, Laura, you *are* sick, darling! Tom, help your sister into the living room, dear! Sit in the living room, Laura—rest on the sofa. Well! (*To* JIM *as* TOM *helps his sister to the sofa in the living room*) Standing over the hot stove made her ill!—I told her that it was just too warm this evening, but— (TOM *comes back to the table.*) Is Laura all right now?

TOM.   Yes.

AMANDA.   What *is* that? Rain? A nice cool rain has come up! (*She gives the gentleman caller a frightened look.*) I think we may—have grace —now . . . (TOM *looks at her stupidly.*) Tom, honey—you say grace!

TOM.   Oh . . . "For these and all thy mercies—" (*They bow their heads,* AMANDA *stealing a nervous glance at* JIM. *In the living room,* LAURA, *stretched on the sofa, clenches her hand to her lips, to hold back a shuddering sob.*) God's Holy Name be praised— (*The scene dims out.*)

SCENE 7

Half an hour later. Dinner is just being finished in the dining room. LAURA *is still huddled upon the sofa, her feet drawn under her, her head resting on a pale blue pillow, her eyes wide and mysteriously watchful. The new floor lamp with its shade of rose-colored silk gives a soft, becoming light to her face, bringing out the fragile, unearthly prettiness which usually escapes attention. There is a steady murmur of rain, but it is slackening and soon stops; the air outside becomes pale and luminous as the moon breaks out. A moment after the curtain rises, the lights in both rooms flicker and go out.*

JIM.   Hey, there, Mr. Light Bulb!

AMANDA (*laughs nervously*).   Where was Moses when the lights went out? Ha-ha. Do you know the answer to that one, Mr. O'Connor?

JIM.   No, Ma'am, what's the answer?

AMANDA.   In the dark! (JIM *laughs appreciatively.*) Everybody sit still. I'll light the candles. Isn't it lucky we have them on the table? Where's a match? Which of you gentlemen can provide a match?

JIM.   Here.

AMANDA.   Thank you, sir.

JIM.   Not at all, Ma'am!

AMANDA.   I guess the fuse has burnt out. Mr. O'Connor, can you tell a burnt-out fuse? I know I can't and Tom is a total loss when it comes to mechanics. (*They rise from the table and go into the kitchenette, from where their voices are heard.*) Oh, be careful you don't bump into something. We don't want our gentleman caller to break his neck. Now wouldn't that be a fine howdy-do?

JIM.   Ha-ha! Where is the fuse box?

AMANDA.   Right here next to the stove. Can you see anything?

JIM.   Just a minute.

AMANDA.   Isn't electricity a mysterious thing? Wasn't it Benjamin Franklin who tied a key to a kite? We live in such a mysterious universe, don't we? Some people say that science clears up all the mysteries for us. In my opinion it only creates more! Have you found it yet?

JIM.   No, Ma'am. All these fuses look okay to me.

AMANDA.   Tom!

TOM.   Yes, Mother?

AMANDA.   That light bill I gave you several days ago. The one I told you we got the notices about?

TOM.   Oh—Yeah.

AMANDA.   You didn't neglect to pay it by chance?

TOM.   Why, I—

AMANDA.   Didn't! I might have known it!

JIM.   Shakespeare probably wrote a poem on that light bill, Mrs. Wingfield.

AMANDA.   I might have known better than to trust him with it! There's such a high price for negligence in this world!

JIM.   Maybe the poem will win a ten-dollar prize.

AMANDA.   We'll just have to spend the remainder of the evening in the nineteenth century, before Mr. Edison made the Mazda lamp!

JIM.   Candlelight is my favorite kind of light.

AMANDA.   That shows you're romantic! But that's no excuse for Tom. Well, we got through dinner. Very considerate of them to let us get through dinner before they plunged us into everlasting darkness, wasn't it, Mr. O'Connor?

JIM.   Ha-ha!

AMANDA.   Tom, as a penalty for your carelessness you can help me with the dishes.

JIM.   Let me give you a hand.

AMANDA.   Indeed you will not!

JIM.   I ought to be good for something.

AMANDA.   Good for something? (*Her tone is rhapsodic.*) You? Why, Mr. O'Connor nobody, *nobody's* given me this much entertainment in years—as you have!

JIM.   Aw, now, Mrs. Wingfield!

AMANDA.   I'm not exaggerating, not one bit! But Sister is all by her lonesome. You go keep her company in the parlor! I'll give you this lovely old candelabrum that used to be on the altar at the church of the Heavenly Rest. It was melted a little out of shape when the church burnt down. Lightning struck it one spring. Gypsy Jones was holding a revival at the time and he intimated that the church was destroyed because the Episcopalians gave card parties.

JIM.   Ha-ha.

AMANDA.   And how about you coaxing Sister to drink a little wine? I think it would be good for her! Can you carry both at once?

JIM.   Sure. I'm Superman!

AMANDA.   Now, Thomas, get into this apron! (JIM *comes into the dining room, carrying the candelabrum, its candles lighted, in one hand and a glass of wine in the other. The door of the kitchenette swings closed on* AMANDA's *gay laughter; the flickering light approaches the portieres.* LAURA *sits up nervously as he enters. Her speech at first is low and breathless from the almost intolerable strain of being alone with a stranger. At first, before* JIM's *warmth overcomes her paralyzing shyness,* LAURA's *voice is thin and breathless, as though she had just run up a steep flight of stairs.* JIM's *attitude is gently humorous. While the incident is apparently unimportant, it is to* LAURA *the climax of her secret life.*)

JIM.   Hello, there, Laura.

LAURA (*faintly*).   Hello. (*She clears her throat.*)

JIM.   How are you feeling now? Better?

LAURA.   Yes. Yes, thank you.

JIM.   This is for you. A little dandelion wine. (*He extends it toward her with extravagant gallantry.*)

LAURA.   Thank you.

JIM.   Drink it—but don't get drunk! (*He laughs heartily.* LAURA *takes the glass uncertainly, laughs shyly.*) Where shall I set the candles?

LAURA.   Oh—oh, anywhere . . .

JIM.   How about here on the floor? Any objections?

LAURA.   No.

JIM.   I'll spread a newspaper to catch the drippings. I like to sit on the floor. Mind if I do?

LAURA.   Oh, no.

JIM.   Give me a pillow?

LAURA.   What?

JIM.   A pillow!

LAURA.   Oh . . . (*Hands him one quickly.*)

JIM.   How about you? Don't you like to sit on the floor?

LAURA.   Oh—yes.

JIM.   Why don't you, then?

LAURA.   I—will.

JIM.   Take a pillow! (LAURA *does. Sits on the other side of the candelabrum.* JIM *crosses his legs and smiles engagingly at her.*) I can't hardly see you sitting way over there.

LAURA.   I can—see you.

JIM.   I know, but that's not fair. I'm in the limelight. (LAURA *moves her pillow closer.*) Good! Now I can see you! Comfortable?

LAURA.   Yes.

JIM.   So am I. Comfortable as a cow! Will you have some gum?

LAURA.   No, thank you.

JIM.   I think I will indulge, with your permission. (*He musingly unwraps it and holds it up.*) Think of the fortune made by the guy that invented the first piece of chewing gum. Amazing, huh? The Wrigley Building is one of the sights of Chicago.—I saw it summer before last when I went up to the Century of Progress.° Did you take in the Century of Progress?

LAURA.   No, I didn't.

JIM.   Well, it was quite a wonderful exposition. What impressed me most was the Hall of Science. Gives you an idea of what the future will be in America, even more wonderful than the present time is! (*There is a pause.* JIM *smiles at her.*) Your brother tells me you're shy. Is that right, Laura?

LAURA.   I—don't know.

JIM.   I judge you to be an old-fashioned type of girl. Well, I think that's a pretty good type to be. Hope you don't think I'm being too personal—do you?

LAURA (*hastily, out of embarrassment*).   I believe I *will* take a piece of gum, if you—don't mind. (*Clearing her throat.*) Mr. O'Connor, have you—kept up with your singing?

JIM.   Singing? Me?

LAURA.   Yes. I remember what a beautiful voice you had.

JIM.   When did you hear me sing?

(*Voice off stage in the pause:*

> O blow, ye winds, heigh-ho,
> A-roving I will go!
> I'm off to my love
> With a boxing glove—
> Ten thousand miles away!)

JIM.   You say you've heard me sing?

Century of Progress: World's Fair in Chicago, 1933–1934

LAURA.   Oh, yes! Yes, very often . . . I—don't suppose—you remember me—at all?

JIM (*smiling doubtfully*).   You know I have an idea I've seen you before. I had that idea soon as you opened the door. It seems almost like I was about to remember your name. But the name that I started to call you—wasn't a name! And so I stopped myself before I said it.

LAURA.   Wasn't it—Blue Roses?

JIM (*springs up. Grinning*).   Blue Roses!—My gosh, yes—Blue Roses! That's what I had on my tongue when you opened the door! Isn't it funny what tricks your memory plays? I didn't connect you with high school somehow or other. But that's where it was; it was high school. I didn't even know you were Shakespeare's sister! Gosh, I'm sorry.

LAURA.   I didn't expect you to. You—barely knew me!

JIM.   But we did have a speaking acquaintance, huh?

LAURA.   Yes, we—spoke to each other.

JIM.   When did you recognize me?

LAURA.   Oh, right away!

JIM.   Soon as I came in the door?

LAURA.   When I heard your name I thought it was probably you. I knew that Tom used to know you a little in high school. So when you came in the door—well, then I was—sure.

JIM.   Why didn't you *say* something, then?

LAURA (*breathlessly*).   I didn't know what to say, I was—too surprised!

JIM.   For goodness sakes! You know, this sure is funny!

LAURA.   Yes! Yes, isn't it, though . . .

JIM.   Didn't we have a class in something together?

LAURA.   Yes, we did.

JIM.   What class was that?

LAURA.   It was—singing—chorus!

JIM.   Aw!

LAURA.   I sat across the aisle from you in the Aud.

JIM.   Aw.

LAURA.   Mondays, Wednesdays and Fridays.

JIM.   Now I remember—you always came in late.

LAURA.   Yes, it was so hard for me getting upstairs. I had that brace on my leg—it clumped so loud!

JIM.   I never heard any clumping.

LAURA (*wincing at the recollection*).   To me it sounded like—thunder!

JIM.   Well, well, well, I never even noticed.

LAURA.   And everybody was seated before I came in. I had to walk in front of all those people. My seat was in the back row. I had to go clumping all the way up the aisle with everyone watching!

JIM.   You shouldn't have been self-conscious.

LAURA.   I know, but I was. It was always such a relief when the singing started.

JIM.   Aw, yes, I've placed you now! I used to call you Blue Roses. How was it that I got started calling you that?

LAURA.   I was out of school a little while with pleurosis. When I came back you asked me what was the matter. I said I had pleurosis — you thought I said Blue Roses. That's what you always called me after that!

JIM.   I hope you didn't mind.

LAURA.   Oh, no—I liked it. You see, I wasn't acquainted with many—people . . .

JIM.   As I remember you sort of stuck by yourself.

LAURA.   I—I—never have had much luck at—making friends.

JIM.   I don't see why you wouldn't.

LAURA.   Well, I—started out badly.

JIM.   You mean being—

LAURA.   Yes, it sort of—stood between me—

JIM.   You shouldn't have let it!

LAURA.   I know, but it did, and—

JIM.   You were shy with people!

LAURA.   I tried not to be but never could—

JIM.   Overcome it?

LAURA.   No, I—I never could!

JIM.   I guess being shy is something you have to work out of kind of gradually.

LAURA (*sorrowfully*).   Yes—I guess it—

JIM.   Takes time!

LAURA.   Yes—

JIM.   People are not so dreadful when you know them. That's what you have to remember! And everybody has problems, not just you, but practically everybody has got some problems. You think of yourself as having the only problems, as being the only one who is disappointed. But just look around you and you will see lots of people as disappointed as you are. For instance, I hoped when I was going to high school that I would be further along at this time, six years later, than I am now—You remember that wonderful write-up I had in *The Torch?*

LAURA.   Yes! (*She rises and crosses to table.*)

JIM.   It said I was bound to succeed in anything I went into! (LAURA *returns with the annual.*) Holy Jeez! *The Torch!* (*He accepts it reverently. They smile across it with mutual wonder.* LAURA *crouches beside him and they begin to turn through it.* LAURA's *shyness is dissolving in his warmth.*)

LAURA.   Here you are in *The Pirates of Penzance!*

JIM (*wistfully*).   I sang the baritone lead in that operetta.

LAURA (*raptly*).   So—beautifully!

JIM (*protesting*).   Aw—

LAURA.   Yes, yes—beautifully—beautifully!

JIM.   You heard me?

LAURA.   All three times!

JIM.   No!

LAURA.   Yes!

JIM.   All three performances?

LAURA (*looking down*).   Yes.

JIM.   Why?

LAURA.   I—wanted to ask you to—autograph my program.

JIM.   Why didn't you ask me to?

LAURA.   You were always surrounded by your own friends so much that I never had a chance to.

JIM.   You should have just—

LAURA.   Well, I—thought you might think I was—

JIM.   Thought I might think you was—what?

LAURA.   Oh—

JIM (*with reflective relish*).   I was beleaguered by females in those days.

LAURA.   You were terribly popular!

JIM.   Yeah—

LAURA.   You had such a—friendly way—

JIM.   I was spoiled in high school.

LAURA.   Everybody—liked you!

JIM.   Including you?

LAURA.   I—yes, I—I did, too— (*She gently closes the book in her lap.*)

JIM.   Well, well, well!—Give me that program, Laura. (*She hands it to him. He signs it with a flourish.*) There you are—better late than never!

LAURA.   Oh, I—what a—surprise!

JIM.   My signature isn't worth very much right now. But some day —maybe—it will increase in value! Being disappointed is one thing and being discouraged is something else. I am disappointed but I am not discouraged. I'm twenty-three years old. How old are you?

LAURA.   I'll be twenty-four in June.

JIM.   That's not old age!

LAURA.   No, but—

JIM.   You finished high school?

LAURA (*with difficulty*).   I didn't go back.

JIM.   You mean you dropped out?

LAURA.   I made bad grades in my final examinations. (*She rises and replaces the book and the program. Her voice is strained.*) How is—Emily Meisenbach getting along?

JIM.   Oh, that kraut-head!

LAURA.   Why do you call her that?

JIM.   That's what she was.

LAURA.   You're not still—going with her?

JIM.   I never see her.

LAURA.   It said in the Personal Section that you were—engaged!

JIM.   I know, but I wasn't impressed by that—propaganda!

LAURA.   It wasn't—the truth?

JIM.   Only in Emily's optimistic opinion!

LAURA.   Oh— (JIM *lights a cigarette and leans indolently back on his elbows smiling at* LAURA *with a warmth and charm which lights her inwardly with altar candles. She remains by the table and turns in her hands a piece of glass to cover her tumult.*)

JIM (*after several reflective puffs on a cigarette*).   What have you done since high school? (*She seems not to hear him.*) Huh? (LAURA *looks up.*) I said what have you done since high school, Laura?

LAURA.   Nothing much.

JIM.   You must have been doing something these six long years.

LAURA.   Yes.

JIM.   Well, then, such as what?

LAURA.   I took a business course at business college—

JIM.   How did that work out?

LAURA.   Well, not very—well—I had to drop out, it gave me—indigestion—

JIM (*laughs gently*).   What are you doing now?

LAURA.   I don't do anything—much. Oh, please don't think I sit around doing nothing! My glass collection takes up a good deal of time. Glass is something you have to take good care of.

JIM.   What did you say—about glass?

LAURA.   Collection I said—I have one— (*She clears her throat and turns away again, acutely shy.*)

JIM (*abruptly*).   You know what I judge to be the trouble with you? Inferiority complex! Know what that is? That's what they call it when someone low-rates himself! I understand it because I had it, too.

Although my case was not so aggravated as yours seems to be. I had it until I took up public speaking, developed my voice, and learned that I had an aptitude for science. Before that time I never thought of myself as being outstanding in any way whatsoever! Now I've never made a regular study of it, but I have a friend who says I can analyze people better than doctors that make a profession of it. I don't claim that to be necessarily true, but I can sure guess a person's psychology, Laura! (*Takes out his gum.*) Excuse me, Laura. I always take it out when the flavor is gone. I'll use this scrap of paper to wrap it in. I know how it is to get it stuck on a shoe. Yep—that's what I judge to be your principal trouble. A lack of confidence in yourself as a person. You don't have the proper amount of faith in yourself. I'm basing that fact on a number of your remarks and also on certain observations I've made. For instance that clumping you thought was so awful in high school. You say that you even dreaded to walk into class. You see what you did? You dropped out of school, you gave up an education because of a clump, which as far as I know was practically non-existent! A little physical defect is what you have. Hardly noticeable even! Magnified thousands of times by imagination! You know what my strong advice to you is? Think of yourself as *superior* in some way!

LAURA.   In what way would I think?

JIM.   Why, man alive, Laura! Just look about you a little. What do you see? A world full of common people! All of 'em born and all of 'em going to die! Which of them has one-tenth of your good points! Or mine! Or anyone else's, as far as that goes—Gosh! Everybody excels in some one thing. Some in many! (*Unconsciously glances at himself in the mirror.*) All you've got to do is discover in *what!* Take me, for instance. (*He adjusts his tie at the mirror.*) My interest happens to lie in electrodynamics. I'm taking a course in radio engineering at night school, Laura, on top of a fairly responsible job at the warehouse. I'm taking that course and studying public speaking.

LAURA.   Ohhhh.

JIM.   Because I believe in the future of television! (*Turning back to her.*) I wish to be ready to go up right along with it. Therefore I'm planning to get in on the ground floor. In fact I've already made the right connections and all that remains is for the industry itself to get under way! Full steam— (*His eyes are starry.*) Knowledge—Zzzzzp! Money —Zzzzzp!—Power! That's the cycle democracy is built on! (*His attitude is convincingly dynamic.* LAURA *stares at him, even her shyness eclipsed in her absolute wonder. He suddenly grins.*) I guess you think I think a lot of myself?

LAURA.   No—o-o-o, I—

JIM. Now how about you? Isn't there something you take more interest in than anything else?

LAURA.   Well, I do—as I said—have my—glass collection— (*A peal of girlish laughter from the kitchenette.*)

JIM.   I'm not right sure I know what you're talking about. What kind of glass is it?

LAURA.   Little articles of it, they're ornaments mostly! Most of them are little animals made out of glass, the tiniest little animals in the world. Mother calls them a glass menagerie! Here's an example of one, if you'd like to see it! This one is one of the oldest. It's nearly thirteen. (*Music: "The Glass Menagerie."* JIM *stretches out his hand.*) Oh, be careful —if you breathe, it breaks!

JIM.   I'd better not take it. I'm pretty clumsy with things.

LAURA.   Go on, I trust you with him! (*Places it in his palm.*) There now—you're holding him gently! Hold him over the light, he loves the light! You see how the light shines through him?

JIM.   It sure does shine!

LAURA.   I shouldn't be partial, but he is my favorite one.

JIM.   What kind of thing is this one supposed to be?

LAURA.   Haven't you noticed the single horn on his forehead?

JIM.   A unicorn, huh?

LAURA.   Mmm-hmmm!

JIM.   Unicorns, aren't they extinct in the modern world?

LAURA.   I know!

JIM.   Poor little fellow, he must feel sort of lonesome.

LAURA (*smiling*).   Well, if he does he doesn't complain about it. He stays on a shelf with some horses that don't have horns and all of them seem to get along nicely together.

JIM.   How do you know?

LAURA (*lightly*).   I haven't heard any arguments among them!

JIM (*grinning*).   No arguments, huh? Well, that's a pretty good sign! Where shall I set him?

LAURA.   Put him on the table. They all like a change of scenery once in a while!

JIM (*stretching*).   Well, well, well, well—Look how big my shadow is when I stretch!

LAURA.   Oh, oh, yes—it stretches across the ceiling!

JIM (*crossing to door*).   I think it's stopped raining. (*Opens fire-escape door.*) Where does the music come from?

LAURA.   From the Paradise Dance Hall across the alley.

JIM.   How about cutting the rug a little, Miss Wingfield?

LAURA.   Oh, I—

JIM.   Or is your program filled up? Let me have a look at it. (*Grasps imaginary card.*) Why, every dance is taken! I'll just have to scratch some out. (*Waltz music: "La Golondrina."*) Ahhh, a waltz! (*He executes some sweeping turns by himself then holds his arms toward* LAURA.)

LAURA (*breathlessly*).   I—can't dance!

JIM.   There you go, that inferiority stuff!

LAURA.   I've never danced in my life!

JIM.   Come on, try!

LAURA.   Oh, but I'd step on you!

JIM.   I'm not made out of glass.

LAURA.   How—how—how do we start?

JIM.   Just leave it to me. You hold your arms out a little.

LAURA.   Like this?

JIM.   A bit higher. Right. Now don't tighten up, that's the main thing about it—relax.

LAURA (*laughing breathlessly*).   It's hard not to.

JIM.   Okay.

LAURA.   I'm afraid you can't budge me.

JIM.   What do you bet I can't? (*He swings her into motion.*)

LAURA.   Goodness, yes, you can!

JIM.   Let yourself go, now, Laura, just let yourself go.

LAURA.   I'm—

JIM.   Come on!

LAURA.   Trying!

JIM.   Not so stiff—Easy does it!

LAURA.   I know but I'm—

JIM.   Loosen th' backbone! There now, that's a lot better.

LAURA.   Am I?

JIM.   Lots, lots better! (*He moves her about the room in a clumsy waltz.*)

LAURA.   Oh, my!

JIM.   Ha-ha!

LAURA.   Oh, my goodness!

JIM.   Ha-ha-ha! (*They suddenly bump into the table.* JIM *stops.*) What did we hit on?

LAURA.   Table.

JIM.   Did something fall off it? I think—

LAURA.   Yes.

JIM.   I hope it wasn't the little glass horse with the horn!

LAURA.   Yes.

JIM.   Aw, aw, aw. Is it broken?

LAURA.   Now it is just like all the other horses.

JIM.   It's lost its—

LAURA.   Horn! It doesn't matter. Maybe it's a blessing in disguise.

JIM.   You'll never forgive me. I bet that was your favorite piece of glass.

LAURA.   I don't have favorites much. It's no tragedy, Freckles. Glass breaks so easily. No matter how careful you are. The traffic jars the shelves and things fall off them.

JIM.   Still I'm awfully sorry that I was the cause.

LAURA (*smiling*).   I'll just imagine he had an operation. The horn was removed to make him feel less—freakish! (*They both laugh.*) Now he will feel more at home with the other horses, the ones that don't have horns . . .

JIM.   Ha-ha, that's very funny! (*Suddenly serious.*) I'm glad to see that you have a sense of humor. You know—you're—well—very different! Surprisingly different from anyone else I know! (*His voice becomes soft and hesitant with a genuine feeling.*) Do you mind me telling you that? (LAURA *is abashed beyond speech.*) I mean it in a nice way . . . (LAURA *nods shyly, looking away.*) You make me feel sort of—I don't know how to put it! I'm usually pretty good at expressing things, but— this is something that I don't know how to say! (LAURA *touches her throat and clears it—turns the broken unicorn in her hands. His voice becomes softer.*) Has anyone ever told you that you were pretty? (*Pause: music.* LAURA *looks up slowly, with wonder, and shakes her head.*)

Well, you are! In a very different way from anyone else. And all the nicer because of the difference, too. (*His voice becomes low and husky.* LAURA *turns away, nearly faint with the novelty of her emotions.*) I wish that you were my sister. I'd teach you to have some confidence in yourself. The different people are not like other people, but being different is nothing to be ashamed of. Because other people are not such wonderful people. They're one hundred times one thousand. You're one times one! They walk all over the earth. You just stay here. They're common as—weeds, but—you—well, you're—*Blue Roses!* (*Music changes.*)

LAURA.   But blue is wrong for—roses . . .

JIM.   It's right for you!—You're—pretty!

LAURA.   In what respect am I pretty?

JIM.   In all respects—believe me! Your eyes—your hair—are pretty! Your hands are pretty! (*He catches hold of her hand.*) You think I'm making this up because I'm invited to dinner and have to be nice. Oh, I could do that! I could put on an act for you, Laura, and say lots of things without being very sincere. But this time I am. I'm talking to you sincerely. I happened to notice you had this inferiority complex that keeps you from feeling comfortable with people. Somebody needs to build your confidence up and make you proud instead of shy and turning away and—blushing—Somebody—ought to—ought to—*kiss* you, Laura! (*His hand slips slowly up her arm to her shoulder. Music swells tumultuously. He suddenly turns her about and kisses her on the lips. When he releases her,* LAURA *sinks on the sofa with a bright, dazed look.* JIM *backs away and fishes in his pocket for a cigarette.*) Stumble-john! (*He lights a cigarette, avoiding her look. There is a peal of girlish laughter from* AMANDA *in the kitchenette.* LAURA *slowly raises and opens her hand. It still contains the little broken glass animal. She looks at it with a tender, bewildered expression.*)

Stumble-john! I shouldn't have done that—That was way off beam. You don't smoke, do you? (*She looks up, smiling, not hearing the question. He sits beside her a little gingerly. She looks at him speechlessly— waiting. He coughs decorously and moves a little farther aside as he considers the situation and senses her feelings, dimly, with perturbation. He speaks gently.*) Would you—care for a—mint? (*She doesn't seem to hear him but her look grows brighter even.*) Peppermint—Life-Saver? My pocket's a regular drug store—wherever I go . . . (*He pops a mint in his mouth. Then gulps and decides to make a clean breast of it. He speaks slowly and gingerly.*) Laura, you know, if I had a sister like you, I'd do the same thing as Tom. I'd bring out fellows and—introduce her to them. The right type of boys of a type to—appreciate her. Only—well—he made a mistake with me. Maybe I've got no call to be saying this. That may not have been the idea in having me over. But what if it was? There's nothing wrong about that. The only trouble is that in my case—I'm not in a situation to—do the right thing. I can't take down your number and say I'll phone. I can't call up next week and—ask for a date. I thought I had better explain the situation in case you—misunderstood it and—hurt your feelings . . . (*Pause. Slowly, very slowly,* LAURA's *look changes, her eyes returning slowly from his to the ornament in her palm.* AMANDA *utters another gay laugh in the kitchenette.*)

LAURA (*faintly*).   You—won't—call again?

JIM.   No, Laura, I can't. (*He rises from the sofa.*) As I was just explaining. I've—got strings on me. Laura, I've—been going steady! I go out all of the time with a girl named Betty. She's a home-girl like you, and Catholic, and Irish, and in a great many ways we—get along fine. I met her last summer on a moonlight boat trip up the river to Alton, on the *Majestic*. Well—right away from the start it was—love! (LAURA *sways slightly forward and grips the arm of the sofa. He fails to notice, now enrapt in his own comfortable being.*) Being in love has made a new man of me! (*Leaning stiffly forward, clutching the arm of the sofa,*

Laura *struggles visibly with her storm. But* Jim *is oblivious; she is a long way off.*) The power of love is really pretty tremendous! Love is something that—changes the whole world, Laura! (*The storm abates a little and* Laura *leans back. He notices her again.*) It happened that Betty's aunt took sick, she got a wire and had to go to Centralia. So Tom—when he asked me to dinner—I naturally just accepted the invitation, not knowing that you—that he—that I— (*He stops awkwardly.*) Huh —I'm a stumble-john! (*He flops back on the sofa. The holy candles in the altar of* Laura's *face have been snuffed out. There is a look of almost infinite desolation.* Jim *glances at her uneasily.*) I wish that you would—say something. (*She bites her lip which was trembling and then bravely smiles. She opens her hand again on the broken glass ornament. Then she gently takes his hand and raises it level with her own. She carefully places the unicorn in the palm of his hand, then pushes his fingers closed upon it.*) What are you—doing that for? You want me to have him—Laura? (*She nods.*) What for?

Laura.   A—souvenir . . . (*She rises unsteadily and crouches beside the victrola to wind it up. At this moment* Amanda *rushes brightly back into the living room. She bears a pitcher of fruit punch in an old-fashioned cut-glass pitcher and a plate of macaroons. The plate has a gold border and poppies painted on it.*)

Amanda.   Well, well, well! Isn't the air delightful after the shower? I've made you children a little liquid refreshment. (*She turns gaily to* Jim.) Jim, do you know that song about lemonade?

"Lemonade, lemonade,
Made in the shade and stirred with a spade—
Good enough for any old maid!"

Jim (*uneasily*).   Ha-ha! No—I never heard it.

Amanda.   Why, Laura! You look so serious!

Jim.   We were having a serious conversation.

Amanda.   Good! Now you're better acquainted!

Jim (*uncertainly*).   Ha-ha! Yes.

Amanda.   You modern young people are much more serious-minded than my generation. I was so gay as a girl!

Jim.   You haven't changed, Mrs. Wingfield.

Amanda.   Tonight I'm rejuvenated! The gaiety of the occasion, Mr. O'Connor! (*She tosses her head with a peal of laughter. Spills lemonade.*) Oooo! I'm baptizing myself!

Jim.   Here—let me—

Amanda (*setting the pitcher down*).   There now. I discovered we had some maraschino cherries. I dumped them in, juice and all!

Jim.   You shouldn't have gone to that trouble, Mrs. Wingfield.

AMANDA.   Trouble, trouble? Why, it was loads of fun! Didn't you hear me cutting up in the kitchen? I bet your ears were burning! I told Tom how outdone with him I was for keeping you to himself so long a time! He should have brought you over much, much sooner! Well, now that you've found your way, I want you to be a frequent caller! Not just occasional but all the time. Oh, we're going to have a lot of gay times together! I see them coming! Mmm, just breathe that air! So fresh, and the moon's so pretty! I'll skip back out—I know where my place is when young folks are having a—serious conversation!

JIM.   Oh, don't go out, Mrs. Wingfield. The fact of the matter is I've got to be going.

AMANDA.   Going, now? You're joking! Why, it's only the shank of the evening, Mr. O'Connor!

JIM.   Well, you know how it is.

AMANDA.   You mean you're a young workingman and have to keep workingmen's hours. We'll let you off early tonight. But only on the condition that next time you stay later.

What's the best night for you? Isn't Saturday night the best night for you workingmen?

JIM.   I have a couple of time-clocks to punch, Mrs. Wingfield. One at morning, another at night!

AMANDA.   My, but you *are* ambitious! You work at night, too?

JIM.   No, Ma'am, not work but—Betty! (*He crosses deliberately to pick up his hat. The band at the Paradise Dance Hall goes into a tender waltz.*)

AMANDA.   Betty? Betty? Who's—Betty! (*There is an ominous cracking sound in the sky.*)

JIM.   Oh, just a girl. The girl I go steady with! (*He smiles charmingly. The sky falls.*)

AMANDA (*a long-drawn exhalation*).   Ohhhh. . . . Is it a serious romance, Mr. O'Connor?

JIM.   We're going to be married the second Sunday in June.

AMANDA.   Ohhhh—how nice! Tom didn't mention that you were engaged to be married.

JIM.   The cat's not out of the bag at the warehouse yet. You know how they are. They call you Romeo and stuff like that. (*He stops at the oval mirror to put on his hat. He carefully shapes the brim and the crown to give a discreetly dashing effect.*) It's been a wonderful evening, Mrs. Wingfield. I guess this is what they mean by Southern hospitality.

AMANDA.   It really wasn't anything at all.

JIM.   I hope it don't seem like I'm rushing off. But I promised Betty I'd pick her up at the Wabash depot, an' by the time I get my jalopy down there her train'll be in. Some women are pretty upset if you keep 'em waiting.

AMANDA.   Yes, I know—The tyranny of women! (*Extends her hand.*) Good-bye, Mr. O'Connor. I wish you luck—and happiness—and success! All three of them, and so does Laura—Don't you Laura?

LAURA.   Yes!

JIM (*taking her hand*).   Good-bye Laura. I'm certainly going to treasure that souvenir. And don't you forget the good advice I gave you. (*Raises his voice to a cheery shout.*) So long, Shakespeare! Thanks again, ladies—Good night! (*He grins and ducks jauntily out. Still bravely grimacing,* AMANDA *closes the door on the gentleman caller. Then she turns back to the room with a puzzled expression. She and* LAURA *don't dare to face each other.* LAURA *crouches beside the victrola to wind it.*)

AMANDA (*faintly*).   Things have a way of turning out so badly. I don't believe that I would play the victrola. Well, well—well—Our gentleman caller was engaged to be married! (*She raises her voice.*) Tom!

TOM (*from the kitchenette*).   Yes, Mother?

AMANDA.   Come in here a minute. I want to tell you something awfully funny.

TOM (*enters with a macaroon and a glass of lemonade*).   Has the gentleman caller gotten away already?

AMANDA.   The gentleman caller has made an early departure. What a wonderful joke you played on us!

TOM.   How do you mean?

AMANDA.   You didn't mention that he was engaged to be married.

TOM.   Jim? Engaged?

AMANDA.   That's what he just informed us.

TOM.   I'll be jiggered! I didn't know about that.

AMANDA.   That seems very peculiar.

TOM.   What's peculiar about it?

AMANDA.   Didn't you call him your best friend down at the warehouse?

TOM.   He is, but how did I know?

AMANDA.   It seems extremely peculiar that you wouldn't know your best friend was going to be married!

TOM.   The warehouse is where I work, not where I know things about people!

AMANDA.   You don't know things anywhere! You live in a dream; you manufacture illusions! (*He crosses to the door.*) Where are you going?

TOM.   I'm going to the movies.

AMANDA.   That's right, now that you've had us make such fools of ourselves. The effort, the preparations, all the expense! The new floor lamp, the rug, the clothes for Laura! All for what? To entertain some other girl's fiancé! Go to the movies, go! Don't think about us, a mother deserted, an unmarried sister who's crippled and has no job! Don't let anything interfere with your selfish pleasure! Just go, go, go—to the movies!

TOM.   All right, I will! The more you shout about my selfishness to me the quicker I'll go, and I won't go to the movies!

AMANDA.   Go, then! Then go to the moon—you selfish dreamer!

(TOM *smashes his glass on the floor. He plunges out of the fire-escape, slamming the door.* LAURA *screams in fright. The dance-hall music becomes louder.* TOM *goes to the rail and grips it desperately, lifting his face in the chill white moonlight penetrating the narrow abyss of the alley.*

(TOM's *closing speech is timed with what is happening inside the house. The interior scene is played as though viewed through soundproof glass.* AMANDA *appears to be making a comforting speech to* LAURA *who is huddled upon the sofa. Now that we cannot hear the mother's speech, her silliness is gone and she has dignity and tragic beauty.* LAURA's *dark hair hides her face until at the end of the speech she lifts it to smile at her mother.* AMANDA's *gestures are slow and graceful, almost dance-like, as she comforts her daughter. At the end of her speech she glances a moment at the father's picture—then withdraws through the portieres. At the close of* TOM's *speech,* LAURA *blows out the candles, ending the play.*)

TOM.   I didn't go to the moon, I went much further—for time is the longest distance between two places—Not long after that I was fired for writing a poem on the lid of a shoe-box. I left Saint Louis. I descended the steps of this fire-escape for a last time and followed, from then on, in my father's footsteps, attempting to find in motion what was lost in space—I traveled around a great deal. The cities swept about me like dead leaves, leaves that were brightly colored but torn away from the branches. I would have stopped, but I was pursued by something. It always came upon me unawares, taking me altogether by surprise. Perhaps it was a familiar bit of music. Perhaps it was only a piece of transparent glass—Perhaps I am walking along a street at night, in some strange city, before I have found companions. I pass the lighted window of a shop where perfume is sold. The window is filled with pieces of colored glass, tiny transparent bottles in delicate colors, like bits of a shattered rainbow. Then all at once my sister touches my shoulder. I turn around and look into her eyes . . . Oh, Laura, Laura, I tried to leave you behind me, but I am more faithful than I intended to be! I reach for a cigarette, I cross the street, I run into the movies or a bar, I buy a drink, I speak to the nearest stranger—anything that can blow your candles out! (LAURA *bends over the candles.*) For nowadays the world is lit by lightning! Blow out your candles, Laura—and so goodbye . . .

(*She blows the candles out.*)

QUESTIONS

1. In presenting Scene 1, the author says: "The scene is memory and is therefore nonrealistic." To whose memory does he refer? Why should memory be nonrealistic? List the different ways in which the play is nonrealistic. What, according to Tom in his opening speech, is the ultimate aim of this nonrealistic method of presentation?

2. How does the kind of language Tom uses as a narrator differ from that he uses as a character? What would happen to the play if Tom used the first kind of language throughout?

3. What is Tom's dilemma? Why is he always quarreling with his mother? What is his attitude toward Laura? Why does he finally leave? Does he ever resolve his dilemma?

4. What qualities possessed by Tom, and by him alone, make him the proper narrator of the play?

5. Laura is the pivotal character in the play, as evidenced by its title and by the fact that the main actions of the play revolve around her. What are the symptoms and causes of her mental condition? Can they all be traced to her physical defect? What qualities make her a sympathetic character? How does her relationship with her mother differ from Tom's?

6. What symbolic meanings has Laura's glass menagerie? What, especially, is symbolized by the unicorn? How and why does her reaction to Jim's breaking the unicorn differ from her reaction to Tom's breaking several pieces at the end of Scene 3? Why does she give the broken unicorn to Jim as a souvenir? What future do you predict for her? What symbolism has her blowing out the candles at the end of the play?

7. The author tells us (page 1153) that "Amanda, having failed to establish contact with reality, continues to live vitally in her illusions." What part of this statement could be applied to Laura as well? What part could not? What are the chief instances in the play of Amanda's having lost "contact with reality"? What are her chief illusions? What are her strengths? How is she both cruel and tender with her children? What qualities has she in common with Jim, the gentleman caller? Why do you suppose her husband left her?

8. The author describes Jim O'Connor as "a nice, ordinary, young man" (page 1153). Tom (in Scene 1) describes him as "the most realistic character, being an emissary from that world of reality that we were set apart from." In what ways is Jim "nice"? In what ways is he "ordinary"? In what ways and in what sense is he more "realistic" than the Wingfields? Does this mean that he is without delusions? What would you predict for his future? Of what is he symbolic?

9. Account for Jim's treatment of Laura in Scene 7.

10. What trait do Laura, Amanda, and Tom all share, which makes Jim more realistic than they? Explain the dramatic irony in Amanda's remark to Tom, in their final dialogue, "You don't know things anywhere! You live in a dream; you manufacture illusions!"

11. What respective claims have Tom, Laura, and Amanda for being considered the protagonist of the play? For which character would it be most
crucial to the success or failure of a production to obtain a highly accomplished actor or actress? Why?

12. The play is set in the 1930s. Of what significance are the many references
throughout the play to its social and historical background? How are these
larger events and the Wingfields' domestic lives related?

13. The play is divided into seven scenes. If you were to produce it with one
intermission, where would you put the intermission? For what reasons?

Luis Valdez
Los Vendidos

Characters

HONEST SANCHO   JOHNNY PACHUCO
SECRETARY   REVOLUCIONARIO
FARMWORKER   MEXICAN-AMERICAN

SCENE: HONEST SANCHO's *Used Mexican Lot and Mexican Curio Shop.
Three models are on display in* HONEST SANCHO's *shop. To the right, there
is a* REVOLUCIONARIO, *complete with sombrero, carrilleras and carabina
30-30.° At center, on the floor, there is the* FARMWORKER, *under a broad
straw sombrero. At stage left is the* PACHUCO, *filero° in hand.* HONEST
SANCHO *is moving among his models, dusting them off and preparing for
another day of business.*

SANCHO. Bueno, bueno, mis monos, vamos a ver a quién
vendemos ahora, ¿no? (*To audience*) ¡Quihubo!° I'm Honest Sancho
and this is my shop. Antes fui contratista, pero ahora logré mi
negocito.° All I need now is a customer. (*A bell rings offstage.*) Ay, a
customer!

SECRETARY (*entering*). Good morning, I'm Miss Jimenez from . . .

SANCHO. Ah, una chicana! Welcome, welcome Señorita Jiménez.

SECRETARY (*Anglo pronunciation*). JIM-enez.

SANCHO. ¿Qué?

SECRETARY. My name is Miss JIM-enez. Don't you speak English?
What's wrong with you?

LOS VENDIDOS First performed in 1967. The title may be translated both "men who
are sold" and "the sellouts," i.e., traitors to the cause. Luis Valdez was born in 1940 in
Delano, California, the son of migrant farmworkers (*campesinos*). Although his early
education was interrupted by the need to work in the fields, he earned a B.A. in
English from San Jose State College in 1964 and then joined the San Francisco
Mime Troupe performing political and satirical plays in public parks. In 1965 he
founded El Teatro Campesino in Delano to present satirical skits (called "Actos") in
support of the farmworkers' cause and as a means of political protest. Like others of
the Actos, *Los Vendidos* was presented free to an audience in a park. Subsequently, in
1972, it won an Emmy in a television production for the Corporation for Public
Broadcasting. At the time of its writing, Ronald Reagan was governor of California
and another former film actor, George Murphy, was a U.S. senator.

carrilleras . . . 30-30: cartridge belts and 30-30 rifle **filero:** switchblade
Bueno . . . Quihubo!: Good, good, my cuties, let's see who we can sell now. What's going
on? **Antes fui . . . negocito:** I used to be a contractor, but now I run my little business.

SANCHO.   Oh, nothing, Señorita JIM-enez. I'm here to help you.

SECRETARY.   That's better. As I was starting to say, I'm a secretary from Governor Reagan's office, and we're looking for a Mexican type for the administration.

SANCHO.   Well, you come to the right place, lady. This is Honest Sancho's Used Mexican Lot, and we got all types here. Any particular type you want?

SECRETARY.   Yes, we were looking for somebody suave . . .

SANCHO.   Suave.

SECRETARY.   Debonaire.

SANCHO.   De buen aire.

SECRETARY.   Dark.

SANCHO.   Prieto.

SECRETARY.   But of course, not too dark.

SANCHO.   No muy prieto.

SECRETARY.   Perhaps, beige.

SANCHO.   Beige, just the tone. Así como cafecito con leche,° ¿no?

SECRETARY.   One more thing. He must be hard-working.

SANCHO.   That could only be one model. Step right over here to the center of the shop, lady. (*They cross to the* FARMWORKER.) This is our standard farmworker model. As you can see, in the words of our beloved Senator George Murphy, he is "built close to the ground." Also, take special notice of his 4-ply Goodyear huaraches,° made from the rain tire. This wide-brimmed sombrero is an extra added feature; keeps off the sun, rain and dust.

SECRETARY.   Yes, it does look durable.

SANCHO.   And our farmworker model is friendly. Muy amable.° Watch. (*Snaps his fingers.*)

FARMWORKER (*lifts up head*).   Buenos días, señorita. (*His head drops.*)

SECRETARY.   My, he is friendly.

SANCHO.   Didn't I tell you? Loves his patrones!° But his most attractive feature is that he's hard-working. Let me show you. (*Snaps fingers.* FARMWORKER *stands.*)

FARMWORKER.   ¡El jale!° (*He begins to work.*)

SANCHO.   As you can see he is cutting grapes.

SECRETARY.   Oh, I wouldn't know.

SANCHO.   He also picks cotton. (*Snaps.* FARMWORKER *begins to pick cotton.*)

SECRETARY.   Versatile, isn't he?

Así . . . leche: Like coffee with milk   **huaraches:** sandals   **Muy amable:** Very friendly   **patrones:** bosses   **El jale:** The job

SANCHO.   He also picks melons. (*Snaps.* FARMWORKER *picks melons.*) That's his slow speed for late in the season. Here's his fast speed. (*Snap.* FARMWORKER *picks faster.*)

SECRETARY.   Chihuahua.° . . . I mean, goodness, he sure is a hardworker.

SANCHO (*pulls the* FARMWORKER *to his feet*).   And that isn't the half of it. Do you see these little holes on his arms that appear to be pores? During those hot sluggish days in the field when the vines or the branches get so entangled, it's almost impossible to move, these holes emit a certain grease that allows our model to slip and slide right through the crop with no trouble at all.

SECRETARY.   Wonderful. But is he economical?

SANCHO.   Economical? Señorita, you are looking at the Volkswagen of Mexicans. Pennies a day is all it takes. One plate of beans and tortillas will keep him going all day. That, and chile. Plenty of chile. Chile jalapeños, chile verde, chile colorado. But, of course, if you do give him chile (*Snap.* FARMWORKER *turns left face. Snap.* FARMWORKER *bends over.*), then you have to change his oil filter once a week.

SECRETARY.   What about storage?

SANCHO.   No problem. You know these new farm labor camps our Honorable Governor Reagan has built out by Parlier or Raisin City? They were designed with our model in mind. Five, six, seven, even ten in one of those shacks will give you no trouble at all. You can also put him in old barns, old cars, riverbanks. You can even leave him out in the field overnight with no worry!

SECRETARY.   Remarkable.

SANCHO.   And here's an added feature: every year at the end of the season, this model goes back to Mexico and doesn't return, automatically, until next spring.

SECRETARY.   How about that. But tell me, does he speak English?

SANCHO.   Another outstanding feature is that last year this model was programmed to go out on STRIKE! (*Snap.*)

FARMWORKER.   ¡Huelga! ¡Huelga! Hermanos, sálganse de esos files.° (*Snap. He stops.*)

SECRETARY.   No! Oh no, we can't strike in the State Capitol.

SANCHO.   Well, he also scabs. (*Snap.*)

FARMWORKER.   Me vendo barato, ¿y qué?° (*Snap.*)

SECRETARY.   That's much better, but you didn't answer my question. Does he speak English?

Chihuahua: Hot damn!   **¡Huelga! . . . files:** Strike! Strike! Brothers, leave those rows.
Me vendo . . . qué?: My price is cheap, so what?

SANCHO.   Bueno . . . no, pero° he has other . . .

SECRETARY.   No.

SANCHO.   Other features.

SECRETARY.   No! He just won't do!

SANCHO.   Okay, okay, pues.° We have other models.

SECRETARY.   I hope so. What we need is something a little more sophisticated.

SANCHO.   Sophisti-qué?

SECRETARY.   An urban model.

SANCHO.   Ah, from the city! Step right back. Over here in this corner of the shop is exactly what you're looking for. Introducing our new 1969 JOHNNY PACHUCO° model! This is our fast-back model. Streamlined. Built for speed, low-riding, city life. Take a look at some of these features. Mag shoes, dual exhausts, green chartreuse paint-job, dark-tint windshield, a little poof on top. Let me just turn him on. (*Snap.* JOHNNY *walks to stage center with a* PACHUCO *bounce.*)

SECRETARY.   What was that?

SANCHO.   That, señorita, was the Chicano shuffle.

SECRETARY.   Okay, what does he do?

SANCHO.   Anything and everything necessary for city life. For instance, survival: he knife fights. (*Snaps.* JOHNNY *pulls out a switchblade and swings at* SECRETARY. SECRETARY *screams.*) He dances. (*Snap.*)

JOHNNY (*singing*).   "Angel Baby, my Angel Baby . . ." (*Snap.*)

SANCHO.   And here's a feature no city model can be without. He gets arrested, but not without resisting, of course. (*Snap.*)

JOHNNY.   En la madre, la placa.° I didn't do it! I didn't do it!

(JOHNNY *turns and stands up against an imaginary wall, legs spread out, arms behind his back.*)

SECRETARY.   Oh no, we can't have arrests! We must maintain law and order.

SANCHO.   But he's bilingual.

SECRETARY.   Bilingual?

SANCHO.   Simón que yes. He speaks English! Johnny, give us some English. (*Snap.*)

JOHNNY (*comes downstage*).   Fuck-you!

SECRETARY (*gasps*).   Oh! I've never been so insulted in my whole life!

SANCHO.   Well, he learned it in your school.

SECRETARY.   I don't care where he learned it.

Bueno . . . pero: Well, no, but   **pues:** then   **Pachuco:** a slang term for an urban tough
En la . . . placa: Oh, oh, the cops

SANCHO.   But he's economical.

SECRETARY.   Economical?

SANCHO.   Nickels and dimes. You can keep Johnny running on hamburgers, Taco Bell tacos, Lucky Lager beer, Thunderbird wine, yesca . . .

SECRETARY.   Yesca?

SANCHO.   Mota.

SECRETARY.   Mota?

SANCHO.   Leños° . . . marijuana. (*Snap.* JOHNNY *inhales on an imaginary joint.*)

SECRETARY.   That's against the law!

JOHNNY (*big smile, holding his breath*).   Yeah.

SANCHO.   He also sniffs glue. (*Snap.* JOHNNY *inhales glue, big smile.*)

JOHNNY.   Tha's too much, man, ése.°

SECRETARY.   No, Mr. Sancho, I don't think this . . .

SANCHO.   Wait a minute, he has other qualities I know you'll love. For example, an inferiority complex. (*Snap.*)

JOHNNY (*to* SANCHO).   You think you're better than me, huh, ése? (*Swings switchblade.*)

SANCHO.   He can also be beaten and he bruises. Cut him and he bleeds, kick him and he . . . (*He beats, bruises and kicks* PACHUCO.) Would you like to try it?

SECRETARY.   Oh, I couldn't.

SANCHO.   Be my guest. He's a great scapegoat.

SECRETARY.   No really.

SANCHO.   Please.

SECRETARY.   Well, all right. Just once. (*She kicks* PACHUCO.) Oh, he's so soft.

SANCHO.   Wasn't that good? Try again.

SECRETARY (*kicks* PACHUCO).   Oh, he's wonderful! (*She kicks him again.*)

SANCHO.   Okay, that's enough, lady. You'll ruin the merchandise. Yes, our Johnny Pachuco model can give you many hours of pleasure. Why, the LAPD just bought twenty of these to train their rookie cops on. And talk about maintenance. Señorita, you are looking at an entirely self-supporting machine. You're never going to find our Johnny Pachuco model on the relief rolls. No, sir, this model knows how to liberate.

SECRETARY.   Liberate?

SANCHO.   He steals. (*Snap.* JOHNNY *rushes to* SECRETARY *and steals her purse.*)

Leños: Joints   **ése:** man

JOHNNY.   ¡Dame esa bolsa, vieja!° (*He grabs the purse and runs. Snap by* SANCHO, *he stops.* SECRETARY *runs after* JOHNNY *and grabs purse away from him, kicking him as she goes.*)

SECRETARY.   No, no, no! We can't have any more thieves in the State Administration. Put him back.

SANCHO.   Okay, we still got other models. Come on, Johnny, we'll sell you to some old lady. (SANCHO *takes* JOHNNY *back to his place.*)

SECRETARY.   Mr. Sancho, I don't think you quite understand what we need. What we need is something that will attract the women voters. Something more traditional, more romantic.

SANCHO.   Ah, a lover. (*He smiles meaningfully.*) Step right over here, señorita. Introducing our standard Revolucionario and/or Early California Bandit type. As you can see, he is well-built, sturdy, durable. This is the International Harvester of Mexicans.

SECRETARY.   What does he do?

SANCHO.   You name it, he does it. He rides horses, stays in the mountains, crosses deserts, plains, rivers, leads revolutions, follows revolutions, kills, can be killed, serves as a martyr, hero, movie star. Did I say movie star? Did you ever see *Viva Zapata? Viva Villa, Villa Rides, Pancho Villa Returns, Pancho Villa Goes Back, Pancho Villa Meets Abbott and Costello?*

SECRETARY.   I've never seen any of those.

SANCHO.   Well, he was in all of them. Listen to this. (*Snap.*)

REVOLUCIONARIO (*scream*).   ¡Viva Villaaaaa!

SECRETARY.   That's awfully loud.

SANCHO.   He has a volume control. (*He adjusts volume. Snap.*)

REVOLUCIONARIO (*mousey voice*).   Viva Villa.

SECRETARY.   That's better.

SANCHO.   And even if you didn't see him in the movies, perhaps you saw him on TV. He makes commercials. (*Snap.*)

REVOLUCIONARIO.   Is there a Frito Bandito in your house?

SECRETARY.   Oh, yes, I've seen that one!

SANCHO.   Another feature about this one is that he is economical. He runs on raw horsemeat and tequila!

SECRETARY.   Isn't that rather savage?

SANCHO.   Al contrario,° it makes him a lover. (*Snap.*)

REVOLUCIONARIO (*to* SECRETARY).   Ay, mamasota, cochota, ven pa 'ca!° (*He grabs* SECRETARY *and folds her back, Latin-lover style.*)

¡**Dame . . . vieja!:** Give me that purse, old lady!   **Al contrario:** On the contrary
Ay . . . pa 'ca: Hey, c'mere, big mama!

SANCHO (*Snap.* REVOLUCIONARIO *goes back upright*).   Now wasn't that nice?

SECRETARY.   Well, it was rather nice.

SANCHO.   And finally, there is one outstanding feature about this model I know the ladies are going to love: he's a genuine antique! He was made in Mexico in 1910!

SECRETARY.   Made in Mexico?

SANCHO.   That's right. Once in Tijuana, twice in Guadalajara, three times in Cuernavaca.

SECRETARY.   Mr. Sancho, I thought he was an American product.

SANCHO.   No, but . . .

SECRETARY.   No, I'm sorry. We can't buy anything but American made products. He just won't do.

SANCHO.   But he's an antique!

SECRETARY.   I don't care. You still don't understand what we need. It's true we need Mexican models, such as these, but it's more important that he be American.

SANCHO.   American?

SECRETARY.   That's right, and judging from what you've shown me, I don't think you have what we want. Well, my lunch hour's almost over, I better . . .

SANCHO.   Wait a minute! Mexican but American?

SECRETARY.   That's correct.

SANCHO.   Mexican but . . . (*A sudden flash.*) American! Yeah, I think we've got exactly what you want. He just came in today! Give me a minute. (*He exits. Talks from backstage.*) Here he is in the shop. Let me just get some papers off. There. Introducing our new 1970 Mexican-American! Ta-ra-ra-raaaa! (SANCHO *brings out the* MEXICAN-AMERICAN *model, a clean-shaven middle-class type in a business suit, with glasses.*)

SECRETARY (*impressed*).   Where have you been hiding this one?

SANCHO.   He just came in this morning. Ain't he a beauty? Feast your eyes on him! Sturdy U.S. Steel frame, streamlined, modern. As a matter of fact, he is built exactly like our Anglo models, except that he comes in a variety of darker shades: naugahyde, leather or leatherette.

SECRETARY.   Naugahyde.

SANCHO.   Well, we'll just write that down. Yes, señorita, this model represents the apex of American engineering! He is bilingual, college educated, ambitious! Say the word "acculturate" and he accelerates. He is intelligent, well-mannered, clean. Did I say clean? (*Snap.* MEXICAN-AMERICAN *raises his arm.*) Smell.

SECRETARY (*smells*).   Old Sobaco, my favorite.

SANCHO (*Snap*. MEXICAN-AMERICAN *turns toward* SANCHO).   Eric? (*To* SECRETARY) We call him Eric García. (*To* ERIC) I want you to meet Miss JIM-enez, Eric.

MEXICAN-AMERICAN.   Miss JIM-enez, I am delighted to make your acquaintance. (*He kisses her hand.*)

SECRETARY.   Oh, my, how charming!

SANCHO.   Did you feel the suction? He has seven especially engineered suction cups right behind his lips. He's a charmer all right!

SECRETARY.   How about boards, does he function on boards?

SANCHO.   You name them, he is on them. Parole boards, draft boards, school boards, taco quality control boards, surf boards, two by fours.

SECRETARY.   Does he function in politics?

SANCHO.   Señorita, you are looking at a political machine. Have you ever heard of the OEO, EOC, COD, WAR ON POVERTY? That's our model! Not only that, he makes political speeches.

SECRETARY.   May I hear one?

SANCHO.   With pleasure. (*Snap.*) Eric, give us a speech.

MEXICAN-AMERICAN.   Mr. Congressman, Mr. Chairman, members of the board, honored guests, ladies and gentlemen. (SANCHO *and* SECRETARY *applaud.*) Please, please. I come before you as a Mexican-American to tell you about the problems of the Mexican. The problems of the Mexican stem from one thing and one thing only: he's stupid. He's uneducated. He needs to stay in school. He needs to be ambitious, forward-looking, harder-working. He needs to think American, American, American, American, American! God bless America! God bless America! God bless America! (*He goes out of control.* SANCHO *snaps frantically and the* MEXICAN-AMERICAN *finally slumps forward, bending at the waist.*)

SECRETARY.   Oh my, he's patriotic too!

SANCHO.   Sí, señorita, he loves his country. Let me just make a little adjustment here. (*Stands* MEXICAN-AMERICAN *up.*)

SECRETARY.   What about upkeep? Is he economical?

SANCHO.   Well, no, I won't lie to you. The Mexican-American costs a little bit more, but you get what you pay for. He's worth every extra cent. You can keep him running on dry Martinis, Langendorf bread . . .

SECRETARY.   Apple pie?

SANCHO.   Only Mom's. Of course, he's also programmed to eat Mexican food at ceremonial functions, but I must warn you, an overdose of beans will plug up his exhaust.

SECRETARY.   Fine! There's just one more question. How much do you want for him?

SANCHO.   Well, I tell you what I'm gonna do. Today and today only, because you've been so sweet, I'm gonna let you steal this model from me! I'm gonna let you drive him off the lot for the simple price of, let's see, taxes and license included, $15,000.

SECRETARY.   Fifteen thousand dollars? For a Mexican!!!!

SANCHO.   Mexican? What are you talking about? This is a Mexican-American! We had to melt down two pachucos, a farmworker and three gabachos° to make this model! You want quality, but you gotta pay for it! This is no cheap run-about. He's got class!

SECRETARY.   Okay, I'll take him.

SANCHO.   You will?

SECRETARY.   Here's your money.

SANCHO.   You mind if I count it?

SECRETARY.   Go right ahead.

SANCHO.   Well, you'll get your pink slip in the mail. Oh, do you want me to wrap him up for you? We have a box in the back.

SECRETARY.   No, thank you. The Governor is having a luncheon this afternoon, and we need a brown face in the crowd. How do I drive him?

SANCHO.   Just snap your fingers. He'll do anything you want. (SECRETARY *snaps*. MEXICAN-AMERICAN *steps forward*.)

MEXICAN-AMERICAN.   ¡Raza querida, vamos levantando armas para liberarnos de estos desgraciados gabachos que nos explotan! Vamos . . .°

SECRETARY.   What did he say?

SANCHO.   Something about taking up arms, killing white people, etc.

SECRETARY.   But he's not supposed to say that!

SANCHO.   Look, lady, don't blame me for bugs from the factory. He's your Mexican-American, you bought him, now drive him off the lot!

SECRETARY.   But he's broken!

SANCHO.   Try snapping another finger. (SECRETARY *snaps*. MEXICAN-AMERICAN *comes to life again*.)

---

gabachos: whites   **¡Raza querida . . . Vamos:** Beloved members of our Mexican race, let's take up arms to free ourselves from those damned whites who exploit us! Let's go . . .

MEXICAN-AMERICAN.   Esta gran humanidad ha dicho basta! ¡Y se
ha puesto en marcha! ¡Basta! ¡Basta! ¡Viva la raza! ¡Viva la causa!
¡Viva la huelga! ¡Vivan los brown berets! ¡Vivan los estudiantes!°
¡Chicano power! (*The* MEXICAN-AMERICAN *turns toward the* SECRETARY,
who gasps and backs up. He keeps turning toward the PACHUCO,
FARMWORKER *and* REVOLUCIONARIO, *snapping his fingers and turning each
of them on, one by one.*)

PACHUCO (*Snap. To* SECRETARY).   I'm going to get you, baby!
¡Viva la raza!

FARMWORKER (*Snap. To* SECRETARY).   ¡Viva la huelga! ¡Viva la
huelga! ¡Viva la huelga!

REVOLUCIONARIO (*Snap. To* SECRETARY).   ¡Viva la revolución!
(*The three models join together and advance toward the* SECRETARY, *who
backs up and runs out of the shop screaming.* SANCHO *is at the other end of
the shop holding his money in his hand. All freeze. After a few seconds of
silence, the* PACHUCO *moves and stretches, shaking his arms and loosening
up. The* FARMWORKER *and* REVOLUCIONARIO *do the same.* SANCHO *stays
where he is, frozen to his spot.*)

JOHNNY.   Man, that was a long one, ése. (*Others agree with him.*)

FARMWORKER.   How did we do?

JOHNNY.   Pretty good, look at all that lana,° man! (*He goes over to*
SANCHO *and removes the money from his hand.* SANCHO *stays where he is.*)

REVOLUCIONARIO.   En la madre, look at all the money.

JOHNNY.   We keep this up, we're going to be rich.

FARMWORKER.   They think we're machines.

REVOLUCIONARIO.   Burros.

JOHNNY.   Puppets.

MEXICAN-AMERICAN.   The only thing I don't like is how come I
always get to play the goddamn Mexican-American?

JOHNNY.   That's what you get for finishing high school.

FARMWORKER.   How about our wages, ése?

JOHNNY.   Here it comes right now, $3,000 for you, $3,000 for you,
$3,000 for you and $3,000 for me. The rest we put back into the
business.

MEXICAN-AMERICAN.   Too much, man. Hey, where you vatos°
going tonight?

FARMWORKER.   I'm going over to Concha's. There's a party.

Esta . . . estudiantes!: This great mass of humanity has done enough talking! It has begun to
march! Enough! Enough! Long live our race! Long live our cause! Long live the strike! Long
live the brown berets! Long live the students!   **lana:** money   **vatos:** guys

JOHNNY. Wait a minute, vatos. What about our salesman? I think he needs an oil job.

REVOLUCIONARIO. Leave him to me. (*The* PACHUCO, FARMWORKER *and* MEXICAN-AMERICAN *exit, talking loudly about their plans for the night. The* REVOLUCIONARIO *goes over to* SANCHO, *removes his derby hat and cigar, lifts him up and throws him over his shoulder.* SANCHO *hangs loose, lifeless. To audience*) He's the best model we got! ¡Ajúa!° (*Exit.*)

QUESTIONS

1. "Honest Sancho" runs his "Used Mexican Lot" like a used car lot. How is this metaphorical context developed in the play? How is the satire directed at both used car salesmen and a Mexican who has sold out his race?
2. Explore the stereotyping that characterizes the "models" that Honest Sancho offers for sale. At whom is the satire directed—the four "models," or people who stereotype others? What is the implication of these men being presented as if they were machines?
3. Of the characters in the play, only Miss Jimenez escapes being portrayed as a machine. Is she therefore treated sympathetically by the play?
4. How effective is the surprise ending?
5. How do you think an audience composed entirely of Mexican Americans would respond to this play? an audience of Anglos? a mixed audience? Would there be differences among these audiences as to how comic the play is?

SUGGESTIONS FOR WRITING

1. Review the chapter on "Characterization" in the Fiction section of this book, paying particular attention to the qualities that contribute to a convincing character. Write an essay demonstrating that one or more characters in one of the plays in the preceding chapter displays those qualities. If you are permitted the space to write a longer essay, extend the essay to include two of these plays, one more realistic than the other.
2. After reviewing the chapter on "Plot" in the Fiction section of this book, write an analysis of the plot of one of the plays in chapter 1. To what extent does plot help to determine whether a play is realistic or nonrealistic?
3. The three plays in this chapter represent a range from realistic to nonrealistic conventions. Using the materials in the opening discussion of those conventions, write an essay on realistic elements in *A Doll House* or *The Glass Menagerie*; or an essay on nonrealistic elements in *The Glass Menagerie* or "Los Vendidos." In each case, consider the way in which the conventions are used to represent human realities and themes.

¡Ajúa!: Wow!

4. In any classification of the plays in chapter 1, Glaspell's "Trifles" would undoubtedly be called realistic, Albee's "The Sandbox" nonrealistic. Write an essay in which you classify any of the other plays in chapter 1 based on the criterion of faithfulness "to the outer appearances of life."

5. In some plays (such as Rivera's "Tape"), the audience only gradually realizes that the incidents are not literally possible. In others (such as Martin's "Beauty" or Ives's "Time Flies"), the play establishes its unreality early on. Using two or threee of the plays presented so far, discuss the advantages and disadvantages of either approach.

6. Write an essay ranking the plays in chapter 1 in terms of their presentation of "life's inner meanings"—their revelation of "human truth."

7. You have had the opportunity to read ten plays thus far. Write an essay in which you use some or all of them to create a hypothesis about the correlation between realistic conventions and significant insights into human behavior.

8. Through the centuries, theatrical producers and writers have sometimes sought to modernize older plays, chiefly by recasting them in the conventions of contemporary theater. Considering the plays you have read so far, and considering the remainder of the plays as you read on in this book, write an essay in which you explore what would be necessary to modernize one of them. Would you find it always appropriate to remove the nonrealistic elements in the play so as to appeal to today's audience—or might you want to adapt the play for that part of the audience that prefers musical dramas?

Tragedy and Comedy

The two masks of drama—one with the corners of its mouth turned down expressing agony or suffering, the other with the corners of its mouth turned up expressing joy or laughter—are familiar everywhere. Derived from masks actually worn by the actors in ancient Greek plays, they symbolize two principal modes of drama. Indeed, just as life gravitates between tears and laughter, they seem to imply that all drama is divided between **tragedy** and **comedy**.

But drama is an ancient literary form; in its development from the beginnings to the present it has produced a rich variety of plays. Can all these plays be classified under two terms? If our answer to this question is Yes, we must define the terms very broadly. If our answer is No, then how many terms do we need, and where do we stop? Polonius, in *Hamlet*, says of a visiting troupe of players that they can act "tragedy, comedy, history, pastoral, pastoral-comical, historical-pastoral, tragical-historical, tragical-comical-historical-pastoral, scene individable, or poem unlimited." Like Polonius himself, his list seems ridiculous. Moreover, even if we adopted these terms, and more, could we be sure that they would accurately classify all plays or that a new play, written tomorrow, would not demand a totally new category?

The discussion that follows proceeds on four assumptions. First, perfect definitions and an airtight system of classification are impossible. There exist no views of tragedy and comedy that have not been challenged and no classification system that unequivocally provides for all examples. Second, it is quite unnecessary that we classify each play we read or see. The most important questions to ask about a play are not "Is this a tragedy?" or "Is this a comedy?" but "Does this play furnish an enjoyable, valid, and significant experience?" Third, the quality of experience furnished by a play may be partially dependent on our perception of its relationship to earlier literary forms, and therefore familiarity with traditional notions of tragedy and comedy is important for our understanding and appreciation of plays. Many of the conventions used in specific plays have been determined by the kind of play the author intended to write. Other plays have been written in deliberate defiance of these conventions. Fourth, whether or not tragedy and comedy be taken as the two all-inclusive dramatic modes, they are certainly, as symbolized by the masks, the two principal ones, and useful points, therefore, from which to begin discussion.

The popular distinctions between comedy and tragedy are fairly simple: comedy is funny; tragedy is sad. Comedy has a happy ending, tragedy an unhappy one. The typical ending for comedy is a marriage; the typical ending for tragedy is a death. There is some truth in these notions, but only some. Some plays called comedies make no attempt to be funny. Successful tragedies, though they involve suffering and sadness, do not leave the spectator depressed. Some funny plays have sad endings: they send the viewer away with a lump in the throat. A few plays usually classified as tragedies do not have unhappy endings but conclude with the protagonist's triumph. In short, the popular distinctions are unreliable. Though we need not abandon them entirely, we must take a more complex view. Let us begin with tragedy.

The first great theorist of dramatic art was Aristotle (384–322 B.C.), whose discussion of tragedy in *Poetics* has dominated critical thought ever since. A very brief summary of Aristotle's view will be helpful.

A tragedy, so Aristotle wrote, is the imitation in dramatic form of an action that is serious and complete, with incidents arousing pity and fear wherewith it effects a **catharsis** of such emotions. The language used is pleasurable and appropriate throughout to the situation. The chief characters are noble personages ("better than ourselves," says Aristotle), and the actions they perform are noble actions. The plot involves a change in the protagonist's fortune, in which he usually, but not always, falls from happiness to misery. The protagonist, though not perfect, is hardly a bad person; his misfortunes result not from character deficiencies but rather from what Aristotle calls **hamartia**, a criminal act committed in ignorance of some material fact or even for the sake of a greater good. A tragic plot has organic unity: the events follow not just *after* one another but *because* of one another. The best tragic plots involve a reversal (a change from one state of things within the play to its opposite) or a discovery (a change from ignorance to knowledge) or both.

In the more extensive account that follows, we will not attempt to delineate the boundaries of tragedy or necessarily describe it at its greatest. Instead, we will describe a common understanding of tragedy as a point of departure for further discussion. Nor shall we enter into the endless controversies over what Aristotle meant by "catharsis" or over which of his statements are meant to apply to all tragedies and which only to the best ones. The important thing is that Aristotle had important insights into the nature of some of the greatest tragedies and that, rightly or wrongly interpreted, his conceptions are the basis for a kind of archetypal notion of tragedy that has dominated critical thought. What are the central features of that archetype? (The following summary retains Aristotle's reference to the tragic protagonist in masculine terms; however, the definitions apply equally to female protagonists such as Sophocles's Antigone and Shakespeare's Cleopatra.)

1. The tragic hero is a man of noble stature. He has a greatness about him. He is not an ordinary man but one of outstanding quality. In Greek and in Shakespearean tragedy, he is usually a prince or a king. We may, if we wish, set down this predilection of former times for kings as tragic heroes as an undemocratic prejudice that regarded some men to be of nobler "blood" than others—preeminent by virtue of their aristocratic birth. But it is only partially that. We may with equal validity regard the hero's kingship as the symbol rather than as the cause of his greatness. He is great not primarily by virtue of his kingship but by his possession of extraordinary powers, by qualities of passion or aspiration or nobility of mind. The tragic hero's kingship is also a symbol of his initial good fortune, the mark of his high position. If the hero's fall is to arouse in us the emotions of pity and fear, it must be a fall from a height. A clumsy man tripping over his shoelace is comic, not tragic—even if it could cause him serious physical pain.

2. The tragic hero is good, though not perfect, and his fall results from his committing what Aristotle calls "an act of injustice" (*hamartia*) either through ignorance or from a conviction that some greater good will be served. This act is, nevertheless, a criminal one, and the good hero is still responsible for it, even if he is totally unaware of its criminality and is acting out of the best intentions. Some later critics ignore Aristotle's insistence on the hero's commission of a guilty act and choose instead to blame the hero's fall on a flaw in his character or personality. Such a notion misrepresents Aristotle's view both of tragedy and of a basically just natural order. It implies a world in which personality alone, not one's actions, can bring on catastrophe.

Aristotle notwithstanding, there is a critical tradition that attributes the fall of the hero to a so-called "tragic flaw"—some fault of character such as inordinate ambition, quickness to anger, a tendency to jealousy, or overweening pride. Conversely, the protagonist's vulnerability has been attributed to some excess of virtue—a nobility of character that unfits him for life among ordinary mortals. But whatever it be—a criminal act, a fault of character, or excessive virtue—the protagonist is personally responsible for his downfall.

3. The hero's downfall, therefore, is his own fault, the result of his own free choice—not the result of pure accident or someone else's villainy or some overriding malignant fate. Accident, villainy, or fate may contribute to the downfall but only as cooperating agents: they are not alone responsible. The combination of the hero's greatness and his responsibility for his own downfall is what entitles us to describe his downfall as tragic rather than as merely pathetic. In common speech these two adjectives are often confused. If a father of ten children is accidentally killed at a street corner, the event, strictly speaking, is pathetic, not tragic. When a weak man succumbs to his weakness and comes to a bad end, the event should be called pathetic, not tragic. The tragic event involves a fall from greatness, brought about, at least partially, by the agent's free action.

4. Nevertheless, the hero's misfortune is not wholly deserved. The punishment exceeds the crime. We do not come away from tragedy with the feeling that "he got what he had coming to him" but rather with the sad sense of a waste of human potential. For what most impresses us about the tragic hero is not his weakness but his greatness. He is, in a sense, "larger than life," or, as Aristotle said, "better than ourselves." He reveals to us the dimensions of human possibility. He is a person mainly admirable, and his fall therefore fills us with pity and fear.

5. Yet the tragic fall is not pure loss. Though it may result in the protagonist's death, it involves, before his death, some increase in awareness, some gain in self-knowledge—as Aristotle puts it, some "discovery"—a change from ignorance to knowledge. On the level of plot, the discovery may be merely learning the truth about some fact or situation of which the protagonist was ignorant, but on the level of character it is accompanied or followed by a significant insight, a fuller self-knowledge, an increase not only in knowledge but in wisdom. Often this increase in wisdom involves some sort of reconciliation with the universe or with the protagonist's situation. He exits not cursing his fate but accepting it and acknowledging that it is to some degree just.

6. Though it arouses solemn emotions—pity and fear, says Aristotle, but compassion and awe might be better terms—tragedy, when well performed, does not leave its audience in a state of depression. Though we cannot be sure what Aristotle meant by his term "catharsis," some sort of emotional release at the end is a common experience of those who witness great tragedies on the stage. They have been greatly moved by pity, fear, and associated emotions, but they are not left emotionally beaten down or dejected. Instead, there may be a feeling almost of exhilaration. This feeling is a response to the tragic action. With the fall of the hero and his gain in wisdom or self-knowledge, there is, besides the appalling sense of human waste, a fresh recognition of human greatness, a sense that human life has unrealized potentialities. Though the hero may be defeated, he at least has dared greatly, and he gains understanding from his defeat.

Is the comic mask laughing or smiling? The question is more important than it may at first appear, for usually we laugh *at* something but smile *with* someone. The laugh expresses recognition of some absurdity in human behavior; the smile expresses pleasure in someone's company or good fortune.

The comic mask may be interpreted both ways. Comedy, Northrop Frye has said, lies between satire and romance. Historically, there have been two chief kinds of comedy—**scornful comedy** and **romantic comedy**, laughing comedy and smiling comedy. Of the two, scornful or satiric comedy is the older and probably still the more dominant.

The most essential difference between tragedy and comedy, particularly scornful comedy, is in their depiction of human nature. Where tragedy emphasizes human greatness, comedy delineates human weakness. Where tragedy celebrates human freedom, comedy points up human limitations. Wherever human beings fail to measure up to their own resolutions or to their own self-conceptions, wherever they are guilty of hypocrisy, vanity, or folly, wherever they fly in the face of good sense and rational behavior, comedy exhibits their absurdity and invites us to laugh at them. Where tragedy tends to say, with Shakespeare's Hamlet, "What a piece of work is a man! how noble in reason! how infinite in faculty! in form and moving how express and admirable! in action how like an angel! in apprehension how like a god!" comedy says, with Shakespeare's Puck, "Lord, what fools these mortals be!"

Because comedy exposes human folly, its function is partly critical and corrective. Where tragedy challenges us with a vision of human possibility, comedy reveals to us a spectacle of human ridiculousness that it makes us want to avoid. No doubt, we should not exaggerate this function of comedy. We go to the theater primarily for enjoyment, not to receive lessons in personality or character development. Nevertheless, laughter may be educative at the same time that it is enjoyable. The comedies of Aristophanes and Molière, of Ben Jonson and Congreve, are, first of all, good fun, but, secondly, they are antidotes for human folly.

Romantic or smiling comedy, as opposed to scornful comedy, and as exemplified by many plays of Shakespeare—*A Midsummer Night's Dream, As You Like It, Twelfth Night, Much Ado About Nothing, The Tempest*, for instance—puts its emphasis upon sympathetic rather than ridiculous characters. These characters—likable, not given up to folly or vanity—are placed in various kinds of difficulties from which, at the end of the play, they are rescued, attaining their ends or having their good fortunes restored. Though different from the protagonists of scornful comedy, however, these characters are not the commanding or lofty figures that tragic protagonists are. They are sensible and good rather than noble, aspiring, and grand. They do not strike us with awe as the tragic protagonist does. They do not so challengingly test the limits of human possibility. In short, they move in a smaller world. Romantic comedies, therefore, do not occupy a different universe from satiric comedies; they simply lie at opposite sides of the same territory. The romantic comedy, moreover, though its protagonists are sympathetic, has usually a number of lesser characters whose folly is held up to ridicule. The satiric comedy, on the other hand, frequently has minor characters—often a pair of young lovers—who are sympathetic and likable. The difference between the two kinds of comedy may be only a matter of whether we laugh at the primary or at the secondary characters.

There are other differences between comedy and tragedy. The norms of comedy are primarily social. Where tragedies tend to isolate their protagonists to emphasize their uniqueness, comedies put their protagonists in the midst of a group to emphasize their commonness. Where tragic protagonists possess overpowering individuality, so that plays are often named after them (for example, *Oedipus Rex, Othello*), comic protagonists tend to be types of individuals, and the plays in which they appear are often named for the type (for example, Molière's *Tartuffe, or The Impostor*, Congreve's *The Double Dealer*). We judge tragic protagonists by absolute moral standards, by how far they soar above society. We judge comic protagonists by social standards, by how well they adjust to society and conform to the expectations of the group.

Finally, comic plots are less likely than tragic plots to exhibit the high degree of organic unity—of logical cause-and-effect progression—that Aristotle required of tragedy. Plausibility, in fact, is not usually the central characteristic of a comic plot. Unlikely coincidences, improbable disguises, mistaken identities—these are the stuff of which comedy is made; and, as long as they make us laugh and, at the same time, help to illuminate human nature and human folly, we need not greatly care. Not that plausibility is no longer important—only that other things are more important, and these other things are often achieved by the most outrageous violations of probability.

This is particularly true regarding the comic ending. *Conventionally*, comedies have a happy ending. The happy ending is, indeed, a *convention* of comedy, which is to say that a comedy ends happily because comedies end happily—that is the nature of the form—not necessarily because a happy ending is a plausible outcome of the events that have preceded it. The greatest masters of comedy—Aristophanes, Shakespeare, Molière—have often been extremely arbitrary in the manner in which they achieved their endings. The accidental discovery of a lost will, rescue by an act of divine intervention (*deus ex machina*), the sudden reform of a mean-spirited person into a friendly person—such devices have been used by the greatest comic writers. And, even where the ending is achieved more plausibly, comedy asks us to forget for the time being that in actuality life has no endings except for death. Marriage, which provides the ending for so many comedies, is really a beginning.

And now, though we do not wish to imitate the folly of Polonius, it is well that we define two additional terms: melodrama and farce. In the two-part classification suggested by the two symbolic masks, melodrama belongs with tragedy, and farce with comedy; but the differences are sufficient to make the two new terms useful.

Melodrama, like tragedy, attempts to arouse feelings of fear and pity, but it does so ordinarily through cruder means. The conflict is an oversimplified one between good and evil depicted in absolute terms. Plot is emphasized at the expense of characterization. Sensational incidents provide the staple of the plot. The young mother and her baby are evicted into a howling storm by the villain holding the mortgage; the heroine is tied to the railroad tracks as the express train approaches. Most important, good finally triumphs over evil, and the ending is happy. Typically, at the end, the hero marries the heroine; villainy is foiled or crushed. Melodrama may, of course, have different degrees of power and subtlety; it is not always as crude as its crudest examples. But in it, moral issues are typically oversimplified, and good is finally triumphant. Melodrama does not provide the complex insights of tragedy. It is usually commercial rather than literary. Much of what television and films present as science fiction, police or medical dramas, and thrillers are examples of melodrama.

Farce, more consistently than comedy, is aimed at rousing explosive laughter. But again the means are cruder. The conflicts are violent and usually at the physical level. Plot is emphasized at the expense of characterization, improbable situations and coincidence at the expense of articulated plot. Comic implausibility is raised to heights of absurd impossibility. Coarse wit, practical jokes, and physical action are staples. Characters trip over benches, insult each other, run into walls, knock each other down, get into brawls. Performed with gusto, farce may be hilariously funny. Psychologically, it may boost our spirits and purge us of hostility and aggression. In content, however, like melodrama, it is usually commercial rather than literary. Contemporary farces are a staple of the movies.

Now we have four classifications—tragedy, comedy, melodrama, farce—the latter two as appendages of the former. But none of these classifications is rigid. They blend into each other and defy exact definition. If we take them too seriously, the tragic mask may laugh, and the comic mask weep.

REVIEWING CHAPTER THREE

1. Summarize the main points of Aristotle's definition of tragedy, indicating where possible how these characteristics arouse responses from the audience.
2. Define the two major types of comedy, satiric and romantic, in terms of their materials and their effects on audiences.
3. Explain how melodrama and farce are related to the major genres of tragedy and comedy.
4. As you read the plays in this chapter, identify any melodramatic events in the tragedies and any farcical elements in the comedies.

Sophocles
Oedipus Rex

The plots of Greek tragedies were based on legends with which Greek audiences were more or less familiar (as American audiences, for example, would be familiar with the major events in a historical play based on the life of Lincoln). These plays often owed much of their impact to the audience's previous knowledge of the characters and their fate, for it enabled the playwright to make powerful use of dramatic irony and allusion. Much of the audience's delight, in addition, came from seeing how the playwright worked out the details of the story. The purpose of this introductory note is therefore to supply such information as the play's first audiences might be presumed to have had.

Because of a prophecy that their new son would kill his father, Laius and Jocasta, King and Queen of Thebes, gave their infant to a shepherd with orders that he be left on a mountainside to die. The shepherd, however, after having pinned the babe's ankles together, took pity on him and gave him instead to a Corinthian shepherd. This shepherd in turn presented him to Polybus and Merope, King and Queen of Corinth, who, childless, adopted him as their own. The child was given the name Oedipus ("Swollen-foot") because of the injury to his ankles.

When grown to manhood at Polybus's court, Oedipus was accused by a drunken guest of not being his father's son. Though reassured by Polybus and Merope, he was still disturbed and traveled to consult the Delphic oracle. The oracle, without answering the question about his parentage, prophesied that Oedipus would kill his father and beget children by his mother. Horrified, resolved to avert this fate, Oedipus determined never to return to Corinth. Traveling from Delphi, he came to a place where three roads met and was ordered off the road by a man in a chariot. Blows were exchanged, and Oedipus killed the man and four of his attendants. Later, on the outskirts of Thebes, he encountered the Sphinx, a monster with the head of a woman, wings of an eagle, and body of a lion, which was terrorizing Thebes by slaying all who failed to answer her riddle ("What goes on four legs in the morning, two legs at noon, and three legs in the evening?"). When Oedipus correctly answered the riddle ("man, for he crawls as an infant, walks erect as a man, and uses a staff in old age"), the Sphinx destroyed herself. As a reward, Oedipus was named King of Thebes to replace the recently slain Laius and was given the hand of Jocasta in marriage. With her, he ruled Thebes successfully for some years and had four children—two sons and two daughters. Then the city was afflicted by a plague. It is at this point that the action of Sophocles's play begins.

The play was first performed in Athens about 430 B.C. In the present version, prepared by Dudley Fitts and Robert Fitzgerald, the translators use spellings for the proper names that are closer to the original Greek than the more familiar Anglicized spellings used in this note. Sophocles (496?–406 B.C.), an active and devoted citizen of Athens during its democratic period, served as an elected general in an Athenian military expedition and held other posts of civic responsibility, but was most importantly its leading and most prolific tragic playwright.

Characters

OEDIPUS, *King of Thebes, supposed son of Polybus and Meropê, King and Queen of Corinth*
IOKASTÊ, *wife of Oedipus and widow of the late King Laïos*
KREON, *brother of Iokastê, a prince of Thebes*
TEIRESIAS, *a blind seer who serves Apollo*
PRIEST
MESSENGER, *from Corinth*

SHEPHERD, *former servant of Laïos*
SECOND MESSENGER, *from the palace*
CHORUS OF THEBAN ELDERS
CHORAGOS, *leader of the Chorus*
ANTIGONE *and* ISMENE, *young daughters of Oedipus and Iokastê. They appear in the Exodus but do not speak.*
SUPPLIANTS, GUARDS, SERVANTS

THE SCENE. *Before the palace of* OEDIPUS, *King of Thebes. A central door and two lateral doors open onto a platform which runs the length of the façade. On the platform, right and left, are altars; and three steps lead down into the orchêstra, or chorus-ground. At the beginning of the action these steps are crowded by suppliants who have brought branches and chaplets of olive leaves and who sit in various attitudes of despair.* OEDIPUS *enters.*

PROLOGUE

OEDIPUS.   My children, generations of the living
In the line of Kadmos,° nursed at his ancient hearth:
Why have you strewn yourselves before these altars
In supplication, with your boughs and garlands?
The breath of incense rises from the city   5
With a sound of prayer and lamentation.
                                        Children,
I would not have you speak through messengers,
And therefore I have come myself to hear you—
I, Oedipus, who bear the famous name.
(*To a* PRIEST) You, there, since you are eldest in the company, 10
Speak for them all, tell me what preys upon you,
Whether you come in dread, or crave some blessing:
Tell me, and never doubt that I will help you
In every way I can; I should be heartless
Were I not moved to find you suppliant here.   15
PRIEST.   Great Oedipus, O powerful king of Thebes!
You see how all the ages of our people
Cling to your altar steps: here are boys
Who can barely stand alone, and here are priests
By weight of age, as I am a priest of God,   20
And young men chosen from those yet unmarried;
As for the others, all that multitude,

2. **Kadmos:** Founder of Thebes

They wait with olive chaplets in the squares,
At the two shrines of Pallas, and where Apollo
Speaks in the glowing embers.
       Your own eyes   25
Must tell you: Thebes is tossed on a murdering sea
And can not lift her head from the death surge.
A rust consumes the buds and fruits of the earth;
The herds are sick; children die unborn,
And labor is vain. The god of plague and pyre   30
Raids like detestable lightning through the city,
And all the house of Kadmos is laid waste,
All emptied, and all darkened: Death alone
Battens upon the misery of Thebes.
You are not one of the immortal gods, we know; 35
Yet we have come to you to make our prayer
As to the man surest in mortal ways
And wisest in the ways of God. You saved us
From the Sphinx, that flinty singer, and the tribute
We paid to her so long; yet you were never   40
Better informed than we, nor could we teach you:
A god's touch, it seems, enabled you to help us.

Therefore, O mighty power, we turn to you:
Find us our safety, find us a remedy,
Whether by counsel of the gods or of men.   45
A king of wisdom tested in the past
Can act in a time of troubles, and act well.
Noblest of men, restore
Life to your city! Think how all men call you
Liberator for your boldness long ago;   50
Ah, when your years of kingship are remembered,
Let them not say *We rose, but later fell*—
Keep the State from going down in the storm!
Once, years ago, with happy augury,
You brought us fortune; be the same again!   55
No man questions your power to rule the land:
But rule over men, not over a dead city!
Ships are only hulls, high walls are nothing,
When no life moves in the empty passageways.
OEDIPUS. Poor children! You may be sure I know 60
All that you longed for in your coming here.
I know that you are deathly sick; and yet,

Sick as you are, not one is as sick as I.
Each of you suffers in himself alone
His anguish, not another's; but my spirit   65
Groans for the city, for myself, for you.

I was not sleeping, you are not waking me.
No, I have been in tears for a long while
And in my restless thought walked many ways.
In all my search I found one remedy,   70
And I have adopted it: I have sent Kreon,
Son of Menoikeus, brother of the queen,
To Delphi, Apollo's place of revelation,
To learn there, if he can,
What act or pledge of mine may save the city.   75
I have counted the days, and now, this very day,
I am troubled, for he has overstayed his time.
What is he doing? He has been gone too long.
Yet whenever he comes back, I should do ill
Not to take any action the god orders.   80
PRIEST.   It is a timely promise. At this instant
    They tell me Kreon is here.
OEDIPUS.   O Lord Apollo!
    May his news be fair as his face is radiant!
PRIEST.   Good news, I gather! he is crowned with bay,
    The chaplet is thick with berries.
OEDIPUS.   We shall soon know;   85
    He is near enough to hear us now. (*Enter* KREON.) O prince:
    Brother: son of Menoikeus:
    What answer do you bring us from the god?
KREON.   A strong one. I can tell you, great afflictions
    Will turn out well, if they are taken well.   90
OEDIPUS.   What was the oracle? These vague words
    Leave me still hanging between hope and fear.
KREON.   Is it your pleasure to hear me with all these
    Gathered around us? I am prepared to speak,
    But should we not go in?
OEDIPUS.   Speak to them all,   95
    It is for them I suffer, more than for myself.
KREON.   Then I will tell you what I heard at Delphi.
    In plain words
    The god commands us to expel from the land of Thebes
    An old defilement we are sheltering.   100

It is a deathly thing, beyond cure;
We must not let it feed upon us longer.
OEDIPUS.   What defilement? How shall we rid ourselves of it?
KREON.   By exile or death, blood for blood. It was
Murder that brought the plague-wind on the city.   105
OEDIPUS.   Murder of whom? Surely the god has named him?
KREON.   My lord: Laïos once ruled this land,
Before you came to govern us.
OEDIPUS.   I know;
I learned of him from others; I never saw him.
KREON.   He was murdered; and Apollo commands us now   110
To take revenge upon whoever killed him.
OEDIPUS.   Upon whom? Where are they? Where shall we find a clue
To solve that crime after so many years?
KREON.   Here in this land, he said. Search reveals
Things that escape an inattentive man.   115
OEDIPUS.   Tell me: Was Laïos murdered in his house,
Or in the fields, or in some foreign country?
KREON.   He said he planned to make a pilgrimage.
He did not come home again.
OEDIPUS.   And was there no one,
No witness, no companion, to tell what happened?   120
KREON.   They were all killed but one, and he got away,
So frightened that he could remember one thing only.
OEDIPUS.   What was that one thing? One may be the key
To everything, if we resolve to use it.
KREON.   He said that a band of highwaymen attacked them   125
Outnumbered them, and overwhelmed the king.
OEDIPUS.   Strange, that a highwayman should be so daring—
Unless some faction here bribed him to do it.
KREON.   We thought of that. But after Laïos's death
New troubles arose and we had no avenger.   130
OEDIPUS.   What troubles could prevent your hunting down the killers?
KREON.   The riddling Sphinx's song
Made us deaf to all mysteries but her own.
OEDIPUS.   Then once more I must bring what is dark to light.
It is most fitting that Apollo shows,   135
As you do, this compunction for the dead.
You shall see how I stand by you, as I should,
Avenging this country and the god as well,
And not as though it were for some distant friend,
But for my own sake, to be rid of evil.   140

Whoever killed King Laïos might—who knows?—
Lay violent hands even on me—and soon.
I act for the murdered king in my own interest.

Come, then, my children: leave the altar steps,
Lift up your olive boughs!
                              One of you go   145
And summon the people of Kadmos to gather here.
I will do all that I can; you may tell them that. (*Exit a* PAGE.)
So, with the help of God,
We shall be saved—or else indeed we are lost.

PRIEST.   Let us rise, children. It was for this we came,   150
And now the king has promised it.
Phoibus° has sent us an oracle; may he descend
Himself to save us and drive out the plague. (*Exeunt* OEDIPUS
and KREON *into the palace by the central door. The* PRIEST *and the*
SUPPLIANTS *disperse right and left. After a short pause the* CHORUS
enters the orchêstra.)

PÁRODOS°

STROPHE 1

CHORUS.   What is God singing in his profound
Delphi of gold and shadow?   155
What oracle for Thebes, the sunwhipped city?
Fear unjoints me, the roots of my heart tremble.
Now I remember, O Healer, your power, and wonder:
Will you send doom like a sudden cloud, or weave it
Like nightfall of the past?   160
Speak to me, tell me, O
Child of golden Hope, immortal Voice.

---

152. Phoibus: Apollo, god of light and truth
Párodos: The song or ode chanted by the chorus on their entry. It is accompanied by dancing
and music played on a flute. The chorus, in this play, represents elders of the city of Thebes.
They remain on stage (on a level lower than the principal actors) for the remainder of the
play. The choral odes and dances serve to separate one scene from another (there was no
curtain in Greek theater) as well as to comment on the action, reinforce the emotion, and
interpret the situation. The chorus also performs dance movements during certain portions of
the scenes themselves. *Strophe* and *antistrophe* are terms denoting the movement and
countermovement of the chorus from one side of their playing area to the other. When the
chorus participates in dialogue with the other characters, their lines are spoken by the
Choragos, their leader.

ANTISTROPHE 1

Let me pray to Athenê, the immortal daughter of Zeus,
And to Artemis her sister
Who keeps her famous throne in the market ring,   165
And to Apollo, archer from distant heaven—
O gods, descend! Like three streams leap against
The fires of our grief, the fires of darkness;
Be swift to bring us rest!
As in the old time from the brilliant house   170
Of air you stepped to save us, come again!

STROPHE 2

Now our afflictions have no end,
Now all our stricken host lies down
And no man fights off death with his mind;
The noble plowland bears no grain,   175
And groaning mothers can not bear—
See, how our lives like birds take wing,
Like sparks that fly when a fire soars,
To the shore of the god of evening.

ANTISTROPHE 2

The plague burns on, it is pitiless,   180
Though pallid children laden with death
Lie unwept in the stony ways,
And old gray women by every path
Flock to the strand about the altars
There to strike their breasts and cry   185
Worship of Phoibus in wailing prayers:
Be kind, God's golden child!

STROPHE 3

There are no swords in this attack by fire,
No shields, but we are ringed with cries.
Send the besieger plunging from our homes   190
Into the vast sea-room of the Atlantic
Or into the waves that foam eastward of Thrace—
For the day ravages what the night spares—
Destroy our enemy, lord of the thunder!
Let him be riven by lightning from heaven!   195

ANTISTROPHE 3

Phoibus Apollo, stretch the sun's bowstring,
That golden cord, until it sing for us,
Flashing arrows in heaven!
                                Artemis, Huntress,
Race with flaring lights upon our mountains!
O scarlet god,° O golden-banded brow,   200
O Theban Bacchos in a storm of Maenads, (*Enter* OEDIPUS, *center*.)
Whirl upon Death, that all the Undying hate!
Come with blinding torches, come in joy!

SCENE 1

OEDIPUS.   Is this your prayer? It may be answered. Come,
Listen to me, act as the crisis demands,   205
And you shall have relief from all these evils.

Until now I was a stranger to this tale,
As I had been a stranger to the crime.
Could I track down the murderer without a clue?
But now, friends,   210
As one who became a citizen after the murder,
I make this proclamation to all Thebans:
If any man knows by whose hand Laïos, son of Labdakos,
Met his death, I direct that man to tell me everything,
No matter what he fears for having so long withheld it.   215
Let it stand as promised that no further trouble
Will come to him, but he may leave the land in safety.
Moreover: If anyone knows the murderer to be foreign,
Let him not keep silent: he shall have his reward from me.
However, if he does conceal it; if any man   220
Fearing for his friend or for himself disobeys this edict,
Hear what I propose to do:

I solemnly forbid the people of this country,
Where power and throne are mine, ever to receive that man
Or speak to him, no matter who he is, or let him   225
Join in sacrifice, lustration, or in prayer.
I decree that he be driven from every house,
Being, as he is, corruption itself to us: the Delphic

---

200. scarlet god: Bacchos, god of wine and revelry; the Maenads were his female attendants.

Voice of Apollo has pronounced this revelation.
Thus I associate myself with the oracle   230
And take the side of the murdered king.
As for the criminal, I pray to God—
Whether it be a lurking thief, or one of a number—
I pray that that man's life be consumed in evil and wretchedness.
And as for me, this curse applies no less   235
If it should turn out that the culprit is my guest here,
Sharing my hearth.
                        You have heard the penalty.
I lay it on you now to attend to this
For my sake, for Apollo's, for the sick
Sterile city that heaven has abandoned.   240
Suppose the oracle had given you no command:
Should this defilement go uncleansed for ever?
You should have found the murderer: your king,
A noble king, had been destroyed!
                        Now I,
Having the power that he held before me,   245
Having his bed, begetting children there
Upon his wife, as he would have, had he lived—
Their son would have been my children's brother,
If Laïos had had luck in fatherhood!
(And now his bad fortune has struck him down)—   250
I say I take the son's part, just as though
I were his son, to press the fight for him
And see it won! I'll find the hand that brought
Death to Labdakos's and Polydoros's child,
Heir of Kadmos's and Agenor's line.°   255
And as for those who fail me,
May the gods deny them the fruit of the earth,
Fruit of the womb, and may they rot utterly!
Let them be wretched as we are wretched, and worse!

For you, for loyal Thebans, and for all   260
Who find my actions right, I pray the favor
Of justice, and of all the immortal gods.
CHORAGOS.   Since I am under oath, my lord, I swear
    I did not do the murder, I can not name

254-55. **Labdakos, Polydoros, Kadmos, and Agenor:** father, grandfather, great-grandfather,
and great-great-grandfather of Laïos

The murderer. Phoibus ordained the search;   265
Why did he not say who the culprit was?
OEDIPUS.   An honest question. But no man in the world
Can make the gods do more than the gods will.
CHORAGOS.   There is an alternative, I think—
OEDIPUS.   Tell me.
Any or all, you must not fail to tell me.   270
CHORAGOS.   A lord clairvoyant to the lord Apollo,
As we all know, is the skilled Teiresias.
One might learn much about this from him, Oedipus.
OEDIPUS.   I am not wasting time:
Kreon spoke of this, and I have sent for him—   275
Twice, in fact; it is strange that he is not here.
CHORAGOS.   The other matter—that old report—seems useless.
OEDIPUS.   What was that? I am interested in all reports.
CHORAGOS.   The king was said to have been killed by highwaymen.
OEDIPUS.   I know. But we have no witness to that.   280
CHORAGOS.   If the killer can feel a particle of dread,
Your curse will bring him out of hiding!
OEDIPUS.   No.
The man who dared that act will fear no curse.
(*Enter the blind seer* TEIRESIAS, *led by a* PAGE.)
CHORAGOS.   But there is one man who may detect the criminal.
This is Teiresias, this is the holy prophet   285
In whom, alone of all men, truth was born.
OEDIPUS.   Teiresias: seer: student of mysteries,
Of all that's taught and all that no man tells,
Secrets of Heaven and secrets of the earth:
Blind though you are, you know the city lies   290
Sick with plague; and from this plague, my lord,
We find that you alone can guard or save us.

Possibly you did not hear the messengers?
Apollo, when we sent to him,
Sent us back word that this great pestilence   295
Would lift, but only if we established clearly
The identity of those who murdered Laïos.
They must be killed or exiled.
                                 Can you use
Birdflight° or any art of divination

---

299. Birdflight: Prophets predicted the future or divined the unknown by observing the flight
of birds.

To purify yourself, and Thebes, and me   300
From this contagion? We are in your hands.
There is no fairer duty
Than that of helping others in distress.

TEIRESIAS.   How dreadful knowledge of the truth can be
When there's no help in truth! I knew this well,   305
But did not act on it: else I should not have come.

OEDIPUS.   What is troubling you? Why are your eyes so cold?

TEIRESIAS.   Let me go home. Bear your own fate, and I'll
Bear mine. It is better so: trust what I say.

OEDIPUS.   What you say is ungracious and unhelpful   310
To your native country. Do not refuse to speak.

TEIRESIAS.   When it comes to speech, your own is neither temperate
Nor opportune. I wish to be more prudent.

OEDIPUS.   In God's name, we all beg you—

TEIRESIAS.   You are all ignorant.
No; I will never tell you what I know.   315
Now it is my misery; then, it would be yours.

OEDIPUS.   What! You do know something, and will not tell us?
You would betray us all and wreck the State?

TEIRESIAS.   I do not intend to torture myself, or you.
Why persist in asking? You will not persuade me.   320

OEDIPUS.   What a wicked old man you are! You'd try a stone's
Patience! Out with it! Have you no feeling at all?

TEIRESIAS.   You call me unfeeling. If you could only see
The nature of your own feelings . . .

OEDIPUS.   Why,
Who would not feel as I do? Who could endure   325
Your arrogance toward the city?

TEIRESIAS.   What does it matter?
Whether I speak or not, it is bound to come.

OEDIPUS.   Then, if "it" is bound to come, you are bound to tell me.

TEIRESIAS.   No, I will not go on. Rage as you please.

OEDIPUS.   Rage? Why not!
                            And I'll tell you what I think: 330
You planned it, you had it done, you all but
Killed him with your own hands: if you had eyes,
I'd say the crime was yours, and yours alone.

TEIRESIAS.   So? I charge you, then,
Abide by the proclamation you have made: 335
From this day forth
Never speak again to these men or me;
You yourself are the pollution of this country.

OEDIPUS.   You dare say that! Can you possibly think you have
    Some way of going free, after such insolence?   340
TEIRESIAS.   I have gone free. It is the truth sustains me.
OEDIPUS.   Who taught you shamelessness? It was not your craft.
TEIRESIAS.   You did. You made me speak. I did not want to.
OEDIPUS.   Speak what? Let me hear it again more clearly.
TEIRESIAS.   Was it not clear before? Are you tempting me?   345
OEDIPUS.   I did not understand it. Say it again.
TEIRESIAS.   I say that you are the murderer whom you seek.
OEDIPUS.   Now twice you have spat out infamy. You'll pay for it!
TEIRESIAS.   Would you care for more? Do you wish to be really angry?
OEDIPUS.   Say what you will. Whatever you say is worthless.   350
TEIRESIAS.   I say you live in hideous shame with those
    Most dear to you. You can not see the evil.
OEDIPUS.   Can you go on babbling like this for ever?
TEIRESIAS.   I can, if there is power in truth.
OEDIPUS.   There is:
    But not for you, not for you,   355
    You sightless, witless, senseless, mad old man!
TEIRESIAS.   You are the madman. There is no one here
    Who will not curse you soon, as you curse me.
OEDIPUS.   You child of total night! I would not touch you;
    Neither would any man who sees the sun.   360
TEIRESIAS.   True: it is not from you my fate will come.
    That lies within Apollo's competence,
    As it is his concern.
OEDIPUS.   Tell me, who made
    These fine discoveries? Kreon? or someone else?
TEIRESIAS.   Kreon is no threat. You weave your own doom.   365
OEDIPUS.   Wealth, power, craft of statesmanship!
    Kingly position, everywhere admired!
    What savage envy is stored up against these,
    If Kreon, whom I trusted, Kreon my friend,
    For this great office which the city once   370
    Put in my hands unsought—if for this power
    Kreon desires in secret to destroy me!

    He has bought this decrepit fortune-teller, this
    Collector of dirty pennies, this prophet fraud—
    Why, he is no more clairvoyant than I am!
                            Tell us: 375
    Has your mystic mummery ever approached the truth?
    When that hellcat the Sphinx was performing here,

What help were you to these people?
Her magic was not for the first man who came along:
It demanded a real exorcist. Your birds—   380
What good were they? or the gods, for the matter of that?
But I came by,
Oedipus, the simple man, who knows nothing—
I thought it out for myself, no birds helped me!
And this is the man you think you can destroy,   385
That you may be close to Kreon when he's king!
Well, you and your friend Kreon, it seems to me,
Will suffer most. If you were not an old man,
You would have paid already for your plot.

CHORAGOS.   We can not see that his words or yours   390
Have been spoken except in anger, Oedipus,
And of anger we have no need. How to accomplish
The god's will best: that is what most concerns us.

TEIRESIAS.   You are a king. But where argument's concerned
I am your man, as much a king as you.   395
I am not your servant, but Apollo's.
I have no need of Kreon or Kreon's name.

Listen to me. You mock my blindness, do you?
But I say that you, with both your eyes, are blind:
You can not see the wretchedness of your life,   400
Nor in whose house you live, no, nor with whom.
Who are your father and mother? Can you tell me?
You do not even know the blind wrongs
That you have done them, on earth and in the world below.
But the double lash of your parents' curse will whip you   405
Out of this land some day, with only night
Upon your precious eyes.
Your cries then—where will they not be heard?
What fastness of Kithairon° will not echo them?
And that bridal-descant of yours—you'll know it then,   410
The song they sang when you came here to Thebes
And found your misguided berthing.
All this, and more, that you can not guess at now,
Will bring you to yourself among your children.

Be angry, then. Curse Kreon. Curse my words.   415
I tell you, no man that walks upon the earth

---

409. Kithairon: the mountain where Oedipus was taken to be exposed as an infant

    Shall be rooted out more horribly than you.

OEDIPUS.   Am I to bear this from him?—Damnation

    Take you! Out of this place! Out of my sight!

TEIRESIAS.   I would not have come at all if you had not asked me.

OEDIPUS.   Could I have told that you'd talk nonsense, that   421

    You'd come here to make a fool of yourself, and of me?

TEIRESIAS.   A fool? Your parents thought me sane enough.

OEDIPUS.   My parents again!—Wait: who were my parents?

TEIRESIAS.   This day will give you a father, and break your heart.   425

OEDIPUS.   Your infantile riddles! Your damned abracadabra!

TEIRESIAS.   You were a great man once at solving riddles.

OEDIPUS.   Mock me with that if you like; you will find it true.

TEIRESIAS.   It was true enough. It brought about your ruin.

OEDIPUS.   But if it saved the town?

TEIRESIAS (*to the* PAGE).   Boy, give me your hand.   430

OEDIPUS.   Yes, boy; lead him away.

                     —While you are here

    We can do nothing. Go; leave us in peace.

TEIRESIAS.   I will go when I have said what I have to say.

    How can you hurt me? And I tell you again:

    The man you have been looking for all this time,   435

    The damned man, the murderer of Laïos,

    That man is in Thebes. To your mind he is foreign-born,

    But it will soon be shown that he is a Theban,

    A revelation that will fail to please.

                     A blind man,

    Who has his eyes now; a penniless man, who is rich now;   440

    And he will go tapping the strange earth with his staff.

    To the children with whom he lives now he will be

    Brother and father—the very same; to her

    Who bore him, son and husband—the very same

    Who came to his father's bed, wet with his father's blood.   445

    Enough. Go think that over.

    If later you find error in what I have said,

    You may say that I have no skill in prophecy.

    (*Exit* TEIRESIAS, *led by his* PAGE. OEDIPUS *goes into the palace.*)

ODE 1

STROPHE 1

CHORUS.   The Delphic stone of prophecies

    Remembers ancient regicide   450

    And a still bloody hand.

That killer's hour of flight has come.
He must be stronger than riderless
Coursers of untiring wind,
For the son° of Zeus armed with his father's thunder   455
Leaps in lightning after him;
And the Furies hold his track, the sad Furies.

ANTISTROPHE 1

Holy Parnassos'° peak of snow
Flashes and blinds that secret man,
That all shall hunt him down: 460
Though he may roam the forest shade
Like a bull gone wild from pasture
To rage through glooms of stone,
Doom comes down on him; flight will not avail him;
For the world's heart calls him desolate,   465
And the immortal voices follow, for ever follow.

STROPHE 2

But now a wilder thing is heard
From the old man skilled at hearing Fate in the wing-beat of a bird.
Bewildered as a blown bird, my soul hovers and can not find
Foothold in this debate, or any reason or rest of mind.   470
But no man ever brought—none can bring
Proof of strife between Thebes' royal house,
Labdakos's line, and the son of Polybos;
And never until now has any man brought word
Of Laïos's dark death staining Oedipus the King.   475

ANTISTROPHE 2

Divine Zeus and Apollo hold
Perfect intelligence alone of all tales ever told;
And well though this diviner works, he works in his own night;
No man can judge that rough unknown or trust in second sight,
For wisdom changes hands among the wise.   480
Shall I believe my great lord criminal
At a raging word that a blind old man let fall?
I saw him, when the carrion woman° faced him of old,
Prove his heroic mind. These evil words are lies.

455. son: Apollo   458. Parnassos: mountain sacred to Apollo
483. carrion woman: the Sphinx

SCENE 2

KREON.   Men of Thebes: 485
I am told that heavy accusations
Have been brought against me by King Oedipus.

I am not the kind of man to bear this tamely.

If in these present difficulties
He holds me accountable for any harm to him   490
Through anything I have said or done—why, then,
I do not value life in this dishonor.
It is not as though this rumor touched upon
Some private indiscretion. The matter is grave.
The fact is that I am being called disloyal   495
To the State, to my fellow citizens, to my friends.
CHORAGOS.   He may have spoken in anger, not from his mind.
KREON.   But did you not hear him say I was the one
Who seduced the old prophet into lying?
CHORAGOS.   The thing was said; I do not know how seriously.   500
KREON.   But you were watching him! Were his eyes steady?
Did he look like a man in his right mind?
CHORAGOS.   I do not know.
I can not judge the behavior of great men.
But here is the king himself. (*Enter* OEDIPUS.)
OEDIPUS.   So you dared come back.
Why? How brazen of you to come to my house,   505
You murderer!
                Do you think I do not know
That you plotted to kill me, plotted to steal my throne?
Tell me, in God's name: am I coward, a fool,
That you should dream you could accomplish this?
A fool who could not see your slippery game?   510
A coward, not to fight back when I saw it?
You are the fool, Kreon, are you not? hoping
Without support or friends to get a throne?
Thrones may be won or bought: you could do neither.
KREON.   Now listen to me. You have talked; let me talk, too.   515
You can not judge unless you know the facts.
OEDIPUS.   You speak well: there is one fact; but I find it hard
To learn from the deadliest enemy I have.
KREON.   That above all I must dispute with you.

OEDIPUS.   That above all I will not hear you deny.   520
KREON.   If you think there is anything good in being stubborn
 Against all reason, then I say you are wrong.
OEDIPUS.   If you think a man can sin against his own kind
 And not be punished for it, I say you are mad.
KREON.   I agree. But tell me: what have I done to you?   525
OEDIPUS.   You advised me to send for that wizard, did you not?
KREON.   I did. I should do it again.
OEDIPUS.   Very well. Now tell me:
 How long has it been since Laïos—
KREON.   What of Laïos?
OEDIPUS.   Since he vanished in that onset by the road?
KREON.   It was long ago, a long time.
OEDIPUS.   And this prophet,   530
 Was he practicing here then?
KREON.   He was; and with honor, as now.
OEDIPUS.   Did he speak of me at that time?
KREON.   He never did,
 At least, not when I was present.
OEDIPUS.   But . . . the enquiry?
 I suppose you held one?
KREON.   We did, but we learned nothing.
OEDIPUS.   Why did the prophet not speak against me then?   535
KREON.   I do not know; and I am the kind of man
 Who holds his tongue when he has no facts to go on.
OEDIPUS.   There's one fact that you know, and you could tell it.
KREON.   What fact is that? If I know it, you shall have it.
OEDIPUS.   If he were not involved with you, he could not say   540
 That it was I who murdered Laïos.
KREON.   If he says that, you are the one that knows it!—
 But now it is my turn to question you.
OEDIPUS.   Put your questions. I am no murderer.
KREON.   First, then: You married my sister?
OEDIPUS.   I married your sister.   545
KREON.   And you rule the kingdom equally with her?
OEDIPUS.   Everything that she wants she has from me.
KREON.   And I am the third, equal to both of you?
OEDIPUS.   That is why I call you a bad friend.
KREON.   No. Reason it out, as I have done.   550
 Think of this first: Would any sane man prefer
 Power, with all a king's anxieties,
 To that same power and the grace of sleep?

Certainly not I.
I have never longed for the king's power—only his rights.   555
Would any wise man differ from me in this?
As the matters stand, I have my way in everything
With your consent, and no responsibilities.
If I were king, I should be a slave to policy.
How could I desire a scepter more   560
Than what is now mine—untroubled influence?
No, I have not gone mad; I need no honors,
Except those with the perquisites I have now.
I am welcome everywhere; every man salutes me,
And those who want your favor seek my ear,   565
Since I know how to manage what they ask.
Should I exchange this ease for that anxiety?
Besides, no sober mind is treasonable.
I hate anarchy
And never would deal with any man who likes it.   570

Test what I have said. Go to the priestess
At Delphi, ask if I quoted her correctly.
And as for this other thing: if I am found
Guilty of treason with Teiresias,
Then sentence me to death. You have my word   575
It is a sentence I should cast my vote for—
But not without evidence!
      You do wrong
When you take good men for bad, bad men for good.
A true friend thrown aside—why, life itself
Is not more precious!
      In time you will know this well: 580
For time, and time alone, will show the just man,
Though scoundrels are discovered in a day.
CHORAGOS. This is well said, and a prudent man would ponder it.
  Judgments too quickly formed are dangerous.
OEDIPUS. But is he not quick in his duplicity?   585
  And shall I not be quick to parry him?
  Would you have me stand still, hold my peace, and let
  This man win everything, through my inaction?
KREON. And you want—what is it, then? To banish me?
OEDIPUS. No, not exile. It is your death I want,   590
  So that all the world may see what treason means.
KREON. You will persist, then? You will not believe me?

OEDIPUS.   How can I believe you?
KREON.   Then you are a fool.
OEDIPUS.   To save myself?
KREON.   In justice, think of me.
OEDIPUS.   You are evil incarnate.
KREON.   But suppose that you are wrong? 595
OEDIPUS.   Still I must rule.
KREON.   But not if you rule badly.
OEDIPUS.   O city, city!
KREON.   It is my city, too!
CHORAGOS.   Now, my lords, be still. I see the queen,
    Iokastê, coming from her palace chambers;
    And it is time she came, for the sake of you both.   600
    This dreadful quarrel can be resolved through her. (*Enter* IOKASTÊ.)
IOKASTÊ.   Poor foolish men, what wicked din is this?
    With Thebes sick to death, is it not shameful
    That you should rake some private quarrel up?
    (*To* OEDIPUS) Come into the house.
                            —And you, Kreon, go now: 605
    Let us have no more of this tumult over nothing.
KREON.   Nothing? No, sister: what your husband plans for me
    Is one of two great evils: exile or death.
OEDIPUS.   He is right.
                    Why, woman I have caught him squarely
    Plotting against my life.
KREON.   No! Let me die   610
    Accurst if ever I have wished you harm!
IOKASTÊ.   Ah, believe it, Oedipus!
    In the name of the gods, respect this oath of his
    For my sake, for the sake of these people here!

STROPHE 1

CHORAGOS.   Open your mind to her, my lord. Be ruled by her, I beg you!
OEDIPUS.   What would you have me do?   616
CHORAGOS.   Respect Kreon's word. He has never spoken like a fool,
    And now he has sworn an oath.
OEDIPUS.   You know what you ask?
CHORAGOS.   I do.
OEDIPUS.   Speak on, then.
CHORAGOS.   A friend so sworn should not be baited so,

In blind malice, and without final proof.   620
OEDIPUS.   You are aware, I hope, that what you say
   Means death for me, or exile at the least.

STROPHE 2

CHORAGOS.   No, I swear by Helios, first in heaven!
              May I die friendless and accurst,
          The worst of deaths, if ever I meant that!   625
          It is the withering fields
              That hurt my sick heart:
          Must we bear all these ills,
              And now your blood as well?
OEDIPUS.   Then let him go. And let me die, if I must,   630
   Or be driven by him in shame from the land of Thebes.
   It is your unhappiness, and not his talk,
   That touches me.
              As for him—
   Wherever he goes, hatred will follow him.
KREON.   Ugly in yielding, as you were ugly in rage!   635
   Natures like yours chiefly torment themselves.
OEDIPUS.   Can you not go? Can you not leave me?
KREON.   I can.
   You do not know me; but the city knows me,
   And in its eyes I am just, if not in yours. (*Exit* KREON.)

ANTISTROPHE 1

CHORAGOS.   Lady Iokastê, did you not ask the King to go to his   640
   chambers?
IOKASTÊ.   First tell me what has happened.
CHORAGOS.   There was suspicion without evidence; yet it rankled
   As even false charges will.
IOKASTÊ.   On both sides?
CHORAGOS.   On both.
IOKASTÊ.   But what was said?
CHORAGOS. Oh let it rest, let it be done with!
   Have we not suffered enough?   645
OEDIPUS.   You see to what your decency has brought you:
   You have made difficulties where my heart saw none.

ANTISTROPHE 2

CHORAGOS.   Oedipus, it is not once only I have told you—
        You must know I should count myself unwise
    To the point of madness, should I now forsake you—   650
        You, under whose hand,
            In the storm of another time,
        Our dear land sailed out free.
          But now stand fast at the helm!
IOKASTÊ.   In God's name, Oedipus, inform your wife as well: 655
    Why are you so set in this hard anger?
OEDIPUS.   I will tell you, for none of these men deserves
    My confidence as you do. It is Kreon's work,
    His treachery, his plotting against me.
IOKASTÊ.   Go on, if you can make this clear to me.   660
OEDIPUS.   He charges me with the murder of Laïos.
IOKASTÊ.   Has he some knowledge? Or does he speak from hearsay?
OEDIPUS.   He would not commit himself to such a charge,
    But he has brought in that damnable soothsayer
    To tell his story.
IOKASTÊ.   Set your mind at rest.   665
    If it is a question of soothsayers, I tell you
    That you will find no man whose craft gives knowledge
    Of the unknowable.
            Here is my proof:
    An oracle was reported to Laïos once
    (I will not say from Phoibus himself, but from   670
    His appointed ministers, at any rate)
    That his doom would be death at the hands of his own son—
    His son, born of his flesh and of mine!

    Now, you remember the story: Laïos was killed
    By marauding strangers where three highways meet;   675
    But his child had not been three days in this world
    Before the king had pierced the baby's ankles
    And left him to die on a lonely mountainside.

    Thus, Apollo never caused that child
    To kill his father, and it was not Laïos's fate   680
    To die at the hands of his son, as he had feared.
    This is what prophets and prophecies are worth!

Have no dread of them.
It is God himself
Who can show us what he wills, in his own way.
OEDIPUS.   How strange a shadowy memory crossed my mind,   685
    Just now while you were speaking; it chilled my heart.
IOKASTÊ.   What do you mean? What memory do you speak of?
OEDIPUS.   If I understand you, Laïos was killed
    At a place where three roads meet.
IOKASTÊ.   So it was said;
    We have no later story.
OEDIPUS.   Where did it happen?   690
IOKASTÊ.   Phokis, it is called: at a place where the Theban Way
    Divides into the roads toward Delphi and Daulia.
OEDIPUS.   When?
IOKASTÊ.   We had the news not long before you came
    And proved the right to your succession here.
OEDIPUS.   Ah, what net has God been weaving for me?   695
IOKASTÊ.   Oedipus! Why does this trouble you?
OEDIPUS.   Do not ask me yet.
    First, tell me how Laïos looked, and tell me
    How old he was.
IOKASTÊ.   He was tall, his hair just touched
    With white; his form was not unlike your own.
OEDIPUS.   I think that I myself may be accurst   700
    By my own ignorant edict.
IOKASTÊ.   You speak strangely.
    It makes me tremble to look at you, my king.
OEDIPUS.   I am not sure that the blind man can not see.
    But I should know better if you were to tell me—
IOKASTÊ.   Anything—though I dread to hear you ask it.   705
OEDIPUS.   Was the king lightly escorted, or did he ride
    With a large company, as a ruler should?
IOKASTÊ.   There were five men with him in all: one was a herald;
    And a single chariot, which he was driving.
OEDIPUS.   Alas, that makes it plain enough!
But who—   710
    Who told you how it happened?
IOKASTÊ.   A household servant,
    The only one to escape.
OEDIPUS.   And is he still
    A servant of ours?
IOKASTÊ.   No; for when he came back at last

And found you enthroned in the place of the dead king,
He came to me, touched my hand with his, and begged   715
That I would send him away to the frontier district
Where only the shepherds go—
As far away from the city as I could send him.
I granted his prayer; for although the man was a slave,
He had earned more than this favor at my hands.   720
OEDIPUS.   Can he be called back quickly?
IOKASTÊ.   Easily.
    But why?
OEDIPUS.   I have taken too much upon myself
    Without enquiry; therefore I wish to consult him.
IOKASTÊ.   Then he shall come.
                        But am I not one also
    To whom you might confide these fears of yours?   725
OEDIPUS.   That is your right; it will not be denied you,
    Now least of all; for I have reached a pitch
    Of wild foreboding. Is there anyone
    To whom I should sooner speak?

    Polybos of Corinth is my father.   730
    My mother is a Dorian: Meropê.
    I grew up chief among the men of Corinth
    Until a strange thing happened—
    Not worth my passion, it may be, but strange.
    At a feast, a drunken man maundering in his cups   735
    Cries out that I am not my father's son!

    I contained myself that night, though I felt anger
    And a sinking heart. The next day I visited
    My father and mother, and questioned them. They stormed,
    Calling it all the slanderous rant of a fool;   740
    And this relieved me. Yet the suspicion
    Remained always aching in my mind;
    I knew there was talk; I could not rest;
    And finally, saying nothing to my parents,
    I went to the shrine at Delphi.   745

    The god dismissed my question without reply;
    He spoke of other things.
                        Some were clear,
    Full of wretchedness, dreadful, unbearable:

As, that I should lie with my own mother, breed
Children from whom all men would turn their eyes;   750
And that I should be my father's murderer.

I heard all this, and fled. And from that day
Corinth to me was only in the stars
Descending in that quarter of the sky,
As I wandered farther and farther on my way   755
To a land where I should never see the evil
Sung by the oracle. And I came to this country
Where, so you say, King Laïos was killed.

I will tell you all that happened there, my lady.

There were three highways   760
Coming together at a place I passed;
And there a herald came towards me, and a chariot
Drawn by horses, with a man such as you describe
Seated in it. The groom leading the horses
Forced me off the road at his lord's command;   765
But as this charioteer lurched over towards me
I struck him in my rage. The old man saw me
And brought his double goad down upon my head
As I came abreast.
                              He was paid back, and more!
Swinging my club in this right hand I knocked him   770
Out of his car, and he rolled on the ground.
                                                I killed him.

I killed them all.
Now if that stranger and Laïos were—kin,
Where is a man more miserable than I?
More hated by the gods? Citizen and alien alike   775
Must never shelter me or speak to me—
I must be shunned by all.
                              And I myself
Pronounced this malediction upon myself!

Think of it: I have touched you with these hands,
These hands that killed your husband. What defilement!   780
Am I all evil, then? It must be so,
Since I must flee from Thebes, yet never again

See my own countrymen, my own country,
For fear of joining my mother in marriage
And killing Polybos, my father.
Ah, 785
If I was created so, born to this fate,
Who could deny the savagery of God?

O holy majesty of heavenly powers!
May I never see that day! Never!
Rather let me vanish from the race of men 790
Than know the abomination destined me!
CHORAGOS.   We too, my lord, have felt dismay at this.
   But there is hope: you have yet to hear the shepherd.
OEDIPUS.   Indeed, I fear no other hope is left me.
IOKASTÊ.   What do you hope from him when he comes?
OEDIPUS.   This much: 795
   If his account of the murder tallies with yours,
   Then I am cleared.
IOKASTÊ.   What was it that I said
   Of such importance?
OEDIPUS.   Why, "marauders," you said,
   Killed the king, according to this man's story.
   If he maintains that still, if there were several, 800
   Clearly the guilt is not mine: I was alone.
   But if he says one man, singlehanded, did it,
   Then the evidence all points to me.
IOKASTÊ.   You may be sure that he said there were several;
   And can he call back that story now? He can not. 805
   The whole city heard it as plainly as I.
   But suppose he alters some detail of it:
   He can not ever show that Laïos's death
   Fulfilled the oracle: for Apollo said
   My child was doomed to kill him; and my child— 810
   Poor baby!—it was my child that died first.

   No. From now on, where oracles are concerned,
   I would not waste a second thought on any.
OEDIPUS.   You may be right.
                     But come: let someone go
   For the shepherd at once. This matter must be settled. 815
IOKASTÊ.   I will send for him.
   I would not wish to cross you in anything.
   And surely not in this.—Let us go in. (*Exeunt into the palace.*)

ODE 2

STROPHE 1

CHORUS.   Let me be reverent in the ways of right,
    Lowly the paths I journey on;   820
    Let all my words and actions keep
    The laws of the pure universe
    From highest Heaven handed down
    For Heaven is their bright nurse,
    Those generations of the realms of light;   825
    Ah, never of mortal kind were they begot,
    Nor are they slaves of memory, lost in sleep:
    Their Father is greater than Time, and ages not.

ANTISTROPHE 1

    The tyrant is a child of Pride
    Who drinks from his great sickening cup   830
    Recklessness and vanity,
    Until from his high crest headlong
    He plummets to the dust of hope.
    That strong man is not strong.
    But let no fair ambition be denied;   835
    May God protect the wrestler for the State
    In government, in comely policy,
    Who will fear God, and on His ordinance wait.

STROPHE 2

    Haughtiness and the high hand of disdain
    Tempt and outrage God's holy law;   840
    And any mortal who dares hold
    No immortal Power in awe
    Will be caught up in a net of pain:
    The price for which his levity is sold.
    Let each man take due earnings, then,   845
    And keep his hands from holy things,
    And from blasphemy stand apart—
    Else the crackling blast of heaven
    Blows on his head, and on his desperate heart.
    Though fools will honor impious men,   850
    In their cities no tragic poet sings.

ANTISTROPHE 2

    Shall we lose faith in Delphi's obscurities,
    We who have heard the world's core
    Discredited, and the sacred wood
    Of Zeus at Elis praised no more?   855
    The deeds and the strange prophecies
    Must make a pattern yet to be understood.
    Zeus, if indeed you are lord of all,
    Throned in light over night and day,
    Mirror this in your endless mind: 860
    Our masters call the oracle
    Words on the wind, and the Delphic vision blind!
    Their hearts no longer know Apollo,
    And reverence for the gods has died away.

SCENE 3

    Enter IOKASTÊ.

IOKASTÊ.   Princes of Thebes, it has occurred to me   865
    To visit the altars of the gods, bearing
    These branches as a suppliant, and this incense.
    Our king is not himself: his noble soul
    Is overwrought with fantasies of dread,
    Else he would consider   870
    The new prophecies in the light of the old.
    He will listen to any voice that speaks disaster,
    And my advice goes for nothing. (*She approaches the altar, right.*)
                    To you, then, Apollo,
    Lycéan lord, since you are nearest, I turn in prayer.
    Receive these offerings, and grant us deliverance   875
    From defilement. Our hearts are heavy with fear
    When we see our leader distracted, as helpless sailors
    Are terrified by the confusion of their helmsman. (*Enter* MESSENGER.)
MESSENGER.   Friends, no doubt you can direct me:
    Where shall I find the house of Oedipus,   880
    Or, better still, where is the king himself?
CHORAGOS.   It is this very place, stranger; he is inside.
    This is his wife and mother of his children.
MESSENGER.   I wish her happiness in a happy house,
    Blest in all the fulfillment of her marriage.   885
IOKASTÊ.   I wish as much for you: your courtesy

Deserves a like good fortune. But now, tell me:
Why have you come? What have you to say to us?
MESSENGER.   Good news, my lady, for your house and your husband.
IOKASTÊ.   What news? Who sent you here?
MESSENGER.   I am from Corinth.   890
The news I bring ought to mean joy for you,
Though it may be you will find some grief in it.
IOKASTÊ.   What is it? How can it touch us in both ways?
MESSENGER.   The word is that the people of the Isthmus
Intend to call Oedipus to be their king.   895
IOKASTÊ.   But old King Polybos—is he not reigning still?
MESSENGER.   No. Death holds him in his sepulcher.
IOKASTÊ.   What are you saying? Polybos is dead?
MESSENGER.   If I am not telling the truth, may I die myself.
IOKASTÊ (*to a* MAIDSERVANT).   Go in, go quickly; tell this to your master. 900
O riddlers of God's will, where are you now!
This was the man whom Oedipus, long ago,
Feared so, fled so, in dread of destroying him—
But it was another fate by which he died. (*Enter* OEDIPUS, *center.*)
OEDIPUS.   Dearest Iokastê, why have you sent for me?   905
IOKASTÊ.   Listen to what this man says, and then tell me
What has become of the solemn prophecies.
OEDIPUS.   Who is this man? What is his news for me?
IOKASTÊ.   He has come from Corinth to announce your father's death!
OEDIPUS.   Is it true, stranger? Tell me in your own words.   910
MESSENGER.   I can not say it more clearly: the king is dead.
OEDIPUS.   Was it by treason? Or by an attack of illness?
MESSENGER.   A little thing brings old men to their rest.
OEDIPUS.   It was sickness, then?
MESSENGER.   Yes, and his many years.
OEDIPUS.   Ah!   915
Why should a man respect the Pythian hearth,° or
Give heed to the birds that jangle above his head?
They prophesied that I should kill Polybos,
Kill my own father; but he is dead and buried,
And I am here—I never touched him, never,   920
Unless he died of grief for my departure,
And thus, in a sense, through me. No. Polybos
Has packed the oracles off with him underground.
They are empty words.

916. Pythian hearth: Delphi

IOKASTÊ.   Had I not told you so?

OEDIPUS.   You had; it was my faint heart that betrayed me.   925

IOKASTÊ.   From now on never think of those things again.

OEDIPUS.   And yet—must I not fear my mother's bed?

IOKASTÊ.   Why should anyone in this world be afraid,
Since Fate rules us and nothing can be foreseen?
A man should live only for the present day.   930

Have no more fear of sleeping with your mother:
How many men, in dreams, have lain with their mothers!
No reasonable man is troubled by such things.

OEDIPUS.   That is true; only—
If only my mother were not still alive!   935
But she is alive. I can not help my dread.

IOKASTÊ.   Yet this news of your father's death is wonderful.

OEDIPUS.   Wonderful. But I fear the living woman.

MESSENGER.   Tell me who is this woman that you fear?

OEDIPUS.   It is Meropê, man; the wife of King Polybos.   940

MESSENGER.   Meropê? Why should you be afraid of her?

OEDIPUS.   An oracle of the gods, a dreadful saying.

MESSENGER.   Can you tell me about it or are you sworn to silence?

OEDIPUS.   I can tell you, and I will.
Apollo said through his prophet that I was the man   945
Who should marry his own mother, shed his father's blood
With his own hands. And so, for all these years
I have kept clear of Corinth, and no harm has come—
Though it would have been sweet to see my parents again.

MESSENGER.   And is this the fear that drove you out of Corinth?   950

OEDIPUS.   Would you have me kill my father?

MESSENGER.   As for that
You must be reassured by the news I gave you.

OEDIPUS.   If you could reassure me, I would reward you.

MESSENGER.   I had that in mind, I will confess; I thought
I could count on you when you returned to Corinth.   955

OEDIPUS.   No: I will never go near my parents again.

MESSENGER.   Ah, son, you still do not know what you are doing—

OEDIPUS.   What do you mean? In the name of God tell me!

MESSENGER.   —If these are your reasons for not going home.

OEDIPUS.   I tell you, I fear the oracle may come true.   960

MESSENGER.   And guilt may come upon you through your parents?

OEDIPUS.   That is the dread that is always in my heart.

MESSENGER.   Can you not see that all your fears are groundless?

OEDIPUS.   Groundless? Am I not my parents' son?
MESSENGER.   Polybos was not your father.
OEDIPUS.   Not my father?   965
MESSENGER.   No more your father than the man speaking to you.
OEDIPUS.   But you are nothing to me!
MESSENGER.   Neither was he.
OEDIPUS.   Then why did he call me son?
MESSENGER.   I will tell you:
     Long ago he had you from my hands, as a gift.
OEDIPUS.   Then how could he love me so, if I was not his?   970
MESSENGER.   He had no children, and his heart turned to you.
OEDIPUS.   What of you? Did you buy me? Did you find me by chance?
MESSENGER.   I came upon you in the woody vales of Kithairon.
OEDIPUS.   And what were you doing there?
MESSENGER.   Tending my flocks.
OEDIPUS.   A wandering shepherd?
MESSENGER.   But your savior, son, that day.   975
OEDIPUS.   From what did you save me?
MESSENGER.   Your ankles should tell you that.
OEDIPUS.   Ah, stranger, why do you speak of that childhood pain?
MESSENGER.   I pulled the skewer that pinned your feet together.
OEDIPUS.   I have had the mark as long as I can remember.
MESSENGER.   That was why you were given the name you bear.   980
OEDIPUS.   God! Was it my father or my mother who did it?
     Tell me!
MESSENGER.   I do not know. The man who gave you to me
     Can tell you better than I.
OEDIPUS.   It was not you that found me, but another?
MESSENGER.   It was another shepherd gave you to me.   985
OEDIPUS.   Who was he? Can you tell me who he was?
MESSENGER.   I think he was said to be one of Laïos's people.
OEDIPUS.   You mean the Laïos who was king here years ago?
MESSENGER.   Yes; King Laïos; and the man was one of his herdsmen.
OEDIPUS.   Is he still alive? Can I see him?
MESSENGER.   These men here   990
     Know best about such things.
OEDIPUS.   Does anyone here
     Know this shepherd that he is talking about?
     Have you seen him in the fields, or in the town?
     If you have, tell me. It is time things were made plain.

CHORAGOS.   I think the man he means is that same shepherd   995
    You have already asked to see. Iokastê perhaps
    Could tell you something.
OEDIPUS.   Do you know anything
    About him, Lady? Is he the man we have summoned?
    Is that the man this shepherd means?
IOKASTÊ.   Why think of him?
    Forget this herdsman. Forget it all.   1000
    This talk is a waste of time.
OEDIPUS.   How can you say that,
    When the clues to my true birth are in my hands?
IOKASTÊ.   For God's love, let us have no more questioning!
    Is your life nothing to you?
    My own is pain enough for me to bear.   1005
OEDIPUS.   You need not worry. Suppose my mother a slave,
    And born of slaves: no baseness can touch you.
IOKASTÊ.   Listen to me, I beg you: do not do this thing!
OEDIPUS.   I will not listen; the truth must be made known.
IOKASTÊ.   Everything that I say is for your own good!
OEDIPUS.   My own good 1010
    Snaps my patience, then; I want none of it.
IOKASTÊ.   You are fatally wrong! May you never learn who you are!
OEDIPUS.   Go, one of you, and bring the shepherd here.
    Let us leave this woman to brag of her royal name.
IOKASTÊ.   Ah, miserable!   1015
    That is the only word I have for you now.
    That is the only word I can ever have. (*Exit into the palace.*)
CHORAGOS.   Why has she left us, Oedipus? Why has she gone
    In such a passion of sorrow? I fear this silence:
    Something dreadful may come of it.
OEDIPUS.   Let it come!   1020
    However base my birth, I must know about it.
    The Queen, like a woman, is perhaps ashamed
    To think of my low origin. But I
    Am a child of Luck; I can not be dishonored.
    Luck is my mother; the passing months, my brothers,   1025
    Have seen me rich and poor.
                If this is so,
    How could I wish that I were someone else?
    How could I not be glad to know my birth?

ODE 3

STROPHE

CHORUS.   If ever the coming time were known
    To my heart's pondering,   1030
    Kithairon, now by Heaven I see the torches
    At the festival of the next full moon,
    And see the dance, and hear the choir sing
    A grace to your gentle shade:
    Mountain where Oedipus was found,   1035
    O mountain guard of a noble race!
    May the god° who heals us lend his aid,
    And let that glory come to pass
    For our king's cradling-ground.

ANTISTROPHE

    Of the nymphs that flower beyond the years,   1040
    Who bore you,° royal child,
    To Pan of the hills or the timberline Apollo,
    Cold in delight where the upland clears,
    Or Hermês for whom Kyllenê's heights° are piled?
    Or flushed as evening cloud,   1045
    Great Dionysis, roamer of mountains,
    He—was it he who found you there,
    And caught you up in his own proud
    Arms from the sweet god-ravisher
    Who laughed by the Muses' fountains?   1050

SCENE 4

OEDIPUS.   Sirs: though I do not know the man,
    I think I see him coming, this shepherd we want:
    He is old, like our friend here, and the men
    Bringing him seem to be servants of my house.
    But you can tell, if you have ever seen him.   1055
    (*Enter* SHEPHERD *escorted by* SERVANTS.)
CHORAGOS.   I know him, he was Laïos's man. You can trust him.

1037. god: Apollo   1041. Who bore you: The chorus is suggesting that perhaps
Oedipus is the son of one of the immortal nymphs and of a god—Pan, Apollo, Hermes, or
Dionysis. The "sweet god-ravisher" (line 1049) is the presumed mother.
1044. Kyllenê's heights: the mountain where Hermes was born

OEDIPUS.   Tell me first, you from Corinth: is this the shepherd
    We were discussing?
MESSENGER.   This is the very man.
OEDIPUS (*to* SHEPHERD).   Come here. No, look at me. You must answer
    Everything I ask.—You belonged to Laïos?   1060
SHEPHERD.   Yes: born his slave, brought up in his house.
OEDIPUS.   Tell me: what kind of work did you do for him?
SHEPHERD.   I was a shepherd of his, most of my life.
OEDIPUS.   Where mainly did you go for pasturage?
SHEPHERD.   Sometimes Kithairon, sometimes the hills near-by.   1065
OEDIPUS.   Do you remember ever seeing this man out there?
SHEPHERD.   What would he be doing there? This man?
OEDIPUS.   This man standing here. Have you ever seen him before?
SHEPHERD.   No. At least, not to my recollection.
MESSENGER.   And that is not strange, my lord. But I'll refresh   1070
    His memory: he must remember when we two
    Spent three whole seasons together, March to September,
    On Kithairon or thereabouts. He had two flocks;
    I had one. Each autumn I'd drive mine home
    And he would go back with his to Laïos's sheepfold.—   1075
    Is this not true, just as I have described it?
SHEPHERD.   True, yes; but it was all so long ago.
MESSENGER.   Well, then: do you remember, back in those days,
    That you gave me a baby boy to bring up as my own?
SHEPHERD.   What if I did? What are you trying to say?   1080
MESSENGER.   King Oedipus was once that little child.
SHEPHERD.   Damn you, hold your tongue!
OEDIPUS.   No more of that!
    It is your tongue needs watching, not this man's.
SHEPHERD.   My king, my master, what is it I have done wrong?
OEDIPUS.   You have not answered his question about the boy.   1085
SHEPHERD.   He does not know . . . He is only making trouble . . .
OEDIPUS.   Come, speak plainly, or it will go hard with you.
SHEPHERD.   In God's name, do not torture an old man!
OEDIPUS.   Come here, one of you; bind his arms behind him.
SHEPHERD.   Unhappy king! What more do you wish to learn?   1090
OEDIPUS.   Did you give this man the child he speaks of?
SHEPHERD.   I did.
    And I would to God I had died that very day.
OEDIPUS.   You will die now unless you speak the truth.

SHEPHERD.   Yet if I speak the truth, I am worse than dead.

OEDIPUS (*to* ATTENDANT).   He intends to draw it out, apparently—   1095

SHEPHERD.   No! I have told you already that I gave him the boy.

OEDIPUS.   Where did you get him? From your house? From somewhere
    else?

SHEPHERD.   Not from mine, no. A man gave him to me.

OEDIPUS.   Is that man here? Whose house did he belong to?

SHEPHERD.   For God's love, my king, do not ask me any more!   1100

OEDIPUS.   You are a dead man if I have to ask you again.

SHEPHERD.   Then . . . Then the child was from the palace of Laïos.

OEDIPUS.   A slave child? or a child of his own line?

SHEPHERD.   Ah, I am on the brink of dreadful speech!

OEDIPUS.   And I of dreadful hearing. Yet I must hear.   1105

SHEPHERD.   If you must be told, then . . .

They said it was Laïos's child;
But it is your wife who can tell you about that.

OEDIPUS.   My wife—Did she give it to you?

SHEPHERD.   My lord, she did.

OEDIPUS.   Do you know why?

SHEPHERD.   I was told to get rid of it.

OEDIPUS.   Oh heartless mother!

SHEPHERD.   But in dread of prophecies . . .   1110

OEDIPUS.   Tell me.

SHEPHERD.   It was said that the boy would kill his own father.

OEDIPUS.   Then why did you give him over to this old man?

SHEPHERD.   I pitied the baby, my king,
And I thought that this man would take him far away
To his own country.

He saved him—but for what a fate!   1115
For if you are what this man says you are,
No man living is more wretched than Oedipus.

OEDIPUS.   Ah God!
It was true!
All the prophecies!
—Now,
O Light, may I look on you for the last time!   1120
I, Oedipus,
Oedipus, damned in his birth, in his marriage damned,
Damned in the blood he shed with his own hand!

(*He rushes into the palace.*)

ODE 4

STROPHE 1

CHORUS.   Alas for the seed of men.
What measure shall I give these generations   1125
That breathe on the void and are void
And exist and do not exist?
Who bears more weight of joy
Than mass of sunlight shifting in images,
Or who shall make his thought stay on   1130
That down time drifts away?
Your splendor is all fallen.
O naked brow of wrath and tears,
O change of Oedipus!
I who saw your days call no man blest—   1135
Your great days like ghósts góne.

ANTISTROPHE 1

That mind was a strong bow.
Deep, how deep you drew it then, hard archer,
At a dim fearful range,
And brought dear glory down!   1140
You overcame the stranger°—
The virgin with her hooking lion claws—
And though death sang, stood like a tower
To make pale Thebes take heart.
Fortress against our sorrow!   1145
True king, giver of laws,
Majestic Oedipus!
No prince in Thebes had ever such renown,
No prince won such grace of power.

STROPHE 2

And now of all men ever known   1150
Most pitiful is this man's story:
His fortunes are most changed; his state
Fallen to a low slave's
Ground under bitter fate.

1141. **stranger:** the Sphinx

O Oedipus, most royal one!   1155
The great door° that expelled you to the light
Gave at night—ah, gave night to your glory:
As to the father, to the fathering son.
All understood too late.
How could that queen whom Laïos won,   1160
The garden that he harrowed at his height,
Be silent when that act was done?

ANTISTROPHE 2

But all eyes fail before time's eye,
All actions come to justice there.
Though never willed, though far down the deep past,   1165
Your bed, your dread sirings,
Are brought to book at last.
Child by Laïos doomed to die,
Then doomed to lose that fortunate little death,
Would God you never took breath in this air   1170
That with my wailing lips I take to cry:
For I weep the world's outcast.
I was blind, and now I can tell why:
Asleep, for you had given ease of breath
To Thebes, while the false years went by.   1175

EXODOS°

Enter, from the palace, SECOND MESSENGER.

SECOND MESSENGER.   Elders of Thebes, most honored in this land,
    What horrors are yours to see and hear, what weight
    Of sorrow to be endured, if, true to your birth,
    You venerate the line of Labdakos!
    I think neither Istros nor Phasis, those great rivers,   1180
    Could purify this place of all the evil
    It shelters now, or soon must bring to light—
    Evil not done unconsciously, but willed.

    The greatest griefs are those we cause ourselves.
CHORAGOS.   Surely, friend, we have grief enough already;   1185
    What new sorrow do you mean?
SECOND MESSENGER.   The queen is dead.

1156. door: Iokastê's womb **Exodos:** final scene

CHORAGOS.   O miserable queen! But at whose hand?
SECOND MESSENGER.   Her own.
  The full horror of what happened you can not know,
  For you did not see it; but I, who did, will tell you
  As clearly as I can how she met her death.   1190

  When she had left us,
  In passionate silence, passing through the court,
  She ran to her apartment in the house,
  Her hair clutched by the fingers of both hands.
  She closed the doors behind her; then, by that bed   1195
  Where long ago the fatal son was conceived—
  That son who should bring about his father's death—
  We heard her call upon Laïos, dead so many years,
  And heard her wail for the double fruit of her marriage,
  A husband by her husband, children by her child.   1200

  Exactly how she died I do not know:
  For Oedipus burst in moaning and would not let us
  Keep vigil to the end: it was by him
  As he stormed about the room that our eyes were caught.
  From one to another of us he went, begging a sword,   1205
  Hunting the wife who was not his wife, the mother
  Whose womb had carried his own children and himself.
  I do not know: it was none of us aided him,
  But surely one of the gods was in control!
  For with a dreadful cry   1210
  He hurled his weight, as though wrenched out of himself,
  At the twin doors: the bolts gave, and he rushed in.
  And there we saw her hanging, her body swaying
  From the cruel cord she had noosed about her neck.
  A great sob broke from him, heartbreaking to hear,   1215
  As he loosened the rope and lowered her to the ground.

  I would blot out from my mind what happened next!
  For the king ripped from her gown the golden brooches
  That were her ornament, and raised them, and plunged them down
  Straight into his own eyeballs, crying, "No more,   1220
  No more shall you look on the misery about me,
  The horrors of my own doing! Too long you have known
  The faces of those whom I should never have seen,
  Too long been blind to those for whom I was searching!

From this hour, go in darkness!" And as he spoke,   1225
He struck his eyes—not once, but many times;
And the blood spattered his beard,
Bursting from his ruined sockets like red hail.
So from the unhappiness of two this evil has sprung,
A curse on the man and woman alike. The old   1230
Happiness of the house of Labdakos
Was happiness enough: where is it today?
It is all wailing and ruin, disgrace, death—all
The misery of mankind that has a name—
And it is wholly and for ever theirs.   1235
CHORAGOS.   Is he in agony still? Is there no rest for him?
SECOND MESSENGER.   He is calling for someone to open the doors wide
So that all the children of Kadmos may look upon
His father's murderer, his mother's—no,
I can not say it!
                      And then he will leave Thebes,   1240
Self-exiled, in order that the curse
Which he himself pronounced may depart from the house.
He is weak, and there is none to lead him,
So terrible is his suffering.
                      But you will see:
Look, the doors are opening; in a moment   1245
You will see a thing that would crush a heart of stone.
(*The central door is opened;* OEDIPUS, *blinded, is led in.*)
CHORAGOS.   Dreadful indeed for me to see.
Never have my own eyes
Looked on a sight so full of fear.

Oedipus!   1250
What madness came upon you, what daemon
Leaped on your life with heavier
Punishment than a mortal man can bear?
No: I can not even
Look at you, poor ruined one.   1255
And I would speak, question, ponder,
If I were able. No.
You make me shudder.
OEDIPUS.   God. God.
Is there a sorrow greater?   1260
Where shall I find harbor in this world?

My voice is hurled far on a dark wind.
What has God done to me?
CHORAGOS.   Too terrible to think of, or to see.

STROPHE 1

OEDIPUS.   O cloud of night,   1265
    Never to be turned away: night coming on,
    I can not tell how: night like a shroud!
    My fair winds brought me here.
                                    O God. Again
    The pain of the spikes where I had sight,
    The flooding pain   1270
    Of memory, never to be gouged out.
CHORAGOS.   This is not strange.
    You suffer it all twice over, remorse in pain,
    Pain in remorse.

ANTISTROPHE 1

OEDIPUS.   Ah dear friend   1275
    Are you faithful even yet, you alone?
    Are you still standing near me, will you stay here,
    Patient, to care for the blind?
                                    The blind man!
    Yet even blind I know who it is attends me,
    By the voice's tone—   1280
    Though my new darkness hide the comforter.
CHORAGOS.   Oh fearful act!
    What god was it drove you to rake black
    Night across your eyes?

STROPHE 2

OEDIPUS.   Apollo. Apollo. Dear   1285
    Children, the god was Apollo.
    He brought my sick, sick fate upon me.
    But the blinding hand was my own!
    How could I bear to see
    When all my sight was horror everywhere?   1290
CHORAGOS.   Everywhere; that is true.
OEDIPUS.   And now what is left?
    Images? Love? A greeting even,

Sweet to the senses? Is there anything?
Ah, no, friends: lead me away.   1295
Lead me away from Thebes.
                                    Lead the great wreck
And hell of Oedipus, whom the gods hate.
CHORAGOS.   Your misery, you are not blind to that.
Would God you had never found it out!

ANTISTROPHE 2

OEDIPUS.   Death take the man who unbound   1300
    My feet on that hillside
    And delivered me from death to life! What life?
    If only I had died,
    This weight of monstrous doom
    Could not have dragged me and my darlings down.   1305
CHORAGOS.   I would have wished the same.
OEDIPUS.   Oh never to have come here
    With my father's blood upon me! Never
    To have been the man they call his mother's husband!
    Oh accurst! Oh child of evil,   1310
    To have entered that wretched bed—
                                    the selfsame one!
    More primal than sin itself, this fell to me.
CHORAGOS.   I do not know what words to offer you.
    You were better dead than alive and blind.
OEDIPUS.   Do not counsel me any more. This punishment   1315
    That I have laid upon myself is just.
    If I had eyes,
    I do not know how I could bear the sight
    Of my father, when I came to the house of Death,
    Or my mother: for I have sinned against them both   1320
    So vilely that I could not make my peace
    By strangling my own life.
                                    Or do you think my children,
    Born as they were born, would be sweet to my eyes?
    Ah never, never! Nor this town with its high walls,
    Nor the holy images of the gods.
                                    For I,   1325
    Thrice miserable!—Oedipus, noblest of all the line
    Of Kadmos, have condemned myself to enjoy
    These things no more, by my own malediction

Expelling that man whom the gods declared
To be a defilement in the house of Laïos.   1330
After exposing the rankness of my own guilt,
How could I look men frankly in the eyes?
No, I swear it.
If I could have stifled my hearing at its source,
I would have done it and made all this body   1335
A tight cell of misery, blank to light and sound:
So I should have been safe in my dark mind
Beyond external evil.
                    Ah Kithairon!
Why did you shelter me? When I was cast upon you,
Why did I not die? Then I should never   1340
Have shown the world my execrable birth.

Ah Polybos! Corinth, city that I believed
The ancient sea of my ancestors: how fair
I seemed, your child! And all the while this evil
Was cancerous within me!
                            For I am sick,   1345
In my own being, sick in my origin.

O three roads, dark ravine, woodland and way
Where three roads met: you, drinking my father's blood,
My own blood, spilled by my own hand: can you remember
The unspeakable things I did there, and the things   1350
I went on from there to do?
                            O marriage, marriage!
The act that engendered me, and again the act
Performed by the son in the same bed—
                            Ah, the net
Of incest, mingling fathers, brothers, sons,
With brides, wives, mothers: the last evil   1355
That can be known by men: no tongue can say
How evil!
            No. For the love of God, conceal me
Somewhere far from Thebes; or kill me; or hurl me
Into the sea, away from men's eyes for ever.

Come, lead me. You need not fear to touch me.   1360
    Of all men, I alone can bear this guilt. (*Enter* KREON.)
CHORAGOS.   Kreon is here now. As to what you ask,

He may decide the course to take. He only
Is left to protect the city in your place.
OEDIPUS.   Alas, how can I speak to him? What right have I   1365
To beg his courtesy whom I have deeply wronged?
KREON.   I have not come to mock you, Oedipus,
Or to reproach you, either.
            (*To* ATTENDANTS)   —You, standing there:
If you have lost all respect for man's dignity,
At least respect the flame of Lord Helios: 1370
Do not allow this pollution to show itself
Openly here, an affront to the earth
And Heaven's rain and the light of day. No, take him
Into the house as quickly as you can.
For it is proper   1375
That only the close kindred see his grief.
OEDIPUS.   I pray you in God's name, since your courtesy
Ignores my dark expectation, visiting
With mercy this man of all men most execrable:
Give me what I ask for—for your good, not for mine.   1380
KREON.   And what is it that you turn to me begging for?
OEDIPUS.   Drive me out of this country as quickly as may be
To a place where no human voice can ever greet me.
KREON.   I should have done that before now—only,
God's will had not been wholly revealed to me.   1385
OEDIPUS.   But his command is plain: the parricide
Must be destroyed. I am that evil man.
KREON.   That is the sense of it, yes; but as things are,
We had best discover clearly what is to be done.
OEDIPUS.   You would learn more about a man like me?   1390
KREON.   You are ready now to listen to the god.
OEDIPUS.   I will listen. But it is to you
That I must turn for help. I beg you, hear me.

The woman in there—
Give her whatever funeral you think proper: 1395
She is your sister.
                —But let me go, Kreon!
Let me purge my father's Thebes of the pollution
Of my living here, and go out to the wild hills,
To Kithairon, that has won such fame with me,
The tomb my mother and father appointed for me,   1400
And let me die there, as they willed I should.

And yet I know
Death will not ever come to me through sickness
Or in any natural way: I have been preserved
For some unthinkable fate. But let that be.   1405

As for my sons, you need not care for them.
They are men, they will find some way to live.
But my poor daughters, who have shared my table,
Who never before have been parted from their father—
Take care of them, Kreon; do this for me.   1410

And will you let me touch them with my hands
A last time, and let us weep together?
Be kind, my lord,
Great prince, be kind!
                    Could I but touch them,
They would be mine again, as when I had my eyes.   1415
(*Enter* ANTIGONE *and* ISMENE, *attended.*)
Ah, God!
Is it my dearest children I hear weeping?
Has Kreon pitied me and sent my daughters?
KREON.   Yes, Oedipus: I knew that they were dear to you
In the old days, and know you must love them still.   1420
OEDIPUS.   May God bless you for this—and be a friendlier
Guardian to you than he has been to me!

Children, where are you?
Come quickly to my hands: they are your brother's—
Hands that have brought your father's once clear eyes   1425
To this way of seeing—
                    Ah dearest ones,
I had neither sight nor knowledge then, your father
By the woman who was the source of his own life!
And I weep for you—having no strength to see you—
I weep for you when I think of the bitterness   1430
That men will visit upon you all your lives.
What homes, what festivals can you attend
Without being forced to depart again in tears?
And when you come to marriageable age,
Where is the man, my daughters, who would dare   1435
Risk the bane that lies on all my children?
Is there any evil wanting? Your father killed

His father; sowed the womb of her who bore him;
Engendered you at the fount of his own existence!
That is what they will say of you.

                            Then, whom   1440
Can you ever marry? There are no bridegrooms for you,
And your lives must wither away in sterile dreaming.
O Kreon, son of Menoikeus!
You are the only father my daughters have,
Since we, their parents, are both of us gone for ever.   1445
They are your own blood: you will not let them
Fall into beggary and loneliness;
You will keep them from the miseries that are mine!
Take pity on them; see, they are only children,
Friendless except for you. Promise me this,   1450
Great prince, and give me your hand in token of it.
(KREON *clasps his right hand.*)
Children:
I could say much, if you could understand me,
But as it is, I have only this prayer for you:
Live where you can, be as happy as you can—   1455
Happier, please God, than God has made your father.
KREON.   Enough. You have wept enough. Now go within.
OEDIPUS.   I must; but it is hard.
KREON.   Time eases all things.
OEDIPUS.   You know my mind, then?
KREON.   Say what you desire.
OEDIPUS.   Send me from Thebes!
KREON.   God grant that I may!   1460
OEDIPUS.   But since God hates me . . .
KREON.   No, he will grant your wish.
OEDIPUS.   You promise?
KREON.   I can not speak beyond my knowledge.
OEDIPUS.   Then lead me in.
KREON.   Come now, and leave your children.
OEDIPUS.   No! Do not take them from me!
KREON.   Think no longer
That you are in command here, but rather think   1465
How, when you were, you served your own destruction. (*Exeunt
into the house all but the* CHORUS; *the* CHORAGOS *chants directly to the
audience.*)
CHORAGOS.   Men of Thebes: look upon Oedipus.

This is the king who solved the famous riddle
And towered up, most powerful of men.
No mortal eyes but looked on him with envy,   1470
Yet in the end ruin swept over him.

Let every man in mankind's frailty
Consider his last day; and let none
Presume on his good fortune until he find
Life, at his death, a memory without pain.   1475

QUESTIONS

1. The oracles had prophesied that Oedipus would kill his father and beget children by his mother. Is Oedipus therefore *made* to do these things? Is the play premised on the notion that Oedipus is bound or free—the puppet of fate or the creator of his own fate? Or some of each?
2. Outline the actions presented on the stage: begin where the play begins, with the people turning to their king for relief from the plague, and disregard for the moment the revelation of incidents that preceded the play. Then summarize the antecedent actions as they are gradually revealed. In what ways are Oedipus's stage actions consistent with his prior actions? In what ways are they different? How do these two sets of actions reveal him to be a person of extraordinary stature?
3. What is Oedipus's primary motivation throughout the action of the play? What were his motives in actions prior to the play? What characters try to dissuade him from pursuing his purpose, and why do they do so? How do his subjects regard him?
4. Is any common pattern of behavior exhibited in Oedipus's encounters with Laïos, with Teiresias, and with Kreon? Is there any justification for his anger with Teiresias? For his suspicion of Kreon? Why?
5. Oedipus's original question, "Who killed Laïos?" soon turns into the question "Who am I?" On the level of plot, the answer is "Son of Laïos and Iokastê, father's murderer, mother's husband." What is the answer at the level of character—that is, in a psychological or philosophical sense?
6. What philosophical issues are raised by Iokastê's judgment on the oracles (Scene 2)? How does the chorus respond to her judgment? How does the play resolve these issues?
7. Why does Oedipus blind himself? Is this an act of weakness or of strength? Why does he ask Kreon to drive him from Thebes? Does he feel that his fate has been just or unjust? Is his suffering, in fact, deserved? Partially deserved? Undeserved?
8. There is a good deal in the play about seeing and blindness. What purpose does this serve? How is Oedipus contrasted with Teiresias? How does Oedipus at the beginning of the play contrast with Oedipus at the end? Why is his blinding himself dramatically appropriate?

9. In what sense may Oedipus be regarded as a better man, though a less fortunate one, at the end of the play than at the beginning? What has he gained from his experience?

10. Some critics have suggested that Oedipus's answer to the Sphinx's riddle was incomplete—that the answer should have been not just man but Oedipus himself—and that Oedipus was as ignorant of the whole truth here as he is when he lays his curse in Scene 1 on the murderer of Laïos. Does this suggestion make sense? On how many legs does Oedipus walk at the end of the play?

11. If the answer to the Sphinx's riddle is not just man but Oedipus himself, may the answer to Oedipus's question "Who am I?" pertain not only to Oedipus but also to man, or at least to civilized Western man? What characteristics of Oedipus as an individual are also characteristics of man in the Western world? Is Sophocles writing only about Oedipus the king, or is he saying something about man's presumed place and his real place in the universe?

12. What purposes are served by the appearance of Antigone and Ismene in the Exodos?

13. What purposes does the chorus serve in the play? Whom does it speak for? Comment on the function of each of the four Odes.

14. What does the final speech of the Choragos tell us about human life?

15. A central formal feature of the play is its use of dramatic irony. Point out speeches by Oedipus, especially in the Prologue and Scene 1, that have a different or a larger meaning for the audience than for Oedipus himself. Sophocles's title literally translates "Oedipus the Tyrant," but the word *tyrant* denoted a ruler who had earned his position through his own intelligence and strength rather than by inheritance—it was not a negative term. Given that, what ironies are suggested by Sophocles's title?

16. The plot of *Oedipus Rex* has been called one of the most perfect dramatic plots ever devised. Why is it admired? What are its outstanding characteristics?

William Shakespeare
Othello, the Moor of Venice

Characters

DUKE OF VENICE
BRABANTIO, *a Senator*
OTHER SENATORS
GRATIANO, *Brabantio's brother*
LODOVICO, *Brabantio's kinsman*
OTHELLO, *a noble Moor in the service of the Venetian state*
CASSIO, *his lieutenant*
IAGO, *his ensign*
MONTANO, *Othello's predecessor in the government of Cyprus*
RODERIGO, *a Venetian gentleman*
CLOWN, *Othello's servant*
DESDEMONA, *Brabantio's daughter and Othello's wife*
EMILIA, *Iago's wife*
BIANCA, *Cassio's mistress*
SAILOR, MESSENGER, HERALD, OFFICERS, GENTLEMEN, MUSICIANS, *and*
    ATTENDANTS

SCENE. *Venice, and a seaport in Cyprus*

OTHELLO, THE MOOR OF VENICE First performed in 1604. The general historical background of the action is probably sometime between 1470 and 1522, a period when Venice, an independent city-state headed by a duke (or doge) elected by the heads of the noble families, was the strongest sea power of the Christian world and included Cyprus and Rhodes among its dominions. Its chief rival for power in the Mediterranean was the Turkish or Ottomite empire. Venetian law required that the commander-in-chief of its forces be an alien, not a Venetian citizen, to prevent political ambition from interfering with his duties. Othello, a black African of royal blood and a soldier of great experience, fulfills the qualifications. The events and characters of the play are fictional, and in any case Shakespeare was not overly concerned with historical accuracy.

William Shakespeare (1564–1616) was born in Stratford-upon-Avon but went to London as a young man and made his fortune as an actor, playwright, and part-owner of the Globe Theatre. He did not supervise the publication of his plays, and the two earliest printings of *Othello*—the quarto of 1622 and the folio of 1623—differ in various ways. Modern editors must rely on judgment and scholarship in reconciling the two to arrive at their texts. The version presented here is that of G. B. Harrison, from *Shakespeare: The Complete Works* (New York: Harcourt, 1952). The editors of this book have selected some notes from Harrison's text and supplemented them with newly created notes.

ACT 1

SCENE 1. Venice. A street.

    Enter RODERIGO *and* IAGO.

RODERIGO.   Tush, never tell me! I take it much unkindly
   That thou, Iago, who hast had my purse
   As if the strings were thine, shouldst know of this.
IAGO.   'Sblood, but you will not hear me.
   If ever I did dream of such a matter,   5
   Abhor me.
RODERIGO.   Thou told'st me thou didst hold him in thy hate.
IAGO.   Despise me if I do not. Three great ones of the city,
   In personal suit to make me his Lieutenant,
   Off-capped to him. And, by the faith of man,   10
   I know my price, I am worth no worse a place.
   But he, as loving his own pride and purposes,
   Evades them, with a bombast circumstance
   Horribly stuffed with epithets of war.
   And, in conclusion,   15
   Nonsuits° my mediators, for, "Certes," says he,
   "I have already chose my officer."
   And what was he?
   Forsooth, a great arithmetician,°
   One Michael Cassio, a Florentine,   20
   A fellow almost damned in a fair wife,°
   That never set a squadron in the field,
   Nor the division of a battle knows
   More than a spinster, unless the bookish theoric,
   Wherein the toged Consuls° can propose   25
   As masterly as he—mere prattle without practice
   Is all his soldiership. But he, sir, had the election.
   And I, of whom his° eyes had seen the proof
   At Rhodes, at Cyprus, and on other grounds
   Christian and heathen, must be beleed° and calmed   30

---

16. Nonsuits: Rejects the petition of   **19. arithmetician:** Contemporary books on military tactics are full of elaborate diagrams and numerals to explain military formations. Cassio is a student of such books.   **21. almost . . . wife:** A much-disputed phrase. There is an Italian proverb, "You have married a fair wife? You are damned." If Iago has this in mind, he means by *almost* that Cassio is about to marry.   **25. toged Consuls:** senators in togas [Eds.]   **28. his:** Othello's [Eds.]   **30. beleed:** placed on the lee (or unfavorable) side

By debitor and creditor. This countercaster,°
He, in good time,° must his Lieutenant be,
And I—God bless the mark!—his Moorship's Ancient.°
RODERIGO.   By Heaven, I rather would have been his hangman.
IAGO.   Why, there's no remedy. 'Tis the curse of service,   35
    Preferment goes by letter and affection,
    And not by old gradation,° where each second
    Stood heir to the first. Now, sir, be judge yourself
    Whether I in any just term am affined°
    To love the Moor.
RODERIGO.   I would not follow him, then.   40
IAGO.   Oh, sir, content you,
    I follow him to serve my turn upon him.
    We cannot all be masters, nor all masters
    Cannot be truly followed. You shall mark
    Many a duteous and knee-crooking knave   45
    That doting on his own obsequious bondage
    Wears out his time, much like his master's ass,
    For naught but provender, and when he's old, cashiered.
    Whip me such honest knaves. Others there are
    Who, trimmed in forms and visages of duty,   50
    Keep yet their hearts attending on themselves,
    And throwing but shows of service on their lords
    Do well thrive by them, and when they have lined their coats
    Do themselves homage. These fellows have some soul,
    And such a one do I profess myself. For, sir,   55
    It is as sure as you are Roderigo,
    Were I the Moor, I would not be Iago.
    In following him, I follow but myself.
    Heaven is my judge, not I for love and duty,
    But seeming so, for my peculiar° end.   60
    For when my outward action doth demonstrate
    The native act and figure of my heart
    In compliment extern, 'tis not long after
    But I will wear my heart upon my sleeve
    For daws to peck at. I am not what I am.   65

31. **countercaster:** calculator (repeating the idea of arithmetician). Counters were used in making calculations.   32. **in good time:** a phrase expressing indignation
33. **Ancient:** Ensign, the third officer in the company of which Othello is Captain and Cassio Lieutenant   36–37. **Preferment . . . gradation:** Promotion comes through private recommendation and favoritism and not by order of seniority.   39. **affined:** tied by affection   60. **peculiar:** personal [Eds.]

RODERIGO.   What a full fortune does the thick-lips owe°
    If he can carry 't thus!°
IAGO.   Call up her father,
    Rouse him. Make after him, poison his delight,
    Proclaim him in the streets. Incense her kinsmen,
    And though he in a fertile climate dwell,   70
    Plague him with flies. Though that his joy be joy,
    Yet throw such changes of vexation on 't
    As it may lose some color.
RODERIGO.   Here is her father's house, I'll call aloud.
IAGO.   Do, with like timorous° accent and dire yell   75
    As when, by night and negligence, the fire
    Is spied in populous cities.
RODERIGO.   What ho, Brabantio! Signior Brabantio, ho!
IAGO.   Awake! What ho, Brabantio! Thieves! Thieves! Thieves!
    Look to your house, your daughter and your bags!°   80
    Thieves! Thieves! (BRABANTIO *appears above, at a window.*)
BRABANTIO.   What is the reason of this terrible summons?
    What is the matter there?
RODERIGO.   Signior, is all your family within?
IAGO.   Are your doors locked?
BRABANTIO.   Why, wherefore ask you this?   85
IAGO.   'Zounds, sir, you're robbed. For shame, put on your gown,
    Your heart is burst, you have lost half your soul.
    Even now, now, very now, an old black ram
    Is tupping your white ewe. Arise, arise,
    Awake the snorting° citizens with the bell,   90
    Or else the Devil° will make a grandsire of you.
                            Arise, I say.
BRABANTIO.   What, have you lost your wits?
RODERIGO.   Most reverend signior, do you know my voice?
BRABANTIO.   Not I. What are you?
RODERIGO.   My name is Roderigo.
BRABANTIO.   The worser welcome.   95
    I have charged thee not to haunt about my doors.
    In honest plainness thou hast heard me say
    My daughter is not for thee, and now, in madness,
    Being full of supper and distempering draughts,

---

66. owe: own   **67. carry 't thus:** i.e., bring off this marriage   **75. timorous:** terrifying
80. bags: moneybags   **90. snorting:** snoring   **91. Devil:** The Devil in old pictures and
woodcuts was represented as black.

Upon malicious bravery° dost thou come   100
To start° my quiet.

RODERIGO.   Sir, sir, sir—

BRABANTIO.   But thou must needs be sure
My spirit and my place have in them power
To make this bitter to thee.

RODERIGO.   Patience, good sir.

BRABANTIO.   What tell'st thou me of robbing? This is Venice,   105
My house is not a grange.°

RODERIGO.   Most grave Brabantio,
In simple and pure soul I come to you.

IAGO.   'Zounds, sir, you are one of those that will not serve God if the
Devil bid you. Because we come to do you service and you think we
are ruffians, you'll have your daughter covered with a Barbary°
horse, you'll have your nephews° neigh to you, you'll have coursers
for cousins,° and jennets° for germans.°   112

BRABANTIO.   What profane wretch art thou?

IAGO.   I am one, sir, that comes to tell you your daughter and the Moor
are now making the beast with two backs.   115

BRABANTIO.   Thou art a villain.

IAGO.   You are—a Senator.

BRABANTIO.   This thou shalt answer. I know thee, Roderigo.

RODERIGO.   Sir, I will answer anything. But I beseech you
If 't be your pleasure and most wise consent,
As partly I find it is, that your fair daughter,   120
At this odd-even° and dull watch o' the night,
Transported with no worse nor better guard
But with a knave of common hire, a gondolier,
To the gross clasps of a lascivious Moor—
If this be known to you, and your allowance,°   125
We then have done you bold and saucy wrongs.
But if you know not this, my manners tell me
We have your wrong rebuke. Do not believe
That, from the sense of all civility,°
I thus would play and trifle with your reverence.   130
Your daughter, if you have not given her leave,
I say again, hath made a gross revolt,

---

100. **bravery:** defiance   101. **start:** startle   106. **grange:** lonely farm   110. **Barbary:**
Moorish   111. **nephews:** grandsons   112. **cousins:** near relations   **jennets:** Moorish
ponies   **germans:** kinsmen   121. **odd-even:** about midnight   125. **your allowance:** by your
permission   129. **from . . . civility:** contrary to all decency [Eds.]

Tying her duty, beauty, wit, and fortunes
In an extravagant° and wheeling° stranger
Of here and everywhere. Straight satisfy yourself.   135
If she be in her chamber or your house,
Let loose on me the justice of the state
For thus deluding you.
BRABANTIO.   Strike on the tinder,° ho!
Give me a taper!° Call up all my people!
This accident is not unlike my dream.   140
Belief of it oppresses me already.
Light, I say! Light! (*Exit above.*)
IAGO.   Farewell, for I must leave you.
It seems not meet, nor wholesome to my place,°
To be produced—as if I stay I shall—
Against the Moor. For I do know the state,   145
However this may gall him with some check,
Cannot with safety cast° him. For he's embarked
With such loud reason to the Cyprus wars,
Which even now stand in act,° that, for their souls,
Another of his fathom they have none   150
To lead their business. In which regard,
Though I do hate him as I do Hell pains,
Yet for necessity of present life
I must show out a flag and sign of love,
Which is indeed but sign. That you shall surely find him,   155
Lead to the Sagittary° the raisèd search,
And there will I be with him. So farewell.
(*Exit* IAGO. *Enter, below,* BRABANTIO, *in his nightgown,*°
and SERVANTS *with torches.*)
BRABANTIO.   It is too true an evil. Gone she is,
And what's to come of my despisèd time
Is naught but bitterness. Now, Roderigo,   160
Where didst thou see her? Oh, unhappy girl!
With the Moor, say'st thou? Who would be a father!
How didst thou know 'twas she? Oh, she deceives me
Past thought! What said she to you? Get more tapers.
Raise all my kindred. Are they married, think you?   165

---

134. extravagant: vagabond   **wheeling:** wandering   **138. tinder:** the primitive method of
making fire, used before the invention of matches   **139. taper:** candle   **143. place:** i.e., as
Othello's officer   **147. cast:** dismiss from service   **149. stand in act:** are under way
[Eds.]   **156. Sagittary:** presumably some inn in Venice [Eds.]   **157. s.d. nightgown:**
dressing-gown [Eds.]

RODERIGO.   Truly, I think they are.

BRABANTIO.   Oh Heaven! How got she out? Oh, treason of the blood!
    Fathers, from hence trust not your daughters' minds
    By what you see them act. Are there not charms°
    By which the property° of youth and maidhood   170
    May be abused?° Have you not read, Roderigo,
    Of some such thing?

RODERIGO.   Yes, sir, I have indeed.

BRABANTIO.   Call up my brother.—Oh, would you had had her!—
    Some one way, some another.—Do you know
    Where we may apprehend her and the Moor?   175

RODERIGO.   I think I can discover him, if you please
    To get good guard and go along with me.

BRABANTIO.   Pray you, lead on. At every house I'll call,
    I may command° at most. Get weapons, ho!
    And raise some special officers of night.   180
    On, good Roderigo, I'll deserve your pains.° (*Exeunt.*)

SCENE 2. *Another street.*

Enter OTHELLO, IAGO, *and* ATTENDANTS *with torches.*

IAGO.   Though in the trade of war I have slain men,
    Yet do I hold it very stuff o' the conscience
    To do no contrivèd murder. I lack iniquity
    Sometimes to do me service. Nine or ten times
    I had thought to have yerked him° here under the ribs.   5

OTHELLO.   'Tis better as it is.

IAGO.   Nay, but he prated
    And spoke such scurvy and provoking terms
    Against your honor
    That, with the little godliness I have,
    I did full hard forbear him. But I pray you, sir,   10
    Are you fast married? Be assured of this,
    That the Magnifico is much beloved,
    And hath in his effect a voice potential
    As double as° the Duke's. He will divorce you,
    Or put upon you what restraint and grievance   15
    The law, with all his might to enforce it on,

---

169. charms: magic spells   **170. property:** nature   **171. abused:** deceived
179. command: find supporters   **181. deserve your pains:** reward your labor
5. yerked him: stabbed Brabantio [Eds.]   **13–14. potential . . . as:** twice as powerful as

Will give him cable.
OTHELLO.   Let him do his spite.
My services which I have done the signiory°
Shall out-tongue his complaints. 'Tis yet to know°—
Which, when I know that boasting is an honor,   20
I shall promulgate—I fetch my life and being
From men of royal siege,° and my demerits°
May speak unbonneted to as proud a fortune
As this that I have reached. For know, Iago,
But that I love the gentle Desdemona,   25
I would not my unhousèd° free condition
Put into circumscription and confine
For the sea's worth. But look! What lights come yond?
IAGO.   Those are the raisèd father and his friends.
You were best go in.
OTHELLO.   Not I, I must be found.   30
My parts, my title, and my perfect soul°
Shall manifest me rightly. Is it they?
IAGO.   By Janus, I think no.
    (*Enter* CASSIO, *and certain* OFFICERS *with torches.*)
OTHELLO.   The servants of the Duke, and my Lieutenant.
The goodness of the night upon you, friends!   35
What is the news?
CASSIO.   The Duke does greet you, General,
And he requires your haste-posthaste appearance,
Even on the instant.
OTHELLO.   What is the matter, think you?
CASSIO.   Something from Cyprus, as I may divine.
It is a business of some heat. The galleys   40
Have sent a dozen sequent messengers
This very night at one another's heels,
And many of the consuls, raised and met,
Are at the Duke's already. You have been hotly called for
When, being not at your lodging to be found,   45
The Senate hath sent about three several° quests
To search you out.
OTHELLO.   'Tis well I am found by you.
I will but spend a word here in the house

18. signiory: state of Venice   19. yet to know: not widely known [Eds.]   22. siege: rank
[Eds.]   demerits: deserts   26. unhousèd: unmarried   31. perfect soul: clear conscience
[Eds.]   46. several: separate

And go with you. (*Exit.*)

CASSIO.   Ancient, what makes he here?

IAGO.   Faith, he tonight hath boarded a land carrack.°   50
    If it prove lawful prize, he's made forever.

CASSIO.   I do not understand.

IAGO.   He's married.

CASSIO.   To who? (*Re-enter* OTHELLO.)

IAGO.   Marry,° to—Come, Captain, will you go?

OTHELLO.   Have with you.

CASSIO.   Here comes another troop to seek for you.

IAGO.   It is Brabantio. General, be advised,   55
    He comes to bad intent.
    (*Enter* BRABANTIO, RODERIGO, *and* OFFICERS *with torches*
        and weapons.)

OTHELLO.   Holloa! Stand there!

RODERIGO.   Signior, it is the Moor.

BRABANTIO.   Down with him, thief!
    (*They draw on both sides.*)

IAGO.   You, Roderigo! Come, sir, I am for you.

OTHELLO.   Keep up° your bright swords, for the dew will rust them.
    Good signior, you shall more command with years   60
    Than with your weapons.

BRABANTIO.   O thou foul thief, where hast thou stowed my
        daughter?
    Damned as thou art, thou hast enchanted her.
    For I'll refer me to all things of sense
    If she in chains of magic were not bound,   65
    Whether a maid so tender, fair, and happy,
    So opposite to marriage that she shunned
    The wealthy curlèd darlings of our nation,
    Would ever have, to incur a general mock,
    Run from her guardage° to the sooty bosom   70
    Of such a thing as thou, to fear, not to delight.
    Judge me the world if 'tis not gross in sense°
    That thou hast practiced on her with foul charms,
    Abused her delicate youth with drugs or minerals
    That weaken motion.° I'll have 't disputed on,°   75
    'Tis probable, and palpable to thinking.

---

50. carrack: large merchant ship   **53. Marry:** a mild oath [Eds.]
59. Keep up: Sheathe   **70. guardage:** guardianship   **72. gross in sense:** obvious [Eds.]
75. motion: sense   **disputed on:** argued in the law courts [Eds.]

I therefore apprehend and do attach° thee
For an abuser of the world, a practicer
Of arts inhibited and out of warrant.°
Lay hold upon him. If he do resist,   80
Subdue him at his peril.

OTHELLO.   Hold your hands,
Both you of my inclining and the rest.
Were it my cue to fight, I should have known it
Without a prompter. Where will you that I go
To answer this your charge?

BRABANTIO.   To prison, till fit time   85
Of law and course of direct session
Call thee to answer.

OTHELLO.   What if I do obey?
How may the Duke be therewith satisfied,
Whose messengers are here about my side
Upon some present business of the state   90
To bring me to him?

FIRST OFFICER.   'Tis true, most worthy signior.
The Duke's in council, and your noble self
I am sure is sent for.

BRABANTIO.   How? The Duke in council?
In this time of the night? Bring him away.
Mine's not an idle cause. The Duke himself,   95
Or any of my brothers of the state,
Cannot but feel this wrong as 'twere their own.
For if such actions may have passage free,
Bondslaves and pagans shall our statesmen be. (*Exeunt.*)

SCENE 3. *A council chamber.*

The DUKE *and* SENATORS *sitting at a table,* OFFICERS *attending.*

DUKE.   There is no composition° in these news°
That gives them credit.

FIRST SENATOR.   Indeed they are disproportioned.
My letters say a hundred and seven galleys.

DUKE.   And mine, a hundred and forty.

SECOND SENATOR.   And mine, two hundred.
But though they jump not on a just account°—   5

---

77. **attach:** arrest   79. **inhibited . . . warrant:** forbidden and illegal [Eds.]   1. **composition:**
agreement   **news:** reports   5. **jump . . . account:** do not agree with an exact estimate

As in these cases, where the aim reports,°
'Tis oft with difference—yet do they all confirm
A Turkish fleet, and bearing up to Cyprus.
DUKE.   Nay, it is possible enough to judgment.
I do not so secure me in the error,°   10
But the main article° I do approve
In fearful° sense.
SAILOR (*within*).   What ho! What ho! What ho!
FIRST OFFICER.   A messenger from the galleys. (*Enter* SAILOR.)
DUKE.   Now, what's the business?
SAILOR.   The Turkish preparation makes for Rhodes.
So was I bid report here to the state   15
By Signior Angelo.
DUKE.   How say you by this charge?
FIRST SENATOR.   This cannot be,
By no assay of reason. 'Tis a pageant
To keep us in false gaze. When we consider
The importancy of Cyprus to the Turk,   20
And let ourselves again but understand
That as it more concerns the Turk than Rhodes,
So may he with more facile question bear it,°
For that it stands not in such warlike brace
But altogether lacks the abilities   25
That Rhodes is dressed in—if we make thought of this,
We must not think the Turk is so unskillful
To leave that latest which concerns him first,
Neglecting an attempt of ease and gain
To wake and wage a danger profitless.   30
DUKE.   Nay, in all confidence, he's not for Rhodes.
FIRST OFFICER.   Here is more news. (*Enter a* MESSENGER.)
MESSENGER.   The Ottomites,° Reverend and Gracious,
Steering with due course toward the isle of Rhodes,
Have there injointed° them with an after-fleet.°   35
FIRST SENATOR.   Aye, so I thought. How many, as you guess?
MESSENGER.   Of thirty sail. And now they do restem°
Their backward course, bearing with frank appearance
Their purposes toward Cyprus. Signior Montano,

---

6. aim reports: i.e., intelligence reports of an enemy's intention often differ in the
details   **10. I . . . error:** I do not consider myself free from danger, because the reports may
not all be accurate.   **11. main article:** general report   **12. fearful:** to be feared
23. with . . . it: take it more easily   **33. Ottomites:** Turks   **35. injointed:** joined
after-fleet: second fleet   **37. restem:** steer again

Your trusty and most valiant servitor,   40
With his free duty recommends° you thus,
And prays you to believe him.
DUKE.   'Tis certain then for Cyprus.
Marcus Luccicos, is not he in town?
FIRST SENATOR.   He's now in Florence.   45
DUKE.   Write from us to him, post-posthaste dispatch.
FIRST SENATOR.   Here comes Brabantio and the valiant Moor.
    (*Enter* BRABANTIO, OTHELLO, IAGO, RODERIGO, *and* OFFICERS.)
DUKE.   Valiant Othello, we must straight employ you
    Against the general enemy Ottoman.
    (*To* BRABANTIO) I did not see you. Welcome, gentle signior,   50
    We lacked your counsel and your help tonight.
BRABANTIO.   So did I yours. Good your Grace, pardon me,
    Neither my place nor aught I heard of business
    Hath raised me from my bed, nor doth the general care
    Take hold on me. For my particular° grief   55
    Is of so floodgate and o'erbearing nature
    That it engluts and swallows other sorrows,
    And it is still itself.
DUKE.   Why, what's the matter?
BRABANTIO.   My daughter! Oh, my daughter!
ALL.   Dead?
BRABANTIO.   Aye, to me.
    She is abused, stol'n from me and corrupted   60
    By spells and medicines bought of mountebanks.
    For nature so preposterously to err,
    Being not deficient, blind, or lame of sense,
    Sans° witchcraft could not.
DUKE.   Whoe'er he be that in this foul proceeding   65
    Hath thus beguiled your daughter of herself
    And you of her, the bloody book of law
    You shall yourself read in the bitter letter
    After your own sense—yea, though our proper° son
    Stood in your action.
BRABANTIO.   Humbly I thank your Grace.   70
    Here is the man, this Moor, whom now, it seems,
    Your special mandate for the state affairs
    Hath hither brought.

41. recommends: advises [Eds.]   **55. particular:** personal   **64. Sans:** Without
69. proper: own

ALL.   We are very sorry for 't.
DUKE (*to* OTHELLO).   What in your own part can you say to this?
BRABANTIO.   Nothing but this is so.   75
OTHELLO.   Most potent, grave, and reverend signiors,
    My very noble and approved good masters,
    That I have ta'en away this old man's daughter,
    It is most true—true, I have married her.
    The very head and front of my offending   80
    Hath this extent, no more. Rude am I in my speech,
    And little blest with the soft phrase of peace,
    For since these arms of mine had seven years' pith
    Till now some nine moons wasted, they have used
    Their dearest action in the tented field;   85
    And little of this great world can I speak,
    More than pertains to feats of broil and battle,
    And therefore little shall I grace my cause
    In speaking for myself. Yet, by your gracious patience,
    I will a round unvarnished tale° deliver   90
    Of my whole course of love—what drugs, what charms,
    What conjuration and what mighty magic—
    For such proceeding I am charged withal—
    I won his daughter.
BRABANTIO.   A maiden never bold,
    Of spirit so still and quiet that her motion   95
    Blushed at herself, and she—in spite of nature,
    Of years, of country, credit,° everything—
    To fall in love with what she feared to look on!
    It is a judgment maimed and most imperfect
    That will confess perfection so could err   100
    Against all rules of nature, and must be driven
    To find out practices of cunning Hell
    Why this should be. I therefore vouch again
    That with some mixtures powerful o'er the blood,
    Or with some dram conjured to this effect,   105
    He wrought upon her.
DUKE.   To vouch this is no proof
    Without more certain and more overt test
    Than these thin habits and poor likelihoods
    Of modern seeming° do prefer against him.

___

90. round . . . tale: direct, unadorned account   **97. credit:** reputation
108–9. thin . . . seeming: superficial, unlikely, and trivial suppositions [Eds.]

FIRST SENATOR.   But, Othello, speak.   110
    Did you by indirect and forcèd courses
    Subdue and poison this young maid's affections?
    Or came it by request, and such fair question
    As soul to soul affordeth?
OTHELLO.   I do beseech you
    Send for the lady to the Sagittary,   115
    And let her speak of me before her father.
    If you do find me foul in her report,
    The trust, the office I do hold of you,
    Not only take away, but let your sentence
    Even fall upon my life.
DUKE.   Fetch Desdemona hither.   120
OTHELLO.   Ancient, conduct them, you best know the place.
    (*Exeunt* IAGO *and* ATTENDANTS.)
    And till she come, as truly as to Heaven
    I do confess the vices of my blood,
    So justly to your grave ears I'll present
    How I did thrive in this fair lady's love   125
    And she in mine.
DUKE.   Say it, Othello.
OTHELLO.   Her father loved me, oft invited me,
    Still° questioned me the story of my life
    From year to year, the battles, sieges, fortunes,
    That I have passed.   130
    I ran it through, even from my boyish days
    To the very moment that he bade me tell it.
    Wherein I spake of most disastrous chances,
    Of moving accidents by flood and field,
    Of hairbreadth 'scapes i' the imminent deadly breach,   135
    Of being taken by the insolent foe
    And sold to slavery, of my redemption thence,
    And portance in my travels' history.
    Wherein of antres° vast and deserts idle,
    Rough quarries, rocks, and hills whose heads touch heaven,   140
    It was my hint to speak—such was the process.
    And of the cannibals that each other eat,
    The anthropophagi,° and men whose heads
    Do grow beneath their shoulders. This to hear
    Would Desdemona seriously incline.   145

128. Still: Always   **139. antres:** caves   **143. anthropophagi:** cannibals

But still the house affairs would draw her thence,
Which ever as she could with haste dispatch,
She'd come again, and with a greedy ear
Devour up my discourse. Which I observing,
Took once a pliant hour and found good means   150
To draw from her a prayer of earnest heart
That I would all my pilgrimage dilate,
Whereof by parcels she had something heard,
But not intentively. I did consent,
And often did beguile her of her tears   155
When I did speak of some distressful stroke
That my youth suffered. My story being done,
She gave me for my pains a world of sighs.
She swore, in faith, 'twas strange, 'twas passing strange,
'Twas pitiful, 'twas wondrous pitiful.   160
She wished she had not heard it, yet she wished
That Heaven had made her such a man. She thanked me,
And bade me, if I had a friend that loved her,
I should but teach him how to tell my story
And that would woo her. Upon this hint° I spake.   165
She loved me for the dangers I had passed,
And I loved her that she did pity them.
This only is the witchcraft I have used.
Here comes the lady, let her witness it.
(*Enter* DESDEMONA, IAGO, *and* ATTENDANTS.)
DUKE.   I think this tale would win my daughter too.   170
Good Brabantio,
Take up this mangled matter at the best.°
Men do their broken weapons rather use
Than their bare hands.
BRABANTIO.   I pray you hear her speak.
If she confess that she was half the wooer,   175
Destruction on my head if my bad blame
Light on the man! Come hither, gentle mistress.
Do you perceive in all this noble company
Where most you owe obedience?
DESDEMONA.   My noble father,
I do perceive here a divided duty.   180
To you I am bound for life and education,

---

165. hint: opportunity [Eds.]   **172. Take . . . best:** Make the best settlement you can of this
confused business.

My life and education both do learn me
How to respect you; you are the lord of duty,
I am hitherto your daughter. But here's my husband,
And so much duty as my mother showed   185
To you, preferring you before her father,
So much I challenge that I may profess
Due to the Moor my lord.

BRABANTIO.   God be with you! I have done.
Please it your Grace, on to the state affairs.
I had rather to adopt a child than get° it.   190
Come hither, Moor.
I here do give thee that with all my heart
Which, but thou hast already, with all my heart
I would keep from thee. For your sake, jewel,
I am glad at soul I have no other child,   195
For thy escape would teach me tyranny,
To hang clogs on them. I have done, my lord.

DUKE.   Let me speak like yourself, and lay a sentence°
Which, as a grise° or step, may help these lovers
Into your favor.   200
When remedies are past, the griefs are ended
By seeing the worst, which late on hopes depended.
To mourn a mischief that is past and gone
Is the next way to draw new mischief on.
What cannot be preserved when fortune takes,   205
Patience her injury a mockery makes.
The robbed that smiles steals something from the thief.
He robs himself that spends a bootless grief.

BRABANTIO.   So let the Turk of Cyprus us beguile,
We lose it not so long as we can smile.   210
He bears the sentence well that nothing bears
But the free comfort which from thence he hears.
But he bears both the sentence and the sorrow
That, to pay grief, must of poor patience borrow.
These sentences, to sugar or to gall,   215
Being strong on both sides, are equivocal.
But words are words. I never yet did hear
That the bruised heart was piercèd through the ear.
I humbly beseech you, proceed to the affairs of state.

---

190 get: beget   **198. sentence:** proverbial saying   **199. grise:** degree

DUKE.   The Turk with a most mightly preparation makes for Cyprus.
     Othello, the fortitude of the place is best known to you, and though
     we have there a substitute° of most allowed sufficiency, yet opinion,
     a sovereign mistress of effects, throws a more safer voice on you. You
     must therefore be content to slubber° the gloss of your new fortunes
     with this more stubborn and boisterous expedition.   225
OTHELLO.   The tyrant custom, most grave Senators,
     Hath made the flinty and steel couch of war
     My thrice-driven bed of down. I do agnize°
     A natural and prompt alacrity
     I find in hardness,° and do undertake   230
     These present wars against the Ottomites.
     Most humbly therefore bending to your state,
     I crave fit disposition for my wife,
     Due reference of place and exhibition,°
     With such accommodation and besort°   235
     As levels with her breeding.
DUKE.   If you please,
     Be 't at her father's.
BRABANTIO.   I'll not have it so.
OTHELLO.   Nor I.
DESDEMONA.   Nor I. I would not there reside,
     To put my father in impatient thoughts
     By being in his eye. Most gracious Duke,   240
     To my unfolding lend your prosperous° ear,
     And let me find a charter in your voice
     To assist my simpleness.
DUKE.   What would you, Desdemona?
DESDEMONA.   That I did love the Moor to live with him,   245
     My downright violence and storm of fortunes
     May trumpet to the world. My heart's subdued
     Even to the very quality° of my lord.
     I saw Othello's visage in his mind,
     And to his honors and his valiant parts°   250
     Did I my soul and fortunes consecrate.
     So that, dear lords, if I be left behind,
     A moth of peace, and he go to the war,
     The rites for which I love him are bereft me,

222. substitute: deputy commander   224. slubber: tarnish   228. agnize: confess
230. hardness: hardship   234. exhibition: allowance   235. besort: attendants
241. prosperous: favorable   248. quality: profession   250. parts: qualities

And I a heavy interim shall support   255
    By his dear absence. Let me go with him.
OTHELLO.   Let her have your voices.
    Vouch with me, Heaven, I therefore beg it not
    To please the palate of my appetite,
    Nor to comply with heat—the young affects   260
    In me defunct°—and proper satisfaction,
    But to be free and bounteous to her mind.°
    And Heaven defend your good souls, that you think
    I will your serious and great business scant
    For she is with me. No, when light-winged toys   265
    Of feathered Cupid seel° with wanton dullness
    My speculative and officed instruments,°
    That my disports° corrupt and taint my business,
    Let housewives make a skillet of my helm,
    And all indign° and base adversities   270
    Make head against my estimation!°
DUKE.   Be it as you shall privately determine,
    Either for her stay or going. The affair cries haste,
    And speed must answer 't. You must hence tonight.
DESDEMONA.   Tonight, my lord?
DUKE.   This night.
OTHELLO.   With all my heart.   275
DUKE.   At nine i' the morning here we'll meet again.
    Othello, leave some officer behind,
    And he shall our commission bring to you,
    With such things else of quality and respect
    As doth import you.
OTHELLO.   So please your Grace, my Ancient,   280
    A man he is of honesty and trust.
    To his conveyance I assign my wife,
    With what else needful your good Grace shall think
    To be sent after me.
DUKE.   Let it be so.
    Good night to everyone. (*To* BRABANTIO) And, noble signior, 285
    If virtue no delighted beauty lack,

260–61. young . . . defunct: in me the passion of youth is dead   262. to . . . mind: Othello
repeats Desdemona's claim that this is a marriage of minds.   266. seel: close up
267. speculative . . . instruments: powers of sight and action; i.e., my efficiency as your
general   268. disports: amusements   270. indign: unworthy   271. estimation: reputation

Your son-in-law is far more fair than black.°
FIRST SENATOR.   Adieu, brave Moor. Use Desdemona well.
BRABANTIO.   Look to her, Moor, if thou hast eyes to see.
　　She has deceived her father, and may thee.　　　　　　　　290
　　(*Exeunt* DUKE, SENATORS, OFFICERS, *etc.*)
OTHELLO.   My life upon her faith! Honest Iago,
　　My Desdemona must I leave to thee.
　　I prithee, let thy wife attend on her,
　　And bring them after in the best advantage.
　　Come, Desdemona, I have but an hour　　　　　　　　295
　　Of love, of worldly matters and direction,
　　To spend with thee. We must obey the time.
　　(*Exeunt* OTHELLO *and* DESDEMONA.)
RODERIGO.   Iago!
IAGO.   What sayest thou, noble heart?
RODERIGO.   What will I do, thinkest thou?　　　　　　　　300
IAGO.   Why, go to bed and sleep.
RODERIGO.   I will incontinently° drown myself.
IAGO.   If thou dost, I shall never love thee after. Why, thou silly
　　gentleman!
RODERIGO.   It is silliness to live when to live is torment, and then have
　　we a prescription to die when death is our physician.　　　306
IAGO.   Oh, villainous! I have looked upon the world for four times
　　seven years, and since I could distinguish betwixt a benefit and an
　　injury I never found man that knew how to love himself. Ere I
　　would say I would drown myself for the love of a guinea hen, I
　　would change my humanity with a baboon.　　　　　　　　311
RODERIGO.   What should I do? I confess it is my shame to be so fond,
　　but it is not in my virtue° to amend it.
IAGO.   Virtue! A fig! 'Tis in ourselves that we are thus or thus. Our
　　bodies are gardens, to the which our wills are gardeners. So that if
　　we will plant nettles or sow lettuce, set hyssop and weed up thyme,
　　supply it with one gender of herbs or distract it with many, either to
　　have it sterile with idleness or manured with industry—why, the
　　power and corrigible° authority of this lies in our wills. If the bal-
　　ance of our lives had not one scale of reason to poise another of
　　sensuality, the blood and baseness of our natures would conduct us

---

286–87. If . . . black: If worthiness is a beautiful thing in itself, your son-in-law, though
black, has beauty.   **302. incontinently:** immediately   **313. virtue:** strength [Eds.]
319. corrigible: correcting, directing

to most preposterous conclusions. But we have reason to cool our raging motions, our carnal stings, our unbitted lusts, whereof I take this that you call love to be a sect or scion.°

RODERIGO.   It cannot be.   325

IAGO.   It is merely a lust of the blood and a permission of the will. Come, be a man! Drown thyself? Drown cats and blind puppies! I have professed me thy friend, and I confess me knit to thy deserving with cables of perdurable toughness. I could never better stead thee than now. Put money in thy purse, follow thou the wars, defeat thy favor with an usurped beard°—I say put money in thy purse. It cannot be that Desdemona should long continue her love to the Moor—put money in thy purse—nor he his to her. It was a violent commencement, and thou shalt see an answerable sequestration°—put but money in thy purse. These Moors are changeable in their wills.°—Fill thy purse with money. The food that to him now is as luscious as locusts shall be to him shortly as bitter as coloquintida.° She must change for youth. When she is sated with his body, she will find the error of her choice. She must have change, she must—therefore put money in thy purse. If thou wilt needs damn thyself, do it a more delicate way than drowning. Make all the money thou canst.° If sanctimony and a frail vow betwixt an erring° barbarian and a supersubtle Venetian be not too hard for my wits and all the tribe of Hell, thou shalt enjoy her— therefore make money. A pox of drowning thyself! It is clean out of the way. Seek thou rather to be hanged in compassing thy joy than to be drowned and go without her.   347

RODERIGO.   Wilt thou be fast to my hopes if I depend on the issue?

IAGO.   Thou art sure of me. Go, make money. I have told thee often, and I retell thee again and again, I hate the Moor. My cause is hearted,° thine hath no less reason. Let us be conjunctive in our revenge against him. If thou canst cuckold him thou dost thyself a pleasure, me a sport. There are many events in the womb of time which will be delivered. Traverse, go, provide thy money. We will have more of this tomorrow. Adieu.   355

RODERIGO.   Where shall we meet i' the morning?

IAGO.   At my lodging.

RODERIGO.   I'll be with thee betimes.

---

324. **sect or scion:** Both words mean a slip taken from a tree and planted to produce a new growth.   330–31. **defeat . . . beard:** disguise your face by growing a beard
334–35. **answerable sequestration:** corresponding separation; i.e., reaction
336. **wills:** desires [Eds.]   338. **coloquintida:** a bitter purgative [Eds.]   342. **Make . . . canst:** Turn all you can into ready cash.   343. **erring:** vagabond   351. **hearted:** heartfelt

IAGO.   Go to, farewell. Do you hear, Roderigo?
RODERIGO.   What say you?   360
IAGO.   No more of drowning, do you hear?
RODERIGO.   I am changed. I'll go sell all my land. (*Exit*.)
IAGO.   Thus do I ever make my fool my purse,
    For I mine own gained knowledge should profane
    If I would time expend with such a snipe   365
    But for my sport and profit. I hate the Moor,
    And it is thought abroad that 'twixt my sheets
    He's done my office. I know not if 't be true,
    But I for mere suspicion in that kind
    Will do as if for surety. He holds me well,   370
    The better shall my purpose work on him.
    Cassio's a proper° man. Let me see now,
    To get his place, and to plume up° my will
    In double knavery—How, how?—Let's see.—
    After some time, to abuse Othello's ear   375
    That he is too familiar with his wife.
    He hath a person and a smooth dispose
    To be suspected,° framed to make women false.
    The Moor is of a free and open nature
    That thinks men honest that but seem to be so,   380
    And will as tenderly be led by the nose
    As asses are.
    I have't. It is engendered. Hell and night
    Must bring this monstrous birth to the world's light. (*Exit*.)

ACT 2

SCENE 1. A seaport in Cyprus. An open place near the wharf.

Enter MONTANO *and two* GENTLEMEN.
MONTANO.   What from the cape can you discern at sea?
FIRST GENTLEMAN.   Nothing at all. It is a high-wrought flood.
    I cannot 'twixt the heaven and the main
    Descry a sail.
MONTANO.   Methinks the wind hath spoke aloud at land,   5
    A fuller blast ne'er shook our battlements.
    If it hath ruffianed so upon the sea,
    What ribs of oak, when mountains melt on them,

---

372. proper: handsome   **373. plume up:** glorify   **377–78. He . . . suspected:** He has an
easy way about him that is naturally suspected.

Can hold the mortise? What shall we hear of this?
SECOND GENTLEMAN.   A segregation° of the Turkish fleet.   10
  For do but stand upon the foaming shore,
  The chidden billow seems to pelt the clouds,
  The wind-shaked surge, with high and monstrous mane,
  Seems to cast water on the burning Bear,
  And quench the guards of the ever-fixèd Pole.°   15
  I never did like molestation view
  On the enchafèd flood.
MONTANO.   If that the Turkish fleet
  Be not ensheltered and embayed, they are drowned.
  It is impossible to bear it out. (*Enter a* THIRD GENTLEMAN.)
THIRD GENTLEMAN.   News, lads! Our wars are done.   20
  The desperate tempest hath so banged the Turks
  That their designment halts. A noble ship of Venice
  Hath seen a grievous wreck and sufferance°
  On most part of their fleet.
MONTANO.   How! Is this true?
THIRD GENTLEMAN.   The ship is here put in,   25
  A Veronesa. Michael Cassio,
  Lieutenant to the warlike Moor Othello,
  Is come on shore, the Moor himself at sea,
  And is in full commission here for Cyprus.
MONTANO.   I am glad on 't. 'Tis a worthy governor.   30
THIRD GENTLEMAN.   But this same Cassio, though he speak of comfort
  Touching the Turkish loss, yet he looks sadly
  And prays the Moor be safe, for they were parted
  With foul and violent tempest.
MONTANO.   Pray Heavens he be,
  For I have served him, and the man commands   35
  Like a full soldier. Let's to the seaside, ho!
  As well to see the vessel that's come in
  As to throw out our eyes for brave Othello,
  Even till we make the main and the aerial blue
  An indistinct regard.
THIRD GENTLEMAN.   Come, let's do so.   40
  For every minute is expectancy
  Of more arrivance. (*Enter* CASSIO.)
CASSIO.   Thanks, you the valiant of this warlike isle

---

10. segregation: separation   **14–15. cast . . . Pole:** drown the constellations [Eds.]
23. sufferance: damage

That so approve the Moor! Oh, let the heavens
Give him defense against the elements,   45
For I have lost him on a dangerous sea.
MONTANO.   Is he well shipped?
CASSIO.   His bark is stoutly timbered, and his pilot
Of very expert and approved allowance.
Therefore my hopes, not surfeited to death,   50
Stand in bold cure.
(*A cry within:* "A sail, a sail, a sail!" *Enter a* FOURTH GENTLEMAN.)
What noise?
FOURTH GENTLEMAN.   The town is empty. On the brow o' the sea
Stand ranks of people and they cry "A sail!"
CASSIO.   My hopes do shape him for the governor. (*Guns heard.*)   55
SECOND GENTLEMAN.   They do discharge their shot of courtesy.
Our friends, at least.
CASSIO.   I pray you, sir, go forth,
And give us truth who 'tis that is arrived.
SECOND GENTLEMAN.   I shall. (*Exit.*)
MONTANO.   But, good Lieutenant, is your General wived?   60
CASSIO.   Most fortunately. He hath achieved a maid
That paragons description and wild fame,
One that excels the quirks of blazoning pens
And in the essential vesture of creation
Does tire the ingener.° (*Re-enter* SECOND GENTLEMAN.)
How now! Who has put in?   65
SECOND GENTLEMAN.   'Tis one Iago, Ancient to the General.
CASSIO.   He has had most favorable and happy speed.
Tempests themselves, high seas, and howling winds,
The guttered rocks, and congregated sands,
Traitors ensteeped to clog the guiltless keel,   70
As having sense of beauty, do omit
Their mortal° natures, letting go safely by
The divine Desdemona.
MONTANO.   What is she?
CASSIO.   She that I spake of, our great Captain's captain,
Left in the conduct of the bold Iago,   75
Whose footing here anticipates our thoughts
A sennight's° speed. Great Jove, Othello guard,

63–65. One . . . ingener: One that is too good for the fancy phrases (*quirks*) of painting pens
(i.e., poets) and in her absolute perfection wearies the artist (i.e., the painter) **ingener:**
inventor   72. mortal: deadly   77. sennight's: week's

And swell his sail with thine own powerful breath,
That he may bless this bay with his tall ship,
Make love's quick pants in Desdemona's arms,   80
Give renewed fire to our extincted spirits,
And bring all Cyprus comfort.
(*Enter* DESDEMONA, EMILIA, IAGO, RODERIGO, *and* ATTENDANTS.)
                                        Oh, behold,
The riches of the ship is come on shore!
Ye men of Cyprus, let her have your knees.
Hail to thee, lady! And the grace of Heaven,   85
Before, behind thee, and on every hand,
Enwheel thee round!
DESDEMONA.   I thank you, valiant Cassio.
    What tidings can you tell me of my lord?
CASSIO.   He is not yet arrived, nor know I aught
    But that he's well and will be shortly here.   90
DESDEMONA.   Oh, but I fear—How lost you company?
CASSIO.   The great contention of the sea and skies
    Parted our fellowship.—But hark! A sail.
    (*A cry within:* "A sail, a sail!" *Guns heard.*)
SECOND GENTLEMAN.   They give their greeting to the citadel.
    This likewise is a friend.
CASSIO.   See for the news. (*Exit* GENTLEMAN.)   95
    Good Ancient, you are welcome. (*To* EMILIA) Welcome, mistress.
    Let it not gall your patience, good Iago,
    That I extend my manners. 'Tis my breeding
    That gives me this bold show of courtesy. (*Kissing her.*)
IAGO.   Sir, would she give you so much of her lips   100
    As of her tongue she oft bestows on me,
    You'd have enough.
DESDEMONA.   Alas, she has no speech.
IAGO.   In faith, too much,
    I find it still when I have list° to sleep.
    Marry, before your ladyship, I grant,   105
    She puts her tongue a little in her heart
    And chides with thinking.
EMILIA.   You have little cause to say so.
IAGO.   Come on, come on. You are pictures° out of doors,
    Bells° in your parlors, wildcats in your kitchens,   110

---

104. list: desire   **109. pictures:** i.e., painted and dumb   **110. Bells:** i.e., ever clacking

Saints in your injuries,° devils being offended,
Players in your housewifery, and housewives in your beds.
DESDEMONA.   Oh, fie upon thee, slanderer!
IAGO.   Nay, it is true, or else I am a Turk.
You rise to play, and go to bed to work.   115
EMILIA.   You shall not write my praise.
IAGO.   No, let me not.
DESDEMONA.   What wouldst thou write of me if thou shouldst praise me?
IAGO.   O gentle lady, do not put me to 't,
For I am nothing if not critical.
DESDEMONA.   Come on, assay.°—There's one gone to the harbor? 120
IAGO.   Aye, madam.
DESDEMONA (aside). I am not merry, but I do beguile
The thing I am by seeming otherwise.—
Come, how wouldst thou praise me?
IAGO.   I am about it, but indeed my invention   125
Comes from my pate as birdlime does from frieze°—
It plucks out brains and all. But my Muse labors,
And thus she is delivered:
If she be fair and wise, fairness and wit,
The one's for use, the other useth it.   130
DESDEMONA.   Well praised! How if she be black° and witty?
IAGO.   If she be black, and thereto have a wit,
She'll find a white° that shall her blackness fit.
DESDEMONA.   Worse and worse.
EMILIA.   How if fair and foolish?   135
IAGO.   She never yet was foolish that was fair,
For even her folly helped her to an heir.
DESDEMONA.   These are old fond paradoxes to make fools laugh i' the
alehouse. What miserable praise hast thou for her that's foul and
foolish?   140
IAGO.   There's none so foul, and foolish thereunto,
But does foul pranks which fair and wise ones do.
DESDEMONA.   Oh, heavy ignorance! Thou praisest the worst best. But
what praise couldst thou bestow on a deserving woman indeed, one
that in the authority of her merit did justly put on the vouch of
very malice itself?°   146

---

111. Saints . . . injuries: Saints when you hurt anyone else   **120. assay:** try   **125–26. my
. . . frieze:** my literary effort (*invention*) is as hard to pull out of my head as frieze (cloth with a
nap)   **131. black:** brunette, dark-complexioned [Eds.]   **133. white:** with a pun on *wight*
(line 157), man, person   **144–46. one . . . itself:** one so deserving that even malice would
declare her good

IAGO.   She that was ever fair and never proud,
    Had tongue at will° and yet was never loud,
    Never lacked gold and yet went never gay,
    Fled from her wish and yet said "Now I may";   150
    She that, being angered, her revenge being nigh,
    Bade her wrong stay and her displeasure fly;
    She that in wisdom never was so frail
    To change the cod's head for the salmon's tail;°
    She that could think and ne'er disclose her mind,   155
    See suitors following and not look behind;
    She was a wight, if ever such wight were—
DESDEMONA.   To do what?
IAGO.   To suckle fools and chronicle small beer.°
DESDEMONA.   Oh, most lame and impotent conclusion! Do not learn
    of him, Emilia, though he be thy husband. How say you, Cassio? Is
    he not a most profane and liberal° counselor?   162
CASSIO.   He speaks home,° madam. You may relish him more in the
    soldier than in the scholar.
IAGO (*aside*).   He takes her by the palm. Aye, well said, whisper. With as
    little a web as this will I ensnare as great a fly as Cassio. Aye, smile
    upon her, do, I will gyve thee in thine own courtship.° You say true,
    'tis so indeed. If such tricks as these strip you out of your Lieuten-
    antry, it had been better you had not kissed your three fingers° so
    oft, which now again you are most apt to play the sir° in. Very good,
    well kissed! An excellent courtesy! 'Tis so indeed. Yet again your
    fingers to your lips? Would they were clyster pipes° for your sake!
    (*Trumpet within.*) The Moor! I know his trumpet.   173
CASSIO.   'Tis truly so.
DESDEMONA.   Let's meet him and receive him.   175
CASSIO.   Lo where he comes! (*Enter* OTHELLO *and* ATTENDANTS.)
OTHELLO.   O my fair warrior!°
DESDEMONA.   My dear Othello!
OTHELLO.   It gives me wonder great as my content
    To see you here before me. O my soul's joy!
    If after every tempest come such calms,   180

---

148. tongue . . . will: a ready flow of words   **154. To . . . tail:** To prefer the tail end of a good thing to the head of a poor thing   **159. suckle . . . beer:** nurse babies and keep petty household accounts (i.e., even the best woman belongs in the nursery and kitchen) [Eds.]   **162. liberal:** gross   **163. home:** bluntly [Eds.]   **167. gyve . . . courtship:** trap you with your own show of courtesy [Eds.]   **169. kissed . . . fingers:** a gesture of gallantry   **170. play the sir:** act the fine gentleman   **172. clyster pipes:** an enema syringe   **177. warrior:** because she is a soldier's wife

May the winds blow till they have wakened death!
And let the laboring bark climb hills of seas
Olympus-high, and duck again as low
As Hell's from Heaven! If it were now to die,
'Twere now to be most happy, for I fear   185
My soul hath her content so absolute
That not another comfort like to this
Succeeds in unknown fate.
DESDEMONA.   The Heavens forbid
But that our loves and comforts should increase,
Even as our days do grow!
OTHELLO.   Amen to that, sweet powers!   190
I cannot speak enough of this content.
It stops me here,° it is too much of joy.
And this, and this, the greatest discords be (*kissing her*)
That e'er our hearts shall make!
IAGO (*aside*).   Oh, you are well tuned now,
But I'll set down the pegs° that make this music,   195
As honest as I am.
OTHELLO.   Come, let us to the castle.
News, friends! Our wars are done, the Turks are drowned.
How does my old acquaintance of this isle?
Honey, you shall be well desired in Cyprus,
I have found great love amongst them. O my sweet,   200
I prattle out of fashion, and I dote
In mine own comforts. I prithee, good Iago,
Go to the bay and disembark my coffers.°
Bring thou the master° to the citadel.
He is a good one, and his worthiness   205
Does challenge much respect. Come, Desdemona,
Once more well met at Cyprus. (*Exeunt all but* IAGO *and* RODERIGO.)
IAGO.   Do thou meet me presently at the harbor. Come hither. If thou
    beest valiant—as they say base men being in love have then a no-
    bility in their natures more than is native to them—list me. The
    Lieutenant tonight watches on the court of guard. First, I must tell
    thee this. Desdemona is directly in love with him.   212
RODERIGO.   With him! Why, 'tis not possible.

_____

192. here: i.e., in the heart   **195. set . . . pegs:** i.e., make you sing out of tune. A stringed
instrument was tuned by the pegs.   **203. coffers:** trunks   **204. master:** captain of the ship

IAGO.   Lay thy finger thus,° and let thy soul be instructed. Mark me with
what violence she first loved the Moor, but for bragging and telling
her fantastical lies. And will she love him still for prating? Let not
thy discreet heart think it. Her eye must be fed, and what delight
shall she have to look on the Devil? When the blood is made dull
with the act of sport, there should be, again to inflame it and to give
satiety a fresh appetite, loveliness in favor,° sympathy in years, manners, and beauties, all which the Moor is defective in. Now, for want
of these required conveniences, her delicate tenderness will find itself abused, begin to heave the gorge, disrelish and abhor the Moor.
Very nature will instruct her in it and compel her to some second
choice. Now, sir, this granted—as it is a most pregnant and unforced
position°—who stands so eminently in the degree of this fortune as
Cassio does? A knave very voluble, no further conscionable° than
in putting on the mere form of civil and humane seeming° for the
better compassing of his salt° and most hidden loose affection? Why,
none, why, none. A slipper° and subtle knave, a finder-out of occasions, that has an eye can stamp and counterfeit advantages,°
though true advantage never present itself. A devilish knave! Besides, the knave is handsome, young, and hath all those requisites in
him that folly and green minds look after. A pestilent complete
knave, and the woman hath found him already.   235
RODERIGO.   I cannot believe that in her. She's full of most blest
condition.°
IAGO.   Blest fig's-end!° The wine she drinks is made of grapes. If she
had been blest, she would never have loved the Moor. Blest
pudding! Didst thou not see her paddle with the palm of his hand?
Didst not mark that?   241
RODERIGO.   Yes, that I did, but that was but courtesy.
IAGO.   Lechery, by his hand, an index and obscure prologue to the his-
tory of lust and foul thoughts. They met so near with their lips that
their breaths embraced together. Villainous thoughts, Roderigo!
When these mutualities so marshal the way, hard at hand comes
the master and main exercise, the incorporate° conclusion. Pish!
But, sir, be you ruled by me. I have brought you from Venice.
Watch you tonight. For the command, I'll lay 't upon you. Cassio
knows you not. I'll not be far from you. Do you find some occasion

---

214. thus: i.e., on the lips   **220. favor:** face   **225–26. pregnant . . . position:** very
significant and probable argument   **227. no . . . conscionable:** who has no more
conscience   **228. humane seeming:** courteous appearance   **229. salt:** lecherous
230. slipper: slippery   **231. stamp . . . advantages:** forge false opportunities
237. condition: disposition   **238. fig's-end:** nonsense [Eds.]   **247. incorporate:** bodily

to anger Cassio, either by speaking too loud, or tainting° his discipline, or from what other course you please which the time shall
more favorably minister.

RODERIGO.   Well.   253

IAGO.   Sir, he is rash and very sudden in choler,° and haply may strike
at you. Provoke him, that he may, for even out of that will I cause
these of Cyprus to mutiny, whose qualification shall come into no
true taste again but by the displanting of Cassio. So shall you have
a shorter journey to your desires by the means I shall then have to
prefer° them, and the impediment most profitably removed without
the which there were no expectation of our prosperity.   260

RODERIGO.   I will do this, if I can bring it to any opportunity.

IAGO.   I warrant thee. Meet me by and by at the citadel. I must fetch
his necessaries ashore. Farewell.

RODERIGO.   Adieu. (*Exit.*)

IAGO.   That Cassio loves her, I do well believe it.   265
That she loves him, 'tis apt and of great credit.°
The Moor, howbeit that I endure him not,
Is of a constant, loving, noble nature,
And I dare think he'll prove to Desdemona
A most dear husband. Now, I do love her too,   270
Not out of absolute lust, though peradventure
I stand accountant for as great a sin,
But partly led to diet° my revenge
For that I do suspect the lusty Moor
Hath leaped into my seat. The thought whereof   275
Doth like a poisonous mineral gnaw my inwards,
And nothing can or shall content my soul
Till I am evened with him, wife for wife.
Or failing so, yet that I put the Moor
At least into a jealousy so strong   280
That judgment cannot cure. Which thing to do,
If this poor trash of Venice, whom I trash
For his quick hunting,° stand the putting-on,
I'll have our Michael Cassio on the hip,
Abuse him to the Moor in the rank garb°—   285
For I fear Cassio with my nightcap too—

---

251. tainting: disparaging   **254. choler:** anger   **259. prefer:** promote   **266. apt . . . credit:**
likely and very creditable   **273. diet:** feed   **282–83. trash . . . hunting:** hold back from
outrunning the pack [Eds.]   **285. rank garb:** gross manner; i.e., by accusing him of being
Desdemona's lover

Make the Moor thank me, love me, and reward me
For making him egregiously an ass
And practicing upon his peace and quiet
Even to madness. 'Tis here, but yet confused.   290
Knavery's plain face is never seen till used. (*Exit.*)

SCENE 2. *A street.*

Enter a HERALD *with a proclamation,* PEOPLE *following.*

HERALD.   It is Othello's pleasure, our noble and valiant General, that
upon certain tidings now arrived, importing the mere perdition° of
the Turkish fleet, every man put himself into triumph°—some to
dance, some to make bonfires, each man to what sport and revels
his addiction leads him. For, besides these beneficial news, it is the
celebration of his nuptial. So much was his pleasure should be proclaimed. All offices° are open, and there is full liberty of feasting
from this present hour of five till the bell have told eleven. Heaven
bless the isle of Cyprus and our noble General Othello! (*Exeunt.*)

SCENE 3. *A hall in the castle.*

Enter OTHELLO, DESDEMONA, CASSIO, *and* ATTENDANTS.
OTHELLO.   Good Michael, look you to the guard tonight.
Let's teach ourselves that honorable stop,
Not to outsport discretion.°
CASSIO.   Iago hath directions what to do,
But notwithstanding with my personal eye   5
Will I look to 't.
OTHELLO.   Iago is most honest.
Michael, good night. Tomorrow with your earliest
Let me have speech with you. (*To* DESDEMONA) Come, my dear love,
The purchase made, the fruits are to ensue—
That profit's yet to come 'tween me and you.   10
Good night. (*Exeunt all but* CASSIO. *Enter* IAGO.)
CASSIO.   Welcome, Iago. We must to the watch.
IAGO.   Not this hour, Lieutenant, 'tis not yet ten o'clock. Our General
cast° us thus early for the love of his Desdemona, who let us not
therefore blame. He hath not yet made wanton the night with her,
and she is sport for Jove.   16

2. **mere perdition:** absolute destruction   3. **put . . . triumph:** celebrate   7. **offices:** the
kitchen and buttery—i.e., free food and drink for all   3. **outsport discretion:** let the fun go
too far.   14. **cast:** dismissed

CASSIO.   She's a most exquisite lady.

IAGO.   And, I'll warrant her, full of game.

CASSIO.   Indeed she's a most fresh and delicate creature.

IAGO.   What an eye she has! Methinks it sounds a parley to   20
    provocation.

CASSIO.   An inviting eye, and yet methinks right modest.

IAGO.   And when she speaks, is it not an alarum to love?

CASSIO.   She is indeed perfection.

IAGO.   Well, happiness to their sheets! Come, Lieutenant, I have a
    stoup of wine, and there without are a brace of Cyprus gallants that
    would fain have a measure to the health of black Othello.   27

CASSIO.   Not tonight, good Iago. I have very poor and unhappy brains
    for drinking. I could well wish courtesy would invent some other
    custom of entertainment.   30

IAGO.   Oh, they are our friends. But one cup—I'll drink for you.

CASSIO.   I have drunk but one cup tonight, and that was craftily quali-
    fied° too, and behold what innovation it makes here. I am unfortu-
    nate in the infirmity, and dare not task my weakness with any more.

IAGO.   What, man! 'Tis a night of revels. The gallants desire it.   35

CASSIO.   Where are they?

IAGO.   Here at the door. I pray you call them in.

CASSIO.   I'll do 't, but it dislikes me. (*Exit.*)

IAGO.   If I can fasten but one cup upon him,
    With that which he hath drunk tonight already,   40
    He'll be as full of quarrel and offense
    As my young mistress' dog. Now my sick fool Roderigo,
    Whom love hath turned almost the wrong side out,
    To Desdemona hath tonight caroused
    Potations pottle-deep, and he's to watch.   45
    Three lads of Cyprus, noble swelling spirits
    That hold their honors in a wary distance,°
    The very elements° of this warlike isle,
    Have I tonight flustered with flowing cups,
    And they watch too. Now, 'mongst this flock of drunkards,   50
    Am I to put our Cassio in some action
    That may offend the isle. But here they come.
    If consequence do but approve my dream,
    My boat sails freely, both with wind and stream.

32–33. **qualified:** diluted [Eds.]   **47. hold . . . distance:** are very sensitive about their honor
[Eds.]   **48. very elements:** typical specimens

(*Re-enter* CASSIO, *with him* MONTANO *and* GENTLEMEN, SERVANTS
    following with wine.)
CASSIO.   'Fore God, they have given me a rouse already.   55
MONTANO.   Good faith, a little one—not past a pint, as I am a soldier.
IAGO.   Some wine, ho! (*Sings*)
            "And let me the cannikin clink, clink
            And let me the cannikin clink.
                A soldier's a man,   60
                A life's but a span.°
            Why, then let a soldier drink."

    Some wine, boys!
CASSIO.   'Fore God, an excellent song.
IAGO.   I learned it in England, where indeed they are most potent in pot-
    ting.° Your Dane, your German, and your swag-bellied Hollander—
    Drink, ho!—are nothing to your English.   67
CASSIO.   Is your Englishman so expert in his drinking?
IAGO.   Why, he drinks you with facility your Dane dead drunk, he
    sweats not to overthrow your Almain,° he gives your Hollander a
    vomit° ere the next pottle can be filled.   71
CASSIO.   To the health of our General!
MONTANO.   I am for it, Lieutenant, and I'll do you justice.
IAGO.   O sweet England! (*Sings*)
            "King Stephen was a worthy peer,   75
                His breeches cost him but a crown.
            He held them sixpence all too dear,
                With that he called the tailor lown.°

            "He was a wight of high renown,
                And thou art but of low degree.   80
            'Tis pride that pulls the country down.
                Then take thine auld cloak about thee."
    Some wine, ho!
CASSIO.   Why, this is a more exquisite song than the other.
IAGO.   Will you hear 't again?   85
CASSIO.   No, for I hold him to be unworthy of his place that does
    those things. Well, God's above all, and there be souls must be
    saved and there be souls must not be saved.

---

61. span: lit., the measure between the thumb and little finger of the outstretched hand;
about 9 inches   **65–66. potting:** drinking   **70. Almain:** German   **gives . . . vomit:** drinks
as much as will make a Dutchman throw up   **78. lown:** lout

IAGO.   It's true, good Lieutenant.

CASSIO.   For mine own part—no offense to the General, nor any man of quality—I hope to be saved.   91

IAGO.   And so do I too, Lieutenant.

CASSIO.   Aye, but, by your leave, not before me. The Lieutenant is to be saved before the Ancient. Let's have no more of this, let's to our affairs. God forgive us our sins! Gentlemen, let's look to our business. Do not think, gentlemen, I am drunk. This is my Ancient, this is my right hand and this is my left. I am not drunk now, I can stand well enough and speak well enough.   98

ALL.   Excellent well.

CASSIO.   Why, very well, then, you must not think then that I am drunk. (*Exit.*)

MONTANO.   To the platform, masters. Come, let's set the watch.   101

IAGO.   You see this fellow that is gone before.
He is a soldier fit to stand by Caesar
And give direction. And do but see his vice.
'Tis to his virtue a just equinox,   105
The one as long as the other. 'Tis pity of him.
I fear the trust Othello puts him in
On some odd time of his infirmity
Will shake this island.

MONTANO.   But is he often thus?

IAGO.   'Tis evermore the prologue to his sleep.   110
He'll watch the horologe a double set,°
If drink rock not his cradle.

MONTANO.   It were well
The General were put in mind of it.
Perhaps he sees it not, or his good nature
Prizes the virtue that appears in Cassio   115
And looks not on his evils. Is not this true? (*Enter* RODERIGO.)

IAGO (*aside to him*). How now, Roderigo! I pray you, after the Lieutenant. Go. (*Exit* RODERIGO.)

MONTANO.   And 'tis great pity that the noble Moor
Should hazard such a place as his own second   120
With one of an ingraft infirmity.
It were an honest action to say
So to the Moor.

IAGO.   Not I, for this fair island.
I do love Cassio well, and would do much

111. watch . . . set: stay awake the clock twice round

To cure him of this evil—But hark! What noise?   125
(*A cry within:* "Help! Help!" *Re-enter* CASSIO, *driving in* RODERIGO.)
CASSIO.   'Zounds! You rogue! You rascal!
MONTANO.   What's the matter, Lieutenant?
CASSIO.   A knave teach me my duty! But I'll beat the knave into a
    wicker bottle.
RODERIGO.   Beat me!   130
CASSIO.   Dost thou prate, rogue? (*Striking* RODERIGO.)
MONTANO.   Nay, good Lieutenant (*staying him*),
                                                            I pray you sir, hold your hand.
CASSIO.   Let me go, sir, or I'll knock you o'er the mazzard.°
MONTANO.   Come, come, you're drunk.
CASSIO.   Drunk! (*They fight.*)   135
IAGO   (*aside to* RODERIGO). Away, I say. Go out and cry a mutiny.
    (*Exit* RODERIGO.)
    Nay, good Lieutenant! God's will, gentlemen!
    Help, ho!—Lieutenant—sir—Montano—sir—
    Help, masters!—Here's a goodly watch indeed! (*A bell rings.*)
    Who's that that rings the bell?—Diablo, ho!   140
    The town will rise. God's will, Lieutenant, hold—
    You will be ashamed forever. (*Re-enter* OTHELLO *and* ATTENDANTS.)
OTHELLO.   What is the matter here?
MONTANO.   'Zounds, I bleed still, I am hurt to death. (*Faints.*)
OTHELLO.   Hold, for your lives!
IAGO.   Hold, ho! Lieutenant—sir—Montano—gentlemen—   145
    Have you forgot all sense of place and duty?
    Hold! The General speaks to you. Hold, hold, for shame!
OTHELLO.   Why, how now, ho! From whence ariseth this?
    Are we turned Turks, and to ourselves do that
    Which Heaven hath forbid the Ottomites?   150
    For Christian shame, put by this barbarous brawl.
    He that stirs next to carve for his own rage
    Holds his soul light, he dies upon his motion.
    Silence that dreadful bell. It frights the isle
    From her propriety. What is the matter, masters?   155
    Honest Iago, that look'st dead with grieving,
    Speak, who began this? On thy love, I charge thee.
IAGO.   I do not know. Friends all but now, even now,
    In quarter and in terms like bride and groom
    Devesting them for bed. And then, but now,   160

133. **mazzard:** head

As if some planet had unwitted men,
Swords out, and tilting one at other's breast
In opposition bloody. I cannot speak
Any beginning to this peevish odds,
And would in action glorious I had lost   165
Those legs that brought me to a part of it!
OTHELLO.   How comes it, Michael, you are thus forgot?°
CASSIO.   I pray you, pardon me, I cannot speak.
OTHELLO.   Worthy Montano, you were wont be civil.
The gravity and stillness of your youth   170
The world hath noted, and your name is great
In mouths of wisest censure.° What's the matter
That you unlace your reputation thus
And spend your rich opinion° for the name
Of a night brawler? Give me answer to it.   175
MONTANO.   Worthy Othello, I am hurt to danger.
Your officer, Iago, can inform you—
While I spare speech, which something now offends me—
Of all that I do know. Nor know I aught
By me that's said or done amiss this night,   180
Unless self-charity° be sometimes a vice,
And to defend ourselves it be a sin
When violence assails us.
OTHELLO.   Now, by Heaven,
My blood begins my safer guides to rule,
And passion, having my best judgment collied,°   185
Assays to lead the way. If I once stir,
Or do but lift this arm, the best of you
Shall sink in my rebuke. Give me to know
How this foul rout began, who set it on,
And he that is approved° in this offense,   190
Though he had twinned with me, both at a birth,
Shall lose me. What! In a town of war,
Yet wild, the people's hearts brimful of fear,
To manage private and domestic quarrel,
In night, and on the court and guard of safety!   195
'Tis monstrous. Iago, who began 't?
MONTANO.   If partially affined or leagued in office,

---

167. are thus forgot: have so forgotten yourself   **172. censure:** judgment   **174. opinion:**
reputation [Eds.]   **181. self-charity:** love for oneself   **185. collied:** darkened
190. approved: proved guilty

Thou dost deliver more or less than truth,
Thou art no soldier.
IAGO.   Touch me not so near.
I had rather have this tongue cut from my mouth   200
Than it should do offense to Michael Cassio.
Yet I persuade myself to speak the truth
Shall nothing wrong him. Thus it is, General.
Montano and myself being in speech,
There comes a fellow crying out for help,   205
And Cassio following him with determined sword
To execute upon him. Sir, this gentleman
Steps in to Cassio and entreats his pause.
Myself the crying fellow did pursue
Lest by his clamor—as it so fell out—   210
The town might fall in fright. He, swift of foot,
Outran my purpose, and I returned the rather
For that I heard the clink and fall of swords,
And Cassio high in oath, which till tonight
I ne'er might say before. When I came back—   215
For this was brief—I found them close together,
At blow and thrust, even as again they were
When you yourself did part them.
More of this matter cannot I report.
But men are men, the best sometimes forget.   220
Though Cassio did some little wrong to him,
As men in rage strike those that wish them best,
Yet surely Cassio, I believe, received
From him that fled some strange indignity,
Which patience could not pass.
OTHELLO.   I know, Iago,   225
Thy honesty and love doth mince this matter,
Making it light to Cassio. Cassio, I love thee,
But never more be officer of mine. (*Re-enter* DESDEMONA, *attended.*)
Look, if my gentle love be not raised up!
I'll make thee an example.
DESDEMONA.   What's the matter?   230
OTHELLO.   All's well now, sweeting. Come away to bed.
(*To* MONTANO, *who is led off.*)
Sir, for your hurts, myself will be your surgeon.
Lead him off.
Iago, look with care about the town,
And silence those whom this vile brawl distracted.   235

     Come, Desdemona. 'Tis the soldier's life
     To have their balmy slumbers waked with strife.
     (*Exeunt all but* IAGO *and* CASSIO.)

IAGO.   What, are you hurt, Lieutenant?

CASSIO.   Aye, past all surgery.

IAGO.   Marry, Heaven forbid!   240

CASSIO.   Reputation, reputation, reputation! Oh, I have lost my
reputation! I have lost the immortal part of myself, and what remains is bestial. My reputation, Iago, my reputation!

IAGO.   As I am an honest man, I thought you had received some bodily
wound. There is more sense in that than in reputation. Reputation
is an idle and most false imposition, oft got without merit and lost
without deserving. You have lost no reputation at all unless you
repute yourself such a loser. What, man! There are ways to recover
the General again. You are but now cast in his mood,° a punishment more in policy° than in malice—even so as one would beat
his offenseless dog to affright an imperious lion.° Sue to him again
and he's yours.   252

CASSIO.   I will rather sue to be despised than to deceive so good a
commander with so slight, so drunken, and so indiscreet an officer. Drunk? And speak parrot°? And squabble? Swagger? Swear?
And discourse fustian° with one's own shadow? O thou invisible
spirit of wine, if thou hast no name to be known by, let us call thee
devil!   258

IAGO.   What was he that you followed with your sword? What had he
done to you?   260

CASSIO.   I know not.

IAGO.   Is 't possible?

CASSIO.   I remember a mass of things, but nothing distinctly—a quarrel,
but nothing wherefore. Oh God, that men should put an enemy in
their mouths to steal away their brains! That we should, with joy,
pleasance, revel, and applause, transform ourselves into beasts!   266

IAGO.   Why, but you are now well enough. How came you thus
recovered?

CASSIO.   It hath pleased the devil drunkenness to give place to the
devil wrath. One unperfectness shows me another, to make me
frankly despise myself.   271

---

249. cast . . . mood: dismissed because he is in a bad mood   **250. in policy:** i.e., because he
must appear to be angry before the Cypriots   **250–51. even . . . lion:** a proverb meaning that
when the lion sees the dog beaten, he will know what is coming to him   **255. speak parrot:**
babble   **256. fustian:** nonsense

IAGO.   Come, you are too severe a moraler. As the time, the place, and the condition of this country stands, I could heartily wish this had not befallen. But since it is as it is, mend it for your own good.

CASSIO.   I will ask him for my place again, he shall tell me I am a drunkard! Had I as many mouths as Hydra, such an answer would stop them all. To be now a sensible man, by and by a fool, and presently a beast! Oh, strange! Every inordinate cup is unblest, and the ingredient is a devil.

IAGO.   Come, come, good wine is a good familiar creature, if it be well used. Exclaim no more against it. And, good Lieutenant, I think you think I love you.   282

CASSIO.   I have well approved it, sir. I drunk!

IAGO.   You or any man living may be drunk at some time, man. I'll tell you what you shall do. Our General's wife is now the General. I may say so in this respect, for that he hath devoted and given up himself to the contemplation, mark, and denotement of her parts and graces. Confess yourself freely to her, importune her help to put you in your place again. She is of so free, so kind, so apt, so blessed a disposition, she holds it a vice in her goodness not to do more than she is re-quested. This broken joint between you and her husband entreat her to splinter° and, my fortunes against any lay° worth naming, this crack of your love shall grow stronger than it was before.   293

CASSIO.   You advise me well.

IAGO.   I protest, in the sincerity of love and honest kindness.

CASSIO.   I think it freely, and betimes in the morning I will beseech the virtuous Desdemona to undertake for me. I am desperate of my fortunes if they check me here.

IAGO.   You are in the right. Good night, Lieutenant, I must to the watch.

CASSIO.   Good night, honest Iago. (*Exit.*)   300

IAGO.   And what's he then that says I play the villain?
    When this advice is free I give and honest,
    Probal° to thinking, and indeed the course
    To win the Moor again? For 'tis most easy
    The inclining Desdemona to subdue   305
    In any honest suit. She's framed as fruitful
    As the free elements. And then for her
    To win the Moor, were 't to renounce his baptism,
    All seals and symbols of redeemèd sin,

---

292. splinter: put in splints   **lay:** bet   **303. Probal:** Probable

His soul is so enfettered to her love   310
That she may make, unmake, do what she list,
Even as her appetite shall play the god
With his weak function.° How am I then a villain
To counsel Cassio to this parallel course,
Directly to his good? Divinity of Hell!   315
When devils will the blackest sins put on,
They do suggest at first with heavenly shows,
As I do now. For whiles this honest fool
Plies Desdemona to repair his fortunes,
And she for him pleads strongly to the Moor,   320
I'll pour this pestilence into his ear,
That she repeals° him for her body's lust,
And by how much she strives to do him good,
She shall undo her credit with the Moor.
So will I turn her virtue into pitch,   325
And out of her own goodness make the net
That shall enmesh them all. (*Enter* RODERIGO.)
                    How now, Roderigo!
RODERIGO.   I do follow here in the chase, not like a hound that hunts
    but one that fills up the cry. My money is almost spent, I have been
    tonight exceedingly well cudgeled, and I think the issue will be I
    shall have so much experience from my pains and so, with no
    money at all and a little more wit, return again to Venice.   332
IAGO.   How poor are they that have not patience!
    What wound did ever heal but by degrees?
    Thou know'st we work by wit and not by witchcraft,   335
    And wit depends on dilatory Time.
    Does 't not go well? Cassio hath beaten thee,
    And thou by that small hurt hast cashiered Cassio.
    Though other things grow fair against the sun,
    Yet fruits that blossom first will first be ripe.   340
    Content thyself awhile. By the mass, 'tis morning.
    Pleasure and action make the hours seem short.
    Retire thee, go where thou art billeted.
    Away, I say. Thou shalt know more hereafter.
    Nay, get thee gone. (*Exit* RODERIGO.)
                    Two things are to be done: 345
    My wife must move for Cassio to her mistress,
    I'll set her on,

---

313. function: mental faculties [Eds.]   **322. repeals**: calls back

Myself the while to draw the Moor apart
And bring him jump° when he may Cassio find
Soliciting his wife. Aye, that's the way.   350
Dull not device by coldness and delay. (*Exit.*)

ACT 3

SCENE 1. *Before the castle.*

Enter CASSIO *and some* MUSICIANS.

CASSIO.   Masters, play here, I will content your pains°—
Something that's brief, and bid "Good morrow, General."°
(*Music. Enter* CLOWN.)
CLOWN.   Why, masters, have your instruments been in Naples, that
they speak i' the nose thus?
FIRST MUSICIAN.   How, sir, how?   5
CLOWN.   Are these, I pray you, wind instruments?
FIRST MUSICIAN.   Aye, marry are they, sir.
CLOWN.   Oh, thereby hangs a tail.
FIRST MUSICIAN.   Whereby hangs a tale, sir?
CLOWN.   Marry, sir, by many a wind instrument that I know. But, mas-
ters, here's money for you. And the General so likes your music that
he desires you, for love's sake, to make no more noise with it.   12
FIRST MUSICIAN.   Well, sir, we will not.
CLOWN.   If you have any music that may not be heard, to 't again. But,
as they say, to hear music the General does not greatly care.   15
FIRST MUSICIAN.   We have none such, sir.
CLOWN.   Then put up your pipes in your bag, for I'll away. Go, vanish
into air, away! (*Exeunt* MUSICIANS.)
CASSIO.   Dost thou hear, my honest friend?
CLOWN.   No, I hear not your honest friend, I hear you.   20
CASSIO.   Prithee keep up thy quillets.° There's a poor piece of gold for
thee. If the gentlewoman that attends the General's wife be stir-
ring, tell her there's one Cassio entreats her a little favor of speech.
Wilt thou do this?
CLOWN.   She is stirring, sir. If she will stir hither, I shall seem to notify
unto her.   26
CASSIO.   Do, good my friend. (*Exit* CLOWN. *Enter* IAGO.)

349. jump: at the moment   1. content your pains: reward your labor
2. bid . . . General.": It was a common custom to play or sing a song beneath the bedroom
window of a distinguished guest or of a newly wedded couple on the morning after their
wedding night.   21. keep . . . quillets: put away your wisecracks

In happy time, Iago.

IAGO.   You have not been abed, then?

CASSIO.   Why, no, the day had broke
 Before we parted. I have made bold, Iago,   30
 To send in to your wife. My suit to her
 Is that she will to virtuous Desdemona
 Procure me some access.

IAGO.   I'll send her to you presently,
 And I'll devise a mean to draw the Moor
 Out of the way, that your convérse and business   35
 May be more free.

CASSIO.   I humbly thank you for 't. (*Exit* IAGO.)
            I never knew
 A Florentine more kind and honest. (*Enter* EMILIA.)

EMILIA.   Good morrow, good Lieutenant. I am sorry
 For your displeasure, but all will sure be well.   40
 The General and his wife are talking of it,
 And she speaks for you stoutly. The Moor replies
 That he you hurt is of great fame in Cyprus
 And great affinity,° and that in wholesome wisdom
 He might not but refuse you. But he protests he loves you, 45
 And needs no other suitor but his likings
 To take the safest occasion by the front
 To bring you in again.

CASSIO.   Yet I beseech you
 If you think fit, or that it may be done,
 Give me advantage of some brief discourse   50
 With Desdemona alone.

EMILIA.   Pray you, come in.
 I will bestow you where you shall have time
 To speak your bosom freely.

CASSIO.   I am much bound to you. (*Exeunt.*)

SCENE 2. *A room in the castle.*

 Enter OTHELLO, IAGO, *and* GENTLEMEN.

OTHELLO.   These letters give, Iago, to the pilot,
 And by him do my duties to the Senate.
 That done, I will be walking on the works.°
 Repair there to me.

---

44. affinity: kindred **3. works:** fortifications

IAGO.   Well, my good lord, I'll do 't.
OTHELLO.   This fortification, gentlemen, shall we see 't?   5
GENTLEMEN.   We'll wait upon your lordship. (*Exeunt.*)

SCENE 3. *The garden of the castle.*

Enter DESDEMONA, CASSIO, *and* EMILIA.

DESDEMONA.   Be thou assured, good Cassio, I will do
   All my abilities in thy behalf.
EMILIA.   Good madam, do. I warrant it grieves my husband
   As if the case were his.
DESDEMONA.   Oh, that's an honest fellow. Do not doubt, Cassio,   5
   But I will have my lord and you again
   As friendly as you were.
CASSIO.   Bounteous madam,
   Whatever shall become of Michael Cassio,
   He's never anything but your true servant.
DESDEMONA.   I know 't. I thank you. You do love my lord.   10
   You have known him long, and be you well assured
   He shall in strangeness stand no farther off
   Than in a politic distance.°
CASSIO.   Aye, but lady,
   That policy may either last so long,
   Or feed upon such nice and waterish diet,   15
   Or breed itself so out of circumstance,
   That, I being absent and my place supplied,
   My General will forget my love and service.
DESDEMONA.   Do not doubt° that. Before Emilia here
   I give thee warrant of thy place. Assure thee,   20
   If I do vow a friendship, I'll perform it
   To the last article. My lord shall never rest.
   I'll watch him tame and talk him out of patience,
   His bed shall seem a school, his board a shrift.°
   I'll intermingle every thing he does   25
   With Cassio's suit. Therefore be merry, Cassio,
   For thy solicitor shall rather die
   Than give thy cause away. (*Enter* OTHELLO *and* IAGO, *at a distance.*)
EMILIA.   Madam, here comes my lord.
CASSIO.   Madam, I'll take my leave.   30

12–13: He . . . distance: i.e., his apparent coldness to you shall only be so much as his official
position demands for reasons of policy   19. doubt: fear   24. shrift: place of confession [Eds.]

DESDEMONA.   Nay, stay and hear me speak.

CASSIO.   Madam, not now. I am very ill at ease,
    Unfit for mine own purposes.

DESDEMONA.   Well, do your discretion. (*Exit* CASSIO.)

IAGO.   Ha! I like not that.   35

OTHELLO.   What dost thou say?

IAGO.   Nothing, my lord. Or if—I know not what.

OTHELLO.   Was not that Cassio parted from my wife?

IAGO.   Cassio, my lord! No, sure, I cannot think it,
    That he would steal away so guilty-like,   40
    Seeing you coming.

OTHELLO.   I do believe 'twas he.

DESDEMONA.   How now, my lord!
    I have been talking with a suitor here,
    A man that languishes in your displeasure.

OTHELLO.   Who is 't you mean?   45

DESDEMONA.   Why, your Lieutenant, Cassio. Good my lord,
    If I have any grace or power to move you,
    His present reconciliation take.°
    For if he be not one that truly loves you,
    That errs in ignorance and not in cunning,   50
    I have no judgment in an honest face.
    I prithee call him back.

OTHELLO.   Went he hence now?

DESDEMONA.   Aye, sooth, so humbled
    That he hath left part of his grief with me,
    To suffer with him. Good love, call him back.   55

OTHELLO.   Not now, sweet Desdemona, some other time.

DESDEMONA.   But shall 't be shortly?

OTHELLO.   The sooner, sweet, for you.

DESDEMONA.   Shall 't be tonight at supper?

OTHELLO.   No, not tonight.

DESDEMONA.   Tomorrow dinner then?

OTHELLO.   I shall not dine at home.
    I meet the captains at the citadel.   60

DESDEMONA.   Why, then tomorrow night or Tuesday morn,
    On Tuesday noon, or night, on Wednesday morn.
    I prithee name the time, but let it not
    Exceed three days. In faith, he's penitent,
    And yet his trespass, in our common reason—   65

---

48. His . . . take: Accept his immediate apology and forgive him.

Save that, they say, the wars must make examples
Out of their best—is not almost° a fault
To incur a private check.° When shall he come?
Tell me, Othello. I wonder in my soul
What you would ask me that I should deny,   70
Or stand so mammering° on. What! Michael Cassio,
That came a-wooing with you, and so many a time
When I have spoke of you dispraisingly
Hath ta'en your part—to have so much to do
To bring him in! Trust me, I could do much—   75
OTHELLO.   Prithee, no more. Let him come when he will.
   I will deny thee nothing.
DESDEMONA.   Why, this is not a boon.
   'Tis as I should entreat you wear your gloves,
   Or feed on nourishing dishes, or keep you warm,
   Or sue to you to do a peculiar profit   80
   To your own person. Nay, when I have a suit
   Wherein I mean to touch your love indeed,
   It shall be full of poise and difficult weight,
   And fearful to be granted.
OTHELLO.   I will deny thee nothing.
   Whereon I do beseech thee grant me this,   85
   To leave me but a little to myself.
DESDEMONA.   Shall I deny you? No. Farewell, my lord.
OTHELLO.   Farewell, my Desdemona. I'll come to thee straight.
DESDEMONA.   Emilia, come. Be as your fancies teach you.
   Whate'er you be, I am obedient.   90
   (*Exeunt* DESDEMONA *and* EMILIA.)
OTHELLO.   Excellent wretch! Perdition catch my soul
   But I do love thee! And when I love thee not,
   Chaos is come again.
IAGO.   My noble lord—
OTHELLO.   What dost thou say, Iago?
IAGO.   Did Michael Cassio, when you wooed my lady,   95
   Know of your love?
OTHELLO.   He did, from first to last. Why dost thou ask?
IAGO.   But for a satisfaction of my thought,
   No further harm.
OTHELLO.   Why of thy thought, Iago?
IAGO.   I did not think he had been acquainted with her.   100

---

67. not almost: hardly   **68. check:** rebuke   **71. mammering:** hesitating

OTHELLO.   Oh yes, and went between us very oft.

IAGO.   Indeed!

OTHELLO.   Indeed! Aye, indeed. Discern'st thou aught in that?
    Is he not honest?

IAGO.   Honest, my lord!

OTHELLO.   Honest! Aye, honest.

IAGO.   My lord, for aught I know.

OTHELLO.   What dost thou think?   105

IAGO.   Think, my lord!

OTHELLO.   Think, my lord! By Heaven, he echoes me
    As if there were some monster in his thought
    Too hideous to be shown. Thou dost mean something.
    I heard thee say even now that thou likedst not that   110
    When Cassio left my wife. What didst not like?
    And when I told thee he was of my counsel
    In my whole course of wooing, thou criedst "Indeed!"
    And didst contract and purse thy brow together
    As if thou then hadst shut up in thy brain   115
    Some horrible conceit. If thou dost love me,
    Show me thy thought.

IAGO.   My lord, you know I love you.

OTHELLO.   I think thou dost,
    And for I know thou'rt full of love and honesty
    And weigh'st thy words before thou givest them breath,   120
    Therefore these stops of thine fright me the more.
    For such things in a false disloyal knave
    Are tricks of custom, but in a man that's just
    They're close delations,° working from the heart,
    That passion cannot rule.

IAGO.   For Michael Cassio,   125
    I dare be sworn I think that he is honest.

OTHELLO.   I think so too.

IAGO.   Men should be what they seem,
    Or those that be not, would they might seem none!°

OTHELLO.   Certain, men should be what they seem.

IAGO.   Why, then I think Cassio's an honest man.   130

OTHELLO.   Nay, yet there's more in this.
    I prithee speak to me as to thy thinkings,
    As thou dost ruminate, and give thy worst of thoughts

---

124. close delations: concealed accusations   **128. seem none:** i.e., not seem to be honest
men

The worst of words.

IAGO.   Good my lord, pardon me.
Though I am bound to every act of duty,   135
I am not bound to that all slaves are free to.
Utter my thoughts? Why, say they are vile and false,
As where's that palace whereinto foul things
Sometimes intrude not? Who has a breast so pure
But some uncleanly apprehensions   140
Keep leets° and law days, and in session sit
With meditations lawful?

OTHELLO.   Thou dost conspire against thy friend, Iago,
If thou but think'st him wronged and makest his ear
A stranger to thy thoughts.

IAGO.   I do beseech you—   145
Though I perchance am vicious in my guess,
As, I confess, it is my nature's plague
To spy into abuses, and oft my jealousy°
Shapes faults that are not—that your wisdom yet,
From one that so imperfectly conceits,°   150
Would take no notice, nor build yourself a trouble
Out of his scattering and unsure observance.°
It were not for your quiet nor your good,
Nor for my manhood, honesty, or wisdom,
To let you know my thoughts.

OTHELLO.   What dost thou mean?   155

IAGO.   Good name in man and woman, dear my lord,
Is the immediate jewel of their souls.
Who steals my purse steals trash—'tis something, nothing,
'Twas mine, 'tis his, and has been slave to thousands—
But he that filches from me my good name   160
Robs me of that which not enriches him
And makes me poor indeed.

OTHELLO.   By Heaven, I'll know thy thoughts.

IAGO.   You cannot, if my heart were in your hand,
Nor shall not, whilst 'tis in my custody.   165

OTHELLO.   Ha!

IAGO.   Oh, beware, my lord, of jealousy.
It is the green-eyed monster which doth mock
The meat it feeds on. That cuckold lives in bliss

---

141. leets: courts   **148. jealousy:** suspicion   **150. conceits:** conceives   **152. observance:** observation

Who, certain of his fate, loves not his wronger.°
But, oh, what damnèd minutes tells he o'er   170
Who dotes, yet doubts, suspects, yet strongly loves!
OTHELLO.   Oh misery!
IAGO.   Poor and content is rich, and rich enough,
But riches fineless° is as poor as winter
To him that ever fears he shall be poor.   175
Good God, the souls of all my tribe defend
From jealousy!
OTHELLO.   Why, why is this?
Think'st thou I'd make a life of jealousy,
To follow still the changes of the moon
With fresh suspicions? No, to be once in doubt   180
Is once to be resolved.° Exchange me for a goat
When I shall turn the business of my soul
To such exsufflicate° and blown surmises,
Matching thy inference.° 'Tis not to make me jealous
To say my wife is fair, feeds well, loves company,   185
Is free of speech, sings, plays, and dances well.
Where virtue is, these are more virtuous.
Nor from mine own weak merits will I draw
The smallest fear or doubt of her revolt,
For she had eyes, and chose me. No, Iago,   190
I'll see before I doubt, when I doubt, prove,
And on the proof, there is no more but this—
Away at once with love or jealousy!
IAGO.   I am glad of it, for now I shall have reason
To show the love and duty that I bear you   195
With franker spirit. Therefore, as I am bound,
Receive it from me. I speak not yet of proof.
Look to your wife. Observe her well with Cassio.
Wear your eye thus, not jealous nor secure.°
I would not have your free and noble nature   200
Out of self-bounty° be abused. Look to 't.

168–69. That . . . wronger: i.e., the cuckold who hates his wife and knows her falseness is
not tormented by suspicious jealousy.   **174. fineless:** limitless   **180–81. to . . . resolved:**
whenever I find myself in doubt I at once seek out the truth.   **182–84. When . . . inference:**
When I shall allow that which concerns me most dearly to be influenced by such trifling
suggestions as yours   **exsufflicate:** blown up like a bubble   **199. secure:** overconfident
201. self-bounty: natural goodness

I know our country disposition well.
In Venice° they do let Heaven see the pranks
They dare not show their husbands. Their best conscience
Is not to leave 't undone, but keep 't unknown.   205

OTHELLO.   Dost thou say so?

IAGO.   She did deceive her father, marrying you,
And when she seemed to shake and fear your looks,
She loved them most.

OTHELLO.   And so she did.

IAGO.   Why, go to, then.
She that so young could give out such a seeming   210
To seel° her father's eyes up close as oak—
He thought 'twas witchcraft—but I am much to blame.
I humbly do beseech you of your pardon
For too much loving you.

OTHELLO.   I am bound to thee forever.

IAGO.   I see this hath a little dashed your spirits.   215

OTHELLO.   Not a jot, not a jot.

IAGO.   I' faith, I fear it has.
I hope you will consider what is spoke
Comes from my love. But I do see you're moved.
I am to pray you not to strain my speech
To grosser issues nor to larger reach   220
Than to suspicion.

OTHELLO.   I will not.

IAGO.   Should you do so, my lord,
My speech should fall into such vile success
As my thoughts aim not at. Cassio's my worthy friend.—
My lord, I see you're moved.

OTHELLO.   No, not so much moved.   225
I do not think but Desdemona's honest.°

IAGO.   Long live she so! And long live you to think so!

OTHELLO.   And yet, how nature erring from itself—

IAGO.   Aye, there's the point. As—to be bold with you—
Not to affect° many proposèd matches   230
Of her own clime, complexion, and degree,
Whereto we see in all things nature tends°—

---

203. In Venice: Venice was notorious for its loose women; the Venetian courtesans were
among the sights of Europe and were much commented upon by travelers.   **211. seel:**
blind   **226. honest:** When applied to Desdemona, "honest" means "chaste," but applied
to Iago it has the modern meaning of "open and sincere."   **230. affect:** be inclined to
232. in . . . tends: i.e., a woman naturally marries a man of her own country, color, and rank.

Foh! One may smell in such a will most rank,°
Foul disproportion, thoughts unnatural.
But pardon me. I do not in position   235
Distinctly speak of her, though I may fear
Her will, recoiling to her better judgment,
May fall to match° you with her country forms,°
And happily° repent.
OTHELLO.   Farewell, farewell.
If more thou dost perceive, let me know more.   240
Set on thy wife to observe. Leave me, Iago.
IAGO (going). My lord, I take my leave.
OTHELLO. Why did I marry? This honest creature doubtless
Sees and knows more, much more, than he unfolds.
IAGO (returning). My lord, I would I might entreat your honor   245
To scan this thing no further. Leave it to time.
Though it be fit that Cassio have his place,
For sure he fills it up with great ability,
Yet if you please to hold him off awhile,
You shall by that perceive him and his means.   250
Note if your lady strain his entertainment°
With any strong or vehement importunity—
Much will be seen in that. In the meantime,
Let me be thought too busy in my fears—
As worthy cause I have to fear I am—   255
And hold her free, I do beseech your Honor.
OTHELLO. Fear not my government.°
IAGO. I once more take my leave. (Exit.)
OTHELLO. This fellow's of exceeding honesty,
And knows all qualities, with a learned spirit,   260
Of human dealings. If I do prove her haggard,°
Though that her jesses° were my dear heartstrings,
I'd whistle her off and let her down the wind
To prey at fortune.° Haply, for° I am black
And have not those soft parts of conversation   265

---

233. will . . . rank: desire most lustful   238. match: compare   country forms: the
appearance of her countrymen, i.e., white men   239. happily: haply, by chance
251. strain his entertainment: urge you to receive him   257. government: self-
control   261. haggard: a wild hawk   262. jesses: the straps attached to a hawk's
legs   261–64. If . . . fortune: Othello keeps up the imagery of falconry throughout. He
means: If I find that she is wild, I'll whistle her off the game and let her go where she will, for
she's not worth keeping.   264. Haply, for: Perhaps, because [Eds.]

That chamberers° have, or for I am declined
Into the vale of years—yet that's not much—
She's gone, I am abused, and my relief
Must be to loathe her. Oh, curse of marriage,
That we can call these delicate creatures ours,   270
And not their appetites! I had rather be a toad
And live upon the vapor of a dungeon
Than keep a corner in the thing I love
For others' uses. Yet, 'tis the plague of great ones,
Prerogatived are they less than the base.   275
'Tis destiny unshunnable, like death.
Even then this forkèd plague° is fated to us
When we do quicken.° Desdemona comes.
(Re-enter DESDEMONA *and* EMILIA.*)*
If she be false, oh, then Heaven mocks itself!
I'll not believe 't.
DESDEMONA.   How now, my dear Othello!   280
    Your dinner, and the generous° islanders
    By you invited, do attend your presence.
OTHELLO.   I am to blame.
DESDEMONA.   Why do you speak so faintly?
    Are you not well?
OTHELLO.   I have a pain upon my forehead here.   285
DESDEMONA.   Faith, that's with watching,° 'twill away again.
    Let me but bind it hard, within this hour
    It will be well.
OTHELLO.   Your napkin° is too little,
    (He puts the handkerchief from him, and it drops.)
    Let it alone. Come, I'll go in with you.
DESDEMONA.   I am very sorry that you are not well.   290
    (Exeunt OTHELLO *and* DESDEMONA.*)*
EMILIA.   I am glad I have found this napkin.
    This was her first remembrance from the Moor.
    My wayward° husband hath a hundred times
    Wooed me to steal it, but she so loves the token,
    For he conjured° her she should ever keep it,   295
    That she reserves it evermore about her

---

266. **chamberers:** playboys   277. **forkèd plague:** i.e., to be a cuckold   278. **quicken:** stir in
our mother's womb   281. **generous:** noble   286. **watching:** lack of sleep   288. **napkin:**
handkerchief   293. **wayward:** unaccountable   295. **conjured:** begged with an oath

To kiss and talk to. I'll have the work ta'en out,°
And give 't to Iago. What he will do with it
Heaven knows, not I.
I nothing know, but for his fantasy.° (*Re-enter* IAGO.)   300
IAGO.   How now! What do you here alone?
EMILIA.   Do not you chide, I have a thing for you.
IAGO.   A thing for me? It is a common thing—
EMILIA.   Ha!
IAGO.   To have a foolish wife.   305
EMILIA.   Oh, is that all? What will you give me now
     For that same handkerchief?
IAGO.   What handkerchief?
EMILIA.   What handkerchief!
     Why, that the Moor first gave to Desdemona,
     That which so often you did bid me steal.   310
IAGO.   Hast stol'n it from her?
EMILIA.   No, faith, she let it drop by negligence,
     And, to the advantage, I being here took 't up.
     Look, here it is.
IAGO.   A good wench. Give it me.
EMILIA.   What will you do with 't, that you have been so earnest 315
     To have me filch it?
IAGO (*snatching it*).   Why, what's that to you?
EMILIA.   If 't be not for some purpose of import,
     Give 't me again. Poor lady, she'll run mad
     When she shall lack it.
IAGO.   Be not acknown on 't,° I have use for it.   320
     Go, leave me. (*Exit* EMILIA.)
     I will in Cassio's lodging lose this napkin,
     And let him find it. Trifles light as air
     Are to the jealous confirmations strong
     As proofs of Holy Writ. This may do something.   325
     The Moor already changes with my poison.
     Dangerous conceits° are in their natures poisons,
     Which at the first are scarce found to distaste,
     But, with a little, act upon the blood,
     Burn like the mines of sulphur. I did say so.°   330
     Look where he comes! (*Re-enter* OTHELLO.)

---

297. work . . . out: pattern copied   **300. fantasy:** whim   **320. Be . . . 't:** Know nothing
about it   **327. conceits:** ideas [Eds.]   **330. I . . . so:** As Iago says this, Othello is seen
approaching, with all the signs of his agitation outwardly visible.

                              Not poppy,° nor mandragora,°
       Nor all the drowsy syrups of the world,
       Shall ever medicine thee to that sweet sleep
       Which thou owedst° yesterday.
OTHELLO.   Ha! Ha! False to me?
IAGO.   Why, how now, General! No more of that.   335
OTHELLO.   Avaunt! Be gone! Thou hast set me on the rack.
       I swear 'tis better to be much abused
       Than but to know 't a little.
IAGO.   How now, my lord!
OTHELLO.   What sense had I of her stol'n hours of lust?
       I saw 't not, thought it not, it harmed not me.   340
       I slept the next night well, was free and merry.
       I found not Cassio's kisses on her lips.
       He that is robbed, not wanting° what is stol'n,
       Let him not know 't and he's not robbed at all.
IAGO.   I am sorry to hear this.   345
OTHELLO.   I had been happy if the general camp,
       Pioners° and all, had tasted her sweet body,
       So I had nothing known. Oh, now forever
       Farewell the tranquil mind! Farewell content!
       Farewell the plumèd troop and the big wars   350
       That make ambition virtue! Oh farewell,
       Farewell the neighing steed and the shrill trump,
       The spirit-stirring drum, the ear-piercing fife,
       The royal banner, and all quality,
       Pride, pomp, and circumstance of glorious war!   355
       And, O you mortal engines,° whose rude throats
       The immortal Jove's dread clamors counterfeit,
       Farewell! Othello's occupation's gone!
IAGO.   Is 't possible, my lord?
OTHELLO.   Villain, be sure thou prove my love a whore,   360
       Be sure of it, give me the ocular proof.
       Or by the worth of man's eternal soul,
       Thou hadst been better have been born a dog
       Than answer my waked wrath!
IAGO.   Is 't come to this?
OTHELLO.   Make me to see 't, or at the least so prove it   365

---

331. **poppy:** opium   **mandragora:** called also mandrake—a root used as a drug to bring
sleep   334. **owedst:** owned   343. **wanting:** missing   347. **Pioners:** Pioneers, the lowest
type of soldier   356. **mortal engines:** deadly cannon

That the probation° bear no hinge nor loop
To hang a doubt on, or woe upon thy life!
IAGO.   My noble lord—
OTHELLO.   If thou dost slander her and torture me,
  Never pray more, abandon all remorse.°   370
  On horror's head horrors accumulate,
  Do deeds to make Heaven weep, all earth amazed,
  For nothing canst thou to damnation add
  Greater than that.
IAGO.   Oh, grace! Oh, Heaven defend me!
  Are you a man? Have you a soul or sense?   375
  God be wi' you, take mine office. O wretched fool,
  That livest to make thine honesty a vice!
  O monstrous world! Take note, take note, O world,
  To be direct and honest is not safe.
  I thank you for this profit, and from hence   380
  I'll love no friend, sith° love breeds such offense.
OTHELLO.   Nay, stay. Thou shouldst be honest.
IAGO.   I should be wise, for honesty's a fool,
  And loses that it works for.
OTHELLO.   By the world,
  I think my wife be honest, and think she is not.   385
  I think that thou are just, and think thou art not.
  I'll have some proof. Her name, that was as fresh
  As Dian's° visage, is now begrimed and black
  As mine own face. If there be cords, or knives,
  Poison, or fire, or suffocating streams,   390
  I'll not endure it. Would I were satisfied!
IAGO.   I see, sir, you are eaten up with passion.
  I do repent me that I put it to you.
  You would be satisfied?
OTHELLO.   Would! Nay, I will.
IAGO.   And may, but how? How satisfied, my lord?   395
  Would you, the supervisor,° grossly gape on?
  Behold her topped?
OTHELLO.   Death and damnation! Oh!
IAGO.   It were a tedious difficulty, I think,
  To bring them to that prospect. Damn them then,
  If ever mortal eyes do see them bolster°   400

---

366. probation: proof   **370. remorse:** pity   **381. sith:** since   **388. Dian:** Diana, goddess of
chastity   **396. supervisor:** looker-on   **400. bolster:** sleep together

More than their own! What then? How then?
What shall I say? Where's satisfaction?
It is impossible you should see this,
Were they as prime° as goats, as hot as monkeys,
As salt° as wolves in pride,° and fools as gross   405
As ignorance made drunk. But yet I say
If imputation° and strong circumstances,
Which lead directly to the door of truth,
Will give you satisfaction, you may have 't.
OTHELLO.   Give me a living reason she's disloyal.   410
IAGO.   I do not like the office.
But sith I am entered in this cause so far,
Pricked to 't by foolish honesty and love,
I will go on. I lay with Cassio lately,
And being troubled with a raging tooth,   415
I could not sleep.
There are a kind of men so loose of soul
That in their sleeps will mutter their affairs.
One of this kind is Cassio.
In sleep I heard him say "Sweet Desdemona,   420
Let us be wary, let us hide our loves."
And then, sir, would he gripe° and wring my hand,
Cry "O sweet creature!" and then kiss me hard,
As if he plucked up kisses by the roots
That grew upon my lips. Then laid his leg   425
Over my thigh, and sighed and kissed, and then
Cried "Cursed fate that gave thee to the Moor!"
OTHELLO.   Oh, monstrous! Monstrous!
IAGO.   Nay, this was but his dream.
OTHELLO.   But this denoted a foregone conclusion.
'Tis a shrewd doubt,° though it be but a dream.   430
IAGO.   And this may help to thicken other proofs
That do demonstrate thinly.
OTHELLO.   I'll tear her all to pieces.
IAGO.   Nay, but be wise. Yet we see nothing done.
She may be honest yet. Tell me this:
Have you not sometimes seen a handkerchief   435
Spotted with strawberries in your wife's hand?
OTHELLO.   I gave her such a one, 'twas my first gift.

---

404. prime: lustful   **405. salt:** eager   **pride:** in heat   **407. imputation:** probability
422. gripe: grip   **430. shrewd doubt:** bitter suspicion

IAGO.   I know not that. But such a handkerchief—
    I am sure it was your wife's—did I today
    See Cassio wipe his beard with.
OTHELLO.   If it be that—   440
IAGO.   If it be that, or any that was hers,
    It speaks against her with the other proofs.
OTHELLO.   Oh, that the slave had forty thousand lives!
    One is too poor, too weak, for my revenge.
    Now do I see 'tis true. Look here, Iago,   445
    All my fond love thus do I blow to Heaven—
    'Tis gone.
    Arise, black Vengeance, from thy hollow cell!
    Yield up, O Love, thy crown and hearted throne
    To tyrannous hate! Swell, bosom, with thy fraught,°   450
    For 'tis of aspics'° tongues!
IAGO.   Yet be content.
OTHELLO.   Oh, blood, blood, blood!
IAGO.   Patience, I say. Your mind perhaps may change.
OTHELLO.   Never, Iago. Like to the Pontic Sea,
    Whose icy current and compulsive course   455
    Ne'er feels retiring ebb but keeps due on
    To the Propontic and the Hellespont;
    Even so my bloody thoughts, with violent pace,
    Shall ne'er look back, ne'er ebb to humble love,
    Till that a capable° and wide revenge   460
    Swallow them up. Now, by yond marble Heaven,
    In the due reverence of a sacred vow (*kneels*)
    I here engage my words.
IAGO.   Do not rise yet. (*Kneels.*)
    Witness, you ever burning lights above,
    You elements that clip° us round about,   465
    Witness that here Iago doth give up
    The execution of his wit,° hands, heart,
    To wronged Othello's service! Let him command,
    And to obey shall be in me remorse,°
    What bloody business ever. (*They rise.*)
OTHELLO.   I greet thy love,   470
    Not with vain thanks, but with acceptance bounteous,
    And will upon the instant put thee to 't.

---

450. fraught: freight   **451. aspics':** asps'   **460. capable:** comprehensive
465. clip: embrace   **467. wit:** mind [Eds.]   **469. remorse:** solemn obligation

Within these three days let me hear thee say
That Cassio's not alive.
IAGO.   My friend is dead. 'Tis done at your request.   475
But let her live.
OTHELLO.   Damn her, lewd minx! Oh, damn her!
Come, go with me apart. I will withdraw,
To furnish me with some swift means of death
For the fair devil. Now art thou my Lieutenant.   480
IAGO.   I am your own forever. (*Exeunt.*)

SCENE 4. BEFORE THE CASTLE.

Enter DESDEMONA, EMILIA, *and* CLOWN.
DESDEMONA.   Do you know, sirrah, where Lieutenant Cassio lies?
CLOWN.   I dare not say he lies anywhere.
DESDEMONA.   Why, man?
CLOWN.   He's a soldier, and for one to say a soldier lies is stabbing.
DESDEMONA.   Go to. Where lodges he?   5
CLOWN.   To tell you where he lodges is to tell you where I lie.
DESDEMONA.   Can anything be made of this?
CLOWN.   I know not where he lodges, and for me to devise a lodging,
and say he lies here or he lies there, were to lie in mine own throat.
DESDEMONA.   Can you inquire him out and be edified by report?°   10
CLOWN.   I will catechize the world for him; that is, make questions and
by them answer.
DESDEMONA.   Seek him, bid him come hither. Tell him I have moved
my lord on his behalf and hope all will be well.
CLOWN.   To do this is within the compass of man's wit, and therefore I
will attempt the doing it. (*Exit.*)   16
DESDEMONA.   Where should I lose that handkerchief, Emilia?
EMILIA.   I know not, madam.
DESDEMONA.   Believe me, I had rather have lost my purse
Full of crusados. And, but my noble Moor   20
Is true of mind and made of no such baseness
As jealous creatures are, it were enough
To put him to ill thinking.
EMILIA.   Is he not jealous?
DESDEMONA.   Who, he? I think the sun where he was born
Drew all such humors from him.
EMILIA.   Look where he comes.   25

10. edified by report: enlightened by the information. Desdemona speaks with mock
pomposity.

DESDEMONA.   I will not leave him now till Cassio
  Be called to him. (*Enter* OTHELLO.)
                How is 't with you, my lord?
OTHELLO.   Well, my good lady. (*Aside*) Oh, hardness to dissemble!
  How do you, Desdemona?
DESDEMONA.   Well, my good lord.
OTHELLO.   Give me your hand. This hand is moist,° my lady.   30
DESDEMONA.   It yet has felt no age nor known no sorrow.
OTHELLO.   This argues fruitfulness and liberal heart.
  Hot, hot, and moist—this hand of yours requires
  A sequester from liberty, fasting and prayer,
  Much castigation, exercise devout.   35
  For here's a young and sweating devil here,
  That commonly rebels. 'Tis a good hand,
  A frank one.
DESDEMONA.   You may indeed say so,
  For 'twas that hand that gave away my heart.
OTHELLO.   A liberal° hand. The hearts of old gave hands,   40
  But our new heraldry is hands, not hearts.°
DESDEMONA.   I cannot speak of this. Come now, your promise.
OTHELLO.   What promise, chuck?°
DESDEMONA.   I have sent to bid Cassio come speak with you.
OTHELLO.   I have a salt and sorry rheum offends me.   45
  Lend me thy handkerchief.
DESDEMONA.   Here, my lord.
OTHELLO.   That which I gave you.
DESDEMONA.   I have it not about me.
OTHELLO.   Not?
DESDEMONA.   No indeed, my lord.
OTHELLO.   That's a fault. That handkerchief
  Did an Egyptian to my mother give.   50
  She was a charmer, and could almost read
  The thoughts of people. She told her while she kept it
  'Twould make her amiable and subdue my father
  Entirely to her love, but if she lost it
  Or made a gift of it, my father's eye   55
  Should hold her loathèd and his spirits should hunt

30. moist: A hot moist palm was believed to show desire.   **40. liberal:** overgenerous
40–41. The . . . hearts: Once love and deeds went together, but now it is all deeds (i.e., faithlessness) and no love.   **43. chuck:** A term of affection, but not the kind of word with which a person of Othello's dignity would normally address his wife. He is beginning to treat her with contemptuous familiarity.

After new fancies. She dying gave it me,
And bid me, when my fate would have me wive,
To give it her. I did so. And take heed on 't,
Make it a darling like your precious eye.   60
To lose 't or give 't away were such perdition
As nothing else could match.
DESDEMONA.   Is 't possible?
OTHELLO.   'Tis true. There's magic in the web of it.
A sibyl that had numbered in the world
The sun to course two hundred compasses   65
In her prophetic fury sewed the work.
The worms were hallowed that did breed the silk,
And it was dyed in mummy which the skillful
Conserved° of maiden's hearts.
DESDEMONA.   Indeed! Is 't true?
OTHELLO.   Most veritable, therefore look to 't well.   70
DESDEMONA.   Then would God that I had never seen 't.
OTHELLO.   Ha! Wherefore?
DESDEMONA.   Why do you speak so startingly and rash?
OTHELLO.   Is 't lost? Is 't gone? Speak, is it out o' the way?
DESDEMONA.   Heaven bless us!   75
OTHELLO.   Say you?
DESDEMONA.   It is not lost, but what an if it were?
OTHELLO.   How!
DESDEMONA.   I say it is not lost.
OTHELLO.   Fetch 't, let me see it.
DESDEMONA.   Why, so I can, sir, but I will not now.   80
This is a trick to put me from my suit.
Pray you let Cassio be received again.
OTHELLO.   Fetch me the handkerchief. My mind misgives.
DESDEMONA.   Come, come,
You'll never meet a more sufficient man.   85
OTHELLO.   The handkerchief!
DESDEMONA.   I pray talk me of Cassio.
OTHELLO.   The handkerchief!
DESDEMONA.   A man that all this time
Hath founded his good fortunes on your love,
Shared dangers with you—
OTHELLO.   The handkerchief!   90
DESDEMONA.   In sooth, you are to blame.

69. Conserved: Prepared

OTHELLO.   Away! (*Exit.*)
EMILIA.   Is not this man jealous?
DESDEMONA.   I ne'er saw this before.
 Sure there's some wonder in this handkerchief.   95
 I am most unhappy in the loss of it.
EMILIA.   'Tis not a year or two shows us a man.°
 They are all but stomachs and we all but food.
 They eat us hungerly, and when they are full
 They belch us. Look you, Cassio and my husband.   100
 (*Enter* CASSIO *and* IAGO.)
IAGO.   There is no other way, 'tis she must do 't.
 And, lo, the happiness!° Go and impórtune her.
DESDEMONA.   How now, good Cassio! What's the news with you?
CASSIO.   Madam, my former suit. I do beseech you
 That by your virtuous means I may again   105
 Exist, and be a member of his love
 Whom I with all the office of my heart
 Entirely honor. I would not be delayed.
 If my offense be of such mortal kind
 That nor my service past nor present sorrows   110
 Nor purposed merit in futurity
 Can ransom me into his love again,
 But to know so must be my benefit.
 So shall I clothe me in a forced content
 And shut myself up in some other course   115
 To Fortune's alms.
DESDEMONA.   Alas, thrice-gentle Cassio!
 My advocation° is not now in tune.
 My lord is not my lord, nor should I know him
 Were he in favor° as in humor altered.
 So help me every spirit sanctified,   120
 As I have spoken for you all my best
 And stood within the blank° of his displeasure
 For my free speech! You must awhile be patient.
 What I can do I will, and more I will
 Than for myself I dare. Let that suffice you.   125
IAGO.   Is my lord angry?
EMILIA.   He went hence but now,

---

97. 'Tis . . . man: It does not take a couple of years to discover the nature of a man; i.e., he
soon shows his real nature. **102. And . . . happiness!:** What good luck, here she is!
117. advocation: advocacy **119. favor:** face [Eds.] **122. blank:** aim

And certainly in strange unquietness.
IAGO.   Can he be angry? I have seen the cannon
When it hath blown his ranks into the air,
And, like the Devil, from his very arm   130
Puffed his own brother, and can he be angry?
Something of moment then. I will go meet him.
There's matter in 't indeed if he be angry.
DESDEMONA.   I prithee do so. (*Exit* IAGO.)
                                    Something sure of state,
Either from Venice, or some unhatched practice   135
Made demonstrable° here in Cyprus to him,
Hath puddled his clear spirit. And in such cases
Men's natures wrangle with inferior things,
Though great ones are their object. 'Tis even so,
For let our finger ache and it indues   140
Our other healthful members even to that sense
Of pain. Nay, we must think men are not gods,
Nor of them look for such observancy
As fits the bridal.° Beshrew me much, Emilia,
I was, unhandsome warrior° as I am,   145
Arraigning his unkindness with my soul,
But now I find I had suborned the witness,°
And he's indicted falsely.
EMILIA.   Pray Heaven it be state matters, as you think,
And no conception nor no jealous toy°   150
Concerning you.
DESDEMONA.   Alas the day, I never gave him cause!
EMILIA.   But jealous souls will not be answered so.
They are not ever jealous for the cause,
But jealous for they are jealous. 'Tis a monster   155
Begot upon itself, born on itself.
DESDEMONA.   Heaven keep that monster from Othello's mind!
EMILIA.   Lady, amen.
DESDEMONA.   I will go seek him. Cassio, walk hereabout.
If I do find him fit, I'll move your suit,   160
And seek to effect it to my uttermost.

135–36. unhatched . . . demonstrable: some plot, not yet matured, which has been
revealed   **144. bridal:** honeymoon   **145. unhandsome warrior:** clumsy soldier. Desdemona
continually thinks of herself as Othello's companion in arms. Cf. 1.3.248 ff.
147. suborned the witness: corrupted the evidence; i.e., misunderstood his behavior
[Eds.]   **150. jealous toy:** silly suspicion

CASSIO.   I humbly thank your ladyship.
   (*Exeunt* DESDEMONA *and* EMILIA. *Enter* BIANCA.)
BIANCA.   Save you, friend Cassio!
CASSIO.   What make you from home?
   How is it with you, my most fair Bianca?
   I' faith, sweet love, I was coming to your house.   165
BIANCA.   And I was going to your lodging, Cassio.
   What, keep a week away? Seven days and nights?
   Eightscore eight hours? And lovers' absent hours,
   More tedious than the dial eightscore times?
   Oh, weary reckoning!
CASSIO.   Pardon me, Bianca.   170
   I have this while with leaden thoughts been pressed,
   But I shall in a more continuate time
   Strike off this score of absence. Sweet Bianca,
   (*Giving her* DESDEMONA's *handkerchief.*)
   Take me this work out.
BIANCA.   O Cassio, whence came this?
   This is some token from a newer friend.   175
   To the felt absence now I feel a cause.
   Is 't come to this? Well, well.
CASSIO.   Go to, woman!
   Throw your vile guesses in the Devil's teeth,
   From whence you have them. You are jealous now
   That this is from some mistress, some remembrance.   180
   No, by my faith, Bianca.
BIANCA.   Why, whose is it?
CASSIO.   I know not, sweet. I found it in my chamber.
   I like the work well. Ere it be demanded—
   As like enough it will—I'd have it copied.
   Take it, and do 't, and leave me for this time.   185
BIANCA.   Leave you! Wherefore?
CASSIO.   I do attend here on the General,
   And think it no addition,° nor my wish
   To have him see me womaned.°
BIANCA.   Why, I pray you?
CASSIO.   Not that I love you not.
BIANCA.   But that you do not love me.   190
   I pray you bring me on the way a little,
   And say if I shall see you soon at night.

---

188. addition: honor   **189. womaned:** with a woman

CASSIO.   'Tis but a little way that I can bring you,
    For I attend here. But I'll see you soon.
BIANCA.   'Tis very good, I must be circumstanced.° (*Exeunt.*)   195

ACT 4

SCENE 1. *Cyprus. Before the castle.*

Enter OTHELLO *and* IAGO.

IAGO.   Will you think so?
OTHELLO.   Think so, Iago!
IAGO.   What,
    To kiss in private?
OTHELLO.   An unauthorized kiss.
IAGO.   Or to be naked with her friend in bed
    An hour or more, not meaning any harm?
OTHELLO.   Naked in bed, Iago, and not mean harm!   5
    It is hypocrisy against the Devil.
    They that mean virtuously and yet do so,
    The Devil their virtue tempts and they tempt Heaven.
IAGO.   So they do nothing, 'tis a venial° slip.
    But if I give my wife a handkerchief—   10
OTHELLO.   What then?
IAGO.   Why, then, 'tis hers, my lord, and being hers,
    She may, I think, bestow 't on any man.
OTHELLO.   She is protectress of her honor too.
    May she give that?   15
IAGO.   Her honor is an essence that's not seen.
    They have it very oft that have it not.
    But for the handkerchief—
OTHELLO.   By Heaven, I would most gladly have forgot it.
    Thou said'st—oh, it comes o'er my memory,   20
    As doth the raven o'er the infected house
    Boding to all°—he had my handkerchief.
IAGO.   Aye, what of that?
OTHELLO.   That's not so good now.
IAGO.   What
    If I had said I had seen him do you wrong?
    Or heard him say—as knaves be such abroad,   25

---

195. **circumstanced:** put off   9. **venial:** pardonable   21–22. **As doth the raven . . . all:** As an evil omen (such as a raven overhead) brings evil tidings to all who live in a plague-infested house [Eds.]

Who having, by their own importunate suit,
Or voluntary dotage of some mistress,
Convincèd or supplied° them, cannot choose
But they must blab—

OTHELLO.   Hath he said anything?

IAGO.   He hath, my lord, but be you well assured,   30
No more than he'll unswear.

OTHELLO.   What hath he said?

IAGO.   Faith, that he did—I know not what he did.

OTHELLO.   What? What?

IAGO.   Lie—

OTHELLO.   With her?

IAGO.   With her, on her, what you will.   34

OTHELLO.   Lie° with her! Lie on her!—We say lie on her when they
belie her. —Lie with her. 'Zounds, that's fulsome!° Handkerchief—
confessions—handkerchief!—To confess, and be hanged for his
labor. First to be hanged, and then to confess. I tremble at it. Nature
would not invest herself in such shadowing passion without some
instruction.° It is not words that shake me thus. Pish! Noses, ears,
and lips. Is 't possible?—Confess?—Handkerchief?—Oh, devil!
(Falls in a trance.)   41

IAGO.   Work on,
My medicine, work! Thus credulous fools are caught,
And many worthy and chaste dames even thus,
All guiltless, meet reproach. What ho! My lord!   45
My lord, I say! Othello! (Enter CASSIO.)
                    How now, Cassio!

CASSIO.   What's the matter?

IAGO.   My lord is fall'n into an epilepsy.
This is his second fit, he had one yesterday.

CASSIO.   Rub him about the temples.

IAGO.   No, forbear,   50
The lethargy° must have his quiet course.
If not, he foams at mouth and by and by
Breaks out to savage madness. Look, he stirs.
Do you withdraw yourself a little while,
He will recover straight. When he is gone,   55

---

28. Convincèd or supplied: Overcome or satisfied their desires   **35–41. Lie . . . devil:**
Othello breaks into incoherent muttering before he falls down in a fit.   **36. fulsome:**
disgusting   **38–40. Nature . . . instruction:** Nature would not fill me with such
overwhelming emotion unless there was some cause.   **51. lethargy:** epileptic fit

I would on great occasion speak with you. (*Exit* CASSIO.)
How is it, General? Have you not hurt your head?°
OTHELLO.   Dost thou mock me?
IAGO.   I mock you! No, by Heaven.
Would you would bear your fortune like a man!
OTHELLO.   A hornèd man's a monster and a beast.   60
IAGO.   There's many a beast, then, in a populous city,
And many a civil monster.
OTHELLO.   Did he confess it?
IAGO.   Good sir, be a man.
Think every bearded fellow that's but yoked°
May draw with you.° There's millions now alive   65
That nightly lie in those unproper beds
Which they dare swear peculiar.° Your case is better.
Oh, 'tis the spite of Hell, the Fiend's arch-mock,
To lip° a wanton in a secure couch°
And to suppose her chaste! No, let me know,   70
And knowing what I am, I know what she shall be.
OTHELLO.   Oh, thou art wise, 'tis certain.
IAGO.   Stand you awhile apart,
Confine yourself but in a patient list.°
Whilst you were here o'erwhelmèd with your grief—
A passion most unsuiting such a man—   75
Cassio came hither. I shifted him away,
And laid good 'scuse upon your ecstasy,°
Bade him anon return and here speak with me,
The which he promised. Do but encave yourself,
And mark the fleers, the gibes, and notable scorns,   80
That dwell in every region of his face.
For I will make him tell the tale anew,
Where, how, how oft, how long ago, and when
He hath and is again to cope° your wife.
I say but mark his gesture. Marry, patience,   85
Or I shall say you are all in all in spleen,
And nothing of a man.
OTHELLO.   Dost thou hear, Iago?

---

57. **Have . . . head?:** With brutal cynicism Iago asks whether Othello is suffering from
cuckold's headache.   64. **yoked:** married   65. **draw with you:** be your yoke fellow
66–67. **That . . . peculiar:** That lie nightly in beds which they believe are their own but
which others have shared   69. **lip:** kiss   **secure couch:** lit., a carefree bed; i.e., a bed which
has been used by the wife's lover, but secretly   73. **patient list:** confines of patience
77. **ecstasy:** fit   84. **cope:** encounter

I will be found most cunning in my patience,
But—dost thou hear?—most bloody.

IAGO.   That's not amiss.
But yet keep time in all. Will you withdraw? (OTHELLO *retires*.) 90
Now will I question Cassio of Bianca,
A housewife° that by selling her desires
Buys herself bread and clothes. It is a creature
That dotes on Cassio, as 'tis the strumpet's plague
To beguile many and be beguiled by one.   95
He, when he hears of her, cannot refrain
From the excess of laughter. Here he comes. (*Re-enter* CASSIO.)
As he shall smile, Othello shall go mad,
And his unbookish° jealousy must construe
Poor Cassio's smiles, gestures, and light behavior   100
Quite in the wrong. How do you now, Lieutenant?

CASSIO.   The worser that you give me the addition°
Whose want even kills me.

IAGO.   Ply Desdemona well, and you are sure on 't.
Now, if this suit lay in Bianca's power,   105
How quickly should you speed!

CASSIO.   Alas, poor caitiff!°

OTHELLO.   Look how he laughs already!

IAGO.   I never knew a woman love man so.

CASSIO.   Alas, poor rogue! I think i' faith, she loves me.

OTHELLO.   Now he denies it faintly and laughs it out.   110

IAGO.   Do you hear, Cassio?

OTHELLO.   Now he impórtunes him
To tell it o'er. Go to. Well said, well said.

IAGO.   She gives it out that you shall marry her.
Do you intend to?

CASSIO.   Ha, ha, ha!   115

OTHELLO.   Do you triumph, Roman?° Do you triumph?

CASSIO.   I marry her! What, a customer!° I prithee bear some charity
to my wit. Do not think it so unwholesome. Ha, ha, ha!

OTHELLO.   So, so, so, so. They laugh that win.

IAGO.   Faith, the cry goes that you shall marry her.   120

CASSIO.   Prithee say true.

---

92. housewife: hussy   **99. unbookish:** unlearned   **102. addition:** title (Lieutenant) which
he has lost   **106. caitiff:** wretch   **116. triumph, Roman:** The word "triumph" suggests
"Roman" because the Romans celebrated their victories with triumphs, elaborate shows, and
processions.   **117. customer:** harlot

IAGO.   I am a very villain else.

OTHELLO.   Have you scored° me? Well.

CASSIO.   This is the monkey's own giving out. She is persuaded I will
    marry her out of her own love and flattery, not out of my
    promise.   126

OTHELLO.   Iago beckons me, now he begins the story.

CASSIO.   She was here even now. She haunts me in every place. I was
    the other day talking on the sea bank with certain Venetians, and
    thither comes the bauble, and, by this hand, she falls me thus about
    my neck—   131

OTHELLO.   Crying "O dear Cassio!" as it were. His gesture imports it.

CASSIO.   So hangs and lolls and weeps upon me, so hales and pulls me.
    Ha, ha, ha!

OTHELLO.   Now he tells how she plucked him to my chamber. Oh, I
    see that nose of yours, but not that dog I shall throw it to.   136

CASSIO.   Well, I must leave her company.

IAGO.   Before me!° Look where she comes.

CASSIO.   'Tis such another fitchew!° Marry, a perfumed one.
    (*Enter* BIANCA.)
    What do you mean by this haunting of me?   140

BIANCA.   Let the Devil and his dam haunt you! What did you mean by
    that same handkerchief you gave me even now? I was a fine fool to
    take it. I must take out the work? A likely piece of work, that you should
    find it in your chamber and not know who left it there! This is some
    minx's token, and I must take out the work? There, give it your hobby-
    horse. Wheresoever you had it, I'll take out no work on 't.   146

CASSIO.   How now, my sweet Bianca! How now! How now!

OTHELLO.   By Heaven, that should be my handkerchief!

BIANCA.   An° you'll come to supper tonight, you may. An you will
    not, come when you are next prepared for. (*Exit.*)   150

IAGO.   After her, after her.

CASSIO.   Faith, I must, she'll rail i' the street else.

IAGO.   Will you sup there?

CASSIO.   Faith, I intend so.

IAGO.   Well, I may chance to see you, for I would very fain speak with
    you.   156

CASSIO.   Prithee, come, will you?

IAGO.   Go to. Say no more. (*Exit* CASSIO.)

---

123. scored: marked, as with a blow from a whip   **138. Before me!:** By my soul!
139. fitchew: polecat   **149. An:** If

OTHELLO (*advancing*). How shall I murder him, Iago?

IAGO.   Did you perceive how he laughed at his vice?   160

OTHELLO.   Oh, Iago!

IAGO.   And did you see the handkerchief?

OTHELLO.   Was that mine?

IAGO.   Yours, by this hand. And to see how he prizes the foolish woman your wife? She gave it him, and he hath given it his whore.   165

OTHELLO.   I would have him nine years a-killing. A fine woman! A fair woman! A sweet woman!

IAGO.   Nay, you must forget that.

OTHELLO.   Aye, let her rot, and perish, and be damned tonight, for she shall not live. No, my heart is turned to stone, I strike it and it hurts my hand. Oh, the world hath not a sweeter creature. She might lie by an emperor's side, and command him tasks.   172

IAGO.   Nay, that's not your way.°

OTHELLO.   Hang her! I do but say what she is, so delicate with her needle, an admirable musician—oh, she will sing the savageness out of a bear—of so high and plenteous wit and invention—   176

IAGO.   She's the worse for all this.

OTHELLO.   Oh, a thousand times. And then, of so gentle a condition!

IAGO.   Aye, too gentle.

OTHELLO.   Nay, that's certain. But yet the pity of it, Iago! O Iago, the pity of it, Iago!   181

IAGO.   If you are so fond over her iniquity, give her patent to offend, for if it touch not you, it comes near nobody.

OTHELLO.   I will chop her into messes.° Cuckold me!

IAGO.   Oh, 'tis foul in her.   185

OTHELLO.   With mine officer!

IAGO.   That's fouler.

OTHELLO.   Get me some poison, Iago, this night. I'll not expostulate with her, lest her body and beauty unprovide my mind again. This night, Iago.   190

IAGO.   Do it not with poison, strangle her in her bed, even the bed she hath contaminated.

OTHELLO.   Good, good. The justice of it pleases. Very good.

IAGO.   And for Cassio, let me be his undertaker.°

You shall hear more by midnight.   195

OTHELLO.   Excellent good. (*A trumpet within.*) What trumpet is that same?

---

173. Nay . . . way: i.e., don't get soft thoughts about her   **184. messes:** mincemeat [Eds.]   **194. be his undertaker:** undertake to manage his business. In Shakespeare's plays the word does *not* mean "mortician."

IAGO.   Something from Venice, sure. 'Tis Lodovico
    Come from the Duke. And see, your wife is with him.
    (*Enter* LODOVICO, DESDEMONA, *and* ATTENDANTS.)
LODOVICO.   God save the worthy General!   200
OTHELLO.   With all my heart, sir.
LODOVICO.   The Duke and Senators of Venice greet you. (*Gives him a
    letter.*)
OTHELLO.   I kiss the instrument of their pleasures.
    (*Opens the letter, and reads.*)
DESDEMONA.   And what's the news, good Cousin Lodovico?
IAGO.   I am very glad to see you, signior.   205
    Welcome to Cyprus.
LODOVICO.   I thank you. How does Lieutenant Cassio?
IAGO.   Lives, sir.
DESDEMONA.   Cousin, there's fall'n between him and my lord
    An unkind breach, but you shall make all well.   210
OTHELLO.   Are you sure of that?
DESDEMONA.   My lord?
OTHELLO (*reads*). "This fail you not to do, as you will—"
LODOVICO.   He did not call, he's busy in the paper.
    Is there division 'twixt my lord and Cassio?   215
DESDEMONA.   A most unhappy one. I would do much
    To atone° them, for the love I bear to Cassio.
OTHELLO.   Fire and brimstone!
DESDEMONA.   My lord?
OTHELLO.   Are you wise?°
DESDEMONA.   What, is he angry?
LODOVICO.   Maybe the letter moved him,
    For, as I think, they do command him home,   220
    Deputing Cassio in his government.
DESDEMONA.   By my troth, I am glad on 't.
OTHELLO.   Indeed!
DESDEMONA.   My lord?
OTHELLO.   I am glad to see you mad.
DESDEMONA.   Why, sweet Othello?
OTHELLO.   Devil! (*Striking her.*)
DESDEMONA.   I have not deserved this.   225
LODOVICO.   My lord, this would not be believed in Venice
    Though I should swear I saw 't. 'Tis very much.
    Make her amends, she weeps.

217. atone: reconcile   **218. Are you wise?:** i.e., in saying you bear love to Cassio

OTHELLO.   O devil, devil!
 If that the earth could teem with a woman's tears,
 Each drop she falls would prove a crocodile.°   230
 Out of my sight!
DESDEMONA.   I will not stay to offend you. (*Going.*)
LODOVICO. Truly, an obedient lady.
 I do beseech your lordship, call her back.
OTHELLO. Mistress!
DESDEMONA. My lord?   235
OTHELLO. What would you with her, sir?
LODOVICO.   Who, I, my lord?
OTHELLO. Aye, you did wish that I would make her turn.
 Sir, she can turn and turn, and yet go on
 And turn again. And she can weep, sir, weep.
 And she's obedient, as you say, obedient,   240
 Very obedient.—Proceed you in your tears—
 Concerning this, sir—oh, well-painted passion!°—
 I am commanded home.—Get you away.
 I'll send for you anon.—Sir, I obey the mandate,
 And will return to Venice.—Hence, avaunt! (*Exit* DESDEMONA.)
 Cassio shall have my place. And, sir, tonight,   246
 I do entreat that we may sup together.
 You are welcome, sir, to Cyprus.—Goats and monkeys! (*Exit.*)
LODOVICO. Is this the noble Moor whom our full Senate
 Call all-in-all sufficient? This the nature   250
 Whom passion could not shake? Whose solid virtue
 The shot of accident nor dart of chance
 Could neither graze nor pierce?
IAGO.   He is much changed.
LODOVICO. Are his wits safe? Is he not light of brain?
IAGO. He's that he is. I may not breathe my censure°   255
 What he might be. If what he might he is not,
 I would to Heaven he were!
LODOVICO.   What, strike his wife!
IAGO. Faith, that was not so well, yet would I knew
 That stroke would prove the worst!
LODOVICO.   Is it his use?

229–30. If . . . crocodile: If the earth could breed from woman's tears, each tear that she lets
fall would become a crocodile. It was believed that the crocodile would cry and sob to attract
the sympathetic passer-by, who was then snapped up. **242. passion:** emotion [Eds.]
255. censure: opinion [Eds.]

Or did the letters work upon his blood,   260
     And new-create this fault?
IAGO.   Alas, alas!
     It is not honesty in me to speak
     What I have seen and known. You shall observe him,
     And his own courses will denote him so
     That I may save my speech. Do but go after,   265
     And mark how he continues.
LODOVICO.   I am sorry that I am deceived in him. (*Exeunt.*)

SCENE 2. *A room in the castle.*

     Enter OTHELLO *and* EMILIA.

OTHELLO.   You have seen nothing, then?
EMILIA.   Nor ever heard, nor ever did suspect.
OTHELLO.   Yes, you have seen Cassio and she together.
EMILIA.   But then I saw no harm, and then I heard
     Each syllable that breath made up between them.   5
OTHELLO.   What, did they never whisper?
EMILIA.   Never, my lord.
OTHELLO.   Nor send you out o' the way?
EMILIA.   Never.
OTHELLO.   To fetch her fan, her gloves, her mask, nor nothing?
EMILIA.   Never, my lord.   10
OTHELLO.   That's strange.
EMILIA.   I durst, my lord, to wager she is honest,
     Lay down my soul at stake. If you think other,
     Remove your thought, it doth abuse your bosom.
     If any wretch have put this in your head,   15
     Let Heaven requite it with the serpent's curse!
     For if she be not honest, chaste, and true,
     There's no man happy, the purest of their wives
     Is foul as slander.
OTHELLO.   Bid her come hither. Go. (*Exit* EMILIA.)
     She says enough. Yet she's a simple bawd   20
     That cannot say as much. This is a subtle whore,
     A closet lock and key of villainous secrets.
     And yet she'll kneel and pray, I have seen her do 't.
     (*Enter* DESDEMONA *with* EMILIA.)
DESDEMONA.   My lord, what is your will?
OTHELLO.   Pray, chuck, come hither.
DESDEMONA.   What is your pleasure?

OTHELLO.   Let me see your eyes.   25
    Look in my face.
DESDEMONA.   What horrible fancy's this?
OTHELLO   (*to* EMILIA). Some of your function,° mistress.
    Leave procreants alone and shut the door,
    Cough, or cry hem, if anybody come.
    Your mystery,° your mystery. Nay, dispatch. (*Exit* EMILIA.)   30
DESDEMONA.   Upon my knees, what doth your speech import?
    I understand a fury in your words,
    But not the words.
OTHELLO.   Why, what art thou?
DESDEMONA.   Your wife, my lord, your true and loyal wife.
OTHELLO.   Come, swear it, damn thyself,   35
    Lest, being like one of Heaven,° the devils themselves
    Should fear to seize thee. Therefore be double-damned.
    Swear thou art honest.
DESDEMONA.   Heaven doth truly know it.
OTHELLO.   Heaven truly knows that thou art false as Hell.
DESDEMONA.   To whom, my lord? With whom? How am I false?   40
OTHELLO.   O Desdemona! Away! Away! Away!
DESDEMONA.   Alas the heavy day! Why do you weep!
    Am I the motive of these tears, my lord?
    If haply you my father do suspect
    An instrument of this your calling-back,   45
    Lay not your blame on me. If you have lost him,
    Why, I have lost him too.
OTHELLO.   Had it pleased Heaven
    To try me with affliction, had they rained
    All kinds of sores and shames on my bare head,
    Steeped me in poverty to the very lips,   50
    Given to captivity me and my utmost hopes,
    I should have found in some place of my soul
    A drop of patience. But, alas, to make me
    A fixèd figure for the time of scorn
    To point his slow unmoving finger at!   55
    Yet could I bear that too, well, very well.
    But there where I have garnered up my heart,
    Where either I must live or bear no life,

---

27. Some . . . function: Get about your business, i.e., prostitution. Othello pretends that
Emilia is keeper of a brothel and Desdemona one of the women.
30. mystery: profession   **36. being . . . Heaven:** because you look like an angel

The fountain from the which my current runs
Or else dries up—to be discarded thence!   60
Or keep it as a cistern for foul toads
To knot and gender in! Turn thy complexion there,
Patience, thou young and rose-lipped cherubin—
Aye, there, look grim as Hell!

DESDEMONA.   I hope my noble lord esteems me honest.   65
OTHELLO.   Oh, aye, as summer flies are in the shambles,°
That quicken even with blowing.° O thou weed,
Who art so lovely fair and smell'st so sweet
That the sense aches at thee, would thou hadst ne'er been born!

DESDEMONA.   Alas, what ignorant sin have I committed?   70
OTHELLO.   Was this fair paper,° this most goodly book,
Made to write "whore" upon? What committed!
Committed! O thou public commoner!°
I should make very forges of my cheeks
That would to cinders burn up modesty   75
Did I but speak thy deeds. What committed!
Heaven stops the nose at it, and the moon winks.
The bawdy wind, that kisses all it meets,
Is hushed within the hollow mine of earth
And will not hear it. What committed!   80
Impudent strumpet!

DESDEMONA.   By Heaven, you do me wrong.
OTHELLO.   Are not you a strumpet?
DESDEMONA.   No, as I am a Christian.
If to preserve this vessel for my lord
From any other foul unlawful touch
Be not to be a strumpet, I am none.   85
OTHELLO.   What, not a whore?
DESDEMONA.   No, as I shall be saved.
OTHELLO.   Is 't possible?
DESDEMONA.   Oh, Heaven forgive us!
OTHELLO.   I cry you mercy, then.
I took you for that cunning whore of Venice
That married with Othello. (*Raising his voice*) You mistress,   90
That have the office opposite to Saint Peter,
And keep the gate of Hell! (*Re-enter* EMILIA.)

---

66. **shambles:** slaughterhouse   67. **quicken . . . blowing:** come to life as soon as the eggs are
laid   71. **fair paper:** i.e., her white body   73. **public commoner:** one who offers herself to all
comers

You, you, aye, you!
We have done our course, there's money for your pains.
I pray you turn the key, and keep our counsel. (*Exit.*)

EMILIA.   Alas, what does this gentleman conceive?   95
How do you, madam? How do you, my good lady?

DESDEMONA.   Faith, half-asleep.

EMILIA.   Good madam, what's the matter with my lord?

DESDEMONA.   With who?

EMILIA.   Why, with my lord, madam.   100

DESDEMONA.   Who is thy lord?

EMILIA.   He that is yours, sweet lady.

DESDEMONA.   I have none. Do not talk to me, Emilia.
I cannot weep, nor answer have I none
But what should go by water.° Prithee tonight
Lay on my bed my wedding sheets. Remember,   105
And call thy husband hither.

EMILIA.   Here's a change indeed! (*Exit.*)

DESDEMONA.   'Tis meet I should be used so, very meet.
How have I been behaved that he might stick
The small'st opinion on my least misuse?°
(*Re-enter* EMILIA *with* IAGO.)

IAGO.   What is your pleasure, madam? How is 't with you?   110

DESDEMONA.   I cannot tell. Those that do teach young babes
Do it with gentle means and easy tasks.
He might have chid me so, for, in good faith,
I am a child to chiding.

IAGO.   What's the matter, lady?

EMILIA.   Alas, Iago, my lord hath so bewhored her,   115
Thrown such despite and heavy terms upon her,
As true hearts cannot bear.

DESDEMONA.   Am I that name, Iago?

IAGO.   What name, fair lady?

DESDEMONA.   Such as she says my lord did say I was.

EMILIA.   He called her whore. A beggar in his drink   120
Could not have laid such terms upon his callet.°

IAGO.   Why did he so?

DESDEMONA.   I do not know. I am sure I am none such.

IAGO.   Do not weep, do not weep. Alas the day!

EMILIA.   Hath she forsook so many noble matches,   125
Her father and her country and her friends,

---

104. go by water: be expressed in tears   **109. misuse:** mistake   **121. callet:** slut [Eds.]

To be called whore? Would it not make one weep?
DESDEMONA.   It is my wretched fortune.
IAGO.   Beshrew him for 't!
    How comes this trick upon him?
DESDEMONA.   Nay, Heaven doth know.
EMILIA.   I will be hanged if some eternal villain,   130
    Some busy and insinuating rogue,
    Some cogging, cozening slave, to get some office,
    Have not devised this slander. I'll be hanged else.
IAGO.   Fie, there is no such man, it is impossible.
DESDEMONA.   If any such there be, heaven pardon him!   135
EMILIA.   A halter pardon him! And Hell gnaw his bones!
    Why should he call her whore? Who keeps her company?
    What place? What time? What form? What likelihood?
    The Moor's abused by some most villainous knave,
    Some base notorious knave, some scurvy fellow.   140
    O Heaven, that such companions° Thou'dst unfold,°
    And put in every honest hand a whip
    To lash the rascals naked through the world
    Even from the east to the west!
IAGO.   Speak withindoor.°
EMILIA.   Oh, fie upon them! Some such squire he was   145
    That turned your wit the seamy side without,
    And made you to suspect me with the Moor.
IAGO.   You are a fool. Go to.°
DESDEMONA.   O good Iago,
    What shall I do to win my lord again?
    Good friend, go to him, for, by this light of Heaven,   150
    I know not how I lost him. Here I kneel.
    If e'er my will did trespass 'gainst his love
    Either in discourse of thought or actual deed,
    Or that mine eyes, mine ears, or any sense
    Delighted them in any other form,   155
    Or that I do not yet,° and ever did,
    And ever will, though he do shake me off
    To beggarly divorcement, love him dearly,
    Comfort forswear me! Unkindness may do much,
    And his unkindness may defeat my life,   160

---

141. companions: low creatures   **unfold:** bring to light   **144. Speak withindoor:** Don't
shout so loud that all the street will hear you.   **148. Go to:** an expression of derision
156. yet: still [Eds.]

But never taint my love. I cannot say "whore,"
It doth abhor me now I speak the word.
To do the act that might the addition° earn
Not the world's mass of vanity° could make me.
IAGO.   I pray you be content, 'tis but his humor.   165
The business of the state does him offense,
And he does chide with you.
DESDEMONA.   If 'twere no other—
IAGO.   'Tis but so, I warrant. (*Trumpets within.*)
Hark how these instruments summon to supper!
The messengers of Venice stay the meat.°   170
Go in, and weep not, all things shall be well.
(*Exeunt* DESDEMONA *and* EMILIA. *Enter* RODERIGO.)
How now, Roderigo!
RODERIGO.   I do not find that thou dealest justly with me.
IAGO.   What in the contrary?
RODERIGO.   Every day thou daffest me with some device, Iago, and
    rather, as it seems to me now, keepest from me all conveniency
    than suppliest me with the least advantage of hope. I will indeed no
    longer endure it, nor am I yet persuaded to put up in peace what al-
    ready I have foolishly suffered.   179
IAGO.   Will you hear me, Roderigo?
RODERIGO.   Faith, I have heard too much, for your words and perfor-
    mances are no kin together.
IAGO.   You charge me most unjustly.
RODERIGO.   With naught but truth. I have wasted myself out of my
    means. The jewels you have had from me to deliver to Desdemona
    would half have corrupted a votarist.° You have told me she hath
    received them, and returned me expectations and comforts of sud-
    den respect and acquaintance, but I find none.   188
IAGO.   Well, go to, very well.
RODERIGO.   Very well! Go to! I cannot go to, man, nor 'tis not very
    well. By this hand, I say 'tis very scurvy, and begin to find myself
    fopped in it.   192
IAGO.   Very well.
RODERIGO.   I tell you 'tis not very well. I will make myself known to
    Desdemona. If she will return me my jewels, I will give over my suit
    and repent my unlawful solicitation. If not, assure yourself I will
    seek satisfaction of you.   197

---

163. addition: title   **164. vanity:** i.e., riches   **170. meat:** serving of supper
186. votarist: nun

IAGO.   You have said now.°

RODERIGO.   Aye, and said nothing but what I protest intendment of doing.

IAGO.   Why, now I see there's mettle in thee, and even from this instant do build on thee a better opinion than ever before. Give me thy hand, Roderigo. Thou hast taken against me a most just exception, but yet I protest I have dealt most directly in thy affair.   204

RODERIGO.   It hath not appeared.

IAGO.   I grant indeed it hath not appeared, and your suspicion is not without wit and judgment. But, Roderigo, if thou hast that in thee indeed which I have greater reason to believe now than ever—I mean purpose, courage, and valor—this night show it. If thou the next night following enjoy not Desdemona, take me from this world with treachery and devise engines° for my life.   211

RODERIGO.   Well, what is it? Is it within reason and compass?

IAGO.   Sir, there is especial commission come from Venice to depute Cassio in Othello's place.

RODERIGO.   Is that true? Why, then Othello and Desdemona return again to Venice.   216

IAGO.   Oh, no. He goes into Mauritania, and takes away with him the fair Desdemona, unless his abode be lingered here by some accident, wherein none can be so determinate as the removing of Cassio.

RODERIGO.   How do you mean, "removing of" him?   220

IAGO.   Why, by making him uncapable of Othello's place, knocking out his brains.

RODERIGO.   And that you would have me to do?

IAGO.   Aye, if you dare do yourself a profit and a right. He sups tonight with a harlotry,° and thither will I go to him. He knows not yet of his honorable fortune. If you will watch his going thence, which I will fashion to fall out between twelve and one, you may take him at your pleasure. I will be near to second your attempt, and he shall fall between us. Come, stand not amazed at it, but go along with me. I will show you such a necessity in his death that you shall think yourself bound to put it on him. It is now high suppertime and the night grows to waste. About it.   232

RODERIGO.   I will hear further reason for this.

IAGO.   And you shall be satisfied. (*Exeunt.*)

---

198. **You . . . now:** or in modern slang, "Oh yeah."   211. **engines:** instruments of torture   225. **harlotry:** harlot

SCENE 3. *Another room in the castle.*

Enter OTHELLO, LODOVICO, DESDEMONA, EMILIA, *and* ATTENDANTS.

LODOVICO.   I do beseech you, sir, trouble yourself no further.
OTHELLO.   Oh, pardon me, 'twill do me good to walk.
LODOVICO.   Madam, good night. I humbly thank your ladyship.
DESDEMONA.   Your Honor is most welcome.
OTHELLO.   Will you walk, sir?
 Oh—Desdemona—   5
DESDEMONA.   My lord?
OTHELLO.   Get you to bed on the instant, I will be returned forthwith.
 Dismiss your attendant there. Look it be done.
DESDEMONA.   I will, my lord.
 (*Exeunt* OTHELLO, LODOVICO, *and* ATTENDANTS.)
EMILIA.   How goes it now? He looks gentler than he did.   10
DESDEMONA.   He says he will return incontinent.°
 He hath commanded me to go to bed,
 And bade me to dismiss you.
EMILIA.   Dismiss me!
DESDEMONA.   It was his bidding, therefore, good Emilia,
 Give me my nightly wearing, and adieu.   15
 We must not now displease him.
EMILIA.   I would you had never seen him!
DESDEMONA.   So would not I. My love doth so approve him
 That even his stubbornness, his checks, his frowns—
 Prithee, unpin me—have grace and favor in them.   20
EMILIA.   I have laid those sheets you bade me on the bed.
DESDEMONA.   All's one. Good faith, how foolish are our minds!
 If I do die before thee, prithee shroud me
 In one of those same sheets.
EMILIA.   Come, come, you talk.
DESDEMONA.   My mother had a maid called Barbary.   25
 She was in love, and he she loved proved mad
 And did forsake her. She had a song of "willow"°—
 An old thing 'twas, but it expressed her fortune,
 And she died singing it. That song tonight
 Will not go from my mind. I have much to do   30
 But to go hang my head all at one side
 And sing it like poor Barbary. Prithee, dispatch.

---

11. incontinent: immediately   **27. willow:** the emblem of the forlorn lover

EMILIA.   Shall I go fetch your nightgown?
DESDEMONA.   No, unpin me here.
     This Lodovico is a proper man.
EMILIA.   A very handsome man.   35
DESDEMONA.   He speaks well.
EMILIA.   I know a lady in Venice would have walked barefoot to Palestine for a touch of his nether lip.
DESDEMONA   (*singing*).
     "The poor soul sat sighing by a sycamore tree,
          Sing all a green willow.   40
     Her hand on her bosom, her head on her knee,
          Sing willow, willow, willow.
     The fresh streams ran by her, and murmured her moans,
          Sing willow, willow, willow.
     Her salt tears fell from her, and softened the stones—"   45
     Lay by these—(*singing*)
          "Sing willow, willow, willow,"
     Prithee, hie thee, he'll come anon.—(*singing*)
          "Sing all a green willow must be my garland.
          Let nobody blame him, his scorn I approve—"   50
     Nay, that's not next. Hark! Who is 't that knocks?
EMILIA.   It's the wind.
DESDEMONA   (*singing*).
          "I called my love false love, but what said he then?
               Sing willow, willow, willow.
          If I court moe° women, you'll couch with moe men."   55
     So get thee gone, good night. Mine eyes do itch.
     Doth that bode weeping?
EMILIA.   'Tis neither here nor there.
DESDEMONA.   I have heard it said so. Oh, these men, these men!
     Dost thou in conscience think—tell me, Emilia—
     That there be women do abuse their husbands   60
     In such gross kind?
EMILIA.   There be some such, no question.
DESDEMONA.   Wouldst thou do such a deed for all the world?
EMILIA.   Why, would not you?
DESDEMONA.   No, by this heavenly light!
EMILIA.   Nor I neither by this heavenly light.
     I might do 't as well i' the dark.   65

55. moe: more

DESDEMONA.   Would thou do such a deed for all the world?

EMILIA.   The world's a huge thing. It is a great price
For a small vice.

DESDEMONA.   In troth, I think thou wouldst not.

EMILIA.   In troth, I think I should, and undo 't when I had done. Marry, I
would not do such a thing for a joint ring,° nor for measures of lawn,°
nor for gowns, petticoats, nor caps, nor any petty exhibition;° but for
the whole world—why, who would not make her husband a cuckold
to make him a monarch? I should venture Purgatory for 't.   73

DESDEMONA.   Beshrew me if I would do such a wrong for the whole
world.

EMILIA.   Why, the wrong is but a wrong i' the world, and having the
world for your labor, 'tis a wrong in your own world and you might
quickly make it right.   78

DESDEMONA.   I do not think there is any such woman.

EMILIA.   Yes, a dozen, and as many to the vantage as would store the
world they played for.
But I do think it is their husbands' faults
If wives do fall. Say that they slack their duties
And pour our treasures into foreign laps,
Or else break out in peevish jealousies,   85
Throwing restraint upon us, or say they strike us,
Or scant our former having in despite,°
Why, we have galls,° and though we have some grace,
Yet have we some revenge. Let husbands know
Their wives have sense like them. They see and smell   90
And have their palates both for sweet and sour,
As husbands have. What is it that they do
When they change us for others? Is it sport?
I think it is. And doth affection breed it?
I think it doth. Is 't frailty that thus errs?   95
It is so too. And have not we affections,
Desires for sport, and frailty, as men have?
Then let them use us well. Else let them know
The ills we do, their ills instruct us so.

DESDEMONA.   Good night, good night. Heaven me such uses send,   100
Not to pick bad from bad, but by bad mend! (*Exeunt.*)

---

70. joint ring: ring made in two pieces, a lover's gift   **measures of lawn:** lengths of finest
linen [Eds.]   **71. petty exhibition:** small allowance of money   **87. scant . . . despite:** for spite
cut down our allowance   **88. galls:** bile, the cause of bitterness

ACT 5

SCENE 1. *Cyprus. A street.*

Enter IAGO *and* RODERIGO.

IAGO.   Here, stand behind this bulk, straight will he come.
Wear thy good rapier bare, and put it home.
Quick, quick, fear nothing. I'll be at thy elbow.
It makes us, or it mars us. Think on that,
And fix most firm thy resolution.   5
RODERIGO.   Be near at hand. I may miscarry in 't.
IAGO.   Here, at thy hand. Be bold, and take thy stand. (*Retires.*)
RODERIGO.   I have no great devotion to the deed,
And yet he hath given me satisfying reasons.
'Tis but a man gone. Forth, my sword. He dies.   10
IAGO.   I have rubbed this young quat° almost to the sense,°
And he grows angry. Now, whether he kill Cassio,
Or Cassio him, or each do kill the other,
Every way makes my gain. Live Roderigo,°
He calls me to a restitution large   15
Of gold and jewels that I bobbed from him
As gifts to Desdemona.
It must not be. If Cassio do remain,
He hath a daily beauty in his life
That makes me ugly,° and besides, the Moor   20
May unfold me to him. There stand I in much peril.
No, he must die. Be 't so. I hear him coming. (*Enter* CASSIO.)
RODERIGO.   I know his gait, 'tis he. Villain, thou diest!
(*Makes a pass at* CASSIO.)
CASSIO.   That thrust had been mine enemy indeed
But that my coat is better than thou know'st.   25
I will make proof of thine. (*Draws, and wounds* RODERIGO.)
RODERIGO.   Oh, I am slain!
(IAGO *from behind wounds* CASSIO *in the leg, and exits.*)
CASSIO.   I am maimed for ever. Help, ho! Murder! Murder!
(*Falls. Enter* OTHELLO.)
OTHELLO.   The voice of Cassio. Iago keeps his word.
RODERIGO.   Oh, villain that I am!

---

11. quat: pimple   **sense:** quick   **14. Live Roderigo:** If Roderigo lives [Eds.]
19–20. He . . . ugly: By comparison with him I am a poor thing. Iago is conscious of his lack
of social graces.

OTHELLO.   It is even so.

CASSIO.   Oh, help, ho! Light! A surgeon!   30

OTHELLO.   'Tis he. O brave Iago, honest and just,
    That hast such noble sense of thy friend's wrong!
    Thou teachest me. Minion,° your dear friend lies dead,
    And your unblest fate hies. Strumpet, I come!
    Forth of my heart those charms, thine eyes, are blotted.   35
    Thy bed lust-stained shall with lust's blood be spotted.
    (*Exit. Enter* LODOVICO *and* GRATIANO.)

CASSIO.   What ho! No watch?° No passage?° Murder! Murder!

GRATIANO.   'Tis some mischance, the cry is very direful.

CASSIO.   Oh, help!

LODOVICO.   Hark!   40

RODERIGO.   Oh, wretched villain!

LODOVICO.   Two or three groan. It is a heavy° night.
    These may be counterfeits. Let's think 't unsafe
    To come in to the cry without more help.

RODERIGO.   Nobody come? Then I shall bleed to death.   45

LODOVICO.   Hark! (*Re-enter* IAGO, *with a light.*)

GRATIANO.   Here's one comes in his shirt, with light and weapons.

IAGO.   Who's there? Whose noise is this that cries on murder?

LODOVICO.   We do not know.

IAGO.   Did not you hear a cry?

CASSIO.   Here, here! For Heaven's sake, help me!

IAGO.   What's the matter? 50

GRATIANO.   This is Othello's Ancient, as I take it.

LODOVICO.   The same indeed, a very valiant fellow.

IAGO.   What are you here that cry so grievously?

CASSIO.   Iago? Oh, I am spoiled, undone by villains! Give me some
    help.   55

IAGO.   Oh me, Lieutenant! What villains have done this?

CASSIO.   I think that one of them is hereabout,
    And cannot make away.

IAGO.   Oh, treacherous villains!
    (*To* LODOVICO *and* GRATIANO) What are you there?
    Come in and give some help.

RODERIGO.   Oh, help me here!   60

CASSIO.   That's one of them.

---

33. Minion: Darling, in a bad sense   **37. watch:** police   **No passage?:** Nobody
passing?   **42. heavy:** thick

IAGO.   Oh, murderous slave! Oh, villain!
    (*Stabs* RODERIGO.)
RODERIGO.   Oh, damned Iago! Oh, inhuman dog!
IAGO.   Kill men i' the dark! Where be these bloody thieves?
    How silent is this town! Ho! Murder! Murder!
    What may you be? Are you of good or evil?   65
LODOVICO.   As you shall prove us, praise us.
IAGO.   Signior Lodovico?
LODOVICO.   He, sir.
IAGO.   I cry your mercy. Here's Cassio hurt by villains.
GRATIANO.   Cassio!   70
IAGO.   How is 't, brother?
CASSIO.   My leg is cut in two.
IAGO.   Marry, Heaven forbid!
    Light, gentlemen. I'll bind it with my shirt. (*Enter* BIANCA.)
BIANCA.   What is the matter, ho? Who is 't that cried?
IAGO.   Who is 't that cried!   75
BIANCA.   Oh, my dear Cassio! My sweet Cassio!
    Oh, Cassio, Cassio, Cassio!
IAGO.   Oh, notable strumpet! Cassio, may you suspect
    Who they should be that have thus mangled you?
CASSIO.   No.   80
GRATIANO.   I am sorry to find you thus. I have been to seek you.
IAGO.   Lend me a garter. Oh, for a chair,
    To bear him easily hence!
BIANCA.   Alas, he faints! Oh, Cassio, Cassio, Cassio!
IAGO.   Gentlemen all, I do suspect this trash   85
    To be a party in this injury.
    Patience awhile, good Cassio. Come, come
    Lend me a light. Know we this face or no?
    Alas, my friend and my dear countryman
    Roderigo? No—yes, sure. Oh Heaven! Roderigo.   90
GRATIANO.   What, of Venice?
IAGO.   Even he, sir. Did you know him?
GRATIANO.   Know him! Aye.
IAGO.   Signior Gratiano? I cry you gentle pardon.
    These bloody accidents must excuse my manners,
    That so neglected you.
GRATIANO.   I am glad to see you.   95
IAGO.   How do you, Cassio? Oh, a chair, a chair!
GRATIANO.   Roderigo!

IAGO.   He, he, 'tis he. (*A chair brought in.*) Oh, that's well said, the chair.
   Some good man bear him carefully from hence.
   I'll fetch the General's surgeon. (*To* BIANCA) For you, mistress,   100
   Save you your labor. He that lies slain here, Cassio,
   Was my dear friend. What malice between you?
CASSIO.   None in the world, nor do I know the man.
IAGO (*to* BIANCA). What, look you pale? Oh, bear him out o' the air.
   (CASSIO *and* RODERIGO *are borne off.*)
   Stay you, good gentlemen. Look you pale, mistress?   105
   Do you perceive the gastness of her eye?
   Nay, if you stare, we shall hear more anon.
   Behold her well, I pray you look upon her.
   Do you see, gentlemen? Nay, guiltiness will speak,
   Though tongues were out of use. (*Enter* EMILIA.)   110
EMILIA.   'Las, what's the matter? What's the matter, husband?
IAGO.   Cassio hath here been set on in the dark
   By Roderigo and fellows that are 'scaped.
   He's almost slain, and Roderigo dead.
EMILIA.   Alas, good gentleman! Alas, good Cassio!   115
IAGO.   This is the fruit of whoring. Prithee, Emilia,
   Go know of Cassio where he supped tonight.
   What, do you shake at that?
BIANCA.   He supped at my house, but I therefore shake not.
IAGO.   Oh, did he so? I charge you, go with me.   120
EMILIA.   Fie, fie upon thee, strumpet!
BIANCA.   I am no strumpet, but of life as honest
   As you that thus abuse me.
EMILIA.   As I! Foh! Fie upon thee!
IAGO.   Kind gentlemen, let's go see poor Cassio dressed.°
   Come, mistress, you must tell's another tale.   125
   Emilia, run you to the citadel,
   And tell my lord and lady what hath happened!
   Will you go on afore? I pray. (*Aside*) This is the night
   That either makes me or fordoes me quite. (*Exeunt.*)

---

124. dressed: i.e., his wound dressed

SCENE 2. A *bedchamber in the castle.* DESDEMONA *in bed asleep, a light burning.*

Enter OTHELLO.

OTHELLO. It is the cause,° it is the cause, my soul.
Let me not name it to you, you chaste stars!
It is the cause. Yet I'll not shed her blood,
Nor scar that whiter skin of hers than snow
And smooth as monumental alabaster.   5
Yet she must die, else she'll betray more men.
Put out the light, and then put out the light.
If I quench thee, thou flaming minister,°
I can again thy former light restore,
Should I repent me. But once put out thy light,   10
Thou cunning'st° pattern of excelling nature,
I know not where is that Promethean heat
That can thy light relume. When I have plucked the rose,
I cannot give it vital growth again,
It needs must wither. I'll smell it on the tree. (*Kissing her*)   15
Ah, balmy breath, that dost almost persuade
Justice to break her sword! One more, one more.
Be thus when thou art dead, and I will kill thee,
And love thee after. One more, and this the last.
So sweet was ne'er so fatal. I must weep,   20
But they are cruel tears. This sorrow's heavenly,
It strikes where it doth love. She wakes.
DESDEMONA. Who's there? Othello?
OTHELLO.   Aye, Desdemona.
DESDEMONA. Will you come to bed, my lord?
OTHELLO. Have you prayed tonight, Desdemona?
DESDEMONA.   Aye, my lord.   25
OTHELLO. If you bethink yourself of any crime
Unreconciled as yet to Heaven and grace,
Solicit for it straight.
DESDEMONA. Alas, my lord, what may you mean by that?
OTHELLO. Well, do it, and be brief. I will walk by.   30
I would not kill thy unprepar̀ed spirit.
No, Heaven forfend! I would not kill thy soul.

---

1. It . . . cause: The meaning of the opening lines of this speech has been much discussed.
The *cause* is Desdemona's supposed faithlessness; Othello, at this moment, sees himself as
embodied justice, the avenger of man betrayed by woman. **8. minister:** servant
11. cunning'st: most skillfully made

DESDEMONA.   Talk you of killing?

OTHELLO.   Aye, I do.

DESDEMONA.   Then Heaven
    Have mercy on me!

OTHELLO.   Amen, with all my heart!

DESDEMONA.   If you say so, I hope you will not kill me.   35

OTHELLO.   Hum!

DESDEMONA.   And yet I fear you, for you are fatal then
    When your eyes roll so. Why I should fear I know not,
    Since guiltiness I know not, but yet I feel I fear.

OTHELLO.   Think on thy sins.

DESDEMONA.   They are loves I bear to you.   40

OTHELLO.   Aye, and for that thou diest.

DESDEMONA.   That death's unnatural that kills for loving.
    Alas, why gnaw you so your nether lip?
    Some bloody passion shakes your very frame.
    These are portents, but yet I hope, I hope,   45
    They do not point on me.

OTHELLO.   Peace, and be still!

DESDEMONA.   I will so. What's the matter?

OTHELLO.   That handkerchief which I so loved and gave thee
    Thou gavest to Cassio.

DESDEMONA.   No, by my life and soul!
    Send for the man, and ask him.

OTHELLO.   Sweet soul, take heed,   50
    Take heed of perjury, thou art on thy deathbed.

DESDEMONA.   Aye, but not yet to die.

OTHELLO.   Yes, presently.°
    Therefore confess thee freely of thy sin,
    For to deny each article with oath
    Cannot remove nor choke the strong conception   55
    That I do groan withal. Thou art to die.

DESDEMONA.   Then Lord have mercy on me!

OTHELLO.   I say amen.

DESDEMONA.   And have you mercy too! I never did
    Offend you in my life, never loved Cassio
    But with such general warranty of Heaven   60
    As I might love. I never gave him token.

OTHELLO.   By Heaven, I saw my handkerchief in 's hand.
    O perjured woman! Thou dost stone° my heart,

---

52. **presently:** at once   63. **stone:** turn to stone

And makest me call what I intend to do
A murder, which I thought a sacrifice.   65
I saw the handkerchief.
DESDEMONA.   He found it, then,
I never gave it him. Send for him hither.
Let him confess a truth.
OTHELLO.   He hath confessed.
DESDEMONA.   What, my lord?
OTHELLO.   That he hath used thee.
DESDEMONA.   How? Unlawfully?
OTHELLO.   Aye.   70
DESDEMONA.   He will not say so.
OTHELLO.   No, his mouth is stopped.
Honest Iago hath ta'en order for 't.
DESDEMONA.   Oh, my fear interprets! What, is he dead?
OTHELLO.   Had all his hairs been lives, my great revenge
Had stomach for them all.   75
DESDEMONA.   Alas, he is betrayed, and I undone!
OTHELLO.   Out, strumpet! Weep'st thou for him to my face?
DESDEMONA.   Oh, banish me, my lord, but kill me not!
OTHELLO.   Down, strumpet!
DESDEMONA.   Kill me tomorrow, let me live tonight!   80
OTHELLO.   Nay, if you strive—
DESDEMONA.   But half an hour!
OTHELLO.   Being done, there is no pause.
DESDEMONA.   But while I say one prayer!
OTHELLO.   It is too late. (*He stifles her.*)
EMILIA (*within*). My lord, my lord! What ho! My lord, my lord!
OTHELLO.   What noise is this? Not dead? Not yet quite dead?   85
I that am cruel am yet merciful,
I would not have thee linger in thy pain.
So, so.
EMILIA (*within*). What ho! My lord, my lord!
OTHELLO.   Who's there?
EMILIA (*within*). Oh, good my lord, I would speak a word with you!
OTHELLO.   Yes, 'tis Emilia. By and by. She's dead.   90
'Tis like she comes to speak of Cassio's death.
The noise was here. Ha! No more moving?
Still as the grave. Shall she come in? Were 't good?
I think she stirs again. No. What's best to do?
If she come in, she'll sure speak to my wife.   95
My wife! My wife! What wife? I have no wife.

Oh, insupportable! Oh, heavy hour!
Methinks it should be now a huge eclipse
Of sun and moon, and that the affrighted globe
Should yawn° at alteration.
EMILIA (*within*).   I do beseech you   100
That I may speak with you, O good my lord!
OTHELLO.   I had forgot thee. Oh, come in, Emilia.
Soft, by and by. Let me the curtains° draw.
What art thou? (*Unlocks the door. Enter* EMILIA.)
                    What's the matter with thee now?
EMILIA.   Oh, my good lord, yonder's foul murders done!   105
OTHELLO.   What, now?
EMILIA.   But now, my lord.
OTHELLO.   It is the very error of the moon.
She comes more nearer earth than she was wont
And makes men mad.   110
EMILIA.   Cassio, my lord, hath killed a young Venetian
Called Roderigo.
OTHELLO.   Roderigo killed!
And Cassio killed!
EMILIA.   No, Cassio is not killed.
OTHELLO.   Not Cassio killed! Then murder's out of tune,
And sweet revenge grows harsh.   115
DESDEMONA.   Oh, falsely, falsely murdered!
EMILIA.   Alas, what cry is that?
OTHELLO.   That! What?
EMILIA.   Out and alas! That was my lady's voice.
Help! Help, ho! Help! O lady, speak again!
Sweet Desdemona! O sweet mistress, speak!   120
DESDEMONA.   A guiltless death I die.
EMILIA.   Oh, who hath done this deed?
DESDEMONA.   Nobody, I myself. Farewell.
Commend me to my kind lord. Oh, farewell! (*Dies.*)
OTHELLO.   Why, how should she be murdered?
EMILIA.   Alas, who knows?   125
OTHELLO.   You heard her say herself it was not I.
EMILIA.   She said so. I must needs report the truth.
OTHELLO.   She's like a liar gone to burning Hell.
'Twas I that killed her.
EMILIA.   Oh, the more angel she,

---

100. **yawn:** split open in an earthquake [Eds.]   103. **curtains:** i.e., of the bed

And you the blacker devil!   130
OTHELLO.   She turned to folly, and she was a whore.
EMILIA.   Thou dost belie her, and thou art a devil.
OTHELLO.   She was false as water.
EMILIA.   Thou art rash as fire to say
    That she was false. Oh, she was heavenly true!
OTHELLO.   Cassio did top her, ask thy husband else.   135
    Oh, I were damned beneath all depth in Hell
    But that I did proceed upon just grounds
    To this extremity. Thy husband knew it all.
EMILIA.   My husband!
OTHELLO.   Thy husband.   140
EMILIA.   That she was false to wedlock?
OTHELLO.   Aye, with Cassio. Nay, had she been true,
    If Heaven would make me such another world
    Of one entire and perfect chrysolite,
    I'd not have sold her for it.
EMILIA.   My husband!   145
OTHELLO.   Aye, 'twas he that told me first.
    An honest man he is, and hates the slime
    That sticks on filthy deeds.
EMILIA.   My husband!
OTHELLO.   What needs this iteration, woman? I say thy husband.
EMILIA.   Oh, mistress, villainy hath made mocks with love!   150
    My husband say that she was false!
OTHELLO.   He, woman.
    I say thy husband. Dost understand the word?
    My friend, thy husband, honest, honest Iago.
EMILIA.   If he say so, may his pernicious soul
    Rot half a grain a day! He lies to the heart.   155
    She was too fond of her most filthy bargain.
OTHELLO.   Ha!
EMILIA.   Do thy worst.
    This deed of thine is no more worthy Heaven
    Than thou wast worthy her.
OTHELLO.   Peace, you were best.   160
EMILIA.   Thou hast not half that power to do me harm
    As I have to be hurt. O gull! O dolt!
    As ignorant as dirt! Thou hast done a deed—
    I care not for thy sword, I'll make thee known,
    Though I lost twenty lives. Help! Help! ho! Help!   165
    The Moor hath killed my mistress! Murder! Murder!

(*Enter* MONTANO, GRATIANO, IAGO, *and others.*)

MONTANO.   What is the matter? How now, General!

EMILIA.   Oh, are you come, Iago? You have done well,
That men must lay their murders on your neck.

GRATIANO.   What is the matter?   170

EMILIA.   Disprove this villain, if thou be'st a man.
He says thou told'st him that his wife was false.
I know thou didst not, thou'rt not such a villain.
Speak, for my heart is full.

IAGO.   I told him what I thought, and told no more   175
Than what he found himself was apt and true.

EMILIA.   But did you ever tell him she was false?

IAGO.   I did.

EMILIA.   You told a lie, an odious, damnèd lie,
Upon my soul, a lie, a wicked lie!   180
She false with Cassio! Did you say with Cassio?

IAGO.   With Cassio, mistress. Go to, charm your tongue.°

EMILIA.   I will not charm my tongue, I am bound to speak.
My mistress here lies murdered in her bed.

ALL.   Oh, Heavens forfend!   185

EMILIA.   And your reports have set the murder on.

OTHELLO.   Nay, stare not, masters. It is true indeed.

GRATIANO.   'Tis a strange truth.

MONTANO.   Oh, monstrous act!

EMILIA.   Villainy, villainy, villainy!
I think upon 't. I think I smell 't. Oh, villainy!   190
I thought so then. I'll kill myself for grief.
Oh, villainy, villainy!

IAGO.   What, are you mad? I charge you, get you home.

EMILIA.   Good gentlemen, let me have leave to speak.
'Tis proper I obey him, but not now.   195
Perchance, Iago, I will ne'er go home.

OTHELLO.   Oh! Oh! Oh! (*Falling on the bed.*)

EMILIA.   Nay, lay thee down and roar,
For thou has killed the sweetest innocent
That e'er did lift up eye.

OTHELLO (*rising*).   Oh, she was foul!
I scarce did know you, Uncle. There lies your niece,   200
Whose breath indeed these hands have newly stopped.
I know this act shows horrible and grim.

---

182. **charm your tongue:** be silent

GRATIANO.   Poor Desdemona! I am glad thy father's dead.
  Thy match was mortal to him, and pure grief
  Shore his old thread in twain. Did he live now,   205
  This sight would make him do a desperate turn—
  Yea, curse his better angel from his side,
  And fall to reprobation.°

OTHELLO.   'Tis pitiful, but yet Iago knows
  That she with Cassio hath the act of shame   210
  A thousand times committed. Cassio confessed it.
  And she did gratify his amorous works
  With that recognizance and pledge of love
  Which I first gave her, I saw it in his hand.
  It was a handkerchief, an antique token   215
  My father gave my mother.

EMILIA.   Oh, Heaven! Oh, heavenly powers!

IAGO.   'Zounds! Hold your peace.

EMILIA.   'Twill out, 'twill out. I peace!
  No, I will speak as liberal as the north.°
  Let Heaven and men and devils, let them all,   220
  All, all, cry shame against me, yet I'll speak.

IAGO.   Be wise, and get you home.

EMILIA.   I will not.

  (IAGO *offers to stab* EMILIA.)

GRATIANO.   Fie!
  Your sword upon a woman!

EMILIA.   O thou dull Moor! That handkerchief thou speak'st of
  I found by fortune and did give my husband,   225
  For often with a solemn earnestness,
  More than indeed belonged to such a trifle,
  He begged of me to steal it.

IAGO.   Villainous whore!

EMILIA.   She give it Cassio! No, alas, I found it,
  And I did give 't my husband.

IAGO.   Filth, thou liest!   230

EMILIA.   By Heaven, I do not, I do not, gentlemen.
  Oh, murderous coxcomb! What should such a fool
  Do with so good a wife!

OTHELLO.   Are there no stones° in Heaven
  But what serve for the thunder? Precious villain!

---

208. reprobation: damnation; i.e., by self-murder **219. liberal . . . north:** as freely as the
north wind, which is loud and bitter **233. stones:** thunderbolts

(*He runs at* IAGO. IAGO, *from behind, stabs* EMILIA, *and exits.*)
GRATIANO.   The woman falls. Sure, he hath killed his wife.   235
EMILIA.   Aye. Aye. Oh, lay me by my mistress' side.
GRATIANO.   He's gone, but his wife's killed.
MONTANO.   'Tis a notorious villain. Take you this weapon,
    Which I have here recovered from the Moor.
    Come, guard the door without, let him not pass,   240
    But kill him rather. I'll after that same villain,
    For 'tis a damnèd slave. (*Exeunt all but* OTHELLO *and* EMILIA.)
OTHELLO.   I am not valiant neither,
    But every puny whipster gets my sword.
    But why should honor outlive honesty?
    Let it go all.
EMILIA.   What did thy song bode, lady?   245
    Hark, canst thou hear me? I will play the swan,
    And die in music. (*Singing*)
                "Willow, willow, willow."
    Moor, she was chaste. She loved thee, cruel Moor,
    So come my soul to bliss as I speak true.
    So speaking as I think, I die, I die. (*Dies.*)   250
OTHELLO.   I have another weapon in this chamber.
    It is a sword of Spain, the ice brook's temper.—
    Oh, here it is. Uncle, I must come forth.
GRATIANO (*within*). If thou attempt it, it will cost thee dear.
    Thou hast no weapon, and perforce must suffer.   255
OTHELLO.   Look in upon me then, and speak with me,
    Or, naked° as I am, I will assault thee. (*Re-enter* GRATIANO.)
GRATIANO.   What is the matter?
OTHELLO.   Behold, I have a weapon,
    A better never did itself sustain
    Upon a soldier's thigh. I have seen the day   260
    That with this little arm and this good sword
    I have made my way through more impediments
    Than twenty times your stop. But, oh, vain boast!
    Who can control his fate? 'Tis not so now.
    Be not afraid, though you do see me weaponed.   265
    Here is my journey's end, here is my butt°
    And very sea mark of my utmost sail.
    Do you go back dismayed? 'Tis a lost fear.
    Man but a rush° against Othello's breast,

257. naked: unarmed   **266. butt:** aim   **269. Man . . . rush:** Attack with only a reed

And he retires. Where should Othello go?   270
Now, how dost thou look now? O ill-starred wench!
Pale as thy smock! When we shall meet at compt,°
This look of thine will hurl my soul from Heaven
And fiends will snatch at it. Cold, cold, my girl!
Even like thy chastity. Oh, cursèd slave!   275
Whip me, ye devils,
From the possession of this heavenly sight!
Blow me about in winds! Roast me in sulphur!
Wash me in steep-down gulfs of liquid fire!
O Desdemona! Desdemona! Dead!   280
Oh! Oh! Oh!

(*Enter* LODOVICO, MONTANO, CASSIO *carried in a chair, and* OFFICERS
    with IAGO, *prisoner.*)

LODOVICO.   Where is this rash and most unfortunate man?
OTHELLO.   That's he that was Othello. Here I am.
LODOVICO.   Where is the viper? Bring the villain forth.
OTHELLO.   I look down toward his feet,° but that's a fable.   285
    If that thou be'st a devil, I cannot kill thee. (*Wounds* IAGO.)
LODOVICO.   Wrench his sword from him.
IAGO.   I bleed, sir, but not killed.
OTHELLO.   I am not sorry neither. I'd have thee live,
    For, in my sense, 'tis happiness to die.
LODOVICO.   O thou Othello, that wert once so good,   290
    Fall'n in the practice° of a damnèd slave,
    What shall be said to thee?
OTHELLO.   Why, anything.
    An honorable murderer, if you will,
    For naught did I in hate, but all in honor.
LODOVICO.   This wretch hath part confessed his villainy.   295
    Did you and he consent in Cassio's death?
OTHELLO.   Aye.
CASSIO.   Dear General, I never gave you cause.
OTHELLO.   I do believe it, and I ask your pardon.
    Will you, I pray, demand that demi-devil   300
    Why he hath thus ensnared my soul and body?
IAGO.   Demand me nothing. What you know, you know.
    From this time forth I never will speak word.
LODOVICO.   What, not to pray?

---

272. **compt:** account; i.e., the Day of Judgment   285. **toward his feet:** i.e., to see if he has
the cloven hoof of a devil   291. **Fall'n . . . practice:** Destroyed by the plotting

GRATIANO.   Torments will ope your lips.

OTHELLO.   Well, thou dost best.   305

LODOVICO.   Sir, you shall understand what hath befall'n,
    Which, as I think, you know not. Here is a letter
    Found in the pocket of the slain Roderigo,
    And here another. The one of them imports
    The death of Cassio to be undertook   310
    By Roderigo.

OTHELLO.   Oh, villain!

CASSIO.   Most heathenish and most gross!

LODOVICO.   Now here's another discontented paper,
    Found in his pocket too. And this, it seems,
    Roderigo meant to have sent this damnèd villain   315
    But that, belike, Iago in the interim
    Came in and satisfied him.

OTHELLO.   Oh, the pernicious caitiff!
    How come you, Cassio, by that handkerchief
    That was my wife's?

CASSIO.   I found it in my chamber.
    And he himself confessed but even now   320
    That there he dropped it for a special purpose
    Which wrought to his desire.

OTHELLO.   O fool! Fool! Fool!

CASSIO.   There is besides in Roderigo's letter
    How he upbraids Iago, that he made him
    Brave° me upon the watch, whereon it came   325
    That I was cast.° And even but now he spake
    After long seeming dead, Iago hurt him,
    Iago set him on.

LODOVICO.   You must forsake this room, and go with us.
    Your power and your command is taken off,   330
    And Cassio rules in Cyprus. For this slave,
    If there be any cunning cruelty
    That can torment him much and hold him long,°
    It shall be his. You shall close prisoner rest
    Till that the nature of your fault be known   335
    To the Venetian state. Come, bring away.

OTHELLO.   Soft you, a word or two before you go.
    I have done the state some service, and they know 't.
    No more of that. I pray you, in your letters,

---

325. Brave: Insult **326. cast:** dismissed **333. long:** i.e., in dying

When you shall these unlucky deeds relate,   340
Speak of me as I am, nothing extenuate,
Nor set down aught in malice. Then must you speak
Of one that loved not wisely but too well;
Of one not easily jealous, but, being wrought,
Perplexed in the extreme; of one whose hand,   345
Like the base Indian, threw a pearl away
Richer than all his tribe; of one whose subdued eyes,
Albeit unusèd to the melting mood,
Drop tears as fast as the Arabian trees
Their medicinable gum. Set you down this,   350
And say besides that in Aleppo once,
Where a malignant and a turbaned Turk
Beat a Venetian and traduced the state,
I took by the throat the circumcisèd dog
And smote him, thus. (*Stabs himself.*)   355
LODOVICO.   Oh, bloody period!
GRATIANO.   All that's spoke is marred.
OTHELLO.   I kissed thee ere I killed thee. No way but this,
    Killing myself, to die upon a kiss. (*Falls on the bed, and dies.*)
CASSIO.   This did I fear, but thought he had no weapon,
    For he was great of heart.
LODOVICO (*to* IAGO).   O Spartan° dog,   360
More fell° than anguish, hunger, or the sea!
Look on the tragic loading of this bed:
This is thy work. The object poisons sight,
Let it be hid.° Gratiano, keep the house,
And seize upon the fortunes of the Moor,   365
For they succeed on you. To you, Lord Governor,
Remains the censure of this hellish villain,
The time, the place, the torture.
Oh, enforce it!
Myself will straight aboard, and to the state   370
This heavy act with heavy heart relate. (*Exeunt.*)

QUESTIONS

1. In what ways is Othello, in the first two acts, shown to be a person of
   extraordinary quality?

---

360. Spartan: i.e., hardhearted   **361. fell:** cruel   **364. Let . . . hid:** At these words the
curtains are closed across the inner stage (or chamber, if this scene was acted aloft),
concealing all three bodies.

2. Is Othello a person jealous "by nature"? Does he show any disposition to jealousy in the first two acts? What does he say about himself in his final soliloquy? (There has been much critical controversy over the psychological probability of Othello's being roused so quickly to such a high pitch of jealousy in Act 3. Some have explained it by attributing a predisposition to jealousy in Othello; others have attributed it to the almost superhuman Machiavellian cleverness of Iago, which would have taken in any husband. In general, however, Shakespeare was less interested in psychological consistency and the subtle tracing of motivation—which are modern interests—than he was in theatrical effectiveness and the orchestration of emotions. Perhaps the question we should properly ask is not "How probable is Othello's jealousy?" but "How vital and effective has Shakespeare rendered it?")

3. Who is more naturally suspicious of human nature—Othello or Iago?

4. Is something of Othello's nobility manifested even in the scale of his jealousy? How does he respond to his conviction that Desdemona has been unfaithful to him? Would a lesser man have responded in the same way? Why or why not?

5. How does Othello's final speech reestablish his greatness?

6. What are Iago's motivations in his actions toward Othello, Cassio, and Roderigo? What is his philosophy? How does his technique in handling Roderigo differ from his technique in handling Othello and Cassio? Why?

7. In rousing Othello's suspicions against Desdemona (3.3), Iago uses the same technique, in part, that he had used with Othello in inculpating Cassio (2.3) and that he later uses with Lodovico in inculpating Othello (4.2). What is this technique? Why is it effective? How does he change his tactics in the opening of 4.1?

8. What opinions of Iago, before his exposure, are expressed by Othello, Desdemona, Cassio, and Lodovico? Is Othello the only one taken in by him? Does his own wife think him capable of villainy?

9. Though Othello is the protagonist, the majority of soliloquies and asides are given to Iago. Why?

10. The difference between Othello and Desdemona that Iago plays on most is that of color, and, reading the play today, we may be tempted to see the play as being centrally about race relations. However, only one other character, besides Othello, makes much of this difference in color. Which one? Is this character sympathetically portrayed? What attitude toward Othello himself, and his marriage, is taken by the Duke, Cassio, Lodovico, Emilia, Desdemona herself? What differences between Othello and Desdemona, besides color, are used by Iago to undermine Othello's confidence in Desdemona's fidelity? What differences between them does Othello himself take into account?

11. What are Desdemona's principal character traits? In what ways are she and Emilia character foils? Is she entirely discreet in pleading Cassio's case to Othello? Why or why not? Why does she lie about the handkerchief (3.4)?

12. Like Sophocles in *Oedipus Rex*, Shakespeare makes extensive use of dramatic irony in this play. Point out effective examples.
13. Unlike *Oedipus Rex*, *Othello* contains comedy. For what purposes is it used? What larger difference in effect between *Othello* and *Oedipus Rex* does this use of comedy contribute to?
14. Find several occasions when chance and coincidence are involved in the plot (for example, Bianca's entry in 4.1). How important are these to the development of the plot? To what extent do they *cause* subsequent events to happen?
15. As much responsible as any other quality for the original popularity and continued vitality of *Othello* is its poetry. What are some of the prominent characteristics of that poetry (language, imagery, rhythm)? What speeches are particularly memorable or effective? Though most of the play is written in blank verse, some passages are written in rhymed iambic pentameter couplets and others in prose. Can you suggest any reasons for Shakespeare's use of these other mediums?
16. How would the effect of the play have been different if Othello had died *before* discovering Desdemona's innocence?

Molière
Tartuffe
or The Impostor

Characters

MADAME PERNELLE, *Orgon's mother*
ORGON, *Elmire's husband*
ELMIRE, *Orgon's second wife*
DAMIS, *Orgon's son, Elmire's stepson*
MARIANE, *Orgon's daughter, Elmire's stepdaughter, in love with Valère*
VALÈRE, *in love with Mariane*
CLÉANTE, *Orgon's brother-in-law, Elmire's brother*
TARTUFFE, *a hypocrite*
DORINE, *Mariane's lady's-maid*
MONSIEUR LOYAL, *a bailiff*
A POLICE OFFICER
FLIPOTE, *Mme. Pernelle's maid*

The scene throughout is a room in Orgon's house in Paris.

ACT 1

SCENE 1

Enter MADAME PERNELLE, FLIPOTE, ELMIRE, DORINE, CLÉANTE, MARIANE, *and* DAMIS.

MADAME PERNELLE.   Come, come, Flipote; it's time I left this place.
ELMIRE.   I can't keep up, you walk at such a pace.

TARTUFFE, OR THE IMPOSTOR First performed in Paris in 1669 (two earlier versions of the play, in 1664 and 1667, were banned by authorities on religious grounds), during the reign of "the Sun King," Louis XIV, a time in social and aristocratic circles when great emphasis was placed on elegance in dress, manners, and taste. Translated by Richard Wilbur. Molière (1622–73) was born Jean-Baptiste Poquelin in Paris and was given excellent schooling by his father, a successful furniture maker with a position at court. He took "Molière" as his stage-name when, at the age of twenty-one, he joined a traveling theater company. The rest of his life was spent in the theater as actor, manager, and author. Though twice sent to prison for debts, and often in trouble with the civil authorities for his satiric writing, he enjoyed a certain amount of royal favor after his establishment in Paris in 1658, when the king provided him with a theater where he worked for the rest of his life. In his productions of *Tartuffe* Molière took the role of Orgon.

MADAME PERNELLE.   Don't trouble, child; no need to show me out.
   It's not your manners I'm concerned about.
ELMIRE.   We merely pay you the respect we owe.   5
   But, Mother, why this hurry? Must you go?
MADAME PERNELLE.   I must. This house appalls me. No one in it
   Will pay attention for a single minute.
   Children, I take my leave much vexed in spirit.
   I offer good advice, but you won't hear it.   10
   You all break in and chatter on and on.
   It's like a madhouse with the keeper gone.
DORINE.   If . . .
MADAME PERNELLE.   Girl, you talk too much, and I'm afraid
   You're far too saucy for a lady's-maid.
   You push in everywhere and have your say.   15
DAMIS.   But . . .
MADAME PERNELLE.   You, boy, grow more foolish every day.
   To think my grandson should be such a dunce!
   I've said a hundred times, if I've said it once,
   That if you keep the course on which you've started,
   You'll leave your worthy father broken-hearted.   20
MARIANE.   I think . . .
MADAME PERNELLE.   And you, his sister, seems so pure,
   So shy, so innocent, and so demure.
   But you know what they say about still waters.
   I pity parents with secretive daughters.
ELMIRE.   Now, Mother . . .
MADAME PERNELLE.   And as for you, child, let me add   25
   That your behavior is extremely bad,
   And a poor example for these children, too.
   Their dear, dead mother did far better than you.
   You're much too free with money, and I'm distressed
   To see you so elaborately dressed.   30
   When it's one's husband that one aims to please,
   One has no need of costly fripperies.
CLÉANTE.   Oh, Madam, really . . .
MADAME PERNELLE.   You are her brother, Sir,
   And I respect and love you; yet if I were
   My son, this lady's good and pious spouse,   35
   I wouldn't make you welcome in my house.
   You're full of worldly counsels which, I fear,
   Aren't suitable for decent folk to hear.
   I've spoken bluntly, Sir; but it behooves us

Not to mince words when righteous fervor moves us.   40
DAMIS.   Your man Tartuffe is full of holy speeches . . .
MADAME PERNELLE.   And practices precisely what he preaches.
    He's a fine man, and should be listened to.
    I will not hear him mocked by fools like you.
DAMIS.   Good God! Do you expect me to submit   45
    To the tyranny of that carping hypocrite?
    Must we forgo all joys and satisfactions
    Because that bigot censures all our actions?
DORINE.   To hear him talk—and he talks all the time—
    There's nothing one can do that's not a crime.   50
    He rails at everything, your dear Tartuffe.
MADAME PERNELLE.   Whatever he reproves deserves reproof.
    He's out to save your souls, and all of you
    Must love him, as my son would have you do.
DAMIS.   Ah no, Grandmother, I could never take   55
    To such a rascal, even for my father's sake.
    That's how I feel, and I shall not dissemble.
    His every action makes me seethe and tremble
    With helpless anger, and I have no doubt
    That he and I will shortly have it out.   60
DORINE.   Surely it is a shame and a disgrace
    To see this man usurp the master's place—
    To see this beggar who, when first he came,
    Had not a shoe or shoestring to his name
    So far forget himself that he behaves   65
    As if the house were his, and we his slaves.
MADAME PERNELLE.   Well, mark my words, your souls would fare far
    better
    If you obeyed his precepts to the letter.
DORINE.   You see him as a saint. I'm far less awed;
    In fact, I see right through him. He's a fraud.   70
MADAME PERNELLE.   Nonsense!
DORINE.   His man Laurent's the same, or worse;
    I'd not trust either with a penny purse.
MADAME PERNELLE.   I can't say what his servant's morals may be;
    His own great goodness I can guarantee.
    You all regard him with distaste and fear   75
    Because he tells you what you're loath to hear,
    Condemns your sins, points out your moral flaws,
    And humbly strives to further Heaven's cause.
DORINE.   If sin is all that bothers him, why is it

He's so upset when folk drop in to visit?   80
Is Heaven so outraged by a social call
That he must prophesy against us all?
I'll tell you what I think: if you ask me,
He's jealous of my mistress' company.

MADAME PERNELLE.   Rubbish! (To ELMIRE) He's not alone, child, in
    complaining   85
Of all your promiscuous entertaining.
Why, the whole neighborhood's upset, I know,
By all these carriages that come and go,
With crowds of guests parading in and out
And noisy servants loitering about.   90
In all of this, I'm sure there's nothing vicious;
But why give people cause to be suspicious?

CLÉANTE.   They need no cause; they'll talk in any case.
Madam, this world would be a joyless place
If, fearing what malicious tongues might say,   95
We locked our doors and turned our friends away.
And even if one did so dreary a thing,
D'you think those tongues would cease their chattering?
One can't fight slander; it's a losing battle;
Let us instead ignore their tittle-tattle.   100
Let's strive to live by conscience' clear decrees,
And let the gossips gossip as they please.

DORINE.   If there is talk against us, I know the source:
It's Daphne and her little husband, of course.
Those who have greatest cause for guilt and shame   105
Are quickest to besmirch a neighbor's name.
When there's a chance for libel, they never miss it;
When something can be made to seem illicit
They're off at once to spread the joyous news,
Adding to fact what fantasies they choose.   110
By talking up their neighbor's indiscretions
They seek to camouflage their own transgressions,
Hoping that others' innocent affairs
Will lend a hue of innocence to theirs,
Or that their own black guilt will come to seem   115
Part of a general shady color-scheme.

MADAME PERNELLE.   All that is quite irrelevant. I doubt
That anyone's more virtuous and devout
Than dear Orante; and I'm informed that she
Condemns your mode of life most vehemently.   120

DORINE.   Oh, yes, she's strict, devout, and has no taint
　　　Of worldliness; in short, she seems a saint.
　　　But it was time which taught her that disguise;
　　　She's thus because she can't be otherwise.
　　　So long as her attractions could enthrall,   125
　　　She flounced and flirted and enjoyed it all,
　　　But now that they're no longer what they were
　　　She quits a world which fast is quitting her,
　　　And wears a veil of virtue to conceal
　　　Her bankrupt beauty and her lost appeal.   130
　　　That's what becomes of old coquettes today:
　　　Distressed when all their lovers fall away,
　　　They see no recourse but to play the prude,
　　　And so confer a style on solitude.
　　　Thereafter, they're severe with everyone,   135
　　　Condemning all our actions, pardoning none,
　　　And claiming to be pure, austere, and zealous
　　　When, if the truth were known, they're merely jealous,
　　　And cannot bear to see another know
　　　The pleasures time has forced them to forgo.   140
MADAME PERNELLE (*initially to* ELMIRE). That sort of talk is what you
　　　　like to hear;
　　　Therefore you'd have us all keep still, my dear,
　　　While Madam rattles on the livelong day.
　　　Nevertheless, I mean to have my say.
　　　I tell you that you're blest to have Tartuffe   145
　　　Dwelling, as my son's guest, beneath this roof;
　　　That Heaven has sent him to forestall its wrath
　　　By leading you, once more, to the true path;
　　　That all he reprehends is reprehensible,
　　　And that you'd better heed him, and be sensible.   150
　　　These visits, balls, and parties in which you revel
　　　Are nothing but inventions of the Devil.
　　　One never hears a word that's edifying:
　　　Nothing but chaff and foolishness and lying,
　　　As well as vicious gossip in which one's neighbor   155
　　　Is cut to bits with epee, foil, and saber.
　　　People of sense are driven half-insane
　　　At such affairs, where noise and folly reign
　　　And reputations perish thick and fast.
　　　As a wise preacher said on Sunday last,   160
　　　Parties are Towers of Babylon, because

The guests all babble on with never a pause;
And then he told a story which, I think . . .
(*To* CLÉANTE) I heard that laugh, Sir, and I saw that wink!
Go find your silly friends and laugh some more!   165
Enough; I'm going; don't show me to the door.
I leave this household much dismayed and vexed;
I cannot say when I shall see you next.
(*Slapping* FLIPOTE) Wake up, don't stand there gaping into space!
I'll slap some sense into that stupid face.   170
Move, move, you slut. (*Exeunt* MADAME PERNELLE, FLIPOTE, ELMIRE,
     MARIANE, *and* DAMIS.)

SCENE 2*

CLÉANTE.   I think I'll stay behind;
     I want no further pieces of her mind.
     How that old lady . . .
DORINE.   Oh, what wouldn't she say
     If she could hear you speak of her that way!
     She'd thank you for the *lady*, but I'm sure   5
     She'd find the *old* a little premature.
CLÉANTE.   My, what a scene she made, and what a din!
     And how this man Tartuffe has taken her in!
DORINE.   Yes, but her son is even worse deceived;
     His folly must be seen to be believed.   10
     In the late troubles, he played an able part
     And served his king with wise and loyal heart,
     But he's quite lost his senses since he fell
     Beneath Tartuffe's infatuating spell.
     He calls him brother, and loves him as his life,   15
     Preferring him to mother, child, or wife.
     In him and him alone will he confide;
     He's made him his confessor and his guide;
     He pets and pampers him with love more tender
     Than any pretty mistress could engender,   20
     Gives him the place of honor when they dine,

---

*In English and in most modern plays, a "scene" is a continuous section of the action in one setting, and acts are not usually divided into scenes unless there is a shift in setting or a shift in time. In older French drama, however, a scene is any portion of the play involving one group of characters, and a new scene begins, without interruption of the action, whenever any important character enters or exits.

Delights to see him gorging like a swine,
Stuffs him with dainties till his guts distend,
And when he belches, cries "God bless you, friend!"
In short, he's mad; he worships him; he dotes;   25
His deeds he marvels at, his words he quotes,
Thinking each act a miracle, each word
Oracular as those that Moses heard.
Tartuffe, much pleased to find so easy a victim,
Has in a hundred ways beguiled and tricked him,   30
Milked him of money, and with his permission
Established here a sort of Inquisition.
Even Laurent, his lackey, dares to give
Us arrogant advice on how to live;
He sermonizes us in thundering tones   35
And confiscates our ribbons and colognes.
Last week he tore a kerchief into pieces
Because he found it pressed in a *Life of Jesus:*
He said it was a sin to juxtapose
Unholy vanities and holy prose.   40

SCENE 3

Enter ELMIRE, MARIANE, *and* DAMIS.

ELMIRE   (*to* CLÉANTE). You did well not to follow; she stood in the door
    And said *verbatim* all she'd said before.
    I saw my husband coming. I think I'd best
    Go upstairs now, and take a little rest.
CLÉANTE.   I'll wait and greet him here; then I must go.   5
    I've really only time to say hello.
DAMIS.   Sound him about my sister's wedding, please.
    I think Tartuffe's against it, and that he's
    Been urging Father to withdraw his blessing.
    As you well know, I'd find that most distressing.   10
    Unless my sister and Valère can marry,
    My hopes to wed *his* sister will miscarry,
    And I'm determined . . .
DORINE.   He's coming. (*Exeunt* ELMIRE, MARIANE,
    and DAMIS.)

SCENE 4

Enter ORGON.

ORGON.   Ah, Brother, good-day.
CLÉANTE.   Well, welcome back. I'm sorry I can't stay.
    How was the country? Blooming, I trust, and green?
ORGON.   Excuse me, Brother; just one moment.
    (*To* DORINE)   Dorine . . .
    (*To* CLÉANTE) To put my mind at rest, I always learn   5
    The household news the moment I return.
    (*To* DORINE) Has all been well, these two days I've been gone?
    How are the family? What's been going on?
DORINE.   Your wife, two days ago, had a bad fever,
    And a fierce headache which refused to leave her.   10
ORGON.   Ah. And Tartuffe?
DORINE.   Tartuffe? Why, he's round and red,
    Bursting with health, and excellently fed.
ORGON.   Poor fellow!
DORINE.   That night, the mistress was unable
    To take a single bite at the dinner-table.
    Her headache-pains, she said, were simply hellish.   15
ORGON.   Ah. And Tartuffe?
DORINE.   He ate his meal with relish,
    And zealously devoured in her presence
    A leg of mutton and a brace of pheasants.
ORGON.   Poor fellow!
DORINE.   Well, the pains continued strong,
    And so she tossed and tossed the whole night long,   20
    Now icy-cold, now burning like a flame.
    We sat beside her bed till morning came.
ORGON.   Ah. And Tartuffe?
DORINE.   Why, having eaten, he rose
    And sought his room, already in a doze,
    Got into his warm bed, and snored away   25
    In perfect peace until the break of day.
ORGON.   Poor fellow!
DORINE.   After much ado, we talked her
    Into dispatching someone for the doctor.
    He bled her, and the fever quickly fell.
ORGON.   Ah. And Tartuffe?
DORINE.   He bore it very well.   30
    To keep his cheerfulness at any cost,

And make up for the blood *Madame* had lost,
He drank, at lunch, four beakers full of port.
ORGON.   Poor fellow!
DORINE.   Both are doing well, in short.
  I'll go and tell *Madame* that you've expressed   35
  Keen sympathy and anxious interest. (*Exit.*)

SCENE 5

CLÉANTE.   That girl was laughing in your face, and though
  I've no wish to offend you, even so
  I'm bound to say that she had some excuse.
  How can you possibly be such a goose?
  Are you so dazed by this man's hocus-pocus   5
  That all the world, save him, is out of focus?
  You've given him clothing, shelter, food, and care;
  Why must you also . . .
ORGON.   Brother, stop right there.
  You do not know the man of whom you speak.
CLÉANTE.   I grant you that. But my judgment's not so weak   10
  That I can't tell, by his effect on others . . .
ORGON.   Ah, when you meet him, you two will be like brothers!
  There's been no loftier soul since time began.
  He is a man who . . . a man who . . . an excellent man.
  To keep his precepts is to be reborn,   15
  And view this dunghill of a world with scorn.
  Yes, thanks to him I'm a changed man indeed.
  Under his tutelage my soul's been freed
  From earthly loves, and every human tie:
  My mother, children, brother, and wife could die,   20
  And I'd not feel a single moment's pain.
CLÉANTE.   That's a fine sentiment, Brother; most humane.
ORGON.   Oh, had you seen Tartuffe as I first knew him,
  Your heart, like mine, would have surrendered to him.
  He used to come into our church each day   25
  And humbly kneel nearby, and start to pray.
  He'd draw the eyes of everybody there
  By the deep fervor of his heartfelt prayer;
  He'd sigh and weep, and sometimes with a sound
  Of rapture he would bend and kiss the ground;   30
  And when I rose to go, he'd run before
  To offer me holy-water at the door.

His serving-man, no less devout than he,
Informed me of his master's poverty;
I gave him gifts, but in his humbleness   35
He'd beg me every time to give him less.
"Oh, that's too much," he'd cry, "too much by twice!
I don't deserve it. The half, Sir, would suffice."
And when I wouldn't take it back, he'd share
Half of it with the poor, right then and there.   40
At length, Heaven prompted me to take him in
To dwell with us, and free our souls from sin.
He guides our lives, and to protect my honor
Stays by my wife, and keeps an eye upon her;
He tells me whom she sees, and all she does,   45
And seems more jealous than I ever was!
And how austere he is! Why, he can detect
A mortal sin where you would least suspect;
In smallest trifles, he's extremely strict.
Last week, his conscience was severely pricked   50
Because, while praying, he had caught a flea
And killed it, so he felt, too wrathfully.

CLÉANTE.   Good God, man! Have you lost your common sense—
Or is this all some joke at my expense?
How can you stand there and in all sobriety . . .   55

ORGON.   Brother, your language savors of impiety.
Too much free-thinking's made your faith unsteady,
And as I've warned you many times already,
'Twill get you into trouble before you're through.

CLÉANTE.   So I've been told before by dupes like you: 60
Being blind, you'd have all others blind as well;
The clear-eyed man you call an infidel,
And he who sees through humbug and pretense
Is charged, by you, with want of reverence.
Spare me your warnings, Brother; I have no fear   65
Of speaking out, for you and Heaven to hear,
Against affected zeal and pious knavery.
There's true and false in piety, as in bravery,
And just as those whose courage shines the most
In battle, are the least inclined to boast,   70
So those whose hearts are truly pure and lowly
Don't make a flashy show of being holy.
There's a vast difference, so it seems to me,
Between true piety and hypocrisy:

How do you fail to see it, may I ask?   75
Is not a face quite different from a mask?
Cannot sincerity and cunning art,
Reality and semblance, be told apart?
Are scarecrows just like men, and do you hold
That a false coin is just as good as gold?   80
Ah, Brother, man's a strangely fashioned creature
Who seldom is content to follow Nature,
But recklessly pursues his inclination
Beyond the narrow bounds of moderation,
And often, by transgressing Reason's laws,   85
Perverts a lofty aim or noble cause.
A passing observation, but it applies.
ORGON.   I see, dear Brother, that you're profoundly wise;
You harbor all the insight of the age.
You are our one clear mind, our only sage,   90
The era's oracle, its Cato too,
And all mankind are fools compared to you.
CLÉANTE.   Brother, I don't pretend to be a sage,
Nor have I all the wisdom of the age.
There's just one insight I would dare to claim: 95
I know that true and false are not the same;
And just as there is nothing I more revere
Than a soul whose faith is steadfast and sincere,
Nothing that I more cherish and admire
Than honest zeal and true religious fire,   100
So there is nothing that I find more base
Than specious piety's dishonest face—
Than these bold mountebanks, these histrios
Whose impious mummeries and hollow shows
Exploit our love of Heaven, and make a jest   105
Of all that men think holiest and best;
These calculating souls who offer prayers
Not to their Maker, but as public wares,
And seek to buy respect and reputation
With lifted eyes and sighs of exaltation;   110
These charlatans, I say, whose pilgrim souls
Proceed, by way of Heaven, toward earthly goals,
Who weep and pray and swindle and extort,
Who preach the monkist life, but haunt the court,
Who make their zeal the partner of their vice—   115
Such men are vengeful, sly, and cold as ice,

And when there is an enemy to defame
They cloak their spite in fair religion's name,
Their private spleen and malice being made
To seem a high and virtuous crusade,   120
Until, to mankind's reverent applause,
They crucify their foe in Heaven's cause.
Such knaves are all too common; yet, for the wise,
True piety isn't hard to recognize,
And, happily, these present times provide us   125
With bright examples to instruct and guide us.
Consider Ariston and Périandre;
Look at Oronte, Alcidamas, Clitandre;
Their virtue is acknowledged; who could doubt it?
But you won't hear them beat the drum about it.   130
They're never ostentatious, never vain,
And their religion's moderate and humane;
It's not their way to criticize and chide:
They think censoriousness a mark of pride,
And therefore, letting others preach and rave,   135
They show, by deeds, how Christians should behave.
They think no evil of their fellow man,
But judge of him as kindly as they can.
They don't intrigue and wangle and conspire;
To lead a good life is their one desire;   140
The sinner wakes no rancorous hate in them;
It is the sin alone which they condemn;
Nor do they try to show a fiercer zeal
For Heaven's cause than Heaven itself could feel.
These men I honor, these men I advocate   145
As models for us all to emulate.
Your man is not their sort at all, I fear:
And, while your praise of him is quite sincere,
I think that you've been dreadfully deluded.
ORGON.   Now then, dear Brother, is your speech concluded?   150
CLÉANTE.   Why yes.
ORGON.   Your servant, Sir. (*He turns to go.*)
CLÉANTE.   No, Brother; wait.
     There's one more matter. You agreed of late
     That young Valère might have your daughter's hand.
ORGON.   I did.
CLÉANTE.   And set the date, I understand.
ORGON.   Quite so.

CLÉANTE.   You've now postponed it; is that true?   155
ORGON.   No doubt.
CLÉANTE.   The match no longer pleases you?
ORGON.   Who knows?
CLÉANTE.   D'you mean to go back on your word?
ORGON.   I won't say that.
CLÉANTE.   Has anything occurred
    Which might entitle you to break your pledge?
ORGON.   Perhaps.
CLÉANTE.   Why must you hem, and haw, and hedge?   160
    The boy asked me to sound you in this affair . . .
ORGON.   It's been a pleasure.
CLÉANTE.   But what shall I tell Valère?
ORGON.   Whatever you like.
CLÉANTE.   But what have you decided?
    What are your plans?
ORGON.   I plan, Sir, to be guided
    By Heaven's will.
CLÉANTE.   Come, Brother, don't talk rot.   165
    You've given Valère your word; will you keep it, or not?
ORGON.   Good day.
CLÉANTE.   This looks like poor Valère's undoing;
    I'll go and warn him that there's trouble brewing. (*Exit.*)

ACT 2

SCENE 1

Enter MARIANE.

ORGON.   Mariane.
MARIANE.   Yes, Father?
ORGON.   A word with you; come here.
MARIANE.   What are you looking for?
ORGON (*peering into a small closet*).   Eavesdroppers, dear.
    I'm making sure we shan't be overheard.
    Someone in there could catch our every word.
    Ah, good, we're safe. Now, Mariane, my child,   5
    You're a sweet girl who's tractable and mild,
    Whom I hold dear, and think most highly of.
MARIANE.   I'm deeply grateful, Father, for your love.
ORGON.   That's well said, Daughter; and you can repay me
    If, in all things, you'll cheerfully obey me.   10

MARIANE.   To please you, Sir, is what delights me best.
ORGON.   Good, good. Now, what d'you think of Tartuffe, our guest?
MARIANE.   I, Sir?
ORGON.   Yes, Weigh your answer; think it through.
MARIANE.   Oh, dear. I'll say whatever you wish me to.
ORGON.   That's wisely said, my Daughter. Say of him, then,   15
  That he's the very worthiest of men,
  And that you're fond of him, and would rejoice
  In being his wife, if that should be my choice.
  Well?
MARIANE.   What?
ORGON.   What's that?
MARIANE.   I . . .
ORGON.   Well?
MARIANE.   Forgive me, pray.
ORGON.   Did you not hear me?
MARIANE.   Of *whom*, Sir, must I say   20
  That I am fond of him, and would rejoice
  In being his wife, if that should be your choice?
ORGON.   Why, of Tartuffe.
MARIANE.   But, Father, that's false, you know.
  Why would you have me say what isn't so?
ORGON.   Because I am resolved it shall be true.   25
  That it's my wish should be enough for you.
MARIANE.   You can't mean, father . . .
ORGON.   Yes, Tartuffe shall be
  Allied by marriage to this family,
  And he's to be your husband, is that clear?
  It's a father's privilege . . .   30

SCENE 2

  Enter DORINE.

ORGON (*to* DORINE).   What are you doing in here?
  Is curiosity so fierce a passion
  With you, that you must eavesdrop in this fashion?
DORINE.   There's lately been a rumor going about—
  Based on some hunch or chance remark, no doubt—   5
  That you mean Mariane to wed Tartuffe.
  I've laughed it off, of course, as just a spoof.
ORGON.   You find it so incredible?
DORINE.   Yes, I do.

I won't accept that story, even from you.

ORGON.   Well, you'll believe it when the thing is done.   10

DORINE.   Yes, yes, of course. Go on and have your fun.

ORGON.   I've never been more serious in my life.

DORINE.   Ha!

ORGON.   Daughter, I mean it; you're to be his wife.

DORINE.   No, don't believe your father; it's all a hoax.

ORGON.   See here, young woman . . .

DORINE.   Come, Sir, no more jokes;   15
    You can't fool us.

ORGON.   How dare you talk this way?

DORINE.   All right, then: we believe you, sad to say.
    But how a man like you, who looks so wise
    And wears a moustache of such splendid size,
    Can be so foolish as to . . .

ORGON.   Silence, please!   20
    My girl, you take too many liberties,
    I'm master here, as you must not forget.

DORINE.   Do let's discuss this calmly; don't be upset.
    You can't be serious, Sir, about this plan.
    What should that bigot want with Mariane?   25
    Praying and fasting ought to keep him busy.
    And then, in terms of wealth and rank, what is he?
    Why should a man of property like you
    Pick out a beggar son-in-law?

ORGON.   That will do.
    Speak of his poverty with reverence.   30
    His is a pure and saintly indigence
    Which far transcends all worldly pride and pelf.
    He lost his fortune, as he says himself,
    Because he cared for Heaven alone, and so
    Was careless of his interests here below.   35
    I mean to get him out of his present straits
    And help him to recover his estates—
    Which, in his part of the world, have no small fame.
    Poor though he is, he's a gentleman just the same.

DORINE.   Yes, so he tells us; and, Sir, it seems to me   40
    Such pride goes very ill with piety.
    A man whose spirit spurns this dungy earth
    Ought not to brag of lands and noble birth;
    Such worldly arrogance will hardly square
    With meek devotion and the life of prayer.   45

. . . But this approach, I see, has drawn a blank;
Let's speak, then, of his person, not his rank.
Doesn't it seem to you a trifle grim
To give a girl like her to a man like him?
When two are so ill-suited, can't you see   50
What the sad consequence is bound to be?
A young girl's virtue is imperilled, Sir,
When such a marriage is imposed on her;
For if one's bridegroom isn't to one's taste,
It's hardly an inducement to be chaste,   55
And many a man with horns upon his brow
Has made his wife the thing that she is now.
It's hard to be a faithful wife, in short,
To certain husbands of a certain sort,
And he who gives his daughter to a man she hates   60
Must answer for her sins at Heaven's gates.
Think, Sir, before you play so risky a role.

ORGON.   This servant-girl presumes to save my soul!
DORINE.   You would do well to ponder what I've said.
ORGON.   Daughter, we'll disregard this dunderhead.   65
Just trust your father's judgment. Oh, I'm aware
That I once promised you to young Valère;
But now I hear he gambles, which greatly shocks me;
What's more, I've doubts about his orthodoxy.
His visits to church, I note, are very few.   70
DORINE.   Would you have him go at the same hours as you,
And kneel nearby, to be sure of being seen?
ORGON.   I can dispense with such remarks, Dorine.
(To MARIANE) Tartuffe, however, is sure of Heaven's blessing,
And that's the only treasure worth possessing.   75
This match will bring you joys beyond all measure;
Your cup will overflow with every pleasure;
You two will interchange your faithful loves
Like two sweet cherubs, or two turtle-doves.
No harsh word shall be heard, no frown be seen,   80
And he shall make you happy as a queen.
DORINE.   And she'll make him a cuckold, just wait and see.
ORGON.   What language!
DORINE.   Oh, he's a man of destiny;
He's *made* for horns, and what the stars demand
Your daughter's virtue surely can't withstand.   85
ORGON.   Don't interrupt me further. Why can't you learn

That certain things are none of your concern?
DORINE.   It's for your own sake that I interfere. (*She repeatedly interrupts*
    ORGON *just as he is turning to speak to his daughter.*)
ORGON.   Most kind of you. Now, hold your tongue, d'you hear?
DORINE.   If I didn't love you . . .
ORGON.   Spare me your affection.   90
DORINE.   I love you, Sir, in spite of your objection.
ORGON.   Blast!
DORINE.   I can't bear, Sir, for your honor's sake,
    To let you make this ludicrous mistake.
ORGON.   You mean to go on talking?
DORINE.   If I didn't protest
    This sinful marriage, my conscience couldn't rest.   95
ORGON.   If you don't hold your tongue, you little shrew . . .
DORINE.   What, lost your temper? A pious man like you?
ORGON.   Yes! Yes! You talk and talk. I'm maddened by it.
    Once and for all, I tell you to be quiet.
DORINE.   Well, I'll be quiet. But I'll be thinking hard.   100
ORGON.   Think all you like, but you had better guard
    That saucy tongue of yours, or I'll . . .
    (*Turning back to* MARIANE)
                            Now, child,
    I've weighed this matter fully.
DORINE (*aside*).   It drives me wild
    That I can't speak. (ORGON *turns his head, and she is silent.*)
ORGON.   Tartuffe is no young dandy,
    But, still, his person . . .
DORINE (*aside*).   Is as sweet as candy.   105
ORGON.   Is such that, even if you shouldn't care
    For his other merits . . .
    (*He turns and stands facing* DORINE, *arms crossed.*)
DORINE (*aside*).   They'll make a lovely pair.
    If I were she, no man would marry me
    Against my inclination, and go scot-free.
    He'd learn, before the wedding-day was over,   110
    How readily a wife can find a lover.
ORGON (*to* DORINE). It seems you treat my orders as a joke.
DORINE.   Why, what's the matter? 'Twas not to you I spoke.
ORGON.   What *were* you doing?
DORINE.   Talking to myself, that's all.
ORGON.   Ah! (*Aside*) One more bit of impudence and gall,   115

And I shall give her a good slap in the face. (*He puts himself in
position to slap her;* DORINE, *whenever he glances at her, stands
immobile and silent.*)
Daughter, you shall accept, and with good grace,
The husband I've selected . . . Your wedding-day . . .
(*To* DORINE) Why don't you talk to yourself?

DORINE.   I've nothing to say.

ORGON.   Come, just one word.

DORINE.   No thank you, Sir. I pass.   120

ORGON.   Come, speak; I'm waiting.

DORINE.   I'd not be such an ass.

ORGON (*turning to* MARIANE). In short, dear Daughter, I mean to be
    obeyed,
    And you must bow to the sound choice I've made.

DORINE (*moving away*). I'd not wed such a monster, even in jest.
    (ORGON *attempts to slap her, but misses.*)

ORGON.   Daughter, that maid of yours is a thorough pest;   125
    She makes me sinfully annoyed and nettled.
    I can't speak further; my nerves are too unsettled.
    She's so upset me by her insolent talk,
    I'll calm myself by going for a walk. (*Exit.*)

SCENE 3

DORINE (*returning*). Well, have you lost your tongue, girl? Must I play
    Your part, and say the lines you ought to say?
    Faced with a fate so hideous and absurd,
    Can you not utter one dissenting word?

MARIANE.   What good would it do? A father's power is great.   5

DORINE.   Resist him now, or it will be too late.

MARIANE.   But . . .

DORINE.   Tell him one cannot love at a father's whim;
    That you shall marry for yourself, not him;
    That since it's you who are to be the bride,
    It's you, not he, who must be satisfied;   10
    And that if his Tartuffe is so sublime,
    He's free to marry him at any time.

MARIANE.   I've bowed so long to Father's strict control,
    I couldn't oppose him now, to save my soul.

DORINE.   Come, come, Mariane. Do listen to reason, won't you?   15
    Valère has asked your hand. Do you love him, or don't you?

MARIANE.   Oh, how unjust of you! What can you mean
    By asking such a question, dear Dorine?

You know the depth of my affection for him;
I've told you a hundred times how I adore him.   20
DORINE.   I don't believe in everything I hear;
Who knows if your professions were sincere?
MARIANE.   They were, Dorine, and you do me wrong to doubt it;
Heaven knows that I've been all too frank about it.
DORINE.   You love him, then?
MARIANE.   Oh, more than I can express.   25
DORINE.   And he, I take it, cares for you no less?
MARIANE.   I think so.
DORINE.   And you both, with equal fire,
Burn to be married?
MARIANE.   That is our one desire.
DORINE.   What of Tartuffe, then? What of your father's plan?
MARIANE.   I'll kill myself, if I'm forced to wed that man.   30
DORINE.   I hadn't thought of that recourse. How splendid!
Just die, and all your troubles will be ended!
A fine solution. Oh, it maddens me
To hear you talk in that self-pitying key.
MARIANE.   Dorine, how harsh you are! It's most unfair   35
You have no sympathy for my despair.
DORINE.   I've none at all for people who talk drivel
And, faced with difficulties, whine and snivel.
MARIANE.   No doubt I'm timid, but it would be wrong . . .
DORINE.   True love requires a heart that's firm and strong.   40
MARIANE.   I'm strong in my affection for Valère,
But coping with my father is his affair.
DORINE.   But if your father's brain has grown so cracked
Over his dear Tartuffe that he can retract
His blessing, though your wedding-day was named,   45
It's surely not Valère who's to be blamed.
MARIANE.   If I defied my father, as you suggest,
Would it not seem unmaidenly, at best?
Shall I defend my love at the expense
Of brazenness and disobedience?   50
Shall I parade my heart's desires, and flaunt . . .
DORINE.   No, I ask nothing of you. Clearly you want
To be Madame Tartuffe, and I feel bound
Not to oppose a wish so very sound.
What right have I to criticize the match?   55
Indeed, my dear, the man's a brilliant catch.
Monsieur Tartuffe! Now, there's a man of weight!

Yes, yes, Monsieur Tartuffe, I'm bound to state,
Is quite a person; that's not to be denied;
'Twill be no little thing to be his bride.   60
The world already rings with his renown;
He's a great noble—in his native town;
His ears are red, he has a pink complexion,
And all in all, he'll suit you to perfection.

MARIANE.   Dear God!

DORINE.   Oh, how triumphant you will feel   65
At having caught a husband so ideal!

MARIANE.   Oh, do stop teasing, and use your cleverness
To get me out of this appalling mess.
Advise me, and I'll do whatever you say.

DORINE.   Ah no, a dutiful daughter must obey   70
Her father, even if he weds her to an ape.
You've a bright future; why struggle to escape?
Tartuffe will take you back where his family lives,
To a small town aswarm with relatives—
Uncles and cousins whom you'll be charmed to meet.   75
You'll be received at once by the elite,
Calling upon the bailiff's wife, no less—
Even, perhaps, upon the mayoress,
Who'll sit you down in the *best* kitchen chair.
Then, once a year, you'll dance at the village fair   80
To the drone of bagpipes—two of them, in fact—
And see a puppet-show, or an animal act.
Your husband . . .

MARIANE.   Oh, you turn my blood to ice!
Stop torturing me, and give me your advice.

DORINE (*threatening to go*). Your servant, Madam.

MARIANE.   Dorine, I beg of you . . . 85

DORINE.   No, you deserve it; this marriage must go through.

MARIANE.   Dorine!

DORINE.   No.

MARIANE.   Not Tartuffe! You know I think him . . .

DORINE.   Tartuffe's your cup of tea, and you shall drink him.

MARIANE.   I've always told you everything, and relied . . .

DORINE.   No. You deserve to be tartuffified.   90

MARIANE.   Well, since you mock me and refuse to care,
I'll henceforth seek my solace in despair:
Despair shall be my counselor and friend,
And help me bring my sorrows to an end. (*She starts to leave.*)

DORINE.   There now, come back; my anger has subsided.   95
    You do deserve some pity, I've decided.
MARIANE.   Dorine, if Father makes me undergo
    This dreadful martyrdom, I'll die, I know.
DORINE.   Don't fret; it won't be difficult to discover
    Some plan of action . . . But here's Valère, your lover.   100

SCENE 4

Enter VALÈRE.

VALÈRE.   Madam, I've just received some wondrous news
    Regarding which I'd like to hear your views.
MARIANE.   What news?
VALÈRE.   You're marrying Tartuffe.
MARIANE.   I find
    That Father does have such a match in mind.
VALÈRE.   Your father, Madam . . .
MARIANE.   . . . has just this minute said   5
    That it's Tartuffe he wishes me to wed.
VALÈRE.   Can he be serious?
MARIANE.   Oh, indeed, he can;
    He's clearly set his heart upon the plan.
VALÈRE.   And what position do you propose to take, Madam?
MARIANE.   Why—I don't know.
VALÈRE.   For heaven's sake—   10
    You don't know?
MARIANE.   No.
VALÈRE.   Well, well!
MARIANE.   Advise me, do.
VALÈRE.   Marry the man. That's my advice to you.
MARIANE.   That's your advice?
VALÈRE.   Yes.
MARIANE.   Truly?
VALÈRE.   Oh, absolutely.
    You couldn't choose more wisely, more astutely.
MARIANE.   Thanks for this counsel; I'll follow it, of course.   15
VALÈRE.   Do, do; I'm sure 'twill cost you no remorse.
MARIANE.   To give it didn't cause your heart to break.
VALÈRE.   I gave it, Madam, only for your sake.
MARIANE.   And it's for your sake that I take it, Sir.
DORINE (*withdrawing to the rear of the stage*).   Let's see which fool will
    prove the stubborner.   20

VALÈRE.   So! I am nothing to you, and it was flat
    Deception when you . . .
MARIANE.   Please, enough of that.
    You've told me plainly that I should agree
    To wed the man my father's chosen for me,
    And since you've deigned to counsel me so wisely,   25
    I promise, Sir, to do as you advise me.
VALÈRE.   Ah, no, 'twas not by me that you were swayed.
    No, your decision was already made;
    Though now, to save appearances, you protest
    That you're betraying me at my behest.   30
MARIANE.   Just as you say.
VALÈRE.   Quite so, And I now see
    That you were never truly in love with me.
MARIANE.   Alas, you're free to think so if you choose.
VALÈRE.   I choose to think so, and here's a bit of news:
    You've spurned my hand, but I know where to turn   35
    For kinder treatment, as you shall quickly learn.
MARIANE.   I'm sure you do. Your noble qualities
    Inspire affection . . .
VALÈRE.   Forget my qualities, please.
    They don't inspire you overmuch, I find.
    But there's another lady I have in mind   40
    Whose sweet and generous nature will not scorn
    To compensate me for the loss I've borne.
MARIANE.   I'm no great loss, and I'm sure that you'll transfer
    Your heart quite painlessly from me to her.
VALÈRE.   I'll do my best to take it in my stride.   45
    The pain I feel at being cast aside
    Time and forgetfulness may put an end to.
    Or if I can't forget, I shall pretend to.
    No self-respecting person is expected
    To go on loving once he's been rejected.   50
MARIANE.   Now, that's a fine, high-minded sentiment.
VALÈRE.   One to which any sane man would assent.
    Would you prefer it if I pined away
    In hopeless passion till my dying day?
    Am I to yield you to a rival's arms   55
    And not console myself with other charms?
MARIANE.   Go then: console yourself; don't hesitate.
    I wish you to; indeed, I cannot wait.
VALÈRE.   You wish me to?

MARIANE.   Yes.
VALÈRE.   That's the final straw.
    Madam, farewell. Your wish shall be my law. (*He starts to*   60
leave, and then returns repeatedly.)
MARIANE.   Splendid.
VALÈRE (*coming back again*).
                This breach, remember, is of your making;
    It's you who've driven me to the step I'm taking.
MARIANE.   Of course.
VALÈRE (*coming back again*).
                  Remember, too, that I am merely
    Following your example.
MARIANE.   I see that clearly.
VALÈRE.   Enough. I'll go and do your bidding, then.   65
MARIANE.   Good.
VALÈRE (*coming back again*).
              You shall never see my face again.
MARIANE.   Excellent.
VALÈRE (*walking to the door, then turning about*).
           Yes?
MARIANE.   What?
VALÈRE.   What's that? What did you say?
MARIANE.   Nothing. You're dreaming.
VALÈRE.   Ah. Well, I'm on my way.
    Farewell, Madame. (*He moves slowly away.*)
MARIANE.   Farewell.
DORINE (*to* MARIANE).   If you ask me,
    Both of you are as mad as mad can be.   70
    Do stop this nonsense, now. I've only let you
    Squabble so long to see where it would get you.
    Whoa there, Monsieur Valère! (*She goes and seizes* VALÈRE *by the*
    arm; he makes a great show of resistance.)
VALÈRE.   What's this, Dorine?
DORINE.   Come here.
VALÈRE.   No, no, my heart's too full of spleen.
    Don't hold me back; her wish must be obeyed.   75
DORINE.   Stop!
VALÈRE.   It's too late now; my decision's made.
DORINE.   Oh, pooh!
MARIANE (*aside*).   He hates the sight of me, it's plain.
    I'll go, and so deliver him from pain.
DORINE (*leaving* VALÈRE, *running after* MARIANE.)

And now *you* run away! Come back.

MARIANE.   No, No.

    Nothing you say will keep me here. Let go!   80

VALÈRE (*aside*). She cannot bear my presence, I perceive.

    To spare her further torment, I shall leave.

DORINE (*leaving* MARIANE, *running after* VALÈRE). Again! You'll not
    escape, Sir; don't you try it.

    Come here, you two. Stop fussing, and be quiet. (*She takes* VALÈRE
    by the hand, then MARIANE, *and draws them together.*)

VALÈRE (*to* DORINE). What do you want of me?

MARIANE (*to* DORINE).   What is the point of this? 85

DORINE. We're going to have a little armistice.

    (*To* VALÈRE) Now weren't you silly to get so overheated?

VALÈRE. Didn't you see how badly I was treated?

DORINE (*to* MARIANE). Aren't you a simpleton, to have lost your head?

MARIANE. Didn't you hear the hateful things he said?   90

DORINE (*to* VALÈRE). You're both great fools. Her sole desire, Valère,
    Is to be yours in marriage. To that I'll swear.

    (*To* MARIANE) He loves you only, and he wants no wife
    But you, Mariane. On that I'll stake my life.

MARIANE (*to* VALÈRE). Then why you advised me so, I cannot see. 95

VALÈRE (*to* MARIANE). On such a question, why ask advice of *me*?

DORINE. Oh, you're impossible. Give me your hands, you two.

    (*To* VALÈRE) Yours first.

VALÈRE (*giving* DORINE *his hand*). But why?

DORINE (*to* MARIANE).   And now a hand from you.

MARIANE (*also giving* DORINE *her hand*).

    What are you doing?

DORINE.   There: a perfect fit.

    You suit each other better than you'll admit. (VALÈRE *and*   100
    MARIANE *hold hands for some time without looking at each other.*)

VALÈRE (*turning toward* MARIANE). Ah, come, don't be so haughty.
    Give a man
    A look of kindness, won't you, Mariane? (MARIANE *turns toward*
    VALÈRE *and smiles.*)

DORINE. I tell you, lovers are completely mad!

VALÈRE (*to* MARIANE). Now come, confess that you were very bad
    To hurt my feelings as you did just now.   105
    I have a just complaint, you must allow.

MARIANE. *You* must allow that you were most unpleasant . . .

DORINE. Let's table that discussion for the present;

Your father has a plan which must be stopped.
MARIANE.   Advise us, then; what means must we adopt?   110
DORINE.   We'll use all manner of means, and all at once.
(*To* MARIANE) Your father's addled; he's acting like a dunce.
Therefore you'd better humor the old fossil.
Pretend to yield to him, be sweet and docile,
And then postpone, as often as necessary,   115
The day on which you have agreed to marry.
You'll thus gain time, and time will turn the trick.
Sometimes, for instance, you'll be taken sick,
And that will seem good reason for delay;
Or some bad omen will make you change the day—   120
You'll dream of muddy water, or you'll pass
A dead man's hearse, or break a looking-glass.
If all else fails, no man can marry you
Unless you take his ring and say "I do."
But now, let's separate. If they should find   125
Us talking here, our plot might be divined.
(*To* VALÈRE) Go to your friends, and tell them what's occurred,
And have them urge her father to keep his word.
Meanwhile, we'll stir her brother into action,
And get Elmire, as well, to join our faction.   130
Good-bye.
VALÈRE (*to* MARIANE).
              Though each of us will do his best,
It's your true heart on which my hopes shall rest.
MARIANE (*to* VALÈRE). Regardless of what Father may decide,
None but Valère shall claim me as his bride.
VALÈRE.   Oh, how those words content me! Come what will . . .   135
DORINE.   Oh, lovers, lovers! Their tongues are never still.
Be off, now.
VALÈRE (*turning to go, then turning back*).
              One last word . . .
DORINE.   No time to chat:
You leave by this door; and *you* leave by that. (DORINE *pushes them,
by the shoulders, toward opposing doors. Exeunt* MARIANE *and*
VALÈRE.)

ACT 3

SCENE 1

Enter DAMIS.

DAMIS.   May lightning strike me even as I speak,
May all men call me cowardly and weak,
If any fear or scruple holds me back
From settling things, at once, with that great quack!.
DORINE.   Now, don't give way to violent emotion.   5
Your father's merely talked about this notion,
And words and deeds are far from being one.
Much that is talked about is left undone.
DAMIS.   No, I must stop that scoundrel's machinations;
I'll go and tell him off; I'm out of patience.   10
DORINE.   Do calm down and be practical. I had rather
My mistress dealt with him—and with your father.
She has some influence with Tartuffe, I've noted.
He hangs upon her words, seems most devoted,
And may, indeed, be smitten by her charm.   15
Pray Heaven it's true! 'Twould do our cause no harm.
She sent for him, just now, to sound him out
On this affair you're so incensed about;
She'll find out where he stands, and tell him, too,
What dreadful strife and trouble will ensue   20
If he lends countenance to your father's plan.
I couldn't get in to see him, but his man
Says that he's almost finished with his prayers.
Go, now. I'll catch him when he comes downstairs.
DAMIS.   I want to hear this conference, and I will.   25
DORINE.   No, they must be alone.
DAMIS.   Oh, I'll keep still.
DORINE.   Not you. I know your temper. You'd start a brawl,
And shout and stamp your foot and spoil it all.
Go on.
DAMIS.   I won't; I have a perfect right . . .
DORINE.   Lord, you're a nuisance! He's coming; get out of sight.   30
(DAMIS *conceals himself in a closet at the rear of the stage*.)

SCENE 2

Enter TARTUFFE.

TARTUFFE (*observing* DORINE, *and calling to his manservant offstage*).
Hang up my hair-shirt, put my scourge in place,

And pray, Laurent, for Heaven's perpetual grace.
I'm going to the prison now, to share
My last few coins with the poor wretches there.
DORINE (*aside*). Dear God, what affectation! What a fake!   5
TARTUFFE.   You wished to see me?
DORINE.   Yes . . .
TARTUFFE (*taking a handkerchief from his pocket*).
                                For mercy's sake,
     Please take this handkerchief, before you speak.
DORINE.   What?
TARTUFFE.   Cover that bosom, girl. The flesh is weak,
     And unclean thoughts are difficult to control.
     Such sights as that can undermine the soul.   10
DORINE.   Your soul, it seems, has very poor defenses,
     And flesh makes quite an impact on your senses.
     It's strange that you're so easily excited;
     My own desires are not so soon ignited;
     And if I saw you naked as a beast,   15
     Not all your hide would tempt me in the least.
TARTUFFE.   Girl, speak more modestly; unless you do,
     I shall be forced to take my leave of you.
DORINE.   Oh, no, it's I who must be on my way;
     I've just one little message to convey.   20
     Madame is coming down, and begs you, Sir,
     To wait and have a word or two with her.
TARTUFFE.   Gladly.
DORINE (*aside*). *That* had a softening effect!
     I think my guess about him was correct.   25
TARTUFFE.   Will she be long?
DORINE.   No: that's her step I hear.
     Ah, here she is, and I shall disappear. (*Exit.*)

SCENE 3

     Enter ELMIRE.

TARTUFFE.   May Heaven, whose infinite goodness we adore,
     Preserve your body and soul forevermore,
     And bless your days, and answer thus the plea
     Of one who is its humblest votary.
ELMIRE.   I thank you for that pious wish. But please,   5
     Do take a chair and let's be more at ease. (*They sit down.*)
TARTUFFE.   I trust that you are once more well and strong?
ELMIRE.   Oh, yes: the fever didn't last for long.

TARTUFFE.   My prayers are too unworthy, I am sure,
    To have gained from heaven this most gracious cure;   10
    But lately, Madam, my every supplication
    Has had for object your recuperation.
ELMIRE.   You shouldn't have troubled so. I don't deserve it.
TARTUFFE.   Your health is priceless, Madam, and to preserve it
    I'd gladly give my own, in all sincerity.   15
ELMIRE.   Sir, you outdo us all in Christian charity.
    You've been most kind. I count myself your debtor.
TARTUFFE.   'Twas nothing, Madam. I long to serve you better.
ELMIRE.   There's a private matter I'm anxious to discuss.
    I'm glad there's no one here to hinder us.   20
TARTUFFE.   I too am glad; it floods my heart with bliss
    To find myself alone with you like this.
    For just this chance I've prayed with all my power—
    But prayed in vain, until this happy hour.
ELMIRE.   This won't take long, Sir, and I hope you'll be   25
    Entirely frank and unconstrained with me.
TARTUFFE.   Indeed, there's nothing I had rather do
    Than bare my inmost heart and soul to you.
    First, let me say that what remarks I've made
    About the constant visits you are paid   30
    Were prompted not by any mean emotion,
    But rather by a pure and deep devotion,
    A fervent zeal . . .
ELMIRE.   No need for explanation.
    Your sole concern, I'm sure, was my salvation.
TARTUFFE (*taking* ELMIRE's *hand and pressing her fingertips*). Quite so;
    and such great fervor do I feel . . .   35
ELMIRE.   Ooh! Please! You're pinching!
TARTUFFE.   'Twas from excess of zeal.
    I never meant to cause you pain, I swear.
    I'd rather . . . (*He places his hand on* ELMIRE's *knee*.)
ELMIRE.   What can your hand be doing there?
TARTUFFE.   Feeling your gown; what soft, fine-woven stuff!
ELMIRE.   Please, I'm extremely ticklish. That's enough. (*She draws* 40
    her chair away; TARTUFFE *pulls his after her*.)
TARTUFFE (*fondling the lace collar of her gown*).   My, my, what lovely
        lacework on your dress!
    The workmanship's miraculous, no less.
    I've not seen anything to equal it.
ELMIRE.   Yes, quite. But let's talk business for a bit.

They say my husband means to break his word   45
And give his daughter to you, Sir. Had you heard?
TARTUFFE.   He did once mention it. But I confess
    I dream of quite a different happiness.
    It's elsewhere, Madam, that my eyes discern
    The promise of that bliss for which I yearn.   50
ELMIRE.   I see: you care for nothing here below.
TARTUFFE.   Ah, well—my heart's not made of stone, you know.
ELMIRE.   All your desires mount heavenward, I'm sure,
    In scorn of all that's earthly and impure.
TARTUFFE.   A love of heavenly beauty does not preclude   55
    A proper love for earthly pulchritude;
    Our senses are quite rightly captivated
    By perfect works our Maker has created.
    Some glory clings to all that Heaven has made;
    In you, all Heaven's marvels are displayed.   60
    On that fair face, such beauties have been lavished,
    The eyes are dazzled and the heart is ravished;
    How could I look on you, O flawless creature,
    And not adore the Author of all Nature,
    Feeling a love both passionate and pure   65
    For you, his triumph of self-portraiture?
    At first, I trembled lest that love should be
    A subtle snare that Hell had laid for me;
    I vowed to flee the sight of you, eschewing
    A rapture that might prove my soul's undoing;   70
    But soon, fair being, I became aware
    That my deep passion could be made to square
    With rectitude, and with my bounden duty.
    I thereupon surrendered to your beauty.
    It is, I know, presumptuous on my part   75
    To bring you this poor offering of my heart,
    And it is not my merit, Heaven knows,
    But your compassion on which my hopes repose.
    You are my peace, my solace, my salvation;
    On you depends my bliss—or desolation;   80
    I bide your judgment and, as you think best,
    I shall be either miserable or blest.
ELMIRE.   Your declaration is most gallant, Sir,
    But don't you think it's out of character?
    You'd have done better to restrain your passion   85
    And think before you spoke in such a fashion.

It ill becomes a pious man like you . . .

TARTUFFE.   I may be pious, but I'm human too:
    With your celestial charms before his eyes,
    A man has not the power to be wise.   90
    I know such words sound strangely, coming from me,
    But I'm no angel, nor was meant to be,
    And if you blame my passion, you must needs
    Reproach as well the charms on which it feeds.
    Your loveliness I had no sooner seen   95
    Than you became my soul's unrivalled queen;
    Before your seraph glance, divinely sweet,
    My heart's defenses crumbled in defeat,
    And nothing fasting, prayer, or tears might do
    Could stay my spirit from adoring you.   100
    My eyes, my sighs have told you in the past
    What now my lips make bold to say at last,
    And if, in your great goodness, you will deign
    To look upon your slave, and ease his pain,—
    If, in compassion for my soul's distress,   105
    You'll stoop to comfort my unworthiness,
    I'll raise to you, in thanks for that sweet manna,
    An endless hymn, an infinite hosanna.
    With me, of course, there need be no anxiety,
    No fear of scandal or of notoriety.   110
    These young court gallants, whom all the ladies fancy,
    Are vain in speech, in action rash and chancy;
    When they succeed in love, the world soon knows it;
    No favor's granted them but they disclose it
    And by the looseness of their tongues profane   115
    The very altar where their hearts have lain.
    Men of my sort, however, love discreetly,
    And one may trust our reticence completely.
    My keen concern for my good name insures
    The absolute security of yours;
    In short, I offer you, my dear Elmire,   120
    Love without scandal, pleasure without fear.

ELMIRE.   I've heard your well-turned speeches to the end,
    And what you urge I clearly apprehend.
    Aren't you afraid that I may take a notion   125
    To tell my husband of your warm devotion,
    And that, supposing he were duly told,
    His feelings toward you might grow rather cold?

TARTUFFE.   I know, dear lady, that your exceeding charity
    Will lead your heart to pardon my temerity;   130
    That you'll excuse my violent affection
    As human weakness, human imperfection;
    And that—O fairest!—you will bear in mind
    That I'm but flesh and blood, and am not blind.
ELMIRE.   Some women might do otherwise, perhaps,   135
    But I shall be discreet about your lapse;
    I'll tell my husband nothing of what's occurred
    If, in return you'll give your solemn word
    To advocate as forcefully as you can
    The marriage of Valère and Mariane,   140
    Renouncing all desire to dispossess
    Another of his rightful happiness,
    And . . .

SCENE 4

DAMIS (*emerging from the closet where he has been hiding*).
        No! we'll not hush up this vile affair;
    I heard it all inside that closet there,
    Where Heaven, in order to confound the pride
    Of this great rascal, prompted me to hide.
    Ah, now I have my long-awaited chance   5
    To punish his deceit and arrogance,
    And give my father clear and shocking proof
    Of the black character of his dear Tartuffe.
ELMIRE.   Ah no, Damis; I'll be content if he
    Will study to deserve my leniency.   10
    I've promised silence—don't make me break my word;
    To make a scandal would be too absurd.
    Good wives laugh off such trifles, and forget them;
    Why should they tell their husbands, and upset them?
DAMIS.   You have your reasons for taking such a course,   15
    And I have reasons, too, of equal force.
    To spare him now would be insanely wrong.
    I've swallowed my just wrath for far too long
    And watched this insolent bigot bringing strife
    And bitterness into our family life.   20
    Too long he's meddled in my father's affairs,
    Thwarting my marriage-hopes, and poor Valère's.
    It's high time that my father was undeceived,

And now I've proof that can't be disbelieved—
Proof that was furnished me by Heaven above.   25
It's too good not to take advantage of.
This is my chance, and I deserve to lose it
If, for one moment, I hesitate to use it.
ELMIRE.   Damis . . .
DAMIS.   No, I must do what I think right.
Madam, my heart is bursting with delight,   30
And, say whatever you will, I'll not consent
To lose the sweet revenge on which I'm bent.
I'll settle matters without more ado;
And here, most opportunely, is my cue.

SCENE 5

Enter ORGON.

DAMIS.   Father, I'm glad you've joined us. Let us advise you
Of some fresh news which doubtless will surprise you.
You've just now been repaid with interest
For all your loving-kindness to our guest.
He's proved his warm and grateful feelings toward you;   5
It's with a pair of horns he would reward you.
Yes, I surprised him with your wife, and heard
His whole adulterous offer, every word.
She, with her all too gentle disposition,
Would not have told you of his proposition;   10
But I shall not make terms with brazen lechery,
And feel that not to tell you would be treachery.
ELMIRE.   And I hold that one's husband's peace of mind
Should not be spoilt by tattle of this kind.
One's honor doesn't require it: to be proficient   15
In keeping men at bay is quite sufficient.
These are my sentiments, and I wish, Damis,
That you had heeded me and held your peace. (*Exit* ELMIRE.)

SCENE 6

ORGON.   Can it be true, this dreadful thing I hear?
TARTUFFE.   Yes, Brother, I'm a wicked man, I fear:
A wretched sinner, all depraved and twisted,
The greatest villain that has ever existed.
My life's one heap of crimes, which grows each minute;   5

There's naught but foulness and corruption in it;
And I perceive that Heaven, outraged by me,
Has chosen this occasion to mortify me.
Charge me with any deed you wish to name;
I'll not defend myself, but take the blame,   10
Believe what you are told, and drive Tartuffe
Like some base criminal from beneath your roof;
Yes, drive me hence, and with a parting curse:
I shan't protest, for I deserve far worse.

ORGON   (to DAMIS). Ah, you deceitful boy, how dare you try   15
   To stain his purity with so foul a lie?

DAMIS.   What! Are you taken in by such a bluff?
   Did you not hear . . . ?

ORGON.   Enough, you rogue, enough!

TARTUFFE.   Ah, Brother, let him speak; you're being unjust.
   Believe his story; the boy deserves your trust.   20
   Why, after all, should you have faith in me?
   How can you know what I might do, or be?
   Is it on my good actions that you base
   Your favor? Do you trust my pious face?
   Ah, no, don't be deceived by hollow shows;   25
   I'm far, alas, from being what men suppose;
   Though the world takes me for a man of worth,
   I'm truly the most worthless man on earth.
   (To DAMIS) Yes, my dear son, speak out now: call me the chief
   Of sinners, a wretch, a murderer, a thief;   30
   Load me with all the names men most abhor;
   I'll not complain; I've earned them all, and more;
   I'll kneel here while you pour them on my head
   As a just punishment for the life I've led.

ORGON   (to TARTUFFE).   This is too much, dear Brother.
   (To DAMIS)   Have you no heart?   35

DAMIS.   Are you so hoodwinked by this rascal's art . . . ?

ORGON.   Be still, you monster.
   (To TARTUFFE)   Brother, I pray you, rise.
   (To DAMIS) Villain!

DAMIS.   But . . .

ORGON.   Silence!

DAMIS.   Can't you realize . . . ?

ORGON.   Just one word more, and I'll tear you limb from limb.

TARTUFFE.   In God's name, Brother, don't be harsh with him.   40
   I'd rather far be tortured at the stake

Than see him bear one scratch for my poor sake.

ORGON *(to* DAMIS*).*   Ingrate!

TARTUFFE.   If I must beg you, on bended knee,
    To pardon him . . .

ORGON *(falling to his knees, addressing* TARTUFFE*).*
                      Such goodness cannot be!
    (To DAMIS*)* Now, *there's* true charity!

DAMIS.   What, you . . . ?

ORGON.   Villain, be still!   45
    I know your motives; I know you wish him ill:
    Yes, all of you—wife, children, servants, all—
    Conspire against him and desire his fall,
    Employing every shameful trick you can
    To alienate me from this saintly man.   50
    Ah, but the more you seek to drive him away,
    The more I'll do to keep him. Without delay,
    I'll spite this household and confound its pride
    By giving him my daughter as his bride.

DAMIS.   You're going to force her to accept his hand?   55

ORGON.   Yes, and this very night, d'you understand?
    I shall defy you all, and make it clear
    That I'm the one who gives the orders here.
    Come, wretch, kneel down and clasp his blessed feet,
    And ask his pardon for your black deceit.   60

DAMIS.   I ask that swindler's pardon? Why, I'd rather . . .

ORGON.   So! You insult him, and defy your father!
    A stick! A stick! *(To* TARTUFFE*)* No, no—release me, do.
    (To DAMIS*)* Out of my house this minute! Be off with you,
    And never dare set foot in it again.   65

DAMIS.   Well, I shall go, but . . .

ORGON.   Well, go quickly, then.
    I disinherit you; an empty purse
    Is all you'll get from me—except my curse! *(Exit* DAMIS.*)*

SCENE 7

ORGON.   How he blasphemed your goodness! What a son!

TARTUFFE.   Forgive him, Lord, as I've already done.
    (To ORGON*)* You can't know how it hurts when someone tries
    To blacken me in my dear Brother's eyes.

ORGON.   Ahh!

TARTUFFE.   The mere thought of such ingratitude   5

Plunges my soul into so dark a mood . . .
Such horror grips my heart . . . I gasp for breath,
And cannot speak, and feel myself near death.

ORGON (*running, in tears, to the door through which he has just driven his*
son). You blackguard! Why did I spare you? Why did I not
Break you in little pieces on the spot?   10
Compose yourself, and don't be hurt, dear friend.

TARTUFFE.   These scenes, these dreadful quarrels, have got to end.
I've much upset your household, and I perceive
That the best thing will be for me to leave.

ORGON.   What are you saying!

TARTUFFE.   They're all against me here;   15
They'd have you think me false and insincere.

ORGON.   Ah, what of that? Have I ceased believing in you?

TARTUFFE.   Their adverse talk will certainly continue,
And charges which you now repudiate
You may find credible at a later date.   20

ORGON.   No, Brother, never.

TARTUFFE.   Brother, a wife can sway
Her husband's mind in many a subtle way.

ORGON.   No, no.

TARTUFFE.   To leave at once is the solution;
Thus only can I end their persecution.

ORGON.   No, no, I'll not allow it; you shall remain.   25

TARTUFFE.   Ah, well; 'twill mean much martyrdom and pain,
But if you wish it . . .

ORGON.   Ah!

TARTUFFE.   Enough; so be it.
But one thing must be settled, as I see it.
For your dear honor, and for our friendship's sake,
There's one precaution I feel bound to take.   30
I shall avoid your wife, and keep away . . .

ORGON.   No, you shall not, whatever they may say.
It pleases me to vex them, and for spite
I'd have them see you with her day and night.
What's more, I'm going to drive them to despair   35
By making you my only son and heir;
This very day, I'll give to you alone
Clear deed and title to everything I own.
A dear, good friend and son-in-law-to-be
Is more than wife, or child, or kin to me.   40
Will you accept my offer, dearest son?

TARTUFFE.   In all things, let the will of Heaven be done.
ORGON.   Poor fellow! Come, we'll go draw up the deed.
   Then let them burst with disappointed greed! (*Exeunt.*)

ACT 4

SCENE 1

   Enter CLÉANTE *and* TARTUFFE.

CLÉANTE.   Yes, all the town's discussing it, and truly,
   Their comments do not flatter you unduly.
   I'm glad we've met, Sir, and I'll give my view
   Of this sad matter in a word or two.
   As for who's guilty, that I shan't discuss;   5
   Let's say it was Damis who caused the fuss;
   Assuming, then, that you have been ill-used
   By young Damis, and groundlessly accused,
   Ought not a Christian to forgive, and ought
   He not to stifle every vengeful thought?   10
   Should you stand by and watch a father make
   His only son an exile for your sake?
   Again I tell you frankly, be advised:
   The whole town, high and low, is scandalized;
   This quarrel must be mended, and my advice is   15
   Not to push matters to a further crisis.
   No, sacrifice your wrath to God above,
   And help Damis regain his father's love.
TARTUFFE.   Alas, for my part I should take great joy
   In doing so. I've nothing against the boy.   20
   I pardon all, I harbor no resentment;
   To serve him would afford me much contentment.
   But Heaven's interest will not have it so:
   If he comes back, then I shall have to go.
   After his conduct—so extreme, so vicious—   25
   Our further intercourse would look suspicious.
   God knows what people would think! Why, they'd describe
   My goodness to him as a sort of bribe;
   They'd say that out of guilt I made pretense
   Of loving-kindness and benevolence—   30
   That, fearing my accuser's tongue, I strove
   To buy his silence with a show of love.
CLÉANTE.   Your reasoning is badly warped and stretched,

And these excuses, Sir, are most far-fetched.
Why put yourself in charge of Heaven's cause?   35
Does Heaven need our help to enforce its laws?
Leave vengeance to the Lord, Sir; while we live,
Our duty's not to punish, but forgive;
And what the Lord commands, we should obey
Without regard to what the world may say.   40
What! Shall the fear of being misunderstood
Prevent our doing what is right and good?
No, no; let's simply do what Heaven ordains,
And let no other thoughts perplex our brains.

TARTUFFE.   Again, Sir, let me say that I've forgiven   45
Damis, and thus obeyed the laws of Heaven;
But I am not commanded by the Bible
To live with one who smears my name with libel.

CLÉANTE.   Were you commanded, Sir, to indulge the whim
Of poor Orgon, and to encourage him   50
In suddenly transferring to your name
A large estate to which you have no claim?

TARTUFFE.   'Twould never occur to those who know me best
To think I acted from self-interest.
The treasures of this world I quite despise;   55
Their specious glitter does not charm my eyes;
And if I have resigned myself to taking
The gift which my dear Brother insists on making,
I do so only, as he well understands,
Lest so much wealth fall into wicked hands,   60
Lest those to whom it might descend in time
Turn it to purposes of sin and crime,
And not, as I shall do, make use of it
For Heaven's glory and mankind's benefit.

CLÉANTE.   Forget these trumped-up fears. Your argument   65
Is one the rightful heir might well resent;
It *is* a moral burden to inherit
Such wealth, but give Damis a chance to bear it.
And would it not be worse to be accused
Of swindling, than to see that wealth misused?   70
I'm shocked that you allowed Orgon to broach
This matter, and that you feel no self-reproach;
Does true religion teach that lawful heirs
May freely be deprived of what is theirs?
And if the Lord has told you in your heart   75

That you and young Damis must dwell apart,
Would it not be the decent thing to beat
A generous and honorable retreat,
Rather than let the son of the house be sent,
For your convenience, into banishment?   80
Sir, if you wish to prove the honesty
Of your intentions . . .
TARTUFFE.   Sir, it is half-past three.
  I've certain pious duties to attend to,
  And hope my prompt departure won't offend you. (*Exit.*)
CLÉANTE.   Damn. (*Starts to leave.*)   85

SCENE 2

Enter ELMIRE, MARIANE, *and* DORINE.

DORINE.   Stay, Sir, and help Mariane, for Heaven's sake!
  She's suffering so, I fear her heart will break.
  Her father's plan to marry her off tonight
  Has put the poor child in a desperate plight.
  I hear him coming. Let's stand together, now,
  And see if we can't change his mind, somehow,
  About this match we all deplore and fear.

SCENE 3

Enter ORGON.

ORGON.   Hah! Glad to find you all assembled here.
  (*To* MARIANE) This contract, child, contains your happiness,
  And what it says I think your heart can guess.
MARIANE (*falling to her knees*).   Sir, by that Heaven which sees me
        here distressed,
  And by whatever else can move your breast,   5
  Do not employ a father's power, I pray you,
  To crush my heart and force it to obey you,
  Nor by your harsh commands oppress me so
  That I'll begrudge the duty which I owe—
  And do not so embitter and enslave me   10
  That I shall hate the very life you gave me.
  If my sweet hopes must perish, if you refuse
  To give me to the one I've dared to choose,
  Spare me at least—I beg you, I implore—
  The pain of wedding one whom I abhor;   15

And do not, by a heartless use of force,
Drive me to contemplate some desperate course.

ORGON   (*feeling himself touched by her*).   Be firm, my soul. No human
    weakness, now.

MARIANE.   I don't resent your love for him. Allow
    Your heart free rein, Sir; give him your property,   20
    And if that's not enough, take mine from me;
    He's welcome to my money; take it, do,
    But don't, I pray, include my person too.
    Spare me, I beg you; and let me end the tale
    Of my sad days behind a convent veil.   25

ORGON.   A convent! Hah! When crossed in their amours,
    All lovesick girls have the same thought as yours.
    Get up! The more you loathe the man, and dread him,
    The more ennobling it will be to wed him.
    Marry Tartuffe, and mortify your flesh!   30
    Enough; don't start that whimpering afresh.

DORINE.   But why . . . ?

ORGON.   Be still, there. Speak when you're spoken to.
    Not one more bit of impudence out of you.

CLÉANTE.   If I may offer a word of counsel here . . .

ORGON.   Brother, in counseling you have no peer;   35
    All your advice is forceful, sound, and clever;
    I don't propose to follow it, however.

ELMIRE   (*to* ORGON). I am amazed, and don't know what to say;
    Your blindness simply takes my breath away.
    You are indeed bewitched, to take no warning   40
    From our account of what occurred this morning.

ORGON.   Madam, I know a few plain facts, and one
    Is that you're partial to my rascal son;
    Hence, when he sought to make Tartuffe the victim
    Of a base lie, you dared not contradict him.   45
    Ah, but you underplayed your part, my pet;
    You should have looked more angry, more upset.

ELMIRE.   When men make overtures, must we reply
    With righteous anger and a battle-cry?
    Must we turn back their amorous advances   50
    With sharp reproaches and with fiery glances?
    Myself, I find such offers merely amusing,
    And make no scenes and fusses in refusing;
    My taste is for good-natured rectitude,
    And I dislike the savage sort of prude   55

Who guards her virtue with her teeth and claws,
And tears men's eyes out for the slightest cause;
The Lord preserve me from such honor as that,
Which bites and scratches like an alley-cat!
I've found that a polite and cool rebuff   60
Discourages a lover quite enough.
ORGON.   I know the facts, and I shall not be shaken.
ELMIRE.   I marvel at your power to be mistaken.
Would it, I wonder, carry weight with you
If I could *show* you that our tale was true?   65
ORGON.   Show me?
ELMIRE.   Yes.
ORGON.   Rot.
ELMIRE.   Come, what if I found a way
To make you see the facts as plain as day?
ORGON.   Nonsense.
ELMIRE.   Do answer me; don't be absurd.
I'm not now asking you to trust our word.
Suppose that from some hiding-place in here   70
You learned the whole sad truth by eye and ear—
What would you say of your good friend, after that?
ORGON.   Why, I'd say . . . nothing, by Jehosophat!
It can't be true.
ELMIRE.   You've been too long deceived,
And I'm quite tired of being disbelieved.   75
Come now: let's put my statement to the test,
And you shall see the truth made manifest.
ORGON.   I'll take that challenge. Now do your uttermost.
We'll see how you make good your empty boast.
ELMIRE (*to* DORINE).   Send him to me.
DORINE.   He's crafty; it may be hard   80
To catch the cunning scoundrel off his guard.
ELMIRE.   No, amorous men are gullible. Their conceit
So blinds them that they're never hard to cheat.
Have him come down. (*Exit* DORINE. *To* CLÉANTE *and* MARIANE)
                              Please leave us, for a bit. (*They leave.*)

SCENE 4

ELMIRE.   Pull up this table, and get under it.
ORGON.   What?
ELMIRE.   It's essential that you be well-hidden.

ORGON.   Why there?
ELMIRE.   Oh, Heavens! Just do as you are bidden.
  I have my plans; we'll soon see how they fare.
  Under the table, now; and once you're there,   5
  Take care that you are neither seen nor heard.
ORGON.   Well, I'll indulge you, since I gave my word
  To see you through this infantile charade.
ELMIRE.   Once it is over, you'll be glad we played.
  (*To her husband, who is now under the table*) I'm going to act
      quite strangely, now, and you   10
  Must not be shocked at anything I do.
  Whatever I may say, you must excuse
  As part of that deceit I'm forced to use.
  I shall employ sweet speeches in the task
  Of making that impostor drop his mask;   15
  I'll give encouragement to his bold desires,
  And furnish fuel to his amorous fires.
  Since it's for your sake, and for his destruction,
  That I shall seem to yield to his seduction,
  I'll gladly stop whenever you decide   20
  That all your doubts are fully satisfied.
  I'll count on you, as soon as you have seen
  What sort of man he is, to intervene,
  And not expose me to his odious lust
  One moment longer than you feel you must.   25
  Remember: you're to save me from my plight
  Whenever . . . He's coming! Hush! Keep out of sight!

SCENE 5

  Enter TARTUFFE.

TARTUFFE.   You wish to have a word with me, I'm told.
ELMIRE.   Yes. I've a little secret to unfold.
  Before I speak, however, it would be wise
  To close that door, and look about for spies.
  (TARTUFFE *goes to the door, closes it, and returns.*)
  The very last thing that must happen now   5
  Is a repetition of this morning's row.
  I've never been so badly caught off guard.
  Oh, how I feared for you! You saw how hard
  I tried to make that troublesome Damis
  Control his dreadful temper, and hold his peace.   10

In my confusion, I didn't have the sense
Simply to contradict his evidence;
But as it happened, that was for the best,
And all has worked out in our interest.
This storm has only bettered your position;   15
My husband doesn't have the least suspicion,
And now, in mockery of those who do,
He bids me be continually with you.
And that is why, quite fearless of reproof,
I now can be alone with my Tartuffe,   20
And why my heart—perhaps too quick to yield—
Feels free to let its passion be revealed.

TARTUFFE.   Madam, your words confuse me. Not long ago,
You spoke in quite a different style, you know.

ELMIRE.   Ah, Sir, if that refusal made you smart,   25
It's little that you know of woman's heart,
Or what that heart is trying to convey
When it resists in such a feeble way!
Always, at first, our modesty prevents
The frank avowal of tender sentiments;   30
However high the passion which inflames us,
Still, to confess its power somehow shames us.
Thus we reluct, at first, yet in a tone
Which tells you that our heart is overthrown,
That what our lips deny, our pulse confesses,   35
And that, in time, all noes will turn to yesses.
I fear my words are all too frank and free,
And a poor proof of woman's modesty;
But since I'm started, tell me, if you will—
Would I have tried to make Damis be still,   40
Would I have listened, calm and unoffended,
Until your lengthy offer of love was ended,
And been so very mild in my reaction,
Had your sweet words not given me satisfaction?
And when I tried to force you to undo   45
The marriage plans my husband has in view,
What did my urgent pleading signify
If not that I admired you, and that I
Deplored the thought that someone else might own
Part of a heart I wished for mine alone?   50

TARTUFFE.   Madam, no happiness is so complete
As when, from lips we love, come words so sweet;

Their nectar floods my every sense, and drains
In honeyed rivulets through all my veins.
To please you is my joy, my only goal;   55
Your love is the restorer of my soul;
And yet I must beg leave, now, to confess
Some lingering doubts as to my happiness.
Might this not be a trick? Might not the catch
Be that you wish me to break off the match   60
With Mariane, and so have feigned to love me?
I shan't quite trust your fond opinion of me
Until the feelings you've expressed so sweetly
Are demonstrated somewhat more concretely,
And you have shown, by certain kind concessions,   65
That I may put my faith in your professions.

ELMIRE   (coughs, to warn her husband). Why be in such a hurry?
    Must my heart
Exhaust its bounty at the very start?
To make that sweet admission cost me dear,
But you'll not be content, it would appear,   70
Unless my store of favors is disbursed
To the last farthing, and at the very first.

TARTUFFE.   The less we merit, the less we dare to hope,
And with our doubts, mere words can never cope.
We trust no promised bliss till we receive it;   75
Not till a joy is ours can we believe it.
I, who so little merit your esteem,
Can't credit this fulfillment of my dream,
And shan't believe it, Madam, until I savor
Some palpable assurance of your favor.   80

ELMIRE.   My, how tyrannical your love can be,
And how it flusters and perplexes me!
How furiously you take one's heart in hand,
And make your every wish a fierce command!
Come, must you hound and harry me to death?   85
Will you not give me time to catch my breath?
Can it be right to press me with such force,
Give me no quarter, show me no remorse,
And take advantage, by your stern insistence,
Of the fond feelings which weaken my resistance?   90

TARTUFFE.   Well, if you look with favor upon my love,
Why, then, begrudge me some clear proof thereof?

ELMIRE.   But how can I consent without offense

To Heaven, toward which you feel such reverence?
TARTUFFE.   If Heaven is all that holds you back, don't worry.   95
    I can remove that hindrance in a hurry.
    Nothing of that sort need obstruct our path.
ELMIRE.   Must one not be afraid of Heaven's wrath?
TARTUFFE.   Madam, forget such fears, and be my pupil,
    And I shall teach you how to conquer scruple.   100
    Some joys, it's true, are wrong in Heaven's eyes;
    Yet Heaven is not averse to compromise;
    There is a science, lately formulated,
    Whereby one's conscience may be liberated,
    And any wrongful act you care to mention   105
    May be redeemed by purity of intention.
    I'll teach you, Madam, the secrets of that science;
    Meanwhile, just place on me your full reliance.
    Assuage my keen desires, and feel no dread:
    The sin, if any, shall be on my head. (ELMIRE *coughs, this time more*
      loudly.)   110
    You've a bad cough.
ELMIRE.   Yes, yes. It's bad indeed.
TARTUFFE   (*producing a little paper bag*). A bit of licorice may be what
    you need.
ELMIRE.   No, I've a stubborn cold, it seems. I'm sure it
    Will take much more than licorice to cure it.
TARTUFFE.   How aggravating.
ELMIRE.   Oh, more than I can say.   115
TARTUFFE.   If you're still troubled, think of things this way:
    No one shall know our joys, save us alone,
    And there's no evil till the act is known;
    It's scandal, Madam, which makes it an offense,
    And it's no sin to sin in confidence.   120
ELMIRE (*having coughed once more*). Well, clearly I must do as
    you require,
    And yield to your importunate desire.
    It is apparent, now, that nothing less
    Will satisfy you, and so I acquiesce.
    To go so far is much against my will;   125
    I'm vexed that it should come to this; but still,
    Since you are so determined on it, since you
    Will not allow mere language to convince you,
    And since you ask for concrete evidence, I
    See nothing for it, now, but to comply.   130

If this is sinful, if I'm wrong to do it,
So much the worse for him who drove me to it.
The fault can surely not be charged to me.
TARTUFFE.   Madam, the fault is mine, if fault there be,
    And . . .
ELMIRE.   Open the door a little, and peek out;   135
    I wouldn't want my husband poking about.
TARTUFFE.   Why worry about the man? Each day he grows
    More gullible; one can lead him by the nose.
    To find us here would fill him with delight,
    And if he saw the worst, he'd doubt his sight.   140
ELMIRE.   Nevertheless, do step out for a minute
    Into the hall, and see that no one's in it. (*Exit* TARTUFFE.)

SCENE 6

ORGON (*coming out from under the table*). That man's a perfect monster,
    I must admit!
    I'm simply stunned. I can't get over it.
ELMIRE.   What, coming out so soon? how premature!
    Get back in hiding, and wait until you're sure.
    Stay till the end, and be convinced completely;   5
    We mustn't stop till things are proved concretely.
ORGON.   Hell never harbored anything so vicious!
ELMIRE.   Tut, don't be hasty. Try to be judicious.
    Wait, and be certain that there's no mistake.
    No jumping to conclusions, for Heaven's sake! (*She places*   10
    ORGON *behind her, as* TARTUFFE *re-enters.*)

SCENE 7

TARTUFFE (*not seeing* ORGON).   Madam, all things have worked out to
    perfection;
    I've given the neighboring rooms a full inspection;
    No one's about; and now I may at last . . .
ORGON (*intercepting him*). Hold on, my passionate fellow, not so fast!
    I should advise a little more restraint.   5
    Well, so you thought you'd fool me, my dear saint!
    How soon you wearied of the saintly life—
    Wedding my daughter, and coveting my wife!
    I've long suspected you, and had a feeling
    That soon I'd catch you at your double-dealing.   10
    Just now, you've given me evidence galore;

It's quite enough; I have no wish for more.

ELMIRE (to TARTUFFE). I'm sorry to have treated you so slyly,
But circumstances forced me to be wily.

TARTUFFE.   Brother, you can't think . . .

ORGON.   No more talk from you;   15
Just leave this household, without more ado.

TARTUFFE.   What I had intended . . .

ORGON.   That seems fairly clear.
Spare me your falsehoods and get out of here.

TARTUFFE.   No, I'm the master, and you're the one to go!
This house belongs to me, I'll have you know,   20
And I shall show you that you can't hurt *me*
By this contemptible conspiracy,
That those who cross me know not what they do,
And that I've means to expose and punish you,
Avenge offended Heaven, and make you grieve   25
That ever you dared order me to leave. (*Exit.*)

SCENE 8

ELMIRE.   What was the point of all that angry chatter?

ORGON.   Dear God, I'm worried. This is no laughing matter.

ELMIRE.   How so?

ORGON.   I fear I understood his drift.
I'm much disturbed about that deed of gift.

ELMIRE.   You gave him . . . ?

ORGON.   Yes, it's all been drawn and signed.   5
But one thing more is weighing on my mind.

ELMIRE.   What's that?

ORGON.   I'll tell you; but first let's see if there's
A certain strong-box in his room upstairs. (*Exeunt.*)

ACT 5

SCENE 1

    Enter ORGON *and* CLÉANTE.

CLÉANTE.   Where are you going so fast?

ORGON.   God knows!

CLÉANTE.   Then wait;
Let's have a conference, and deliberate
On how this situation's to be met.

ORGON.   That strong-box has me utterly upset;

This is the worst of many, many shocks.   5
CLÉANTE.   Is there some fearful mystery in that box?
ORGON.   My poor friend Argas brought that box to me
        With his own hands, in utmost secrecy;
        'Twas on the very morning of his flight.
        It's full of papers which, if they came to light,   10
        Would ruin him—or such is my impression.
CLÉANTE.   Then why did you let it out of your possession?
ORGON.   Those papers vexed my conscience, and it seemed best
        To ask the counsel of my pious guest.
        The cunning scoundrel got me to agree   15
        To leave the strong-box in his custody,
        So that, in case of an investigation,
        I could employ a slight equivocation
        And swear I didn't have it, and thereby,
        At no expense to conscience, tell a lie.   20
CLÉANTE.   It looks to me as if you're out on a limb.
        Trusting him with that box, and offering him
        That deed of gift, were actions of a kind
        Which scarcely indicate a prudent mind.
        With two such weapons, he has the upper hand,   25
        And since you're vulnerable, as matters stand,
        You erred once more in bringing him to bay.
        You should have acted in some subtler way.
ORGON.   Just think of it: behind that fervent face,
        A heart so wicked, and a soul so base!   30
        I took him in, a hungry beggar, and then . . .
        Enough, by God! I'm through with pious men:
        Henceforth I'll hate the whole false brotherhood,
        And persecute them worse than Satan could.
CLÉANTE.   Ah, there you go—extravagant as ever!   35
        Why can you not be rational? You never
        Manage to take the middle course, it seems,
        But jump, instead, between absurd extremes.
        You've recognized your recent grave mistake
        In falling victim to a pious fake;   40
        Now, to correct that error, must you embrace
        An even greater error in its place,
        And judge our worthy neighbors as a whole
        By what you've learned of one corrupted soul?
        Come, just because one rascal made you swallow   45
        A show of zeal which turned out to be hollow,

Shall you conclude that all men are deceivers,
And that, today, there are no true believers?
Let atheists make that foolish inference;
Learn to distinguish virtue from pretense,   50
Be cautious in bestowing admiration,
And cultivate a sober moderation.
Don't humor fraud, but also don't asperse
True piety; the latter fault is worse,
And it is best to err, if err one must,   55
As you have done, upon the side of trust.

SCENE 2

Enter DAMIS.

DAMIS.   Father, I hear that scoundrel's uttered threats
    Against you; that he pridefully forgets
    How, in his need, he was befriended by you,
    And means to use your gifts to crucify you.
ORGON.   It's true, my boy. I'm too distressed for tears.   5
DAMIS.   Leave it to me, Sir; let me trim his ears.
    Faced with such insolence, we must not waver.
    I shall rejoice in doing you the favor
    Of cutting short his life, and your distress.
CLÉANTE.   What a display of young hotheadedness!   10
    Do learn to moderate your fits of rage.
    In this just kingdom, this enlightened age,
    One does not settle things by violence.

SCENE 3

Enter MADAME PERNELLE, DORINE, MARIANE, *and* ELMIRE.

MADAME PERNELLE.   I hear strange tales of very strange events.
ORGON.   Yes, strange events which these two eyes beheld.
    The man's ingratitude is unparalleled.
    I save a wretched pauper from starvation,
    House him, and treat him like a blood relation,   5
    Shower him every day with my largesse,
    Give him my daughter, and all that I possess;
    And meanwhile the unconscionable knave
    Tries to induce my wife to misbehave;
    And not content with such extreme rascality,   10
    Now threatens me with my own liberality,
    And aims, by taking base advantage of

The gifts I gave him out of Christian love,
To drive me from my house, a ruined man,
And make me end a pauper, as he began.   15
DORINE.   Poor fellow!
MADAME PERNELLE.   No, my son, I'll never bring
  Myself to think him guilty of such a thing.
ORGON.   How's that?
MADAME PERNELLE.   The righteous always were maligned.
ORGON.   Speak clearly, Mother. Say what's on your mind.
MADAME PERNELLE.   I mean that I can smell a rat, my dear.   20
  You know how everybody hates him, here.
ORGON.   That has no bearing on the case at all.
MADAME PERNELLE.   I told you a hundred times, when you were small,
  That virtue in this world is hated ever;
  Malicious men may die, but malice never.   25
ORGON.   No doubt that's true, but how does it apply?
MADAME PERNELLE.   They've turned you against him by a clever lie.
ORGON.   I've told you, I was there and saw it done.
MADAME PERNELLE.   Ah, slanderers will stop at nothing, Son.
ORGON.   Mother, I'll lose my temper . . . For the last time,   30
  I tell you I was witness to the crime.
MADAME PERNELLE.   The tongues of spite are busy night and noon,
  And to their venom no man is immune.
ORGON.   You're talking nonsense. Can't you realize
  I saw it; saw it; saw it with my eyes?   35
  Saw, do you understand me? Must I shout it
  Into your ears before you'll cease to doubt it?
MADAME PERNELLE.   Appearances can deceive, my son. Dear me,
  We cannot always judge by what we see.
ORGON.   Drat! Drat!
MADAME PERNELLE.   One often interprets things awry;   40
  Good can seem evil to a suspicious eye.
ORGON.   Was I to see his pawing at Elmire
  As an act of charity?
MADAME PERNELLE.   Till his guilt is clear,
  A man deserves the benefit of the doubt.
  You should have waited, to see how things turned out.   45
ORGON.   Great God in Heaven, what more proof did I need?
  Was I to sit there, watching, until he'd . . .
  You drive me to the brink of impropriety.
MADAME PERNELLE.   No, no, a man of such surpassing piety
  Could not do such a thing. You cannot shake me.   50

I don't believe it, and you shall not make me.
ORGON.   You vex me so that, if you weren't my mother,
    I'd say to you . . . some dreadful thing or other.
DORINE.   It's your turn now, Sir, not to be listened to;
    You'd not trust us, and now she won't trust you.   55
CLÉANTE.   My friends, we're wasting time which should be spent
    In facing up to our predicament.
    I fear that scoundrel's threats weren't made in sport.
DAMIS.   Do you think he'd have the nerve to go to court?
ELMIRE.   I'm sure he won't: they'd find it all too crude   60
    A case of swindling and ingratitude.
CLÉANTE.   Don't be too sure. He won't be at a loss
    To give his claims a high and righteous gloss;
    And clever rogues with far less valid cause
    Have trapped their victims in a web of laws.   65
    I say again that to antagonize
    A man so strongly armed was most unwise.
ORGON.   I know it; but the man's appalling cheek
    Outraged me so, I couldn't control my pique.
CLÉANTE.   I wish to Heaven that we could devise   70
    Some truce between you, or some compromise.
ELMIRE.   If I had known what cards he held, I'd not
    Have roused his anger by my little plot.
ORGON (to DORINE, as M. LOYAL enters). What is that fellow looking
        for? Who is he?
    Go talk to him—and tell him that I'm busy.   75

SCENE 4

MONSIEUR LOYAL.   Good day, dear sister. Kindly let me see
    Your master.
DORINE.   He's involved with company,
    And cannot be disturbed just now, I fear.
MONSIEUR LOYAL.   I hate to intrude; but what has brought me here
    Will not disturb your master, in any event.   5
    Indeed, my news will make him most content.
DORINE.   Your name?
MONSIEUR LOYAL.   Just say that I bring greetings from
    Monsieur Tartuffe, on whose behalf I've come.
DORINE (to ORGON). Sir, he's a very gracious man, and bears
    A message from Tartuffe, which, he declares,   10
    Will make you most content.

CLÉANTE.   Upon my word,
    I think this man had best be seen, and heard.
ORGON.   Perhaps he has some settlement to suggest.
    How shall I treat him? What manner would be best?
CLÉANTE.   Control your anger, and if he should mention   15
    Some fair adjustment, give him your full attention.
MONSIEUR LOYAL.   Good health to you, good Sir. May Heaven confound
    Your enemies, and may your joys abound.
ORGON (*aside, to* CLÉANTE). A gentle salutation: it confirms
    My guess that he is here to offer terms.   20
MONSIEUR LOYAL.   I've always held your family most dear;
    I served your father, Sir, for many a year.
ORGON.   Sir, I must ask your pardon; to my shame,
    I cannot now recall your face or name.
MONSIEUR LOYAL.   Loyal's my name; I come from Normandy,   25
    And I'm a bailiff, in all modesty.
    For forty years, praise God, it's been my boast
    To serve with honor in that vital post,
    And I am here, Sir, if you will permit
    The liberty, to serve you with this writ . . .   30
ORGON.   To—*what?*
MONSIEUR LOYAL.   Now, please, Sir, let us have no friction:
    It's nothing but an order of eviction.
    You are to move your goods and family out
    And make way for new occupants, without
    Deferment or delay, and give the keys . . .   35
ORGON.   I? Leave this house?
MONSIEUR LOYAL.   Why yes, Sir, if you please.
    This house, Sir, from the cellar to the roof,
    Belongs now to the good Monsieur Tartuffe,
    And he is lord and master of your estate
    By virtue of a deed of present date,   40
    Drawn in due form, with clearest legal phrasing . . .
DAMIS.   Your insolence is utterly amazing!
MONSIEUR LOYAL.   Young man, my business here is not with you,
    But with your wise and temperate father, who,
    Like every worthy citizen, stands in awe   45
    Of justice, and would never obstruct the law.
ORGON.   But . . .
MONSIEUR LOYAL.   Not for a million, Sir, would you rebel
    Against authority; I know that well.

You'll not make trouble, Sir, or interfere
With the execution of my duties here.   50
DAMIS.   Someone may execute a smart tattoo
On that black jacket of yours, before you're through.
MONSIEUR LOYAL.   Sir, bid your son be silent. I'd much regret
Having to mention such a nasty threat
Of violence, in writing my report.   55
DORINE (aside). This man Loyal's a most disloyal sort!
MONSIEUR LOYAL.   I love all men of upright character,
And when I agreed to serve these papers, Sir,
It was your feelings that I had in mind.
I couldn't bear to see the case assigned   60
To someone else, who might esteem you less
And so subject you to unpleasantness.
ORGON.   What's more unpleasant than telling a man to leave
His house and home?
MONSIEUR LOYAL.   You'd like a short reprieve?
If you desire it, Sir, I shall not press you,   65
But wait until tomorrow to dispossess you.
Splendid. I'll come and spend the night here, then,
Most quietly, with half a score of men.
For form's sake, you might bring me, just before
You go to bed, the keys to the front door.   70
My men, I promise, will be on their best
Behavior, and will not disturb your rest.
But bright and early, Sir, you must be quick
And move out all your furniture, every stick:
The men I've chosen are both young and strong,   75
And with their help it shouldn't take you long.
In short, I'll make things pleasant and convenient,
And since I'm being so extremely lenient,
Please show me, Sir, a like consideration,
And give me your entire cooperation.   80
ORGON (aside). I may be all but bankrupt, but I vow
I'd give a hundred louis, here and now,
Just for the pleasure of landing one good clout
Right on the end of that complacent snout.
CLÉANTE.   Careful; don't make things worse.
DAMIS.   My bootsole itches   85
To give that beggar a good kick in the breeches.
DORINE.   Monsieur Loyal, I'd love to hear the whack
Of a stout stick across your fine broad back.

MONSIEUR LOYAL.   Take care: a woman too may go to jail if
　　She uses threatening language to a bailiff.   90
CLÉANTE.   Enough, enough, Sir. This must not go on.
　　Give me that paper, please, and then begone.
MONSIEUR LOYAL.   Well, *au revoir*. God give you all good cheer!
　　(*Leaving.*)
ORGON.   May God confound you, and him who sent you here!

SCENE 5

ORGON.   Now, Mother, was I right or not? This writ
　　Should change your notion of Tartuffe a bit.
　　Do you perceive his villainy at last?
MADAME PERNELLE.   I'm thunderstruck. I'm utterly aghast.
DORINE.   Oh, come, be fair. You mustn't take offense   5
　　At this new proof of his benevolence.
　　He's acting out of selfless love, I know.
　　Material things enslave the soul, and so
　　He kindly arranged your liberation
　　From all that might endanger your salvation.   10
ORGON.   Will you not ever hold your tongue, you dunce?
CLÉANTE.   Come, you must take some action, and at once.
ELMIRE.   Go tell the world of the low trick he's tried.
　　The deed of gift is surely nullified
　　By such behavior, and public rage will not   15
　　Permit the wretch to carry out his plot.

SCENE 6

　　Enter VALÈRE.

VALÈRE.   Sir, though I hate to bring you more bad news,
　　Such is the danger that I cannot choose.
　　A friend who is extremely close to me
　　And knows my interest in your family
　　Has, for my sake, presumed to violate   5
　　The secrecy that's due to things of state,
　　And sends me word that you are in a plight
　　From which your one salvation lies in flight.
　　That scoundrel who's imposed upon you so
　　Denounced you to the King an hour ago   10
　　And, as supporting evidence, displayed
　　The strong-box of a certain renegade

Whose secret papers, so he testified,
You had disloyally agreed to hide.
I don't know just what charges may be pressed,   15
But there's a warrant out for your arrest;
Tartuffe has been instructed, furthermore,
To guide the arresting officer to your door.
CLÉANTE.   He's clearly done this to facilitate
His seizure of your house and your estate.   20
ORGON.   That man, I must say, is a vicious beast!
VALÈRE.   Quick, Sir; you mustn't tarry in the least.
My carriage is outside, to take you hence;
This thousand louis should cover all expense.
Let's lose no time, or you shall be undone;   25
The sole defense, in this case, is to run.
I shall go with you all the way, and place you
In a safe refuge to which they'll never trace you.
ORGON.   Alas, dear boy, I wish that I could show you
My gratitude for everything I owe you.   30
But now is not the time; I pray the Lord
That I may live to give you your reward.
Farewell, my dears; be careful . . .
CLÉANTE.   Brother, hurry.
We shall take care of things; you needn't worry.

SCENE 7

Enter TARTUFFE *conducting a* POLICE OFFICER.

TARTUFFE.   Gently, Sir, gently; stay right where you are.
No need for haste; your lodging isn't far.
You're off to prison, by order of the Prince.
ORGON.   This is the crowning blow, you wretch; and since
It means my total ruin and defeat,   5
Your villainy is now at last complete.
TARTUFFE.   You needn't try to provoke me; it's no use.
Those who serve heaven must expect abuse.
CLÉANTE.   You are indeed most patient, sweet, and blameless.
DORINE.   How he exploits the name of Heaven! It's shameless. 10
TARTUFFE.   Your taunts and mockeries are all for naught;
To do my duty is my only thought.
MARIANE.   Your love of duty is most meritorious,
And what you've done is little short of glorious.
TARTUFFE.   All deeds are glorious, Madam, which obey   15

The sovereign Prince who sent me here today.
ORGON.   I rescued you when you were destitute;
    Have you forgotten that, you thankless brute?
TARTUFFE.   No, no, I well remember everything;
    But my first duty is to serve my King.   20
    That obligation is so paramount
    That other claims, beside it, do not count;
    And for it I would sacrifice my wife,
    My family, my friend, or my own life.
ELMIRE.   Hypocrite!
DORINE.   All that we most revere, he uses   25
    To cloak his plots and camouflage his ruses.
CLÉANTE.   If it is true that you are animated
    By pure and loyal zeal, as you have stated,
    Why was this zeal not roused until you'd sought
    To make Orgon a cuckold, and been caught?   30
    Why weren't you moved to give your evidence
    Until your outraged host had driven you hence?
    I shan't say that the gift of all his treasure
    Ought to have damped your zeal in any measure;
    But if he is a traitor, as you declare,   35
    How could you condescend to be his heir?
TARTUFFE (*to the* OFFICER). Sir, spare me all this clamor; it's
    growing shrill.
    Please carry out your orders, if you will.
OFFICER.   Yes, I've delayed too long, Sir. Thank you kindly.
    You're just the proper person to remind me.   40
    Come, you are off to join the other boarders
    In the King's prison, according to his orders.
TARTUFFE.   Who? I, Sir?
OFFICER.   Yes.
TARTUFFE.   To prison? This can't be true!
OFFICER.   I owe an explanation, but not to you.
    (*To* ORGON) Sir, all is well; rest easy, and be grateful.   45
    We serve a Prince to whom all sham is hateful,
    A Prince who sees into our inmost hearts,
    And can't be fooled by any trickster's arts.
    His royal soul, though generous and human,
    Views all things with discernment and acumen;   50
    His sovereign reason is not lightly swayed,
    And all his judgments are discreetly weighed.
    He honors righteous men of every kind,

And yet his zeal for virtue is not blind,
Nor does his love of piety numb his wits   55
And make him tolerant of hypocrites.
'Twas hardly likely that this man could cozen
A King who's foiled such liars by the dozen.
With one keen glance the King perceived the whole
Perverseness and corruption of his soul,   60
And thus high Heaven's justice was displayed:
Betraying you, the rogue stood self-betrayed.
The King soon recognized Tartuffe as one
Notorious by another name, who'd done
So many vicious crimes that one could fill   65
Ten volumes with them, and be writing still.
But to be brief: our sovereign was appalled
By this man's treachery toward you, which he called
The last, worst villainy of a vile career,
And bade me follow the impostor here   70
To see how gross his impudence could be,
And force him to restore your property.
Your private papers, by the King's command,
I hereby seize and give into your hand.
The King, by royal order, invalidates   75
The deed which gave this rascal your estates,
And pardons, furthermore, your grave offense
In harboring an exile's documents.
By these decrees, our Prince rewards you for
Your loyal deeds in the late civil war,   80
And shows how heartfelt is his satisfaction
In recompensing any worthy action,
How much he prizes merit, and how he makes
More of men's virtues than of their mistakes.
DORINE.   Heaven be praised!
MADAME PERNELLE.   I breathe again, at last.   85
ELMIRE.   We're safe.
MARIANE.   I can't believe the danger's past.
ORGON (*to* TARTUFFE). Well, traitor, now you see . . .
CLÉANTE.   Ah, Brother, please,
　　Let's not descend to such indignities.
　　Leave the poor wretch to his unhappy fate,
　　And don't say anything to aggravate   90
　　His present woes; but rather hope that he
　　Will soon embrace an honest piety,

And mend his ways, and by a true repentance
Move our just King to moderate his sentence.
Meanwhile, go kneel before your sovereign's throne   95
And thank him for the mercies he has shown.
ORGON.   Well said: let's go at once and, gladly kneeling,
Express the gratitude which all are feeling.
Then, when that first great duty has been done,
We'll turn with pleasure to a second one,   100
And give Valère, whose love has proven so true,
The wedded happiness which is his due.

QUESTIONS

1. The title character does not appear on the stage until Act 3, though he is the topic of all conversation preceding his entrance. How has he gained entrance to Orgon's household, and what is his function there? What expectations do you have about him before he appears? Do his actions hold any surprises for you?

2. Orgon as protagonist is preyed upon by his antagonist Tartuffe, but also displays characteristics that make him easily victimized. What are these, and how are they revealed not only in his dealings with Tartuffe but in other actions? What kinds of internal conflicts does he have?

3. The romantic subplot of Mariane and Valère suffers the traditional difficulties of a "blocking" father and a lovers' quarrel. Trace how these difficulties are overcome, and discuss the ways in which the subplot is integrated into the major plot. How is it more than an amusing contrast to the plot of Tartuffe's rise and fall?

4. What are Mme. Pernelle's complaints about her son's family? What set of values does she uphold? How does the first act define the moral and social values of the society in which the play is set?

5. A *raisonneur* is a character in a play who speaks for the author, providing commentary and correcting the mistaken ideas of others. How do Cléante and Dorine represent normative values? How are they more than mere mouthpieces for Molière?

6. This play employs some of the devices of farce. Identify these, and indicate how they support characterization, plot, and meaning in the play. In particular, how does the scene in which Orgon is hidden under the table (4.5) provide physical action that parallels meaning?

7. How does the scene with M. Loyal provide a miniature version of Tartuffe's relations with Orgon?

8. One early version of the play was called *Tartuffe, or The Hypocrite*. What implications does that title have, and how do they differ from those of the present title? Which more accurately captures the themes of the play?

9. Is the king's intervention in the final scene plausible? It resolves the conflicts between the antagonist and the protagonist, but to what extent does it provide a conclusion to the themes the play has raised?

10. Acts 1–3 flow continuously without any breaks in time. How much time is presumed to have elapsed between Acts 3 and 4, and between Acts 4 and 5? What is the effect of a play's action taking no more time than its stage performance? How closely do other plays in this book match this use of time?

11. Early versions of the play were suppressed because they were thought to satirize religion. Is that an accurate estimation of this play? Why, or why not? Aside from Tartuffe's actions and speeches, what information does the play provide about religious belief and behavior?

12. Aside from the use of poetry for dialogue, would you judge this play to be more realistic or nonrealistic?

Beth Henley
Am I Blue

Characters

JOHN POLK RICHARDS, *seventeen*
ASHBE WILLIAMS, *sixteen*
HILDA, *a waitress, thirty-five*
STREET PEOPLE: BARKER, WHORE, BUM, CLAREECE

SCENE. *A bar, the street, the living room of a run-down apartment.*
TIME. *Fall 1968.*

The scene opens on a street in the New Orleans French Quarter on a rainy, blue bourbon night. Various people—a WHORE, BUM, STREET BARKER, CLAREECE—*appear and disappear along the street. The scene then focuses on a bar where a piano is heard from the back room playing softly and indistinctly* "Am I Blue?" *The lights go up on* JOHN POLK, *who sits alone at a table. He is seventeen, a bit overweight and awkward. He wears nice clothes, perhaps a navy sweater with large white monograms. His navy raincoat is slung over an empty chair. While drinking John Polk concentrates on the red and black card that he holds in his hand. As soon as the scene is established,* ASHBE *enters from the street. She is sixteen, wears a flowered plastic raincoat, a white plastic rain cap, red galoshes, a butterfly barrette, and jeweled cat-eye glasses. She is carrying a bag full of stolen goods. Her hair is very curly. Ashbe makes her way cautiously to John Polk's table. As he sees her coming, he puts the card into his pocket. She sits in the empty chair and pulls his raincoat over her head.*

ASHBE. Excuse me . . . do you mind if I sit here please?
JOHN POLK (*looks up at her—then down into his glass*). What are you doing hiding under my raincoat? You're getting it all wet.
ASHBE. Well, I'm very sorry, but after all it is a raincoat. (*He tries to pull off coat.*) It was rude of me I know, but look I just don't want them to recognize me.
JOHN POLK (*looking about*). Who to recognize you?

AM I BLUE First performed in 1972 by SMU Theatre at Southern Methodist University where the author was an undergraduate in a playwriting class; first professional performance in New York in 1981. Beth Henley was born in Jackson, Mississippi, in 1952. After completing her degree at SMU she studied acting at the University of Illinois. Her first full-length play, *Crimes of the Heart* (1979), won a Pulitzer Prize for drama and was later adapted by Henley as a successful film, and she has written several other screenplays and more than a half dozen plays.

ASHBE.   Well, I stole these two ashtrays from the Screw Inn, ya know
    right down the street. (*She pulls out two glass commercial ashtrays
    from her white plastic bag.*) Anyway, I'm scared the manager saw me.
    They'll be after me I'm afraid.

JOHN POLK.   Well, they should be. Look, do you mind giving me back
    my raincoat? I don't want to be found protecting any thief.

ASHBE (*coming out from under coat*). Thief—would you call Robin
    Hood a thief?

JOHN POLK.   Christ.

ASHBE (*back under coat*). No, you wouldn't. He was valiant—all the
    time stealing from the rich and giving to the poor.

JOHN POLK.   But your case isn't exactly the same, is it? You're stealing
    from some crummy little bar and keeping the ashtrays for yourself.
    Now give me back my coat.

ASHBE (*throws coat at him*). Sure, take your old coat. I suppose I should
    have explained—about Miss Marcey. (*Silence.*) Miss Marcey, this
    cute old lady with a little hump in her back. I always see her in her
    sun hat and blue print dress. Miss Marcey lives in the apartment
    building next to ours. I leave all the stolen goods, as gifts on her
    front steps.

JOHN POLK.   Are you one of those kleptomaniacs? (*He starts checking his
    wallet.*)

ASHBE.   You mean when people all the time steal and they can't help it?

JOHN POLK.   Yeah.

ASHBE.   Oh, no. I'm not a bit careless. Take my job tonight, my very
    first night job, if you want to know. Anyway, I've been planning it
    for two months, trying to decipher which bar most deserved to be
    stolen from. I finally decided on the Screw Inn. Mainly because of
    the way they're so mean to Mr. Groves. He works at the magazine
    rack at Diver's Drugstore and is really very sweet, but he has a
    drinking problem. I don't think that's fair to be mean to people
    simply because they have a drinking problem—and, well, anyway,
    you see I'm not just stealing for personal gain. I mean, I don't even
    smoke.

JOHN POLK.   Yeah, well, most infants don't, but then again, most
    infants don't hang around bars.

ASHBE.   I don't see why not, Toulouse Lautrec did.

JOHN POLK.   They'd throw me out.

ASHBE.   Oh, they throw me out too, but I don't accept defeat. (*Slowly
    moves into him.*) Why it's the very same with my pickpocketing.
    (JOHN POLK *sneers, turns away.*) It's a very hard act to master. Why
    every time I've done it, I've been caught.

JOHN POLK.   That's all I need, is to have some slum kid tell me how good it is to steal. Everyone knows it's not.

ASHBE   (about his drink). That looks good. What is it?

JOHN POLK.   Hey, would you mind leaving me alone—I just wanted to be alone.

ASHBE.   Okay, I'm sorry. How about if I'm quiet? (JOHN POLK shrugs. He sips drink, looks around, catches her eye, she smiles and sighs.) I was just looking at your pin. What fraternity are you in?

JOHN POLK.   S.A.E.

ASHBE.   Is it a good fraternity?

JOHN POLK.   Sure, it's the greatest.

ASHBE.   I bet you have lots of friends.

JOHN POLK.   Tons.

ASHBE.   Are you being serious?

JOHN POLK.   Yes.

ASHBE.   Hmm. Do they have parties and all that?

JOHN POLK.   Yeah, lots of parties, booze, honking horns, it's exactly what you would expect.

ASHBE.   I wouldn't expect anything. Why did you join?

JOHN POLK.   I don't know. Well, my brother . . . I guess it was my brother . . . he told me how great it was, how the fraternity was supposed to get you dates, make you study, solve all your problems.

ASHBE.   Gee, does it?

JOHN POLK.   Doesn't help you study.

ASHBE.   How about dates? Do they get you a lot of dates?

JOHN POLK.   Some.

ASHBE.   What were the girls like?

JOHN POLK.   I don't know—they were like girls.

ASHBE.   Did you have a good time?

JOHN POLK.   I had a pretty good time.

ASHBE.   Did you make love to any of them?

JOHN POLK   (to self). Oh, Christ . . .

ASHBE.   I'm sorry . . . I just figured that's why you had the appointment with the whore . . . cause you didn't have anyone else . . . to make love to.

JOHN POLK.   How did you know I had the, ah, the appointment?

ASHBE.   I saw you put the red card in your pocket when I came up. Those red cards are pretty familiar around here. The house is only about a block or so away. It's one of the best though, really very plush. Only two murders and a knifing in its whole history. Do you go there often?

JOHN POLK.   Yeah, I like to give myself a treat.

ASHBE.   Who do you have?

JOHN POLK.   What do you mean?

ASHBE.   I mean which girl. (JOHN POLK *gazes into his drink.*) Look, I just
thought I might know her is all.

JOHN POLK.   Know her, ah, how would you know her?

ASHBE.   Well, some of the girls from my high school go there to work
when they get out.

JOHN POLK.   G.G., her name is G.G.

ASHBE.   G.G. . . . Hmm, well, how does she look?

JOHN POLK.   I don't know.

ASHBE.   Oh, you've never been with her before?

JOHN POLK.   No.

ASHBE   (*confidentially*).   Are you one of those kinds that likes a lot of
variety?

JOHN POLK.   Variety? Sure, I guess I like variety.

ASHBE.   Oh, yes, now I remember.

JOHN POLK.   What?

ASHBE.   G.G., that's just her working name. Her real name is Myrtle
Reims, she's Kay Reims' older sister. Kay is in my grade at school.

JOHN POLK.   Myrtle? Her name is Myrtle?

ASHBE.   I never liked the name either.

JOHN POLK.   Myrtle, oh, Christ. Is she pretty?

ASHBE   (*matter of fact*).   Pretty, no she's not real pretty.

JOHN POLK.   What does she look like?

ASHBE.   Let's see . . . she's, ah, well, Myrtle had acne and there are a
few scars left. It's not bad. I think they sort of give her character.
Her hair's red, only I don't think it's really red. It sort of fizzles out
all over her head. She's got a pretty good figure . . . big top . . . but
the rest of her is kind of skinny.

JOHN POLK.   I wonder if she has a good personality.

ASHBE.   Well, she was a senior when I was a freshman; so I never really
knew her. I remember she used to paint her fingernails lots of
different colors . . . pink, orange, purple. I don't know, but she kind
of scares me. About the only time I ever saw her true personality
was around a year ago. I was over at Kay's making a health poster
for school. Anyway, Myrtle comes busting in, screaming about how
she can't find her spangled bra anywhere. Kay and I just sat on the
floor cutting pictures of food out of magazines while she was
storming about slamming drawers and swearing. Finally, she found
it. It was pretty garish—red with black and gold sequined G's on
each cup. That's how I remember the name—G.G. (*As* ASHBE
illustrates the placement of the G's she spots HILDA, *the waitress,*

approaching. ASHBE *pulls the raincoat over her head and hides on the floor.* HILDA *enters through the beaded curtains spilling her tray.* HILDA *is a woman of few words.*)

HILDA.   Shit, damn curtain. Nuther drink?

JOHN POLK.   Mam?

HILDA (*points to drink*). Vodka coke?

JOHN POLK.   No, thank you. I'm not quite finished yet.

HILDA.   Napkins clean. (ASHBE *pulls her bag off the table.* HILDA *looks at* ASHBE *then to* JOHN POLK. *She walks around the table, as* ASHBE *is crawling along the floor to escape.* ASHBE *runs into* HILDA'S *toes.*)

ASHBE.   Are those real gold?

HILDA.   You again. Out.

ASHBE.   She wants me to leave. Why should a paying customer leave? (*Back to* HILDA.) Now I'll have a mint julep and easy on the mint.

HILDA.   This pre-teen with you?

JOHN POLK.   Well, I . . . No . . . I . . .

HILDA.   I.D.'s.

ASHBE.   Certainly, I always try to cooperate with the management.

HILDA (*looking at* JOHN POLK'S *I.D.*). I.D., 11-12-50. Date: 11-11-68.

JOHN POLK.   Yes, but . . . well, 11-12 is less than two hours away.

HILDA.   Back in two hours.

ASHBE.   I seem to have left my identification in my gold lamé bag.

HILDA.   Well, boo-hoo. (*Motions for* ASHBE *to leave with a minimum of effort. She goes back to table.*). No tip.

ASHBE.   You didn't tip her?

JOHN POLK.   I figured the drinks were so expensive . . . I just didn't . . .

HILDA.   No tip!

JOHN POLK.   Look, Miss, I'm sorry. (*Going through his pockets.*) Here would you like a . . . a nickel . . . wait, wait, here's a quarter.

HILDA.   Just move ass, sonny. You too, Barbie.

ASHBE.   Ugh, I hate public rudeness. I'm sure I'll refrain from ever coming here again.

HILDA.   Think I'll go in the back room and cry. (ASHBE *and* JOHN POLK *exit.* HILDA *picks up tray and exits through the curtain, tripping again.*) Shit. Damn curtain.
        (ASHBE *and* JOHN POLK *are now standing outside under the awning of the bar.*)

ASHBE.   Gee, I didn't know it was your birthday tomorrow. Happy birthday! Don't be mad. I thought you were at least twenty or twenty-one, really.

JOHN POLK.   It's o.k. Forget it. (*As they begin walking, various blues are heard coming from the nearby bars.*)

ASHBE.   It's raining.

JOHN POLK.   I know.

ASHBE.   Are you going over to the house now?

JOHN POLK.   No, not till twelve.

ASHBE.   Yeah, the red and black cards—they mean all night. Midnight till morning. (*At this point a street* BARKER *beckons the couple into his establishment. Perhaps he is accompanied by a* WHORE.)

BARKER.   Hey mister, bring your baby on in, buy her a few drinks, maybe tonight ya get lucky.

ASHBE.   Keep walking.

JOHN POLK.   What's wrong with the place?

ASHBE.   The drinks are watery rot gut, and the show girls are boys . . .

BARKER.   Up yours, punk!

JOHN POLK   (*who has now sat down on a street bench*). Look, just tell me where a cheap bar is. I've got to stay drunk, but I don't have much money left.

ASHBE.   Yikes, there aren't too many cheap bars around here, and a lot of them check I.D.'s.

JOHN POLK.   Well, do you know of any that don't?

ASHBE.   No, not for sure.

JOHN POLK.   Oh, God, I need to get drunk.

ASHBE.   Aren't you?

JOHN POLK.   Some, but I'm losing ground fast. (*By this time a* BUM *who has been traveling drunkenly down the street falls near the couple and begins throwing up.*)

ASHBE.   Oh, I know! You can come to my apartment. It's just down the block. We keep one bottle of rum around. I'll serve you a grand drink, three or four if you like.

JOHN POLK   (*fretfully*). No, thanks.

ASHBE.   But look, we're getting all wet.

JOHN POLK.   Sober too, wet and sober.

ASHBE.   Oh, come on! Rain's blurring my glasses.

JOHN POLK.   Well, how about your parents? What would they say?

ASHBE.   Daddy's out of town and Mama lives in Atlanta; so I'm sure they won't mind. I think we have some cute little marshmallows (*Pulling on him.*) Won't you really come?

JOHN POLK.   You've probably got some gang of muggers waiting to kill me. Oh, all right . . . what the hell, let's go.

ASHBE.   Hurrah! Come on. It's this way. (*She starts across the stage, stops, and picks up an old hat.*) Hey, look at this hat. Isn't something! Here, wear it to keep off the rain.

JOHN POLK (*throwing hat back onto street*). No, thanks, you don't know who's worn it before.

ASHBE (*picking hat back up*). That makes it all the more exciting. Maybe it was a butcher's who slaughtered his wife or a silver pirate with a black bird on his throat. Who do you guess?

JOHN POLK.   I don't know. Anyway what's the good of guessing? I mean you'll never really know.

ASHBE (*trying the hat on*). Yeah, probably not. (*At this point* ASHBE *and* JOHN POLK *reach the front door.*) Here we are. (ASHBE *begins fumbling for her key.* CLAREECE, *a teeny-bopper, walks up to* JOHN POLK.)

CLAREECE.   Hey, man, got any spare change?

JOHN POLK (*looking through his pockets*). Let me see . . . I . . .

ASHBE (*coming up between them, giving* CLAREECE *a shove*). Beat it, Clareece. He's my company.

CLAREECE (*walks away and sneers*). Oh, shove it, Frizzels.

ASHBE.   A lot of jerks live around here. Come on in. (*She opens the door. Lights go up on the living room of a run-down apartment in a run-down apartment house. Besides being merely rundown the room is a malicious pig sty with colors, paper hats, paper dolls, masks, torn up stuffed animals, dead flowers and leaves, dress-up clothes, etc., thrown all about.*) My bones are cold. Do you want a towel to dry off?

JOHN POLK.   Yes, thank you.

ASHBE (*picks up a towel off the floor and tosses it to him*). Here. (*He begins drying off, as she takes off her rain things; then she begins raking things off the sofa.*) Please do sit down. (*He sits.*) I'm sorry the place is disheveled, but my father's been out of town. I always try to pick up and all before he gets in. Of course, he's pretty used to messes. My mother never was too good at keeping things clean.

JOHN POLK.   When's he coming back?

ASHBE.   Sunday, I believe. Oh, I've been meaning to say . . .

JOHN POLK.   What?

ASHBE.   My name's Ashbe Williams.

JOHN POLK.   Ashbe?

ASHBE.   Yeah, Ashbe.

JOHN POLK.   My name's John Polk Richards.

ASHBE.   John Polk? They call you John Polk?

JOHN POLK.   It's family.

ASHBE (*putting on socks*). These are my favorite socks, the red furry ones. Well, here's some books and magazines to look at while I fix you something to drink. What do you want in your rum?

JOHN POLK.   Coke's fine.

ASHBE.   I'll see if we have any. I think I'll take some hot Kool-Aid myself. (*She exits to the kitchen.*)

JOHN POLK.   Hot Kool-Aid?

ASHBE.   It's just Kool-Aid that's been heated; like hot chocolate or hot tea.

JOHN POLK.   Sounds great.

ASHBE.   Well, I'm used to it. You get so much for your dime, it makes it worth your while. I don't buy presweetened, of course, it's better to sugar your own.

JOHN POLK.   I remember once I threw up a lot of grape Kool-Aid when I was a kid. I've hated it ever since. Hey, would you check on the time?

ASHBE (*enters carrying a tray with several bottles of food coloring, a bottle of rum, and a huge glass*). I'm sorry we don't have Coke. I wonder if rum and Kool-Aid is good? Oh, we don't have a clock either. (*She pours a large amount of rum into the large glass.*)

JOHN POLK.   I'll just have it with water then.

ASHBE (*finds an almost empty glass of water somewhere in the room and dumps it in with the rum*). Would you like food coloring in the water? It makes a drink all the more aesthetic. Of course, some people don't care for aesthetics.

JOHN POLK.   No, thank you, just plain water.

ASHBE.   Are you sure? The taste is entirely the same. I put it in all my water.

JOHN POLK.   Well . . .

ASHBE.   What color do you want?

JOHN POLK.   I don't know.

ASHBE.   What's your favorite color?

JOHN POLK.   Blue, I guess. (*She puts a few blue drops into the glass. As she has nothing to stir with, she blows into the glass turning the water blue.*)

JOHN POLK.   Thanks.

ASHBE (*Exits. She screams from kitchen*). Come on, say come on, cat, eat your fresh, good milk.

JOHN POLK.   You have a cat?

ASHBE (*off*). No.

JOHN POLK.   Oh.

ASHBE (*enters carrying a tray with a cup of hot Kool-Aid and Cheerios and colored marshmallows*). Here are some Cheerios and some cute, little, colored marshmallows to eat with your drink.

JOHN POLK.   Thanks.

ASHBE.   I one time smashed all the big white marshmallows in the plastic bag at the grocery store.

JOHN POLK.   Why did you do that?

ASHBE.   I was angry. Do you like ceramics?

JOHN POLK.   Yes.

ASHBE.   My mother makes them. It's sort of her hobby. She is very talented.

JOHN POLK.   My mother never does anything. Well, I guess she can shuffle the bridge deck okay.

ASHBE.   Actually, my mother is a dancer. She teaches at a school in Atlanta. She's really very talented.

JOHN POLK   (*indicates ceramics*). She must be to do all these.

ASHBE.   Well, Madeline, my older sister, did the blue one. Madeline gets to live with Mama.

JOHN POLK.   And you live with your father.

ASHBE.   Yeah, but I get to go visit them sometimes.

JOHN POLK.   You do ceramics too?

ASHBE.   No, I never learned . . . but I have this great potholder set. (*Gets up to show him.*) See, I make lots of multicolored potholders and send them to Mama and Madeline. I also make paper hats. (*Gets material to show him.*) I guess they're more creative, but making potholders is more relaxing. Here, would you like to make a hat?

JOHN POLK.   I don't know, I'm a little drunk.

ASHBE.   It's not hard a bit. (*Hands him material.*) Just draw a real pretty design on the paper. It really doesn't have to be pretty, just whatever you want.

JOHN POLK.   It's kind of you to give my creative drives such freedom.

ASHBE.   Ha, ha, ha, I'll work on my potholder set a bit.

JOHN POLK.   What time is it? I've really got to check on the time.

ASHBE.   I know. I'll call the time operator. (*She goes to the phone.*)

JOHN POLK.   How do you get along without a clock?

ASHBE.   Well, I've been late for school a lot. Daddy has a watch. It's 11:03.

JOHN POLK.   I've got a while yet. (ASHBE *twirls back to her chair, drops, and sighs.*) Are you a dancer, too?

ASHBE (*delighted*). I can't dance a bit, really. I practice a lot is all, at home in the afternoon. I imagine you go to a lot of dances.

JOHN POLK.   Not really, I'm a terrible dancer. I usually get bored or drunk.

ASHBE.   You probably drink too much.

JOHN POLK.   No, it's just since I've come to college. All you do there is drink more beer and write more papers.

ASHBE.   What are you studying for to be?

JOHN POLK.   I don't know.

ASHBE.   Why don't you become a rancher?

JOHN POLK.   Dad wants me to help run his soybean farm.

ASHBE.   Soybean farm. Yikes, that's really something. Where is it?

JOHN POLK.   Well, I live in the Delta, Hollybluff, Mississippi. Anyway, Dad feels I should go to business school first; you know, so I'll become, well, management-minded. Pass the blue.

ASHBE.   Is that what you really want to do?

JOHN POLK.   I don't know. It would probably be as good as anything else I could do. Dad makes good money. He can take vacations whenever he wants. Sure it'll be a ball.

ASHBE.   I'd hate to have to be management-minded. (JOHN POLK *shrugs.*) I don't mean to hurt your feelings, but I would really hate to be a management mind. (*She starts walking on her knees, twisting her fists in front of her eyes, and making clicking sounds as a management mind would make.*)

JOHN POLK.   Cut it out. Just forget it. The farm could burn down, and I wouldn't even have to think about it.

ASHBE   (*after a pause*). Well, what do you want to talk about?

JOHN POLK.   I don't know.

ASHBE.   When was the last dance you went to?

JOHN POLK.   Dances. That's a great subject. Let's see, oh, I don't really remember—it was probably some blind date. God, I hate dates.

ASHBE.   Why?

JOHN POLK.   Well, they always say that they don't want popcorn, and they wind up eating all of yours.

ASHBE.   You mean, you hate dates just because they eat your popcorn? Don't you think that's kind of stingy?

JOHN POLK.   It's the principle of the thing. Why can't they just say, yes, I'd like some popcorn when you ask them. But, no, they're always so damn coy.

ASHBE.   I'd tell my date if I wanted popcorn. I'm not that immature.

JOHN POLK.   Anyway, it's not only the popcorn. It's a lot of little things. I've finished coloring. What do I do now?

ASHBE.   Now you have to fold it. Here . . . like this: (*She explains the process with relish.*) Say, that's really something.

JOHN POLK.   It's kind of funny looking. (*Putting the hat on.*) Yeah, I like it, but you could never wear it anywhere.

ASHBE.   Well, like what anyway?

JOHN POLK.   Huh?

ASHBE.   The things dates do to you that you don't like, the little things.

JOHN POLK.   Oh, well, just the way they wear those false eyelashes and put their hand on your knee when you're trying to parallel park, and keep on giggling and going off to the bathroom with their girl friends. It's obvious they don't want to go out with me. They just want to go out so that they can wear their new clothes and won't have to sit on their ass in the dormitory. They never want to go out with me. I can never even talk to them.

ASHBE.   Well, you can talk to me, and I'm a girl.

JOHN POLK.   Well, I'm really kind of drunk, and you're a stranger . . . well, I probably wouldn't be able to talk to you tomorrow. That makes a difference.

ASHBE.   Maybe it does. (*A bit of a pause and then extremely pleased by the idea she says.*) You know we're alike because I don't like dances either.

JOHN POLK.   I thought you said you practiced . . . in the afternoons.

ASHBE.   Well, I like dancing. I just don't like dances. At least not like . . . well, not like the one our school was having tonight . . . they're so corny.

JOHN POLK.   Yeah, most dances are.

ASHBE.   All they serve is potato chips and fruit punch, and then this stupid baby band plays and everybody dances around thinking they're so hot. I frankly wouldn't dance there. I would prefer to wait till I am invited to an exclusive ball. It doesn't really matter which ball, just one where they have huge, golden chandeliers and silver fountains, and serve delicacies of all sorts and bubble blue champagne. I'll arrive in a pink silk cape. (*Laughing.*) I want to dance in pink!

JOHN POLK.   You're mixed up. You're probably one of those people that live in a fantasy world.

ASHBE.   I do not. I accept reality as well as anyone. Anyway, you can talk to me, remember. I know what you mean by the kind of girls it's hard to talk to. There are girls a lot that way in the small clique at my school. Really tacky and mean. They expect everyone to be as stylish as they are, and they won't even speak to you in the hall. I don't mind if they don't speak to me, but I really love the orphans, and it hurts my feelings when they are so mean to them.

JOHN POLK.   What do you mean—they're mean to the "orpheens"? (*Giggles to himself at the wordplay.*)

ASHBE.   Oh, well, they sometimes snicker at the orphans' dresses. The orphans usually have hand-me-down, drab, ugly dresses. Once Shelly Maxwell wouldn't let Glinda borrow her pencil, even though she had two. It hurt her feelings.

JOHN POLK.   Are you best friends with these orphans?

ASHBE.   I hardly know them at all. They're really shy. I just like them a lot. They're the reason I put spells on the girls in the clique.

JOHN POLK.   Spells, what do you mean, witch spells?

ASHBE.   Witch spells? Not really, mostly just voodoo.

JOHN POLK.   Are you kidding? Do you really do voodoo?

ASHBE.   Sure, here I'll show you my doll. (*Goes to get doll, comes back with straw voodoo doll. Her air as she returns is one of frightening mystery.*) I know a lot about the subject. Cora, she used to wash dishes in the Moonlight Cafe, told me all about voodoo. She's a real expert on the subject, went to all the meetings and everything. Once she caused a man's throat to rot away and turn almost totally black. She's moved to Chicago now.

JOHN POLK.   It doesn't really work. Does it?

ASHBE.   Well, not always. The thing about voodoo is that both parties have to believe in it for it to work.

JOHN POLK.   Do the girls in school believe in it?

ASHBE.   Not really, I don't think. That's where my main problem comes in. I have to make the clique believe in it, yet I have to be very subtle. Mainly, I give reports in English class or Speech.

JOHN POLK.   Reports?

ASHBE.   On voodoo.

JOHN POLK.   That's really kind of sick, you know.

ASHBE.   Not really. I don't cast spells that'll do any real harm. Mainly, just the kind of thing to make them think . . . to keep them on their toes. (*Blue drink intoxication begins to take over and* JOHN POLK *begins laughing.*) What's so funny?

JOHN POLK.   Nothing. I was just thinking what a mean little person you are.

ASHBE.   Mean! I'm not mean a bit.

JOHN POLK.   Yes, you are mean . . . (*Picking up color.*) . . . and green too.

ASHBE.   Green?

JOHN POLK.   Yes, green with envy of those other girls; so you play all those mean little tricks.

ASHBE.   Envious of those other girls, that stupid, close-minded little clique!

JOHN POLK.   Green as this marshmallow. (*Eats marshmallow.*)

ASHBE.   You think I want to be in some group . . . a sheep like you? little sheep like you that does everything when he's supposed to do it!

JOHN POLK.   Me a sheep . . . I do what I want!

ASHBE.   Ha! I've known you for an hour and already I see you for the sheep you are!

JOHN POLK.   Don't take your green meanness out on me.

ASHBE.   Not only are you a sheep, you are a NORMAL sheep. Give me back my colors! (*Begins snatching colors away.*)

JOHN POLK (*pushing colors at her*). Green and mean! Green and mean! Green and mean!

ASHBE (*throwing marshmallows at him*). That's the reason you're in a fraternity and the reason you're going to manage your mind. And dates . . . you go out on dates merely because it's expected of you even though you have a terrible time. That's the reason you go to the whorehouse to prove you're a normal man. Well, you're much too normal for me.

JOHN POLK.   Infant bitch. You think you're really cute.

ASHBE.   That really wasn't food coloring in your drink, it was poison! (*She laughs, he picks up his coat to go, and she stops throwing marshmallows at him.*) Are you going? I was only kidding. For Christ sake, it wasn't really poison. Come on, don't go. Can't you take a little friendly criticism?

JOHN POLK.   Look, did you have to bother me tonight? I had enough problems without . . . (*Phone rings. Both look at phone, it rings for the third time. He stands undecided.*)

ASHBE.   Look, wait, we'll make it up. (*She goes to answer phone.*) Hello . . . Daddy. How are you? . . . I'm fine . . . Dad, you sound funny . . . What? . . . Come on, Daddy, you know she's not here. (*Pause.*) Look, I told you I wouldn't call anymore. You've got her number in Atlanta. (*Pause, as she sinks to the floor.*) Why have you started again? . . . Don't say that. I can tell it. I can. Hey, I have to go to bed now, I don't want to talk anymore, okay? (*Hangs up phone, then softly to self.*) Goddamnit.

JOHN POLK (*he has heard the conversation and is taking off his coat*). Hey, Ashbe . . . (*She looks at him blankly, her mind far away.*) You want to talk?

ASHBE.   No. (*Slight pause.*) Why don't you look at my shell collection? I have this special shell collection. (*She shows him collection.*)

JOHN POLK.   They're beautiful, I've never seen colors like this. (ASHBE *is silent, he continues to himself.*) I used to go to Biloxi a lot when I was a kid . . . One time my brother and I, we camped out on the beach. The sky was purple. I remember it was really purple. We ate pork and beans out of a can. I'd always kinda wanted to do that.

Every night for about a week after I got home, I dreamt about these waves foaming over my head and face. It was funny. Did you find these shells or buy them?

ASHBE.   Some I found, some I bought. I've been trying to decipher their meaning. Here, listen, do you hear that?

JOHN POLK.   Yes.

ASHBE.   That's the soul of the sea. (*She listens.*) I'm pretty sure it's the soul of the sea. Just imagine when I decipher the language. I'll know all the secrets of the world.

JOHN POLK.   Yeah, probably you will. (*Looking into the shell.*) You know, you were right.

ASHBE.   What do you mean?

JOHN POLK.   About me, you were right. I am a sheep, a normal one. I've been trying to get out of it, but now I'm as big a sheep as ever.

ASHBE.   Oh, it doesn't matter. You're company. It was rude of me to say.

JOHN POLK.   No, because it was true. I really didn't want to go into a fraternity, I didn't even want to go to college, and I sure as hell don't want to go back to Hollybluff and work the soybean farm till I'm eighty.

ASHBE.   I still say you could work on a ranch.

JOHN POLK.   I don't know. I wanted to be a minister or something good, but I don't even know if I believe in God.

ASHBE.   Yeah.

JOHN POLK.   I never used to worry about being a failure. Now I think about it all the time. It's just I need to do something that's . . . fulfilling.

ASHBE.   Fulfilling, yes, I see what you mean. Well, how about college? Isn't it fulfilling? I mean, you take all those wonderful classes, and you have all your very good friends.

JOHN POLK.   Friends, yeah, I have some friends.

ASHBE.   What do you mean?

JOHN POLK.   Nothing . . . well, I do mean something. What the hell, let me try to explain. You see it was my "friends," the fraternity guys that set me up with G.G., excuse me, Myrtle, as a gift for my eighteenth birthday.

ASHBE.   You mean, you didn't want the appointment?

JOHN POLK.   No, I didn't want it. Hey, ah, where did my blue drink go?

ASHBE (*as she hands him the drink*). They probably thought you really wanted to go.

JOHN POLK.   Yeah, I'm sure they gave a damn what I wanted. They
never even asked me. Hell, I would have told them a handkerchief,
a pair of argyle socks, but, no, they have to get me a whore just
because it's a cool-ass thing to do. They make me sick. I couldn't
even stay at the party they gave. All the sweaty T-shirts, and
moron sex stories . . . I just couldn't take it.

ASHBE.   Is that why you were at the Blue Angel so early?

JOHN POLK.   Yeah, I needed to get drunk, but not with them. They're
such creeps.

ASHBE.   Gosh, so you really don't want to go to Myrtle's?

JOHN POLK.   No, I guess not.

ASHBE.   Then are you going?

JOHN POLK   (pause). Yes.

ASHBE.   That's wrong. You shouldn't go just to please them.

JOHN POLK.   Oh, that's not the point anymore, maybe at first it was,
but it's not anymore. Now I have to go for myself . . . to prove to
myself that I'm not afraid.

ASHBE.   Afraid? (Slowly, as she begins to grasp his meaning.) You mean,
you've never slept with a girl before?

JOHN POLK.   Well, I've never been in love.

ASHBE   (in amazement). You're a virgin?

JOHN POLK.   Oh, God.

ASHBE.   No, don't feel bad, I am too.

JOHN POLK.   I thought I should be in love . . .

ASHBE.   Well, you're certainly not in love with Myrtle. I mean, you
haven't even met her.

JOHN POLK.   I know, but, God, I thought maybe I'd never fall in love.
What then? You should experience everything . . . shouldn't you?
Oh, what's it matter, everything's so screwed.

ASHBE.   Screwed? Yeah, I guess it is. I mean, I always thought it would
be fun to have a lot of friends who gave parties and go to dances all
dressed up. Like the dance tonight . . . it might have been fun.

JOHN POLK.   Well, why didn't you go?

ASHBE.   I don't know. I'm not sure it would have been fun. Anyway,
you can't go . . . alone.

JOHN POLK.   Oh, you need a date?

ASHBE.   Yeah, or something.

JOHN POLK.   Say, Ashbe, ya wanna dance here?

ASHBE.   No, I think we'd better discuss your dilemma.

JOHN POLK.   What dilemma?

ASHBE.   Myrtle. It doesn't seem right you should . . .

JOHN POLK.   Let's forget Myrtle for now. I've got a while yet. Here have some more of this blue-moon drink.

ASHBE.   You're only trying to escape through artificial means.

JOHN POLK.   Yeah, you got it. Now come on. Would you like to dance? Hey, you said you liked to dance.

ASHBE.   You're being ridiculous.

JOHN POLK (*winking at her*). Dance?

ASHBE.   John Polk, I just thought . . .

JOHN POLK.   Hmm?

ASHBE.   How to solve your problem . . .

JOHN POLK.   Well . . .

ASHBE.   Make love to me!

JOHN POLK.   What?!

ASHBE.   It all seems logical to me. It would prove you weren't scared, and you wouldn't be doing it just to impress others.

JOHN POLK.   Look, I . . . I mean, I hardly know you . . .

ASHBE.   But we've talked. It's better this way, really. I won't be so apt to point out your mistakes.

JOHN POLK.   I'd feel great, stripping a twelve-year-old of her virginity.

ASHBE.   I'm sixteen! Anyway I'd be stripping you of yours just as well. I'll go put on some Tiger Claw perfume. (*She runs out.*)

JOHN POLK.   Hey, come back! Tiger Claw perfume, Christ.

ASHBE (*entering*). I think one should have different scents for different moods.

JOHN POLK.   Hey, stop spraying that! You know I'm not going to . . . well, you'd get neurotic, or pregnant, or some damn thing. Stop spraying, will you!

ASHBE.   Pregnant? You really think I could get pregnant?

JOHN POLK.   Sure, it'd be a delightful possibility.

ASHBE.   It really wouldn't be bad. Maybe I would get to go to Tokyo for an abortion. I've never been to the Orient.

JOHN POLK.   Sure getting cut on is always a real treat.

ASHBE.   Anyway, I might just want to have my dear baby. I could move to Atlanta with Mama and Madeline. It'd be wonderful fun. Why I could take him to the supermarket, put him in one of those little baby seats to stroll him about, I'd buy peach baby food and feed it to him with a tiny golden spoon. Why I could take colored pictures of him and send them to you through the mail. Come on . . . (*Starts putting pillows onto the couch.*) Well, I guess you should kiss me for a start. It's only etiquette, everyone begins with it.

JOHN POLK.   I don't think I could even kiss you with a clear conscience. I mean, you're so small with those little cat-eye glasses and curly hair . . . I couldn't even kiss you.

ASHBE.   You couldn't even kiss me? I can't help it if I have to wear glasses. I got the prettiest ones I could find.

JOHN POLK.   Your glasses are fine. Let's forget it, okay?

ASHBE.   I know, my lips are too purple, but if I eat carrots, the dye'll come off and they'll be orange.

JOHN POLK.   I didn't say anything about your lips being too purple.

ASHBE.   Well, what is it? You're just plain chicken, I suppose . . .

JOHN POLK.   Sure, right, I'm chicken, totally chicken. Let's forget it. I don't know how, but, somehow, this is probably all my fault.

ASHBE.   You're darn right it's all your fault! I want to have my dear baby or at least get to Japan. I'm so sick of school I could smash every marshmallow in sight! (*She starts smashing.*) Go on to your skinny pimple whore. I hope the skinny whore laughs in your face, which she probably will because you have an easy face to laugh in.

JOHN POLK.   You're absolutely right, she'll probably hoot and howl her damn fizzle red head off. Maybe you can wait outside the door and hear her, give you lots of pleasure, you sadistic little thief.

ASHBE.   Thief! Was Robin Hood . . . Oh, what's wrong with this world? I just wasn't made for it, is all. I've probably been put in the wrong world, I can see that now.

JOHN POLK.   You're fine in this world.

ASHBE.   Sure, everyone just views me as an undesirable lump.

JOHN POLK.   Who?

ASHBE.   You, for one.

JOHN POLK (*pause*). You mean because I wouldn't make love to you?

ASHBE.   It seems clear to me.

JOHN POLK.   But you're wrong, you know.

ASHBE (*to self, softly*). Don't pity me.

JOHN POLK.   The reason I wouldn't wasn't that . . . it's just that . . . well, I like you too much to.

ASHBE.   You like me?

JOHN POLK.   Undesirable lump, Jesus. Your cheeks they're . . . they're . . .

ASHBE.   My cheeks? They're what?

JOHN POLK.   They're rosy.

ASHBE.   My cheeks are rosy?

JOHN POLK.   Yeah, your cheeks, they're really rosy.

ASHBE.   Well, they're natural, you know. Say, would you like to dance?

JOHN POLK.   Yes.

ASHBE.   I'll turn on the radio. (*She turns on radio. Ethel Waters is heard singing "Honey in the Honeycomb."* ASHBE *begins snapping her fingers.*) Yikes, let's jazz it out. (*They dance.*)

JOHN POLK.   Hey, I'm not good or anything . . .

ASHBE.   John Polk.

JOHN POLK.   Yeah?

ASHBE.   Baby, I think you dance fine! (*They dance on, laughing, saying what they want till end of song. Then a radio announcer comes on and says the 12:00 news will be in five minutes. Billie Holiday, or Terry Pierce, begins singing, "Am I Blue?"*)

JOHN POLK.   Dance?

ASHBE.   News in five minutes.

JOHN POLK.   Yeah.

ASHBE.   That means five minutes till midnight.

JOHN POLK.   Yeah, I know.

ASHBE.   Then you're not . . .

JOHN POLK.   Ashbe, I've never danced all night. Wouldn't it be something to . . . to dance all night and watch the rats come out of the gutter?

ASHBE.   Rats?

JOHN POLK.   Don't they come out at night? I hear New Orleans has lots of rats.

ASHBE.   Yeah, yeah, it's got lots of rats.

JOHN POLK.   Then let's dance all night and wait for them to come out.

ASHBE.   All right . . . but, but how about our feet?

JOHN POLK.   Feet?

ASHBE.   They'll hurt.

JOHN POLK.   Yeah.

ASHBE (*smiling*). Okay, then let's dance. (*He takes her hand, and they dance as lights black out and the music soars and continues to play.*) End.

QUESTIONS

1. What actions and attitudes characterize Ashbe and John Polk? Are they realists? Are they realistically presented?

2. Both characters have problems with their families. What are these? Both characters have problems with their peers. What are these?

3. Ashbe says "Oh, what's wrong with this world? I just wasn't made for it, is all." Is that an appropriate statement of the theme of the play?

4. To what extent are the actions of Ashbe and John Polk defensive? What are they defending themselves against?

5. Would the play be improved or damaged if John Polk had accepted Ashbe's offer of sex?

6. "Am I Blue?" with a question mark is the name of a blues love song. Why does the title of the play omit the question mark?

7. The action of the play is precisely stated—November 11, 1968. After researching major events in the country that year, can you relate the action of the play to larger public issues? How "blue" was the national mood?

SUGGESTIONS FOR WRITING

1. One of the structural devices regularly used by Shakespeare is contrast in tone, content, or effect. In tragedies, he follows a scene of high seriousness with a comic scene (commonly called **comic relief**, because like a "relief map," it delineates for us by contrast the heights of emotion that we have just experienced). Conversely, in comedies, we often encounter actions that threaten dire consequences or remind the audience of the less pleasant side of life (no one has labeled this "tragic relief," though that might be an appropriate term). Using "Time Flies," "Los Vendidos," *Tartuffe*, or *A Midsummer Night's Dream*, write an essay that explores the emotional effects of these contrasts.

2. Using one of the plays in this chapter, write an essay demonstrating the idea that the conclusion of a tragedy or of a comedy has a mixed effect on the audience—that tragedy does not produce unmitigated woe and depression, that comedy leaves its audience not only laughing but with a renewed sense of its own limitations.

3. Explore the emotional effects of the conclusions of one or more of the following: Glaspell's "Trifles," Albee's "The Sandbox," Ibsen's *A Doll House*, Williams's *The Glass Menagerie*.

4. Write an essay about one of the ten plays in chapters 1 and 2 showing it to be an example of one of the four dramatic categories defined in this chapter—tragedy, comedy, melodrama, or farce. If your choice does not wholly fit into one of the categories, explore the ways in which it has characteristics of more than one of them.

Plays for
Further Reading

Arthur Miller

Death of a Salesman

Certain Private Conversations in Two Acts and a Requiem

Characters

WILLY LOMAN	CHARLEY, *a neighbor*
LINDA, *his wife*	BERNARD, *Charley's son*
BIFF ⎱ *his sons*	JENNY, *Charley's secretary*
HAPPY ⎰	STANLEY, *a waiter*
UNCLE BEN, *his older brother*	MISS FORSYTHE ⎱ *young women*
HOWARD WAGNER, *his employer*	LETTA ⎰
THE WOMAN	

The action takes place in WILLY LOMAN's house and yard and in various places he visits in the New York and Boston of today.

ACT 1

A melody is heard, played upon a flute. It is small and fine, telling of grass and trees and the horizon. The curtain rises.

Before us is the Salesman's house. We are aware of towering, angular shapes behind it, surrounding it on all sides. Only the blue light of the sky falls upon the house and forestage; the surrounding area shows an angry glow of orange. As more light appears, we see a solid vault of apartment houses around the small, fragile-seeming home. An air of the dream clings to the place, a dream rising out of reality. The kitchen at center seems actual enough, for there is a kitchen table with three chairs, and a refrigerator. But no other fixtures are seen. At the back of the kitchen there is a draped entrance, which leads to the living-room. To the right of the kitchen, on a level raised two feet, is a bedroom furnished only with a brass bedstead and a straight chair. On a shelf over the bed a silver athletic trophy stands. A window opens onto the apartment house at the side.

DEATH OF A SALESMAN   First performed in 1949. Arthur Miller (1915–2005) was born in New York City, the son of a well-to-do manufacturer whose financial losses in the Depression forced a move to Brooklyn in 1929. Here Miller graduated from high school and worked in an automobile parts warehouse for two years before entering the University of Michigan, where he won three drama prizes. After graduation in 1938, he returned to Brooklyn, married, and fathered a son and daughter. *Death of a Salesman* was his third Broadway play.

Behind the kitchen, on a level raised six and a half feet, is the boys' bedroom, at present barely visible. Two beds are dimly seen, and at the back of the room a dormer window. (This bedroom is above the unseen living-room.) At the left a stairway curves up to it from the kitchen.

The entire setting is wholly, or, in some places, partially transparent. The roofline of the house is one-dimensional; under and over it we see the apartment buildings. Before the house lies an apron, curving beyond the forestage into the orchestra. This forward area serves as the back yard as well as the locale of all WILLY's imaginings and of his city scenes. Whenever the action is in the present the actors observe the imaginary wall-lines, entering the house only through its door at the left. But in the scenes of the past these boundaries are broken, and characters enter or leave a room by stepping "through" a wall onto the forestage.

From the right, WILLY LOMAN, the Salesman, enters, carrying two large sample cases. The flute plays on. He hears but is not aware of it. He is past sixty years of age, dressed quietly. Even as he crosses the stage to the doorway of the house, his exhaustion is apparent. He unlocks the door, comes into the kitchen, and thankfully lets his burden down, feeling the soreness of his palms. A word-sigh escapes his lips—it might be "Oh, boy, oh, boy." He closes the door, then carries his cases out into the living-room, through the draped kitchen doorway.

LINDA, his wife, has stirred in her bed at the right. She gets out and puts on a robe, listening. Most often jovial, she has developed an iron repression of her exceptions to WILLY's behavior—she more than loves him, she admires him, as though his mercurial nature, his temper, his massive dreams and little cruelties, served her only as sharp reminders of the turbulent longings within him, longings which she shares but lacks the temperament to utter and follow to their end.

LINDA (*hearing* WILLY *outside the bedroom, calls with some trepidation*).   Willy!

WILLY.   It's all right. I came back.

LINDA.   Why? What happened? (*Slight pause.*) Did something happen, Willy?

WILLY.   No, nothing happened.

LINDA.   You didn't smash the car, did you?

WILLY (*with casual irritation*).   I said nothing happened. Didn't you hear me?

LINDA.   Don't you feel well?

WILLY.   I'm tired to the death. (*The flute has faded away. He sits on the bed beside her, a little numb.*) I couldn't make it. I just couldn't make it, Linda.

LINDA (*very carefully, delicately*).   Where were you all day? You look terrible.

WILLY.   I got as far as a little above Yonkers. I stopped for a cup of coffee. Maybe it was the coffee.

LINDA.   What?

WILLY (*after a pause*).   I suddenly couldn't drive any more. The car kept going off onto the shoulder, y'know?

LINDA (*helpfully*).   Oh. Maybe it was the steering again. I don't think Angelo knows the Studebaker.

WILLY.   No, it's me, it's me. Suddenly I realize I'm goin' sixty miles an hour and I don't remember the last five minutes. I'm—I can't seem to—keep my mind to it.

LINDA.   Maybe it's your glasses. You never went for your new glasses.

WILLY.   No, I see everything. I came back ten miles an hour. It took me nearly four hours from Yonkers.

LINDA (*resigned*).   Well, you'll just have to take a rest, Willy, you can't continue this way.

WILLY.   I just got back from Florida.

LINDA.   But you didn't rest your mind. Your mind is overactive, and the mind is what counts, dear.

WILLY.   I'll start out in the morning. Maybe I'll feel better in the morning. (*She is taking off his shoes.*) These goddam arch supports are killing me.

LINDA.   Take an aspirin. Should I get you an aspirin? It'll soothe you.

WILLY (*with wonder*).   I was driving along, you understand? And I was fine. I was even observing the scenery. You can imagine, me looking at scenery, on the road every week of my life. But it's so beautiful up there, Linda, the trees are so thick, and the sun is warm. I opened the windshield and just let the warm air bathe over me. And then all of a sudden I'm goin' off the road! I'm tellin' ya, I absolutely forgot I was driving. If I'd've gone the other way over the white line I might've killed somebody. So I went on again—and five minutes later I'm dreamin' again, and I nearly—(*He presses two fingers against his eyes.*) I have such thoughts, I have such strange thoughts.

LINDA.   Willy, dear. Talk to them again. There's no reason why you can't work in New York.

WILLY.   They don't need me in New York. I'm the New England man. I'm vital in New England.

LINDA.   But you're sixty years old. They can't expect you to keep traveling every week.

WILLY.   I'll have to send a wire to Portland. I'm supposed to see Brown and Morrison tomorrow morning at ten o'clock to show the line. Goddammit, I could sell them! (*He starts putting on his jacket.*)

LINDA (*taking the jacket from him*).   Why don't you go down to the place tomorrow and tell Howard you've simply got to work in New York? You're too accommodating, dear.

WILLY.   If old man Wagner was alive I'd a been in charge of New York now! That man was a prince, he was a masterful man. But that boy of his, that Howard, he don't appreciate. When I went north the first time, the Wagner Company didn't know where New England was!

LINDA.   Why don't you tell those things to Howard, dear?

WILLY (*encouraged*).   I will, I definitely will. Is there any cheese?

LINDA.   I'll make you a sandwich.

WILLY.   No, go to sleep. I'll take some milk. I'll be up right away. The boys in?

LINDA.   They're sleeping. Happy took Biff on a date tonight.

WILLY (*interested*).   That so?

LINDA.   It was so nice to see them shaving together, one behind the other, in the bathroom. And going out together. You notice? The whole house smells of shaving lotion.

WILLY.   Figure it out. Work a lifetime to pay off a house. You finally own it, and there's nobody to live in it.

LINDA.   Well, dear, life is a casting off. It's always that way.

WILLY.   No, no, some people—some people accomplish something. Did Biff say anything after I went this morning?

LINDA.   You shouldn't have criticized him, Willy, especially after he just got off the train. You mustn't lose your temper with him.

WILLY.   When the hell did I lose my temper? I simply asked him if he was making any money. Is that a criticism?

LINDA.   But, dear, how could he make any money?

WILLY (*worried and angered*).   There's such an undercurrent in him. He became a moody man. Did he apologize when I left this morning?

LINDA.   He was crestfallen, Willy. You know how he admires you. I think if he finds himself, then you'll both be happier and not fight any more.

WILLY.   How can he find himself on a farm? Is that a life? A farmhand? In the beginning, when he was young, I thought, well, a young man, it's good for him to tramp around, take a lot of different jobs. But it's more than ten years now and he has yet to make thirty-five dollars a week!

LINDA.   He's finding himself, Willy.

WILLY.   Not finding yourself at the age of thirty-four is a disgrace!

LINDA.   Shh!

WILLY.   The trouble is he's lazy, goddammit!

LINDA.   Willy, please!

WILLY.   Biff is a lazy bum!

LINDA.   They're sleeping. Get something to eat. Go on down.

WILLY.   Why did he come home? I would like to know what brought him home.

LINDA.   I don't know. I think he's still lost, Willy. I think he's very lost.

WILLY.   Biff Loman is lost. In the greatest country in the world a young man with such—personal attractiveness, gets lost. And such a hard worker. There's one thing about Biff—he's not lazy.

LINDA.   Never.

WILLY (*with pity and resolve*).   I'll see him in the morning; I'll have a nice talk with him. I'll get him a job selling. He could be big in no time. My God! Remember how they used to follow him around in high school? When he smiled at one of them their faces lit up. When he walked down the street . . . (*He loses himself in reminiscences.*)

LINDA (*trying to bring him out of it*).   Willy, dear, I got a new kind of American-type cheese today. It's whipped.

WILLY.   Why do you get American when I like Swiss?

LINDA.   I just thought you'd like a change—

WILLY.   I don't want change! I want Swiss cheese. Why am I always being contradicted?

LINDA (*with a covering laugh*).   I thought it would be a surprise.

WILLY.   Why don't you open a window in here, for God's sake?

LINDA (*with infinite patience*).   They're all open, dear.

WILLY.   The way they boxed us in here. Bricks and windows, windows and bricks.

LINDA.   We should've bought the land next door.

WILLY.   The street is lined with cars. There's not a breath of fresh air in the neighborhood. The grass don't grow any more, you can't raise a carrot in the back yard. They should've had a law against apartment houses. Remember those two beautiful elm trees out there? When I and Biff hung the swing between them?

LINDA.   Yeah, like being a million miles from the city.

WILLY.   They should've arrested the builder for cutting those down. They massacred the neighborhood. (*Lost*) More and more I think of those days, Linda. This time of year it was lilac and wisteria. And then the peonies would come out, and the daffodils. What fragrance in this room!

LINDA.   Well, after all, people had to move somewhere.

WILLY.   No, there's more people now.

LINDA.   I don't think there's more people. I think—

WILLY.   There's more people! That's what's ruining this country! Population is getting out of control. The competition is maddening! Smell the stink from that apartment house! And another one on the other side . . . How can they whip cheese?

(*On* WILLY's *last line,* BIFF *and* HAPPY *raise themselves up in their beds, listening.*)

LINDA.   Go down, try it. And be quiet.

WILLY (*turning to* LINDA, *guiltily*).   You're not worried about me, are you, sweetheart?

BIFF.   What's the matter?

HAPPY.   Listen!

LINDA.   You've got too much on the ball to worry about.

WILLY.   You're my foundation and my support, Linda.

LINDA.   Just try to relax, dear. You make mountains out of molehills.

WILLY.   I won't fight with him any more. If he wants to go back to Texas, let him go.

LINDA.   He'll find his way.

WILLY.   Sure. Certain men just don't get started till later in life. Like Thomas Edison, I think. Or B. F. Goodrich. One of them was deaf. (*He starts for the bedroom doorway.*) I'll put my money on Biff.

LINDA.   And Willy—if it's warm Sunday we'll drive in the country. And we'll open the windshield, and take lunch.

WILLY.   No, the windshields don't open on the new cars.

LINDA.   But you opened it today.

WILLY.   Me? I didn't. (*He stops.*) Now isn't that peculiar! Isn't that a remarkable—(*He breaks off in amazement and fright as the flute is heard distantly.*)

LINDA.   What, darling?

WILLY.   That is the most remarkable thing.

LINDA.   What, dear?

WILLY.   I was thinking of the Chevvy. (*Slight pause.*) Nineteen twenty-eight . . . when I had that red Chevvy—(*Breaks off.*) That's funny! I coulda sworn I was driving that Chevvy today.

LINDA.   Well, that's nothing. Something must've reminded you.

WILLY.   Remarkable. Ts. Remember those days? The way Biff used to simonize that car? The dealer refused to believe there was eighty thousand miles on it. (*He shakes his head.*) Heh! (*To* LINDA) Close your eyes, I'll be right up. (*He walks out of the bedroom.*)

HAPPY (*to* BIFF).   Jesus, maybe he smashed up the car again!

LINDA (*calling after* WILLY).   Be careful on the stairs, dear! The cheese is on the middle shelf! (*She turns, goes over to the bed, takes his jacket, and goes out of the bedroom.*)

(*Light has risen on the boys' room. Unseen,* WILLY *is heard talking to himself, "Eighty thousand miles," and a little laugh.* BIFF *gets out of bed, comes downstage a bit, and stands attentively.* BIFF *is two years older than his brother* HAPPY, *well built, but in these days bears a worn air and seems less self-assured. He has succeeded less, and his dreams are stronger and less acceptable than* HAPPY's. HAPPY *is tall, powerfully made. Sexuality is like a visible color on him, or a scent that many women have discovered. He, like his brother, is lost, but in a different way, for he has never allowed himself to turn his face toward defeat and is thus more confused and hard-skinned, although seemingly more content.*)

HAPPY (*getting out of bed*).   He's going to get his license taken away if he keeps that up. I'm getting nervous about him, y'know, Biff?

BIFF.   His eyes are going.

HAPPY.   No, I've driven with him. He sees all right. He just doesn't keep his mind on it. I drove into the city with him last week. He stops at a green light and then it turns red and he goes. (*He laughs.*)

BIFF.   Maybe he's color-blind.

HAPPY.   Pop? Why he's got the finest eye for color in the business. You know that.

BIFF (*sitting down on his bed*).   I'm going to sleep.

HAPPY.   You're not still sour on Dad, are you, Biff?

BIFF.   He's all right, I guess.

WILLY (*underneath them, in the living-room*).   Yes, sir, eighty thousand miles—eighty-two thousand!

BIFF.   You smoking?

HAPPY (*holding out a pack of cigarettes*).   Want one?

BIFF (*taking a cigarette*).   I can never sleep when I smell it.

WILLY.   What a simonizing job, heh!

HAPPY (*with deep sentiment*).   Funny, Biff, y'know? Us sleeping in here again? The old beds. (*He pats his bed affectionately.*) All the talk that went across those two beds, huh? Our whole lives.

BIFF.   Yeah. Lotta dreams and plans.

HAPPY (*with a deep and masculine laugh*).   About five hundred women would like to know what was said in this room. (*They share a soft laugh.*)

BIFF.   Remember that big Betsy something—what the hell was her name—over on Bushwick Avenue?

HAPPY (*combing his hair*).   With the collie dog!

BIFF.   That's the one. I got you in there, remember?

HAPPY.   Yeah, that was my first time—I think. Boy, there was a pig! (*They laugh, almost crudely.*) You taught me everything I know about women. Don't forget that.

BIFF.   I bet you forgot how bashful you used to be. Especially with girls.

HAPPY.   Oh, I still am, Biff.

BIFF.   Oh, go on.

HAPPY.   I just control it, that's all. I think I got less bashful and you got more so. What happened, Biff? Where's the old humor, the old confidence? (*He shakes* BIFF's *knee.* BIFF *gets up and moves restlessly about the room.*) What's the matter?

BIFF.   Why does Dad mock me all the time?

HAPPY.   He's not mocking you, he—

BIFF.   Everything I say there's a twist of mockery on his face. I can't get near him.

HAPPY.   He just wants you to make good, that's all. I wanted to talk to you about Dad for a long time, Biff. Something's—happening to him. He—talks to himself.

BIFF.   I noticed that this morning. But he always mumbled.

HAPPY.   But not so noticeable. It got so embarrassing I sent him to Florida. And you know something? Most of the time he's talking to you.

BIFF.   What's he say about me?

HAPPY.   I can't make it out.

BIFF.   What's he say about me?

HAPPY.   I think the fact that you're not settled, that you're still kind of up in the air . . .

BIFF.   There's one or two other things depressing him, Happy.

HAPPY.   What do you mean?

BIFF.   Never mind. Just don't lay it all to me.

HAPPY.   But I think if you just got started—I mean—is there any future for you out there?

BIFF.   I'll tell ya, Hap, I don't know what the future is. I don't know—what I'm supposed to want.

HAPPY.   What do you mean?

BIFF.   Well, I spent six or seven years after high school trying to work myself up. Shipping clerk, salesman, business of one kind or another. And it's a measly manner of existence. To get on that subway on the hot mornings in summer. To devote your whole life to keeping stock, or making phone calls, or selling or buying. To suffer fifty weeks of the year for the sake of a two-week vacation, when all you really desire is to be outdoors, with your shirt off. And always to have to get ahead of the next fella. And still—that's how you build a future.

HAPPY.   Well, you really enjoy it on a farm? Are you content out there?

BIFF (*with rising agitation*).   Hap, I've had twenty or thirty different kinds of jobs since I left home before the war, and it always turns out the same. I just realized it lately. In Nebraska when I herded cattle, and the Dakotas, and Arizona, and now in Texas. It's why I came home now, I guess, because I realized it. This farm I work on, it's spring there now, see? And they've got about fifteen new colts. There's nothing more inspiring or—beautiful than the sight of a mare and a new colt. And it's cool there now, see? Texas is cool now, and it's spring. And whenever spring comes to where I am, I suddenly get the feeling, my God, I'm not gettin' anywhere! What the hell am I doing, playing around with horses, twenty-eight dollars a week! I'm thirty-four years old, I oughta be makin' my future. That's when I come running home. And now, I get here, and I don't know what to do with myself. (*After a pause.*) I've always made a point of not wasting my life, and everytime I come back here I know that all I've done is to waste my life.

HAPPY.   You're a poet, you know that, Biff? You're a—you're an idealist!

BIFF.   No, I'm mixed up very bad. Maybe I oughta get married. Maybe I oughta get stuck into something. Maybe that's my trouble. I'm like a boy. I'm not married, I'm not in business, I just—I'm like a boy. Are you content, Hap? You're a success, aren't you? Are you content?

HAPPY.   Hell, no!

BIFF.   Why? You're making money, aren't you?

HAPPY (*moving about with energy, expressiveness*).   All I can do now is wait for the merchandise manager to die. And suppose I get to be merchandise manager? He's a good friend of mine, and he just built a terrific estate on Long Island. And he lived there about two months and sold it, and now he's building another one. He can't enjoy it once it's finished. And I know that's just what I would do. I don't know what the hell I'm workin' for. Sometimes I sit in my apartment—all alone. And I think of the rent I'm paying. And it's crazy. But then, it's what I always wanted. My own apartment, a car, and plenty of women. And still, goddammit, I'm lonely.

BIFF (*with enthusiasm*).   Listen, why don't you come out West with me?

HAPPY.   You and I, heh?

BIFF.   Sure, maybe we could buy a ranch. Raise cattle, use our muscles. Men built like we are should be working out in the open.

HAPPY (*avidly*).   The Loman Brothers, heh?

BIFF (*with vast affection*).   Sure, we'd be known all over the counties!

HAPPY (*enthralled*).   That's what I dream about, Biff. Sometimes I want to just rip my clothes off in the middle of the store and outbox that goddam merchandise manager. I mean I can outbox him, outrun, and outlift anybody in that store, and I have to take orders from those common, petty sons-of-bitches till I can't stand it any more.

BIFF.   I'm tellin' you, kid, if you were with me I'd be happy out there.

HAPPY (*enthused*).   See, Biff, everybody around me is so false that I'm constantly lowering my ideals . . .

BIFF.   Baby, together we'd stand up for one another, we'd have someone to trust.

HAPPY.   If I were around you—

BIFF.   Hap, the trouble is we weren't brought up to grub for money. I don't know how to do it.

HAPPY.   Neither can I!

BIFF.   Then let's go!

HAPPY.   The only thing is—what can you make out there?

BIFF.   But look at your friend. Builds an estate and then hasn't the peace of mind to live in it.

HAPPY.   Yeah, but when he walks into the store the waves part in front of him. That's fifty-two thousand dollars a year coming through the revolving door, and I got more in my pinky finger than he's got in his head.

BIFF.   Yeah, but you just said—

HAPPY.   I gotta show some of those pompous, self-important executives over there that Hap Loman can make the grade. I want to walk into the store the way he walks in. Then I'll go with you, Biff. We'll be together yet, I swear. But take those two we had tonight. Now weren't they gorgeous creatures?

BIFF.   Yeah, yeah, most gorgeous I've had in years.

HAPPY.   I get that any time I want, Biff. Whenever I feel disgusted. The only trouble is, it gets like bowling or something. I just keep knockin' them over and it doesn't mean anything. You still run around a lot?

BIFF.   Naa. I'd like to find a girl—steady, somebody with substance.

HAPPY.   That's what I long for.

BIFF.   Go on! You'd never come home.

HAPPY.   I would! Somebody with character, with resistance! Like Mom, y'know? You're gonna call me a bastard when I tell you this. That girl Charlotte I was with tonight is engaged to be married in five weeks. (*He tries on his new hat.*)

BIFF.   No kiddin'!

HAPPY.   Sure, the guy's in line for the vice-presidency of the store. I don't know what gets into me, maybe I just have an overdeveloped sense of competition or something, but I went and ruined her, and furthermore I can't get rid of her. And he's the third executive I've done that to. Isn't that a crummy characteristic? And to top it all, I go to their weddings! (*Indignantly, but laughing*) Like I'm not supposed to take bribes. Manufacturers offer me a hundred-dollar bill now and then to throw an order their way. You know how honest I am, but it's like this girl, see. I hate myself for it. Because I don't want the girl, and, still, I take it and—I love it!

BIFF.   Let's go to sleep.

HAPPY.   I guess we didn't settle anything, heh?

BIFF.   I just got one idea that I think I'm going to try.

HAPPY.   What's that?

BIFF.   Remember Bill Oliver?

HAPPY.   Sure, Oliver is very big now. You want to work for him again?

BIFF.   No, but when I quit he said something to me. He put his arm on my shoulder, and he said, "Biff, if you ever need anything, come to me."

HAPPY.   I remember that. That sounds good.

BIFF.   I think I'll go to see him. If I could get ten thousand or even seven or eight thousand dollars I could buy a beautiful ranch.

HAPPY.   I bet he'd back you. 'Cause he thought highly of you, Biff. I mean, they all do. You're well liked, Biff. That's why I say to come back here, and we both have the apartment. And I'm tellin' you, Biff, any babe you want . . .

BIFF.   No, with a ranch I could do the work I like and still be something. I just wonder though. I wonder if Oliver still thinks I stole that carton of basketballs.

HAPPY.   Oh, he probably forgot that long ago. It's almost ten years. You're too sensitive. Anyway, he didn't really fire you.

BIFF.   Well, I think he was going to. I think that's why I quit. I was never sure whether he knew or not. I know he thought the world of me, though. I was the only one he'd let lock up the place.

WILLY (*below*).   You gonna wash the engine, Biff?

HAPPY.   Shh! (BIFF *looks at* HAPPY, *who is gazing down, listening.* WILLY *is mumbling in the parlor.*) You hear that? (*They listen.* WILLY *laughs warmly.*)

BIFF (*growing angry*).   Doesn't he know Mom can hear that?

WILLY.   Don't get your sweater dirty, Biff! (*A look of pain crosses* BIFF's *face.*)

HAPPY.   Isn't that terrible? Don't leave again, will you? You'll find a job here. You gotta stick around. I don't know what to do about him, it's getting embarrassing.

WILLY.   What a simonizing job!

BIFF.   Mom's hearing that!

WILLY.   No kiddin', Biff, you got a date? Wonderful!

HAPPY.   Go on to sleep. But talk to him in the morning, will you?

BIFF (*reluctantly getting into bed*).   With her in the house. Brother!

HAPPY (*getting into bed*).   I wish you'd have a good talk with him. (*The light on their room begins to fade.*)

BIFF (*to himself in bed*).   That selfish, stupid . . .

HAPPY.   Sh . . . Sleep, Biff.

(*Their light is out. Well before they have finished speaking,* WILLY's *form is dimly seen below in the darkened kitchen. He opens the refrigerator, searches in there, and takes out a bottle of milk. The apartment houses are fading out, and the entire house and surroundings become covered with leaves. Music insinuates itself as the leaves appear.*)

WILLY.   Just wanna be careful with those girls, Biff, that's all. Don't make any promises. No promises of any kind. Because a girl, y'know, they always believe what you tell 'em, and you're very young, Biff, you're too young to be talking seriously to girls. (*Light rises on the kitchen.* WILLY, *talking, shuts the refrigerator door and comes downstage to the kitchen table. He pours milk into a glass. He is totally immersed in himself, smiling faintly.*) Too young entirely, Biff. You want to watch your schooling first. Then when you're all set, there'll be plenty of girls for a boy like you. (*He smiles broadly at a kitchen chair.*) That so? The girls pay for you? (*He laughs.*) Boy, you must really be makin' a hit. (WILLY *is gradually addressing—physically—a point offstage, speaking through the wall of the kitchen, and his voice has been rising in volume to that of a normal conversation.*) I been wondering why you polish the car so careful. Ha! Don't leave the hubcaps, boys. Get the chamois to the hubcaps. Happy, use newspaper on the windows, it's the easiest thing. Show him how to do it, Biff! You see, Happy? Pad it up, use it like a pad. That's it, that's it, good work. You're doin' all right, Hap. (*He pauses, then nods in approbation for a few seconds, then looks upward.*) Biff, first thing we gotta do when we get time is clip that big branch over the house. Afraid it's gonna fall in a storm and hit the roof. Tell you what. We get a rope and sling her around, and then we climb up there with a couple of saws and take her down. Soon as you finish the car, boys, I wanna see ya. I got a surprise for you, boys.

BIFF (*offstage*).   Whatta ya got, Dad?

WILLY.   No, you finish first. Never leave a job till you're finished— remember that. (*Looking toward the "big trees"*) Biff, up in Albany I saw a beautiful hammock. I think I'll buy it next trip, and we'll hang it right between those two elms. Wouldn't that be something? Just swingin' there under those branches. Boy, that would be . . . (YOUNG BIFF *and* YOUNG HAPPY *appear from the direction* WILLY *was addressing.* HAPPY *carries rags and a pail of water.* BIFF, *wearing a sweater with a block "S," carries a football.*)

BIFF (*pointing in the direction of the car offstage*).   How's that, Pop, professional?

WILLY.   Terrific. Terrific job, boys. Good work, Biff.

HAPPY.   Where's the surprise, Pop?

WILLY.   In the back seat of the car.

HAPPY.   Boy! (*He runs off.*)

BIFF.   What is it, Dad? Tell me, what'd you buy?

WILLY (*laughing, cuffs him*).   Never mind, something I want you to have.

BIFF (*turns and starts off*).   What is it, Hap?

HAPPY (*offstage*).   It's a punching bag!

BIFF.   Oh, Pop!

WILLY.   It's got Gene Tunney's signature on it! (HAPPY *runs onstage with a punching bag.*)

BIFF.   Gee, how'd you know we wanted a punching bag?

WILLY.   Well, it's the finest thing for the timing.

HAPPY (*lies down on his back and pedals with his feet*).   I'm losing weight, you notice, Pop?

WILLY (*to* HAPPY).   Jumping rope is good too.

BIFF.   Did you see the new football I got?

WILLY (*examining the ball*).   Where'd you get a new ball?

BIFF.   The coach told me to practice my passing.

WILLY.   That so? And he gave you the ball, heh?

BIFF.   Well, I borrowed it from the locker room. (*He laughs confidentially.*)

WILLY (*laughing with him at the theft*).   I want you to return that.

HAPPY.   I told you he wouldn't like it!

BIFF (*angrily*).   Well, I'm bringing it back!

WILLY (*stopping the incipient argument, to* HAPPY).   Sure, he's gotta practice with a regulation ball, doesn't he? (*To* BIFF) Coach'll probably congratulate you on your initiative!

BIFF.   Oh, he keeps congratulating my initiative all the time, Pop.

WILLY.   That's because he likes you. If somebody else took that ball there'd be an uproar. So what's the report, boys, what's the report?

BIFF.   Where'd you go this time, Dad? Gee, we were lonesome for you.

WILLY (*pleased, puts an arm around each boy and they come down to the apron*).   Lonesome, heh?

BIFF.   Missed you every minute.

WILLY.   Don't say? Tell you a secret, boys. Don't breathe it to a soul. Someday I'll have my own business, and I'll never have to leave home any more.

HAPPY.   Like Uncle Charley, heh?

WILLY.   Bigger than Uncle Charley! Because Charley is not— liked. He's liked, but he's not—well liked.

BIFF.   Where'd you go this time, Dad?

WILLY.   Well, I got on the road, and I went north to Providence. Met the Mayor.

BIFF.   The Mayor of Providence!

WILLY.   He was sitting in the hotel lobby.

BIFF.   What'd he say?

WILLY.   He said, "Morning!" And I said, "You got a fine city here, Mayor." And then he had coffee with me. And then I went to Waterbury. Waterbury is a fine city. Big clock city, the famous Waterbury clock. Sold a nice bill there. And then Boston—Boston is the cradle of the Revolution. A fine city. And a couple of other towns in Mass., and on to Portland and Bangor and straight home!

BIFF.   Gee, I'd love to go with you sometime, Dad.

WILLY.   Soon as summer comes.

HAPPY.   Promise?

WILLY.   You and Hap and I, and I'll show you all the towns. America is full of beautiful towns and fine, upstanding people. And they know me, boys, they know me up and down New England. The finest people. And when I bring you fellas up, there'll be open sesame for all of us, 'cause one thing, boys: I have friends. I can park my car in any street in New England, and the cops protect it like their own. This summer, heh?

BIFF *and* HAPPY (*together*).   Yeah! You bet!

WILLY.   We'll take our bathing suits.

HAPPY.   We'll carry your bags, Pop!

WILLY.   Oh, won't that be something! Me comin' into the Boston stores with you boys carryin' my bags. What a sensation! (BIFF *is prancing around, practicing passing the ball.*) You nervous, Biff, about the game?

BIFF.   Not if you're gonna be there.

WILLY.   What do they say about you in school, now that they made you captain?

HAPPY.   There's a crowd of girls behind him everytime the classes change.

BIFF (*taking* WILLY'*s hand*).   This Saturday, Pop, this Saturday— just for you, I'm going to break through for a touchdown.

HAPPY.   You're supposed to pass.

BIFF.   I'm takin' one play for Pop. You watch me, Pop, and when I take off my helmet, that means I'm breakin' out. Then you watch me crash through that line!

WILLY (*kisses* BIFF).   Oh, wait'll I tell this in Boston! (BERNARD *enters in knickers. He is younger than* BIFF, *earnest and loyal, a worried boy.*)

BERNARD.   Biff, where are you? You're supposed to study with me today.

WILLY.   Hey, looka Bernard. What're you lookin' so anemic about, Bernard?

BERNARD.   He's gotta study, Uncle Willy. He's got Regents° next week.

HAPPY (*tauntingly, spinning* BERNARD *around*).   Let's box, Bernard!

BERNARD.   Biff! (*He gets away from* HAPPY.) Listen, Biff, I heard Mr. Birnbaum say that if you don't start studyin' math he's gonna flunk you, and you won't graduate. I heard him!

WILLY.   You better study with him, Biff. Go ahead now.

BERNARD.   I heard him!

BIFF.   Oh, Pop, you didn't see my sneakers! (*He holds up a foot for* WILLY *to look at.*)

WILLY.   Hey, that's a beautiful job of printing!

BERNARD (*wiping his glasses*).   Just because he printed University of Virginia on his sneakers doesn't mean they've got to graduate him, Uncle Willy!

WILLY (*angrily*).   What're you talking about? With scholarships to three universities they're gonna flunk him?

BERNARD.   But I heard Mr. Birnbaum say—

WILLY.   Don't be a pest, Bernard! (*To his* BOYS) What an anemic!

Regents: a statewide proficiency examination administered in New York high schools

BERNARD.   Okay, I'm waiting for you in my house, Biff. (BERNARD *goes off. The* LOMANS *laugh.*)

WILLY.   Bernard is not well liked, is he?

BIFF.   He's liked, but he's not well liked.

HAPPY.   That's right, Pop.

WILLY.   That's just what I mean. Bernard can get the best marks in school, y'understand, but when he gets out in the business world, y'understand, you are going to be five times ahead of him. That's why I thank Almighty God you're both built like Adonises. Because the man who makes an appearance in the business world, the man who creates personal interest, is the man who gets ahead. Be liked and you will never want. You take me, for instance. I never have to wait in line to see a buyer. "Willy Loman is here!" That's all they have to know, and I go right through.

BIFF.   Did you knock them dead, Pop?

WILLY.   Knocked 'em cold in Providence, slaughtered 'em in Boston.

HAPPY (*on his back, pedaling again*).   I'm losing weight, you notice, Pop? (LINDA *enters, as of old, a ribbon in her hair, carrying a basket of washing.*)

LINDA (*with youthful energy*).   Hello, dear!

WILLY.   Sweetheart!

LINDA.   How'd the Chevvy run?

WILLY.   Chevrolet, Linda, is the greatest car ever built. (*To the* BOYS) Since when do you let your mother carry wash up the stairs?

BIFF.   Grab hold there, boy!

HAPPY.   Where to, Mom?

LINDA.   Hang them up on the line. And you better go down to your friends, Biff. The cellar is full of boys. They don't know what to do with themselves.

BIFF.   Ah, when Pop comes home they can wait!

WILLY (*laughs appreciatively*).   You better go down and tell them what to do, Biff.

BIFF.   I think I'll have them sweep out the furnace room.

WILLY.   Good work, Biff.

BIFF (*goes through wall-line of kitchen to doorway at back and calls down*).   Fellas! Everybody sweep out the furnace room! I'll be right down!

VOICES.   All right! Okay, Biff.

BIFF.   George and Sam and Frank, come out back! We're hangin' up the wash! Come on, Hap, on the double! (*He and* HAPPY *carry out the basket.*)

LINDA. The way they obey him!

WILLY. Well, that's training, the training. I'm tellin' you, I was sellin' thousands and thousands, but I had to come home.

LINDA. Oh, the whole block'll be at that game. Did you sell anything?

WILLY. I did five hundred gross in Providence and seven hundred gross in Boston.

LINDA. No! Wait a minute, I've got a pencil. (*She pulls pencil and paper out of her apron pocket.*) That makes your commission . . . Two hundred—my God! Two hundred and twelve dollars!

WILLY. Well, I didn't figure it yet, but . . .

LINDA. How much did you do?

WILLY. Well, I—I did—about a hundred and eighty gross in Providence. Well no—it came to—roughly two hundred gross on the whole trip.

LINDA (*without hesitation*).   Two hundred gross. That's . . . (*She figures.*)

WILLY. The trouble was that three of the stores were half closed for inventory in Boston. Otherwise I woulda broke records.

LINDA. Well, it makes seventy dollars and some pennies. That's very good.

WILLY. What do we owe?

LINDA. Well, on the first there's sixteen dollars on the refrigerator—

WILLY. Why sixteen?

LINDA. Well, the fan belt broke, so it was a dollar eighty.

WILLY. But it's brand new.

LINDA. Well, the man said that's the way it is. Till they work themselves in, y'know. (*They move through the wall-line into the kitchen.*)

WILLY. I hope we didn't get stuck on that machine.

LINDA. They got the biggest ads of any of them!

WILLY. I know, it's a fine machine. What else?

LINDA. Well, there's nine-sixty for the washing machine. And for the vacuum cleaner there's three and a half due on the fifteenth. Then the roof, you got twenty-one dollars remaining.

WILLY. It doesn't leak, does it?

LINDA. No, they did a wonderful job. Then you owe Frank for the carburetor.

WILLY. I'm not going to pay that man! That goddam Chevrolet, they ought to prohibit the manufacture of that car!

LINDA. Well, you owe him three and a half. And odds and ends, comes to around a hundred and twenty dollars by the fifteenth.

WILLY.   A hundred and twenty dollars! My God, if business don't pick up I don't know what I'm gonna do!

LINDA.   Well, next week you'll do better.

WILLY.   Oh, I'll knock 'em dead next week. I'll go to Hartford. I'm very well liked in Hartford. You know, the trouble is, Linda, people don't seem to take to me. (*They move onto the forestage.*)

LINDA.   Oh, don't be foolish.

WILLY.   I know it when I walk in. They seem to laugh at me.

LINDA.   Why? Why would they laugh at you? Don't talk that way, Willy. (WILLY *moves to the edge of the stage.* LINDA *goes into the kitchen and starts to darn stockings.*)

WILLY.   I don't know the reason for it, but they just pass me by. I'm not noticed.

LINDA.   But you're doing wonderful, dear. You're making seventy to a hundred dollars a week.

WILLY.   But I gotta be at it ten, twelve hours a day. Other men—I don't know—they do it easier. I don't know why—I can't stop myself —I talk too much. A man oughta come in with a few words. One thing about Charley. He's a man of few words, and they respect him.

LINDA.   You don't talk too much, you're just lively.

WILLY (*smiling*).   Well, I figure, what the hell, life is short, a couple of jokes. (*To himself*) I joke too much! (*The smile goes.*)

LINDA.   Why? You're—

WILLY.   I'm fat. I'm very—foolish to look at, Linda. I didn't tell you, but Christmas time I happened to be calling on F. H. Stewarts, and a salesman I know, as I was going in to see the buyer I heard him say something about—walrus. And I—I cracked him right across the face. I won't take that. I simply will not take that. But they do laugh at me. I know that.

LINDA.   Darling . . .

WILLY.   I gotta overcome it. I know I gotta overcome it. I'm not dressing to advantage, maybe.

LINDA.   Willy, darling, you're the handsomest man in the world—

WILLY.   Oh, no, Linda.

LINDA.   To me you are. (*Slight pause.*) The handsomest. (*From the darkness is heard the laughter of a woman.* WILLY *doesn't turn to it, but it continues through* LINDA's *lines.*) And the boys, Willy. Few men are idolized by their children the way you are. (*Music is heard as, behind a scrim to the left of the house,* THE WOMAN, *dimly seen, is dressing.*)

WILLY (*with great feeling*).   You're the best there is, Linda, you're a pal, you know that? On the road—on the road I want to grab you sometimes and just kiss the life outa you.

(*The laughter is loud now, and he moves into a brightening area at the left, where* THE WOMAN *has come from behind the scrim and is standing, putting on her hat, looking into a "mirror" and laughing.*)

WILLY.   'Cause I get so lonely—especially when business is bad and there's nobody to talk to. I get the feeling that I'll never sell anything again, that I won't make a living for you, or a business, a business for the boys. (*He talks through* THE WOMAN'*s subsiding laughter;* THE WOMAN *primps at the "mirror."*) There's so much I want to make for—

THE WOMAN.   Me? You didn't make me, Willy. I picked you.

WILLY (*pleased*).   You picked me?

THE WOMAN (*who is quite proper-looking,* WILLY'*s age*).   I did. I've been sitting at that desk watching all the salesmen go by, day in, day out. But you've got such a sense of humor, and we do have such a good time together, don't we?

WILLY.   Sure, sure. (*He takes her in his arms.*) Why do you have to go now?

THE WOMAN.   It's two o'clock . . .

WILLY.   No, come on in! (*He pulls her.*)

THE WOMAN.   . . . my sisters'll be scandalized. When'll you be back?

WILLY.   Oh, two weeks about. Will you come up again?

THE WOMAN.   Sure thing. You do make me laugh. It's good for me. (*She squeezes his arm, kisses him.*) And I think you're a wonderful man.

WILLY.   You picked me, heh?

THE WOMAN.   Sure. Because you're so sweet. And such a kidder.

WILLY.   Well, I'll see you next time I'm in Boston.

THE WOMAN.   I'll put you right through to the buyers.

WILLY (*slapping her bottom*).   Right. Well, bottoms up!

THE WOMAN (*slaps him gently and laughs*).   You just kill me, Willy. (*He suddenly grabs her and kisses her roughly.*) You kill me. And thanks for the stockings. I love a lot of stockings. Well, good night.

WILLY.   Good night. And keep your pores open!

THE WOMAN.   Oh, Willy!

(THE WOMAN *bursts out laughing, and* LINDA'*s laughter blends in.* THE WOMAN *disappears into the dark. Now the area at the kitchen table brightens.* LINDA *is sitting where she was at the kitchen table, but now is mending a pair of her silk stockings.*)

LINDA.   You are, Willy. The handsomest man. You've got no reason to feel that—

WILLY (*coming out of* THE WOMAN'*s dimming area and going over to* LINDA).   I'll make it all up to you, Linda. I'll—

LINDA.   There's nothing to make up, dear. You're doing fine, better than—

WILLY (*noticing her mending*).   What's that?

LINDA.   Just mending my stockings. They're so expensive—

WILLY (*angrily, taking them from her*).   I won't have you mending stockings in this house! Now throw them out! (LINDA *puts the stockings in her pocket.*)

BERNARD (*entering on the run*).   Where is he? If he doesn't study!

WILLY (*moving to the forestage, with great agitation*).   You'll give him the answers!

BERNARD.   I do, but I can't on a Regents! That's a state exam! They're liable to arrest me!

WILLY.   Where is he? I'll whip him, I'll whip him!

LINDA.   And he'd better give back that football, Willy, it's not nice.

WILLY.   Biff! Where is he? Why is he taking everything?

LINDA.   He's too rough with the girls, Willy. All the mothers are afraid of him!

WILLY.   I'll whip him!

BERNARD.   He's driving the car without a license! (THE WOMAN's *laugh is heard.*)

WILLY.   Shut up!

LINDA.   All the mothers—

WILLY.   Shut up!

BERNARD.   (*backing quietly away and out*). Mr. Birnbaum says he's stuck up.

WILLY.   Get outa here!

BERNARD.   If he doesn't buckle down he'll flunk math! (*He goes off.*)

LINDA.   He's right, Willy, you've gotta—

WILLY (*exploding at her*).   There's nothing the matter with him! You want him to be a worm like Bernard? He's got spirit, personality . . . (*As he speaks,* LINDA, *almost in tears, exits into the living-room.* WILLY *is alone in the kitchen, wilting and staring. The leaves are gone, it is night again, and the apartment houses look down from behind.*) Loaded with it. Loaded! What is he stealing? He's giving it back, isn't he? Why is he stealing? What did I tell him? I never in my life told him anything but decent things. (HAPPY *in pajamas has come down the stairs;* WILLY *suddenly becomes aware of* HAPPY's *presence.*)

HAPPY.   Let's go now, come on.

WILLY (*sitting down at the kitchen table*).   Huh! Why did she have to wax the floors herself? Everytime she waxes the floors she keels over. She knows that!

HAPPY.   Shh! Take it easy. What brought you back tonight?

WILLY.   I got an awful scare. Nearly hit a kid in Yonkers. God! Why didn't I go to Alaska with my brother Ben that time! Ben! That man was a genius, that man was success incarnate! What a mistake! He begged me to go.

HAPPY.   Well, there's no use in—

WILLY.   You guys! There was a man started with the clothes on his back and ended up with diamond mines!

HAPPY.   Boy, someday I'd like to know how he did it.

WILLY.   What's the mystery? The man knew what he wanted and went out and got it! Walked into a jungle, and comes out, the age of twenty-one, and he's rich! The world is an oyster, but you don't crack it open on a mattress.

HAPPY.   Pop, I told you I'm gonna retire you for life.

WILLY.   You'll retire me for life on seventy goddam dollars a week? And your women and your car and your apartment, and you'll retire me for life! Christ's sake, I couldn't get past Yonkers today! Where are you guys, where are you? The woods are burning! I can't drive a car! (CHARLEY *has appeared in the doorway. He is a large man, slow of speech, laconic, immovable. In all he says, despite what he says, there is pity, and, now, trepidation. He has a robe over pajamas, slippers on his feet. He enters the kitchen.*)

CHARLEY.   Everything all right?

HAPPY.   Yeah, Charley, everything's . . .

WILLY.   What's the matter?

CHARLEY.   I heard some noise. I thought something happened. Can't we do something about the walls? You sneeze in here, and in my house hats blow off.

HAPPY.   Let's go to bed, Dad. Come on. (CHARLEY *signals to* HAPPY *to go.*)

WILLY.   You go ahead, I'm not tired at the moment.

HAPPY (*to* WILLY).   Take it easy, huh? (*He exits.*)

WILLY.   What're you doin' up?

CHARLEY (*sitting down at the kitchen table opposite* WILLY). Couldn't sleep good. I had a heartburn.

WILLY.   Well, you don't know how to eat.

CHARLEY.   I eat with my mouth.

WILLY.   No, you're ignorant. You gotta know about vitamins and things like that.

CHARLEY.   Come on, let's shoot. Tire you out a little.

WILLY (*hesitantly*).   All right. You got cards?

CHARLEY (*taking a deck from his pocket*).   Yeah, I got them. Someplace. What is it with those vitamins?

WILLY (*dealing*).   They build up your bones. Chemistry.

CHARLEY.   Yeah, but there's no bones in a heartburn.

WILLY.   What are you talkin' about? Do you know the first thing about it?

CHARLEY.   Don't get insulted.

WILLY.   Don't talk about something you don't know anything about. (*They are playing. Pause.*)

CHARLEY.   What're you doin' home?

WILLY.   A little trouble with the car.

CHARLEY.   Oh. (*Pause.*) I'd like to take a trip to California.

WILLY.   Don't say.

CHARLEY.   You want a job?

WILLY.   I got a job, I told you that. (*After a slight pause*) What the hell are you offering me a job for?

CHARLEY.   Don't get insulted.

WILLY.   Don't insult me.

CHARLEY.   I don't see no sense in it. You don't have to go on this way.

WILLY.   I got a good job. (*Slight pause.*) What do you keep coming in here for?

CHARLEY.   You want me to go?

WILLY (*after a pause, withering*).   I can't understand it. He's going back to Texas again. What the hell is that?

CHARLEY.   Let him go.

WILLY.   I got nothin' to give him, Charley, I'm clean, I'm clean.

CHARLEY.   He won't starve. None a them starve. Forget about him.

WILLY.   Then what have I got to remember?

CHARLEY.   You take it too hard. To hell with it. When a deposit bottle is broken you don't get your nickel back.

WILLY.   That's easy enough for you to say.

CHARLEY.   That ain't easy for me to say.

WILLY.   Did you see the ceiling I put up in the living-room?

CHARLEY.   Yeah, that's a piece of work. To put up a ceiling is a mystery to me. How do you do it?

WILLY.   What's the difference?

CHARLEY.   Well, talk about it.

WILLY.   You gonna put up a ceiling?

CHARLEY.   How could I put up a ceiling?

WILLY.   Then what the hell are you bothering me for?

CHARLEY.   You're insulted again.

WILLY.   A man who can't handle tools is not a man. You're disgusting.

CHARLEY.   Don't call me disgusting, Willy. (UNCLE BEN, *carrying a valise and an umbrella, enters the forestage from around the right corner of the house. He is a stolid man, in his sixties, with a mustache and an authoritative air. He is utterly certain of his destiny, and there is an aura of far places about him. He enters exactly as* WILLY *speaks.*)

WILLY.   I'm getting awfully tired, Ben. (BEN's *music is heard.* BEN *looks around at everything.*)

CHARLEY.   Good, keep playing; you'll sleep better. Did you call me Ben? (BEN *looks at his watch.*)

WILLY.   That's funny. For a second there you reminded me of my brother Ben.

BEN.   I only have a few minutes. (*He strolls, inspecting the place.* WILLY *and* CHARLEY *continue playing.*)

CHARLEY.   You never heard from him again, heh? Since that time?

WILLY.   Didn't Linda tell you? Couple of weeks ago we got a letter from his wife in Africa. He died.

CHARLEY.   That so.

BEN (*chuckling*).   So this is Brooklyn, eh?

CHARLEY.   Maybe you're in for some of his money.

WILLY.   Naa, he had seven sons. There's just one opportunity I had with that man . . .

BEN.   I must make a train, William. There are several properties I'm looking at in Alaska.

WILLY.   Sure, sure! If I'd gone with him to Alaska that time, everything would've been totally different.

CHARLEY.   Go on, you'd froze to death up there.

WILLY.   What're you talking about?

BEN.   Opportunity is tremendous in Alaska, William. Surprised you're not up there.

WILLY.   Sure, tremendous.

CHARLEY.   Heh?

WILLY.   There was the only man I ever met who knew the answers.

CHARLEY.   Who?

BEN.   How are you all?

WILLY (*taking a pot, smiling*).   Fine, fine.

CHARLEY.   Pretty sharp tonight.

BEN.   Is Mother living with you?

WILLY.   No, she died a long time ago.

CHARLEY.   Who?

BEN.   That's too bad. Fine specimen of a lady, Mother.

WILLY (*to* CHARLEY).   Heh?

BEN.   I'd hoped to see the old girl.

CHARLEY.   Who died?

BEN.   Heard anything from Father, have you?

WILLY (*unnerved*).   What do you mean, who died?

CHARLEY (*taking a pot*).   What're you talkin' about?

BEN (*looking at his watch*).   William, it's half-past eight!

WILLY (*as though to dispel his confusion he angrily stops* CHARLEY's *hand*).   That's my build!

CHARLEY.   I put the ace—

WILLY.   If you don't know how to play the game I'm not gonna throw my money away on you!

CHARLEY (*rising*).   It was my ace, for God's sake!

WILLY.   I'm through, I'm through!

BEN.   When did Mother die?

WILLY.   Long ago. Since the beginning you never knew how to play cards.

CHARLEY (*picks up the cards and goes to the door*).   All right! Next time I'll bring a deck with five aces.

WILLY.   I don't play that kind of game!

CHARLEY (*turning to him*).   You ought to be ashamed of yourself!

WILLY.   Yeah?

CHARLEY.   Yeah! (*He goes out.*)

WILLY (*slamming the door after him*).   Ignoramus!

BEN (*as* WILLY *comes toward him through the wall-line of the kitchen*).   So you're William.

WILLY (*shaking* BEN's *hand*).   Ben! I've been waiting for you so long! What's the answer? How did you do it?

BEN.   Oh, there's a story in that. (LINDA *enters the forestage, as of old, carrying the wash basket.*)

LINDA.   Is this Ben?

BEN (*gallantly*).   How do you do, my dear?

LINDA.   Where've you been all these years? Willy's always wondered why you—

WILLY (*pulling* BEN *away from her impatiently*).   Where is Dad? Didn't you follow him? How did you get started?

BEN.   Well, I don't know how much you remember.

WILLY.   Well, I was just a baby, of course, only three or four years old—

BEN.   Three years and eleven months.

WILLY.   What a memory, Ben!

BEN.   I have many enterprises, William, and I have never kept books.

WILLY.   I remember I was sitting under the wagon in—was it Nebraska?

BEN.   It was South Dakota, and I gave you a bunch of wild flowers.

WILLY.   I remember you walking away down some open road.

BEN (*laughing*).   I was going to find Father in Alaska.

WILLY.   Where is he?

BEN.   At that age I had a very faulty view of geography, William. I discovered after a few days that I was heading due south, so instead of Alaska, I ended up in Africa.

LINDA.   Africa!

WILLY.   The Gold Coast!

BEN.   Principally diamond mines.

LINDA.   Diamond mines!

BEN.   Yes, my dear. But I've only a few minutes—

WILLY.   No! Boys! Boys! (YOUNG BIFF *and* HAPPY *appear*.) Listen to this. This is your Uncle Ben, a great man! Tell my boys, Ben!

BEN.   Why, boys, when I was seventeen I walked into the jungle, and when I was twenty-one I walked out. (*He laughs.*) And by God I was rich.

WILLY (*to the* BOYS).   You see what I been talking about? The greatest things can happen!

BEN (*glancing at his watch*).   I have an appointment in Ketchikan Tuesday week.

WILLY.   No, Ben! Please tell about Dad. I want my boys to hear. I want them to know the kind of stock they spring from. All I remember is a man with a big beard, and I was in Mamma's lap, sitting around a fire, and some kind of high music.

BEN.   His flute. He played the flute.

WILLY.   Sure, the flute, that's right! (*New music is heard, a high, rollicking tune.*)

BEN.   Father was a very great and a very wild-hearted man. We would start in Boston, and he'd toss the whole family into the wagon, and then he'd drive the team right across the country; through Ohio and Indiana, Michigan, Illinois, and all the Western states. And we'd stop in the towns and sell the flutes that he'd made on the way. Great inventor, Father. With one gadget he made more in a week than a man like you could make in a lifetime.

WILLY.   That's just the way I'm bringing them up, Ben—rugged, well liked, all-around.

BEN.   Yeah? (*To* BIFF) Hit that, boy—hard as you can. (*He pounds his stomach.*)

BIFF.   Oh, no, sir!

BEN (*taking boxing stance*).   Come on, get to me! (*He laughs.*)

WILLY.   Go to it, Biff! Go ahead, show him!

BIFF.   Okay! (*He cocks his fists and starts in.*)

LINDA (*to* WILLY).   Why must he fight, dear?

BEN (*sparring with* BIFF).   Good boy! Good boy!

WILLY.   How's that, Ben, heh?

HAPPY.   Give him the left, Biff!

LINDA.   Why are you fighting?

BEN.   Good boy! (*Suddenly comes in, trips* BIFF, *and stands over him, the point of his umbrella poised over* BIFF's *eye.*)

LINDA.   Look out, Biff!

BIFF.   Gee!

BEN (*patting* BIFF's *knee*).   Never fight fair with a stranger, boy. You'll never get out of the jungle that way. (*Taking* LINDA's *hand and bowing*) It was an honor and a pleasure to meet you, Linda.

LINDA (*withdrawing her hand coldly, frightened*).   Have a nice—trip.

BEN (*to* WILLY).   And good luck with your—what do you do?

WILLY.   Selling.

BEN.   Yes. Well . . . (*He raises his hand in farewell to all.*)

WILLY.   No, Ben, I don't want you to think . . . (*He takes* BEN's *arm to show him.*) It's Brooklyn, I know, but we hunt too.

BEN.   Really, now.

WILLY.   Oh, sure, there's snakes and rabbits and—that's why I moved out here. Why, Biff can fell any one of these trees in no time! Boys! Go right over to where they're building the apartment house and get some sand. We're gonna rebuild the entire front stoop right now! Watch this, Ben!

BIFF.   Yes, sir! On the double, Hap!

HAPPY (*as he and* BIFF *run off*).   I lost weight, Pop, you notice? (CHARLEY *enters in knickers, even before the* BOYS *are gone.*)

CHARLEY.   Listen, if they steal any more from that building the watchman'll put the cops on them!

LINDA (*to* WILLY).   Don't let Biff . . . (BEN *laughs lustily.*)

WILLY.   You shoulda seen the lumber they brought home last week. At least a dozen six-by-tens worth all kinds a money.

CHARLEY.   Listen, if that watchman—

WILLY.   I gave them hell, understand. But I got a couple of fearless characters there.

CHARLEY.   Willy, the jails are full of fearless characters.

BEN (*clapping* WILLY *on the back, with a laugh at* CHARLEY).   And the stock exchange, friend!

WILLY (*joining in* BEN's *laughter*).   Where are the rest of your pants?

CHARLEY.   My wife bought them.

WILLY.   Now all you need is a golf club and you can go upstairs and go to sleep. (*To* BEN) Great athlete! Between him and his son Bernard they can't hammer a nail!

BERNARD (*rushing in*).   The watchman's chasing Biff!

WILLY (*angrily*).   Shut up! He's not stealing anything!

LINDA (*alarmed, hurrying off left*).   Where is he? Biff, dear! (*She exits.*)

WILLY (*moving toward the left, away from* BEN).   There's nothing wrong. What's the matter with you?

BEN.   Nervy boy. Good!

WILLY (*laughing*).   Oh, nerves of iron, that Biff!

CHARLEY.   Don't know what it is. My New England man comes back and he's bleedin', they murdered him up there.

WILLY.   It's contacts, Charley, I got important contacts!

CHARLEY (*sarcastically*).   Glad to hear it, Willy. Come in later, we'll shoot a little casino. I'll take some of your Portland money. (*He laughs at* WILLY *and exits.*)

WILLY (*turning to* BEN).   Business is bad, it's murderous. But not for me, of course.

BEN.   I'll stop by on my way back to Africa.

WILLY (*longingly*).   Can't you stay a few days? You're just what I need, Ben, because I—I have a fine position here, but I—well, Dad left when I was such a baby and I never had a chance to talk to him and I still feel—kind of temporary about myself.

BEN.   I'll be late for my train. (*They are at opposite ends of the stage.*)

WILLY.   Ben, my boys—can't we talk? They'd go into the jaws of hell for me, but I—

BEN.   William, you're being first-rate with your boys. Outstanding, manly chaps!

WILLY (*hanging on to his words*).   Oh, Ben, that's good to hear! Because sometimes I'm afraid that I'm not teaching them the right kind of—Ben, how should I teach them?

BEN (*giving great weight to each word, and with a certain vicious audacity*).   William, when I walked into the jungle, I was seventeen. When I walked out I was twenty-one. And, by God, I was rich! (*He goes off into the darkness around the right corner of the house.*)

WILLY.   . . . was rich! That's just the spirit I want to imbue them with! To walk into a jungle! I was right! (BEN *is gone, but* WILLY *is still speaking to him as* LINDA, *in nightgown and robe, enters the kitchen, glances around for* WILLY, *then goes to the door of the house, looks out and sees him. Comes down to his left. He looks at her.*)

LINDA.   Willy, dear? Willy?

WILLY.   I was right!

LINDA.   Did you have some cheese? (*He can't answer.*) It's very late, darling. Come to bed, heh?

WILLY (*looking straight up*).   Gotta break your neck to see a star in this yard.

LINDA.   You coming in?

WILLY.   Whatever happened to that diamond watch fob? Remember? When Ben came from Africa that time? Didn't he give me a watch fob with a diamond in it?

LINDA.   You pawned it, dear. Twelve, thirteen years ago. For Biff's radio correspondence course.

WILLY.   Gee, that was a beautiful thing. I'll take a walk.

LINDA.   But you're in your slippers.

WILLY (*starting to go around the house at the left*).   I was right! I was! (*Half to* LINDA, *as he goes, shaking his head*) What a man! There was a man worth talking to. I was right!

LINDA (*calling after* WILLY).   But in your slippers, Willy! (WILLY *is almost gone when* BIFF, *in his pajamas, comes down the stairs and enters the kitchen.*)

BIFF.   What is he doing out there?

LINDA.   Sh!

BIFF.   God Almighty, Mom, how long has he been doing this?

LINDA.   Don't, he'll hear you.

BIFF.   What the hell is the matter with him?

LINDA.   It'll pass by morning.

BIFF.   Shouldn't we do anything?

LINDA.   Oh, my dear, you should do a lot of things, but there's nothing to do, so go to sleep. (HAPPY *comes down the stairs and sits on the steps.*)

HAPPY.   I never heard him so loud, Mom.

LINDA.   Well, come around more often; you'll hear him. (*She sits down at the table and mends the lining of* WILLY's *jacket.*)

BIFF.   Why didn't you ever write me about this, Mom?

LINDA.   How would I write to you? For over three months you had no address.

BIFF.   I was on the move. But you know I thought of you all the time. You know that, don't you, pal?

LINDA.   I know, dear, I know. But he likes to have a letter. Just to know that there's still a possibility for better things.

BIFF.   He's not like this all the time, is he?

LINDA.   It's when you come home he's always the worst.

BIFF.   When I come home?

LINDA.   When you write you're coming, he's all smiles, and talks about the future, and—he's just wonderful. And then the closer you seem to come, the more shaky he gets, and then, by the time you get here, he's arguing, and he seems angry at you. I think it's just that maybe he can't bring himself to—to open up to you. Why are you so hateful to each other? Why is that?

BIFF (*evasively*).   I'm not hateful, Mom.

LINDA.   But you no sooner come in the door than you're fighting!

BIFF.   I don't know why. I mean to change. I'm tryin', Mom, you understand?

LINDA.   Are you home to stay now?

BIFF.   I don't know. I want to look around, see what's doin'.

LINDA.   Biff, you can't look around all your life, can you?

BIFF.   I just can't take hold, Mom. I can't take hold of some kind of a life.

LINDA.   Biff, a man is not a bird to come and go with the springtime.

BIFF.   Your hair . . . (*He touches her hair.*) Your hair got so gray.

LINDA.   Oh, it's been gray since you were in high school. I just stopped dyeing it, that's all.

BIFF.   Dye it again, will ya? I don't want my pal looking old. (*He smiles.*)

LINDA.   You're such a boy! You think you can go away for a year and . . . You've got to get it into your head now that one day you'll knock on this door and there'll be strange people here—

BIFF.   What are you talking about? You're not even sixty, Mom.

LINDA.   But what about your father?

BIFF (*lamely*).   Well, I meant him, too.

HAPPY.   He admires Pop.

LINDA.   Biff, dear, if you don't have any feeling for him, then you can't have any feeling for me.

BIFF.   Sure I can, Mom.

LINDA.   No. You can't just come to see me, because I love him. (*With a threat, but only a threat, of tears*) He's the dearest man in the world to me, and I won't have anyone making him feel unwanted and low and blue. You've got to make up your mind now, darling, there's no leeway any more. Either he's your father and you pay him that respect, or else you're not to come here. I know he's not easy to get along with—nobody knows that better than me—but . . .

WILLY (*from the left, with a laugh*).   Hey, hey, Biffo!

BIFF (*starting to go out after* WILLY).   What the hell is the matter with him? (HAPPY *stops him.*)

LINDA.   Don't—don't go near him!

BIFF.   Stop making excuses for him! He always, always wiped the floor with you. Never had an ounce of respect for you.

HAPPY.   He's always had respect for—

BIFF.   What the hell do you know about it?

HAPPY (*surlily*).   Just don't call him crazy!

BIFF.   He's got no character—Charley wouldn't do this. Not in his own house—spewing out that vomit from his mind.

HAPPY.   Charley never had to cope with what he's got to.

BIFF.   People are worse off than Willy Loman. Believe me, I've seen them.

LINDA.   Then make Charley your father, Biff. You can't do that, can you? I don't say he's a great man. Willy Loman never made a lot of money. His name was never in the paper. He's not the finest character that ever lived. But he's a human being, and a terrible thing is happening to him. So attention must be paid. He's not to be allowed to fall into his grave like an old dog. Attention, attention must be finally paid to such a person. You called him crazy—

BIFF.   I didn't mean—

LINDA.   No, a lot of people think he's lost his—balance. But you don't have to be very smart to know what his trouble is. The man is exhausted.

HAPPY.   Sure!

LINDA.   A small man can be just as exhausted as a great man. He works for a company thirty-six years this March, opens up unheard-of territories to their trademark, and now in his old age they take his salary away.

HAPPY (*indignantly*).   I didn't know that, Mom.

LINDA.   You never asked, my dear! Now that you get your spending money someplace else you don't trouble your mind with him.

HAPPY.   But I gave you money last—

LINDA.   Christmas time, fifty dollars! To fix the hot water it cost ninety-seven fifty! For five weeks he's been on straight commission, like a beginner, an unknown!

BIFF.   Those ungrateful bastards!

LINDA.   Are they any worse than his sons? When he brought them business, when he was young, they were glad to see him. But now his old friends, the old buyers that loved him so and always found some order to hand him in a pinch—they're all dead, retired. He used to be able to make six, seven calls a day in Boston. Now he takes his valises out of the car and puts them back and takes them out again and he's exhausted. Instead of walking he talks now. He drives seven hundred miles, and when he gets there no one knows him any more, no one welcomes him. And what goes through a man's mind, driving seven hundred miles home without having earned a cent? Why shouldn't he talk to himself? Why? When he has to go to Charley and borrow fifty dollars a week and pretend to me that it's his pay? How long can that go on? How long? You see what I'm sitting here and waiting for? And you tell me he has no character? The man who never worked a day but for your benefit? When does he get the medal for that? Is this his reward—to turn around at the age of sixty-three and find his sons, who he loved better than his life, one a philandering bum—

HAPPY.   Mom!

LINDA.   That's all you are, my baby! (*To* BIFF) And you! What happened to the love you had for him? You were such pals! How you used to talk to him on the phone every night! How lonely he was till he could come home to you!

BIFF.   All right, Mom, I'll live here in my room, and I'll get a job. I'll keep away from him, that's all.

LINDA.   No, Biff. You can't stay here and fight all the time.

BIFF.   He threw me out of this house, remember that.

LINDA.   Why did he do that? I never knew why.

BIFF.   Because I know he's a fake and he doesn't like anybody around who knows!

LINDA.   Why a fake? In what way? What do you mean?

BIFF.   Just don't lay it all at my feet. It's between me and him—that's all I have to say. I'll chip in from now on. He'll settle for half my pay check. He'll be all right. I'm going to bed. (*He starts for the stairs.*)

LINDA.   He won't be all right.

BIFF (*turning on the stairs, furiously*).   I hate this city and I'll stay here. Now what do you want?

LINDA.   He's dying, Biff. (HAPPY *turns quickly to her, shocked.*)

BIFF (*after a pause*).   Why is he dying?

LINDA.   He's been trying to kill himself.

BIFF (*with great horror*).   How?

LINDA.   I live from day to day.

BIFF.   What're you talking about?

LINDA.   Remember I wrote you that he smashed up the car again? In February?

BIFF.   Well?

LINDA.   The insurance inspector came. He said that they have evidence. That all these accidents in the last year—weren't—weren't—accidents.

HAPPY.   How can they tell that? That's a lie.

LINDA.   It seems there's a woman . . . (*She takes a breath as*—)

{ BIFF (*sharply but contained*).   What woman?

{ LINDA (*simultaneously*).   . . . and this woman . . .

LINDA.   What?

BIFF.   Nothing. Go ahead.

LINDA.   What did you say?

BIFF.   Nothing. I just said what woman?

HAPPY.   What about her?

LINDA.   Well, it seems she was walking down the road and saw his car. She says that he wasn't driving fast at all, and that he didn't skid. She says he came to that little bridge, and then deliberately smashed into the railing, and it was only the shallowness of the water that saved him.

BIFF.   Oh, no, he probably just fell asleep again.

LINDA.   I don't think he fell asleep.

BIFF.   Why not?

LINDA.   Last month . . . (*With great difficulty*) Oh, boys, it's so hard to say a thing like this! He's just a big stupid man to you, but I tell you there's more good in him than in many other people. (*She chokes, wipes her eyes.*) I was looking for a fuse. The lights blew out, and I went down to the cellar. And behind the fuse box—it happened to fall out—was a length of rubber pipe—just short.

HAPPY.   No kidding?

LINDA.   There's a little attachment on the end of it. I knew it right away. And sure enough, on the bottom of the water heater there's a new little nipple on the gas pipe.

HAPPY (*angrily*).   That—jerk.

BIFF.   Did you have it taken off?

LINDA.   I'm—I'm ashamed to. How can I mention it to him? Every day I go down and take away that little rubber pipe. But, when he comes home, I put it back where it was. How can I insult him that way? I don't know what to do. I live from day to day, boys. I tell you, I know every thought in his mind. It sounds so old-fashioned and silly, but I tell you he put his whole life into you and you've turned your backs on him. (*She is bent over in the chair, weeping, her face in her hands.*) Biff, I swear to God! Biff, his life is in your hands!

HAPPY (*to* BIFF).   How do you like that damned fool!

BIFF (*kissing her*).   All right, pal, all right. It's all settled now. I've been remiss. I know that, Mom. But now I'll stay, and I swear to you, I'll apply myself. (*Kneeling in front of her, in a fever of self-reproach*) It's just—you see, Mom, I don't fit in business. Not that I won't try. I'll try, and I'll make good.

HAPPY.   Sure you will. The trouble with you in business was you never tried to please people.

BIFF.   I know, I—

HAPPY.   Like when you worked for Harrison's. Bob Harrison said you were tops, and then you go and do some damn fool thing like whistling whole songs in the elevator like a comedian.

BIFF (*against* HAPPY).   So what? I like to whistle sometimes.

HAPPY.   You don't raise a guy to a responsible job who whistles in the elevator!

LINDA.   Well, don't argue about it now.

HAPPY.   Like when you'd go off and swim in the middle of the day instead of taking the line around.

BIFF (*his resentment rising*).   Well, don't you run off? You take off sometimes, don't you? On a nice summer day?

HAPPY.   Yeah, but I cover myself!

LINDA.   Boys!

HAPPY.   If I'm going to take a fade the boss can call any number where I'm supposed to be and they'll swear to him that I just left. I'll tell you something that I hate to say, Biff, but in the business world some of them think you're crazy.

BIFF (*angered*).   Screw the business world!

HAPPY.   All right, screw it! Great, but cover yourself!

LINDA.   Hap, Hap!

BIFF.   I don't care what they think! They've laughed at Dad for years, and you know why? Because we don't belong in this nuthouse of a city! We should be mixing cement on some open plain, or—or carpenters. A carpenter is allowed to whistle! (WILLY *walks in from the entrance of the house, at left.*)

WILLY.   Even your grandfather was better than a carpenter. (*Pause. They watch him.*) You never grew up. Bernard does not whistle in the elevator, I assure you.

BIFF (*as though to laugh* WILLY *out of it*).   Yeah, but you do, Pop.

WILLY.   I never in my life whistled in an elevator! And who in the business world thinks I'm crazy?

BIFF.   I didn't mean it like that, Pop. Now don't make a whole thing out of it, will ya?

WILLY.   Go back to the West! Be a carpenter, a cowboy, enjoy yourself!

LINDA.   Willy, he was just saying—

WILLY.   I heard what he said!

HAPPY (*trying to quiet* WILLY).   Hey, Pop, come on now . . .

WILLY (*continuing over* HAPPY's *line*).   They laugh at me, heh? Go to Filene's, go to the Hub, go to Slattery's, Boston. Call out the name Willy Loman and see what happens! Big shot!

BIFF.   All right, Pop.

WILLY.   Big!

BIFF.   All right!

WILLY.   Why do you always insult me?

BIFF.   I didn't say a word. (*To* LINDA) Did I say a word?

LINDA.   He didn't say anything, Willy.

WILLY (*going to the doorway of the living-room*).   All right, good night, good night.

LINDA.   Willy, dear, he just decided . . .

WILLY (*to* BIFF).   If you get tired hanging around tomorrow, paint the ceiling I put up in the living-room.

BIFF.   I'm leaving early tomorrow.

HAPPY.   He's going to see Bill Oliver, Pop.

WILLY (*interestedly*).   Oliver? For what?

BIFF (*with reserve, but trying, trying*).   He always said he'd stake me. I'd like to go into business, so maybe I can take him up on it.

LINDA.   Isn't that wonderful?

WILLY.   Don't interrupt. What's wonderful about it? There's fifty men in the City of New York who'd stake him. (*To* BIFF) Sporting goods?

BIFF.   I guess so. I know something about it and—

WILLY.   He knows something about it! You know sporting goods better than Spalding, for God's sake! How much is he giving you?

BIFF.   I don't know, I didn't even see him yet, but—

WILLY.   Then what're you talkin' about?

BIFF (*getting angry*).   Well, all I said was I'm gonna see him, that's all!

WILLY (*turning away*).   Ah, you're counting your chickens again.

BIFF (*starting left for the stairs*).   Oh, Jesus, I'm going to sleep!

WILLY (*calling after him*).   Don't curse in this house!

BIFF (*turning*).   Since when did you get so clean?

HAPPY (*trying to stop them*).   Wait a . . .

WILLY.   Don't use that language to me! I won't have it!

HAPPY (*grabbing* BIFF, *shouts*).   Wait a minute! I got an idea. I got a feasible idea. Come here, Biff, let's talk this over now, let's talk some sense here. When I was down in Florida last time, I thought of a great idea to sell sporting goods. It just came back to me. You and I, Biff—we have a line, the Loman Line. We train a couple of weeks, and put on a couple of exhibitions, see?

WILLY.   That's an idea!

HAPPY.   Wait! We form two basketball teams, see? Two water-polo teams. We play each other. It's a million dollars' worth of publicity. Two brothers, see? The Loman Brothers. Displays in the Royal Palms—all the hotels. And banners over the ring and the basketball court: "Loman Brothers." Baby, we could sell sporting goods!

WILLY.   That is a one-million-dollar idea!

LINDA.   Marvelous!

BIFF.   I'm in great shape as far as that's concerned.

HAPPY.   And the beauty of it is, Biff, it wouldn't be like a business. We'd be out playin' ball again . . .

BIFF (*enthused*).   Yeah, that's . . .

WILLY.   Million-dollar . . .

HAPPY.   And you wouldn't get fed up with it, Biff. It'd be the family again. There'd be the old honor, and comradeship, and if you wanted to go off for a swim or somethin'—well, you'd do it! Without some smart cooky gettin' up ahead of you!

WILLY.   Lick the world! You guys together could absolutely lick the civilized world.

BIFF.   I'll see Oliver tomorrow. Hap, if we could work that out . . .

LINDA.   Maybe things are beginning to—

WILLY (*wildly enthused, to* LINDA).   Stop interrupting! (*To* BIFF) But don't wear sport jacket and slacks when you see Oliver.

BIFF.   No, I'll—

WILLY.   A business suit, and talk as little as possible, and don't crack any jokes.

BIFF.   He did like me. Always liked me.

LINDA.   He loved you!

WILLY (*to* LINDA).   Will you stop! (*To* BIFF) Walk in very serious. You are not applying for a boy's job. Money is to pass. Be quiet, fine, and serious. Everybody likes a kidder, but nobody lends him money.

HAPPY.   I'll try to get some myself, Biff. I'm sure I can.

WILLY.   I see great things for you kids, I think your troubles are over. But remember, start big and you'll end big. Ask for fifteen. How much you gonna ask for?

BIFF.   Gee, I don't know—

WILLY.   And don't say, "Gee," "Gee" is a boy's word. A man walking in for fifteen thousand dollars does not say "Gee!"

BIFF.   Ten, I think, would be top though.

WILLY.   Don't be so modest. You always started too low. Walk in with a big laugh. Don't look worried. Start off with a couple of your good stories to lighten things up. It's not what you say, it's how you say it—because personality always wins the day.

LINDA.   Oliver always thought the highest of him—

WILLY.   Will you let me talk?

BIFF.   Don't yell at her, Pop, will ya?

WILLY (*angrily*).   I was talking, wasn't I?

BIFF.   I don't like you yelling at her all the time, and I'm tellin' you, that's all.

WILLY.   What're you, takin' over this house?

LINDA.   Willy—

WILLY (*turning on her*).   Don't take his side all the time, goddammit!

BIFF (*furiously*).   Stop yelling at her!

WILLY (*suddenly pulling on his cheek, beaten down, guilt ridden*). Give my best to Bill Oliver—he may remember me. (*He exits through the living-room doorway.*)

LINDA (*her voice subdued*).   What'd you have to start that for? (BIFF *turns away.*) You see how sweet he was as soon as you talked hopefully? (*She goes over to* BIFF.) Come up and say good night to him. Don't let him go to bed that way.

HAPPY.   Come on, Biff, let's buck him up.

LINDA.   Please, dear. Just say good night. It takes so little to make him happy. Come. (*She goes through the living-room doorway, calling upstairs from within the living-room.*) Your pajamas are hanging in the bathroom, Willy!

HAPPY (*looking toward where* LINDA *went out*).   What a woman! They broke the mold when they made her. You know that, Biff?

BIFF.   He's off salary. My God, working on commission!

HAPPY.   Well, let's face it: he's no hot-shot selling man. Except that sometimes, you have to admit, he's a sweet personality.

BIFF (*decidedly*).   Lend me ten bucks, will ya? I want to buy some new ties.

HAPPY.   I'll take you to a place I know. Beautiful stuff. Wear one of my striped shirts tomorrow.

BIFF.   She got gray. Mom got awful old. Gee, I'm gonna go in to Oliver tomorrow and knock him for a—

HAPPY.   Come on up. Tell that to Dad. Let's give him a whirl. Come on.

BIFF (*steamed up*).   You know, with ten thousand bucks, boy!

HAPPY (*as they go into the living-room*).   That's the talk, Biff, that's the first time I've heard the old confidence out of you! (*From within the living-room, fading off*) You're gonna live with me, kid, and any babe you want just say the word . . . (*The last lines are hardly heard. They are mounting the stairs to their parents' bedroom.*)

LINDA (*entering her bedroom and addressing* WILLY, *who is in the bathroom. She is straightening the bed for him*).   Can you do anything about the shower? It drips.

WILLY (*from the bathroom*).   All of a sudden everything falls to pieces! Goddam plumbing, oughta be sued, those people. I hardly finished putting it in and the thing . . . (*His words rumble off.*)

LINDA.   I'm just wondering if Oliver will remember him. You think he might?

WILLY (*coming out of the bathroom in his pajamas*).   Remember him? What's the matter with you, you crazy? If he'd've stayed with Oliver he'd be on top by now! Wait'll Oliver gets a look at him. You don't know the average caliber any more. The average young man today —(*he is getting into bed*)—is got a caliber of zero. Greatest thing in the world for him was to bum around. (BIFF *and* HAPPY *enter the bedroom. Slight pause.* WILLY *stops short, looking at* BIFF.) Glad to hear it, boy.

HAPPY.   He wanted to say good night to you, sport.

WILLY (*to* BIFF).   Yeah. Knock him dead, boy. What'd you want to tell me?

BIFF.   Just take it easy, Pop. Good night. (*He turns to go.*)

WILLY (*unable to resist*).   And if anything falls off the desk while you're talking to him—like a package or something—don't you pick it up. They have office boys for that.

LINDA.   I'll make a big breakfast—

WILLY.   Will you let me finish? (*To* BIFF) Tell him you were in the business in the West. Not farm work.

BIFF.   All right, Dad.

LINDA.   I think everything—

WILLY.   (*going right through her speech*). And don't undersell yourself. No less than fifteen thousand dollars.

BIFF (*unable to bear him*).   Okay. Good night, Mom. (*He starts moving.*)

WILLY.   Because you got a greatness in you, Biff, remember that. You got all kinds of greatness . . . (*He lies back, exhausted.* BIFF *walks out.*)

LINDA (*calling after* BIFF).   Sleep well, darling!

HAPPY.   I'm going to get married, Mom. I wanted to tell you.

LINDA.   Go to sleep, dear.

HAPPY (*going*).   I just wanted to tell you.

WILLY.   Keep up the good work. (HAPPY *exits*.) God . . . remember that Ebbets Field° game? The championship of the city?

LINDA.   Just rest. Should I sing to you?

WILLY.   Yeah. Sing to me. (LINDA *hums a soft lullaby*.) When that team came out—he was the tallest, remember?

LINDA.   Oh, yes. And in gold. (BIFF *enters the darkened kitchen, takes a cigarette, and leaves the house. He comes downstage into a golden pool of light. He smokes, staring at the night*.)

WILLY.   Like a young god. Hercules—something like that. And the sun, the sun all around him. Remember how he waved to me? Right up from the field, with the representatives of three colleges standing by? And the buyers I brought, and the cheers when he came out—Loman, Loman, Loman! God Almighty, he'll be great yet. A star like that, magnificent, can never really fade away! (*The light on* WILLY *is fading. The gas heater begins to glow through the kitchen wall, near the stairs, a blue flame beneath the red coils*.)

LINDA (*timidly*).   Willy dear, what has he got against you?

WILLY.   I'm so tired. Don't talk any more. (BIFF *slowly returns to the kitchen. He stops, stares toward the heater*.)

LINDA.   Will you ask Howard to let you work in New York?

WILLY.   First thing in the morning. Everything'll be all right. (BIFF *reaches behind the heater and draws out a length of rubber tubing. He is horrified and turns his head toward* WILLY's *room, still dimly lit, from which the strains of* LINDA's *desperate but monotonous humming rise.* WILLY *stares through the window into the moonlight*.) Gee, look at the moon moving between the buildings! (BIFF *wraps the tubing around his hand and quickly goes up the stairs*.)

ACT 2

Music is heard, gay and bright. The curtain rises as the music fades away. WILLY, *in shirt sleeves, is sitting at the kitchen table, sipping coffee, his hat in his lap.* LINDA *is filling his cup when she can.*

WILLY.   Wonderful coffee. Meal in itself.

LINDA.   Can I make you some eggs?

Ebbets Field: A baseball stadium, the home of the Brooklyn Dodgers, torn down in 1960. Because it was used primarily for baseball, its locker rooms were called clubhouses.

WILLY.   No. Take a breath.

LINDA.   You look so rested, dear.

WILLY.   I slept like a dead one. First time in months. Imagine, sleeping till ten on a Tuesday morning. Boys left nice and early, heh?

LINDA.   They were out of here by eight o'clock.

WILLY.   Good work!

LINDA.   It was so thrilling to see them leaving together. I can't get over the shaving lotion in this house!

WILLY (*smiling*).   Mmm—

LINDA.   Biff was very changed this morning. His whole attitude seemed to be hopeful. He couldn't wait to get downtown to see Oliver.

WILLY.   He's heading for a change. There's no question, there simply are certain men that take longer to get—solidified. How did he dress?

LINDA.   His blue suit. He's so handsome in that suit. He could be a —anything in that suit! (WILLY *gets up from the table*. LINDA *holds his jacket for him.*)

WILLY.   There's no question, no question at all. Gee, on the way home tonight I'd like to buy some seeds.

LINDA (*laughing*).   That'd be wonderful. But not enough sun gets back there. Nothing'll grow any more.

WILLY.   You wait, kid, before it's all over we're gonna get a little place out in the country, and I'll raise some vegetables, a couple of chickens . . .

LINDA.   You'll do it yet, dear. (WILLY *walks out of his jacket*. LINDA *follows him.*)

WILLY.   And they'll get married, and come for a weekend. I'd build a little guest house. 'Cause I got so many fine tools, all I'd need would be a little lumber and some peace of mind.

LINDA (*joyfully*).   I sewed the lining . . .

WILLY.   I would build two guest houses, so they'd both come. Did he decide how much he's going to ask Oliver for?

LINDA (*getting him into his jacket*).   He didn't mention it, but I imagine ten or fifteen thousand. You going to talk to Howard today?

WILLY.   Yeah. I'll put it to him straight and simple. He'll just have to take me off the road.

LINDA.   And, Willy, don't forget to ask for a little advance, because we've got the insurance premium. It's the grace period now.

WILLY.   That's a hundred . . . ?

LINDA.   A hundred and eight, sixty-eight. Because we're a little short again.

WILLY.   Why are we short?

LINDA.   Well, you had the motor job on the car . . .

WILLY.   That goddam Studebaker!

LINDA.   And you got one more payment on the refrigerator . . .

WILLY.   But it just broke again!

LINDA.   Well, it's old, dear.

WILLY.   I told you we should've bought a well-advertised machine. Charley bought a General Electric and it's twenty years old and it's still good, that son-of-a-bitch.

LINDA.   But, Willy—

WILLY.   Whoever heard of a Hastings refrigerator? Once in my life I would like to own something outright before it's broken! I'm always in a race with the junkyard! I just finished paying for the car and it's on its last legs. The refrigerator consumes belts like a goddam maniac. They time those things. They time them so when you finally paid for them, they're used up.

LINDA (*buttoning up his jacket as he unbuttons it*).   All told, about two hundred dollars would carry us, dear. But that includes the last payment on the mortgage. After this payment, Willy, the house belongs to us.

WILLY.   It's twenty-five years!

LINDA.   Biff was nine years old when we bought it.

WILLY.   Well, that's a great thing. To weather a twenty-five year mortgage is—

LINDA.   It's an accomplishment.

WILLY.   All the cement, lumber, the reconstruction I put in this house! There ain't a crack to be found in it any more.

LINDA.   Well, it served its purpose.

WILLY.   What purpose? Some stranger'll come along, move in, and that's that. If only Biff would take this house, and raise a family . . . (*He starts to go.*) Good-by, I'm late.

LINDA (*suddenly remembering*).   Oh, I forgot! You're supposed to meet them for dinner.

WILLY.   Me?

LINDA.   At Frank's Chop House on Forty-eighth near Sixth Avenue.

WILLY.   Is that so! How about you?

LINDA.   No, just the three of you. They're gonna blow you to a big meal!

WILLY.   Don't say! Who thought of that?

LINDA.   Biff came to me this morning, Willy, and he said, "Tell Dad, we want to blow him to a big meal." Be there six o'clock. You and your two boys are going to have dinner.

WILLY.   Gee whiz! That's really somethin'. I'm gonna knock Howard for a loop, kid. I'll get an advance, and I'll come home with a New York job. Goddammit, now I'm gonna do it!

LINDA.   Oh, that's the spirit, Willy!

WILLY.   I will never get behind a wheel the rest of my life!

LINDA.   It's changing, Willy, I can feel it changing!

WILLY.   Beyond a question. G'by, I'm late. (*He starts to go again.*)

LINDA (*calling after him as she runs to the kitchen table for a handkerchief*).   You got your glasses?

WILLY (*feels for them, then comes back in*).   Yeah, yeah, got my glasses.

LINDA (*giving him the handkerchief*).   And a handkerchief.

WILLY.   Yeah, handkerchief.

LINDA.   And your saccharine?

WILLY.   Yeah, my saccharine.

LINDA.   Be careful on the subway stairs. (*She kisses him, and a silk stocking is seen hanging from her hand.* WILLY *notices it.*)

WILLY.   Will you stop mending stockings? At least while I'm in the house. It gets me nervous. I can't tell you. Please. (LINDA *hides the stocking in her hand as she follows* WILLY *across the forestage in front of the house.*)

LINDA.   Remember, Frank's Chop House.

WILLY (*passing the apron*).   Maybe beets would grow out there.

LINDA (*laughing*).   But you tried so many times.

WILLY.   Yeah. Well, don't work hard today. (*He disappears around the right corner of the house.*)

LINDA.   Be careful! (*As* WILLY *vanishes,* LINDA *waves to him. Suddenly the phone rings. She runs across the stage and into the kitchen and lifts it.*) Hello? Oh, Biff! I'm so glad you called, I just . . . Yes, sure, I just told him. Yes, he'll be there for dinner at six o'clock, I didn't forget. Listen, I was just dying to tell you. You know that little rubber pipe I told you about? That he connected to the gas heater? I finally decided to go down the cellar this morning and take it away and destroy it. But it's gone! Imagine? He took it away himself, it isn't there! (*She listens.*) When? Oh, then you took it. Oh—nothing, it's just that I'd hoped he'd taken it away himself. Oh, I'm not worried, darling, because this morning he left in such high spirits, it was like the old days! I'm not afraid any more. Did Mr. Oliver see you? . . . Well, you wait there then. And make a nice impression on him, darling. Just don't perspire too much before you see him. And have a nice time with Dad. He may have big news too! . . . That's right, a New York job. And be sweet to him tonight, dear. Be loving to him. Because he's only a little boat looking for a harbor. (*She is trembling with sorrow and joy.*) Oh, that's wonderful, Biff, you'll save his life. Thanks, darling. Just put your arm around him when he comes into the restaurant. Give him a smile. That's the boy . . . Good-by, dear . . . You got your comb? . . . That's fine. Goodby, Biff dear.

(*In the middle of her speech,* HOWARD WAGNER, *thirty-six, wheels on a small typewriter table on which is a wire-recording machine and proceeds to plug it in. This is on the left forestage. Light slowly fades on* LINDA *as it rises on* HOWARD. HOWARD *is intent on threading the machine and only glances over his shoulder as* WILLY *appears.*)

WILLY.   Pst! Pst!

HOWARD.   Hello, Willy, come in.

WILLY.   Like to have a little talk with you, Howard.

HOWARD.   Sorry to keep you waiting. I'll be with you in a minute.

WILLY.   What's that, Howard?

HOWARD.   Didn't you ever see one of these? Wire recorder.

WILLY.   Oh. Can we talk a minute?

HOWARD.   Records things. Just got delivery yesterday. Been driving me crazy, the most terrific machine I ever saw in my life. I was up all night with it.

WILLY.   What do you do with it?

HOWARD.   I bought it for dictation, but you can do anything with it. Listen to this. I had it home last night. Listen to what I picked up. The first one is my daughter. Get this. (*He flicks the switch and "Roll Out the Barrel" is heard being whistled.*) Listen to that kid whistle.

WILLY.   That is lifelike, isn't it?

HOWARD.   Seven years old. Get that tone.

WILLY.   Ts, ts. Like to ask a little favor of you . . . (*The whistling breaks off, and the voice of* HOWARD's *daughter is heard.*)

HIS DAUGHTER.   "Now you, Daddy."

HOWARD.   She's crazy for me! (*Again the same song is whistled.*) That's me! Ha! (*He winks.*)

WILLY.   You're very good! (*The whistling breaks off again. The machine runs silent for a moment.*)

HOWARD.   Sh! Get this now, this is my son.

HIS SON.   "The capital of Alabama is Montgomery; the capital of Arizona is Phoenix; the capital of Arkansas is Little Rock; the capital of California is Sacramento . . ." (*and on, and on*).

HOWARD (*holding up five fingers*).   Five years old, Willy!

WILLY.   He'll make an announcer some day!

HIS SON (*continuing*).   "The capital . . ."

HOWARD.   Get that—alphabetical order! (*The machine breaks off suddenly.*) Wait a minute. The maid kicked the plug out.

WILLY.   It certainly is a—

HOWARD.   Sh, for God's sake!

HIS SON.   "It's nine o'clock, Bulova watch time. So I have to go to sleep."

WILLY.   That really is—

HOWARD.   Wait a minute! The next is my wife. (*They wait.*)

HOWARD'S VOICE.   "Go on, say something." (*Pause.*) "Well, you gonna talk?"

HIS WIFE.   "I can't think of anything."

HOWARD'S VOICE.   "Well, talk—it's turning."

HIS WIFE (*shyly, beaten*).   "Hello." (*Silence.*) "Oh, Howard, I can't talk into this . . ."

HOWARD (*snapping the machine off*).   That was my wife.

WILLY.   That is a wonderful machine. Can we—

HOWARD.   I tell you, Willy, I'm gonna take my camera, and my bandsaw, and all my hobbies, and out they go. This is the most fascinating relaxation I ever found.

WILLY.   I think I'll get one myself.

HOWARD.   Sure, they're only a hundred and a half. You can't do without it. Supposing you wanna hear Jack Benny, see? But you can't be at home at that hour. So you tell the maid to turn the radio on when Jack Benny comes on, and this automatically goes on with the radio . . .

WILLY.   And when you come home you . . .

HOWARD.   You can come home twelve o'clock, one o'clock, any time you like, and you get yourself a Coke and sit yourself down, throw the switch, and there's Jack Benny's program in the middle of the night!

WILLY.   I'm definitely going to get one. Because lots of time I'm on the road, and I think to myself, what I must be missing on the radio!

HOWARD.   Don't you have a radio in the car?

WILLY.   Well, yeah, but who ever thinks of turning it on?

HOWARD.   Say, aren't you supposed to be in Boston?

WILLY.   That's what I want to talk to you about, Howard. You got a minute? (*He draws a chair in from the wing.*)

HOWARD.   What happened? What're you doing here?

WILLY.   Well . . .

HOWARD.   You didn't crack up again, did you?

WILLY.   Oh, no. No . . .

HOWARD.   Geez, you had me worried there for a minute. What's the trouble?

WILLY. Well, tell you the truth, Howard, I've come to the decision that I'd rather not travel any more.

HOWARD. Not travel! Well, what'll you do?

WILLY. Remember, Christmas time, when you had the party here? You said you'd try to think of some spot for me here in town.

HOWARD. With us?

WILLY. Well, sure.

HOWARD. Oh, yeah, yeah. I remember. Well, I couldn't think of anything for you, Willy.

WILLY. I tell ya, Howard. The kids are all grown up, y'know. I don't need much any more. If I could take home—well, sixty-five dollars a week, I could swing it.

HOWARD. Yeah, but Willy, see I—

WILLY. I tell ya why, Howard. Speaking frankly and between the two of us, y'know—I'm just a little tired.

HOWARD. Oh, I could understand that, Willy. But you're a road man, Willy, and we do a road business. We've only got a half-dozen salesmen on the floor here.

WILLY. God knows, Howard, I never asked a favor of any man. But I was with the firm when your father used to carry you in here in his arms.

HOWARD. I know that, Willy, but—

WILLY. Your father came to me the day you were born and asked me what I thought of the name of Howard, may he rest in peace.

HOWARD. I appreciate that, Willy, but there just is no spot here for you. If I had a spot I'd slam you right in, but I just don't have a single solitary spot. (*He looks for his lighter.* WILLY *has picked it up and gives it to him. Pause.*)

WILLY (*with increasing anger*).   Howard, all I need to set my table is fifty dollars a week.

HOWARD. But where am I going to put you, kid?

WILLY. Look, it isn't a question of whether I can sell merchandise, is it?

HOWARD. No, but it's a business, kid, and everybody's gotta pull his own weight.

WILLY (*desperately*).   Just let me tell you a story, Howard—

HOWARD. 'Cause you gotta admit, business is business.

WILLY (*angrily*).   Business is definitely business, but just listen for a minute. You don't understand this. When I was a boy—eighteen, nineteen—I was already on the road. And there was a question in my mind as to whether selling had a future for me. Because in those days I had a yearning to go to Alaska. See, there were three gold strikes in one month in Alaska, and I felt like going out. Just for the ride, you might say.

HOWARD (*barely interested*).   Don't say.

WILLY.   Oh, yeah, my father lived many years in Alaska. He was an adventurous man. We've got quite a little streak of self-reliance in our family. I thought I'd go out with my older brother and try to locate him, and maybe settle in the North with the old man. And I was almost decided to go, when I met a salesman in the Parker House. His name was Dave Singleman. And he was eighty-four years old, and he'd drummed merchandise in thirty-one states. And old Dave, he'd go up to his room, y'understand, put on his green velvet slippers—I'll never forget—and pick up his phone and call the buyers, and without ever leaving his room, at the age of eighty-four, he made his living. And when I saw that, I realized that selling was the greatest career a man could want. 'Cause what could be more satisfying than to be able to go, at the age of eighty-four, into twenty or thirty different cities, and pick up a phone, and be remembered and loved and helped by so many different people? Do you know? when he died—and by the way he died the death of a salesman, in his green velvet slippers in the smoker of the New York, New Haven and Hartford, going into Boston—when he died, hundreds of salesmen and buyers were at his funeral. Things were sad on a lotta trains for months after that. (*He stands up.* HOWARD *has not looked at him.*) In those days there was personality in it, Howard. There was respect, and comradeship, and gratitude in it. Today, it's all cut and dried, and there's no chance for bringing friendship to bear—or personality. You see what I mean? They don't know me any more.

HOWARD (*moving away, to the right*).   That's just the thing, Willy.

WILLY.   If I had forty dollars a week—that's all I'd need. Forty dollars, Howard.

HOWARD.   Kid, I can't take blood from a stone, I—

WILLY (*desperation is on him now*).   Howard, the year Al Smith° was nominated, your father came to me and—

HOWARD (*starting to go off*).   I've got to see some people, kid.

WILLY (*stopping him*).   I'm talking about your father! There were promises made across this desk! You mustn't tell me you've got people to see—I put thirty-four years into this firm, Howard, and now I can't pay my insurance! You can't eat the orange and throw the peel away—a man is not a piece of fruit! (*After a pause.*) Now pay attention. Your father—in 1928 I had a big year. I averaged a hundred and seventy dollars a week in commissions.

HOWARD (*impatiently*).   Now, Willy, you never averaged—

Al Smith: Four-term governor of New York and the 1928 Democratic nominee for president, who lost to Herbert Hoover.

WILLY (*banging his hand on the desk*).   I averaged a hundred and seventy dollars a week in the year of 1928! And your father came to me —or rather, I was in the office here—it was right over this desk—and he put his hand on my shoulder—

HOWARD (*getting up*).   You'll have to excuse me, Willy, I gotta see some people. Pull yourself together. (*Going out*) I'll be back in a little while. (*On HOWARD's exit, the light on his chair grows very bright and strange.*)

WILLY.   Pull myself together! What the hell did I say to him? My God, I was yelling at him! How could I! (*WILLY breaks off, staring at the light, which occupies the chair, animating it. He approaches this chair, standing across the desk from it.*) Frank, Frank, don't you remember what you told me that time? How you put your hand on my shoulder, and Frank . . . (*He leans on the desk and as he speaks the dead man's name he accidentally switches on the recorder, and instantly*)

HOWARD'S SON.   ". . . of New York is Albany. The capital of Ohio is Cincinnati, the capital of Rhode Island is . . ." (*The recitation continues.*)

WILLY (*leaping away with fright, shouting*).   Ha! Howard! Howard! Howard!

HOWARD (*rushing in*).   What happened?

WILLY (*pointing at the machine, which continues nasally, childishly, with the capital cities*).   Shut it off! Shut it off!

HOWARD (*pulling the plug out*).   Look, Willy . . .

WILLY (*pressing his hands to his eyes*).   I gotta get myself some coffee. I'll get some coffee . . . (*WILLY starts to walk out. HOWARD stops him.*)

HOWARD (*rolling up the cord*).   Willy, look . . .

WILLY.   I'll go to Boston.

HOWARD.   Willy, you can't go to Boston for us.

WILLY.   Why can't I go?

HOWARD.   I don't want you to represent us. I've been meaning to tell you for a long time now.

WILLY.   Howard, are you firing me?

HOWARD.   I think you need a good long rest, Willy.

WILLY.   Howard—

HOWARD.   And when you feel better, come back, and we'll see if we can work something out.

WILLY.   But I gotta earn money, Howard. I'm in no position to—

HOWARD.   Where are your sons? Why don't your sons give you a hand?

WILLY.   They're working on a very big deal.

HOWARD.   This is no time for false pride, Willy. You go to your sons and tell them that you're tired. You've got two great boys, haven't you?

WILLY.   Oh, no question, no question, but in the meantime . . .

HOWARD.   Then that's that, heh?

WILLY.   All right, I'll go to Boston tomorrow.

HOWARD.   No, no.

WILLY.   I can't throw myself on my sons. I'm not a cripple!

HOWARD.   Look, kid, I'm busy this morning.

WILLY (*grasping* HOWARD'*s arm*).   Howard, you've got to let me go to Boston!

HOWARD (*hard, keeping himself under control*).   I've got a line of people to see this morning. Sit down, take five minutes, and pull yourself together, and then go home, will ya? I need the office, Willy. (*He starts to go, turns, remembering the recorder, starts to push off the table holding the recorder.*) Oh, yeah. Whenever you can this week, stop by and drop off the samples. You'll feel better, Willy, and then come back and we'll talk. Pull yourself together, kid, there's people outside. (HOWARD *exits, pushing the table off left.* WILLY *stares into space, exhausted. Now the music is heard—*BEN'*s music—first distantly, then closer, closer. As* WILLY *speaks,* BEN *enters from the right. He carries valise and umbrella.*)

WILLY.   Oh, Ben, how did you do it? What is the answer? Did you wind up the Alaska deal already?

BEN.   Doesn't take much time if you know what you're doing. Just a short business trip. Boarding ship in an hour. Wanted to say good-by.

WILLY.   Ben, I've got to talk to you.

BEN (*glancing at his watch*).   Haven't the time, William.

WILLY (*crossing the apron to* BEN).   Ben, nothing's working out. I don't know what to do.

BEN.   Now look here, William. I've bought timberland in Alaska and I need a man to look after things for me.

WILLY.   God, timberland! Me and my boys in those grand outdoors!

BEN.   You've a new continent at your doorstep, William. Get out of these cities, they're full of talk and time payments and courts of law. Screw on your fists and you can fight for a fortune up there.

WILLY.   Yes, yes! Linda, Linda! (LINDA *enters as of old, with the wash.*)

LINDA.   Oh, you're back?

BEN.   I haven't much time.

WILLY.   No, wait! Linda, he's got a proposition for me in Alaska.

LINDA.   But you've got—(*To* BEN) He's got a beautiful job here.

WILLY.   But in Alaska, kid, I could—

LINDA.   You're doing well enough, Willy!

BEN (*to* LINDA).   Enough for what, my dear?

LINDA (*frightened of* BEN *and angry at him*).   Don't say those things to him! Enough to be happy right here, right now. (*To* WILLY, *while* BEN *laughs*) Why must everybody conquer the world? You're well liked, and the boys love you, and someday—(*to* BEN)—why, old man Wagner told him just the other day that if he keeps it up he'll be a member of the firm, didn't he, Willy?

WILLY.   Sure, sure. I am building something with this firm, Ben, and if a man is building something he must be on the right track, mustn't he?

BEN.   What are you building? Lay your hand on it. Where is it?

WILLY (*hesitantly*).   That's true, Linda, there's nothing.

LINDA.   Why? (*To* BEN) There's a man eighty-four years old—

WILLY.   That's right, Ben, that's right. When I look at that man I say, what is there to worry about?

BEN.   Bah!

WILLY.   It's true, Ben. All he has to do is go into any city, pick up the phone, and he's making his living and you know why?

BEN (*picking up his valise*).   I've got to go.

WILLY (*holding* BEN *back*).   Look at this boy! (BIFF, *in his high-school sweater, enters carrying suitcase.* HAPPY *carries* BIFF's *shoulder guards, gold helmet, and football pants.*) Without a penny to his name, three great universities are begging for him, and from there the sky's the limit, because it's not what you do, Ben. It's who you know and the smile on your face! It's contacts, Ben, contacts! The whole wealth of Alaska passes over the lunch table at the Commodore Hotel, and that's the wonder, the wonder of this country, that a man can end with diamonds here on the basis of being liked! (*He turns to* BIFF.) And that's why when you get out on that field today, it's important. Because thousands of people will be rooting for you and loving you. (*To* BEN, *who has again begun to leave*) And Ben! when he walks into a business office his name will sound out like a bell and all the doors will open to him! I've seen it, Ben, I've seen it a thousand times! You can't feel it with your hand like timber, but it's there!

BEN.   Good-by, William.

WILLY.   Ben, am I right? Don't you think I'm right? I value your advice.

BEN.   There's a new continent at your doorstep, William. You could walk out rich. Rich! (*He is gone.*)

WILLY.   We'll do it here, Ben! You hear me? We're gonna do it here! (YOUNG BERNARD *rushes in. The gay music of the* BOYS *is heard.*)

BERNARD.   Oh, gee, I was afraid you left already!

WILLY.   Why? What time is it?

BERNARD.   It's half-past one!

WILLY.   Well, come on, everybody! Ebbets Field next stop! Where's the pennants? (*He rushes through the wall-line of the kitchen and out into the living-room.*)

LINDA (*to* BIFF).   Did you pack fresh underwear?

BIFF (*who has been limbering up*).   I want to go!

BERNARD.   Biff, I'm carrying your helmet, ain't I?

HAPPY.   No, I'm carrying the helmet.

BERNARD.   Oh, Biff, you promised me.

HAPPY.   I'm carrying the helmet.

BERNARD.   How am I going to get in the locker room?

LINDA.   Let him carry the shoulder guards. (*She puts her coat and hat on in the kitchen.*)

BERNARD.   Can I, Biff? 'Cause I told everybody I'm going to be in the locker room.

HAPPY.   In Ebbets Field it's the clubhouse.

BERNARD.   I meant the clubhouse, Biff!

HAPPY.   Biff!

BIFF (*grandly, after a slight pause*).   Let him carry the shoulder guards.

HAPPY (*as he gives* BERNARD *the shoulder guards*).   Stay close to us now. (WILLY *rushes in with the pennants.*)

WILLY (*handing them out*).   Everybody wave when Biff comes out on the field. (HAPPY *and* BERNARD *run off.*) You set now, boy? (*The music has died away.*)

BIFF.   Ready to go, Pop. Every muscle is ready.

WILLY (*at the edge of the apron*).   You realize what this means?

BIFF.   That's right, Pop.

WILLY (*feeling* BIFF's *muscles*).   You're comin' home this afternoon captain of the All-Scholastic Championship Team of the City of New York.

BIFF.   I got it, Pop. And remember, pal, when I take off my helmet, that touchdown is for you.

WILLY.   Let's go! (*He is starting out, with his arms around* BIFF, *when* CHARLEY *enters, as of old, in knickers.*) I got no room for you, Charley.

CHARLEY.   Room? For what?

WILLY.   In the car.

CHARLEY.   You goin' for a ride? I wanted to shoot some casino.

WILLY (*furiously*).   Casino! (*Incredulously*) Don't you realize what today is?

LINDA.   Oh, he knows, Willy. He's just kidding you.

WILLY.   That's nothing to kid about!

CHARLEY.   No, Linda, what's goin' on?

LINDA.   He's playing in Ebbets Field.

CHARLEY.   Baseball in this weather?

WILLY.   Don't talk to him. Come on, come on! (*He is pushing them out.*)

CHARLEY.   Wait a minute, didn't you hear the news?

WILLY.   What?

CHARLEY.   Don't you listen to the radio? Ebbets Field just blew up.

WILLY.   You go to hell! (CHARLEY *laughs. Pushing them out*) Come on, come on! We're late.

CHARLEY (*as they go*).   Knock a homer, Biff, knock a homer!

WILLY (*the last to leave, turning to* CHARLEY).   This is the greatest day of his life.

CHARLEY.   Willy, when are you going to grow up?

WILLY.   Yeah, heh? When this game is over, Charley, you'll be laughing out the other side of your face. They'll be calling him another Red Grange.° Twenty-five thousand a year.

CHARLEY (*kidding*).   Is that so?

WILLY.   Yeah, that's so.

CHARLEY.   Well, then, I'm sorry, Willy. But tell me something.

WILLY.   What?

CHARLEY.   Who is Red Grange?

WILLY.   Put up your hands. Goddam you, put up your hands! (CHARLEY, *chuckling, shakes his head and walks away, around the left corner of the stage.* WILLY *follows him. The music rises to a mocking frenzy.*) Who the hell do you think you are, better than anybody else? You don't know everything, you big, ignorant, stupid . . . Put up your hands!

(*Light rises, on the right side of the forestage, on a small table in the reception room of* CHARLEY's *office. Traffic sounds are heard.* BERNARD, *now mature, sits whistling to himself. A pair of tennis rackets and an overnight bag are on the floor beside him.*)

WILLY (*offstage*).   What are you walking away for? Don't walk away! If you're going to say something say it to my face! I know you laugh at me behind my back. You'll laugh out of the other side of your goddam face after this game. Touchdown! Touchdown! Eighty thousand people! Touchdown! Right between the goal posts.

(BERNARD *is a quiet, earnest, but self-assured young man.* WILLY's *voice is coming from right upstage now.* BERNARD *lowers his feet off the table and listens.* JENNY, *his father's secretary, enters.*)

JENNY (*distressed*).   Say, Bernard, will you go out in the hall?

BERNARD.   What is that noise? Who is it?

Red Grange: famous All-American running back at the University of Illinois (1923–1925)

JENNY.   Mr. Loman. He just got off the elevator.

BERNARD (*getting up*).   Who's he arguing with?

JENNY.   Nobody. There's nobody with him. I can't deal with him any more, and your father gets all upset everytime he comes. I've got a lot of typing to do, and your father's waiting to sign it. Will you see him?

WILLY (*entering*).   Touchdown! Touch—(*He sees* JENNY.) Jenny, Jenny, good to see you. How're ya? Workin'? Or still honest?

JENNY.   Fine. How've you been feeling?

WILLY.   Not much any more, Jenny. Ha, Ha! (*He is surprised to see the rackets.*)

BERNARD.   Hello, Uncle Willy.

WILLY (*almost shocked*).   Bernard! Well, look who's here! (*He comes quickly, guiltily, to* BERNARD *and warmly shakes his hand.*)

BERNARD.   How are you? Good to see you.

WILLY.   What are you doing here?

BERNARD.   Oh, just stopped by to see Pop. Get off my feet till my train leaves. I'm going to Washington in a few minutes.

WILLY.   Is he in?

BERNARD.   Yes, he's in his office with the accountant. Sit down.

WILLY (*sitting down*).   What're you going to do in Washington?

BERNARD.   Oh, just a case I've got there, Willy.

WILLY.   That so? (*Indicating the rackets*) You going to play tennis there?

BERNARD.   I'm staying with a friend who's got a court.

WILLY.   Don't say. His own tennis court. Must be fine people, I bet.

BERNARD.   They are, very nice. Dad tells me Biff's in town.

WILLY (*with a big smile*).   Yeah, Biff's in. Working on a very big deal, Bernard.

BERNARD.   What's Biff doing?

WILLY.   Well, he's been doing very big things in the West. But he decided to establish himself here. Very big. We're having dinner. Did I hear your wife had a boy?

BERNARD.   That's right. Our second.

WILLY.   Two boys! What do you know!

BERNARD.   What kind of deal has Biff got?

WILLY.   Well, Bill Oliver—very big sporting goods man—he wants Biff very badly. Called him in from the West. Long distance, carte blanche, special deliveries. Your friends have their own private tennis court?

BERNARD.   You still with the old firm, Willy?

WILLY (*after a pause*).   I'm—I'm overjoyed to see how you made the grade, Bernard, overjoyed. It's an encouraging thing to see a young man really—really—Looks very good for Biff—very—(*He breaks off, then*) Bernard—(*He is so full of emotion, he breaks off again.*)

BERNARD.   What is it, Willy?

WILLY (*small and alone*).   What—what's the secret?

BERNARD.   What secret?

WILLY.   How—how did you? Why didn't he ever catch on?

BERNARD.   I wouldn't know that, Willy.

WILLY (*confidentially, desperately*).   You were his friend, his boyhood friend. There's something I don't understand about it. His life ended after that Ebbets Field game. From the age of seventeen nothing good ever happened to him.

BERNARD.   He never trained himself for anything?

WILLY.   But he did, he did. After high school he took so many correspondence courses. Radio mechanics; television; God knows what, and never made the slightest mark.

BERNARD (*taking off his glasses*).   Willy, do you want to talk candidly?

WILLY (*rising, faces* BERNARD).   I regard you as a very brilliant man, Bernard. I value your advice.

BERNARD.   Oh, the hell with the advice, Willy. I couldn't advise you. There's just one thing I've always wanted to ask you. When he was supposed to graduate, and the math teacher flunked him—

WILLY.   Oh, that son-of-a-bitch ruined his life.

BERNARD.   Yeah, but, Willy, all he had to do was go to summer school and make up that subject.

WILLY.   That's right, that's right.

BERNARD.   Did you tell him not to go to summer school?

WILLY.   Me? I begged him to go. I ordered him to go!

BERNARD.   Then why wouldn't he go?

WILLY.   Why? Why! Bernard, that question has been trailing me like a ghost for the last fifteen years. He flunked the subject, and laid down and died like a hammer hit him!

BERNARD.   Take it easy, kid.

WILLY.   Let me talk to you—I got nobody to talk to. Bernard, Bernard, was it my fault? Y'see? It keeps going around in my mind, maybe I did something to him. I got nothing to give him.

BERNARD.   Don't take it so hard.

WILLY.   Why did he lay down? What is the story there? You were his friend!

BERNARD.   Willy, I remember, it was June, and our grades came out. And he'd flunked math.

WILLY.   That son-of-a-bitch!

BERNARD.   No, it wasn't right then. Biff just got very angry, I remember, and he was ready to enroll in summer school.

WILLY (*surprised*).   He was?

BERNARD.   He wasn't beaten by it at all. But then, Willy, he disappeared from the block for almost a month. And I got the idea that he'd gone up to New England to see you. Did he have a talk with you then? (WILLY *stares in silence.*) Willy?

WILLY (*with a strong edge of resentment in his voice*).   Yeah, he came to Boston. What about it?

BERNARD.   Well, just that when he came back—I'll never forget this, it always mystifies me. Because I thought so well of Biff, even though he'd always taken advantage of me. I loved him. Willy, y'know? And he came back after that month and took his sneakers—remember those sneakers with "University of Virginia" printed on them? He was so proud of those, wore them every day. And he took them down in the cellar, and burned them up in the furnace. We had a fist fight. It lasted at least half an hour. Just the two of us, punching each other down the cellar, and crying right through it. I've often thought of how strange it was that I knew he'd given up his life. What happened in Boston, Willy? (WILLY *looks at him as at an intruder.*) I just bring it up because you asked me.

WILLY (*angrily*).   Nothing. What do you mean, "What happened?" What's that got to do with anything?

BERNARD.   Well, don't get sore.

WILLY.   What are you trying to do, blame it on me? If a boy lays down is that my fault?

BERNARD.   Now, Willy, don't get—

WILLY.   Well, don't—don't talk to me that way! What does that mean, "What happened?" (CHARLEY *enters. He is in his vest, and he carries a bottle of bourbon.*)

CHARLEY.   Hey, you're going to miss that train. (*He waves the bottle.*)

BERNARD.   Yeah, I'm going. (*He takes the bottle.*) Thanks, Pop. (*He picks up his rackets and bag.*) Good-by, Willy, and don't worry about it. You know, "If at first you don't succeed . . ."

WILLY.   Yes, I believe in that.

BERNARD.   But sometimes, Willy, it's better for a man just to walk away.

WILLY.   Walk away?

BERNARD.   That's right.

WILLY.   But if you can't walk away?

BERNARD (*after a slight pause*).   I guess that's when it's tough. (*Extending his hand*) Good-by, Willy.

WILLY (*shaking* BERNARD's *hand*).   Good-by, boy.

CHARLEY (*an arm on* BERNARD's *shoulder*).   How do you like this kid? Gonna argue a case in front of the Supreme Court.

BERNARD (*protesting*).   Pop!

WILLY (*genuinely shocked, pained, and happy*).   No! The Supreme Court!

BERNARD.   I gotta run. 'By Dad!

CHARLEY.   Knock 'em dead, Bernard! (BERNARD *goes off.*)

WILLY (*as* CHARLEY *takes out his wallet*).   The Supreme Court! And he didn't even mention it!

CHARLEY (*counting out money on the desk*).   He don't have to— he's gonna do it.

WILLY.   And you never told him what to do, did you? You never took any interest in him.

CHARLEY.   My salvation is that I never took any interest in anything. There's some money—fifty dollars. I got an accountant inside.

WILLY.   Charley, look . . . (*With difficulty*) I got my insurance to pay. If you can manage it—I need a hundred and ten dollars. (CHARLEY *doesn't reply for a moment; merely stops moving.*) I'd draw it from my bank but Linda would know, and I . . .

CHARLEY.   Sit down, Willy.

WILLY (*moving toward the chair*).   I'm keeping an account of everything, remember. I'll pay every penny back. (*He sits.*)

CHARLEY.   Now listen to me, Willy.

WILLY.   I want you to know I appreciate . . .

CHARLEY (*sitting down on the table*).   Willy, what're you doin'? What the hell is goin' on in your head?

WILLY.   Why? I'm simply . . .

CHARLEY.   I offered you a job. You can make fifty dollars a week. And I won't send you on the road.

WILLY.   I've got a job.

CHARLEY.   Without pay? What kind of a job is a job without pay? (*He rises.*) Now, look, kid, enough is enough. I'm no genius but I know when I'm being insulted.

WILLY.   Insulted!

CHARLEY.   Why don't you want to work for me?

WILLY.   What's the matter with you? I've got a job.

CHARLEY.   Then what're you walkin' in here every week for?

WILLY (*getting up*).   Well, if you don't want me to walk in here—

CHARLEY.   I am offering you a job.

WILLY.   I don't want your goddam job!

CHARLEY.   When the hell are you going to grow up?

WILLY (*furiously*).   You big ignoramus, if you say that to me again I'll rap you one! I don't care how big you are! (*He's ready to fight. Pause.*)

CHARLEY (*kindly, going to him*).   How much do you need, Willy?

WILLY.   Charley, I'm strapped. I'm strapped. I don't know what to do. I was just fired.

CHARLEY.   Howard fired you?

WILLY.   That snotnose. Imagine that? I named him. I named him Howard.

CHARLEY.   Willy, when're you gonna realize that them things don't mean anything? You named him Howard, but you can't sell that. The only thing you got in this world is what you can sell. And the funny thing is that you're a salesman, and you don't know that.

WILLY.   I've always tried to think otherwise, I guess. I always felt that if a man was impressive, and well liked, that nothing—

CHARLEY.   Why must everybody like you? Who liked J. P. Morgan? Was he impressive? In a Turkish bath he'd look like a butcher. But with his pockets on he was very well liked. Now listen, Willy, I know you don't like me, and nobody can say I'm in love with you, but I'll give you a job because—just for the hell of it, put it that way. Now what do you say?

WILLY.   I—I just can't work for you, Charley.

CHARLEY.   What're you, jealous of me?

WILLY.   I can't work for you, that's all, don't ask me why.

CHARLEY (*angered, takes out more bills*).   You been jealous of me all your life, you damned fool! Here, pay your insurance. (*He puts the money in* WILLY's *hand.*)

WILLY.   I'm keeping strict accounts.

CHARLEY.   I've got some work to do. Take care of yourself. And pay your insurance.

WILLY (*moving to the right*).   Funny, y'know? After all the highways, and the trains, and the appointments, and the years, you end up worth more dead than alive.

CHARLEY.   Willy, nobody's worth nothin' dead. (*After a slight pause.*) Did you hear what I said? (WILLY *stands still, dreaming.*) Willy!

WILLY.   Apologize to Bernard for me when you see him. I didn't mean to argue with him. He's a fine boy. They're all fine boys, and they'll end up big—all of them. Someday they'll all play tennis together. Wish me luck, Charley. He saw Bill Oliver today.

CHARLEY.   Good luck.

WILLY (*on the verge of tears*).   Charley, you're the only friend I got. Isn't that a remarkable thing? (*He goes out.*)

CHARLEY.   Jesus!

(CHARLEY *stares after him a moment and follows. All light blacks out. Suddenly raucous music is heard, and a red glow rises behind the screen at right.* STANLEY, *a young waiter, appears, carrying a table, followed by* HAPPY, *who is carrying two chairs.*)

STANLEY (*putting the table down*).   That's all right, Mr. Loman, I can handle it myself. (*He turns and takes the chairs from* HAPPY *and places them at the table.*)

HAPPY (*glancing around*).   Oh, this is better.

STANLEY.   Sure, in the front there you're in the middle of all kinds a noise. Whenever you got a party, Mr. Loman, you just tell me and I'll put you back here. Y'know, there's a lotta people they don't like it private, because when they go out they like to see a lotta action around them because they're sick and tired to stay in the house by theirself. But I know you, you ain't from Hackensack. You know what I mean?

HAPPY (*sitting down*).   So how's it coming, Stanley?

STANLEY.   Ah, it's a dog's life. I only wish during the war they'd a took me in the Army. I coulda been dead by now.

HAPPY.   My brother's back, Stanley.

STANLEY.   Oh, he come back, heh? From the Far West.

HAPPY.   Yeah, big cattle man, my brother, so treat him right. And my father's coming too.

STANLEY.   Oh, your father too!

HAPPY.   You got a couple of nice lobsters?

STANLEY.   Hundred per cent, big.

HAPPY.   I want them with the claws.

STANLEY.   Don't worry, I don't give you no mice. (HAPPY *laughs.*) How about some wine? It'll put a head on the meal.

HAPPY.   No. You remember, Stanley, that recipe I brought you from overseas? With the champagne in it?

STANLEY.   Oh, yeah, sure. I still got it tacked up yet in the kitchen. But that'll have to cost a buck apiece anyways.

HAPPY.   That's all right.

STANLEY.   What'd you, hit a number or somethin'?

HAPPY. No, it's a little celebration. My brother is—I think he pulled off a big deal today. I think we're going into business together.

STANLEY. Great! That's the best for you. Because a family business, you know what I mean?—that's the best.

HAPPY. That's what I think.

STANLEY. 'Cause what's the difference? Somebody steals? It's in the family. Know what I mean? (*Sotto voce*) Like this bartender here. The boss is goin' crazy what kinda leak he's got in the cash register. You put it in but it don't come out.

HAPPY (*raising his head*). Sh!

STANLEY. What?

HAPPY. You notice I wasn't lookin' right or left, was I?

STANLEY. No.

HAPPY. And my eyes are closed.

STANLEY. So what's the—?

HAPPY. Strudel's comin'.

STANLEY (*catching on, looks around*). Ah, no, there's no—(*He breaks off as a furred, lavishly dressed girl enters and sits at the next table. Both follow her with their eyes.*) Geez, how'd ya know?

HAPPY. I got radar or something. (*Staring directly at her profile*) Ooooooo . . . Stanley.

STANLEY. I think that's for you, Mr. Loman.

HAPPY. Look at that mouth. Oh, God. And the binoculars.

STANLEY. Geez, you got a life, Mr. Loman.

HAPPY. Wait on her.

STANLEY (*going to the* GIRL's *table*). Would you like a menu, ma'am?

GIRL. I'm expecting someone, but I'd like a—

HAPPY. Why don't you bring her—excuse me, miss, do you mind? I sell champagne, and I'd like you to try my brand. Bring her a champagne, Stanley.

GIRL. That's awfully nice of you.

HAPPY. Don't mention it. It's all company money. (*He laughs.*)

GIRL. That's a charming product to be selling, isn't it?

HAPPY. Oh, gets to be like everything else. Selling is selling, y'know.

GIRL. I suppose.

HAPPY. You don't happen to sell, do you?

GIRL. No, I don't sell.

HAPPY. Would you object to a compliment from a stranger? You ought to be on a magazine cover.

GIRL (*looking at him a little archly*). I have been. (STANLEY *comes in with a glass of champagne.*)

HAPPY.   What'd I say before, Stanley? You see? She's a cover girl.

STANLEY.   Oh, I could see, I could see.

HAPPY (*to the* GIRL).   What magazine?

GIRL.   Oh, a lot of them. (*She takes the drink.*) Thank you.

HAPPY.   You know what they say in France, don't you? "Champagne is the drink of the complexion"—Hya, Biff! (BIFF *has entered and sits with* HAPPY.)

BIFF.   Hello, kid. Sorry I'm late.

HAPPY.   I just got here. Uh, Miss—?

GIRL.   Forsythe.

HAPPY.   Miss Forsythe, this is my brother.

BIFF.   Is Dad here?

HAPPY.   His name is Biff. You might've heard of him. Great football player!

GIRL.   Really? What team?

HAPPY.   Are you familiar with football?

GIRL.   No, I'm afraid I'm not.

HAPPY.   Biff is quarterback with the New York Giants.

GIRL.   Well, that is nice, isn't it? (*She drinks.*)

HAPPY.   Good health.

GIRL.   I'm happy to meet you.

HAPPY.   That's my name. Hap. It's really Harold, but at West Point they called me Happy.

GIRL (*now really impressed*).   Oh, I see. How do you do? (*She turns her profile.*)

BIFF.   Isn't Dad coming?

HAPPY.   You want her?

BIFF.   Oh, I could never make that.

HAPPY.   I remember the time that idea would never come into your head. Where's the old confidence, Biff?

BIFF.   I just saw Oliver—

HAPPY.   Wait a minute. I've got to see that old confidence again. Do you want her? She's on call.

BIFF.   Oh, no. (*He turns to look at the* GIRL.)

HAPPY.   I'm telling you. Watch this. (*Turning to the* GIRL) Honey? (*She turns to him.*) Are you busy?

GIRL.   Well, I am . . . but I could make a phone call.

HAPPY.   Do that, will you, honey? And see if you can get a friend. We'll be here for a while. Biff is one of the greatest football players in the country.

GIRL (*standing up*).   Well, I'm certainly happy to meet you.

HAPPY.   Come back soon.

GIRL.   I'll try.

HAPPY.   Don't try, honey, try hard. (*The* GIRL *exits.* STANLEY *follows, shaking his head in bewildered admiration.*) Isn't that a shame now? A beautiful girl like that? That's why I can't get married. There's not a good woman in a thousand. New York is loaded with them, kid!

BIFF.   Hap, look—

HAPPY.   I told you she was on call!

BIFF (*strangely unnerved*).   Cut it out, will ya? I want to say something to you.

HAPPY.   Did you see Oliver?

BIFF.   I saw him all right. Now look, I want to tell Dad a couple of things and I want you to help me.

HAPPY.   What? Is he going to back you?

BIFF.   Are you crazy? You're out of your goddam head, you know that?

HAPPY.   Why? What happened?

BIFF (*breathlessly*).   I did a terrible thing today, Hap. It's been the strangest day I ever went through. I'm all numb, I swear.

HAPPY.   You mean he wouldn't see you?

BIFF.   Well, I waited for six hours for him, see? All day. Kept sending my name in. Even tried to date his secretary so she'd get me to him, but no soap.

HAPPY.   Because you're not showin' the old confidence, Biff. He remembered you, didn't he?

BIFF (*stopping* HAPPY *with a gesture*).   Finally, about five o'clock, he comes out. Didn't remember who I was or anything. I felt like such an idiot, Hap.

HAPPY.   Did you tell him my Florida idea?

BIFF.   He walked away. I saw him for one minute. I got so mad I could've torn the walls down! How the hell did I ever get the idea I was a salesman there? I even believed myself that I'd been a salesman for him! And then he gave me one look and—I realized what a ridiculous lie my whole life has been! We've been talking in a dream for fifteen years. I was a shipping clerk.

HAPPY.   What'd you do?

BIFF (*with great tension and wonder*).   Well, he left, see. And the secretary went out. I was all alone in the waiting-room. I don't know what came over me, Hap. The next thing I know I'm in his office— paneled walls, everything. I can't explain it. I—Hap, I took his fountain pen.

HAPPY.   Geez, did he catch you?

BIFF.   I ran out. I ran down all eleven flights. I ran and ran and ran.

HAPPY.   That was an awful dumb—what'd you do that for?

BIFF (*agonized*).   I don't know, I just—wanted to take something, I don't know. You gotta help me, Hap, I'm gonna tell Pop.

HAPPY.   You crazy? What for?

BIFF.   Hap, he's got to understand that I'm not the man somebody lends that kind of money to. He thinks I've been spiting him all these years and it's eating him up.

HAPPY.   That's just it. You tell him something nice.

BIFF.   I can't.

HAPPY.   Say you got a lunch date with Oliver tomorrow.

BIFF.   So what do I do tomorrow?

HAPPY.   You leave the house tomorrow and come back at night and say Oliver is thinking it over. And he thinks it over for a couple of weeks, and gradually it fades away and nobody's the worse.

BIFF.   But it'll go on forever!

HAPPY.   Dad is never so happy as when he's looking forward to something! (WILLY *enters.*) Hello, scout!

WILLY.   Gee, I haven't been here in years! (STANLEY *has followed* WILLY *in and sets a chair for him.* STANLEY *starts off but* HAPPY *stops him.*)

HAPPY.   Stanley! (STANLEY *stands by, waiting for an order.*)

BIFF (*going to* WILLY *with guilt, as to an invalid*).   Sit down, Pop. You want a drink?

WILLY.   Sure, I don't mind.

BIFF.   Let's get a load on.

WILLY.   You look worried.

BIFF.   N-no. (*To* STANLEY) Scotch all around. Make it doubles.

STANLEY.   Doubles, right. (*He goes.*)

WILLY.   You had a couple already, didn't you?

BIFF.   Just a couple, yeah.

WILLY.   Well, what happened, boy? (*Nodding affirmatively, with a smile*) Everything go all right?

BIFF (*takes a breath, then reaches out and grasps* WILLY'*s hand*).   Pal . . . (*He is smiling bravely, and* WILLY *is smiling too.*) I had an experience today.

HAPPY.   Terrific, Pop.

WILLY.   That so? What happened?

BIFF (*high, slightly alcoholic, above the earth*).   I'm going to tell you everything from first to last. It's been a strange day. (*Silence. He looks around, composes himself as best he can, but his breath keeps breaking the rhythm of his voice.*) I had to wait quite a while for him, and—

WILLY.   Oliver?

BIFF.   Yeah, Oliver. All day, as a matter of cold fact. And a lot of —instances—facts, Pop, facts about my life came back to me. Who was it, Pop? Who ever said I was a salesman with Oliver?

WILLY.   Well, you were.

BIFF.   No, Dad, I was a shipping clerk.

WILLY.   But you were practically—

BIFF (*with determination*).   Dad, I don't know who said it first, but I was never a salesman for Bill Oliver.

WILLY.   What're you talking about?

BIFF.   Let's hold on to the facts tonight, Pop. We're not going to get anywhere bullin' around. I was a shipping clerk.

WILLY (*angrily*).   All right, now listen to me—

BIFF.   Why don't you let me finish?

WILLY.   I'm not interested in stories about the past or any crap of that kind because the woods are burning, boys, you understand? There's a big blaze going on all around. I was fired today.

BIFF (*shocked*).   How could you be?

WILLY.   I was fired, and I'm looking for a little good news to tell your mother, because the woman has waited and the woman has suffered. The gist of it is that I haven't got a story left in my head, Biff. So don't give me a lecture about facts and aspects. I am not interested. Now what've you got to say to me? (STANLEY *enters with three drinks. They wait until he leaves.*) Did you see Oliver?

BIFF.   Jesus, Dad!

WILLY.   You mean you didn't go up there?

HAPPY.   Sure he went up there.

BIFF.   I did. I—saw him. How could they fire you?

WILLY (*on the edge of his chair*).   What kind of a welcome did he give you?

BIFF.   He won't even let you work on commission?

WILLY.   I'm out! (*Driving*) So tell me, he gave you a warm welcome?

HAPPY.   Sure, Pop, sure!

BIFF (*driven*).   Well, it was kind of—

WILLY.   I was wondering if he'd remember you. (*To* HAPPY) Imagine, man doesn't see him for ten, twelve years and gives him that kind of a welcome!

HAPPY.   Damn right!

BIFF (*trying to return to the offensive*).   Pop look—

WILLY.   You know why he remembered you, don't you? Because you impressed him in those days.

BIFF.   Let's talk quietly and get this down to the facts, huh?

WILLY (*as though* BIFF *had been interrupting*).   Well, what happened? It's great news, Biff. Did he take you into his office or'd you talk in the waiting-room?

BIFF.   Well, he came in, see, and—

WILLY (*with a big smile*).   What'd he say? Betcha he threw his arm around you.

BIFF.   Well, he kinda—

WILLY.   He's a fine man. (*To* HAPPY) Very hard man to see, y'know.

HAPPY (*agreeing*).   Oh, I know.

WILLY (*to* BIFF).   Is that where you had the drinks?

BIFF.   Yeah, he gave me a couple of—no, no!

HAPPY (*cutting in*).   He told him my Florida idea.

WILLY.   Don't interrupt. (*To* BIFF) How'd he react to the Florida idea?

BIFF.   Dad, will you give me a minute to explain?

WILLY.   I've been waiting for you to explain since I sat down here! What happened? He took you into his office and what?

BIFF.   Well—I talked. And—and he listened, see?

WILLY.   Famous for the way he listens, y'know. What was his answer?

BIFF.   His answer was—(*He breaks off, suddenly angry.*) Dad, you're not letting me tell you what I want to tell you!

WILLY (*accusing, angered*).   You didn't see him, did you?

BIFF.   I did see him!

WILLY.   What'd you insult him or something? You insulted him, didn't you?

BIFF.   Listen, will you let me out of it, will you just let me out of it!

HAPPY.   What the hell!

WILLY.   Tell me what happened!

BIFF (*to* HAPPY).   I can't talk to him!

(*A single trumpet note jars the ear. The light of green leaves stains the house, which holds the air of night and a dream.* YOUNG BERNARD *enters and knocks on the door of the house.*)

YOUNG BERNARD (*frantically*).   Mrs. Loman, Mrs. Loman!

HAPPY.   Tell him what happened!

BIFF (*to* HAPPY).   Shut up and leave me alone!

WILLY.   No, no! You had to go and flunk math!

BIFF.   What math? What're you talking about?

YOUNG BERNARD.   Mrs. Loman, Mrs. Loman! (LINDA *appears in the house, as of old.*)

WILLY (*wildly*).   Math, math, math!

BIFF.   Take it easy, Pop!

YOUNG BERNARD.   Mrs. Loman!

WILLY (*furiously*).   If you hadn't flunked you'd've been set by now!

BIFF.   Now, look, I'm gonna tell you what happened, and you're going to listen to me.

YOUNG BERNARD.   Mrs. Loman!

BIFF.   I waited six hours—

HAPPY.   What the hell are you saying?

BIFF.   I kept sending in my name but he wouldn't see me. So finally he . . . (*He continues unheard as light fades low on the restaurant.*)

YOUNG BERNARD.   Biff flunked math!

LINDA.   No!

YOUNG BERNARD.   Birnbaum flunked him! They won't graduate him!

LINDA.   But they have to. He's gotta go to the university. Where is he? Biff! Biff!

YOUNG BERNARD.   No, he left. He went to Grand Central?

LINDA.   Grand— You mean he went to Boston!

YOUNG BERNARD.   Is Uncle Willy in Boston?

LINDA.   Oh, maybe Willy can talk to the teacher. Oh, the poor, poor boy! (*Light on house area snaps out.*)

BIFF (*at the table, now audible, holding up a gold fountain pen*)   . . . so I'm washed up with Oliver, you understand? Are you listening to me?

WILLY (*at a loss*).   Yeah, sure. If you hadn't flunked—

BIFF.   Flunked what? What're you talking about?

WILLY.   Don't blame everything on me! I didn't flunk math—you did! What pen?

HAPPY.   That was awful dumb, Biff, a pen like that is worth—

WILLY (*seeing the pen for the first time*).   You took Oliver's pen?

BIFF (*weakening*).   Dad, I just explained it to you.

WILLY.   You stole Bill Oliver's fountain pen!

BIFF.   I didn't exactly steal it! That's just what I've been explaining to you!

HAPPY.   He had it in his hand and just then Oliver walked in, so he got nervous and stuck it in his pocket!

WILLY.   My God, Biff!

BIFF.   I never intended to do it, Dad!

OPERATOR'S VOICE.   Standish Arms, good evening!

WILLY (*shouting*).   I'm not in my room!

BIFF (*frightened*).   Dad, what's the matter? (*He and* HAPPY *stand up.*)

OPERATOR.   Ringing Mr. Loman for you!

WILLY.   I'm not there, stop it!

BIFF (*horrified, gets down on one knee before* WILLY).   Dad, I'll make good, I'll make good. (WILLY *tries to get to his feet.* BIFF *holds him down.*) Sit down now.

WILLY.   No, you're no good, you're no good for anything.

BIFF.   I am, Dad, I'll find something else, you understand? Now don't worry about anything. (*He holds up* WILLY'S *face.*) Talk to me, Dad.

OPERATOR.   Mr. Loman does not answer. Shall I page him?

WILLY (*attempting to stand, as though to rush and silence the* OPERATOR).   No, no, no!

HAPPY.   He'll strike something, Pop.

WILLY.   No, no . . .

BIFF (*desperately, standing over* WILLY).   Pop, listen! Listen to me! I'm telling you something good. Oliver talked to his partner about the Florida idea. You listening? He—he talked to his partner, and he came to me . . . I'm going to be all right, you hear? Dad, listen to me, he said it was just a question of the amount!

WILLY.   Then you . . . got it?

HAPPY.   He's gonna be terrific, Pop!

WILLY (*trying to stand*).   Then you got it, haven't you? You got it! You got it!

BIFF (*agonized, holds* WILLY *down*).   No, no. Look, Pop. I'm supposed to have lunch with them tomorrow. I'm just telling you this so you'll know that I can still make an impression, Pop. And I'll make good somewhere, but I can't go tomorrow, see?

WILLY.   Why not? You simply—

BIFF.   But the pen, Pop!

WILLY.   You give it to him and tell him it was an oversight!

HAPPY.   Sure, have lunch tomorrow!

BIFF.   I can't say that—

WILLY.   You were doing a crossword puzzle and accidentally used his pen!

BIFF.   Listen, kid, I took those balls years ago, now I walk in with his fountain pen? That clinches it, don't you see? I can't face him like that! I'll try elsewhere.

PAGE'S VOICE.   Paging Mr. Loman!

WILLY.   Don't you want to be anything?

BIFF.   Pop, how can I go back?

WILLY.   You don't want to be anything, is that what's behind it?

BIFF (*now angry at* WILLY *for not crediting his sympathy*).   Don't take it that way! You think it was easy walking into that office after what I'd done to him? A team of horses couldn't have dragged me back to Bill Oliver!

WILLY.   Then why'd you go?

BIFF.   Why did I go? Why did I go! Look at you! Look at what's become of you! (*Off left,* THE WOMAN *laughs.*)

WILLY.   Biff, you're going to go to that lunch tomorrow, or—

BIFF.   I can't go. I've got no appointment!

HAPPY.   Biff, for . . . !

WILLY.   Are you spiting me?

BIFF.   Don't take it that way! Goddammit!

WILLY (*strikes* BIFF *and falters away from the table*).   You rotten little louse! Are you spiting me?

THE WOMAN.   Someone's at the door, Willy!

BIFF.   I'm no good, can't you see what I am?

HAPPY (*separating them*).   Hey, you're in a restaurant! Now cut it out, both of you! (*The* GIRLS *enter.*) Hello, girls, sit down. (THE WOMAN *laughs, off left.*)

MISS FORSYTHE.   I guess we might as well. This is Letta.

THE WOMAN.   Willy, are you going to wake up?

BIFF (*ignoring* WILLY).   How're ya, miss, sit down. What do you drink?

MISS FORSYTHE.   Letta might not be able to stay long.

LETTA.   I gotta get up very early tomorrow. I got jury duty. I'm so excited! Were you fellows ever on a jury?

BIFF.   No, but I been in front of them! (*The* GIRLS *laugh.*) This is my father.

LETTA.   Isn't he cute? Sit down with us, Pop.

HAPPY.   Sit him down, Biff!

BIFF (*going to him*).   Come on, slugger, drink us under the table. To hell with it! Come on, sit down, pal. (*On* BIFF's *last insistence,* WILLY *is about to sit.*)

THE WOMAN (*now urgently*).   Willy, are you going to answer the door! (THE WOMAN's *call puts* WILLY *back. He starts right, befuddled.*)

BIFF.   Hey, where are you going?

WILLY.   Open the door.

BIFF.   The door?

WILLY.   The washroom . . . the door . . . where's the door?

BIFF (*leading* WILLY *to the left*).   Just go straight down. (WILLY *moves left.*)

THE WOMAN.   Willy, Willy, are you going to get up, get up, get up, get up? (WILLY *exits left.*)

LETTA.   I think it's sweet you bring your daddy along.

MISS FORSYTHE.   Oh, he isn't really your father!

BIFF (*at left, turning to her resentfully*).   Miss Forsythe, you've just seen a prince walk by. A fine, troubled prince. A hard-working, unappreciated prince. A pal, you understand? A good companion. Always for his boys.

LETTA.   That's so sweet.

HAPPY.   Well, girls, what's the program? We're wasting time. Come on, Biff. Gather round. Where would you like to go?

BIFF.   Why don't you do something for him?

HAPPY.   Me!

BIFF.   Don't you give a damn for him, Hap?

HAPPY.   What're you talking about? I'm the one who—

BIFF.   I sense it, you don't give a good goddam about him. (*He takes the rolled-up hose from his pocket and puts it on the table in front of* HAPPY.) Look what I found in the cellar, for Christ's sake. How can you bear to let it go on?

HAPPY.   Me? Who goes away? Who runs off and—

BIFF.   Yeah, but he doesn't mean anything to you. You could help him—I can't! Don't you understand what I'm talking about? He's going to kill himself, don't you know that?

HAPPY.   Don't I know it! Me!

BIFF.   Hap, help him! Jesus . . . help him . . . Help me, help me, I can't bear to look at his face! (*Ready to weep, he hurries out, up right.*)

HAPPY (*starting after him*).   Where are you going?

MISS FORSYTHE.   What's he so mad about?

HAPPY.   Come on, girls, we'll catch up with him.

MISS FORSYTHE (*as* HAPPY *pushes her out*).   Say, I don't like that temper of his!

HAPPY.   He's just a little overstrung, he'll be all right!

WILLY (*off left, as* THE WOMAN *laughs*).   Don't answer! Don't answer!

LETTA.   Don't you want to tell your father—

HAPPY.   No, that's not my father. He's just a guy. Come on, we'll catch Biff, and, honey, we're going to paint this town! Stanley, where's the check! Hey, Stanley! (*They exit,* STANLEY *looks toward left.*)

STANLEY (*calling to* HAPPY *indignantly*).   Mr. Loman! Mr. Loman! (STANLEY *picks up a chair and follows them off. Knocking is heard off left.* THE WOMAN *enters, laughing.* WILLY *follows her. She is in a black slip; he is buttoning his shirt. Raw, sensuous music accompanies their speech.*)

WILLY.   Will you stop laughing? Will you stop?

THE WOMAN.   Aren't you going to answer the door? He'll wake the whole hotel.

WILLY.   I'm not expecting anybody.

THE WOMAN.   Whyn't you have another drink, honey, and stop being so damn self-centered.

WILLY.   I'm so lonely.

THE WOMAN.   You know you ruined me, Willy? From now on, whenever you come to the office, I'll see that you go right through to the buyers. No waiting at my desk any more, Willy. You ruined me.

WILLY.   That's nice of you to say that.

THE WOMAN.   Gee, you are self-centered! Why so sad? You are the saddest, self-centeredest soul I ever did see-saw. (*She laughs. He kisses her.*) Come on inside, drummer boy. It's silly to be dressing in the middle of the night. (*As knocking is heard*) Aren't you going to answer the door?

WILLY.   They're knocking on the wrong door.

THE WOMAN.   But I felt the knocking. And he heard us talking in here. Maybe the hotel's on fire!

WILLY (*his terror rising*).   It's a mistake.

THE WOMAN.   Then tell him to go away!

WILLY.   There's nobody there.

THE WOMAN.   It's getting on my nerves, Willy. There's somebody standing out there and it's getting on my nerves!

WILLY (*pushing her away from him*).   All right, stay in the bathroom here, and don't come out. I think there's a law in Massachusetts about it, so don't come out. It may be the new room clerk. He looked very mean. So don't come out. It's a mistake, there's no fire. (*The knocking is heard again. He takes a few steps away from her, and she vanishes into the wing. The light follows him, and now he is facing* YOUNG BIFF, *who carries a suitcase.* BIFF *steps toward him. The music is gone.*)

BIFF.   Why didn't you answer?

WILLY.   Biff! What are you doing in Boston?

BIFF.   Why didn't you answer? I've been knocking for five minutes, I called you on the phone—

WILLY.   I just heard you. I was in the bathroom and had the door shut. Did anything happen home?

BIFF.   Dad—I let you down.

WILLY.   What do you mean?

BIFF.   Dad . . .

WILLY.   Biffo, what's this about? (*Putting his arm around* BIFF) Come on, let's go downstairs and get you a malted.

BIFF.   Dad, I flunked math.

WILLY.   Not for the term?

BIFF.   The term. I haven't got enough credits to graduate.

WILLY.   You mean to say Bernard wouldn't give you the answers?

BIFF.   He did, he tried, but I only got sixty-one.

WILLY.   And they wouldn't give you four points.

BIFF.   Birnbaum refused absolutely. I begged him, Pop, but he won't give me those points. You gotta talk to him before they close the school. Because if he saw the kind of man you are, and you just talked to him in your way, I'm sure he'd come through for me. The class came right before practice, see, and I didn't go enough. Would you talk to him? He'd like you, Pop. You know the way you could talk.

WILLY.   You're on. We'll drive right back.

BIFF.   Oh, Dad, good work! I'm sure he'll change it for you!

WILLY.   Go downstairs and tell the clerk I'm checkin' out. Go right down.

BIFF.   Yes, sir! See, the reason he hates me, Pop—one day he was late for class so I got up at the blackboard and imitated him. I crossed my eyes and talked with a lithp.

WILLY (*laughing*).   You did? The kids like it?

BIFF.   They nearly died laughing!

WILLY.   Yeah? What'd you do?

BIFF.   The thquare root of thixty twee is . . . (WILLY *bursts out laughing;* BIFF *joins him*). And in the middle of it he walked in! (WILLY *laughs and* THE WOMAN *joins in off-stage.*)

WILLY (*without hesitation*).   Hurry downstairs and—

BIFF.   Somebody in there?

WILLY.   No, that was next door. (THE WOMAN *laughs off-stage.*)

BIFF.   Somebody got in your bathroom!

WILLY.   No, it's the next room, there's a party.

THE WOMAN (*enters, laughing. She lisps this*).   Can I come in? There's something in the bathtub, Willy, and it's moving! (WILLY *looks at* BIFF, *who is staring open-mouthed and horrified at* THE WOMAN.)

WILLY.   Ah—you better go back to your room. They must be finished painting by now. They're painting her room so I let her take a shower here. Go back, go back . . . (*He pushes her.*)

THE WOMAN (*resisting*).   But I've got to get dressed, Willy, I can't—

WILLY.   Get out of here! Go back, go back . . . (*Suddenly striving for the ordinary*) This is Miss Francis, Biff, she's a buyer. They're painting her room. Go back, Miss Francis, go back . . .

THE WOMAN.   But my clothes, I can't go out naked in the hall!

WILLY (*pushing her off-stage*).   Get outa here! Go back, go back! (BIFF *slowly sits down on his suitcase as the argument continues off-stage.*)

THE WOMAN.   Where's my stockings? You promised me stockings, Willy!

WILLY.   I have no stockings here!

THE WOMAN.   You had two boxes of size nine sheers for me, and I want them!

WILLY.   Here, for God's sake, will you get outa here!

THE WOMAN (*enters holding a box of stockings*).   I just hope there's nobody in the hall. That's all I hope. (*To* BIFF) Are you football or baseball?

BIFF.   Football.

THE WOMAN (*angry, humiliated*).   That's me too. G'night. (*She snatches her clothes from* WILLY *and walks out.*)

WILLY (*after a pause*).   Well, better get going. I want to get to the school first thing in the morning. Get my suits out of the closet. I'll get my valise. (BIFF *doesn't move.*) What's the matter? (BIFF *remains motionless, tears falling.*) She's a buyer. Buys for J. H. Simmons. She lives down the hall—they're painting. You don't imagine—(*He breaks off. After a pause*) Now listen, pal, she's just a buyer. She sees merchandise in her room and they have to keep it looking just so . . . (*Pause. Assuming command*) All right, get my suits. (BIFF *doesn't move.*) Now stop crying and do as I say. I gave you an order. Biff, I gave you an order! Is that what you do when I give you an order? How dare you cry! (*Putting his arm around* BIFF) Now look, Biff, when you grow up you'll understand about these things. You mustn't—you mustn't overemphasize a thing like this. I'll see Birnbaum first thing in the morning.

BIFF.   Never mind.

WILLY (*getting down beside* BIFF).   Never mind! He's going to give you those points. I'll see to it.

BIFF.   He wouldn't listen to you.

WILLY.   He certainly will listen to me. You need those points for the U. of Virginia.

BIFF.   I'm not going there.

WILLY.   Heh? If I can't get him to change that mark you'll make it up in summer school. You've got all summer to—

BIFF (*his weeping breaking from him*).   Dad . . .

WILLY (*infected by it*).   Oh, my boy . . .

BIFF.   Dad . . .

WILLY.   She's nothing to me, Biff. I was lonely, I was terribly lonely.

BIFF.   You—you gave her Mama's stockings! (*His tears break through and he rises to go.*)

WILLY (*grabbing for* BIFF).   I gave you an order!

BIFF.   Don't touch me, you—liar!

WILLY.   Apologize for that!

BIFF.   You fake! You phony little fake! You fake! (*Overcome, he turns quickly and weeping fully goes out with his suitcase.* WILLY *is left on the floor on his knees.*)

WILLY.   I gave you an order! Biff, come back here or I'll beat you! Come back here! I'll whip you! (STANLEY *comes quickly in from the right and stands in front of* WILLY, *who shouts at him.*) I gave you an order . . .

STANLEY.   Hey, let's pick it up, pick it up, Mr. Loman. (*He helps* WILLY *to his feet.*) Your boys left with the chippies. They said they'll see you home. (*A second waiter watches some distance away.*)

WILLY.   But we were supposed to have dinner together. (*Music is heard,* WILLY's *theme.*)

STANLEY.   Can you make it?

WILLY.   I'll—sure. I can make it. (*Suddenly concerned about his clothes*) Do I—I look all right?

STANLEY.   Sure, you look all right. (*He flicks a speck off* WILLY's *lapel.*)

WILLY.   Here—here's a dollar.

STANLEY.   Oh, your son paid me. It's all right.

WILLY (*putting it in* STANLEY's *hand*).   No, take it. You're a good boy.

STANLEY.   Oh, no, you don't have to . . .

WILLY.   Here's some more, I don't need it any more. (*After a slight pause.*) Tell me—is there a seed store in the neighborhood?

STANLEY.   Seeds? You mean like to plant? (*As* WILLY *turns,* STANLEY *slips the money back into his jacket pocket.*)

WILLY.   Yes. Carrots, peas . . .

STANLEY.   Well, there's hardware stores on Sixth Avenue, but it may be too late now.

WILLY (*anxiously*).   Oh, I'd better hurry. I've got to get some seeds. (*He starts off to the right.*) I've got to get some seeds, right away. Nothing's planted. I don't have a thing in the ground. (WILLY *hurries out as the light goes down.* STANLEY *moves over to the right after him, watches him off. The other waiter has been staring at* WILLY.)

STANLEY (*to the waiter*).   Well, whatta you looking at?

(*The waiter picks up the chairs and moves off right.* STANLEY *takes the table and follows him. The light fades on this area. There is a long pause, the sound of the flute coming over. The light gradually rises on the kitchen, which is empty.* HAPPY *appears at the door of the house, followed by* BIFF. HAPPY *is carrying a large bunch of long-stemmed roses. He enters the kitchen, looks around for* LINDA. *Not seeing her, he turns to* BIFF, *who is just outside the house door, and makes a gesture with his hands, indicating "Not here, I guess." He looks into the living-room and freezes. Inside,* LINDA, *unseen, is seated,* WILLY's *coat on her lap. She rises ominously and quietly and moves toward* HAPPY, *who backs up into the kitchen, afraid.*)

HAPPY.   Hey, what're you doing? (LINDA *says nothing but moves toward him implacably.*) Where's Pop? (*He keeps backing to the right, and now* LINDA *is in full view of the doorway to the living-room.*) Is he sleeping?

LINDA.   Where were you?

HAPPY (*trying to laugh it off*).   We met two girls, Mom, very fine types. Here, we brought you some flowers. (*Offering them to her*) Put them in your room, Ma. (*She knocks them to the floor at* BIFF's *feet. He has now come inside and closed the door behind him. She stares at* BIFF, *silent.*) Now what'd you do that for? Mom, I want you to have some flowers—

LINDA (*cutting* HAPPY *off, violently to* BIFF).   Don't you care whether he lives or dies?

HAPPY (*going to the stairs*).   Come upstairs, Biff.

BIFF (*with a flare of disgust, to* HAPPY).   Go away from me! (*To* LINDA) What do you mean, lives or dies? Nobody's dying around here, pal.

LINDA.   Get out of my sight! Get out of here!

BIFF.   I wanna see the boss.

LINDA.   You're not to go near him!

BIFF.   Where is he? (*He moves into the living-room and* LINDA *follows.*)

LINDA (*shouting after* BIFF).   You invite him to dinner. He looks forward to it all day—(BIFF *appears in his parents' bedroom, looks around, and exits*)—and then you desert him there. There's no stranger you'd do that to!

HAPPY.   Why? He had a swell time with us. Listen, when I— (LINDA *comes back into the kitchen*)—desert him I hope I don't outlive the day!

LINDA.   Get out of here!

HAPPY.   Now look, Mom . . .

LINDA.   Did you have to go to women tonight? You and your lousy rotten whores! (BIFF *re-enters the kitchen.*)

HAPPY.   Mom, all we did was follow Biff around trying to cheer him up! (*To* BIFF) Boy, what a night you gave me!

LINDA.   Get out of here, both of you, and don't come back! I don't want you tormenting him any more. Go on now, get your things together! (*To* BIFF) You can sleep in his apartment. (*She starts to pick up the flowers and stops herself.*) Pick up this stuff, I'm not your maid any more. Pick it up, you bum, you! (HAPPY *turns his back to her in refusal.* BIFF *slowly moves over and gets down on his knees, picking up the flowers.*)

LINDA.   You're a pair of animals! Not one, not another living soul would have had the cruelty to walk out on that man in a restaurant!

BIFF (*not looking at her*).   Is that what he said?

LINDA.   He didn't have to say anything. He was so humiliated he nearly limped when he came in.

HAPPY.   But, Mom, he had a great time with us—

BIFF (*cutting him off violently*).   Shut up! (*Without another word,* HAPPY *goes upstairs.*)

LINDA.   You! You didn't even go in to see if he was all right!

BIFF (*still on the floor in front of* LINDA, *the flowers in his hand; with self-loathing*).   No. Didn't. Didn't do a damned thing. How do you like that, heh? Left him babbling in a toilet.

LINDA.   You louse. You . . .

BIFF.   Now you hit it on the nose! (*He gets up, throws the flowers in the wastebasket.*) The scum of the earth, and you're looking at him!

LINDA.   Get out of here!

BIFF.   I gotta talk to the boss, Mom. Where is he?

LINDA.   You're not going near him. Get out of this house

BIFF (*with absolute assurance, determination*).   No. We're gonna have an abrupt conversation, him and me.

LINDA.   You're not talking to him! (*Hammering is heard from outside the house, off right.* BIFF *turns toward the noise.* LINDA *is suddenly pleading.*) Will you please leave him alone?

BIFF.   What's he doing out there?

LINDA.   He's planting a garden!

BIFF (*quietly*).   Now? Oh, my God! (BIFF *moves outside,* LINDA *following. The light dies down on them and comes up on the center of the apron as* WILLY *walks into it. He is carrying a flashlight, a hoe, and a handful of seed packets. He raps the top of the hoe sharply to fix it firmly, and then moves to the left, measuring off the distance with his foot. He holds the flashlight to look at the seed packets, reading off the instructions. He is in the blue of night.*)

WILLY.   Carrots . . . quarter-inch apart. Rows . . . one-foot rows. (*He measures it off.*) One foot. (*He puts down a package and measures off.*) Beets. (*He puts down another package and measures again.*) Lettuce. (*He reads the package, puts it down.*) One foot—(*He breaks off as* BEN *appears at the right and moves slowly down to him.*) What a proposition, ts, ts. Terrific, terrific. 'Cause she suffered, Ben, the woman has suffered. You understand me? A man can't go out the way he came in. Ben, a man has got to add up to something. You can't, you can't— (BEN *moves toward him as though to interrupt.*) You gotta consider, now. Don't answer so quick. Remember, it's a guaranteed twenty-thousand-dollar proposition. Now look, Ben, I want you to go through the ins and outs of this thing with me. I've got nobody to talk to, Ben, and the woman has suffered, you hear me?

BEN (*standing still, considering*).   What's the proposition?

WILLY.   It's twenty-thousand dollars on the barrelhead. Guaranteed, gilt-edged, you understand?

BEN.   You don't want to make a fool of yourself. They might not honor the policy.

WILLY.   How can they dare refuse? Didn't I work like a coolie to meet every premium on the nose? And now they don't pay off? Impossible!

BEN.   It's called a cowardly thing, William.

WILLY.   Why? Does it take more guts to stand here the rest of my life ringing up a zero?

BEN (*yielding*).   That's a point, William. (*He moves, thinking, turns.*) And twenty-thousand—that *is* something one can feel with the hand, it is there.

WILLY (*now assured, with rising power*).   Oh, Ben, that's the whole beauty of it! I can see it like a diamond shining in the dark, hard and rough, that I can pick up and touch in my hand. Not like—like an appointment! This would not be another damned-fool appointment, Ben, and it changes all the aspects. Because he thinks I'm nothing, see, and so he spites me. But the funeral—(*Straightening up*) Ben, that funeral will be massive! They'll come from Maine, Massachusetts, Vermont, New Hampshire! All the old-timers with the strange license plates—that boy will be thunderstruck, Ben, because he never realized —I am known! Rhode Island, New York, New Jersey—I am known, Ben, and he'll see it with his eyes once and for all. He'll see what I am. He's in for a shock, that boy!

BEN (*coming down to the edge of the garden*).   He'll call you a coward.

WILLY (*suddenly fearful*).   No, that would be terrible.

BEN.   Yes. And a damned fool.

WILLY.   No, no, he mustn't, I won't have it! (*He is broken and desperate.*)

BEN.   He'll hate you, William. (*The gay music of the BOYS is heard.*)

WILLY.   Oh, Ben, how do we get back to all the great times? Used to be so full of light, and comradeship, the sleigh-riding in winter and the ruddiness of his cheeks. And always some kind of good news coming up, always something nice coming up ahead. And never let me carry the valises in the house, and simonizing, simonizing that little red car! Why, why can't I give him something and not have him hate me?

BEN.   Let me think about it. (*He glances at his watch.*) I still have a little time. Remarkable proposition, but you've got to be sure you're not making a fool of yourself. (BEN *drifts off upstage and goes out of sight.* BIFF *comes down from the left.*)

WILLY (*suddenly conscious of* BIFF, *turns and looks up at him, then begins picking up the packages of seeds in confusion*).   Where the hell is that seed? (*Indignantly*) You can't see nothing out here! They boxed in the whole goddam neighborhood!

BIFF.   There are people all around here. Don't you realize that?

WILLY.   I'm busy. Don't bother me.

BIFF (*taking the hoe from* WILLY).   I'm saying good-by to you, Pop. (WILLY *looks at him, silent, unable to move.*) I'm not coming back any more.

WILLY.   You're not going to see Oliver tomorrow?

BIFF.   I've got no appointment, Dad.

WILLY.   He put his arms around you, and you've got no appointment?

BIFF.   Pop, get this now, will you? Every time I've left it's been a fight that sent me out of here. Today I realized something about myself and I tried to explain it to you and I—I think I'm just not smart enough to make any sense out of it for you. To hell with whose fault it is or anything like that. (*He takes* WILLY's *arm.*) Let's just wrap it up, heh? Come on in, we'll tell Mom. (*He gently tries to pull* WILLY *to left.*)

WILLY (*frozen, immobile, with guilt in his voice*).   No, I don't want to see her.

BIFF.   Come on! (*He pulls again, and* WILLY *tries to pull away.*)

WILLY (*highly nervous*).   No, no, I don't want to see her.

BIFF (*tries to look into* WILLY's *face, as if to find the answer there*). Why don't you want to see her?

WILLY (*more harshly now*).   Don't bother me, will you?

BIFF.   What do you mean, you don't want to see her? You don't want them calling you yellow do you? This isn't your fault; it's me, I'm a bum. Now come inside! (WILLY *strains to get away.*) Did you hear what I said to you? (WILLY *pulls away and quickly goes by himself into the house.* BIFF *follows.*)

LINDA (*to* WILLY).   Did you plant, dear?

BIFF (*at the door, to* LINDA).   All right, we had it out. I'm going and I'm not writing any more.

LINDA (*going to* WILLY *in the kitchen*).   I think that's the best way, dear. 'Cause there's no use drawing it out, you'll just never get along. (WILLY *does not respond.*)

BIFF.   People ask where I am and what I'm doing, you don't know, and you don't care. That way it'll be off your mind and you can start brightening up again. All right? That clears it, doesn't it? (WILLY *is silent, and* BIFF *goes to him.*) You gonna wish me luck, scout? (*He extends his hand.*) What do you say?

LINDA.   Shake his hand, Willy.

WILLY (*turning to her, seething with hurt*).   There's no necessity to mention the pen at all, y'know.

BIFF (*gently*).   I've got no appointment, Dad.

WILLY (*erupting fiercely*).   He put his arm around . . . ?

BIFF.   Dad, you're never going to see what I am, so what's the use of arguing? If I strike oil I'll send you a check. Meantime forget I'm alive.

WILLY (*to* LINDA).   Spite, see?

BIFF.   Shake hands, Dad.

WILLY.   Not my hand.

BIFF.   I was hoping not to go this way.

WILLY.   Well, this is the way you're going. Good-by. (BIFF *looks at him a moment, then turns sharply and goes to the stairs.* WILLY *stops him with*) May you rot in hell if you leave this house!

BIFF (*turning*).   Exactly what is it that you want from me?

WILLY.   I want you to know, on the train, in the mountains, in the valleys, wherever you go, that you cut down your life for spite!

BIFF.   No, no.

WILLY.   Spite, spite, is the word of your undoing! And when you're down and out, remember what did it. When you're rotting somewhere beside the railroad tracks, remember, and don't you dare blame it on me!

BIFF.   I'm not blaming it on you!

WILLY.   I won't take the rap for this, you hear? (HAPPY *comes down the stairs and stands on the bottom step, watching.*)

BIFF.   That's just what I'm telling you!

WILLY (*sinking into a chair at the table, with full accusation*).   You're trying to put a knife in me—don't think I don't know what you're doing!

BIFF.   All right, phony! Then let's lay it on the line. (*He whips the rubber tube out of his pocket and puts it on the table.*)

HAPPY.   You crazy—

LINDA.   Biff! (*She moves to grab the hose, but* BIFF *holds it down with his hand.*)

BIFF.   Leave it there! Don't move it!

WILLY (*not looking at it*).   What is that?

BIFF.   You know goddam well what that is.

WILLY (*caged, wanting to escape*).   I never saw that.

BIFF.   You saw it. The mice didn't bring it into the cellar! What is this supposed to do, make a hero out of you? This supposed to make me sorry for you?

WILLY.   Never heard of it.

BIFF.   There'll be no pity for you, you hear it? No pity!

WILLY (*to* LINDA).   You hear the spite!

BIFF.   No, you're going to hear the truth—what you are and what I am!

LINDA.   Stop it!

WILLY.   Spite!

HAPPY (*coming down toward* BIFF).   You cut it out now!

BIFF (*to* HAPPY).   The man don't know who we are! The man is gonna know! (*To* WILLY) We never told the truth for ten minutes in this house!

HAPPY.   We always told the truth!

BIFF (*turning on him*).   You big blow, are you the assistant buyer? You're one of two assistants to the assistant, aren't you?

HAPPY.   Well, I'm practically—

BIFF.   You're practically full of it! We all are! And I'm through with it. (*To* WILLY) Now hear this, Willy, this is me.

WILLY.   I know you!

BIFF.   You know why I had no address for three months? I stole a suit in Kansas City and I was in jail. (*To* LINDA, *who is sobbing*) Stop crying. I'm through with it. (LINDA *turns away from them, her hands covering her face.*)

WILLY.   I suppose that's my fault!

BIFF.   I stole myself out of every job since high school!

WILLY.   And whose fault is that?

BIFF.   And I never got anywhere because you blew me so full of hot air I could never stand taking orders from anybody! That's whose fault it is!

WILLY.   I hear that!

LINDA.   Don't, Biff!

BIFF.   It's goddam time you heard that! I had to be boss big shot in two weeks, and I'm through with it!

WILLY.   Then hang yourself! For spite, hang yourself!

BIFF.   No! Nobody's hanging himself, Willy! I ran down eleven flights with a pen in my hand today. And suddenly I stopped, you hear me? And in the middle of that office building, do you hear this? I stopped in the middle of that building and I saw—the sky. I saw the things that I love in this world. The work and the food and time to sit and smoke. And I looked at the pen and said to myself, what the hell am I grabbing this for? Why am I trying to become what I don't want to be? What am I doing in an office, making a contemptuous, begging fool of myself, when all I want is out there, waiting for me the minute I say I know who I am! Why can't I say that, Willy? (*He tries to make* WILLY *face him, but* WILLY *pulls away and moves to the left.*)

WILLY (*with hatred, threateningly*).   The door of your life is wide open!

BIFF.   Pop! I'm a dime a dozen, and so are you!

WILLY (*turning on him now in an uncontrolled outburst*).   I am not a dime a dozen! I am Willy Loman, and you are Biff Loman! (BIFF *starts for* WILLY, *but is blocked by* HAPPY. *In his fury,* BIFF *seems on the verge of attacking his father.*)

BIFF.   I am not a leader of men, Willy, and neither are you. You were never anything but a hard-working drummer who landed in the ash can like all the rest of them! I'm one dollar an hour, Willy! I tried seven states and couldn't raise it. A buck an hour! Do you gather my meaning? I'm not bringing home any prizes any more, and you're going to stop waiting for me to bring them home!

WILLY (*directly to* BIFF).   You vengeful, spiteful mutt! (BIFF *breaks from* HAPPY. WILLY, *in fright, starts up the stairs.* BIFF *grabs him.*)

BIFF (*at the peak of his fury*).   Pop, I'm nothing! I'm nothing, Pop. Can't you understand that? There's no spite in it any more. I'm just what I am, that's all. (BIFF's *fury has spent itself, and he breaks down, sobbing, holding on to* WILLY, *who dumbly fumbles for* BIFF's *face.*)

WILLY (*astonished*).   What're you doing? What're you doing? (*To* LINDA) Why is he crying?

BIFF (*crying, broken*).   Will you let me go, for Christ's sake? Will you take that phony dream and burn it before something happens? (*Struggling to contain himself, he pulls away and moves to the stairs.*) I'll go in the morning. Put him—put him to bed. (*Exhausted,* BIFF *moves up the stairs to his room.*)

WILLY (*after a long pause, astonished, elevated*).   Isn't that—isn't that remarkable? Biff—he likes me!

LINDA.   He loves you, Willy!

HAPPY (*deeply moved*).   Always did, Pop.

WILLY.   Oh, Biff! (*Staring wildly*) He cried! Cried to me. (*He is choking with his love, and now cries out his promise.*) That boy—that boy is going to be magnificent! (BEN *appears in the light just outside the kitchen.*)

BEN.   Yes, outstanding, with twenty thousand behind him.

LINDA (*sensing the racing of his mind, fearfully, carefully*).   Now come to bed, Willy. It's all settled now.

WILLY (*finding it difficult not to rush out of the house*).   Yes, we'll sleep. Come on. Go to sleep, Hap.

BEN.   And it does take a great kind of man to crack the jungle. (*In accents of dread,* BEN's *idyllic music starts up.*)

HAPPY (*his arm around* LINDA).   I'm getting married, Pop, don't forget it. I'm changing everything. I'm gonna run that department before the year is up. You'll see, Mom. (*He kisses her.*)

BEN.   The jungle is dark but full of diamonds, Willy. (WILLY *turns, moves, listening to* BEN.)

LINDA.   Be good. You're both good boys, just act that way, that's all.

HAPPY.   'Night, Pop. (*He goes upstairs.*)

LINDA (*to* WILLY).   Come, dear.

BEN (*with greater force*).   One must go in to fetch a diamond out.

WILLY (*to* LINDA, *as he moves slowly along the edge of the kitchen, toward the door*).   I just want to get settled down, Linda. Let me sit alone for a little.

LINDA (*almost uttering her fear*).   I want you upstairs.

WILLY (*taking her in his arms*).   In a few minutes, Linda. I couldn't sleep right now. Go on, you look awful tired. (*He kisses her.*)

BEN.   Not like an appointment at all. A diamond is rough and hard to the touch.

WILLY.   Go on now. I'll be right up.

LINDA.   I think this is the only way, Willy.

WILLY.   Sure, it's the best thing.

BEN.   Best thing!

WILLY.   The only way. Everything is gonna be—go on, kid, get to bed. You look so tired.

LINDA.   Come right up.

WILLY.   Two minutes. (LINDA *goes into the living-room, then reappears in her bedroom.* WILLY *moves just outside the kitchen door.*) Loves me. (*Wonderingly*) Always loved me. Isn't that a remarkable thing? Ben, he'll worship me for it!

BEN (*with promise*).   It's dark there, but full of diamonds.

WILLY.   Can you imagine that magnificence with twenty thousand dollars in his pocket?

LINDA (*calling from her room*).   Willy! Come up!

WILLY (*calling into the kitchen*).   Yes, yes. Coming! It's very smart, you realize that, don't you, sweetheart? Even Ben sees it. I gotta go, baby. 'By! 'By! (*Going over to* BEN, *almost dancing*) Imagine? When the mail comes he'll be ahead of Bernard again!

BEN.   A perfect proposition all around.

WILLY.   Did you see how he cried to me? Oh, if I could kiss him, Ben!

BEN.   Time, William, time!

WILLY.   Oh, Ben, I always knew one way or another we were gonna make it, Biff and I!

BEN (*looking at his watch*).   The boat. We'll be late. (*He moves slowly off into the darkness.*)

WILLY (*elegiacally, turning to the house*).   Now when you kick off, boy, I want a seventy-yard boot, and get right down the field under the ball, and when you hit, hit low and hit hard, because it's important, boy. (*He swings around and faces the audience.*) There's all kinds of important people in the stands, and the first thing you know . . . (*Suddenly realizing he is alone*) Ben! Ben, where do I . . . ? (*He makes a sudden movement of search.*) Ben, how do I . . . ?

LINDA (*calling*).   Willy, you coming up?

WILLY (*uttering a gasp of fear, whirling about as if to quiet her*).   Sh! (*He turns as if to find his way; sounds, faces, voices, seem to be swarming in upon him and he flicks at them, crying*) Sh! Sh! (*Suddenly music, faint and high, stops him. It rises in intensity, almost to an unbearable scream. He goes up and down on his toes, and rushes off around the house.*) Shhh!

LINDA.   Willy? (*There is no answer.* LINDA *waits.* BIFF *gets up off his bed. He is still in his clothes.* HAPPY *sits up.* BIFF *stands there listening.* LINDA, *with real fear*) Willy, answer me! Willy! (*There is the sound of a car starting and moving away at full speed.*) No!

BIFF (*rushing down the stairs*).   Pop!

(*As the car speeds off, the music crashes down in a frenzy of sound, which becomes the soft pulsation of a single cello string.* BIFF *slowly returns to his bedroom. He and* HAPPY *gravely don their jackets.* LINDA *slowly walks out of her room. The music has developed into a dead march. The leaves of day are appearing over everything.* CHARLEY *and* BERNARD, *somberly dressed, appear and knock on the kitchen door.* BIFF *and* HAPPY *slowly descend the stairs to the kitchen as* CHARLEY *and* BERNARD *enter. All stop a moment when* LINDA, *in clothes of mourning, bearing a little bunch of roses, comes through the draped doorway into the kitchen. She goes to* CHARLEY *and takes his arm. Now all move toward the audience, through the wall-line of the kitchen. At the limit of the apron,* LINDA *lays down the flowers, kneels, and sits back on her heels. All stare down at the grave.*)

REQUIEM

CHARLEY.   It's getting dark, Linda. (LINDA *doesn't react. She stares at the grave.*)

BIFF.   How about it, Mom? Better get some rest, heh? They'll be closing the gate soon. (LINDA *makes no move. Pause.*)

HAPPY (*deeply angered*).   He had no right to do that. There was no necessity for it. We would've helped him.

CHARLEY (*grunting*).   Hmmm.

BIFF.   Come along, Mom.

LINDA.   Why didn't anybody come?

CHARLEY.   It was a nice funeral.

LINDA.   But where are all the people he knew? Maybe they blame him.

CHARLEY.   Naa. It's a rough world, Linda. They wouldn't blame him.

LINDA.   I can't understand it. At this time especially. First time in thirty-five years we were just about free and clear. He only needed a little salary. He was even finished with the dentist.

CHARLEY.   No man only needs a little salary.

LINDA.   I can't understand it.

BIFF.   There were a lot of nice days. When he'd come home from a trip; or on Sundays, making the stoop; finishing the cellar; putting on the new porch; when he built the extra bathroom; and put up the garage. You know something, Charley, there's more of him in that front stoop than in all the sales he ever made.

CHARLEY.   Yeah. He was a happy man with a batch of cement.

LINDA.   He was so wonderful with his hands.

BIFF.   He had the wrong dreams. All, all, wrong.

HAPPY (*almost ready to fight* BIFF).   Don't say that!

BIFF.   He never knew who he was.

CHARLEY (*stopping* HAPPY's *movement and reply. To* BIFF).   Nobody dast blame this man. You don't understand: Willy was a salesman. And for a salesman, there is no rock bottom to the life. He don't put a bolt to a nut, he don't tell you the law or give you medicine. He's a man way out there in the blue, riding on a smile and a shoeshine. And when they start not smiling back—that's an earthquake. And then you get yourself a couple of spots on your hat, and you're finished. Nobody dast blame this man. A salesman is got to dream, boy. It comes with the territory.

BIFF.   Charley, the man didn't know who he was.

HAPPY (*infuriated*).   Don't say that!

BIFF.   Why don't you come with me, Happy?

HAPPY.   I'm not licked that easily. I'm staying right in this city, and I'm gonna beat this racket! (*He looks at* BIFF, *his chin is set.*) The Loman Brothers!

BIFF.   I know who I am, kid.

HAPPY.   All right, boy. I'm gonna show you and everybody else that Willy Loman did not die in vain. He had a good dream. It's the only dream you can have—to come out number-one man. He fought it out here and this is where I'm gonna win it for him.

BIFF (*with a hopeless glance at* HAPPY, *bends toward his mother*). Let's go, Mom.

LINDA.   I'll be with you in a minute. Go on, Charley. (*He hesitates.*) I want to, just for a minute. I never had a chance to say good-by. (CHARLEY *moves away, followed by* HAPPY. BIFF *remains a slight distance up and left of* LINDA. *She sits there, summoning herself. The flute begins, not far away, playing behind her speech.*) Forgive me, dear. I can't cry. I don't know what it is, but I can't cry. I don't understand it. Why did you ever do that? Help me, Willy, I can't cry. It seems to me that you're just on another trip. I keep expecting you. Willy, dear, I can't cry. Why did you do it? I search and search and I search, and I can't understand it, Willy. I made the last payment on the house today. Today, dear. And there'll be nobody home. (*A sob rises in her throat.*) We're free and clear. (*Sobbing more fully, released*) We're free. (BIFF *comes slowly toward her.*) We're free . . . We're free . . .

(BIFF *lifts her to her feet and moves out up right with her in his arms.* LINDA *sobs quietly.* BERNARD *and* CHARLEY *come together and follow them, followed by* HAPPY. *Only the music of the flute is left on the darkening stage as over the house the hard towers of the apartment buildings rise into sharp focus, and the curtain falls.*)

QUESTIONS

1. Critics have disagreed as to whether *Death of a Salesman* can be called a tragedy. Most of the debate centers on whether or not Willy Loman has the stature of a tragic hero. How would you answer this question? What admirable characteristics does Willy have? Could any of his desires or motivations be called noble? Consider particularly Willy's motivations in committing suicide. In what respect are they to be admired? In what respect are they mistaken? Does Willy make any "discovery" before his death? If so, does it involve an increased self-knowledge?

   Miller himself has said that he did not set out to "write a tragedy" in this play, but "to show the truth" as he saw it. It is nevertheless clear from his various comments about the play that he regards it as a tragedy, with Willy as its hero. In his article "Tragedy and the Common Man" he has written that "the tragic feeling is evoked in us when we are in the presence of a character who is ready to lay down his life, if need be, to secure one thing—his sense of personal dignity." Is this remark applicable to Willy Loman?

2. Regardless of your answers to question 1, there can be little doubt that Willy Loman is the victim of a "tragic flaw." Can you isolate that flaw? Is it Willy's own tragic flaw that causes his downfall? Is it society's? Is it a combination of both?

3. Willy is generally assumed to be the protagonist of *Death of a Salesman*, but a case can also be made for its being Biff's play. Consider the play in terms of both interpretations. If Willy is the protagonist, who or what constitutes the antagonistic force? Is the antagonist the same if one considers Biff as protagonist? Explain.

4. Which characters change during the course of the play? In what respects?

5. Some critics have viewed *Death of a Salesman* entirely as a social commentary. To what extent do you consider this evaluation valid or invalid?

6. Discuss the interaction of the characters in *Death of a Salesman*. What effect has Willy had upon his sons' lives? They on his? Linda has been described as "the perfect wife." Do you find her so? What has been her effect on the lives of her husband and children? Willy's brother Ben is in many ways a character foil to Willy. To what extent, if any, has Ben's "success" contributed to Willy's failure? What is Ben's role in the play? What function do Charley and Bernard serve in the play?

7. What purposes are served by the Requiem? What ironies does it contain? What would be lost by its omission from the play?

8. To what extent is *Death of a Salesman* a realistic play? To what extent is it nonrealistic? Describe as precisely as you can the nonrealistic devices used by Miller in the play, and comment on their purpose.

William Shakespeare

A Midsummer Night's Dream

Characters

THESEUS, *Duke of Athens*

HIPPOLYTA, *Queen of the Amazons, conquered by Theseus and betrothed to him*

PHILOSTRATE, *Theseus's Master of the Revels*

EGEUS, *an Athenian nobleman, Hermia's father*

HERMIA, *Egeus's daughter in love with Lysander*

HELENA, *a young Athenian in love with Demetrius*

LYSANDER, *a young Athenian in love with Hermia*

DEMETRIUS, *a young Athenian in love with Hermia and Egeus's choice for her*

OBERON, *King of the Fairies*

TITANIA, *Queen of the Fairies*

PUCK (or ROBIN GOODFELLOW), *Oberon's jester and henchman*

PEASEBLOSSOM, COBWEB, MOTH, MUSTARDSEED, *Titania's attendant fairies*

PETER QUINCE, *a carpenter who acts the role of* PROLOGUE

NICK BOTTOM, *a weaver who acts the role of* PYRAMUS

FRANCIS FLUTE, *a bellows mender who acts the role of* THISBE

TOM SNOUT, *a tinker who acts the role of* WALL

A MIDSUMMER NIGHT'S DREAM   There is no recorded first performance, but the play is customarily dated 1594–95. It combines story material from Greek mythology (the marriage of Theseus and Hippolyta), typical confusions, frustrations, and fulfillments of young love (Hermia and Lysander, Helena and Demetrius), folklore about fairies and elves (Titania, Oberon, and Puck), a drama of star-crossed lovers drawn from Latin literature (the Pyramus and Thisbe play-within-a-play), and down-to-earth, uneducated working men familiar to Shakespeare's audiences. While its multiple plots amply illustrate that "the course of true love never did run smooth," it completes the promise of its title by making dreams come true. Mixing references to midsummer festivals and May Day rituals, the play evokes an atmosphere of superstition and celebration, while at the same time displaying the sophistication of courtly behavior. Appropriate to the presence of the mythical Theseus and Hippolyta, the location of the action is "Athens," but there is no attempt to represent an actual time or geographical place.

This play was first printed in a quarto in 1600, and a subsequent quarto in 1619 and the folio of 1623 are based on that first printing. The present text has been edited from the first quarto and adopts some suggestions from several of Shakespeare's earliest editors. For a brief summary of Shakespeare's life, see the note introducing *Othello, the Moor of Venice* (page 1273).

SNUG, *a joiner who acts the role of* LION
ROBIN STARVELING, *a tailor who acts the role of* MOONSHINE
Other FAIRIES *and* ATTENDANTS

SCENE. *Athens and the woods near it.*

ACT 1

SCENE 1. *The court of Theseus.*

    Enter THESEUS, HIPPOLYTA, PHILOSTRATE, *and* ATTENDANTS.

THESEUS.   Now, fair Hippolyta, our nuptial hour
    Draws on apace. Four happy days bring in
    Another moon; but, O, methinks, how slow
    This old moon wanes! She lingers° my desires,
    Like to a stepdame or a dowager   5
    Long withering out a young man's revenue.°
HIPPOLYTA.   Four days will quickly steep° themselves in night;
    Four nights will quickly dream away the time;
    And then the moon, like to a silver bow
    New bent in heaven, shall behold the night   10
    Of our solemnities.
THESEUS.   Go, Philostrate,
    Stir up the Athenian youth to merriments.
    Awake the pert and nimble spirit of mirth.
    Turn melancholy forth to funerals:
    The pale companion is not for our pomp.°   15
    (*Exit* PHILOSTRATE.)
    Hippolyta, I wooed thee with my sword
    And won thy love doing thee injuries;
    But I will wed thee in another key,
    With pomp, with triumph, and with reveling.
    (*Enter* EGEUS, *his daughter* HERMIA, LYSANDER, *and* DEMETRIUS.)
EGEUS.   Happy be Theseus, our renownèd Duke!   20
THESEUS.   Thanks, good Egeus. What's the news with thee?
EGEUS.   Full of vexation come I, with complaint
    Against my child, my daughter Hermia.—
    Stand forth, Demetrius.—My noble lord,

---

4. lingers: delays   **5–6. Like . . . revenue:** i.e., like a stepmother or widowed mother who
controls her son's inheritance   **7. steep:** absorb   **15. pomp:** celebration

This man hath my consent to marry her.— 25
Stand forth, Lysander.—And, my gracious Duke,
This man hath bewitched the bosom of my child.
Thou, thou Lysander, thou hast given her rhymes
And interchanged love tokens with my child.
Thou hast by moonlight at her window sung 30
With feigning voice verses of feigning° love,
And stol'n the impression of her fantasy°
With bracelets of thy hair, rings, gauds, conceits,
Knacks,° trifles, nosegays, sweetmeats—messengers
Of strong prevailment in° unhardened youth. 35
With cunning hast thou filched my daughter's heart,
Turned her obedience, which is due to me,
To stubborn harshness. And, my gracious Duke,
Be it so° she will not here before Your Grace
Consent to marry with Demetrius, 40
I beg the ancient privilege of Athens:
As she is mine, I may dispose of her,
Which shall be either to this gentleman
Or to her death, according to our law
Immediately° provided in that case. 45
THESEUS.   What say you, Hermia? Be advised, fair maid.
To you your father should be as a god,
One that composed your beauties, yea; and one
To whom you are but as a form in wax
By him imprinted, and within his power 50
To leave the figure or disfigure it.°
Demetrius is a worthy gentleman.
HERMIA.   So is Lysander.
THESEUS.   In himself he is;
But in this kind,° wanting° your father's voice,
The other must be held the worthier. 55
HERMIA.   I would my father looked but with my eyes.
THESEUS.   Rather your eyes must with his judgment look.
HERMIA.   I do entreat Your Grace to pardon me.

---

31. feigning . . . feigning: The words imply both pretending and yearning.   **32. And . . . fantasy:** And made a deceitful impression on her imagination   **33–34. gauds . . . Knacks:** insignificant presents and compliments   **35. prevailment in:** influence on   **39. Be it so:** If   **45. Immediately:** Expressly   **51. leave . . . or disfigure it:** let it be or destroy it   **54. kind:** case   **wanting:** without

I know not by what power I am made bold,
Nor how it may concern my modesty°   60
In such a presence here to plead my thoughts;
But I beseech Your Grace that I may know
The worst that may befall me in this case
If I refuse to wed Demetrius.
THESEUS.   Either to die the death or to abjure   65
Forever the society of men.
Therefore, fair Hermia, question your desires,
Know of your youth, examine well your blood,
Whether, if you yield not to your father's choice,
You can endure the livery of a nun,   70
For aye° to be in shady cloister mewed,°
To live a barren sister all your life,
Chanting faint hymns to the cold fruitless moon.
Thrice blessèd they that master so their blood
To undergo such maiden pilgrimage;   75
But earthlier° happy is the rose distilled°
Than that which, withering on the virgin thorn,
Grows, lives, and dies in single blessedness.
HERMIA.   So will I grow, so live, so die, my lord,
Ere I will yield my virgin patent° up   80
Unto his lordship, whose unwishèd yoke
My soul consents not to give sovereignty.
THESEUS.   Take time to pause, and by the next new moon—
The sealing day betwixt my love and me
For everlasting bond of fellowship—   85
Upon that day either prepare to die
For disobedience to your father's will,
Or else to wed Demetrius, as he would,
Or on Diana's altar to protest°
For aye austerity and single life.   90
DEMETRIUS.   Relent, sweet Hermia, and, Lysander, yield
Thy crazèd° title to my certain right.
LYSANDER.   You have her father's love, Demetrius;
Let me have Hermia's. Do you marry him.
EGEUS.   Scornful Lysander! True, he hath my love,   95

---

60. concern my modesty: seem to be inappropriate for an unmarried young woman
71. for aye: forever   **mewed:** caged up   **76. earthlier:** in worldly terms   **distilled:** plucked
and made into perfume   **80. virgin patent:** the privilege of my virginity   **89. protest:** swear
an oath   **92. crazèd:** flawed

And what is mine my love shall render him.
And she is mine, and all my right of her
I do estate° unto Demetrius.
LYSANDER.   I am, my lord, as well derived° as he,
    As well possessed;° my love is more than his;   100
    My fortunes every way as fairly ranked,
    If not with vantage,° as Demetrius';
    And, which is more than all these boasts can be,
    I am beloved of beauteous Hermia.
    Why should not I then prosecute my right?   105
    Demetrius, I'll avouch it to his head,°
    Made love to° Nedar's daughter, Helena,
    And won her soul; and she, sweet lady, dotes,
    Devoutly dotes, dotes in idolatry
    Upon this spotted and inconstant° man.   110
THESEUS.   I must confess that I have heard so much,
    And with Demetrius thought to have spoke thereof;
    But, being overfull of self-affairs,
    My mind did lose it. But, Demetrius, come,
    And come, Egeus, you shall go with me;   115
    I have some private schooling for you both.
    For you, fair Hermia, look you° arm yourself
    To fit your fancies to your father's will,
    Or else the law of Athens yields you up—
    Which by no means we may extenuate—   120
    To death or to a vow of single life.
    Come, my Hippolyta. What cheer, my love?
    Demetrius and Egeus, go along.
    I must employ you in some business
    Against° our nuptial, and confer with you   125
    Of something nearly that° concerns yourselves.
EGEUS.   With duty and desire we follow you.
    (*Exeunt all but* HERMIA *and* LYSANDER.)
LYSANDER.   How now, my love, why is your cheek so pale?
    How chance the roses there do fade so fast?
HERMIA.   Belike° for want of rain, which I could well   130
    Beteem° them from the tempest of my eyes.

---

98. **estate:** bestow   99. **as well derived:** equal in rank   100. **well possessed:** equally
wealthy   102. **vantage:** superiority   106. **avouch . . . head:** declare it to his face
107. **Made love to:** Courted, pursued   110. **spotted and inconstant:** immoral and
unfaithful   117. **look you:** take care to   125. **Against:** In preparation for   126. **nearly
that:** that privately   130. **Belike:** Probably   131. **Beteem:** Send forth

LYSANDER.   Ay me! For aught that I could ever read,
    Could ever hear by tale or history,
    The course of true love never did run smooth;
    But either it was different in blood—°   135
HERMIA.   O cross! Too high to be enthralled to low.
LYSANDER.   Or else misgraffèd in respect of years—°
HERMIA.   O spite! Too old to be engaged to young.
LYSANDER.   Or else it stood upon the choice of friends—°
HERMIA.   O hell, to choose love by another's eyes!   140
LYSANDER.   Or if there were a sympathy in choice,
    War, death, or sickness did lay siege to it,
    Making it momentany° as a sound,
    Swift as a shadow, short as any dream,
    Brief as the lightning in the collied° night   145
    That in a spleen unfolds° both heaven and earth,
    And ere a man hath power to say "Behold!"
    The jaws of darkness do devour it up.
    So quick° bright things come to confusion.°
HERMIA.   If then true lovers have been ever crossed,°   150
    It stands as an edict in destiny.
    Then let us teach our trial patience,
    Because it is a customary cross,
    As due to love as thoughts, and dreams, and sighs,
    Wishes, and tears, poor fancy's followers.°   155
LYSANDER.   A good persuasion. Therefore, hear me, Hermia:
    I have a widow aunt, a dowager
    Of great revenue, and she hath no child.
    From Athens is her house remote seven leagues;
    And she respects me as her only son.   160
    There, gentle Hermia, may I marry thee,
    And to that place the sharp Athenian law
    Cannot pursue us. If thou lovest me, then,
    Steal forth thy father's house tomorrow night;
    And in the wood, a league without° the town,   165
    Where I did meet thee once with Helena
    To do observance to a morn of May,°

---

135. blood: hereditary rank   **137. misgraffèd . . . years:** badly matched in age
139. friends: kinsmen   **143. momentany:** momentary   **145. collied:** black as coal
146. in a spleen unfolds: reveals in a sudden flash   **149. quick:** living (as well as
quickly) **confusion:** destruction   **150. ever crossed:** always thwarted   **155. fancy's
followers:** love's accompaniments   **165. without:** outside   **167. do . . . May:** observe May
Day rituals

There will I stay for thee.
HERMIA.   My good Lysander!
   I swear to thee, by Cupid's strongest bow,
   By his best arrow° with the golden head,   170
   By the simplicity of Venus' doves,°
   By that which knitteth souls and prospers loves,
   And by that fire which burned the Carthage queen
   When the false Trojan under sail was seen,°
   By all the vows that ever men have broke,   175
   In number more than ever women spoke,
   In that same place thou hast appointed me
   Tomorrow truly will I meet with thee.
LYSANDER.   Keep promise, love. Look, here comes Helena.
   (*Enter* HELENA.)
HERMIA.   God speed, fair Helena! Whither away?   180
HELENA.   Call you me fair? That "fair" again unsay.
   Demetrius loves your fair.° O happy fair!°
   Your eyes are lodestars,° and your tongue's sweet air°
   More tunable than lark to shepherd's ear
   When wheat is green, when hawthorn buds appear.   185
   Sickness is catching. O, were favor° so,
   Yours would I catch, fair Hermia, ere I go;
   My ear should catch your voice, my eye your eye,
   My tongue should catch your tongue's sweet melody.
   Were the world mine, Demetrius being bated,°   190
   The rest I'd give to be to you translated.
   O, teach me how you look and with what art
   You sway the motion° of Demetrius' heart.
HERMIA.   I frown upon him, yet he loves me still.
HELENA.   O, that your frowns would teach my smiles such skill! 195
HERMIA.   I give him curses, yet he gives me love.
HELENA.   O, that my prayers could such affection move!
HERMIA.   The more I hate, the more he follows me.
HELENA.   The more I love, the more he hateth me.
HERMIA.   His folly, Helena, is no fault of mine.   200

---

170. best arrow: Cupid shot two kinds of arrows, golden-headed to cause love and leaden-headed to cause hatred.   **171. simplicity . . . doves:** Innocent doves pulled the chariot of Venus.   **173–74. Carthage . . . seen:** Dido, Queen of Carthage, burned herself to death when she was deserted by her Trojan lover Aeneas.   **182. your fair:** your beauty   **happy fair:** you fortunate beauty   **183. lodestars:** guiding stars, attracting Demetrius's look   **air:** music   **186. favor:** appearance, good looks   **190. bated:** excepted   **193. sway the motion:** control the inclination

HELENA.   None, but your beauty. Would that fault were mine!
HERMIA.   Take comfort. He no more shall see my face.
    Lysander and myself will fly this place.
    Before the time I did Lysander see
    Seemed Athens as a paradise to me.°   205
    O, then, what graces in my love do dwell,
    That he hath turned a heaven unto a hell?
LYSANDER.   Helen, to you our minds we will unfold.
    Tomorrow night, when Phoebe° doth behold
    Her silver visage in the watery glass,°   210
    Decking with liquid pearl the bladed grass,
    A time that lovers' flights doth still° conceal,
    Through Athens' gates have we devised to steal.
HERMIA.   And in the wood, where often you and I
    Upon faint primrose beds were wont to lie,   215
    Emptying our bosoms of their counsel sweet,
    There my Lysander and myself shall meet,
    And thence from Athens turn away our eyes
    To seek new friends and stranger companies.
    Farewell, sweet playfellow. Pray thou for us,   220
    And good luck grant thee thy Demetrius!
    Keep word, Lysander. We must starve our sight
    From lovers' food till morrow deep midnight.
LYSANDER.   I will, my Hermia. (*Exit* HERMIA.) Helena, adieu.
    As you on him, Demetrius dote on you! (*Exit.*)   225
HELENA.   How happy some o'er other some° can be!
    Through Athens I am thought as fair as she.
    But what of that? Demetrius thinks not so;
    He will not know what all but he do know.
    And as he errs, doting on Hermia's eyes,   230
    So I, admiring of his qualities.
    Things base and vile, holding no quantity,°
    Love can transpose to form and dignity.
    Love looks not with the eyes, but with the mind,
    And therefore is winged Cupid painted blind.   235
    Nor hath Love's mind of any judgment taste;°

204–5. Before . . . me: Before I fell in love with Lysander (and thus ran into all the problems with my father and Demetrius), Athens was a heavenly place to me.   **209. Phoebe:** Diana, goddess of chastity, identified with the moon   **210. watery glass:** reflective surface of lakes, etc.   **212. still:** always   **226. o'er . . . some:** in contrast to others   **232. holding no quantity:** having no shape or proportion   **236. Nor . . . taste:** i.e., love has no ability to judge

Wings and no eyes figure° unheedy haste.
And therefore is Love said to be a child,
Because in choice he is so oft beguiled.
As waggish boys in game themselves forswear,   240
So the boy Love is perjured everywhere.
For ere Demetrius looked on Hermia's eyne,°
He hailed down oaths that he was only mine;
And when this hail some heat from Hermia felt,
So he dissolved, and showers of oaths did melt.   245
I will go tell him of fair Hermia's flight.
Then to the wood will he tomorrow night
Pursue her; and for this intelligence
If I have thanks, it is a dear expense.°
But herein mean I to enrich my pain,   250
To have his sight thither and back again. (*Exit.*)

SCENE 2. *Peter Quince's house in Athens.*

Enter PETER QUINCE *the carpenter,* NICK BOTTOM *the weaver,* SNUG *the joiner,* FLUTE *the bellows mender,* SNOUT *the tinker, and* STARVELING *the tailor.*

QUINCE.   Is all our company here?

BOTTOM.   You were best to call them generally,° man by man, according to the scrip.°

QUINCE.   Here is the scroll of every man's name which is thought fit, through all Athens, to play in our interlude° before the Duke and the Duchess on his wedding day at night.   6

BOTTOM.   First, good Peter Quince, say what the play treats on, then read the names of the actors, and so grow to a point.

QUINCE.   Marry,° our play is "The most lamentable comedy and most cruel death of Pyramus and Thisbe."   10

BOTTOM.   A very good piece of work, I assure you, and a merry. Now, good Peter Quince, call forth your actors by the scroll. Masters, spread yourselves.

QUINCE.   Answer as I call you. Nick Bottom, the weaver.

BOTTOM.   Ready. Name what part I am for, and proceed.   15

QUINCE.   You, Nick Bottom, are set down for Pyramus.

---

237. **figure:** represent   242. **eyne:** eyes   249. **dear expense:** something that costs a lot (Either Demetrius will find it difficult to repay her by thanking her, or she will be paying a lot for the little thanks she gets.)   2. **generally:** Bottom means "individually," but uses a word that means the opposite.   3. **scrip:** scrap of paper (Bottom means "script.")   5. **interlude:** play   9. **Marry:** Indeed (originally a mild oath, "by the Virgin Mary")

BOTTOM.   What is Pyramus? A lover or a tyrant?

QUINCE.   A lover, that kills himself most gallant for love.

BOTTOM.   That will ask some tears in the true performing of it. If I do
it, let the audience look to their eyes. I will move storms; I will
condole° in some measure. To the rest—yet my chief humor° is for
a tyrant. I could play Ercles° rarely, or a part to tear a cat in, to
make all split.°   23

> "The raging rocks
>   And shivering shocks   25
>   Shall break the locks
>   Of prison gates;
>   And Phibbus' car°
>   Shall shine from far
> And make and mar   30
>   The foolish Fates."

This was lofty! Now name the rest of the players. This is Ercles' vein, a
tyrant's vein. A lover is more condoling.

QUINCE.   Francis Flute, the bellows mender.

FLUTE.   Here, Peter Quince.   35

QUINCE.   Flute, you must take Thisbe on you.

FLUTE.   What is Thisbe? A wandering knight?

QUINCE.   It is the lady that Pyramus must love.

FLUTE.   Nay, faith, let not me play a woman. I have a beard coming.

QUINCE.   That's all one. You shall play it in a mask, and you may speak
as small° as you will.   41

BOTTOM.   An° I may hide my face, let me play Thisbe too. I'll speak
in a monstrous little voice: "Thisne, Thisne!" "Ah, Pyramus, my
lover dear! Thy Thisbe dear, and lady dear!"

QUINCE.   No, no, you must play Pyramus, and Flute, you Thisbe.   45

BOTTOM.   Well, proceed.

QUINCE.   Robin Starveling, the tailor.

STARVELING.   Here, Peter Quince.

QUINCE.   Robin Starveling, you must play Thisbe's mother. Tom
Snout, the tinker.   50

SNOUT.   Here, Peter Quince.

---

21. condole: express grief   **humor:** temperament, inclination   **22. Ercles:** Hercules,
portrayed in old plays as a ranting character   **to tear . . . split:** to rant and bluster, and cause
great commotion in the audience   **28. Phibbus' car:** the chariot of Phoebus the sun
god   **41. small:** in a shrill voice   **42. An:** If

QUINCE.   You, Pyramus' father; myself, Thisbe's father; Snug, the joiner, you, the lion's part; and I hope here is a play fitted.

SNUG.   Have you the lion's part written? Pray you, if it be, give it me, for I am slow of study.   55

QUINCE.   You may do it extempore, for it is nothing but roaring.   5

BOTTOM.   Let me play the lion too. I will roar that I will do any man's heart good to hear me. I will roar that I will make the Duke say, "Let him roar again, let him roar again."   59

QUINCE.   An you should do it too terribly, you would fright the Duchess and the ladies, that they would shriek; and that were enough to hang us all.

ALL.   That would hang us, every mother's son.   63

BOTTOM.   I grant you, friends, if you should fright the ladies out of their wits, they would have no more discretion but to hang us; but I will aggravate° my voice so that I will roar you as gently as any sucking dove;° I will roar you an 'twere any nightingale.   67

QUINCE.   You can play no part but Pyramus; for Pyramus is a sweet-faced man, a proper° man as one shall see in a summer's day, a most lovely gentlemanlike man. Therefore you must needs play Pyramus.   71

BOTTOM.   Well, I will undertake it. What beard were I best to play it in?

QUINCE.   Why, what you will.

BOTTOM.   I will discharge it in either your straw-color beard, your orange-tawny beard, your purple-in-grain° beard, or your French-crown-color° beard, your perfect yellow.   76

QUINCE.   Some of your French crowns° have no hair at all, and then you will play barefaced. But, masters, here are your parts. And I am to entreat you, request you, and desire you to con° them by tomorrow night, and meet me in the palace wood, a mile without the town, by moonlight. There will we rehearse; for if we meet in the city, we shall be dogged with company, and our devices known. In the meantime I will draw a bill of properties, such as our play wants. I pray you, fail me not.   84

BOTTOM.   We will meet, and there we may rehearse most obscenely° and courageously. Take pains, be perfect. Adieu.

---

66. aggravate: He intends to mean "moderate."   **67. sucking dove:** a combination of two symbols of innocence and mildness, "sitting dove" and "sucking lamb"   **69. proper:** handsome   **75. purple-in-grain:** dyed a deep red color   **75–76. French-crown-color:** gold-colored (after the French coin)   **77. crowns:** heads (gone bald from syphilis, the "French disease")   **79. con:** learn, memorize   **85. obscenely:** Bottom probably means "seemly," properly.

QUINCE.   At the Duke's oak we meet.
BOTTOM.   Enough. Hold, or cut bowstrings.° (*Exeunt.*)

ACT 2
SCENE 1. *A wood near Athens.*

Enter from opposite sides of the stage a FAIRY *and* PUCK.

PUCK.   How now, spirit, whither wander you?
FAIRY.   Over hill, over dale,
   Thorough bush, thorough brier,
   Over park, over pale,°
    Thorough flood, thorough fire,   5
   I do wander everywhere,
   Swifter than the moon's sphere;
   And I serve the Fairy Queen,
   To dew her orbs° upon the green.
   The cowslips tall her pensioners° be.   10
   In their gold coats spots you see;
   Those be rubies, fairy favors;
   In those freckles live their savors.
   I must go seek some dewdrops here
   And hang a pearl in every cowslip's ear.   15
   Farewell, thou lob° of spirits; I'll be gone.
   Our Queen and all her elves come here anon.
PUCK.   The King doth keep his revels here tonight.
   Take heed the Queen come not within his sight.
   For Oberon is passing fell and wrath,°   20
   Because that she as her attendant hath
   A lovely boy, stolen from an Indian king;
   She never had so sweet a changeling.°
   And jealous Oberon would have the child
   Knight of his train, to trace° the forests wild. 25
   But she perforce° withholds the lovèd boy,
   Crowns him with flowers, and makes him all her joy.
   And now they never meet in grove or green,

---

88. Hold . . . bowstrings: An unexplained phrase, possibly from archery; Bottom's meaning is apparently "Either we do this well, or we give up on it." (Characteristically, Bottom insists on having the last word.)   **4. pale:** fence   **9. orbs:** "fairy rings," circles of darker grass in a meadow   **10. pensioners:** the Queen's bodyguards   **16. lob:** lout, bumpkin   **20. passing . . . wrath:** extremely fierce in his anger   **23. changeling:** a child stolen by fairies   **25. trace:** roam through   **26. perforce:** by force

By fountain clear, or spangled starlight sheen,
But they do square,° that all their elves for fear   30
Creep into acorn cups and hide them there.
FAIRY.   Either I mistake your shape and making quite,
Or else you are that shrewd and knavish sprite
Called Robin Goodfellow. Are not you he
That frights the maidens of the villagery,   35
Skim milk,° and sometimes labor in the quern,°
And bootless° make the breathless huswife churn,
And sometimes make the drink to bear no barm,°
Mislead night wanderers, laughing at their harm?
Those that "Hobgoblin" call you, and "Sweet Puck,"   40
You do their work, and they shall have good luck.
Are you not he?
PUCK.   Thou speakest aright;
I am that merry wanderer of the night.
I jest to Oberon and make him smile
When I a fat and bean-fed horse beguile,   45
Neighing in likeness of a filly foal;
And sometimes lurk I in a gossip's° bowl
In very likeness of a roasted crab,°
And when she drinks, against her lips I bob
And on her withered dewlap° pour the ale.   50
The wisest aunt, telling the saddest° tale,
Sometimes for three-foot stool mistaketh me;
Then slip I from her bum, down topples she,
And "Tailor" cries, and falls into a cough;
And then the whole quire° hold their hips and laugh,   55
And waxen° in their mirth, and neeze,° and swear
A merrier hour was never wasted there.
But, room,° fairy! Here comes Oberon.
FAIRY.   And here my mistress. Would that he were gone!
(*Enter from one side* OBERON, *the King of the Fairies with his train, and
from the other side* TITANIA, *the Queen of the Fairies with her train.*)
OBERON.   Ill met by moonlight, proud Titania.   60

---

30. square: quarrel, argue   **36. Skim milk:** Steal the cream   **quern:** handmill for grinding
grain   **37. bootless:** in vain (because the cream won't turn to butter)   **38. barm:** yeast
(preventing the ale from fermenting)   **47. gossip's:** old woman's   **48. crab:** crab apple,
added to a drink for flavor   **50. dewlap:** loose skin under the chin   **51. saddest:** most
serious   **55. quire:** company   **56. waxen . . . neeze:** laugh loudly and sneeze   **58. room:**
make room, stand aside

TITANIA.   What, jealous Oberon? Fairies, skip hence.
    I have forsworn his bed and company.
OBERON.   Tarry, rash wanton.° Am not I thy lord?
TITANIA.   Then I must be thy lady; but I know
    When thou hast stolen away from Fairyland   65
    And in the shape of Corin° sat all day,
    Playing on pipes of corn and versing love
    To amorous Phillida.° Why art thou here
    Come from the farthest step of India,
    But that, forsooth, the bouncing Amazon,   70
    Your buskined° mistress and your warrior love,
    To Theseus must be wedded, and you come
    To give their bed joy and prosperity.
OBERON.   How canst thou thus for shame, Titania,
    Glance at my credit° with Hippolyta,   75
    Knowing I know thy love to Theseus?
    Didst not thou lead him through the glimmering night
    From Perigenia,° whom he ravishèd?
    And make him with fair Aegles° break his faith,
    With Ariadne° and Antiopa?°   80
TITANIA.   These are the forgeries of jealousy;
    And never, since the middle summer's spring,
    Met we on hill, in dale, forest, or mead,
    By pavèd fountain or by rushy brook,
    Or in the beachèd margent° of the sea,   85
    To dance our ringlets° to the whistling wind,
    But with thy brawls thou hast disturbed our sport.
    Therefore the winds, piping to us in vain,
    As in revenge, have sucked up from the sea
    Contagious fogs which, falling in the land,   90
    Hath every pelting° river made so proud
    That they have overborne their continents.°
    The ox hath therefore stretched his yoke° in vain,
    The plowman lost his sweat, and the green corn°
    Hath rotted ere his youth attained a beard;   95
    The fold° stands empty in the drownèd field,

---

63. wanton: willful creature   **66, 68. Corin, Phillida:** typical names in pastoral poetry
71. buskined: wearing hunting boots   **75. Glance . . . credit:** Insult my good name
78–80. Perigenia, Aegles, Ariadne, Antiopa: various amorous conquests of Theseus
85. margent: margin   **86. ringlets:** round dances   **91. pelting:** paltry, insignificant
92. overborne . . . continents: flooded over their banks   **93. stretched his yoke:** dragged
heavily on its yoke in plowing   **94. corn:** wheat or other grain   **96. fold:** sheep pen

And crows are fatted with the murrain° flock;
The nine-men's morris° is filled up with mud,
And the quaint mazes° in the wanton° green
For lack of tread are undistinguishable.   100
The human mortals want their winter° here;
No night is now with hymn or carol blessed.
Therefore° the moon, the governess of floods,
Pale in her anger, washes all the air,
That rheumatic diseases do abound.   105
And thorough this distemperature° we see
The seasons alter: hoary-headed frosts
Fall in the fresh lap of the crimson rose,
And on old Hiems'° thin and icy crown
An odorous chaplet of sweet summer buds   110
Is, as in mockery, set. The spring, the summer,
The childing° autumn, angry winter, change
Their wonted liveries,° and the mazèd° world
By their increase now knows not which is which.
And this same progeny of evils comes   115
From our debate, from our dissension.
We are their parents and original.
OBERON.   Do you amend it, then. It lies in you.
Why should Titania cross her Oberon?
I do but beg a little changeling boy   120
To be my henchman.
TITANIA.   Set your heart at rest.
The fairy land buys not the child of me.
His mother was a vot'ress of my order,°
And in the spicèd Indian air by night
Full often hath she gossiped by my side   125
And sat with me on Neptune's yellow sands,
Marking th' embarkèd traders on the flood,°
When we have laughed to see the sails conceive

---

97. murrain: killed by the plague   **98. nine-men's morris:** a lawn marked out for playing a game of this name   **99. quaint mazes:** a series of paths laid out for another kind of game   **wanton:** growing luxuriantly   **101. want their winter:** miss the sports and festivities of wintertime   **103. Therefore:** As a result (of our quarreling)   **106. distemperature:** natural disturbance   **109. Hiems':** Winter's   **112. childing:** pregnant (ready for harvesting)   **113. wonted liveries:** normal appearances   **mazèd:** confused, amazed   **123. vot'ress . . . order:** devoted follower, as if a nun worshipping me   **127. embarkèd . . . flood:** merchant ships beginning their voyage

And grow big-bellied with the wanton wind;
Which she, with pretty and with swimming gait,   130
Following—her womb then rich with my young squire—
Would imitate, and sail upon the land
To fetch me trifles, and return again
As from a voyage, rich with merchandise.
But she, being mortal, of that boy did die;   135
And for her sake do I rear up her boy,
And for her sake I will not part with him.
OBERON.   How long within this wood intend you stay?
TITANIA.   Perchance till after Theseus' wedding day.
If you will patiently dance in our round°   140
And see our moonlight revels, go with us;
If not, shun me, and I will spare° your haunts?
OBERON.   Give me that boy, and I will go with thee.
TITANIA.   Not for thy fairy kingdom. Fairies, away!
We shall chide° downright, if I longer stay.   145
(*Exeunt* TITANIA *with her train.*)
OBERON.   Well, go thy way. Thou shalt not from this grove
Till I torment thee for this injury.
My gentle Puck, come hither. Thou rememb'rest
Since once I sat upon a promontory,
And heard a mermaid on a dolphin's back   150
Uttering such dulcet and harmonious breath°
That the rude sea grew civil at her song,
And certain stars shot madly from their spheres
To hear the sea-maid's music?
PUCK.   I remember?
OBERON.   That very time I saw, but thou couldst not,   155
Flying between the cold moon and the earth
Cupid, all armed. A certain aim he took
At a fair vestal° thronèd by the west,
And loosed his love shaft smartly from his bow
As it should pierce a hundred thousand hearts;   160
But I might see young Cupid's fiery shaft
Quenched in the chaste beams of the watery moon,
And the imperial vot'ress passèd on,
In maiden meditation, fancy-free.°

---

140. round: circle dance   **142. spare:** avoid   **145. chide:** quarrel   **151. dulcet . . . breath:**
sweet and melodious song   **158. fair vestal:** beautiful vestal virgin (presumably a compliment
to Elizabeth, "the Virgin Queen")   **164. fancy-free:** not touched by sexual desire

Yet marked I where the bolt° of Cupid fell: 165
It fell upon a little western flower,
Before milk-white, now purple with love's wound,
And maidens call it love-in-idleness.°
Fetch me that flower; the herb I showed thee once.
The juice of it on sleeping eyelids laid   170
Will make or man or° woman madly dote
Upon the next live creature that it sees.
Fetch me this herb, and be thou here again
Ere the leviathan° can swim a league.
PUCK.   I'll put a girdle round about the earth°   175
 In forty minutes. (*Exit.*)
OBERON.   Having once this juice,
 I'll watch Titania when she is asleep
 And drop the liquor of it in her eyes.
 The next thing then she waking looks upon,
 Be it on lion, bear, or wolf, or bull,   180
 On meddling monkey, or on busy ape,
 She shall pursue it with the soul of love.
 And ere I take this charm from off her sight,
 As I can take it with another herb,
 I'll make her render up her page to me.   185
 But who comes here? I am invisible,
 And I will overhear their conference.
 (*Enter* DEMETRIUS *followed by* HELENA.)
DEMETRIUS.   I love thee not; therefore pursue me not.
 Where is Lysander and fair Hermia?
 The one I'll slay; the other slayeth me.   190
 Thou toldst me they were stol'n unto this wood;
 And here am I, and wode° within this wood;
 Because I cannot meet my Hermia.
 Hence, get thee gone, and follow me no more.
HELENA.   You draw me, you hardhearted adamant!°   195
 But yet you draw not iron, for my heart
 Is true as steel. Leave you° your power to draw,
 And I shall have no power to follow you.

---

165. bolt: arrow   168. love-in-idleness: popular name for the pansy   171. or . . . or: either
. . . or   174. leviathan: whale   175. put . . . earth: fly around the world
192. wode: frantic, insane   195. adamant: a very hard magnetic stone   197. Leave you: If
you will give up

DEMETRIUS.   Do I entice you? Do I speak you fair?°
    Or rather do I not in plainest truth   200
    Tell you I do not nor I cannot love you?
HELENA.   And even for that do I love you the more.
    I am your spaniel; and, Demetrius,
    The more you beat me I will fawn on you.
    Use me but as your spaniel, spurn me, strike me,   205
    Neglect me, lose me, only give me leave,
    Unworthy as I am, to follow you.
    What worser place can I beg in your love—
    And yet a place of high respect with me—
    Than to be usèd as you use your dog?   210
DEMETRIUS.   Tempt not too much the hatred of my spirit,
    For I am sick when I do look on thee.
HELENA.   And I am sick when I look not on you.
DEMETRIUS.   You do impeach° your modesty too much
    To leave the city and commit yourself   215
    Into the hands of one that loves you not,
    To trust the opportunity of night
    And the ill counsel of a desert° place
    With the rich worth of your virginity.
HELENA.   Your virtue is my privilege.° For that   220
    It is not night when I do see your face,
    Therefore I think I am not in the night;
    Nor doth this wood lack worlds of company,
    For you, in my respect,° are all the world.
    Then how can it be said I am alone   225
    When all the world is here to look on me?
DEMETRIUS.   I'll run from thee and hide me in the brakes,°
    And leave thee to the mercy of wild beasts.
HELENA.   The wildest hath not such a heart as you.
    Run when you will. The story shall be changed: 230
    Apollo flies and Daphne holds the chase,°
    The dove pursues the griffin,° the mild hind°
    Makes speed to catch the tiger—bootless° speed,
    When cowardice pursues and valor flies!

---

199. speak you fair: speak kindly to you   **214. impeach:** discredit, call into question
218. desert: wild and uninhabited   **220. Your . . . privilege:** Your goodness will defend
me.   **224. in my respect:** to me   **227. brakes:** bushes, thickets   **231. Apollo . . . chase:**
Reversing the mythical story, the pursuer and pursued change roles.   **232. griffin:** a mythical
monster, half-eagle and half-lion   **hind:** female deer   **233. bootless:** fruitless

DEMETRIUS.   I will not stay thy questions.° Let me go!   235
    Or if thou follow me, do not believe
    But I shall do thee mischief in the wood.
HELENA.   Ay, in the temple, in the town, the field,
    You do me mischief. Fie, Demetrius!
    Your wrongs do set a scandal on my sex.   240
    We cannot fight for love, as men may do;
    We should be wooed and were not made to woo.
    (*Exit* DEMETRIUS.)
    I'll follow thee and make a heaven of hell,
    To die upon the hand I love so well. (*Exit*.)
OBERON.   Fare thee well, nymph. Ere he do leave this grove   245
    Thou shalt fly him, and he shall seek thy love.
    (*Enter* PUCK.)
    Hast thou the flower there? Welcome, wanderer.
PUCK.   Ay, there it is.
OBERON.   I pray thee, give it me.
    I know a bank where the wild thyme blows,°
    Where oxlips and the nodding violet grows,   250
    Quite overcanopied with luscious woodbine,
    With sweet muskroses and with eglantine.
    There sleeps Titania sometime of the night,
    Lulled in these flowers with dances and delight;
    And there the snake throws her enameled skin,°   255
    Weed° wide enough to wrap a fairy in.
    And with the juice of this I'll streak her eyes
    And make her full of hateful fantasies.
    Take thou some of it, and seek through this grove.
    A sweet Athenian lady is in love   260
    With a disdainful youth. Anoint his eyes,
    But do it when the next thing he espies
    May be the lady. Thou shalt know the man
    By the Athenian garments he hath on.
    Effect it with some care, that he may prove   265
    More fond° on her than she upon her love;
    And look thou meet me ere the first cock crow.
PUCK.   Fear not, my lord, your servant shall do so. (*Exeunt*.)

---

235. stay thy questions: listen to your arguments   **249. blows:** blooms   **255. throws . . .
skin:** sheds its shiny skin   **256. Weed:** Garment   **266. fond:** foolishly doting

SCENE 2. *Another part of the wood.*

Enter TITANIA *with her train.*

TITANIA.   Come, now a roundel° and a fairy song;
　　　Then, for the third part of a minute, hence,
　　　Some to kill cankers° in the muskrose buds,
　　　Some war with reremice° for their leathern wings
　　　To make my small elves coats, and some keep back　　　　5
　　　The clamorous owl, that nightly hoots and wonders
　　　At our quaint spirits. Sing me now asleep,
　　　Then to your offices, and let me rest.
　　　(FAIRIES *sing and dance.*)
FIRST FAIRY.   You spotted snakes with double tongue,
　　　　Thorny hedgehogs, be not seen;　　　　　　　　　10
　　　Newts and blindworms,° do no wrong;
　　　　Come not near our Fairy Queen!
CHORUS (*dancing*). Philomel,° with melody
　　　　Sing in our sweet lullaby;
　　　Lulla, lulla, lullaby, lulla, lulla, lullaby.　　　　　　15
　　　　Never harm
　　　　Nor spell nor charm
　　　Come our lovely lady nigh.
　　　So good night, with lullaby.
FIRST FAIRY.   Weaving spiders, come not here;　　　　　20
　　　　Hence, you long-legged spinners, hence!
　　　Beetles black, approach not near;
　　　　Worm nor snail, do no offense.
CHORUS (*dancing*). Philomel, with melody
　　　　Sing in our sweet lullaby;　　　　　　　　　　25
　　　Lulla, lulla, lullaby, lulla, lulla, lullaby.
　　　　Never harm
　　　　Nor spell nor charm
　　　Come our lovely lady nigh.
　　　So good night, with lullaby.　　　　　　　　　　30
　　　(TITANIA *sleeps.*)
SECOND FAIRY.   Hence, away! Now all is well.
　　　One aloof stand sentinel.

---

1. **roundel:** round dance   3. **cankers:** cankerworms or other parasites   4. **reremice:**
bats 11. **Newts . . . blindworms:** varieties of lizard erroneously considered venomous
13. **Philomel:** the nightingale, so called from a tale in Ovid's *Metamorphoses*

(*Exeunt* FAIRIES, *leaving one as sentinel. Enter* OBERON, *who squeezes the flower on* TITANIA'*s eyelids.*)

OBERON.   What thou seest when thou dost wake,
    Do it for thy true love take;
    Love and languish for his sake.   35
    Be it ounce,° or cat, or bear,
    Pard,° or boar with bristled hair,
    In thy eye that shall appear
    When thou wak'st, it is thy dear.
    Wake when some vile thing is near. (*Exit.*)   40
(*Enter* LYSANDER *and* HERMIA.)

LYSANDER.   Fair love, you faint with wandering in the wood;
    And to speak truth, I have forgot our way.
    We'll rest us, Hermia, if you think it good,
    And tarry for the comfort of the day.

HERMIA.   Be it so, Lysander. Find you out a bed,   45
    For I upon this bank will rest my head.

LYSANDER.   One turf shall serve as pillow for us both;
    One heart, one bed, two bosoms, and one troth.°

HERMIA.   Nay, good Lysander, for my sake, my dear,
    Lie further off yet. Do not lie so near.   50

LYSANDER.   O, take the sense,° sweet, of my innocence!
    Love takes the meaning in love's conference.°
    I mean that my heart unto yours is knit,
    So that but one heart we can make of it;
    Two bosoms interchainèd with an oath—   55
    So then two bosoms and a single troth.
    Then by your side no bed-room me deny,
    For lying so, Hermia, I do not lie.

HERMIA   Lysander riddles very prettily.
    Now much beshrew° my manners and my pride   60
    If Hermia meant to say Lysander lied.
    But, gentle friend, for love and courtesy
    Lie further off, in human modesty.
    Such separation as may well be said
    Becomes a virtuous bachelor and a maid,   65
    So far be distant, and good night, sweet friend.
    Thy love ne'er alter till thy sweet life end!

---

36. ounce: lynx   **37. Pard:** Leopard   **48. troth:** pledged faithfulness   **51. take the sense:** understand the meaning   **52. Love . . . conference:** Lovers can understand each other.
60. beshrew: condemn

LYSANDER.   Amen, amen, to that fair prayer, say I,
    And then end life when I end loyalty!
    Here is my bed. Sleep give thee all his rest!   70
HERMIA.   With half that wish the wisher's eyes be pressed!
    (*They sleep apart. Enter* PUCK.)
PUCK.   Through the forest have I gone,
    But Athenian found I none
    On whose eyes I might approve°
    This flower's force in stirring love.   75
    Night and silence.—Who is here?
    Weeds of Athens he doth wear.
    This is he, my master said,
    Despisèd the Athenian maid;
    And here the maiden, sleeping sound,   80
    On the dank and dirty ground.
    Pretty soul, she durst not lie
    Near this lack-love, this kill-courtesy.
    Churl, upon thy eyes I throw
    All the power this charm doth owe.°   85
    When thou wak'st, let love forbid
    Sleep his seat on thy eyelid.
    So awake when I am gone,
    For I must now to Oberon. (*Exit.*)
    (*Enter* DEMETRIUS *running, pursued by* HELENA.)
HELENA.   Stay, though thou kill me, sweet Demetrius!   90
DEMETRIUS.   I charge thee, hence, and do not haunt me thus.
HELENA.   O, wilt thou darkling° leave me? Do not so.
DEMETRIUS.   Stay, on thy peril! I alone will go. (*Exit.*)
HELENA.   O, I am out of breath in this fond chase!
    The more my prayer, the lesser is my grace.°   95
    Happy is Hermia, wheresoe'er she lies,
    For she hath blessèd and attractive eyes.
    How came her eyes so bright? Not with salt tears;
    If so, my eyes are oftener washed than hers.
    No, no, I am as ugly as a bear,   100
    For beasts that meet me run away for fear.
    Therefore no marvel though Demetrius
    Do, as a monster,° fly my presence thus.
    What wicked and dissembling glass of mine

74. approve: test **85. owe:** own **92. darkling:** in the dark **95. my grace:** the favor he gives me **103. as a monster:** as if I were a monster

Made me compare with Hermia's sphery eyne?°   105
But who is here? Lysander, on the ground?
Dead, or asleep? I see no blood, no wound.
Lysander, if you live, good sir, awake!
LYSANDER (*awaking*). And run through fire I will for thy sweet sake.
Transparent° Helena! Nature shows art,   110
That through thy bosom makes me see thy heart.
Where is Demetrius? O, how fit a word
Is that vile name to perish on my sword!
HELENA.   Do not say so, Lysander; say not so.
What though he love your Hermia? Lord, what though?   115
Yet Hermia still loves you. Then be content.
LYSANDER.   Content with Hermia? No! I do repent
The tedious minutes I with her have spent.
Not Hermia but Helena I love.
Who will not change a raven for a dove?   120
The will° of man is by his reason swayed,
And reason says you are the worthier maid.
Things growing are not ripe until their season;
So I, being young, till now ripe not to reason.
And, touching now the point of human skill,°   125
Reason becomes the marshal to my will
And leads me to your eyes, where I o'erlook°
Love's stories written in love's richest book.
HELENA.   Wherefore° was I to this keen mockery born?
When at your hands did I deserve this scorn?   130
Is 't not enough, is 't not enough, young man,
That I did never—no, nor never can—
Deserve a sweet look from Demetrius' eye,
But you must flout my insufficiency?
Good troth, you do me wrong, good sooth, you do,   135
In such disdainful manner me to woo.
But fare you well. Perforce I must confess
I thought you lord of more true gentleness.°
O, that a lady, of one man refused,
Should of° another therefore be abused! (*Exit.*)   140
LYSANDER.   She sees not Hermia. Hermia, sleep thou there,

---

105. sphery eyne: starlike eyes   **110. Transparent:** Radiant, honest, and clear   **121. will:** passion   **125. touching . . . skill:** now having reached full judgment   **127. o'erlook:** read   **129. Wherefore:** Why   **138. lord . . . gentleness:** a more courteous man **139–40. of . . . of:** by . . . by (also in line 148)

And never mayst thou come Lysander near!
For as a surfeit of the sweetest things
The deepest loathing to the stomach brings,
Or as the heresies that men do leave   145
Are hated most of those they did deceive,°
So thou, my surfeit and my heresy,
Of all be hated, but the most of me!
And, all my powers, address your love and might
To honor Helen and to be her knight! (*Exit.*)   150
HERMIA (*awaking*). Help me, Lysander, help me! Do thy best
   To pluck this crawling serpent from my breast!
   Ay me, for pity! What a dream was here!
   Lysander, look how I do quake with fear.
   Methought a serpent ate my heart away,   155
   And you sat smiling at his cruel prey.
   Lysander! What, removed? Lysander! Lord!
   What, out of hearing? Gone? No sound, no word?
   Alack, where are you? Speak, an if you hear;
   Speak, of all loves!° I swoon almost with fear.   160
   No? Then I well perceive you are not nigh.
   Either death, or you, I'll find immediately.
   (*Exit.* TITANIA *remains, asleep.*)

ACT 3

SCENE 1. *The scene continues, with* TITANIA *still sleeping.*

Enter BOTTOM, QUINCE, SNOUT, STARVELING, FLUTE, *and* SNUG.

BOTTOM.   Are we all met?
QUINCE.   Pat, pat; and here's a marvelous convenient place for our
   rehearsal. This green plot shall be our stage, this hawthorn brake
   our tiring-house,° and we will do it in action as we will do it before
   the Duke.   5
BOTTOM.   Peter Quince?
QUINCE.   What sayest thou, bully° Bottom?
BOTTOM.   There are things in this comedy of Pyramus and Thisbe that
   will never please. First, Pyramus must draw a sword to kill himself,
   which the ladies cannot abide. How answer you that?   10
SNOUT.   By 'r lakin, a parlous fear.°
STARVELING.   I believe we must leave the killing out, when all is done.

145–46. as . . . deceive: as men who give up heretical beliefs are most extreme in denouncing
their former heresies   **160. of all loves:** for the sake of love   **3–4. brake . . . tiring-house:**
thicket our dressing room   **7. bully:** admirable fellow   **11. By . . . fear:** By the Virgin, a
fearful danger

BOTTOM.   Not a whit. I have a device to make all well. Write me° a prologue, and let the prologue seem to say, we will do no harm with our
swords, and that Pyramus is not killed indeed; and for the more
better assurance, tell them that I, Pyramus, am not Pyramus but Bottom the weaver. This will put them out of fear.   17

QUINCE.   Well, we will have such a prologue, and it shall be written in
eight and six.°

BOTTOM.   No, make it two more: let it be written in eight and eight.°

SNOUT.   Will not the ladies be afeard of the lion?   21

STARVELING.   I fear it, I promise you.

BOTTOM.   Masters, you ought to consider with yourself, to bring in—
God shield us!—a lion among ladies is a most dreadful thing. For
there is not a more fearful wildfowl than your lion living, and we
ought to look to 't.   26

SNOUT.   Therefore another prologue must tell he is not a lion.

BOTTOM.   Nay, you must name his name, and half his face must be
seen through the lion's neck, and he himself must speak through,
saying thus or to the same defect:° "Ladies," or "Fair ladies, I would
wish you," or "I would request you," or "I would entreat you, not to
fear, not to tremble; my life for yours.° If you think I come hither
as a lion, it were pity of my life. No, I am no such thing; I am a man
as other men are." And there indeed let him name his name, and
tell them plainly he is Snug the joiner.   35

QUINCE.   Well, it shall be so. But there is two hard things: that is, to
bring the moonlight into a chamber; for, you know, Pyramus and
Thisbe meet by moonlight.

SNOUT.   Doth the moon shine that night we play our play?

BOTTOM.   A calendar, a calendar! Look in the almanac. Find out
moonshine, find out moonshine.   41

QUINCE.   Yes, it doth shine that night.

BOTTOM.   Why then may you leave a casement of the great chamber
window where we play open, and the moon may shine in at the
casement.   45

QUINCE.   Ay, or else one must come in with a bush of thorns and a
lantern° and say he comes to disfigure° or to present the person of
Moonshine. Then there is another thing: we must have a wall in
the great chamber; for Pyramus and Thisbe, says the story, did talk
through the chink of a wall.   50

---

13. Write me: I suggest you write ("me" does not imply "for me to speak")   **19–20. eight and
six, eight and eight:** refers to numbers of syllables per line in poetry   **30. defect:** he means
"effect"   **32. my . . . yours:** I'd give my life rather than see you harmed.
46–47. bush . . . lantern: In popular lore, the "man in the moon" was not the round face we
see there but a man carrying a lantern and a bundle of thorn branches, accompanied by his
dog.   **47. disfigure:** he means "figure," represent

SNOUT.   You can never bring in a wall. What say you, Bottom?

BOTTOM.   Some man or other must present Wall. And let him have
some plaster, or some loam,° or some roughcast° about him, to signify wall; or let him hold his fingers thus, and through that cranny
shall Pyramus and Thisbe whisper.   55

QUINCE.   If that may be, then all is well. Come, sit down, every
mother's son, and rehearse your parts. Pyramus, you begin. When
you have spoken your speech, enter into that brake, and so everyone according to his cue. (*Enter* PUCK.)

PUCK (*aside*).   What hempen homespuns° have we swaggering here
So near the cradle of the Fairy Queen?   61
What, a play toward?° I'll be an auditor;
An actor, too, perhaps, if I see cause.

QUINCE.   Speak, Pyramus. Thisbe, stand forth.

BOTTOM (*as Pyramus*).   "Thisbe, the flowers of odious savors sweet—"

QUINCE.   Odors, odors.   66

BOTTOM.   "—Odors savors sweet;
So hath thy breath, my dearest Thisbe dear.
But hark, a voice! Stay thou but here awhile,
And by and by I will to thee appear." (*Exit.*)   70

PUCK.   A stranger Pyramus than e'er played here. (*Exit.*)

FLUTE.   Must I speak now?

QUINCE.   Ay, marry, must you; for you must understand he goes but to
see a noise that he heard, and is to come again.

FLUTE (*as Thisbe*).   "Most radiant Pyramus, most lily-white of hue,
Of color like the red rose on triumphant brier,   76
Most brisky juvenal° and eke° most lovely Jew,°
As true as truest horse that yet would never tire.
I'll meet thee, Pyramus, at Ninny's tomb."

QUINCE.   "Ninus'° tomb," man. Why, you must not speak that yet.
That you answer to Pyramus. You speak all your part at once, cues
and all. Pyramus, enter. Your cue is past; it is "never tire."   82

FLUTE.   O—"As true as truest horse, that yet would never tire."
(*Enter* PUCK, *and* BOTTOM *wearing an ass's head.*)

BOTTOM.   "If I were fair, Thisbe, I were only thine."

---

53. loam, roughcast: materials used to plaster walls   **60. hempen homespuns:** men who dress
in coarse, homemade fabrics—poor louts   **62. toward:** being prepared   **77. brisky juvenal:**
lively young man   **eke:** also   **Jew:** a meaningless echo of the first syllable of "juvenal"
80. Ninus: mythical founder of Ninevah

QUINCE. O, monstrous! O, strange! We are haunted!   85
    Pray, masters! Fly, masters! Help!
    (*Exeunt* QUINCE, SNOUT, STARVELING, FLUTE, *and* SNUG.)
PUCK. I'll follow you, I'll lead you about a round,
      Thorough bog, thorough bush, thorough brake,
        thorough brier.
    Sometimes a horse I'll be, sometimes a hound,
      A hog, a headless bear, sometimes a fire;   90
    And neigh, and bark, and grunt, and roar, and burn,
    Like horse, hound, hog, bear, fire, at every turn. (*Exit.*)
BOTTOM. Why do they run away? This is a knavery of them to make
    me afeard.
    (*Enter* SNOUT.)
SNOUT. O Bottom, thou art changed! What do I see on thee?   95
BOTTOM. What do you see? You see an ass head of your own, do you?
    (*Exit* SNOUT. *Enter* QUINCE.)
QUINCE. Bless thee, Bottom, bless thee! Thou art translated.° (*Exit.*)
BOTTOM. I see their knavery. This is to make an ass of me, to fright
    me, if they could. But I will not stir from this place, do what they can. I
    will walk up and down here, and will sing, that they shall hear I am
    not afraid (*he sings*):   101
              The ouzel° cock so black of hue,
                  With orange-tawny bill,
              The throstle° with his note so true,
                The wren with little quill—°   105
TITANIA (*awaking*). What angel wakes me from my flowery bed?
BOTTOM (*sings*).
              The finch, the sparrow, and the lark,
                The plainsong° cuckoo gray,
            Whose note full many a man doth mark,
                And dares not answer nay—°   110
    For indeed, who would set his wit to° so foolish a bird? Who would
    give a bird the lie,° though he cry "cuckoo" never so?
TITANIA. I pray thee, gentle mortal, sing again.
    Mine ear is much enamored of thy note;
    So is mine eye enthrallèd to thy shape;   115

---

97. translated: transformed   **102. ouzel:** blackbird (in England, a songbird)
104. throstle: thrush   **105. little quill:** piping song   **108. plainsong:** a simple, repetitive
melody   **110. dares . . . nay:** cannot deny that he is a cuckold (which the song of the cuckoo
seems to reveal)   **111. set his wit to:** attempt to answer   **112. give . . . lie:** call the bird
a liar

And thy fair virtue's force° perforce doth move me
On the first view to say, to swear, I love thee.
BOTTOM.   Methinks, mistress, you should have little reason for that.
And yet to say the truth, reason and love keep little company to-
gether nowadays—the more the pity that some honest neighbors
will not make them friends. Nay, I can gleek° upon occasion.   121
TITANIA.   Thou art as wise as thou art beautiful.
BOTTOM.   Not so, neither. But if I had wit enough to get out of this
wood, I have enough to serve mine own turn.°
TITANIA.   Out of this wood do not desire to go.   125
Thou shalt remain here, whether thou wilt or no.
I am a spirit of no common rate.°
The summer still doth tend upon my state,°
And I do love thee. Therefore, go with me.
I'll give thee fairies to attend on thee,   130
And they shall fetch thee jewels from the deep,
And sing while thou on pressèd flowers dost sleep.
And I will purge thy mortal grossness so
That thou shalt like an airy spirit go.
Peaseblossom, Cobweb, Moth, and Mustardseed!   135
(*Enter* PEASEBLOSSOM, COBWEB, MOTH,° *and* MUSTARDSEED.)
PEASEBLOSSOM.   Ready.
COBWEB.   And I.
MOTH.   And I.
MUSTARDSEED.   And I.
ALL.   Where shall we go?
TITANIA.   Be kind and courteous to this gentleman.
Hop in his walks and gambol in his eyes;
Feed him with apricots and dewberries,   140
With purple grapes, green figs, and mulberries;
The honey bags steal from the humble-bees,
And for night tapers crop their waxen thighs
And light them at the fiery glowworms' eyes,
To have my love to bed and to arise;   145
And pluck the wings from painted butterflies
To fan the moonbeams from his sleeping eyes.
Nod to him, elves, and do him courtesies.

---

116. fair . . . force: the power of your beauty   **121. gleek:** make a witty joke
124. serve . . . turn: take care of myself   **127. rate:** rank   **128. still . . . state:** always attends
upon me   **136 s.d. MOTH:** Pronounced like "mote," the word may refer to a speck or to the
insect.

PEASEBLOSSOM.   Hail, mortal!

COBWEB.   Hail!   150

MOTH.   Hail!

MUSTARDSEED.   Hail!

BOTTOM.   I cry your worships mercy,° heartily. I beseech your
worship's name.

COBWEB.   Cobweb.   155

BOTTOM.   I shall desire you of more acquaintance, good Master Cobweb. If I cut my finger,° I shall make bold with you.—Your name,
honest gentleman?

PEASEBLOSSOM.   Peaseblossom.

BOTTOM.   I pray you, commend me to Mistress Squash,° your mother,
and to Master Peascod,° your father. Good Master Peaseblossom, I
shall desire you of more acquaintance too.—Your name, I beseech
you, sir?   163

MUSTARDSEED.   Mustardseed.

BOTTOM.   Good Master Mustardseed, I know your patience well. That
same cowardly, giantlike ox-beef° hath devoured many a gentleman of your house. I promise you, your kindred hath made my eyes
water ere now. I desire you of more acquaintance, good Master
Mustardseed.

TITANIA.   Come wait upon him; lead him to my bower.   170
    The moon methinks looks with a watery eye;
And when she weeps, weeps° every little flower,
    Lamenting some enforcèd° chastity.
    Tie up my lover's tongue; bring him silently.
(*Exeunt.*)

SCENE 2. *The scene continues.*

Enter OBERON.

OBERON.   I wonder if Titania be awaked,
    Then, what it was that next came in her eye,
    Which she must dote on in extremity. (*Enter* PUCK.)
    Here comes my messenger. How now, mad spirit?
    What night-rule° now about this haunted° grove?   5

153. cry . . . mercy: I beg pardon of your worships (assuming the Fairies to be important
dignitaries) for asking presumptuous questions.   **157. cut my finger:** cobwebs were used to
stop bleeding from a cut   **160, 161. Squash, Peascod:** names for an unripe and a ripe pea
pod   **166. ox-beef:** mustard is a common condiment for beef   **172. weeps:** causes
dew   **173. enforcèd:** violated   **5. night-rule:** mischief, night's sport   **haunted:** much
visited

PUCK.   My mistress with a monster is in love.
　　Near to her close and consecrated bower,
　　While she was in her dull and sleeping hour,
　　A crew of patches,° rude mechanicals,°
　　That work for bread upon Athenian stalls,°   10
　　Were met together to rehearse a play
　　Intended for great Theseus' nuptial day.
　　The shallowest thickskin of that barren° sort,
　　Who Pyramus presented, in their sport
　　Forsook his scene and entered in a brake.   15
　　When I did him at this advantage take,
　　An ass's noll° I fixèd on his head.
　　Anon his Thisbe must be answerèd,
　　And forth my mimic° comes. When they him spy,
　　As wild geese that the creeping fowler° eye,   20
　　Or russet-pated choughs,° many in sort,
　　Rising and cawing at the gun's report,
　　Sever themselves and madly sweep the sky,
　　So, at his sight, away his fellows fly;
　　And, at our stamp, here o'er and o'er one falls;   25
　　He "Murder!" cries and help from Athens calls.
　　Their sense thus weak, lost with their fears thus strong,
　　Made senseless things begin to do them wrong,
　　For briers and thorns at their apparel snatch;
　　Some, sleeves—some, hats; from yielders all things catch.   30
　　I led them on in this distracted fear
　　And left sweet Pyramus translated there,
　　When in that moment, so it came to pass,
　　Titania waked and straightway loved an ass.
OBERON.   This falls out better than I could devise.   35
　　But hast thou yet latched° the Athenian's eyes
　　With the love juice, as I did bid thee do?
PUCK.   I took him sleeping—that is finished too—
　　And the Athenian woman by his side,
　　That, when he waked, of force° she must be eyed.   40
　　(*Enter* HERMIA *followed by* DEMETRIUS.)
OBERON.   Stand close. This is the same Athenian.
PUCK.   This is the woman, but not this the man.

---

9. **patches:** clowns   **mechanicals:** workingmen   10. **stalls:** market shops
13. **barren:** empty-headed   17. **noll:** head   19. **mimic:** actor   20. **fowler:** bird hunter   21. **russet-pated choughs:** gray-headed crow-like birds   36. **latched:** caught,
snared   40. **of force:** necessarily

DEMETRIUS.   O, why rebuke you him that loves you so?
    Lay breath so bitter on your bitter foe.
HERMIA.   Now I but chide, but I should use thee worse,   45
    For thou, I fear, hast given me cause to curse.
    If thou hast slain Lysander in his sleep,
    Being o'er shoes in blood, plunge in the deep
    And kill me too.
    The sun was not so true unto the day   50
    As he to me. Would he have stolen away
    From sleeping Hermia? I'll believe as soon
    This whole earth may be bored, and that the moon
    May through the center creep, and so displease
    Her brother's noontide with th' Antipodes.°   55
    It cannot be but thou hast murdered him,
    So should a murderer look, so dead,° so grim.
DEMETRIUS.   So should the murdered look, and so should I,
    Pierced through the heart with your stern cruelty.
    Yet you, the murderer, look as bright, as clear   60
    As yonder Venus in her glimmering sphere.
HERMIA.   What's this to my Lysander? Where is he?
    Ah, good Demetrius, wilt thou give him me?
DEMETRIUS.   I had rather give his carcass to my hounds.
HERMIA.   Out, dog! Out, cur! Thou driv'st me past the bounds   65
    Of maiden's patience. Hast thou slain him, then?
    Henceforth be never numbered among men.
    O, once tell true, tell true, even for my sake!
    Durst thou have looked upon him being awake?
    And hast thou killed him sleeping? O brave touch!   70
    Could not a worm, an adder, do so much?
    An adder did it; for with doubler° tongue
    Than thine, thou serpent, never adder stung.
DEMETRIUS.   You spend your passion on a misprised° mood.
    I am not guilty of Lysander's blood,   75
    Nor is he dead, for aught that I can tell.
HERMIA.   I pray thee, tell me then that he is well.
DEMETRIUS.   And if I could, what should I get therefor?
HERMIA.   A privilege never to see me more.
    And from thy hated presence part I so.   80
    See me no more, whether he be dead or no. (*Exit.*)

---

55. Her . . . Antipodes: The sun shining on the opposite side of the earth
57. dead: deadly   **72. doubler:** twice as deceitful   **74. misprised:** mistaken

DEMETRIUS.   There is no following her in this fierce vein,
    Here therefore for a while I will remain.
    So sorrow's heaviness doth heavier grow
    For debt that bankrupt sleep doth sorrow owe,   85
    Which now in some slight measure it will pay,
    If for his tender here I make some stay.°
    (*He lies down and sleeps.*)
OBERON.   What hast thou done? Thou hast mistaken quite
    And laid the love juice on some true love's sight!
    Of thy misprision must perforce ensue   90
    Some true love turned, and not a false turned true.
PUCK.   Then fate o'errules, that, one man holding troth,
    A million fail, confounding oath on oath.°
OBERON.   About the wood go swifter than the wind,
    And Helena of Athens look thou find.   95
    All fancy-sick° she is and pale of cheer°
    With sighs of love that cost the fresh blood dear.
    By some illusion see thou bring her here.
    I'll charm his eyes against she do appear.°
PUCK.   I go, I go, look how I go,   100
    Swifter than arrow from the Tartar's bow. (*Exit.*)
OBERON (*applying the flower juice to* DEMETRIUS' *eyes*).
           Flower of this purple dye,
           Hit with Cupid's archery,
           Sink in apple of his eye.
           When his love he doth espy,   105
           Let her shine as gloriously
           As the Venus of the sky.
           When thou wak'st, if she be by,
           Beg of her for remedy. (*Enter* PUCK.)
PUCK.   Captain of our fairy band,   110
           Helena is here at hand,
           And the youth, mistook by me,
           Pleading for a lover's fee.°
           Shall we their fond pageant° see?
           Lord, what fools these mortals be!   115

84–87. So . . . stay: A man in sorrow cannot sleep, even when the sorrow increases his need for sleep, but I will try to let sleep give me ease by lying here.   **92–93. one . . . oath:** for one man true in love there are a million who fail, breaking oath after oath   **96. fancy-sick:** lovesick   **cheer:** face   **99. against . . . appear:** to prepare for her arrival   **113. fee:** reward   **114. fond pageant:** display of foolishness

OBERON.   Stand aside. The noise they make
                 Will cause Demetrius to awake.
PUCK.   Then will two at once woo one;
                 That must needs be sport alone.
                 And those things do best please me   120
                 That befall preposterously.
(OBERON *and* PUCK *stand aside. Enter* HELENA *followed by* LYSANDER.)
LYSANDER.   Why should you think that I should woo in scorn?
        Scorn and derision never come in tears.
     Look when I vow, I weep, and vows so born,
        In their nativity all truth appears.°   125
     How can these things in me seem scorn to you,
     Bearing the badge of faith to prove them true?
HELENA.   You do advance your cunning more and more.
        When truth kills truth,° O, devilish-holy fray!
     These vows are Hermia's. Will you give her o'er?   130
        Weigh oath with oath, and you will nothing weigh.
     Your vows to her and me, put in two scales,
     Will even weigh, and both as light as tales.
LYSANDER.   I had no judgment when to her I swore.
HELENA.   Nor none, in my mind, now you give her o'er.   135
LYSANDER.   Demetrius loves her, and he loves not you.
DEMETRIUS (*awaking*).   O Helen, goddess, nymph, perfect, divine!
     To what, my love, shall I compare thine eyne?
     Crystal is muddy.° O, how ripe in show
     Thy lips, those kissing cherries, tempting grow!   140
     That pure congealèd white, high Taurus° snow,
     Fanned with the eastern wind, turns to a crow
     When thou hold'st up thy hand.° O, let me kiss
     This princess of pure white, this seal° of bliss!
HELENA.   O spite! O hell! I see you all are bent   145
     To set against me for your merriment.
     If you were civil and knew courtesy,
     You would not do me thus much injury,
     Can you not hate me, as I know you do,
     But you must join in souls to mock me too?   150

124–25. vows . . . appears: vows made by a weeping person are always sincere
129. truth kills truth: one vow cancels the other—he has sworn love to both Helena and
Hermia   **139. Crystal is muddy:** Compared to her eyes, crystal would look opaque.
141. Taurus: a mountain range in Asia Minor   **142–43. turns . . . hand:** seems black
compared to her white hand   **144. seal:** guarantee

If you were men, as men you are in show,
You would not use a gentle lady so,
To vow, and swear, and superpraise my parts,
When I am sure you hate me with your hearts.
You both are rivals and love Hermia,   155
And now both rivals to mock Helena.
A trim° exploit, a manly enterprise,
To conjure tears up in a poor maid's eyes
With your derision! None of noble sort
Would so offend a virgin and extort°   160
A poor soul's patience, all to make you sport.

LYSANDER.   You are unkind, Demetrius. Be not so.
For you love Hermia, this you know I know.
And here, with all good will, with all my heart,
In Hermia's love I yield you up my part;   165
And yours of Helena to me bequeath,
Whom I do love, and will do till my death.

HELENA.   Never did mockers waste more idle breath.

DEMETRIUS.   Lysander, keep thy Hermia, I will none.
If e'er I loved her, all that love is gone.   170
My heart to her but as guestwise sojourned,°
And now to Helen is it home returned,
There to remain.

LYSANDER.   Helen, it is not so.

DEMETRIUS.   Disparage not the faith thou dost not know,
Lest, to thy peril, thou aby° it dear.   175
Look where thy love comes; yonder is thy dear.

(*Enter* HERMIA.)

HERMIA.   Dark night, that from the eye his function takes,
The ear more quick of apprehension makes;
Wherein it doth impair the seeing sense,
It pays the hearing double recompense.   180
Thou art not by mine eye, Lysander, found;
Mine ear, I thank it, brought me to thy sound.
But why unkindly didst thou leave me so?

LYSANDER.   Why should he stay, whom love doth press to go?

HERMIA.   What love could press Lysander from my side?   185

LYSANDER.   Lysander's love, that would not let him bide—
Fair Helena, who more engilds the night

---

157. trim: fine   **160. extort:** torture   **171. My . . . sojourned:** My heart only made a short
visit to her   **175. aby:** pay for

Than all yon fiery oes and eyes of light.°
Why seek'st thou me? Could not this make thee know
The hate I bear thee made me leave thee so?   190
HERMIA.   You speak not as you think. It cannot be.
HELENA.   Lo, she is one of this confederacy!
    Now I perceive they have conjoined all three
    To fashion this false sport, in spite of me.°
    Injurious Hermia, most ungrateful maid!   195
    Have you conspired, have you with these contrived
    To bait° me with this foul derision?
    Is all the counsel that we two have shared—
    The sisters' vows, the hours that we have spent
    When we have chid the hasty-footed time   200
    For parting us—O, is all forgot?
    All schooldays' friendship, childhood innocence?
    We, Hermia, like two artificial° gods
    Have with our needles created both one flower,
    Both on one sampler, sitting on one cushion,   205
    Both warbling of one song, both in one key,
    As if our hands, our sides, voices, and minds
    Had been incorporate.° So we grew together,
    Like to a double cherry, seeming parted,
    But yet an union in partition,   210
    Two lovely berries molded on one stem;
    So, with two seeming bodies but one heart,
    Two of the first, like coats in heraldry,
    Due but to one and crownèd with one crest.°
    And will you rend our ancient love asunder   215
    To join with men in scorning your poor friend?
    It is not friendly, 'tis not maidenly.
    Our sex, as well as I, may chide you for it,
    Though I alone do feel the injury.
HERMIA.   I am amazèd at your passionate words.   220
    I scorn you not. It seems that you scorn me.
HELENA.   Have you not set Lysander, as in scorn,
    To follow me and praise my eyes and face?
    And made your other love, Demetrius,

188. oes . . . light: stars   194. in spite of me: to spite me   197. bait: tease or
torment   203. artificial: artistically creative   208. incorporate: one single body
213–14. Two . . . crest: As if we were a married couple whose separate coats of arms were
merged into a single one.

Who even but now did spurn me with his foot,   225
To call me goddess, nymph, divine, and rare,
Precious, celestial? Wherefore speaks he this
To her he hates? And wherefore doth Lysander
Deny your love, so rich within his soul,
And tender me, forsooth, affection,   230
But by your setting on, by your consent?
What though I be not so in grace as you,
So hung upon with love, so fortunate,
But miserable most, to love unloved?
This you should pity rather than despise.   235

HERMIA.   I understand not what you mean by this.

HELENA.   Ay, do! Persever,° counterfeit sad° looks,
Make mouths upon me when I turn my back,
Wink each at other, hold the sweet jest up,
This sport, well carried, shall be chronicled.°   240
If you have any pity, grace, or manners,
You would not make me such an argument.°
But fare ye well. 'Tis partly my own fault,
Which death, or absence, soon shall remedy.

LYSANDER.   Stay, gentle Helena; hear my excuse,   245
My love, my life, my soul, fair Helena!

HELENA.   O excellent!

HERMIA (*to* LYSANDER).   Sweet, do not scorn her so.

DEMETRIUS (*to* LYSANDER).   If she cannot entreat, I can compel.

LYSANDER.   Thou canst compel no more than she entreat.
Thy threats have no more strength than her weak prayers.   250
Helen, I love thee, by my life, I do!
I swear by that which I will lose for thee,
To prove him false that says I love thee not.

DEMETRIUS (*to* HELENA).   I say I love thee more than he can do.

LYSANDER.   If thou say so, withdraw, and prove it° too.   255

DEMETRIUS.   Quick, come!

HERMIA.   Lysander, whereto tends all this?

LYSANDER.   Away, you Ethiope!°

DEMETRIUS.   No, no; he'll
Seem to break loose; take on as you° would follow,
But yet come not. You are a tame man. Go!

---

237. **Persever:** Keep the game going   **sad:** serious   240. **chronicled:** written in history
books   242. **argument:** subject for a story   255. **prove it:** i.e., by fighting a duel
257. **Ethiope:** exaggerating the comparative darkness of Hermia's complexion and
hair   258. **take on as you:** pretend you are trying to

LYSANDER (*to* HERMIA).   Hang off, thou cat, thou burr! Vile thing, let
    loose,   260
  Or I will shake thee from me like a serpent!
HERMIA.   Why are you grown so rude? What change is this,
    Sweet love?
LYSANDER.   Thy love? Out, tawny Tartar, out!
    Out, loathèd med'cine!° O hated potion, hence!
HERMIA.   Do you not jest?
HELENA.   Yes, sooth, and so do you.   265
LYSANDER.   Demetrius, I will keep my word with thee.
DEMETRIUS.   I would I had your bond,° for I perceive
    A weak bond° holds you. I'll not trust your word.
LYSANDER.   What, should I hurt her, strike her, kill her dead?
    Although I hate her, I'll not harm her so.   270
HERMIA.   What, can you do me greater harm than hate?
    Hate me? Wherefore? O me, what news, my love?
    Am not I Hermia? Are not you Lysander?
    I am as fair now as I was erewhile.°
    Since night you loved me; yet since night you left me.   275
    Why, then you left me—O, the gods forbid!—
    In earnest, shall I say?
LYSANDER.   Ay, by my life!
    And never did desire to see thee more.
    Therefore be out of hope, of question, of doubt;
    Be certain, nothing truer. 'Tis no jest   280
    That I do hate thee and love Helena.
HERMIA (*to* HELENA).   O me! You juggler! You cankerblossom!°
    You thief of love! What, have you come by night
    And stol'n my love's heart from him?
HELENA.   Fine, i' faith!
    Have you no modesty, no maiden shame,   285
    No touch of bashfulness? What, will you tear
    Impatient answers from my gentle tongue?
    Fie, fie! You counterfeit, you puppet,° you!
HERMIA.   "Puppet"? Why, so! Ay, that way goes the game.
    Now I perceive that she hath made compare   290
    Between our statures; she hath urged her height,
    And with her personage, her tall personage,

---

264. med'cine: poison   **267–68. bond; bond:** written agreement; Hermia's grasp
274. erewhile: a short while ago   **282. cankerblossom:** worm that destroys the bud of a
flower   **288. puppet:** little doll (referring to Hermia's shortness)

    Her height, forsooth, she hath prevailed with him.
    And are you grown so high in his esteem
    Because I am so dwarfish and so low?   295
    How low am I, thou painted maypole? Speak!
    How low am I? I am not yet so low
    But that my nails can reach unto thine eyes.
HELENA.   I pray you, though you mock me, gentlemen,
    Let her not hurt me. I was never curst;°   300
    I have no gift at all in shrewishness;
    I am a right maid° for my cowardice.
    Let her not strike me. You perhaps may think,
    Because she is something lower than myself,
    That I can match her.
HERMIA.   Lower? Hark, again!   305
HELENA.   Good Hermia, do not be so bitter with me.
    I evermore did love you, Hermia,
    Did ever keep your counsels, never wronged you,
    Save that, in love unto Demetrius,
    I told him of your stealth unto this wood.   310
    He followed you; for love I followed him.
    But he hath chid me hence and threatened me
    To strike me, spurn me, nay, to kill me too.
    And now, so° you will let me quiet go,
    To Athens will I bear my folly back   315
    And follow you no further. Let me go.
    You see how simple and how fond I am.
HERMIA.   Why, get you gone. Who is 't that hinders you?
HELENA.   A foolish heart, that I leave here behind.
HERMIA.   What, with Lysander?
HELENA.   With Demetrius.   320
LYSANDER.   Be not afraid; she shall not harm thee, Helena.
DEMETRIUS.   No, sir, she shall not, though you take her part.
HELENA.   O, when she is angry, she is keen and shrewd.°
    She was a vixen when she went to school,
    And though she be but little, she is fierce.   325
HERMIA.   "Little" again? Nothing but "low" and "little"?
    Why will you suffer her to flout me thus?
    Let me come to her.

---

300. curst: fierce, sharp-tongued   **302. right maid:** truly feminine   **314. so:** if
323. keen and shrewd: fierce and sharp-tongued

LYSANDER.   Get you gone, you dwarf!
    You minimus,° of hindering knotgrass° made!
    You bead, you acorn!
DEMETRIUS.   You are too officious   330
    In her behalf that scorns your services.
    Let her alone. Speak not of Helena;
    Take not her part. For, if thou dost intend
    Never so little show of love to her,
    Thou shalt aby it.
LYSANDER.   Now she holds me not.   335
    Now follow, if thou dar'st, to try whose right,
    Of thine or mine, is most in Helena. (*Exit.*)
DEMETRIUS.   Follow? Nay, I'll go with thee, cheek by jowl. (*Exit*)
HERMIA.   You, mistress, all this coil° is 'long of you.°
    Nay, go not back.
HELENA.   I will not trust you, I,   340
    Nor longer stay in your curst company.
    Your hands than mine are quicker for a fray;
    My legs are longer, though, to run away. (*Exit.*)
HERMIA.   I am amazed and know not what to say. (*Exit.*)
OBERON.   This is thy negligence. Still thou mistak'st,   345
    Or else committ'st thy knaveries willfully.
PUCK.   Believe me, king of shadows, I mistook.
    Did not you tell me I should know the man
    By the Athenian garments he had on?
    And so far blameless proves my enterprise   350
    That I have 'nointed an Athenian's eyes;
    And so far am I glad it so did sort,
    As this their jangling I esteem a sport.
OBERON.   Thou seest these lovers seek a place to fight.
    Hie therefore, Robin, overcast the night;   355
    The starry welkin° cover thou anon°
    With drooping fog as black as Acheron,°
    And lead these testy rivals so astray
    As one come not within another's way.
    Like to Lysander sometimes frame thy tongue,   360
    Then stir Demetrius up with bitter wrong,

---

329. **minimus:** tiniest creature   **knotgrass:** a weed supposed to be able to stunt one's
growth   339. **coil:** fighting   **'long of you:** your fault   356. **welkin:** sky
anon: immediately   357. **Acheron:** river of Hades

And sometimes rail thou like Demetrius.
And from each other look thou lead them thus,
Till o'er their brows death-counterfeiting sleep
With leaden legs and batty wings doth creep.   365
Then crush this herb into Lysander's eye,
Whose liquor hath this virtuous property,
To take from thence all error with his might
And make his eyeballs roll with wonted sight.°
When they next wake, all this derision   370
Shall seem a dream and fruitless vision,
And back to Athens shall the lovers wend
With league whose date till death shall never end.°
Whiles I in this affair do thee employ,
I'll to my queen and beg her Indian boy;   375
And then I will her charmèd eye release
From monster's view, and all things shall be peace.

PUCK.   My fairy lord, this must be done with haste,
For night's swift dragons cut the clouds full fast,
And yonder shines Aurora's harbinger,°   380
At whose approach ghosts, wand'ring here and there,
Troop home to churchyards. Damnèd spirits all,
That in crossways and floods have burial,
Already to their wormy beds are gone.°
For fear lest day should look their shames upon,   385
They willfully themselves exile from light
And must for aye° consort with black-browed night.

OBERON.   But we are spirits of another sort.°
I with the Morning's love have oft made sport,
And, like a forester, the groves may tread   390
Even till the eastern gate, all fiery red,
Opening on Neptune with fair blessèd beams,
Turns into yellow gold his salt green streams.
But notwithstanding, haste, make no delay.
We may effect this business yet ere day. (*Exit.*)   395

PUCK.   Up and down, up and down,
I will lead them up and down.
I am feared in field and town.

367–69. hath . . . sight: has the power to remove his mistaken vision and make him see as he
used to   373. With . . . end: Everlastingly united   379–80. night's . . . harbinger: The
dragons that draw night's chariot are speeding away, and the precursor of dawn, the morning
star Venus, has risen.   382–84. Damnèd . . . gone: The ghosts of those who were damned for
their suicide have ceased their night wandering.   387. for aye: forever   388. of another
sort: not damned, and so able to function in daylight as well as night

Goblin,° lead them up and down.
Here comes one. (*Enter* LYSANDER.)   400
LYSANDER.   Where art thou, proud Demetrius? Speak thou now.
PUCK (*imitates* DEMETRIUS' *voice*).   Here, villain, drawn° and ready.
    Where art thou?
LYSANDER.   I will be with thee straight.
PUCK.   Follow me, then,
    To plainer ground. (LYSANDER *follows the voice. Enter* DEMETRIUS.)
DEMETRIUS.   Lysander! Speak again!
    Thou runaway, thou coward, art thou fled?   405
    Speak! In some bush? Where dost thou hide thy head?
PUCK (*imitates* LYSANDER's *voice*).   Thou coward, art thou bragging to
        the stars,
    Telling the bushes that thou look'st for wars,
    And wilt not come? Come, recreant,° come, thou child,
    I'll whip thee with a rod. He is defiled   410
    That draws a sword on thee.
DEMETRIUS.   Yea, art thou there?
PUCK.   Follow my voice. We'll try° no manhood here.
    (*Exeunt all three.* LYSANDER *returns.*)
LYSANDER.   He goes before me and still dares me on.
    When I come where he calls, then he is gone.
    The villain is much lighter-heeled than I.   415
    I followed fast but faster he did fly,
    That fallen am I in dark uneven way,
    And here will rest me. Come, thou gentle day!
    For if but once thou show me thy gray light,
    I'll find Demetrius and revenge this spite.   420
    (*He lies down and sleeps. Enter* PUCK *leading* DEMETRIUS.)
PUCK.   Ho, ho, ho! Coward, why com'st thou not?
DEMETRIUS.   Abide° me, if thou dar'st, for well I wot°
    Thou runn'st before me, shifting every place,
    And dar'st not stand nor look me in the face.
    Where art thou now?
PUCK.   Come hither. I am here.   425
DEMETRIUS.   Nay, then, thou mock'st me. Thou shalt buy this dear,°
    If ever I thy face by daylight see.
    Now go thy way. Faintness constraineth me
    To measure out my length on this cold bed.

---

399. Goblin: Puck refers to himself, using one of his names, "Hobgoblin."   **402. drawn:** with
my sword in my hand   **409. recreant:** traitor, coward   **412. try:** test   **422. Abide:** Wait
for   **wot:** know   **426. buy this dear:** pay plenty for this

By day's approach look to be visited.   430
(*He lies down and sleeps. Enter* HELENA.)
HELENA.   O weary night, O long and tedious night,
     Abate° thy hours! Shine comforts from the east,
That I may back to Athens by daylight
     From these that my poor company detest;
And sleep, that sometimes shuts up sorrow's eye,   435
Steal me awhile from mine own company.
(*She lies down and sleeps.*)
PUCK.   Yet but three? Come one more;
                    Two of both kinds makes up four.
                    Here she comes, curst° and sad.
                    Cupid is a knavish lad,   440
                    Thus to make poor females mad. (*Enter* HERMIA.)
HERMIA.   Never so weary, never so in woe,
     Bedabbled with the dew and torn with briers,
     I can no further crawl, no further go;
     My legs can keep no pace with my desires.   445
Here will I rest me till the break of day.
Heavens shield Lysander, if they mean a fray!
(*She lies down and sleeps.*)
PUCK.   On the ground
     Sleep sound.
     I'll apply   450
     To your eye,
Gentle lover, remedy. (*He squeezes the juice on* LYSANDER's *eyes.*)
     When thou wak'st,
     Thou tak'st
     True delight   455
     In the sight
Of thy former lady's eye;
And the country proverb known,
That every man should take his own,
In your waking shall be shown: 460
     Jack shall have Jill;
     Naught shall go ill;
The man shall have his mare again, and all shall be well. (*Exit. The
four lovers remain, asleep.*)

---

432. Abate: Shorten   **439. curst:** ill-tempered

ACT 4

SCENE 1. *The action continues, with the four lovers still asleep on the ground.*

Enter TITANIA, BOTTOM, *and* FAIRIES, *and behind them* OBERON.

TITANIA.   Come, sit thee down upon this flowery bed,
    While I thy amiable° cheeks do coy,°
And stick muskroses in thy sleek smooth head,
    And kiss thy fair large ears, my gentle joy.

BOTTOM.   Where's Peaseblossom?   5

PEASEBLOSSOM.   Ready.

BOTTOM.   Scratch my head, Peaseblossom. Where's Monsieur° Cobweb?

COBWEB.   Ready.

BOTTOM.   Monsieur Cobweb, good monsieur, get you your weapons in your hand, and kill me a red-hipped humble-bee on the top of a thistle; and, good monsieur, bring me the honey bag. Do not fret yourself too much in the action, monsieur; and, good monsieur, have a care the honey bag break not. I would be loath to have you over-flown with a honey bag, signor. (*Exit* COBWEB.) Where's Monsieur Mustardseed?   16

MUSTARDSEED.   Ready.

BOTTOM.   Give me your neaf,° Monsieur Mustardseed. Pray you, leave your courtesy,° good monsieur.

MUSTARDSEED.   What's your will?   20

BOTTOM.   Nothing, good monsieur, but to help Cavalery° Cobweb to scratch. I must to the barber's, monsieur, for methinks I am mar-velous hairy about the face; and I am such a tender ass, if my hair do but tickle me I must scratch.

TITANIA.   What, wilt thou hear some music, my sweet love?   25

BOTTOM.   I have a reasonable good ear in music. Let's have the tongs and the bones.° (FAIRIES *play rustic music.*)

TITANIA.   Or say, sweet love, what thou desirest to eat.

BOTTOM.   Truly, a peck of provender. I could munch your good dry oats. Me thinks I have a great desire to a bottle° of hay. Good hay, sweet hay, hath no fellow.°   31

---

2. **amiable:** lovely   **coy:** caress   7, 21. **Monsieur, Cavalery:** terms appropriate for addressing French and Italian gentlemen ("Cavalery" for "Cavaliere")   18. **neaf:** fist
18–19. **leave . . . courtesy:** there's no need to keep bowing   26–27. **tongs . . . bones:** crude rustic musical instruments, both creating monotone percussion effects
30. **bottle:** bundle   31. **fellow:** equal

TITANIA.   I have a venturous fairy that shall seek
    The squirrel's hoard, and fetch thee new nuts.
BOTTOM.   I had rather have a handful or two of dried peas. But, I pray
    you, let none of your people stir me. I have an exposition° of sleep
    come upon me.   36
TITANIA.   Sleep thou, and I will wind thee in my arms.
    Fairies, begone, and be all ways away. (*Exeunt* FAIRIES.)
    So doth the woodbine the sweet honeysuckle
    Gently entwist; the female ivy so   40
    Enrings the barky fingers of the elm.
    O, how I love thee! How I dote on thee!
    (*They sleep. Enter* PUCK.)
OBERON (*coming forward*). Welcome, good Robin. Seest thou this
        sweet sight?
    Her dotage now I do begin to pity.
    For, meeting her of late behind the wood   45
    Seeking sweet favors for this hateful fool,
    I did upbraid her and fall out with her.
    For she his hairy temples then had rounded
    With coronet of fresh and fragrant flowers;
    And that same dew, which sometime on the buds   50
    Was wont to swell like round and orient pearls,
    Stood now within the pretty flowerets' eyes
    Like tears that did their own disgrace bewail.
    When I had at my pleasure taunted her,
    And she in mild terms begged my patience,   55
    I then did ask of her her changeling child,
    Which straight she gave me, and her fairy sent
    To bear him to my bower in Fairyland.
    And, now I have the boy, I will undo
    This hateful imperfection of her eyes.   60
    And, gentle Puck, take this transformèd scalp
    From off the head of this Athenian swain,
    That he, awaking when the other do,
    May all to Athens back again repair,°
    And think no more of this night's accidents   65
    But as the fierce vexation of a dream.
    But first I will release the Fairy Queen.

---

35. exposition: Bottom means "disposition" or "inclination." **64. repair:** return

(*He applies the antidote to* TITANIA's *eyes.*)
 Be as thou wast wont to be;
 See as thou wast wont to see.
 Dian's bud o'er Cupid's flower°   70
 Hath such force and blessèd power.
Now, my Titania, wake you, my sweet queen.
TITANIA (*awaking*). My Oberon! What visions have I seen!
 Methought I was enamored of an ass.
OBERON. There lies your love?
TITANIA.   How came these things to pass? 75
 O, how mine eyes do loathe his visage now!
OBERON. Silence awhile. Robin, take off this head.
 Titania, music call, and strike more dead
 Than common sleep of all these five the sense.°
TITANIA. Music, ho! Music, such as charmeth sleep! (*Music.*) 80
PUCK (*to* BOTTOM, *removing the ass's head from him*).
 Now, when thou wak'st, with thine own fool's eyes peep.
OBERON. Sound, music! Come, my queen, take hands with me,
 And rock the ground whereon these sleepers be.
 (*They dance.*)
 Now thou and I are new in amity,
 And will tomorrow midnight solemnly   85
 Dance in Duke Theseus' house triumphantly,
 And bless it to all fair prosperity.
 There shall the pairs of faithful lovers be
 Wedded, with Theseus, all in jollity.
PUCK. Fairy King, attend, and mark: 90
 I do hear the morning lark.
OBERON. Then, my queen, in silence sad,°
 Trip we after night's shade.
 We the globe can compass soon,
 Swifter than the wandering moon.   95
TITANIA. Come, my lord, and in our flight
 Tell me how it came this night
 That I sleeping here was found
 With these mortals on the ground.
 (*Exeunt* TITANIA, OBERON, *and* PUCK. *Hunting horns sound, and enter*
 THESEUS *with his train,* HIPPOLYTA, *and* EGEUS.)

---

70. Dian's . . . flower: a flower sacred to the goddess of chastity Diana, over the flower
transformed by the arrow of Cupid (the pansy) **78–79. strike . . . sense:** put all five of them
(Bottom and the four lovers) into a deeper sleep than normal **92. sad:** serious

THESEUS.   Go, one of you, find out the forester,   100
  For now our observation° is performed;
  And since we have the vaward° of the day,
  My love shall hear the music of my hounds.
  Uncouple° in the western valley; let them go.
  Dispatch, I say, and find the forester.   105
  (*Exit an* ATTENDANT.)
  We will, fair queen, up to the mountain's top
  And mark the musical confusion
  Of hounds and echo in conjunction.
HIPPOLYTA.   I was with Hercules and Cadmus once
  When in a wood of Crete they bayed° the bear   110
  With hounds of Sparta. Never did I hear
  Such gallant chiding,° for, besides the groves,
  The skies, the fountains, every region near
  Seemed all one mutual cry. I never heard
  So musical a discord, such sweet thunder.   115
THESEUS.   My hounds are bred out of the Spartan kind,
  So flewed, so sanded;° and their heads are hung
  With ears that sweep away the morning dew;
  Crook-kneed, and dewlapped° like Thessalian bulls;
  Slow in pursuit, but matched in mouth like bells,   120
  Each under each.° A cry more tunable
  Was never holloed to nor cheered with horn
  In Crete, in Sparta, nor in Thessaly.
  Judge when you hear. But soft! What nymphs are these?
EGEUS.   My lord, this is my daughter here asleep,   125
  And this Lysander; this Demetrius is;
  This Helena, old Nedar's Helena.
  I wonder of their being here together.
THESEUS.   No doubt they rose up early to observe
  The rite of May, and hearing our intent,   130
  Came here in grace of our solemnity.°
  But speak, Egeus. Is not this the day
  That Hermia should give answer of her choice?
EGEUS.   It is, my lord.

---

101. observation: May morning ritual   **102. vaward:** earliest part
104. Uncouple: Unleash   **110. bayed:** brought to bay   **112. chiding:** barking
117. flewed, sanded: with hanging cheeks, sand-colored   **119. dewlapped:** with folds of skin
hanging under their chins   **120–21. matched . . . each:** barking in harmony, like bells, from
high to low   **131. in . . . solemnity:** to honor our marriage ceremony

THESEUS.   Go bid the huntsmen wake them with their horns.   135
(*Exit an* ATTENDANT. *Shouting and horns sounding off-stage. The four
lovers start up.*)
Good morrow, friends. Saint Valentine° is past.
Begin these woodbirds but to couple now?
LYSANDER.   Pardon, my lord. (*They kneel.*)
THESEUS.   I pray you all, stand up. (*They stand.*)
    I know you two are rival enemies;
    How comes this gentle concord in the world,   140
    That hatred is so far from jealousy°
    To sleep by hate and fear no enmity?
LYSANDER.   My lord, I shall reply amazedly,
    Half sleep, half waking; but as yet, I swear,
    I cannot truly say how I came here.   145
    But, as I think—for truly would I speak,
    And now I do bethink me, so it is—
    I came with Hermia hither. Our intent
    Was to be gone from Athens, where we might,
    Without the peril° of the Athenian law—   150
EGEUS.   Enough, enough, my lord; you have enough.
    I beg the law, the law, upon his head.
    They would have stol'n away; they would, Demetrius,
    Thereby to have defeated you and me,
    You of your wife and me of my consent,   155
    Of my consent that she should be your wife.
DEMETRIUS.   My lord, fair Helen told me of their stealth,
    Of this their purpose hither to this wood,
    And I in fury hither followed them,
    Fair Helena in fancy following me.   160
    But, my good lord, I wot not by what power—
    But by some power it is—my love to Hermia,
    Melted as the snow, seems to me now
    As the remembrance of an idle gaud°
    Which in my childhood I did dote upon;   165
    And all the faith, the virtue of my heart,
    The object and the pleasure of mine eye,
    Is only Helena. To her, my lord,
    Was I betrothed ere I saw Hermia,

---

136. **Saint Valentine:** the day on which birds were thought to choose a mate
141. **jealousy:** suspicion or fear of danger   150. **Without the peril:** Beyond the
danger   164. **idle gaud:** worthless toy

But like a sickness did I loathe this food;   170
But, as in health, come to my natural taste,
Now I do wish it, love it, long for it,
And will forevermore be true to it.

THESEUS.   Fair lovers, you are fortunately met.
Of this discourse we more will hear anon.   175
Egeus, I will overbear your will;
For in the temple, by and by, with us
These couples shall eternally be knit.
And, for the morning now is something worn,
Our purposed hunting shall be set aside.   180
Away with us to Athens. Three and three,
We'll hold a feast in great solemnity.
Come, Hippolyta.

(*Exeunt* THESEUS, HIPPOLYTA, EGEUS, *and train.*)

DEMETRIUS.   These things seem small and undistinguishable,
Like far-off mountains turnèd into clouds.   185

HERMIA.   Methinks I see these things with parted° eye,
When everything seems double.

HELENA.   So methinks;
And I have found Demetrius like a jewel,
Mine own, and not mine own.

DEMETRIUS.   Are you sure
That we are awake? It seems to me   190
That yet we sleep, we dream. Do not you think
The Duke was here, and bid us follow him?

HERMIA.   Yea, and my father.

HELENA.   And Hippolyta.

LYSANDER.   And he did bid us follow to the temple.

DEMETRIUS.   Why, then, we are awake. Let's follow him,   195
And by the way let us recount our dreams.

(*Exeunt the four lovers.*)

BOTTOM (*awaking*). When my cue comes, call me, and I will answer. My
next is "Most fair Pyramus." Heigh-ho! Peter Quince! Flute, the
bellows mender! Snout, the tinker! Starveling! God's my life,°
stolen hence and left me asleep! I have had a most rare vision. I
have had a dream, past the wit of man to say what dream it was.
Man is but an ass if he go about to expound this dream. Methought
I was—there is no man can tell what. Methought I was—and

186. **parted:** out of focus   199. **God's my life:** God save me.

methought I had—but man is but a patched fool° if he will offer to say what methought I had. The eye of man hath not heard, the ear of man hath not seen, man's hand is not able to taste, his tongue to conceive, nor his heart to report,° what my dream was. I will get Peter Quince to write a ballad° of this dream. It shall be called "Bottom's Dream," because it hath no bottom,° and I will sing it in the latter end of a play, before the Duke. Peradventure, to make it the more gracious, I shall sing it at her° death. (*Exit.*)   211

SCENE 2. *Athens.* QUINCE's *house.*

Enter QUINCE, FLUTE, SNOUT, *and* STARVELING.

QUINCE.   Have you sent to Bottom's house? Is he come home yet?
STARVELING.   He cannot be heard of. Out of doubt he is transported.°
FLUTE.   If he come not, then the play is marred. It goes not forward. Doth it?
QUINCE.   It is not possible. You have not a man in all Athens able to discharge Pyramus but he.   6
FLUTE.   No, he hath simply the best wit° of any handicraft man in Athens.
QUINCE.   Yea, and the best person° too, and he is a very paramour for a sweet voice.   10
FLUTE.   You must say "paragon." A paramour is, God bless us, a thing of naught.° (*Enter* SNUG.)
SNUG.   Masters, the Duke is coming from the temple, and there is two or three lords and ladies more married. If our sport had gone forward, we had all been made men.°   15
FLUTE.   O sweet bully Bottom! Thus hath he lost sixpence a day during his life;° he could not have scaped sixpence a day. An the Duke had not given him sixpence a day for playing Pyramus, I'll be hanged. He would have deserved it. Sixpence a day in Pyramus, or nothing. (*Enter* BOTTOM.)
BOTTOM.   Where are these lads? Where are these hearts?   20
QUINCE.   Bottom! O most courageous day! O most happy hour!

204. **patched fool:** a court jester in motley   205–7. **The eye . . . report:** Bottom typically mixes up senses and what they report.   208. **ballad:** Printed poems related the latest sensational (and sometimes fictitious) news, a sixteenth-century version of supermarket tabloids.   209. **hath no bottom:** is profound beyond measuring (also, has no basis in reality)   211. **her:** presumably, Thisbe's   2. **transported:** stolen away by the fairies   7. **wit:** intelligence   9. **best person:** handsomest   12. **of naught:** immoral   15. **made men:** men who have made it in life   16–17. **sixpence . . . life:** a generous royal pension, equivalent to a craftsman's daily wage

BOTTOM.   Masters, I am to discourse wonders.° But ask me not what;
for if I tell you, I am no true Athenian. I will tell you everything,
right as it fell out.

QUINCE.   Let us hear, sweet Bottom.   25

BOTTOM.   Not a word of me. All that I will tell you is that the Duke
hath dined. Get your apparel together, good strings° to your beards,
new ribbons to your pumps;° meet presently at the palace; every
man look o'er his part; for the short and the long is, our play is preferred.° In any case, let Thisbe have clean linen; and let not him
that plays the lion pare his nails, for they shall hang out for the
lion's claws. And, most dear actors, eat no onions nor garlic, for we
are to utter sweet breath; and I do not doubt but to hear them say it
is a sweet comedy. No more words. Away! Go, away! (*Exeunt.*)   34

ACT 5

SCENE 1. *Athens. The palace of* THESEUS.

Enter THESEUS, HIPPOLYTA, PHILOSTRATE, LORDS, *and* ATTENDANTS.

HIPPOLYTA.   'Tis strange, my Theseus, that these lovers speak of.

THESEUS.   More strange than true. I never may believe
These antique fables nor these fairy toys.°
Lovers and madmen have such seething brains,
Such shaping fantasies,° that apprehend°   5
More than cool reason ever comprehends.°
The lunatic, the lover, and the poet
Are of imagination all compact.°
One sees more devils than vast hell can hold;
That is the madman. The lover, all as frantic,   10
Sees Helen's beauty in a brow of Egypt.°
The poet's eye, in a fine frenzy rolling,
Doth glance from heaven to earth, from earth to heaven;
And as imagination bodies forth
The forms of things unknown, the poet's pen   15

---

22. am . . . wonders: have wonderful things to tell you   **27. good strings:** for tying on their
beards   **28. pumps:** shoes   **29. preferred:** accepted for consideration, "on the short list"
3. fairy toys: trivial fairy stories   **5. fantasies:** imaginations   **apprehend:** perceive,
imagine   **6. comprehends:** understands   **8. Are . . . compact:** Are composed entirely of
imagination   **11. Helen's . . . Egypt:** the beauty of Helen of Troy in the (ugly) face of a gypsy

Turns them to shapes and gives to airy nothing
A local habitation and a name.
Such tricks hath strong imagination
That if it would but apprehend some joy,
It comprehends some bringer° of that joy;   20
Or in the night, imagining some fear,
How easy is a bush supposed a bear!
HIPPOLYTA.   But all the story of the night told over,
And all their minds transfigured so together,
More witnesseth than fancy's images°   25
And grows to something of great constancy;°
But, howsoever, strange and admirable.°
(*Enter* LYSANDER, DEMETRIUS, HERMIA, *and* HELENA.)
THESEUS.   Here come the lovers, full of joy and mirth.
Joy, gentle friends! Joy and fresh days of love
Accompany your hearts!
LYSANDER.   More than to us   30
Wait in your royal walks, your board, your bed!
THESEUS.   Come now, what masques,° what dances shall we have
To wear away this long age of three hours
Between our after-supper and bedtime?
Where is our usual manager of mirth?   35
What revels are in hand? Is there no play
To ease the anguish of a torturing hour?
Call Philostrate.
PHILOSTRATE.   Here, mighty Theseus.
THESEUS.   Say, what abridgment° have you for this evening?
What masque? What music? How shall we beguile   40
The lazy time, if not with some delight?
PHILOSTRATE (*giving him a paper*).   There is a brief° how many sports
      are ripe.
Make choice of which Your Highness will see first.
THESEUS (*reads*).   "The battle with the Centaurs,° to be sung
By an Athenian eunuch to the harp"?   45
We'll none of that. That have I told my love,
In glory of my kinsman Hercules.

---

20. comprehends . . . bringer: invents some cause   **25. More . . . images:** Seems evidence of
more than just imaginary things   **26. constancy:** consistency, certainty
27. admirable: wonderful   **32. masques:** courtly entertainments   **39. abridgment:** pastime,
entertainment   **42. brief:** summary list   **44. battle . . . Centaurs:** probably refers to a
mythical story in which the centaurs (half human, half horse) attempted to steal a bride from
her husband, but were defeated with the help of Hercules

(*He reads.*) "The riot of the tipsy Bacchanals,
Tearing the Thracian singer in their rage"?°
That is an old device; and it was played   50
When I from Thebes came last a conqueror.
(*He reads.*) "The thrice three Muses mourning for the death
Of Learning, late deceased in beggary"?
That is some satire, keen and critical,
Not sorting with° a nuptial ceremony.   55
(*He reads.*) "A tedious brief scene of young Pyramus
And his love Thisbe; very tragical mirth"?
Merry and tragical? Tedious and brief?
That is, hot ice and wondrous strange snow.
How shall we find the concord of this discord?   60
PHILOSTRATE.   A play there is, my lord, some ten words long,
Which is as brief as I have known a play.
But by ten words, my lord, it is too long,
Which makes it tedious. For in all the play
There is not one word apt, one player fitted.   65
And tragical, my noble lord, it is,
For Pyramus therein doth kill himself,
Which, when I saw rehearsed, I must confess,
Made mine eyes water; but more merry tears
The passion of loud laughter never shed.   70
THESEUS.   What are they that do play it?
PHILOSTRATE.   Hardhanded men that work in Athens here,
Which never labored in their minds till now,
And now have toiled their unbreathed° memories
With this same play, against° your nuptial.   75
THESEUS.   And we will hear it.
PHILOSTRATE.   No, my noble lord,
It is not for you. I have heard it over,
And it is nothing, nothing in the world—
Unless you can find sport in their intents,
Extremely stretched° and conned° with cruel pain,   80
To do you service.
THESEUS.   I will hear that play;
For never anything can be amiss
When simpleness and duty tender it.
Go, bring them in, and take your places, ladies.
(*Exit* PHILOSTRATE.)

48–49. The riot . . . rage: The poet Orpheus was torn to pieces by a mob of drunken women
(worshippers of the god of wine Bacchus).   **55. sorting with:** appropriate to
74. unbreathed: inexperienced, undeveloped   **75. against:** in preparation for
80. stretched: strained   **conned:** memorized

HIPPOLYTA.   I love not to see wretchedness o'ercharged,°   85
   And duty in his service° perishing.
THESEUS.   Why, gentle sweet, you shall see no such thing.
HIPPOLYTA.   He says they can do nothing in this kind.
THESEUS.   The kinder we, to give them thanks for nothing.
   Our sport shall be to take what they mistake;   90
   And what poor duty cannot do, noble respect
   Takes it in might, not merit.°
   Where I have come, great clerks° have purposèd
   To greet me with premeditated welcomes,
   Where I have seen them shiver and look pale,   95
   Make periods in the midst of sentences,
   Throttle their practiced accent in their fears,
   And in conclusion dumbly have broke off,
   Not paying me a welcome. Trust me, sweet,
   Out of this silence yet I picked a welcome,   100
   And in the modesty of fearful duty
   I read as much as from the rattling tongue
   Of saucy and audacious eloquence.
   Love, therefore, and tongue-tied simplicity
   In least speak most, to my capacity.°   105
   (*Enter* PHILOSTRATE.)
PHILOSTRATE.   So please Your Grace, the Prologue is addressed.°
THESEUS.   Let him approach.
   (*Flourish of trumpets. Enter* QUINCE *for the Prologue.*)
PROLOGUE.   If we offend, it is with our good will.
   That you should think, we come not to offend,
   But with good will. To show our simple skill,   110
   That is the true beginning of our end.
   Consider, then, we come but in despite.
   We do not come, as minding° to content you,
   Our true intent is. All for your delight
   We are not here. That you should here repent you,   115
   The actors are at hand, and, by their show,
   You shall know all that you are like to know.
THESEUS.   This fellow doth not stand upon points.°

---

85. **wretchedness o'ercharged:** poor men trying to do too much   86. **in his service:** in
attempting to serve   91–92. **noble . . . merit:** i.e., a noble mind is more concerned with the
good intention than with the poor performance   93. **great clerks:** learned scholars
105. **In . . . capacity:** Are most eloquent when they say less, in my judgment
106. **addressed:** ready   113. **minding:** intending   118. **stand upon points:** pay attention to
punctuation marks (and thus, doesn't make his points clearly)

LYSANDER.   He hath rid his prologue like a rough colt; he knows not
the stop.° A good moral, my lord: it is not enough to speak, but to
speak true.

HIPPOLYTA.   Indeed, he hath played on his prologue like a child on a
recorder:° a sound, but not in government.°

THESEUS.   His speech was like a tangled chain: nothing impaired, but
all disordered. Who is next?   125

(*Enter* BOTTOM *as* PYRAMUS, FLUTE *as* THISBE, SNOUT *as* WALL,
STARVELING *as* MOONSHINE, *and* SNUG *as* LION.)

PROLOGUE.   Gentles, perchance you wonder at this show,
>   But wonder on, till truth make all things plain.
This man is Pyramus, if you would know.
>   This beauteous lady Thisbe is, certain.
This man with lime and roughcast doth present   130
>   Wall, that vile wall which did these lovers sunder,
And through Wall's chink, poor souls, they are content
>   To whisper. At the which let no man wonder.
This man, with lantern, dog, and bush of thorn,
>   Presenteth Moonshine; for, if you will know,   135
By moonshine did these lovers think no scorn°
>   To meet at Ninus' tomb, there, there to woo.
This grisly beast, which Lion hight° by name,
>   The trusty Thisbe coming first by night
Did scare away, or rather did affright;   140
>   And as she fled, her mantle she did fall,°
Which Lion vile with bloody mouth did stain.
>   Anon comes Pyramus, sweet youth and tall,°
And finds his trusty Thisbe's mantle slain;
>   Whereat, with blade, with bloody, blameful blade,   145
He bravely broached his boiling bloody breast.
>   And Thisbe, tarrying in mulberry shade,
His dagger drew, and died. For all the rest,
>   Let Lion, Moonshine, Wall, and lovers twain
At large discourse, while here they do remain.   150

(*Exeunt* PROLOGUE, PYRAMUS, THISBE, MOONSHINE, *and* LION.)

THESEUS.   I wonder if the lion be to speak.

DEMETRIUS.   No wonder, my lord. One lion may, when many asses do.

WALL.   In this same interlude° it doth befall

---

120. **stop:** reining in an untrained colt, and punctuation mark   123. **recorder:** a wind
instrument like a flute   **government:** control   136. **think no scorn:** not regard it as
disgraceful   138. **hight:** is named   141. **did fall:** dropped   143. **tall:** brave
153. **interlude:** play

That I, one Snout by name, present a wall,
And such a wall as I would have you think   155
That had in it a crannied hole or chink,
Through which the lovers, Pyramus and Thisbe,
Did whisper often, very secretly.
This loam, this roughcast, and this stone doth show
That I am that same wall; the truth is so.   160
And this the cranny is, right and sinister,°
Through which the fearful lovers are to whisper.

THESEUS.   Would you desire lime and hair to speak better?

DEMETRIUS.   It is the wittiest partition that ever I heard discourse,
my lord. (*Enter* PYRAMUS.)   165

THESEUS.   Pyramus draws near the wall. Silence!

PYRAMUS.   O grim-looked night! O night with hue so black!
O night, which ever art when day is not!
O night, O night! Alack, alack, alack,
I fear my Thisbe's promise is forgot!   170
And thou, O wall, O sweet, O lovely wall,
That stand'st between her father's ground and mine,
Thou wall, O wall, O sweet and lovely wall,
Show me thy chink, to blink through with mine eyne. (WALL
holds up his fingers.)
Thanks, courteous wall. Jove shield thee well for this.   175
But what see I? No Thisbe do I see.
O wicked wall, through whom I see no bliss!
Cursed be thy stones for thus deceiving me!

THESEUS.   The wall, methinks, being sensible,° should curse again.°

PYRAMUS.   No, in truth, sir, he should not. "Deceiving me" is Thisbe's
cue: she is to enter now, and I am to spy her through the wall. You
shall see, it will fall pat° as I told you. Yonder she comes. (*Enter*
THISBE.)

THISBE.   O wall, full often hast thou heard my moans   183
For parting my fair Pyramus and me.
My cherry lips have often kissed thy stones,
Thy stones with lime and hair knit up in thee.

PYRAMUS.   I see a voice. Now will I to the chink,
To spy an I can hear my Thisbe's face.
Thisbe!

THISBE.   My love! Thou art my love, I think.

---

161. right and sinister: running from right to left, horizontal   **179. sensible:** capable of
feeling   **curse again:** curse back at him   **182. fall pat:** happen precisely

PYRAMUS.   Think what thou wilt, I am thy lover's grace,   190
    And like Limander° am I trusty still.
THISBE.   And I like Helen,° till the Fates me kill.
PYRAMUS.   Not Shafalus° to Procrus° was so true.
THISBE.   As Shafalus to Procrus, I to you.
PYRAMUS.   O, kiss me through the hole of this vile wall!   195
THISBE.   I kiss the wall's hole, not your lips at all.
PYRAMUS.   Wilt thou at Ninny's tomb meet me straightway?
THISBE.   'Tide° life, 'tide death, I come without delay.
    (*Exeunt* PYRAMUS *and* THISBE.)
WALL.   Thus have I, Wall, my part dischargèd so,
    And, being done, thus Wall away doth go. (*Exit.*)   200
THESEUS.   Now is the mural down between the two neighbors.
DEMETRIUS.   No remedy, my lord, when walls are so willful to hear
    without warning.°
HIPPOLYTA.   This is the silliest stuff that ever I heard.
THESEUS.   The best in this kind are but shadows,° and the worst are no
    worse, if imagination amend them.   206
HIPPOLYTA.   It must be your imagination then, and not theirs.
THESEUS.   If we imagine no worse of them than they of themselves,
    they may pass for excellent men. Here come two noble beasts in, a
    man and a lion.   210
    (*Enter* LION *and* MOONSHINE.)
LION.   You, ladies, you, whose gentle hearts do fear
    The smallest monstrous mouse that creeps on floor,
    May now perchance both quake and tremble here,
      When lion rough in wildest rage doth roar.
    Then know that I, as Snug the joiner, am   215
    A lion fell,° nor else no lion's dam;
    For, if I should as lion come in strife
    Into this place, 'twere pity on my life.°
THESEUS.   A very gentle beast, and of a good conscience.
DEMETRIUS.   The very best at a beast, my lord, that e'er I saw.   220
LYSANDER.   This lion is a very fox for his valor.°
THESEUS.   True, and a goose for his discretion.°

191–93. Limander, Helen, Shafalus, Procrus: mangled references to famous pairs of lovers—
Leander and Hero (not Helen), Cephalus and Procris   **198. 'Tide:** Betide, come
203. without warning: i.e., without telling the parents of the elopement
205. shadows: mere representations, not true-to-life   **216. fell:** fierce
218. 'twere . . . life: it would cost me my life   **221. is . . . valor:** his valor is chiefly just
craftiness   **222. goose . . . discretion:** more foolish than he is discreet

DEMETRIUS.   Not so, my lord, for his valor cannot carry his discretion, and the fox carries the goose.

THESEUS.   His discretion, I am sure, cannot carry his valor, for the goose carries not the fox. It is well. Leave it to his discretion, and let us listen to the moon.   227

MOON.   This lanthorn doth the hornèd moon present—

DEMETRIUS.   He should have worn the horns on his head.°

THESEUS.   He is no crescent, and his horns are invisible within the circumference.°   231

MOON.   This lanthorn doth the hornèd moon present;
     Myself the man i' the moon do seem to be.

THESEUS.   This is the greatest error of all the rest. The man should be put into the lanthorn. How is it else the man i' the moon?   235

DEMETRIUS.   He dares not come there for the candle, for you see it is already in snuff.°

HIPPOLYTA.   I am aweary of this moon. Would he would change!

THESEUS.   It appears, by his small light of discretion, that he is in the wane; but yet, in courtesy, in all reason, we must stay the time.   240

LYSANDER.   Proceed, Moon.

MOON.   All that I have to say is to tell you that the lanthorn is the moon, I, the man i' the moon, this thornbush my thornbush, and this dog my dog.

DEMETRIUS.   Why, all these should be in the lanthorn, for all these are in the moon. But silence! Here comes Thisbe. (*Enter* THISBE.)   246

THISBE.   This is old Ninny's tomb. Where is my love?

LION (*roaring*). O!

DEMETRIUS.   Well roared, Lion.

     (THISBE *runs off, dropping her mantle.*)

THESEUS.   Well run, Thisbe.   250

HIPPOLYTA.   Well shone, Moon. Truly, the moon shines with a good grace.

     (LION *shakes* THISBE's *mantle, drops it, and exits.*)

THESEUS.   Well moused,° Lion. (*Enter* PYRAMUS.)

DEMETRIUS.   And then came Pyramus.

LYSANDER.   And so the lion vanished.   255

PYRAMUS.   Sweet Moon, I thank thee for thy sunny beams;
     I thank thee, Moon, for shining now so bright;

---

229. **on his head:** a cuckold was said to sprout horns   230–31. **He . . . circumference:** The horns of a crescent moon are not visible when the moon is full.   237. **in snuff:** smoking, in need of having its wick trimmed   253. **moused:** shaken, as a cat shakes a mouse

For, by thy gracious, golden, glittering gleams,
        I trust to take of truest Thisbe sight.
        But stay, O spite!   260
        But mark, poor knight,
    What dreadful dole° is here?
        Eyes, do you see?
        How can it be?
    O dainty duck! O dear!   265
        Thy mantle good,
        What, stained with blood?
    Approach, ye Furies fell!°
        O Fates,° come, come,
    Cut thread and thrum;°   270
    Quail,° crush, conclude, and quell!°
THESEUS.   This passion, and the death of a dear friend, would go near
    to make a man look sad.°
HIPPOLYTA.   Beshrew my heart, but I pity the man.
PYRAMUS.   O, wherefore, Nature, didst thou lions frame?   275
    Since lion vile hath here deflowered my dear,
    Which is—no, no, which was—the fairest dame
    That lived, that loved, that liked, that looked with cheer.
        Come, tears, confound,
        Out, sword, and wound   280
    The pap° of Pyramus;
        Ay, that left pap,
        Where heart doth hop. (*Stabs himself.*)
    Thus die I, thus, thus, thus.
        Now am I dead,   285
        Now am I fled;
    My soul is in the sky.
        Tongue, lose thy light;
        Moon, take thy flight. (*Exit* MOONSHINE.)
        Now die, die, die, die, die. (*Dies.*)   290
DEMETRIUS.   No die, but an ace, for him; for he is but one.°
LYSANDER.   Less than an ace, man; for he is dead, he is nothing.

---

262. **dole:** grievous sight   268. **Furies fell:** fierce avenging goddesses of Greek mythology   269. **Fates:** the three Greek goddesses who spun, drew out, and cut the thread of
life   270. **Cut thread and thrum:** i.e., destroy everything   271. **Quail:** Overpower
quell: slay   272–73. **This . . . sad:** i.e., this acting of violent sorrow is so absurd that you
could only be sad if you had some genuine cause (such as the death of a friend) to add to it
281. **pap:** breast   291. **No . . . one:** Bottom is not even a whole die (singular of dice), only
the side of the cube with one spot on it.

THESEUS.   With the help of a surgeon he might yet recover, and yet
  prove an ass.°
HIPPOLYTA.   How chance Moonshine is gone before Thisbe comes
  back and finds her lover?   296
THESEUS.   She will find him by starlight. (*Enter* THISBE.)
  Here she comes; and her passion ends the play.
HIPPOLYTA.   Methinks she should not use a long one for such a Pyra-
  mus. I hope she will be brief.   300
DEMETRIUS.   A mote° will turn the balance, which Pyramus, which
  Thisbe, is the better: he for a man, God warrant us; she for a
  woman, God bless us.
LYSANDER.   She hath spied him already with those sweet eyes.
DEMETRIUS.   And thus she means,° videlicet:°   305
THISBE.   Asleep, my love?
      What, dead, my dove?
      O Pyramus, arise!
        Speak, speak. Quite dumb?
        Dead, dead? A tomb   310
      Must cover thy sweet eyes.
        These lily lips,
        This cherry nose,
      These yellow cowslip cheeks,
        Are gone, are gone!   315
        Lovers, make moan.
      His eyes were green as leeks.
        O Sisters Three,°
        Come, come to me,
      With hands as pale as milk;   320
        Lay them in gore,
        Since you have shore°
      With shears his thread of silk.
        Tongue, not a word.
        Come, trusty sword,   325
      Come, blade, my brest imbrue.° (*Stabs herself.*)
        And farewell, friends.
        Thus Thisbe ends.
      Adieu, adieu, adieu. (*Dies.*)
THESEUS.   Moonshine and Lion are left to bury the dead.   330
DEMETRIUS.   Ay, and Wall too.

294. ass: similar in pronunciation to "ace" in Shakespeare's time   **301. mote:** speck
305. means: moans   **videlicet:** (Latin) as follows   **318. Sisters Three:** the Fates
322. shore: cut   **326. imbrue:** make bloody

BOTTOM (*starting up, as* FLUTE *does also*).   No, I assure you, the wall is down that parted their fathers. Will it please you to see the epilogue, or to hear a Bergomask° dance between two of our company?   334
(*The other players enter.*)

THESEUS.   No epilogue, I pray you; for your play needs no excuse. Never excuse; for when the players are all dead, there need none to be blamed. Marry, if he that writ it had played Pyramus and hanged himself in Thisbe's garter, it would have been a fine tragedy; and so it is, truly, and very notably discharged. But, come, your Bergomask. Let your epilogue alone. (*A dance.*) The iron tongue° of midnight hath told twelve.   341
Lovers, to bed, 'tis almost fairy time.
I fear we shall outsleep the coming morn
As much as we this night have overwatched.°
This palpable-gross° play hath well beguiled   345
The heavy° gait of night. Sweet friends, to bed.
A fortnight hold we this solemnity,
In nightly revels and new jollity. (*Exeunt.*)
(*Enter* PUCK *carrying a broom.*)

PUCK.   Now the hungry lion roars,
    And the wolf behowls the moon,   350
Whilst the heavy° plowman snores,
    All with weary task fordone.°
Now the wasted brands do glow,°
    Whilst the screech owl, screeching loud,
Puts the wretch that lies in woe   355
    In remembrance of a shroud.
Now it is the time of night
    That the graves, all gaping wide,
Every one lets forth his sprite,°
    In the church-way paths to glide.   360
And we fairies, that do run
    By the triple Hecate's team°
From the presence of the sun,
    Following darkness like a dream,
Now are frolic.° Not a mouse   365
    Shall disturb this hallowed house.

---

334. **Bergomask:** a rough country dance   340–341. **iron tongue:** bell   344. **overwatched:** stayed awake too long   345. **palpable-gross:** obviously crude   346. **heavy:** dull
351. **heavy:** exhausted   352. **fordone:** overcome   353. **wasted . . . glow:** burned out logs are now only embers   359. **sprite:** ghost   362. **triple Hecate's team:** the dragons that pull the chariot of the moon (The goddess Hecate had three forms: Luna or Cynthia in the heavens, Diana on the earth, and Proserpina in the underworld.)   365. **frolic:** merry

I am sent with broom before,
To sweep the dust behind° the door.
(*Enter* OBERON *and* TITANIA *with all their train of* FAIRIES.)
OBERON.   Through the house give glimmering light,
   By the dead and drowsy fire;   370
  Every elf and fairy sprite
   Hop as light as bird from brier;
  And this ditty, after me,
  Sing, and dance it trippingly.
TITANIA.   First, rehearse° your song by rote,   375
  To each word a warbling note.
  Hand in hand, with fairy grace,
  Will we sing, and bless this place.
  (*Song and dance.*)
OBERON.   Now, until the break of day,
  Through this house each fairy stray.   380
  To the best bride-bed will we,
  Which by us shall blessèd be;
  And the issue there create°
  Ever shall be fortunate.
  So shall all the couples three   385
  Ever true in loving be;
  And the blots of Nature's hand
  Shall not in their issue stand;
  Never mole, harelip, nor scar,
  Nor mark prodigious,° such as are   390
  Despisèd in nativity,
  Shall upon their children be.
  With this field dew consecrate,°
  Every fairy take his gait,°
  And each several° chamber bless,   395
  Through this palace, with sweet peace;
  And the owner of it blest
  Ever shall in safety rest.
  Trip away; make no stay;
  Meet me all by break of day.   400
  (*Exeunt* OBERON, TITANIA, *and* FAIRIES.)

---

368. behind: from behind (where presumably a sloppy housekeeper has missed it)
375. rehearse: perform   **383. issue there create:** children conceived there
390. mark prodigious: monstrous birthmark   **393. consecrate:** blessed
394. take his gait: go his way   **395. several:** separate

PUCK (*to the audience*).   If we shadows have offended,
   Think but this, and all is mended,
   That you have but slumbered here
   While these visions did appear.
   And this weak and idle theme,   405
   No more yielding but° a dream,
   Gentles, do not reprehend.
   If you pardon, we will mend.°
   And, as I am an honest Puck,
   If we have unearnèd luck   410
   Now to scape the serpent's tongue,°
   We will make amends ere long;
   Else the Puck a liar call.
   So, good night unto you all.
   Give me your hands,° if we be friends,   415
   And Robin shall restore amends.° (*Exit.*)

QUESTIONS

1. The play contains six love plots, all resolved by the conclusion of the drama. Trace each of these plots from their origins to their resolutions: (1) Hippolyta and Theseus; (2) Hermia and Lysander; (3) Helena and Demetrius; (4) Titania and Oberon; (5) Titania and Bottom; and (6) "Pyramus and Thisbe." Be sure to include any expository material that precedes the action of the play.

2. In addition to the love plots, the play includes the plot of Quince, Bottom, and the other craftsmen preparing their play. How are the goals of these men like and unlike the goals displayed in the lovers' plots?

3. In what ways does the play make the two young men and the two young women similar in characterization? What is the thematic importance of this similarity?

4. There are two pairs of mature lovers—Hippolyta and Theseus, and Titania and Oberon. Sometimes in staging the play, the same actress takes the role of Hippolyta and Titania, the same actor Theseus and Oberon. What thematic ideas might be reinforced by this double casting?

5. Explore the nonrealistic elements of the play. Consider the following: (1) the mythological characters; (2) the supernatural characters; (3) the magical potions; (4) the elapsed time of the play, and its identification with "midsummer" (June 20–21). What truths are being expressed by these nonrealistic means? In particular, what unpleasant or grim realities are alluded to in the dialogue of the fairies?

---

406. No . . . but: Yielding no more than   408. mend: improve   411. serpent's tongue: hissing of the audience   415. Give . . . hands: Applaud   416. restore amends: give future satisfaction in return

6. Of the seven plots identified in questions 1 and 2 above, which is most realistic in terms of motivation and character, and which is least realistic? When considering this question, disregard the supernatural or mythological identifications and explore the characters as human beings.

7. The word "dream" has two relevant meanings in the play: (1) an imaginary event that occurs while sleeping, and (2) the hope, ambition, or aspiration that motivates a person's actions. Explore the occurrences of both kinds of "dream" (and include in your investigation the synonymous word "vision"). What universal dream about love and marriage lies at the center of the play? (See Oberon's blessing at the end of 5.1 and Puck's jingle about Jack and Jill at 3.3.458–63).

8. Until the triple marriage preceding Act 5, there is only one married couple in the play—Titania and Oberon. How does their relationship cast doubt on the universal dream you identified in the preceding question?

9. "The course of true love never did run smooth," says Lysander (1.1.134). Is this a sufficient statement of the themes of the play? Of the various obstacles that interfere with the smooth course of love, which are imposed upon the lovers by outside forces, and which arise from within the lovers' own feelings? Do the external or the internal obstacles play a larger role?

10. This play contains elements of both "smiling" and "laughing" comedy (see pages 1223–1224). Identify these as fully as you can, and determine which type predominates.

11. We often leave the performance of a comedy with mixed feelings—pleasure arising from seeing the success of sympathetic characters overcoming obstacles to their happiness, and a renewed sense that such success does not often occur in real life but depends upon the conventions of comic drama. How does this play explicitly remind the audience of these limitations in real life?

August Wilson

Fences

Characters

TROY MAXSON
JIM BONO, *Troy's friend*
ROSE, *Troy's wife*
LYONS, *Troy's oldest son by previous marriage*
GABRIEL, *Troy's brother*
CORY, *Troy and Rose's son*
RAYNELL, *Troy's daughter*

The setting is the yard which fronts the only entrance to the Maxson household, an ancient two-story brick house set back off a small alley in a big-city neighborhood. The entrance to the house is gained by two or three steps leading to a wooden porch badly in need of paint.

A relatively recent addition to the house and running its full width, the porch lacks congruence. It is a sturdy porch with a flat roof. One or two chairs of dubious value sit at one end where the kitchen window opens onto the porch. An old-fashioned icebox stands silent guard at the opposite end.

The yard is a small dirt yard, partially fenced, except for the last scene, with a wooden sawhorse, a pile of lumber, and other fence-building equipment set off to the side. Opposite is a tree from which hangs a ball made of rags. A baseball bat leans against the tree. Two oil drums serve as garbage receptacles and sit near the house at right to complete the setting.

FENCES   First produced in 1985. The setting is a black neighborhood in Pittsburgh, reminiscent of the author's childhood home where he was one of six children raised by their mother in the absence of their white father. August Wilson (1945–2005) quit the football team and dropped out of high school when he was sixteen but continued his education by reading in the public library, where he developed the goal of being a writer. After a series of jobs, he moved to St. Paul, Minnesota, and became involved with the Playwrights Center in Minneapolis. *Fences* is one of ten plays dealing with African American experience in the twentieth century (one play for each decade). The action of the play begins ten years after Jackie Robinson (1919–1972) became the first black to play major league baseball. Prior to that time blacks were limited to playing in the Negro Leagues; two of the legendary players in the Leagues were Josh Gibson (1911–1947), called "the Babe Ruth" of the Negro Leagues, and the venerable Satchel Paige (1906–1982). Probably the most celebrated black athlete of the first half of the century was the heavyweight boxing champion Joe Louis (1914–1981).

Near the turn of the century, the destitute of Europe sprang on the city with tenacious claws and an honest and solid dream. The city devoured them. They swelled its belly until it burst into a thousand furnaces and sewing machines, a thousand butcher shops and bakers' ovens, a thousand churches and hospitals and funeral parlors and money-lenders. The city grew. It nourished itself and offered each man a partnership limited only by his talent, his guile, and his willingness and capacity for hard work. For the immigrants of Europe, a dream dared and won true.

The descendants of African slaves were offered no such welcome or participation. They came from places called the Carolinas and the Virginias, Georgia, Alabama, Mississippi, and Tennessee. They came strong, eager, searching. The city rejected them and they fled and settled along the riverbanks and under bridges in shallow, ramshackle houses made of sticks and tarpaper. They collected rags and wood. They sold the use of their muscles and their bodies. They cleaned houses and washed clothes, they shined shoes, and in quiet desperation and vengeful pride, they stole, and lived in pursuit of their own dream: that they could breathe free, finally, and stand to meet life with the force of dignity and whatever eloquence the heart could call upon.

By 1957, the hard-won victories of the European immigrants had solidified the industrial might of America. War had been confronted and won with new energies that used loyalty and patriotism as its fuel. Life was rich, full, and flourishing. The Milwaukee Braves won the World Series, and the hot winds of change that would make the sixties a turbulent, racing, dangerous, and provocative decade had not yet begun to blow full.

ACT 1

SCENE 1

It is 1957. TROY and BONO enter the yard, engaged in conversation. TROY is fifty-three years old, a large man with thick, heavy hands; it is this largeness that he strives to fill out and make an accommodation with. Together with his blackness, his largeness informs his sensibilities and the choices he has made in his life.

Of the two men, BONO is obviously the follower. His commitment to their friendship of thirty-odd years is rooted in his admiration of TROY's honesty, capacity for hard work, and his strength, which BONO seeks to emulate.

It is Friday night, payday, and the one night of the week the two men engage in a ritual of talk and drink. TROY is usually the most talkative and at times he can be crude and almost vulgar, though he is capable of rising to profound heights of expression. The men carry lunch buckets and wear or carry burlap aprons and are dressed in clothes suitable to their jobs as garbage collectors.

BONO.   Troy, you ought to stop that lying!

TROY.   I ain't lying! The nigger had a watermelon this big. (*He indicates with his hands.*) Talking about . . . "What watermelon, Mr. Rand?" I liked to fell out! "What watermelon, Mr. Rand?" . . . And it sitting there big as life.

BONO.   What did Mr. Rand say?

TROY.   Ain't said nothing. Figure if the nigger too dumb to know he carrying a watermelon, he wasn't gonna get much sense out of him. Trying to hide that great big watermelon under his coat. Afraid to let the white man see him carry it home.

BONO.   I'm like you . . . I ain't got no time for them kind of people.

TROY.   Now what he look like getting mad cause he see the man from the union talking to Mr. Rand?

BONO.   He come to me talking about . . . "Maxson gonna get us fired." I told him to get away from me with that. He walked away from me calling you a troublemaker. What Mr. Rand say?

TROY.   Ain't said nothing. He told me to go down the Commissioner's office next Friday. They called me down there to see them.

BONO.   Well, as long as you got your complaint filed, they can't fire you. That's what one of them white fellows tell me.

TROY.   I ain't worried about them firing me. They gonna fire me 'cause I asked a question? That's all I did. I went to Mr. Rand and asked him, "Why? Why you got the white mens driving and the colored lifting?" Told him, "what's the matter, don't I count? You think only white fellows got sense enough to drive a truck. That ain't no paper job! Hell, anybody can drive a truck. How come you got all whites driving and the colored lifting?" He told me "take it to the union." Well, hell, that's what I done! Now they wanna come up with this pack of lies.

BONO.   I told Brownie if the man come and ask him any questions . . . just tell the truth! It ain't nothing but something they done trumped up on you cause you filed a complaint on them.

TROY.   Brownie don't understand nothing. All I want them to do is change the job description. Give everybody a chance to drive the truck. Brownie can't see that. He ain't got that much sense.

BONO.   How you figure he be making out with that gal be up at Taylors' all the time . . . that Alberta gal?

TROY.   Same as you and me. Getting just as much as we is. Which is to say nothing.

BONO.   It is, huh? I figure you doing a little better than me . . . and I ain't saying what I'm doing.

TROY.   Aw, nigger, look here . . . I know you. If you had got anywhere near that gal, twenty minutes later you be looking to tell somebody. And the first one you gonna tell . . . that you gonna want to brag to . . . is me.

BONO.   I ain't saying that. I see where you be eyeing her.

TROY.   I eye all the women. I don't miss nothing. Don't never let nobody tell you Troy Maxson don't eye the women.

BONO.   You been doing more than eyeing her. You done bought her a drink or two.

TROY.   Hell yeah, I bought her a drink! What that mean? I bought you one, too. What that mean cause I buy her a drink? I'm just being polite.

BONO.   It's all right to buy her one drink. That's what you call being polite. But when you wanna be buying two or three . . . that's what you call eyeing her.

TROY.   Look here, as long as you known me . . . you ever known me to chase after women?

BONO.   Hell yeah! Long as I done known you. You forgetting I knew you when.

TROY.   Naw, I'm talking about since I been married to Rose?

BONO.   Oh, not since you been married to Rose. Now, that's the truth, there. I can say that.

TROY.   All right then! Case closed.

BONO.   I see you be walking up around Alberta's house. You supposed to be at Taylors' and you be walking up around there.

TROY.   What you watching where I'm walking for? I ain't watching after you.

BONO.   I seen you walking around there more than once.

TROY.   Hell, you liable to see me walking anywhere! That don't mean nothing cause you see me walking around there.

BONO.   Where she come from anyway? She just kinda showed up one day.

TROY.   Tallahassee. You can look at her and tell she one of them Florida gals. They got some big healthy women down there. Grow them right up out the ground. Got a little bit of Indian in her. Most of them niggers down in Florida got some Indian in them.

BONO.   I don't know about that Indian part. But she damn sure big and healthy. Woman wear some big stockings. Got them great big old legs and hips as wide as the Mississippi River.

TROY.   Legs don't mean nothing. You don't do nothing but push them out of the way. But them hips cushion the ride!

BONO.   Troy, you ain't got no sense.

TROY.   It's the truth! Like you riding on Goodyears!

(ROSE *enters from the house. She is ten years younger than* TROY; *her devotion to him stems from her recognition of the possibilities of her life without him: a succession of abusive men and their babies, a life of partying and running the streets, the Church, or aloneness with its attendant pain and frustration. She recognizes* TROY's *spirit as a fine and illuminating one and she either ignores or forgives his faults, only some of which she recognizes. Though she doesn't drink, her presence is an integral part of the Friday night rituals. She alternates between the porch and the kitchen, where supper preparations are under way.*)

ROSE.   What you all out here getting into?

TROY.   What you worried about what we getting into for? This is men talk, woman.

ROSE.   What I care what you all talking about? Bono, you gonna stay for supper?

BONO.   No, I thank you, Rose. But Lucille says she cooking up a pot of pigfeet.

TROY.   Pigfeet! Hell, I'm going home with you! Might even stay the night if you got some pigfeet. You got something in there to top them pigfeet, Rose?

ROSE.   I'm cooking up some chicken. I got some chicken and collard greens.

TROY.   Well, go on back in the house and let me and Bono finish what we was talking about. This is men talk. I got some talk for you later. You know what kind of talk I mean. You go on and powder it up.

ROSE.   Troy Maxson, don't you start that now!

TROY (*puts his arms around her*).   Aw, woman . . . come here. Look here, Bono . . . when I met this woman . . . I got out that place, say, "Hitch up my pony, saddle up my mare . . . there's a woman out there for me somewhere. I looked here. Looked there. Saw Rose and latched on to her." I latched on to her and told her—I'm gonna tell you the truth—I told her, "Baby, I don't wanna marry, I just wanna be your man." Rose told me . . . tell him what you told me, Rose.

ROSE.   I told him if he wasn't the marrying kind, then move out the way so the marrying kind could find me.

TROY.   That's what she told me. "Nigger, you in my way. You blocking the view! Move out the way so I can find me a husband." I thought it over two or three days. Come back—

ROSE.   Ain't no two or three days nothing. You was back the same night.

TROY.   Come back, told her . . . "Okay, baby . . . but I'm gonna buy me a banty rooster and put him out there in the backyard . . . and when he see a stranger come, he'll flap his wings and crow . . ." Look here, Bono, I could watch the front door by myself . . . it was that back door I was worried about.

ROSE.   Troy, you ought not talk like that. Troy ain't doing nothing but telling a lie.

TROY.   Only thing is . . . when we first got married . . . forget the rooster . . . we ain't had no yard!

BONO.   I hear you tell it. Me and Lucille was staying down there on Logan Street. Had two rooms with the outhouse in the back. I ain't mind the outhouse none. But when that goddamn wind blow through there in the winter . . . that's what I'm talking about! To this day I wonder why in the hell I ever stayed down there for six long years. But see, I didn't know I could do no better. I thought only white folks had inside toilets and things.

ROSE.   There's a lot of people don't know they can do no better than they doing now. That's just something you got to learn. A lot of folks still shop at Bella's.

TROY.   Ain't nothing wrong with shopping at Bella's. She got fresh food.

ROSE.   I ain't said nothing about if she got fresh food. I'm talking about what she charge. She charge ten cents more than the A&P.

TROY.   The A&P ain't never done nothing for me. I spends my money where I'm treated right. I go down to Bella, say, "I need a loaf of bread, I'll pay you Friday." She give it to me. What sense that make when I got money to go and spend it somewhere else and ignore the person who done right by me? That ain't in the Bible.

ROSE.   We ain't talking about what's in the Bible. What sense it make to shop there when she overcharge?

TROY.   You shop where you want to. I'll do my shopping where the people been good to me.

ROSE.   Well, I don't think it's right for her to overcharge. That's all I was saying.

BONO.   Look here . . . I got to get on. Lucille going be raising all kind of hell.

TROY.   Where you going, nigger? We ain't finished this pint. Come here, finish this pint.

BONO.   Well, hell, I am . . . if you ever turn the bottle loose.

TROY (*hands him the bottle*).   The only thing I say about the A&P is I'm glad Cory got that job down there. Help him take care of his school clothes and things. Gabe done moved out and things getting tight around here. He got that job. . . . He can start to look out for himself.

ROSE.   Cory done went and got recruited by a college football team.

TROY.   I told that boy about that football stuff. The white man ain't gonna let him get nowhere with that football. I told him when he first come to me with it. Now you come telling me he done went and got more tied up in it. He ought to go and get recruited in how to fix cars or something where he can make a living.

ROSE.   He ain't talking about making no living playing football. It's just something the boys in school do. They gonna send a recruiter by to talk to you. He'll tell you he ain't talking about making no living playing football. It's a honor to be recruited.

TROY.   It ain't gonna get him nowhere. Bono'll tell you that.

BONO.   If he be like you in the sports . . . he's gonna be all right. Ain't but two men ever played baseball as good as you. That's Babe Ruth and Josh Gibson. Them's the only two men ever hit more home runs than you.

TROY.   What it ever get me? Ain't got a pot to piss in or a window to throw it out of.

ROSE.   Times have changed since you was playing baseball, Troy. That was before the war. Times have changed a lot since then.

TROY.   How in hell they done changed?

ROSE.   They got lots of colored boys playing ball now. Baseball and football.

BONO.   You right about that, Rose. Times have changed, Troy. You just come along too early.

TROY.   There ought not never have been no time called too early! Now you take that fellow . . . what's that fellow they had playing right field for the Yankees back then? You know who I'm talking about, Bono. Used to play right field for the Yankees.

ROSE.   Selkirk?

TROY.   Selkirk! That's it! Man batting .269, understand? .269. What kind of sense that make? I was hitting .432 with thirty-seven home runs! Man batting .269 and playing right field for the Yankees! I saw Josh Gibson's daughter yesterday. She walking around with raggedy shoes on her feet. Now I bet you Selkirk's daughter ain't walking around with raggedy shoes on her feet! I bet you that!

ROSE.   They got a lot of colored baseball players now. Jackie Robinson was the first. Folks had to wait for Jackie Robinson.

TROY.   I done seen a hundred niggers play baseball better than Jackie Robinson. Hell, I know some teams Jackie Robinson couldn't even make! What you talking about Jackie Robinson. Jackie Robinson wasn't nobody. I'm talking about if you could play ball then they ought to have let you play. Don't care what color you were. Come telling me I come along too early. If you could play . . . then they ought to have let you play. (TROY *takes a long drink from the bottle.*)

ROSE.   You gonna drink yourself to death. You don't need to be drinking like that.

TROY.   Death ain't nothing. I done seen him. Done wrassled with him. You can't tell me nothing about death. Death ain't nothing but a fastball on the outside corner. And you know what I'll do to that! Lookee here, Bono . . . am I lying? You get one of them fastballs, about waist high, over the outside corner of the plate where you can get the meat of the bat on it . . . and good god! You can kiss it goodbye. Now, am I lying?

BONO.   Naw, you telling the truth there. I seen you do it.

TROY.   If I'm lying . . . that 450 feet worth of lying! (*Pause.*) That's all death is to me. A fastball on the outside corner.

ROSE.   I don't know why you want to get on talking about death.

TROY.   Ain't nothing wrong with talking about death. That's part of life. Everybody gonna die. You gonna die, I'm gonna die. Bono's gonna die. Hell, we all gonna die.

ROSE.   But you ain't got to talk about it. I don't like to talk about it.

TROY.   You the one brought it up. Me and Bono was talking about baseball . . . you tell me I'm gonna drink myself to death. Ain't that right, Bono? You know I don't drink this but one night out of the week. That's Friday night. I'm gonna drink just enough to where I can handle it. Then I cuts it loose. I leave it alone. So don't you worry about me drinking myself to death. 'Cause I ain't worried about Death. I done seen him. I done wrestled with him.

Look here, Bono . . . I looked up one day and Death was marching straight at me. Like Soldiers on Parade! The Army of Death was marching straight at me. The middle of July, 1941. It got real cold just like it be winter. It seem like Death himself reached out and touched me on the shoulder. He touch me just like I touch you. I got cold as ice and Death standing there grinning at me.

ROSE.   Troy, why don't you hush that talk.

TROY.   I say . . . what you want, Mr. Death? You be wanting me? You done brought your army to be getting me? I looked him dead in the eye. I wasn't fearing nothing. I was ready to tangle. Just like I'm ready to tangle now. The Bible say be ever vigilant. That's why I don't get but so drunk. I got to keep watch.

ROSE.   Troy was right down there in Mercy Hospital. You remember he had pneumonia? Laying there with a fever talking plumb out of his head.

TROY.   Death standing there staring at me . . . carrying that sickle in his hand. Finally he say, "You want bound over for another year?" See, just like that . . . "You want bound over for another year?" I told him, "Bound over hell! Let's settle this now!"

It seem like he kinda fell back when I said that, and all the cold went out of me. I reached down and grabbed that sickle and threw it just as far as I could throw it . . . and me and him commenced to wrestling.

We wrestled for three days and three nights. I can't say where I found the strength from. Every time it seemed like he was gonna get the best of me, I'd reach way down deep inside myself and find the strength to do him one better.

ROSE.   Every time Troy tell that story he find different ways to tell it. Different things to make up about it.

TROY.   I ain't making up nothing. I'm telling you the facts of what happened. I wrestled with Death for three days and three nights and I'm standing here to tell you about it. (*Pause.*) All right. At the end of the third night we done weakened each other to where we can't hardly move. Death stood up, throwed on his robe . . . had him a white robe with a hood on it. He throwed on that robe and went off to look for his sickle. Say, "I'll be back." Just like that. "I'll be back." I told him, say, "Yeah, but . . . you gonna have to find me!" I wasn't no fool. I wasn't going looking for him. Death ain't nothing to play with. And I know he's gonna get me. I know I got to join his army . . . his camp followers. But as long as I keep my strength and see him coming . . . as long as I keep up my vigilance . . . he's gonna have to fight to get me. I ain't going easy.

BONO.   Well, look here, since you got to keep up your vigilance . . . let me have the bottle.

TROY.   Aw hell, I shouldn't have told you that part. I should have left out that part.

ROSE.   Troy be talking that stuff and half the time don't even know what he be talking about.

TROY.   Bono know me better than that.

BONO.   That's right. I know you. I know you got some Uncle Remus° in your blood. You got more stories than the devil got sinners.

TROY.   Aw hell, I done seen him too! Done talked with the devil.

ROSE.   Troy, don't nobody wanna be hearing all that stuff.

(LYONS *enters the yard from the street. Thirty-four years old,* TROY's *son by a previous marriage, he sports a neatly trimmed goatee, sport coat, white shirt, tieless and buttoned at the collar. Though he fancies himself a musician, he is more caught up in the rituals and "idea" of being a musician than in the actual practice of the music. He has come to borrow money from* TROY, *and while he knows he will be successful, he is uncertain as to what extent his lifestyle will be held up to scrutiny and ridicule.*)

LYONS.   Hey, Pop.

TROY.   What you come "Hey, Popping" me for?

LYONS.   How you doing, Rose? (*He kisses her.*) Mr. Bono. How you doing?

BONO.   Hey, Lyons . . . how you been?

TROY.   He must have been doing all right. I ain't seen him around here last week.

ROSE.   Troy, leave your boy alone. He come by to see you and you wanna start all that nonsense.

TROY.   I ain't bothering Lyons. (*Offers him the bottle.*) Here . . . get you a drink. We got an understanding. I know why he come by to see me and he know I know.

LYONS.   Come on, Pop . . . I just stopped by to say hi . . . see how you was doing.

TROY.   You ain't stopped by yesterday.

ROSE.   You gonna stay for supper, Lyons? I got some chicken cooking in the oven.

LYONS.   No, Rose . . . thanks. I was just in the neighborhood and thought I'd stop by for a minute.

TROY.   You was in the neighborhood all right, nigger. You telling the truth there. You was in the neighborhood cause it's my payday.

LYONS.   Well, hell, since you mentioned it . . . let me have ten dollars.

TROY.   I'll be damned! I'll die and go to hell and play blackjack with the devil before I give you ten dollars.

BONO.   That's what I wanna know about . . . that devil you done seen.

Uncle Remus: black narrator of folk tales in a series of books by Joel Chandler Harris (1848–1908)

LYONS.   What . . . Pop done seen the devil? You too much, Pops.

TROY.   Yeah, I done seen him. Talked to him too!

ROSE.   You ain't seen no devil. I done told you that man ain't had nothing to do with the devil. Anything you can't understand, you want to call it the devil.

TROY.   Look here, Bono . . . I went down to see Hertzberger about some furniture. Got three rooms for two-ninety-eight. That what it say on the radio. "Three rooms . . . two-ninety-eight." Even made up a little song about it. Go down there . . . man tell me I can't get no credit. I'm working every day and can't get no credit. What to do? I got an empty house with some raggedy furniture in it. Cory ain't got no bed. He's sleeping on a pile of rags on the floor. Working every day and can't get no credit. Come back here—Rose'll tell you—madder than hell. Sit down . . . try to figure what I'm gonna do. Come a knock on the door. Ain't been living here but three days. Who know I'm here? Open the door . . . devil standing there bigger than life. White fellow . . . white fellow . . . got on good clothes and everything. Standing there with a clipboard in his hand. I ain't had to say nothing. First words come out of his mouth was . . . "I understand you need some furniture and can't get no credit." I liked to fell over. He say, "I'll give you all the credit you want, but you got to pay the interest on it." I told him, "Give me three rooms worth and charge whatever you want." Next day a truck pulled up here and two men unloaded them three rooms. Man what drove the truck give me a book. Say send ten dollars, first of every month to the address in the book and everything will be all right. Say if I miss a payment the devil was coming back and it'll be hell to pay. That was fifteen years ago. To this day . . . the first of the month I send my ten dollars, Rose'll tell you.

ROSE.   Troy lying.

TROY.   I ain't never seen that man since. Now you tell me who else that could have been but the devil? I ain't sold my soul or nothing like that, you understand. Naw, I wouldn't have truck with the devil about nothing like that. I got my furniture and pays my ten dollars the first of the month just like clockwork.

BONO.   How long you say you been paying this ten dollars a month?

TROY.   Fifteen years!

BONO.   Hell, ain't you finished paying for it yet? How much the man done charged you?

TROY.   Ah hell, I done paid for it. I done paid for it ten times over! The fact is I'm scared to stop paying it.

ROSE.   Troy lying. We got that furniture from Mr. Glickman. He ain't paying no ten dollars a month to nobody.

TROY.   Aw hell, woman. Bono know I ain't that big a fool.

LYONS.   I was just getting ready to say . . . I know where there's a bridge for sale.

TROY.   Look here, I'll tell you this . . . it don't matter to me if he was the devil. It don't matter if the devil give credit. Somebody has got to give it.

ROSE.   It ought to matter. You going around talking about having truck with the devil . . . God's the one you gonna have to answer to. He's the one gonna be at the Judgment.

LYONS.   Yeah, well, look here, Pop . . . let me have that ten dollars. I'll give it back to you. Bonnie got a job working at the hospital.

TROY.   What I tell you, Bono? The only time I see this nigger is when he wants something. That's the only time I see him.

LYONS.   Come on, Pop, Mr. Bono don't want to hear all that. Let me have the ten dollars. I told you Bonnie working.

TROY.   What that mean to me? "Bonnie working." I don't care if she working. Go ask her for the ten dollars if she working. Talking about "Bonnie working." Why ain't you working?

LYONS.   Aw, Pop, you know I can't find no decent job. Where am I gonna get a job at? You know I can't get no job.

TROY.   I told you I know some people down there. I can get you on the rubbish if you want to work. I told you that the last time you came by here asking me for something.

LYONS.   Naw, Pop . . . thanks. That ain't for me. I don't wanna be carrying nobody's rubbish. I don't wanna be punching nobody's time clock.

TROY.   What's the matter, you too good to carry people's rubbish? Where you think that ten dollars you talking about come from? I'm just supposed to haul people's rubbish and give my money to you cause you too lazy to work. You too lazy to work and wanna know why you ain't got what I got.

ROSE.   What hospital Bonnie working at? Mercy?

LYONS.   She's down at Passavant working in the laundry.

TROY.   I ain't got nothing as it is. I give you that ten dollars and I got to eat beans the rest of the week. Naw . . . you ain't getting no ten dollars here.

LYONS.   You ain't got to be eating no beans. I don't know why you wanna say that.

TROY.   I ain't got no extra money. Gabe done moved over to Miss Pearl's paying her the rent and things done got tight around here. I can't afford to be giving you every payday.

LYONS.   I ain't asked you to give me nothing. I asked you to loan me ten dollars. I know you got ten dollars.

TROY.   Yeah, I got it. You know why I got it? 'Cause I don't throw my money away out there in the streets. You living the fast life . . . wanna be a musician . . . running around in them clubs and things . . . then, you learn to take care of yourself. You ain't gonna find me going and asking nobody for nothing. I done spent too many years without.

LYONS.   You and me is two different people, Pop.

TROY.   I done learned my mistake and learned to do what's right by it. You still trying to get something for nothing. Life don't owe you nothing. You owe it to yourself. Ask Bono. He'll tell you I'm right.

LYONS.   You got your way of dealing with the world . . . I got mine. The only thing that matters to me is the music.

TROY.   Yeah, I can see that! It don't matter how you gonna eat . . . where your next dollar is coming from. You telling the truth there.

LYONS.   I know I got to eat. But I got to live too. I need something that gonna help me to get out of the bed in the morning. Make me feel like I belong in the world. I don't bother nobody. I just stay with the music 'cause that's the only way I can find to live in the world. Otherwise there ain't no telling what I might do. Now I don't come criticizing you and how you live. I just come by to ask you for ten dollars. I don't wanna hear all that about how I live.

TROY.   Boy, your mamma did a hell of a job raising you.

LYONS.   You can't change me, Pop. I'm thirty-four years old. If you wanted to change me, you should have been there when I was growing up. I come by to see you . . . ask for ten dollars and you want to talk about how I was raised. You don't know nothing about how I was raised.

ROSE.   Let the boy have ten dollars, Troy.

TROY (*to* LYONS).   What the hell you looking at me for? I ain't got no ten dollars. You know what I do with my money. (*To* ROSE) Give him ten dollars if you want him to have it.

ROSE.   I will. Just as soon as you turn it loose.

TROY (*handing* ROSE *the money*).   There it is. Seventy-six dollars and forty-two cents. You see this, Bono? Now, I ain't gonna get but six of that back.

ROSE.   You ought to stop telling that lie. Here, Lyons. (*She hands him the money.*)

LYONS.   Thanks, Rose. Look . . . I got to run . . . I'll see you later.

TROY.   Wait a minute. You gonna say, "thanks, Rose" and ain't gonna look to see where she got that ten dollars from? See how they do me, Bono?

LYONS.   I know she got it from you, Pop. Thanks. I'll give it back to you.

TROY.   There he go telling another lie. Time I see that ten dollars . . . he'll be owing me thirty more.

LYONS.   See you, Mr. Bono.

BONO.   Take care, Lyons!

LYONS.   Thanks, Pop. I'll see you again. (LYONS *exits the yard.*)

TROY.   I don't know why he don't go and get him a decent job and take care of that woman he got.

BONO.   He'll be all right, Troy. The boy is still young.

TROY.   The *boy* is thirty-four years old.

ROSE.   Let's not get off into all that.

BONO.   Look here . . . I got to be going. I got to be getting on. Lucille gonna be waiting.

TROY (*puts his arm around* ROSE).   See this woman, Bono? I love this woman. I love this woman so much it hurts. I love her so much . . . I done run out of ways of loving. So I got to go back to basics. Don't you come by my house Monday morning talking about time to go to work . . . 'cause I'm still gonna be stroking!

ROSE.   Troy! Stop it now!

BONO.   I ain't paying him no mind, Rose. That ain't nothing but gin-talk. Go on, Troy. I'll see you Monday.

TROY.   Don't you come by my house, nigger! I done told you what I'm gonna be doing. (*The lights go down to black.*)

SCENE 2

The lights come up on ROSE *hanging up clothes. She hums and sings softly to herself. It is the following morning.*

ROSE (*sings*).   Jesus, be a fence all around me every day

           Jesus, I want you to protect me as I travel on my way.

           Jesus, be a fence all around me every day.

(TROY *enters from the house.*)

           Jesus, I want you to protect me

           As I travel on my way.

(*To* TROY) 'Morning. You ready for breakfast? I can fix it soon as I finish hanging up these clothes.

TROY.   I got the coffee on. That'll be all right. I'll just drink some of that this morning.

ROSE.   That 651 hit yesterday. That's the second time this month. Miss Pearl hit for a dollar . . . seem like those that need the least always get lucky. Poor folks can't get nothing.

TROY.   Them numbers don't know nobody. I don't know why you fool with them. You and Lyons both.

ROSE.   It's something to do.

TROY.   You ain't doing nothing but throwing your money away.

ROSE.   Troy, you know I don't play foolishly. I just play a nickel here and nickel there.

TROY.   That's two nickels you done thrown away.

ROSE.   Now I hit sometimes . . . that makes up for it. It always comes in handy when I do hit. I don't hear you complaining then.

TROY.   I ain't complaining now. I just say it's foolish. Trying to guess out of six hundred ways which way the number gonna come. If I had all the money niggers, these Negroes, throw away on numbers for one week—just one week—I'd be a rich man.

ROSE.   Well, you wishing and calling it foolish ain't gonna stop folks from playing numbers. That's one thing for sure. Besides . . . some good things come from playing numbers. Look where Pope done bought him that restaurant off of numbers.

TROY.   I can't stand niggers like that. Man ain't had two dimes to rub together. He walking around with his shoes all run over bumming money for cigarettes. All right. Got lucky there and hit the numbers . . .

ROSE.   Troy, I know all about it.

TROY.   Had good sense, I'll say that for him. He ain't throwed his money away. I seen niggers hit the numbers and go through two thousand dollars in four days. Man bought him that restaurant down there . . . fixed it up real nice . . . and then didn't want nobody to come in it! A Negro go in there and can't get no kind of service. I seen a white fellow come in there and order a bowl of stew. Pope picked all the meat out the pot for him. Man ain't had nothing but a bowl of meat! Negro come behind him and ain't got nothing but the potatoes and carrots. Talking about what numbers do for people, you picked a wrong example. Ain't done nothing but make a worser fool out of him than he was before.

ROSE.   Troy, you ought to stop worrying about what happened at work yesterday.

TROY.   I ain't worried. Just told me to be down there at the Commissioner's office on Friday. Everybody think they gonna fire me. I ain't worried about them firing me. You ain't got to worry about that. (*Pause.*) Where's Cory? Cory in the house? (*Calls*) Cory?

ROSE.   He gone out.

TROY.   Out, huh? He gone out 'cause he know I want him to help me with this fence. I know how he is. That boy scared of work. (GABRIEL *enters. He comes halfway down the alley and, hearing* TROY's *voice, stops.*) He ain't done a lick of work in his life.

ROSE.   He had to go to football practice. Coach wanted them to get in a little extra practice before the season start.

TROY.   I got his practice . . . running out of here before he get his chores done.

ROSE.   Troy, what is wrong with you this morning? Don't nothing set right with you. Go on back in there and go to bed . . . get up on the other side.

TROY.   Why something got to be wrong with me? I ain't said nothing wrong with me.

ROSE.   You got something to say about everything. First it's the numbers . . . then it's the way the man runs his restaurant . . . then you done got on Cory. What's it gonna be next? Take a look up there and see if the weather suits you . . . or is it gonna be how you gonna put up the fence with the clothes hanging in the yard.

TROY.   You hit the nail on the head then.

ROSE.   I know you like I know the back of my hand. Go on in there and get you some coffee . . . see if that straighten you up. 'Cause you ain't right this morning. (TROY *starts into the house and sees* GABRIEL. GABRIEL *starts singing.* TROY's *brother, he is seven years younger than* TROY. *Injured in World War II, he has a metal plate in his head. He carries an old trumpet tied around his waist and believes with every fiber of his being that he is the Archangel Gabriel. He carries a chipped basket with an assortment of discarded fruits and vegetables he has picked up in the strip district and which he attempts to sell.*)

GABRIEL(*singing*).   Yes, ma'am, I got plums
       You ask me how I sell them
       Oh ten cents apiece
       Three for a quarter
       Come and buy now
       'Cause I'm here today
       And tomorrow I'll be gone

(GABRIEL *enters the yard.*) Hey, Rose!

ROSE.   How you doing, Gabe?

GABRIEL.   There's Troy . . . Hey, Troy!

TROY.   Hey, Gabe. (*Exit into kitchen.*)

ROSE (*to* GABRIEL).   What you got there?

GABRIEL.   You know what I got, Rose. I got fruits and vegetables.

ROSE (*looking in basket*).   Where's all these plums you talking about?

GABRIEL.   I ain't got no plums today, Rose. I was just singing that. Have some tomorrow. Put me in a big order for plums. Have enough plums tomorrow for St. Peter and everybody. (TROY *reenters from kitchen, crosses to steps.*) Troy's mad at me.

TROY.   I ain't mad at you. What I got to be mad at you about? You ain't done nothing to me.

GABRIEL.   I just moved over to Miss Pearl's to keep out from in your way. I ain't mean no harm by it.

TROY.   Who said anything about that? I ain't said anything about that.

GABRIEL.   You ain't mad at me, is you?

TROY.   Naw . . . I ain't mad at you, Gabe. If I was mad at you I'd tell you about it.

GABRIEL.   Got me two rooms. In the basement. Got my own door too. Wanna see my key? (*He holds up a key.*) That's my own key! Ain't nobody else got a key like that. That's my key! My two rooms!

TROY.   Well, that's good, Gabe. You got your own key . . . that's good.

ROSE.   You hungry, Gabe? I was just fixing to cook Troy his breakfast.

GABRIEL.   I'll take some biscuits. You got some biscuits? Did you know when I was in heaven . . . every morning me and St. Peter would sit down by the gate and eat some big fat biscuits? Oh, yeah! We had us a good time. We'd sit there and eat us them biscuits and then St. Peter would go off to sleep and tell me to wake him up when it's time to open the gates for the judgment.

ROSE.   Well, come on . . . I'll make up a batch of biscuits. (*Exits into the house.*)

GABRIEL.   Troy . . . St. Peter got your name in the book. I seen it. It say . . . Troy Maxson. I say . . . I know him! He got the same name like what I got. That's my brother!

TROY.   How many times you gonna tell me that, Gabe?

GABRIEL.   Ain't got my name in the book. Don't have to have my name. I done died and went to heaven. He got your name though. One morning St. Peter was looking at his book . . . marking it up for the judgment . . . and he let me see your name. Got it in there under M.

Got Rose's name . . . I ain't seen it like I seen yours . . . but I know it's in there. He got a great big book. Got everybody's name what was ever been born. That's what he told me. But I seen your name. Seen it with my own eyes.

TROY.   Go on in the house there. Rose going to fix you something to eat.

GABRIEL.   Oh, I ain't hungry. I done had breakfast with Aunt Jemimah. She come by and cooked me up a whole mess of flapjacks. Remember how we used to eat them flapjacks?

TROY.   Go on in the house and get you something to eat now.

GABRIEL.   I got to sell my plums. I done sold some tomatoes. Got me two quarters. Wanna see? (*He shows* TROY *his quarters.*) I'm gonna save them and buy me a new horn so St. Peter can hear me when it's time to open the gates. (GABRIEL *stops suddenly. Listens.*) Hear that? That's the hellhounds. I got to chase them out of here. Go on get out of here! Get out! (GABRIEL *exits singing.*)

> Better get ready for the judgment
> Better get ready for the judgment
> My Lord is coming down

(ROSE *enters from the house.*)

TROY.   He's gone off somewhere.

GABRIEL (*offstage*).   Better get ready for the judgment

> Better get ready for the judgment morning
> Better get ready for the judgment
> My God is coming down.

ROSE.   He ain't eating right. Miss Pearl say she can't get him to eat nothing.

TROY.   What you want me to do about it, Rose? I done did everything I can for the man. I can't make him get well. Man got half his head blown away . . . what you expect?

ROSE.   Seem like something ought to be done to help him.

TROY.   Man don't bother nobody. He just mixed up from that metal plate he got in his head. Ain't no sense for him to go back into the hospital.

ROSE.   Least he be eating right. They can help him take care of himself.

TROY.   Don't nobody wanna be locked up, Rose. What you wanna lock him up for? Man go over there and fight the war . . . messin' around with them Japs, get half his head blown off . . . and they give him a lousy three thousand dollars. And I had to swoop down on that.

ROSE.   Is you fixing to go into that again?

TROY.   That's the only way I got a roof over my head . . . 'cause of that metal plate.

ROSE.   Ain't no sense you blaming yourself for nothing. Gabe wasn't in no condition to manage that money. You done what was right by him. Can't nobody say you ain't done what was right by him. Look how long you took care of him . . . till he wanted to have his own place and moved over there with Miss Pearl.

TROY.   That ain't what I'm saying, woman! I'm just stating the facts. If my brother didn't have that metal plate in his head . . . I wouldn't have a pot to piss in or a window to throw it out of. And I'm fifty-three years old. Now see if you can understand that! (TROY *gets up from the porch and starts to exit the yard.*)

ROSE.   Where you going off to? You been running out of here every Saturday for weeks. I thought you was gonna work on this fence?

TROY.   I'm gonna walk down to Taylors'. Listen to the ball game. I'll be back in a bit. I'll work on it when I get back. (*He exits the yard. The lights go to black.*)

SCENE 3

The lights come up on the yard. It is four hours later. ROSE *is taking down the clothes from the line.* CORY *enters carrying his football equipment.*

ROSE.   Your daddy like to had a fit with you running out of here this morning without doing your chores.

CORY.   I told you I had to go to practice.

ROSE.   He say you were supposed to help him with this fence.

CORY.   He been saying that the last four or five Saturdays, and then he don't never do nothing, but go down to Taylors'. Did you tell him about the recruiter?

ROSE.   Yeah, I told him.

CORY.   What he say?

ROSE.   He ain't said nothing too much. You get in there and get started on your chores before he gets back. Go on and scrub down them steps before he gets back here hollering and carrying on.

CORY.   I'm hungry. What you got to eat, Mama?

ROSE.   Go on and get started on your chores. I got some meat loaf in there. Go on and make you a sandwich . . . and don't leave no mess in there. (CORY *exits into the house.* ROSE *continues to take down the clothes.* TROY *enters the yard and sneaks up and grabs her from behind.*) Troy! Go on, now. You liked to scared me to death. What was the score of the game? Lucille had me on the phone and I couldn't keep up with it.

TROY.   What I care about the game? Come here, woman. (*He tries to kiss her.*)

ROSE.   I thought you went down Taylors' to listen to the game. Go on, Troy! You supposed to be putting up this fence.

TROY (*attempting to kiss her again*).   I'll put it up when I finish with what is at hand.

ROSE.   Go on, Troy. I ain't studying you.

TROY (*chasing after her*).   I'm studying you . . . fixing to do my homework!

ROSE.   Troy, you better leave me alone.

TROY.   Where's Cory? That boy brought his butt home yet?

ROSE.   He's in the house doing his chores.

TROY (*calling*).   Cory! Get your butt out here, boy! (ROSE *exits into the house with the laundry.* TROY *goes over to the pile of wood, picks up a board, and starts sawing.* CORY *enters from the house.*) You just now coming in here from leaving this morning?

CORY.   Yeah, I had to go to football practice.

TROY.   Yeah, what?

CORY.   Yessir.

TROY.   I ain't but two seconds off you noway. The garbage sitting in there overflowing . . . you ain't done none of your chores . . . and you come in here talking about "Yeah."

CORY.   I was just getting ready to do my chores now, Pop . . .

TROY.   Your first chore is to help me with this fence on Saturday. Everything else come after that. Now get that saw and cut them boards. (CORY *takes the saw and begins cutting the boards.* TROY *continues working. There is a long pause.*)

CORY.   Hey, Pop . . . why don't you buy a TV?

TROY.   What I want with a TV? What I want one of them for?

CORY.   Everybody got one. Earl, Ba Bra . . . Jesse!

TROY.   I ain't asked you who had one. I say what I want with one?

CORY.   So you can watch it. They got lots of things on TV. Baseball games and everything. We could watch the World Series.

TROY.   Yeah . . . and how much this TV cost?

CORY.   I don't know. They got them on sale for around two hundred dollars.

TROY.   Two hundred dollars, huh?

CORY.   That ain't that much, Pop.

TROY.   Naw, it's just two hundred dollars. See that roof you got over your head at night? Let me tell you something about that roof. It's been over ten years since that roof was last tarred. See now . . . the snow come this winter and sit up there on that roof like it is . . . and it's gonna seep inside. It's just gonna be a little bit . . . ain't gonna hardly notice it. Then the next thing you know, it's gonna be leaking all over the house. Then the wood rot from all that water and you gonna need a whole new roof. Now, how much you think it cost to get that roof tarred?

CORY.   I don't know.

TROY.   Two hundred and sixty-four dollars . . . cash money. While you thinking about a TV, I got to be thinking about the roof . . . and whatever else go wrong here. Now if you had two hundred dollars, what would you do . . . fix the roof or buy a TV?

CORY.   I'd buy a TV. Then when the roof started to leak . . . when it needed fixing . . . I'd fix it.

TROY.   Where you gonna get the money from? You done spent it for a TV. You gonna sit up and watch the water run all over your brand new TV.

CORY.   Aw, Pop. You got money. I know you do.

TROY.   Where I got it at, huh?

CORY.   You got it in the bank.

TROY.   You wanna see my bankbook? You wanna see that seventy-three dollars and twenty-two cents I got sitting up in there.

CORY.   You ain't got to pay for it all at one time. You can put a down payment on it and carry it on home with you.

TROY.   Not me. I ain't gonna owe nobody nothing if I can help it. Miss a payment and they come and snatch it right out your house. Then what you got? Now, soon as I get two hundred dollars clear, then I'll buy a TV. Right now, as soon as I get two hundred and sixty-four dollars, I'm gonna have this roof tarred.

CORY.   Aw . . . Pop!

TROY.   You go on and get you two hundred dollars and buy one if ya want it. I got better things to do with my money.

CORY.   I can't get no two hundred dollars. I ain't never seen two hundred dollars.

TROY.   I'll tell you what . . . you get you a hundred dollars and I'll put the other hundred with it.

CORY.   All right, I'm gonna show you.

TROY.   You gonna show me how you can cut them boards right now. (CORY *begins to cut the boards. There is a long pause.*)

CORY.   The Pirates won today. That makes five in a row.

TROY.   I ain't thinking about the Pirates. Got an all-white team. Got that boy . . . that Puerto Rican boy . . . Clemente. Don't even half-play him. That boy could be something if they give him a chance. Play him one day and sit him on the bench the next.

CORY.   He gets a lot of chances to play.

TROY.   I'm talking about playing regular. Playing every day so you can get your timing. That's what I'm talking about.

CORY.   They got some white guys on the team that don't play every day. You can't play everybody at the same time.

TROY.   If they got a white fellow sitting on the bench . . . you can bet your last dollar he can't play! The colored guy got to be twice as good before he get on the team. That's why I don't want you to get all tied up in them sports. Man on the team and what it get him? They got colored on the team and don't use them. Same as not having them. All them teams the same.

CORY.   The Braves got Hank Aaron and Wes Covington. Hank Aaron hit two home runs today. That makes forty-three.

TROY.   Hank Aaron ain't nobody. That what you supposed to do. That's how you supposed to play the game. Ain't nothing to it. It's just a matter of timing . . . getting the right follow-through. Hell, I can hit forty-three home runs right now!

CORY.   Not off no major-league pitching, you couldn't.

TROY.   We had better pitching in the Negro leagues. I hit seven home runs off of Satchel Paige. You can't get no better than that!

CORY.   Sandy Koufax. He's leading the league in strikeouts.

TROY.   I ain't thinking of no Sandy Koufax.

CORY.   You got Warren Spahn and Lew Burdette. I bet you couldn't hit no home runs off of Warren Spahn.

TROY.   I'm through with it now. You go on and cut them boards. (*Pause.*) Your mama tell me you done got recruited by a college football team? Is that right?

CORY.   Yeah. Coach Zellman say the recruiter gonna be coming by to talk to you. Get you to sign the permission papers.

TROY.   I thought you supposed to be working down there at the A&P. Ain't you suppose to be working down there after school?

CORY.   Mr. Stawicki say he gonna hold my job for me until after the football season. Say starting next week I can work weekends.

TROY.   I thought we had an understanding about this football stuff? You suppose to keep up with your chores and hold that job down at the A&P. Ain't been around here all day on a Saturday. Ain't none of your chores done . . . and now you telling me you done quit your job.

CORY.   I'm going to be working weekends.

TROY.   You damn right you are! And ain't no need for nobody coming around here to talk to me about signing nothing.

CORY.   Hey, Pop . . . you can't do that. He's coming all the way from North Carolina.

TROY.   I don't care where he coming from. The white man ain't gonna let you get nowhere with that football noway. You go on and get your book-learning so you can work yourself up in that A&P or learn how to fix cars or build houses or something, get you a trade. That way you have something can't nobody take away from you. You go on and learn how to put your hands to some good use. Besides hauling people's garbage.

CORY.   I get good grades, Pop. That's why the recruiter wants to talk with you. You got to keep up your grades to get recruited. This way I'll be going to college. I'll get a chance . . .

TROY.   First you gonna get your butt down there to the A&P and get your job back.

CORY.   Mr. Stawicki done already hired somebody else 'cause I told him I was playing football.

TROY.   You a bigger fool than I thought . . . to let somebody take away your job so you can play some football. Where you gonna get your money to take out your girlfriend and whatnot? What kind of foolishness is that to let somebody take away your job?

CORY.   I'm still gonna be working weekends.

TROY.   Naw . . . naw. You getting your butt out of here and finding you another job.

CORY.   Come on, Pop! I got to practice. I can't work after school and play football too. The team needs me. That's what Coach Zellman say . . .

TROY.   I don't care what nobody else say. I'm the boss . . . you understand? I'm the boss around here. I do the only saying what counts.

CORY.   Come on, Pop!

TROY.   I asked you . . . did you understand?

CORY.   Yeah . . .

TROY.   What?!

CORY.   Yessir.

TROY.   You go on down there to that A&P and see if you can get your job back. If you can't do both . . . then you quit the football team. You've got to take the crookeds with the straights.

CORY.   Yessir. (*Pause.*) Can I ask you a question?

TROY.   What the hell you wanna ask me? Mr. Stawicki the one you got the questions for.

CORY.   How come you ain't never liked me?

TROY.   Liked you? Who the hell say I got to like you? What law is there say I got to like you? Wanna stand up in my face and ask a damn fool-ass question like that. Talking about liking somebody. Come here, boy, when I talk to you. (CORY *comes over to where* TROY *is working. He stands slouched over and* TROY *shoves him on his shoulder.*) Straighten up, goddammit! I asked you a question . . . what law is there say I got to like you?

CORY.   None.

TROY.   Well, all right then! Don't you eat every day? (*Pause.*) Answer me when I talk to you! Don't you eat every day?

CORY.   Yeah.

TROY.   Nigger, as long as you in my house, you put that sir on the end of it when you talk to me!

CORY.   Yes . . . sir.

TROY.   You eat every day.

CORY.   Yessir!

TROY.   Got a roof over your head.

CORY.   Yessir!

TROY.   Got clothes on your back.

CORY.   Yessir.

TROY.   Why you think that is?

CORY.   'Cause of you.

TROY.   Ah, hell I know it's 'cause of me . . . but why do you think that is?

CORY (*hesitant*).   'Cause you like me.

TROY.   Like you? I go out of here every morning . . . bust my butt . . . putting up with them crackers every day . . .'cause I like you? You are the biggest fool I ever saw. (*Pause.*) It's my job. It's my responsibility! You understand that? A man got to take care of his family. You live in my house . . . sleep you behind on my bedclothes . . . fill you belly up with my food . . .'cause you my son. You my flesh and blood. Not 'cause I like you! 'Cause it's my duty to take care of you. I owe a responsibility to you! Let's get this straight right here . . . before it go along any further . . . I ain't got to like you. Mr. Rand don't give me my money come payday 'cause he likes me. He give me 'cause he owe me. I done give you everything I had to give you. I gave you your life! Me and your mama worked that out between us. And liking your black ass wasn't part of the bargain. Don't you try and go through life worrying about if somebody like you or not. You best be making sure they doing right by you. You understand what I'm saying, boy?

CORY.   Yessir.

TROY.   Then get the hell out of my face, and get on down to that A&P. (ROSE *has been standing behind the screen door for much of the scene. She enters as* CORY *exits.*)

ROSE.   Why don't you let the boy go ahead and play football, Troy? Ain't no harm in that. He's just trying to be like you with the sports.

TROY.   I don't want him to be like me! I want him to move as far away from my life as he can get. You the only decent thing that ever happened to me. I wish him that. But I don't wish him a thing else from my life. I decided seventeen years ago that boy wasn't getting involved in no sports. Not after what they did to me in the sports.

ROSE.   Troy, why don't you admit you was too old to play in the major leagues? For once . . . why don't you admit that?

TROY.   What do you mean too old? Don't come telling me I was too old. I just wasn't the right color. Hell, I'm fifty-three years old and can do better than Selkirk's .269 right now!

ROSE.   How's was you gonna play ball when you were over forty? Sometimes I can't get no sense out of you.

TROY.   I got good sense, woman. I got sense enough not to let my boy get hurt over playing no sports. You been mothering that boy too much. Worried about if people like him.

ROSE.   Everything that boy do . . . he do for you. He wants you to say "Good job, son." That's all.

TROY.   Rose, I ain't got time for that. He's alive. He's healthy. He's got to make his own way. I made mine. Ain't nobody gonna hold his hand when he get out there in that world.

ROSE.   Times have changed from when you was young, Troy. People change. The world's changing around you and you can't even see it.

TROY (slow, methodical).   Woman . . . I do the best I can do. I come in here every Friday. I carry a sack of potatoes and a bucket of lard. You all line up at the door with your hands out. I give you the lint from my pockets. I give you my sweat and my blood. I ain't got no tears. I done spent them. We go upstairs in that room at night . . . and I fall down on you and try to blast a hole into forever. I get up Monday morning . . . find my lunch on the table. I go out. Make my way. Find my strength to carry me through to the next Friday. (Pause.) That's all I got, Rose. That's all I got to give. I can't give nothing else. (TROY exits into the house. The lights go down to black.)

SCENE 4

It is Friday. Two weeks later. CORY starts out of the house with his football equipment. The phone rings.

CORY (calling).   I got it! (He answers the phone and stands in the screen door talking.) Hello? Hey, Jesse. Naw . . . I was just getting ready to leave now.

ROSE (*calling*).   Cory!

CORY.   I told you, man, them spikes is all tore up. You can use them if you want, but they ain't no good. Earl got some spikes.

ROSE (*calling*).   Cory!

CORY (*calling to* ROSE).   Mam? I'm talking to Jesse. (*Into phone*) When she say that? (*Pause.*) Aw, you lying, man. I'm gonna tell her you said that.

ROSE (*calling*).   Cory, don't you go nowhere!

CORY.   I got to go to the game, Ma! (*Into the phone*) Yeah, hey, look, I'll talk to you later. Yeah, I'll meet you over Earl's house. Later. Bye, Ma. (CORY *exits the house and starts out the yard.*)

ROSE.   Cory, where you going off to? You got that stuff all pulled out and thrown all over your room.

CORY (*in the yard*).   I was looking for my spikes. Jesse wanted to borrow my spikes.

ROSE.   Get up there and get that cleaned up before your daddy get back in here.

CORY.   I got to go to the game! I'll clean it up when I get back. (CORY *exits.*)

ROSE.   That's all he need to do is see that room all messed up. (ROSE *exits into the house.* TROY *and* BONO *enter the yard.* TROY *is dressed in clothes other than his work clothes.*)

BONO.   He told him the same thing he told you. Take it to the union.

TROY.   Brownie ain't got that much sense. Man wasn't thinking about nothing. He wait until I confront them on it . . . then he wanna come crying seniority. (*Calls*) Hey, Rose!

BONO.   I wish I could have seen Mr. Rand's face when he told you.

TROY.   He couldn't get it out of his mouth! Liked to bit his tongue! When they called me down there to the Commissioner's office . . . he thought they was gonna fire me. Like everybody else.

BONO.   I didn't think they was gonna fire you. I thought they was gonna put you on the warning paper.

TROY.   Hey, Rose! (*To* BONO) Yeah, Mr. Rand like to bit his tongue. (TROY *breaks the seal on the bottle, takes a drink, and hands it to* BONO.)

BONO.   I see you run right down to Taylors' and told that Alberta gal.

TROY (*calling*).   Hey Rose! (*To* BONO) I told everybody. Hey, Rose! I went down there to cash my check.

ROSE (*entering from the house*).   Hush all that hollering, man! I know you out here. What they say down there at the Commissioner's office?

TROY.   You supposed to come when I call you, woman. Bono'll tell you that. (*To* BONO) Don't Lucille come when you call her?

ROSE.   Man, hush your mouth. I ain't no dog . . . talk about "come when you call me."

TROY (*puts his arm around* ROSE).   You hear this, Bono? I had me an old dog used to get uppity like that. You say, "C'mere, Blue!" . . . and he just lay there and look at you. End up getting a stick and chasing him away trying to make him come.

ROSE.   I ain't studying you and your dog. I remember you used to sing that old song.

TROY (*he sings*).   Hear it ring! Hear it ring! I had a dog his name was Blue.

ROSE.   Don't nobody wanna hear you sing that old song.

TROY (*sings*).   You know Blue was mighty true.

ROSE.   Used to have Cory running around here singing that song.

BONO.   Hell, I remember that song myself.

TROY (*sings*).   You know Blue was a good old dog.
          Blue treed a possum in a hollow log.
That was my daddy's song. My daddy made up that song.

ROSE.   I don't care who made it up. Don't nobody wanna hear you sing it.

TROY (*makes a song like calling a dog*).   Come here, woman.

ROSE.   You come in here carrying on, I reckon they ain't fired you. What they say down there at the Commissioner's office?

TROY.   Look here, Rose . . . Mr. Rand called me into his office today when I got back from talking to them people down there . . . it come from up top . . . he called me in and told me they was making me a driver.

ROSE.   Troy, you kidding!

TROY.   No I ain't. Ask Bono.

ROSE.   Well, that's great, Troy. Now you don't have to hassle them people no more. (LYONS *enters from the street.*)

TROY.   Aw hell, I wasn't looking to see you today. I thought you was in jail. Got it all over the front page of the *Courier* about them raiding Sefus's place . . . where you be hanging out with all them thugs.

LYONS.   Hey, Pop . . . that ain't got nothing to do with me. I don't go down there gambling. I go down there to sit in with the band. I ain't got nothing to do with the gambling part. They got some good music down there.

TROY.   They got some rogues . . . is what they got.

LYONS.   How you been, Mr. Bono? Hi, Rose.

BONO.   I see where you playing down at the Crawford Grill tonight.

ROSE.   How come you ain't brought Bonnie like I told you? You should have brought Bonnie with you, she ain't been over in a month of Sundays.

LYONS.   I was just in the neighborhood . . . thought I'd stop by.

TROY.   Here he come . . .

BONO.   Your daddy got a promotion on the rubbish. He's gonna be the first colored driver. Ain't got to do nothing but sit up there and read the paper like them white fellows.

LYONS.   Hey, Pop . . . if you knew how to read you'd be all right.

BONO.   Naw . . . naw . . . you mean if the nigger knew how to *drive* he'd be all right. Been fighting with them people about driving and ain't even got a license. Mr. Rand know you ain't got no driver's license?

TROY.   Driving ain't nothing. All you do is point the truck where you want it to go. Driving ain't nothing.

BONO.   Do Mr. Rand know you ain't got no driver's license? That's what I'm talking about. I ain't asked if driving was easy. I asked if Mr. Rand know you ain't got no driver's license.

TROY.   He ain't got to know. The man ain't got to know my business. Time he find out, I have two or three driver's licenses.

LYONS (*going into his pocket*).   Say, look here, Pop . . .

TROY.   I knew it was coming. Didn't I tell you, Bono? I know what kind of "Look here, Pop" that was. The nigger fixing to ask me for some money. It's Friday night. It's my payday. All them rogues down there on the avenue . . . the ones that ain't in jail . . . and Lyons is hopping in his shoes to get down there with them.

LYONS.   See, Pop . . . if you give somebody else a chance to talk sometimes, you'd see that I was fixing to pay you back your ten dollars like I told you. Here . . . I told you I'd pay you when Bonnie got paid.

TROY.   Naw . . . you go ahead and keep that ten dollars. Put it in the bank. The next time you feel like you wanna come by here and ask me for something . . . you go on down there and get that.

LYONS.   Here's your ten dollars, Pop. I told you I don't want you to give me nothing. I just wanted to borrow ten dollars.

TROY.   Naw . . . you go on and keep that for the next time you want to ask me.

LYONS.   Come on, Pop . . . here go your ten dollars.

ROSE.   Why don't you go on and let the boy pay you back, Troy?

LYONS.   Here you go, Rose. If you don't take it I'm gonna have to hear about it for the next six months. (*He hands her the money.*)

ROSE.   You can hand yours over here too, Troy.

TROY.   You see this, Bono. You see how they do me.

BONO.   Yeah, Lucille do me the same way. (GABRIEL *is heard singing offstage. He enters.*)

GABRIEL.   Better get ready for the Judgment! Better get ready for . . . Hey! . . . Hey! There's Troy's boy!

LYONS.   How are you doing, Uncle Gabe!

GABRIEL.   Lyons . . . The King of the Jungle! Rose . . . hey, Rose. Got a flower for you. (*He takes a rose from his pocket.*) Picked it myself. That's the same rose like you is!

ROSE.   That's right nice of you, Gabe.

LYONS.   What you been doing, Uncle Gabe?

GABRIEL.   Oh, I been chasing hellhounds and waiting on the time to tell St. Peter to open the gates.

LYONS.   You been chasing hellhounds, huh? Well . . . you doing the right thing, Uncle Gabe. Somebody got to chase them.

GABRIEL.   Oh, yeah . . . I know it. The devil's strong. The devil ain't no pushover. Hellhounds snipping at everybody's heels. But I got my trumpet waiting on the judgment time.

LYONS.   Waiting on the Battle of Armageddon, huh?

GABRIEL.   Ain't gonna be too much of a battle when God get to waving that Judgment sword. But the people's gonna have a hell of a time trying to get into heaven if them gates ain't open.

LYONS (*putting his arm around* GABRIEL).   You hear this, Pop. Uncle Gabe, you all right!

GABRIEL (*laughing with* LYONS).   Lyons! King of the Jungle.

ROSE.   You gonna stay for supper, Gabe? Want me to fix you a plate?

GABRIEL.   I'll take a sandwich, Rose. Don't want no plate. Just wanna eat with my hands. I'll take a sandwich.

ROSE.   How about you, Lyons? You staying? Got some short ribs cooking.

LYONS.   Naw, I won't eat nothing till after we finished playing. (*Pause.*) You ought to come down and listen to me play, Pop.

TROY.   I don't like that Chinese music. All that noise.

ROSE.   Go on in the house and wash up, Gabe . . . I'll fix you a sandwich.

GABRIEL (*to* LYONS, *as he exits*).   Troy's mad at me.

LYONS.   What you mad at Uncle Gabe for, Pop?

ROSE.   He thinks Troy's mad at him 'cause he moved over to Miss Pearl's.

TROY.   I ain't mad at the man. He can live where he want to live at.

LYONS.   What he move over there for? Miss Pearl don't like nobody.

ROSE.   She don't mind him none. She treats him real nice. She just don't allow all that singing.

TROY.   She don't mind that rent he be paying . . . that's what she don't mind.

ROSE.   Troy, I ain't going through that with you no more. He's over there 'cause he want to have his own place. He can come and go as he please.

TROY.   Hell, he could come and go as he please here. I wasn't stopping him. I ain't put no rules on him.

ROSE.   It ain't the same thing, Troy. And you know it. (GABRIEL *comes to the door.*) Now, that's the last I wanna hear about that. I don't wanna hear nothing else about Gabe and Miss Pearl. And next week . . .

GABRIEL.   I'm ready for my sandwich, Rose.

ROSE.   And next week . . . when that recruiter come from that school . . . I want you to sign that paper and go on and let Cory play football. Then that'll be the last I have to hear about that.

TROY (*to* ROSE *as she exits into the house*).   I ain't thinking about Cory nothing.

LYONS.   What . . . Cory got recruited? What school he going to?

TROY.   That boy walking around here smelling his piss . . . thinking he's grown. Thinking he's gonna do what he want, irrespective of what I say. Look here, Bono . . . I left the Commissioner's office and went down to the A&P . . . that boy ain't working down there. He lying to me. Telling me he got his job back . . . telling me he working weekends . . . telling me he working after school . . . Mr. Stawicki tell me he ain't working down there at all!

LYONS.   Cory, just growing up. He's just busting at the seams trying to fill out your shoes.

TROY.   I don't care what he's doing. When he get to the point where he wanna disobey me . . . then it's time for him to move on. Bono'll tell you that. I bet he ain't never disobeyed his daddy without paying the consequences.

BONO.   I ain't never had a chance. My daddy came on through . . . but I ain't never knew him to see him . . . or what he had on his mind or where he went. Just moving on through. Searching out the New Land. That's what the old folks used to call it. See a fellow moving around from place to place . . . woman to woman . . . called it searching out the New Land. I can't say if he ever found it. I come along, didn't want no kids. Didn't know if I was gonna be in one place long enough to fix on them right as their daddy. I figured I was going searching too. As it turned out I been hooked up with Lucille near about as long as your daddy been with Rose. Going on sixteen years.

TROY.   Sometimes I wish I hadn't known my daddy. He ain't cared nothing about no kids. A kid to him wasn't nothing. All he wanted was for you to learn how to walk so he could start you to working. When it come time for eating . . . he ate first. If there was anything left over, that's what you got. Man would sit down and eat two chickens and give you the wing.

LYONS.   You ought to stop that, Pop. Everybody feed their kids. No matter how hard times is . . . everybody care about their kids. Make sure they have something to eat.

TROY.   The only thing my daddy cared about was getting them bales of cotton in to Mr. Lubin. That's the only thing that mattered to him. Sometimes I used to wonder why he was living. Wonder why the devil hadn't come and got him. "Get them bales of cotton in to Mr. Lubin" and find out he owe him money . . .

LYONS.   He should have just went on and left when he saw he couldn't get nowhere. That's what I would have done.

TROY.   How he gonna leave with eleven kids? And where he gonna go? He ain't knew how to do nothing but farm. No, he was trapped and I think he knew it. But I'll say this for him . . . he felt a responsibility toward us. Maybe he ain't treated us the way I felt he should have . . . but without that responsibility he could have walked off and left us . . . made his own way.

BONO.   A lot of them did. Back in those days what you talking about . . . they walk out their front door and just take on down one road or another and keep on walking.

LYONS.   There you go! That's what I'm talking about.

BONO.   Just keep on walking till you come to something else. Ain't you never heard of nobody having the walking blues? Well, that's what you call it when you just take off like that.

TROY.   My daddy ain't had them walking blues! What you talking about? He stayed right there with his family. But he was just as evil as he could be. My mama couldn't stand him. Couldn't stand that evilness. She run off when I was about eight. She sneaked off one night after he had gone to sleep. Told me she was coming back for me. I ain't never seen her no more. All his women run off and left him. He wasn't good for nobody.

When my turn come to head out, I was fourteen and got to sniffing around Joe Canewell's daughter. Had us an old mule we called Greyboy. My daddy sent me out to do some plowing and I tied up Greyboy and went to fooling around with Joe Canewell's daughter. We done found us a nice little spot, got real cozy with each other. She about thirteen and we done figured we was grown anyway . . . so we down there enjoying ourselves . . . ain't thinking about nothing. We didn't know Greyboy had got loose and wandered back to the house and my daddy was looking for me. We down there by the creek enjoying ourselves when my daddy come up on us. Surprised us. He had them leather straps off the mule and commenced to whupping me like there was no tomorrow. I jumped up, mad and embarrassed. I was scared of my daddy. When he commenced to whupping on me . . . quite naturally I run to get out of the way. (*Pause.*) Now I thought he was mad 'cause I ain't done my work. But I see where he was chasing me off so he could have the gal for himself. When I see what the matter of it was, I lost all fear of my daddy. Right there is where I become a man . . . at fourteen years of age. (*Pause.*) Now it was my turn to run him off. I picked up them same reins that he had used on me. I picked up them reins and commenced to whupping on him. The gal jumped up and run off . . . and when my daddy turned to face me, I could see why the devil had never come to get him . . . 'cause he was the devil himself. I don't know what happened. When I woke up, I was laying right there by the creek, and Blue . . . this old dog we had . . . was licking my face. I thought I was blind. I couldn't see nothing. Both my eyes were swollen shut. I laid there and cried. I didn't know what I was gonna do. The only thing I knew was the time had come for me to leave my daddy's house. And right there the world suddenly got big. And it was a long time before I could cut it down to where I could handle it.

Part of that cutting down was when I got to the place where I could feel him kicking in my blood and knew that the only thing that separated us was the matter of a few years. (GABRIEL *enters from the house with a sandwich.*)

LYONS.   What you got there, Uncle Gabe?

GABRIEL.   Got me a ham sandwich. Rose gave me a ham sandwich.

TROY.   I don't know what happened to him. I done lost touch with everybody except Gabriel. But I hope he's dead. I hope he found some peace.

LYONS.   That's a heavy story, Pop. I didn't know you left home when you was fourteen.

TROY.   I didn't know nothing. The only part of the world I knew was the forty-two acres of Mr. Lubin's land. That's all I knew about life.

LYONS.   Fourteen's kinda young to be out on your own. (*Phone rings.*) I don't even think I was ready to be out on my own at fourteen. I don't know what I would have done.

TROY.   I got up from the creek and walked on down to Mobile. I was through with farming. Figured I could do better in the city. So I walked the two hundred miles to Mobile.

LYONS.   Wait a minute . . . you ain't walked no two hundred miles, Pop. Ain't nobody gonna walk no two hundred miles. You talking about some walking there.

BONO.   That's the only way you got anywhere back in them days.

LYONS.   Shhh. Damn if I wouldn't have hitched a ride with somebody!

TROY.   Who you gonna hitch it with? They ain't had no cars and things like they got now. We talking about 1918.

ROSE (entering).   What you all out here getting into?

TROY (to ROSE).   I'm telling Lyons how good he got it. He don't know nothing about this I'm talking.

ROSE.   Lyons, that was Bonnie on the phone. She say you supposed to pick her up.

LYONS.   Yeah, okay, Rose.

TROY.   I walked on down to Mobile and hitched up with some of them fellows that was heading this way. Got up here and found out . . . not only couldn't you get a job . . . you couldn't find no place to live. I thought I was in freedom. Shhh. Colored folks living down there on the riverbanks in whatever kind of shelter they could find for themselves. Right down there under the Brady Street Bridge. Living in shacks made of sticks and tarpaper. Messed around there and went from bad to worse. Start stealing. First it was food. Then I figured, hell, if I steal money I can buy me some food. Buy me some shoes too! One thing led to another. Met your mama. I was young and anxious to be a man. Met your mama and had you. What I do that for? Now I got to worry about feeding you and her. Got to steal three times as much. Went out one day looking for somebody to rob . . . that's what I was, a robber. I'll tell you the truth. I'm ashamed of it today. But it's the truth. Went to rob this fellow . . . pulled out my knife . . . and he pulled out a gun. Shot me in the chest. I felt just like somebody had taken a hot branding iron and laid it on me. When he shot me I jumped at him with my knife. They told me I killed him and they put me in the penitentiary and locked me up for fifteen years. That's where I met Bono. That's where I learned how to play baseball. Got out that place and your mama had taken you and went on to make life without me. Fifteen years was a long time for her to wait. But that fifteen years cured me of that robbing stuff. Rose'll tell you. She asked me when I met her if I had gotten all that foolishness out of my system. And I told her, "Baby, it's you and baseball all what count with me." You hear me, Bono? I mean it too. She say, "Which one comes first?" I told her, "Baby, ain't no doubt it's baseball . . . but you stick and get old with me and we'll both outlive this baseball." Am I right, Rose? And it's true.

ROSE.   Man, hush your mouth. You ain't said no such thing. Talking about, "Baby, you know you'll always be number one with me." That's what you was talking.

TROY.   You hear that, Bono. That's why I love her.

BONO.   Rose'll keep you straight. You get off the track, she'll straighten you up.

ROSE.   Lyons, you better get on up and get Bonnie. She waiting on you.

LYONS (*gets up to go*).   Hey, Pop, why don't you come on down to the Grill and hear me play?

TROY.   I ain't going down there. I'm too old to be sitting around in them clubs.

BONO.   You got to be good to play down at the Grill.

LYONS.   Come on, Pop . . .

TROY.   I got to get up in the morning.

LYONS.   You ain't got to stay long.

TROY.   Naw, I'm gonna get my supper and go on to bed.

LYONS.   Well, I got to go. I'll see you again.

TROY.   Don't you come around my house on my payday.

ROSE.   Pick up the phone and let somebody know you coming. And bring Bonnie with you. You know I'm always glad to see her.

LYONS.   Yeah, I'll do that, Rose. You take care now. See you, Pop. See you, Mr. Bono. See you, Uncle Gabe.

GABRIEL.   Lyons! King of the Jungle! (LYONS *exits.*)

TROY.   Is supper ready, woman? Me and you got some business to take care of. I'm gonna tear it up too.

ROSE.   Troy, I done told you now!

TROY (*puts his arm around* BONO).   Aw hell, woman . . . this is Bono. Bono like family. I done known this nigger since . . . how long I done know you?

BONO.   It's been a long time.

TROY.   I done know this nigger since Skippy was a pup. Me and him done been through some times.

BONO.   You sure right about that.

TROY.   Hell, I done know him longer than I known you. And we still standing shoulder to shoulder. Hey, look here, Bono . . . a man can't ask for no more than that. (*Drinks to him.*) I love you, nigger.

BONO.   Hell, I love you too . . . I got to get home see my woman. You got yours in hand. I got to go get mine. (BONO *starts to exit as* CORY *enters the yard, dressed in his football uniform. He gives* TROY *a hard, uncompromising look.*)

CORY.   What you do that for, Pop? (*He throws his helmet down in the direction of* TROY.)

ROSE.   What's the matter? Cory . . . what's the matter?

CORY.   Papa done went up to the school and told Coach Zellman I can't play football no more. Wouldn't even let me play the game. Told him to tell the recruiter not to come.

ROSE.   Troy . . .

TROY.   What you Troying me for. Yeah, I did it. And the boy know why I did it.

CORY.   Why you wanna do that to me? That was the one chance I had.

ROSE.   Ain't nothing wrong with Cory playing football, Troy.

TROY.   The boy lied to me. I told the nigger if he wanna play football . . . to keep up his chores and hold down that job at the A&P. That was the conditions. Stopped down there to see Mr. Stawicki . . .

CORY.   I can't work after school during the football season, Pop! I tried to tell you that Mr. Stawicki's holding my job for me. You don't never want to listen to nobody. And then you wanna go and do this to me!

TROY.   I ain't done nothing to you. You done it to yourself.

CORY.   Just 'cause you didn't have a chance! You just scared I'm gonna be better than you, that's all.

TROY.   Come here.

ROSE.   Troy . . . (CORY *reluctantly crosses over to* TROY.)

TROY.   All right! See. You done made a mistake.

CORY.   I didn't even do nothing!

TROY.   I'm gonna tell you what your mistake was. See . . . you swung at the ball and didn't hit it. That's strike one. See, you in the batter's box now. You swung and you missed. That's strike one. Don't you strike out! (*Lights fade to black.*)

ACT 2

SCENE 1

The following morning. CORY *is at the tree hitting the ball with the bat. He tries to mimic* TROY, *but his swing is awkward, less sure.* ROSE *enters from the house.*

ROSE.   Cory, I want you to help me with this cupboard.

CORY.   I ain't quitting the team. I don't care what Poppa say.

ROSE.   I'll talk to him when he gets back. He had to go see about your Uncle Gabe. The police done arrested him. Say he was disturbing the peace. He'll be back directly. Come on in here and help me clean out the top of this cupboard. (CORY *exits into the house.* ROSE *sees* TROY *and* BONO *coming down the alley.*) Troy . . . what they say down there?

TROY.   Ain't said nothing. I give them fifty dollars and they let him go. I'll talk to you about it. Where's Cory?

ROSE.   He's in there helping me clean out these cupboards.

TROY.   Tell him to get his butt out here. (TROY *and* BONO *go over to the pile of wood.* BONO *picks up the saw and begins sawing. To* BONO) All they want is the money. That makes six or seven times I done went down there and got him. See me coming they stick out their *hands.*

BONO.   Yeah. I know what you mean. That's all they care about . . . that money. They don't care about what's right. (*Pause.*) Nigger, why you got to go and get some hard wood? You ain't doing nothing but building a little old fence. Get you some soft pine wood. That's all you need.

TROY.   I know what I'm doing. This is outside wood. You put pine wood inside the house. Pine wood is inside wood. This here is outside wood. Now you tell me where the fence is gonna be?

BONO.   You don't need this wood. You can put it up with pine wood and it'll stand as long as you gonna be here looking at it.

TROY.   How you know how long I'm gonna be here, nigger? Hell, I might just live forever. Live longer than old man Horsely.

BONO.   That's what Magee used to say.

TROY.   Magee's a damn fool. Now you tell me who you ever heard of gonna pull their own teeth with a pair of rusty pliers.

BONO.   The old folks . . . my granddaddy used to pull his teeth with pliers. They ain't had no dentists for the colored folks back then.

TROY.   Get clean pliers! You understand? Clean pliers! Sterilize them! Besides we ain't living back then. All Magee had to do was walk over to Doc Goldblum's.

BONO.   I see where you and that Tallahassee gal . . . that Alberta . . . I see where you all done got tight.

TROY.   What you mean "got tight"?

BONO.   I see where you be laughing and joking with her all the time.

TROY.   I laughs and jokes with all of them, Bono. You know me.

BONO.   That ain't the kind of laughing and joking I'm talking about. (CORY *enters from the house.*)

CORY.   How you doing, Mr. Bono?

TROY.   Cory? Get that saw from Bono and cut some wood. He talking about the wood's too hard to cut. Stand back there, Jim, and let that young boy show you how it's done.

BONO.   He's sure welcome to it. (CORY *takes the saw and begins to cut the wood.*) Whew-e-e! Look at that. Big old strong boy. Look like Joe Louis. Hell, must be getting old the way I'm watching that boy whip through that wood.

CORY.   I don't see why Mama want a fence around the yard noways.

TROY.   Damn if I know either. What the hell she keeping out with it? She ain't got nothing nobody want.

BONO.   Some people build fences to keep people out . . . and other people build fences to keep people in. Rose wants to hold on to you all. She loves you.

TROY.   Hell, nigger, I don't need nobody to tell me my wife loves me. Cory . . . go on in the house and see if you can find that other saw.

CORY.   Where's it at?

TROY.   I said find it! Look for it till you find it! (CORY *exits into the house*.) What's that supposed to mean? Wanna keep us in?

BONO.   Troy . . . I done known you seem like damn near my whole life. You and Rose both. I done know both of you all for a long time. I remember when you met Rose. When you was hitting them baseball out the park. A lot of them old gals was after you then. You had the pick of the litter. When you picked Rose, I was happy for you. That was the first time I knew you had any sense. I said . . . My man Troy knows what he's doing . . . I'm gonna follow this nigger . . . he might take me somewhere. I been following you too. I done learned a whole heap of things about life watching you. I done learned how to tell where the shit lies. How to tell it from the alfalfa. You done learned me a lot of things. You showed me how to not make the same mistakes . . . to take life as it comes along and keep putting one foot in front of the other. (*Pause.*) Rose a good woman, Troy.

TROY.   Hell, nigger, I know she a good woman. I been married to her for eighteen years. What you got on your mind, Bono?

BONO.   I just say she a good woman. Just like I say anything. I ain't got to have nothing on my mind.

TROY.   You just gonna say she a good woman and leave it hanging out there like that? Why you telling me she a good woman?

BONO.   She loves you, Troy. Rose loves you.

TROY.   You saying I don't measure up. That's what you trying to say. I don't measure up 'cause I'm seeing this other gal. I know what you trying to say.

BONO.   I know what Rose means to you, Troy. I'm just trying to say I don't want to see you mess up.

TROY.   Yeah, I appreciate that, Bono. If you was messing around on Lucille I'd be telling you the same thing.

BONO.   Well, that's all I got to say. I just say that because I love you both.

TROY.   Hell, you know me . . . I wasn't out there looking for nothing. You can't find a better woman than Rose. I know that. But seems like this woman just stuck onto me where I can't shake her loose. I done wrestled with it, tried to throw her off me . . . but she just stuck on tighter. Now she's stuck on for good.

BONO.   You's in control . . . that's what you tell me all the time. You responsible for what you do.

TROY.   I ain't ducking the responsibility of it. As long as it sets right in my heart . . . then I'm okay. 'Cause that's all I listen to. It'll tell me right from wrong every time. And I ain't talking about doing Rose no bad turn. I love Rose. She done carried me a long ways and I love and respect her for that.

BONO.   I know you do. That's why I don't want to see you hurt her. But what you gonna do when she find out? What you got then? If you try and juggle both of them . . . sooner or later you gonna drop one of them. That's common sense.

TROY.   Yeah, I hear what you saying, Bono. I been trying to figure a way to work it out.

BONO.   Work it out right, Troy. I don't want to be getting all up between you and Rose's business . . . but work it so it come out right.

TROY.   Ah hell, I get all up between you and Lucille's business. When you gonna get that woman that refrigerator she been wanting? Don't tell me you ain't got no money now. I know who your banker is. Mellon don't need that money bad as Lucille want that refrigerator. I'll tell you that.

BONO.   Tell you what I'll do . . . when you finish building this fence for Rose . . . I'll buy Lucille that refrigerator.

TROY.   You done stuck your foot in your mouth now! (*Grabs up a board and begins to saw.* BONO *starts to walk out of the yard.*) Hey, nigger . . . where you going?

BONO.   I'm going home. I know you don't expect me to help you now. I'm protecting my money. I wanna see you put that fence up by yourself. That's what I want to see. You'll be here another six months without me.

TROY.   Nigger, you ain't right.

BONO.   When it comes to my money . . . I'm right as fireworks on the Fourth of July.

TROY.   All right, we gonna see now. You better get out your bankbook. (BONO *exits, and* TROY *continues to work.* ROSE *enters from the house.*)

ROSE.   What they say down there? What's happening with Gabe?

TROY.   I went down there and got him out. Cost me fifty dollars. Say he was disturbing the peace. Judge set up a hearing for him in three weeks. Say to show cause why he shouldn't be recommitted.

ROSE.   What was he doing that cause them to arrest him?

TROY.   Some kids was teasing him and he run them off home. Say he was howling and carrying on. Some folks seen him and called the police. That's all it was.

ROSE.   Well, what's you say? What'd you tell the judge?

TROY.   Told him I'd look after him. It didn't make no sense to recommit the man. He stuck out his big greasy palm and told me to give him fifty dollars and take him on home.

ROSE.   Where's he at now? Where'd he go off to?

TROY.   He's gone about his business. He don't need nobody to hold his hand.

ROSE.   Well, I don't know. Seem like that would be the best place for him if they did put him into the hospital. I know what you're gonna say. But that's what I think would be best.

TROY.   The man done had his life ruined fighting for what? And they wanna take and lock him up. Let him be free. He don't bother nobody.

ROSE.   Well, everybody got their own way of looking at it I guess. Come on and get your lunch. I got a bowl of lima beans and some cornbread in the oven. Come and get something to eat. Ain't no sense you fretting over Gabe. (*Turns to go into the house.*)

TROY.   Rose . . . got something to tell you.

ROSE.   Well, come on . . . wait till I get this food on the table.

TROY.   Rose! (*She stops and turns around.*) I don't know how to say this. (*Pause.*) I can't explain it none. It just sort of grows on you till it gets out of hand. It starts out like a little bush . . . and the next thing you know it's a whole forest.

ROSE.   Troy . . . what is you talking about?

TROY.   I'm talking, woman, let me talk. I'm trying to find a way to tell you . . . I'm gonna be a daddy. I'm gonna be somebody's daddy.

ROSE.   Troy . . . you're not telling me this? You're gonna be . . . what?

TROY.   Rose . . . now . . . see . . .

ROSE.   You telling me you gonna be somebody's daddy? You telling your *wife* this? (GABRIEL *enters from the street. He carries a rose in his hand.*)

GABRIEL.   Hey, Troy! Hey, Rose!

ROSE.   I have to wait eighteen years to hear something like this.

GABRIEL.   Hey, Rose . . . I got a flower for you. (*He hands it to her.*) That's a rose. Same rose like you is.

ROSE.   Thanks, Gabe.

GABRIEL.   Troy, you ain't mad at me is you? Them bad mens come and put me away. You ain't mad at me is you?

TROY.   Naw, Gabe, I ain't mad at you.

ROSE.   Eighteen years and you wanna come with this.

GABRIEL (*takes a quarter out of his pocket*).   See what I got? Got a brand new quarter.

TROY.   Rose . . . it's just . . .

ROSE.   Ain't nothing you can say, Troy. Ain't no way of explaining that.

GABRIEL.   Fellow that give me this quarter had a whole mess of them. I'm gonna keep this quarter till it stop shining.

ROSE.   Gabe, go on in the house there. I got some watermelon in the Frigidaire. Go on and get you a piece.

GABRIEL.   Say, Rose . . . you know I was chasing hellhounds and them bad mens come and get me and take me away. Troy helped me. He come down there and told them they better let me go before he beat them up. Yeah, he did!

ROSE.   You go on and get you a piece of watermelon, Gabe. Them bad mens is gone now.

GABRIEL.   Okay, Rose . . . gonna get me some watermelon. The kind with the stripes on it. (GABRIEL *exits into the house.*)

ROSE.   Why, Troy? Why? After all these years to come dragging this in to me now. It don't make no sense at your age. I could have expected this ten or fifteen years ago, but not now.

TROY.   Age ain't got nothing to do with it, Rose.

ROSE.   I done tried to be everything a wife should be. Everything a wife could be. Been married eighteen years and I got to live to see the day you tell me you been seeing another woman and done fathered a child by her. And you know I ain't never wanted no half nothing in my family. My whole family is half. Everybody got different fathers and mothers . . . my two sisters and my brother. Can't hardly tell who's who. Can't never sit down and talk about Papa and Mama. It's your papa and your mama and my papa and my mama . . .

TROY.   Rose . . . stop it now.

ROSE.   I ain't never wanted that for none of my children. And now you wanna drag your behind in here and tell me something like this.

TROY.   You ought to know. It's time for you to know.

ROSE.   Well, I don't want to know, goddamn it!

TROY.   I can't just make it go away. It's done now. I can't wish the circumstance of the thing away.

ROSE.   And you don't want to either. Maybe you want to wish me and my boy away. Maybe that's what you want? Well, you can't wish us away. I've got eighteen years of my life invested in you. You ought to have stayed upstairs in my bed where you belong.

TROY.   Rose . . . now listen to me . . . we can get a handle on this thing. We can talk this out . . . come to an understanding.

ROSE.   All of a sudden it's "we." Where was "we" at when you was down there rolling around with some godforsaken woman? "We" should have come to an understanding before you started making a damn fool of yourself. You're a day late and a dollar short when it comes to an understanding with me.

TROY.   It's just . . . She gives me a different idea . . . a different understanding about myself. I can step out of this house and get away from the pressures and problems . . . be a different man. I ain't got to wonder how I'm gonna pay the bills or get the roof fixed. I can just be a part of myself that I ain't never been.

ROSE.   What I want to know . . . is do you plan to continue seeing her. That's all you can say to me.

TROY.   I can sit up in her house and laugh. Do you understand what I'm saying? I can laugh out loud . . . and it feels good. It reaches all the way down to the bottom of my shoes. (*Pause.*) Rose, I can't give that up.

ROSE.   Maybe you ought to go on and stay down there with her . . . if she's a better woman than me.

TROY.   It ain't about nobody being a better woman or nothing. Rose, you ain't the blame. A man couldn't ask for no woman to be a better wife than you've been. I'm responsible for it. I done locked myself into a pattern trying to take care of you all that I forgot about myself.

ROSE.   What the hell was I there for? That was my job, not somebody else's.

TROY.   Rose, I done tried all my life to live decent . . . to live a clean . . . hard . . . useful life. I tried to be a good husband to you. In every way I knew how. Maybe I come into the world backwards, I don't know. But . . . you born with two strikes on you before you come to the plate. You got to guard it closely . . . always looking for the curve ball on the inside corner. You can't afford to let none get past you. You can't afford a call strike. If you going down . . . you going down swinging. Everything lined up against you. What you gonna do? I fooled them, Rose. I bunted. When I found you and Cory and a halfway decent job . . . I was safe. Couldn't nothing touch me. I wasn't gonna strike out no more. I wasn't going back to the penitentiary. I wasn't gonna lay in the streets with a bottle of wine. I was safe. I had me a family. A job. I wasn't gonna get that last strike. I was on first looking for one of them boys to knock me in. To get me home.

ROSE.   You should have stayed in my bed, Troy.

TROY.   Then when I saw that gal . . . she firmed up my backbone. And I got to thinking that if I tried . . . I just might be able to steal second. Do you understand after eighteen years I wanted to steal second.

ROSE.   You should have held me tight. You should have grabbed me and held on.

TROY.   I stood on first base for eighteen years and I thought . . . well, goddamn it . . . go on for it!

ROSE.   We're not talking about baseball! We're talking about you going off to lay in bed with another woman . . . and then bring it home to me. That's what we're talking about. We ain't talking about no baseball.

TROY.   Rose, you're not listening to me. I'm trying the best I can to explain it to you. It's not easy for me to admit that I been standing in the same place for eighteen years.

ROSE.   I been standing with you! I been right here with you, Troy. I got a life too. I gave eighteen years of my life to stand in the same spot with you. Don't you think I ever wanted other things? Don't you think I had dreams and hopes? What about my life? What about me. Don't you think it ever crossed my mind to want to know other men? That I wanted to lay up somewhere and forget about my responsibilities? That I wanted someone to make me laugh so I could feel good? You not the only one who's got wants and needs. But I held on to you, Troy. I took all my feelings, my wants and needs, my dreams . . . and buried them inside you. I planted a seed and watched and prayed over it. I planted myself inside you and waited to bloom. And it didn't take me no eighteen years to find out the soil was hard and rocky and it wasn't never gonna bloom.

But I held on to you, Troy. I held you tighter. You was my husband. I owed you everything I had. Every part of me I could find to give you. And upstairs in that room . . . with the darkness falling in on me . . . I gave everything I had to try and erase the doubt that you wasn't the finest man in the world. And wherever you was going . . . I wanted to be there with you. 'Cause you was my husband. 'Cause that's the only way I was gonna survive as your wife. You always talking about what you give . . . and what you don't have to give. But you take too. You take . . . and don't even know nobody's giving! (*Turns to exit into the house;* TROY *grabs her arm.*)

TROY.   You say I take and don't give!

ROSE.   Troy! You're hurting me!

TROY.   You say I take and don't give!

ROSE.   Troy . . . you're hurting my arm! Let go!

TROY.   I done give you everything I got. Don't you tell that lie on me.

ROSE.   Troy!

TROY.   Don't you tell that lie on me! (CORY *enters from the house.*)

CORY.   Mama!

ROSE.   Troy. You're hurting me.

TROY.   Don't you tell me about my taking and giving.   (CORY *comes up behind* TROY *and grabs him.* TROY, *surprised, is thrown off balance just as* CORY *throws a glancing blow that catches him on the chest and knocks him down.* TROY *is stunned, as is* CORY.)

ROSE.   Troy. Troy. No! (TROY *gets to his feet and starts at* CORY.) Troy . . . no. Please! Troy! (ROSE *pulls on* TROY *to hold him back.* TROY *stops himself.*)

TROY (*to* CORY).   All right. That's strike two. You stay away from around me, boy. Don't you strike out. You living with a full count. Don't you strike out. (TROY *exits out the yard as the lights go down.*)

SCENE 2

It is six months later, early afternoon. TROY *enters from the house and starts to exit the yard.* ROSE *enters from the house.*

ROSE.   Troy, I want to talk to you.

TROY.   All of a sudden, after all this time, you want to talk to me, huh? You ain't wanted to talk to me for months. You ain't wanted to talk to me last night. You ain't wanted no part of me then. What you wanna talk to me about now?

ROSE.   Tomorrow's Friday.

TROY.   I know what day tomorrow is. You think I don't know tomorrow's Friday? My whole life I ain't done nothing but look to see Friday coming and you got to tell me it's Friday.

ROSE.   I want to know if you're coming home.

TROY.   I always come home, Rose. You know that. There ain't never been a night I ain't come home.

ROSE.   That ain't what I mean . . . and you know it. I want to know if you're coming straight home after work.

TROY.   I figure I'd cash my check . . . hang out at Taylors' with the boys . . . maybe play a game of checkers . . .

ROSE.   Troy, I can't live like this. I won't live like this. You livin' on borrowed time with me. It's been going on six months now you ain't been coming home.

TROY.   I be here every night. Every night of the year. That's 365 days.

ROSE.   I want you to come home tomorrow after work.

TROY.   Rose . . . I don't mess up my pay. You know that now. I take my pay and I give it to you. I don't have no money but what you give me back. I just want to have a little time to myself . . . a little time to enjoy life.

ROSE.   What about me? When's my time to enjoy life?

TROY.   I don't know what to tell you, Rose. I'm doing the best I can.

ROSE.   You ain't been home from work but time enough to change your clothes and run out . . . and you wanna call that the best you can do?

TROY.   I'm going over to the hospital to see Alberta. She went into the hospital this afternoon. Look like she might have the baby early. I won't be gone long.

ROSE.   Well, you ought to know. They went over to Miss Pearl's and got Gabe today. She said you told them to go ahead and lock him up.

TROY.   I ain't said no such thing. Whoever told you that is telling a lie. Pearl ain't doing nothing but telling a big fat lie.

ROSE.   She ain't had to tell me. I read it on the papers.

TROY.   I ain't told them nothing of the kind.

ROSE.   I saw it right there on the papers.

TROY.   What it say, huh?

ROSE.   It said you told them to take him.

TROY.   Then they screwed that up, just the way they screw up everything. I ain't worried about what they got on the paper.

ROSE.   Say the government send part of his check to the hospital and the other part to you.

TROY.   I ain't got nothing to do with that if that's the way it works. I ain't made up the rules about how it work.

ROSE.   You did Gabe just like you did Cory. You wouldn't sign the paper for Cory . . . but you signed for Gabe. You signed that paper. (*The telephone is heard ringing inside the house.*)

TROY.   I told you I ain't signed nothing, woman! The only thing I signed was the release form. Hell, I can't read, I don't know what they had on that paper! I ain't signed nothing about sending Gabe away.

ROSE.   I said send him to the hospital . . . you said let him be free
. . . now you done went down there and signed him to the hospital for
half his money. You went back on yourself, Troy. You gonna have to
answer for that.

TROY.   See now . . . you been over there talking to Miss Pearl. She
done got mad 'cause she ain't getting Gabe's rent money. That's all it is.
She's liable to say anything.

ROSE.   Troy, I seen where you signed the paper.

TROY.   You ain't seen nothing I signed. What she doing got papers
on my brother anyway? Miss Pearl telling a big fat lie. And I'm gonna
tell her about it too! You ain't seen nothing I signed. Say . . . you ain't
seen nothing I signed. (ROSE *exits into the house to answer the telephone.*
Presently she returns.)

ROSE.   Troy . . . that was the hospital. Alberta had the baby.

TROY.   What she have? What is it?

ROSE.   It's a girl.

TROY.   I better get on down to the hospital to see her.

ROSE.   Troy . . .

TROY.   Rose . . . I got to go see her now. That's only right . . .
what's the matter . . . the baby's all right, ain't it?

ROSE.   Alberta died having the baby.

TROY.   Died . . . you say she's dead? Alberta's dead?

ROSE.   They said they done all they could. They couldn't do
nothing for her.

TROY.   The baby? How's the baby?

ROSE.   They say it's healthy. I wonder who's gonna bury her.

TROY.   She had family, Rose. She wasn't living in the world by
herself.

ROSE.   I know she wasn't living in the world by herself.

TROY.   Next thing you gonna want to know if she had any
insurance.

ROSE.   Troy, you ain't got to talk like that.

TROY.   That's the first thing that jumped out your mouth. "Who's
gonna bury her?" Like I'm fixing to take on that task for myself.

ROSE.   I am your wife. Don't push me away.

TROY.   I ain't pushing nobody away. Just give me some space.
That's all. Just give me some room to breathe. (ROSE *exits into the house.*
TROY *walks about the yard. With a quiet rage that threatens to consume*
him.) All right . . . Mr. Death. See now . . . I'm gonna tell you what I'm
gonna do. I'm gonna take and build me a fence around this yard. See?
I'm gonna build me a fence around what belongs to me. And then I
want you to stay on the other side. See? You stay over there until you're

ready for me. Then you come on. Bring your army. Bring your sickle. Bring your wrestling clothes. I ain't gonna fall down on my vigilance this time. You ain't gonna sneak up on me no more. When you ready for me . . . when the top of your list say Troy Maxson . . . that's when you come around here. You come up and knock on the front door. Ain't nobody else got nothing to do with this. This is between you and me. Man to man. You stay on the other side of that fence until you ready for me. Then you come up and knock on the front door. Anytime you want. I'll be ready for you. (*The lights go down to black.*)

SCENE 3

The lights come up on the porch. It is late evening three days later. ROSE *sits listening to the ball game waiting for* TROY. *The final out of the game is made and* ROSE *switches off the radio.* TROY *enters the yard carrying an infant wrapped in blankets. He stands back from the house and calls.*

ROSE *enters and stands on the porch. There is a long, awkward silence, the weight of which grows heavier with each passing second.*

TROY.   Rose . . . I'm standing here with my daughter in my arms. She ain't but a wee bittie little old thing. She don't know nothing about grownups' business. She innocent . . . and she ain't got no mama.

ROSE.   What you telling me for, Troy? (*She turns and exits into the house.*)

TROY.   Well . . . I guess we'll just sit out here on the porch. (*He sits down on the porch. There is an awkward indelicateness about the way he handles the baby. His largeness engulfs and seems to swallow it. He speaks loud enough for Rose to hear.*) A man's got to do what's right for him. I ain't sorry for nothing I done. It felt right in my heart. (*To the baby*) What you smiling at? Your daddy's a big man. Got these great big old hands. But sometimes he's scared. And right now your daddy's scared 'cause we sitting out here and ain't got no home. Oh, I been homeless before. I ain't had no little baby with me. But I been homeless. You just be out on the road by your lonesome and you see one of them trains coming and you just kinda go like this . . . (*He sings as a lullaby.*)

> Please, Mr. Engineer let a man ride the line
> Please, Mr. Engineer let a man ride the line
> I ain't got no ticket please let me ride the blinds

(ROSE *enters from the house.* TROY, *hearing her steps behind him, stands and faces her.*) She's my daughter, Rose. My own flesh and blood. I can't deny her no more than I can deny them boys. (*Pause.*) You and them boys is my family. You and them and this child is all I got in the world. So I guess what I'm saying is . . . I'd appreciate it if you'd help me take care of her.

ROSE.   Okay, Troy . . . you're right. I'll take care of your baby for you . . . 'cause . . . like you say . . . she's innocent . . . and you can't visit the sins of the father upon the child. A motherless child has got a hard time. (*She takes the baby from him.*) From right now . . . this child got a mother. But you a womanless man. (ROSE *turns and exits into the house with the baby. Lights go down to black.*)

SCENE 4

It is two months later. LYONS *enters from the street. He knocks on the door and calls.*

LYONS.   Hey, Rose! (*Pause.*) Rose!

ROSE (*from inside the house*).   Stop that yelling. You gonna wake up Raynell. I just got her to sleep.

LYONS.   I just stopped by to pay Papa this twenty dollars I owe him. Where's Papa at?

ROSE.   He should be here in a minute. I'm getting ready to go down to the church. Sit down and wait on him.

LYONS.   I got to go pick up Bonnie over her mother's house.

ROSE.   Well, sit it down there on the table. He'll get it.

LYONS (*enters the house and sets the money on the table*).   Tell Papa I said thanks. I'll see you again.

ROSE.   All right, Lyons. We'll see you. (LYONS *starts to exit as* CORY *enters.*)

CORY.   Hey, Lyons.

LYONS.   What's happening, Cory? Say man, I'm sorry I missed your graduation. You know I had a gig and couldn't get away. Otherwise, I would have been there, man. So what you doing?

CORY.   I'm trying to find a job.

LYONS.   Yeah I know how that go, man. It's rough out here. Jobs are scarce.

CORY.   Yeah, I know.

LYONS.   Look here, I got to run. Talk to Papa . . . he know some people. He'll be able to help you get a job. Talk to him . . . see what he say.

CORY.   Yeah . . . all right, Lyons.

LYONS.   You take care. I'll talk to you soon. We'll find some time to talk. (LYONS *exits the yard.* CORY *wanders over to the tree, picks up the bat, and assumes a batting stance. He studies an imaginary pitcher and swings. Dissatisfied with the result, he tries again.* TROY *enters. They eye each other for a beat.* CORY *puts the bat down and exits the yard.* TROY *starts into the house as* ROSE *exits with* RAYNELL. *She is carrying a cake.*)

TROY.   I'm coming in and everybody's going out.

ROSE.   I'm taking this cake down to the church for the bake sale. Lyons was by to see you. He stopped by to pay you your twenty dollars. It's laying in there on the table.

TROY (*going into his pocket*).   Well . . . here go this money.

ROSE.   Put it in there on the table, Troy. I'll get it.

TROY.   What time you coming back?

ROSE.   Ain't no use in you studying me. It don't matter what time I come back.

TROY.   I just asked you a question, woman. What's the matter . . . can't I ask you a question?

ROSE.   Troy, I don't want to go into it. Your dinner's in there on the stove. All you got to do is heat it up. And don't you be eating the rest of them cakes in there. I'm coming back for them. We having a bake sale at the church tomorrow. (ROSE *exits the yard.* TROY *sits down on the step, takes a pint bottle from his pocket, opens it, and drinks. He begins to sing.*)

TROY.   Hear it ring! Hear it ring!
   Had an old dog his name was Blue
   You know Blue was mighty true
   You know Blue was a good old dog
   Blue trees a possum in a hollow log
   You know from that he was a good old dog. (BONO *enters the yard.*)

BONO.   Hey, Troy.

TROY.   Hey, what's happening, Bono?

BONO.   I just thought I'd stop by to see you.

TROY.   What you stop by and see me for? You ain't stopped by in a month of Sundays. Hell, I must owe you money or something.

BONO.   Since you got your promotion I can't keep up with you. Used to see you every day. Now I don't even know what route you working.

TROY.   They keep switching me around. Got me out in Greentree now . . . hauling white folks' garbage.

BONO.   Greentree, huh? You lucky, at least you ain't got to be lifting them barrels. Damn if they ain't getting heavier. I'm gonna put in my two years and call it quits.

TROY.   I'm thinking about retiring myself.

BONO.   You got it easy. You can *drive* for another five years.

TROY.   It ain't the same, Bono. It ain't like working the back of the truck. Ain't got nobody to talk to . . . feel like you working by yourself. Naw, I'm thinking about retiring. How's Lucille?

BONO.   She all right. Her arthritis get to acting up on her sometime. Saw Rose on my way in. She going down to the church, huh?

TROY.   Yeah, she took up going down there. All them preachers looking for somebody to fatten their pockets. (*Pause.*) Got some gin here.

BONO.   Naw, thanks. I just stopped by to say hello.

TROY.   Hell, nigger . . . you can take a drink. I ain't never known you to say no to a drink. You ain't got to work tomorrow.

BONO.   I just stopped by. I'm fixing to go over to Skinner's. We got us a domino game going over his house every Friday.

TROY.   Nigger, you can't play no dominoes. I used to whup you four games out of five.

BONO.   Well, that learned me. I'm getting better.

TROY.   Yeah? Well, that's all right.

BONO.   Look here . . . I got to be getting on. Stop by sometime, huh?

TROY.   Yeah, I'll do that, Bono. Lucille told Rose you bought her a new refrigerator.

BONO.   Yeah, Rose told Lucille you had finally built your fence . . . so I figured we'd call it even.

TROY.   I knew you would.

BONO.   Yeah . . . okay. I'll be talking to you.

TROY.   Yeah, take care, Bono. Good to see you. I'm gonna stop over.

BONO.   Yeah. Okay, Troy. (BONO *exits.* TROY *drinks from the bottle.*)

TROY.   Old Blue died and I dig his grave
     Let him down with a golden chain
     Every night when I hear old Blue bark
     I know Blue treed a possum in Noah's Ark.
     Hear it ring! Hear it ring!

(CORY *enters the yard. They eye each other for a beat.* TROY *is sitting in the middle of the steps.* CORY *walks over.*)

CORY.   I got to get by.

TROY.   Say what? What's you say?

CORY.   You in my way. I got to get by.

TROY.   You got to get by where? This is my house. Bought and paid for. In full. Took me fifteen years. And if you wanna go in my house and I'm sitting on the steps . . . you say excuse me. Like your mama taught you.

CORY.   Come on, Pop . . . I got to get by. (CORY *starts to maneuver his way past* TROY. TROY *grabs his leg and shoves him back.*)

TROY.   You just gonna walk over top of me?

CORY.   I live here too!

TROY (*advancing toward him*).   You just gonna walk over top of me in my own house?

CORY.   I ain't scared of you.

TROY.   I ain't asked if you was scared of me. I asked you if you was fixing to walk over top of me in my own house? That's the question. You ain't gonna say excuse me? You just gonna walk over top of me?

CORY.   If you wanna put it like that.

TROY.   How else am I gonna put it?

CORY.   I was walking by you to go into the house 'cause you sitting on the steps drunk, singing to yourself. You can put it like that.

TROY.   Without saying excuse me??? (CORY *doesn't respond.*) I asked you a question. Without saying excuse me???

CORY.   I ain't got to say excuse me to you. You don't count around here no more.

TROY.   Oh, I see . . . I don't count around here no more. You ain't got to say excuse me to your daddy. All of a sudden you done got so grown that your daddy don't count around here no more . . . Around here in his own house and yard that he done paid for with the sweat of his brow. You done got so grown to where you gonna take over. You gonna take over my house. Is that right? You gonna wear my pants. You gonna go in there and stretch out on my bed. You ain't got to say excuse me 'cause I don't count around here no more. Is that right?

CORY.   That's right. You always talking this dumb stuff. Now, why don't you just get out my way?

TROY.   I guess you got someplace to sleep and something to put in your belly. You got that, huh? You got that? That's what you need. You got that, huh?

CORY.   You don't know what I got. You ain't got to worry about what I got.

TROY.   You right! You one hundred percent right! I done spent the last seventeen years worrying about what you got. Now it's your turn, see? I'll tell you what to do. You grown . . . we done established that. You a man. Now, let's see you act like one. Turn your behind around and walk out this yard. And when you get out there in the alley . . . you can forget about this house. See? 'Cause this is my house. You go on and be a man and get your own house. You can forget about this. 'Cause this is mine. You go on and get yours 'cause I'm through with doing for you.

CORY.   You talking about what you did for me . . . what'd you ever give me?

TROY.   Them feet and bones! That pumping heart, nigger! I give you more than anybody else is ever gonna give you.

CORY.   You ain't never gave me nothing! You ain't never done nothing but hold me back. Afraid I was gonna be better than you. All you ever did was try and make me scared of you. I used to tremble every time you called my name. Every time I heard your footsteps in the house. Wondering all the time . . . what's Papa gonna say if I do this? . . . What's he gonna say if I do that? . . . What's Papa gonna say if I turn on the radio? And Mama, too . . . she tries . . . but she's scared of you.

TROY.   You leave your mama out of this. She ain't got nothing to do with this.

CORY.   I don't know how she stand you . . . after what you did to her.

TROY.   I told you to leave your mama out of this! (*He advances toward* CORY.)

CORY.   What you gonna do . . . give me a whupping? You can't whup me no more. You're too old. You just an old man.

TROY (*shoves him on his shoulder*).   Nigger! That's what you are. You just another nigger on the street to me!

CORY.   You crazy! You know that?

TROY.   Go on now! You got the devil in you. Get on away from me!

CORY.   You just a crazy old man . . . talking about I got the devil in me.

TROY.   Yeah, I'm crazy! If you don't get on the other side of that yard . . . I'm gonna show you how crazy I am! Go on . . . get the hell out of my yard.

CORY.   It ain't your yard. You took Uncle Gabe's money he got from the army to buy this house and then you put him out.

TROY (*advances on* CORY).   Get your black ass out of my yard! (TROY's *advance backs* CORY *up against the tree.* CORY *grabs up the bat.*)

CORY.   I ain't going nowhere! Come on . . . put me out! I ain't scared of you.

TROY.   That's my bat!

CORY.   Come on!

TROY.   Put my bat down!

CORY.   Come on, put me out. (*Swings at* TROY, *who backs across the yard.*) What's the matter? you so bad . . . put me out! (TROY *advances toward* CORY. *Backing up*) Come on! Come on!

TROY.   You're gonna have to use it! You wanna draw that bat back on me . . . you're gonna have to use it.

CORY.   Come on! . . . Come on! (CORY *swings the bat at* TROY *a second time. He misses.* TROY *continues to advance toward him.*)

TROY.   You're gonna have to kill me! You wanna draw that bat back on me. You're gonna have to kill me. (CORY, *backed up against the tree, can go no farther.* TROY *taunts him. He sticks out his head and offers him a target.*) Come on! Come on! (CORY *is unable to swing the bat.* TROY *grabs it.*) Then I'll show you. (CORY *and* TROY *struggle over the bat. The struggle is fierce and fully engaged.* TROY *ultimately is the stronger and takes the bat from* CORY *and stands over him ready to swing. He stops himself.*) Go on and get away from around my house. (CORY, *stung by his defeat, picks himself up, walks slowly out of the yard and up the alley.*)

CORY.   Tell Mama I'll be back for my things.

TROY.   They'll be on the other side of that fence. (CORY *exits.*) I can't taste nothing. Hallelujah! I can't taste nothing no more. (TROY *assumes a batting posture and begins to taunt Death, the fastball on the outside corner.*) Come on! It's between you and me now! Come on! Anytime you want! Come on! I be ready for you . . . but I ain't gonna be easy. (*The lights go down on the scene.*)

SCENE 5

The time is 1965. The lights come up in the yard. It is the morning of TROY's *funeral. A funeral plaque with a light hangs beside the door. There is a small garden plot off to the side. There is noise and activity in the house as* ROSE *and* BONO *have gathered. The door opens and* RAYNELL, *seven years old, enters dressed in a flannel nightgown. She crosses to the garden and pokes around with a stick.* ROSE *calls from the house.*

ROSE.   Raynell!

RAYNELL.   Mam?

ROSE.   What you doing out there?

RAYNELL.   Nothing. (ROSE *comes to the door.*)

ROSE.   Girl, get in here and get dressed. What you doing?

RAYNELL.   Seeing if my garden growed.

ROSE.   I told you it ain't gonna grow overnight. You got to wait.

RAYNELL.   It don't look like it never gonna grow. Dag!

ROSE.   I told you a watched pot never boils. Get in here and get dressed.

RAYNELL.   This ain't even no pot, Mama.

ROSE.   You just have to give it a chance. It'll grow. Now you come on and do what I told you. We got to be getting ready. This ain't no morning to be playing around. You hear me?

RAYNELL.   Yes, mam. (ROSE *exits into the house.* RAYNELL *continues to poke at her garden with a stick.* CORY *enters. He is dressed in a Marine corporal's uniform, and carries a duffel bag. His posture is that of a military man, and his speech has a clipped sternness.*)

CORY (*to* RAYNELL).   Hi. (*Pause.*) I bet your name is Raynell.

RAYNELL.   Uh huh.

CORY.   Is your mama home? (RAYNELL *runs up on the porch and calls through the screen door.*)

RAYNELL.   Mama . . . there's some man out here. Mama? (ROSE *comes to the door.*)

ROSE.   Cory? Lord have mercy! Look here, you all! (ROSE *and* CORY *embrace in a tearful reunion as* BONO *and* LYONS *enter from the house dressed in funeral clothes.*)

BONO.   Aw, looka here . . .

ROSE.   Done got all grown up!

CORY.   Don't cry, Mama. What you crying about?

ROSE.   I'm just so glad you made it.

CORY.   Hey Lyons. How you doing, Mr. Bono. (LYONS *goes to embrace* CORY.)

LYONS.   Look at you, man. Look at you. Don't he look good, Rose. Got them Corporal stripes.

ROSE.   What took you so long?

CORY.   You know how the Marines are, Mama. They got to get all their paperwork straight before they let you do anything.

ROSE.   Well, I'm sure glad you made it. They let Lyons come. Your Uncle Gabe's still in the hospital. They don't know if they gonna let him out or not. I just talked to them a little while ago.

LYONS.   A Corporal in the United States Marines.

BONO.   Your daddy knew you had it in you. He used to tell me all the time.

LYONS.   Don't he look good, Mr. Bono?

BONO.   Yeah, he remind me of Troy when I first met him. (*Pause.*) Say, Rose, Lucille's down at the church with the choir. I'm gonna go down and get the pallbearers lined up. I'll be back to get you all.

ROSE.   Thanks, Jim.

CORY.   See you, Mr. Bono.

LYONS (*with his arm around* RAYNELL).   Cory . . . look at Raynell. Ain't she precious? She gonna break a whole lot of hearts.

Rose.   Raynell, come and say hello to your brother. This is your brother, Cory. You remember Cory?

Raynell.   No, Mam.

Cory.   She don't remember me, Mama.

Rose.   Well, we talk about you. She heard us talk about you. (*To* Raynell) This is your brother, Cory. Come on and say hello.

Raynell.   Hi.

Cory.   Hi. So you're Raynell. Mama told me a lot about you.

Rose.   You all come on into the house and let me fix you some breakfast. Keep up your strength.

Cory.   I ain't hungry, Mama.

Lyons.   You can fix me something, Rose. I'll be in there in a minute.

Rose.   Cory, you sure you don't want nothing? I know they ain't feeding you right.

Cory.   No, Mama . . . thanks. I don't feel like eating. I'll get something later.

Rose.   Raynell . . . get on upstairs and get that dress on like I told you. (Rose *and* Raynell *exit into the house.*)

Lyons.   So . . . I hear you thinking about getting married.

Cory.   Yeah, I done found the right one, Lyons. It's about time.

Lyons.   Me and Bonnie been split up about four years now. About the time Papa retired. I guess she just got tired of all them changes I was putting her through. (*Pause.*) I always knew you was gonna make something out yourself. Your head was always in the right direction. So . . . you gonna stay in . . . make it a career . . . put in your twenty years?

Cory.   I don't know. I got six already, I think that's enough.

Lyons.   Stick with Uncle Sam and retire early. Ain't nothing out here. I guess Rose told you what happened with me. They got me down the workhouse. I thought I was being slick cashing other people's checks.

Cory.   How much time you doing?

Lyons.   They give me three years. I got that beat now. I ain't got but nine more months. It ain't so bad. You learn to deal with it like anything else. You got to take the crookeds with the straights. That's what Papa used to say. He used to say that when he struck out. I seen him strike out three times in a row . . . and the next time up he hit the ball over the grandstand. Right out there in Homestead Field. He wasn't satisfied hitting in the seats . . . he want to hit it over everything! After the game he had two hundred people standing around waiting to shake his hand. You got to take the crookeds with the straights. Yeah, Papa was something else.

CORY.   You still playing?

LYONS.   Cory . . . you know I'm gonna do that. There's some fellows down there we got us a band . . . we gonna try and stay together when we get out . . . but yeah, I'm still playing. It still helps me to get out of bed in the morning. As long as it do that I'm gonna be right there playing and trying to make some sense out of it.

ROSE (*calling*).   Lyons, I got these eggs in the pan.

LYONS.   Let me go on and get these eggs, man. Get ready to go bury Papa. (*Pause.*) How you doing? You doing all right? (CORY *nods*. LYONS *touches him on the shoulder and they share a moment of silent grief.* LYONS *exits into the house.* CORY *wanders about the yard.* RAYNELL *enters.*)

RAYNELL.   Hi.

CORY.   Hi.

RAYNELL.   Did you used to sleep in my room?

CORY.   Yeah . . . that used to be my room.

RAYNELL.   That's what Papa call it. "Cory's room." It got your football in the closet. (ROSE *comes to the door.*)

ROSE.   Raynell, get in there and get them good shoes on.

RAYNELL.   Mama, can't I wear these? Them other ones hurt my feet.

ROSE.   Well, they just gonna have to hurt your feet for a while. You ain't said they hurt your feet when you went down to the store and got them.

RAYNELL.   They didn't hurt then. My feet done got bigger.

ROSE.   Don't you give me no backtalk now. You get in there and get them shoes on. (RAYNELL *exits into the house.*) Ain't too much changed. He still got that piece of rag tied to that tree. He was out here swinging that bat. I was just ready to go back in the house. He swung that bat and then he just fell over. Seem like he swung it and stood there with this grin on his face . . . and then he just fell over. They carried him on down to the hospital, but I knew there wasn't no need . . . why don't you come on in the house?

CORY.   Mama . . . I got something to tell you. I don't know how to tell you this . . . but I've got to tell you . . . I'm not going to Papa's funeral.

ROSE.   Boy, hush your mouth. That's your daddy you talking about. I don't want to hear that kind of talk this morning. I done raised you to come to this? You standing there all healthy and grown talking about you ain't going to your daddy's funeral?

CORY.   Mama . . . listen . . .

ROSE.   I don't want to hear it, Cory. You just get that thought out of your head.

CORY.   I can't drag Papa with me everywhere I go. I've got to say no to him. One time in my life I've got to say no.

ROSE.   Don't nobody have to listen to nothing like that. I know you and your daddy ain't seen eye to eye, but I ain't got to listen to that kind of talk this morning. Whatever was between you and your daddy . . . the time has come to put it aside. Just take it and set it over there on the shelf and forget about it. Disrespecting your daddy ain't gonna make you a man, Cory. You got to find a way to come to that on your own. Not going to your daddy's funeral ain't gonna make you a man.

CORY.   The whole time I was growing up . . . living in his house . . . Papa was like a shadow that followed you everywhere. It weighed on you and sunk into your flesh. It would wrap around you and lay there until you couldn't tell which one was you anymore. That shadow digging in your flesh. Trying to crawl in. Trying to live through you. Everywhere I looked, Troy Maxson was staring back at me . . . hiding under the bed . . . in the closet. I'm just saying I've got to find a way to get rid of that shadow, Mama.

ROSE.   You just like him. You got him in you good.

CORY.   Don't tell me that, Mama.

ROSE.   You Troy Maxson all over again.

CORY.   I don't want to be Troy Maxson. I want to be me.

ROSE.   You can't be nobody but who you are, Cory. That shadow wasn't nothing but you growing into yourself. You either got to grow into it or cut it down to fit you. But that's all you got to make life with. That's all you got to measure yourself against that world out there. Your daddy wanted you to be everything he wasn't . . . and at the same time he tried to make you into everything he was. I don't know if he was right or wrong . . . but I do know he meant to do more good than he meant to do harm. He wasn't always right. Sometimes when he touched he bruised. And sometimes when he took me in his arms he cut.

When I first met your daddy I thought . . . Here is a man I can lay down with and make a baby. That's the first thing I thought when I seen him. I was thirty years old and had done seen my share of men. But when he walked up to me and said, "I can dance a waltz that'll make you dizzy," I thought, Rose Lee, here is a man that you can open yourself up to and be filled to bursting. Here is a man that can fill all them empty spaces you been tipping around the edges of. One of them empty spaces was being somebody's mother.

I married your daddy and settled down to cooking his supper and keeping clean sheets on the bed. When your daddy walked through the house he was so big he filled it up. That was my first mistake. Not to make him leave some room for me. For my part in the matter. But at that time I wanted that. I wanted a house that I could sing in. And that's what your daddy gave me. I didn't know to keep up his strength I had to give up little pieces of mine. I did that. I took on his life as mine and mixed up the pieces so that you couldn't hardly tell which was which anymore. It was my choice. It was my life and I didn't have to live it like that. But that's what life offered me in the way of being a woman and I took it. I grabbed hold of it with both hands.

By the time Raynell came into the house, me and your daddy had done lost touch with one another. I didn't want to make my blessing off of nobody's misfortune . . . but I took on to Raynell like she was all them babies I had wanted and never had. (*The phone rings.*) Like I'd been blessed to relive a part of my life. And if the Lord see fit to keep up my strength . . . I'm gonna do her just like your daddy did you . . . I'm gonna give her the best of what's in me.

RAYNELL (*entering, still with her old shoes*).   Mama . . . Reverend Tollivier on the phone. (ROSE *exits into the house.*)

RAYNELL.   Hi.

CORY.   Hi.

RAYNELL.   You in the Army or the Marines?

CORY.   Marines.

RAYNELL.   Papa said it was the Army. Did you know Blue?

CORY.   Blue? Who's Blue?

RAYNELL.   Papa's dog what he sing about all the time.

CORY.   (*singing*). Hear it ring! Hear it ring!

I had a dog his name was Blue
You know Blue was mighty true
You know Blue was a good old dog
Blue treed a possum in a hollow log
You know from that he was a good old dog.
Hear it ring! Hear it ring! (RAYNELL *joins in singing.*)

CORY *and* RAYNELL.   Blue treed a possum out on a limb
Blue looked at me and I looked at him
Grabbed that possum and put him in a sack
Blue stayed there till I came back
Old Blue's feets was big and round
Never allowed a possum to touch the ground.
Old Blue died and I dug his grave
I dug his grave with a silver spade
Let him down with a golden chain
And every night I call his name
Go on Blue, you good dog you
Go on Blue, you good dog you

RAYNELL. Blue laid down and died like a man
   Blue laid down and died . . .
BOTH. Blue laid down and died like a man
   Now he's treeing possums in the Promised Land
   I'm gonna tell you this to let you know
   Blue's gone where the good dogs go
   When I hear old Blue bark
   When I hear old Blue bark
   Blue treed a possum in Noah's Ark
   Blue treed a possum in Noah's Ark.
(ROSE *comes to the screen door.*)
   ROSE. Cory, we gonna be ready to go in a minute.
   CORY (*to* RAYNELL). You go on in the house and change them
shoes like Mama told you so we can go to Papa's funeral.
   RAYNELL. Okay, I'll be back. (RAYNELL *exits into the house.* CORY
gets up and crosses over to the tree. ROSE *stands in the screen door watching
him.* GABRIEL *enters from the alley.*)
   GABRIEL (*calling*). Hey, Rose!
   ROSE. Gabe?
   GABRIEL. I'm here, Rose. Hey Rose, I'm here! (ROSE *enters from
the house.*)
   ROSE. Lord . . . Look here, Lyons!
   LYONS. See, I told you, Rose . . . I told you they'd let him come.
   CORY. How you doing, Uncle Gabe?
   LYONS. How you doing, Uncle Gabe?
   GABRIEL. Hey, Rose. It's time. It's time to tell St. Peter to open
the gates. Troy, you ready? You ready, Troy. I'm gonna tell St. Peter to
open the gates. You get ready now. (GABRIEL, *with great fanfare, braces
himself to blow. The trumpet is without a mouthpiece. He puts the end of it
into his mouth and blows with great force, like a man who has been waiting
some twenty-odd years for this single moment. No sound comes out of the
trumpet. He braces himself and blows again with the same result. A third
time he blows. There is a weight of impossible description that falls away and
leaves him bare and exposed to a frightful realization. It is a trauma that a
sane and normal mind would be unable to withstand. He begins to dance. A
slow, strange dance, eerie and life-giving. A dance of atavistic signature and
ritual.* LYONS *attempts to embrace him.* GABRIEL *pushes* LYONS *away. He
begins to howl in what is an attempt at song, or perhaps a song turning back
into itself in an attempt at speech. He finishes his dance and the gates of
heaven stand open as wide as God's closet.*) That's the way that go!

QUESTIONS

1. Construct a chronological biography of Troy Maxson. How naturally do the expository materials figure into the conversations where they are revealed (that is, what reasons does Troy have for summarizing his past at various points in the play)?
2. Describe the condition of the marriage of Rose and Troy at the opening of the play. What are their habits? How well-meshed are they? What about their marriage has made Troy discontented?
3. What are Troy's relationships to the other characters—Bono, Lyons, Gabriel? Show how these are compounded of both conflict and congruence of feelings.
4. Define the conflicts between Cory and Troy, showing how they develop. In what ways do they resemble those between Troy and his father? What does Troy want to protect Cory from, and what direction does he want him to take? What unspoken dangers does Cory face as a Marine in 1965?
5. Explore the various meanings of the title, from the literal fence Troy is building (why is he? what purpose will it serve?) to the more figurative fences, the obstacles that Troy has faced and overcome. What does the title have to do with Troy's career as a baseball player? How are Troy's victories ironic? (For example, he achieves his wish to become a driver, but what effect does that have on his relationship with Bono? Does it bring him happiness?)
6. What similarities and contrasts exist between this play and *Death of a Salesman?* How is Troy like and unlike Willy Loman in his situations and in his temperament? What is his attitude toward the importance of being "liked"? Does Troy lie to himself or to others?
7. What aspects of this play make it convincingly realistic in its conventions? What qualities of African American urban life in the late fifties does it capture? What universal themes are conveyed within this restricted, specific milieu?

Terrence McNally

Andre's Mother

Characters

CAL, *a young man*
ARTHUR, *his father*
PENNY, *his sister*
ANDRE'S MOTHER

SCENE. *Now. New York City, Central Park*

Four people—Cal, ARTHUR, PENNY, *and* ANDRE'S MOTHER—*enter. They are nicely dressed and each carries a white helium-filled balloon on a string.*

CAL.   You know what's really terrible? I can't think of anything terrific to say. Goodbye. I love you. I'll miss you. And I'm supposed to be so great with words!

PENNY.   What's that over there?

ARTHUR.   Ask your brother.

CAL.   It's a theatre. An outdoor theatre. They do plays there in the summer. Shakespeare's plays. (*To* ANDRE'S MOTHER.) God, how much he wanted to play Hamlet again. He would have gone to Timbuktu to have another go at that part. The summer he did it in Boston, he was so happy!

PENNY.   Cal, I don't think she . . . ! It's not the time. Later.

ARTHUR.   Your son was a . . . the Jews have a word for it . . .

PENNY (*quietly appalled*).   Oh my God!

ARTHUR.   Mensch, I believe it is, and I think I'm using it right. It means warm, solid, the real thing. Correct me if I'm wrong.

PENNY.   Fine, Dad, fine. Just quit while you're ahead.

ANDRE'S MOTHER   First performed in 1988, broadcast on television in 1990. Terrence McNally was born in 1939 in St. Petersburg, Florida and raised in Corpus Christi, Texas. He graduated Phi Beta Kappa from Columbia University in 1956. After working as a stage manager, editor, and film critic, he established himself as a playwright, writing theatrical plays, screenplays, and books for musicals. McNally has won several major awards for his work, including four Tonys, an Emmy, and two Guggenheim Fellowships. Many of his plays explore gay themes.

ARTHUR.   I won't say he was like a son to me. Even my son isn't always like a son to me. I mean . . . ! In my clumsy way, I'm trying to say how much I liked Andre. And how much he helped me to know my own boy. Cal was always two handsful but Andre and I could talk about anything under the sun. My wife was very fond of him, too.

PENNY.   Cal, I don't understand about the balloons.

CAL.   They represent the soul. When you let go, it means you're letting his soul ascend to Heaven. That you're willing to let go. Breaking the last earthly ties.

PENNY.   Does the Pope know about this?

ARTHUR.   Penny!

PENNY.   Andre loved my sense of humor. Listen, you can hear him laughing. (*She lets go of her white balloon.*) So long, you glorious, wonderful, I-know-what-Cal-means-about-words . . . *man*! God forgive me for wishing you were straight every time I laid eyes on you. But if any man was going to have you, I'm glad it was my brother! Look how fast it went up. I bet that means something. Something terrific.

ARTHUR (*lets his balloon go*).   Goodbye. God speed.

PENNY.   Cal?

CAL.   I'm not ready yet.

PENNY.   Okay. We'll be over there. Come on, Pop, you can buy your little girl a Good Humor.

ARTHUR.   They still make Good Humor?

PENNY.   Only now they're called Dove Bars and they cost twelve dollars. (PENNY *takes* ARTHUR *off.* CAL *and* ANDRE'S MOTHER *stand with their balloons.*)

CAL.   I wish I knew what you were thinking. I think it would help me. You know almost nothing about me and I only know what Andre told me about you. I'd always had it in my mind that one day we would be friends, you and me. But if you didn't know about Andre and me . . . If this hadn't happened, I wonder if he would have ever told you. When he was sick, if I asked him once I asked him a thousand times, tell her. She's your mother. She won't mind. But he was so afraid of hurting you and of your disapproval. I don't know which was worse. (*No response. He sighs.*) God, how many of us live in this city because we don't want to hurt our mothers and live in mortal terror of their disapproval. We lose ourselves here. Our lives aren't furtive, just our feelings toward people like you are! A city of fugitives from our parents' scorn or heartbreak. Sometimes he'd seem a little down and I'd say, "What's the matter, babe?" and this funny sweet, sad smile would cross his face and he'd say, "Just a little homesick, Cal, just a little bit." I always accused him of being a country boy just playing at being a hotshot, sophisticated New Yorker. (*He sighs.*) It's bullshit. It's all bullshit. (*Still no response.*) Do you remember the comic strip *Little Lulu?* Her mother had no name, she was so remote, so formidable to all the children. She was just Lulu's mother. "Hello, Lulu's Mother," Lulu's friends would say. She was almost anonymous in her remoteness. You remind me of her. Andre's mother. Let me answer the questions you can't ask and then I'll leave you alone and you won't ever have to see me again. Andre died of AIDS. I don't know how he got it. I tested negative. He died bravely. You would have been proud of him. The only thing that frightened him was you. I'll have everything that was his sent to you. I'll pay for it. There isn't much. You should have come up the summer he played Hamlet. He was magnificent. Yes, I'm bitter. I'm bitter I've lost him. I'm bitter what's happening. I'm bitter even now, after all this, I can't reach you. I'm beginning to feel your disapproval and it's making me ill. (*He looks at his balloon.*) Sorry, old friend. I blew it. (*He lets go of the balloon.*) Good night, sweet prince, and flights of angels sing thee to thy rest!° (*Beat.*) Goodbye, Andre's mother. (*He goes.* ANDRE'S MOTHER *stands alone holding her white balloon. Her lips tremble. She looks on the verge of breaking down. She is about to let go of the balloon when she pulls it down to her. She looks at it awhile before she gently kisses it. She lets go of the balloon. She follows it with her eyes as it rises and rises. The lights are beginning to fade.* ANDRE'S MOTHER'*s eyes are still on the balloon. The lights fade.*)

QUESTIONS

1. In this brief play there is little time for characterization. How much can you infer about the personalities and past lives of the four characters?
2. Is Penny younger or older than Cal? What evidence can you find, and what is the relevance to the play?
3. Penny suggests that her father's definition of "Mensch" is not completely true. What does the term mean? From what we learn about Andre, was he a mensch?
4. In his long speech to Andre's mother, Cal says that many homosexuals move to New York to conceal their orientation from their mothers out of fear that they will be hurt by the knowledge, or will disapprove—"heartbreak" or "scorn." Contrast that assumption with Cal's relationship with his family. What accounts for the difference?
5. Discuss the symbolism of the white balloons.
6. Why is this play not called "Andre"? Like Miss Y in "The Stronger," the title character never speaks. Does her final gesture constitute a response to Cal's monologue?

Good . . . rest! Horatio's last words to his dead friend Hamlet (Act 5, scene 2)

Glossary of Terms

These definitions sometimes repeat and sometimes differ in language from those in the text. Where they differ, the intention is to give a fuller sense of the term's meaning by allowing the reader a double perspective on it. Page numbers refer to the discussions in the text, which in most but not all cases are fuller than those in the glossary. Multiple page references may indicate separate discussions in the various sections of this book—Fiction, Poetry, Drama.

Absurd, Drama of the   A type of drama, allied to *comedy*, radically nonrealistic in both content and presentation, that emphasizes the absurdity, emptiness, or meaninglessness of life. **(page 1069)**

Accent   In this book, the same as *stress*. A syllable given more prominence in pronunciation than its neighbors is said to be accented. **(page 835)**

Allegory   A narrative or description that has a second meaning beneath the surface, often relating each literal term to a fixed, corresponding abstract idea or moral principle; usually, the ulterior meanings belong to a pre-existing system of ideas or principles. **(pages 291–292, 734)**

Alliteration   The repetition at close intervals of the initial consonant sounds of accented syllables or important words (for example, map–moon, kill–code, preach–approve). Important words and accented syllables beginning with vowels may also be said to alliterate with each other inasmuch as they all have the same lack of an initial consonant sound (for example, "*Inebriate* of *Air*—*am I*"). **(page 820)**

Allusion   A reference, explicit or implicit, to something in previous literature or history. (The term is reserved by some writers for implicit references only, such as those in "in Just—," **[page 776]**; and "On His Blindness," **[page 777]**, but the distinction between the two kinds of reference is not always clear-cut.) **(pages 772–775)**

Anapest   A metrical foot consisting of two unaccented syllables followed by one accented syllable (for example, ŭn-dĕr-stánd). **(page 839)**

Anapestic meter   A *meter* in which a majority of the feet are anapests. (But see *Triple meter*.) **(page 839)**

Anaphora   Repetition of an opening word or phrase in a series of lines. **(page 829)**

Antagonist   Any force in a story or play that is in conflict with the *protagonist*. An antagonist may be another person, an aspect of the physical or social environment, or a destructive element in the protagonist's own nature. **(page 104)** See *Conflict*.

Apostrophe   A figure of speech in which someone absent or dead or something nonhuman is addressed as if it were alive and present and could reply. **(page 711)**

Approximate rhyme (also known as *imperfect rhyme*, *near rhyme*, *slant rhyme*, or *oblique rhyme*)   A term used for words in a rhyming pattern that have some kind of sound correspondence but are not perfect rhymes. See *Rhyme*. Approximate rhymes occur occasionally in patterns where most of the rhymes are perfect (for example, *push-rush* in "Leda and the Swan," **[page 783]**), and sometimes are used systematically in place of perfect rhyme (for example, "The last Night that She lived," **[page 643]**).

Artistic unity   That condition of a successful literary work whereby all its elements work together for the achievement of its central purpose. In an artistically unified work nothing is included that is irrelevant to the central purpose, nothing is omitted that is essential to it, and the parts are arranged in the most effective order for the achievement of that purpose. **(page 109)**

Aside   A brief speech in which a character turns from the person being addressed to speak directly to the audience; a dramatic device for letting the audience know what a character is really thinking or feeling as opposed to what the character pretends to think or feel. **(page 1024)**

Assonance   The repetition at close intervals of the vowel sounds of accented syllables or important words (for example, hat–ran–amber, vein–made). **(page 820)**

Aubade   A poem about dawn; a morning love song; or a poem about the parting of lovers at dawn. **(page 984)**

Ballad   A fairly short narrative poem written in a songlike *stanza* form. Examples: "Ballad of Birmingham," **(page 645)**; "La Belle Dame sans Merci," **(page 980)**.

Blank verse   Unrhymed iambic pentameter. **(page 849)**

Cacophony   A harsh, discordant, unpleasant-sounding choice and arrangement of sounds. **(page 865)**

Caesura   A speech pause occurring within a line. See *Grammatical pause* and *Rhetorical pause*. **(page 836)**

Catharsis   A term used by Aristotle to describe some sort of emotional release experienced by the audience at the end of a successful tragedy. **(pages 1220–1222)**

Chance   The occurrence of an event that has no apparent cause in antecedent events or in predisposition of character. **(pages 109–110)**

Character   Any of the persons presented in a story or play. **(page 163)**

    Developing (or *dynamic*) *character*   A *character* who during the course of a work undergoes a permanent change in some distinguishing moral qualities or personal traits or outlook. **(pages 164–165)**

    Flat character   A *character* whose distinguishing moral qualities or personal traits are summed up in one or two traits. **(pages 163–164)**

    Foil character   A minor character whose situation or actions parallel those of a major character, and thus by contrast sets off or illuminates the major character; most often the contrast is complimentary to the major character.

    Round character   A *character* whose distinguishing moral qualities or personal traits are complex and many-sided. **(pages 163–164)**

    Static character   A *character* who is the same sort of person at the end of a work as at the beginning. **(page 164)**

    Stock character   A stereotyped character: one whose nature is familiar to us from prototypes in previous literature. **(page 164)**

Characterization   The various literary means by which characters are presented. **(pages 161–165)**

Chorus   A group of actors speaking or chanting in unison, often while going through the steps of an elaborate formalized dance; a characteristic device of Greek drama for conveying communal or group emotion. **(pages 1086, 1232)**

Climax   The turning point or high point in a *plot*. **(page 110)**

Coincidence   The chance concurrence of two events having a peculiar correspondence between them. **(pages 109–110)**

Comedy   A type of drama, opposed to *tragedy*, having usually a happy ending, and emphasizing human limitation rather than human greatness. **(pages 1219–1220, 1223–1226)**

    Scornful comedy   A type of *comedy* whose main purpose is to expose and ridicule human folly, vanity, or hypocrisy. **(page 1223)**

    Romantic comedy   A type of *comedy* whose likable and sensible main characters are placed in difficulties from which they are rescued at the end of the play, either attaining their ends or having their good fortunes restored. **(pages 1223–1224)**

Comic relief   In a *tragedy*, a comic scene that follows a scene of seriousness and by contrast intensifies the emotions aroused by the serious scene. **(page 1445)**

Commercial fiction   Fiction written to meet the taste of a wide popular audience and relying usually on tested formulas for satisfying such taste. **(pages 61–66)**

Conflict   A clash of actions, desires, ideas, or goals in the *plot* of a story or drama. Conflict may exist between the main *character* and some other person or persons; between the main character and some external force—physical nature, society, or "fate"; or between the main character and some destructive element in his or her own nature. **(pages 104–105)**

Connotation   What a word suggests beyond its basic dictionary definition; a word's overtones of meaning. **(pages 674–676)**

Consonance   The repetition at close intervals of the final consonant sounds of accented syllables or important words (for example, book–plaque–thicker). **(page 820)**

Continuous form   That *form* of a poem in which the lines follow each other without formal grouping, the only breaks being dictated by units of meaning. **(page 881)**

Couplet   Two successive lines, usually in the same *meter*, linked by *rhyme*. **(page 885)**

Dactyl   A metrical foot consisting of one accented syllable followed by two unaccented syllables (for example, mér-ri-lў). **(page 839)**

Dactylic meter   A *meter* in which a majority of the feet are dactyls. (But see *Triple meter*.) **(page 839)**

Denotation   The basic definition or dictionary meaning of a word. **(pages 674–676)**

Denouement   That portion of a *plot* that reveals the final outcome of its conflicts or the solution of its mysteries.

Deus ex machina ("god from the machine")   The resolution of a *plot* by use of a highly improbable chance or coincidence (so named from the practice of some Greek dramatists of having a god descend from heaven at the last possible minute—in the theater by means of a stage machine—to rescue the *protagonist* from an impossible situation). **(pages 109, 1225)**

Developing character   See *Character*.

Didactic writing   Poetry, fiction, or drama having as a primary purpose to teach or preach. **(page 904)**

Dilemma   A situation in which a *character* must choose between two courses of action, both undesirable. **(page 106)**

Dimeter   A metrical line containing two feet. **(page 839)**

Direct presentation of character   That method of *characterization* in which the author, by exposition or analysis, tells us directly what a *character* is like, or has someone else in the story do so. **(pages 162–163)**

Double rhyme   A rhyme in which the repeated vowel is in the second last syllable of the words involved (for example, *politely–rightly–sprightly*); one form of *feminine rhyme*. **(pages 820, 825)**

Dramatic convention   Any dramatic device which, though it departs from reality, is implicitly accepted by author and audience as a means of representing reality. **(pages 1085–1087)**

Dramatic exposition   The presentation through dialogue of information about events that occurred before the action of a play, or that occur offstage or between the staged actions; this may also refer to the presentation of information about individual characters' backgrounds or the general situation (political, historical, etc.) in which the action takes place.

Dramatic framework   The situation, whether actual or fictional, realistic or fanciful, in which an author places his or her characters in order to express the *theme*. **(page 663)**

Dramatic irony   See *Irony*.

Dramatic point of view   See *Point of view*.

Dramatization   The presentation of character or of emotion through the speech or action of characters rather than through exposition, analyses, or description by the author. See *Indirect presentation of character*. **(pages 163–164)**

Duple meter   A *meter* in which a majority of the feet contain two syllables. *Iambic* and *trochaic* are both duple meters. **(page 839)**

Dynamic character   See *Character*.

Editorializing   Writing that departs from the narrative or dramatic mode and instructs the reader how to think or feel about the events of a story or the behavior of a *character*. **(page 337)**

End rhyme   Rhymes that occur at the ends of lines. **(page 821)**

End-stopped line   A line that ends with a natural speech pause, usually marked by punctuation. **(page 836)**

English (or *Shakespearean*) *sonnet*   A *sonnet* rhyming *ababcdcdefefgg*. Its content or structure ideally parallels the rhyme scheme, falling into three coordinate *quatrains* and a concluding *couplet*; but it is sometimes structured, like the *Italian sonnet*, into *octave* and *sestet*, the principal break in thought coming at the end of the eighth line. **(page 885)**

Epiphany   A moment or event in which a *character* achieves a spiritual insight into life or into her or his own circumstances. **(page 165)**

Euphony   A smooth, pleasant-sounding choice and arrangement of sounds. **(page 865)**

Expected rhythm   The rhythmic expectation set up by the basic *meter* of a poem. **(page 847)**

Extended figure (also known as *sustained figure*)   A *figure of speech* (usually *metaphor*, *simile*, *personification*, or *apostrophe*) sustained or developed through a considerable number of lines or through a whole poem. **(pages 716–717)**

Extended metaphor   See *Extended figure*.

Extended simile   See *Extended figure*.

Extrametrical syllables   In metrical verse, extra unaccented syllables added at the beginnings or endings of lines; these may be either a feature of the metrical *form* of a poem (example, "Is my team plowing," odd-numbered lines **[page 662]**) or occur as exceptions to the *form* (example, "Virtue," lines 9 and 11 **[page 840]**). In *iambic* lines, they occur at the end of the line; in *trochaic*, at the beginning. **(page 840)**

Falling action   That segment of the *plot* that comes between the *climax* and the conclusion. **(page 110)**

Fantasy   A kind of fiction that pictures creatures or events beyond the boundaries of known reality. **(pages 292–295)**

Farce   A type of drama related to *comedy* but emphasizing improbable situations, violent conflicts, physical action, and coarse wit over *characterization* or articulated *plot*. **(pages 1225–1226)**

Feminine rhyme   A rhyme in which the repeated accented vowel is in either the second or third last syllable of the words involved (for example, *ceiling–appeal–ing*; *hurrying–scurrying*). **(page 820)**

Figurative language   Language employing *figures of speech*; language that cannot be taken literally or only literally. **(page 705)**

Figure of speech   Broadly, any way of saying something other than the ordinary way; more narrowly (and for the purposes of this book) a way of saying one thing and meaning another. **(pages 705–715)**

First-person point of view   See *Point of view*.

Fixed form   A *form* of poem in which the length and pattern are prescribed by previous usage or tradition, such as *sonnet*, *villanelle*, and so on. **(pages 883–884)**

Flat character   See *Character*.

Foil character   See *Character*.

Folk ballad   A narrative poem designed to be sung, composed by an anonymous author, and transmitted orally for years or generations before being written down. It has usually undergone modification through the process of oral transmission. **(page 646)**

Foot   The basic unit used in the *scansion* or measurement of verse. A foot usually contains one accented syllable and one or two unaccented syllables (the *spondaic foot* is a modification of this principle). **(page 838)**

Form   The external pattern or shape of a poem, describable without reference to its content, as *continuous form*, *stanzaic form*, *fixed form* (and their varieties), *free verse*, and *syllabic verse*. See *Structure*. **(page 881)**

Free verse   Nonmetrical poetry in which the basic rhythmic unit is the line, and in which pauses, line breaks, and formal patterns develop organically from the requirements of the individual poem rather than from established poetic forms. **(page 836)**

Grammatical pause (also known as *caesura*)   A pause introduced into the reading of a line by a mark of punctuation. **(page 848)**

Hamartia   In Greek tragedy, a criminal act committed in ignorance of some material fact or even for the sake of a greater good. **(page 1220)**

Happy ending   An ending in which events turn out well for a sympathetic *protagonist*. **(pages 107–108)**

Heard rhythm   The actual *rhythm* of a metrical poem as we hear it when it is read naturally. The heard rhythm mostly conforms to but sometimes departs from or modifies the *expected rhythm*. **(page 847)**

Hexameter   A metrical line containing six feet. **(page 839)**

Iamb   A metrical *foot* consisting of one unaccented syllable followed by one accented syllable (for example, rĕ-heárse). **(page 839)**

Iambic meter   A *meter* in which the majority of feet are *iambs*. The most common English meter. **(page 839)**

Imagery   The representation through language of sense experience. **(pages 689–692)**

Indeterminate ending   An ending in which the central problem or *conflict* is left unresolved. **(pages 108–109)**

Indirect presentation of character   That method of *characterization* in which the author shows us a *character* in action, compelling us to infer what the character is like from what is said or done by the character. **(pages 162–163)**

Internal rhyme   A rhyme in which one or both of the rhyme-words occurs *within* the line. **(pages 820–821)**

Irony   A situation or a use of language involving some kind of incongruity or discrepancy. **(pages 334–337, 753–758)** Three kinds of irony are distinguished in this book:

>   *Verbal irony*   A *figure of speech* in which what is said is the opposite of what is meant. **(pages 334, 753–754)**

>   *Dramatic irony*   An incongruity or discrepancy between what a *character* says or thinks and what the reader knows to be true (or between what a character perceives and what the author intends the reader to perceive). **(pages 335, 756–757)**

>   *Irony of situation*   A situation in which there is an incongruity between appearance and reality, or between expectation and fulfillment, or between the actual situation and what would seem appropriate. **(pages 336–337, 757)**

Italian (or *Petrarchan*)   *sonnet* A *sonnet* consisting of an *octave* rhyming *abbaabba* and of a *sestet* using any arrangement of two or three additional rhymes, such as *cdcdcd* or *cdecde*. **(pages 884)**

Literary fiction   Fiction written with serious artistic intentions, providing an imagined experience yielding authentic insights into some significant aspect of life. **(pages 61–66)**

Masculine rhyme (also known as *single rhyme*)   A rhyme in which the repeated accented vowel sound is in the final syllable of the words involved (for example, *dance-pants*, *scald-recalled*). **(page 820)**

Melodrama   A type of drama related to *tragedy* but featuring sensational incidents, emphasizing *plot* at the expense of *characterization*, relying on cruder conflicts (virtuous *protagonist* versus villainous *antagonist*), and having a *happy ending* in which good triumphs over evil. **(page 1225)**

Metaphor   A *figure of speech* in which an implicit comparison is made between two things essentially unlike. It may take one of four forms: (1) that in which the literal term and the figurative term are *both named*; (2) that in which the literal term is *named* and the figurative term *implied*; (3) that in which the literal term is *implied* and the figurative term *named*; (4) that in which *both* the literal and the figurative terms are *implied*. **(pages 705–708)**

Meter   The regular patterns of accent that underlie metrical verse; the measurable repetition of accented and unaccented syllables in poetry. **(pages 837–838)**

Metonymy   A *figure of speech* in which some significant aspect or detail of an experience is used to represent the whole experience. In this book the single term *metonymy* is used for what are sometimes distinguished as two separate figures: *synecdoche* (the use of the part for the whole) and *metonymy* (the use of something closely related for the thing actually meant). **(pages 712–713)**

Metrical variations   Departures from the basic metrical pattern (see *substitution, extrametrical syllables*). **(page 840)**

Monometer   A metrical line containing one *foot*. **(page 839)**

Moral   A rule of conduct or maxim for living expressed or implied as the "point" of a literary work. Compare *Theme*. **(page 636)**

Motivation   The incentives or goals that, in combination with the inherent natures of characters, cause them to behave as they do. In *commercial fiction* actions may be unmotivated, insufficiently motivated, or implausibly motivated. **(page 163)**

Mystery   An unusual set of circumstances for which the reader craves an explanation; used to create *Suspense*. **(pages 105–106)**

Narrator   In drama a *character*, found in some plays, who, speaking directly to the audience, introduces the action and provides a string of commentary between the dramatic scenes. The narrator may or may not be a major character in the action itself. **(page 1086)**

Nonrealistic drama   Drama that, in content, presentation, or both, departs markedly from fidelity to the outward appearances of life. **(pages 1083–1087)**

Objective point of view   See *Point of view*.

Octave   (1) an eight-line *stanza*. (2) the first eight lines of a *sonnet*, especially one structured in the manner of an *Italian sonnet*. **(page 884)**

Omniscient point of view   See *Point of view*.

Onomatopoeia   The use of words that supposedly mimic their meaning in their sound (for example, *boom, click, plop*). **(page 863)**

Overstatement (or *hyperbole*)   A *figure of speech* in which exaggeration is used in the service of truth. **(pages 750–751)**

Oxymoron   A compact verbal paradox in which two successive words seemingly contradict one another. **(page 900)**

Paradox   A statement or situation containing apparently contradictory or incompatible elements. **(page 749)**

Paradoxical situation   A situation containing apparently but not actually incompatible elements. The celebration of a fifth birthday anniversary by a twenty-year-old man is paradoxical but explainable if the man was born on February 29. The Christian doctrines that Christ was born of a virgin and is both God and man are, for a Christian believer, paradoxes (that is, apparently impossible but true). **(page 749)**

Paradoxical statement (or *verbal paradox*)   A *figure of speech* in which an apparently self-contradictory statement is nevertheless found to be true. (**page 749**)

Paraphrase   A restatement of the content of a poem designed to make its *prose meaning* as clear as possible. (**pages 658–660**)

Pentameter   A metrical line containing five feet. (**page 839**)

Personification   A *figure of speech* in which human attributes are given to an animal, an object, or a concept. (**pages 708–710**)

Petrarchan sonnet   See *Italian sonnet.*

Phonetic intensive   A word whose sound, by an obscure process, to some degree suggests its meaning. As differentiated from *onomatopoetic* words, the meanings of phonetic intensives do not refer explicitly to sounds. (**pages 863–864**)

Playwright   A maker of plays. (**page 1023**)

Plot   The sequence of incidents or events of which a story or play is composed. (**page 103**)

Plot manipulation   A situation in which an author gives the *plot* a twist or turn unjustified by preceding action or by the characters involved. (**page 109**)

Poeticizing   Writing that uses immoderately heightened or distended language to sway the reader's feelings. (**page 337**)

Point of view   The angle of vision from which a story is told. (**page 237**) The four basic points of view are as follows:

Omniscient point of view   The author tells the story using the third person, knowing all and free to tell us anything, including what the characters are thinking or feeling and why they act as they do. (**pages 238–239**)

Third-person limited point of view   The author tells the story using the third person, but is limited to a complete knowledge of one *character* in the story and tells us only what that one character thinks, feels, sees, or hears. (**pages 239–240**)

First-person point of view   The story is told by one of its characters, using the first person. (**pages 240–241**)

Objective (or *Dramatic*) *point of view*   The author tells the story using the third person, but is limited to reporting what the characters say or do; the author does not interpret the characters' behavior or tell us their private thoughts or feelings. (**pages 241–242**)

Prose meaning   That part of a poem's *total meaning* that can be separated out and expressed through *paraphrase.* (**page 785**)

Prose poem   Usually a short composition having the intentions of poetry but written in prose rather than *verse*. (**page 837**)

Protagonist   The central *character* in a story or play. (**page 104**)

Quatrain   (1) A four-line *stanza*. (2) A four-line division of a *sonnet* marked off by its rhyme scheme. (**page 885**)

Realistic drama   Drama that attempts, in content and in presentation, to preserve the illusion of actual, everyday life. (**pages 1083–1087**)

Refrain   A repeated word, phrase, line, or group of lines, normally at some fixed position in a poem written in *stanzaic form*. (**page 822**)

Rhetorical pause (also known as *caesura*)   2A natural pause, unmarked by punctuation, introduced into the reading of a line by its phrasing or syntax. (**page 848**)

Rhetorical poetry   Poetry using artificially eloquent language, that is, language too high-flown for its occasion and unfaithful to the full complexity of human experience. (**page 903**)

Rhetorical stress   In natural speech, as in prose and poetic writing, the stressing of words or syllables so as to emphasize meaning and sentence structure. (**page 836**)

Rhythm   Any wavelike recurrence of motion or sound. (**page 835**)

Rhyme   The repetition of the accented vowel sound and all succeeding sounds in important or importantly positioned words (for example, *old–cold*, *vane–reign*, *court–report*, *order–recorder*). The above definition applies to *perfect rhyme* and assumes that the accented vowel sounds involved are preceded by differing consonant sounds. If the preceding consonant sound is the same (for example, *manse–romance*, *style–stile*), or if there is no preceding consonant sound in either word (for example, *aisle–isle*, *alter–altar*), or if the same word is repeated in the rhyming position (for example, *hill–hill*), the words are called *identical rhymes*. Both perfect rhymes and identical rhymes are to be distinguished from *approximate rhymes*. (**pages 820–821**)

Rhyme scheme   Any fixed pattern of rhymes characterizing a whole poem or its stanzas. (**page 882**)

Rising action   That development of *plot* in a story or play that precedes and leads up to the climax. (**page 110**)

Romantic comedy   See *Comedy*.

Round character   See *Character*.

Run-on line   A line which has no natural speech pause at its end, allowing the sense to flow uninterruptedly into the succeeding line. (**page 836**)

Sarcasm Bitter or cutting speech; speech intended by its speaker to give pain to the person addressed. **(page 753)**

Satire A kind of literature that ridicules human folly or vice with the purpose of bringing about reform or of keeping others from falling into similar folly or vice. **(page 753)**

Scansion The process of measuring metrical verse, that is, of marking accented and unaccented syllables, dividing the lines into feet, identifying the metrical pattern, and noting significant variations from that pattern. **(page 840)**

Scornful comedy See *Comedy*.

Sentimentality Unmerited or contrived tender feeling; that quality in a work that elicits or seeks to elicit tears through an oversimplification or falsification of reality. **(pages 337–338, 903)**

Sentimental poetry Poetry that attempts to manipulate the reader's emotions in order to achieve a greater emotional response than the poem itself really warrants. (A sentimental novel or film is sometimes called, pejoratively, a "tearjerker.") **(page 903)**

Sestet (1) A six-line *stanza*. (2) The last six lines of a *sonnet* structured on the Italian model. **(page 884)**

Setting The context in time and place in which the action of a story occurs.

Shakespearean sonnet See *English sonnet*.

Simile A *figure of speech* in which an explicit comparison is made between two things essentially unlike. The comparison is made explicit by the use of some such word or phrase as *like, as, than, similar to, resembles,* or *seems*. **(page 705)**

Single rhyme See *Masculine rhyme*.

Situational irony See *Irony*.

Soliloquy A speech in which a *character*, alone on the stage, addresses himself or herself; a soliloquy is a "thinking out loud," a dramatic means of letting an audience know a character's thoughts and feelings. **(page 1024)**

Sonnet A *fixed form* of fourteen lines, normally iambic pentameter, with a rhyme scheme conforming to or approximating one of two main types—the *Italian* or the *English*. **(page 884)**

Spondee A metrical *foot* consisting of two syllables equally or almost equally accented (for example, *trúe–blúe*). **(page 839)**

Stanza A group of lines whose metrical pattern (and usually its rhyme scheme as well) is repeated throughout a poem. **(pages 840, 882)**

Stanzaic form   The *form* taken by a poem when it is written in a series of units having the same number of lines and usually other characteristics in common, such as metrical pattern or rhyme scheme. **(page 882)**

Static character   See *Character.*

Stock character   See *Character.*

Stream of consciousness   Narrative that presents the private thoughts of a *character* without commentary or interpretation by the author. **(page 240)**

Stress   In this book, the same as *Accent.* But see page 835 (footnote).

Structure   The sequential arrangement of plot elements in fiction or drama. **(page 103)** In poetry, the internal organization of content (see *Form*). **(page 881)**

Substitution   In metrical verse, the replacement of the expected metrical *foot* by a different one (for example, a *trochee* occurring in an *iambic* line). **(page 840)**

Surprise   An unexpected turn in the development of a *plot.* **(page 107)**

Surprise ending   A completely unexpected revelation or turn of *plot* at the conclusion of a story or play. **(page 107)**

Suspense   That quality in a story or play that makes the reader eager to discover what happens next and how it will end. **(pages 105–107)**

Sustained figure   See *Extended figure.*

Syllabic verse   *Verse* measured by the number of syllables rather than the number of feet per line. **(page 854)**

Symbol   Something that means *more* than what it is; an object, person, situation, or action that in addition to its literal meaning suggests other meanings as well. **(pages 284–295, 726–730)**

Synecdoche   A *figure of speech* in which a part is used for the whole. In this book it is subsumed under the term *Metonymy.* **(pages 712–713)**

Synesthesia   Presentation of one sense experience in terms usually associated with another sensation. **(page 871)**

Tercet   A three-line *stanza* exhibited in *terza rima* and *villanelle* as well as in other poetic forms. **(pages 687, 886)**

Terza rima   An interlocking rhyme scheme with the pattern *aba bcb cdc,* etc. **(page 895)**

Tetrameter   A metrical line containing four feet. **(page 839)**

Theme   The central idea or unifying generalization implied or stated by a literary work. **(pages 191–197, 658)**

Third-person limited point of view   See *Point of view*.

Tone   The writer's or speaker's attitude toward the subject, the audience, or herself or himself; the emotional coloring, or emotional meaning, of a work. **(pages 800–805)**

Total meaning   The total experience communicated by a poem. It includes all those dimensions of experience by which a poem communicates—sensuous, emotional, imaginative, and intellectual—and it can be communicated in no other words than those of the poem itself. **(page 785)**

Tragedy   A type of drama, opposed to *comedy*, which depicts the causally related events that lead to the downfall and suffering of the *protagonist*, a person of unusual moral or intellectual stature or outstanding abilities. **(pages 1219–1223)**

Trimeter   A metrical line containing three feet. **(page 839)**

Triple meter   A *meter* in which a majority of the feet contain three syllables. (Actually, if more than 25 percent of the feet in a poem are triple, its effect is more triple than duple, and it ought perhaps to be referred to as triple meter.) *Anapestic* and *dactylic* are both triple meters. **(page 839)**

Trochaic meter   A *meter* in which the majority of feet are trochees. **(page 839)**

Trochee   A metrical foot consisting of one accented syllable followed by one unaccented syllable (for example, bár-tĕr). **(page 839)**

Truncation   In metric verse, the omission of an unaccented syllable at either end of a line (for example, "Introduction to *Songs of Innocence*," [page 851]). **(page 840)**

Understatement   A *figure of speech* that consists of saying less than one means, or of saying what one means with less force than the occasion warrants. **(page 751)**

Unhappy ending   An ending that turns out unhappily for a sympathetic *protagonist*. **(page 108)**

Verbal irony   See *Irony*.

Verse   Metrical language; the opposite of *prose*.

Villanelle   A nineteen-line *fixed form* consisting of five tercets rhymed *aba* and a concluding quatrain rhymed *abaa*, with lines 1 and 3 of the first *tercet* serving as refrains in an alternating pattern through line 15 and then repeated as lines 18 and 19. **(pages 886–887)**

Copyrights
and Acknowledgments

Chinua Achebe, "Civil Peace" from *Girls at War*. Copyright © 1972, 1973 by Chinua Achebe. Used by permission of Doubleday, a division of Random House, Inc. and the Emma Sweeney Literary Agency, LLC.

Kim Addonizio, "Sonnenizio on a Line from Drayton" from *What Is This Thing Called Love*. Copyright © 2004 by Kim Addonizio. Used by permission of W.W. Norton & Company, Inc.

Edward Albee, THE SANDBOX. Copyright © 1959 and renewed 1987 by Edward Albee. All rights reserved. CAUTION: Professionals and amateurs are hereby warned that "The Sandbox" is subject to a royalty. It is fully protected under the copyright laws of the United States of America and of all countries covered by the International Copyright Union (including the Dominion of Canada and the rest of the British Commonwealth), the Berne Convention, the Pan-American Copyright Convention and the Universal Copyright Convention as well as all countries with which the United States has reciprocal copyright relations. All rights, including professional/amateur stage rights, motion picture, recitation, lecturing, public reading, radio broadcasting, television, video or sound recording, all other forms of mechanical or electronic reproduction, such as CD-ROM, CD-I, information storage and retrieval systems and photocopying, and the rights of translations in foreign languages, are strictly reserved. Particular emphasis is laid upon the matter of readings, permission for which must be secured from the author's agent in writing. Inquiries concerning rights should be addressed to: William Morris Agency, LLC, 1325 Avenue of the Americas, New York, NY 10019, Attn: Eric Lupfer.

Maya Angelou, "The Health-Food Diner" from *Shaker, Why Don't You Sing?*. Copyright © 1983 by Maya Angelou. "Harlem Hopscotch" from *Just Give Me a Cool Drink of Water 'Fore I Die*. Copyright © 1971 by Maya Angelou. "Africa" and "The Telephone" from *Oh Pray My Wings Are Gonna Fit Me Well*. Copyright © 1975 by Maya Angelou. "Lady Luncheon Club" and "Woman Work" from *And Still I Rise*. Copyright © 1978, 1983, 1993 by Maya Angelou. All used by permission of Random House, Inc.

Margaret Atwood, "Siren Song" from *Selected Poems 1965–1975*. Copyright © 1976 by Margaret Atwood. Reprinted with the permission of Houghton Mifflin Company and Oxford University Press Canada. All rights reserved. "Landcrab I" from *Selected Poems II: Poems Selected and New 1976–1987*. Copyright © 1987 by Margaret Atwood. Reprinted with the permission of Houghton Mifflin Company and Oxford University Press Canada. All rights reserved. "Rape Fantasies" from *Dancing Girls and Other Stories*. Copyright © 1977, 1982 by Margaret Atwood. Reprinted with the permission of Phoebe Larmore Literary Agency and McClelland & Stewart Ltd., the Canadian publishers.

W. H. Auden, "That night when joy began," "The Unknown Citizen," and "Musée des Beaux Arts" from *W. H. Auden: Collected Poems*, edited by Edward Mendelson. Copyright 1937, 1940 and renewed © 1965, 1968 by W. H. Auden. Used by permission of Random House, Inc.

Jimmy Santiago Baca, "Main Character" from *Black Mesa Poems*. Copyright © 1989 by Jimmy Santiago Baca. Reprinted with the permission of New Directions Publishing Corp.

D.C. Berry, "On Reading Poems to a Senior Class at South High" from *Divorce Boxing*. Reprinted with the permission of Eastern Washington University Press.

Elizabeth Bishop, "One Art," "The Fish," and "Manners" from *The Complete Poems 1927–1979*. Copyright 1950 by Elizabeth Bishop. Reprinted with the permission of Farrar, Straus & Giroux, LLC.

Gwendolyn Brooks, "Kitchenette Building," "We Real Cool," and "Sadie and Maude" from *Blacks*. Copyright © 1991 by Gwendolyn Brooks Blakely. "a song in the front yard" from *Selected Poems*. Copyright © 1963 by Gwendolyn Brooks. "Tornado at Talladega" from *The Near-Johannesburg Boy*. Copyright © 1988 by Gwendolyn Brooks. All reprinted by Consent of Brooks Permissions.

Albert Camus, "The Guest" from *The Exile and the Kingdom*, translated by Justin O'Brien. Copyright © 1957, 1958 by Alfred A. Knopf, a division of Random House, Inc. Used by permission of Alfred A. Knopf, a division of Random House, Inc.

Gladys Cardiff, "Combing" from *To Frighten a Storm* (Port Townsend, Wash: Copper Canyon Press, 1976). Copyright © 1976 by Gladys Cardiff. Reprinted with the permission of the author.

John Cheever, "The Swimmer" from *The Stories of John Cheever*. Copyright © 1978 by John Cheever. Used by permission of Alfred A. Knopf, a division of Random House, Inc.

Lucille Clifton, "in the inner city" and "good times" from *Good Woman: Poems and a Memoir, 1969–1980*. Copyright © 1987 by Lucille Clifton. Reprinted with the permission of BOA Editions Ltd., www.boaeditions.org.

Billy Collins, "Introduction to Poetry" and "My Number" from *The Apple that Astonished Paris*. Copyright © 1988 by Billy Collins. Reprinted with the permission of the University of Arkansas Press, www.uapress.com. "Sonnet" from *Sailing Alone Around the Room*. Copyright © 2001 by Billy Collins. Used by permission of Random House, Inc. "The History Teacher" and "Weighing the Dog" from *Questions About Angels*. Copyright © 1991 by Billy Collins. Reprinted with the permission of the University of Pittsburgh Press. "Picnic, Lightning" from *Picnic, Lightning*. Copyright © 1998 by Billy Collins. Reprinted with the permission of University of Pittsburgh Press.

Richard Connell, "The Most Dangerous Game." Copyright 1924 by Richard Connell, renewed 1952 by Louise Fox Connell. Reprinted by permission of Brandt & Hochman Literary Agents, Inc.

Hart Crane, "Voyages I" from *Complete Poems of Hart Crane*, edited by Marc Simon. Copyright 1933, © 1958, 1966 by Liveright Publishing Corporation. Copyright © 1986 by Marc Simon. Used by permission of Liveright Publishing Corporation.

Countee Cullen, "Incident" and "Yet Do I Marvel" from *Color*. Copyright 1925 by Harper & Brothers, renewed 1953 by Ida M. Cullen. Copyrights held by the Amistad Research Center, Tulane University, administered by Thompson and Thompson, Brooklyn, NY.

E. E. Cummings, "in Just—," "the Cambridge ladies who live in furnished souls," and "Spring is like a perhaps hand" from *Complete Poems 1904–1962*. Copyright 1923, 1925, 1951, 1953, © 1991 by the Trustees for the E. E. Cummings Trust. Copyright © 1976 by George James Firmage. Used by permission of Liveright Publishing Corporation.

Edwin Denby, "I had heard it's a fight. At the first clammy touch" from *The Collected Poems of Edwin Denby* (New York: Full Court Press, 1975). Reprinted with the permission of Yvonne Jacquette Burckhardt.

Emily Dickinson, "The last night that She lived," "There's been a Death, in the opposite house," "There is no Frigate like a Book," "I felt a Funeral, in my Brain," "It sifts from Leaden Sieves," "I taste a liquor never brewed," "Because I could not stop for Death," "Much Madness is divinest Sense," "I never saw a moor," "'Faith' is a fine invention," "Apparently with no surprise," "One dignity delays for all," "'Twas warm —at first—like Us," "As imperceptibly as grief," "I heard a Fly buzz—when I died," "These are the days when the Birds come back," "I like to see it lap the Miles," "There's a certain slant of light," "A Light exists in Spring," "A narrow Fellow in the Grass," "I died for Beauty—but was scarce," and "I like a look of Agony" from *The Poems of Emily Dickinson*, edited by Thomas H. Johnson. Copyright 1945, 1951, © 1955, 1979, 1983 by the President and Fellows of Harvard College. Reprinted with the permission of The Belknap Press of Harvard University Press.

Rita Dove, "Persephone, Falling" from *Mother Love*. Copyright © 1995 by Rita Dove. Used by permission of the author and W. W. Norton & Company, Inc. "Nexus" from *The Yellow House on the Corner* (Pittsburgh: Carnegie Mellon University Press, 1980). Copyright © 1980 by Rita Dove. Reprinted with the permission of the author.

Richard Eberhart, "For a Lamb" from *Collected Poems 1930–1986*. Copyright © 1988 by Richard Eberhart. Reprinted with the permission of the author and Oxford University Press, Ltd.

T. S. Eliot, "The Journey of the Magi" from *T. S. Eliot: The Complete Poems and Plays 1909–1950*. Copyright 1925, 1927 1941 by T. S. Eliot. Reprinted with the permission of Harcourt, Inc. and Faber & Faber, Ltd. "The Love Song of J. Alfred Prufrock" from *T. S. Eliot: The Complete Poems and Plays 1909–1950*. Reprinted with the permission of Faber & Faber, Ltd.

Mari Evans, "When in Rome" from *I Am A Black Woman* (New York: William Morrow, 1970). Reprinted with the permission of the author.

William Faulkner, "A Rose for Emily" from *Collected Stories of William Faulkner*. Copyright 1930 and renewed © 1958 by William Faulkner. Used by permission of Random House, Inc.

Lawrence Ferlinghetti, "Constantly risking absurdity" and "Christ climbed down" from *A Coney Island of the Mind*. Copyright © 1958 by Lawrence Ferlinghetti. Reprinted with the permission of New Directions Publishing Corp.

F. Scott Fitzgerald, "A New Leaf" from *The Short Stories of F. Scott Fitzgerald*, edited by Matthew J. Bruccoli. Copyright 1931 by The Curtis Publishing Co. Copyright renewed © 1959 by Frances Scott Fitzgerald Lanahan. Reprinted by permission of Scribner, a division of Simon & Schuster Adult Publishing.

Carolyn Forché, "The Colonel" from *The Country Between Us*. Copyright © 1981 by Carolyn Forché. Reprinted with the permission of HarperCollins Publishers.

Robert Francis, "Pitcher" from *The Orb Weaver*. Copyright © 1960 by Robert Francis. Reprinted with the permission of Wesleyan University Press, www.wesleyan.edu/wespress.

Robert Frost, "Desert Places," "After Apple-Picking," "Bereft," "The Road Not Taken," "Fire and Ice," "A Considerable Speck," "Out, Out—," "Stopping by Woods on a Snowy Evening," "Design," "Nothing Gold Can Stay," "The Aim Was Song," "Tree at My Window," "Acquainted with the Night," "Home Burial," "Birches," "Mending Wall," and "Once by the Pacific" from *The Poetry of Robert Frost*, edited by Edward Connery Lathem. Copyright 1923, 1928, 1930, 1939, 1947, © 1969 by Henry Holt and Co., Inc. Copyright 1936, 1942, 1944, 1951, © 1956, 1958 by Robert Frost. Copyright © 1964, 1967, 1970, 1975 by Lesley Frost Ballantine. Reprinted with the permission of Henry Holt and Company LLC.

Tim Gautreaux, "Welding with Children" from *Welding with Children*. Copyright © 1999 by Tim Gautreaux. Reprinted with the permission of Sterling Lord Literistic, LLC.

Allen Ginsberg, "A Supermarket in California" from *Collected Poems 1947–1980*. Copyright © 1984 by Allen Ginsberg. Reprinted with the permission of HarperCollins Publishers.

Nadine Gordimer, "Once upon a Time" from *Jump and Other Stories*. Copyright © 1991 by Felix Licensing, B.V. Reprinted with the permission of Farrar, Straus & Giroux, LLC and Penguin Group (Canada), a division of Pearson Canada Inc.

Graham Greene, "The Destructors" from *Collected Stories of Graham Greene*. Copyright © 1955, 1983 by Graham Greene. Reprinted with the permission of Viking Penguin, a division of Penguin Group (USA) Inc. and David Higham Associates, Ltd.

Thom Gunn, "The Man with Night Sweats" and "From the Wave" from *Collected Poems*. Copyright © 1979 by Thom Gunn. Reprinted with the permission of Farrar, Straus & Giroux, LLC and Faber & Faber Ltd.

R. S. Gwynn, "Snow White and the Seven Deadly Sins" from *No Word of Farewell: Selected Poems 1970–2000* (Ashland Oregon: Story Line Press, 2001). Copyright © 2001 by R.S. Gwynn. Reprinted with the permission of the author.

Daniel Halpern, "On the Death of a Child" from *Foreign Neon*. Copyright © 1991 by Daniel Halpern. Used by permission of Alfred A. Knopf, a division of Random House, Inc.

Robert Hayden, "The Whipping" and "Those Winter Sundays" from *Angle of Ascent: New and Collected Poems*. Copyright © 1966 by Robert Hayden. Used by permission of Liveright Publishing Corporation.

Seamus Heaney, "The Forge" and "Digging" from *Selected Poems*. Copyright © 1998 by Seamus Heaney. "An August Night," "Mid-Term Break," "Villanelle for an Anniversary," and "Follower" from *Opened Ground*. Copyright © 1998 by Seamus Heaney. All reprinted with the permission of Farrar, Straus & Giroux, LLC and Faber & Faber, Ltd.

Ernest Hemingway, "Hills Like White Elephants" from *The Short Stories of Ernest Hemingway*. Copyright 1927 by Charles Scribner's Sons, renewed © 1955 by Ernest Hemingway. Reprinted by permission of Scribner, a division of Simon & Schuster Adult Publishing Group.

Mary Beth Henley, *AM I BLUE?* Copyright © 1992 by Beth Henley. All rights reserved. CAUTION: Professionals and amateurs are hereby warned that *AM I BLUE?* is subject to a royalty. It is fully protected under the copyright laws of the United States of America and of all countries covered by the International Copyright Union (including the Dominion of Canada and the rest of the British Commonwealth), the Berne Convention, the Pan-American Copyright Convention and the Universal Copyright Convention as well as all countries with which the United States has reciprocal copyright relations. All rights, including professional/amateur stage rights, motion picture, recitation, lecturing, public reading, radio broadcasting, television, video or sound recording, all other forms of mechanical or electronic reproduction, such as CD-ROM, CD-I, information storage and retrieval systems and photocopying, and the rights of translations in foreign languages, are strictly reserved. Particular emphasis is laid upon the matter of readings, permission for which must be secured from the author's agent in writing. Inquiries concerning rights should be addressed to: William Morris Agency, LLC, 1325 Avenue of the Americas, New York, NY 10019, Attn: Eric Lupfer.

Langston Hughes, "Suicide's Note," "Cross," "Harlem (A Dream Deferred)," "The Weary Blues," "Theme for English B," "Aunt Sue's Stories," and "Negro Servant" from *Collected Poems of Langston Hughes.* Copyright © 1994 by the Estate of Langston Hughes. Used by permission of Alfred A. Knopf, a division of Random House, Inc.

Ted Hughes, "Thistles" from *Wodwo.* Copyright © 1961 by Ted Hughes. Reprinted with the permission of HarperCollins Publishers and Faber & Faber, Ltd.

Henrik Ibsen, "A Doll House," translated by Otto Reinert, from *Thirteen Plays: An Introductory Anthology,* edited by Otto Reinert and Peter Arnott. Copyright © 1977 by Otto Reinert. Reprinted with the permission of the translator.

David Ives, "Time Flies" from *Time Flies and Other Short Plays.* Copyright © 2001 by David Ives. Reprinted with the permission of Grove/Atlantic, Inc.

Shirley Jackson, "The Lottery" from *The Lottery and Other Stories.* Copyright 1948, 1949 by Shirley Jackson. Copyright renewed © 1976, 1977 by Laurence Hyman, Barry Hyman, Mrs. Sarah Webster, and Mrs. Joanne Schnurer. Reprinted with the permission of Farrar, Straus & Giroux, LLC.

Randall Jarrell, "The Death of the Ball Turret Gunner" from *Complete Poems.* Copyright © 1969 by Mary von Schrader Jarrell. Reprinted with the permission of Farrar, Straus & Giroux, LLC.

Jenny Joseph, "Warning" from *Selected Poems* (Bloodaxe Books, 1992). Copyright © 1992 by Jenny Joseph. Reprinted with the permission of Johnson & Alcock, Ltd.

Donald Justice, "In Memory of the Unknown Poet, Robert Bardman Vaughn" from *New and Selected Poems.* Copyright © 1995 by Donald Justice. Used by permission of Alfred A. Knopf, a division of Random House, Inc. "Men at Forty" from *The Summer Anniversaries.* Copyright © 1967 by Donald Justice. Reprinted with the permission of Wesleyan University Press, www.wesleyan.edu/wespress.

Ellen Kay, "Pathedy of Manners" from *A Local Habitation* (Chicago: Swallow Press, 1958). Copyright © 1958 by Ellen Kay. Reprinted with the permission of the author.

Galway Kinnell, "Blackberry Eating" from *Mortal Acts, Mortal Words.* Copyright © 1980 by Galway Kinnell. Reprinted with the permission of Houghton Mifflin Company. All rights reserved.

Jhumpa Lahiri, "Interpreter of Maladies" from *Interpreter of Maladies*. Copyright © 1999 by Jhumpa Lahiri. Reprinted with the permission of Houghton Mifflin Company. All rights reserved.

Philip Larkin, "A Study of Reading Habits" from *The Whitsun Weddings*. Copyright © 1964 by Philip Larkin. Reprinted with the permission of Farrar, Straus & Giroux, LLC and Faber & Faber, Ltd. "Toads" and "Church Going" from *The Less Deceived*. Copyright © 1955 by Philip Larkin. Reprinted with the permission of The Marvell Press, England and Australia. "Aubade" from *Collected Poems*, edited by Anthony Thwaite. Copyright © 1988 by The Estate of Philip Larkin. Reprinted with the permission of Farrar, Straus & Giroux, LLC and Faber & Faber, Ltd.

D. H. Lawrence, "The Rocking-Horse Winner" from *Complete Short Stories of D. H. Lawrence*. Copyright 1933 by The Estate of D. H. Lawrence, renewed © 1961 by Angelo Ravagli and C. M. Weekley, Executors of the Estate of Frieda Lawrence. Reprinted with the permission of Viking Penguin, a division of Penguin Group (USA) Inc.

Ursula K. Le Guin, "The Ones Who Walk Away from Omelas" from *The Wind's Twelve Quarters*. First appeared in *New Dimensions 3* (1973). Copyright © 1973, 2001 by Ursula K. Le Guin. Reprinted with the permission of the author and the author's agents, the Virginia Kidd Agency, Inc.

Denise Levertov, "The Blind Man's House at the Edge of the Cliff" from *A Door in the House*. Copyright © 1990 by Denise Levertov. Reprinted with the permission of New Directions Publishing Corp.

Philip Levine, "Animals Are Passing from Our Lives" from *Not This Pig*. Copyright © 1968 by Philip Levine. Reprinted with the permission of Wesleyan University Press, www.wesleyan.edu/wespress.

Archibald MacLeish, "Ars Poetica" from *Collected Poems 1917–1982*. Copyright 1926 by Archibald MacLeish. Copyright © 1985 by The Estate of Archibald MacLeish. Reprinted with the permission of Houghton Mifflin Company. All rights reserved.

Katherine Mansfield, "Miss Brill" from *The Short Stories of Katherine Mansfield*. Copyright 1923 by Alfred A. Knopf, Inc. and renewed 1951 by John Middleton Murry. Used by permission of Alfred A. Knopf, a division of Random House, Inc.

Gabriel Garcia Marquez, "A Very Old Man with Enormous Wings" from *Leaf Storm and Other Stories*, translated by Gregory Rabassa. Copyright © 1971 by Gabriel Garcia Marquez. Reprinted with the permission of HarperCollins Publishers.

Jane Martin, "Beauty." Reprinted with the permission Jane Martin, c/o Alexander Speer, Actors Theatre of Louisville. CAUTION: Professionals and Amateurs are hereby warned that BEAUTY is subject to a royalty. It is fully protected under the copyright laws of the United States of America, the British Commonwealth, including Canada, and all other countries of the Copyright Union. All rights, including professional, amateur, motion pictures, recitation, lecturing, public reading, radio broadcasting, television, and the rights of translation into foreign languages are strictly reserved, In its present form the play is dedicated to the Reading Public only. Particular emphasis is laid on the question of amateur or professional readings, permission and terms for which must be secured in writing from Samuel French, Inc., 45 West 25th Street, New York, NY 10010.

William Matthews, "Puberty" from *Selected Poems and Translations, 1969–1991*. Copyright © 1992 by William Matthews. Reprinted with the permission of Houghton Mifflin Company. All rights reserved.

Terrence McNally, *ANDRE'S MOTHER*. Copyright © 1995 by Terrence McNally. All Rights reserved. CAUTION: Professionals and amateurs are hereby warned that *ANDRE'S MOTHER* is subject to a royalty. It is fully protected under the copyright laws of the United States of America and of all countries covered by the International Copyright Union (including the Dominion of Canada and the rest of the British Commonwealth), the Berne Convention, the Pan-American Copyright Convention and the Universal Copyright Convention as well as all countries with which the United States has reciprocal copyright relations. All rights, including professional/amateur stage rights, motion picture, recitation, lecturing, public reading, radio broadcasting, television, video or sound recording, all other forms of mechanical or electronic reproduction, such as CD-ROM, CD-I, information storage and retrieval systems and photocopying, and the rights of translations in foreign languages, are strictly reserved. Particular emphasis is laid upon the matter of readings, permission for which must be secured from the author's agent in writing. Inquiries concerning rights should be addressed to: William Morris Agency, LLC, 1325 Avenue of the Americas, New York, NY 10019, Attn: Eric Lupfer.

Arthur Miller, "Death of a Salesman" from *Death of a Salesman*. Copyright 1949, renewed © 1977 by Arthur Miller. Reprinted with the permission of Viking Penguin, a division of Penguin Group (USA) Inc.

Molière, "Tartuffe, or The Impostor" from *Tartuffe: Comedy in Five Acts*, translated by Richard Wilbur. Copyright © 1963, 1962, 1961, and renewed 1991, 1990, 1989 by Richard Wilbur. Reprinted with the permission of Harcourt, Inc. CAUTION: Professionals and amateurs are hereby warned that this translation, being fully protected under the copyright laws of the United States of America, the British Empire, including the Dominion of Canada, and all other countries which are signatories of the Universal Copyright Convention, is subject to royalty. All rights, including professional, amateur, motion picture, recitation, lecturing, public reading, radio broadcasting, and the rights of translation into foreign languages, are strictly reserved. Particular emphasis is laid on the question of readings, , permission for which must be secured from the author's agent in writing. Inquiries on professional rights (except amateur) should be addressed to Mr. Gilbert Parker, William Morris Agency, 1325 Avenue of the Americas, New York, NY 10019; inquiries on translation rights should be addressed to Harcourt, Inc. Permissions Department, Orlando, FL 32887-6777.

Marianne Moore, "Silence" from *Collected Poems*. Copyright 1935 by Marianne Moore, renewed © 1963 by Marianne Moore and T. S. Eliot. Reprinted by permission of Scribner, an imprint of Simon & Schuster Adult Publishing. All rights reserved.

Harryette Mullen, "Dim Lady" from *Sleeping with the Dictionary*. Copyright © 2002 by Harryette Mullen. Reprinted with the permission of the University of California Press.

Alice Munro, "How I Met My Husband" from *Something I've Been Meaning to Tell You*. Originally published by McGraw-Hill Ryerson, copyright © 1974 by Alice Munro. Reprinted with the permission of William Morris Agency, LLC.

Ogden Nash, "The Turtle" from *Verses 1929*. Originally from *The New Yorker* (1930). Copyright 1930 by Ogden Nash. Reprinted with the permission of Curtis Brown, Ltd.

Lynn Nottage, "Poof!" from *Crumbs from the Table of Joy, and Other Plays* (New York: Theatre Communications Group, 2004). Copyright © 2004 by Lynn Nottage. Reprinted with permission.

Joyce Carol Oates, "Life After High School" and "June Birthing" from *Will You Always Love Me?*. Copyright © 1996 by The Ontario Review, Inc. "Where Are You Going, Where Have You Been?" from *Where Are You Going, Where Have You Been?: Selected Early Stories*. Copyright © 1993 by The Ontario Review, Inc. All reprinted with the permission of John Hawkins & Associates, New York.

Flannery O'Connor, "Everything That Rises Must Converge" from *Everything That Rises Must Converge*. Copyright © 1964, 1965 by The Estate of Flannery O'Connor. Reprinted with the permission of Farrar Straus & Giroux, LLC. "A Good Man Is Hard to Find" from *A Good Man Is Hard to Find and Other Stories*. Copyright 1953 by Flannery O'Connor and renewed © 1981 by Regina O'Connor, Reprinted with the permission of Harcourt, Inc. "Greenleaf" from *The Complete Stories*. Copyright © 1971 by the Estate of Mary Flannery O'Connor. Reprinted with the permission of Farrar, Straus & Giroux, LLC.

Frank O'Connor, "The Drunkard" from *Collected Stories*. Copyright © 1981 by Harriet O'Donovan Sheehy, Executrix of the Estate of Frank O'Connor. Used by permission of Alfred A. Knopf, a division of Random House, Inc. and Lyons & Pande International LLC as agent for the proprietor.

Sharon Olds, "35/10," "Rite of Passage," and "The Victims" from *The Dead and the Living*. Copyright © 1987 by Sharon Olds. "My Son the Man" and "The Planned Child" from *The Wellspring*. Copyright © 1995 by Sharon Olds. "I Go Back to May 1937" from *The Gold Cell*. Copyright © 1987 by Sharon Olds. All used by permission of Alfred A. Knopf, a division of Random House, Inc.

Mary Oliver, "Music Lessons" from *Twelve Moons*. Copyright © 1979 by Mary Oliver. Reprinted with the permission of Little, Brown and Company.

Dorothy Parker, "Résumé" from *The Portable Dorothy Parker*, introduction by Brendan Gill. Originally published in *Enough Rope*. Copyright 1926, 1928 and renewed 1954, © 1956 by Dorothy Parker. Reprinted with the permission of Viking Penguin, a division of Penguin Group (USA) Inc.

Linda Pastan, "Ethics" from *Waiting for My Life*. Copyright © 1981 by Linda Pastan. "To a Daughter Leaving Home" from *The Imperfect Paradise*. Copyright © 1988 by Linda Pastan. Both used by permission of W.W. Norton & Company, Inc.

Marge Piercy, "Barbie doll" and "A work of artifice" from *Circles on the Water*. Copyright © 1982 by Marge Piercy. Used by permission of Alfred A. Knopf, a division of Random House, Inc.

Sylvia Plath, "Mirror," "Metaphors," and "Wuthering Heights" from *Crossing the Water*. Copyright © 1960 and renewed 1988 by Ted Hughes. "Old Ladies' Home" from *The Collected Poems*, edited by Ted Hughes. Copyright © 1960, 1965, 1971, 1981 by the Estate of Sylvia Plath. Editorial material copyright © 1981 by Ted Hughes. "Mad Girl's Love Song" from *The Bell Jar*. Copyright © 1971 by Harper & Row, Publishers, Inc. All reprinted with the permission of HarperCollins Publishers

and Faber & Faber, Ltd. "Spinster" from *The Colossus and Other Poems*. Copyright ©
1962 by Sylvia Plath. Used by permission of Alfred A. Knopf, a division of Random
House, Inc. and Faber & Faber, Ltd.

Katherine Anne Porter, "The Jilting of Granny Weatherall" from *Flowering Judas
and Other Stories*. Copyright 1930 and renewed © 1958 by Katherine Anne Porter.
Reprinted with the permission of Harcourt, Inc.

Ezra Pound, "Salutation" from *Personae*. Copyright 1926 by Ezra Pound. Reprinted
with the permission of New Directions Publishing Corp.

Dudley Randall, "Ballad of Birmingham" from *Cities Burning*. Copyright © 1968 by
Dudley Randall. Reprinted with the permission of Broadside Press.

John Crowe Ransom, "Here Lies a Lady" from *Selected Poems, Revised Edition*.
Copyright 1924, 1927 by Alfred A. Knopf, Inc., renewed 1952, © 1955 by John
Crowe Ransom. Used by permission of Alfred A. Knopf, a division of Random
House, Inc.

Henry Reed, "Naming of Parts" from *Henry Reed: Collected Poems*, edited by Jon
Stallworthy. Copyright © 1991. Reprinted with the permission of Oxford University
Press, Ltd.

Adrienne Rich, "Poetry: I" from *Your Native Land, Your Life*. Copyright © 1986 by
Adrienne Rich. "Storm Warnings," "Living in Sin," "Aunt Jennifer's Tigers," and
"Diving into the Wreck" from *The Fact of a Doorframe: Poems Selected and New,
1950–1984*. Copyright © 1984, 1981 by Adrienne Rich. Copyright © 1978, 1975 by
W. W. Norton & Company, Inc. "Ghost of a Chance" from *Collected Early Poems:
1950–1970*. Copyright © 1993, 1955 by Adrienne Rich. All used by permission of
the author and W. W. Norton & Company, Inc.

Elisavietta Ritchie, "Sorting Laundry" from *The Arc of the Storm* (Chapel Hill:
Signal Books, 1998). Originally published in *Poetry* (1989). Copyright © 1998 by
Elisavietta Ritchie. Reprinted with the permission of the author.

Jose Rivera, "Tape" from *Giants Have Us In Their Books: Six Naive Plays* (New York:
Broadway Play Publishing, 1997). Copyright © 1997 by Jose Rivera. Reprinted with
permission.

Theodore Roethke, "The Waking," "I Knew a Woman," "My Papa's Waltz," and
"Root Cellar" from *Collected Poems of Theodore Roethke*. Copyright 1942 by Hearst
Magazines, Inc., renewed © 1969 by Beatrice Roethke Lushington. Used by
permission of Doubleday, a division of Random House, Inc.

Anne Sexton, "Young" from *Complete Poems*. Copyright © 1981 by Linda Gray
Sexton and Loring Conant, Jr., Executors of the will of Anne Sexton. Reprinted
with the permission of Houghton Mifflin Company. All rights reserved.

William Shakespeare, *Othello, the Moor of Venice* from *Shakespeare: The Complete
Works*, edited by G B Harrison. Copyright 1952 by Harcourt Brace & Company,
renewed © 1980 by G. B. Harrison. Reprinted with the permission of Harcourt, Inc.

Charles Simic, "Watermelons" from *Selected Poems 1963–1983*. Copyright © 1974
by Charles Simic. Reprinted with the permission of George Braziller, Inc.

Stevie Smith, "Not Waving but Drowning" from *Collected Poems of Stevie Smith*.
Copyright © 1972 by Stevie Smith. Reprinted with the permission of New
Directions Publishing Corp.

Sophocles, "Oedipus Rex" from *Sophocles, The Oedipus Cycle: An English Version*, translated by Dudley Fitts and Robert Fitzgerald. Copyright 1949 by Harcourt Brace & Company and renewed © 1977 by Cornelia Fitts and Robert Fitzgerald. Reprinted with the permission of Harcourt, Inc.

Gary Soto, "Small Town with One Road" from *New and Selected Poems*. Copyright © 1995 by Gary Soto. Used with permission of Chronicle Books, LLC, San Francisco. Visit ChronicleBooks.com.

William Stafford, "Traveling Through the Dark" from *The Way It Is: New and Selected Poems*. Copyright © 1962, 1977, 1991, 1998 by the Estate of William Stafford. Reprinted with the permission of Graywolf Press, Saint Paul, Minnesota.

Wallace Stevens, "The Course of a Particular" from *The Palm at the End of the Mind: Selected Poems and a Play*. Copyright © 1967, 1969, 1971 by Holly Stevens. "The Death of a Soldier," from *The Collected Poems of Wallace Stevens*. Copyright 1954 by Wallace Stevens and renewed © 1982 by Holly Stevens. Both used by permission of Alfred A. Knopf, a division of Random House, Inc.

May Swenson, "Question" from *Nature: Poems Old and New*. Copyright © 1994 by May Swenson. Reprinted with the permission of Houghton Mifflin Company. All rights reserved.

Dylan Thomas, "Do Not Go Gentle into That Good Night" and "Fern Hill" from *The Poems of Dylan Thomas*. Copyright 1945 by The Trustees for the Copyrights of Dylan Thomas. Copyright 1952 by Dylan Thomas. Reprinted with the permission of New Directions Publishing Corp.

John Updike, "A&P" from *Pigeon Feathers and Other Stories*. Copyright © 1962 and renewed 1990 by John Updike. Used by permission of Alfred A. Knopf, a division of Random House, Inc.

Luis Valdez, "Los Vendidos" from *Luis Valdez—Early Works: Actos, Bernabe, Pensamiento Serpentino*. Copyright © 1971 by Luis Valdez. Reprinted with the permission of Arte Publico Press-University of Houston.

Derek Walcott, "The Virgins" from *Sea Grapes*. Copyright © 1976 by Derek Walcott. Reprinted with the permission of Farrar, Straus & Giroux, LLC.

Alice Walker, "Everyday Use" from *In Love and Trouble: Stories of Black Women*. Copyright © 1973 by Alice Walker. Reprinted with the permission of Harcourt, Inc.

Eudora Welty, "A Worn Path" from *A Curtain of Green and Other Stories*. Copyright 1941 and renewed © 1969 by Eudora Welty. Reprinted with the permission of Harcourt, Inc.

Edith Wharton, "Roman Fever" from *Roman Fever and Other Stories*. Copyright 1934 by Liberty Magazine, renewed © 1962 by William R. Tyler. Reprinted by permission of Scribner, an imprint of Simon & Schuster Adult Publishing.

Richard Wilbur, "Mind" from *The Things of This World*. Copyright © 1956 and renewed 1984 by Richard Wilbur. "The Writer" from *The Mind-Reader*. Copyright © 1971 by Richard Wilbur. Both reprinted with the permission of Harcourt, Inc.

C. K. Williams, "The Critic" from *Flesh and Blood*. Copyright © 1987 by C. K. Williams. Reprinted with the permission of Farrar, Straus & Giroux, LLC.

Tennessee Williams, *The Glass Menagerie*. Copyright 1945 by The University of the South. Reprinted by permission of Georges Borchardt, Inc. for the Tennessee Williams Estate.

William Carlos Williams, "The Red Wheelbarrow," "The Widow's Lament in Springtime," "Poem," and "Spring and All" from *Collected Poems: 1909–1939, Volume 1*. Copyright 1938 by New Directions Publishing Corp. "The Dance" from *Collected Poems: 1939–1962, Volume II*. Copyright 1944 by William Carlos Williams. All reprinted with the permission of New Directions Publishing Corp.

August Wilson, "Fences" from *Fences*. Copyright © 1986 by August Wilson. Reprinted with the permission of Dutton Signet, a division of Penguin Group (USA) Inc.

Yvor Winters, "The Slow Pacific Swell" and "A Summer Commentary" from *Collected Poems*. Copyright © 1960 by Yvor Winters. Reprinted with the permission of Swallow Press/Ohio University Press, www.ohioswallow.com.

Tobias Wolff, "Hunters in the Snow" from *In the Garden of the North American Martyrs*. Copyright © 1981 by Tobias Wolff. Reprinted with the permission of HarperCollins Publishers.

James Wright, "A Blessing" from *Collected Poems*. Copyright © 1971 by James Wright. Reprinted with the permission of Wesleyan University Press, www.wesleyan.edu/wespress.

Richard Wright, "The Man Who Was Almost a Man" from *Eight Men*. Copyright 1940, © 1961 by Richard Wright, renewed © 1989 by Ellen Wright. Reprinted with the permission of HarperCollins Publishers.

William Butler Yeats, "Leda and the Swan" and "Sailing to Byzantium" from *The Poems of W. B. Yeats: A New Edition*, edited by Richard J. Finneran. Copyright 1928 by The Macmillan Company, renewed © 1956 by Georgie Yeats. Reprinted with the permission of Scribner, an imprint of Simon & Schuster Adult Publishing Group. All rights reserved.

Index of Authors, Titles, and First Lines

Author's names appear in capitals, titles of selections in italics. A number in bold face indicates the page of the selection, and number in roman type indicate the pages where the selection is discussed.

S0-BSV-592

SCALE 1:24000

QUADRANGLE LOCATION

SANDY HOOK, N. J.—N. Y.

N4022.5—W7358.33/7.5x9.17

1954

CONTOUR INTERVAL 20 FEET
DATUM IS MEAN SEA LEVEL
DEPTH CURVES AND SOUNDINGS IN FEET—DATUM IS MEAN LOW WATER
SHORELINE SHOWN REPRESENTS THE APPROXIMATE LINE OF MEAN HIGH WATER
THE MEAN RANGE OF TIDE IS 3·8 FEET

INTERIOR—GEOLOGICAL SURVEY, WASHINGTON, D. C.—1962-NS
MR 1227

INTRODUCTION TO PHYSICAL GEOGRAPHY

COVER PHOTOGRAPH

The earth presented a gibbous phase to astronauts aboard the Apollo 10 spacecraft when this photograph was taken. The circle of illumination, or terminator, lies in a plane normal to the sun's rays, while the north polar end of the earth's axis is inclined toward the left. The sun's declination on this date, about a month before summer solstice, is such that the sub-solar point at noon falls on the 20th parallel north, while all of the region poleward of the 80th parallel north is under perpetual sunlight. The Arabian Peninsula is clearly outlined at the center of the earth-disk, with the Gulf of Aden and the Somali region of Africa directly below it. (National Aeronautics and Space Administration.)

FACING TITLE PAGE

Sixteenth century globe. (Cosmographia Petri Apiani, 1551.)

ARTHUR N. *ewell* STRAHLER

INTRODUCTION TO PHYSICAL GEOGRAPHY

SECOND EDITION

JOHN WILEY & SONS, INC.

New York · London · Sydney · Toronto

STATEN ISLAND COMMUNITY COLLEGE LIBRARY
STATEN ISLAND, NEW YORK 10301

GB
56
.S74
1970

Copyright © 1965, 1970, by John Wiley & Sons, Inc.

All rights reserved. No part of this book may be reproduced by any means, nor transmitted, nor translated into a machine language without the written permission of the publisher.

Library of Congress Catalogue Card Number: 73-91648

SBN 471 83168 9

Printed in the United States of America

10 9 8 7 6 5 4 3 2

STATEN ISLAND COMMUNITY COLLEGE LIBRARY
STATEN ISLAND, NEW YORK 10301

10-15-70

Preface

FIRST published in 1965, *Introduction to Physical Geography* met the need for a shortened version of its parent work, *Physical Geography*, 1960, which was then in its second edition. The requisite abbreviation was accomplished by deletion of entire topics and chapters dealing with certain aspects of astronomy, geophysics, geodesy, and cartography. At the same time, new material was added in fields of plant ecology, distribution of natural vegetation, climatology, and soil hydrology. Climatic and pedogenic regimes were introduced and related to the soil-water budget.

Since the publication of *Introduction to Physical Geography*, the parent volume has itself been revised. The appearance of new material on the atmosphere and its heat budget, soils, and world landform classification in the third edition of *Physical Geography*, 1969, as well as the introduction of color in the line drawings, made imperative this second edition of *Introduction to Physical Geography*.

We have taken as a basic premise that the aim of physical geography is an understanding of man's physical environment. Of primary importance is the thin planetary zone in which most human beings have lived and have developed their economic, political, and cultural structures. Thus the near-surface layer of the lands has first priority; it requires concentration of study upon climates, landforms, surface waters, soils, and vegetation. First attention has been given to those topics which will prove most directly enlightening to the student when he proceeds to a course in human geography. With regret, much natural science of the earth's crust and interior, the oceans and their basins, the upper and outer atmosphere, and planetary space is omitted from this abbreviated textbook.

New material includes separate chapters for a survey of the earth's atmosphere as a layered structure and the heating and cooling of the atmosphere as viewed from the standpoint of a global radiation budget. New world maps of surface air temperatures, pressures, and winds are a major improvement. A full-color plate of representative soil profiles greatly improves the appreciation of great soil groups, while a brief review of the *Seventh Approximation* system of soil classification, written by Dr. Roy W. Simonson, allows the student to learn what changes are in store in that field.

Introduction of Dr. Richard E. Murphy's worldwide system of landform classification, together with his map, *Landforms of the World* (reproduced in full color as Plate 5), fills a gap that has long existed in the world geography of landforms.

To compensate for the added pages required by the new material, the lengthy appendix of climatic data has been deleted. However, the appendix dealing with topographic map reading has been retained and strengthened.

Over a period of many years, many helpful suggestions have been sent in by colleagues and students who have used the foregoing editions of my physical geography textbooks. It is a source of regret that I cannot acknowledge individually the aid of these many contributors. Their total effort has played a major role in strengthening this newest work and making it more useful in the teaching of physical geography.

Columbia University
November, 1969
                                        Arthur N. Strahler

Contents

Color Plates Bound at End of Book

Plate 1 Mean Annual Precipitation of the World

Plate 2 Climates of the World

Plate 3 Great Soil Groups of the World

Plate 4 Natural Vegetation Regions of the World

Plate 5 Landforms of the World

World Population Distribution

World Political Division

End Papers

Front: U.S.G.S. Topographic Map and Legend

Back: Weather Map Symbols

INTRODUCTION TO PHYSICAL GEOGRAPHY

Introduction

WHAT is physical geography? As a first step in understanding this term we might well expand it to read "the physical basis of geography," for physical geography is simply the study and unification of a number of earth sciences which give general insight into the nature of man's environment. Not in itself a distinct branch of science, physical geography is a body of basic principles of natural science selected with a view to including primarily the environmental influences that vary from place to place over the earth's surface.

What, then, are the individual sciences that comprise physical geography, and why are they selected? First and most fundamental are the form of the earth, a concern of the science of *geodesy*, and the relationship between earth and sun, a part of *astronomy*. Much of astronomy is beyond the concern of the geographer, for only two bodies, the sun and the moon, appreciably affect life on earth. Because all energy for sustaining life, all motive power for streams, winds, and ocean currents, comes by radiant emanation from the sun, and because the intensity of this energy changes through daily and annual cycles, an understanding of the motions of the earth in its orbit about the sun is a prime essential. The moon, as the body that controls ocean tides, enters into physical geography only in a minor way.

Because data of the earth sciences are often best represented by maps, and perhaps many are impossible to describe without maps, the science of maps, *cartography*, is an essential ingredient of physical geography. True, cartography is really a science of technique, rather than a basic earth science, but it deserves a place early in the list of topics so that it may provide a means for representing the information to follow.

Man, though he lives on the earth's solid surface, is an air-breather *in* the atmosphere and owes his very survival to favorable conditions of weather and climate. The sciences of *meteorology* and *climatology*, which treat these topics, are thus a major concern of the physical geographer. Lying between the atmosphere and the land masses of the earth is a thin layer, the soil, which reflects the influence of both climate and topography. Soil science, or *pedology*, is thus another constituent of physical geography. The structure and distribution of natural vegetation types, though a botanical rather than a physical-science subject, must be included for consideration in physical geography because plants are important features of the landscape and are remarkably consistent indicators of climate, soils, and landforms. Thus the science of *plant geography* is taken into the fold of physical geography.

In our concern for the lands of the earth we should not overlook the oceans of the globe. *Physical oceanography*, which includes a study of ocean waves, currents, and tides, finds its way into physical geography inevitably because man uses the oceans for intercontinental communication, for naval and air operations, and as a source of food as well.

The topographic features, or landforms, of the earth's surface are of prime concern to man because they influence the placement of his agricultural lands, his cities, his lines of communication. The science of *geomorphology* treats the origin and systematic development of all types of landforms and is a major part of physical geography. Very often landforms express the varieties and structures of rocks under the surface, so that a certain minimum knowledge of the principles of *geology* is included. An understanding of geological principles will have the further value of explaining the origin and distribution of the principal types of mineral deposits—coal, petroleum, natural gas, metallic ores, building stones, and many others. Closely involved with geomorphology is the science of *hydrology*, which treats the earth's surface and underground waters, including rivers, lakes, springs, and marshes. Fresh water, a basic essential for man's survival, thus looms as an important element of the physical basis of geography.

The professional physical geographer will usually be a specialist in only one of the several fields involved, such as climatology, geomorphology, or soil science. Besides carrying out original research in his chosen specialty, to which he may be making important scientific contributions, the physical geographer attempts to keep informed on important developments as they occur in the other fields of specialization. He is thus able to assemble and integrate pertinent fragments of knowledge into a unified picture of the natural environment of man at any place on the globe at any season of year.

1

CHAPTER 1

The Geographic Grid and Its Projections

THE spherical form of the earth is one of the facts of our physical environment, which children learn at an early age, but probably few people give much thought to some of the simple proofs of the earth's sphericity. For example, the evidence that people have repeatedly sailed or flown completely around the globe is tacitly assumed to prove the sphericity of the earth, whereas it means only that the earth is a solid body. Circumnavigation could also be performed on a cubical or cylindrical earth.

Even without optical instruments we can get some inkling that the earth's surface curves downward away from us through the observation that sunlight illuminates the tops of high clouds after sunset and before sunrise.

One proof of the earth's sphericity may be had from observations at sea. As a ship recedes farther and farther into the distance, it appears to sink slowly beneath the water level (Figure 1.1). Seen through binoculars or a telescope the sea surface will appear to rise until the decks are awash, then gradually to submerge the funnel and the masts, leaving finally only smoke visible above the horizon. The explanation obviously lies in the fact that the sea surface curves downward away from us. To prove that this curvature is spherical would require numerous observations in which measurements were made of the amount of apparent sinking of a vessel per unit of distance in many different directions away from the observing point.

A second proof is found in the observation that in all lunar eclipses, at which time the earth's shadow falls on the moon, the edge of the shadow appears as an arc of a circle. It can be shown by geometrical proof that a sphere is the only body that will always cast a circular shadow upon another sphere. Because at the time of these eclipses the earth is rarely turned in just the same position, we may conclude that, no matter what earth profile is cast on the moon, the circular shadows are all alike and the earth must be spherical.

Photographs taken from rockets and earth satellites (such as the *Tiros* weather satellites) at extremely high altitudes show the horizon as a curved line (Figure 1.2). Because the curvature appears to be the same in many widely separated parts of the earth, a series of such photographs provides us with a third proof of the earth's spherical form.

A fourth proof may be had from observation of the position of Polaris, the north star. To the observer at the equator Polaris is on the horizon, but as he travels toward the north pole the star seems to be located higher and higher in the sky, until, at the north pole, it is directly overhead in the sky. It would be found that Polaris rises 1° higher in the sky for every 69 mi (111 km) of northward travel by the observer. A similar condition would hold for travel from the equator to the south pole if a star nearly in line with the earth's axis in the southern sky could be observed. Thus we can prove that all north-south lines drawn from pole to pole (e.g., meridians) are arcs of circles, and that the earth is spherical.

A fifth proof of the earth's sphericity comes from the observation that an object near sea level will weigh very nearly the same amount on a spring type of scales at any place on the globe. Knowing that the weight depends upon the pull of gravity, we conclude that the object weighs the same everywhere because all points on the earth's sur-

Figure 1.1 Seen through a telescope, a distant ship seems to be partly submerged.

Figure 1.2 Curvature of the earth's horizon shows clearly on this photograph of the southwestern United States and northern Mexico, taken from a Navy Viking-12 rocket at an altitude of 143 mi (230 km). On the left are Lower California and the Gulf of California. To the right the view extends as far as the Los Angeles area. (Official U.S. Navy Photograph.)

face are equidistant from its center, hence, the earth is a sphere.

Now, a pendulum clock will also serve to measure the force of gravity. If the pendulum is kept of exactly constant length the clock will keep constant time so long as it is acted upon by a constant gravity. Thus, if a pendulum clock is found to keep good time at all points at sea level over the earth, the spherical form is proved. Extremely precise calculations based upon this principle, however, show slight variations in gravity, which, as will be explained later, led to the discovery that the earth's true form is not a perfect sphere.

As a last proof it may be noted that modern navigation methods are based on the assumption that the earth is a sphere. When we consider that, for more than a century, positions of vessels have been correctly determined innumerable times by these methods, it becomes obvious that the correctness of the assumption has been established many times over.

Although the ancient Greeks, among them Pythagoras (540 B.C.) and associates of Aristotle (384–322 B.C.), believed the earth to be spherical and had speculated upon its circumference, it remained until 200 B.C. for Eratosthenes, librarian at Alexandria, to perform a direct measurement of the earth's circumference. He obtained a value believed to be equivalent to about 26,660 statute miles (42,900 km), somewhat larger than the true value, which is not far from 25,000 mi (40,000 km). Arabs of the ninth century, using measure-

ments of the positions of stars combined with direct ground-distance measurements, also arrived at estimates of the earth's size. Their measurements were probably much more accurate than those of Eratosthenes, but because the units of measure are not known in modern equivalents, their work cannot be checked.

The earth as an oblate ellipsoid

In 1671 a French astronomer, Jean Richer, was sent by Louis XIV to the Island of Cayenne, French Guiana, to make certain astronomical observations. His clock had been so adjusted that its pendulum, slightly over 39 in (99 cm) long, beat the exact seconds in Paris. Upon arriving in Cayenne, which is near the equator, Richer found the clock to be losing about two and one-half minutes per day. As soon as Newton's laws of gravitation and motion were published (1686) it became possible to attribute the slowing of the clock at Cayenne to a somewhat reduced force of gravity near the equator. It was soon realized that this phenomenon could be accounted for by supposing that the equatorial portions of the earth's surface lie further from the earth's center than do more northerly places.

Refined measurements have since revealed that the true form of the earth is more like a sphere which has been compressed along the polar axis and made to bulge slightly around the equator (Figure 1.3). This form is known as an *oblate ellipsoid*. A cross section through the poles gives an *ellipse* rather than a circle. The equator remains a circle and is the largest possible circumference on the ellipsoid. The earth's oblateness is attributed to the centrifugal force of the earth's rotation, which deforms the somewhat plastic earth into a form in equilibrium with respect to the forces of gravity and rotation.

Rounding off the earth's dimensions to the nearest whole mile, the equatorial diameter is 7927 mi (12,757 km), whereas the length of polar axis is 7900 mi (12,714 km), a difference of about 27 mi (43 km). The *oblateness* of the earth ellipsoid, or *flattening of the poles*, is the ratio of this difference to the equatorial diameter, or roughly 27/7927, which reduces to a fraction only slightly larger than 1/300. Thus we can say that the earth's polar axis is about 1/300 shorter than the equatorial diameter. Using these figures the earth's equatorial circumference is about 24,900 mi (40,075 km). For rough calculations the figure of 25,000 mi (40,000 km) is close enough.

Great and small circles

For many purposes of physical geography the earth can be treated as if it were a true sphere. Generally, flattening of the poles can be disregarded in order to simplify an understanding of the important concepts of the earth as an object turning under the sun's rays.

If a sphere is divided exactly in half by a plane passed through the center, the intersection of the plane with the sphere is the largest circle that can be drawn on the sphere and is known as a *great circle* (Figure 1.4). Circles produced by planes passing through a sphere anywhere except through the center are smaller than great circles and are designated *small circles*.

Become thoroughly familiar with the following properties of great circles, because they frequently enter into such global subjects as meridians, navigation, illumination of the globe, and map projections:

1. A great circle always results when a plane passes through the center of a sphere, regardless of the attitude of the plane.

2. A great circle is the largest possible circle that can be drawn on the surface of a sphere.

3. An infinite number of great circles can be drawn on a sphere.

4. One and only one great circle can be found that will pass through two given points on the surface of the sphere (unless the two points are at the extremities of the same diameter, in which case an infinite number of great circles can be drawn through them).

5. An arc of a great circle is the shortest surface distance between any two points on a sphere.

Figure 1.3 **Dimensions of the earth according to the International Ellipsoid of Reference (Hayford, 1909).**

6. Intersecting great circles always bisect each other.

One use of great circles that may be elaborated on here is in navigation. Wherever ships must travel over vast expanses of open ocean between distant ports, or planes must make long flights, it is desirable in the interests of saving fuel and time to follow the great-circle arc between the two points, provided, of course, that there are no obstacles or other deterring factors preventing the use of the great-circle path. Navigators use special types of maps which have the property of always showing great-circle arcs as straight lines. These are known as *great-circle sailing charts* and are discussed more fully under the subject of map projections. To plot the shortest course between any two points it is necessary only to draw a straight line between the two points on such a chart.

Great-circle courses may easily be found on a small globe by using only a piece of thin string or a rubber band (Figure 1.5). The string can be held in such a way that it is stretched tightly against the surface of the globe between the two thumbnails, each of which is on one of the points

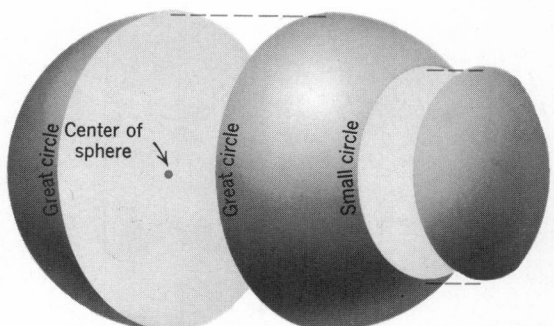

Figure 1.4 **Great circle and small circle.**

Figure 1.5   A great-circle course. (Charles Phelps Cushing.)

between which the great-circle course is desired. If a rubber band is used, a complete great circle can be shown; it is of special value for points on opposite sides of the globe. Many globes show great-circle routes between distant ports on the Pacific, Atlantic, or Indian oceans. These may readily be checked by the stretched piece of string.

Meridians and parallels

The spinning of the earth on its axis provides two natural points—the poles—upon which to base the *geographic grid*, a network of intersecting lines inscribed upon the globe for purposes of fixing the location of surface features. The grid consists of a set of north-south lines connecting the poles—the *meridians*—and a set of east-west

lines running parallel with the equator—the *parallels* (Figure 1.6).

All meridians are halves of great circles, whose ends coincide with the earth's north and south poles. Though it is true that opposite meridians taken together comprise a complete great circle, it is well to remember that a single meridian is only half of a great circle and contains 180° of arc. Additional characteristics of meridians are:

1. All meridians run in a true north-south direction.
2. Meridians are spaced farthest apart at the equator and converge to common points at the poles.
3. An infinite number of meridians may be drawn on a globe. Thus a meridian exists for any point selected on the globe. For representation on maps and globes, however, meridians are selected at suitable equal distances apart.

Parallels are entire small circles, produced by passing planes through the earth parallel to the plane of the equator. They possess the following characteristics:

1. Parallels are always parallel to one another. Although they are circular lines, they always remain equal distances apart.
2. All parallels represent true east-west lines.
3. Parallels intersect meridians at right angles. This fact holds true for any place on the globe, except the two poles, despite the fact that the parallels are strongly curved near the poles.
4. All parallels except the equator are small circles; the equator is a complete great circle.
5. An infinite number of parallels may be drawn on the globe. Therefore, every point on the globe, except the north or south pole, lies on a parallel.

Longitude

The location of points on the earth's surface follows a system in which lengths of arc are meas-

Figure 1.6   *A*, Meridians.

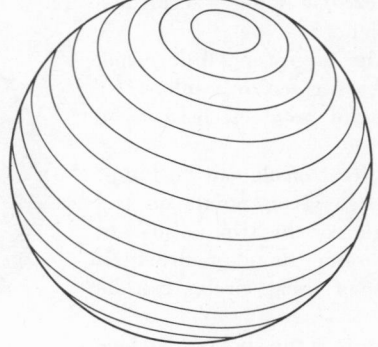

B, Parallels.

ured along meridians and parallels (Figure 1.7). Taking the equator as the starting line, arcs are measured north or south to the desired points. Taking a selected meridian, or *prime meridian*, as a reference line, arcs are measured eastward or westward to the desired points.

Longitude of a place may be defined as the arc, measured in degrees, of a parallel between that place and the prime meridian (Figure 1.7). The prime meridian is almost universally accepted as that which passes through the Royal Observatory at Greenwich, near London, England, and is often referred to as the *meridian of Greenwich*. This meridian has the value 0° longitude. The longitude of any given point on the globe is measured eastward or westward from this meridian, whichever is the shorter arc. Longitude may thus range from 0° to 180°, either east or west. It is commonly written in the following form: *long. 77° 03′ 41″ W*, which may be read "longitude 77 degrees, 3 minutes, 41 seconds west of Greenwich."

If only the longitude of a point is stated we cannot tell its precise location because the same arc of measure applies to an entire meridian. For this reason, a meridian might be defined as a line representing all points having the same longitude. This definition explains why the expression "a meridian of longitude" is often used. Confusion may arise because of the statement that longitude is measured along a parallel of latitude, but this may be clarified by the realization that in order to measure the arc between a point and the prime meridian it is necessary to follow eastward or westward along one of the parallels (Figure 1.7).

The actual length, in miles or kilometers, of a degree of longitude will depend upon where it is measured. At the equator this distance may be computed by dividing the earth's circumference by 360°:

$$\frac{24{,}900 \text{ mi}}{360°} = 69 \text{ statute miles (approx.)}$$

$$\frac{40{,}075 \text{ km}}{360°} = 111 \text{ kilometers (approx.)}$$

Because of the rapid convergence of the meridians northward or southward, care should be taken not to employ this equivalent inadvertently except close to the equator. It is a further useful item of knowledge that the length of 1° of longitude is reduced to about one-half as much at the 60th parallels, or about $34\frac{1}{2}$ mi ($55\frac{1}{2}$ km).

Latitude

Latitude of a place may be defined as the arc, measured in degrees, of a meridian between that place and the equator (Figure 1.7). Latitude may thus range from 0° at the equator to 90° north

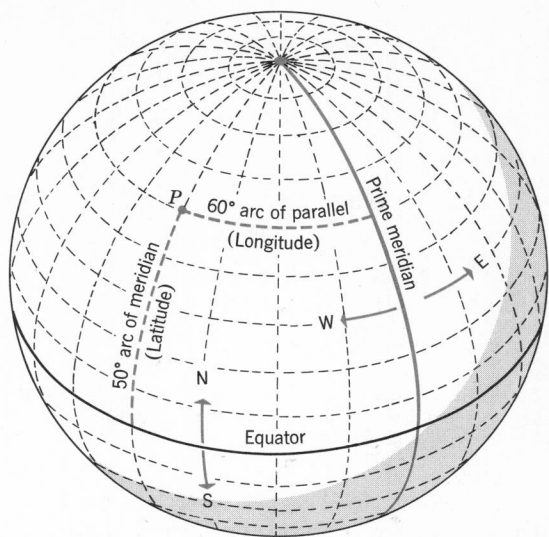

Figure 1.7 The point *P* has a latitude of 50° N, a longitude of 60° W.

or south at the poles. The latitude of a place, written as *lat. 34° 10′ 31″ N*, may be read "latitude 34 degrees, 10 minutes, 31 seconds north." When both the latitude and longitude of a place are given, it is accurately and precisely located with respect to the geographic grid.

For most purposes of physical geography we consider the earth to be a sphere, and therefore the parallels of latitude are taken to be exactly equidistantly spaced if they are drawn on a globe for unit amounts of arc, as, for example, every 10 degrees. The length of a degree of latitude is almost the same as the length of a degree of longitude at the equator, so that the value of 69 mi (111 km) per degree may be used for ordinary purposes.

To be very precise, and take into account the oblateness of the earth, it must be recognized that a degree of latitude changes slightly in length from equator to poles. Using figures of the Clarke ellipsoid of 1866, the length of 1° of latitude at the equator is 68.704 statute miles (110.569 km); at the poles it is 69.407 mi (111.700 km), or 0.7 mi (1.1 km) longer. One degree at the poles is 1 percent longer than at the equator. The difference is by no means trivial and must be taken into account in construction of large-scale maps.

The explanation of this variation in length of a degree of latitude may be had from a diagram showing how degrees of latitude are determined (Figure 1.8). Because of the earth's oblateness, the surface curvature is less strong near the poles than at the equator. That is to say, a smaller circle can be fitted to the curvature near the equator than at the poles, as shown in Figure 1.8. A single degree

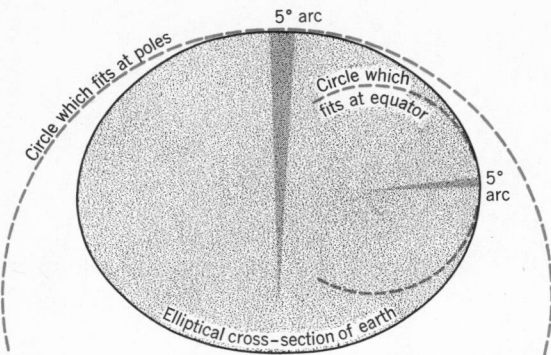

Figure 1.8 The length of a degree of latitude is very slightly greater at the poles than at the equator.

on the largest circle has a greater length of arc than a degree on the smallest circle. Hence the length of a single degree of latitude will be greatest near the poles and least near the equator. In order to obtain the correct values for specific latitudes, it is necessary to consult prepared tables. Table 1.1 gives the lengths of single degrees of both latitude and longitude for various latitudes.

Statute mile and nautical mile

Both marine and air navigation use the *nautical mile* as the unit of length or distance. Meteorology (weather science) of the upper atmosphere has also adopted as the unit of wind speed the mariner's *knot*, which is a velocity of one nautical mile per hour. It is therefore worthwhile for the geographer to understand the nautical mile.

On July 1, 1954, the U.S. Department of Defense adopted the *international nautical mile*, defined as exactly equivalent to 1852 international meters, or 6076.103333 feet (the digit 3 is repeated indefinitely). Therefore, dividing this value in feet by 5280, the number of feet per *statute mile*, we arrive at the equivalent: 1 international nautical mile = 1.150777 statute miles. For ordinary calculations, then, the value of 1.15 statute miles (1.85 km) per nautical mile is quite satisfactory.

At what place on the earth does the international nautical mile equal the length of one minute of arc of the earth ellipsoid? This can be computed by first multiplying 1.150777 by 60 to give 69.04663 statute miles per degree of arc. Next, consulting Table 1.1, this figure is seen to be very close to the length of one degree of latitude at 45°, which is given as 69.054 miles according to the Clarke ellipsoid of reference. Furthermore, if all of the values of the middle column of Table 1.1 are added and the average value computed, it will be found to be 69.055. This leads to the conclusion that the international nautical mile very closely approximates the average length of one

minute of latitude, or that it is the $\frac{1}{5400}$ part of the length of a meridian between equator and pole.

Map projections

A map projection is an orderly system of parallels and meridians used as a basis for drawing a map on a flat surface. The fundamental problem is to transfer the geographic grid from its actual spherical form to a flat surface in such a way as to present the earth's surface or some part of it in the most advantageous way possible for the purposes desired.

One way to avoid the map-projection problem is to use only a globe. Unfortunately a globe has shortcomings. First, we can see only one side of a globe at a time. Second, a globe is on too small a scale for many purposes. On globes ranging from a few inches to two or three feet in diameter, only the barest essentials of geography can be shown. The few large globes in existence, those several feet in diameter, may show considerable detail, but they serve also to accentuate a third shortcoming of globes—their lack of portability. Flat maps printed on paper can be folded compactly so that many may be carried in a small pocket, whereas even the smallest globe is a cumbersome and delicate object. Ease of reproduction greatly favors maps over globes. Making a quality globe requires not only that a map be printed but also that the map be trimmed and carefully pasted onto a spherical shell.

The problem of map projection must therefore be squarely faced in an endeavor to learn what types of networks of parallels and meridians are best suited to illustration of various portions of the earth's surface. It is well to point out, however, that no map projection will ever substitute fully for a globe to show general world relations, and use of a globe is to be recommended in conjunction with flat maps.

Developable geometric surfaces

Certain geometric surfaces are said to be *developable* because by cutting along certain lines they can be made to unroll or unfold to make a flat sheet. Two such forms are the *cone* and the *cylinder* (Figure 1.9). Were the earth conical or cylindrical, the map-projection problem would be solved once and for all by using the developed surface. No distortion of surface shapes or areas would occur, although it is true that the surface would be cut apart along certain lines. The earth belongs to a group of geometric forms said to be *undevelopable*, because, no matter how they are cut, they cannot be unrolled or unfolded to lie flat. It is possible to draw a true straight line in

TABLE 1.1[a]

Latitude, Degrees	Length of 1° of Latitude		Length of 1° of Longitude	
	Statute Miles	Kilometers	Statute Miles	Kilometers
0	68.704	110.569	69.172	111.322
5	68.710	110.578	68.911	110.902
10	68.725	110.603	68.129	109.643
15	68.751	110.644	66.830	107.553
20	68.786	110.701	65.026	104.650
25	68.829	110.770	62.729	100.953
30	68.879	110.850	59.956	96.490
35	68.935	110.941	56.725	91.290
40	68.993	111.034	53.063	85.397
45	69.054	111.132	48.995	78.850
50	69.115	111.230	44.552	71.700
55	69.175	111.327	39.766	63.997
60	69.230	111.415	34.674	55.803
65	69.281	111.497	29.315	47.178
70	69.324	111.567	23.729	38.188
75	69.360	111.625	17.960	28.904
80	69.386	111.666	12.051	19.394
85	69.402	111.692	6.049	9.735
90	69.407	111.700	0.000	0.000

[a]Based on Clarke ellipsoid of 1866, from *U.S. Geological Survey Bulletin* 650, "Geographic Tables and Formulas," by S. S. Gannett, 1916, pp. 36–37.

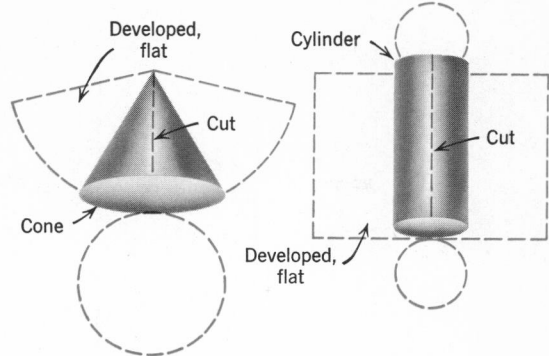

Figure 1.9 The cone and cylinder are developable geometric forms.

one or more directions on the surface of a developable solid, but nowhere can this be done on an undevelopable form such as a spherical surface. In order to make the parts of a spherical surface lie perfectly flat, it must be stretched—more in some places than in others. Thus, it is impossible to make a perfect map projection.

When a map is made of a very small part of the earth's surface, for example, an area four miles across, the map-projection problem can be ignored. If the meridians and parallels are drawn as straight lines, intersecting at right angles and correctly spaced apart, the actual error present is probably so small as to fall within the width of the lines drawn and is not worth correcting. As the area included on the map is increased, however, the problem gains in importance. When an attempt is made to show the whole globe, very serious trouble develops. Only by some compromise can the distortion be reduced to a reasonable degree over important parts of the earth's surface.

Although for purposes of simplicity this chapter treats projections of a spherical globe upon a flat map, it is well to point out that in precise plotting of a map projection the earth ellipsoid is the geometrical form that is actually used. But because the earth's oblateness is slight, the earth can be assumed a true sphere for an elementary and descriptive study of map projections.

Map scale

All globes and maps depict the earth's features in much smaller size than the true features which they attempt to represent. Globes are intended in principle to be perfect models of the earth itself, differing from the earth only in size, but not in shape. The *scale* of a globe is therefore the ratio between the size of the globe and the size of the earth, where size is expressed by some measure of length or distance (but not area or volume). Take, for example, a globe 10 inches in diameter representing the earth, whose diameter is about 8000 miles. The scale of the globe is therefore the ratio between 10 inches and 8000 miles. Dividing both figures by 10, this reduces to a scale stated as: *1 inch represents 800 miles*, a relationship that holds true for distances between any two points on the globe. (Stated in metric units, the scale of this globe would be the ratio of 25 cm to 12,900 km, or *1 centimeter represents 516 kilometers*.)

Scale is more usefully stated as a simple fraction, termed the *fractional scale*, or *representative fraction* (*R.F.*), which can be obtained by reducing both map and globe distances to the same unit of measure, thus:

$$\frac{1 \text{ in. on globe}}{800 \text{ mi on earth}} = \frac{1 \text{ in.}}{800 \times 63,360 \text{ in. (per mile)}}$$

$$= \frac{1 \text{ in.}}{50,688,000 \text{ in.}} = \frac{1}{50,688,000}$$

This fraction may be written as 1:50,688,000 for convenience in printing. The advantage of the representative fraction is that it is entirely free of any specified units of measure, such as the foot, mile, meter, or kilometer. Persons of any nationality understand the fraction, regardless of the language or units of measure used in their nation, provided only that the arabic numerals are understood.

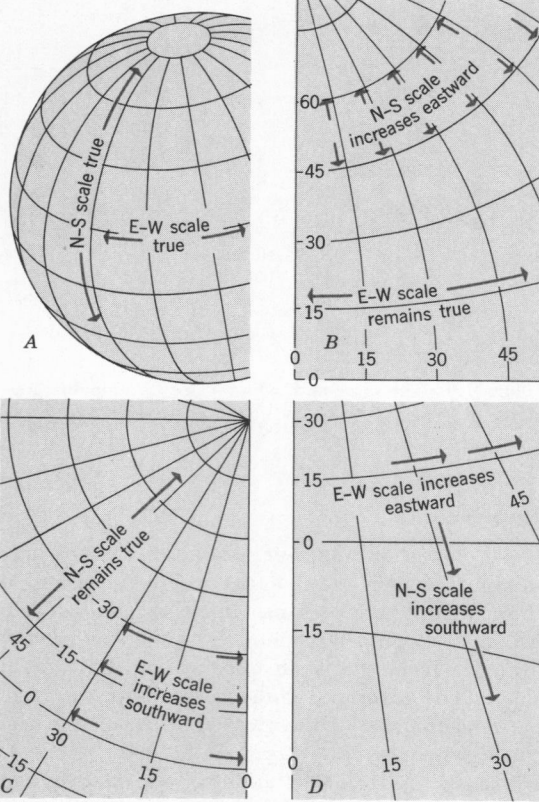

Figure 1.10 *A*, Scale true in all directions on a globe. *B*, Scale true along all parallels but not along all meridians. *C*, Scale true along all meridians but not along all parallels. *D*, Scale changes along both parallels and meridians.

A globe is a *true-scale model* of the earth, in that the same scale of miles applies to any distances on the globe, regardless of the latitude or longitude, and regardless of the compass direction of the line whose distance is being considered (Figure 1.10*A*). This is to say that the scale remains constant over the entire globe. Map projections, however, cannot have the uniform-scale property of a globe, no matter how cleverly devised. In flattening the curved surface of the sphere to conform to a flat plane, all map projections stretch the earth's surface in a nonuniform manner, so that the scale changes from place to place. Thus, we cannot say about a map of the world: "the scale of this map is 1:50,000,000," for the statement is false for any form of projection.

It is quite possible, however, to have the scale of a flat map remain true, or constant, in certain specified directions. For example, one type of projection preserves constant scale along all parallels, but not along the meridians. This condition is illustrated in Figure 1.10*B*. Another type of projection keeps scale constant along all meridians,

but not along parallels, as shown in Figure 1.10*C*. Still other projections have changing scale along both meridians and parallels, as illustrated in Figure 1.10*D*.

Preserving areas on map projections

Because a globe is a true-scale model of the earth, given areas of the earth's surface are shown to correct relative size everywhere over its surface. If we should take a small wire ring, say one inch in diameter, and place it anywhere on the surface of the ten-inch globe, the area enclosed will represent an equal amount of area of the earth's surface. But a similar procedure would not enclose constant areas on all parts of most map projections, only on those having the special property of being *equal-area* projections.

At this point a good question arises. If, as stated above, no projection preserves a true, or constant, scale of distances in all directions over the projection, how can circles of equal diameter placed on the map enclose equal amounts of earth area? The answer is suggested in Figure 1.11. The square, one mile on a side, encloses one square mile between two meridians and two parallels. The square can be deformed into rectangles of different shapes, but if the dimensions are changed in an inverse manner, each will still enclose one square mile. The scale has been changed in one direction to compensate for change in another in just the right way to preserve equal areas of map between corresponding parts of intersecting meridians and parallels. Hence, any small square or circle moved about over the map surface will enclose a piece of the map representing a constant quantity of area of the earth's surface. Projections shown in Figure 1.23 and 1.24 have the equal-area property, but it is also obvious that these networks have had distortions of shape, particularly near the outer edges of the map.

Preserving shapes on map projections

A map projection is said to be *conformal* when any small piece of the earth's surface has the same

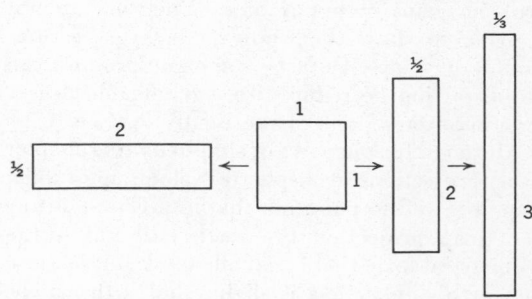

Figure 1.11 Areas can be preserved even though scales and shapes change radically.

shape on the map as it does on a globe. Thus, the appearance of small islands or countries is faithfully preserved by a conformal map. One characteristic of a conformal projection is that parallels and meridians cross each other at right angles everywhere on the map, just as they do on the globe. However, not all projections whose parallels and meridians cross at right angles are conformal.

Another way of saying that parallels and meridians intersect at right angles is that *shearing* of areas does not occur. Figure 1.12 illustrates the meaning of shearing. For projections consisting of straight parallels and meridians, shearing gives parallelograms formed of acute and obtuse angles. For projections with curved meridians and parallels, straight lines are drawn tangent to the curves at the point of intersection. If these tangent lines cross at right angles, the projection is not sheared; but if the tangents form obtuse and acute angles, shearing is present. Conformal maps are not sheared, but not all maps without shearing are conformal. A conformal map cannot have equal-area properties besides, so that some areas are greatly enlarged at the expense of others. Generally speaking, areas near the margin of a conformal map have a much larger scale than central ones.

Whether a conformal or equal-area projection is to be selected depends on what is to be shown. Where the surface extent of something, such as grain crops, or forest-covered lands, is to be shown, an equal-area projection is needed. For most general purposes a conformal type is preferable because physical features most nearly resemble their true shapes on the globe. Many map projections are neither perfectly conformal nor equal area, but represent a compromise between the two. This compromise may be desired either to achieve a map of more all-around usefulness or because the projection has some other very special property that makes its use essential for certain purposes.

Classification of map projections

Map projections may be classified according to the following groups: (1) *zenithal (azimuthal)*, (2) *conic*, (3) *cylindric*, and (4) individual, or unique types.

The *zenithal*, or *azimuthal*, group of projections includes all types that are centered about a point and have a radial, or wheel-like, symmetry. Some zenithal projections can actually be demonstrated in the laboratory by the following method. (See Figure 1.13.) A wire replica of the earth, in which the wires represent parallels and meridians, is used. A tiny light source, such as a flashlight bulb or an arc light, is placed at the center of the wire globe (or at any one of several prescribed positions). In a darkened room the shadow of the wire

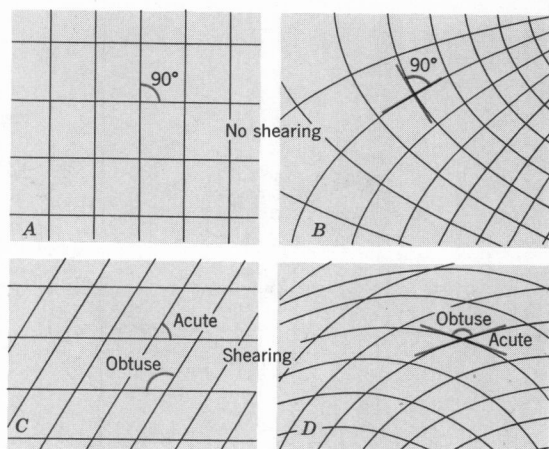

Figure 1.12   Shearing of areas.

globe is cast upon a screen or upon the wall or ceiling. This shadow is a true geometric projection. All projections made with this apparatus are of the zenithal type, which are characterized by the following properties (Figure 1.14).

1. A line drawn from center point of the map to any other point gives the true compass direction taken by a great circle as it leaves the center point, headed for the outer point.

2. When a complete globe or hemisphere is shown, the map is circular in outline. Because any map can be trimmed down to have a circular outline, this feature is not a reliable criterion of the zenithal class.

3. The map possesses a center point around which all its properties are grouped. All changes

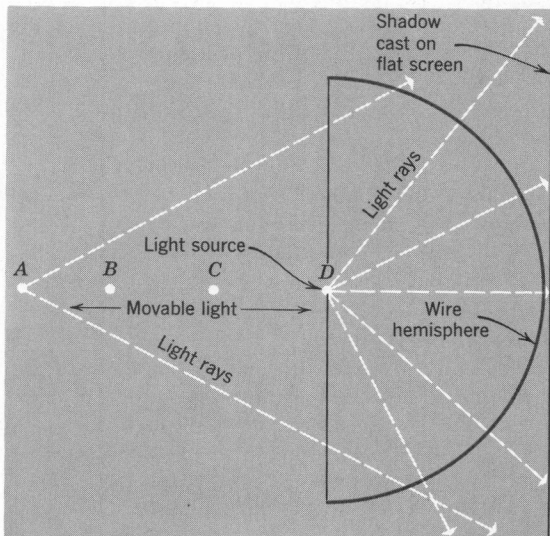

Figure 1.13   Principle of zenithal projections.

Figure 1.14 Properties of zenithal projections.

Figure 1.15 Principle of the conic projections.

of scale and distortion of shapes occur uniformly (concentrically) outward from this center.

4. All points equidistant from the center lie on a circle, known as the *horizon circle.* When the entire globe is shown by a zenithal map, the circular edge of the map represents the opposite point, or *antipode,* on the globe. When a hemisphere is shown, the outer edge of the map represents a great circle, everywhere equidistant from the point on which the projection is centered.

5. All great circles which pass through the center point of the projection appear as straight lines on the map. Likewise, all straight lines drawn through the center point of the map are true great circles.

Zenithal projections appear in three positions, or orientations: (1) *polar,* (2) *equatorial,* and (3) *oblique* or *tilted,* illustrated in Figures 1.17, 1.18, and 1.19. In the polar position, the center of the projection coincides with the north or south pole; in the equatorial position, the center is somewhere on the equator; in the oblique position, the center is at any desired point intermediate between the equator and poles. Although the equatorial and oblique types may not seem to be radially symmetrical, they nevertheless possess, just as truly as the polar type, the five characteristics described above.

The *conic* group of projections is based on the principle of transferring the geographic grid from a globe to a cone, then developing the cone to a flat map. This principle, too, can be demonstrated in the laboratory with the wire globe and a point source of light (Figure 1.15). Instead of a vertical flat screen, however, a translucent cone of stiff paper is seated on the wire globe, much as a

lampshade is seated on a lamp. The shadow of the wires cast upon the conical shade gives a conic projection. If this shadow were traced in pencil or ink and the cone unrolled, a true conic projection would result. Simple conic projections possess the following features (Figure 1.21). All meridians are straight lines, converging to a common point

Figure 1.16 Principle of the cylindric projections.

at the north (or south) pole. All parallels are arcs of concentric circles, whose common center lies at the north (or south) pole. A complete conic projection is a sector of a circle, never a complete circle. A conic projection cannot show the whole globe and usually shows little more than the northern (or southern) hemisphere.

Cylindric projections are based on the principle of transferring the geographic grid first onto a cylinder wrapped about the earth, then unrolling the cylinder to make a flat map (Figure 1.16). Simple cylindric projections are easy to draw because they consist of intersecting horizontal and vertical lines. (See Figure 1.22.) The completed map is rectangular in outline, and the whole circumference of the globe can be shown. When the cylinder is tangent to the equator, meridians are equally spaced vertical lines. Parallels are spaced in various ways, according to the particular projection desired.

Many other kinds of map projections exist, each based upon some unique principle.

Several important map projections have been selected to illustrate the wide range of qualities available. Included are conformal and equal-area types, as well as those with unique properties.

1. *Orthographic projection.* The *orthographic* projection belongs to the zenithal class and employs a principle of construction illustrated in Figure 1.17. Parallel rays, or lines, are used to

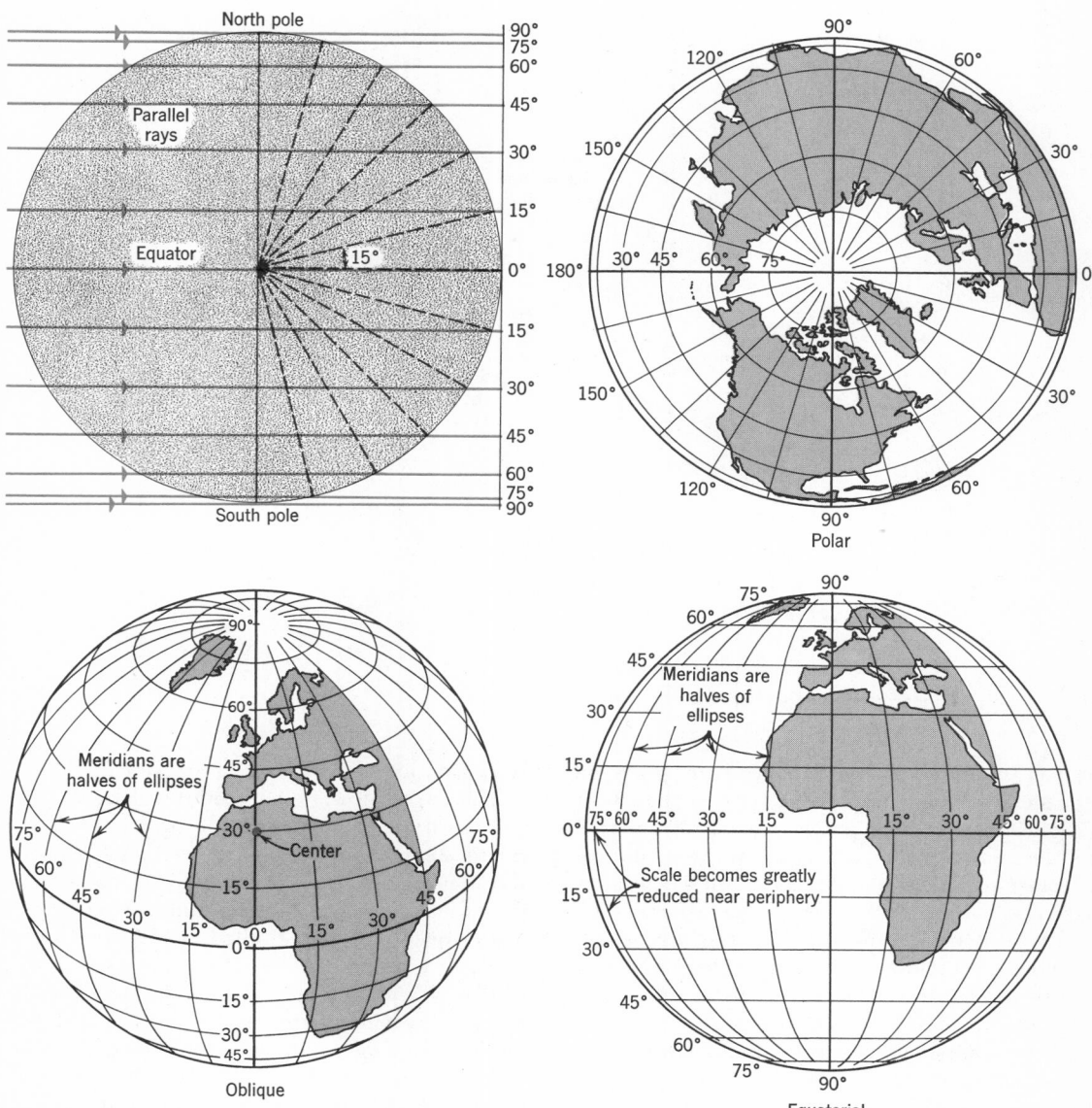

Figure 1.17   The orthographic projection.

Figure 1.18   The stereographic projection.

project the geographic grid of one hemisphere on a plane touching the globe at pole, equator, or at some intermediate point. The projection can also be imagined as resulting when the shadow of a hemispherical wire globe is cast on a screen by light rays coming from a very distant source, such as the sun. In the polar position the parallels of latitude crowd close together near the outer margin. In the equatorial position, the meridians are parts of true ellipses and show close crowding near the outer margin, whereas the parallels are straight, horizontal lines, spaced more closely near the poles. In the oblique position, the closer crowding of meridians and parallels near the outer margin

is also noticeable.

The largest possible portion of a globe that can be shown on the orthographic projection is one hemisphere. The projection is neither equal area nor conformal. The scale of miles is much larger near the center than near the outer edges. Use of this projection is quite limited, but it gives a visual effect of a globe in three dimensions and is very similar to a photograph taken of a globe. For this reason it often appears to illustrate articles or books on global political or military strategic problems. It gives a true picture of relations between countries or continents which are located near the central point of the projection. A little

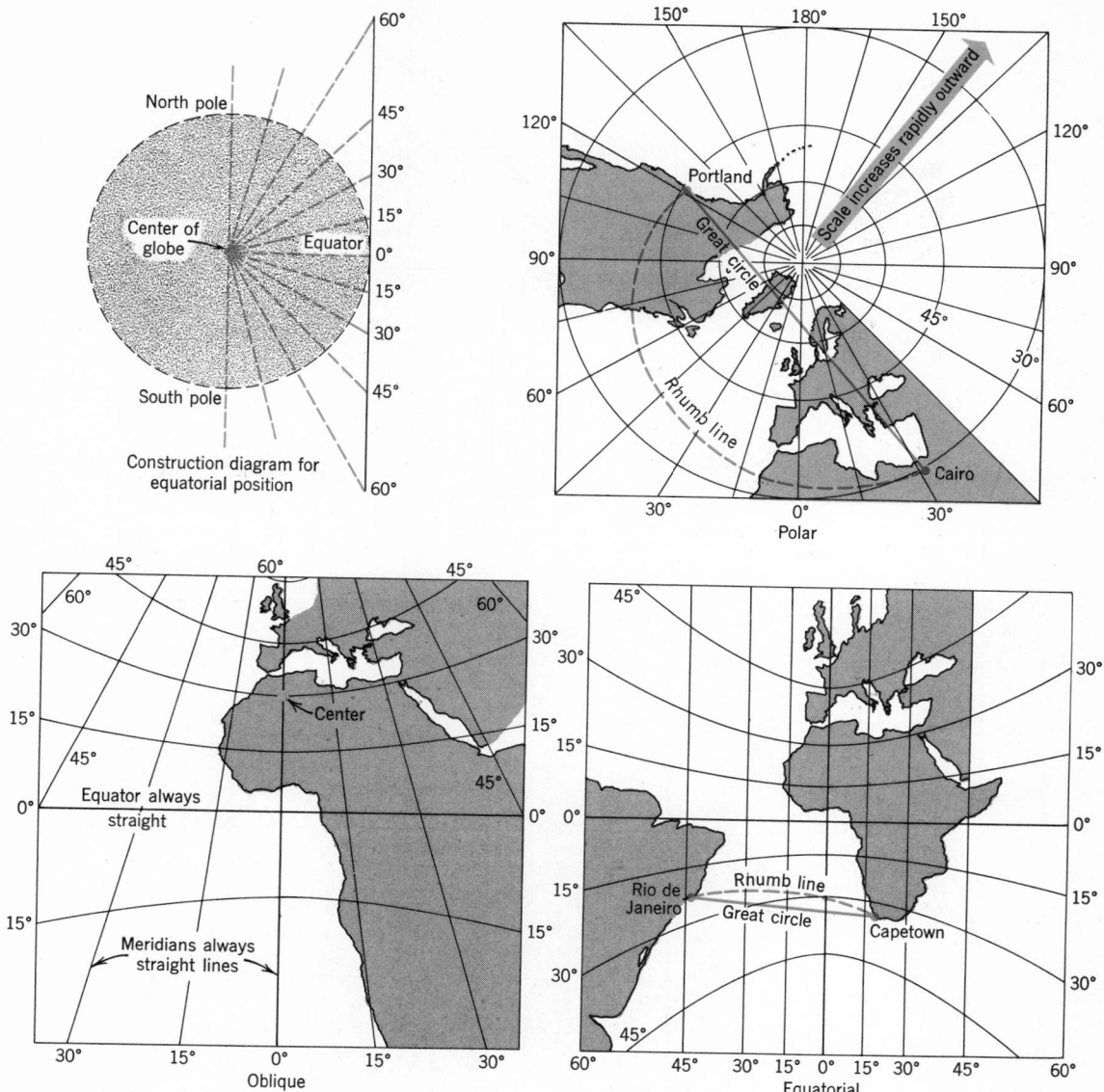

Figure 1.19 The gnomonic projection.

shading added to the map accentuates the perspective effect.

2. *Stereographic projection.* In the *stereographic* projection, a zenithal type, the point from which construction lines, or rays, emanate is located on the globe at a point diametrically opposite to the point where a plane touches the globe (Figure 1.18). Whereas the orthographic projection gives a map of exactly the same diameter as the original globe used, the stereographic projection gives a much larger map than the original globe. Furthermore, the stereographic net can show much more than one hemisphere, although it cannot show the whole globe. The principal

distinguishing characteristic of this projection is evident in all three of its positions: parallels and meridians show closer spacing near the map center and increasingly wider spacing toward the outer margins. On any stereographic projection the parallels and meridians are either straight lines or arcs of circles. No other kinds of curved lines occur. The reason for this is that the stereographic projection is truly conformal. All lines that are circles on the globe are shown as circles on the map. The scale of miles, however, always increases from the map center toward the periphery.

With the enormous growth in importance of polar regions in the age of scientific discovery and

Figure 1.20   The equidistant projection.

of long-range missile and aircraft operation, the polar stereographic projection has assumed great importance.

World Aeronautical Charts issued by the U.S. Coast and Geodetic Survey are based on a polar stereographic projection for latitudes 80° to 90°. The data of scientific observations of the Arctic Ocean and Antarctic continent are usually shown on this projection. The U.S. Weather Bureau's daily weather map is printed on a polar stereographic projection.

3. *Gnomonic projection (great-circle sailing chart)*. The *gnomonic* projection, a zenithal type, is made by drawing rays from a point at the center of the globe, as illustrated in Figure 1.19. The resulting network is easily recognized because the spacing of meridians and parallels increases enormously outward from the map center and results in great distortion of shapes of land areas in the outer part of the map. For geometrical reasons evident from the construction lines in Figure 1.19, it is impossible to show a complete hemisphere; it is even impractical to include the greater part of a hemisphere. For this reason, a gnomonic map is usually trimmed to a rectangular shape.

The gnomonic projection, with its grotesque distortions of both scale and shapes, would find little use were it not for one unique and important property: On a gnomonic map all straight lines are great circles. Conversely, all great circles appear as straight lines. Note that on all three of the projections illustrated in Figure 1.19, all meridians and the equator are straight lines, regardless of where they are located on the map. For navigational purposes the plotting of great-circle courses is accomplished by merely connecting with a straight line any two desired points. For this reason the gnomonic projection goes by the name *great-circle sailing chart* when adapted to navigational uses. Illustrations of great-circle routes plotted on a gnomonic net are shown in Figure 1.19 on the polar and equatorial maps. (Refer to Figure 1.22 to see these same routes plotted on the Mercator projection.)

4. *Equidistant projection*. Fourth of the zenithal types is the *equidistant* projection (Figure 1.20). As its name implies, this network is made by spacing the meridians (or parallels) equidistantly outward from the map center. Moreover, there is nothing to stop the cartographer from extending the map to include the whole globe. The opposite pole, or *antipode*, is then shown as a circle surrounding the map. Thus constructed the scale of miles remains constant along all radial straight lines emanating from the map center. This gives the map a specialized use for air navigation. When centered on a particular city or airport,

great-circle routes can easily be laid off and measured by drawing a line from the central point to any desired point on the map and finding the distance on a graphic scale having equally spaced units.

The equidistant net is often used for small-scale hemispherical maps. The polar position makes a pleasing map to show grouping of the world's principal land areas about the Arctic Ocean.

5. *Conic projection*. The conic projection is based on the principle that a cone can be placed over a globe in such a way as to have its apex directly over the north pole and to touch the globe along a single parallel (Figure 1.15). If the parallels and meridians are then projected upon the cone by drawing rays from the globe's center, and the cone is unrolled to a flat surface, a conic map results (Figure 1.21). Meridians are straight lines radiating from the pole; parallels are arcs of concentric circles, centered on the pole. The conic projection makes a fairly good general-purpose map, without shearing of areas but can effectively show little more than the northern hemisphere. Certain improved types, notably the Lambert conformal conic, are in wide use.

6. *Mercator projection*. Perhaps the best known of all map projections is the *Mercator* net, devised by Gerardus Mercator in 1569 (Figure 1.22). It is based upon a mathematical formula. The principle, however, can be explained without mathematical expression, as follows. On any cylindrical projection in which the meridians are straight vertical lines, equidistantly spaced, the meridians have had to be spread apart. (See right side of Figure 1.22.) Only along the equator are they the same distance apart as on a globe of the same equatorial scale. In order to maintain them as parallel lines, the normally converging meridians have had to be spread apart in a greater and greater ratio as the poles are approached. At 60° N and S lat., the meridians are spread apart twice as far as originally, because at that place a degree of longitude is only half what it is at the equator. At the poles the spreading is infinitely greater, because the poles themselves are infinitely tiny points. Now, to maintain the map as a truly conformal map, we must space the parallels increasingly far apart toward the poles, using the same ratio of increase that resulted when the meridians were spread to make vertical lines. For example, near the 60th parallel north, parallels must be spread twice as far apart as on the globe because, as explained above, the meridians here are also spread twice as far apart. At 80° latitude the scale is enlarged almost six times. Near the poles the spacing of parallels increases enormously and rapidly approaches infinity. Because an enormous

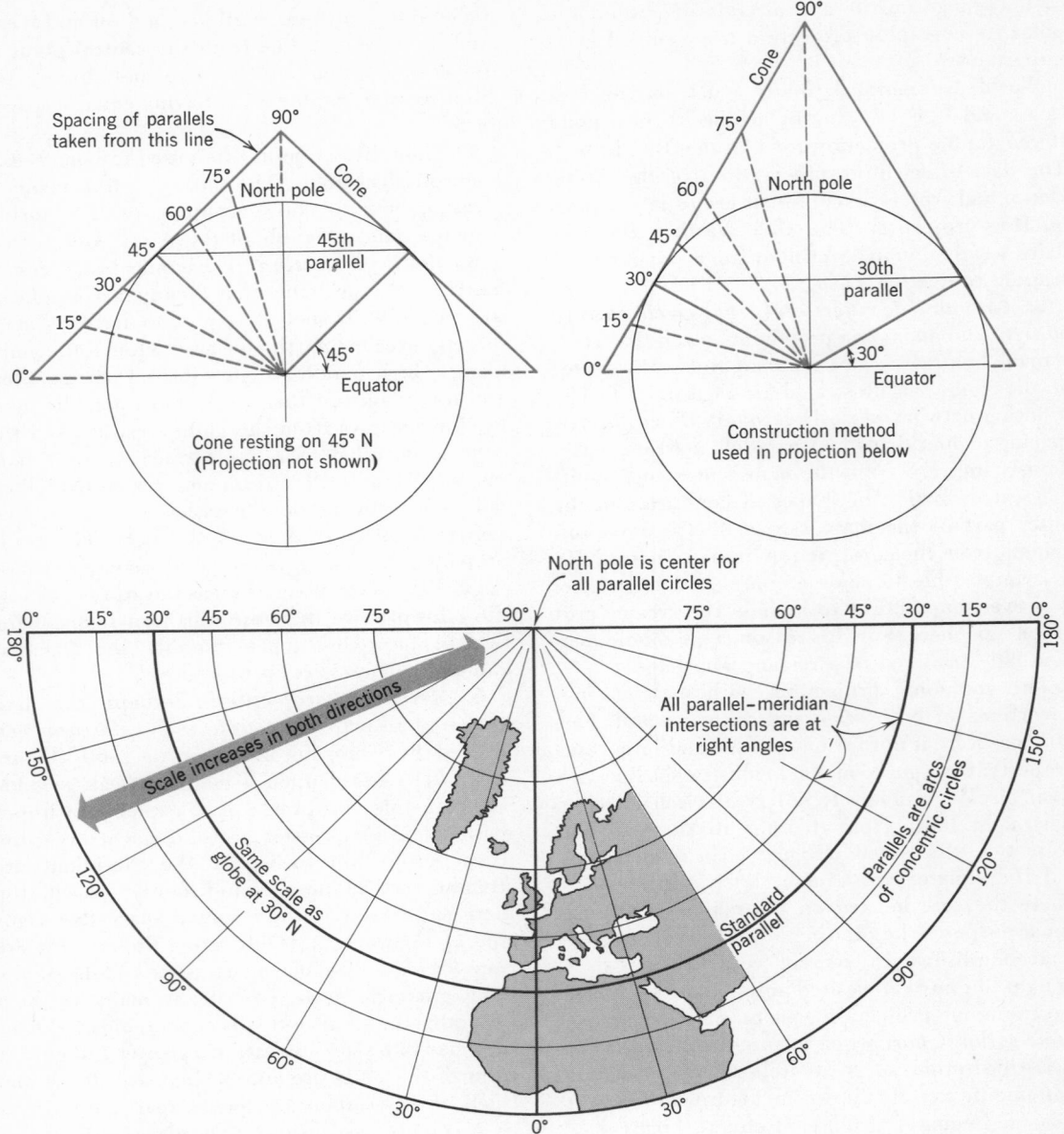

Figure 1.21 The conic projection.

sheet of paper would be needed to show extreme polar regions, the Mercator map is usually cut off about 80° or 85° N and S lat. The poles can never be shown.

The Mercator chart is a true conformal projection. Any small island or country is shown in its true shape. The scale of the map, however, becomes enormously greater toward the poles.

The really important, unique feature of an equatorial Mercator projection is that a straight line drawn anywhere on the map, in any direction desired, is a line of constant compass bearing. Such a line is known to navigators as a *rhumb line*, or

loxodrome (Figure 1.22). If this line is followed, the ship's (or plane's) compass will show that the course is always at a constant angle with respect to geographic north. Once the proper compass bearing is determined, the ship is kept on the same bearing throughout the voyage, if the rhumb line is to be followed. The Mercator chart is the only one of all known projections on which all rhumb lines are true straight lines, and vice versa. A protractor can be used with reference to any meridian on the map, and the compass bearing of any straight line can be measured off directly.

The relation of great-circle routes to rhumb lines

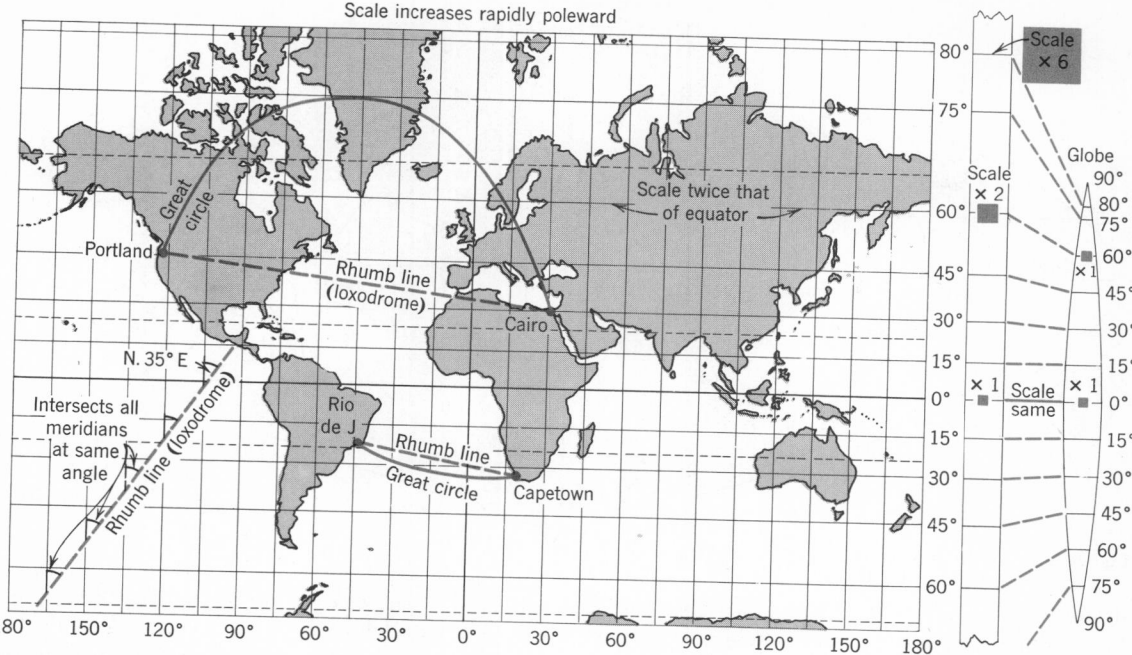

Figure 1.22 The Mercator projection.

is shown by two examples on Figures 1.19 and 1.22. Note that on the gnomonic map great circles are straight and rhumb lines curved, whereas on the Mercator chart rhumb lines are straight and great circles curved. Along the equator and all meridians (but only on these lines) rhumb lines and great circles are identical and are straight lines on both charts.

Although indispensable for navigational uses, the equatorial Mercator projection has serious shortcomings for use as a world map to show geographical information dealing with areas of distribution. Except for equatorial regions, for which it provides an excellent grid, distortions of scale are very serious. Because of infinite stretching toward the poles, this map fails completely to show how the land areas of North America, Asia, and Europe are grouped around the polar sea. In the

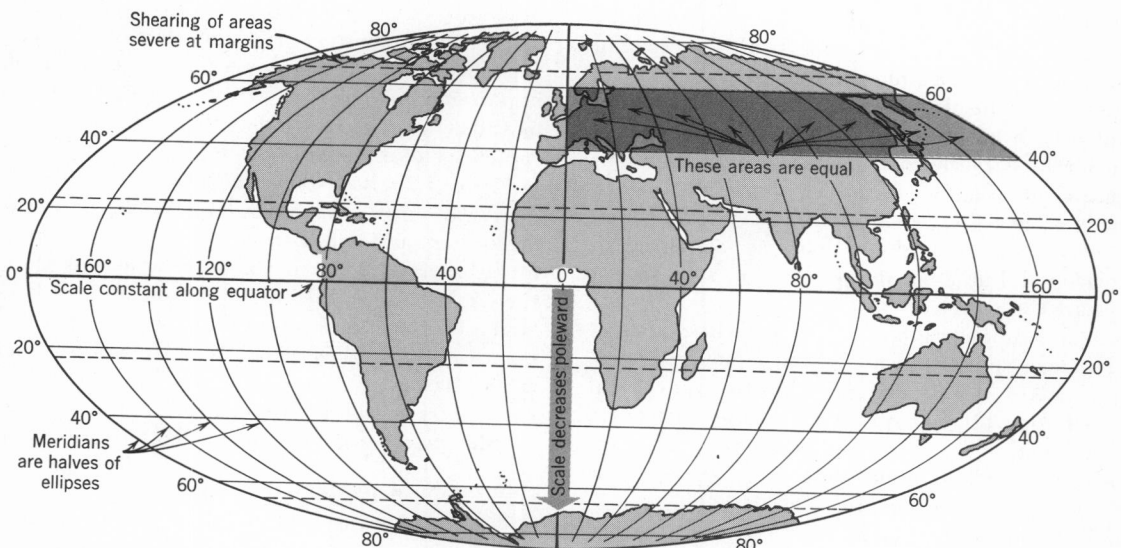

Figure 1.23 The Mollweide homolographic projection.

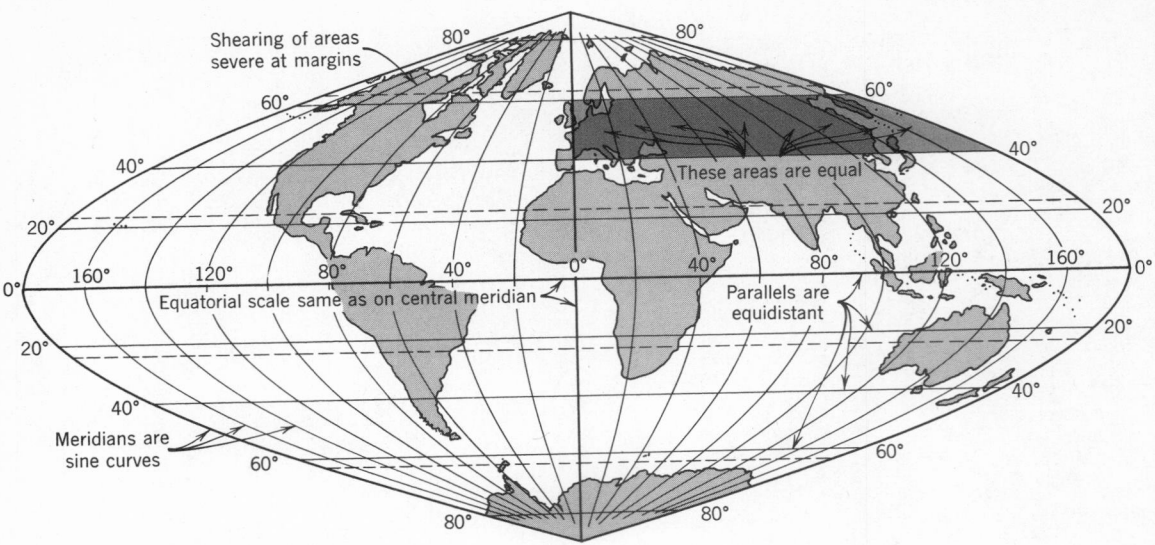

Shearing of areas severe at margins

80° 80°

60° 60°

40° 40°

These areas are equal

20° 20°

160° 120° 80° 40° 0° 40° 80° 120° 160° 0°
Equatorial scale same as on central meridian

Parallels are equidistant

20° 20°

40° 40°

Meridians are sine curves

60° 60°

80° 80°

Figure 1.24   The sinusoidal projection.

mind of an inexperienced user it may enhance a false sense of isolation between inhabitants of these lands.

On the other hand, certain forms of geographical information are best shown on the Mercator projection. Because of its accurate depiction of the compass directions of lines, the Mercator net is preferred for maps of direction of flow of ocean currents and winds, direction of pointing of the compass needle, or lines of equal value of air pressure and air temperature. Examples of such uses of the Mercator projection will be seen in later chapters.

7.   *Homolographic projection.* One projection rather widely used by geographers to show the entire globe is the *homolographic* projection (Figure 1.23). "Homolographic" is a word often used to mean "equal area," a property this projection possesses. One hemisphere is outlined by a circle; the other hemisphere is divided into two parts and added with an elliptical outline to either side of the circle. All other meridians, except the straight central meridian, are halves of ellipses. The equator is twice as long as the central meridian, which is also true on a globe. Parallels are straight, horizontal lines, becoming more closely spaced toward the poles.

The homolographic projection has distinct advantages and disadvantages. Its equal-area property makes it valuable for showing the global distribution of geographical properties that cover areas, such as crops, soil types, or political units. Severe distortion in the polar regions, however, has hindered its wider use.

8.   *Sinusoidal projection.* In some ways the *sinusoidal* projection is similar to the homolographic projection. It is an equal-area projection

with straight central meridian and horizontal straight parallels (Figure 1.24). The difference lies in the type of curve used in meridians. Whereas the homolographic net uses ellipses, the sinusoidal net uses a type of line known as a *sine curve*.

The same advantages and disadvantages apply to the sinusoidal projection. Distortion in polar areas is not quite so great in the sinusoidal net but is nevertheless offensive.

9.   *Homolosine projection.* The *homolosine* projection, invented by Dr. Paul Goode in 1923, is a combination of the homolographic and sinusoidal types (Figure 1.25). The sinusoidal projection is used between 40° N and S lat., the homolographic for the remaining poleward parts.

In both homolographic and sinusoidal projections the shearing of polar areas is especially marked to the extreme right and left of the map. This distortion can be reduced by centering each important land area on its own straight central meridian and fitting together the parts. The *interrupted* form of the homolosine projection, shown in Figure 1.25, has North America, Eurasia, South America, Africa, and Australia, each based on the best-suited meridian. Because the map cannot thus fit together between the land areas, except along the equator, large gaps occur. If our interest is in land areas only, as, for example, if we wish to show the areas under wheat cultivation, the interruption is not serious. To show oceans of the world we may center the oceans on central meridians, making the interruptions occur on land areas.

Summary of projections

Nine projections have been described and illustrated. This should serve to give the geography student a good start into map-projection principles.

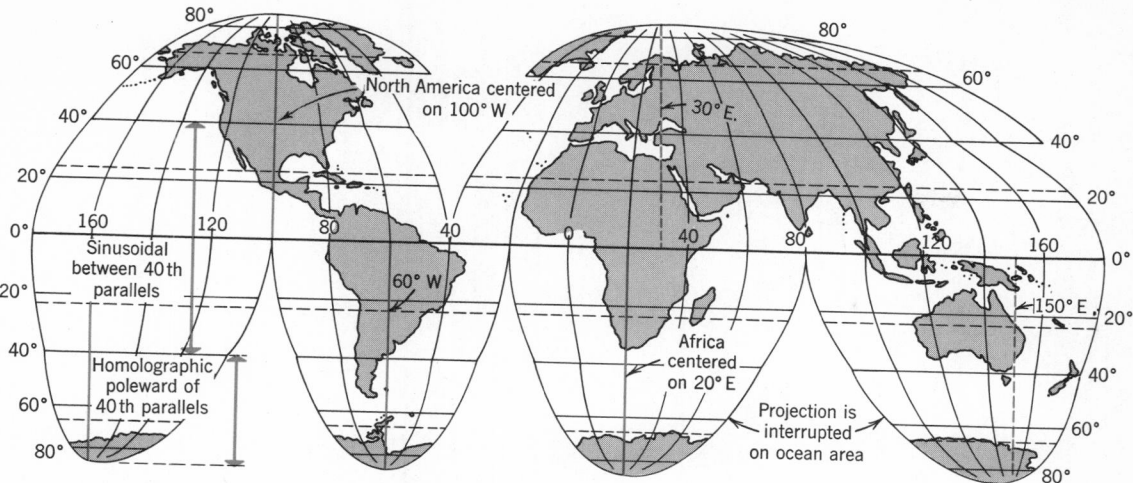

Figure 1.25 Goode's interrupted homolosine projection. (Based on Goode Base Map. Copyright by the University of Chicago. Used by permission of the University of Chicago Press.)

But, because more than 200 projections have been invented, unfamiliar types will frequently be encountered.

The following admonitions may serve to point out some of the principles of selecting a projection:

Where a map is required, select the projection best suited to the need. For example, use an equal-area map to show the areal distribution of things. Always choose a conformal projection to show lines whose compass directions are important and cannot be distorted. Use pole-centered maps for high latitudes.

Certain properties of interest to geographers change systematically from the equator toward either pole. That is to say, the properties depend on latitude. Examples are world temperatures, climates, soils, or vegetation types. To show such properties, choose a map with horizontal, straight parallels so that the eye can easily follow a given latitude zone.

Before you begin to draw conclusions and analyze geographical factors from a map, be sure that you know the qualities of the projection, whether equal-area, conformal, or neither. If in doubt, compare two or more projections of the same areas

and see what possible erroneous concepts each might give. The more of the earth's surface a map shows, the greater should your caution become.

Consult a good globe whenever points or areas are to be related in distance and direction. There is no satisfactory substitute for a true-scale model of the earth's surface features as a study aid to understanding the problems and principles of geography.

REFERENCES FOR FURTHER STUDY

Deetz, C. H. and O. S. Adams (1945), Elements of map projection, *Special Publ.* 68, U.S. Dept. Commerce, U.S. Govt. Printing Office, Washington, D.C., 226 pp.

Chamberlin, W. (1947), *The round earth on flat paper*, Nat. Geog. Soc., Washington, D.C., 126 pp.

Raisz, E. (1948), *General cartography*, McGraw-Hill Book Co., New York, 354 pp.

Robinson, A. H. and R. D. Sale (1969), *Elements of cartography*, third edition, John Wiley and Sons, New York, 343 pp.

Strahler, A. N. (1969), *Physical geography*, third edition, John Wiley and Sons, New York, 733 pp. See Chapters 1 and 2.

REVIEW QUESTIONS

1. Offer at least five proofs of the earth's approximate sphericity.

2. How did Richer contribute evidence that the earth is an oblate ellipsoid rather than a true sphere?

3. What geometrical form has a cross section of the earth cutting through the poles? What is the oblateness of the earth? What fraction approximately expresses the oblateness?

4. What is a great circle? How is it formed? How many great circles can be drawn upon the surface of a sphere? What is a small circle?

5. List six properties of great circles. Of what practical importance are great circles?

6. What is a meridian? How are meridians formed on a globe? List the characteristics of meridians.

7. What is a parallel? How are parallels formed? List the characteristics of parallels.

8. Define and explain longitude. How is longitude written? Give an example. What is a prime meridian? Where is the Greenwich meridian? How long is a degree of longitude, in miles, at the equator? at 60° latitude? at the poles?

9. Define and explain latitude. How is latitude written? Give an example. How long is a degree of latitude, in miles? Does it vary from equator to poles? How much? Why?

10. What is a nautical mile? A knot? At what latitude is the international nautical mile most nearly equal to the length of one minute of arc of the ellipsoid?

11. What is a map projection? What is the basic problem of map projection?

12. For what purposes is a globe inferior to a flat map? For what purposes is a globe preferable to a flat map?

13. Explain the concept of map scale. What is the representative fraction? Do any map projections pre-serve constant scale in all places and directions over the map?

14. What is an equal-area map projection? Name two equal-area types.

15. What is a conformal map projection? Name two conformal types.

16. Are projections which are neither equal-area nor conformal of any value? Illustrate with a specific example.

17. For what purposes might you select the orthographic projection?

18. Why is the stereographic projection favored for polar regions? Why is it a good base for the U.S. Weather Bureau daily weather maps?

19. Explain how a navigator uses the gnomonic projection. Why is it often called a great-circle sailing chart?

20. How would you go about constructing an equidistant projection? For what purpose might it be used? What properties has the simple conic projection?

21. Explain the principle of the Mercator projection. Is this an equal-area or conformal projection? What shape has a complete Mercator map showing the entire globe? How does the map scale at 60° latitude compare with the equatorial scale?

22. What is a rhumb line? What is a loxodrome? What projection shows all rhumb lines as straight lines? What use is made of rhumb lines and great circles in navigation?

23. Compare the homolographic and sinusoidal projections in appearance. Are these projections equal-area, conformal, or neither?

24. What advantages has Goode's interrupted homolosine projection over the homolographic and sinusoidal projections?

CHAPTER 2
Seasons and Time

OF the utmost importance to man is the relation between the earth and the sun's rays. The angles at which rays strike the earth at different latitudes and at different times of day and year determine the apparent path of the sun in the sky, the lengths of day and night, and the occurrence of seasons. Rhythmic variations in the rates of receipt of solar energy by different parts of the earth at different times act as fundamental controls of atmospheric temperatures, which in turn have a major effect on air pressure, winds, precipitation, storms, and oceanic circulation—all of which taken together make up the earth's varied climates. That is why one must thoroughly master earth-sun relationships before going ahead to the subjects of weather and climate. Because the earth is turning on its axis at the same time that it is moving in a path about the sun, and because the earth's axis is tilted with respect to the plane of its orbit, these relationships are often difficult to understand. We must learn to think in terms of three dimensions, to imagine ourselves viewing the earth from various vantage points in space; then imagine the same situations as they would appear to an observer standing at various points on the earth.

Rotation of the earth

The spinning of the earth on its polar axis is termed *rotation*. In this study of earth-sun relationships we use the period of rotation, the *mean solar day*, consisting of 24 mean solar hours. This day is the average time required for the earth to make one complete turn in respect to the sun.

Direction of earth rotation can be determined by applying one of the following rules. (*a*) If we imagine ourselves to be looking down upon the north pole of the earth, the direction of turning is counterclockwise. (*b*) If we place a finger upon a point on a globe near the equator and push the finger eastward, it will cause the globe to rotate in the correct direction (Figure 2.1). This demonstrates a common expression, "eastward rotation of the earth." (*c*) Direction of earth rotation is opposite that of the apparent motion of the sun, moon, and stars. Because these bodies appear to travel westward across the sky the earth must be turning in an eastward direction.

The velocity of earth rotation, defined as rate of travel of a point on the earth's surface in a circular path due to rotation alone, may easily be computed by dividing the length of parallel at the latitude of the point in question by 24, the approximate period of rotation. Thus at the equator, where the circumference is about 25,000 mi (40,000 km), the velocity of an object on the surface is about 1050 mi (1700 km) per hour. At the 60th parallel the velocity is half this amount, or about 525 mi (850 km) per hour. At the poles it is, of course, zero. We are unaware of this motion because the rotation is at an almost perfectly constant rate.

Two important physical phenomena result from the decrease in rotational velocity with increase in latitude. First, there is a *centrifugal force* generated by the earth's turning which gives surface objects a faint tendency to fly off into space. Because the force of gravity is 289 times greater than this centrifugal force at the equator, objects cannot leave the surface, but the practical effect is to reduce the weight of objects slightly. Near the equator, where the centrifugal force is strongest, this effect is most marked. For example, an object which would weigh 289 pounds at the equator if the earth were not turning actually weighs 1 pound less.

Another effect of the decreasing rotational velocity with increasing latitude is to cause objects in motion to be deflected slightly to the right or left of their paths. This effect will be more fully treated under the subject of the earth's wind systems.

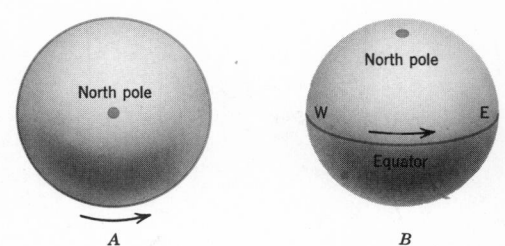

Figure 2.1 Direction of rotation is (*A*) counterclockwise at the north pole, and (*B*) eastward at the equator.

Proof of the earth's rotation

The several kinds of proofs offered for the earth's rotation are beyond the needs of the student of physical geography but one proof in particular, the *Foucault experiment*, is so outstanding as to warrant study. It has been described as follows.[1]

In 1851, the French physicist, M. Leon Foucault, suspended from the dome of the Pantheon, in Paris, a heavy iron ball by wire 200 feet long. A pin was fastened to the lowest side of the ball so that when swinging it traced a slight mark in a layer of sand placed beneath it. Carefully the long pendulum was set swinging. It was found that the path gradually moved around toward the right. [see Figure 2.2.] Now either the pendulum changed its plane or the building was gradually turned around. By experimenting with a ball suspended from a ruler one can readily see that turning the ruler will not change the plane of the swinging pendulum. If the pendulum swings back and forth in a north and south direction, the ruler can be entirely turned around without changing the direction of the pendulum's swing. If at the north pole a pendulum was set swinging toward a fixed star, say Arcturus, it would continue swinging toward the same star and the earth would thus be seen to turn around in a day. The earth would not seem to turn but the pendulum would seem to deviate toward the right, or clockwise.

At first thought it might seem as though the floor would turn completely around under the pendulum in a day, regardless of the latitude. It will be readily seen, however, that it is only at the pole that the earth would make one complete rotation under the pendulum in one day, or show a deviation of 15° in an hour. At the equator the pendulum will show no deviation, and at intermediate latitudes the rate of deviation varies.

Table 2.1 gives the hourly change in direction of the pendulum's swing and the total time re-

[1] W. E. Johnson, *Mathematical geography*, American Book Co., New York, 1907, pp. 54–57.

TABLE 2.1

Latitude	Hourly Change in Pendulum Direction, Degrees	Total Time for 360° Change in Direction, Hours
0°	None	None
5	1.31	275
10	2.60	138
15	3.88	93
20	5.13	70
25	6.34	57
30	7.50	48
35	8.60	42
40	9.64	37
45	10.61	34
50	11.49	31
55	12.29	29
60	12.99	28
65	13.59	26.5
70	14.10	25.6
75	14.49	24.9
80	14.77	24.5
85	14.94	24.1
90	15.00	24.0

quired for the direction to change through 360°.

Another proof of the earth's rotation lies in the oblate ellipsoidal form of the earth. In order to explain the bulging at the equator and shortening of the polar axis, centrifugal force due to rotation on an axis is required.

Revolution of the earth

The motion of the earth in its orbit around the sun is termed *revolution*. The period of revolution, or *year*, is the time required for the earth to complete one circuit around the sun. The year is, however, defined in different ways. For example, the time required for the earth to return to a given point in its orbit with reference to the fixed stars is called the *sidereal year*.

For earth-sun relationships we use the *tropical year*, which is the period of time from one vernal equinox to the next, and has a length of approximately $365\frac{1}{4}$ days. Every four years the extra one-fourth day difference between the tropical year and the calendar year of 365 days accumulates to nearly one whole day. By inserting a 29th day in February every leap year we are able to correct the calendar with respect to the tropical year. Further minor corrections are necessary to perfect this system.

In its orbit the earth moves in such a direction that if we imagine ourselves in space, looking down upon the earth and sun so as to see the north pole of the earth, the earth is traveling counterclockwise around the sun (Figure 2.3). This is the same direction of turning as the earth's rotation.

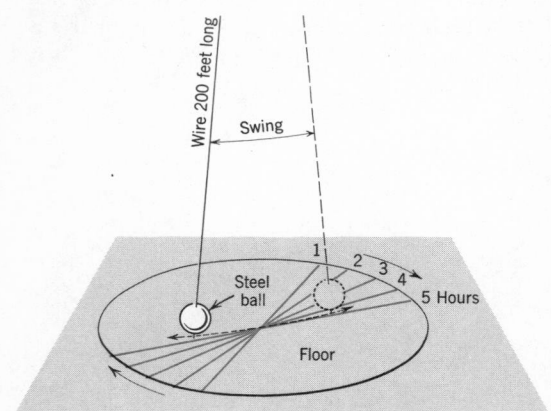

Figure 2.2 The Foucault pendulum.

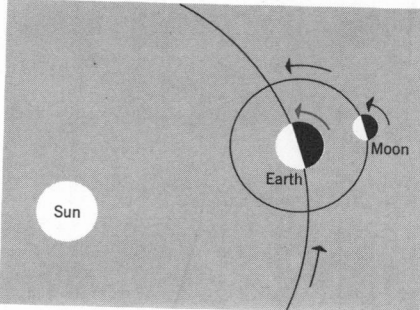

Figure 2.3   Direction of earth rotation and revolution.

Earth's orbit

The earth's orbit is an ellipse, rather than circle, although the *ellipticity,* or degree of flattening of the ellipse, is very slight. The sun occupies one *focus* of the ellipse. Ellipses of various shapes are easily constructed using only a drawing board, two pins or thumb tacks, a piece of thread or thin string, and a pencil, as illustrated in Figure 2.4. The thread is made into a loop which passes around the two pins and serves to guide the pencil point. By this device we maintain the sum of the distances from pencil point to each pin always the same. Each pin is located at one *focus* of the ellipse. The two *foci* lie on a line which is the maximum diameter of the ellipse and is called the *major axis.* The shortest diameter, drawn at right angles to the major axis, is known as the *minor axis.* The size of the ellipse may be controlled by the length of the loop of thread, whereas the ellipticity may be controlled by changing the distance between the two foci.

Perihelion and aphelion

The average distance between earth and sun is about 93 million miles (150 million km), but

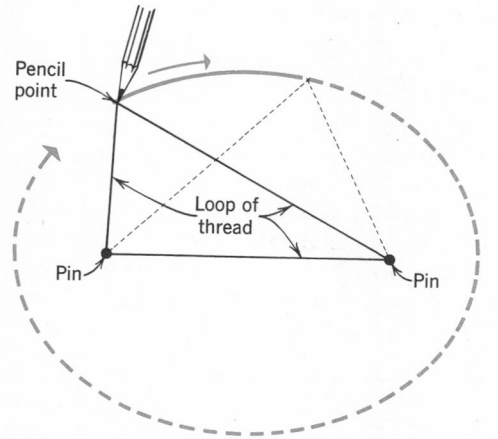

Figure 2.4   Construction of an ellipse.

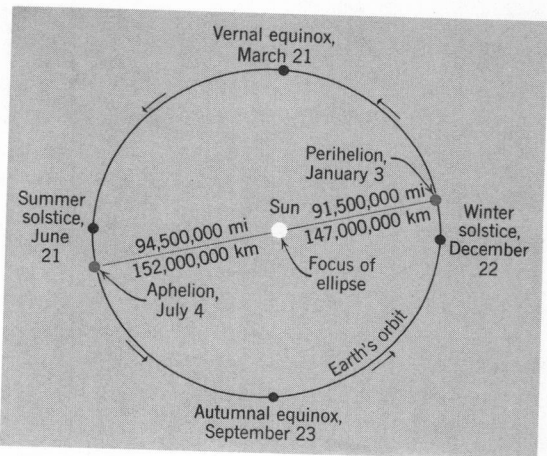

Figure 2.5   Earth's orbit and seasons.

because of the ellipticity of the orbit the distance may be $1\frac{1}{2}$ million miles (2.5 million km) greater or less than this figure (Figure 2.5). The distance is least, or about $91\frac{1}{2}$ million miles (147 million km), on about January 3, at which time the earth is said to be in *perihelion* (from the Greek *peri,* around or near; and *helios,* the sun). On about July 4 the earth is at its farthest point from the sun, or in *aphelion* (from the Greek *ap,* away from; *helios,* sun), at a distance of $94\frac{1}{2}$ million miles (152 million km).

These differences in distance do cause some differences in the amount of solar energy received by the earth, but they are not the cause of summer and winter seasons. This is obvious because perihelion, when the earth should receive most heat, falls at the coldest time of year in the northern hemisphere. Moreover, opposite seasons are present simultaneously in the northern and southern hemispheres, proving that another cause exists. In theory, however, summers and winters should be slightly intensified in the southern hemisphere and slightly moderated in the northern hemisphere as a result of the relation of the dates of perihelion and aphelion to the summer and winter seasons.

Inclination of the earth's axis

Most globes that are made to rotate on the polar axis are fixed in a tilted position. So accustomed are we to seeing the earth represented this way that a globe with its axis vertical seems unnatural. In this position the globe may be used to illustrate the fact that the plane of the equator is inclined $23\frac{1}{2}°$ with the plane of the orbit. The earth's axis makes an angle of $66\frac{1}{2}°$ with plane of the orbit, and is tilted $23\frac{1}{2}°$ from a line perpendicular to that plane (Figure 2.6). No other single fact connected with earth-sun relationships is so important as the inclination of the earth's axis.

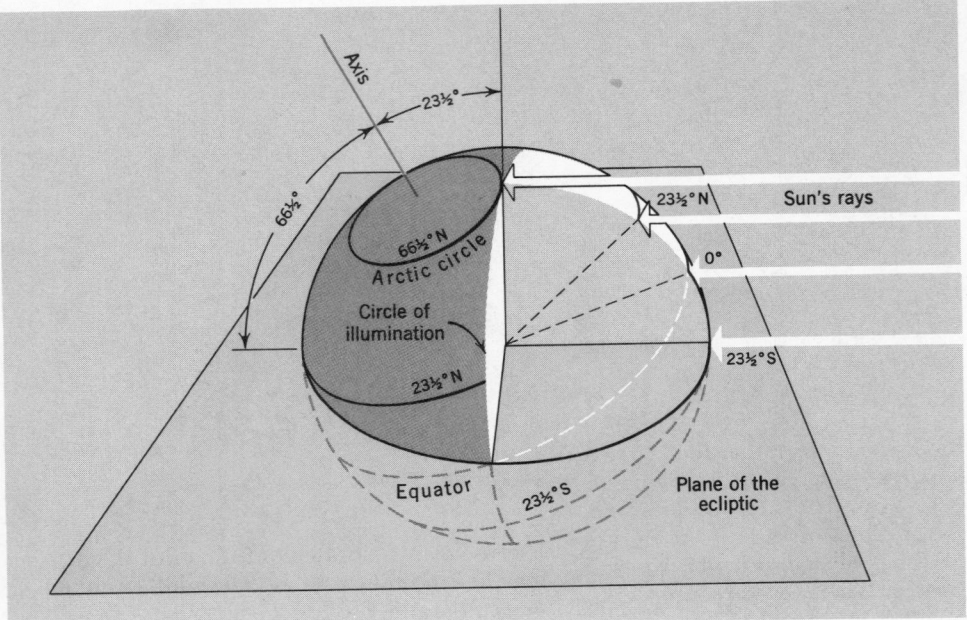

Figure 2.6 Inclination of the earth's axis. (After A. N. Strahler, *The Earth Sciences*, Harper and Row, New York.)

The earth's axis, although always making the angle $66\frac{1}{2}°$ with the plane of the orbit, maintains a fixed orientation with respect to the stars. That is to say, the earth's axis constantly points to the same spot in the heavens as it makes its yearly circuit around the sun. To help in visualizing this movement hold a globe so as always to keep the axis tilted at $66\frac{1}{2}°$ with horizontal. Move the globe in a small horizontal circle, representing the orbit, at the same time keeping the axis pointed at the same point on the ceiling (Figure 2.7).

As a direct consequence of the facts (1) that the earth's axis keeps a fixed angle with the plane of the orbit and (2) that the axis always points to the same place among the stars, it will be seen that at one point in its orbit the earth's axis leans toward the sun, that at an opposite point in the orbit the axis leans away from the sun, and at the two intermediate points the axis leans neither toward, nor away from, the sun (Figure 2.7). Here again, a globe, or, better still, four globes, may be used to aid in visualizing the facts.

Solstice and equinox

On June 21 or 22 the earth is so located in its orbit that the north polar end of its axis leans at the full $23\frac{1}{2}°$ angle toward the sun. The northern hemisphere is tipped toward the sun, and the southern hemisphere is tipped away from the sun. This condition is named the *summer solstice*. Six months later, on December 21 or 22, the earth is in an equivalent position on the opposite point

in its orbit. At this time, known as the *winter solstice*, the axis again leans the full $23\frac{1}{2}°$ directly toward the sun, but now it is the southern hemisphere that is tipped toward the sun.

Midway between the dates of the solstices occur the *equinoxes*, at which time the earth's axis makes a right angle with a line drawn to the sun, and neither the north nor south pole has any inclination toward the sun. The *vernal equinox* occurs on March 20 or 21; the *autumnal equinox* on September 22 or 23.[2] Conditions are identical on the two equinoxes as far as earth-sun relationships are concerned, whereas on the two solstices, the conditions of one hemisphere are the exact reverse of the other. For this reason it is necessary to consider each solstice separately, whereas the equinoxes can be treated together.

Winter solstice

Conditions at the winter solstice, December 21 or 22, are best studied with the aid of diagrams. Figure 2.8 is a cross-sectional representation to show the angles at which the sun's rays strike the earth. Keep in mind that "winter" applies only to the northern hemisphere and that the southern hemisphere is experiencing its summer season.

The great circle which at all times marks the

[2] The exact time of solstices and equinoxes ranges into two calendar days because of the one-fourth day difference in the tropical year and the calendar year, which builds up to one whole day every fourth year and is corrected by adding one day in leap year.

Figure 2.7   The seasons.

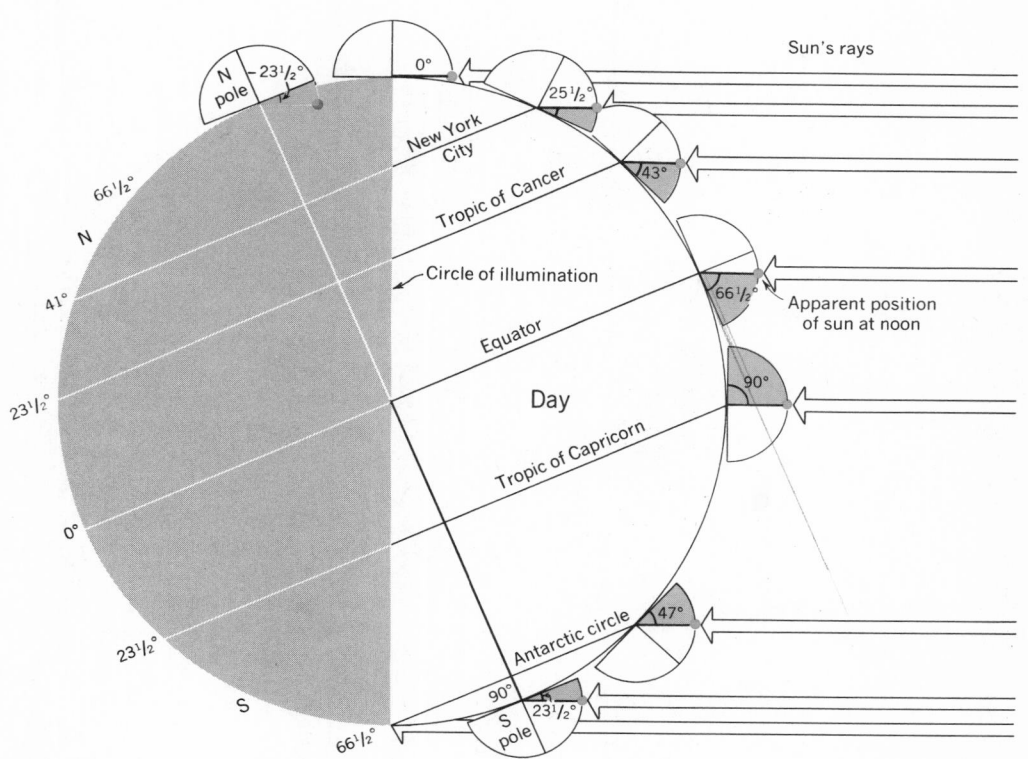

Figure 2.8   Winter solstice. (From A. N. Strahler, *The Earth Sciences*, Harper and Row, New York.)

boundary between sunlit and shadowed halves of the earth is called the *circle of illumination*. At the winter solstice it divides all parallels of latitude which it crosses except the equator into unequal parts. The circle of illumination is tangent to the *Arctic Circle* (66½° N lat.) and the *Antarctic Circle* (66½° S lat.). This occurrence explains why the two parallels are given special designation on the globe. The circle of illumination bisects the equator

in accordance with the law that any two intersecting great circles bisect each other.

Because of the position of the circle of illumination at the winter solstice, day and night are unequal in length over most of the globe. This inequality may be estimated from Figure 2.8 by noting what proportions of a given parallel lie on either side of the circle of illumination. The following facts are evident.

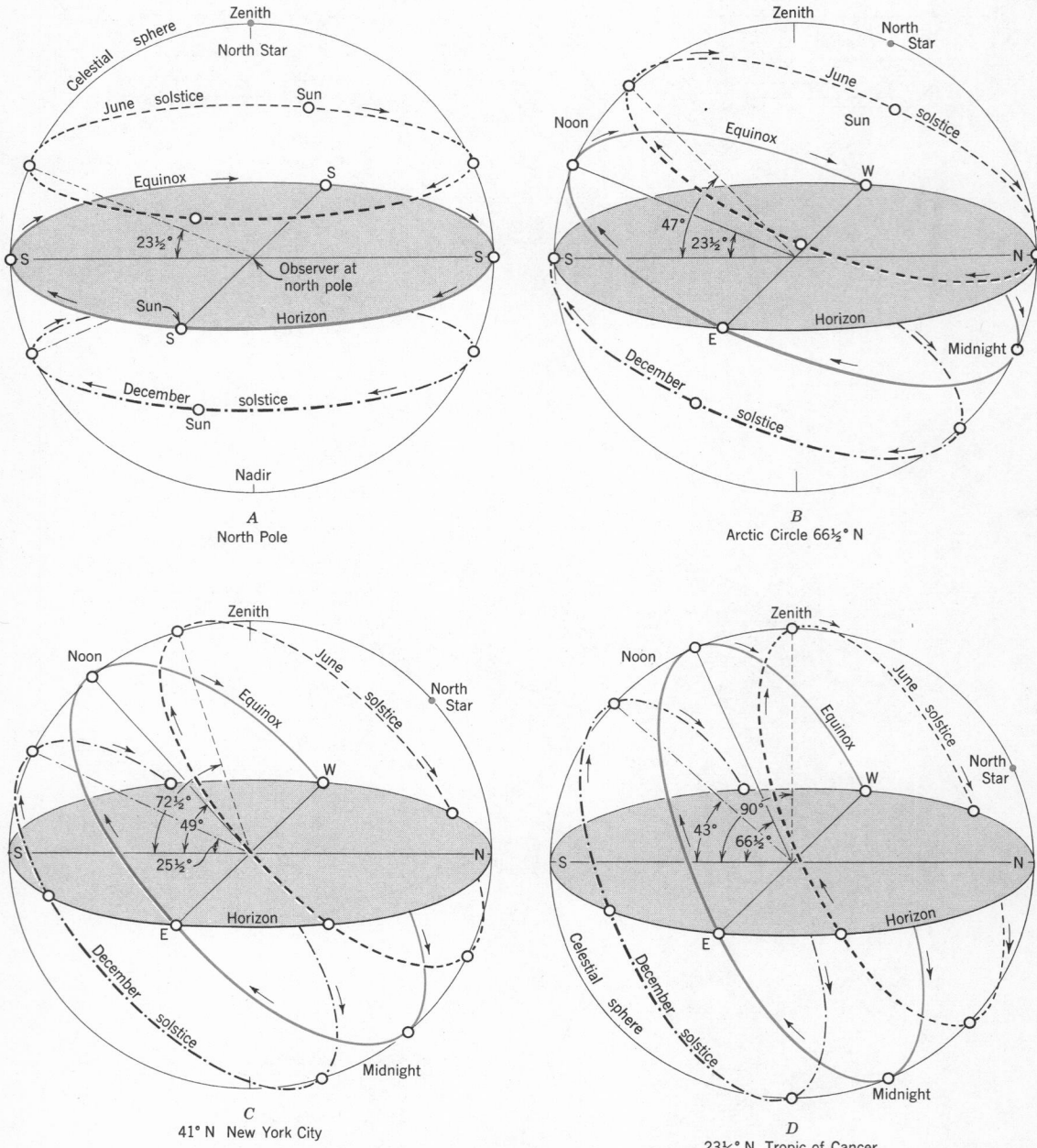

Figure 2.9 To the earth-bound observer the earth's surface is a flat, horizontal disc. The sun, moon, and stars seem to travel on the inner surface of a hemispherical dome above him. The path of the sun in the sky at various latitudes is shown here for the equinox and both solstices.

(a) Night is longer than day in the northern hemisphere.

(b) Day is longer than night in the southern hemisphere.

(c) The inequality between day and night increases from the equator poleward.

(d) At corresponding latitudes north and south of the equator the relative lengths of day and night are in exact opposite relation.

(e) Between the Arctic Circle, $66\frac{1}{2}$° N, and the north pole, night lasts the entire 24 hours.[3] This fact is evident from Figure 2.8 because the entire polar area north of the Arctic Circle lies on the shaded side of the circle of illumination and hence will not come into the sun's rays even though the earth turns through 360°.

[3]This statement does not take into account *twilight*, which provides considerable light near the Arctic Circle.

E
Equator
0° Lat.

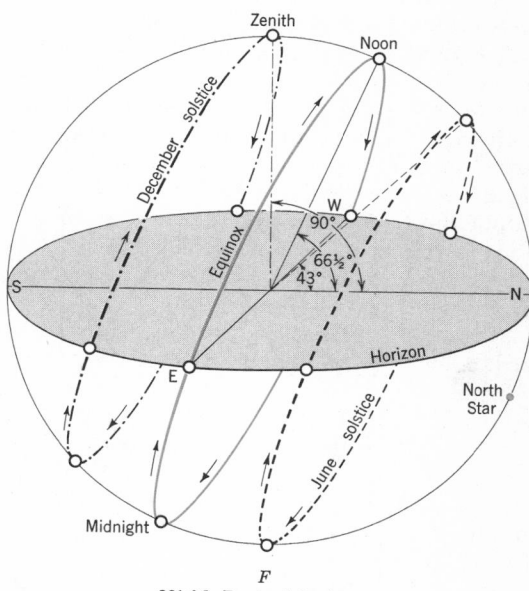

F
$23\frac{1}{2}$° S Tropic of Capricorn

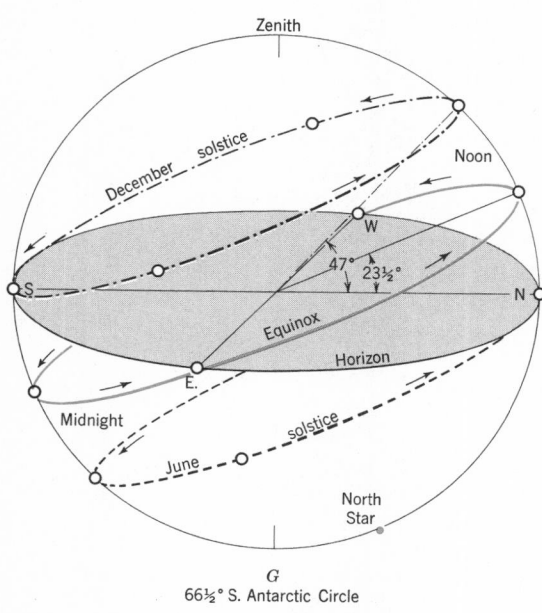

G
$66\frac{1}{2}$° S. Antarctic Circle

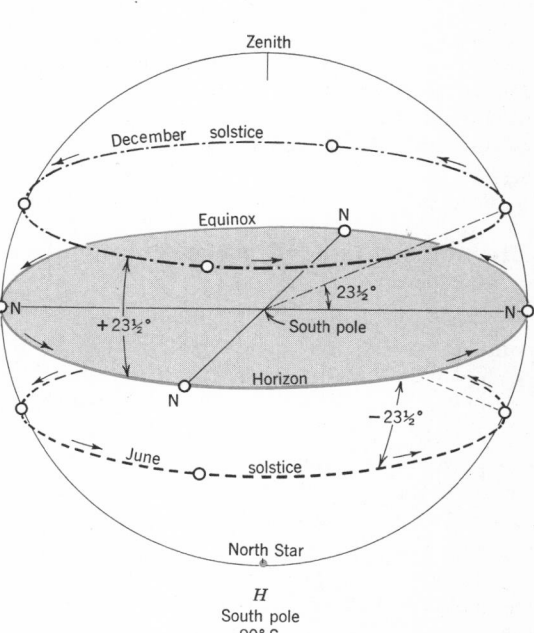

H
South pole
90° S

(*f*) Between the Antarctic Circle, 66½° S, and the south pole day lasts the entire 24 hours, because the earth's turning fails to bring any part of this area into the zone of darkness.

Solar noon occurs when the sun reaches its highest point in the sky. Noon occurs simultaneously at all points having the same longitude, that is, for all points lying on a single meridian. The vertical angle of the sun above the horizon at noon, designated the *sun's noon altitude*, may be determined from Figure 2.8 by measuring the angle between a ray from the sun and a line tangent to the globe at a selected latitude. Sun's noon altitude in degrees is given for various latitudes on the right-hand side of Figure 2.8. Although the earth's surface is curved, the apparent world in which we, as tiny individuals, live is a flat world. Within the limits of vision the horizon appears to make a circle on a flat plane. This explains why a straight tangent line may be used for measuring the altitude angle on the diagram.

At lat. 23½° S the sun's rays at noon strike the earth at an angle of 90° above the horizon. Thus the sun is exactly in the center of the sky, or *zenith*. The parallel 23½° S has therefore been designated the *Tropic of Capricorn*. At the Arctic Circle, 66½° N, the sun at noon is exactly on the horizon. At the south pole, the noon sun has an altitude of 23½° above the horizon, and maintains this angle throughout the full 24 hours.

The path of the sun in the sky at the winter solstice is illustrated for various latitudes in Figure 2.9. The horizon is drawn as a circle lying in a horizontal plane, and the sky is visualized as a hemispherical celestial dome. Below the horizon is the opposite celestial hemisphere, the two hemispheres together comprising the *celestial sphere*. The sun daily completes an entire circle inscribed on the celestial sphere. On certain occasions, as on the equinoxes, these circular paths are great circles on the celestial sphere; otherwise they are small circles.

Direction and time of sunrise and sunset at solstice

The compass direction of sunrise and sunset points on the horizon varies greatly with latitude, as shown in Figure 2.9. At the Antarctic Circle on the December solstice, sunrise and sunset occur at the same instant—midnight—at a point due south on the horizon. At all places between the Antarctic Circle and the Arctic Circle, the sun rises at some point between south and east, and sets at a point between south and west.

To determine approximately the length of day and night and times of sunrise and sunset at solstice for various latitudes, a small globe and a rubber

band can be used (Figure 2.10). Proceed as follows:

Winter solstice. Place the rubber band so as to represent the circle of illumination (great circle) crossing the equator at the 90° meridians west and east, and just tangent to the Arctic and Antarctic Circles where they cross the Greenwich and 180th meridians. Now select a particular latitude, for example, 40° N. Taking the Greenwich meridian as noon, count 15° of longitude to the hour, westward along the 40th parallel, until the rubber band is reached. This number of hours subtracted from 12:00 noon gives the approximate time of sunrise (local apparent solar time), and added to 12:00 noon gives the time of sunset. The lengths of day and night can be obtained by simple calculation. The shorter arc in this case gives the length of day; the longer arc, by way of the Pacific, gives length of night.

Summer solstice. Turn the globe around and use the Pacific side, leaving the rubber band in the same position as before. Be sure that the rubber band maintains a great circle and cuts the equator at the 90th meridians west and east.

Solstice conditions at the poles

At the poles the path of the sun in the sky is the most extraordinary of all places on the earth (Figure 2.9*A,H*). Here the sun does not rise and sink in a slanting path with respect to the horizon, as at other latitudes. Instead it follows a horizontal circle, remaining parallel with the horizon throughout the day. (In actuality this path is spiral, but so low a spiral that it cannot be detected by

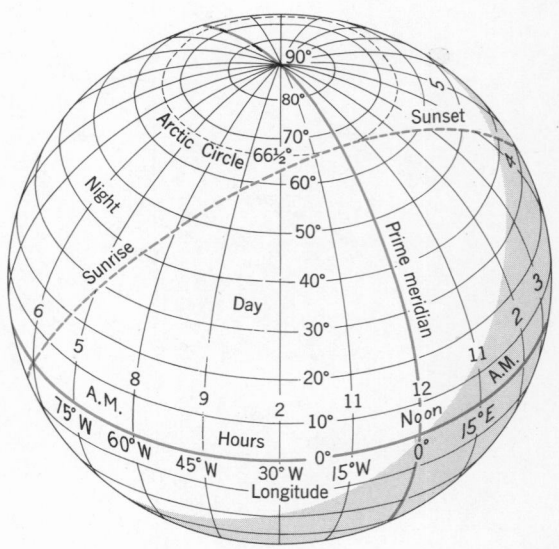

Figure 2.10 A small globe can be used as a graph for determining the lengths of day and night at any latitude.

Figure 2.11 This photograph of the sun was taken at midnight at Hammerfest, Norway, 70°40′ N. lat., during the summer solstice period. The sun has reached its lowest point in the sky. (Photograph by A. Kalland, Hammerfest.)

ordinary observation.) At the December solstice the sun at the north pole remains $23\frac{1}{2}°$ below the horizon throughout the day, while at the south pole it is constantly $23\frac{1}{2}°$ above the horizon. At the south pole we would have no natural way of determining when noon would occur because the sun's altitude remains constant. Moreover, all meridians converge to a point at the pole so that we could not refer the time to any local meridian.

Summer solstice

In almost every way the conditions at summer solstice, June 21 or 22, are the exact reverse of winter solstice conditions. At this time the north polar end of the earth's axis is inclined directly toward the sun and the northern hemisphere enjoys the same conditions of increased sunshine that the southern hemisphere had during the winter solstice (Figure 2.11). Instead of a special diagram to show the relation of sun's rays to the earth, it is suggested that Figure 2.8 be turned upside down, exchanging "north" for "south," "Arctic" for "Antarctic," and "Tropic of Cancer" for "Tropic of Capricorn." The various statements made in the previous pages concerning circle of illumination, length of day and night, and the sun's noon altitude at the winter solstice may be reread, with suitable changes to fit the reversed conditions of the summer solstice.

The path of the sun in the sky on June 21 is

shown in Figure 2.9. For all latitudes between the Arctic and Antarctic Circles the sun rises on the northeastern horizon, and sets on the northwestern horizon.

The equinoxes

On March 20 or 21 and September 22 or 23, the vernal and autumnal equinoxes, respectively, the relation of earth to sun's rays is identical and the two dates may be treated jointly. Figure 2.7 shows the general situation. Although the earth's axis is, as always, inclined $66\frac{1}{2}°$ to the plane of the orbit, the inclination is so oriented that it is neither toward nor away from the sun. The sun's rays make an angle of 90° with the earth's axis. Further details of the equinoctial conditions are shown in Figure 2.12.

The circle of illumination at the equinoxes passes through the poles and hence coincides with the meridians as the earth turns.

As evident from Figure 2.12, the parallels are divided into equal halves by the circle of illumination. Hence day and night are of exactly equal length, twelve hours each, at all latitudes.[4] Conditions are the same for both northern and southern hemispheres. Sunrise occurs at 6:00 A.M. (local

[4]This explains the word equinox, from the Latin aequus, equal; and nox, night. We are not taking into account twilight, which extends the period of daylight before sunrise and after sunset.

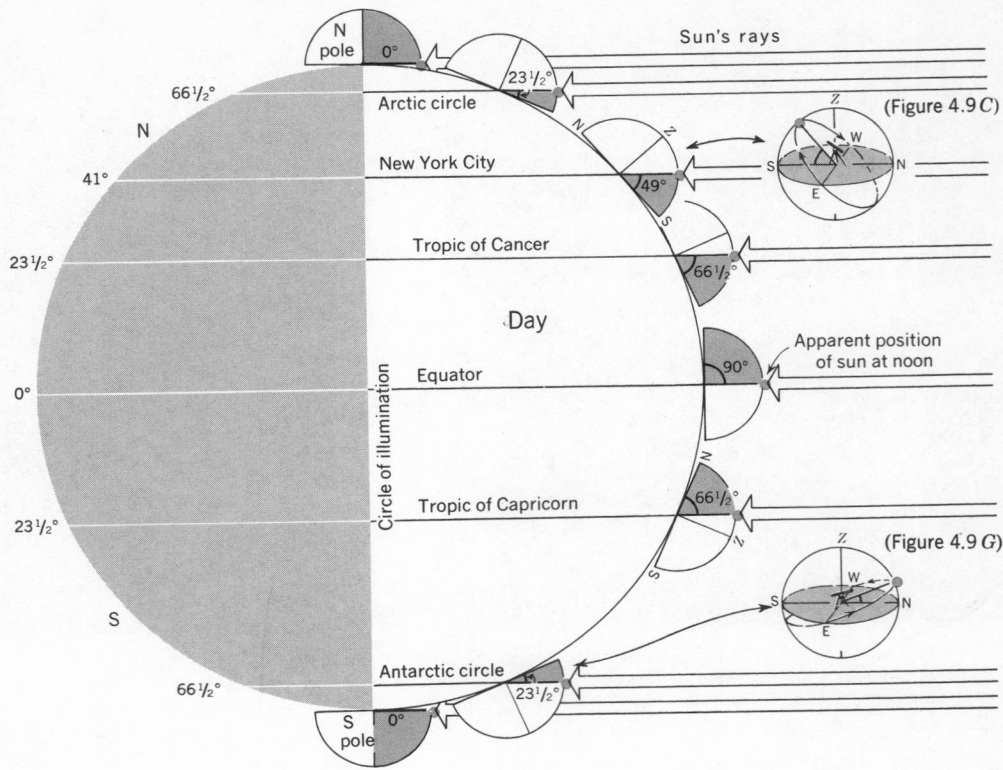

Figure 2.12 Equinox. (From A. N. Strahler, *The Earth Sciences*, Harper and Row, New York.)

solar time), sunset at 6:00 P.M., at all places on the globe, except at the poles, where special conditions prevail.

The sun's noon altitude is found by direct measurement of the angle between the sun's parallel rays and tangent lines drawn at selected points (Figure 2.12). A few such measurements should reveal that the altitude is always the *colatitude*, or 90° minus the latitude. Thus, on the equinoxes, but not for any other time of year, the sun's noon altitude may be computed by a single simple subtraction, if only the latitude is given. Although the altitude is the same for similar latitudes both north and south of the equator, it should be remembered that the angle is measured from the southern horizon in the northern hemisphere, from the northern horizon in the southern hemisphere.

The path of the sun in the sky at the equinoxes is illustrated in Figure 2.9. In each case the path is midway between the paths at the solstices. The sun rises at a point due east on the horizon and sets at a point due west on the horizon at all latitudes except at the two poles. At the poles, the sun remains on the horizon all day long, traveling one complete circuit of the horizon in 24 hours. Note, however, that the direction of apparent movement of the sun is opposite for the two poles.

At the equator the sun has an altitude of 90° at noon; moreover, its path is in a plane perpendicular to the horizon plane. For this reason the sun changes altitude 15° per hour throughout the day at the equator on the equinoxes. Furthermore, at the equator on these dates the shadow of any vertical rod will point due west from 6:00 A.M. to noon, will disappear precisely at noon, and will point due east from noon until 6:00 P.M.

Time

The need for understanding global time relationships and the various kinds of time in use scarcely needs emphasis in this modern day of instantaneous communication and high-speed travel. Before the coming of the telegraph, problems of time differences were of little or no concern to people who lived most of their lives in one community. Even the traveler was caused only the inconvenience of resetting his watch to the time used by local communities. The amount of time consumed in getting from one place to another was so much more than the difference in watch time between the two places that the difference was of little practical consequence.

When it became possible to transmit messages

instantaneously by telegraph, differences in local time resulting from differences in longitudinal position were immediately apparent. With the development of rapid means of travel it became important to correct schedules for the gain or loss of time incurred by passage across the meridians. East-to-west flight in the middle latitudes can now approximate the speed necessary to keep pace with the sun. For example, a plane leaving New York at 12:00 noon, Eastern Standard time, can by traveling about 800 mph (1300 km per hr) arrive in San Francisco at 12:00 noon, Pacific Standard time.

Longitude and time

To avoid confusion and make the study of time relations as simple as possible it is necessary to think of the earth as standing still and of the sun as completing one circuit about the earth every 24 hours. This is a perfectly permissible concept inasmuch as earth-sun relationships are purely relative. Imagine that a meridian is free to sweep westward around the globe and that it constantly maintains such a speed as to be located always where the sun's rays strike the earth's surface at the highest possible angle. This line we shall call the *noon meridian* (Figure 2.13). Directly opposite this meridian, on the other side of the globe, is the *midnight meridian.* It, too, sweeps westward over the globe and remains constantly 180° of longitude apart from the noon meridian. Whereas the noon meridian separates the forenoon and afternoon of the same calendar day, the midnight meridian is the dividing line between one calendar

day and the next.

Because the noon meridian sweeps over 360° of longitude every 24 hours, it must cover 15° of longitude every hour, or 1° of longitude every 4 minutes. We therefore find it convenient to state that one hour of time is the equivalent of 15° of longitude. This equality forms the basis for all calculations concerning time belts of the globe. For example, if the noon meridian reaches one place on the globe 4 hours after it leaves another place, the two places are separated by 60° of longitude.

Enlarging this concept of time meridians still further, let it be imagined that in addition to the noon and midnight meridians there are 22 hour circles, each one a half great circle, 15° of longitude apart from its neighbor. The hour circles are equidistantly spaced between the noon and midnight meridians (Figure 2.13). Each hour circle will then represent a given hour of the day and can be labeled with a specific hour number which it keeps permanently. Together with the noon and midnight meridians, the hour circles can be imagined to form a birdcagelike net enclosing the globe and attached only at the north and south poles. As a further convenience in analyzing global time relations, it is most helpful if the globe used has meridians drawn for every 15°. If so, wherever the noon meridian of the time net coincides with the Greenwich meridian, all other hour circles coincide with true meridians on the globe.

A working model of global time relations is illustrated in Figure 2.14. If a small globe is available, make a cardboard girdle to fit about the equator and mark upon the cardboard the posi-

Figure 2.13 Hour circles.

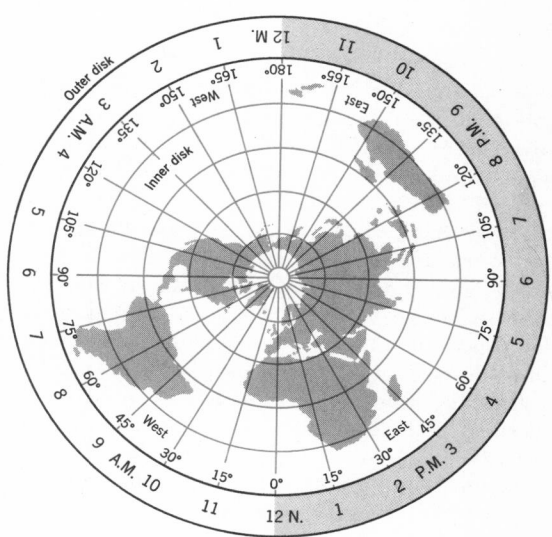

Figure 2.14 A working model of global time.

tions of the time meridians. If no globe is available, make two cardboard discs of different radius and attach them at their centers in such a way that one disc can be turned while the other remains still. On the inner disc draw radii to represent 15° meridians of a globe seen from a point above the north pole. On the outer disc draw similar radii, but label them in hours to represent the time net. As a further refinement, the inner disc may consist of a hemispherical world map.

People sometimes become confused when trying to decide whether the watch time of places to the east (or west) of them is ahead or behind their own watch time. This is especially evident where the problem is to calculate when a radio or television program will be on the air in different parts of the country, or to decide whether to set one's watch ahead or behind one hour when traveling from one standard time zone to another. To avoid confusion let the time meridians be visualized as moving westward around the globe. Then consider, for example, that you are in New York City and the time there is 12:00 noon. The noon meridian which is at New York left Greenwich, England, five hours earlier. Therefore, in England five hours must have elapsed since noon and it must be 5 P.M. in that country. From this we get the general rule: *places that lie east of you have a later hour.* Again, consider that the noon meridian is at New York City. It will take that meridian about three hours to travel westward to reach San Francisco. Hence it must be 9:00 A.M. in that city. This gives a counterpart of the rule stated above, namely: *places that lie west of you have an earlier hour.* Both rules are subject to qualifications where the International Date Line lies between the places.

Local time

One means of establishing a time system for a small community is to take the meridian of longitude that passes through some central point in the town or city, as for example the courthouse or a cathedral. All clocks of the community are set to read 12:00 noon when the sun is directly over that meridian, that is to say, when a shadow cast by a vertical rod points due north. The sun is an erratic timekeeper, and it would be necessary to take the mean value of the sun's noon position, but this need not concern us now. The time system thus derived is called *local time* and may be defined as mean solar time based on the local meridian. All places located on the same meridian, regardless of how far apart they may be, have the same local time, whereas all places located on different meridians have unlike local times, differing by four minutes for every degree of longitude between them.

Standard time

The undesirability of using local time systems in each community of a highly populated country in our modern day is obvious. American railroads, about 1870, introduced a standardized system covering considerable belts of territory, but this system was developed by the railroad companies for their own convenience. Consequently, if several railroads met or passed in a single town, the inhabitants might have had to contend with several different kinds of railroad time in addition to their own local time. It is said that before 1883 as many as five different time systems were used in a single town and that the railroads of the United States altogether followed 53 different systems of time.

The obvious solution to such problems is *standard time,* based on a *standard meridian,* whose local time is arbitrarily given to wide strips of country on both sides. Thus, all clocks within the belt are set to a single time. It is evident that if standard meridians are 15° apart, adjacent zones will have standard times differing by exactly one hour. Furthermore, if these meridians represent longitudes which are multiples of 15, for example, 60°, 75°, 90°, or 105°, each successive standard time zone will differ from the standard time of Greenwich, England, by whole hour units. This is the system of standard time zones employed over most of the globe.

Standard time in the United States

The present system of standard time in the United States was placed in operation on November 18, 1883, but it was not until March 19, 1918, that Congress passed legislation directing the Interstate Commerce Commission to determine timezone boundaries. The standard meridians and boundaries are shown on Figure 2.15. The six time zones and their meridians are as follows:

Eastern standard time	75th meridian
Central standard time	90th meridian
Mountain standard time	105th meridian
Pacific standard time	120th meridian
Alaskan standard time	150th meridian
Hawaiian standard time	150th meridian

If it had been carried out precisely, the system would have resulted in belts extending exactly $7\frac{1}{2}$° east and west of each standard meridian, but a glance at the map shows that great liberties have been taken in locating the boundaries. Wherever the time-zone boundary could conveniently be located along some already existing and widely recognized line, this was done. Natural physiographic boundaries have been used. For example, the Eastern time-Central time boundary line follows Lake Michigan down its center, and the Mountain

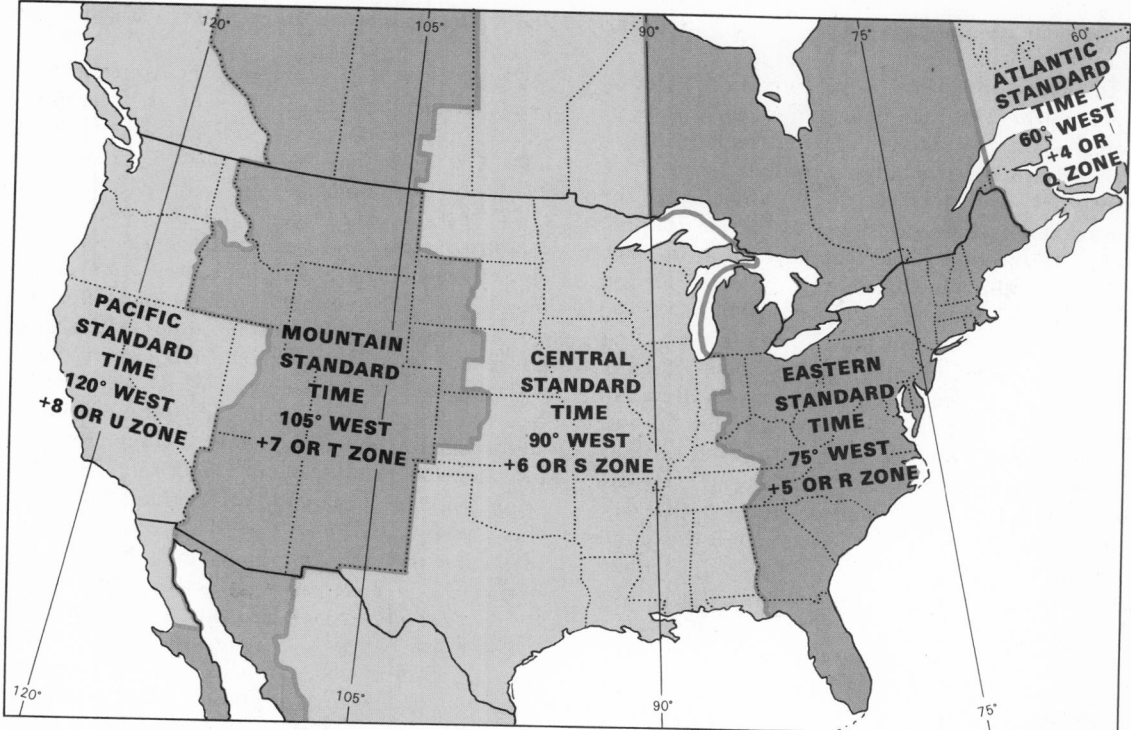

Figure 2.15 Time-zone map of the United States and southern Canada. (Based on data by Interstate Commerce Commission and Department of Transportation.)

time-Pacific time boundary follows a ridge-crest line also used by the Idaho-Montana state boundary. Most frequently, the time-zone boundary follows state and county boundaries. For example, before 1941, the Eastern time-Central time boundary passed north to south through Georgia, but in that year the ICC held hearings in Georgia and officially moved the time-zone boundary westward to the Alabama-Georgia state line, thus bringing all of Georgia into the Eastern standard zone.

The time belts are by no means equally distributed on both sides of the standard meridians, as a glance at the map will show. An extreme example is found in western Texas, where the Central time-Mountain time boundary follows the western boundary of Texas, even crossing west of the standard meridian (105° W) of the Mountain time zone. Although such deviations may seem odd, they cause little difficulty when the boundaries are once well established. The advantage gained by extreme deviations of the boundaries is in permitting entire states to operate under one kind of time. In some places the determining factor was a railroad division point junction or terminal. Where the line was drawn through such a point, as for example at Ogden or Salt Lake City, divisions east and west of the city each ran under a single time.

Daylight saving time and War time

Because many human activities, especially in cities and manufacturing areas, start well after sunrise but continue long after sunset, it would seem desirable to set forward the hours of daylight so as to utilize them to best advantage. A considerable saving in electric power would be made if the early morning daylight period, wasted while people are still in bed and offices and factories are closed, were transferred to the early evening when the large majority of persons are awake and busy. The adjusted time system is known as *daylight saving time* and is obtained by setting ahead all timepieces by one hour. Thus, when the sun is over the standard meridian (i.e., noon by the mean sun), all clocks in that time zone read 1:00 P.M. Sunrise and sunset at the equinoxes or equator, instead of occurring at 6:00 A.M. and 6:00 P.M., would occur at 7:00 A.M. and 7:00 P.M., respectively.

In terms of the standard time system, we may describe daylight saving time as based on the standard meridian lying 15° of longitude east of the standard meridian normally giving the standard time to that zone. For example, Eastern daylight saving time is the same as standard time of the meridian 60° W long.; Central daylight saving time is the same as Eastern standard time, both being based on the meridian 75° W long.

Daylight saving time was adopted in the United States during the First World War, and by act of Congress was put into effect from the last Sunday in April to the last Sunday in September of 1918. After that war it was used locally throughout the United States where authorized by local legislation. During the Second World War, daylight saving time was used nationally throughout the entire period of February 1942, to October 1945, and was known as War time. England during the same war period employed a double daylight saving time in which clocks were running two hours ahead of Greenwich civil time. This was desirable because of the unusually long summer days which England enjoys as a result of her relatively far northerly latitude. Many European countries normally use daylight saving time, which goes under the name *summer time*, during a part of the year. Nations whose time is advanced by an hour throughout the entire year are Great Britain, Ireland, Spain, France, the Netherlands, Belgium, and the USSR.

In April 1966, The United States Congress passed the *Uniform Time Act*, which requires that daylight saving time be applied uniformly throughout each state, unless the legislature of that state has voted to remain instead on standard time. In the latter case, standard time must be applied uniformly throughout the entire state. Daylight time goes into effect at 2:00 A.M. of the last Sunday of April and continues until 2:00 A.M. of the last Sunday of October. The Uniform Time Act is administered by the Department of Transportation, which also has authority to adjust time-zone boundaries.

World time zones

In 1884 an international congress was held in Washington to consider the subject of world standard time. As a result, standard times of countries throughout the world are based on standard meridians, which are multiples of the unit 15° and thus differ from one another by whole hourly amounts. In all global time calculations, the prime meridian of Greenwich, England, is taken as the reference meridian. All time zones of the globe are described in terms of the number of hours' difference between the standard meridian of that zone and the Greenwich meridian. In order to distinguish whether the time zones lie east or west of the Greenwich meridian the time is designated *fast* for all places east of Greenwich (east longitude), and *slow* for all places west of Greenwich (west longitude). U.S. Eastern Standard time, for example, is said to be "5 hours slow."

An alternative system of designating world time

zones uses letters of the alphabet, as shown in Figures 2.15 and 2.16.

Figure 2.16 is a world map on which the 24 principal standard time zones of the world are shown. Fifteen-degree meridians are in black lines; $7\frac{1}{2}$° meridians, which form large elements of the zone boundaries, are indicated in color lines. Within each time zone is inscribed the number of hours' difference between the zone time and Greenwich time. Careful examination of this map brings out a number of interesting facts. Some small countries or islands lie about midway between 15° meridians. Under such circumstances a standard meridian is chosen which lies halfway between the two and is thus a multiple of $7\frac{1}{2}$°. The standard time of the country is therefore fast or slow by some multiple of a half hour. Iran ($3\frac{1}{2}$ hours fast) and Surinam ($3\frac{1}{2}$ hours slow) illustrate this point. India, for a large country, is unusual in having the time $5\frac{1}{2}$ hours fast. The country having the greatest east-west extent is the Soviet Union, with eleven standard time zones, but these are all advanced by one hour with respect to the standard time meridians in each zone, to give a perpetual daylight saving time. Canada occupies six time zones. Notice that Newfoundland and Labrador use the time $3\frac{1}{2}$ hours fast.

Although virtually all countries today have standard times related by whole hours or half hours to Greenwich Civil time, it was not so long ago that many countries determined their standard times by meridians of the capital cities or those passing through local observatories. For example, in 1905, all of France used the local time of the meridian passing through the Paris Observatory. This gave a time which was $0^h 9^m 20.9^s$ fast. India in 1905 used the local time of the Madras Observatory, which is $5^h 20^m 59.1^s$ fast of Greenwich Civil time. Ireland in 1905 was using the time $0^h 25^m 21.1^s$ slow, which is the local time of the Dublin meridian.

By 1970, only a few small nations or colonies persisted in the use of odd local meridians for their standard time. These were Liberia ($0^h 44\frac{1}{2}^m$ slow), Guyana ($3^h 45^m$ slow), Chatham Island ($12^h 45^m$ fast), Saudi Arabia, and Mongolia. An up-to-date list of world standard times will be found in *The Air Almanac*.

The International Date Line

If we were to take a world map or globe on which 15° meridians are drawn and count them in an eastward direction, starting with the Greenwich meridian as 0, we would find that the 180th meridian is number 12, and that the time of this meridian is, therefore, 12 hours fast. Counting in a similar manner westward from the Greenwich

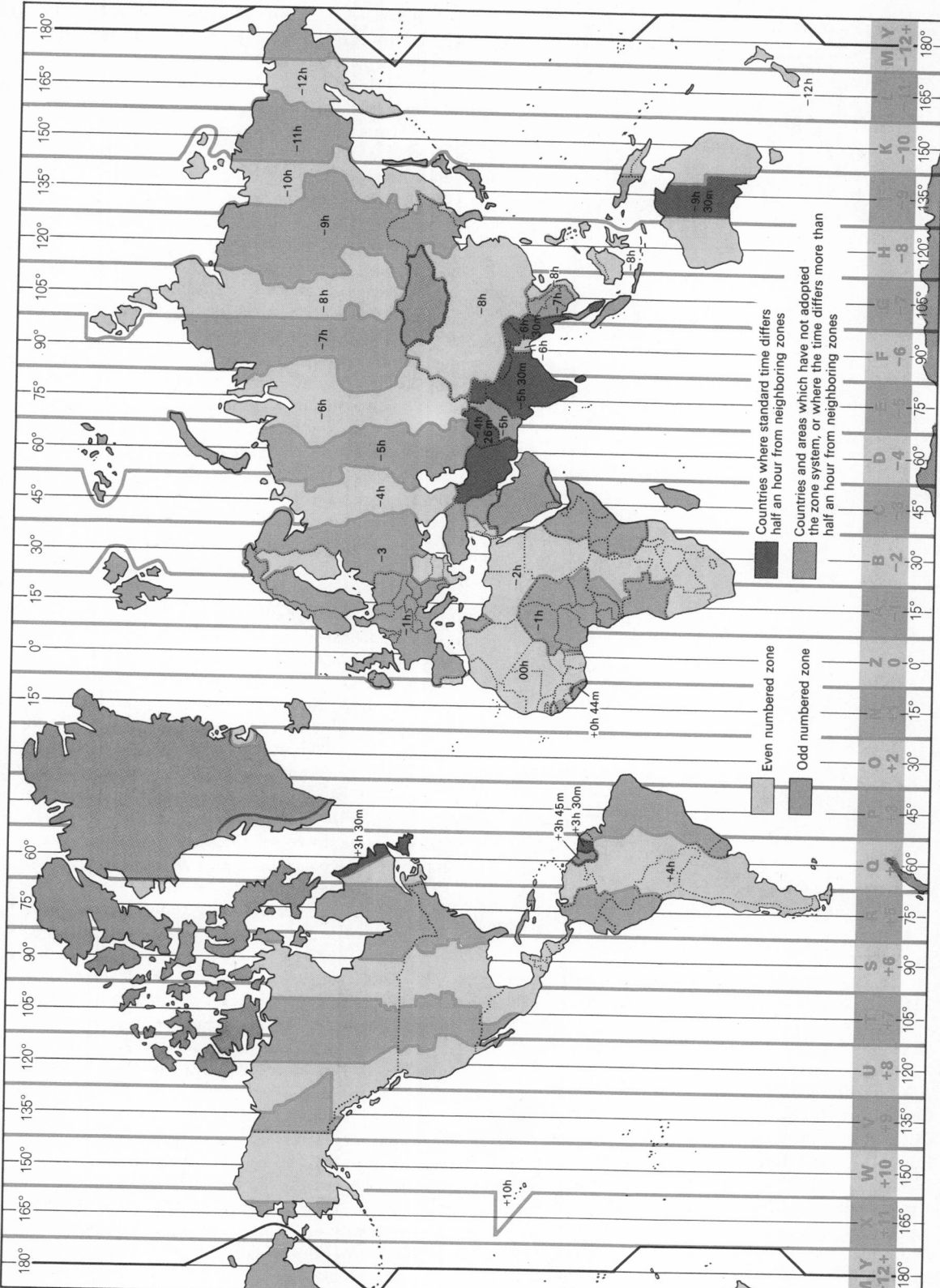

Figure 2.16 Time-zone map of the world. (After U.S. Navy Oceanographic Office, No. 5192.)

Countries where standard time differs
half an hour from neighboring zones

Countries and areas which have not adopted
the zone system, or where the time differs more than
half an hour from neighboring zones

Even numbered zone

Odd numbered zone

Figure 2.17 The International Date Line.

on the east (American) side. For example, if it is Monday on the Asiatic side of the 180th meridian, it is Sunday on the American side. Confusion can be avoided and the correct dates consistently obtained if it is remembered that by counting hours from the Greenwich meridian eastward around the globe by way of Asia, the 180th meridian has the time 12 hours fast, hence that the Asiatic side of the meridian must be a day ahead of the other side.

In the days of very slow trans-Pacific travel by sailing vessel and low-powered steamship, an entire calendar day was merely omitted on a westbound voyage and an entire day repeated on an eastbound voyage. The change was made at any convenient place and time in midocean and usually planned so as to have neither two Sundays in one week nor a week without a Sunday.[5]

It was due to their failure to advance the calendar by a whole day that the crew of Magellan's only surviving ship, reaching Seville after circumnavigating the globe in a westward direction, found that in Spain it was September 8, 1522, whereas by their own reckoning it was only September 7 of that year.

When traveling across the Pacific in today's high-speed jet aircraft, the 24-hour correction is made at the time the 180th meridian is crossed. Suppose that the plane is traveling eastward toward North America and crosses the meridian at 4:00 P.M., (standard time 12 hours fast) on a Tuesday. At the instant of crossing, the time becomes 4:00 P.M. Monday. When traveling westward to the Orient the time moves ahead by a full day. For example, if the meridian is crossed at 9:30 A.M. Wednesday, the time becomes 9:30 A.M. Thursday.

Because of these peculiar properties, the 180th meridian was designated the *International Date Line* by the International Meridian Conference held in Washington, D.C., in 1884 (Figure 2.17). It is one of the fortuitous occurrences of modern civilization that, after the Greenwich meridian had come into widespread use in English-speaking countries as the international basis for the reckoning of longitude, the 180th meridian should have been found to fall in an almost ideal location—squarely in the middle of the world's largest expanse of ocean. Nevertheless, the International Date Line has had to deviate both eastward and westward to permit certain land areas and groups of islands to have the same calendar day (Figure 2.17). By an eastward bulge passing through Bering Strait, the easternmost part of Siberia is included in the Asiatic side, and a westward deflection of the line allows the Aleutian Islands to be included

[5]Willis E. Johnson, 1907, *Mathematical geography*, American Book Co., New York. See pp. 96–103.

meridian, we find that the 180th meridian is again number 12, but that the time is 12 hours slow. Both results are, of course, correct; and the explanation becomes obvious when we note that the difference in time between 12 hours fast and 12 hours slow is 24 hours, or a full day. At the precise instant when the noon meridian coincides with the Greenwich meridian, the 180th meridian coincides with the midnight hour meridian. At this instant, and only at this instant, the same calendar day exists on both sides of the meridian. At all other times the calendar day on the west (Asiatic) side of the 180th meridian is one day ahead of that with the Alaskan peninsula. A few degrees south of the equator the date line is shifted eastward $7\frac{1}{2}°$ and thus avoids cutting through the Ellice, Wallis, Fiji, and Tonga island groups, which have the same day as New Zealand.

Duration of days on the globe

One of the most curious aspects of global time is the manner in which calendar days appear and disappear on the globe. If a day lasts 24 hours for a specific place on the earth, and the same series of hours reaches places lying farther west at a later time, it follows that a calendar day exists more than 24 hours for the earth as a whole. To develop this idea fully use the following visual aids:

Holding a small globe in your hands so that the Pacific Ocean is before you, imagine that the international date line is a narrow slit extending from pole to pole on the 180th meridian. (For the time being let it be assumed that the line has no deviations from the meridian.) Imagine further that calendar days—Monday, Tuesday, etc.—issue from the long slit and spread westward over the globe like a thin film. The leading edge of this film extends from pole to pole and corresponds to the midnight time meridian. The film, which is now issuing from the slit, can be designated Monday, and all global areas which it covers have the calendar day Monday. Traveling at the rate of 15° of longitude per hour, the midnight meridian, or leading edge of the film, will require twelve hours to arrive at the Greenwich meridian. At this precise moment it is midnight in England and the calendar day Monday covers the eastern hemisphere. The western hemisphere still has the calendar day Sunday, which may be pictured as retreating ahead of Monday. Twelve hours later the imaginary film which we are calling Monday has spread over the entire globe and the edge of the film has reached the slit at the 180th meridian.

At this precise instant Monday envelops the entire earth and is the only calendar day present anywhere.

Because no calendar day can ever cross the date line, we will have to picture Monday as disappearing into the slit whence it had begun to issue 24 hours earlier. As it does so, the next calendar day, Tuesday, is beginning to issue from the slit and to spread across the Pacific Ocean toward Asia, just as Monday had done earlier. Now we are prepared to answer the intriguing question: what is the total number of hours that the calendar day Monday, whose progress we are observing, will exist on the globe? The answer is that Monday will exist 48 hours. It has required 24 hours for the film representing Monday to spread around and completely cover the earth, and it requires an additional 24 hours for it to disappear back into the slit. Thus Monday is present on the earth's surface for a continuous period of 48 hours, although for any specified place on the globe it can last only 24 hours.

REFERENCES FOR FURTHER STUDY

Hosmer, G. L. and J. M. Robbins (1948), *Practical astronomy*, fourth edition, John Wiley and Sons, New York, 355 pp. See Chapters 1 and 5.

Mehlin, T. G. (1959), *Astronomy*, John Wiley and Sons, New York, 391 pp.

Strahler, A. N. (1969), *Physical geography*, third edition, John Wiley and Sons, New York, 733 pp. See Chapters 4, 5.

Royal Astronomical Society of Canada, *The observer's handbook*, issued annually, Univ. of Toronto Press.

U.S. Naval Observatory, *The air almanac*, issued annually, U.S. Govt. Printing Office, Washington, D.C.

World Journal Tribune, *The world almanac and book of facts*, issued annually, Newspaper Enterprise Association, New York.

REVIEW QUESTIONS

1. Why are earth-sun relationships important in the study of geography?

2. What is meant by rotation of the earth? What is the period of rotation with reference to the sun?

3. What is the direction of rotation of the earth? Does the earth's rotation have any observable effects on objects at or near the earth's surface aside from the astronomical effects?

4. Describe and explain the Foucault pendulum experiment. What does it prove? Could you determine your latitude by means of a Foucault pendulum? How?

5. What is meant by revolution of the earth? In what two ways can the length and starting point of a year be reckoned? Which one is used in our calendar system? How long is this type of year? How must it be periodically corrected to fit our calendar? What is the direction of the earth's revolution?

6. What form has the earth's orbit? What is perihelion? What is aphelion? On what dates do they occur? What distances separate earth and sun at perihelion and at aphelion? What effect does this have on the seasons?

7. Describe the way in which the earth's axis is tilted with respect to the plane of the earth's orbit. What is the angle of tilt? Does this angle change throughout the year?

8. Describe each of the two solstice and two equinox positions of the earth with respect to the sun, giving the dates of each in correct sequence.

9. What is the circle of illumination? Where is the circle of illumination located on the date of equinox? On December solstice? On June solstice?

10. Describe the conditions of global illumination, length of day and night, and path of sun in the sky at June solstice. Give details for the equator, Tropics of Cancer and Capricorn, Arctic and Antarctic Circles, and poles.

11. Describe the conditions of global illumination, length of day and night, and path of sun in the sky at equinox. Give details for the equator, Tropics of Cancer and Capricorn, Arctic, and Antarctic Circles,

and poles. How is the sun's noon altitude related to latitude on the date of equinox?

12. Describe the path of the sun in the sky throughout the year at the north pole. How do conditions differ at the south pole?

13. Describe the path of the sun in the sky at the Arctic Circle at equinox and at each solstice.

14. Describe in a general way how the compass direction of sunrise and sunset varies with season of year and with latitude.

15. Explain how longitude is related to time. How many degrees of longitude are the equivalent of one hour of time? How many hour meridians are there on the globe? In which direction do they travel?

16. Do places located east of you have a time that is earlier or later than your time?

17. What is local time? On what is it based? Can places that differ in longitude have the same local time? Can places that differ in latitude have the same local time?

18. What is standard time? Explain the system of standard time used in the United States. Which meridians are used?

19. How are boundaries between standard time zones determined? Give examples of various kinds of boundaries used in the United States.

20. What is daylight saving time? Why is it used? When is it used?

21. Explain the system of world time zones now in general use. On what prime meridian is it based? What is fast time? Slow time? What advantages are there in conforming to the world time zone system?

22. What is the International Date Line? Describe its location and form. Explain the difference in calendar days on the two sides of this line. Which side has the earlier days? Is it possible for the same day to exist simultaneously on both sides of the line?

23. How long does a given calendar day exist on the globe? Describe the life history of one calendar day as it envelopes the globe and then disappears.

CHAPTER *3*

The Earth's Atmosphere

MAN lives at the bottom of an ocean of air; he is an air-breather dependent upon favorable conditions of pressure, temperature, and chemical composition of the atmosphere that surrounds him. He also lives on the solid outer surface of the earth, upon which he is dependent for food, clothing, shelter, and means of movement from place to place. But the air and the land are not two entirely separate realms; they constitute an interface across which there is a continual flux of matter and energy. Man's surface environment is a shallow but highly complex zone in which atmospheric conditions exert control upon the land surface, while at the same time the surface of the land exerts an influence upon the properties of the immediately adjacent atmosphere.

Essentially the same statements apply with respect to the surface of the oceans and the atmospheric layer above it. Man utilizes the surface of the sea as a source of food and a means of transportation. There is a continual flux of energy and matter between the sea surface and the lower layer of the atmosphere. Here, again, we find an interface of vital concern to Man. The sea influences the atmosphere above it while the atmosphere influences the sea beneath it.

Our object in this book is to examine the atmosphere and oceans with particular reference to air-land and air-sea interfaces which are so vital to Man. To the geographer, the distributions of physical properties of the ocean and atmosphere are matters of special interest, concerned as he is with spatial relationships on a global scale. The physical geographer seeks to describe and explain the manner in which the environmental elements of weather and climate change with latitude and season, and with geographical position in relation to oceans and continents. The geographer seeks out the broad patterns of similar regions and attempts to define their boundaries and organize them into systems of classification.

States of matter

Study of the atmosphere, ocean, and land requires continual application of the principles relating to three basic states of matter: *gaseous state*, *liquid state*, and *solid state*. A *gas* is a substance that expands easily to fill any small empty container, is readily compressible, and usually much less dense than liquids and solids of the same chemical composition. While the atmosphere is largely in the gaseous state, it also contains varying amounts of substances in the liquid and solid states.

A *liquid* is a substance that flows freely in response to unequal stresses, but characteristically maintains a free upper surface. Liquids are compressed only slightly with strong stresses. Liquids have densities closely comparable with solids of the same composition.

Although the world ocean is largely composed of water in the liquid state, it also contains substances in the gaseous and solid states. Both gases and liquids belong to the class of *fluids*. Layers of fluids tend to assume positions of equilibrium at rest in which a less dense fluid overlies a more dense fluid.

Solids are substances that resist changes of shape and volume and are typically capable of withstanding large unequal stresses without yielding. When yielding occurs, it is usually by sudden breakage. Although the earth's crust is largely in the solid state, it also contains substances in both gaseous and liquid states.

A further observation concerning states of matter is that a *change of state* is possible and occurs frequently in the world of nature. Most important and widespread is the change of state of water from water vapor (a gas) to liquid water and *vice versa*, and from liquid water to ice (solid state) and *vice versa* (Chapter 6). These changes of state require either an input of heat energy or the disposal of heat energy, depending upon the direction of the change.

The broad generalizations and principles that have been set down here concerning states of matter are further refined, explained, qualified, and applied in the ensuing chapters of this book.

Composition of the atmosphere

The earth's atmosphere consists of a mixture of various gases surrounding the earth to a height of many miles. Held to the earth by gravitational attraction, this envelope of air is densest at sea level and thins rapidly upward. Although almost all of the atmosphere (97 percent) lies within 18 mi (29 km) of the earth's surface, the upper limit of the atmosphere can be drawn approximately at a height of 6000 mi (10,000 km), a distance approaching the diameter of the earth itself. The science of *meteorology* deals with the physics of this atmosphere.

From the earth's surface upward to an altitude of about 50 mi (80 km) the chemical composition of the atmosphere is highly uniform throughout in terms of the proportions of its component gases. The name *homosphere* has been applied to this lower, uniform layer, in contrast to the overlying *heterosphere*, which is nonuniform in an arrangement of spherical shells.

Pure, dry air of the homosphere consists largely of *nitrogen* (78.084 percent by volume) and *oxygen* (20.946 percent). Nitrogen does not easily enter into chemical union with other substances, and can be thought of as primarily a neutral filler substance. In contrast, oxygen is highly active chemically and combines readily with other elements in the process of *oxidation*. Combustion of fuels represents a rapid form of oxidation, whereas certain forms of rock decay (weathering) represent very slow forms of oxidation.

The remaining 0.970 percent of the air is mostly *argon* (0.934 percent). *Carbon dioxide*, although constituting only about 0.033 percent, is a gas of great importance in atmospheric processes because of its ability to absorb heat and thus to allow the lower atmosphere to be warmed by heat radiation coming from the sun and from the earth's surface.

Green plants, in the process of *photosynthesis*, utilize carbon dioxide from the atmosphere, converting it with water into solid hydrocarbons. A pronounced rise in the carbon dioxide content of the atmosphere has been noted since 1900 and is a possible result of Man's combustion of vast quantities of wood, coal, petroleum, and natural gas. In this change, we may find an example of Man's impact upon his environment, for an increase in carbon dioxide, as well as in atmospheric dusts, can result in appreciable increases in average atmospheric temperatures.

The remaining gases of the homosphere are *neon, helium, krypton, xenon, hydrogen, methane,* and *nitrous oxide,* listed in decreasing order of percentage by volume. Altogether, these constituents total slightly less than 0.003 percent by volume. All of the component gases of the homosphere are perfectly diffused among one another, so as to give the pure, dry air a definite set of physical properties, just as if it were a single gas.

The heterosphere

The heterosphere, encountered at about 55 mi (90 km) above the earth's surface, consists of four gaseous layers, each of distinctive composition (Figure 3.1). Lowermost is the *molecular nitrogen layer* consisting dominantly of molecules of nitrogen (N_2) and extending upward to about 125 mi (200 km). Above this height lies the *atomic oxygen layer,* consisting dominantly of oxygen atoms (O). Between about 700 mi (1100 km) and 2200 mi (3500 km) lies the *helium layer,* composed dominantly of helium atoms (He). Above this region lies the *atomic hydrogen layer,* consisting of hydrogen atoms (H). No definite outer limit can be set to the hydrogen layer. A height of 6000 mi (10,000 km) may perhaps be taken as an arbitrary limit, for here the density of the hydrogen atoms is approximately the same as that found throughout interplanetary space. However, hydrogen atoms rotating with the earth, and hence belonging to the earth's atmosphere, may exist as far out as 22,000 mi (35,000 km).

It should be noted that the four layers described above have transitional boundary zones, rather than sharply defined surfaces of separation. The arrangement of gases is in order of their weights: molecular nitrogen, the heaviest, is lowest; atomic hydrogen, the lightest, is outermost. It should further be kept in mind that, at the extremely high altitudes of the heterosphere, the density of the

Figure 3.1 Homosphere and heterosphere. (Based on data of R. Jastrow, N.A.S.A., and M. Nicolet.)

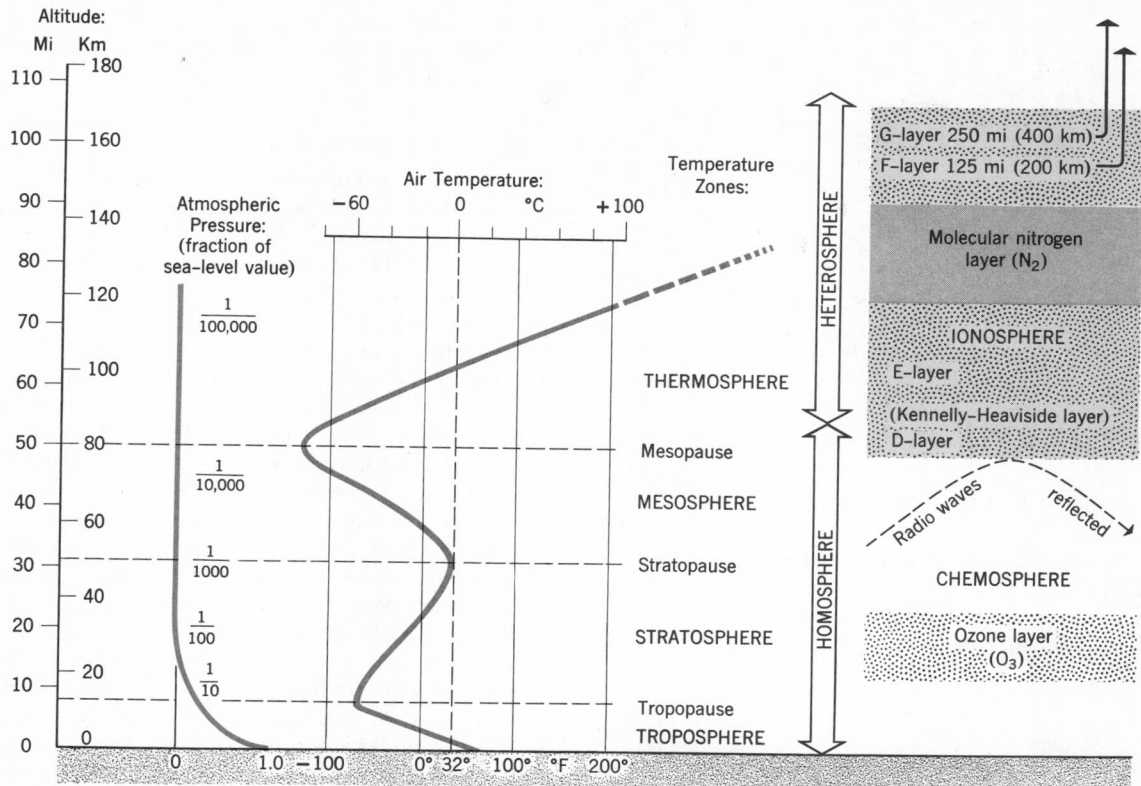

Figure 3.2 Structure of the atmosphere. (After A. N. Strahler, *The Earth Sciences*, Harper and Row, New York.)

gases molecules and atoms is extremely low. For example, at 60 mi (96 km) close to the base of the heterosphere, the atmosphere has a density of only about one millionth that at sea level. Atoms and molecules of the heterosphere are neutral in charge and turn with the earth's rotation.

Subdivisions of the homosphere

The atmosphere has been subdivided into layers according to temperatures and zones of temperature change. Three temperature zones lie within the homosphere; a fourth is assigned to the lower heterosphere. Figure 3.2 shows how temperature is related to altitude. Starting at the earth's surface, temperature falls steadily with increasing altitude at the fairly uniform average rate of $3\frac{1}{2}$ F° per 1000 ft (6.4 C° per km). This rate of temperature drop is known as the *normal temperature lapse rate*. Departures from this rate will be observed, depending upon geographical location and season of year. The layer in which the normal lapse rate applies is known as the *troposphere*, the properties of which are discussed in detail below. Figure 3.3 shows details of a typical atmospheric sounding in middle latitudes.

The normal lapse rate gives way rather abruptly

at a height of 8 to 9 mi (12.5 to 15 km) to a layer, known as the *stratosphere*, in which temperature holds essentially constant with increasing height (see Figure 3.3). The level at which the troposphere gives way to the stratosphere is termed the *tropopause*. Figure 3.4 shows that the elevation of the tropopause is least at the poles, 5 to 6 mi (8 to 10 km), whereas at the equator, the tropopause is encountered at 10 mi (17 km). If the troposphere is thought of as a complete surface in three dimensions, it resembles an oblate ellipsoid with a polar flattening and an equatorial bulge.

Seasonal changes in the elevation of the tropopause are marked in middle and high latitudes. For example, at 45° latitude the average altitude in January is 8 mi (12.5 km), but rises to 9 mi (15 km) in July. Temperatures at the tropopause are markedly lower at the equator than at the poles, as shown in Figure 3.4. At first glance, this relationship may seem strange, accustomed as we are to considering the equatorial region to be hot and the poles cold. However, with a constant temperature lapse rate assumed, the higher the tropopause, the colder will be the air.

Upward through the stratosphere there is a

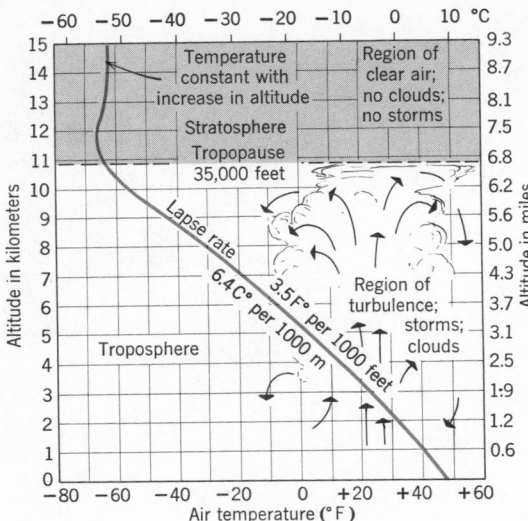

Figure 3.3 A typical lapse rate curve.

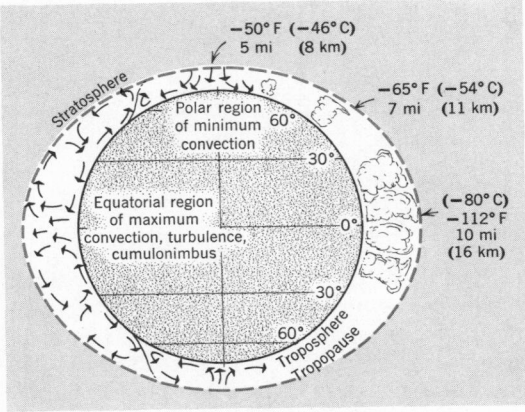

Figure 3.4 Schematic cross section of the troposphere. Figures give height and temperature of the tropopause.

slow rise in temperature until a value of about 32°F (0°C) is reached at about 30 mi (50 km). Here, at the *stratopause*, a reversal to falling temperature sets in. Temperature decreases through the overlying *mesosphere*, a layer extending upward to about 50 mi (80 km), where a low point of −120°F (−83°C) is reached. This level of temperature minimum and reversal is termed the *mesopause*. With further increasing elevation, a steep climb in temperature is observed within the *thermosphere*. As previously noted, the thermosphere lies within the heterosphere. Hence, the mesopause may be regarded as coincident with the upper limit of the homosphere. Within the thermosphere, temperatures reach 2000 to 3000°F (1100 to 1650°C), but such figures have little meaning when we consider that the density of the

air is so slight as to approach a vacuum. Very little heat can be held or conducted by air of such low density.

The troposphere and Man

It is the lowermost atmospheric layer, the troposphere, that is of most direct importance to Man in his environment at the bottom of the atmosphere. Virtually all phenomena of weather and climate that materially affect Man take place within the troposphere.

In addition to pure dry air, the troposphere contains *water vapor*, a colorless, odorless gaseous form of water which mixes perfectly with the other gases of the air. The degree to which water vapor is present is designated as the *humidity* and is of primary importance in weather phenomena. Water vapor can condense into clouds and fog. If condensation is excessive, rain, snow, hail, or sleet, collectively termed *precipitation*, may result. Where water vapor is present only in small proportions, extreme dryness of air typical of the hot deserts results. There is, in addition, a most important function performed by water vapor. Like carbon dioxide, it is capable of absorbing heat, which penetrates the atmosphere in the form of radiant energy from the sun and earth. Water vapor gives to the troposphere the qualities of an insulating blanket, which prevents the rapid escape of heat from the earth's surface.

The troposphere contains myriads of tiny dust particles, so small and light that the slightest movements of the air keep them aloft. They have been swept into the air from dry desert plains, lake beds and beaches, or explosive volcanoes. Strong winds blowing over the ocean lift droplets of spray into the air. These may dry out, leaving as residues extremely minute crystals of salt which are carried high into the air. Forest and brush fires are yet another important source of atmospheric dust particles. Countless meteors, vaporizing from the heat of friction as they enter the upper layers of air, have contributed dust particles.

Dust in the troposphere contributes to the occurrence of twilight and the red colors of sunrise and sunset, but the most important function of dust particles is not observable and is rarely appreciated. Certain types of dust particles serve as *nuclei*, or centers, around which water vapor condenses to produce cloud particles. This is illustrated in the air over industrial cities which discharge much chemically active dust into the air. So effective are these dusts in causing moisture to collect around them that almost perpetual dense haze, or *smog*, hangs over the city.

The stratosphere and higher layers are virtually free of water vapor and dust. Clouds are rare and storms are absent in the stratosphere, although winds of high speed are observed.

Atmospheric pressure

Although we are not constantly aware of it, air is a tangible, material substance. At sea level, the atmosphere exerts a pressure of about 15 lb per square inch (about 1 kg per square centimeter) on every solid or liquid surface exposed to it. Because this pressure is exactly counterbalanced by the pressure of air within liquids, hollow objects, or porous substances, its ever-present weight creates no special concern. The pressure on one square inch of surface can be thought of as the actual weight of a column of air one inch in cross section extending upward to the outer limits of the atmosphere. Air is readily compressible. That which lies lowest is most greatly compressed and is, therefore, densest. In an upward direction, both density and pressure of the air fall off rapidly.

The meteorologist uses another method of stating the pressure of the atmosphere, based on a classic experiment of physics first performed by Torricelli in the year 1643. A glass tube about 3 ft (1 m) long, sealed at one end, is completely filled with mercury. The open end is temporarily held closed. Then the tube is inverted and the end is immersed into a dish of mercury. When the opening is uncovered, the mercury in the tube falls a few inches, but then remains fixed at a level about 30 in (76 cm) above the surface of the mercury in the dish (Figure 3.5). Atmospheric pressure now balances the weight of the mercury column.

Figure 3.6 Top and base of standard mercurial barometer. (U.S. Weather Bureau.)

Should the air pressure increase or decrease, the mercury level will rise or fall correspondingly. Here, then, is an instrument for measuring air pressure and its variations.

Any instrument that measures atmospheric pressure is a *barometer*. The type devised by Toricelli is known as the *mercurial barometer*. With various refinements over the original simple device it has become the standard instrument (Figure 3.6). Pressure may be read in inches or centimeters of mercury, the true measure of the height of the mercury column. Standard sea-level pressure is 29.92 in. on this scale. In metric units this is 76 cm (760 mm).

Another unit has been introduced by meteorologists. This is the *millibar* (mb). One inch of mercury is equivalent to about 33.9 mb. Standard sea-level pressure is 1013.2 mb, and each $\frac{1}{10}$ inch of mercury is equal to about 3 mb (0.1 in. = 3.39 mb). In this book, both systems of stating air pressure will be used.

Another type of barometer is the *aneroid barometer* (Figure 3.7). It consists of a hollow metal chamber partly emptied of air and sealed. The walls of the chamber are flexible, so that the chamber expands and contracts as the outside air pressure varies. These movements operate a hand

Figure 3.5 Principle of the mercurial barometer.

Vacuum

Mercury

Height of mercury column 29.92 inches (76 cm)

Glass tube

Dish

Figure 3.7 Aneroid barometer (above) and schematic diagram of workings (below). (Photograph by U.S. Weather Bureau. Diagram after Wold, *College Physics*.)

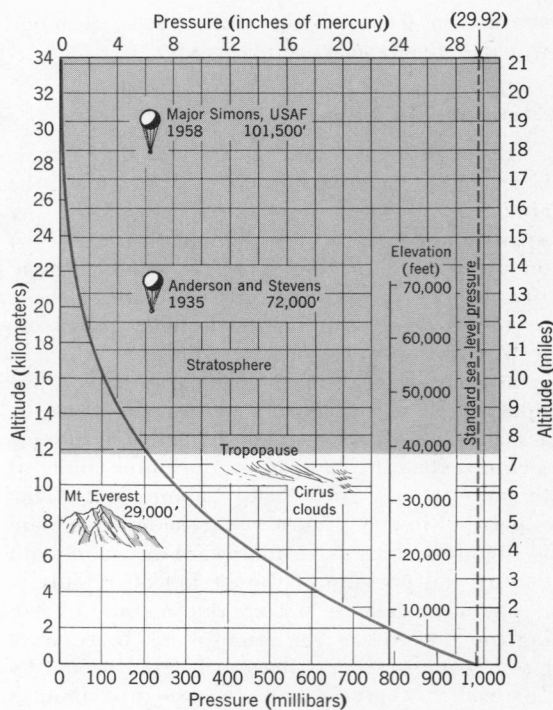

Figure 3.8 Decrease of air pressure with elevation. (Data from Humphreys, *Physics of the Air*.)

which is read against a calibrated circular dial. The aneroid is compact and easily carried in a plane or on the person.

Vertical distribution of pressure

Figure 3.8 shows how pressure falls with increasing altitude. For every 900 ft (275 m) of rise in elevation, the mercury column falls $\frac{1}{30}$ of its height. As the graph shows (by a steepening of the curve), the rate of drop of the mercury becomes less and less with increasing altitude until, beyond a height of 30 mi (50 km), decrease is extremely slight.

The effects of decreased air pressure upon human physiology, upon the boiling point of water, and upon the gain and loss of atmospheric heat are treated in Chapter 12.

Phenomena of the outer atmosphere

Man continues to extend his activities into more distant layers of the atmosphere. Of particular interest to students of geography are advances in use of communications satellites and remote sensing instruments which scan the earth's surface. Weather satellites continually orbit the earth, providing photographs that materially assist in weather forecasting and in the early detection of tropical storms. Certain physical phenomena of the outer atmospheric regions are thus of importance in the broad framework of physical geography.

Of particular interest in the development of radio communication on a global scale is a layer known as the *ionosphere*, located in the altitude range of 50 to 250 mi (80 to 400 km). Notice that this position coincides with the bottom of the heterosphere in which the molecular nitrogen layer and the atomic oxygen layer are found (see Figure 3.2). Furthermore, the ionosphere is essentially identical in position with the lower thermosphere. The ionosphere consists of a number of layers in which the process of *ionization* takes place. Here highly energetic gamma rays and X-rays from the solar radiation spectrum are absorbed by molecules and atoms of nitrogen and oxygen. In the absorption process, each molecule or atom gives up an electron, becoming a positively charged *ion*. The electrons thus released form an electric current that flows freely on a global scale within the ionosphere. Of particular interest in the geography of radio communication is the ability of the layers of ions to reflect radio waves and thus to turn them back toward the earth. Most of the important reflection of long-wave radio waves takes place in the lower part of the ionosphere, which bears the name of *Kennelly-Heaviside layer*. Without such reflection, long-distance radio communication would not be possible. Because the process of ionization requires direct solar radiation, the ionospheric layers, of which there are five, are developed on the sunlight side of the earth (Figure 3.9). On the dark side, under nighttime conditions, the layers tend to weaken and disappear.

Yet another phenomenon, one of vital concern to Man and all other life forms on earth, is the presence of an *ozone layer* largely occurring in the region from 12 to 21 mi (20 to 35 km) elevation, but also extending upward to an elevation of 30 to 35 mi (50 to 55 km) (see Figure 3.2). The ozone layer thus extends from the upper stratosphere into the mesosphere. The ozone layer is a region of concentration of the form of oxygen molecule known as *ozone*, (O_3), in which three oxygen atoms are combined instead of the usual two atoms (O_2). Ozone is produced by the action of ultraviolet rays upon ordinary oxygen atoms. The ozone layer thus serves as a shield, protecting the troposphere and

earth's surface from most of the ultraviolet radiation found in the sun's radiation spectrum. If these ultraviolet rays were to reach the earth's surface in full intensity, all exposed bacteria would be destroyed and animal tissues severely burned. Thus the presence of the ozone layer is an essential element in Man's environment. It is also interesting to note that the high temperatures of the mesosphere are produced by the absorption of the ultraviolet rays in the upper part of the ozone layer. The level of greatest ozone concentration is at its highest altitude in low latitudes (28 mi; 48 km), but descends to the lowest altitude in arctic latitudes (22 mi; 35 km). There are also marked seasonal variations in altitude in middle latitudes.

The magnetosphere

The earth can be thought of as a simple bar magnet, the axis of which approximately coincides with the earth's geographic axis (Figure 3.10). Magnetism is generated within the earth's metallic core, a central spherical body about half of the earth's diameter. The earth's magnetic axis is inclined several degrees with respect to the geographic axis. Hence the north and south *magnetic poles* do not coincide with the geographic north and south poles, nor does the *magnetic equator* coincide with the earth's geographic equator.

Lines of force of the earth's magnetic field,

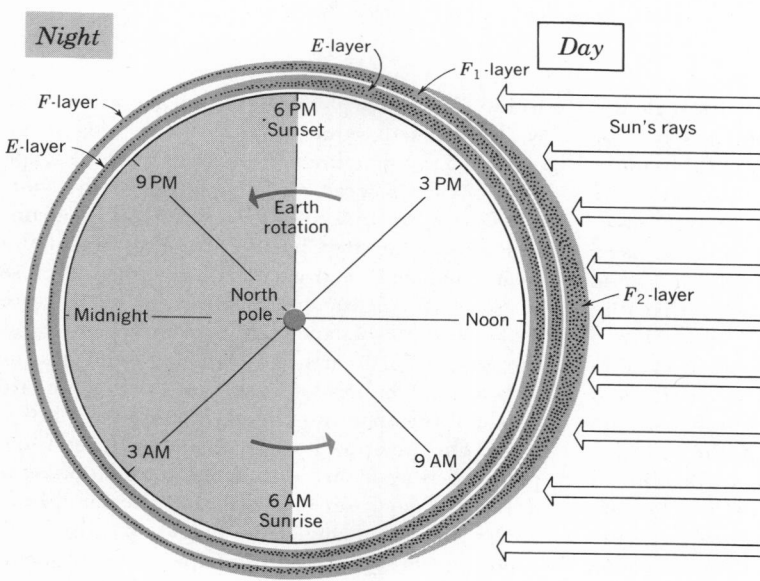

Figure 3.9 This diagram of the ionospheric layers is a cross section through the earth's equator. The observer looks down upon the cross section from a point over the north pole. (Based on a figure by B. F. Howell, Jr., 1959, *Introduction to Geophysics*, McGraw-Hill, N.Y. From A. N. Strahler, *The Earth Sciences*, Harper and Row, N.Y.)

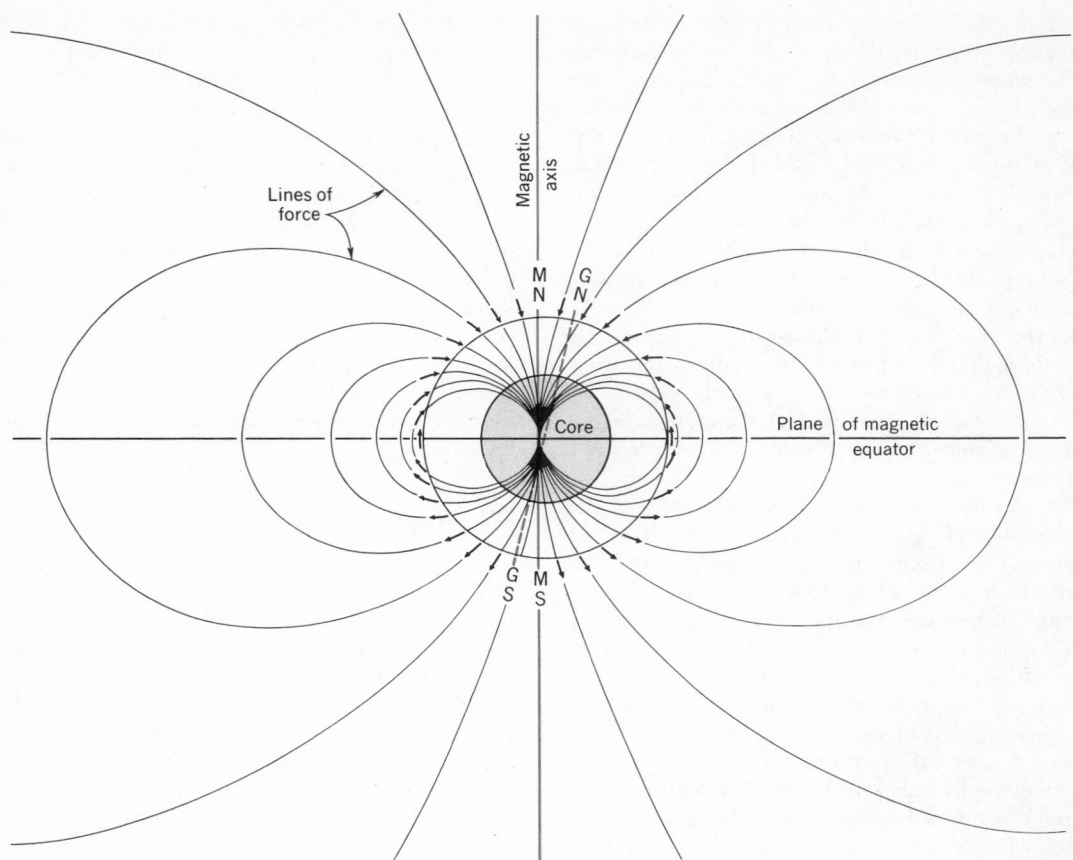

Figure 3.10 Lines of force of the earth's magnetic field are shown diagrammatically in a cross section drawn through the magnetic and geographic poles. The small arrows show the inclination of lines of force at surface points over the globe. (From A. N. Strahler, *The Earth Sciences*, Harper and Row, N.Y.)

shown in Figure 3.10, pass outward through the earth's surface and into surrounding space. A magnetic compass needle, which is nothing more than a delicately balanced bar magnet, orients itself in a position of rest parallel with the lines of force. The lines of force, which extend out into space, comprise the earth's *external magnetic field.* If we assume, for purposes of comparison, that the earth's atmosphere extends outward to a distance equal to twice its own radius, or 8000 mi (13,000 km) it becomes evident that the magnetic field extends far beyond the outermost limits of the atmosphere. The effective limit of the external magnetic field lies perhaps 40,000 to 80,000 mi (64,000 to 130,000 km) from the earth. All of the region within this limit is described as the *magnetosphere;* its outer boundary, the *magnetopause.*

The simplest geometrical model for the shape of the magnetosphere would be a doughnut-shaped ring surrounding the earth. The plane of the ring would lie in the plane of the magnetic equator, while the earth would occupy the opening in the center of the doughnut. Actually, this ideal shape does not exist because of the action of the *solar wind,* a more or less continual flow of electrons and protons emitted by the sun. Pressure of the solar wind acts to press the magnetopause close to the earth on the side nearest the sun (Figure 3.11). Here the distance to the magnetopause is on the order of 10 earthradii (about 40,000 mi, or 64,000 km). Lines of force in this region are crowded together and the magnetic field is intensified. On the opposite side of the earth, in a line pointing away from the sun, the magnetopause is drawn far out from the earth and the force lines are greatly attenuated. The extent of this "tail" is not known, but the entire shape of the magnetosphere has been described as resembling a comet. Length of the magnetic tail has been estimated to be at least 4 million miles (6,400,000 km) and is possibly vastly longer.

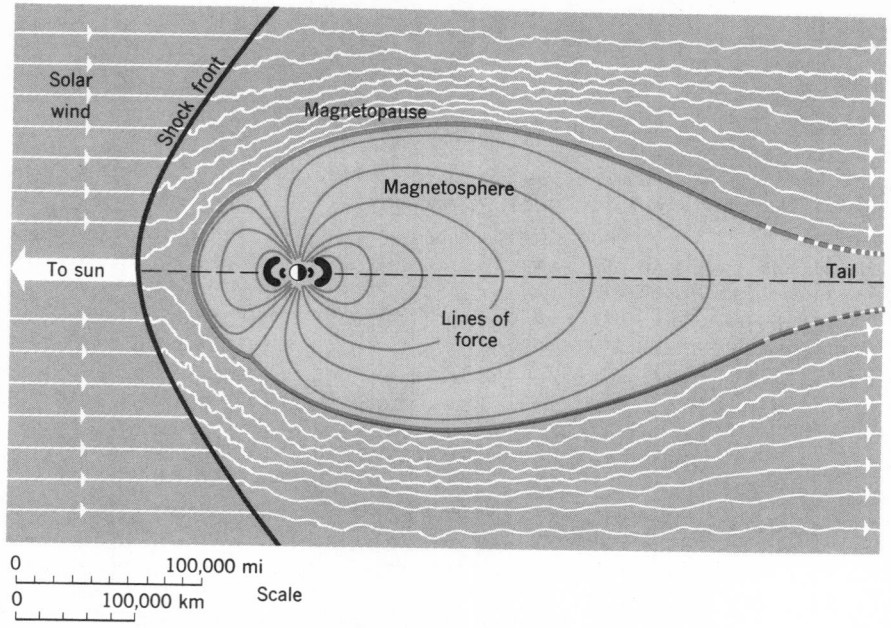

Figure 3.11 Magnetosphere and magnetopause. The Van Allen radiation belts are shown as black areas on either side of earth. (After C. O. Hines, *Science*, 1963, and B. J. O'Brien, *Science*, 1965.)

Radiation belts

In 1958, satellites *Explorer I* and *III*, carrying Geiger counters, sent to earth information concerning the existence of a region of intense radioactivity within the magnetosphere. It was soon discovered that two ring-shaped belts of radiation existed, one lying within the other (Figure 3.11). These rings were named the *Van Allen radiation belts*, after the physicist who first described them. An inner belt was found to lie about 2300 mi (2600 km) from the earth's surface; an outer and much more intense belt at about 8000 to 12,000 mi (13,000 to 19,000 km) distance.

The Van Allen radiation belts represent concentrations of charged particles—protons and electrons—trapped within lines of force of the earth's external magnetic field. These highly energetic particles are derived from the sun and are trapped upon entering the magnetopause. Intensity of trapped radiation fluctuates over a wide range. Solar flares from the sun's surface, occurring at irregular intervals, send bursts of ion clouds toward the earth. At such times, the intensity of trapped particle radiation is greatly increased. One manifestation of such events is the *aurora*, which is most intense over arctic and antarctic latitudes. On earth, severe disturbances to the magnetic field, known as *magnetic storms*, accompany the arrival of ion clouds from solar flares and seriously disrupt radio communication.

REFERENCES FOR FURTHER STUDY

Nelson, J. H., L. Hurwitz, and D. G. Knapp (1962), *Magnetism of the earth*, Coast and Geodetic Survey, Publ. 40–1, U.S. Govt. Printing Office, Washington, 79 pp.

Jacobs, J. A. (1963), *The earth's core and geomagnetism*, The Macmillan Company, New York, 137 pp. See Chapters 5 and 6.

Bates, D. R. (1964), *The planet earth*, second edition, Pergamon Press, Oxford, 370 pp.

Riehl, H. (1965), *Introduction to the atmosphere*, McGraw-Hill Book Co., New York, 365 pp.

Craig, R. A. (1968), *The edge of space, exploring the upper atmosphere*, Doubleday and Co., New York, 150 pp.

1. Describe Man's environment on earth in terms of the realms of land, sea, and air. In what way is physical geography concerned with sciences that treat the atmosphere and oceans?

2. Describe the gaseous, liquid, and solid states of matter. Do these states of matter comprise three complete separate and distinct realms of planet Earth? How are energy changes related to changes of state?

3. Compose definitions of the terms *atmosphere* and *meteorology*. What is the basis for subdividing the atmosphere into the homosphere and the heterosphere?

4. List the nonvarying component gases of the homosphere in order of decreasing proportion by volume, giving approximate percentages for each. Evaluate each gas in terms of its importance to plant and animal life on earth.

5. Describe the layers of the heterosphere in order from lowest to highest. Are the layers sharply divided from one another? Explain the development of layers. How far from earth does the atmosphere extend?

6. Describe the subdivisions of the homosphere. What conditions of temperature prevail in each zone? At what altitude is the tropopause encountered over the equator? over the poles? over middle latitudes? What changes in altitude of the tropopause take place throughout the year?

7. Why is the troposphere of special interest to geographers? What are the constituents of the troposphere, in addition to gases of the pure, dry air? What importance has each constituent?

8. What is the cause of atmospheric pressure? How is pressure measured? Describe Torricelli's experiment and explain the principle involved. Describe a mercurial barometer.

9. What value is given to standard sea-level pressure in inches and centimeters of mercury? What is the equivalent value in millibars? Give a good reason for choosing to use millibars instead of inches or centimeters of mercury.

10. Explain the principle of the aneroid barometer. What advantages has this type over the mercurial barometer? Explain how the aneroid barometer can be used as an altimeter for determining elevation in aircraft.

11. At what rate does air pressure diminish with increasing altitude? Is the rate constant? Does the pressure-altitude curve reveal the position of the tropopause? Explain how air density is related to air pressure.

12. Explain the formation of the ionosphere. At what level does the ionosphere occur? What relation exists between intensity of development of ionospheric layers and the exposure of the atmosphere to sunlight? How does the ionosphere promote long-distance radio communication? What is the Kennelly-Heaviside layer?

13. What is the ozone layer? At what altitude is it found? How is ozone produced? How does the ozone layer influence the environment of plant and animal life at the earth's surface?

14. Describe the earth's magnetic field. Define the magnetic poles and magnetic equator.

15. Describe the magnetosphere. What is the magnetopause? How is the shape of the magnetosphere influenced by the solar wind?

16. What are the Van Allen radiation belts? How were they first discovered? What is the source of radioactivity in these belts? In what way does the activity of the charged particles of the radiation belts differ from that of the gas atoms and molecules of the heterosphere? In what way are aurorae and magnetic storms related to the magnetosphere and to the Van Allen radiation belts?

CHAPTER 4
Heating and Cooling of the Earth's Surface

THE physical geographer seeks to describe and explain the conditions of Man's natural environment. So far as the atmospheric influences are concerned, it is the elements of weather and climate that directly concern Man. These subjects are descriptive and explanatory phases of the sciences of meteorology and climatology.

Weather may be defined as the state of the atmosphere at a given point in time and may be described for a single observing station or for any specified area of the earth's surface. In contrast, *climate* is the characteristic condition of the atmosphere deduced from long periods of repeated observations. Climate includes not only an analysis of average values, but also the departures from those averages and the probabilities of recurrence of particular sets of observations. It follows then that information about climate is derived from weather information; that the former represents a generalization, whereas the latter deals with the specific event.

A statement of weather is a summation of a number of descriptive parameters, often referred to as *weather elements*, falling into several groups, as follows: (1) *air temperature*; (2) *air pressure*; (3) *winds*—the direction and speed of horizontal air movement; and (4) *atmospheric moisture*, including (*a*) *humidity* (measure of water vapor content), (*b*) *clouds* and *fog*, when present, and (*c*) *precipitation*, the falling of liquid or solid water particles. Determination of the weather elements is made by instrumental and direct visual observations at a fixed station on the ground and can be extended upward by means of instrument packages raised by balloon. Ideally, a complete picture of the weather must be three dimensional, extending vertically through the troposphere as well as horizontally over a network of stations. The area between observing stations is treated by means of *interpolation*, and consists of the drawing of lines of equal value (*isopleths*) to show the estimated values of the various weather elements over an entire region and the directions and rates of change of those values from one place to another. Preparation of *weather maps*, which show the simultaneous weather conditions by means of station data and isopleths, constitutes a branch of weather science known as *synoptic meteorology*. Weather maps can be constructed not only for the ground surface but also for various altitude levels.

A statement of climate is based upon the same groups of elements that comprise weather. However, certain categories of information receive major emphasis. In many systems of climate, air temperatures and precipitation amounts are the sole basis of defining climate types and differentiating one from another. The nature of climate data is treated in detail in Chapter 8.

Concept of a global heat budget

This chapter deals primarily with the weather element of air temperature and with related temperatures of land and water surfaces. Everyone is familiar with the measurement of air temperature by thermometer. Most of us routinely receive and interpret air temperature readings as a guide to planning our dress and outdoor activities. Yet we must remember that the air temperature is simply an indicator of the quantity of heat energy within the air. This heat, which may be called *sensible heat*, exists by reason of the *kinetic energy* (energy of motion) of gas molecules. As temperature rises, the energy of molecular motion increases. Therefore attention must be focused upon heat energy and the manner in which it is received and transmitted, exchanged with liquid and solid surfaces, and stored in latent form.

We are all familiar with the cyclic nature of temperature changes. There is a daily rhythm of rise and fall of temperature as well as a seasonal rhythm. There are also systematic average changes in air temperatures from equatorial to polar latitudes as well as from oceanic to continental surfaces. Correspondingly, the lower atmosphere and the surfaces of the lands and oceans must be receiving and giving up heat energy in daily and seasonal cycles. There must also be great differences in the quantities of heat received and given up as one travels from low latitudes to high latitudes.

Despite the existence of thermal cycles and latitudinal contrasts in temperature, human history as well as the geologic record indicate an overall uniformity of the global thermal environment through time. It is apparent that the earth as a planet maintains a *heat balance*, for if this were not the case, the gradual drift toward either increasing heat or decreasing heat would ultimately render the earth's surface too hot or too cold to support life.

For all practical calculations, the sole source of heat energy of the earth's surface is the sun. Minute quantities of heat that flow toward the earth's surface from internal radioactive and volcanic sources can be disregarded as inconsequential. Solar heat is intercepted by our spherical planet and the level of heat energy tends to be raised. At the same time, our planet radiates heat into outer space, a process that tends to diminish the level of heat energy. Incoming and outgoing processes are simultaneously in action. In one place and time more heat is being gained than lost; in another place and time more heat is being lost than gained.

These considerations lead to the concept of a global *heat budget*, analogous in many respects to the money budget of a complex institution such as a large corporation or a government. A first premise of the heat-budget concept is that, over a long period of time, the average level of heat energy for the system as a whole remains absolutely constant. All departures from the average, whether in cycles of short period or long period are balanced out by equal and opposite departures. Furthermore, because equatorial regions receive much more heat than is lost directly to space and polar regions lose much more heat than is received, there must be included in the system mechanisms of heat transfer adequate to export excess heat from one region and to import heat into a region of deficiency. On our planet, motions of the atmosphere and oceans act as heat-transfer mechanisms. Thus a study of the earth's heat budget will not be complete until the patterns of global air and water circulation are described and explained in Chapter 5.

Storage of heat energy in the latent form is an important part of the earth's heat budget. It was noted, in the introduction to Chapter 3, that changes of state between gaseous, liquid, and solid states are accompanied by the taking up of heat energy or release of heat energy. Water in its three states—as water vapor in the atmosphere and as liquid and solid water in the oceans and over the land surfaces—absorbs and liberates heat as it changes from one state to another. Consequently, a study of the earth's heat budget will not be complete until the processes of change of state of water in the atmosphere are examined in Chapters 6, 7, and 9.

Upon reflection, it becomes apparent that the movement of water through atmosphere, oceans, and upon the lands comprises a system of equal importance to the flow of heat and that the activities of these two systems are closely intermeshed. The concept of a *water budget* with a *water balance* can be developed and takes its place beside the heat budget (Chapters 9 and 20). The heat budget can be thought of as dealing with energy and the water budget with matter. Together, these two great systems of energy and matter form a single, grand planetary system and permit us to relate and explain many of the environmental phenomena of our earth within a single unified framework.

A systematic approach to the earth's heat budget begins with an examination of the input, or source, of energy from solar radiation. This radiation is traced as it penetrates the earth's atmosphere and is absorbed or transformed. We then turn to the mechanism of output of heat energy by the earth as a secondary radiator.

Solar radiation

Our sun, a star of about medium mass and temperature, as compared with the overall range of stars, has a surface temperature of about 11,000°F (6000°C). The highly heated, incandescent gas that comprises the sun's surface emits a form of energy known as *electromagnetic radiation*. This form of energy transfer can be thought of as a collection, or *spectrum*, of waves of a wide range of lengths traveling at the uniform velocity of 186,000 mi (300,000 km) per second. The energy travels in straight lines radially outward from the sun, and requires about $9\frac{1}{3}$ minutes to travel the 93 million miles (150 million kilometers) from sun to earth. Although the solar radiation travels through space without energy loss, the intensity of radiation within a beam of given cross section (such as one square inch) decreases inversely as the square of the distance from the sun. The earth thus intercepts only about one two-billionth of the sun's total energy output.

The solar radiation spectrum consists of (*a*) X-rays, gamma rays, and ultraviolet rays, carrying about 9 percent of the total energy, (*b*) visible light rays, 41 percent, and (*c*) invisible infrared and heat rays, 50 percent. Table 4.1 gives the wavelengths in microns, of the various parts of the spectrum. A micron is equivalent to one ten-thousandth of a centimeter. Hereafter, the term *shortwave* radiation is applied to the visible and ultraviolet portion of the spectrum (wavelengths less than 0.7 microns) as distinct from the *infrared* portion (wavelengths longer than 0.7 microns). We see that the total energy of the radiation spectrum is about

TABLE 4.1

	Wavelength	Total Energy (%)
(Shortest)		
X-rays and gamma rays	1/2000 to 1/100 micron	9
Ultraviolet rays	0.2 to 0.4 micron	
Visible light rays	0.4 to 0.7 micron	41
(Longest)		
Infrared rays	0.7 to 3000 microns	50

equally divided between shortwave and infrared portions.

The source of solar energy is in the sun's interior where, under enormous confining pressure and high temperature, hydrogen is converted to helium. In this fusion process, a vast quantity of heat is generated and finds its way by convection and conduction to the sun's surface. Because the rate of production of energy is constant, the output of solar radiation is also unvarying, to the best of scientific knowledge. Hence, at the average distance from the sun, the amount of solar energy received upon a unit area of surface held at right angles to the sun's rays is also unvarying. Known as the *solar constant*, this radiation rate has a value of 2 gram calories per square centimeter per minute. It is assumed, of course, that the radiation is measured beyond the limits of the earth's atmosphere so that none has been lost. One gram calorie per square centimeter constitutes a unit measure of heat energy termed the *langley*. Therefore, we can say that the solar constant is equal to 2 langleys per minute. In English heat units, the solar constant is equivalent to 430 Btu per square foot per hour. Orbiting space satellites equipped with suitable instruments for measuring electromagnetic radiation intensity have provided precise data on the solar constant.

Insolation over the globe

Because the earth is a sphere (disregarding oblateness), only one point on earth—that upon which the sun's noon rays are perpendicular—presents a surface at right angles to the sun's rays. In all directions away from this point, the earth's curved surface becomes turned at a decreasing angle with respect to the rays until the circle of illumination is reached. Along that great circle the rays are parallel with the surface. (See Chapter 2 for a discussion of the relation between the earth and the sun's rays throughout the year.)

Let us now assume that the earth is a perfectly uniform sphere with no atmosphere. Only at the subsolar point will solar energy be intercepted at the maximum rate of 2 langleys per minute. (Hereafter the term *insolation* will be used to mean the interception of solar energy by an exposed surface.) At any particular place on the earth, the quantity of insolation received in one day will then depend upon two factors: (1) the angle at which the sun's rays strike the earth, and (2) the length of time of exposure to the rays. These factors are varied by latitude and by the seasonal changes in the path of the sun in the sky.

Figure 4.1 shows that intensity of insolation is greatest where the sun's rays strike vertically, as they do at noon at the latitude equal to the sun's declination ranging between the tropics of Cancer and Capricorn. With diminishing angle, the same amount of solar energy spreads over a greater area of ground surface. Hence, on the average, the polar regions receive the least heat per unit area. This fact helps to explain the general distribution of average air temperatures over the globe, from a maximum at low latitudes to a minimum near either pole.

We have seen in Chapter 2 that, because of the inclination of the earth's axis, the angle of the sun's noon rays shifts through a total range 47° from one solstice to the next. This cycle does not make the yearly total of insolation for the entire globe different from an ideal situation in which the earth's axis would not be inclined, but it does cause a great difference in both latitudinal and seasonal distribution of the insolation.

Consider first that, if the earth's axis were perpendicular to the orbital plane, the poles would not receive any insolation, regardless of time of year, whereas the equator would receive an unvarying maximum. In other words, equinox conditions (shown in Figures 2.9 and 2.12) would apply every

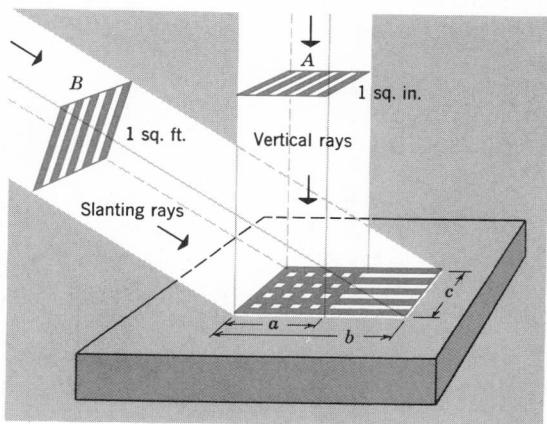

Figure 4.1 The angle of the sun's rays determines the intensity of insolation upon the ground.

day of the year. The earth's inclination, by exposing the poles alternately to the sun, redistributes the yearly total insolation toward higher latitudes, but deducts somewhat from the equatorial zone.

Second, the earth's inclination produces seasonal differences in insolation at any given latitude, and these differences increase toward the poles, where the ultimate in opposites (six months of day; six of night) is reached. Along with the variation in angle of the sun's rays operates another factor, the duration of daylight. At the season when the sun's path is highest in the sky, the length of time it is above the horizon is correspondingly greater. The two factors thus work hand in hand to intensify the contrast between amounts of insolation at opposite solstices.

A three-dimensional diagram (Figure 4.2) shows how insolation varies with latitude and with season of year. Figure 4.3 shows graphs of insolation at various selected latitudes from equator to north pole. These diagrams show insolation at the outer limits of the atmosphere and thus would apply at the ground surface only for an earth imagined to have no atmosphere to absorb or reflect radiation. Notice that the equator receives two maximum periods (corresponding with the equinoxes, when the sun is overhead at the equator) and two minimum periods (corresponding to the solstices, when the sun's declination is farthest north and south of the equator). At the Arctic Circle, $66\frac{1}{2}°$ N, insolation is reduced to nothing on the day of the winter solstice, and with increasing latitude poleward this period of no insolation becomes longer. All latitudes between the Tropics of Cancer and Capricorn have two maxima and two minima, but one maximum becomes dominant as the tropic is approached. From $23\frac{1}{2}°$ to $66\frac{1}{2}°$ there is a single continuous insolation cycle with maximum at one solstice, minimum at the other.

Figure 4.4 presents these insolation data in yet another way. Lines of equal total daily solar radia-

Figure 4.3 Insolation at various latitudes in the northern hemisphere. (From A. N. Strahler, *The Earth Sciences*, Harper and Row, New York.)

tion are drawn upon a graph in which latitude and the yearly calendar form the coordinates. This graph may be thought of as the base upon which the three-dimensional diagram of Figure 4.2 is constructed, while the curves in Figure 4.3 may be thought of as cross sections taken across Figure 4.4 at specified latitudes.

World latitude zones

The sun's path in the sky, which determines the flow of solar energy reaching the earth's surface—and hence governs the thermal environment of Man—provides a basis for dividing the globe into latitude zones (Figure 4.5). It is not intended that the specified zone limits be taken as absolute and binding, but rather that the system be considered as a convenient terminology for referring to world areas throughout this text.

The *equatorial zone* lies astride the equator and extends to 10° latitude north and south. Within this zone, the sun throughout the year provides intense insolation, while day and night are of roughly equal duration. Astride the Tropics of Cancer and Capricorn are the *north tropical zone* and *south tropical zone* respectively, spanning the latitude belts 10° to 25° north and south. In this zone, the sun takes a path close to the zenith at one solstice and is appreciably lower at the opposite solstice. Thus a marked seasonal cycle exists, but is combined with a potentially large total annual insolation. The geography student should note that literary usage and some geographical

Figure 4.2 Insolation at various latitudes and seasons. (After W. M. Davis.)

Figure 4.4 Solar radiation received on a horizontal surface outside the earth's atmosphere. (Data after S. Fritz, 1951, *Compendium of Meteorology*. From A. N. Strahler, *The Earth Sciences*, Harper and Row, New York.)

works differ from what is described here, for the word *tropics* has been widely used to denote the entire belt of 47 degrees of latitude between the tropics of Cancer and Capricorn. Such, indeed, is the definition of "tropics" found in most dictionaries, but that usage, if classically correct, ill fits the needs of physical geography, as will become apparent in the study of climate, soil, and natural vegetation.

Immediately poleward of the tropical zones are transitional regions which have become widely accepted among geographers as the *subtropical zones*. For convenience, these zones are here assigned the latitude belts 25° to 35° north and south, but it is understood that the adjective "subtropical" as applied to geographical regions may extend a few degrees farther poleward or equatorward of these parallels.

The *middle-latitude zones*, lying between 35°

and 55° north and south latitude represent regions in which the sun's path shifts through a relatively large range of noon altitudes, so that seasonal contrasts in incoming solar energy are strong. Strong seasonal differences in lengths of day and night exist as compared with the tropical zones.

Bordering the middle-latitude zones on the poleward side are the *subarctic zones*, 55° to 60° north and south latitudes, transitional between middle-latitude and arctic zones.

Astride the Arctic and Antarctic circles, 66½° north and south latitudes, lie the *arctic zones*, which may be further differentiated, if desired, into an *arctic zone* and an *antarctic zone*. The latitudinal extent of the arctic zones is here specified as 60° to 75° north and south, but these limits should not be imposed severely. The arctic zones have an extremely large yearly variation in lengths of day and night, yielding enormous contrasts in

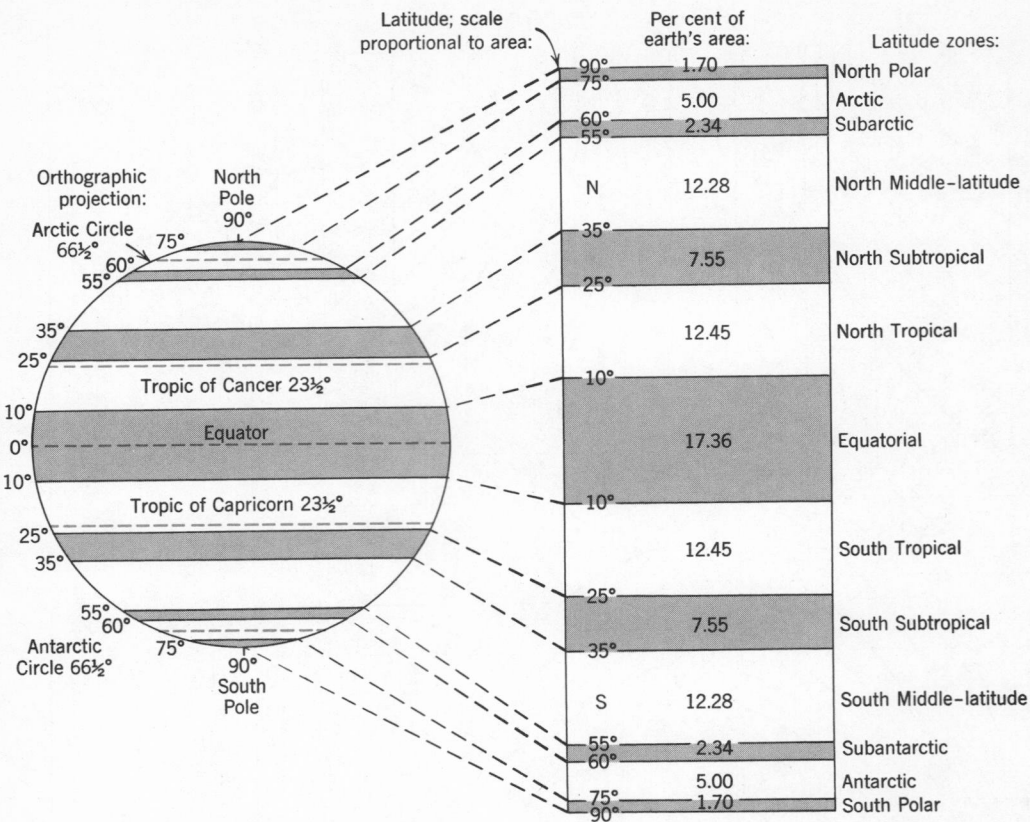

Latitude; scale proportional to area:	Per cent of earth's area:	Latitude zones:
90° / 75°	1.70	North Polar
	5.00	Arctic
60° / 55°	2.34	Subarctic
N	12.28	North Middle-latitude
35°	7.55	North Subtropical
25°	12.45	North Tropical
10°	17.36	Equatorial
10°	12.45	South Tropical
25°	7.55	South Subtropical
35°		
S	12.28	South Middle-latitude
55° / 60°	2.34	Subantarctic
	5.00	Antarctic
75° / 90°	1.70	South Polar

Orthographic projection:
North Pole 90°
Arctic Circle 66½° — 75° — 60° — 55°
35° — 25°
Tropic of Cancer 23½°
10° — Equator — 0° — 10°
Tropic of Capricorn 23½°
25° — 35°
55° — 60° — 75°
Antarctic Circle 66½° — 90° South Pole

Figure 4.5 A geographical system of latitude zones.

incoming solar energy from solstice to solstice. Notice that classical usage, as found in standard dictionaries, considers the "arctic" or "arctic region" as the entire area from arctic circle to north pole, and "antarctic" in a corresponding sense for the southern hemisphere. As with "tropics," "arctic" and "antarctic" in the literary sense are not well suited to the needs of physical geography.

The *polar zones*, north and south, are circular areas between 75° latitude and the poles. Here the polar solar regime of a six-month day and six-month night is predominant and yields the ultimate in seasonal contrasts of incoming solar energy.

Insolation losses in the atmosphere

As the sun's radiation penetrates the earth's atmosphere, a series of selective depletions and diversions of energy take place. At an altitude of 95 mi (150 km), the radiation spectrum possesses almost 100 percent of its original energy, but in penetration to an altitude of 55 mi (88 km) absorption of X-rays is almost complete and some of the ultraviolet radiation has been absorbed as well. As noted in Chapter 3, the ionosphere is

developed in this region of the atmosphere by the effect of the highly energetic X-rays, gamma rays, and ultraviolet rays upon molecules and atoms of nitrogen and oxygen.

As solar radiation penetrates into deeper and denser atmospheric layers, gas molecules cause the visible light rays to be turned aside in all possible directions, a process known as *Rayleigh scattering*. Where dust particles are encountered in the troposphere, further scattering occurs. The total process may be described as *diffuse reflection*. That the clear sky is blue in color is explained by Rayleigh scattering of the shorter visible wavelengths. These predominantly blue light waves reach our eyes indirectly from all parts of the sky. The red wavelengths and infrared rays are less subject to scatter and largely continue in a straight-line path toward earth. The setting sun appears red because a part of the red rays escape deflection from the direct line of sight.

As a result of all forms of shortwave scattering, some solar energy is returned to space and forever lost, while at the same time some scattered short-wave energy also is directed earthward. The latter is referred to as *diffuse sky radiation*, or *down scatter.* An additional but minor cause of energy loss is that which occurs in the ozone layer (see Chapter 3), as oxygen molecules are broken into atoms and reformed into ozone molecules.

Another form of energy loss takes place as the sun's rays penetrate the atmosphere. Both carbon dioxide and water vapor are capable of directly absorbing infrared radiation. Absorption results in a rise of sensible temperature of the air. Thus some direct heating of the lower atmosphere takes place during incoming solar radiation. Although carbon dioxide is a constant quantity in the air (0.033 percent by volume) the water vapor content varies greatly from place to place, being as low as 0.02 percent under desert conditions to as high as 1.8 percent in humid equatorial regions. Absorption correspondingly varies from one global environment to another.

All forms of direct absorption listed above, namely X-ray, gamma ray, and ultraviolet absorption in the ionosphere and ozone layer, combined with direct longwave absorption by carbon dioxide, water vapor, and other gas molecules and dust particles, is estimated to average as little as 10 percent for conditions of clear, dry air, to as high as 30 percent when a cloud cover exists.

Figure 4.6 shows in a highly diagrammatic way the range of values of the various forms of reflection and absorption that may occur. When skies are clear, reflection and absorption combined may total about 20 percent, leaving as much as 80 percent to reach the ground.

Yet another form of energy loss must be brought into the picture. The upper surfaces of clouds are extremely good reflectors of shortwave radiation. Air travelers are well aware of how painfully brilliant the sunlit upper surface of a cloud deck can be when seen from above. Cloud reflection can account for a direct turning back into space of from 30 to 60 percent of total incoming radiation (Figure 4.6). Thus we see that, under conditions of a heavy cloud layer, the combined reflection and absorption from clouds alone can account for a loss of from 35 to 80 percent of the incoming radiation and allow from 45 to 0 percent to reach the ground.

The surfaces of the land and ocean reflect some shortwave radiation directly back into the atmosphere. This quantity, which is very small, may be combined with cloud reflection in evaluating total reflective losses.

The percentage of radiant energy reflected back by a surface is termed the *albedo*. This is an important property of the earth's surface because it determines the relative rate of heating of the surface when exposed to insolation. Albedo of a water surface is very low (2 percent) for nearly vertical rays, but high for low-angle rays. It is also extremely high for snow or ice (45 to 85 percent). For fields, forests, and bare ground the albedos

Figure 4.6   Losses of incoming solar energy by scattering, reflection and absorption. (From A. N. Strahler, *The Earth Sciences*, Harper and Row, New York.)

STATEN ISLAND COMMUNITY COLLEGE LIBRARY
STATEN ISLAND, NEW YORK 10301

TABLE 4.2[a]

	Percent	Langleys per Minute
Total incoming energy lost or absorbed in atmosphere	100	0.485
LOST OR ABSORBED IN ATMOSPHERE		
Absorption by atmosphere, including clouds	19	0.092
Diffuse reflection loss to space	9	0.044
Cloud and ground reflection loss	25	0.121
Total losses	53	0.257
RECEIVED AT GROUND		
From direct penetration	41	0.199
From diffuse sky radiation	6	0.029
Total received at ground	47	0.228
RETURNED TO ATMOSPHERE		
By long-wave radiation (net value)	14	0.069
By latent heat transfer (evaporation and condensation)	23	0.111
By conduction (net value)	10	0.048
Total returned by ground	47	0.228

[a] Data from H. G. Houghton, 1954, "On the Annual Heat Balance of the Northern Hemisphere," *Journal of Meteorology*, Vol. 11, pp. 1–9.

are of intermediate value, ranging from as low as 3 percent to as high as 25 percent.

Attempts have been made to calculate average annual values for percentage of losses of incoming solar radiation in the northern hemisphere. One such estimate is given in the upper part of Table 4.2.

Ground radiation and atmospheric heating

Any substance that possesses heat sends out energy of electromagnetic radiation from its surface. The amount of radiant energy thus sent out is directly proportional to the fourth power of the absolute temperature of the substance. Also, the lower the temperature of the radiating material, the longer are the wavelengths of the rays emitted.

The ground or ocean surface, possessing heat derived originally from absorption of the sun's rays, continually radiates this energy back into the atmosphere, a process known as *ground radiation* or *terrestrial radiation*. This infrared radiation consists of wavelengths longer than 3 or 4 microns and is referred to here as *longwave radiation*. The atmosphere also radiates energy both toward the

earth and outward into space where it is lost. Note that longwave radiation is quite different from reflection, in which the rays are turned back directly without being absorbed. Longwave radiation from both ground and atmosphere continues during the night, when no solar radiation is being received.

Energy radiated from the ground is easily absorbed by the atmosphere because it consists largely of very long wavelengths (4 to 30 microns), in contrast to the visible light rays (0.4 to 0.7 microns) and shorter infrared rays (0.7 to 3.0 microns) which make up almost all of the entering solar radiation. Absorption of longwave radiation by water vapor and carbon dioxide takes place largely in wavelengths from 4 to 8 microns and 12 to 20 microns. However, radiation in the range of wavelengths between 8 and 12 microns passes freely through the earth's atmosphere and into outer space. From one-quarter to one-third of the longwave radiation that is directed outward leaves the atmosphere in this manner. Thus the atmosphere receives heat by an indirect process in which the radiant energy in shortwave form is permitted to pass through, but that in longwave form is not all permitted to escape. For this reason, the lower atmosphere with its water vapor and carbon dioxide acts as a blanket which returns heat to the earth and helps to keep surface temperatures from dropping excessively during the night or in winter at middle and high latitudes. Somewhat the same principle is employed in greenhouses and in homes using the solar-heating method (Figure 4.7). Here the glass permits entry of shortwave energy. Accumulated heat cannot escape by mixing with cooler air outside. The expression *greenhouse effect* has been used by meteorologists to describe the atmospheric heating principle.

Returning to consideration of the earth's total heat budget, it is a requirement of a heat balance that just as much energy, on the average, over long periods of time is sent out from the entire planet Earth into space as is received from the sun. It can also be inferred that the earth's total surface (including both land and water surfaces) on the yearly average must return to the atmosphere just as much energy as it receives, otherwise the surface temperature would rise to intense heat or sink to extreme cold.

The earth's surface gives back heat energy to the atmosphere not only by longwave ground radiation, described above, but also by two other heat-transfer mechanisms. The first of these is by *latent heat* associated with evaporation and subsequent condensation of water. As water evaporates from water surfaces and moist soil, heat energy enters into a latent (stored) form in water vapor. This water vapor diffuses and mixes with the lower atmosphere, carrying the latent heat with it. Condensation in clouds and precipitation in the form of rain and snow releases the latent heat into sensible heat form, raising the temperature of the atmosphere. (This process is treated in further detail in Chapters 6 and 9.)

The second additional mechanism for transfer of heat energy from ground to atmosphere is by direct conduction. Heat is transferred directly from land or sea surfaces to the air in contact with it. Turbulent air motions accompanying winds mix the heated air with higher layers. Of course, when the ground is colder than the air above it, conduction acts in reverse and the ground receives heat from the air.

The estimate in Table 4.2 gives 47 percent as the proportion of incoming solar energy received at the earth's surface as an annual average for the northern hemisphere. Table 4.2 also gives corresponding estimates of the proportions whereby this 47 percent is disposed of. We see that the net loss upward from longwave radiation is 14 percent. By net loss is meant here the difference between upward and downward longwave radiation. From latent heat transfer the loss upward is 23 percent; the net loss from direct conduction of sensible heat is 10 percent.

Although the budget has been stated in percentage units of the original 100 percent of incoming energy, it is easily possible to use absolute units of energy flow, namely, langleys per minute. Our 100 units of incoming solar energy are equivalent

Figure 4.7   Principle of solar heating of a house.

to an average annual value of 0.485 langleys per minute for the northern hemisphere. The figure of 47 percent is equivalent to 0.228 langleys per minute. The remaining equivalents are listed in Table 4.2.

Effect of latitude

Thus far, in examining the total heat budget of the earth, including its atmosphere, consideration has not been given to the effect of latitude. Obviously, an annual average for one entire hemi-

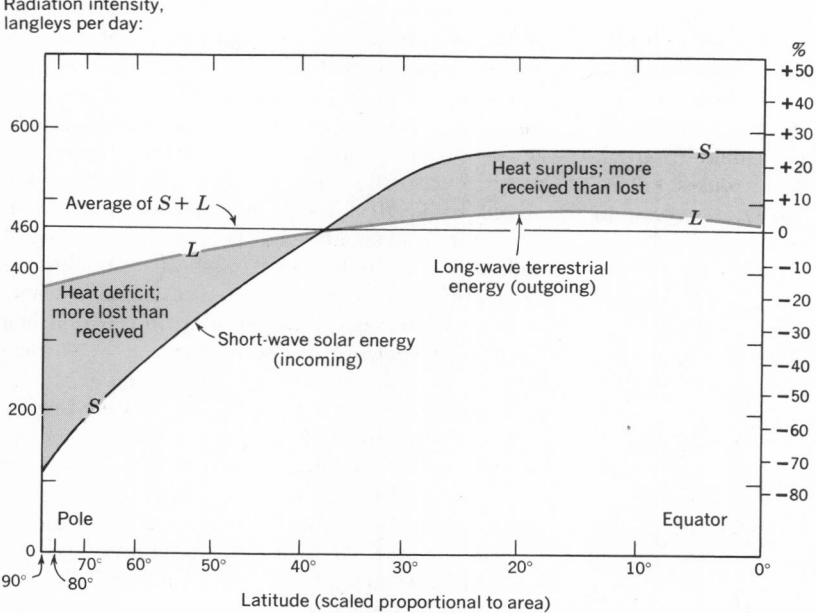

Figure 4.8   The earth's heat budget. (Data after H. G. Houghton, 1954. From A. N. Strahler, *The Earth Sciences*, Harper and Row, New York.)

sphere does not reveal the fact that low latitudes have a large annual radiation surplus, while high latitudes have a large annual deficit. Figure 4.8 is an attempt to evaluate the imbalances of incoming and outgoing energy according to latitude for the earth's surface and the entire atmosphere. On this graph, latitude is scaled on the horizontal axis in proportion to the earth's surface area between any two given parallels of latitude. The vertical axis is on a percentage basis. A plus value represents a radiation surplus relative to the average value, which is the zero line. A negative value represents a deficit. One curve is for incoming shortwave energy; another is for outgoing longwave radiation. The areas lying between these two lines represent the amounts of surplus and deficit; the two areas are equal. Equatorward of about 38° latitude, an annual surplus of radiation exists; poleward of that parallel is an equal deficit. The radiation deficit increases to a maximum at the pole.

It is obvious that moderate temperatures cannot be maintained over the entire globe unless heat is transferred from low to high latitudes. Such heat transfer, in fact, does occur through the action of wind and ocean current systems. These vast movements are discussed in Chapter 5.

Seasonal imbalances in the heat budget

Just as the annual seasonal cycle of incoming radiation shows increasing summer-to-winter contrasts as it is followed from equatorial to polar regions (Figure 4.3), so the radiation budget incurrs increasing summer surpluses and winter deficits from low to high latitudes. Figure 4.9 is a graph in which the difference between incoming and outgoing radiation is plotted against latitude. One curve represents July, the other January. Close to the equator, a heat surplus is shown for both seasons. Poleward of about 20° latitude, the winter season yields a negative value, or deficit, which increases to either pole. Summer surpluses, behaving somewhat differently with latitude, increase to

maxima at 30 to 35° latitude, then fall off with high latitude. The curves actually show negative values in summer, poleward of about 65° latitude. When we look for that latitude at which the summer surplus just equals the winter deficit, it will be found to lie between 35° and 40° north and south. Referring back to Figure 4.8, the latitude at which incoming and outgoing curves cross is 38° N, which agrees well with Figure 4.9. We must keep in mind that the data of Figures 4.8 and 4.9 are generalizations and estimates based upon highly incomplete global data.

Land and water differences

As a final consideration in analyzing the earth's heat budget, it is necessary to introduce the fact that land and water surfaces have quite different properties in absorption and radiation of heat. The general law may be stated as follows. Land surfaces are rapidly and intensely heated under the sun's rays, whereas water surfaces are only slowly and moderately heated. On the other hand, land surfaces cool off more rapidly and reach much lower temperatures than water surfaces when solar radiation is cut off. Temperature contrasts are therefore great over land areas, but only moderate over water areas. It is further true that the larger the mass of land, the greater are seasonal temperature contrasts. Because the heating of ground and water surfaces controls heating of the atmosphere above, the same observations apply to air temperature as to surface temperature.

An explanation of the law of land and water contrasts may be found in the application of certain simple principles of physics (Figure 4.10). Water is transparent and permits heat rays to penetrate many feet, thus distributing the heat through a thickness of several feet of water. The ground surface, being opaque, absorbs heat only at the surface, which thus attains a higher temperature than the water surface. Ocean waters are mixed by vertical rising and sinking motions in the surface layer, allowing heat to be distributed and stored through a great mass of water, but no such movement can occur in the ground. Water surfaces permit continual evaporation, which is a cooling process and serves to alleviate the surface heat. Ground surfaces, which are commonly moist and covered by vegetation, also permit cooling by evaporation, but to a lesser degree than ocean surfaces. As a further cause of contrast, water must absorb almost five times as much heat energy in order to rise in temperature the same amount as dry soil or rock. If heat is being applied equally to both substances, the ground will attain a high temperature long before the water will; *specific heat* of the water is said to be great, that of rock or soil to be small.

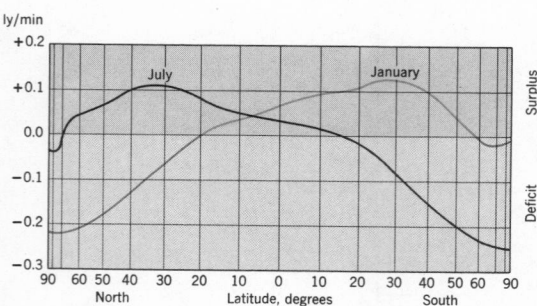

Figure 4.9 Net radiation from pole to pole for January and July. (Data by G. C. Simpson, 1929. After B. Haurwitz and J. M. Austin, 1944, *Climatology,* **McGraw-Hill Book Company, N.Y.)**

Figure 4.10 Contrasts in heating of land and water.

Measurement of air temperature

The remainder of this chapter deals with the surface thermal environment, specifically, with sensible heat expressed in air temperatures. At every recording weather station, the temperature of the air is read at regular intervals from thermometers mounted inside a boxlike shelter built several feet off the ground (Figure 4.11). The instruments are protected from direct sunlight, but air is allowed to circulate freely through the shelter. Standard equipment consists of a pair of *maximum-minimum* thermometers, one of which shows the maximum temperature, the other the minimum, that have occurred in the period since last reset. In addition, an automatic recording thermometer, called a *thermograph,* may be used to draw a continuous temperature record on a piece of graph paper (Figure 4.12).

Throughout this book, the *Fahrenheit* temperature scale is used—the common everyday scale among the general public in the United States. Freezing temperature is 32°; the boiling point is 212° on this scale (Figure 4.13). The U.S. Weather Bureau uses this scale, as do many descriptive elementary textbooks of weather and climate published in this country. One advantage of this scale is that the general reader can relate Fahrenheit temperatures to degrees of bodily comfort or discomfort. The *Centigrade,* or *Celsius,* temperature scale, in which 0° is freezing point and 100° the boiling point, is favored in England and on

Figure 4.11 Standard U.S. Weather Bureau shelter. Rain gauge at left. (U.S. Weather Bureau.)

the European continent and is normally used in physics, chemistry, and advanced meteorology. Fahrenheit and Centigrade (Celsius) measurements are distinguished by the letter "F" or "C" following the figure.

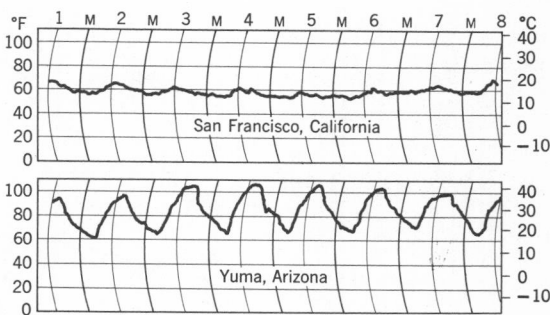

Figure 4.12 Thermograph trace sheets show temperatures for one week. (After Kincer, U.S. Dept. of Agriculture.)

Figure 4.13 Fahrenheit and Centigrade (Celsius) temperature scales.

Annual cycle of air temperature

In order to build statistical information about temperatures for longer periods of time than a single day, a unit known as the *mean daily temperature* is used. The U.S. Weather Bureau follows a very simple method of obtaining the mean daily temperature, using readings made once a day from the maximum-minimum thermometers. The maximum and minimum temperatures for one day are added together and divided by 2. If the mean daily temperatures are collected for many years and averaged for each calendar day or month, then plotted on a graph, a smooth curve of annual temperature is obtained. Figure 4.14 shows such curves for two places at about 40° latitude. Concordia, Kansas, has a midcontinent location; San Luis Obispo, California, at about the same latitude, is near a great ocean body.

Although insolation reaches a maximum at summer solstice, the hottest part of the year on land is about a month later, owing to the lag of peak output of heat energy from the ground beyond the time of peak insolation. One contributing cause of this lag lies in the absorption of heat early in the summer by the soil layer. Air temperature maximum, closely coinciding with maximum ground output of heat, is correspondingly delayed. (Bear in mind that this cycle applies to middle and high latitudes, but not to the region between Tropics of Cancer and Capricorn.) Simi-

larly, the coldest time of year for land areas is January, about a month after winter solstice, because the ground surface continues to lose heat even after insolation begins to rise.

Over the oceans there are two differences. (1) Maximum and minimum temperatures are reached about a month later than on land—in August and February, respectively—because water bodies heat or cool much more slowly than land areas. (2) The yearly range is less than over land, following the law of temperature differences between land and water surfaces. Coastal regions are usually influenced by the oceans to the extent that maximum and minimum temperatures occur later than in the interior. This principle shows nicely for the summer maximum at San Luis Obispo (Figure 4.14).

Several other monthly temperature figures are required for a complete statement of the annual cycle of temperature characteristics of a place. These are named and illustrated in Figure 4.15.

Air temperature maps

The distribution of air temperatures over large areas can best be shown by a map composed of *isotherms*. Similar to topographic contours, whose meaning and construction are discussed at length in Appendix II, isotherms are drawn to connect all points having the same temperature. Figure 4.16 shows a weather map upon which the observed air temperatures have been recorded in the

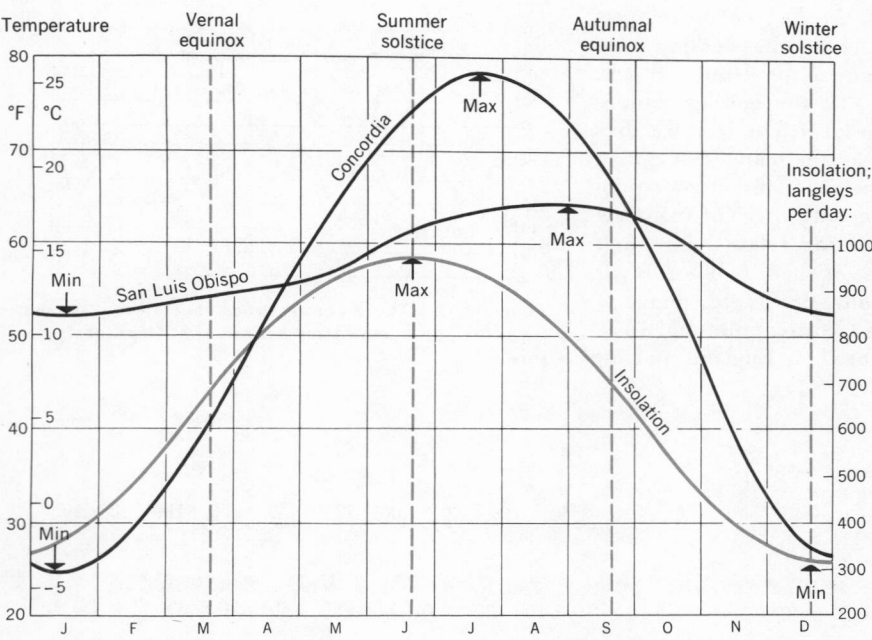

Figure 4.14 The annual cycle of temperature in middle latitudes. (Data of U.S. Dept. of Agriculture. From A. N. Strahler, *The Earth Sciences*, Harper and Row, New York.)

Figure 4.15 Seven annual temperature curves. (After J. B. Kincer, U.S. Dept. of Agriculture.)

Figure 4.16 Construction of isotherms.

correct places. These may represent single readings taken at the same time everywhere, or they may represent the averages of many years of records for a particular day or month of a year, depending upon the purposes of the map. Usually, isotherms representing 5° or 10° differences are chosen, but they can be drawn for any selected temperatures. The isotherms pass through the observing stations only when the station readings coincide with the value selected for an isotherm. Otherwise it is necessary to draw the isotherms by estimating their proper position between stations. The value of isothermal maps is that they make clearly visible the important characteristics of the prevailing temperatures. Centers of high or low temperature are clearly outlined. Zones of gradation are readily seen. From a mere mass of figures on a map, these features are not easily grasped.

World temperature distribution

Isothermal maps of the world for January and July are shown in Figures 4.17 and 4.18. Annual temperature range is shown in Figure 4.19. Isotherms have a general east-west trend around the earth because of the general decrease of insolation from equator to polar regions. The east-west trend and parallelism of isotherms are best developed in the southern hemisphere, south of the 25th parallel, where land areas are small. In the northern hemisphere, isotherms show wide northward and southward deflections where they pass from

a land area to an ocean area, particularly in January, when land and ocean surface temperatures are brought most strongly into contrast.

The land-water effect is represented diagrammatically in Figure 4.20, for the northern hemisphere. The January isotherm is deflected southward over the land, northward over the water. Temperatures along a single parallel are low on land but high on water. In July the reverse is true, with the isotherm pushed far north over the continent.

Throughout the year, isotherms shift through several degrees of latitude, following the declination of the sun but lagging behind a month or so in time. Over large water areas, such as the south Pacific, the annual shift amounts to only about five degrees of latitude, whereas over landmasses, such as Africa, this shift is as much as 20° latitude. (Examine the change in position of the 70°F (21°C) isotherms over Africa.) This difference in amount of latitude shift is also explained by the rapidity and intensity with which lands are heated and cooled as compared with ocean areas.

Certain definite centers of high and low temperature occur and are shown by isotherms which are completely closed to form oval or irregular-shaped enclosures. Notice that all of them are over landmasses. In July, high-temperature centers occur over the southwestern United States, North Africa, and southwestern Asia. In January, a continental center of low temperature occurs over Siberia and is strongly developed with the average January temperatures lower than −50°F (−46°C). A corresponding region of low temperature, marked off by the closed isotherm of −30°F (−34°C), occurs in northernmost North America. It is not so well developed as that of Asia because of the presence of considerable areas of Arctic Ocean among the islands of the northern fringe of the landmass and the smaller size of the North American landmass.

Permanent centers of low temperature exist over

JANUARY
MEAN TEMPERATURE
IN FAHRENHEIT DEGREES

C.	F.
43°	110°
27°	80°
10°	50°
−7°	20°
−23°	−10°
−40°	−40°
−57°	−70°

NORTH POLE

Figure 4.17 (*above and left*)   January temperatures in degrees Fahrenheit. (Compiled by John E. Oliver from data by World Climatology Branch, Meteorological Office, *Tables of Temperature*, 1958, Her Majesty's Stationery Office, London; U.S. Navy, 1955, *Marine Climatic Atlas*, Washington, D.C.; and P. C. Dalrymple, 1966, American Geophysical Union. Cartography by John Tremblay.)

Greenland and Antarctica, the two regions of massive icecaps. Temperatures over Greenland do not, however, reach the extreme low of northern Siberia in January, although the annual average temperature of the icecap is much lower. Analyzed from the polar projection in Figure 4.17, the January region of extreme cold is a distorted ellipse with its long axis extending across the Arctic Ocean from eastern Siberia to northern Canada, but with a sharp, deep reentrant over Greenland. By contrast, the Antarctic region yields concentric isotherms neatly centered on the south pole.

A comparison of winter temperatures at the two poles is instructive, since one lies in a region of deep ocean and the other in the heart of a continent at high elevation. Because of heat conduction through the floating sea ice, not more than 15 ft (5 m) thick, north-polar January mean temperature is probably about −30°F (−35°C). By contrast, the July average at the south pole is about −75°F (−60°C), partly because heat which radiates rapidly from the elevated plateau is not replaced from below. The true cold pole of the antarctic continent is centered 7° to 8° distant from the geographic south pole (Figure 4.18). Here the July mean is below −90°F (−68°C).

The annual range of monthly mean temperatures

JULY
MEAN TEMPERATURE
IN FAHRENHEIT DEGREES

Figure 4.18 (*above and left*)   July temperatures in degrees Fahrenheit. (Data sources same as Figure 4.17.)

at any desired location may be roughly computed from the January and July maps but is more conveniently analyzed on a world map of annual temperature ranges (Figure 4.19). The lines on this map are drawn through points of equal range and may be called *corange lines*. In northern Siberia, the range is about 110 F° (61 C°), greatest of any place on earth. Next are north-central Canada, just west of Hudson Bay, and Greenland with ranges of 70 F° (40 C°). The Arctic Ocean and surrounding continental fringes have a comparable range. Then follow Africa, South America, and Australia, with maximum ranges of about 30 F° (17 C°). An equatorial belt, about 35° of latitude in width over the oceans and about 10° wide across Africa and South America, has an annual range of 5 F°

(2.8 C°) or less.

Ocean currents locally exert a noticeable modification upon the isotherms. The North Atlantic current, which runs northeastward close to the British Isles and the Norwegian coast, causes a sharp northeastward bend of isotherms in winter, when temperature contrasts are generally most marked. An opposite, or equatorward, deflection of isotherms occurs along the western coasts of South America, North America (July), and Africa, where cold currents cause the air temperatures to be lower than usual for tropical latitudes.

Daily cycle of air temperature

If a thermometer is read every hour or half hour throughout 24 hours and the readings are plotted

JANUARY–JULY
TEMPERATURE RANGE
IN FAHRENHEIT DEGREES

C.		F.
0°		0°
11°		20°
22°		40°
33°		60°
44°		80°
56°		100°
67°		120°

Legend (top right of figure):

JANUARY-JULY
TEMPERATURE RANGE
IN FAHRENHEIT DEGREES

C.	F.
0°	0°
11°	20°
22°	40°
33°	60°
44°	80°

Figure 4.19 (*above and left*) Annual range of air temperature. (Same data source as in Figures 4.17 and 4.18.)

on a graph, the curve for a clear day typically shows one low point near sunrise and one high point in midafternoon with a fairly smooth curve throughout. This rhythmic rise and fall of air temperature is termed the *daily*, or *diurnal*, *air temperature cycle*.

Figure 4.21 relates the typical diurnal air temperature curve (bottom) with cycles of both incoming and outgoing heat energy. The diagrams are schematic and apply to a typical middle-latitude location (40° to 45° latitude). We assume equinox conditions (March 21 or September 23), with the time of sunrise and sunset as 6:00 A.M., and 6:00 P.M., respectively. The uppermost graph shows incoming shortwave radiation throughout a clear day. Both direct and indirect shortwave energy are included. Disregarding small amounts of indirect shortwave energy before sunrise and after sunset, the curve begins at 6:00 A.M., reaches a maximum at noon, and ends at 6:00 P.M.

The middle graph shows the net radiation of energy to and from the ground surface. All wavelengths are included. We see here only the difference between incoming and outgoing radiant energy. Where the curve is above the zero line, excess energy is passing upward from ground to atmosphere; where it is below the zero line, excess energy is passing from atmosphere to ground. These positive and negative values are labeled *surplus* and *deficit*, respectively. When a surplus is present, the temperature of the air layer above the ground tends to rise; when a deficit exists, the air tends

Daily Cycle of Air Temperature | 69

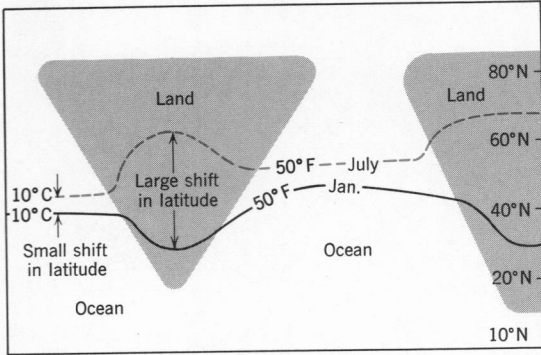

Figure 4.20 Seasonal shift of an isotherm.

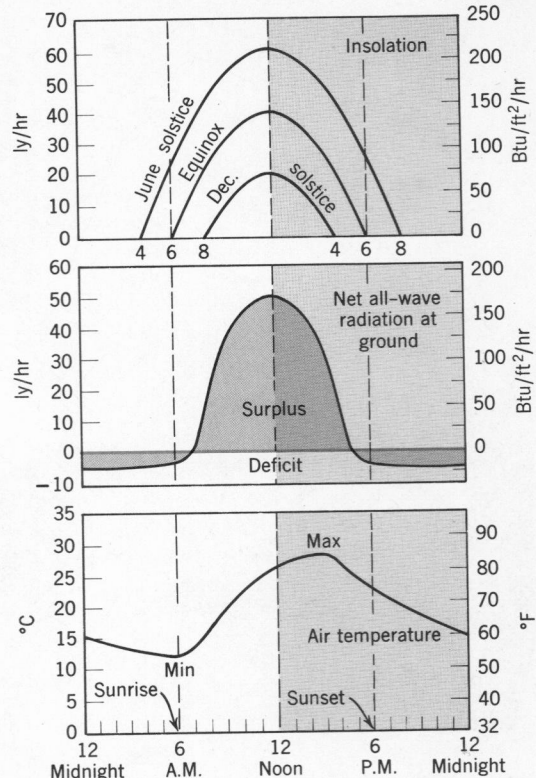

Figure 4.21 Relation of diurnal air temperature curve to insolation and net ground radiation, middle latitudes at equinox.

to be cooled. The net all-wave radiation curve tends to be symmetrical with respect to noon (the maximum point) and to be nearly flat during hours of darkness. As the graph shows, a surplus normally sets in about one hour after sunrise and thereafter increases rapidly. A deficit sets in about an hour or so before sunset.

The typical diurnal air temperature curve, shown in the lowermost graph of Figure 4.21, is not symmetrical. The minimum point occurs at about sunrise. Temperature rises steeply as the radiation surplus increases rapidly. Air temperature continues to rise past noon, for the radiation surplus, although beginning to diminish, is still large. The air temperature maximum typically occurs between 2:00 and 4:00 P.M. Thereafter, the air temperature begins to fall, even though a radiation surplus exists, as the middle curve shows. If air temperature depended only upon ground radiation, the maximum temperature would occur later in the day, perhaps at about 5:00 P.M. under the equinox conditions illustrated. However, another factor has entered the picture. During the early afternoon, mixing of the lower air in turbulent motions increases in intensity, carrying the heated air upward and replacing it with cooler air. The effect of this mixing is to cause the air temperature curve to begin to drop long before the radiation surplus has ended.

Under conditions of June solstice, incoming solar radiation is greatly increased (upper graph in Figure 4.21); the insolation commences much earlier and ends much later. The surplus part of the net ground radiation curve (not shown) is similarly broadened and raised in height. The hour of minimum temperature is set back correspondingly to perhaps 4:00 A.M. However, the hour of maximum temperature remains essentially the same. At December solstice, corresponding reductions of incoming energy and a narrowing and lowering of the part of the surplus radiation curve occur. The time of minimum temperature is ad-

vanced correspondingly.

Figure 4.22 shows the average diurnal cycle of air temperature at two places, one of interior continental location in a dry climate, the other very close to the ocean water on a windward coast. Notice that the hour of minimum temperature changes with solstice and equinox, but that the hour of maximum temperature remains fairly constant. These two graphs show the contrasting effects of water and land in controlling the daily and annual temperature ranges.

Temperature inversion and frost

Although air temperature typically falls with increasing elevation, weather conditions at night in the lower air on land are typically such that, instead of falling, the temperature first rises with increasing height above ground before beginning to drop off into the normal lapse rate (Figure 4.23). This condition is termed *temperature inversion* and signifies that warmer air overlies colder air.

Low-level temperature inversion, or *ground inversion*, commonly results at night from rapid heat loss by radiation from the ground surface and basal air layer upward into space. Rapid radiation

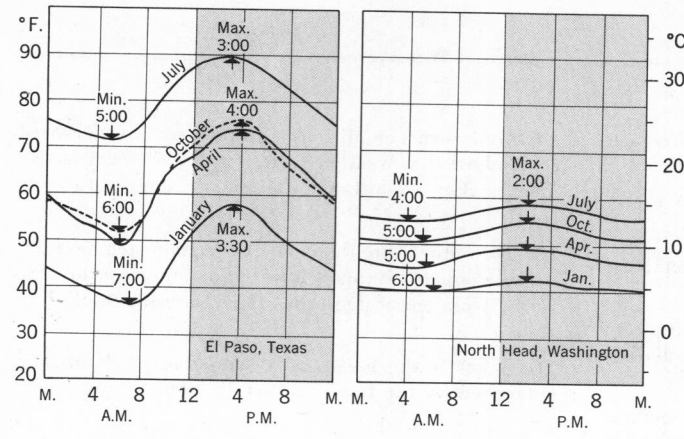

Figure 4.22 The average daily march of air temperatures for two stations. (After J. B. Kincer, U.S. Dept of Agriculture.)

loss is favored by calm air and clear skies. Over snow-covered surfaces on clear winter nights, inversion is particularly marked. If the heat loss is great during a night in spring or early fall, the air temperature close to the ground may drop below freezing, resulting in a killing frost which damages sensitive crops. There are other causes and varieties of both temperature inversions and killing frosts, but these involve movements of masses of air and are not phenomena of heat radiation.

Killing frost may be prevented in orchards and citrus groves by causing a circulation of air that mixes the warmer air above with the cold-air layer near the ground. Where the cold-air layer is thin this effect may be accomplished by the use of powerful motor-driven propellors that circulate air much as does a fan in a room.

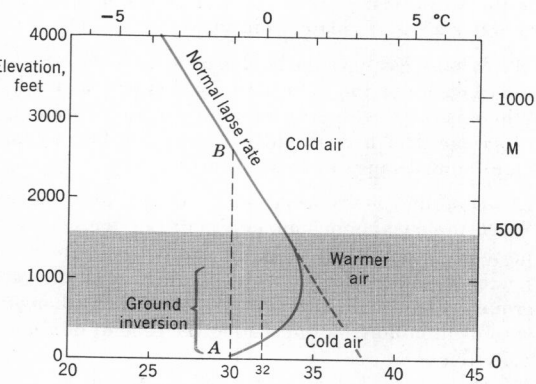

Figure 4.23 A low-level temperature inversion.

REFERENCES FOR FURTHER STUDY

Kincer, J. B. (1928), Temperature, sunshine and wind, *Atlas of American Agriculture*, U.S. Govt. Printing Office, Washington, D.C., 40 pp.

Johnson, J. C. (1954), *Physical meteorology*, Technology Press of M.I.T. and John Wiley and Sons, New York, 393 pp.

Gates, D. M. (1962), *Energy exchange in the biosphere*, Harper and Row, New York, 151 pp.

Geiger, R. (1965), *The climate near the ground*, fourth edition, Harvard University Press, Cambridge, Mass., 611 pp.

Sellers, W. D. (1965), *Physical climatology*, University of Chicago Press, 272 pp.

Petterssen, S. (1969), *Introduction to meteorology*, edition, McGraw-Hill Book Co., New York, 333 pp.

1. Define weather and climate. What is the difference between the two?

2. List the weather elements. How does synoptic meteorology treat the weather elements?

3. Explain the concept of the earth's heat budget. How can the earth maintain a heat balance?

4. From what source does the earth's atmosphere receive its heat energy? Describe the solar radiation spectrum. What is the solar constant?

5. What factors determine the amount of insolation received each day at a given place on the earth? On the average, throughout the year, how is insolation related to latitude?

6. How does the occurrence of the seasons (changing declination of the sun) affect insolation in equatorial latitudes? in middle latitudes (40° to 50°)? in near-polar regions?

7. Name the world latitude zones in order from equator to poles. Give the approximate latitude span and insolation conditions for each zone.

8. Describe the losses in solar radiation in the troposphere. Why should insolation received at the ground surface vary from day to day?

9. How is the earth's atmosphere heated? What has ground radiation to do with atmospheric heating? Is direct reflection from the earth's land or water surfaces important in atmospheric heating?

10. What is the principle of solar heating in a home? What is the greenhouse effect?

11. What effect has latitude upon the annual totals of heat surplus and heat deficit?

12. Describe the seasonal imbalances in heat budget components in middle and high latitudes.

13. Explain the basic differences of land and water surfaces as regards their properties for absorbing and transmitting insolation. How may these differences be expected to influence air temperatures over continental areas as contrasted with ocean areas?

14. Under what conditions is air temperature measured at standard U.S. Weather Bureau stations? What instrument makes a continuous automatic temperature record?

15. How do Fahrenheit and Centigrade temperature scales compare? Explain how temperature can be converted from one scale to the other. Describe the Kelvin scale.

16. What is the mean daily temperature? How is it computed by the U.S. Weather Bureau?

17. How does the annual temperature curve for a middle-latitude place with an inland location differ from that of a place located on a seacoast? Is there a difference in the times at which maximum and minimum temperatures normally occur in these two locations? Why?

18. What are isotherms? How are they drawn? In what way are isothermal maps more useful in the study of weather and climate than maps showing only the temperature figures?

19. What is the general trend of isotherms on the globe? What influence has the changing sun's declination upon the isotherms of monthly mean temperatures? Is the latitudinal shift of isotherms greater over land or water areas? Explain your answer.

20. What effect have the land masses of North America and Asia upon the isotherms for January and July? Where is the earth's greatest annual temperature range experienced? Where would you expect to find a minimum annual range of temperature?

21. Describe the normal daily temperature curve. When are maximum and minimum air temperatures normally reached? How is the air temperature cycle related to the cycle of insolation and to net all-wave ground radiation? Describe the effect of changing seasons in middle latitudes upon the time of minimum daily temperature.

22. What is temperature inversion? Explain how a ground inversion occurs. How are killing frosts produced by radiation of heat?

CHAPTER 5
Winds and the Global Circulation

UP to this point in our study of the atmosphere, little or nothing has been said of air in motion. In Chapter 3 the structure of the atmosphere was described as if motion were absent. In Chapter 4 the daily and seasonal rhythms of heating and cooling were examined, but without explanation of the air motions that such thermal imbalances produce. We therefore turn next to the subject of winds and the global circulation.

The basic principles involved in motion of the earth's atmosphere are these: Nonuniform heating and cooling of the earth's atmosphere sets up nonuniform horizontal distributions of barometric pressure, which in turn tend to set the air in motion. When air motion occurs, heat is transferred from one place to another. Heat exchange by such atmospheric mixing is of great significance in the world patterns of weather and climate, and in the earth's heat budget. Air in motion also transports water vapor from place to place, and this process is likewise of great significance in weather and climate. The role of water with its changes of state in the atmosphere is treated in Chapter 6.

Horizontal distribution of air pressure

Although the vertical decrease of barometric pressure described in Chapter 3 is of interest and importance in many phases of weather science and aviation, it is not the vital element in understanding weather conditions at ground level or world climate types and their distribution. Weather stations that are appreciably above sea level, as most are, have their barometer readings corrected in such a way as to reduce them to sea-level equivalents. Thus, surface weather maps and most climate charts show pressure conditions as if the earth's surface were all at sea level. This adjustment is necessary in order to reveal pressure differences due to factors other than elevation. The recording barograph makes a continuous record of pressure and is an important instrument in weather observing stations (Figure 5.1).

Comparison of barometric pressures (reduced to sea level) recorded simultaneously at several different observing stations, or a comparison of a sequence of pressure readings taken several hours apart at the same station will show small differences that are of great importance in analyzing weather conditions. If 1013 mb (29.92 in., 76 cm) is taken as standard sea-level pressure, readings higher than this will frequently be observed in middle latitudes, occasionally up to 1040 mb (30.7 in., 78 cm) or higher. These pressures are designated as *high*. Pressures ranging down to 982 mb 29 in., 74 cm) or below are *low*. As explained later, low-pressure centers normally are commonly associated with unsettled, cloudy, or stormy weather conditions, whereas high-pressure centers generally have fair, dry weather. This explains why mariners have always regarded a falling barometer as a sign of approaching bad weather.

During winter in middle latitudes, a series of observations taken at one locality will reveal that spells of cold dry weather are commonly accompanied by high pressures, warm or mild spells with cloudiness and precipitation, by low pressures.

Isobaric maps

Pressure conditions can be shown on a map by means of *isobars*, which are lines connecting all places having the same barometric pressure. On the daily weather map, which shows conditions

Figure 5.1   Recording barograph. (U.S. Weather Bureau.)

JANUARY
ATMOSPHERIC PRESSURE
IN MILLIBARS

INCHES	MILLIBARS
29.1	987
29.4	996
29.7	1005
29.9	1014
30.2	1023
30.5	1032
30.7	1041

← Prevailing winds

Figure 5.2 (*above and left*) Average January barometric pressures (millibars, reduced to sea level) and surface winds. Wind arrows in polar regions largely inferred from isobars. (Compiled by John E. Oliver from data by Y. Mintz, G. Dean, R. Geiger, and J. Blüthagen. Cartography by John Tremblay.)

for a specified time only, the isobars are essential in showing the location of moving centers of high or low pressure. On climate maps the isobars show average pressures, computed from the accumulated data of many years. It is to the average world conditions that attention is now directed. Figures 5.2 and 5.3 show conditions in January and July, the months in which temperature extremes are reached.

Figure 5.4 will be useful in converting millibars to inches.

World pressure belts

In the equatorial zone is a belt of somewhat lower than normal pressure, between 1011 and 1008 mb (29.9 and 29.8 in., 76 and 75.7 cm), which is known as the *equatorial trough*. Lower pressure is made conspicuous by contrast with belts of higher pressure lying to the north and south and centered on about latitudes 30° N and S. These are the *subtropical belts of high pressure*. In the southern hemisphere this belt is clearly defined but contains centers of high pressure, termed *pressure cells*. In the northern hemisphere in summer the high-pressure belt is dominated by two oceanic cells, one over the eastern Pacific, the other over the eastern North Atlantic. Average pressures exceed 1026 mb (30.3 in., 77.0 cm) in the centers of the cells.

Poleward of the subtropical high-pressure belts

JULY
ATMOSPHERIC PRESSURE
IN MILLIBARS

INCHES	MILLIBARS
29.4	996
29.7	1005
29.9	1014
30.2	1023
30.5	1032

← Prevailing winds

Figure 5.3 (*above and left*) Average July barometric pressures and winds. (See Figure 5.2 for sources.)

Mb	948		952		956		960		964		968		972		976		980		984		988		992		996		1000		1004		1008

In	28.0	28.1	28.2	28.3	28.4	28.5	28.6	28.7	28.8	28.9	29.0	29.1	29.2	29.3	29.4	29.5	29.6	29.7	29.8

Mb	996	1000	1004	1008	1012	1016	1020	1024	1028	1032	1036	1040	1044	1048	1052	1056

In	29.4	29.5	29.6	29.7	29.8	29.9	30.0	30.1	30.2	30.3	30.4	30.5	30.6	30.7	30.8	30.9	31.0	31.1	31.2

Figure 5.4 Scale for conversion of millibars to inches.

are broad belts of low pressure, extending roughly from the middle-latitude zone to the arctic zone but centered and intensified in the subarctic zone at about the 60th parallels of latitude. In the southern hemisphere, over the continuous expanse of southern ocean the *subantarctic low-pressure belt* is especially defined with average pressures as low as 984 mb (29.1 in., 73.9 cm). The polar zones have permanent centers of high pressure known as the *polar highs*, better illustrated by the south polar zone where the high contrasts strongly with the encircling subantarctic low.

The pressure belts shift seasonally through several degrees of latitude, just as do the isotherm belts that accompany them. More attention will be given this shift in the explanation of climates.

Northern hemisphere pressure centers

The vast landmasses of North America and Asia, separated by the North Atlantic and North Pacific oceans, exert such a powerful control over pressure conditions in the northern hemisphere that the belted arrangement typical of the southern hemisphere is absent.

Land areas develop high-pressure centers at the same time that winter temperatures fall far below those of adjacent oceans. In summer, land areas develop low-pressure centers, at which season land-surface temperatures rise sharply above temperatures over the adjoining oceans. Ocean areas show centers of pressure opposite to those on the lands, as seen in the January and July isobaric maps. In winter, pressure contrasts are greater, just as temperature contrasts are greater. Over north central Asia is developed the *Siberian high*, with pressure average exceeding 1035 mb (30.6 in., 77.7 cm). Over central North America is a clearly defined, but much less intense, ridge of high pressure, called the *Canadian high*. Over the oceans are the *Aleutian low* and the *Icelandic low*, named after the localities over which they are centered. These two low-pressure areas have much cloudy, stormy weather in winter, whereas the continental highs characteristically have a large proportion of clear, dry days.

Figure 5.5 shows diagrammatically the pressure centers as they appear grouped around the north pole. Highs and lows occupy opposite quadrants.

In summer, pressure conditions are exactly the opposite of winter conditions. Asia and North America develop lows, but the low in Asia is more intense. It is centered in southern Asia where it is fused with the equatorial low-pressure belt. Over the Atlantic and Pacific oceans are two well-developed cells of the subtropical belt of high pressure, shifted northward of their winter position and considerably expanded. These are termed the

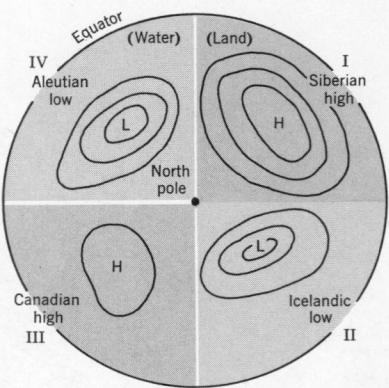

Figure 5.5 Northern hemisphere pressure centers in January.

Azores (or *Bermuda*) *high* and the *Hawaiian high* respectively.

Relation of winds to barometric pressure

Figure 5.6 is an isobaric map, showing centers of high and low pressure. From the center of the high there is progressively lower pressure, or a *barometric slope*, outward in any direction from the center. This slope is also termed the *pressure gradient*. Direction of pressure gradient, indicated by broad arrows, is always at right angles to the isobars. Whether there are pressure centers or belts, a pressure gradient always exists, running from higher to lower pressure. Closely spaced isobars indicate that the gradient is strong and that pressure changes occur rapidly within a short horizontal distance. Widely spaced isobars indicate a weak gradient.

The widespread and persistent winds of the earth are those movements of air set up in response to pressure differences. A *pressure gradient force*, acting in the direction of the pressure gradient, tends to start the flow of air from higher to lower pressure. Strong pressure gradients, indicated by

Figure 5.6 Relation of winds to isobars.

closely crowded isobars on the map, cause strong winds, whereas widely spaced isobars can be expected to yield weak winds. Calms exist in the centers of high pressure.

The Coriolis force and its effect on winds

If the earth did not rotate upon its axis, winds would follow the direction of pressure gradient. Instead, earth rotation produces another force, the *Coriolis force*, which tends to turn the flow of air. The direction of action of the Coriolis force is stated in Ferrel's law: Any object or fluid moving horizontally in the northern hemisphere tends to be deflected to the right of its path of motion, regardless of the compass direction of the path. In the southern hemisphere a similar deflection is toward the left of the path of motion. The Coriolis force is absent at the equator but increases progressively poleward.

On Figure 5.7 the various arrows show how an initial straight line of motion is modified by the deflective force. Note especially that the compass direction is not of any consequence. If we face down the direction of motion, turning will always be toward the right hand in the northern hemisphere. Because the deflective force is very weak, it is normally apparent only in freely moving fluids such as air or water. Ocean current patterns are greatly affected by it, and streams occasionally will show a tendency to undercut their right-hand banks in the northern hemisphere. Driftwood floating in rivers at high northerly latitudes con-

centrates along the right-hand edge of the stream. Rifle bullets are slightly deflected over long ranges.

Applying these principles to the relation of winds to pressure (Figure 5.8), the gradient force (acting in the direction of the pressure gradient) and the Coriolis force (acting to the right of the path of flow) quickly reach a balance, or equilibrium, when the wind has been turned to the point that it flows in a direction at right angles to the pressure gradient, that is, parallel with the isobars. The ideal wind in this state of balance with respect to the two forces is termed the *geostrophic wind* for cases in which the isobars are straight. Where isobars are curved, centrifugal force must also be taken into account, but, in general, air flow at high altitudes parallels the isobars (Figure 5.8). The rule for the relation of wind to pressure in the northern hemisphere is known as *Ballot's law*; it states: Stand with your back to the wind and the low pressure will be on your left, the high on your right.

Near the earth's surface, at levels from the ground upward to about 2000 or 3000 ft (600 or 900 m), yet another force modifies the wind direction. This is the force of friction of the air with the ground. It acts in such a way as to counteract in part the Coriolis force and to prevent the wind from being deflected until parallel with the isobars. Instead, the wind blows obliquely across the iso-

Detail of above map:

Figure 5.7 Deflective force of the earth's rotation.

Figure 5.8 Wind follows isobars at high levels.

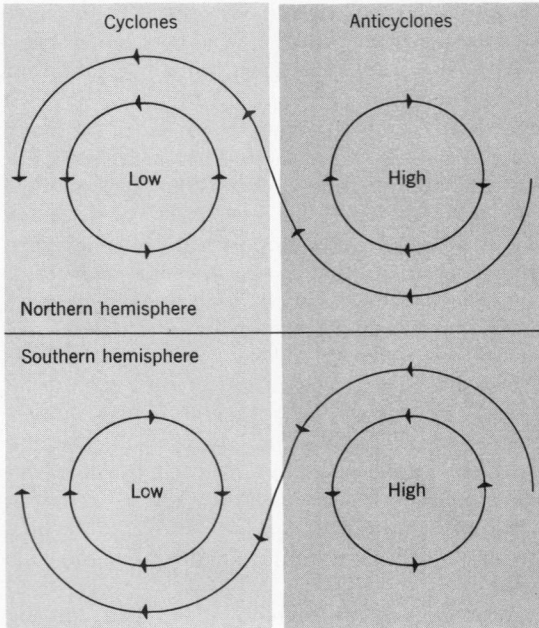

Figure 5.9 Winds at high elevation around cyclones and anticyclones.

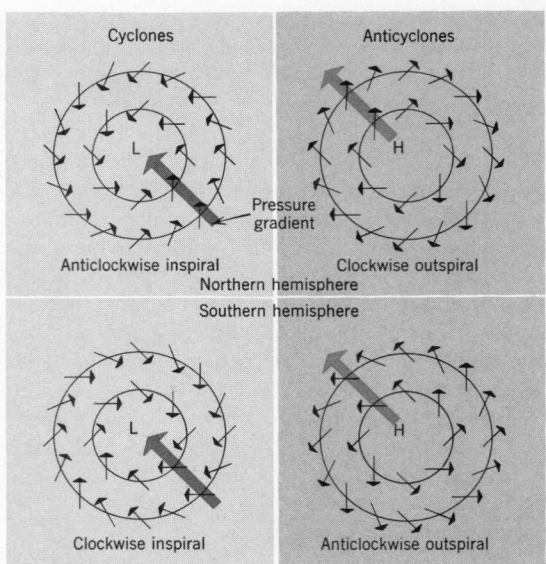

Figure 5.10 Surface winds within cyclones and anticyclones.

bars, the angle being from 20° to 45°. Figure 4.9 illustrates surface winds and is typical of conditions found on the surface weather map. The angle is large for rugged terrain; small for smooth surfaces, such as water or a flat plain. Wind speed is reduced in proportion to ground friction.

Cyclones and anticyclones

In the language of meteorology and climatology, a center of low pressure is designated a *cyclone*; a center of high pressure is an *anticyclone*. Cyclones and anticyclones may be of the stationary, or semipermanent type, such as the Aleutian low and Siberian high described under the topic of global pressure centers, or they may be rapidly moving pressure centers such as create the weather disturbances described in Chapter 6. It will be of great help to the student of weather and climate to have a clear picture of the pattern of winds in cyclones and anticyclones of both northern and southern hemispheres.

As shown in Figure 5.8 air moving at high elevations, where surface friction does not act, parallels the isobars. We can thus give the rule that in the northern hemisphere winds move anticlockwise (counterclockwise) about a cyclone; clockwise about an anticyclone. In the southern hemisphere these patterns are exactly reverse: clockwise about a cyclone; anticlockwise about an anticyclone. The simple upper-air map in Figure 5.9 shows how these rules apply.

For surface winds, which move obliquely across the isobars, the systems for cyclones and anticyclones in both hemispheres are shown in Figure 5.10. To construct the wind arrows, first draw a long arrow to show the direction of pressure gradient. Next, draw short, straight arrows through the point where the gradient arrow crosses each isobar. Be sure that the wind arrows are deflected to the right in the northern hemisphere and to the left in the southern. After carrying out this operation on four sides of a pressure center the pattern will emerge and can easily be completed. To avoid confusion, keep the wind arrows short and straight, as they are on weather maps. When the pattern is complete, it will be seen that the winds in a cyclone in the northern hemisphere show an anticlockwise inspiral; in an anticyclone, a clockwise outspiral. Note the reversal between the labels "anticlockwise" and "clockwise" in the southern hemisphere. In both hemispheres the surface winds spiral inward upon the center of the cyclone, hence the air is *converging* upon the center and must also rise to be disposed of. For the anticyclone, by contrast, surface winds spiral out from the center, which represents a *diverging* of air flow and must be accompanied by a sinking (subsidence) of air in the center of the anticyclone to replace the outmoving air.

Measurement of winds

A description of winds requires measurement of two quantities, direction and speed. Direction is easily determined by a *wind vane*, known to all because it is frequently mounted on rooftops and is one of the commonest of the amateur weather instruments. Wind direction is stated in terms of the direction from which the wind is coming. Thus an east wind comes from the east, but the direction of air movement is toward the west. The direction of movement of low clouds is an excellent indicator of wind direction and can be observed without the aid of instruments.

Speed of wind is measured by an *anemometer*. There are several types. The commonest one seen at weather stations is the *cup anemometer*. It consists of three or four hemispherical cups mounted as if at the ends of spokes of a horizontal wheel (Figure 5.11). The cups travel with a speed proportional to that of the wind. Other types of anemometers depend on measuring the force exerted by the wind upon an exposed surface.

For wind velocities at higher levels a small hydrogen-filled balloon, whose rate of ascent is known, is released into the air and observed through a telescope. Knowing the balloon's vertical position by measuring the elapsed time, an observer can calculate the horizontal drift of the balloon downwind. For modern, upper-air measurements of wind velocity and direction the balloon carries a target that reflects radar waves and can thus be followed when the sky is overcast.

Conventional symbols have been established to show wind direction and speed on weather and climate maps. For single observations, such as those on a daily weather map, an arrow of the type shown in Figure 5.12 is used. The circle takes the place of the arrow point and is centered on the observing station. Attached to the shaft of the

Figure 5.12 Standard weather map symbols.

arrow are short lines, or feathers, and pennants, whose numbers show wind speed in knots (nautical miles per hour) according to a predetermined code.

For wind observations collected over a long period of time a device known as a *wind rose* is constructed. One is illustrated in Figure 5.13. Wind directions are reduced to eight compass sectors shown by lines radiating from the central point. The percentage of total length of time during which wind blows from these sectors of the compass is indicated by length of the lines. On charts showing wind roses there is printed on the margin a scale from which the percentages may be measured. Small feather lines attached to the ends of the radial lines are used to show the average wind speed during the period for which the wind rose is constructed. The Beaufort scale of wind force is used.

Earth's surface wind systems

Prevailing surface winds during the months of January and July are suggested by arrows on the pressure maps, Figures 5.2 and 5.3. A highly diagrammatic representation of the wind systems

Figure 5.11 A cup-type anemometer. (Courtesy of U.S. Weather Bureau.)

Figure 5.13 The wind rose.

in Figure 5.14 shows the earth as if no land areas existed to modify the belted arrangement of pressure zones.

In the equatorial trough of low pressure, intense solar heating causes the moist air to break into great convection columns, so that there is a general rise of air. This region, lying roughly between 5° S and 5° N lat., was long called the *equatorial belt of variable winds and calms*, or the *doldrums*. There are no prevailing surface winds here, but a fair distribution of directions around the compass (Figure 5.15). Calms prevail as much as a third of the time. Violent thunderstorms with strong squall winds are common. Centrally located on a belt of low pressure, this zone has no strong pressure gradients to induce a persistent flow of wind.

North and south of the doldrums are the *trade wind* belts, covering roughly the zones lying between 5° and 30° N and S. The trades are a result of a pressure gradient from the subtropical belt of high pressure to the equatorial trough of low pressure. In the northern hemisphere, air moving equatorward is deflected by the earth's rotation to turn westward. Thus, the prevailing wind is from the northeast and the winds are termed the *northeast trades*. In the southern hemisphere, deflection of the moving air to the left causes the *southeast trades*. Trade winds are noted for their steadiness

and directional persistence. Figure 5.15 shows wind roses within the trade wind belts. Note that most winds come from one quarter of the compass.

The system of doldrums and trades shifts seasonally north and south, through several degrees of latitude, as do the pressure belts that cause them. Because of the large land areas of the northern hemisphere, there is a tendency for these belts to be shifted farther north in the northern hemisphere in summer (July) than they are shifted south in winter (January). The trades are best developed over the Pacific and Atlantic oceans, but are upset in the Indian Ocean region by the proximity of the great Asiatic landmass.

The trade winds provided a splendid avenue for westward travel in the days of sailing vessels. Steadiness of wind and generally clear weather made this a favorite zone of mariners. Crossing of the doldrums was hazardous because of the possibility of being becalmed for long periods and because of the uncertainty of wind direction. The trade wind belts are not altogether favorable for navigation and flying, however, because over certain oceanic portions, at certain seasons of the year, terrible tropical storms known as hurricanes or typhoons occur (Chapter 7).

Between latitudes 30° and 40° are what have long been called the *subtropical belts of variable*

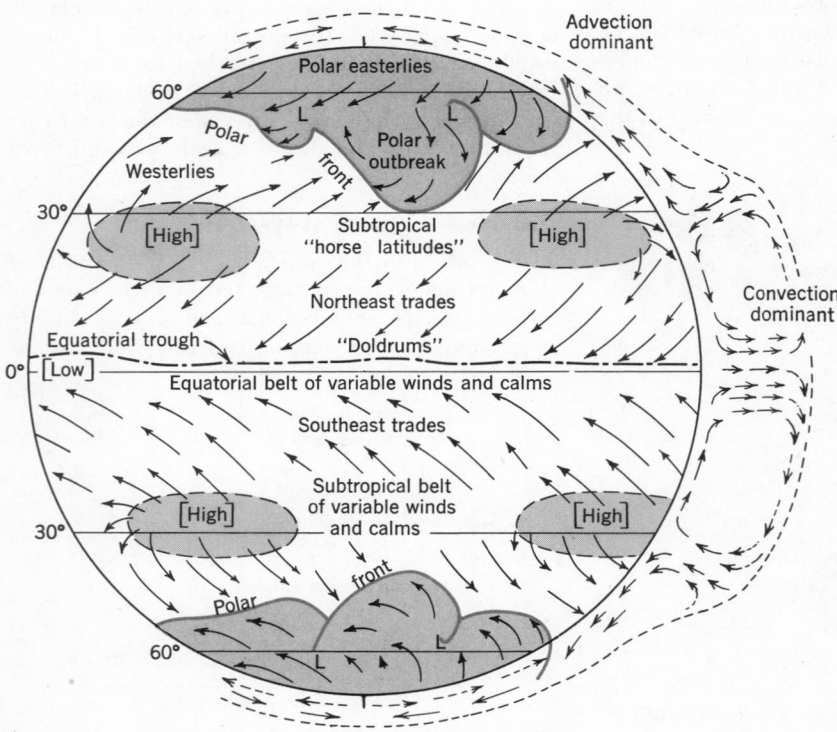

Figure 5.14 The general scheme of atmospheric circulation.

Figure 5.15 This portion of an Oceanographic Office pilot chart of the North Atlantic for July shows parts of both the northeast and southeast trade wind belts, with the narrow doldrum belt lying between. The area shown here extends from 5°S lat. to 20° N lat. Wind roses occupy 5° squares. (U.S. Navy Oceanographic Office, Chart 1400.)

Figure 5.16 Semi-permanent centers of high pressure and surface winds.

winds and calms, or horse latitudes, coinciding with the subtropical high-pressure belt. Instead of being continuous even belts, however, the high-pressure areas are concentrated into distinct anticyclones or cells, located over the oceans. Figure 5.16 shows anticyclones in the northern and southern hemisphere and the resultant surface winds. The apparent outward spiraling movement of air is directed equatorward into the easterly trade wind system; poleward into the westerly wind system. The cells of high pressure are most strongly developed in the summer (January in the southern hemisphere, July in the northern). There is also

a latitudinal shifting following the sun's declination. This amounts to less than 5° in the southern hemisphere, but it is about 8° for the strong Hawaiian high located in the northeastern Pacific.

Wind roses for the horse latitudes are shown in Figure 5.17. Winds are distributed around a considerable range of compass directions. Calms prevail as much as a quarter of the time. The cells of high pressure have generally fair, clear weather, with a strong tendency to dryness. Most of the world's great deserts lie in this zone and in the adjacent trade wind belt. An explanation of the dry, clear weather lies in the fact that the anticyclonic cells are centers of descending air, settling from higher levels of the atmosphere and spreading out near the earth's surface. Descending air, as explained more fully in the next chapter, becomes increasingly dry.

Between latitudes 35° and 60°, both N and S, is the belt of the westerlies, or prevailing westerly winds. Moving from the subtropical anticyclones toward the subarctic lows, these surface winds are shown on Figure 5.14 to blow from a southwesterly quarter in the northern hemisphere, from a northwesterly quarter in the southern hemisphere. This generalization is somewhat misleading, however, because winds from polar directions are frequent and strong. It is more accurate to say that within the westerly wind belt, winds blow from any direction of the compass, but that the westerly components are definitely predominant. Storm winds are common in this belt, as are frequent cloudy days with continued precipitation. Weather is highly changeable.

In the northern hemisphere, landmasses cause considerable disruption of the westerly wind belt, but in the southern hemisphere, between the latitudes 40° and 60° S, there is an almost unbroken belt of ocean. Here the westerlies gain great strength and persistence, giving rise to the mariner's expressions, "the roaring forties," "the furious fifties," and "the screaming sixties." This belt was extensively used for sailing vessels traveling eastward from the South Atlantic Ocean to Australia, Tasmania, New Zealand, and the southern

Pacific islands. From these places it was then easier to continue eastward around the world to return to European ports. Rounding Cape Horn was relatively easy on an eastward voyage, but in the opposite direction, in the face of prevailing stormy westerly winds, was fraught with great danger.

Although the westerly wind belts no longer exert a strong influence over the routes of modern ocean vessels, they are important in long-distance flying. Transoceanic and transcontinental flights in the easterly direction require less fuel and a shorter time. On westward flights, strong head winds may eat dangerously into the fuel supply on the plane and in any event necessitate reduced pay loads.

A wind system often termed the *polar easterlies* has been described as characteristic of the arctic and polar zones (Figure 5.14). The concept is greatly oversimplified, if not actually erroneous, for winds in these regions take a variety of directions, as dictated by local weather disturbances. Perhaps in Antarctica, where an icecapped landmass rests squarely upon the pole and is surrounded by a vast oceanic expanse, the outward spiraling flow of polar easterlies is a valid concept. Deflected to the left in the southern hemisphere, the radial winds would spiral counterclockwise, producing a system of southeasterly winds.

Monsoon winds of Asia and North America

Frequent reference has been made to the powerful control which Asia and North America exert upon conditions of temperature and pressure in the northern hemisphere. Because pressure conditions control winds, it is obvious that these areas must develop wind systems relatively independent of the belted system of earth winds so well illustrated in the southern hemisphere.

In summer, southern Asia develops a cyclone into which there is a considerable flow of air. This may be a *heat low*, or *thermal low*, limited to the lower levels of the atmosphere (Figure 5.18). From the Indian Ocean and the southwestern Pacific warm, humid air moves northward and northwestward into Asia, passing over India, Indochina, and China (See Figure 5.3.) This air flow constitutes the *summer monsoon*, which is accompanied by heavy rainfall in southeastern Asia.

In winter, Asia is dominated by a strong center of high pressure, from which there is an outward flow of air reversing that of the summer monsoon (see Figures 5.2, 5.18). Blowing southward and southeastward toward the equatorial oceans, this *winter monsoon* brings dry, clear weather for a period of several months.

North America, being smaller in extent, does not have the remarkable extremes of monsoon winds experienced by southeastern Asia, but there

Figure 5.17 The subtropical belt of variable winds and calms (horse latitudes) lies in the center of this portion of an Oceanographic Office pilot chart of the South Atlantic for June–July–August. To the north are the steady southeast trades; to the south, the variable northwesterlies. The area shown here extends from 10° to 40° S lat. Wind roses occupy 5° squares. (U.S. Navy Oceanographic Office, Chart 2600.)

Figure 5.18   Monsoon winds over the Indian Peninsula. (Data from U.S. Navy Oceanographic Office and Blanford.)

is nevertheless an alternation of temperature and pressure conditions between winter and summer. Analysis of wind records shows that in summer there is a prevailing tendency for air originating in the Gulf of Mexico to move northward across the central and eastern part of the United States, whereas in winter there is a prevailing tendency for air to move southward from sources in Canada (Figures 5.2 and 5.3). Australia, too, shows a monsoon effect, but being south of the equator it reverses the conditions of Asia.

Global circulation systems

The surface wind systems thus far described represent only a shallow basal air layer a few thousands of feet thick, whereas the troposphere is from 5 to 12 mi (8 to 20 km) thick. What is the nature of air flow at these higher levels? Since the Second World War, a vast network of observing stations has been taking upper-air observations extending up to 80,000 ft (25,000 m) or higher by means of the *radiosonde*, a compact set of weather instruments that automatically sends back information on pressure, temperature, and humidity by code from a self-contained radio transmitter. Carried aloft by a gas-filled balloon, the radiosonde transmitter can be tracked by means of a radio direction finder. From observations taken simultaneously at many places, a weather map of upper air conditions can be drawn. It has been found that there are slowly moving high- and

low-pressure systems aloft, but that these are generally simple in pattern with smoothly curved isobars. Winds, which may be extremely strong and follow the isobars closely, move counterclockwise around the lows (northern hemisphere), but clockwise around the highs, as shown in Figure 5.8.

The general or average pattern of upper air flow is sketched in Figure 5.19. Two systems dominate.

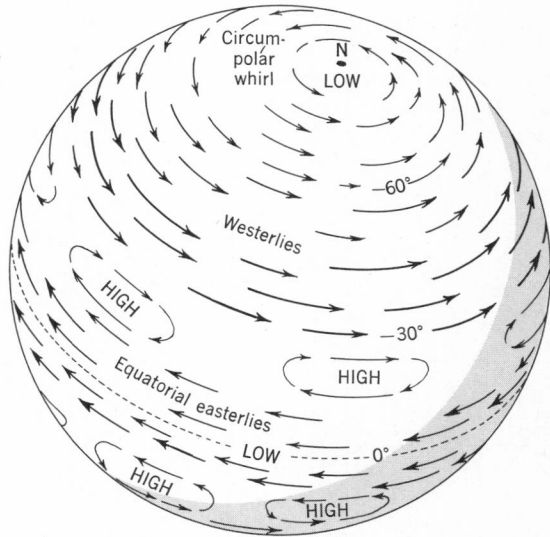

Figure 5.19   Schematic representation of circulation in the upper part of the troposphere, 20,000 to 40,000 ft (6 to 12 km).

One is the system of *westerlies* blowing in a complete circuit about the earth from about latitude 20° almost to the poles. At high latitudes these westerlies constitute a *circumpolar whirl*, coinciding with a great polar low-pressure center. Toward low latitudes the pressure rises steadily at a given altitude, to form two high-pressure ridges at latitudes 15° to 20° N and S. These are the high-altitude parts of the subtropical highs, but are shifted somewhat equatorward. In the high-pressure zones, wind velocities are low, just as in the horse latitudes at sea level. Between the high-pressure ridges is a trough of weak low pressure, in which the winds are easterly, comprising the second major circulation system of the globe, termed the *equatorial easterlies*. At lower elevation their influence spreads into somewhat higher latitudes as the trade winds.

The jet stream

The upper-air westerlies tend to form somewhat serpentine or meandering paths, giving rise to slowly moving *upper air waves*, in which the winds are turned first equatorward, then poleward (Figure 5.20). Associated with the development of such upper air waves at altitudes of 30,000 to 40,000 ft (10,000 to 12,000 m) are narrow zones in which wind streams attain velocities up to 200 to 250 knots (350–450 km per hr). This phenomenon, named the *jet stream*, consists of pulselike movements of air following a broadly curving track (Figure 5.20). In cross section the jet may be likened to a stream of water moving through a hose, the center line of highest velocity being surrounded by concentric zones of less rapidly moving fluid, as pictured in Figure 5.21.

It is by means of the upper air waves that warm air of the tropics is carried far north at the same time that cold air of polar regions is brought equatorward. In this way horizontal mixing, or *advection*, develops on a gigantic scale and serves to provide heat exchange between regions of high and low insolation.

Figure 5.21   The jet stream. (From U.S. Weather Bureau.)

Local winds

In certain favorable localities, *local winds* are generated by immediate influences of the surrounding terrain, rather than by the large-scale pressure systems that produce global winds and large traveling storms. Local winds are important to the geographer interested in climates, because the characteristic repetition of occurrence of a local wind is itself an important aspect of the local climate.

One simple system of local winds, widely occurring along coasts, is the *land and sea breeze* (Figure 5.22), in which the wind blows from sea to land during the day, but from land to sea at night. The daytime wind, or sea breeze, is caused by a landward-sloping barometric pressure gradient developed as a result of daytime heating of the lower air layer over the land. Because the adjacent sea surface is not so intensely heated it remains relatively cooler. In response to the local pressure gradient, air flows landward at low level. The sea breeze is comparatively cool and brings pleasant relief to a narrow coastal belt on hot summer afternoons. At night the temperature differences are reversed because of more rapid cooling of the land surface. The pressure gradient is now from

Figure 5.20   The jet stream, shown by lines of equal wind speed. (After U.S. Weather Bureau.)

land to sea, causing a seaward flow of air—the land breeze.

Mountain and *valley winds* are local winds following a daily alternation of direction in a manner similar to the land and sea breezes. The air moves from valleys, upward over rising mountain slopes, toward the summits during the day, when slopes are intensely heated by the sun. The air then moves valleyward, down the ground slopes, when the same slopes have been cooled at night by radiation of heat from ground to air. These winds are therefore responding to local pressure gradients set up by heating or cooling of the lower air.

Still another group of local winds are known as *drainage winds*, or *katabatic winds*, in which cold air flows under the influence of gravity from higher to lower regions. Such cold, dense air may accumulate in winter over a high plateau or high interior valley. When general weather conditions are favorable some of this cold air spills over low divides or through passes to flow out upon adjacent lowlands as a strong, cold wind. Drainage winds occur in many mountainous regions of the world and go by various local names. The *bora* of the northern Adriatic coast and the *mistral* of southern France are well-known examples. In southern California there issues on occasion from the Santa Ana Valley a strong, dry east wind, the *Santa Ana*, which blows across the coastal lowland. This air is of desert origin and may carry much dust and silt in suspension. On the icecaps of Greenland and Antarctica, powerful katabatic winds move down the gradient of the ice surface and are funneled through coastal valleys to produce powerful blizzards lasting for days at a time.

Still other types of local winds, bearing such names as *foehn* and *chinook*, result when strong regional winds passing over a mountain range are forced to descend on the lee side with the result that the air is heated and dried. These winds are explained in Chapter 6.

Ocean currents

The circulation of the oceans is a matter of great interest to the geographer seeking an understanding of climates. Warm water currents bring a moderating influence to coasts in arctic latitudes; cool currents greatly alleviate the heat of tropical deserts along narrow coastal belts.

The direction of motion of surface ocean currents is stated in terms of compass direction toward which the water is moving. Much information on the direction and velocity of currents has been gained from *drift bottles*, sealed bottles containing return-addressed cards, set adrift in the hope that the bottle will be found at a distant point and the card returned. To measure currents, anchored vessels may put down *current meters* which tell the direction and speed of water flow. These devices look much like the current meter used in stream gauging (Figure 20.8). Much of our knowledge of currents has been built up from navigational observations. The direction and speed of a current can be computed when a ship's actual position is determined astronomically after a day's run. The true position is compared with the supposed position reckoned from the known rate and direction of course held through the preceding day. The difference in the two positions gives a measure of oblique drifting as a result of traveling at an angle to the current direction. (Figure 5.23).

Virtually all of the important surface currents of the oceans are set in motion by prevailing surface winds. Energy is transferred from wind to water by the frictional drag of the air blowing over the water surface. Because of the Coriolis force, the water drift is impelled toward the right of its

Figure 5.23 Calculation of drift.

path of motion (northern hemisphere), and therefore the current at the water surface is in a direction about 45° to the right of the wind direction. Under the influence of winds, currents may tend to bank up the water close to the coast of a continent, in which case the force of gravity, tending to equalize the water level, will cause other currents to be set up.

Density differences may also cause flow of ocean water. Such differences arise from greater heating by insolation, or greater cooling by radiation, in one place than another. Thus, surface water chilled in the arctic and polar seas will sink to the ocean floor, spreading equatorward and displacing upward the less dense, warmer water.

Still another controlling influence upon water movements is the configuration of the ocean basins and coasts. Currents initially caused by winds impinge upon a coast and are locally deflected to a different path or confined in straits or gulfs.

The combined action of wind and density differences sets up an oceanic circulation system including not only horizontal motions, but upwelling and down-sinking motions besides. In this introductory study, emphasis is on the currents of a shallow surface water zone, inasmuch as these motions directly affect marine navigation and have a strong climatic influence upon the overlying layer of atmosphere.

Generalized scheme of ocean currents

To illustrate surface water circulation an idealized ocean extending across the equator to latitudes of 60° or 70° on either side may be taken for illustration (Figure 5.24). Perhaps the most outstanding features are the circular movements, or *gyres,* around the subtropical highs, centered about 25° to 30° N and S. An *equatorial current* marks the belt of the trades. Whereas the trades blow to the southwest and northwest, obliquely across the parallels of latitude, the water movement follows the parallels. Thus, ocean currents trend at an angle of about 45° with the prevailing surface winds, because of the deflective force of the earth's rotation.

A slow eastward movement of water over the zone of the westerly winds is named the *west-wind drift.* It covers a broad belt between 35° and 45° in the northern hemisphere, and between 30° or 35° and 70° in the southern where open ocean exists in the higher latitudes.

The equatorial currents are separated by an *equatorial countercurrent.* This is well developed in the Pacific, Atlantic, and Indian oceans (Figure 5.25).

Along the west sides of the oceans in low latitudes the equatorial current turns poleward, form-

Figure 5.24   Schematic map of system of ocean currents.

ing a warm current paralleling the coast. Examples are the *Gulf Stream* (*Florida* or *Caribbean* stream), the *Japan current* (*Kuroshio*) and the *Brazil current,* which bring higher than average temperatures along these coasts. This is illustrated in Figure 4.18 by the southward bulge of the 70°F (21°C) July isotherm along the west side of the South Atlantic.

The west-wind drift, upon approaching the east side of the ocean, is deflected both south and north along the coast. The equatorward flow is a cool current, produced by upwelling of colder water from greater depths. It is well illustrated by the *Humboldt current* (Peru current) off the coast of Chile and Peru; by the *Benguela current* off the southwest African coast; by the *California current* off the west coast of the United States; and by the *Canaries current,* off the Spanish and North African coast. Note that this cold upwelling causes a marked equatorward deflection of the isotherms, illustrated in Figure 4.17 by the northward bend in the 70°F (21°C) January isotherm along the east side of the South Pacific and South Atlantic oceans.

In the northern eastern Atlantic Ocean, the westwind drift is deflected poleward as a relatively warm current. This is the *North Atlantic current,* which spreads around the British Isles, into the North Sea, and along the Norwegian coast. The

Figure 5.25   Surface drifts and currents of the oceans (January). (After U.S. Navy Oceanographic Office.)

ice-free port of Murmansk, on the Arctic Circle, has year-round navigability by way of this coast. Note that in Figure 4.17 isotherms are deflected northward where they cross this current. In winter this effect is much more pronounced than in summer.

In the northern hemisphere, where the polar sea is largely landlocked, cold water flows equatorward along the west side of the large straits connecting the Arctic Ocean with the Atlantic basin. Three principal cold currents are the *Kamchatka current*, flowing southward along the Kamchatka Peninsula and Kurile Islands; the *Greenland current*, flowing south along the east Greenland coast through the Denmark Strait; and the *Labrador current*, moving south from the Baffin Bay area through Davis Strait to reach the coasts of Newfoundland, Nova Scotia, and New England.

In both the north Atlantic and Pacific oceans the Icelandic and Aleutian lows in a very rough way coincide with two centers of counterclockwise circulation involving the cold arctic currents and the west-wind drifts.

The antarctic region has a relatively simple current scheme consisting of a single *antarctic*

circumpolar current moving clockwise around the antarctic continent in latitudes 50° to 65° S, where a continuous expanse of open ocean occurs.

Oceanographers today recognize that oceanic circulation involves the complex motions of water masses of different temperature and salinity characteristics. The very simple outline of surface currents given here does not take into account the movements of these water masses at different depths.

REFERENCES FOR FURTHER STUDY

Cotter, C. H. (1965), *The physical geography of the oceans*, American Elsevier Publ. Co., New York, 317 pp. See Chapters 10, 12, and 13.

Donn, W. L. (1965) *Meteorology*, third edition, McGraw-Hill Book Co., New York, 484 pp.

Riehl, H. (1965), *Introduction to the atmosphere*, McGraw-Hill Book Co., New York, 365 pp.

Reiter, E. R. (1967), *Jet streams*, Doubleday and Co., New York, 189 pp.

Petterssen, S. (1969), *Introduction to meteorology*, third edition, McGraw-Hill Book Co., New York, 333 pp.

1. What range of sea-level air pressures is normally found to occur from day to day and season to season at a given place? What is considered high pressure? What is low pressure?

2. What are isobars? Explain how an isobaric map is prepared.

3. Describe the principal pressure belts of the globe, giving the latitude and approximate pressures for each.

4. Why do the pressure belts shift in latitude throughout the year? Is this shift over as great a latitude as the sun's declination?

5. Why do the landmasses of North America and Asia disrupt the belted pressure pattern of the globe? What pressures occur on these land areas in the winter solstice season? In the summer solstice season?

6. What pressure centers dominate the North Atlantic and North Pacific oceans during the summer months? During the winter months? Give the names of the lows and highs.

7. Explain the relation of pressure gradient to isobars and to the production of winds. What is the Coriolis force? State Ferrel's law. How are wind directions modified near the earth's surface?

8. What is a cyclone? An anticyclone? Describe the pattern of surface winds in cyclones and anticyclones in both northern and southern hemispheres.

9. With what instruments are winds measured? What information is needed about winds? How is the direction of a wind designated? How can wind direction and speed in the upper air levels be determined?

10. Explain how a wind rose is constructed. What symbols are used on weather maps to show surface winds? To show winds at high levels?

11. What conditions of winds and calms prevail in the equatorial trough? Why are steady, prevailing winds absent here?

12. Describe the trade winds. Which way do they blow in the northern hemisphere? In the southern hemisphere? Explain the direction of the trade winds. How were the trade winds used by mariners in the days of sailing vessels?

13. What are the subtropical belts of variable winds and calms? Describe the cells of high pressure of which this belt is composed. How do they shift in latitude seasonally?

14. Describe the westerly wind belts. How do the westerlies compare with the trades for constancy of direction and strength? How does the westerly wind belt influence transoceanic sailing and flying?

15. Describe the monsoon wind systems of southeastern Asia. What general type of weather condition is associated with the summer monsoon? With the winter monsoon? Why is a monsoon system not so strongly developed on other continents, such as Africa?

16. How is weather information obtained from the upper levels of the troposphere? How are winds related to isobars at high levels? How does air circulate around a center of low pressure? Around a high?

17. Describe the general global circulation in the middle and upper troposphere. What are the westerlies? The equatorial easterlies? What is the circumpolar whirl? With what barometric pressure is it associated?

18. Describe the jet stream and its relation to upper air waves of the westerlies.

19. What are local winds? Explain the land and sea breeze; the mountain and valley breeze. Where are katabatic (drainage) winds found? Give examples.

20. How are the direction and velocity of ocean currents measured? Discuss the causes of surface ocean currents. Show how the Coriolis force modifies the direction of flow.

21. Sketch a hypothetical ocean modeled after the Pacific or Atlantic and indicate the general scheme of surface currents. Label fully.

22. List three warm currents and three cool currents, giving the location and direction of flow of each. What effect have these currents upon isotherms of air temperatures?

23. What current systems conduct very cold water into the northern Atlantic Ocean? What current prevails in the southern ocean?

CHAPTER 6
Moisture, Clouds, and Precipitation

THE physical nature and *importance* of *water vapor* in the atmosphere has already been touched upon in an earlier chapter, in which the capacity of water vapor to absorb radiant heat energy was described. We will consider here the proportions in which water vapor is held in the air and the manner in which vapor may condense to form clouds, fog, rain, and snow.

The *amount* of *water vapor* that may be present in the *air* at a given time varies widely from place to place. It ranges from virtually nothing in the cold, dry air of arctic regions in winter to as much as 4 or 5 percent of a given volume of the atmosphere in humid, hot tropical areas.

Water vapor enters the atmosphere by *evaporation* from exposed water surfaces such as oceans, lakes, rivers, or moist ground. Some is supplied by plants which *transpire* water as a physiological function (Chapter 15). With large expanses of ocean and densely forested humid lands over the globe, there is no lack of evaporating surfaces.

Water states and heat

Water occurs in three states, (1) frozen as ice, a crystalline *solid*, (2) *liquid* as water, and (3) *gaseous* as water vapor (Figure 6.1). From the gaseous vapor state, molecules may pass into the liquid state by *condensation,* or, if temperatures are below the freezing point, they can pass by *sublimation* directly into the solid state to form ice crystals. By *evaporation*, molecules can leave a water surface to become gas molecules in water vapor. The analogous change from ice directly into water vapor is also designated sublimation. Then, of course, water may pass from liquid to solid state by *freezing*, and from solid state to liquid state by *melting*. All of this can be represented by a triangle in which the three states of water form the corners. Arrows show the six possible changes of state.

Of great importance in weather science are the exchanges of heat energy accompanying changes of state. For example, when water evaporates, *sensible heat*, which we can feel and measure by thermometer, passes into a hidden form held by the water vapor and known as the *latent heat of vaporization.* This results in a drop in temperature of the remaining liquid. The cooling effect produced by

evaporation of perspiration from the skin is perhaps the most obvious example. For every gram of water that is evaporated, about 600 calories change into the latent form. In the reverse process of condensation, an equal amount of energy is released to become sensible heat and the temperature rises correspondingly. Similarly, the freezing process releases heat energy in the amount of about 80 calories per gram of water, whereas melting absorbs an equal quantity of heat. This is referred to as the *latent heat of fusion.* When sublimation occurs, the heat absorbed by vaporization, or released by crystallization, is still greater for each gram of water, for the latent heats of vaporization and fusion are added together.

Humidity

The term *humidity* simply refers to the degree to which water vapor is present in the air. For any specified temperature there is a definite limit to the quantity of moisture that can be held by the air. This limit is known as the *saturation point.* The proportion of water vapor present relative to the maximum quantity is the *relative humidity*, expressed as a percentage. At the saturation point, relative humidity is 100 percent; when half of the total possible quantity of vapor is present, relative humidity is 50 percent, and so on.

Figure 6.1 Three states of water. (After C.A.A., U.S. Dept. Commerce.)

A change in relative humidity of the atmosphere can be caused in one of two ways. If an exposed water surface is present, the humidity can be increased by evaporation. This is a slow process, requiring that the water vapor diffuse upward through the air. The other way is through a change of temperature. Even though no water vapor is added, a lowering of temperature results in a rise of relative humidity. This is automatic and is a logical consequence of the fact that the capacity of the air to hold water vapor has been lowered by cooling; thus the existing amount of vapor represents a higher percentage of the total capacity of the air. Similarly, a rise of *air temperature* results in decreased relative humidity, even though no water vapor has been taken away. The principle of *relative humidity change caused by temperature change* is illustrated by a graph of these two properties throughout the day (Figure 6.2). As air temperature rises, relative humidity falls, and vice versa.

A simple example may be given to illustrate these principles. At a certain place the temperature of the air is 60°F (16°C), the relative humidity 50 percent. Should the air become warmed by the radiant energy from the sun and ground surface to 90°F (32°C), the relative humidity automatically drops to 20 percent, which is very dry air. Should the air become chilled during the night and its temperature fall to 40°F (5°C), the relative humidity will automatically rise to 100 percent, the saturation point. Any further cooling will cause condensation of the excess vapor into liquid form. As the air temperature continues to fall, the humidity remains at 100 percent, but condensation continues. This may take the form of minute droplets of dew or fog. If the temperature falls below freezing, condensation occurs as frost upon exposed surfaces.

The term *dew point* is applied to the critical temperature at which the air is fully saturated, and below which *condensation* normally occurs. An excellent illustration of condensation due to cooling is seen in summertime when beads of moisture form on the outside surface of a pitcher or glass filled with ice water. Air immediately adjacent to the cold glass or metal surface is sufficiently chilled to fall below the dew point temperature, causing moisture to condense on the surface of the glass.

In understanding the relationships between atmospheric temperature and relative humidity, a very homely analogy may prove helpful. An ordinary sponge, if left to soak up water, will take up moisture to its full capacity. This is analogous to the manner in which air will gradually increase its humidity to the saturation point, if allowed to stand over a water surface and to maintain a constant temperature. If the sponge is now lifted out of the water and held carefully in the hand it will continue to hold the absorbed water. Suppose now the sponge is slowly squeezed. Water is expelled. In a like manner, the lowering of temperature below dew point of the saturated air expels moisture by condensation of the excess water vapor. After most of the water has been squeezed from the sponge it may be released, but not permitted to touch the water. This is analogous to a rise of air temperature back to the previous starting point, but without being permitted to take up water. This condition would prevail over an interior desert region. The air, like the sponge, is now holding only a small fraction of its total possible moisture content. If it is again cooled no condensation will result from the air until a temperature below the previous minimum is reached, just as no water will be released from the sponge until it is squeezed even harder than previously.

Absolute humidity

Although relative humidity is an important indicator of the state of water vapor in the air, it is a statement only of the relative quantity with respect to a saturation quantity. The actual quantity of moisture present is denoted by *absolute humidity*, defined as the weight of water vapor contained in a given volume of air. Weight is stated in grams, volume in cubic meters. For any specified air temperature, there is a maximum weight of water vapor that a cubic meter of air can hold (the saturation quantity). Figure 6.3 is a graph showing this maximum moisture content of air for a wide range of temperatures.

In a sense, the absolute humidity is a geographer's yardstick of a basic natural resource—water—to be applied from equatorial to polar regions. It is a measure of the quantity of water that can be extracted from the atmosphere as precipitation. Cold air can supply only a small quantity of rain or snow; warm air is capable of supplying huge quantities.

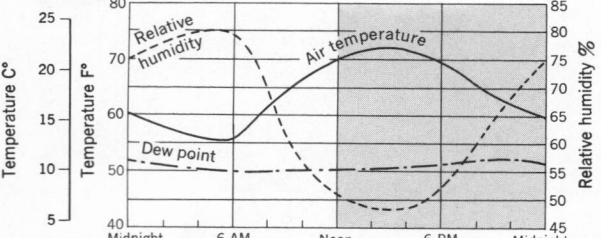

Figure 6.2 Relative humidity, temperature, and dew point for May at Washington, D.C. (After U.S. Weather Bureau; from A. N. Strahler, *The Earth Sciences*, Harper and Row, New York.)

Vapor pressure

In Chapter 3, it is explained that the weight of a column of atmosphere counterbalances the mercury column in a barometer and that variations in mercury height measure changes in air pressure. When water vapor is added to otherwise pure, dry air, the water molecules diffuse perfectly among the other gas molecules. That part of the total barometric pressure that is due to the water vapor alone is termed the *vapor pressure*. For cold, dry air, the vapor pressure may be as low as 0.05 in (0.013 cm); for very warm, moist air of the equatorial regions, it may be as high as 0.80 in (2 cm).

Figure 6.3 shows the maximum possible vapor pressure for air of a range of temperatures from very cold to very warm. Both vapor pressure and absolute humidity tell the quantity of water vapor present in the air, but in somewhat different ways.

One disadvantage of using absolute humidity in the study of atmospheric moisture is that when air rises or sinks in elevation, it undergoes corresponding volume changes of expansion or compression. Thus the absolute humidity cannot remain a constant figure for the same body of air. Modern meteorology therefore makes use of another measure of moisture content, *specific humidity*, which is the ratio of weight of water vapor to weight of moist air (including the water vapor). This ratio

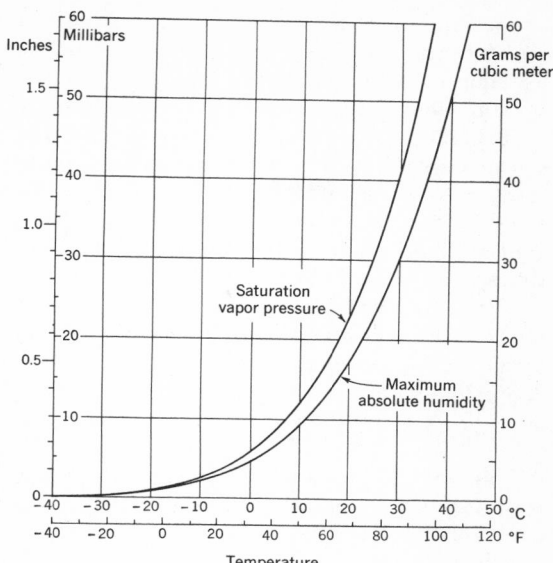

Figure 6.3 Maximum vapor pressure and absolute humidity. (From A. N. Strahler, *The Earth Sciences*, Harper and Row, New York.)

is stated in units of grams of water vapor per kilogram of moist air. When a given parcel of air is lifted to higher elevations without gain or loss of moisture the specific humidity remains constant, despite volume increase.

Figure 6.4 Relation of relative humidity to latitude (above) and of mixing ratio to latitude (below). Values of mixing ratio are numerically similar to values of specific humidity. (After Haurwitz and Austin, 1944, *Climatology*.)

Specific humidity is often used to describe the moisture characteristics of a large mass of air. For example, extremely cold, dry air over arctic regions in winter may have a specific humidity of as low as 0.2 grams per kilogram, whereas extremely warm moist air of tropical regions may hold as much as 18 grams per kilogram. The total natural range on a world-wide basis is such that the largest values of specific humidity are from 100 to 200 times as great as the least.

Figure 6.4 is a graph of average specific *humidity and latitude*, showing that the warm air of equatorial regions normally holds vastly more water vapor than cold air of arctic and polar regions.

How humidity is measured

Humidity of the air can be measured in two ways. An instrument known as a *hygrometer* indicates relative humidity on a calibrated dial. One simple type uses a strand of human hair which lengthens and shortens according to the relative humidity and thereby activates the dial (Figure 6.5). A continuous record of humidity can be obtained by means of a recording *hygrograph*. Using the same basic mechanism as the hygrometer, a continuous, automatic record is drawn by a pen on a sheet of paper attached to a rotating drum.

A different principle is applied in the *sling psychrometer*. This instrument is simply a pair of *thermometers* mounted side by side (Figure 6.6). One is of the ordinary type; the other has a piece

Figure 6.6   Sling psychrometer. (U.S. Weather Bureau.)

of wet cloth around the bulb. If the air is fully saturated (relative humidity 100 percent), there will be no evaporation from the wet cloth and both thermometers will read the same. If, however, the air is not fully saturated, evaporation will occur, cooling the cloth-covered thermometer below the temperature shown on the ordinary thermometer. Because the rate of evaporation depends on *dryness* of the air, the difference in temperature shown by the two thermometers will increase as relative humidity decreases.

Standard tables are available to show the relative humidity for a given combination of *wet- and dry-bulb temperatures*. In order to be sure that maximum possible evaporation is taking place, the two thermometers are attached by a swivel joint to a handle by which the thermometers can be swung around in a circle by hand. Other types have a fan to blow air past the wet thermometer bulb.

How *condensation* occurs

Falling rain, snow, sleet, or hail, referred to collectively as *precipitation*, can result only where large masses of air are experiencing a steady drop in temperature below the dew point. This condition cannot be brought about by the simple process of chilling of the air through loss of heat by long-wave radiation during the night. Instead, it is necessary that the large mass of air be rising to higher elevations. This statement requires that a new principle of weather science be explained.

One of the most important laws of meteorology is that rising air experiences a drop in temperature, even though no heat energy is lost to the outside (Figure 6.7). The drop of temperature is a result of the decrease in air pressure at higher elevations, permitting the rising air to expand. Individual molecules of the gas are more widely diffused and do not strike one another so frequently, hence imparting a lower sensible temperature to the gas. When no condensation is occurring, the rate of drop of temperature, termed the *dry adiabatic rate*, is about $5\frac{1}{2}$ F° per 1000 feet of vertical rise of air. In metric units the rate is 1 C° per 100 meters. The dew point also declines with rise of air; the rate is 1 F° per 1000 ft (0.2 C° per 100 m).

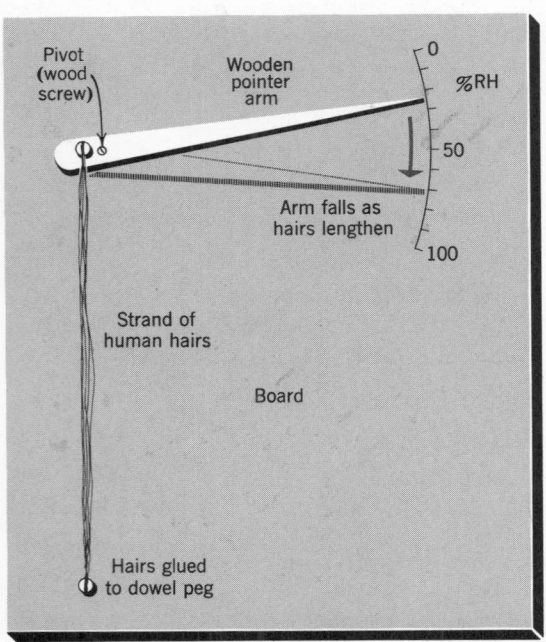

Figure 6.5   A simple hygrometer.

Pivot (wood screw)

Wooden pointer arm

0

%RH

50

Arm falls as hairs lengthen

100

Strand of human hairs

Board

Hairs glued to dowel peg

If water vapor in the air is condensing, the adiabatic rate is less, about 3.2 F° per 1000 ft (0.6 C° per 100 m), owing to the partial counteraction of temperature loss through the liberation of latent heat during the condensation process. This modified rate is referred to as the *wet adiabatic*, or *saturation adiabatic* rate (Figure 6.7). Adiabatic cooling rate should not be confused with the normal lapse rate, explained in Chapter 3. The normal lapse rate applies only to still air whose temperature is measured at successively higher levels.

Where *condensation* is occurring directly in the form of snow (ice crystals), the *adiabatic rate* is intermediate in value between dry and saturated rates (Figure 6.7).

The various ways in which large masses of air are induced to rise to higher elevations are treated more fully in a later paragraph. Because the actual fall of rain, snow, or other forms of precipitation is preceded by the formation of clouds, it is desirable first to consider the various types of clouds and their significance.

Clouds

Clouds consist of extremely tiny *droplets* of water, 0.0008 to 0.0024 in (0.02 to 0.06 mm) in diameter, or minute crystals of ice. These are sustained by the slightest upward movements of air. In order for cloud droplets to form, it is

necessary that microscopic dust particles serve as centers, or *nuclei*, of *condensation. Dusts* with a high affinity for water are abundant throughout the atmosphere.

Where the air temperature is well below freezing, clouds may form of tiny crystals. Water in such minute quantities can remain liquid far below normal freezing temperatures. Thus, water droplets exist at temperatures down to 10°F (−12°C); a mixture of water droplets and ice crystals from 10° to −20°F (−12 to −30°C) or even lower; and predominantly *ice crystals* below −20°F (−30°C). Below −40°F (−40°C) all of the cloud is ice. *Clouds* appear *white* when thin or when the sun is shining upon the outer surface. When dense and thick, clouds appear gray or black underneath simply because this is the shaded side.

Cloud types may be classified on the basis of two characteristics: general form and altitude. On the basis of form there are two major groups: *stratiform* or layered types, and *cumuliform* or massive, globular types (Figure 6.8).

The stratiform clouds are blanketlike, often covering vast areas, but are fairly thin in comparison to horizontal dimensions. Stratiform clouds are subdivided according to the level of elevation at which they lie. The highest type is the *cirrus* cloud and its related forms, *cirrostratus* and *cirrocumulus* (Figures 6.8 and 6.9). These are roughly within the altitude range of 20,000 to 40,000 ft (6000

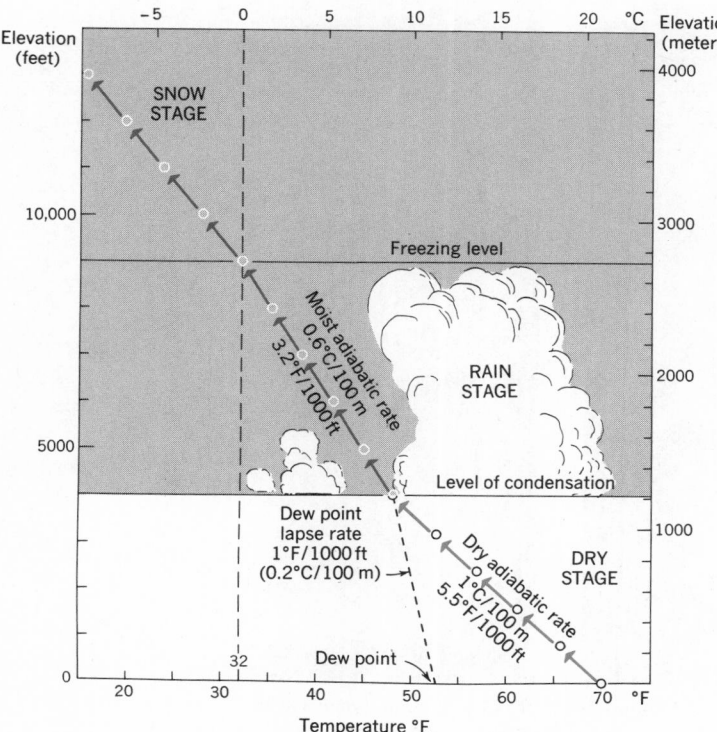

Figure 6.7 Adiabatic changes of temperature in a rising air mass. (From A. N. Strahler, *The Earth Sciences*, Harper and Row, New York.)

Figure 6.8 Cloud types are grouped into *families* according to height range and form.

to 12,000 m) and are composed of *ice crystals*. *Cirrus* is a delicate, wispy cloud, often forming streaks or stringers across the sky. It does not interfere with the passage of sunlight or moonlight and appears to the ground observer to be moving very slowly, if at all. *Cirrostratus* is a more com-

plete layer of cloud, producing a *halo* about the sun or moon. Where the layer consists of closely packed globular pieces of cloud, arranged in groups or lines, the name cirrocumulus is given. This is the *mackerel sky* of popular description.

At *intermediate height range*, from 6500 to

A. Cirrus in parallel trails and small patches. (Photograph by F. Ellerman. Courtesy of U.S. Weather Bureau.)

B. Cirrocumulus (*above*) with tufted cirrus (*below*). (Photograph by F. Ellerman. Courtesy of U.S. Weather Bureau.)

C. Thin altostratus with fractostratus patches below. (Photograph by G. A. Clarke. Courtesy of U.S. Weather Bureau.)

D. Altocumulus; active form. (Photograph by C. F. Brooks. Courtesy of U.S. Weather Bureau.)

E. Stratus, a uniform layer extending below the level of the hilltop, with shreds of fractostratus visible against the hillside. (Photograph by G. A. Clarke. Courtesy of U.S. Weather Bureau.)

F. Stratocumulus in irregular horizontal rolls. (Photograph by W. J. Humphreys. Courtesy of U.S. Weather Bureau.)

G. Cumulus of fair weather. (Photograph by H. T. Floreen. Courtesy of U.S. Weather Bureau.)

Figure 6.9 (*above and left*)   Cloud types.

H. Cumulonimbus, an isolated thunderstorm showing rain falling from base. (Photograph by Air Service, U.S. Navy. Courtesy of U.S. Weather Bureau.)

20,000 ft (2000 to 6000 m), are the *altostratus* and *altocumulus* clouds. Altostratus is a blanket layer, often smoothly distributed over the entire sky. It is grayish in appearance, usually has a smooth underside, and will often show the sun as a bright spot in the cloud. Altocumulus is a layer of individual cloud masses, fitted closely together in geometric pattern. The masses appear white, or somewhat gray on the shaded sides, and blue sky is seen between individual patches or rows. Altostratus is commonly associated with the development of bad weather, whereas altocumulus is usually characteristic of generally fair conditions.

In the low cloud group, from ground level to 6500 ft (2000 m), are *stratus*, *nimbostratus*, and *stratocumulus* clouds. Stratus is a dense, low-lying dark-gray layer (Figure 6.9E). If rain or snow is falling from this cloud, it is termed nimbostratus, the prefix *nimbo* merely meaning that precipitation is coming from the cloud. Stratocumulus is a low-lying cloud layer consisting of distinct grayish masses of cloud between which is open sky. The individual masses often take on the form of long rolls of cloud, oriented at right angles to the direction of wind and cloud motion. Stratocumulus is generally associated with fair or clearing weather, but sometimes rain or snow flurries issue from individual cloud masses.

Fog is simply a form of stratus cloud lying very close to the ground. One type, known as a *radiation fog*, is formed at night when temperature of the basal air falls below the dew point. Another type, *advection fog*, results from the movement of warm, moist air over a cold or snow-covered ground surface. Losing heat to the ground, the air layer undergoes a drop of temperature below the dew point, and condensation sets in. A similar type of advection fog is formed over *oceans* where air from over a warm *current* blows across the cold surface of an adjacent cold current. Fogs of the Grand Banks off Newfoundland are largely of this origin because here the cold *Labrador current* comes in contact with warm waters of *Gulf Stream* origin.

The cumuliform clouds tend to display a height as great as, or greater than, their horizontal dimensions. *Cumulus* is a white, woolpack cloud mass, often showing a flat base and a bumpy upper surface somewhat resembling a head of cauliflower (Figure 6.9G). These clouds look pure white on the side illuminated by the sun, but may be gray or black on the shaded or underneath side. Small cumulus clouds are associated with fair weather. Under different conditions, discussed below, individual masses grow into *cumulonimbus*, the *thunderstorm cloud* mass of enormous size which brings heavy rainfall, thunder and lightning, and gusty winds (Figure 6.9H). A large cumulonimbus cloud may extend from a height of 1000 to 2000 ft (300 to 600 m) at the base up to 30,000 or 40,000 ft (9000 to 12,000 m). When seen from a great distance, the top of the cumulonimbus cloud is pure white, but to observers beneath, the sky may be darkened to almost nighttime blackness. More will be said of this cloud in connection with thunderstorms.

Forms of *precipitation*

Precipitation results when condensation is occurring rapidly within a cloud. *Rain* is formed when cloud droplets in large numbers are caused to coalesce into drops too large to remain suspended in the air. The drops may then grow by colliding with other drops and joining with them to become as large as 0.25 in (7 mm) in diameter; but above this size they are unstable and break into smaller drops. Falling droplets less than 0.02 in (0.5 mm) in diameter make a *drizzle*.

Sleet, as the term is used in the United States, consists of pellets of ice produced from freezing of rain. The raindrops form in an upper, warmer layer, but fall into an underlying cold air layer. (Elsewhere in the English-speaking world sleet means a mixture of rain and snow.)

Snow consists of masses of crystals of ice, grown directly from the water vapor of the air, where air temperature is below freezing. Individual *snow crystals*, which can be carefully caught upon a black surface and examined with a strong magnifying glass, develop in six-sided, flat crystals, or as prisms. They display infinite variations in their beautiful symmetrical patterns (Figure 6.10).

Hail consists of rounded lumps of ice, having an internal structure of concentric layers, much like an onion. Ordinarily the ice is not clear but has a frosted appearance. *Hailstones* range from 0.2 to 2 in (0.5 to 5 cm) in diameter and may be extremely destructive to crops and light buildings (Figure 6.11). Hail occurs only from the cumulonimbus cloud type, inside of which are extremely strong updrafts of air. Raindrops are carried up to high altitudes, are frozen into ice pellets, then fall again through the cloud. Suspended in powerful updrafts, the hail stone grows by the attachment and freezing of droplets, much as ice accumulates on the leading edge of an airplane wing. Eventually the hailstone escapes from the updrafts and falls to earth.

When rain falls upon a ground surface that is covered by an air layer of below-freezing temperature, the water freezes into clear ice after striking the ground or other surfaces such as trees, houses, or wires (Figure 6.12). The coating of ice that results is called a *glaze*, and an *icing storm* is said

Figure 6.10 *Snowflakes.* (Photograph by Ewing Galloway.)

to have occurred. Actually no ice falls, so that ice glaze is not a form of precipitation. Icing storms cause great damage, especially to telephone, telegraph, and power wires and to tree limbs. Roads and sidewalks are made extremely hazardous.

How *precipitation is measured*

Precipitation is generally stated in units of inches or centimeters that fall per unit of time. One inch of rainfall, for example, is a quantity sufficient to cover the ground to a *depth* of one

inch, provided that none is lost by runoff, evaporation, or sinking into the ground. A simple form of *rain gauge* can be operated merely by setting out a straight-sided, flat-bottomed pan and measuring the depth to which water accumulates during a particular period. Unless this period is short, however, evaporation seriously upsets the results. Furthermore, very small amounts of rainfall, such as 0.1 in (0.25 cm), would make too thin a layer to be accurately measured. To avoid this difficulty, as well as to reduce evaporation loss, good rain gauges are made in the form of a cylinder whose base is a funnel leading into a narrow pipe (Figure 6.13). A small amount of rainfall will fill the narrow pipe to a considerable height, thus making it easy to read accurately, once a simple scale has been provided for the pipe. This gauge requires frequent emptying unless it is equipped with automatic devices for this purpose.

Snowfall is *measured* by melting a sample column of snow and reducing it to an equivalent in water. Thus, rainfall and snowfall records may be combined for purposes of comparison. Ordinarily, a ten-inch layer of snow is assumed to be equivalent to one inch of rainfall, but this ratio may range from 30 to 1 in very loose snow to 2 to 1 in old, partly melted snow.

Precipitation-producing conditions

Thus far it has been stated that precipitation results when air rises and is adiabatically cooled

Figure 6.11 These hailstones, larger than hens' eggs (arrow), fell at Girard, Illinois, on August 13, 1929. (U.S. Weather Bureau.)

Figure 6.12 Heavily coated wires and branches caused heavy damage in eastern New York State in January 1943, as a result of this icing storm. (Courtesy of U.S. Weather Bureau, and New York Power and Light Co., Albany, N.Y.)

Figure 6.13 A tipping-bucket rain gauge. (U.S. Weather Bureau.)

below the dew point so rapidly that not only do clouds form, but rain, snow, or hail is produced as well. Consider, then, how large masses of air are actually induced to rise to higher elevations. The three possible ways are (1) *convectional*, (2) *orographic*, and (3) *cyclonic* or *frontal*.

Convectional precipitation results from a *convection cell*, which is simply an updraft of warmer air, seeking higher altitude because it is lighter than surrounding air (Figure 6.14). The cell is completed by a downdraft of cooler, denser air. Suppose that on a clear, warm summer morning the sun is shining upon a landscape consisting of patches of open fields and woodlands. Certain of these types of surfaces, such as the bare ground, heat more rapidly and transmit radiant heat to the overlying air. Air over a warmer patch is thus warmed more than adjacent air and begins to rise in a tall column, much as hot air and smoke rise in a chimney. Vertical currents of this type are often called *thermals* by sailplane pilots who use them to obtain lift.

As the air rises, it is cooled adiabatically so that eventually it will reach the same temperature as the surrounding air and come to rest. Before this happens, however, it may be cooled below the dew point. At once condensation begins, and the rising air column appears as a cumulus cloud whose flat base shows the critical level above which *condensation* is occurring (Figure 6.14). The bulging "cauliflower" top of the cloud represents the top of the rising warm air column, pushing into higher levels of the atmosphere. Should this convection column continue to develop, the cloud may grow to a *cumulonimbus* mass, or *thunderstorm*, from which heavy rain will issue.

The picture outlined above contains a serious defect. Any alert person will wonder why convection continues vigorously after the cloud has grown so large as to shade the ground, or after the cloud has drifted downwind away from the originally heated spot on the ground. Actually, the unequal heating of the ground served only as a trigger effect to release a spontaneous updraft, fed by *latent heat* energy liberated from the *condensing* water vapor. Recall that for every gram of water formed by condensation 600 calories of *heat* are released.

The graph of Figure 6.15*A* is a plot of altitude against air temperature. The small circles represent a small parcel of air being forced to rise steadily higher, following the same *dry adiabatic rate of cooling* shown in Figure 6.7. To the right of this line is a solid line showing the temperature of the undisturbed surrounding air; it is the normal lapse rate, such as is shown in Figure 3.3. Suppose that the air parcel is lifted from a point near the ground, where its temperature is 90°F (32°C). After the air parcel has been carried up 2000 ft (600 m), its temperature has fallen about 11 F° (6 C°) and is now 79°F (26°C); whereas the surrounding air is cooler by only about 7 F° (4 C°), and has a temperature of 83°F (28°C). The air parcel would thus be cooler than the surrounding air at 2000 ft (600 m), and if no longer forcibly carried upward, would tend to sink back to the ground. These conditions represent *stable* air, not likely to produce convection cells, because the air would resist lifting.

Figure 6.14 Convectional rainfall.

Figure 6.15 A, Forced ascent of stable air. B, Spontaneous rise of unstable air.

When the air layer near the ground is excessively heated by the sun, the lapse rate is increased (solid line reclines to lower slope, Figure 6.15B). The air parcel near the ground begins to rise spontaneously because it is lighter than air over adjacent, less intensely heated ground areas. Although cooled adiabatically while rising, the air parcel at 1000 ft (300 m) has a temperature of 85°F (29°C), but this is well above the temperature of the surrounding still air. The air parcel, therefore, is lighter than the surrounding air and continues its rise. At 2000 ft (600 m), the dew point is reached and condensation sets in. Now the rising air parcel is cooled at the reduced *wet adiabatic rate* of 3.2 F° per 1000 feet (0.6 C° per 100 m), because the *latent heat* liberated in condensation offsets the rate of drop due to expansion. At 3000 ft (900 m), the rising air parcel is still several degrees warmer than the surrounding air, and therefore continues its spontaneous rise.

The air described here as spontaneously rising during condensation is *unstable* in properties. In such air the updraft tends to increase in intensity as time goes on, much as a bonfire blazes with increasing ferocity as the updraft draws in greater supplies of oxygen. Of course, at very high altitudes, the bulk of the water vapor having condensed and fallen as precipitation, the energy source is gone; the convection cell then weakens and air rise finally ceases.

Unstable air, given to spontaneous convection in the form of heavy *showers* and *thunderstorms*, is most likely to be found in warm, humid areas such as the equatorial and tropical oceans and their bordering lands throughout the year, and the middle-latitude regions during the summer season.

The second precipitation-producing mechanism is described as *orographic*, which means "related to mountains." Prevailing winds or other moving masses of air may be forced to flow over mountain ranges (Figure 6.16). As the air rises on the windward side of the range, it is cooled at the adiabatic rate. If cooling is sufficient, precipitation will result. After passing over the mountain summit, the air will begin to descend the lee side of the

Figure 6.16 Forced ascent of oceanic air masses, producing precipitation and a rainshadow desert. (From A. N. Strahler, *The Earth Sciences*, Harper and Row, New York.)

range. Now it will undergo a warming through the same adiabatic process and, having no source from which to draw up moisture, will become very dry. A belt of dry climate, often called a *rainshadow*, may exist on the lee side of the range. Several of the important dry deserts of the earth are of this type.

Dry, warm *foehn winds* (Europe) and *chinook winds* (northwestern United States), which occur on the lee side of a mountain range, may cause extremely rapid evaporation of snow or soil moisture. These winds result from turbulent mixing of lower and upper air in the lee of the range. The upper air, which has little moisture to begin with, is greatly dried and heated when swept down to low levels.

An excellent illustration of orographic precipitation and rainshadow occurs in the far west of the United States. Prevailing westerly winds bring moist air from the Pacific Ocean over the coast ranges of central and northern California and the great Sierra Nevada Range, whose summits rise to 14,000 ft (4000 m) above sea level. (See Figure 12.15.) Heavy rainfall is experienced on the windward slopes of these ranges, nourishing great forests. Passing down the steep eastern face of the Sierras, air must descend nearly to sea level, even below sea level in Death Valley. The adiabatic heating thus caused, and a consequent drop in humidity, produces part of America's great desert zone, covering a strip of eastern California and all of Nevada.

Much orographic rainfall is actually of the convectional type, in that it takes the form of heavy convectional showers and thunderstorms. The storms are induced, however, by the forced ascent of unstable air as it passes over the mountain barrier.

A third type of precipitation is *cyclonic*. This topic cannot be fully understood until the entire subject of cyclonic storms and fronts has been developed. It will suffice here to note that in middle and high latitudes much of the precipitation occurs in cyclonic storms or eastward-moving centers of low pressure into which air is converging and being forced to rise.

Thunderstorms

A *thunderstorm* is an intense local storm associated with a large, dense cumulonimbus cloud in which there are very strong updrafts of air (Figures 6.9*H*, 6.14). *Thunder* and *lightning* normally accompany the storm, and rainfall is heavy, often of cloudburst intensity, for a short period. Violent surface winds may occur at the onset of the storm. A thunderstorm is not the cyclonic type of storm described in Chapter 7 because there is no inspiraling wind system. Instead, it may be described as a *convective storm* because it is essentially a powerful updraft of air seeking a higher elevation. The cause of precipitation and spontaneous rise of air has been explained in the discussion of unstable air and convectional precipitation.

Thunderstorm development has been studied by coordinated use of aircraft, ground weather stations, radiosonde stations, and long-range radar. Most thunderstorms consist of several *cells*, each cell being an updraft, usually with an associated downdraft. Individual cells pass through a life cycle as shown in Figure 6.17, and a storm may contain cells in various stages of development. First of three stages is the *cumulus stage*, in which the cell is a simple updraft with a steadily rising cloud top. The updraft tends to draw in air from the sides as it rises. In the *mature stage*, falling rain has created a downdraft by frictional drag on the air. Reaching the ground and spreading out, this air is cool. Upon first arriving at the ground, the

Figure 6.17   Stages in the development of thunderstorm cell. (After Horace R. Byers, 1949.)

downdraft produces strong gusts which are normally felt before or during the start of the rain.

The *dissipating stage* of the thunderstorm cell is reached after the *downdraft* has spread across the lower levels of the cell and updraft has ceased. The upper part of the *cloud* has now taken on a mushroom or *anvil form* and continues to spread out, forming an altostratus or cirrostratus layer. In a large, complex thunderstorm new cells are forming while others are dissipating, thus maintaining the storm in a condition of constant activity as it drifts along with the regional air movement.

The principal *updraft*, or chimney, of a thunderstorm cell may have amazingly rapid flow of air. The fact that 3 in (8-cm) *hailstones* require updrafts of 120 mi (200 km) per hour in order to be kept aloft while forming indicates something of the intensity. Updrafts of 70 mi (112 km) per hour are not unusual in the mature stage of the storm. In general, warm air is required for thunderstorms because only warm air can hold large quantities of water vapor. Thus thunderstorms are commonest at low latitudes and are virtually absent in polar regions. In middle latitudes thunderstorms are commonest during the summer.

Thunderstorms may be classified into several types, based on the mechanism or cause of initial lift of the air column that sets off the spontaneous growth of the storm. One common type is the *thermal*, or *air mass thunderstorm*, which is set off by thermal convection caused by solar heating of the ground and lower air layer. Figure 6.14 illustrates the process. Storms of this type are often widely scattered over a large region covered by warm, moist air. The time of occurrence is typically in the late afternoon because air temperatures near the ground reach their highest levels at this time.

In the *orographic thunderstorm*, air is forced to rise over a mountain barrier, as shown in Figure 6.16. If the air is warm and moist, with unstable properties, it readily breaks into heavy showers and thunderstorms. The torrential *monsoon rains* of the Asiatic and East Indian mountain ranges are largely of this type. For example, Cherrapunji, a hill station facing the summer monsoon air drift in northeast India, averages 426 in (1082 cm) of rainfall annually. In the arid southwestern United States, isolated mountain ranges and high plateaus receive abundant summer rain in the form of thunderstorms orographically induced. Here rich forests grow while the surrounding lower areas are barren or sparsely vegetated deserts.

Still other types of thunderstorms are set off by the forced rise of a layer of warm air over a layer of cold air. Such storms, which may be described as *frontal thunderstorms*, are explained in the following chapter.

World distribution of rainfall

Average annual rainfall for the earth is shown in Plate 1 (folded map at end of book). Lines termed *isohyets* have been drawn through places having the same annual average rainfall. This map shows how the principles of precipitation are applied to world regions.

Rainfall is very heavy, more than 80 in (200 cm), in the *equatorial zone*, where high temperatures and great oceanic expanses provide large amounts of water vapor and generally unstable atmospheric conditions. Virtually all this rainfall is convectional in origin, although the presence of mountainous belts serves locally to add the orographic effect.

Rainfall is very light over the subtropical high-pressure belts, or cells, owing to the general pattern of subsiding air warmed adiabatically and thus made extremely dry. The *deserts* of North Africa, Arabia, and Iran lie along this zone as well as those of Australia, South Africa, and the west coast of South America. This zone of aridity is extended equatorward into the trade wind belt.

The *trade winds* should not be thought of as necessarily dry winds. Wherever they blow from the ocean across a coastal belt which is hilly or mountainous, fairly heavy orographic precipitation is caused. One good illustration is Central America, another is Madagascar. In both places the eastern, or windward, coasts receive rainfall of more than 80 in (200 cm) annually.

On the east side of the oceanic subtropical highs are dry coastal belts, such as the Peruvian coast of South America and the Namib Desert of southwest Africa. Here air subsides and is adiabatically heated.

The *monsoon* winds of Asia largely control *rainfall* of the southeastern part of that continent. In summer the flow of moist tropical air from the Indian Ocean and western Pacific encounters various mountain chains to give very heavy orographic precipitation. This is vividly illustrated by the narrow strips having precipitation over 80 in (200 cm), coinciding with the Himalayas in northern India and their southeastward extensions into Burma and Malaya, and with the high western edge of the Deccan Plateau along the west coast of peninsular India. The rugged mountain chains of the East Indies receive *orographic rainfall* associated with both sets of monsoon winds which blow between Australia and Asia.

Precipitation in the middle latitudes shows clearly the effect of the prevailing westerly winds. Western continental coasts within the latitude range 35° to 60° appear as narrow strips of heavy precipitation. Most striking are the British Columbia-southeastern Alaska coast in the northern hemisphere, and the Chilean coast of southernmost South America. Here, copious orographic precipitation is induced by coastal ranges which force a rise of moist air moving in from the Pacific Ocean. The effect is less striking on the Atlantic coast of Europe and the British Isles where relief is less, but it is nevertheless clearly evident. Note, too, that New Zealand, south of 40° S lat., has a marked zoning of precipitation from west to east.

Rainshadow deserts are developed in the westerly wind belt, in the lee of coastal ranges. The best illustration is the desert Great Basin of Nevada, already cited as an example of the principle of rainshadow development. A similar relation exists in southernmost South America but is not so well developed. Even the Iberian Peninsula shows semiaridity in its eastern half, as compared with a moist western coast. The vast continent of Eurasia exhibits a generally increasing aridity from west to east. Not only is moist air from the Atlantic dried as it travels eastward, but moist tropical air from the Indian Ocean is blocked by mountain barriers on the south.

Both the eastern United States and the eastern part of Asia, including much of China, Japan, Korea, and Manchuria, are moist, even though located on the eastern, or lee, side of the continents. This is explained by the prevalence of humid masses of air which move northward from the subtropical oceans during the summer months as a part of the monsoon circulation.

In arctic regions, precipitation is very small in terms of annual total, as the map clearly shows. The atmosphere here is at prevailingly low temperatures and thus does not hold large quantities of water vapor from which precipitation can be produced. At the same time, low temperatures reduce evaporation to such an extent that there is generally abundant soil moisture and surface water in summer and snow and ice in winter.

REFERENCES FOR FURTHER STUDY

Byers, H. R. and R. R. Braham, Jr. (1949), *The thunderstorm*, U.S. Dept. of Commerce, Weather Bureau, U.S. Govt. Printing Office, Washington, D.C., 287 pp.

World Meteorological Organization (1956), *International cloud atlas*, 2 volumes, English language edition, Geneva, Switzerland.

Byers, H. R. (1959), *General meteorology*, McGraw-Hill Book Co., New York, 540 pp. See Chapters 8, 18, 20.

Battan, L. J. (1962), *Cloud physics and cloud seeding*, Doubleday and Co., New York, 144 pp.

U.S. Dept. of Commerce and Federal Aviation Agency (1965), *Aviation Weather*, U.S. Govt. Printing Office, Washington, D.C., 299 pp.

Petterssen, S. (1969), *Introduction to meteorology*, third edition, McGraw-Hill Book Co., New York, 333 pp. See Chapters 4–8.

REVIEW QUESTIONS

1. In what ways is the presence of water vapor in the air important in weather and climate? What are the sources of atmospheric moisture?

2. Describe the three states in which water may exist. How, and in what amounts, is heat liberated or absorbed as water passes from one state to another?

3. Define relative humidity. What effect has a change of air temperature upon the relative humidity of the air? What is the dew point temperature? Explain the phenomenon of condensation of water vapor.

4. What is absolute humidity? Vapor pressure? Specific humidity? What use have these measures of water vapor? What ranges of specific humidity may be expected from equatorial to polar regions?

5. How is humidity of the air measured? Explain the principle of the hygrometer and psychrometer.

6. Explain the process whereby condensation and precipitation occur as a result of the lifting of a mass of air. What is the adiabatic rate? How does this differ from the normal lapse rate?

7. Of what are clouds composed? How are clouds classified? Name the common cloud types, give their height ranges, and describe their forms. What are stratiform and cumuliform clouds?

8. Name and describe the various forms of precipitation. Is an icing storm a form of precipitation? How does hail form?

9. In what units is rainfall measured? Describe a rain gauge. How is snowfall measured? How does 1 foot of snow compare with 1 foot of rainfall for relative amounts of water?

10. What are the three ways in which precipitation can occur on a large scale? Describe how a convection column of air operates to produce rainfall. What keeps the updraft in operation during a convectional storm? What is an unstable air mass?

11. Explain how orographic precipitation occurs. Why is there often a dry area, or rainshadow, on the lee side of a mountain chain? Is the air which has reached a rainshadow area normally warmer or cooler than it was at the same elevation over the coastal zone from which it came? Explain.

12. Describe the internal meteorological conditions of a thunderstorm. What size and height do these storms commonly attain? How is hail formed in a thunderstorm? What keeps a thunderstorm active? What is the source of energy?

13. Name three common types of thunderstorms. What can be said about time of day and geographical regions of occurrence of thunderstorms?

14. How can rainfall distribution be represented on a map? Briefly summarize the distribution of annual rainfall over the globe, using the pressure and wind belts as a basis for your discussion. What regions are most favorably located for heavy rainfall? How do the arctic regions compare in total annual precipitation with the equatorial and tropical regions?

CHAPTER 7
Cyclonic Storms, Air Masses, Weather Fronts

MUCH of the unsettled, cloudy weather experienced in middle and high latitudes is associated with traveling cyclones. The convergence of masses of air toward these centers is accompanied by lift of air and adiabatic cooling, which, in turn, produces cloudiness and precipitation. By contrast, much fair, sunny weather is associated with traveling anticyclones in which the air tends to subside and spread outward, causing adiabatic warming, a process that is unfavorable to the development of clouds and precipitation.

Cyclones may be very mild in intensity, passing with little more than a period of cloud cover and light rain or snow. On the other hand, if the pressure gradient is strong, winds ranging in strength from moderate to gale force may accompany the cyclone. In such a case, the disturbance may be called a *cyclonic storm*.

Moving cyclones fall into three general classes. (1) The *middle-latitude cyclone* (or *extratropical cyclone*) is typical of middle and high latitudes. It ranges in severity from a weak disturbance to a powerful storm. (2) The *tropical cyclone* is found in low latitudes over ocean areas. It ranges from a mild disturbance to the terribly destructive *hurricane*, or *typhoon*. (3) The *tornado*, although a very small storm, is an intense cyclonic vortex of enormously powerful winds. It is on a very much smaller scale of magnitude than other types of cyclones and must be treated separately.

The thunderstorm, described in Chapter 6, is a localized disturbance connected with a large cumulonimbus cloud in which there is a rapid convectional rise of air. It lacks the cyclonic spiral flow of winds. Thunderstorms often occur in large numbers within a single cyclonic storm, and occasionally tornadoes develop within the thunderstorms at the same time.

Middle-latitude cyclones

Before the advent of modern weather theory it was well known that within the middle latitudes, 35° to 65° N and S, weather changes are associated with moving centers of low and high barometric pressure, which can be drawn on the weather map and followed from day to day in the course of their eastward travel.

Lows, or cyclones, consist of oval-shaped concentric isobars, usually elongate on a northeast to southwest axis. The lows travel 25 to 30 mi (40 to 50 km) per hour, on the average, and have diameters of 500 to 1000 mi (800 to 1600 km). Cloudiness and precipitation generally are located in the eastern or southeastern half, and the northwestern part is usually a zone of clearing weather.

Between successive lows occur anticyclones, or simply *highs*, bringing cool, fair weather with distinctly drier air than in the lows. In the United States, the highs characteristically move in from the north, whereas the lows more often develop in southerly areas and move northeast, although there are many exceptions.

With the aid of periodic weather maps showing the positions of highs and lows, successful weather forecasting was carried on by experienced men who had come to know the habits of lows as a result of many years of observing their behavior. It was known that lows follow certain common paths, such as moving along the St. Lawrence Valley.

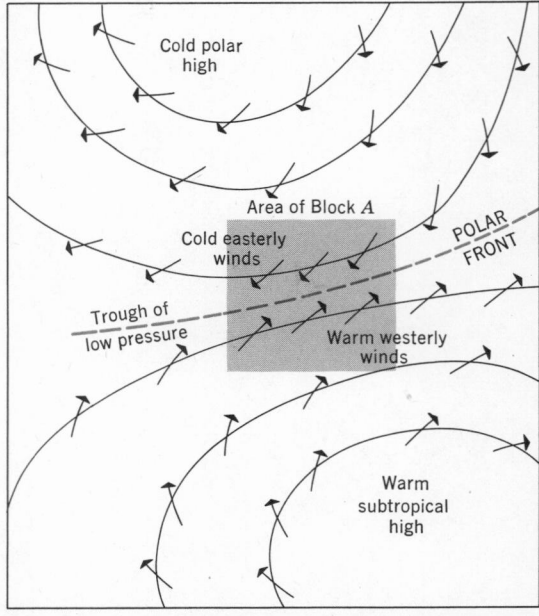

Figure 7.1 The trough between two high-pressure regions is a likely zone for development of a wave cyclone.

Wave theory of cyclones

The simple analysis of weather outlined above leaves many puzzling things unexplained. During the First World War a Norwegian meteorologist, J. Bjerknes, brought forward a new theory to explain moving cyclones and anticyclones. In middle latitudes, there exists a line of contact between cold air of arctic or polar origin and warm air of subtropical origin. This fluctuating line of contact was named the *polar front* (Figure 7.1). To any large body of the lower atmosphere having fairly uniform conditions of temperature and moisture, the term *air mass* was applied. We can say that a front separates two air masses of unlike properties.

The term *front*, used by Bjerknes, was particularly apt because of the resemblance of this feature to the fighting fronts in western Europe, then active. Just as vast armies met along a sharply defined front which moved back and forth, so masses of cold polar air meet in conflict with warm, moist air from the subtropical regions. Instead of mixing freely, these unlike air masses remain clearly defined, but interact along the polar front in great whorls whose structure is not unlike the form of an ocean wave seen in cross section.

A series of individual blocks, Figure 7.2 shows the various stages in the life history of an extra-tropical (middle-latitude) cyclone. At the start of the cycle the polar front is simply a smooth boundary along which air of unlike qualities is moving in opposite directions, as shown in Figure 7.1. In Block *A* of Figure 7.2, the polar front shows a bulge, or *wave*, beginning to form. Cold air is turned in a southerly direction, warm air in a northerly direction, as if each would penetrate the domain of the other. The situation is very much as if two individuals enter a revolving door from opposite sides. Pivoting on a center pin, the door permits each to pass into the area vacated

Figure 7.2 The development of a middle-latitude cyclone.

by the other. It is now necessary to digress from the series of diagrams of Figure 7.2 to consider what occurs when cold air moves into an area of warm air, or vice versa.

Cold and warm fronts

The structure of a frontal contact zone in which cold air is invading the warm-air zone is shown in Figure 7.3. A front of this type is termed a *cold front*. The colder air mass, being heavier, remains in contact with the ground and forces the warmer air mass to rise over it. The slope of the cold front surface is greatly exaggerated in the figure, being actually of the order of slope of 1 in 40 to 1 in 80 (meaning that the slope rises 1 foot vertically for every 80 feet of horizontal distance). Cold fronts are associated with strong atmospheric disturbance; the warm air thus lifted often breaks out in violent thunderstorms. In some instances these violent thunderstorms occur along a line well in advance of the cold front, a *squall line*. Such lines of thunderstorms can be seen on the radar screen (Figure 7.4).

Figure 7.5 illustrates a *warm front* in which warm air is moving into a region of colder air. Here, again, the cold air mass remains in contact with the ground, and the warm air mass is forced to rise as if ascending a long ramp. Warm fronts have lower slopes than cold fronts, being of the order of 1 in 80 to as low as 1 in 200. Moreover, warm fronts are commonly attended by stable atmospheric conditions and lack the turbulent air motions of the cold front. Of course, if the warm air is unstable, it will develop convection cells and there will be heavy showers and thunderstorms. To the list of thunderstorm types described in Chapter 6 can now be added the thunderstorms of both cold front and warm front origin.

Cold fronts normally move along the ground at a faster rate than warm fronts. Hence, when both types are in the same neighborhood, as they are

Figure 7.4 Photograph of a radar screen on which lines of thunderstorms show as bright patches. The heavy circles are spaced 50 nautical miles (80 km) apart. (Courtesy of U.S. Weather Bureau.)

in the cyclonic storm, the cold front may overtake the warm front. A curious combination known as an *occluded front* then results (Figure 7.6). The colder air of the fast-moving cold front remains next to the ground, forcing both the warm air and the less cold air to rise over it. The warm air mass is lifted completely free of the ground. The relations between warm, cold, and occluded fronts will now be introduced into the life history of the cyclone.

In Figure 7.2*B* the wavelike disturbance along the polar front has deepened and intensified. Cold air is now actively pushing southward along a cold front; warm air is actively moving northeastward along a warm front. Each front is convex in the direction of motion. The zone of precipitation is

Figure 7.3   A cold front.

Figure 7.5   A warm front.

Figure 7.6 An occluded warm front.

now considerable, but wider along the warm front than along the cold front. In a still later stage the more rapidly moving cold front has reduced the zone of warm air to a narrow sector. In Block *C*, the cold front has overtaken the warm front, producing an occluded front and forcing the warm air mass off the ground, isolating it from the parent region of warm air to the south. The source of moisture and energy thus cut off, the cyclonic storm gradually dies out and the polar front is reestablished as originally (Block *D*).

Cyclones on the daily weather map

Further details and characteristics of a wave cyclone are illustrated in Figure 7.7, in which two weather maps are shown. These have been redrawn with only slight changes from the U.S. Weather Bureau daily maps for April 3 and 4, 1963. Map *A* shows a cyclone in a stage approximately equivalent to Block *B* of Figure 7.2. The storm is centered over western Minnesota and is moving northeastward. Note the following points: (*a*) Isobars of the low are closed to form an oval-shaped pattern. (*b*) Isobars make a sharp V where crossing cold and warm fronts. (*c*) Wind directions, indicated by arrows, are at an angle to the trend of the isobars and form a pattern of counterclockwise inspiraling. (*d*) In the warm-air sector there is northward flow of warm, moist tropical air toward the direction of the warm front. (*e*) There is a sudden shift of wind direction accompanying the passage of the cold front, as indicated by the widely different wind directions at stations close to the cold front, but on opposite sides. (*f*) There is a severe drop in temperature accompanying the passage of the cold front, as shown by differences in temperature readings at stations on either side of the cold front. (*g*) Precipitation, shown by shading, is occurring over a broad zone near the warm front and in the central area of the cyclone, but extends as a thin band down the length of

the cold front. (*h*) Cloudiness, shown by degree of blackness of station circles, is great over the entire cyclone. (*i*) The low is followed on the west by a high (anticyclone) in which low temperatures and clear skies prevail. (*j*) The 32°F (0°C) isotherm crosses the cyclone diagonally from northeast to southwest, showing that the southeastern part is warmer than the northwestern part.

A cross section through Map *A* along the line AA′ shows how the fronts and clouds are related. Along the warm front is a broad area of stratiform clouds. These take the form of a wedge with a thin leading edge of cirrus. Westward this thickens to altostratus, then to stratus, and finally to nimbostratus with steady rain. Within the warm air mass sector the sky may partially clear with scattered cumulus. Along the cold front are violent thunderstorms with heavy rains, but this is along a narrow belt that passes quickly.

The second weather map, Map *B*, shows conditions 24 hours later. The cyclone has moved rapidly northeastward into Canada, its path shown by the line labeled *storm track*. The center has moved about 800 mi (1300 km) in 24 hours, a speed of just over 40 mi (65 km) per hour. The cyclone has occluded. An occluded front replaces the separate warm and cold fronts in the central part of the disturbance. The high-pressure area, or tongue of cold polar air, has moved in to the west and south of the cyclone, and the cold front is passing over the eastern and Gulf Coast states. Within closed isobars around the anticyclone the skies are clear and winds are weak. In another day the entire storm will have passed out to sea, leaving the eastern United States in the grip of cold but clear weather. A cross section below the map shows conditions along the line BB′, cutting through the occluded part of the storm. Note that the warm air mass is being lifted higher off the ground and is giving heavy precipitation.

Long observation on the movements of cyclones and anticyclones has revealed that certain tracks are most commonly followed. Figure 7.8 is a map of the United States showing these common paths. Notice that whereas some cyclonic storms travel across the entire United States from places of origin in the North Pacific, such as the Aleutian low, others originate in the Rocky Mountain region, the central states, or the Gulf Coast. Most tracks converge toward the northeastern United States and pass out into the North Atlantic, where they tend to concentrate in the region of the Icelandic low. General world distribution of paths of cyclonic storms is shown in Figure 7.9. Notice the heavy concentration in the neighborhood of the Aleutian and Icelandic lows. Extratropical cyclones commonly form in succession to travel in a chain across the north Atlantic and north

Figure 7.7 A middle-latitude cyclone shown on surface weather maps for successive days.
Pressures are given in millibars; temperatures in degrees Fahrenheit. Areas experiencing

110 | *Cyclonic Storms, Air Masses, Weather Fronts*

STATEN ISLAND COMMUNITY COLLEGE LIBRARY
STATEN ISLAND, NEW YORK 10301

precipitation are shaded. See Figure 5.12 for explanation of wind symbols. (Modified and simplified from Daily Weather Map of the U.S. Weather Bureau.)

Figure 7.8 Common tracks taken by middle-latitude cyclones passing across the United States. (After Bowie and Weightman.)

Figure 7.9 Principal tracks of middle-latitude cyclones are shown by solid lines; those of tropical cyclones by dashed lines. (After Petterssen, *Introduction to Meteorology*.)

Pacific oceans. Figure 7.10, a world weather map, shows several such *cyclone families*.

In the southern hemisphere, storm tracks are more nearly along a single lane, following the parallels of latitude. This appears to be the result of uniform ocean surface throughout the middle latitudes, only the southern tip of South America breaking the monotonous oceanic expanse. Furthermore, the polar-centered icecap of Antarctica provides a centralized source of polar air.

Air masses and source regions

The wave theory of extratropical cyclones places much emphasis upon the interaction of air masses, which differ in physical properties but which are essentially of uniform nature internally. The general subdivision of air masses of middle latitudes into two major groups, *polar* and *tropical*, has already been emphasized in explaining the development of the cyclonic storms. The distinctive prop-

erties of an air mass are developed when the air layer lies stagnant over a body of land or ocean, the *source region*. As the air mass leaves the source region, to travel across other kinds of land or ocean surfaces, the air is cooled or heated, and gains or loses moisture, as the case may be. Thus, an air mass evolves or changes as it follows a characteristic path, or *trajectory*, which may take it thousands of miles from the source region.

The polar air masses are divided into *maritime* and *continental* types. The continental polar air masses of North America (symbol, cP) originate over north-central Canada and are characterized by low temperature and low moisture content (Figure 7.11). These air masses form tongues of cold air, which periodically extend south and east from the source region to produce anticyclones accompanied, in winter, by low temperatures and clear skies. Over the North Pacific and Bering Straits originate the maritime polar air masses

Figure 7.10 A daily weather map of the world for a given day during July or August might look like this map, which is a composite of typical weather conditions. (After M. A. Garbell.)

Figure 7.11 North American air mass source regions and trajectories. (After Haynes, U.S. Dept. Commerce.)

(symbol, MP). With ample opportunity to absorb moisture both over the source region and throughout their travel southeastward to the west coast of North America, these air masses are characteristically cool and moist, with a tendency in winter to become unstable, giving heavy precipitation over coastal ranges. Note that the polar air masses (MP, cP) originate in the subarctic latitude zone (Figure 4.5), not in the polar latitude zone. The meteorological definition of the word "polar" for air masses has long been in use and has international acceptance, hence cannot be changed to conform with the latitude zones defined in Chapter 4.

Another maritime polar air mass of the North American region originates over the North Atlantic Ocean (Figure 7.11). It, too, is cool and moist. Because of its location, east of the North American continent, it only occasionally reaches the United States when drawn in over New England by a favorably placed cyclone lying south of New England. This situation brings on a *northeaster*, a storm characterized by northeast winds, penetrating cold, and misting rain. The northeaster is restricted to the northeastern states.

Of the tropical air masses, there are also maritime and continental types. The commonest visitor to the central and eastern states is the maritime tropical air mass (symbol, MT) from the Gulf of Mexico (Figure 7.11). It moves northward, bringing warm, moist, unstable air over the eastern part of the country. In the summer, particularly, this air mass brings hot, sultry weather to the east. It gives frequent thunderstorms. Closely related is a maritime tropical air mass from the Atlantic Ocean east of Florida, over the Bahamas. It has characteristics similar to those of the tropical Gulf air mass and brings similar weather conditions.

During the summer there originates over northern Mexico, western Texas, New Mexico, and Arizona a tropical continental air mass (symbol, cT) which is hot and dry. This air mass does not travel widely, but governs weather conditions over the source region.

Over the Pacific Ocean in the cell of high pressure located to the southwest of Lower California is a source region of another maritime tropical air mass. It visits the United States only in winter and affects only the southern coast of California.

Besides the air masses of middle latitudes already described, there are additional groups typical of polar and equatorial locations. Over the Arctic Ocean and its bordering lands of the arctic zone there develops the arctic air mass (symbol, A) which is extremely cold and stable. When this air mass invades the United States, it produces a severe cold wave. The Antarctic continent provides a source region for extremely cold air masses, designated as antarctic air masses (symbol, AA).

Over equatorial oceans, in the trough of low pressure toward which the trade winds converge, air becomes very moist, warm, and unstable. It is then classified as an equatorial air mass (symbol, mE). Invasion of southeastern Asia by equatorial air masses occurs during the wet monsoon season and constitutes the source of moisture for torrential rains.

Tropical and equatorial weather

As the study of weather conditions has been extended along modern lines into the low latitudes of the globe, largely as a result of enormously increased aircraft operation during the Second World War, a much clearer picture has emerged of the relations of air masses and storms in these regions.

Figure 7.10 shows a typical set of weather conditions in the subtropical and equatorial parts of the world, in addition to showing the general scheme of traveling cyclonic waves in middle and high latitudes.

Fundamentally the arrangement consists of two rows of high-pressure cells, one or two cells to each land or ocean body. The northern row lies approximately along the Tropic of Cancer; the southern row, along the Tropic of Capricorn. Between the subtropical highs lies the equatorial trough of low pressure. Toward this trough converge the north-

east and southeast trade winds. For this reason the trough is called the *Intertropical convergence zone*. At higher levels in the troposphere, the air flow is almost directly from east to west in the form of persistent *tropical easterlies*, described in Chapter 4.

One of the simplest forms of weather disturbance is an *easterly wave*, a slowly moving trough of low pressure within the belt of tropical easterlies. These waves occur in a zone 5° to 30° latitude over oceans both north and south of the equator, but not over the equator itself. Figure 7.12 is a simplified weather map of an easterly wave, showing isobars, winds, and the zone of rain. The wave is simply a series of indentations in the isobars to form a shallow pressure trough. Note that it travels westward, perhaps 200 to 300 mi (325 to 500 km) per day. Air flow tends to converge on the eastern, or rear, side of the wave axis. This causes the moist air to be lifted and to break out into scattered showers and thunderstorms. The rainy period may last for a day or two.

Another related disturbance is an *equatorial wave*, or *weak equatorial low*, which forms in the center of the equatorial trough (Figure 7.13). Although the normal air flow is from east to west, there develops an eddy in the tropical easterlies.

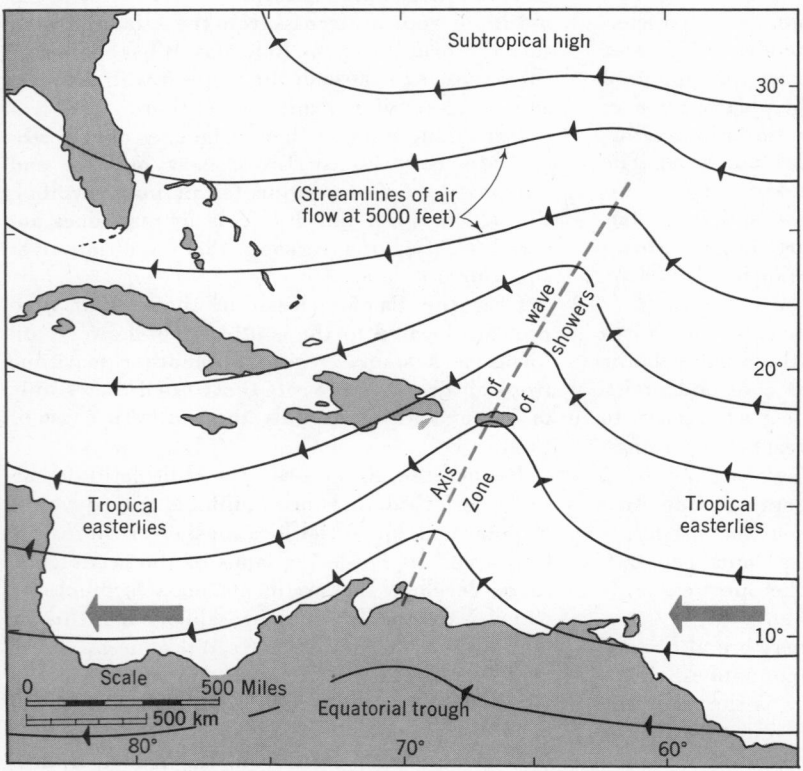

Figure 7.12   An easterly wave passing over the West Indies. (After Riehl.)

Figure 7.13   An equatorial wave. (After Riehl.)

Here air flow is locally reversed and tends to run opposite to the main stream. The result is a weak low-pressure center, the equatorial wave, into which moist equatorial air masses converge, causing rainfall from many individual convectional storms within the low. Several such weak lows are shown on the world weather map (Figure 7.10), lying along the equatorial trough. Because the map is for a day in July or August, the trough is shifted well north of the equator.

Another distinctive feature of tropical weather is the occasional penetration of powerful tongues of cold polar air from the middle latitudes into very low latitudes. These are known as *polar outbreaks* and bring unusually cool, clear weather with strong, steady winds moving behind a cold front with squalls. The polar outbreak is best developed in the Americas. Outbreaks which move southward from the United States over the Caribbean Sea and Central America are called *northers* or *nortes*; those which move north from Patagonia into tropical South America are called *pamperos* or *friagems*. One such outbreak is shown over South America on the world weather map (Figure 7.10).

Tropical cyclones

One of the most powerful and destructive types of cyclonic storms is the *tropical cyclone*, otherwise known as the *hurricane* or *typhoon*. The storm develops over oceans in latitudes 8° to 15° N and S, but not close to the equator, where the Coriolis force is extremely weak. In many cases an easterly wave simply deepens and intensifies, growing into a deep, circular low. High sea-surface temperatures which are over 80°F (27°C) in these latitudes, are of basic importance in the environ-

ment of storm origin. Warming of air at low level creates instability and predisposes toward storm formation. Once formed, the storm moves westward through the trade wind belt. It may then curve northwest and north, finally penetrating well into the belt of westerly winds. The tropical cyclone is an almost circular storm center of extremely low pressure into which winds are spiraling with great speed, accompanied by very heavy rainfall (Figure 7.14). The diameter of the storm may be 100 to 300 mi (150 to 500 km); the wind velocities range from 75 to 125 mi (120 to 200 km) per hour, sometimes much more; and the barometric pressure in the center commonly falls to 965 mb (28.5 in, 72.4 cm) or lower (Figure 7.15).

A brief description of the passage of a tropical cyclone at sea might be as follows. During the day

Figure 7.14   A hurricane (tropical cyclone) of the West Indies.

Figure 7.15 Trace sheet from a barograph at Galveston, Texas, during the hurricane of July 27, 1943. (U.S. Weather Bureau.)

preceding the storm the air is generally calm, the pressure somewhat above normal, and the sky shows cirrus clouds in long streamers, seeming to originate from a distant point on the horizon. The cirrus may be veil-like, giving a halo to the sun or moon and producing a red sunset. A long swell is felt on the sea, this being the train of dying storm waves that have outrun the slowly moving storm center. As the storm approaches, the barometer begins to fall. Wind springs up. A great dark wall of cloud approaches. When this envelopes the ship, torrential rainfall begins. The wind rises quickly to terrifying intensity. Great waves break over the vessel; the spray blows in continuous sheets which reduce visibility almost to zero.

This terrible storm continues for several hours and is abruptly followed by total calm and clearing skies, and sometimes by a sharp rise in temperature. The barometer has now reached its lowest point and the vessel is in the calm *central eye* of the storm. This is merely a hollow vortex produced by the rapid spiraling of air in the storm, comparable to the funnel-like air hole in the center of a vortex of water passing down a drain. Although the air is clear and calm, seas are mountainous and rise in great peaklike masses which are of gravest peril to the vessel. The period of calm may last a half hour. Then a great dark wall of cloud strikes the vessel and winds of high velocity again set in, but this time, in reverse direction to those of the first half of the storm. For several hours more the full fury of the storm rages, then gradually the winds abate, the clouds break, and fair weather returns.

World distribution of tropical cyclones is limited to six regions, all of them over tropical and subtropical oceans (Figure 7.16): (1) West Indies, Gulf of Mexico, and Caribbean Sea; (2) western North Pacific, including the Philippine Islands, China Sea, and Japanese Islands; (3) Arabian Sea and Bay of Bengal; (4) eastern Pacific coastal region off Mexico and Central America; (5) south Indian Ocean, off Madagascar; and (6) western South Pacific, in the region of Samoa and Fiji Islands and the east coast of Australia, Curiously enough, these storms are unknown in the South Atlantic. Tropical cyclones never originate over land, although they often penetrate the margins of continents.

Paths, or tracks, of tropical cyclones of the North Atlantic (Figure 7.17) show that most of the storms originate at 10° to 20° latitude, travel westward and northwestward through the trades, then turn northeast at about 30° to 35° latitude into the zone of the westerlies. Here the intensity lessens and the storms change into typical middle-latitude cyclones. In the trade wind belt the cyclones travel some 6 to 12 mi (10 to 20 km) per hour, in the westerlies, from 20 to 40 mi (30 to 60 km) per hour.

The occurrence of tropical cyclones is restricted to certain seasons of year, depending on the global location of the storm region. Those of the West

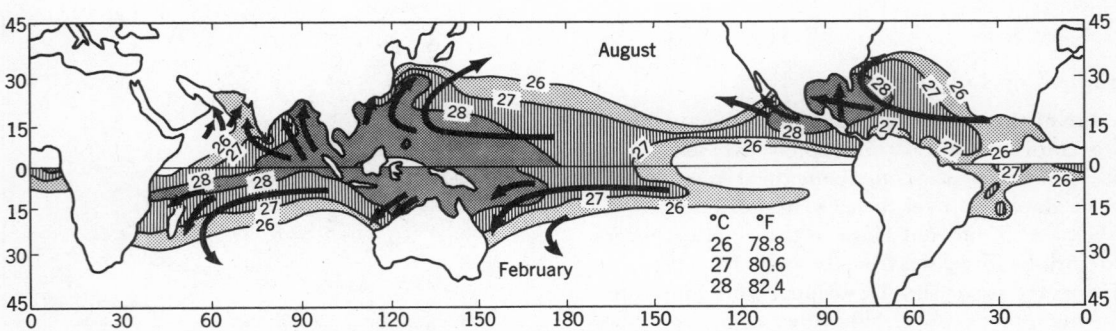

Figure 7.16 Typical paths of tropical cyclones in relation to sea surface temperatures (°C) in summer of the respective hemisphere. (After Palmen, 1948).

Figure 7.17 Tracks of some typical hurricanes occurring during August. (After U.S. Navy Oceanographic Office.)

Figure 7.18 This devastation along the south coast of Haiti was caused by Hurricane Flora on October 3, 1963. (Miami News photo by Chief Photographer Jay Spencer.)

Indies, and off the western coast of Mexico, occur largely from May through November, with maximum frequency in late summer or early autumn. Those of the western North Pacific, Bay of Bengal, and Arabian Sea are spread widely through the year but are dominant from May through November. Those of the South Pacific and south Indian oceans occur from October through April. Thus, they are restricted to the warm season in each hemisphere.

The geographical importance of tropical cyclones lies in their tremendously destructive effect upon island and coastal habitations (Figure 7.18). Wholesale destruction of cities and their inhabitants has been reported on several occasions. A terrible hurricane which struck Barbados in the West Indies in 1780 is reported to have torn stone buildings from their foundations, destroyed forts, and carried cannon more than a hundred feet from their locations. Trees were torn up and stripped of their bark. More than 6000 persons perished there.

Coastal destruction by storm waves and greatly raised sea level is perhaps the most serious effect of tropical cyclones. Where water level is raised by strong wind pressure, great breaking storm waves attack ground ordinarily far inland of the limits of wave action. A sudden rise of water level, known as a *storm surge*, may take place as the hurricane moves over a coastline. Ships are lifted bodily and carried inland to become stranded. If high tide accompanies the storm the limits reached by inundation are even higher. The terrible hurricane disaster at Galveston, Texas, in 1900 was wrought largely by a sudden storm surge inundating the low coastal city and drowning about 6000 persons. At the mouth of the Hooghly River on the Bay of Bengal, 300,000 persons died as a result of inundation by a 40-foot (12-meter) storm surge which accompanied a severe tropical cyclone in 1737. Low-lying coral atolls of the western Pacific may be entirely swept over by wind-driven sea water, washing away palm trees and houses and drowning the inhabitants.

Of importance, too, is the large quantity of rainfall produced by tropical cyclones. A considerable part of the summer rainfall of certain coastal regions can often be traced to a few such storms.

Tornadoes

The smallest but most violent of all known storms is the *tornado*. It seems to be a typically

Figure 7.19 This funnel cloud was photographed by William L. Males at Amarillo, Oklahoma, on May 4, 1961. The tornado was less than one mile from the observer when the picture was taken.

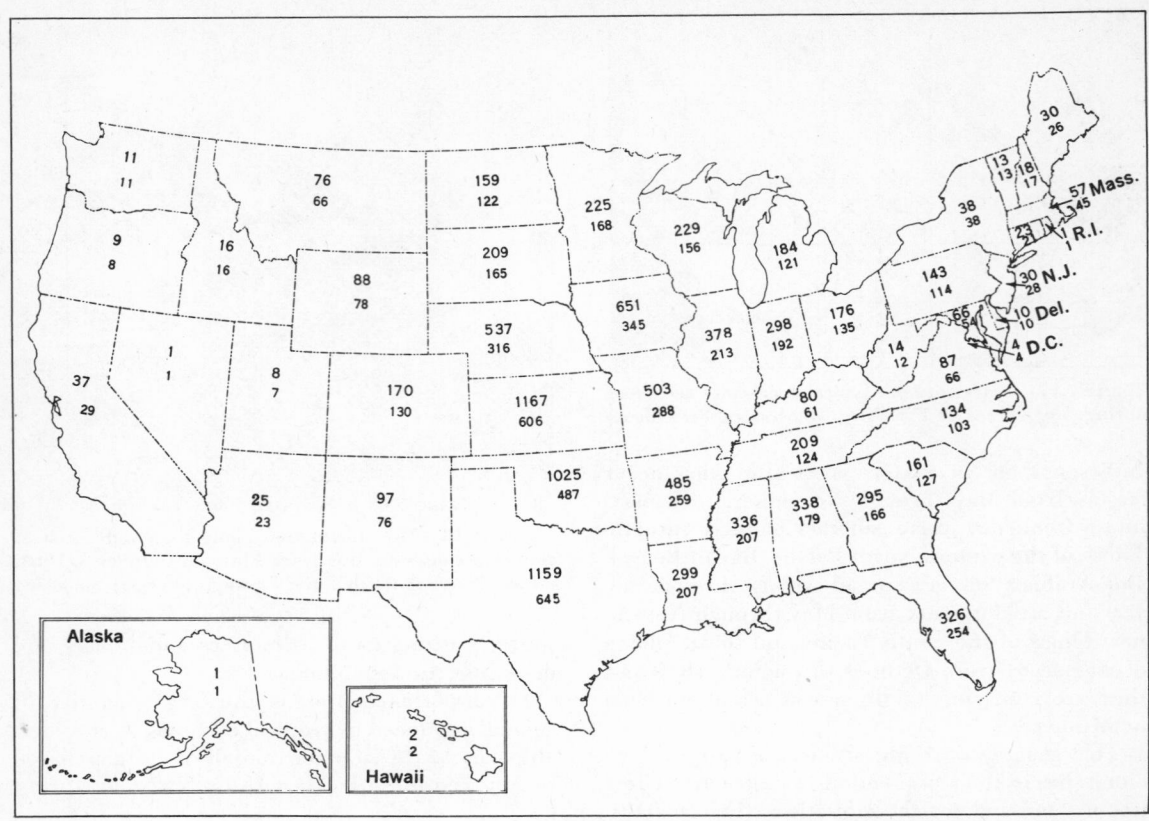

Figure 7.20 Tornado frequency by states for the period 1916–1960. The upper figure shows the total number of tornadoes reported in each state during the 45-year period; the lower figure shows the total number of days in the same period on which one or more tornadoes were reported in some part of the state. (From U.S. Weather Bureau.)

American storm, being most frequent and violent in the United States, although occurring in Australia in substantial numbers and reported occasionally in other places in middle latitudes. Tornadoes are also known throughout tropical and subtropical regions of the globe.

The tornado is a small, intense cyclone in which the air is spiraling at tremendous velocity. It appears as a dark *funnel cloud* (Figure 7.19), hanging from a large cumulonimbus cloud. At its lower end the funnel may be from 300 to 1500 ft (90 to 460 m) in diameter. The funnel appears dark because of the density of condensing moisture, dust, and debris swept up by the wind.

Wind speeds in a tornado exceed anything known in other storms. Estimates of wind speed run to as high as 500 mi (800 km) per hour. There is, in addition, a violent updraft in the funnel. As the tornado moves across the country the funnel writhes and twists. The end of the funnel cloud may alternately sweep the ground, causing complete destruction of anything in its path, and rise in the air to leave the ground below unharmed. Tornado destruction occurs both from the great

wind stress and from the sudden reduction of air pressure in the vortex of the cyclonic spiral. Closed houses literally explode. It is even reported that the corks will pop out of empty bottles, so great is the difference in air pressure.

Tornadoes occur as parts of powerful cumulonimbus clouds in the squall line that travels in advance of a cold front. They seem to originate where turbulence is greatest. They are commonest in the spring and summer but occur in any month. Where maritime polar (mP) air lifts warm, moist tropical (mT) air on a cold front, conditions may become favorable for tornadoes. They occur in greatest numbers in the Mississippi Valley region and are rare over mountainous and forested regions. They are almost unknown from the Rocky Mountains westward and are relatively few on the eastern seaboard (Figures 7.20 and 7.21).

Devastation from a tornado is complete within the narrow limits of its path (Figure 7.22), but fortunately the storms are uncommon and the total danger small. Even in states having the most tornadoes, deaths from automobile and other accidents are a very much more serious danger.

Figure 7.21 Average number of tornadoes reported in each month in the United States for the period 1916–1960. (From U.S. Weather Bureau.)

Figure 7.22 Tornado devastation at Ionia, Iowa, on April 23, 1948, included this store in which two persons were killed. (Courtesy of U.S. Weather Bureau and *Des Moines Register*.)

Storm cellars built completely below ground provide satisfactory protection if they can be reached in time. Although a tornado can often be seen or heard approaching, a cold front passing during the hours of darkness, as it often does, may present no warning. The U.S. Weather Bureau maintains a tornado forecasting and warning system. Whenever weather conditions conspire to favor tornado development, the danger area is alerted and systems for observing and reporting a tornado are set in readiness. Communities in the paths of tornadoes may thus be warned in time for inhabitants to take shelter.

Waterspouts are similar in structure to tornadoes but form at sea under cumulonimbus clouds. They are smaller and less powerful than tornadoes. Sea water may be lifted 10 ft (3 m) above the sea surface, and the spray is carried higher. Water-spouts are commonly found in subtropical waters of the Gulf of Mexico and off the southeastern coast of the United States and seem to result from air turbulence occurring when continental air masses spread out over these oceans.

REFERENCES FOR FURTHER STUDY

Flora, S. D. (1954), *Tornadoes of the United States*, Univ. of Oklahoma Press, Norman, 221 pp.

Flora, S. D. (1956), *Hailstorms of the United States*, Univ. of Oklahoma Press, Norman, 201 pp.

Battan, L. J. (1961), *The nature of violent storms*, Anchor Science Study Series, Doubleday and Co., New York, 158 pp.

Dunn, G. E. and B. I. Miller (1964), *Atlantic hurricanes*, Louisiana State Univ. Press, Baton Rouge, 377 pp.

Riehl, H. (1965), *Introduction to the atmosphere*, McGraw-Hill Book Co., New York, 365 pp.

Helm, T. (1967), *Hurricanes: weather at its worst*, Dodd, Mead and Co., New York, 234 pp.

REVIEW QUESTIONS

1. What varieties of cyclonic storms exist? Is the thunderstorm a cyclonic storm?

2. Describe the weather conditions associated with a middle-latitude cyclone, or low, in the central and eastern United States. Include discussion of the pressure pattern, winds, cloudiness and precipitation areas, temperatures, size, and rate of travel.

3. Describe the weather conditions associated with an anticyclone, or high, such as might normally follow the cyclone mentioned in the previous question.

4. Explain the wave theory of middle-latitude weather which was originated by J. Bjerknes. What is the polar front? What is an air mass?

5. How does a cyclone develop and change along the polar front? Explain a cold front and the air mass relationships involved in it. In a similar manner, describe and explain a warm front and an occluded front.

6. Describe the changes in wind direction and strength, cloudiness and precipitation, and temperature that an observer experiences when a middle-latitude cyclone passes with its center north of the observer. Do the same for a cyclone in which the center passes south of the observer.

7. What is the prevailing direction of movement of cyclonic storms in the United States? Do storm tracks show any tendency to concentrate at particular places in the northern hemisphere? If so, where? Do you think this may explain the average pressure conditions in these areas as shown on the world pressure maps?

8. How are air masses classified and designated? Discuss the air masses of North America, giving their source regions, paths of movement, and generally associated weather characteristics. What air masses are found over polar regions? over the equatorial belt?

9. What is an easterly wave? What weather does it bring? What is an equatorial wave? What weather does it bring?

10. Describe polar outbreaks of tropical regions. What names do these outbreaks have locally in the Central American area? in South America?

11. Describe the weather elements in a tropical cyclone, or hurricane. Where do these storms originate? What paths do they normally follow? Explain the calm central eye of a tropical cyclone.

12. Name the regions of the world where tropical cyclones occur. Tell the seasons of occurrence of storms in each locality. How is season of storms related to position of the equatorial trough?

13. Describe some of the destructive effects of tropical cyclones along low-lying coasts. How is ocean level affected by these storms?

14. What is a tornado? Where and how does it occur? What wind velocities are thought to exist in a tornado? Why are tornadoes in the United States commonest in the spring? What is a waterspout?

CHAPTER 8
Climate Classification and Climatic Regimes

THE importance of climate as a geographical factor is so marked, and reaches into so many aspects of human life, that overemphasis would be difficult.

Climate determines to a large extent the type of soil and natural vegetation in a given region and hence influences the utilization of the land, whether for crop cultivation, forest, or grazing. Together with terrain factors of relief and steepness of slope, then, climate in part determines the ability of land to support a population. To be sure, the introduction of engineering works has provided irrigation and power where it might not otherwise be available, but the distribution of world population still reflects strongly the advantages of favorable climate and terrain.

Climate exerts an important influence on physiology. Cold weather, particularly that involving alternations of cold and mild periods with varying degrees of cloudiness, precipitation, and windiness, is believed to stimulate human mental and physical activity.

A contributing factor to economic development in middle latitudes is that freezing temperatures reduce the activity of many organisms responsible for disease. In warm, humid tropical and equatorial zones a great variety of parasitic organisms thrives, together with numerous host animals necessary in their life cycles. Malaria and yellow fever, borne by the mosquito, and sleeping sickness, carried by the tsetse fly, are well-known examples. Fungi in excessively humid, warm areas hasten the corrosion and decay of clothing, furniture, and machines.

Classification of climate

As in dealing with all other natural phenomena, the scientist attempts to devise schemes of classification that will include all variations in climate, yet permit them to be placed in several clearly defined and easily distinguished groups. Success is only partially achieved. Nature resists simple categorical schemes.

Maps showing the extent of climate zones are often misleading in that a solid, thin line separates two zones whose shading or color pattern is uniform to the line of contact. Actually, most of these boundaries are transitional, so that intergradation of patterns or colors might be more suitable. Only where the abrupt face of a mountain range creates a sharp climate boundary are the conventional map symbols appropriate. A second misleading quality of most climate maps and classifications is the restriction of the climate zones to land areas. Oceans, though having smaller contrasts in climate, nevertheless can be fitted into the general scheme.

If the weather elements—temperature, pressure, winds, and precipitation—are taken as bases of classification, some useful systems may be devised. The distribution of natural vegetation and soils might suggest still other types of classifications.

Temperature as a basis of climate classification

The general parallelism of isotherms with parallels of latitude has already been pointed out in an earlier chapter and was perhaps the first basis of climate classification. In Chapter 4 a series of latitude zones was defined: equatorial, tropical, subtropical, middle-latitude, subarctic, arctic, and polar (Figure 4.5). Unfortunately, because of the contrasting thermal properties of land and water bodies, we cannot correlate temperature regimes directly with latitude zones.

With intelligent application temperature has been made a fundamental factor in most climate classifications. Three major climate groups can be defined: (1) winterless climates of low latitudes, (2) climates of middle latitudes with both a summer and a winter season, and (3) summerless climates of high latitudes. A winterless climate is commonly defined as one in which no month of the year has a monthly mean temperature lower than 64.4°F (18°C). The approximate position of the appropriate isotherm is shown on a world map (Figure 8.1). Note that the isotherm shows a considerable latitude range, bending equatorward over the cool west-coast ocean currents and over the land in north Africa and Australia.

A summerless climate is commonly defined as one in which no month has a monthly mean temperature higher than 50°F (10°C). The appropriate isotherm, shown in Figure 8.1, has a wide latitude range in the northern hemisphere, being

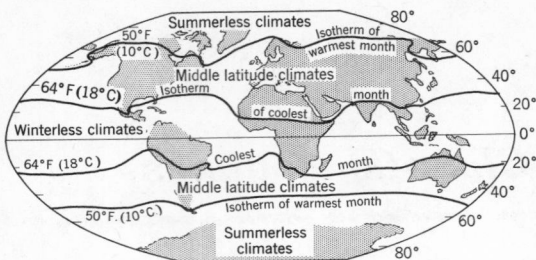

Figure 8.1   Climate groups based on temperature.

farthest poleward over the landmasses of North America and Eurasia, but dipping to middle latitudes over the intervening oceans. The 50°F (10°C) isotherm of the warmest month closely coincides with the northernmost limit of tree growth, hence it separates the regions of boreal forests from the treeless arctic tundra. Here then, is an example of a thermal climatic boundary selected to coincide with a natural vegetation boundary.

Climates having both a summer and a winter season lie in the regions between the two boundary isotherms described above and constitute a middle-latitude group.

Temperature alone as a basis of climate classification is unsatisfactory because humid and desert regions receive no distinction. An obvious remedy is a further subdivision according to precipitation.

Precipitation as a basis for climate classification

The profound effect of precipitation on nature of vegetation, drainage systems, soil moisture, and ground water, makes it desirable to consider the amount and seasonal distribution of rainfall and snowfall as a basis of climate classification.

Five precipitation ranges are as follows:

Climatic Type	Rainfall Type	Annual Rainfall Inches	Cm
Arid	Scanty	0–10	0–25
Semi-arid	Light	10–20	25–50
Subhumid	Moderate	20–40	50–100
Humid	Heavy	40–80	100–200
Very wet	Very heavy	More than 80	More than 200

A climate map on this basis would be the same as the mean annual rainfall map (Plate 1). An important refinement of this classification would be the subdivision of classes according to distribution of precipitation throughout the year, whether uniform or seasonal.

As a useful climate classification this one fails because it groups cold arctic climates together with the hot deserts of low latitudes. Evaporation, which determines what proportion of the rainfall

will remain in the ground, is controlled by air temperature. In general, cold climates are effectively humid with the same meager precipitation that produces very dry deserts in hot subtropical and tropical latitudes. It would seem, then, that a useful climate system must combine temperature and precipitation classes. Although such combining will increase the number of climate types recognized, each type will be an effective description of a distinctive environment.

An example of intelligent combination of monthly mean temperature and precipitation data to derive climatic zones is illustrated in Table 8.1. The temperature units are fixed in equal increments of 10 C° (18 F°), whereas the precipitation range is varied to suit temperature range. Consequently, "humid" denotes 4 to 12 in (10 to 30 cm) of precipitation in a month when monthly mean temperature is above 86°F (30°C), but denotes only 1 to 3 in (2.5 to 7.5 cm) when temperature mean is between 14° and 32°F (−10° and 0°C). Climate is described according to such combinations of forms as "warm-dry," "cool-humid," or "cold-dry." Because this system is applied to a given month of the year, a world climate map based upon it shows conditions only for the specified month (Figure 8.2). Twelve such maps would be needed to give an analysis of world climate throughout the year. The system was used by the U.S. Air Force for a set of northern hemisphere monthly climatic maps published in 1947.

TABLE 8.1   CLIMATIC ZONES BASED ON AVERAGES OF A GIVEN MONTH[a]

Above 30°C	Dry	Humid	Wet	Hot (Above 86°F)
	Under 4 in (10 cm)	4–12 in (10–30.5 cm)	Over 12 in (30.5 cm)	
30°C				86°F
	Under 3 in (7.5 cm)	3–12 in (7.5–30.5 cm)	Over 12 in (30.5 cm)	Warm
20°C				68°F
	Under 2 in (5 cm)	2–8 in (5–20 cm)	Over 8 in (20 cm)	Mild
10°C				50°F
	Under 1 in (2.5 cm)	1–5 in (2.5–12.7 cm)	Over 5 in (12.7 cm)	Cool
0°C				32°F
	Under 1 in (2.5 cm)	1–3 in (2.5–7.5 cm)	Over 3 in (7.5 cm)	Cold
−10°C				14°F
		Very cold (−4° to 14°F)		
−20°C		−4°F		
		Extreme cold (−40° to −4°F)		
−40°C		−40°F		
		Ultra cold (Below −40°F)		

[a]After U.S. Air Force, Aeronautical Chart Service, 1947.

June climate zones:

Hot–dry

Warm–dry

Mild–dry

Cool–dry

Cold–dry

Warm–humid

Mild–humid

Cool–humid

Cold–humid

Warm–wet

Mild–wet

Figure 8.2 June climate zones of North America, using the combinations of precipitation and temperature given in Table 8.1. (After Aeronautical Chart Service, U.S. Air Force, 1947.)

Vegetation and soils as a basis of climate classification

Botanists and geographers have long been aware that plants are highly responsive to differences in climate. With each plant species is associated a particular combination of climatic elements most favorable to its growth, as well as certain extremes of heat, cold, or drought beyond which it cannot survive. Plants tend to adapt their physical forms to meet the stresses of climate, hence we find that there is a wide range of forms taken by assemblages of the dominant plant species, and that the overall form patterns or habits closely reflect climate. These subjects are treated in Chapters 15 and 16.

There is much to recommend a climate classification based on the different forms taken by groups of plants. On the other hand, such plant forms represent responses to climate, rather than causes of global climate variation. A fundamental principle of scientific classification is that the setting up of classes of things is better done according to the causes of the class differences than according to the effects that such differences produce.

Since the late nineteenth century, soil scientists have recognized that the several fundamental classes of mature soils, seen on a world-wide scope, are more strongly controlled by climatic elements than by any other single factor. (See Chapters 13 and 14.) But plants also contribute to determining the properties of the very soils upon which they depend. Thus, as in the case of vegetation, soils reflect differences in climate but do not cause those differences. A climate classification based upon soils would be highly meaningful, but not scientifically as desirable as a climate classification based upon causes.

The Köppen climate classification system

The foregoing concepts of devising climate classes that combine temperature and precipitation characteristics, but of setting limits and boundaries fitted into known vegetation and soil distributions, were actually carried out in 1918 by Dr. Wladimir Köppen of the University of Graz in Austria. The classification was subsequently revised and extended by Köppen and his students to become the most widely used of climatic classifications for geographical purposes.

The Köppen system is strictly empirical. This is to say that each climate is defined according to fixed values of temperature and precipitation, computed according to the averages of the year or of individual months. In such a classification, no concern whatever need be given to the causes of the climate in terms of pressure and wind belts, air masses, fronts, or storms. It is possible to assign a given place to a particular climate subgroup solely on the basis of the records of temperature and precipitation of that place, provided, of course, that the period of record is long enough to yield meaningful averages. Air temperature and precipitation are the most easily obtainable surface weather data, requiring only simple equipment and a very elementary observer education. A climate system based on these data has a great advantage, in that the areas covered by each subtype of

climate can be computed or estimated for large regions of the world.

The Köppen system features a shorthand code of letters designating major climate groups, subgroups within the major groups, and further subdivisions to distinguish particular seasonal characteristics of temperature and precipitation.

Five major climate groups are designated by capital letters as follows (Figure 8.3). Groups A, C, and D have sufficient heat and precipitation for growth of high-trunk trees (e.g., forest and woodland).

A *Tropical climates.* Average temperature of every month is above 64.4°F (18°C). These climates have no winter season. Annual rainfall is large and exceeds annual evaporation.

B *Dry climates.* Potential evaporation exceeds precipitation on the average throughout the year. No water surplus; hence no permanent streams originate in B climate zones.

C *Warm temperate (mesothermal)*[3] *climates.* Coldest month has an average temperature under 64.4°F (18°C), but above 26.6°F (−3°C); at least one month has an average temperature above 50°F (10°C). The C climates thus have both a summer and a winter season.

D *Snow (microthermal)*[4] *climates.* Coldest month average temperature under 26.6°F (−3°C). Average temperature of warmest month above 50°F (10°C), that isotherm coinciding approximately with poleward limit of forest growth.

E *Ice climates.* Average temperature of warmest month below 50°F (10°C). These climates have no true summer.

Note that four of these five groups (A, C, D, and E) are defined by temperature averages, whereas one (B) is defined by precipitation-to-evaporation ratios. This may seem to be a fundamental inconsistency.

Subgroups within the five major groups are designated by a second letter according to the following code:

S *Steppe climate:* A semi-arid climate with about 15 to 30 in (38 to 76 cm) of rainfall annually at low latitudes. Exact rainfall boundary determined by formula taking temperature into account.

W *Desert climate:* Arid climate. Most regions included have less than 10 in (25 cm) of rainfall annually.

---

[3]The middle latitudes are anything but "temperate" in seasonal and day-to-day weather. *Mesothermal* is widely substituted for *temperate* to imply intermediate temperatures as compared with the extreme heat of dry deserts and the extreme cold of polar and arctic climates.

[4]The term *microthermal*, meaning "small heat," is widely substituted in the United States, along with *mesothermal*, in the titles of Köppen groups D and C, respectively.

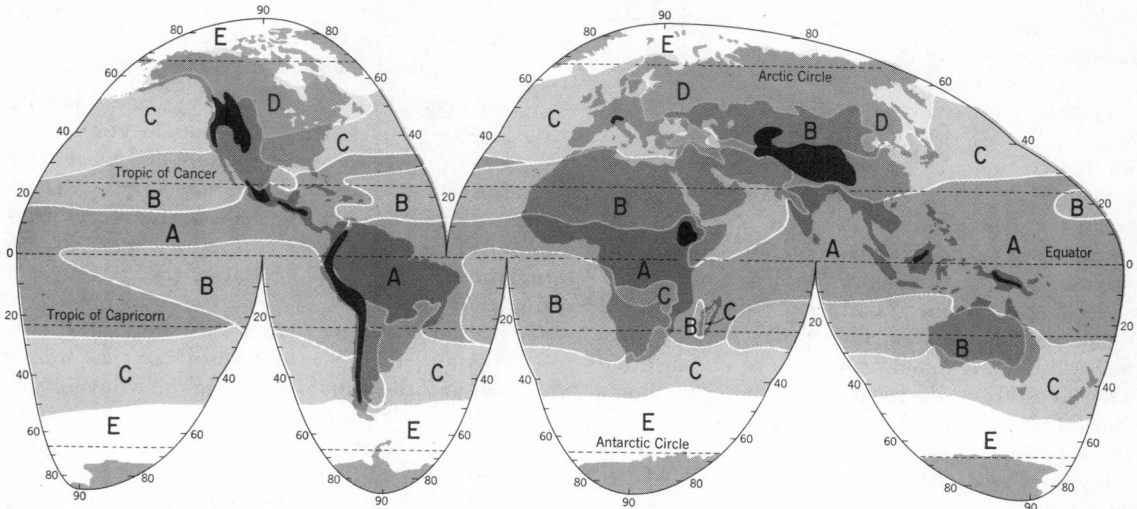

Figure 8.3 Highly generalized world map of major climatic regions according to the Köppen classification. Highland areas in black. (Based on Goode Base Map. Copyright by the University of Chicago. Used by permission of the University of Chicago Press.)

Exact boundary with steppe climate determined by formula.

(The letters *S* and *W* are applied only to the dry *B* climates, yielding two combinations, *BS* and *BW*.)

f   Moist. Adequate precipitation in all months. No dry season. This modifier is applied to *A*, *C*, and *D* groups.

w   Dry season in winter of the respective hemisphere (low-sun season).

s   Dry season in summer of the respective hemisphere (high-sun season).

m   Rainforest climate despite short, dry season in monsoon type of precipitation cycle. Applies only to *A* climates.

From combinations of the two letter groups, eleven distinct climates emerge as follows:

Af   Tropical rainforest (Also *Am*, a variant of *Af*).
Aw   Tropical savanna.
BS   Steppe climate.
BW   Desert climate.
Cw   Temperate rainy (humid mesothermal) climate with dry winter.
Cf   Temperate rainy (humid mesothermal) climate moist all seasons.
Cs   Temperate rainy (humid mesothermal) climate with dry summer.
Df   Cold snowy forest (humid microthermal) climate moist in all seasons.
Dw   Cold snowy forest (humid microthermal) climate with dry winter.
ET   Tundra climate.
EF   Climates of perpetual frost (icecaps).

To differentiate still more variations in temperature or other weather elements. Köppen added a third letter to the code group. Meanings are as follows:

a   With hot summer; warmest month over 71.6°F (22°C) (*C* and *D* climates).

b   With warm summer; warmest month below 71.6°F (22°C) (*C* and *D* climates).

c   With cool, short summer; less than four months over 50°F (10°C) (*C* and *D* climates).

d   With very cold winter; coldest month below −36.4°F (−38°C) (*D* climates only).

h   Dry-hot; mean annual temperature over 64.4°F (18°C) (*B* climates only).

k   Dry-cold; mean annual temperature under 64.4°F (18°C) (*B* climates only).

As an example of a complete Köppen climate code, *BWk* would refer to *cool desert climate, Dfc* would refer to *cold, snowy forest climate with cool, short summer*. The complete list of climate code designations is included in the summary table of climates to follow. A world map of climates following a later revision of the Köppen system (the Köppen-Geiger system) appears as Plate 2.

An explanatory-descriptive climate system

Earlier chapters on weather elements, global circulation, air mass properties and source regions, and cyclonic storms have armed the reader with many principles concerning the causes of weather patterns and their seasonal variations. It would be a pity if this knowledge were left unused with no application in the systematic study of world climates, in favor of a purely empirical system based on temperature and precipitation averages expressed by code letters.

The most satisfying systems of natural science classification are those described as *genetic*, meaning that the genesis, or origin, of the phenomena is put first in designing the classification units. Because a genetic system gives an explanation of the things classified, it may be considered as *explanatory*. If the explanation is carried out largely in verbal statements (as distinct from numerical or mathematical statements) it may be labeled as *descriptive*. This general approach to classification can therefore be designated as *explanatory-descriptive* in contrast to the *empirical-quantitative* approach followed in the Köppen system.

In the chapters to follow, world climates are treated by an explanatory-descriptive system based on causes and effects. It will not be difficult to introduce the Köppen code symbols into such a system by way of interrelating the two. In fact, it will soon become apparent that the explanatory-descriptive system is simply providing a reasonable scientific explanation for the existence of Köppen's climate groups and subgroups.

Air mass source regions and frontal zones as a basis of classification

The system of climate analysis used in the succeeding chapters is based on the location of air mass source regions and the nature and movement of air masses, fronts, and cyclonic storms. A schematic global diagram, Figure 8.4, shows the principles of the classification. A world map, Figure 8.5, shows the general locations of each of fourteen fundamental types.

Three major climate groups are shown in Figure 8.4. Group I includes the tropical air mass source regions and the equatorial trough or convergence zone between. *Equatorial* is here defined as pertaining to the latitude zone within a few degrees north and south of the equator; *tropical* is defined as referring to the two latitude zones included within a few degrees north and south of the tropics of Cancer and Capricorn (Figure 4.5).

Climates of Group I are controlled by the dynamic subtropical high-pressure cells, or anticyclones, which are regions of air subsidence and are basically dry, and by the great equatorial trough of convergence that lies between them.

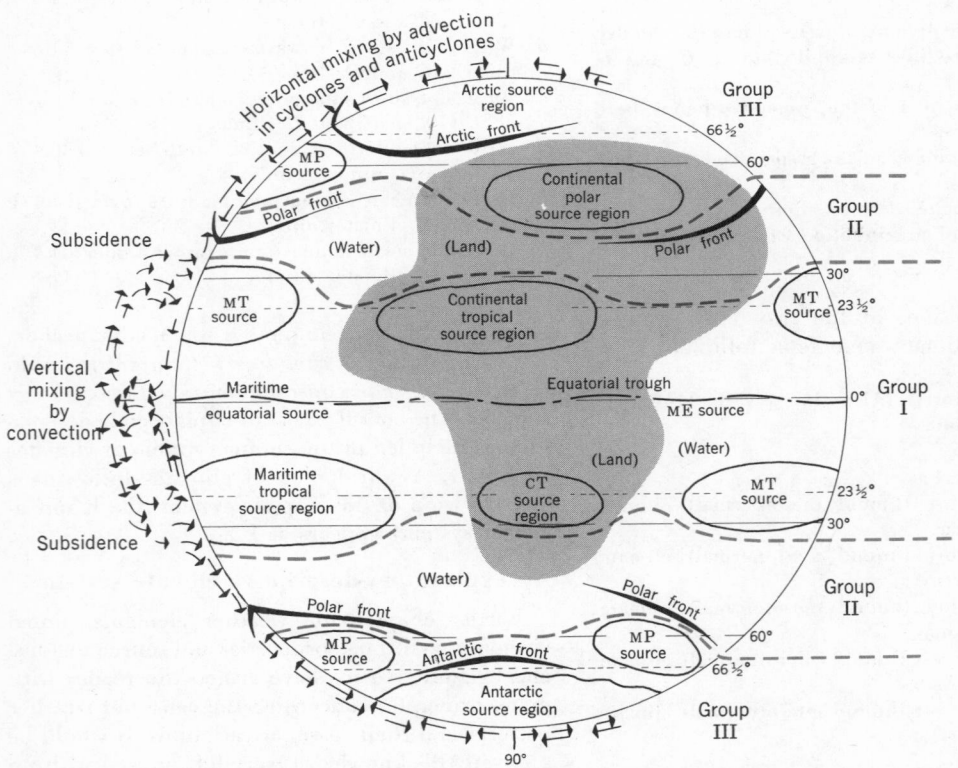

Figure 8.4   Global diagram of major climate groups. (After Petterssen and others.)

Though it is true that air of polar origin occasionally invades the tropical and equatorial latitudes, it may be said of the climates of Group I that they are almost wholly dominated by tropical and equatorial air masses.

Climates of Group II are in a zone of intense interaction between unlike air masses: the *polar front zone*. Tropical air masses moving poleward and polar air masses moving equatorward are in conflict in this zone, which contains a procession of eastmoving cyclonic storms. Locally and seasonally either tropical or polar air masses may dominate in these regions, but neither has exclusive control.

Climates of Group III are dominated by polar and arctic (including antarctic) air masses. The two polar continental air mass source regions of northern Canada and Siberia fall into this group,

but there is no southern hemisphere counterpart to these continental centers. In the belt of the 60th to 70th parallels, air masses of arctic origin meet polar continental air masses along an *arctic front zone*, creating a series of east-moving cyclones.

Fourteen major climate types are listed below. Where a compound climate type is formed by the alternation of two simple types, it follows them on the list. Simple names are applied to these climate types following common usage among geographers. Numbers correspond with those in Figure 8.5. Köppen symbols are added to the table to show close correspondence of these fourteen types with his eleven climates and their subtypes. Note, however, that the Köppen symbols and climate types can be completely disregarded without affecting the explanatory-descriptive treatment in terms of air masses and frontal zones.

GROUP I: LOW-LATITUDE CLIMATES (CONTROLLED BY EQUATORIAL AND TROPICAL AIR MASSES)

Climate Name	Köppen Symbol		Air Mass Source Regions and Frontal Zones, General Climate Characteristics
1. Wet Equatorial Climate 10° N–10° S lat. (Asia 10°–20° N)	*Af*	Tropical rainforest climate, and	Equatorial trough (convergence zone) climates are dominated by warm, moist tropical maritime (mT) and equatorial (mE) air masses yielding heavy rainfall through convectional storms. Remarkably uniform temperatures prevail throughout the year.
	Am	Tropical rainforest climate, monsoon type	
2. Trade Wind Littoral Climate 10°–25° N and S lat.	*Af-Am*	Included in climates	Tropical easterlies (trades) bring maritime tropical (mT) air masses from moist western sides of oceanic subtropical high-pressure cells to give narrow east-coast zones of heavy rainfall and uniformly high temperatures. Rainfall shows strong seasonal variation.
3. Tropical Desert and Steppe Climates 15°–35° N and S lat.	*BWh*	Desert climate, hot, and	Source regions of continental-tropical (cT$_s$) air masses in high-pressure cells at high level over lands astride the Tropics of Cancer and Capricorn give arid to semi-arid climate with very high maximum temperatures and moderate annual range.
	BSh	Steppe climate, hot	
4. West Coast Desert Climate 15°–30° N and S lat.	*BWk*	Desert climate, cool, and	On west coasts bordering the oceanic subtropical high-pressure cells, subsiding maritime tropical (mT$_s$) air masses are stable and dry. Extremely dry, but relatively cool, foggy desert climates prevail in narrow coastal belts. Annual temperature range is small.
	BWh	Desert climate, hot (*BWn* in earlier versions, *n* meaning frequent fog)	
5. Tropical Wet-Dry Climate 5°–25° N and S lat.	*Aw*	Tropical rainy climate, savanna; also	Seasonal alternation of moist mT or mE air masses with dry cT air masses gives climate with wet season at time of high sun, dry season at time of low sun.
	Cwa	Temperate rainy (Humid mesothermal) climate, dry winter, hot summer	

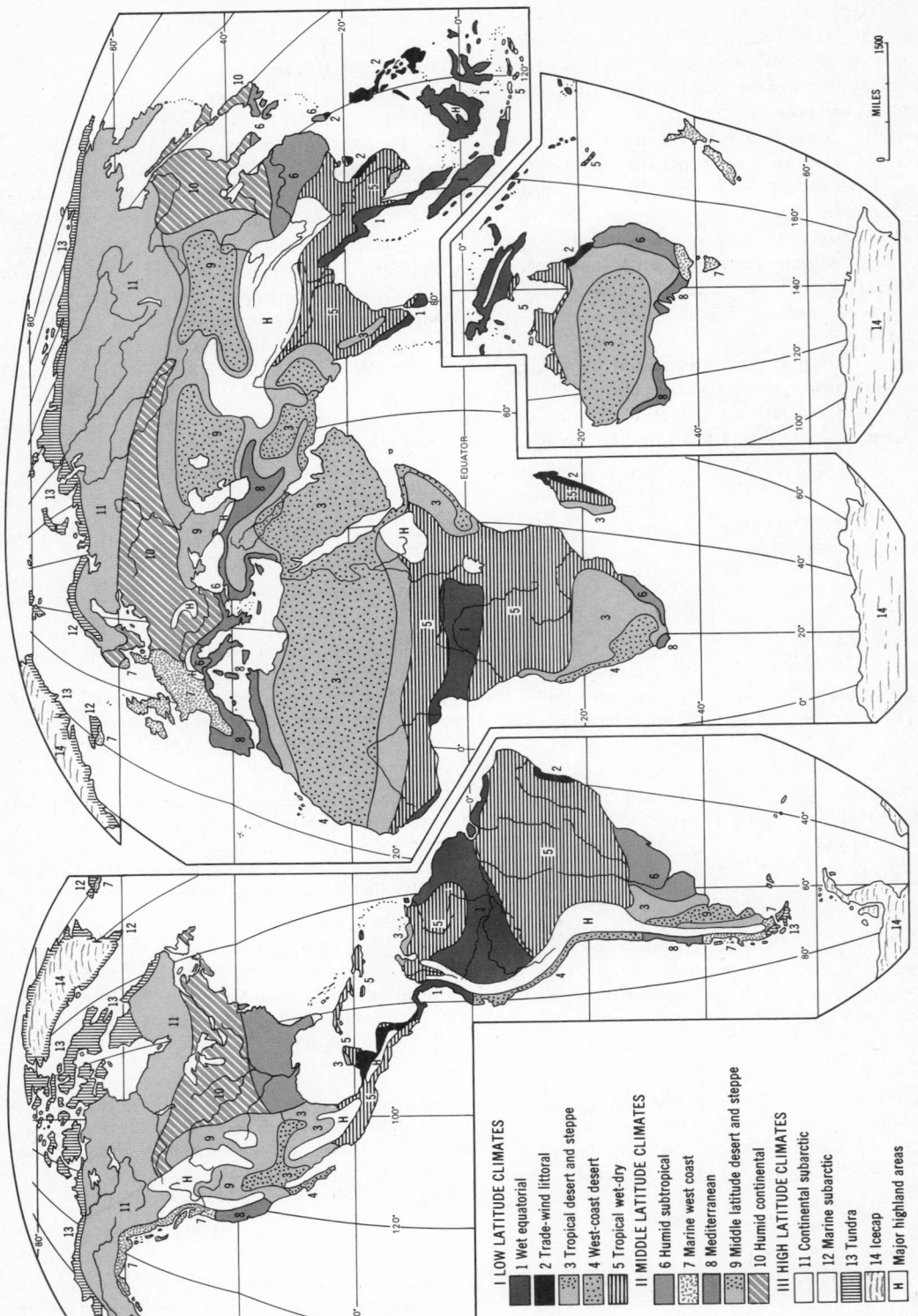

Figure 8.5 Generalized and simplified world map showing distribution of fourteen climates. In many respects, these climate regions correspond with regions as defined by G. T. Trewartha. (Aitoff's equal-area projection adapted by V. C. Finch.)

GROUP II: MIDDLE-LATITUDE CLIMATES (CONTROLLED BY BOTH TROPICAL AND POLAR AIR MASSES)

6. Humid Subtropical Climate 20°–35° N and S lat.	Cfa	Temperate rainy (Humid mesothermal) climate, hot summers	Subtropical, eastern continental margins dominated by moist maritime (MT) air masses flowing from the western sides of oceanic high-pressure cells. In high-sun season, rainfall is copious and temperatures warm. Winters are cool with frequent continental polar (cP) air mass invasions. Frequent cyclonic storms.
7. Marine West Coast Climate 40°–60° N and S lat.	Cfb	Temperate rainy (Humid mesothermal) climate, warm summers, and	Windward, middle-latitude west coasts receive frequent cyclonic storms with cool, moist maritime polar (MP) air masses. These bring much cloudiness and well-distributed precipitation, but the winter maximum. Annual temperature range is small for middle latitudes.
	Cfc	same but cool, short summers	
8. Mediterranean Climate 30°–45° N and S lat.	Csa	Temperate rainy (Humid mesothermal) climate, dry, hot summer, and	This wet-winter, dry-summer climate results from seasonal alternation of conditions causing climates 4 and 7; MP air masses dominate in winter with cyclonic storms and ample rainfall, MT_s air masses dominate in summer with extreme drought. Moderate annual temperature range.
	Csb	same, but dry, warm summer	
9. Middle-latitude Desert and Steppe Climates 35°–50° N and S lat.	BWk	Desert climate, cool	Interior, middle-latitude deserts and steppes of regions shut off by mountains from invasions of maritime air masses (MT or MP), but dominated by continental tropical (cT) air masses in summer and continental polar (cP) air masses in winter. Great annual temperature range; hot summers, cold winters.
	BWk′	same, but cold; and	
	BSk	Steppe climate, cool	
	BSk′	same, but cold	
10. Humid Continental Climate 35°–60° N lat.	Dfa	Cold, snowy forest (Humid microthermal) climate, moist all year, hot summers, and	Located in central and eastern parts of continents of middle latitudes, these climates are in the polar front zone, the battle ground of polar and tropical air masses. Seasonal contrasts are strong and weather highly variable. Ample precipitation throughout the year is increased in summer by invading maritime tropical (MT) air masses. Cold winters are dominated by continental polar (cP) air masses invading frequently from northern source regions.
	Dfb	same, but warm summers; also	
	Dwa	Cold, snowy forest (Humid microthermal) climate, dry winters, hot summers, and	
	Dwb	same, but warm summers	

GROUP III: HIGH-LATITUDE CLIMATES (CONTROLLED BY POLAR AND ARCTIC AIR MASSES)

11. Continental Sub-arctic Climate 50°–70° N lat.	Dfc	Cold, snowy forest (Humid microthermal) climate, moist all year, cool summers, and	This climate lies in source region of continental polar (cP) air masses, which in winter are stable and very cold. Summers are short and cool. Annual temperature range is enormous. Cyclonic storms, into which maritime polar (MP) air is drawn, supply light precipitation, but evaporation is small and the climate is therefore effectively moist.
	Dfd	Same, but very cold winters, also	
	Dwc	Cold, snowy forest (Humid microthermal) climate, dry winter, cool summer, and	
	Dwd	same, but very cold winter	
12. Marine Subarctic Climate 50°–60° N and 45°–60° S lat.	ET	Polar, tundra climate	Located in the arctic frontal zones of the winter season, these windward coasts and islands of subarctic latitudes are dominated by cool MP air masses. Precipitation is relatively large and annual temperature range small for so high a latitude.
13. Tundra Climate North of 55° N South of 50°S	ET	Polar, tundra climate	The arctic coastal fringes lie along a frontal zone, in which polar (MP, cP) air masses interact with arctic (A) air masses in cyclonic storms. Climate is humid and severely cold with no warm season or summer. Moderating influence of ocean water prevents extreme winter severity as in Climate 11.
14. Icecap Climate (Greenland, Antarctica)	EF	Polar climate, perpetual frost	Source regions of arctic (A) and antarctic (AA) air masses situated upon the great continental icecaps have climate with annual temperature average far below all other climates and no above-freezing monthly average. High altitudes of ice plateaus intensify air mass cold.
Highland Climates			Cool to cold moist climates, occupying high-altitude zones of the world's mountain ranges, are localized in extent and not included in classification system.

Climatic regimes

Whatever system of climate classification a geographer may choose to adopt, a study of the combined monthly temperature and precipitation characteristics will reveal that a climate expresses one or more of seven basic *regimes*. These regimes are of particular importance in an understanding of soils and plant geography because each regime induces a characteristic response from soils and vegetation.

The climatic regimes are particularly well displayed by means of a *thermohyet diagram* (see Figure 8.6). Similar diagrams have been previously referred to as *climographs*. The thermohyet diagram shows the monthly means of air temperature and precipitation plotted in combination as points representing each month of the year. The months are connected by lines to show the cycle of monthly averages throughout the year. The thermohyet diagram used throughout this chapter has temperature and precipitation scales of special design to expand the low-precipitation range and compress the low-temperature range in order to give more space on the graph where it is most needed. Data used on the thermohyet diagram are for the most part the averages of many years of record and thus provide an expression of the characteristic yearly regime, or climatic cycle.

1. Middle-latitude equable regime

One concept of climate description, expressed in the words *equability* and *inequability*, relates to the degree of uniformity and lack of uniformity, respectively, in the temperature and precipitation characteristics of a station. An *equable climate* exhibits a small annual range in monthly means of temperatures or of precipitation, or of both. On the thermohyet diagram, equability is expressed by a diagram covering a small surface area. Several examples are shown in Figure 8.6.

Because temperature and precipitation are largely independent constituents of climate, equability might conceivably be present (1) in both monthly mean temperature and monthly mean precipitation, (2) in temperature, but not in precipitation; and (3) in precipitation, but not in temperature. The first case, which can be described as one of *total equability*, is rare in nature, but can be found in middle latitudes in certain insular or windward coast locations. The five examples shown in Figure 8.6*A–E* (Auckland, Punta Arenas, Hasselbough Bay, South Orkneys, and Los Evangelistas) are all in regions of prevailing westerlies and are exposed constantly to moist maritime air masses. They represent the *middle-latitude equable regime* of climate.

The equability of Hasselbough Bay, Macquarie Islands, is truly remarkable, with its annual range of only 10 F° (6 C°); but the record of Los Evangelistas, Chile, is almost unbelievable. This station lies close to sea level on a small island off the west coast of South America at about 52½° S. latitude. Its annual temperature range is only 7½ F° (4 C°), while the total annual precipitation of 119 in (300

cm) is so evenly distributed that no month averages less than 8 in (20 cm) or more than 12 in (30 cm)! Below freezing temperatures are rare despite an annual mean temperature of 43°F (6°C). No month of the year averages fewer than 20 days with more than 0.04 in (0.1 cm) of precipitation; which is to say that it rains about two days out of three on the average throughout the year.

These examples of total equability are all the more remarkable when we consider that in middle latitudes the annual cycle of insolation shows a wide range (Figure 4.3), tending to cause a strong annual temperature range. In all five cases shown in Figure 8.6*A–E*, the moderating influence of the vast Southern Ocean effectively suppresses the insolation cycle.

2. Equatorial regime

Great uniformity of monthly mean temperatures, but rarely of monthly precipitation means, is characteristic of the equatorial belt, which may be said to possess a high degree of thermal equability. The climatic regime associated with these very low latitudes is the *equatorial regime*. Two examples, Figure 8.6 *F, G*, are selected for exceptionally low annual ranges in monthly mean rainfall. Figure 8.7 shows the more commonly observed conditions, consisting of exceptional thermal equability superimposed upon a wide range in monthly rainfall averages. The result is a thermohyet diagram which is almost a horizontal

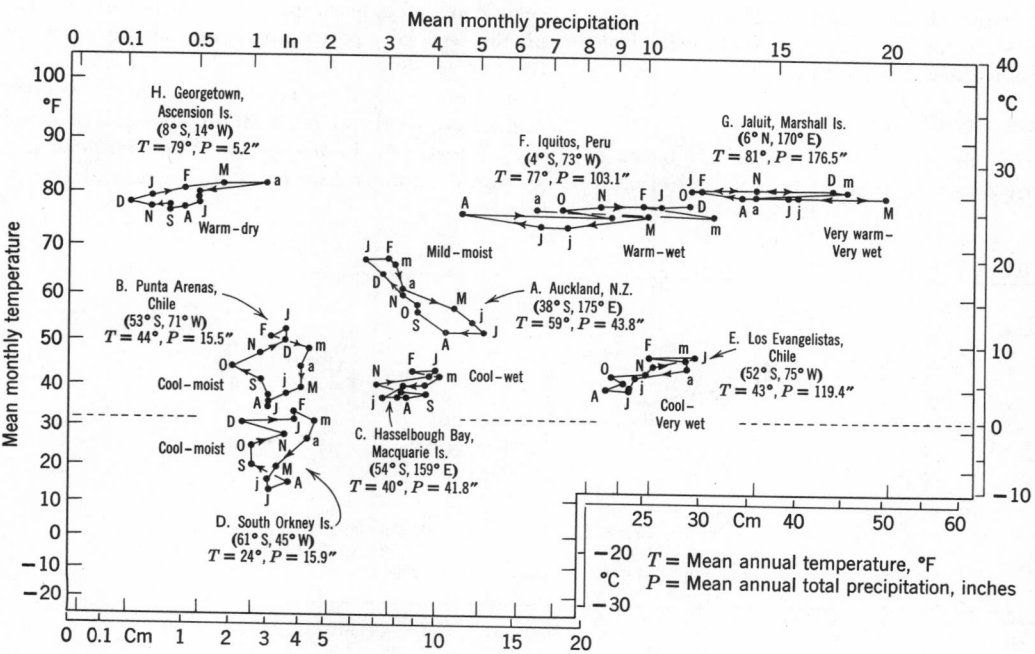

Figure 8.6 Selected examples of highly equable climatic regimes shown by thermohyet diagrams. (Data from Meterological Office of Great Britain and G. T. Trewartha.)

Figure 8.7 Examples of stations exhibiting the wet equatorial climatic regime. (Data from Meteorological Office of Great Britain.)

straight line on the graph. Note the wide ranges in monthly rainfalls, combined with large annual totals.

With increasing altitude the entire cycle is pushed down and to the left on the graph, but otherwise little changed, as shown in succession by Takengön, Sumatra; Quito, Ecuador; and Jauja, Peru (Figure 8.7, *B*, *C*, *D*).

Equability in temperature but not in precipitation is found only in the very dry deserts and is treated below under the desert regime. Georgetown, Ascension Island (Figure 8.6*H*), is an exceptional case of total equability in equatorial latitudes, but with a very dry climate.

3. Tropical wet-dry regime

A *tropical wet-dry regime* is distinctive because a very rainy season at time of high sun alternates

with a very dry season at time of low sun, usually to the accompaniment of a moderate seasonal range in temperatures. Thermohyets of tropical wet-dry stations are shown in Figure 8.8. Paraná, Brazil, tends toward thermal equability, but this equability is offset by the great contrast in drought and rains. Kano, Nigeria, is in many respects the most extreme of low-latitude examples, for it has a rainless period when the sun's declination is most southerly. In striking contrast is the extremely wet period following summer solstice. Obviously, a regime of such great precipitation contrasts will place a severe stress upon plants and animals in the dry season.

A noteworthy feature of the tropical wet-dry regime is a thermal peak about during April and May (northern hemisphere). The temperatures moderate somewhat after May, because of arrival

Figure 8.8 Examples of stations exhibiting the tropical wet-dry climatic regime. (Data from Meteorological Office of Great Britain.)

of cloud cover and the cooling effect of falling rain and its evaporation. Thus we find a three-season cycle in certain tropical regions: cool-dry, hot-dry, warm-wet. In north India, particularly, the thermohyet diagram forms a figure-eight loop of distinctive shape, as shown in the data for Allahabad, India (Figure 8.8*C*). Here the thermal range is exaggerated by the higher latitude and is superimposed on a strong Asiatic monsoon.

4. Mediterranean regime

The *Mediterranean regime (dry-summer subtropical regime)* is characterized by a very dry, warm summer alternating with a wet, mild winter. The precipitation extremes of dry and wet season are not greatly different from those of the tropical wet-dry regime, but are in exactly opposite phase in terms of the sun's declination. Moreover, the thermal cycle of the Mediterranean regime tends to be rather equable because of a west coast location in the zone of prevailing westerlies.

Thermohyet diagrams (Figure 8.9) show two varieties of the Mediterranean regime. Santiago, Chile, illustrates the cooler, drier variety found along the west coasts of continents. Siracuse, Sicily, is a warmer, wetter variety with greater temperature range and warmer summers. A distinctive feature of the thermohyet diagram is that the loop takes the form of an ellipse whose long axis is inclined downward to the right. The same tendency is found in thermohyet diagrams of any west coast station in the belt of westerly winds, whether a dry season exists or not. (See Vancouver, B.C., Figure 8.9*C* and Auckland, N.Z., Figure 8.6*A*.)

As in the case of the tropical wet-dry regime, the Mediterranean regime places a severe stress upon plants and animals during the almost rainless summer, but in neither regime is cold an important stress.

5. Continental regime

The *continental regime* is dominated by a large annual temperature range, often accompanied by a severely cold winter. The thermohyet diagrams of Figure 8.10 show a distinctive elongation and are diagonally oriented, running from upper right to lower left. The significance of the diagonal trend of the diagram is that the warm season has appreciably greater precipitation than the cold season. The continental regime thus usually exhibits seasonal contrasts both in temperature and precipitation. There is, however, a considerable difference in overall aridity or humidity of climate from one position or another within a continent.

As Figure 8.10 shows, the centers of the continents tend to be dry (Yakutsk, U.S.S.R.) whereas the more easterly locations have increasingly more precipitation throughout the year (Omaha, Nebraska; Shanghai, China). As we would expect, increased latitude brings a marked overall lowering of the temperatures and at the same time increases the annual range. In one respect the continental regime resembles the tropical wet-dry regime: the greatest precipitation falls in the high-sun period. One might thus expect a complete gradation of the tropical wet-dry regime poleward into the continental regime, where the climate is traced along the central and eastern parts of a continent from tropical into middle-latitude zones.

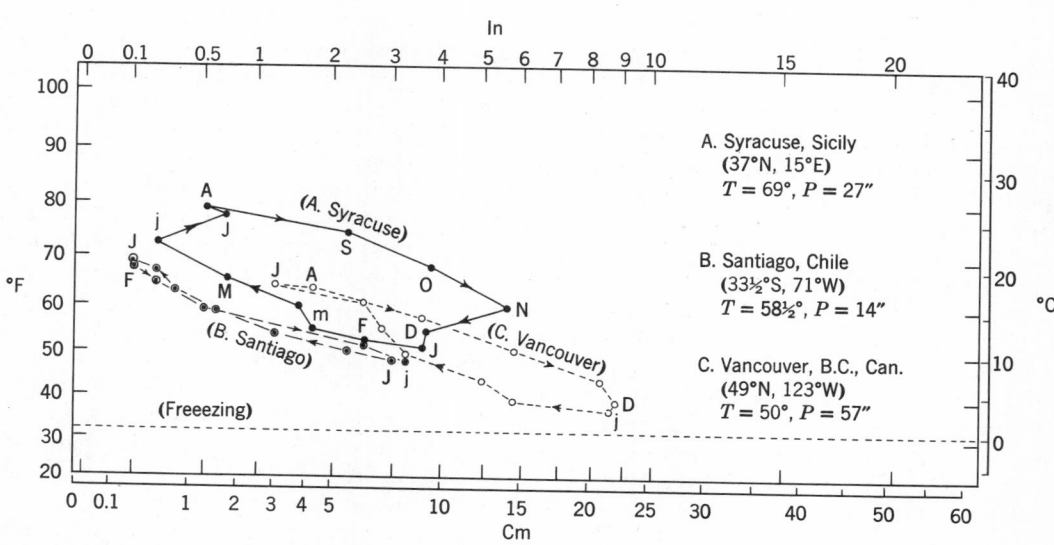

Figure 8.9 Examples of stations exhibiting the Mediterranean climatic regime. (Data from Meteorological Office of Great Britain.)

Figure 8.10 Examples of stations exhibiting the continental climatic regime. (Data from G. T. Trewartha and Meteorological Office of Great Britain.)

Figure 8.11 Examples of stations exhibiting desert and polar climatic regimes. (Data from G. T. Trewartha and Meteorological Office of Great Britain.)

6. Polar regime

A *polar regime* exists poleward of the Arctic and Antarctic circles in both hemispheres. This regime is, of course, one of year-round low temperatures. Only three or four months may have means above freezing. The thermohyet diagrams of representative stations from the Arctic coastal fringes are thus situated far down on the left of the chart (Figure 8.11*A, B, C*). Precipitation is measurable but small in all months. The extreme range in intensity of insolation throughout the year is responsible for a large annual temperature range of 40 to 50 F° (22 to 28 C°), but this range is greatly exceeded in the continental regime at lower latitudes in Canada and Siberia (see Yakutsk, Figure 8.10*B*).

By far the most intense polar regime is found at high altitudes in the interiors of the great icecaps of Greenland and Antarctica. The thermohyet of one year's record at Eismitte, over 9000 ft (2700 m) in elevation in central Greenland, shows that only two monthly means were above 0°F (−18°C), whereas four months averaged −40°F (−40°C) or below! Because no plant life can survive under icecap conditions, this icecap

form of the polar regime constitutes a total cold desert.

7. Desert regime

The *desert regime* combines extremely low precipitation with temperatures ranging from warm to very hot. As a result, a typical thermohyet diagram lies to the far left and generally rather high up (Figure 8.11*D, E, F*). The annual cycles of many desert stations have no month with more than 0.2 in (0.5 cm) average rainfall. Rainfall is sporadic, so that an average of 0.1 in (0.25 cm) for a given month may represent the precipitation of a single storm preceded and followed by many years in which that month was rainless. With regard to temperatures, the desert regime shows the influence of one of the other three regimes: Effect of the continental regime is felt in the interiors of large landmasses, as seen in the thermohyet diagram for Stuart, Australia; here the annual range is 30 F° (17 C°).

Effect of the Mediterranean regime is seen on the diagram for Cairo, Egypt, which has a rainless summer but a marked rainfall maximum in winter. Thermal equability of low latitudes is seen in the thermohyet diagram of Iquique, Chile, with only 11 F° (7 C°) range. The desert regime is one of great stress upon plants and animals, primarily because of the unavailability of water throughout the year, and also, in many locations because of the extremely great heat of air and soil at time of high sun.

Combinations of climatic regimes

The seven climatic regimes have specific areas of optimum development and might be said to form a world climate classification of seven basic types—each one readily understood in terms of the annual cycle of insolation, the properties of land and water bodies, the prevailing winds, and the interplay of air masses and their conflicts in fronts and storms. On the other hand, large land areas lie in intermediate regimes, comprised of two or more of the seven basic regimes. It is for this reason that we have chosen a climate classification with fourteen classes, rather than seven.

Where a region possesses a climatic regime combining two or more of the basic regimes, we can use modifying phrases derived from the names of the seven regimes. For example, Cairo, Egypt (Figure 8.11D), has "a desert regime showing a Mediterranean tendency"; Allahabad, India (Figure 8.8C), has "a tropical wet-dry regime with a marked continental influence"; Yakutsk, Siberia (Figure 8.10B) has "a continental regime with a polar influence."

As explained in Chapter 16, structure and distribution of the several basic forms of natural vegetation strongly reflect the influences of the seven basic climatic regimes. Soil development is similarly influenced. This close association of natural vegetation and soils with climate is ample justification for an analysis of world climates in terms of the fundamental regimes.

REFERENCES FOR FURTHER STUDY

Kendrew, W. G. (1953), *The climates of the continents*, Oxford University Press, London, 607 pp.

Köppen-Geiger (1954), Klima der Erde (map), Justus Perthes, Darmstadt, Germany; American distributor, A. J. Nystrom and Co., Chicago.

Dansereau, Pierre (1957), *Biogeography, an ecological perspective*, The Ronald Press Co., New York, 394 pp. See Chapter 2.

Koeppe, E., and G. C. DeLong (1958), *Weather and climate*, McGraw-Hill Book Co., New York, 341 pp.

Trewartha, G. T. (1968), *An introduction to climate*, fourth edition McGraw-Hill Book Co., New York, 408 pp.

Petterssen, S. (1969), *Introduction to meteorology*, third edition McGraw-Hill Book Co., New York, 333 pp. See Chapter 17.

REVIEW QUESTIONS

1. Discuss the importance of climate as a force influencing soils, natural vegetation, agriculture, physiology, disease, and other factors that affect human life.

2. What difficulties stand in the way of devising satisfactory climate classifications? In what way can climate maps be misleading?

3. Explain how temperature can be used as a basis for a climate classification. Why is this element alone unsatisfactory as a basis for a climate system?

4. How can annual precipitation be used as a basis for a climate classification? Why does the factor of evaporation make this classification of limited value?

5. Why is it that the distribution of natural vegetation types forms a workable basis for distinguishing climate zones?

6. Explain the basic principles underlying the Köppen climate system. What are the five major climate groups? What code system is used to designate eleven climates? Name these and give symbols for each.

7. What do each of the following letters mean in the Köppen system: *a, b, c, d, h, k?*

8. Explain how a climate classification system can be based on the air mass source regions, patterns of air mass flow, and frontal zones. What advantage has a natural science classification that is based on origin of the things classified as against one that is based on numerical values?

9. How may the climates of the globe be classified into three major groups on the basis of air mass types?

10. What five climates comprise the group controlled by equatorial and tropical air masses? How are they related to the system of pressure and wind belts? What Köppen climates are equivalent?

11. What five climates are controlled by both tropical and polar air masses? Explain briefly how each type is determined. What Köppen climates are equivalent?

12. What four climates are controlled by polar and arctic air masses? Explain how the large northern hemisphere landmasses and icecaps control these climates. What is the arctic front zone? Is there a comparable front zone in the southern hemisphere? What are the equivalent Köppen climates?

13. Explain what is meant by "climatic regimes." Why is the study of climatic regimes a matter of importance in geography?

14. Name the six climatic regimes. For each regime state the essential characteristics and global location.

15. What is a "thermohyet diagram"? What climate information is given on the horizontal and vertical scales of this diagram? Why are the units not uniformly spaced on these scales?

16. Can the climate of a given place show the influence of more than one basic regime? Give examples.

CHAPTER 9
Soil Water and the Water Balance

A FUNDAMENTAL concept of climatology now coming increasingly under consideration by geographers is that the availability of water to plants and animals is a more important factor in classifying climates than precipitation itself, which is only the amount of water received from the sky. Much of the water received as precipitation is lost in a variety of ways and is not usable for plants and animals. Just as in a fiscal budget, when the monthly or yearly loss of moisture exceeds the precipitation a budgetary deficit results; when precipitation exceeds the losses, a budgetary surplus results. An analysis of the water balance, or water budget, of a given area of the earth's surface is actually arrived at in much the same way as the understanding of a fiscal budget and requires only additions and subtractions of amounts within fixed periods of time, such as the calendar month or year. On the other hand, to understand why such gains and losses occur involves study of the physical processes affecting water in its vapor, liquid, and solid states not only in the atmosphere but also in the soil and rock and in exposed water of streams, lakes, and glaciers. The science of *hydrology* treats such relationships of water as a complex but unified system on the earth. In this chapter, our primary concern is with the hydrology of the soil zone.

Surface and subsurface water

We may classify water according to whether it is *surface water*, flowing exposed or ponded upon the land, or *subsurface water*, occupying openings in the soil, overburden, or bedrock. That which is held in the soil within a few feet of the surface is termed *soil water*, and is the particular concern of the botanist, soil scientist, and agricultural engineer. That which is held in the openings of the bedrock or deep within thick layers of transported overburden is usually referred to as *ground water*, studied by the geologist, who is concerned with the storage and flow of this water in various kinds of rocks and structures. Surface water in streams, lakes, and glaciers, and the geologic aspects of ground water and wells are considered in later chapters.

The hydrologic cycle

Water of oceans, atmosphere, and lands moves in a great series of continuous interchanges of both geographic position and physical state, known as the *hydrologic cycle* (Figure 9.1). A particular molecule of water might, if we could trace it continuously, travel through any one of a number of possible circuits involving alternately the water vapor state and the liquid or solid state. A good place to start the description of the hydrologic cycle would be the oceans, which cover nearly three-quarters of the globe. It has been estimated that some 80,000 cu mi (335,000 cu km) of water are evaporated each year from the oceans, and another 15,000 cu mi (65,000 cu km) from the lakes and moist land surfaces of the continents. The total yearly evaporation figure 95,000 cu mi (400,000 cu km) must exactly balance, on the average, the total quantity of water restored to the earth's surface by condensation from the atmosphere. About 24,000 cu mi (100,000 cu km) of water falls as precipitation upon the earth's land surfaces each year—enough to cover an area the

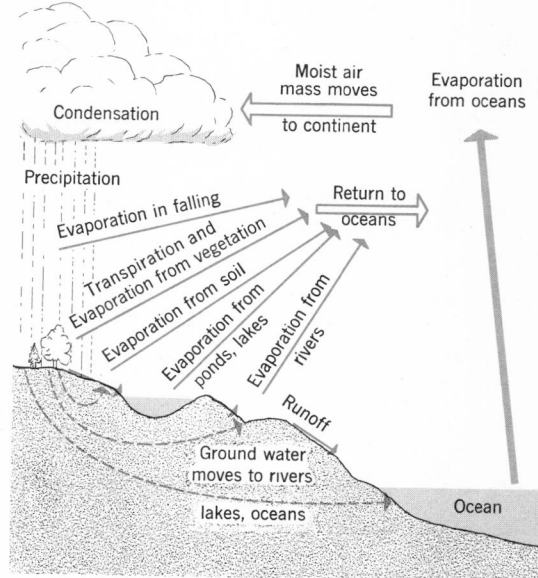

Figure 9.1   The hydrologic cycle. (After Holtzman.)

size of Texas to a depth of 475 ft (145 m). We see that considerably more water falls upon the lands than is returned to the atmosphere by evaporation from the lands. Therefore, much of what falls returns to the sea in liquid form.

Those parts of the hydrologic cycle dealing with water vapor, its movement toward the lands in maritime air masses, and eventual precipitation from clouds, has been treated in Chapters 6 and 7 as a phase of meteorology. Some of the falling precipitation evaporates directly before reaching the ground. Part of that which reaches the ground may be quickly returned to the atmosphere in water vapor form by evaporation from vegetative and soil surfaces, but if rainfall is heavy and long continued, much will soak in to the soil to become a part of the soil water. If close to the ground surface, soil water may be returned to the atmosphere by plants which take up the water through their roots and release it into the air through their leaves. Some soil water will evaporate directly into the soil air, which permeates soil openings.

Should rain continue to fall, water will percolate through the soil under gravitational pull and will reach the bedrock, or will penetrate deep deposits of transported overburden. This ground water moves very slowly but at length emerges in streams, lakes, or even from the ocean floor in the form of seepages and springs.

If the ability of the soil to receive and transmit heavy and long-continued rainfall is exceeded, surface flow occurs, conducting the water directly down slopes into streams and lakes. From these exposed surfaces the water may evaporate directly into the atmosphere or may reach the oceans by stream flow. We have now traced water through its full hydrologic cycle.

Evaporation and the earth's heat budget

The annual heat budget of the earth is outlined in Chapter 4. In Table 4.2, under the heading of energy returned to the atmosphere, the amount returned through the process of latent heat transfer (evaporation from ground and subsequent condensation in atmosphere) is given as 23 percent of total incoming energy, equivalent to 0.111 langleys per minute for the northern hemisphere. The importance of this heat-exchange process becomes evident when we note from Table 4.2 that the quantity of energy involved is almost twice that of longwave ground radiation (14 percent) and more than twice that transferred by conduction (10 percent).

Attempts have been made to estimate energy loss by latent heat transfer over the entire global surface. Such maps are not complete, but reveal striking differences from place to place. Table 9.1 lists some representative values for heat loss from evaporation in various global environments. Data have been reduced to equivalents in langleys per minute, to correspond with Table 4.2.

Knowledge of world distribution of isotherms, belts of pressure and winds, and air mass regions (Chapters 4 through 7) can be put to good use in interpreting the information in Table 9.1. Highest values of latent heat transfer by evaporation occur in the equatorward parts of the subtropical high-pressure cells. Here dry air in combination with intense insolation and a warm ocean surface gives maximum yearly evaporation rates. Evaporation over equatorial oceans, although higher than average, is less than over tropical oceans because the equatorial air holds a large amount of water vapor and there is greater cloud cover. In contrast,

TABLE 9.1[a]

Region	Latitude Belt	Energy Flux (Langleys Per Minute)
Equatorial oceans	5° S to 5° N	0.11 to 0.15
Tropical South Indian and South Pacific oceans	10 to 20° S	0.23 to 0.27
Tropical North Atlantic and North Pacific oceans	15 to 25° N	0.15 to 0.19
Tropical North Africa and Arabian peninsula	20 to 30° N	Under 0.02
Middle-latitude oceans	40 to 60° N, S	0.04 to 0.11
Middle-latitude interior of North America and Asia	40 to 60° N	0.02 to 0.04
Arctic and polar regions	Above 60° N, S	Under 0.02

[a] Data from M. I. Budyko, 1958.

the tropical deserts give very low values because soil is dry and there is almost no surface water to be evaporated. Continental interiors of middle latitudes are also low in annual evaporation, partly because of long cold winters. Arctic and polar regions have very low values because of prevailingly low air and ground temperatures.

Infiltration and runoff

Most soil surfaces in their undisturbed, natural states are capable of absorbing the water from light or moderate rains, a process known as *infiltration*. Such soils have natural passageways between poorly fitting soil particles, as well as larger openings, such as earth cracks resulting from soil drying, borings of worms and animals, cavities left from decay of plant roots, or openings made by heaving and collapse of soil as frost crystals alternately grow and melt. A mat of decaying leaves and stems breaks the force of falling drops and helps to keep these openings clear. If rain falls too rapidly to be passed downward through these soil openings the excess amount flows as a surface water film or sheet down the direction of ground slope, a runoff process termed *overland flow* (Figure 9.2).

As stated in Chapter 6, rainfall is measured in units of inches or centimeters per hour. This is the depth to which water will accumulate in each hour if rain is caught in a flat-bottomed, straight-sided container, assuming none to be lost by evaporation or splashing out. Similarly, infiltration is stated in inches or centimeters per hour and might be thought of as the rate at which the water level in the same container might drop if the water were leaking through a porous base. Runoff, also stated in inches (cm) per hour, may be thought of as the amount of overflow of the container per hour when rain falls too fast to be disposed of by leaking through the base.

Now, it is an important fact about soils that their *infiltration capacity*, or ability to infiltrate rainfall, is usually great at the start of a rain which has been preceded by a dry spell, but drops rapidly as the rain continues to fall and to soak into the soil. After several hours the soil's infiltration capacity becomes almost constant. The reason for the high starting value and its rapid drop is, of course, that the soil openings rapidly become clogged by particles brought from above, or tend to close up as the colloidal clays take up water and swell. From this we can easily reason that a sandy soil with little or no clay will not suffer so great a drop in infiltration capacity, but will continue to let the water through indefinitely at a generous rate. In contrast, the clay-rich soil is quickly sealed to the point that it allows only a very slow rate of infiltration. This principle is

Figure 9.2 Rainfall, infiltration, and overland flow. (From A. N. Strahler, *The Earth Sciences*, Harper and Row, New York.)

Figure 9.3 Infiltration rates vary greatly according to soil texture and land use. (Data from Sherman and Musgrave; Foster.)

illustrated by the graph in Figure 9.3*A* showing the infiltration curves of two soils, one sandy, one rich in clay.

It also follows that a sandy soil may be able to infiltrate even a heavy, long-continued rain without any surface runoff occurring, whereas the clay soil must divert much of the rain into overland flow, a process that may lead to erosion by gullies. Many forms of artificial disturbance of natural soils tend to decrease the infiltration capacity and to increase the amount of surface runoff (Figure 9.3*B*, *C*). Cultivation tends to leave the soil exposed so that rain beat quickly seals the soil pores. Fires, by destroying the protective vegetation and surface litter, also expose the soil to rain beat. Trampling by livestock will tamp the porous soil into a dense, hard layer. It is little wonder, then, that man has, through his farming and grazing practices, radically changed the original proportions of infiltration to runoff in such a way as to result in severe erosion damage and at the same time to decrease the reserves of soil moisture which might otherwise sustain plant growth and stream flow in droughts.

Evaporation and transpiration

Between periods of rain, water held in the soil is gradually given up by a twofold drying process. First, direct evaporation into the open air occurs at the soil surface and progresses downward. Air also enters the soil freely and may actually be forced alternately in and out of the soil by atmospheric pressure changes. Even if the soil did not "breathe" in this way, there would be a slow diffusion of water vapor surfaceward through the open soil pores. Ordinarily only the first foot (30 cm) of soil is dried by evaporation in a single dry season, but in the prolonged drought of deserts, drying will extend to depths of many feet. Second, plants draw the soil water into their systems through vast networks of tiny rootlets. This water, after being carried upward through the trunk and branches into the leaves, is discharged in the form of water vapor, through leaf pores into the atmosphere, a process termed *transpiration*. Further details of plant transpiration are given in Chapter 15.

In studies of climatology and hydrology it is convenient to use the term *evapotranspiration* to cover the combined moisture loss from direct evaporation and the transpiration of plants. The rate of evapotranspiration slows down as soil moisture supply becomes depleted during a dry summer period because plants employ various devices to reduce transpiration. In general, the less moisture remaining, the slower is the loss through evapotranspiration. Consequently, it is necessary to

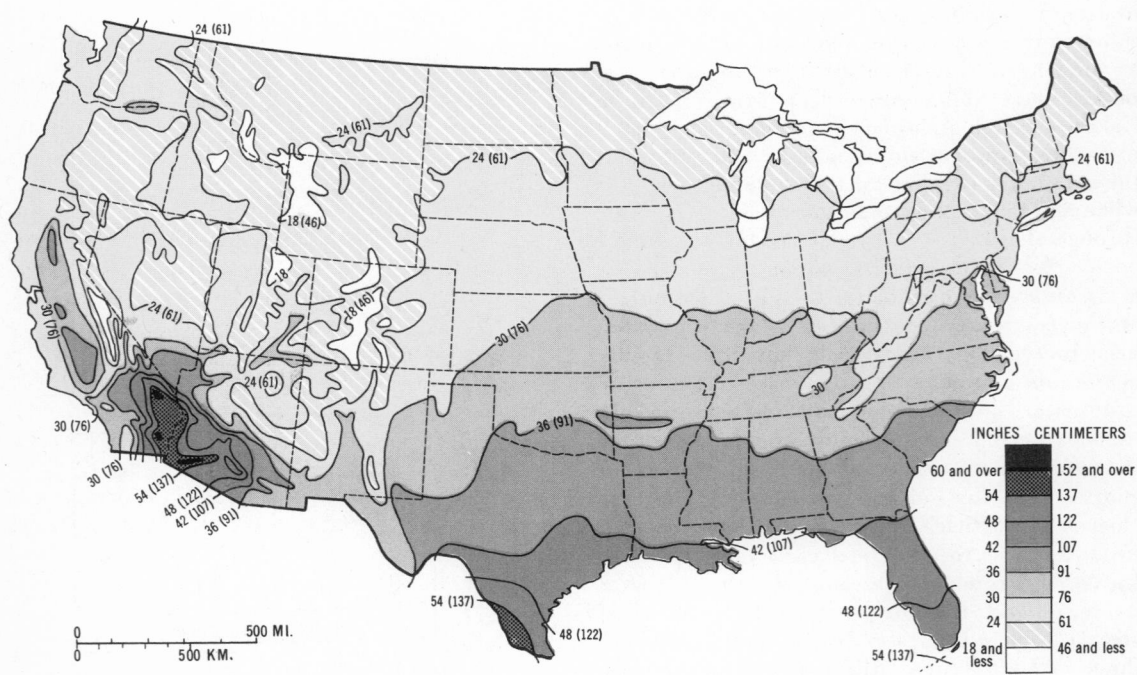

Figure 9.4 Average annual potential evapotranspiration in the United States. (Courtesy of *The Geographical Review*, vol. 38, 1948. Copyrighted by the American Geographical Society of New York.)

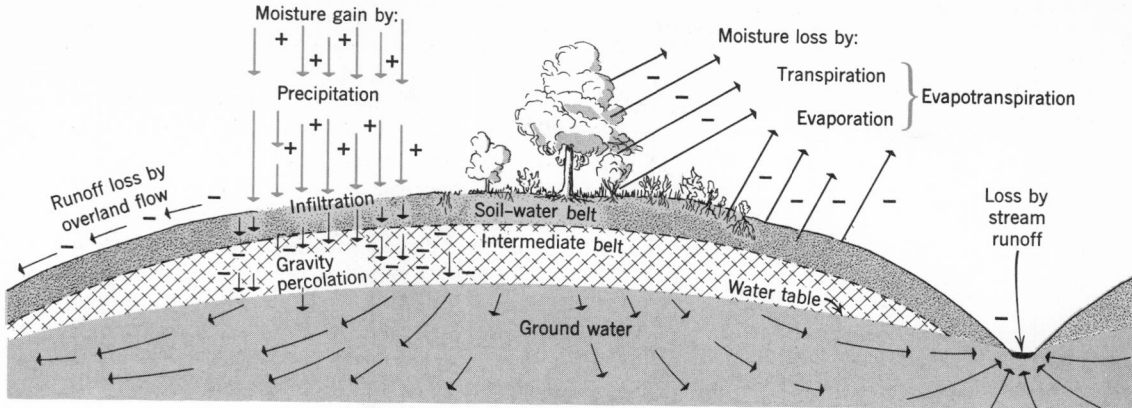

Figure 9.5 The soil-water belt occupies an important position in the hydrologic cycle.

define two forms of evapotranspiration: (1) *Potential evapotranspiration* is the maximum loss of water possible under the given conditions of plant cover and climatic factors, assuming that we can continue to supply the soil by irrigation with all of the water which the plants can use and the soil pores can hold. (2) *Actual evapotranspiration* is the true or observed quantity of evapotranspiration, decreasing in rate as the soil moisture is depleted. Figure 9.4 is a map of the United States showing the average annual potential evapotranspiration. This map is based on air temperatures and latitude; it does not take into account wind or varying humidities. The quantities shown have, nevertheless, been found to agree rather well with direct measurements of evapotranspiration made in irrigated areas, and with estimates derived from data on stream flow.

Figure 9.5 shows diagrammatically the various terms explained up to this point and serves to give a more detailed picture of that part of the hydrologic cycle involving the soil. As the plus signs show, the soil belt gains water through precipitation and infiltration. As the minus signs show, the soil loses water through transpiration, evaporation, and overland flow, and by gravity percolation downward through the soil to the ground water zone below.

Moisture in the soil

When infiltration occurs during heavy and prolonged rains (or when a snow cover is melting) the water is drawn downward by gravity through the soil pores, wetting successively lower layers. Soon the soil openings are filled with water moving downward, except for some air entrapped in the form of bubbles. Then the percolation continues downward into the bedrock. Suppose now that the rain stops and a period of several days of dry weather follows. The excess soil water continues to drain downward, but some water clings to the

soil particles and completely resists the pull of gravity through the force of *capillary tension*. We are all familiar with the way in which a water droplet seems to be enclosed in a "skin" of surface molecules, drawing the droplet together into a rounded outline, so that it clings to the side of a glass indefinitely without flowing down. Similarly, tiny films of water adhere to the soil grains, particularly at the points of grain contacts, and will stay until disposed of by evaporation or by absorption into plant rootlets.

When a soil has first been saturated by water, then allowed to drain under gravity until no more water moves downward, the soil is said to be holding its *field capacity* of water. This takes no more than two or three days for most soils. Most is drained out within one day. Field capacity is measured in units of depth, usually inches or centimeters, just as with precipitation. This means that for a given cube of soil, say 12 in on a side (1 cu ft), if we were to extract all of the field moisture, it might form a layer of water 3-in deep in a pan 1-ft square. This would be equivalent to complete absorption of a 3-in rainfall by a completely dry 12-in layer of soil. (Metric units of volume and depth may be substituted.)

Field capacity of a given soil depends largely on its texture. Sandy soil has a very low field capacity; clay soil has high field capacity. This effect is shown in Figure 9.6, a graph in which field capacity is plotted against soil texture, from coarse to fine. It should also be noted that sandy soils reach their field capacity very quickly, both because of the ease with which the water penetrates and the low quantity required. Clay soils take long rain periods to reach field capacity because the infiltration is slow and the total quantity required to be absorbed is great.

Agricultural scientists also use a measure of soil moisture termed the *wilting point*. This is the quantity of soil water below which plants will be

Figure 9.6 Field capacity and wilting point. (After Smith and Ruhe, *Yearbook of Agriculture*, 1955.)

changes in this example, the cycle it shows can be considered generally representative of conditions in humid, middle-latitude climates where there is a strong temperature contrast between winter and summer. Let us start with the early spring (March). At this time the evaporation rate is low, because of low temperatures. The abundance of melting snows and rains has restored the soil moisture to a surplus quantity. For two months the quantity of water percolating through the soil and entering the ground water keeps the soil pores nearly filled with water. This is the time of year when one encounters soft, muddy ground conditions, whether driving on dirt roads or walking across country. This, too, is the season when runoff is heavy and major floods may be expected on larger streams and rivers. In terms of the soil water budget, a *water surplus* exists.

By May, the rising air temperatures, increasing evaporation, and the full growth of plant foliage, bringing on heavy transpiration, have reduced the soil moisture to a quantity below field capacity, although it may be restored temporarily by unusually heavy rains in some years. By midsummer, a state of heavy *water deficiency* exists in the water budget. Even the occasional heavy thunderstorm rains of summer cannot restore the water lost by steady and heavy evapotranspiration. Small springs and streams dry up, the soil becomes firm and dry. By November (and sometimes in September), however, the soil moisture again begins to increase. This is because the plants go into a dormant state, sharply reducing transpiration losses, while, at the same time, falling air temperatures reduce evaporation. By late winter, usually in February at this location, the field capacity of the soil is again restored.

unable to extract further moisture from the soil and the foliage will wilt. As Figure 9.6 shows, the wilting point also depends upon particle size.

The soil water cycle

Equipped with the foregoing explanations of processes and terms relating to water gains and losses in the soil, we can turn next to consider the annual water budget of the soil, involving principles of great concern not only in plant geography and agriculture, but in the further study of ground water, surface runoff, stream flow, and therefore of the sculpturing of land slopes.

Figure 9.7 shows the annual cycle of soil water for the year 1944 at an agricultural experiment station in Coshocton, Ohio. If we follow the

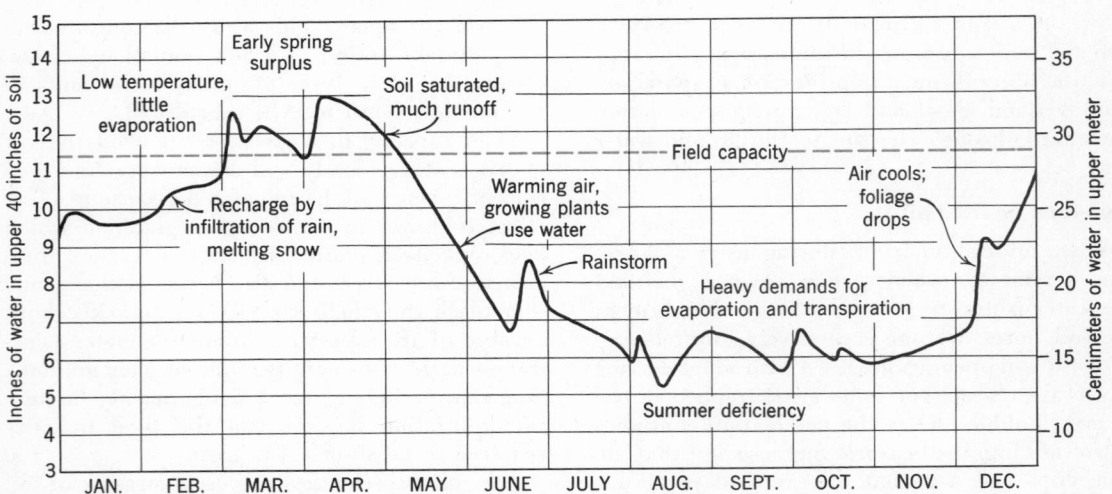

Figure 9.7 Annual cycle of soil moisture. (After Thornthwaite and Mather, *The Water Balance*, 1955.)

The water budget

With the above example of soil moisture changes throughout a year's time, we turn to a more generalized concept of the water budget in terms of the two essential parts of the budget: (1) precipitation, representing the income, and (2) potential evapotranspiration, representing the expenditure. These two quantities will be considered on a month-to-month basis throughout the year, but average monthly values for a record of many years' duration will be used instead of the data of but a single year.

Figure 9.8 shows the water budget for Seattle, Washington, a typical station of the marine west-coast climate. Two graphs are superimposed: (A) average monthly precipitation (solid line), and (B) average monthly potential evapotranspiration (hollow line). Each graph takes a series of steps up and down across the twelve-month period. (Essentially, these are bar graphs whose height can be read against the scale of inches or centimeters on the side of the diagram.) Note first that the precipitation is highest in the months of November through February but declines to low values in summer. In almost completely opposite phase, the evapotranspiration rises from low values in winter to maximum values in summer. This form is just what would be expected in middle latitudes because potential evapotranspiration increases with rising air temperatures and with increased number of hours that the sun is in the sky.

Starting in January, the graph shows that precipitation is much greater in that month than potential evapotranspiration. There exists a large *water surplus*, and this escapes by percolating down through the soil or flows over the ground to the nearest stream. As spring progresses, potential evapotranspiration rises rapidly, while precipitation declines. In May potential evapotranspiration is the larger value, requiring that the supply of stored soil moisture be drawn upon. In a sense, soil moisture is like a savings bank account, to be drawn upon when monthly expenses exceed income. Through June the soil moisture is sufficient to make up the lack of precipitation. But soil moisture is limited to 4 in (10 cm) of water and is entirely used up by early July.[1] Here, on the graph, a vertical line has been drawn and marks the beginning of a *water deficiency*. In terms of one's personal money budget, the water deficiency corresponds to going in debt, but with the reasonable assurance that a surplus later in the year will enable the loan to be paid back. Altogether, a

[1] It is assumed here for simplicity that the soil moisture is used at a steady rate equal to the potential evapotranspiration rate until it is all gone, whereas actually the rate of use declines as the remaining quantity declines.

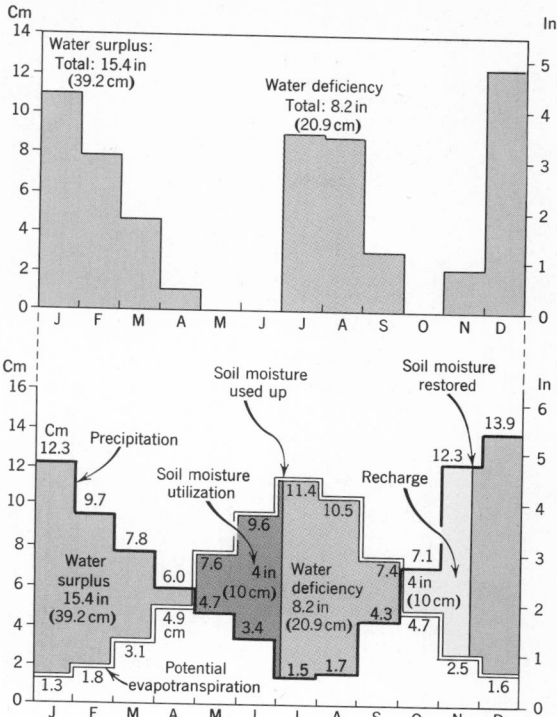

Figure 9.8   The water budget for Seattle, Washington. (After C. W. Thornthwaite, *Geographical Review*, 1948.)

water deficiency of about 8 in (21 cm) is incurred by the end of September. In October the monthly precipitation is again greater than potential evapotranspiration. Now the excess is used to restore, or *recharge*, the soil moisture, but it is not until late in November that this is accomplished (vertical line on graph) and a water surplus is resumed. Returning to an analogy with one's personal budget, the savings account has been restored before beginning repayment on the loan.

Summarizing the annual water budget at Seattle, it is evident that the climatic regime it represents is one of both a surplus and a deficiency, occurring in opposite seasons. On a separate graph in the upper part of Figure 9.8 are shown the monthly surpluses and deficiencies together with the totals of each. The total surplus was 15.4 in (39.2 cm); the total water deficiency was 8.2 in (20.9 cm). Obviously, considerable irrigation is needed in July, August, and September, if plant growth is to be sustained at the maximum possible rate. The analysis which we have made of the water budget at Seattle is, therefore, of great practical value to gardeners and farmers in that area.

These water budget principles with concepts of moisture deficiencies and surpluses were developed by Dr. C. Warren Thornthwaite, a climatologist who applied his knowledge to practical problems of agriculture as well as to a world-wide system

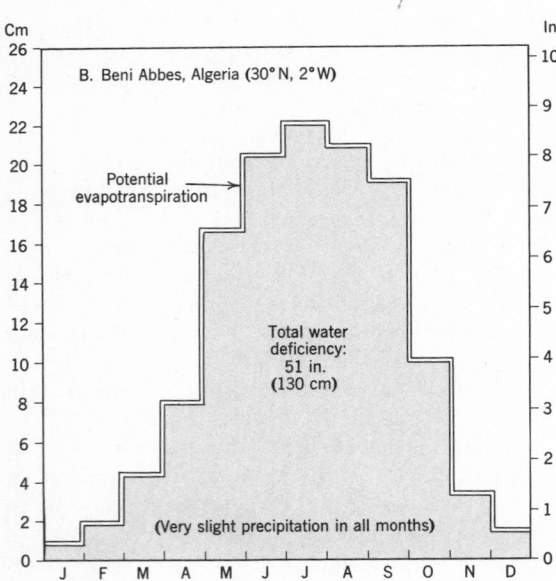

Figure 9.9 Water budgets for eight stations representing a wide variety of climatic regimes. (Data from C. W. Thornthwaite, 1948, and Douglas B. Carter, 1954 and 1956.)

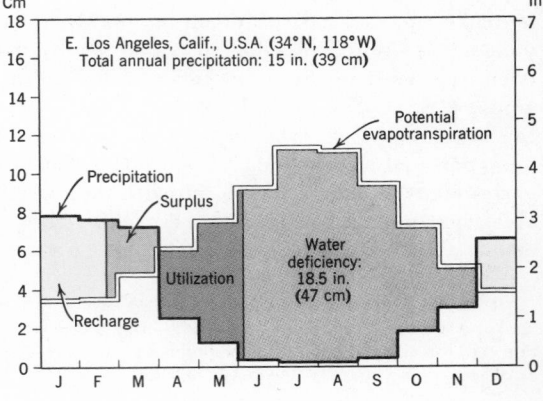

of climate classification based on the relations between precipitation and evapotranspiration. Some further refinements have been made in estimating the amount of soil moisture remaining as the deficiency sets in, but these are beyond the scope of the present discussion.

Climatic regimes and the water budget

Water budgets for some other representative climatic regimes are shown in Figure 9.9. These give some idea of the great contrasts that are possi-

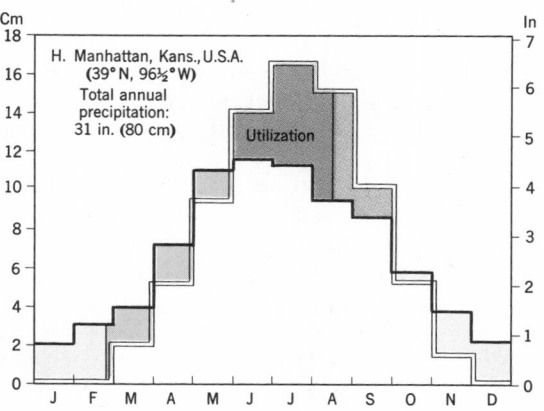

ble in water surpluses and deficiencies. The vast water surplus of a wet equatorial climate is illustrated by data for Kribi, Cameroon, an African west coast station at 3° N lat. (Figure 9.9A). Rainfall totals about 116 in (295 cm) for the year and has two strong maxima, one in the period April through June, the other in September and October. During these periods large water surpluses occur, the annual total surplus being 64 in (162 cm). The graph of potential evapotranspiration shows only a small annual variation because of uniformly high air temperatures.

Although soil moisture is drawn upon in December and January, no water deficiency occurs. Obviously in such a climatic regime soil moisture will be plentiful for plant growth year-around; runoff to streams will be copious.

A tropical desert regime is seen in the data for Beni Abbes, Algeria, at 30° N lat. (Figure 9.9B). Here the total annual precipitation averages about 1 in (2.5 cm). Throughout the entire year potential evapotranspiration greatly exceeds rainfall; a large water deficiency prevails—over 50 in (127 cm).

The tropical wet-dry climatic regime of low latitudes is illustrated by Yambio, Sudan, at 4½° N lat. (Figure 9.9C). Potential evapotranspiration here follows a cycle much like that of Kribi, but the dry season of low sun brings on a large water deficiency. Rains of the high-sun period make a substantial water surplus. Agra, India, at 27° N lat. illustrates the wet-dry regime with Asiatic monsoon influence (Figure 9.9D). The potential evapotranspiration cycle closely resembles that of Beni Abbes, which lies about at the same latitude. The summer monsoon at Agra brings rainfall of 8 to 9 in (20 to 30 cm) per month in July and August, sufficient to exceed potential evapotranspiration and bring a short period of soil moisture recharge. This soil moisture is used up in September. No water surplus can develop, whereas the water deficiency, totaling 33 in (86 cm), prevails for more than nine months of the year.

The Mediterranean (dry-summer subtropical) regime is illustrated by Los Angeles, California (Figure 9.9E). Here the large summer deficiency of 18.5 in (47 cm) results from the fact that the high summer rate of potential evapotranspiration coincides with the summer precipitation minimum. The small surplus of 1.4 in (3.6 cm) endures little over a month's time. The overall plan of the Los Angeles water budget resembles that of Seattle (Figure 9.8) so far as the phase of the cycles is concerned, but with a major contrast in water surpluses.

Ankara, Turkey, illustrates a water budget having the same phasing and roughly the same values of surplus and deficiency as seen in the Mediterranean regime of Los Angeles, but with important differences in precipitation distribution. The cold winter months at Ankara have little or no potential evapotranspiration.

Continentality of climatic regime is seen in the water budgets of Ulm, Germany, and Manhattan, Kansas (Figure 9.9*G*, *H*). Both localities have a summer maximum of precipitation coinciding with a summer maximum of potential evapotranspiration. The result is that there is no water deficiency at Ulm and only a small deficiency at Manhattan. Both places show a small water surplus in late winter and early spring.

Each type of climate has its own characteristic annual water budget. To attempt to present the full spectrum of budgets would go far beyond the scope of this brief survey. From the examples shown, however, the importance of Thornthwaite's system of analysis of soil water conditions should be evident. The method is quantitative, giving definite estimates of the amounts of water gained and lost, and thereby making possible realistic estimates of the water available or needed for use in agriculture, as well as of the water surpluses which may be drawn upon for irrigation and hydroelectric systems. Thornthwaite's system of water-balance evaluation is particularly effective in estimating the stress (or lack of it) which climate exerts upon vegetation, as will be shown in Chapter 16.

Ground water

Water that is drawn downward by gravity through the soil zone to lower levels becomes part of the ground water body, the relations of which are shown in Figure 9.10. Strictly speaking, *ground*

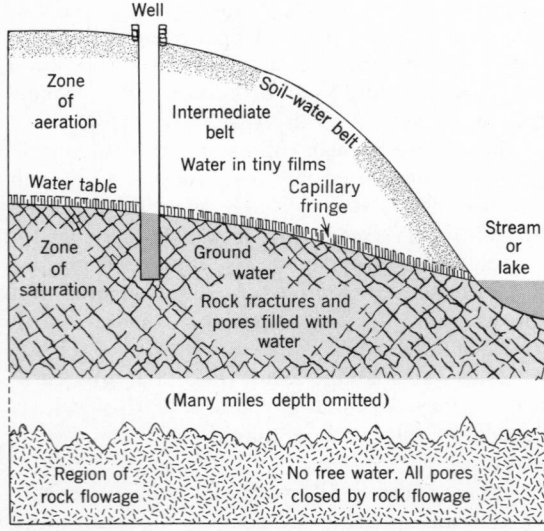

Figure 9.10 Ground-water and soil-water belts and zones. (After Ackerman, Colman and Ogrosky.)

water is that part of subsurface water which fully saturates the pore spaces of the rock or its overburden and which behaves in response to gravitational force. The ground water occupies the *zone of saturation*. Above it is the *zone of aeration*, in which water does not fully saturate the pores. We have seen that the soil water belt is the uppermost layer of the zone of aeration and that moisture is held in this belt by capillary force in tiny films adhering to the soil particles. A similar condition prevails through the underlying *intermediate belt*. The sole basis for distinguishing these two belts is that the soil belt represents a shallow zone of moisture usable by plants, whereas the intermediate belt is too deep for capillary water to be returned to the atmosphere by either direct evaporation or transpiration. The depth of the zone of aeration may be very shallow or missing (when the ground water is close to the surface in low, flat regions), or up to several hundred feet thick in hilly or mountainous regions with low ground water level.

At the base of the zone of aeration is the *capillary fringe*, a thin layer in which the water has been drawn upward from the ground water body through capillary force. The action is much like the rise of kerosene in a lamp wick, or of water in a blotter whose edge is immersed. Water in the capillary fringe largely fills the soil pores, hence, is continuous with the ground water body. Thickness of the capillary fringe depends on the soil texture, because capillary rise is higher when the openings are smaller. Thus, in a silty material the capillary fringe may be 2 ft (0.6 m) thick, but only a fraction of an inch (1 cm) thick in coarse sand or fine gravel with large pore spaces.

Ground water in the zone of saturation moves under the force of gravity and therefore its upper surface, the *water table*, tends to become a horizontal surface, just as with a free water body such as a lake. But because water moves very slowly through the rock, the water table actually maintains a sloping surface, highest under the hill tops and divides, lowest in valleys. Ground water is discussed further in Chapter 20.

Effluent and influent streams

An important contrast between regions of arid and humid climates lies in the nature of stream flow. The manner in which the channels of streams and their associated landforms differ in the contrasting climates is discussed in later chapters on geomorphology. From the standpoint of soils and the physical environments of natural vegetation, an important consideration is the manner in which the water enters and leaves a stream channel.

In a humid region with a high water table sloping toward the stream channels, ground water

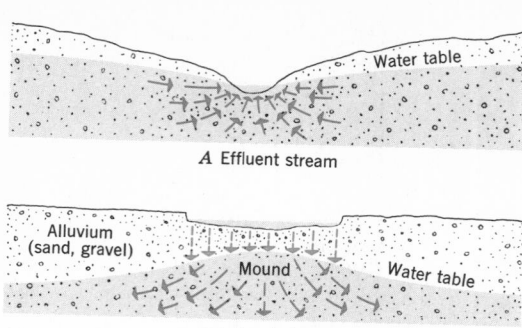

A Effluent stream

Alluvium (sand, gravel)

Mound

Water table

B Influent stream

Figure 9.11 Effluent and influent streams. (From. A. N. Strahler, *The Earth Sciences*, Harper and Row, New York.)

moves steadily toward the channels, into which it seeps, producing permanent, or *perennial* streams. Such streams are described as *effluent* (Figure 9.11*A*). Surplus water in a humid region— both that which flows over the ground in wet weather, and that which seeps into the channel from the ground water table—escapes by through-flowing channels to regions of lower elevation and eventually to the sea. In the course of such drainage, dissolved substances (ions and colloids) that have been removed from the soil are taken out of the region, permanently removing them from the soil (Chapter 13).

In arid regions, where streams flow across plains of gravel and sand, water is lost from the channels by seepage to a water table that lies below the level of the streams. Such streams are designated as *influent* (Figure 9.11*B*). This water gradually moves away from the zone of the channel and eventually returns to the surface in flat-floored basins known as *playas* (Chapter 22), where evaporation takes place and salts are left behind to form the saline soils and salt crusts.

Water-table lakes, marshes, and bogs

In humid climates with a large annual surplus in the water budget and with generally high water tables, the various events of geologic history, such as erosion and deposition by wind and by ice sheets of the most recent glacial stage, have created natural depressions with floors at or below the water table elevation. Seepage of ground water, as well as direct runoff of precipitation, maintains these free water surfaces permanently throughout the year. Examples of fresh water-table ponds are found widely distributed in North America and Europe where plains of glacial sand and gravel contain natural pits and hollows left by the melting of stagnant ice masses. (See Chapter 23.) Figure 9.12 is a portion of a topographic map of a number of small fresh-water ponds on Cape Cod, within a mile or two (2–3 km) of the Atlantic Ocean. The surface elevation of these ponds is 8 ft (2.5 m) and is maintained by the supply of fresh ground water which excludes salt water by causing the ground water to flow gradually from land to ocean.

Many former fresh-water water-table ponds have, since they were formed by glacial ice, become partially or entirely filled by the organic matter from growth and decay of water-loving plants. The result is a *bog* whose surface lies close to water table (Chapter 15).

Marshes and swamps, where water stands at or

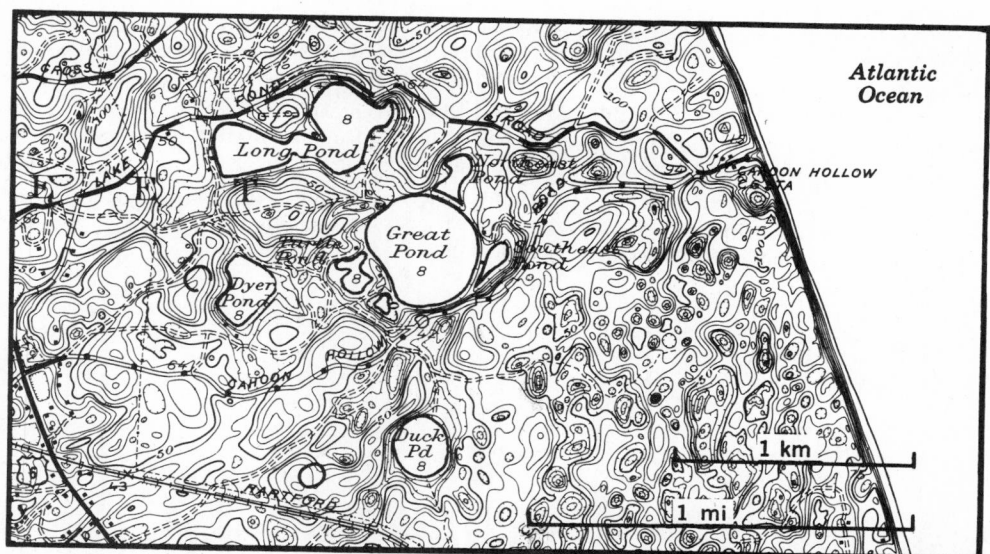

Figure 9.12 Portion of a topographic map of Cape Cod, Mass., showing freshwater ponds close to the ocean shoreline. The figure in each pond gives elevation in feet. (U.S. Geological Survey.)

close to the ground surface over a broad area, represent the appearance of the water table at the surface. Such areas of poor surface drainage have a variety of origins. For example, the broad, shallow fresh-water marshes of the Atlantic and Gulf coastal plain represent regions only recently emerged from the sea. Others are created by the shifting of river channels on floodplains (Chapter 21).

REFERENCES FOR FURTHER STUDY

Thornthwaite, C. W. (1948), An approach toward a rational classification of climate, *Geographical Review*, Vol. 38, pp. 55–94.

Thornthwaite, C. E., and J. R. Mather (1955), *The water balance*, Drexel Institute of Technology, Laboratory of Climatology, Publ. in *Climatology*, vol. 8, No. 1, Centerton, N.J., 86 pp.

U.S. Dept. Agriculture (1955), *Water; Yearbook of Agriculture, 1955*, U.S. Govt. Printing Office, Washington, D.C., 751 pp.

Todd, D. K. (1959), *Ground water hydrology*, John Wiley and Sons, New York, 336 pp.

Chang, Jen-Hu (1968), *Climate and agriculture; an ecological survey*, Aldine Publ. Co., Chicago, 304 pp. See Chapters 12, 13, and 19.

REVIEW QUESTIONS

1. Why is an understanding of soil water important to the student of soils? Of plant geography? Of economic geography?

2. Distinguish between surface water and subsurface water; between soil water and ground water.

3. Give a complete general account of the hydrologic cycle. What quantities of water are evaporated annually from the oceans? From the lands? How is this balanced by precipitation and runoff?

4. What is infiltration? What is overland flow? In what units is each stated? How does infiltration capacity change when rain falls? Explain. How do soils differ in this respect? In what ways does man alter infiltration capacity?

5. To what depth does soil moisture evaporate? How do atmospheric pressure changes assist in this process?

6. Explain the process of transpiration by plants. What quantities of soil water are thus lost? To what depth does this loss extend? Define evapotranspiration. Distinguish between potential and actual evapotranspiration.

7. How is soil water held in place? What is the source of soil moisture? What is field capacity? How does it vary with soil texture? What is the wilting point?

8. Describe the annual cycle of soil water in humid, middle-latitude climates. When and why do water surpluses and deficits occur?

9. Sketch a typical annual water budget cycle by months, showing precipitation and potential evapotranspiration. Label water surpluses and deficiencies. When is irrigation needed?

10. How does the annual water budget differ between regions of tropical desert climate and those of a tropical wet-dry climate? Describe other climate contrasts as shown in their respective water budgets.

11. Define ground water. How does one distinguish between zones of saturation and aeration? Between soil water and intermediate water belts? What is the capillary fringe? How does its thickness vary with soil texture? What is the water table?

12. Describe effluent and influent streams and their relation to climate. How are soil-forming processes tied in with such streams?

13. What are water-table lakes? Do they show great seasonal changes of water level? What is a bog? A marsh?

CHAPTER 10
Equatorial and Tropical Climates

CLIMATES of group I are those of low latitudes. They are controlled largely by equatorial and tropical air masses.

1. Wet equatorial climate (Af, Am)

Bringing together the information on global pattern of weather elements contained in previous chapters and focusing attention on the equatorial belt of the earth, it will be seen that within 5° of latitude north and south of the equator the following conditions prevail:

(*a*) Temperatures average close to 80°F (27°C) for every month (Figures 4.17 and 4.18), so that the annual range is extremely small.

(*b*) Air pressures average between 1009 and 1012 mb, or slightly less than normal sea-level pressure (Figures 5.2 and 5.3).

(*c*) The general flow of air is from east to west in the tropical easterlies at high altitude, but somewhat more equatorward in the surface trade winds, which originate in the subtropical high-pressure cells. Here, then, is a region of converging warm, unstable air masses meeting along the equatorial trough (Chapter 7).

(*d*) Examination of the world rainfall map (Plate 1) shows this to be a belt of heavy rainfall, exceeding 80 in (200 cm) annually for the most part. This belt has been explained in Chapter 7 as convectional rainfall from great cumulonimbus masses in weak, slowly moving easterly waves and equatorial lows.

From the above information we can compile a description of the wet equatorial climate. Average annual temperatures are close to the 80°F(27°C) mark; seasonal range of temperature is so slight as to be imperceptible because the sun is high throughout the year. Rainfall is heavy during the entire year, but with considerable differences in monthly averages because of the seasonal shifting of the equatorial convergence zone and a consequent variation in air mass characteristics.

Figure 10.1 is a monthly average temperature-rainfall graph for Iquitos, Peru, a typical wet equatorial station located at about 3° S lat. in the broad basin of the Amazon River. Note that the annual range in temperature is only 4 F° (2.2 C°)

Figure 10.1   Climograph for Iquitos, Peru, 3½° S. lat., upper Amazon River basin. (Data from Blair.)

and that the annual rainfall total is more than 100 in (250 cm). In all but one month the monthly rainfall averages more than 6 in (15 cm). According to Köppen's definition of this *Af* climate, no month averages less than 2.4 in (6 cm) of rainfall.

Some idea of the extreme monotony of the daily temperature cycle in this climate can be had from Figure 10.2, which shows minimum and maximum daily temperatures for two months at Panama, 9° N lat. An especially noteworthy feature is that the daily range is normally from 15 to 20 F° (8 to 11 C°), a vastly greater range than the annual range of monthly mean temperatures. In other words, daily variations far exceed seasonal variations in the wet equatorial climate. The thermohyet diagram for Belém, Brazil (Figure 8.7*A*) illustrates well the extreme equability of temperature to be expected.

An illustration of month-to-month differences in average monthly rainfall in the wet equatorial climate is given in Figure 10.3. All the stations shown here lie within a few degrees of the equator

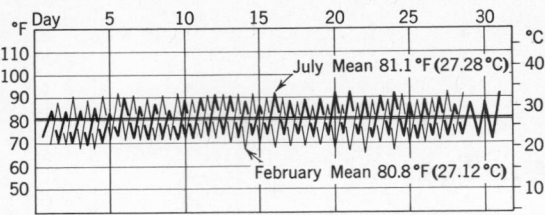

Figure 10.2 July and February temperatures at Panama, 9° N lat. (After Mark Jefferson, *Geographical Review*.)

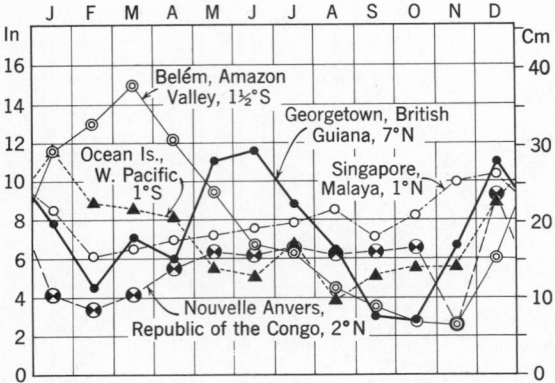

Figure 10.3 Monthly rainfall averages for stations in wet equatorial climates. (Data from Trewartha.)

and are basically similar in climate. The fact that some stations show one maximum and one minimum in the rainfall graph, whereas others have two maxima and two minima is not easily explained, but is probably attributable to a rather complex series of seasonal changes in air mass movements and positions of the equatorial trough.

Because of the abundant rainfall and prevailingly warm temperatures, the equatorial region is characterized by growth of *rainforest*, or *selva*, described in detail in Chapter 16, a vegetation type unexcelled for luxuriance of tree growth and numbers of species (Figures 16.2, 16.3, 16.4). Broadleaf trees rise to heights of 100 to 150 ft (30–45 m), forming a dense leaf canopy through which little sunlight can reach the ground. Giant *lianas* (woody vines) hang from the trees. The forest is evergreen, although individual species have a rhythm of leaf-shedding (Figure 10.4).

Rainforest is the home of the small forest animals, of which the monkeys are perhaps the best representatives, taking advantage of the continuous forest canopy for living and traveling. Birds, too, are numerous in species and spectacularly plumaged.

With copious rainfall and prevailingly high temperatures, chemical processes are continuously active on the rocks and soils in the wet equatorial regions. Leaching out of all soluble constituents

of the deeply decayed rock results in a distinctive type of soil, termed a *latosol* (color plate). Reddish or yellowish, and often containing irregular nodules of reddish iron hydroxides, this soil is especially rich in hydroxides of iron, manganese, and aluminum. These have been left behind in the soil after the soluble minerals (including silica) have been carried down through the soil and into the streams and rivers. Large concentrations of the iron, manganese, or aluminum minerals occurring as lenses or layers in the soil are termed *laterite*. These minerals may be extracted as ores of commercial value. *Bauxite* is the foremost ore of aluminum in use today, being extracted, for example, from the Guiana coast of South America (Figure 10.5). Manganese ores are likewise of great value, but lateritic iron ore is as yet not so widely exploited because of iron ore abundance in other forms.

Vegetation and climate work hand in hand to make lateritic soils and ore bodies. The soil-forming regime of laterization is discussed in Chapter 13. At the prevailingly warm temperatures, bacteria in the upper soil layer are unusually vigorous and consume virtually all dead vegetation. Thus *humus*, the black, partially decomposed plant matter present in most soils of middle-latitude and arctic climates, is almost entirely absent on well-drained sites. Rotting and decay of bedrock may be very deep in wet equatorial regions of low topographic relief. It is reported that even to depths as great as 300 ft (90 m) the rock has been found to be soft and crumbly from chemical action.

Stream flow tends to be fairly constant and extremely copious because a large water surplus exists throughout much of the year and provides ample runoff (Figure 9.9A). River channels are lined along the banks with dense vegetation. Sand bars or sand banks are not so conspicuous as in drier regions. Floodplains have meanders and many swampy sloughs where the river channels have shifted their courses (Figure 10.4). Although water is abundant, river systems such as the Amazon carry relatively little material in chemical solution. This has been explained as resulting from the thorough leaching of soils, which have little soluble mineral matter left to contribute.

Human transportation is by streams whose sluggish courses can be utilized by dugout canoes or shallow-draft river steamers. The use of light aircraft has, however, greatly simplified long-distance transportation. Villages are characteristically built close to the river banks.

Not all equatorial rainforest areas are of low topographic relief. Hilly or mountainous belts have very steep slopes, on which flows, slides, and

Figure 10.4   This air view over the rainforest of the Amazon Basin shows the Rio Negro, a tributary of the Amazon River. The view is southward from a point about 0°23' S, 64°05' W. (Photograph by Colonel Richmond, courtesy of the American Geographical Society.)

Figure 10.5   Bauxite mining in British Guiana. These thick layers of bauxite ore accumulated as sediments derived from the erosion of lateritic soils of interior uplands. (Photograph by courtesy of Aluminium Limited, Canada.)

Figure 10.6 Climograph for Cochin, India, 10° N. lat. (Data from Clayton, Smithsonian Institution.)

avalanches of soil and rock frequently occur, stripping away all forest and soil down to the bedrock.

Of economic importance are several forest products. Hardwood lumber, such as mahogany, ebony, or rosewood, is a valuable tropical product. Quinine, cocaine, and other drugs come from the bark and leaves of tropical plants; cocoa comes from the seed kernel of the cacao plant. Rubber, made from the sap of the rubber tree, is now largely an economic product of Malaya, Sumatra, and Ceylon, although the tree comes from South America, where it was first exploited.

Although most of the wet equatorial climate lies in a belt 10° of latitude on either side of the equator, the Malabar coast of India and the coasts of Burma and Thailand, located between 10° and 25° N lat., have a warm, wet climate with large annual total of rainfall, which also supports rainforest. This Asiatic climate may be considered as a special wet monsoon type. Under the Köppen system it is designated by the symbol *Am*, with the stipulation that the average rainfall of the driest month shall be less than 2.4 in (6 cm). (See Figure 10.21.) Figure 10.6 shows the temperature-precipitation graph of a wet monsoon climate. A short dry season occurs in the low-sun season, when the winter monsoon is in effect and continental air masses move southward from interior Asia. This dry period is too brief to deplete soil moisture and ground water reserves. Rainforest therefore thrives. Note that the summer (rainy) monsoon brings enormous quantities of rainfall in June and July. This rain is derived from convectional storms

within moist maritime equatorial air masses moving northward from the Indian Ocean.

2. Trade-wind littoral climates (var. of Af and Am)

A study of the world rainfall map, Plate 1, shows that along the east coasts of Central and South America, Madagascar, Indochina, the Philippines, and northeastern Australia, in latitudes 10° to 25°, there are narrow belts of heavy rainfall. These are coasts exposed to moist maritime tropical air masses brought by the tropical easterlies, or trade winds, from the oceanic subtropical highs. These air masses are abundantly supplied with moisture, as is typical of maritime tropical air on the western sides of the high-pressure cells. When these air masses encounter the hill and mountain slopes of the coasts, a heavy orographic precipitation results. Easterly waves cause periods of rainy weather. In addition, the high-sun solstice period sees the onset of tropical cyclones, to which these coasts are vulnerable.

Because of its coastal position with respect to the easterlies, this climate may be called a *trade-wind littoral climate*. Under the Köppen system it is included with the rainforest climates *Af* and *Am*. It is treated as a separate climate here because the precipitation characteristics differ from the wet equatorial climate, and the temperatures show a somewhat more pronounced annual range.

The temperature and rainfall graph for a representative station of this climate is shown in Figure 10.7. Belize, British Honduras, is located in Cen-

Figure 10.7 Climograph for Belize, British Honduras, 17° N. lat. (Data from Trewartha.)

tral America at 17° N lat. The total rainfall is great, almost 80 in (200 cm) annually, and rain is abundant in most months. A tendency toward dryness, typical of the tropical wet-dry climates (which generally elsewhere lie at this same latitude), is seen in the low rainfall of February, March, and April. The temperature cycle has a range of only 9 F° (5 C°) because of the moderating influence of the nearby ocean but this range is conspicuously greater than that of the wet equatorial climate.

The warm, wet climates of trade-wind coasts support a tropical rainforest vegetation, somewhat similar to the equatorial rainforest. Differences are explained in Chapter 16.

3. Tropical desert and steppe climates (BWh, BSh)

In strong contrast to the wet equatorial climate are the very dry climates controlled by subsiding, outwardly moving air of the continental high-pressure cells which dominate much of the earth's land areas in the latitude belts 15° to 35°, roughly centered on the Tropics of Cancer and Capricorn. Here lie the source regions of the continental tropical (cTs) air masses. The vast deserts of north Africa, Arabia, Iran, and West Pakistan exemplify this climate type, as do also the Sonoran Desert of the southwestern United States and northern Mexico, the interior Kalahari Desert of South Africa, and the Australian Desert.

Within this region of general aridity we can recognize the truly arid zones, or *deserts* (BWh), in which annual rainfall is less than 10 in (4 cm), and the semi-arid zones, or *steppes* (BSh), in which rainfall is from 10 to 30 in (4 to 12 cm) annually.

In the continental interiors in these tropical regions, far removed from oceanic sources of moisture, extreme aridity prevails. Average annual rainfall is often less than 5 in (2 cm); at some localities a period of several years may pass without measurable rainfall. As an example, at In Salah, Algeria, the average annual rainfall for a 15-year record was 0.6 in (1.5 cm). Other Algerian stations had even less. Because these are regions of subsiding air in the general global scheme of circulation, adiabatic heating reduces the relative humidity of the air to low levels much of the time. At the drier stations in the Sahara Desert, relative humidity at 1:00 P.M. averages 25 to 30 percent for the year, but from 15 to 20 percent in the hottest months. Although in the summer low pressure due to ground-surface heating develops over the tropical landmasses (as seen in Figures 5.2 and 5.3), this is only a low-level condition, with the permanent highs persisting at higher levels of the atmosphere.

Figure 10.8 Annual evaporation (inches) from a free water surface in the United States. (After Mead.)

The capacity of tropical desert air for evaporation of exposed water surfaces is enormous (Figure 10.8). In the Sonoran Desert, annual evaporation from a free water surface exceeds 90 to 100 in (230 or 250 cm) annually, or about twenty times as much as falls in rain. It is obvious that the full amount of evaporation that is possible does not take place in the tropical deserts. Once the stream channels and soil have become dry after a rain, further evaporation is limited to a small amount of moisture slowly brought to the surface locally by capillary movement from moist soil or rock at depth. Figure 9.9B shows the water balance for Beni Abbes, Algeria, and illustrates well the prevailing water deficiency of the tropical desert climate.

Although dryness is the dominant characteristic of the continental tropical air mass source regions, sporadic heavy rainfall does occur from violent convectional storms. Penetration of maritime tropical or equatorial air may be responsible for such storms. During a single cloudburst confined to an area of a few square miles, the major portion of rainfall of one or more year's total may fall, producing debris floods in the stream channels.

The concept of variability in rainfall is an important one in climate study. By variability we mean the degree to which the rainfall of the individual years differs from the average value computed over a long period of years. Figure 10.9 illustrates this principle. The yearly amounts of rainfall are shown by bars for three stations for a period of many years. At the top the record for Padang, Sumatra, gives data for a wet equatorial climate; the bottom graph gives rainfall for Abbassia, Egypt (near Cairo), a tropical desert station. The middle graph is of a combined climate type (tropical wet-dry climate). We say that the rainfall variability of the wet equatorial climate is small because the individual yearly amounts were, in this case, never more than twice the average or less

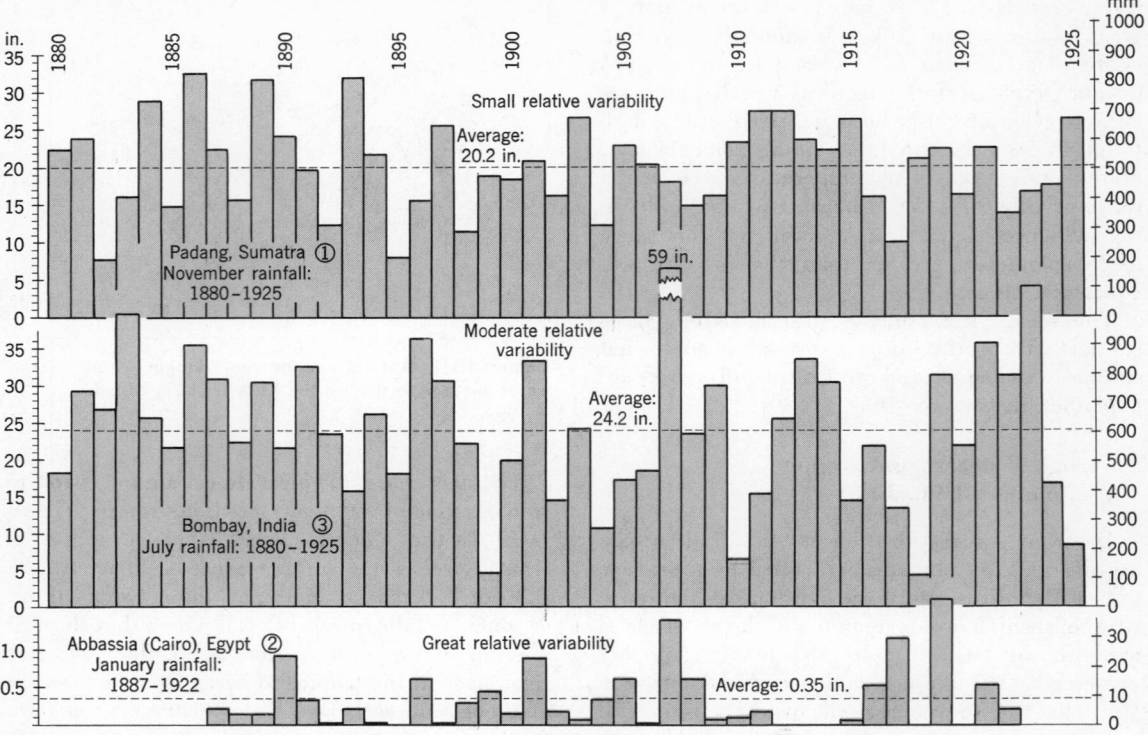

Figure 10.9 These three graphs illustrate the concept of variability of rainfall by showing the actual amount of rain received each year during the month which, on the average, is the rainiest month at that place. (Data from H. H. Clayton, Smithsonian Institution.)

than a third of the average. On the other hand, Abbassia shows great variability because, although several years had no rainfall at all, five of the years had more than twice the average amount and two of the years had four or more times the average.

Rainfall variability has been estimated for the world in terms of percentage departure from the normal value (Figure 10.10). As would be expected, the tropical desert areas lying near the tropics of Cancer and Capricorn have the highest variability; the equatorial belt of heavy rainfall, the least variability of the low-latitude part of the globe.

Consider next the temperature conditions of the dry continental tropical air mass source regions. Figure 10.11 shows the yearly march of temperatures at Yuma, Arizona, a representative North American station of the tropical desert (*BWh*) climate type. Two points are noteworthy: (*a*) temperatures are very high during the period of high sun; (*b*) annual range is moderately strong. Normally the annual range of temperature (hottest month average minus coolest month average) in these climates is 30 to 40 F° (17 to 22 C°) and is directly related to the height of the sun in the sky.

For those who consider southern Arizona to be a hot desert, the data of Bou-Bernous, Algeria, may

be enlightening (Figure 10.12). Here the mean daily temperature averaged over 100°F (38°C) in July—a full 10 F° (5.5 C°) higher than Yuma, Arizona.

More interesting, perhaps, than annual range is the normal daily range of temperatures in the tropical deserts. Figure 10.13 shows maximum and minimum daily readings for the months of January and July at Phoenix, Arizona. Note that the daily range is often as much as 35 F° (22 C°), the average daily range about 30 F° (17 C°). In no other climate does so great a daily range occur. This is explained by the rapid nightly heat loss from the ground and lower air layers because of the low water-vapor content of the air. On the other hand, insolation during the day is extremely intense and air temperatures soar to great heights. An all-time record range was recorded in Bir Milrha in the Sahara Desert, south of Tripoli, where 31°F and 99°F (−0.6°C and 37.2°C) were recorded on the same day, a range of 68 F° (37.8 C°).[1]

The world's highest temperatures are recorded in certain parts of the continental tropical deserts.

---

[1] G. T. Trewartha, *An Introduction to Weather and Climate*, McGraw-Hill Book Co., New York, 1943, p. 367.

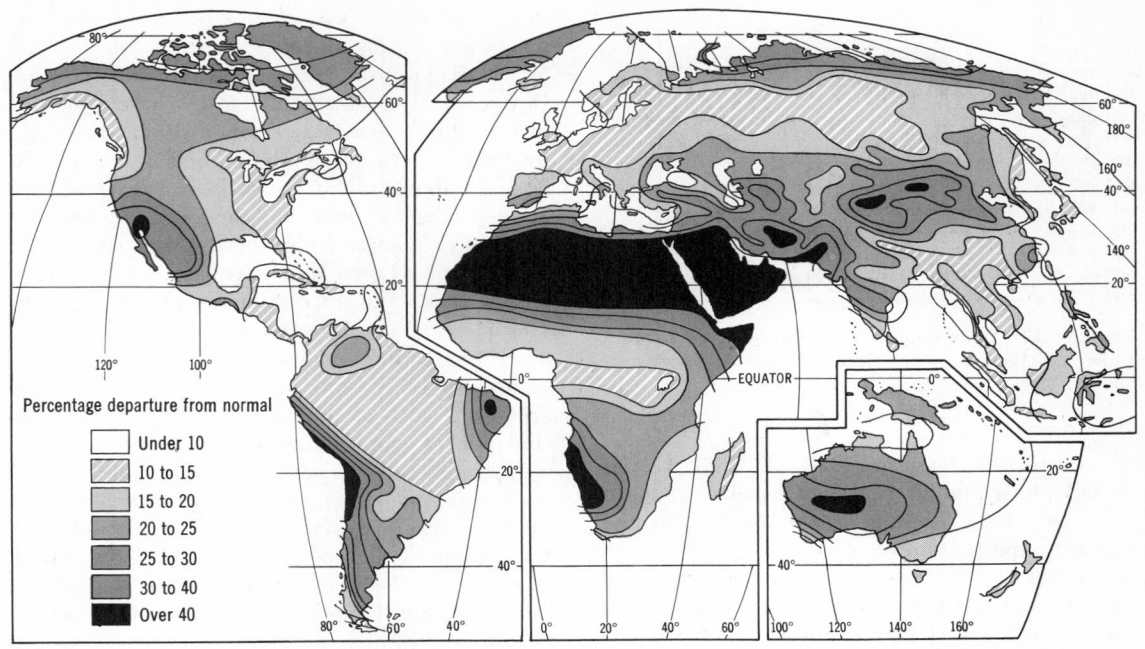

Figure 10.10 Precipitation variability map of the world. (After William Van Royen, 1954, *Atlas of the World's Agricultural Resources*, Prentice-Hall, Englewood Cliffs, N.J.)

Figure 10.11 Climograph for Yuma, Arizona, 33° N. lat. (Data from Trewartha.)

Figure 10.12 Air temperature data for Bou-Bernous, Algeria, 27°17′ N, 02°53′ W, elevation 1509 ft (460m). (Data from Meteorological Office of Great Britain.)

3. Tropical Desert and Steppe Climates (BWh, BSh) | 155

Figure 10.13 Daily temperatures for July and January at Phoenix, Arizona. (After Mark Jefferson, *Geographical Review.*)

A world record maximum of 136.4°F (58°C) was officially observed in the shade under standard shelter at Azizia, Tripoli. Figure 10.14 shows the highest temperatures ever observed in the western United States. The Sonoran Desert region of the lower Colorado River valley clearly surpasses all other areas for high temperatures.

In the extremely dry deserts (*BWh*), virtually the entire land surface appears to be free of vegetation and consists of bare rock, stream gravels and sands, or drifting dune sands. This does not mean

Figure 10.14 The highest temperatures (Fahrenheit) ever observed during the period 1899 to 1938. (After J. B. Kincer, U.S. Dept. of Agriculture, *Yearbook of American Agriculture*, 1941.)

that vegetation is wholly absent, rather, that the plants are thinly scattered over the surface and lack foliage to protect or obscure the bare ground. Desert plants are adapted to long drought periods by thick, fleshy leaves and stems, which store water for long periods of time but which do not permit loss of water through the surface. Representative of desert vegetation are the cacti and other shrubs seen in the Sonoran Desert of southwestern United States and northern Mexico (Figure 16.29). Chapter 15 treats the adaptation of plants to a dry (xerophytic) environment; Chapter 16 describes desert vegetation and its distribution.

Soils of the deserts are lacking in humus and are of a grayish or reddish color, depending upon the type of iron compound present to produce staining. These soils contain excessive amounts of calcium carbonate and other salts, which are left near the ground surface by evaporating water. In the centers of shallow lakes, the salts concentrate to form white saltflats, entirely sterile and almost perfectly smooth. Soil-forming processes of deserts are discussed in Chapter 13, the great soil groups of deserts in Chapter 14.

For a discussion of landforms of the mountainous desert topography, the student is referred to Chapter 22 on the fluvial cycle of landmass denudation.

Tropical steppe climate (*BSh*) borders the tropical deserts on both north and south, and in places on the east as well. Locally because of altitude, plateaus and high plains within what would otherwise be desert have the semi-arid steppe climate. Steppe zones lying equatorward of the deserts are transitional into the tropical wet-dry climate (*Aw*) and resemble it in many ways (Figure 10.15). Steppes on the poleward fringes of the tropical deserts grade into the Mediterranean climate (*Cs*) in many places. Steppes typically are grasslands of short grasses and other herbs, and with locally developed shrub and woodland (see Chapter 16). These areas are able to support limited numbers of grazing animals but are not generally moist enough for crop cultivation without irrigation. Soils are commonly of the *brown soil* and *chestnut soil* groups, containing some humus (Chapter 14).

4. West coast desert climate (BWk, BWh)

Again referring to the world rainfall map, Plate 1, it will be seen that all west coasts in latitudes 15° to 30° are extremely dry, generally with less than 10 in (25 cm) of rainfall annually. The Atacama desert of Chile and the Namib Desert of coastal southwest Africa are perhaps the most celebrated of these deserts, but they exist also in Lower California, the Morrocan coast of Africa, and the west coast of Australia. The arid belt

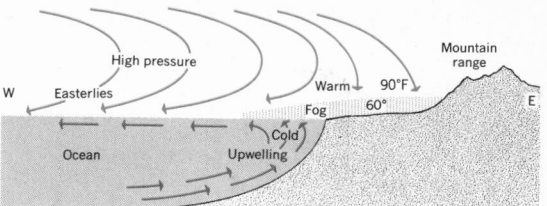

Figure 10.16 Subsiding air above a coastal temperature inversion. (From A. N. Strahler, *The Earth Sciences*, Harper and Row, New York.)

Figure 10.15 Climograph for Kayes, Mali, 14½° N lat. (Data from Trewartha.)

extends continuously eastward to inland continental tropical deserts.

Does it not seem strange that extreme dryness exists immediately along the shores of the oceans, close to possible sources of moist maritime air masses? The interior tropical deserts, already discussed, are logically explained by land-centered high-pressure cells into which moist air masses cannot easily drift, but the dry west coast strips are located between the oceanic and continental high-pressure cells where we might expect to find some development of fronts and convergence of air masses. The key to this problem seems to lie in the fact that the oceanic subtropical high-pressure cells are inherently dry on their east sides. The circulation in these cells is thought to be such that the air on the east sides is subsiding as it moves outward, hence, is adiabatically heated and its humidity reduced. The result is dry, stable air masses that bring an arid zone not only to the coast but extending far seaward as well. Strangely enough, there are dry deserts over the oceans in these tropical latitudes (Figure 10.16).

In what respects do the dry west coasts differ in climate from the interior continental deserts which they adjoin? The principal difference is in temperature. The coastal deserts are relatively cool, with annual average temperatures around 65°F (18°C), whereas the interior continental deserts average some 10 F° (5 C°) higher. The presence of cool upwelling and equatorward-flowing currents, such as the Humboldt and Benguela currents, explains the lowered temperatures. (See

Chapter 5.) The annual range of temperature in the coastal deserts is very low, as illustrated in Figure 10.17 by the temperature graph of Iquique, Chile (20° S), on the dry Atacama Desert coast of South America. The annual range is only 11 F° (6 C°). In contrast, the temperature cycle of Aswan, Egypt (24° N), shows both a higher average and a greater range.

Although the cool west coast desert climate is treated here as a separate climate from the tropical desert climate, not all climate classifications make the distinction. In the original Köppen classification, the cooler desert west coasts are designated by the symbol *BWn*, in which *n* means *frequent fog* (from the German, *nebel*, meaning fog). Persistent coastal fog banks form in the cool lower air layer overlying the cool ocean water (Figure 10.16). In the latest versions of the Köppen climate system, the symbols *BWh* and *BWk* are applied to the west coast deserts. The *BWk* climate is limited to the South American and southwest African coasts in latitudes 20° to 32° S, where the cool ocean currents are most influential.

Vegetation and soils of the cool west coast deserts are essentially similar to those of the interior deserts. An unusually high incidence of fog on these coasts leads to growth of some specialized

Figure 10.17 Temperature conditions compared for coastal and interior tropical desert locations. (Data from H. H. Clayton, Smithsonian Institution, and Trewartha.)

plants which can exist on condensed moisture close to the shore.

5. Tropical wet-dry climate (Aw, also Cwa)

We have thus far considered two extreme climate types. One, a wet climate lying in the equatorial zone, the other a desert climate arranged in two belts along the Tropics of Cancer and Capricorn. What of the intermediate zones where these two climate types come together? Knowing from previous study that the pressure and wind belts of the globe migrate northward at June solstice season and southward at December solstice season, we can infer that the intermediate zones in question will have climates that combine the characteristics of the first two types in a seasonal alternation. This results in the tropical wet-dry (Aw) climate, which has a wet season controlled by moist, warm equatorial and maritime tropical air masses at time of high sun and a dry season controlled by the continental tropical air masses at time of low sun.

The latitude belts in which tropical wet-dry climate is found lie roughly between 5° and 25° latitude, throughout Central and South America, Africa, and Australia. In southeast Asia this zone is pushed northward to latitudes 10° to 30° because the continental tropical air mass source region in summer is necessarily situated farther north to conform to the Asiatic landmass.

Climate characteristics of the tropical wet-dry climate can be judged from Figure 10.18, which gives temperature and rainfall data for a representative west African station. This can be studied in conjunction with Figure 10.19, which shows seasonal air mass and flow patterns. Timbo lies closer to the equator than Kayes, representing the tropical steppe (BSh) climate (Figure 10.15), hence has a longer wet season and a more even temperature cycle. Note especially the fact that maximum temperatures occur in March, April, or May, rather than in July, because the onset of the rains brings a cloud cover and cooler air temperatures. The water budget of an African tropical wet-dry station, Yambio, Sudan, is shown in Figure 9.9C. Here both a surplus and a deficiency occur in the cycle.

The Asiatic tropical wet-dry climate is somewhat different in that the monsoon controls are strong and bring an extreme contrast of wet and dry conditions. If we now look at the record of Allahabad, India, 25° N lat. (Figure 10.20), the basic similarity to Kayes and Timbo in western Africa (Figures 10.15 and 10.18), is very marked. The higher latitude of Allahabad results in much cooler January temperatures, and a greater annual range, but otherwise the temperature curves show the same dip during the rainy season. Köppen places Allahabad and a large belt of southeastern Asia in latitudes 20° to 25° in the Cwa climate (temperate, rainy climate, dry winter, hot summer). The Cw climate is a poleward extension of the Aw climate both here and in Africa and South and Central America. The two are here treated under the tropical wet-dry climate because tropical air masses dominate and the regime is basically of one pattern. Figure 8.8 shows the characteristic distorted figure-eight loop of the Indian wet-dry regime. Allahabad, India, is a Cwa station and shows a marked continental effect in its annual range. Paraná, a Brazilian Aw station, shows the thermal equability we associate with the wet equatorial climate but has a marked dry season.

The Köppen system provides an exact basis for the distinction between Am and Aw climates, both of which have a dry season. The Am-Aw boundary varies according to both total annual rainfall and driest-month rainfall, as shown by a graph (Figure 10.21). In the annual rainfall range between 40 in (100 cm) and 100 in (250 cm) the Am climate can exist with progressively lower values of driest-month rainfall, beginning with 2.4 in (6 cm) and declining to zero. Thus an Am station might have one month with no rainfall whatsoever, provided it has an annual total of more than 100 in (250 cm).

The contrast in wet and dry season rainfall in the tropical wet-dry climate is further illustrated in Figure 10.22. Here the rainfall of the one rainest month is compared with the total for the three consecutive driest months for a number of typical stations. Rainfall is not so reliable in the tropical

Figure 10.18 Climograph for Timbo, Republic of Guinea, 10°40′ N lat. (Data from Trewartha.)

Figure 10.19 These maps of Africa and southern Asia illustrate one interpretation of the air-mass source regions and circulation patterns that govern the equatorial and tropical climates. (Modified after M. A. Garbell, *Tropical and Equatorial Meteorology*, New York, 1947. Based on a Goode Base Map. Copyright by the University of Chicago. Used by permission of the University of Chicago Press.)

wet-dry climate as in the wet equatorial climate but is more reliable than in the very dry tropical deserts. This can be seen from the record of Bombay, India, in Figure 10.9, and is also apparent from the world variability map, Figure 10.10.

Alternation of wet and dry seasons results in the growth of a distinctive vegetation known generally as the *tropical savanna*. This is characterized by open expanses of tall grasses, interspersed with hardy, drought-resistant shrubs and trees (Figure 16.20). Other areas have savanna woodland, monsoon forest, thornbush, and tropical scrub, all of which are formation classes grouped on Plate 4 under the heading "Raingreen." These formation

classes are described in Chapter 16. Grasses in this climate are dried to straw and many tree species shed their leaves in the dry season. Other trees and shrubs have thorns and small leaves or hard, leathery leaves that resist water loss.

Soils of the wet-dry tropical climates are mostly yellowish or reddish latosols, similar to those described in connection with the wet equatorial climate. (See Chapter 14.) Excessive leaching is again the result of the heavy rainfall and high temperatures. In general, these residual soils of uplands are not fertile and are little cultivated in South America and Africa. Locally, rich floodplain alluvium is highly productive. Stream flow in these

Figure 10.20   Climograph for Allahabad, India, 25° N lat. (Data from H. H. Clayton, Smithsonian Institution.)

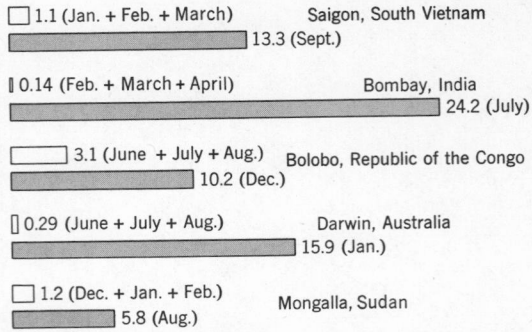

Figure 10.22   Rainfall (inches) of the one wettest month is shown contrasted with the total rainfall of the three consecutive driest months for five wet-dry tropical climate stations. (Data from Clayton and Trewartha.)

Africa are the natural home of such herbivores as wildebeest, gazelle, deer, antelope, buffalo, rhinoceros, zebra, giraffe, and elephant. On them feed the lion, leopard, hyena, and jackal. Some of the herbivores depend upon fleetness of foot to escape the predators. Others, such as the rhinoceros, buffalo, and elephant, defend themselves by their size, strength, or armor-thick hide. The giraffe is a peculiar adaptation to savanna woodlands; his long neck permits browsing upon the higher foliage of scattered trees.

The dry season brings a severe struggle for existence to animals of the African savanna. As streams and hollows dry up, the few muddy waterholes must supply all drinking water. Danger of attack by carnivores is greatly increased.

The Indian savanna, woodland, and thornforest have a somewhat similar assemblage. Deer and antelope are especially abundant, with some water buffalo and a few rhinoceroses. The tiger replaces the lion as the principal carnivore. The Indian elephant, however, is largely restricted in natural habitat to the rainforest coastal strips of Burma, the Malabar coast, and Ceylon.

REFERENCES FOR FURTHER STUDY

Gautier, E. F., tr. by D. F. Mayhen (1935), *Sahara, the great desert*, Columbia Univ. Press, New York, 264 pp.

Lee, D. H. K. (1957), *Climate and economic development in the tropics*, Harper and Row, New York, 182 pp.

Church, R. J. H. (1961), *West Africa, a study of environment and man's use of it*, John Wiley and Sons, New York, 547 pp.

Trewartha, G. T. (1961) *The earth's problem climates*, Univ. of Wisconsin Press, Madison, Methuen and Co., London, 334 pp.

Hills, E. S., ed. (1966), *Arid lands; a geographical appraisal*, Methuen and Co., London, 461 pp.

Meigs, P. (1966), *Geography of coastal deserts*, UNESCO Publications Center, New York, 140 pp.

Figure 10.21   This graph shows how *Aw* climates are distinguished from *Am* climates in the Köppen system. (After Haurwitz and Austin.)

regions contrasts greatly with that of the wet equatorial climate, in that the former has a very strong seasonal fluctuation. From flood conditions with extensive low-lying areas under water in the rainy season, the streams pass to a regime of little or no flow in the dry season, when channel bottoms of sand and gravel are exposed and mud flats dry out.

Closely related to vegetation and climate is the natural animal life of the savanna grasslands and woodlands. These are the regions of the carnivorous game animals and a vast multitude of grazing animals on which they feed. The grasslands of

1. What conditions of temperature, pressure, and rainfall prevail in the equatorial belt? What air masses are present? Under what conditions does heavy precipitation occur? How does the equatorial trough change position throughout the year?

2. Describe the annual temperature curve for a typical station in the wet equatorial (*Af*) climate zone. What range is usually found? How does the daily temperature range compare with the annual range?

3. Approximately how great is the average annual rainfall of the wet equatorial climate? How is rainfall distributed throughout the year? Is variability of rainfall great or small?

4. What is rainforest? Of what types of vegetation is it composed? (See Chapter 16.)

5. What is a lateritic soil (latosol)? What processes are responsible for development of lateritic soils. Of what economic importance are laterites? (See Chapter 14.)

6. Is there much humus in lateritic soils (latosols)? Explain how temperature and bacterial activity affect the accumulation of decomposed vegetation in the hot equatorial regions as contrasted with cold regions.

7. Is the chemical decay of rock relatively small or great in the wet equatorial climate? Explain.

8. What can be said about stream flow in the wet equatorial climate? In what way are rivers of importance to native inhabitants of these regions?

9. In what way does the wet, monsoon-dominated climate of the southern Asiatic coasts (*Am*) differ from that close to the equator (*af*)?

10. Why is there heavy precipitation on east coast belts in latitudes 10° to 25°? What climate occurs here? What type of climate occurs at inland locations in this same latitude belt?

11. What causes the tropical deserts in latitudes 15° to 35°? Explain these deserts in terms of the global pattern of air circulation. What kind of air mass has its source over these areas?

12. Distinguish between desert and steppe climates. What Köppen symbols denote these climates?

13. Discuss the evaporation of moisture in the tropical deserts. How great is evaporation from a free water surface? What influence has this factor upon streams and the ground water table?

14. What type of rainfall occurs in the tropical deserts? Is it widespread or localized? Is rainfall variability in these deserts great or small?

15. What is the nature of the annual temperature cycle in the tropical deserts? Explain these characteristics. What is the nature of the daily cycle of temperature? How does it compare with that of the wet equatorial climate?

16. What kind of vegetation is native to the tropical deserts? To what extent does it afford cover to the ground? What kinds of soils are typical of these deserts?

17. Explain the west coast deserts in latitudes 15° to 30°. How are these related to the subtropical high pressure cells? Why is the air dry in these locations?

18. What is the outstanding feature of the annual temperature cycle of the west coast deserts? Why is the range small? Why are the temperatures abnormally low for this latitude? Why is fog abundant along these coasts?

19. Explain the characteristic seasonal features of the wet-dry tropical climate in terms of air masses and seasonal shifting of the pressure and wind belts of the globe.

20. How do annual precipitation and its distribution throughout the year change if we start with the wet equatorial climate zone and examine the rainfall records for stations progressively farther north until the Sahara Desert is reached?

21. Describe the annual temperature cycle of the tropical wet-dry climate. When is the maximum reached? Why does this not coincide with the time of highest sun?

22. In what way does the Asiatic wet-dry tropical climate differ from that of Africa or South America? Explain. How does Köppen distinguish the climate of north India from the climate of peninsular India?

23. What is the natural vegetation of the wet-dry tropical climate? What are the characteristics of the wild animal life of these regions? What type of soil is generally present? What effect has the seasonal contrast of dry and wet periods upon stream flow?

CHAPTER 11
Middle-Latitude Climates

CLIMATES of group II are those of middle latitudes occupying the polar front zone in which both tropical and polar air masses play an important part. The latitude belt in which these climates lie is subject to cyclonic storms; most of the precipitation in these climates occurs along fronts within these cyclones.

6. Humid subtropical climate (Cfa)

The moist nature of the west sides of the oceanic subtropical high-pressure cells has already been discussed in Chapter 6. Maritime tropical (мT) air in this part of the anticyclonic cell is engaged in a slight ascending motion combined with its flow toward higher latitudes. The air mass has a steep lapse rate. Moisture that enters the air mass by evaporation from the warm ocean surface is distributed to great heights. As this moist, unstable maritime tropical air mass moves over the eastern continental coasts in latitudes 25° to 35° and drifts inland, it brings the necessary moisture and latent heat energy for heavy precipitation. Lifting occurs along warm and cold fronts where the tropical air encounters polar air. This general pattern of climate, here called the *humid subtropical climate*, is exemplified by the southern Atlantic and Gulf Coast states of the United States; corresponding regions are found in the Argentina-Uruguay-southern Brazil area of South America, in eastern China and southern Japan, along a small part of the southeastern coast of Africa, and on the east Australian coast.

In the Köppen system, these areas lie in the *Cfa* climate, described as a temperate rainy climate with hot summers. Temperature specifications of the *C* climates have been stated in Chapter 8. The *Cfa* climate has no dry season, and even the driest summer month receives more than 1.2 in (3 cm) of rain. The hot summer specified by the letter *a* is one in which the average temperature of the warmest month is over 71.6°F (22°C).

For an analysis of the temperature and precipitation characteristics of this moist, subtropical climate, we may refer to the record for Charleston, South Carolina (Figure 11.1). Rainfall is ample at all times of the year, but is distinctly greater during the summer when the oceanic high strengthens and the flow of maritime tropical air is increased. Thunderstorms are especially frequent in summer (Figure 11.2). They may be of the thermal (heat) type, or of squall-line or cold front origin. An occasional tropical cyclone may strike the coastal area, bringing very heavy rains. Winter precipitation, some of it in the form of snow, is of frontal type in the frequent middle-latitude cyclones that sweep over these regions. Not all stations in the humid subtropical climate show a summer maximum. For example, Atlanta, Georgia, has a winter maximum, but a secondary peak in midsummer. Typically the annual precipitation totals more than 40 in (100 cm).

Temperatures show a moderately strong range, of very much the same magnitude as in the tropical deserts, but without the extreme heat in summer. Humidity is, of course, very high, in marked contrast to the deserts, and summer climate on the humid east coasts is at times similar to the wet equatorial climate in temperature, rainfall, and

Figure 11.1 Climograph for Charleston, South Carolina, 33° N. lat. (Data from Trewartha.)

162

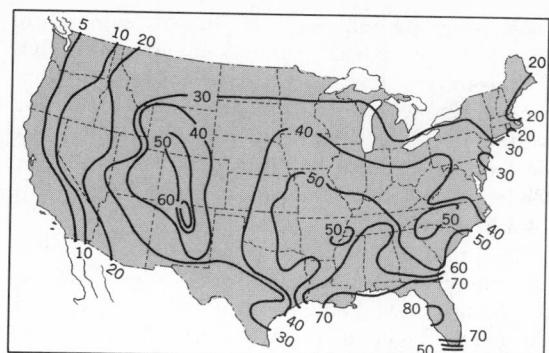

Figure 11.2 Average annual number of days with thunderstorms, based on records of the period 1899 to 1938. (After J. B. Kincer, U.S. Dept. of Agriculture.)

humidity. Winters show the influence of outbursts of polar air masses, which frequently penetrate into subtropical latitudes and bring below-freezing weather with killing frosts. We might say that this climate type is shared to some extent by both tropical and polar air masses, but that the tropical air masses prevail most of the time and dominate in summer.

In southeast Asia the humid subtropical climate is somewhat modified by intensive monsoon development. Winter air masses from interior Asia are very dry, and a winter scarcity of precipitation develops, whereas maritime air masses in summer, together with occasional typhoons, cause a strongly accentuated maximum in the summer. This shows clearly in the precipitation cycle of Shanghai, China (Figure 11.3), which has a winter both drier and cooler than that of Charleston.

With reference to climatic regime, the humid subtropical climate usually shows a pronounced continentality, as in the case of the thermohyet diagram for Shanghai, China, in Figure 8.10C.

Soils of the moister, warmer parts of the humid subtropical regions are strongly leached red-yellow soils related to the latosols of the humid tropical and equatorial climates. Rich in iron and aluminum oxides, these soils are poor in many of the plant nutrients essential for successful agricultural production.

Forest is the natural vegetation of most of the areas having the humid subtropical climate. Plate 4 shows temperate rainforest to be the dominant type, but with some areas of tropical rainforest occupying the coastal belts in lower latitudes. Much of the sandy coastal region of the southeastern United States today has a second growth forest of longleaf, loblolly, and slash pine, whereas the inland region has summer-green deciduous forest. (These forest types are treated in Chapter 16.) Toward higher latitudes forest gives way to tall-grass prairie such as the *Pampa* of Argentina

and Uruguay, and the prairies of Oklahoma and Missouri. Here the soils are of dark prairie and chernozem groups, typical of a dry continental climate. These grasslands occupy regions that are *subhumid*, i.e., best considered transitional to the semi-arid steppes, for they have less than 40 in (100 cm) annual precipitation and a marked dryness of the winter season.

7. Marine west coast climate (Cfb, Cfc)

Shifting attention now toward higher latitudes, and using the information about air masses, fronts, and cyclones presented in Chapter 7, we might expect to find that western coasts in the belt of cyclonic storms would receive ample rainfall from maritime polar air masses and would have rather moderate temperature variations because of the proximity to the oceans from which the air masses tend to drift landward.

These conditions are fulfilled in west coasts of landmasses lying between 40° or 45° and 60° latitude. Situated too far poleward to be dominated by the dry influence of the subtropical oceanic high-pressure cells, these climates lack a dry season. Because continental polar air masses tend to drift eastward, they rarely move westward to visit the west coasts; hence severe dry-cold conditions are uncommon.

Köppen classifies the marine west coast climate as *Cfb*, a temperate rainy climate with warm summers. The average temperature of the warmest month is under 71.6°F (22°C) and at least four

Figure 11.3 Climograph for Shanghai, China, 31° N lat. (Data from Meteorological Office of Great Britain.)

months average 50°F (10°C) or more. The cool summer variety *Cfc* has fewer than four months with averages over 50°F (10°C).

Climate of the middle-latitude west coasts is illustrated by the graphs for Brest, France (Figure 11.4), located at 49° N lat. on the Brittany coast. Precipitation is well distributed throughout the year, but shows a distinct reduction during the summer months. This feature is also found on rainfall graphs for coastal stations on the Pacific northwest coast of the United States. Why should this reduction occur? In summer, the oceanic subtropical high is most strongly developed and moves farthest north, bringing its arid influence to bear just enough to make a distinct decrease in summer rainfall. In other words, this is a manifestation of the same mechanism that causes a west coast desert in low latitudes.

Although the total rainfall for Brest and similar marine west coast stations over much of Europe is not great, judged by tropical or equatorial standards, the cooler air temperatures reduce evaporation and produce a very damp, humid climate with much cloud cover. Nearness to the ocean makes for a small annual temperature range, just as it does in lower latitudes on the west coast deserts. Mild winters and relatively cool summers are characteristic. Winters which are severely cold at the same latitudes in mid-continent and east-continent positions are by contrast surprisingly mild on the west coasts.

In terms of climatic regime, the marine west coast climate combines equability of temperature with a Mediterranean regime. Vancouver, B.C., has a thermohyet diagram with the typical Mediterranean shape, but is displaced to a colder and wetter position (Figure 8.9*C*). Auckland, New Zealand, is depicted in Figure 8.6*A* as equable in tendency, its annual temperature range being only 14.5 F° (8 C°).

The influence of coastal ranges upon rainfall is extremely marked in middle latitudes. Whereas low-lying coasts, such as in northern France or southern England, receive only 30 to 40 in (75–100 cm) of precipitation annually, mountainous coasts of British Columbia, Alaska, Norway, and Chile get 60 to 80 in (150–200 cm) and over. This has been a major factor in the development of fiords along the seacoasts. (See Chapter 23.) Heavy snows in the glacial period nourished vigorous valley glaciers which descended to the sea, scouring deep troughs below sea level at their lower ends.

Natural vegetation of the marine west coast climate is forest, but of widely different classes from one world locality to another. Western Europe has a summer-green deciduous forest whereas that of west coast North America is of the needleleaf class. On coast ranges of the Pacific northwest, Douglas fir, red cedar, and spruce grow in magnificent forests (Figure 16.14). Forests of the marine west coast climate belts of Chile and New Zealand are of the temperate rainforest class (Chapter 16).

Soils of the marine west coast climate regions bearing needleleaf forests are of a strongly leached type, the *podzols*, and are acid in nature. Under cool temperatures, bacterial activity is slow, in contrast to the warm tropics, so that vegetative matter is not consumed and forms a heavy surface deposit. Organic acids from the decomposing vegetation react with the soil compounds, resulting in removal of such bases as calcium, sodium, and potassium. Soils of western Europe are of the *gray-brown podzolic* group, typically associated with deciduous forests in middle latitudes. This soil is not so strongly leached and is suited to diversified forms of agriculture.

8. Mediterranean climate (dry summer subtropical climate) (Csa, Csb)

Situated on west coasts between latitudes 30° and 45° is a zone subject to alternate wet and dry seasons because it is located in the transitional zone between the dry west coast tropical desert (on the equatorward side) and the wet west coast climate (on the poleward side). Because these two climate types have been analyzed and described in previous pages, we need only substitute the information to derive a distinctive compound climate type.

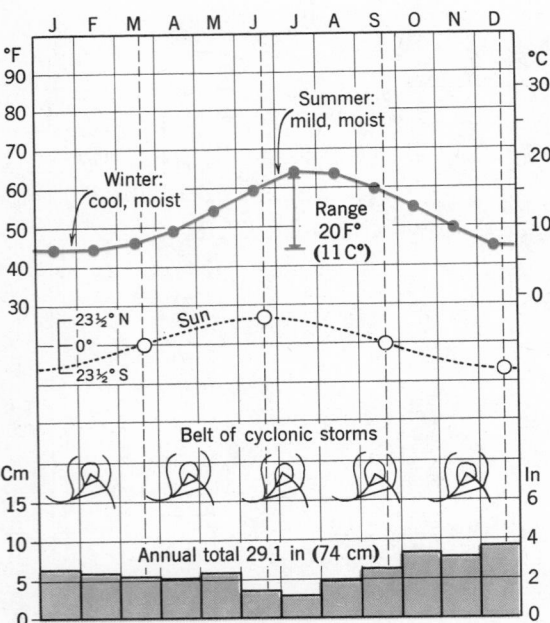

Figure 11.4   Climograph for Brest, France, on the coast of Brittany, 49° N lat. (Data from Blair.)

Consider the climate of Monterey, California, as an example (Figure 11.5). In summer, when the oceanic subtropical high is most powerfully developed and farthest north, the same desert conditions that prevail permanently farther south take over control of the climate and bring a severe drought. However, the proximity of the ocean with its cool current keeps summer temperatures to a mild 60°F (16°C) average. In winter, the humid regime of middle-latitude cyclones and moist maritime polar (MP) air masses is felt in the ample precipitation.

The dry-summer subtropical climate is particularly extensive in the Mediterranean lands. Hence, the name *Mediterranean climate* is commonly used for this climate. The unique regime of the Mediterranean climate has been described in Chapter 8. The thermohyet forms an elliptical figure slanting down to the right (Figure 8.9*A*, *B*).

Köppen classifies the climate of the Mediterranean lands as *Csa*, a temperate rainy climate with dry, hot summers. Those narrow coastal belts directly bordering the cool currents of the open Atlantic, Pacific, and Indian oceans, Köppen designates as *Csb*, distinguished by a markedly cooler summer than the *Csa* climate. Thus Monterey, California, represents a *Csb* climate.

An example of a *Csa* station in the Mediterranean lands is Naples, Italy (Figure 11.6). The annual temperature range here is 28.5 F° (16 C°), which is over twice that at Monterey. The summer is not rainless, but monthly averages are very low

Figure 11.6   Climograph for Naples, Italy, 40½° N lat. (Data from Meteorological Office of Great Britain.)

in June and July. Annual precipitation is double that of Monterey. In short, the equable influence of the cool west coast desert is replaced by a continental influence.

It is apparent that if one travels from the Mediterranean shore into North Africa, he will pass from the Mediterranean climate into the tropical steppe climate of the Sahara. A transition climate type intermediate between the two is nicely shown by the record for Bengasi, Tripoli, at lat. 32° N (Figure 11.7). Note that the temperature record resembles that of the tropical dry climates, although not so hot, but the rainfall distribution is distinctly of the same type as the Mediterranean rainfall, though not so copious.

The Mediterranean climate, its drought coinciding with the high temperatures of summer, incurs a large water deficiency in middle and late summer (Figure 9.9*E*). Winter rains quickly restore the moisture deficiency and a surplus is developed by early spring.

The occurrence of a wet winter and a dry summer is unique among climate types and results in a distinctive natural vegetation of hardleaved evergreen trees and shrubs, known as *sclerophyll forest* (Chapter 16). Various forms of sclerophyll woodland and scrub are also typical (Figures 16.16, 16.17). Trees and shrubs must withstand the severe summer drought of two to four rainless months and intense evaporation.

Soils of the Mediterranean climate are not readily subject to simple classification. Reddish-chestnut and reddish-brown soils typical of semi-

Figure 11.5   Climograph of Monterey, California, 36½° N lat. (Data from Blair.)

Figure 11.7 Climograph for Bengasi, Tripoli, 32° N lat., on the North African coast. (Data from Trewartha.)

arid climates are generally present (Plate 3). In the Mediterranean lands *terra rossa*, a red soil formed on limestone, occurs in various locations.

9. Middle-latitude desert and steppe climates (BWk, BSk)

The interiors of North America and Asia, in latitudes 35° to 50°, and, to a limited extent, that of southernmost South America have desert and steppe climates of somewhat complex origin. Three basic air mass controls operate. (1) In summer, when pressure and wind belts are shifted poleward, these regions temporarily become the source regions for continental tropical air masses, developed because of intense heating of the large continental interiors. (2) In winter, the intense development of the Siberian and Canadian highs, which are the source areas for continental polar air masses, causes frequent invasions of relatively dry continental air. (3) Mountain ranges separate these deserts from moist maritime polar and maritime tropical air masses which supply abundant rainfall to the west and southeast coasts. Through forced ascent over these ranges, followed by adiabatic heating upon descending the lee slopes (see Chapter 6), the maritime air masses are deprived of their moisture and raised in temperature as well. Thus the regions in question are poorly situated for obtaining precipitation. Because of the prevailing westerly winds in these latitudes, maritime tropical air masses cannot easily reach these areas from the east. In southern Asia, the northward flow of moist tropical

air from the Indian Ocean is blocked by the great Himalayan chain.

Under the Köppen system, two climate varieties are recognized, the semi-arid steppes, *BSk*, and the true desert, *BWk* (Plate 2). The letter *k* signifies a cool climate, with average annual temperature below 64.4°F (18°C). Where the letter *k'* is used, a cold climate is indicated, with the warmest month average below 64.4°F (18°C).

Only a small proportion of the area covered by dry middle-latitude climates is extremely dry: the Turkestan and Gobi deserts of central Asia and parts of the Great Basin in Nevada and Utah (Plate 1). The principal respect in which these deserts differ from the tropical deserts of lower latitudes is that their annual temperature range is much greater and the winter temperatures much lower. Astrakhan, USSR, at 46° N lat., illustrates this feature nicely (Figure 10.17). The enormous annual range of 58 F° (32 C°) is almost double that of Aswan, Egypt; the January mean temperature is a severe 20°F (−7°C), as compared with 60°F (16°C) for Aswan; and the July maximum is only 15 F° (8 C°) less than for Aswan.

Of considerably greater importance geographically than the deserts are the vast semi-arid steppe lands of the middle-latitude dry climates. Partly because of higher elevation, which increases the precipitation, or because of location nearer to maritime air mass invasions, these regions receive from 10 to 20 in (25 to 50 cm) of precipitation annually (Plate 1).

Continentality is the dominant climatic regime of the middle-latitude steppes and deserts. A repre-

Figure 11.8 Temperature regimes of highland steppe climates. (Data from Trewartha.)

Figure 11.9 Climograph for Pueblo, Colorado, 38° N lat. (Data from Blair.)

sentative thermohyet diagram, that of Omaha, Nebraska (Figure 8.10*A*), has an elongate figure with a diagonal axis trending from upper right to lower left. As winter temperatures are lowered with increasing latitude the figure is drawn lower on the left side. This effect is seen when the semi-arid steppes are followed from subtropical highlands in Mexico to middle latitudes, the annual temperature cycles show not only progressively lower temperatures but also greatly increased annual ranges (Figure 11.8). A typical steppe climate of intermediate position is that of Pueblo, Colorado (Figure 11.9). Compared with the Mediterranean climate of Monterey, California (Figure 11.5), which lies at about the same latitude, the annual temperature range of Pueblo is very much greater, the precipitation cycle is just reversed, with the summer maximum clearly marked. In summer large highs drifting over the central United States produce a northerly return flow of air on their western sides, spreading moist tropical air from the Gulf of Mexico far northward and westward into the continental interior. This air is unstable and readily produces thunderstorms when lifted over a mountain range or along a cold front.

Steppes support a short-grass vegetation cover suited to grazing of cattle and sheep, but inadequate for farming without irrigation or special dry-farming methods. Special attention is given by geographers and climatologists to the boundary between dry and humid climates, particularly because the limits of agriculture without irrigation are drawn by nature as a fluctuating line over a hazardous frontier zone. Here, productivity may

in some years be high; in others, drought brings disastrous failures. Figure 11.10 is a map showing precipitation and temperature data for the boundary between dry and humid climates in the Great Plains region of the United States. Let us define a humid climate as one in which the precipitation on the average exceeds evaporation, so as to give permanently flowing streams and a generally moist soil; a dry climate as one in which evaporation on the average exceeds precipitation, so as to give ephemeral streams and a generally dry soil. The humid-arid boundary cannot be permanently located, but its average position runs somewhere along the dashed north-south line in Figure 11.10. Note that in North Dakota, the boundary cuts the 15-in (38-cm) annual isohyet but in southern Texas runs close to the 25-in (64-cm) isohyet. This shift is explained by the temperatures, which are higher

In.	Cm	°C	°F
10	25	35	95
15	38	40	104
20	51	45	113
25	64	50	122
30	76	55	131
35	89	60	140
40	102	65	149
45	114	70	158
50	127		
55	140		
60	152		

Figure 11.10 On this map, the boundary zone between semiarid and subhumid climates runs north-south. Superimposed are isotherms of average annual Fahrenheit temperature (solid lines) and lines of equal average annual precipitation in inches (broken lines). (After J. B. Kincer, U.S. Dept. of Agriculture.)

in the south and result in greater evaporation losses.

Middle-latitude steppes are characterized by short-grass prairie and by local occurrences of woodland and semi-desert shrubs (Plate 4, Figure 16.27). (This vegetation is described in Chapter 16.) Middle-latitude steppes now constitute the great sheep and cattle ranges of the world. On the vast expanses of the High Plains, the American bison lived in great numbers until almost exterminated by hunters. Likewise, the short-grass veldt of South Africa supported much game at one time. Steppe grasses do not form a complete sod cover, and loose, bare soil is exposed between grass clumps. For this reason, overgrazing or a series of dry years often reduces the hold of grasses enough to permit destructive soil erosion and gullying from heavy local downpours.

Soils of the steppe lands are deficient in humus. They belong to the group of brown soils in the less dry parts; elsewhere they are reddish or gray desert soils. Calcium carbonate is present in excess quantities and may form nodules in the soil. Encrustations of calcium carbonate make a hard, whitish crust termed *caliche* in the southwestern United States. These calcium-rich soils are highly fertile in terms of bases favorable to grain crops, such as wheat, but unless irrigation is employed the advantage is lost. Traced toward humid-climate zones which adjoin the steppes, the soils become darker brown in color, denoting the increasing amounts of humus from heavier growth of grasses. Thus the gray or red desert and steppe soils grade into the rich, dark brown and black chestnut and chernozem soils of the prairies (Plate 3).

10. Humid continental climate (Dfa, Dfb, Dwa, Dwb)

Consider a vast region located in a middle latitude, say between 40° and 55° N, extending from the continental interior to the east coast. North America and Asia are, of course, the areas that we have in mind. The location is intermediate between the source region of polar continental air masses on the north and maritime or continental tropical air masses on the south and southeast. In this polar-front zone, maximum interaction between polar and tropical air masses can be expected along warm and cold fronts associated with east-moving cyclones. In winter, the continental polar air masses dominate and much cold weather prevails; in summer, tropical air masses dominate and high temperatures prevail. Thus, strong seasonal temperature contrasts must be expected in this region. Precipitation is ample throughout the year, because the region lies in a frontal zone. Strong contrasts in air masses result in strong frontal

activity and highly changeable weather. This climate may be described as both humid and continental in properties.

The climate picture drawn above applies well to the north-central and northeastern United States and southeastern Canada as well as to northern China, southern Manchuria, Korea, and northern Japan. Very similar climatic conditions also hold for much of central and eastern Europe, the Balkan countries, and Russia, but this third region differs from the first two in that it is influenced by a great source region of continental-tropical air masses lying to the south and southeast, instead of the oceanic source regions of maritime tropical air masses.

Four varieties of climate, according to Köppen, are found in the regions that we are grouping together as having the humid continental climate. *Dfa* and *Dfb* are cold, snowy, forest climates, the first with a hot summer, the second with a warm summer. The precise definitions of *a* and *b* are as previously given. *Dwa* and *Dwb* climates, found in eastern Siberia, Manchuria, and northern Korea, are cold, snowy forest climates with a dry winter. Letters *a* and *b* refer to hot and warm summers, respectively. The winter dryness, typical of all climates of eastern Asia, is explained below.

We are also including here under the humid continental climate the northern part of Köppen's *Cf* climate region in the eastern United States. (Compare Plate 2 and Figure 8.5.) Recall that Köppen used as his *C-D* boundary the isotherm

Figure 11.11 A comparison of climates at New York and Omaha, both in the humid continental climate zone. (Data from H. H. Clayton, Smithsonian Institution.)

Figure 11.12 Climograph for Moscow, USSR, 56° N lat. (Data from Blair.)

of 26.6°F (−3°C) of the coldest month. Thus, for example, Köppen places New Haven and Cleveland in the same *Cfa* climate as New Orleans and Tampa, despite obvious contrasts in January mean temperatures, soil groups, and natural vegetation between these northern and southern zones.

Some characteristic features of the humid continental climate can be seen from the temperature-precipitation graphs of four stations: Omaha and New York City (Figure 11.11), Moscow, USSR (Figure 11.12), and Peiping, China (Figure 11.13). All four stations have similar temperature curves. Yearly range is near 55 F° (33 C°) for all but New York City, which is moderated by its near-ocean location. Omaha and Peiping, located at the same latitude (40° N), have almost identical temperatures; Moscow, being more than 1000 mi (620 km) farther north 56° N), has a temperature cycle which runs 10 F° (5.5 C°) lower than that of Omaha or Peiping.

Precipitation records of the four stations illustrated show certain marked dissimilarities which require explanation. A summer maximum is apparent in all four but is very weakly defined in New York City because maritime air masses, both polar and tropical, have ready access to the eastern seaboard at all times of the year. Omaha and Moscow have well-defined summer maxima and winter minima, reflecting the predominance of tropical air masses in summer and continental-polar air masses in the winter. Moscow, being farther north, near to the source region of polar continental air masses, has less precipitation than

the other stations. Peiping shows a very strong summer maximum and a winter drought. This contrast is characteristic of the east Asiatic middle-latitude stations and reflects the powerful monsoon control, whereby dry continental air masses dominate in winter.

Continentality is the dominant climatic regime expressed by the above stations. The thermohyet diagrams (Figure 8.10) are elongate in the vertical axis, but inclined to the right, reflecting a summer precipitation maximum.

The general temperature pattern of middle-latitude climates is well illustrated by daily temperature graphs of three stations at about the same latitude across North America (Figure 11.14). Victoria, British Columbia, on the west coast, occupies a windward position with respect to maritime polar air masses from the Pacific. Consequently, the contrasts between July and February (the two extreme months of the year) are small. Moreover, the daily ranges are small, especially in winter. The graph of Winnipeg, Manitoba, shows maximum continental influence with strong annual and daily contrasts. Note especially the wide fluctuations in winter, with outbursts of polar and arctic air bringing very low temperatures. St. Johns, Newfoundland, occupies a leeward position with respect to the continent and is accessible to maritime air masses from the Atlantic. It therefore has only a moderate annual temperature range, but the continental influence is nevertheless clearly marked in the sharply fluctuating daily temperature record.

Figure 11.13 Climograph for Peiping, China, 40° N lat. (Data from Trewartha.)

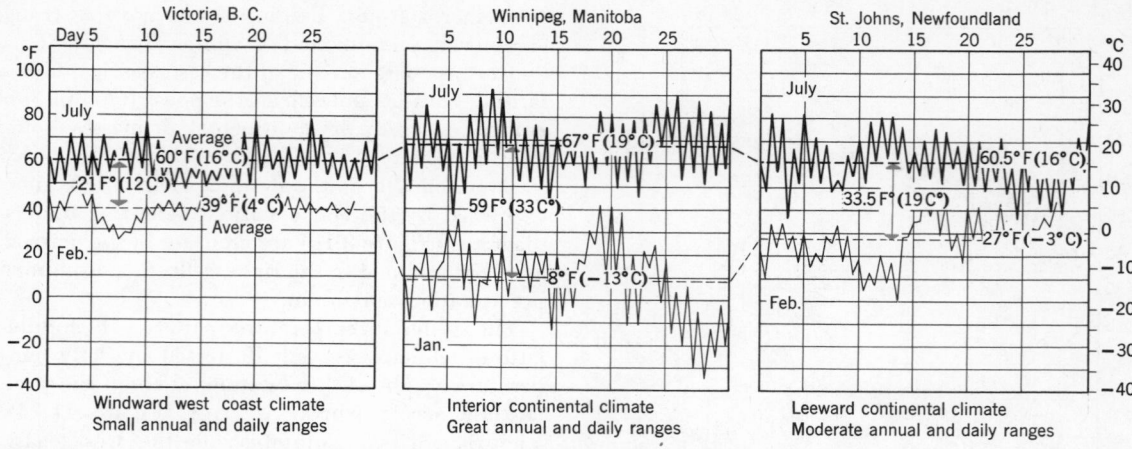

Figure 11.14 Along the 50th parallel in North America lie widely differing climate types. Averages are for months actually shown on graphs. (After Mark Jefferson, *Geographical Review*.)

Three major types of natural vegetation and their associated soils may be recognized in the humid continental climate. The distribution is well illustrated in North America. (See Plates 3 and 4.)

In the more humid eastern sections, including the warmer parts of the humid continental climate zone (*Dfa*), natural vegetation is summergreen deciduous forest (Figure 16.11). Here soils are of the *brown forest* and *gray-brown podzolic* types, rich in humus and moderately leached so as to have a distinct light-colored leached zone under the upper dark layer. In this region, diversified farming and dairying are the most successful uses of the land where topography is favorable.

A northern belt of needleleaf evergreen forest (Figure 16.12) extends along the entire length of the colder northern parts of the humid continental climate zone (*Dfb*). To this may be added the mountain regions of the Adirondacks and northern New England. Here soils are of the *podzol* type, strongly leached, but with an upper layer of humus (Chapter 14). Cool temperatures inhibit bacterial activity which would destroy this organic matter in tropical regions. Podzols are deficient in calcium, potassium, and magnesium, and are, in general, acid in chemical nature. Thus they are not highly productive for crop farming, even though adequate rainfall is generally assured. The podzols are, however, well suited to the growth of conifers.

The drier plains areas of the humid continental climate support a natural tall-grass prairie (Figure 16.26), which grades into the drier steppe regions of short grasses to the west. The prairie soils and chernozem soils, two major soil groups of these grasslands, are typically dark in color and consist of a single, thick upper layer grading into the parent soil material below (Chapter 14). These soils contain abundant calcium, magnesium, and potassium because rainfall is here distinctly less than farther eastward and leaching is less active as a soil-forming process.

REFERENCES FOR FURTHER STUDY

U.S. Dept. Agriculture (1941), *Yearbook of Agriculture, 1941*, U.S. Govt. Printing Office, Washington, D.C. See: C. O. Sauer, "The settlement of the humid East," pp. 157–176; C. W. Thornthwaite, "Climate and settlement in the Great Plains," pp. 177–196; J. Leighly, "Settlement and cultivation in the summer-dry climates," pp. 197–204.

White, G. F., ed. (1956), *The future of arid lands*, Am. Assoc. Advancement of Sci., Publ. 43, Washington, D.C., 453 pp.

Jaeger, E. C. (1957), *The North American deserts*, Stanford Univ. Press, Stanford, Calif., 308 pp.

Trewartha, G. T. (1961), *The earth's problem climates*, The Univ. of Wisconsin Press, Madison, Methuen and Co., London, 334 pp.

1. Explain the occurrence of a moist climate in subtropical latitudes (25° to 35°) along the eastern continental margins. What air masses prevail over this region? What is the nature of these air masses?

2. Describe the annual cycle of temperature and precipitation at a typical humid subtropical climate (*Cfa*) station on the southeastern Atlantic Coast or eastern Gulf Coast of the United States. When is precipitation at a maximum? Why? Are thunderstorms common or rare?

3. What are the characteristics of climate on the southeastern Asiatic coast in the subtropical latitudes? How does the precipitation cycle differ from that in comparable localities in the southeastern United States? Why is there a difference?

4. What is the natural vegetation of the humid subtropical climate of east coasts in latitudes 25° to 35°? What is a characteristic feature of the soils in this climate zone? To what other groups of soils are they most closely related?

5. What are the important characteristics of the climates of west coasts in middle latitudes (40° to 60°)? What air masses are dominant? From what direction do most air masses and cyclonic storms approach these coasts? How is this reflected in the annual temperature cycle?

6. Why does the marine west coast climate (*Cfb*) show a marked reduction in rainfall during the summer, especially between 40° and 50° latitude?

7. What type of forest vegetation is developed on windward mountain slopes in the marine west coast belts. In what way is orographic rainfall related to the development of these forests and their associated soils?

8. Describe and explain the Mediterranean climate (*Csb*) which prevails on west coasts between 30° and 40° latitude. What is unique about the annual precipitation graph of this climate? How does it compare with graphs of the tropical savanna climate (*Aw*)?

9. What is the natural vegetation of the Mediterranean climate (*Csa, Csb*)?

10. Why are dry climates developed in middle latitudes in interior continental locations? Are they related to the presence of mountain barriers? Give examples. Explain the principle of the rainshadow desert.

11. What distinction is made between extremely arid regions and semi-arid regions or steppes? What is the natural vegetation of steppes? Of the very dry middle-latitude deserts (*BWk*)?

12. How does altitude influence the degree of aridity in the dry middle-latitude regions?

13. What is noteworthy about the annual temperature cycle of the middle-latitude steppes (*BSk*) and deserts (*BWk*)? How does this cycle differ from that of the tropical deserts?

14. How may the boundary between dry and humid climates be determined? Is it a fixed line, or does it fluctuate? Of what economic importance is this boundary?

15. Of what economic value are the middle-latitude steppe lands of the world? What types of soils underlie these regions? Is the soil suitable for grain crops? What is caliche? How does it form?

16. Describe the climate located in middle latitudes in the central and eastern parts of the continents. What air masses are involved in this climate? How does season of year determine which air masses are dominant?

17. Describe the annual temperature cycle of a typical station in the humid continental climate zone (*Dfa, Dfb*). Is the range great or small? Explain. Is the average temperature of the coldest month below freezing?

18. What can be said about the day-to-day temperature fluctuations in the humid continental climate? How do these variations reflect the conflict in air masses?

19. Discuss the natural vegetation and soils of the humid continental climate (*Dfa, Dfb*) in middle latitudes. How do southerly and northerly locations differ in this respect? How do easterly and westerly locations differ?

CHAPTER **12**
Polar, Arctic, and Highland Climates

CLIMATES of group III, located at high latitudes, are controlled largely by polar and arctic air masses. They have low temperatures, usually low precipitation, and low evaporation.

11. Continental subarctic climate (Dfc, Dfd, Dwc, Dwd)

In the two great landmasses of North America and Eurasia, a vast expanse of interior continental area lies between 50° and 70° N lat. Here are the source regions for the continental polar air masses.

In winter, when excessive heat loss by radiation has resulted in the formation of the prevailing Siberian and Canadian highs, severely cold air temperatures develop over snow-covered surfaces, forming a cold, dense air mass. Typically, a severe temperature inversion prevails in winter, so that the air at, say, 5000 ft (1500 m) may be 10 F° (5 C°) warmer than air at the ground level. Low in moisture content, this air mass is stable and normally clear.

In summer, the source region is shifted farther north; air mass temperatures rise to moderately high levels, but the moisture content, although

Figure 12.1 Climographs for Ft. Vermilion, Alberta, and Yakutsk, USSR. (Data from Trewartha.)

much greater in summer, is still small by comparison with that of maritime tropical air masses.

We might expect, therefore, a climate type showing very great seasonal temperature range, with extremely severe winters and a small annual total precipitation concentrated in the warm months. This climate, called here the *continental subarctic climate*, includes four of Köppen's climate types. The largest area, including belts from Alaska to Labrador and from Scandinavia to Siberia, is classified as *Dfc*, a cold, snowy forest climate, moist all year, with cool, short summers. Less than four months of the year have averages over 50°F (10°C). A still colder climate, *Dfd*, found in northern Siberia only, has very cold winters in which the average of the coldest months is below −36.4°F (−38°C). Climates *Dwc* and *Dwd* are also cold, snowy forest climates, but with a dry winter. They are found only in northeastern Asia. The letters *c* and *d* denote a cool summer and a very cold winter, respectively.

The continental subarctic climate (*Dfc*) is well illustrated by the graph of Ft. Vermilion, Alberta, at 58° N lat. (Figure 12.1). The annual range of 74 F° (41 C°) is remarkable enough, but it is greatly exceeded by that of Yakutsk, USSR, lying in the *Dwd* climate type. The annual temperature range of the continental subarctic climate is the greatest of any on earth, reaching 110 F° (61 C°) in Siberia. Even in central Antarctica, which has the lowest temperatures on earth, the annual range is not over 65 F° (36 C°).

Absolute minimum temperatures of −70° to −80°F (−57° to −62°C) are recorded in northwestern Canada, the lowest being −81.4°F (−63°C) at Snag, Yukon on February 3, 1947. Perhaps the coldest place in the northern hemisphere is Verkhoyansk, USSR, which lies in this climate zone and has a January mean of −59°F (−51°C) and an absolute minimum recorded temperature of −93°F (−69°C).

Summer in the subarctic climate regions is very short. The warmest month average may not greatly exceed 50°F (10°C), and frosts can occur at any time during the summer. Daily maximum temperatures, however, commonly reach 70°F (21°C). At these high latitudes the sun is above the horizon

172

Figure 12.2   Distribution of permafrost in the northern hemisphere, and representative cross sections in Alaska and Asia. (From Robert F. Black, "Permafrost," Chapter 14 of P. D. Trask's *Applied Sedimentation*, John Wiley and Sons, New York, 1950.)

for sixteen to eighteen hours from May through August. (See graph on Figure 12.1.) The long hours of sunshine so accelerate the growth of plants that agriculture may be possible despite a very short growing season.

Winter is the dominant season of the continental subarctic climate. Because subfreezing monthly average temperatures occur for six or seven consecutive months, all moisture in the soil and subsoil is solidly frozen to depths of many feet. (See Figure 12.6.) Summer warmth is insufficient to thaw more than the upper few feet so that a condition of perennially frozen ground, or *permafrost*, prevails over large parts of this and the tundra regions to the north. Seasonal thaw penetrates from 2 to 14 ft (0.6–4m), depending on location and nature of the ground. This shallow zone of alternate freeze and thaw is termed the *active zone*.

The distribution of permafrost in the northern hemisphere is shown in Figure 12.2. Three zones are recognized. Continuous permafrost, which extends without gaps or interruptions under all topographic features, coincides largely with the tundra climate (*ET*), but also includes a large part of the continental subarctic climate (*Dfc, Dfd, Dwd*) in Siberia. Discontinuous permafrost, which occurs in patches separated by frost-free zones under lakes and rivers, occupies much of the continental subarctic climate (*Dfc*) zone of North America and Eurasia. Sporadic occurrence of permafrost in small patches extends into the southern limits of the continental subarctic climate.

Depth of permafrost reaches 1000 to 1500 ft (300 to 450 m) in the continuous zone near latitude 70° (Figure 12.2). Much of this permanent frost is an inheritance from more severe conditions of the last ice age, but some permafrost bodies may be growing under existing climate conditions.

Permafrost presents problems of great concern in engineering and building construction in these cold regions. Buildings must be insulated underneath to protect the ground moisture beneath from melting; otherwise, the building might literally be engulfed in mud. Another serious problem is in the behavior of streams in winter. As the surface of streams or springs freezes over, the water beneath bursts out from place to place, freezing into huge accumulations of ice. Highways are thus made impassable. Scraping of insulating peat, forest litter, and vegetative cover from the frozen ground to make roads and air fields may result in dire consequences. The summer sun thaws the bare ground, which turns into a liquid mud, often growing into sizable lake basins by melting and sapping around the edges of the exposed areas.

Most of the source areas of the continental polar air masses are in regions of less than 20 in (50 cm) of precipitation annually, whereas the northerly portions have less than 10 in (25 cm). Although this amount would result in dry deserts at low latitudes, evaporation is greatly reduced by prevailingly low temperatures. Thus, essentially humid moisture conditions of air and soil prevail.

Precipitation is largely cyclonic in type and shows a very definite maximum in the summer months. Snowfall, although conspicuous in winter because it remains upon the ground, accounts for only a fraction of an inch of precipitation per month in the coldest months. Cyclonic storms crossing these areas bring little precipitation at this season. In summer, cyclonic rains are frequent, although thunderstorms are few.

The continental regime of climate modified by a polar influence is dominant in the continental subarctic climate. The thermohyet diagram of Yakutsk, Siberia (Figure 8.10*B*) is a good illustration.

The subarctic climate zone coincides with a great belt of needleleaf forest, often referred to as *boreal forest* (Figure 16.12), and open lichen woodland, the *taiga* (Figure 16.25). Trees tend to be small, so that they are economically of less value for lumber than for pulpwood.

Soils of the *podzol* group are associated with the arctic needleleaf forest. As explained before, these soils are strongly leached and of acid type. They are light gray and have a very distinct leached layer beneath the uppermost layer of humus and forest litter. These soils are extremely poor from the standpoint of agriculture. Added to the natural inadequacy of soils of this region is a great prevalence of swamps and lakes left by the departed ice sheets (Figure 23.16). Some rock surfaces were scoured by ice which stripped off the soil entirely. Elsewhere rock basins were formed, or previous stream courses dammed, making countless lakes. Insufficient geologic time has elapsed for good drainage even to begin to be reestablished over large areas.

12. Marine subarctic climate (EM)

In Chapter 8, the remarkable properties of the middle-latitude equable climatic regime were described. When traced farther poleward into the subarctic latitude zone, so as to span the latitude range 45° to 65°, the equable regime constitutes a distinct climate type, the *marine subarctic climate*, marked by unusually large total annual precipitation and an unusually small annual temperature range for such high latitudes.

The marine subarctic climate is dominated by maritime polar (mP) air masses throughout the year. The climate distribution actually coincides rather well with the mP air mass source regions in the North Atlantic, North Pacific, and the Southern Ocean. Important in defining the characteristics of this climate is the persistence of cloudy skies and strong winds, and the high percentage of days with precipitation.

The marine subarctic climate is not designated as a separate variety in the Köppen system, which includes it in the tundra climate (*ET*). Recent recognition by geographers of the marine subarctic climate has been coupled with the suggestion that it be entered in the Köppen system with the symbol *EM*, the letter "M" to mean an equable marine regime.

The marine subarctic climate is found on limited stretches of windward coasts, on islands, and over wide expanses of ocean in latitudes 50° to 60° in the Bering Sea, and latitudes 55° to 75° in the North Atlantic, touching points on the south Greenland coast, north Iceland, and extreme northern Norway. In the southern hemisphere, the marine subarctic climate occupies almost no land. The few representative stations are found in the southernmost tip of South America, the Falkland Islands, South Georgia Island, and a number of other small islands.

Representative stations in the marine subarctic climate qualify as belonging in the E climates of Köppen, for the warmest-month means are all below 50°F (10°C). In contrast to the typical tundra climate (ET) the annual ranges are all much smaller, the winters much milder, and the annual precipitation totals much larger. These contrasts are brought out strikingly in the comparison of two stations in Figure 12.3. Coldest month temperature mean is not below 20°F (−7°C).

Thermohyet diagrams of marine subarctic stations are shown in Figure 8.6 (C,E); they occupy a unique position well to the right of the cold climates and well below the rainy climates of lower latitudes. Combined with low evaporation rates, the large precipitation yields a large water surplus.

Soils and vegetation of the marine subarctic climate are essentially of the same tundra varieties associated with the tundra climate, treated below. The landscape is treeless and gives the impression of great barrenness, but it is nevertheless surprisingly rich in the variety of plant species that exist in the layer close to the ground.

13. Tundra climate (ET)

The northern continental fringes of North America and Eurasia from the Arctic Circle to about the 75th parallel lie within the outer zone of control of arctic-type air masses, whose source region covers the Arctic Ocean and Greenland. To the south lie the continental polar (cP) and maritime polar (mP) air mass source regions. The land fringes are thus in a frontal zone, which has been known as the *arctic front*, but which may be more simply identified as belonging to a widely shifting polar front, well developed over the northern Pacific and Atlantic oceans. Here many intense east-moving cyclonic storms are developed, and much bad weather may be expected.

These conditions produce a *tundra climate*, described by Köppen with the symbol *ET*. This is a polar climate in which the average temperature of the warmest month is below 50°F (10°C), but above 32°F (0°C).

The tundra climate is illustrated by the temperature-precipitation graph of Upernivik at 73° N lat.

Figure 12.3 Climographs for Upernivik, Greenland, 73° N lat. and Cumberland Bay, South Georgia Island, 54° S lat. (Data from Blair and Meteorological Office of Great Britain.)

on the west Greenland coast (Figure 12.3). Note that (*a*) temperature range is large, but not nearly as great as in the continental subarctic climate; (*b*) the warmest month averages are just over 40°F (4°C) and the coldest month average is well below 0°F (−18°C); and (*c*) precipitation total is less than 10 in (25 cm), with an increased amount falling during and after the warm season. Nearness to the Arctic Ocean explains the somewhat more moderate temperature range and minimum, compared to the continental centers. Coolness of the summer is explained by the nearness to the large ocean body, keeping air temperatures down despite large receipts of solar energy at this latitude near summer solstice. Possibly a more persistent cloud cover is also a factor.

Thermohyet diagrams of the tundra climate combine the continental and polar regimes, as seen in the diagrams for Grønfjorden, Spitzbergen, and Barrow Point, Alaska (Figure 8.11B,C). Tundra climate of the southern hemisphere is more equable, lacking the continental influence, as seen in the thermohyet diagram for the South Orkney Islands (Figure 8.6D).

Vegetation of the treeless tundra consists of grasses, sedges, and lichens, along with shrubs of willow (Figure 16.28). Traced southward the vegetation changes into birch-lichen woodland, then into the needleleaf forest. In some places a distinct tree line separates the forest and tundra. Coinciding approximately with the 50° isotherm of the warmest month, this line has been used by Köppen as a boundary between *Df* and *ET* climates.

Tundra soils are noteworthy in that the soil particles are produced almost entirely by mechanical breakup of the parent rock and have suffered little or no chemical alteration. Grayish loam and blue-gray clay layers are present with much peat. Continual freezing and thawing of soil moisture has been responsible for disintegration of the soil particles. Like the soils of the northern continental interiors, soils of the tundra are affected by the permanently frozen, or permafrost, condition (Figure 12.2). The permafrost layer is more than 1000 ft (300 m) thick over most of this region; seasonal thaw reaches only 4 to 24 in (10–60 cm) below the surface.

Geomorphic processes have a somewhat distinctive pattern in the tundra regions, and a variety of curious landforms results. Under a protective sod of small plants, the soil water melts in summer, producing a thick mud which may flow downslope to create bulges and terraces without breaking through the surface. This process is known as *solifluction*, or *sludging*, and forms *solifluction terraces* and *lobes* on slopes (Figures 12.4 and 19.19). In the desert tundra, solifluction occurs without the confining cover and may be described as a layer of thick mud creeping down the slopes. Observers who have studied this flowage find that it is most rapid at midday, the mud flowing at a rate of several feet per hour and carrying along large blocks of rock (Figure 19.21).

The freeze and thaw of water in the soil gives

Figure 12.5 Ice-wedge polygons on Wollaston Peninsula, Victoria Island (lat. 70° N. long. 112° W), viewed from the air. (Photograph by A. L. Washburn, Arctic Institute of North America.)

rise to a curious system of polygonal cracks in flat ground (Figure 12.5). They may result from the shrinkage of the clay as water is withdrawn to form ice crystals in lenses or layers within the soil (Figure 12.6). The resulting pattern is termed *polygonal ground*. On hill and mountain summits the cracks are filled with stones, which seem to be gradually sorted and pushed to the sides of each

Figure 12.4 Solifluction, a slow soil flowage, has produced this lobate form on a tundra slope on Mt. Pelly, Victoria Island (lat. 69° N, long. 104° W). Surface of lobe stands about 6 ft (1.8 m) above surrounding slope. (Photograph by A. L. Washburn, Arctic Institute of North America.)

Figure 12.6 This vertical river-bank exposure near Livengood, Alaska, in the subarctic climate region reveals a V-shaped ice wedge surrounded by layered silt of alluvial origin. (Photograph by T. L. Péwé, U.S. Geological Survey.)

polygon during alternate freeze and thaw of soil water. These forms are called *stone rings*, or *stone polygons*. On slopes, the stone rings are drawn downslope to produce *stone stripes*, appearing from the air like giant hachures on the ground.

14. Icecap climate (EF)

Three vast regions of ice exist on the earth. These are the Greenland and Antarctic continental icecaps and the large area of floating sea ice in the Arctic Ocean (Figures 23.9 and 12.9). The continental icecaps differ in various ways, both physically and climatically, from the polar sea ice and can be separately treated. Glacial and topographic features of Greenland and Antarctica are treated in Chapter 23.

Icecap climate has by far the lowest average annual temperature of all global climates. Designated by Köppen *EF*, or polar climate of perpetual frost, this climate has no monthly average above freezing (32°F, 0°C). Available records indicate mean annual temperatures of −20° to −30°F (−30° to −35°C) for the Greenland icecap, but about −9°F (−23°C) for the Arctic Ocean. Compare this with the 10° to 25°F (−12° to −4°C) mean annual temperature of the tundra climate. The higher Arctic Ocean temperature is due to its sea-level altitude and the moderating influence of the ocean water, which can supply a continuous amount of heat conducted through the floating ice to the air.

The annual temperature graph for a Greenland icecap station, "Eismitte," is shown in Figure 12.7. This information was gathered by a German expedition under the direction of Alfred Wegener in the years 1929 through 1931. Note that only in three months of the year did the mean monthly temperatures rise above 0°F (−18°C), and then only to a July maximum of 12°F (−11°C). The coldest month was February, with −53°F (−47°C), making an annual range of 65F° (36C°).

A shallow layer of air over the ice sheet is chilled severely and at times flows downslope under the influence of gravity toward the margins as a severe blizzard wind. It is reported that so great is the chill of the ice upon the air that tiny ice crystals sometimes form within a few feet of the ground. These may make a "snowstorm," above which the head and shoulders of a man rise clear. Driving blizzard winds pack the sandlike snow into a hard, smooth pavement.

Cyclonic storms frequently penetrate Greenland, bringing precipitation to the icecap. The principal nourishment of the ice sheet is from this source.

Climate of the Antarctic icecap was little understood until a number of weather stations were maintained in the International Geophysical Year of 1957–1958. Temperatures in the interior have

Figure 12.7 Temperature graphs for five icecap stations. (Data from Trewartha; *I. G. Y. Bulletin*; and Weatherwise, vol. 16, 1963.)

proved to be far lower than any place on earth. The Russian meteorological station "Vostok," located about 800 mi (1300 km) from the south pole at an elevation of 11,440 ft (3488 m), may be the world's coldest spot (Figure 12.7). Here a record low of −125.3°F (−87.4°C) was observed on August 25, 1958. Note that this minimum value occurred near the end of the long polar night. At the pole itself (Amundsen-Scott Station), July, August, and September of 1957 had averages about −76°F (−60°C) (Figure 12.7). Temperatures run roughly 40 F° (22 C°) higher, month for month, at Little America Station because it is located close to the Ross Sea and is at low elevation.

A remarkable feature of the high, antarctic interior is the intense chilling of air close to the snow surface. A strong temperature inversion develops in winter, so that the air near the surface may be 50 to 60 F° (28 to 33 C°) colder than air a few hundred feet higher. Downslope flow of this heavy, cold air layer causes blizzard winds to develop in favorable valley locations.

Sea ice

Greatly increased utilization and study of high latitudes by both military forces and civilian scientist research groups has brought to attention the

Figure 12.8 The U.S. Coast Guard icebreaker Northwind forces a passage through McClure Strait, Banks Island, Canadian Northwest Territory, in mid-August. To the left is an open lead. Cutting across from left to right is a rugged zone of pressure ridges. (Official U.S. Coast Guard photo.)

phenomenon of floating sea ice. Supply of arctic and antarctic outposts by ship, maintenance of observing stations on floating ice masses, and submarine operation in the polar sea are forms of activity influenced by sea ice.

The oceanographer distinguishes *sea ice*, formed by direct freezing of ocean water, from *icebergs*, and *ice islands*, which are bodies of land ice broken free from tide-level glaciers and continental ice shelves. Aside from differences in origin, a major difference between sea ice and floating masses of land ice is in thickness. Sea ice, which begins to form when the surface water is cooled to temperatures of about $28\frac{1}{2}°$ F ($-2°$ C) is limited in thickness to about 15 ft (5 m), because heat is supplied from the underlying water as rapidly as it is lost upward, once an insulating layer of floating ice has been formed.

Pack ice is the name given to ice that completely covers the sea surface (Figure 12.8). Under the forces of wind and currents, pack ice breaks up into individual patches, termed *ice floes*. The narrow strips of open water between such floes are *leads*. Where ice floes are forcibly brought together by winds, the ice margins buckle and turn upward into pressure ridges resembling walls or irregular hummocks (Figure 12.8). The difficulties of travel on foot across the polar sea ice are made extreme by the presence of such obstacles. The surface zone of sea ice is composed of fresh water, the salt having been excluded in the process of freezing.

The Arctic Ocean, which is surrounded by landmasses, is normally covered by pack ice throughout the year, although open leads are numerous in the summer (Figure 12.9). The relatively warm North Atlantic drift maintains an ice-free zone off the northern coast of Norway. The situation is quite different in the antarctic,

Figure 12.9 Sea ice of the Arctic Ocean. Common tracks of icebergs are shown by arrows. A tilted homolographic projection is used for this map. (Based on data of the National Research Council. From A. N. Strahler, *The Earth Sciences*, Harper and Row, New York.)

where a vast open ocean bounds the sea ice zone on the equatorward margin (Figure 12.10). Because the ice floes can drift freely north into warmer waters, the antarctic ice pack does not spread far beyond 60° S lat. in the cold season. In March, close to the end of the warm season, the ice margin shrinks to a narrow zone bordering the Antarctic continent.

Icebergs and ice islands

Icebergs, formed by the breaking off, or *calving*, of blocks from a valley glacier or tongue of an icecap, may be as thick as several hundred feet. Being only slightly less dense than sea water, the iceberg floats very low in the water, about five-sixths of its bulk lying below water level (Figure 12.11). The ice is fresh, of course, since it is formed of compacted and recrystallized snow.

In the northern hemisphere, icebergs are derived largely from glacier tongues of the Greenland icecap (Figure 12.9). They drift slowly south with the Labrador and Greenland currents and may find their way into the North Atlantic in the vicinity of the Grand Banks of Newfoundland. Icebergs

Figure 12.10 Sea ice of the antarctic region. (Data from National Academy of Sciences and American Geographical Society. From A. N. Strahler, *The Earth Sciences*, Harper and Row, New York.)

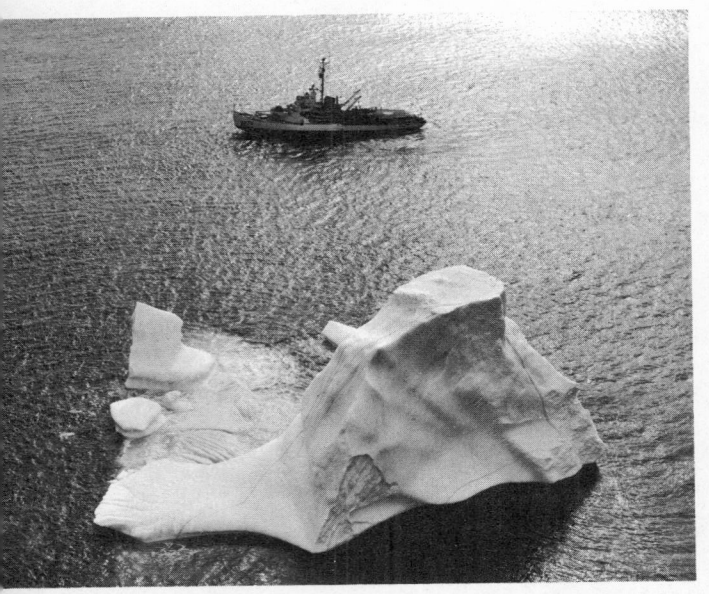

Figure 12.11 This great iceberg in the east Arctic Ocean dwarfs the U.S. Coast Guard icebreaker Eastwind. (Official U.S. Coast Guard photo.)

of the antarctic are distinctly different. Whereas those of the North Atlantic are irregular in shape and therefore present rather peaked outlines above water, the antarctic icebergs are commonly *tabular* in form, with flat tops and steep clifflike sides (Figure 12.12). This is because tabular bergs are parts of ice shelves, the great, floating platelike extensions of the continental icecap (Chapter 23). In dimensions, a large tabular berg of the antarctic may be tens of miles broad and over 2000 ft (600 m) thick, with an ice wall rising 200 to 300 ft (60 to 90 m) above sea level.

Somewhat related in origin to the tabular bergs of the antarctic are *ice islands* of the North Polar Sea. These huge plates of floating ice may be 20 mi (32 km) across and have an area of 300 sq mi (800 sq km). The bordering ice cliff, 20 to 30 ft (6 to 10 m) above the surrounding pack ice, indicates an ice thickness of 200 ft (60 m) or more. The few ice islands known are probably derived from a shelf of land-fast glacial ice attached to Ellesmere Island, about 83° N lat. (Figure 12.9). The ice islands move slowly with the water drift of the Arctic Ocean and a charting of their tracks reveals much about circulation in that ocean. (See path of T-3 in Figure 12.9). As permanent and sturdy platforms, ice islands serve as bases of

Figure 12.12   This tabular iceberg was observed near the Bay of Whales, Little America, Antarctica, in January 1947. (Official U.S. Coast Guard photo.)

scientific researches from which observations of oceanography, meteorology, and geophysics can be carried out over long periods.

Highland climates

As explained in earlier chapters, increasing elevation brings a great reduction in both pressure and temperature. Thus, climates change greatly within a vertical range of a few thousand feet. In a general way, a rise of altitude is equivalent to an increase in latitude, so that the tundra and icecap climate equivalents can be found among the glaciers of a mountain mass above timber line. In one major respect, however, the analogy is inadequate. Whereas intensity of insolation is progressively less toward the poles, it is increased at higher altitudes. Thus, daily temperature ranges are excessive at high altitudes in middle and low latitudes, but are much less pronounced in equivalent arctic climates.

Pressure and temperature

As stated in Chapter 3, for every 900 ft (275 m) of increased elevation the barometric pressure falls $\frac{1}{30}$ of its value (Figure 3.8).

The physiological effects of a pressure decrease are well known from the experiences of flying and mountain climbing. The principal influence is through an insufficient amount of oxygen to supply the blood through the lungs. At altitudes of 10,000 to 15,000 ft (3000 to 4500 m) mountain sickness (altitude sickness) occurs, characterized by weakness, headache, nosebleed, or nausea. Persons who remain at these altitudes for a day or two normally adjust to the conditions, but physical exertion is always accompanied by shortness of breath.

At reduced pressures the boiling point of water or other liquids is reduced so that cooking time of various foods is greatly lengthened.

The table gives some data on pressure and boiling point relationships. From these figures it is evident that the use of pressure cookers will be of great value about 5000 ft (1500 m) wherever the cooking involves boiling of water.

Elevation		Pressure		Boiling Temperature	
Ft	M	In	Cm	°F	°C
Sea level	0	29.9	76	212	100
1000	300	28.8	73	210	99
3000	900	26.8	68	206	97
5000	1500	24.9	63	203	95
10,000	3000	20.7	53	194	90

From the standpoint of weather and climate, reduced atmospheric pressure is principally effective in that the thinner atmosphere, with relatively less carbon dioxide, water vapor, and dust, absorbs and deflects less solar energy and thus permits a high intensity of insolation at the ground.

Increasing intensity of insolation at higher elevation has a profound influence upon temperature relations. Surfaces exposed to sunlight heat rapidly and intensely, shaded surfaces are quickly and severely cooled. This results in rapid air heating during the day and rapid cooling at night at high-mountain locations (Figure 12.13). Thus at mountain vacation resorts not only is the air pure and the landscape features sharply outlined as if washed clean, but the cool nights and warm days are stimulating physically.

The contrast between exposed and shaded surfaces is particularly noteworthy at high altitudes. It is said that temperatures of objects in the sun and in the shade differ by as much as 40 to 50 F° (22 to 28 C°).

Increased intensity of insolation is accompanied by an increase in intensity of violet and ultraviolet rays. Sunburn is very much more rapid above 5000 ft (1500 m) than at sea level, as many a person has learned by unfortunate experience. The red and infrared rays of the spectrum, on the other hand, are relatively less intensified by increased elevation because they are better able to pass through a dense atmosphere.

A general decrease in air temperature with elevation has been discussed in Chapter 3, where

Figure 12.13 Daily maximum and minimum temperatures for mountain stations in Peru, 15° S lat. (After Mark Jefferson, *Geographical Review.*)

it was stated that the average lapse rate is about 3½ F° per 1000 ft (2 C° per 300 m). Thus, we might expect a station 10,000 ft (3000 m) in elevation to have a temperature about 35 F° (20 C°) below that of a nearby sea-level station. Actually it is somewhat less than this.

In high altitudes of the equatorial regions, annual range of temperature is very small, much as in the wet equatorial rainforest climates which surround these tropical mountains at low elevations (Figure 12.14). The range at Quito, Ecuador, is thus only 0.7 F° (0.4 C°) for the year. Compare this with Figure 10.1.

The effect of increasing altitude at low latitude is seen in the thermohyet diagrams of Figure 8.7. A high degree of thermal equability is maintained as the diagram is shifted down and to the left.

In middle and high latitudes, on the other hand, a wide annual temperature variation is to be expected, following the marked variations of insolation from summer to winter, as the Longs Peak graph shows (Figure 12.14).

Precipitation

The general influence of increased elevation is first to bring an increase in precipitation, at least for the first few thousand feet of elevation. This is due to the production of orographic rainfall, generated by the forced ascent of air masses and the resultant cooling of the air. (See Chapter 6.) Above elevations of 6000 to 10,000 ft (1800 to 3000 m), which form the zone of heaviest rainfall in low latitudes, precipitation increase begins to slacken with elevation, owing to the inability of air at the lower temperatures to hold, and therefore to give up, as much moisture.

Generally speaking, mountains and plateaus are humid climate zones. This is particularly striking in an arid or semi-arid region, where the mountains form islands of humid climate surrounded by desert or steppe. Reduction in temperatures results in reduced evaporation, so that a humid condition prevails.

The influence of mountains upon precipitation is strikingly illustrated by the state of California (Figure 12.15), whose topography is greatly diversified. Note that in the Great Valley and Death Valley precipitation is less than 10 in (25 cm), but on the west slopes of the Sierra Nevada and Klamath Mountains it is over 70 in (175 cm).

From the standpoint of river flow and floods, mountain climates are of greatest importance in middle latitudes. The higher ranges serve as snow storage areas, keeping back the precipitation until early or midsummer, releasing it slowly through melting, and thus aiding in the maintenance of continuous river flow. As melting proceeds to successively higher levels, the meltwater is supplied

Figure 12.14 A comparison of rainfall and temperature characteristics of two mountain stations. (Data from Trewartha.)

Figure 12.15 The effect of mountain topography on rainfall is well shown by the state of California. Isohyets in inches. (Rainfall map after U.S. Dept. of Agriculture, *Yearbook of American Agriculture*, 1941.)

to the drainage basin. Among the snow-fed rivers of the United States are the Columbia, Snake, Missouri, Platte, Arkansas, and Colorado. In the eastern United States, the Appalachians serve in a similar but less pronounced fashion for the Ohio and other rivers. Here, however, the snow is melted in late spring and has no influence in the middle and late summer.

Vegetation and life zones

It has been observed that increased elevation brings climatic conditions approximately equivalent to those encountered by increase in latitude. Consequently there exist distinct zones of natural vegetation which, in a general way, recapitulate the vegetation types of increasingly high latitudes.

Effects of increasing altitude on vegetation in wet equatorial lands are illustrated by an example from southern Peru (Figure 12.16*A*). Two other important regions besides the Andes of South America are the Ruwenzori Range of central Africa and the central mountain range of New Guinea. Where exposed to prevailing winds (trades) or to seasonal winds (wet monsoon) which bring moisture of maritime air masses (mT, mE) precipitation increases greatly with elevation.[1] As a result, rainforest extends high up the mountain slopes. Between 4000 and 6000 ft (1200 and 1800 m) the rainforest gradually changes into *montane forest*, which resembles the temperate rainforest found at low elevations farther poleward (Chapter 16). Montane forest is lower and less dense than equatorial rainforest and becomes still lower with increasing altitude. Tree ferns and bamboos are conspicuous. Epiphytes (air plants) are abundant. Mosses increase with altitude, giving what is termed *mossy forest* in the zone of persistent mists and high relative humidities. Near its upper limit the montane forest trees become dwarfed, constituting *elfin forest*, and are densely festooned with mosses. Above the forest limit, which occurs about at 12,000 ft (3600 m), there sets in a treeless vegetation which may be alpine tundra, scrub, grassland, or heath. (See Chapter 16 for a description of these vegetation forms.) Still higher, the alpine zone gives way to the zone of perpetual snow (Figure 12.16*A*). The snow line lies at about 16,000 ft (5000 m) in central Peru; about at 15,000 ft (4600 m) in the Ruwenzori Range.

In middle latitudes, where steppe or desert exist at low elevations, the zonation is particularly striking. Figure 12.16*B* shows the vegetation zones of the Colorado Plateau region of northern Arizona and adjacent states. Zone names, elevations, dominant forest trees, and annual precipitation data are given in the figure. Ecologists have set up a series of *life zones*, whose names suggest the similarities of these zones with latitude zones encountered in poleward travel on a meridian. The Hudsonian zone, 9500 to 11,500 ft (2900 to 3500 m), bears a needleleaf forest essentially similar to subarctic needleleaf (boreal) forest. Soils are similarly of podzolic type. As the limit of forest, or tree line, is approached the coniferous trees take on a stunted appearance and decrease in height to low shrublike forms.

A vegetation zone of *alpine meadows* (alpine tundra) lies above tree line and resembles in many ways the arctic tundra. The snow line is encountered at about 9000 to 10,000 ft (2750 to 3000 m)

---

[1] Altitude stations shown in the thermohyet diagrams of Figure 8.7 are in leeward positions and do not show this effect.

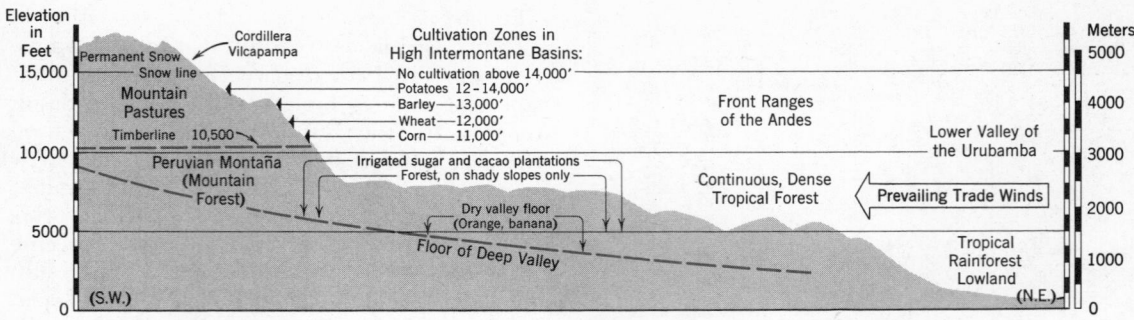

Figure 12.16A Altitude zoning of climates in the equatorial Andes of southern Peru, 10°-15° S lat. (After Isaiah Bowman, *The Andes of Southern Peru*, 1916.)

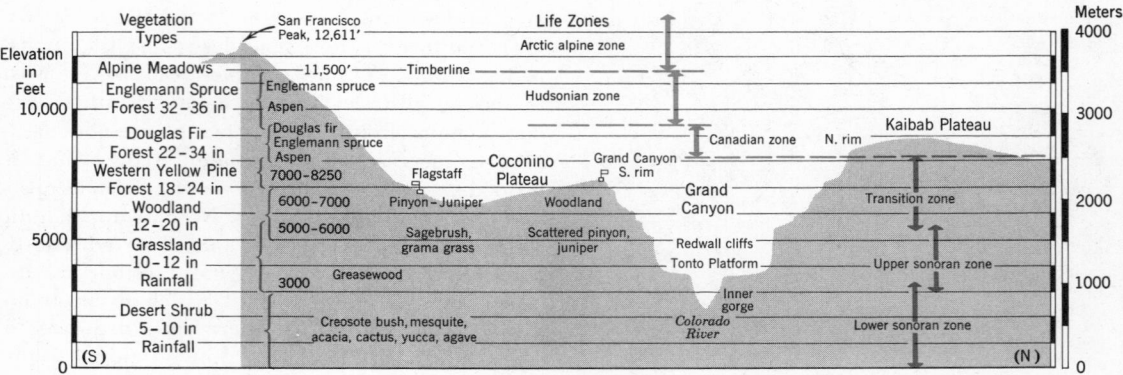

Figure 12.16B Altitude zoning of mountain and plateau climates in the arid southwestern United States. Grand Canyon-San Francisco Mountain district of northern Arizona. (After G. A. Pearson, C. H. Merriam, and A. N. Strahler.)

in these middle latitudes, which is of course much lower than at the equator. Poleward the snow line decreases in altitude, eventually reaching sea level in the vicinity of the Arctic Circle.

REFERENCES FOR FURTHER STUDY

Bowman, I (1916), *The Andes of Peru*, Henry Holt and Co., New York, 336 pp.

Peattie, R. (1936), *Mountain geography. A critique and field study*, Harvard Univ. Press, Cambridge, Mass., 257 pp.

Kimble, G. H. T. and D. Good, eds. (1955), *Geography of the Northlands*, Amer. Geog. Soc., Special Publ. No. 32, John Wiley and Sons, New York, 534 pp.

Baird, P. D. (1964), *The polar world*, John Wiley and Sons, New York, 328 pp.

Bird, J. B. (1967), *The physiography of arctic Canada*, The Johns Hopkins Press, Baltimore, Md., 336 pp.

REVIEW QUESTIONS

1. Summarize and explain the characteristics of the continental subarctic climate. How do the Köppen symbols *Dfc*, *Dfd*, *Dwc*, and *Dwd* distinguish varieties of this climate? What is particularly noteworthy about the annual temperature cycle? Explain the excessively low winter temperatures. Where is the coldest place in the northern hemisphere?

2. What is perennially frozen ground, or permafrost? What is the origin of permafrost? How great a depth of ground is thawed during the summers in the continental subarctic climate? What are some of the engineering problems associated with permafrost?

3. How does the annual total of precipitation in the northern continental centers compare with that in the tropical deserts? How does evaporation compare in these two regions?

4. Describe the boreal forest and lichen woodland. What is the taiga? What types of soils are found in the continental subarctic climate regions? How has glaciation affected the surfaces of these regions?

5. What are the characteristics of the marine subarctic climate? How is the equability of this climate explained? Compare the marine subarctic climate with the tundra climate.

6. Describe the tundra climate along continental fringes between 65° and 75° N lat. What air masses interact in this zone? In what two regions is cyclonic activity strongly concentrated?

7. Compare the annual temperature cycle of the tundra climate with that of the continental subarctic climate? Compare ranges, warmest month averages, and coldest month averages.

8. What is the tundra? What types of plants are found on the tundra? What kinds of soils are developed here? Describe permafrost conditions in the tundra regions. To what depth is the soil moisture frozen over most of this area? To what depth does the annual summer thaw extend?

9. What is the tree line of the arctic regions? With what monthly isotherm is it approximately identified?

10. What are some of the unusual geomorphic processes active in the tundra regions? Explain the following terms: solifluction, solifluction terraces, polygonal ground, stone rings, stone stripes.

11. What are the essential characteristics of icecap climate? Describe temperature conditions throughout the year. With what air mass source regions is this climate associated?

12. Describe briefly the Greenland and Antarctic icecaps. How is the Greenland icecap nourished, that is, where does the moisture for the snow fields come from?

13. How is sea ice different from ice of icebergs and ice islands? What is the thickness of sea ice? Why is it limited? Describe pack ice, ice floes, leads, and pressure ridges.

14. Explain how the distribution of sea ice differs between the Arctic Ocean and the Antarctic Ocean.

15. How are icebergs formed? What proportion is submerged? Compare the form and source of bergs found in the North Atlantic with those of the antarctic region.

16. What is an ice island? What is its origin? How may it serve the purposes of scientific research?

17. Discuss the influence of increasing altitude upon air pressure. Describe the effects of high altitudes upon physiological processes and upon the boiling point of liquids.

18. What is the effect of increasing altitude upon air temperature? How are maximum and minimum daily temperatures affected? How is the mean annual temperature affected? Is the annual range significantly changed by increased elevation?

19. What influence has increased elevation upon precipitation? Explain this effect. Cite examples of variation of precipitation with elevation.

20. Explain how snow storage in high mountains affects the flow of rivers. Name some snow-fed rivers of the United States.

21. Describe the influence of increased altitude upon natural vegetation and crop cultivation in equatorial regions, using the Andes of Peru as an illustration. What is montane forest? Mossy forest?

22. Describe the influence of increased altitude upon vegetation in the southwestern United States, using the Grand Canyon-San Francisco Mountains region as an illustration. How does the elevation of the alpine meadow zone here compare with that of the upper limit of pastures in the Andes?

23. At what elevation is the snow line encountered near the equator? In middle latitudes? In high latitudes?

CHAPTER 13
Soils and Soil-Forming Processes

AN understanding of fundamental principles of soil science, or *pedology*, is indispensable to a geographer. Soils constitute a major geographical factor, influencing by their fertility and special qualities, not only whether a population can be fed, clothed, and housed but also the particular types of food and fiber or lumber products that can be obtained from a region. The systematic study of soils logically follows a study of climates because climate is a primary factor in soil making.

The soil as a dynamic body

Many persons think of the soil as a lifeless, residual layer, which has somehow accumulated over a long period of time and which merely holds a supply of things necessary for plant growth. As soil science has developed, however, it has become known that the soil is a dynamic layer in which many complex chemical, physical, and biological activities are going on constantly. Far from being a static, lifeless zone, it is a changing and developing body. We know now that soils become adjusted to conditions of climate, landform, and vegetation and will change internally when those controlling conditions change.

Figure 13.1   Bedrock, residual overburden, and true soil.

The soil scientist restricts the word *soil*, or *solum*, to the surface material, which, over a long period of years, has come to have distinctive layers, or horizons (Figure 13.1). A soil has certain distinctive physical, chemical, and biological qualities, which permit it to support plant growth and which set it off from the infertile substratum, which may consist of *overburden* or solid *bedrock* lying beneath. (See Chapter 17.) The true soil is composed both of mineral and organic particles, whereas the underlying material may be, and usually is, wholly mineral matter.

Soil is made up of substances existing in three states: solid, liquid, and gaseous. For plant growth a proper balance of all three states of matter is necessary.

The solid portion of soil is both inorganic and organic. Weathering of rock produces the inorganic particles that give a soil the main part of its weight and volume (Figure 13.1). These fragments range from gravel and sand down to tiny colloidal particles too small to be seen by an optical microscope. The organic solids consist of both living and decayed plant and animal materials, most being plant roots, fungi, bacteria, worms, insects, and rodents. Colloidal particles of organic matter share with inorganic colloidal particles an important function in soil chemistry.

The liquid portion of soil, the *soil solution*, is a complex chemical solution necessary for many important activities that go on in the soil. Soil without water cannot have these chemical reactions, or can it support life. Gases in the open pore spaces of the soil form the third essential component. They are principally the gases of the atmosphere, together with gases liberated by biological and chemical activity in the soil.

For an understanding of soils, information is needed about (1) the physical-chemical properties and materials of soils, and (2) processes that make and maintain soils.

Physical-chemical make-up of soils

Although a minor factor in itself, *soil color* is perhaps the characteristic that is first noticed about a soil. Color can tell much about how a soil is formed and what it is made of. Soil horizons are

TABLE 13.1 SOIL TEXTURE GRADES

(U.S. Department of Agriculture)

Name of Grade	Diameter, In	Diameter, Mm
Coarse gravel	Above 0.08	Above 2
Fine gravel	0.04–0.08	1–2
Coarse sand	0.02–0.04	0.5–1
Medium sand	0.01–0.02	0.25–0.5
Fine sand	0.004–0.01	0.1–0.25
Very fine sand	0.002–0.004	0.05–0.1
Silt	0.000,08–0.002	0.002–0.05
Clay	Below 0.000,08	Below 0.002

Figure 13.3 Typical compositions of five soil texture classes. These examples are shown as lettered points on Figure 13.2. (After U.S. Dept. of Agriculture, *Yearbook of American Agriculture*, 1938.)

usually distinguishable by color differences. One sequence of colors ranges from white, through brown, to black as a result of an increasing content of *humus* which is finely divided, partially decomposed organic matter. Abundance of humus depends in a general way on luxuriance of vegetation and upon intensity of microbial activity, which in turn depend on climate. Thus we find that in middle latitudes, soils range from black or dark brown in the cool, humid areas to light brown or gray in the semi-arid steppe lands and deserts.

Desert soils have little humus.

Reds and yellows are common colors in soils and are the result of small quantities of iron compounds. The red color is particularly associated with *sesquioxide of iron* (Fe_2O_3), whereas the yellow color may indicate the presence of this same iron compound combined with water (*hydrated iron oxide*). Red color indicates that the soil is well drained, but locally the color may be

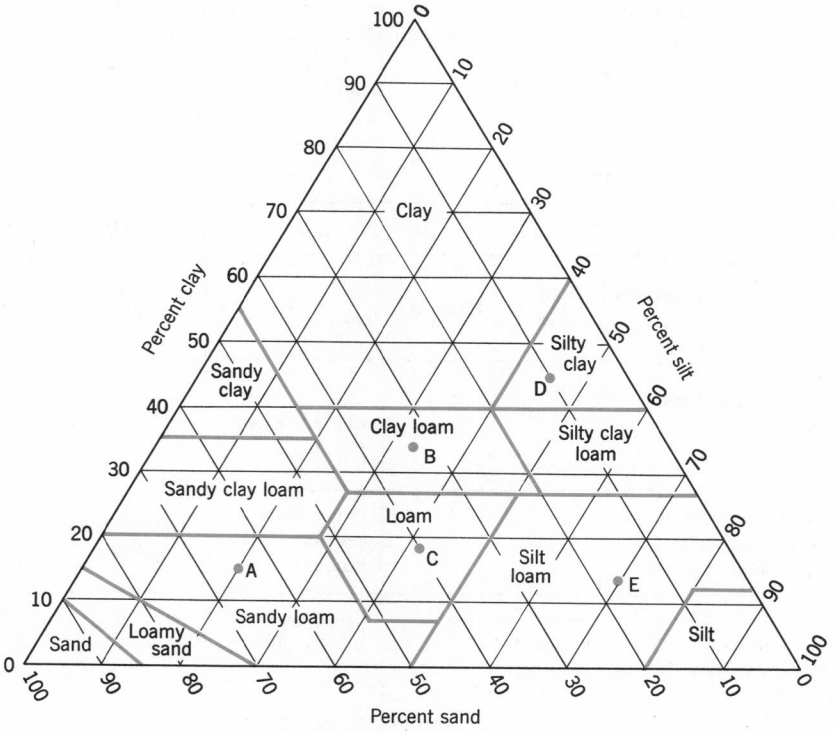

Figure 13.2 Texture classes shown as areas bounded by heavy lines on a triangular graph. (See also Figure 13.3.) (From U.S. Department of Agriculture and Millar, Turk, and Foth, *Fundamentals of Soil Science*, John Wiley and Sons, New York.)

derived from a red source rock such as a red shale or sandstone.

Grayish and bluish colors in soils of humid climates often mean the presence of reduced iron compounds (such as FeO) in the soil and indicate poor drainage or bog conditions. Grayish soils in dry climates mean a meager amount of humus; a white color may be a result of the deposit of salts in the soil. Although some recently formed soils retain the color of the parent overburden or bedrock, the color of fully developed soils is independent of what lies beneath.

Soil texture, a major characteristic of the soil, refers to particle sizes composing the soil. Particles are classified as various grades of gravel, sand, silt, and clay, in decreasing order of size (Table 13.1).

The U.S. Department of Agriculture has set up standard definitions of soil-texture classes in which the proportions of sand, silt and clay are given in percentages. Rather than to attempt to list these classes and give the limiting percentages for each, the information is given in a triangular diagram (Figure 13.2), which enables the percentages of all three components to be shown simultaneously. The corners of the triangle represent 100% of each of the three grades of particles—sand, silt, or clay. The word *loam* refers to a mixture in which no one of the three grades dominates over the other two. Loams therefore appear in the central region of the triangle. A particular soil whose components give it a position at Point *A* in the triangle has 65% sand, 20% silt, and 15% clay; it falls into a texture class known as *sandy loam*. Another soil,

whose texture is represented by Point *B* has $33\frac{1}{3}$% sand, $33\frac{1}{3}$% silt, and $33\frac{1}{3}$% clay; it falls into the class of a *clay loam*. Figure 13.3 gives five examples of soil textures; their positions are shown on Figure 13.2.

Texture is important because it largely determines the water retention and transmission properties of the soil as explained later in this chapter. Sand may drain too rapidly; in a clay soil the individual pore spaces are too small for adequate drainage. Where clay and silt proportions are high, root penetration is difficult. Generally speaking, the loam textures are best for plant growth.

Included in the clay grade, smaller than 0.002 mm (0.000,08 in), are mineral soil colloids. Colloid particles are so small that they cannot be seen by optical microscope and will remain suspended indefinitely in water. Individual particles are in the form of thin flakes in the size range 0.001 to 1.0 microns[1] diameter. Finely divided humus provides another class of soil colloids, which may be referred to as *humus colloids,* or *organic colloids.*

Unusual chemical properties of colloids result from their very vast surface area for a given weight. Colloids have the property of being electrically charged and can therefore attract and hold *ions,* the unit chemical particles of dissolved substances. Ions of calcium, magnesium, and potassium are known in soil science as *bases.* These bases may be given up by the colloids to plants, which require them for growth, by a process known as *base*

[1] One micron = 0.001 mm = 0.00004 in.

TABLE 13.2   SOIL ACIDITY AND ALKALINITY[a]

pH	4.0 4.5	5.0	5.5	6.0 6.5 6.7 7.0	8.0	9.0	10.0 11.0
Acidity	Very strongly acid	Strongly acid	Moderately acid	Slightly acid	Neutral	Weakly alkaline	Alkaline	Strongly alkaline	Excessively alkaline
Lime requirements	Lime needed except for crops requiring acid soil	Lime needed for all but acid-tolerant crops		Lime generally not required	No lime needed			
Occurrence	Rare	Frequent	Very common in cultivated soils of humid climates			Common in subhumid and arid climates	Limited areas in deserts	
Soil groups		Podzols	Gray-brown podzolic soils Tundra soils	Brown forest soils Prairie soils Latosols		Chestnut and brown soils Tropical black earths	Black alkali soils	

[a] Based on data of C. E. Millar, L. M. Turk, and H. D. Foth (1958), *Fundamentals of soil science,* third edition, John Wiley and Sons, New York, 526 pp. See Chart 4.

A. Platy B. Prismatic

C. Blocky D. Granular

Figure 13.4   Four basic soil structures are illustrated here. The black bar on each photograph represents one inch. (Photographs *A* and *C* by Roy W. Simonson; *B* and *D* by C. C. Nikiforoff. Courtesy of Division of Soil Survey, U.S. Dept. of Agriculture.)

exchange. On the other hand, the *hydrogen ion* in the soil solution makes for an *acid* condition. The concentration of hydrogen ions in the soil solution, relative to hydroxyl ions, is known as the pH of the soil, and is a measure of soil acidity or alkalinity. Hydrogen ions are held also by the soil colloids in exchange positions. In soils a value of 7.0 in the pH scale is *neutral*, whereas values are below 7.0 (4.0 to 7.0) in *acid soils* but above 7.0 (7.0 to 10.0) in *alkaline soils.* Table 13.2 will help to explain the scale of acidity and alkalinity as applied by agronomists to soils.

Soil colloids also are useful in holding water in the soil. When present in large quantities colloids

may make the soil sticky and tough so that it is difficult to cultivate.

Soil structure refers to the way in which soil grains are grouped together into larger pieces held together by soil colloids (Figure 13.4). Irregular pieces with sharp corners and edges give a *blocky* or nutlike structure. More or less spherical pieces make *granular* and *crumb* structure. Some soils have *columnar* and *prismatic* structure, made up of vertical columns or prisms 0.2 to 4 in (0.5 to 10 cm) across. *Platy* soil structure consists of plates, or flat pieces, in a horizontal position. Soil structure influences the rate at which water is absorbed by the soil, the susceptibility of the soil

Figure 13.5   Horizons of the soil profile. (After U.S. Dept. of Agriculture, 1938.)

to erosion, and the ease of soil cultivation.

Another constituent of the soil is *soil air*, which occupies the pore spaces of the soil when it is not saturated with water. Soil air has been analyzed and found to contain an excess of carbon dioxide, but a deficiency of oxygen and nitrogen.

Soil water, the water temporarily held in the soil, is in reality a complex chemical solution. It is a dilute solution of such substances as bicarbonates, sulfates, chlorides, nitrates, phosphates, and silicates of calcium, magnesium, potassium, sodium, and iron.

The term *soil profile* denotes the arrangement of the soil into layerlike *horizons* of differing texture, color, and consistency (Figure 13.5). Soils are recognized and classified into broad groups on the basis of the parts of the profile that are present. Basically there are three parts to the soil profile. Horizons *A* and *B* represent the true soil, or *solum*; horizon *C* is the subsoil, or weathered parent body. Below this is the parent bedrock or other underlying rock, designated as horizon *D*. The *A* horizon in humid climates is composed of two very different parts. The upper, or A_1, horizon is rich in organic matter and is dark colored. The lower, or A_2, horizon is a zone of leaching. The *B* horizon is usually a zone of accumulation of soil colloids and is dark in contrast to the A_2 horizon above it. These processes and the horizons they produce are discussed more fully in later pages.

Soil-forming processes and factors

Many types of processes and influences, known altogether as *soil formers*, act together to develop a soil. Some of these are *passive* conditions; others are *active* agents. Five principal soil formers are (1) parent material, (2) landform, (3) time, (4) climate, and (5) biological activity.

The first of the passive soil formers is *parent material*, the residual or transported overburden of disintegrated rock making up the bulk of the soil. Certain of the original rock forming minerals have been thoroughly changed chemically into new compounds and reduced to colloidal size. Although many people think that the type of parent material alone determines the kind of soil that is present, this is an inaccurate concept. For example, the same granite forms the bedrock in the Piedmont region in both Maryland and Georgia, but because of climatic differences the soils of these two states are somewhat different. On the other hand, soils of the same major groups may be found to overlie two different types of overburden or bedrock.

An exception to the general rule that soil type is independent of parent material origin is found in young soils that have not had enough time to develop, and in some limestone areas where the influence of the rock is especially strong. Parent material may locally exert a strong control over the soil texture. For example, on the sandy cuestas of the New Jersey coastal plain, the soil consists largely of quartz sand and is very porous. On glacial clays of the Hudson Valley the soil is unusually sticky and dense, deterring rainfall from seeping through.

Another passive soil former is *landform*, or ground-surface configuration (Figure 13.6). Where slope is steep, surface erosion by runoff is more rapid and water penetration is less than on gentle slopes. As a result, the soil will be thinner on steeper slopes. Flat upland areas accumulate a thick soil that has a thick layer of dense clay (clay pan) and is excessively leached. There the products of weathering tend to remain in place. Flat bottom lands likewise have thick soils, but they are poorly drained and dark colored. Here, constant saturation retards decay of vegetation and allows organic matter to accumulate. Gentle slopes where drainage is good but erosion is slow are considered the norm for soil formation. Slow, continuous erosion is a normal geologic soil process whereby the removal balances the formation of new soil from the parent material. Only when this erosion is greatly accelerated does it become harmful to the soil.

Another influence of landform is the slope aspect or direction of exposure of the surface to the slanting rays of the sun. In middle latitudes it is common to find that south-facing slopes, exposed to the warming and drying effects of sunlight, have different conditions of vegetation and soils from north-facing slopes, which retain cold and moisture longer.

A third passive factor in soil formation is *time*. A soil is said to become *mature* when it has been acted upon by all soil-forming processes for a sufficient long time to have developed a profile that changes only imperceptibly with further passage of time. Soils that are evolving from recently deposited river alluvium or glacial till, for example, are considered *young*. In young soils the characteristic horizons are absent or poorly developed. No age in terms of years can be given to all mature soils because the rate at which a mature soil is developed depends on many other factors. Some soils of humid regions in sandy localities may require 100 to 200 years to develop, whereas more commonly, several thousand years may be needed to produce a mature soil. Some soils of tropical and equatorial regions are thought to be as old as one to six million years, or of Pliocene geologic age. As with development of landforms, age of soils is purely relative. Another way of defining a mature soil might be to say that it is in equilibrium with the many processes and forces acting upon it.

Climate and soil

Of the active soil formers, climate is perhaps the most important. Climatic elements involved in soil development are (1) *moisture conditions* affecting the soil (precipitation, evaporation, and humidity), (2) *temperature*, and (3) *wind*.

Precipitation provides the soil water, without which chemical and biological activities are not possible. When soluble chemicals are dissolved in water they ionize, or dissociate into positively and negatively charged particles. Without ionization the many complex chemical interchanges of elements necessary to soil development and plant growth cannot take place. An excess of precipita-

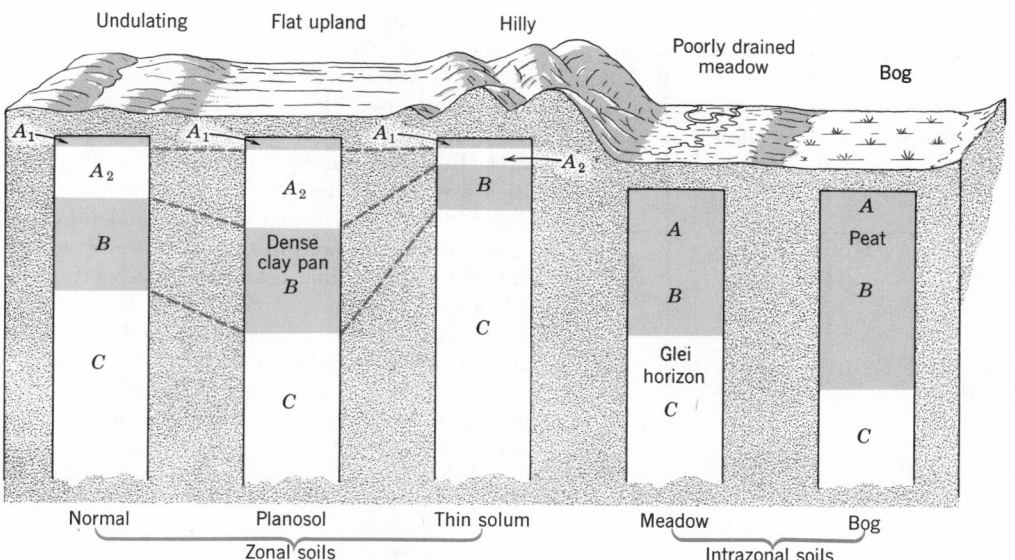

Figure 13.6 Topography as a factor in soil development. (After U.S. Dept. of Agriculture, *Yearbook of American Agriculture*, 1938.)

tion, however, tends to leach away the colloids and ions. This process of downward migration of soil components by waters percolating through the soil is known as *eluviation*. A distinctive leached horizon of the soil, the A_2 horizon, results from this process. (See Figure 13.5). The deposition of colloids and bases in the underlying B horizon is a process known as *illuviation*.

In warm climates where rainfall is extremely heavy, silica (SiO_2) is largely removed from the soil and carried off in streams. This process is termed *desilication*. Thus soils in the wet equatorial rain-forest belts are deficient in silica as well as in such bases as calcium, sodium, magnesium, and potassium, and are generally low in fertility.

In dry climates, evaporation exceeds precipitation and the soil is dry for long periods. Ground water is slowly brought to the surface by capillary attraction and evaporates in the soil, leaving behind the salts that were dissolved in the water. Calcium carbonate, the commonest of these deposits, forms a whitish crust, or *hardpan*, in the soil. In the southwestern United States this material is called *caliche*, and in places it makes the soil as hard and resistant to erosion as if it were a limestone. Gypsum (hydrous calcium sulfate) forms similar encrustations. In intermediate precipitation zones, such as the humid eastern border of the middle-latitude steppes, calcium carbonate appears as small nodules in the soil.

Rainfall and evaporation controls result in the formation of two major groups of soils (Figure 13.7). (1) *Pedalfer soils* show pronounced leaching and occur in the eastern United States where the rainfall is more than 25 in (60 cm) annually. (2) *Pedocal soils* have an excess of calcium carbonate and occur in the western United States where rainfall is less than 25 in (60 cm). The names are coined from the chemical content of the soil. The syllables *al* and *fer* in pedalfer refer to aluminum and iron, respectively, and were chosen because

excessive leaching leaves behind the aluminum and iron oxides as residual substances which thus become important in quantity. The syllable *cal* in pedocal refers, of course, to calcium, which is present in the carbonate form in all pedocal soils.

Temperature is another important climatic factor in soil formation. It acts in two ways. (1) Chemical activity is generally increased by higher temperatures but reduced by cold,[2] and it ceases when soil water is frozen. Thus, tropical soils have a parent material which is thoroughly altered chemically, whereas soils of the frozen tundra have a parent material which is composed largely of mechanically broken minerals. (2) Bacterial activity is increased by warmer soil temperatures. Where bacteria thrive, as in the humid tropics, they consume all dead plants that lie upon the ground. Thus there is no layer of decomposing vegetation on the ground and little humus within the soils of the humid tropics. In cold continental climates, bacterial action is reduced, and a generous layer of decomposing vegetation (leaf mold) covers the ground under forests. Hence, raw humus is preserved at the soil surface and is important in the upper part of the mature soil profile.

Wind is of minor importance as a climatic factor in soil development. Winds may increase the evaporation from soil surfaces and may remove surface soil in arid regions lacking a plant cover. Windblown dust may accumulate and thereby provide the parent material of a soil.

Biological soil formers

Both plants and animals profoundly influence soil development. The plant kingdom consists of the *macroflora* (trees, shrubs, and herbs) and *microflora* (bacteria and fungi).

Grasses and trees require somewhat different chemical substances for growth. Trees, particularly the conifers, use little calcium and magnesium. Hence they thrive well in the pedalfer soils from which these substances have been leached and which are usually acid. Grasses and small grains (wheat, oats, barley) need abundant calcium and magnesium and do well in the pedocal soils of the semi-arid and marginal lands. For grasses to grow well in acid pedalfers, calcium must be added to the soil in the form of lime or crushed limestone. Plants tend to maintain the fertility of soil by bringing the bases (calcium, magnesium, potassium) from lower layers of the soil into the plant stems and leaves, then releasing them to the soil surfaces as the plant decomposes.

[2] The process of *carbonation*, or reaction of carbonic acid (H_2CO_3) upon minerals, is believed to be quite active at low temperatures because the concentration of carbonic acid is greater in cold water than in warm.

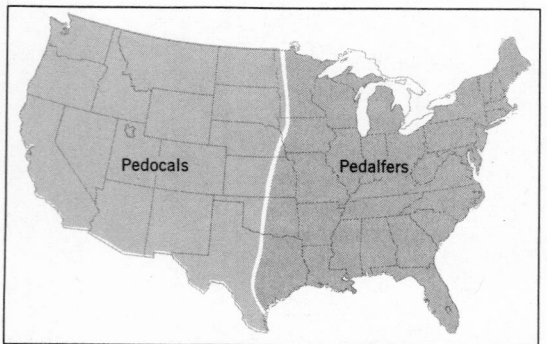

Figure 13.7 Major soil classes of the United States. (After C. F. Marbut.)

Dead plants provide *humus,* the finely-divided organic matter of the soil. Humus gives a dark brown or black color to the soil, as already noted. Humus particles of colloidal size act in the same way as mineral colloids in holding ions in the soil. The process of humus development, or *humification,* is essentially the slow oxidation, or burning, of the vegetative matter. Acids, known as the *organic acids,* are formed during humification. They aid in decomposing the minerals of the parent soil material. The hydrogen ions of the acid solution tend to replace the ions of potassium, calcium, magnesium, and sodium, which are removed in the leaching process. Soils of the cold humid climates are therefore deficient in the bases and are consequently of low fertility for crop farming.

Turning now to the microflora, or bacteria and fungi, we find that bacteria consume humus. In cold climates bacterial growth is slow, hence, humus may accumulate on and in the soil. Soils of the subarctic and tundra climates have much undecomposed organic matter, which locally forms layers of peat, but in humid tropical and equatorial climates, bacterial action is intense and all dead vegetation is rapidly oxidized by the bacteria. Here humus content of the soil is low. The organic acids formed by humus are therefore also lacking, and certain bases such as aluminum, iron, and manganese accumulate in a large proportion relative to silica. In this way the fundamental differences in soils of cold and warm climates can be traced back to intensity of bacterial activity.

Figure 13.8 shows the relation between mean annual air temperature and the relative rate of production and destruction of organic matter by macroflora and microflora, respectively. In the colder climate regimes production exceeds destruction and humus accumulates. Above a mean annual temperature of 77°F (25°C) destruction exceeds production and humus is absent.

Another function of some bacteria and other soil organisms (algae) is to take gaseous nitrogen from the air and convert it into a chemical form that can be used by plants. This process is known as *nitrogen fixation.* One kind of bacteria (*Rhizobium*) lives in the root nodules of leguminous plants and there fixes nitrogen beneficial to the plant host.

The influence of animals in the soil is largely mechanical, but nevertheless important. Earthworms are a particularly important agent in humid regions. They not only continually rework the soil by burrowing, but also change the texture and chemical composition of the soil as it passes through their digestive systems. Ants and termites bring large quantities of soil from lower horizons to the surface. Such burrowing animals as prairie

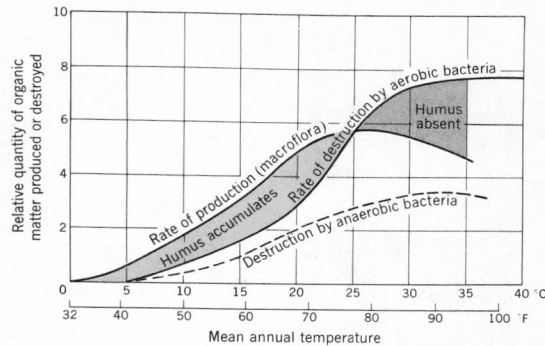

Figure 13.8 Relative rates of production and destruction of organic matter. (After M. W. Senstius, from A. N. Strahler, *The Earth Sciences,* Harper and Row, New York.)

dogs, gophers, ground squirrels, moles, and field mice disturb and rearrange the soil. Digging of burrows brings soil of lower horizons to the surface; collapse of burrows carries surface soil into lower horizons.

The pedogenic regimes

The foregoing analysis of soil-forming processes has been piecemeal in the sense that each factor and activity has been considered separately and in serial order. If the topics seemed in some cases to be out of order and some repetition occurred, it was because the soil-forming processes act in concert and affect the action of one another. To bring the study of soils into a more unified perspective we may concentrate upon several basic trends in soil development, each leading to formation of a distinctive major soil group under the control of a particular climatic regime. Such basic trends may be referred to as *pedogenic regimes.*

The regime of *podzolization* dominates in climates having sufficient cold to inhibit bacterial action, but sufficient moisture to permit larger green plants (macroflora) to thrive (Figure 13.9). Such conditions exist only in middle and high latitudes, and at high altitudes. The corresponding climatic regime may be equable, provided that it is prevailingly cool (marine west coast climates, poleward of 40° latitude), or it may be a continental regime which has cold winters and adequate precipitation distributed throughout the year (humid continental climate; continental subarctic climate). In its extreme development podzolization is associated with coniferous trees (spruce, fir, hemlock, pine). These plants do not require the bases (calcium, magnesium, and potassium) and hence do not restore them to the soil surface. The result is that humic acids, produced from the abundant leaf mold and humus, leach the upper soil strongly of bases, colloids, and the oxides of iron and aluminum, leaving a characteristic ashgray

Figure 13.9 Soil profile development under four pedogenic regimes.

A_2 soil horizon composed largely of silica (SiO_2) (Figure 14.1). Colloids, humus, and oxides of iron carried out of the A_2 horizon accumulate in the B horizon, which may be dark in color, dense in structure, and in some cases hardened to rocklike consistency (*ortstein*).

The pedogenic regime of *laterization* is in some respects a warm-climate relative of podzolization, in that both are associated with climatic regimes of ample precipitation and with forests. Laterization takes place in a warm climate having copious rainfall well distributed throughout the year (equatorial rainforest climate; tropical wet-dry climate with long wet season; humid subtropical climate). A high mean annual temperature and a lack of severe winter season permit sustained bacterial action which destroys dead vegetation as rapidly as it is produced. Consequently little or no humus is found upon or in the soil (Figure 13.9B). In the absence of humic acids the sesquioxides of iron (Fe_2O_3) are insoluble and accumulate in the soil as red clays, nodules, and rocklike layers (*laterite*). Silica, on the other hand, is leached out of the soil and disposed of eventually by stream flow in the process of *desilication*. No distinctive soil horizons are developed. In the absence of silicate colloids the soil tends to be firm and porous rather than sticky and plastic, and will transmit water readily. Laterization results in very low soil fertility because bases are not held in the soil and humus is lacking.

Calcification is a pedogenic regime of climates

in which evaporation on the average exceeds precipitation. Calcification is associated with a continental climatic regime with low total annual precipitation (middle-latitude steppe climate) and with a tropical wet-dry climatic regime with a short wet season (tropical steppe climate). Rainfall is not enough to leach out the bases, so that calcium and magnesium ions remain in the soil (Figure 13.9C). Grasses, which use these bases, restore them to the soil surface. Colloids remain essentially in place and are not leached out, but are in a dense (flocculated) state and hold the soil into aggregate structures. Calcium carbonate, brought upward by capillary water films and evaporated in dry periods, is precipitated in the B horizon of the soil in the form of nodules, slabs, and even dense stony layers (caliche). Microbial activity is restricted and humus may be abundantly distributed throughout the A and B horizons. Humus occurs in progressively smaller amounts as one traces the soil into climate zones of increasing aridity. Calcification is characteristically associated with grasslands—the steppes and semi-deserts.

The pedogenic regime of *gleization* is characteristic of poorly drained (but not saline) environments under a moist and cool or cold climate. Gleization is thus associated with the climatic regime of polarization (tundra climate) but is also effective in bog environments of continental climates with cold winters. Low temperatures permit heavy accumulations of organic matter to form a surface layer of peaty material (Figure 13.9D). Beneath this is the *glei horizon*, a thick layer of compact, sticky, structureless clay of bluish-gray color. The glei horizon lies generally within the zone of ground water saturation; consequently the iron is in a partially reduced condition and imparts the bluish-gray color.

Finally, there is the pedogenic regime of *salinization*, or accumulation of highly soluble salts in the soil. Salinization is associated with the desert climatic regime and takes place in poorly drained locations where surface runoff evaporates. Such locations are typically low-lying valley floors, flats, and basins in the continental interiors; and coastal flats in arid climates. Sulphates and chorides of calcium and sodium are common salts in such soils.

The pedogenic regimes form the basis for classifying the soils of the world into a number of great soil groups, discussed in Chapter 14. The pedogenic regimes also underlie, or are closely interrelated with the geography of plants and constitute one of the major classes of environmental influences upon plants.

REFERENCES FOR FURTHER STUDY

U.S. Dept. of Agriculture (1938), *Soils and men; yearbook of agriculture 1938*, U.S. Government Printing Office, Washington, D.C., 1232 pp.

Robinson, G. W. (1959), *Soils; their origin, constitution and classification*, third edition, John Wiley and Sons, New York, 573 pp.

Bunting, B. T. (1965), *The geography of soil*, Aldine Publ. Co., Chicago, 213 pp.

Millar, C. E., L. M. Turk, and H. D. Foth (1965), *Fundamentals of soil science*, fourth edition, John Wiley and Sons, New York, 491 pp.

Money, D. C. (1965), *Climate, soils, and vegetation*, University Tutorial Press, Ltd., London, 272 pp.

Eyre, S. R. (1968), *Vegetation and soils; a world picture*, second edition, Aldine Publishing Co., Chicago, 328 pp.

1. In what way is the soil a dynamic, rather than a lifeless, static body? To what general influences does the soil respond?

2. How is the term *soil* defined by the soil scientist? Of what three states of matter is soil made up? Are all three necessary for plant growth? Describe the types of substances that make up the soil.

3. What is the significance of soil color? What are some of the common soil colors, and what do they mean? In general, what relationship does soil color bear to climate?

4. What is meant by soil texture? What are the various soil textures recognized by the U.S. Department of Agriculture? What influence has soil texture upon agricultural use of the land?

5. What are some of the common soil structures? Describe four structures. How does soil structure influence the rate at which water is absorbed and transmitted by the soil?

6. What is meant by soil constitution? What properties are included in this term? Of what importance is soil constitution?

7. What are soil colloids? Explain how colloids hold ions. What are the bases commonly present in soils? What is base exchange? What is the relation of hydrogen ion concentration to acidity of the soil? What is meant by pH of the soil?

8. What is soil air? In what way is it different from normal air of the free atmosphere? What are some of the substances commonly found in soil water?

9. Describe an idealized soil profile containing *A*, *B*, and *C* horizons. Which of these horizons constitute the true soil?

10. List the five principal soil formers, including both passive conditions and active agents.

11. From what types of parent material can soils be derived? Does the type of parent material strongly control the characteristics of a fully developed soil profile? Give examples to illustrate. How may young soils strongly reflect the nature of the parent materials? Give examples.

12. How does landform influence development of the soil profile? Explain how various degrees of slope influence thickness of the profile. What conditions of slope are best for the development of soils suited to agriculture?

13. What is a mature soil? Does a mature soil profile continue to evolve through a series of changing forms? How long does it take for a mature soil to develop?

14. What influence has precipitation upon the soil profile? What is eluviation? What is illuviation? What horizons of the soil are affected by these processes? What is meant by desilication? Where is this process most intensively developed?

15. How do soils of dry climates differ fundamentally from soils of humid climates? What two major soil classes have been recognized on this basis?

16. How does temperature affect soil formation? Explain the control exerted by temperature over the type of weathering of the parent material and upon the accumulation of organic matter.

17. How are the needs of different plant groups suited to particular groups of soils? Are plants essential in maintaining the profile of a mature soil?

18. Explain the importance of humus in soil development. What is humification? What acids are formed during humification? What is the action of these acids in the soil? How does bacterial activity determine the amount of humus in the soil? How does this factor determine the fundamental difference between soils of equatorial and arctic regions?

19. What is meant by nitrogen fixation? How is it accomplished?

20. What important influence have earthworms, ants, termites, and burrowing animals upon the soil?

21. Name the basic pedogenic regimes and give the climatic regime in which each develops.

22. Describe and explain the soil profile characteristics associated with each pedogenic regime.

REPRESENTATIVE EXAMPLES OF PROFILES
OF THE GREAT SOIL GROUPS

Terminology and classification are according to the U.S. Department of Agriculture, 1938. Given in parentheses below are approximate equivalents from the U.S. Department of Agriculture, Soil Conservation Service, *Soil Classification, A Comprehensive System, 7th Approximation,* 1960 and 1967. Scale units are in feet. (Photographs were provided by the Soil Conservation Service, U.S. Department of Agriculture, courtesy of Dr. Guy D. Smith, Director, Soil Survey Investigations, Soil Conservation Service.)

ZONAL ORDER

A *Podzol (Humod)* Humus podzol, Fontainbleu, France.

B *Gray-Brown Podzolic Soil (Udalf)*, Minnesota.

C *Yellow Podzolic Soil (Udult)*, Puerto Rico.

D *Terra Rossa (Xeralf)*, Portugal.

E *Latosol (Orthox)*, Puerto Rico.

F *Prairie Soil* or *Brunizem Soil (Udoll)*, Story County, Iowa.

G *Chernozem Soil (Udic Boroll)*, Spink County, South Dakota.

H *Chestnut Soil (Typic Boroll)*, Raymon, Saskatchewan.

I *Reddish Brown Soil (Ustalf)*, Vernon, Texas.

J *Brown Soil (Aridic Boroll)*, Scobey, Montana.

K *Sierozem* or *Gray Desert Soil (Calciorthid)*, Escalante, Utah.

L *Red Desert Soil (Argid)*, Tucson, Arizona.

INTRAZONAL ORDER

M *Bog Soil (Fibrist)*, Sphagnum peat, Minnesota.

N *Meadow Soil* or *Humic Glei Soil (Aquoll)*, Union County, Iowa.

O *Solonchak* or *Saline Soil (Salorthid)*, Virgin River, Nevada. White horizon is salt.

P *Rendzina (Rendoll)*, Puerto Rico. Developed on marl.

SOIL PROFILES

A Podzol

B Gray-brown
podzolic soil

C Yellow
podzolic soil

D Terra rossa

E Latosol

F Prairie soil

G Chernozem

H Chestnut soil

SOIL PROFILES

I Reddish brown
     soil

J Brown soil

K Sierozem
     (gray desert soil)

L Red desert
     soil

M Bog soil

N Meadow soil
     (Humic glei soil)

O Solonchak

P Rendzina

CHAPTER 14
The Great Soil Groups

THE soil scientist recognizes that all soils can be subdivided into three orders, known as *zonal, intrazonal,* and *azonal* orders. Zonal soils, formed under conditions of good soil drainage through the prolonged action of climate and vegetation, are by far the most important and widespread of the three orders. Intrazonal soils are simply those formed under conditions of very poor drainage (such as in bogs, flood-plain meadows, or in the playa lake basins of the deserts) or upon limestones whose influence is dominant.

Azonal soils have no well-developed profile characteristics, either because they have had insufficient time to develop or because they are on slopes too steep to allow profile development. Azonal soils include thin, stony mountain soils of the earth's mountain regions (*lithosols*), freshly laid alluvial materials, or dune sands (*regosols*). These usually have poorly developed profiles and cannot be easily classified, whereas the zonal and intrazonal soils have distinctive profile characteristics as the result of long development.

The great soil groups

A widely used classification of soils is illustrated in Table 14.1. The U.S. Department of Agriculture in 1938 recognized about 30 *great soil groups,* but these can be simplified into about 18 principal varieties, including both zonal and intrazonal orders, that have world-wide distributions under similar climatic and geomorphic conditions. Various zonal soil groups have already been mentioned and briefly discussed in earlier chapters describing climates. Combining knowledge of the pedogenic processes and regimes gained in Chapter 13 with an understanding of climatic elements, we can proceed to a systematic study of each of the great soil groups. Some of the soil groups bear Russian names, applied by soil scientists of Russia who pioneered in this field.

The founder of modern theories of soil origin and classification was V. V. Dokuchaiev, a Russian geologist; his studies between 1882 and 1900 led him to the concept that soil is an independent body whose character is determined primarily by climate and vegetation. A Russian follower of Dokuchaiev, K. D. Glinka, expanded the concepts

of horizons in the soil profile. For the development of modern soil science in the United States during the 1920's and 1930's, much credit is given to C. F. Marbut, who served for many years as chief of the Soil Survey Division of the United States Department of Agriculture. Marbut translated Glinka's work into English, borrowed and modified the Russian pedologic views and ultimately created a comprehensive system of soil classification for the United States. It is Marbut's system, with further modifications, that is presented here.

Podzol soils

Of the zonal soils of cool humid climates the most widely distributed are the *podzol soils* (or simply, the *podzols*), found closely associated with the subarctic climate, the more northerly parts of the humid continental climate, and the cooler parts of the marine west coast climate. Podzol soils require a cold winter and adequate precipitation distributed throughout the year. (Plate 3 is a world soils map which may be referred to in conjunction with the world maps of climate and vegetation, Plates 2 and 4.) The pedogenic regime is that of podzolization (Chapter 13).

The podzol profile (Figure 14.1 and color plate, *A*) is the soil profile from which the various soil horizons were originally named. At the very top, lying on the soil surface, is a layer of leaf mold and acid humus termed the A_0 horizon. Below this is the first soil layer, designated as the A_1 horizon. It is a thin, acid layer, rich in humus and varying in color from gray through yellowish brown to a reddish brown. The A_1 horizon is rich in colloids and is a zone of interaction between acids and bases.

Below the A_1 horizon is a distinctive light-colored zone called the A_2 horizon. This is the strongly leached horizon from which colloids and bases have been carried down. It sometimes has a bleached ash-gray or whitish-gray color because coloring agents such as the iron oxides and colloidal humus have been removed. Leaching such as occurs in the A_2 horizon constitutes eluviation, explained in Chapter 13.

Below the A_2 horizon of the podzol profile is the B horizon, a brownish zone that is enriched by the colloids and bases brought down from the A_2 horizon. The process of accumulation is one of illuviation (Chapter 13). The colloids give a heavy, clayey consistency to the B horizon. Excessive deposit of oxides may cause the soil particles in this horizon to become strongly cemented into stony material known as *hardpan*, or, in European soil terminology, *ortstein*. Nodules of soil in the B horizon formed by the same process as hardpan are termed *concretions*. They may be composed of clay cemented by *limonite*, a hydrous iron oxide compound. Altogether the A and B horizons of the podzol profile total less than 3 ft (1 m) in thickness.

In the United States (Figure 14.2), the podzols are found in the northern Great Lakes states, the Adirondacks, and mountainous parts of New England. Here the ample precipitation combined with

TABLE 14.1 CLASSIFICATION OF SOILS[a]

ZONAL ORDER	
Suborders	Great Soil Groups

Light-colored podzolized soils of forested regions	PODZOL SOILS
	  Brown podzolic soils
	GRAY-BROWN PODZOLIC SOILS
	RED-YELLOW PODZOLIC SOILS
	  (Incl. *terra rossa*)

Lateritic soils of warm, moist subtropical, tropical, and equatorial regions	LATOSOLS
	  Reddish-brown lateritic soils
	  Black and dark-gray tropical soils

Soils of the forest-grassland transition	Degraded chernozem soils
Dark-colored soils of the semi-arid, subhumid, and humid grasslands	PRAIRIE SOILS (BRUNIZEM SOILS) Reddish prairie soils CHERNOZEM SOILS CHESTNUT SOILS REDDISH-CHESTNUT AND REDDISH-BROWN SOILS
Light-colored soils of arid regions	BROWN SOILS GRAY DESERT SOILS (SIEROZEM SOILS) RED DESERT SOILS
Soils of the cold zone	TUNDRA SOILS Arctic brown forest soils
INTRAZONAL ORDER	
Hydromorphic soils of marshes, swamps, bogs, and flat uplands	BOG SOILS MEADOW SOILS (WIESENBÖDEN) Alpine meadow soils PLANOSOLS
Halomorphic soils of poorly-drained arid regions and coastal deposits	SALINE SOILS (SOLONCHAK) ALKALI SOILS (SOLONETZ) Soloth
Calcimorphic soils	RENDZINA SOILS
AZONAL ORDER	
LITHOSOLS	
REGOSOLS	Alluvial soils Sands (dry)

[a]Based on U.S. Department of Agriculture (1938), *Soils and men; Yearbook of Agriculture 1938*, U.S. Govt. Printing Office, Washington, D.C. See pp. 993–995.

Figure 14.1 Podzol profile developed beneath pine forest. (From S. R. Eyre: *Vegetation and Soils*, Aldine Publishing Company. Copyright © 1963 by S. R. Eyre.)

long, cold winters favors surface accumulation of decomposed vegetation. Organic acids cause a strong leaching of the A_2 horizon. Islands of podzolic soil are found in the Allegheny Mountains, where high altitude gives a cooler climate, and in the sandy New Jersey and Long Island coastal plain belt, where leaching is intense in the porous sand. Podzols of the United States are but the small southern fringe of a great podzol belt corresponding with the needleleaf evergreen forest of the subarctic climate zones in Canada and Eurasia (Figure 14.3 and Plate 3). This forest is dominated by conifers which promote the process of podzolization.

Podzol soils are low in fertility. Leaching of important plant constituents is shown by the association of coniferous forest with this soil. Conifers need little of the calcium, magnesium, potassium, and phosphorus which many other plants require. Consequently the trees do not bring these bases to the ground surface from which they can be restored to the upper soil horizons. Certain species of oaks have a similar lack of use of the bases. The Pine Barrens on podzol soils of the New Jersey coastal plain are examples of adaptation of pine and oak forest to podzol soils.

The podzols cannot produce the crops to feed a large population. Addition of lime and fertilizers to the soil will largely correct soil acidity and replenish the leached bases, but the favorable areas for such treatment are limited by the effects of continental glaciation. Bouldery morainal topography interspersed with swamps and lakes still renders much of the podzol soil area unfit for farming.

Gray-brown podzolic soils

The second major great soil group of humid climates consists of the *gray-brown podzolic soils*. They differ from the podzols in that leaching is less intense and the soil color is brownish. The various soil horizons correspond with those of the podzols (Figures 14.4 and color plate, *B*). The A_1 horizon is a moderately acid humus layer. The A_2 horizon is a grayish-brown leached zone. It is less intensely leached than in the podzols and, consequently, is neither so light colored nor so distinctly limited. The *B* horizon is thick and yellowish brown to light reddish brown in color. Like the podzols, it has concentrated colloids and bases.

The gray-brown podzolic soils contain more of the important bases than the podzols but are nevertheless somewhat acid. Deciduous forests (maple, beech, oak) grow luxuriantly on the forest soils (Figure 14.3). These trees bring the bases up from the *B* horizon, returning them to the surface as dead leaves and branches. Thus the soil is replenished by these bases in a way not found in the podzols.

When treated with lime and fertilizers, the gray-brown podzolic soils make highly productive farms on which diversified crop farming and dairying are well developed. This is seen from the distribution of the gray-brown podzolic soils in the eastern-central United States where rainfall is 35 to 40 in (90 to 100 cm) yearly in the humid continental climate. Note that southern Wisconsin, southern Michigan, Indiana, Ohio, Kentucky, New York, Pennsylvania, and Maryland, and southern New England are largely underlain by these soils (Figure 14.2). These are states noted for the value of their diversified crop production. Gray-brown podzolic soils are also found in the Pacific northwest and on summit areas in the Rocky Mountains.

The gray-brown podzolic soils are also found over much of western Europe in both the marine west coast climate and humid continental climate. Smaller areas occur in the humid continental climate of northern China and northern Japan. Summer-green deciduous forest is associated with these areas of gray-brown podzolic soils.

Of relatively minor extent are the *brown podzolic soils* (Table 14.1), found in southern New England (Figure 14.2). These are transitional between podzols and gray-brown podzolic soils. The brown podzolic soils have only a very thin leached A_2 horizon. Although acid, they can be highly productive when heavily limed and fertilized.

Red-yellow podzolic soils

Farther south than the gray-brown podzolic soils, in a zone of increasingly warmer climate but

ZONAL SOILS

Pz   Podzol soils
G   Gray wooded soils (Canada)
BP   Brown podzolic soils
GB   Gray-brown podzolic soils
RY   Red and yellow podzolic soils
Pr   Prairie soils
RPr Reddish prairie soils
Cz   Chernozem soils
Cs   Chestnut soils
RCh Reddish chestnut soils
Br   Brown soils
RBr Reddish brown soils
NC   Noncalcic brown (Shantung brown) soils

Sz   Sierozem (Gray desert) soils
RD   Red desert soils

INTRAZONAL SOILS

Pl   Planosols
Rz   Rendzina soils
So   Solonchak and solonetz soils
W   Wiesenböden, ground-water podzol, and half
     bog soils
Bg   Bog soils

AZONAL SOILS

L   Lithosols and shallow soils, sands, lava beds
A   Alluvial soils

Figure 14.2   Soils of the contiguous 48 United States and southern Canada. (Modified and simplified from map of soil associations of the United States by U.S. Department of Agriculture, Soil Survey Division, in *Yearbook of American Agriculture, 1938,* U.S. Government Printing Office, Washington, D.C., 1938, and *Atlas of Canada,* 1957, Plate No. 35, Canada Dept. of Mines and Technical Surveys.)

with equally abundant precipitation, lies a great area of *red-yellow podzolic soils* (Figure 14.2). These soils occupy the southern United States from Texas to the Atlantic, and coincide fairly well with the extent of the humid subtropical climate. A similar geographic relation holds in Japan, while in southern Brazil and southeastern Paraguay there is also a substantial area of these soils at comparable latitudes (Plate 3). Smaller coastal zones of red-yellow podzolic soils are found in South Africa, Australia, and New Zealand.

The red-yellow soils are of the podzolic type

and show the same characteristic leaching of the A_2 horizon (color plate, *C*). Warm summers and mild winters favor bacterial action. Humus content is low. Thus, both podzolization and laterization act in concert as pedogenic processes. The typical red and yellow colors are a staining in the form of hydroxides of iron. The yellow soils are the more strongly leached of the two and are found on sandy coastal plain belts. Aluminum hydroxides are also abundant in these soils, a condition typical of tropical soils in warm, humid regions.

Deciduous forest was the natural vegetation of

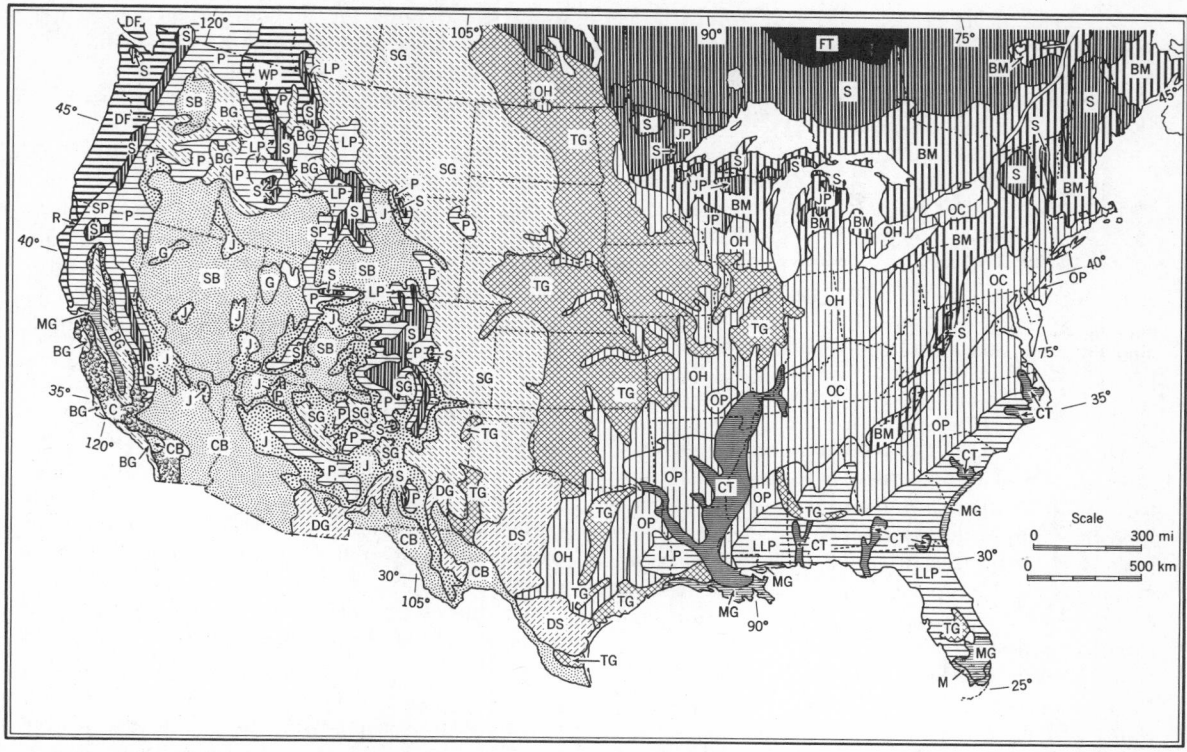

EASTERN FOREST VEGETATION

FT   Subarctic forest-tundra transition (Canada)
S   Spruce-fir (Northern coniferous forest)
JP   Jack, red, and white pines (Northeastern pine forest)
BM   Birch-beech-maple-hemlock (Northeastern hardwoods)
Oak forest (Southern hardwood forest):
     OC   Chestnut-chestnut oak-yellow poplar
     OH   Oak-hickory
     OP   Oak-pine
CT   Cypress-tupelo-red gum (River bottom forest)
LLP Longleaf-loblolly-slash pines (Southeastern pine forest)
M   Mangrove (Subtropical forest)

WESTERN FOREST VEGETATION

S   Spruce-fir (Northern coniferous forest)
Cedar-hemlock (Northwestern coniferous forest):
     WP   Western larch-western white pine
     DF   Pacific Douglas fir
     R   Redwood

Yellow pine-Douglas fir (Western pine forest)
     Sp   Yellow pine-sugar pine
     P   Yellow pine-Douglas fir
     LP   Lodgepole pine
J   Pinon-Juniper (Southwestern coniferous woodland)
C   Chaparral (Southwestern broad-leaved woodland)

DESERT SHRUB VEGETATION

SB   Sagebrush (Northern desert shrub)
CB   Creosote bush (Southern desert shrub)
G   Greasewood (Salt desert shrub)

GRASS VEGETATION

TG   Tall grass (Prairie grassland)
SG   Short grass (Plains grassland)
DG   Mesquite-grass (Desert grassland)
DS   Mesquite and desert grass savanna (Desert savanna)
BG   Bunch grass (Pacific grassland)
MG   Marsh grass (Marsh grassland)
Alpine meadow (Not shown)

Figure 14.3   Vegetation of the contiguous 48 United States and southern Canada. (Modified and simplified from maps of H. L. Shantz and Raphael Zon, in *Atlas of American Agriculture*, 1929, U.S. Government Printing Office, Washington, D.C. and Canada Department of Forestry, Bulletin 123, 1963.)

Figure 14.4 Brown forest soil profile formed beneath oak forest. (From S. R. Eyre: *Vegetation and Soils*, Aldine Publishing Company. Copyright © 1963 by S. R. Eyre.)

the northern part of the red soil belt in the United States. Soils of these southern states, though low in plant nutrients, respond well to fertilizers and have been important producers of tobacco, cotton, peanuts, soybeans, corn, sweet potatoes, cowpeas, and many other crops. Yellow soils, owing to their strong leaching, support forests of longleaf, loblolly, and slash pine (Figure 14.3). The pitch pine of the coastal belt is an important source of turpentine and resin; the slash pine is a good pulpwood tree.

In the other world regions of red-yellow podzolic soils noted above, natural vegetation is dominantly rainforest, of both tropical and temperate classes (Plate 4).

A great soil group related to the red podzolic soils is the *terra rossa* of Mediterranean lands (Plate 3). This red soil, poor in humus, is rich in sesquioxide of iron (Fe_2O_3) to which it largely owes its color. The origin of terra rossa is the source of much speculation. Perhaps it represents a soil that was once much richer in humus, but which has lost that humus because of the destruction of forest cover by man and his grazing animals over the course of many centuries. In some areas of its occurrence, terra rossa is associated with limestone as the parent matter, suggesting that its properties are inherited from a calcareous subsoil.

Latosols

Soils of the humid tropical and equatorial zones are called *latosols*, or *lateritic soils* (color plate, E). They are characterized as follows: (1) Chemical and mechanical decomposition of the parent rock is complete, owing to the favorable conditions of moisture and heat. (2) Silica has been almost entirely leached from the soil. (3) Sesquioxides of iron and aluminum have accumulated in the soil as abundant and permanent residual materials. (4) Humus is almost or entirely lacking because of the rapidity of bacterial action in the prevailingly warm temperatures. (5) The soil is distinctively reddish because of the presence of sesquioxides of

iron. The reasons for the development of these conditions have been explained in Chapter 13 under the pedogenic regime of *laterization*. Loss of silicate clay minerals renders the latosols relatively low in plasticity (stickiness) and remarkably porous. Consequently rainfall sinks readily into these soils.

True latosols are found only in warm, humid regions and, hence, correspond closely with the wet equatorial climate and the tropical wet-dry climate. Though the red-yellow podzolic soils show the effects of laterization, they are not true latosols.

Latosols quickly lose their fertility under crop cultivation because excessive leaching has removed the plant nutrients in all but a thin surface layer. However, the soil is favorable for the luxuriant growth of broadleaf evergreen rainforest (Plate 4). Other large areas have the raingreen forest and woodland associated with the tropical wet-dry climatic regime.

An interesting feature of latosols is the local development of accumulations of iron and aluminum sesquioxides into layers that can be cut out as building bricks. The material is termed *laterite*. On exposure to the drying effects of the air, these blocks become very hard. In Indochina, particularly, laterite bricks have been much used as a building material.

Valuable mineral deposits occur as laterites. These are thick layers of such minerals as *bauxite* (hydrous aluminum oxide), *limonite* (hydrous iron oxide), and *manganite* (manganese oxide). They are known as *residual ores* because they are not soluble in soil water and have continued to accumulate as the parent rock has weathered away and the silica and other soluble constituents have been removed. Important bauxite deposits of the Guianas of northern South America and of western India are of this type. (See Figure 10.5.) Valuable resources of manganese are in laterite deposits.

By no means all soils of the humid tropical and equatorial climates are latosols of the type described above. Variations of the latosols have been described as *yellowish-brown lateritic* and *reddish-brown lateritic* soils. Large upland areas of Africa and India within the tropical wet-dry climate regime have *black* and *dark-gray tropical soils*. The extent of these is given in Plate 3. These dark soils may be related to special conditions of underlying bedrock. For example, the dark soils of peninsular India shown in Plate 3 coincide rather well with the Deccan Plateau, underlain by basalts.

Hydromorphic soils (intrazonal)

Hydromorphic soils are soils associated with marshes, swamps, bogs, or poorly drained flat uplands. All are considered intrazonal soils because of poor drainage.

Bog soils are formed under bog vegetation in regions of cool, moist continental climates. Continental glaciation in North America and Europe left countless basins that have since been largely filled by a succession of water-loving plants (Chapter 15). Here the soil is saturated most of the time and plant decay is greatly retarded. The partly decomposed plants of the bog therefore accumulate into an upper peat layer 3 to 4 ft (1 m) thick (color plate, *M*). Below this is a horizon of sticky, structureless clay, known to soil scientists as the *glei* (also *gley*) horizon. It is of gray-blue color and is largely impervious to water seepage. The process of *gleization* was discussed in Chapter 13.

Meadow soils (*wiesenböden*) are formed on the flood plains of streams where drainage is somewhat better than in the bogs, but is nevertheless poor. These areas are extensively used in the humid middle-latitude climates as pastures because the grass grows rapidly and densely. A thick, humus-rich layer is developed, overlying a sticky gley horizon (color plate, *N*). A similar process of soil development takes place on poorly drained sites at the bases of hill slopes where there is a tendency for water to collect.

The name *humic-glei soils* has been proposed for the meadow soils in combination with half-bog soils.

At high altitudes, where the alpine tundra climate prevails, *alpine meadow soils* are found. Dark in color, these soils support a growth of grasses, sedges, and flowering plants.

Strongly leached soils developed on flat or gently sloping, elevated surfaces are known as *planosols*. The soil horizons are abnormally thick because of slow removal by erosion. Planosols have a thick, dense clay horizon in humid climates. In subhumid climates planosols have a dense, cemented horizon.

Tundra soils

Soils of the arctic tundra are so widespread (Plate 3) that they may be considered a zonal type along with the podzols, gray-brown forest soils, red-yellow soils, and latosols, but because they are poorly drained they are sometimes classified as intrazonal.

Climate conditions favorable for tundra soils have been described under tundra climates of the northern continental fringes, Chapter 12. Intensely cold, long winters cause soil moisture to be frozen during many months of the year. Under these cold conditions chemical alteration of the minerals is slow, and much of the parent material of the soil consists of mechanically broken particles. The slow rate of plant decomposition results in the presence of much raw humus, or peat. The tundra soils do not have simple, distinctive soil profiles, but consist of thin layers of sandy clay and raw humus. The surface may be covered with a sod of lichens, mosses, and herbaceous plants.

In the tundra regions of Siberia and North America, the condition of permanently frozen ground, or *permafrost*, is widespread. (See Chapter 12.) Curious lenses, layers, and vertical wedgelike bodies of ice are present under the soil.

In parts of central Alaska, principally in the valleys of the Yukon and Tanana rivers, are dark-colored soils which have been given great-soil group status as the *arctic brown forest soils* (Plate 3). The profiles of these soils have a thick, dark A_1 horizon rich in organic matter. Downward through lower horizons the soils grade into lighter brown colors and finally to gray in the C horizon. These soils may have originated in a surface layer of loess (wind-blown silt).

Chernozem soils

Of the zonal soils in a semi-arid climate among the most distinctive and widely distributed types are the *chernozem soils*, or *black earths* (color plate, *G*). A typical chernozem profile appears to consist essentially of two layers. Immediately beneath a grass sod is a black layer, the A horizon, 2 to 3 ft (0.6 to 1 m) thick and rich in humus. In this layer the structure is a crumb or nut. The A horizon grades downward into a B horizon of brown or yellowish-brown color, then, with a sharp line of demarcation, into a light-colored C horizon. As in the podzolic soils, in the B horizon colloids and bases accumulate by downward percolation through the A horizon, but unlike the podzols, the chernozem soils have no leached A_2 horizon.

Chernozem soils are rich in calcium, which appears in excess as calcium carbonate precipitated in the lower B horizon or just beneath the B horizon. It has been noted that chernozem soils develop in parent material rich in calcium carbonate. The origin and distribution of chernozem soils have long attracted the soil scientist. Russian investigators in particular have been intensely interested in chernozem soils because they occupy a large area in the Ukraine, surrounding the Black Sea on its west, north, and east sides (Plate 3) and continuing in a great belt eastward along the 55th parallel into the heart of Asia.

Chernozem soils are important in the United States and Canada, where they form a north-south belt starting in Alberta and Saskatchewan and running through the Great Plains of the United States to central Texas. A similar area lies in Argentina. Other areas are mapped in Australia and Manchuria (Plate 3).

Climate has long been thought to be a determining factor in the development of chernozem soils. Comparison of soil and climate maps shows that the middle-latitude chernozems, in the Americas and Europe, lie on the more arid western side of the humid continental climates and with decreasing latitude extend over into the middle-latitude steppe climates. Aridity is therefore a definite contributing cause. The continental location of chernozem areas makes for hot summers and cold winters. Drought periods with strong evaporation dry out the soil, and forests cannot exist. Instead, grasses, which can withstand drought readily and which are tolerant to soils with excesses of mineral salts, flourish on chernozem soils. Steppe grasslands and prairies are the natural vegetation of the middle-latitude chernozem soils.

An important factor in development of the middle-latitude chernozem soils is their occurrence on *loess*, the wind-transported dust so extensively deposited during the glacial period. (See Chapter 25.) Though chernozem soils are not limited to such areas, the texture and lime content of loess, together with the plains topography, have been especially favorable to chernozem development.

Geographically, perhaps the outstanding point of importance regarding the chernozem soils is their productivity for small grain crops—wheat, oats, barley, and rye. Great grain surpluses are exported from chernozem areas in the United States, Canada, and the Ukraine and Argentine, causing them to be described as breadbaskets of the world.

Where forests invade the chernozem soil grasslands, some influence of podzolization is felt and there develops a faint A_2 horizon. Such soils are known as *degraded chernozem soils*. They are transitional to the gray-brown podzolic soils and occupy a geographical position adjacent to them. One particularly large region of degraded chernozem soils lies northwest of the Black Sea and extends from the Danube River of Rumania to the southern Ukraine (Plate 3).

Prairie soils (brunizem soils)

Examination of the soil map (Figure 14.2) will show that between the chernozems and gray-brown podzolic soils in the United States lies a zone of *prairie soils* (or *brunizem soils*). Rainfall is 25 to 40 in (60 to 100 cm) and diminishes greatly across this belt (Figure 11.10). This soil group is similar to the chernozems in general profile and appearance, but differs in that it lacks the excess calcium carbonate of the chernozems (color plate, *F*). The prairie soil is, therefore, a transitional type between the major soil divisions: pedocal and pedalfer.

Of special interest in the United States has been the origin of natural tall-grass prairies of the upper Mississippi Valley and the Great Plains states: Illinois, Iowa, eastern Nebraska, southern Minnesota, northern Missouri, and eastern Kansas (Figure 14.3). Here forests were lacking over vast expanses at the time of the coming of white men. Although many explanations have been offered for the existence of the prairies, including the possibility of deforestation by burning, it seems likely that a major contributing factor has been that the prairie soils become almost completely dry between summer rains down to a depth of a foot or so (0.3 m) as a result of the dryness and heat of summer air masses. Although the prairie grasses can survive these conditions, deciduous forests, which border the prairies on the east, cannot.

Prairie soils are extremely productive, combining the fertility of the chernozems with somewhat moister climate. Perhaps the outstanding crop associated with the prairie-soil belt is corn. The corn belt is practically identical with the prairie-soil belt, although the corn belt actually extends eastward into the gray-brown forest soils of Indiana and Ohio. Corn requires not only high temperatures during the growing season but ample moisture as well. This last requirement is met by periods of summer thunderstorms interspersed with hot, dry periods.

South of the prairie soils in the United States lies a small area of *reddish prairie soils*, located south of the Arkansas River in Kansas, Oklahoma, and Texas (Figure 14.2). The reddish prairie soils are essentially like the prairie soils, but of reddish-brown color. They support a prairie grassland vegetation.

Chestnut soils and brown soils

To the arid side of the chernozem belt lies the belt of *chestnut soils* or *dark brown soils*. They occupy the semi-arid middle-latitude steppe lands, in North America and Asia (Plate 3). The chestnut-soil profile is generally similar to the chernozem, but contains less humus and hence is not so dark in color. The soil structure tends to be prismatic in the *B* horizon.

The chestnut soils are fertile under conditions of adequate rainfall or irrigation, but lie in a hazardous marginal belt in which years of drought and adequate rainfall are alternated. Bordering on the productive chernozem wheat belt of the Great Plains, the chestnut-soil belt of the United States offers a temptation for expanded wheat cultivation. Under special cultivation practices that conserve soil moisture, a period of moist years brings high grain yields to these marginal belts; but a series of drought years can bring repeated crop failures and poverty.

Toward still more arid regions the chestnut soils give way to the *brown soils*, generally similar, but with still less humus and consequently a lighter color (Figure 14.5 and color plate, *J*). In the western United States, the brown soils occupy basins in the central Rockies of Wyoming, the Colorado Piedmont, and parts of the Colorado Plateaus in Colorado, Utah, Arizona, and New Mexico.

The brown soils are typical of the middle-latitude steppes and support a light growth of grasses suitable for livestock grazing. With irrigation they are productive, but farming is not attempted without.

Reddish-chestnut and reddish-brown soils

Widespread in semi-arid and subhumid tropical and subtropical regions of the world are soils of reddish brown surface color which grade downward into a heavier dull-red or reddish-brown subsoil, then into a zone of lime accumulation. These are classified as *reddish-chestnut* and *reddish-brown soils* and grouped with the reddish prairie soils on the world soils map (Plate 3).

Comparison of the distribution of these reddish soils with the distribution of climate and natural vegetation (Plates 2 and 4) suggest that these soils are found in regions of tropical wet-dry climates with a short wet season and with their bordering tropical steppes. They also occupy regions of Asiatic monsoon wet-dry climate and regions of Mediterranean climates in Australia, North Africa, and the Middle East. Vegetation associated with reddish-chestnut and reddish-brown soils is varied, being tall-grass prairie, short-grass steppe, rain-green savanna and scrub, or monsoon forest. All of the areas of reddish-chestnut and reddish-brown soils have in common a marked degree of aridity of climate, whether associated with an annual cycle or drought in the winter (low-sun season) or in the summer (high-sun season). Very high air temperatures and a severe water deficiency occur at one season of the year. Otherwise, in terms of latitude, these reddish soils occupy the same global positions as areas of latosols and lateritic soils, into which the reddish soils grade in Central and South America, Africa, southern Asia, and Australia.

Aridity in the seasonal climatic cycle explains the occurrence of calcium carbonate in lower layers of the reddish-brown and reddish-chestnut soils, for this is a characteristic of the pedocal soils. Red color is evidence of an abundance of the sesquioxides of iron, which accumulate in warm climates where organic acids are not produced in quantity.

Gray desert soils (sierozem) and red desert soils

Soils of the middle-latitude deserts and tropical deserts fall into two great soil groups on the basis

Figure 14.5 Profile of a brown soil formed from loess in Colorado. The *B* horizon has good prismatic structure. Depths in feet. (Photograph by C. C. Nikiforoff. Courtesy of Soil Conservation Service, U.S. Dept. of Agriculture.)

of color. (1) *gray desert soils*, or *sierozem*, and (2) *red desert soils*.

The gray desert soils, or sierozem, are well developed in Wyoming and in the deserts of Nevada, western Utah, and southern portions of Oregon and Idaho (Figure 14.2). This latter region is sometimes referred to as the Great Basin because of the prevalence of interior drainage systems ending in evaporating basins. It corresponds approximately with the middle-latitude desert climate and has northward extensions into the middle-latitude steppe climate.

The gray desert soils contain little humus because of the sparse growth of vegetation, such as sagebrush and bunchgrass. Color ranges from light gray to grayish brown (color plate, *K*). Horizons are present, but being only slightly differentiated are not conspicuous. Excessive amounts of calcium carbonate are present at depths of less than one foot (0.3 m) in the form of *lime crust*, or *caliche*, a deposit of calcium carbonate or hydrous calcium sulfate. In places this deposit has the appearance of a hard rock layer and may even resist erosion in such a way as to produce small mesas or platforms. Gravels deposited by streams are often thus cemented into a conglomerate rock. Lime crust forms during prolonged dry periods when ground waters rise slowly surfaceword by capillary attraction and evaporate near the surface, leaving the salts behind in the soil.

In the more arid, hotter tropical deserts are found the *red desert soils* (Plate 3). These range from a pale reddish gray to a pronounced deep red (color plate, *L*). Humus is reduced to the minimum, there being only a scattered growth of desert shrubs. Thus the activity of plants as soil formers reaches its lowest point in the red desert soils, as does also the activity of animals. Color is derived from small amounts of oxides of iron. Horizons are poorly developed; texture is often coarse, with many fragments of parent rock throughout the soil. Deposits of lime carbonate are present, as with the gray desert soils.

The gray and red desert soils are suitable for cultivation only where they are fine textured, as along the floodplain terraces of exotic streams and on the outer slopes of alluvial fans. Irrigation is essential, whether water is diverted from a river or obtained from wells penetrating the ground water reserves in alluvial fans.

Altitude and soils

As explained in Chapter 12, climate zoning in mountains tends to reproduce world climates in a series of vertical zones, the effect of increasing altitude being much the same as that of increasing latitude. Because climate is a major determining factor in soils, we might also expect increasing altitude to result in a series of great soil groups. Such a series is illustrated by soils of the Big Horn Mountains in Wyoming (Figure 14.6). Starting with gray desert soils at the lowest elevation, the series progresses through the zonal soils of dry climates through prairie soils to podzols at the high elevations.

Compare these altitude changes with Figure 14.7, which summarizes the profile changes along an imaginary traverse line from the southwestern desert of the United States, eastward across the high plains region, then north into the Lake Superior region.

Halomorphic soils (intrazonal)

In the steppes and deserts, evaporation on the average greatly exceeds precipitation and there are many topographic depressions that have no outlet to external drainage systems. Here the products of rock weathering are brought by intermittent flowing streams in times of flood and left behind on the basin floor. Along with clay, silt and sand are the dissolved mineral salts that crystallize out as the water evaporates.

Shallow lake basins, or *playas*, of extreme flatness are often covered with only a thin film of water which evaporates rapidly, leaving its salts on the surface. Most persons are familiar with the salt flats of Great Salt Lake in Utah, on which so many automobile speed records have been set. Salts found in the various playa lakes of the southwestern United States are *soda* (Na_2CO_3), *borax* ($Na_2B_4O_7$), *calcium carbonate* ($CaCO_3$), various sulfates (Na_2SO_4, $MgSO_4$, K_2SO_4), chlorides ($NaCl$, $CaCl_2$, $MgCl_2$), and many others. Where salts are thick and pure in the inner parts of the playas there is no soil in the true sense of the word. The term *halomorphic soil* is properly applied to marginal areas where silts and clays make up a large proportion of the body of the soil.

The pedogenic process in the development of halomorphic soils is salinization (Chapter 13). Two major groups of halomorphic soils are recognized: *saline soils* (*solonchak*) and *alkali soils* (*solonetz*). Halomorphic soils are classed as intrazonal because of their poor drainage and limited extent.

Saline soils (solonchak, or *white alkali soils*) contain chlorides, sulfates, carbonates, and bicar-

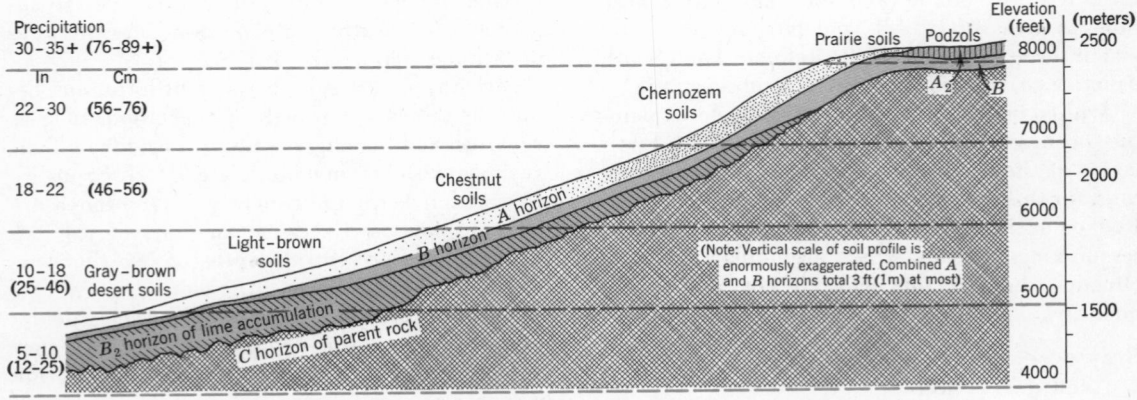

Figure 14.6 This schematic diagram shows the gradation of soils from a dry steppe-climate basin (left) to a cool, humid climate (right) as one ascends the west slopes of the Bighorn Mountains, Wyoming. (After J. Thorp, 1931.)

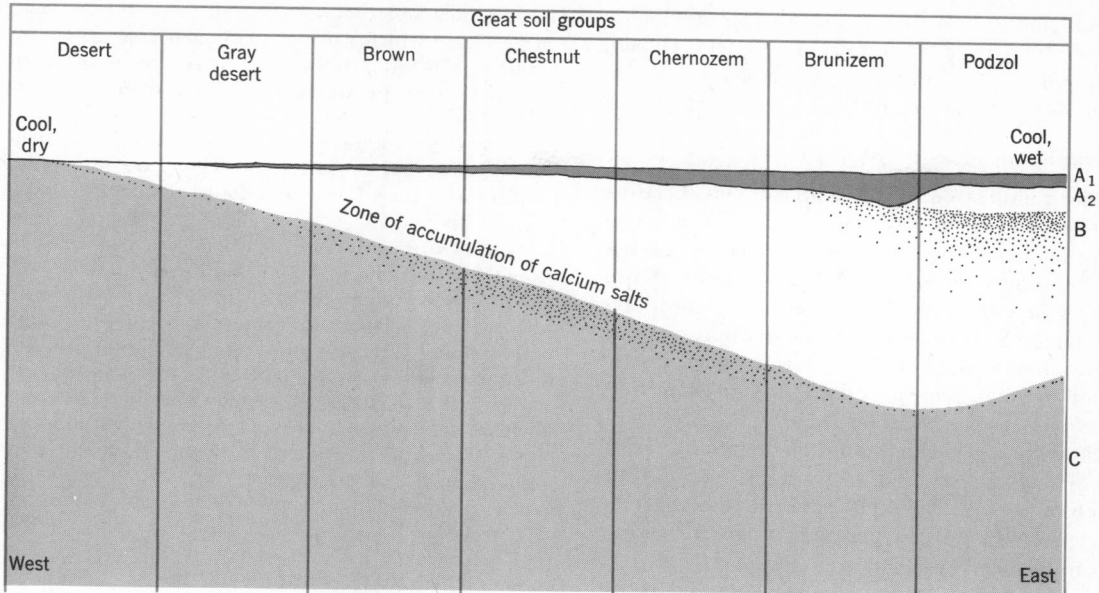

Figure 14.7 Schematic diagram of the relationships among profiles of the great soil groups, traced from dry to humid climates. (After C. E. Millar, L. M. Turk, and H. D. Foth, *Fundamentals of Soil Science*, John Wiley and Sons, New York, 1958.)

bonates of sodium, calcium, magnesium, and potassium. These soils are light colored and show poorly developed horizons (color plate, *O*). Although there are many species of plants adapted to saline soils the plant cover is at best sparse. Plants which are salt-tolerant are known as *halophytic* plants. They include grasses, shrubs, and some trees. Agriculture is not possible on saline soils unless they are flushed out with large quantities of irrigation water to remove the salts. This has been done to advantage to reclaim much good agricultural land in the southwestern United States.

In the second major group of halomorphic soils, the alkali soils (solonetz or *black alkali soils*), sodium salts predominate, especially sodium carbonate ($NaCO_3$). The soil profile is characterized by the presence of a dark, hard, columnar layer, i.e., a layer with prismatic structure (Figure 13.4*B*). Although salts of the alkali soils are of somewhat different chemical properties from salts of the saline soils, both soils occur in the same areas. Alkali soils occupy areas of somewhat better drainage than the saline soils and may be derived from the latter by the removal of more soluble salts (desalinization). Grass and shrub vegetation is found on alkali soils, but the species are particularly alkali-resistant.

With improved drainage—whether by man's intervention or by natural processes—solonetz is transformed by leaching of salts into *soloth*, a halomorphic soil of light-colored, slightly acid surface layer and a heavy-textured, dark brown *B* horizon with columnar structure.

Calcimorphic soils

Another class of intrazonal soils consists of the *calcimorphic soils*. These are soils whose characteristics are strongly related to the presence of lime-rich parent material. The process of *calcification* (introduction of calcium) is dominant in the formation of calcimorphic soils. An important example of the calcimorphic soils are the *rendzina soils*.

Rendzina soils have dark-gray or black surface layers overlying soft, light-gray or white material which is highly calcareous (lime-rich) (color plate, *P*). The parent matter of rendzina soils may be marl (a lime mud), soft limestone, or chalk, all of which are forms of calcium-carbonate. The soil profile is regarded as immature. The natural vegetation is typically grassland, which results in a well-distributed humus in the upper layers and imparts the dark color to the soils, just as in the chernozem.

Distribution of rendzina soils in the United States is fragmented into a number of geologically favorable areas. Substantial areas of these soils are found in undulating prairies of central and northeastern Texas and central-southern Oklahoma (Blackland Prairie and Grand Prairie). Another geographically important area is the Black Belt of Alabama and Mississippi, a lowland underlain by soft limestone. These areas are in the humid subtropical climate. Other rendzina areas occur on a high limestone plateau in northwestern Arizona, and in the Mediterranean climate regime of southern California.

Rendzina soils of the humid subtropical climate are productive agriculturally and yield cotton, corn, and alfalfa. In more arid grassland environments, uses are for grazing and some dry-farming.

A newer soil classification

Since publication of the 1938 soil classification, soil scientists of the Soil Survey, U.S. Department of Agriculture, have engaged in intensive review and modification of the 1938 system. Major changes in soil categories and nomenclature have been made. For students wishing to appraise these developments, there follows a general review of the new system, known as the *7th Approximation*. This review was written by Dr. Roy W. Simonson, Director, Soil Classification and Correlation, Soil Survey, U.S. Department of Agriculture, Soil Conservation Service. Excerpts from the review article are reprinted below by permission of both author and publisher.[1] Reprinted as Appendix I is a map of the United States showing patterns of soil orders and suborders, with explanatory legend and explanation of nomenclature.

History, purpose, and basic objectives of the 7th Approximation

Because it can be no better than the state of knowledge in the soil science of its day, any scheme must eventually be modified or replaced. This is the only way whereby new data or improved understanding of available data can be reflected in soil classification. The need for modifying or replacing old schemes was evident in the several reports on work in progress made to the Seventh International Congress of Soil Science in 1960.

The scheme presented by American pedologists to the 1960 congress has been carried through a succession of stages over a period of years. For purposes of identification, these stages have been numbered, and the stage presented to the 1960 congress is identified as the 7th Approximation of a comprehensive system of soil classification.[2] This approximation is currently being tested, as were earlier stages, and some modifications are likely to follow. These are expected to be modifications in details of the scheme, however, rather than in general structure. Hence, it seems that the scheme embodied in the 7th Approximation will be adopted, with minor changes, in this country within the next few years.

The scheme of soil classification now being developed in the United States differs from earlier schemes prepared in this country and elsewhere in several ways which are important. This scheme reflects evolution in the concept of soil itself. Basic to the scheme is the

[1] Simonson, Roy W., 1962, "Soil Classification in the United States," *Science*, Vol. 137, pp. 1027–1034. Copyright © by the American Association for the Advancement of Science.

[2] Soil Survey Staff, *Soil classification, a comprehensive system—7th Approximation*, U.S. Department of Agriculture Soil Conservation Service, Washington, D.C. 1960.

concept that soil comprises a continuum on the land surface, one which can be subdivided into classes in a variety of ways. Also basic to the scheme is an effort to achieve more quantitative definitions than have been devised heretofore. Definitions of classes at every categoric level are expressed in terms of properties that can be observed or measured. These are important departures from schemes developed earlier for classifying soils.

The basic objectives of the classification scheme are essentially the same as those of earlier schemes, despite the differences in approach. The scheme must first of all organize, define, and name classes in the lowest category, and it must group these classes into progressively broader classes in higher categories and provide names for these classes. Its general purpose is to make the characteristics of soils easier to remember, to bring out relationships among soils and between the soils and other elements of the environment, and to provide a basis for developing principles of soil genesis and soil behavior that have prediction value.

Concept of the pedon

The approach toward solution of this problem followed in the 7th Approximation differs from earlier approaches in several ways. An attempt is being made to define a small volume of soil as the basic entity, one for which the term *pedon* (plural, *pedons*) has been suggested. *Pedon* is proposed as a generic term for small volumes of soil, each large enough for the study of horizons and their interrelationships within the profile and having a roughly circular lateral cross section of between 1 and 10 square meters.

A group of contiguous pedons belonging to a single class of the lowest category (soil series) in the 7th Approximation is identified as a "soil individual" in the monograph. Since the monograph was prepared it has seemed that use of some other term to identify such groups of contiguous pedons would be desirable. Consequently, the term *polypedon* (plural, *polypedons*) has been proposed. A single polypedon is defined as a group of pedons contiguous within the soil continuum and having a range in characteristics within the limits of a single soil series.

Categories within the new system

Like other schemes developed earlier in this country, the 7th Approximation is a multiple-category system. Six categories are used in the scheme. These are identified, from top to bottom, as *orders, suborders, great groups, subgroups, families,* and *series.* Among these categories, that of the soil series has been used in the United States for a long time. The concept of the soil series has been changed over the years, but further change is not proposed in the 7th Approximation. In contrast to the category of the soil series, other categories in the scheme do not correspond exactly in level of generalization to any that have been used previously in this country or elsewhere, so far as is known. The "suborder" category in the 7th Approximation does approach in level of abstraction the category of the great soil group currently in use in this country, but the two are not fully equivalent.

Some measure of the span in properties permitted within classes is indicated by the numbers of classes in the categories. The 7th Approximation provides for the recognition of ten classes in the "order" category. The numbers of classes in the other categories (in rounded numbers) are as follows: suborders, 40; great groups, 120; subgroups, 400; families, 1500; and series, 7000. It should be mentioned that the totals for the three lowest categories cover only the soils of the United States. These totals would be appreciably larger if soils of other continents were included. On the other hand, the total number of each of the orders, suborders, and great groups is expected to remain the same, or virtually so, whether the scheme is applied to the United States or to the world as a whole. The intent has been to provide a place in the scheme for all known soils in the world, though this goal may not have been reached. In the construction of the scheme it is recognized that soils not known to the authors of the scheme may have been omitted. It is also recognized that modification of this scheme or its replacement will eventually become necessary as the knowledge and understanding of soils continue to grow.

Definitions of the classes in the different categories of the 7th Approximation are in terms of morphology and composition of the soils—that is in terms of soil characteristics themselves. Moreover, an attempt is made to have the definitions as nearly quantitative as currently available data will permit.

Nomenclature

The nomenclature proposed in the 7th Approximation represents a marked departure from past practice in soil classification. A new nomenclature is proposed for the classes in each of the four highest categories. The proposed names for classes in the order, suborder, great group, and subgroup categories consist of coined terms in which Greek and Latin roots are largely used. (See Appendix I.) The names are distinctive for the classes in each category, so that a name itself will indicate the category to which a given class belongs. Moreover, the names are designed so that each subgroup may be identified, by its name, with the great group, suborder, and order in which it is classified.

Several objectives have been kept in mind in developing the proposed nomenclature. Efforts were made to devise names that were distinctive and could be easily remembered, would suggest a few characteristics of the soils in each class, would identify the categorical level to which a class belonged, would fit into the existing pattern of language readily, and would provide convenient adjective as well as substantive forms. An effort to reach all of these objectives simultaneously is ambitious, and the several are not compatible in all cases. Hence, it is not surprising that some defects have already been noted in the proposed nomenclature.

The ten orders

The names of the ten orders consist of three or four syllables, and every name ends in the suffix *sol*. The names of the ten orders are "entisols," "vertisols," "inceptisols," "aridisols," "mollisols," "spodosols," "alfisols," "ultisols," "oxisols," and "histosols" (the letter *s* is added for the plural form). (See Appendix I.)

The ten orders are set apart on the basis of one or more of the following factors: gross composition, degree of horizonation, the presence or absence of certain horizons, and what is in effect a combined index of weathering and weatherability of minerals. The characteristics selected to distinguish the orders are believed to reflect major differences in paths of horizon differentiation, in stages reached in horizon differentiation, or in both. To state this another way, the intent has been to choose as differentiating characteristics properties that reflect major differences in genesis of the soils. Whether the selections have been successful for this purpose, and if they have been, to what degree, will become evident only after the scheme has been tested for a time.

The bases for distinguishing ten orders may be made clearer by some illustrations. Full definitions will not be given here for any of the orders, but the principal differentiae for the histosols, entisols, mollisols, and spodosols will be sketched briefly.

The histosols are organic soils, mainly those known as peats and mucks. these are distinguished from soils of the other nine orders by differences in gross composition: histosols are high in organic matter (20 percent or more). The balance among processes of horizon differentiation in soils so high in organic matter is very different from that in dominantly mineral soils.

The entisols are mineral soils with low degrees of horizonation, mainly those that have been identified as lithosols, regosols, and alluvial soils in the United States in recent years. The entisols have few and faint horizons in their profiles. These soils are in early stages of horizon differentiation. Some are forming in regoliths consisting of highly resistant minerals; others in areas where accretions of fresh materials keep pace with horizon differentiation; still others in areas where removal by erosion keeps pace with horizon differentiation.

The mollisols are mineral soils which have a characteristic known as a *mollic epipedon*. This is a darkened surface layer of considerable thickness, relatively high in organic matter, high in base saturation, and friable. For identification as a mollic epipedon, minimum requirements for thickness, color, base saturation, level of organic matter, and consistence are given. Unlike the histosols and entisols, mollisols tend to occur within certain geographic zones. Such soils are the major ones of the Corn Belt and Great Plains in the United States. Mollisols have been formed almost entirely under prairie vegetation in semiarid-to-subhumid climates. Included in the mollisols are the chernozems, studied almost a century ago by Dokuchaiev in Russia.

The spodosols are mineral soils which have a characteristic known as a spodic horizon. This is a subsurface horizon of illuvial accumulation of humus, usually in conjunction with accumulation of iron or aluminum, or both. The spodic horizon corresponds closely to the *B* horizon of podzols, as those soils have been described in North America and western Europe.

Like the mollisols, and spodosols tend to be associated with certain climatic and vegetation types. These soils are found in cool, humid regions, for the most part, and they are formed mainly under coniferous forest or under vegetation dominated by plants such as heather. The spodosols occur extensively in eastern Canada, in New England and the northern Lake States, and in the taiga region of the Soviet Union. Such soils often have strikingly different horizons in the same profile, and this may be why they were among the first to be studied with care.

Suborders

The basic approach followed in defining orders in the 7th Approximation is carried down to the suborder and great-group categories, though the same characteristics are not used as criteria. Additional characteristics of the soil are introduced as criteria for distinguishing classes at each level.

The kinds of characteristics used in differentiating suborders within orders are moisture regimes, temperature, mineralogy, and specific kinds of horizons. One suborder is set apart in each of eight orders because of the evidence of wetness in the morphology of the soils. In two of the orders, one pair of suborders is distinguished mainly on the basis of temperature. The mineralogy of the soil—for example, very high levels of quartz, dominance of allophone, or high proportions of calcium carbonate—provides criteria for recognizing at least one suborder in each of four orders. Characteristics such as an argillic horizon, a cambic horizon, and the tonguing of an albic horizon into an argillic horizon are definitive for at least one suborder in each of five orders.

The name of each suborder is a two-syllable rather than a three- or four-syllable term. Each name consists of a prefix syllable with a specific connotation plus a syllable from the name of the order in which the suborder is classified. Fourteen formative elements are used as prefixes in the construction of suborder names. Thus, for example, suborders in the order of entisols are identified as "aquents," "ustents," and "udents." (See Appendix I.)

Great groups and subgroups

The setting apart of great groups within suborders is based on the same kinds of criteria as is the distinguishing of suborders within orders. Great groups are distinguished within suborders by the presence or absence of characteristic horizons or other features, the occurrence of horizons extraneous to the sequence required for the suborder, and temperature. The range of definitive characteristics within individual classes has been reduced step by step in coming down the ladder from the order to the suborder to the great group. Thus, the soils of a great group are more homogeneous in their characteristics than are soils of classes in higher categories. For each great group, the soils have the same kinds of horizons in the same sequence within pedons, except for surface horizons, which may be obliterated by plowing or by erosion.

The approach in defining subgroups differs from that followed in defining classes in higher categories. As explained earlier, a typifying subgroup is first defined for each great group and identified by the term *orthic* preceding the great-group name. This subgroup has the median expression of the definitive characteristics of the great group. In addition to the orthic subgroup, other subgroups are set apart as intergrade or extragrade subgroups. Intergrade subgroups have some characteristics definitive of another great group, either in the same order or in some other order. Extragrade subgroups have some properties that are not definitive of any known great group. In both intergrade and extragrade subgroups, however, the soils are more like the orthic or central subgroup of the great group to which each belongs than to any other known kind of soil. Recognition of orthic, intergrade, and extragrade subgroups is one device for recognizing that the soil mantle forms a continuum in which changes are gradational rather than abrupt.

REFERENCES FOR FURTHER STUDY

U.S. Dept. of Agriculture (1938), *Soils and men; yearbook of agriculture 1938*, U.S. Govt. Printing Office, Washington, D.C., 1232 pp.

Robinson, G. W. (1959), *Soils, their origin, constitution and classification*, third edition, John Wiley and Sons, New York, 573 pp.

Bunting, B. T. (1965), *The geography of soil*, Aldine Publ. Co., Chicago, 213 pp.

Millar, C. E., L. M. Turk, and H. D. Foth (1965), *Fundamentals of soil science*, fourth edition, John Wiley and Sons, New York, 491 pp.

Money, D. C. (1965), *Climate, soils, and vegetation*, University Tutorial Press, Ltd., London, 272 pp.

Eyre, S. R. (1968), *Vegetation and soils; a world picture*, second edition, Aldine Publishing Co., Chicago, 328 pp.

REVIEW QUESTIONS

1. What are the three orders into which all soils can be classified? Under what conditions is each of these orders developed? What kinds of soils are included under the azonal order?

2. How did our present system of soil classification develop? What basic concepts underlie the classification? Name persons who made important contributions to this field.

3. Describe the profile of a typical podzol soil. What climatic conditions are required for the development of soils of this group? What is the natural vegetation of this great soil group? How do these soils rate in terms of agricultural productivity? In what ways do they require treatment?

4. How do the gray-brown podzolic soils differ from the podzol soils? How do the climatic factors differ? What geographic positions do the gray-brown podzolic soils have with respect to the podzols? How does natural vegetation of the two soil groups differ? Which soil group is better for agricultural purposes? Why?

5. What are the essential characteristics of the red-yellow soils? With what climate are they associated? Explain how temperature and precipitation determine the features of these soils. What types of forest are found on the red-yellow soils?

6. What is terra rossa? Where is it found? What ideas have been advanced as to the origin of terra rossa?

7. What are latosols (lateritic soils)? What are their essential characteristics? What is meant by laterization? How do latosols rate in terms of agricultural productivity?

8. How can laterite be used as a building material? What are some of the residual ores obtained from laterites?

9. Describe other soils of humid tropical and equatorial climates.

10. What are hydromorphic soils? Why are the bog and meadow soils classed as intrazonal? What is the appearance of the profiles of these soils? What is the glei horizon? How do meadow soils differ from bog soils?

11. What are planosols? To what order do they belong? Where do planosols develop, and what is different about their profiles as compared with associated zonal soils?

12. Describe a tundra soil. In what respect does it differ from the podzol soils? What effect has excessive cold upon the composition of the parent material of the soil? Where are the arctic brown forest soils found?

13. What are the chernozem soils? Where were these soils first studied? Where are they best developed? Describe the chernozem profile.

14. What is the essential difference between the chernozems and the podzolic soils? With what climatic characteristics are the chernozem regions associated?

15. What is the natural vegetation of chernozem soils? How is loess associated with the chernozem?

16. In what way are the prairie soils related to both the chernozems and the gray-brown podzolic soils? What is the nature of the geographic and climatic location of the prairie soils?

17. What are the tall-grass prairies? What theories have been advanced for the absence of forests in these areas? With what crops are the prairie regions now associated in the central United States? Where are reddish prairie soils found?

18. Where are the chestnut soils (dark-brown soils) located in relation to the chernozems? With what climatic conditions are they associated?

19. How do the brown soils differ from the chestnut soils? What is distinctive about the *B* horizon of a brown soil?

20. Describe reddish-chestnut and reddish-brown soils. Where are they found, and with what climates and natural vegetation types are they associated?

21. Describe the gray-desert soils and red-desert soils. How do these two groups differ in geographic location and in climatic controls? Are horizons well developed in these soils? What forms do excessive calcium carbonate and hydrous calcium sulfate take in these soils?

22. How does altitude influence the development of soil types? In an arid region in middle latitudes, what succession of soil groups might be encountered in passing from an intermontane basin to a lofty mountain summit?

23. What are halomorphic soils? Where do saline soils form? What are some of the salts found in playa lakes of the dry deserts? How do the alkali soils differ from the saline soils?

24. What are calcimorphic soils? Describe rendzina soils and give locations of three occurrences. Why are rendzina soils regarded as intrazonal?

Structure and Environment of Vegetation

VEGETATION on the lands of the earth is of prime concern to the geographer. Plants, as stationary objects possessing distinctive physical properties, are an element of the landscape just as fully as landforms, soils, and hydrographic features. That the physical forms of individual plants and of their assemblages vary in some systematic way with latitude, elevation, and continental position excites the interest of the geographer and causes him to inquire more closely into the interrelations of vegetation, soils, landforms, and climate. Plants, as consumable and renewable sources of food, fuel, clothing, shelter and many other categories of life-essentials, form a great natural resource base essential to man. The ways in which man has used these resources to his advantage—or has been hindered by plants in his progress—throughout human history forms a vital part of historical geography; the present and future development and management of plant resources is a part of the fabric of many studies of economic and political geography.

Our concern here is with *natural vegetation*, that is, vegetation which develops without appreciable interference and modification by man. The widespread activities of man in agriculture, herding, forest-cropping, and urbanization guarantee that a considerable proportion of the earth's land surfaces does not bear a natural vegetation. Nevertheless, from the study of islandlike remnants of protected plant life and historical records, the plant geographer can achieve some success in the global mapping of broad units of natural vegetation. (See Chapter 16.) Such maps represent the vegetation that might be expected eventually to return through a series of stages, if man's interference with the natural regimen were to be suspended.

Floristic or structural approach?

Our selection of study topics is extremely limited in terms of the scope of the science of botany and even of plant geography as a specialized field within botany. Emphasis here is not upon a *floristic* approach, that is an approach primarily concerned with the *flora*. Should we describe the flora of a region, we would produce a list of the plant species found there. But such a list would tell us little about the relative abundance of the species; their physical forms; and their characteristic arrangements as landscape elements.

To be sure, where the trees of a forest consist largely of two or three dominant species, it will be desirable to name these species and to designate the forest accordingly. For example, one finds in the plateaus of Arizona and Utah a woodland in which the tree population consists almost exclusively of pinyon pine (*Pinus edulis*) and juniper (*Juniperus utahensis*). Through our knowledge of the characteristic height, branching habit, and foliage of these species we gain a true picture of the physical form of the woodland. Such a terse forest description by floristic means would be impossible in an equatorial forest composed of scores of different species. Instead, the forest must be described according to its *structure*, that is, by the way in which the living parts of the plants are shaped and distributed in space. Generally, in the classification of the world's natural vegetation, the structural approach is most meaningful to follow.

Bioclimatology and ecology

Our study of plant geography will not be concerned with the historical aspects, that is, with the evolution of plants and the spread and decline of floras through geologic time. On the other hand, we will be greatly interested in the *bioclimatological* aspects of plant geography in which the responses of plants to light, heat, and moisture are studied and the knowledge of climate elements and their global distribution is brought into play. If we choose, the bioclimatological approach can be narrowed to the response of a single species to a single meteorological element.

A quite different approach to the question of a plant's relation to its environmental influences is to consider together all the organisms—plant and animal—living in one place at one time in terms of their total environment and of their adjustments to both the environment and to each other. Such a whole dynamic system is referred to as an *ecosystem*; the study of an ecosystem is *plant ecology*. The ecosystem represents the combined use by plants and animals of the resources provided, in one place at one time, by the surroundings. Air, water, nutrients, heat, and light are variously utilized, transformed, stored, and returned to the nonliving state.

The biosphere and its subdivision

To fix the place of natural vegetation units in the scheme of life on earth we begin with the total system, or *biosphere*, which encompasses the entire near-surface zone of the earth favorable to life in one form or another. The biosphere may be subdivided into three environmental divisions, or *biocycles*: (1) *salt water* (oceans), (2) *fresh water* (streams, lakes, ponds), and (3) *land* (soil and the air in contact with it). We are interested primarily in the land biocycle, although the geographer's concern extends into the fresh water and salt water biocycles as well.

The land biocycle is divided into ecological systems of decreasing size and complexity, schematically represented in Figure 15.1*A*. Four great *biochores* comprise the land biocycle: (*a*) *forest*, (*b*) *savanna*, (*c*) *grassland*, and (*d*) *desert*. (See Figure 16.1). These four classes of vegetation are separated on the basis of the structure of the plant assemblages and represent the fundamental re-

sponse of vegetation to global climate controls, principally available moisture (precipitation and evaporation), but secondarily light, heat, and winds. The four biochores comprise systems too vast in area and having too wide a variation within each biochore to use in the mapping of world vegetation. Therefore, within the biochores are *formation classes*—altogether from 15 to 20 or more in number, depending upon the judgment of the plant geographer whose classification system is used. Thus there are clearly several varieties of forests (e.g., rainforest, deciduous forest, needleleaf forest) each responding to the climate regime to which it is subjected. Definitions of such terms as "forest," "woodland," and "grassland" are given in the discussion of the individual formation classes in Chapter 16. The distinction among the several biochores and their included formation classes is made on the basis of the plant structure, rather than species. Thus classification is structural, rather than floristic.

Plant habitats and communities

As we all know from direct experience, vegetation is strongly influenced by landforms and soil. Vegetation on an upland, that is, on relatively high ground of moderate surface slope and thick soil,

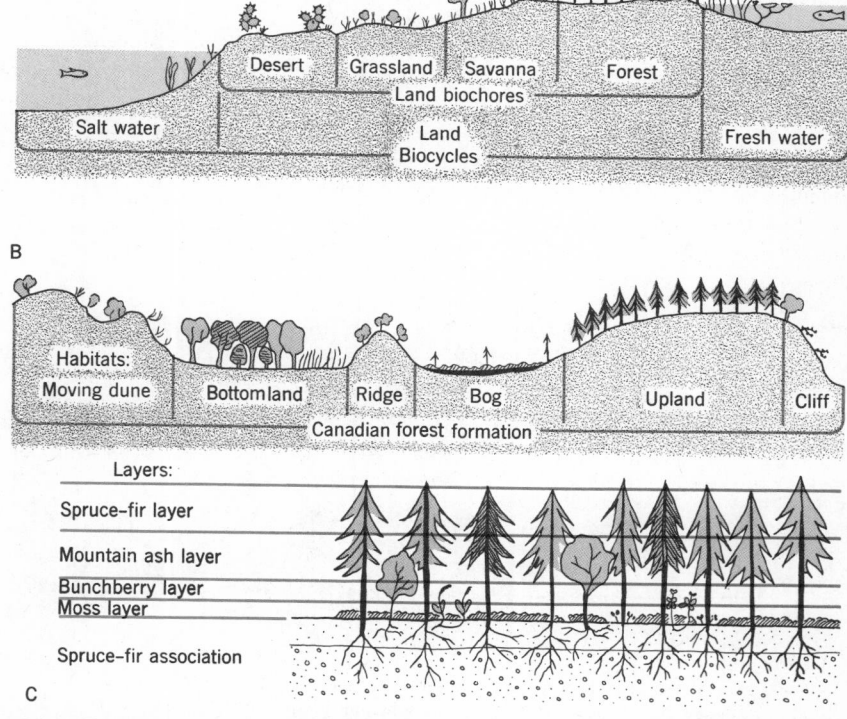

Figure 15.1 Dimensions of the environment. *A*, the biocycles and biochores. *B*, Habitats in the Canadian forest formation. *C*, Detail of spruce-fir upland association. (From Pierre Dansereau, 1951, *Ecology*, Vol. 32.)

is quite different from that on an adjacent valley floor where water lies near the surface much of the time. Vegetation is also strikingly different in form on rocky ridges and on steep cliffs where water drains away rapidly and soil is thin or largely absent.

Thus, each region which we assign to a given formation class is actually a mosaic of smaller units reflecting the inequalities in conditions of slope, elevation, and soil type. Such subdivisions of the plant environment are described as *habitats* (Figure 15.1*B*). In the example shown, the Canadian needleleaf forest (a formation class) actually comprises at least six habitats: upland, bog, bottomland, ridge, cliff, and active dune. Just where each habitat is located and how large an area it occupies depends largely upon the geologic history of the region, e.g., what processes of erosion and deposition have acted in the past to shape the landforms. The patterns of landforms from such processes are in turn influenced by the ancient geologic history which brought about varied combinations of arrangements of weak and resistant rocks. In the final part of this book, the evolution of landforms is explained in some detail.

Closely tied in with the effect of landform upon habitat is the distribution of water in the soil and rock, a topic also treated in later chapters. Finally, each habitat has characteristic soil properties which are determined not only by the conditions of slope and water, but in part by the plants themselves.

Adjacent habitats may possess strikingly different vegetation structures so that the question arises as to which habitat shall be selected as that for which the formation class is named. For this purpose the upland habitat, with its well-drained surface, moderate surface slopes, and well-developed soil, is usually taken as the reference standard.

The vegetation structure found in the upland habitat is thus what we have in mind when naming and describing a formation class (Figure 15.1*C*).

Within a given habitat will be found a smaller unit of ecosystem, the *plant community*, composed of rather definite proportions of organisms which are more or less interdependent and which use the resources of their habitat in such a way as to either maintain the habitat or modify it. No particular dimensions and boundary limits can be set for plant communities; these properties will depend on the changing habitat patterns. Within a given plant community can be recognized a structure of vegetation which is distinctive and a certain floristic composition, which may seem more or less fixed, or which may be gradually changing with time.

Structural description of vegetation

If the plant geographer is to describe vegetation according to its structure, or physical properties and outward forms, he must set up a number of categories of information, each designed to contribute an essential element to the description of the vegetation. Six categories are used in a system set up by Dr. Pierre Dansereau.[1] These six categories of information tell us about the growth-form of the plants, their size and stratification, the degree to which they cover the ground, their time functions, and their leaf forms.

1. *Life-form.* Plants can be classified according to their life-forms. The first two forms, *trees* and *shrubs* are erect, woody plants (Figure 15.2). The word "tree" means a perennial plant having a single upright main trunk, often with few branches

[1] Dansereau, Pierre (1957), *Biogeography, an ecological perspective*, The Ronald Press Co., New York. See pp. 147–154.

Figure 15.2   Schematic diagram of life forms in a beech-maple-hemlock forest. The tree layer consists of sugar maple (As), ash (Fa), beech (Fg), and hemlock (Tc) and includes a liana (Cs). The shrub layer includes elder (Sp), dogwood (Ca), and a young hemlock (Tc). An epiphyte (Ul) grows upon the hemlock. Plants designated Te, Mr, Cb, and Cu form the herb layer. Moss (Du) forms the lowest layer. (From Pierre Dansereau, 1951, *Ecology*, Vol. 32.)

Figure 15.3 A stand of mature sugar maples, 160 to 200 years old, in the Allegheny National Forest, Pennsylvania, 1939. (U.S. Forest Service photograph.)

Figure 15.4 Lianas of the equatorial rainforest, near Belém, Brazil. (Photograph by Otto Penner. Courtesy of Instituto Agronómico do Norte.)

in the lower part, but branching in the upper part to a crown which, in the mature individual, contributes to one of the upper layers of vegetation (Figure 15.3). The word "shrub" generally refers to a woody plant having several stems branching near the ground, so as to place the foliage in a mass starting close to ground level. Next are recognized woody vines which climb up on trees: the *lianas* (Figure 15.4). These may climb upon mature plants, or may be lifted during the growth of young trees to which they have become attached. Although the term "liana" is usually associated with woody vines of tropical forests, the meaning may be broadened to include woody vines of middle-latitude forests, such as the poison ivy and Virginia creeper. Thus it is apparent that the life-form classes cut across the taxonomic categories of the plant world. For example, palms and tree ferns look much alike outwardly but are of entirely different plant orders.

Fourth of the life-forms is the plant group known as the *herbs*. These are usually small tender plants, lacking woody stems. They occur in a wide variety of forms and leaf structures; including annuals and perennials, and broad-leaved plants as well as the grasses. Broad-leaved herbs are termed *forbs* in distinction with grasses. The adjective *herbaceous* is applied to this life-form. The herbaceous layer will normally occupy a low position in a layered or stratified plant community. Smaller, and lying in close contact with the ground or attached to tree trunks are the *bryoids,* a life-form named for a plant phylum which includes the mosses and liverworts.

Finally, among the life-forms are the *epiphytes*, plants which use other plants as supporting structures and thus live above the ground level, out of contact with soil (Figure 15.5). Familiar to all are the tropical orchids that live high upon tree limbs and are sometimes referred to as "air plants." Ferns also commonly exist as epiphytes (see Figure 16.5).

Not included in our list of life-forms are lower forms of plants, grouped under the name of *thallophytes*. These include bacteria, algae, molds, and fungi—all of which are plants lacking true roots, stems, and leaves. *Lichens*, plant forms in which algae and fungi live together to form a single plant structure, are included within the life-form classification of bryoids. Lichens occur as tough, leathery coatings or crusts and as leaflike masses attached to rocks and tree trunks (Figure 15.6). In arctic and alpine environments lichens may grow in profusion and dominate the vegetation in the near absence of more conspicuous plant forms.

Figure 15.5 An epiphyte, or air plant. This *Bromeliad* is attached to a limb of the host tree by a mass of fibrous roots. The plant leaves form an urn-shaped structure that collects and holds rainfall. About $\frac{1}{7}$ natural size. (After W. H. Brown, 1935, *The Plant Kingdom*, courtesy of Blaisdell Publishing Co., a Division of Ginn and Co.)

Figure 15.6 A lichen (*Stereocaulon vulcani*) growing on a rough lava surface, Waiakea Forest Reserve, Maua, Hawaii. (Photograph by Pierre Dansereau.)

2. *Size and stratification.* Each of the life-forms described above may be classified according to size. The words "tall," "medium," and "low" may be given definite limits for each life-form. For example, a tree higher than 25 meters (82 feet) is "tall"; from 10 to 25 meters (33 to 82 feet) is "medium"; 8 to 10 meters (26 to 33 feet), "low." For the smaller life-forms different limits are set (Table 15.1). Such standardization of size enables the plant geographer to make precise descriptions of vegetation. Further standardization is achieved by setting height limits for a series of layers, numbered successively from the ground up (Table 15.1).

3. *Coverage.* The degree to which the foliage of individual plants of a given life-form cover the ground beneath them is designated the *coverage.* We may use four terms descriptive of the coverage: barren or very sparse; discontinuous; in tufts or groups; and continuous. For example, the trees may be of discontinuous coverage whereas the herb layer is continuous, or vice versa.

4. *Function, or periodicity.* Of primary importance in the classification of forms of natural vegetation is the response of the plant foliage to the annual climatic cycle. *Deciduous* plants shed their leaves and become dormant in an unfavorable season, which is either too cold or too dry to permit growth. *Evergreen* plants retain green foliage year-around, although in some cases becoming almost dormant in a cold or dry season. Where the climate is equable (that is, moist and not cold throughout the year) evergreen plants grow continuously. A third class, the *semideciduous* plants, are those which shed their leaves at intervals not in phase with a season. Thus a semideciduous forest would not at any one time have all of its individuals devoid of foliage. As a fourth class we recognize *evergreen-succulent* and *evergreen-leafless* plants, those with very thick fleshy leaves, which retain their foliage year-around, and those with fleshy stems but no functional leaves, such as the cacti.

5. *Leaf shape and size.* Recognition of the leaf form of a plant constitutes an essential part of the structural description (Figure 15.7). One form is the *broadleaf*, familiar to us in such common trees as the maple, beech, and rhododendron. In contrast is the *needleleaf*, also familiar in the pine, spruce, fir, and hemlock. A similar form is the *spine*, which in some plants represents the transformation of the entire leaf. The slender, tapering leaves of grass are referred to as *graminoid* in form. We may also recognize the *small leaf-form*, as in the birch or holly; and the *compound leaf*, as in the hickory and ash.

6. *Leaf texture.* Leaf textures range widely according to the climate and habitat, because of the different degrees to which the water loss from the leaf into the air must be controlled. Leaves of average thickness are described as *membranous;* those which are thin and delicate (as in the maidenhair fern) are described as *filmy.* Leaves which are hard, thick, and leathery are *sclerophyllous;* a forest dominated by trees and shrubs having such

TABLE 15.1 PLANT SIZE AND
STRATIFICATION OF VEGETATION[a]

Plant Size

TALL:	Tree	Over 82 ft (25 m)
	Shrub	6.6 to 26 ft (2 to 8 m)
	Herb	Over 6.6 ft (2 m)
MEDIUM:	Tree	33 to 82 ft (10 to 25 m)
	Shrub	1.6 to 6.6 ft (0.5 to 2 m)
	Herb	1.6 to 6.6 ft (0.5 to 2 m)
	Bryoid	Over 4 in (10 cm)
LOW:	Tree	26 to 33 ft (8 to 10 m)
	Shrub	Under 1.6 ft (0.5 m)
	Herb	Under 1.6 ft (0.5 m)
	Bryoid	Under 4 in (10 cm)

Stratification

LAYER NUMBER	RANGE
7	Over 82 ft (25 m)
6	33 to 82 ft (10 to 25 m)
5	26 to 33 ft (8 to 10 m)
4	6.6 to 26 ft (2 to 8 m)
3	1.6 to 6.6 ft (0.5 to 2 m)
2	4 in to 1.6 ft (10 cm to 0.5 m)
1	0 to 4 in (0 to 10 cm)

[a] After Pierre Dansereau, 1958, Botanical Institute of the University of Montreal, *Contributions* No. 72, pp. 31–32.

Figure 15.7 Leaf shapes. *A*, Large thin leaf (sycamore). *B*, Needle leaf (pine). *C*, Spine. *D*, Graminoid leaf (grass). *E*, Small leaf. *F*, Compound leaf (fern). *G*, Succulent stem (cactus).

leaves is termed a *sclerophyll forest*. Very greatly thickened leaves, capable of holding much water in their spongy structure, are described as *succulent*.

Environmental factors in plant ecology

With some information now at our disposal concerning the structure of vegetation and its organization into plant communities, associations, formation-classes, and biochores, we can study the environmental factors which require vegetation to assume such varied forms.

The four main classes of environmental factors are (1) *climatic*, (2) *geomorphic* (related to land-form), (3) *edaphic* (related to soil), and (4) *biotic* (related to living organisms). Although we treat each of these classes of factors in turn and examine each factor separately, it must be kept in mind that the basic concept of ecology is that many factors act simultaneously and that factors affect one another in a most complex interrelationship. The very plants that are affected by environmental factors may react in such a way as to modify the environment and thus change the factors themselves.

In considering how various factors of the physical environment influence plant structures and distributions, two scale ranges can be treated. One is essentially the global scale and consists of such climatic factors as the seasonal and latitudinal patterns of insolation, light and darkness, temperature, precipitation, and prevailing winds. The other scale of consideration is that of variations of the physical environment found within a relatively small habitat and between adjacent habitats. Thus, although there are vast global climate patterns of deserts and humid regions, we may also find within a region of generally humid climate a few small habitats (such as a dune or cliff) which are extremely dry places for plants to live. We may also find in a large desert some small habitats which are extremely wet most of the time (such as a seep or spring).

Water needs of plants

The need for water is perhaps the dominating consideration in analyzing the physical environment of plants. In conjunction with their growth processes, leaf-bearing plants give off large quantities of water into the atmosphere, a process termed *transpiration*, which is essentially a form of evaporation from water films upon the exposed surfaces of plant cells. A relatively small amount of water is also required by green plants in the process of *photosynthesis* in which the energy of light is used together with carbon dioxide and water to produce carbohydrates. The dominant source of water needed for transpiration and photosynthesis is from the soil, where it is taken up into the plant roots.

The rate of transpiration varies greatly according to the type of plant and the prevailing atmospheric conditions. High temperatures, low humidities, and winds favor high rates of transpiration. The plant structure, particularly of the leaf, largely determines the rate of water loss. Plants with large total foliage surfaces composed of broad, thin leaves have higher rates of loss than plants bearing needle leaves, spines, or small thick leaves (sclerophylls). Under conditions of critical water supply but high rates of evaporation, only those plants can survive that minimize transpiration losses by their special leaf structures and by their small size.

The adaptation of plant structures to water budgets with large water deficiencies is of particular interest to the plant geographer. Transpiration occurs largely from specialized leaf pores, called *stomata*, which are openings in the *epidermis* (outer cell layer) and *cuticle* (an outermost protective layer) through which water vapor and other gases can pass into and out of the leaf (Figure 15.8). Surrounding the openings of the stomata are *guard cells* which can open and close the openings and thus to some extent regulate the flow of water vapor and other gases. Although most of the transpiration occurs through the stomata, some may pass through the cuticle. This latter form of loss is reduced in some plants by thickening of the outer layers of cells or by the deposition of wax or waxlike material on or near the leaf surface. Thus many desert plants have thickened cuticle or wax-coated leaves, stems, or branches.

Another means of reducing transpiration is the development of stomata deeply sunken into the leaf surface that retard outward diffusion of water vapor into dry air, and the restriction in location of stomata to the shaded undersurfaces of leaves. A plant may also adapt to a desert environment by greatly reducing the leaf area, or by bearing no leaves at all. Thus needle-leaves and spines representing leaves greatly reduce loss from transpiration. In cacti the foliage leaf is not present and transpiration is limited to fleshy stems.

In addition to developing leaf structures that reduce water loss by transpiration, plants in a water-scarce environment improve their means of obtaining water and of storing it. Roots become greatly extended to reach soil moisture at increased depth. In cases where the roots reach to the ground water table, a steady supply of water is assured. Plants drawing from such a source are termed *phreatophytes* and may be found along dry channels (draws) and alluvial valley floors in desert regions. Other desert plants produce a widespread but shallow root system enabling them to absorb the maximum quantity of water from sporadic desert downpours which saturate only the uppermost soil layer. Stems of desert plants are commonly greatly thickened by a spongy tissue in which much water can be stored. As already noted, such plants would be described as *succulents*.

A quite different adaptation to extreme aridity is seen in many species of small desert plants that complete a very short cycle of germination, leafing,

Figure 15.8 Cell structure of a foliage leaf. (After W. W. Robbins and T. E. Weier, 1950, *Botany*, John Wiley and Sons.)

flowering, fruiting, and seed dispersal immediately following a desert downpour.

Classification of plants by water need

Habitats of the land biocycle are differentiated primarily with reference to the degree of saturation of the soil by water. So important is this factor that plants may be classified according to their water requirements. The terminology associated with the water factor is built upon three simple prefixes of Greek roots: *xero-*, dry; *hygro-(hydro)*, wet; and *meso-*, intermediate or middle. Thus a habitat may be prevailing wet (*hygric*); prevailingly dry (*xeric*), or of intermediate degree of wetness (*mesic*). Those plants which grow in dry habitats are *xerophytes*; those which grow in water or in wet habitats are *hygrophytes* (*hydrophytes*); those of habitats of an intermediate degree of wetness and relatively uniform water availability are *mesophytes*.

The xerophytes are highly tolerant of drought and can survive in habitats which dry quickly following rapid drainage of precipitation, for example, on sand dunes, beaches, and bare rock surfaces. The plants typical of dry climates (deserts) are also xerophytes; cactus is an example. The hygrophytes are tolerant of excessive water and may be found in shallow streams, lakes, marshes, swamps, and bogs; an example is the water lily. The mesophytes are found in upland habitats in regions of ample rainfall. Here the drainage of precipitation is good and moisture penetrates deeply where it can later be used by the plants. On such upland locations the soil may be of intermediate texture—not too coarse or too fine—and is usually thickly and uniformly present.

Certain of the climatic regimes, such as the tropical wet-dry regime (including monsoon climates) and the continental regime where moist but not too cold, have a yearly cycle with one season in which water is unavailable to plants because of lack of precipitation or because the soil water is frozen. This season alternates with one in which there is abundant water. Plants adapted to such regimes are termed *tropophytes*, from the Greek word *trophos*, meaning change, or turn. Tropophytes may meet the impact of the season of unavailable water by dropping their leaves and becoming dormant. When water is again available, they leaf out and grow at a rapid rate. Trees and shrubs which seasonally shed their leaves are said to be *deciduous*; in distinction with *evergreen* trees which retain most of their leaves in a green state throughout the year.

Other climatic factors

The factor of light is of importance in plant ecology. Within the habitat of a given plant association or community the degree of light available will depend in large part upon position of the plant. Tree crowns of the upper layer receive maximum light, but correspondingly reduce the amount available to lower layers. In extreme cases forest trees so effectively cut off light that the forest floor is almost free of shrubs and herbaceous plants. In certain deciduous forests of middle latitudes, the period of early spring, before the trees are in leaf, is one of high light intensity at ground level, permitting certain herbaceous plants to go through a rapid growth cycle. In summer these plants will largely disappear as the leaf canopy is completed. Other herbaceous plants in the same habitat require shade and do not appear until later in the summer.

Treated on a global basis, the factor of light available for plant growth is varied by latitude. Duration of daylight in summer increases rapidly with higher latitude and reaches its maximum poleward of the arctic and antarctic circles, where the sun may be above the horizon for 24 hours (Chapter 2). Thus, although the growing season for plants is greatly shortened at high latitudes by frost, the rate of plant growth in the short frost-free summer is greatly accelerated by the prolonged daylight. But in still higher, subarctic latitudes plant growth is greatly slowed by the low heat budget, despite perpetual summer daylight.

In middle latitudes, where vegetation is of a deciduous type, the annual rhythm of increasing and decreasing periods of daylight determines the timing of budding, flowering, fruiting, leaf-shedding, and other vegetation activities. As to the importance of light intensity itself, it is generally believed that even on overcast days there is sufficient light to permit plants to carry out photosynthesis at their maximum rates and that direct sunlight constitutes a considerable excess of light.

Temperature, another of the important climatic factors in plant ecology, acts directly upon plants through its influence upon the rates at which the physiological processes take place. In general, we can say that each plant species has an optimum temperature associated with each of its functions, such as photosynthesis, flowering, fruiting, or seed germination, and that there exist some overall optimum yearly temperature conditions for its growth in terms of size and numbers of individuals. There are also limiting lower and upper temperatures for the individual functions of the plant as well as for its total survival. Temperature acts as an indirect factor in many other ways. Higher air temperatures increase the water-vapor capacity of the air and thus induce greater plant transpiration as well as greater rates of evaporative loss of moisture from the soil.

In general, the colder the climate, the fewer

Figure 15.9 Bioclimatic limits of the sugar maple (*Acer saccharophorum*) in eastern North America. The shaded area represents the distribution of the sugar maple. Line 1, 30 in (76 cm) annual precipitation. Line 2, −40°F (−40°C) mean annual minimum temperature. Line 3, eastern limit of yearly boundary between arid and humid climates. Line 4, 10 in (25 cm) mean annual snowfall. Line 5, 16°F (−10°C) mean annual minimum temperature. (Based on *Biogeography—An Ecological Perspective*, by Pierre Dansereau. Copyright © 1957, The Ronald Press Company.)

numbers of species that are capable of surviving. A large number of tropical plant species cannot survive below-freezing temperatures. In the severely cold arctic and alpine environments of high latitudes and high altitudes only a few species can survive. Application of this principle explains why a forest in the equatorial zone has many species of trees, whereas a forest of the subarctic zone may be dominantly of one, two, or three tree species. Tolerance to cold is closely tied up with the ability of the plant to withstand the physical disruption that accompanies the freezing of water. If the plant has no means of disposing of the excess water in its tissues, the freezing of that water will damage the cell tissue.

On the basis of preference for, or tolerance to, temperatures, plant geographers distinguish the following: *megatherms*, plants favoring warm regions; *microtherms*, favoring cold regions; and *mesotherms*, favoring regions of intermediate temperatures.

It is a law of bioclimatology that there is a critical level of climatic stress beyond which a plant species cannot survive; hence that there will exist a geographical boundary that will mark the limits of its distribution. Such a boundary may also be referred to as a *frontier*. Although the frontier is determined by a complex of climatic elements, it is sometimes possible to single out one climatological element that coincides with the plant frontier. An example is seen in the limits of growth of the sugar maple (*Acer saccharophorum*) in North America (Figure 15.9). Here the boundaries on the north, west, and south are found to coincide roughly with selected values of annual precipitation, mean annual minimum temperature, and mean annual snowfall. Another example is seen in the distribution of the yellow pine (*Pinus ponderosa*) of western North America (Figure 15.10). In this mountainous region annual rainfall varies sharply with elevation. The 20 in (50 cm) isohyet of annual total precipitation encloses most of the upland areas having the yellow pine. It is the parallelism of the isohyet with forest boundary that is significant, rather than actual degree of coincidence.

Wind is seen as an important environmental factor in the structure of vegetation in highly exposed positions. Close to timber line in high mountains and along the northern limits of tree growth in the arctic zone trees will be found to be deformed so that the branches project from the lee side of the trunk only (flag shape), or the trunk and branches are bent to near-horizontal attitude, facing away from the prevailing wind direction (Figure 15.11). In such habitats the effect of wind is to cause excessive drying on the exposed side of the plant. The tree limit on mountainsides thus varies in elevation with degree of exposure of the slope to strong prevailing winds and will extend higher on lee slopes and in sheltered pockets.

Geomorphic factors

Geomorphic, or landform, factors influencing plant forms include such elements as *slope steepness* (the angle which the ground surface makes with respect to the horizontal), *slope aspect* (the orientation of a sloping ground surface with respect to geographic north), and *relief* (the difference in elevation of divides and adjacent valley bottoms). In a much broader sense, the geomorphic factor includes the entire sculpturing of the landforms of a region by processes of erosion, transportation and deposition by streams, waves, wind, and ice, and by forces of vulcanism and mountain building. The unique landform assemblage found in any one region is understood in terms of geomorphic processes; these are treated in Chapters 19 through 28. An infinite variety of plant habitats can be ascribed to the geomorphic processes and their individual landforms.

Slope steepness acts indirectly by its influence upon the rate at which precipitation is drained from the surface. On steep slopes surface runoff is rapid and the water does not long remain available to plants. On gentle slopes much of the precipitation can penetrate the soil and become available for prolonged plant use. More rapid erosion on steep slopes may result in thin soil, whereas that on gentler slopes is thicker. Slope aspect has a direct influence upon plants by increasing or decreasing the exposure to sunlight and to prevailing winds. Slopes facing the sun have a warmer, drier environment than slopes facing away from the sun and therefore lying in shade for much longer periods of the day. In middle latitudes these slope-aspect contrasts may be so strong as to produce quite different plant formations on north-facing and south-facing slopes (Figure 15.12.)

Geomorphic factors are in part responsible for the dryness or wetness of the plant habitat within a region having essentially the same overall climate. Each plant community has its own microclimate. Upon divides, peaks, and ridge crests the soil tends to dryness because of rapid drainage of water away from such places and because the surfaces are more exposed to sunlight and to drying winds. By contrast, the valley floors tend to wetness because surface runoff over the ground and into streams causes water to converge there. In humid climates the ground water table may lie close to the ground in the valley floors or may actually coincide with the ground surface to produce marshes and swamps. Watertable ponds and bogs may also occur. Hygrophytic plants thus form distinctive plant communities in the valley floors in humid climates while at the same time mesophytic or xerophytic communities occupy the intervalley surfaces.

Edaphic factors

Edaphic factors are those related to the soil. In Chapter 13 principles of soil development (pedogenesis) have been taken up systematically. In

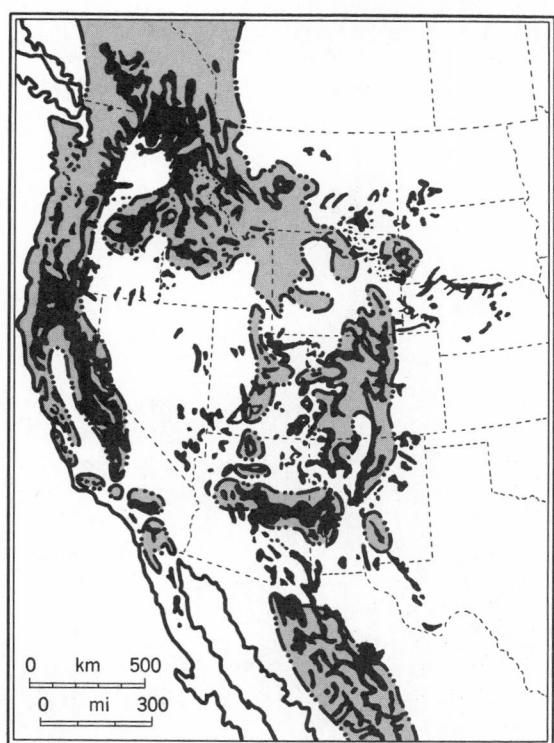

Figure 15.10 Areas of yellow pine (*Pinus ponderosa*) in western North America are shown in solid black. Edge of the shaded area represents the isohyet of 20 in (50 cm) annual precipitation. (Based on *Biogeography—An Ecological Perspective*, by Pierre Dansereau. Copyright © 1957, The Ronald Press Company.)

0   km   500

0   mi   300

Figure 15.11 Trees deformed by the effects of cold, dry winds. Timberline scene in Arapaho National Forest, Colorado, 1946. (U.S. Forest Service photograph.)

terms of plant geography we can look at soils in two perspectives. One views broad patterns of the great soil groups, reflecting the pedogenic regimes of podzolization, laterization, calcification, gleization, and salinization. These pedogenic regimes are largely controlled by the climatic regimes and will be found closely correlated with the global patterns of the vegetation formation classes. These broad relationships will be taken up together in Chapter 16. A second view point is in terms of plant habitats—the small-scale mosaic of place-to-place variations of the earth's surface. Here the edaphic factors also act as important controls.

Among the edaphic factors treated in Chapter 13 are: soil texture and structure, humus content; presence or absence of soil horizons; soil alkalinity, acidity, or salinity; and the activity of bacteria and animals in the soil.

Although this book treats the systematic principles of soil science ahead of those of natural vegetation, a good argument might be made for reversing this order of treatment on the grounds that vegetation plays a leading role in the development of soil characteristics. Given a barren habitat, recently formed by some geologic event such as the outpouring of lava or the emergence of a

Figure 15.12 Contrasts in vegetation on opposing valley-side slopes. The heavily wooded slope on the left faces northeast and is in shade during the afternoon. The sparsely wooded slope on the right, facing southwest, receives intense insolation when air temperatures are highest. Long Canyon of the Rio Hondo, Carson National Forest, New Mexico. (U.S. Forest Service photograph.)

coastal zone from beneath the sea, the gradual evolution of a soil profile goes hand in hand with the occupance of the habitat by a succession of plant communities. The plants profoundly alter the soil by such processes as contributing organic matter, or by producing acids which act upon the mineral matter. Animal life, feeding upon the plant life, also makes its contribution to physical and chemical processes of soil evolution. We will give further attention to this topic under the subject of dynamics of vegetation.

Biotic factors

The sustained activity within a particular plant community functioning as a stable ecosystem and the gradual modification of the vegetation at a given place with time throughout a succession of stages require that the plants and animals within that community contribute to its operation through their own physical and chemical processes and through their life cycles of growth and subsequent decay. So vast and complex are these biotic factors that we can do no more here than to suggest by examples what is meant by biotic influence.

Among the biotic factors may be mentioned the activity of bacteria in consuming the dead tissue of larger plants; of earthworms in altering and aerating the soil; of insects and herbivorous animals which attack and consume plants; and of insects and birds which perform such functions as pollination of plants and the dispersal of seeds. A whole realm of biotic influence lies in the diseases of plants, the spread of which may drastically alter the plant associations over wide areas. The geographer is particularly interested in the way in which large herds of grazing and browsing animals, whether wild or domesticated, have contributed to the development of certain formation classes of vegetation. To what extent, say, have herds of American bison been responsible for the maintenance of grasslands against the spread of woodland and forest?

Man is himself perhaps the most potent biotic factor influencing vegetation over the globe today. His role has been dominantly destructive with respect to the plant associations and formation classes that might otherwise be expected to cover the lands in response to the various factors of climate, soil, and geomorphology that we have thus far reviewed.

Dynamics of vegetation

One of the main themes of plant geography is that the vegetation at a particular place evolves with time, usually starting with very simple plant communities, then leading gradually to more complex communities, and ultimately to the establish-ment of a relatively stable plant community—the *climax*. Starting with a newly formed ground surface, or one that has been denuded of vegetation, the process of *succession* takes place, in which one plant community invades the area and is followed in turn by other plant communities in an orderly sequence, or *sere*, culminating in the vegetation climax.

A new site for the development of vegetation may have one of several origins: a sand dune, a sand beach, the surface of a new lava flow or of a freshly fallen layer of volcanic ash, or the deposits of silt on the inside of a river bend which is gradually shifting. Such a site will not have a true soil with horizons; rather it may be a lithosol—perhaps little more than a deposit of coarse mineral fragments. In other cases, such as that of the floodplain silt deposits, the surface layer may represent redeposited soil endowed with substantial proportions of soil colloids and bases. Ground surfaces from which vegetation has been destroyed by fire will have the soil profile largely intact.

The first stage of a succession is a *pioneer stage*, consisting of a few plant species unusually well adapted to adverse conditions of rapid water drainage and drying of soil, and to excessive exposure to sunlight, wind, and extreme ground and lower air temperatures. As these plants grow, their roots penetrate the soil; their subsequent decay adds humus to the soil. Fallen leaves and stems add an organic layer to the ground surface. Bacteria and animals begin to live in the soil in large numbers. Soon conditions are favorable for other plant species which *invade* the area and displace the pioneers. The new arrivals may be larger plant forms providing more extensive cover of foliage over the ground. In this case the climate near the ground, or *microclimate*, is considerably altered toward one of less extreme air and soil temperatures, higher humidities, and less intense insolation. Now still other species can invade and thrive in the modified environment.

When the succession has finally run its course, there will exist a stable community consisting of certain definite proportions of the various species, each of which contributes to the total structure of the vegetation. This climax stage represents an ideal model for the so-called natural vegetation of a region. Doubt exists as to whether a climax, unchanging with time, can truly be maintained. Some plant geographers consider that the climax must be followed by disturbance leading to a *regression*, or return to one of the earlier stages of the succession, so that a type of self-repeating cycle is the rule. There is also the possibility that climatic change prevents the climax from being maintained in one place.

One type of succession is that in which the

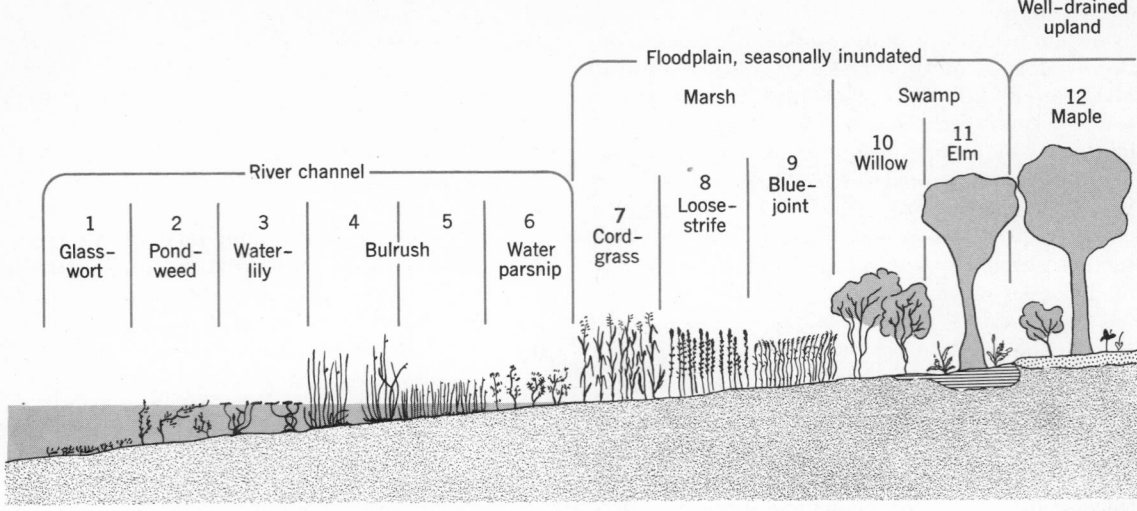

Figure 15.13 Allogenic succession on the bank of the St. Lawrence River. Twelve vegetation belts, each characterized by a plant association, shift gradually from right to left as bank deposition continues. (After Pierre Dansereau, 1956, *Revue Canadienne de Biologie*, Vol. 15.)

normal geomorphic processes build new ground continuously, as on a floodplain, delta, or sandspit. The succession associated with such continuous accretion of ground is described as *allogenic*. An example is shown in Figure 15.13, representing the zonation of vegetation along the St. Lawrence River. The twelve zones shift gradually to the left as silting by the river raises the level of the ground surface and shifts the water line to the left. Here we see the hygrophytes, living largely submerged, giving way to plants which thrive under conditions of intense sunlight on ground that is alternately exposed and inundated. Higher upon the bank are

successive forest zones: willow, elm, and finally maple, representing the climax of mesophytic trees.

Another form of succession, described as *autogenic*, results from the alteration of the environment by the plants themselves, and not by outside agencies (such as the silt accumulation from flood stages of a river). The gradual covering of a sand dune by small plants, then by forest, would illustrate autogenic succession. Another illustration is provided by the evolution of a shallow pond or lake of glacial origin in the regions of cold continental climate such as prevail in Canada and northern Europe (Figure 15.14). This *bog succession* is illustrated by stages beginning with the lake as it was left following disappearance of glacial ice, perhaps 10,000 to 15,000 years ago. A remarkable feature of the bog succession is that the organic matter produced by the growth and partial decay of the plants accumulates to such thickness that the open water is actually replaced by an organic mass of a substance known as *peat*. At the water's edge is a zone of sedges, followed by rushes (Figure 15.15). These construct a floating layer that encroaches upon the open water. There follows a zone of sphagnum (peat moss), which eventually completely fills the lake. Now the peat deposit supports hygrophytic trees (largely spruce) which produce a woody peat. This community may in turn be replaced by mesophytic trees, marking the climax stage. In the shallower upland ponds, shown on either side of the profile, the mesophytic growth is achieved much earlier than over the larger water body.

In terms of the vast scope and depth of the

Figure 15.14 Bog succession in Emmet County, Michigan. A bog mat lies at the edge of the lake, a black spruce forest in background. (Photograph by Pierre Dansereau.)

Vegetation:

Rushes	Sedges	Sphagnum	Heaths	Mesophytic shrubs	Hygrophytic trees	Mesophytic trees

Peats:

Rush	Sedges	Sphagnum	Woody

Figure 15.15 Autogenic bog succession typical of the Laurentian shield area of Canada. (After Dansereau and Segadas-Vianna, 1952, *Canadian Journal of Botany*, Vol. 30.)

science of plant geography, this chapter must be taken as a greatly simplified review touching upon only a few essential topics. As with all other subjects which we call collectively "physical geography," plant geography can be seriously approached only through intensive study of principles of botany, including the classification of plants (taxonomy), their evolution and floristic distribution, plant morphology, and the chemistry and physics of plant physiology.

REFERENCES FOR FURTHER STUDY

Dansereau, Pierre (1957), *Biogeography; an ecological perspective*, The Ronald Press, New York, 394 pp.

Daubenmire, R. F. (1959), *Plants and environment: a textbook of plant autecology*, second edition, John Wiley and Sons, New York, 422 pp.

Oosting, H. J. (1956), *The study of plant communities; an introduction to plant ecology*, second edition, W. H. Freeman, San Francisco, 440 pp.

Polunin, Nicholas (1960), *Introduction to plant geography and some related sciences*, McGraw-Hill Book Co., New York, 640 pp.

Robbins, W. W., T. E. Weier, and C. R. Stocking, (1964), *Botany: an introduction to plant science*, third edition, John Wiley and Sons, New York, 480 pp.

REVIEW QUESTIONS

1. How does vegetation act as a geographic factor? To what other branches of physical geography is plant geography most closely related?

2. What is meant by natural vegetation? What does a map of natural vegetation attempt to portray?

3. Compare floristic with structural approach in the study of natural vegetation. Which approach is most useful in physical geography and why?

4. What is bioclimatology? Define an ecosystem. What is the subject of plant ecology?

5. Name the three environmental divisions of the biosphere. Into what four great biochores is the land biocycle divided? Explain the basis of this subdivision.

6. What are formation-classes? How many formation classes are commonly recognized? On what basis are formation classes set up?

7. How does habitat influence the structure of vegetation? What six habitats can be recognized within the Canadian needleleaf forest? What is the cause of differing habitats? On the basis of what type of habitat are the formation classes defined? What is a plant community?

8. What six categories have been used to form a system of description of the structure of vegetation? Define each category and give the units of subdivision within each.

9. How is a tree distinguished from a shrub? What are lianas? What kind of plants fall within the category of herbs? What are forbs? Bryoids? Epiphytes? Lichens? What kinds of plants are included within the thallophytes?

10. Distinguish deciduous from evergreen plants. What are semideciduous plants? Name the principal leaf forms and give examples from common plants.

11. What are the varieties of leaf textures? What is a sclerophyll forest? What are succulent leaves?

12. List the four main classes of environmental factors in plant ecology. What two scale ranges of phenomena are included in the environment?

13. How do plants use water? What factors affect the rate of transpiration? How are plants adapted to reduce water loss? How do some plants improve their means of obtaining and storing water? What are phreatophytes?

14. Explain how plants are classified according to water need. Name and define the three plant groups so classified. What are tropophytes?

15. Discuss the climatic factors of light, air temperature, and wind as they apply to plant ecology. How do numbers of plant species in a region depend upon temperature conditions? Distinguish megatherms, microtherms, and mesotherms.

16. What bioclimatological law relates a plant species to the level of climatic stress imposed upon it? Give an example of a plant frontier.

17. Discuss the geomorphic factors in plant ecology and show how each factor acts to influence vegetation.

18. What are edaphic factors? What two points of view can be taken in treating the edaphic controls? How do plants themselves modify the soils upon which they grow?

19. Discuss the biotic factors in plant ecology. Give specific examples of the way in which animal life affects vegetation. What is the role of man as a biotic factor in our present day?

20. What is the process of succession in development of vegetation? Define sere and climax. What kinds of new sites may become available for plant successions? What is the pioneer stage? What is meant by a regression following climax?

21. Distinguish allogenic from autogenic succession and give one example of each type.

CHAPTER 16
Distribution of Natural Vegetation

THE principles of description of vegetation in terms of its structure, and the organization of vegetation into plant assemblages of various orders of magnitude (biochore, formation class, association, community), have been treated in Chapter 15. Using these principles in combination with our understanding of the climatic regimes, pedogenic regimes, and the soil-water budget, we are now prepared to analyze the world-wide distribution of vegetation and to explain its variations with latitude, continental position, and altitude.

The great biochores

All natural vegetation of the lands falls into four major structural subdivisions, the *biochores*, illustrated schematically in Figure 16.1. First is the *forest biochore*. We define a *forest* as a plant formation consisting of trees growing close together and forming a layer of foliage that largely shades the ground. Forests often show stratification, with more than one layer. Shading of the ground gives a distinctly different microclimate than that which would be found over open ground. Forests require a relatively large annual precipitation, but it does not need to be uniformly distributed throughout the year. No single value of precipitation can be stated because the effectiveness of the precipitation depends upon the water loss by evapotranspiration, and this in turn depends upon air temperature and humidity. Consequently, the forest biochore spans a great climatic range, from wet equatorial to cold subarctic.

The *savanna biochore* is a formation consisting of a combination of trees and grassland in various proportions. The appearance of the vegetation can be described as parklike, with trees spaced singly or in small groups and surrounded by, or interspersed with, surfaces covered by grasses, or by some other plant life form, such as shrubs or annuals in a low layer. The savanna biochore indicates a climate of limited total annual precipitation with an uneven distribution throughout the year.

The *grassland biochore* consists of an upland vegetation largely or entirely of herbs, which may include grasses, grasslike plants, and forbs (broadleaf herbs). Degree of coverage may range from continuous to discontinuous and there may be stratification. The grassland biochore may include trees in moister habitats of valley floors and along stream courses where ground water is available. The grassland biochore is typical of a climate which has small total annual precipitation, but otherwise the climate may range from one of extreme heat to one of extreme cold.

The *desert biochore*, associated with climates of extreme aridity, has thinly dispersed plants and hence a high percentage of bare ground exposed to direct insolation and to the forces of wind and water erosion or to freeze-thaw action. Although essentially treeless, the desert biochore may have scattered woody plants. Typically, however, the plants are small, e.g., herbs, bryoids, lichens. Because the desert biochore includes climates ranging from extremely hot tropical desert to extremely cold arctic desert, a great range in plant communities and habitats is spanned by the biochore.

In describing the four great biochores, emphasis has been placed on the vast range of climates spanned by each. Essentially, the biochores are determined by the degree to which moisture is available to plants in a scale ranging from abundant (forest biochore) to almost none (desert biochore). But within each biochore conditions of temperature are vastly different from low to high latitudes and from low to high altitudes. Consequently, there is need to subdivide each biochore into a number of formation classes.

The formation classes

The description of world vegetation in terms of formation classes was first developed fully by Professor A. F. W. Schimper whose monumental work in two volumes entitled *Plant Geography on a Physiological Basis* was first published in German in 1903. This work was subsequently revised by Professor F. C. von Faber and published in 1935. A somewhat similar approach to structural classification of world vegetation was taken by Professor Eduard Rübel who published a major volume in 1930. The classification system described below follows in many respects the recent work of Professor Pierre Dansereau [1] and is based

[1] Dansereau, Pierre (1957), *Biogeography, an ecological perspective*, The Ronald Press Co., New York, 394 pp.

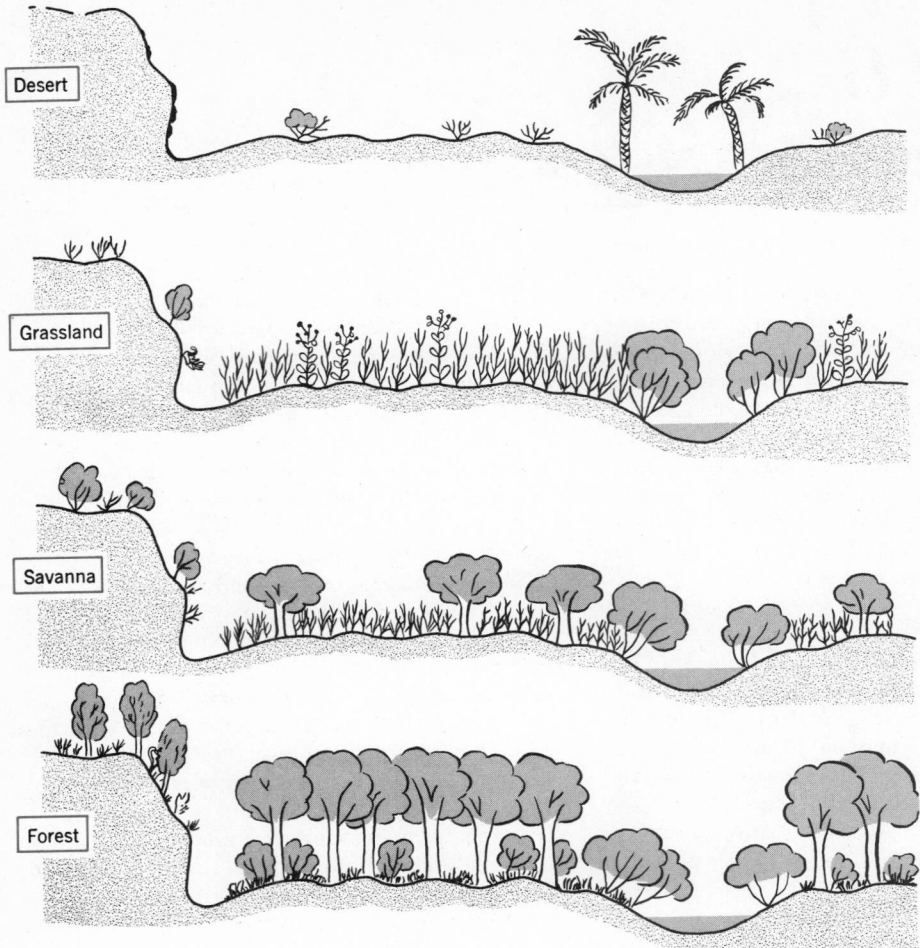

Figure 16.1 Diagrammatic representation of the four great biochores. Well-drained upland is shown in the middle of each profile; steep cliffs on the left; wet or poorly drained ground on the right. Note that the vertical scale of the grassland biochore is exaggerated in comparison with the other three. (From *Biogeography—An Ecological Perspective,* by Pierre Dansereau. Copyright © 1957, The Ronald Press Company.)

essentially on Schimper's and Rübel's principles. The world map of vegetation, Plate 4, follows Rübel's system in showing the distribution of ten map units, designated here by the letters *A* through *J.* The eighteen formation classes listed in this chapter are all included within Rübel's ten map units so that in certain cases two to four formation classes are combined into a single map unit. The map is thus simplified in appearance and brings out broad world patterns that are obviously related to the climate regimes.

Table 16.1 lists eighteen formation classes within the four biochores and gives the corresponding world map units of Plate 4. On the map legend is a similar table in reverse, giving the ten map units and listing the formation classes which are included in each.

Forest biochore

1. *Equatorial rainforest*[2] consists of tall, closely set trees whose crowns form a continuous canopy of foliage and provide dense shade for the ground and lower layers (Figure 16.2). The trees are characteristically smooth barked and unbranched in the lower two-thirds. Trunks commonly are buttressed at the base by radiating, wall-like roots (Figure 16.3). Tree leaves are large and evergreen; from this characteristic the equatorial rainforest is often described as "broadleaf evergreen forest." Crowns of the trees tend to form into two or three layers, or strata, of which the highest layer consists of scattered emergent crowns rising to 130 ft (40 m) and protruding conspicuously above a second

---

[2]Called *tropical rainforest* by Dansereau and others.

TABLE 16.1   THE FORMATION CLASSES

I Forest Biochore		Equivalent map units (Plate 4)
1. Equatorial rainforest		
2. Tropical rainforest	A.	Equatorial and tropical rainforest
3. Monsoon forest	C.	Raingreen forest, woodland, scrub, and savanna.
4. Temperate rainforest	B.	Temperate rainforest or Laurel forest
5. Summergreen deciduous forest	E.	Summergreen deciduous forest
6. Needleleaf forest	F.	Needleleaf forest
7. Evergreen-hardwood forest (Sclerophyll forest)	D.	Evergreen-hardwood forest (Sclerophyll forest)

II Savanna Biochore		
8. Savanna woodland		
9. Thornbush and tropical scrub	C.	Raingreen forest, woodland, scrub, and savanna
10. Savanna		
11. Semidesert	H.	Dry desert and semidesert
12. Heath		(Heath not shown on map)
13. Cold woodland	I.	Tundra

III Grassland Biochore		
14. Prairie		
15. Steppe	G.	Steppe and Prairie grasslands
16. Grassy tundra	I.	Tundra

IV Desert Biochore		
17. Dry desert	H.	Dry desert and Semidesert
18. Arctic fell field	I.	Tundra

layer, 50 to 100 ft (15 to 30 m) which is continuous (Figure 16.4). A third, lower layer consists of small, slender trees 15 to 50 ft (5 to 15 m) high with narrow crowns (Figure 16.4).

Typical of the equatorial rainforest are lianas, thick woody vines supported by the trunks and branches of trees. Some are slender, like ropes, others reach thicknesses of 8 in (20 cm). They rise to heights of the upper tree levels where light is available and may have profusely branched crowns. Lianas may depend upon a growing tree to be carried upward, where the liana has no devices with which to climb by itself. Other woody climbers rise by winding about the tree trunk. Epiphytes are numerous in the equatorial rainforest. These plants are attached to the trunk, branches and foliage of trees and lianas, using the "host" solely as a means of physical support. Epiphytes are of many plant classes and include ferns, orchids, mosses, and lichens (Figure 16.5). Some epiphytes are *stranglers*. These woody vines send down their roots to the soil and may eventually surround the tree, perhaps ultimately replacing it. The *strangling fig* (*Ficus*) is an example (Figure 16.6). Other stranglers begin as lianas.

A particularly important botanical characteristic of the equatorial rainforest is the large number of species of trees that coexist. It is said that as many as 3000 species may be found in a square mile. Individuals of a species are thus widely separated. Consequently, if a particular tree species is to be extracted from the forest for commercial uses, considerable labor is involved in seeking out the trees and transporting them from their isolated positions. Representative trees of the rainforest of the Amazon valley are the Brazilnut (*Bertholletia excelsa*) and the silk-cotton tree (species of *Bombax*).

The floor of the equatorial rainforest is usually so densely shaded that plant foliage is sparse close to the ground and gives the forest an open aspect, making it easy to traverse. The ground surface is covered only by a thin litter of leaves. Rapid consumption of dead plant matter by bacterial action results in the absence of humus upon the soil surface and within the soil profile. As explained in Chapter 13, these conditions are typical of the pedogenic process of laterization, with which the rainforest is identified.

Equatorial rainforest is a response to an equable climatic regime which is continuously warm, frost-free, and has abundant precipitation in all months of the year (or, at most, only one or two dry months). A large water surplus characterizes the annual water budget (see Figure 9.9A), so that soil moisture is adequate at all times and the export of large amounts of stream runoff allows permanent removal of bases and silica from the soils of the region. In the absence of a cold or dry season, plant growth goes on continuously throughout the year. Individual species have their own seasons of leaf shedding, possibly caused by slight changes in the light period.

Variations in the equatorial rainforest structure are found in specialized habitats and where man has disturbed the vegetation. Where the forest has been cleared by cutting and burning (as for small-plot agriculture or highways), the returning plant growth is low and dense and may be described as *jungle.* Jungle can consist of a tangled growth of lianas, bamboo scrub, thorny palms, and thickly branching shrubs, constituting an impenetrable

Figure 16.3 Buttress roots at the base of a large tree (*Bombacopsis fendleri*) of the rainforest on Barro Coloradi Island, Canal Zone. (Courtesy of the American Museum of Natural History.)

Figure 16.2 Equatorial rainforest near Belém, Brazil. This forest of tall broad-leaved evergreen trees and numerous lianas is on the relatively high ground (*terra firme*) of the Amazon lowland. (Photograph by Otto Penner, courtesy of Instituto Agronómico do Norte.)

barrier to travel, in contrast to the open floor of the climax rainforest.

Coastal vegetation in areas of equatorial rainforest is highly specialized. Coasts which receive suspended sediment (mud) from river mouths, and where water depths are shallow, typically have *mangrove swamp forest,* consisting of stilted trees (Figure 16.7). The mangrove prop-roots serve to trap sediment from ebb and flood tidal currents, so that the land is gradually extended seaward. Mangroves commonly consist of several shoreward belts of the red (*Rhizophora*), the black (*Avicennia*), and the white (*Laguncularia*) mangrove. Another common coastal salt-marsh plant of the humid tropics is the screw-pine (*Pandanus*). Typical of recently formed coastal deposits are belts of palms, such as the cocoanut palm (*Cocos nucifera*) (Figure 16.8).

World distribution of equatorial rainforest is shown on the vegetation map, Plate 4, by those areas of rainforest (Class *A*) located close to the equator. The principal world areas are: the Amazon lowland of South America; the Congo lowland of Africa and a coastal zone extending westward from Nigeria to Guinea; and the East Indian region, from Sumatra on the west to the islands of the western Pacific on the east. Poleward borders of these equatorial rainforest regions are, of course, transitional into rainforest of higher latitudes, particularly that found on tropical windward coasts and that of coastal monsoon rainforest belts of south and southeast Asia.

2. *Tropical rainforest* is in many respects structurally similar to equatorial rainforest but has distinct differences imposed upon it by its location, which is on windward coasts, roughly from 10° latitude to the tropics of Cancer and Capricorn

Figure 16.4 Diagram of the structure of tropical rainforest in Trinidad, British West Indies. A representative species of the tallest trees is *Mora exelsa*. (After J. S. Beard, 1946, *The Natural Vegetation of Trinidad*, Clarendon Press, Oxford.)

Figure 16.5 A tree limb covered by epiphytic ferns. Upland rainforest of Kenya, Africa. (Courtesy of the American Museum of Natural History.)

Figure 16.6 This strangler fig has surrounded the trunk of a cabbage palm in southernmost Florida. (Photograph by Bob Haugen, Everglades National Park.)

($23\frac{1}{2}°$). Here we find a distinct annual precipitation cycle, consisting of a long wet season alternating with a season of reduced rainfall, if not actual drought. There is also a marked annual temperature cycle resulting from the variations in height of the sun's path in the sky in tropical latitudes. The cooler temperatures, coinciding approximately with the period of reduced rainfall, impose some stress upon the plants. As a result, there are fewer species and fewer lianas. Epiphytes are, however, abundant because of continued exposure to humid air and cloudiness of the maritime tropical air masses which impinge upon the coastal hill and mountain slopes.

In terms of global distribution, the tropical rainforest is represented on the world map (Plate 4) by those areas of rainforest (Class *A*) which lie between 10° and 25° latitude. The Carribean lands represent one important area of tropical rainforest, although the rainforest is predominantly limited to windward locations. Of interest to American students is the fact that the Everglades of southernmost Florida contains small isolated communities of tropical rainforest, termed *hammocks*, in which one finds the mahogany tree and strangler fig, along with abundant epiphytes. The coast of this same area has extensive mangrove forest and scrub.

In southern and southeastern Asia tropical rainforest is extensive in coastal zones and highlands which have heavy monsoon rainfall and a very short dry season. The Western Ghats of India and the coastal zone of Burma have tropical rainforest supported by orographic rains of the southwest monsoon. In the zone of combined northeast trades and Asiatic summer monsoon are rainforests of the coasts of Vietnam and the Philippine Islands. In the southern hemisphere belts of tropical rainforest extend down the eastern Brazilian coast, the Madagascar coast, and the coast of northeastern Australia.

As is the equatorial rainforest, the tropical rainforest is associated with a pedogenic regime of laterization under an equable climatic regime. It is common practice among plant geographers to combine the equatorial and tropical rainforests into a single formation class, because their points of similarity greatly outweigh their points of difference.

Figure 16.8   A grove of cocoanut palms (*Cocos nucifera*) along a sandy beach in the Solomon Islands. Wave action is undermining the trees. (Courtesy of the American Museum of Natural History.)

3. *Monsoon forest* presents a more open tree growth than the equatorial and tropical rainforests. Consequently, there is less competition among trees for light but a greater development of vegetation in the lower layers. Maximum tree heights range from 40 to 100 ft (12 to 35 m), which is less than in the equatorial rainforest. Many tree species are present and may number 30 to 40 species in a small tract. Tree trunks are massive; the bark is often thick and rough. Branching starts at comparatively low level and produces large round crowns. Perhaps the most important feature of the monsoon forest is the deciduousness of most of the tree species present, e.g., the abundance of tropophytes. The shedding of leaves results from the stress of a long dry season which occurs at time of low sun and cooler temperatures. Thus the forest in the dry season has somewhat the dormant winter aspect of deciduous forests of middle latitudes (Figure 16.9). Some writers use the name "tropical deciduous forest" for monsoon forest, emphasizing the deciduousness rather than the climate regime. A representative example of a monsoon forest tree is the teakwood tree. (*Tectona grandis*).

Lianas and epiphytes are locally abundant in monsoon rainforest but are fewer and smaller than in the equatorial rainforest. Undergrowth is often a dense shrub thicket. Where second-growth vegetation has formed, it is typically jungle. Clumps of bamboo are an important part of the vegetation in climax teakwood forest.

As already noted, monsoon forest is a response to a wet-dry tropical climate regime in which a long rainy season with a large total precipitation alternates with a dry, rather cool season. Such

Figure 16.7   Mangrove growing in salt water, Harney's River, Florida. (Courtesy of the American Museum of Natural History.)

conditions are most strongly developed in the Asiatic monsoon climate, but are not limited to that area. Perhaps the type regions of monsoon forest are in Burma (inland from the coastal tropical rainforest belt) and in Thailand and Cambodia. Large areas of deciduous and semideciduous tropical forest occur in west Africa and in central and South America, bordering the equatorial and tropical rainforests into which there is a gradation. Areas of monsoon forest or related types are also described in Indonesia (especially Java and Celebes), in northern Australia, and in western Madagascar. World vegetation maps and standard reference works do not agree closely on the location and extent of the monsoon, or deciduous tropical forest areas. In Plate 4, monsoon forests are included in Class *C*, the raingreen vegetation of the wet-dry tropics, which also represents other formation classes.

The prevailing pedogenic regime of monsoon forest areas is that of laterization. Despite the dry season, a substantial water surplus is developed during the warm rainy season. Humus does not accumulate; leaching of bases and silica is the dominant soil-forming process.

4. *Temperate rainforest*, also referred to as *temperate evergreen forest* and *laurel forest*, differs from the equatorial and tropical rainforests in having relatively few species of trees, and hence large populations of individuals of a species. Trees are not as tall as in the low-latitude rainforests; the leaves tend to be smaller and more leathery; the leaf canopy less dense. Among the trees commonly found in the temperate rainforests of southern Japan and the southeastern United States are evergreen oaks (such as *Quercus virginiana*) and members of the laurel and magnolia families (such as *Magnolia grandiflora*). A quite different temperate rainforest flora is found in New Zealand and consists of large tree ferns, large conifers such as the kauri tree (*Agathis australis*), podocarp trees (*Podocarpus*), and small-leaved southern beeches (*Nothofagus*) (Figure 16.10). Another important type of temperate rainforest, found in the Azores and Canary island groups, is the Canary laurel forest, which formerly covered Europe in the Miocene geological epoch.

Temperate rainforests tend to have a well-developed lower stratum of vegetation that, in different places, may include tree ferns, small palms, bamboos, shrubs, and herbaceous plants. Lianas and epiphytes are abundant. Particularly striking at higher elevations where fog and cloud are persistent is the sheathing of tree trunks and branches by mosses. An example of conspicuous epiphyte accumulation at low elevation is the Spanish "moss" (*Tillandsia usneoides*) which festoons the Evangeline oak, bald cypress, and other trees of

Figure 16.9 Monsoon forest in Chieng Mai Province, northern Thailand. Scale is indicated by a line of porters crossing the clearing. (Photograph by Robert L. Pendleton, courtesy of the American Geographical Society.)

the gulf coast of the southeastern United States.

Temperate rainforest represents a response to an equable climatic regime in which the annual range of temperature is small or moderate and rainfall is abundant and well distributed throughout the year. Such conditions are met in three quite different geographical locations: (1) at higher altitudes in the equatorial and tropical zones; (2) along eastern continental margins and on islands in the latitude belt 25° to 35° or 40°; (3) on west coasts from 35° to 55°. In the first location the effect of higher elevation is to reduce temperatures and evaporation and thereby to increase the moisture available to plants.

Figure 16.10 This podocarp forest illustrates a variety of temperate rainforest in a marine west-coast climate, Hari Hari, western coast of South Island of New Zealand. (Photograph by Pierre Dansereau.)

A word about the vegetation of the coastal region of the southeastern United States may save misunderstanding. On forest maps of the United States (Figure 14.3), and on a number of maps of world vegetation, this coastal zone is shown as having needleleaf evergreen or coniferous forest, whereas on Plate 4, it is shown as temperate rainforest. It is true that large areas of sandy upland bear forests of loblolly and slash pine and that bald-cypress is a dominant tree in swamps, but such vegetation represents xerophytic and hydrophytic forms in excessively dry or wet habitats, or the second-growth forest following fire and deforestation. The climax vegetation of mesophytic habitats is nevertheless the evergreen-oak and magnolia forest.

Temperate rainforest spans two pedogenic regimes: laterization and podzolization. In lower

Figure 16.11 This stand of beech and hemlock in the Allegheny National Forest, Pennsylvania, illustrates mixed summergreen deciduous forest and needleleaf forest in the northeastern United States. (U.S. Forest Service photograph.)

latitudes laterization is characteristic, and this grades through regimes in which both laterization and podzolization are effective (red-yellow soils), to the cool higher latitude regions of podzolization.

5. *Summergreen deciduous forest,* sometimes called *temperate deciduous forest,* is familiar to inhabitants of eastern North America and western Europe as a native forest type. It is dominated by tall, broadleaf trees which provide a continuous and dense canopy in summer but shed their leaves completely in the winter (Figure 16.11). Lower layers of small trees and shrubs are weakly developed. In spring a luxuriant low layer of herbs quickly develops, but this is greatly reduced after the trees have reached full foliage and shaded the ground.

Summergreen deciduous forest is almost entirely limited to the middle-latitude landmasses of the northern Hemisphere (Plate 4, Class *E*). Common trees of the deciduous forests of eastern North America, southeastern Europe, and eastern Asia (all in the humid-continental climate) are oak (*Quercus*), beech (*Fagus*), birch (*Betula*), hickory (*Carya*), walnut (*Juglans*), maple (*Acer*), basswood (*Tilia*), elm (*Ulmus*), ash (*Fraximus*), tulip tree (*Liriodendron*), sweet chestnut (*Castanea*), and hornbeam (*Carpinus*). In western and central Europe, under a marine west coast climate dominant trees are mostly oak and ash, with beech (*Fagus sylvatica*) in cooler and moister areas.

In poorly drained habitats, the deciduous forest consists of such trees as alder, willow, ash, and elm, and many hygrophytic shrubs. Where the deciduous forests have been cleared in lumbering, pines readily develop as second-growth vegetation.

The summergreen deciduous forest represents a response to a continental climatic regime which at the same time receives adequate precipitation in all months. There is a strong annual temperature cycle with a cold winter season and a warm summer. Precipitation is markedly greater in the summer months (especially so in eastern Asia) and thus increases at the time of year when evapotranspiration is great and the moisture demands are high. Only a small water deficit is incurred in the summer, while a large surplus normally develops in spring. In eastern Asia the winter is exceptionally dry, but this factor is compensated for by cold.

The pedogenic process associated with summergreen deciduous forest is that of podzolization, but moderated by the warm wet summers. As a result, the soils are characteristically of the gray-brown forest group. Toward lower latitudes the tendency to laterization becomes stronger and red-yellow podzolic soils are encountered; toward the continental interiors the tendency to calcification sets in and the deciduous forest extends into regions of darker soils of the grasslands (prairie and chernozem soils). In the summergreen deciduous forests a thick layer of fallen leaves covers the ground and there is abundant humus in the soil.

Because the regions of summergreen deciduous forest have for centuries been the areas of dense populations, few remnants of a primeval forest have survived. Instead, most existing forests are modified by practices of tree farming. Large areas are completely and permanently removed from forest growth by farming, urban development, and roadways.

6. *Needleleaf forest* is composed largely of straight-trunked, conical trees with relatively short branches, and small, narrow, needlelike leaves. These trees are conifers (Figure 16.12). Where evergreen, the needleleaf forest provides continuous and deep shade to the ground so that lower layers of vegetation are sparse or absent, except for a thick carpet of mosses in many places. Species are few and large tracts of forest consist almost entirely of but one or two species.

Reference to the world vegetation map (Plate 4, Class *F*) will show that needleleaf forest is predominantly in two great continental belts, one in North America and one in Eurasia, which span the landmasses from west to east in latitudes 45° to 75°. The needleleaf forest of North America, Europe, and western Siberia is composed of evergreen conifers, such as spruce (*Picea*), fir (*Abies*), and pine (*Pinus*), whereas that of north-central and eastern Siberia is dominantly of larch (*Larix*) which sheds its needles in winter and comprises a deciduous forest (Figure 16.13). Associated with the needleleaf trees is mountain ash. Aspen and balsam poplar (*Populus*), willow, and birch tend to take over rapidly in areas of needleleaf forest

Figure 16.13 Woodland of larch (*Larix dahurica*), Tompo River region, about latitude 64° N, Yakutsk, A.S.S.R. This scene shows the larch tree near the northern limit of its growth. (Photograph by I. D. Kild'ushevsky, courtesy of Professor B. A. Tikhomirov, Komarov Botanical Institute, Leningrad.)

which have been burned over, or can be found bordering streams and in open places.

Needleleaf evergreen forest extends into lower latitudes wherever mountain ranges and high plateaus exist. Thus in western North America this formation class extends southward into the United States on the Cascade, Sierra Nevada, and Rocky Mountain ranges and over parts of the higher plateaus of the southwestern states. In Europe, needleleaf evergreen forests flourish on all of the higher mountain ranges, and well into Scandinavia.

The needleleaf evergreen forests of British Columbia and California are of particular interest. Here, under a regime of heavy orographic precipitation and prevailing high humidities, are perhaps the densest of all coniferous forests, with the world's largest trees. Forests of coastal redwood (*Sequoia sempervirens*), big tree (*Sequoiadendron giganteum*) and Douglas fir (*Pseudotsuga taxifolia*) are particularly remarkable (Figure 16.14). Individuals of redwood and big tree attain heights of over 325 ft (100 m) and girths of over 65 ft (20 m) (Figure 16.15).

As much of the area of needleleaf evergreen forest in North America and Europe was subjected to glaciation in the Wisconsin stage of the Pleistocene epoch, there abound lakes and poorly drained depressions. These bear the hygrophytic vegetation, described in Chapter 15 as forming a bog succession, and leading to large, thick peat accumulations known in Canada as *muskeg*.

Podzolization, the pedogenic regime of the needleleaf forests, is a direct result of a climatic

Figure 16.12 Spruce forest, Upper Peribonka River, Quebec, Canada. (Photograph by Pierre Dansereau.)

regime of continentality with a strong polar influence. As explained in Chapter 13, the conifers require little of the bases and these are leached from the soil, which is characteristically acidic.

7. *Evergreen-hardwood forest,* also termed *sclerophyll forest,* consists of low trees with small, hard, leathery leaves. Typically the trees are low-branched and gnarled, with thick bark. The formation class includes much *woodland,* an open forest in which the canopy coverage is only 25 to 60%. Also included are extensive areas of *scrub,* a plant formation type consisting of shrubs having

Figure 16.15 A grove of Sequoia trees, Sequoia National Park, California. The largest tree measures 51 ft (15m) in circumference. A man can be seen standing at the right of this tree (look for hat). (Courtesy of the American Museum of Natural History.)

Figure 16.14 This mixed stand of white pine. Douglas fir, and Englemann spruce is on the western slopes of the Cascade Range in Washington. (U.S. Forest Service photograph.)

a canopy coverage of perhaps 50% (Figure 16.16). The trees and shrubs are evergreen, their thickened leaves being retained despite a severe annual drought. There is little stratification in the sclerophyll forest and scrub, although there may be a spring herb layer.

Evergreen hardwood forest is closely associated with the dry-summer subtropical (Mediterranean) climate and hence quite narrowly limited in geographical extent—primarily to west coasts between 30° and 40° or 45° latitude (Plate 4, Class *D*). In the Mediterranean lands the hardwood forest forms a narrow peripheral coastal belt. Here the woodland consists of such trees as cork oak (*Quercus suber*), live oak (*Quercus ilex*), Aleppo pine (*Pinus halepensis*), stone pine (*Pinus pinea*), and olive (*Olea europaea*). What may have once been luxuriant forests of such trees were greatly disturbed by man over the centuries and reduced to woodland or entirely destroyed. Instead, large areas consist of dense scrub termed *maquis* which includes many species, some of them very spiny. The other northern hemisphere region of evergreen hardwood forest is that of the California coast ranges. Some of this is a woodland composed largely of the live oak (*Quercus agrifolia*) and white oak (*Quercus lobata*). Much of the vegetation is a scrub or "dwarf forest" known as *chaparral*, which varies in composition with elevation and exposure (Figure 16.17). Chaparral may contain wild lilac (*Ceanothus*), manzanita (*Arctostaphylos*), mountain mahogany (*Cercocarpus*), "poison oak" (*Rhus diversiloba*), and live oak. The evergreen hardwood forest is represented in central Chile and in the Cape region of South Africa by a maquislike scrub vegetation which is, however, of quite different flora from those of the northern hemisphere. Important areas of sclerophyll forest, woodland, and scrub are found in southeast, southcentral, and southwest Australia, including several species of eucalypts and acacias (Figure 16.18).

The dry-summer subtropical (Mediterranean) regime of the evergreen hardwood forest is one of great environmental stress because the severe drought season coincides with high air temperatures. Thus a large water deficit occurs in the summer (see Figure 9.9E). The wet, mild winter is, by contrast, highly favorable to rapid plant growth. The pedogenic regime is one associated with semi-aridity, namely calcification, and results in soils with some precipitated calcium carbonate in the B horizon. Much of the area of the evergreen hardwood forest, woodland, and scrub is classified as having reddish-chestnut, reddish-prairie, and reddish-brown soils, and in the Mediterranean lands, *terra rossa*.

Savanna biochore

8. *Savanna woodland* consists of trees spaced rather widely apart, permitting development of a dense lower layer, which may be of grasses or shrubs. This formation class is sometimes referred to as "parkland" because of the open, parklike appearance of the vegetation. Savanna woodland is associated with a climate regime in which aridity is sufficiently developed to prevent the tree growth from forming a closed canopy.

Many geographers associate savanna woodland closely with the tropical wet-dry climate. It is this tropical variety of woodland that is implied in the world vegetation map (Plate 4) by the inclusion of savanna woodland with Class *C* vegetation. However, from the standpoint of the vegetation structure itself, the definition of savanna woodland can be broadened to include woodlands of middle latitudes, such as the open stands of yellow pine and of pinyon pine and juniper which, in the western United States, occur in an elevation zone

Figure 16.16 Chaparral on steep mountain slopes of the San Dimas Experimental Forest, near Glendora, California, 1953. This vegetation has been protected from burning for many years. (Photograph by A. N. Strahler.)

above that of the sagebrush scrub and below that of the needleleaf forests. One might also include in this formation class the Eucalyptus woodlands of southern Australia, which we have elsewhere placed in the formation class of evergreen-hardwood forest.

Figure 16.17 Detail of chaparral vegetation, San Dimas Experimental Forest (see Figure 16.16). A tilted rain gauge, 8 in (20 cm) in diameter, rests on bare ground at the left. (Photograph by A. N. Strahler.)

Figure 16.18 Eucalyptus woodland, Darling Range, Western Australia, about 1930. (Photograph by Agent General for Western Australia, courtesy of the American Geographical Society.)

Referring now to the tropical savanna woodland, the trees are of medium height, the crowns flattened or umbrella-shaped, and the trunks have thick, rough bark (see Figure 16.20). The trees tend toward xerophytic forms with small leaves and thorns, or may be deciduous, shedding their leaves in the dry season. In this respect, tropical savanna woodland is closely akin to monsoon forest, into which it grades. The trees are of species capable of withstanding fires which sweep through the lower layer in dry season; thus many rainforest tree species which might otherwise grow in the wet-dry climate regime are prevented by fires from invading.

Tropical savanna woodland is found widely throughout Africa, South America, southeast Asia, northern Australia, and in Central America and the Carribean Islands (Plate 4, Class *C*). The pedogenic process usually dominant is laterization.

9. *Thornbush and tropical scrub* (which may be treated as two different formation classes) consist of xerophytic trees and shrubs responding to a climate with a very long dry season and only a short, but intense, rainy season. Thornbush, also referred to as "thorn forest," and "thornwoods," consists of tall, closely spaced woody shrubs commonly bearing thorns and largely deciduous (Figure 16.19). Cacti may also be present. The lower layer of herbs may consist of annuals which largely disappear in the dry season, or of grasses. In the drier areas the lower layer may consist only of scattered grass clumps with much bare ground

between. One example of the thornbush is the *caatinga* of northeastern Brazil, an open thorn forest of the dry highlands. Another is the *dornveld* of South Africa.

Tropical scrub is a dense growth of low woody shrubs which may occur in patches or clumps separated by barren ground. Scrub may develop in stony, sandy, or gravelly sites in areas of thornbush.

Thornbush and tropical scrub have been included in Class *C* of the world vegetation map (Plate 4) as formation classes of the wet-dry tropical climate regime. Thornbush and tropical scrub are found in many parts of the world where the wet-dry tropical climatic regime is transitional into the tropical desert regime. Soils show the influence of aridity and are subject to calcification, and (in poorly drained sites) of salinization. Reddish-brown and reddish-chestnut soils occur in much of the area of these formation classes.

10. *Savanna* is a vegetation consisting of widely scattered trees rising from a more or less continuous lower layer dominated typically by grasses. Although the term "savanna" most commonly refers to a vegetation in tropical and subtropical latitudes, structurally similar vegetation can be found in the subarctic lands of the northern hemisphere—the *taiga*. (See "cold woodland.") As discussed here, savanna is that of low latitudes, included in Class *C* in the world vegetation map (Plate 4) as a relative of the tropical savanna woodland, monsoon forest, and thornbush and tropical scrub. Like its relatives, the tropical sa-

Figure 16.19 Thornbush in the region of the Tona River, central Africa. (Photograph of the Akeley Expedition, courtesy of the American Museum of Natural History.)

vanna is a response to a wet-dry tropical climate regime in which the severe drought period is one of relatively cooler temperature but which experiences great heat just preceding the onset of the rains.

As with the savanna woodland, the tropical savanna supports trees and shrubs which are xerophytic or deciduous. In some localities the trees are palms, giving a "palm savanna." Grasses in the tropical savanna are characteristically tall, with stiff coarse blades, commonly higher than the height of a man, and even up to 12 ft (4 m) high. In the dry season these grasses form a yellowish straw mat that is highly flammable and subject to periodic burning. It is widely held that, to a greater or lesser degree, periodic burning of the savanna grasses is responsible for the maintenance of the grassland against the invasion of forest. Fire does not kill the underground parts of grass plants, but limits tree growth to a few individuals of fire-resistant species. The browsing of animals, which kills many young trees, is also a factor in maintaining grassland at the expense of forest.

The African savanna is perhaps the most celebrated of the tropical grasslands, spanning the continent from west to east in two great belts, centered about on the 10th parallels of latitude north and south, and connected in east Africa by a broad north-south belt (Figure 16.20). In equatorial latitudes the African savanna replaces the rainforest because of the aridity associated with highlands in Sudan, Kenya, and Tanzania. Characteristic are the flat-topped acacia trees (*Acacia*), and the grotesque baobab (*Adansonia digitata*), which has a large barrel-shaped water-storing trunk (Figure 16.21). Elephant grass (*Pennisetum pur-*

Figure 16.21   Baobab tree (*Adansonia digitata*), near Nairobi, Kenya, Africa. (Photograph of the Akeley Expedition, courtesy of the American Museum of Natural History.)

pureum), forming almost inpenetrable thickets, may grow to heights of 16 ft (5 m).

Savanna in South America is exemplified in the *campo cerrado* of the interior Brazilian Highlands (Figure 16.22). Here the trees are largely evergreen, deep-rooted, and capable of tapping lower levels of soil moisture not available to the grasses during the dry season.

Other important savanna areas occur in northern Australia, India, and southeast Asia. The mesquite savanna of Texas provides an American example. Of interest to American students is the small patch

Figure 16.20   African tall-grass savanna in Kenya. (Photograph by Richard U. Light, courtesy of American Geographical Society.)

Figure 16.22   The *campo cerrado* at Pirassununga, Sao Paulo, Brazil. (Photograph by Pierre Dansereau.)

of rather specialized (edaphic) tropical savanna in southern Florida—the Everglades. Underlain by a limestone formation, the extremely low, flat plain of the Everglades is flooded by a shallow layer of runoff from summer rains and becomes a swamp. In winter the area becomes extremely dry. Coarse saw grass (*Cladium effusum*) covers much of the plain. Scattered trees are represented by palms and, on higher ground, by pines.

The pedogenic process most closely associated with tropical savanna is laterization, promoted by the high temperatures associated with the rainy season. However, laterization gives way to calcification as the savanna is traced toward higher latitudes where thornbush and, ultimately, steppe grasslands are encountered.

11. *Semidesert* (also called *half desert*) is a xerophytic shrub vegetation with a poorly developed herbaceous lower layer. Trees are generally absent. Semidesert shrub vegetation is well developed in subtropical and middle-latitude dry climates having a small annual total rainfall and high summer temperatures. An example is the sagebrush (*Artemisia tridentata*) vegetation of the middle and southern Rocky Mountain region and Colorado Plateau (Figure 16.23). Semidesert shrub vegetation seems recently to have expanded widely into areas of the western United States that were formerly steppe grasslands, as a result of overgrazing and trampling by livestock.

On the world map of vegetation, Plate 4, semidesert is included with dry-desert vegetation. The xerophytic shrub vegetation is to be expected along the less arid margins of the deserts and in favorable highland locations within the desert. Pedogenic processes are calcification, producing brown soils,

Figure 16.24 Lowland heath, mostly heather (*Calluna vulgaris*), on moraine, North Norfolk. (Photograph by S. R. Eyre.)

and gray desert soils. Salinization is found in poorly drained sites.

12. *Heath* is a low, dense layer of shrubs commonly not more than 10 in (25 cm) in height, which occurs in regions of highly equable but cool climate in middle and high latitudes (Figure 16.24). The shrubs are usually dominated by members of the Heath family (*Ericaceae*); mosses are also important. A common plant of heath vegetation is heather (*Calluna vulgaris*). In very cold climates heath includes small shrubby birches and willows.

Distribution of heath is not shown on the world vegetation map (Plate 4) but is found in small areas in Classes *E* and *I*. A cool, marine west coast climate is favorable to development of heath. Well-distributed precipitation and a temperature regime with small annual range are required. The pedogenic process is podzolization and soils are acidic. Examples of heath vegetation are seen in Ireland and other exposed west coasts of the British Isles (*moors*) and in western and north-central Europe.

13. *Cold woodland*, the last on our list of formation classes in the savanna biochore, is a form of vegetation limited to very cold subarctic and tundra climates. Trees are low in height and well spaced apart; a shrub layer may be well developed. The ground cover of lichens and mosses is distinctive. Cold woodland is essentially equivalent to what is widely referred to as *taiga*,[3] and occurs along the northern fringes of the high-latitude, needleleaf forests. Cold woodland is thus transitional into the treeless tundra and arctic heath.

In North America representative trees of the

Figure 16.23 Sage-brush semidesert, Vermilion Cliffs, near Kanab, Utah, 1906. (Photograph by Douglas Johnson.)

[3]The term "taiga" is commonly used to include also needleleaf forest, needleleaf woodland, and needleleaf savanna.

cold woodland are black spruce (*Picea mariana*) and tamarack (*Larix laricina*). In northern Scandinavia a scrubby birch (*Betula odorata*) forms a woodland with a low layer of lichens, such as reindeer "moss" (*Cladonia rangiferina*) (Figure 16.25). In Siberia larch (*Larix*) is the woodland tree. Birch-lichen woodland is also found in the subarctic regions of northwestern Canada and Alaska.

Cold woodland is dominated by the polar climatic regime with its long and severe winters in which all soil moisture is frozen for many months of the year. A shallow depth of thaw accompanies the short "summer," when insolation continues throughout much of the day. The pedogenic process is toward gleization in the poorly drained sites; toward podzolization on upland sites.

Cold woodland is not shown separately on the world vegetation map (Plate 4) but can be found in the tundra areas (Class *I*) along the boundary with needleleaf forest (Class *F*).

Grassland biochore

14. *Prairie* consists of tall grasses, comprising the dominant herbs, and subdominant forbs (broadleaved herbs) (Figure 16.26). Trees and shrubs are almost totally absent but may occur in the same region as forest or woodland patches in valleys and other topographic depressions. The grasses are deeply rooted and form a continuous and dense sward. The grasses flower in spring and early

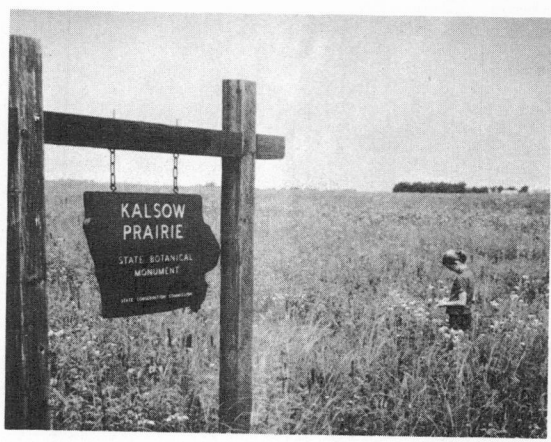

Figure 16.26   Kalsow Prairie, Iowa, has been set aside as an example of virgin prairie. (Photograph by courtesy of State Conservation Commission of Iowa.)

summer; the forbs, in late summer. In Iowa, a representative region of tall-grass prairie, typical grasses are big bluestem (*Andropogon gerardi*) and little bluestem (*A. scoparius*), a typical forb is black-eyed Susan (*Rudbeckia nitida*).

The tall-grass prairies are typically associated with continental, middle-latitude climates described as *subhumid*, that is, in which evapotranspiration and precipitation are almost balanced on an average yearly basis and range between 20 and 40 in (50–100 cm). In summers air and soil temperatures are high, so that on uplands soil moisture is not adequate for tree growth and deeper water sources are beyond reach of tree roots. The North American Prairies are found in a broad belt extending from Illinois, northwestward to southern Alberta and Saskatchewan. On the world map of vegetation (Plate 4) the North American prairie includes the eastern and northern parts of Class *G*. Areas of forest are mixed with areas of prairies in a transitional belt between forest and prairie regions.

Because the tall-grass prairies grade into shortgrass prairies and eventually into steppe grasslands in the direction of increasing aridity, it is not practical to try to list all world regions of tall-grass prairies. In Europe, a typical region of tall-grass prairie is the *puszta* of Hungary. The Argentine *pampa* is often cited as a region of prairie vegetation, as are areas in north China.

The pedogenic process associated with prairie vegetation is calcification and results in development of prairie and chernozem soil profiles.

15. *Steppe*, sometimes called *short-grass prairie*, is a formation class consisting of short grasses tending to be bunched and sparsely distributed (Figure 16.27). Scattered shrubs and low trees may be found in the steppe and there exist all grada-

Figure 16.25   Lichen woodland (open boreal forest) on a sand plain of the Hamilton River delta, Labrador. Black spruce and a few small white birch are widely spaced. The floor is covered by lichen (*Cladonia*). (Photograph by F. Kenneth Hare, courtesy of the American Geographical Society.)

Figure 16.27 Short-grass vegetation of the Great Plains, South Dakota. (Photograph by Douglas Johnson.)

tions into semidesert and woodland formation classes. Ground coverage is small and much bare soil is exposed. Many species of grasses and other herbs occur; a typical grass of the American steppe is buffalo grass (*Buchloe dactyloides*), other typical plants are the sunflower (*Helianthus rigidus*) and loco weed (*Oxytropis lambertii*).

The world distribution of steppe vegetation is extremely wide in terms of latitude, ranging in location from the equator to 55° N and 45° S (Plate 4, Class *G*). Steppes of low latitudes are transitional from vegetation of the wet-dry tropical climates into the dry deserts. Steppes of North Africa are transitional from Mediterranean climate, with its sclerophyll forest, to the African desert. Steppes of middle latitudes are associated with a semi-arid continental climatic regime in which, despite a summer rainfall maximum, evaporation exceeds precipitation on the average. Winters in the middle-latitude steppes are cold and dry; the summers warm to hot. In this climatic regime the dominant pedogenic process is calcification, with salinization in poorly drained sites. Soils contain a large excess of precipitated calcium carbonate and are very rich in bases. Brown soils are typical. Humus content is relatively small because of the sparseness of the vegetation.

16. *Grassy tundra* (including *alpine meadow*) is a grassland biochore formation limited to very cold climates having ample available moisture and often saturated soils. Grassy tundra of the arctic regions flourishes under a regime of long summer days during which time the ground ice melts only in a shallow surface layer. The frozen ground beneath (permafrost) remains impermeable and melt water cannot readily escape. Consequently, in summer a marshy condition prevails for at least a short time over wide areas. Humus accumulates in a well-developed layer.

Plants of the arctic grassy tundra are low and mostly herbaceous, although dwarf willow (*Salix herbacea*) occurs in places. Sedges, grasses, mosses, and lichens dominate the tundra in a low layer (Figure 16.28). Typical species are ridge sedge (*Carex bigelowii*), arctic meadow grass (*Poa arctica*), cottongrasses (*Eriophorum*), and snow lichen (*Cetraria nivalis*). There are also many species of forbs which flower brightly in the summer. Considerable variations in composition of the tundra are seen in the range from wet to well-drained habitats. One form of tundra consists of sturdy hummocks of plants with low, water-covered ground between. In the regions of grassy tundra will also be found areas of arctic scrub vegetation composed of willows and birches.

Under the subarctic climate and a condition of poor soil-water drainage, the pedogenic regime tends toward gleization. Size of plants is in part limited by the mechanical rupture of roots during freeze and thaw of the surface layer of soil, producing shallow-rooted plants. In winter drying winds and mechanical abrasion by wind-driven snow tend to reduce any portions of a plant that project above the snow.

In all latitudes, where altitude is sufficiently high, an alpine tundra is developed above the limit of tree growth and below the vegetation-free zone of barren rock and perpetual snow. Alpine tundra resembles arctic tundra in many physical respects.

Desert biochore

17. *Dry desert* is a formation class of xerophytic plants widely dispersed and providing almost negligible ground cover. In dry periods (which are the rule) the visible vegetation consists of small hard-leaved or spiny shrubs, succulent plants (cacti), or hard grasses. Many species of small annuals may be present, but appear only after a rare but heavy rain has saturated the soil.

Desert floras differ greatly from one part of the

Figure 16.28 Cotton-grass meadows, Arctic coastal plain of Alaska. (Photograph by William R. Farrand.)

Figure 16.29 Shrub vegetation of the Sonoran Desert, southwestern Arizona. Ocotillo plant in the left foreground; saguaro cactus plants in left distance. (Photograph by A. N. Strahler.)

world to another. In the Mohave-Sonoran deserts of the southwestern United States, plants are often large and in places give a near-woodland appearance (Figure 16.29). Well known are the treelike saguaro cactus (*Carnegiea gigantea*), the prickly-pear cactus (*Opuntia imbricata*), the ocotillo (*Fouquiera splendens*), creosote bush (*Larrea tridentata*) and smoke tree (*Dalea spinosa*). Much of the "desert" of the southwestern United States is in fact scrub, thorn scrub, savanna, or steppe grassland (Figure 14.2). In the Sahara desert (most of it very much drier than in the American desert) a typical plant is a hard grass (*Stipa*); another, found along the dry beds of watercourses, is tamarisk (*Tamarix*). The coastal desert of southwest Africa is known for the strange tumboa plant (*Welwitschia mirabilis*) with strap-shaped leaves radiating from a central tap root which penetrates deep into the ground (Figure 16.30).

Much of the area assigned to dry-desert vegetation has no plants of visible dimensions, being composed of shifting dune sands, or almost sterile salt flats.

Distribution of dry deserts is shown in the world vegetation map, Plate 4, as Class *H*. As a study of climate will show, three variations of the desert trend exist. The true tropical-continental deserts have not only extreme aridity but also extremely high air and soil temperatures; the middle-latitude deserts (30° to 35° lat.) have both aridity and a great annual temperature range including extremes of winter cold; the tropical west coast deserts have

remarkable uniformity and relative coolness of temperature along with persistent coastal fog. A dominant pedogenic process of dry deserts is salinization, locally producing areas of salt crust where only salt-loving (halophytic) plants can survive. Calcification is conspicuous on well-drained uplands; encrustations and deposits of calcium carbonate (caliche) are commonplace. Humus is lacking and soils are pale gray or red in color, e.g., sierozems and red-desert soils.

18. *Arctic fell field* is the arctic equivalent of the dry desert, being found in the extremely cold tundra and icecap climates. The arctic fell field consists of rocky ground surfaces, produced by

Figure 16.30 The tumboa plant (*Welwitschia mirabilis*) on a sandy plain in the Kalahari Desert of southwestern Africa. (Photograph by Robert J. Rodin.)

Figure 16.31 Arctic fell-field vegetation, Etah, Greenland. On the left is *Dryas integrifolia*; on the right, *Cerastium alpinium*. (Photograph of Crockerland Expedition, courtesy of the American Museum of Natural History.)

intense frost shattering and having only small patches of finetextured mineral soil. Vegetation is very sparse and consists mostly of lichens, mosses, and a few small shrubs (Figure 16.31). For example, in northern Baffin Island, typical plants are a small polar willow (*Salix polaris*), purple saxifrage (*Saxifraga oppositifolia*), and woolly moss (*Rhacomitrium lanuginosum*).

Arctic fell field can be found as far north as the extreme limits of land, namely up to 84° N latitude and southward to ice-free parts of Antarctica. Soil-forming processes consist of little more than rock disintegration by frost action, manifested in the formation of stone polygons in which finer particles are sorted from the coarse into patches. On the world vegetation map, Plate 4, arctic fell field is included in Class *I* along with grassy tundra and arctic scrub.

This attempt to classify world vegetation into a number of formation classes and to show their distribution by means of a map can be only partly successful, at best. The infinite variations in structure of vegetation defy a simple categorical system. Moreover, no two authorities in the field of plant geography will set up the same array of classes or produce closely corresponding maps. An appreciation of broad systems of plant formation classes in response to the restraints and freedoms of the spectrum of climatic regimes should be foremost in the mind of the geographer and he must stress the underlying principles and distributional aspects that most systems show in common, rather than be diverted by the seeming contradictions and complexities he frequently encounters.

REFERENCES FOR FURTHER STUDY

Shantz, H. L., and R. Zon (1924), *Natural vegetation*, Atlas of American Agriculture, Section E, U.S. Department of Agriculture, U.S. Govt. Printing Office, Washington, D.C., 29 pp.

Newbigin, Marion I. (1948), *Plant and animal geography*, second edition, E. P. Dutton and Co., New York, 298 pp.

Brockmann-Jerosch, H. (1951), *Vegetation of the earth* (wall map), Justus Perthes, Gotha.

American Geographical Society (1956), *A world geography of forest resources*, edited by Haden-Guest, Wright, and Teclaff, The Ronald Press Co., New York, 736 pp.

Dansereau, Pierre (1957), *Biogeography; an ecological perspective*, The Ronald Press Co., New York, 394 pp.

Polunin, Nicholas (1960), *Introduction to plant geography*, McGraw-Hill Book Co., New York, 640 pp.

Küchler, A. W. (1964), Potential natural vegetation of the conterminous United States (map and manual), Amer. Geographical Soc., Special Publ. No. 36, 116 pp.

Eyre, S. R. (1968), *Vegetation and soils; a world picture*, second edition, Aldine Publ. Co., Chicago, 328 pp.

REVIEW QUESTIONS

1. What are the four great biochores? Describe each briefly and give its general climatic associations.

2. What investigators were responsible for developing the system of vegetation formation classes commonly followed today? Discuss some of the problems that might be connected with preparing a useful world map of natural vegetation.

3. Describe the equatorial rainforest in terms of structure. What is the importance of lianas in this rainforest? Of epiphytes? Comment on the numbers of species of trees found in the equatorial rainforest. Name two representative trees. What climatic and pedogenic regimes are associated with the equatorial rainforest?

4. What coastal vegetation forms may be expected in regions of equatorial rainforest? Describe particularly the mangrove coasts.

5. How does tropical rainforest differ from equatorial rainforest and in what respects is it similar? In what geographic regions is tropical rainforest found? Explain.

6. What are the unique characteristics of the monsoon forest as compared with other low-latitude forests? What accounts for the deciduousness of the trees? Relate the monsoon forest to a particular climatic regime and describe its world distribution pattern.

7. How does temperate rainforest differ in structure and geographic location from equatorial and tropical rainforests? Describe temperate rainforests of America, Asia, and New Zealand. What is particularly noteworthy of the development of epiphytes in the temperate rainforest?

8. What three types of world locations favor temperate rainforest? What climatic and pedogenic regimes are associated with temperate rainforest?

9. Describe the summergreen deciduous forest as to structure and seasonal development. Name common trees of the deciduous forests of eastern North America and Europe. In what ways does the summergreen deciduous forest represent a response to the continental climatic regime? What is the associated pedogenic process?

10. Describe a needleleaf forest in terms of vegetation structure. Define the major world regions of occurrence of needleleaf forest and name common trees of these belts.

11. How does topography influence the extension of needleleaf forests into lower latitudes? Describe the needleleaf forests of the Pacific coastal regions of North America. What is the dominant pedogenic regime in areas of needleleaf forest?

12. Describe the evergreen-hardwood (sclerophyll) forest in terms of vegetation structure. With what climatic regime is this formation class closely associated and how is this association seen in the world geographical distribution of sclerophyll forest, woodland, and scrub? Name some representative sclerophyll forest plants of the Mediterranean region, California, and Australia.

13. What is savanna woodland? With what climatic regime is it most commonly associated? What are the life-form characteristics of trees and shrubs of the tropical savanna woodland?

14. Describe thornbush and tropical scrub as vegetation classes. What is the *caatinga* of Brazil? The *dornveld* of South Africa?

15. How does savanna differ from savanna woodland? Describe the vegetation soils, climate, and animal life associated with tropical savanna, with particular reference to Africa. What is the *campo cerrado* of Brazil?

16. What is semidesert vegetation? Describe semidesert in the southwestern United States.

17. What is heath? What common plants are associated with heath? Describe the conditions of climate and geographic location favorable to occurrence of heath.

18. Describe cold-woodland vegetation. Is *taiga* an equivalent designation for this formation class? What are some representative plants of the cold woodland of North America? Of Scandinavia? Of Siberia?

19. What plants comprise prairie as a vegetation formation class? Name representative examples from the tall-grass prairie of Iowa. With what climatic and pedogenic regimes is prairie vegetation associated? Explain. What is the *puszta* of Hungary? The *pampa* of Argentina?

20. Compare steppe (short-grass prairie) with tall-grass prairie in terms of vegetation structure and climatic regime.

21. Describe the grassy tundra of cold climates, giving names of typical plants. With what conditions of climate, drainage, and pedogenic process is the grassy tundra associated? Compare alpine tundra with grassy tundra of low elevations.

22. Describe dry desert as a plant formation class. Name some typical desert plants of the southwestern United States, the Sahara, and southwest Africa. What is the dominant pedogenic process of the dry desert?

23. What relation does arctic fell field bear to other formation classes of the cold lands in high latitudes? Explain how freeze and thaw of soil water plays a dominant role in the landscape associated with arctic fell field.

CHAPTER 17

Landforms and Earth Materials

LANDFORMS, the distinctive geometric configurations of the earth's land surface, are of primary concern to the geographer because they exert far-reaching and fundamental influence on the patterns of human activity. The direct influences are obvious to any thoughtful person. A mountain chain is an effective barrier between groups of people who live in adjacent lowlands. A plain, on the other hand, may be densely populated, rich in agricultural resources, and unified culturally and politically by a network of good roads and railroads that permit people with common interests to intercommunicate freely. One coast line, deeply indented with excellent natural harbors but bordered by a rocky rugged coastal belt, may produce a community of seafaring humans, adapted to fishing, ocean commerce, and shipbuilding. Another coast line, whose simple plan and shallow bottom provide not a single good natural harbor, may be bordered by a low, fertile coastal plain. Here human activity turns naturally to agriculture.

Examples of the direct effect of landforms, or topographic relief features, on human beings could be cited almost without end, but there are, in addition, indirect geographical influences to be considered. As we have seen in the study of rainfall distribution, a high mountain range profoundly influences climate in adjacent areas. If it shields a nearby lowland from prevailing moisture-bearing winds, a desert results. On mountain slopes, climates become cooler and moister with increased altitude, bringing a changing succession of agricultural and forest conditions, which, in turn, determine to what extent occupation is possible and what natural products can be obtained. Steepness of slopes is closely associated with fertility of soils. Hill and mountain slopes have thin, relatively poor soils, readily subject to devastating soil erosion when exposed by axe or plow. Plains may have thick, rich soils, not easily eroded even under poor farming practices.

Geomorphology

The systematic study of topographic relief features is known as geomorphology (*geo*, earth; *morph*, form; *ology*, science), but for simplicity may well be called "the study of landforms." Landscape features must be sorted out into classes or groups of those essentially similar both in outward form and in origin. The geomorphologist is equally interested in forms and in the processes and stages of development of those forms. This book will treat landforms in terms of how they came about. Landscape features pass through an orderly series of changes, just as do human beings in their life span. Once these life stages are known, any landscape feature can be related to a particular event in the life cycle of landforms, thereby lending order and natural law to our concepts of landform development.

Genetic landform description

It is possible, of course, to describe all landscape features by tabulating their size, shape, angles of slope, and orientation without thought to their origin or development. This is an *empirical* approach to natural science. Volumes of figures and other factual data would be required to convey the proper description of even the simplest assemblages of landforms.

If, on the other hand, the development of landforms is carefully examined, it is seen that the same series of forms is repeated with remarkable similarity over and over again in nature. In order to classify and describe a complex assemblage of forms in terms of orderly sequences of development, we need only a single brief statement giving (a) the *structure* of the rock mass beneath, (b) the *process* which sculptured the landform and (c) the *stage* of its development. Such a description is *genetic* because it emphasizes genesis, or origin. The person who hears or reads such a description, knowing what the ideal forms are like, can relate any particular landform to its proper place in the natural scheme.

The systematic study of landforms according to their origin and stage of development was introduced by Professor William Morris Davis, of Harvard University, about 1890. His influence has been so profound that many English-speaking geomorphologists follow the basic plans that he laid down.

A. Mountain block created: an initial landform

Earth's crust fractured, dislocated by internal earth forces

B. Mountain block carved into sequential landforms
(a) Erosional (canyon) (divide)
(b) Depositional (fan)

Earth forces dormant

Figure 17.1   Initial and sequential landforms.

Initial and sequential landforms

In terms of the grand scale of geological processes there are two fundamental classes of landforms. First, there are the original crustal masses raised by internal earth forces and by volcanic eruptions. These comprise the *initial landforms* (Figure 17.1*A*). Second, there are the landforms made by agents of denudation. Because these follow the initial forms and occur in orderly sequences, they are called collectively the *sequential landforms* (Figure 17.1*B*).

Any landscape is really nothing more than the existing stage in a great struggle or contest. The internal earth forces spasmodically elevate parts of the crust to create initial landforms. The external agents patiently keep wearing these masses down and carving them into vast numbers of smaller sequential landforms.

All stages of this struggle can be seen in various parts of the world. Where high, rugged mountains exist, the internal earth forces have recently dominated. Where certain kinds of low plains exist today, denudational forces have finally triumphed. All intermediate stages can be found. Because the internal earth forces act repeatedly, new landmasses keep coming into existence as old ones are subdued. Judging from conditions in various periods of the geologic past, we are now in a time when continents stand relatively high above sea level. This suggests that internal forces were active relatively recently, geologically speaking.

Agents of land sculpture

Sequential landforms are products of one or more of the land-sculpturing agents, running water, waves, ice, and wind. These erosional agents, aided by processes of rock decay and downslope move-

ments of soil and rock under gravitational force, attack from the outside all continental rock masses that become elevated by mountain-making upheavals or warping of the earth's solid crust. No part of the land surface is immune from attack. As soon as any rock mass comes to be exposed to the air or to wave attack it is set upon by these denudational agents and processes. They work to one ultimate goal—wearing away the landmass until it becomes a low plain, which is then slowly consumed by waves and perhaps finally covered by ocean waters. The disintegration products are spread over the sea floors surrounding the continents. The processes act with extreme slowness, to be sure, but geologic time is enormously great. Streams and waves seen in action today have had millions of years to do their work. Geologists believe that all sequential landforms can be explained as results of processes that can be seen acting at the present time.

In the wearing down of landmasses, a great variety of sequential landforms results. Where rock is eroded away, valleys or topographic depressions of one sort or another are formed. Between the eroded depressions are ridges, hills, or mountains representing unconsumed parts of landmasses. All such sequential landforms shaped by progressive removal of the bedrock mass are designated *erosional landforms.*

Rock and soil fragments that were removed are deposited elsewhere to make an entirely different set of topographic features, the *depositional landforms.* Figure 17.2 illustrates these two groups of landforms. The ravine, canyon, peak, spur, col and bluffs are erosional landforms; the fan, built of rock fragments below the mouth of the ravine, is a depositional landform. The floodplain, built of material transported by a stream, is also a depositional landform.

Bedrock, soil, and residual overburden

Examination of a freshly cut cliff, such as that in a new highway cut or quarry wall, will reveal several kinds of earth materials, shown in Figure 17.3. Solid, hard rock which is still in place and

Peak
Shoulder
Col
Ravine
Canyon
Spur
Fan
Bluffs
Floodplain

Figure 17.2   Erosional and depositional landforms.

Figure 17.3   Residual and transported overburden.

relatively unchanged is called *bedrock*. It grades upward into a zone where the rock has become decayed and has disintegrated into clay, silt, and sand particles. This may be called the *weathered overburden*, or *residual overburden*. At the top is a layer of true *soil*, often called *topsoil* by farmers and gardeners. Soil properties, soil-forming processes, and soil classification were treated in Chapters 13 and 14. Over the soil may be a protective layer of grass, shrubs, or trees.

One or more of these zones may be missing. Sometimes everything is stripped off down to the bedrock, which then appears at the surface as an *outcrop*. Sometimes following cultivation or forest fires the true soil only is eroded away, leaving exposed the overburden, which is infertile and may become scored by deep gullies. The thickness of soil and overburden is quite variable. Although the true soil is rarely more than a few feet thick, the residual overburden of decayed and fragmented rock may extend down tens or even hundreds of feet. Formation of the overburden is greatly aided by the presence of innumerable bedrock cracks termed *joints* (Figure 17.3), along which water can move easily to promote rock decay.

Transported overburden

Another variety of overburden that may be found covering the bedrock is *transported overburden*. It consists of such materials as stream-laid gravels and sands, floodplain silts, clays of lake bottoms, beach and dune sands, or rubble left by a melting glacier. All types have in common a history of having been transported by streams, ice, waves, or wind.

Whereas residual overburden, formed in place by disintegration of bedrock below it, is of local origin, transported overburden consists of rock and mineral varieties from distant sources and may be quite unlike the underlying minerals and rocks. Figure 17.3 shows stream valley deposits, called *alluvium*, which would be designated as transported overburden in contrast to residual overburden of the adjacent hill slope. Once deposited, transported overburden may remain undisturbed for many thousands of years, in which case a true soil is formed in its uppermost layer.

In a broad sense all of the materials of which the depositional landforms are built up are of transported overburden. In later chapters many kinds of depositional landforms are described and explained in terms of the processes by which the particles are carried.

Influence of rocks on landforms

Bedrock strongly influences shape, size, and development of the erosional landforms. In some places, rock takes the form of thin layers, lying horizontally, tilted, folded, or broken, as the case may be. Elsewhere it consists of thick, irregular masses extending down to great depths. Some varieties of rock are soft and are readily washed away by streams and waves; others are extremely resistant to all agents of weathering and erosion. To a considerable degree the weakness or resistance of rocks is determined by their origin and age. When varied rocks lie side by side near the surface of the earth's crust the agents of denudation etch them out according to their degree of resistance, the weak rock tending to form valleys or other types of depressions, the resistant ones standing out in bold relief as hills, mountains, or plateaus. Consequently, landforms reflect closely the shape and arrangement of the original rock masses and will show certain distinctive qualities whereby they may be referred to an orderly classification.

The first step in approaching geomorphology is,

therefore, to learn the fundamental facts about rocks of the earth's crust, their composition, physical and chemical properties, characteristic forms of occurrence, processes of origin, and geologic age. A knowledge of common rocks and the predominant minerals which comprise them is of further value to the geographer because rocks and minerals have intrinsic value to man as ores, fuels, and construction materials. An evaluation of the natural resources of a region is thus in part a question of geology.

Igneous rocks

Rocks may be divided into three major classes: (1) *igneous*, (2) *sedimentary*, and (3) *metamorphic*, according to their origin. *Igneous rocks* solidify from a molten state. The highly heated fluid rock, termed *magma*, originates at considerable depths beneath the earth's surface and is forced by great internal pressures to penetrate the solid, brittle outer crust of the earth (Figure 17.4). It should not be supposed that the whole interior of the earth is molten. It seems more likely that local pockets of magma, lying at depths of 20 mi (30 km) or more, are formed in various places and eventually are forced toward the surface.

The nature and origin of molten rocks bodies and the forces that control their behavior comprise a highly speculative phase of geology. Unlike the study of landforms, in which both the landform and the erosional process can be observed in their entirety, the study of deep-seated igneous rock masses cannot be made during their formation, but can only be interpreted in the light of the appearance and composition of the rock after it has cooled and become solidified, then exposed to the surface by long ages of landmass denudation.

Intrusive and extrusive igneous rocks

Molten masses that do not reach the surface but solidify in spaces that they have made by pushing the surrounding rock apart, or melting, or dissolving it are termed *intrusive* igneous rocks (Figure 17.4). They do, in fact, intrude or invade the

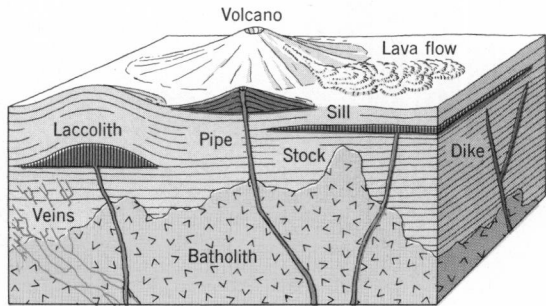

Figure 17.4   Igneous rock bodies.

previously formed rock. Where the intrusion has been violent the surrounding rocks may show breaking, crushing, folding, or uparching around the newly formed rock body. Where the intrusion has been gradual and the surrounding rock slowly melted or dissolved, no disturbance of the adjoining rock may result.

A second class of igneous rock, termed *extrusive*, is that which reaches the ground surface, issuing from a pipe or crack and pouring out upon the ground, then quickly solidifying into a hard rock. Volcanoes and lava flows are the principal products of igneous rock extrusion (Figure 17.4).

Intrusive rocks differ from extrusive rocks considerably in both gross outward form and details of internal structure and texture. Intrusive rocks commonly occur in enormous masses, termed *batholiths*, covering areas as great as an entire state and extending many miles down (Figure 17.4). The adjective *plutonic* is commonly used for this and other deep-seated intrusive rock bodies. Such large masses cooled very slowly; consequently, the individual mineral crystals of which the rock is composed are relatively large (Figure 17.5), commonly measuring 0.1 to 0.5 in (0.25 to 1.5 cm) across. Crystal grains of intrusive igneous rock interlock closely so as to produce a dense, strong rock, free of cavities.

Minerals

A *mineral* is a naturally occurring, inorganic substance that has a definite or fairly definite chemical composition and usually exhibits a characteristic crystal form, together with certain distinctive qualities of color, hardness, luster, and fracture habit. Although a few kinds of rocks consist almost wholly of a single mineral variety, most rock types are aggregates or physical mixtures of two or more minerals. Both the mineral varieties present and the proportions in which they are mixed determine the name and properties of a given rock variety.

Mineralogy, the study of minerals, and *petrology*, the study of rocks, are important branches of geology. Several thousand mineral varieties have been identified and named; the list of rock varieties runs into the hundreds. Fortunately, only a few minerals are so abundant in volume and worldwide distribution as to combine into major rock types. This introductory study goes little further than to describe a few of the commonest igneous rocks and to name the principal constituent minerals.

Common varieties of intrusive rocks

One of the most abundant and best known of the intrusive rocks is *granite*, composed of a

Figure 17.5 Seen close up, this granite, a coarse-grained intrusive rock, proves to be made of tightly interlocking crystals of a few kinds of minerals.

mixture of these minerals: *quartz* (silicon dioxide), *potash feldspar* (an aluminum silicate of potassium), *hornblende* (an aluminum silicate of iron and magnesium), and *biotite mica* (a complex aluminum silicate with manganese and iron) (Figure 17.6). Because quartz and feldspar, which together may comprise three-quarters of the rock, are light-colored, whereas hornblende and biotite mica are black, granite has a speckled appearance when closely examined (Figure 17.5).

The potash feldspar grains will be identified by their opacity, blocklike outlines, and shiny luster on cleavage surfaces. In some granites this feldspar is almost white, producing gray granite; in others, the feldspar is salmon pink, producing pink granite. The quartz grains are clear and appear glassy beside the feldspar grains. Quartz grains tend to have irregular outlines and break irregularly, after the manner of glass. Both hornblende and biotite crystals are black, but the biotite mica is soft and can be split into thin flakes with the point of a knife or needle.

A second variety of intrusive igneous rock is

Figure 17.6 Various combinations of light and dark minerals produce the igneous rocks.

diorite. Not nearly so widespread in occurrence as granite, it illustrates a rock of more limited mineral composition, in that quartz is entirely lacking and only two minerals dominate: (1) *plagioclase feldspar* (soda-lime feldspar), which is an aluminum silicate mineral with varying proportions of sodium and calcium, and (2) a dark mineral, which may be either hornblende or *pyroxene.* The plagioclase feldspar, which is milky white to gray in color, with vitreous luster on its cleavage surfaces, makes up about three-fourths of the rock. Both hornblende and pyroxene are commonly black and are extremely difficult to tell apart without the aid of a microscope. Pyroxene, like hornblende, is a silicate mineral with magnesium, iron, and calcium, but pyroxene is often lacking in aluminum.

A third intrusive igneous rock of importance is *gabbro,* composed primarily of two minerals, plagioclase feldspar and pyroxene. The difference between this rock and diorite is largely in the proportions of the two minerals. Feldspar dominates in diorite, but makes up only about 50 percent in gabbro. Another mineral, *olivine,* is commonly present in gabbro. Olivine, a silicate of magnesium and iron, is commonly green in color. Gabbro is a coarse-grained, plutonic rock like granite or diorite and also occurs in great masses.

A fourth intrusive rock variety is *peridotite,* a dense, dark rock composed largely of pyroxene and olivine. Little or no feldspar is present. Peridotite is found usually in small masses or dikes, not in vast batholiths such as granite.

Granitic and basaltic rock groups

As Figure 17.6 shows, the four examples of intrusive igneous rocks have been placed in an orderly arrangement, such that the light-colored minerals, quartz and feldspar, decrease in proportion while the dark-colored minerals increase in proportion. In granite and diorite there is a preponderance of quartz and feldspar, which are light-colored minerals of low density. A cube of granite will weigh about 2.6 times as much as a similar volume of water; its relative density, or *specific gravity,* is therefore stated as 2.6. Igneous rocks containing largely light-colored minerals of low density, rich in aluminum silicate combined with potassium, sodium, and calcium (as in the feldspars), are said to belong to the *granitic group.* Geologists often refer to these rocks collectively as *sial,* a word coined from *si,* for silica, and *al,* for alumina.

Gabbro and peridotite, on the other hand, are composed predominately of minerals rich in magnesium and iron, the so-called *ferromagnesian minerals.* These minerals are relatively dense, so that peridotite, for example, may have a specific

gravity over 3.2, which is roughly 25 percent greater than granite. Rocks composed largely of the dense ferromagnesian minerals belong to the *basaltic group* (or *basic* group). The word *sima,* coined for these rocks collectively in distinction to sial, is taken from *si* for silica and *ma* for magnesium. The importance of granitic and basaltic (or sialic and simatic) groups of rocks in the great layers of the earth's crust is discussed in Chapter 18.

Extrusive igneous rocks

The extrusive igneous rocks take two forms: (*a*) fluid magma flows in the form of thin tongues or sheets, called *lava flows,* and (*b*) solid or near-solid pieces blown violently from volcanic vents and collectively termed *volcanic ejecta.* (See Figure 28.9.) Some lava flows may have a rough, blocky surface; others a smooth billowy surface. Usually flows are dark red or black in surface color. Because of the rapid cooling, mineral crystals have little or no opportunity to develop during the

Figure 17.7 Above: The outer surface of lava has wrinkles produced by flowage. Below: A frothy, gaseous lava solidifies into a light, porous scoria (left). Rapidly cooled lava may form a dark volcanic glass (right).

solidification and cannot be detected with the unaided eye. Expanding gases may fill the rock with countless bubblelike cavities, producing a texture of rock called *scoria* (Figure 17.7). Where solidification is extremely rapid, a glass is formed. This glass goes by the name *obsidian*, or simply *volcanic glass* (Figure 17.7).

Lavas may be similar in composition to the various kinds of intrusive igneous rocks, inasmuch as the same magma may reach the surface in one place but not in another. The lava that corresponds to granite is *rhyolite* (Figure 17.6). That which corresponds to diorite is *andesite.* These rocks are both rather light gray or pink on freshly broken surfaces. Even close study will show only a dull rock surface, the crystals being too fine to see with the naked eye. In some lavas, however, there is a sprinkling of large crystals of feldspar easily seen in outline against the fine-grained background.

The extrusive equivalent of diabase is *basalt,* a dense black rock which is perhaps the commonest and most widespread of the lavas. Areas of huge size, such as the Columbia River plateaus in Washington, Oregon, and Idaho and the Deccan region of western India, are underlain by thousands of feet of thickness of basalt lavas, poured out in tremendous upwellings through long cracks known as *fissures.* A horizontal layer of basalt, upon cooling, shrinks somewhat and forms into four-, five-, or six-sided columns which stand vertically. The structure is termed *columnar jointing* and gives a most striking appearance to cliffs of basalt (Figure 17.8).

Volcanic ejecta come in various sizes and shapes. Very fine material is termed *volcanic dust* or *volcanic ash.* Coarser particles, up to 2 or 3 in (5 or 8 cm) across, are termed *cinder* and resemble the clinkers from a coal furnace. Still larger masses are *volcanic bombs* (Figure 28.9). These may be still plastic when blown from a volcanic vent and become shaped into rounded masses resembling a loaf of bread. Volcanic ejecta result from the presence of large amounts of gas under high pressure in the magma. As it approaches the surface the gas is released from confining pressure and expands, frothing the magma into a bubbly foam and producing the violent explosions that blow the fragments into the air. One particularly spongy, foamlike variety of lava is *pumice,* which is so light that it floats on water.

Sedimentary rocks

Those rocks that are composed of particles derived from previously existing rock, then laid down after transportation by streams, ocean or wave currents, wind, or ice are *sedimentary rocks.* Rocks of any origin may be the parent material for sediment. In addition, sediment may result

Figure 17.8   This cliff of old lava has weathered away, revealing the columnar jointing system formed during cooling. (Photograph by Gifford.)

from chemical reaction and precipitation. As the solid particles settle out, a layer is formed. Should the size or composition of the particles change repeatedly, the result will be a series of layers of varied type. Thus a series of muds or clays, sands, or gravels might be deposited upon an ocean or lake bottom, or upon land if the material is deposited from streams, winds, or glaciers. In their original state, these sediments are soft, but in time they become hardened into rocks as we are accustomed to seeing them. Hardening occurs both because of pressure compaction driving out water, and because chemical deposits of calcium carbonate or silicon dioxide form between the particles, causing them to be cemented together.

Sedimentary rocks are distinguished from igneous rocks by the usual presence of layers resulting from changing size and composition of sediment. The layers are termed *strata*, or simply *beds*. The planes of separation between successive layers are *planes of stratification*, or *bedding planes*. The rock is said to be *stratified* or *bedded*. (See Figures 26.14, 26.15, 26.16.) Bedding planes in their original condition are nearly horizontal but may be tilted to any angle by subsequent movements of the earth's crust (Figure 17.9).

Groups of contiguous rock strata having some common properties of rock variety or geologic age or both are designated as *formations* and are usually named for the geographic locality at which they are well displayed for study, or were first described by the geologist. For example, the *Mesa Verde Formation* is a sandstone named for its striking cliff exposures at Mesa Verde, in southwestern Colorado, yet it is found in several states and is believed to have been once a vast, continuous layer of sands laid down in the floor of an ancient shallow sea.

Clastic sediments

One great class of sedimentary rocks is described as *clastic*, meaning that the particles are produced by disintegration of previous rocks through the combined weathering processes (Chapter 19). Processes of transportation in water or wind tend to sort the particles into various size grades, from which the clastic sedimentary rocks are named as follows:

Rock Name	Particle Name	Diameter or Fineness of grains
Conglomerate	Boulders	Over 10 in (25 cm)
	Cobbles	$2\frac{1}{2}$ to 10 in (6 to 25 cm)
	Pebbles (gravel)	$\frac{1}{16}$ to $2\frac{1}{2}$ in (2 mm to 6 cm)
Sandstone	Sand	10 to 1000 per inch (0.02 to 2 mm)
Siltstone	Silt	1000 to 10,000 per inch (0.002 to .02 mm)
Shale	Clay	Finer than 10,000 per inch (Under 0.002 mm)

Conglomerate, although named for the presence of boulders, cobbles, or pebbles, has a large proportion of sand filling the interstices. The larger particles are usually well rounded from tumbling on stream beds or in the surf zone of beaches (Figure 17.10). In fact, conglomerates may be thought of as fossil gravel bars or beaches of ancient rivers or shorelines. Where the large fragments are angular, instead of rounded, the rock is called a *breccia*, rather than a conglomerate. Breccia might be formed of rock fragments rolled

Figure 17.9 These limestone strata in Oklahoma were steeply tilted long after being laid down. (Photograph by Lofman. Courtesy of Standard Oil Co., New Jersey.)

from a cliff, crushed within a landslide, or swept from a steep ravine in a brief torrential flood.

Sandstone and *siltstone* grade into one another and are distinguished much as coarse sandpaper is distinguished from very fine. The grains of sandstone may be of any durable mineral, such as those described in the foregoing section on igneous rocks. Nevertheless, the long distance of travel of the grains in rivers or along shores eliminates the soft, easily powdered minerals and allows chemical decay to turn others, such as the feldspars and ferromagnesian minerals, into soft clay. Therefore, the commonest mineral of sandstones is quartz, whose resistance to mechanical and chemical attack is phenomenal. A few grains of dark minerals may be present, as well as tiny gleaming mica flakes.

Sandstone, siltstone, and conglomerate owe their hardness to cementation following deposition.

Figure 17.10 Conglomerate is a mixture of pebbles and sand cemented into a hard rock.

Gradually, in the vast spans of geologic time that follow deposition and burial, deposits of silica (SiO_2) or calcium carbonate ($CaCO_3$) accumulate in the pore spaces between sand grains, producing a solid, strong rock. The cementing substances are carried in solution by slowly moving underground water. Cementing material rarely fills all of the openings of a sandstone, so that the rock can hold large stores of fluids such as water or oil. We depend on sandstones as reservoirs of our natural gas, petroleum, and in many cases of ground water supplies as well (Chapters 20 and 26).

Shale is compacted clay or mud, greatly increased in density and hardness by the application of pressure from overlying strata. Clays commonly consist of submicroscopic flakes of mineral matter. Such particles behave as colloids, which have a strong affinity for water. Under sufficient pressure, the excess water is largely driven off; an extremely dense rock results. Whereas a clay or mud will soften and swell when soaked for a short time in water, shale will not. Shales are gray, earth-red, or black. The red color is due to presence of iron oxides; black may indicate the presence of finely divided organic matter in the form of carbon compounds. Shales have a soft, smooth feel in contrast to the gritty surface texture of sandstones. Furthermore, shale is mechanically weak and can easily be shattered into thin flakes and plates. For this reason shale plays the geomorphic role of a weak rock, easily carved away by the agents of land erosion to produce valleys and broad lowlands.

Pyroclastic rocks

A special class of clastic rocks results from the violent eruption of volcanoes, where fine ash is belched from the vent in great clouds. Sediment settling from the air during such explosions is described as *pyroclastic* material. An important variety of pyroclastic rock is *tuff*, a fine-grained, light-gray rock composed of compacted volcanic ash. Scattered small crystals of igneous minerals, blown from the vent, are sometimes visible in the tuff. If the ash has been picked up by streams and carried into a body of standing water, the tuff may be reformed into a distinctly stratified sedimentary rock. Other volcanic ash outbursts were carried by gases of such high temperature that the ash was fused into a hard rock known as *welded tuff*.

Organic and chemical sedimentary rocks

A second important class of sedimentary rocks, described as *organic*, consists of rock matter produced by the growth activities of plants and animals. A sedimentary rock variety of major importance is *limestone* (Figure 17.9), much of which is formed from the limy parts of such organisms as corals, algae, foraminifera, clams, and snails. The

organic origin is obvious where large shell fragments have been cemented into a variety of limestone termed *coquina*.

Limestone in its pure state consists of *calcite* (calcium carbonate), a mineral easily scratched with the sharp point of a knife and responding by vigorous effervescence when a drop of dilute hydrochloric acid is placed on its surface. Limestones may be pure white, as in the case of a very soft variety termed *chalk*, or gray to black in the more common dense varieties. Limestone may also form by direct chemical precipitation from waters of lakes or oceans heavily charged with lime in solution. The soft lime mud thus formed is termed *marl*. Because of its susceptibility to weak acids present in the rain water, soil water, and streams, limestone is rapidly eaten away in regions of humid climates, forming valleys and broad lowlands.

Many limestones have considerable amounts of the mineral *dolomite* (calcium-magnesium carbonate) incorporated with the calcite. Where the mineral dolomite predominates, the rock itself is called *dolomite*.

Quite different from limestone is another organic type of sedimentary rock, *coal*, formed of vast bog accumulations of partly decayed plant matter. In the early stages of its formation, coal passes through the stage of *peat*, a soft brown, combustible mass of plant fragments. Through later burial and compaction, water and certain volatile compounds are slowly driven off, yielding dense, black, rocklike layers of coal which contain a high proportion of fixed carbon.

Of great importance economically, though not abundant in comparison with limestone, are a group of chemical sediments termed *evaporites*. These are salts that have been precipitated from waters of shallow desert lakes or constricted bays of the ocean, where evaporation of the water is rapid. One evaporite which is found in rock layers of wide extent is *anhydrite* (calcium sulfate). Closely related is *gypsum* (hydrous calcium sulfate), a soft white mineral. Gypsum is often found interlayered with shales and limestones. Another evaporite familiar to all is rock salt, occurring as the mineral *halite* (sodium chloride), which forms thick sedimentary rock layers along with shales in a few localities.

Sedimentary rocks as landform controls

Figure 17.11 shows five types of sedimentary rock together with a mass of much older igneous rock upon which the sediments were laid. Their usual landform habit, whether to form valleys or mountains, is indicated, together with the conventional symbols used on cross sections by geologists. These rock strata have been strongly tilted and deeply eroded, so that there is maximum oppor-

Figure 17.11 Many landscape features originate through the slow erosional removal of weaker rock, leaving the more resistant rock standing as ridges or mountains.

tunity for the development of relief as a consequence of the different degrees of resistance offered to denudational processes.

Metamorphic rocks

Any of the types of igneous or sedimentary rocks may be altered by the tremendous pressures and high temperatures that accompany mountain-building movements of the earth's crust. The result is a rock so greatly changed in appearance and composition as to be classified as a *metamorphic rock*. Generally speaking, metamorphic rocks are harder and more compact than their original types, except when the latter are igneous rocks. Moreover, the kneading action and baking that metamorphic rocks have undergone produces new structures and even new minerals. Each sedimentary and igneous rock has an equivalent metamorphic rock. The term *metasediment* conveniently covers all metamorphic rocks derived from sedimentary strata.

Shale, on being squeezed and sheared under mountain-making forces, turns into *slate*, a gray or brick-red rock that splits neatly into thin plates so familiar to all as roofing shingles and flagstones of patios and walks. The planes of splitting form a structure called *slaty cleavage*. This is a new structure imposed upon the rock during the process of internal slippage during metamorphism, not merely stratification or bedding. Slate is fine textured and of rather dull surface texture. It can be distinguished from shale by the fact that a thin slab of slate rings when struck sharply.

With continued application of pressure and internal shearing, slate changes into *schist*, the most advanced grade of metamorphic rock. Schist has a structure termed *foliation*, consisting of thin but rough and irregularly curved planes of parting in the rock. Schist is set apart from slate and phyllite by the coarse texture of the mineral grains, the abundance of mica, and the presence of scattered large crystals of new minerals such as *garnet* and *staurolite*, which have grown during the proc-

ess of internal shearing of the rock (Figure 17.12).

Slates and schists are relatively resistant to the processes of denudation and tend to form hills and uplands. In comparison with granite, however, these rocks are less resistant, so that granites will usually form markedly higher mountain masses.

The metamorphic equivalent of conglomerate, sandstone, and siltstone is *quartzite*, formed by the addition of silica (SiO_2) to fill completely the interstices between grains, most of which are normally quartz (also silica). This process is carried out by the slow movement of underground waters carrying the silica into the sandstone, where it is deposited. Pressure and kneading of the rock is not essential in producing a quartzite, but may deform the quartz grains. When a quartzite is fractured, as with a hammer blow, the break will cut across sand grains and pebbles in the rock. In this way, quartzite can be distinguished from a sandstone, which usually breaks around the grains, leaving them mostly intact. The extreme hardness of quartzite, combined with its high immunity to chemical decay, makes it the most resistant of all rocks. Many prominent ridge crests and peaks in a region of metamorphic rock will be found to be composed of quartzite.

Limestone, upon metamorphism, becomes *marble*, commonly a white rock of sugary texture when freshly broken. During the process of internal shearing, the calcite mineral of the limestone has reformed into larger, more uniform crystals than before. Bedding planes are obscured and masses of mineral impurities are drawn out into swirling streaks and bands. Like limestone, marble is easily decomposed by weak acids in the soil water and streams, hence, is usually found occupying valleys and lowlands.

Finally, the important metamorphic rock,

Figure 17.12 This fragment of schist, 6 in (15 cm) long, has a glistening, undulating surface (above) consisting largely of mica flakes. An edgewise view (below) of the same specimen shows the wavy foliation planes.

Figure 17.13   Gneiss shows a banded surface.

Figure 17.15   Strike and dip.

gneiss, may be formed either from intrusive igneous rocks, or as a metasediment from strata that have been in close contact with intrusive magmas.

A single description will not fit all gneisses, which vary considerably in appearance, mineral composition, and structure. One common variety is *granite gneiss*, formed directly by flowage of granite in a somewhat plastic state. Granite gneiss resembles granite in its massiveness, general texture, and mineral components, but possesses a streaked appearance, called *lineation*, produced by parallelism of dark minerals which have been drawn out into long, pencil-like shapes in the direction of flow.

Still other gneisses are strongly banded into light and dark layers or lenses (Figure 17.13), which may be contorted into wavy folds. It is possible that in some instances these bands, which have differing mineral compositions, may be the relics of sedimentary strata such as shale and sandstone to which new mineral matter has been added from nearby intrusive rocks. Gneisses are strong, resistant rocks, which, like granite, generally form bold highlands or mountain chains. Figure 17.14 shows the topographic expressions we would expect in regions where various metamorphic rocks rest side by side and have been acted upon for vast spans of time by the agents of landmass denudation.

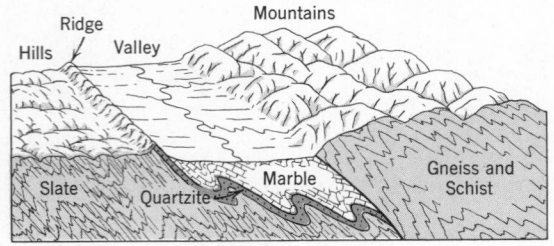

Figure 17.14   Metamorphic rocks tend to form elongate, parallel belts of valleys and mountains.

Dip and strike

Because natural planes are characteristic of the structure of each type of rock, the geologist requires a system of geometry to enable him to measure and describe the attitude of these natural planes and to indicate them on maps. Examples of such planes are the bedding layers of sedimentary strata, the sides of a dike, the upper and lower surfaces of a sill, slaty cleavage of slates, and the joints in a granite. Rarely are these planes truly horizontal.

The acute angle formed between a natural rock plane and an imaginary horizontal plane is termed the *dip*, and is stated in degrees ranging from 0° for a horizontal plane to 90° for a vertical plane. Figure 17.15 shows the dip angle for an outcropping layer of sandstone, against which rests a horizontal water surface.

The compass direction, or bearing, of the line of intersection between the inclined rock plane and an imaginary horizontal plane is the *strike*. In Figure 17.15 the strike is north.

REFERENCES FOR FURTHER STUDY

Dunbar, C. O. and J. Rodgers (1957), *Principles of stratigraphy*, John Wiley and Sons, New York, 356 pp.

Pettijohn, F. J. (1957), *Sedimentary rocks*, second edition, Harper and Row, New York, 718 pp.

Spock, L. E. (1962), *Guide to the study of rocks*, Harper and Row, New York, 298 pp.

Leet, L. D. and S. Judson (1965), *Physical geology*, third edition, Prentice-Hall, Inc., Englewood Cliffs, N.J., 406 pp. See Chapters 4, 5, 6, 8, and 18.

Gilluly, J., A. C. Waters, and A. O. Woodford (1968), *Principles of geology*, third edition, W. H. Freeman and Co., San Francisco, 687 pp. See Chapters 2, 3, 17, and 18.

Longwell, C. R., R. F. Flint, and J. E. Sanders (1969), *Physical geology*, John Wiley and Sons, New York, 685 pp. See Chapters 3, 4, 16, and 20.

1. What are landforms? What is geomorphology? Of what importance are landforms to the geographer? Cite several examples.

2. What is a genetic system of description? How does it differ from an empirical description?

3. What advantage is there to describing and classifying landforms according to structure, process, and stage? Explain these terms.

4. What is the basis for dividing all landforms into initial and sequential groups?

5. What are the agents of land sculpture? Toward what goal do they work?

6. Explain what is meant by the terms *erosional landforms* and *depositional landforms*.

7. Explain how a landscape reflects the work of both internal and external earth forces and processes.

8. Define bedrock, overburden, and soil. What is an outcrop?

9. What is the distinction between transported and residual overburden? What is the relation between transported overburden and the depositional landforms?

10. In what way is an understanding of rocks and their structures necessary in explaining landforms?

11. What are igneous rocks? What is a magma? What is the difference between intrusive and extrusive igneous rocks? How does each type occur? What difference is there in the texture of extrusive and intrusive rocks? Why?

12. What is a mineral? How does a mineral differ from a rock? What name is given to the science of minerals? Of rocks?

13. What is granite? Of what minerals is it composed? Give the names and mineral components of at least two other intrusive igneous rocks.

14. What minerals tend to make an igneous rock light in color and low in specific gravity? What minerals tend to make an igneous rock dark and high in specific gravity? How do the words *sial* and *sima* serve to distinguish two major divisions of igneous rocks?

15. What forms do extrusive igneous rocks take? What is lava? How does the texture of lava differ from that of the intrusive igneous rocks? Why? Through what kind of passages do extrusive rocks reach the earth's surface? What is columnar jointing?

16. How are volcanic ejecta classified according to the sizes of the fragments? How are pyroclastic sedimentary rocks related to volcanic ejecta?

17. What is a sedimentary rock? How are the sedimentary materials hardened into rock? What are the sources of sediment? Define strata; stratification planes.

18. On what basis are formations set apart as units in sedimentary rock?

19. Name in order of size the particles that make up clastic sediments and the rock name for each grade. In what way is conglomerate different from breccia? What is the principal mineral of sandstone? What characterizes the shape and properties of particles which make up shale? Name a pyroclastic rock and explain how it is formed.

20. How does limestone differ from the clastic sedimentary rocks? In what ways may limestone be formed? What is chalk? What is marl? What mineral composes pure limestone? How does dolomite differ from limestone in chemical composition?

21. How are peat and coal produced? What class of sedimentary rocks do they illustrate? Explain how an evaporite forms. Name two common evaporites and give their compositions.

22. How do the various kinds of sedimentary rocks influence the development of landforms? Which form valleys? Which form mountains and ridges? How do the sedimentary rocks compare with the igneous rocks in this respect?

23. What are metamorphic rocks? How are they formed? From what other rocks may they be derived? Describe slate, schist, quartzite, marble, and gneiss. Which of these rock types generally form valleys? Which form ridges or mountains?

24. Explain how dip and strike tell the orientation in space of an inclined rock plane.

The Earth's Crust and Its Relief Forms

THE geographer concerned largely with man's occupation of the earth's surface may justifiably feel little need to study those branches of geology dealing with the earth's interior, the subsurface structures of the continents, the relief features of the ocean floor, and the events of ancient geologic history. It is true that the remoteness of these things—whether in place or in time—relegate them to indirect or remote roles in man's economic, social, and cultural processes, inasmuch as few immediate or direct environmental effects can be established. Nevertheless, it is worthwhile for the student of physical geography to place the surficial elements of the lands, atmosphere, and oceans in the broader setting of global geology.

Internal structure of the earth

Man's direct observation of the composition and physical properties of the earth's interior is limited by mining and drilling operations to depths of a few miles at best, so that he must turn to indirect means of obtaining information. The science of *geophysics* is concerned largely with obtaining information about the physical properties of the earth by means of instruments that measure earthquake waves, earth magnetism, and

the force of gravity. Interpretation of these data through established laws of physics has yielded surprisingly detailed knowledge of the earth's structure and properties.

Figure 18.1 is a cutaway diagram of the earth to show its major parts. The earth is an almost spherical body approximately 3960 mi (6370 km) in equatorial radius. The center is occupied by the *core*, a spherical zone about 2160 mi (3475 km) in radius. Because of the sudden change in behavior of earthquake waves upon reaching this zone, it has been concluded that the outer core has the properties of a liquid, in abrupt contrast to a solid mass which surrounds it. However, the innermost part of the core with a radius of 780 mi (1255 km) may be solid, or crystalline.

Through astronomical calculations it can be shown that the earth has a specific gravity of about $5\frac{1}{2}$, whereas the surface rocks average 3 or less (Chapter 17). This observation must mean that specific gravity increases greatly toward the interior, where it may be about from 10 to 15. Iron, with a small proportion of nickel, is considered as the probable substance comprising the liquid core. This conclusion is supported by the fact that many meteorites, representing disrupted fragments of our solar system, are of iron-nickel composition. Temperatures in the earth's core may lie between 4000° and 5000°F (2200° and 2750°C); pressures are as high as three to four million times the pressure of the atmosphere at sea level.

Outside of the core lies the *mantle*, a layer about 1800 mi (2895 km) thick, composed of mineral matter in a solid state. Judging from the behavior of earthquake waves, the mantle is probably composed largely of the mineral olivine (magnesium iron silicate), which comprises a basic rock variety called *dunite*. This rock, which may be in a glassy state, exhibits qualities of great rigidity and high density in response to sudden stresses of earthquake waves which pass through it. On the other hand, the mantle rock can also adjust by slow flowage to unequal forces which act over great periods of time. In this respect it is somewhat like cold tar, which is hard and shatters easily if struck, but which will slowly flow downhill if left undisturbed for a long time.

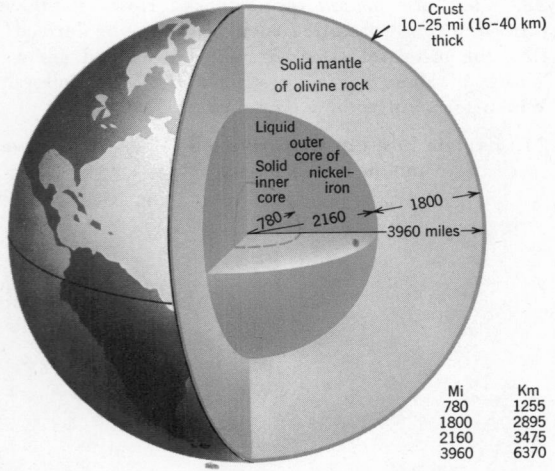

Figure 18.1   **Concentric zones make up the earth's interior.**

The crust

Outermost and thinnest of the earth zones is the *crust*, a layer some 5 to 25 mi (8 to 40 km) thick. Formed of crystalline rocks, largely igneous in classification, the crust exhibits properties of brittleness when subjected to mountain-building forces and therefore may break along great faults. The base of the crust, where it contacts the mantle, is sharply defined, a fact known because earthquake waves change velocity abruptly at that level (Figure 18.2*A*). The surface of separation between crust and mantle is called the *Moho*, a simplification of Mohoroviçić, the name of the seismologist who discovered it.

From a study of earthquake waves it is concluded that the crust consists of two layers: (1) a lower, continuous layer of basaltic rock otherwise termed *sima* (see Chapter 17); (2) an upper layer of granitic rock, otherwise termed *sial*, which constitutes the continents. The granitic layer is therefore discontinuous in areal extent, being absent over the ocean basins. Figure 18.2*B* shows schematically a small part of the crust near the margin of a continent. The sedimentary strata of the continents are on the average merely a thin skin, not shown on this diagram, although locally they are several thousand feet thick.

Those parts of the crust forming the continents are much thicker than the crust under the ocean basins, and may be likened to vast icebergs floating in the sea with only a small part visible above the water, but with a great bulk deeply submerged. The glassy rock of the earth's mantle has yielded by slow flowage, much like a very viscous fluid; this has permitted the lighter, rigid, continental plates of the crust to come to rest in the manner of the floating iceberg.

Distribution of continents and ocean basins

The first-order relief features of the earth are the continents and oceans basins. From a globe or atlas we can compute that about 29% of the globe is land; 71% oceans. If, however, the seas were to drain away, it would become apparent that broad areas lying close to the continental shores are actually covered by shallow water, less than 600 ft (180 m) deep. From these relatively shallow *continental shelves* the ocean floor drops rapidly to depths of thousands of feet. In a sense, then, the ocean basins are brimful of water and have even spread over the margins of ground that would more reasonably be assigned to the continents. If the ocean level were to drop by 600 ft (180 m) the surface area of continents would increase to 35%; the ocean basins decrease to 65%; figures which we may regard as representative of the true relative proportions.

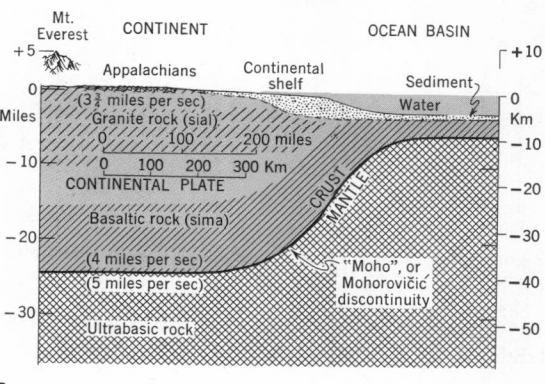

Figure 18.2 The earth's crust is much thicker under continents than beneath the ocean basins.

Figure 18.3 shows graphically the percentage distribution of the earth's surface area with respect to elevation both above and below sea level. Note that most of the land surface of the continents is less than 3300 ft (1 km) above sea level. There is a rapid drop off from about −3000 to −10,000 ft (−1 to −3 km) until the ocean floor is reached. A predominant part of the ocean floor lies between 10,000 and 20,000 ft (3 and 6 km) below sea level. Disregarding the earth's curvature, the continents can be visualized as platformlike masses; the oceans as broad, flat-floored basins.

Scale of the earth's landforms

Before turning to a description of the major subdivisions of the continents and ocean basins, it is revealing to consider the true scale of the earth's landforms in comparison with the earth as a sphere. Most of the relief globes and pictorial relief maps seen commonly in magazines and atlases are greatly exaggerated in vertical scale. For a true-scale profile around the earth we might draw a chalk-line circle 21 ft (6.4 m) in diameter, representing the earth's circumference on a scale of 1 : 2,000,000. A chalk line 3/8 in (0.15 cm) wide would include within its limits not only the highest point on the earth, Mt. Everest, +29,000 feet (+8840 m) but also the deepest known ocean trenches, below −35,000 feet (−10,700 m).

Figure 18.4 shows profiles correctly curved and scaled to fit a globe whose diameter is 21 ft (6.4 m). The topographic profile is drawn to natural scale, without vertical exaggeration. Although the most imposing landforms of Asia and North

Figure 18.3 Distribution of the earth's solid surface in successively lower altitude zones.

America are shown, they seem little more than trivial irregularities on the great global circle.

Second-order relief features of the ocean basins

The North Atlantic Ocean illustrates certain typical features of the ocean basins and the continental margins. Three major units of the North Atlantic are (1) the *continental margin*, (2) the *ocean basin floor*, and (3) the *mid-oceanic ridge* (Figure 18.5). These units may be regarded as second-order relief features of the earth's surface.

Along the eastern margin of North America lies the *continental shelf*, a fairly smooth, sloping plain 75 to 100 mi (120 to 160 km) wide and reaching a depth of 600 ft (180 m) at the outer edge. This shelf, a part of the continental margin, is essentially a zone of deposition of sedimentary rock layers built of material brought from the eastern United

States by streams and spread over the sea floor by currents. At its outer edge, the shelf abruptly gives way to a descending *continental slope* leading down to the true ocean basin floor at a depth of about 12,000 ft (3700 m).

The slope is scored by strange *submarine canyons* (Figure 18.6), whose origin has been strongly debated. The canyons seem to be the work of eroding streams, very likely flows of muddy water, called *turbidity currents*, which are produced when storms or earthquake shocks disturb soft sediment at the canyon heads. These flows travel swiftly down the continental slope because their density is greater than that of the surrounding sea water. Spreading out upon the deep sea floor, turbidity currents come slowly to rest. The sediment is spread in broad layers which have accumulated over millions of years, gradually burying the irregular topographic features of the sea floor and

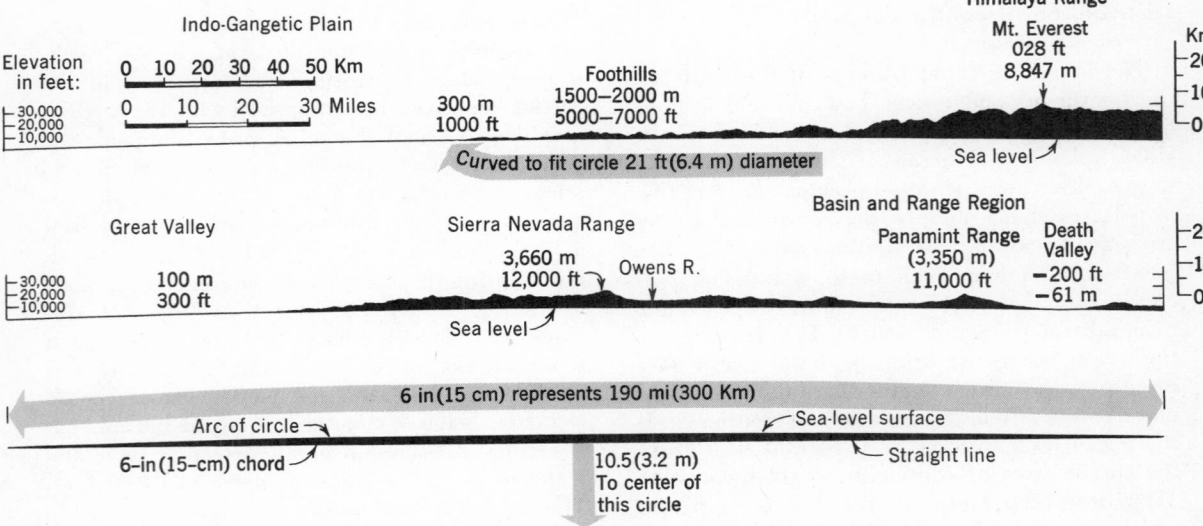

Figure 18.4 These profiles show the earth's great relief features in true scale with sea-level curvature fitted to a globe 21 ft (6.4 m) in diameter.

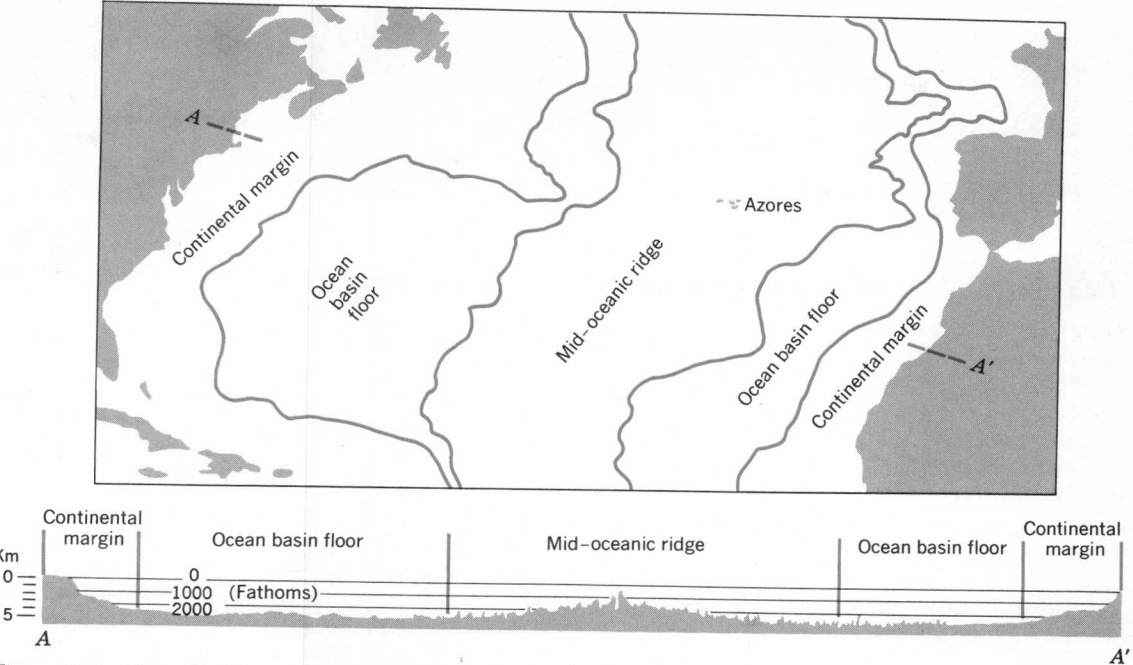

Figure 18.5 Major divisions of the North Atlantic Ocean basin (above), and a representative profile from New England to the coast of Africa (below). Profile exaggeration is about 40 times. (Data of B. C. Heezen, M. Tharp, and M. Ewing, 1959, from A. N. Strahler, *The Earth Sciences,* Harper and Row, New York.)

producing vast, flat *abyssal plains* lying within the ocean basin floor (Figure 18.7). The broad basin of the North Atlantic thus has a remarkably smooth floor over large areas at a depth of about 18,000 ft (5500 m). Rising abruptly from the floor are isolated submarine mountains, named *seamounts*, some of which may be ancient volcanoes.

In the center of the Atlantic lies a great submarine mountain range, the *Mid-Atlantic Ridge,* comparable with the Rocky Mountain chain in size and relief but entirely submerged except for the

Azores Islands. This ridge is merely a part of a single, continuous mid-ocean ridge traced through the South Atlantic, Indian, South and East Pacific, and Arctic oceans. It is the expression of a major fracture system of the earth's crust (Figure 18.8). The oceanic crust is in process of being pulled apart along the mid-ocean ridge, causing a *rift valley* to lie along the center line of the ridge (see profile of Figure 18.5). At the same time mantle rock is being pushed up to elevate the ridge.

Evidence in support of crustal spreading in the

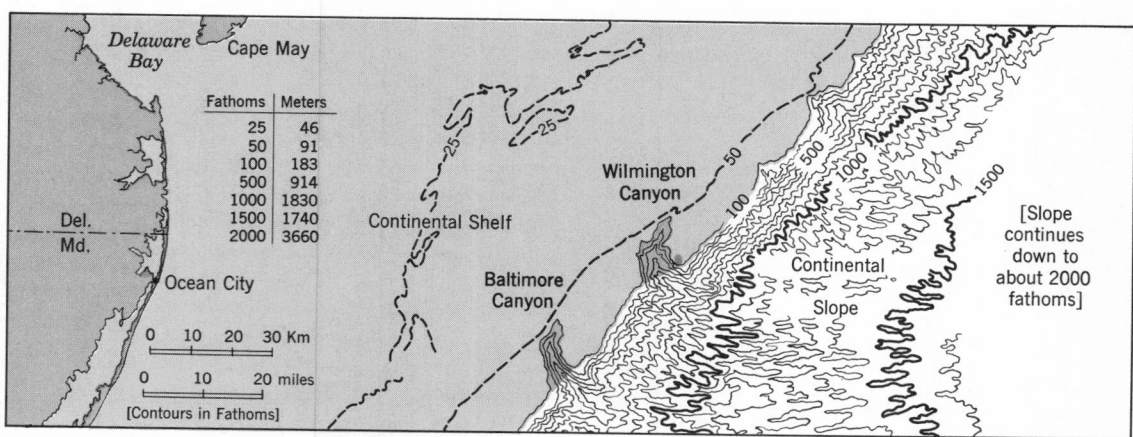

Figure 18.6 Two submarine canyons notch the outer edge of the Atlantic continental shelf off the Delaware-Maryland coast. (After Veatch and Smith.)

Figure 18.7 Profiles across the Atlantic Ocean basin reveal continental shelf and slope, abyssal plain, trench, and various minor irregularities. (After Bruce C. Heezen, Lamont Geological Observatory of Columbia University.)

mid-ocean ridge zone has come from studies of magnetic properties of the basalt rock in belts adjacent to the ridge. Rate of separation of the crustal masses on either side of the mid-ocean ridge has been estimated to be about 0.8 in (2 cm) per year in the North Atlantic region. Separation affects the continents lying east and west of the Atlantic ocean basin and constitutes a geologic process known as *continental drift*. Present-day scientific opinion strongly supports the hypothesis that North and South America were formerly joined to the African and Eurasian landmasses. If so, the basaltic rocks underlying the floor of the Atlantic Ocean basin are much younger than the

bulk of rocks comprising the crust of the drifted continents.

Other features of the ocean floor are *trenches* or *foredeeps*—long, narrow depressions whose bottoms reach depths of 24,000 to 30,000 ft (7500 to 10,000 m) or more (Figure 18.7 and 18.9). The trenches are thought by geologists to represent downfolded zones associated with recent mountain-building movements. Accumulation of sediment on the trench floors has been so slow that these depressions are not filled in, as they would be if above sea level.

Geologists and geophysicists have long been convinced that the continental crustal masses have

Figure 18.8 World map of the mid-ocean ridge system and its transverse fracture zones. (Based on data of B. C. Heezen, 1962, from A. N. Strahler, *The Earth Sciences*, Harper and Row, New York.)

endured throughout all recorded geologic time and have not exchanged places with the ocean basins by crustal warping. Evidence for this belief lies in the fact that most sedimentary rocks of past geologic ages seen on the continents are of types deposited in fairly shallow depths, whereas the very fine-grained deep-sea clays, or *oozes*, which settle out upon seamounts and isolated submarine

Figure 18.10 This map of the western Pacific shows trenches (solid black), island arcs (dashed lines), active volcanoes (black dots), and deep-focus earthquake centers (circles). (After H. H. Hess.)

Figure 18.9 The great Mindanao Trench, lying east of the Philippines, reaches a maximum depth of 34,218 ft (10, 430 m) which is considerably deeper than Mt. Everest is high. (After H. H. Hess, Hydrographic Office Chart 5485.)

ridges, are absent from geological strata of the continents. Sample submarine cores, penetrating more than 50 ft (15 m) into such oozes, show thin clay layers dating back as far as 100 million years and indicating that the rain of sediment from the overlying ocean water has been extremely slow as compared to deposition on continental shelves and in shallow inland seas. The lower, deeper parts of the ocean basins have, however, received the deposition of thousands of feet of layered clay and sand carried by turbidity currents from continental margins.

Present-day mountain building near the margins of the ocean basins is distributed along long, narrow, curving zones, known as *island arcs* (Figure 18.10). Each arc represents a zone of sharp crustal folding or compression and is associated with active volcanoes and earthquakes. The great ocean deeps generally lie along the outer side of the island arcs.

Second-order relief features of the continents

Just as with the ocean basins, the continents can be subdivided into second-order relief units. Essentially, the continents consist of two fundamental kinds of geologic units: (1) *shields* and (2) *moun-*

tain belts, or *orogenic belts*. The shields are the heartlands of the continental plates and consist of extremely ancient rocks. The age of the shield rocks is *Precambrian*, that is, older than 600 million years. Most of the shield rock is much older than one billion years and some has been dated as $3\frac{1}{2}$ billion years old. Several periods of mountain-making, or *orogeny*, affected the shields throughout the Precambrian era of geologic time and there was much metamorphism of ancient sedimentary rocks as well as many large intrusions of granitic rock in the form of batholiths (Chapter 17). Whereas great mountain ranges existed at various times during the Precambrian era, processes of erosion effectively reduced those mountains to their roots and leveled the ancient continents to nearly featureless plains. The shields today are therefore largely plains and low plateaus and are highly stable parts of the earth's continental crust.

Crustal movements of the shields in later geologic time have been of a type known as *epeirogenic* movements; that is, rising or sinking of the crust over broad areas without appreciably breaking or bending the rocks. Epeirogenic movements reflect crustal stability generally, in contrast to compressional and tensional orogenic movements affecting unstable zones.

When epeirogenic movements were of a negative, or sinking, type, large parts of the shields became submerged as shallow seas and continental shelves. This inundation gave opportunity for sedimentary strata to be deposited on the old metamorphic and igneous rocks. Later, positive, or rising, epeirogenic movements brought the sedimentary cover above sea level where it has since been carved up by streams into hills and plateaus.

Shields of the northern hemisphere are shown in Figure 18.11. North America's geological heartland is the *Canadian Shield*; that of Europe is the *Russian-Baltic Shield*, also called the *Fenno-Scandian Shield*. Rocks in both of these regions date back to the oldest era of geologic time, from one to three billion years ago. In the southern hemisphere, similar shield areas occupy parts of Australia, South Africa, and the Antarctic.

The mountain belts of the continents are long, narrow orogenic zones in which the crust has been compressed and forced to buckle into tight folds and at the same time to be strongly elevated. Two basic ages of mountain belts are distinguished. The first includes mountains produced in the Paleozoic and early Mesozoic (200 million to 600 million years ago). Now inactive, these ancient mountain ranges in some places still possess rugged relief and moderately high elevations; elsewhere, they are reduced to hill belts. The second age group of mountain belts belongs to the late Mesozoic and Cenozoic eras of geologic time (younger than about 150 million years) and are characterized by bold relief and great altitude. Those ranges produced in the last, or Cenozoic, era are in many places still active zones of crustal deformation and volcanic activity; they rise as spectacular alpine mountains.

The geologic time scale

To discuss the development of relief features of the continents requires reference to events of the geologic past. Even the explanation of landforms produced in the more recent of the geological periods requires some knowledge of the length and sequence of geologic time units. The economic geographer interested in the occurrence and distribution of ores and mineral fuels will find that a knowledge of historical geology will be extremely helpful in gaining understanding of the occurrence of economic mineral deposits in various parts of the world. Table 18.1, therefore, outlines the important events and subdivisions of geologic history. Note that the upper part of the table, representing the younger or more recent events, subdivides geologic time into small intervals, whereas with increasing age the units are larger and more generalized. This is because the geologic record is most fragmentary for the oldest ages but becomes generally more detailed as recent time is approached.

Absolute ages given in the table have been verified by means of chemical analyses of radioactive mineral substances and are generally accepted by geologists, subject to a small percentage of error. In every period of geologic time, there were widespread accumulations of sedimentary strata; in fact, the strata comprise the record itself and constitute sole evidence of the climatic and geomorphic conditions of the time, as well as containing the fossil remains of plant and animal life.

Generally speaking, each major time unit was brought to a close by orogeny, also called *revolution*, disrupting the sequence of sediment deposition. As already noted, the largest time unit is the *era* of which the last three are *Cenozoic, Mesozoic,* and *Paleozoic*, in order of increasing age. All time before this is designated as belonging to the *Precambrian* time. Eras have been recognized within the Precambrian, but the record tends to be fragmentary and confused. The second order of time unit is the *period*, of which the Paleozoic era has seven; the Mesozoic era, three; and the Cenozoic, two. *Epochs* are still shorter units of time, listed on the table only for the Cenozoic era.

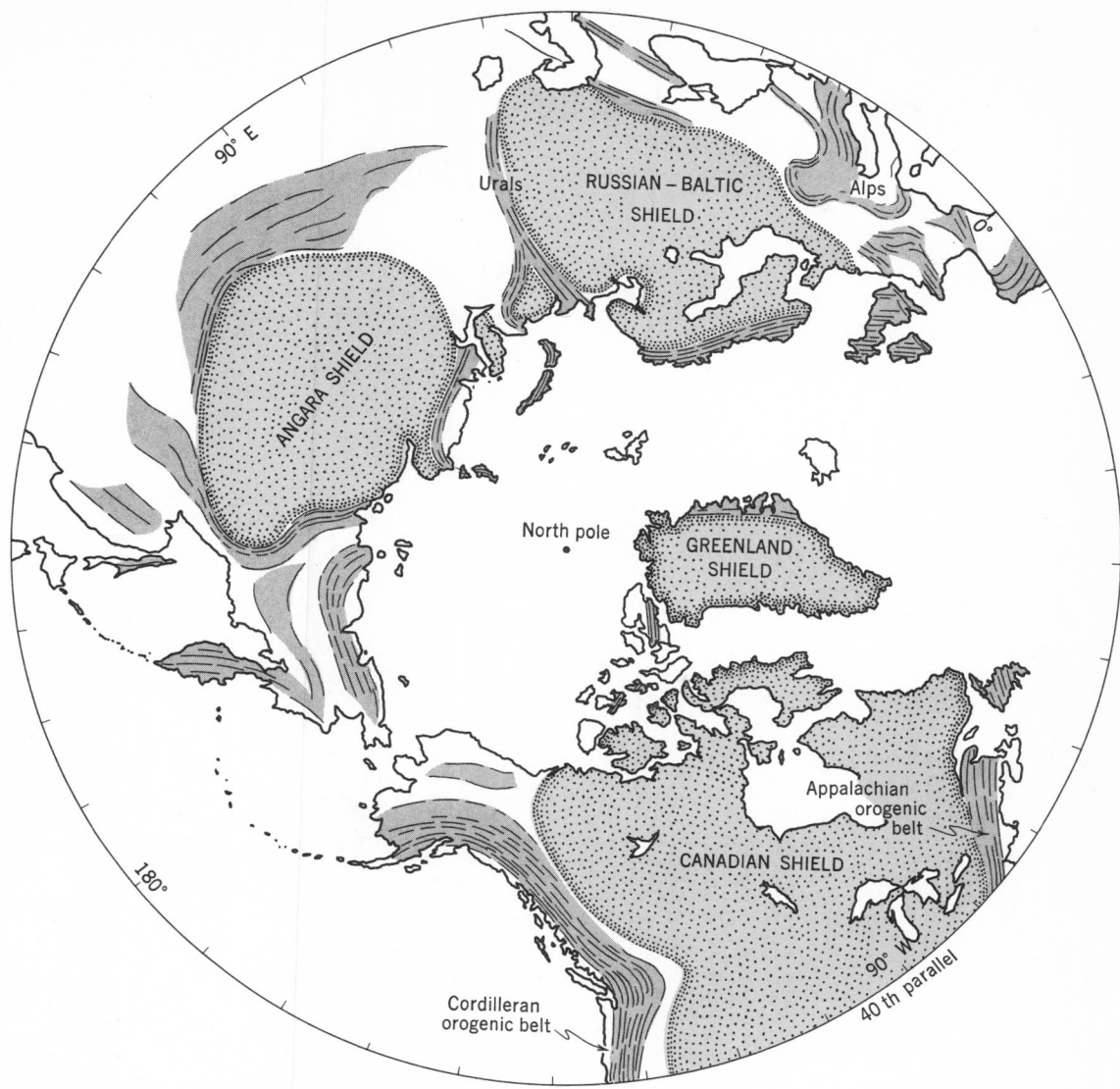

Figure 18.11 Shields are bounded by mountain belts (dashed lines) of Paleozoic and younger age. Shield areas include sedimentary covers. (After A. J. Eardley, *Structural Geology of North America.*)

Scheme of major geologic events

It is beyond the scope of this volume to treat physical and historical geology. But some brief insight into a general scheme of geologic events which has been repeated many times in the past may be had from the diagrams of Figure 18.12. These represent certain inferred events in the development of the Hudson Valley region throughout the Paleozoic, Mesozoic, and Cenozoic eras encompassing approximately the last 600 million years.

In block *A* the region is shown as a Paleozoic seaway in which thousands of feet of sedimentary strata had accumulated. An inland seaway deposit of this nature is called a *geosyncline*. The source of sediment was in large part from a chain of volcanic islands lying to the east. The Paleozoic era was brought to a close by a great orogeny, the *Appalachian Revolution*. Sedimentary strata of the geosyncline were severely crumpled, as well as broken into slices which slid over one another (block *B*). As a result, a great mountain range stood where formerly there had been a seaway. The bending of the strata is generally referred to as *folding*, and the corrugated structures thus produced are simply termed *folds*. The slanting surfaces upon which sliding occurred are termed

TABLE 18.1   TABLE OF GEOLOGICAL HISTORY

ERA	PERIOD	EPOCH	Absolute age in years before present	Major geologic events in United States given in order of increasing age	Distinctive features of plant and animal life	
CENOZOIC	QUATERNARY	Recent (HOLOCENE)		Minor changes in land forms by work of streams, waves, wind	Rise of civilizations	Age of Man
			10,000			
		PLEISTOCENE		Four stages of spread of continental ice sheets and mountain glaciers	Development of man; extinction of large mammals	
			1,000,000	Cascadian orogeny: Cascade and Sierra Nevada ranges uplifted; volcanoes built	Early evolution of man; dominance of elephants, horses, and large carnivores	Age of Mammals
	TERTIARY	PLIOCENE				
			13,000,000	Marine sediments deposited on Atlantic and Gulf coastal plain; stream deposits spread over Great Plains and Rocky Mountain basins; thick marine sediments deposited in Pacific coastal region	Development of whales, bats, monkeys	
		MIOCENE				
			25,000,000		Rise of anthropoids	
		OLIGOCENE	36,000,000			
		EOCENE			Development of primitive mammals; rise of grasses, cereals, fruits	
			58,000,000			
		PALEOCENE			Earliest horses	
			63,000,000	Laramide orogeny: Rocky Mountains formed		
MESOZOIC	CRETACEOUS			Marine sediment deposition over Atlantic and Gulf coastal plain and in geosyncline of Rocky Mountain region	Extinction of dinosaurs; development of flowering plants	Age of Reptiles
			135,000,000	Nevadian orogeny: Intrusion of batholith of Sierra Nevada region		
	JURASSIC			Marine sediment deposition in seas of western United States; desert sands deposited in Colorado Plateau	Culmination of dinosaurs; first birds appear	
			180,000,000	Palisadian disturbance: Block faulting in eastern United States		
	TRIASSIC			Deposition of red beds in fault basins of eastern United States and in shallow basins of western United States	First dinosaurs; first primitive mammals; spread of cycads and conifers	
			230,000,000	Appalachian orogeny: Folding of Paleozoic strata of Appalachian geosyncline		
PALEOZOIC	PERMIAN			Deposition of red shales and limestones in southwestern United States; much salt and gypsum (glaciation of southern hemisphere continents)	Conifers abundant; reptiles developed; spread of insects and amphibians; trilobites become extinct.	Age of Amphibians
			280,000,000			
	CARBONIFEROUS PENNSYLVANIAN			Deposition of coal-bearing strata in eastern and central United States	Widespread forests of coal-forming spore-bearing plants; first reptiles; abundant insects	
			310,000,000			
	CARBONIFEROUS MISSISSIPPIAN			Deposition of limy, shaly sediments in widespread, shallow seas of central and eastern United States	Spread of sharks; culmination of crinoids	
			345,000,000	Acadian orogeny: Folding and igneous rock intrusion in New England		
	DEVONIAN			Deposition of thick marine strata in geosynclines of eastern and western United States	First amphibians; many corals; earliest forests spread over lands	Age of Fishes
			405,000,000			
	SILURIAN				First land plants and air-breathing animals; development of fishes	
			425,000,000	Taconian orogeny: Folding of rocks in eastern United States, Nevada, and Utah		
	ORDOVICIAN			Deposition of thick marine strata in geosynclines of eastern and western United States	Life only in seas; spread of molluscs; culmination of trilobites	Age of Marine Invertebrates
			500,000,000			
	CAMBRIAN				Trilobites predominant; many marine invertebrates	
			600,000,000			
	Precambrian time; age goes back to over four billion years			Many periods of sediment deposition alternating with orogeny	Earliest known forms of life; few fossils known	

overthrust faults, the process being known as *overthrusting*. Mountain topography thus produced by folding and thrusting is composed of initial landforms, as explained in Chapter 17. The agents of denudation are nevertheless shown to be dissecting the initial mountain forms even before the folding and thrusting have ceased.

After the Appalachian Revolution, the region shown here remained essentially stable and quiescent for many millions of years. The mountains were reduced by the denudational processes to a land surface of very faint relief termed a *peneplain*. The peneplain is shown in block *C*. Notice that the oldest rock, a gneiss of Precambrian age, is exposed in the core of the mountain belt, whereas the youngest sedimentary layers, of Paleozoic age, remain in the zone of least disturbance, at the left end of the diagram.

In Figure 18.12*D*, The region is shown to have been again subjected to crustal movement, but of a quite different nature from previous movements. This was the *Palisadian disturbance*, which began in the Triassic period. The region has been broken into a series of blocks, each tilted with respect to its neighbor. The fractures are a type of fault, but are different from overthrust faults by having nearly vertical inclination of the breaks and by the absence of any pronounced crustal compression and shortening. The entire breakage scheme may be termed *block faulting*. The peneplain made before faulting forms the smooth, sloping surfaces of the fault blocks.

In block *E*, the region has again been reduced to a peneplain, indicating another prolonged period of relative stability of the earth's crust lasting into the Tertiary period. The more resistant gneiss, granite, conglomerate, and sandstone rise as low hills between broad, flat lowlands underlain by shale.

The region next experienced still another crustal movement, of epeirogenic nature. This was a very simple rising, or upwarping. No faulting or folding occurred. Consequently, the peneplain of Figure 18.12*E* was merely uplifted about 2000 ft (600 m). Streams and other agents of land denudation again set to work and excavated the weaker rocks to form valleys. The resistant sandstones, conglomerates, granites, and gneisses were left as ridges and mountain masses, as shown in diagram *F*, representing the present. The topography of today is solely the result of different rates of downwasting of the ground surface upon complex rock structures formed through a long series of geologic events.

Chapters 26 to 28 treat the individual peculiarities of landforms developed on flat-lying strata, folded strata, domed strata, block faults, and the extrusive and intrusive igneous rocks.

A world-wide system of landform classification

World-wide classification systems for climates, great soil groups, and natural vegetation types are developed in earlier chapters. Plates 2 to 4 present the results of those classifications. It is essential for the geographer to add a fourth classification system—that of landforms—to complete his analysis of global distribution of the four basic elements of physical geography: climates, soils, vegetation, and landforms.

A classification system which is based in part upon the genesis (origin) of landforms and in part upon the actual configuration of the land surface is both appropriate and meaningful in terms of the explanatory-descriptive system of landform analysis described in Chapter 17. Such a classification system has been devised and applied by Dr. Richard E. Murphy[1] and has led to the world map of landforms reproduced as Plate 5 (folding plate inside back cover). Description of the system as given below conforms with definitions set forth by Dr. Murphy in 1967.[2]

The Murphy system of landform classification uses three levels, or categories, of information in successive application to identify a landform type in terms of its geologic origin and rock composition (structural regions), the configuration of its surface (topography), and finally the nature of the geomorphic process by which it has been shaped (erosional or depositional landscapes). The threefold basis of the genetic approach to landform study—structure, process, and stage—is included in the first and third categories of the classification system. A particularly valuable attribute of the genetic approach is that a highly trained and experienced geomorphologist can use his background of knowledge to predict or anticipate many characteristic details of the landforms that are not implicitly stated in the definitions of the various classes.

The empirical ingredient of the Murphy system is found in the second level of classification, namely topography. Here subdivision of geometrical properties of the land surface follows strict numerical definitions. Elevation above sea level and local relief (difference in elevation between highest and lowest points in adjacent locations) form the basis for defining classes. The empirical

[1] Richard E. Murphy, 1968, *Landforms of the world*, Annals Map Supplement Number Nine, Annals, Association of American Geographers, **58**(1).

[2] Richard E. Murphy, 1967, *A spatial classification of landforms based on both genetic and empirical factors—a revision*, Annals, Association of American Geographers, Vol. 57, No. 1, pp. 185–186. Material from the text of Dr. Murphy's paper is quoted here with the author's permission.

A

Devonian—
Silurian   Cambro-Ordovician

B

Granite   Precambrian
gneiss

C

D

E

Pocono-Catskill   Hudson
Plateau   Shawangunk Mtn.   River   Hudson
                     Great Valley   Schunemunk   Highlands
F   Mtn.

Figure 18.12 A sequence of events which has been generally repeated throughout geologic
time over the continents of the globe is well illustrated in the Hudson Valley region. In these
diagrams northwest is to the left, southeast to the right. *A*, A shallow inland seaway accumulated
thousands of feet of sediments during the Paleozoic era. *B*, Mountain-making at the end of the
Paleozoic era produced a series of folds and thrust faults. A general uplifting brought a large
mass above sea level. *C*, Following a long period of erosion, a peneplain was produced. *D*,
Faulting in the Triassic period produced these gently tilted blocks. *E*, A second long period
of erosion resulted in another peneplain. *F*, The region today owes its relief to different rates
of removal of the various kinds of rocks (From A. N. Strahler, *The Earth Sciences*, Harper
and Row, New York.)

approach to description of the topography lends an element of useful and unambiguous information to the classification system.

The entire system uses three sets of letter symbols, the first to represent structural regions, the second to represent topographical classes, and the third to indicate the kinds of erosional or depositional landscapes.

Structural regions

Seven structural regions are recognized and are designated by the capital letters *A, C, G, L, R, S,* and *V,* defined as follows.

A   *Alpine system.* World-girdling system of mountain chains formed since the Jurassic period. Faulted areas, plateaus, basins, and coastal plains enclosed by such ranges are included in the system.

C   *Caledonian (or Hercynian or Appalachian) remnants.* Remains of mountain chains and ranges formed during the Paleozoic and Mesozoic eras, prior to the Cretaceous period and experiencing no orogeny since then, although epeirogenic movements may (and often have) occurred. In some cases, only worn-down roots remain. Faulted areas, plateaus, basins, and coastal plains enclosed by these remnants are included with them.

G   *Gondwana shields.* Areas of stable, massive blocks of the earth's sialic crust, lying south of the great east-west portion of the Alpine system, where Precambrian rocks form either the entire surface rock or where Precambrian rocks form an encircling enclosure with no gap of more than 200 mi (320 km) between outcroppings or covering extrusives and within which crystalline rocks form more than 50 percent of the surface rock. These shields have not been subject to orogeny since the Cambrian period.

L   *Laurasian shields.* Areas of stable, massive blocks of the earth's sialic crust lying north of the great east-west portion of the Alpine system. (Remainder of definition same as in *G,* above.)

R   *Rifted shield areas.* Block-faulted areas of shields forming grabens together with associated horsts and volcanic features.

S   *Sedimentary covers.* Areas of sedimentary layers which have not been subjected to orogeny and which lie outside either the crystalline rock enclosures of the shields or the enclosing mountains and hills of the Alpine or older orogenic systems. These areas of sedimentary rock form continuous covers over underlying structures.

V   *Isolated volcanic areas.* Areas of volcanoes, active or extinct, with associated volcanic features, lying outside the Alpine or older mountain systems and outside the rifted shield areas.

Figure 18.13 shows the distribution of the seven structural regions, together with major oceanic rift and fault lines, undersea axial connections of the Alpine system, and continental shelf areas.

Topographical regions

Six classes of topography, represented by the capital letters *P, H, T, M, W,* and *D,* are defined as follows (metric equivalents are approximate).

P   *Plains.* Surfaces with local relief less than 325 ft (100 m). On the marine side the surface slopes gently to the sea. Plains rising continuously inland may attain elevations of high plains, over 2000 ft (600 m).

H   *Hills and low tablelands.* Hill areas have local relief more than 325 ft (100 m) but less than 2000 ft (600 m). At the oceanic shoreline, however, local relief may be as low as 200 ft (60 m). A low tableland is an area less than 5000 ft (1500 m) in elevation, with local relief less than 325 ft (100 m), but which (unlike plains) either does not reach the sea or, where it does, terminates in a bluff at least 200 ft (60 m) high. A tableland may also terminate in a similar bluff overlooking a low coastal plain.

T   *High tablelands.* Upland surfaces over 5000 ft (1500 m) in elevation having local relief less than 1000 ft (300 m), except where cut by widely separated canyons.

M   *Mountains.* Areas of steep slopes with local relief more than 2000 ft (600 m).

W   *Widely spaced mountains.* Mountains which are discontinuous and stand in isolation with intervening areas having local relief less than 500 ft (150 m).

D   *Depressions.* Basins surrounded by mountains, hills, or tablelands which abruptly delimit the basins.

Figure 18.14 shows the distribution of the six topographical regions.

Erosional and depositional landforms

The kind of geomorphic process acting currently, or relatively recently in geologic time, to shape the landscape into its present form provides the basis for five classes of areas, indicated by lower-case letters *h, d, g, w,* and *i,* and defined as follows.

h   *Humid landform areas.* Areas in which the pattern of permanent streams has a density of at least one stream in every 10 mi (16 km) traverse distance, and which have not been subject to glaciation since the beginning of the Pleistocene epoch.

d   *Dry landform areas.* Areas in which the pattern of stream density is more sparse than one stream in 10 mi (16 km), and which have not been subject to glaciation since the beginning of the Pleistocene epoch. Some karst as well as arid areas are included in this category.

g   *Glaciated areas.* Areas covered by glacial ice at some time since the beginning of the Pleistocene epoch, but earlier than the Wisconsin and Würm glaciations. The symbol *g* is also used for undifferentiated glaciated areas.

STRUCTURAL REGIONS

A	Alpine system
C	Caledonian and Hercynian remnants
G	Gondwana shields
L	Laurasian shields
R	Rifted shield areas
V	Isolated volcanic areas
S	Sedimentary covers outside shield exposures
– · –	Major oceanic rift and fault lines
· · · ·	Undersea axial connections of the Alpine system
	Continental shelf

Figure 18.13 World structural regions. (From R. E. Murphy, 1968, Annals, A.A.G., Map Supplement No. 9. Based on Goode Base Map. Copyright by the University of Chicago. Used by permission of the University of Chicago Press.)

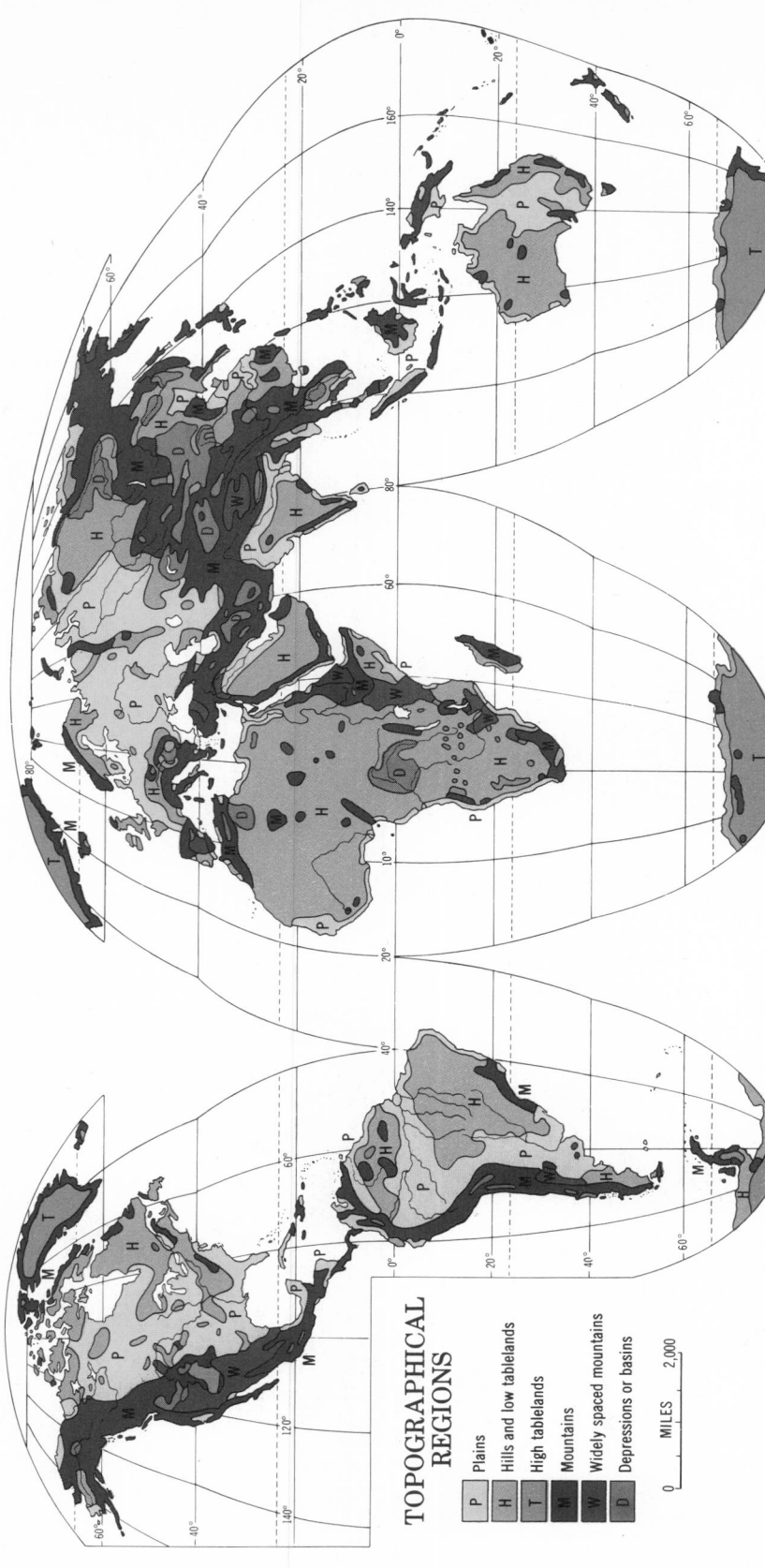

TOPOGRAPHICAL
REGIONS

P	Plains
H	Hills and low tablelands
T	High tablelands
M	Mountains
W	Widely spaced mountains
D	Depressions or basins

MILES
0   2,000

Figure 18.14 World topographical regions. (From R. E. Murphy, 1968, Annals, A.A.G., Map Supplement No. 9. Based on Goode Base Map. Copyright by the University of Chicago. Used by permission of the University of Chicago Press.)

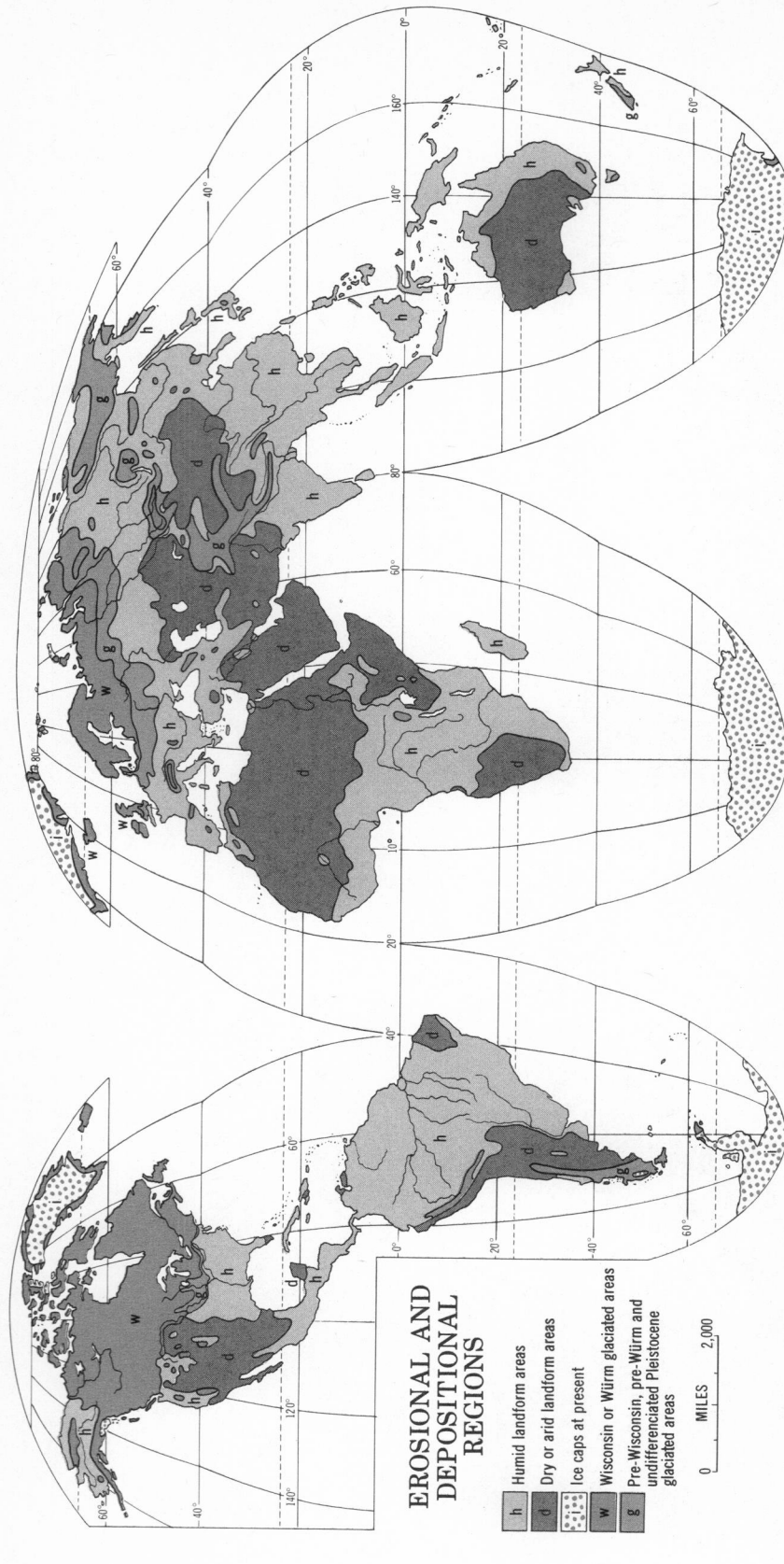

EROSIONAL AND DEPOSITIONAL REGIONS

h	Humid landform areas
d	Dry or arid landform areas
⋰	Ice caps at present
w	Wisconsin or Würm glaciated areas
g	Pre-Wisconsin, pre-Würm and undifferenciated Pleistocene glaciated areas

0   MILES   2,000

Figure 18.15 World distribution of erosional and depositional landforms. (From R. E. Murphy, 1968, Annals, A.A.G., Map Supplement No. 9. Based on Goode Base Map. Copyright by the University of Chicago. Used by permission of the University of Chicago Press.)

w Wisconsin and Würm glaciated areas. Areas covered by glacial ice during or since the Wisconsin and Würm glaciations but now free of glacial ice.

i Icecaps. Areas covered by glacial ice at present.

Figure 18.15 shows the distribution of the five classes of erosional and depositional landforms.

Combined landform classes

Under the Murphy system, the three categories of classification are superimposed to yield a complete world landform map (Plate 5). To designate a particular area within the complete system, the code letter of each category is stated in sequence. For example, the Colorado Plateau is symbolized as *ATd*, meaning that it is an elevated tableland over 5000 ft (1500 m) in elevation, enclosed within the Alpine system, and characterized by landforms developed under conditions more arid than humid. The Congo basin is symbolized as *GDh*, indicating a depression in the Gondwana shield subject to geomorphic processes of a humid climate. Central Poland is designated as *SPg*, a sedimentary plain which has been subjected to Pleistocene glaciation.

As with all attempted classifications of climates, soils, and natural vegetation types, any classification of landforms is difficult to implement in the form of a world map because of lack of sufficient information. Over vast areas of the continents information on bedrock geology and surface topography is only generalized and of questionable reliability because of the reconnaissance nature of field surveys. Consequently, as new information of increasing detail of scale and accuracy becomes available, the world map must be modified. In the light of new information, minor changes in the categories and their definitions may also be desirable. Nevertheless, the existing world landform map (Plate 5) represents a vast quantity of soundly established geologic and topographic information, organized into a logical and meaningful classification system.

REFERENCES FOR FURTHER STUDY

Guilcher, A. (1958), *Coastal and submarine morphology*, John Wiley and Sons, New York, 274 pp. See Part II.

Heezen, B. C., M. Tharp, and M. Ewing (1959), *The floors of the oceans*, Geological Society of America, Special Paper 65, 122 pp.

Dunbar, C. (1960), *Historical geology*, second edition, John Wiley and Sons, New York, 500 pp.

Shepard, F. P. (1963), *Submarine geology*, second edition, Harper and Row, New York, 557 pp.

Kay, M. and E. H. Colbert (1965), *Stratigraphy and life history*, John Wiley and Sons, New York, 736 pp.

Woodford, A. O. (1965), *Historical geology*, W. H. Freeman and Co., San Francisco, 512 pp.

1. Describe the earth's core and mantle, giving dimensions, mineral composition, and physical properties. What type of evidence is used to obtain this information? What temperatures and pressures may be expected at the earth's center?

2. What is the earth's crust? How thick is it? How can it be distinguished in properties from the underlying mantle? Of what two rock layers does the crust consist? What is the general distribution of sima and sial over the earth?

3. Describe the general form of the continents and ocean basins as regards the levels of concentration of surface areas. If sea level were lowered by 600 ft (180 m), what percentage of the earth would be land?

4. On a globe 21 ft (6.4 m) in diameter, how far would the greatest relief features of the earth depart from a perfect circle drawn to represent sea level?

5. What are the principal second-order relief features of the ocean basins?

6. What is a continental shelf? By what type of rock material is it underlain? What is a continental slope? What relation do submarine canyons bear to these features?

7. What are turbidity currents? What work do they perform? What deposits do they build?

8. What kinds of relief features are found on the floors of the ocean basins? Describe seamounts, trenches (foredeeps), and submarine mountain ledges.

9. Describe the mid-ocean ridge system. What feature marks the central line of the ridge? How do geologists account for the mid-ocean ridge system?

10. With what sort of crustal deformation are the island arcs and deep trenches of the ocean basins associated?

11. Why are the ocean basins thought to have remained as permanent features throughout known geologic history? What is the evidence?

12. What are the second-order relief features of the continents? What are shields? What are orogenic belts?

13. What are epeirogenic crustal movements? Contrast orogenic movements with epeirogenic movements.

14. Name the eras of geologic time and give the total duration of each in years. For each of the eras, name the periods of geologic time. Into what epochs is the Tertiary period subdivided? What great events occurred during the Pleistocene epoch?

15. What type of geologic event has brought to a close each era and many of the periods? What is the known duration of Precambrian time? How much longer is Precambrian time than all of post-Cambrian time?

16. Explain the general scheme of geologic events in which sedimentary rocks are deposited, then deformed, and finally reduced by erosion. What is a geosyncline? What is a revolution?

17. What is meant by folding and overthrusting of strata? Do these deformations require compression or tension of the earth's outer crust?

18. What is a peneplain? At what level do peneplains form? How long a period of time is required to reduce a mountain range to a peneplain?

19. What is faulting? How does block faulting differ from overthrust faulting? Why would you not expect both types to occur simultaneously in the same region?

20. When a peneplain is upwarped, what type of landform development follows? What happens to the peneplain?

21. Describe the system of landform classification devised by Dr. Richard E. Murphy. Compare this system with the Köppen system of climate classification. Compare it with systems of great soil groups and structural classes of vegetation used in this book.

22. What are the seven structural regions that comprise the first category of the Murphy system? Describe the broad patterns of worldwide distribution of the mountain and shield classes.

23. How is the empirical approach used by Murphy in defining six classes of topography? What advantages does an empirical approach offer?

24. How are geomorphic processes reflected in the third category of classification in the Murphy system? Of what value is this type of information to the geographer?

The Wasting of Slopes

THE term *slope*, as used throughout the science of geomorphology, designates some small element or area of the land surface which is inclined from the horizontal. Thus, we speak of "mountain slopes," "hill slopes," or "valley-side slopes" with reference to the inclined ground surfaces extending from divides and summits down to valley bottoms.[1]

Slopes are required for the flow of surface water under the influence of gravity. Therefore, slopes are fitted together to form drainage systems in which surface water flow converges into stream channels, these, in turn, conduct the water and rock waste to the oceans to complete the hydrologic cycle. Nature has so completely provided the earth's land surfaces with slopes that perfectly horizontal or vertical surfaces are extremely rare.

Our concern in this chapter is with the wasting of land slopes under the dominant influence of water acting in conjunction with gravity. Emphasis is on the slow processes whereby bedrock is transformed into residual overburden. This material in turn moves down the slopes to channels where it can be taken by stream flow to still more distant, lower areas. Slopes are also shaped by other processes—glaciers, winds, and waves—which are treated in later chapters.

Weathering and mass wasting

Weathering is the combined action of all processes whereby rock is decomposed and disintegrated because of exposure at or near the earth's surface. Weathering normally changes hard, massive rock into finely fragmented, soft residual overburden, the parent matter of the soil. For this reason, weathering is often described as the preparation of rock materials for transportation by the agents of land erosion—flowing water, glacial ice, waves, and wind. Because gravity exerts its force on all matter, both bedrock and the products of weathering tend to slide, roll, flow, or creep down all slopes in a variety of types of earth and rock movements grouped under the term *mass wasting*.

[1] *Slope* is also used to mean inclination from the horizontal, measured as in *dip* (Chapter 17); or it is used as a verb *to slope*, meaning *to incline*.

Weathering processes may be subdivided into two large groups, *physical (mechanical) weathering* and *chemical weathering*. Although these processes are extremely complex and act in combinations that are hard to separate into simple concepts, we shall attempt to identify the most important individual changes and to show what landforms or surface features of the rock and soil are caused by each.

Geometry of rock breakup

Before examining weathering processes, it is well to introduce four terms applied to the geometrical manner in which bedrock breaks into smaller pieces. In so doing we are not considering the possible forces involved, merely the shapes of the rock fragments as they appear to the eye.

Rocks composed of rather coarse mineral grains (intrusive igneous rocks of granitoid texture and coarse clastic sedimentary rocks) commonly fall apart grain by grain, a form of breakup termed *granular disintegration* (Figure 19.1). The product is a gravel or sand in which each grain consists of a single mineral particle separated from its fellows along the original crystal or grain boundaries. *Exfoliation* is the formation of curved rock shells which separate in succession from the original rock mass, leaving behind successively smaller spheroidal bodies (Figure 19.11). This type of breakup is also called *spalling*.

Where a rock has numerous joints produced previously by mountain-making pressures or by shrinkage during cooling from a magma, the common form of breakup is by *block separation* (Figure 19.1). Obviously, comparatively weak forces can separate such blocks, whereas great forces are required to make fresh fractures through solid rock. In sedimentary rocks the planes of stratification, or bedding planes, comprise one set of planes of weakness commonly cutting at right angles to the joints. Figures 19.7 and 19.9 show joint blocks being separated by weathering forces. Of course, it is quite possible that a single, solid joint block will later break up either by granular disintegration or by exfoliation.

Shattering is the disintegration of rock along new surfaces of breakage in otherwise massive,

Granular disintegration

Exfoliation

Block separation

Shattering

Figure 19.1　Rock breakup takes various forms.

strong rock, to produce highly angular pieces with sharp corners and edges (Figure 19.1). The surface of fracture may pass between individual mineral crystals or grains, or may cut through them. Blocks seen in Figure 19.2 are joint blocks, many of which have been shattered into smaller pieces.

Figure 19.2　A felsenmeer atop Medicine Bow Peak, Snowy Range, Wyoming, at 12,000 ft (3650 m) elevation. The rock is quartzite. (Photograph by A. N. Strahler.)

Physical weathering processes and forms

The physical, or mechanical, processes of weathering produce fine particles from massive rock by the exertion of stresses sufficient to fracture the rock, but do not change its chemical composition. One of the most important physical weathering processes in cold climates is *frost action*, the repeated growth and melting of ice crystals in the pore spaces or fractures of soil and rock. As water in joints freezes, it forms needlelike ice crystals extending across the openings. As these ice needles grow, they exert tremendous force against the confining walls and can easily pry apart the joint blocks. Even massive rocks can be shattered by the growth of ice crystals created from water that has previously soaked into the rock. Where soil water freezes, it tends to form ice layers parallel with the ground surface, *heaving* the soil upward in an uneven manner.

Freezing water strongly affects soil and rock in all middle- and high-latitude regions having a cold winter season, but its effects are most striking in high mountains, above the timberline. Here the separation and shattering of joint blocks may produce an extensive ground surface littered with angular blocks (Figure 19.2). Such a surface is termed a *felsenmeer* (rock sea), or *boulder field*. Where cliffs of bare rock exist at high altitudes, fragments fall from the cliff face, building up piles of loose blocks into conical forms, termed *talus cones* (Figure 19.27).

Closely related to the growth of ice crystals is the weathering process of rock disintegration by growth of salt crystals. This process operates extensively in dry climates and is responsible for many of the niches, shallow caves, rock arches, and pits in sandstone formations. During long drought periods, ground water is drawn to the surface of the rock by capillary force. As evaporation of the water takes place in the porous outer zone of the sandstone, tiny crystals of salts are left behind. The growth force of these crystals is capable of producing granular disintegration of the sandstone, which crumbles into a sand and is swept away by wind and rain. Especially susceptible are zones of rock lying close to the base of a cliff, for here the ground water tends to seep outward, perhaps prevented from further downward percolation by impervious layers below (Figure 19.3). In the southwestern United States, many of the deep niches thus formed were occupied by Indians, whose cliff dwellings obtained protection from the elements as well as safety from armed attack (Figure 19.4).

An important but little appreciated process of physical weathering is the continual swelling and shrinking of soils as the particles of fine silt and

Figure 19.3 Seepage of water from the cliff base localizes development of niches through rock weathering.

clay absorb or give up soil water in alternate periods of rain and drought. Shrinkage forms soil cracks in dry periods, making the infiltration of rainfall much more rapid in early stages of an ensuing rain. In clay-rich sedimentary rocks such as shales, the swelling is largely responsible for a spontaneous breakup known as *slaking*, in which the shale crumbles into small chips or pencil-like fragments when exposed to the air.

Most crystalline solids, such as the minerals of rocks, tend to expand when heated and to contract when cooled. Where rock surfaces are exposed daily to the intense heating of the sun alternating with nightly cooling, the resulting expansion and contraction exerts powerful forces upon the rock. Given sufficient time (tens of thousands of such daily alternations), even the strongest rocks may develop fractures. Breakage can take the form of exfoliation or granular disintegration.

A curious but widespread process related to physical weathering results from *unloading*, the relief of confining pressure, as rock is brought nearer to the earth's surface through the erosional removal of overlying rock. Geologists think that rock formed at great depth beneath the earth's surface (particularly igneous and metamorphic rock) is in a slightly contracted state because of the tremendous pressures applied during mountain-making crustal deformations. On being brought to the surface, the rock expands slightly in volume and, in so doing, great shells of rock break free from the parent mass below. The new surfaces of fracture are a form of joint termed *sheeting structure* and show best in massive rocks such as granite and marble, because in a closely jointed rock the expansion would be taken up among the blocks. The rock sheets or shells produced by unloading generally parallel the ground surface and therefore tend to dip valleyward. On granite coasts the shells are found to dip seaward at all points along the shore. Sheeting structure is well seen in quarries, where it greatly facilitates the removal of rock (Figure 19.5).

Where sheeting structure has formed over the top of a single large body of massive rock, an *exfoliation dome* is produced (Figure 19.6). These are among the largest of the landforms due primarily to weathering. In the Yosemite Valley region, California, where domes are spectacularly displayed, the individual rock shells may be as thick as 20 to 50 ft (6 to 15 m).

Other large, smooth-sided rock domes lacking in shells are not true exfoliation domes, but are formed by granular disintegration of a single body of hard, coarse-grained intrusive igneous rock lacking in joints. Examples are the Sugar Loaf of Rio de Janeiro and Stone Mountain, Georgia (Figure 22.4), which rise prominently above surrounding areas of weaker rock.

Finally, in this list of physical weathering processes, the wedging of plant roots deserves consideration as a possible mechanism whereby joint blocks may be separated. We have all seen at one time or another a tree whose lower trunk and roots are firmly wedged between two great joint blocks of massive rock (Figure 19.7). Whether the tree has actually been able to spread the blocks farther apart is doubtful at best. However, it is certain that the growth of tiny rootlets in joint fractures must be of great importance in loosening countless small rock scales and grains, particularly when a rock has already been softened by decay or fractured by frost action.

Figure 19.4 White House Ruin occupies a deep niche in the sandstone wall of Canyon de Chelly, Arizona. (Photograph by Ray Atkeson.)

Figure 19.5 Sheeting of granite, a large scale form of exfoliation, facilitates quarrying operations. (Photograph by courtesy of Smith Quarry Division of Rock of Ages Corporation, Barre, Vermont.)

Chemical weathering processes and forms

Chemical weathering denotes changes in chemical compositions of rock-forming minerals to produce new minerals better suited to existing in equilibrium with the relatively low temperatures and pressures found at the earth's surface. One group of these changes involves addition of oxygen and water, both of which are abundantly available in the soil and bedrock. A second group of changes is the reaction of natural acids of the soil solution with rock-forming minerals to yield salts which are readily carried away by ground water movement. Third, certain salts of the type known as *evaporites* (see Chapter 17), found in layers in sedimentary strata, are readily dissolved without change in chemical composition and are carried away in ground water flow. The first two groups of chemical processes are considered in somewhat more detail.

Water enters into a permanent chemical union with many common rock-forming minerals in a chemical change termed *hydrolysis*. The igneous rocks are particularly susceptible. Potash feldspar commonly turns to a clay mineral known as *kaolin*. When this happens in a granite, in which potash feldspar is an important constituent, the granite will undergo granular disintegration. Not only is the kaolin a soft mineral, but it tends to swell and thus to burst the grains apart. Similarly, the iron-magnesium minerals such as hornblende and biotite decompose and soften, causing disintegration of basic rocks such as gabbro or basalt. The iron thus released unites with oxygen and water to form *limonite*, a soft, yellowish mineral that is responsible for much of the staining of rock surfaces with earth-red colors.

Figure 19.6 North Dome and Basket Dome in Yosemite National Park, California, are exfoliation domes developed from huge masses of solid igneous rock. (Photograph by Douglas Johnson.)

Figure 19.7 Jointing in sandstone resembles pavement blocks at Artists View, Catskill Mountains, New York. (Photograph by A. N. Strahler.)

Figure 19.8 Weathering converts rectangular blocks into rounded forms. (Drawn by E. Raisz.)

Figure 19.9 Egg-shaped granite boulders are produced from joint blocks by granular disintegration in a semiarid climate near Prescott, Arizona. (Photograph by A. N. Strahler.)

The hydrolysis of granite, with accompanying granular disintegration and some exfoliation of thin scales, produces many interesting boulder and pinnacle forms by rounding of angular joint blocks (Figures 19.8, 19.9, 19.10). These forms are particularly conspicuous in arid regions because of the absence of any thick cover of soil and vegetation. There is ample moisture in most deserts for hydrolysis to act, given sufficient time. Hydrolysis in fine-grained basic igneous rocks, such as basalt, commonly gives small-scale exfoliation of a type called *spheroidal weathering* (Figure 19.11).

In warm, humid climates, hydrolysis of susceptible rocks goes on below the soil and may result in the deep decay or rotting of igneous and metamorphic rocks to depths as much as 100 to 300 ft (30 to 90 m). Geologists who first studied this deep rock decay in the Southern Appalachian region termed the rotted layer *saprolite*. To the engineer, occurrences of deep weathering are of major importance in construction of highways, dams, or other heavy structures. Advantageous as is the property of softness of the saprolite, so as to be removable by power shovels with little blasting, there is serious danger in the weakness of the material in bearing heavy loads, as well as undesirable plastic properties because of a high content of clay minerals.

Of the acid reactions affecting rock-forming minerals, perhaps the most important is that caused by *carbonic acid*, a weak acid formed when carbon dioxide gas of the atmosphere is dissolved in soil and ground water. Particularly susceptible is limestone, formed of the mineral calcite (calcium carbonate). The action of carbonic acid on limestone produces a salt (calcium bicarbonate) which is readily carried off in the flow of ground water and streams. Because limestone is a common rock, this process is of major importance in land-

Figure 19.10 Stages in the development of egg-shaped boulders from rectangular joint blocks. (After W. M. Davis.)

Figure 19.11 Spheroidal weathering, shown here, has produced many thin concentric shells in a basaltic igneous rock. Lucchetti Dam, Puerto Rico. (Photograph by C. A. Kaye, U.S. Geological Survey.)

form development. Surfaces of limestones are commonly deeply pitted and grooved (Figure 19.12). More important is the removal of vast amounts of rock in underground locations to produce cavern systems into which surface water disappears. The landforms associated with cavern development are explained in Chapter 26.

Figure 19.12 Solution rills in limestone, west of Las Vegas, Nevada. Scale is indicated by pocket knife in center. (Photograph by John S. Shelton.)

Those who have studied the rate at which carbonic acid acts have estimated that in a humid climate, such as that of the eastern United States, the ground surface of a limestone region may be lowered at the average rate of 1 ft (0.3 m) in 10,000 years through this process alone.

In any soil rich in decaying plant matter, a variety of organic acids is formed in the soil solution, and these also react with mineral surfaces to produce chemical weathering. The salts that are products of such reactions are carried down through the soil into the ground water zone, then eventually to streams.

The weathering processes reviewed above, both physical and chemical, work universally but produce few distinctive large landforms or spectular activities that would draw the attention of the average person. Nevertheless, these processes are of enormous importance in slope development in that they prepare the bedrock for soil formation and for erosional removal by the agents of land sculpture. Without the weathering processes, vegetation could not thrive as we know it today, or could the great continental land masses be easily reduced by the agents of denudation.

Mass wasting

Everywhere on the earth's surface, gravity pulls continually downward on all materials. Bedrock is usually so strong and well supported that it remains fixed in place, but should a mountain slope become too steep through removal of rock at the base, bedrock masses break free, falling or sliding to new positions of rest. In cases where huge masses of bedrock are involved, the result may be catastrophic in loss to life and property in towns and villages in the path of the slide. Soil and overburden, being poorly held together, are much more susceptible to gravity movements. There is abundant evidence that on most slopes at least a small amount of downhill movement is going on at all times. Much of this is imperceptible, but sometimes the overburden slides or flows rapidly.

Taken altogether, the various kinds of downslope movements occurring under the pull of gravity, which we have collectively termed mass wasting, constitute an important process in slope wasting and denudation of the lands. A few of the commoner kinds of gravity movements and resulting landforms are described here.

Soil creep

On almost any moderately steep, soil-covered slope, some evidence may be found of extremely slow downslope movement of soil and overburden, a process called *soil creep*. Figure 19.13 shows some of the evidence that the process is going on.

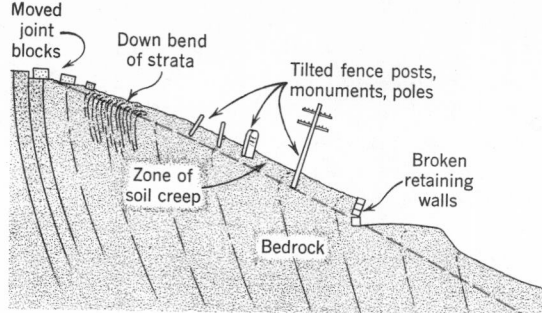

Figure 19.13 Slow, downhill creep of soil and weathered overburden. (After C. F. S. Sharpe.)

Joint blocks of distinctive rock types are found moved far downslope from the outcrop. In some layered rocks such as shales or slates, edges of the strata seem to bend in the downhill direction. This is not true plastic bending, but is the result of slight movement on many small joint cracks (Figure 19.14). Fence posts and telephone poles lean downslope and even shift measurably out of line. Retaining walls of road cuts lean and break outward under pressure of soil creep from above.

What causes soil creep? Heating and cooling of the soil, growth of frost needles, alternate drying and wetting of the soil, trampling and burrowing by animals, and shaking by earthquakes all produce some disturbance of the soil and mantle. Because gravity exerts a downhill pull on every such rearrangement that takes place, the particles are urged progressively downslope.

Creep affects rock masses enclosed in the soil or lying upon bare bedrock. Huge boulders which have gradually crept down a mountain side in large numbers may accumulate at the mountain base to produce a boulder field containing blocks the size of a house. Creep also affects the rock pieces in a talus slope, causing the angle of the talus surface gradually to become flatter. In some alpine mountains, high above timberline, sheets of frost-shattered rock fragments creep slowly down the valleys, making curious tonguelike bodies which in many ways resemble a glacier of ice. These forms are called *rock glaciers* (Figure 19.15). Among the best examples are those from mountain ranges in Alaska, where a single rock glacier may be 1 to 2 mi (1.5 to 3 km) long and 0.25 mi (0.4 km) wide.

Earthflow

In humid climate regions, if slopes are steep, masses of water-saturated soil, overburden, or weak

Figure 19.14 Slow creep has caused this down hill bending of steeply dipping sandstone layers. (Photograph by courtesy of Ward's Natural Science Establishment.)

Figure 19.15 Its wrinkled surface suggesting internal flowage, this rock glacier descends a steep mountain slope in the Copper River Region of Alaska. (Photograph by Bradford Washburn.)

Earth Flow | 281

Figure 19.16   Two varieties of earthflow. (After E. Raisz.)

bedrock may slide downslope during a period of a few hours in the form of *earthflows*. Figures 19.16 and 19.17 are sketches of earthflows showing how the material slumps away from the top, leaving steplike terraces bounded by arcuate scarps, and flows down to form a bulging "toe" in which wrinkles are curved convexly downslope.

Shallow earthflows, affecting only the soil and residual overburden, are common on sod-covered slopes that have been saturated by heavy rains. An earthflow may affect a few square yards, or it may cover an area of several acres. If the bedrock is rich in clay (shale or deeply weathered igneous rocks), earthflow sometimes include millions of tons of bedrock, moving by plastic flowage like a great mass of thick mud.

A special variety of earth flowage characteristic of arctic regions is *solifluction* (from Latin words meaning *soil* and *to flow*. In late spring and early summer, when thawing has penetrated the upper few feet, soil is fully saturated with water which cannot escape downward because of the underlying impermeable frozen mass (permafrost). Flowing almost imperceptibly, this saturated soil forms terraces and lobes that give the mountain slope a stepped appearance (Figure 19.19).

Figure 19.17   Earthflows in a mountainous region. (After W. M. Davis.)

Mudflow

One of the most spectacular forms of mass wasting is the *mudflow*, a mud stream of fluid consistency which pours down canyons in mountainous regions (Figure 19.20). In deserts, where vegetation does not protect the mountain soils, violent local storms produce rain much faster than it can be absorbed by the soil. As the water runs down the slopes it forms a thin mud, which flows down to the canyon floors. Following stream courses, the mud continues to flow until it becomes so thickened that it must stop. Great boulders are carried along, buoyed up in the mud. Roads, bridges, and houses in the canyon floor are engulfed and destroyed. If the mudflow emerges from the canyon and spreads across a piedmont plain, property damage and loss of life can result, because in desert regions the plains lying at the foot of a mountain range which supplies irrigation water may be heavily populated.

Mudflows also occur on the slopes of erupting volcanoes. Freshly fallen volcanic ash and dust is turned into mud by heavy rains and flows down the slopes of the volcano. Herculaneum, a city at the base of Mt. Vesuvius, was destroyed by a mudflow during the eruption of 79 A.D., when the neighboring city of Pompeii was buried under volcanic ash.

Still other mudflows, usually of small size, occur in high mountains and in arctic tundra regions during periods of thaw when excess water is produced by melting of snow and soil ice (Figure 19.21).

Landslide

Landslide is the rapid sliding of large masses of rock with little or no flowage of the materials as in the previous types. Two basic forms of landslide are (*a*) *rockslide*, in which the bedrock mass slips on a relatively flat inclined rock plane, such as a fault or bedding plane, and (*b*) *slump*, in which there is backward rotation on a curved up-concave slip plane (Figure 19.22).

Wherever steep mountain slopes occur, there is a possibility of great and disastrous rockslides. In Switzerland, Norway, or the Canadian Rockies, for example, villages built on the floors of steep-sided valleys are sometimes destroyed and their inhabitants killed by the sliding of millions of cubic yards of rock, set loose without any warning (Figures 19.23 and 19.24). Certain kinds of artificial excavations, made in connection with the building of dams, railroads, or highways, may undermine rock masses, causing troublesome landslides. Aside from occasional great catastrophes, rockslides do not have strong geographical influences because of their sporadic occurrence in thinly populated

Figure 19.18 The great earthflow in Slumgullion Gulch, in the San Juan Mountains of Colorado, dammed a river to produce Lake San Cristobal. (Photograph by C. W. Cross, U.S. Geological Survey.)

Figure 19.19 Solifluction lobes cover this Alaskan mountain slope in the tundra climate region. (Photograph by P. S. Smith, U.S. Geological Survey.)

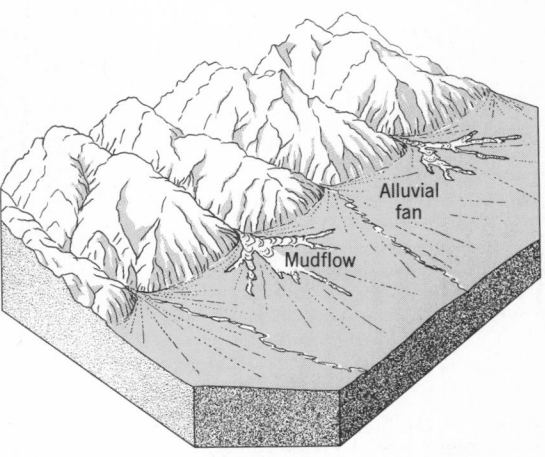

Figure 19.20 Thin streamlike mudflows commonly issue from canyon mouths in arid regions, spreading out upon the piedmont alluvial fan slopes.

Landslide | 283

Figure 19.21 A small mudflow resulting from summer thaw in a tundra climate, De Salis Bay, Banks Island (lat. 71½° N, long. 122° W). The inner channel is about 2 ft (0.6 m) wide. (Photograph by A. L. Washburn, Arctic Institute of North America.)

Figure 19.22 Landslides may involve (A) slip on a nearly plane surface or (B) slump with rotation on a curved plane.

mountainous regions. Small slides may, however, repeatedly block or break an important mountain highway or railway line.

Because rockslides are characteristic of over-steepened topography formed by glaciers, streams, and waves, and of regions having certain geologic characteristics, the basic reasons for the existence of steep slopes favorable to landsliding will be clarified in later chapters.

The second form of landslide produces *slump blocks,* great masses of bedrock or overburden that slide downward from a cliff, at the same time rotating backward on a horizontal axis (Figure 19.25). Wherever massive sedimentary strata, usually sandstones or limestones, or lava beds, rest upon weak clay or shale formations, a steep cliff

Figure 19.23 A classic example of a great, disastrous landslide is the Turtle Mountain slide, which took place at Frank, Alberta, in 1903. A huge mass of limestone slid from the face of Turtle Mountain between South and North peaks, descended to the valley, then continued up the low slope of the opposite valley side until it came to rest as a great sheet of bouldery rock debris. (After Canadian Geological Survey, Dept. of Mines.)

Figure 19.24 The debris of a landslide in Yellowstone Park, Wyoming, consists of rock masses of all sizes tumbled in a disordered fashion. (Photograph by Douglas Johnson.)

Figure 19.25 Slump blocks rotate backward as they slide from a cliff.

tends to be formed by erosion. As the weak rock is eroded from the cliff base, the cap rock is undermined. When a point of failure is reached, a large block breaks off, sliding down and tilting back along a curving plane of slip. Slump blocks may be as much as 1 to 2 mi (1.5 to 3 km) long and 500 ft (800 m) thick. A single block appears as a ridge at the base of the cliff. A closed depression or lake basin may lie between the block and the cliff.

Slumping commonly occurs on a small scale wherever weak overburden, such as floodplain alluvium or a glacial deposit, is cut away, hence it is seen in caving river banks or along a sea cliff.

Rockfall and talus

Most rapid of all mass wasting processes is *rockfall*, the free falling or rolling of single masses of rock from a steep cliff. Individual fragments may be as small as sand grains, or as large as a

city block, depending upon the overall scale of the cliff and the manner in which the rock breaks up. Large blocks disintegrate upon falling, strewing the slope below with rubble and leaving a conspicuous scar on the upper cliff face (Figure 19.26).

Rockfall goes on continuously over long periods of time, yielding a rain of countless individual small fragments at the cliff base. These accumulate in a distinctive landform, the *talus cone*, already referred to as a by-product of rapid frost disintegration on exposed cliff faces at high altitudes or in arctic regions (Figure 19.27). A talus slope, or *scree slope*, as it is often called, has a remarkably constant slope angle of about 34° or 35°. So long as the talus slope is freshly formed and contains little very fine material mixed in with the coarse, the angle is constant within one or two degrees of variation, regardless of the rock type or the shape of the blocks.

Most cliffs are notched by narrow ravines which funnel the fragments into individual tracks, so as to produce conelike talus bodies arranged side by side along the cliff. Where a large range of sizes of particles is supplied, the larger pieces, by reason of their greater momentum and ease of rolling, travel to the base of the cone, whereas the tiny

Figure 19.26 This rockfall on the Palisades of the Hudson River, just north of the George Washington Bridge, took place in November 1955. About 1200 tons of broken rock fragments resulted from the fall of a large columnar joint block of diabase. (Photograph by Bergen Evening Record.)

Figure 19.27 Talus cones at the base of a frost-shattered cirque headwall. Moraine Lake in the Canadian Rockies. (Photograph by Ray Atkeson.)

grains lodge in the apex. This tends to sort the fragments by size, progressively finer from base to apex (Figure 19.28).

Most fresh talus slopes are unstable, so that the disturbance created by walking across the slope, or dropping of a large rock fragment from the cliff above, will easily set off a sliding of the surface layer of particles. The upper limiting angle to which coarse, hard, well-sorted rock fragments will stand is termed the *angle of repose*. Other examples of this critical angle of slope are seen in the leeward surfaces (slip faces) of sand dunes and on the side slopes of small volcanic cones.

REFERENCES FOR FURTHER STUDY

Matthes, F. E. (1930), Geologic history of Yosemite Valley, *U.S. Geol. Prof. Paper 160*, 137 pp. See pp. 114–116.

Sharpe, C. F. S. (1938), *Landslides and related phenomena*, Columbia University Press, New York, 137 pp.

Lobeck, A. K. (1939), *Geomorphology*, McGraw-Hill Book Co., New York, 731 pp. See Chapter 3.

Reiche, P. (1950), *A survey of weathering processes and products*, University of New Mexico Press, 95 pp.

Highway Research Board (1958), *Landslides and engineering practice*, Special Report 29, N.A.S.—N.R.C. Publication 544. Washington, D.C., 232 pp.

Thornbury, W. D. (1969), *Principles of geomorphology*, second edition, John Wiley and Sons, New York, 594 pp. See chapter 4.

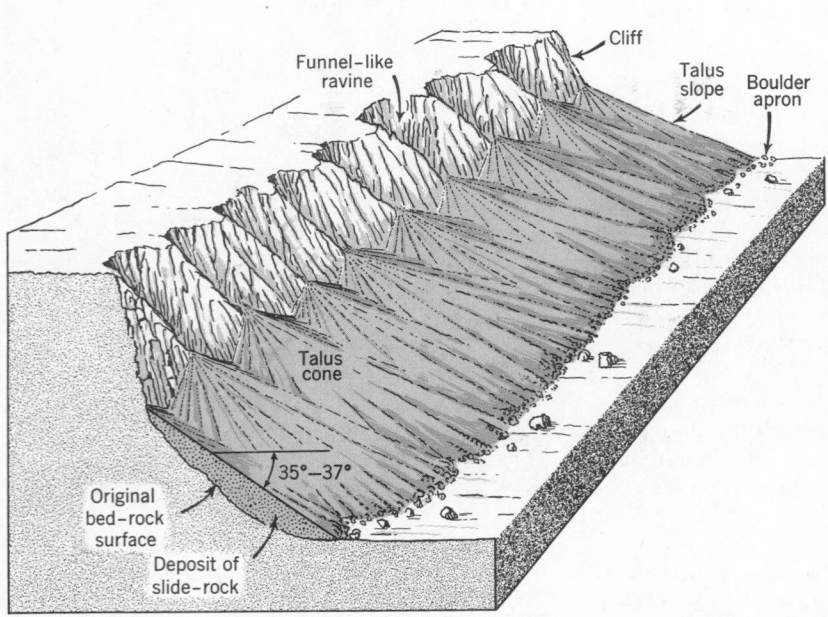

Figure 19.28 Idealized diagram of talus cones formed at the base of a cliff, which might be 200 to 500 ft (60 to 150 m) high.

REVIEW QUESTIONS

1. What is the meaning of the term slope? In what way do slopes contribute to the functioning of the hydrologic cycle?

2. Define and distinguish between weathering and mass wasting. Into what two large groups can the weathering processes be divided?

3. Describe four common geometrical forms of rock breakup. For each, name two or three common rock types in which the particular form of breakup might be expected.

4. List the physical processes of weathering. Of these, which require water to be present? Which do not? Which are controlled by changes in air temperature? Which can act deep in the soil or bedrock? Which cannot?

5. What are felsenmeer and talus? Under what climatic environment would they be formed? What process of weathering dominates in such places?

6. How can the growth of salt crystals cause rock disintegration? What climatic conditions favor this process? What forms result?

7. Under what conditions can temperature changes alone cause rock disintegration? What evidence is available that the process is effective?

8. Explain how sheeting structure and exfoliation domes result from unloading. What rock type is most likely to exhibit such structure? Name a locality famous for the display of exfoliation domes.

9. Comment on the effectiveness of plant growth forces in producing the disintegration of rock.

10. What three groups of changes come under the general heading of chemical weathering processes?

11. What is the nature of changes in minerals when hydrolysis takes place? How does hydrolysis promote weathering? What rocks are most susceptible to this type of decay? What are some of the visible forms resulting from hydrolysis in granitic rocks? In basic rocks? How deep in the ground do the effects of hydrolysis extend?

12. How is carbonic acid formed and how does it act on rock? What type of rock is most susceptible? What surface forms are produced? What other acids are commonly found in soil water?

13. What role does mass wasting play in the denudation of the lands? List the evidences of soil creep. What general type of mechanism causes soil creep? Are large rock masses also affected by creep? Explain.

14. Describe an earthflow. How large are earthflows? Under what conditions of season and climate might earthflows be expected to take place? Describe and explain the special features of solifluction.

15. Under what topographic and climatic conditions do mudflows occur? Point out the similarities and differences between a mudflow and a stream.

16. To what kinds of movement and earth material is landslide restricted? Distinguish between rockslide and slump as two basic types of landslide. Describe the topographic and geologic conditions favorable to each of these types.

17. What is rockfall? What sizes of rock masses may be included? How is a talus cone produced and what angle of slope does it normally have? How may the particles of a talus cone be arranged in order of size from apex to base? Explain.

CHAPTER **20**

Runoff and Ground Water

IN earlier chapters we followed the hydrologic cycle from the water vapor phase in air masses through precipitation and evapotranspiration to infiltration as subsurface water. Chapter 9 treated in detail the part of the cycle dealing with soil moisture and the water budget. Study of the cycle is now resumed by a consideration of *runoff*, which consists of all surface water flow, both over the land slopes and in streams. Runoff may be derived directly from excessive precipitation which cannot infiltrate the soil, or it may originate as the outflow of ground water along lines where the water table intersects the earth's surface.

Seeking to escape to progressively lower levels and eventually to the sea, runoff becomes organized into *drainage systems*, which we may describe as more or less pear-shaped areas bounded by divides, within which ground slopes and branching stream networks are adjusted to dispose as efficiently as possible of the runoff and its contained load of mineral particles, and thus to lower the land surfaces progressively toward the ultimate goal of the processes of denudation—reduction to a nearly featureless plain close to sea level. Most drainage systems possess a constricted exit, normally the mouth of the master stream, where it meets a large body of water. Thus, a drainage system is a converging mechanism funneling and integrating the weaker and more diffuse forms of runoff into progressively deeper and more intense paths of activity.

The study of drainage systems brings us in contact with two fields of science, hydrology and geology. Much of the study of the water itself, particularly as to the quantities of water involved in runoff and their variations in response to precipitation, is done by hydrologists, who are affiliated with the profession of civil engineering. The study of streams in eroding and transporting rock materials, so as to shape the landforms of drainage systems, is done by geologists. In the United States, both groups pool their efforts in the analysis and solution of problems of both runoff and ground water under the Water Resources Division of the U.S. Geological Survey, to which is given the responsibility for assessing the surface and ground water resources of the nation. Many facets of the work of that agency will be touched upon in this chapter; also the work of the Forest Service, which studies problems of runoff in the nation's forests, and the Soil Conservation Service, which is concerned with the effects of runoff in causing land erosion and related agricultural problems. Runoff problems concerned with the improvement of irrigation works and navigable waterways are dealt with by engineers and scientists of the Bureau of Reclamation and the U.S. Army Corps of Engineers.

Runoff, ground water, and geography

For the geography student, runoff and ground water are subjects of vital concern as comprising a basic natural resource upon which agricultural and industrial development are heavily dependent. Runoff held in reservoirs behind dams provides water supplies for great urban centers, such as New York City and Los Angeles; diverted from large rivers, it provides irrigation water for highly productive lowlands in arid lands, such as the Imperial Valley of California and the Nile Valley of Egypt. To these uses are added hydroelectric power, where the drop of the river is steep; or routes of inland navigation, where the drop is gentle.

Available sources of both surface and ground water are fast being fully exploited in heavily populated areas. More and more attention is being paid to reducing various forms of waste of useful water, making a larger proportion available for man's productive use. In underdeveloped lands, many proposed improvements in the agricultural and industrial economy require development of surface and ground water resources. A geographer analyzing the potential of such regions needs to understand certain principles of hydrology and geology if he is to make realistic appraisals of the available water resources.

Forms of overland flow

Runoff that flows down the slopes of the land in more or less broadly distributed films, sheets, or rills is referred to as *overland flow* in distinction with *channel flow*, or *stream flow*, in which the water occupies a narrow trough confined by lateral banks. Within this broad definition, overland flow can take many forms. It may be a continuous thin film, called *sheet flow*, where the soil or rock surface is extremely smooth, or a series of tiny rivulets connecting one water-filled hollow with another, where the ground is rough or pitted. On a grass-covered slope, overland flow is subdivided into countless tiny threads of water, passing around the stems. Even in a heavy and prolonged rain, overland flow in full progress on a sloping lawn may not be visible to the casual observer. On heavily forested slopes bearing a thick mat of decaying leaves and many fallen branches and tree trunks, overland flow may pass almost entirely concealed beneath this cover.

Intermediate in classification between overland flow and channel flow is flow in shallow *shoestring rills*, which may score the hillside surface as a system of long, parallel lines (Figure 20.4). In some cases, shoestring rills are merely seasonal features, developed during periods of torrential rain in the spring and summer, but healing over as ground frost heaves the soil during the winter season. Again, shoestring rills may actually represent a permanent change brought on by deforestation or cultivation, in which new stream channels are in the process of formation.

Progress of overland flow

Imagine that a hillside slope which has been thoroughly drained of moisture in a period of drought is subjected to a period of rain. What are the successive stages in the production of overland flow? If heavy vegetation such as forest is present, much of the rain at the beginning is held in droplets on the leaves and plant stems, a process termed *interception*. This water may be returned directly to the atmosphere by evaporation, so that if the rainfall is brief, little water reaches the ground.

As explained in Chapter 9, the ground surface is capable of absorbing by infiltration even a heavy rain in the early stages of a rain period. Therefore, unless the rain continues for an hour or so, no overland flow may be expected. Soon, however, the soil passages are sealed or obstructed, dropping the infiltration rate to a low, but constant value. Any excessive precipitation now remains on the ground surface, first accumulating in small puddles or pools which occupy natural hollows in the rough ground surface or are held behind tiny check dams formed by fallen leaves and twigs (Figure 20.1). *Surface detention* is the term applied to the holding of water on a slope by such small natural containers. Assuming that the rain continues to fall with sufficient intensity, water then overflows from hollow to hollow, becoming true overland flow.

Because any given square unit of ground on a hill side must receive the overland flow from the

Figure 20.1   Precipitation and overland flow.

entire strip of ground of that width lying upslope of it, we may expect the rate of discharge (volume of water passing across a given line in a given unit of time) to increase in direct proportion to the length of the total path of flow. Depth of the flowing layer might therefore be expected to increase the farther downslope it progresses, but this increase may be small because the flow velocity will also be increasing down the slope. Figure 20.2 shows heavy runoff at the base of a long slope, where the accumulated overland flow has converged into broad shallow streams spreading across the slope.

At the base of a hill slope, overland flow is disposed of by passing into a stream channel or lake, or by sinking into the ground, should a highly permeable layer of sand, gravel, or blocky slide rock be encountered.

Overland flow is measured in inches or centimeters of water per hour, just as for precipitation and infiltration. Therefore, a simple formula expresses the rate at which overland flow will be produced by a given unit of ground surface as follows:

Rate of production of overland flow = rate of precipitation − rate of infiltration

For example, if the rate of infiltration became constant at a value of 0.4 inches per hour, and the rate of rainfall was a steady 0.6 inches per hour (a heavy rain), the runoff would be produced at a rate of 0.2 inches per hour, assuming none to be returned to the atmosphere by evaporation.

Accelerated land erosion

Overland flow, by exerting a dragging force over the soil surface, picks up particles of mineral matter ranging in size from fine clay to coarse sand or gravel, depending on the speed of the flow and the degree to which the particles are bound by

Figure 20.2 Overland flow running down an 8 percent slope following a heavy thunderstorm. The ditch in the foreground receives the runoff and conducts it away as channel flow. (Soil Conservation Service photograph.)

plant rootlets or held down by a mat of leaves. Added to this solid matter is dissolved mineral matter produced by acid reactions or direct solution. Such slow removal of soil is part of the natural geological process of landmass denudation and is both inevitable and universal. Under stable, natural conditions, the erosion rate in a humid climate is slow enough that a soil with distinct horizons is formed and maintained, enabling vegetation to maintain itself. Soil scientists refer to this state of activity as the *geologic norm*.

By contrast, the rate of soil erosion may be enormously speeded up through man-made activities or rare natural events to result in a state of *accelerated erosion*, removing the soil much faster than it can be formed. This condition comes about most commonly from a change in the conditions of vegetative cover and physical state of the ground surface. Destruction of vegetation by clearing of land for cultivation, or by forest fires, directly causes great changes in the relative proportions of infiltration to runoff. Interception of rain by foliage is ended; protection afforded by a ground cover of fallen leaves and stems is removed. Consequently the rain falls directly upon the mineral soil.

Direct force of falling drops (Figure 20.3) causes a geyserlike splashing in which soil particles are lifted and then dropped into new positions, a process termed *splash erosion*. It is estimated that a violent rainstorm has the ability to disturb as much as 100 tons of soil per acre (225 metric tons per hectare). On a sloping ground surface, splash erosion tends to shift the soil slowly downhill. A more important effect is to cause the soil surface to become much less able to infiltrate water because the natural soil openings become sealed by particles shifted by raindrop splash. Reduced infiltration permits a much greater proportion of overland flow to occur from rain of given intensity and duration. The depth and velocity of overland flow then increase greatly, intensifying the rate of soil removal.

Another effect of destruction of vegetation is to reduce greatly the resistance of the ground surface to the force of erosion under overland flow. On a slope covered by grass sod, even a deep layer of overland flow causes little soil erosion because the energy of the moving water is dissipated in friction with the grass stems, which are tough and elastic. Similarly on a heavily forested slope, countless check dams made by leaves, twigs, roots, and fallen tree trunks take up the force of overland flow. Without such vegetative cover the eroding force is applied directly to the bare soil surface, easily dislodging the grains and sweeping them downslope.

Summarizing these things, we may state that the eroding capacity of overland flow is directly proportional to the rate of precipitation and length of slope, but inversely proportional to both the infiltration capacity of the soil and the resistance of the surface. To complete this equation, we need only to add the effect of the steepness of ground slope. Obviously, the steeper the slope of ground, the faster is the flow and the more intense the erosion. We therefore add that the eroding capacity of overland flow increases directly with angle of slope. As the slope angle approaches the vertical, however, erosion will become less intense from overland flow because the ground surface intercepts much less of the vertically falling rain.

Forms of accelerated erosion

When a plot of ground is first cleared of forest and ploughed for cultivation, little erosion will occur until the action of rain splash has broken down the soil aggregates and sealed the larger opening. Following this, overland flow begins to remove the soil in rather uniform thin layers, a process termed *sheet erosion*. Because of seasonal cultivation, the effects of sheet erosion are often little noticed until the upper horizons of the soil (*A* and *B* horizons) are removed or greatly thinned. Reaching the base of the slope, where the angle of surface is rapidly reduced to meet the valley bottom, soil particles come to rest and accumulate in a thickening layer termed *colluvium*, or simply *slope wash*. This, too, has a sheetlike distribution and may be little noticed, except where it can be seen that fence posts or tree trunks are being slowly buried.

Material that continues to be carried by overland flow to reach a stream in the valley axis is then carried further down valley and may be built up into layers on the valley floor, where it becomes

Figure 20.3 A large raindrop (above) lands on a wet soil surface, producing a miniature crater (below). Grains of clay and silt are thrown into the air and the soil surface is disturbed. (Official U.S. Navy photograph.)

alluvium, a word applied generally to any stream-laid deposits. Colluvium and alluvium together are described as products of *sedimentation*, the opposite process from erosion. In many ways, sedimentation at the base of slopes and in valley bottoms is a process equally serious to erosion from the agricultural standpoint, because it results in burial of soil horizons under relatively infertile, sandy layers and may choke the valleys of small streams, causing the water to flood broadly over the valley bottoms.

Where slopes are exceptionally steep and runoff from storms is exceptionally heavy, sheet erosion progresses into a more intense activity, that of *rill erosion*, or *rilling* (Figure 20.4), in which innumerable, closely spaced channels, already referred to as *shoestring rills*, are scored into the soil and subsoil. If these rills are not destroyed by soil tillage, they may soon begin to integrate into still larger channels, termed *gullies*. This transformation comes about as the more active rills deepen more rapidly than their neighbors and incorporate

Figure 20.4 Shoestring rills on a barren slope. (Soil Conservation Service photograph.)

the adjacent drainage areas. Erosive action thus is concentrated into a few large channels which deepen into steep-walled, canyonlike trenches whose upper ends grow progressively upslope (Figure 20.5).

Ultimately, a rugged, barren topography, resembling the badland forms of the arid climates, may result from accelerated soil erosion allowed to proceed unchecked. Curative measures developed by the Soil Conservation Service have proved effective in stopping accelerated soil erosion and permitting the return to slow erosion rates approaching the geologic norm. These measures

Figure 20.5 This great gully, eroded into deeply weathered overburden, was typical of certain parts of the Piedmont region of South Carolina and Georgia before remedial measures were applied. (Soil Conservation Service photograph.)

include construction of terraces to reduce slope angle and distance of overland flow, permanent restoration of overly steep slope belts to dense vegetative cover, and the healing of gullies by placing check dams in the gully floors.

Stream channels

The channel of a stream may be thought of as a long, narrow trough, shaped by the forces of flowing water to be most effective in moving the quantities of water and sediment supplied from the drainage basin or watershed. Channels may be so narrow that a person can jump across them, or as wide as one mile (1.5 km) for great rivers such as the Mississippi. Taking the entire range of natural channel widths as between one foot and one mile, a 5000-fold difference in size can exist.

Hydraulic engineers who must measure stream dimensions and flow rates have adopted a set of terms to describe channel geometry (Figure 20.6). *Depth*, in feet or meters, is measured at any specified point in the stream as the vertical distance from surface to bed. *Width* is the distance across the stream from one water's edge to the other. *Cross-sectional area*, A, is the area in square feet or square meters of a vertical slice across the stream at any specified place. *Wetted perimeter*, P, is the length of the line of contact between the water and the channel, as measured from the cross section. An important characteristic of streams is the *hydraulic radius*, R, which is defined as the cross-sectional area, A, divided by the wetted perimeter, P, or $R = A/P$.

Another important ratio expressing channel geometry is *form ratio*, defined as depth, d, divided by width, w, or d/w. Form ratio is commonly stated as a simple fraction such as 1/100 or 1:100, meaning that the stream channel is 100 times as wide as it is deep. Finally, a most important measure is *slope*, S (or *gradient*), which is the angle between the water surface and the horizontal plane. Slope can be stated in feet per mile or meters per kilometer. Thus a slope of five feet per mile means that the stream surface undergoes a vertical drop of five feet for each mile of horizontal distance downstream. Slope can also be given in terms of *per cent grade*, a common practice in engineering. A grade of 3 percent, or 0.03, means that the stream drops 3 feet for every 100 feet of horizontal distance.

Stream flow

Gravity acts upon the water of a stream to exert pressure against the confining walls. A small part of the gravitational force is aimed downstream parallel with the surface and bed, causing flow. Resisting the force of downstream flow is the force

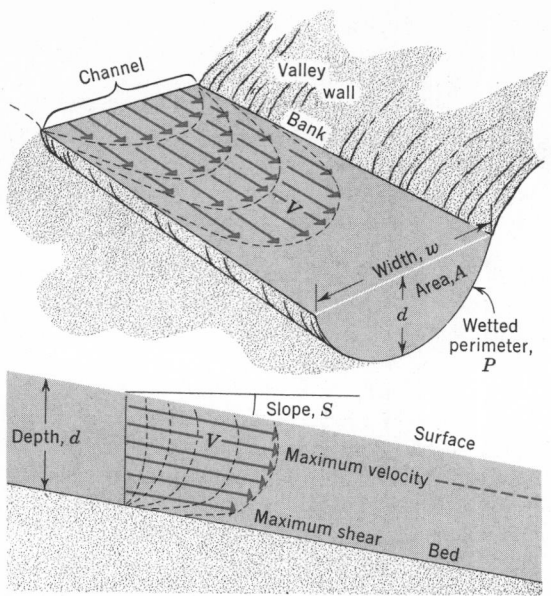

Figure 20.6 Geometry of a stream channel.

Because the average velocity at a given point in a stream differs greatly according to whether it is being measured close to the banks and bed, or out in the middle line, a single figure, the *mean velocity*, is computed for the entire cross section to express the activity of the stream as a whole. Mean velocity in streams is commonly equal to about six-tenths of the maximum velocity, but depends on the relative depth of the stream.

The last and most important measure of stream flow is *discharge*, Q, defined as the volume of water passing through a given cross section of the stream in a given unit of time. Commonly, discharge is stated in cubic feet per second, abbreviated to *cfs*. Sometimes the hydraulic engineer simply states this quantity as *second feet*. In metric units discharge is stated in cubic meters per second (cms). Discharge may be obtained by taking the mean velocity V, and multiplying it by cross-sectional area, A. This relationship is stated by the important equation, $Q = AV$, sometimes referred to as "the equation of continuity of flow."

Stream gauging

An important activity of the U.S. Geological Survey is the measurement, or gauging, of stream flow in the United States. In cooperation with states and municipalities this organization maintains over 6000 river-measurement stations on principal streams and their tributaries. The figures on discharge thus obtained are published by the Geological Survey in a series of *Water-Supply Papers*. Information on daily discharge and flood discharges is essential for planning the distribution

of resistance, or friction, between the water and the floor and sides of the channel. As a result, water close to the bed and banks moves slowly; that in the deepest and most centrally located zone flows fastest. Figure 20.6 indicates by dotted lines the manner in which flow takes place, or the *velocity distribution*. We can imagine that each dot is a given drop of water and that we observe its subsequent positions at equal time intervals. The single line of highest velocity is located in midstream, if the channel is straight and symmetrical, but about one-third of the distance down from surface to bed.

The above statements about velocity need to be qualified. Actually, in all but the most sluggish streams, the water is affected by *turbulence*, a system of innumerable eddies that are continually forming and dissolving. Therefore, a particular molecule of water, if we could keep track of it, would actually describe a highly irregular, corkscrew path as it is swept downstream. Motions would include upward, downward, and sideward directions. Turbulence in streams is extremely important because of the upward elements of flow that lift and support fine particles of sediment. The murky, turbid appearance of streams in flood is ample evidence of turbulence, without which sediment would remain near the bed. Only if we measure the water velocity at a certain fixed point for a long period of time, say several minutes, will the average motion at that point be downstream and in a line parallel with the surface and bed. It is such average values that are shown by the arrows in Figure 20.6.

Figure 20.7 This stilling tower on Fish Creek, near Duarte, California, houses gauges for recording stream flow. (U.S. Geological Survey photograph.)

Figure 20.8 In gauging large rivers, the current meter is lowered on a cable by a power winch. Earphones, connected by wires to the meter, receive a series of clicks whose frequency indicates water velocity. (U.S. Geological Survey photograph.)

is to be recorded. More useful is an automatic-recording gauge, which is mounted in a *stilling tower* built beside the river bank (Figure 20.7). The tower is simply a hollow masonry shaft filled by water which enters through a pipe at the base. By means of a float connected by cable to a recording mechanism above, a continuous ink-line record of the stream stage is made on a graph paper attached to a slowly rotating drum.

To measure stream discharge, it is necessary to determine both the area of cross section of the stream and the mean velocity. This requires that a *current meter* (Figure 20.8) be lowered into the stream at closely spaced intervals so that the velocity can be read at a large number of points evenly distributed in a grid pattern through the stream's cross section (Figure 20.9). A bridge often serves as a convenient means of crossing over the stream; otherwise a cable car or small boat is used. The current meter has a set of revolving cups whose rate of turning is proportional to current velocity. The Price current meter, pictured in Figure 20.8, is in general use by the Geological Survey and will measure velocities from 0.2 to 20 ft (0.06 to 6 m) per second. As the velocities are being measured from point to point, a profile of the river bed is also made by sounding the depth. Thus, a profile is drawn and the cross-sectional area is measured from the profile. Mean velocity is computed by summing all individual velocity readings and dividing by the number of readings. Discharge can then be computed using the formula, $Q = AV$.

Stream flow and precipitation

By studying the records of stream discharge in relation to precipitation on a given watershed, the hydrologist has developed a set of basic principles applying to the variations in stream discharge with different lengths and intensities of storms and with different sizes of watersheds.

Figure 20.10 shows the water graph, or *hydrograph*, of Sugar Creek, Ohio, with a watershed area of 310 sq mi (805 sq km). Sugar Creek basin, a part of the much larger Muskingum River watershed, is outlined in Figure 20.11, a map showing

and development of surface waters as well as for design of flood-protection structures and for the prediction of floods as they progress down a river system.

A stream gauging station requires a device for measuring the height of the water surface, or *stage* of the stream. Simplest to install is a *staff gauge*, which is simply a graduated stick permanently attached to a post or bridge pier. This must be read directly by an observer whenever the stage

Figure 20.9 Idealized diagram of stream gauging installation.

Figure 20.10　Four days of flow of Sugar Creek, Ohio. (After Hoyt and Langbein, *Floods*.)

by isohyetal lines the rainfall during the twelve-hour storm of August 6–7, 1935, for which the hydrograph was constructed. Over the area of Sugar Creek the average total rainfall was 6.3 in (16 cm) for the entire storm, but the total quantity discharged by Sugar Creek was only 3.0 in (7.5 cm). This means that 3.3 in (8.5 cm), or more than half of the rainfall, was retained on the watershed, having infiltrated to become part of the soil and ground water, or had evaporated.

Studying the rainfall and runoff graphs in Figure 20.10, we see that prior to the onset of the storm, Sugar Creek was carrying a small discharge. This was being supplied by the seepage of ground water into the channel and is termed *base flow*. After

Figure 20.11　Isohyets of Sugar Creek Watershed, Ohio. Centimeter equivalents in parentheses. (After Hoyt and Langbein, *Floods*.)

the heavy rainfall began several hours elapsed before the stream gauge at the basin mouth began to show a rise in discharge. This time interval is known as the *lag* and indicated that the branching system of channels was acting as a temporary reservoir, receiving inflow more rapidly than it could be passed down the channel system to the stream gauge. The term *channel storage* is applied to runoff delayed in this manner during the early period of a storm.

The peak of flow in Sugar Creek was reached almost 24 hours after the rain began, or about 6 hours after the cessation of rainfall. Note also that the rate of decline in discharge was much slower than the rate of rise. In general, the larger a watershed, the longer is the lag of time between peak rainfall and peak discharge; the more gradual is the rate of decline of discharge after the peak has passed. Because much rainfall had entered the ground and had reached the water table, a slow but distinct rise is seen in the amount of discharge contributed by base flow.

Base flow and surface water flow

In regions of humid climates, where the water table is high and normally intersects the important stream channels, the hydrographs of larger streams will show clearly the effects of two sources of water: (*a*) *base flow* and (*b*) *surface water flow*. Figure 20.12 is a hydrograph of the Chattahoochee River, Georgia, a large river draining a watershed of some 3350 sq mi (8700 sq km), much of it in the humid southern Appalachian Mountains. The sharp, abrupt fluctuations in discharge are produced by overland flow following rain periods of one to three days duration. These are each similar to the hydrograph of Figure 20.10, except that they are here shown much compressed by the time scale.

After each rain period the discharge falls off rapidly, but if another storm occurs within a few

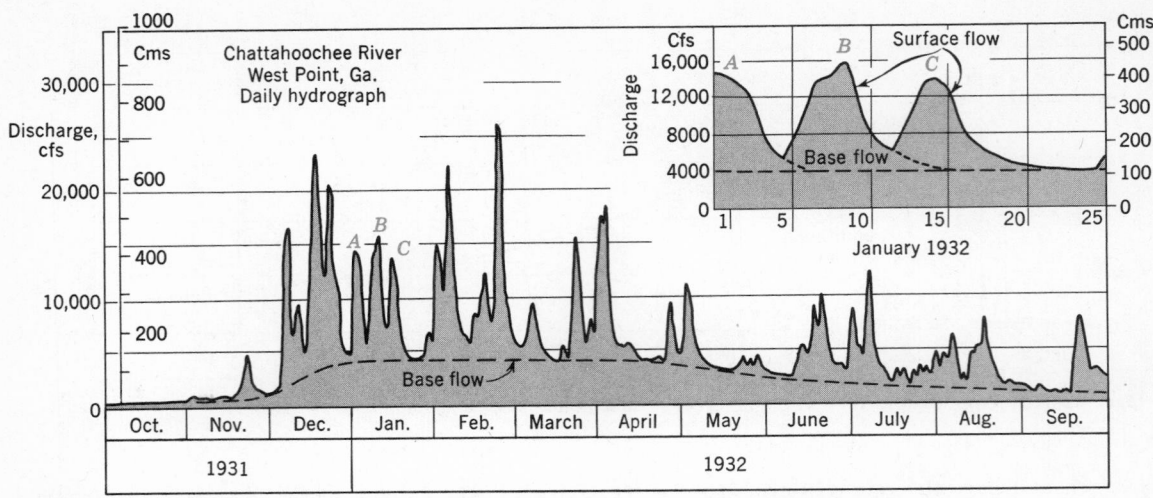

Figure 20.12   Flow peaks of the Chattahoochee River. (After E. E. Foster, *Rainfall and Runoff.*)

days, the discharge rises to another peak. The enlarged inset graph, showing details of the month of January, reveals how this effect occurs. Where a long period intervenes between storms, the discharge falls to a low value, the base flow, where it levels off. Throughout the year the base flow, which represents ground water inflow into the stream, undergoes a marked annual cycle. During the period of recharge (winter and early spring), water table levels are raised and the rate of inflow into streams is increased. For the Chattahoochee River, the rate of base flow during January, February, March, and April holds uniform at about 4000 cfs (110 cms). As the heavy evapotranspiration losses of spring reduce soil water, and therefore cut off the recharge of ground water by downward percolation (see Chapter 9), the base flow falls steadily. The decline continues through the summer, reaching by the end of October a low of about 1000 cfs (30 cms) supplied entirely from base flow.

Finally, examine the hydrograph of the Missouri River at Omaha, Nebraska, from October 1940, to September 1942 (Figure 20.13). This great river, draining 322,800 sq mi (840,000 sq km) of water-

shed, is a major tributary of the Mississippi River. Note that the discharge, ranging from 10,000 to 100,000 cfs (280 to 2800 cms), is many times greater than the discharges of smaller streams considered thus far. High rates of flow are chiefly from snowmelt, which occurs on the High Plains in spring and in the Rocky Mountain headwater areas in early summer. This event explains the sudden high discharges from April through June. During midwinter, when soil moisture is frozen and total precipitation small over the watershed as a whole, the discharge rises little above the base flow. Ground water recharge occurring in the spring raises summer levels of base flow to about 20,000 cfs (570 cms), or two to three times the winter base flow.

Floods

In our modern day of newspapers, movies, and television, everyone has seen enough pictures of river floods to have a good idea of the appearance of flood waters and the havoc wrought by their erosive power and by the silt and clay that they leave behind. Nevertheless, even the hydraulic engineer may not be fully satisfied that he can

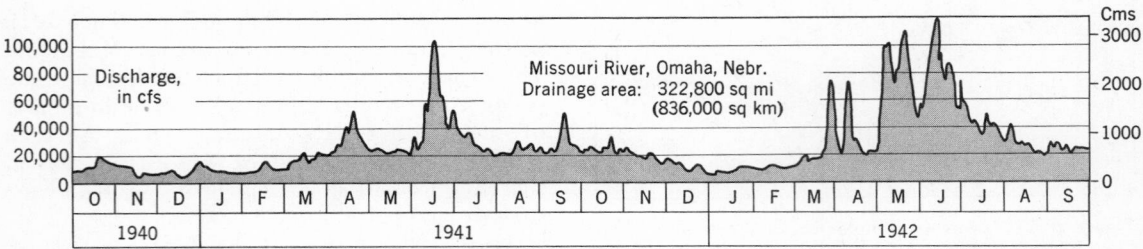

Figure 20.13   Discharge of the Missouri River. (After E. E. Foster, *Rainfall and Runoff.*)

exactly define the term *flood*. Perhaps it is enough to say that a condition of flood exists when the discharge of a river cannot be accommodated within the margins of its normal channel, so that the water spreads over adjoining ground upon which crops or forests are able to flourish.

Most larger streams of humid climates have a *floodplain*, a belt of low flat ground bordering the channel on one or both sides inundated by stream waters about once a year, at the season when abundant supplies of surface water combine with effects of a high water table and ample soil moisture to supply more runoff than can stay within the heavily scoured troughlike channel (Figure 20.14). Such annual inundation is considered a flood, even though its occurrence is expected and does not prevent the cultivation of crops after the flood has subsided, or does it interfere with the growth of dense forests which are widely distributed over low, marshy floodplains in all humid regions of the world. Still higher discharges of water, the rare and disastrous floods which may occur as infrequently as a decade or longer, inundate ground lying above the floodplain, principally affecting broad steplike expanses of ground known as *terraces* (Figure 20.15).

For practical purposes, the U.S. Weather Bureau, which provides a flood-warning service, designates a particular stage of gauge height at a given place as the *flood stage*, implying that the critical level has been reached above which overbank flooding may be expected to set in. Immediately at or below flood stage the river may be described as being in the *bank-full stage*, the flow being entirely within the limits of the heavily scoured channel.

Downstream progress of a flood wave

The rise of a river stage to its maximum height, or *crest*, followed by a gradual lowering of stage, is termed the *flood wave*. The flood wave is simply a large-sized rise and fall of river discharge of the type already analyzed in earlier paragraphs, and follows the same principles. Figure 20.16*A* shows the downstream progress of a flood on the Chattooga-Savannah river system. In the Chattooga River near Clayton, Georgia, the flood peak or crest was quickly reached—one day after the storm—and quickly subsided. On the Savannah River, 65 mi (105 km) downstream at Calhoun Falls, South Carolina, the peak flow occurred a day later, but the discharge was very much larger because of the larger area of watershed involved. Downstream another 95 mi (153 km), near Clyo, Georgia, the Savannah River crested five days after the initial storm with a discharge of over 60,000 cfs (1700 cms). This set of three hydrographs

Figure 20.14 The Wabash River in flood near Delphi, Indiana, February 1954. An ice dam clogs the river channel, while lines of trees mark the crest of the bordering natural levees. The floodplain itself is inundated on both sides of the channel and reaches to the base of the bluff, at left. (U.P.I. Telephoto.)

shows that (*a*) the time lag in occurrence of the crest increases downstream, (*b*) the entire period of rise and fall of flood wave becomes longer downstream, and (*c*) the discharge increases greatly downstream as watershed area increases.

Figure 20.16*B* is a somewhat different presentation of the same flood data, in that the discharge is given in terms of a common unit of area, the square mile, thus eliminating the effect of increase in discharge downstream and showing us only the shape or form of the flood crest.

Flood prediction

The U.S. Weather Bureau operates a River and Flood Forecasting Service through 85 selected offices located at strategic points along major river systems of the United States. Each office issues river and flood forecasts to the communities within

Figure 20.15   The city of Hartford was partly inundated by the Connecticut River flood of March 1936. The river channel is to the left, its banks marked by a line of trees. (Official Photograph, 8th Photo Section, A. C., U.S. Army.)

the associated district, which is laid out to cover one or more large watersheds. Flood warnings are publicized by every possible means. Close co-operation is maintained with such agencies as the American Red Cross, the U.S. Army Corps of Engineers, and the U.S. Coast Guard, in order to plan evacuation of threatened areas, and the re-moval or protection of vulnerable property.

Long and intensive study of stream flow data enables the U.S. Weather Bureau to prepare graphs of flood stages telling the likelihood of occurrence of given stages of high water for each month of the year. Figure 20.17 shows expectancy graphs for four selected stations. The meaning of the strange looking bar symbols is explained in the

key. The Mississippi River at Vicksburg illustrates a great river corresponding largely to spring floods so as to yield a simple annual cycle. The Colorado River at Austin, Texas, is chosen to illustrate a river draining largely semi-arid plains. Summer floods are produced directly by torrential rains from invading moist tropical air masses. Floods of the late summer and fall are often attributable to tropical storms (hurricanes) moving inland from the Gulf of Mexico. The Sacramento River at Red Bluff, California, has a winter flood season when rains are heavy, but a sharp dip to low stages in late summer, which is the very dry period for the California coastal belt. The flood expectancy graph for the Connecticut River at Hartford shows two

Figure 20.16 The downstream progress of a flood wave. (After Hoyt and Langbein, *Floods*.)

seasons of floods. The more reliable of the two is the early spring, when snowmelt is rapid over the mountainous New England terrain; the second, in the fall, when rare but heavy rainstorms, some of hurricane origin, bring exceptional high stages.

Flood control

In the face of repeated disastrous floods, vast sums of money have been spent on a wide variety of measures to reduce and control floods. The economic, social, and political aspects of flood control are beyond the scope of this book, but mention can be made of certain physical principles applied to the problem. Two basic forms of control are: (*a*) to detain and delay runoff by various means on the ground surfaces and in smaller tributaries of the watershed; (*b*) to modify the lower reaches of the river where floodplain inundation is expected.

The first form of control is aimed at treatment of watershed slopes, usually by reforestation or planting of other vegetative cover so as to increase the amount of infiltration and reduce the rate of overland flow. This type of treatment, together with construction of many small flood-storage dams

in the valley bottoms, may greatly reduce the flood crests and allow the discharge to pass into the main stream over a longer period of time.

Under the second type of flood control, designed to protect the floodplain areas directly, two quite different theories can be practiced. First, the building of *levees*, or *dikes*, parallel with the river channel on both sides can function to contain the overbank flow and prevent inundation of the adjacent floodplain (Figure 20.18). Such levees are broad embankments built of earth and must be designed with great care, not only to possess the physical resistance to water pressures, but must be high enough to contain the greatest floods; otherwise they will be breached rapidly by great gaps, termed *crevasses*, at the points where water spills over (Figure 20.19). Under the control of the Mississippi River Commission, which began in 1879, a vast system of levees was built along the Mississippi River in the expectation of containing all floods. Figure 20.18 shows such a levee during the flood of 1903, when it was necessary in Louisiana to add to the top of the levee by means of planks and sand-filled bags for a distance of 71 mi (114 km) to prevent overflow. Levees have been continuously improved and now total more than 2500 mi (4000 km) in length and in places are as high as 30 ft (10 m). Additional levees on the lower, or deltaic, alluvial plain form floodways, by means of which excessive discharges can be diverted in time of flood and passed directly to the sea.

The second theory, practiced in more recent years on the Mississippi River by the U.S. Army Corps of Engineers, is to shorten the river course by cutting channels directly across the great meander loops to provide a more direct river flow. Shortening has the effect of increasing the river slope, which in turn increases the mean velocity. Greater velocity enables a given flood discharge to be moved through a channel of smaller cross-sectional area; the flood stage is correspondingly reduced. Channel improvement has had a measurable effect in reducing flood crests along the lower Mississippi and the levees are thus not in such great danger of being overtopped. Certain parts of the floodplain are also set aside as temporary basins into which the river is to be diverted according to plan to reduce the flood crest. This planned flooding can make use of the least populated parts of the floodplain.

Ground water

The relation of soil water to ground water, and the distinction between zones of aeration and saturation were treated briefly in Chapter 9. We turn now to consider the distribution and move-

Figure 20.17   The highest water stage that occurred in each month is given in terms of percentages on these graphs of four rivers. (After U.S. Weather Bureau.)

Figure 20.18 This old photograph shows the artificial levee of the Mississippi River near Greenville, Mississippi, during the great flood of March 1903. A crevasse, or break, at the distant point, *x*, is discharging flood water into the lower flood plain on the left. (Mississippi River Commission photograph.)

ment of ground water and its geologic and economic aspects.

Table 20.1 summarizes the earth's water resources and shows how the total quantity of soil and ground water (subsurface water) compares with that held as surface water on the lands, as glacial ice, as atmospheric moisture, and as water in the world ocean. Note that the volume of ground water is vastly greater than that held in lakes and streams, but is itself less than one-third of the volume held as ice of icecaps and glaciers. Ground water is subdivided into that less than a half-mile (0.8 km) in depth, which is largely extractable for man's use, and that below a half-mile, much of which is not economically recoverable.

Figure 20.19 This air view taken in April 1952, shows a break in the artificial levee adjacent to the Missouri River in western Iowa. Water is spilling from the high river level at right to the lower floodplain level at left. (Photograph by Forsythe, U.S. Department of Agriculture.)

Pore spaces in the ground water zone

Ground water can saturate a great variety of geological materials ranging from relatively soft overburden, of both residual and transported types, to hard bedrock of any origin. The term

TABLE 20.1   DISTRIBUTION OF THE WORLD'S ESTIMATED WATER[a]

Location	Surface Area		Water Volume		Percent of Total
	Sq Mi	Sq Km	Cu Mi	Cu Km	
SURFACE WATER					
Fresh-water lakes	330,000	860,000	30,000	125,000	0.009
Saline lakes and inland seas	270,000	700,000	25,000	104,000	0.008
Average in stream channels	—	—	300	1,250	0.0001
SUBSURFACE WATER					
Soil moisture and intermediate-zone (vadose) water	50,000,000	130,000,000	16,000	67,000	0.005
Ground water within 0.5 mi (0.8 km) depth	50,000,000	130,000,000	1,000,000	4,200,000	0.31
Ground water, deep-lying	50,000,000	130,000,000	1,000,000	4,200,000	0.31
Total liquid water in land areas	50,600,000	132,000,000	2,070,000	8,630,000	0.635
ICECAPS AND GLACIERS	6,900,000	18,000,000	7,000,000	29,200,000	2.15
ATMOSPHERE	197,000,000	510,000,000	3,100	13,000	0.001
WORLD OCEAN	139,500,000	360,000,000	317,000,000	1,322,000,000	97.2
Totals (rounded)			326,000,000	1,360,000,000	100

[a] Data from Dr. Raymond L. Nace, U.S. Geological Survey, 1964.

porosity refers to the total volume of pore space present in a given volume of rock. The amount of water that can be held in storage in a rock is measured by its porosity. A knowledge of rocks enables us to understand something of the variation in porosity that might be expected in rocks. Among the sedimentary rocks, the coarse-grained clastic rocks, such as sandstone or conglomerate, can have large porosity. Similarly, any transported overburden consisting of sands and gravels laid down by streams or shore currents will have large porosity. Shale, because of its dense compaction, has relatively low porosity, but soft clay or mud, by contrast, has high porosity even though the pores are extremely tiny. Limestones may have large openings, such as caverns, produced by solution of the rock. Scoriaceous lavas commonly have great porosity.

Dense, massive rocks, such as the igneous and metamorphic types, have little or no pore space between the individual mineral crystals, but the presence of numerous fractures, such as joints and faults, offers a large number of interconnected openings in which water can be stored and through which it can move. In sedimentary strata the bedding planes may provide additional openings.

How far down into the earth does the ground water zone extend? No single depth can be stated in answer to this question, but it is certain from experience with deep wells that water becomes very scanty at depths of more than 2 mi (3.2 km). Furthermore, geologists have evidence that at depths greater than about 10 mi (16 km), rock is under such great pressure that it yields by slow flowage, tightly closing any natural openings in the rock and preventing any water from entering or remaining in the rock. We may call this the *region of rock flowage* and say that it limits the extent of the ground water body in depth.

Still another property besides porosity determines whether ground water will move through a rock mass. This is *permeability*, or the ease with which water may be forced through the rock. Obviously, pore spaces in a rock, even though large, may offer no free passage to water if each pore is sealed off from its neighbors by mineral matter. Thus the degree to which openings are interconnected is important in determining permeability.

Second, the size of the openings exerts a strong influence upon rate of flow. Coarse sands or gravels permit rapid flow and are therefore rated as highly permeable materials. The microscopic pores of a clay impede flow of water so effectively that clays and rocks containing much clay are commonly *impermeable* (not permeable), at least for practical purposes of obtaining useful flow of water from them. Although intrusive igneous rocks are highly impermeable where massive and not decomposed, they may actually constitute highly permeable bodies if broken by numerous, closely set systems of joints and fractures.

The water table

Ground water is extracted for man's use from wells dug or drilled to reach the ground water zone. In the ordinary shallow well, water rises to the same height as the ground water table (not including the capillary fringe). The upper limit of saturation is actually at the upper limit of the capillary fringe (Chapter 9).

If wells are numerous in an area, the position of the water table can be mapped in detail by plotting the water heights and noting the trends in elevation from one well to the other. When this is done it is usually seen that the water table is highest under the highest areas of surface, namely, hilltops and divides, but descends toward the valleys where it may appear at the surface close to streams, lakes, or marshes (Figure 20.20). The reason for such a configuration of the water table is that water percolating down through the zone of aeration tends to raise the water table, whereas seepage into streams, swamps, and lakes tends to draw off ground water and to lower its level.

Because ground water moves extremely slowly, a difference in water table level, or *head*, is built up and maintained between areas of high elevation and those of low elevation. In periods of excessive rainfall this head is increased by rise in water table over divide areas; in drought periods the water table slowly falls (Figure 20.20). Large fluctuations such as these are usually seen only in periods of excessive rain or drought lasting several years, but in humid, middle-latitude regions of strong seasonal contrasts, a distinct annual cycle of rise and fall of water table is present. This cycle is illus-

Figure 20.20 The water table conforms to surface topography.

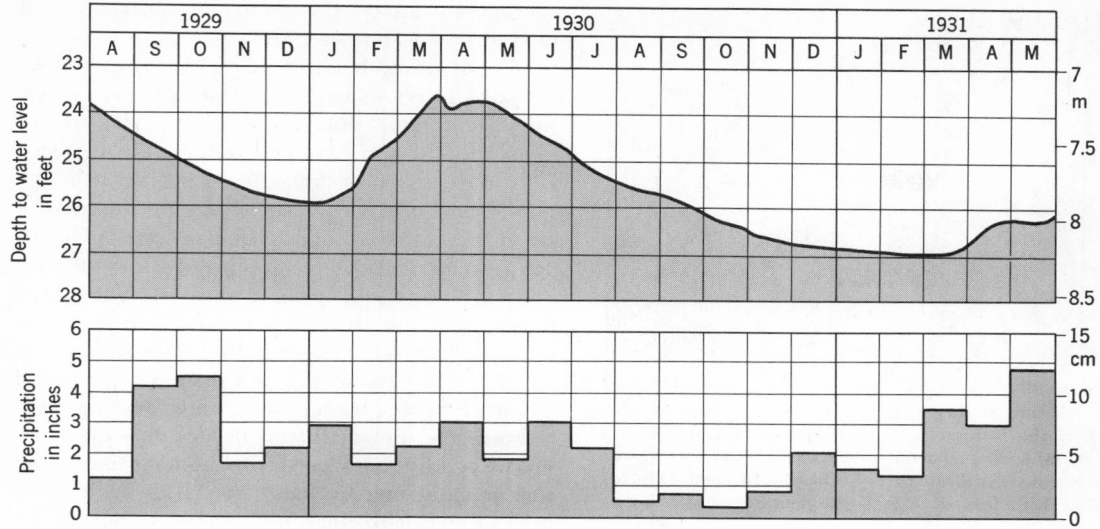

Figure 20.21   Water level in an observation well at Washington, D.C. (After Meinzer.)

trated in the graphical record of water table and precipitation by months based on the level of an observation well at Washington, D.C., extending from 1929 to 1931 (Figure 20.21). These were unusually dry years. Note that the water table dropped steadily in the latter part of 1929, even though considerable rain fell in September and October. This continued drop is explained by the fact that the soil belt and intermediate belt absorbed and held all of the water which infiltrated the surface, allowing none to get down to the water table. By late winter, however, considerable amounts of water were reaching the ground water zone, because the overlying belts in the zone of aeration had taken up all the water they could hold. Such a rise in water table illustrates the *recharge* of ground water supplies by percolation of surface water.

Aquifers, aquicludes, perched water tables, and artesian wells

Where rock layers lie nearly horizontal, or in gently inclined positions, the ground water relations may be quite different from the simple pattern illustrated in Figure 20.20 in which completely uniform geologic materials were assumed to exist. Suppose, for example, that the region is one of sedimentary strata with beds of sandstone alternating with beds of shale (Figure 20.22). Sandstone is commonly both porous and permeable, providing a large ground water storage reservoir through which water may move easily. Such a rock body is termed an *aquifer*. By contrast, a shale bed with low permeability virtually prevents flow of ground water and is called an *aquiclude*. In the particular case shown in Figure 20.22, a

thin bed of shale has effectively blocked the downward percolation of water to the main water table below, creating a *perched water table*, separated from the main water table by a zone of aeration. Where the perched water table meets the valley side a *seep* or *spring* (that is, a slow flow of water emerging from the ground) is formed.

Most natural springs are mere trickles of water, unseen and unnoticed under a cover of dense vegetation. A few springs, however, discharge enormous volumes of water where an unusually good aquifer, abundantly fed from a large source area, is exposed in a deep valley or canyon (Figure 20.23).

Where strata are inclined (dipping) a favorable situation may exist for development of an *artesian* spring or well, one in which the water flows upward toward the surface through its own pressure. In Figure 20.24 we see a highly diagrammatic representation of such conditions, the vertical exaggeration being very great merely to show the principle. The eroded edge of a sandstone aquifer is exposed to intake of water at a high position.

Figure 20.22   A perched water table.

Figure 20.23 Thousand Springs, Idaho, emerges from the north side of the Snake River Canyon, opposite the mouth of the Salmon River. The spring extends for 0.5 mi (0.8 km) and issues from a scoriaceous basalt layer with a nearly constant discharge of 500 cfs (14 cms). (Photograph by I. C. Russell, U.S. Geological Survey.)

Figure 20.24 Geological conditions for artesian flow.

Water entering here passes deep underground to a position below the valley floor, at which point the water is under a strong pressure, or head, from the weight of the overlying water. This pressure is sufficient to force water up to the surface in a well drilled down through the impervious shale layer into the aquifer. Similar flow as an artesian spring may occur naturally if there are faults in the strata which permit water to seep upward through the shale layer.

Pumping, drawdown, and recharge of wells

Of increasing importance in economic geography is the effect on the water table of man's withdrawals of ground water. The drilling of vast numbers of wells, from which water is forced out in great volumes by powerful pumps, has profoundly altered nature's balance of ground water recharge and loss, which is a part of the hydrologic cycle. Increased urban populations and industrial developments require larger water supplies, needs

that cannot always be met from construction of new surface water reservoirs.

In agricultural lands of the semi-arid and desert climates, heavy dependence is placed upon irrigation water from pumped wells, especially since many of the major river systems have already been fully developed for irrigation from surface supplies. Wells can be drilled within the limits of a given agricultural or industrial property, and hence can provide immediate supplies of water without need to construct expensive canals or aqueducts. A few of the physical principles of water wells are treated here to aid the geography student in understanding the basis of complex economic and legal problems arising from ground water development.

Formerly the small well needed to supply domestic and livestock needs of a home or farmstead was actually dug by hand as a large cylindrical hole, lined with masonry where required. By contrast, the modern well put down to supply irrigation and industrial water is drilled by powerful machinery which may bore a hole 12 to 16 in (30 to 40 cm) or more in diameter to depths of 1000 ft (300 m) or more, although much smaller-scaled wells and well-boring machines suffice for domestic purposes. Drilled wells are sealed off by metal casings which exclude impure near-surface water and prevent clogging of the tube by caving of the walls. Near the lower end of the hole, where it enters the aquifer, the casing is perforated so as to admit the water through a considerable surface area. Rate of flow of a well or spring is stated in units of gallons or liters per minute or per day. The yields of single wells range from as low as a few gallons per day in a domestic well to many millions of gallons per day for large, deep industrial or irrigation wells.

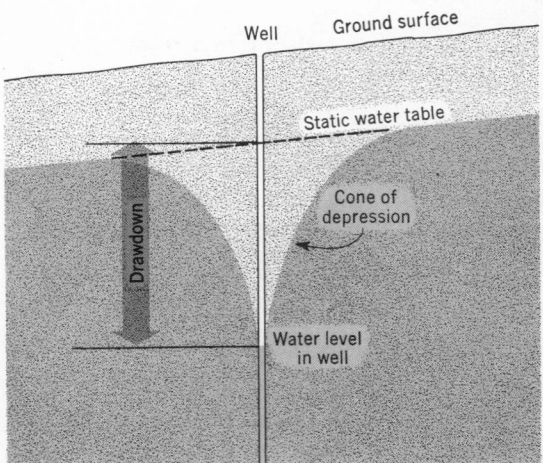

Figure 20.25 Drawdown and cone of depression in a pumped well.

In most wells, powerful pumps can easily bring water to the surface more rapidly than it can enter the well, so that the delivery of ground water is limited by the properties of the aquifer rather than by the mechanical equipment. Figure 20.25 shows the effects of rapid pumping. The rate at which water can enter the well depends on the permeability of the aquifer, which limits the rate of flow of water through the aquifer from the surrounding area. Flow of ground water is extremely slow, in any case, compared to flow of streams. It is estimated that ground water may move at a speed of 5 ft (1.5 m) per day through a formation in which wells of good yield are developed, that in exceptional cases of coarse gravels the velocity may reach 30 to 60 ft (10 to 20 m) per day. In dense clays and shales the rate may be immeasurably slow.

When rate of pumping of the well exceeds the rate at which water can enter, the level of water in the well drops and the surrounding water table is lowered in the shape of a conical surface, termed the *cone of depression*, the height of which is termed the *drawdown* (Figure 20.25). By producing a steeper gradient of the water table, the flow of ground water toward the well is also increased, so that the well will yield more water. This holds only for a limited amount of drawdown, beyond which the yield fails to increase. The cone of depression may extend as far out as 8 to 10 mi (13 to 16 km) or more from a well where very heavy pumping is continued. Where many wells are in operation, their intersecting cones produce a general lowering of the water table.

Depletion often greatly exceeds the rate at which the ground water of the area is recharged by percolation from rain or from the beds of streams. In an arid region, much of the ground water for irrigation is from wells driven into thick sands and gravels which are lowland deposits of transported overburden of a type termed *alluvium*. (These features are described in Chapter 21.) Recharge of such deposits depends on the seasonal flows of water from streams heading high in adjacent mountain ranges. Where such highly permeable materials exist, the extraction of ground water by pumping can greatly exceed the recharge by stream flow. Cones of depression deepen and widen; deeper wells and more powerful pumps are then required. Overdrafts of water accumulate and the result is exhaustion of a natural resource not renewable except by long lapses of time. In humid areas where annual rainfall is copious—from 30 to 50 in (75 to 125 cm) annually—natural recharge is by general percolation over the ground area surrounding the well. Here the prospects of achieving a balance of recharge and withdrawal are highly favorable through the control of pumping

and the return of waste waters or stream waters to the ground water table by means of other wells in which water flows down, rather than up.

Natural discharge of ground water

The subsurface phase of the hydrologic cycle is completed when the ground water emerges along lines or zones where the water table intersects the ground surface. Such places are the channels of streams and the floors of marshes and lakes. By slow seepage and spring flow the water must emerge in sufficient quantity to balance that which enters the ground water table by percolation through the zone of aeration.

Contrary to what the average person might predict, all of the ground water does not move directly from divides to the lines of seepage by flow close to the top of the water table. If such were the case, the lower parts of the ground water body would be stagnant. Certain geological phenomena, such as the cementation of rocks and the transfer of dissolved mineral matter from place to place, would not take place without some ground water flow, even though extremely slow.

Figure 20.26 shows the theoretical paths of flow of ground water as calculated by use of basic principles of the physics of fluids. Water follows paths curved concavely upward. Water entering the slope midway between divide and stream flows rather directly. Close to the divide point on the water table, however, the flow lines go almost straight down to great depths in the earth from which they recurve upward to points under the streams. Progress along these deep paths would be incredibly slow; that near the surface would be faster. The most rapid flow is encountered close to the line of discharge in the stream, where the arrows are shown to converge.

Of considerable interest in economic geography of coastal regions is the problem of the relation of fresh ground water to salt ground water, because wells put down close to the shore may encounter salt water, or may, through overdraft, cause salt

Figure 20.26 Theoretical paths of ground-water movement under divides and valleys. (After M. K. Hubbert.)

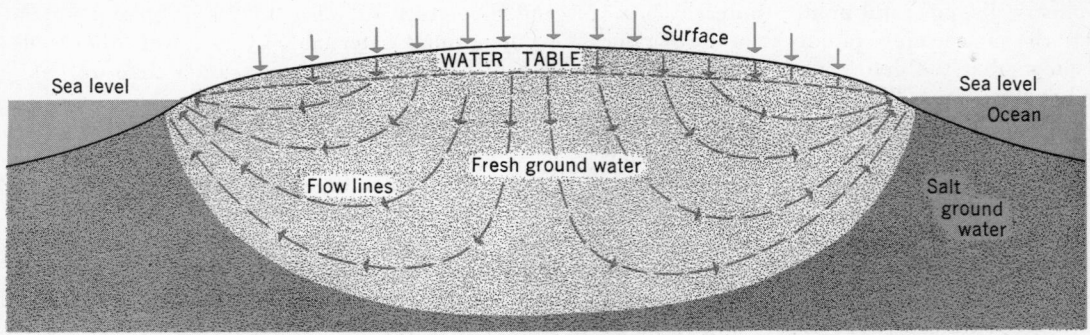

Figure 20.27   Fresh-water and salt-water relations in an island or peninsula. (After G. Parker.)

water to be drawn into the well and render it unfit for use. Figure 20.27 shows an idealized diagram through an island or a narrow peninsula. The body of fresh ground water takes the shape of gigantic lens with convex faces, except that the upper surface has only a broad curvature whereas the lower surface, in contact with the salt ground water, bulges deeply downward. Because fresh water is less dense than salt, we can think of this fresh water lens as floating upon the salt water, pushing it down much as the hull of an ocean liner pushes aside the surrounding water. The ratio of densities of fresh water to salt water is as 40 to 41. Hence, if the water table is, say, 10 feet above sea level, the bottom of the fresh water lens will be located 400 feet below sea level, or forty times as deep as the water table is high with respect to sea level.

The fresh ground water extends seaward some distance beyond the shoreline. Although the salt ground water is stagnant, the fresh water travels in the curved paths shown by arrows in Figure 20.27. If water is pumped excessively from wells close to the coast, the contact of salt with fresh ground water shifts landward, where it may intersect the wells and contaminate the fresh water.

When such a condition exists, the only cure is to cease pumping and allow the fresh water slowly to push the contact back toward its original seaward position, or to create a fresh water recharge barrier between the wells and the coastline. Resumed pumping must then be regulated to a lower rate.

REFERENCES FOR FURTHER STUDY

Foster, E. E. (1948), *Rainfall and runoff*, The Macmillan Co., New York, 487 pp.

Thomas, H. E. (1951), *The conservation of ground water*, McGraw-Hill Book Co., New York, 321 pp.

Leopold, L. and T. Maddock, Jr. (1954), *The flood control controversy*, The Ronald Press Co., New York, 255 pp.

Bennett, H. H. (1955), *Elements of soil conservation*, second edition, McGraw-Hill Book Co., New York, 358 pp.

Hoyt, W. G. and W. B. Langbein (1955), *Floods*, Princeton University Press, Princeton, N.J., 469 pp.

U.S. Dept. of Agriculture (1955), *Water; yearbook of agriculture 1955*, U.S. Govt. Printing Office, Washington, D.C., 751 pp.

Todd, D. K. (1959), *Ground water hydrology*, John Wiley and Sons, New York, 336 pp.

1. What are the general characteristics of a natural drainage system? What is the shape of the drainage basin?

2. What branches of earth science deal with runoff and drainage systems? What governmental agencies take responsibility for various phases of this study? In what ways is a knowledge of principles of runoff of value to the student of geography?

3. Distinguish between overland flow and channel flow. To what extent is overland flow observable? How does flow in shoestring rills fit into this classification of types of flow?

4. Describe the development of overland flow, beginning with the onset of rainfall. What is interception? Surface detention? What equation relates overland flow to precipitation and infiltration?

5. How does the geologic norm of soil erosion differ from accelerated soil erosion? What is the role of splash erosion? What forms of land surface treatment bring about accelerated land erosion? Explain. How is the degree of ground slope a factor in intensity of soil erosion?

6. Describe the successively more severe forms of accelerated soil erosion. What happens to the eroded soil? Distinguish between *colluvium* and *alluvium*. In what ways is sedimentation harmful?

7. List the various geometrical elements of a stream channel, state how each is defined and measured. Explain the meaning of "percent of grade."

8. Describe the manner in which velocity varies throughout a stream, both across the channel and in vertical section. Why is the velocity not the same in all parts of the stream?

9. What is stream turbulence? What role does it play in stream transportation?

10. What is the mean velocity of a stream? State and explain in words the equation relating discharge to area and mean velocity.

11. Describe the methods and equipment used in stream gauging. What governmental agency is responsible for stream gauging in the United States? How is mean velocity actually measured and computed?

12. What is a hydrograph? Describe the manner in which runoff occurs following a rainstorm on a watershed. Why is there a time lag between rainfall and runoff? For larger drainage basins, how do these relationships differ?

13. What is base flow? What supplies base flow? What is channel storage and how does it affect the hydrograph of a large watershed?

14. Describe the annual changes in base flow and surface water contributions in a watershed typical of the humid southeastern United States.

15. How is a flood defined? How can the normal channel of a river be distinguished from the adjacent floodplain? What is the bank-full stage of a stream flow?

16. Describe the progress of a flood crest down a large river. How does discharge change with increasing distance downstream? How does the form of the flood wave change?

17. What government agency supplies river and flood forecasts? How are its activities organized and what is their function?

18. How do flood expectancies differ for the Mississippi River at Vicksburg, Mississippi, and the Colorado River at Austin, Texas? Explain.

19. What basic forms of flood control are used? What principles lie behind each? What are the advantages and disadvantages of constructing extensive levee systems? How can channels be modified to reduce flood crests?

20. How does the volume of ground water on earth compare with the average volume of water held in lakes and streams? With that held in glacial ice?

21. Distinguish between porosity and permeability of rocks. Cite varieties of rocks and transported overburden to illustrate extremes of porosity and permeability. What conditions exist in the region of rock flowage?

22. Describe the form of the water table under a hilly topography. What fluctuations may be expected in the water table? What is ground water recharge and how does it take place?

23. Explain how layered rocks can cause a perched water table. How can springs be so formed? What geologic conditions are required for artesian wells and springs?

24. How does pumping cause drawdown of water table? What is the cone of depression? How far may it extend from a well? How rapidly is ground water recharged from alluvial deposits of arid regions?

25. Where is ground water discharged from the ground to become runoff? Describe the paths of ground water flow from divide to stream.

26. Describe and explain the relation of a fresh ground water body to the salt ground water beneath an island. What physical principle governs the relation of water table elevation to depth of fresh water? How is salt water contamination of wells caused?

CHAPTER 21
Landforms Made by Streams

FAR from being mere systems for disposal of excess runoff, streams are important agents of land sculpture—the principal carriers of mineral matter from the lands to the oceans. Not only is this denudational role of interest to the geomorphologist, who studies the landforms produced, but also to the student of historical geology for whom the sedimentary strata of past geologic eras can be interpreted in many instances as the deposits brought by streams from ancient land masses.

Geologic work of streams

The geologic work of streams consists of three closely interrelated activities: *erosion, transportation*, and *deposition*. Erosion by a stream is the progressive removal of mineral material from the floor and sides of the channel, whether this be carved in bedrock, or in residual or transported overburden.

Transportation consists of movement of the eroded particles by dragging along the bed, by suspension in the body of the stream, or in solution. Deposition is the progressive accumulation of transported particles upon the stream bed and floodplain, or on the floor of a standing body of water into which the stream empties. Obviously, erosion cannot occur without some transportation taking place, and the transported particles must eventually come to rest. Therefore, erosion, transportation, and deposition are simply three phases of a single activity.

Stream erosion

Streams erode in various ways, depending on the nature of the channel materials and the tools with which the current is armed. The force of the flowing water alone, exerting impact and a dragging action upon the bed, can erode poorly consolidated alluvial materials such as gravel, sand, silt, and clay, a process termed *hydraulic action*. Where rock particles carried by the swift current strike against bedrock channel walls, chips of rock are detached. The rolling of cobbles and boulders over the stream bed will further crush and grind smaller grains to produce an assortment of grain sizes. These processes of mechanical wear are combined under the term *corrasion*, or *abrasion*, which is the principal means of erosion in bedrock too strong to be affected by simple hydraulic action. Finally, the chemical processes of rock weathering—acid reactions and solution—are effective in removal or rock from the stream channel and may be designated as *corrosion*. Effects of corrosion are most marked in limestone, which is a hard rock not easily carved by abrasion, but yielding readily to the action of carbonic acid in solution in the stream water.

One interesting form produced by stream abrasion is the *pothole*, a cylindrical hole carved into the hard bedrock of a swiftly moving stream (Figure 21.1). Potholes range in diameter from a few inches to several feet; the larger ones may be many feet deep. Often a spherical or discus-shaped stone is found in the pothole and is apparently the tool, or *grinder*, with which the pothole was deepened. A spiraling flow of water in the pothole causes the grinder to be rotated at the base of the hole, thus boring gradually into the rock. Many other features of abrasion, such as plunge pools, chutes, and troughs lend variety to the rock channel of a swift mountain stream.

Stream transportation

The load of a stream is carried in three forms. Dissolved matter is transported invisibly in the

Figure 21.1 These potholes have been carved in granite in the channel of the James River, Henrico County, Virginia. (Photograph by C. K. Wentworth, U.S. Geological Survey.)

form of chemical ions. All streams carry some dissolved salts resulting from rock decomposition. Clay and silt are carried in *suspension*, that is, held up in the water by the upward elements of flow in turbulent eddies in the stream. This fraction of the transported matter is termed the *suspended load*. Sand, gravel, and still larger fragments move as *bed load* close to the channel floor by rolling or sliding and an occasional low leap.

The load carried by a stream varies enormously in the total quantity present and the size of the fragments, depending on the discharge and stage of the river. In flood, when velocities of 20 ft (6 m) per second or more are produced in large rivers, the water is turbid with suspended load. Boulders of great size may be moving over the stream bed, if the river gradient is steep. Frederick S. Dellenbaugh, a member of Major Powell's boat party which descended the Grand Canyon of the Colorado River in 1871 and 1872, wrote that as the men rested beside the river at night they could feel and hear the dull, thundering impacts of huge boulders rolled over and over on the channel bottom in the swift rapids.

The hydraulic action of flood waters is capable of excavating enormous quantities of unconsolidated materials in a short time (Figure 21.2). Not only is the channel often greatly deepened in flood, but the undermining of the banks causes huge masses of alluvium to slump into the river where the particles are quickly separated and become a part of the stream's load. This process, known as *bank caving*, is an important source of sediment during high river stages, and is associated with rapid sidewise shifts in channel position on the outsides of river bends.

Suspended loads of large rivers

The load carried by a large river is of considerable importance in planning for construction of large storage dams and in the construction of canal systems for irrigation. Sediment will be trapped in the reservoir behind a dam, eventually filling the entire basin and ending the useful life of the reservoir as a storage body. At the same time, depriving the river of its sediment in the lower course below the dam may cause serious upsets in river activity. Resulting deep scour of the bed and lowering of river level may upset the grades of irrigation systems. In designing for canal systems, the forms of artificial channels must be adjusted to the size and quantity of sediment carried by the water, otherwise obstruction by deposition or abnormal scour may follow.

The table at right gives comparative figures on the sediment loads of rivers in various stages.[1]

[1] Data from G. H. Matthes, "Paradoxes of the Mississippi," *Scientific American*, Vol. 184, pp. 19–23, 1951.

Figure 21.2 A river in flood eroded this huge trench at Cavendish, Vermont, in November 1927. An area 1 mi (1.6 km) wide and 3 mi (4.8 km) long, once occupied by eight farms, was cut away by the flood waters. Damage was great because the material consisted of sand and gravel which offered little resistance. (Photograph by Wide World Photos.)

Although information is scanty on quantity of sediment moved as bed load, the proportion of suspended load is generally very high. For the Mississippi, 90 per cent of the total load is carried in suspension. The table below shows that rivers draining semi-arid or arid lands (Missouri and Colorado) have very high suspended loads because

	Suspended Sediment Parts per Million	Fraction by Weight
Mississippi River		
Yearly average	500 to 600	1/1800 to 1/1660
Flood stage up to 2,000,000 cfs (56,600 cms)	2,600	1/400
Low stage 70,000 cfs (2,000 cms)	50 (water blue, clear)	1/2000
Missouri River		
Flood stage	20,000	1/50
Colorado River (before Hoover Dam)		
Flood stage 50,000 to 70,000 cfs (1400 to 2000 cms)	40,000	1/25
Yellow River, China		
Flood stage	Weight of solids may be greater than weight of water	

of the large expanses of barren soil from which sediment is easily swept by overland flow into the stream channels.

How channels change in flood

We tend to think of a river in flood as changing largely through increase in height of water surface, which causes channel overflow and inundation of the adjoining floodplain. Because of the turbidity of the water we cannot see the changes taking place on the stream bed, but these can be determined by sounding the river depth during stream-gauging measurements (Figure 21.3). At first the bed may be built up by large amounts of bed load supplied to the stream during the first phases of heavy runoff. This is soon reversed, however, and the bed is actively deepened by scour as stream stage rises. Thus, in the period of highest stage, the river bed is at its lowest elevation. When the discharge then starts to decline, the level of the stream's surface drops and the bed is built back up by the deposition of alluvium. In the example shown in Figure 21.3, about 10 ft (3 m) of thickness of alluvium was *reworked*, that is, moved about in the complete cycle of rising and falling stages.

Alternate deepening by scour and shallowing by deposition of load are responses to changes in the stream's ability to transport its load. The maximum quantity, or load, of debris that can be carried by a stream is a measure of the stream's *capacity*. Load is usually stated in terms of the weight of material moved through a given stream cross section in a given unit of time, commonly in units of tons per day. Total load includes both the bed load and the suspended load.

If a stream is flowing in a channel of hard bedrock, it may not be able to pick up enough alluvial material to supply its full capacity for bed load. Such conditions exist in streams occupying deep gorges and having steep gradients, so that

when flood occurs, the channel cannot be quickly deepened in response. In an alluvial river, however, where thick layers of silt, sand, gravel, and boulders underlie the channel, the rising river easily picks up and sets in motion all of the material that it is capable of moving. In other words, the increasing capacity of the stream for load is easily satisfied.

Capacity for load increases sharply with the stream's velocity, because the swifter the current the more intense is the turbulence and the stronger is the dragging force against the bed. Capacity to move bed load goes up about as the third to fourth power of the velocity. Thus, if a stream's velocity is doubled in flood, its ability to transport bed load is increased from eight to sixteen times. It is small wonder, then, that most of the conspicuous changes in the channel of a stream, such as sidewise shifting of the course, occur in flood stage, with very few important changes occurring in low water stages.

When the flood crest has passed and the discharge begins to decrease, the stream's capacity to transport load also declines. Therefore, some of the particles that are in motion must come to rest on the bed in the form of sand and gravel bars. First the largest boulders and cobblestones will cease to roll, then the pebbles and gravel, then the sand. Fine sand and silt carried in suspension can no longer be sustained, and settle to the bed. In this way the stream adjusts to its falling capacity. When restored to low stage the water may become quite clear, with only a few grains of sand rolling along the bed where the current threads are fastest.

Life history of a stream

Throughout its life history, a stream passes through a series of stages, each with certain definite characteristics (Figure 21.4). The initial stage

Figure 21.3 Changes in channel form of the San Juan River near Bluff, Utah, during the progress of a flood. (After Leopold and Maddock, U.S. Geological Survey.)

A. In the initial stage a stream has lakes, waterfalls, and rapids.

B. By middle youth the lakes are gone, but falls and rapids persist along the narrow incised gorge.

C. Early maturity brings a smoothly graded profile without rapids or falls, but with the beginnings of a flood plain.

D. Approaching full maturity, the stream has a flood plain almost wide enough to accommodate its meanders.

E. Full maturity is marked by a broad flood plain and freely developed meanders. *L* = levee; *O* = oxbow lake; *Y* = yazoo stream; *A* = alluvium; *B* = bluffs; *F* = flood plain.

Figure 21.4   Stages in the life history of a stream. (After E. Raisz.)

occurs as soon as a new land surface is created by uplift and dislocation of a portion of the earth's crust. It is assumed here for simplicity of discussion that the surface was formerly under ocean level and has now become exposed for the first time. The landscape is thus composed entirely of initial landforms. Rain falling upon the land will produce overland flow. This must flow down the initial slopes, whatever their form. Water flow will be concentrated where slight depressions exist in the slopes, thus causing the development of stream channels, which are quickly deepened by erosive

action of the water and any loose rock particles it carries. Depressions will fill up with water, making lakes. Overflow at the lowest points on the rims of these lake basins will serve to make a connected system of drainage from higher to lower lakes. Thus the initial stream system comes into existence. It is characterized by falls, rapids, and lakes along its course (Figure 21.4*A*).

Once formed, the stream enters upon the stage of *youth*. Deepening of the channel is the principal activity of a young stream, whose capacity for load exceeds the load available to it. Lake outlets are cut through, draining the lakes and extending the stream across the old lake floors. Waterfalls are cut down at the lip until they are nothing more than rapids. A deepening *gorge* or *canyon* is perhaps the most striking landform associated with a young stream. The gorge is steep-walled and has a V-shaped cross section. The stream occupies all the bottom of the gorge. From the steep walls much weathered rock material is shed into the stream. Landslides occur frequently, large fallen masses sometimes temporarily damming the stream. Talus slopes of loose rock fragments may here and there extend down into the water. Because of rapid denudation of the steep valley walls, bedrock outcrops are conspicuous, locally forming bold cliffs (Figure 21.4*B*).

The geographic importance of a young river valley can be readily imagined. There is no room for roads or railroads between the stream and the

Figure 21.6 Niagara Falls is formed where the river passes over the eroded edge of a massive limestone layer. Continual undermining of weak shales at the base keeps the fall steep. (After G. K. Gilbert and E. Raisz.)

valley sides; hence road beds must be cut or blasted at great expense and hazard from the valley sides. Maintenance is expensive because of undercutting by the stream and the sliding and falling of rock, which can wipe out or damage the road bed. Yet a young gorge may afford the only passage through a mountain range. The Royal Gorge of the Arkansas River, in the Rocky Mountain Front Range of southern Colorado, is a striking example (Figure 21.5).

Another geographic consideration is that a young stream is not navigable, even though it might otherwise have a sufficient discharge.

The steep gradients of young streams, especially at waterfalls, sometimes make them important sources of hydroelectric power (Figures 21.6, 21.7). Most large young rivers, however, do not possess abrupt drops in gradient, and so it is necessary to build dams in order to create artificially the vertical drop necessary for turbine operation. An example is the Hoover Dam, behind which lies Lake Mead occupying the canyon of the young Colorado River.

As a stream progresses through the stage of youth it removes falls and rapids from its course, creating a smooth, even gradient. Deepening of the valley becomes greatly retarded, allowing the canyon or gorge walls to be worn down to more moderate slopes (Figure 21.8).

Stream equilibrium

The stage of *maturity* is reached when the stream has completed its phase of rapid downcutting and has prepared itself a smoothly graded course. It is now in a state of balance, or *equilibrium*, in which the average rate of supply of rock waste to the stream from all its tributaries and their

Figure 21.5 The Royal gorge of the Arkansas River in the Colorado Rockies illustrates the canyon of a young river with a steep gradient. Seen above is a suspension bridge, 1053 ft (321 m) above river level. (Photograph by Josef Muench.)

Figure 21.7 This air view of Victoria Falls of the Zambezi River shows that the river has excavated a long cleft in the bedrock, probably along a fault or other zone of weakness. (Photographer not known.)

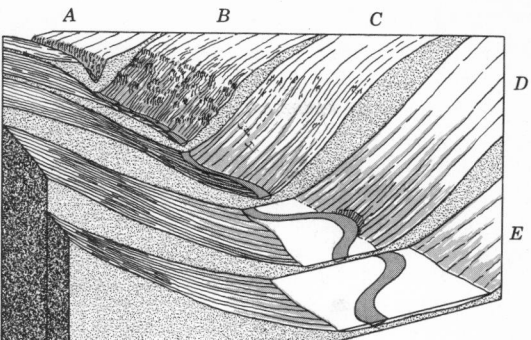

Figure 21.8 As a stream progresses from youth to maturity, its valley walls become more gentle in slope and the bedrock is covered by soil and weathered rock. (After W. M. Davis.)

slopes is equal to the average rate at which the stream can transport the load. In other words, the stream's capacity is satisfied by the load supplied.

The longitudinal profile, representing the stream channel from upper to lower end, is a profile of equilibrium (Figure 21.9). It may also be said that the stream is *graded*, which simply means that it possesses a profile of equilibrium.

It is important to understand that the balance between load and a stream's capacity exists only as an average condition over periods of many years. As already explained, streams scour their channels in flood and deposit load when in low stage. Thus in terms of conditions of the moment, a stream is rarely in equilibrium; but over long periods of time, the graded stream maintains its level by restoring those channel deposits temporarily removed by the excessive energy of flood flows.

Having attained this state of balance, the stream continues to cut sidewise on the outsides of banks. It cannot continue to cut down without destroying the equilibrium condition, but the lateral cutting does not materially affect the equilibrium (Figure 21.4C).

Figure 21.9 Longitudinal profiles of the Arkansas and Canadian rivers. The middle and lower parts of the profiles are for the most part smoothly graded, whereas the poorly graded upper parts reflect rock inequalities and glacial modifications within the Rocky Mountains. (From Gannett, U.S. Geological Survey.)

Floodplain development

Immediate evidence of the earliest stage of maturity is the beginning of development of a flat valley floor. During enlargement of a bend, the river channel shifts toward the outer part of the bend, leaving a strip of relatively flat land, or *floodplain*, on the inner side of the bend (Figure 21.10). The flood plain is built of bars composed largely of sand and gravel brought as bed load scoured from the outsides of bends immediately upstream. Innundation of the floodplain approximately yearly in frequency allows finer silt and clay to settle out over the surface, adding to the floodplain height and covering the coarser alluvium beneath.

As lateral cutting by the stream continues, floodplain strips grow wider and presently join to form more or less continuous belts along either side of the stream (Figure 21.11). The stream bends are now larger and more smoothly rounded. When the bends are developed into smooth, sinuous curves they are termed *meanders*. As valley development progresses the flood plain becomes wide enough to accommodate the meanders without cramping their form. The stream has then passed from *early maturity* to *full maturity* (Figure 21.4*E*).

The stage of early maturity of a stream is significant geographically. The floodplain, though narrow, will accommodate roads or railroads. The graded stream profile assures low, smooth grades for the roadbeds. Agriculture, impossible on the steep walls of a young valley, can be practiced on the narrow floodplain strips. With advanced maturity, the floodplain valley assumes more and more importance as a productive belt and is occupied by relatively greater numbers of persons than the upland areas between the valleys.[2] Furthermore, the absence of rapids in the stream channels

---

[2] We are speaking figuratively here, because the changes in stage of a stream's life cycle take tens or hundreds of thousands of years.

Figure 21.11 Widening of a valley by lateral cutting of a graded stream permits the free growth and cutoff of meander bends. (After W. M. Davis.)

permits navigation, although streams in the early mature stage require locks to assure navigability.

After a stream has reached full maturity, its principal activity is to widen the floodplain. Eventually the floodplain attains a width several times as great as the meander belt. By *meander belt* is meant the area included by two lines, each one drawn on the side of the meandering stream in such a way as to connect the outermost points of the bends. It is common practice for the hydraulic engineer to apply the term *alluvial river* to a freely meandering stream with a broad floodplain.

The ultimate goal to which the stream profile is being lowered is an imaginary inland extension of a sea-level surface. Below this level, which the

Figure 21.10 A graded stream cuts sidewise against the outside of a bend, leaving a flood-plain belt on the inside. (After W. M. Davis.)

Figure 21.12 This vertical air photograph, taken from an altitude of about 20,000 ft (6100 m) shows meanders, cutoffs, oxbow lakes and swamps, and flood-plain of the Hay River, Alberta (lat. 58° 55′ N, long. 118° 10′ W). (Copyright photograph by Air Photo Division, Canadian Government Department of Energy, Mines and Resources.)

geologist calls *base level*, the valleys could not be deepened. The mouth of every stream that empties into the sea is at base level. Although theoretically the remainder of the stream might eventually reach base level, all alluvial rivers have a slight gradient, due to the fact that the lands within each drainage basin still stand well above sea level, and

are shedding sediment which requires a sloping stream bed for transport.

Meanders of alluvial rivers

The floodplains of large alluvial streams have many special features of interest to the geographer (Figures 21.4*E* and 21.12). Meander bends grow as the stream undercuts the bank on the outside of the bend and deposits alluvium on the inside of the bend. These two sides of the bend are called the *undercut* and *slipoff slopes*, respectively. The bars of alluvium built on the slipoff slope are referred to as *point-bar deposits*.

The bends grow larger and larger until the channels meet, causing the intervening meander loop to be pinched off and abandoned. An occurrence of this type is called a *cutoff* (Figure 21.13). On a large river, such as the Mississippi, Missouri, or Arkansas, cutoffs are of considerable geographical importance. Where a state boundary is defined as the midline of a river, cutoffs cause portions of land within the cutoff bends to be transferred from one state to another, automatically altering

Figure 21.14 The Missouri-Kansas boundary was originally surveyed along the midline of the Missouri River, but the river has since shifted to a new course. (After U.S. Geological Survey.)

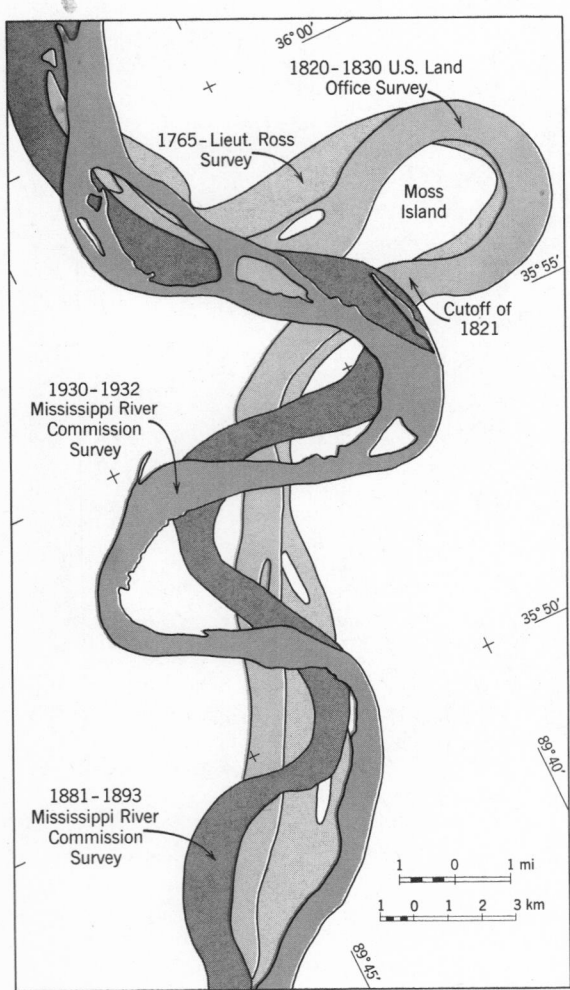

Figure 21.13 A series of four surveys of the Mississippi River shows considerable changes in the position of the channel and the form of the meander bends. Note that one meander cutoff has occurred (1821) and new bends are being formed. (After U.S. Army Corps of Engineers.)

the legal residences of persons who live on these lands and making them subject to laws and taxes of the other state. This difficulty can be overcome by fixing the boundary at a given time and maintaining it despite river changes. As a result, some maps show the old boundary meandering along a former river course quite different from the present course (Figure 21.14).

Along the Mississippi, towns grew up at many places along the steep undercut banks of meander bends. Here a river steamer could safely come close to the bank, dropping its gangplank directly upon the shore. If the meander bend was cut off the river took a new channel and the town immediately felt the effects of economic strangulation. Lakes formed by sealing off of the cutoff bend are called *oxbow lakes* (Figure 21.4E). Several oxbow lakes and marshes can be identified in Figure 21.12.

Natural levees

A floodplain, as the name implies, is normally inundated by flood stages. Unless protected by artificial levees (Chapter 20), a floodplain experiences inundation about once annually, at the season of highest runoff. Although the whole plain, from one valley wall, or *bluff*, to the other, is under water at such times (Figure 20.14), the water current is most rapid along the deep line of the river channel. Silt-bearing water, which spreads out and mingles with shallow flood waters on either side, quickly loses velocity, and much of the silt and mud settles out. Because the greatest amount of sediment settles out adjacent to the river channel there is built up by many such floods a belt of slightly higher ground, known as a *natural levee,* on both sides of the river (Figure 21.4*E*). The levee surface slopes gently downward away from the river to lower portions of the floodplain. Strangely enough, then, the highest ground on the floodplain is along the natural levees, immediately adjacent to the river. This narrow strip of ground may remain above water in all but the highest floods and is the safest place, aside from the floodplain bluffs themselves, of any on the floodplain.

Streams entering upon the floodplain cannot directly join the main river because of the levees; hence they flow down valley, parallel to the river, considerable distances until a point of entry can be found. Streams of this type are called *yazoo streams* (Figure 21.4*E*), after the Yazoo River of the Mississippi River floodplain. Heightening of the natural levees by artificial levees may prevent the river from overflowing its banks in most floods. Once the water breaks through, however, it is difficult or impossible to control and the whole floodplain between levee and bluffs is inundated (Chapter 20).

The extensive, flat lands of a broad floodplain are usually highly productive and densely populated agricultural regions. The natural levee slopes are intensively cultivated; ditches assist in the natural surface water drainage away from the river bank. Farther from the river, in the lower parts of the floodplain and in oxbows and other sections of abandoned channels, are swamps that support a dense forest of trees adapted to the wet environment. Because of natural and artificial levees, the river channel is often slowly built up to appreciably higher level than the floodplain, making these "bottom lands," as they are called, subject to repeated inundations and consequent heavy loss of life and property. Floodplains of many of the world's great rivers present serious problems of this type. In China, in 1887, the Hwang Ho inundated an area of 50,000 sq mi (130,000 sq km), causing the direct death of a million people and the indirect death of a still greater number through ensuing famine.

Braided streams and alluvial fans

When a stream is supplied with more rock waste than it can carry, the excess material is spread along the channel bottom. This is done by the stream to increase its gradient, which will in turn increase its velocity of flow and therefore increase its capacity to transport load. The process of building up the channel is termed *aggradation;* it is the opposite of *degradation,* the normal downcutting process so marked in young streams.

Aggradation gives a distinctive broad, shallow form to stream channels. The stream divides and subdivides into two, three, four, or more threads, which come together and redivide in a manner suggestive of the braided strands of rope. The term *braided stream* is, in fact, used to describe the pattern of an aggrading stream. The reason for braiding and constant shifting of the channels is that deposition of sand and gravel bars on the channel floor causes the stream to split into two or more channels which shift sideways toward lower adjacent ground. The stream thus forces itself out of its own channel. Aggrading streams are commonest in dry regions where stream flow is small, but where large quantities of rock waste are swept into stream valleys from relatively bare, unprotected valley slopes.

One very common landform built by braided, aggrading streams is the *alluvial fan,* a low cone of alluvial sands and gravels resembling in outline an open Japanese fan (Figure 21.15). The apex, or central point of the fan, lies at the mouth of a canyon, ravine, or gully and is built out upon an adjacent plain. Alluvial fans are of many sizes, ranging from tiny miniature fans a foot or two across, such as the ones seen alongside a roadcut, to huge fans many miles across.

Fans are built by young streams carrying heavy loads of coarse rock waste out from a mountain or upland region. Where the stream flows out upon the gentle slope of the plain, the current velocity is greatly reduced, thus forcing the stream to aggrade. The braided channel shifts constantly but, because it is firmly fixed in position at the canyon mouth, must sweep back and forth like the wagging

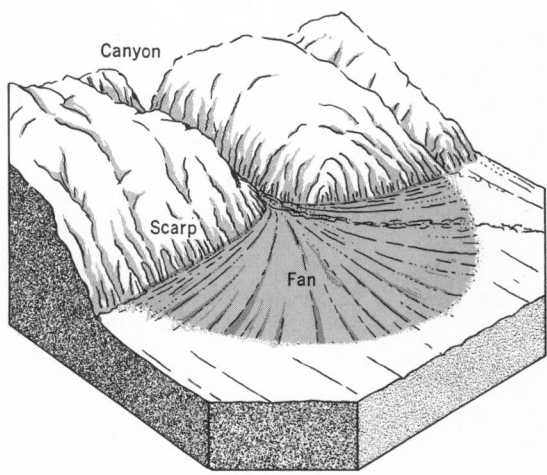

Figure 21.15 A simple alluvial fan.

Figure 21.16   A great alluvial fan in Death Valley, built of debris swept out of a large canyon.
Observe the braided stream channels. (Copyrighted Spence Air Photos.)

tail of a gigantic dog. This fixed apex accounts for the semicircular form and the downward slope in all radial directions from the apex (Figure 21.16).

Fans are of considerable geographic importance. In many mountainous regions, populations and cities are concentrated on the gentler outer fringes of alluvial fans near the base of a mountain range. Water for irrigation is diverted from the streams that issue from the canyon mouths. Artesian water can be had from wells drilled into the permeable alluvial material of which the fan is made.

A striking example of fan utilization is found in the Los Angeles basin of southern California. Flash floods have been a serious menace to such communities as Burbank, Glendale, Montrose, and Pasadena, whose favored residential districts are on the higher, inner slopes of these fans. These *debris floods*, as they are called by engineers, are distinctive in that the sediment load is very great and may include large boulders as well as sand,

silt, and clay. The floods arise on the steep slopes of mountain watersheds, especially where brush fires have destroyed protective vegetation.

Terraces

If a stream aggrades its valley for a long time the alluvial deposits may reach a thickness of many tens of feet, as Diagram *A* of Figure 21.17 shows. Among several possible causes of aggradation is the onset of a more arid climate, which reduces stream discharge and requires streams to steepen their gradients by building up their channels. A steeper gradient enables a stream to increase its ability to move coarse bed load shed from slopes unprotected by vegetative cover. Perhaps the commonest cause of aggradation in fairly recent geologic time in North America has been the advance and wasting away of great ice sheets. (See Chapter 23). Melting water from the ice was heavily charged with rock debris, which caused virtually all streams near the ice front to fill their valleys with alluvium.

With return to normal conditions of reduced load, a stream will cut down through its alluvial deposit and eventually sweep most of it out of the valley. During this degradation a series of *alluvial terraces* is formed. A terrace is a relatively flat strip of ground bounded on one side by a steeply descending slope and on the other side by a steeply rising slope. A series of alluvial terraces resembles a flight of rather broad, low steps (Figure 21.18). As indicated in Diagrams B and C of Figure 21.17, terraces are made by the stream swinging from one side of the valley to the other as it slowly cuts down through the material. As each terrace is cut, the width of the next one above it is reduced.

All older terraces would be destroyed were it not that bedrock of the valley wall here and there projects through the alluvium and protects higher terraces. In Diagram C, the valley alluvium has been largely removed, but some *rock-defended terraces* remain on the valley sides, protected from stream attack by the rock which outcrops at the points labeled R. Notice that the scarps separating terraces are curved in broad arcs concave toward the valley. The curvature is easily explained as the result of cutting of the scarps by curved meander bends.

Terraces are of geographical importance similar to that of river floodplains. The relatively flat terrace surfaces are suitable for cultivation and make good sites for towns and cities, highways, and railroads. In all these utilizations terraces have one advantage over floodplains: their surfaces may

Figure 21.17 Alluvial terraces form when a graded stream slowly cuts away the alluvial fill in its valley.

Figure 21.18 Terraces of the Shoshone River near Cody, Wyoming, indicate former positions of the river flood plain. (Photograph by Frank J. Wright.)

Figure 21.19 This air view of the Kander delta in Switzerland shows a tongue of silt-ladened water being projected into Lake Thun. (Swissair photo.)

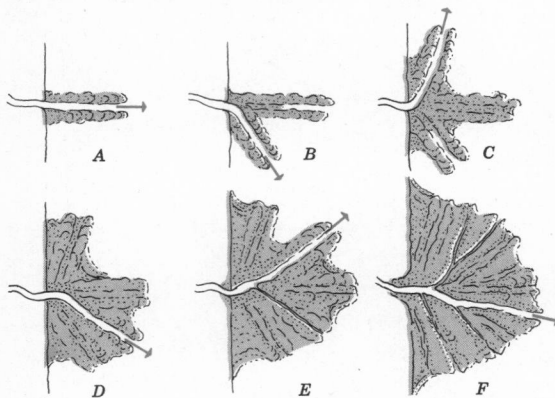

Figure 21.20 Stages in the formation of a simple delta. (After G. K. Gilbert.)

be well above the level of even the highest floods, whereas floodplains are normally subject to frequent inundation.

Deltas

The deposit of mud, silt, sand, or gravel made by a stream where it flows into a body of standing water is known as a *delta* (Figure 21.19). Deposition is caused by rapid reduction in velocity of the stream current as it pushes out into the standing water (Figure 21.20). The coarse particles settle out first; the fine clays continue out farthest and eventually come to rest in fairly deep water (Figure 21.21). Contact of fresh with salt water causes the finest clays to clot into larger aggregates which settle to the sea floor.

Deltas show a variety of shapes. The Nile delta, whose resemblance to the Greek letter "delta" suggested the name for this type of landform, has many *distributaries* which branch out in a radial arrangement (Figure 21.22*A*). Because of its broadly curving shoreline, causing it to resemble in outline an alluvial fan, this type may be described as an *arcuate* delta. The Mississippi River delta presents a very different sort of picture (Figure 21.22*B*). It is said to be of the *bird-foot* type because of the long, projecting fingers which grow far out into the water at the ends of each distributary. Where a river empties out upon a fairly straight shoreline along which wave attack is vigorous, the sediment brought out by the stream is spread along the shore in both directions from the river mouth, giving a pointed delta with curved sides. Because of its resemblance to a sharp tooth, this type is called a *cuspate* delta (Figure 21.22*C*). Where a river empties into a long, narrow estuary, the delta is confined to the shape of the estuary (Figure 21.22*D*). This type can be called an *estuarine* delta.

Figure 21.21 Structure of a simple delta shown in a vertical section. (After G. K. Gilbert.)

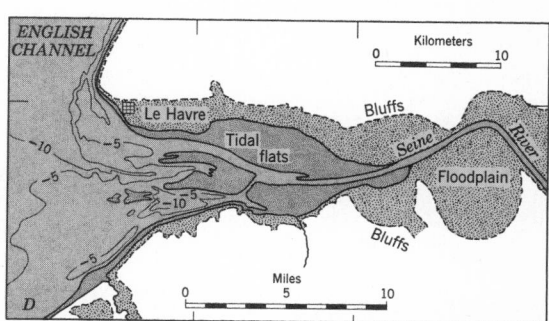

Figure 21.22 Deltas. *A*, The Nile delta has an arcuate shoreline and is triangular in plan. *B*, The Mississippi delta is of the branching, bird-foot type with long passes. *C*, The Tiber delta on the Italian coast is pointed, or cuspate, because of strong wave and current action. *D*, The Seine delta is filling in a narrow estuary.

Deltas of large rivers have been of great geographic importance from earliest historical times because their extensive flat areas support dense agricultural populations. Important coastal cities, linking ocean and river traffic, are often situated on or near deltas, as Alexandria on the Nile, Calcutta on the Ganges-Brahmaputra, Amsterdam and Rotterdam on the Rhine, Shanghai on the Yangtze, Marseilles on the Rhone, and New Orleans on the Mississippi, to mention but a few. Delta growth is often rapid, ranging from about 10 ft (3 m) per year for the Nile to 200 ft (60 m) per year for the Po and Mississippi rivers. Thus, some cities and towns that were at river mouths several hundred years ago are today several miles inland. An important engineering problem is to keep an open channel for ocean-going vessels which have to enter the delta distributaries to reach port. The ends of the Mississippi River delta distributaries, known as *passes*, have been extended by the con-struction of jetties, between which the narrowed stream is forced to move faster, thereby scouring a deep channel (Figure 21.22*B*).

Rejuvenated streams and entrenched meanders

A mature stream, which has developed a graded profile with respect to a fixed sea level at its mouth, may experience a marked change if the land rises or the sea level falls. In either event, the base level of the stream is lowered and the stream is caused to begin rapid downcutting in order to reestablish its graded profile at a lower level. This process, termed *rejuvenation*, begins as a series of rapids at the stream's mouth, where the water passes from the former mouth down to the lowered sea level. The rapids quickly shift upstream, and soon the entire stream valley is being trenched to form a new, youthful valley.

If rejuvenation occurs when a stream has

Figure 21.23 The winding valley of this stream resulted from entrenchment of the meandering river shown in Figure 21.4E. (After E. Raisz.)

Figure 21.25 The Moselle River has a winding entrenched-meandering gorge through the Eifel district of Western Germany. (Portion of German 1:100,000 topographic map, 1890.)

reached maturity, the effect is to give a steep-walled inner gorge, on either side of which lies the former floodplain, now a flat terrace high above river level (Figures 21.23 and 21.24). Meanders which the river had formed on its floodplain have now become impressed into the bedrock and give the inner gorge a meandering pattern. These sinuous bends are termed *entrenched meanders* to distinguish them from the common floodplain meanders.

Figure 21.24 The Goose-Necks of the San Juan River in Utah are entrenched river meanders in horizontal sedimentary strata. (Spence Air Photos.)

Although entrenched meanders are not free to shift about as floodplain meanders, they can enlarge slowly so as to produce cutoffs. Cutoff of an entrenched meander leaves a high, round hill surrounded on three sides by the deep abandoned river channel and on the fourth by the shortened river course. As might be guessed these hills form ideal natural fortifications. Many European fortresses of the Middle Ages were built on such cutoff meander spurs. A good example is Verdun, near the Meuse River.

Under unusual circumstances, where the bed rock includes a strong, massive sandstone formation, meander cutoff leaves a *natural bridge*, formed by the narrow meander neck (Figure 21.23). One well-known example is Rainbow Bridge at Navajo Mountain, in southeastern Utah; other fine examples can be seen in Natural Bridges National Monument at White Canyon in San Juan County, Utah.

Entrenched meanders do not offer ideal locations for railroads and highways, but in a few instances they have been the best available choices for arteries of travel. This point is well illustrated by the Moselle River, whose winding entrenched meanders through the Ardennes mountain upland of Belgium and Western Germany have been utilized (Figure 21.25). Engineers have even cut tunnels through the narrow meander necks to shorten the distance of travel.

REFERENCES FOR FURTHER STUDY

Powell, J. W. (1875), *Exploration of the Colorado River of the West and its tributaries*, U.S. Govt. Printing Office, Washington, D.C. 291 pp.

Lobeck, A. K. (1939), *Geomorphology*, McGraw-Hill Book Co., 731 pp. See Chapters 5, 6, 7.

Davis, W. M. (1954), *Geographical essays*, Dover Publications, New York, 777 pp. See pp. 514–580, 587–616.

Leopold, L. B., M. G. Wolman, and J. P. Miller (1964), *Fluvial processes in geomorphology*, W. H. Freeman, San Francisco, 522 pp.

Morisawa, M. (1968), *Streams: their dynamics and morphology*, McGraw-Hill Book Co., New York, 175 pp.

REVIEW QUESTIONS

1. What three geologic activities are carried on by a stream? Explain the ways in which stream erosion occurs. What is a pothole and how is it formed?

2. What are the modes of stream transportation? What sizes of particles are carried in each? When is bank caving of great importance?

3. How is the quantity of suspended sediment load of a stream stated? How does it vary in large rivers? Why?

4. Explain the changes in cross section of the channel of an alluvial river during a cycle of rising and falling discharge. Define stream capacity. What causes capacity to vary in a stream?

5. Describe the very first events in the formation of a new stream.

6. What features characterize the stage of youth of a stream? What is the geographical importance of young streams?

7. What event marks the attainment of the stage of maturity of streams? What is the profile of equilibrium? What is a graded stream? What is the form of the longitudinal profile of a graded stream?

8. Describe the floodplain and meanders of an alluvial river. What is the geographical importance of a floodplain?

9. Explain the following terms: undercut and slipoff slopes, point-bar deposits, cutoffs, oxbow lakes, natural levees, yazoo streams.

10. What is the lower limit to which a stream can eventually degrade its channel? What stage of stream development would be found on a peneplain?

11. When does aggradation take place in a stream? Does aggradation change the stream gradient? Explain. What is a braided stream?

12. Describe and explain the development of an alluvial fan. Where and why are alluvial fans of great importance to human beings?

13. Explain how stream terraces are formed. How did the advance and retreat of the continental ice sheet cause terraces to form in the northeastern United States?

14. Describe the stages in growth of a simple delta. What internal structures has a simple delta? How is the sediment sorted according to particle size?

15. Describe and explain the various forms commonly assumed by deltas of large rivers. Cite examples of the rates of growth of deltas.

16. How can a mature, graded river become rejuvenated? How do entrenched meanders form?

CHAPTER 22
The Cycle of Landmass Denudation

THUS far, individual types of landforms produced by weathering, mass wasting, overland flow, and streams have been examined. Consider now the entire aspect of denudation of a large region under the combined attack of these agents. Imagine an area, such as a continent or a large portion of a continent, which is elevated by internal earth movements to provide a new landmass. This elevation will constitute the *initial* stage of a grand *cycle of landmass denudation*, in which the region passes through youth, maturity, and old age. For the sake of simplicity, it must be assumed that the elevation of the landmass occurs rapidly and that further crustal deformation then ceases, leaving the denudational agents a long period of uninterrupted activity.

A single, ideal cycle of landmass denudation will not cover all occurrences. There is a difference between landform development in humid climates and that in arid climates. It is consequently necessary to describe two cycles, one for each climate. Furthermore, some initial landmasses are relatively smooth surfaced, representing an even sea floor broadly uparched by epeirogenic crustal movement. Others are mountainous because of breaking and bending of the rock during orogeny. For our purposes, two combinations will be discussed: (1) a smooth-surfaced landmass in a region of humid climate; (2) a rugged, mountainous landscape in an arid climate.

Cycle of landmass denudation in a humid climate

A landmass formed by uparching of a relatively smooth sea floor would have gentle slopes dipping seaward from the high central area. A portion of this slope is shown in Block *A* of Figure 22.1; it is said to be in the *initial stage*. Overland flow upon the new surface would drain off in the most convenient downslope direction and would soon develop initial streams. In the manner already explained in connection with the life history of a stream, these would begin to trench youthful V-shaped valleys into the initial landmass. Marshes and lakes occupying shallow depressions in the initial surface would soon be drained.

Block *B* shows a stage of *early youth* in the cycle of landmass denudation. The *relief* of the area—that is, the difference in elevation between valley bottoms and divide summits—is now increasing rapidly because the streams are cutting down rapidly, whereas between the streams there remain relatively flat portions of the initial land surface (Figure 22.2). As the valleys deepen they also widen, because rock waste is swept down the valley sides into the streams. The unconsumed areas between valleys thus are reduced in proportionate area, while the steep valley slopes increase in extent. Small tributary valleys branch out from the larger streams, further cutting into the initial landmass.

Block *C* of Figure 22.1 shows remnants of the initial land surface, between which are well-developed valley systems, but the remnants shrink in area until the greater proportion of the region consists of steep valley slopes, a stage that may be termed *late youth*. Relief has been steadily increasing as the streams have been actively downcutting. Next, however, conditions show a marked change. When the larger streams become graded and begin to form their floodplains, the increase in relief is halted. The remaining flat remnants of the initial surface are finally consumed, and the valley slopes intersect in narrow divides.

When relief has reached the maximum, the stage of *maturity* is attained (Block *D*, Figure 22.1 and Figure 22.3). From this time on, the valley floors are lowered with extreme slowness, whereas the interstream divides are rapidly lowered. Thus the relief of the region decreases steadily. Slopes become progressively lower in angle (Block *E*, Figure 22.1). Sheet wash and gravity movements no longer are so active as in previous stages.

Base level and peneplain

After a period of time much longer than was required for maturity to be reached, the landscape is reduced to a low rolling surface and may be said to have entered the stage of *old age* (Block *F*, Figure 22.1). By this time most of the streams have extremely low gradients and extensive floodplains. The ultimate goal, which would be reached if infinite time were available for its accomplishment, would be the reduction of the land to a

Figure 22.1 The cycle of land-mass denudation in a humid climate. (After E. Raisz.) *A*, In the initial stage, relief is slight, drainage poor. *B*, In early youth, stream valleys are narrow, uplands broad and flat. *C*, In late youth, valley slopes predominate but some interstream uplands remain. *D*, In maturity, the region consists of valley slopes and narrow divides. *E*, In late maturity, relief is subdued, valley floors broad. *F*, In old age, a peneplain with monadnocks is formed. *G*, Uplift of the region brings on a rejuvenation, or second cycle of denudation, shown here to have reached early maturity.

surface coinciding with sea level projected inland. To this imaginary surface is applied the word *base level*, for it is both a base toward which denudation is progressing and a water-level surface. Although the base level is attainable only in theory, a fairly close approach to it has been made in various parts of the world throughout eras of the geologic past. The word *peneplain* is given to a land surface of faint relief produced in the old-age stage of a cycle of denudation.

A peneplain is not perfectly flat but has gentle slopes. Because the streams are sluggish and the land slopes low, further denudation is extremely slow. It is not easy to set a particular figure for the number of years required for a region to pass from initial stage to old age, because this depends

upon how high the landmass was elevated to begin with and how resistant the rocks are to weathering and erosion. Perhaps it would be safe to say that in known cases in the geologic record, several million years have been required to reduce a mountain mass to a peneplain.

Sometimes a region contains zones or patches of rock far more resistant to weathering and erosion than the rock of the region as a whole. As the cycle progresses through maturity into old age, these harder rocks are left standing in prominent hills or isolated mountains, which rise conspicuously above the surrounding peneplain (Figure 22.4). To a residual hill or mountain of this type is given the name *monadnock* , named for Mount Monadnock in southern New Hampshire.

Figure 22.2   The Grand Canyon of the Yellowstone River, viewed from over Inspiration Point, illustrates a youthful canyon carved into the initial surface of a lava plateau. (U.S. Army Air Service Photograph.)

Rejuvenation

Once formed, a peneplain is usually elevated again by crustal movement. This follows the principle, stated earlier, that the internal earth forces act spasmodically, and that periods of extreme stability of a particular part of the world are ended by uparching or severe deformation.

A peneplain that is badly folded or fractured during orogeny is quickly obliterated in the erosion cycle that follows. If, however, the region is merely elevated by epeirogenic movements of a few hundred or a few thousand feet, remains of the peneplain persist for a considerable period. In Block G of Figure 22.1 this occurrence is illustrated. Similarity between this and the young stage illustrated in Block C is marked. The principal difference between the two is that the initial land surface in Block C is a former sea floor, whereas the "initial" surface in Block G is the uplifted peneplain. Drainage on the uplifted peneplain is already well established, so that the streams are merely rejuvenated and cut deep V-shaped valleys into their old shallow courses. When maturity of the second cycle is reached, the former peneplain is completely consumed, but its influence is seen generally in the accordant summits of hilltops over the region as a whole. There is no particular limit to the number of cycles a region can undergo. In some regions three or four previous cycles can be interpreted from a study of the topography.

Figure 22.3   This air view of a maturely dissected region shows a complex of stream channels and small drainage basins. (Spence Air Photos.)

Geographic aspects of the erosion cycle

The geographic importance of stage in the cycle of landmass denudation is very great. Regions in the initial stage of the cycle are relatively flat plains on which drainage is poor and marsh lands often extensive. Sandy beach deposits left by waves as the land surface emerged from beneath the sea usually produce infertile soils. An excellent example is the coastal plain region of Georgia and northern Florida. The great Okefenokee Swamp occupies a shallow depression in the former sea floor whereas long sandy strips of higher land parallel the coast. The porous sands permit plant nutrients to be leached out of the soil.

Not all regions in an initial stage have emerged from the sea; some, such as the High Plains of eastern Colorado, western Kansas, and northern Texas, were built by aggrading streams and, although remarkably flat, are well drained and do not have extensive marshes. The High Plains possess a high productivity in wheat, not only because the soil and climate are favorable but also because the flatness of the land permits enormous grain fields to be cultivated and harvested by machines.

Still other areas of initial land surface are formed by lava flows, poured out profusely to inundate the previous topography and produce a high, undulating lava plateau. This is the origin of the plateau into which the Yellowstone River

Figure 22.4 Stone Mountain, on the Piedmont upland near Atlanta, Georgia, is a striking monadnock about 1.5 mi (2.4 km) long and rising 650 ft (193 m) above the surrounding Piedmont peneplain surface. The rock is a light-gray granite, almost entirely free of joints, and has been rounded into a smooth dome by weathering processes. (Photograph by U.S. Army Air Service.)

has carved its gorge (Figure 22.2). The Snake River Plain of southern Idaho is another example. A region in youth of the cycle supports its population on the relatively flat areas between deep V-shaped valleys. Because these valleys are in a young stage they have no floodplains; hence, roads, railroads, cities, and farms are situated on the uplands. A mature region, on the other hand, has no flat uplands remaining, hence is not favorable to habitation, agriculture, or transportation. Many of the world's mountain regions are in the stage of maturity in the erosion cycle. Extremely great relief and steep slopes are the result of recent, high uplift of those portions of the earth's crust. A coastal region, on the other hand, elevated only 200 or 300 ft (60 to 90 m) above sea level, can never attain really mountainous relief because the streams can cut into the mass no more deeply than the mass itself rises above sea level. In some maturely dissected regions, the larger streams have already reached full maturity in their own individual life cycles and have sizable floodplains at the same time that the surrounding region is

extremely rugged. Under such circumstances, human activity is concentrated in the valley floors.

Regions with a humid climate in late maturity or old age of the cycle are usually favorable to agriculture. Slopes are moderate or low and are well drained. Soils tend to be thick. Destructive soil erosion can be held in check. Roads and railroads cross the rolling surface without great difficulty or follow extensively developed floodplains.

Much of the Amazon Basin is a peneplain, but because of the heavy rainfall a dense forest vegetation renders the region passable only at the cost of great labor. Low, floodplain areas bordering the mature rivers are forbidding morasses.

Peneplains that have been uplifted and trenched by valleys in a new cycle are comparable geographically to regions in young stages of the cycle of landmass denudation.

Drainage networks

Much of the earth's land surface consists of landforms produced in the cycle of denudation in a humid climate, although little is in the initial and early youth stages of the cycle because of the short duration of those stages. Thus, well-developed drainage systems characterize vast areas of the continents. Even in deserts, where a somewhat different cycle is followed by the landmass as a whole, the mountains and plateaus are dominated by drainage systems quite like those of the cycle in humid climates. It is therefore important to devote some attention to the form development, or *morphology*, of stream networks and the associated systems of slopes and drainage basins by which they are fed.

If we place a sheet of tracing paper over a topographic map, the network of stream channels can be traced and examined, as in Figure 22.5. Only the larger streams are shown on topographic maps by actual lines, but most are clearly indicated by the sharp V-bends of contours. A larger-scaled map would probably show many more small finger-tip branches than are drawn on Figure 22.5, but even a generalized map illustrates the fundamental principles. Major divides have also been drawn (dashed lines) to show the outlines of the larger watersheds.

Ground slopes converge upon the head of each channel, bringing overland flow in sufficient quantities during heavy rains to produce channel flow and keep the channel well scoured, free of soil and vegetation which might otherwise tend to

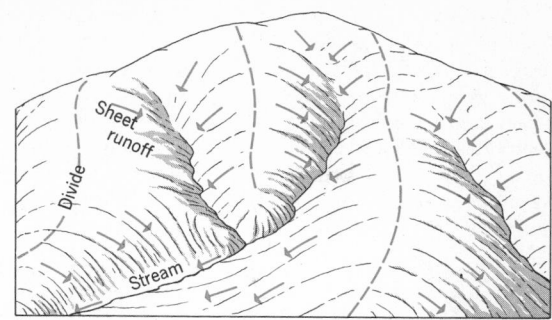

Figure 22.6 Overland flow from slopes in the headwater area of a stream system supplies water and rock debris to the smallest elements of the channel network.

obstruct and obliterate the channel (Figure 22.6). Over a long period of time, as the landmass cycle evolved through youth into maturity, the available ground has been apportioned to the individual small channels so that each receives the amount of runoff required to sustain it. Ground slopes and channel gradients have become mutually adjusted so that the rates of erosion are neither so rapid that a channel lengthens at the expense of its neighbor, nor is it so deficient in area of runoff that it becomes choked with debris of which it cannot dispose. Slow down-cutting of channels and slow lowering of slopes and divides continues, but with a general uniformity over the entire region.

Each finger-tip channel joins another, or enters a larger channel, in such a way that watersheds of increasing size are formed; exit channels are progressively larger in dimensions and discharge. Most stream junctions form acute angles, so that the discharge is carried in the general direction of the larger trunk streams in as direct a manner as possible and with as few channels as possible while, at the same time, providing each element of the stream network with an adequate area of surface runoff.

Playfair's law

Prior to about 1800 there was a widespread belief among naturalists that stream valleys and other landforms were the products of a great cataclysmic upheaval, or rending, of the earth's crust. It was supposed that streams later occupied the valleys produced in this manner, hence, that the valleys came first and were not the work of the streams themselves.

To John Playfair, an English geologist, is attributed the first clear and convincing statement of beliefs universally accepted today concerning streams and their valleys. In 1802, he published the following statement, now known as *Playfair's law*:

Figure 22.5 A drainage system consists of many small basins, each adjusted in size and shape to the magnitude of the stream it serves. Streams are shown by solid lines; divides by dashed lines.

Every river appears to consist of a main trunk, fed from a variety of branches, each running in a valley proportioned to its size, and all of them together forming a system of valleys connecting with one another, and having such a nice adjustment of their declivities that none of them join the principal valley on too high or too low a level; a circumstance which would be infinitely improbable if each of these valleys were not the work of the stream which flows in it.

The three main points of this law, restated in abstract form, are (1) valleys are proportioned in size to streams flowing in them; (2) stream junctions are accordant in level; (3) therefore, valleys are carved by the streams flowing in them, because both (1) and (2) would be "infinitely improbable" on the basis of chance alone. Exceptions occur in nature. Sometimes a tributary stream passes over a waterfall to reach the level of the master stream. Sometimes small streams occupy very large valleys. But for each of these exceptions, closer study reveals unusual or special conditions that have locally prevailed. Regions of homogeneous bedrock, which have been eroded by streams over a long period of time, invariably bear out the truth of Playfair's law.

Drainage density and texture of topography

If we study an area of badlands, the intricately eroded forms which develop in barren areas of soft clays in arid climates (Figure 22.7), we cannot fail to be impressed with the way that the landforms resemble miniature mountains. Innumerable tiny

Figure 22.7 This vertical air photograph of an area of one square mile in the Big Badlands of South Dakota illustrates ultrafine texture. (U.S. Dept. of Agriculture.)

channels carve tiny valleys to reproduce on a small scale the same great canyon and ridge forms seen in a rugged mountain range, such as the San Gabriel Range of California, or the Great Smoky Mountains of North Carolina. Evidently nature follows certain laws of geometry regardless of whether the smallest unit drainage basin is so small that one can stand astride it, or whether it is a full mile across. Because such similarity of geometry prevails in maturely eroded landmasses, it is necessary to have some means of describing and measuring the scale of magnitude of the forms.

If, for the drainage network map of Figure 22.5, we should measure the total length in miles of all channels, and divide this figure by the total area in square miles of the entire map or watershed, the *drainage density* is found:

$$\text{Drainage density} = \frac{\text{total length of streams (miles)}}{\text{area (square miles)}}$$

Suppose that a drainage density value of 12 is obtained; this is interpreted as meaning that there are twelve miles of channel for every square mile of land surface.[1]

Low drainage density, averaging three to four miles of channel per square mile, is typical of a region underlain by massive, hard, sandstone beds and under heavy forest cover. Such a region of low drainage density may be described as having *coarse texture*, since the individual elements of the topography are very large, or gross.

Medium drainage density, averaging 12 to 16, is typical of an area underlain by thin-bedded sandstones and thick shales, relatively easily eroded, but under a heavy deciduous forest cover. It is typical of large parts of the humid eastern United States where the stage of landmass erosion is mature. (See Figure 26.18.)

High drainage density, or *fine texture*, is developed in easily eroded, weak sedimentary strata where vegetative cover is sparse. Drainage density runs from 30 to 40 under such conditions. Much higher values of drainage density are found in badlands, where there may be from 200 to 500 or more miles of channel per square mile. Such topography would be described as *ultra-fine texture* (Figure 22.7).

What factors control drainage density? One highly important control is rock type. Hard, resistant rocks, such as intrusive granitic rock, gneiss, sandstone, and quartzite, tend to give low drainage density (coarse texture). This is because stream erosion is difficult and only a relatively large channel can maintain itself. In weak rocks, such as

[1]Metric units of length and area might also be used. To convert to kilometers per square kilometer multiply drainage density values by 0.62.

shales and clays, even a small watershed can supply enough runoff for channel erosion. A second factor is the relative ease of infiltration of precipitation into the ground surface and downward to the water table (see Chapter 9). Highly permeable materials, such as sand or gravel, tend to give low drainage density because infiltration is great and little water is available as surface runoff to maintain channels. Clays and shales, on the other hand, have a high proportion of surface runoff and this combines with their weakness to give high drainage density. A third major factor is the presence or absence of vegetative cover. A weak rock will have much lower drainage density in a humid climate, where a strong, dense, cover of forest or grass protects the underlying material, than in an arid region where no protective cover exists. For this reason, badlands are characteristic of arid climates, and the drainage density there tends to be markedly higher on all rock types, even the most resistant.

Cycle of landmass denudation in an arid climate

The general appearance of desert regions is strikingly different from that of humid regions, reflecting differences in both vegetation and landforms. It should be emphasized that rain falls in dry climates as well as in moist and that most landforms of desert regions are formed by running water. A particular locality in a dry desert may experience heavy rain only once in several years, but when it does fall, stream channels carry water and perform the same work as the constantly flowing streams of moist regions. Excess water runs off from the valley slopes into the streams, washing down rock particles into the channels, just as in the moister regions. We may even go further and say that, although running water is a rather rare phenomenon in dry deserts, it works with more spectacular effectiveness on the fewer occasions when it does act. This is explained by the meagerness of vegetation in dry deserts. The few small shrubs and herbs that survive offer little or no protection to soil or bedrock. Without a thick vegetative cover to protect the ground and hold back the swift downslope flow of water, excessive quantities of coarse rock debris are swept into the streams. A dry channel is transformed in a few minutes into a raging flood of muddy water, heavily charged with rock fragments.

From these statements it might be inferred that rainfall in desert regions is heavier and more violent than in moist regions. This is not true. In dry deserts, almost all rainfall is of the thunderstorm type, which is localized and intense, affecting only a small area directly under the storm. In humid middle-latitude climates there are even more frequent and heavier thunderstorm downpours, but also many prolonged periods of steady, light rain during which the soil takes in moisture and becomes fully saturated. Furthermore, the air of humid regions tends to be moist, thus reducing evaporation from the ground. Under such conditions, vegetation can grow densely and maintain its protective hold upon the ground. Water tables are high and streams are fed in part by base flow. It is true that in the humid tropics most of the rainfall is of the violent thunderstorm type, but this occurs so frequently that dense vegetation can flourish. In a dry desert the periods between rains are so prolonged that only a few species of extremely hardy plants can grow.

Because desert rainfall is so localized, a stream flowing into an adjacent dry area will evaporate rapidly, leaving its load upon the stream bed. One of the most important generalizations made about streams in desert regions is that "the streams are shorter than the slopes." Instead of long, continuously flowing streams extending to the sea, streams of desert regions are often short and terminate in alluvial fans and shallow, dry lake floors where rock waste accumulates.

A cycle of landmass denudation in an arid region is illustrated in Figure 22.8. In this ideal cycle we imagine a mountainous region formed by folding or fracturing of the earth's crust and lying in an interior part of the continent (Block *A*). Relief is at the maximum in the initial stage and diminishes throughout successive stages. Numerous large depressions exist between mountain ranges. These do not fill up with water to form lakes, as in a moist climate, but remain dry because of excessive evaporation in the hot, dry climate. The flat central parts of such depressions provide the beds of temporary lakes and are known as *playas*. Playas lakes are shallow and fluctuate considerably in level, often disappearing entirely for long periods. Because they have no outlets, playa lakes contain salt water often more strongly saline than ocean water.

Throughout the erosion cycle, the intermontane depressions become filled with rock waste as alluvial fans are built out from the adjoining mountain masses (Figure 22.9). When the basins are filled with alluvium and the mountains masses are cut up into an intricate set of canyons, divides, and peaks, the region is said to be in the *mature stage* (Block *B*, Figure 22.8). As maturity progresses, the mountains are worn lower, at the same time shrinking in size as the alluvium of the fans encroaches progressively farther inward upon the mountain base.

When *old age* is reached the mountains are represented by small islandlike remnants of their former selves (Block *C*). Eventually even these

D — Fault depression

A — Alluvium
F — Fan slopes
M — Mountains
L — Playa
R — Mountain remnants
P   Pediment

Figure 22.8   The cycle of land-mass denudation in a mountainous desert. *A*, In the initial stage, relief made by crustal deformation is at the maximum. *B*, In the mature stage, the mountains are completely dissected and the basins are filled with alluvial fan material and playa deposits. *C*, In the old stage, relief is low and alluvial deposits have largely buried the eroded mountain masses, whose remnants project here and there as islandlike groups.

remnants, which may be compared to monadnocks on a peneplain, are eroded away and a vast plain remains. This surface is a type of peneplain, but it has not been developed with reference to sea level as a base because no streams drain out to the sea, and it may, therefore, even lie many hundreds of feet above sea level. It contains shallow depressions occupied by playas rather than by floodplains of meandering rivers. Wind action in a dry climate is effective in eroding shallow depressions and in making dunes of shifting sand.

Pediments

In most deserts, the sloping surfaces of boulders, gravel, and sand which extend from the abrupt base of steep mountain faces to the flat ground

Figure 22.9 This air view of Death Valley, California, shows a mature desert landscape comparable to that shown in Figure 22.8*B*. (Copyrighted Spence Air Photos.)

of the playas are alluvial fans, underlain by thick deposits of alluvium shed by the mountains. In some places, however, this alluvium, although outwardly taking the form alluvial fans, is nothing more than a veneer perhaps 10 to 20 ft (3 to 6 m) thick, overlying a smooth sloping floor of solid bedrock. To such a rock surface, fringing a desert mountain range or cliff line, the term *pediment* is applied. On the righthand cross section of Blocks *B* and *C*, Figure 22.8, pediment surfaces are shown in profile in a narrow zone between the thick basin alluvium and the rugged mountain masses.

Because the pediment gradient is approximately the same as that of the alluvial cover upon it, and because the alluvial cover is composed of the bedload deposits of graded streams issuing from canyons in the mountain front, it is reasonable to suppose that the pediment is carved by water erosion. The larger streams will be actively down-cutting (youthful) in their upper reaches, deep within the mountain ranges. In their lower reaches, where the streams meet the flat basin floor, they are aggrading, or depositing. Therefore, in a narrow intermediate zone which lies close to the mouth of the canyon, the stream will be graded and can shift laterally to undercut the rock of adjacent mountain slopes, much as a saw blade might act

if turned on its side. This process, termed *lateral planation*, is a normal activity of any stream and is the same process by which floodplains are widened by alluvial rivers of humid climates.

Other processes of removal are believed to be important in carving pediments, the relative importance of each depending upon the location and type of bedrock. Between the larger canyons are smaller streams, issuing from steep-walled narrow ravines, while still smaller channels, which may be termed *rills*, drain the mountain slope and are important in removing weathered rock and wearing back the slope. These forms of running water must also adjust their gradients to conform to the gradients of the larger streams which they join, hence, can extend the pediment as a continuous rock floor with only minor undulations.

Once a pediment or alluvial fan is formed, flood flows from the canyons easily fill the shallow, braided channels to overflowing and spread as a more or less uniform layer, termed a *sheetflood*, over the entire graded slope. Some geologists consider that the erosive power of sheetfloods is an important agent in shaping pediments.

Because a pediment is normally veneered by alluvium while it is being formed, the only way to be certain that a pediment exists is to see the

Figure 22.10 Bedrock is widely exposed over this pediment surface at the foot of the Dragoon Mountains near Benson, Arizona. (Photograph by Douglas Johnson.)

bedrock widely exposed to view by later erosion. Thus, the pediment shown in Figure 22.10 has been cut into by stream action, exposing bedrock in numerous outcrops. The cause of stream rejuvenation in this case is not certain, but it may have been brought about by renewed faulting of the mountain block or by a climate change which upset the graded condition of the streams.

Because the old-age surface of the arid climate landmass cycle consists in part of pediments, the term *pediplain* has been introduced as equivalent to the term "peneplain" in the humid climate landmass cycle. A pediplain consists of alluvial fan and playa surfaces as well as pediments; it is thus partly erosional and partly depositional.

Geographical aspects of the arid cycle

The geographical aspects of mountainous deserts are well illustrated by the vast basin-and-range region which includes Nevada, southern California, western Utah, and the southern halves of Arizona and New Mexico. Here, excellent examples of various stages in the cycle can be observed as one travels through the desert on the main transcontinental highways, railroads, and airways. Sparseness of population goes hand in hand with sparseness of vegetation. In 1960, the state of Nevada, which lies wholly within this region, had only about 285,000 inhabitants in its 110,000 sq mi (286,000 sq km). Contrast this with Pennsylvania, whose 45,000 sq mi (117,000 sq km) contained over 11,000,000 persons. The vastness of waste land in this region can be partly appreciated when we realize that the explosion of the first test atom bomb was kept a secret within a single intermontane basin in New Mexico.

To the traveler, this landscape of mountainous deserts seems to be composed of three distinctive elements: (1) intensely rugged and inhospitable mountains; (2) broad sloping pediments and alluvial fans scored with innumerable shallow dry stream channels, or *washes;* and (3) perfectly flat playa lake floors, covered with shallow water or white salt deposits. In the rugged mountains occur valuable mineral deposits, which are an outstanding source of economic wealth. The alluvial fan slopes are virtually worthless except in the few places where wells bring in a flow of water for the needs of isolated communities. The playas provide mineral wealth of a different sort. Various salts of calcium, sodium, and potassium are often present in sufficient quantities to exploit.

REFERENCES FOR FURTHER STUDY

Lobeck, A. K. (1939), *Geomorphology*, McGraw-Hill Book Co., New York, 731 pp. See Chapter 5.

Cotton, C. A. (1941), *Landscape*, Cambridge University Press, Cambridge, England, 301 pp. See Chapters 7, 14, 17, 18, 19, 20.

Cotton, C. A. (1942), *Climatic accidents in landscape-making*, Whitcombe and Tombs, Christchurch, N.Z. 354 pp. See Section I.

Davis, W. M. (1954), *Geographical essays*, Dover Publications, New York, 777 pp. See pp. 249–278, 296–322, 350–380, 381–412.

Thornbury, W. D. (1969), *Principles of geomorphology*, second edition, John Wiley and Sons, New York, 594 pp. See Chapters 5, 6, 8, 11.

REVIEW QUESTIONS

1. Explain the concept of the cycle of landmass denudation. What possible combinations of initial relief and climate may be considered?

2. Describe the various stages in the landmass denudation cycle in a humid climate. Include discussion of the development of the drainage system, valley slopes and divides, and topographic relief. Which stage has greatest relief?

3. Describe the appearance of a peneplain. What is a monadnock? If elevation of the land causes a new cycle to begin, what happens to the peneplain?

4. Describe the appearance of a drainage network. How is it adapted to efficient discharge of runoff and sediment load?

5. State Playfair's law. What other view was held in Playfair's time? Does the law have any exceptions? Explain.

6. Define drainage density and give a series of typical values found in nature. Discuss the factors that control drainage density.

7. How does the role of running water in arid regions differ from that in humid climates? Contrast the forms of stream channels in humid and arid climates. Explain the statement that in deserts "streams are shorter than slopes."

8. Describe the stages of a landmass cycle in mountainous deserts. Compare this cycle, stage by stage, with the cycle of landmass denudation in a humid climate. Compare a peneplain with a pediplain.

9. Describe a pediment. How does it resemble an alluvial fan? How does it differ from an alluvial fan? What processes are considered to produce pediments?

10. Discuss the economic geographical aspects of mountainous deserts. What physical factors in the environment tend to limit human occupation of such areas?

CHAPTER 23
Landforms Made by Glaciers

MOST of us know ice only as a brittle, crystalline solid because we are accustomed to seeing it only in small quantities. Where a great thickness of ice exists, let us say 200 to 300 ft (60 to 90 m) or more, the ice at the bottom behaves as a plastic material and will slowly flow in such a way as to spread out the mass over a larger area, or to cause it to move downhill, as the case may be. This behavior characterizes *glaciers*, which may be

Figure 23.1 The Eklutna Glacier, Chugach Mountains, Alaska, seen from the air. A deeply crevassed ablation zone with a conspicuous medial moraine (foreground) contrasts with the smooth-surfaced firn zone (background). (Photograph by Steve McCutcheon, Alaska Pictorial Service.)

defined as any large natural accumulations of land ice affected by present or past motion.

Conditions requisite to the accumulation of glacial ice are simply that snowfall of the winter shall, on the average, exceed the amount of melting and evaporation of snow that occurs in summer. (The term *ablation* is used by glaciologists to include both evaporation and melting of snow and ice.) Thus, each year a layer of snow is added to what has already accumulated. As the snow compacts, by surface melting and refreezing, it turns into a granular ice, then is compressed by overlying layers into hard crystalline ice. When the ice becomes so thick that the lower layers become plastic, outward or downhill flow commences, and an active glacier has come into being.

At sufficiently high altitudes, whether in high or low latitudes, glaciers form both because air temperature is low and mountains receive heavy orographic precipitation (Chapter 6). Glaciers that form in high mountains are characteristically long and narrow because they occupy previously formed valleys and bring the plastic ice from small collecting grounds high upon the range down to lower elevations, and consequently warmer temperatures, where the ice disappears by ablation (Figure 23.1). Such *valley glaciers*, or *alpine glaciers*, are distinctive types.

In arctic and polar regions, prevailing temperatures are low enough that ice can accumulate over broad areas, wherever uplands exist to intercept heavy snowfall. As a result, areas of many thousands of square miles may become buried under gigantic plates of ice whose thickness may reach several thousand feet. The term *icecap* is usually applied to an ice plate limited to high mountain and plateau areas. During glacial periods an icecap spreads over surrounding lowlands, enveloping all landforms it encounters and ceasing its spread only when the rate of ablation at its outer edge balances the rate at which it is spreading. This extensive type of ice mass is called a *continental glacier* or *ice sheet*.

Figure 23.2 illustrates a number of features of alpine glaciers. The center illustration is of a simple glacier occupying a sloping valley between steep rock walls. Snow is collected at the upper

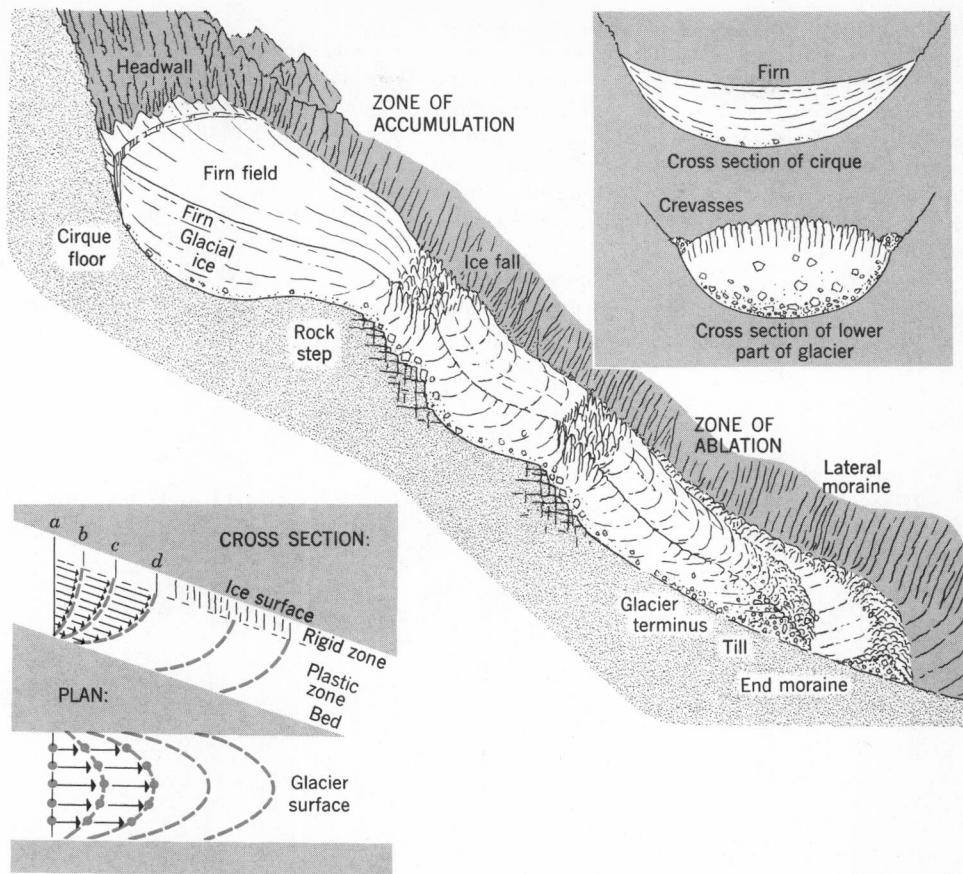

Figure 23.2 Structure and flowage of a simple alpine glacier.

end in a bowl-shaped depression, the *cirque*. The upper end constitutes the *zone of accumulation.* Layers of snow in the process of compaction and recrystallization constitute the *firn* (or *névé*). The smooth *firn field* is slightly concave up in profile (upper right). Flowage in the glacial ice beneath carries the excess ice out of the cirque, down valley. An abrupt steepening of the grade comprises a *rock step*, over which the rate of ice flow is accelerated and produces deep crevasses (gaping fractures) which form an *ice fall.* The lower part of the glacier lies in the *zone of ablation.* Here the rate of ice wastage is rapid and old ice is exposed at the glacier surface, which is extremely rough and deeply crevassed. The glacier *terminus*, or *snout* is heavily charged with rock debris. The lower part of the glacier is usually of upwardly convex cross-profile, the center being higher than the sides (upper right).

The uppermost layer of a glacier, perhaps 200 ft (60 m) in thickness is brittle and fractures readily into crevasses, whereas the ice beneath behaves as a plastic substance and moves by slow flowage (lower left). If one were to place a line of stakes across the glacier surface, the glacier flow would gradually deform the line into a parabolic curve, indicating that rate of movement is fastest in the center and diminishes toward the sides.

Altogether, a simple glacier forms a system that readily establishes a dynamic equilibrium in which the rate of accumulation at the upper end balances the rate of ablation at the lower end. Ice is transferred by flowage to maintain the glacier at approximately a given length and cross-sectional area. Equilibrium is easily upset by changes in the average annual rates of nourishment or wastage.

Rate of flowage of both alpine and continental glaciers is very slow indeed, amounting to a few inches per day for large ice sheets and for the more sluggish valley glaciers, up to several feet per day for an active valley glacier.

Glacial erosion

Most glacial ice is heavily charged with rock fragments, ranging from pulverized rock flour to huge angular boulders of fresh rock. This material is derived from the rock floor upon which the ice moves, or in alpine glaciers, from material that slides or falls from valley walls. Glaciers are capable of great erosive work, both by *abrasion*, erosion caused by ice-held rock fragments that scrape and grind against the bedrock, and by *plucking*, in which the moving ice lifts out blocks of bedrock that have been loosened by freezing of water in joint fractures. The process of plucking out of joint blocks is illustrated in Figure 23.2, at the rock steps.

The debris thus obtained must eventually be left stranded at the outer edge or lower end of a glacier when the ice is dissipated. Thus there are two glacial activities to consider, erosion and deposition. Both result in distinctive landforms, which in some cases are further differentiated according to the type of glacier, whether alpine or continental.

Landforms made by alpine glaciers

Landforms made by alpine glaciers can best be studied by a series of diagrams (Figure 23.3), in which a previously unglaciated mountainous

A. Before glaciation sets in, the region has smoothly rounded divides and narrow, V-shaped stream valleys.

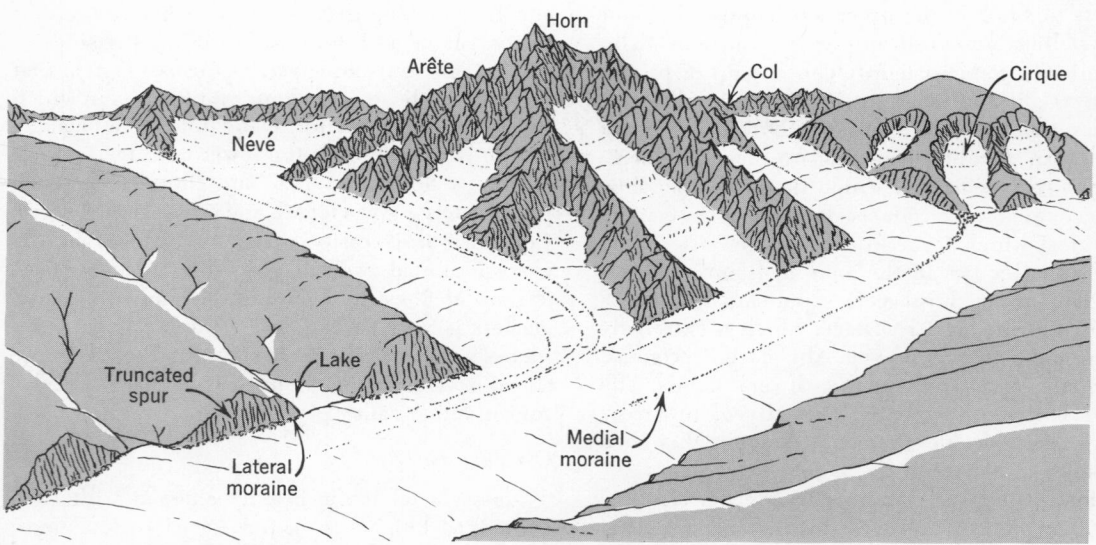

B. After glaciation has been in progress for thousands of years new erosional forms are developed.

Figure 23.3   Landforms produced by alpine glaciers. (After W. M. Davis and A. K. Lobeck.)

region is imagined to be attacked and modified by glaciers, after which the glaciers disappear and the remaining landforms are exposed to view.

Block *A* shows a mountainous region sculptured entirely by weathering, mass wasting, and streams. The mountains have a smooth, full-bodied appearance, with rather rounded divides. Although this is not always true, it is typical of the appearance of mountains in humid regions, for example, the Great Smoky Mountains of the southern Appalachians. Imagine now a climatic change in which the average annual temperature becomes several degrees lower and results in the accumulation of snow in the heads of most of the valleys high upon the mountain sides. An early stage of glaciation is shown at the right hand side of Block *B*, where snow is collecting and cirques are being carved by the outward motion of the ice and by intensive frost shattering of the rock near the masses of compacted snow.

In Block *B*, glaciers have filled the valleys and are integrated into a system of tributaries that feed a trunk glacier just as in a stream system. Glaciers are, of course, enormously thicker than streams, because the extremely slow rate of ice motion requires a great cross section if a glacier is to maintain a discharge equivalent to a swiftly flowing stream. Tributary glaciers join the main glacier with smooth, accordant junctions, but, as we shall see later, the bottoms of their channels are quite discordant in level.

Vigorous freezing and thawing of melt water from snows lodged in crevices high upon the walls of the cirque shatters the bare rock into angular fragments, which fall or creep down upon the snowfield and are incorporated into the glacier.

Figure 23.4   The Swiss Alps appear from the air as a sea of sharp arêtes and toothlike horns. In the foreground is a cirque. (Swissair Photo.)

Frost shattering also affects the rock walls against which the ice rests. The cirques thus grow steadily larger. Their rough, steep walls soon replace the smooth, rounded slopes of the original mountain mass. Where two cirque walls intersect from opposite sides, a jagged, knifelike ridge, called an *arête*, results. Where three or more cirques grow together, a sharp-pointed peak is formed by the intersection of the arêtes. The name *horn* is applied to such peaks in the Swiss Alps (Figure 23.4). One of the best known is the striking Matterhorn. Where the intersection of opposed cirques has

C. **With the disappearance of the ice a system of glacial troughs is exposed.**

Figure 23.5 This maturely dissected mountain mass presents a sea of cirques, arêtes, and horns. A lake occupies the cirque floor near center. San Juan Mountains, Colorado. (Photograph by Frank Jensen.)

been excessive, a pass or notch, called a *col*, is formed.

Glacier flow constantly deepens and widens its channel so that after the ice has finally disappeared there remains a deep, steep-walled *glacial trough*, characterized by a relatively straight or direct course and by the U-shape of its transverse profile (Block *C*, Figure 23.3). Tributary glaciers likewise carve U-shaped troughs, but they are smaller in cross section, with floors lying high above the floor level of the main trough, so are called *hanging troughs*. Streams, which later occupy the abandoned trough systems, form scenic waterfalls and cascades where they pass down from the lip of a hanging trough to the floor of the main trough. These streams quickly cut a small V-shaped notch in the trough bottom.

Valley spurs that formerly extended down to the main stream before glaciation occurred have been beveled off by ice abrasion and are termed *truncated spurs* (Block *B*). Under a glacier the bedrock is not always evenly excavated, so that the floors of troughs and cirques may contain *rock basins*

and *rock steps*. Cirques and upper parts of troughs thus are occupied by numerous small lakes, called *tarns* (Figure 23.5). The major troughs frequently contain large, elongate *trough lakes*, sometimes referred to as *finger lakes*. Landslides are numerous because glaciation leaves oversteepened trough walls. In glaciated countries such as Switzerland and Norway slides are a major type of natural disaster, because most towns and cities lie in the trough floors where they are readily destroyed by mudflows and landslides (Chapter 19).

Debris may be carried by an alpine glacier within the ice, or it may be dragged along between the ice and the valley wall as a *lateral moraine* (Figures 23.2 and 23.3*B*). Where two ice streams join, this marginal debris is dragged along to form a *medial moraine*, riding upon the ice in midstream (Figure 23.1). At the terminus of a glacier debris accumulates in a heap known as a *terminal moraine*, or *end moraine*. This heap is usually in the form of a curved embankment lying across the valley floor and bending upvalley along each wall of the trough to merge with the lateral moraines (Figures 23.2 and 23.6). As the end of the glacier wastes back, scattered debris is left behind. Should irregularities in the rate of glacier wasting cause the front temporarily to stand still, another moraine ridge will be built. Successive halts in ice

Figure 23.6 Moraines of a former valley glacier appear as looped embankments marking successive positions of the ice margins. (After W. M. Davis.)

Figure 23.7 Development of a glacial trough. (After E. Raisz.) *A*, During maximum glaciation, the U-shaped trough is filled by ice to the level of the small tributaries. *B*, After glaciation, the trough floor may be occupied by a stream and lakes. *C*, If the main stream is heavily
loaded, it may fill the trough floor with alluvium. *D*, Should the glacial trough have been
deepened below sea level, it will be occupied by an arm of the sea, or fiord.

retreat produce successive moraines, termed *recessional moraines.*

Glacial troughs and fiords

Many large glacial troughs now are nearly flat-
floored because aggrading streams that issued from
the receding ice front were heavily laden with
rock fragments. Figure 23.7 shows a comparison
between a trough with little or no fill and another
with alluvial-filled bottom. The deposit of alluvium
extending down valley from a melting glacier is
the *valley train.*

When the floor of a trough open to the sea lies
below sea level, the sea water will enter as the ice
front recedes, thus producing a narrow estuary
known as a *fiord* (Figure 23.8). Fiords may originate either by submergence of the coast or by
glacial erosion to a depth below sea level. Most
fiords are explained in the second way because ice
is of such a density that, when floating, from
three-fourths to nine-tenths of its mass lies below
water level. Therefore, a glacier several hundred
feet thick could erode to considerable depth below
sea level before the buoyancy of the water reduced
its erosive power where it entered the open water.

Fiords are observed to be opening up today along
the Alaskan coast, where some glaciers are melting
back rapidly and the fiord waters are being extended along the troughs. Fiords are found largely
along mountainous coasts in latitudes 50° to 70° N
and S. The explanation of this distribution lies in
climate and is treated under the discussion of
marine west coast climate (Chapter 11).

Geographical aspects of alpine glaciation

In general, the ruggedness of fully glaciated
mountains such as the Alps, Pyrenees, Himalayas,
or Sierra Nevada makes for sparseness of population and difficulty of access. Land above timber
line is useless for any purpose except summer
pastures and the extraction of such minerals as may
lie in the rocks. Locally, recreational uses—mountain climbing and winter sports—are intensively
developed.

Below timber line are rich forests. U-shaped
glacial troughs provide broad, accessible strips of
land at relatively low levels. These are utilized for
town sites, for winter pasture, and as arteries of
transportation. In the Italian Alps several great
flat-floored glacial troughs extend from the heart

Figure 23.8 This Norwegian fiord has the steep rock walls of a deep glacial trough. (Photograph by Mittet and Co.)

of the Alps southward to the plain of northern Italy. These are important geographic controls because they provide smooth and easy access into the heart of the Alps and to the principal Alpine passes. The Brenner Pass lies at the head of a magnificent trough of this type, the Adige River valley.

The steep-walled troughs contain many waterfalls and rapids readily used for hydroelectric plants. Electrification of railroads and industry is highly advanced in Switzerland and Norway.

Ice sheets of the present

Two enormous accumulations of glacial ice are the Greenland and Antarctic icecaps. These may be imagined as huge plates of ice, several thousand feet thick in the central areas, resting upon landmasses of subcontinental size. The Greenland icecap has an area of 670,000 sq mi (1,740,000 sq km) and occupies about seven-eighths of the entire island of Greenland (Figure 23.9). Only a narrow, mountainous coastal strip of land is exposed.

The Antarctic icecap covers about 5,000,000 sq mi (13,000,000 sq km) and in places spreads out into the ocean to form floating *ice shelves* (Figure 23.10). One significant point of difference between these two icecaps is their position with reference to the poles. Whereas the antarctic ice rests almost squarely upon the south pole, the Greenland icecap is considerably offset from the north pole, with its center about at 75° N lat. This position illustrates a fundamental principle; that a large area of high land is essential to the accumulation of a great icecap. No land exists near the north pole; ice accumulation there is restricted to a thin layer of floating sea ice.

Contours drawn upon the surface of the Greenland icecap show that it is in the form of very broad, smooth domes. From a high point of about 10,000 ft (3000 m) elevation east of the center there is a gradual slope outwards in all directions. The rock floor of the icecap lies close to sea level under the central region, but is higher near the edges. Accumulating snows add layer upon layer of ice to the surface, while at great depth the plastic ice slowly flows outward toward the edges. At the outer edge of the sheet the ice thins down to a few hundreds of feet. Continual loss through ablation keeps the position of the ice margin relatively steady where it is bordered by a coastal belt of land. Elsewhere the ice extends in long tongues, called *outlet glaciers*, to reach the sea at the heads of fiords. From the floating glacier edge huge masses of ice break off and drift out to open sea with tidal currents. The breakup of the ice front is known as *calving* and is brought about by strains caused by the rise and fall of tide level as well as by the undercutting and melting at and below the water line. The calving of floating glacier fronts is an extremely rapid process compared to ablation of ice fronts on land. Consequently, ice-caps are limited in their seaward extent and rarely extend far into the ocean beyond the limits of bays and shallow continental shelves.

Ice thickness in Antarctica is even greater than that of Greenland. For example, on Marie Byrd Land a thickness of 14,000 ft (4250 m) was measured, the rock floor lying 8200 ft (2500 m) below sea level. On Victoria Land Plateau at an elevation of 8900 ft (2700 m) above sea level, the ice was found to be 13,000 ft (4000 m) thick. This means that the rock floor over certain parts of the Antarctic continent lies below sea level.

An important glacial feature of Antarctica is the presence of great plates of floating glacial ice, termed *ice shelves* (Figure 23.10). The largest of these is the Ross Ice Shelf with an area of about 200,000 sq mi (520,000 sq km) and a surface elevation averaging about 225 ft (70 m) above the sea. Ice shelves are fed by the icecap, but also accumulate new ice through the compaction of snow.

Ice sheets of the Pleistocene epoch

As if the vast ice sheets of Greenland and Antarctica do not seem fantastic enough, geologists have brought to light abundant and convincing evidence that much of North America and Europe and parts of northern Asia and southern South America were covered by enormous ice sheets in a period of time designated the Pleistocene epoch (see Chapter 18). Despite the fact that this ice age ended 10,000 to 15,000 years ago with the rapid wasting away of the ice sheets, the glacial epoch is the most recent major episode in geologic his-

Figure 23.9 Generalized map of Greenland. (After R. F. Flint, *Glacial and Pleistocene Geology.*)

tory. Landforms made by the last ice advance and recession are very little modified by erosional agents.

Figures 23.11 and 23.12 show the extent to which North America and Europe were covered at the maximum known spread of the last advance of the ice. In the United States, all the land lying north of the Missouri and Ohio rivers was covered, as well as northern Pennsylvania and all of New York and New England. In Europe, the ice sheet centered upon the Baltic Sea, covering the Scandinavian countries and spreading as far south as central Germany. The British Isles were almost covered by an icecap that had several centers on highland areas and spread outward to coalesce with the Scandinavian ice sheet. The Alps at the same time were heavily inundated by enlarged alpine glaciers, fused into a single icecap. All high mountain areas of the world underwent greatly intensified alpine glaciation at the time of maximum ice-sheet advance. Today, only small remnant alpine glaciers exist as vestiges of these great valley glaciers. In less favorable mountain regions no glaciers remain.

Proof of the former great extent of ice sheets has been carefully accumulated since the middle of the nineteenth century when the great naturalist

Figure 23.10   Antarctica. (John P. Tremblay, cartographer.)

Louis Agassiz first announced the bold theory. In general, the evidence of past glaciation lies in the recognition throughout North America and Europe of landforms identical with those now seen near the margins of the Greenland icecap and other glaciers. Although Agassiz's pronouncement was greeted with much skepticism a century ago, continental glaciation of the Pleistocene epoch is now universally accepted among scientists. Moreover, careful study of the deposits left by the ice has led to the knowledge that not one but four major advances and retreats occurred, spaced over a total period of about a million years. It is the deposits of the last advance, known as the *Wisconsin stage*, that form fresh and conspicuous landforms. For the most part, then, the discussion of glacial landforms will concern these most recent deposits.

Glacial stages

The four principal glacial stages of North America are matched by corresponding stages of Europe, as deciphered in the Alps. Together with the interglacial stages (periods of mild climate during which the ice sheets disappeared), these glacial stages in order of increasing age are:

North American Stages (Northcentral U.S.)	European Stages (Alps)
Wisconsin glacial	Würm glacial
Sangamon interglacial	Riss-Würm interglacial
Illinoian glacial	Riss glacial
Yarmouth interglacial	Mindel-Riss interglacial
Kansan glacial	Mindel glacial
Aftonian interglacial	Günz-Mindel interglacial
Nebraskan glacial	Günz glacial

Figure 23.13 shows the limit of southerly spread of ice of each glacial stage in the north-central United States. Where older limits were overridden by younger, the boundaries are conjectural. Notice that an area in Wisconsin (the *Driftless Area*) was surrounded by ice but never inundated.

The absolute age and duration in years of the Pleistocene epoch and its stages are extremely difficult to fix, even though the relative order of events is well established. The last ice disappeared 10,000 to 15,000 years ago from the north-central United States. The Wisconsin stage may have endured 60,000 years. The earliest onset of glacial advance (Nebraskan) may have occurred 300,000 to 600,000 years ago, although the beginning of the Pleistocene epoch of geologic time is commonly set by geologists as about one million years before present.

Cause of continental glaciation

It should not be inferred that the occurrence of an ice age as the last event of geologic history

Figure 23.11 Pleistocene ice sheets of North America at their maximum spread reached as far south as the present Ohio and Missouri rivers. (After R. F. Flint.)

Figure 23.12 The Scandinavian ice sheet dominated northern Europe during the Pleistocene glaciations. Solid line shows limits of ice in the last glacial stage; dotted line on land shows maximum extent at any time. (After R. F. Flint.)

means that the earth as a planet is cooling off. There is excellent evidence in the form of rock deposits of similar periods of glaciation in the early part of the earth's geologic history. But, beyond the fact that glaciations are occasional events in geologic history, knowledge concerning the cause of glaciation is speculative. Obviously a prolonged

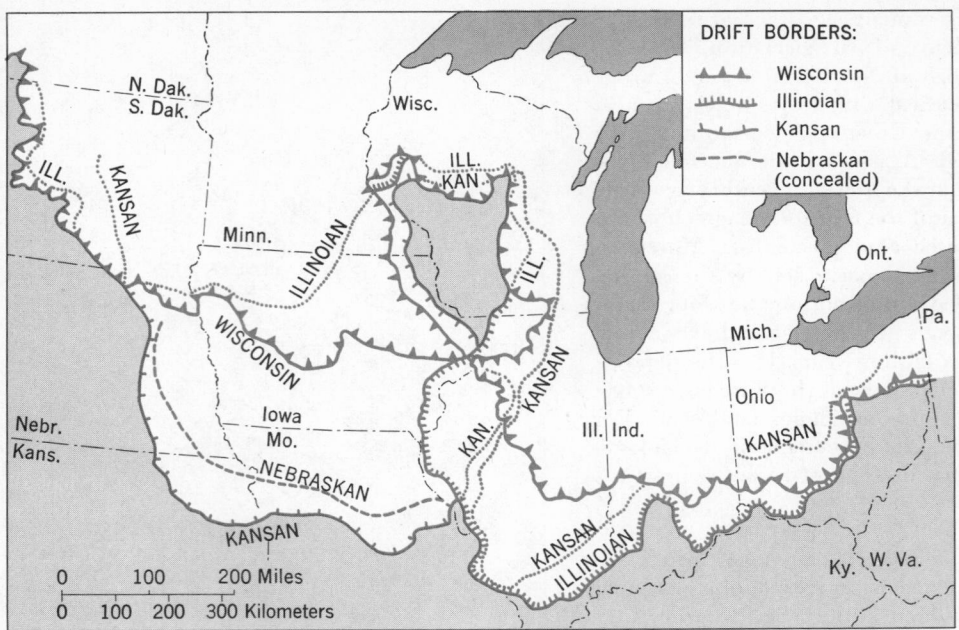

Figure 23.13   In each glacial stage, the ice sheet reached a different line of maximum advance. (After R. F. Flint, *Glacial and Pleistocene Geology*.)

period of colder climate with ample snowfall brings on the growth of ice sheets.

One possible contributing cause of glaciation is a decrease in the quantity of solar radiation intercepted by the earth. It has been reasoned that, should this quantity of energy have diminished somewhat at the beginning of the Pleistocene epoch, the average temperature of the earth's atmosphere would have dropped to a lower level. Providing that this change did not also diminish the quantity of snowfall, the reduced ablation of snowfields would increase the quantity of snow turned into glacial ice, with resultant growth and spread of icecaps. A second factor, possibly working in harmony with the first, is the known increase in elevation of large parts of the continents during the Pliocene and early Pleistocene epochs as a result of widespread mountain making (orogeny), as well as broad uparching of continental interiors (epeirogenic uplift). That mountains intercept large quantities of precipitation has already been explained (Chapter 6) in the discussion of orographic precipitation. The combined effects of reduced solar energy and increased altitude of continents would bring on colder climates with increased snowfall over favorable areas of the continents, such as the Laurentian Upland of eastern Canada and the Scandinavian peninsula. This composite theory of cause of glaciation may be called the *solar-topographic theory*.

An important and widely held theory attributes glaciation to a reduction of the carbon dioxide content of the atmosphere. The role of carbon dioxide in absorbing long-wave radiation and thus warming the atmosphere has been explained in Chapter 4. It is estimated that if the carbon dioxide content of the atmosphere, which is now 0.03 percent by volume, were reduced by half that amount, the earth's average surface temperature would drop about 7 F° (4 C°). Such a reduction in carbon dioxide content might be postulated in combination with increased continental altitude to bring on the growth of ice sheets.

Other theories invoke quite different mechanisms. It has been postulated that increased quantities of volcanic dust in the atmosphere might bring about a glacial period because more solar energy would be reflected back into space, permitting less to enter the lower atmosphere. Along with the reduced air temperature would be the increase in numbers of tiny dust particles to serve as nuclei for the condensation of moisture, thus favoring increased precipitation. Another group of theories propose shifts in the positions of the continents with respect to the poles, bringing various parts of the landmasses into favorable geographical positions for the growth of ice sheets. Still another theory requires that changes in oceanic currents, specifically the diversion or blocking of such warm currents as the Gulf Stream, would have brought colder climates to the subarctic regions. Variations in the earth's orbit, causing changes in the amounts of solar energy received by the earth, have also been considered as the cause of glacial periods.

Erosion by ice sheets

Like alpine glaciers, ice sheets are effective eroding agents. The slowly moving ice may scrape and grind away much solid bedrock, leaving behind smoothly rounded rock masses bearing countless minute abrasion marks. Scratches, or *striations*, trend in the general direction of ice movement (Figure 23.14), but variations in ice direction from time to time often result in intersecting lines. Certain kinds of rock were susceptible to deep grooving (Figure 23.15).

Where a strong, sharp-pointed piece of rock was held by the ice and dragged over the bedrock surface, there resulted a series of curved cracks fitted together along the line of ice movement. These *chatter marks*, and closely related *crescentic gouges*, whose curvature is the opposite, are good indicators of the direction of ice movement (Figure 23.14). Some very hard rocks have acquired highly polished surfaces from the rubbing of fine clay particles against the rock. The evidences of ice erosion described here are common throughout the northeastern United States. They may be seen on almost any exposed hard rock surface. Once understood, they may be recognized by any alert observer.

Commonly bearing the above abrasion marks is a type of conspicuous knob of solid bedrock that has been shaped by the moving ice (Figure 23.16). One side, that from which the ice was approaching, is characteristically smoothly rounded and shows a striated and grooved surface. This is termed the *stoss* side. The other, or *lee* side, where the ice plucked out angular joint blocks, is irregular, blocky, and steeper than the stoss side. The quaint term *roches moutonnées* has long been applied by glaciologists to such glaciated rock knobs.

Vastly more important than the minor abrasion forms are enormous excavations that the ice sheets made in some localities where the bedrock is of a weak variety and the ice current was accentuated by the presence of a valley paralleling the direction of ice flow. Under such conditions the ice sheet behaved much as a valley glacier, scooping out a deep, U-shaped trough. As fine examples may be cited the Finger Lakes of western New York State. Here a set of former stream valleys lay parallel to southward spread of the ice, which scooped out a series of deep troughs. Blocked at the north ends by glacial debris the basins now hold elongated lakes. Many hundreds of lake basins were created in a similar manner all over the glaciated portion of North America and Europe. Countless small lakes of Minnesota, Canada, and Finland occupy rock basins scooped out by ice action (Figure 23.17). Irregular debris deposits left by the ice are also important in causing lake basins.

Figure 23.14 Glacial striations and fracture marks, mostly crescentic gouges, cover the smoothly rounded surface of this rock knob. These marks were made by the East Twin Glacier, Alaska. The ice moved in a direction away from the photographer. (Photograph by Maynard Miller.)

Figure 23.15 Unusually smooth, deep glacial grooves were carved in limestone by the ice action on Kelley's Island near the south shore of Lake Erie. (Photograph by State of Ohio, Department of Industrial and Economic Development.)

Figure 23.16 A glacially abraded rock knob. (From A. N. Strahler, *The Earth Sciences*, Harper and Row, New York.)

Figure 23.17 Seen from the air, this esker in the Canadian shield area appears as a narrow embankment crossing the terrain of glacially eroded lake basins. (Photograph by Canadian Department of Mines, Geological Survey.)

Deposits left by ice sheets

The term *glacial drift* has long been applied to include all varieties of rock debris deposited in close association with glaciers. Drift is of two major types: (1) *Stratified drift* consists of layers of sorted and stratified clays, silts, sands, or gravels deposited by melt-water streams or in bodies of water adjacent to the ice. (2) *Till* is a heterogeneous mixture of rock fragments ranging in size from clay to boulders and is deposited directly from the ice without water transport. Moraines of valley glaciers, previously described, are composed largely of till, whereas the valley train is composed of stratified drift.

Over those parts of the United States formerly covered by Pleistocene ice sheets, glacial drift averages from 20 ft (6 m) thick over mountainous terrain such as New England, to 50 ft (15 m) and more thick over the lowlands of the north-central United States. Over Iowa, drifts are from 150 to 200 ft (45 to 60 m) thick; over Illinois, it averages more than 100 ft (30 m) thick. Locally, where deep stream valleys existed prior to glacial advance, as in Ohio, drift may be several hundred feet deep.

In order to understand the form and composition of deposits left by ice sheets, it is desirable to consider the conditions prevailing at the time of existence of the ice, as shown in Figure 23.18. Block *A* shows a region partly covered by an ice sheet with a relatively stationary front edge. This condition occurs when the rate of ice ablation balances the amount of ice brought forward by spreading of the ice sheet. Any increase in ice movement would cause the ice to shove forward to cover more ground; an increase in the rate of wasting would cause the edge to recede and the ice surface to become lowered. Although the Pleistocene ice fronts did advance and recede in many minor and major fluctuations, there were considerable periods when the front was essentially stable. This condition is represented in Block *A*.

The transportational work of an ice sheet may be likened to that of a great conveyor belt. Anything carried on the belt is dumped off at the end and if not constantly removed will pile up in increasing quantity. Rock fragments brought within the ice are deposited at the edge as the ice evaporates or melts. There is no possibility of return transportation.

Glacial till that accumulates at the immediate ice edge forms an irregular, rubbly heap known as a *terminal moraine*. After the ice has disappeared, as in Diagram *B*, the moraine appears as a belt of knobby hills interspersed with basinlike hollows, some of which hold small lakes. The term *knob and kettle topography* is often applied to morainal belts (Figure 23.19). Terminal moraines tend to form great curving patterns, the convex form of curvature being directed southward and indicating that the ice advanced as a series of great *lobes*, each with a curved front (Figure 23.20). Where two lobes came together, the moraines curved back and fused together into a single moraine pointed northward. This is termed an *interlobate moraine* (Figure 23.18, Block *B*). In its general recession accompanying disappearance, the ice front paused for some time along a number of lines, causing morainal belts similar to the terminal moraine belt to be formed. These belts, known as *recessional moraines* (Figures 23.18 and 23.20), run roughly parallel with the terminal moraine but are often thin and discontinuous.

Figure 23.18, Block *A*, shows a smooth, sloping plain lying in front of the ice margin. This is the *outwash plain*, formed of stratified drift left by braided streams issuing from the ice. Their deposits are in reality great alluvial fans upon which are spread layer upon layer of sands and gravels. The adjective *glaciofluvial* is often applied to stream-laid stratified drift.

Large streams issue from tunnels in the ice, particularly when the ice for many miles back from the front has become stagnant, without forward movement. Tunnels then develop throughout the ice mass, serving to carry off the melt water. After the ice has gone (Block *B*, Figure 23.18) the outwash plain remains in its original form, but may be bounded on the iceward side by a steep slope which is the mold of the ice against which the outwash was built. Such a slope is called an *ice-contact slope*. Farther back, behind the terminal moraine, the position of a former ice tunnel is marked by a long, sinuous ridge known as an *esker*. The esker is the deposit of sand and gravel for-

T – tunnel	*ML* – marginal lake
BS – braided stream	*I* – iceberg
OP – outwash plain	*D* – delta
IB – ice blocks	*O* – lake outlet

A. With the ice front stabilized and the ice in a wasting, stagnant condition, various depositional features are built by melt water.

TM – Terminal moraine	*D* – Delta
RM – Recessional moraine	*DK* – Delta kame
IM – Interlobate moraine	*S* – Shoreline
GM – Ground moraine	*LB* – Lake bottom
E – Esker	*OP* – Outwash plain
DR – Drumlins	*K* – Kettle

B. After the ice has wasted completely away, a variety of new landforms made under the ice is exposed to view.

Figure 23.18   Marginal landforms of continental glaciers.

Figure 23.19 Rugged topography of small knobs and kettles characterizes this interlobate moraine northeast of Elkhart Lake, Sheboygan County, Wisconsin. (Photograph by W. C. Alden, U.S. Geological Survey.)

merly laid upon the floor of the ice tunnel. Inasmuch as ice formed the sides and roof of the tunnel, its disappearance left merely the stream-bed deposit, which now forms a ridge (Figure 23.21). Eskers are often many miles long; in parts of Maine a few are more than 100 mi (160 km) long. Some have branches just as streams do. Because the esker is made of highly porous sand and gravel, the rapid draining away of water from the crest may prevent the growth of trees along the top of some eskers, which look as if artificially cleared of forest (Figure 23.17).

Another curious glacial form is the *drumlin*, a smoothly rounded, oval hill resembling the bowl of an inverted teaspoon. It consists of glacial till (Figure 23.22). Drumlins invariably lie in a zone behind the terminal or recessional moraines. They commonly occur in groups or swarms, which may number in the hundreds. The long axis of each drumlin parallels the direction of ice movement, and the drumlins thus point toward the terminal moraines and serve as indicators of direction of ice movement. From a study of the composition and structure of drumlins, it has been generally agreed that they were formed under moving ice by a kind of plastering action in which layer upon layer of bouldery clay was spread upon the drumlin. This would have been possible only if the ice were so heavily choked with debris that the excess had to be left behind. Furthermore, some sort of knob or surface irregularity may have been required to start the plastering action and localize its occurrence.

Between the terminal, recessional, and interlobate moraines, the surface left by the ice is usually overspread by a cover of glacial till known as *ground moraine*. This cover is often inconspicuous because it forms no prominent or recognizable topographic feature. Nevertheless, the ground moraine may be thick and may obscure or entirely bury the hills and valleys that existed before glaciation. Where thick and smoothly spread, the ground moraine forms an extensive, level till plain, but this condition is likely only in regions already fairly flat to start with. In more dissected regions, the preglacial valleys and hills retain their same general outlines despite glaciation.

Deposits built into standing water

Where the general land slope is toward the front of an ice sheet, a natural topographic basin is formed between the ice front and the rising ground. Valleys that may have opened out northward are blocked by ice. Under such conditions, *marginal glacial lakes* form along the ice front (Figure 23.18, Block *A*). These lakes overflow along the lowest available channel, which lies between the ice and the ground slope or over some low pass along a divide. Into marginal lakes streams of melt water from the ice build *glacial deltas*, similar in most respects to deltas formed by any stream flowing into a lake. Streams from the land likewise build deltas into the lake. When the ice has disap-

Figure 23.20 Moraine belts of the north-central United States have a festooned pattern left by ice lobes. (After R. F. Flint and others, *Glacial Map of North America*, 1945.)

peared the lake drains away, exposing the bottom upon which layers of fine clay and silt have been laid. These fine-grained strata, which have settled out from suspension in turbid lake waters, are called *glaciolacustrine* sediments and are a variety of stratified drift. The layers are commonly of banded appearance, with alternating dark and light layers, termed *varves*. Glacial lake plains are extremely flat, with meandering streams and extensive areas of marshland.

Deltas, built with a flat top at what was formerly the lake level, are now curiously isolated, flat-topped landforms known as *delta kames*. Delta and stream channel deposits built between a stagnant ice mass and the wall of a valley become *kame terraces*, whose steep scarps are ice-contact slopes (Figure 23.23). Kame terraces are difficult to distinguish from the uppermost member of a series of alluvial terraces, but most kames have undrained depressions or pits produced by the melting of enclosed ice blocks. Built of very well-washed and sorted sands and gravels, kames commonly show the steeply dipping foreset beds characteristic of deltas (Figure 23.24).

Geographical aspects of glacial landforms

Because much of Europe and North America was glaciated by the Pleistocene ice sheets, landforms associated with the ice are of fundamental geographical importance in influencing the activity of human beings. Agricultural influences of glaciation are both favorable and unfavorable, depending on preglacial topography and whether the ice eroded or deposited heavily. In hilly or mountainous regions, such as New England, the glacial till is thinly distributed and extremely stony. Cultivation is made difficult by countless boulders and stones in the soil. Along morainal belts the steep slopes, irregularity of topography, and abundance of boulders and stones in the till are unfavorable to cultivation. These same features, however, make morainal belts extremely desirable as suburban residential areas. A pleasing variety of hills, depressions, and small lakes makes ideal locations for large estates.

Extensive till plains, outwash plains, and lake plains, on the other hand, make for some of the most productive agricultural land in the world. In this class belong the prairie lands of Indiana, Illinois, Iowa, Nebraska, and Minnesota.

Glaciofluvial deposits are of great economic value. The sands and gravels of outwash plains, kames, and eskers provide the aggregate necessary for concrete and other building purposes (Figure 23.25). The purest sands may be used for molds needed for metal castings. Huge quantities of ground water are contained in glaciofluvial deposits. Where deep, preglacial valleys were filled

Figure 23.21 This esker has developed a cover of soil and vegetation, concealing the coarse gravel that lies within it. Dodge County, Wisconsin. (Photograph by W. C. Alden, U.S. Geological Survey.)

Figure 23.22 This small drumlin, located south of Sodus, New York, shows a tapered form from upper right to lower left, indicating that the ice moved in that direction (north to south). (Photograph by Ward's Natural Science Establishment, Inc., Rochester, N.Y.)

Figure 23.23 Kames may originate as stream or lake deposits laid between a stagnant ice mass and the valley sides. (After R. F. Flint.)

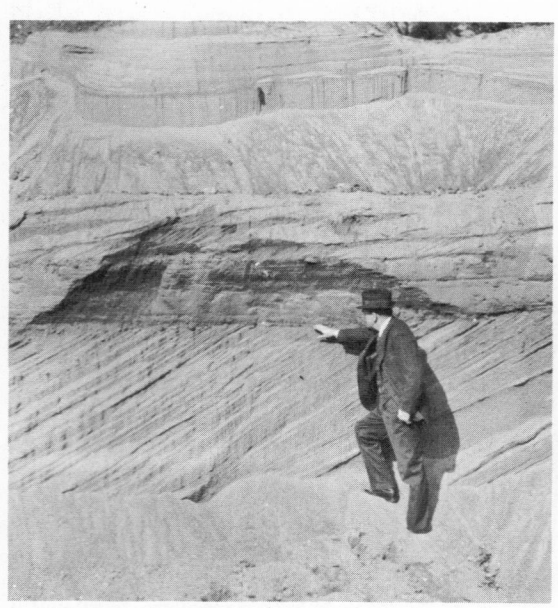

Figure 23.24 These cross-bedded, sorted sands were laid down in a glacial delta near North Haven, Connecticut. (Photograph by R. J. Lougee.)

Figure 23.25 Thick layers of outwash sands and gravels such as these on the north shore of Long Island are excavated in great quantities for use in highway and building construction. The dark layer at the top is a bed of glacial till, left by a glacial advance. Boulders in the foreground are glacial erratics that have rolled down from the till bed. (Photograph by A. K. Lobeck.)

with such materials, large quantities of water can be pumped from wells penetrating the deposit. In this way, many large cities and industrial plants in Ohio, Pennsylvania, and New York obtain their water supplies.

REFERENCES FOR FURTHER STUDY

Lobeck, A. K. (1939), *Geomorphology*, McGraw-Hill Book Co., New York, 731 pp. See Chapters 8 and 9.

Davis, W. M. (1954), *Geographical essays*, Dover Publications, New York, 777 pp. See pp. 617–634.

Flint, R. F. (1957), *Glacial and Pleistocene geology*, John Wiley and Sons, New York, 553 pp.

Hough, J. L. (1958), *Geology of the Great Lakes*, University of Illinois Press, Urbana, 313 pp.

Dyson, J. L. (1962), *The world of ice*, A. A. Knopf, New York, 292 pp.

Schultz, Gwen (1963), *Glaciers and the Ice Age*, Holt, Rinehart and Winston, New York, 128 pp.

Wright, H. E., and D. G. Frey, eds. (1965), *The Quaternary of the United States*, Princeton University Press, Princeton, N.J., 922 pp.

Thornbury, W. D. (1969), *Principles of geomorphology*, second edition, John Wiley and Sons, New York, 594 pp. See Chapters 14, 15, 16.

REVIEW QUESTIONS

1. What is a glacier? What conditions are necessary for the formation of glaciers? Define ablation. What is firn? What is the distinction between alpine and continental glaciers?

2. Describe a simple alpine glacier and explain how it operates. What is glacier equilibrium? How fast does a glacier flow?

3. How do glaciers erode their channels? Compare alpine glaciers with streams in regard to erosion and transportation activities.

4. How do alpine glaciers modify mountain topography? Describe and explain the following features: cirque, arête, horn, col, glacial trough, hanging trough, rock basin, rock step, tarn, finger lake.

5. What is the form of a glacial trough? How does this form differ from that of a normally eroded stream valley? Explain how a fiord is formed. Where are fiords found?

6. Describe the various kinds of deposits made by a valley glacier. What are the location and form of the following types of moraines: medial, lateral, terminal, and recessional? What is a valley train?

7. Where are the icecaps of the world today? About how thick is the ice in the central parts of these icecaps? Explain how an icecap is fed and how the ice moves. What are ice shelves? Outlet glaciers? What is calving?

8. Describe the extent of ice sheets of the Pleistocene epoch in North America and Europe. Describe the southern glacial limit in the United States. What great scientist was largely responsible for convincing the scientific world that the Pleistocene glaciation actually occurred?

9. Name in order the glacial and interglacial stages of North America. How long ago did the last glacial ice disappear from the United States?

10. Review the principal theories that attempt to explain the occurrence of glacial periods.

11. What erosional features on rock surfaces give evidence of the former presence of an ice sheet? How can the direction of ice movement be inferred?

12. How can the direction of ice movement be inferred from the shapes of a glaciated rock knobs (roches moutonnées)? How were the Finger Lakes of western New York State formed?

13. What is glacial drift? What is the distinction between stratified drift and till?

14. Describe and explain the various depositional forms associated with the margin of an ice sheet.

15. What kinds of moraines are left by ice sheets? What is a glacial outwash plain? Describe the surface topography of an outwash plain.

16. How is an esker formed? How long are eskers? Of what material are they composed?

17. What is a drumlin? Of what material is it composed? How is it formed? Where are most drumlins found in relation to the terminal moraine?

18. What is a till plain? How is it formed?

19. Explain how marginal glacial lakes are formed. What types of deposits are formed in them? What is a delta kame? A kame terrace? What are varves?

20. Discuss the geographical aspects of glacial landforms.

CHAPTER 24
Landforms Made by Waves and Currents

OCEAN waves work unceasingly to transform the shores of continents and islands. Waves travel across the deep ocean with only gradual loss of energy, but when shallow water is reached, the wave form changes radically and new water motions are developed. These motions take the form of powerful surges and currents capable of performing great erosive and transportational work.

Most shorelines have a rather smooth, sloping bottom extending out beneath the water level. As waves approach this shallow zone, wave velocity becomes less and wave crests become more closely spaced (Figure 24.1). Wave height and steepness increase rapidly until the crest rolls forward to make a *breaker* (Figure 24.2). After the breaker has collapsed, a foamy, turbulent sheet of water rides up the beach slope. This *swash*, or *uprush*, is a powerful surge causing a landward movement of sand and gravel on the beach. When the force of the swash has been spent against the slope of the beach, the return flow, or *backwash*, pours down the beach, but much disappears by infiltration into the permeable beach sand. Sands and gravels are swept seaward by the backwash.

Wave erosion

In times of relative calm or moderate winds, waves do little erosional work but tend instead to build beaches and sand bars out of sand and gravel. In times of storm, when enormous waves break

Figure 24.2   A breaking wave.

and throw tons of water against the shoreline, erosion is rapid (Figure 24.3). The violent uprush hurls cobbles and boulders against exposed bedrock along the shore, causing fragments to be broken free. A continual crushing and grinding action goes on as the stones are jostled together. The products of this breaking up are sorted according to size. Fine particles are carried out to sea, where they eventually come to rest in deep, quiet water to form silt and clay layers. Sands and gravels remain close to shore, forming beaches and bars.

Should the shoreline consist of hard rock, erosion will be slow and the storms of many years' time will make little visible change. Where soft materials, such as glacial moraines or outwash plains, form the shoreline, erosion is very rapid. The force of the water alone is sufficient to erode such deposits, and the sea cliff may recede many feet in a single storm (Figure 24.4). Some of the particular forms produced by wave erosion are described and explained in a later paragraph.

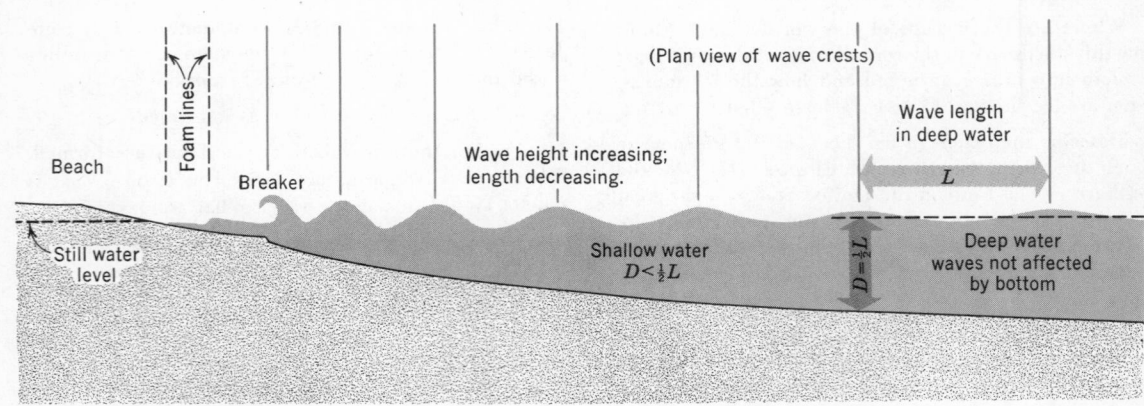

Figure 24.1   As waves enter shallow water the form changes until breaking occurs.

Figure 24.3 Tremendous forward thrust is evident in these storm waves breaking against a sea wall at Hastings, England. (Photographer not known.)

Shore and beach drifting

The unceasing alternate shifting of materials with swash and backwash of breaking waves results not only in movements of rock fragments in seaward and landward directions on the beach, but also in a sidewise movement known as *beach drifting* (Figure 24.5). Wave fronts usually approach the shore with a slight obliquity rather than directly head on. The swash is therefore directed obliquely up the beach, and the sand, gravel, and cobbles are consequently moved obliquely up the slope. After the water has spent its energy, the backwash flows down the slope of the beach, being controlled by the pull of gravity which urges it in the most direct downhill direc-

Figure 24.4 Storm waves breaking against a coast underlain by weak sand quickly undermined this shore home at Seabright, New Jersey. The barrier of wooden pilings (right) proved ineffective in preventing cutting back of the cliff. (Photograph by Douglas Johnson.)

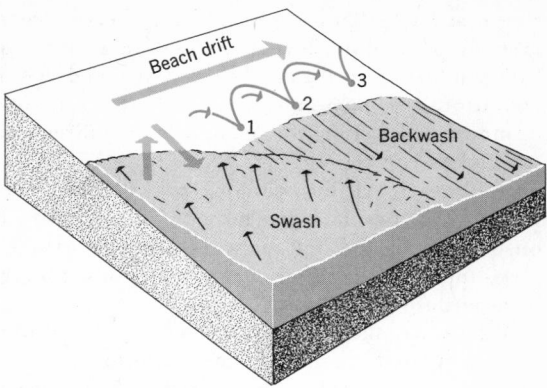

Figure 24.5 Swash and backwash.

tion. The particles are therefore dragged directly seaward and come to rest at a position to one side of the starting place. Because, on a particular day, wave fronts approach consistently from the same direction this movement is repeated many times. Individual rock particles thus travel a considerable distance along the shore. Multiplied many thousands of times to include the numberless particles of the beach, this form of mass transport is a major process in shoreline development.

Although the word *beach* is in common language use, it would be well at this point to define a beach as a deposit of sand, gravel, or cobbles formed inshore from the zone of breaking waves by the action of swash and backwash. If the sand is arriving at a particular section of the beach more rapidly than it can be carried away, the beach is widened and built shoreward, a change called *progradation*. If sand is leaving a section of beach more rapidly than it is being brought in, the beach is narrowed and the shoreline moves landward, a change called *retrogradation*.

A process related to beach drifting is *longshore drifting*. When waves approach a shoreline under the influence of strong winds, the water level is slightly raised near shore by a slow shoreward drift of water. There is thus an excess of water pushed

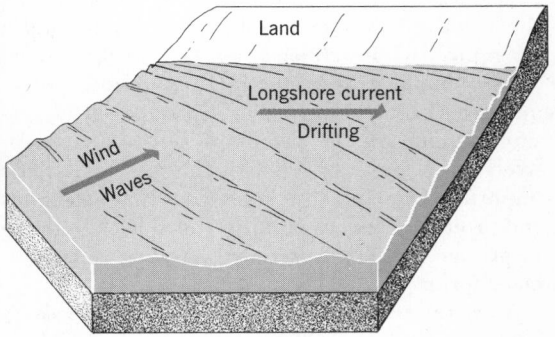

Figure 24.6 Longshore current drifting.

shoreward, which must escape. A *longshore current* is set up parallel to shore in a direction away from the wind (Figure 24.6). When wave and wind conditions are favorable, this current is capable of moving sand along the sea bottom in a direction parallel to the shore.

Both beach drifting and longshore drifting move particles in the same direction for a given set of onshore winds and oblique wave fronts and therefore supplement each other's influence in sediment transportation.

Tidal currents are still another type of water movement that causes the transportation of rock particles. The nature of these currents is discussed in a later paragraph. They are particularly effective in narrow bays and estuaries, but of little importance where a shoreline is fairly straight.

Wave refraction

The phenomenon of change in direction, or bending, of wave fronts as they approach the shore is known as *wave refraction*. Figure 24.7 shows a shoreline with bays and promontories. Successive positions of a wave are indicated by the lines numbered 1, 2, 3, etc. In deep water the wave fronts are parallel. As the shore is neared, the retarding influence of shallow water is felt first in the areas in front of the promontories. Shallowing of water reduces speed of wave travel at those places, but in the deeper water in front of the bays the retarding action has not yet occurred. Consequently, the wave front is bent, or *refracted*, in rough conformity with the shoreline. If the shoreline pattern consists of broad, open curves, the waves may break everywhere along the shore at the same time, but this is unusual. The wave ordinarily will break first upon the promontory and on the bay head last, as indicated in Figure 24.7.

Particularly important in understanding the development of embayed shorelines is the distribution of wave energy along the shore. On Figure 24.7, dashed lines (lettered *a, b, c, d,* etc.) divide the wave at position 1 into equal parts, which may be taken to include equal amounts of energy. Along the headlands the energy is concentrated into a short piece of shoreline; along the bays it is spread over a much greater length of shoreline. Consequently, the breaking waves act as powerful erosional agents on the promontories, but are relatively weak and ineffective at the bay heads. The important principle thus revealed is that headlands and promontories are rapidly eroded back, tending to produce a simple, straight shoreline as an ultimate form.

Wave refraction also occurs where oblique waves approach a perfectly straight shore (Figure 24.8). They are turned so as to break almost parallel with

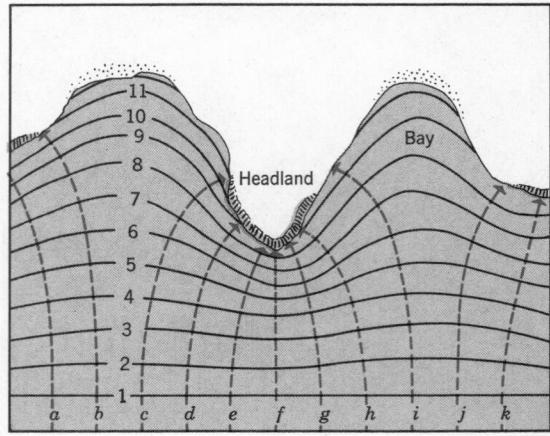

Figure 24.7 Wave refraction along an embayed coast.

the beach. Wave-refraction patterns can be studied from air photographs and may provide valuable information regarding the form of the bottom in the vicinity of the shoreline.

Development of sea cliffs

Where a steeply sloping land surface descends below the water the development of steep cliffs bordering the shoreline is especially favored. Such a condition may come about by a sinking of the land or a rise of ocean level, bringing the water line against what were formerly the steep slopes of mountains or hills.

Figure 24.9 illustrates the development of sea cliffs. Block *A* shows an early stage, termed the *nip stage*, in which wave attack has carved out a small cliff in the hard bedrock. At the base of the cliff is a small rock platform sloping seaward and lying just below water level. Disintegrated rock fragments are swept seaward because wave energy is excessive and will not permit sand and gravel to remain as a beach.

Block *B* shows a cliff developed to considerable height, because, as the cliff is cut back, the rise of land slope causes its height to increase. The

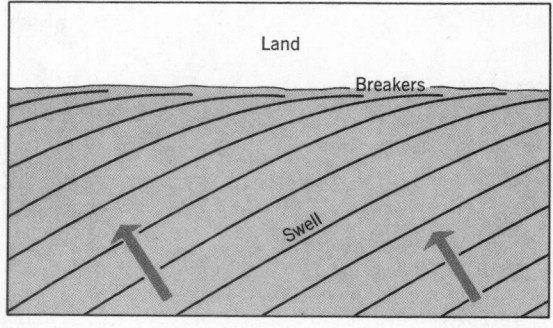

Figure 24.8 Wave refraction on a straight shoreline.

Figure 24.9 Development of sea cliffs. (After E. Raisz.) *A.* Breaking waves first cut out a small cliff, or nip. *B.* As the cliff is cut back it develops undercut notches, arches, stacks, and crevices. At the same time, an abrasion platform is cut and a terrace built. *A* = arch: *S* = stack: *C* = cave: *N* = notch: *P* = abrasion platform: *T* = shore face terrace: *B* = beach: and *R* = crevice. *C.* When equilibrium has been reached a broad platform is present and the cliff is no longer actively undermined.

waves have sought out points of comparative weakness in the rock, penetrating to form crevices and *sea caves.* Some more solid portions of rock project seaward. Where attached to the mainland they may form *sea arches;* where detached, they rise as *stacks* (Figure 24.10). At this stage, the cliff line has reached its greatest degree of irregularity. It is still being vigorously undercut, as evidenced by a wave-cut *notch* at the cliff base. The sloping rock-floored platform at the cliff base, known as the *abrasion platform* is now relatively wide. The inner edge is covered by water only at times of high tide or storm. A beach of sand or cobblestones may be present, but is transitory and may disappear during a single storm, to be built back very slowly. At the outer edge of the rock-abrasion platform, the slope is extended in a deposit of sand and larger rock particles known as the *shore-face terrace,* derived from ground-up rock that the waves have eroded from the cliff.

Streams that formerly flowed to the sea in valleys whose lower ends were at sea level may now be shortened and left as *hanging valleys*

(Figure 24.11), having been unable to deepen their valleys with sufficient rapidity to keep pace with the retreating sea cliff. If the rock material is of an unstable variety, large masses may slump or slide from the cliff (Figure 24.12).

A late stage in the development of sea cliffs, shown in Block *C* of Figure 24.9, may be considered the *mature stage.* The abrasion platform has been so greatly widened that all, or almost all, wave energy is expended in friction as the waves travel over the shallow platform, and in shifting sand across the beach. Consequently, wave attack upon the cliff base is greatly reduced. Weathering and rainbeat acting upon the cliff face wear it down to a lower slope. Irregularities such as sea caves and crevices disappear. The beach may now be broad and deep with little bedrock appearing at the surface.

The geographical influence of marine cliffs is felt in several ways. The coast may be inaccessible because of the high cliffs. In military operations this is especially significant, because a landing is hazardous and a beachhead difficult to expand where a sheer cliff parallels the beach. If the stream valleys are hanging, there are few points where access may be had to the coastal region. Along such coasts, which tend to be fairly straight, the only natural harbors are at the mouths of large streams that have been able to cut down to an accordant junction with the sea (Figures 24.10 and 24.11). This condition prevails along parts of the French channel coast.

A shore bordered by a marine cliff may be of limited value for summer beach use because of the inaccessibility of the shore from the land back of the cliff and because the beach may be thin or rocky even if present. At high tide, the abrasion platform is sometimes inundated to the cliff base, making the shore a dangerous place where bathers can be trapped by rising tide.

Sand bars and sand spits

Where the continued abrasion of a marine cliff has produced an ample supply of sand, or where the delta of a stream furnishes a sand supply, the sand is moved by shore drifting away from the source toward regions of less intense wave action in more sheltered locations. In the case of a straight shoreline indented by a deep bay, as shown in Figure 24.13, shore drifting extends the beach in a more or less direct line into the open water of the bay to produce a *sand spit.* Spits are usually curved toward the land at their extremities, and are described as *recurved spits.* Ultimately, a sand spit will join with another spit developed from the opposite side of the bay and will form a continuous sand bar, or *baymouth bar,* separating the bay from the open water body (Figure 24.14).

Figure 24.10 The chalk cliffs of Normandy, along the French channel coast, show stacks, arches, and sea caves. (Photographer not known.)

Figure 24.11 When a marine cliff is cut back rapidly, hanging valleys appear as notches in the cliff. The large stream at the right has been able to maintain an accordant junction with the sea level and provides a small harbor. (After W. M. Davis.)

Figure 24.12 Coastal landslides in weak sedimentary strata are the result of oversteepening of a marine cliff by wave attack. (After W. M. Davis.)

Shore drift from an island commonly forms a *tombolo*, which is a sand bar connecting the island with the mainland (Figure 24.15). Drift of sand along a shore from opposing directions results in the building of a pointed sand-bar deposit known as a *cuspate bar* (Figure 24.16). Long-continued deposition, adding one beach upon another in a ribbed arrangement, produces a prominent *cuspate foreland* (Figure 24.17).

Tidal currents

Most marine coasts are to some degree influenced by the *tide*, or rhythmic rise and fall of sea level under the influence of changing attractive forces of moon and sun upon the rotating earth. Where tides are great, the effects of changing water level and the currents thus set in motion are of

Figure 24.13 Shore drifting producing a sand spit in a bay. (From A. N. Strahler. *The Earth Sciences*, Harper and Row, New York.)

Figure 24.14 These baymouth bars have sealed off two bays. (After W. M. Davis.)

Figure 24.16 This cuspate bar, which has enclosed a triangular lagoon, receives drifted beach materials from both sides. (After E. Raisz.)

Figure 24.15 Two tombolos have connected this island with the mainland. (After W. M. Davis.)

Figure 24.17 Dungeness Foreland, on the Dover Straits of southeastern England, is a large cuspate foreland with curving beach ridges.

major importance in shaping the coastal landforms.

Without going into the causes of ocean tides and their many variations, some of the important principles of tidal action can be understood by considering the common type of *tide curve* in which the cycle of rise and fall is *semidaily* (*semidiurnal*), taking approximately 12½ hours to complete. If we make half-hourly observations of the position of water level against a measuring stick or tide staff attached to a pier or sea wall, we can plot the changes of water level and thus draw the tide curve. Figure 24.18 is a tide curve for Boston Harbor covering a day's time. The water reached its maximum height, or *high water*, at the 12-ft (3.7-m) mark on the tide staff, then fell to its minimum height, or *low water*, occurring about 6¼ hours later. A second high water occurred about 12½ hours after the previous high water, completing a single semidaily tide cycle.

The *range of tide*, or difference between heights of successive high and low waters, is about 9 ft (2.7 m) for the example shown in Figure 24.18. The tide range and the form of the tide curve vary throughout the lunar month of about 29½ days. Twice during the month the range is greater than average, comprising *spring tides;* one week later the range is less than average, comprising *neap tides.*

The importance of tides along a coast lies in the currents set up by the changing water level and by the fact that at high water the swash of breaking waves reaches high up on the beach, whereas at low water the waves act only upon the foot of the beach.

The rising tide sets in motion in bays and estuaries a landward current of water known as the *flood current.* When the tide begins to fall this flood current slackens. Flow ceases about the time when the water is midway between high and low water (*midtide*), a condition known as *slack water.* As the tide continues to fall, a seaward current, the *ebb current,* begins to flow and gains in strength to attain a maximum speed about at low tide. The relationships between tidal-current speed and the tide curve are shown in Figure 24.19, which is based on observations at the mouth of New York Harbor. Note that the ebb current is stronger than the flood current, a condition explained by the fact that the Hudson River contributes a considerable discharge of fresh water from the land which must escape to the sea. This stream discharge augments the ebb current but opposes the flood current.

Tidal current deposits

Ebb and flood currents generated by tides perform several important functions along a shoreline. First, the currents that flow into and out of bays through narrow inlets are very swift and can scour the inlet strongly to keep it open despite the tendency of shore drifting processes to close the inlet with sand. Second, the tidal currents carry much fine silt and clay in suspension, derived from streams which enter the bays or from bottom muds agitated by storm wave action. This fine sediment tends to become clotted into small aggregates (process of *flocculation*) where fresh water mixes with salt water. The sediment then settles to the floors of the bays and estuaries where it accumulates in layers and gradually fills the bays. Much organic matter is normally present in such sediment.

In time, tidal sediments fill the bays and produce *mud flats*, which are barren expanses of silt and clay exposed at low tide but covered at high tide (Figure 24.20). Next, there takes hold upon the mud flat a growth of salt-tolerant plants (such as the genus *Spartina*). The plant stems entrap more sediment and the flat is built up to approximately the level of high tide, becoming a *salt marsh* (Figure 24.21). Tidal currents maintain their flow through the salt marsh by means of a highly complex network of sinuous *tidal streams* in which the water alternately flows seaward and landward (Figure 24.22).

Salt marsh is of interest to geographers because it is land that can be drained and made agriculturally productive. The salt marsh is first cut off from the sea by construction of an embankment of earth, a *dike*, in which gates are installed to allow the fresh water drainage of the land to exit

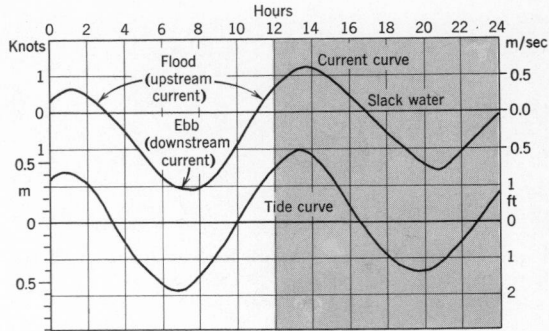

Figure 24.19 Ebb and flood currents at the entrance to New York Harbor. (After H. A. Marmer.)

in ebb flow but to prevent the ingress of salt water during flood flow. Gradually the salt water is excluded and soil water of the diked land becomes fresh. Such diked lands are intensively developed in Holland (*polders*) and southeast England (*fenlands*). Over many decades the surface of reclaimed salt marsh subsides because of compaction of the underlying peat layers and may come to lie well below mean sea level. The threat of flooding by salt water, when storm waves breach the dikes, hangs constantly over the inhabitants of such low areas. The reclamation of salt marsh by dike construction and drainage was practiced by New World settlers in New England and Nova Scotia.

Shoreline classification

Because shorelines display a wide variety of forms, it is desirable to have a classification to group them according to their origin and development. Five major classes of shorelines have been found to include most known types (Figure 24.23).

1. *Shorelines of submergence.* Wherever a sinking down of the earth's crust occurs near the border of a land area, or there is a rise of sea level, the new shoreline takes a position along what was approximately a former contour of the land surface. Below this level all the surface formerly exposed to the air is now submerged beneath the sea. In this way, the term *shoreline of submergence* is applicable.

It is possible to subdivide shorelines of submergence into subgroups, depending on the type of topography that existed before the submergence. Wherever a region was dissected by streams into a system of valleys and divides, submergence produces highly irregular, embayed shoreline termed a *ria shoreline*. Former valleys become deep embayments; former hilltops produce islands; former divides between valleys produce promontories or peninsulas. Variations in ria shoreline form depend on the stage of dissection and relief

Figure 24.18 Height of water at Boston Harbor measured every half hour. (After H. A. Marmer.)

Figure 24.20 Viewed from the air at low tide these tidal mud flats near Yarmouth, Nova Scotia, show a well-adjusted branching system of tidal streams. The area shown is 1.5 mi (2.4 km) wide. (Royal Canadian Air Force Photograph.)

Figure 24.21 Salt marsh at low tide, Green Harbor, Boston Bay region, Massachusetts. Distant houses are on a higher sand ridge separating the salt marsh from the sea. (Photograph by Douglas Johnson.)

Figure 24.22 This broad tidal marsh along the east coast of Florida is laced with serpentine tidal channels. (Aerial photograph by Laurence Lowry.)

of the land immediately before submergence. Two possibilities, one a mountainous region (*1A*), the other a coastal plain of very low relief (*1B*), are illustrated in Figure 24.23.

Some coastal regions have been heavily eroded by valley glaciers, whose troughs were excavated below sea level. After the glaciers have disappeared, a *fiord shoreline* results (Figure 24.23, *1C*). (See also Chapter 23.) Such shorelines are distinctive because of the steepness of the fiord walls, the great depth of water, and the great inland extent of the fiords.

Other subtypes of shorelines of submergence result from the submergence of landscapes formed by continental glaciation (Figure 24.23, *1D*).

2. *Shorelines of emergence.* Wherever a rising of the earth's crust has occurred near the border of a continent, or the sea level has fallen, a *shoreline of emergence* is created. The water line takes a position against what was formerly a slope of the sea floor. Above the new shoreline lies a new coastal land belt which has emerged from the sea. Withdrawal of water to form extensive continental

Figure 24.23 Classification of shorelines. (1) *Shorelines of Submergence:* 1A, submerged mountainous coast; 1B, submerged coastal plain, low relief; 1C, fiord coast; 1D, submerged glacial deposits (drumlins). (2) *Shorelines of Emergence:* 2A, coastal plain type, low relief; 2B, steeply sloping type, strong relief. (3) *Neutral Shorelines:* 3A, alluvial fan shoreline; 3B, delta shoreline; 3C, volcano shoreline; 3D, coral reef shoreline. (4) *Fault Shorelines.*

ice sheets is an effective cause of sea-level lowering. It is likely that shorelines of emergence were widely distributed during the time of maximum glacier advance in the Pleistocene epoch.

Most sea floors that have been submerged for a long period of geologic time near the margins of continents have been receiving layered deposits of muds, sands, and gravels derived from erosion of the lands and distributed by ocean currents. These continental shelves have a relatively smooth surface and gentle slope away from the continents. When a continental shelf is exposed by emergence it produces a low, smooth, gently sloping coastal plain, bounded by a simple, even shoreline, which may be termed a *coastal-plain shoreline* (Figure 24.23, *2A*).

Along some coastal belts, the submarine topography contains steep slopes. The shoreline of emergence here differs from that of the coastal-plain shoreline in that deep water lies close offshore and the coastal belt may be relatively mountainous to within a short distance of the shore (Figure 24.23, *2B*). No simple name has been given to this subtype, but it may be designated a *steeply sloping shoreline of emergence*. Old wave-cut cliffs and benches at various levels above the sea indicate that emergence was spasmodic.

3. Neutral shorelines. Wherever a shoreline has been formed as a result of new materials being built out into the water, it is classified as a *neutral shoreline*. The word "neutral" implies that there need be no relative change between the level of the sea and the coastal region of the continent.

Several types of neutral shorelines are known. Each type is easily understood when referred to the agent responsible for building out the material into the water (Figure 24.23, *3A, 3B, 3C, 3D*). An *alluvial fan shoreline*, curved in outline, is built by braided streams building a fan in the manner already explained in Chapter 21. Very similar are shorelines formed by building of a glacial outwash plain into the sea where the ice front stood near the shore. A *delta shoreline* is built of material brought out by a stream system (Chapter 21). Where a volcanic eruption has occurred, the slope of a volcano or the edge of a lava flow may compose the shore, which is then classified as a *volcano shoreline*. A *coral-reef shoreline* is built by marine organisms in the shallow-water zones of tropical seas.

4. Fault shorelines. An unusual type of shoreline is produced by faulting of the earth's crust in such a way that there is a dropping down of a segment of the crust on the seaward side of the break and corresponding rising up of the landward side. Should the downdropped block subside below sea level, the shoreline will come to rest against the steeply sloping land surface which is the sur-

face of the plane of faulting, and can be termed a *fault shoreline* (Figure 24.23, *4*). A similar result would be obtained where a crustal mass bounded by fault planes arises from beneath the sea.

5. Compound shorelines are those that show the forms of two of the previous classes combined, for example, submergence followed by emergence, or vice versa.

Life history of a shoreline of submergence

A shoreline of submergence of the ria type passes through a series of developmental stages, as illustrated in Figure 24.24. In the initial stage, submergence has just occurred to modify the shoreline. The coast is deeply bayed, with long peninsulas or promontories. Numerous islands lie offshore.

In the stage of early youth, wave attack is vigorous upon the headlands and upon the seaward sides of islands. Wave refraction brings maximum attack to these points. Wave-cut cliffs form such minor features as sea caves, stacks, and arches. The term *cliffed headland* is applied to the beveled peninsulas. Rock abrasion platforms develop at the cliff base, but beaches are thin or absent.

In the stage of late youth, the cliffs have increased in height and have been cut back considerably. Some of the smaller islands have been entirely planed off by wave abrasion and the larger ones have lost considerable area. In this stage, large numbers of depositional forms begin to appear. They are built of sand and gravel by the processes of beach and longshore drifting, described earlier, and represent a series of sequential landforms built out of the waste products of wave abrasion against the cliffs.

Fronting the cliffed headlands are *headland beaches*. From these sources sands have drifted out across the bay mouths to produce spits extending into open water. These spits will normally be recurved, or bent toward the land. Continued growth may add new curved portions to the end of a recurved spit, forming a *compound recurved spit*. Should waves generated within the waters of the bay break upon the spit on its landward side, a secondary spit may be built by shore drifting, forming a complex spit.

As shoreline development continues the spits join to produce baymouth bars, which cut off the bays from the open ocean. A variety of other types of bars also forms along the coast. Tombolos connect islands with the mainland. Between an island and mainland may lie a harbor suitable for small craft. Sometimes a double tombolo is formed, enclosing a lagoon of quiet water between island and mainland (Figure 24.15). A *looped bar* may grow along the landward side of an island as a result of the drift of materials around the lee side

Figure 24.24   Development of the shoreline of submergence. T = tombolo; S = spit; RS = recurved spit; CS = complex spit; CT = complex tombolo; LB = looped bar; CH = cliffed headland; DT = double tombolo; HB = headland beach; BMB = baymouth bar; CB = cuspate bar; BHB = bayhead beach; BSB = bayside beach; BHD = bayhead delta; L = lagoon; I = inlet; CD = cuspate delta.

of the island from the cliffed portion on the seaward side.

Along the sides and ends of the bays are formed *bayside beaches* and *bayhead beaches*. These grow as a result of the drift of sand along the shore from the headlands. Because the bay heads are places of minimum wave attack, the sand tends to accumulate there. If the bays are long and narrow, curving bars will be built across the bay. If located in the middle portion of the bay, they are called *midbay bars;* if near the bay heads, *bayhead bars*. These bars are always smoothly curved, the concave part of the curve facing seaward and merging smoothly with the line of the bayside beaches. A cuspate bar, described in an earlier paragraph, sometimes forms along the side of a bay or on the outer shoreline (Figure 24.16).

At bay heads, deltas may be built into water, thus aiding in the process of filling the bays.

As the stage of youth draws to a close, the outlying islands are completely consumed and the cliffed headlands begin to form a fairly straight line. Baymouth bars carry the smooth line of the shore from headland to headland.

With the attainment of a simple, smooth shoreline the stage of early maturity is reached. This coast consists alternately of cliffed headlands and baymouth bars. The point of fundamental importance is that throughout the life cycle thus far described, a highly irregular shoreline has been replaced by a nearly straight shoreline. The bays now become filled in by delta materials supplied by streams and by deposition of silts as the tide rises and falls, and the tide-induced currents flow in and out through narrow passes in the baymouth bars. Some small bays lack any passes in the baymouth bars, but the permeability of the sand is sufficient to permit runoff to escape into the sea. Ultimately the bays are occupied by tide flats and salt marsh.

Throughout early maturity the shoreline continues to retreat landward. The sea cliffs are progressively cut back while the baymouth bars are pushed back to keep in a straight line. Eventually a position is reached where the shoreline coincides with the original line of the bay heads. The baymouth bars and all other depositional features except the outer beach disappear, and the cliff of bedrock extends along the entire shoreline, which is then said to have attained full maturity (Figure 24.24). No further major development occurs, aside from the continued landward retreat of the shoreline. This retrogression will, however, become a very slow process, as the increased relief of the land causes the cliffs to be heightened and to supply more detritus to the shore.

Geographical aspects of shorelines of submergence

The influence of shorelines on human activity is strong, especially that of shorelines of submergence. The deep embayments of the youthful shoreline make splendid natural harbors. Much of the shoreline of Scandinavia, France, and the British Isles is thus provided with harbor facilities. Consequently, these peoples have a strong tradition of fishing, ship-building, ocean commerce, and marine activity generally. Mountainous relief of ria and fiord coasts makes agriculture difficult or impossible, forcing the people to turn to the sea for a livelihood. Rich forests and cheap hydroelectric power have, however, stimulated lumbering and manufacturing. New England and the Maritime Provinces of Canada have a youthful shoreline of submergence with abundant good harbors. The influence of this environment has been to foster the same development of fishing, whaling, ocean commerce, shipbuilding, and manufacturing seen in the British Isles and Scandinavian countries.

A mature shoreline of submergence has few natural harbors but extensive sheer marine cliffs. Portions of the channel coast of France illustrate this development (Figure 24.10).

Development of barrier-island coasts

In contrast to ria and fiord coasts, with their bold relief and deeply embayed outlines, are coasts of low relief from which the land slopes gently beneath the sea. The coastal plain of the Atlantic and Gulf coasts of the United States presents a particularly fine example of such a gently-sloping surface. As explained in Chapter 26, this coastal plain is a belt of relatively young sedimentary strata, formerly accumulated beneath the sea as deposits on the continental shelf. Emergence as a result of repeated crustal uplifts of epeirogenic nature has characterized this coastal plain during the latter part of the Cenozoic era and into recent time. There exist various elevated marine features, such as wave-cut scarps and platforms, extensive sand beaches, and lagoonal deposits of tide-water origin, lying many miles inland and at elevations of many tens of feet.

Such evidence points toward the conclusion that the shoreline of the Atlantic and gulf coastal plain is one of emergence, but on closer examination we find that the lower portions of stream valleys along the entire coast are drowned by a rise of sea level and that tidal channels and tidal marshes extend in many places for miles inland in the valley bottoms. (See Figure 26.6.) Clearly the last event has been one of a rise of sea level, occasioned by the melting of the Pleistocene ice sheets, and has produced many characteristics of a shoreline of submergence.

Along with the rise of sea level there has developed along much of the Atlantic and Gulf coast shoreline a *barrier island*, which is a low ridge of sand built by waves and further increased in height by the growth of dunes shaped from beach sands by wind action. Behind the barrier island lies a *lagoon*, which is a broad expanse of shallow water, often several miles wide, and in places largely filled with tidal deposits. (See Figure 26.10.)

The manner in which barrier islands may have come into existence along gently sloping coasts of the world since the end of the last glacial stage is illustrated in Figure 24.25 which represents the Gulf coast of Texas. At the time when ice sheets were at their maximum extent over the continents, sea level was drawn down to perhaps as much as 330 ft (100 m) below present sea level. The shoreline then was many miles farther seaward than today and a broad sloping plain lay exposed. Streams draining the land were extended across this plain and carved deep trenches into it. Then, as the ice began to melt rapidly some 10,000 to 12,000 years ago, the sea level began its rise and the shoreline rapidly shifted landward. The forward part of the block diagram in Figure 24.25 shows conditions about 5000 years ago. A low barrier island was formed of beach sands derived from the shallow sea floor and from longshore drift. As the sea level rose, the waves continued to add material to the crest of the barrier, building it up to keep pace with rise of water level. Correspondingly, the lagoon widened and the inner

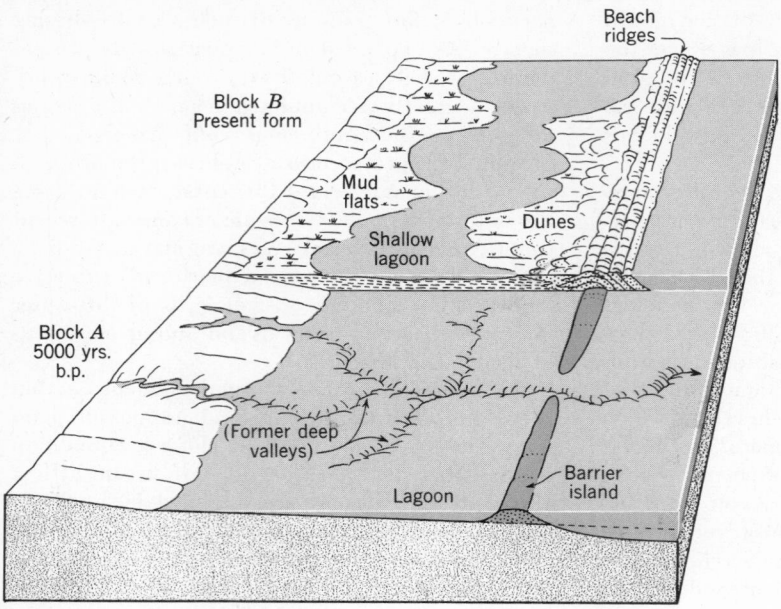

Figure 24.25 Upbuilding of a barrier island during post-glacial rise in sea level is an essential part of the history of the Texas Gulf Coast. (Based on data of H. N. Fisk, From A. N. Strahler, *The Earth Sciences*, Harper and Row, New York.)

shoreline encroached farther upon the gently sloping land surface. Today, as shown in the rear part of the block in Figure 24.25, the barrier island is a complex structure consisting of several wave-built beach ridges and of dunes which have widened the island on the landward side. The lagoon is partly filled by tidal muds.

Other examples of barrier-island coasts are found where glacial outwash plains were built out into the sea to produce a gently sloping plain. Post-glacial rise of sea level has partly submerged these outwash plains while at the same time a barrier beach has formed and produced a lagoon. A particularly striking example is the south shore of Long Island, New York, along which Fire Island separates Great South Bay, a lagoon over 5 mi (8 km) wide, from the Atlantic Ocean.

Tidal inlets and tidal deltas

A characteristic feature of most barrier islands—and of many baymouth bars as well—is the presence of gaps, known as *tidal inlets*, through which strong currents flow alternately seaward and landward as the tide rises and falls, building *tidal deltas*.

The spacing of tidal inlets in a barrier beach depends in part on the average range of tides along the coast, the spacing being closer where the range is greater. In heavy storms, the barrier may be breached by new inlets (Figure 24.26). Tidal currents will subsequently tend to keep a new inlet open, but it may be closed by shore drifting of sand. Among these opposing activities a sort of balance is maintained, so that neither too many nor too few inlets exist.

Geographical aspects of barrier-island shorelines

Shallow water results in generally poor natural harbors along barrier-island shorelines. The lagoon itself may serve as a harbor if channels and dock areas are dredged to sufficient depths. Ships enter and leave through one of the passes in the barrier island, but artificial sea walls and jetties are required to confine the current and thereby keep sufficient channel depth. Frequently the major port cities are located where a large river empties into the lagoon. Drowning of the lower courses of large rivers provides tidal channels which may be dredged to accommodate large vessels and thus make seaports of cities many miles inland.

One of the finest examples of a barrier island and lagoon is along the Gulf coast of Texas. Here the island is unbroken for as much as 100 mi (160 km) at a stretch and passes are few. The lagoon is 5 to 10 mi (8 to 16 km) wide, indicating that the original slope of the sea bottom was very slight. Galveston is built upon the barrier island adjacent to an inlet connecting Galveston Bay with the sea. Most other Texas ports, however, are located on the mainland shore. Submergence has caused an embayed inner shoreline with extensive estuaries marking the mouths of the larger streams. Corpus Christi, Rockport, Texas City, Lavaca, and other

Figure 24.26 East Moriches Inlet was cut through Fire Island, a barrier island off the Long Island shoreline, during a severe storm in March 1931. This aerial photograph, taken a few days after the breach occurred, shows the underwater tidal delta being built out into the lagoon (right) by currents. The entire area shown is about 1 mi (1.6 km) long. North is to the right; the open Atlantic Ocean on the left. (U.S. Army Air Forces Photograph.)

Figure 24.27 The horizontal step seen in the mountain base is a wave-cut bench with associated gravel deposits. It represents a high stand of ancient Lake Bonneville, which occupied the Great Salt Lake basin during the glacial period. (Photograph by Hal Rumel. Utah Travel Council.)

ports are located along the shores of these embayments. (See Figure 26.10.)

Still another good illustration of the geographical aspects of a barrier-island shoreline is seen in the Atlantic coast of New Jersey, Delaware, Maryland, Virginia, and North Carolina. (See Figure 26.5.) Virtually the entire coast from Sandy Hook to Cape Lookout is bordered by a barrier beach. Extensive post-glacial submergence has caused vast embayments such as Chesapeake Bay and Delaware Bay. Great port cities, such as Baltimore, Wilmington, and Philadelphia are situated at the heads of these tidal estuaries. Along the New Jersey coast, however, the old inner shoreline of the lagoon is remarkably straight and shows vestiges of earlier wave cutting. The lagoon is largely filled now and forms a flat plain through which wander sinuous tidal creeks. The barrier beach makes a splendid resort and has been fully utilized with the building of such cities as Atlantic City and Asbury Park.

Elevated shorelines

A shoreline may, at any stage in its development, be raised above water level so as to become a land feature. At the same time, a new shoreline, which is a true shoreline of emergence, is produced at the new position of the water line. The raised shoreline, or *elevated shoreline*, is not a shoreline of emergence; in fact, it is not a true shoreline at all because it is no longer associated with wave and current action. Having once been elevated, it is attacked by weathering, mass wasting, and streams and will eventually be destroyed.

Elevated shorelines result either from crustal uplift along a coastal belt such as that of Alaska or California coast, which are subject to faulting and earthquakes, or from a falling of sea or lake level.

Lake Bonneville, the ancestor of the present Salt Lake in Utah, rose to a maximum level in the Pleistocene epoch when rainfall was greater and evaporation less than now. Excellent illustrations of elevated shorelines are to be found on the lower slopes of the mountain ranges in the Salt Lake region (Figure 24.27). From a study of these ancient wave-cut benches with their associated beaches, spits, and bars, it has been possible to reconstruct the history of the old lake and to make inferences as to climates of the past.

Where lake level falls steadily, or coastal regions rise steadily, the elevated shorelines become *strand lines* resembling natural contours of the land (Figure 24.28). Crustal rise of this continual and rather uniform nature has been occurring in the Baltic Sea area and along the Arctic coast of North America as a result of the recovery of the crust following its depression under the load of Pleistocene ice sheets.

Figure 24.28 This great succession of elevated strand lines bordering the shore of Hudson Bay documents the almost-continuous post-glacial rise of the earth's crust which has followed the removal of ice load. (Photograph by Canadian Government Department of Energy, Mines, and Resources; Air Photo Division.)

Where elevated wave-cut platforms stand but a few feet above mean sea level, as they do on many islands of the Pacific (Figure 24.29), we have difficulty in deciding whether there has been a rise of land level or a sinking of sea level, inasmuch as the result would be the same in either event.

Extreme emergence of a coast may expose a wide belt of former sea floor (Figure 24.30). This new land is a coastal plain (Chapter 26) and is veneered with recently formed sedimentary layers.

Coral-reef shorelines

As a variety of neutral shoreline, coral-reef shorelines are unique in that the addition of new land is made by organisms: *corals*, which secrete lime to form their skeletons, and *algae*, plants that also make limy encrustations. Corals are colonial types of animals, that is, they occur in large colonies of individuals. As coral colonies die, new ones are built upon them, thus developing a coral limestone made up of the strongly cemented limy

skeletons. Coral fragments torn free by wave attack and pulverized may be deposited to form beaches, spits, and bars, which later are cemented into a limestone.

Coral-reef shorelines occur in warm, tropical water between the limits 30° N and 25° S lat. Water temperatures above 68° F (20°C) are necessary for dense reef coral growth. Furthermore, reef corals live near the water surface, down to limiting depths of about 200 ft (60 m). Water must be free of suspended sediment and well aerated for vigorous coral growth; hence corals thrive in positions exposed to wave attack from the open sea. Because muddy water prevents coral growth, reefs are missing opposite the mouths of muddy streams. Coral reefs are remarkably flat on top (Figure 24.31) and have a level approximately equal to the upper one-third mark of the range of tide. Thus they are exposed at low tide and covered at high tide.

Three general types of coral reefs may be recog-

Figure 24.29 This wave-cut rock bench (*B*) on the shore of Tutuila in the Samoan Islands is about 10 ft (3 m) above mean sea level and may indicate a recent drop of sea level or a recent rise of the island. (After W. M. Davis.)

Figure 24.31 A fringing reef on the south coast of Java forms a broad bench between surf zone (left) and a white coral-sand beach. Inland is rainforest. (Photograph by Luchtvaart-Afdeeling, Bandung.)

nized: (1) fringing reefs, (2) barrier reefs, and (3) atolls. *Fringing reefs* are built as platforms attached to shore (Figure 24.32). They are widest in front of headlands where wave attack is strongest, and the corals receive clean water with abundant food supply. Fringing reefs are usually absent near the mouths and deltas of streams, where the water is muddy. This is a fact of great military importance where the problem is to find reef-free places for landing of troops and supplies. Fringing reefs may be from 0.25 to 1.5 mi (0.4 to 2.5 km) wide, depending on the length of time that the reef has been developing.

Barrier reefs lie out from shore and are separated from the mainland by a lagoon which may range from 0.5 to 10 mi (2.5 to 16 km) or more in width (Figure 24.33). The reef itself may be from 20 to 3000 ft (6 to 900 m) wide. The lagoon is shallow and flat-floored, usually 120 to 240 ft (35 to 75 m) deep. There are, however, many towerlike columns of coral in the lagoon. *Passes*, which occur at intervals in barrier reefs, are narrow gaps through which excess water from breaking

Figure 24.30 A coastal-plain strip 40 mi (65 km) wide and more than 1000 mi (1600 km) long indicates emergence along the east coast of peninsular India. The present shoreline is a young shoreline of emergence; the former shoreline, now of the elevated type, appears as a steep mountain front rising abruptly from a plain. (After W. M. Davis and S. W. Cushing.)

waves is returned from the lagoon to the open sea. They sometimes occur opposite deltas on the mainland shore, because of the inhibiting effect of mud on coral growth. Passes are of geographical and military importance because they provide the only means of entrance by ship into the lagoon.

Atolls are more or less circular coral reefs enclosing a lagoon, but without any land inside (Figure 24.34). In all other respects they are similar to barrier reefs. On large atolls, parts of the reef have been built up by wave action and wind to form low island chains, connected by the reef. A cross section of an atoll shows that the lagoon is flat-floored and shallow, and that the outer slopes are steep, often descending thousands of feet to great ocean depths.

Several plausible theories have been advanced for the origin of atolls and barrier reefs. To explain each one and discuss the advantages and disadvantages of each would take many pages. One interesting theory of origin, which has been popular since it was first outlined by a great scientist, Charles Darwin, in 1842, may be called the *subsidence theory* (Figure 24.35). He supposed that small islands, such as volcanoes, slowly subsided in a general downwarping of the earth's crust over parts of the ocean basin. Coral reefs, which were originally fringing reefs attached to the island shores, continued to build upward as the island subsided. Thus the area of the island shrank and a lagoon formed, creating a barrier reef. Finally the island sank out of sight, but the reef persisted, maintained at sea level by vigorous coral and algal growth.

Coral-Reef Shorelines | 369

Figure 24.32 Fringing reefs are widest in front of headlands and may be absent near the mouths of streams. (After W. M. Davis.)

Figure 24.34 Bikini Atoll in the Pacific, scene of early atom bomb tests, is thought to consist of a great thickness of reef deposits resting on a sea mountain of volcanic rock. (After M. Dobrin, et al.)

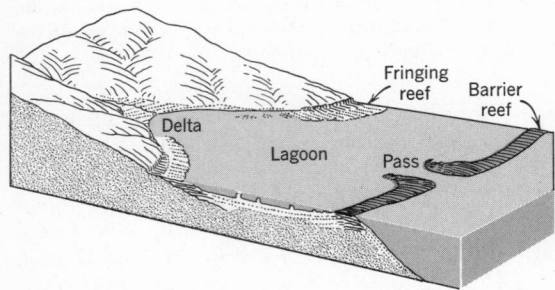

Figure 24.33 A barrier reef is separated from the mainland by a shallow lagoon. (After W. M. Davis.)

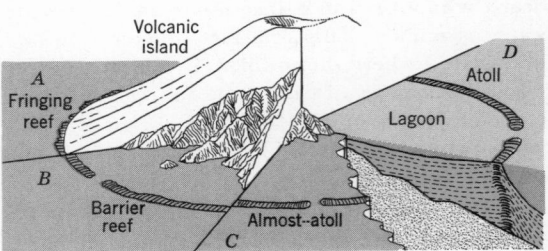

Figure 24.35 The subsidence theory of barrier-reef and atoll development is shown in four stages, beginning with a fringing reef attached to a volcanic island and ending with a circular reef. (After W. M. Davis.)

The geographical aspects of atoll islands are unique in some respects. First, there is no rock other than coral limestone, composed of calcium carbonate. This means that trees requiring other minerals, such as silica, cannot be cultivated without the aid of fertilizers or some outside source of rock from a larger island composed of volcanic or other igneous rock. The palm tree is native to atoll islands because it thrives on brackish water, and the seed, or palm nut, is distributed widely by floating from one island to another. Native inhabitants have cultivated the cocoanut palm to provide food, clothing, fibers, and building materials. Fresh water is scarce on small atoll islands because there is not enough surface area for the collection of rainfall, and the land is so low that a high water table of fresh water is not present to supply springs, streams, and wells. Rainfall must be caught in open vessels or catchment basins and carefully conserved. Fish and other marine animals are an important part of the human diet on atoll islands. Calm waters of the lagoon make a good place for fishing and for beaching canoes. Coral islands of the western Pacific stand in continual danger of devastation by tropical cyclones (typhoons). Breaking waves wash over the low-lying ground, sweeping away palm trees and houses and drowning the inhabitants. There is no high ground for refuge. In the same way, great seismic sea waves of unpredictable occurrence may inundate atoll islands.

Mangrove coasts are of great extent in tropical and equatorial regions, where an abundance of fine sediment in suspension prevents coral reef growth. Mangrove as a form of natural vegetation is discussed in Chapter 16.

REFERENCES FOR FURTHER STUDY

Johnson, D. W. (1919), *Shore processes and shoreline development*, John Wiley and Sons, New York, 584 pp. Reprinted in 1965, Hafner Publ., New York.

Lobeck, A. K. (1939), *Geomorphology*, McGraw-Hill Book Co., New York, 731 pp. See Chapter X and XII.

Guilcher, A. (1958), *Coastal and submarine morphology*, John Wiley and Sons, New York, 274 pp.

King, C. A. M. (1960), *Beaches and coasts*, St. Martin's Press, New York, 403 pp.

Shephard, F. P. (1963), *Submarine geology*, second edition, Harper and Row, New York, 557 pp. See Chapters 6, 7, and 12.

Bascomb, W. (1964), *Waves and beaches*, Doubleday and Co., New York, 260 pp.

Thornbury, W. D. (1969), *Principles of geomorphology*, second edition, John Wiley and Sons, New York, 594 pp. See Chapter 17.

REVIEW QUESTIONS

1. Why do breakers form in shallow water? What do the terms *swash* and *backwash* mean? How are beach materials moved by these currents?

2. Under what conditions do waves do the greatest amount of shore erosion? When are beaches built?

3. Explain beach drifting and longshore drifting. What forms are built by these processes? What is a longshore current, and how is it caused?

4. Describe the phenomenon of wave refraction. Why does refraction occur? When waves are refracted along an embayed coast where is the energy of wave erosion concentrated? Where is it least? What important result does this have on the form of the shoreline?

5. Describe the development of sea cliffs, beginning with a newly submerged slope and continuing through to a mature sea cliff. Explain the following terms: nip, sea cave, sea arch, stack, wave-cut notch, abrasion platform, beach, shore-face terrace hanging valley.

6. What are sand spits? How and where do they form? What shape characterizes the end of a spit?

7. Explain the formation of baymouth bars, tombolos, and cuspate bars. How does a cuspate foreland differ from a cuspate bar?

8. Describe the rise and fall of water level in a simple semidaily tide cycle. What are spring and neap tides?

9. How are tidal currents produced? Define flood current, slack water, and ebb current.

10. What deposits of sediment are associated with tidal currents in bays and estuaries? Describe these deposits as to form and composition. How are salt marshes utilized by man?

11. How can shorelines be classified? Name the five principal classes.

12. What kinds of shorelines of submergence are recognized? Name and explain the subdivisions.

13. Describe the changing coastal landforms of a shoreline of submergence as it passes through its development cycle.

14. What is a barrier-island coast? How are barrier islands formed? How are tidal inlets related to barrier islands?

15. How have shorelines of submergence exerted an influence on human activities?

16. Discuss the geographical aspects of barrier-island shorelines. Compare harbor facilities of a barrier-island shoreline with those of a young shoreline of submergence.

17. Name several kinds of neutral shorelines.

18. What is meant by an elevated shoreline? How does it differ from a shoreline of emergence? Where may some excellent elevated shorelines be seen today?

19. How are coral reefs formed? Under what conditions do reef-building corals flourish?

20. What three general types of reefs are formed? Describe each type. Explain Darwin's subsidence theory of atolls.

CHAPTER **25**
Landforms Made by Wind

WIND, the fourth of the agents of erosion thus far discussed, produces a variety of interesting sequential landforms, both erosional and depositional. In terms of total mass of material thereby removed or deposited, however, it ranks below mass wasting, running water, waves, and ice, except in certain desert regions especially favorable to its action. In humid regions, with ample soil moisture and dense vegetative cover, there are few evidences of the work of wind. These usually are coastal sand dunes. Elsewhere, vegetation holds the ground in place unless man has laid it bare.

Erosion by wind

Wind performs two kinds of erosional work. Loose particles lying upon the ground surface may be lifted into the air or rolled along the ground. This process is *deflation*. Where the wind drives sand and dust particles against an exposed rock or soil surface, causing it to be worn away by the impact of the particles, the process is *abrasion*. Abrasion requires cutting tools carried by the wind; deflation is accomplished by air currents alone.

Deflation acts wherever the ground surface is thoroughly dried out and is littered with small, loose particles derived by rock weathering or previously deposited by running water, ice, or waves.

Thus, dry river courses, beaches, and areas of recently formed glacial deposits are highly susceptible to deflation. In dry climates, virtually the entire ground surface is subject to deflation because the soil or rock is everywhere bare. Wind is selective in its deflational action. The finest particles, those which constitute clay and silt, are lifted most easily and raised high into the air. Sand grains are moved only by moderately strong winds and tend to travel close to the ground. Gravel fragments and rounded pebbles up to 2 or 3 in (5 to 8 cm) in diameter may be rolled over flat ground by strong winds but do not travel far. They become easily lodged in hollows or between their fellows. Consequently, where a mixture of sizes of

Figure 25.1   This blowout hollow on the plains of Nebraska contains a remnant column of the original material, thus providing a natural yardstick for the depth of material removed by deflation. (Photograph by N. H. Darton, U.S. Geological Survey.)

particles is present on the ground, the finer sizes are removed; the coarser particles remain behind.

The principal landform produced by deflation is a shallow depression termed a *blowout*, or *deflation hollow*. This depression may be from a few yards to a mile or more in diameter, but is usually only a few feet deep. Blowouts form in plains regions in dry climates. Any small depression in the surface of the plain, particularly where the grass cover is broken through, may develop into a blowout. Rains fill the depression, creating a shallow pond or lake. As the water evaporates the mud bottom dries out and cracks, forming small scales or pellets of dried mud which are lifted out by the wind. In grazing lands, cattle may trample the margins of the depression into a mass of mud, breaking down the protective grass-root structure and facilitating removal when dry. Thus the depression is progressively enlarged (Figure 25.1). Blowouts are also found on rock surfaces where the rock is being disintegrated by weathering.

In the great deserts of southeastern California, Arizona, and New Mexico, the floors of intermontane basins are subject to deflation. The flat floors of the vast, shallow playas have in some places been reduced by deflation as much as several feet over areas of many square miles.

Where deflation has been active on a ground surface littered with loose fragments of a wide range of sizes, the pebbles that remain behind tend to accumulate until they cover the entire surface (Figure 25.2). By rolling or jostling about as the fine particles are blown away, the pebbles may become closely fitted together, forming a *desert pavement*. In North Africa such a pebble-covered surface is called a *reg*. The precipitation of calcium carbonate, gypsum, and other salts near the surface, as ground water is drawn to the surface and evaporated in dry weather, tends to cement the pebbles together, forming a highly effective protection against further deflation.

The sandblast action of wind against exposed rock surfaces is limited to the basal few feet of a cliff, hill, or other rock mass rising above a relatively flat plain, because sand grains do not rise high into the air. Wind abrasion produces pits, grooves, and hollows in the rock. Where a small rock mass projects above the plain it may be cut away at the base to make a *pedestal rock*, delicately balanced upon a thin stem. Most pedestal rocks, or *mushroom rocks*, are, however, produced by weathering processes.

Dust storms and sand storms

In dry seasons over plains regions, strong, turbulent winds lift great quantities of fine dust into the air, forming a dense, high cloud called a *dust storm*. The dust storm is generated where ground

Figure 25.2 This desert pavement of quartzite fragments was formed by action of both wind and water on the surface of an alluvial fan in the desert of southeastern California. Fragments range in size from 1 to 12 in (2.5 to 33 cm). Silt underlies the layer of stones. (Photograph by C. S. Denny, U.S. Geological Survey.)

surfaces have been stripped of protective vegetative cover by cultivation or grazing, or where they naturally carry no vegetation cover because of extreme aridity of the climate. A dust storm approaches as a great dark cloud extending from the ground surface to heights of several thousand feet (Figure 25.3). Within the dust cloud deep gloom or even total darkness prevails. visibility is cut to a few yards, and a fine choking dust penetrates everywhere.

It has been estimated that as much as 4000 tons of dust may be suspended in a cubic mile of air (875 metric tons per cubic kilometer). On this basis, a dust storm 300 mi (500 km) in diameter might be carrying more than 100 million tons (90 million metric tons) of dust—enough to make a

Figure 25.3 Front of an approaching dust storm, Coconino Plateau, Arizona. (Photograph by D. L. Babenroth.)

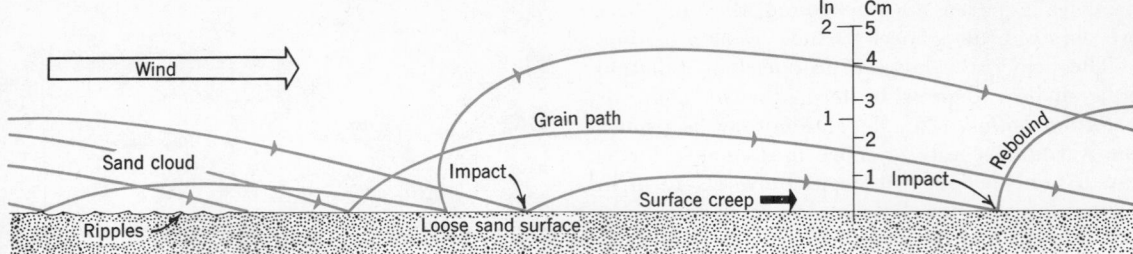

Figure 25.4   Sand particles travel in a series of long jumps.   (After R. A. Bagnold.)

hill 100 ft (30 km) high and 2 mi (3 km) across the base.[1] A region that supplied the dust for thousands of such storms would thus lose a considerable mass over a span of thousands of years. Whether during the same period streams would remove more material from the same area is difficult to say, but in all probability they would remove much more.

Dust travels enormous distances in the air. That of individual dust storms is often traceable as far as 2500 mi (4000 km). Volcanoes erupt much extremely fine dust into the air. The renowned eruption of the volcano Krakatoa in Indonesia in the year 1883 cast out an enormous quantity of dust, some of which was caught by atmospheric circulation at high levels and carried around the entire earth. It is said that unusually brilliantly colored sunsets occurred in the British Isles in the years following 1883 as a result of the presence of the Krakatoa dust in the atmosphere. These were referred to as the "Chelsea sunsets," and were a favorite subject for paintings by English artists of the period.

The true desert *sandstorm* is a low cloud of moving sand that rises usually only a few inches

[1]A. K. Lobeck, *Geomorphology*, McGraw-Hill Book Co., New York. 1939, 731 pp., p. 380.

Figure 25.5   Barchans, or crescentic dunes. Arrow indicates wind direction.

and at most 6 ft (2 m) above the ground. It consists of sand particles driven by a strong wind. Those who have experienced sandstorms report that a man standing upright may have his head and shoulders entirely above the limits of the sand cloud. The reason why the sand does not rise higher is that the individual particles are engaged in a leaping motion, termed *saltation* (Figure 25.4). Grains describe a curved path of travel and strike the ground with considerable force but at a low angle. The impact causes the grain to rebound into the air. At the same time, the surface layer of sand grains creeps downwind as the result of the constant impact of the bouncing grains.

The erosional effect of blown sand is thus concentrated on surfaces exposed less than a foot or two (0.3 to 0.6 m) above the flat ground surface. Telephone poles on wind-swept sandy plains are quickly cut through at the base unless a protective metal sheathing or heap of large stones is placed around the base.

Sand dunes

A *dune* is any hill or accumulation of sand shaped by the wind. Dunes may be active, or *live*, when bare of vegetation and constantly changing form under wind currents. They may be inactive, or *fixed*, dunes, covered by vegetation that has taken root and serves to prevent further shifting of the sand.

Several common varieties of dunes are treated here. The *crescentic dune*, or *barchan* (also spelled barcan, barkhan, or barchane), is an isolated dune, which in plan view resembles a blunted crescent (Figure 25.5). The broadly rounded ends of the crescent point downwind and indicate the direction of dune motion and prevailing winds. On the windward side of the crest the sand slope is gentle, being the slope up which the sand grains move. On the lee side of the dune, within the crescent, is a steep curving dune slope, the *slip face*, which maintains an angle of about 35° from the horizontal (Figure 25.6). Sand grains fall or slide down the steep face after being blown free of the crest. When a strong wind is blowing, the flying sand makes a perceptible cloud at the crest. The term

Figure 25.6 Barchan dunes at Biggs, Oregon (Photograph by G. K. Gilbert, U.S. Geological Survey.)

smoking crest has been used for this feature. Crescentic dunes rest upon a flat, pebble-covered ground surface. The sand may originate as a drift in the lee of some obstacle, such as a small hill, rock, or clump of brush. Once a sufficient mass of sand has formed it begins to move downwind, taking the form of a crescent dune. Thus the dunes are commonly arranged in chains extending downwind from the source drifts.

Where sand is so abundant that it completely covers the ground, dunes take the form of wavelike ridges separated by troughlike furrows. The dunes are called *transverse dunes* because their crests trend at right angles to direction of wind (Figure 25.7). The entire area may be called a *sand sea*, for it resembles a storm-tossed sea suddenly frozen to immobility. The term *erg*, referring to any large expanse of dunes in the Sahara Desert, has been

Figure 25.7 This air photograph of a sand-dune field between Yuma, Arizona, and Calexico, California, shows a sand sea of transverse dunes in the background and a field of crescentic barchan dunes in the foreground. (Copyrighted Spence Air Photos.)

Sand Dunes | 375

A. Coastal blowout dunes with saucerlike depressions.

C. Parabolic dunes of hairpin form.

B. Parabolic blowout dunes on an arid plain.

D. Longitudinal dune ridges on a desert plain.

Figure 25.8   Four types of dunes. Prevailing wind, shown by arrow, is the same for all diagrams.

Figure 25.9   At Beaufort Harbor, near Cape Lookout, North Carolina, coastal sand dunes are inundating a forest of live oak. (Photograph by J. A. Holmes, U.S. Geological Survey.)

adopted by geographers for this type of landscape. Individual sand ridges have sharp crests and are asymmetrical, the gentle slope being on the windward, the steep slope on the lee side. Deep depressions lie between the dune ridges. Sand seas require huge quantities of sand, often derived from weathering of a sandstone formation underlying the ground surface, or from adjacent alluvial plains. Still other transverse dune belts form adjacent to beaches which supply abundant sand and have strong onshore winds (Figure 25.10).

Another group of dunes belongs to a family in which the curve of the dune crest is bowed convexly downwind, the opposite of the curvature of crests in the barchan and transverse dunes. These may be described as *parabolic* in form. A common representative of this class, the *coastal blowout dune*, is formed adjacent to beaches, where large supplies of sand are available and are blown landward by prevailing winds (Figure 25.8A). A saucer-shaped depression is formed by deflation; the sand is heaped in a great curving ridge resembling a

Figure 25.10 The arrows on this photograph point to elongate blowout dunes of hairpin form, which once advanced from the beach and have since become stabilized by vegetation. Active transverse dunes are overriding the blowout dunes in a fresh wave, San Luis Obispo Bay, California. (Spence Air Photos.)

horseshoe in plan. On the landward side is a steep slip face which advances over the lower ground and buries forests, killing the trees (Figure 25.9). Coastal blowout dunes are well displayed along the southern and eastern shore of Lake Michigan, those of the southern shore being set aside for public use as the Indiana Dunes State Park.

In arid plains and plateaus, where vegetation is sparse and winds strong, groups of *parabolic blow-out dunes* develop to the lee of shallow deflation hollows (Figure 25.8B). Sand is caught by low bushes and accumulates in a broad, low ridge. These dunes have no steep slip faces, and may remain relatively immobile. In some cases, however, the dune ridge migrates downwind, drawing the parabola into a long, narrow form with parallel sides

(Figure 25.8C). This form resembles a hairpin in plan; hence has been named a *hairpin dune*, although it is a member of the parabolic family. Hairpin dunes stabilized by vegetative growth are seen in Figure 25.10.

Still another class of dunes is described as *longitudinal* because the dune ridges run parallel with the wind direction. On desert plains and plateaus, where sand supply is meager but winds are strong from one direction, *longitudinal dune ridges* are formed (Figure 25.8D). These are usually only a few feet high, but may be several miles long. In some areas, at least, the longitudinal dune is produced by extreme development of the hairpin dune, such that the parallel side ridges become the dominant form.

Figure 25.11 This oblique air photograph shows longitudinal sand-dune ridges reaching as far as the eye can see. Simpson Desert, southeast of Alice Springs, Australia. (Photograph by George Silk, *Life Magazine*, © Time, Inc.)

Figure 25.12 Longitudinal sand drifts appear on this air photograph as sharp-crested bladelike streamers of sand drawn out to the lee of a hill. Several barchan dunes are present in the lower left-hand corner. Width of area shown is about 0.75 mi (1.2 km). Air photomosaic of portion of Chao-Virú-Moche area, Peru. (Courtesy Ministerio de Fomento.)

Longitudinal dune ridges, oriented parallel with dominant winds, occupy vast areas of central Australia referred to as *sand-ridge deserts* (Figure 25.11). Ridges average 30 to 50 ft (10 to 15 m) in height, are spaced 0.25 to 1.5 mi (0.4 to 2.4 km) apart, and run in continuous length as much as 25 to 50 mi (40 to 80 km).

Also longitudinally oriented with respect to the wind, but not a true dune, is the *sand drift*, which is a long, tapering sharp-crested ridge of sand extending downwind from some topographic obstacle, such as a hill that might rise above a desert plain (Figure 25.12). Sand moving in saltation passes over or around the obstacle, lodging to the leeward and gradually building the drift until the zone of quiet air is filled.

Although the dunes described above are representative of types found in the United States, many other types have been described. In the vast deserts of North Africa, Arabia, and southern Iran are large, complex dune forms apparently not represented in the United States. One of these is the *seif dune*, or *sword dune*, which is a huge tapering sand ridge whose crestline rises and falls in alternate peaks and saddles and whose side slopes are indented by crescentic slip faces. Seif dunes may be a few hundred feet high and tens of miles long. Another Saharan type is the *star dune*, *pyramidal dune*, or *heaped dune*, a great hill of sand whose base resembles a many-pointed star in plan (Figure 25.13). Radial ridges of sand rise toward the dune center, culminating in sharp peaks as high as 300 ft (100 m) or more above the base. Star dunes seem to remain fixed in position for centuries and can serve as reliable landmarks for desert travelers.

Loess

In several parts of the world the ground is underlain by deposits of wind-transported silt, which has settled out from dust storms over many thousands of years. The material thus formed is known as *loess*. It generally has a uniform buff color and lacks any visible layering or other banding. Loess has a tendency to break, or *cleave*, along vertical cliffs wherever it is exposed by the cutting of a stream or by man (Figure 25.14). The cleavage is possibly produced by a slight shrinkage of the entire mass as it has compacted after being laid down.

Perhaps the greatest deposits of loess are in China, where thicknesses over 100 ft (30 m) are common and a maximum of 300 ft (90 m) has been measured. It covers many hundreds of square miles in northern China and appears to have been derived from the interior of Asia, out of which blow dry winter winds. Loess deposits are also important in central Europe, Argentina, and New Zealand, but not so extensive or thick as in China.

Figure 25.13   Seen from an altitude of 6 mi (10 km), these sand dunes of the Libyan desert appear as irregular patches which rise to star-shaped central peaks 300 to 600 ft (90 to 180 m) higher than the intervening flat ground. Width of the photograph represents about 7 mi (11 km). (Photograph by courtesy of Aero Service Corporation.)

In the United States, important loess deposits lie in the Mississippi River valley (Figure 25.15). Much of the prairie plains region of Illinois, Iowa, Missouri, Nebraska, and Kansas is underlain by a loess layer ranging in thickness from 3 to 100 ft (1 to 30 m). There are also extensive deposits along the lands bordering the lower Mississippi River floodplain on its east side, throughout Tennessee and Mississippi (Figure 25.14). Still other loess deposits are in northeast Washington and western Idaho. The American and European loess deposits are directly related to the continental glaciers of the Pleistocene epoch. At the time when the ice covered much of North America and Europe, it

is possible that a generally dry winter climate prevailed in the land bordering the ice sheets and that strong winds blew southward and eastward over the bare ground, picking up silt from the floodplains of braided streams which discharged the melt water from the ice. This dust settled upon the ground between streams, gradually building up to produce a smooth, level ground surface. The loess is particularly thick along the eastern sides of the valleys because of prevailing westerly winds, and is well exposed along the bluffs of most streams flowing through the region today (Figure 25.16).

The importance of loess in world agricultural resources cannot be easily overestimated. Loess

Figure 25.14 This perpendicular road cut in loess south of Vicksburg is typical of thick glacial loess accumulations on the eastern bluffs of the Mississippi River. (Photograph by Orlo Childs.)

Figure 25.16 Thickness of loess in Illinois. (After R. F. Flint.)

plains and plateaus have developed rich, black soils especially suited to cultivation of grains. These are the prairie, chernozem, chestnut, and brown soils described in Chapter 14. The highly productive plains of southern Russia, the Argentine Pampa, and the rich grain region of north China are underlain by loess. In the United States, corn is extensively cultivated on the loess plains in those states, such as Iowa and Illinois, where rainfall is sufficient; wheat is grown farther west on loess plains of Kansas and Nebraska and in the Palouse region of eastern Washington.

Because loess forms vertical walls along valley sides and is able to resist sliding or flowage, but at the same time is easily dug into, it has been

Figure 25.15 Loess deposits of the central United States (After E. T. Apfel.)

Figure 25.17 Road sunken deeply into loess, Shensi, China. (Photograph by Frederick G. Clapp, courtesy of The Geographical Review.)

widely used for cave dwellings both in China and in Central Europe. In China, old trails and roads in the loess have become deeply sunken into the ground as a result of the pulverization of the loess of the road bed and its removal by wind and water (Figure 25.17).

REFERENCES FOR FURTHER STUDY

Gautier, E. F. (1935), *Sahara: The great Desert*, translated by D. F. Mayhen, Columbia University Press, New York, 264 pp.

Lobeck, A. K. (1939), *Geomorphology*, McGraw-Hill Book Co., New York, 731 pp. See Chapter 11.

Bagnold, R. A. (1941), *The physics of blown sand and desert dunes*, Methuen and Co., London, 265 pp.

Cotton, C. A. (1942), *Climatic accidents in landscape-making*, Whitcombe and Tombs, Christchurch, N.Z., 354 pp. See Chapters 1 and 9.

Flint, R. F. (1957), *Glacial and Pleistocene geology*, John Wiley and Sons, New York, 533 pp. See Eolian features, pp. 176–194.

Thornbury, W. D. (1969), *Principles of geomorphology*, second edition, John Wiley and Sons, New York, 591 pp. See Chapter 12.

REVIEW QUESTIONS

1. Explain the processes of deflation and abrasion by wind.

2. What conditions favor deflation? What topographic forms are produced?

3. What is a desert pavement? How does it form? What is a reg?

4. What forms does wind abrasion produce?

5. How do dust storms originate? How much material might be carried in a single dust storm? How far does the dust travel?

6. How do sand grains travel in a sandstorm? How high do the grains rise? At what level is abrasion concentrated?

7. What are sand dunes? What is the distinction between live dunes and fixed dunes?

8. Describe a crescentic, or barchan, dune. In which direction does it move?

9. What are transverse dunes? What is a sand sea? What is the source of the sand? What places would be most favorable for the development of dune areas? What is an erg landscape?

10. Describe a coastal blowout dune, a parabolic blowout dune and a hairpin dune. How does each develop?

11. Describe longitudinal sand dunes and drifts. What do they indicate as to the direction of prevailing winds?

12. Where are seif dunes and star dunes found?

13. What is loess? How is it formed? What structure has loess?

14. Describe the distribution of loess throughout the world. What origin has the loess of northern China?

15. What states of the Mississippi-Missouri river region have loess deposits? Of what economic importance is loess?

Coastal Plains, Horizontal Strata, Domes

THE foregoing chapters on landforms produced by weathering, mass wasting, streams, ice, waves, and wind have given little or no account of the manner in which variations in rock composition and structure are capable of exerting a powerful control upon the shapes and sizes of landforms. Instead, by assuming that all bedrock is of uniform composition throughout, it has been possible to describe the simple, ideal erosional landforms produced by each agent of denudation. There are, it is true, large land areas where bedrock is fairly uniform throughout, and it is in such areas that the denudational agents can produce the ideal forms. Elsewhere, sedimentary rocks are tilted, folded, domed, or faulted; metamorphic rocks are arranged in belted patterns; intrusive igneous rocks have solidified in a variety of bodies. It is with such structures and their topographic expression that these chapters deal.

Classification of landmasses

As illustrated in Figure 26.1, landmasses fall into several groups, distinguished according to the structure and composition of the bedrock comprising the mass.

A. **Undisturbed structures.**
 1. **Coastal plains.** Recently emerged coastal belts underlain by sedimentary rock layers which lap over older rocks of the continents.
 2. **Horizontal strata.** Sedimentary strata, essentially horizontal in attitude, which have been raised over a large area, but not otherwise seriously disturbed. Horizontal lava flows of great thickness and extent may be included in this group.
B. **Disturbed structures.**
 3. **Domes and basins.** Circular or oval zones of uplift or depression causing sedimentary layers to be convexly or concavely bent.
 4. **Folds.** Sedimentary strata that have been deformed by mountain-making crustal movements into long belts of wavelike folds. The folds may be broad and open or tightly compressed, depending on the degree of crustal compression.
 5. **Fault blocks.** Crustal masses of any rock type or structure broken by faulting into sharply cut

blocks that have been displaced in relation to one another. Some tilting usually accompanies the faulting.
 6. **Homogeneous crystallines.** Masses of intrusive igneous rock or metamorphic rock which are essentially uniform throughout as regards their resistance to weathering and erosion.
 7. **Belted metamorphics.** Narrow zones of metamorphic rocks forming parallel mountain and valley belts (Figure 17.14).
 8. **Complex structures.** Crustal masses that have suffered a combination of folding, faulting, or intrusion by igneous rocks so as to make a mass of irregular and complicated structures.
C. **Volcanoes and related forms.**
 All types of rock masses resulting from the extrusion of molten rock. These include various types of volcanoes and lava flows.

There is a significant difference in the initial appearance of the undisturbed and the disturbed structures. The former have surfaces of low relief (plains or plateaus) before erosional modification sets in. The disturbed structures and volcanic forms, on the other hand, usually have bold, mountainous relief in the initial stage. Relief is greatest at the beginning of their life history, and the masses are ultimately reduced to surfaces of faint relief.

Each one of the structural types described above passes through an orderly series of erosional stages, patterned after the general cycle of landmass denudation already explained. For regions of horizontal strata or homogenous crystalline rocks, this cycle is very similar to the ideal general cycle because these rock masses are of uniform composition and structure in every direction horizontally. Folds, fault blocks, domes, and volcanoes, however, have life cycles quite different, not only from the ideal cycle, but also from one another, because the rock variations or initial shapes have a dominant control upon the denudational rates.

Coastal plains

Coastal plains pass through a series of stages illustrated in Figure 26.2. In Block *A* the region has recently emerged from beneath the sea, where

Figure 26.1   Land masses can be classified according to the groups illustrated here. Belted metamorphics are shown in Figure 17.14. Classification is based on variety and structure of rock.

it was formerly a shallow continental shelf accumulating successive layers of sediment brought from the land and distributed by currents. On the initial surface, streams flow directly seaward, down the slope of the new surface. A stream of this origin is a *consequent stream*, defined as any stream whose course is controlled by the initial slope of land surface. Consequent streams occur on many landforms, such as volcanoes, fault blocks, or beds of drained lakes. Streams that formerly drained the land surface inland from the coastal plain, but that now have become extended across it to reach the new shoreline, are called *extended consequent streams.* The term *oldland* is applied to the area

of older rock lying inland from the coastal plain. If the oldland had prominent hills upon its surface before the submergence which allowed sediments to be deposited, the hills may project through the coastal-plain layers as *mendips* (named after the Mendip Hills of southern England), or *inliers.*

In the mature stage of coastal-plain development a new series of streams and topographic features has developed (Block *B*). Where more easily eroded strata (usually clay or shale) are exposed, denudation is rapid, making *lowlands.* Between them rise broad low ridges or belts of hills comprising *cuestas.* The lowland lying between the oldland and the first cuesta is called the *inner*

A. Initial stage; plain recently emerged.

B. Mature stage; cuestas and lowlands developed. *S* = subsequent: *C* = consequent; *O* = obsequent; *R* = resequent.

C. Late mature or old stage; relief very low.

Figure 26.2   Development of a broad coastal plain. (After A. K. Lobeck.)

Figure 26.3   This sharply defined cuesta in the Paris basin of northern France has its steep face to the east (left), a very gentle slope westward from the crest. (Photograph by Douglas Johnson.)

lowland. Cuestas are commonly underlain by sand, sandstone, limestone, or chalk. They have a fairly steep slope on the landward side, or *inface*, because the edge of the eroded layer is exposed on this side. The seaward slope, or *backslope*, of the cuesta is gentle because it follows the top surface of the gently inclined harder layer. Where the resistant layer is very hard and is underlain by a weak layer, the cuesta face is often steep with occasional rock cliffs, as in the limestone cuesta near Rheims, France (Figure 26.3). More commonly, however, the cuesta is merely a belt of low hills.

Streams that develop along the trend of the lowlands, parallel with the shoreline, are of a class

Figure 26.4 Four kinds of streams are associated with eroded dipping sedimentary layers. These form a trellis drainage pattern.

obsequent streams. Their direction of flow is opposite to the seaward slope of the strata, as well as opposite to the direction of flow of the consequent streams. Streams that came into existence on the backslopes of cuestas, but which were not originally present as consequent streams, are termed *resequent streams.* They flow in the same direction as the original consequent streams, but develop only as the backslope of the cuesta comes into being by removal of the weaker overlying layers (Figure 26.4).

The drainage lines on a maturely dissected coastal plain combine to form a *trellis* pattern (Figure 26.4), consisting of consequent, subsequent, obsequent, and resequent streams.

Diagram *C*, Figure 26.2, shows the coastal plain reduced to a peneplain in the stage of old age. The trellis drainage pattern persists, and the cuestas still show as faint hills rising above the nearly flat lowlands.

Coastal plains of the United States and England

Splendid examples of coastal plains are present along the Atlantic and Gulf coasts of the United States, in southeastern England, and in the Paris Basin region of north-central France.

The coastal plain of the United States is by far the largest of these, ranging in width from 100 to 300 mi (160 to 500 km) and extending for 2000 mi (3000 km) along the Atlantic and Gulf coasts. Strata are of Cretaceous and Tertiary age, the former being exposed nearest to the inner margin of the coastal plain because they lie directly upon the oldland rocks of Paleozoic and Precambrian age. The coastal plain starts at Long Island, which is a partly submerged cuesta, and widens rapidly southward so as to include much of New Jersey, Delaware, Maryland, and Virginia (Figure 26.5). Throughout this portion the coastal plain has but one cuesta, that which forms the Atlantic Highlands, Mt. Laurel, Pine Hills, and similar hill groups. The cuesta is underlain by a porous sand formation of Tertiary and Cretaceous age, which resists erosion by absorbing rainwater rapidly and thereby minimizing overland flow. The inner lowland is a continuous broad valley developed on a weak clay formation of Cretaceous age.

In Alabama and Mississippi the coastal plain is maturely dissected in all but the coastal area, which has recently emerged from the sea. Cuestas and lowlands run in belts roughly parallel with the coast (Figure 26.6). Hence the term *belted coastal plain* is applied to these regions. The cuestas tend to be underlain by sandy formations and support a growth of pines. Limestone forms fertile lowlands such as the Black Belt in Alabama.

known as *subsequent* streams. They take their position along any belt or zone of weak rock and therefore follow closely the pattern of rock exposure. Subsequent streams occur in many regions and will be mentioned frequently in the discussion of folds, domes, and fault blocks.

Streams that flow down the inface of a cuesta to join the subsequent stream in a lowland are

Figure 26.5 The coastal plain of the Atlantic seaboard states shows little cuesta development except in New Jersey. The inner limit of the coastal plain is marked by a series of fall-line cities. (After A. K. Lobeck.)

Figure 26.6 The Alabama-Mississippi coastal plain is belted by a series of sandy cuestas and shale or marl lowlands. (After A. K. Lobeck.)

Figure 26.7 Southeastern England is a broadly curved mature coastal plain. L = London; K = Cretaceous chalk cuesta; C = Cambridge; O = Oxford; H = Humber River; Y = York; N = Nottingham; S = Severn River; B = Bristol; D = Dartmoor; W = Wales; M = Manchester; L = Liverpool; P = Pennine Range: T = Jurassic limestone cuesta. (After W. M. Davis.)

The principal steams cross the belted topography with little regard for lowlands and cuestas, suggesting that they originated as extended consequents. The shoreline of the Gulf Coast is one of fairly recent emergence, as explained in an earlier chapter.

The entire southeastern portion of England is a mature coastal plain (Figure 26.7). Two cuestas dominate the topography. The innermost is of Jurassic limestone and is locally named the Cotswold Hills. In England, the term *wold* is applied to a cuesta, *vale* to an intercuesta lowland. The outer or southeastern cuesta is of white chalk of Cretaceous age and includes the Chiltern Hills. Between cuestas is a lowland in which lie Oxford and Cambridge; hence it is called the Educational Lowland. An extensive inner lowland runs between the inner cuesta and the oldland rock masses of Cornwall, Wales, and the Pennine Range. In the inner lowland are the important cities of Bristol, Gloucester, Birmingham, Nottingham, Lincoln, and York, as well as extensive farm lands. This lowland is drained by a number of subsequent streams the Severn, Avon, Trent, and Ouse.

Geographical aspects of coastal plains

Broad coastal plains, such as those of the eastern United States and southeastern England, show intensive agricultural development because of the fertility and easy cultivation of broad lowlands. Although important seaport cities have developed on coastal plains there was not the same impelling necessity toward marine occupations that was induced by mountainous coastal belts bordered by shorelines of submergence.

Cuestas provide valuable forests, as in England and Europe and in the southern United States. Where excessively porous sands occur, as in the New Jersey coastal plain, pine and oak are supported.

Transportation tends to follow the lowlands and to connect the larger cities located there. For example, important roads and railroads connect New York with Trenton, Philadelphia, Baltimore and Washington, all of which are situated in an inner lowland. Cuesta topography, however, is rarely so rugged as to interfere seriously with the location of communication lines.

The seaward dip of sedimentary strata in a coastal plain provides a structure favorable to the development of artesian water wells. Water penetrates deeply into a sandy cuesta stratum, which is overlain by shales or clays impervious to the flow of underground waters. When a well is drilled into the sand formation considerably seaward of its surface exposure, water under hydraulic pressure reaches the surface (Figure 26.8). Artesian water in large quantities is available in many parts of the Atlantic and gulf coastal plains, although

Figure 26.8 An artesian well requires a dipping sandstone layer. (After E. Raisz.)

Figure 26.9 Oil pools can form in the fringes of sand formations which pinch out in the up-dip direction.

it is no longer sufficient to supply the demands of densely populated and industrialized localities.

The Gulf Coastal Plain of the United States contains petroleum and natural gas accumulations of enormous economic value. Oil occurs in *stratigraphic traps*, which are layers or lenses of permeable sand or sandstone capped by impermeable shales or clays. One kind of stratigraphic trap is the *pinch out*, illustrated in Figure 26.9. A sandstone formation in the coastal plain sequence of strata thins in the updip (landward) direction to a feather edge, where it disappears, whether through lack of deposition, or by later erosion that

preceded deposition of the next younger beds. Capped above by impermeable beds, the sandstone wedge forms a trap for oil migrating updip. Figure 26.10 show two curving bands of oil *pools* of this type in the Gulf Coast of Texas.

Another quite different type of oil pool common in coastal plains and other regions of thick sedimentary strata occurs on *salt domes*, or *salt plugs* (Figure 26.11). These strange, stalklike bodies of rock salt project upward through coastal plain strata. Apparently they were forced up by slow plastic flowage from thick salt formations lying in deep lower layers of the coastal plain. Surrounding strata are sharply bent up and faulted against the side of the salt plug, making traps for petroleum. Salt plugs commonly have a cap rock of limestone resting upon a plate of gypsum and anhydrite. Oil

Figure 26.10 Two zones of oil pools on up-dip pinchouts of sands of Eocene age (AA') and Oligocene age (BB'). (After A. I. Levorsen.)

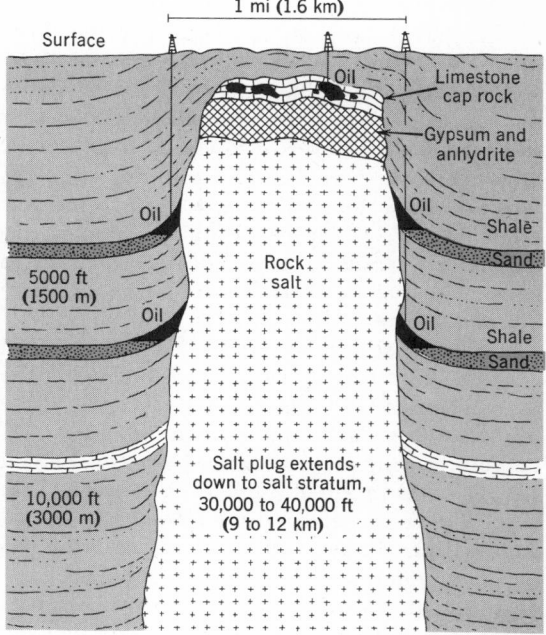

Figure 26.11 Idealized structure section of a salt dome.

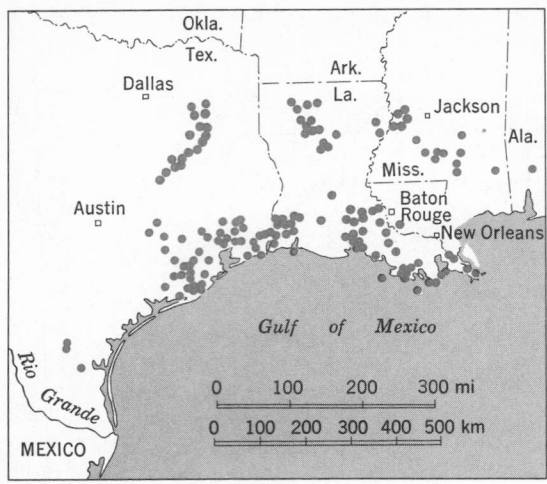

Figure 26.12 Distribution of salt domes of the Gulf Coast region is indicated by dots. (After K. K. Landes.)

Figure 26.13 Erosional development of horizontal sedimentary strata. The development of cliffs is accentuated here, as typical of an arid climate. (After E. Raisz.)

may collect in cavities in the limestone. Distribution of salt domes of the Gulf Coast is shown in Figure 26.12. The salt dome should not be confused with sedimentary domes discussed later in this chapter.

Other mineral deposits of economic importance in coastal plains include: *sulfur,* occuring in the coastal plain of Louisiana and Texas; *phosphate* beds, found in Florida; *lignite* (a low-grade, woody coal), used as a fuel in Alabama, Mississippi, and Texas; and *clays,* used in manufacture of pottery, tile, and brick in New Jersey and the Carolinas.

Horizontal strata

Considerable areas of the continental shields are covered by thick sequences of sedimentary-rock layers, which at one time in the geologic past were the bottom deposits of shallow inland seas or were stream deposits spread over vast alluvial plains. Strata of all three post-Cambrian geologic eras are represented. When uplifted with little disturbance other than a faint warping or minor faulting, these sedimentary strata pass through a series of stages of erosion such as those illustrated in the series of block diagrams of Figure 26.13.

In the initial stage the land is fairly smooth and is drained by consequent streams following the gentle slope of the surface. If the elevation of the initial surface is high, these streams soon cut deep canyons, leaving plateau surfaces between. Should the region have initially low elevation above sea level, the streams are prevented by the base level from cutting deeply, and hence strong relief can never develop in the region. Throughout the stage of youth, the region, whether of great or small relief, is dissected by streams whose valley network develops at the expense of the initial land surface.

When the initial land surface is entirely or almost entirely consumed and the region has reached its most rugged character, the stage of maturity has been reached. Throughout the remainder of the erosion cycle the relief diminishes and the slopes perhaps tend to become more gentle. In old age the region is reduced to a rolling plain upon which the larger streams have broad, flat floodplains. A few remnants of harder rock strata may remain as monadnocks.

The horizontal attitude of the rock layers gives rise to distinctive landforms where the layers are of alternately weak and resistant nature (Figure 26.14). The resistant layers, usually of sandstone and limestone (the latter particularly in arid cli-

Figure 26.14 In arid climates, a distinctive set of landforms develops in flat-lying sedimentary formations.

mates), form *cliffs* or steep slopes. The weak layers, usually of shale, clay, or marl, are easily washed away from beneath the lower edges of the resistant layers, hence serving to accentuate the cliffs above them and form smoothly descending slopes at each cliff base. In dry climates, where vegetation is scant and the action of rainwash especially effective, sharply defined topographic forms develop. They comprise what may be described as *scarp-slope-shelf* topography, because the normal sequence of forms is a cliff, or scarp, at the base of which is a smooth slope. This in turn flattens out to make a shelf, terminated at the outer edge by the cliff of the next lower set of forms. In the walls of the great canyons of the Colorado Plateau region in Colorado, Utah, Arizona, and New Mexico, these forms are wonderfully displayed (Figure 26.15).

In plateau regions underlain by horizontal strata, the erosion processes tend to strip successive layers from the plateau surface. Cliffs, capped by hard rock layers, retreat as near-perpendicular surfaces because the weak clay or shale formations exposed at the cliff base are rapidly washed away by storm runoff and channel erosion. Thus undermined, the rock in the upper cliff face repeatedly breaks away along vertical fractures. Where a cliff has thus retreated a considerable distance from a canyon, there remains a broad, flat bench which is the exposed surface of the next layer below. The bench

so formed is termed an *esplanade* (Figure 26.15). Should the entire plateau surface be formed by the complete or almost complete removal of a rock series, leaving a plateau capped by a resistant layer, the plateau is termed a *stripped surface* or *stratum plain*.

In the later stages of erosion the landscape in an arid region has many *mesas* (Figure 25.14), tabletopped hills or mountains bordered on all sides by cliffs and representing the remnant of a formerly extensive layer of resistant rock. Often a mesa is capped by a lava flow, which is generally more resistant than the sedimentary rocks over which it once flowed. As a mesa is reduced in area by retreat of the cliffs that border it, it maintains its flat top and altitude. Before its complete consumption the final stage is a small, steep-sided hill or peak known as a *butte* (Figure 26.16).

Where extremely weak clays or shales, lacking a protective vegetative cover, are exposed to rainwash and gully erosion in dry regions, a very rugged topography resembling miniature mountains develops. Such areas are termed *badlands* (Figures 26.14 and 26.17).

In humid climates the elements described above, namely, scarp-slope-shelf topography, stripped surfaces, mesas, and buttes, are present only in greatly subdued aspect. This is due to the thick cover of vegetation that protects the ground from

Figure 26.15   This panoramic drawing by the noted geologist-artist, W. H. Holmes, published in 1882, shows the Grand Canyon at the mouth of the Toroweap. In this part of the canyon, rarely seen by tourists, a broad bench called The Esplanade is well developed. (From Dutton, *Atlas to accompany Monograph II*, U.S. Geological Survey.)

Figure 26.16 This early photograph shows a butte of horizontal red sandstones capped by a gypsum layer, near Cambria, Wyoming. (Photograph by N. H. Darton, U.S. Geological Survey.)

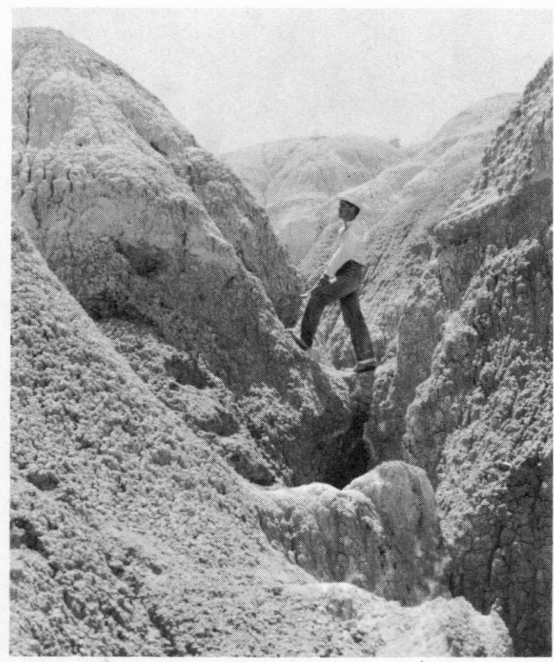

Figure 26.17 Badlands, such as these in the Petrified Forest National Monument, Arizona, are like minature mountain topography on bare clay formations. (Photograph by B. Mears, Jr.)

rapid rainwash and permits a layer of soil and residual overburden to cloak the bedrock. Nevertheless, occasional lines of cliffs do form, and mesalike hills and mountains are developed. Vast areas in Pennsylvania, New York, Ohio, West Virginia, Kentucky, Tennessee, and Alabama consist of maturely dissected horizontal strata. Much of this land is mountainous and heavily forested (Figure 26.18).

In a maturely dissected region of horizontal strata the stream system forms a *dendritic drainage pattern*, in which the smaller streams show no predominant directional orientation or control (Figure 22.5). This pattern has been likened to the branching of an apple tree. Usually the larger trunk streams show a rough parallelism, because they were the original consequent streams which followed a perceptible slope of the region as a whole. The smaller streams, whose pattern is dendritic, are said to be *insequent* in origin. An insequent stream is controlled in its growth by very minor inequalities of rock resistance and slope which are not themselves systematically oriented. On the whole, therefore, the direction of branching is very much a matter of chance.

Figure 26.18 Seen from the air, the maturely dissected Allegheny Plateau of West Virginia appears largely forested. Relief of 700 to 800 ft (210 to 240 m) is here developed on shales of Devonian age. (Photograph by J. L. Rich, Courtesy of the *Geographical Review*.)

In addition to regions underlain by sedimentary rocks, the regions of horizontal strata may be made to include thick accumulations of lava flows. In some parts of the world, such as the Columbia Plateau region of eastern Washington and Oregon, or the Deccan Plateau of western India, the vast outpourings of highly fluid basalt lavas now cover thousands of square miles and are several thousand feet thick. Interbedded with the lavas are lake and stream deposits of sands, gravels, and clays, as well as much volcanic ash and dust. Consequently, the structure exhibits alternately weak and resistant layers in which erosion produces landforms very similar to those of sedimentary strata.

Geographical aspects of horizontal strata

Generalizations cannot readily be made about the utilization of areas underlain by horizontal strata because of the great variations in surface relief that exist. On initial and old surfaces, where the topography is plainlike, agriculture is widely developed. On the high plains of western Kansas and Nebraska, eastern Wyoming and Colorado, New Mexico, and Texas, wheat farming is the predominant activity. Here the plain is in its initial or very early stage of erosion. Despite elevations of 3000 to 5000 ft (900 to 1500 m), the plain is trenched only by a few major through-flowing streams.

Some regions of horizontal strata in the interior United States, including much of Illinois, Indiana,

Ohio, Missouri, Montana, Kansas and Iowa, are maturely dissected but a mantle of glacial drift has reduced relief so that slopes are gentle and are highly cultivated. Where relief is strong, as in the mountain areas of the Alleghenies or the Cumberland Mountains, cultivation is limited to a few small tracts, such as the floodplain belts of larger streams, despite the favorable humid climate (Figure 26.18). In the canyon lands of the Colorado Plateau an extremely low population density exists, not only because the high relief and aridity do not favor agriculture, but also because human access is virtually impossible across the network of sheer-walled canyons.

As with coastal plains, regions of horizontal strata have only those minerals and rocks of economic value that are associated with sedimentary rocks (or lavas). Building stone, such as the Bedford limestone in Indiana or the Berea sandstone in Ohio, is a valuable product. Limestone may be quarried for use in manufacture of portland cement or as flux in iron smelting. Some important deposits of lead, zinc, and iron ores occur in sedimentary rocks. For example, the lead and zinc mines of the Tristate district (Missouri, Kansas, Oklahoma) are in horizontal limestones.

Perhaps the greatest mineral resources occurring in sedimentary strata are coal and petroleum. Where the strata are undisturbed, coal is of the *bituminous*, or soft, variety and lies in horizontal layers from a few inches to several feet thick and hundreds of square miles in extent. Where the relief of the region is great, coal seams outcrop along the valley walls into which mine openings termed *drifts* can be tunneled to obtain the coal. This is common practice in the bituminous field of western Pennsylvania, eastern Ohio, and West Virginia. Where the coal seams are not exposed at the surface they must be reached by vertical shafts, as in the Illinois coal fields. Anywhere that a rich coal seam is found outcropping in a hillside or lies near the surface it can be reached by removing the overlying of rock and soil with powerful earth-moving machines. This process, termed *strip mining*, leaves great gashes and adjacent embankments of rock debris.

Petroleum occurs within permeable sandstone layers, in which the oil is trapped by overlying impermeable shales. Because the strata are not perfectly horizontal, but are affected by minor warpings and faults as well as by changes in thickness and character of the sandstone layers, there are many structures in which petroleum is localized into pools. Stratigraphic traps, similar in principle to those of coastal plains, form important pools. Traps also result from faulting, which offsets the edges of the strata (Figure 27.16).

Figure 26.19 As a cavern system develops, surface stream flow is diverted to underground flow. (After A. K. Lobeck.)

Figure 26.20 Outcrops of horizontal limestone strata show in the walls of this deep sinkhole on the Kaibab Plateau of northern Arizona. Because of high elevation, 8500 ft (2500 m), the climate here is cool and humid, favoring limestone solution. (Photograph by A. N. Strahler.)

Limestone caverns

Limestone, composed of calcium and magnesium carbonate, is readily dissolved by weak solutions of carbonic acid present in soil and ground water. Ground waters carry away the dissolved carbonates, leaving elaborate systems of subterranean caverns. Most persons are familiar with the names of famous caverns, such as Mammoth Cave, Carlsbad Caverns, Luray Caverns, or Cave of the Winds, and many Americans have visited one or more of these famous tourist attractions. Although caverns may develop in folded, faulted, and steeply dipping limestone layers, most caverns occur in areas of flat-lying strata, so that it is appropriate to take up the subject at this point.

The development of a cavern system is illustrated in Figure 26.19. According to one widely held theory of cavern formation, it is necessary that a thick limestone formation be present and that the region be an elevated one with the valleys of the larger rivers deeply cut so as to provide topographic relief. At first (Stage A) the limestone is solid and is covered by a sandstone layer. The water drains off by means of surface streams. As the large river cuts more deeply, water percolating downward toward the lowered water table flows through joint cracks in the limestone to emerge at the river bank (Stage B). The passageways in the limestone become larger and deeper as time goes on (Stage C). By now, all surface water pours down into cavities known as *sinkholes* (Figure 26.20). These are usually filled at the surface by broken rock and soil through which the water filters. Occasionally they are enlarged by collapse so as to make a gaping hole. In Stage D the sinkholes are enlarged into small valleys and the cavern system is fully developed, with many passageways and shafts. On the lowest level run underground rivers, which emerge at the banks of the main river. Abandoned caves at higher levels may be dry except for the localized dripping of water.

A second theory of cavern development holds that the removal of carbonate rock takes place below the water table. As water slowly moves in the paths shown in Figure 20.26, the dissolved solids are brought to streams and carried off. This

A. Entrance to caves.

C. A drip curtain.

B. A stalagmite.

D. A travertine terrace.

Figure 26.21   The Jenolan Caves of New South Wales, Australia, have remarkably fine displays of cavern deposits. (Courtesy N. S. W. Government Printer.)

explanation, termed the *phreatic-water theory*, accounts for many cavern features not explained by the first theory. Once formed, the caverns come to lie above the water table as the adjacent stream valleys are carved to greater depths.

Cave deposits (or "formations," as they are usually called by tourist guides in our American caverns) are encrustations of calcium carbonate or gypsum formed after the cavern is fully enlarged and is no longer the site of rapid solution. The slow drip of water from the ceilings is accompanied by evaporation so that a small amount of calcium carbonate is left behind. Many beautiful forms result. Some of these are pictured in Figure 26.21. Spikelike forms hanging from the ceilings are *stalactites* (*D*); blunt columns growing up from the floor are *stalagmites* (*B*). Where the water drips from a long joint crack on the ceiling, a *drip curtain* results (*C*). Stalactites and stalagmites join to form *columns*; and rows of columns formed under a large joint crack may coalesce to make a *wall*. Among the blocks of stone that litter the cavern floor, pools of water overflow from one to another, making *travertine terraces* (*D*).

The geographical importance of caves is felt in several ways. Throughout man's early development, caves were an important habitation. Now we find the skeletal remains of these people, together with their implements and cave drawings, preserved through the centuries in caves in many parts of the world. Today, with increasing destructiveness of weapons of warfare, caverns are achieving importance as possible sites for storage of valuable materials, as living quarters, and as factories for important types of production.

Caverns have provided some valuable deposits of *guano*, the excrement of birds or bats, which is rich in nitrates and is used in the manufacture of fertilizers and explosives. Bat guano was taken from Mammoth Cave for making gunpowder during the war of 1812. Much more recently a valuable guano deposit in a limestone cavern in the wall of the Grand Canyon of the Colorado River has been mined and lifted to the canyon rim by cable car.

Karst landscapes

Where limestone solution has been especially active there results a landscape with many unique landforms. This is especially true along the Dalmatian coastal area of Yugoslavia, where the topography is termed *karst*. The term may be applied to the topography of any limestone area where sinkholes are numerous and small surface streams nonexistent. Four stages of development of a karst landscape are shown in Figure 26.22. Exposed limestone surfaces are deeply grooved and fluted

Figure 26.22 Stages of evolution of a karst landscape show increased relief and cavern development followed by decreasing relief and the removal of the limestone mass. (Drawn by E. Raisz.)

into *lapiés* (*A*). Deep, steep-walled funnel-like sinkholes, called *dolines* (*B*), are numerous. In places, these have coalesced to make open, flat-floored valleys termed *poljes* (*C*). Here surface streams flow and the soil may be suitable for agriculture.

Some other regions of karst or karstlike topography are the Mammoth Cave region of Kentucky, the Causses region of France, the Yucatan Peninsula, and parts of Cuba and Puerto Rico.

Domes and basins

Sedimentary layers in many places show a warping into broad domelike or basinlike structures, which may range from 100 to 200 mi (160 to 325 km) in diameter, but in which the strata are

Figure 26.23   The Weald region of southeastern England is a broad dome of sedimentary strata from which the top has been removed. (After A. K. Lobeck.)

nowhere inclined more than 1° or 2° from the horizontal. Such domes and basins tend to form concentric cuestas when dissected. An example is the Weald Uplift of southeastern England (Figure 26.23). As the central part of the dome is eroded away, older rock layers are exposed. As each layer is cut through, it is eroded back from the center. Thus the cuestas have their steep inface toward

the center of the dome and retreat away from the center. An example of a broad, shallow basin structure is the Paris Basin. The cuestas have their steep infaces outward, and as erosion progresses the cuestas retreat toward the center of the basin.

Domes may also be steep-sided and high, differing from the broad, low type in that the strata on the flanks dip outward at angles up to 25° or more. Thus the dome forms a conspicuous hill or mountain and, when maturely dissected, may constitute a truly rugged mass of peaks. To distinguish this type of dome it will be referred to as a *mountainous dome*. Basins of comparable development are not known because, although the strata may be strongly domed up by the intrusion of molten rock under great pressure, there is no geologic mechanism by which the strata can be sharply punched down.

The erosion of a mountainous dome is shown in the diagrams of Figure 26.24. In the stage of early youth a series of consequent streams drains outward in a *radial* drainage pattern. These streams entrench the flanks of the dome and quickly expose the underlying layers. As erosion progresses, the resistant strata begin to stand out

Figure 26.24   Stages in the development of a mountainous dome. *C* = consequent stream; *S* = subsequent stream; *F* = flatiron; *P* = plateau in center of dome; *M* = mountains of crystalline rock; *H* = horizontal strata surrounding dome; *R* = resequent stream.

Figure 26.25   In this air photo, the Virgin River is seen cutting across a hogback of steeply dipping strata on the flank of the Virgin anticline in southwestern Utah. (Photograph by Frank Jensen.)

as sharp-crested ridges, or *hogbacks*, encircling the dome (Figure 26.25). Hogbacks are very striking landforms; they owe their development to the rapid removal of weaker shale or clay beds on either side (Figure 26.26). A concentric arrangement of alternate hogback ridges and valleys develops on the mature dome. Streams occupying the weak rock valleys are subsequent in origin, forming a concentric, or *annular*, drainage pattern (Figure 26.27). Tributaries that flow down from the in-

tervening hogback ridges are resequent and obsequent streams, the former flowing outward, the latter inward.

As dome erosion progresses, older and deeper rocks are exposed in the center. If geologic conditions are favorable, erosion may reveal in the center a core of intrusive igneous rock representing material that was forced up to produce the dome. In this event the igneous rock is younger than the sedimentary rock of the dome. One variety of

Figure 26.26 Hogbacks may gradually merge into cuestas, the cuestas into plateaus and esplanades, if the dip of the strata becomes less from one place to another. *S* = subsequent stream; *H* = hogback ridge; *Cu* = cuesta; *M* = mesa; *E* = esplanade; *Cl* = cliff; *P* = plateau. (After W. M. Davis.)

Figure 26.27   The drainage pattern on a maturely eroded dome combines annular and radial elements. It resembles a trellis pattern bent into a circle.

Figure 26.28 Navajo Mountain, Utah, is thought to be a laccolith whose igneous rock core is still covered by sedimentary strata. (After H. E. Gregory.)

intrusive dome is the *laccolith*, a convex but flat-bottomed mass of igneous rock which came up between strata and spread out, forcing the overlying layers to rise (Figure 26.28). In other domes the central core is of ancient rock, much older than even the sedimentary layers, and represents the rock upon which those sediments were deposited. It shows through in the dome core because the strata are not thick enough to cover it when the dome is fully dissected.

The last sedimentary rock layer to be stripped from the central core of crystalline rock clings to the sides of the core in triangular patches known

Figure 26.29 The Black Hills consist of a broad, flat-topped dome, deeply eroded to expose a core of crystalline rock.

as *flatirons.* The flatirons cap the ends of mountain spurs and are separated by V-shaped canyons (Figure 26.24).

In the old-age stage, a mountainous dome has been reduced to a peneplain on which the hogback ridges are represented by faint rows of hills. In the central core, a few monadnock masses may rise conspicuously above the peneplain level.

Geographical aspects of domes

For broad, low domes and basins the human-geographic and economic features are essentially those of coastal plains or regions of horizontal strata. Mountainous domes, however, have some unique features. These are illustrated by the great Black Hills dome of western South Dakota and eastern Wyoming (Figure 26.29).

The annular subsequent valleys that encircle the dome are splendid locations for railroads and highways. Thus it is natural that towns and cities should grow in these valleys. In the Black Hills dome, one annular valley in particular, the Red Valley, is continuously developed around the entire dome and has been termed the Race Track because of its shape. It is underlain by a weak shale which is easily washed away. In the Red Valley lie such towns as Rapid City, Spearfish, and Sturgis. On the outer side of the Red Valley is a high, sharp hogback of Dakota sandstone, known simply as the Hogback Ridge. It rises some 400 to 500 ft (120 or 150 m) above the level of the Red Valley. Farther out toward the margins of the dome the strata are less steeply inclined and form a series of cuestas. Artesian water is obtained from wells drilled in the surrounding plain.

The eastern central part of the Black Hills consists of a mountainous core of intrusive and metamorphic rocks. These mountains are richly forested, whereas the intervening valleys are beautiful open parks. Thus the region is attractive as a summer resort area. Harney Park, elevation 7242 ft (2207 m), is highest of the peaks of the core. In the northern part of the central core, in the vicinity of Lead and Deadwood, are valuable ore deposits. At Lead is the fabulous Homestake Mine, one of the world's richest gold-producing mines. In the southern part of the central crystalline area, at Pennington, is the Etta Mine, known widely for its enormous pegmatite crystals of spodumene, a source of lithium. These occurrences illustrate the principle that the interior cores of mature domes may be favorable places for mineral deposits.

The western central part of the Black Hills consists of a limestone plateau deeply dissected by streams. The original dome has a flattened summit. The limestone plateau represents one of the last remaining sedimentary rock layers to be stripped from the core of the dome.

Figure 26.30   The Dominguez Hills, a low dome in an early stage of erosion, has beneath it a valuable oil pool. (After H. W. Hoots and U.S. Geological Survey.)

The subject of economic importance of domes cannot be passed by without mention of the important accumulations of oil and gas in many domes of sedimentary strata. Although not illustrated in the Black Hills themselves, many domes of the Rocky Mountain region have been important petroleum producers, for example, the Rock Springs Dome and Teapot Dome in Wyoming. Oil tends to accumulate in the domed sandstone layers which are overlain by impervious shales. An example of a very low dome in the initial stage of development, which is a valuable producer of oil, is the Dominguez Hills dome in the Los Angeles Basin (Figure 26.30).

REFERENCES FOR FURTHER STUDY

Dutton, C. E. (1882), *Tertiary history of the Grand Canyon district,* U.S. Geological Survey, Monograph 2, 264 pp.

Johnson, D. W. (1921), *Battlefields of the World War,* Amer. Geog. Soc. Research Series, No. 3, 684 pp.

Fenneman, N. M. (1931), *Physiography of the western United States,* McGraw-Hill Book Co., New York, 534 pp.

Fenneman, N. M. (1938), *Physiography of the eastern*

United States, McGraw-Hill Book Co., New York, 691 pp.

Lobeck, A. K. (1939), *Geomorphology*, McGraw-Hill Book Co., New York, 731 pp. See Chapters 13, 14, and 15.

Thornbury, W. D. (1965), *Regional geomorphology of the United States*, John Wiley and Sons, New York, 609 pp.

Hunt, C. B. (1967), *Physiography of the United States*, W. H. Freeman and Co., San Francisco, 480 pp.

REVIEW QUESTIONS

1. What groups of geologic structures make up the bedrock landmasses of the earth? Name and describe briefly each variety.

2. What is the basic difference in surface relief of the undisturbed and disturbed structural groups of landmasses in the initial stages of their respective erosion cycles?

3. How is a coastal plain formed? By what rock types is it underlain? What is a consequent stream? Where and how does it form on a new coastal plain?

4. What is the oldland? What is a mendip?

5. Describe the topography of a mature coastal plain. Name the component parts as they appear along a profile line beginning on the oldland and extending to the sea.

6. What is a subsequent stream? An obsequent stream? A resequent stream? Show by a sketch map how these stream types are related in a trellis drainage pattern.

7. Describe the coastal plain of the Atlantic and gulf coast states. What is notable about the drainage pattern of the Gulf coastal plain? What kind of shoreline is associated with the Gulf coastal plain?

8. Briefly state the salient features of the coastal plain topography of southeastern England.

9. How are agriculture and transportation influenced by coastal-plain topography? Explain how artesian wells can function on a coastal plain.

10. What are some of the mineral products of coastal plains? Which of these is most important in the United States?

11. Describe the stages of erosional development of a region of horizontal strata. What determines the maximum relief that can occur?

12. What special features develop during erosion of horizontal layers of shale and sandstone in an arid climate? Explain the following: mesa, butte, esplanade, stripped surface (stratum plain), badlands.

13. What is a dendritic drainage pattern? Of what kind of streams is it composed? How does a dendritic drainage pattern develop?

14. How can horizontal lava flows result in topography similar to that on horizontal sedimentary strata? Where are great lava plateaus found today?

15. How does the topography of a region of horizontal strata in the various stages of the erosion cycle influence agriculture and human settlements? What are the principal economic mineral products of regions of horizontal strata?

16. In what kind of rock are caverns formed? Why? What are sinkholes? Describe stalactites, stalagmites, drip curtains, and columns. What is travertine? What is guano?

17. What is karst? From what region does this term originate? Describe lapiés, dolines, and poljes. Name some regions of karst topography.

18. Describe the various kinds of dome and basin structures that occur in regions underlain by sedimentary rock formations. What variations may be found in the sizes of these structures and the steepness of dip of the strata?

19. Outline the systematic changes in topography that occur as a mountainous dome is eroded through the stages of youth, maturity, and old age. What type of drainage pattern is formed? Of what kinds of streams is this pattern composed? Compare this pattern with that of a coastal plain.

20. What is a hogback? How is it formed? What are flatirons?

21. Describe a laccolith. How does it differ from a batholith?

22. Describe briefly the important structural and topographical features of the Black Hills. In what ways are these features related to the economic products of the Black Hills?

23. How can domes act as traps for petroleum? Give examples of domes that have become valuable oil producers.

Folds, Faults, and Fault Blocks

REGIONS of sedimentary strata that have been compressed into sets of parallel, wavelike folds pass through a series of stages illustrated in the diagrams of Figure 27.1. Short consequent streams drain the flanks of the folds to join major consequent streams that follow the axes of the troughs.

In geological terminology, a downfold is known as a *syncline;* an upfold, an *anticline* (Block *A*). It may help in remembering these terms to know that the root word *clino* means "lean," as, for example, in the word *incline.* The prefix *syn* means "together." Hence, a syncline is a structure in which strata dip toward the center line of the trough. *Anti*, meaning against or opposite, implies that in an anticline the layers dip away from the center line. In the initial stages of the development of folds, anticlines are identical with the mountains, or ridges; synclines, with the valleys.

Block *A* (Figure 27.1) shows erosion of anticlines occurring during the last stages of folding. Synclines are being filled with alluvial fan materials swept down from the adjacent anticlines. After folding has ceased the upper layers of soft, unconsolidated rock are removed until, as shown in Block *B*, a hard, well-cemented sandstone layer is exposed, reflecting the full amplitude of the folding. Coinciding with synclines are *synclinal valleys;* with anticlines, *anticlinal mountains.*

Streams that drain the flanks of the anticlines quickly cut deep ravines, exposing the underlying layers. The breaching spreads rapidly to the crest of the anticline, where a long, narrow valley is opened out along the summit (Block *B*). This valley is occupied by a subsequent stream excavating a belt of weak rock and is known as an *anticlinal valley,* because it lies upon the center line of the anticline. As this valley grows in length, depth, and breadth it replaces the original anticlinal mountain. A reversal of topography thus occurs. The synclinal valley, which originally contained the major stream, is now shrunken between the growing anticlinal valleys on either side. Moreover, the anticlinal valleys are the more rapidly deepened because of the core of weak rock exposed to attack, so that eventually the syncline becomes a mountain ridge, termed a *synclinal mountain* (Block *C*). This change of landform might well bring to mind the words of the prophet, Isaiah,

"Every valley shall be exalted, and every mountain and hill shall be made low." At this stage, which is that of maturity of the folds, the original topography has been completely reversed. The drainage pattern is a trellis type, similar in most respects to the trellis pattern of a mature coastal plain, but different in that the major subsequent streams are more closely spaced and the obsequent and resequent tributaries are shorter (Figure 27.2).

Here and there in a belt of folds, a principal stream crosses several folds at nearly right angles, passing through the sharply defined ridges by narrow *watergaps.* These streams are likely to have existed previously to the folding and to have maintained themselves as the folds were formed. The term *antecedent* has been applied to such streams. Some are illustrated in Block *B* of Figure 18.12, crossing the series of folds produced in the Appalachian revolution of Permian time.

As the dissection of the folded strata progresses, there is a continuous change in the form and position of the various types of ridges and valleys. Following the reversal of topography shown in Block *C*, Figure 27.1, the synclinal ridges will be completely removed by erosion. Meanwhile, new ridges are appearing in the centers of the anticlinal valleys. These form as a result of the uncovering of still older resistant strata which were folded along with the rest, but which previously lay below the general level of the land surface. The new ridges, which may be thought of as second-generation *anticlinal ridges*, grow in height as the weak rock is stripped from both sides. In time the anticlinal ridges, like the original anticlines of the initial land surface, are breached by streams and finally are transformed into anticlinal valleys. Thus an inversion of topography is again accomplished. The hard sandstone layers stand as narrow, sharp ridges separated by long, parallel valleys. Where the strata in a ridge dip in one direction only, representing one flank of an anticline or syncline, the ridge is termed a *homoclinal ridge* (Block *C*). Likewise, a valley of weak shales or limestones in which the layers all dip in one direction is termed a *homoclinal valley.*

In summary, mature topography developed on alternately resistant and weak sedimentary strata may have three types of ridges, or mountains: anticlinal, synclinal, and homoclinal; and three types of valleys: anticlinal, synclinal, and homoclinal.

Ultimately the belt of folds is reduced to a peneplain (Figure 27.1, Block *D*). Even here, the ridges rise as rows of low hills and the streams maintain their trellis drainage pattern.

Zigzag ridges and plunging folds

The folds illustrated in Figure 27.1 are continuous and even-crested, hence they produce ridges that are approximately parallel in trend and continue for great distances. In some fold regions, however, the folds are not continuous and level-crested but instead have crests that rise or descend from place to place. When maturely dissected, such folds give rise to a zigzag line of ridges (Figure 27.3).

The topographic form of a syncline whose trough descends, or *plunges*, differs from that of an anticline which plunges in the same direction, when both are maturely dissected. Figure 27.3 compares the two forms. The plunging syncline is represented by a ridge with a slightly concave summit but steeply descending cliffs on the end and sides. Along the direction of plunge of the

Figure 27.2 A trellis drainage pattern on folds. This resembles Figure 26.4, but opposing sets of tributaries are shorter and of more nearly equal length than on cuesta topography.

fold center line, or *axis*, this ridge develops an increasing concavity, then separates into two diverging homoclinal ridges. The plunging anticline is represented by a ridge that points in a direction opposite to the plunging synclinal mountain. The end is smoothly rounded and descends gradually to the level of the valley in the direction of plunge. In the opposite direction the mountain splits into

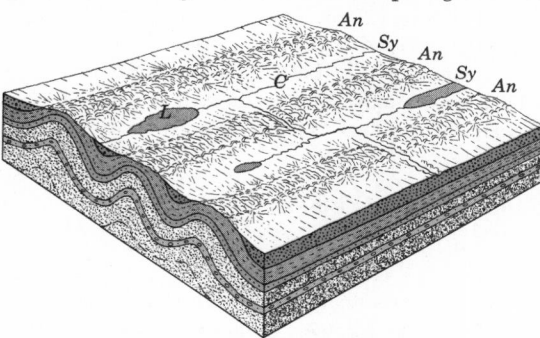

A. While folding is still in progress, erosion cuts down the anticlines; alluvium fills the synclines, keeping relief low. *An* = anticline; *Sy* = syncline; *C* = consequent stream; *L* = lake.

B. Long after folding has ceased, erosion exposes a highly resistant layer of sandstone or quartzite. *AV* = anticlinal; *SV* = synclinal valley; *C* = consequent stream; *WG* = water-gap; *R* = resequent stream.

C. Continued erosion partly removes the resistant formation but reveals another below it. *AM* = anticlinal mountain; *SM* = synclinal mountain; *HM* = homoclinal ridge; *HV* = homoclinal valley: *O* = obsequent stream; *S* = subsequent stream.

D. Peneplanation reduces the fold belt to low relief, but the hard-rock ridges still show.

Figure 27.1   Stages in the erosional development of folded strata.

two homoclinal ridges. Enclosed is a valley bounded by steep cliffs (Figure 27.3). The end of this valley, where the cliff line swings around, is often termed an *anticlinal cove*. In comparing the two forms it is apparent that the cliff slope faces outward on a plunging syncline, but faces inward in a plunging anticline.

Geographical aspects of fold regions

Some of the human-geographical and economic aspects of maturely dissected fold regions are illustrated by the Appalachians of south-central and eastern Pennsylvania (Figure 27.4). The ridges, of resistant sandstones and conglomerates, rise boldly to heights of 500 to 2000 ft (150 to 600 m) above broad lowlands underlain by weak shales and limestones. Major highways run in the valleys, crossing from one valley to another through the watergaps of streams that have cut through the ridges. Important cities may be situated near the watergaps of major streams. An example is Harrisburg, where the Susquehanna River issues from a series of watergaps cut in Blue Mountain, Second Mountain, and Peters Mountain (Figure 27.4). Where no watergaps are conveniently located, the roads must climb in long, steep grades over the ridge crests. The ridges are heavily forested; the valleys are rich agricultural belts. Fire towers are situated upon the ridge crests and command splendid views of distant ridges.

In various fold regions of the world, for example, in the Pennsylvania Appalachians, an important resource is *anthracite*, or hard coal (Figure 27.5). This occurs in strata that have been folded and squeezed. Pressure has converted the coal from bituminous into anthracite. Because of extensive erosion, all coal has been removed except that which lies in the central parts of synclines. The coal seams dip steeply; workings penetrate deeply to reach the coal that lies in the bottoms of the synclines. Seams near the surface are worked by strip mining.

Broad, gentle anticlinal folds may form impor-

tant traps for the accumulation of petroleum. The principle is the same as in low domes of sedimentary strata (Figure 26.30). Oil migrates in permeable sandstone beds to the anticlinal crest, where it is trapped by an impervious cap rock of shale. Many of the oil and gas pools of western Pennsylvania, where petroleum production first succeeded, are on low anticlines.

Pressures which created folds also changed shales into slates of considerable commercial value. The slate quarries of Pennsylvania occur in rows paralleling the base of a great sandstone ridge. Limestone, if of satisfactory quality for the manufacture of portland cement, is quarried along narrow belts where a steeply dipping bed appears at the surface.

Not all fold regions contain as extensive agricultural valleys as the Pennsylvania Appalachians. In parts of Maryland, West Virginia, and Virginia the ridges are predominant and form a great rugged mountain belt difficult to cross and thinly populated.

Other fold regions somewhat like the Appalachians are the Ouachita Mountains of Arkansas and the Jura Mountains of the Swiss and French Alps region (Figure 27.6). The Jura Mountains consist almost entirely of anticlinal limestone ridges. Good illustrations of fold belts likewise occur in North Africa, principally in Tunisia and Algeria, and in the Union of South Africa, not far north of Capetown.

Faults and fault blocks

A *fault* is a break in the brittle surficial rocks of the earth's crust as a result of unequal stresses. Faulting is accompanied by a slippage or displacement along the plane of breakage. Faults are often of great horizontal extent, so that the *fault line* can be traced along the ground for many miles,

Figure 27.4 A great synclinal fold involving three resistant quartzite-conglomerate formations and thick intervening shales has been eroded to form bold ridges through which the Susquehanna River has cut a series of watergaps. (After A. K. Lobeck.)

Figure 27.3 Folds with crests that plunge downward give zigzag ridges when maturely eroded. (After E. Raisz.)

Figure 27.5 Anthracite coal basins of central Pennsylvania correspond with areas of Pennsylvania strata, downfolded into long synclinal troughs.

Age of Strata:
- Pennsylvanian
- Mississippian
- Devonian
- Silurian

sometimes even 100 mi (160 km) or more. Little is known of what happens to faults at depth, but in all probability most extend down for at least several thousands of feet.

Faulting occurs in sudden slippage movements which generate *earthquakes*, the wavelike ground tremors that start in the zone of maximum movement. A particular fault movement may result in a slippage of as little as an inch (2.5 cm) or as much as 25 or 50 ft (8 or 15 m). Successive

movements may occur many years apart, even many tens of hundreds of years apart, but aggregate total displacements of hundreds or thousands of feet. In some places clearly recognizable sedimentary rock layers are offset on opposite sides of a fault and the amount of displacement can be accurately measured.

According to the nature and relative direction of the displacement, several types of faults can be recognized (Figure 27.7). A *normal fault* has a steep or nearly vertical *fault plane*. Movement is predominantly in a vertical direction, so that one side is raised or *upthrown* relative to the other, which is *downthrown*. A normal fault results in a steep, straight *fault scarp*, whose height is an approximate measure of the vertical element of displacement (Figure 27.8). Fault scarps range in height from a few feet to a few thousand feet. Their length is measurable in miles; often they attain lengths of 100 to 200 mi (160 to 320 km). Normal faulting is an expression of tension in the earth's outer crust. It is an evident geometric observation that sliding upon an inclined surface of the type indicated in Figure 27.7 *A* must result in a spreading apart of points situated on opposite sides of the fault.

In a *reverse fault* the inclination of the fault plane is such that one side rides up over the other and a crustal shortening occurs (Figure 27.7*B*). Reverse faults produce fault scarps similar to those of normal faults, but the possibility of landsliding is greater because an overhanging scarp tends to be formed.

A *strike-slip fault* is unique in that the movement is predominantly in a horizontal direction

Figure 27.6 The Jura Mountains of France and Switzerland, a foothill range lying northwest of the Alps, are formed of a series of folded limestones. Almost all the mountains are anticlinal. Streams have cut valleys through these ridges to make deep watergaps. (Drawn by E. Raisz.)

Faults and Fault Blocks | 403

Figure 27.7 Four types of faults and their topographic expression.

(Figure 27.7*C*). Hence no scarp results, or a very low one at most. Instead, only a thin line is traceable across the surface. Streams sometimes turn and follow the fault line for a short distance. Sometimes a narrow trench, or *rift*, marks the fault line (Figure 27.17).

Figure 27.8 Formation of this fresh fault scarp in alluvial materials accompanied the Hebgen Lake earthquake of August 17, 1959, in Gallatin County, Montana. Displacement was about 19 ft (6 m) at the maximum point. Vehicle stands on the upthrown side of the fault. (Photograph by J. G. Stacy, U.S. Geological Survey.)

A *low-angle overthrust fault* (Figure 27.7*D*) likewise involves predominantly horizontal movement, but the fault plane is in a horizontal position and one slice of rock rides up over the adjacent ground surface. A thrust slice may be a few hundred or thousand feet thick but up to 25 or 50 mi (40 to 80 km) wide. Overthrusting of this type is generally associated with strong crustal compression in which intense folding also occurs. The scarp produced by low-angle overthrusting is not straight or smooth, as in normal and reverse faults; instead in may be irregular in plan.

Normal faults are not always simple, clean breaks. The fault may be split in such a manner that the end of one fault is overlapped by the end of another (Figure 27.9). Between the overlapping ends a sloping ramp, or *fault splinter*, is formed. Paradoxically, it is thus possible to go from the downthrown to the upthrown block without crossing any fault!

Normal faults may occur as a series of parallel, closely set fractures between which the rock is broken into thin slices (Figure 27.9). At the surface a series of steplike levels occurs, giving rise to the term *step faulting* for this multiple-fault arrangement.

Closely related to normal faulting is *monoclinal flexing* (Figure 27.10), in which sedimentary layers are sharply bent between the upthrown and downthrown sides instead of being fractured. A monocline passes through a series of stages of erosion quite similar to an anticline, except that only half the anticline is represented.

Faults rarely are isolated features. More often they occur in multiple arrangements, commonly

Figure 27.9 Normal faults.

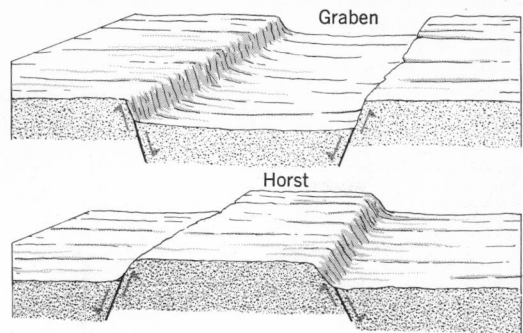

Figure 27.11 Graben and horst.

as a parallel series of faults. This gives rise to a grain or pattern of rock structure and topography. A narrow block dropped down between two normal faults is a *graben* (Figure 27.11). A narrow block elevated between two normal faults is a *horst*. Grabens make conspicuous topographic trenches, with straight, parallel walls. Horsts make blocklike plateaus or mountains, often with a fairly flat top, but steep, straight sides.

Erosional development of a fault scarp

Some of the various stages and forms attained by normal faults throughout the erosional period that follows their formation are illustrated in Figure 27.12. At the rear part of the block is the original fault scarp, produced directly by crustal movement, and therefore belonging to the group of initial landforms. Stage *A* is a *young fault scarp* in which the scarp is still straight and smooth, with only a few stream-cut canyons and some talus cones and alluvial fans built along the scarp base.

Stage *B* is a *mature fault scarp.* Weathering and erosion have caused the scarp to retreat from the original line and to become highly irregular.

In Stage *C* the scarp results entirely through erosion and is designated a *fault-line scarp.* In Stage *D* the region has been reduced to a peneplain and the scarp obliterated entirely.

In Stage *E* further erosion has revealed still another fault-line scarp. In appears because the weak shale formation has been stripped from both sides of the fault, revealing a basement of resistant igneous rocks upon which the shale was once deposited (Figure 27.13).

Fault-block mountains

In regions where normal faulting is on a grand scale, with displacements up to several thousands of feet, huge mountain masses are produced. In general, these faulted mountain blocks can be classed as *tilted* and *lifted* (Figure 27.14). A tilted block has one steep face, the fault scarp, and one gently sloping side. The initial divide lies near the top of the fault scarp and is hence situated over to one side of the block. A lifted block, which is a type of horst, is bound by steep slopes on both sides.

Figure 27.15 shows stages in the life history of a tilted fault block. Most numerous good examples of fault-block ranges are in the desert of the western United States. It should not be supposed,

Figure 27.12 Erosional stages of a fault line.

Figure 27.10 A monocline.

Figure 27.13 Fault-line scarp, MacDonald Lake, near Great Slave Lake, Northwest Territories, Canada. (Royal Canadian Air Force Photograph.)

Figure 27.14 Fault block mountains may be of tilted type (left) or lifted type (right). (After W. M. Davis.)

however, that block mountains and arid climates necessarily go hand in hand.

In youth, the fault block is asymmetrical and has generally even sides, despite the presence of numerous small stream valleys that have been developing as the fault block was elevated.

In maturity (Figure 27.15), the range is dissected into a great number of divides, spurs, and peaks separated by deep canyons. The main crest line of the range is now pushed back to a more nearly central position and the simple blocklike aspect of the mountain range has disappeared. Along the base of the fault scarp, between canyon mouths, remain some parts of the original fault scarp. These make *triangular facets*, aligned nicely along the base line (Figure 27.15). Fans are more extensive than in early youth. The adjoining basins are filled higher with alluvium. In a humid climate, a rolling landscape of moderate relief develops in late maturity, whereas in old age the range is reduced to a subdued peneplain surface.

Geographical aspects of faults and block mountains

Faults are of economic and human-geographic significance for both geologic and topographic reasons. Fault planes are usually zones along which the rock has been pulverized, or at least considerably fractured. This has the effect of permitting ore-forming chemical solutions to rise along fault planes. Many important ore deposits lie in fault planes or in rocks that faults have broken across.

Another related phenomenon is the easy rise of underground water along fault planes. Springs, both cold and hot, are commonly situated along fault lines. They occur along the bases of young

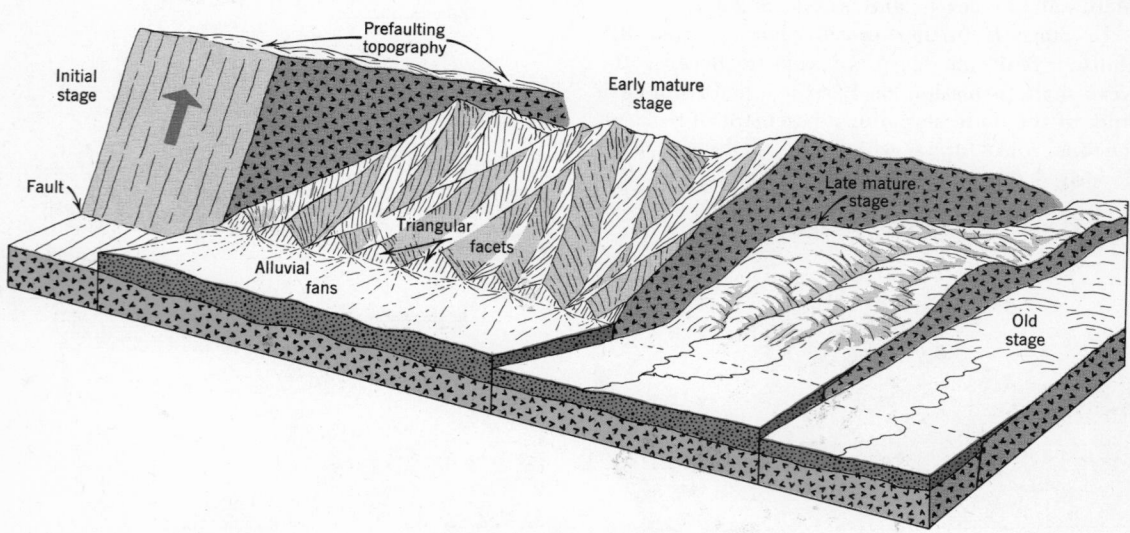

Figure 27.15 Stages in the erosion of a tilted fault block. (After W. M. Davis.)

fault-block mountains, as, for example, Arrowhead Springs along the base of the San Bernardino Range and Palm Springs along the foot of the San Jacinto Mountains, both in southern California.

Petroleum, too, finds its way along fault planes where the rocks have been rendered permeable by crushing, or it becomes trapped in porous beds that have been faulted against impervious shale beds (Figure 27.16). Some of the most intensive searches for oil center about areas of faulted sedimentary strata because of the great production that has been achieved from pools of this type.

Fault scarps and fault-line scarps may form imposing topographic barriers across which it is difficult to build roads and railroads. The great Hurricane Ledge of southern Utah is a feature of this type, in places a steep wall 2500 ft (760 m) high.

Active faults, those on which repeated fault movements are in progress, may impose serious threat of earthquake damage to cities, bridges, aqueducts, and other structures located on or near the fault lines. The California coastal belt is faced with such problems. Through the San Francisco Bay area passes the famed San Andreas fault (Figure 27.17). The devastating earthquake of 1906 resulted from slippage along this fault, which is of the strike-slip type. The San Andreas fault, 600 mi (965 km) long, extends southward and is in places represented by a rift valley, elsewhere by a normal fault bordering the San Bernardino mountain block. Where the Los Angeles aqueduct crosses this fault line and is particularly vulnerable to breakage through fault movement, special structures have been prepared to assure rapid repair in the event of damage. Vulnerability of the urban communities in the San Francisco and Los Angeles areas to earthquake shock is especially great be-

Figure 27.17 The valley followed by the road is the San Andreas Rift, California, marking a strike-slip type of fault along which earthquake-generating movements occur from time to time. In the foreground is Grant Lake. The view is southeast toward Palo Prieto Pass. (Spence Air Photos.)

cause the alluvial materials of the plains shake with great violence in an earthquake which might otherwise cause little disturbance to solid bedrock.

Grabens may be of such size as to form broad lowlands. An illustration is the Rhine graben of Western Germany. Here a belt of rich agricultural land, 20 mi (32 km) wide and 150 mi (240 km) long, lies between the Vosges and Black Forest ranges, both of which are block mountains faulted up in contrast with the downdropped Rhine graben block.

REFERENCES FOR FURTHER STUDY

Fenneman, N. M. (1931), *Physiography of the western United States*, McGraw-Hill Book Co., New York, 534 pp.

Johnson, Douglas (1931), *Stream sculpture on the Atlantic slope*, Columbia University Press, New York, 142 pp.

Figure 27.16 An oil pool has accumulated in the permeable sandstone beds and is prevented from escaping by the impermeable shales faulted against the edge of the sandstone layer.

Fenneman, N. M. (1938), *Physiography of the eastern United States*, McGraw-Hill Book Co., New York, 691 pp.

Lobeck, A. K. (1939), *Geomorphology*, McGraw-Hill Book Co., New York, 731 pp., See Chapters 16 and 17.

Davis, W. M. (1954), *Geographical essays*, Dover Pub-lications, New York, 777 pp. See pp. 413–484, 725–772.

Thornbury, W. D. (1965), *Regional geomorphology of the United States*, John Wiley and Sons, New York, 609 pp.

Hunt, C. B. (1967), *Physiography of the United States*, W. H. Freeman and Co., San Francisco, 480 pp.

REVIEW QUESTIONS

1. What is an anticline? A syncline? How are these features related in a series of folds?

2. What is an anticlinal valley? A synclinal valley? How does reversal of topography normally occur in the process of erosion of a fold region?

3. How are watergaps formed in a fold region? Of what geographic importance are watergaps? What is an antecedent stream? How might antecedent streams develop in a fold region?

4. What type of drainage pattern is developed in a maturely dissected region of folds? Of what types of streams is this pattern composed?

5. How do homoclinal ridges and valleys differ from anticlinal and synclinal ridges and valleys? Show all these types by simple cross-sectional diagrams.

6. What effect does a downplunge of fold axes have upon the forms of ridges and valleys? How can a plunging synclinal mountain be distinguished from a plunging anticlinal mountain?

7. Discuss the geographical aspects of fold regions of rugged ridge-and-valley topography. What economic mineral products are important in fold regions?

8. What is a fault? What is a fault line? Explain how earthquakes are related to faults.

9. Describe a normal fault, and explain how it differs from a reverse fault. What kind of topographic feature is produced by these types of faulting? Explain how fault splinters and fault steps are associated with normal faults.

10. What is a strike-slip fault? How does it differ in topographic expression from a normal fault? What is a rift? Describe the San Andreas fault of California. Is this an active fault line at the present time?

11. Describe a low-angle overthrust fault. With what kind of crustal deformation is it associated? What topographic expression does an overthrust fault have?

12. How does monoclinal flexing differ from faulting? Are the two structures basically related?

13. Distinguish between a graben and a horst. Briefly describe the Rhine graben region as an illustration of graben and horst forms.

14. Why is it necessary to distinguish between a fault scarp and a fault-line scarp? Which form comes first? What varieties of fault-line scarps are recognized?

15. What kinds of block mountains can be formed? Compare the stages of youth and maturity of a large, tilted fault-block mountain. What are the triangular facets? How do they differ from flatirons?

16. In what ways do faults influence the occurrence of ground water and springs? How is petroleum concentrated by fault structures? Why are fault zones favorable for occurrences of ore minerals?

Crystalline Masses and Volcanic Forms

THE term *crystalline rock* is useful in referring collectively to intrusive igneous rock and the metamorphic rocks, such as schists and gneisses. It is of value in understanding regional landform assemblages to recognize the range of landmass types possible under the general class of crystalline rocks, even though distinct subgroups cannot always be separated.

Homogeneous crystallines

Intrusive igneous rocks, such as granites (Figure 17.4), generally occur in enormous batholiths. One batholith in Idaho is exposed over an area of 16,000 sq mi (40,000 sq km), a region almost as large as New Hampshire and Vermont combined. The rock seems to extend down many thousands of feet, and for practical purposes may be considered bottomless. A smaller body of igneous rock less than 40 sq mi (100 sq km) in surface extent is termed a *stock*.

Batholiths and stocks do not reach the surface of the earth when formed, hence produce no initial landforms and have no initial stage in the erosional development cycle. They appear only after prolonged erosion has stripped away the older, overlying rock when the landmass is in a mature or old stage of denudation (Figure 28.1). An additional illustration of the process of exposure of deep-seated rocks was given in the discussion of the manner in which the central core of a dome becomes exposed (Chapter 26).

Topography developed on batholiths varies somewhat according to texture and composition of the rock and whether or not the mass has been faulted. Where the rock is quite uniform and free of strong faults, it is eroded into a maze of canyons and ravines which follow no predominant trend (Figure 28.2). The drainage pattern is dendritic and is composed of insequent streams just as for horizontal sedimentary strata. In fact, the two patterns may be virtually indistinguishable.

Where faulting has occurred, making a series of intersecting zones of crushed and weakened rock, the drainage follows the fault lines and forms a rectangular pattern (Figure 28.3). The streams are of subsequent type because they developed in the zones of weakness.

Certain areas of metamorphic rocks, such as gneisses and schists, also develop a dendritic drainage pattern of insequent streams because the vari-

Figure 28.1 Deep-seated igneous rocks appear at the surface only after long-continued erosion has removed thousands of feet of overlying rocks. (After Longwell, Knopf, and Flint.)

Figure 28.2 This dendritic drainage pattern is developed on the maturely dissected Idaho batholith.

Figure 28.3   A rectangular drainage pattern.

ations in rock texture and composition seem to have little influence upon valley development. The topography of such areas may be identical with that of batholiths. Therefore it is convenient to use the term *homogeneous crystallines* to include both the igneous intrusive and metamorphic rock masses.

Belted metamorphics

Regions of metamorphic rock normally show a strong grain in the topography. Ridges tend to be elongate in one direction and to be separated by long, roughly parallel valleys (see Figure 17.14). Neither ridges nor valleys have the sharpness of folded sedimentary strata, but the drainage pattern is clearly of trellis or rectangular form. Regions of this type may be classed as *belted metamorphics* because the topography is a reflection of different rates of denudation of parallel belts of metamorphic rocks, such as schist, slate, quartzite, and marble. Marble tends to form distinctive valleys; slate and schist make belts of medium to strong relief; quartzite usually stands out boldly and may produce conspicuous narrow hogback ridges. Furthermore, most metamorphic rocks have been broken by reverse and overthrust faults which run parallel with the different belts and often separate one rock type from another. Subsequent stream valleys occupying these fault lines help bring out the grain of the topography. Much of New England, particularly the Taconic and Green Mountains, illustrates these principles well. The larger valleys trend north and south and are underlain by marble. These are flanked by ridges of gneiss, schist, slate, or quartzite. The highlands of the Hudson and of northern New Jersey continue this belted pattern southward where it joins the Blue Ridge. Near Harpers Ferry, Maryland, quartzite ridges rise prominently above broad valley belts of schist.

Areas of complex structure

Some parts of the earth's crust, particularly the continental shields, have undergone several periods of folding, faulting, intrusion, and volcanism. As each event occurred, new rocks or new structures were added to the mass, so that it may appear today as a region of *complex structure* (Figure 28.4). Because of the variety of rock types and structures, the landforms show a variety of forms.

Figure 28.5 shows by a series of diagrams the cycle of erosion in a geologically complex region. In the initial stage, mountains result from faulting, folding, doming, and volcanic activity. In the mature stage, a highly irregular drainage pattern develops. The rugged topography consists of fault and fault-line scarps, hogbacks, old volcanoes, and other landform types. Intrusive and sedimentary rocks of various ages and shapes are exposed. In the old-age stage, the region is reduced to a peneplain, but the harder rock masses stand out as monadnocks.

Geographical aspects of batholiths, metamorphic belts, and complex areas

Regions of intrusive igneous rock, metamorphic rock, and complex structure are often rich in mineral wealth. Where igneous intrusion occurred repeatedly, metallic ores were deposited. Examples from the Rocky Mountains are the copper, silver, gold, and lead of Butte, Montana; the silver and lead of the Coeur d'Alene District in Idaho; and the lead, zinc, and silver of Leadville, Colorado.

Metamorphic rocks, such as slates, quartzites, marbles, and schists, are not likely to contain metallic ores of importance, unless intrusive rocks have penetrated them. They do, however, have economic value for the slate or marble which can be quarried from them. Vermont has these rocks, along with intrusive granites which are quarried as well.

Among the foreign examples of valuable metallic mineral deposits occurring in igneous, meta-

Figure 28.4 Complexly folded and faulted strata of Precambrian age, northern Rockies of Glacier National Park, Montana. (Photograph by Chapman, U.S. Geological Survey.)

morphic, and complex rocks might be cited the tin deposits of the Katanga district, Republic of the Congo.

Much of the batholithic, metamorphic, and complex areas of the world are mountainous, hence, heavily forested and thinly populated. Examples are the Salmon River Mountains, underlain by the great Idaho batholith; the Great Smoky Mountains of North Carolina, Georgia, and Tennessee underlain by intrusive and metamorphic rocks in generally complex arrangement; or the Taconic and Green mountain ridges of belted metamorphics in Vermont and Massachusetts. Lumber is thus an important resource of these regions, in addition to their mineral wealth. At the same time, transportation is often difficult, and in the absence of agricultural land the population is thinly distributed if not actually absent from large areas.

Other extensive regions of intrusive or metamorphic rocks are of low relief—the continental shields—having been reduced to peneplains and only slightly dissected in the present erosion cycle. Much of eastern Canada is of this type of topog-

raphy, as are parts of Sweden and Finland. Not only are they similar in rock conditions, but these regions because of glaciation have countless lakes, and because of similar climate support a needleleaf evergreen forest.

In the United States, the outstanding example of a peneplain on intrusive and metamorphic rocks is the Piedmont Upland of Virginia, the Carolinas, and Georgia. A rolling landscape of monotonously uniform hill-top level extends in a vast belt between the Blue Ridge Mountains on the west and the Coastal Plain on the east. Above this surface rise a few monadnocks. On the Piedmont, soils are thick, slopes are low enough to permit agriculture, and transportation is easy between most points.

Volcanoes and associated landforms

Volcanoes are built by the eruption of molten rock and heated gases under pressure from a relatively small pipe, or *vent*, leading from a magma reservoir at depth. Both explosive and quiet types of eruption occur, the forms built differing for the two types.

Figure 28.5   Stages in the development of a region of highly complex structure. (Drawn by
E. Raisz.)

Figure 28.6   Seen in this oblique air view, a fresh cinder cone and its associated basaltic lava flow (left) have partially blocked a valley. Dixie State Park, about 17 mi (27 km) northwest of St. George, Utah. (Photograph by Frank Jensen.)

Volcanoes of explosive eruption are *cinder cones* and *composite cones;* those formed by relatively quiet outflow of lava are *lava domes.* Quiet eruption of lava, if issuing from extensive cracks, or *fissures,* in sufficient quantities may make great plains or plateaus of lava, classified with horizontal strata (Chapter 26).

Cinder cones

Smallest of the volcanoes are the cinder cones, built entirely of pieces of solidified lava thrown from a central vent. They form where a high proportion of gas in the molten rock causes it to froth into a bubbly mass and to be ejected from a vent with great violence. The froth breaks up into small fragments which solidify as they are ejected and fall as solid particles near the vent (Figure 28.6). The fragments resemble clinkers and ash taken from a coal furnace. Large pieces up to several tons in weight are *volcanic bombs;* they may be somewhat plastic when ejected. Smaller pieces, a fraction of an inch up to an inch or two

(1 to 5 cm) in size, are *cinders;* these make up the bulk of the cinder cone. Still finer particles are termed *ash* and *volcanic dust.* The ash falls like snow upon the ground within a few miles of the eruption (see Figure 28.9). Finer dust is carried by winds to distant regions and may settle out only after years of drifting in the atmosphere.

Figure 28.7   A cinder cone with its lava flows has dammed a valley, making a lake. Farther down valley, in the distance, another lava mass has made a second dam. (After W. M. Davis.)

Cinder cones rarely grow to more than 500 or 1000 ft (150 to 300 m) in height. Growth is rapid. Monte Nuovo, near Naples, Italy, grew to a height of 400 ft (120 m) in the first week of its existence. Paricutin, in Mexico, started as a cinder cone and reached a height of 1000 ft (300 m) in the first three months. The angle of slope of a recently formed cinder cone ranges between 26° and 30°. So loose is the material that it absorbs heavy rain without permitting surface runoff. Erosion is thus delayed until weathering produces a soil which fills the interstices.

Cinder cones normally have proportionately large central craters (Figure 28.6). The rim is often much higher on one side than the other, as the prevailing wind blows the finer cinders and ash to one side of the vent.

Lava flows sometimes issue from the same vent as a cinder cone. They may burst apart the side of the cone but more commonly do not alter its form. Cinder cones may erupt in almost any conceivable topographic location, on ridges, on slopes, and in valleys (Figure 28.7). Cinder cones usually occur in groups, often many dozens in an area of a few tens of square miles. They sometimes show an alignment parallel with fault lines in the underlying rock.

Composite volcanoes

Most of the world's great volcanoes are composite cones. They are built of layers of cinder and ash alternating with layers of lava, and for this reason have been called *strato-volcanoes* by some writers. The steep-sided form is governed by the angle at which the cinder and ash stands, whereas the lava layers provide strength and bulk to the volcano (Figure 28.8). Among the outstanding examples of recently formed composite volca-

Figure 28.8 Looking into the crater of an active stratovolcano, Mt. Spurr, el. 11,070 ft (3535 m). West side of Cook Inlet, near Anchorage, Alaska. (Steve McCutcheon, Alaska Pictorial Service)

A. This distant view of Sakurajima shows the great cauli-flower cloud of volcanic gases and condensed steam.

C. Reaching the sea, the hot lava makes clouds of steam.

B. A blocky lava flow is advancing slowly over a ground surface littered with volcanic bombs and ash.

D. Volcanic ash has buried this village.

Figure 28.9   Sakurajima, a Japanese volcano, erupted violently in 1914. These pictures show various scenes from the eruption. (Photograph by T. Nakasa.)

noes are Fujiyama in Japan, Mayon in the Philippines, Mt. Hood in Oregon, and Shishaldin in the Aleutians. Other famous ones, less perfectly formed, are Vesuvius, Etna, and Stromboli in Italy and Sicily. Heights of several thousand feet and slopes of 20° to 30° are characteristic.

Many composite volcanoes lie in a great belt, the *circum-Pacific ring*, extending from the Andes in South America, through the Cascades and the Aleutians, into Japan; thence south into the East Indies and New Zealand. (See Figure 18.13.) There is also an important Mediterranean group, mentioned above, which includes active volcanoes of Italy and Sicily. Otherwise, Europe has no active volcanoes.

The eruption of large composite volcanoes is usually accompanied by explosive issue of steam, cinders, bombs, and ash, and by lava flows (Figure 28.9). The crater may change form rapidly, both

from demolition of the upper part and from new accumulation.

Calderas

One of the most catastrophic of natural phenomena is a volcanic explosion so violent as to destroy the entire central portion of the volcano. There remains only a great central depression, termed a *caldera*. Whether the upper part of the volcano is largely blown outward in fragments or subsides into the ground beneath the volcano is not certain. Although calderas have been formed in historic time, conditions near the volcano do not permit observation of the process. Vast quantities of ash and dust are emitted and fill the atmosphere for many hundreds of square miles around.

Krakatoa, a volcanic island in Indonesia, exploded in 1883, leaving a great caldera. It is estimated that 18 cu mi (75 cu km) of rock disappeared during the explosion. Great seismic sea waves, or *tsunamis*, generated by the explosion killed many thousands of persons living on low coastal areas of Java and Sumatra. Another historic explosion was that of Katmai, on the Alaskan Peninsula, in 1912. A caldera more than 2 mi (3 km) wide and 2000 to 3700 ft (600 to 1100 m) deep was produced at this time. The explosion was heard at Juneau, 750 mi (1200 km) distant, while at Kodiak, 100 mi (160 km) away, the ash formed a layer 10 in (25 cm) deep.[1]

A classic example of a caldera produced in prehistoric time is Crater Lake, Oregon (Figure 28.10). Mt. Mazama, the former volcano, is estimated to have risen 4000 ft (1200 m) higher than the present rim. Valleys previously cut by streams and glaciers into the flanks of Mt. Mazama were beheaded by the explosive subsidence of the central portion and now form distinctive notches in the rim. Wizard Island, a recent volcano with associated flows, has since grown in the floor of the caldera.

Erosion cycle of volcanoes

Figure 28.11 shows successive stages in the erosion of volcanoes, lava flows, and a caldera. In

[1]A. K. Lobeck, *Geomorphology*, McGraw-Hill Book Co., New York, 1939, p. 685.

the first block are active volcanoes in the process of building. These are in their initial stage. Lava flows issuing from the volcanoes have spread down into a stream valley, following the downward grade of the valley and forming a lake behind the lava dam.

In the next block some changes have taken place, the most conspicuous of which is the destruction of the largest volcano to produce a caldera. A lake occupies the caldera, and a small cone has been built inside. One of the other volcanoes, formed earlier, has become extinct. It has been dissected by streams, losing the initial form, and may be said to be in a stage of late youth. Smaller, neighboring volcanoes are still active, and the contrast in form is marked. The examples of large, beautifully formed volcanoes cited above are all in their initial or very young stage.

The drainage pattern of streams upon a volcanic cone is of necessity *radial* in pattern. Because these streams take their positions upon a slope of an initial land surface they are of consequent origin. It is often possible to recognize volcanoes from a drainage map alone (Figure 28.12) because of the perfection of the radial pattern. Where a well-formed crater exists, small streams flow from the crater rim toward the bottom of the crater. Here the water is absorbed in the porous layers of ash

Figure 28.10 Crater Lake, Oregon, is an outstanding illustration of a caldera, now holding a lake. A great composite volcano which existed here was destroyed in prehistoric time by violent explosion. (After E. Raisz.)

Initial

(Caldera formed)

Caldera

Lava mesa

Mature

Necks, dikes

Old

Mesa

Figure 28.11   Stages in the erosional development of volcanoes and lava flows. (Drawn by E. Raisz.)

within the cone, or is conducted outward by means of a single gap in the crater rim. This inward drainage, described as *centripetal,* often adds to the certainty of interpreting a volcano from a drainage pattern.

In the third block, Figure 28.11, all volcanoes are extinct and have been eroded into the stage of maturity. The caldera lake has been drained and the rim worn to a low, circular ridge. The lava flows which formerly flowed down stream valleys have been able to resist erosion far better than the rock of the surrounding area and have come to stand as mesas high above the general level of the region.

An example of a maturely dissected volcano is Mt. Shasta in the Cascade Range (Figure 28.13).

Figure 28.12 Radial drainage patterns of volcanoes in the East Indies. (After Verbeck and Fennema.)

Figure 28.13 Mt. Shasta in the Cascade Range is a maturely dissected volcano. The bulge on the left-hand slope is a more recent subsidiary cone, Shastina. (Infrared photograph by Eliot Blackwelder.)

Figure 28.14 Shiprock, New Mexico, is a volcanic neck. Radiating from it are dikes. (Spence Air Photos.)

A smaller subsidiary cone of more recent date, named Shastina, is attached to the side of the mountain.

Figure 28.11 shows the old-age stage of erosion of volcanoes. There remains now only a small sharp peak, or *volcanic neck*, representing the solidified lava in the pipe, or neck, of the volcano. Radiating from this are wall-like *dikes*, formed of lava, which previously filled fractures around the base of the volcano. Perhaps the finest illustration of a volcanic neck with radial dikes is Ship Rock, New Mexico (Figure 28.14). Because the central neck and radial dikes extend to great depths in the rock below the base of the volcano, they may persist as landforms long after the cone and its associated flows have been removed.

Lava domes or shield volcanoes

A very important type of volcano, differing greatly in form from those already discussed, is the *lava dome* or *shield volcano*. The best examples are from the Hawaiian Islands, which consist entirely of lava domes (Figure 28.15).

Lava domes are characterized by gently rising, smooth slopes which tend to flatten near the top, producing a broad-topped volcano. The Hawaiian domes range to elevations up to 13,000 ft (4,000 m) above sea level, but including the basal portion lying below sea level they are more than twice that high. In width they range from 10 to 50 mi (16 to 80 km) at sea level and up to 100 mi (160 km) wide at the submerged base.

Lava domes, as the name implies, are built by repeated outpourings of lava. Explosive behavior and emission of fragments are not important, as they are for cinder cones and composite cones. The lava, which in the Hawaiian lava domes is of a dark basaltic type, is highly fluid and travels far down the low slopes, which do not usually exceed 4° or 5°.

Instead of the explosion crater, lava domes have a wide, steep-sided *central depression*, or *sink*, which may be 2 mi (3.2 km) or more wide and several hundred feet deep. These large depressions are a type of caldera produced by subsidence accompanying the removal of molten lava from beneath. Molten basalt is actually seen in the floors of deep *pit craters*, steep-walled depressions 0.25 to 0.5 mi (0.4 to 0.8 km) wide or smaller, which occur on the floor of the sink or elsewhere over the surface of the lava dome (Figure 28.16). Most lava flows issue from cracks, or *fissures*, on the sides of the volcano.

Lava domes of the Hawaiian islands are in various stages of erosion (Figure 28.15). Active volcanoes such as Kilauea and Mauna Loa are in the initial stage and have smooth slopes. Others, such as East Maui, are partly dissected by deep canyons but still possess sizable parts of the original surface. Still others, such as West Maui, are fully dissected. Rising from the sea are some steep-walled stacks representing the last vestiges of old domes; and there exist submarine banks some 250 ft (75 m) below sea level, representing the final stage in destruction.

Geographical aspects of volcanoes

Volcanic eruptions count among the earth's great natural disasters. Wholesale loss of life and destruction of towns and cities are frequent in the history

Figure 28.15 Lava domes in various stages of erosion make up the Hawaiian Islands. (Data from Stearns and Macdonald.) *A.* Initial dome with central depression and fresh flows issuing from radial fissure lines. *B,* Young stage with deeply eroded valley heads. *C,* Mature stage with steep slopes and great relief.

Figure 28.16 Halemaumau, a pit crater on Mauna Ioa, with a fire fountain of molten lava on its floor, 1952. (National Park Service, U.S. Dept. of the Interior.)

of peoples who live near active volcanoes. Loss occurs principally from sweeping clouds of incandescent gases that descend the volcano slopes like great avalanches; from lava flows whose relentless advance engulfs whole cities; from the descent of showers of ash, cinders, and bombs; from violent earthquakes associated with the volcanic activity; and from mudflows of volcanic ash saturated by heavy rain. For habitations along lowlying coasts there is the additional peril of great seismic sea waves, generated by submarine earth faults. These do not necessarily accompany volcanic activity and may occur without warning in the ocean basins which are bordered by belts of active mountain-making.

The surfaces of volcanoes and lava flows remain barren and sterile for long periods after their formation. Certain types of lava surfaces are extremely rough and difficult to traverse; the Spaniards who encountered such terrain in the southwestern United States named it *malpais* (bad ground). Most volcanic rocks in time produce highly fertile soils that are extensively cultivated.

Volcanic ash may have a remarkably beneficial effect upon productivity of soil where the ash fall is relatively light. The eruption of Sunset Crater, near Flagstaff, Arizona, about 800 A.D., spread a layer of sandy volcanic ash over the barren reddish soil of the surrounding region and caused it to become highly productive because of the moisture-conserving effect of the ash, which acted as a mulch in the semi-arid climate. Because Hopi Indian corn grows well in sand, this development attracted Indians, who settled the area thickly. As the ash was gradually washed off of the slopes by heavy summer rains or blown into thick dunes by wind, the fertility declined and after about 200 years of occupation the region was abandoned to its previous state.

Young and mature volcanoes possess most of the geographical attributes of rugged mountains of any sort. Steep slopes prevent extensive agriculture, although providing valuable timber resources. Thus the San Francisco Mountains, a group of maturely dissected volcanoes in northern Arizona, are clothed in what is perhaps the finest known western yellow pine forest (ponderosa pine). A lumber industry centered about the towns of Flagstaff and Williams has flourished for many years.

As scenic features of great beauty, attracting a heavy tourist trade, few landforms outrank volcanoes. National parks have been made of Mt. Rainier, Mt. Lassen, and Crater Lake in the Cascade Range. Mt. Vesuvius and Fujiyama also attract many visitors.

Mineral resources, particularly the metallic ores, are conspicuously lacking in volcanoes and lava flows, unless later geologic events have resulted in the injection or diffusion of ore minerals into the volcanic rocks. The gas-bubble cavities in some ancient lavas have become filled with copper or other ores. The famed *kimberlite* rock of South Africa, source of diamonds, is the pipe of an ancient volcano.

As a source of crushed rock for concrete aggregate or railroad ballast, and other engineering purposes, lava rock is often extensively used. Thus the ancient lava layers that make up the Watchung ridges of northern New Jersey have in places been virtually leveled in quarrying operations continued over several decades.

REFERENCES FOR FURTHER STUDY

Tyrell, G. W. (1931), *Volcanoes*, Butterworth and Co., London, 252 pp.

Lobeck, A. K. (1939), *Geomorphology*, McGraw-Hill Book Co., New York, 731 pp. See Chapters 18 and 19.

Williams, H. (1941), *Crater Lake, the story of its origin*, University of California Press, Berkeley and Los Angeles, 97 pp.

Cotton, C. A. (1944), *Volcanoes as landscape formers*, Whitcombe and Tombs, Christchurch, N.Z., 416 pp.

Jaggar, T. A. (1945), *Volcanoes declare war*, Paradise of the Pacific, Honolulu, 166 pp.

Bullard, F. M., (1962), *Volcanoes in history, in theory, in eruption*, University of Texas Press, Austin, 441 pp.

REVIEW QUESTIONS

1. What is a batholith? A stock? How large are these features? Of what kind of rock is a batholith composed? What kind of topography does it produce in a mature stage?

2. What is the meaning of a rectangular drainage pattern in a region underlain by homogeneous crystalline rock of a batholith?

3. What kind of topography develops in regions of belted metamorphic rocks such as gneiss, schist, slate, marble, and quartzite? Which of these rock types would form valleys? Which would form narrow ridges; which broad ridges?

4. What are some of the varieties of rocks and structure that might be found in a region of complex structure? From the standpoint of geologic time would a complex region be ancient or comparatively recent in development? Would it be a likely region for mineral deposits of economic value?

5. What types of volcanoes are recognized? How do they differ?

6. Describe a cinder cone. Of what material is it formed? What size is normally attained by cinder cones? How fast do they form? How are groups of cinder cones arranged in plan?

7. How is a composite type of volcano formed? Name several famous large composite volcanoes. Along what belts are most of the world's active, or recently active, large volcanoes located?

8. What is a caldera? What volcanic activity occurred at Krakatoa (1883) and at Katmai (1912)? Describe Crater Lake as an illustration of a caldera.

9. Describe the stages of youth, maturity, and old age in the erosion of a large volcano. What form of drainage pattern is typically present on volcanoes?

10. Describe a volcanic neck with radial dikes. Give an example.

11. Discuss the form and development of large lava domes, or shield volcanoes, as exemplified by the Hawaiian Islands. What feature of a lava dome corresponds to the crater of a composite volcano?

12. Discuss the geographical aspects of volcanic landforms. In what way are soils and vegetation affected by volcanic forms?

APPENDIX *I*

Soil Orders of the United States

U. S. DEPARTMENT OF AGRICULTURE

SOIL CONSERVATION SERVICE

PATTERNS OF SOIL ORDERS AND SUBORDERS OF THE UNITED STATES

Generalized from 1967 Soil Map,
Scale 1:7,500,000, U. S. Atlas

SLOPE CLASSES

Gently sloping = slopes mainly less than 10 percent

Moderately sloping = slopes mainly between 10 and 25 percent

Steep = slopes mainly steeper than 25 percent

Scale 1:17,000,000

100 0 100 200 300 400 Miles

LEGEND

Only the dominant orders and suborders are shown. Each delineation has many inclusions of other kinds of soil. General definitions for the orders and suborders follow. For complete definitions see Soil Survey Staff, Soil Classification, A Comprehensive System, 7th Approximation, Soil Conservation Service, U. S. Department of Agriculture, 1960 (for sale by U. S. Government Printing Office) and the March 1967 Supplement (available from Soil Conservation Service, U. S. Department of Agriculture). Approximate equivalents in the modified 1938 soil classification system are indicated for each suborder.

ALFISOLS . . . Soils with gray to brown surface horizons, medium to high base supply, and subsurface horizons of clay accumulation; usually moist but may be dry during warm season

A1 AQUALFS (seasonally saturated with water) gently sloping; general crops if drained, pasture and woodland if undrained (Some Low–Humic Gley soils and Planosols)

A2 BORALFS (cool or cold) gently sloping; mostly woodland, pasture, and some small grain (Gray Wooded soils)

A2S BORALFS steep; mostly woodland

A3 UDALFS (temperate or warm, and moist) gently or moderately sloping; mostly farmed, corn, soybeans, small grain, and pasture (Gray–Brown Podzolic soils)

A4 USTALFS (warm and intermittently dry for long periods) gently or moderately sloping; range, small grain, and irrigated crops (Some Reddish Chestnut and Red–Yellow Podzolic soils)

A5S XERALFS (warm and continuously dry in summer for long periods, moist in winter) gently sloping to steep; mostly range, small grain, and irrigated crops (Noncalcic Brown soils)

ARIDISOLS . . . Soils with pedogenic horizons, low in organic matter, and dry more than 6 months of the year in all horizons

D1 ARGIDS (with horizon of clay accumulation) gently or moderately sloping; mostly range, some irrigated crops (Some Desert, Reddish Desert, Reddish–Brown, and Brown soils and associated Solonetz soils)

D1S ARGIDS gently sloping to steep

D2 ORTHIDS (without horizon of clay accumulation) gently or moderately sloping; mostly range and some irrigated crops (Some Desert, Reddish Desert, Sierozem, and Brown soils, and some Calcisols and Solonchak soils)

D2S ORTHIDS gently sloping to steep

ENTISOLS . . . Soils without pedogenic horizons

E1 AQUENTS (seasonally saturated with water) gently sloping; some grazing

E2 ORTHENTS (loamy or clayey textures) deep to hard rock; gently to moderately sloping; range or irrigated farming (Regosols)

E3 ORTHENTS shallow to hard rock; gently to moderately sloping; mostly range (Lithosols)

E3S ORTHENTS shallow to hard rock; steep; mostly range

E4 PSAMMENTS (sand or loamy sand textures) gently to moderately sloping; mostly range in dry climates, woodland or cropland in humid climates (Regosols)

HISTOSOLS . . . Organic soils

H1 FIBRISTS (fibrous or woody peats, largely undecomposed) mostly wooded or idle (Peats)

H2 SAPRISTS (decomposed mucks) truck crops if drained, idle if undrained (Mucks)

INCEPTISOLS . . . Soils that are usually moist, with pedogenic horizons of alteration of parent materials but not of accumulation

I1S ANDEPTS (with amorphous clay or vitric volcanic ash and pumice) gently sloping to steep; mostly woodland; in Hawaii mostly sugar cane, pineapple, and range (Ando soils, some Tundra soils)

I2 AQUEPTS (seasonally saturated with water) gently sloping; if drained, mostly row crops, corn, soybeans, and cotton; if undrained, mostly woodland or pasture (Some Low–Humic Gley soils and Alluvial soils)

I2P AQUEPTS (with continuous or sporadic permafrost) gently sloping to steep; woodland or idle (Tundra soils)

I3 OCHREPTS (with thin or light–colored surface horizons and little organic matter) gently to moderately sloping; mostly pasture, small grain, and hay (Sols Bruns Acides and some Alluvial soils)

I3S OCHREPTS gently sloping to steep; woodland, pasture, small grains

I4S UMBREPTS (with thick dark–colored surface horizons rich in organic matter) moderately sloping to steep; mostly woodland (Some Regosols)

MOLLISOLS . . . Soils with nearly black, organic–rich surface horizons and high base supply

M1 AQUOLLS (seasonally saturated with water) gently sloping; mostly drained and farmed (Humic Gley soils)

M2 BOROLLS (cool or cold) gently or moderately sloping, some steep slopes in Utah; mostly small grain in North Central States, range and woodland in Western States (Some Chernozems)

M3 UDOLLS (temperate or warm, and moist) gently or moderately sloping; mostly corn, soybeans, and small grains (Some Brunizems)

M4 USTOLLS (intermittently dry for long periods during summer) gently to moderately sloping; mostly wheat and range in western part, wheat and corn or sorghum in eastern part, some irrigated crops (Chestnut soils and some Chernozems and Brown soils)

M4S USTOLLS moderately sloping to steep; mostly range or woodland

M5 XEROLLS (continuously dry in summer for long periods, moist in winter) gently to moderately sloping; mostly wheat, range, and irrigated crops (Some Brunizems, Chestnut, and Brown soils)

M5S XEROLLS moderately sloping to steep; mostly range

SPODOSOLS . . . Soils with accumulations of amorphous materials in subsurface horizons

S1 AQUODS (seasonally saturated with water) gently sloping; mostly range or woodland; where drained in Florida, citrus and special crops (Ground–Water Podzols)

S2 ORTHODS (with subsurface accumulations of iron, aluminum, and organic matter) gently to moderately sloping; woodland, pasture, small grains, special crops (Podzols, Brown Podzolic soils)

S2S ORTHODS steep; mostly woodland

ULTISOLS . . . Soils that are usually moist with horizon of clay accumulation and a low base supply

U1 AQUULTS (seasonally saturated with water) gently sloping; woodland and pasture if undrained, feed and truck crops if drained (Some Low–Humic Gley soils)

U2S HUMULTS (with high or very high organic–matter content) moderately sloping to steep; woodland and pasture if steep, sugar cane and pineapple in Hawaii, truck and seed crops in Western States (Some Reddish–Brown Lateritic soils)

U3 UDULTS (with low organic–matter content; temperate or warm, and moist) gently to moderately sloping; woodland, pasture, feed crops, tobacco, and cotton (Red–Yellow Podzolic soils, some Reddish–Brown Lateritic soils)

U3S UDULTS moderately sloping to steep; woodland, pasture

U4S XERULTS (with low to moderate organic–matter content, continuously dry for long periods in summer) range and woodland (Some Reddish–Brown Lateritic soils)

VERTISOLS . . . Soils with high content of swelling clays and wide deep cracks at some season

V1 UDERTS (cracks open for only short periods, less than 3 months in a year) gently sloping; cotton, corn, pasture, and some rice (Some Grumusols)

V2 USTERTS (cracks open and close twice a year and remain open more than 3 months); general crops, range, and some irrigated crops (Some Grumusols)

AREAS with little soil . . .

X1 Salt flats

X2 Rockland, ice fields

NOMENCLATURE

The nomenclature is systematic. Names of soil orders end in sol (L. solum, soil), e. g., ALFISOL, and contain a formative element used as the final syllable in names of taxa in suborders, great groups, and sub–groups.

Names of suborders consist of two syllables, e. g., AQUALF. Formative elements in the legend for this map and their connotations are as follows:

and — Modified from Ando soils; soils from vitreous parent materials

aqu — L. aqua, water; soils that are wet for long periods

arg — Modified from L. argilla, clay; soils with a horizon of clay accumulation

bor — Gr. boreas, northern; cool

fibr — L. fibra, fiber; least decomposed

hum — L. humus, earth; presence of organic matter

ochr — Gr. base of ochros, pale; soils with little organic matter

orth — Gr. orthos, true; the common or typical

psamm — Gr. psammos, sand; sandy soils

sapr — Gr. sapros, rotten; most decomposed

ud — L. udus, humid; of humid climates

umbr — L. umbra, shade; dark colors reflecting much organic matter

ust — L. ustus, burnt; of dry climates with summer rains

xer — Gr. xeros, dry; of dry climates with winter rains

Topographic Map Reading

Topographic maps

SEVERAL methods have been used to show accurately the configuration of the land surface on topographic maps: *plastic shading, altitude tints, hachures,* and *contours* (Figure II.1). The first three processes give a strong visual effect of three dimensions so that even untutored persons can grasp the essential character of the landscape features without preliminary explanation. But, as compensation for ease of understanding, such methods of showing relief are inadequate because they do not tell the reader the elevation above sea level of all points on the map, or how steep the slopes are. The method of topographic contours, however, gives this information and makes the most useful type of topographic map.

Plastic shading

Maps using plastic shading to show relief look very much like photographs taken down upon a plaster relief model of the land surface illuminated from directly above or from an oblique angle (Figure II.1). They may also be likened to air photographs taken when the sun's rays are striking the earth at a fairly low angle (Figure II.2). The effect of relief is produced by gray or brown tones applied according to one of two principles. In the *oblique illumination* method, light rays are imagined as coming from a point in the northwestern sky somewhere intermediate between the horizon and zenith. Thus all slopes facing southwest receive the heaviest shades and are darkest where the slopes are steepest (Figure II.3).

Altitude tints

In its simplest form, altitude tinting consists of assigning a certain color, or a certain depth of tone of a color, to all areas on the map lying within a specified range of elevation. Schoolroom wall maps commonly show low areas by deep green, intermediate ranges of elevations by successive shades of buff and light brown, and high mountain elevations in darker shades of brown or red. The method is effective for small-scale maps that are viewed at some distance.

Hachures

Hachures are tiny, short lines arranged in such a way as to look as if someone had placed thousands of match sticks side by side into roughly parallel rows. Each hachure line lies along the direction of the steepest slope and represents the direction that would be taken by water flowing down the surface.

A precise system of hachures, adapted to representation of detailed topographic features on accurate, large-scale maps, was invented by a Saxon army officer, Major J. G. Lehmann (1765–1811), and was widely used on military maps of European countries throughout the nineteenth century. In the Lehmann system, steepness of slope is indicated by thickness of the hachure line.

Because hachures do not tell the elevation of surface points, it is necessary to print numerous elevation figures on hilltops, road intersections, towns, and other strategic locations. These numbers are known as *spot heights*. Without them a hachure map would be of little practical value.

Contour lines

A *contour line* may be defined as an imaginary line on the ground, every point of which is at the same altitude, or elevation, above sea level. Contour lines on a map are simply the graphic representations of ground contours, drawn for each of a series of specified elevations such as 10, 20, 30, 40, or 50 feet or meters above sea level or any other chosen base, known as a *datum plane*. The resulting line pattern not only gives a visual impression of topography to the experienced student of maps but also supplies accurate information about true elevations and slopes.

In order to clarify the contour principle, various commonplace things can be used for illustration. Imagine, for example, a small island, as shown in Figure II.5. the shoreline is a natural contour line because it is a line connecting all points having zero elevation. Suppose that sea level could be made to rise exactly ten feet (or that the island could be made to sink exactly ten feet); the water would come to rest along the line labeled "10."

Figure AII.1 Various ways in which relief can be shown are, from top to bottom: (1) perspective diagram or terrain sketch, (2) hachures, (3) contours, (4) hachures and contours combined, and (5) plastic shading and contours combined. (Drawn by E. Raisz.)

Figure AII.2 A vertical air photograph (above) is a kind of topographic map, showing all relief details but lacking elevation information. The contour topographic map (below) covers the same area and shows a small side canyon of the Grand Canyon. North is toward the bottom of these maps to give the proper effect of relief in the photograph. (U.S. Forest Service and U.S. Geological Survey.)

This would be the 10-foot contour because it connects all points on the island that are exactly ten feet higher than the original shoreline. By successive rises in water level, each exactly ten feet more than the last, the positions of the remaining contours would be fixed.

Contour interval and slope

Contour interval is the vertical distance separating successive contours. The interval remains constant over the entire map, except in special cases where two or more intervals are used on the map sheet.

Because the vertical contour interval is fixed, horizontal spacing of contours on a given map varies with changes in land slope. The general rule is: close crowding of contour lines represents a steep slope; wide spacing represents a gentle slope. Figure II.6 shows a small island, one side of which is a steep, clifflike slope. From the summit point *B* to the cliff base at *A* the contours are crossed within a short horizontal distance and therefore appear closely spaced on the map. From *B* to the shore at *C* the same total vertical descent is made, but because the slope is gentle, the horizontal

Figure AII.3 Plastic shading combined with contours greatly enhances the visual effect of relief. (Portion of U.S. Geological Survey, Kitzmiller, Md.–W. Va., topographic quadrangle. scale 1:24,000.)

distance is much greater. Hence, the contours between *B* and *C* are widely spaced on the map.

Selection of contour interval depends both on relief of the land and on scale of the map. Topographic maps showing regions of strong relief require a large interval, such as 50, 100, or 200 ft (10, 25, or 50 m); regions of moderate relief, intervals such as 10 or 25 ft (2 or 5 m).

Because by far the greatest parts of the earth's land surfaces are sculptured by streams flowing in valleys, special note should be made of how contours behave when crossing a stream valley. Figure II.7 is a small contour sketch map illustrating some stream valleys. Notice that each contour is bent into a V whose apex lies on the stream and points in an upstream direction.

Determining elevations by means of contours

Figure 11.7 can be used to illustrate the determination of elevations. Point *B* is easy to determine because it lies exactly on the 1300-foot contour. Point *C* requires interpolation. Because it lies midway between the 1100- and 1200-foot lines, its elevation is likewise the midvalue of the vertical interval, or 1150 feet. Point *D* lies about

one-fifth of the distance from the 1000 to the 1100-foot contours. Inasmuch as one-fifth of the contour interval is 20 feet, point *D* has an approximate elevation of 1020 feet. For the last two points only a guess has been made as to the true elevation, but if the ground is not too irregular the error will probably be small. Determination of the summit elevation, point *A*, involves still more uncertainty. It is certain that the summit point is more than 1700 feet and less than 1800 because the 1700-foot contour is the highest one shown. Because a sizable area is included within the 1700-foot contour, it may be supposed that the summit rises appreciably higher than 1700. A guess would place the true elevation at about 1750 feet.

On many topographic maps the elevation of hilltops, road intersections, bridges, lakes, etc., is printed on the map to the nearest foot or meter. These spot heights do away with the need for estimating elevations at key points.

Federal agencies, such as the U.S. Coast and Geodetic Survey and the U.S. Geological Survey, in mapping an area carefully determine elevation and position of convenient reference points. These are known as *bench marks*. On the map they are

Figure AII.6 On the steep side of this island the contours appear more closely spaced.

Figure AII.4 A portion of the Metz sheet is shown above to correct scale. This map is one of the French 1:80,000 topographic series using black hachures and spot heights. The Lehmann system of hachuring, shown below, varies the thickness of hachure line according to ground slope.

Figure AII.7 Stream valleys produce V-shaped indentations of the contours.

designated by the letters B.M., together with the elevation stated to the nearest foot.

Depression contours

A special type of contour is used where the land surface has basinlike hollows, or *closed depressions,* which would make small lakes if they could be filled with water. This is the *hachured contour,* or *depression contour.* Figure II.8 is a sketch of a depression in a gently sloping plain. Below it is the corresponding contour map. Hachured contours have the same elevations and contour intervals as regular contours on the same map.

Topographic profiles

In order to get a better idea of the nature of the relief, *topographic profiles* are sometimes drawn. These are lines that show the rise and fall of the land surface along a selected line crossing the map. Figure II.9 illustrates the construction of a profile. A line, *XY,* is lightly drawn across

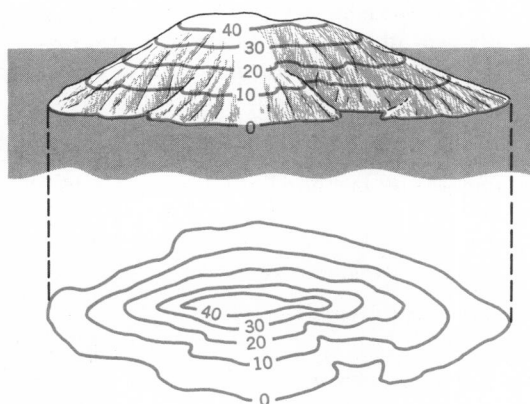

Figure AII.5 Contours on a small island.

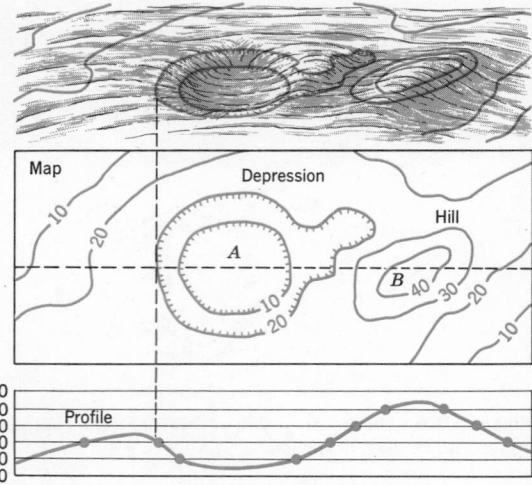

Figure AII.8 Contours which close in a circular manner show either closed depressions or hills.

the map at the desired location. A piece of paper, ruled with horizontal lines, is placed so that its top edge lies along the line *XY*.

Each horizontal line represents a contour level and is so numbered along the left-hand side. Starting at the left, a perpendicular is dropped from the point *a* where the map contour intersects the profile line, *XY*, down to the corresponding horizontal level. A point *a'* is marked on the horizontal line. Next, the procedure is repeated for the 400-foot contour at point *b*, and so on, until all points have been plotted. A smooth line is then drawn through all the points, completing the profile. Where contours are widely spaced, some judgment is required in drawing of the profile.

Figure AII.9 A topographic profile can be constructed from a contour map along any desired line.

Figure II.11 shows two profiles, both of which are drawn along the same line *XY*. The difference is one of degree of exaggeration of the vertical scale. In this illustration, horizontal map scale is 1 inch to 10,000 feet, or 1:120,000, whereas the vertical scale of the upper profile is 1 inch to 1000 feet, or 1:12,000. The vertical scale is thus ten times as large as the horizontal map scale, and the profile is said to have a *vertical exaggeration* of ten times. In the lower profile the horizontal scale remains the same, of course, but the vertical scale is 1 inch to 2000 feet, or 1:24,000. The vertical exaggeration is therefore five times. Some degree of vertical exaggeration is usually needed to bring out the nature of the topography. A *natural scale* profile, one in which the vertical and horizontal scales are the same, would give a profile with such tiny fluctuations as to be not only difficult to read but also difficult to draw or reproduce.

Map scale

Distance between-points shown on a map depends on the scale of the map—the ratio between map distances and the actual ground distances which the map represents (Chapter 1). Given a fractional scale (representative fraction, or R.F.) on which to draw his map, the cartographer must convert this fraction to units of measurement, for he must use a ruler scaled in inches or centimeters to measure lengths of line on the map to represent ground distances in miles or kilometers.

For example, if the map scale is given as 1/63,360, or 1:63,360, as explained in Chapter 1, this fractional scale may be interpreted as "one inch on the map represents one mile on the ground." A map scale of 1:100,000 could be read as "one centimeter represents one kilometer."

Most maps of small areas carry a fractional scale printed on the map margin. Conversion to equivalent ratios of inches to miles or centimeters to kilometers is left to the reader to compute. For practical map use, however, a *graphic scale* is printed on the map margin. This is a length of line divided off into numbered segments (Figure II.10). The units are in conventional terms of measurement, such as feet, yards, and miles, or meters and kilometers. To use the graphic scale, a piece of paper with a straight edge is held along the line to be measured on the map and the distance marked on the edge of the paper. The paper is then placed along the graphic scale and the length of the line read directly.

Large-scale and small-scale maps

The relative size of two different scales is determined according to which fraction is the larger and which the smaller. For example, a scale of 1:10,000 is twice as large as a scale of 1:20,000.

Figure AII.10 The distance between two points on a map can be read directly from a graphic scale. (Portion of U.S. Geological Survey map.)

Maps with scales ranging from 1:600,000 down to 1:100,000,000 or smaller are known as *small-scale maps*. Those of scale 1:600,000 to 1:75,000 are *medium-scale* maps; those of scale greater than 1:75,000 are *large-scale* maps.

For representing details of the earth's surface configuration, large-scale maps are needed and the area of land surface shown by an individual map sheet must necessarily be small. A topographic sheet 10 by 20 inches, on a scale of 1,63,360 (1 inch to 1 mile) would, of course, include an area 10 by 20 miles, or 200 square miles. Of the common sets of topographic maps published by national governments for general distribution, most fall within the scale range of 1:20,000 to 1:250,000.

Relation between scales and areas

Assuming that two maps, each on a different scale, have the same dimensions, what is the relation between the ground areas shown by each? In Figure II.11 are shown three maps, each having the same dimensions, but representing scales of 1:20,000, 1:10,000 and 1:5,000, respectively, from left to right. Although map B is on twice the scale of map A, it shows a ground area only one-fourth as great. Map C is on four times as large a scale as map A, yet it covers a ground area only one-sixteenth as much. From this example can be deduced the following rule: the ground area that is represented by a map of given outside dimensions varies inversely with the square of the change in scale. Thus, if the scale is reduced to one-third its original value, the area that can be shown on a map of fixed dimensions increases to nine times the original value.

Map orientation and declination of the compass

It is a well-known convention to draw large-scale topographic maps in such a way that north is in a direction toward the top of the map, south to the bottom of the map, and east and west to the right- and left-hand sides, respectively.

The geographic north pole, to which all meridians converge, forms a reference point for the *true north*, or *geographic north*, direction. There is, however, another place, the *magnetic north pole*, to which magnetic compasses point (Figure II.12). The magnetic north pole is located in the

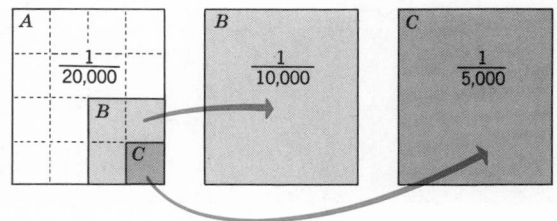

Figure AII.11 Area shown on a map decreases as scale increases.

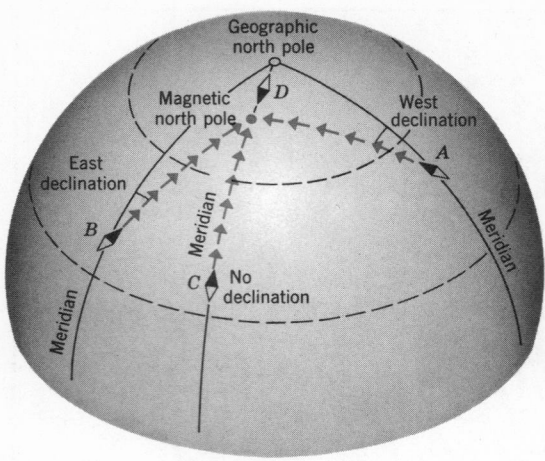

Figure AII.12 Whether declination is east or west depends on the observer's global position with respect to the magnetic and geographic north poles. (From A. N. Strahler, *The Earth Sciences*, Harper and Row, Inc., N.Y.)

point. One arrow designates true north, the other one *magnetic north*. The angular distance between the two directions is known as the *magnetic declination*.

Magnetic declination varies greatly in different parts of the world, depending principally on one's position relative to the geographic and magnetic poles. Lines on a map drawn through all places having the same compass declination are known as *isogonic lines* (Figure II.13). The line of zero declination (*agonic line*) runs through the eastern United States. Anywhere along this line the compass points to true geographic north, and no adjustment is required.

Magnetic declination changes appreciably with the passage of years. The amount of annual change in declination is usually stated on the margin of a good map.

Bearings and azimuths

In using maps it is frequently necessary to state the direction followed by a road or stream, or to describe the direction that can be taken to locate a particular object with respect to some known reference point. In air and marine navigation the direction from one point to another must be stated.

Northwest Territories of Canada on Prince of Wales Island about lat. 73° N, long. 100° W. Most published large-scale maps have printed on the margin two arrows stemming from a common

Figure AII.13 On this world isogonic map, declination is given in intervals of ten degrees. (Based on data of U.S. Navy Oceanographic Office. From A. N. Strahler, *The Earth Sciences*, Harper and Row, Inc., N.Y.)

A. Compass quadrant bearings

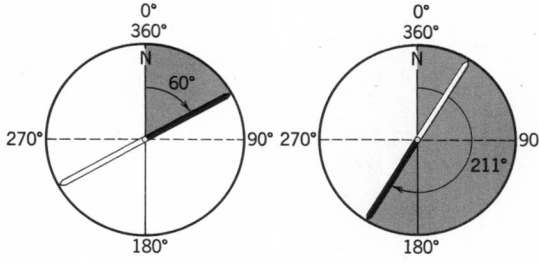

B. Azimuths

Figure AII.14 Directions expressed as bearings or azimuths.

For these purposes the angle that the given line makes with a north-south line is measured. The unit of angular measurement most common in map work is the *degree*, 360 of which comprise a complete circle, but other systems of angular measurement, such as the *mil* (of which there are 6400 in a complete circle), are sometimes preferable for special applications.

Two systems of stating directions with respect to north can be used (Figure II.14). (*a*) *Compass quadrant bearings* are angles measured eastward or westward of either north or south, whichever happens to be the closer. Examples are shown in Figure II.14*A*. The direction from a given point to some object on the map is thus written as "N 49° E" or "S 70° W." All bearings range between 0° and 90°. Compass bearings may be magnetic bearings, related to magnetic north, or true bearings, related to geographic north. Unless specifically stated otherwise, a bearing should be assumed to be a true bearing.

(*b*) *Azimuths* are used by military services and in air and marine navigation generally. As shown in Figure II.14*B*, all azimuths are read in a clockwise direction from north and therefore range between 0° and 360°. Azimuths are usually measured from either magnetic north or true north, referred to as *magnetic azimuth* and *true azimuth*, respectively.

Topographic quadrangles

Any system whereby points on the earth's surface are located with reference to a previously determined set of intersecting lines can be called

a *coordinate system*. The system of parallels and meridians used throughout the world, and the designation of any point on the earth's surface in terms of latitude and longitude are treated in Chapter 1. The system of *geographic coordinates* constitutes the commonest of the coordinate systems in general use. Two other systems are the *military grid* and the *township grid of U.S. Land Office Survey*.

Most published sets of large-scale topographic maps use the geographic grid to determine the position and size of individual map sheets in a series. A single map sheet, or *quadrangle*, is bounded on the right- and left-hand margins by meridians, and on the top and bottom by parallels, which are a specified number of minutes or degrees apart. Thus, individual sheets may be fitted together to form unified groups.

Seven standard scales comprise the National Topographic Map Series:

Series	R.F.	Unit Equivalents
7.5 minute	1:24.000	1 inch to 2000 feet
7.5 minute	1:31,680	1 inch to one-half mile
15 minute	1:62,500	1 inch to about 1 mile
Alaska	1:63,360	1 inch to 1 mile
30 minute	1:125,000	1 inch to about 2 miles
1:250,000	1:250,000	1 inch to about 4 miles
1:1,000,000	1:1,000,000	1 inch to about 16 miles

Figures II.15 and II.16 compare the coverages and sizes of standard quadrangles on several of these series.

The United States Land Office Survey

Topographic maps of the central and western United States show the civil divisions of land according to the United States Land Office Survey.

In 1785, Congress authorized a survey of the territory lying north and west of the Ohio River. To avoid the irregular and unsystematic type of land subdivision that had grown up in seaboard states during colonial times, Congress specified that the new lands should be divided into six-mile squares, now called *congressional townships*, and that the grid of townships should be based upon a carefully surveyed east-west base line, designated the "geographer's line." Meridians and parallels laid off at six-mile intervals from the base line were to form the boundaries of the townships. This general plan, believed to have been proposed by Thomas Jefferson, was subsequently carried out to cover the balance of the central and western states.

The *principal meridians* and *base lines*, from which rows of townships were laid off, are shown in Figure II.17. Principal meridians run north or

Figure AII.15 Large-scale maps of the U.S. Geological Survey are bounded by parallels and meridians to form quadrangles. The four quadrangles shown here represent the scales and areas commonly used in the United States, exclusive of Alaska.

south, or both, from selected points whose latitude and longitude were calculated by astronomical means. Some 32 principal meridians have been surveyed. Westward from the Ohio-Pennsylvania boundary these are numbered from 1 through 6, after which they are designated by names.

Through the initial point selected for starting the principal meridian, an east-west base line was run, corresponding to a parallel of latitude through that point. North and south from the base line, horizontal tiers of townships were laid off and numbered accordingly. Vertical rows of townships, called *ranges,* were laid off to the right and left of the principal meridians, and were numbered accordingly (Figure II.18).

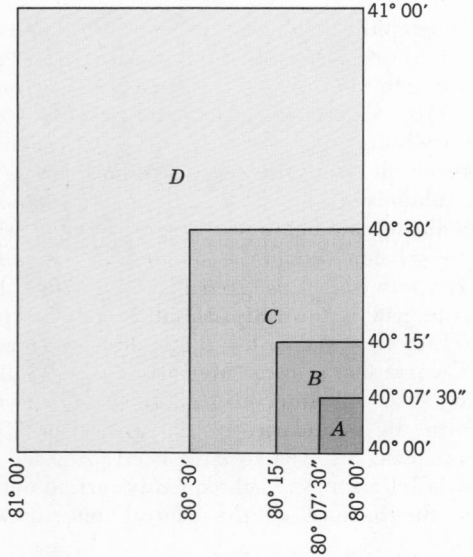

Figure AII.16 If the four quadrangles of Figure AII.15 were reduced to the same scale, their areas would compare as shown here.

The area governed by one principal meridian and its base line is restricted to a particular section of country, usually about as large as one or two states. Where two systems of townships meet, they do not correspond, because each system was built up independently of the others.

Because the range lines, on eastern and western boundaries of townships, are meridians converging slightly as they are extended northward, the width of townships is progressively diminished in a northward direction. In order to avoid a considerable reduction in township widths in the more northerly tiers, new base-lines, known as *standard parallels,* are surveyed for every four tiers of townships. They are designated 1st, 2nd, 3rd Standard Parallel N, etc. (Figure II.18). The ranges will be found to offset at the standard parallels, and in consequence, roads which follow range lines make an offset or jog when crossing standard parallels.

Subdivisions of the township are square-mile *sections,* of which there are 36 to the township. These are usually numbered as illustrated in Figure II.19. Each section may be subdivided into halves, quarters, and half-quarters, or even smaller units. These divisions, together with the number of acres contained in each, are illustrated in Figure II.20.

Topographic map symbols

Large-scale topographic maps of the U.S. Geological Survey use a standard set of symbols to show many kinds of features that cannot be represented to true scale. Reproduced on the front end paper of this book is the set of symbols used by the U.S. Geological Survey on its most recent series of large-scale topographic maps, together with a representative example of a recent map on the scale of 1:24,000.

In general, it is conventional to show relief

Figure AII.17 Base lines and principal meridians of these two portions of the United States are representative of the system used by the U.S. Land Office. (After U.S. Dept. Interior, General Land Office Map of the United States, 1937.)

features in brown, hydrographic (water) features in blue, vegetation in green, and cultural (man-made) features in black or red.

Geologic maps and structure sections

The *areal geologic map* shows by means of colors or patterns the surface distribution of each rock unit with special emphasis upon the lines of contact of rocks unlike in variety or age. Faults are shown as lines. Strikes and dips of strata are added by special symbols.

Figure II.21 is a simple geologic map of the same area shown by a perspective diagram in

R. 6 W.

6	5	4	3	2	1
7	8	9	10	11	12
18	17	16	15	14	13
19	20	21	22	23	24
30	29	28	27	26	25
31	32	33	34	35	36

T. 2 S.

Figure AII.19 A township is divided into 36 sections, each one a square mile.

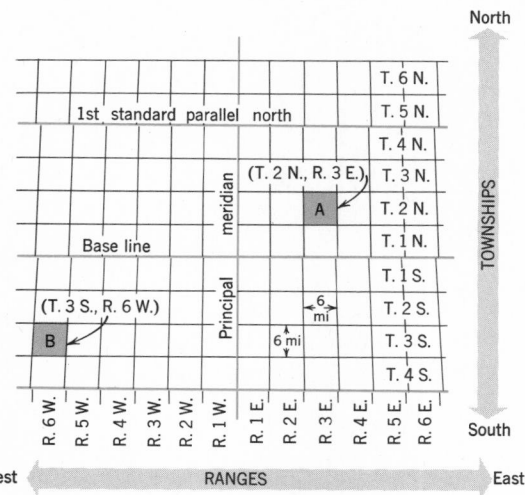

Figure AII.18 Designation of townships and ranges.

Figure AII.20 A section may be subdivided into many units. (After Willis E. Johnson.)

Rock units in order of age:

Shale (youngest)

Conglomerate

Limestone

Sandstone

Shale

Granite (oldest)

Vertical structure section

Figure AII.21   A geologic map shows the surface distribution of rocks and structures. The structure section shows rocks at depth.

Figure 17.11. If map reproduction is limited to black and white, patterns are applied to differentiate the rock units. Shorthand letter combinations may be added as a code to set apart formations of different ages. Small T-shaped symbols, seen on the map, tell strike-and-dip. The long bar gives direction of strike; the short bar which abuts it at right angles show direction of dip. Amount of dip in degrees is given by a figure beside the symbol. A small fault, cutting across the northwest corner of the map, is shown by a solid line. The letters D and U indicate which side slipped downward, which upward.

To show the internal geologic structure of an area the geologist resorts to the *structure section*, an imaginary vertical slice through the rocks. A structure section is illustrated in the lower part of Figure II.21. The upper line of the section is a topographic profile.

Index

Epeirogenic movements, 264
  and landmass cycle, 324, 326
Epidermis of leaf, 218
Epipedon, mollic, 209
Epiphytes, 215, 229, 231, 233
  in montane forest, 183
Epoch of geologic time, 264
Equability of climate, 131
Equal-area map projection, 10
Equator, geographic, 6, 7
  magnetic, 47
Equatorial belt of variable winds
    and calms, 82
Equatorial countercurrent, 88
Equatorial current, 88
Equatorial easterlies, 86
Equatorial rainforest, 228
Equatorial trough, 75, 114
Equatorial wave, 114
Equatorial zone, 54
Equidistant map projection, 17
Equilibrium, of glacier, 337
  of stream, 312
Equinox, 26, 31
  and air temperatures, 70
  autumnal, 26
  vernal, 26
Era of geologic time, 264
Eratosthenes, 4
Erg landscape, 375
Ericaceae, 240
Eriophorum, 242
Erosion, accelerated, 290, 291
  glacial, 174, 337
  by ice sheets, 347
  of soil, 290
  by streams, 308
  and vegetation, 290
  by waves, 354
  by wind, 372, 374
Erosion cycle, *see* Denudation
Esker, 348, 351
Esplanade, 389
Eucalyptus, 237
Evaporation, 91, 140
  and air temperature, 94
  and climate, 122
  in deserts, 153
  and heat budget, 138
  and latent heat, 58
  from leaves, 140
  from oceans, 137
  of precipitation, 138
  and salt crystal growth, 276
  from soil, 140
  world total, 137
Evaporites, 254, 278
Evapotranspiration, 140
  actual, 141
  average annual, 141
  potential, 141
  and recharge, 143
Everglades of Florida, 232, 240
Evergreen-hardwood forest, 165, 236
Evergreen forest, broadleaf, 228
  hardwood, 165, 236
  needleleaf, 235
Evergreen plants, 216
  leafless, 216
Evergreen-succulent plants, 216

Evolution of plants and animals, 266
Exfoliation, 275
Exfoliation dome, 277
Explorer satellites, 49
Extrusive igneous rocks, 251
Eye of tropical cyclone, 116

Fagus, 234
  F. sylvaticus, 234
Fahrenheit scale, 61
Fall Line, 385
Falls, 311
Fan, alluvial, 317
Fault-block mountains, 405
  erosional development, 405
  geographical aspects, 406
Fault blocks, 382, 402
  life history, 405
  lifted, 405
  tilted, 405
Fault line, 402
Fault-line scarp, 405, 407
Fault plane, 403
Faulting, 267
Faults, 402, 409
  active, 407
  block, 267
  dimensions, 403
  displacement, 403
  and earthquakes, 403, 407
  geographical aspects, 406
  on maps, 436
  multiple, 404
  normal, 403
  overthrust, 267, 404, 410
  reverse, 403, 410
  rift, 404
  strike-slip, 403
Fault scarp, 403
  erosional development, 405
  mature, 405
  young, 405
Fault shoreline, 363
Fault splinter, 404
Fault trap, 407
Feldspar, 250
  plagioclase, 251
  potash, 250
  weathering, 278
Fell field, arctic, 243
Felsenmeer, 276
Fenlands, 360
Fenno-Scandian Shield, 264
Ferns, 215
Ferrel's law, 79
Ferromagnesian minerals, 251
Ficus, 229
Field capacity of soils, 141
Finger lake, 340, 347
Finger Lakes, 347
Fiords, 341, 361
Fiord shoreline, 361
Firn, 337
Firn field, 337
Fir tree, 235
Fissure, volcanic, 252, 413, 419
Flatiron, 398
Flattening of poles, 5
Flocculation, 360
Floes of ice, 178

Flood control, 299
Flood current of tide, 359
Floodplain, 150, 297, 314, 324
  inundation, 317
  in landmass cycle, 324, 238
  and loess, 379
Floods, 296
  and bank erosion, 309
  channel changes, 310
  control, 299
  crest, 297
  debris, 318
  expectancy, 298
  forecasting, 297
  and natural levees, 316
  prediction, 297
  and snowmelt, 182, 299
Flood stage, 297
Flood-storage dam, 299
Flood wave, 297
Flora, 212
Florida stream, 88
Flows, *see* Lava flows
Fluid, 41
Focus of ellipse, 25
Foehn wind, 87, 102
Fog, 51, 98
  advection, 98
  of desert west coasts, 157
  and forests, 233
  radiation, 98
Folding, of strata, 265
  crustal, 263
Folds of strata, 265, 382
  axes, 401
  erosional development, 400
  geographical aspects, 402
  plunging, 401
Foliation of rock, 255
Forbs, 215, 241, 242
Foredeep, 262
Foreland, cuspate, 358
Foreset beds, 351
Forest biochore, 213, 227, 228
Forests, 227
  boreal, 174
  broadleaf deciduous, 234
  broadleaf evergreen, 202, 228
  chaparral, 237
  coastal, 365
  coniferous, 235
  on cuestas, 386
  deciduous, 163, 164, 170, 199, 200,
      232, 234
  dwarf, 237
  elfin, 183
  equatorial, 150, 152, 228
  eucalyptus, 237
  evergreen, 150, 170, 228, 233, 235
  evergreen hardwood, 236
  evergreen oak, 233
  hardwood, 236
  larch, 235
  laurel, 233
  magnolia, 233
  mangrove swamp, 230
  monsoon, 232
  montane, 183
  mossy, 183
  of mountains, 183

Ice-contact slope, 348
Ice crystals, and rock weathering, 276
Ice fall, 337
Ice floes, 178
Ice islands, 178, 180
Icelandic low, 78, 109
  and ocean currents, 89
Ice sheets, 336, 342
  deposits, 348, 350
  erosion by, 347
  of Pleistocene, 343
  of present, 342
  transportation by, 348
Ice shelves, 342, 343
Ice-wedge polygons, 176
Icing storm, 98
Igneous rocks, 249, 382, 396, 409
  extrusive, 249, 251
  forms, 249
  intrusive, 249
  weathering of, 275
Illinoian glacial stage, 345
Illuviation, 192
Inceptisol, 209
Inface of cuesta, 384
Infiltration capacity, 139
Infiltration of precipitation, 139, 289
  and drainage density, 331
  rates, 139
  and runoff, 140
  and soil texture, 139
Infrared radiation, 52
Infrared rays, 52
Initial stage, of landmass cycle, 324
  of stream, 310
Inlet, tidal, 366
Inlier, 383
Inner lowland, 383
Insequent stream, 390, 409
Inolation, 53
  and altitude, 181
  daily cycle, 69
  and latitude, 53
  losses in atmosphere, 56
  and seasons, 54
Interception of precipitation, 289
Interlobate moraine, 348
International Date Line, 36
International ellipsoid of 1909, 5
International Meridian Conference, 38
International nautical mile, 8
Intertropical convergence zone, 114
Intrazonal soil order, 197
Intrusion of rock, 382, 410
Intrusive rock, 382, 409
Inversion of air temperature, 70
  antarctic, 177
  and frost, 70
  ground, 70
  subarctic, 172
Ion clouds, 49
Ionization, 46, 191
Ionosphere, 46, 56
Ions, atmospheric, 47
  hydrogen, 189, 193
  hydroxyl, 189
  in soil solution, 188, 191
Iron hydroxides, 150, 200
Iron ore, 391
Iron oxide, hydrated, 187

Iron oxide, reduced, 188
  in soil, 192, 194
Island arcs, 263
Isobars, 73
  on fronts, 109
  in lows, 106, 109
  and winds, 78
Isogonic line, 432
Isogonic map, 432
Isohyet, 103
Isopleth, 51
Isotherms, 62
  annual shift, 63
  and climate boundaries, 121
  construction, 63
  deflection, 67

Japan current, 88
Jet stream, 86
Joint blocks, 275
  creep of, 281
  plucking, 338
Joints in rock, 248, 275
  columnar, 252
Juglans, 234
Jungle, 230, 232
Juniper, 212
Juniperus utahensis, 212
Jura Mountains, 402
Jurassic period, 266

Kalahari Desert, 153
Kamchatka current, 89
Kame, 351
Kame terrace, 351
Kansan glacial stage, 345
Kaolin, 278
Karst, 394
Karst landscape, 394
Katabatic winds, 87
Katmai volcano, 416
Kauri tree, 233
Kennelly-Heaviside layer, 46
Kettle, glacial, 348
Kimberlite, 421
Knob and kettle topography, 348
Knot, 8
Köppen climate system, 124
Köppen, Wladimir, 124
Krakatoa volcano, 374, 415
Krypton, 42
Kuroshio, 88

Labrador current, 89, 98
Laccolith, 397
Lagoon, 363, 365
  coral reef, 369, 370
Laguncularia, 230
Lake Bonneville, 367
Lakes, caldera, 416
  desert, 206
  finger, 340, 347
  glacial, 147, 174, 340, 347, 350
  initial, 311, 324
  kettle, 348, 351
  marginal, 350
  oxbow, 316
  playa, 206
  tarn, 340
  trough, 340, 347

Lakes, volume, 301
  water table, 147
Land biocycle, 213
Land breeze, 86
Land erosion, 289
  accelerated, 290, 291
  geologic norm, 290
  by gullies, 291
  by rills, 291
  by splash, 290
Landform classification, 267
  Murphy system, 267
Landforms, 246
  and bedrock, 248
  classification, 267
  depositional, 247, 269
  description, 246
  of dry areas, 269
  erosional, 247, 269
  explanatory-descriptive system, 246
  genetic description, 246
  of glaciated areas, 269, 338, 348, 351
  of humid areas, 269
  initial, 247
  and Man, 246
  Murphy classification, 267
  and plants, 221
  and process, 246
  and rock structure, 248, 382
  scale on globe, 259
  sequential, 247
  of shorelines, 354
  and soils, 191
  and stage, 246
  of streams, 308
  structural regions, 267
  and structure, 246
  study of, 246
  topographical classes, 269
  of weathering, 276
  of wind action, 372
  world classification, 267
  world map, 273
Landmass classification, 382
Landmass denudation, 324
  agents, 324
  cycle, 324
    in arid climate, 324, 331
    geographical aspects, 327, 334
    in humid climate, 324
  processes, 247
  products, 247
  stages, 382
Land sculpture, agents, 247
Landslides, 282, 312, 340
  coastal, 357
  on fault scarp, 403
Langley, 53
Lapiés, 394
Lapse rate of temperature, 43
  dew point, 94
  normal, 43, 182
Larch tree, 235, 241
Larch woodland, 241
Larix, 235, 241
  L. laricina, 241
Larrea tridentata, 243
Latent heat, 58, 91
  of fusion, 91
  and global heat balance, 138

MEAN ANNUAL PRECIPITATION OF THE WORLD

Simplified and modified from Plate 3, World Climatology,
Volume I, The Times Atlas, Editor John Bartholomew,
The Times Publishing Company, Ltd., London, 1958

Inches	0	4	12	20	40	80	200	above 200
Centimeters	0	10	30	50	100	200	500	above 500

Isohyets labeled in inches (approximate), centimeters in parentheses.

MILES

0   1,000   2,000   3,000

(True distances on mid – meridians and parallels 0 to 40)

Based on Goode Base Map, copyright by the University of Chicago;
used by permission of the University of Chicago Press. Prepared by
J. P. Tremblay, cartographer, for John Wiley and Sons, Inc., Publishers.

TROPIC OF CANCER

TROPIC OF CAPRICORN

Plate 1
MEAN ANNUAL PRECIPITATION
OF THE WORLD

KÖPPEN-GEIGER SYSTEM OF CLIMATE CLASSIFICATION

After R. Geiger and W. Pohl (1953)

Key to letter code designating climate regions:

FIRST LETTER

A C D Sufficient heat and precipitation for growth of high-trunked trees.

A Tropical climates. All monthly mean temperatures over 64.4° F (18° C).

B Dry climates. Boundaries determined by formula using mean annual temperature and mean annual precipitation (see graphs).

C Warm temperate climates. Mean temperature of coldest month: 64.4° F (18° C) down to 26.6° F (−3° C).

D Snow climates. Warmest month mean over 50° F (10° C) Coldest month mean under 26.6° F (−3° C).

E Ice climates. Warmest month mean under 50° F (10° C)

SECOND LETTER

S Steppe climate. ⎫
W Desert climate. ⎬ Boundaries determined by formulas (See graphs).

f Sufficient precipitation in all months.

m Rainforest despite a dry season (i.e., monsoon cycle).

s Dry season in summer of the respective hemisphere.

w Dry season in winter of the respective hemisphere.

THIRD LETTER

a Warmest month mean over 71.6° F (22° C).

b Warmest month mean under 71.6° F (22° C). At least 4 months have means over 50° F (10° C).

c Fewer than 4 months with means over 50° F (10° C).

d Same as c, but coldest month mean under −36.4° F (−38° C).

h Dry and hot. Mean annual temperature over 64.4° F (18° C).

k Dry and cold. Mean annual temperature under 64.4° F (18° C).

H Highland climates.

MILES

| 0 | 1,000 | 2,000 | 3,000 |

(True distances on mid-meridians and parallels 0 to 40)

Based on Goode Base Map, copyright by the University of Chicago; used by permission of the University of Chicago Press. Prepared by J. P. Tremblay, cartographer, for John Wiley and Sons, Inc., Publishers.

Plate 2
CLIMATES OF THE WORLD

BOUNDARIES OF DRY CLIMATES

Precipitation evenly distributed throughout year

Precipitation concentrated in summer (high-sun) season

Precipitation concentrated in winter (low-sun) season

R = MEAN ANNUAL PRECIPITATION, INCHES

GREAT SOIL GROUPS OF THE WORLD

Simplified and modified from a world map of soils by
A. C. Orvedal in Goode's World Atlas 11th edition,
1960, Edward B. Espenshade, Jr. Editor.
Used by permission of Rand McNally & Company,
Chicago, Illinois.

Color Significance: Podzolization-blues . Laterization-reds . Calcification-browns.
Salinization-yellows . Gleization-greens.

SOILS OF PLAINS AND HILLS

1 Alluvial

2 Tundra
(including lithosol and marsh)

3 Arctic brown forest

4 Podzol and weakly podzolized

5 Gray-brown podzolic

6 Red-yellow podzolic-latosolic

7 Degraded chernozem.

8 Prairie and chernozem

9 Chestnut and brown

10 Reddish prairie, reddish chestnut,
and reddish brown

11 Sierozem and desert
(including lithosol and sand)

12 Red desert
(including lithosol and sand)

13 Black and dark gray soils of
wet-dry tropics

14 Terra rossa, brown forest,
and rendzina

15 Latosolic soils of wet-dry tropics

16 Latosolic soils of continuously
humid tropics

SOILS OF MOUNTAINS
(including some hill areas with steep slopes)

17 Mountain soils of tundra zone
with lithosols.

18 Mountain soils of podzolic soil zones
with lithosols, including islands of
tundra and alpine meadow soils at
high elevations.

19 Mountain soils of chernozem,
chestnut, reddish chestnut, brown
and reddish brown soil zones with
lithosols, including islands of podzol,
alpine meadow or tundra soils at high
altitudes.

20 Mountain soils of sierozem, desert, and red desert
soil zones with lithosols, including islands of brown,
reddish brown, chestnut, reddish chestnut, or
chernozem soils at high elevations.

21 Mountain soils of latosolic soil zones with lithosols,
including islands of podzolic and alpine meadow
soils at high elevations.

22 Mountain soils of desert and latosolic soil zones
with lithosols, including reddish brown, reddish
chestnut and black soils of tropics at intermediate
elevations and islands of alpine meadow soils at high elevat

23 Mountain soils of brown forest, terra rossa and ren
soil regions with lithosols, including podzolic and a
meadow soils at high elevations.

Plate 3
GREAT SOIL GROUPS
OF THE WORLD

IRCLE

EQUATOR

TROPIC OF CAPRICORN

ARCTIC CIRCLE

MILES

1,000   3,000

(True distances on mid-meridians and parallels 0 to 40)
Based on Goode Base Map, copyright by the University of Chicago;
used by permission of the University of Chicago Press. Prepared by
J. P. Tremblay, cartographer, for John Wiley and Sons, Inc., Publishers.

NATURAL VEGETATION REGIONS OF THE WORLD

Simplified and modified from a world vegetation map by H. Brockmann Jerosch, 1951, showing vegetation-classes according to the classification of Eduard Rübel.

	Map classes	Equivalent formation classes
1	A. EQUATORIAL & TROPICAL RAINFOREST	1. Equatorial rainforest 2. Tropical rainforest
2	B. TEMPERATE RAINFOREST (LAUREL FOREST)	4. Temperate rainforest (Laurel forest)
4	C. RAINGREEN FOREST, WOODLAND, SCRUB, & SAVANNA	3. Monsoon forest (Tropical deciduous forest) 8. Savanna-woodland 9. Thornbush & Tropical scrub 10. Savanna
3	D. EVERGREEN-HARDWOOD FOREST	7. Evergreen-hardwood forest (Sclerophyll forest)
7	E. SUMMER-GREEN DECIDUOUS FOREST	5. Summer-green deciduous forest
8	F. NEEDLELEAF FOREST	6. Needleleaf forest
5	G. STEPPE & PRAIRIE GRASSLANDS	14. Prairie 15. Steppe
6	H. DRY DESERT & SEMI-DESERT	17. Dry desert 11. Semi-desert
9	I. TUNDRA (ARCTIC & ALPINE)	16. Grassy tundra 17. Cold woodland 18. Arctic fell-field
10	J. ICE-CAPS & GLACIERS	
	Highland areas with sufficiently high elevation to have alpine tundra.	

TROPIC OF CANCER

MILES

0   1,000   2,000   3,000

(True distances on mid—meridians and parallels 0 to 40)

Based on Goode Base Map, copyright by the University of Chicago; used by permission of the University of Chicago Press. Prepared by J. P. Tremblay, cartographer, for John Wiley and Sons, Inc., Publishers.

Plate 4
NATURAL VEGETATION REGIONS
OF THE WORLD

LANDFORMS OF THE WORLD
by Richard E. Murphy, Ph.D.

ALPINE SYSTEM
- AM
- AW
- AT
- AH
- AD
- AP

CALEDONIAN AND HERCYNIAN (OR APPALACHIAN) REMNANTS
- CM
- CW
- CT
- CH
- CD
- CP

GONDWANA SHIELDS
- GM
- GW
- GT
- GH
- GD
- GP

LAURASIAN SHIELDS
- LM
- LT
- LH
- LD
- LP

RIFTED SHIELD AREAS
- RM
- RW
- RT
- RH
- RD
- RP

SEDIMENTARY COVERS OUTSIDE SHIELD EXPOSURES
- SM
- SW
- ST
- SH
- SD
- SP

ISOLATED VOLCANIC AREAS
- VM
- VH

M-Mountains
W-Widely spaced mountains
T-High tablelands
H-Hills and low tablelands
D-Depressions or basins
P-Plains

.... i-Ice caps at present
— — — w-Wisconsin or Würm glaciated areas
— · — · g-Pre-Wisconsin, pre-Würm and undifferentiated Pleistocene glaciated areas
h-Humid landform areas
d-Dry or arid landform areas
——— Division between humid and dry landform areas

Continental shelf

- - - - Undersea axial connections of the Alpine system

⌐ Major oceanic rift and fault lines

TROPIC OF CANCER

ANTARCTIC CIRCLE

Plate 5
LANDFORMS OF THE WORLD

CHi

CIRCLE
SMw

SPw

SPh

SPg

SHh

AMg

ADd

SPd

AMh

SHd

GHh

SHd

GHh

EQUATOR

70°

80°

90°

100°

110°

120°

60°

GMh

GHd

SPd

CHh

TROPIC OF CAPRICORN

AMh

AMg

GHd

SMh

GTi

GTi

60°

50°

40°

30°

20°

10°

10°

20°

30°

40°

50°

60°

70°

10° 20° 30° 40° 50° 60° 70°

100° 110° 120° 130° 140° 150° 160° 170°

Map supplement number 9,
Annals of the Association of
American Geographers
Volume 58, number 1, March 1968.

Based on Goode's base map,
copyright by the University of Chicago;
used by permission of the University of
Chicago Press.
Prepared by J. P. Tremblay, cartographer,
for John Wiley and Sons, Incorporated,
Publishers.

0 500 1000 1500
MILES
(True distances on mid-meridians
and parallels 0 to 40)

WORLD POPULATION DISTRIBUTION

INHABITANTS

Per square kilometer	Per square mile
Under 2	Under 2
1 to 9	2 to 24
10 to 24	25 to 59
25 to 49	60 to 124
50 to 100	125 to 250
Over 100	Over 250

○ Cities with 1,000,000 to 2,500,000 population
● Cities with over 2,500,000 population

0   1,000   2,000
MILES
True distances on mid-meridians and parallels 0 to 40

TROPIC OF CANCER

TROPIC OF CAPRICORN

80°
70°
60°
50°
40°
30°
20°
10°
0°
-10°

140° 130° 120° 110° 100°

Montreal
Detroit
Chicago
New York
Philadelphia
Los Angeles
Guadalajara
Mexico D.F.

Caracas
Bogota
Lima
Recife
Rio de Janeiro
São Paulo
Santiago
Buenos Aires
Montevideo

Glas
Birmin
Barce
Madrid
Casablanca

70° 90° 80° 60° 50° 40° 30°

WORLD
POPULATION DISTRIBUTION

Based on Goode Base Map,
copyright by the University of Chicago;
used by permission of the University of Chicago Press.
Prepared by J. P. Tremblay, cartographer,
for John Wiley and Sons, Inc., Publishers.

WORLD POLITICAL DIVISIONS

ARCTIC OCEAN

BARENTS SEA
North Cape

FINLAND
Helsinki

kholm

pest

UMANIA
Bucharest

BUL

BLACK SEA

TURKEY
Ankara

Nicosia
CYPRUS
LEBANON
Beirut
ISRAEL
Cairo
Jerusalem
Damascus
SYRIA
Amman
JORDAN

U.A.R.
(EGYPT)
A

SUDAN
Khartoum

HEJAZ
SAUDI ARABIA
ASIR
Riyadh

YEMEN
Sana
SOUTH YEMEN

TERRITORY OF THE
AFARS & ISSAS
(France)
Djibouti
Medina al Eshaab
SOCOTRA
(South Yemen)
Addis Ababa
ETHIOPIA

SOMALI REPUBLIC

UGANDA
Kampala
RWANDA
Kigali
BURUNDI
Buiumbura
Victoria
HE
NGO
KENYA
Nairobi
L. Tanganyika
Mogadiscio
TANZANIA
Dar-es-Salaam
PEMBA
ZANZIBAR

ZAMBIA
usaka
MALAWI
L. Nyasa
Salisbury
RHODESIA
Zomba

WANA
ees
Mbabane
toria
SWAZILAND
LESOTHO
Maseru
Lourenço Marques

MOCAMBIQUE
(Portugal)
MADAGASCAR
MALAGASY REPUBLIC
Tananarive

COMORO ISLANDS

Mozambique Channel

SIBERIA

UNION OF SOVIET SOCIALIST REPUBLICS
Moscow

NOVAYA ZEMLYA

KARA SEA

LAPTEV SEA

NEW SIBERIAN ISLANDS
EAST SIBERIAN SEA

80°
70°
60°

Yenisey
Lena
Ob

ARAL SEA
CASPIAN SEA
Syr Darya
Amu Darya
Lake Balkhash

AFGHANISTAN
Kabul
Rawalpindi
Tehran
IRAN
IRAQ
Baghdad
KUWAIT
Neutral zone
BAHREIN
QATAR
TRUCIAL STATES
Muscat
MUSCAT AND OMAN

Persian Gulf

WEST PAKISTAN
KASHMIR
Delhi

TIBET
Brahmaputra

NEPAL
Katmandu
SIKKIM
BHUTAN
Ganges

INDIA

EAST PAKISTAN

BURMA
Rangoon

MONGOLIA
Ulan Bator

SINKIANG-UIGUR

CHINA
Peking
Yellow
Yangtze
Hsi

MANCHURIA

NORTH KOREA
Pyongyang
Seoul
SOUTH KOREA

Amur

OKHOTSK SEA

SAKHALIN

HOKKAIDO

SEA OF JAPAN

JAPAN
HONSHU
Tokyo
SHIKOKU
KYUSHU

RYUKYU ISLANDS

EAST CHINA SEA

Taipei
TAIWAN

MACAO (Port.)
HONGKONG (U.K.)
Hanoi
NORTH VIETNAM
Vientiane
LAOS
HAINAN

THAILAND
Bangkok
CAMBODIA
Phnom Penh
SOUTH VIETNAM
Saigon

Gulf of Siam

SOUTH CHINA SEA

LUZON
Manila
THE PHILIPPINES
SAMAR
MINDANAO

GUAM (U.S.A.)
YAP
PALAU
U.S.A. Trusteeship

BERING SEA

PACIFIC OCEAN

50°
40°
30°
20°
10°

70°
60°

ARABIAN SEA

LACCADIVE ISLANDS (India)

BAY OF BENGAL

ANDAMAN ISLANDS (India)

Colombo
CEYLON
MALDIVE ISLANDS
Malé

NICOBAR ISLANDS (India)

Kuala Lumpur
MALAYSIA
SINGAPORE
BRUNEI (U.K.)
SABAH
BORNEO
CELEBES

SUMATRA
Djakarta
JAVA
INDONESIA
WEST IRIAN
Portugal
TIMOR

INDIAN OCEAN

EQUATOR

SEYCHELLES (U.K.)

60°

80°
110°
120°
130°
140°

TERRITORY OF NEW GUINEA
WEST IRIAN
N.E. NEW GUINEA (Australia)
PAPUA (Australia)

0°
10°

CORAL SEA

NEW HEBRIDES (U.K., France)
FIJI ISLANDS
Suva

NEW CALEDONIA (France)

AUSTRALIA
Canberra

TASMAN SEA

NORTH ISLAND
NEW ZEALAND
Wellington
SOUTH ISLAND

TASMANIA

INDIAN OCEAN

30°

50°

60°

70°

40°
50°
60°
90°
100°
110°
120°
130°
140°
150°
160°
170°

RCTICA

ANTARCTICA

Based on Goode Base Map, copyright by the University of Chicago; used by permission of the University of Chicago Press.
Prepared by J. P. Tremblay, cartographer, for John Wiley and Sons, Inc., Publishers.

SO-AEK-497

WITHDRAWN

Brunswick County Library
109 W. Moore Street
Southport NC 28461

WITHDRAWN

PRAISE FOR

JUST DOWN THE ROAD

"A welcome return packed with cameos from familiar characters." —*Publishers Weekly*

"This book is like once again visiting old friends while making new ones and will leave readers eager for the next visit. A pure joy to read."
—**RT Book Reviews**

"An addictive read that fills you with some strong emotions as you watch those you have come to love fight through the pitfalls of life. I love how human Ms. Thomas's characters are." —*Smexy Books*

THE COMFORTS OF HOME

"Even for readers new to the series, the intricate relationships between these affable men and eccentric women are easy to follow and even easier to love. Thomas skillfully juggles the many subplots, and the relationship between Ronelle and Marty, which inspires both to trust again, is especially touching." —*Publishers Weekly*

continued . . .

"There's always something brewing in Harmony and each story just adds to the richness of depth of the characters and town. If you haven't had a chance to meet the fine folks of Harmony, Texas, what are you waiting for?" —*Fallen Angel Reviews*

"If you're a fan of small-town settings, heartwarming tales, and out-of-the-ordinary characters, you don't want to miss this book."
—Petit Fours and Hot Tamales

SOMEWHERE ALONG THE WAY

"A delightful story with as much love and warmth as there is terror and fear . . . This is terrific reading from page one to the end. Jodi Thomas is a passionate writer who puts real feeling into her characters."
—Fresh Fiction

"Thomas once again brings to life this fascinating little Texas town and its numerous characters. The reader is expertly drawn into their lives and left eager to know what happens next." —*RT Book Reviews*

"Thomas continues her contemporary small-town saga with a large helping of suspense, vibrant (if eccentric) characters, and Texas humor to spice it up."
—Booklist

WELCOME TO HARMONY

"The characters are delightful, and a subplot about mysterious fires balances the sweet stories about being and becoming family."   —*Publishers Weekly*

"A fast-moving, engaging tale that keeps you turning pages . . . Thomas's characters become as familiar as family or friends."   —*Fresh Fiction*

"A heartwarming tale, with plenty of excitement, *Welcome to Harmony* is Jodi Thomas all the way—super characters, lots of riveting subplots, and the background of a realistic Texas town. Don't miss this terrific novel."   —*Romance Reviews Today*

ADDITIONAL PRAISE FOR THE NOVELS OF JODI THOMAS

"Compelling and beautifully written, it is exactly the kind of heart-wrenching, emotional story one has come to expect from Jodi Thomas."
—Debbie Macomber, #1 *New York Times* bestselling author

continued . . .

"Jodi Thomas is a masterful storyteller. She grabs your attention on the first page, captures your heart, and then makes you sad when it is time to bid her wonderful characters farewell. You can count on Jodi Thomas to give you a satisfying and memorable read."
—Catherine Anderson, *New York Times* bestselling author

HICKMANS

Can't Stop Believing

Jodi Thomas

**Doubleday Large Print
Home Library Edition**

Brunswick County Library
109 W. Moore Street
Southport NC 28461

BERKLEY BOOKS, NEW YORK

This Large Print Edition, prepared especially for
Doubleday Large Print Home Library, contains
the complete, unabridged text of the original
Publisher's Edition.

THE BERKLEY PUBLISHING GROUP
Published by the Penguin Group
Penguin Group (USA) Inc.
375 Hudson Street, New York,
New York 10014, USA

USA | Canada | UK | Ireland | Australia |
New Zealand | India | South Africa | China

Penguin Books Ltd., Registered Offices:
80 Strand, London WC2R 0RL, England
For more information about the Penguin Group,
visit penguin.com.

CAN'T STOP BELIEVING

A Berkley Book / published by arrangement
with the author

Copyright © 2013 by Jodi Koumalats.
Excerpt from *Promise Me Texas* by Jodi Thomas
copyright © by Jodi Koumalats.
All rights reserved. No part of this book may be
reproduced, scanned, or distributed in any printed
or electronic form without permission. Please do
not participate in or encourage piracy of copyrighted
materials in violation of the author's rights.
Purchase only authorized editions.

BERKLEY® is a registered trademark of
Penguin Group (USA) Inc.
The "B" design is a trademark of
Penguin Group (USA) Inc.

ISBN: 978-1-62490-436-3

PRINTED IN THE UNITED STATES OF AMERICA

Cover art by Jim Griffin.
Cover design by George Long.
Interior text design by Kristin del Rosario.

This is a work of fiction. Names, characters, places,
and incidents either are the product of the

author's imagination or are used fictitiously, and
any resemblance to actual persons, living or dead,
business establishments, events, or locales
is entirely coincidental.
The publisher does not have any control over
and does not assume any responsibility for author
or third-party websites or their content.

**This Large Print Book carries the
Seal of Approval of N.A.V.H.**

**For Sally Cottrell.
A woman whose bravery
will always make her a hero in my heart.**

Chapter 1

MARCH 2012
HARMONY, TEXAS

CORD MCDOWELL FELT SWEAT TRICKLING down his back as he worked in the pit beneath the semitruck's engine. He ignored the heat along with all the sounds and smells around him. His hands were black with oil and dirt, but he didn't dare take a break. Old Man Whitaker had been itching for a reason to fire him since the day he'd come to work three years ago.

Tannon Parker might own the trucking company, but Whitaker ran the shop. The old ex-Marine had told the boss he'd take Cord McDowell on, but he'd also fire the convict the first time he messed up. Like a vulture, he'd been waiting and watching for his chance. Cord made a habit of being early to work and last to leave. He ignored jabs from the other mechanics and never talked to anyone unless he had reason. Cord worked alone, here and on his farm.

As long as he worked here he had a chance of keeping his farm, and as long as he had his farm, he held on to one dream. The last dream.

When Cord had been arrested nine years ago, his folks had a couple hundred thousand in reserve to cover bad years of farming, but when he got out of prison there was no seed money in any account and they'd both been buried long enough for weeds to grow up around their graves.

"McDowell!" Whitaker yelled from above. "You dead down there?" He barked a laugh. "'Cause if you're dead, we might as well just fill in the hole with dirt and move on. No one will waste time trying to haul that big body of yours out."

Cord fought down a curse and pulled

himself up. "I'm about finished. Another two hours if I work through lunch." He knew that would make the old man happy. He liked having his men work the noon hour without an extra hour's pay, and Cord didn't really mind. The work was easier than sitting in the box of a break room while men talked around him but rarely to him.

"Never mind the truck, McDowell. There's a lady out front who wants you to work on her Jeep. Says she won't have another man even open the hood."

Cord wiped his hands on a rag almost as dirty. "Since when do we work on anything but Parker trucks?"

Whitaker looked like he was irritated to even have to talk to Cord, but for once he didn't sound angry when he answered, "That's what I told Mr. Parker when he called saying he was sending her over, but Parker isn't a man to argue with. If he wants his shop to work on a Jeep, we'll work on a Jeep, even if the damn thing looks like it should have been scrapped twenty years ago."

Cord remembered how quiet he'd been when he'd met the owner of Parker Trucking. Cord had just stood in front of the massive desk and waited for Tannon Parker to read his application. The trucking company was the fifth place he'd applied that day. Every other shop had taken one look at where he'd learned his skills, Huntsville Prison, and said they'd call if they had an opening. One guy had glanced up at Cord and simply said their business hadn't had anything stolen in five years and he planned to keep it that way.

Parker, however, had studied Cord's application for a few minutes, then walked around the table and offered his hand like the part about Cord being in prison for six years hadn't mattered.

"We need good mechanics," Tannon Parker said. "Welcome to the company, McDowell."

Parker was the first person who'd treated him like an equal in years. Cord had been so shocked he barely remembered how to shake hands. He'd made up his mind that day that when he earned enough money to quit, he'd go back into Parker's office, shake hands with him again, and thank the owner for giving him a chance.

As he followed Old Man Whitaker through the maze of hallways toward the front office, Cord reminded himself he worked for Tannon Parker and not for Whitaker.

The sun almost blinded Cord as he stepped out the front door and into the cool morning air. There was a March chill, but he could feel spring coming. In another few weeks he'd need to have seed in the ground.

"Over there." Whitaker pointed with his head.

When Cord raised his gaze toward a beat-up old Jeep parked at the end of the drive, Whitaker swore, mumbling something about wasting time.

Cord pulled his worn baseball cap from his back pocket, combed his sandy blond hair back with one rake of his hand, and crammed the hat on his head. He followed the foreman over to a woman leaning against a piece of junk that looked like it had seen its best days thirty years ago.

As he neared, he recognized Nevada Britain. His farm bordered her huge ranch. He'd watched her from a distance riding her horses full out across her land or driving down the county road past his place at twice the speed limit, but it had been years since he'd seen her up close. If possible she was even more beautiful than she'd been at sixteen.

Only today, she was stone cold sober, a far cry from the wild, drunk teen he'd once watched.

Whitaker took on his official role as shop manager. "What seems to be the problem, little lady?"

Cord hung back, staring at Nevada Britain beneath the shadow of his cap. A smile twitched at the corner of his mouth as he saw that she hadn't liked being called "little lady." Whitaker didn't pick up on it and was therefore destined to make the mistake again.

She was taller than Whitaker's five feet six inches and looked like she was dressed for a funeral in her expensive charcoal suit and high heels. Only her white blouse was unbuttoned just enough to show a hint of lace when she straightened.

Maybe the wild teen hadn't completely vanished, Cord thought.

No, she wasn't quite funeral proper, and she knew it. From all he'd read, Nevada Britain hadn't been proper in years. If Harmony, Texas, had a tabloid, she'd be the centerfold.

She was beautiful, he'd give her that. Darn near perfect as far as he could tell from looking, but from what he'd heard, she was no lady. Some said she had her mother's beauty and her father's ruthlessness. Cord had never figured Nevada Britain out. She looked like she'd always gotten everything she wanted, but it never seemed enough. She'd even called the sheriff on him once for flying too low over her horses. People like her even thought they owned the air.

Harmony was a small town, and he'd heard about her wild parties and parade of loser husbands. Apparently she fought to outdo her three crazy brothers.

Technically, he was her neighbor, but she didn't even wave when she passed him. She lived five miles down from him, but it might as well have been another planet. The Britains called themselves ranchers, but mostly they were from old oil money. When he was in prison, his mother used to send him clippings of their court battles and wild ways. He'd seen pictures of her in the Founders Day parade and riding one of her fine horses at some big horse show. Like all the other pictures of her, she wasn't smiling, so it didn't surprise him that she didn't smile now.

When he went to prison there had been four Britain children, all sent to private school back east after they aged into double digits. By the time he got out of Huntsville, two were dead. One from an overdose and one from a drunken boating accident.

Nevada was the youngest, and probably the only person in the county disliked more than he was. Folks said, to the Britains' way of thinking, there was only one way— their way. Like pit bulls, they were bred to be hot-tempered scrappers and all the money in the world couldn't wash away heredity.

"How can I help you, Miss Britain?" Cord asked as Whitaker moved aside. He'd seen Parker Trucking's rigs going onto her land and could guess why Tannon Parker had said yes to having his men look at her little Jeep. Business was business. Parker probably shipped all the cattle they raised.

She frowned at him. "Is that you, Cord McDowell, under all that dirt and grease?"

"It's me." He was surprised she remembered him. They hadn't talked since he'd been arrested ten years ago, and they hadn't been friends then. Cord braced himself for the insult or questions to come. Something about how he had liked prison or how he was wasting his life.

"I heard you were working here." She leaned her head sideways as if studying him. "Tannon says you're the best mechanic he's got."

Looking surprised that Cord and Nevada were talking, Old Man Whitaker said something about getting back before the whole damn shop fell apart and left the two of them to work things out.

"I don't work on Jeeps much." Cord kept his voice low. Nevada wasn't afraid of him, which was more than he could say about most women in town. They all seemed to think that since he'd been in prison, he might go ballistic any minute and murder the whole town.

"I know," she pouted, like the spoiled woman she probably was. "I've been to every garage in town. Nobody knows how to fix it. Half of them wouldn't even take a look."

"You could take it into Amarillo. There'd probably be someone there." He couldn't help but wonder if the other shops didn't want to deal with her, or the Jeep. He'd heard that her father had bankrupted the company who'd sold his son the speed-boat years ago.

She pulled off her sunglasses and looked up at him with tears in her beautiful blue eyes. Cord had no trouble seeing why she'd had three husbands and wasn't out of her twenties. Any man would have trouble saying no to her.

"Please take a look at it, Cord," she said, as if she knew him well. She patted the old piece of junk as if it were her pet. "She was my grandfather's, and if she gives out, I'll lose the last part of him."

Cord knew how she felt. Sometimes things get attached to the love left behind when someone dies. Maybe that happens to leftover love when there's no one to pass it along to. He had one of those "things" taking up half of the old barn on his farm. His grandfather had loved the old biplane, and he couldn't bear to junk it.

"All right," he said. "If you'll leave it with me for a few hours, I'll see what I can do."

She handed him her keys. "You'll handle her with care?"

Her hand touched his for a moment as he answered, "As if she were my own."

He stood next to the Jeep watching Nevada walk away. For the first time in longer than he could remember, he wished for more than he had.

Chapter 2

MARTHA Q PATTERSON DROVE AWAY FROM Parker Trucking with the image of Cord McDowell and Nevada Britain stuck in her mind. Like she always did on her morning errands, she watched people, and those two were saying more with their body language in a few minutes than most people say aloud in a week.

For a few blocks she let the plot of a steamy novel play out in her thoughts. Tough guy in working clothes talking to society girl who'd been wild since she started wearing a bra. The lines from a song about a man not fitting into her highbrow world drifted through the imagined scene. Martha Q might be older than the two of them put together, but she could remember romantic times she'd once had in a garage with her fourth husband.

Or maybe it was her second. It was hard to keep track, but the smell of motor oil still turned her on even though her engine never got a chance to run these days.

Everyone in town knew Nevada Britain. The girl was on her way to breaking Martha Q's record for number of husbands. Just seeing her standing beside Cord, good-looking trouble that he was, made Martha Q start writing love scenes in her head as she drove. Ever since she'd signed up for the creative writing class at the library, Martha Q couldn't stop building backstories in her mind. The habit was getting so dominant that she sometimes confused what was real and what she'd made up.

Occupational habit, she decided. All great writers have the same problem. Or at least she thought they did. Take George Hatcher, owner of the used bookstore; she'd provided him with a far more interesting past than he'd probably ever manage on his own. Martha Q waved at him as she made the square on Main and headed toward her huge old house that she'd turned into a bed-and-breakfast after her last husband died.

Once she'd made up a story about dear old George Hatcher being a time traveler come back a hundred years to collect period pieces for the History Channel. Martha Q couldn't seem to be completely truthful with the man who smelled like mildewed old paperbacks. She even left out one of the ingredients to her apricot scones just in case he planned to take it back to the future someday.

As she turned into the oldest neighborhood in Harmony, Texas, Martha Q let her mind drift back to the way Cord McDowell had tipped his greasy ball cap like it was a top hat when he'd said good-bye to Nevada in her tailored suit and she'd tried to look him in the eye. He was a gentleman, Martha Q decided, beneath all that dirt. It didn't matter what folks said about him.

Some claimed he'd gone wild one night and almost killed a deputy, but Martha Q figured there was more to the story. She considered herself an expert on crime because she had a pen pal in prison who grew more handsome in her eyes with every letter.

A moment later she was ripped from her fantasy when she almost slammed into the black hearse parked in her driveway.

Martha Q opened her door and wiggled out of her boat of a car before the engine finished its usual death rattle. As always, she'd parked too far to the left of the thin sliver of concrete and had to fight the budding elm branches to move around her car. "I'm going to cut that thing down before . . ."

She stopped when she noticed someone was listening to her talk to herself. Martha Q never minded the habit, but she hated others eavesdropping.

"Tyler Wright," she yelled at the man on the porch as she waddled toward him. "I told you not to come before eleven. I get my nails done on Mondays and I need time for them to dry before I can have a proper conversation." She waved her fingers in the air while her purse, looped to her elbow, battered her ample breast.

The chubby funeral director just smiled as he watched her heading toward him. "It *is* eleven, but I'll be happy to come back if you like." He bowed slightly. In his black suit he looked funeral ready.

She frowned. Agreeable men always bothered her. She'd preferred the yellers and fighters. They made the best lovers, that was a fact. Course, they always turned into ex-husbands who either cried or stalked her. She'd figured out one fact about men years ago: Most couldn't do two things at once. It didn't matter if they were having sex or yelling, they didn't seem to be able to think at the same time.

Tyler Wright smiled as she neared, obviously having no idea what she was thinking, thank goodness.

"No, don't leave." Martha Q grabbed the railing and pulled herself onto the porch. "I need to talk to you, Tyler, and it has to be before noon. The widows will be back as soon as they finish the early-bird lunch at the Mexican Hat."

She motioned for him to take one of the wicker chairs on the wide porch of the Winter's Inn Bed-and-Breakfast. "I don't want you coming back, or staying too long for that matter. The neighbors will get the idea I've died and rush over to start picking at my bones."

"Now, Martha Q." Tyler sat beside her. "You know they'd do no such thing."

"I *don't* know." Strike two, she thought. She didn't like being corrected even when they both knew she was wrong. To argue her case, she added, "I think one of them stole my new rake. It was here, right by the porch, all last fall and then one day it was gone. Thought about turning it in to the sheriff, but she sometimes pats my hand. I decided rake theft was probably a hand-patting crime."

When Tyler laughed, Martha Q huffed up. "Just you wait about twenty years, Mr. Wright. Once you're into your sixties, folks start patting on you like they're testing to see if you bite before they step closer."

He rocked back in his chair. "I'm feeling older every day. Too old to be a father for the first time. Kate and I will both be forty-six by the time this baby comes in a few months. We'll be signing up for Medicare about the same time he enrolls in college."

"He?"

Tyler grinned. "He. Doc says for sure. I'm going to have a son."

Martha Q couldn't resist reaching over and patting his hand. "The next generation to run the Wright Funeral Home. He'll be the fifth. Think of the history."

Tyler shook his head. "Kate and I have both promised we won't push him that direction. She says all her family has been career military. He might pick that road instead."

They both rocked in silence for a few minutes, Tyler lost in his future and Martha Q lost in fiction. She'd made a rule to never live in the past and did her best to stay out of problems in the present, but one was bothering her and it was time she got down to business.

"Tyler, I asked you here because you're Joni Rosen's friend. She and the two other widows you sent over last month seemed to think they can homestead here at my place."

The funeral director straightened, knowing the visiting was over. "Is something wrong with Mrs. Rosen? Has she been ill? Has she caused problems?"

"No, but she ain't right. Her husband died four months ago, and everyone understood when she stayed at my place after the funeral, but I'm not a boardinghouse.

She needs to go home. Her place is so close she could walk, but instead, she's now entertaining the other two widows. I swear if they stay much longer I'll have to rename the place Widows' Inn. They play cards and watch movies until almost midnight, then wake me before nine tromping up and down the stairs."

"I wouldn't have thought she'd tromp," he whispered to himself. As always, Tyler looked concerned. Martha Q wasn't sure whether he felt it or had just developed a habit over twenty years in the burying business.

"Does she still pay her bill?" he finally said. "Her husband left her a nice insurance policy and she has her teacher retirement."

"Yes, but that's not the point. I'm used to folks coming and going, not coming and staying. I've had to get up and put on my makeup every morning for four months and now, with three of them, I'm running to the store more often for food and having to wake up the housekeeper regularly to keep the place clean. I only got two more rooms to rent and honeymooners aren't likely to book with three women in black sitting on the front porch knitting like happy Halloween decorations."

Tyler smiled.

"Don't you dare laugh. Being this beautiful at my age takes a lot of time and money. I'd like to sleep in, put on my oldest jogging suit, and read all day, but no, I have to be the innkeeper." When he didn't offer an answer, she prodded. "You got to talk to her about getting on with her life. She's young, not even fifty-five yet. At that age I still had two or three good tries at marriage in me."

Tyler stood. "When will she be back?"

"I never know. I have to stay dressed all day just in case. She sometimes goes the ten blocks over to her place to do her laundry on Mondays. I keep thinking she'll just decide to stay, but she doesn't."

"I'll talk to her," Tyler frowned. "I have to anyway about her husband's headstone."

Martha Q stood. "Good." She was halfway to the door when she remembered her car still parked behind Tyler's hearse. "Thanks for coming over. I'll drive back out so you can leave."

Tyler walked beside her to his car. "I'll let you know when the baby comes."

"You won't have to. Everyone in town will be talking about it. It wouldn't surprise me if the hospital sold tickets to the waiting room. Give Kate a hug if you can still get your arms around her."

He nodded as he climbed in his long black car and waited for her to back out.

"Babies." Martha Q shook her head, and then an idea of adding a secret baby to her romance plot came to her and she couldn't wait to get back to her study and write. She might go thirty, maybe even forty minutes before her lunch break. Long writing spells always made her hungry.

Chapter 3

McDOWELL FARM

FROM THE SHADE OF HIS PORCH, CORD MC-
Dowell watched the road with mounting
anger. His neighbor, Nevada Britain, was
driving up his dirt drive like she was drag
racing. The little Jeep he'd spent hours
working on left a half-mile trail of dirt behind as it roared toward him.

He knew the second she spotted him.
She slowed and he wondered if she was
surprised to see him home before dark.
There were always a dozen chores on the

farm he needed to get to even after he stopped plowing. Only tomorrow morning he wanted to be at the bank when it opened, so he'd come in early. After three years of saving every dime he could, he was still five thousand short on paying off the loan he'd gotten the week he'd walked out of prison. Some said no one would give a convict a loan, but the bank hadn't hesitated when he put up his farm as collateral. If he couldn't pay, they'd make twenty to one on their money.

He'd dress in his best jeans and head for town at first light, hoping they'd give him three more months to pay. One more season. Then, if it rained and the bugs didn't find his spring crop and the tractor held out, he might be able to come up with the money. Swearing under his breath, he watched Nevada come closer, feeling like he was Moses waiting for the next plague to strike.

Cord shoved what money he planned to pay on the loan deeper into his pocket and watched his beautiful, spoiled, selfish neighbor approach. Whitaker had been the one to hand her the keys after the Jeep had been repaired, and she hadn't even bothered to walk to where Cord worked in the garage to thank him.

There was little hope that she'd driven over after three days to say thanks, so Cord figured he must have done something wrong. Hell, she'd probably come to threaten to sue him for stirring up too much dirt while he plowed too near her fence line.

He watched her stop halfway between his barn and his parents' old house and look around as she climbed out. He hadn't had the time or the money to fix up the place, but right now it seemed to look worse than he thought. Imagining his farm through her eyes made him wish for more hours in the day, more days in the week, more time, period. Then he could have painted the barn, fixed up the fence, replaced the steps.

Only it was too late to worry about it now.

She was dressed western from her red boots to her leather vest. If some women are shiny-penny pretty, Nevada was silver-dollar beautiful.

Near as he could remember, he'd watched her every chance he'd gotten since the day she was born. They'd gone to school together, ridden the same bus home a few times when her mom didn't pick her up, and then in the fifth grade she'd disappeared. She'd gone away to school and he'd only seen her riding her horses now and then during vacations. When her dad let her start driving, even though she was a year away from being legal, everyone on Sunset Road tried to stay out of her way.

Fighting down a grin, Cord remembered the half dozen cars she'd wrecked before she got driving down pat. One she'd rolled in the drainage ditch. Her parents had left it there a month, probably just to make her pass it every time she went to town. He doubted the lesson had taken.

Pulling off her sunglasses, she tossed her long blond hair back like it was a mane and she was ready to run. He liked the way she moved, all fast and headstrong, like she owned the world—and, as near as he could tell, her family did. Talk was that when her parents died her brother, Barrett Britain, cleaned out the family bank accounts and bought a villa in France. He left her with the ranch and the oil business, saying the next time he came to Texas he'd be in a pine box. She'd taken over everything, and as she walked toward Cord, he realized he didn't even know how to talk to her.

"You're home," she said, as she stormed the porch with a large envelope in one hand and her hat in the other.

"Yep," he said without explaining, knowing it would irritate her. He wasn't disappointed.

She glared at him, as if considering turning around and leaving.

If he wanted her to stay, even a minute, he'd better think of something. "Why are you here, Nevada? Looks like the Jeep is still running."

She surprised him by saying, "I was in a hurry the other day or I would have stopped in to say thanks. You got it running better than I ever remember."

"Guess I should be glad you didn't bring the sheriff." She'd called in a complaint two years ago and he'd almost been fined. If the sheriff had sent deputies, he'd have been cuffed and hauled in before they even bothered to ask questions. Every lawman in the county except Sheriff Alexandra Matheson had dropped by to warn Cord that they'd be watching him.

Alexandra wasn't friendly, but he guessed she was fair. She'd asked questions first.

"I can't believe you're still upset about that. If I hadn't sent the sheriff, you know you wouldn't have listened to me, Cord. I left three messages on your phone before I called Sheriff Matheson. You can't just go flying that old plane around over my land. It stampeded my horses."

"I don't answer my phone." He shrugged, accepting an ounce of the blame.

Before he could step back into their two-year-old feud, she stopped him with an open palm like she was a crossing guard for his front porch.

"I didn't drive out here to talk about that. I came to ask a favor."

Every drop of anger and frustration went out of him even though he didn't move an inch. "A favor?" The Britains had never asked the McDowells for anything in three generations. His grandfather said once that they started out with bad blood over the boundary between the two ranches, and the wound it left would take a hundred years to heal.

"I'm not selling," he said, the first thought that came to his mind. She could probably already smell blood in the water, but he'd lose to the bank before he'd sell to her.

"I'm not asking," she snapped, none too friendly for a woman asking for a favor.

He remembered a time when she'd been home for Christmas break when they were in high school. He asked her for a date and she'd turned him down so fast it took him several heartbeats for his mind to catch up with his ears. They'd both changed a great deal in ten years. She'd grown from a skinny girl to a beautiful woman, and he'd turned into stone. Even now, if he'd been brave or wild enough to pull her against him, she'd feel no heart. Any kindness, any caring, had been beat out of him in Huntsville.

She straightened, all proper. "What I'm offering is a business deal that could benefit us both."

"I'm not interested in doing business with a Britain, and I'm fresh out of favors." He looked down at her and was surprised to find that she wasn't looking at him. He'd always pictured her as straightforward and demanding, a queen in her realm. Now he wasn't so sure. He didn't know her well enough to be able to tell if she was being shy or simply taking a moment to plan her strategy.

He'd watched her drive past his land. He'd seen her in town a few times, but they'd never been close enough to speak. Two years ago she'd called the sheriff on him. She hadn't even given him time to tell her he'd been having engine trouble and was flying low, praying he'd make it to his land before he crashed the plane.

Her hands tightened into fists, and she slowly raised her head. "I knew I'd be wasting my time coming over here. Since you went to prison, everyone says you've been nothing but mean. You don't have a friend in this world, Cord McDowell, and as near as I can see, you never will. You live out on this dry, worthless land and work all day seven days a week and for what? So you can die alone? I'll probably be the one who finds the body and has to see about the funeral, and I don't like you, either. If you weren't my last choice, I wouldn't be here, so you're going to have to listen to me for a minute before I leave and never step on your land again."

Cord felt a lecture coming on, so he sat down in one of the metal chairs that had been spray-painted a dozen times. While she paced, planning her next attack, he studied her. Watching Nevada storm was better than watching anything on TV.

Finally, she stopped and placed the envelope she'd carried onto the porch railing. "I came all this way and I'd like you to at least consider my offer. What I have to say is too important to give up on."

"All right," he said, knowing he wasn't buying or selling, but listening he could afford.

She stared out at the open land as she lowered her voice to almost a whisper. "I can't explain any of the why, so don't ask. Just hear me out and then say yes or no."

"Fair enough." He propped his long legs on the railing beside the manila envelope. "Tell me, Miss Britain, why'd you come out here?"

"I'm prepared to offer you the three hundred acres of my land that borders your land."

"In exchange for what?" Cord knew, as well as she did probably, that she was offering him the same plot of land their great-grandfathers had fought over. "I fear the price may be more than I can afford." The rich land was worth more than his farm, and he doubted the five hundred in his pocket would buy more than a few rocks.

For the first time she didn't look sure of herself, but she plowed forward. "I can't tell you why, but I promise you there will be no disadvantage to you. I'll sign the deed over to you when we're at the courthouse and our bargain is sealed. The land will be yours free and clear from that time on."

He frowned as he rocked back in his chair. "What's my part of the bargain?"

"Your name," she said simply. "The land is yours if you'll marry me and agree to live on my ranch for as long as we're married. I think eight months should about do it. That should be enough time to get a crop in, increase the herd and stock for winter."

The front two legs of his chair hit the floor. "I'm sorry; I thought I just heard you ask me to marry you?"

She looked down. "I told you I can't explain, but I've had my lawyer draw up a prenuptial agreement. Your land will remain yours, along with the three hundred acres, when we separate. Mine will remain mine, along with all Britain holdings." She squared her shoulders as if preparing to fight. "All I'm asking for is eight months. From now until the first hard freeze should do it. After that either of us can file for divorce and, as stated in the prenup, we both agree not to contest the divorce. All profits from both ranches will be combined for the length of the marriage and split evenly when we separate."

Cord felt like laughing out loud for the first time in years. Ideas this crazy only appear in jokes, or con schemes. Just for the hell of it, he asked, "What makes you think we'll separate?"

"I've been married three times before, and all three cost me dearly. This time I'll know the price going in. If you want, you can have total control of the farming and ranching on both places, but anything dealing with the horses or the oil business is mine. It's part of the agreement. I'll hand over the ranch business and accounts to you and trust you to run them wisely, since half of the profit for the term we're married will be yours. The horses are not part of the bargain, and no one can sell them or move them without my permission. I've seen the way you work, the way you run this place, and I think you'd be able to handle both my land and yours."

"What else?" He knew she was either crazy or trying to pull one over on him, but he'd hear her out.

"You'll have to quit your day job at Parker Trucking, but when we split, half of my ranch's income should compensate you for the loss of wages."

"What does your spread pull down?"

"A quarter million in profit on a down year when the ranch is worked. Since my dad got sick and died it hasn't been worked. If all goes well, we clear over half a million on a good year. The ranch is in my name only, so I can bargain with it and I've got enough funds to make it work."

He would have tried to look disappointed, but his jaw was open too far to fake it. She'd just offered him nearly a quarter of a million to stay married to her for eight months.

This had to be some kind of sick joke. She was playing a game, probably. "Why should I believe a word you've said?"

"Look at the agreement," she said as her fingers tapped the envelope. "Talk to your lawyers, then let me know what you decide. The only thing I ask is that we keep this agreement to ourselves. As far as everyone knows, you're just the next man I fell in love with and brought home. Most folks won't ask any questions."

"Are you crazy, lady?" He had to ask, though it occurred to him that either way she'd answer no.

"Don't call me lady or honey, or darling, or babe—"

"Got it." He stopped her before she went on. "You're not dying, are you?" It was the only reason he could think of that a woman like her would want to marry him. She might still die, but maybe she figured being married to him would make the time she had left seem longer.

"I said I wasn't answering questions, Cord, so don't bother asking. It's yes or no." She turned to leave. "I'll be at the courthouse all morning. If you show up before noon, the deal is on; if not, don't bother ever speaking to me again."

"If I say yes, I want one thing added." He figured he'd push a little to see how far she was willing to take this prank.

"What?" She looked back at him.

"If I play your husband, I want you sleep-

ing beside me every night until it's over."
He guessed sleeping next to him would
shock her out of this game she seemed to
be playing.

"Why?"

He smiled. "No questions why. Do we
agree or not?"

He thought she'd keep walking, but as
always, she surprised him. She turned and
walked back until she stood a foot in front
of him, her boot almost touching his.

"I've married and slept with three men I
thought I knew and didn't. One more added
to the list won't matter. I agree. Only, I warn
you, if you ever hit me, I'll shoot first and
wait for an apology later."

He studied her cold blue eyes and wondered if she'd been hit in the past. He'd
bet on it.

"Just look over the papers, Cord. I swear
I'm not trying to pull anything over on you."

"All right. I'll look at them." He doubted
he'd have the time.

"As soon as possible," she added, pushing just a little.

"As soon as possible," he agreed.

She was doing a good job of acting like

this mattered to her. If this was real, maybe he was just the lesser of two evils she had to pick between.

She straightened and took a long breath. "I'll make plans to meet you at the courthouse. My lawyer's office number is on the envelope. If you show up, we'll sign everything there and the three hundred acres will be yours."

He nodded once. "I'll be there by eleven if I come."

She gave him a jerky nod. A fighter realizing the fight was over.

For a moment he thought he saw fear in her eyes. Not of him, but of something beyond tomorrow if he didn't come. "Are you sure about this?" he said in little more than a whisper.

"No," she whispered back, "but it's the only plan I have."

Without another word, she walked away. No good-bye, no hello-next-husband kiss. To her this was a business deal, and he had no idea why she needed him. He'd be signing away eight months of his life if he showed up tomorrow, but he'd given away time before. Six years in fact.

This time, no matter how bad it was, if

he took her offer, he could be walking away a rich man. He could farm the three hundred acres for a good profit alone this summer and, with just eight months of her farm income, he could afford the right equipment to make his land pay when he moved back home.

Cord picked up the envelope and began to read. Somehow this was too good to be true. She'd even included bank statements. He wouldn't be taking over a rundown ranch with everything falling apart. The account could easily buy whatever he'd need to get started. He'd driven by her land, and most of it that he could see from the road wasn't being used as farm or ranchland.

The sun was down by the time he finished reading every line twice. All the facts were there, except for the sleeping arrangements. Even if she planned to torture him for eight months, it would be worth it for enough money to really start farming. Once he was making money on his land, it wouldn't matter that no one spoke to him. He could come back here and live alone in peace.

He'd never been a gambler, but this time he might just roll the dice.

After cleaning out the refrigerator, he packed the one old suitcase he owned and set it by the door, then lay awake in bed until five thinking of all the reasons she might have asked him to marry her. None made any sense.

He called himself every kind of fool, but he'd always said he'd never had a chance. What if his crazy neighbor was offering him a chance? One slim chance to change his life. Did he really want to toss it away?

He got up, drank the last of the milk, and took a shower. It wouldn't hurt to go see if she was really waiting for him at the courthouse.

On his way out, he picked up his mother's thin gold ring and slipped it on his little finger, then locked up the house and headed for town in his pickup, with a rusty trailer pulling the one horse he owned.

While he drove toward town, he went over the contract one more time in his mind, looking for the deep well he was sure he'd fall into. All the details Nevada had talked about were there. From the day they married he'd have control of the Britain ranch as well as keep total control of his own property. If the marriage lasted eight months, he'd receive half the profits from both ranches. Since his would be lucky to make twenty thousand over the summer, he wasn't taking much of a risk compared to her. There was enough money in her accounts to buy several hundred more head, and the grass was already up high enough to feed them. They'd have a good season with cattle alone, not counting the crops he planned to get in the ground.

The deed to the three hundred acres had been folded in the envelope. It already had his name on it. All it needed was her signature. She'd even included a title company's notarized statement saying she was the sole owner of Britain land.

He headed to the town square deciding he must be dreaming. Tomorrow he'd wake up and find himself back in the grease pit working. *But today*, he thought, *I might as well ride this dream out.* Maybe her insanity was spreading.

On impulse, he stopped in at Bailey Brothers and bought a suit. When Cord walked out in his new clothes, he couldn't seem to get comfortable. He felt like he was wearing a costume, trying to pretend to be someone he wasn't, but there was no turning back now.

He walked across the street to the post office. If he was really going to be getting married in a few minutes, he might as well change his address.

"Morning," the bashful woman behind the counter greeted him.

"Morning, Ronny," he answered, remembering the time he'd dropped in and asked her who'd paid for the postage on all the newspapers he got in prison after his folks died. She'd looked so shy and embarrassed; he'd left without waiting for the answer.

Since then he'd learned her name was Ronny Logan and he had a faint memory of her from school, only she was very timid and he'd been wild, running with a group of boys who called themselves "The Outlaws." She was still shy and he'd learned to avoid people, so that kind of made them alike. Not that it would be likely that their types would ever get together and form a club, but they had something in common, it seemed.

He picked up the change-of-address packet and headed out.

"Cord." Her soft voice stopped him.

"Yeah," he said, surprised she'd called his name.

"You look real nice today."

"Thanks, Ronny."

Stepping back out into the morning air, Cord straightened. Compliments were so rare he could almost feel them raw on his face, but he stood taller as he walked back toward the courthouse square.

Chapter 4

COURTHOUSE

NEVADA BRITAIN WATCHED FROM THE THIRD-floor window of the courthouse as Cord McDowell walked into the building. Her heart pounded faster and faster. She had hoped he'd come, but she hadn't believed he would.

He was bigger than any of her former husbands and solid as a rock, and handsome in a keep-your-distance kind of way. But his looks and his manner had nothing to do with why she'd asked him to marry her.

She knew she was taking a gamble that might get her killed, but she'd let others stop her from doing what she knew was right before and lived to regret it. If Cord was a cold man able to kill in rage, she'd know it soon enough. In a few minutes she'd be betting her life on one trait McDowell did show. He was a survivor.

Cord might turn out to be as mean as a snake like folks said, but he was easy on the eyes and she'd developed an instinct about when to run. She liked the power in his movements, like he was a giant trying to walk among fairies. When he wasn't in public, his shoulders were straight and he seemed taller, but now, while people were watching, he kept his head low and his shoulders rounded to pull his six-foot-five frame down a few inches.

When he stepped off the elevator and moved to where she stood by the windows, Nevada noticed his old boots had been polished and the suit was so new it still had wrinkles from hanging on the rack. His tan skin warmed against the white of his open-collared shirt.

"You came," she said, more to herself than him.

"I forgot to buy a tie. I'm sorry." He looked as uncomfortable as she felt. When she didn't say anything, he added, "I brought the contract."

"My lawyer had another copy. We'll stop in his office first." She forced a smile she didn't feel. "Don't worry about the tie. You look fine." *A knight in not-so-shining armor*, she thought, *or a killer who'd honed his skills in prison.* Either way, her troubles would be over.

He just stood there looking at her. Finally, he said, "I know you said you don't want to tell me why you're doing this, but before we take another step I have to know what I'm getting into. Not all, maybe, but some."

She managed a nod. He was right. He should know. "I've got problems with the drilling business. I need to be at the office. The ranch is losing money. If I don't turn it around I might lose it too."

He met her eyes, and she knew that fighting for her land was something he understood.

She rushed on before she lost her nerve. "And I've got an ex who wants to make life miserable for me. If he knows I'm married again, he might move on." Nevada closed her eyes, knowing that she was leaving out boulders and talking about pebbles but she wasn't used to sharing her troubles.

"Fair enough." Cord seemed satisfied. "Let's do this."

They walked down the hallway, and he cleared his throat twice before he said, "I've got a thousand questions about the ranch, but we can talk about them later." He seemed to be fighting to keep his voice conversational, to just talk to her like they were two normal people going to get married. "I jotted down some ideas I want to go over with you."

"I hope I know the answers. I gave everyone on the Boxed B the weekend off so we'd have time to look at the books and ride the land. You're not taking on an easy job, I got to warn you. I've tried to keep everything going, but half the ranch hands quit and the other half seem to be waiting around doing nothing until I fire them. I can't handle both the oil business and the ranch, so you'll be in charge there."

She wanted to add more about trouble sure to come, but it would be best to bring him in a little at a time. Letting him believe her biggest problem was the ranch would be the safest plan. If he knew more, he'd bolt on her.

They reached the office door. "Work doesn't scare me," he said before he turned the knob. "I didn't figure it would be easy. Nothing in my life ever has been."

She nodded, thinking they had more in common than he knew. "From this point on, I'll trust you, Cord, if you'll trust me. It's the only promise I can make, but you have my word." The lie only stung a little on her tongue as she told herself omitting a problem isn't lying. "I need you far more than you need me in this deal, and the strip of land between our places is a small price to pay. With you by my side I may still lose it all, but at least with you I have a fighting chance."

"I'll try trusting." He touched her arm. "But I'm not long on practice in that area."

The white-headed lawyer in a thousand-dollar suit rushed to greet them. "Welcome." He grinned. "We're ready for you, Miss Britain."

Nevada straightened, moving into her planned speech. "Call me Mrs. McDowell, and this is my husband-to-be, Cord. I've never given up Britain to take a husband's name, but I think I'll take this one. I'd like people in this town to know I'm married to Cord McDowell."

The lawyer grinned as if he thought she was joking. When she didn't say anything, he rushed on. "I'm happy to meet you, Mr. McDowell. If you'll just step this way, we'll get the papers signed and witnessed. Your bride tells me you both are in a hurry. The judge who'll marry you is already waiting in the conference room."

Nevada tried to keep her breathing slow, but it wasn't easy. She knew the routine. Said all the right words. Signed all the papers. Only she hadn't expected Cord to slip a thin gold ring on her finger when he said, "I, Cordell Harrison McDowell, take you, Nevada Britain, to be my wife."

The judge didn't say *You may kiss the bride* when he finished. She guessed he figured she'd already been kissed enough.

Cord didn't move toward her, and she couldn't even bring herself to look at him. She'd rushed him into this only half believing he'd agree.

Now he shook the hands of the lawyer and the judge. He seemed in a hurry to be out of the office, but once they were in the hallway, he stood silent, looking at the rug beneath his boots while she tried to think of something to say. They'd been neigh-bors all their lives, but she knew little about him outside the young boy she'd once seen in school and the time he'd spent in prison since then. She'd heard that his parents had been quiet people already into their forties when he was born. Some-one said his mother died of cancer and his father followed her in death a year later of a heart attack.

"You hungry?" Cord finally spoke as they waited for the elevator. "I didn't bother to eat supper or breakfast, so I could eat half a beef."

"All right." She wasn't sure she could keep anything down, but at least he had a suggestion. If he planned to wait for her to come up with something, they'd be grow-ing along with the grass on the courthouse lawn.

"Where do you like to eat?" He waited for her to step into the elevator. When the door closed she became very much aware of him in the small space.

"I don't usually eat out in town. I have a great cook at the ranch."

"I like the diner across the street and down a few doors. I eat there now and then. Whatever's on the daily special is usually good."

She nodded, making note that he wasn't particular about his food, or apparently his clothes. The pant legs of the suit were an inch shorter than they should be, and with his light brown hair, the gray suit washed him out like a camera shot out of focus.

"I need to check in at the office, then I'll meet you there," she said as she moved outside.

"Fine," he answered. "There's something I need to take care of too. Thirty minutes?"

"Thirty minutes," she said, and almost ran to her car. As she drove the few blocks to her offices, she noticed him walking toward Parker Trucking and guessed he was going to quit.

Thirty minutes later, it was almost noon and the Blue Moon Diner was packed when they met at the door and walked in. Several people looked up, but no one spoke. She recognized a few of the town's folks but couldn't call them by name. The Britains didn't mix with the locals, never had.

"Friendly group," Cord mumbled as he slid into the booth across from her. "Must be you. I can't think of a thing I've done wrong lately."

She smiled. "If you weren't married to me, you probably wouldn't speak to me either."

"You got that right." He surprised her when he winked at her.

Nevada laughed. He was being honest, just like she'd asked. Suddenly it didn't matter that folks thought the Britains were uppity or that Cord was an ex-con. "If I weren't married to you I wouldn't talk to you either, Mr. McDowell."

"Sounds like a great way to start a marriage, Mrs. McDowell."

She caught the corner of his mouth lifting slightly before he raised his menu and said, "It's going to be a conversation-packed marriage. I can already tell."

Staring at her menu, she fought down a giggle. Maybe, just maybe, this marriage might be tolerable. At least until he got to know her. Then, like all the other husbands, he'd begin to pick her apart. Thanks to her father, her brothers, and three ex-husbands, she'd learned the hard way that something—no, maybe everything as far as they were concerned—was wrong with her. Only this time, after the eight months was up, she wouldn't stay around for the insults. This time she'd planned her escape ahead of time. She'd walk away with a working ranch, and he'd have money for a fresh start at his old place. If trouble didn't come, they might just both survive until winter.

They ordered, then sat in silence for a while. Absently, she played with the wedding band. "Thanks for thinking of the ring," she finally said.

"It was my mother's," he answered. "When you pull it off, Nevada, I'll pack. No discussion. No argument. Fair enough?"

"Fair enough." He'd just answered one of her worries as if he'd read her mind. Now all that she could hope for was that he might truly be a man of his word. "I'll give it back when we're over, but it was a nice gesture."

"I won't need it again."

She felt sad somehow for him. "You never know. You might marry again one day and want your wife to have the ring."

"I don't think so. You're the only woman who's come down the road asking in three years. What are the odds of it happening again?"

She laughed. "After being married to me for a while, you'll probably swear off women forever."

"You that much of a tornado, Nevada?"

She stared straight into his brown eyes. "And if I am?"

He didn't turn away. "I've always liked the wind."

She relaxed slightly. For the first time since she'd walked up to his porch last night, she felt like they just might have a chance of making this contract work for both of them.

They ate their meal in silence. The waitress brought the bill and he pulled cash from his pocket and paid. From the way he looked at his money, she guessed there was no reserve in his pocket.

When he stood to leave, he offered her his hand. She felt his strong grip around her fingers, and a bit of the nervousness that had kept her awake all night returned. For the hundredth time she wondered if she'd made the right decision. In a lifetime of turning the wrong way at every corner, fate had to let her make a right turn some-time, and maybe this was it.

He didn't let go of her hand until they were past all the people and out in the street.

"We need to stop at the bank," she said. "I called them this morning. They'll have everything ready."

He nodded, as if he knew what she was talking about.

When she walked in, she was halfway to the president's office before she real-ized Cord had turned off at the first teller.

She waited, trying to look patient until he joined her. "Have to stop and visit, did you?" The young teller was still smiling at Cord and acting like she didn't even no-tice Nevada.

"No." He didn't explain what he'd been doing. "You jealous already?"

The question was so ridiculous she al-most laughed. "No, but I hate to be kept waiting. You might want to remember that. Let's get this done."

She marched into the president's office and they began to sign papers again. Nevada couldn't keep from watching him shift slightly when the banker told Cord that he'd have sole control of the Boxed B Ranch accounts.

Somehow they'd managed to get him a leather folder of business checks with his name engraved along the bottom and the Boxed B brand just below.

"Nevada can still sign on the accounts, but she tells me you'll be handling them. If you have any questions, Mr. McDowell, just let me know. The general account has bonds in reserve, but if you need money for a short run, we'll be happy to extend you a line of credit."

The banker passed him a money bag. "This is the cash Nevada said you'd need to keep on hand at the ranch." He handed Cord a debit card. "This draws off the checking account for any little expenses. I'm afraid if you need more than a thousand in one day you'll need to write a check." He grinned. "I'm guessing you're going to pay off what's left of that loan on your farm today."

Cord raised his head slowly from the debit card. "You're guessing wrong. I'll be in next month with another payment if you've no

objection. That's my land, my responsibility. I'll pay it off with my money."

"But . . ."

Cord put on his hat. "Thank you for the
help, but we need to be getting home."

To her surprise, Cord offered his arm to
her. When she took it, he walked out of the
bank as if he didn't notice everyone staring. Half the people in the bank must have
figured out that they were married, and
they couldn't have looked more shocked if
she'd hitched up with one of her daddy's
prize longhorns.

As before, when they were outside, he
let go of her hand. "Is that all we have to
do?"

"Yes."

"Good. I've had enough of town."

"Me too." They agreed on something.

"I'll follow you back to your place," he
said, pulling off his suit jacket as they
walked toward the parking lot.

"Is that your trailer with a horse inside?"
The old blue pickup she'd seen on their
road was now hooked to the oldest horse
trailer she'd ever seen.

"Yeah. I had to bring him along. I couldn't

leave him behind, not knowing when I'd get back to feed him, and the pasture fences wouldn't hold him."

She ran to the trailer and looked inside. A powerful gray stallion stomped and pushed against the trailer wall. "Cord, he's beautiful." She hadn't expected that he'd bring more than a suitcase to her land and certainly not a fine horse.

Cord stood beside her and smiled. "His mother was my horse when I was a kid. Only horse we ever had on the farm. My dad wasn't fond of them, but my mother thought I should have a horse, so my dad found a gentle mare. When I went to prison, my dad just turned her to pasture. He wrote me a year later and said she'd had a colt. By the time I got out he was grown and wild."

"But who was . . ."

"They say mustangs run deep in the canyon, but I've never seen them. More than likely, one of your stallions jumped the fence and found my mare."

"My horses would never have come over uninvited. They're all thoroughbreds." She laughed. "What do you call him?"

"Devil. My grandfather told me once that

his father said the finest horse he'd ever seen was named Devil, so I thought I'd call him that."

"Well, he's welcome to come over to stay, but I'll not have him mixing with my mares. I'll bet he doesn't even have papers."

Cord shrugged. "Nope, neither do I. You sure you want to take us in?"

"I'm sure about the horse. The jury's still out on you." A man who loved his horse couldn't be all bad, she decided. "I only ask one favor: If you come home with me, you've got to let me buy the right clothes for your life as a rancher. That suit looks like Bailey Brothers pulled it off a rack they had in the basement from the 1980s."

"I don't care much about clothes, and picking this suit out was pure torture. Knock yourself out. I'll wear whatever you want me to as long as it's not orange. I hate that color. Mr. Bailey, back in the store, insisted on taking my measurements, so he should know the sizes. I don't plan on going in for a fitting again in this lifetime. Most clothes I've ever bought, I just held them up to see if they'd fit."

She stepped away from the trailer and

hurried to her car. They'd just settled their first agreement in marriage. Maybe things would go smoothly for a change. She had a world of problems lurking like spiders in the shadows, and Cord might just take one of them off her hands.

Her last husband, rich with his family's oil money, wanted her ranch and thought she came with it. With the ranch crumbling from neglect and poor management, he might have had a chance to buy it, but if Cord could turn the Boxed B around, it would remain hers. She'd bought her brother's share when their father died and she planned to keep it, only Bryce Galloway had fought the divorce and kept her in court long enough to drain her reserves. She knew she had only one summer's stake left to make the ranch pay.

Driving onto her land, Nevada smiled. This was her home, and she'd never give it up without a fight. This land was not something her ex-husband could have just because he wanted it. It wasn't for sale, and neither was she. Bryce Galloway would just have to get used to the fact that there were some things no amount of money would buy.

She remembered Cord gripping her hand when the banker went over the accounts. It must have looked like a great deal of money for running a ranch, but it would be needed to make a profit this year.

Five hours later, she was frustrated and Cord was furious. They'd gone over the books, and even she could see that a ranch with the best equipment and finest stock around was losing money. It didn't appear that any of the three bookkeepers she'd had in the past year had embezzled, but all the part-time foremen were obviously wasting money and showing little profit.

"I'll go put on some coffee." She headed toward the kitchen. To her surprise, he followed her.

Without asking, he began opening cabinets.

"Looking for something?"

"Food," he answered, without stopping his search. "I've developed this habit. I like to eat at least a couple times a day." He pulled out a dozen eggs and a skillet. "Hand me the butter and cheese."

Before she knew it she was chopping up a salad while he scrambled eggs. She asked if he wanted her to open a bottle of wine, but he shook his head and poured two glasses of milk.

They ate in a comfortable silence, both calming down from the stress of the day. All afternoon Cord had asked her questions about the ranch, and her answer was always the same: *I don't know.* She had all she could handle taking care of her prize horses and running the trust as well as the oil corporation. At the end of the day there was never any time to study ranch business. The place had been running itself for two years, and it hadn't been running well. Since her longtime foreman had been fired by her last husband, the men who stepped into the job seemed to be progressing steadily into incompetence.

"Tell me how the house runs." He finally broke the silence. "I don't want to be in the way."

She thought about saying that it was the staff's job to stay out of his way, but she just stated the facts. "My cook usually comes about nine. I don't eat breakfast. She does the light cleaning, the laundry, and the cooking. She leaves about five unless I have guests and need her to stay.

When I entertain, the bunkhouse cook, who is also her husband, usually helps her. A couple comes in once a week for the heavy cleaning and the yard work in the courtyard, but Ora Mae, my cook, has an herb garden off the back porch."

Cord listened as he ate.

"Ten years ago, before she ran off, my dad's last wife insisted on a courtyard, and somehow we've managed to keep it up."

"What time is breakfast at the bunk-house?"

"Seven, I think."

"Monday morning we'll have breakfast in the bunkhouse with the men. After the hands settle into the fact that I'm running the ranch, you can sleep in if you like, but I'll eat with them every morning. After Monday, breakfast will always be served at dawn in the bunkhouse until fall."

He finished off her last bite of egg and added, "Ready to get back to the books? I thought when we're finished I'd like to see maps. As you know, I've flown over your land a few times, but I need to know every inch of it."

She groaned but followed him back to the massive old study she'd always thought of as her father's even though he'd been dead for two years.

After answering a dozen more questions, she tugged off her shoes and curled into her father's old leather chair. It still smelled of his pipe tobacco and the right arm had worn from years of balancing a whiskey glass. She didn't miss her father or mother, but now and then she missed the parents they might have been. She missed having just one memory of her father reading to her in this chair. Just one simple memory would have been something to hold on to.

An hour later she fell asleep wondering if this strange man she'd just married would ever stop working.

Chapter 5

DUPLEX NEAR THE TOWN SQUARE

RONNY LOGAN STOOD IN THE DARK SHADOWS of the front yard of the duplex she'd rented for two years. As the lights of the old town square blinked a shadowy yellow, memories flowed around her in the cool breeze. She felt like she'd been asleep the first twenty-seven years of her life, a shy child dominated by an overbearing mother. Through childhood she'd believed she was loved and her mother was trying to mold her into the perfect little girl, but during her teens she realized she'd never pass Dallas

Logan's scrutiny. Her mother saw her as not just flawed, but damaged. By Ronny's twentieth birthday, her mother had convinced her that she was worthless.

Her father had simply been Dallas's first victim, and he hadn't done much better than his daughter. When he died, however, he left his half of the house to his only child. Since she finished school, Ronny had worked at the post office, as silent and invisible as a midnight mouse. She'd believed nothing would ever change, and then one day while making a delivery, she met a handsome man in a wheelchair, and her world moved from gray to bright colors.

Within a few months she bloomed, and when Marty Winslow left Harmony one night without saying good-bye, she ran away from home and moved into his old apartment. Dallas disowned her ungrateful daughter of twenty-seven years, and Ronny decided she'd survive better on her own. Marty Winslow might not have stayed around, but he'd believed in her, and one person believing is a long way from none. He gave her hope.

Only now, standing with the moonlight breeze blowing her long brown hair as the gentle sounds of Harmony surrounded her, Ronny Logan knew her life was about to change again, and this time was far more frightening than leaving home.

"You all right out here?" Beau Yates, her neighbor, startled her as he rounded the corner. Like her, he always dressed in a black jacket and dark jeans to move through the streets after dark.

"I'm fine," she answered as he seemed to materialize from the shadows. He was younger than her and always kind, even though with his black hair and late hours she often thought him more vampire than human. "I thought you were playing at the bar tonight."

"I am. I just ran home to pick up my new guitar. It seemed easier than driving the few blocks. My lungs could use the fresh air." He opened the unlocked side of the duplex and grabbed a case that must have been waiting at the door for him. "I have to get back before the break is over. The thought of Border playing on his own scares me." Beau laughed. "There's only a dozen drunks still in there tonight, but they'd give their best try at murdering him if he played."

Ronny didn't laugh at his joke, so he slowed, trying to see her in the poor light. "You sure you're all right, Ronny?"

"I'm all right, Beau." She couldn't think of a lie, and he didn't seem to need one. When you're twenty, nothing about life makes sense so you don't bother questioning.

He leaned against the wall as if sensing she needed to not be alone for a moment. "I like the stillness of this time of night. One of these days I'm going to write a song. I think I'm going to call it 'Between Heartbeats' because that's kind of what it feels like."

When she didn't say anything, he pushed away from the side of the house and headed toward the road with a wave and a flash of a smile.

As she listened to him jogging back toward the bar, she grinned at him even though he'd gone. Beau and his roommate, Border Biggs, made her life easier. Her neighbors reminded her of two pups, always getting into trouble, always hungry. They never went to bed before two and burned everything they cooked, but Beau could play and sing good enough to make you believe heaven was piped with country music, and Border was always there backing him up on stage and off.

Ronny closed her eyes and thought about what the kid had said about the night. She could almost feel the stillness, like daytime was for the heartbeats and the night seemed the silence in between.

A long black Lincoln turned onto her street and pulled up in front of her house, drawing Ronny's attention back to the present.

She looked toward town, making sure no one else was on the street. Her mother had been known to drive by, but never this late.

No one moved in the night. Beau and Border would be at least another two hours practicing their music at the bar. When they came in, they'd see her dark quarters and assume she'd gone to bed. No one would miss her if she disappeared for a while.

She walked toward the car as the driver stepped out and opened the back door for her. He nodded politely but didn't look up at her. Once she was inside, he climbed back into the driver's seat, put on music she knew someone had selected for her to listen to, and silently drove away.

As they left the lights of Harmony, she pulled the blanket from the seat beside her and leaned her head back. She had a long drive with little hope of finding happiness at the end. She'd made it before only to be turned away, but maybe tonight would be different. Closing her eyes, she wished for what might have been.

Ronny had no idea how long she'd slept, but the bright parking lot lights of a huge hospital woke her. As she straightened, the car pulled to a side entrance where a tall man in black waited. He was rail thin and his hair looked silver in the harsh light. When she'd seen him once before, he hadn't stepped closer; he'd only shaken his head as if to say *I'm sorry* and slipped back inside the hospital, closing the door so she couldn't have followed.

This time the driver remained in place as the tall man moved forward and opened her door. "Good evening, Miss Logan. I'm glad you agreed to come."

"I'll always come. Mr. Carleon, right?" she said, wondering if anyone else visited at this time of night.

"Yes. I'm the one who sent you the note. I feel as if I know you, miss."

They reached the hospital door and this time it stood open, waiting for her.

"If you'll follow me." Mr. Carleon moved swiftly. "He's expecting you this time and we have no roadblocks."

Ronny straightened and fought back tears. Two years without a word from Marty Winslow, and then a registered letter asking her to be ready an hour before midnight and to trust Carleon to make the plans. *I'll be waiting. Marty* was all the personal note she'd gotten from a man who'd stolen her heart just by being kind to her. He'd never pretended to be more than a friend, but for a woman starved of all love, it had been enough for her to build a world of dreams on.

"I'm sorry about last time, miss." Mr. Carleon kept his voice low as they walked the darkened back hallway. "There had been a shift change I hadn't been aware of."

She didn't care about the wasted journey

she'd made a month ago. All that mattered was that Marty Winslow had contacted her. "How is he?"

"Weak, miss. Very weak."

Mr. Carleon moved from one hallway to another until they came to a freight elevator. When the man finally faced her, she saw kindness in his pale eyes and gray-salted hair that had once been black. He could have been anywhere between forty and seventy, but there was strength about him, a stillness that must have come with age.

"I've been with Mr. Winslow since he was ten. I was waiting at the base when the skiing accident paralyzed him almost four years ago." The older man's face wilted with sadness. "He's very near death, miss. This last surgery took all he had, and now infection has set in. The doctors are doing all they can, pumping him with drugs, monitoring him constantly. His parents are dead, but his older brother has taken charge. Daniel insists Marty suffer no pain, but if he takes all the pills, he'll sleep his last hours away."

A vision of how Marty had looked the day she'd met him flashed into her mind. He was alone and angry but very much a

man in his chair. With his dark hair and fiery eyes, she'd thought he was a devil,
and he'd been angry enough at the world
to almost make her believe it.

"How long?"

Mr. Carleon shook his head. "I can only
allow you an hour. Maybe a few minutes
more."

"No." She didn't care how long the visit
would be. "How long does he have left to
live?"

"A few days. A week at the most, the
doctors say. Even if the infection clears,
his body is beginning to shut down. One
of his doctors suggested flying him somewhere else for a therapy, but his brother
was told he might not even survive the
journey. So Daniel finally said no. Two
years, five operations, and a dozen hospitals is enough. With Marty here, he'll be
home when the end comes. The brother
and doctors decided that's all they can do
for him. He's out of time, miss."

Ronny fought back her scream. Marty
had been there for her when she came
alive, and if he asked her to, she'd be there
for him when he died.

She had a hundred other questions, but

Mr. Carleon opened a door and she stepped into a private room lined with machines.

For a moment she didn't recognize him. Marty was thin and pale, as though he were fading away. She remembered how his strong arms had held her and how his laughter could fill a room.

It took all her strength to move to his bed and take his hand. Leaning close to his ear, she whispered, "One heartbeat past forever. That's how long I'll love you."

Marty didn't open his eyes.

Mr. Carleon pulled up a chair and offered it to her, but Ronny couldn't sit down. She stood like a soldier as one by one her memories of Marty faced the firing squad until the only reality left was the man in front of her barely breathing. His hand that had once set fire to her with a touch was now cold and limp. His lips that had taught her to kiss were almost white and thinned in pain. His laughter, his teasing, his loving words were all drowned out by the rattle of machines that played an out-of-tune death march through the night.

Minutes ticked by, but she refused to move. She stared, hungry for a sign from him. She took the pain of how little of him remained. A hundred things passed through her mind that she needed to tell him. She'd almost finished her degree in finance. She'd learned to cook. She'd bought a new car. She'd made friends in town. Like he told her to, she'd grown.

But she'd missed him every day that he'd been gone. It took her a while, but she finally figured it out. There was no forgetting Marty, no getting over him. She'd love him forever.

"Miss?" Mr. Carleon whispered beside her. "Miss, you have to go. The hour is up."

"But he didn't wake." She tightened her grip on Marty's hand, hoping he'd at least squeeze her fingers back.

"I was afraid he wouldn't," Carleon said, too calmly to betray any emotion. "I think he knows you're here, though. His breathing has calmed since you took his hand. I've been watching. His heartbeat is steady."

"Can I stay longer, please?"

"Miss, it would mean my job if Daniel knew I brought you here."

"Then why did you?" Never seeing Marty again would have been less painful. "He won't even know I'm here."

"Every time he wakes, he waits until

only the two of us are in the room, then motions me near. I lean close and he whispers your name." Mr. Carleon stared at Marty. "I know you're always in his thoughts. I know his brother thinks I work for him, but I work for Marty Winslow and I will until the day he dies."

"Can I come back?" She kissed Marty's hand as she pulled her fingers away.

"I'll send the car every night I can an hour before midnight. It will wait ten minutes. If you can't make the trip, I'll understand. If I don't meet you at the back door of the hospital, you'll understand. There are very few people I can trust."

"I'll come if the car is there." She walked to the door, not daring to look back. The only man who'd ever thought she was beautiful was dying, and she was allowed only an hour a night to see him, with nothing but a promise of a next time.

As she rode back toward Harmony, tears ran unchecked down her cheeks, and she knew that when Marty Winslow died, so would she.

Chapter 6

ALMOST DAWN
DUPLEX

BEAU YATES LEANED AGAINST THE WINDOWSILL, his body so slim and still he almost looked like a part of the frame. He watched his neighbor step out of a late-model Lincoln and walk slowly toward the porch they shared.

He couldn't help but wonder where she'd been. If Ronny Logan had been another kind of woman, wild or even normal, he would have guessed she'd had a wild night out, but she wasn't the type. Ronny was warm hot chocolate on a cold night. She was kittens and apple pie and all the kind of things he thought of as pure good. He'd never heard her say a bad word or claim she hated anyone. She didn't even complain about her witch of a mother, who flew by now and then on her broom just to remind her only child that she still hated her.

Beau picked up his guitar as his neighbor went into her side of the duplex without raising her head. Somehow, she had a secret. He didn't know what it was, but he knew it was good. Maybe she prayed at church all night?

As his fingers began to play across the strings, he smiled, thinking of his secret life. He also climbed into a car now and then with a girl he called Trouble, and they raced the moonlight. It seemed the only time in his twenty years of life that he didn't feel like he was waiting for something to happen. With the girl in the ponytail, he just relaxed and breathed in life.

Slowly, he picked out the melody to a song about how most folks while their life away waiting for lightning to strike and set the dullness of their days afire, when all they'd have to do is pull the box of matches from their pocket and strike one.

Maybe Ronny was doing just that.

Beau smiled, thinking that he was one of the waiting ones. His father, a preacher to the bone, was convinced Beau lived in sin. He'd left home. He played in a bar. He shared an apartment with a guy who had tattoos and drove a motorcycle. He stayed up all night writing songs.

Setting the guitar down, Beau watched the first pale light of dawn. With luck, he could be sound asleep before full sunup reached Harmony. At least he'd break the bad habit of staying up all night his father thought he had.

Pulling off his shirt as he walked toward his bed, he thought of Trouble in her car as she let the night wind blow her hair. If she ever came around again, he could get used to her as a keeper in the bad-habit column of his life.

Chapter 7

BOXED B RANCH

CORD WORKED UNTIL AFTER MIDNIGHT, THEN turned off the study lights and carried his sleeping bride to what he hoped was their room in the rambling old ranch house. She'd set his suitcase by an empty closet door, but she hadn't bothered with a tour of the place.

He pulled back the cover on one side of the king-size bed and laid her down. Slowly, he tugged the tie from her hair and let the long white-blond strands spread out across the pillow in streams of gold. With a hun-

CAN'T STOP BELIEVING 79

ger for something he'd never known, he watched her breathe. She was so lovely, this wife of his, and fragile despite all her tough-girl attitude. For a few minutes he just studied her, learning the curve of her face and the beauty of her hands as he wondered if he'd ever know her better than he did right now.

Neither of them had said a kind word all evening. He'd asked questions and she'd answered, pouting when she didn't know the answer, sharp when he pushed, but always honest. He didn't have to tell her what a mess the ranch was in; she saw it same as he had. If the spending continued without any profit coming in, the Boxed B wouldn't last another year, and she obviously had no one to turn to if she'd come to him.

He doubted she even liked him, but she needed him, and he planned to be there for her—though they both knew they'd be counting this marriage in months.

In one evening with her he'd figured out two things. He already knew more about the ranch than she did, and no other man besides her father had left his fingerprints on the maps in the study. No brother of hers. No husband had cared about the ranch. He'd be the first since her father to take charge, and that was one question he hadn't had the nerve to ask why.

He told himself that the ranch was why she'd brought him here, but deep down he knew there was more she wasn't talking about. He felt it. A shadow hung over the ranch like an aging dragon waiting to fight one final battle.

When he'd asked about the oil business, she'd said she almost bankrupted it buying her brother's half of the ranch. He'd walked away with millions and left her with two lame businesses about to fail.

She's a fighter, Cord thought as he covered her and went to the other side of the bed. The night was warm enough that he spread out on top of the covers and fell asleep to the soft sound of her breathing.

When he woke it was after nine. The glare of full daylight shocked him awake. Cord had gotten up early for so long, he felt disoriented at first.

He didn't see the note on the pillow between them until he stood.

Gone shopping. Be back at noon. She'd

signed her initials, like he might not know who'd left the note.

He walked around the room, unsure what to do. When he realized he was alone in the house, he went through each room. Five bedrooms, each with a bath. All but the master looked to have been closed off years ago. Two living areas, two dining rooms, one small, one huge. A breakfast nook off the ranch kitchen and a big bathroom next to the back door. The wide office they'd worked in had windows facing west.

Two facts about it tumbled in his mind. One, he could almost see his farm if he stared hard enough, and two, a loaded Colt rested in the bottom drawer of the massive desk. Maybe Nevada kept her father's Colt there to remember him, or maybe she felt there was a need to be armed.

When they knew each other better, he'd act like he'd just noticed it and ask. Maybe. His headstrong wife was afraid of something . . . something more than him. She was skittish as a pony who'd heard a rattler.

Cord found another office upstairs next

to an exercise room and a game room. The pool table looked as if it had never been used, but animal heads covered the walls and full gun racks braced each corner. Most of the weapons were classic Remingtons that looked like they'd never been fired.

Cord felt a little like a robber casing the place, but he needed to know the house and he wasn't sure she cared enough to show him around.

The upstairs study was cluttered with papers and books. This was Nevada's world. He could almost feel her here. It looked newly painted in pale blues and greens with sketches of horses covering the wall. When he moved closer he saw dates on each frame along with *N.B.* scribbled in the corner of each. She'd been painting pictures of horses since she was seven, each year getting better and better. Her office was the only room he felt reluctant to leave. The only room that wasn't cold and aged.

He knew without asking that this place might be her house, but she had never made it her home. There were no pictures of family, no trophies, nothing that looked like it might have belonged to any one person.

By the time he got to know the house and showered, Nevada was back. She walked into the bedroom as he buttoned his Levi's. When he looked up she was standing in the door, her arms loaded down with bags and her blue eyes watching him.

He'd never thought of himself as shy, but darn if he didn't feel himself blush. "Any chance you bought me a shirt? The only dress shirt I own is pretty wrinkled after I slept in it." On this full day together he didn't want to wear one of his old work shirts.

She popped out of her trance. "I did. Most of what I bought is being altered or ordered, but I did pick up a few things. You're about the same size as my brother, but I tossed all his clothes when he left." Like a rabid squirrel, she dropped the bags and began rummaging, then proudly showed her prize to him.

"Thanks," he managed to say as she stared at his chest. "You finished looking?"

She ducked her head. "Yes," she mumbled as she went back to digging in the bags.

While he pulled the pins and cardboard out of an eighty-dollar pale blue shirt with pearl snaps, she lined up socks atop a boot box. "I just told the Bailey brothers to load me up with a week's worth of work clothes. They said that after forty years in the business they can guess a man's sizes down to his underwear when he walks in the door."

Cord pulled on the finest shirt he'd ever owned, thinking that she thought it was a work shirt. The cotton had to be blended with silk or something. He thought of telling her a twenty-dollar shirt would do fine, but he'd already agreed she could dress him, so he might as well play along. Shopping was something she probably had made pro in before she was out of high school.

Five minutes later he realized the boots fit perfectly as well. They had an inch heel and the leather was soft. When he faced her, he held up his hands, feeling a little like the world's largest paper doll. "Do I pass?"

"You passed, Cord, when you were just wearing your jeans, but now you look like a man who runs a ranch. Ready to see the place?"

"No," he said. "First we eat. I've already missed breakfast and it's almost noon."

"This feeding you might be a problem. When Ora Mae shows up Monday, I may have to give her a raise."

"Come on, Princess. I'll show you how to make sandwiches. We can eat once we're in the saddle. I plan to see every square mile of this place before dark."

"Let me change first. You can put your things in that closet while you wait." She pointed to the closet where she'd left his suitcase as she crossed the room to the other walk-in closet and bathroom. "And," she yelled over her shoulder, "don't call me Princess."

"Fine," he answered as he stepped into what was now his closet. "This place is bigger than my bedroom at home and there's a dresser built in here."

She didn't answer, and he hoped she hadn't heard. He was sounding like a hick. The walls began closing in on him and he fought to keep them at bay. Years of living in a cell so small he could almost touch the walls played on his mind and made him crave open spaces. Even a closet this big wasn't a place he wanted to spend any time in.

Dropping the bags, he moved back to

the door and took a deep breath. Air. He needed fresh air.

In three long strides he was at the wall of windows and noticed that none were built to open. What kind of idiot builds windows that don't open?

Looking toward her closet door, he saw her standing among her colorful clothes. She'd stripped off her dress and was tugging on her jeans. The bra and panties were little more than lace.

Cord gave up breathing altogether. He'd seen pictures of women nude, movies with beautiful bodies, but nothing had ever affected him like the sight of Nevada. He couldn't have turned away if she'd threatened death.

He watched her button her pants and then pull on a white T-shirt that fit like a second skin. Over the tee, she wiggled into an oversized sweater that hung off one shoulder. Turning, she looked up and smiled. "Finished looking?"

He'd lost the power of speech, so he just stood as still as a tree.

What few brain cells he had left knew he should probably apologize, or something, but all he could get out was, "I . . . I . . ."

She walked past him and picked up her hat. "Look, Cord, we're going to be living together for a while. We might as well get used to each other. I've never been shy and it's nothing I'm sure you haven't seen before."

When he didn't move, she added, "I'll pack up some water and fruit while you collect your thoughts."

With that she was gone. He felt like he was one of those backward people on *Star Trek* who got beamed up on the teleporter of the starship *Enterprise*. He couldn't understand what was going on. Had she just told him it was all right for him to watch her dress? Hell, he felt a habit coming on.

When he finally found the new hat she'd bought him and made it to the front door, she was waiting for him. They were saddled up and riding full out before he could clear the vision of her standing in her underwear from his mind.

Nevada had obviously gotten over the view of him much faster, because she was rattling off facts about the ranch. She might not know anything about the day-to-day running of the place, but she knew its history.

She also knew how to ride across the open land and where all the watering holes and roads were. She could recite facts about the oil production that had been going on since long before she was born.

Again and again he climbed down to feel the earth. The land was good, but very little of it was being used. Except for the pasture where her twenty prize horses roamed, most of the pastureland was empty, if you didn't count jackrabbits. The land that had been plowed under for crops had been abandoned years ago to weeds, and he'd seen records of where hay had been hauled in for winter feed even though there were more than enough barns to hold a home-grown supply.

"There's a great deal to be done." He saw potential.

"Hire who you need," she said. "The money you put in the safe last night should pay any day labor, but the regulars draw ranch checks. I've been advertising for a new bookkeeper for the ranch. You might as well do the hiring. Ora Mae will call those who applied for interviews when you have time. You'll meet all the staff on Monday."

"Who pays the hands?"

"I have been for the last four months since the last bookkeeper quit. Cattle started disappearing about that time, and lately I've noticed the men hanging around the bunkhouse kitchen waiting for orders. Some are good men, I think, but they need a leader. They're not comfortable handling things."

"How many foremen you been through since your dad got ill and stopped running the place?"

"Four. The last one was just a hand, but he tried. Mostly he made mistakes and I wasn't much help to him."

"How many bookkeepers?"

"Three." She didn't need him to say more. "I know. I've got a problem. I have to take off work at the office to show them around, and then about the time they learn everything, they leave. I think someone is buying them away, offering more money. No matter what I do, I can't keep more than the cleaning staff and a handful of cowhands."

Cord swore he saw a tear slide over her cheek, and he had no doubt that she had tried. "I'll make mistakes too. Lots of them." He stared at the sky, giving her time to relax. She'd acted as if he might criticize her for not making a go of two businesses at once. "Can I count on you standing with me, right or wrong? I don't want men going around me and you changing things I'm setting up. If you don't like something I'm doing, I expect you to tell me first."

"You have my word." She climbed down and pulled a water bottle from her pack. "I love this place, but Dad never thought I needed to know ranch business. He didn't even like me showing up at the roundups. To him the ranch was my brothers', and the oil business was a place he'd let me work. It didn't matter that they all three hated it. When my two oldest brothers died, Dad just doubled his efforts to force Barrett to take over. I think Barrett left a week after the funeral, fearing that somehow the land might trap him even with Dad gone. He signed it over to me, and I gave him all cash on hand along with stock in the oil. Sometimes I think I paid too dearly for land I don't even know how to run. I sometimes think maybe the only reason I wanted it was because of my horses, and maybe because Dad didn't want me having any part of it."

"It's beautiful country," Cord said as he

swung out of the saddle and took the drink she offered. "You could show a good profit, and you're right—one good season is all you need to turn this place around."

"No. I can't. I've tried." She looked up at him. "But you can." She looked straight at him. "You should know there are those who do not wish you well."

He walked his horse closer to her and whispered, "What else is new?"

The wind blew a few strands of her hair from the clamp she'd twisted back as they mounted up.

"Bring it on," he smiled.

She smiled back at him. "Bring it on," she repeated as they kicked their mounts into action and rode straight into the wind.

Chapter 8

AN HOUR BEFORE MIDNIGHT
DUPLEX

WITHOUT A SINGLE WORD, RONNY LOGAN climbed into the black Lincoln and closed her eyes. This was her third ride on the interstates to Marty's hospital room. Each night she thought the car might not come for her, or Mr. Carleon might not meet her at the door. Marty might not still be alive.

She felt like a zombie, walking the waking world but not part of it. Each morning she'd manage to do her job and study. She could sleep in the back of the post office at noon instead of eating, but no matter how tired, she would be waiting in the dark. Each night she dressed in her best clothes and waited for the black car.

The second night she'd been awake enough to realize they were heading toward Oklahoma City, but mostly she slept in the car with its smooth music and warm blanket. Last night after she'd left without Marty waking yet again, she'd felt herself crying in her sleep, but it didn't matter. All that mattered was Marty and the tiny hope that she'd be there when he opened his eyes.

Tonight Mr. Carleon was there, his hand offering to help her from the car, his face blank of emotions. There was no time for greetings as he rushed her through the hallways and up the elevator.

"How is he?" she asked, not expecting Carleon to say anything.

"He's awake," Mr. Carleon whispered as he opened the hospital room door, "but I don't know for how long."

She moved to Marty's side, afraid to even breathe.

"Hello, beautiful," he said, in a low voice that wrapped her in love as it had once before.

"Hello." All the things she'd thought she would say to him vanished when she realized it was enough just to hear him.

"You wouldn't want to crawl up here and sleep with me, would you?" His voice was barely more than a whisper, but his hand gripped hers. "God, how I've missed you."

She glanced at Mr. Carleon standing in the shadows. He'd told her Marty was dying, not from the illness but from the cures they'd tried. Even the family composed of one brother and a handful of cousins had given up hope weeks ago. Now, his brother checked with the doctors a few times a day but didn't bother to visit a man sleeping away his last hours. Daniel had left orders to be notified if there was a change, and a few of the cousins still brought flowers but didn't stay.

Having her near had been his last wish, and Mr. Carleon was there to help. If nothing else, he'd block the door tonight.

The older man nodded slightly, and she carefully leaned down beside Marty and laid her hand gently over his heart. "I'll love you one heartbeat past forever," she whispered, and thought she saw him smile just before he drifted back into a drug-induced sleep.

After three nights of midnight rides, Ronny felt her body relax. She knew she was probably breaking every rule the hospital had, but she closed her eyes and took the ounce of happiness in her world without love. Her friends had told her to move on after Marty left, find someone else, but how could she settle? She'd rather hold on to a memory.

As machines ticked the minutes away, she let tears flow, wondering if every person just has so many they have to cry in a lifetime. If so, she must be near her quota. Once, Marty's hand touched her hair, moving through it slowly as if remembering every minute he'd touched her in those few months they'd known one another.

Mr. Carleon nudged her gently an hour later and woke her. "It's time to go, miss."

She nodded and moved slowly away as Marty remained sleeping. For the first time, on the way home, she didn't cry.

She slept and worked and ate . . . and waited for the night.

At eleven the next night the car ride

seemed endless, but when she walked into the room, Marty was waiting. His dark eyes slowly moved over her, and then he raised his hand. "You finally got here, honey. I've been waiting."

She sat on the edge of his bed, not knowing what to say and very much aware of Mr. Carleon listening.

Marty wove his fingers between hers. "Tell me about Harmony, beautiful. Tell me about your life. Tell me about your day and every day you've had since I walked out on you."

She could see pain in his dark eyes and wondered if he'd declined the pain meds so that he could be awake with her. If so, she needed to make their time count.

"I moved into your duplex after you left. It's still like what you described once, a cuddly dump." She had so many questions she wanted to ask, but she didn't know if he was up to answering. Did where he'd been really matter? He was here now. "I found the money you left with the cookbook and used it to enroll in online courses. I love the computer you sent. Every time I turn it on, I think of you."

Marty smiled. "I knew you'd need it."

"It's become my life. I carry a full load of classes online, and with each class I make friends going to school in their pajamas. Now I have friends all over the world."

"How's the post office?"

"The same. My route that started with your house and the fire department is the whole downtown square now. It takes me an hour to walk it after I've sorted all the incoming mail. I love walking it, watching the seasons change."

"Do you talk to the people now?" He studied her hand in his as he spoke.

"Some." She remembered how shy she'd been, thinking every stranger might be the one who would harm her. "There are a few that I'm just on nodding terms with."

One by one, Marty asked about all the people who had been in his world when he'd lived in Harmony. Summer, the friend of Ronny's who'd let her room with her when Ronny first left home. Tyler Wright, the funeral director who had always been kind to her. The Biggs brothers, who lived in the other half of the duplex, and Beau Yates, who'd moved in with them.

They were people from a sliver of his past, but she had the feeling he cared about each one. Until the accident he'd lived an exciting life: the best schools, the most thrilling vacations. Money had never been a problem. She knew he'd come to Harmony to hide out in his wheelchair, but somehow he'd found a peace there, and he'd found her.

When she paused, he gripped her hand tighter. "I always meant to come back to you, honey. I swear."

Ronny couldn't answer. She didn't know if he meant it or not. It didn't matter. She believed it, she always had.

"Tell me more," he whispered. "Hearing you makes me forget about the pain."

He fell asleep as she talked about learning to cook.

Mr. Carleon moved to her side. "It's time to go, miss."

She nodded. "I wish I could do something."

"You did, miss. You helped a great deal. You gave Mr. Winslow peace for an hour. You let him go back to Harmony to visit, something neither his brother nor the doctors thought would be wise."

Ronny looked up at the thin man. "Why'd you let me come here?"

"Because he never stops asking about you or for you. He's been all over the world seeing doctors. His brother persuaded him to concentrate on getting better. At first when he asked to see you and his few close friends, the caretakers put up roadblocks by promising only delays. It wasn't hard. He wanted to walk, and the thought of walking back to see you kept him going.

"By the time he realized Daniel wasn't going to allow him any visitors, his cell phone and computer were gone and a nurse guarded him all hours. He had no way to get to you. Two months ago, after yet another surgery, he was confined to bed, unable to manage even the wheel-chair. I watched him turn inward, not wanting the world to see him, but still he'd ask for me to check on you.

"Once we settled in here, Daniel didn't stay around much and the few cousins he never really talked to lost interest in doing their family duty. They had lives to get back to. Hour visits became five-minute drop-bys, and daily trips stretched into weekly stops."

"But you stayed?"

"I stayed. When he ran to Harmony two years ago, I thought his family was right—if I didn't go to help, he'd come back. But now I know I was wrong. If I had gone with him then, he might have made a life even in the chair and not had to go through all the cures that didn't work."

She looked around the room. "You live here, don't you?"

Mr. Carleon nodded. "I leave to sleep a few hours in the morning and shower, then I'm back. I won't leave him again. Even when the private nurses were hired, I remained."

Ronny raised an eyebrow. "The invisible private nurse?"

Carleon smiled. "With all the machines and nurses just down the hall, the private nurse saw no need to sleep in a chair. I played along with her conspiracy to slip away about midnight and sleep across the street in a hotel where I provided her a room. She's always back by five, and I've promised I'll be here with him and notify her of any change. On weekends I hired her friend under the same arrangements. Both know I'm near if there is any problem, but he sleeps through the night and most days away."

"Thank you," she said as he opened the back door of the hospital. "For being his friend."

Mr. Carleon nodded once. "I wish I'd known you, miss. I would have made the arrangements earlier, but I believed what the doctors and Daniel kept saying about distractions impeding his progress."

She had to ask. "Will you let me know if something happens? I don't think I could bear it if the car just didn't come one night and I never knew."

"I promise." His smile was sad as he closed the door and she stepped into the waiting Lincoln.

Chapter 9

MONDAY
BOXED B RANCH

BY THE THIRD NIGHT OF HIS MARRIAGE TO Nevada, Cord decided they'd developed a habit. He worked until he was dead tired. She fell asleep watching him. He carried her to bed. Then he lay three feet away from her and tried not to think about her or the way she smelled, or how she moved, or how the shadowy outline of her body curved beneath the covers. From the looks of things he would have to learn not to think at all if she was within fifty feet of him. He had a feeling if he complimented her she'd fly into that tornado he'd been expecting since they'd left the courthouse.

Nevada Britain wasn't like what he thought. She didn't seem as wild or crazy as people said. She just seemed lonely and, of course, spoiled. She was a hard worker, not much for talking unless he mentioned her horses, and cold in a way he never thought a woman who'd had lovers would ever be.

Near as he could tell Nevada didn't trust anyone, but for some reason she'd been forced into trusting him with her land. Other than that, she didn't even seem to like him most of the time or want him involved in her life. They talked about the ranch and nothing more. If he mentioned her family, she'd fire up and say she didn't want to talk about them, or her ex-husbands for that matter.

Like they had the first night, Sunday night they'd cooked a simple meal together, and then he'd eaten and she'd picked at her food. When she'd pulled on her riding boots, he'd followed. They'd saddled up and ridden under the evening sky, not getting back until full dark and not having said more than a dozen words to one another.

He helped her with her horse in the new barn for just her herd, and then they rode double over to the main barn, where she watched him take care of Devil. Without a word, he took her hand and they crossed the last forty feet to the back gate of the main house. He guessed they were both tired and maybe a little nervous, but he couldn't think of anything to say as he followed her into the house and back to their bedroom.

They'd settled into a few habits that he didn't mind at all. Neither made any pretense of not watching when the other dressed or undressed. She even rushed into his closet wearing only her underthings to lecture him about maybe burning the clothes he'd brought with him to the ranch. They finally agreed on his packing them in the old suitcase he'd brought and promising to try wearing only the clothes that she bought him. In truth, he'd gotten used to the luxury of well-fitting clothes.

Cord thought of telling her she should never argue with him wearing only a bra and panties, but then she might take his advice and he'd hate that. He fell asleep each night planning what he'd do tomorrow and wishing that he could touch her.

When he woke Monday, she was already in the shower in her bathroom. It seemed strange for a room to have two complete bathrooms, but he'd figured out two days ago that the whole place had been designed by idiots. Half the windows didn't open. Most of the rooms had no use, and if the huge fireplace in the living room was ever lit it would warm all the ranch and half of western Oklahoma.

She came out of the bathroom with a thin robe plastered around her damp body. "I'll be ready in ten for the breakfast with the boys, but I can predict they won't be happy to see us. As far as I know, a Britain has never eaten with them."

"I'm not a Britain."

She frowned as if she wished she'd thought to add that into the contract. "They just won't like it." She lifted her arms to pull off the towel covering her hair. Her short robe moved up a few inches.

"Not my problem," he managed to mumble before stepping into his bathroom, all of his body now fully awake.

After a quick shower, Cord pulled another one of his new shirts from the rack and decided to try a pair of jeans that she'd picked out for him. He wanted to look like he knew what he was doing this morning when he faced the men for the first time. The jeans fit snugger than he usually wore, with a boot cut on the cuffs that was just right.

When he walked past the mirror to grab his hat, Cord noticed his reflection. A rancher, not a farmer, looked back. In this case, he hoped clothes made the man if he was to have any chance at pulling this charade off.

Nevada was waiting for him at the door. To his surprise, she wore a business suit. Her beautiful blond hair, which he'd gotten used to watching sway over the weekend, was now tied atop her head in a little knot that he hated. Everything about her was all business.

"I'll drive you over and introduce you to the men, then I have to get to the office." Nevada straightened her jacket. "I have a board meeting at nine and I need to go over a few things at the office first with my staff."

"You work all day?" Somehow he thought she mostly shopped and had lunch.

"Eight to five, sometimes later." She shrugged. "Between husbands I managed to get a business degree with a minor in law. Never finished in law, but it comes in handy in dealing with contracts and leases."

He didn't miss the sadness in her blue eyes when she added, "I love being here with my horses, but I understand oil." She handed him a small cell phone. "If you need me, just hold down two and I'll answer. I'm the only one who has your number, so unless you give it to someone else, it'll be me calling if the phone rings."

"Fair enough."

The smile on her now-painted lips didn't reach her eyes. "You ready to go face the world as husband and wife? When we step out of this door we've got to make them believe it, and with my record with men it won't be easy. Remember, no one is to know of our agreement. As far as anyone knows, including the staff and ranch hands, we married for love and you're here to stay."

He thought about yelling, *No way can we pull this off*, but something in her stare stopped him. She was silently pleading, begging him to go along with her plan, and he couldn't let her down. He had no idea why it was so important to her, but he'd keep his word. A bargain was a bargain. Until now he'd thought running the ranch was the most important part of the bargain, but now he realized that to her, their playing the happily married couple might be.

Taking her hand, he walked her to her car and they drove to a long bunkhouse a few hundred yards away from the main house. The ranch headquarters was built like a small town with the big house in the center. Trails, two tracks wide, joined most of the buildings like wagon spokes, and he noticed a few four-wheelers around that were probably used to haul goods from one building to another.

Beyond the bunkhouse was a small gravel lot that had been empty when they'd ridden by yesterday but now held several cars and trucks. Nevada had already explained that all but a few cowhands drove into work every morning. The rest went home on weekends but stayed over during the week. Her housekeeper and the bunkhouse cook had a small cabin on the property but spent their weekends at a lake cabin over near Twisted Creek.

Three men stood on the porch watching as Cord and Nevada walked up to the bunkhouse that looked big enough to be a small hotel. One tipped his hat slightly; the other two just stared. None spoke.

Cord tensed, realizing they might not know him, but they had no respect for Nevada. He knew without hearing that these men had talked about her, probably even joked about her behind her back. One of the silent men looked at her with hunger in his eyes as if she were not the boss but a streetwalker passing by.

Cord opened the door for her and waited until she stepped in. When he followed he took in the room slowly.

A dozen more ranch hands were in a great room with a long table that could easily seat thirty on one side of the room and comfortable leather chairs on the other. A middle-aged man with an apron stepped from the kitchen and smiled at Nevada. His was the only smile in the room.

"Morning, Little Miss," the cook said.

"Morning, Galem. I'd like you to meet my

new husband." She brushed Cord's arm, showing the first affection she'd ever shown. Her sudden caress made him jerk slightly. "Honey." She leaned into him slightly. "This is the bunkhouse cook and a friend. He's been with the ranch for twenty-three years."

Galem wiped his hand on his apron and offered it to Cord. "Nice to meet you, Mr. McDowell. I heard you were coming. My youngest daughter works at the court-house and said Nevada married Friday."

Galem might be thin and balding, but his smile was warm and a kind of friendly Cord had rarely seen. Open. Trusting. Ac-cepting.

Cord managed a nod as he sized up all that Galem hadn't said. He hadn't men-tioned that she'd married for the fourth time, even though he must have known. He also hadn't told the others, for several in the room coughed. And last, he hadn't lied about hearing about the wedding.

"Galem, if you'll call the others, I'd like to hold a meeting over coffee this morning." Cord moved into his planned speech. "It will only take a few minutes and then the men can ask any questions while we eat.

I'll be here for breakfast every morning at dawn, and any man who is tired of working for the Boxed B won't need to join us. Any man coming in after breakfast has missed a day's work."

Galem smiled. He didn't need to call anyone; the men scattered in every direction. Some ran to get the others; some took their seats at the table. Change was on the wind and they all knew it.

"You like it black, Mr. McDowell?" Galem guessed.

"I do, and call me Cord. We've got a long day and no time for extra words."

Galem nodded once at Cord, but Cord didn't miss the wink he gave Nevada. To his surprise he felt a bit jealous, especially when she winked back.

She'd just flirted with the cook more than she'd flirted with him all weekend.

Putting his arm around his wife, Cord turned her toward the door. "I can handle it from here, Nevada. You probably need to get on to the office."

She agreed, and by the speed of her walk, he guessed she wasn't comfortable among the men filling the room. Not one man said a word to her, and she called none by name.

As soon as they were out of anyone's hearing, she whispered, "Galem likes you. Can you believe it? He likes you. I can tell."

"Stop winking at the cook," Cord ordered, but she wasn't listening.

"He never liked any of the others. Wouldn't even speak to my first husband. Spilled boiling coffee on the second, and the third was afraid to go out to the bunkhouse when my brother told him that number two had his privates so scalded he was in constant pain for a week. You'd think Bryce would have known better than to believe my brother; they'd roomed together in college."

"You care about what the cook thinks, Nevada?" Cord's brain was still focusing on the wink.

"Of course. When I was little and he started working here, he was my guardian angel. More than once he stopped my brothers from picking on me. A few years ago he married Ora Mae, and she took over managing the house. He adopted her three daughters, but you'd never know they weren't his blood from the way he brags about them. I've always thought Galem and Ora Mae made a cute couple. You'd think they were in their twenties and not their forties."

Cord relaxed as he opened her car door.

She stood next to him. "I think we fooled even Galem. He seemed to really believe we were a couple. He won't inform on any ranch hand, but he won't lie for them either. If he thinks we're real, so will the others."

"Then this should help seal the deal," Cord said as he put his hands on Nevada's waist and pulled her to him.

Before he could change his mind, he kissed her full on the mouth. She hesitated, trying to pull away for only a few seconds before she seemed to understand. To his surprise, she wrapped her arms around his neck and kissed him back.

He lifted her off the ground as he straightened, letting her body mold along his. The taste of her, the feel of her, the hint of apricots from her shampoo almost buckled his knees.

When she pulled away, she touched his jaw. "That should do it. Thank you for thinking of it."

"You're welcome," he whispered against her cheek.

He lowered her back to the ground and she added, as cold and formal as if the kiss hadn't just happened, "Don't wait up for me. I may not be home until late."

Cord watched her drive away, thinking about how kissing her for real had felt so much better than he'd thought it would. He figured he'd shock her if she knew that when he dreamed of loving, he dreamed of her. He'd even hung the clipping of her riding in a parade on his cell wall once. She'd fascinated him with what his life might have been like if they'd gone on that date ten years ago.

The clipping had lasted only a few months before his cellmate tore it down and told him to stay in the real world for a change. The picture and the dreams had lasted about as long as this marriage probably would, but while it lasted he could feel like, for once, he didn't need to dream.

He walked back to the bunkhouse knowing everyone inside was staring at him.

When he took the seat at the head of the table, Galem came from the kitchen with a steaming cup of coffee. Cord watched as the cook set the cup down carefully in front of him.

"Thanks," Cord said to the cook as the last of the cowhands took their places.

While Galem served coffee, Cord started, "I've studied the books. No one here has had a raise in two years. That ends today. Next, we work with the sun, not on the clock, and every man stops at six unless I've asked for overtime. We'll run a five-man crew on weekends from now on, and any who want to work then will draw time and a half. When it's cold we'll start later, and we'll end earlier when the weather turns bad, but you'll still draw the same pay. Fair enough?"

No one said a word. A few looked shocked, but most looked like they were calculating next month's paycheck. Cord knew that raising wages on a failing ranch was risky, but these men would bring the place back to life.

"I want to talk to each one of you and see what you like doing best, but understand, until we get this ranch in working order, we all do what needs to be done. If you can't do a job, let me know when it's assigned, not when you fail."

"I count twenty men. We'll need forty, so if you know someone who's honest and wants work, bring him to breakfast tomorrow. If I hire him, he needs to be ready to work. If not, he'll have had a meal for his trouble."

As he talked, Galem put food on the table. By the time they began eating, four men had walked out and the others were asking questions and making suggestions. Most, he figured, were hands who had been around for at least a few years and were happy to have someone finally ask for their opinion on the running of the ranch. By nine, Cord was in the saddle and working. Everything had to be ready to get crops in the ground and cattle in the pastures as fast as possible.

About two the phone in his pocket sounded. Cord walked away from the corral so he could hear Nevada. It seemed like days since he'd seen her, not hours.

"How are things going?" she asked. "This is the first break I've had."

"Fine," he answered, surprised at how

fast the morning had gone. "Four men quit. I fired three others." The man who'd glared at her had been one Cord let go. "We're trying to get ready to move what cattle you have left to the north pasture. I'm planning to buy at least a hundred new head tomorrow. The auction is in the morning, and Tannon Parker says he can have any cattle I buy delivered before dark. I've got a crew mending fences now."

"Not the ranch, Cord, how are you doing?"

"I'm good." He thought about saying that he was great. Inside he felt like he was walking in boots that didn't quite fit, but he was giving being boss his best try. One of the men he'd fired had cussed him out, calling him nothing but a con. Normally he would have gotten mad, but Cord knew it was coming. He'd planned what he'd say and how he'd walk away. He had a ranch to run and didn't have time to talk about the past.

"I hired three brothers who rodeo on weekends. They may cut out on me early on Fridays, but they know cattle. Galem calls them the presidents since they're named Johnson, Jefferson, and Jackson."

"Oh," she said, sounding as if she were only half interested. He could hear papers shuffling in the background.

All he could think to say to her now was, "Did you eat lunch?"

"I rarely eat lunch at work. I live on coffee."

He growled like a bear, and she laughed.

"Everyone cooperating?" She changed the subject.

"Everyone except Ora Mae. I went in about an hour ago to grab something for lunch and she ran me out with the broom. Said if I wanted a noon meal she'd serve me on the porch. I told her I didn't have time to sit down, so she threw a couple of apples at me and told me she'd have supper ready at six after I cleaned up. Now I know why you got that room off the back of the kitchen. Your housekeeper won't let anyone in who smells like a cow or is dripping dirt."

"She likes you too." Nevada laughed through the phone. "If she didn't, she wouldn't have tossed apples."

"I don't think so. I'm thinking lunch around this place may be hazardous to my health."

"Of course she does. She threw skillets

at my last husband. When he told her he only wanted green for lunch, she mowed the yard and served it up."

"I like her better now." In truth, he liked that Nevada was talking to him about her past. "I'll give Ora Mae another chance, but it'll be from a distance." He hung up and walked back to the corral. As soon as he got more men hired, he'd move a few to his land and get a crop in the ground. The cowhands had been cold at first, but as the day aged and they saw that he had a plan, they chipped in to help. Some of them even took up a challenge to keep up with him and work as hard as he did.

When he walked past the bunkhouse a little before six, a lanky stranger stepped off the porch. His legs were slightly bowed and he wore his hat low. Cord decided he could have stepped out of the past, a cowboy from a hundred years ago just getting in from a trail drive. The sound of his spurs clinking reached Cord, and he stopped and waited to see if the man was flesh and blood.

"I'm Zeb Darnell." The stranger offered his hand, rough with calluses and scars.

"Galem called me and said I might want to work for the new boss on the Boxed B. Said you had plans and might could use a cowhand."

Cord nodded and shook hands. "I told men applying to come to breakfast."

"I know, but I've worked here before. I'm a good hand, but I was no foreman. Nevada's last husband fired me 'cause I couldn't read the notes he kept leaving me when I took over the job."

Cord waited, giving the man rope.

"I understand you're buying cattle tomorrow. That's why I came tonight. I've been working at the stockyard, but I'd like to hire on here. I think I could be some help at the auction tomorrow. If you're interested in me working, I'd need to quit there and be started here before the show opens. I know cattle, Mr. McDowell, and I can help you with the buy."

Cord realized he'd learned a great deal about reading men in prison. If Zeb was lying, he was far better at it than any man Cord had come across. Also, he wasn't the type to brag. If he said he knew cattle, he probably did. "I'll see you at the stockyards tomorrow. You're hired."

"I'll go there early to quit." Zeb smiled. "I'll have the stock checked before you get there."

"Fair enough. You're working for the Boxed B now, and I'd like to pick up a hundred head tomorrow. You think we can manage that?"

Zeb tipped his hat. "Yes, sir. Thanks, Mr. McDowell, you won't be sorry."

"Call me Cord, and I'm the one who needs to thank you for coming out tonight. Once we're finished with the buy, we'll eat lunch and wait for the trucks. I'd like you riding back in the trucks with the cattle. You'll know where to tell the drivers to unload if you worked here before."

"I was planning on riding back. I brought my horse here tonight just in case I got the job." He touched his hat. "See you tomorrow."

The man walked toward the parking area at the side of the bunkhouse as Galem stepped onto the porch.

Cord waited until Zeb's old pickup pulled away before he said, "You being my guardian angel, Galem?"

The cook smiled. "Maybe. That cowhand knows cattle better than any man I've ever seen. He's honest too, but he won't work for a fool like Bryce Galloway, who only wanted to play at ranching. When Nevada married Bryce, I knew Zeb wouldn't hang around long, and he didn't."

"He can't read." Cord's words were a statement, not a question.

"No," Galem answered, "but the cows don't notice."

Cord laughed. "Thanks. He'll be a big help walking me through the sale tomorrow. I'm pretty green."

"He needs a job on land, not in feedlots, and he'll help you build the herd. I think he was nervous coming out, being fired once from this place."

"Tell the men that they all start fresh with me when they hire on. No past hanging on."

Galem nodded. "No past," he echoed.

Cord turned toward the house, knowing Nevada had been right about Galem. The cook had just filled a weak spot Cord had been worried about. He knew farming and land, but he didn't know enough about cattle. Zeb wouldn't need to read, just point at what to buy to build the best herd that had ever roamed the ranch.

After a few steps, he stopped and looked

back at Galem. "Any chance you know a bookkeeper?"

"Nope, but you might ask around."

Cord almost laughed out loud. He didn't have anyone he knew to ask. If he asked anyone in town they'd probably have him arrested for speaking to them.

After a shower and a shave, he walked into the dining room in clean clothes. The table was set for one. Ora Mae had left a note. *Little Miss's food is in warmer. She said to tell you to go ahead and eat, she won't be in until late.*

He read the note twice, noticing Ora Mae had used the same nickname as Galem had for Nevada. He figured he'd have to hang around a lot longer than eight months before she'd let him use one, if ever.

Cord took his plate to the study and looked over past cattle buys. Every bone in his body hurt from work. He'd pushed the men, but he'd pushed himself twice as hard. At ten he could keep his eyes open no longer. He stripped down to his underwear and crawled into his side of the bed. He was asleep before his head hit the pillow.

Deep into the night he felt the bed shift

and knew Nevada had climbed in on her side. She might run around half the night, but she'd kept her word. She'd come home to sleep in his bed.

Chapter 10

MARCH 14
WINTER'S INN BED-AND-BREAKFAST

MARTHA Q PATTERSON WAS EXHAUSTED. WHEN the funeral director's little talk with Joni Rosen didn't seem to work, Martha Q knew she had to think of another plan for emptying her house of widows. She liked the idea of being an innkeeper. It somehow sounded romantic when she started, but since then she'd heard that the two happiest days of an innkeeper's life are the day he opens his doors to the public and the day he closes them.

She needed rest, not more work, but the three widows showed no sign of leaving.

Even worse than having to get dressed and put on her face each day was the problem of writer's block. They were slowing down her great career as the next top writer of sexy, intriguing, apocalyptic murder mysteries. She'd decided from the first to write a book with everything in it. Masochistic shape shifters who time-traveled into Rome as it fell. They ran around producing zombies in togas while they became wine experts. Her book would hit the best seller lists, she was sure of it.

Martha Q thumped her own forehead. She was getting off track again. She needed to plan.

Maybe ants or termites. The widows would hate that.

Red ants would send the ladies running. Or bedbugs. People hated bedbugs, thanks to the idiot who'd blown them up to puppy size and put them on the Internet. If the bugs had just been butterfly cute, no one would have minded. They'd just toss back the covers and smile as feathery bedbugs flew by.

Off track again.

Martha Q considered hiring a prowler, or a Peeping Tom. She grinned. That would make an interesting story if a Peeping Tom fell in love with an exhibitionist. They'd be neighbors. He'd wear out the grass between their houses and she'd save enough money on window blinds to replant. Every night, no matter the weather, he'd pull on his coat and stand in the flower beds until she turned out the lights after blinking three times, their secret code for *I love you.*

"Off track again," she mumbled as she reached for her bowl of chocolate-covered peanuts.

Half a bowl later she realized every single plan she came up with to send the widows away would also hurt her business. She liked people, with their secrets and stories, coming into her home, making her feel as if she had a big family and wasn't alone.

But she also admitted she was a fair-weather liker of people. It was grand when they came on weekends or even odd days of the week. It was the every-day thing that bothered her. She needed a vacation. Maybe she'd drive up to Kansas and stay at someone else's bed-and-breakfast.

The doorbell pulled her out of her worrying and away from the now-empty candy bowl.

"Darlene," she yelled up the stairs where she thought the newest housekeeper might be. "Stop eating my candy."

"Yes, ma'am. I'll be down in a minute to fill it back up."

"Thank you," Martha Q said over her shoulder as she rushed to the door. One of the widows probably forgot her key, or maybe a few of the half dozen things she'd ordered from the shopping channel had arrived. Every time she couldn't sleep it cost her twenty-nine ninety-five plus shipping. The cleaning products, Christmas lights, and one-size-fits-all cuddle pillows never looked the same in daylight as they had at two in the morning, but the anticipation kept her hoping.

She pulled open the heavily carved door as she plastered on her best smile.

The nice-looking man on her porch didn't appear as if he came as part of any midnight deal. Tall, well built, thirty-five maybe.

"Yes?" Martha Q straightened to her proprietor pose. "May I help you?"

He ducked his head slightly as he faced

her; a smile sparkled in bedroom eyes. "I'm sorry I didn't call ahead, Mrs. Patterson, but I hoped you might have a room for a weary traveler. I'm here on business for a few days. I was told this was the best place in town, though I never had a chance to visit during the short time I lived here a few years ago."

After seven husbands, Martha Q had learned to mistrust flattery, but the sound of his whiskey-smooth voice made her wish she hadn't given up drinking. "We do have a room, but I'm afraid it's on the third floor."

"I could use the exercise." He smiled again, and she thought he might be an actor playing a part. She knew she could read people, even if she sometimes read them wrong. That didn't change the fact that she could usually read them, and this one seemed to be printed in smaller type than normal. Like the last crossword puzzle in the book, he wouldn't be easy to figure out.

Maybe he was a famous actor; after all, if he hadn't appeared on *Gunsmoke*, she probably wouldn't have seen him. Maybe he was here scoping out sites for a new series or a reality show based on innkeepers.

Martha Q rattled her head, hoping to shake a few brain cells awake. This guy had *never worked a day in his life* written all over him. "I'll show you the room. Mr.—"

"No need to look it over. I'll take it," he answered, a bit too fast.

She noticed his leather hand-tooled bag already at his feet. Cocky, she decided, like her first boyfriend, who'd always carried three condoms in his pocket. But this one was much better-looking than any guy she'd ever dated, and he was dressed like he had his clothes made just for him. "Come on in, Mr. . . ." She tried again for the name.

"Bryce." He smiled with his too-perfect teeth. "Bryce Galloway."

"Any chance you play loud music and stay up all night smoking and swearing?"

"No. I'm pretty quiet."

Martha Q sighed. "I was afraid of that. I take two nights in advance. Every third night is free and breakfast is at eight thirty." She opened the door wider and invited him in, having no faith that he'd have any effect on the widows. He was too young and too smooth for them to give him a second look. Widows like a man who's lived long enough to have a few bad habits and rough corners they can work on. The first husband might be married for love or even lust, but the second one was usually a fixer-upper.

The good news was that now the inn had only one room left vacant. The bad news, she'd be the first woman in history to scrub her nose off trying to get her makeup removed every night.

Bryce Galloway might be easy on the eyes, but having another guest would simply mean more work.

When she walked into the kitchen to tell her cook that there would be another mouth to feed for breakfast, Martha Q was surprised to see Mrs. Biggs's grandson Border sitting at the kitchen table.

"Is it Sunday night already?" Martha Q said, as if she were really asking a question.

Border, unlike his friend Beau Yates, never knew how to take her. "No, Mrs. Patterson, it's only Wednesday. I just came over to say hello to my grandmother."

Martha Q frowned. The idiot thought she was senile. *This day was going downhill. A change of subject was needed.*

She sat down and cut herself a slice of

the pie Border had already had half of. "Border, did you know that I was thinking about becoming a great writer?"

"No, Mrs. Patterson. That's really something. I've never known a writer before. What are you working on?"

Martha Q hated questions about her work. "Well, I haven't worked much yet. First comes the thinking."

"Of course." Border actually looked interested. "That's the part I would have trouble with."

"I have no doubt, but you know Beau and he writes songs. How does he get his inspiration?"

Border shrugged. "He says sometimes he feels like they're already in his head and he's just fighting to get them out. Like the other day I asked him about this girl who sometimes picks him up after work, and he said she'd been on the back roads of his mind. I found out later that them words were in an old song. I swear, he don't just write songs, he talks them too."

Martha Q knew she would get little help from Border. She finished off her slice of pie. "Mrs. Biggs," she said to the cook.

"Have you got an extra pie to send the boys? Maybe it'd help Beau write."

"I'll do that." Mrs. Biggs smiled at her tattooed, two-hundred-pound, shaved-headed grandson like he was adorable.

Martha Q decided the pair were proof that love is blind, and with that thought came an idea for a story about a beauty who fell in love with an ugly beast of a man.

She made the mistake of telling Border her idea, and he said he loved that movie even if it was a cartoon.

Martha Q marched off, frustrated that a storyteller had stolen her great idea before she could even get it down on paper.

Chapter 11

MARCH 15

THE LINCOLN HADN'T SHOWN UP IN FRONT OF the duplex on Monday night, but Ronny trusted Mr. Carleon. On Tuesday when it came, she saw that Marty was still alive but too weak to wake. On Wednesday, he talked a few moments then drifted off. By Thursday, she wasn't sure she'd find him alive. The week had been a roller coaster with little sleep. Even Cord McDowell told her she looked pale when he came in to mail Boxed B letters.

She sometimes wondered if Cord had

guessed she was the one who made sure he got a newspaper mailed to him in prison after his folks died. She couldn't think of another reason for him to make a point of speaking to her when he came in while he ignored everyone else. They were two usually invisible people who saw each other.

With the days at work and the nights at the hospital, Ronny realized she was wearing down, but she couldn't stop. When someone is in the hospital, everyone around them dies a little. Each night she saw Marty, she felt his pain as she watched his life slipping away.

The newest rumor Ronny's mother had started was that Ronny's living alone, when everyone knows a girl should live with her mother until marriage no matter how late in life, had led to an unwanted pregnancy. Dallas Logan had a hard time pulling off the rumor because Ronny looked like she was losing weight, not gaining. Plus folks talked to Dallas Logan only long enough to plot their escape.

Ronny no longer worried what her mother told people. She'd said she never wanted to speak to Ronny again, and Ronny planned to do her best to honor that request. Dallas Logan didn't miss having a daughter; she simply missed having someone to control and lecture. Marty had given Ronny the strength to walk away from her mother two years ago, and she'd silently thanked him every day. He'd pulled her out of hell, and even if she hadn't fallen in love with him, she still owed him.

When the black Lincoln arrived an hour before midnight on Thursday, Ronny let out a long breath she hadn't realized she'd been holding and walked to the open door, letting all her worries and problems slip away. Seeing Marty was all that mattered.

Mr. Carleon met her at the back door of the hospital, his face as stony as always.

"How is he?" She braced herself for bad news.

"He's awake but in pain," Mr. Carleon whispered as he moved down the back hallways with her, almost running to keep up.

Ronny felt both happy and sad. She knew Marty had skipped some of his medicine so he could see her. Being awake meant pain.

She almost ran into his room but took a

moment to calm, preparing herself for whatever might happen. Reason told her that one night he'd be gone, but reason didn't reach her heart.

When she entered, three men blocked her path to Marty's bed. They were all three tall and lean like runners. One, the oldest at about forty, wore khakis and a bomber jacket. Another, maybe five years younger, was dressed like a hunter, and the third seemed just as comfortable as the others in his suit.

All three stood shoulder to shoulder in front of Marty's bed. They'd been waiting for her, for they showed no surprise. The urge to run washed over her, but she stood her ground. If they wanted her out of the room, they'd have to use force.

"You Ronny Logan?" the one in the suit asked, as if he were quizzing a witness.

"Yes," she answered.

The man who looked like a bush pilot took a step toward her. His eyes were steel and his face weathered past his years. "You sure she can handle this, Marty? The little lady looks like a frightened mouse."

The suit raised an eyebrow. "I don't know

about this one, Marty. She looks like she'd break under pressure. You need a bull-dog, partner."

Ronny had had enough. She might not be brave enough to talk to them, but she could try pushing through the line.

Bumping the suit's shoulder and the hunter's arm, she darted between them and rushed to the bed. Marty's smile was all she needed to calm.

His fingers closed over her hand as he said, "She can handle whatever comes along. She made it through you three clowns, didn't she?"

Ronny could see the pain in his eyes, but Marty smiled at her. "Honey, these are my three best friends. They were with me when I tumbled off the mountain. The one in the jacket is Ross. He thinks he's the best pilot ever born. Ivan may look dumb in that suit, but he's the best lawyer Austin has to offer. And last is Glen. He's half mountain man, but he did manage to make it through med school even after I dropped out and stopped helping him, so we call him Doc. They said they'd come if I ever needed them, so I called."

"We're here to try and talk Marty out of

his craziest idea yet." Doc's voice was low and flavored from the deep South.

"What's that?" Ronny squeezed Marty's hand, letting him know she was on his side no matter what the idea.

Ivan, the lawyer, took over. "He says he wants to go home with you, if you'll have him. Wants to set up housekeeping in Nowhere, Texas."

Ronny couldn't speak. She just stared at the three men.

Doc took over again. "He's rallied the past few days since I've seen him. I'll give you credit for that. And, considering his condition, if the move doesn't kill him, then his chances aren't that much different here or in Harmony. If he dies, he'll die where he wants to be. While he's living, he'll be with you."

"Right. You might want to think about this and join our side of the debate." Ivan tugged off his suit jacket and stared at Ronny as if he thought she might not be stable. "If he lives longer than expected, you'll be stuck with him, Miss Logan. Our Marty's not an easy man to live with when he's healthy, and when he's in pain, he's the devil. We should know. We carried him off the mountain after he broke his back. More than once we considered knocking him out with a right cross. If he wasn't cussing, he was giving directions and pushing all of us."

They all three agreed. The doctor picked up the debate. "He'll need home nursing, round the clock, and machines. More as time goes on and his body begins to shut down. Near as I can tell, all the hospital is doing right now is trying to make his last days as painless as possible. It looks like the doctors and his brother are just waiting."

"Have you given up on him?" she whispered, knowing that Marty was hearing every word even though he'd closed his eyes.

"No, Miss Logan, we didn't give up on him on the mountain. It took us three days to get down to him and dig him out, then we lashed our skis together and carried him out. We know Marty like no one else knows him. He's a fighter. This move may shorten his life, but he's willing to take that chance. At the worst, it'll make his last few days happier being with you. At the best, it might add some time, but you got to understand from the first, we're counting time in days, not weeks."

"Don't listen to him, honey," Marty whispered. "He's an OB and pediatrician in a little town that makes Harmony look like the big city. Bottom of his class. I'm betting he's wrong."

Doc laughed. "I just might be wrong and I wouldn't have been at the bottom, Marty, if you'd stayed in school. But I'm a realist and don't believe in lying to a patient or a friend."

Marty squeezed her hand. "I'm down, Ronny, but not for the count. Not yet. If Doc's right and I only have a few days, I want to spend it in Harmony with you. But I want to be straight with you from the first. I knew these guys would make sure you understood before you said yes."

Everyone was silent for a moment as Ronny leaned over Marty. Her kiss on his cheek was all the answer they seemed to be waiting for.

Ivan pulled a paper from his briefcase. "When he stopped e-mailing us last year, the three of us stayed in touch with Marty through Mr. Carleon. I believe we've figured out how to make this all happen if it's what he, and you, Miss Logan, really want. The discussion stops here if you're not

willing to sign these papers." He straightened. "And as your lawyer, almost, I'd suggest you do not sign. If Marty's brother
gets mad and finds a way to cut him off,
you could end up going bankrupt trying to
care for him. You wouldn't be able to work."

"I've got enough money of my own to
ride this out," Marty whispered between
clenched teeth.

Ronny thought about it. The only thing
she had of value was half of the house her
mother lived in. She'd gladly sell it to stay
home and care for Marty. "Where do I
sign?" She grinned.

"You'll want to take a few days to think
about it," Doc added in his slow southern
tone. "You'd be taking over legal and medical power of attorney for him. We'll help
all we can, but I know his brother. Daniel
Winslow won't make it easy on you."

She looked at the three men. They were
Marty's true friends. At one time he would
have stood equal in strength to them. All
three looked like they had doubts about
Marty's plan.

"What do you think, Ross?" she asked
the man in the leather jacket. His arms

were crossed and he'd been frowning the whole time the other two had talked.

"I think I'd rather live a day near someone I love than a lifetime without them. You're going to be taking on hard times, girl, but you got to ask yourself how hard it'll be to walk away."

Ronny could have kissed the pilot right there in front of everyone. He'd turned the problem around. It wasn't Marty's choice or even just what Marty wanted. It was her decision. Her choice. Her life.

Marty didn't seem to be listening. He'd drifted into the twilight between pain and reality, but his hand still held hers.

"I'll sign the papers." There was no pull to walk away. One day, one week, one month, she'd take it. "When can I take him home?"

Ross smiled. "Saturday morning. Doc and I will start for Harmony before dawn by plane. We'll have a day to make arrangements to get all the right equipment installed and a nurse on call at all hours. He'll also meet with a local doctor and fill him in on Marty's condition. If you'll hand us your keys tomorrow, we'll have everything set up by the time the ambulance brings him to your place. Marty told us once that the place is not big. We'll knock out walls if we have to, but we'll have it ready."

Ronny tightened her grip on Marty's hand. "Is this what you really want, to go back to Harmony?"

His answer came in a slight nod and a whisper: "In a perfect world, I'd come home to you."

"Where do I sign?" she said again. She was no child. She knew what she'd be getting into. A battle to keep him alive. A possible battle with his brother. It wouldn't be easy, but she had friends who'd help her.

As she moved through the papers, she planned. "I'll go to work tomorrow and ask for a vacation. I've got enough days not to have to worry about working for a while. I'll move all the furniture into the bedroom and kitchen. You can put his bed and the machines in the living area."

The three men nodded as if they'd already talked everything out with Marty.

When Mr. Carleon walked her to the waiting Lincoln, he said simply, "If you want to come back tomorrow night, miss, you can ride down with Marty in the private ambulance. Ivan and a medic will be with you and I'll follow in a van with his personal items. We'll have you both back in Harmony by one. I'll stay with you until you feel comfortable and the nurse is satisfactory, but I'd like to get a room nearby. Then I can sit with him some and run errands for you both to make this time easier. Do you have a suggestion where I can stay?"

Ronny couldn't stop smiling. After all he'd done, he was talking as if they were simply planning to visit. "There's a bed-and-breakfast close. In fact, Martha Q Patterson owns the duplex I rent. I'm sure she'll have a room."

He nodded as he opened the back door for her. "I'll be in touch with her about the lodging. Try to get some sleep. I'll send the car tomorrow night."

"I'll be waiting. I'd like to ride down with him."

Ronny turned toward Carleon as she stepped out into the night air. "So, you come with this bargain?"

"I'm afraid so." He bowed slightly like the butler he probably had been. "I promise no inconvenience on your part. I hope to be of service."

She leaned over and kissed his cheek. "Thanks. I'm sure you will be a great help."

He took the kiss with a slight nod and opened her car door. "Until tomorrow," he said as she slid into the Lincoln.

This time she sat in the dark backseat and cried with joy and fear and hope as the Lincoln pulled away from the hospital.

Marty Winslow was coming back to Harmony.

Chapter 12

FOR THE FOURTH DAY IN A ROW NEVADA WOKE with her husband already gone. They were passing in the night, and that deep pit of loneliness she sometimes felt seemed to be settling in again.

She told herself he had the ranch and she had her work. That was the way she'd wanted it from the beginning. He was only following the rules of the bargain. Each called the other a few times a day, but the conversations were short and usually formal, since others were in her office or he had men working nearby. No unnecessary words, never any endearments.

Unbelievably, Nevada could already see changes in the ranch. He'd hired a dozen more men and an independent contractor to repair roads crossing the Boxed B land. Trucks and tractors were on the farm roads now, and more horses were in the main barn. Cattle roamed land she hadn't seen grazed in years. She'd told him every day to remind the new guys to stay away from her horses. Her mares had their own stable and pastures. She'd handpicked the trainer who drove out from town to work with them every morning. Her one rule was that no one else was ever to go near her horses. Her very sanity depended on it, she sometimes thought.

She wished she could be home to watch over things, but she was needed in the office. Lawsuits were still coming in claiming her father had promised something he hadn't delivered, or he'd forgotten to pay a bill near the end of his days, but that was not Cord's problem. It was all hers.

Bryce Galloway had also contacted her, reminding her that he'd be happy to take the ranch off her hands at a rock-bottom price. He could afford to pay more, but he wanted to humiliate her. He thought of her as weak. When he'd left her before her father died and her brother ran, he'd thought she would crumble and come begging to him for help, but instead she'd served him with divorce papers. The divorce was final before she'd inherited the land.

Bryce knew she loved the ranch, and he wanted to hurt her by taking it from her. Almost from the first she'd known that Bryce wanted her, not to love, but to control. Even after two years he still thought she was his to play with and taunt for fun.

None of this was Cord's problem. She wanted to keep it from him mainly because if he knew she'd married a man like Bryce, he'd think her a spoiled fool who only saw the Galloway money. The reason was far darker. She'd married Bryce and put up with him for months, not out of a need for money, or even love, but simply because she thought she didn't deserve anything better. He'd reminded her every day he'd lived on the ranch that a tramp like her was lucky he married her. He was good-looking, rich, from a powerful family, and she was simply his.

Nevada had worked hard to prove him wrong. She was worth more, she told herself. She deserved better.

The first Monday after she'd married Cord, she'd made up an explanation as to why she was often late getting home, but Cord had never asked. When she left in the morning she sometimes saw him from a distance, but he was never close enough to speak to. He never kissed her again. She didn't know whether to be happy or sad about it. She only knew that to protect herself she needed to stay away, not just from Cord, but from all men.

As the days passed, one fact became more and more evident. He hadn't let her down. Cord was holding up his half of the bargain. She only prayed he would continue to do so if trouble stormed. She could feel problems mounting at the office; she just couldn't gauge where they might spill over next and who among her staff of thirty might be feeding the fire. Bryce's lawyers seemed to know where her business was weakest and kept striking with offers to buy or rumors of poor management of her business.

Right now her ex-husband was playing

with her like she was no more than a mouse and he was a cat that hadn't gotten hungry enough to eat her yet. She guessed he hadn't heard about her marriage to Cord, and to say he wouldn't be happy was an understatement. Even the day he'd left her, Bryce had sworn he'd be back to take over the ranch. Now, with Cord there, the take-over wouldn't be as easy as he might have planned.

Cuddling into the warm covers, she forced aside Bryce Galloway and the memory of his fist slamming into her face the last time they'd met and concentrated on Cord. In many ways she thought of him as a simple man, not dumb or backward, but simple in his needs. He worked, he slept, and he ate. That seemed enough. He talked of plans for the ranch and his little farm, but he never mentioned dreams or goals for himself. He didn't seem to care about how he dressed, but he worried about her eating, like she was a child who might starve if he didn't pay attention.

She'd never be attracted to a man who didn't have grand dreams, but she liked the way Cord looked and the polite, almost hesitant way he sometimes acted around her. And, of course, she loved the way he wore the clothes she bought. The way he moved and, most of all, the times when he was perfectly still, as if he'd paused just to treasure something like the morning air, or his first bite of a sandwich, or her as she dressed. A simple man in a complicated world. Life could never be so easy. Not for her.

If it hadn't been for the kiss and the looks he gave her when he watched her change clothes, she'd think he wasn't attracted to her. But he had to be. She knew men, and no man looked at a woman like that who didn't want her. No man kissed like he had without wanting more.

If he was only pretending, he should win an Oscar.

Kicking her way out of the covers, Nevada stretched and leaned her head back to shake her tangled mass of hair behind her. They'd been married a week today. Her plan was working. Galem had kept her up on what was happening. Cord was a hard boss, but the men respected him. He never talked about anything but the ranch and he listened to all suggestions. Zeb Darnell, a loyal hand who'd been fired a few years ago, had now become Cord's right-hand man. Zeb's knowledge seemed to fill in the gaps in Cord's knowledge of ranching.

She had to give Cord credit. He'd shown good sense to hire Zeb.

As she dressed, Nevada wondered if there was any kindness or loving left in Cord. Prison must have been hard. She'd asked Tannon Parker a year ago how Cord was doing at work, and Tannon had said simply that he was a shell of a man. All he did was work, and it didn't seem to matter if he was on his land or hers; Cord was determined to work himself to death.

Maybe Tannon was right. She'd hoped for a man but got only a shell. She could live with that for eight months. She'd learned she could live with almost anything. Only this time, living with Cord might gain her the one thing she'd never had . . . security. By the first hard freeze she'd be so solid no one would ever take anything from her. No one would hurt her.

When she stepped from her bathroom, she almost collided with the object of her thoughts.

"Cord," she managed to say as she pulled her blouse around her.

Mud covered one side of his body and his hat was missing. "Didn't mean to startle you. I took a fall and decided it would be easier to change clothes than to beat myself to death trying to brush off."

She laughed. "You do look like a mud man." For the first time in a week she thought he looked adorable, like a big kid who'd rolled in the corral. "How'd you get past Ora Mae?"

"Came in the courtyard door. It's never locked. Keep your voice down so I can get cleaned up before she sees me."

"Of course," she whispered. "I'd hate for my housekeeper to murder you for tracking in mud after I left for work."

He raised an eyebrow and glanced down at her open blouse. "You don't look ready to leave."

She didn't bother to button the blouse together. "I took the day off. I wanted to work with my horses and I've got shopping in town. I thought we could have dinner together tonight if you've no other plans."

"That would be a change." He began stripping off his clothes and tossing them into the sink.

She leaned against his bathroom door

and watched. "Ora Mae says you go through two sets of clothes a day, sometimes three."

"If I were home I'd just hose off in the yard and drip dry, but I figure you'd be upset. If I stripped outside, Ora Mae would have a heart attack. She thinks I'm not housebroke because I drink out of the cartons of milk and juice, but when I lived alone there wasn't much need for glasses."

"I'll pick up more clothes today. I wouldn't want everyone seeing you strip."

"There's no need. I can make do."

"I don't mind. I'll be in town anyway, and you're right, I do like the way you look in the clothes I buy." She hesitated and added, "As well as without them. You've got a fine body, Cord."

He unbuttoned his trousers. "If you don't turn around, Nevada, you're about to see the without view right now."

She didn't move.

He took the challenge and finished stripping. Once he was in the shower, he yelled, "I expect the same views."

She laughed. "Dream on." Even through the glass door she watched the frosted shadow of his frame. He wasn't all tanned and perfect like a male model. He had muscles hard from work and parts of his body that had never seen sunlight. He had hair on his chest and scars. A scrape ran the length of his arm from elbow to wrist and she guessed he hadn't simply rolled in the mud when he'd taken the fall.

"You fall off your horse?" she asked as she reached for the first-aid kit.

"No, he actually tumbled out from under me. Zeb talked me into trying his cutting horse, and the mare shifted faster than I could move. I tried to tell Zeb that until a week ago I was a farmer, but those new clothes must have convinced him otherwise."

"What did he do when you fell off?"

"Laughed over my cussing."

She heard the shower go off. When he stepped out, he'd pulled a towel around his waist as he kept talking. "I'm thinking of having a long talk with that horse."

"Put your arm on the counter."

"It's nothing." Cord looked at the scrape, now bubbling fresh blood. "It'll scab over."

She blocked his bathroom door and repeated, "Put your arm on the counter."

For a few seconds they stared at each

other, and she wasn't sure which one would win this argument. She wasn't even sure why she was fighting. If the man wanted to bleed, let him bleed.

Without breaking his stare, he lowered his arm, scab side up, and she watched the muscles of his arm tighten as she neared.

Nevada dabbed the blood, sprayed antiseptic, and wrapped the scrape from elbow to wrist with first gauze and then tape. "There, that wasn't so bad. Now at least it will stay clean. You can unwrap it when you get home and let it air."

She looked up and found him still staring at her.

Feeling very mothering, she shooed him with her hands. "Now go back out and play."

A slow smile finally tugged his lip up. "I'd better dress first." He moved to his closet and pulled out the first shirt and jeans he saw.

"I hadn't noticed," she lied as she ran across the room. By the time she'd pulled on trousers and her boots, he was gone without another word.

That night at dinner she was still thinking about how good he'd looked nude. They were little more than polite strangers, but they were getting to know one another. He never complained or asked too many questions. He didn't try to keep up with her or boss her around. This might be the best marriage she'd had so far. Of course, if it lasted eight months it would break a record.

She pushed her food around on the plate as she thought of the morning and how they'd almost been a normal couple for a few minutes.

"I can't get the windows around this place open," he said from across the table.

"What?" She realized she hadn't been listening. "Oh, yes, the windows. You told me."

"I like to sleep in fresh air, and whoever built this place forgot to buy working windows."

She thought of telling him that windows were the dumbest dinner conversation subject she'd ever heard. She'd known the man a week and he'd never bothered to ask her what books she liked, or what was her favorite movie, or even who she voted for. At this rate they'd never learn each other. "Well," she said, trying not to sound bored, "just knock one open."

"Or we could just move the bed out in the courtyard. There's plenty of fresh air out there among all those strange flowers."

"My stepmother, who lasted one summer around here, had the flowers brought in from all over the South. My father wouldn't let her redecorate the house. I like the courtyard, but I'm not sleeping outside."

"You are if I do." His words were a challenge.

"Right. Our bargain. For eight months I sleep with you, right?"

"Right."

Ora Mae walked in to say she was leaving, and the discussion dropped. He talked about what he'd done on the ranch, and she talked about a problem at the office. Neither understood much of what the other one was saying.

When they went to bed, he sat in a chair by the sealed windows and pulled off his boots as he watched her. She always turned her back to him when she slipped off her bra and tugged on her nightshirt. If he'd asked her to turn around, she told herself she would, but he'd have to ask. Otherwise, she had no intention of putting on a show.

When she crawled into bed he walked

over to her side and flipped off her light, then pulled the cover to her shoulder, and she had the feeling he'd done the same thing every night they'd been married. One week.

Nevada lay awake waiting for him to say something. She guessed he wasn't a man who asked for things, and she wasn't a woman who waited for what she wanted.

After ten minutes she was still wide awake and waiting. "I've had it," she broke the silence. "I'm tired of lying over here every night waiting for you to reach over and touch me. If you're gay, that's fine, but if you're not, I'd like to know why you're not attracted to me like every boy I've known since I was old enough to car-date."

Practically every man she'd spoken to since she'd been fifteen had hit on her. Before she became the CEO of Britain Oil and Drilling, almost every male in the office had brushed against her, or acted drunk and made a pass. But Cord had been sleeping three feet away and hadn't even tried. She'd never played hard to get. He must know that.

"When I suggested marriage I meant it as a business arrangement." She tried to calm. "I knew you'd be good at running the ranch, but then you added the bit about my sleeping in your bed and I thought, great, he's just like all men, he wants a piece of me. I've given away so many pieces in the last ten years I didn't figure one more would matter. Then you marry me and I do my part of the bargain and crawl into bed with you, and you don't even bother to touch me. I'm lying here wondering night after night when you're going to pounce on me. I swear, it's downright exhausting."

"You coming up for air anytime soon, Nevada?" Cord sounded more concerned than interested in her crisis.

She sat up and tried to glare at him, but the room was too dark to pull it off. "I see you looking at me, taking off my clothes with your eyes. But when I'm right here all night long, you don't cross the three feet of bed between us. We might as well be sleeping in cots, or better yet have a bundling pillow between us like the Victorians did. I don't know why you asked me to be here anyway. We'd probably both be more comfortable in separate rooms; after all, you've got four others to pick from. Which reminds me, you don't make a sound all night or move. You just fall into bed like you were shot and sleep without even pulling covers. Corpses don't lie as still as you do at night, Cord McDowell, and I can tell you for a fact it's unnerving. Twice last night I woke up and couldn't even hear you breathing. I lay there thinking, great, I'm in bed with a dead man."

He got out of bed and circled round to her side. "You finished?"

She shrugged, thinking she'd made a fool of herself, but she'd always had a problem slowing down once she got rolling. He was about to be husband number four to tell her to shut up. She'd really outdone herself in finding something wrong with this one. Why couldn't she just have been happy with his plain conversation and simple ways? It wasn't like he had habits hard to put up with. The man didn't even leave his socks on the floor.

Cord sat down beside her and turned her shoulders until they were facing each other. "I'm an only child. I've always slept alone. When I went to prison I slept alone. Since I came home three years ago, I've never shared a bed with anyone."

Her vision adjusted to the light enough

to see his face. "You asked me to be in your bed because you didn't want to be alone? That's it! I don't know if I'm more insulted or confused."

"It seemed like a good idea." He sounded tired, not at all like a man who planned to take his turn listing her faults. "I didn't know your sleeping in my bed came with touching." His big hand moved down her arm. "But I could get used to the idea if it bothers you so much."

"Oh, it's all right now that I understand; forget about it. I was just feeling rejected. Now that I know you wanted to sleep, I'm fine, really." She pushed his hand away and turned her back to him.

He sat on the bed awhile, but she wasn't about to start rattling on again.

She felt him stand and heard him walk to the windows. The drapes swished as he opened them, and she guessed he was looking out into the night. Another one of his simple habits, she thought. Something scraped across the floor.

Glass shattered with a crash vibrating like a gunshot through the room.

Preparing for flight, Nevada jumped to her knees on the bed. His broad-shouldered body shadowed across a seven-foot window, now without glass. The heavy iron luggage rack she'd always hated now rested upside down atop one of the rosebushes.

Cool night air flowed gently around her as the room settled back into silence. "What do you think you're doing?" she whispered, afraid to confront him too strongly.

"Opening a window," he answered as he walked back to her side of the bed.

"Have you lost your mind? You've probably broken half the branches on that rosebush, and it will be a mess cleaning up all the glass."

"Stop talking, Nevada, and lie back." He lifted her covers and she leaned back against the pillows. Without another word, he moved in beside her, pushing her over to allow himself room. With one arm around her shoulders, he pressed his body along hers. "I don't want you to feel rejected. I'm not going to pounce and attack you, but I think I might like to be close enough to touch you for a while."

They were both nervous, but neither one moved away. She told herself she wasn't afraid of him, but the man had just knocked open a floor-to-ceiling window. She corrected her evaluation of him from simple to unpredictable.

He placed his hand on her waist and pressed his cheek against her hair.

"I like the way your hair smells." He pulled the covers over them both.

She wiggled to a more comfortable spot beside him, deciding that she might need his warmth now that they had cool air coming in. "You going to touch me while I'm asleep?"

"I might. You got any objections?"

"No. I guess not."

It took a while, but slowly both calmed and she fell asleep.

Their night together set a pattern. Whoever went to bed first picked the side, and the other cuddled in. If he explored her body during the night, she wasn't aware of it. As the days passed, she realized that if they'd had sex she would have felt wanted, but by gently holding her Cord had made her feel cherished, and she'd never felt cherished. Somehow it was more intimate than sex. She'd never had a lover who'd held her all night.

In the mornings he moved away from her. With a light kiss on the cheek, he vanished. If she saw him before she went to work, she made a point to walk over to wherever he was and kiss him good-bye. He'd always cup the back of her head and stare down at her as if he wanted one last look before she left. Days passed, drifting into spring, and one by one all the windows were fitted with windows that opened.

On cool evenings they always rode, Cord on his gray horse named Devil and Nevada on one of the mares from her own private stable. Slowly, they grew used to the other's touch. The way he put his hand on her leg when he checked the stirrup. The light touch of his fingers against her back when they walked. Her pats on his forearm when she wanted his full attention.

There were no words of endearment between them except when they knew others were listening, but there were few words of anger. He was stubborn about running the ranch and seemed to trust his judgment more and more. She rarely came home in time to eat dinner with him, and he was often gone before she woke up.

At night, she'd bring her dinner into the study and watch him work at her father's old desk. Once in a while he'd tell her about something that happened at the ranch. She'd usually fall asleep watching the news and he'd carry her to bed. The next morning she'd wake up with her clothes still on and raccoon eyes from sleeping in her makeup. And . . . she'd smile, remembering that she'd slept soundly in his arms.

The only time he slowed his routine was when he watched her dress, and she made sure that was as often as possible. She liked the idea that she affected this cold man. Sometimes, if they went to bed at the same time, he'd just sit in the chair with a clear view of her closet and watch. Sometimes he'd stand at the door and study her as she changed into riding clothes after work.

They were like two people occupying the same space, but in different dimensions. If she hadn't felt his warmth against her at night, she would have wondered if maybe he was simply a machine and not a man.

As she cuddled next to Cord, Nevada told herself that a machine was exactly what she needed to marry. She was no good with people . . . with relationships, and neither was he. If there was no passion,

she could live with it. He apparently didn't
have any for her, and she'd learned from
others that what she'd thought was passion had been simply lust. Once lust cools,
it shrivels into indifference to the point of
cruelty. Her last husband's bruises had
taken weeks to heal.

Bryce liked to play rough with her, half
teasing, half cruel, to prove he was stronger and in control. At first he'd said he was
sorry when he hurt her in his play before
he took her to bed, but after a few months
he stopped caring. He only wanted control, and if she didn't respond fast enough,
he made her pay.

When she'd shown her bruises to her
father, he'd told her to stop lying; Bryce
had already told him she'd been drinking
again and that he'd had to restrain her
when she'd gone wild. By the time her father grew ill, she knew Bryce thought he'd
broken her. She'd followed his every rule
and she'd learned to curl into a ball if he
raised his hand. Most of the time, he'd
laugh and forget about hitting her.

He thought he'd take charge of everything but couldn't stand the depression of

watching her father wither away, so he'd left, thinking to make her suffer without him. But while he partied in Vegas, she'd served him with divorce papers. He hadn't thought she would go through with it, so he'd ignored the court date. The divorce was final before he could contest it.

The last words Bryce said to her when he'd collected his things had been that she'd never belong to anyone else. Even knowing that he was miles away didn't keep the shiver of fear away. Bryce wasn't finished toying with her. He'd been wealthy and worthless all his life. Like a big-game hunter who kills for the thrill, Bryce wanted her. He told her once that she was beautiful and he wanted everyone to know that she was his. At the time, she'd been flattered, not realizing he saw her only as a toy.

His words would have been funny later in the marriage, if she hadn't felt his anger so many times. In truth, she'd never belonged to Bryce, or anyone else.

At first, when Bryce had been courting, she'd noticed pats that were a bit too hard, always followed by apologies. She told herself he was showing off in front of her brother, proving he was the boss. Then after they married, even his grip often left bruises. She'd been a fool not to see the signs early, but he'd always talked his way around her hurt and anger, until finally he no longer cared and hurting her became pure entertainment when no one was around to see. He'd always been attentive in public, explaining her bruises as drunken accidents as he served her another drink.

Bryce didn't want her, not then and not now. He'd made it plain within days after they married, but he did like playing the rancher.

She'd married Cord McDowell for more than his help on the ranch. She married him to be a barrier between her and the man who swore he'd finish the job of killing her one day. It wasn't fair to Cord. Much as she hated herself for it, Cord was just one more wall she'd built to feel safe.

She'd realized when the bargain first occurred to her that she might be putting him in danger, but there had been no family, no friends to turn to. She'd told herself the risk was worth taking. After all, if she hadn't picked Cord, he might have lost his farm. Only now, she felt guilty for not telling him more about Bryce. He had a right to know. She'd only been thinking of herself.

As worry swirled in her mind, she pulled her hand from the covers and moved her fingers slowly over Cord's bare shoulder. "I'll protect you," she whispered, hoping that she could find a way to make it true.

A memory surfaced in her tired mind.

She'd been more drunk than sober years ago when a group of her friends gathered for a party at the lake one July Fourth. In the shadows she watched a man coming toward the camp, flashing his light like a weapon and shouting orders. Then he grabbed a kid's arm and jerked him up.

The kid came up swinging and the invader crumpled after one blow. The reflection of a badge on his shirt blinked in the flashlight's beam. Then Nevada remembered running into the shadows, leaving the kid and the deputy behind.

She rested her head on Cord's arm, knowing the kid she'd seen that night had been him. Not one of the dozen teenagers drinking around the campfire came forward the next day to testify to what happened. She'd tried to talk to a cop that night, but he didn't seem interested in listening to a drunk sixteen-year-old. When she'd wanted to go in the next morning, her father had demanded she remain silent.

The deputy claimed he'd been attacked, and there was no one to say otherwise.

Chapter 13

MARTHA Q PATTERSON THOUGHT SHE MIGHT have a stroke before she got up all the steps at the front of Wright Funeral Home. If she did, Tyler better do her funeral for half price, since he insisted she come over to his place to talk.

She knew she'd called him three times in less than two weeks, but she needed someone to talk to. Since he'd be getting her business someday, he might as well earn it now. Only this time he'd said he couldn't leave his pregnant wife even for ten minutes, so here she was climbing Heart Attack Hill. It occurred to her that some of Tyler's business might walk in and go out boxed.

Martha Q knew she wouldn't complain. She cared about Kate Wright, so she came to Tyler's office this time. In a strange way they were in the same business, innkeepers and funeral directors. They both laid people to rest.

Martha Q was laughing at her own joke when Tyler opened the door.

"Good morning." He made a slight bow of his head, as if she were the queen come to call. Martha Q would have been flattered, but Tyler pretty much treated everyone like royalty.

"How is Kate?" Martha Q wasn't in the mood to waste words and any more energy. She needed answers and a chair.

"My Kate is resting. She won't admit it, but I think this pregnancy has been hard on her these last few months. She said something about how going into a war zone was nothing compared to carrying a baby." He motioned for her to follow him into his office.

"Well, see that you two don't get in this situation again," Martha Q huffed. "There are ways to prevent this disease from happening again."

Tyler laughed. "You sound like you're talking to two kids. Once Tyler Two is born, I think we'll be happy with one child. Kate and a son are far more than I'd hoped for in this lifetime."

Martha Q squealed. "Please, Lord, don't tell me that's what you're naming the poor child?"

"No," he grinned. "That's just what Kate calls him."

As always, Tyler's love for his wife showed in his face. For years the man hadn't been able to get a date in town, what with his occupation and his build, and then he found Kate. Martha Q had heard several women wishing they'd given him a chance before he went off the market. Nothing makes a man more handsome than when he cherishes his wife.

Martha Q moved into Tyler's messy office, mumbling that she hoped the kid had his father's sense of humor and his mother's looks.

Tyler acted like he didn't hear her as he offered her a seat beside the windows. "When you called, I asked Autumn to make a fresh pot of coffee for us. With the cool morning I thought you might like a cup.

Kate always tells me how nice Winter's Inn was when she stayed there before we married. She said you'd have tea every afternoon in the style of a grand lady. I'm afraid all we can manage here is coffee and scones from the bakery. Autumn's been too busy to bake lately."

She straightened. In one lifetime she'd gone from being called the town slut to being called a great lady. Of course she was smart enough to know that a fine tea set doesn't make a lady any more than fishnet hose make a slut.

As Tyler always did, he lowered his voice and asked, "How may I be of help to you?"

Martha Q finished off a corner of her scone before she stated her first fact. "I think we got one of those serial killers living right here in Harmony. Nobody knows it, and by the time they do, there'll be a line of bodies waiting at your back door."

Tyler frowned. "Who?" He said the word so slowly it sounded like a hum.

"A good-looker named Bryce Galloway. About thirty-five, all fancy, real nice. Too nice. You know, the kind whose neighbors are all interviewed after he's arrested and they all comment on how 'polite' he was."

"Bryce Galloway? Wasn't he married to Nevada Britain a season or two? Seems like she got divorced right before her father died. If I remember correctly, he was from old oil money down near Houston or Dallas. Folks said he was crazy about her the minute he saw her."

"You know him?"

Tyler shook his head. "He didn't help Nevada with the funeral arrangements. Far as I know he didn't even attend. Her only brother refused to come too, said he hated the old man. She looked so alone there in the family pew, her back straight, her eyes staring ahead like she saw nothing but trouble coming to blow her over."

"I'm not surprised he didn't help. Probably wouldn't have even if they'd still been married. He has that none-of-my-family-has-worked-in-three-generations look about him, but I'd bet his Italian loafers he's never worn out a pair of boots."

Tyler nodded as if he knew what she was talking about.

"And besides"—Martha Q pointed her finger at some invisible point floating between her and Tyler—"who *wasn't* married to Nevada Britain? Just split the population of Harmony and you'll hit the number she's planning on stopping at. Somehow I heard she talked Cord McDowell into marrying her the other day. Not that anyone else would want him, but—"

Tyler raised his eyebrow. He was not a man to gossip . . . at least not for long. "What makes you think Bryce is up to something illegal?"

She thought of mentioning how the man sometimes, when he thought no one was looking, would huff and puff as if fighting to control rage. He ate strange too. Eggs with no yolks, bread with no flour, milk that didn't come from a cow. Everything else had to be fat, sugar, and caffeine free. The last time he gave the cook, Mrs. Biggs, his order for breakfast, she told him to just gnaw on the table until she got back. Martha Q didn't usually pay much attention to the breakfast part of her business, but since Mr. Galloway arrived she'd been running to the store to pick up food that wasn't even real.

There was no way out; she had to be honest with Tyler Wright. He'd know what to do. "It's just a feeling," she began. "It's not any one thing he does or says. It's more like the pieces of him just don't fit together. I get the feeling I'll be that person interviewed about how well I knew him." She leaned forward. "I know men, Tyler, and I'm telling you this one is not right."

"You want me to have the sheriff evict him from your place? I'm not sure how she'd do it, but you might be able to say you had folks coming in who needed the room."

"No. I don't want to make him mad. I just want you to tell Alex and a few of her deputies to keep an eye on him. He only lived here when he was married to Nevada, so he's not one of us. I keep wondering what kind of business brought him back. Now think about it, Tyler; if you were rich and could live anywhere, would you move back to a little town and stay on the third floor of a bed-and-breakfast just to be next to an ex-wife who probably wishes you were dead?"

"How do you know that?"

Martha Q raised an eyebrow as if questioning his IQ. "Most ex-wives do; it's a fact."

Tyler shook his head. "If you don't like having him under your roof, something needs to be done."

"I'll call Rick Matheson and take the

lawyer to lunch. He'll tell me how I can get him out of my inn with the least trouble." They both nodded as if something had been settled.

Martha Q figured Tyler just thought he'd listened to the latest in a long line of problems she'd made up, and maybe he had. Since she didn't have a quiet house to write in, she might as well make up drama in real life.

She finished off her coffee, tucked the rest of her scone into her purse for later, and made Tyler promise to talk to the sheriff. It shouldn't be much of an inconvenience; he had breakfast with Hank and Alex once a week at the diner. Hank was the fire department chief, and his wife was the sheriff. Between the three of them they knew everything happening in Harmony.

When she drove back to the B&B, a man dressed in black was sitting on her porch steps. He was tall and thin, and for a moment, before he noticed Martha Q, he seemed to have the weight of the world on his shoulders.

Martha Q swore. She was starting to feel like her place was the pound for lost singles.

To the man's credit, he stood when she headed toward him. A formal kind of stance, like a military man or butler. She'd guess him near sixty with beautiful silver-gray hair.

"Mrs. Patterson, I presume?"

"Correct." He didn't look like he was selling anything, but if she'd been a few years younger she might have been interested in buying. "I'm Martha Q Patterson."

"I'm Anthony Carleon. I work for Marty Winslow, who I believe rented half of a duplex you own a few years back."

"It's rented right now, if he's thinking of coming back." Martha Q frowned. If Marty could afford to hire a man like this to work for him, surely he could get a better place than her duplex to live. It had been a dump when she and her first husband bought it almost forty years ago.

Anthony Carleon smiled. "Mrs. Patterson, if you'll allow me a bit of time, I'll try to explain the situation, but first I must ask if you have a room available here." He motioned toward the house behind him. "I'm in need of lodging."

"I have one left, but it's on the third floor. Marty would never be able to get his wheelchair up there."

"No, the room is for me. Marty will be staying at the duplex with your current tenant, Ronny Logan. Of course, we'll expect you to increase the rent and we'll check with you about upgrading or painting."

Martha Q unlocked her door and turned back to Carleon. "This sounds like a sit-down story. Won't you step into the parlor, Mr. Carleon?"

Half an hour later she handed Carleon the key to the third-floor bedroom next to Bryce Galloway. As her latest boarder moved up the stairs with his one suitcase, she thought of calling Dallas Logan and giving her a heart attack. The old bag had been making up stories about her poor homely daughter ever since she moved out. When Dallas heard that her only child had a man living with her, Dallas would take it like a full-power Taser jolt.

Chapter 14

RONNY LOGAN WASN'T SURE SHE'D SLEPT AT all after signing the papers and leaving the hospital. Her world was about to change. She'd always dreamed Marty Winslow would come back to her, but she'd never thought it would be to die.

As she stepped out of the Lincoln one last time, she wondered if the long black car would be coming with them. Somehow she doubted it.

Ross and Ivan called and said all was ready at her place by the time Ronny walked into the front of the huge hospital. They told her Doc had already sent a nurse with all the equipment needed. Mr. Carleon, of course, had driven over yesterday to make arrangements, then driven back to the hospital to see that Marty's things were loaded properly. A little after dawn he'd be following the ambulance toward Harmony.

As she walked down the front hallway for the first time, Ronny answered Ross's questions on her cell and added, "I think it would be nice if Marty could see out the front windows from his bed."

"We already got it, Ronny. Mr. Carleon found a few extra chairs and a cot for the nurse on the night shift. We'll have everything ready by the time you arrive."

Ronny clicked the phone off as she reached Marty's hospital room door.

"Ready?" Mr. Carleon interrupted as he stepped into the hall. "If we leave soon, his brother isn't likely to confront us."

Ronny nodded. The sooner she got him away, the better.

Marty was either asleep or drugged so heavily he didn't make a sound when the EMTs moved him. Even with Doc running the show, moving a man from this hospital was like prodding a near-frozen snake along. One minute everyone at the hospital thought they were in charge and needed to be checked with, and the next no one was responsible for anything.

Once they were on the road, Doc insisted she sit in the chair next to the driver, and within minutes Ronny drifted to sleep to the low sounds of the machines just behind her and the rhythm of the road beating out the miles until she was home.

She sometimes dreamed that Marty had never been hurt and they'd fallen in love and married just like all happy couples. Only even in her dreams she knew she would have never met him if he hadn't been crippled and hiding away in Harmony.

A small part of her wondered if she wasn't more needed than loved. If he'd been walking, running a business, wheeling and dealing, she never would fit into his world. Only now with him hurt and dying, she'd made room for him in her world.

She remembered he'd said something that always echoed in her memories of their days together. "In a perfect world," he'd said, "I know we would find each other. Some people are just meant to cross paths."

Chapter 15

Boxed B Ranch

Cord pulled the powerful pickup behind the house and parked next to his twenty-year-old truck. He'd driven his pickup only once since the day they married. Galem had handed him the keys to the special-edition Ford F-450 Platinum and said, "You'll need the power, Boss."

Cord smiled, remembering how he'd driven out to a dirt road and spent an hour reading the owner's manual. The learning curve around this place was huge. Surprisingly, a few of the courses he'd taken in prison helped. The auto mechanics and computer classes along with the two he'd taken on bookkeeping were wonderful, but he still hadn't figured out how to work the cell phone. Not that it mattered. The only person he wanted to call was Nevada.

She'd been home all day and he'd been working. So many little things were going wrong on the land, like fences cut and gates left open, that he was starting to wonder if a few of the men he'd fired weren't coming back to pester him. Today, even though it was Sunday, he'd been out driving the roads, checking. At noon he hadn't made it in for lunch because a farmer wanted to meet him to buy off the last of Cord's equipment on his parents' place.

The money was enough to pay off the loan on his land, but Cord knew if the marriage didn't make the eight-month mark he'd be hurting. Owning the land, even the three hundred acres Nevada had signed over, wouldn't help if he had no money to buy what he needed to farm.

When he walked into the house, he grabbed an apple and ate it as he ambled around looking for Nevada. His mind was on an idea he'd had of using the new land to raise horses. A stream ran through the land most months, and two windmills would serve the dry times. He didn't want to have fancy horses like she raised, but good strong ranch horses. He might even use Devil for stud.

Cord found her in her little upstairs study. She was so engrossed in painting she didn't even notice him watching her until he crunched down on the apple.

"Want to tell me what you're doing?" he asked.

"Nope," she answered. "Want to tell me where you've been?"

"Nope," he echoed. If he told her of some of the problems, she'd just worry, and he was doing enough of that for them both.

He watched her a minute, wondering how this angry woman could possibly be the same person he cuddled with at night. Something was bothering her, but he had no idea what. She went back to painting and he stood at the door. He hadn't been invited in.

She signed the painting and smiled. "Finished," she said as she turned the canvas to face him.

Cord grinned. "Very good." A horse standing in a pasture. It was nice, real nice, but what kept him smiling was that she'd signed her initials *NM*, not *NB*. She'd meant it when she'd said she wanted his name.

"Want to go into town and have supper? We could walk the town square."

She made a face. "Sounds charming."

Cord frowned. "Does that mean yes or no?"

She was out of her chair so fast he didn't have time to get out of the doorway before she bumped her way around him and headed downstairs. "Yes. I'll go. Why not?"

Cord figured he'd pushed conversation to the limit, so he just waited downstairs. He didn't have long to review their confusing conversation before she stormed out of the bedroom with her jacket and purse. When she bumped past him on her way outside, he decided he was no more than a turnstile.

He followed and was surprised to see her climb into his truck instead of her little car she usually drove back and forth to town, but he didn't ask questions. He just headed to town.

They were halfway there before she spoke. "There's something I should tell you. I've heard that my ex-husband is in town. Has been for a few days, I think."

"I'm not giving you back," Cord said simply, and winked at her.

To his surprise, she laughed. "Don't worry, I wouldn't go back."

Cord decided now was as good a time to ask as any. "How do you think we're doing?"

"Good. I'm happy with the agreement. You?"

He thought about it for a while before answering. "It's different than I thought it would be. The days are long and the work is hard, but you and me, we seem to be getting by." From the way she'd cuddled close last night, he could have no complaints. "We mostly just stay out of each other's way."

He stopped at a Mexican food place she claimed she'd never noticed. She ordered a salad and he ordered a platter. It was so noisy they barely talked, but he felt a little of the tension leave her. While they waited for the check, he rested his hand over hers, and she didn't pull away. He had no idea if she liked it, but touching her hand made him feel more normal, like they were just another couple out for dinner.

When they walked out, all four tires on his truck had been slashed.

Cord walked around the truck twice, swearing to himself. When he passed her the second time, he asked, "Got any idea who might do this?"

"Several," she said. "One of the men you fired. Any one of my three ex-husbands. Wild kids causing damage just for the hell of it. Some guy who thought you got his parking place."

Cord rolled his shoulders to relax. "In other words, anyone."

"Pretty much."

Nevada wanted to call the sheriff's office, but Cord didn't want them involved. The chances were slim they'd catch whoever did it, but he'd bet the cop coming out would know him and give him a hard time. He didn't care about the cop, or the hard time, but he didn't want Nevada to see him as all the cops around saw him. An ex-con. A wild kid who'd sent a sheriff's deputy to the hospital with one punch. Cord would have to keep his gaze to the ground and be extra polite, but they'd still talk to him like they knew he must be doing something illegal.

"I could call Galem," Nevada suggested. "If you insist on not calling the sheriff."

"Galem and Ora Mae are at their cabin at the lake. He said they didn't plan to drive in until early tomorrow."

"We could walk home." She began to pace.

"Not in those heels, you can't. I'd end up carrying you the last few miles."

"I could call a cab," she smiled.

"Or we could catch the subway." He bought into her joke. The closest thing Harmony had to mass transit was the little Joy bus that picked up folks at the nursing homes on Sunday for church.

A tall man dressed in a black suit walked past them. He paused, and in the twilight Cord saw intelligent eyes take in the crime and understand.

Cord expected him to walk on. No one in town ever spoke to him, and Nevada didn't speak to anyone she didn't have to. But the man turned toward them as formal as a royal guard.

"Pardon me for interrupting, but do you two need a lift? I have to drop off a takeout order to my employer a few blocks away, but if you don't mind waiting, I'd be glad to take you somewhere."

Cord could already see Nevada shaking her head, but he answered, "We'd be much obliged, but we live a few miles out of town."

"No problem." The man smiled as if happy to be of service.

They crammed into the front of a U-Haul van with takeout orders in their laps. Nevada looked like she thought she was being kidnapped, but Cord relaxed.

When the tall man started the van, Cord listened as he shifted and said, "Sounds like the transmission is going out."

"I fear you may be right. As soon as I get time to unload it, I plan to turn it in. This was a sudden move, and I had to take whatever they had. My employer is very ill, so his needs have to come first before the unpacking or my frustration."

They drove a few blocks toward downtown before he pulled up at an old duplex. Nevada held on to Cord's leg as if she feared death coming. He spread his hand over hers, but she didn't relax. He wished he could tell her that he'd seen enough bad guys in his life to know the gentleman in black wasn't one of them.

"I'll be a few minutes dropping these off." The man added, "I hope you don't mind waiting."

The thin fellow was so polite, Cord felt bad for adding to what was obviously a long day for him. "If you don't mind me taking a look under the hood, maybe I can make sure this engine lasts until you get it turned in."

Carleon straightened, then smiled. "I would be much obliged." He said the words with the same Texas drawl that Cord had used. "I'll just deliver these to the people inside and make sure the night nurse has arrived."

Nevada pouted while Cord looked at the engine. Finally, she got tired of waiting and climbed out to stand next to him. "We should have just called someone," she whispered. "Who knows how long we'll be stuck here? One of the guys at the bunkhouse could have come into town and picked us up."

"Sorry, Princess."

"Don't call me that, and why do I have to be nice to this stranger? I've never seen him before and I'll probably never see him again."

"You don't know how to be nice, do you, Princess?" Cord didn't bother to look at her. He knew she was pouting.

She caught him on the shoulder with a jab that surprised him so much he jerked up, banging his head on the open hood.

When he stepped back, rubbing his scalp, the tall man stood three feet away.

"Everything all right?"

"Yeah, I was just having a discussion with my wife. She tends to storm." Cord winked at her as if they'd been playing.

Nevada looked at him like she might swing again.

Lowering the hood, he said, "I think this thing will make a few more miles."

Carleon nodded. "I need to get one box out of the back, and then we can be on our way. There will be plenty of time to unload the rest when I return."

To Cord's shock, Nevada smiled at the very proper gentleman raising the back door of the van. "Please, allow us to help. We'll be happy to move the boxes onto the porch for you. It'll save you time."

Carleon started to protest, but Nevada

picked up a box and headed for the porch. Cord had no choice but to follow. She matched him trip after trip, taking her share of the load. He knew she couldn't be comfortable in high heels, but she never complained. She was too busy proving that she wasn't a princess.

On one of the last trips Cord thought he saw Ronny Logan standing just inside the window of the duplex. She didn't seem to notice him, but Cord couldn't help but wonder if the boss Carleon had said was so ill had something to do with why the lady from the post office looked so sad.

By the time Mr. Carleon took them home, it was long past dark and they were exhausted. Without a word they moved to their separate bathrooms and showered. Cord could hear her drying her hair as he tumbled into bed. He was almost asleep when she cuddled next to him.

With her warm and in his arms, he whispered, "That was a good thing you did tonight." When she didn't say anything, he added, "I'm proud of you."

He knew she wasn't asleep, but she didn't move. After a few long breaths he felt a tear roll off her cheek and onto his arm.

The next morning, Cord got the men started working and headed into town in his old truck to get his tires fixed on the Ford. He stopped by the garage and paid for four new tires with the cash in his wallet, something he'd never imagined being able to do. The salesman said they'd put them on at the restaurant parking lot and then drive his truck over to the shop to have them balanced. No one argued when Cord said he'd be back in an hour to pick up his truck. They simply answered, "Yes, sir."

His next stop was the post office. He didn't have to ask about Ronny Logan; one of the postmen was complaining about her taking a few days off and now everyone had to help get the mail sorted.

Cord left the post office and drove to the duplex. The U-Haul was gone, and so were the boxes that they'd left on the porch.

He felt like a fool, sticking his nose in someone else's business, but Ronny Logan was as close to a friend as he had in this town. He needed to know she was all right.

He tapped on the duplex door and was surprised when Ronny opened it so fast she must have seen him walk up.

She didn't say a word, just stared at him with big brown eyes red-rimmed from crying.

"I'm sorry to bother you," he stuttered. "I just came to see if you're all right or if I can help." It didn't come naturally to him to offer help, but he had a feeling she'd never ask, no matter how dearly she needed it.

Ronny nodded and opened the screen door. He backed up as she moved outside.

For a minute, they just stood there. Two people who hardly ever talked to anyone were about to have a conversation.

Finally, she blew her nose on a ball of a tissue and said, "You know how to build a ramp for a wheelchair?"

A hundred questions came to mind, but Cord simply said, "Yes. Where do you want it?"

She took a deep breath and walked around to the back of the house. He saw the remains of a ramp that didn't look like it had been built solid enough to stand one winter.

"The doctors think my friend, Marty, came here to die. None of them, not even Mr. Carleon, believes he'll ever sit in a chair again, but I believe and, if I had the ramp, Marty might believe."

Cord looked at the rotting lumber that would no longer hold a wheelchair. "I'll have you one built by tomorrow."

"I can pay," she whispered.

He shook his head. "I'm happy to help. I'll worry about this. You worry about getting that friend of yours well enough to use it."

He put on his hat and headed for his pickup. When he backed out, Ronny was standing on the porch staring at him. She didn't wave or say a word, but he thought he saw a hint of a smile.

Within thirty minutes he'd collected supplies and called Galem to tell him to round up Jefferson and Jackson. Johnson, the youngest of the president brothers, could help Zeb with the cattle, but he needed the other two and Galem. "Meet me at the hardware store. Tell them to wear carpenter belts fully loaded for work."

Galem didn't ask questions; he just said, "We're on our way."

Cord closed the phone and smiled. They were seasoned ranch hands. The two could handle pretty much any job, and he had no doubt Galem would keep advice flowing until they were finished.

When they arrived, pickups were loaded with supplies and they headed back to the duplex. Cord saw no sign of anyone inside either side of the place, so he set to work.

Halfway through the job, Martha Q Patterson pulled up in her old car, which rattled to a stop. Everyone in town knew the owner of the bed-and-breakfast. She'd been so wild in her youth that folks still told stories about her.

"Cord McDowell?" she yelled as she rushed toward him.

He straightened and reached for the shirt he'd pulled off half an hour ago. "Yes, Mrs. Patterson."

She was out of breath by the time she reached him. "What in the hell do you think you're doing?" Her eyes never left his chest.

"I'm building a ramp for Ronny."

Martha Q folded her arms and finally looked up at him. "You want to tell me why?"

"She asked me to." He didn't see any need to tell her more. Cord didn't like questions and never gave more than a short answer. He stared down at the lady, wishing she'd go away.

To his surprise, the tall, thin man who'd offered them a lift yesterday stepped out the back door of the duplex and rushed to Martha Q like she was an old friend. "I'm so glad you came by," he said to Martha Q before offering his hand to Cord. "Mr. McDowell, I don't think I properly introduced myself to you last night. I'm sorry; exhaustion is my only excuse. I'm Anthony Carleon, and, if you've no objection, I'd love to explain to Mrs. Patterson exactly what is happening here."

Cord nodded once and went back to work, happy to be out of the conversation. Hell, he didn't really know what he was doing here. This had nothing to do with his farm or Nevada's ranch. He had plenty of work to do on both, but, strange as it would sound to most folks in town, he and Ronny were friends. Ever since he'd gotten out of prison he could count on her saying "Good morning" to him or talking about the weather when he came in to get his mail. When no one talks to you for days, such a small kindness meant something. It meant even more when he watched and saw that she was so shy she barely looked at others.

As he worked, he listened to the man who'd called himself Mr. Carleon explain that some guy named Marty Winslow might one day be able to sit in a wheelchair, and Ronny promised him when he did that she'd wheel him out of the house and they'd take a walk.

When Martha Q finally drove off, Cord thanked the man, and Mr. Carleon laughed. "She only wanted to be part of what was going on," he said. "Despite her bluster, she thinks very highly of you."

"She does?" He didn't think someone like Martha Q would even remember him.

"Yes," Carleon smiled. "She was telling one of the other boarders at the inn just this morning that your wife had picked a fine man this time." Carleon looked around at the ramp. "From your work, I would have to agree. This looks like it will still be standing when the house falls down."

"Thanks." Cord wasn't sure for what— for passing on the compliment, or for his work. "If you're staying here, you'll let me know if Ronny needs anything?"

Carleon straightened but didn't answer.

Cord knew he'd have to say more. "She's a friend. I'd like to help if I can."

The older man must have believed him, for he said, "I will. But I work for Mr. Winslow. I board at the inn. Marty, my employer, has round-the-clock nurses to help him, and I'm here to run errands, but I'm guessing Ronny could always use a friend. I hope you'll stop by often. I'm here whenever I'm needed."

He pointed at the dried-up creek that ran behind the duplex. "If I cross the creek, I'm actually very close. Thanks to Mr. Galloway for pointing out the shortcut."

Cord stopped breathing. "Bryce Galloway?"

Carleon answered casually, "Why, yes, do you know him? He's one of the boarders at the inn."

"No, but I've heard of him. My wife thought he might be in town, but I thought he was just passing through." Bryce Galloway had just moved to the top of his list of who might have slashed his tires.

Chapter 16

MARCH 21

AS THE DAYS ROLLED INTO SPRING, MARTHA Q and Mr. Carleon developed a habit of sitting on the porch after supper. They found that both enjoyed watching the day age into evening. She decided he was a pleasant man. At her age, pleasant men could fill the lonely hours sometimes far more than women friends.

She'd learned that he'd lost his wife to cancer twenty years ago and had no children. Which, to her way of thinking, was a blessing for her. Everyone she knew had not only children, but grandchildren, and they were simply boring when Martha Q knew she had no chance of one-upping them with a better story.

As they took their places among the wicker furniture, Martha Q began. "It's a really nice night tonight, Mr. Carleon, don't you think?"

"I do." He waited until she was settled in her chair before he sat down. "Here among all your huge old elms, it reminds me of New England."

"Me too," she answered, even though she'd never been to New England. In fact, she wasn't even sure where it was. Up north somewhere, but all the states got fuzzy past the Mississippi.

"How was Marty today?" Martha Q figured she'd better change the subject before he asked where in New England she'd visited.

"He's weak. Very weak. I can't say I was much for moving him, but like his friends, I couldn't just stand around and watch him die. Now at least when he wakes up, he smiles through the pain. His first word is always *Ronny*." Carleon stared out at the trees' shadows crawling toward the house.

"I don't know if he loves her so much as the dream of what might have been between them, but she is very dear to him."

"She's a good girl, I can tell you. I've known her all her life. Some say a man like him wouldn't be loving her if he were healthy, but I say it doesn't matter why he loves her. The important thing is, he does. Having a special man like that care about her will make all the difference in her life. In her later years, she'll have him to remember and know that, even for a moment, she was special to someone."

Mr. Carleon nodded. "I see their love more every day. Each time he stays awake an hour longer or manages to move his arms to do a few simple exercises, her face lights up like Christmas morning. I don't think she believes he's going to die. That'll make it harder on her when it happens."

"There is no easy where death's involved."

"How right you are."

They grew silent as Bryce Galloway walked up the walk-way. Unlike the other boarders, Galloway never bought the simple supper at the inn. He usually went into town or to the bar for his dinner, unless of course it rained; then he drove the black Rover he'd rented to a drive-through and bought a bag of junk food. The smell of fast food often drifted down all the way to the first floor from his room. For a man who insisted his food be cooked with no dairy, fat, or sugar, Bryce sure brought a great many greasy bags in.

Martha Q had no idea where Bryce went, but he seemed a busy man for someone who never mentioned a job or friends in town. His rental car looked like it was built for off-road travel. But he seemed more the type who thought he was roughing it if he stayed anywhere without a golf course connected to the property.

"Evening," Galloway said with a wide smile that flashed for only a moment when he looked up.

Mr. Carleon leaned forward and welcomed him without a smile. "Evening."

Bryce didn't bother with small talk. At some point he'd quit trying to make an impression on them. Maybe because he knew they'd already figured him out. He simply tipped an imaginary hat and went into the bed-and-breakfast.

Martha Q waited until she heard him

tromping up the stairs before she said, "If I were writing a mystery right now, that man would be the character who did it."

Mr. Carleon laughed. "I believe you're right; though I don't have a single fact to back up my opinion of him, I'd bet a month's pay that he's up to something."

Joni Rosen, dressed in her usual black, joined them on the porch. Martha Q didn't mind, except that Widow Joni was petite, and little women always made her feel bigger. She solved the problem by moving to the swing and covering up with a blanket, which she really didn't need.

Joni had that sadness that hangs around after a funeral. At a certain age Martha Q decided it makes people over fifty feel comfortable around each other. They've all spent time in that well and know it.

Martha Q knew the only way to cheer Joni up was to gossip. The little woman never started gossip, but she didn't mind spreading it along. She and Joni filled Mr. Carleon in on what they knew of Bryce Galloway. He'd shown up in town two or three years ago like he'd just bought the place at a half-price sale. He was friendly and outgoing, becoming buddies with everyone right away—or at least with all the people he thought counted.

Barrett Britain, Nevada's brother, introduced him to everyone as the man who would someday take over the Boxed B. They'd been roommates in college, but Bryce had never visited Harmony before. He came one summer to ride dirt bikes, but he stayed fascinated with Nevada.

Strange thing was, no one in town ever saw him with Nevada until they saw the wedding announcement in the paper. By the time he married her a few months later, you would have thought she was the outsider, judging from all the hugs he got. Of course, the wedding was at the country club with all the important people attending. Martha Q heard all about it because some guests stayed at the inn and felt the need to fill her in on what she'd missed.

Joni explained how Nevada went right on being her wild self even after the wedding, and folks started feeling sorry for the city boy who'd moved in and tried to handle her. She was always wrecking a car or making a scene. Word was she was once so drunk, she fell down a flight of stairs and bruised up one whole side of her body.

The poor man had to nurse her back because nobody in town wanted to go out to the Boxed B with her there drinking and the old man dying.

The marriage was over after a few months. Bryce left saying they'd get back together, but it never happened.

When Joni went in for cocoa, Mr. Carleon told Martha Q about the look he'd seen on Cord McDowell's face when he'd mentioned Bryce.

Martha Q returned the honesty by saying there was something about the polished Bryce Galloway that bothered her. "I've taken to locking my bedroom door at night and hinted that the widows do the same. He hasn't done one thing wrong, but something about him doesn't add up."

"Maybe we should keep an eye on Galloway," Mr. Carleon suggested. "I have a friend on the Houston police force. I might just give him a call tomorrow. He might be rich, but probably not rich enough to make police records disappear. If he had problems, they'd be filed somewhere."

"Would you?" Martha Q squealed with excitement. She was living a real-life mystery.

Joni Rosen picked that moment to step back outside and insisted on knowing what was going on.

Martha Q had to include her; after all, it would have been rude not to.

With their heads together over cocoa, the three planned to set up their own neighborhood watch on Bryce Galloway.

The next morning at breakfast they enlisted the other two widows. While the ladies went out to buy trench coats and black hats, Mr. Carleon crossed the creek and went to work for Marty Winslow. He'd already decided that their little spy game was harmless and would be something interesting to tell Marty when he woke. He might even go with Martha Q to her writers' meeting at the library. Maybe he'd hear a few bits Marty would find interesting. Carleon had always thought him a brilliant young man.

When he stepped on the porch of the duplex, Carleon almost collided with the big kid next door named Border Biggs. His head was freshly shaved so even more tattoos were visible than usual.

"Morning," Border said in almost a growl. "Mr. Carleon, ain't it? I heard you came with Marty when he arrived."

"Yes," Carleon smiled, remembering that the tattooed biker was, hard as it might be to believe, sweet Mrs. Biggs's grandson. "And you must be Border. Your grandmother makes the best pancakes I've ever tasted."

The big thug raised an eyebrow and nodded. "She's something, ain't she?"

"Yes. I'm enjoying the breakfasts she makes immensely." Carleon knew he hadn't won the kid over by simply one compliment.

In an offer of friendship, or at least peace, Carleon pulled up his sleeve. "What do you think of that?"

On the older man's arm was an eagle in full flight with an American flag between his claws. "I got it in 'Nam. I don't remember why, but it seemed a good idea at the time."

Border didn't look less frightening when he smiled. "That's so cool, man. Really cool."

Somehow they were no longer strangers. The kid stepped off the porch and headed toward his Harley. "See you later, man."

Mr. Carleon buttoned his cuff. "See you later, Border."

As he walked into Ronny's little apartment, he thought about how this was the strangest town. He was part of the widows' detective agency, hunting a man they thought looked like he might do something wrong, and he was also friends with the local Hells Angel. No wonder his boss, Marty Winslow, loved this place.

Chapter 17

MARCH 23

FRUSTRATED AND EXHAUSTED, NEVADA CAME home later than usual. She'd spent an hour longer at the office than she'd planned. Bryce had dropped by the office as if he thought he'd be welcomed back after two years. Though he'd been polite to all, it set her nerves on edge and she couldn't get back to work for an hour after he'd left.

When no one was near enough to overhear, he'd whispered, "You about ready for me to come back, Nevada? You know you can't handle the ranch and this business without me. I've grown up in the oil business and I like the idea of playing rancher."

"I'm married," she said, holding out her hand with Cord's mother's ring.

"Yeah, how long will that last? Even an ex-con is too good for you. He wouldn't put up with you for long. You're the kind of woman who needs a strong hand." He stared at her. "He'll be gone soon and you'll need me back."

Despite his family's deep pockets, she'd heard that he'd failed at several ventures since he'd left her. Maybe he figured running a ranch was easy. She really didn't know or care what he thought. "We'll never be together again, Bryce. Never."

He smiled that playboy smile that she'd loved when she'd first seen it. "Don't be too sure about that, Nevada. I haven't been able to get you out of my mind, and I'm a man used to getting exactly what he wants."

"Not me. I'm married."

He smiled. "What's he going to do to stop me? If McDowell lays a hand on me, he'll be in prison the rest of his life. All I'd probably have to do was say he threatened me and there are cops in this county who'd lock him up."

Nevada felt a chill. She told herself Bryce was lying, but she wasn't so sure. The thought of how gently Cord held her at night crossed her mind, and she decided she'd keep this problem with Bryce between them. She didn't want Cord involved or hurt.

Bryce made a polite bow and left her office, probably knowing just how badly he'd frightened her. Before their honeymoon was over, he'd begun playing a game with her. He liked to plant the seed of trouble or place a threat as if casually making a bet that he knew he'd collect on later.

The *later* always came after he'd had a few drinks and they were alone.

When Nevada left the office after sunset, she asked security to walk her to her car. Bryce wouldn't try anything in public, that wasn't his style, but she wasn't sure what she'd do if she had to face him alone.

Storm. She thought of the word Cord had used when she got angry. He'd said it so simply. *"My wife tends to storm."* Like it was something she just did from time to time. Cord had said it as if storming were a part of her character that he didn't mind at all.

Nevada could never remember knowing that kind of acceptance in her life. It seemed every day of her life someone had been trying to change her, mold her, control her.

She'd always worked hard, even when her father didn't notice, but all he'd ever done was criticize her. When he died, she walked into the company her grandfather had built and took over without missing a step. There had been no one to pat her on the back and say *Good job*, but for every mistake she made there were whispers.

Only now, Bryce was back in town and the constant feeling that she was being watched fed a bad mood she'd had all week. Bryce thought he'd keep pushing, keep pestering, until she caved.

He didn't know her as well as he thought he did, she decided. All she needed was the weekend off and she'd come back fighting. She wanted to relax at home and ride her horses, and sleep without an alarm. Maybe she'd even say she was sorry for barely speaking to Cord, if he ever stopped working long enough to listen.

Her short-term husband deserved better.

Bryce Galloway would eventually go away. She didn't like the idea that he'd come to Harmony. Maybe he thought his downhill slide started when he walked out on her to teach her a lesson. She knew he hadn't expected her to go through with the divorce. Even now, he hadn't fully accepted that they were over, forever and ever over.

She wasn't afraid of him anymore. He might hit her, if he got the chance, but he'd never own her again. No man ever would. Two years ago her father was dying, her brother was planning his escape from the ranch he hated, and Bryce had left her to deal with it all. It was the lowest point in her life. Strange thing about dropping to the bottom of a deep well—you've got nowhere to go but up. She had begun to climb.

The only thing that did frighten her was how he might try to hurt Cord.

As she walked into her cool home, Nevada set her packed briefcase on the nearest chair. *Home*, she thought, *I'm finally home*.

Her day had started out a disaster. The designer briefcase she always carried back and forth to the office had toppled over that morning when she was leaving, and she hadn't had time to get all the papers back in order. Then she had to deal with a lightning fire at one of the rig work sites. Her secretary had called in sick, something Bridget never did, and from there the day dropped even lower when Bryce came in. Now, she just wanted to forget about everything and relax.

When she walked by the kitchen, she almost didn't notice Cord sitting at the breakfast nook table, his meal half finished.

"About time you got in, Babe." He sounded cold, almost angry.

She stopped. He'd never questioned her hours and he'd never called her Babe.

"I told you several times, I don't like nicknames. Maybe it's time to test your hearing." She moved closer to the table. "And . . ." She drew a breath, knowing that she had to nip his questions about her time in the bud. "It's none of your concern where I've been. I told you from the start I often work late."

"I waited dinner for you."

"Why, so we could have another meal not talking?" She was being bitchy, but she didn't care. Her head hurt. Her feet hurt. Her emotions had been shredded like cheap confetti.

"Don't pick another fight when we're in

the middle of this one." Cord's cold eyes drilled into her. "You weren't late working. I called your office. You weren't there. No one was. Even the answering machine must have taken off early."

"You could have called my cell. We've been getting some odd calls at the office. I have the systems turned off at five so no one can get through." She didn't add that it was her ex-husband she feared would call late.

He didn't look away. He only asked, "So you could lie to me and tell me you were working late. I don't care what you do or where you go, Nevada, I just hate being lied to."

This is it, she thought. *This is where the marriage starts to turn. From now on it will start to rot and nothing can be done to save it.* She held her ground. "I don't want to lie to you, Cord, but it's none of your concern. I thought we had that understanding from the first. I don't want you worrying about me; that's just one step from controlling me."

She expected him to accuse her of having an affair or of drinking or even shopping too much, but he said simply, "Want to tell me about the odd phone calls?"

She shook her head. "No. It's just business." She felt terrible for lying. He didn't deserve it. He'd been straight with her, but she saw no point in telling him about Bryce. There was nothing he could do.

He stood and walked to her. For a second she flinched, a tiny part of her bracing for a hit. Cord was bigger than Bryce. If he hit her, it would break bones.

But he only walked around her and pulled her plate from the microwave. When he'd set her food on the table, he pulled out her chair and waited for her to join him.

She took the offered seat, unsure where she stood with this husband she rarely talked to.

While she picked at her food, he pulled a note from his pocket and slowly unfolded it. Before he placed it between them, she knew what it was. A note from Bryce. Three had come to the office, always addressed personally to her. Always the same.

She didn't pick up the paper.

"You know what it says?" Cord asked. "I wasn't prying. I found it on the floor next to where you always leave your briefcase. It must have fallen out."

"I know what it says. It says the same

thing as the odd phone messages I've been receiving at work." She couldn't lie anymore. Not to him.

Just to have something to do, she picked up the note and saw four words written in bold print. *Missing you. Coming soon.*

She expected Cord to accuse her of having a lover, but he just waited. "It's not a love note. It's a threat, and I've taken measures at the office. It's not something you have to worry about, Cord."

To her shock he seemed to believe her. He took the note, folded it back into his pocket, and said simply, "You'll tell me when it is?"

She thought about hugging him for not asking more. This was her problem, and she'd made up her mind after talking to Bryce that she'd do her best to keep Cord out of it. "I promise." She'd dealt with Bryce two years ago, and she could deal with him now.

"Then let's eat, Babe." He smiled. "And I thought we'd talk at meals from now on. Maybe not rattle on, but it doesn't have to be so silent."

She realized he was dropping the subject. No drilling of questions. No yelling. All he asked for was that she didn't lie. "Back to argument number two. Don't call me Babe."

Now, when the argument turned to nothing of importance, he frowned. "I like calling you Babe, but I could change to Honey. Honey sounds a little too sweet for you. Darling or Sweetie wouldn't be right. No, Babe has to be it."

"*No*," she yelled. "Babe is the name of a pig."

Cord thought about it. "Yeah, I know, but it was a cute pig."

She took a bite of pot roast, chewed while she thought about him, and then said, "Are you trying to pick a fight?"

He smiled. "Maybe, Babe. I like to see you fired up. It's better than worried."

She considered hitting him with her baked potato, but she doubted it was hot enough to do any real damage.

He read her mind. "If you toss one bite of that food I swear I'll—"

"You'll what?" Even play-fighting with him could get her hurt.

He grinned. "I'll think of a worse name to call you than Babe."

She smiled, settling into the nearness of him like she always did. "If you call me Babe, I'll call you Pa because it fits you. I swear, Cord, you look young but you've got the ways of an old man." She guessed he'd had very little time in his life to have fun.

Then it hit her. He'd gone to prison about the time he turned eighteen. He'd never had time to flirt or act silly. The man was almost thirty and he'd never flirted with a woman. Even when he'd asked her out once when they were still both kids, he'd just asked, no smiling or *How are you doing*, just "You want to go out?" She'd said no more because of the way he asked than because she didn't want to date him.

"Cord," she said, before he thought of another topic to bug her with tonight. "How about we go sit on the couch and watch a movie?"

"Why?" He looked like he smelled a trap.

"I could pop some popcorn and we could hold hands and pretend we're at the movies on a date. You're right. I need to leave my worries for a while and relax. You're the only one around, so I guess that makes you my date."

He stood and collected the plates. "You pick the movie, I'll pop the corn. It sounds like a dumb idea, but I'll go along with it."

When they were settled on the couch and had munched on half a bowl of popcorn, she took his hand in hers. For a few minutes he didn't seem to know what to do, and then hesitantly he began to move his thumb over her palm. When she shifted and pushed her shoulder against him, he lifted his arm and pulled her to him.

Halfway through the movie he lowered the volume and whispered, "I wasn't checking up on you today. One of the men said he found you one night a few years ago between here and town. You'd totaled your car. He claimed you must have taken the curve at sixty instead of thirty. I called because I thought you might have had car trouble or wrecked another car. I tried your cell first but you didn't answer."

"I remember that night. I don't know how fast I was going, I only remember crying so hard I couldn't see the road." She leaned her head back against his arm. "Funny, I don't remember why I was crying."

"I was worried about you tonight."

"I know," she answered, "but don't expect me to report in. Just know I'll always be coming home as soon as I can. I'll keep my promise to sleep in your bed every night."

"Fair enough." He kissed her cheek.

"And, anytime you call, always leave a message. Sometimes I step out of my office and forget to take the phone." When he didn't look like he understood, she added, "You know, to the ladies' room."

"Oh."

She swore he blushed.

She placed her hand on his jaw and turned his head toward her. The kiss was soft, gentle, like a first kiss. Neither seemed to want it to end, but neither pushed for more. For now, it was enough. This wasn't a peck on the cheek or a kiss for show. This kiss was real and they both knew it.

When she finally pulled away, he smiled and turned the movie back up. A settling had passed between them and an acceptance that neither one had ever felt. It took her a long while to realize what had happened, to recognize the feeling blanketing over them both.

It was simply a trust unlike anything she'd ever felt. He trusted her without questioning when she'd given no answer. All he'd asked for was not to be lied to, and she swore she never would. She'd keep her secrets, but she would no longer wrap them in lies.

When the movie ended, he took her hand and they walked to the bedroom without a word. He stripped off his clothes, watching her do the same. Neither bothered to turn on a light. The open blinds and windows let in enough moonlight to see.

He pulled back the covers on his side of the bed and waited for her to climb in. When she did, he moved in beside her and kissed her lightly. "The movie wasn't such a bad idea after all," he whispered against her ear. "I wouldn't mind having a date with you again."

She stretched, letting her body settle against his. All the stress of the day moved away, and she finally felt safe. She wouldn't have cared if he kissed her again, but he only whispered, "Good night, Babe."

She poked him gently in the ribs and felt his laughter against her throat.

Chapter 18

MARCH 24
DUPLEX

RONNY SLIPPED OUT THE BACK DOOR OF HER little apartment and into the cool night air. She had to force herself to think about what day it was. The twenty-fourth, she thought. One week since Marty had moved in with her. The days, even the hours flowed together. There was so much to be done, and time passed not from morning to night, but from the precious hours Marty was awake.

They'd almost lost him the second day.

She didn't sleep for more than thirty hours as she stayed by his side. Something in her tired mind said she'd lose him if she didn't keep watch. Finally he calmed, and she slept for twelve hours only to find him smiling at her when she ran in to check on him.

Mr. Carleon tried to keep time in balance. He insisted she eat breakfast even when she didn't notice it was morning. Beau Yates, next door, played his guitar every evening he didn't work, and Marty would hold her hand as if they were at a great concert.

Dr. Addison Spencer came every day to check on him. She kept close records and tried to balance his pain medicine so that he could keep his wits about him. Ronny teased him that the doctor was fighting a lost cause because after falling off a mountain he didn't have many wits left.

Marty, in his usual superior way, claimed he'd been born double-witted and could stand to lose a few. The first time he laughed, everyone in the room stopped. Ronny fought back tears as she realized teasing him just might be the magic that helped him live one day longer.

As always, Marty complained. He didn't like the food or it was too hot or cold in the room or the sun bothered him or the room was drab. He even complained about the color of the paint.

Ronny frowned at him. "Well, in a perfect world, what color would this room be?"

"Green," he said. "Deep forest green."

That afternoon, while he slept, everyone grabbed a paintbrush, and when he woke up the room was green. Of course, he reminded them all that it was the worst paint job he'd ever seen, but no one listened.

Tonight was the end of his eighth day and he was still alive. She walked to the ramp Cord and his men had built for a wheelchair. Marty was no closer to being able to sit in a chair than he'd been the day he came, but seeing the ramp brought her promise.

Someday, she hoped, she'd roll him down the ramp and they'd go the block to Main Street. They'd go past all the stores and look at the courthouse. Maybe they'd stop at the diner for lunch or go over to Buffalo's Bar and Grill and have a beer. She'd sit beside his chair and they'd hold hands as they listened to Beau and his partner in the band play. It would be like a real date, something they'd had very few of.

Marty would always say that Beau was a dreamer, his head full of songs, and she'd argue that it might not be a bad way to go through life.

Ronny wasn't a big dreamer. She'd never wanted a great passion or riches or to travel the world. All she'd ever wanted was for someone to love her. She wanted to hold someone's hand and smile. She wanted one person to care when she had a cold or lost weight or cut her hair.

"I don't want much, God," she whispered into the silent night around her. "If you could see your way to give us just a little more time."

Marty was asleep and the night called her out for a walk.

The sudden sound of a car moving slowly down the street made her move back into the shadows of the duplex. In the foggy glow of the streetlight half a block away, she watched her mother's car circle the block. Once. Twice.

On impulse, Ronny walked to the curb. If her mother wanted to say something to her, Ronny decided she'd listen. She no longer had any energy left to be angry at Dallas Logan for kicking her out. In truth, it had been the start of her awakening, and she knew, even if asked, she'd never go back.

When Dallas's old Buick circled one more time, she made it almost even with Ronny before she gunned the engine and sped away.

Ronny smiled at the taillights as she buttoned her coat and tied back her hair with a band she kept in her coat pocket. She was sure her mother thought the gesture of driving away fast would hurt Ronny. One more insult. One more time that Dallas could reject her child.

Only Ronny no longer felt it. She knew she was loved and needed by the man inside, and her mother's anger no longer mattered. She moved silently through the streets, no more than another layer of shadow between the streetlights. She liked the night when she could disappear and let the darkness hold her for a while.

When she went back inside, Marty was awake. He must have been watching her from the window. "Come here, honey." Not only did his eyes show the pain he felt inside, but he seemed sad for her as well.

She walked to the chair that always sat close to his bed. "You saw my mother's car?"

"I did. If I could I'd take away all the bad memories of your growing up with that woman, but I've come to believe that the bad only makes us appreciate the good, and you are the best thing that ever came into my life."

"Really?"

"You're the only person who ever needed me. I wish I could always be here for you. When I was away, every day I tried to remember details about you. The way your hair moved. The way you stood up to me that first day we met even though I was yelling at you. I even remember that funny hat you used to wear when you delivered the mail. I thought it was the ugliest hat I'd ever seen, but you were cute as a bug wearing it. Funny, no matter what was going on when I was away, the thought of that hat would always make me smile."

She laced her hand in his. They'd agreed days ago not to waste time saying things like "How do you feel?" or "You need to rest" to one another. They took the short periods of time they had. It was all that was left and somehow, it had to be enough.

"Tell me about your adventures," she said, curling against the bed so that she was as close as the machines would allow her. "Tell me about the world you've seen."

He began telling her of mountain climbing and hang gliding and skiing in the Alps. For a moment, as she listened, he wasn't a frail man in a hospital bed. He was the man she had met and fallen in love with. He was whole again, pulling her along with him on his adventures . . . pulling her into a perfect world.

Chapter 19

APRIL 4

THEY'D BEEN MARRIED ALMOST A MONTH WHEN Cord woke Nevada at dawn with a rough kiss. They'd kissed good night for over a week—soft, gentle kisses—but this was different. This tasted of passion.

"I can't hold out any longer, Babe." His hand spread wide along her side. "I got to get closer to you, so if you don't want this, you'd better stop me now."

She stared up into his warm eyes, still half asleep. He looked more like a man being tortured than someone about to make love to his wife. His jaw was set. His gaze never left hers as his hand moved down her, hungry for the feel of her. The silk nightgown bunched and tugged against his callused hands. He wasn't holding her, only brushing over her, as if learning her every curve.

"You're so soft," he whispered against her ear. "So soft."

She didn't budge as he pulled off her short gown and moved above her. The feel of his body pressing over her warmed her as he shifted her arms and spread her blond hair across the pillow. For a minute he waited, matching his breathing to balance hers, letting his warmth blanket hers.

He braced his elbows on either side of her face and kissed her with feather kisses along her cheek. With each breath his hard chest lowered and pressed against her as his lips trailed over her skin. When he returned to her mouth, she opened to his hunger and moaned as the kiss turned molten.

The kiss was deep, and neither thought to breathe. When he finally broke away, she gulped for air and waited for him to pull her into heaven.

His big hands moved into her hair and

tugged her gently as he tasted the flesh of her throat like a man starving for her.

She could feel her whispered moans of pleasure pushing him beyond reason.

If she didn't tell him how she felt, he'd move away and she'd never know this man she'd married any better than she knew him now. Pressing her lips against his ear, she whispered, "Make love to me, Cord. Just love me."

He pulled away and looked into her eyes, then lowered his mouth to hers with one last gentle kiss before passion consumed them both.

Without a word he made love to her with great tenderness. The only sound was her soft cry when he entered her. He wasn't taking, but giving in loving touches and slow kisses that moved over her skin like warm water. What he lacked in polish, he made up for in gentleness. He hesitated at times, giving her moments to anticipate pure pleasure and rushed at others as if he couldn't wait to be closer to her. His body never smothered or dominated, but comforted and sheltered her from all the world except his touch.

As he moved over her, so close they

became one, she had the sense of coming home, of being complete.

When they were finished and both too tired to do more than breathe, he pulled her against his chest and floated the covers over them both without saying a word.

Even in the shadows of passion, he held her as no man had ever held her. His hand moved slowly down her body, cherishing one last touch before he fell asleep.

Tears dripped down her cheeks. She'd wondered what making love to him would be like. Violent, savage, wild, but it was none of those. He'd made no promises. Whispered no endearments. Told no lies. But his every touch told of caring deeply, so deeply he'd lost himself in satisfying her.

An hour later, he was dressed by the time she woke and crawled from the bed. For a minute they just looked at each other. He wore his jeans and western-cut shirt with the snaps, all pressed and starched. His winter-wheat hair was still wet from a shower and she could smell the shaving cream he'd just used. Down to his hand-made boots he looked every bit a successful, powerful rancher.

She stood before him with wild straw

hair and a gown strap hanging to her elbow. The top of one breast showed, but after he'd handled her so completely at dawn she didn't think it would matter much.

"About this morning . . ." He finally broke the silence.

"Don't you dare apologize," she interrupted.

He raised an eyebrow but didn't move any closer.

She crossed half the distance between them. "No one's ever made love to me like that. Not ever. You made me feel like I was special. Like I was priceless, and I'll not have you ruin it by saying you're sorry or that we shouldn't have done it."

A slow smile spread across his face. "I was going to ask you if it really happened or if I was just dreaming. Either way I had no intention to apologize."

She felt like a fool for her outburst. "It happened," was all she could manage.

"So, I take it, you've no objection to it happening again sometime."

"I'm looking forward to it." Crossing her arms, she tried to look proper. "In fact, I wouldn't mind at all if it became a habit between us."

She wanted to run to him and kiss him, but something in the way he stood told her he wanted to keep everything in a compartment, even her.

For a man who never touched anyone, he had certainly touched her before dawn. Even now she could still feel his big hands sliding down her body, moving her gently so that he could satisfy every part of her.

"I have to get over to the bunkhouse." He pulled her back from her thoughts.

"All right," she answered, not knowing how to talk about how perfectly they'd made love.

He nodded once and walked to the door. "You might want to go shopping for more of those little gowns that aren't long enough to cover anything or thick enough to hide anything. I like them."

Looking down at the silk slip of a gown, she smiled. It had cost her a hundred dollars, and until last night she hadn't thought he'd noticed. She'd order half a dozen online today and have them sent overnight.

Chapter 20

AT NINE IN THE MORNING MARTHA Q FOUND herself totally alone in the inn. All the widows went to the first-day sale at the Sears outlet store. Mr. Carleon left to stay with Marty in one of his usual pressed black suits. Bryce Galloway said he would be gone all day, and the housekeeper took Mrs. Biggs grocery shopping.

Martha Q wasn't sure what to do. She hadn't had the run of the house, completely alone, in months. She told herself she wasn't a nosy person, but it seemed like a good time to look in every room. After all, it was her house.

She collected the master keys and decided to start on the third floor. Mr. Carleon's room was perfect. Three black suits, an overcoat, and a half dozen white shirts were lined up in his closet. No color, she observed. All his personal things were lined up neatly in the three dressers. Underwear. Handkerchiefs. Socks. A black shaving kit. Several books were on the shelf by the bed, all in order of size. The man even made his own bed. He folded his underwear and left a thin bookmark in the paperback he was reading. No excitement, no surprises.

In Bryce Galloway's room, she found the opposite. Nothing was picked up or cleaned. Dirty clothes scattered on the floor, the suitcase left open atop the dresser as if he didn't realize he had drawers he could have used. The maid had already complained that his was the hardest room to clean. He'd left shaving cream and stubble in the sink, towels on the floor, water stains where his glass sat on the nightstand, and crumbs on the desk along with dirty dishes he'd carried up from the kitchen.

Leaving the door open so she could hear anyone coming up the stairs, she

went through his belongings like a spy.
Papers were piled on the desk, but they all
looked like legal documents or geographic
maps, except for one that had simple times
written down. *6:10, 6:22, 7:03. All in by 7:15*,
and so on. There was another list of times
with initials beside them, but they made
even less sense. Each time had an *A* or *B*
before it, like he was keeping a log on two
people or two houses at the same time.
Galloway was watching people come and
go, but who and from where had not been
written down.

Martha Q fought the urge to call Tyler
Wright again and fill him in on the details.
Since the man had found out he was going to be a father, he didn't seem to give
his full attention so easily, but the funeral
director was the only man she could think
of who might be able to solve the riddle.
Bryce Galloway didn't belong here. He
wasn't one of them. From the look of him,
he had enough money to stay at a grand
hotel, not a little bed-and-breakfast in the
old part of town.

Harmony had its share of nuts and odd
characters, but Bryce was different. If
there was a town somewhere where he'd

fit in, Martha Q didn't want to go there. Tyler Wright would listen to her and probably pat her hand and tell her she didn't have anything to worry about. He'd be gone soon. After all, if he'd planned to stay, wouldn't he have bought a house and not stayed at the inn?

She grinned, remembering how she'd driven by the funeral home a few days ago and seen Tyler helping his Kate out of the car. For a moment in the quiet morning air when they thought no one else was around, he'd kissed her cheek as he'd spread his hand across her swollen belly. If Hallmark could get that emotion of pure love on a card, they'd sell a million.

As she walked down the stairs, Martha Q decided she'd have to depend on the widows' detective agency to find out more about Bryce. She'd put one of them on him from the time he left after breakfast until he returned. No, she'd better make them go in twos. One was bound to get distracted. Martha Q wanted to know where he went, who he talked to.

At the bottom of the stairs, the fat cat swore in cat talk when Martha Q tripped over him. Martha Q swung in an attempt to kick the cat, but Mr. Dolittle just walked away mumbling to himself. If cats really were reincarnated people, he must have been a bachelor. No woman would put up with him if he weighed more than twenty pounds.

"I might as well get dressed," she said to no one. "I may have to do some investigating of my own. I'll have to stop by the bookstore and buy a tablet first. He's not the only one who can keep records." If Bryce was keeping track of someone's comings and goings, she'd bet it was for no good.

Chapter 21

APRIL 4

CORD SPENT THE MORNING TRYING TO KEEP HIS mind on work. No matter how hard he pushed, there never seemed enough hours in the day, and now he had a feeling there wouldn't be enough hours at night either. If Nevada was ever agreeable to it again, and she seemed to be, he'd die of exhaustion before he'd give up making love to her. At one point he was so wrapped in passion that lightning could have set fire to the bed and he wouldn't have noticed.

But as the day aged, he told himself he

didn't have time to think about her and what they'd done at dawn. The ranch had more than its share of problems. One of the fences was down in the north pasture and cattle were everywhere, even on the county road. Galem said men had to stop their trucks and shoo a dozen cows away before they could get to work. An hour later they discovered that the pump to one of the main water supplies had broken.

To make matters worse, the day turned cloudy about eleven and so did his mood. Try as he did, he couldn't keep his mind away from thoughts of Nevada. There were probably words he should have said to her before he left, but he had no idea what they would be. He found himself wishing for the night as thunder rolled in the distance. Wishing it could be just the two of them in the world again. She'd looked so adorable with her hair all wild and her little nightgown half falling off.

The thought of how Nevada felt in his arms returned again and again like a merry-go-round of pleasure circling in his mind. She'd lain back on the pillows and let him touch her, only moving slightly now and then when she showed her pleasure.

He'd taken his time, learning every part of her. The softest spot just beneath her breasts and the way she laughed when he brushed his fingers down her spine. He loved the smell of her when she was warm and wrapped in the sheets. He loved the taste of her throat as he felt her pulse against his open mouth.

"You asleep, Cord?" Galem shouted above the thunder.

Cord jumped out of the way of a cow coming down the branding chute. A few men smothered laughter until Cord laughed at himself, and then full all-out teasing began.

"You'd think the boss was on his honeymoon," one said.

"He does look like he needs sleep."

"Got that calf-eyed look about him."

"We'd better watch out for him or he's liable to get trampled."

"Maybe you should consider taking a nap somewhere besides where five hundred pounds of beef can knock you down."

Cord grumbled, but he couldn't hide the smile or even fake anger at the time they were wasting. Let them laugh; in a few hours he'd be going home to Nevada and it wouldn't take long to get her back between the sheets.

"Let's get back to work," he ordered, and added to himself, "We've got loads to do before it rains."

The men went back to business, and Cord forced his mind to focus on what he was doing.

Around one o'clock he ordered everyone to take a break. Galem handed him one of the sandwiches he'd packed for the men. They were too far from headquarters to go in, so sandwiches and lukewarm water would hold hunger at bay. The men broke into groups, most talking about plans for the weekend, while Cord sat down beside Galem.

"Wouldn't do you no good to go back to headquarters for lunch anyway, Cord," Galem said. "Ora Mae went to Amarillo with Little Miss. Phoned an hour ago to tell me they were in the middle of a shopping spree and would be lucky to make it in by six."

Shaking his head, Cord admitted, "I don't see why she likes to shop. I always hated it."

"Ora Mae told me once that Nevada's mother only showed her any attention when they shopped. She liked to dress the little girl up. I guess that was her way of showing love."

Cord almost mentioned that Nevada was probably shopping for him, but he doubted she considered it a show of love in his case.

He took another sandwich. "Why do you call her Little Miss? She's five seven before she puts on her heels. She's not exactly a little miss." He smiled, thinking of how his chin touched the top of her head.

"I know, but I remember the skinny little girl who followed me around when I came to work at the Boxed B. I was still in my teens when I quit school, my folks kicked me out of the nest. Helping out in the bunkhouse wasn't just my first job, it was my only home. Back then Nevada's father was running the place and he wanted men at the bunkhouse day and night. We didn't just work hours, we signed on for the season. He was always pushing his three grown sons to cowboy up, but he ignored his half-grown daughter. Near as I could see, the boys followed his lead. I never saw them do anything but tease her or tell her how dumb she was 'cause she couldn't keep up with them."

Galem took a bite of his sandwich and continued, "I never heard the old man say a kind word to anyone. He mostly yelled at everyone, except Little Miss. To him, she wasn't even there. He told me once that she was something his wife wanted, like she was nothing but a pet around the place. I didn't know a lot, but I taught her to ride and tried to teach her to cook. Cooking lessons were a waste of time, but I never saw a kid love horses like she did and still does. She'd come home every summer and nag her mom until she got a new mare. She always said she'd raise horses to sell as show horses. Her mom gave in to her, kind of the anything-you-want-as long-as-you-go-away brand of raising a kid. By the time she was fifteen she was showing horses and winning every trophy around."

"I've never seen a single trophy around the house," Cord commented. "You would have thought they'd let her put them up somewhere."

"That stepmother she had one summer tossed them all out, I bet. She even tried to get the old man to sell off Nevada's horses. Only her daddy had promised Nevada's mother before she died that he wouldn't mess with them, and the old man kept his word. Maybe he figured as long as Nevada had the horses she wouldn't spend much time at home. I swear that summer the step-witch was here, Nevada slept more in the barn than she did in the house."

"Thanks for telling me." Cord realized Galem must trust him to so openly talk about Nevada. "And thanks for yelling. That steer almost bloodied one of these shirts Nevada bought me. I was daydreaming on the job."

"No thanks needed," Galem answered. "I'm guessing you got a problem on your mind."

"Right," he managed to say as he looked up and saw the *problem* headed straight toward him in her grandfather's old Jeep.

Swearing, Cord swung over the fence thinking he should have stripped all the gears except first so she couldn't go over twenty. He headed toward the spot he hoped would be where she stopped before hitting the corral.

Her own little cloud of dust swirled

around her as she hit the brakes and slid to within three feet of him.

Cord waited. He knew it wouldn't be long.

She climbed out of the Jeep talking. It took his mind a few beats to catch up with her.

"Hold on now, Nevada. Take a long breath and start over."

"What is the matter with you? Didn't you hear what I said?" She folded her arms over her chest and stared at him as if he were brain dead. "I swear if I have to tell you everything twice, we'll never finish a conversation."

Cord moved closer and lowered his voice so none of the men could hear. "I just need time to get over the sight of you before I can think. You're beautiful even when you're upset."

He fought the urge to kiss her. "I thought you weren't on the ranch. I heard something about you going shopping." He grinned. "You do look great in that sundress." He closed his mouth and his eyes. He was starting to sound as scattered as she always did. Maybe being brain dead and chattering on about nothing was catching.

"The men are staring at us," she whispered. Thunder rattled the air and the first raindrops plopped in the dirt, but she didn't move.

"They're staring at you and that cotton dress." He'd thought she looked and felt great in silk, but now he couldn't imagine anything finer than cotton brushing her legs.

"We need to talk. Something happened in town that I should tell you about." She took his arm and pulled him toward the Jeep. "Go for a drive with me."

"I can't," he started, as huge drops splattered around him. The sky darkened as if someone had turned down the dimmer switch on the world. Big drops of rain hit the hood of the Jeep like tiny bombs spraying inch-wide circles across the hot metal. "We need to finish here."

Horses danced nervously as lightning flashed and the men scrambled for the rain slickers tied to their saddles. This wasn't just a light afternoon shower coming; something strong was blowing in.

Cord turned back to his men. "Close it down, boys, and call it a day." Even if the rain stopped soon, it would be too muddy to get much work done. He saw Zeb running for one of the horse trailers as the cowhands loaded up their mounts. Riding home in this storm might get horse and rider killed.

He put his arm over Nevada's shoulder. "All right, let's go talk, but I drive." In the drafty old Jeep they'd both be soaked in minutes if they didn't find cover fast.

As he circled the corral, he made sure all cowhands were loaded into trucks, horses were ready to move, and gates were closed. Cord didn't want to come back in the morning to find fifty head of cattle wandering the west side of the ranch. He'd had enough accidents happen lately. So many, in fact, he was starting to think someone had it in for him, making trouble run double time. In the back of his mind the name of Bryce Galloway kept echoing even though he didn't have an ounce of proof. He wouldn't put it past the ex-husband to try to make things hard for Cord just for the fun of it.

Since Cord was closer to his farm than the ranch house, he headed down the dirt road toward his home place. He'd sold his old tractor and his horse trailer, hoping to make enough money to pay off the last of his loan. The buyer was supposed to pick both up yesterday. He'd left them parked in the yard between the house and the barn and had planned to drive over to his place today anyway just to make sure they were gone.

As they drove he could feel them racing the edge of the storm, and he guessed if he slowed it would catch them. Rolling down the window, he let damp air fly past him as lightning danced along the horizon. In this country it paid to watch the weather.

Nevada chatted about her trip to Amarillo and all she'd bought as he drove. He knew she wasn't talking about what she needed to. She was nervous about something more than the lightning. Like him, she grew up with the sudden storms and knew to take cover.

When they turned onto his land, he slowed. The storm hadn't caught up to them yet, and the last thing he wanted to do was accidentally flip the old Jeep in a pothole. He knew his place needed repairs, but somehow the Boxed B always drew his attention.

"You need to get the crew out working

on this road." She voiced his thoughts. "I don't want you neglecting your farm. I always thought this was a nice place, like one of those pictures of what folks in cities think farmhouses should look like."

He'd never thought of it that way. It had always been just a house. Even though he grew up there, it still seemed more his folks' place than his.

"That's not what you came out to talk to me about." Cord was ready to hear whatever she had to say. "What brought you back from town so early?"

"There was another note on my car when I stopped at the mall. We weren't there long and I saw no sign of him, but Bryce left it. I know he did."

"Same words."

She nodded. "Ora Mae said we'd better get back to the ranch. I was glad I wasn't alone. I swear I could feel him watching us. It spooked us both."

"You won't be alone again. Until this guy stops *missing you*, me or one of the men will drive you anywhere you want to go." He glanced her way and saw her open her mouth to argue, then stop.

"Agreed?" he pushed, knowing it sounded

more like an order than a request, but he couldn't just talk about her safety, he had to do what he could.

"You're right. If I know Bryce, we won't have long to wait. He had the attention span of a mosquito sucking tequila. He'll either show up soon or move on. I should warn you, he's a master at causing distraction and walking away like the victim. Once when he blacked my eye, Galem taught him a lesson. On the way to the hospital to get a few stitches, Bryce swore he'd see Galem in jail. When I begged him not to, he ran off the road. I was barely conscious when he shoved me behind the wheel and called 911. My injuries, as well as his, were written up as a car accident. The sheriff thought I was driving blind drunk, and he said he'd gone along hoping to stop me." Nevada shook her head. "He put on such a show of begging the sheriff not to book me, even promising to hide the keys on the nights I drank."

"Were you over the limit?"

"Probably, but I hadn't been the one driving. Luckily, we were still on the ranch when the wreck happened. Private property saved me from a DWI."

"You could have told the truth."

"I wouldn't have been believed. It would have been my word against his, and Bryce has this way of telling lies that suckers everyone in. After that night he was the long-suffering husband and I was the wild spoiled brat who had totaled yet another car."

Cord remembered reading about the wreck. Even the local paper had run it more as a "see what the Britain girl has done now" story than a news report. They'd even reported the injuries suffered by the passenger, her husband.

"That where you got the little scar just over your left eyebrow?"

Surprise pulled her out of her depression. "You noticed that."

"I notice everything about you, Babe."

He'd managed to make her smile. "Apparently you do, except that I hate being called Babe."

When he pulled up to his place and cut the engine, he thought his farm looked abandoned. With the farm equipment and the trailer gone, the house and barn looked even more run down. Tumbleweeds were caught along the fence line and one of the chairs had blown off the porch. Far to

the right he could see the first crop breaking the soil by a few inches. Thanks to the
Boxed B's huge tractors, they'd plowed
and planted in days instead of weeks. Cord
had even bought mobile irrigation units,
almost guaranteeing a good crop. When
their marriage ended, he'd haul the irrigation system over to her place.

Glancing down at her finger, he saw the
thin band of gold. She was still wearing it,
so today wouldn't be the last day. After a
month, he'd thought they were working well
together, but now he wasn't so sure. After
all, he had made love to her just before
dawn without them even talking it over first.

She hadn't exactly invited him to make
love to her, but she hadn't objected. He'd
thought she enjoyed it as much as he had.
She'd come home in the middle of the day
and pulled him away from work, saying
she needed to talk. A note left on a car
didn't seem that urgent. Something else
was bothering her.

Maybe he'd stepped over that invisible
trip wire he'd been looking for since they
walked out of the courthouse . . . maybe
he'd tripped the switch that was about to
blow up everything.

"So, I finally heard what Ora Mae had been trying to tell me. That woman would drive to heaven in a wheelbarrow to get her point across."

"What did she tell you?" He'd dropped out of the conversation at some point. He had enough frightening things in his past. The housekeeper wouldn't have to make something up. Whatever it was, he knew he'd found the real problem that had made her drive across half the ranch to find him.

Nevada huffed as if she'd been asked to say everything again. "She told me that you're not comfortable in the house. She says you go around opening drapes and turning on lights. She says every door you walk through, you leave open, and you're forever roaming through the kitchen looking for something to eat."

Cord relaxed. She was complaining about his habits. He could fix that. "I like light and fresh air. I like being able to eat whenever I'm hungry, but if it bothers you I can change." He could learn to live in the cavelike rooms with their thick drapes and closed windows. He could eat on a timetable; he had in prison.

"It doesn't bother me." Now, after he

gave in, she sounded angry. "If you want light and air, we can work on that. I told Ora Mae to leave a basket of fruit and snacks out on the counter and clean the wine cooler out and stock it with individual milks you can take with you or whatever kind of drinks you like. Since our marriage I seem to have given up the habit of wine with dinner anyway."

Now he was confused. She was giving in. He climbed out of the Jeep and ran the few feet to the overhang at the side of his parents' home. "What are we talking about, Nevada?"

She followed him to the corner of the porch and sat down, propping her boots up on the steps. "We're talking about making you happy, you idiot, so stop making a big deal of it and tell Ora Mae what you want her to do. She'll stock up on whatever you like. We'll turn off the air conditioner and keep the windows open as long as the wind is under forty. W—"

He knelt to her level on the thick grass that had always grown on the shady side of the porch. "One more time. What are we talking about, Nevada? This isn't about me turning on lights or what I want to drink.

You didn't drive out to talk about Ora Mae's worries, did you? What are we really talking about here? Say what you want to say, Babe," he asked again, and then waited.

For a while she didn't look at him, and he just listened to the rain playing on the tin porch roof of the old house. He'd grown up in this quiet farmhouse where no one talked out their problems. He didn't want it to be like that between him and Nevada. He'd rather face trouble head on than wonder what was bothering her.

When she finally did look up, her beautiful eyes were swimming in tears. "Why'd you make love to me like that, Cord?"

Of all the things he thought might be on her mind, bothering her, making her nervous and angry, their dawn loving had finally made it to the top of the list.

He cupped the side of her face and brushed a tear away with his thumb. "Like what? Did I do something wrong?" He wanted to scream that he could change, he could get it right next time, only in his life there were very few second chances and maybe she wasn't willing to give him one.

Her hand covered his, pressing his palm

against her cheek. "I didn't expect it, not knowing the kind of man you are. I didn't expect you to be so tender." She gulped down a sob. "No one's ever made love to me like that. Like I was special, like I was made of fine china."

He stood and looked down at her, wondering how any man could touch her in any other way. The thought that someone had made his gut knot.

She straightened, lifting her chin. "We agreed to be honest, so here goes. I've had more lovers than I can count. I gave it away to half a dozen on my sixteenth birthday just to show my dad that I could party even if he forgot to say *happy birthday* to me. I've had one-night stands where I couldn't remember the guy's name in the morning. I had three husbands, one who thought that wild sex was an every-night rodeo and one who used it to dominate and control. If I didn't want to, he'd torture me insisting on it and, if I agreed too easily, he'd say that I was a tramp and deserved to be treated like one."

She held to her pride, and he saw all her invisible scars for the first time.

"I've had sex in the back of pickups and

penthouse suites, coatrooms and bathroom bars, but I've never, ever had what you offered this morning."

He circled his arms around her and pulled her gently against his chest. "What do you want?"

She pressed her forehead against his chest. "I want that kind of loving again, but I don't want to have to ask or beg for it. I don't want it to be part of the negotiation between us. I don't want it to be a game between you and me. Not this. I need to know that this one thing is real between us."

He turned her head up and kissed her before whispering, "I've never done it in a pickup or a penthouse, or a bathroom bar. In fact, except for a few awkward times before I left for prison, I've never made love at all, so I guess if you put us together we average out to about even."

"But how?"

He laughed. "I dreamed of making love a lot, and always when I did, I dreamed that it was with you."

She pulled away. "You're kidding."

He shook his head. "That's why it came so easy last night. I'd practiced in my mind a thousand times."

He kissed her again, this time with passion. When he finally broke the kiss, his hands still moved over her. "Making love to you was never part of any game. Whenever you want to again, just touch me. There will be no negotiating or bargaining." He kissed her ear. "Or holding back. Any time. Any place."

"Now," she whispered, then laughed when he stumbled backward into the rain.

She wrapped her arms around him and held on tight, not caring that big cold raindrops splattered around her. Her first kiss was almost shy.

He moved his hands over her bottom and lifted her as she wrapped her legs around his waist. Moving toward the house, they were lost to everything around but each other. Without a word, he kicked in the door, climbed the narrow stairs, and walked into his old room. The storm made it seem like night, and the rain blocked out all the world.

Pulling the dust cover off the bed, he lowered with her still in his arms. "I want to take that dress off you real slow. Any objections?"

He tugged the tie free at the back of her

neck. "Then, I'm going to take my time learning every curve of you, Babe, all over again."

She giggled as if it were her first time to be truly loved.

Within minutes their clothes were piled on the dusty floor, but neither noticed. They were too wrapped in each other. As the storm pounded the little farmhouse, passion flowed between them in long kisses and easy strokes. In the shadowy light he watched her face, loving knowing how much he made her feel . . . loving knowing what his touch did to her.

In his dreams he'd hadn't heard the way she sighed softly when she was happy and how she cried out when lost in passion. Now, every sound she made washed over him in sweet melody. Loving her was as easy as breathing, and he never wanted to stop. Even when he was exhausted and she lay sleeping on his shoulder, he couldn't keep from touching her.

As he drifted to sleep, he dreamed of loving her and woke to find her still in his arms.

When they finally got dressed and started home, the rain had stopped and the sun was setting. He turned the Jeep toward his old barn. "Want to go for a ride in my grandfather's old plane?"

She looked worried.

"I'm a safe pilot." He laughed. "I swear."

She slipped her hand in his and nodded, making him feel like he could almost fly without the plane. She was trusting him, something it seemed like he'd had very little of in his life.

They flew over their land with the wind blowing in their faces. They watched the sunset and night move over the fields. The smell of spring brushed past them, making the night seem newborn.

When he set the plane down, she climbed out and into his arms.

"Can we do it again?"

"Babe, we can do everything again, and again, and again."

Nevada laughed free and unguarded.

They talked of nothing when they pushed the plane back into the barn, then held hands as they walked to the Jeep.

He drove slowly, not wanting the world to catch up to them again. Twice, he stopped in the center of the road to pull her close and kiss her.

"I already want you again," he whispered, and loved the way she laughed as she moved her fingers into his hair.

When she finished kissing him, she pulled away and added, "We'd better get home fast. Maybe we should have flown the plane home."

He saw her need for him in her blue eyes and felt like his heart might explode.

The ranch house was dark when they finally made it home, and he noticed she turned on every light as she walked through to the kitchen. Then, like starving children, they collected everything that looked edible and camped out in the breakfast nook. They talked of nothing and ate ice cream over cereal topped with chocolate sauce.

He felt like he'd gone to prison before he'd finished growing. He never remembered allowing himself to act silly, but tonight the air seemed enchanted. They fought over every cherry he pulled from the jar. She tickled him, then giggled when he refused to tickle her back. Though he wanted to hold her tight against him, he kept his embrace light, easy for her to move in and out.

When they crawled into bed, they settled in the middle, making love one more time as if both knew eventually this day had to end. After she fell asleep on his chest, Cord lay awake thinking that if he had only one day of heaven coming to him in this lifetime, this one day was enough.

He kissed the top of her head. "I love you," he whispered, wondering if he'd ever say the words to her when she was awake. Nevada didn't believe in forever.

She didn't believe in love.

He knew the seven months of married life they had left wouldn't be long enough, but he'd take the time and do all he could to become the one person in her life that she couldn't do without.

He'd become the habit she couldn't break. Even if she never said the words, she'd love him, and when their time was over, she'd remain in his bed. She'd sleep with him through the first frost.

"Sleep, Babe," he whispered as he bumped his chin against her forehead.

She moaned and wiggled closer to him for warmth.

He moved his hand down her back, pressing her against him. "I'm going to make love to you again at dawn."

"Promise," she mumbled, more asleep than awake. "It'd be a great start to the day."

"Promise," he answered, knowing that Nevada already loved him and didn't even know it. "Tomorrow and every morning," he added, smiling.

Chapter 22

APRIL 5

THE DOCTORS WARNED RONNY THAT MARTY Winslow would have good days and bad, but the good days were always too short and the bad days were growing worse. Sometimes he didn't wake for more than an hour, and when he did, he didn't seem to see the world.

His brother and cousins who had been waiting for him to die seemed content to stay away and let Mr. Carleon and Ronny handle the work of the last few days. With the nurses on eight-hour shifts around the clock and the doctor coming every day, there was still plenty of work to keep both Mr. Carleon and Ronny rushing.

Mr. Carleon read to him from adventure books he knew Marty loved, and Beau would still play for him in the evenings. A hundred times Ronny checked and swore Marty was less with them than he had been the day before. The machines were working, counting off breaths and heart-beats, but he seemed to be leaving an inch at a time.

Ronny found her escape in long walks when she knew he was resting well. Time lost all meaning. She would move like a ghost through the town in the early morn-ing and again when the moon was high. People she sometimes passed were no more alive than the mannequins in the windows of the stores on Main.

She kept her phone close, knowing that Mr. Carleon would call her if anything changed, but sometimes she feared she wouldn't hear it because she didn't hear anything. The world, her world, was grow-ing silent.

Cord McDowell dropped by on Thurs-day morning, just to see if she needed

anything. He was a quiet man trying to be kind, and she knew being sociable didn't come any easier for him than it did for her. On impulse, Ronny invited him in. Marty was awake and might enjoy the company.

Cord didn't seem to know how to make small talk. When Marty asked him about the ranching business, he told him some of the problems he was having trying to run a ranch after spending most of his adult years in prison.

To Ronny's surprise, Cord and Marty talked with a kind of honesty that few people bother to use. No frills or stories just to entertain. Marty's mind seemed to sharpen. He knew nothing of ranching, but he knew business. Like a man working a puzzle, Marty asked the right questions, drawing Cord down logical roads.

"If you'll bring your books over," Marty finally said, "I'll take a look at them. I stayed in college long enough to get a minor in everything and a major in fun."

"I don't want to be a bother, but thank you for the offer." Cord smiled at Ronny, and she knew he saw what she saw in Marty, not the frail man in the bed, but a bright mind with little tolerance for fools.

"It's no bother," Marty said. "You've given me something to think about besides dying. I'm asking more for my sanity than your need."

"I have to come to town tomorrow. Would that be too soon for you to start answering a few questions? I swear I can't make heads or tails of the books, and I don't know how to figure out exactly what the profit margin is on the cattle. I'd interview for a bookkeeper, but I don't even know what questions to ask."

"Sure." Marty sounded excited. "If I can't figure it out, Ronny might be able to help."

Cord picked up his hat and backed out of the room. She knew without asking that having people be kind to him was still too new for the man to take it for granted. She kissed Marty on the cheek and followed Cord out.

"Thanks for coming. Your visit did him a world of good."

Cord looked embarrassed. "He's a good man. I wish I knew half of what he does."

"He is a good man and you'll learn fast with his help. I think I loved him from the first, even when he was angry and yelling

at me. One thing I love about him is that he never stops growing."

Cord reached into his pocket and pulled out a scrap of paper. "This is my cell number. If you need me just call."

She looked at the note. "It's an easy number to remember. With the two sets of thirteen, it's like a double bad luck number."

"Yeah, that's probably what my wife thought when she picked up the phone."

"I'll bet she searched for an easy one to remember."

Cord agreed. "You're probably right, because she calls me several times a day." As if on cue, his phone rang.

Cord pulled it from his pocket. "Hello." He paused for a moment. "Yes, I'm in town. I'll pick you up." He closed the phone and smiled. "She wants to have lunch. Like I have time for lunch."

"You're going, aren't you?"

"Of course. I'll make time. She's meeting me at the diner. Lied and told me she couldn't wait to try the daily special."

Ronny smiled as he walked away. He didn't have to say a word. She knew Cord McDowell was in love.

The next night, Ronny pulled on her black coat and walked along the dried-up creek that crossed through the heart of town. She forced herself to listen to the crunch of leaves and twigs beneath her feet. She was fighting to stay positive, but she knew deep inside she was already grieving what would never be.

Marty had enjoyed a good day. They'd talked and watched the dawn together, and then he'd slept most of the morning. Cord, as he had promised, showed up around one with a pie his housekeeper had made and a folder full of accounts. They all ate a slice of pie while he showed Marty the mess he'd made of keeping books. Marty talked in "big picture" terms of running a business, teaching gently, while Ronny pored over the books. After all her boring finance and bookkeeping classes, she finally saw reason in the lessons.

While Marty slept the afternoon away, she worked on Cord's books, loving having something to fill her mind as she sat next to Marty, watching over him.

After supper, they had their time together. He talked about what life would have been like if they had years and not days. After all

his traveling and adventures, Marty saw paradise as living here in Harmony with her. They could open a business. They'd build a funny house with round rooms and a skylight in every ceiling. They'd invite friends in for dinner and go to the movie every Friday night no matter how bad the film. They'd make love on a blanket in the backyard and pretend they were in the Amazon.

He fell asleep holding her hand, and she sat for a long while in the darkness, lit only by lights from the machines, and cried for what might have been and never would be.

When the shift nurse took her place, Ronny pulled on her jacket and went for a walk. Days, even the good ones, were sometimes too sweet to relive. She just wanted to stretch her muscles and feel the night. She crossed the calm darkness of sleeping streets, heading in no particular direction.

As she paused to get her bearings, she heard footsteps behind her. Suddenly her numb body came awake.

Someone was following her.

With quick steps, she ran to the opening between the trees that led her out of the creek. No one was ever out at this time of night. In all the years she'd been walking, she'd never crossed paths with another so late. And this other wasn't just walking, he was following her, for she heard his steps rushing toward her as she climbed.

When she reached the road, she darted across to the park, where shadows layered and no one would see her. The grass was slippery and damp, but she didn't stop running until she passed behind the trees, leaning against an old cottonwood to listen.

Nothing.

Slowly, she looked around the tree. The foggy glow of a streetlight a hundred yards away showed nothing. For a long time, she stood, listening, waiting.

Nothing moved. Maybe she'd just been hearing the echo of her own steps. Maybe she'd let her imagination run away. When she'd been little, her mother had always filled her head with evil men roaming the world in search of little girls to kill.

Ronny pushed away from the tree. She wouldn't live in fear. She wouldn't base her life on her mother's irrationality. She wouldn't hide.

With sure steps she marched to the

road and headed toward Buffalo's Bar. She could just make out the outline of Beau's ancient car. She didn't want to re-trace her path back to the duplex. Within minutes she stepped into the old bar.

It looked like it had been packed tonight. Bottles of beer were stacked on the tables along with empty red baskets that had once held wings and burgers. Even the floor was snowy with napkins and the place smelled of aging grease.

"We're closed," the bartender said.

"I just came to see Beau."

"He's—"

The bartender's words were flooded by Border yelling from the cage. "Ronny. You need a ride home? We were just closing up."

Ronny hurried over to the boys who were her neighbors. "I was just out walking and thought I might catch a ride. It looks like it might rain," she lied.

Beau picked up his case. "How's Marty? I got a new song I want him to hear."

"He's asleep." They'd agreed days ago to stop giving medical reports to everyone who asked.

Border climbed out of the cage of a stage.

"You want to go over to the truck stop for enchiladas?"

"I thought they fed you here?"

"Harley does, but that was ten o'clock." Border glanced at Beau. "You coming tonight?"

"Sure," Beau answered as he shoved his black hair out of his eyes. "If Trouble doesn't show up."

Border grinned and interpreted. "Trouble is this girl he knows. She comes in now and then. When she does, he drops me like I was his ugly half sister."

Border was the only one who laughed at his own joke.

They walked out of the bar with both guys talking at once about everything that had happened that night. Border swore he had two women beg him to go home with them. Beau reminded his friend that both bar lizards had been old enough to be his mother. They talked about one woman who got so drunk she started stripping on the dance floor, and Harley had to carry her out with half the bar cheering and the other half booing.

Ronny let them convey her along, needing the time to just be normal for an hour even though she felt a twinge of guilt at not being home with Marty.

As they drove to the truck stop, she texted the nurse and learned all was quiet. Marty was sleeping calmly through the night.

They ordered three enchilada plates with rice and beans on the side. While they waited, Border showed her how one lady had danced like an upright snake, and Beau claimed another guy always danced like he was a rooster strutting around the yard.

Ronny laughed and breathed and relaxed, but Marty never left her thoughts. By the time they paid, she found herself in a hurry to get back home, and the ghost who'd followed her along the dried-up creek bed was forgotten.

Chapter 23

APRIL 7

MARTHA Q PATTERSON HEADED UP TO HER study on the second floor Saturday morning before anyone woke. She had a house full of paying guests who were keeping her from doing any writing. Stories bounced around in her head like Ping-Pong balls, and she planned to get a few of them on paper before they dribbled out.

On the third step her left sock stuck to something. She wasn't awake enough to investigate, but when her right foot stepped on something that pushed through the wool to her toe, Martha Q decided to sit down and check it out.

Mud. There was mud on her stairs. Not dirt, but mud. Because she locked the doors after everyone had retired to their room, and she was the first one up, she saw only one answer. One of her boarders was sneaking out. And worse, tracking in mud.

Pulling off her socks to hold the evidence, she tiptoed upstairs. The three widows were on the second floor, but the mud droppings continued up the next flight of steps. Reason told her Mr. Carleon, with his neat habits, would never commit such a crime. That left Bryce Galloway, the well-dressed snob who didn't bother washing his whiskers out of the sink. He was guilty as sin in her mind, and she didn't plan to stand for it.

Thirty minutes later she was waiting when Mr. Carleon came down the stairs. "Morning," she managed with a nod.

"Morning," Mr. Carleon answered with a polite smile.

Martha was so angry she couldn't return his smile. "Is Mr. Galloway awake yet?"

"I didn't hear a sound. I like to be up and out of the bathroom before he wakes."

"I don't blame you. My housekeeper tells me what a mess he leaves. I wouldn't want to be in there after him."

Mr. Carleon smiled. "Sharing a bath is only a slight inconvenience for being so close to Marty. I enjoy the walk over and back every day as well as your company and conversation each evening."

She led him into the breakfast nook, where he and the widows usually took their morning coffee while Mrs. Biggs prepared the dining room breakfast buffet.

"I've something to talk to you about while we're alone, Mr. Carleon."

He waited until she wiggled into the nook, then sat down across from her. "I hope there is no problem with my lodging here?"

"Oh, no, but you may find my question a bit personal."

"Ask away, dear lady. I'll answer if I can."

Martha Q had to fight down a giggle to remain in her innkeeper mode. "May I ask if you left the house last night after I locked the door? I know you might be called back to attend to Marty at any hour."

He frowned. "I did not, but if I'd been called, I would have gone, of course. If that happens, Mrs. Patterson, I assure you I'll lock the door behind me."

"I know you would, Mr. Carleon. Just as I know you would not leave mud on the stairs."

He nodded in understanding. "I stopped to pick up a few chunks that were not quite dry on my way down a few minutes ago." He leaned closer, obviously enjoying the conversation. "You think Galloway went out last night and didn't come in early enough to have his muddy footprints dry before dawn."

"That is exactly what I think. I also think that it is strange for a man to go out after ten at night and not take his car parked in my drive. Bryce Galloway doesn't strike me as the type for midnight walks."

Mr. Carleon took a slow drink of his coffee. "The man wears Italian loafers. A man who wears that kind of shoes doesn't walk in mud."

"Good point. Just as a man who goes for a walk at night would be most likely to stay on the sidewalks or even in the street, where the lights would be bright enough to show any mud holes."

They both sat in silence. Martha Q wiggled her eyebrows at him, loving that they were sharing something so intimate together. A conspiracy, maybe. A plot perhaps.

Finally, he said, "I'm sure there is a simple explanation for this."

"So am I, but I got a feeling it's not one we're going to like."

She made up her mind. "If he goes out tonight, I think one of us should follow him. I noticed a scrap of paper he carries has times in and times out. I'm guessing he's watching someone who doesn't know he's watching."

"Agreed. But who?"

"Maybe his ex-wife? I heard rumors that she didn't play fair in the divorce. 'Course, that was from someone who played golf with Bryce when he was married to Nevada."

Mr. Carleon shook his head. "Surely he's not bothering her. She's remarried to a nice guy. Cord McDowell's been by the duplex a few times. Judging from the measure of the man, I think Bryce Galloway would be a fool to mess with him."

Martha Q laughed. "It's been my experience that ex-husbands turn into fools quite easily, and you're right—if Bryce steps in Cord's way, he won't be the last one standing."

Mr. Carleon reached across the table and laid his hand over Martha Q's. "What is our plan, dear lady?"

Martha Q almost giggled, and she hadn't giggled in years. At that moment she really didn't much care what the plan was or what Bryce was up to. She loved the game they were playing at the breakfast nook, and she planned to make sure it continued. Her blood hadn't been this warm since the summer it reached 107 and half the air conditioners in town seemed to break at the same time.

"I think we should think all this out. I'll ask my hairdresser. She'll know all the gossip on Bryce Galloway. If you've no objection, I suggest we meet tonight over hot cocoa on the porch."

Mr. Carleon raised one eyebrow. "Should we include the widows in our discussion?"

"Not just yet," Martha Q answered with a sly smile. If she had anything to do with it, the widows would be out for the evening.

As if they'd heard their names called, all

three of the women hurried in. Before the good mornings were said, Mrs. Biggs opened the door to the dining room and announced that breakfast was served.

Martha Q closed her fingers over the hand that Mr. Carleon had held briefly and decided she'd have not only her hair done, but a manicure and pedicure as well. She might even have a facial . . . all in the name of gathering information, of course.

Chapter 24

APRIL 9

"YOU MAKE HER HAPPY, CORD, YOU KNOW THAT, don't you?" Galem said as he poured coffee while both men stood in the bunkhouse kitchen. Dawn was just turning the sky. The ranch hands were already gathering around the table for breakfast.

Cord had come over early to check out the day's work schedule with the cook. He looked over at the man who was quickly becoming more a friend than an employee of the ranch. "Who?"

Galem smiled. "Nevada, of course. You make her happy."

"Maybe." Cord hid a smile behind his coffee cup as he remembered the pleasure they'd shared less than an hour ago. "She seems to like the changes around here." He tried to get his mind on the ranch and not the way his wife's body had felt against his in the shower. "I think we'll finish all the roads on the Boxed B today, and I'll send the crews over to work on my farm for a week or so. The crop's coming in, so a good road would help with moving the equipment we're going to need come harvest."

Galem frowned. "She does like the changes, but that's not what I'm talking about. Little Miss has got her share of problems at work, but it does my heart good to see her light up every time she sees you."

Before Cord could comment, the cook added, "Hell if I know why. You never say more than a few words to her. Let me give you some advice. They like that. A woman also likes to be complimented now and then, talked to, even when you don't see a need. They're funny creatures that way."

"I'll work on it." Cord had given up suggesting Galem stop offering him advice. It seemed to come with breakfast, and Galem, having been married for years, thought he had all the answers.

Galem smiled. "Good. Now, next time you see her, be sure and tell her how nice she looks. With all the time she spends shopping, it's bound to be important to her."

Before Cord had to swear he would, the back door of the bunkhouse flew open and a ranch hand, covered in mud, bolted in at a full run.

"We got trouble, Boss." Jackson gulped for air as he took off his hat. "One of your wife's horses is down in the front pasture. I tried to get her up, but . . ."

Both men grabbed their hats and followed the messenger out as he kept talking. "I drove past a few minutes ago and thought the black mare looked strange. I might have just thought she was resting if I hadn't seen the fence down. White wooden planks scattered all over the road."

"Nevada's horses are boarded in stalls at night. Never left in the field." Galem voiced what both Cord and Jackson already knew.

They all three grabbed anything they thought they might need from the tack room as they moved toward the truck. "What happened?" Cord shouted over the noise they made.

"Looks like someone rammed the fence." Jackson picked up a couple of gallons of water and climbed into the bed of the truck. "I could see tire tracks in the mud by the road."

"The horse?" Cord would worry about the downed fence later. He tossed in blankets and a toolbox along with a few ropes and a first-aid kit. Nevada wouldn't be happy if he had to rope one of her horses, no matter how crazy the mare might be acting.

"The mare's alive, but barely moving. I couldn't get her to raise her head, much less stand. When I saw how bad the horse was, I figured running for help was the best thing I could do." Jackson looked tortured. "Man, I hate like hell to see a horse in pain."

Cord glanced at Galem. The cook had read his mind; he was already talking to the vet as he climbed in the passenger side.

Taking the curves toward Nevada's private horse barn and pasture at sixty with rocks flying everywhere, Cord ordered Galem, "Have him meet us there as fast as possible. Then try to get ahold of the trainer who cares for her horses. Nevada won't want us touching the horse without the trainer there."

"He's usually there by now." Galem punched numbers on his cell. "She likes to stop by on her way to work now and then to talk to him. Joey comes in early, but he seems to think as soon as he finishes, his eight-hour day is over. He's never around when she comes past there after work. But he wouldn't have let the horse out this early. It's not part of his routine."

Pulling his phone from his vest pocket, Cord punched two and waited for Nevada to answer. She'd gone in before dawn, saying she had a meeting over some big problem at one of the drill sites.

No answer. Maybe she hadn't made it in to the office yet. Cord left a message for her to call him, then tried to remember her general office number. He hadn't bothered to key it into his phone, thinking that if he needed her he could always call the cell.

Cord was parked and walking toward

the downed mare when Galem got Nevada's secretary on his cell. The cook passed his phone to Cord.

"This is Cord McDowell. Tell my wife to call me," Cord shouted into the phone.

When the secretary stuttered, he added, "Now!"

Then, without waiting for an answer, he handed Galem's phone back and knelt down beside the beautiful star-marked black mare laboring for every breath.

Jackson had been right. Something was very wrong with the horse. Cord pulled off his gloves and slowly moved his hands over the animal. Huge wild eyes watched him as she fought for air. The powerful muscles of her hind legs jerked slightly as if longing to run, but the horse didn't get up.

"It's going to be all right," Cord said, more to himself than the mare. "We're here now. We'll take care of you."

Galem hauled blankets and water. He tried to pour water into the horse's mouth, but she wouldn't take it. "She's burning up," he said.

Cord spread one of the blankets over

the horse's head and wet it down with water. He had no idea if he was doing the right thing, but he knew that the dark would calm the horse, and hopefully the cool wet blanket would help.

"The doc's on his way," Galem said as his phone chimed. "He'll be here in five."

Jackson, the rough cowhand whom Cord had rarely seen say more than three words without one of them being a swear word, now sat patting the horse's neck and whispering softly as if he were talking to a baby.

Cord stood, feeling helpless. He didn't know horses. He only knew if something happened to one of Nevada's beautiful animals she would be crushed. For some reason they seemed to mean more to her than people.

The vet drove over the downed fence and hopped out of his truck running, bag in hand. His clothes were wrinkled and he was at least three days away from his last shave, but Doc Freeman was a welcome sight.

Cord felt so relieved he almost hugged the man. Within minutes the doc was shouting orders to everyone and working with the skill of an emergency room specialist. He might look like a down-on-his-luck cowboy, but the vet knew what he was doing.

Other hands arrived, circling around the animal, watching, worrying, whispering guesses of what might be wrong. Cord sent a few up to the barn to check on the other horses, fearing that the mare might be the first to be coming down with something deadly.

But as he paced, he knew no illness had caused what was happening. It hadn't taken much to figure out that the fresh tire tracks had come from the barn, crossed the pasture, and broken out. The shattered remains of the fence had been scattered on the road, not in the grass. Whoever did this was in a hurry to get away.

"Maybe we should call the sheriff?" Galem asked.

"Let's see what we're dealing with first. We take care of the animal, then call. When I worked at Parker Trucking I used to pass the sheriff heading for work a little after seven thirty. If we wait a few minutes we'll get her and not some deputy who's been up all night."

Whoever did this knew the property, and he knew how much the act would hurt Nevada. Cord could think of only one man who might have done it. Any fired hand could have slashed the tires on his car, but hurting a horse would cut deep. Bryce Galloway crossed his mind, and he decided that whether Nevada liked him in her business or not, he planned to find out more about the trouble between his wife and her last husband.

Moving among the men, Cord asked each one what time he'd driven by the fence. Was it down when they passed? Did they see lights heading toward town?

A few didn't remember noticing because it was dark, but three swore the fence had been intact when they turned onto the road about fifteen minutes before Jackson had discovered it. He'd been running late. He was the last cowhand to head in from the main road. If he hadn't overslept, they might not have found the horse for hours.

Cord also knew the fence had been up when Nevada drove past to go to work. She would have noticed. He'd seen her look toward the barn every time they passed, no matter the hour.

As Cord walked back, the doc stood. "No maybe about it. This horse has been poisoned. If we'd reached her ten minutes later, we'd be looking at a dead animal right now."

"But that barn is kept locked with the horses inside every night," Galem said. "Since the day it was built, I don't ever remember a single horse left in open pasture."

The vet lifted his bag. "If someone will stay with the mare, I'll go check the other horses. By the time I get back, the shot I gave her will be working and she'll be in less pain." He walked toward Cord, scrubbing hair that hadn't been combed in days. "Someone needs to notify the sheriff, and Cord, I'd appreciate it if you'd get a trailer up here for me to transport the mare to my clinic. Pad the sides as heavy as we can. I've got a strap in my pickup that will keep her standing once we get her in."

Cord nodded at the doctor as he ordered several men to follow the vet. Galem and Jackson went for the trailer.

When all were busy, he walked back to his truck and spread his hands out wide on the hood, trying to calm down. Nevada hadn't called, but she would. When she did, she'd panic at the news.

Several minutes passed as he waited for Nevada to call and the sheriff to arrive. The vet reported that no other horses seemed to have been poisoned, and the mare had managed to stand on her own. When he helped Dr. Freeman load the mare, he realized the trainer was late. As the vet drove away, Cord pulled Zeb and one other man he trusted aside.

"Either of you have any idea where the trainer lives?"

Zeb nodded. "I was working here when he first came. Nevada wanted him to live on the ranch, but he insisted she rent him a house in town. Her husband at the time sided with the trainer. Me and another fellow were ordered to go help him move in. I think I can find the place without much trouble."

"Good. Go find out why he didn't show up for work this morning. If he's not sick, he's fired." He paused, then added, "Check his car for damages by a fence." Cord doubted the trainer would run the fence;

whoever did this must have known he had little time before being spotted where he didn't belong.

When Zeb was out of hearing distance, Galem said, "I'll wait for the sheriff." Everyone knew Cord hadn't called in a crime when his tires had been slashed.

"All right," Cord answered. "You stay, but right now, I've got to get to Nevada before she hears about this from someone else. Tell the sheriff I'll be happy to give a statement. She's welcome to investigate anywhere on the land she needs to, and she'll have full cooperation from every man."

Galem walked with Cord toward the door of his truck. "If Nevada's not in her office, you might try the rig site out by Rattler Creek. Ora Mae said she wore her boots this morning." Galem frowned. "She always wears her boots when she heads out there. She's hated snakes ever since her big brothers used to tease her with little garden snakes."

"I'll do that." Cord climbed in his truck. "Keep me informed on anything here. I'll be back as soon as I can."

He headed toward town, trying to think how he could break the bad news to

Nevada. She didn't have to tell him how she loved the horses; he knew. He'd seen the way she patted them and cared for them. They were her children, her family.

When he pulled into her office parking lot, he'd decided telling her straight out would be the only way.

He walked in beneath a six-foot-tall gold plaque bearing the Boxed B brand. This was her world, all business and professional. The day he'd picked her up for lunch, it had taken her ten minutes to relax and talk at a normal speed. She might complain about it, but her father had groomed her to take over this business. Cord couldn't help but wonder what the old man had done to make sure she knew oil. He must have thought she was his last chance after failing to make any of his sons ranchers.

Cord rushed toward the main set of offices. Her office door stood dead center among them. The huge double doors had the Boxed B brand burned into the wood. Everything reminded him that she was a Britain, yet when they'd married, she'd insisted on taking his name.

A receptionist jumped in his way with

the look of a startled rabbit. "May I help you, sir?" she said, near panic when he didn't slow. "These are private offices."

"I'm here to see my wife. I'm Cord McDowell."

"Yes, sir," she said, trying to get ahead of him. "Miss Britain is in an important meeting, but I'll tell her you're here."

When she glanced at a closed double door, Cord knew he'd be wasting his time bothering with the receptionist. "I'll tell her myself and her name is no longer Britain, it's McDowell."

He opened the door and walked in before he changed his mind or the rabbit thought of pouncing on him.

Half a room away, Nevada stood talking to two men in suits. All three held papers in their hands, but the gray-haired suit looked like he'd paused in midsentence.

Cord made it three more steps before he heard security rushing toward him from a side door. For a blink, they reminded him of the prison guards, beefy and determined. Only now, Cord wouldn't back down. He stood his ground as they advanced.

Nevada raised her hand before they reached him. "It's all right. Don't touch him."

Every one of her employees looked confused.

"Gentlemen," she said calmly, "this is my husband, and if he's here, I'm sure it's something important, so I'll have to ask you all to step out for a moment."

The older lawyer looked bothered, but he walked out, closing the door behind him with a bang.

Cord stood, facing Nevada from five feet away. Here in her tailored pantsuit and her hair tied up in a knot, she looked hard as stone. *This* woman could handle anything he had to tell her. It crossed his mind that he would have never fallen in love with Nevada if this were all he knew of her, but Cord knew the woman inside all the polish and ice.

"What is it?" She seemed impatient, but not unkind. "I've got a full schedule this morning, but you obviously have something to say that can't wait. So tell me."

He stared into her eyes, wondering where the woman he'd made love to only

hours ago had gone. Maybe she was always like this at work. He'd stepped into
her world. He'd stepped into where he
didn't belong and hadn't been invited.

"One of your mares was found down
this morning. She'd been poisoned."

For a heartbeat, she didn't move. She
just stared at him.

He forced it all out, knowing the blow
would be no lighter if delayed. "Someone
broke into your barn about dawn."

Color drained from her face. "Is the
mare dead?"

"No. Not yet. The vet says she's got better than a fifty-fifty chance, but there may
be internal damage."

He hadn't realized he was moving toward her until he reached to brush her
arms. "We loaded her up and sent her to
the vet's. He'll watch over her. Galem called
while I was driving in and said whoever did
it didn't know horses. He bloodied the
mare's lip forcing down the poison."

She backed away from Cord and gulped
for air, then raised her arms at him. At first,
he thought she was trying to block his
words, but then she swung at him.

Cord didn't move. Didn't try to defend against the blows as she pounded on him. The pain in her eyes was so great, he barely felt the hits. She was lost in a horror she'd always feared would come true.

"I told you never to move my horses."

She sobbed so deeply he could barely understand her. He knew the blows were not aimed at him, but at the world. "No one touches my horses. No one hurts them. My daddy promised. Never again."

Engulfing her in a bear hug, he held on tightly as she struggled against him and swore, calling him names. As she cried, he knew her pain was bleeding through an old wound that had never healed. All he could do was stand and let her rage.

After a while, she stopped and, leaning her head on his shoulder, cried.

"It's all right, Babe," he whispered. "It's going to be all right." His hand pulled the pins from her hair and dug his fingers into the golden strands. "I didn't want you to hear it from anyone but me. I couldn't let the horse die without a fight. You've got to trust that we did all we could, and the vet is still working."

She pushed her forehead against him. "You came because you didn't want me killing any messenger you sent."

He relaxed a bit and smiled. "Well, there was that. I figured you could kill me and no one would care. Hell, no one likes me anyway." He kissed her forehead. "Besides, I had a pretty good idea how you'd react, and if my wife is going to pound on anyone, it better be me."

"That part of the 'for better or worse' section of our contract?"

"Something like that." His hold gentled and she rocked slowly in his arms, letting her breathing slow to normal.

"Now that you know what's happened, we can go over to the vet's together. I'm right here, Nevada. We'll figure out who did this in time, but right now we'll worry about the horse."

She nodded and stepped away to blow her nose. The office door opened.

"Are you all right?" The gray-haired lawyer was back. "I heard crying and shouting. I've got security out here and we've called the sheriff."

"I'm fine," Nevada said, as she pulled

herself together as calmly as she straightened her jacket.

Cord stepped in front of her. "My wife is upset. One of her prize horses was hurt this morning." He forced his fists to relax. "I appreciate your concern." Now that he knew Nevada was back in control, there was no reason to keep the facts a secret. "I called the sheriff before I left the ranch." He looked at the rabbit of a receptionist. "If you'll call her office and tell her we'll meet her at the ranch, I'd appreciate it."

The girl jumped to the door and vanished. The old lawyer, if possible, looked even more angry. "Nevada, you know who did this. You know."

Nevada moved to Cord's side and leaned into him. He widened his stance to brace her.

"We don't know for sure. Bryce is too clever to leave any clues. Even if he's doing it, he's planning on me firing up and doing something stupid. This time I'm not falling into his trap."

She slipped her hand into Cord's. "I want to check on my horse and then talk to the sheriff. If you gentlemen will excuse me, I'll reschedule this meeting for later today."

Nevada held it together until they were in his truck, and then she leaned against him and cried all the way to the vet's clinic.

Chapter 25

NEVADA SAT BESIDE STARLIGHT AS DOC FREE-
man talked about the damage done by the
poison. Tears fell unchecked when he said
the mare had already lost the colt she carried. Between the loss of blood and the
injuries, it would be an uphill climb.

"I don't usually suggest this," the vet
said, "but she's in a great deal of pain. If
you want me to, I'll put her down."

Nevada couldn't speak. She just shook
her head and heard Cord telling the doc
to do all he could first. "We don't want her
to suffer, but if she's got a chance to pull
through, we want to give her that chance."

Starlight hadn't been her first horse, but Nevada was more girl than woman when she bought her. At first her mother had insisted that only the trainer ride the horse, but within two weeks Nevada was sneaking away from the house and taking Starlight for midnight runs in the pasture. To her the horses were her friends, each very different, each loved for different reasons.

When she was eight, her father moved her first three ponies to the back pasture with the cattle. During a storm, two had frozen to death. Only one had survived, just barely. Nevada had cried for weeks. She swore at the time she would never care that much again for anything or anyone, but she couldn't stop herself. She loved horses. And now, someone hated her enough to hurt her again by hurting one of them.

Nevada pressed her face into Starlight's mane and felt as if she might lose an old friend. People always let her down, but her horses never had.

When Cord offered his hand to help her up, she shook her head. "I'll stay awhile. I don't want to leave her alone."

"We need to talk to the sheriff." Cord's

voice was low and calm. Not an order, just a fact.

"You go. I'll be here when you get back."

He touched her shoulder. "Call if you need me. I'll be back as soon as I can."

She nodded and laid her head down next to the mare just as she had once before when she was eight. The last pony was still alive when they found him that winter, but her father shot him, claiming the pony wasn't strong enough to make it back to the barn. The first bullet hadn't killed the animal.

Nevada dropped to the pony and hugged him as if she could help.

When her father saw the damage he'd done to his daughter, he'd pulled Nevada off the animal, angry both at himself and at the child for making such a scene.

She'd heard the second shot as Galem carried her away from her pet. She cried for days and refused to eat. Her mother promised her another horse, then a barn of her own. But it was her father's promise never to go near her horses again that finally stopped the crying.

He hated that he'd given in to his tiny daughter, but he kept his word. Even let her put up wooden fences in her pasture and breed her horses. By the time his wife died and he could have gone back on his word about the horses, Nevada had her own money for their care and her father had other worries to occupy his time.

Kneeling down close she brushed the mare's warm neck. Through all her life she'd known that she was only a play toy to her mother and a bother to her father, but to her horses, she was a friend. She loved them and they loved her back, without question. Without judgment.

She closed her eyes and envisioned herself riding Starlight across the midnight pastures.

"Nevada?" The vet's voice woke her.

"Sorry, I didn't realize I'd fallen asleep."

"Your mare's resting easy now. If she holds on, I think she might just make it."

She smiled up at the doc. He was one of the few people she knew who loved horses as much as she did. "You mind if I stay a little longer? My husband will be back for me soon."

Dr. Freeman smiled. "I have no doubt. I never saw a man look so worried when I pulled up to the mare. It took me a while to figure out that it was you and not the horse he was worried about. You might love this animal, but that man loves you. He couldn't stand the notion that something might hurt you."

Nevada shook her head. The doc was wrong. She almost told him that all they had was a pretend marriage. But they'd agreed to play it like it was real, and she'd keep that promise.

"He was just afraid of how angry I'd be. He says I tend to storm, and I guess he's right."

"Nope. He's not afraid of your anger. A man don't walk right into what he's afraid of. As soon as we'd done all we could in the field, he said he was headed to you. He didn't want anyone telling you but him. That doesn't sound like a man afraid."

Chapter 26

CORD DROVE TOWARD THE RANCH WHILE HE got an update from Galem on the phone. The cook told him that Zeb had reported back that the trainer, Joey Mason, wasn't at home. They pounded so hard on his door that the neighbor came out to say that if his car wasn't in the drive, they were probably wasting their time.

So far the trainer's only crime was coming in late to work, and he'd like to keep it that way.

As soon as he closed the phone, Cord swung the truck around in the center of the road and headed toward the old part of Harmony. An idea had been dancing in his mind since he first thought that Bryce Galloway might have something to do with not only the horse, but other trouble they'd had lately. He needed help from someone who'd walked both sides of the law all his life, and Cord could think of only one man who might fit the bill.

Minutes later he pulled up in front of the duplex where Ronny Logan lived. She was taking groceries out of her car when he arrived. Cord jumped out and hurried up to her.

As he neared, Mr. Carleon stepped out of the house and took the grocery bags.

Cord couldn't hear what Ronny said, but the man nodded a hello and vanished back inside.

"How's Marty?" Cord asked as he neared. He didn't know Marty well, but he liked the man. Plus, anyone Ronny obviously loved so much had to be worth liking.

"About the same. Addison gave him something new for the pain and he seems to be resting easier this morning." Ronny smiled her shy smile. "But you look like hell, Cord."

"It's been a hard morning." He didn't

have time to explain, but he did try to dust a little of the dirt off his jeans. "I came to ask a favor if you've got a minute for me to pick your brain."

"I'll help any way I can."

Cord started with the facts. "The first few months, when I was in prison, there was another guy in my unit who said he was from Harmony. He was only there awhile, but I remember one of the guards saying that once he was free he'd disappear. They called him Cam and I don't remember his last name."

Ronny shook her head, telling Cord he might be wasting his time, but he pushed on.

"One of the cons claimed he'd left Harmony to work a crew on a small-time movie production company. He ended up settling down in the Dallas area and between working on film crews, he turned to crime. He would move into a nice neighborhood, blend in with everyone, rob the houses one by one in daylight, and then disappear without anyone being able to give the cops a good description of him. The guy said he never got caught because he was the most bland, plain-vanilla person who mixed into a crowd.

No marks, no scars, no accent, nothing stood out about the man."

Ronny smiled. "What did he look like in prison?"

Cord shrugged. "I don't really remember. Not tall or short. Medium build. Nothing specific. The guy hung around like faded wallpaper. When I met him, he had his earlobe bandaged because he said his new wife had ripped out his earring in the fight before she called the cops on him. Mumbled something about living a life of crime and ending up in prison because the one woman he loved forgot to love him back.

"He was only there for a few months, so everyone figured she must have dropped the charges against him. But, like some guys do, he bragged about the jobs he'd pulled to the other cons."

Ronny waited, listening to every word.

"I was wondering if there is any chance you know where Cam Whatever might be. Doesn't the postal service know everyone? I'm guessing he didn't go back to Dallas to reconnect with his wife, and if he's gone straight, he's probably working around town. The one time I talked to him he told me he loved Harmony, so I figure he might have come back."

Ronny frowned. "The sheriff might know, but I can't think of anyone. Lots of people look like that, I guess, just customers on the other side of the desk. I don't pay much attention sometimes."

She shrugged. "There's one guy who comes to mind that I've waited on a few times. Only thing about him I thought strange was the round sunglasses he wore. You know, like he thought he was Truman Capote. Sorry I couldn't be of more help."

"If you think of more, let me know." He started to walk away, then paused. "If you need me—"

"I know. I'll call." Her smile was sad, as if she knew the time was coming.

Cord climbed back into his truck and headed for the ranch. He'd deal with the sheriff and help any way he could and then go back after Nevada. He hated thinking about her lying in the hay beside the horse. He'd never seen her like this. Broken. He had no idea how to help.

When he reached the barn where she kept her horses, several cars he didn't recognize were clustered around the front. One was a sheriff's cruiser. The silent flashing lights brought back bad memories of ten years ago when the lights had flashed in the dark stillness of midnight.

It had been hot that night and the air so dry it seemed to suck the moisture out of everything. A dozen of what had been Harmony's wild crowd in high school had gone out to celebrate the Fourth of July by setting off fireworks at the lake. They knew it was illegal in the drought of summer, but they all figured they could see a cop car coming from far enough away to vanish before they got caught.

Cord didn't remember much about the night. A campfire. Couples scattered around in the dark. He was two weeks away from being eighteen and thought he was bulletproof after half a bottle of whiskey. He must have passed out after complaining to anyone who would listen that his dad was going to make him go to college.

What he thought was a stick woke him with a hard poke in the stomach. Someone was yelling at him, screaming for him to get up and shining a flashlight right in his face.

He came up swinging and connected solidly with the intruder's jaw. The stick that had stabbed Cord turned out to be the barrel of a rifle. When the shadow's head flew back from the blow, the rifle fired wild, lighting the night. For a blink Cord watched a man in a uniform fall on the rocky shoreline.

For months after that, through the trial and going to prison, Cord would relive that one moment over and over in dreams. The cop shouting in pain. The night so black. And then always in the background the voice from several feet away whispering into radio static. "Officer down. Send backup with an ambulance." Finally, a flashlight's beam passing back and forth across the camp as if on guard until more help arrived.

The rest of that night was a blur. He'd knelt beside the downed cop trying to see where he was hurt, but it had been too dark. The voice that had radioed for help ordered him to raise his hands or he'd shoot. Cord felt warm blood on the cop's face and threw up while he felt his hands being cuffed behind him. The other cop grabbed him by the shoulder and shoved Cord down into the dirt spotted with vomit and blood.

"Cord?" A woman's voice drew him out of his nightmare. "Cord McDowell."

He cut the truck's engine and climbed out. Despite the sun, he removed his hat. "Sheriff Matheson. I'm sorry. I was thinking about something."

The slender sheriff walked closer.

She smiled. "You looked a million miles away. I haven't seen enough of you lately to recognize you, but my message box was full of people telling me you wanted to see me. I came as fast as I could and we're already working the crime scene."

He had to make himself raise his eyes from the ground. Too many years of not looking at guards directly made it a hard habit to break. "I know this was just a horse—"

"Stop right there, Cord." The sheriff started walking toward the barn and he followed along beside her. "I'm from ranch folks and am married to a man who loves horses. There is no such thing as 'just a horse.' You and I come from generations of people who know the importance of horses. In fact, it wasn't so long ago when stealing a man's horse was a hanging offense, so don't you think we're going to take this lightly."

"Thanks," he said, feeling good that he'd had Galem call her. Sheriff Alex Matheson was as good an officer of the law as he'd ever seen. When he'd first gotten out, she'd been the only law officer who hadn't threatened to keep an eye on him.

She paused and turned to look at Cord. "We've brought in a Texas Ranger to help with the investigation. He's a brand inspector and knows cattle and horses better than most. He's been working a rustling problem nearby and offered to help."

Cord saw a stout man dressed in a tan shirt and pants heading toward him. He was a few inches shorter but seemed all business. His Stetson shadowed his face as he offered his hand to Cord.

Cord took the offered hand in a strong grip as the ranger looked up and said, "Ranger Travis Salem."

For a moment both men froze.

Cord hadn't seen *Deputy* Salem in almost ten years. Memories of a young cop in his late twenties with a bandage over his eye were nothing like the ranger in his late thirties with graying hair and fifty pounds added to his build.

"Cord McDowell," the ranger said without emotion. "I wouldn't have recognized you."

The sheriff seemed unaware of the two men's past as she watched the movements of her deputies and the cowhands still surrounding the barn. "We've found a few clues, but your boys didn't make it easy, tromping all over my crime scene before I got here. One even picked up the bucket of poison, ruining any chance of fingerprints."

Travis Salem moved closer to Cord and lowered his voice before he loosened his grip and the handshake died. "We've got a man killing horses to deal with right now, McDowell, but when this is over, I'd like it if you and I could talk."

Cord didn't move. This man's testimony had sent him to prison. He said Cord had attacked, and there were no witnesses to stand with Cord when he said he swung wild without knowing it was an officer of the law. The patch over Salem's eye had been a constant reminder to the jury of the damage Cord had done.

"You don't have to talk to me, Cord," Ranger Salem added. "I can't order you to, but I think it's something that needs to be done."

All the times guards had ordered him around or asked him to do something when he knew he had no choice in the matter piled up in his throat. There were no *yes, sirs* left in him. "I'll think about it," Cord answered. "Right now, all that's on my mind is protecting my wife's horses."

The ranger seemed to understand. He pulled out a notepad and began rattling off facts. The sheriff joined them.

"I've got two of my deputies out looking for the trainer," she said. "He may have just left for a day off, but it seems strange that he'd go missing on the same day someone tries to kill a horse."

"My wife has a standing order that if the trainer takes a weekday off, he calls in to Galem. We've got the third key to the barn hanging in the bunkhouse and Galem comes out to feed the horses if Nevada has to stay late in town. Other than them, no one is allowed near the barn."

"What about you, McDowell? Don't you

have a key to the barn? You run the ranch, don't you?" Salem wasn't too friendly.

"I do run the ranch as well as my farm to the south, but we've only been married a few weeks and I've never needed to get in here before." He felt the need to add, "When we ride together, I always come back here and help Nevada brush her mount down, then we ride double back to the main barn. So I know where everything is in here and I know the horses are all well taken care of. At least until today."

"So these horses are not part of the ranch?"

"They belong here. Nevada breeds and trains them. Most of the colts go for several thousand. They're fine show horses."

"Seems like a waste of time and money on a working ranch," the ranger said, as if talking to himself.

Cord didn't miss the fact that a few of his hands, including Jackson and his brothers, were standing behind him as if ready to back him up.

The ranger paced, then twirled as if he planned to say something dramatic. "Any of your cowhands come to work in shoes and not boots?"

"No."

Salem held one finger up. "Your wife. Does she have big feet and wear loafers?"

"No, she doesn't. She wears heels to her office and boots on the ranch."

"Are you sure about that, McDowell?"

Cord tried not to let any anger show, but he stood his ground. "My wife is afraid of snakes. If she walks the land, she has boots on."

Galem, never a quiet man, broke from the crowd growing behind Cord. "I can back the boss up. I've known her for near twenty years and I've never seen her without her boots if she goes beyond the shadow of the house."

"You telling me your boss is an honest man and I can trust his word?"

Cord heard the men behind him shift as if widening their stance.

Galem did the same. "He is, mister, and I'll fight any man that says he ain't, including you if you'll take off that star on your pocket."

Alex Matheson obviously had had enough of the tough talk. She stepped between the men and stared at the ranger. "I brought you here to help, Ranger Salem.

This is McDowell's land. He's got a right to be here. You, however? I'm not sure this case is even in your jurisdiction."

The ranger smiled. "You're right, Sheriff, I was out of line. I just needed to know fast what kind of boss we were dealing with. Most of the time when something like this happens, it's one of the hands trying to get a dig in at his boss." Salem looked at Cord with his men standing firm behind him. "I got my answer. To the man, they stand with him. So I'll tell you what I know."

The tension in Cord's shoulders relaxed and the men gathered around to listen.

"First, we're dealing with someone from the outside who knows the ranch. He's walked this land at least once before today. He knew what time the men arrived and that there would be time to drive in, poison the horses, and leave before anyone passed down the road again. My guess is, he waited somewhere along the road to town for Nevada to pass, then counted the cars of cowhands coming to work. Only somehow he missed Jackson."

"That's because I usually ride in with my brothers, but when I wasn't ready, they left me."

Ranger Salem took notes, then added, "The man we're looking for also knew the barn was locked and brought a key along. I saw no sign of forced entry. My guess is if we check we'll find one of the three keys missing."

"I got mine right here," Galem offered, now willing to help the ranger, since he appeared to finally be making sense. "Nevada keeps hers on her keychain. That only leaves the little trainer's key."

The ranger nodded his approval of Galem's logic. "Third, I found a few prints of a man's size shoe among all the bootprints. One in the soft dirt by the door and another near the first stall. Whoever poisoned the mare wasn't wearing boots."

Everyone began offering possibilities. No one had ever seen the trainer, Joey Mason, in anything but the polished riding boots he must have worn during his days as a jockey.

Cord's phone sounded, and everyone paused.

"It's my wife," he said as he looked at the ID. "I have—"

Before he could finish, all the ranch

hands chimed in with what he always said, "to take this call."

Cord would have sworn he was too old to blush, but he stepped a few feet away and didn't bother lowering his voice when he said hello.

No one made any pretense of not trying to listen. When he said, "That's good news. Starlight is out of danger." The men were cheering and only the ranger heard Cord add, "Come on home, Babe. I'll be at the barn."

Fifteen minutes later, when one of the vet's assistants dropped her off and Nevada ran into Cord's arms, no one on the ranch doubted how dearly he cared for her. He lifted her off the ground into a hug.

Salem stayed around to ask her questions, but he was polite, calling her Mrs. McDowell and thanking her for her time.

Cord walked the ranger to his car. "What was between us was between us. It has nothing to do with the ranch or my wife."

The ranger nodded. "We'll talk maybe, if you agree, but right now you'll have my best effort to help find this guy."

"Thanks," Cord managed. "And when

this is over I'll meet you for coffee one morning at the diner." Cord was making it plain that whatever happened between them would be aboveboard and in daylight. There'd be no two versions of the story this time.

He noticed the long, thin scar just above the ranger's eyes as Travis offered his hand. "Fair enough."

As he drove away Cord knew they'd never be friends, not in this lifetime, but hatred no longer festered between them.

He walked back into the barn as men left. Nevada was moving among her horses, touching each as if reassuring them.

Galem was the last to leave. He'd made it to the door when Cord yelled, "Mind asking Ora Mae to bring my supper out here? I've decided I'm sleeping in the barn tonight."

Galem nodded. "I'll drive her out. She goes nuts on that four-wheeler. I don't trust her more than ten feet in that thing. How about you, Little Miss? You want me to give you a lift to the house?"

"No, if Cord's sleeping here, so am I." She smiled at Cord, as if knowing he was doing this just for her.

Galem walked away mumbling some-thing that sounded like, *Why am I not sur-prised?'*

An hour later they'd eaten dinner on pa-per plates and were sitting in the loft open-ing watching the sunset. Nevada had been so quiet, Cord began to worry. He wanted to pull her close, but he guessed she needed time to let her nerves settle.

"You still mad at me for moving the horse?"

"No."

He decided she wasn't going to say any-thing, but then she whispered, "If you found out I did something to hurt you, would you hate me?"

"I didn't move the horse to hurt you, Babe."

"I know. I was just thinking. Cord, if I hurt you, would you forgive me if I asked you to?"

He thought about it a minute and pulled her against his side to whisper, "I don't know what you've got on your mind, but I've already forgiven you. No matter what. You can stop worrying about it right now." He'd done a few things he wasn't proud of. He'd ended up in prison, and not once had she held his past against him. "If you're thinking the pounding you gave me hurt, forget about it. Seeing you in pain was far more torture."

"I wasn't thinking of that," she said, "but now you mention it, I shouldn't have taken it out on you. Give me a little time, Cord, I've never learned to rein in emotion."

He kissed the top of her head. "I know, Babe, that's why I'm looking forward to rolling in the hay with you tonight."

She pulled away. "We're not having sex in front of my horses."

"I'll blindfold them all if you like." He laughed. "But, Babe, we are having that roll in the hay."

Chapter 27

RONNY KNELT BESIDE MARTY'S BED, WISHING she could talk God into trading her life for Marty's. He was so smart. He had so much to offer the world and she had nothing. No one would miss a postal clerk, but everyone who met him thought he was brilliant. Even ill, he'd helped Beau handle his finances and begin savings. Marty had given Cord advice about making a better profit at the Boxed B. He'd changed her life—no, he'd started her life, because the years before him all ran together into dull days of just existing.

She curled back in her chair and began

to think of the little things she used to do at the post office to help pass the time. She'd sign up folks who never got mail for free gifts and secretly help people out when they didn't pay the right postage or forgot to forward their mail. When she'd mailed Cord the Harmony paper, she guessed he would enjoy it, but he'd told her it kept him sane some days.

As she turned through the people in her mind, an average-looking man in his forties who sometimes came in to ask about his mail crossed her thoughts. One magazine about the ins and outs of Hollywood wouldn't fit in his box. She'd always leave a note and he'd ask for it, not by his name, but by the box number.

She thought it was strange that he took that magazine until one day the postmaster told her he worked at the old movie theater down on Main. "The waitress over at the diner said he must love movies if he watched them all day. Said he told her he once worked on a film set."

Ronny could almost see the name on the magazine, not Cam, but Cameron. He might be the man Cord was looking for.

She pulled out her phone and remembered the way she'd thought of his number as double bad luck, two sets of thirteens.

Foster Harrison, one of the nurses, came on duty just as she moved to the kitchen to talk to Cord. Foster gently touched her arm, silently telling her not to worry, Marty was sleeping easy tonight and he'd take the midnight watch while she slept.

Ronny thanked the kind nurse with a nod.

"Hello," Cord snapped, as if he were in the middle of something important.

"I remembered someone," she whispered.

"Ronny?" he lowered his voice. "Good."

"There's a man who runs the movie house. If it's him, and I'm not saying it is, I might have an idea of where he lives. Years ago the Palace used to do live performances, and there were rooms behind the stage. You might find your Cam there."

"Thanks."

She hung up before he could ask about Marty and she had to try to think of something to say. Waving at Foster, she pulled on her jacket, thinking she'd take a walk before she went to bed. The day had been hard and endless.

Unlike a few nights ago, she stayed to the street, walking down the center and heading toward the old downtown area. Since the night she'd heard someone following her, she hadn't felt safe, but she needed the exercise and there seemed to be no other time. So she kept to the pavement where she could see. Buffalo's Bar would still be open, and the men would be hanging out at the fire station if she needed to run for help. This way wasn't as quiet a walk, but it was safer.

When she turned down Main, she thought she saw movement half a block away. Someone else was on the streets tonight.

She rounded toward the fire station. If someone else was out walking, they were keeping to the shadows. The night didn't feel right. Something or someone was out there watching her. A few times she'd passed Beau walking home from the bar, but even dressed in black, they'd both seen each other.

As she reached the firehouse, she glanced upstairs, where a few firemen usually slept. The windows were dark tonight, but the bright lights over the huge doors out front lit the street.

Ronny jogged across to the sheriff's offices and relaxed when she saw Deputy Phil Gentry sitting outside on the steps talking on his cell phone. He waved and called, "Any problem, Ronny?"

"No, sir, just walking."

He shoved his phone into his pocket and stood. "How about I walk a block with you? I'm on a break and this time of night it's either eat or exercise. Some nights around town are so calm I think I'll have to lock myself up to keep from going crazy."

She was happy for the company. Phil had been around for as long as she could remember and liked to visit. Some folks said if he ever retired, the paper would have to double to keep everyone up on what was going on.

As they walked, he told her what had happened at the Boxed B that morning, and Ronny understood why Cord had looked so upset when he stopped by. He must have thought she had her own share of problems, so he hadn't mentioned his.

Phil reached the bridge that crossed

onto her street. "You can almost see your house from here. I think I'd better be getting back." He handed her his flashlight. "Take this. You can bring it back to the station on your next walk."

Ronny didn't really need a flashlight, but she took it just because Phil always wanted to help. So she thanked him and shoved it into her pocket.

As she strolled the short block to her duplex, her mind was full of all that had to be done. Taking care of Marty was far harder than she thought it would be and she couldn't forget, or leave out a single detail. His life depended on it.

A tear bubbled over and dripped down her cheek. If she did everything right he might live one more day, or maybe one more week. He'd already beaten the odds the doctors at the hospital had given him. But nothing she could do would change the fact that his body was shutting down, turning off like old Christmas lights left up until spring. One light burning out at a time until one day soon there would be no light left in the world.

She stepped to the side of the duplex so she could circle around to the back entrance. Ronny caught a movement out of the corner of her eye. More reaction than action, she ducked as someone reached toward her.

Instinct took over. She moved away from the house as she pulled the flashlight out of her pocket. The shadow moved again, reaching but not willing to step out of the blackness. She fumbled with the flashlight switch but couldn't make it work. As she took a step backward, the uneven ground tripped her.

She fell, hitting the side of the ramp with her shoulder and crying out in pain.

Fighting the need to curl into a ball, she lifted the flashlight and threw it toward the shadow above her.

It hit the mark and Ronny heard a muttered oath. The back door rattled open. Foster clicked the porch light back and forth trying to make it come on. "Ronny," he whispered, not wanting to wake Marty. "Ronny, is that you? Is something wrong?"

The shadow vanished in the dark behind the house. Bushes along the dry creek bed rustled as he ran.

"Ronny?" Foster tried again as he moved down the back ramp.

"I'm here," she said, standing slowly. "Someone tried to attack me."

Foster helped her into the house and insisted on checking her shoulder as she called the sheriff's office.

Phil Gentry was at the back door before she finished talking to the dispatcher. While Foster wrapped her shoulder, the deputy asked the same questions the dispatcher had. "What happened? What did you see? Tell me everything that happened. Every detail, no matter how small."

Ronny went slowly through every detail she could remember from the first movement to the sound of the weeds when he ran. Phil took notes and asked that no one go in or out the back door until sunup and he had a chance to look for evidence.

This wasn't a chance happening. Someone knew she was out walking and waited for her in the darkness.

"Whoever did this has been watching you." Phil finally stated the one fact he knew.

Ronny told him about having the feeling that she was being followed a few nights before.

"I'll ask the sheriff to come out first thing," the deputy said.

Since Mr. Carleon and the nurses always entered through the front door, Ronny knew there would be no problem. She'd muddied her hands when she'd tumbled, so there might be a chance they would find something out back.

After the deputy left, Ronny sat with Marty and tried to calm down while Foster cleaned up in the kitchen. The deputy had wanted to take her to the hospital to be checked, but she trusted Foster's care and she couldn't leave Marty. Not now.

When she'd fallen, her shoulder had been cut. A thin line now ran along her arm, and the place where she'd hit the ramp would leave a bad bruise, but no bones were broken. She'd been lucky.

A few hours before dawn Marty woke and asked about the bandage. Ronny told him every detail calmly.

"You shouldn't have been out there," he said, sounding more worried than angry.

"No," she smiled. "He shouldn't have been out there."

"Right," Marty agreed. "In another world

I would have rushed out there and beat the guy to a pulp."

"In another world Gentry wouldn't have given me his flashlight and the attacker would have gotten in a few more blows. Then I'd be buried beside you." The words were out before she could stop them. After no sleep, the filter on her thoughts no longer worked.

With effort, he took her hand. "In a perfect world we'd live long lives and then lie side by side in a garden of stone. Only we both know the world's not perfect. I want you to live, Ronny, really live, and then someday when your hair is white and your bones are brittle, I want you to go to sleep beside me. I'll be waiting."

Ronny laid her cheek against his hand. "I love you so much. I never said it, but I felt it."

"I know. I love you too. It doesn't matter how much time we have. Tonight we have time, and I want to spend every waking minute talking to you. We'll make up memories that will stay with us forever. You'll have them here and I'll have them in the next life to think about while I'm waiting for you."

She cried softly as he began to talk of taking her down the Nile and getting lost in a rain forest. He talked as if they'd had their time and all he said were shared memories. "Remember when I had to kick you out of the sleeping bag so you'd make coffee, because you know I can't make coffee that's fit to drink on a campfire?"

Slowly she began to see what he was doing. Marty was weaving together his adventures to include her.

"Remember that time we got lost in the subways of New York? You wanted to go to the Bronx Zoo, and between us we couldn't read the map on the subway car. I was never so glad to climb out of that hole and see daylight. Even the New York air smelled good."

She smiled. "It wasn't my fault; you said you could read the map. You're the great adventurer who knows every continent."

He laughed. "I can read a map. Well, usually I can. My favorite part that day was buying hot dogs in Central Park and ending up feeding the buns to the squirrels."

"A few of those squirrels looked like huge rats." She laughed, remembering that once he'd told her about the rats in Central Park.

"I like the times we went skiing in the Alps. Remember the Black Forest and how you wanted that stupid cuckoo clock, but I knew I'd have to make room in my backpack for it? After we lugged it around for days, it never did keep time."

"We threw it away in Paris, didn't we?"

"Yeah, in that little village we found when we were biking. Remember the one where no one spoke English and we had to get by on what little I learned in one semester of French back in high school?"

"Your French is terrible."

"I know; I'll work on it before we go again."

"I hated the cold, but I loved the lodge." She smiled, remembering a picture she'd seen of a farm in France. "Didn't you say the place we stayed was three hundred years old?"

"Four, I think, and judging from the bed we slept in, the mattress was the same age."

Ronny raised her head. "I can't remember, Marty, did we make love there?"

"We did, great passionate love. The kind that left both of us mindless for a while. Your body was made for loving, Ronny. The best part of loving you is spooning with you afterward when you're all warm against me, like we're not two people but two parts of one."

"Like salt and pepper shakers that fit together."

He laughed. "The next time we travel let's buy some of those funny sets. They'd look great on that shelf in the kitchen, and they'd be a lot easier to get home than that damn clock."

She nodded, not telling him that she'd taken the shelf down to paint two years ago and forgotten to put it back.

He fell asleep telling her that when he woke they'd remember the time they took a train from Chicago to Albuquerque and made love in every empty private car along the way.

Ronny sat in the silence with the blinking machines surrounding her and realized she'd never gone more than a few hundred miles in her life, but she'd carry the memories of everything they'd talked about as if they were the only memories she possessed.

A little before dawn, she fell asleep thinking of the other adventures he'd tell her that they'd shared when he woke. She'd ask him to describe how they made love and if they ever fought. She'd ask him about the food they ate in the jungle and in Paris when they slept beside a bridge because he lost his wallet. That would be a fun memory to build.

Only Marty never woke. He left her while she slept, holding his hand.

He left her with the memories of a perfect world.

Chapter 28

APRIL 10

TYLER WRIGHT WOKE MARTHA Q BEFORE EIGHT the next morning to ask her if Mr. Carleon would mind coming to the phone. He said he didn't have the man's cell number or he wouldn't have bothered Martha Q.

She trudged up the stairs and knocked on Mr. Carleon's door, then waited in the hallway when he took the call.

She listened to Carleon talking to the funeral director long enough to guess what had happened, then rushed to her room to dress in one of her best jogging suits. When

Mr. Carleon came back down the stairs to leave ten minutes later, Martha Q was ready.

"If you've no objection, I'd like to go with you, Anthony." It was the first time she'd used his Christian name, but she thought it was about time. "Tyler wouldn't have called you unless there has been a death, and I can think of only one that would concern you. I'd like to go to help, if you've no objection. Ronny is as dear to me as a daughter." Since she had no daughter, Martha Q had no idea how dear that was, but it sounded good.

"That's very kind of you, Martha," he said. "I'm sure Ronny can use a friend right now."

"And you," she added. "Marty was your friend too. I want you to know I'll be there for you as well if you need a shoulder to cry on."

"Thank you. I'll miss him, you know. We've been talking of this day for months. Marty Winslow was a brilliant man who never seemed to plan his life, but he did plan his death. I have many details to put into action before I have time to grieve the loss of a friend and an employer."

As they walked out the door, Martha Q added, "I'll do whatever I can. Ronny will take this hard, I'm afraid. I was there when she thought she lost him two years ago." She handed Carleon her keys. "I hope you don't mind driving?"

"Of course not." He opened the car door for her. "Should we call her mother to be with her at this time?"

"No, there's no need to make it harder than it has to be. Dallas Logan complains she's dying every few months. If we ask her to come over, all she'll talk about is her funeral. Says she has no reason to live now that her Howard is gone and her daughter ran away. I try to tell Dallas that daughters who are twenty-seven don't run away, they just leave, but she doesn't listen."

Martha Q knew Mr. Carleon couldn't be counted on to keep up the conversation, so she'd help him out by talking as he drove. "If you ask me, Howard Logan is up in heaven on his knees every single morning praying that the Lord will let Dallas live a long life so he'll have a little more peace in the hereafter."

Mr. Carleon didn't say a word. He just drove the few blocks to the duplex.

Tyler and the sheriff were already there sitting on the front porch.

Martha Q greeted them with a nod and asked if she could see Ronny. She really didn't feel like she needed permission to enter a place she owned, but it pays to be respectful at times of grief.

When she went in, Ronny was sitting beside Marty's bed. He looked like he was sleeping, but all the machines were off.

Martha Q waited until Ronny looked up at her and then whispered, "You said your good-bye to him, child?"

Ronny nodded.

"Well then, there's much that needs doing. How about I walk you through the beginning until you get your footing?"

Ronny stood, moving so slowly she looked like she'd aged overnight. She leaned over Marty and kissed him one last time, then went with Martha Q to her bedroom.

Without a word Martha Q helped her into the shower and stood waiting until she finished. Then, wrapped in a towel, Ronny sat and let the older woman comb her hair. She looked hollow, as if someone had carved the insides out of her and left only the shell.

Martha Q talked about how pretty Ronny's

hair was and how the day would seem endless, but the night would come just as
the morning would tomorrow. She had
no idea if Ronny heard her, but it didn't
matter.

The morning nurse came in and reban-
daged Ronny's arm. The cut was no more
than a thin line of scab; bruises ran from
shoulder to elbow. Both women helped
her dress in a simple navy dress.

"You can do this, Ronny," Martha Q whispered as they moved back into the living
room. "Death knocks on all doors whether
we want it to come or not. The only advice
I can give you is to not think about anything
but putting one foot in front of the other.
You'll make the hard climb one step at a
time. That's what survivors do."

Tyler Wright had taken Marty's body
away and most of the machines had been
shoved against the far wall. Someone had
set up chairs around the fireplace even
though it wasn't cold enough to light the
fire. Coffee percolated in the kitchen.

Mr. Carleon took Ronny's hand and sat
beside her, explaining all the details Marty
had already taken care of concerning what

he wanted at his funeral. He insisted that he wanted to be buried here in Harmony in a simple graveside service. Marty had instructed Mr. Carleon to buy two plots in the Harmony Cemetery the day after he arrived.

"He said"—Carleon picked his words carefully—"that you could leave the space beside him empty. If you married and wanted to be buried elsewhere, you might consider putting up a bench so you could sit beside him now and then. He said he liked the idea of watching you growing old and knowing that you hadn't forgotten him."

Ronny nodded, but she didn't ask questions. When she looked up at the silver-haired man who'd been with Marty for years, he seemed to read her mind.

"I'll stay for as long as you need me. He would have wanted me to, and I find I've grown very fond of you and this little town. I'll make sure everything is taken care of before I leave."

Finally, Ronny seemed to wake from her trance. "Where will you go?" she asked, as if suddenly her family were falling apart.

"I don't know. When I left with Marty to

come here, the Winslows terminated my employment within hours, but don't you worry, I've got enough money saved to live comfortably just about anywhere in the world."

Martha Q, who was listening, suddenly realized that if Mr. Carleon left, she'd miss him. The fact shocked her. She hadn't missed a man in years. In fact, the last few husbands she had been looking forward to missing for months before they finally left.

Throughout the morning people came and went from the duplex. The preacher. The postmaster, who'd heard the news. The boys next door. As the word spread around town, people came bringing food and flowers as if they'd known Marty for years. Even the three widows Martha Q was boarding came. They'd never met Marty, but they cried just the same.

The only person who didn't come was Dallas Logan. Her only child had just lost the love of her life, and Dallas couldn't set aside her anger long enough to comfort Ronny.

It made Martha Q so mad she hugged Ronny every chance she got while she plotted to thump Dallas Logan a good one if she ever saw the woman again.

In the evening, the cook at the funeral home, stopped in with her baby. She asked Ronny to come back to her apartment in the back of the funeral home. The girls had shared it once before, and Martha Q guessed it was as close as Ronny had to a home that she'd want to go to.

Summer talked Ronny into taking a walk, leaving Martha Q and Mr. Carleon alone in the little duplex apartment.

"It's been a long day," she said as she sat next to him on the porch. "And tomorrow won't be any shorter."

Anthony nodded. "You were a great help today, Martha."

"I try to be," Martha Q lied. Help was rarely something she tried.

"I feel a bit lost," he admitted. "I don't think there has been a minute I haven't had Marty on my mind in two years. Most of my energy has been spent taking care of him, and now I'm not sure what to do with myself."

She'd been watching Anthony Carleon all day. He was organized, always thoughtful, and as pure a gentleman as she'd ever seen, but the man lived on coffee and nothing else. "It's been my experience, Anthony, that the only cure for feeling lost is home-cooked food. How about we go back to my place and raid the fridge?"

He offered a tired smile. "That sounds like a good idea, my dear."

A few minutes later when they climbed the steps of the bed-and-breakfast, the three little widows were waiting for them. All three were so angry they looked like they'd been wound up too tight and couldn't stop jittering.

The trio had been told by the sheriff to quit following Bryce Galloway, but they were determined, even if threatened at gunpoint, to continue their quest. They'd followed him into the cleaners and asked to see the jacket he turned in.

The little lady behind the counter didn't understand why. Joni Rosen, the leader, made up a story about being Bryce's mother and said she'd put something in his pocket at church and he must have forgotten it was there.

Martha Q thought the story lacked her

own natural creativity, but she nodded and encouraged Joni to continue. "And did you find your missing valuable?"

Joni smiled. "No, but we found this."

She held up one piece of straw. "Talk's all over town about how someone tried to poison one of Nevada Britain's horses. Well, ladies and gentleman, I have the proof right here."

"You mean Nevada McDowell's horses. She's married, you know." Martha Q liked to use the right name. She always hated it when people called her by the wrong last name. Usually when it happened, she had to fight down the urge to hit them up the side of their head and tell them to read the paper now and then. She'd made the front page in her wedding dress all seven times.

"Whatever," Joni said. "Back to the find. A clue. Horses hang out in barns. This proves Bryce was in a barn, therefore he was probably the one who tried to kill the horse."

Martha Q doubted one piece of straw would do the trick, but she decided to do all she could to keep the widows off spying and out of the house. "This is great, ladies. Keep up the good work."

About that time Bryce pulled up out front and the widows scattered.

Martha Q and Anthony remained on the porch.

Bryce whistled as he walked up the steps. "Good evening," he said, obviously in a good mood.

"Evening," Martha Q offered in return. "Had a busy day?"

"Not particularly." Bryce passed them without stopping to talk. "Just looking over some investments."

He'd disappeared inside before she could ask any questions.

Anthony leaned close and whispered, "My friend in Houston checked on him. Nothing. He'd been questioned twice about fights he'd been in, but charges were never filed."

"Money bought him out of trouble," she whispered back, loving being so close to Mr. Carleon.

They stood, listening to Bryce run up the stairs. Finally, when the third-floor door slammed, Anthony offered his arm. "I believe, Martha, we have a date waiting in the kitchen."

"A date?" Martha Q grinned as she curled

her hand around his arm. "Does it come with a good-night kiss?"

Anthony looked more relaxed in the porch light's glow than she'd ever seen him. "It just might, dear lady. It just might."

Chapter 29

APRIL 10

CORD LEFT NEVADA SLEEPING ON THE BLAN-
kets in the hay and moved to the door of
the barn loft. It was sunup and he should
be at the bunkhouse giving the men orders for the day, but he didn't want to leave
her. Even after he'd held her close all night,
he was still hungry for the feel of her against
him. She was quickly becoming an addiction that went all the way to the bone. It
occurred to him that if he'd known her, really known her, before he went to prison,
he would have died of starvation for the

feel of her in the six years he'd been behind bars.

She'd teased him about having a girlfriend when Ronny called concerning the
man Cord was trying to find, but Nevada
would have to be blind to not see that
she was the only woman he looked at.
Cord was falling hard for his temporary wife.
He already knew that when their time was
over and he had to leave, his heart would
be staying behind.

He'd held her all night long. He'd always
thought of her as headstrong and wild.
Only yesterday he'd seen her broken, and
he never wanted to see her like that again.
Whoever poisoned the horse must have
known how it would hurt her. Someone
wanted her shattered, unable to fight, but
why? Surely not over land? If Bryce was to
blame, he wouldn't have needed to break
her to get her to sell the land. His family
was rich enough to buy half the ranches in
Texas.

He pulled out his cell and called Galem,
passing along what needed to be done on
the ranch. Then Cord asked if Galem
would tell Jackson and his brothers to wait
for him in the bunkhouse kitchen. When

Galem confirmed his order, Cord added that he wanted Zeb to pack lunch and a rifle and be at the horse barn in ten minutes. Cord was taking no chance of anyone who didn't belong stepping foot in the place again.

"If Zeb sees a stranger's car turn off the county road onto the ranch, tell him to fire off a couple of shots. I want no one stepping on the Boxed B that doesn't belong."

"Will do," Galem answered. "He'll be on his way to act as guard in a few minutes."

The horse barn was a good place to station a guard. From the loft opening one man could see the land all the way to where their road hooked up to the county road. The only other entrance into the ranch was eight miles farther down, and Cord planned to bust the dam at that end. Within an hour the dirt road would be so muddy not even a tank could get down it.

"You know, Galem, this trouble isn't over." Cord needed to be honest, with himself and the cook. "We may have hard times coming."

"I know. We all know, Boss. Only I'm thinking you may be wrong about Bryce Galloway being behind all this trouble. He ain't got the balls. I think he wants Nevada back, but he won't face you."

Cord hadn't met the man, but from what Nevada had told him, he didn't like Bryce. Maybe Galem was right; the ex-husband did seem to be more the type to bully Nevada, or even frighten her, to get what he wanted, than to come straight on. "I'm not taking any chances."

"I agree. Nevada's old man made his share of enemies, and even you made a few when you fired men those first few days. In Harmony you'll be hard-pressed to find a dozen people who like the Britains, and most would question your sanity for marrying one. They'll wonder why you'd want to step between Nevada and her ex."

"They don't know me." Cord grinned, thinking no one would ever understand how he felt about Nevada.

Galem laughed. "You got a point, but the men here are with you."

"Then we make our stand here."

Cord walked to where Nevada slept. When he tried to wake her with a touch, she only curled deeper into the blanket.

He gave up and lifted her, blanket and all. He carried her to his truck and nestled her beside him as he drove the short distance to their house. Without trying to wake her, he walked into their bedroom and placed her in the middle of the king-size bed. She'd had an emotional day yesterday, and maybe she'd sleep the morning away.

When she didn't move, he closed the curtains for the first time since he'd moved in with her and left the room dark. As he walked through the kitchen, he told Ora Mae not to wake her.

Cord hesitated a moment and added, "When she does wake up, tell her I have one of my boys at her barn and he's staying."

"She won't like that." Ora Mae never stated more than the facts.

"I don't care. If she's got a problem with it, tell her to talk to me." He checked the phone in his pocket. "Of course. she'll have to find me first."

By the time he was out of the house, Cord's mind was focusing in on what had to be done. A few minutes later he was eating breakfast as Jackson filled him in on every detail he and Zeb could find out about the trainer. He'd been hired while

Nevada was married to Bryce. He wasn't from Harmony, and as near as they could find out he'd made no attempts to fit into the community. He was a loner who liked it that way, but Nevada had never complained about his work.

When Jackson finished the report, Cord simply said, "Find him."

Jackson smiled. "That's the same thing the sheriff said she planned to do."

When Jackson left, Galem poured himself a cup of coffee and sat down across from Cord. "You can't afford to do anything illegal. You know that ranger and half the cops in this part of the state are watching you. Waiting for you to make one wrong move."

"I know, Mother." Cord smiled.

Galem got the hint. "I'm just saying that if you're planning anything the least bit shady, you got to let me do it. I've got this innocent face. Everyone trusts me."

Cord almost choked on his coffee as he laughed. Galem's face was weathered and pockmarked. He'd admitted to having his nose broken once by a bull and then straightened with another break in a fight. A few of the men kidded him once, saying they were surprised Galem ever found a woman willing to marry him, since he was so homely even the cattle noticed. Galem had answered that great lovers are always handsome in the dark.

"I'll stay legal, I promise." Cord set his cup down. "Watch over the ranch for a few hours; I need to go to town and set a few things in motion."

Galem raised an eyebrow but nodded.

Cord drove to town, pulled through the bank's drive-through window for cash, and headed to the movie theater. He couldn't believe Cameron had been in town and he hadn't noticed him, but then, no one ever noticed the man. Plus, Cord hadn't been on this end of Main more than a dozen times in the three years he'd been back, and he'd never gone to the movies.

He found Cameron, older but still as bland-looking as ever, emptying the trash out back of the theater. His hair was gray and in need of a cut, his clothes baggy.

"Remember me?" Cord said as he walked up.

"Nope." The man turned to go back inside, showing no interest in talking.

Cord was a long way from the kid he'd

been when he met Cameron in prison. Cord had grown a few inches since then and put on fifty pounds. "We met once almost ten years ago. You told me you were from Harmony and would be headed back as soon as you got out. I probably said I was never coming back here if I ever got out of prison."

Cameron stopped and slowly turned around. He took the time to study Cord, from his expensive boots to the monogrammed initials on his cuff and the western-cut leather jacket. "I've tried to forget that time in prison, and I'm guessing you have too. I thought you looked familiar, but I'm trying never to remember anyone I met behind bars."

Cord guessed he had about thirty seconds to make his point. "It doesn't matter if you remember me. You interested in a job that pays good money?" He pulled the cash from his pocket. "Nothing illegal. I just need someone watched and I don't want him to spot you. A few of the guys used to say you were good at moving around without folks noticing. All you got to do is tail him."

"I used to be good at not being noticed." Cameron straightened a little taller with pride. "I could shadow anyone right into their own house without them spotting me. I'm strictly legit now, but there's no harm in watching someone, I guess. I could really use the money. My boss wants to sell this place, and if he closes I'll have trouble finding another job. You want them tailed day and night, I'm your man—Cord?"

"You do remember me?"

Cameron smiled. "Nothing slips by me. I've seen you around town a few times; surprised you noticed me."

"I didn't, but I hoped you were here. A friend helped me out with your address, but that's not the problem. I'd like to hire you starting now and going until I get the information I need. I'm guessing it won't be more than a two- or three-day job, with a bonus at the end if you learn something helpful."

"It'll cost you three hundred a day, and all I do is watch and report. Nothing more. I'm too old to get in the middle of anything."

"If you're spotted, you're fired."

"Fair enough, but if I get what you want, the bonus is a thousand. I can work till Friday, then if you still want me, I can call in sick here. I got a kid who can fill in and run the projector. I stay on this guy until you call me off, or get what you want in the way of information."

Cord nodded. "Be ready in thirty minutes. I'll pick you up here in the alley."

Cameron disappeared into the theater and Cord drove over to the mall. He bought a phone with prepaid minutes, a camera with extra batteries, and a pocket tape recorder from a secondhand shop. When he circled back by the theater, Cameron was waiting for him with a toolbox and a clipboard in one hand and a work jacket in the other. The old guy had changed into dark blue trousers stained on one knee and a denim work shirt.

As he climbed into Cord's special-edition Ford, he whispered to himself, "If I'd known you drove a 450, I would have doubled my price. You've done well for yourself since prison. Heard folks talking about you and some rancher's daughter marrying. I don't have to take the paper; I just listen to folks talk before the movies."

"I married money," Cord answered flatly.

Cameron laughed, like he thought Cord was kidding.

The little man took notes as Cord rattled off the facts about Bryce Galloway. "He's probably eating over at the bed-and-breakfast about now. From there I have no idea where he goes or who he talks to"—Cord glanced at Cameron, who had started playing with all his new toys—"but I will after today. I'll expect details for my money."

"You'll get them." Cameron shoved everything into his toolbox. "I'll need all your numbers and I might call at any hour. I can't step away to talk to you until I know this guy is set somewhere."

"I only have one number, and it's already in the phone. Don't talk to anyone but me. Don't call me until you have something important to say. I'll call you if I hear anything you need to know about this guy."

Cameron nodded. "If I don't answer, I'll call back as soon as I can. This ain't the kind of job that allows visiting."

"I understand." He handed over the five bills. "I'll pay the balance when the job is over."

"Drop me off a few houses from the Winter's Inn. I don't want anyone seeing me with you." Cameron shoved his notes into his vest pocket.

Cord pulled to the curb. "You planning on just walking in?"

Cameron smiled. "No, I'll be invited in. I may have given up crime, but I still watch what's going on. The old lady who owns the B&B drives a boat of a car. I see her cruising Main like some of the kids do. Since it's not parked in the drive, she's not home. I'm guessing there will be a cook or housekeeper to let the gas inspector in." He pulled a faded ID tag from his pocket and clipped it to his coat. "Folks never read the tag; just having one is all you need if you smile and act all polite."

"Be careful, Cameron. This guy could be dangerous."

"I figured that or you wouldn't be hiring me." The little man winked like he was about to have the time of his life.

Cord let him out, then pulled across the street and watched Cameron walk straight up to the front door. He talked to a lady who looked like the housekeeper for a minute, and then she opened the door to let him in.

Smiling, Cord noticed a rental car parked to the side. He'd bet it was Bryce's, and Cameron was probably watching him eat breakfast right now. The con man might just be worth the money.

On his way over to the sheriff's office he called the house and wasn't surprised to hear Nevada was still asleep.

Circling by Ronny's old duplex, he noticed Tyler Wright wheeling a body down the ramp he'd made. Marty had passed. He'd finally used the ramp.

A boat of a car was parked beside the undertaker, so Cord didn't stop. He had his share of trouble today, but he couldn't help worrying about his friend. He hoped she'd remember to call if she needed him.

Alex Matheson was out of her office when Cord walked into the sheriff's station, but Travis Salem had taken over the small conference room next to the sheriff's office. Cord tried to back out without the ranger seeing him, but Salem looked up.

"McDowell," he yelled. "Come on in. I need to talk to you."

Cord didn't bother taking off his hat as he stepped a few feet into the room. He didn't like being this close to Salem. He didn't trust him, even if he was a Texas Ranger. His memories were washed in whiskey from the night they'd first met out by the lake, but Cord didn't remember going at the man in a wild rage like then-Deputy Travis Salem had testified.

One of the older sheriff's deputies saw Cord and offered him a cup of coffee. Cord was glad when the deputy stayed in the room to hear what the ranger had to say. Cord didn't know Phil Gentry very well, but he couldn't start avoiding folks he didn't know or he'd have to be a hermit.

Ranger Salem pointed to a pile of papers. "The way this is stacking up, McDowell, we don't have enough hard evidence to charge anyone, even if you and your wife think you know who poisoned the horse. That ex-husband of your wife's could just say he dropped by the barn one day for old times' sake. Even if we could prove it was his footprint, we don't have enough to charge Bryce Galloway."

Cord wasn't surprised. He hadn't expected Travis Salem to help him.

"Galloway, you say," Phil lowered his coffee. "I just took a complaint from him. He claims he's being stalked."

Cord froze. He'd left Cameron fifteen minutes ago. Surely he wasn't already caught?

He hadn't earned a dollar of the five hundred.

Phil laughed. "Yeah, the guy claims three little widows staying at the bed-and-breakfast tail him everywhere he goes. He says losing them usually takes half the morning, but he's tired of the hassle."

Cord relaxed. Just for a minute. Until he realized the women's interest in the man might mess up Cameron's tracking possibilities.

"Why would they be following Bryce?" Travis asked, without showing much interest.

"I don't know. He's a good-looking man. Maybe they're all three in love." Phil poked his cheek with his tongue. "Come to think of it, if I go over there they'll take one look at Bryce and start following me around. A man with a little gray in his hair is far more attractive to the widow types." Phil shrugged. "Don't see how we can charge them with anything. Eating at the same café as Bryce or driving down the same street isn't a crime that I know of."

Travis Salem looked like the deputy was interfering with important police work, but since he was a guest in the office he probably figured he shouldn't start giving orders. The ranger stood politely and waited for Gentry to finish his one-sided conversation.

Cord listened to the deputy while he watched Salem out of the corner of his eye. The ranger didn't seem any more comfortable around him than he was around the ranger. Surely the guy wasn't afraid Cord might swing at him again. More than likely, he decided, Travis Salem worried that the lie he'd told ten years ago that had sent Cord to prison might somehow surface.

Only no one had believed Cord's side of the story back then, and if Cord was guessing, he'd say no one would believe it now.

Cord finished his coffee and headed out. "Let me know if you find anything," he said to the ranger, then smiled at Phil Gentry, deciding he liked the old deputy. After all, Gentry was one of the few lawmen who hadn't suggested he leave town permanently. "Good luck with the band of widows. You might think about arresting them to keep them out of trouble."

Gentry nodded as if he were considering the idea.

Cord made it to the bottom of the front steps before Gentry caught up to him. "Mr. McDowell, you're a friend of Ronny Logan, aren't you?"

"I am."

"I thought I should tell you she was attacked out behind her house last night. Someone hiding in the shadows tried to grab hold of her and she fell backing away. Luckily, she was only bruised, but I tell you, I can't think of why anyone would do such a thing. The poor girl's got her basket full of troubles already. With Marty dying, she's got other things on her mind today, but I'm filing a full report."

Cord asked a few details, but Gentry didn't know any more.

"It don't make any sense." Phil shook his head. "Everyone likes Ronny, except maybe her mother, and I can't see that old witch trying to kill her only child. Who would she have to complain about?"

Cord climbed into his truck. Gentry was right. No one would go after Ronny. Unless . . . unless they thought by hurting her they'd be hurting someone else.

When he made it back to the ranch, Nevada was dressed and reading the paper as she nibbled on a muffin. He stood in the kitchen doorway for a moment watching her. When she finally looked up he asked, "Should I run?"

She smiled. "No, I've decided to let you live."

"I'm not backing down on the guard at your barn. I want a man I can trust there." He figured he might as well face the problem head-on. "The guard stays no matter what you say."

"Okay," she said, shocking him.

"No storm?"

"No storm," she answered. "I think after a month of living with you I've figured out that, for the first time in longer than I can remember, I've got someone on my side."

"Want to go with me to make a round of the ranch? I want to check fences and change the codes on all the locked gates going to where your oil rigs are. If someone's out to cause hell on the Boxed B, I plan to make it as hard on them as I can."

To his surprise she said yes and pulled on her boots. "Let's take the old Jeep; I haven't driven it in a week. If I go much longer it won't start."

"Fair enough, but I drive."

He rested his arm lightly on her shoulder as they walked out behind the barn, where she always parked the Jeep in an old shed that looked like her grandfather had probably built it. More boards were missing from the sides than on it.

"I'm doubling the security at my office. Everything else that has happened lately could be written off as an accident, but not Starlight."

Cord agreed. "I feel like we're under attack."

She smiled up at him. "And we fight, right?"

He kissed the top of her head. "Right, Babe."

As she moved beside him, he fought the urge to kiss her again. She was becoming a part of him. Everyone he'd ever cared about had turned their backs or died on him. Cord knew she'd do the same when their bargain was finished. She had her secrets and she'd leave before she'd let him any closer, but right now she needed him.

Nevada always left the keys in the ignition and the windows rolled up. Most of the paint was gone on the roof of the Jeep, but Cord guessed it had once been blue, or maybe army green. He couldn't be sure.

He pulled the driver's door open as she smiled and swung into the passenger side.

Everything happened in a flash, like lightning hit several places at once.

Nevada screamed.

Cord heard the familiar tick-tick-tick of a rattler's tail. He'd already extended his hand toward the wheel and felt the hard sudden stab of fangs going into his wrist before he could pull back. When he did step away, the snake came along, attached to his wrist.

The rattlesnake had to be near six feet long and held on as Cord tried to swing it free. His skin ripped when he finally slung the snake a few feet away. More out of instinct than logic, Cord slammed his boot straight down an inch below the snake's head, pinning it in the dirt.

The body of the snake whipped and coiled around his legs.

Nevada continued to scream for help. She'd managed to climb out of the Jeep, but he couldn't tell if she'd been bitten.

Cord ground hard, but the dirt around the shed was too soft to kill the snake.

He couldn't move. If he did, the snake

might try to strike again, or worse, slither off. Tightening his fist, he could already feel the numbness moving into his wrist. This was not a dry bite. The snake had injected venom.

Ora Mae came running from the back door of the house as two cowhands rushed from the barn. Like a warrior of old, Ora Mae raised her garden hoe and swung.

Cord closed his eyes, figuring if she missed he would not only have a snakebite to deal with but also a few missing toes.

The hoe hit the rattler just behind the head and severed the body.

Cord stared down, afraid to move. He had no idea if his heart was pounding in his throat because of the venom pumping in his blood or because, for the first time since he got out of prison, he was terrified.

The cowhands reached them just as another snake slithered from the open door of the Jeep. One of the men borrowed Ora Mae's hoe and killed the second snake with one whack.

Cord moved to Nevada's side. "Are you bit?" he yelled.

She shook her head as she gulped for air and moved closer to him.

They watched silently as four more snakes were pulled from the Jeep. All were longer than four feet. This was no nest. They'd been planted in the hot vehicle and they didn't look too happy about it. The windows had been rolled up. Towels for them to hide in had been piled in the back-seat.

When Cord pulled off his belt and tied it around his forearm, Nevada saw the bite marks as blood stained his cuff. "We need to get you to the hospital."

"You drive. I'm not sure I won't pass out."

They headed to his truck. He'd only seen one man with a snakebite before. He was a day laborer on his dad's farm. Cord had been about seven, but he re-membered how sick the man looked be-fore they got him to town.

Nevada stopped shaking as anger built in her. She drove so fast he figured a poi-sonous snakebite might be the least of his problems. Neither talked. They both knew what was at stake.

She pulled into the emergency room drive before either said a word.

"Can you make it in?"

"I can." Cord was giving serious consideration to a prayer of thanks for surviving the drive. One good thing, she'd taken his mind off the bite. He'd read in books that anyone bitten should remain calm. Fat chance of that. He took a deep breath, testing to see if he had any trouble breathing. No problem, but his arm was starting to swell and he had no feeling in his hand.

She jumped out of the truck and ran around to help him out, then pushed him into the empty emergency room.

While the nurse took him back, Nevada stopped to fill out paperwork. He could tell she didn't want to leave him, but she was starting to make him more nervous than the dripping blood from the two bite marks.

"I'll be fine, Babe," he yelled over his shoulder as they led him away.

"You'd better be." He could hear the anger in her words and knew if he died on her she'd never forgive him for breaking their bargain.

Dr. Addison Spencer was waiting for him with shots ready and a list of instructions taped to the wall.

He took one look at the shot and said, "I didn't know you were a gunslinger, Doc."

She smiled in that *this is going to hurt you more than it does me* kind of way as she pulled his already unbuttoned shirt off his shoulder and shot him.

Cord flinched. "Hey, Doc, aren't you supposed to say 'Make a fist' or something?"

"I didn't want to waste time. Snake venom can restrict your air passages."

"After that shot, it's going to take me a while to breathe normal." Cord watched her carefully in case she reloaded.

While she worked, a conversation passed through the curtain that acted as a door to the emergency area. One woman's voice said, "Strange couple, if you ask me."

Another said, "I've heard he's violent. Almost killed a deputy about ten years back."

The first laughed. "Well, I heard she tried to kill her last husband, so they're probably evenly matched."

Cord growled.

The first voice from the hallway added, "I'm surprised a rattler would even bite him. They usually don't attack their own."

Dr. Spencer laughed, drawing Cord's attention. "You that mean, cowboy?"

"Probably," he answered, realizing she

was far too bright to buy into gossip. "I'm working on it."

"My fiancé, Tinch Turner, was over at the vet's this morning working with your horse. He said the vet told a different story. Said he heard you and your wife slept with the horses to make sure they were all right."

Cord frowned. "Don't tell those ladies, you'll ruin my rep."

"Your secret's safe with me, cowboy." Without another word, she began cleaning the wound.

Cord decided he liked this no-nonsense doctor.

When Nevada found him fifteen minutes later, he'd already had two shots and the wound had been cleaned and bandaged. He'd been ordered to wait on the examining table, and the nurse would be back to check his heart rate.

He felt like a fool with his feet swinging off the table and his shirt open. They'd offered him a hospital gown, but he told them he'd as likely wear pink PJs as a gown. In truth, he felt fine. He hadn't even wanted to lie down. Once the fear wore off, Cord felt like everyone was making a big deal over

JODI THOMAS

nothing. His arm ached, but it was no longer swelling and he had most of the feeling back in his hand.

For the first time he realized how frightened Nevada looked. "I'm all right, but they cut up the sleeve of the shirt you bought me. I really liked the way you put my initials on the cuff. I'm sorry about messing it up."

Nevada pressed as close as she could get to him. "I don't care about the shirt, Cord. I care about you, you idiot."

He looked up into her beautiful blue eyes and smiled. "You do?"

The meaning behind her words seemed to hit them both at the same time. Somehow during the past month they'd changed from two almost-strangers who'd made a bargain to something different, and neither really knew what it was.

She leaned down and kissed his lips softly. "Don't you dare die on me. I didn't really think I would, but I like having you around, Cord McDowell."

It wasn't exactly a declaration of love, but he'd take it. He slid his unbandaged hand into the hair at the back of her neck, pulled her close, and kissed her soundly, then whispered, "I thought about it, but I figured you'd really storm if I cut out on the bargain."

Her hand moved through the hair on his chest as her cheek rubbed against his. They didn't know how to say the right words about how much the other meant to them. He'd never used a word like *love* much, and she'd used it so often it no longer held any meaning.

She moved between his legs and wrapped her arms around his neck. He circled her waist with his bandaged wrist and pulled her close enough to feel her heart beat against his. When he caressed her soft breasts beneath the silk of her blouse, he decided if the poison wasn't out of his system it was probably running double time through his veins about now.

"I thought I'd die when I saw that snake; then when you were bit I swear my heart completely stopped." She gulped for air. "I think I finally found something more frightening than snakes. It's thinking about you hurt and knowing that it's somehow all my fault." She pulled his face close to hers. "This is my fault, Cord. I know it."

"No. It's not. Whoever's doing this may want to hurt you, but it's not your fault. We're going to get through this. Me and you, Babe." Any doubt that they were in this fight together was gone, and they both knew it.

She leaned into him and kissed him softly on the mouth. A thank-you kiss. A promise. A bonding of their own special kind of loving.

Cord forced the words. "As soon as my heart slows down a few hundred beats a minute, how about we go back to those blankets in the barn?" He could think of one place where they had no trouble communicating. "Or, I think it looks like rain. We might want to take a nap over at my farm."

"I don't want to sleep." She smiled.

"Me either," he answered.

She tortured him by wiggling against him again. "Are you saying you want my body?"

"I want all of you." *Including your heart*, he thought as his hand moved over her hip. "It'd take more than a snakebite to slow me down." He needed to be alone with her more than he needed air right now. "How about we go back and send Ora Mae home? We could tell her the doctor ordered bed rest."

Nevada kissed him tenderly, but her body seemed to be begging to be handled with passionate touches. They'd made love enough to know what the other liked, and right now Cord was thinking he liked everything about her. Something about being scared half to death made him feel totally alive. He could read every move she made, and he had no doubt he could give her just what she wanted.

Cord was almost lost in pleasure when he heard boots stomping their way down the hall and knew their time together was about to end.

He managed to push her away a few inches before the room filled with half a dozen of his men. They were all talking and cussing at once. Most had been out working cattle when they heard about the snakebite. Cord swore the smell of cows followed them into the hospital room.

Jackson slapped his hat against his leg. "Someone's trying to kill you, Boss, and we're not going to stand around and let that happen."

"No, not me," he answered. "They weren't trying to kill me."

He looked at Nevada, who paled seeing the truth in his words. "No one drives the old Jeep but me," she whispered as her hand gripped his shoulder. "The snakes were meant for me."

If she'd taken the Jeep by herself, it would have been midmorning and no one would be around to help. Two or three bites and she might not have gotten to help in time. Before, everything had seemed like accidents, but no longer.

"The snakes had to be brought in from somewhere else," one of the men volunteered. "We haven't seen a rattler that big around the ranch in years. And four of them together. It wouldn't make sense. Someone took the time to catch them and put them in there."

Everyone started talking at once about what needed to be done. Cord listened as he thought. They were right, of course; the snakes had been planted, but by whom? Again the same facts came back that he'd faced yesterday after the horse had been poisoned. Whoever did this knew the ranch, knew that Nevada drove the Jeep, maybe even knew she was afraid of snakes. If she hadn't noticed the rattlers for a few minutes, she might have been driving; fast, of course. Then the Jeep would flip on the narrow road and kill her. The snakes might even crawl away before anyone reached her.

He made his mind go through all the men who'd been fired the first day he came. They'd been mad at him, not at her. A few had cussed when he'd fired them, but none looked like he wanted a fight. What would be the point? Cord wasn't likely to hire them back.

That left only one person: Bryce Galloway, or maybe someone he'd paid to plant the snakes. Galem had mentioned once that Bryce said once that he'd never let her go. Maybe he'd always thought they'd get back together eventually. When Cord married her, that option vanished.

Cord thought about how Nevada had asked him to marry her. She hadn't wanted a husband; she said she wanted his last name. Could she have been that afraid of Galloway? Was that the real reason she'd married him? The reason she said she wouldn't explain?

Only Bryce came from a wealthy family. He had relatives in the state senate and an uncle who was a judge. Everyone in the state thought she married up on her third try, and half the people in town still thought that Nevada and her wild ways drove Bryce away. Maybe she thought Cord was the only man who'd be on her side if a fight came. Remembering the way the cowhands had ignored her when she'd walked into the bunkhouse that first Monday after they married, Cord decided maybe Nevada had guessed right.

But why him? She could have hired bodyguards and lawyers. Even though the ranch was losing money, she still had resources. Why marry the dirt-poor farmer next door? What had made her take a chance and believe that an ex-con would stand with her when trouble came?

If she knew it was coming at all?

He looked at Nevada, knowing that sometime soon he was going to have to ask the one question she'd told him never to ask. Why'd she marry him?

Dr. Spencer came into the examining room and demanded that all the cowhands leave. They were polite, even respectful, but reluctant to move. When she finally promised she'd let Cord go as soon as she was through examining him, they wandered off. Two offered to take his place if she'd examine them, and one asked her for a date before Cord reminded him that the doc was engaged to Tinch Turner.

All the town knew of Tinch's ability with his fists. The hospital had seen its share of his sparring partners after a bar fight. Only Tinch had settled down once he met the doctor. The cowboy and the city-girl doctor were an odd couple. Almost as odd as Cord and Nevada, Cord thought.

Finally only Cord, the doc, and Nevada were in the room.

"He'll need to take it easy for a few hours," Dr. Spencer said. "If his arm starts to swell or he experiences chills or sweats, I want him back in here."

"You treat a lot of snakebites, Doc?" Cord asked, just so she'd stop reading from a printout he felt sure she'd hand him when he walked out.

"You're my first. Most people who see snakes walk around them."

Cord reached for his hat. "I'm fine, Doc. You did a great job and I'll take your advice from now on, but I got to get back to work."

She looked like she might argue with him, but then she smiled as if she'd dealt with stubborn fools before. "Get some rest, Cord."

He put his arm around his wife and said, "I'll do that, Doc. My wife is taking me straight home to bed, aren't you, Babe?"

Chapter 30

April 11

Martha Q didn't like the idea of leaving Ronny in her grief, but the girl was in good hands with Mr. Carleon watching over her. They were busy notifying all of Marty's friends and relatives that the graveside service would be at dawn tomorrow. After his accident and long stays in the hospital, most of those he knew had drifted away. Except for three men, all others made excuses as to why they couldn't come. But the three friends who'd carried him off the mountain after his fall said they were on their way. Mr. Carleon called them Marty's knights.

Ronny looked like she was moving through water. Her face was pale and her hand shook now and then. Only she kept busy, as though if she were to stop and take a deep breath the sorrow would catch up to her and smother her completely. Nothing anyone said or did would take the pain away. Mr. Carleon was doing what he could. He walked with her through the hardest day of her life.

Martha Q had never known great love like that, and as she watched Ronny, she felt both thankful and cheated. She'd known passion and lust, but *love* was mostly just a word she used. She hadn't cried when her father died until she found out her sister inherited everything. Her mother passed on after ten years of swearing she was "about to." Martha Q felt like she'd been holding her breath for years waiting for death to show up, so when her mother stopped breathing it came as no surprise. Two of her husbands had died after long illnesses, leaving her more relieved than heartbroken. She had no children or pets she liked. So grief was something usually a few pounds of sweets could cure.

And there was certainly no time for a great love in her life now, Martha Q decided. She needed to get back to her place and have a talk with the three little widows. The sheriff had told her about Bryce's complaint, and it was only a matter of time before one of the widows broke and spilled the beans that Martha Q had come up with the idea to follow Bryce Galloway.

Martha Q's part in the plot would be exposed. Bryce would probably sue her, or worse, kill her. After all, he had to start somewhere, and she was always around. She still had the feeling he was secretly a serial killer in training. He might act all sweet and polite, but she wasn't fooled. She'd played that part herself now and then and knew all the lines.

It would be an even greater crime if he killed her right at a point in her life when she'd found a man who might be interested in her. It had been years since her last real flirtation. Her pen pal in prison really didn't count, since half of his love letters were blacked out. She thought about asking if they could send the deleted half to her anonymously so she could at least dream, but she doubted the correctional system had much interest in her longings.

Martha Q knew she was getting ahead of herself thinking that Mr. Carleon might be interested. After all, all he'd ever touched of her was her hand and, at her size, that didn't amount to even five percent if she measured interest by the pound. The kiss he'd hinted at after their almost-date in the kitchen was no more than a peck on her cheek.

She knew she shouldn't, but she just had to drive over to the funeral home and talk to Tyler. He was busy planning all the details for Marty's graveside funeral, but surely he'd have a few minutes to visit with her. First, he was the only man who would listen to her problems, and second, she wanted to check on Kate. The woman must be insane to get pregnant in her forties. Didn't Kate realize that Martha Q was too old to have a friend who was having a baby? Hell, as her best friend, Martha Q should probably give her a shower.

She was thinking about having a stay-at-home shower when she pulled up to Wright Funeral Home. She'd invite women over forty and tell them if they didn't want to come, they could send two gifts and stay at home. Kate would get a ton of gifts and Martha Q wouldn't have to waste time thinking of dumb games to play.

She climbed out, already making her list of who wouldn't come to the shower. Of course, she would leave Dallas Logan off the list, even if they did go to high school together. There was no excuse for Dallas disowning her only child, Ronny. The woman had always had rocks for brains, and now they were mold-covered.

Not feeling like the climb up the front steps, Martha Q went around to the kitchen door and tapped. Autumn, the housekeeper and cook, answered the door, a fat little baby in her arms.

Martha Q grunted. The world was exploding. If people didn't stop having kids, Harmony would have to change the population sign again.

"Morning, Mrs. Patterson. How can I help you?"

The girl was just too cheery for Martha

Q's liking. People in funeral homes should at least look respectfully sad, not like they'd just been laughing.

"I need to see Mr. Wright." Martha Q pushed her way in. The smell of warm gingerbread made her offer a quick smile to the cook.

"He's not here, but you could talk to Kate. I was just about to make her lunch, and I know she'd be happy if you joined her. It's no trouble to make an extra plate."

Martha Q decided she always did like Autumn. Even if she did have a baby, at least she had the good sense to be able to cook. "What are you having for lunch?"

"Chicken salad, made with walnuts and grapes, on homemade wheat bread with a slice of red velvet cake I made this morning for dessert. It's still too warm to cut, but by the time lunch is over, it should be ready."

"I thought I smelled ginger?" Martha Q examined the organized kitchen. They'd added a baby cage in the corner. She knew people called them playpens, but she'd never seen a child actually playing in one.

"Oh, you did. I'm making cookies for the fire department meeting tonight. You're welcome to have a few as an appetizer with lunch."

Martha Q reevaluated her opinion of the girl. Perhaps Autumn should breed; after all, she was obviously brilliant as well as talented.

Martha Q plopped her purse down on one of the stools. If the designer purse got any bigger or heavier, it would need rollers on the bottom; but fashion was fashion and the shopping network claimed orange went with everything this year. "Well, I guess I could keep Kate company for a while." She'd decided years ago that food she hadn't made or paid for was calorie free. "I might even have lunch just to make sure she eats. She needs to keep up her strength for the birthing due next week."

Five minutes later she sat in the breakfast area of the warm kitchen eating with Kate and told her of the problem with a full house at the bed-and-breakfast.

Unfortunately, unlike Tyler, Kate wasn't one to just listen. She talked, asked questions, made suggestions. Martha Q liked the woman, but she often found her exhausting. Tyler listened to her problems, but Kate tried to solve them.

Finally, as if she were no match for interrogation, Martha Q told Kate of her worries about Bryce Galloway and, to her surprise, Kate said that if a woman who knows men as well as Martha Q did thought there was something wrong with the man, it was worth investigating.

Then Martha Q told her about the widows getting caught trailing the man. It seemed he wasn't willing to believe they just happened to eat at the same place he did for lunch and walk in the park at the same time of day. He not only noticed them, but he'd tattled on them to the sheriff. Everyone in town knew the sheriff had more important things to do than haul in three widows for interrogation.

When her water broke, Kate lost interest in Martha Q's story. All at once Martha Q's problem was pushed aside, and everyone rallied around Kate like there hadn't been a few billion babies already born in the world. Tyler was called and told to meet them at the hospital. Autumn ran out with two baby bags and said she had to drop off her little girl with Willie at the fire station, and then she'd meet Kate at the hospital. The secretary, two guys from the basement, and Kate all piled into one of the vans and disappeared without even waving good-bye.

To Martha Q's surprise, she was left in charge of the funeral home. She felt like she hadn't been invited to the party. No one needed to go except for Kate, and she'd looked plenty calm enough to drive herself the few blocks. The two guys from the basement didn't need to go, or the secretary. And Autumn probably had snacks in the second baby bag. Everyone was over in the waiting room laughing it up, while Martha Q was alone in a building full of rooms where dead people normally hung out.

After waiting by the phone for fifteen minutes, during which no dead people called needing business, Martha Q locked up the front and let herself out the back door. She'd go to the hospital when all the screaming and blood was over.

She headed home, needing a nap after all the excitement.

When she pulled into her drive at the bed-and-breakfast, Beau Yates sat on the steps to her porch looking like the ghost of a young Johnny Cash in his black clothes and hat.

Martha Q swore. Lobbies in this town got less wear than her front porch. Every time she left, someone seemed to be waiting for her to return. It was downright nerve-racking.

Rolling down her window, she yelled, "Can you drive?"

Beau stood. "Of course."

"Well, get in. I need a cherry lime from Sonic to wash down all the ginger cookies I ate at the funeral home." After everyone left, Martha Q had been nervous about being in charge and munched the firehouse cookies down from three dozen to two.

Beau took off his cowboy hat and climbed into the driver's side like he was saddling up for a wild ride while she tried to slide across the bench seat. All her body parts didn't seem to follow willingly. Once on the passenger side, she had to take a few moments to regroup her layers of fat.

Beau put the car in reverse and pulled out of the drive. "You should get you a new car, Mrs. Q. This one rattles worse than Leon's old ice cream truck."

She ignored his insult. "My name is not Mrs. Q and you know it. I swear it's hard to believe you're the brighter of that nest of bums living in my duplex. If I didn't happen to talk to Border now and then, I'd find it impossible to believe. His bulb's not only dim, someone forgot to flip the switch on. I have a feeling his reading list consists of only his tattoos."

Beau smiled. "Having a good day, are you, Mrs. Q?"

She glared at him. "No, I'm not." She glanced up and noticed Dallas Logan, Ronny's mother, coming out of the bank. "Run that woman over, would you, Beau? It'll cheer me up."

Beau gunned the engine. "All right, if you say so."

Dallas Logan saw him coming, squealed like a pig before jumping to the curb, and then started yelling like she'd been robbed, raped, and run over all at the same time.

"You nitwit," Martha Q swore. "You missed her by a mile. Turn around and try again."

Beau looked at her as if he thought she might have finally lost her mind. "Come on, Mrs. Q, you can't be serious. Who was that woman anyway?"

"That was Ronny's mother."

"Oh, why didn't you say so?" He turned the car around in the middle of Main Street.

By the time they got back to the spot, Dallas Logan was gone. Martha Q laughed so hard she cried, and Beau seemed to catch the disease from her.

As soon as she could draw a breath, she yelled, "Damn if that wasn't the most fun I've ever had with my clothes on. It was worth risking prison to see her mouth open so wide her whole face turned into wrinkles."

"You're not thinking of taking your clothes off, are you?" Beau paled.

"No, I think you'll have to settle for a float at Sonic. I'm not putting on any show. Those days are over."

When he looked relieved, she thought of hitting him, but since he was the one driving that might not be a good idea.

They sat at the drive-in and had their drinks with Tater Tots and mustard. Then she asked him to drive her out to the cemetery so she could see where Marty was going to be buried.

The drive cheered her up. Martha Q liked the Harmony Cemetery. The very air seemed peaceful and most of her enemies rested there below ground.

Beau held her arm as they walked

through the grass to the empty grave along the north side where tall cedars grew. Tyler Wright and his crew had everything ready. The fake grass over the mound of dirt. The folding chairs beneath a flapping green tent. The empty racks for flowers.

She sat in one of the chairs while Beau stared into the hole and frowned like he thought he might see right into hell.

Martha Q guessed Beau was lost in a song that played in his head. Much as she teased him, she knew talent dripped off him like sweat. She wanted to tell him to go for the dream he always talked about. Don't let anything stop him. Don't back down. Don't make promises or fall in love or be dishonest even with himself. Head straight for his dream and don't let any roadblock get in his way.

Only, maybe it was the things that got in the way that mattered. Maybe it was the turns in life that made it worth the living, not the goals or the dreams.

She pulled a tissue from her pocket and blew her nose. She was getting way too deep. Maybe it was this creative energy running through her. If she'd given up sex ten years earlier, she could have had the energy to outrun Nora Roberts on the charts. She would have a limo driving her around, not some kid who couldn't remember her name. She'd have so many servants she'd have to call them by number because, after all, a great writer couldn't be expected to remember real people's names.

"You ready to go?" Beau broke into her daydream.

"Sure. I'll be renting space in this place soon enough."

They walked back to the car.

"Why were you waiting on my porch? Mrs. Biggs finally wise up to you guys and lock you out of her kitchen?"

"No, I came to see you." He opened her car door. "I need to ask you what you think I should do."

Martha Q wiggled into her seat. "So many people want advice from me lately, I'm thinking of moving to a mountaintop and becoming a sage. If it wasn't for having to wear robes and put up with eagles flying low, I'd probably be gone tomorrow."

Beau slid behind the wheel. "Can we make this about someone else besides you for a moment, Mrs. Q?"

"Of course." She thought of pouting, but at some point her round, plump face started to look pumpkin-fat when she even thought about twisting her lips together.

Beau turned so he could face her when he said, "I think whoever reached for Ronny last night wasn't going after her, but he might have been wanting to talk to me."

"What?" She was sure her eyebrows went so far up they moved into her hairline. "How in the world did you come up with that? Even people who hate country music don't want to grab the singer."

"No. Hear me out. We live in the same place, just different sides. Ronny's tall, almost exactly my height. We both wear black coats. In fact, we got them mixed up the other night when Border and I took her out after we played."

"Okay, black coats. Same height. It's not exactly a *CSI* plot."

"We both walk at night in the shadows. She does it even more, I think, since Marty came back. Last night, when she was walking, it was about the time I usually take my break. I sometimes walk for a few minutes just to enjoy the clear air and the silence from the bar."

"You both walk. Not much to make me believe your theory, Beau."

"All right, how about this? Can you think of one reason anyone would want to hurt Ronny Logan?"

"No, I can't."

"Well, Harley, the guy who owns the bar I play in, said he saw two beefy types hanging out behind Buffalo's Bar late one night last week. He said they were staring at my old car. He tried to talk to them and they claimed they just needed to talk to me. When he started to ask more questions, they disappeared."

"Maybe they wanted your autograph?"

Beau tried again. "Not likely. Harley said they were sober. If they were fans, wouldn't they have been inside listening?"

Martha Q studied him. "Be honest with me. Are you seeing some woman? Maybe another man's wife or a rich rancher's only daughter? These guys could have just wanted to tell you to get lost."

Beau shrugged. "Yeah, I kind of am seeing someone, but nobody knows about it."

"If what you're saying is true, then I think there is a good chance someone does know about it. They might not want you seeing whoever you're seeing. Maybe the rich daddy hates the thought of long-haired grandsons, or the husband just hates. You might ask this secret lady if she's married and her husband wants you beat to a pulp. It's been my experience that affairs usually stop about the time the couple starts to talk."

Beau nodded. "So you're agreeing with me that maybe these guys did want to talk to me, and I'm thinking they got Ronny last night instead."

"Maybe. Anyone else you know who might be waiting in the dark to have a talk with you?"

"My dad. He tells everyone I've gone over to the dark side. I've heard his sermons usually have me in them somewhere as the bad example."

Martha Q's head was starting to pound from too much figuring. She didn't even like mystery shows. She was always worn out by the time they solved the murder. Sometimes she'd flip channels during the commercials and miss the show's ending. Then she'd stay up half the night wondering who did it.

"We'd better get home, Beau. You probably need to practice, and I need a nap.
We'll worry about this tomorrow. Problems
never seem so bad when they're warmed
over."

Chapter 31

APRIL 12

AT HALF PAST MIDNIGHT THE FIFTH GENERATION of Wrights in Harmony came into the world. He weighed six pounds, fourteen ounces, and his daddy, Tyler Wright, thought he was the most beautiful baby ever to be born.

McAllens, Mathesons, and one Truman filled the waiting room. The three families who'd built Harmony stood ready to welcome Jonathan Henry Wright to town, just as they'd welcomed his great-grandfather almost a hundred and fifty years ago.

Tyler walked through the double doors

of the delivery room with little Henry in his arms, knowing that they all wished the first Wright born in forty-six years well. He also hoped that "Hank" would grow up to watch over the people just as he had, and his father, and his father, and his father.

"My Kate says if you want to hold the baby, you got to wash your hands and put on a mask first."

Noah McAllen shouted, "The kid'll think he's been born into a band of outlaws. Come on, Mr. Wright, we just want to look at the little fellow."

A few others grumbled.

"That's Kate's orders. She says when he cries I'm to bring him right back, so some of you better get to scrubbing." Tyler looked down at the bundle. "Now, son, try to remember everyone's name when I introduce you. You'll be needing to know."

He passed the baby over to Adam McAllen, the oldest of the McAllen family. The tall, lean cattleman had silver in his hair but was smiling wide. They'd brought a saddle to the hospital for little Henry Wright.

The Matheson women made a quilt for the baby, and the sheriff and her husband gave him his first spurs. Tyler lost track of all the trucks and baby clothes. It didn't matter. He was thankful for the friends more than the gifts.

Reagan Truman hauled a five-foot apple tree right into the hospital foyer for her gift. She said by the time he could climb, the tree would be ready for him.

Tyler was glad a few minutes later when Hank let out a yell and the doc said visiting hours were over. He wanted to take the baby back to his Kate.

All the people in the waiting room waved the newborn good-bye, as if he'd notice. Tyler fought back tears of joy.

If a man's heart could burst with love, he knew his might. He'd never considered himself good-looking, or smart, or talented in any way, but he always tried to be kind. Maybe that was the secret, because he could ask for no more in life than what he had.

In the morning, a little after dawn, there would be a funeral for Marty Winslow. Tyler would leave Kate and go by the home to change clothes, and then he'd do his job as he had all his adult life. But his family would never be out of his thoughts. From now on, no matter how sad the day, he'd be heading home smiling. Kate would be waiting, and they planned to spend their days watching Jonathan Henry grow.

Maybe that was how his great-grandfather had felt when he'd nailed a hand-painted sign on the fence by the road after his crops failed. The sign said simply: WILL UNDERTAKE ANY HONEST WORK. The first Henry Wright hadn't set out to become an undertaker; he'd just wanted to feed his family, and he'd found a way to help the entire community.

"Tyler," Kate whispered as she held the baby close against her. "Now, we begin."

"Yes, my Kate, now we begin."

Chapter 32

APRIL 12
HARMONY CEMETERY

CORD STOOD STONE STILL AS HE WATCHED THE hearse winding slowly up the hill. He couldn't remember attending a funeral before he went to prison, and he hadn't been able to attend either of his parents' burials. This was his first time.

He'd expected only a few people, but there were at least forty. Most folks didn't know Marty, but they knew Ronny and they'd stand beside her this day.

The long black funeral car stopped in

the middle of the road and Tyler Wright climbed out. He opened the back and six men slowly pulled out a plain wooden casket. Three tall businessmen in their early forties on one side and the Biggs brothers on the other, with Beau Yates sandwiched between them.

As they moved up the hill the last few feet, Cord felt Nevada's hand slip into his. He wondered if she had any idea how much he wanted to run. He was twenty-eight and staring eye to eye at death for the first time. When he'd been told his mom and then his dad had died, he hadn't reacted at all. He'd been too hard by then to care. Nothing changed. The next day was the same hell as the day before. So Cord guessed their deaths didn't seem real. Nothing did back then. He'd shut down, turned off all emotion. After a few months in prison, a light went out that he thought would never turn back on.

Only it had. One thing had happened that made him care if he lived or died. Cord felt like he was standing in death's garden coming alive again cell by cell.

He tried to remember the exact moment it happened. Not when he got out of prison.

Not when he went back home. Cord Mc-
Dowell had come alive the day that Nevada
had driven up on his land and asked him
to marry her. He couldn't name the exact
moment his heart started beating again,
but it was around the time he realized he
was going to take her offer no matter what
the conditions.

Before that day he should have been
taking his pulse every morning just to
make sure he was among the living.

Nevada tugged on his hand and they
began to follow the others toward the
grave. Ronny sat in the front row with Mr.
Carleon on one side and Martha Q on the
other. Cord had no problem telling which
were Marty's family and friends and which
were there for Ronny.

City folks and country folks, he thought.
Someone had said that Marty's brother
had been in London and told them to go
ahead with the funeral without him. There
were a few fashion statements there who
looked bored and antsy to leave. They
must have been his cousins from Oklahoma City. Ronny's friends looked truly
sad as they huddled near her; most had
their work clothes on because as soon as

the funeral was over they'd head back to work.

Beau opened his guitar case and pulled out an old Gibson. He began to play. For a while the music filled the dawn air like a scented breeze, and then his low words blended with the notes. He sang a song about the "never weres" in life, the things we never do, the words we never say, and how we pile them up over the years we walk this earth so we'll have something new to do in heaven. When he finished, everyone had tears in their eyes. There didn't seem a need for any eulogy, any prayer. Beau's song had done it all.

Cord didn't hear most of the rest of the service. He was too wrapped in his own thoughts. The bad thing about coming alive after ten years was that now he thought about dying. He'd never been afraid of dying. First he'd been too young, and then in prison he hadn't cared. He'd seen more than one inmate carried out on a stretcher with a blanket over him, and all he'd thought was that the guy was free.

When everyone stood and began hugging, Cord pulled Nevada to him so hard she whispered, "Let me breathe, Cord."

He loosened his grip and kissed the top of her head. "Sorry. I thought this was the hugging time."

Last night had been the first time they hadn't made love in a week, and somehow the night had been sweeter. She'd fretted over his snakebite and been worried about her horses. He was sad because of Marty and frustrated that Cameron hadn't reported in. So they crawled into bed and just held each other.

She'd whispered about how she wanted to change the locks on the barn and what time she needed to get to work and a hundred other things Cord didn't really care about, but he loved listening to her whispering in the darkness. It was almost like she was singing him a good-night song.

He also liked the way he could put his hand on her and she didn't pull away. Sometimes, while she talked, she would reach up and move his hand from one place to another as she wiggled into just the right spot beside him. He didn't care; touching any part of her felt just as good. He'd never be able to tell her how much her sleeping next to him meant to him.

Hoping to clear his mind, Cord tried to focus on where they were, but it was impossible. Nevada was branded into his thoughts and heart too deep.

When people began to head back to their cars, Cord walked her to her car and asked if she wouldn't mind waiting while he told Ronny to call if she needed anything. He had no idea what was proper to say, but he needed to talk to her.

To Cord's surprise, Nevada pulled a card from her purse and handed it to him. "Tell her the same goes for me. I'm in town. If she needs me I could run over to her place."

Cord winked at his wife. Maybe he wasn't the only one coming alive.

As he glanced down the line of cars parked in single file all the way to the gate, he noticed a round little woman storming the hill like an invader.

Looking back, he saw Ronny curling down in the grass beside the grave. Crying. Beau knelt beside her, trying to offer comfort, and the three friends of Marty's stood behind the grave looking sad and helpless.

Border Biggs and his older brother were headed toward Cord, but most others who attended the funeral were pulling away in their cars.

"We got to stop that woman." Border's words were low, deadly serious as he reached Cord. "That's Ronny's mother, and she's here to cause trouble."

Cord noticed a few other people trying to delay the woman's climb, but she didn't stop to talk with them. She kept coming. He stood his ground, not sure what was going on, but if they were somehow protecting Ronny, he'd join the brigade.

"Get out of my way," the woman shouted as she reached the path leading up to the grave. "I got to get to my daughter. She's making a fool of herself lying in the grass."

Cord moved, blocking the woman. "I don't think anyone needs to bother her, Mrs. Logan. Maybe later when she's rested."

Border's brother brushed Cord's shoulder on one side; Mr. Carleon was on the other.

"If Ronny wants to mourn beside his grave all day, I'd say she has that right. You'll not disturb her." Cord wouldn't touch the woman, but he wouldn't move out of her way either. He doubted she'd climb the uneven grass just off the path, even in her practical two-inch heels.

Dallas Logan took a step back and looked like she planned to fight. She obviously was a woman used to bullying her way through life.

Cord had no idea what he'd do if the old woman stormed the line. Marty's three friends in suits joined behind him, looking like they felt sorry for Mrs. Logan, but still they couldn't let her hurt Ronny. Others backtracked from their cars as if hearing a call to arms. The postmaster, two mailmen, a waitress from the diner, two men who wore fire department shirts, a sheriff's deputy in a suit too small for him. An army of friends stood between Dallas and the grave.

A standoff. Dallas just glared at them.

To Cord's surprise, the undertaker walked around them all and reached Dallas Logan.

"I'm so very sorry you were late for the service, Mrs. Logan," Tyler said, as if he'd just noticed Dallas in the crowd. "I know you wanted to be with your daughter in her time of sorrow. It was a beautiful service and a fine morning to walk into heaven, I think."

Dallas looked shocked as Tyler took her elbow with one hand and wrapped his free arm around her shoulder. "Why don't you ride along with me? I'd hate to think of you walking all that way back down to your car. If you took a fall, I'd never forgive myself." He started moving, leaving her no choice but to follow. "These old roads can be slippery in the morning dew. I've got a thermos of hot coffee in my Cadillac. It'll warm you up and give you time to think about what you need to say to Ronny to help her get through this hard time."

When the dragon lady halted, he continued, "I remember when your dear husband died. It was such a nice service and all those yellow roses the postmen sent from all over the state made the chapel look so grand. He was much loved, I could tell that right away."

Dallas broke into sniffles and Tyler patted her.

Everyone watched in amazement as the chubby little funeral director guided her off without stopping his account of the funeral long enough for her to get in a word.

"Man," Border whispered, "that Mr. Wright is my hero. Did you see how he walked right into the mess that I don't think most bomb squads would have tackled?"

"It's his job," added someone from behind Cord.

"No," another said, "he's truly gifted."

Cord broke from the others and climbed back up to where Ronny lay in the grass. He could hear her sobs even as she tried to keep them inside. The sound hurt his heart to listen.

"She won't get up," Beau whispered. "She says she wants to stay here with him."

Border and Big Biggs joined them as all others moved away, maybe because they couldn't bear to see her pain or maybe because they didn't know what to do. Marty's three friends seemed to be finding their purpose in shuffling Winslow relatives back in their rented cars.

Cord knelt down and put his hand on her back. "Come on, Ronny. Marty would have wanted you to lean on your friends. Maybe that's one of the reasons he came home, knowing he was dying. He wanted to be with you and he didn't want you to be alone when his time was up."

She didn't seem to hear him.

Cord didn't know her well, but he couldn't stand to see her so shattered. He tried to think about what a friend should do, wishing he'd had a little more practice in being one.

He waited as the cemetery cleared of all cars except for a few. "Ronny, it's time to go. Marty's not there, he's gone to another world."

She looked up. "There is no perfect world, you know."

"I know."

Without a word, he lifted her off the ground. She came to him like a child, too broken to protest.

With the Biggs brothers on either side, Cord walked toward the cars still parked along the road. He turned away from the black funeral car with Ronny's mother inside talking to Tyler.

"I'll take her home," Big volunteered. "Put her in my truck." He pointed to the nearest pickup.

A tall young woman waited by the old white truck. She opened the door to the passenger side as Cord walked closer.

He lifted Ronny inside. The woman crawled in beside her and wrapped Ronny in a blanket. Big climbed in the other side while Border swung into the bed of the truck.

Big slowly drove away.

"Don't worry, mister," Beau said when he neared. "We'll take care of her. Big's girl said she'd stay with her tonight after Mr. Carleon leaves if she needs someone to."

Cord smiled. "She's lucky to be surrounded by friends."

"We're just strays nobody wants, but when we get together we make a pretty good family." Beau waved and headed to his old car.

Cord walked back to Nevada, thinking he fit in that category too, or he would in a few months when the marriage was over. He had no one, and Nevada only had her brother Barrett, who she said called once last year just to tell her he was never coming back. He'd cleaned out all the accounts, sold the ranch to her for all she could raise, and vanished, saying he never wanted a sister anyway.

"Let's go home," Cord said to her as he slipped into the passenger seat of her car, very much aware that her place wasn't really his home.

How would it be to look across his fields and see Nevada's land after he'd moved back to the farm? She'd made it plain that she'd only wanted him and his name until the first frost. By then the crops would be in, the cattle sold for a good profit.

Then, like she had after every marriage ended, she'd go back to being Nevada Britain. She'd be back in her world and he'd be back in his. Suddenly the money he would walk away with didn't seem nearly as important as the fact that he'd have to sleep alone again. The clear difference from before would be that he'd miss her every night for the rest of his life.

How could he tell her that he didn't want this marriage to end? She'd think he was just playing her like the three husbands before. He couldn't break the bargain they'd agreed on. He'd have to live each day as they'd agreed until the day he walked away.

That day, he'd be just as dead as Marty Winslow was now. They might as well put him in the ground.

"You going into town to your office?" Cord had to concentrate on what had to be done. He forced his entire body to harden because if he didn't, he'd fall apart. "I've got work in the south pasture. I told the men to start on it after breakfast and I'd be out as soon as I could. I'd like to have the fence ready to hold about a hundred head by next week. Sooner we get the cattle on the land, the fatter they'll be for winter."

"I don't want to go in," she whispered, almost like a child begging. "Take me flying, Cord, please. If you can spare the time?"

"Of course." He lifted his arm and stretched it behind her shoulders. "I'll be happy to. Maybe it will do us good to get away for an hour. I'll take you up where the air is pure. I need to clear my head."

Neither said a word as she drove to his place. He was surprised how clean the yard looked on his parents' old farm. The road crew must have carried away some of the weeds and trash that had blown up with the last storm. The house almost looked lived in and not abandoned. Someone had even replaced the missing boards on the porch steps. The place had been his only home growing up, and he'd fought like hell the past three years to hang on to the farm, but nothing about the house drew him. No sense of coming home. No longing to be there. It was just a place where two quiet people lived with a son who never asked for much, even love.

Nevada parked beneath the old oak halfway between the house and the barn.

They pulled out his grandfather's old plane and flew, crossing back and forth over their land. Now and then she'd tap him on the shoulder and point to something below she wanted him to see. The crops coming up, the cattle, her horses.

When they flew along the back of Britain property where the land was rocky and uneven, Cord noticed black spots in places, like shadows of clouds. Only the sky was clear. When he flew lower, he could tell the grass had burned. Maybe fires set by lightning and put out by the rain. Maybe not.

Nevada didn't comment on the charred spots, so Cord didn't say anything, but he made a mental note to drive out as soon as the earth dried enough to cross open field.

His mind and body slowly relaxed as childhood memories of flying with his grand-dad drifted back. He'd let Cord fly the plane when he turned twelve and by sixteen he'd had his license. The old man moved into a home the next year, his body crippling with arthritis, his mind dulling.

Cord felt his grandfather's loss. School, the farm, even his horse didn't really matter once the old guy left. A few times Cord tried going to the nursing home to talk, but his grandfather was too drugged up. Each time less of the man he'd loved was there and only a shell remained.

Cord began to run with a wild crowd looking for excitement, looking to feel alive. He wasn't old enough to understand why, but he knew he had to run fast because he'd seen what was coming at the end. One day his grandfather could fly and it seemed the next he couldn't even feed himself.

Part of Cord was glad his grandfather didn't know where he'd been headed that last summer. Gramps wouldn't have been proud of him, and it would have torn Cord up to know he'd discovered his only grandson had gone to prison. Cord's parents hadn't even written to tell Cord of the old man's death. Cord had read the Harmony paper's obituary to learn the truth.

He'd written asking his father to save the plane for him.

His father had sent a note saying simply, "Will do."

They'd never talked about it again, but the plane was waiting in the barn when Cord came home, the only thing that welcomed him. Flying now was like drifting through time, weightless among memories of the past.

When they finally touched down, he helped Nevada from the plane and couldn't resist pulling her against him. He needed to hold on to someone, to her, to one spark of happiness in life while it still burned.

"You feel so good, Babe," he whispered as he smelled the wind in her wild hair.

When he kissed her, it occurred to him that this was one less day they'd spend together.

The kiss deepened, not out of passion,

or need, but just with the pure pleasure of knowing that she welcomed his touch. He knew she'd had many other lovers, but it didn't matter; right now she was his.

When he finally lowered her feet to the ground, she smiled as if she understood how he felt. "Thanks for taking me away. It was nice."

"You're welcome. Anytime." He took her hand and they headed toward the car.

A picnic basket sat on the farmhouse porch when they walked close. He wanted to keep her beneath his arm even though the day was more cool than cold, but Nevada laughed when she spotted the red basket and ran to open it like it was the first gift Christmas morning.

"Ora Mae must be getting used to the idea that she might need to find us now and then to feed us." He watched Nevada pulling out food wrapped in plastic. "I feel like I'm a free-range diner around this place."

"She probably didn't notice we were back, since she's always in the house, but I'll bet Galem did. He's the one who guessed where to leave the basket." Nevada grinned.

"I'm starving. Want to eat inside or out here?"

Cord didn't care. He wasn't ready to go back to the world just yet. Work, his and hers, could wait an hour. He liked having her all to himself. "It's dusty in there."

"Not on the bed," she said, smiling as if she knew a secret.

He picked up the basket and followed her in and up the stairs to his old room. He moved through the shadows, watching her drop clothes as she rushed toward his bedroom. Her jacket, her shoes, her blouse. He barely noticed that someone had cleaned his room, adding fresh linens and a colorful bedspread.

"You been in here?" he managed to say as she unsnapped her skirt.

"I wanted to surprise you," she said, stripping down to her bra and panties. "I thought we might want to use your place as our getaway cabin. Since we spent the afternoon here the other day I think of it as special, like an enchanted cottage where we are just ourselves and the world can't interfere."

He knew how she felt. The ranch house

of hers seemed heavy with unhappy memories and stale like old velvet flowers in a winter window box.

She pulled the covers back and climbed in, standing on her knees to tell him, "I want to paint this room blue and maybe take out that wall so the upstairs area is one huge bedroom. Since college I've never had the opportunity to redecorate more than my study, but I didn't figure you'd mind if I had some fun with your place. It's a wonderful old house that's got great bones."

"I don't care what you do around here. Knock yourself out." He thought of his closet full of clothes he'd never have time to wear and figured he was releasing a monster. But she was a cute monster, especially in pale blue underwear with lace that almost wasn't there.

"I've been thinking this place could be great with a few coats of paint and a dozen carpenters hammering away. We could knock out part of the roof and you'd have skylights over your bed. Then I'd start on the kitchen. Really could use some—"

"Hush, Babe. Talking time is over." He pulled her to him as he popped the last button on his shirt. He needed them skin on skin. "We'll talk while we eat, and we'll eat later." The sight of her body was driving him crazy.

Nevada giggled. "I thought you'd never take the hint."

Hours later, Cord lay back watching moonlight drift through the cloudy sky. Nevada was curled against him fast asleep, wearing one of his old T-shirts they'd found in his drawer. They'd made a slow kind of love that drifted like a song, beautiful. Then they'd taken a shower together in the tiny bathroom off his room and eaten everything in the red basket as if they were starving. Still on the bed, huddled in blankets, they talked about everything and nothing.

All afternoon they touched, unable to get enough of each other. Maybe it was the fact that they'd been to the funeral, or maybe he was growing on her the way she was on him. Neither talked of love or forever. They wanted the now to stretch as long as it could.

Like a windup toy, she fell asleep in midsentence, not even noticing that he was still touching her, moving his hand beneath the covers and over her body.

"I can't give you up," he whispered as he kissed her hair.

He saw right through her tough-girl attitude and her temper tantrums. He saw the beauty of her, inside and out. The only problem was he couldn't seem to figure out why she'd picked him. Right now *he* was the one thing in her world that didn't make sense. She could have hired a foreman and bodyguards if she thought she needed them. Hell, she probably could have found a better lover than him.

He grinned suddenly, remembering how she couldn't have had any complaints today. She'd dropped back on her pillows after they'd made love and demanded, "Just kill me now because it'll never be any better than that."

He'd laughed and promised to work on making her statement a lie.

Once she'd asked him if he'd forgive her anything, and he hadn't known what to say. Now he knew he would. No matter how wild she'd been. No matter what she'd said or done. He'd forgive her. She didn't even need to bother to ask. The lives they'd lived before didn't matter, not when they were together like this.

Cord watched her sleep, wishing he could wake her and relive the afternoon. But the cell phone in his pocket buzzed before he could carry out his plan.

Rolling from the bed as carefully as he could, he pulled on his jeans and moved to the hallway.

"Hello," he whispered.

"Cord," a gravelly voice said. "I got some information."

"What is it?" Cord moved down the stairs, wondering what Cameron had managed to find as he followed Bryce Galloway. Whatever the news, Cord knew it wouldn't be good. Nothing about the guy was.

"I'll show you if you can meet me at the theater after midnight. Come alone to the back door. I don't want anyone to even know I know you."

"I'll be there," Cord answered, and hung up knowing that his time in paradise was over.

He carried his sleeping wife home. He stayed in bed with her for more than an hour to make sure she was sound asleep, then finished dressing in the bathroom off the kitchen without waking Nevada. He had to handle this alone, and he knew he'd touch her if he went back in the bedroom they shared.

Cameron's information might change everything. If Bryce Galloway was hurting Nevada, Cord wasn't sure he could hold his rage.

Chapter 33

<small>APRIL 13</small>

BEAU WOKE FRIDAY MORNING TO THE SMELL OF rain and the constant beat of thunder rumbling in the background like a low drumroll.

"Beau?" Border yelled from the other bedroom. "Is it raining in your room?"

Beau sat up in bed and felt drops drip on his head and shoulders. "Yeah," he said, knowing that Border could hear him through the thin walls. Indoor rain was one of the thousand complaints he had about this place.

Border showed up with their only two

good pots. "I already used all the bowls for my room."

They moved the bed and began to catch water in every container they could find. By eight the place had a tinkling sound like the opening to a children's ballet. Beau covered the equipment with tarps, dressed in sweats, and talked Border into running across the creek to Martha Q's place. It might be muddy, but Beau reasoned that it was half as far as using the road, so they'd only get half as wet.

Martha Q looked at them like they were two homeless wet dogs at her back door, but she let them in. "Take off your shoes and just drip there till I get some towels."

"Thanks," Border said, then took a deep breath as if he could smell a few hundred calories of breakfast cooking.

"I've been meaning to get that roof fixed, but I don't think of it till it rains." Martha Q looked like she'd been out partying all night. Her lipstick had slid off one side of her mouth, and one fake eyelash was missing. Surprisingly, she had the nerve to look at them as if they were the ones who looked strange.

"If you boys will clean up and dry off I'll

let you eat with my guest. Mrs. Biggs can add a little water to the gravy and we'll have plenty. We always have hot biscuits on Friday."

After she left to go put her face on, Border whispered, "She's just feeling guilty because she doesn't fix our roof. If we never, ever mention it, maybe she'll forget again and we can guilt her out of a few more breakfasts."

Beau accepted a towel from Border's grandmother and tried to dry off without taking his clothes off. "I hope she never marries again. If she does, and forgets to take her makeup off again, her husband will wake up and think he's on a *Night of the Zombies* rerun."

Mrs. Biggs tried not to smile at the comment. "I've got a couple of old raincoats that workmen left here a year ago when crews came in to build a fast-food place over by the mall. You boys can wear them home. They'll cover you from head to toe."

"Thanks, Granny." Border kissed her cheek.

Beau did the same even though he found it hard to believe that such a sweet lady could be related to the Biggs boys.

JODI THOMAS

Must have been grandbabies switched at birth.

She waved them both away. "Go sit down in the dining room, but no eating until all the guests have filled their plates. If we run out, it should be you two who have to wait until I can scramble more."

Beau moved into the formal little dining room with one wall of windows facing east. Normally the place was sunny this time of day, but this morning it was gray with water tapping against the glass.

One man sat drinking coffee at the end of the table. Dressed in a white shirt and plum-colored sweater, he looked out of place among the mismatched table and chairs Martha Q must have found at a secondhand store.

"Morning," Beau offered. "Nice day." The guy was in his thirties. He stared at Beau with a bored expression that must have taken years to practice.

"Morning," he finally said. "Don't tell me you're other guests. I thought the place was packed."

Beau poured himself a cup of coffee and sat down as far from the man as possible. "No. I was just invited to breakfast.

Heard it's biscuits and gravy. I love the way Mrs. Biggs puts those big hunks of sausage in her gravy."

The man sighed as if talking to call waiting. "I don't eat flour, or milk products, or pig."

"I'm sure the chickens are sorry to hear that."

The stranger just stared at him. "I don't eat any meat products." He had that why-am-I-telling-this-idiot-anything look about him.

Border backed his way into the room with cookies in both hands.

While he set his appetizer on the table-cloth, Beau thought he'd try the introductions. "Border, this is one of the guests. He's a vegetarian."

Border smiled. "That's great. My grandmother is a Presbyterian."

Beau grinned. Border had figured out people often took one look at his tattoos and assumed he was dumb. He played it up to the hilt.

Border smiled at the guy. "I'm Border Biggs, mister. I was just pulling your leg."

"Bryce Galloway," the man said, without offering a hand. "I've heard about you two. You play in a band over at Buffalo's Bar."

"That's right," Beau said. "You should come hear us some night."

Bryce lifted his cup. "I might drop by tonight. It's been a long time since I've heard that country twang."

There was no more time to talk. The three widows, staying at the place, hurried in. They'd all met Beau and Border, so they made a fuss over them like they were company and ignored the strange man at the end of the table. When all were seated, Beau didn't miss the fact that the seats on either side of Bryce Galloway remained empty.

Joni, the chatty one of the three, chimed in as if she'd raised her hand and it was her time to talk. "Are you gentlemen aware you all have names starting with *B*? Border even has two. Would one of you consider changing?"

All three men said no at the same time, and the room went back into silence as if a sign had dropped down demanding it.

Martha Q came in as they were finishing up and said she'd drive the boys back to their place because she planned to take breakfast to Mr. Carleon and Ronny. He'd gone over early to help with the moving of all the medical machines remaining in the duplex.

Beau was glad for the ride and happy to be out of the same room with Galloway. Something about the man bothered him. All his appearance was polished, but Beau had to fight the urge to check and make sure his wallet was still in his pocket when he walked away from the man.

As the day aged, he couldn't get Bryce Galloway out of his mind. He didn't feel like practicing, so he slept and read one of the books Marty had lent him.

Ronny invited them over to eat some of the food that folks had dropped off. She looked heartbroken, but at least she'd stopped crying. Beau had heard her most of the night and wished the walls were thicker. It seemed to him that sorrow always passed through thin walls, but joy never did.

When they left for the bar just after dark, it was raining so hard they wrapped the guitars beneath their thick raincoats and ran for Beau's car.

The mood of the day filtered over into the

night. Few came in for drinks or food, and those who did seemed more in the mood to talk than dance. Beau missed watching the people who usually tried to dance.

About eleven a girl with a blond ponytail walked in and sat at the last booth closest to the band cage.

"There's your girl," Border whispered.

Beau lifted his head and winked at her, then continued to play.

She watched them for a while. When Beau took a break and walked by her, he whispered, "Hello, Trouble." He had no idea what her real name was, but she'd been driving over and picking him up now and then for months. They never talked, they just drove through the night.

"My top's up on the convertible," she said with a smile, "but you still think you'd want to go for a drive?"

"Sure." Within ten minutes he'd talked Border into taking his car home and convinced Harley that the band should quit early.

When she left, she pointed to the front door, telling him where she'd be waiting.

Border pulled on the oversized slicker his grandmother had given him that morning. "Go ahead. I'll load up. You parked so close out back I won't get anything wet. I can load everything, drive home, and have most of the food Ronny left us eaten before you can say good-bye to the little lady."

"Save me one slice of the chocolate pie." Beau knew if he didn't pick something, Border would finish off everything. They had no use for a garbage disposal at the apartment.

Border was tangled in the cords when he looked back. Beau ran to the front. He couldn't remember when he'd needed a ride with Trouble more than tonight. Between the funeral and the rain, sunshine seemed a long way away.

Chapter 34

CAMERON WAITED FOR CORD AT THE BACK door of the old theater like a leftover ghost of movies past. Cord didn't even see the man until his headlights flashed across him. Without bothering with a greeting, they walked through the narrow theater aisles that smelled of stale popcorn and dust. The seats were in poor shape and the floor sticky, just as Cord remembered it from when he was a kid.

The little guy had made living quarters out of three dressing rooms off the stage. Cord saw into one that looked like a small apartment kitchen with a table and a single chair. He walked into another that must serve as the office for the theater. It had a huge old scarred desk that took up half the space and a file cabinet so full the drawers wouldn't close.

"I thought I'd better tell you what I found. You need to see the whole picture here." Cameron jumped up on the desk and smiled, as if delighted to have a guest in his place.

Cord remained standing. He wasn't afraid, but he felt his whole body go on guard as if from some primal instinct. "Go on," Cord said, wanting to get the meeting over with.

"I followed Bryce for two days, learning only that he was scum. Both days he left the B&B after breakfast and wandered around like he had no purpose. Coffee shops, bakeries, bookstores, diners. All he bought in each was coffee, and he didn't even buy that in the used bookstore. The owner of the store talked to him, asking questions. Galloway never gave him a straight answer."

Cameron rubbed the bridge of his nose with his index finger. "That rented Rover wasn't too hard to follow. He'd stop at each place and usually strike up a conversation with whoever was around, like he was building an alibi. Then he'd sit somewhere, the park mostly, and make calls. I couldn't get close enough to hear, but I could tell he was frustrated, and even angry, at whoever was on the other end."

"Have any idea who he was talking to?" Cord asked.

"Nope." Cameron lit a cigarette with nervous hands. "The first day he had these three ladies following him. I was so busy watching them tail him, I lost him for a few hours. Picked him up at the bar out by the truck stop. You know, the one with three Xs on the roof. He parked in the back, but so does everyone who hangs out in that dump. Of course I followed him in, but I didn't have to worry about him spotting me. It was so dark I could have picked his pocket and he wouldn't have seen me.

"He mostly just drank and flirted with the ugly girls who were over-made-up and underdressed. I saw him go back behind the curtain with a few of them for a private dance. He always came back smiling like a goon, and they came back looking disgusted. I heard one girl say she wouldn't give him anything extra no matter how much he paid."

Cord thought he could guess what was happening. Nevada had mentioned once that her ex liked to hurt her where the bruises wouldn't show.

Cameron continued, enjoying himself. "When he left there, he drove back to town by way of the road running next to your ranch."

"My ranch isn't on the way back from the truck stop."

"I know. I thought that was strange, but it got stranger. He ate at the diner, making a point to talk loud enough for everyone in the place to notice him. Then he headed over to the show at the mall. After that, he returned to the bed-and-breakfast. The guy seemed to have no purpose, no friends, no life. He's drifting."

"Did he go out later?"

"Nope. I slept so close to his car, he couldn't have started it without waking me up."

"He could have walked," Cord snapped, tired of the rambling.

"He could have, but he didn't seem the type. I thought he was the most boring guy I'd ever followed until this afternoon, when he bought a ticket to the same movie for the third time. I followed him in instead of waiting outside."

Cameron smiled. "I know my way around dark theaters. He never saw me even when I sat three rows behind him. About halfway through the movie, some guy came in the rear door and sat down beside him. For a second I thought it might be you: same tall build, comfortable in his western clothes. They whispered for a few minutes and then left out the back. I followed them across the alley to a little dump of a house behind the mall. I could see them through the dirty window and took a chance moving closer to hear what they said, but it was muffled."

Cord fought not to shake the man to get facts. "What happened next?"

"When the stranger opened the front door, I was so close to them the door almost hit me in the nose. I heard Bryce say something about how the guy's paycheck would never happen because Bryce said he had to do the dirty work himself."

"Did the man answer? Any clue what it was he didn't do?"

Cameron shook his head. "The stranger just swore and walked off cussing."

Cord couldn't help but wonder, since the man was dressed western, if killing a horse was the one thing he wouldn't do. "What happened next?"

"Galloway picked up a book, big like a photo album, and walked out the back door. He went straight across the alley and back into the theater. When I followed five minutes later, I took the time to take the tape off the lock. Nothing bothers me more than people sneaking in without paying."

"What next?"

"Oh, Galloway watched the movie, drove by a takeout place, and went back to the B&B. I hung around until ten, but he never left the place. I thought of driving back to the dump of a house, but I figure it was just where they met to talk. Then I remembered Bryce hadn't taken the album in. It took me a while, but I unlocked the rental car door and found it under the front seat."

Cameron pulled an old photo album out from under papers on his desk. "I thought you should see this. I'll get it back before dawn so Bryce will never know."

Cord slowly opened the book and began to turn the pages. Photo after photo. All of them were grainy, but he had no problem seeing that they were of Nevada. Riding. Swimming. Walking. Smiling on the steps of her home. He couldn't see much detail. They were probably taken with a cell phone and blown up on a computer before being run off on plain paper. In a few she looked younger by a few years and her hair was shorter than it was now.

"Bryce is collecting pictures of my wife?" Cord whispered after a few minutes. The last one in the book was of her standing next to him at Marty's funeral. In the center of the picture, where her arm linked his, someone had cut a hole in the picture.

Cameron frowned. "Someone is obsessed with her. I heard that her ex-husband was in town to try and buy her ranch, but he doesn't want the ranch back, he wants her."

"But why would he be causing trouble around the ranch?"

"Maybe he thinks she'll turn to him?" Cameron shrugged. "If the ranch fails, are your pockets deep enough to bail her out?"

"I don't even have pockets." Again the reason she'd married him drifted across his thoughts. She'd said she was low on money and needed a good season or she might lose the ranch. Cord had a feeling that if she'd gone to Bryce, she would have given up far more than the land.

Bryce Galloway wanted her back, and he seemed willing to do whatever it took to get her.

"My only question to you is, which one of these guys do you want me to follow tomorrow?"

"Bryce. The other must be just working for him, and from the sound of it Bryce tried to push him too far." Cord flipped back through the book, noticing there were pictures of Nevada in every spot on the ranch. "But why the pictures? He was married to her. He knows what she looks like."

"Not part of my job, figuring out nutcases, but if I was guessing I'd say Bryce is waiting for her to be in the wrong place at the wrong time. He wants her in his sights. That much is obvious. Maybe he just wants to talk her into leaving you and going with him. He strikes me as the type who's always gotten whatever he wants, when he wants it, and you are pushing him, making him go to extremes."

"Maybe he'll get tired and quit?"

Cameron shook his head. "He's like an addict and your wife is his drug. Maybe she's the only one who ever said no to him. Maybe he thinks she belongs to him. I've been around a lot of druggies in my life. If he thinks he has to have your wife, he's not stopping."

Cord nodded and moved to the door.

"One other thing," Cameron added. "I found a couple of high-powered rifles hidden in the trunk of Bryce's car. They were new, looked like they'd never even been tested."

"Lots of men in this part of the country hunt," Cord said, without turning around.

"Yeah." Cameron's answer wasn't reassuring.

Cord walked out of the old downtown theater with more questions than answers. He drove around for a while after he left Cameron. He even stopped in front of the house Cameron had described behind the mall. It was easy to guess which one it was. Just an abandoned house with an old dirt bike parked among the trash near a crumbling carport, a perfect meeting place. No one passing. Not any occupied houses close enough to see a light.

An hour later when Cord slipped back into bed, Nevada rolled in his direction. He held her to him until dawn, knowing that trouble was riding full out toward them and he couldn't do anything to stop it. He didn't have enough proof to go to the sheriff, and Cord knew without asking that Nevada wouldn't run for cover.

But what Bryce didn't know was that he'd have to go through Cord to get to her.

At dawn, while she dressed, Cord kept his voice casual. "What are your plans today?"

She wiggled into her jeans. "I'm staying around the house this morning."

He wondered if she was trying to act normal, the same way he was. "I've got to go check a few things. If you'll wait here, I'll go into the vet's with you in an hour."

"Make it two or three hours. I want to start a painting of Starlight for my study. Then we can go check on her and have lunch in town. I'm starting to like the daily special at the diner."

She moved into his arms, laughing as she kissed him lightly. "I'm getting used to a lot of things lately."

He tightened his arms around her, wanting to keep the conversation easy but unable to hide how much he needed her close. Part of him could almost understand Bryce being obsessed with her. The woman was addictive. He wasn't sure that leaving her wouldn't break him as well. Only, unlike Bryce, if she said good-bye to him, Cord would walk away. He didn't want to own her or control her; he only wanted to love her.

"I'll be back before noon," he whispered against her hair. "Wait here for me."

"You'd better be back." She pulled away so she could smile at him. "I'm already starving."

He could tell by the look in her beautiful blue eyes that her starvation had nothing to do with the special at the diner. He grabbed his hat to stop himself from undressing her. "Bye, Babe."

He ran from the house, not in a hurry to be away, but in a hurry to be back.

Cord drove out to where he'd seen the dark spots on the earth when they'd flown over. The sun had dried the ground, but he knew he was still leaving tracks an inch deep. Whenever he crossed open land he hated the way his truck tires scarred the earth, even temporarily. The only good thing seemed to be that the land always went back to nature.

Cord spotted burn spots in what had been tall natural grasses. Too many circles of blackened grass for it to have been lightning strikes.

When he walked the burned area, he found a charred pack of matches, as though someone had struck them all aflame and dropped the pack. The grass must have caught fire and burned across the rocky uneven ground, and then stopped suddenly. The only reason he could think of was that rain had put the fires out.

As Cord drove back to town he went over the details. All he knew was that whoever set the fires had done so on a stormy night, hoping the fire would be blamed on the lightning, only they hadn't planned on a rain coming so soon. Cord grew up with prairie fires. On backland like this they could spread for miles before anyone noticed, and by then they'd be so wide a hundred men couldn't stop them from spreading. Someone might have noticed Bryce's rental roaming over the land, but no one would have paid much attention to a man on horseback. Maybe the man Cameron had described as a cowboy had set the fires. He could have parked his truck and trailer on a back road and ridden in from the border of the property.

He drove into Harmony hoping to talk to the sheriff but found Travis Salem in her office instead. The ranger looked the same as he had when he'd investigated the horse poisoning, but Cord no longer found him frightening. For a second when Cord first saw him that day, he stepped back to being seventeen again, but now he remembered who he was. The boy no longer existed.

"McDowell," the ranger yelled when he saw Cord walk past the dispatcher's desk. "Glad you came in."

Cord couldn't think of any person he wanted to see less. But other than being rude, he couldn't turn and leave. "Salem. I thought you'd be back in Fort Worth by now."

"I was just packing up. No leads on your wife's case. I'll let you both know if anything turns up. We did find Joey Mason, the trainer, last night. I was planning to call you before I headed back. The trainer showed up on a flight passenger list at DFW and about panicked when he found out every-one was looking for him."

Cord waited for Salem to get around to the facts.

"Security talked to him but didn't hold him. He said he'd gotten a letter firing him as of last week. It was on Boxed B statio-nery and included a thousand in cash if he'd go quietly. Joey said he went over, cleaned out his gear, and left. The secu-rity officer faxed me the letter if you want to see it."

"Who signed the letter?"

Salem dug in a box and handed him the fax. "You did."

Cord glared at the paper. "Not my—"

"I figured that. I asked to have the origi-nal sent, but it's probably been handled so much there won't be any fingerprints on it that can help with the investigation."

"I understand."

"Joey Mason didn't question it. He claimed he never fit in on the ranch and was glad to leave. You said you hadn't got-ten around to meeting him."

Cord didn't argue. "I should have. I'd seen him from a distance several times." If he hadn't listened to Nevada's rule, he would have ridden over to her barn and met Joey.

"We never had that cup of coffee," Travis Salem finally said as he folded his glasses and slid them in the case clipped to his vest pocket. "Any chance you got time for it now?"

Cord wanted to say no, but he hoped somehow he could let go of some of the anger that had kept him breathing all the years he'd been locked up.

"I'll be at the Blue Moon Diner as soon as I leave a message for Sheriff Matheson. If you want to talk, I've got time for one cup of coffee."

Salem nodded and returned to boxing up papers.

Cord walked away. He headed straight for the dispatcher and asked if Alex would contact him as soon as she had a few free minutes. No emergency. He wasn't sure what he could tell her. Cameron had stolen the photo album, and the letter to Joey still didn't make enough to arrest Bryce.

Cord drove to the diner and parked out

front. When he walked in, the breakfast rush was over, so the place looked deserted except for dirty tables. He took a seat in the first clean booth and ordered a cup of coffee. If the ranger wasn't there before he finished, there would be no next time.

Cord's cup was half empty when Travis Salem entered. Even though he'd put on a stomach the size of a basketball, Salem looked so much smaller than he had that night at the lake. That night he'd had a rifle in one hand and a flashlight in the other. That night Cord had been more kid than man.

"Thanks for waiting," the ranger said as he slid in and motioned to the waitress that he'd have a cup.

Cord was silent. He had nothing he wanted, or needed, to say.

Salem took a few deep breaths. "I've been needing to say something to you for a long time. It took me a while to figure everything out. I was madder than hell at you for years. When I finally got up the nerve to talk, I drove out to the prison and they said you'd been released. After that, I guessed I'd be the last person you wanted to see."

Cord held the coffee cup so tightly he

was surprised the mug didn't shatter in his hands.

Salem thanked the waitress for his coffee and waited until she walked away. "I lost ninety percent of the sight in my left eye that night. I thought my life was over. All I'd ever wanted to be was a deputy sheriff, and you ended that dream."

Cord stared at the man, not knowing whether to feel guilty or angry. Did he think he was the only one who lost something that night?

"I sat at home recovering and feeling sorry for myself for months. One day, out of the blue, your parents showed up at my door. I figured they were going to beg me to help get you out early, but all they wanted to do was give me your college fund. Said they'd had an argument with you over going to college, and that was probably why you were drinking that night."

Cord didn't breathe. Memories poured like liquid lead over him. His parents not listening to him, the argument, the feeling that they didn't care what he wanted.

The ranger continued, "I took the money and, more out of anger than want, I decided to go back to school and use every dime of it. Four years of school and two eye surgeries later, I walked out with a master's degree and enough sight in my left eye to pass the test to try out for the Texas Rangers. They saw me as a hero, injured in the line of duty. I got a job I never would have worked my way up to on my own. It's more business and paperwork. Not the fun of being out there fighting crime, but I've settled into it and surprisingly I'm good at it."

"You got a point to this?" Cord asked. "I'm almost finished with my coffee."

"Yeah." Salem stared at his cup, still untouched. "One of the first things I did after becoming a ranger was go back and look at the file we had on you. I listened to the tape of your testimony and heard something I hadn't heard before. You sounded scared. I ran what you said over and over in my mind. I remember walking into the camp of drunks and kids high on who knows what. It was dark and the smell of fireworks reminded me of the army when I was nineteen and deployed straight into hell. That same kind of terror filled my mind that night at the lake. I must have been yelling as I headed toward you."

"What are you saying?"

Salem straightened, and Cord knew no apology would be coming. He didn't expect one. He didn't want one. What good would it do now?

The ranger's voice hardened slightly. "I found a note in the file. Apparently, a teenage girl had come forward, to one of the other deputies, after I was sent to the hospital and you were arrested. She claimed I came at them with a bright light and in charge mode like I was ready for a fight. No one knew who I was. They didn't even know it was the cops. She said she thought I either stepped on your leg or kicked you, and you came up swinging wildly."

Cord froze. Exactly the story he'd told. The story no one believed.

Salem shrugged. "The deputy who took the statement told her to come by the station the next morning, but she never did. When they checked on her, her father swore she'd never been out of the house that night. Since she was a minor, her statement was dropped."

"Why tell me now?" It was too late to change anything. "I don't care who she was or what she said. She didn't help when it counted."

"Oh, I figured you knew who she was." Salem raised his eyebrow in surprise. "You married her."

Cord didn't remember saying good-bye to the ranger. He sat in the diner for an hour in the dungeon of his thoughts.

When he drove back to the ranch, he went straight to the bunkhouse, gathered up equipment, and headed for the south pasture.

At sundown, he was still working as hard as he could, pounding in fence posts across the uneven ground when Galem found him.

"Putting in a hard day, aren't you, Boss?" the cook shouted, without getting out of his pickup.

"Shouldn't you and Ora Mae be gone to the lake?" Cord stopped long enough to wipe the sweat off his face with a shirt he'd ruined hours ago.

"We decided to stay here this weekend. Ora Mae says she don't think she can eat another bite of fish or one more hush puppy for a while. I took her into town for Mexican food, and when we got back I noticed your truck was still gone. If I hadn't seen your headlights shining out here, I never would have found you."

Cord pulled the next fence post from his truck.

"You plan on stringing barbed wire in the glow of your headlights?"

"I might." Cord didn't want to talk any more than he wanted to think. "You want to help?"

"Nope." Galem shoved his hat back. "You want to talk about what's bothering you?"

"Nope," Cord answered.

Galem took the hint and shifted into gear. "Well, I'll see you back at headquarters. I'm guessing if your battery don't run down, you'll be finished about dawn. Anything you want me to tell Little Miss?"

"Nope."

Galem pulled his hat back down almost to his eyebrows. "Well, nice talking to you."

Cord didn't stop to wave as the cook drove off.

Chapter 35

SEVERAL HOURS LATER CORD DIDN'T HAVE TO look up to know his wife's Jeep was flying across the land at twice the speed she should be driving. He could hear her coming, and dread filled him to the core.

He watched her as she shot out of her seat without turning off the engine or the lights. She headed right toward him. Storming, he thought, there was no doubt.

"Cord, what do you think you're doing out here in the middle of the night? The wire is dangerous enough to pull from post to post in daylight."

"There's work to be done," he said, without stopping the pounding. "That's what you married me for, isn't it? To work your ranch. Don't worry, you don't have to come out to sleep with me, because I don't plan on sleeping. In fact, I'm thinking I might just work until I drop dead. Then you could be a widow for a change."

She stormed around in and out of the beams of light like a moth. He guessed she had to be pretty confused right now. The last time she saw him, he'd kissed her good-bye so deeply she'd tried to tug him back to bed. She didn't know about the pictures or the trouble she might be in or that someone was setting fires in the back pastures hoping to burn the entire ranch down. She didn't know what Salem had told him. She didn't know that he knew she hadn't bothered to even try to keep him out of prison. Her silence had ruined his life just as Salem's lies had.

His whole body and mind were being drawn and quartered into pieces. Six years he'd sat in prison because not one person had come forward to back up his story. Of course the jury took the deputy's side. Cord had known there were others around the campfire, but he'd figured they all ran. Nevada must have stayed long enough to see what happened to him. She even talked to the other deputy, but she hadn't said a word when he needed someone to back him up.

She marched back to her Jeep and pulled out something, then marched back. "Galem said you ruined your shirt. I brought you another one. At least take the time to put it on."

"You spend too much time worrying about what I wear. Don't you have anything better to do?" He twisted the wire around, nicking his hand for the tenth time. Cord barely noticed. "What difference does it make anyway?"

She waited for him to take the shirt. He could hear her pouting like she always did when things weren't going her way.

He stuck the wire cutters in his back pocket and reached out for the denim shirt. In the lights he could see her face and hated himself for making her so unhappy. She'd grown up on a ranch. She knew he was putting himself in danger to be out here alone after dark. She'd probably worried for hours before finally coming out.

"You got a gun with you? There are wild hogs on this back land."

"No. It's been my experience that people are far more likely to hurt me than wild animals."

She walked halfway back to the Jeep, then turned to face him. "I hate it when you're like this, Cord, all closed off and cold."

He almost said he hated it when she wasn't honest. She played him and he didn't even know the rules.

Hell, he hated them both. What kind of game were they playing anyway? If she wouldn't stand up for him, why would she marry him?

Suddenly, he remembered one detail about the night at the lake. One fact he'd stored back in his whiskey-washed head drifted forward. Cord remembered the cop who'd cuffed him and shoved him down in Salem's blood and his own vomit. When he jerked him up to frisk him, he had ripped Cord's shirt. By the time they made it to the office it had fallen completely off.

Cord forced his anger to settle. Before he said a word, he saw panic flash in her eyes. She was afraid of him. He'd never hurt her, never raised his hand to her. But her blue eyes couldn't hide the fear as she stared at him. She thought she was watching a wild animal. Maybe she thought he'd snap and hurt her like all the folks in town seemed to think he might. After all, he was an ex-con.

Slowly, he took the shirt and pulled it over tired shoulders. "Thanks." His voice sounded hoarse even to him. "You were there at the lake ten years ago, weren't you, Nevada? You saw the cop tear off my shirt, because he was certain that I had a weapon. That's why you buy all those shirts. You're trying to replace that one from ten years ago."

She didn't answer.

"I talked to Salem this morning. He told me a girl told the officer left at the scene about what happened, but she wouldn't testify. The next day, her father swore she wasn't there." Cord let out a long breath and felt his muscles relax. "It was his word against a cop who'd seen her in the dark, and nobody thought to question your daddy's word; after all, he was a big rancher."

Nevada crumpled, disappearing from the lights of his truck and her Jeep. For a moment it was as if she just vanished.

Cord stepped toward where she'd been. On the third step, his leg bumped against her. He knelt, feeling her shoulders as she crouched, curled into a ball. His grip was rough as he pulled her up, needing to see her face. Her body was stiff in his grip, as if she were preparing for a blow.

Her tears cracked the wall of anger he'd been building inside all day. He circled her with his arms and pulled her close. All the times when she'd talked to him. All the nights she'd rattled on about nothing and suddenly his wife couldn't say a word.

"We're going to talk about this," he finally whispered as his hands stroked up and down her back. "It's not going to stand between us anymore. We're going to get it all out, right now."

He felt her nod against his shoulder. Before all the wrong words came between them and the fragile peace they'd known was forever broken, he kissed her one last time. Her lips were salty with tears, but she kissed him back. He felt her lip tremble and her hand rest hesitantly over his heart, but she gave him what he needed, one last kiss.

When he finally pulled away, he lifted her and walked to the bed of the pickup. It was dark there, but maybe what they had to say needed to be said in the shadows. After all, that was where it had happened.

He set her down and rested his hands on either side of her knees. "Tell me the truth. I've got a right to know. Did you marry me out of guilt? Was it some kind of sick joke?"

She gulped back a sob, and he understood.

"Before you start, let's get one thing straight. I'm not going to hurt you, Babe. No matter what you tell me, I swear, I'm not going to hurt you. I'm not going to leave you either. No matter what is said here, I go back with you and we finish what we've started. We make it to the first frost. We make the ranch pay."

She nodded, but he couldn't be sure she believed him. He fought the urge to touch her, but he knew if he did, they'd never work this out. The attraction between them was the only thing he knew was real.

She wrapped her arms around her sides,

making the shadow of her seem smaller. "I saw what happened that July Fourth. I tried to tell the cop writing down names of who was there, but I could tell he wasn't buying my story even if he did write it in his notes. He kept asking if I was with you and would I lie just to help you."

Cord waited, giving her all the time she needed.

"When I got home, my dad exploded. He slapped me so hard my ears rang. He said everyone already hated the Britains, and if I got mixed up in your problem it would only be worse. He threatened all kinds of things if I spoke up again and convinced me that they wouldn't take my statement anyway. All the time he was talking, he was jerking me around, slapping me just to make sure I got the point of every word he said.

"If my mother hadn't stepped in, I think he might have beat me senseless that night." She stared at her fingers twisted together in her lap. "My brother Barrett was there. He just stood watching and smiling, like it was about time someone taught me a lesson. I knew that night I was nothing to my dad, and my brother would never come to my rescue. I wanted to help you, but I couldn't fight them all, and I didn't believe a drunk minor's statement would be of much help."

Cord knew she was probably right. He waited for the rest.

Finally, she said, "For years, even after you got out, Barrett teased me that you were going to come over and kill me some night. He said if you weren't a bad guy when you went to prison, you would be when you got out. He had me afraid to drive down the road past your farm."

"How do you know I'm not?"

"I didn't, but that day you worked on the Jeep, I was at the end of my rope. Another year of poor management and I would lose the ranch. My ex had been promising to come back. When my father was dying and Barrett was packing to make his break, Bryce grew tired of all the problems and took off, thinking that I'd be begging for his help in a few months. He didn't take my calls or answer my mail. By the time he found out about the divorce it was almost final. He couldn't stop it, but he swore I'd come back to him begging for his help one day. Even after the divorce was final, he whispered that when I begged him to take me back, I'd have to come on his terms."

"So you married me before Bryce could get to you?"

"No. I needed your name to prove I'd moved on. I don't know, maybe I was tired of fighting him alone. I thought he'd back away if you were in the picture. I told Bryce that if he stepped foot on my land I'd shoot him, and I meant it. I married you because . . ." She hesitated, then put her hand on his arm. "When I saw how you took care of the Jeep that day and how no one gave you any credit for doing it, I wanted to make you the man you would have been if you hadn't gone to prison. The man you should have become."

Cord pulled back. He hadn't expected her to say something like that.

"I saw it in you, Cord, and I was right. You were a good man, broken and hollow, forced into a hard life. I thought I was helping, but I'm not sure if I haven't brought you more trouble than you had before."

He didn't touch her when he whispered, "Don't you know? You brought me to life." He couldn't lie to her, couldn't play any games.

He brushed his fingers over her hair. "I told you once that I'd forgive you anything, but this, it's nothing to forgive. I fell into hell, but you were going through it too."

"You don't hate me?"

"How could I hate someone I love so much? Somehow you crawled into my heart, and I'd have to cut the thing out of my body to stop caring."

He lifted her up and swung her into the light.

She smiled, seeing him open for the first time. All at once she was crying and laughing at the same time.

As he lowered her in front of him, a shot rang out in the night.

Cord reacted on instinct, taking her with him to the ground between the two sets of headlights.

Another shot. Then another as Cord pulled her deeper into the darkness.

"Follow me," he whispered. "Stay away from the light."

He heard one of the bullets kick up dirt. Another hit a rock three feet away. Whoever was firing was guessing. They were too far from town or the ranch to make it on foot, and it was unlikely anyone on the ranch would hear the shots. Their only chance was to make it to the Jeep.

He pulled her close, trying to shield her as much as he could with his body. "Move toward the Jeep and slip into the driver's side," he whispered. Another shot rang out. The shooter was spraying the area between the two lights, hoping to hit something.

Silently, he pulled the wire cutters from his back pocket and tossed them toward his pickup.

They hit the roof and rattled off onto the hood.

Three rapid-fire shots shattered the night air. All hit the truck. One smacked a light. Another broke the windshield.

Cord ran for the Jeep, hoping Nevada had made it before him.

When he climbed in the open window, he heard her shift and gun the engine. Like a rocket the little Jeep went backward for a quarter mile, then spun around and flew toward the main road.

He heard a few more shots, but he guessed they were out of range by the time whoever was shooting at them figured out what was happening.

"Where?" Nevada yelled.

"Straight to town. If we head to the ranch house, we might be followed." As she drove faster than he thought the old Jeep could possibly go, he dialed Galem and told him what had happened.

"Stay inside until light. Tell anyone at the bunkhouse to do the same. I don't want him picking anyone off. Call all the guys and tell them not to come in tomorrow until I send the order. We have to know it's safe before we step out."

Cord listened, then hung up. "Galem thinks the shooter might have followed you out to me. He said he passed a car on the county road that looked abandoned. When you went past, the shooter could have left his lights off and followed you. This Jeep makes so much noise neither of us would have heard another car."

"But he would have to know this ranch very well to know where I turned off the road onto the land. There's only a ten-foot hole in the fence."

Cord thought of the pictures. "He does know the ranch well."

Nevada turned onto the main road, and within a few minutes they saw the lights of Harmony.

When they got to the sheriff's department, the night shift was still working. Phil Gentry took all the notes but wanted to wait for daylight and the sheriff. "Not much we can do for a few hours. Alex will be in about eight if she doesn't get a call on the way into work. As long as you've got your people inside and safe, there's not much we can do about a shooter on your land. It would take a few dozen men to even find him, and we'd never be able to round them up this time of night."

"Once it's light, I can fly and tell you if he's on my land." Cord was already forming a plan.

"That might work. Alex and a few of us can be on the ground. We'll get the highway patrol to block the roads in and out of your place. If you spot him, you can direct us to him."

"I can do that." Cord fought down a yawn.

Phil shook his head. "You folks look beat. Why don't you go over to the diner and get some breakfast and a pot of coffee? I think they open at five."

"I could use a few hours' sleep if I'm going to be flying soon." Cord's muscles were sore from the hard work he'd done and he hadn't had anything to eat since breakfast yesterday, but most of all he needed to sleep.

"I got a couple of empty cells. You're welcome to your pick."

"No, thanks. I'll sleep standing up before I step foot in a cell. How about that couch in the sheriff's office?"

Phil waved them into her dark office. "It's not much better than the bunk in the cell, and with the glass door there's no privacy. What about you, Mrs. McDowell? What can I get you?"

"I stay with Cord," she whispered.

"I understand. You've both had quite a night, but don't worry, I'll be right outside on duty. You're safe here. You won't need an alarm clock. When the day shift comes on they make enough noise to wake even the dispatcher."

Cord tugged off his boots as she closed the door and found a blanket folded in a corner. He stretched out on the couch and she moved in beside him. The milky glass on the door made the pale light in the room almost moonlight.

"There's not enough room," she whispered, pushing him over.

He tugged her against him, already half asleep. "Where I sleep—"

"I know," she answered.

After a few minutes, she whispered, "Did you mean what you said back there?"

"When?"

"Before the shots were fired. Did you mean what you said about loving me?"

He took a deep breath and answered, knowing that there would be no going back, "I did. I think I always have, but Babe, I've got to admit, you're not an easy woman to love."

She rested her head on his shoulder and wrapped her arm across his chest. "I know. Haven't you heard that nothing worth doing is ever easy?"

He kissed the top of her head. "Well, at least it's not boring."

Chapter 36

RONNY TALKED MARTHA Q INTO TAKING MR. Carleon to the hospital to see the new baby. Mr. Carleon didn't seem all that interested, but when Ronny said she needed to take a nap, the proper gentleman understood.

"There are some papers I need to go over with you when you feel up to it," he said.

"I'll call you when I wake," Ronny promised as she waved.

She moved into her apartment as they drove away. To her surprise, he seemed to enjoy Martha Q's company. He lived a very ordered life, and Martha Q had never even organized her thoughts. Maybe opposites do attract.

Ronny looked around her place. Everything had been put back in order as if Marty had never been there. But she saw the little differences and she knew he'd always be with her. This time he hadn't left her; he'd gone on ahead.

Mr. Carleon had left a folder at the kitchen table where he often did his work. This was the first time he hadn't put every paper away in his case, and she had no doubt that the folder was for her.

Absently, she looked at it, knowing this was what he planned to talk to her about when she was ready.

On the top of a stack of papers was a plane ticket to Paris for September third. Scribbled in Marty's bold hand was a note. *You have to see Paris in the fall.*

She moved her thumb over the words he'd written before turning the page.

Next was a two-week cruise down the Rhine and another for the Mediterranean. Complete with luggage tags and agendas for each day.

Next, clipped together were all that was needed for traveling down the Nile.

Ronny turned over another ticket, then another, each dated, planned, organized.

Each trip moved into the next until finally, the last was a flight to New York for December twenty-third. *Promise you'll stay to ring in the New Year*, a note said.

Beneath the last ticket was a key and a final note. *My apartment in Manhattan. Stay as long as you like.*

Next, she noticed page after page of details. Tours, dinners, plays, concerts all marked paid in full on the agendas. *There is plenty to do in New York until spring. Walk in Central Park when the gardens start to green and feel my love walking with you.*

Ronny smiled. Marty was giving her the world. She would trade it all for one more day with him, but that wasn't possible, so he'd given her memories.

He'd also given her time to mourn. By the fall he wanted her traveling.

She pulled on her jacket and walked the blocks to the cemetery, loving the cool morning air. The tent was gone and hundreds of flowers now lay across his grave.

Ronny didn't cry; she just sat in the grass beside him and remembered.

"In a perfect world, you'll be with me," he'd said, and someday she would be, but now wasn't her time to die. Now was the time to live so when they did meet again, they could compare notes on all they'd seen.

After a while, she stood and walked home, thinking of all the things she had to do to be ready to travel. She wanted to finish her last two classes online and get her degree. Marty would have liked that. She would have to train someone to take over at the post office. She'd have to shop for clothes.

Her mother was waiting in front of her house when she came back from the cemetery. Ronny walked past her window expecting to see Dallas race off at any moment to prove she still wasn't speaking to her child.

Only Dallas rolled down the window. "I won't come in," she said, as if she'd been invited. "I just came to tell you that you can come home. I hate the thought of everyone seeing you falling apart in public over some man who wouldn't marry you but came to live with you."

"He came to die." Ronny was surprised how calm she felt. Her mother's words didn't bother her at all. She could almost see Marty smiling at her from the front window.

"Well, what are you going to do with yourself? Never a wife, not a widow. He didn't leave you any money, did he?" She answered her own question. "Of course not. If he had money he wouldn't have moved in with you so you could be a free nurse to him."

"He didn't leave me a dime, but I've saved a little and I think I may travel for a while."

Dallas laughed. "You travel? You don't even know how to drive on the interstate. Except for that time your father insisted we go to Kansas, you've never even stayed in a hotel. You'll get as far as Dallas or Oklahoma City and turn around, crying all the way home."

"Maybe. I'll send you a postcard if I don't turn around."

"You always were a fool, Ronny. Why would you want to travel alone when you can come home and keep me company?"

Ronny turned away and was halfway up

the steps before she looked back. "Good-bye, Mother."

Dallas gunned the car and drove off without a word.

Smiling, Ronny could almost see Dallas's reaction when a card from a different country arrived every week. She'd go on the trip Marty planned and, who knows, maybe she would stay in New York long after the new year.

Chapter 37

CORD WAS IN THE AIR BY TEN, CROSSING BACK and forth over the land. Nevada wanted to go with him, but he knew she'd be safer with the sheriff. They all agreed that the shooter had wanted to kill.

He flew low, looking for a car that didn't belong, or even tracks in the pastures. The area where he'd been putting up fence last night bordered government land that was too rocky for much of anything. A man would have to know the land, know what he was doing, to track across that land. He'd also have to be a good shot to fire on them at night.

Nevada told him Bryce had been a hunter since he could tag along with his dad, but that wasn't exactly damning evidence. Many men in Texas could say the same.

Which left Cord with only one answer. The man trying to kill Nevada might be Bryce Galloway, but he didn't have the proof he needed. Bryce might threaten her now and have knocked her around when they were married, but Cord couldn't prove anything.

He kept his phone close, hoping Cameron would call in with facts.

Another piece of information kept rolling around in his head. Bryce spent his days building alibis. The kind of folks he was talking to wouldn't be able to remember if they talked to him on a certain day of the week by the time they were questioned. In a week he'd probably be able to produce someone who swore he was in town all day, every day. So far everything he'd done to try to harm Nevada had been at night, but he might have to act during the day if he wanted to get closer. Which would mean that he'd have to come on the ranch in daylight.

Cord had told the cowhands to search in groups of two. They were all armed with rifles, standard for any man in the saddle. Cord guessed he was the only man on the ranch not armed. Nevada must have taken the Colt from the office drawer because it had been missing since the snakes visited.

The now-familiar feeling of trouble thundering in rattled through his body. He had to protect her. He had to do the right thing. He had to follow the law.

He crossed one more time over the place where he'd been working last night. His truck, with the windshield missing, looked abandoned. Knowing Nevada, she'd probably ordered him a new one. He'd never known anyone to spend money faster than she did.

As he circled back to his farm to refuel, he spotted the sheriff's cruiser parked near the field he used as his landing strip. Cord rolled to a stop and climbed out.

"Nothing?" she said.

"Nothing," he answered.

"I was afraid of that." She walked with him toward his old pickup. "I found your truck out in the south pasture earlier. It was shot up, just like you said. The crime team came over from Amarillo to work the evidence."

Cord pulled out two bottles of water from the cooler in the bed of his truck and offered her one. "They find anything?"

"Yeah, your truck was shot to hell."

Cord smiled because she'd used his exact words when he'd told her where to find the truck. "I should have gone into law enforcement."

"Something else. The bullets used were hollow point. Not as accurate from a distance, but if they'd hit one of you, they would have done some serious damage."

"Which means?"

"Which means whoever was firing at you wanted you dead, not just hurt."

Cord leaned against the old pickup. Between digging holes in hard earth all day and half the night and then sleeping on the sheriff's couch, he felt like a pretzel left out to dry.

Alex took a drink and added, "We're not dealing with just a mad ex-husband. If you're right and it is Bryce Galloway, he means to kill you both. Maybe he figures if he can't have Nevada, no one should."

"I figured that out up there." He pointed at the sky. "I think he tried to pay someone else to bother us, but when he got serious, he decided to do the dirty work himself. Nevada said that as far as she knows he'd always gotten everything and everyone he wanted until her."

Alex followed his logic. "Who stands to benefit from her dying?"

"Me, I guess. The lawyer asked us if we had wills, and we said we'd worry about it later. So if she dies, I inherit." He hardened. "That makes me a suspect."

Alex smiled. "You forgot one thing. Whoever was shooting last night was shooting at you both. I'd think that pretty well takes you out of the lineup."

Alex let her words sink in, then continued, "Nevada and you are both in danger. This isn't about the ranch, it's about you two."

"I'm not worried about me."

She smiled. "I could have guessed that, but *I* am. I don't like the idea of someone killing anyone in my town."

"Even me?" He wasn't sure he believed her.

"Even you." She laughed. "You're starting

to grow on me. How about we go find Nevada?"

Cord tossed his empty water bottle in the bed of the pickup. "She's at the ranch house."

Alex straightened. "No. I was just there. I even tried her cell. No answer."

Without a word they both jumped into their vehicles and raced toward the ranch.

Five minutes later Cord hit the kitchen door first. Ora Mae looked up from pulling a pie from the oven and glared at him.

"Where's Nevada?" He didn't have time for her to remind him to wipe his feet or tell him what time it was. Any time he walked in early, that always seemed to be her first response.

Ora Mae nodded at the sheriff as Alex stepped beside Cord. She answered formally as if testifying. "She got a call about twenty minutes ago saying one of her horses was acting sick."

"Who called?"

"I don't know, but Nevada took off in that old Jeep." She looked from Cord to the sheriff. "I'm sure she's safe. Her barn is not that far from the house and you've got an armed guard posted over there."

Alex didn't answer the housekeeper. She just lifted her phone and hit a number. "I need all deputies on the roads into the Boxed B. No one, and I mean no one, leaves this land unless I say so. Then ask the highway patrol to log all cars on county roads that border the ranch."

Cord walked beside her as she moved to her cruiser. "We may be overreacting—"

"We're not," he snapped.

Cord looked in the direction of the barn where Nevada kept her horses. He couldn't see it, but what he saw stopped his heart.

A few thin lines of smoke rose, widening in the air and disappearing.

Cord ran toward his truck.

Chapter 38

Nevada stared at the fire growing in the center stall of her barn. She could hear the horses moving, kicking at their stalls, making low sounds of fear. They knew something was wrong; they could smell the fire.

"You can't do this!" she screamed toward the loft above her. "Leave me here, but get the horses out. Please don't kill them!" Hot tears rolled down her face. She fought against the rope binding her hands and feet.

"Why?" Bryce's angry voice came from above. "What do I care if they die—these pets of yours? You've made a fool of me,

Nevada. I thought when you divorced me I'd go back to my life, but I couldn't. Not when you didn't get what you deserved."

He tossed a bale of hay on the fire he'd started a few minutes before. "My friends back home, even my family made fun of me. *Where's the little wife, Bryce? Lose her, did you?* I couldn't stand the jabs. Even when I tried dating, it never worked. They weren't as pretty as you. They didn't crumble as easily. I was treated like damaged goods. If you didn't want me, no one else seemed to. I finally figured out I'd have to deal with you before I could move on."

He glared down at her from above. "Only you messed it all up. I thought I could frighten you and you'd give in like you did when we were married, but you married someone else. You belong to me, Nevada. You have since I first saw you. After seeing the way your father and brother treated you, I knew you were made for me. I'd have no problem with control." He swore at her, then added, "Only you tricked me, and you'll pay by dying with the screams of your beloved horses in your head."

Bryce laughed. "Poor little unloved Nevada. Once you're gone I'll think of myself as a widower; after all, I will have lost the one woman I ever wanted."

Smoke began to fill the barn, and the horses' cries ripped at her mind. "Please," she said, knowing that he wasn't listening. "Please let the horses out."

Bryce started down the ladder at the far wall. He stopped to watch the fire as smoke fogged the air inside the barn. "I thought I could whip you into shape, but you were stronger than I thought. You didn't take the bit like you should have."

She struggled, wishing she could reach her duster only a few feet away. Deep in the pocket was her father's old Colt.

"You never cared for me," she said, more to herself than him. She'd known more love in the weeks married to Cord than she'd known all her life.

"You got that right, but I wanted you."

Nevada coughed. The smoke was getting thicker. "You'll never get away with it."

He laughed. "Who's going to stop me? The fire in your barn was an accident. I made sure it looked like the guard you left upstairs was smoking. He tossed a few cigars out the loft opening, and the fire department will find them and think one must have started the fire."

Nevada had been so shocked to see Bryce waiting for her in the barn, she hadn't thought of the guard. Johnson, the youngest of the brothers, was on duty today. "Where's the kid?"

"Oh, he's dead"—Bryce almost giggled— "or he will be soon. The smoke's getting thicker and thicker up there. I knocked him over the head and tossed the body in the back of the loft. They'll find his body during the cleanup. What a mess this place is going to be. In fact, I'd better hurry if I want to get out alive. I parked a bike out behind the barn, so I'll be miles away before anyone gets here."

Nevada steadied her voice. "You are really going to leave me here to burn to death?"

"Oh no, dear. I couldn't do that." He pulled her to her feet and shoved her toward the horse now going wild in the first stall. "I want you to be near your horse. You always worried more about them than you ever did me. I've even locked the barn door and plan to leave out the back. By the time anyone sees the fire and breaks in, it will be too late."

Nevada stumbled, unable to move her feet.

He jerked her forward, half dragging her with him. The ropes cut into her wrists, but she barely noticed.

"I'm going to let the horse kill you. Fitting, don't you think?"

He pulled her hands free of the ropes as he shoved her inside and pushed the bolt closed. "One more thing," he yelled above the horses' screams. "I shot this one full of a steroid. Even you won't be able to calm her, but don't worry, I'll wait until you stop screaming before I leave."

The mare shoved against Nevada, knocking her off her feet. She tried to reach the rope binding her feet, but the horse was too near, too threatening. All she could do was twist out of her way.

Nevada rolled against the stall as the animal raged, fighting to get out. A hoof slammed against her leg, snapping the bone just above the knee.

Nevada screamed and fought to press flat against the stall wall. She heard Bryce laugh as smoke blurred her sight.

If she couldn't see anything, neither could he. She clamped her mouth closed so tight she feared her teeth might crack, but she didn't make a sound. Let him think she was dead; she would be in seconds. If the horse didn't trample her, the smoke would suffocate her before the fire even reached her.

She waited for death, listening to the screams of her horses. She'd ride into the hereafter with them.

Chapter 39

BY THE TIME CORD REACHED THE BARN, SMOKE was coming from the roof. He didn't slow the old pickup as he raced toward the barn door, closed and locked.

The Ford hit the huge doors hard and Cord hit the brakes as lumber tumbled around him. Bellows of smoke escaped with waves of heat that felt like opening an oven an inch from his face.

By the time he was out of the truck and running, his face felt sunburned.

He reached the first stall and threw the bolt. The horse almost ran over him.

As he ran for the second stall, he heard

Alex yelling for everyone to stay away, but the cowboys came barging in, their bandannas around their faces, like bandits of old. One by one the stall doors were flung open and the horses were herded out. A few of the hands grabbed fire extinguishers and tried to fight the fire, but it had spread too far.

"Nevada!" Cord yelled, but there was no answer.

He moved to the next stall, where a mare was bleeding from fighting so hard to get out. When the horse ran past him, he saw a dark movement in the back of the stall. For a second, he thought it might be a colt, and then Nevada's blond hair brushed across the bloody floor.

Men were shouting all around him, but the world went silent. All he saw, all he could think about was the woman curled on the floor.

"Everyone get out now!" Galem shouted. "The roof is about to fall!"

Cord knelt, knowing he wouldn't leave her. Carefully, as if she were a newborn, he lifted her up. Her arm was bleeding and a gash on her head poured blood over her beautiful hair. One leg twisted at an odd angle. He knew it was broken. "Come on, Babe," he said as he pulled her against his chest. "Let's go home."

She cried out once as he moved her, but she never let go of him.

He carried her through the burning barn with fire flying around him. All the horses were gone, but the flames seemed to be laughing in victory.

Ten feet out of the barn he cleared the smoke, and a cheer went up. He knew they were safe.

A fire truck and an ambulance were pulling up as everyone backed away from the burning barn.

Medics ran toward Nevada. They both had packs of supplies and a stretcher balanced between them.

Cord slowly laid her on the stretcher. He looked up at the barn, now completely engulfed in flames. Only the charred outline of his truck showed at what had once been the opening. The cowboys were standing back several yards. Galem bandaged one man's hand and Ora Mae passed out water bottles.

The adrenaline slowly drained from Cord's body. Everyman on the ranch must have seen the smoke and come running. Pickups and trucks were parked along the road and in the pasture like scattered toys.

"She's stable," a medic said. "Looks like we're dealing with a broken arm and a compound fracture of the leg. Got to have the doc check that head wound as well. We need to transport her. You coming along, sir?"

Cord didn't answer. He knelt beside Nevada and smiled when he saw her blue eyes open. "You all right, Babe?"

"I will be. Thanks to you."

He smiled. "We got an agreement; you have to sleep with me every night. I couldn't let you die and back out on that."

She tried a smile but couldn't manage one. He had a feeling the shot the medic had given her was taking the edge off the pain. "Tell the sheriff it was Bryce who did this."

Alex moved closer. "You don't have to tell me. We found him behind the barn."

The medics moved in, lifting Nevada's stretcher. "Are you coming with her, sir?" he asked again.

"No." Cord looked at Nevada. "I'm going to stay here and end this now."

His wife nodded as if she understood. "I'll be waiting when you're finished."

When he leaned in to kiss her cheek, she added in a sleepy whisper, "I love you, you know."

He straightened. "I know."

As the ambulance pulled away, Cord followed the sheriff around the barn to the horse tank.

Johnson sat on the ground, while Dr. Freeman looked at his head. "I need to get to the horses and check on them, son. I don't have time to thump on you, but if you were a horse I'd say you're fine. Not too bright, of course, to drop out of a twenty-foot loft door."

Johnson grinned. "I had this guy to break my fall. I was coming to when I heard him say he was leaving out the back, so I held my breath and waited just above the little door. He didn't even look up, but he must have thought he was hit by a falling train."

Cord looked over at a man in handcuffs standing beside the sheriff's cruiser.

"If you're thinking of killing him, forget it." Alex walked up behind Cord.

"He tried to kill my wife," Cord said simply.

"He's going with me and he'll be locked away for a long time."

Cord smiled at the sheriff. "That's worse than anything I could do to him. I know. He's all yours, Sheriff." He took a few steps and added, "Remind him a few times on the drive in that Nevada is fine and she's with me."

"I'll do that, Cord."

Jackson and Jefferson straightened from where they'd been hovering over their brother. Jackson balled his fists. "He tried to kill my kid brother, Sheriff. Mind if I pound on him a little?"

"Sorry. I can't let you do that, but look at the bright side. Johnson had to get out of that barn. Bryce here saved him a broken bone or two by giving him something to land on."

Neither Jackson nor Jefferson looked happy about having to settle for nonviolence, but they respected the sheriff. "Would you let him know that if he ever gets out, one of us will be waiting for him?"

"Sure." Alex headed toward her car. "Johnson, if your boss has no objections, I'd like you to come on in and give a full statement. Then I'll get Nevada's as soon as the doctor gets finished with her."

As they moved around what was left of the barn, Galem offered, "Boss, you might want to ride along with me. Your truck wasn't in too good of shape the last time I saw it. It appears trucks have a very short life around you. At this rate you might single-handedly keep Ford in business."

Cord laughed. "Yeah, I keep parking them in the wrong spot."

Chapter 40

MARTHA Q PULLED INTO HER DRIVE, TRYING NOT to touch the steering wheel any more than necessary with wet fingernails. Looking up, she swore.

Two cowboys and a sheriff's deputy looking like they'd just had a run in with Smokey the Bear were sitting on her front porch.

"I'm going to chop that porch off and drag it into the creek bed." She climbed out of her car, forgetting all about her nails. As she headed up the walk, she yelled, "I'm full up, boys. No more room in the inn."

Amid all the dirt and soot, she recognized Cord McDowell. "And you, Cord, you need to go home to that wife of yours." She was at the steps when she added, "But take a bath first. You smell like a campfire."

"My wife is in the hospital with a few broken bones. She got trampled by a horse an hour ago." Nothing in Cord's tone was conversational. He was simply stating facts. "We're just coming along with the deputy. He's got a search warrant and we thought we'd give him a hand."

"Bryce Galloway in some kind of trouble?"

Phil Gentry stepped around Cord. "Galloway is under arrest for trying to kill Cord's wife."

Martha Q raised her eyebrow, surprised at being right.

Squeals came from just inside. The widows, if she were guessing.

Cord turned to Martha Q. "Would you mind if we went up?"

She wouldn't dream of saying no. This was the most exciting thing that had happened in months. While they tromped up the stairs, she called Anthony and told him to hurry over.

As he walked up to the porch, three gray-headed women rushed out, all chattering about there being too much excitement at the inn. Joni paused only long enough to give her notice of leaving to Martha Q.

"You've got a free night coming," Martha Q suggested.

"No, thanks," Joni said as she rushed away. "I'm going home."

Mr. Carleon stepped up beside Martha Q. "Is everything all right, dear?"

"Yes, Anthony, but we'd better step away from the door. I'll explain as they carry Bryce Galloway's things out. You won't have to worry about sharing a bathroom again."

He smiled as he took his chair on the porch. "Tell me all about it, dear."

They rocked in the porch chairs as the deputy and two cowboys carried out everything that had belonged to Bryce Galloway.

"I'm glad he's gone. I think Bryce was the one who grabbed Ronny the night before Marty died. Maybe he was just angry and wanted to take it out on someone, or maybe he knew she was Cord's friend and thought by hurting her, he'd get to Cord."

"Have you any proof?" Martha Q asked.

"No, just a hunch."

Martha Q shook her head. "Sometimes I'm afraid to be alone in this big old house."

She shivered, and he took her hand. "But you don't need to worry. I've decided to stay awhile, if the room's still available."

"It is for you, Anthony."

"Thank you, Martha," he added, without letting go of her hand. "I like it here."

"Here in Harmony, or here with me?"

He winked at her, and Martha Q giggled as if she were on her first date.

Chapter 41

Cord CLEANED UP AT THE SHERIFF'S OFFICE before going over to the hospital. He looked terrible, but he didn't care. His wife was going to be all right. Bryce was locked away, and this time there were plenty of witnesses who could back Cord up on exactly what happened. Thanks to Cameron, the sheriff found the rifles Bryce had used in the abandoned house behind the mall. No amount of family money would buy him out of this mess.

When Cord called to check on Nevada, the nurse on duty told him to come quick, she was throwing a fit wanting to get out.

He wasn't surprised. On a good day she didn't react well to stress. He had to get to her quick. Galem was waiting to drive him over, and then the cook said he needed to get back to the ranch. Cord knew he'd be back if needed, but it was a husband's place next to his wife now.

Five minutes later, she looked up from the forms she was filling out, Cord smiled down at her. "Hi, Babe."

"How are my horses?" she asked. "If one of them is hurt, I'll—"

"The horses are fine. Aren't you worried about me?"

"Why? You seem in one piece, except it looks like you've ruined another shirt."

"Sorry about that," he shrugged. "When are you getting out of that bed and coming home to sleep with me?"

Nevada frowned. "Are you crazy? What's not burned on you looks dirty."

"Well, if you'd stayed put in the house like I told you, I'd only be dirty and not burned."

The nurse darted from the room as if she thought a fight might break out any minute.

Cord and Nevada both laughed, and then Nevada cried in pain. He comforted her with his easy touch on the part of her arm not covered by a cast.

"She's out there telling everyone how mean we are to each other," Nevada said.

"I don't care."

"Me either. If I want to storm at my husband, I will."

He leaned so close she could feel his words against her cheek. "I love you, storms and all."

"I love you too," she answered. "Maybe even more than I love my horses, but don't you dare tell them that."

He grinned, knowing just how great a love that must be.

Epilogue

OCTOBER 27

CORD WORKED UNTIL SUNSET WORRYING ABOUT winter coming on. They'd made a good profit on the cattle, but he'd kept quite a few head to increase the herd. The winter crops should have already been planted, so he'd have men working all weekend.

Any day the first frost would hit. For months he'd kept thinking that the work would slow down, but it never did. His list of things that needed to be done grew longer every day. He'd finished the rebuilding of the barn for Nevada's horses, but there

were still things that needed doing and
never enough hours in the day.

His mind was full of everyday problems
when he stepped into his old farmhouse
after dark. Nevada said she wanted to
meet him there. He knew she'd been talking about remodeling the place, but Cord
didn't have time to listen to all the details.

The doctor said it would give her something to do while she recovered. The arm
healed quickly, but the leg had to have therapy. He'd slept beside her for more than a
month before she'd begged him to touch
her. Making love to her the day she got her
cast off was like making love to her for the
first time. He was afraid he'd hurt her and
she was afraid he wouldn't be attracted to
her, but in truth Cord didn't even see the
scars. They didn't matter.

When he reached for the light switch
just inside the kitchen door of his old place,
he noticed candles on the table. For a moment, he just stood staring, thinking maybe
he'd walked into the wrong house. The
place looked nothing like it had. Like everything she did, Nevada must have rushed
into decorating full steam ahead.

Nevada, wearing one of the cotton

dresses he loved, stepped from the shadows with only a slight limp.

"Hi, Babe," he said. "What's this all about?"

"Our bargain is up. The weatherman says it'll come a hard freeze tonight." She held up the paper. "We made it all through the season."

He hadn't even had time to think about the bargain. Between work and getting her well, his days had been too full to count.

"I want you to move back to your place, so I fixed it up. Ora Mae and I even moved your clothes over this morning."

Cord couldn't seem to force air into his lungs. She couldn't be serious. They hadn't talked about the contract they'd signed the day they married since she'd been hurt. She'd told him she loved him a hundred times. Whispered it in his ear when others were near and screamed it out loud when they made love. He'd thought they'd go on forever.

She moved into the soft candlelight. "I don't have to sleep where you sleep anymore."

He nodded once. If he said a word, he was afraid he'd never stop. Maybe he hadn't made it plain how much he loved her, but it never crossed his mind that he would just be the next husband on her list to leave.

"So, since I'm free of that part of the bargain, I can sleep wherever I want." She took one more step, careful not to limp. "And from now on I'm sleeping with my husband in this house. In his house."

Kissing him softly, she whispered, "Because I love him dearly."

He pulled her against him as his tender kisses welcomed her and his heart started beating again. She was making it plain she wanted no bargain between them; only love would hold them together now.

Finally, he pulled back and smiled down at her. "I'm nothing but mean, you know. You might want to reconsider. I work too hard and I don't talk things over enough."

"There is nothing to reconsider. I found you, Cord, and I'm not letting you go. Not ever."

"You sure you won't get mad one day and storm off down the road to your place?"

She smiled. "I gave the ranch house to Galem and Ora Mae today. If you don't keep me, I'll have to go live in Martha Q's inn."

"Oh, don't worry, Mrs. McDowell. I'm keeping you." He picked her up. "How about you show me the house, starting with our room."

"Don't you want to eat dinner first?"

He moved up the stairs. "Later. I want to see the stars through those skylights over our bed first, Babe."

She grinned. "I didn't think you were listening. I love you, Cord."

"And I love you."

HICKMANS

Brunswick County Library
109 W. Moore Street
Southport NC 28461